International Directory of
COMPANY
HISTORIES

International Directory of
COMPANY
HISTORIES

VOLUME 72

Editor

Tina Grant

ST. JAMES PRESS

An imprint of Thomson Gale, a part of The Thomson Corporation

Detroit • New York • San Francisco • San Diego • New Haven, Conn. • Waterville, Maine • London • Munich

THOMSON

GALE

International Directory of Company Histories, Volume 72
Tina Grant, Editor

Project Editor
Miranda H. Ferrara

Editorial
Virgil Burton, Donna Craft, Louise Gagné,
Peggy Geeseman, Julie Gough, Linda Hall,
Sonya Hill, Keith Jones, Lynn Pearce,
Maureen Puhl, Holly Selden,
Justine Ventimiglia

Imaging and Multimedia
Randy Bassett, Lezlie Light

Manufacturing
Rhonda Dover

Product Manager
Gerald L. Sawchuk

LIBRARY OF CONGRESS CATALOG NUMBER 89-190943
ISBN: 1-55862-547-X

BRITISH LIBRARY CATALOGUING IN PUBLICATION DATA
International directory of company histories. Vol. 72
I. Tina Grant
33.87409

Printed in the United States of America
10 9 8 7 6 5 4 3 2 1

CONTENTS

Preface . . . . page vii
List of Abbreviations ix

Company Histories

Adolfo Dominguez S.A. 3
Altadis S.A. 6
The Austin Company. 14
Banca Nazionale del Lavoro SpA 19
Behr GmbH & Co. KG 22
Belk, Inc. 26
Bettys & Taylors of Harrogate Ltd. 30
BigBen Interactive S.A. 33
Billing Concepts, Inc. 36
Bonhams 1793 Ltd. 40
The Branch Group, Inc. 43
Brigham's Inc. 46
CACI International Inc. 49
Camaïeu S.A. 54
Caritas Internationalis 57
Carl Allers Etablissement A/S 60
Cazenove Group plc 63
Cia Hering 66
Cincinnati Lamb Inc. 69
Clougherty Packing Company. 72
Colorado Baseball Management, Inc. 75
Combe Inc. 79
Dallah Albaraka Group 83
Debeka Krankenversicherungsverein auf
    Gegenseitigkeit 87
Duron Inc. 91
E.W. Howell Co., Inc. 94
Éditions Gallimard. 97
Electronics Boutique Holdings
    Corporation 102
Embrex, Inc. 106
Empire Resorts, Inc. 109
Engelhard Corporation. 113
Eschelon Telecom, Inc. 119
Ezaki Glico Company Ltd. 123
Farmacias Ahumada S.A. 126

F5 Networks, Inc. 129
Fisk Corporation 132
5 & Diner Franchise Corporation 135
FLSmidth & Co. A/S 138
Friendly Ice Cream Corporation 141
Galardi Group, Inc. 145
Gilman & Ciocia, Inc. 148
Grand Piano & Furniture Company 151
Greatbatch Inc. 154
Groupe Monnoyeur 157
Hammacher Schlemmer & Company Inc. 160
Harris Teeter Inc. 163
HDOS Enterprises 167
Health Communications, Inc. 170
Hensel Phelps Construction Company 174
Homasote Company. 178
Howard Johnson International, Inc. 182
Intermec Technologies Corporation 187
Ipsen International Inc. 192
J.L. Hammett Company. 196
Jo-Ann Stores, Inc. 200
Johnson Publishing Company, Inc. 204
KraftMaid Cabinetry, Inc. 208
Kumon Institute of Education Co., Ltd. 211
Malayan Banking Berhad 215
Manutan International S.A. 219
Marchex, Inc. 222
Memry Corporation 225
Michigan Sporting Goods Distributors, Inc. . . . 228
The Monarch Cement Company 231
Natural Ovens Bakery, Inc. 234
New York Health Care, Inc. 237
Nigerian National Petroleum Corporation. . . . 240
Nippon Yusen Kabushiki Kaisha (NYK) 244
NOF Corporation 249
NSF International. 252

Orion Oyj. 256
Orthofix International NV 260
Pall Corporation. 263
Parque Arauco S.A. 267
Perfetti Van Melle S.p.A. 270
Pernod Ricard S.A. 274
Petrobras Energia Participaciones S.A. 278
PMP Ltd. 282
Pure World, Inc. 285
PZ Cussons plc 288
R.C. Willey Home Furnishings 291
Ratner Companies 294
Renal Care Group, Inc. 297
Ryoshoku Ltd. 300
Schreiber Foods, Inc. 303
Schwebel Baking Company. 307
Screen Actors Guild. 310
Seiko Corporation 314
Sekisui Chemical Co., Ltd. 319

Shearer's Foods, Inc. 323
Shoe Carnival Inc. 326
SNC-Lavalin Group Inc. 330
Spinnaker Exploration Company. 334
Stein Mart Inc. 337
Stoddard International plc 340
Taco Cabana, Inc. 344
Tiger Aspect Productions Ltd. 348
Turkish Airlines Inc.
        (Türk Hava Yollari A.O.) 351
UAW (International Union, United
        Automobile, Aerospace and Agricultural
        Implement Workers of America). 354
Utz Quality Foods, Inc. 358
Velcro Industries N.V. 361
ViewSonic Corporation 365
Walter Industries, Inc. 368
Wirtz Corporation 374
ZiLOG, Inc. 377

Index to Companies 381
Index to Industries 561
Geographic Index 607
Notes on Contributors. 649

PREFACE

The St. James Press series *The International Directory of Company Histories (IDCH)* is intended for reference use by students, business people, librarians, historians, economists, investors, job candidates, and others who seek to learn more about the historical development of the world's most important companies. To date, *IDCH* has covered over 7,500 companies in 72 volumes.

Inclusion Criteria

Most companies chosen for inclusion in *IDCH* have achieved a minimum of US$25 million in annual sales and are leading influences in their industries or geographical locations. Companies may be publicly held, private, or nonprofit. State-owned companies that are important in their industries and that may operate much like public or private companies also are included. Wholly owned subsidiaries and divisions are profiled if they meet the requirements for inclusion. Entries on companies that have had major changes since they were last profiled may be selected for updating.

The *IDCH* series highlights 10% private and nonprofit companies, and features updated entries on approximately 50 companies per volume.

Entry Format

Each entry begins with the company's legal name, the address of its headquarters, its telephone, toll-free, and fax numbers, and its web site. A statement of public, private, state, or parent ownership follows. A company with a legal name in both English and the language of its headquarters country is listed by the English name, with the native-language name in parentheses.

The company's founding or earliest incorporation date, the number of employees, and the most recent available sales figures follow. Sales figures are given in local currencies with equivalents in U.S. dollars. For some private companies, sales figures are estimates and indicated by the abbreviation *est.* The entry lists the exchanges on which a company's stock is traded and its ticker symbol, as well as the company's NAIC codes.

Entries generally contain a *Company Perspectives* box which provides a short summary of the company's mission, goals, and ideals, a *Key Dates* box highlighting milestones in the company's history, lists of *Principal Subsidiaries, Principal Divisions, Principal Operating Units, Principal Competitors,* and articles for *Further Reading.*

American spelling is used throughout *IDCH*, and the word "billion" is used in its U.S. sense of one thousand million.

Sources

Entries have been compiled from publicly accessible sources both in print and on the Internet such as general and academic periodicals, books, annual reports, and material supplied by the companies themselves.

Cumulative Indexes

IDCH contains three indexes: the **Index to Companies**, which provides an alphabetical index to companies discussed in the text as well as to companies profiled, the **Index to Industries**, which allows researchers to locate companies by their principal industry, and the **Geographic Index**, which lists companies alphabetically by the country of their headquarters. The indexes are cumulative and specific instructions for using them are found immediately preceding each index.

Suggestions Welcome

Comments and suggestions from users of *IDCH* on any aspect of the product as well as suggestions for companies to be included or updated are cordially invited. Please write:

The Editor
International Directory of Company Histories
St. James Press
27500 Drake Rd.
Farmington Hills, Michigan 48331-3535

AB	Aktiebolag (Finland, Sweden)
AB Oy	Aktiebolag Osakeyhtiot (Finland)
A.E.	Anonimos Eteria (Greece)
AG	Aktiengesellschaft (Austria, Germany, Switzerland, Liechtenstein)
A.O.	Anonim Ortaklari/Ortakligi (Turkey)
ApS	Amparteselskab (Denmark)
A.Š.	Anonim Širketi (Turkey)
A/S	Aksjeselskap (Norway); Aktieselskab (Denmark, Sweden)
Ay	Avoinyhtio (Finland)
B.A.	Buttengewone Aansprakeiijkheid (The Netherlands)
Bhd.	Berhad (Malaysia, Brunei)
B.V.	Besloten Vennootschap (Belgium, The Netherlands)
C.A.	Compania Anonima (Ecuador, Venezuela)
C. de R.L.	Compania de Responsabilidad Limitada (Spain)
Co.	Company
Corp.	Corporation
CRL	Companhia a Responsabilidao Limitida (Portugal, Spain)
C.V.	Commanditaire Vennootschap (The Netherlands, Belgium)
G.I.E.	Groupement d'Interet Economique (France)
GmbH	Gesellschaft mit beschraenkter Haftung (Austria, Germany, Switzerland)
Inc.	Incorporated (United States, Canada)
I/S	Interessentselskab (Denmark); Interesentselskap (Norway)
KG/KGaA	Kommanditgesellschaft/Kommanditgesellschaft auf Aktien (Austria, Germany, Switzerland)
KK	Kabushiki Kaisha (Japan)
K/S	Kommanditselskab (Denmark); Kommandittselskap (Norway)
Lda.	Limitada (Spain)
L.L.C.	Limited Liability Company (United States)
Ltd.	Limited (Various)
Ltda.	Limitada (Brazil, Portugal)
Ltee.	Limitee (Canada, France)
mbH	mit beschraenkter Haftung (Austria, Germany)
N.V.	Naamloze Vennootschap (Belgium, The Netherlands)
OAO	Otkrytoe Aktsionernoe Obshchestve (Russia)
OOO	Obschestvo s Ogranichennoi Otvetstvennostiu (Russia)
Oy	Osakeyhtiö (Finland)
PLC	Public Limited Co. (United Kingdom, Ireland)
Pty.	Proprietary (Australia, South Africa, United Kingdom)
S.A.	Société Anonyme (Belgium, France, Greece, Luxembourg, Switzerland, Arab speaking countries); Sociedad Anónima (Latin America [except Brazil], Spain, Mexico); Sociedades Anônimas (Brazil, Portugal)
SAA	Societe Anonyme Arabienne
S.A.R.L.	Sociedade Anonima de Responsabilidade Limitada (Brazil, Portugal); Société à Responsabilité Limitée (France, Belgium, Luxembourg)
S.A.S.	Societá in Accomandita Semplice (Italy); Societe Anonyme Syrienne (Arab speaking countries)
Sdn. Bhd.	Sendirian Berhad (Malaysia)
S.p.A.	Società per Azioni (Italy)
Sp. z.o.o.	Spólka z ograniczona odpowiedzialnoscia (Poland)
S.R.L.	Società a Responsabilità Limitata (Italy); Sociedad de Responsabilidad Limitada (Spain, Mexico, Latin America [except Brazil])
S.R.O.	Spolecnost s Rucenim Omezenym (Czechoslovakia
Ste.	Societe (France, Belgium, Luxembourg, Switzerland)
VAG	Verein der Arbeitgeber (Austria, Germany)
YK	Yugen Kaisha (Japan)
ZAO	Zakrytoe Aktsionernoe Obshchestve (Russia)

$	United States dollar	ISK	Icelandic krona
£	United Kingdom pound	ITL	Italian lira
¥	Japanese yen	JMD	Jamaican dollar
AED	Emirati dirham	KPW	North Korean won
ARS	Argentine peso	KRW	South Korean won
ATS	Austrian shilling	KWD	Kuwaiti dinar
AUD	Australian dollar	LUF	Luxembourg franc
BEF	Belgian franc	MUR	Mauritian rupee
BHD	Bahraini dinar	MXN	Mexican peso
BRL	Brazilian real	MYR	Malaysian ringgit
CAD	Canadian dollar	NGN	Nigerian naira
CHF	Swiss franc	NLG	Netherlands guilder
CLP	Chilean peso	NOK	Norwegian krone
CNY	Chinese yuan	NZD	New Zealand dollar
COP	Colombian peso	OMR	Omani rial
CZK	Czech koruna	PHP	Philippine peso
DEM	German deutsche mark	PKR	Pakistani rupee
DKK	Danish krone	PLN	Polish zloty
DZD	Algerian dinar	PTE	Portuguese escudo
EEK	Estonian Kroon	RMB	Chinese renminbi
EGP	Egyptian pound	RUB	Russian ruble
ESP	Spanish peseta	SAR	Saudi riyal
EUR	euro	SEK	Swedish krona
FIM	Finnish markka	SGD	Singapore dollar
FRF	French franc	THB	Thai baht
GRD	Greek drachma	TND	Tunisian dinar
HKD	Hong Kong dollar	TRL	Turkish lira
HUF	Hungarian forint	TWD	new Taiwan dollar
IDR	Indonesian rupiah	VEB	Venezuelan bolivar
IEP	Irish pound	VND	Vietnamese dong
ILS	new Israeli shekel	ZAR	South African rand
INR	Indian rupee	ZMK	Zambian kwacha

International Directory of

COMPANY
HISTORIES

Adolfo Dominguez S.A.

Pol Ind San Cibrao das Vinas, Ru
San Cibrao das Vinas
E-32901
Spain
Telephone: +34 988 39 87 05
Fax: +34 988 24 67 61
Web site: http://www.adolfo-dominguez.com

Public Company
Incorporated: 1952
Employees: 1,111
Sales: EUR 130.07 million ($176 million) (2004)
Stock Exchanges: Madrid
Ticker Symbol: ADZ
NAIC: 448120 Women's Clothing Stores; 315220 Men's
    and Boys' Cut and Sew Apparel Manufacturing;
    315230 Women's and Girls' Cut and Sew Apparel
    Manufacturing; 442299 All Other Home Furnishings
    Stores; 448110 Men's Clothing Stores; 448150
    Clothing Accessories Stores

Adolfo Dominguez S.A. is one of Spain's leading and most well-known fashion groups. The Oreste-region company designs and produces a full range of clothing for men's, women's, and youth segments. The company markets its clothing under the AD and Linea U brands, among others. In addition to producing clothing, Adolfo Dominguez also produces a range of accessory items and footwear, much of which is developed under license by third parties. Similarly, the company has its own line of perfumes to support its major labels, developed and produced by fragrance specialist Myrurgia. Adolfo Dominguez is a vertically integrated company, a position that has enabled the company to produce high-quality, fashion-oriented clothing at attractive price points. The company's vertical integration extends into the retail sector. Since the early 1980s, the company has built up a strong, internationally operating retail network of more than 300 stores. Of this total, 142 stores are company owned, with the remaining stores operated as franchises. Spain remains the company's biggest market, where it operates 93 company-owned stores and 137 franchise locations. Europe is the company's largest region, with 32 company-owned stores, and most of the group's 23 foreign franchised stores. France is the group's primary international market, but the company also has a presence in Germany and the Benelux markets, and elsewhere. Founded in the 1950s as a small tailor's shop, the company remains under the control of the Dominguez family, including longtime Chairman and CEO Adolfo Dominguez, the founder's son. The Dominguez family retains a controlling stake in the company, which was listed on the Madrid Stock Exchange in 1997. In 2004, the company posted total sales of EUR 130 million.

Expanding the Family Store in the 1970s

Adolfo Dominguez, Sr., opened a tailor's shop in Orense, Spain in the early 1950s, and remained a small, family-owned affair into the 1970s. By then, the elder Dominguez established a strong reputation in the Orense region for the quality of his men's suits.

Yet, the death of Adolfo Dominguez, Sr., in the mid-1970s placed the family-owned business at a crossroads. Dominquez's eldest son Adolfo Dominguez Fernandes had until then exhibited more interest for cinema and literature than for clothing, and had gone on to study filmmaking, and spent time in London. Yet, after his father's death, Dominguez returned to Orense and took over the business. As Dominguez told the *Daily News Record:* "I didn't have a special vocation to be a designer. I loved literature, art and cinema, but I realized that you had to do something in order to live, so I decided to become an entrepreneur."

Dominguez decided to extend the company's business beyond just tailoring. In 1976, Dominguez established a new clothing business, Adolfo Dominguez, specializing in high-end, although somewhat classically styled, men's clothing designs. Dominguez, then just 25, was joined by wife Elena, who became an important part of the young company's design team.

Dominguez's production at first targeted Spain's multi-brand retailers. The company sold its clothing through third-party commercial agents who brought its designs to the country's stores, and its shoppers. Into the 1980s, the company began to acquire a

Key Dates:

1950: Adolfo Dominguez, Sr., founds a tailor shop in Orense, Spain.

1976: Adolfo Dominguez, Jr., takes over the business and launches a men's designer clothing label.

1982: The company opens its first two retail stores, in Madrid and Barcelona.

1985: The company opens its first international store in Paris.

1986: A franchising agreement is reached with Taka-Q in Japan; a women's clothing line is launched.

1991: After fire destroys the factory, the company launches new production techniques and a low-pricing policy.

1994: The company opens its first store in Portugal.

1995: The company launches the sportswear label, Golf.

1997: A public offering is made on the Madrid Stock Exchange; the company enters Belgium.

2001: The company launches the youth-oriented label, Linea U.

2002: The company opens a store in Miami, Florida.

2005: The company operates more than 300 company-owned and franchised stores worldwide.

name for itself among Spanish consumers, and its reputation for the high quality of its clothing grew.

At the time, the designer brand trend had not yet taken hold in Spain. Dominguez became an industry pioneer, especially in his willingness to use advertising to establish the brand. In 1982, the company launched a highly successful advertising campaign, proclaiming that "wrinkles are beautiful." As a result, the Dominguez name became one of the most recognized names in high-end fashion in Spain.

The campaign coincided with Dominguez's launch into the retail sector. In 1982, Dominguez opened its first store in Madrid—becoming one of the first Spanish design houses to place its name on its own shop. The success of that opening, backed by the enthusiastic response to the company's advertising campaign, encouraged the company to open a second store in Barcelona by the end of that year.

Into the mid-1980s, Dominguez continued to play the role of Spanish fashion pioneer. Not content with its expanding sales in Spain, the company became determined to launch itself as an international design label. For this, the company turned toward the fashion capitals of London, Paris, and New York, opening designer showrooms in each market. The Paris store was the first to open, in 1985, followed soon after by the others. The company also began promoting its label to other retailers. In Italy, for example, the company placed its designs in more than 100 stores. The United States proved much more difficult to crack, however, and by the end of the decade, the company decided to shut its New York store.

If Dominguez's designs failed to inspire the Americans, the company had much more luck with the Japanese. In 1986, the company signed a two-year licensing agreement with Japan's Taka-Q to import the Dominguez label into that country. The agreement with Taka-Q turned into a full-scale partnership, as Taka-Q began opening the first franchised stores in Japan. In 1988, the two companies renewed their agreement, and Taka-Q added some 16 Adolfo Dominguez stores to its network.

Expanding Lines for the New Century

Dominguez had in the meantime expanded beyond its core menswear collections. In 1986, the company entered the women's fashion sector as well, releasing its first collection that year. Dominguez also began to extend the brand into a full range of accessories, including footwear, handbags, jewelry, and, in a licensing deal with Myrugia, perfumes. The company itself handled most of its accessories production, contracting out only for silks, from China.

By the early 1990s, Adolfo Dominguez had boosted its sales to more than $55 million, and its number of company-owned stores past 12, and franchised stores to 15. The company also had greatly expanded its Orense facility, adding four new factories to support its diversified production. At the same time, Dominguez expanded its labels, adding the casual look Dominguez Basico, and new line of men's clothing, Almacen Dominguez, featuring printed shirts, sweaters, and sportscoats.

Yet, disaster struck the company in 1991, when a fire destroyed its Orense headquarters. The company was forced to restructure and lay off nearly one-third of its employees. But Dominguez soon turned the disaster to its advantage. The company decided to adopt a vertically integrated structure—including taking on its own distribution, eliminating its wholesaler middlemen—and adopting just-in-time manufacturing techniques in its rebuilt factories.

Of importance, Dominguez also decided to convert the substantial cost savings gained through its restructuring into lower pricing policies for its clothing. Most of the company's clothing now could be sold for 30–40 percent less than before the restructuring, and even up to half the price. Yet the company was careful not to sacrifice its reputation for quality. These decisions helped Dominguez flourish despite the onset of a long economic recession in its core European and overseas markets.

Dominguez expanded strongly through the 1990s—by the mid-2000s, its Spanish retail network had grown to 93 company-owned stores, with nearly 140 more franchised stores. Into the mid-1990s, the company's foreign presence remained limited to its London and Paris stores. The company, with its reduced pricing in place, launched a renewed international expansion at this time, starting with the opening of its first store in Portugal in 1994. The company continued to build up its European presence, notably in France, then entered Belgium in 1997.

The company also began an expansion deeper into the Asian market, signing agreements to introduce its designs via a number of third-party retailers in Malaysia, Singapore, and Taipei. In 1997, the company attempted a return to the United States, this time through the opening of a number of in-store "corners." In the meantime, the company abandoned the Almacen Dominguez label in favor of a new casual label, Golf, launched in 1995.

Dominguez went public in 1997 in order to fuel its further expansion. The highly successful initial public offering was oversubscribed some 300 percent, and placed some 70 percent of the group's stock on the public market. Adolfo Dominguez himself kept his 30 percent stake and, together with allies, controlled a majority block of more than 50 percent of the company's stock.

This controlling block came into good stead in 2001, when rival Spanish clothing group Cortefiel launched a takeover attempt for Dominguez. In the end, however, Adolfo Dominguez and other shareholders rejected the offer, for some EUR 78 million ($72 million), as too low.

Dominguez now turned its attention to future growth. In 2001, the company launched a new youth-oriented label, Linea U, to compete with fast-growing competitor brands such as Zara, owned by Inditex, and Cortefiel. The company also continued in its attempt to add new markets, entering Argentina with its first store in the early 2000s. In 2002, the company again returned to the United States, this time opening a store in Miami. By then, the company had added operations in Mexico, China, and Luxembourg.

Like most retailers, Dominguez was hit hard by the global recession at the beginning of the 2000s. Nonetheless, the company remained one of Spain's leading fashion labels, backed by an international network of more than 300 company-owned and franchised stores. By the end of 2004, Dominguez had boosted its sales to EUR 130 million ($176 million). With Adolfo Dominguez remaining at the helm, the company set its sights on new growth in the new century.

Principal Subsidiaries

Adolfo Dominguez Arg. S.A. (Argentina); Adolfo Dominguez Belgique; Adolfo Dominguez GmbH (Germany); Adolfo Dominguez Japan Ltd.; Adolfo Dominguez Ltd. (United Kingdom); Adolfo Dominguez Lux. S.A. (Luxembourg); Adolfo Dominguez Moda Ltd. (Portugal); Adolfo Dominguez S.A.R.L. (France); Adolfo Dominguez USA Inc.; Trespass S.A. de C.V. (Mexico).

Principal Competitors

The Gap Inc.; Hennes & Mauritz AB; Benetton Group S.p.A.; Vivarte; Gruppo Coin S.p.A.; Kiabi S.A.; Inditex Industria de Diseno Textil S.A.; Somfy International S.A.; Cortefiel S.A.; Mango S.A.

Further Reading

Aguiilar, Lupita, "Adolfo Dominguez: Un intelectual en la moda," *Reforma,* June 29, 2002, p. 3.

Deeny, Godfrey, "Spanish Eyes: Adolfo Dominguez Is Looking to the Future," *Daily News Record,* October 4, 1991, p. 4.

Elkin, Mike, "Cortefiel Pulls Hostile Bid for Rival," *Daily Deal,* April 17, 2001.

Hernandez, Itxaso, "Adolfo Dominguez Introduces U for Men," *Cosmetics International,* November 21, 2003, p. 12.

Kleinman, Rebecca, and Merri Grace McLeroy, "AD from A to Z," *WWD,* March 27, 2002, p. 60S.

Toledo, Fernando, "Adolfo Dominguez: Al puro estilo gallego," *El Norte,* December 13, 2003, p. 2?.

——, "15 razones para querer a Adolfo Dominguez," *Palabra,* February 10, 2005, p. 7.

—M.L. Cohen

Altadis S.A.

Eloy Gonzalo, 10
28010 Madrid
Spain
Telephone: +34 91 360 90 00
Fax: +34 91 360 91 00
Web site: http://www.altadis.com

Public Company
Incorporated: 1926 as Service d'exploitation industrielle
    des tabacs and 1945 as Tabacalera Sociedad Anónima,
    Compañía Gestora del Monopolio de Tabacos y
    Servicios Anejos
Employees: 21,786
Sales: £6.68 billion (2003)
Stock Exchanges: Madrid Paris
Ticker Symbol: ALT
NAIC: 312221 Cigarette Manufacturing; 312229 Other
    Tobacco Product Manufacturing; 424940 Tobacco and
    Tobacco Product Merchant Wholesalers

Altadis S.A., formed from the 1999 merger of the French and Spanish state tobacco monopolies SEITA and Tabacalera, is the third largest European tobacco company and the world's largest cigar producer. It is also a major distributor of tobacco and other products in Western Europe. Tabacalera, established in the seventeenth century as the tobacco monopoly of the Spanish empire, and Seita, which was incorporated from the remains of the Bourbon kings' tobacco monopoly by Napoleon I in the nineteenth century, joined operations to protect themselves from takeover by such tobacco giants as Philip Morris and to bolster their ability to make acquisitions and expand their power in the world marketplace.

History of SEITA

Tobacco was first introduced to France in the 16th century by the French monk Andre Thevet, but it was Jean Nicot, France's ambassador to the court of Portugal, who would give his name to the plant's active ingredient in 1560. The cultivation of tobacco—in particular, a "brown" variant of the plant that would dominate French tobacco tastes until the late 20th century—soon centered in the Savoy and southern regions. Touted for its medicinal properties, tobacco was first distributed by pharmacies and was used as an ingredient in a variety of syrups, balms, and ointments, as well as a snuff; it was not long, however, before smoking became the most popular usage of tobacco. By the mid-17th century sales of tobacco had reached significant levels.

Toward the end of the 17th century tobacco began to take on a new, and lasting, role: that of a "tax collector" for the state. France's war with Holland in that century had exhausted the country's treasury. In 1674, during the reign of Louis XIV, tobacco sales were placed under control of a "tobacco farm" (Ferme des tabacs) by Jean-Baptiste Colbert, the French king's controller-general of finances. Seven years later Colbert extended the royal monopoly to the fabrication of tobacco products, particularly cigars, as well. The farm's control over tobacco and tobacco products was to last for more than a century.

Sales of tobacco remained largely nonspecialized through the 17th century. Merchants developed signs to indicate that they were selling tobacco; while signs in the shape of pipes were common, another symbol became the most popular. Called the "carotte," the symbol represented the bundle of tobacco leaves tied and twisted together that the merchants used to prepare the pipe and snuff tobaccos for their clients. At the beginning of the 18th century the first dedicated tobacconists appeared, marking a new method of tobacco distribution. The oldest of these, the Civette, opened in 1716 in Paris, was still in operation (and under the same family ownership) in the 1990s. As the trend toward tobacconist shops developed, the carotte was adopted as an official symbol and, at the beginning of the 20th century, the use of the carotte became obligatory.

Tobacco became a favorite of France's nobility. The monopoly control of tobacco and the heavy taxes imposed on its sale, however, placed tobacco beyond the reach of the country's poor—soon to enter history as the sans-culottes. Meanwhile, a lively contraband succeeded in popularizing tobacco beyond the ruling class. In 1791 the French Revolution abolished the Tobacco Farm and liberated the cultivation, fabrication, and sale of tobacco and tobacco products. Yet this freedom would not last long.

Once again, tobacco represented an important source of potential revenues for a state in dire need of funds. In 1810 Napoleon Bonaparte reestablished monopoly control over the cultivation, production, and sale of tobacco and tobacco products, setting up a state agency, the Direction des Tabacs, to govern the monopoly. At the same time, the distribution of tobacco was regulated as well, with merchants placed under direction of the tax office. These merchants, particularly bar and newsstand operators, were required to fulfill other distribution functions, such as the sale of postage and fiscal stamps. The 19th century would see a number of important developments in tobacco use in France. Pipe smoking, which had long achieved popularity in northern Europe, came into fashion in France at the beginning of the 1800s. In 1825 a new tobacco product made its appearance in France. Greeted with disdain by "serious" cigar smokers, the little cigar, or cigarette, was considered little more than a fad that would quickly fade. Under Emperor Napoleon III, a dedicated smoker, cigarettes achieved a fashionable status. The period was marked also by the arrival of the first rolling papers, which, perfumed or tinted to match the smokers' clothing, brought a new elegance to smoking.

For most of the 19th century, cigarettes were handmade by artisans. In 1860 these manufacturers, as well as manufacturers of other tobacco products, were brought under the control of a new state body, the Executive Office for State Production, formed by the French Finance Ministry. Cigarette production remained rather limited—a skilled artisan was capable of producing as much as 1,200 cigarettes per day. The Industrial Revolution soon caught up to cigarette production: in 1878 the first industrial cigarette machinery was introduced in France, with production runs of more than 3,500 cigarettes per hour. Cigarette machinery would continue to be refined; by the 1990s machines were producing cigarettes at a rate of 9,000 per minute. The greater supply and lower cost of production began the rise of cigarettes as the dominant form of tobacco product.

Although certain names in cigars had long enjoyed popularity (the Morlaix site, still in operation in the 1990s, began producing cigars under Louis XV), brand names would play an important role in building the tobacco market in the 20th century. A step in this direction had been made in the 1850s, when the first cigar bands, bearing the manufacturer's or a prominent personality's name, appeared. The rise of production volumes enabled the packaging of cigarettes, leading in turn to the first branded cigarettes. In France the government tobacco

body introduced two brands in 1910, Gitanes and Gauloises. Based on blends of brown tobacco, both would prove to have lasting appeal for the French smoker—indeed, they would become synonyms for cigarettes themselves—and achieve an international reputation. Distribution of tobacco products, through a growing network of merchants placed under separate government control, took a step forward when adoption of the "carotte" became mandatory in 1906. In France the sale of tobacco products became strictly limited to these merchants, a system common in much of southern Europe, as opposed to the northern European countries where tobacco distribution was more flexible (vending machines, supermarkets, etc.).

The modernization of the government tobacco monopoly would begin in the 1920s. To aid France's economy, devastated after the First World War, the French premier Raymond Poincaré established a new organization for managing the tobacco monopoly in 1926. Called the Service d'Exploitation industrielle des tabacs, or SEIT, the new body once again fulfilled an old function, that of reimbursing public debt. Yet the SEIT represented a first step toward eventual independence, functioning as an autonomous body.

Cigarette sales continued to rise, becoming the tobacco product of choice in the 20th century. The SEIT's flagship brands also began to develop their logos (Gitanes with its silhouette of a gypsy dancer; Gauloises with its winged helmet of a Gaul warrior) in the 1920s and 1930s. With the monopoly on the French market, including France's colonies in Africa, Southeast Asia, the Middle East, and Latin America, the SEIT had little difficulty imposing its brands. Yet even after the introduction of competing brands, Gauloises and Gitanes maintained their appeal. SEITA added the final initial to its name in 1935 when the production of matches (allumettes) was placed under its monopoly control as well.

Cigarette smoking gained in popularity and, by the end of the World War II, had become immensely popular. In 1953 SEITA launched a third brand of cigarettes, the Royale. Growing concerns over health issues related to tobacco use prompted SEITA's research and development wing to develop a method of reducing the tar levels in its cigarettes. From 35 mg per cigarette in 1953, tar levels would eventually be mandated, by the European Community, down to just 12 mg per cigarette in 1998. The formation of the European Community in the postwar years would lead to changes in the nature of SEITA as well. In 1959 SEITA's status was adjusted to that of a state-owned industrial/commercial concern (an Etablissement Public à Caractere Industriel et Commercial). The following year the European Community took the first steps in opening its internal borders, allowing the importation of cigarettes among member countries. In 1962 SEITA's employees, formerly classified as civil servants, were granted independent legal status.

While the importation of foreign cigarette brands was slowly liberalized, their distribution in France remained under the exclusive control of the network of merchants established under Napoleon I. In 1964 that monopoly system, sorely in need of modernization, was also placed under SEITA's direction. As such, SEITA found itself in a new role, that of a "tax collector" for the French state. Other changes were in store as the European countries worked toward the formation of the European

---

Key Dates:

1636: Estanco de Tabaco, the Spanish royal monopoly on tobacco, is established.

1674: The French tobacco industry is nationalized by Louis XIV.

1791: The French national tobacco monopoly is abolished during the Revolution.

1810: The French state tobacco monopoly is re-established by Napoleon.

1825: The cigarette is invented.

1887: Management of the Spanish state tobacco monopoly is leased to Arrendataria de Tabacos.

1926: Service d'Exploitation industrielle des tabacs (SEIT) is established as the government tobacco monopoly in France.

1935: Production of matches (alumettes) is added to the French tobacco monopoly, which is renamed SEITA.

1945: Tabacalera, Sociedad Anonima, Compañia Gestora del Monopolio de Tabacos y Servicios Anejos is formed, and the Spanish government assumes control of the tobacco monopoly again.

1959: SEITA's status is adjusted to that of a state-owned industrial/commercial concern.

1960: The European Economic Community (EEC) eases import strictures on cigarettes and other products among member states.

1962: SEITA employees are no longer considered civil servants.

1964: SEITA is given monopoly over tobacco distribution in France.

1970: SEITA loses monopoly on tobacco cultivation in France.

1971: Foreign cigarette brands are given free access to French market.

1972: SEITA loses monopoly on import of EEC-produced matches.

1976: SEITA loses monopoly on tobacco importation and distribution; warning labels are required on French cigarette packs; cigarette advertising is banned in France.

1986: Tabacalera is partially privatized when Spain joins the EEC. The company diversifies into food products.

1990: Nearly all forms of tobacco advertising are banned in Spain.

1994: After diversifying too quickly, Tabacalera divests most of its food brands; by 1996 the company divests all of its non-tobacco, non-distribution operations.

1995: Tabacalera buys General Cigar Company.

1995: SEITA, renamed Seita, is privatized.

1999: Seita and Tabacalera merge to form Altadis; the company buys a controlling stake in the Cuban cigar monopoly Corporación Habanos and becomes the world leader in cigar production.

2003: Altadis purchases 80 percent control of the Moroccan state tobacco monopoly.

2004: Altadis acquires Etinera, the former logistics division of the onetime Italian state tobacco monopoly.

Economic Community (EEC). In 1968 SEITA introduced its first "foreign" brand, adding the production, under license, of Pall Mall cigarettes. Two years later the common market countries took down the customs barriers among member states; at the same time, SEITA lost its monopoly on tobacco cultivation—French tobacco farmers could now sell their produce on the worldwide market. The following year, another of the EEC barriers fell, when foreign brands were granted free access to the French market. SEITA, however, conserved its monopoly on the importation and distribution of these cigarettes. Yet, in 1972, SEITA lost the monopoly on the importation of EEC-produced matches.

In 1976 SEITA lost its importation and distribution monopoly—in name, at least. In practice, the company's continued direction of the country's nearly 40,000 tobacco retailers, the largest retail network in France, meant that its competitors were still required to contract with SEITA for distribution of their products. That same year, however, held a more substantial blow to the company's marketing endeavors, when the growing strength of the anti-smoking forces succeeded in placing warning labels on cigarette packages and in instituting a ban on advertisements for cigarettes. This move came at the same time as imported cigarettes, particularly the lighter-flavored, blond "American" brands, were finding increasing acceptance among French smokers. SEITA faced a similar situation beyond its borders. While the U.S., British, and Dutch markets traditionally had favored, almost exclusively, blond tobaccos, other countries, notably West Germany, Italy, and Belgium, were also turning

more and more to blond tobacco products. By the end of the 1970s blond tobacco had captured as much as 95 percent of these markets as well. Gauloises, which had ranked as the sixth largest selling brand in the world, steadily lost market share, tumbling to 15th place by the mid-1980s.

While France and its former colonies, as well as Spain and Switzerland, continued to favor brown tobacco, the increasing popularity of blond tobacco among female smokers and, most important, among young smokers, forced SEITA to adapt. In 1979 the company began producing light versions of its brown tobacco cigarettes; the following year the company introduced, rather unsuccessfully, its own "American" cigarette, News. In that same year SEITA began producing under license the Lucky Strike brand for the French market. More successful for the company was the 1984 launch of Gauloises Blondes, which enabled the company to hold on to its market leadership in France. SEITA's de facto control over cigarette distribution in France, meanwhile, allowed it to continue to profit from its competitors' success.

By the mid-1980s, however, SEITA was bleeding. As a government-controlled organization, SEITA was criticized for its slow response to the changing marketplace. As foreign brands grew in popularity (while cigarette consumption itself began to decline), SEITA's losses would rise to some FRF 4.5 billion per year by the end of the decade. Yet the government, content to collect taxes on tobacco sales (of some FRF 30 billion in sales, some FRF 24 billion went to the state), was ill-inspired to take action. Nonetheless, SEITA slowly began to change its status. A first step was made in 1980, when SEITA was transformed from a "service" to a nationalized company as a "société nationale." In 1984 SEITA's character was again changed to that of a shareholder society, with the sole shareholder remaining the French state. This change, however, enabled the company to diversify its activities for the first time.

The company's new organization, which included a reorganization of its production capacity and the ability to lay off employees, enabled it to become profitable by the beginning of the 1990s. At the same time, the company managed to recapture much of the French market, with Gauloises Blondes becoming the second largest selling cigarette. In 1991, on post tax revenues of nearly FRF 13 billion, SEITA earned a net profit of FRF 226 million.

A significant change for the company would come in the mid-1990s. In 1993 SEITA was included in the list of national companies to be privatized, and in February 1995 SEITA (now Seita) became a privatized company, listing as a public company on the Paris stock exchange. As such, the company faced head-to-head competition with tobacco giants such as BAT Industries and Philip Morris, in a worldwide market where Seita's share was as little as one percent. Yet with its leadership position in the French market remaining stable, enhanced by its privileged position with the country's 35,000-strong retail network, Seita could begin to take steps toward international growth. In 1995 the company acquired Poland's third largest cigarette producer, ZPT Radom. In 1996 the company began expanding its exports into other Eastern European markets, including Slovakia and Slovenia. In July 1996 Seita made moves to expand into China, the world's single largest cigarette market, when it signed a technical cooperation agreement with the Chengdu cigarette factory.

After privatization, Seita's sales continued to rise, passing FRF 17 billion in 1996, for net profits of FRF 786 million. Seita continued to play the role of a tax collector for the French government, a position that came to the company's aid in 1997. With Seita facing a price war to maintain market share (as a result of a foreign brand's dumping its cigarettes on the French market), the government imposed a new tax on tobacco products in late 1997, a tax calculated against Seita's price structure. A giant at home, Seita remained a minor player on the international tobacco market in 1998. Yet with Gauloises's status as one of the world's most recognized brands, Seita maintained an attractive future, certainly to a potential suitor to the company's key French retail network.

History of Tabacalera

Tabacalera is one of the oldest companies in the world, with its roots in the period of Spanish colonization of Central and South America. Tobacco was one of many substances unknown in Europe before being discovered by the conquistadors as they pushed the new boundaries of Spanish domination south from their first settlements in Mexico during the 16th century. Regarded initially as a curiosity with supposedly medicinal properties when ground and inhaled, tobacco was used in Europe only in small quantities during the 16th century.

One of the main features of Spanish colonial expansion was the government's determination to retain tight control of the economic traffic between the colonies and Spain. Aimed mainly at ensuring a steady flow of mineral wealth from American mines, this policy limited the number of ports in the colonies that could ship goods to Spain, while also limiting the number of ports in Spain that could receive the goods. At the Spanish end, the government designated Seville as the central port for trade with the colonies, and it was controlled by the Casa de Contratacion—the hiring house for seafarers—which was established in 1504. Because of this designation, Seville became the center of tobacco imports from the Americas, and was one of the first places in Europe where the tobacco plant was cultivated. In the early 17th century, a factory for processing tobacco was built on the banks of the Guadalquivir River near Seville to cater to the growing popularity of snuff (powdered tobacco) among Sevillans.

In 1636, the Spanish government moved to ensure its control of the growing tobacco trade by establishing a monopoly over the production and sale of tobacco in the kingdoms of Castille and Leon. The government decreed that tobacco trade would be controlled by a newly formed body, the Estanco del Tabaco. Despite considerable changes to its structure and powers in the following three and a half centuries, the Estanco del Tabaco formed the foundation of what became present-day Tabacalera, S.A.

Tobacco use grew steadily during the late 17th and early 18th centuries, and in 1725 the Estanco del Tabaco decided to build a new factory in Seville to accommodate the increasing demand. Although construction began in 1728, disputes over the plans and other problems delayed completion of the new factory until 1770. Upon completion, however, the size of the new Royal Tobacco Factory of Seville, along with its proximity to the tobacco port, made it the most important tobacco manufacturing plant in the world at the time.

As popular tobacco tastes changed in the early 19th century, the Royal Tobacco Factory in Seville restructured its operations to begin producing cigars in addition to powdered snuff tobacco, which had been produced exclusively for years. The shift to cigar manufacture, brought on by changes in consumer tastes, required a highly labor-intensive process and demanded a large, cheap work force to hand-roll the tobacco leaves. This demand was satisfied by using large numbers of women in the factory, marking one of the first instances of women's large-scale involvement in Spanish industry. This provided the inspiration for the main character in Merimee's novella *Carmen*, which in turn inspired Bizet's opera of the same name.

The demand created by the emergence of cigars as a popular form of tobacco prompted the Estanco del Tabaco to invest heavily in expanding its production capacity during the 19th century. With a second factory already established at Cadiz, the Estanco opened nine more new factories throughout Spain during the 19th century, creating one of the country's biggest and most productive industrial enterprises.

In the mid-19th century, the Spanish government began looking for ways to change the managerial structure of the company. It wished to take advantage of the more sophisticated economic environment, in which direct state control appeared outdated and seemed to hamper delivery of the highest possible profit to the state. Beginning in 1844, various proposals were put forward until finally the operations were placed under the control of a strictly corporate entity in 1887. At that time, the state transferred its monopoly to the central bank, the Bank of Spain, which formed a company called the Compañia Arrendataria de Tabacos. This company leased the management of the monopoly from the bank. The new corporate structure was aimed at achieving the greatest efficiency from the operation by distancing it from the government, while at the same time ensuring the continued supply of revenue to the state from the tobacco operations.

The leasing company controlled the tobacco monopoly for the next 60 years, throughout the tumultuous Spanish Civil War of the 1930s and the final victory of the fascists in 1938. When the contract between the company and the bank came up for its regular review in the early 1940s, the government changed the legal structure of the company once again, opting this time to turn it into a company wholly owned by the state. Thus, in March of 1945 a limited company was formed: Tabacalera, Sociedad Anonima, Compañia Gestora del Monopolio de Tabacos y Servicios Anejos was formed. This change set in place the corporate structure that the company retains today.

After three-and-a-half centuries of operating in the comfortable environment of a state-enforced monopoly, Tabacalera was presented with one of its greatest challenges in January 1986, when Spain opted to join the European Economic Community (EEC). As part of the requirements for joining the community, the Spanish government was obliged to relinquish its monopoly of tobacco production and sales. This process involved the partial privatization of Tabacalera, S.A. The state transferred all of its assets and acquired rights in the tobacco monopoly to Tabacalera, in exchange for shares issued by the company that left the state with a 53 percent controlling stake of the company's capital.

Under the new laws of the EEC, Spain's wholesale import and tobacco trading activities were liberalized, giving anybody the right to carry out these activities, but under strict guidelines. Although Tabacalera continued to manage the Spanish monopoly for tobacco products manufactured outside the EEC, and although the state retained control of the retail sales monopoly through its concessionaires, the breaking of the local production monopoly struck at the heart of Tabacalera's operations. This fundamental change, coupled with the upcoming single European market, made it clear that the company had to do more than simply continue making and selling tobacco products if it was to survive. The urgency of change was made even more pressing by signs that tobacco sales could no longer be counted on to rise due to heightened anti-smoking sentiment worldwide.

In 1987, under the presidency of Candido Velazquez Gaztelu, Tabacalera launched a wide-ranging diversification plan aimed at ensuring the company's future in the less secure post-monopoly commercial environment. Velazquez pushed the company into two new areas—food manufacturing and retail distribution—on the basis that these two sectors were best suited to Tabacalera's existing operational structure.

Tabacalera took its first tentative step into the food industry in 1986 by setting up a snack foods operation, Nabisco Brands España y Portugal, as a joint venture with RJR Nabisco. Two years later, Tabacalera actually purchased the company when Kohlberg Kravis Roberts took over RJR Nabisco. In the same time period, Tabacalera bought a group of companies controlled by the Spanish food group Instituto Nacional de Industria. These companies gave Tabacalera access to a wide range of food markets, such as Spain's leading milk concentrate and liquid milk producer, Lactaria Española (LESA); meat and preserves company Carnes y Conservas Españolas S.A. (CARCESA); deep-frozen foods producer Frioalimentos (FRIDARAGO); and Congelados Ibericos S.A. (COISA). Tabacalera also bought a controlling share in a pulses company, Comercial Industrial Fernandez (COIFER S.A.), and a stake in a marine cultivation company, called Acuicultura. Tabacalera also made a strong move into retail distribution, purchasing 75 percent of retailing business Distribuciones Reus S.A. (DIRSA), a company with 325 supermarkets and over 500 franchised shops. DIRSA was also the owner of another company with a chain of more than 100 supermarkets.

The diversification program made Tabacalera one of Spain's leading producers of items such as biscuits, powdered and concentrated desserts, and milk packaging, while it also gave the company a leading position in the tomato sauces, pulps, conserves, juices, and pulses markets and control of one of the largest networks of retail outlets in Spain.

Unfortunately, rather than assure Tabacalera a secure hold on a broader range of operations, the swiftness of the diversification program brought with it a number of serious problems. Namely, in the rush to acquire new businesses, the company had bought a number of operations which were heavy loss-makers. Tabacalera planned to use the economies of scale provided by such a large group to turn the troubled subsidiaries around, but after two years it became clear that the worst of them were largely unsalvageable and would only hamper the group's efforts to become more flexible.

Therefore, Velazquez's successor as chairman, Miguel Angel del Valle Inclan, took office in 1989 and began a process of rationalizing the group's food and distribution activities. He described Velazquez's diversification program as "too ambitious," as reported by *Reuters News Service* on June 21, 1990. The new aim was to keep only the profitable food subsidiaries, divest the rest, and acquire businesses in other sectors so that the company's revenue from non-tobacco activities would match its tobacco revenue.

Accompanying these moves into different markets, Tabacalera also updated its core tobacco operations during the 1980s to account for changes in the market. Spanish smokers had begun to give up their traditional preference for black tobacco in favor of blond Virginian tobacco. By 1985, Virginian tobacco sales in Spain had already risen to 44 percent of the total tobacco sales, and were on the verge of surpassing those of black tobacco. Tabacalera responded by reorganizing its cultivation and processing operations to produce more Virginian tobacco, which provided a higher profit margin. The company took consideration of this consumption change when it began building a new factory at Cadiz in 1984, much bigger and more efficient than the company's existing plants. Furthermore, in preparation for the challenges likely to emerge due to the upcoming single European market in 1993, the company signed an agreement with Tabaqueira de Portugal in 1989 to allow cross-marketing of the two companies' brands in their respective countries. In December 1990 Tabacalera also announced a modernization plan, which would involve the termination of 1,500 jobs to produce a leaner company in time for the advent of the single market.

In 1990, Tabacalera sold the DIRSA retail chain for ESP 12 billion to the French Promodes group, after owning it for only two years. In the same year, the company sold its interest in FRIDARAGO, and gave up its management of the Tabacos de Filipinas company, which had incurred losses of ESP 1.4 billion in 1989 and 1990.

The main problem brought on by the diversification was the milk company, LESA, which continued to lose money despite Tabacalera's investment of large sums to improve it. The company provided more than ESP 8 billion to LESA in the two years following the purchase, but by 1990 the milk producer still showed a huge loss of ESP 5.2 billion. Tabacalera put LESA up for sale, and by April 1991 was holding advanced talks with the French group Union Laitiere Normande over the sale of the subsidiary. Also in 1991, Tabacalera changed the name of its Nabisco Brands subsidiaries to Royal Brands.

After cleaning out the bulk of its unprofitable food operations, Tabacalera attempted to consolidate the lucrative remaining businesses by merging the Royal Brands subsidiary with the Carcesa operation to create a more efficient food division. Under del Valle, the company also began to diversify into other areas: particularly real estate and tourism. In 1990, Tabacalera took a 33 percent stake in a joint venture to build a ESP 10 billion tourist complex in the Canary Islands. It also began to take advantage of its widespread real estate holdings by leasing them out, as well as by using its distribution network to deliver other companies' products. The most lucrative of these contracts was that of the West German company Quelle, Europe's biggest mail-order house, which chose to use Tabacalera's trucks for its Spanish deliveries.

The changes brought about by Spain joining the EEC, combined with the challenges posed by the European single market, caused the question of Tabacalera's relationship with the state to be raised once again. In August 1990, del Valle had stated his belief that the arrival of the single market was a good time to consider whether the state should continue to be the company's major shareholder. The question was sharpened when Spanish legislation was passed in 1990 banning almost all forms of tobacco advertising. Later that year, Spanish newspapers reported that Tabacalera desired a reduction in the state's stake, which would allow the company to be quoted on Spanish stock exchanges by the end of 1992.

The growing debate reached its peak in April 1991, when del Valle was forced out of office in what the *Financial Times* (April 10, 1991) described as "the climax of a political confrontation with the Finance Ministry." He was replaced by German Calvillo Urabayen, president of another government-controlled body: Fomento de Comercio Exterior. Meanwhile, many news sources were giving the impression that the Spanish government was actually considering the idea of selling a portion of its stake in Tabacalera, as well as its stakes in other large state-controlled companies, as a means of earning money to reduce the country's deficit.

By 1993, however, Tabacalera remained a company that was primarily held and controlled by the government. Rather than wait to see if a government business privatization plan would affect the company and help generate growth, Tabacalera instead focused its attention once again on continued restructuring efforts. It entered into a joint venture with RJR Nabisco Holdings Corporation in July 1993, in which each company held a 50 percent stake in the Royal Brands food operations. The deal was structured so that RJR Nabisco would have the option of purchasing the remaining 50 percent of Royal Brands in early 1994, which it did in May of that year. In selling Royal Brands off, Tabacalera signaled its renewed focus on its tobacco products and its desire to continue divesting other peripheral operations acquired in the 1980s.

The following year, Tabacalera was facing a mature market in its homeland of Spain. Although existing Spanish laws gave the company unique distribution rights which translated to a monopoly of sorts, the company knew that it needed to expand globally in order to sustain growth. Therefore, it purchased a 51 percent stake in Culbro Corporation's General Cigar Company, which gave Tabacalera an entry into the United States' cigar market, which was one of the world's largest and fastest-growing markets. The purchase helped Tabacalera position itself for future growth and distribution expansion, even in the face of the fact that Spain's government was still see-sawing on the idea of relinquishing a portion of its controlling stock in Tabacalera to the public.

By mid-1996, Tabacalera had made moves to sell off the remainder of its food businesses and focus solely on the production and distribution of tobacco, the product it began with over three centuries earlier. The company launched a new cigarette brand in France, called Montecristo, in its continued effort to expand distribution beyond the borders of Spain.

Despite the initial difficulties caused by an over-zealous diversification program a decade earlier, by the closing years of the 20th century Tabacalera appeared to have emerged in a good position to face the more competitive environment of a single European market. Its profits were healthy, its core tobacco business was reorganized to accommodate a changing market, and its expansion into other less lucrative sectors was successfully abandoned. The question of the company's future relationship with the state remained the only unresolved issue, but posed no immediate problems.

The Late 1990s Merger

In 1999, SEITA and Tabacalera announced that they would merge under the new name Altadis, which is an acronym in French and Spanish for "alliance in tobacco and distribution." The move was billed as a merger of equals, but the deal was structured as a friendly takeover of SEITA by Tabacalera. Under the acquisition agreement, SEITA shareholders received 19 Tabacalera shares and EUR 5 for every six SEITA shares, a deal that was estimated at EUR 6.7 billion ($3.3 billion). The stated goals of the merger agreement were to protect SEITA and Tabacalera from takeover, to increase turnover from EUR 692 million to EUR 1 billion by 2001, and to realize "financial synergies" that would result in a combined profit of EUR 70 million to EUR 100 million by 2003. Altadis' official headquarters were placed in Madrid, and the company's operational headquarters were situated in Paris. The chairmen of the former companies would act as co-chairs of the new conglomerate. Shareholders were less than sanguine about the deal. As one commentator wrote in *The Economist* of December 21, 2000, the merger "combines two small, fat and badly managed companies. The signs are that it will produce one large, fat and badly managed company." Both companies' stocks took a beating after the merger was announced, whereas they had been on the rise before the merger was announced due to speculation about possible takeover attempts from larger competitors.

The new company set about looking for acquisitions to secure a larger stake in the rapidly consolidating world tobacco market while trimming back on redundant and outdated operations in its home countries. On both fronts, the going proved tough. Shortly after its merger, Altadis was able to buy a 50 percent share in the Cuban state cigar monopoly, Corporación Habanos, which added leading premium cigar brands including Montecristo and Romeo y Julieta to Altadis' portfolio and vaulted the conglomerate to the lead position in the world cigar market. A 2002 bid to acquire the German tobacco company Reemstra was no match for the big money put up by U.K. competitor Imperial Tobacco, however. Altadis also lost out in the bidding for the state tobacco monopolies in Italy, where British American Tobacco won control, and Austria, which sold its tobacco business to UK competitor Gallaher. In 2003, the company scored a major coup by acquiring an 80 percent stake in the Moroccan national tobacco monopoly Régie des Tabacs Marocains (RTM) for EUR 1.29 billion ($1.51 billion) in cash outbidding both Philip Morris and British American Tobacco. The deal bought Altadis a well-managed company of tobacco farms and manufactories located on a continent where smoking was on the rise, giving it a foothold for further African acquisition attempts and market expansion. The deal angered some shareholders who believed that the company had overpaid for RTM in an attempt to compensate for its poor bidding strategy in the competition for Reemstra.

In 2002, Altadis opened a new cigarette factory in Alicante, Spain, that took over production from closed factories in Valencia, Madrid, San Sebastian, and an older plant in Alicante. In autumn 2003 a new factory in Cantabria replaced production from shuttered factories in Managa, Dijon, and Santander. Opposition from unions and workers over closure of factories—some of which were centuries old—brought protests in France and Spain in 2003. Although workers managed to win some concessions in the form of social programs intended to help displaced people find new jobs, Altadis eliminated 1,276 jobs and closed cigarette factories in Lille, France, and Tarragona, Spain; a threshing plant in Tenneins, France; and the 400-year-old cigar workshop in Seville, Spain.

The largest growing segment of Altadis' business was its logistics division, which produced 20 percent of the company's revenues. In 2004 it purchased Etinera, the logistics division of the former Italian tobacco monopoly, from British American Tobacco, strengthening its position as a distributor of sweets, stationery, magazines, and other non-tobacco merchandise in the European Union. Although Altadis' cigarette division produced 56 percent of company revenues, and its cigar division was responsible for a quarter of world cigar sales, the tobacco market worldwide was shrinking. The logistics division, known as Logista, provided a stable basis for future growth as consumers became more aware of the dangers of smoking and nations campaigned to reduce or eliminate smoking within their borders.

Principal Competitors

Altria Group Inc.; British American Tobacco plc; Japan Tobacco Inc.

Further Reading

"Altadis to Make More Closures," *World Tobacco* 196, September 2003, p. 10.

Apted, Emma, "Altadis Sees Safety in Acquisitions," *World Tobacco*, March 2001, p. 23.

Brown, Jonathan, "Altadis Extends North African Presence," *Duty-Free News International*, July 1, 2003, p. 9.

"Bullish Opening in Pamplona," *World Tobacco*, May 2002, p. 28.

Campo, Silvia, "Altadis to Benefit from Restructuring," *World Tobacco,* March 2002, p. 26.

Campo, Silvia, "One Factory Replaces Three," *World Tobacco*, July 2002, p. 35.

"Cashing in on Africa's Smokers," *Asia Africa Intelligence Wire,* June 13, 2003.

Crawford, Leslie, "The Tobacco Group where Everything Rolls out Two-by-Two," *Financial Times*, December 21, 2000, p. 28.

"Cuban Cigar Production Drops as World Demand Slumps," *Cuba News*, November 2000, p. 3.

Du Bois, Peter C., "A U.K. Analyst is Bullish on Spain," *Barron's,* July 3, 1989, p. 36.

Fitere, Anne-Laurence, "Riche, Vieille, et Jolie," *L'Expansion,* January 6, 1994, p. 82.

Fortson, Danny, "Altadis Smokes Rivals in Morocco Auction," *Daily Deal,* June 3, 2003, n.p.

Haggman, Matthew, "Cigar Giant Fights Counterfeit Smokes," *Miami Daily Business Review* 78, no. 47, August 15, 2003, p. A1.

Iskander, Samer, "Altadis to Buy Back 5% of Its Shares," *Financial Times,* December 6, 1999, p. 26.

Kaupp, Katia D., "Chique et Choc Chez S.E.I.T.A.," *Le Nouvel Observateur,* April 1984, p. 65.

"Merger between SEITA and Tabacalera Cleared," *European Report,* December 8, 1999.

Mulligan, Mark, "Altadis Profits Hit by Slower French Sales," *Financial Times,* September 1, 2004, p. 24.

Phalon, Richard, "Smoke Rings," *Forbes,* August 28, 1995, p. 92.

"Prête pour une Guerre des Prix," *La Vie Française,* May 24, 1997, p. 29.

"Rich Raise Count of Montecristos," *Sunday Business* (London), November 26, 2000, p. C7.

Ridgway, Laurence, "Altadis Shares Down on Acquisition News," *World Tobacco*, July 2003, p. 8.

Rigsby, G.G., "Job Cuts Planned in Hav-A-Tampa Merger," *Business Journal* (Tampa, Fla.), June 23, 2000, p. 3.

"RJR Nabisco Buys Full Stake in Spain's Royal Brands," *Reuter Business Report,* May 9, 1994.

Routier, Airy, "Seita: Cap sur la Distribution," *L'Expansion,* December 21, 1989, p. 70.

Schwimmer, Anne, "Spanish Issues Expected," *Pensions & Investments,* October 28, 1991, p. 38.

"Seita: Profil," *Fusions et Acquisitions,* April 1996, p. 4.

Selva, Meera, "Spanish Tobacco Firm Favourite to Gain Cigarette Maker," *Sunday Business* (London), September 22, 2002.

Simpson, David, "Gauloises: To Oxford and the Middle East," *Tobacco Control,* June 2001, p. 92.

"Smoke in Your Eyes," *Economist,* October 9, 1999, p. 83.

"Spain: A Striking Protest," *World Tobacco,* November 2003, p. 5.

"Tabac: une Taxe Speciale Seita," *Le Nouvel Observateur,* December 4, 1997, p. 92.

"Tabacalera, Selling Stakes in Food Firms, Focuses on Tobacco," *Wall Street Journal,* September 20, 1996, p. B5C.

Torres Mulas, R. & D. Hortas, *Tabacalera: 350 Años Despues,* Madrid: Tabacalera, 1987.

"Ups and Downs in Euroland's Cigarettes," *Tobacco Europe,* March-April 2002, p. 6.

Welling, Kathryn M., "Ahead of the Herd," *Barron's,* February 13, 1995, p. 22.

Wherry, Rob, "Merger Mentality," *Forbes Global,* April 14, 2003, p. 946.

White, David, "Tobacco Partners in Cuban Cigar Deal," *Financial Times,* December 10, 1999, p. 29.

—M.L. Cohen; Richard Brass
—updates: Laura E. Whiteley; Jennifer Gariepy

THE AUSTIN COMPANY

The Austin Company

6095 Parkland Boulevard
Cleveland, Ohio 44124
U.S.A.
Telephone: (440) 544-2600
Fax: (440) 544-2684
Web site: http://www.theaustin.com

Private Company
Incorporated: 1904 as The Samuel Austin & Son Company
Employees: 2,100
Sales: $2.23 billion (1992)
NAIC: 54131 Architectural Services; 54133 Engineering
    Services

From roots extending back well into the 19th century, The Austin Company grew into one of the largest and most sophisticated design, engineering, and construction companies in the world. With 40 offices in ten countries on five continents, including eight regional operating units in the United States, the Cleveland-based company boasts a history of world records for building size and technological innovation. Austin's triumphs include the design, engineering, and construction of the industrial facilities that broke world records for size, including the Boeing Company's manufacturing and assembly complex in Everett, Washington. In 1992–93, Austin constructed the Asia and Pacific Trade Center in Osaka, Japan, one of the world's largest international exhibition facilities.

19th-Century Origins

The Austin story began with a young English carpenter who came to America in 1872 to find work rebuilding Chicago after that city's great fire. The carpenter, Samuel Austin, never made it to Chicago. When he arrived in the United States, he chose to work in Cleveland, building residences with a contractor and, over the course of the next six years, building a reputation for solid workmanship. He then set off to carry on his work alone, meeting with enough success to build a shop for his business in 1880.

A contract to construct a new savings bank building in 1889 marked Samuel Austin's debut into commercial work. Industry executives who banked in the new Broadway Savings Bank admired Austin's work and soon offered him work to construct their factories. In 1895 Austin won the contract to build Cleveland's first electric lamp factory; a series of contracts from the National Electric Lamp Association soon followed. Also in 1895, when the Western Mineral Wool Company decided to branch out and begin production in Chicago, it called on Samuel Austin to build their factory. The Western Mineral Wool contract represented Austin's first work outside of Cleveland. Ironically, the work was in the same location—Chicago—that he had originally intended to reach after emigrating to America 23 years earlier.

When Samuel Austin's son, Wilbert J. Austin, graduated from the Case School of Applied Sciences (now part of Case Western Reserve University) in 1904 with a degree in engineering, the father and son established The Samuel Austin & Son Company. Wilbert Austin brought to the business the innovative concept of combining full-service engineering and construction into one operation. This approach came to be known as "The Austin Method" and would distinguish the firm throughout the United States and eventually around the world.

The Austin Method transformed the traditional process of contracting by including in one contract the responsibility for the architecture, engineering, and construction of an entire project. By integrating these three services into one process, the Austin Method enabled the contractor to complete the project more quickly, thus saving the client both time and money. Armed with the prototype concept of an integrated engineering and construction contract, Samuel Austin & Son began its long history of firsts that carried the company to national and international prominence.

In 1907 Samuel Austin & Son built the first reinforced concrete structure in Cleveland for the H. Black Company. The building initially housed the region's largest women's clothing factory, the Wooltex Cloak Company, then served as offices for a series of tenants, including Tower Press, Inc., a printing company. (The Black Company building, located on Superior Avenue, was designated a Cleveland landmark in 1963.)

In 1911 Samuel Austin & Son engineered and constructed the first campus-type, industrial research facility for the Na-

Company Perspectives:

The Austin Company is committed to world leadership as a premier complete-service architecture, engineering and construction firm. Through service, technology, growth and enterprise, The Austin Company will continue to set the highest standards in the industry for quality, service, professionalism and innovation.

tional Electric Lamp Association. This facility is now known as Nela Park, General Electric's principal research complex, located in suburban East Cleveland. A contract for the design and construction of another large lamp manufacturing plant about one mile away accompanied the contract for the research complex. Since these two contracts were the two largest that Samuel Austin & Son had worked on to date, the Company moved its offices closer to the sites, specifically to Euclid and Noble Roads, where the company's headquarters remained until 1960.

Incorporation and Growing the Business in the Early 1900s

While applying their new design and construction methodology on these two projects, the Austins developed a keener awareness of the economic problems of planning new industrial plants. In 1916, then, Austin & Son introduced standard building designs for the quick delivery of prefabricated packaged industrial building concepts. Refining and standardizing the Austin Method, the company enjoyed successes in factories of all types in New England, the Midwest, and the West Coast. Samuel Austin & Son was incorporated as The Austin Company in 1916, which soon opened district offices across the country to handle scores of new contracts. The Austin Company had gained a national reputation.

With its stature established, Austin strove over the succeeding decades to become one of the nation's leading architectural, engineering, and construction organizations. To that end, Austin branched into design and construction services for a variety of different industries, researched and developed cutting-edge engineering and construction concepts, and continually innovated new kinds of building concepts.

One of the earliest and longest-running lines of business that Austin diversified into was the defense industry. Many of the plants that had been designed and built earlier by Austin were producing arms for the Allies during World War I. When the United States entered the war in 1917, an enormous demand emerged virtually overnight for additional war materiel. Manufacturers immediately turned to Austin for new facilities.

The Austin Company's involvement in these and other industries remained constant across the decades, continuing on beyond the lives of its founders. By the end of 1940, both Samuel Austin and Wilbert J. Austin had died. Under the leadership of the new president, George A. Bryant, however, Austin continued its work in war plants as well as other, non-defense, industries. During World War II, according to The Austin Story, Austin designed and constructed crucial facilities for the war, including "mammoth aircraft production plants, military airports, air force

training stations and naval facilities" for the U.S. government and "a variety of industrial defense plants" for private industry. Austin also constructed chemical-processing plants for the defense industry during the war. Austin's work for the government in its war efforts resumed in the early 1990s.

As innovators in the design and construction of automated distribution centers for use by the retail-merchandising and manufacturing industries, Austin in 1990 developed the U.S. Army's Eastern Distribution Center in New Cumberland, Pennsylvania. That 1.6-million-square-foot facility was designed to deliver supplies to military installations in the United States, Europe, and the Middle East. It fulfilled crucial logistical functions during the Persian Gulf War in 1991.

Austin's contribution to U.S. defense efforts was largely the result of its success, based on technological developments, in a host of civilian industries. The fields of industry in which Austin achieved leadership in facilities design and construction were few, but important. The company expanded into a limited number of industries, such as aviation, broadcasting, food processing, newspaper publishing, and pharmaceutical manufacturing. At the same time, Austin developed expertise in operations centers, research and development centers, automated distribution centers, computer-controlled manufacturing and processing plants, and "intelligent" office buildings.

Austin's work in aviation stemmed from government contracts garnered during World War I, when Austin built aviation support facilities at many of the nation's airports. Following the war, Austin continued its work in aviation. In the late 1920s, Austin designed and constructed hangars, maintenance facilities, and administration and terminal buildings, including those for the Cleveland Municipal Airport (now Cleveland Hopkins International Airport). Under the direction of Wilbert Austin, who had succeeded his father as company president in 1925 when Samuel Austin became chairman, the company perfected the original canopy door for wide-span hangars. Austin's new hangar design became the prototype for many succeeding hangar-door designs.

Moreover, an enduring business relationship with the Boeing Company, begun in the mid-1920s, led to a world record in building size in the early 1990s. Austin began constructing facilities for the Boeing Company in 1924; during 1966–67, Austin designed and constructed a 2.2-million-square-foot facility to assemble the 747 jumbo jet. In 1991 Austin was awarded a contract from Boeing to expand that Everett, Washington, manufacturing plant for the production of the new 777 aircraft; with the addition of 1.7 million square-feet in mid-1993, the plant became the largest-volume industrial structure in the world.

This building was not Austin's first record-breaker, however. In 1927 the company erected what was then the world's largest building, a manufacturing plant for the Oakland Motor Car Company in Pontiac, Michigan. Austin continued its work in the automotive industry since that time. In 1930 a historically significant international contract called for a $60 million integrated automobile manufacturing complex and workers' city located in the former Soviet town of Gorki (now known as Nizhny Novgorod, Russia). The project incorporated infrastructure to accommodate 50,000 people.

Key Dates

1904: Austin incorporates with his son Wilbert as Samuel Austin & Son Company.

1907: Austin builds the first prestressed concrete building in Cleveland.

1911: Austin designs and builds the first campus-type industrial research facility in the world.

1918: Austin builds the world's largest manufacturing facility for Curtiss Aeroplane and Motor Company.

1927: The world's largest building, a factory for the Oakland Motor Car Company of Pontiac, Michigan, is built by Austin.

1928: The company constructs the world's first commercial building with an all-welded structural steel frame.

1929: The first "controlled conditions" building in the world is designed and built by Austin.

1936: Samuel Austin dies.

1940: Wilbert J. Austin dies in a plane crash.

1950s: Company develops specialty practices for television studios and newspaper production plants.

1967: Austin completes Boeing's 2.2 million square foot 747 jumbo jet assembly plant.

1984: Austin is bought by National Gypsum Company.

1990: National Gypsum files for bankruptcy in the wake of asbestos-related damage suits.

1993: Ownership of Austin is turned over to a trust that pays damages to asbestos claimants. The company posts a loss for the year.

1995: Austin is sold back to National Gypsum.

1997: Austin's management buys the company from National Gypsum.

In addition to the automobile industry, Austin distinguished itself in design and construction for the communications industry. The company designed Hollywood's first sound stages and film studios in the 1920s, NBC's famous Radio City of the West in Hollywood in 1938, and 50 of the first 75 local television stations that went on the air across the country after World War II.

Postwar Era

Austin's experience in newspaper publishing dated back to 1921, when it created the Warren Tribune's newspaper production plant. *The Austin Story* recounts that in 1959, the newspaper publishing trade journal, Editor & Publisher credited one of Austin's creations as "probably the most efficiently laid out plant ever constructed for a major newspaper in the United States." Austin's client list included more than 100 of the country's leading dailies, including The Austin Company's hometown newspaper, the *Cleveland Plain Dealer*.

Austin's expertise in engineering cutting-edge buildings manifested itself also in operations centers and research and development centers. While Austin designed computer operating centers for public utilities and airlines, its most significant computer facilities have been sophisticated computer data processing centers for institutions of finance. Notable earlier experience in this area accrued to Austin as a result of its design and construction of the largest computer center in Ohio during the mid-1960s, a six-story facility completed in 1964 for Cleveland Trust, subsequently absorbed into Society Corporation. More recently, Austin designed and constructed a 180,000-square-foot computer center in Cleveland in 1991 for Society Corporation, parent of Society National Bank. This center processed all of the bank's collections of data.

Advanced research centers represent a similarly complex area of building design. Austin has gained experience in such facilities through its work for clients in the industries of food, petroleum, and pharmaceuticals, among several others. In 1992 Austin completed one of the world's largest pharmaceutical research centers for the Upjohn Company, located in Kalamazoo, Michigan.

The design and construction of these complex structures, as well as the company's reputation in serving such a broad range of industries, were a direct result of Austin's long-standing practice of researching and innovating new building technologies. During the late 1920s and 1930s, construction of vast automotive and farming implements factories demanded immense tonnages of riveted steel. Austin saw an opportunity to improve the assembly of steel-framed plants, and launched experiments into steel fabrication using electric-arc welding.

In 1928 The Austin Company designed and constructed at its own expense the Upper Carnegie Building using arc welding technology developed by the Lincoln Electric Company. The Upper Carnegie was the world's first commercial building with an all-welded steel structural framework. Across the street from the Upper Carnegie, Austin constructed the prestigious Carnegie Medical Building, using similar technology, in 1931.

Austin's research achievements are diverse and numerous. 1929, for instance, marked the beginning of research that led to the design of the world's first "controlled-conditions" building, for the Simmonds Saw and Steel Company at Fitchburg, Massachusetts. This factory, from which windows were entirely eliminated, made possible the control of all internal environmental conditions—temperature, humidity, light, and sound. In the late 1930s, Austin pioneered the installation of fluorescent lighting in industrial buildings and championed the efficiency of single-story factories. When business slowed during the 1930s, Austin intensified its research and diversified its business. It established a division in 1933 devoted to the design and construction of insulated steel structures. The division eventually produced packaged, pre-fabricated, porcelain-enamel service stations for major oil corporations across the nation.

Beginning in 1980, Austin also gained considerable experience in building computer-controlled logistics facilities such as automated distribution centers. By the early 1990s, Austin had assumed a position as a leader in the design and construction of such facilities; its clientele included both the U.S. Army and the U.S. Postal Service.

Austin engineered one of the most sophisticated "intelligent" buildings in the world, the Information Systems Building for the Salt River Project public utility in Phoenix, Arizona. In an "intelligent" building, every operation and function is completely computerized, automated, and electronically controlled.

Austin has built similar facilities in other locations such as Los Angeles and Madrid, Spain, as well.

Extreme Challenges in the 1980s–90s

While The Austin Company ownership remained stable throughout most of its lifetime, in the 1980s its corporate identity began to shift. In 1984 the National Gypsum Company, a gypsum wallboard manufacturer, acquired Austin. National Gypsum underwent a leveraged buyout in 1988, after fending off take-over bids from The Wickes Cos. of Santa Monica, Drexel Burnham Lambert Inc., and Ivan F. Boesky. National Gypsum thus became a centerpiece of the largest insider trading lawsuits ever filed by the Securities and Exchange Commission against brokers and investment bankers.

National Gypsum filed for voluntary bankruptcy in 1990. Austin was not included in the bankruptcy filing, however. In March 1993 a bankruptcy court judge confirmed National Gypsum's reorganization plan, thus preparing NGC to emerge from bankruptcy. As part of the reorganization plan, a trust was established to pay the claims of thousands of plaintiffs who had sued National Gypsum and other former asbestos manufacturers for injuries allegedly derived from asbestos. The trust became the legal owner of The Austin Company's stock, as well as insurance policies intended to compensate the asbestos claimants. Austin operated independently as a private company under the trust.

The Austin Company currently has two specialized divisions, Austin Consulting and Austin Process, as well as a general contracting subsidiary, Ragnar Benson Inc. Austin Consulting provides services to clients in the area of manufacturing and logistics operations. Austin Process offers engineering and construction services for the process industries, particularly in the fields of agrichemicals, chemicals, fermentation, food processing, petrochemicals, and pharmaceuticals. Ragnar Benson, Inc., a subsidiary of Austin, provides general contracting and construction management services for clients. RBI projects include commercial buildings, facilities for public power utilities, corporate headquarters, and manufacturing plants.

Internationally, Austin maintains permanent offices in Japan, Australia, Belgium, Canada, Mexico, the Netherlands, Spain, and the United Kingdom. Associated companies operate in Argentina, Brazil, and Italy. Internationally, Austin has won six major contracts in Japan since 1990. Most recently, an Austin-Japanese consortium won the bid to construct a wing of the Asia and Pacific Trade Center at Osaka, which, after completion, will house one of the world's largest international trading facilities. Austin has maintained an office in Tokyo since 1972, and since then has gradually built credibility among major Japanese corporations and the Japanese government. Austin hopes to continue expanding its international operations while maintaining its stature in the U.S. marketplace.

Several factors intervened in this course of action. Due to a drop in construction projects, especially in Europe, Austin went through a period of downsizing. Sales dropped from $2 billion in 1990 to $365 million in 1994. In 1992 and 1993, the company reportedly posted losses. All of Austin's international subsidiaries except its U.K. company were sold off or closed down in the early 1990s, and the company refocused its efforts on the U.S. market. In 1995, the asbestos settlement trust decided to get rid of the ailing construction company by selling it back to the reorganized National Gypsum Company for $125 million—$70 million for the actual purchase of Austin and a $55 million tax-deductible donation to the trust. Austin suffered another setback in 1996 when the U.S. Department of Justice sued the company for overcharging for federal construction work. According to Jeffery Raday, vice-president of sales and marketing, the intricacies of accounting practices and federal regulations concerned in the matter led to the suit. "There was nothing intentional here," he told Mark Rollenhagen of the *Cleveland Plain Dealer*, "but because these are complex regulations and subject to a lot of interpretation, we just decided it was best to settle it." Austin agreed to pay the federal government $4 million to resolve claims of alleged padding in costs relating to employee pension funds.

Into a New Century

The dispute coincided with National Gypsum's efforts to sell off the construction company. Deals with the defense-contractor giant Raytheon, which maintained its own design, engineering, and construction business, and another unnamed buyer fell through, however, and National Gypsum decided to offer the company to its employees. In September 1997 J. William Meslop, president and CEO of Austin, and 21 other members of senior management purchased the company for an undisclosed sum, which was said to be the same price the second buyer would have paid had the earlier deal gone through. Under its new ownership, Austin upgraded its technology. During the slump years of the early 1990s, Meslop told Dan Harkins of *Ohio Business,* adding "the investment in new plants and equipment was at the lowest level in 40 years." M. Glenn Hobratschk, Austin's executive vice-president and chief financial officer, remarked to Thomas W. Gerdel of the *Cleveland Plain Dealer,* "we've invested heavily in technology, and that allows us to do resource sharing much more efficiently than we did previously. We've been able to maintain or increase our volume in recent years with a much smaller head count." Such innovations as web cameras on construction sites that provide photo updates on construction progress at 15-minute intervals have cut time and staff needed to keep projects on track. "We used to take job photos and do reviews on a monthly basis," Philip J. Todd, vice-president of Austin's Cleveland district told Gerdel. "Now it's an update on the Internet," he noted. The company's health bounced back sufficiently to allow them to construct a new headquarters in Mayfield Heights, Ohio, to replace their long-time Cleveland Heights office. Austin's award-winning large projects of the early 2000s included an aircraft paint hangar in Oklahoma City for the U.S. Air Force, an Emergency Operations Center at Los Alamos National Laboratories in New Mexico, the Boeing Rocket Center in Decatur, Alabama, and broadcast centers for WGCL-TV and WSB-TV, both in Atlanta, Georgia. As of 2005, the company reported 300 employees and a 2003 sales volume of $640 million.

Principal Subsidiaries

Ragnar Benson Inc.; The Austin Co. of U.K. Ltd.

Principal Competitors

The Haskell Company; Hensel Phelps Construction Co.; Washington Group International Inc.

Further Reading

"Austin, Designer of PD Plant, Molds City's Skyline," *Cleveland Plain Dealer,* January 5, 1992.

The Austin Story, Cleveland: Austin, May 11, 1993.

"Bankruptcy Court Judge Confirms Reorganization," *Wall Street Journal,* March 10, 1993, p. A4.

Bullard, Stan, "Austin Co. To Leave Its Longtime Home: Firm To Anchor New Mayfield Hts. Complex," *Crain's Cleveland Business,* January 11, 1999, p. 1.

——, "Raytheon May Acquire Austin Co.," *Crain's Cleveland Business,* April 8, 1996, p. 1.

The Challenge of Change, Rosemont, Ill.: Austin Consulting, 1991.

"Court Approves National Gypsum's Agreement with Trust," *PR Newswire,* May 1, 1995.

Creators of Facilities for Global Competition, Cleveland: Austin, 1993.

Facilities for Tomorrow's Global Marketplace, Cleveland: Austin, 1993.

"4 Companies Agree to Settle Asbestos Case in Maryland," *New York Times,* July 6, 1992, p. D2.

Gerdel, Thomas W., "Austin Co. Focuses on U.S.: New Management Takes over Cleveland Heights Design Firm," *Cleveland Plain Dealer,* June 10, 1997, p. 1C.

Harkins, Dan, "Bricks and Mortar," *Ohio Business,* 2003.

Holden, Ted, and Zachary Schiller, "Building a Doorway to Japan," *Business Week,* December 31, 1990, p. 50.

"Management Buys Back Company," *Building Design & Construction,* September 1997, p. 12.

"National Gypsum Agrees to Settle with NGC Settlement Trust," *PR Newswire,* March 29, 1995.

Paltrow, Scot J., "The Anatomy of 3 Alleged Insider Deals," *Los Angeles Times,* September 9, 1988, Sec. 4, p. 1.

Rollenhagen, Mark, "Austin Co. Will Pay $4 Million for Claims of Overcharging U.S.," *Cleveland Plain Dealer*, August 27, 1996, p. 5C.

—Nicholas S. Patti
—update: Jennifer Gariepy

Banca Nazionale del Lavoro SpA

Via Vittorio Veneto 119
Roma I-00187
Italy
Telephone: (+39) 06 4702139
Fax: (+39) 06 4702844539
Web site: http://www.bnl.it

Public Company
Incorporated: 1913 as Istituto di Credito per la
    Cooperazione;
Employees: 18,000
Total Assets: EUR 78.89 billion ($101 billion) (2004)
Stock Exchanges: Milan
Ticker Symbol: BNL
NAIC: 522110 Commercial Banking

Banca Nazionale del Lavoro SpA (BNL) is Italy's fifth-largest bank and one of the top 100 banks in the world with total assets of nearly EUR 80 billion ($110 billion). Formerly controlled by the Italian government, BNL is also Italy's most national bank, operating more than 700 branch offices in every region and every major provincial city in Italy. BNL offers services in commercial banking; capital market and treasury operations; asset management, through subsidiary BNL Gestioni; and credit and debit cards; as well as insurance (BNL Vita), leasing (Locafit SpA), and factoring (Ifitalia SpA). Privatized in 1998, BNL failed to complete a merger with Banca Monte dei Paschi di Siena that would have placed it at the top of Italy's banking industry. Instead, BNL has since become tabbed as a prime takeover target by foreign banks seeking entry into the Italian market. In April 2005, major shareholder Banco Bilbao Vizcaya Argentaria (BBVA) of Spain launched an effort to take full control of BNL. A merger of BNL into BBVA would then create one of Europe's first and largest cross-border banking groups, leading the way to a truly European banking market. In June 2005, however, the BBVA bid was challenged by rumors of an impending bid by Italy's Unipol Compagnia Assicuratice SpA, possibly with the backing of Deutsche Bank. BNL is listed on the Milan Stock Exchange and is led by president Luigi Abete.

Becoming a National Bank in the 1920s

Banca Nazionale del Lavoro can trace its origins to the Italian banking cooperative movement. Italian banking cooperatives, stimulated by the economic ideas of Luigi Luzzatti, among others, had begun to grow strongly amid the economic and trade reforms instituted in the early years of Italian democracy. Until then, the country's banking sector had been largely dominated by banking foundations controlled by religious entities, such as the Banca Monte dei Paschi di Siena.

In order to provide a solid foundation for the growth of Italy's new banking cooperatives and for the cooperative movement in general, Luzzatti and others called for the creation of a central organization as a coordinator of funding and loans to the cooperatives, using funds and loans from the Italian government and other sources. That body was created in 1913 under the auspices of Giovanni Giolitti as Istituto Nazionale di Credito per la Cooperazione (INCC). Arturo Osio became the INCC's first director. From the start, the INCC's focus was the national market, a feature that set it apart from the country's largely locally and at best regionally focused banks.

By the 1920s, the INCC's future was threatened by the rise of the fascists to political power. As fascist groups raided and plundered the country's workers associations and cooperatives, which were associated with communist and socialist parties, the INCC's base shrunk dramatically. The bank was finally rescued by the Italian government, which recognized the need for a bank operating on a national scale.

Toward the end of the decade, the Italian government decided to take over the INCC, still under Osio's direction, and convert it to a state-owned, publicly operating company. The banks range of operations were also expanded, adding commercial banking functions. In 1929, the INCC was formally converted to the status of a commercial bank. At that time, the bank took on its new name, Banca Nazionale del Lavoro.

Italy's banking sector plunged deeper into crisis during the 1930s and by mid-decade bordered on complete collapse. In 1936, the Italian government enacted a new Banking Law that placed the country's 24 largest banks under direct government control. Among other features, the banking reform established a separation between short-term lending on the one hand, and medium- and long-term lending on the other. The reforms also placed BNL in the privileged position of using special credit instruments, such as government-subsidized loans. In this way, BNL was able to capture a growing share of the market, and by the end of the decade represented some 5 percent of Italy's total banking market.

During this time, BNL restructured its operations, creating a number of new, more or less autonomous divisions focused on specialty operations. In this way, the bank was able to respond more directly to the market. The restructuring into business units helped pioneer the emergence of modern banking structures in the Italian banking industry overall.

Repositioning: Postwar Era through the 1990s

The Italian capitulation to the Allied forces during World War II put BNL's operations on temporary hold. In the 1950s, however, BNL came to play an important role in the reconstruction of the country. During this period, BNL was given ''special banking'' status which enabled it expand its operations beyond its traditional support of the country's cooperative movement. As such, BNL was permitted to begin lending to the country's small and mid-sized business sector, as well as to the public utilities sector. Among BNL's favorite lending targets were the country's film and tourist industries, both of which enjoyed massive international success in the 1950s and 1960s. Another initiative of the bank was its ''Green Plan,'' which provided funding to the agricultural sector in the 1950s.

BNL's growth remained steady through the 1960s. The bank played a leading role in supporting Italy's economic boom, particularly by supporting the growth of many of the country's private and publicly owned companies. By the end of the decade, BNL counted among Italy's top banks, and had also established a position for itself among the larger European banks.

In the 1970s, however, new banking reforms, including the introduction of a single treasury department in the Italian government, placed BNL under pressure. As the new treasury took over much of BNL's former core operations of lending to government agencies and government-owned companies, BNL was forced to look elsewhere to maintain its growth.

BNL then began the slow process of repositioning itself away from its legacy as a provider of funding and loan support to Italy's cooperatives and businesses. Through the 1970s and 1980s, BNL began building up new operations in the retail banking sector, before emerging as a full-fledged commercial bank in the 1990s. As part of the group's repositioning, it established an extensive network of branch offices in Italy. By the early 2000s, BNL boasted the country's most national network, with more than 700 branches covering every region and major provincial city in the country. BNL also expanded internationally during this time, notably in the Latin American countries of Brazil and Argentina.

Takeover Target in the 2000s

During the 1980s, BNL became embroiled in a series of scandals, including what some consider the greatest banking scandal of all time. BNL's problems began when it became involved in a scheme with Banco Ambrosiano, soon to collapse in 1982, to fund the secretive right-wing group Propaganda Due, linked to terrorist attacks in the 1970s.

The late 1980s then saw BNL make international headlines when it was revealed that its branch office in Atlanta, Georgia, had secretly funneled some $3 billion in loans to Iraq. The extent of the scandal was so great that it was listed in the Guinness Book of World Records. As a result, BNL was forced to shut down its Atlanta office in 1994 and generally cut back its U.S. operations.

By then, BNL had begun to move toward its privatization. In 1992, the Italian government, amid a new restructuring of the country's banking sector, converted BNL into a private corporation. The bank nonetheless remained controlled by the Italian government at more than 80 percent. Leading the newly privatized, and money-losing, bank was Mario Sarcinelli, who, as a general deputy in the late 1970s, had been among those who had initiated the investigation into the Propaganda Due scandal.

BNL's privatization itself was carried out in 1998, when the government floated the bank on the Milan Stock Exchange. The offering was highly successful and gave the bank such major shareholders as Instituto Nazionale delle Assicurazioni (INA), Banca Popolare, and, in 1999, Assicurazioni Generali, which acquired INA's stake. Another major early investor in BNL was Spain's Banco Bilbao Vizcaya Argentaria (BBVA). That bank made no secret of its ambitions to become a leader in what many observers saw as an impending wave of cross-border mergers as part of a process of creating a truly European banking industry.

In the run-up to this larger European consolidation, many of Italy's largest banks launched into a series of mergers, creating a new set of market leaders. BNL, too, sought out a partner for a merger that would enable it to maintain its status among the sector's leaders. In the early 2000s, BNL appeared certain to merge with Banca Monte dei Paschi di Siena. Yet by 2002, after the two sides were unable to reach an agreement on terms of the merger, the marriage was called off.

Instead, BBVA stepped up to announce its interest in acquiring full control of BNL. By April 2005, BBVA had tabled its offer, in a bid worth more than EUR 9 billion. Yet the offer soon appeared to have hit a roadblock when a group of BNL shareholders, the so-called ''counter-pact'' led by businessman Vito Bonsignore, declared its refusal to sell its 25 percent stake in BNL to BBVA.

Key Dates:

1913: Istituto di Credito per la Cooperazione is founded in order to provide funding for the Italian cooperative movement.

1929: The bank is taken over by the Italian government, which converts it to a corporation and changes its name to Banca Nazionale del Lavoro (BNL).

1972: BNL begins expanding its operations to include private banking services.

1992: BNL is converted to a corporation that is more than 80 percent owned by the Italian government.

1998: BNL is privatized and listed on the Milan Stock Exchange.

2002: BNL abandons merger talks with Monte Pasche di Siena.

2004: BNL completes its exit from the South American banking sector.

2005: Banco Bilbao Vizcaya Argentaria of Spain launches a takeover offer for BNL.

As the two sides searched for a compromise in order to resolve the situation, a new suitor for BNL appeared. In June 2005, industry rumors had begun to circulate that Italy's Unipol Compagnia Assicuratice SpA, possibly with the backing of Deutsche Bank, was preparing a bid for NBL. Both sides denied the rumor, however.

While waiting for the outcome of questions surrounding its future owners, BNL launched a streamlining effort in an attempt to stop its losses, which topped EUR 34 million in 2004. As part of that effort, the company exited its Latin American markets, selling off its businesses in Brazil and Argentina. BNL's focus on its domestic market made it an attractive target for foreign banks seeking entry into Italy in the mid-2000s.

Principal Subsidiaries

BNL International (Luxembourg); Hesse Newman & Co. AG (Germany); Lavoro Bank AG (Switzerland); Artigiancassa SpA; BNL Finance SpA; BNL Fondi Immobiliari Sgr; BNL Gestioni Sgr; BML International Investments S.A. (Luxembourg); BNL Multiservizi SpA; Coopercredito SpA; Ifitalia-Int.Factors Italia SpA; Lavoro Bank Overseas (Curacao); Locafit SpA; Servizio Italia SpA; BNL E–Banking SpA; BNL Partecipazioni SpA; BNL Vita SpA.

Principal Competitors

Banca Intesa SpA; Sanpaolo IMI SpA; Banca d'Italia; Banca Monte Parma SpA; Banca Mediolanaum SpA; Banca Monte dei Paschi di Siena SpA; Banca di Roma SpA; Banco Popolare di Verona e Novara.

Further Reading

Barber, Tony, and Mulligan, Mark, "Hostile Fight Looms for Spanish Bank," *Financial Times*, March 30, 2005, p. 26.

Bickerton, Ian, and Crawford, Leslie, "Foreign Banks Mean Business in Italy," *Financial Times*, March 21, 2005, p. 23.

"BNL Is Vulnerable to Takeover," *Banker*, October 2000, p. 48.

"BNL's Problems Threaten Merger Plans," *Retail Banker International*, May 28, 2002, p. 4.

"BNL Quits Brazil," *LatinFinance*, July 2004, p. 5.

Edmonson, Gail, "Will the Walls Tumble Down?" *Business Week*, April 4, 2005, p. 87.

Gumbel, Peter, "Cross-border Bank Raid," *Time International*, April 4, 2005, p. 14.

Tran, Tini, "Italian Exchange Suspends BNL Shares Ahead of Expected Takeover Bid," *America's Intelligence Wire*, March 29, 2005.

—M.L. Cohen

BEHR

Behr GmbH & Co. KG

Mauserstr. 3
D-70469 Stuttgart
Germany
Telephone: (+49) 711 896-0
Fax: (+49) 711 896-4000
Web site: http://www.behrgroup.com

Private Company
Incorporated: 1907 as Süddeutsche Kühlerfabrik Julius
   Fr. Behr
Employees: 17,000
Sales: EUR 3 billion ($3.9 billion) (2004)
NAIC: 336391 Motor Vehicle Air-Conditioning
   Manufacturing; 333415 Air-Conditioning and Warm
   Air Heating Equipment and Commercial and
   Industrial Refrigeration Equipment Manufacturing

Headquartered in Stuttgart, Germany, Behr GmbH & Co. KG (Behr Group) is a globally present original equipment manufacturer of air conditioning and engine cooling systems for passenger cars and commercial vehicles. Behr maintains 30 production plants and ten development centers all around the world. Roughly 60 percent of the group's sales are generated outside of Germany. Engine cooling is Behr's most important activity in terms of sales. According to the company, roughly every fourth vehicle manufactured in Europe is equipped with a Behr cooling system. About half of the group's revenues stem from the air conditioning division. Behr's industry division supplies cooling and air conditioning systems for buses, trains, ships, airplanes, and special vehicles as well as for machinery used in construction, agriculture, and industry. It also manufactures fuel tanks, body sections, and wheels for motorcycles. The company is majority-owned by heirs of the company founder Julius Fr. Behr.

Success in the Early 20th Century

In 1905, 33-year-old inventor Julius Fr. Behr joined Veigel and Zoller, a small workshop in Stuttgart, Germany, that manufactured radiators and tachometers for passenger cars and cake tins for pastry shops. When one of the partners, Andreas Veigel, left the partnership, Behr became a partner with Gustav Zoller and the firm was renamed Behr & Zoller. Two years later, Zoller left as well and Behr became the sole owner of the enterprise, which was then renamed Süddeutsche Kühlerfabrik Julius Fr. Behr (Southern German Radiator Factory Julius Fr. Behr). Envisioning the bright future of motorized transportation in general and of the automobile in particular, Julius Fr. Behr decided to drop the cake tin production and to concentrate on the manufacture of radiators. Not only did he have a constant drive to find new and better technical solutions, Behr also had a sense for emerging markets. Besides radiators, he soon began to develop fin systems for airplanes and added coolers for special vehicles to the company's product range in 1917. While the number of competitors in the emerging market for passenger cars quickly multiplied, Behr's strong determination to succeed kept his enterprise ahead of the competition. By 1910, Süddeutsche Kühlerfabrik (S.K.F.) had won many of the renowned early car makers as customers, including Opel, Benz, Neckarsulmer Fahrzeugwerke AG (NSU), and Saurer. Even the legendary Zeppelin airships had coolers from S.K.F. on board. Soon the enterprise outgrew the available space in its small workshop. In 1911, S.K.F. moved into a large factory building in nearby Feuerbach. Two years later, the company employed 85 workers, most of whom made radiators by hand. By 1916, the factory's workforce had doubled again. To better use production capacity, S.K.F. began to manufacture hose clamps for use in cars, airplanes, breweries, and the telegraph industry in 1914. In 1926, the company started making steel doors, an operation that ceased after about a decade.

During the first years of building his enterprise, Julius Fr. Behr applied for many patents. To stay at the cutting edge of technical developments, Julius Fr. Behr connected with renowned technical pioneers and stayed in close contact with them. Research and development became an important part of Behr's efforts to distinguish his own products from those of several dozen competitors. As early as 1907, the company leader conducted aerodynamic as well as thermodynamic tests on his radiators. Behr learned from those tests that heat dissipation was highly influenced by the design of the radiator's front side. To further explore his insights, Behr began to cooperate

Company Perspectives:

Climate control-differentiation potential in international competition. *The automotive future is climate controlled. By the year 2005, two out of three vehicles produced in Europe will be equipped with air conditioning. This obvious trend means automobile manufacturers worldwide are increasingly demanding air-conditioning systems which offer enhanced driver benefits, reduce technical and, consequently, economical expense and consistently improve environment-friendly performance. Only on this basis can the differentiation potential between climate control systems be fully utilized in the internationally competitive automobile industry and standards from top automobile ranges also be used in vehicles of lower-price categories. We are meeting this challenge as a systems integrator who sees its key competence in a consistent integral approach and methodology.* Optimum solutions today for the cooling technology of tomorrow. *The same also applies to our cooling technology which is subjected to the ever increasing demands of modern engine generations. Compact solutions in the Behr core competences of coolant, charge air, oil and exhaust gas cooling, as well as Visco fans, repeatedly prove the compatibility of top engine performance, reduced emissions and considerate use of natural resources. We save space by combining technical functions, reduce weight and fuel consumption, use recyclable materials and appropriately control thermo-management of the engine according to performance requirements. No more and no less.*

with the Aerodynamics Institute for Aircraft Craftsmanship at Dresden's Technical University, where Behr's radiators underwent even more thorough scientific testing. As a result, Behr developed more sophisticated technical solutions. For example, in 1915 Behr was awarded a patent for his standard element radiator, which consisted of standard-sized elements that could be replaced individually with new ones without having to replace the whole radiator, a technical milestone in the history of the field. Another example was Behr's pointed radiators for motor vehicles, which were not only practical but also decorative and quickly gained a considerable market in Switzerland and the Netherlands. In the early 1920s, when the domestic economy was suffering from massive currency devaluation through hyperinflation, the revenues in foreign currencies from abroad helped the company not only manage to survive these difficult times but also to pay for the construction of a brand-new administrative building. In 1926, Behr traveled to the United States, where he studied cutting-edge technologies used by major American auto makers and met with inventor Thomas Edison and entrepreneur Henry Ford. A few years later, in 1930, Julius Fr. Behr died at age 58.

Generational Change and Expansion in the 1930s

Manfred Behr, the son of Julius Fr. Behr, was 21 years old when his father died. His mother, Helene Behr, together with other family members and the support of experienced S.K.F. managers, took over her husband's business while her son finished his studies in mechanical engineering. In 1931, Manfred Behr became a member of the executive management board and

officially joined the company as technical director in 1935. Seven years later, he became the company's CEO. Manfred Behr continued to put a high emphasis on innovation and new product development, pushed diversification forward, and initiated the company's massive international expansion after World War II.

The early 1930s brought the Great Depression to Germany, resulting in numerous bankruptcies and rapidly rising unemployment. In contrast, S.K.F. invested heavily in new machinery and built a second production plant in Feuerbach. A result of Julius Fr. Behr's negotiations in the late 1920s, the company was awarded a supplier contract to deliver radiators to the Berlin plant of the Ford Motor Company. Beginning in 1930, about 90 radiators were shipped daily to Berlin. Due to the efforts of the company founder, which were continued by Manfred Behr, by the mid-1930s S.K.F. radiators and coolers could be found in most major means of transportation: passenger cars and trucks, motorcycles, locomotives, and airplanes. In the second half of the 1930s, the company enjoyed healthy growth. Within only two years, the number of S.K.F. employees grew by over 50 percent, from 615 in 1936 to 939 in 1938, while revenues in 1938 exceeded those from two years earlier by 85 percent.

As technical director Manfred Behr was the driving force behind the company's stream of innovations. The mechanical engineer followed in the footsteps of his father in terms of inventions. His 1934 dissertation "The Automatically Ventilated Cooler Installed in the Vehicle Interior" solved the problem of putting a radiator in the rear of a car instead of the front. The new radiator was first installed in the 130/170 H rear-engine vehicle developed by German automaker Daimler-Benz. Behr was also involved in development work for the first Volkswagen and a sensational new racing car developed by Auto Union, another leading German car manufacturer. During the 1930s, when the expansion of Germany's freeway system called for faster cars, S.K.F. began to set up scientific testing facilities to further improve radiator performance. Most notably, in 1937 a wind tunnel began measuring the cooling performance of S.K.F. radiators at the Stuttgart plant, one of the first of its kind in the world. It complemented the obligatory road tests and made test results more comparable because conditions could be influenced by research engineers. The testing facility was also used by car manufacturer Daimler-Benz to measure the circulation of cooling water and oil in vehicles under development.

Heating and Air-Conditioning Systems after World War II

As Germany initiated World War II in September 1939, S.K.F. became an important part of Hitler's war machine. The company supplied coolers for tanks, airplanes, and half-track vehicles, as well as charge-air coolers and heat exchangers for high-speed launches. A new development of that time was a cooler for aircraft made out of aluminum, which was manufactured in increasing numbers for Germany's air force. As more and more S.K.F. employees were drawn into the military, the company began to use forced laborers to keep production going during the war.

The years that immediately followed Germany's defeat demanded creativity and determination from the 240 remaining

---

Key Dates:

1907: Julius Fr. Behr becomes the sole owner of a radiator firm in Stuttgart.

1915: Behr receives a patent for standard element radiators.

1924: The company develops the first heavy-duty cooling aggregate for diesel locomotives.

1942: Süddeutsche Kühlerfabrik (S.K.F.) is transformed into a limited partnership.

1949: The company begins to manufacture heaters for motor vehicles.

1965: S.K.F. starts the serial production of air conditioners for passenger cars.

1969: The first subsidiaries abroad are set up in France and the United States.

1980: Dr. Heinz Breuer is the first non-family member to become CEO.

1990: The company is renamed Behr GmbH & Co. KG after Manfred Behr's death.

1993: Behr of America merges with U.S. truck cooler manufacturer McCord.

1999: The company enters two joint ventures with German automotive component supplier Hella.

2000: Two joint ventures are set up in Japan.

2003: Behr enters three joint ventures in China.

S.K.F. employees. With the production of motorized vehicles such as cars and airplanes practically non-existent and raw materials extremely hard to come by, they began to manufacture cookware and milking buckets with the last supplies of aluminum that survived the war. These goods were exchanged for coke and carbine, which they used to generate the gas necessary for repairing war-damaged radiators for the American occupation troops. Beginning in 1946, a limited number of radiators were manufactured again, and two years later the serial production of radiators for passenger cars resumed. The introduction of a new currency in 1948 marked the end of the postwar reconstruction years and the beginning of an unprecedented economic boom in Western Germany. By 1949, radiator production at S.K.F. was back at 75,000 per year. In the following decades, production capacity for radiators was constantly expanded and modernized.

The year 1949 marked a new era for S.K.F. In that year, the company entered a market that perfectly complemented the existing product range. In addition to coolers, S.K.F. began to build heaters for motorized vehicles. Manfred Behr pioneered the field with his fresh air heater that used warm water from the radiator to heat the passenger cabins of cars, truck, and buses. The 1950s also saw new developments in the radiator division. In 1951, S.K.F. issued a license to India Radiators Ltd. which consequently began to manufacture S.K.F. radiators on the subcontinent. A number of innovations were introduced by the company during the decade, including cooling units for trucks and buses with hydrostatic fans and a hydraulic fan drive equipped cooling system for diesel locomotives. In addition, the company began in the 1950s to develop air-conditioning systems, which were already widely used in the United States. In 1957, the first Hydraulic Ventilation and Air Conditioning

System (HVAC) went into serial production at S.K.F. and was built into the Mercedes-Benz 300 passenger car. In the same year, the company resumed cooler production for airplanes and built an adjustable climatic wind tunnel for testing heating and cooling systems, the first of its kind in Europe.

In the 1960s, S.K.F. began to manufacture Visco clutches and fans under license. The company refined production technologies using plastics in heaters and introduced salt-bath dip brazing of aluminum heat exchangers. New production facilities were built at several locations to keep up with the sharply growing demand during the so-called "economic miracle" years. In 1966, air conditioner and fuel heater development and production became a separate business division.

Global Systems Supplier: 1980s to the Mid-2000s

As his father did in the early days, Manfred Behr recognized the importance of international markets. Under his leadership, the German parts supplier S.K.F. took the first steps towards becoming a global systems supplier. In 1969, two foreign subsidiaries were established in major markets: one in France and one in the United States. Entering a period of liberalization of global trade, major automakers began to move production closer to markets abroad as well as to low-cost locations around the world. S.K.F. followed suit. During the 1970s, the company took over the Spanish firm Frape S.A. and acquired a share in India Radiators Ltd.

In the 1980s, S.K.F. made the transition from family to external management and underwent a number of organizational changes in the 1990s. In 1980, Dr. Heinz Breuer, who had been with the company for many years, succeeded Manfred Behr as CEO. Five years later, the son of the company founder retired from participation in day-to-day business and became the head of a newly established advisory board. In 1988, Horst Geidel, another S.K.F. manager who knew the company from the inside out, took over as CEO. After Manfred Behr's death in 1990, the company was renamed Behr GmbH & Co. KG. In the same year, all business activities besides those concerning the automobile industry were united in the new division Behr Industrietechnik (Behr Industrial Tech). After the reunification of East and West Germany, the company acquired the East German firm Fahrzeugheizungen Kirchberg GmbH, a manufacturer of heaters for motorized vehicles. Important organizational changes in the 1990s included the establishment of customer centers, teamwork models in all production areas, technology that allowed the combination of standardized modules in various ways according to customer specifications, and a "Total Quality and People Orientation" project.

During the 1990s and in the early years of the 21st century, Behr followed its customers to Asia, South America, and Eastern Europe, creating new production subsidiaries and customer centers in Brazil, Japan, the Czech Republic, Korea, and China. In addition, breaking into the North American market became the company's primary focus. In 1993, the merger of Behr America and McCord, a subsidiary of Cummins Engine Corporation and the number one producer of coolers for trucks in the United States, established the new market leader in the truck segment, Behr America. First successes in the passenger car market followed in 1998 when Behr began to supply engine cooling units for General Motors' Saturn model and for BMW's Z3. In 2002, Behr acquired Ohio-based Dayton Thermal Products from DaimlerChrysler and built a center for technical research in Troy, Michigan. Two years later, the company received DaimlerChrysler's Global Supplier Award for outstanding performance.

In the late 1990s, Behr began to enter a number of strategic alliances to further strengthen the company's capabilities in a highly competitive global market. In 1999, Behr teamed up with German vehicle lighting and accessory supplier Hella KG Hueck & Co. and set up two joint ventures, Hella-Behr Thermocontrol and Hella-Behr Vehicle Systems. In Japan, joint ventures were established with the country's number three radiator maker, Toyo, and with compressor manufacturer Sanden Corporation in 2000. In 2003 and 2004, Behr entered three joint ventures aimed at the Chinese market with Sanden Corporation and with the two Chinese manufacturers Shanghai Automotive and Dongfeng. By 2005, three-fifths of Behr's total labor force worked abroad, up from about two-fifths a decade earlier.

Although the Behr family had handed over management of the business to "outsiders," the company still carried the founder's family name. After the two great-grandsons of company founder Julius Fr. Behr sold their shares in the business in 1996, Baden-Württembergische Kapitalanlagegesellschaft (BWK), a holding company, became a minority shareholder. However, other Behr family members, including Manfred Behr's daughter, granddaughter, and nephew still owned a majority in the motor heating and cooling specialist that celebrated its 100th anniversary in 2005. Under the leadership of Dr. Markus Flik, a former MIT professor in mechanical engineering, Behr aimed at remaining an independent global player firmly based in Germany and at becoming a global performance leader in its major markets.

Principal Subsidiaries

Behr GmbH & Co. KG (Germany); Behr France S.A.R.L.; Behr Lorraine S.A.R.L. (France); Behr South Africa (Pty.); Ltd. Behr India Ltd.; Behr Thermot-tronik Korea Ltd.; Behr America, Inc. (United States); Behr Climate Systems, Inc. (United States); Behr Heat Transfer Systems, Inc. (United States); Behr Dayton Thermal Products, LLC (United States); Behr Thermot-tronik Prettl (Mexico); Frape Behr S.A. (Spain); Behr Czech s.r.o.; Behr Japan K.K.; Behr Brasil Ltda.; Behr Italia S.R.L.

Principal Competitors

Valeo Group; Visteon Corporation; Delphi Corp.; DENSO Corporation.

Further Reading

"Behr Earns GM 2004 Supplier of the Year Award," *PR Newswire*, April 25, 2005.

Behr 100, Stuttgart, Germany: Behr GmbH & Co. KG, 2005, 79 p.

Chew, Edmund, "Behr Starts Second Joint Venture in China," *Automotive News Europe*, February 23, 2004, p. 14.

"ContiTech Takes Control at Kuhner in Air Con Deal," *European Rubber Journal*, February 2000, p. 3.

Cummins, Andrew, "Tricky Weather? Behr's New Climate Tunnel Helps the Supplier Increase Its Testing Capacity," *Automotive Industries*, August 2002, p. 14.

Flik, Markus, "Behr CEO Focused on Growth in America, Asia," *Automotive News*, May 17, 2004, p. 24N.

Meiners, Jens, "Behr, SAIC Join Forces; China Venture Will Produce AC, Engine Cooling Products," *Automotive News Europe*, November 17, 2003, p. 6.

Miel, Rhoda, "Plastic Omnium Joins in on Hella-Behr JV," *Plastics News*, January 19, 2004, p. 1.

Murphy, Tom, "Front-End Module Demand Just Beginning," *Ward's Auto World*, April 1, 2005, p. 27.

Wrigley, Al, "Behr Takes Wheel, But Chrysler Seated for Long Haul," *American Metal Market*, March 18, 2002, p. 11.

—Evelyn Hauser

belk.com

Belk, Inc.

2801 West Tyvola Road
Charlotte, North Carolina 28217-4500
U.S.A.
Telephone: (704) 357-1000
Toll Free: (866) 235-5443
Fax: (704) 357-1876
Web site: http://www.belk.com

Private Company
Incorporated: 1891 as Belk Brothers Company
Employees: 17,900
Sales: $2.45 billion (2005)
NAIC: 452110 Department Stores

Belk, Inc., is the largest privately held department store chain in the United States. The company is headquartered in Charlotte in the middle of its traditional stronghold of North and South Carolina. While it has flagship stores at large malls, the company has opened many stores in smaller cities. In all, there are 225 Belk stores in 14 states.

Belk, Inc. was formed in 1998 from a network of more than 100 separate businesses that had been built up over the previous century. Still operated by descendants of the founding Belk brothers, Belk is one of the few large family-owned retail entities remaining in the United States. Though privately held, Belk, Inc. has filed earnings statements with the Securities and Exchange Commission since its 1998 restructuring because it has some public debt.

Late 19th-Century Origins

In 1888, William Henry Belk opened a small bargain store in Monroe, North Carolina. The store, New York Racket, was financed with a loan from a local widow, Belk's savings, and goods on consignment. The goods' prices were clearly marked and not negotiated with customers, an idea that was just becoming accepted in retailing. Within seven months, Belk had gone from being over $4,000 in debt to earning a $3,300 profit.

In 1891, the founder approached his brother, John Belk, to become a partner in the prospering store. Thus the Belk Broth-

ers Company was formed. A second store was opened in 1893 in Chester, South Carolina. A third opened in Union, South Carolina, in 1894, and the following year William Belk moved to Charlotte, North Carolina, to open the company's fourth store. His brother John remained to manage the Monroe store until his death in 1928. The brothers' stores were doing so well by 1895 that other merchants even began to copy its straight-talking slogans like "Cheap Goods Sell Themselves" and "The Cheapest Store on Earth."

William Belk's success resulted from some retailing ideas that were innovative for the time. In 1897, he combined the purchasing power of the four stores, plus two others in which the brothers had no financial interest, and formed a loose cooperative buying network. This allowed them to purchase goods in bulk quantity at favorable prices. All purchases and sales were cash. Belk also made extensive use of advertising. In 1899, the brothers opened a store in Greensboro, North Carolina.

Rapid Expansion Begins in the Early 20th Century

In the early 1900s, Charlotte was a boom town, expanding along with the textile industry, and was the state's largest city by 1910. That year, Belk sales approached $1 million, and a new five-story building was erected to house the Charlotte store. The company's greatest expansion followed World War I, as the southern economy received a boost. Cotton prices went up, and soldiers came home. Between 1918 and 1920, Belk stores' total sales more than doubled to $12 million a year. In 1920, Will Leggett, John Belk's nephew by marriage, opened a store with the Belks in Burlington, North Carolina. His brother, Fred Leggett, opened a store in Danville, Virginia, that same year, the Belk-Leggett. The Belk brothers often added managers' names to their own on new stores.

Boom days and postwar prosperity gave way to recession, however, and the Belks retrenched, not opening any stores between 1922 and 1925. In 1925, however, they opened three more stores and three again in 1926. In 1927, the Belks and the Leggett brothers agreed that the Leggetts would own 80 percent of the stores they opened, with Belk Brothers Company owning the remaining 20 percent. In the past, the Belks had always owned the majority of their stores. This arrangement formed the foundation of Belk's unusual organizational scheme.

Company Perspectives:

The mission of Belk is to be the leader in their markets in selling merchandise that meets customers' needs for fashion, quality, value and selection; to offer superior customer service; and to make a reasonable profit.

Reflecting the beliefs of its founders of the various Belk corporations, Belk stores want their customers to have a feeling of confidence that they will receive honest and fair treatment, that they will get full value for every dollar, and that they will be satisfied in every respect so that they will want to shop with Belk stores again. Belk stores have a responsibility to the people who make their growth and success possible. They are committed to maintaining relationships of integrity, honesty, and fairness with customers, associates, vendors, other business partners, stockholders, and with all people in every community they serve. Vision: The vision of Belk is to be dominant in selling fashion merchandise that meets customers' needs for value, quality and service.

Opportunistic Growth During the Great Depression

The years between 1910 and 1930 were prosperous for retailing. Competition, however, began to creep up on the Belks. Then the stock market crash of 1929 slowed Belk's sales growth, but its stores stayed open. Belk took advantage of other companies' misfortune by acquiring defunct stores, netting 22 stores in 1930 and 1931. In 1934, Belk opened a record 27 stores, expanding geographically into Tennessee and Georgia in the process. Charlotte was once again becoming a booming center of commerce in the South, and Belk expanded its headquarters store in that city. This location evolved into the organization's operational headquarters, consolidating purchasing, assisting with taxes and merchandise distribution, and providing other services for all affiliated stores. By 1938, Belk was doing business in 162 locations in seven states.

In response to growing competition from such national chains as JC Penney, Montgomery Ward, and Sears and Roebuck, which were thriving in larger cities, Belk stores were remodeled and expanded. Belk Stores Association had formed in the 1920s, gathering the new store managers for quarterly meetings. By the late 1930s, the group was too large to gather for meetings four times a year, so it met at annual conventions. Belk Buying Service was formally set up in 1940. World War II defense spending enhanced the economy, and, by the war's end, sales were two-and-one-half times what they had been in 1941. This helped pay off Depression debts and feed expansion. The Belks opened 25 stores in 1945 alone and achieved a net increase of more than 60 stores between the end of World War II and the close of the decade. In 1952, founder William Belk died at the age of 89. He had worked as the head of the company up until the time of his death.

Second Generation of Managers in the Postwar Era

After William Belk's death, his son Henry took his place. The founder's other sons, John and Tom, were also active in the company. Six months after his father's death, Henry opened the company's first shopping center store in Florida. This store

marked a dramatic break from Belk traditions: a New York design firm created a fancy interior, music was played, and merchandise was displayed for self-service. This contrasted sharply with the Belk stores' trademark features of spare, no-nonsense decor and an army of well-trained sales clerks. Henry opened several more stores afterward without consulting his family, and by 1955 legal disputes were brewing among family members and other shareholders. Although lawsuits were filed, they eventually were dropped. Later that year, Belk Stores Services, Inc., was established to make a formal organization out of what had long been an operating entity. The BSS board then elected John Belk as president, leaving Henry to his Florida venture, the Belk-Lindsey Company. Though BSS cut all ties with Henry's chain of department stores in November 1955, family feuding would continue throughout the next four decades. John would later advance to chairman of BSS, with Tom as president.

The Belks' private-label business was now thriving, and by 1959 it accounted for a major share of the buying office's inventory. In the late 1950s, the Belks department stores had nearly peaked in the South, with 325 stores in 16 states. In 1956, Belk acquired its only viable competitor in the region, the Efird department stores.

Modernization Program Begins in the 1960s

During the 1960s, the company had to adjust to a changing retail environment in the South. Stores that could once count on their reputations as local institutions found themselves in the midst of a highly mobile population that was attracted to the offerings of big-city stores. The largely autonomous and divergent stores making up the Belk group were not prepared to compete. A more mobile society, newly popular shopping centers, and the South's expanding economy presented BSS with the task of uniting its network of stores.

In 1958, there were 380 stores in 17 states. By 1963, the stores were, for the first time, presented to the public as a unit instead of a string of independent operations. Change was still slow, however. At a time when more buyers were using credit, 87 percent of Belk's sales were still cash. In 1967, extensive meetings were held by BSS and its long-range planning committees to chart the company's future.

Meanwhile, more stores were added to the fold: 14 opened in 1969 and 16 in 1970. The new stores were larger and used modern management techniques, such as computerized payrolls and centralized personnel departments. As planning and coordination gained in importance, so did BSS's role. By assuming more leadership, it accelerated the changes as the stores moved from budget to fashion merchandise. Expansion continued, and between 1972 and 1975 more than 50 stores were opened. Several of the company's signature downtown stores were closed in favor of stores in the prospering outlying malls. Credit and data processing systems were centralized and upgraded. Another change was Belk's pursuit of upscale brand names. Estée Lauder, a brand of cosmetics, was aggressively wooed until it was added to product lines in 1975. Even Belk stores in smaller towns upgraded their look and merchandise. This served to add new customers to an already loyal clientele.

Under the direction of president and CEO Thomas Belk, the company succeeded in transforming its operations in order to meet the demands of style-conscious shoppers during the

Key Dates:

1888: William Henry Belk opens a discount store in Monroe, North Carolina.
1891: Belk Brothers Company is formed, and John Belk becomes a partner.
1910: The chain's sales approach $1 million.
1921: Leggett brothers begin opening stores in partnership with the Belks.
1940: Belk Buying Service is established.
1952: The first shopping center store is opened in Florida.
1955: Belk Stores Services, Inc. is formed.
1956: Rival Efird department stores is acquired.
1983: Belk hosts its first New York fashion buying show as its emphasis shifts to style.
1988: A huge office complex is opened in Charlotte, North Carolina.
1996: Belk Corporation acquires a controlling interest in affiliate Leggett Stores Inc.
1998: Belk, Inc. is formed from 112 existing Belk companies.
2001: Belk.com is launched.
2004: John M. Belk retires after 50 years as CEO.

1980s, as opposed to catering strictly to a clientele looking for thrift, durability, and value. For example, Belk hosted its first fashion buying show in New York in 1983, and within four years representatives from the nation's top fashion lines were competing for representation in the show. This further consolidated buying and proved Belk's place in the fashion retail market. Marking the change from bargain chain to fashion stores was top designer Oscar de la Renta's appearance at a grand reopening of a Belk store in 1986. Though some stores retained the small-town, bargain-budget flavor of Belk's founder's vision, others moved to suburban malls and shopping centers. The company celebrated its 100th birthday in 1988 while opening a huge new BSS office complex in Charlotte. The company would later close its New York office and consolidate buying operations at the new facility.

Transitions in the 1990s

Though the retail industry in general and the department store segment in particular were disrupted by recession, competition from mega-discounters, mergers, and multi-billion-dollar bankruptcies in the early 1990s, one observer characterized Belk Stores as "a rock of stability." The company achieved this constancy through a series of well-considered divestments and acquisitions. In an effort to focus on its strongest markets, the company sold a few stores in marginal markets, maintaining its strongholds in North and South Carolina. Hot on the heels of rumors that longtime affiliate Leggett Stores Inc. was negotiating a merger with Dillard Department Stores Inc., Belk's parent company purchased a controlling interest in the Virginia-based chain in the fall of 1996. The addition of Leggett's more than 40 stores increased Belk Corporation's amalgamation of stores by nearly 20 percent and, perhaps more importantly, ensured the continuation of Leggett's long-running affiliation with Belk Stores Services.

Belk Stores withstood an unplanned management transition in January 1997 when 71-year-old Thomas Belk died following gall bladder surgery. His three sons, Thomas M. "Tim" Belk, Jr., H.W. McKay Belk, and John R. Belk shared the title of president and divided merchandising and operating responsibilities among themselves. Strategies for the future included cost reduction, consolidation of operations with a special focus on inventory management, and a continuing emphasis on the customer.

Belk, Inc. Formed in 1998

The Belk Companies posted earnings of $64.5 million on sales of $1.8 billion in the fiscal year ending February 1, 1997. Taken as a whole, Belk was the country's largest privately held department store chain, with 29,000 employees at 225 stores in 13 states. Half of the stores were located in North and South Carolina. The company closed more than three dozen stores, including a series of discount outlets known as Tags.

The 112 companies that made up the Belk stores were consolidated into one corporation, Belk, Inc., on May 2, 1998. According to an official history, *Belk, Inc.: The Company and the Family That Built It*, the initial filing with the Securities and Exchange Commission (SEC) had 7,358 pages and was more than three feet in height. However, the consolidation spared the owners from having to file more than 100 separate tax returns every year. While Belk remained privately held, it began filing returns with the SEC in 1998 due to the fact that it carried public debt.

A number of new projects refined the business in the late 1990s. The Belk National Bank was launched in Lawrenceville, Georgia, in 1998 to boost the company's credit card business. Belk tried installing in-store kiosks for online sales in 1999 but failed to generate much interest beyond the wedding registry. Two years later, Belk began selling merchandise over the Internet through its Web site, Belk.com.

The company also experimented with the size of its stores. A 2,000-square-foot "Belk Express" store stocked with lipstick and pantyhose was a success among professional women in downtown Charlotte. A series of 50,000-square-foot "smart stores" proved a manageable size for small towns. Belk was stepping up its marketing to younger customers through new private labels such as J. Khaki and Z Universe.

Expanding in 2000 and Beyond

In 2000, Belk opened a new distribution center in Blythewood, South Carolina. This facility replaced a half-dozen smaller warehouses. Sales were more than $2 billion and growing, though margins suffered in the weakening economy. The company fared relatively well in the very difficult shopping season following the 9/11 terrorist attacks on the United States.

Belk was expanding, adding plenty of retail space on the home front and in new territories. In 2002, the company added 40,000 square feet to its store at Charlotte's SouthPark Mall and opened a 180,000-square-foot location near Durham's Research Triangle Park. (Another 180,000-square-foot store had opened in Charleston two years earlier.) Belk consolidated its merchandising, formerly handled by the four divisions, into one central buying office during the year.

Texas was another focus of expansion beginning in 2001. Here as elsewhere, Belk preferred to open stores in smaller cities such as McKinney, Kerrville, and Waco. The chain's history in the state dated back to the 1950s when a store was opened in Paris, Texas. It ventured into Mississippi in 2003.

John M. Belk, son of the company's founder, retired in May 2004. He was succeeded as chairman and CEO by Thomas M. "Tim" Belk, Jr., who had previously been Belk, Inc.'s president of store divisions, human resources, real estate, and visual presentation. Tim Belk's brothers H.W. McKay and John R. Belk were appointed chief merchandising officer and chief operating officer, respectively, and remained co-presidents with Tim Belk.

John Belk left a company in good shape. Profits were up almost a third in the January 2004 fiscal year, to $111.5 million, as sales approached $2.3 billion. Sales were nearly $2.5 billion in fiscal 2005 as income climbed 11 percent to $124.1 million.

Principal Subsidiaries

Belk Administration Company; The Belk Center, Inc.; Belk Gift Card Company LLC; Belk International, Inc.; Belk National Bank; Belk-Simpson Company; Belk Stores Services, Inc.; Belk Texas Holdings LLC; Belk Texas LP; United Electronic Services, Inc.

Principal Divisions

Central; Northern; Southern; Western.

Principal Competitors

Dillard's Inc.; JC Penney Co.; Federated Department Stores; May Department Stores Co.; Saks Inc.

Further Reading

"Battling Belks: Maul in the Family," *Business North Carolina*, December 1993, pp. 14–15.

"Belk Corp. Buying Majority Stake in Leggett Chain," *Daily News Record*, September 16, 1996, p. 13.

Blueweiss, Herbert, "Belk's . . . Beginning the Next 100 Years," *Daily News Record*, January 16, 1989, p. 48.

Blythe, LeGette, *William Henry Belk, Merchant of the South*, Chapel Hill: University of North Carolina Press, 1950; enlarged edition, 1958.

Covington, Howard, *Belk: A Century of Retail Leadership*, Chapel Hill: University of North Carolina Press, 1988.

Covington, Howard E., Jr., *Belk, Inc.: The Company and the Family That Built It*, Charlotte: Belk, Inc., 2002.

Dyer, Leigh, "Head of Charlotte, N.C.-Based, Family-Owned Retail Powerhouse to Retire," *Charlotte Observer*, March 12, 2004.

Halkias, Maria, "Department Store Chain Belk to Expand Texas Presence," *Dallas Morning News*, October 13, 2003.

Jean, Sheryl, "Belk Department Stores Returns to Columbia, S.C.," *State* (Columbia, South Carolina), July 15, 1998.

"John M. Belk Announces Retirement as Chairman and Chief Executive Officer of Belk, Inc.; Thomas M. Belk Jr., H.W. McKay Belk and John R. Belk Elected to New Corporate Positions," *PR Newswire*, March 11, 2004.

Karr, Arnold J., "Markdowns Hurt Belk in Year," *DNR*, May 7, 2001, p. 1.

Lee, Georgia, "Tom Belk: After Drought, Women's Seeing Revival," *WWD*, September 13, 1995, p. 18.

Lee, Georgia, and David Moin, "Thomas M. Belk, 71, Belk Stores President, Dies in Charlotte," *WWD*, January 28, 1997, pp. 1–2.

Palmieri, Jean E., "Many Department Stores Still Clicking; Belk," *Daily News Record*, January 17, 1990, p. 10.

Postman, Lore, "Belk Stores' Revenue, Profits Lag Competitors' Results," *Charlotte Observer*, January 4, 1998.

"Three Belk Brothers Promoted," *Daily News Record*, March 3, 1997, p. 2.

Ward, Leah Beth, "Belk Department Store Chain Shareholders Approve Reorganization," *Charlotte Observer*, April 18, 1998.

—Carol I. Keeley
—updates: April D. Gasbarre; Frederick C. Ingram

Bettys & Taylors of Harrogate Ltd.

1 Parliament Street
Harrogate
North Yorkshire HG1 2QU
United Kingdom
Telephone: (+44) 1423 877 300
Fax: (+44) 1423 877 301
Web site: http://www.bettysandtaylors.co.uk

Private Company
Incorporated: 1886
Employees: 900
Sales: $85.3 million (2003)
NAIC: 722213 Snack and Nonalcoholic Beverage Bars

Bettys & Taylors of Harrogate Ltd. is a company with roots in two long-established family businesses: tea and cake. The company, owned by Frederick Belmont's third-generation descendants, bakes its own breads and cakes, makes its own chocolates and pastries, roasts its own coffees, and imports teas from all over the world that it blends and packages on the premises. There are three divisions to the business: five tea rooms, a bakery, and a tea and coffee blending factory.

Origins

In 1907, Frederick Belmont, a native of Bern, Switzerland, arrived in England unable to speak a word of English. Belmont, the son of a miller, had trained as a baker and discovered that his passion and talent lay in working as a confectioner and chocolatier. Although he intended to settle on the south coast of England, Bern mistakenly boarded a train for Yorkshire. Finding work and love there, he married his landlady's daughter, Clare, and settled in Harrogate.

In 1919, Belmont opened his own business, a Continental-style tea room, called Bettys Café Tea Room, in Harrogate. The Belmonts' business was an instant success and came "Under Royal and Distinguished Patronage" as the place where Crown Princes and Princesses on the Grand Tour stopped to take their tea. Throughout the 1920s and 1930s, Belmont opened three additional Bettys in York, Ilkley, and Northallerton, Yorkshire. He also built a craft bakery in Harrogate, where all of the breads, cakes, pastries, and chocolates for the company's tea rooms were made. The inspiration for the Bettys York came from Belmont's experiences on the maiden voyage of the Queen Mary in 1936. Returning to Harrogate, he commissioned the ship's interior designers to turn a dilapidated furniture store into tea rooms with huge curved windows, wood paneling, and ornate mirrors to resemble one of the state rooms of the luxury ocean liner.

The business grew as a local concern throughout the 1940s and 1950s. Bettys Bar was a favorite haunt of the airmen who were stationed in the Vale of York. Then, in 1962, the company purchased rival company C.E. Taylor & Co. when Charles Taylor died, and Bettys & Taylors of Harrogate began.

C.E. Taylor & Co. was owned by Charles Taylor, who began his career in southwest England in the last quarter of the nineteenth century, buying and blending teas that grocers could promote as their own house blend. Taylor had a flair for creating tea blends that were specially suited to the local water and enjoyed searching for and purchasing new types of teas.

After being fired for making a too risky purchase, Charles and his brother, Llewellyn Taylor, went out on their own as tea and coffee merchants and founded C.E. Taylor & Co. in a small warehouse in Leeds in 1886. The business was successful, especially after the brothers opened several local Kiosk Coffee Houses where they roasted coffee daily and created their own house blends of exotic teas, suited, of course, to the local water.

In 1926, Jim Raleigh, nephew of the Taylors, became the buyer for C.E. Taylor's warehouse, which by then supplied the best retailers and hotels in West Riding with coffees and teas. The company also had its own chain of Imperial Tea Shops and Kiosk Coffee Houses. Grocers from across Yorkshire used to visit C.E. Taylor, bringing with them samples of their local water so that Raleigh could blend tea especially for them. In 1928, "new-fangled" teas from Kenya arrived, and Raleigh began including African tea in his blends. C.E. Taylor, like Bettys, struggled during World War II but continued to serve its clientele throughout the 1940s and 1950s.

Company Perspectives:

Our unique business is devoted to many of life's pleasures; handmade cakes, mouth-watering chocolates, beautiful Café Tea Rooms, rare and exclusive coffees and fine teas. It's a business that cares about the communities it trades with and develops staff to reach their potential.

Bettys & Taylors: 1962–90

Having acquired C.E. Taylor, the newly formed Bettys and Taylors now had tea rooms, a craft bakery, and a tea and coffee blending business. Almost a decade after the merger, in the 1970s, Bettys & Taylors moved the company's tea and coffee importing business to Harrogate and began marketing what would become its famous Yorkshire Tea, a proprietary blend of black tea, with different versions to suit different waters.

The company's coffee business grew in the 1980s under the direction of coffee buyer Tony Wild, a member of the Belmont family, who had a degree in English and a love of travel. Having worked his way around the London importing houses, where he learned the language and skills of the professional coffee taster, Wild determined to turn a competent regional roaster into "the moral high ground of the British coffee world," according to a 1991 *Independent* article.

In a nation where 91 percent of the coffee consumed was instant, Wild deliberately set about to find unusual coffees to introduce the British population to the diverse possibilities of the coffee bean. At the time, Wild explained to the *Independent,* there was only "gold blend, ordinary coffee, and . . . Jamaican Blue Mountain."

Social and Environmental Responsibility: 1990–2005

By 1990, Taylors was moving 500 tons of coffee, selling its beans in retail shops, Marks & Spencer department stores, and through catering outlets, as well as at Bettys, which had exclusives on three of its coffees. The company made a commitment in the early 1990s to support the quality of life of those involved in its coffee business. It trained all of its buyers in line with the Ethical Trade Institute Codes of Conduct for international labor, entered into long-term relationships with its coffee suppliers, and instituted "buying principles" to pay sustainable prices for all its coffees and uncouple the price of beans from world commodity prices. Taylors covered farmers' direct costs and added a profit margin to enable them to continue to grow their crop and secure their livelihood. "We are determined not to exploit the people we work with in other countries and they know they can rely on us to buy from them every season and to pay premium prices for the best quality," explained Fiona Hunter, the company's sales manager, in a 2001 *Marketing* article.

Bettys & Taylors also partnered with Oxfam in 1990 to start its Tree for Life campaign after Jonathan Wild, chairman of the company, promised his children that he would find a way to plant one million trees. Between 1990 and 2005, the company planted three million trees in Ethiopia, Kenya, India, Indonesia, Brazil, Guatemala, Ecuador, and other countries. In addition to planting trees, Trees for Life also became involved in addressing broader Third World community needs, building wells, teaching agriculture skills, and educating children about the importance of trees. Turning its attention closer to home, it replanted native woodland and repaired footpaths and dry-stone walls in the Yorkshire Moors and Dales in cooperation with the National Trust. It also worked with the Woodland Trust to plant 10,000 trees.

The late 1990s saw the end of one era in the United Kingdom and the beginning of a new one. In 1998, the last weekly tea auction in London took place, and London's commercial tea dealers began to buy directly from plantations or at auction in Calcutta and Mombasa. London had been the center of the world's tea trade since the weekly auction began around 1835. Taylors of Harrogate paid £24,000, £555 pounds per kilogram, for 44 kilograms of Ceylon Flowery Pekoe tea worth abut £50 pounds, outbidding Twinings at the last historic auction for tea. Another new era began at Bettys & Taylors in 1999 when the company began trading via the Internet and launched a new line of organic green teas. In 2000, it built a new craft bakery.

The emphasis on social responsibility continued to be a distinguishing characteristic at Bettys & Taylors. In 2001, the company was named to the United Kingdoms's first list of Britain's Best Companies to Work For and also won the Queen's Award for Enterprise for Sustainable Development in recognition of its commitment to environmental and social initiatives in the counties where it engaged in business. The company also made a point of treating its employees well, providing them with outstanding benefits and getting to know each one individually.

The company's new Feelgood tea and coffee lines debuted in 2002. These lines ensured fair prices and a sharing of profits with suppliers. Believing that its responsible business practices led to its success, Bettys & Taylors made a point of donating 30,000 pounds to local charities each year and sent staff to primary schools to share their expertise. "When we work with local children we are helping them, but also working with our future customers and staff. When we plant trees around the world we are securing the future of the communities we rely on to produce our tea and coffee," explained the company's sales manager in a 2001 *Marketing* article.

By 2003, nine million cups of Taylors' Yorkshire Tea were drunk each day. At Bettys, where 12 different teas were on the menu, including two exclusive teas, 400,000 pots of tea were ordered a year. Traditional teas were still the biggest sellers, but specialty teas had grown to account for 25 percent of all sales. Tea still ranked as the most popular warm beverage in Britain; with 165 million cups of tea drunk each day, it accounted for 42 percent of all adult fluid intake. However, most traditional tea rooms were finding it hard to compete with other leisure activities, and only 14 percent of the tea drunk in the United Kingdom was consumed in cafes and restaurants.

By 2004, Bettys & Taylors had six outlets, all in Yorkshire, turnover of £50 million, and 900 employees. China joined Taylors' list of 30 countries to which it exported its tea blends in 2004 when Taylors shipped 30,000 pounds of specialty blends to Shanghai via its Taiwanese distribution partner. The year

---

Key Dates:

1886: Charles Taylor and his brother found C.E. Taylor & Co.
1919: Belmont opens Bettys Café Tea Rooms.
1962: C.E. Taylor & Co. merges with Bettys to form Bettys & Taylors of Harrogate.
1990: The company launches its Trees for Life campaign.
1998: The last tea auction takes place in London.
2000: The company opens a new craft bakery.
2001: The company is named to the United Kingdom's first list of Britain's Best Companies to Work For and wins the Queen's Award for Enterprise for Sustainable Development.
2004: The company begins shipping tea to China.

2004 was also a record-breaking fundraising year for Bettys & Taylors, whose staff held auctions, raffles, and other events to raise money for seven Yorkshire charities, primarily in the field of healthcare and research. The company also launched its Fairtrade Organic line of coffees whose beans came from a small farmers' cooperative in Matagalpa, Nicaragua, where the company helped to build a new health clinic and a well and to put environmentally friendly stoves into homes.

As Bettys & Taylors of Harrogate looked to the future, it placed a strong emphasis on tradition, from using wood-burning ovens in its bakery to focusing on the people who made up its family of workers. The company, which had been featured as one of the *Sunday Times'* "100 Best Companies to Work For" every year since the list's inception in 2001, made a point of cele-brating "individual craft skills, so the business' success is everyone's success," according to a 2004 *Employee Benefits* article.

"People say we are mad not to have Bettys teashops on every high street, but we are not mad, we're wise," was the opinion of Jonathan Wild in a 2004 *Director* article. The company's decision to limit growth was based on its belief that its strong team and hands-on, family culture would not survive geographic expansion. "That culture is central to our success and the starting point for what we have identified as sustainable growth. You ignore that at your peril, however tempting it might be to open in London, Edinburgh or anywhere else."

Principal Competitors

Twinings.

Further Reading

Arnold, Mathew, "CRM Shows Its Winning Ways—The Business in the Community Awards for Excellence Saw Just How Valuable CRM Activity Can Be," *Marketing*, July 19, 2001. p. 19.
Blythman, Joanna, "Waiter, There's a Wolf in My Cup of Coffee," *Independent*, April 27, 1991, p. 32.
"Bread Fit For a Prince!," *Harrogate Adviser*, February 18, 2003.
Harmer, Janet, "The Nation's Favourite?," *Caterer and Hotelkeeper*, April 24, 2003, p. 72.
"Jim Raleigh," *Times*, February 4, 2000.
Judge, Elizabeth, "Now It's the Small Firms' Turn to Be Good Neighbors," *Times*, May 27, 2003, p. 22.
Mead, Gary, "Tradition Ends with a Chest of Flowery Pekoe Tea," *Financial Times*, June 30, 1998, p. 23.
Pike, J., "Bettys & Taylors Hitting the Sweet Spot," *Employee Benefits*, April 1, 2004, p.46.
Simms, Jane, "No-Grow Area," *Director*, April 2004, p. 54.

—Carrie Rothburd

BigBen Interactive S.A.

Rue de la Voyette
Centre de Gros No. 1
Lesquin F-59818 Cedex
France
Telephone: (+33) 3 20 90 72 00
Fax: (+33) 3 20 90 72 34
Web site: http://www.bigben.fr

Public Company
Incorporated: 1981
Employees: 397
Sales: EUR 135.85 million ($180 million) (2004)
Stock Exchanges: Euronext Paris
Ticker Symbol: 7407
NAIC: 423430 Computer and Computer Peripheral
   Equipment and Software Merchant Wholesalers

BigBen Interactive S.A. is France's leading developer and distributor of video game console peripherals and a leading distributor of video gaming consoles and software in the French, Benelux, and German markets. BigBen operates in four primary areas: video game accessories and peripherals, non-exclusive video console and software distribution, exclusive software distribution, and the company's original operation, wholesale distribution of watches, gifts, promotional items, and electronic goods. The company's youngest and fastest growing activity is the design, marketing, and distribution of peripherals and accessories for the video console market, with products including a line of carrying cases for the Nintendo DS and the Body Pad gaming controller. The company carried out research and development for this category at its Hong Kong subsidiary, which was opened in 2000. BigBen's non-exclusive video console and software business includes its acquisition of the entire European stock of the discontinued Sega Dreamcast in 2001 and the non-exclusive distribution of software and video game consoles in France and the Benelux markets. In addition, the company acts as an exclusive distributor for a number of smaller software publishers, including deals with the Netherlands' 3Pi, the 3DO in the United States, and Jester Interactive

in the United Kingdom. BigBen's smallest operation, the wholesaling business, is also its oldest, launched at the company's founding by Alain Falc in 1981. Falc remains the Euronext Paris-listed company's chairman and largest shareholder, with a 49 percent stake. Difficult trading conditions have forced the company to shut down its U.K. subsidiary in 2005. The company's sales, at EUR 135.85 million in March 2005, represented a drop of some 26 percent from the previous year.

Beginnings in the 1980s

In 1981, at the age of 20, Alain Falc founded a business selling watches at wholesale from his town of Lesquin, near Lille in the north of France. Falc named his company BigBen, in reference to the famous clock tower in London. Early on, Falc became a distributor for a number of watch brands, including Patrick Arnaud and Yves Bertelin Zeon, serving primarily the wholesaler circuit.

Through the 1980s, BigBen expanded its range of offerings, adding a variety of electronics goods, as well as gifts and promotional items. For the most part, however, the company remained close to its original focus on timepieces. By the early 1990s, Falc had put into place a thriving regional business. Lille's position near the Belgian border also gave BigBen an entry into the Benelux market.

The boom in the consumer electronics market at the beginning of the 1990s, especially the development of the video gaming console market, led BigBen to further expand its operations to include a wider array of products. Falc's recognition of the potential for the video gaming market enabled the company to become an early player in what was to become one of the world's largest-selling leisure sectors.

The company's background in distribution helped it win non-exclusive distribution deals with a number of fast-rising companies in the video game sector, including Acclaim, Nintendo, Sony, and Electronic Arts. With this catalog of heavy hitters, BigBen quickly became one of the leading distributors in the French video game market. BigBen counted among its customers such major retailing groups as Auchan, Carrefour, and Casino, as well as specialist retailers including Toys "R"

Key Dates:

1981: Alan Falc launches BigBen as a wholesaler for branded wristwatches and other timepieces and gradually expands into gifts, promotional items, and consumer electronics.

1993: BigBen begins focusing on the distribution of video game consoles, software, accessories and peripherals and begins developing its own peripherals and accessories, as well as building up its own video game retail distribution network under the Game's and Espace 3 names.

1999: The company goes public with a listing on the Euronext Paris secondary market.

2000: The company establishes a research and development subsidiary in Hong Kong, launches a distribution subsidiary in Germany, and acquires Atoll Soft in Belgium and Planet Distribution in the United Kingdom.

2001: European stock and rights for Dreamcast consoles, accessories, and software titles are acquired.

2002: BigBen signs a pan-European distribution agreement with the Jester Interactive as part of the company's extension into exclusive distribution channel.

2005: The company shuts down its money-losing U.K. operations and gains development and distribution licensing for upcoming Xbox 3D from Microsoft.

Us and Fnac. At the same time, BigBen itself moved into the retail market, adding a chain of stores specializing in video games and consoles under the names Game's and Espace 3 and building a network of 14 stores by the end of the decade.

BigBen's involvement with the video game sector rapidly overtook the company's original wholesaling operations. Nonetheless, BigBen continued to distribute wristwatches and other timepieces, gifts, and promotional goods.

Designing for the Turn of the 21st Century

As the market for video gaming consoles developed, and the technology driving each new generation of consoles advanced, BigBen recognized a new market opportunity, that of peripherals and accessories. Following the initial purchase of a console, consumers often sought to enhance the gaming experience with new peripheral equipment, such as steering wheels for driving games or joysticks providing "feedback." These peripherals were also particularly prone to wear and tear and often needed to be replaced. At the same time, the console market generated demand for accessories, such as stands to hold the consoles or carrying cases and displays for the games themselves.

BigBen quickly moved into the design area as well, developing an increasing number of accessories and peripherals for the consoles. The company began releasing a line of memory cards, wired and wireless analog and digital controllers, cable links, and steering wheels, as well as its own accessories. By the end of the 1990s, the company had become the market leader for the consoles peripherals sector in France. In 2000, in support of this

activity, BigBen launched a dedicated research and development subsidiary in Hong Kong, which in turn contracted for the group's manufacturing needs. The company rapidly became a market leader in innovative products, developing such peripherals as an LCD (Liquid Crystal Display) screen for the PS One or a vibrating steering wheel that provided interactive feedback for racing games.

Acquisitions played a role in BigBen's growth at the end of the 1990s and into the 2000s. The company established itself in the Benelux market with the purchase of Atoll Soft in 1999. That acquisition gave BigBen the leading position in the video console distribution market in Belgium and the Netherlands. The company also moved into Germany, establishing a dedicated German subsidiary in 2000.

Fueling the company's expansion was its public offering, with a listing on the Euronext Paris Stock Exchange's Secondary Market in October 1999. Falc nonetheless maintained a 49 percent stake in the company. In addition to its expansion into the German and Benelux markets, BigBen also targeted the market in the United Kingdom. In April 2000, the company acquired Planet Distribution, one of the United Kingdom's leading independent video game distributors. This operation was renamed BigBen Interactive UK. Yet BigBen was less successful in the United Kingdom than it had been in other countries. In 2005, after years of steady losses, the company placed the U.K. subsidiary into receivership.

Struggles and Successes in the 2000s

A major step forward for the company came in 2001, when BigBen acquired the entire European market for Sega's Dreamcast console system and video game software titles. Sega, hammered by the release of the Playstation II and the Nintendo GameCube, had decided to exit the console business. With control of distribution for the format, BigBen not only boosted its sales but added several years of steady profits.

The company maintained its multi-faceted growth strategy into the middle of the decade. In 2002, BigBen boosted its retail network with the addition of a new format, King Games, adding ten stores that year. The company also moved into a new area, that of the exclusive software distribution segment. Unlike the group's distribution operations for gaming consoles and major games publishers, which were performed on a non-exclusive basis, the company had recognized an opportunity to establish exclusive distribution agreements with smaller publishers, usually on a time-limited and regional basis. In this way, BigBen enjoyed sole control over potentially popular titles, while the smaller publisher achieved access to the larger distribution circuit through BigBen's established relationships.

The company quickly put into place a number of strategic exclusive agreements, such as the 2002 rights to the Super Trucks games series and the rights to distribute Manic Miner, a game for the Game Boy Advance. The company captured European exclusive distribution rights for titles from the United Kingdom's Jester Interactive in 2002. The company also negotiated a number of regional exclusives, such as a deal with the newly formed U.K. outfit Midas Interactive and the American company 3DO. In 2003, the company added

JoWood AG, based in Austria, giving it the right to market that company's catalog of 21 titles in Germany, France, the Benelux countries, and Switzerland.

The winding down of the Dreamcast market in the mid-2000s, coupled with the company's own growing pains, contributed to a decline in company revenues, which dropped from more than EUR 225 million in 2002 to EUR 186 million in 2003, then to just under EUR 136 million in 2004. As Falc himself explained to *Challenges:* "We'd experienced a very sharp growth in 2001–2002. We didn't have the capacity to manage sales that strong!"

In response, the company began restructuring, including shutting down its money-losing U.K. operations at the beginning of 2005. The company focused on reducing debt and cutting down on investments in order to balance its books. At the same time, BigBen placed its international expansion on hold.

Despite its difficulties, BigBen remained the leader in the French market for video console accessories, beating out even Sony with rising sales at the end of 2004 and into 2005. The company prepared a new stream of peripherals for the 2005 season, such as the Multitap for the Playstation 2 and Action Replays for the Grand Turismo 4 and Metal Gear Solid 3 titles. BigBen's future also brightened when the company announced that it had received a license to develop a complete range of accessories and peripherals for the upcoming Xbox 360 from Microsoft Corporation.

Principal Subsidiaries

Atoll Soft Nederland BV (Netherlands); Atoll Software SA (Belgium); BigBen Interactive (HK) Limited (Hong Kong); BigBen Interactive GMBH (Germany); Espace 3 Game's SAS; Yves Bertelin SAS.

Principal Competitors

Sony Corporation; Nintendo Corporation; Guillemot International SA; Innelec SA.

Further Reading

"BigBen Interactive: va quitter la Grande-Bretagne," *Investir.fr*, April 13, 2005.
"Infogrames, BigBen unveil operations," *Echos*, February 16, 2000, p. 17.
Libeskind, Jerome, "Interview: Alain Falc, president de BigBen Interactive," *Investir.fr*, April 24, 2001.
Rousseau, Anna, "Alain Falc," *Challenges*, November 18, 2004, p. 10.
Shannon, Victoria, "Sega Teams up with BigBen," *International Herald Tribune*, April 6, 2001, p. 15.

—M.L. Cohen

Billing Concepts, Inc.

7411 John Smith Drive, Suite 200
San Antonio, Texas 78229-4898
U.S.A.
Telephone: (210) 949-7000
Fax: (210) 696-0270
Web site: http://www.billingconcepts.com

Wholly Owned Subsidiary of ABRY Partners LLC
Incorporated: 1985 as U.S. Long Distance Corporation
Employees: 115
Sales: $10 million (2004 est.)
NAIC: 541219 Other Accounting Services; 518111
  Internet Service Providers; 518210 Data Processing,
  Hosting, and Related Services

Billing Concepts, Inc. (BCI) bills itself as the "authentic, proven, trusted" billing clearinghouse for the telecommunications industry. Together with ACI Billing Services Inc., Billing Concepts forms the Billing Services Group of parent ABRY Partners LLC, providing a comprehensive billing system that collects long distance charges from telephone users on behalf of more than 1,300 local telephone companies. The company also provides these services to wireless carriers and Internet Service Providers (ISPs). One of the fastest growing and most profitable companies of its kind in the late 1990s, Billing Concepts was streamlined and restructured in the early 2000s when its software businesses were divested and the billing operations and company moniker were acquired by the investment firm of ABRY Partners.

Deregulation of Telecommunications: 1984–96

The 1984 breakup of American Telephone & Telegraph (AT&T) and of the Bell System revolutionized the operation of the telecommunications industry. Local telephone companies that made up the Regional Bell Operating Companies (also known as the Baby Bells) had to provide billing and collections on a nondiscriminatory basis to all carriers that supplied telecommunication services to their end-user customers. Only the largest long distance carriers, such as AT&T, MCI Telecommunications Corporation, and Sprint Incorporated, could afford the cost of agreements with local telephone companies for direct billing. Several entrepreneurs recognized an opportunity for establishing companies that would enter into these billing and collection agreements to aggregate telephone-call records for local exchange carriers and long distance carriers.

Furthermore, with the 1986 advent of technology that allowed zero-plus dialing (ZPD), customers could use an automated credit card for long distance calls or use the prefix 1 before a telephone number to make zero-minus calls (collect, third-party billing, operator-assisted calling card, or person-to-person calls). These calls were routed away from AT&T to a competitive long distance services provider. Typically, the billing information resided with the billed person's local telephone company. In order to bill for ZPD and zero-minus calls, a long distance services provider either had to obtain billing and collection agreements with LECs or use the services of third-party clearinghouses.

The Telecommunications Act of 1996 dramatically changed the ground rules for competition and regulation in virtually all sectors of the communications industry. After promulgation of the 1984 antitrust consent decree that dismantled the Bell System, major strides had been made in relaxing federal regulation and in ensuring fair competition in the long distance telephone market. But emerging technology for telecommunications led to conflicting interpretations of the Communication Act of 1934 that had prevailed for 62 years. With the Telecommunications Act, Congress set a course that clearly adopted competition as the basic charter for all telecommunications markets for the next five years. The Telecommunications Act cleared market-entry barriers for entrepreneurs and other small businesses in the provision and ownership of telecommunications services.

Origins: 1985–95

While the telecommunications industry was taking shape, in 1985 Parris H. Holmes, Jr., invested $50,000 to start a small pay-phone business in his Houston garage. However, Holmes was not comfortable with the Texas regulatory environment for billing services and he switched into the long distance business by founding a company named U.S. Long Distance Corporation, later known as USLD Communications Corporation. Ac-

Company Perspectives:

Utilizing state-of-the-art systems technology, Billing Concepts built a platform enabling the future of billing, clearing and settlement services including authentication and authorization, mediation, invoicing, collection and settlements. Billing Concepts, Inc. (BCI) offers outsourced billing solutions through a wide range of proprietary LEC processing products and wireless Internet clearing and settlement services.

cording to Don Sheron's 1997 article in the *San Antonio Express News,* "from 1986–87 Holmes raised $9.2 million from people who had known him for a long time." Within a few years USLD acquired 11 companies.

Among these acquisitions was the 1988 purchase of Zero Plus Dialing, Inc., which brought with it a portfolio of billing and collection agreements with several local telephone companies. Using these agreements, USLD billed and collected from the local telephone companies for its own operator services. Billing and collection agreements were subsequently made with additional LECs, including GTE and the Baby Bells. Furthermore, USLD marketed its billing and collection services to LECs, arguing that outsourcing the administration of these operations would save time and money. The company also began to offer its third-party clearinghouse services to other operator services that did not have proprietary agreements with the local telephone companies.

By 1989 USLD was a $200,000-a-year business. The company continued its rapid expansion through the early 1990s, especially through the profitable operations of US Billing, Inc., and Enhanced Services Billing, Inc.—companies acquired in 1993 and 1994, respectively. However, the disparate functions of these subsidiaries raised concerns among clients and industry analysts. Was USLD a telecommunications company or a billing company, and was the financial data acquired through billing operations available for USLD to use against its competitors? To allay concerns, USLD separated its business into two groups that functioned independently of each other: The Billing Group and The Telecommunications Group.

Meanwhile, USLD improved its information management services with the 1990 development of a comprehensive information management system capable of processing, tracing, recording, and accounting for telephone-call transactions. USLD was also the first third-party billing clearinghouse to offer an advance funding program for its customers' accounts receivable. In 1992 the company began to offer LEC billing services to providers of direct-dial long distance services. From 1993 to 1995 the company offered enhanced clearinghouse billing and information management services to other businesses, including providers of telecommunications equipment and information, as well as other providers of nonregulated communication services and products (for example, 900 access pay-per-call transactions, cellular long distance services, paging services, voicemail services, and equipment for Caller ID and other telecommunications applications). The billing of nonregulated telecommunication products and services became a significant factor in the

successful evolution of USLD's business. Revenues grew steadily reaching $33.16 million in 1992, $46.46 million in 1993, $57.75 million in 1994, and $80.85 million in 1995.

Two New Public Companies Emerge in the Mid-1990s

By 1996, USLD's two Groups (Billing and Telecommunications) operated profitably in their respective markets. According to Sheron in the *San Antonio Express News,* Parris Holmes later commented that the Groups "simply outgrew the marriage. This was just a healthy growth situation." On July 10, 1996, USLD's board of directors approved the spinoff of the commercial billing clearinghouse and information management services into a public company. The Billing Group Business became Billing Information Concepts Corporation, and on February 27, 1998, was renamed Billing Concepts Corporation (BCC). The Telecommunications Business Group remained the focus of the new USLD, later renamed USLD Communications Corporation (USLD), which in 1998 was acquired as a subsidiary by Qwest Communications International, the nation's fourth largest long distance provider.

Holmes remained Chairman/CEO of USLD until June 1997. "I felt like the separation process had been completed," said Holmes in a December 1997 interview with Diane Mayoros in the *Wall Street Corporate Reporter.* "It was a natural progression to move on to focus my time and energy" as chairman and CEO of Billing Concepts Corporation.

Holmes focused on getting a head start for building the information infrastructure of the 21st century by tapping into the opportunities opened up by the Telecommunications Act, which allowed local, long distance, and cable service providers to enter each other's markets. BCC also strengthened its presence in billing services through the June 1997 acquisition of Computer Resources Management, Inc., a company that developed software systems for the direct billing of telecommunication services and was already performing billing for the utility industry. As a single-source, direct-billing solution (also referred to as convergent billing or one-stop billing) for long distance and cellular calls, PCS, paging, cable and satellite television, Internet, and utilities, Computer Resources Management software aggregated all bills on one invoice. In September this new acquisition was reorganized into Billing Concepts as a subsidiary called Billing Concepts Systems, Inc. (BCS); it offered software licensing, equipment sales, service-bureau billing, custom programming, and other ancillary services. Since Billing Concepts Systems was a Premier Business Partner of IBM, the acquisition also brought BCC an alliance that allowed for immediate expansion of its technological resources.

BCC relocated 528 employees to new headquarters, added three industry professionals to its senior management team, and doubled its technical staff. The company defined its products and services as four separate lines of business: Local Exchange Carrier Billing, Direct Billing, Software Licensing and Developing, and Back-Office Services. LEC Billing, the company's core product, consisted of three distinct divisions: U.S. Billing, Inc., Zero Plus Dialing, Inc., and Enhanced Services Billing, Inc.

U.S. Billing was BCC's fastest-growing division and accounted for more than half of the company's annual revenue. The

---

Key Dates:

1985: U.S. Long Distance Corporation founded; Billing Concepts is a subsidiary.
1988: Billing Concepts Corporation is launched as separate company.
1998: Company acquires CommSoft.
1999: Company spins off three divisions as Aptis.
2000: Company acquired by Platinum Equity Holdings; becomes Billing Concepts, Inc.
2003: ABRY Partners acquires company.
2004: Company is merged with ACI Billing Services, Inc., under the ABRY umbrella.

---

division served carriers of direct-dial, long distance companies. This service consisted of billing "1+" long distance telephone calls to individual residential customers and small commercial accounts. The growing volume of these telephone calls soon placed long distance carriers in the position of having to increase their collection rates if they billed through the local telephone companies. U.S. Billing offered these carriers a more effective way to bill and receive payment from residential customers.

Zero Plus Dialing was devoted exclusively to billing and information management services for operator-assisted calls (known as zero-plus/zero-minus calls), such as third-party calls, collect calls, and credit card calls. Zero Plus's customers included private-pay telephone owners, hotels, universities, airports, and prisons. This service was BCC's original form of LEC billing and drove the development of the systems and infrastructure used by all of the company's LEC billing services. Enhanced Services Billing, founded in 1994, billed local telephone companies for nonregulated and enhanced telecommunications services. These businesses included providers of telecommunications equipment and Internet providers; paging and voicemail services; cellular and PCS long distance services; caller ID and premium pay-per-call services (900-prefixed calls), such as weather, sports, and information services. Enhanced Services Billing's profit margins were significantly higher than those of BCC's other core products because fees could be based on a percentage of revenue rather than charged to each processed record.

At the request of its customers, BCC spent the last months of 1996 and the greater part of 1997 developing invoice-ready billing, a product that gave BCC's customers—long distance companies and providers of operator-assisted services—the ability to prepare a customized bill statement. This product was more than a generic statement on which BCC's customers could place their name; it allowed them to personalize the statement with their name, their logo, and/or marketing messages. BCC was the first company, outside of the "big three" AT&T, MCI, and Sprint, to market this product. The first invoice-ready bill was produced in October 1997.

For many of its LEC customers, BCC processed the tax records associated with telephone-call records and other transactions and files, as well as certain federal excise, state, and local telecommunications-related tax returns covering these records and transactions. The company submitted over 1,800 tax returns each month on behalf of its customers and provided

customer service to end-users inquiring about calls for which they were billed.

BCC's 1997 acquisition of Billing Concepts Systems (BCS) gave it a head start to bundle services in a direct billing environment. As early as 1988 the subsidiary company had developed billing and customer care solutions. When the Telecommunications Act of 1996 allowed providers of local, long distance, and cable services to enter each other's markets, BCS positioned itself to become a competitive player in the market as a one-stop supplier of convergent telecommunications products and services. BCS developed state-of-the-art billing software, dubbed Modular Business Applications (MBA), to provide a single-source, direct-billing solution that allowed billing for multiple products such as local, long distance, cellular, PCS, paging, cable/satellite TV, Internet, and even utilities. The convergent-billing platform had the capability to produce a "universal bill" whereby multiple services and products could be billed directly to the end-user on one consolidated billing statement. MBA was offered as a service-bureau (back office) or in-house software solution utilizing the IBM AS/400 as the operational platform. BCS was ready for the not-too-distant future when long distance carriers would enter the $100 billion local markets, and when LECs would enter the $80 billion long distance markets.

In addition to billing services, BCC offered customer service, accounting services and reports, data processing, tax filings, and an advance funding program. The customer service center handled over 30,000 calls per day during fiscal 1997. As many as nine taxes could accrue for each long distance call. Each quarter, BCC's tax department prepared over 5,000 tax returns on behalf of its customers. Furthermore the company, predominantly with its own cash, funded a program that proved to be very valuable to customers who could not afford to wait the typical 60-day billing cycle to receive their payments from the local telephone companies. After qualification for this advance funding program, participants were advanced up to 80 percent of their receivables within five days of submitting their call records. When Billing Concepts received payment from the LECs for these call records, the company submitted the balance to customers, less its fees and incurred interest. BCC maintained a $50 million revolving line of credit to fund any growth in this program.

At the end of fiscal 1997, BCC revenues of $122.84 million and net income of $21.86 million were up 18 percent and 22 percent, respectively, from the revenues and net income of 1996.

Toward the 21st Century

On January 30, 1998, BCC distributed a one-for-one stock dividend to its shareholders of record. During the third quarter, actions by the FCC and the Regional Bell Operating Companies on "slamming and cramming" issues led to a temporary interruption in the revenue growth of BCC's business. "Slamming" refers to the unauthorized switching of consumers' long distance provider and "cramming" refers to the practice of billing consumers for unauthorized charges, such as the Universal Service Charge, a new federal tax added to phone bills to fund library and school access to the Internet.

However, for the first nine months of fiscal 1998, BCC reported that total revenues increased 37.4 percent to $119.7 million from $87.1 million during the comparable period of fiscal 1997. Chairman/CEO Holmes said that BCC was conducting its billing business "in a manner consistent with what the FCC was to publish in its upcoming "Best Billing Practices' document." Furthermore, seven major industry analysts went on record as supporting BCC's strong position in its specialized niche and its ability to maintain a revenue growth rate of at least 25 percent annually over the next several years.

"BCC's energies," Holmes emphasized, "are being focused on competitive local exchange carriers and telecommunication carriers who are diversifying their product and service offerings. . . . Our competitive advantage is time-to-market and a highly marketable convergent billing solution. . . . We remain focused on our long-term goals and are excited about our opportunities."

BCC continued to seize opportunities for expansion by providing add-on services to both new and existing customers and by acquiring new business. For instance, during the second quarter of 1998, BCC announced that Intermedia Communications, a provider of integrated telecommunications solutions, chose BCS's Modular Billing Application to replace a number of its billing systems. Another significant event occurred when LCI International Telecommunications Corporation, a subsidiary of Qwest Communications and one of the nation's fastest-growing major telecommunication companies, signed a multi-year agreement for BCC to provide billing services for customers of LCI's operator-assisted services while LCI provided long distance and 800 services for BCC's customers. During the third quarter, BCC signed 26 new accounts and received renewal of 18 contracts. BCS also continued to add new business by selling three in-house systems and signing two service-bureau agreements.

Then, in July 1998, WinStar Communications, Inc., chose BCS to consolidate its multiple billing platforms onto the MBA system, thereby receiving a complete solution set to support WinStar's long distance, local resale, calling card, and enhanced services for retail and wholesale customers. In August of the same year, Philadelphia-based Eagle Communications, entered into a five-year contract for BCC's entire suite of product offerings, which included MBA, BCC's customer service and billing software, and back-office support. Also in August, BCC signed an agreement to acquire 22 percent of the capital stock of Princeton Telecommunications Corporation (PTC), a private company specializing in electronic-bill publishing over the Internet and advanced payment solutions. According to Chairman/CEO Holmes, "this association with PTC is a key to our on-going strategy to grow our solution set. Consumers are rapidly embracing the ability to pay their bills over the Internet and this phenomenon is causing vendors to publish their bills electronically. . . . Instead of developing these services, we will deliver them through PTC." He went on to say that this way of sharing billing strategies "will not only enhance our investment in PTC, but will catapult Billing Concepts into the emerging Internet market."

In 1998 Billing Concepts purchased CommSoft, a telecommunications software company, for $36 million. CommSoft and two other company divisions were spun off under the name of Aptis in 1999.

Changes in Ownership in the Early 2000s

The new century saw many changes at Billing Concepts. In 2000 the company sold three of its divisions, including Billing Concepts, Inc. (BCI), to Platinum Equity Holdings, a $4 billion holding firm based in Los Angeles. Subsequently, the corporate shell of Billing Concepts Corporation changed its name to New Century Equity Holdings Corporation and got out of the billing services and software industry. It was now essentially an investment firm specializing in technology companies. In 2003 ABRY Partners, a private equity fund based in Boston, acquired Billing Concepts, Inc., Enhanced Services Billing, Inc., and Avery Communications, Inc. Those three companies were then merged together under the name Billing Concepts, Inc. In 2004 BCI was joined with ACI Billing Services, Inc., under the name Billing Services Group LLC, owned by ABRY Partners. The new company was expected to bill and settle over $1 billion annually.

Several new services were also added. In 2001 BCI began offering Revenue Recovery Service, a system in which telecom service providers could collect charges from customers whose local exchange carriers no longer handled local service. In 2003 BCI introduced one of its most promising new services, eZ-Wi. The new service allowed customers with existing ISP accounts to access the Internet from participating hotspots. The hotspot charges would appear automatically on the customer's regular ISP bill. The eZ-Wi service quickly caught the attention of several leading ISPs. Among the companies who signed up for eZ-Wi were Grande Communications, Pacific Information Exchange, and NetNearU Corporation.

BCI remained the leading force in LEC billing. In August 2004, BCI integrated traffic from its sister company, ACI Billing Services, to a common platform. The result meant that the two companies were capturing about 85 percent of the LEC billing market.

Principal Competitors

Syniverse Holdings, Inc.; CallVision Inc.; Telesoft Corporation; Billing Services Group LLC.

Further Reading

"CompTel /Ascent Member Profiles," *CompTel Connection,* July 14, 2003.
Cullen, Lisa Reilly, "How You Can Make Money in Telecommunications Without Getting Tangled in Turf Wars," *Money,* April 1988, pp. 60–62.
"A Man and His Company," *Capital District Business Review,* February 26, 2001, p. 18.
Mayores, Diane, "Market Will Explode: Interview with Parris H. Holmes," *Wall Street Corporate Reporter,* December 8–14, 1997.
Mensheha, Mark, "Billing Firm Lines Up Credit Package," *San Antonio Business Journal,* January 31, 1997, pp. 1–2.
Moorse, Alan, "Billing Concepts Sells Aptis Software Division," *Capital District Business Review,* October 30, 2000, p. 5.
——, "Billing Concepts to Sell Aptis, Two Other Divisions," *Capital District Business Review,* September 25, 2000, p. 7.
Much, Marilyn, "The New America," *Investor's Business Daily,* November 17, 1997, p. 1.
Sheron, Don, "Billing Concepts Corp. Proves It Can Stand Alone," *San Antonio Express News,* August 17, 1997, pp. 1H, 5H.
Weiss, Sebastian, "Corpus [Christi] Gains Call Center Due to Tight Labor Market Here," *San Antonio Business Journal,* May 15, 1998, p. 5.

—Gloria A. Lemieux
—update: Thomas Wiloch

Bonhams 1793 Ltd.

101 New Bond Street
London W1S 1SR
United Kingdom
Telephone: 44 (0)207 447 7447
Fax: 44 (0)20 7447 7400
Web site: http://www.bonhams.com

Private Company
Incorporated: 1793
Employees: 250
Revenues: $400 million (2004)
NAIC: 453998 Auction Houses; 453920 Art Dealers;
453998 453920 Art Dealers;
454111 Electronic Shopping; 454112 Electronic Auctions

Bonhams 1793 Ltd. is one of the world's oldest and the third largest and fastest-growing auction house in the world. Bonhams offers more sales than any of its rivals, through two major salerooms in London: New Bond Street and Knightsbridge, and another ten throughout the United Kingdom, including one in Edinburgh, Scotland. Sales also take place in San Francisco, Los Angeles, New York, and Boston in the United States, and in Switzerland, France, Monaco, and Australia. In addition, Bonhams has a worldwide network of offices and regional representatives offering sales advice and valuation services in 14 countries.

Origins

Little has been published on the history of Bonhams. Thomas Dodd, a renowned antique print dealer, and Walter Bonham, a book specialist, founded Bonhams in London in 1793. At the time, they were just one of several auction houses in Georgian London. The company eventually expanded and by the 1850s Bonhams was handling all categories of antiques, including jewelry, porcelain, furniture, arms and armor, and fine wines. In the 1950s, the Bonham family purchased some land in London's Knightsbridge district and erected a salesroom there, and as the auction house increased its specialties and business another salesroom was opened in Chelsea. By the early 1980s, Bonhams, along with Christie's, Sotheby's, and Phillips, was considered one of England and Europe's "Big Four" auction houses.

After enjoying decades of a solid reputation and profitability, however, by the late 1980s the company's fortunes had experienced a reversal. Many of the auction house's experts had been lured away by Christie's and Sotheby's and therefore its reputation and revenues were slipping. In an effort to turn things around, in 1987 the company brought in Christopher Elwes as its new leader. Elwes, who had earlier helped Christie's set up its highly successful South Kensington showroom, directed Bonhams to focus on its smaller departments and become a specialist in such fields as contemporary ceramics, musical instruments, portrait miniatures, and rock ephemera. "The bigger departments at Sotheby's and Christie's were all looked after," he recalled in a 1997 *Management Today* article, adding "but smaller ones tended to feel rather neglected. As a smaller company, we could give these areas much more attention." This move provided Bonhams with ownership of the sorts of niches that the bigger players in the auction market had overlooked. One such niche was that of ceramic art. Bonhams established this department in 1988 and by the early 1990s had conducted several major sales of ceramics, including some works by Picasso.

The late 1990s were a difficult time for England's auction houses as they contended with changes initiated by the European Union, specifically a 2.5 percent temporary import tax on all objects brought into the United Kingdom for sale. In addition, the opening of the Paris auction market in the late 1990s took business away from the London auction houses. As these changes occurred in Europe, the United States went from selling almost nothing to having auction sales equal to or exceeding those of the United Kingdom. "Finding foreign buyers is the new buzz word in all the auction houses nowadays," explained Elwes in 1997 in *Management Today*.

Fortunately, Bonhams—unlike the others in the Big Four, all of which traded overseas—did most of its business in its home country, and thus was relatively insulated from these changes. In 1996, Bonhams sales were around $65 million.

Mid-1990s–2000s: New Markets and Mergers

Much of Bonhams' increase in business was due to its initiation of the first genuinely public auction in Japan, held in downtown Tokyo in early 1996. The commodity sold at this auction was the popular memorabilia of The Beatles, including the Fab Four's velvet capes and Sir Paul McCartney's birth certificate. Bonhams' Tokyo sale was remarkable for its theatricality (It used a satellite link to coordinate bidding between Tokyo and London.), its extensive press coverage, and the excitement it generated. This quality led to ''prices that were far higher than we might otherwise have expected them to be,'' according to Elwes, again in *Management Today.* Bonhams' next Tokyo auction, devoted to the memorabilia of Elvis Presley, was also a success.

With an emphasis on taking on the big auction houses—Sotheby's and Christie's—Bonhams joined forces with two other smaller houses—Tajan of France and Dorotheum of Austria—in 1997 to hold a successful modern art auction of nearly 300 lots. The following year, an interactive TV auction by Bonhams sold other pop memorabilia, including underwear from an all-girl rock band.

There were risks involved in coming to be known as the fun auction house, as Elwes acknowledged also in *Management Today:* ''Being known as the auctioneers who sold Paul McCartney's birth certificate does not necessarily help you when you're pitching to sell Old Master pictures of 18th-century furniture.'' Bonhams' pop specialist, an aging 1960s rocker, was not an expert or connoisseur in the traditional sense. Moreover, creating a market for a commodity was a chancier undertaking than dealing in objects that had an established record in the salesroom.

However, Bonhams was not dissuaded from moving in new directions. In 2000, the company merged with another auction house known as Brooks, founded in 1989 by Christie's veteran Robert Brooks. Brooks specialized in the sale of vintage motorcars, and Bonhams had been collaborating with Brooks on a Web site called supergavel. Together, sales at the new Bonhams & Brooks were reported at £75 annually.

In 2001, Bonhams & Brooks merged with the U.K. operations of Phillips, de Pury & Luxombourg, itself a subsidiary of luxury conglomerate LVMH. Acquisition activity continued, and by 2002, the year in which it purchased Butterfields for $21.8 million, Bonhams had replaced competitor Phillips, de Pury & Luxombourg in the number three slot of the Big Four, posting $304 million in auction sales for the year. Bonhams changed Butterfields' name to Bonhams & Butterfields, and Malcolm Barber, formerly of Brooks, became the chief executive officer of the American subsidiary. Bonhams remained the company's brand name outside of the United States.

Butterfields itself had a long and colorful history. The company dated back to 1865, when William Butterfield retired as a

sheriff and took up his auctioneer's gavel at Marble Head Auctioneers in San Francisco. At the time, Marble Head catered to Gold Rush Californians and offered mostly surplus goods consigned by sailing ships entering the San Francisco harbor. As the Golden Gate city became more prosperous and sophisticated with the arrival of the Victorian era, there developed a demand for fine art and furnishings. Butterfield, who by now owned the business, adapted his auction house to meet people's need for a place where they could buy and sell their possessions.

Fred R. Butterfield, William Butterfield's son, joined the firm in 1914. Fred's ambition was to place his family's company on a par with the greatest auction houses of London. Immediately following his arrival, there was a great upsurge in the auction market as the nation entered World War I. Fred's son, Reeder Butterfield, joined the business, now called Butterfield & Butterfield, in 1935 and took its helm after his father's death. Reeder developed Butterfield & Butterfield's European and Asian markets by acquiring consigned goods and attracting collectors from outside the United States. Under his direction, Butterfield & Butterfield became one of the strongest auction houses in the world.

Internet auctioneer eBay, in 1999, purchased Butterfield & Butterfield, which had auction showrooms in San Francisco and Los Angeles, for $260 million in stock as part of its ongoing attempts to tap the fine art auction market. Butterfields, as the company came to be known, was supposed to funnel sale items to eBay's Web site in a category known as ''Premier.'' However, the company's revenues fell under eBay's stewardship because shoppers refused to buy high-end paintings, antique furniture, and ceramics online without first seeing them. ''I think we had just been slightly off target in understanding the change in consumer buying habits,'' said a spokesman for eBay in the *San Francisco Chronicle*, adding ''We thought it would happen at a more accelerated pace.'' Scores of staff were laid off, and Butterfields' entertainment memorabilia, photography, and art deco departments were jettisoned. Live auctions in Butterfields Chicago branch ended in 2000. Nearly 70 percent of Butterfields sales were still offline when it was sold to Bonhams in 2002.

More International Activity in the Early 2000s

In 2003, Bonhams moved further onto the international stage when it joined with Sydney auctioneer Goodmans to create Bonhams & Goodman based in Sydney, Australia. Goodmans, which had been in business since 1994, accounted for about 20 percent of sales in the Australian auction market. At the time, the Australian auction market was still dominated by Sotheby's, Christie's, and Deutscher-Menzies, which together accounted for 75 percent of its sales.

By the end of 2003, Bonhams had grown to encompass more than 800 sales annually, more than 665 employees, and annual sales of $304 million. The company's worldwide network of sales included two major London venues, nine additional U.K. locations, and sales rooms in Switzerland, Monaco, Germany, Los Angeles, San Francisco, and Sydney.

Bonhams & Butterfields conducted its first East Coast sale in 2003 with an auction of Edwin C. Jameson's collection of

Key Dates:

1793: Thomas Dodd and Walter Bonham found Bonhams.
1865: William Butterfield founds Marble Head Auctioneers.
1987: Elwes takes charge of Bonhams Auctioneers.
1999: eBay acquires Butterfields.
2000: Bonhams merges with Brooks to become Bonhams & Brooks.
2001: Bonhams & Brooks merges with the U.K. operations of Phillips, de Pury & Luxombourg.
2001: eBay closes Butterfields' Chicago office.
2002: Bonhams purchases Butterfields.
2003: Bonhams acquires Goodmans Auctioneers.
2004: Bonhams New York opens a permanent salesroom.

classic cars and antiques in Massachusetts. Bonhams & Butterfields also developed a strong presence in fine jewelry and Asian art, and strove to become the world leader in ethnographic art. In addition, it had a strong presence in the following markets: arms and armor; American, Western, and California paintings; natural history; modern furniture; and decorative arts markets. Back in the United Kingdom, Bonhams set a world record for sales of British marine paintings by artists Robert Dodd and Thomas Butterworth and for paintings by American artist Aldro T. Hibbard, as well as fetching top dollar for works by Americans Andy Warhol and Roy Lichtenstein.

In 2004, Bonhams & Butterfields, with operations in New York, Los Angeles, and San Francisco, expanded its presence to New York City with the establishment of a permanent salesroom and offices known as Bonhams New York. Its inaugural New York City auction featured 20th century furniture and decorative arts. Bonhams & Butterfields, which specialized in the appraisal and disposition, through auction, of fine art, antiques, collectibles, and decorative objects, also provided consignment management and insurance services.

In 2005, Bonhams New York held auctions in jewelry, 20th-century decorative arts, and American paintings. In an attempt to capture a broader spectrum of buyers, Bonhams & Butterfields took part in San Francisco's South of Market (SoMa) and Los Angeles' Sunset sales. These monthly auctions introduced Bonhams & Butterfields to selling moderately-valued estate property, fine art and furnishings in the $400 to $4,000 range, and opened yet more avenues for profit to the already well-established multinational company.

Bonhams 1793 Ltd. had a ways to go before challenging the likes of Christies and Sotheby's, but it had certainly closed the gap in recent years under the direction of Chairman Robert Brooks. With its Bonhams & Butterfields presence in the United States, and its move into Australia with Bonhams & Goodman, the U.K.-based company was quick to proclaim its role as "not only the world's fastest growing auction house, [but] also the world's oldest and largest auctioneer of fine art and antiques still in British ownership."

Principal Operating Units

Bonhams & Butterfields (United States); Bonhams & Goodman (Australia).

Principal Competitors

Christie's International plc; Phillips, de Pury & Luxembourg; Sotheby's Holdings Inc.

Further Reading

Darwent, Charles, "Bonhams Breaks With Tradition," *Management Today*, July 1997, p. 56.
Kopytoff, Verne, "eBay's Offline Plan Fails, Butterfields Sold," *San Francisco Chronicle*, August 1, 2002, p. B1.
"London Auction Houses Join to Become More Competitive," *Daily Mail* (London), September 13, 2000.
Menon, Jon, "French Tycoon Proposes Merger of Two Auction Houses," *Sunday Business* (London), July 8, 2001.
Meyers, Laura, "Bonhams Goes Global," *Art Business News*, January 2004, p. 42.
Moeran, Brian, "Jousting at Bonhams, London," *Ceramics Monthly*, January 1990, p. 18.
Stanbridge, Philip, "A Hot London Summer," *Ceramics Monthly*, October 1991, p. 28.
Windsor, John, "Stop Press! Art Market Says Size Does Matter," *Independent*, May 8, 1993, p. 34.

—Carrie Rothburd

The Branch Group, Inc.

442 Rutherford Avenue
Roanoke, Virginia 24016
U.S.A.
Telephone: (540) 982-1678
Fax: (540) 982-4217
Web site: http://www.branchgroup.com

Private Company
Incorporated: 1963 as Branch & Associates, Inc.
Employees: 750
Sales: $250 million (2003 est.)
NAIC: 233000 Building, Developing, and General
Contracting

The Branch Group, Inc., is a Roanoke, Virginia-based regional building construction company offering general contracting, design-build, and construction management services to the Mid-Atlantic region of the United States. The firm also maintains offices in Winston-Salem, North Carolina, and Virginia Beach, Virginia. Branch is comprised of four wholly owned subsidiary operating companies. Branch & Associates, Inc. is a general contractor for both public and private buildings, including hotels and resorts; institutional, educational, industrial, and health care facilities; and multi-family housing. The subsidiary operates out of Roanoke and Winston-Salem. Branch Highways, Inc., based in Roanoke and serving the Mid-Atlantic region, handles both public and private clients, offering a full range of highway, bridge, airport, infrastructure, and site development capabilities. E.V. Williams, Inc., based in Virginia Beach, Virginia, is also a paving specialist, doing public highway work as well as private site development projects. Finally, G.J. Hopkins, Inc. offers complete mechanical and electrical construction services, including design capabilities, for both public and private clients, primarily in the healthcare, higher education, and industrial construction areas. Also based in Roanoke, Hopkins serves the western Virginia market. Since 1982, the Branch Group has been owned by its employees through an Employee Stock Ownership Plan, an arrangement that has motivated the work force and been a key factor in the company's strong growth over the last 20 years.

Establishing a Construction Company: 1950s–80s

The Branch Group bears the name of its founder, Billy H. Branch. He was born in 1928 in Bells, Tennessee, the son of a railroad worker. He attended David Lipscomb College in Nashville for one year before transferring to Georgia Tech University, where he graduated in 1950 with a degree in electrical engineering. He took a job with Southeast Underwriters, putting his engineering training to use for an insurance company. He was then transferred to Roanoke, Virginia, and first became familiar with the area, but his time there was cut short by the Korean War and a call to service. He was assigned to the Army Ordinance Corp and stationed in Washington, D.C., from 1951 to 1952. It was during this time that he met his wife, Betty McAlister, who also came from Roanoke. After the war, the couple moved to Georgia, where Branch went to work for South Wire Company, maker of electrical wiring and related products. Because it was a young company, he took on a wide range of operational roles, including office manager, purchasing agent, and production manager. After about two and a half years, he was asked to help set up a subsidiary for South Wire, but he elected instead to go into business with his father-in-law, Claude W. McAlister, who had been involved in the construction industry in Roanoke and had recently lost his partner. At this point, McAlister had some equipment but no business. Although close to retirement age, he had no interest in giving up working. His tales about building the West Virginia Turnpike had always intrigued Branch, who was also attracted to the idea of entering a risky yet challenging business, one that was very much a boom-or-bust proposition. Moreover, the experience and skills the two men possessed complemented each other. McAlister's background was in the field, while Branch possessed both the necessary engineering knowledge as well as the operational experience he picked up at South Wire to run a construction business. Thus, in 1955, McAlister and Branch formed a partnership called McAlister Construction Company.

McAlister Construction started out doing work for home builders and general contractors in the Roanoke area, digging basements and building roads for housing subdivisions. It was the road building that quickly became the company's focus. In the second year of doing business, McAlister Construction landed its first highway contract, paving a six-mile stretch in

Company Perspectives:

Our primary goal is to continuously improve our profitability in order to grow stockholder wealth.

Buchanan County, Virginia. Construction turned out to be a profitable enterprise for the company's two partners, as the company grew about 20 percent each year from 1955 to 1963. At this point, McAlister was ready to retire and Branch, eager to stand entirely on his own, bought him out. In 1963, the business was reorganized and incorporated as Branch & Associates, Inc.

Initially, little changed after McAlister's departure. The company was primarily a highway builder and remained so until the 1970s, when Billy Branch became involved in real estate. As he described it, he was buying "holes and hills." He would fill in the holes, level off the hills, and on the level ground construct buildings that he could then turn around and sell. He tried to line up buyers before he began construction on a project, but he found it difficult to accurately estimate the costs to maximize his profits. As a result, he changed his strategy so that he leased the buildings rather than sold them. Using this approach, Branch & Associates built a number of structures that became fast food restaurants, finer restaurants, and office buildings. However, it did not take long before the company turned its attention to larger jobs, becoming interested in whatever projects could be found on the bid market for both public and private clients. As a result, the company began building schools and taking on various construction projects for Virginia Tech University and the University of Virginia. Other major building projects over the ensuing years included the Roanoke Airport Marriott Hotel, the Snowshoe and Silver Creek ski resorts in West Virginia, a Buckingham County prison, and an addition to the Roanoke Memorial Hospital. What began as a sideline to highway construction became large enough in the 1970s to become a separate division. Thus, Branch & Associates was now comprised of a highway division and a building division.

A third division would also grow out of the building business: mechanical contracting. A major factor in construction was the cost of plumbing, heating, air conditioning, and electrical, so it made sense to bring that work in house rather than rely on subcontractors. The Branch Group's current chief executive officer, James C. Harrison, who had started out as a surveyor for the highway division, approached Billy Branch about starting the mechanical unit in the late 1970s and was given permission to proceed. The unit was intended to work on Branch projects but in short order it began taking on outside work. In 1984, this business was expanded through the acquisition of G.J. Hopkins, Inc., a Roanoke mechanical and electrical contractor. It was founded in 1958 by Garland Hopkins as a mechanical contractor and added electrical capabilities in 1963. The company further added a sheet metal shop. According to Billy Branch, when Garland Hopkins approached him about buying the business, he said it was losing about $50,000 a month. Branch also speculated that Hopkins might have had some health concerns that prompted him to seek a buyer. Despite the problems at G.J. Hopkins, Branch agreed to buy the business and folded his smaller operation into it. Hopkins stayed on to run the unit, but his health soon failed and he passed away.

Restructuring for the Future: 1980s and 1990s

The Branch Group was formed as a holding company in 1985, and Branch Associates and the other units now became subsidiaries. The company, which at this stage was doing about $40 million worth of work each year, was also in the process of changing its ownership structure. In 1982, Branch launched a profit-sharing plan, which allowed the company to contribute pre-tax dollars into a fund that the employees would share. Billy Branch then elected to use the profit-sharing fund as a mechanism to create an Employee Stock Ownership Plan (ESOP), so that the employees would eventually become the owners of the business. Billy Branch cited three reasons why he decided to pursue an ESOP. It served as an incentive for employees, helping to make a more productive company. It allowed him, as he was nearing retirement age, to withdraw from the business while saving on taxes. Finally, as he said in a 2004 interview, "It was a nice thing to do for the employees." Aside from growing a successful construction business, Billy Branch had also gained a reputation for philanthropy. He raised considerable sums of money for Young Life and its network of Christian youth camps, and he would also serve as chairman for the Habitat for Humanity home-construction program. Unlike many ESOPs, Branch employees took on no debt. Instead, profit sharing money was put into a trust fund, which gradually bought up Billy Branch's stock in the company.

By 1993, the employees had bought about 80 percent of Billy Branch's stock and were well on the way to gaining a 100 percent stake. Also during this time, Branch began turning over many of the day-to-day responsibilities to his management team, while he oversaw the business as chairman of the board. In April 1993, at age 65, he decided to retire as chairman as well, telling the *Roanoke Times & World News,* "I've delegated myself out of a job." Nevertheless, he stayed on as a board member for another 11 years and, far from devoting himself to a life of leisure, he continued his interest in real estate development, running Branch Management. This business grew and took up so much of his time that in the spring of 2004 he resigned from the Branch Group board to focus on his new endeavors. His successor as chairman of Branch Group was Ralph Shivers, a longtime executive of the firm, who along with chief financial officer Kelly Speas was a key player in the growth of the Branch Group, which by 1993 was generating approximately $100 million in annual revenues, a far cry from the $1.3 million in annual business the company was generating in 1972.

Internal and External Growth: 1990s and Beyond

Branch looked to consolidate its operations in the early 1990s. The Hopkins unit had outgrown its 11,000-square-foot facility, as did Branch Highways with its 6,000-square-foot building. In 1993, the company paid $800,000 for a 19,000-square-foot building in Roanoke, the former manufacturing plant for Clarke-America Checks Inc. After a year of remodeling, which took place even as the Branch operations were moving in, the facility was enlarged to 26,000 square feet, offering office space as well as a modern shop.

Branch took another major step in its growth in February 1997 with the acquisition of E.V. Williams Inc., a Tidewater area contractor that specialized in road building. It was founded

Key Dates:

1955: McAlister Construction Company is founded by Claude McAlister and Billy Branch.
1963: Branch buys out McAlister to form Branch & Associates.
1984: G.J. Hopkins, Inc. is acquired.
1985: The Branch Group is formed as a holding company.
1993: Billy Branch retires.
1997: E.V. Williams Inc. is acquired.
2003: The company celebrates its 40th anniversary and is now generating $250 million a year in revenue.

in 1941 by Elmer Virginius Williams to operate as a local road grading company. After acquiring a paving company in 1945, it took advantage of a highway building boom that occurred in the United States in the Cold War years after World War II, a time when the construction of a national highway system was a vital defense initiative. In 1948, Williams paved a 45-mile section of the Pennsylvania Turnpike. The business expanded in 1952 with the acquisition of Portsmouth Paving Company, which operated a pair of asphalt plants in Portsmouth and Chesapeake, Virginia. With its increased capabilities, Williams completed paving projects throughout the Mid-Atlantic States. In addition to highways, it did work on airports, military bases, and deep-water ports. The company also began operating borrow pits in the Tidewater area as well as a major public landfill.

Branch Group also grew internally during the late 1990s. In 1998, Hopkins added design and build capabilities. A year later, Hopkins launched two subdivisions, offering industrial automation and data communications cabling design and installation services. When Branch Group celebrated its 40th anniversary in 2003, it was a $250 million business and well positioned for ongoing growth.

Principal Subsidiaries

Branch & Associates, Inc.; Branch Highways Inc.; G.J. Hopkins, Inc.; E.V. Williams Inc.

Principal Competitors

Bechtel Group, Inc.; Fluor Corporation; The Turner Corporation.

Further Reading

Edwards, Greg, "Company to Show Quarters After a Year of Renovation," *Roanoke Times & World News*, July 28, 1994, p. B10.
Kegley, George, "A Quiet Departure," *Roanoke Times & World News*, April 18, 1994, p. F1

—Ed Dinger

Brigham's Inc.

30 Mill Street
Arlington, Massachusetts 02476
U.S.A.
Telephone: (781) 648-9000
Toll Free: (800) 274-4426
Fax: (781) 646-0507
Web site: http://www.brighams.com

Private Company
Founded: 1914
Employees: 350
Sales: $50 million (2004 est.)
NAIC: 311520 Ice Cream and Frozen Dessert
    Manufacturing

Brigham's, Inc., is a privately owned, Arlington, Massachusetts-based company that produces ice cream and frozen yogurt under the Brigham's and premium Elan brands, as well as for regional private labels. A tradition in New England, Brigham's vanilla ice cream is the number one selling frozen food in the region. The company also maintains 27 full-service restaurants in Massachusetts, offering sandwiches as well as ice cream.

Early 1900s Origins

Brigham's traces its history to 1914 when the Durrand Company, founded by the Symmes brothers, opened a shop in Boston's Post Office Square to sell candy and ice cream. The man who would lend his name to the company, Edward L. Brigham, opened his own ice cream shop, called ''The Little Shop,'' in the Newton Highlands section in 1924. He made his own candies and ice cream in the backroom, relying on private recipes, including the one for vanilla ice cream that would be passed down to the present age. All that would be revealed about the formula was that it began with vanilla extract imported from Madagascar. In addition to producing delicious ice cream, The Little Shop also became known for serving generous portions of its five and ten cent cones and 20 cent sundaes. On summer weekends, according to company lore, the crowds were so thick around The Little Shop that police were called in

to maintain order. Brigham was so successful that after five years, in 1929, he merged his business with the Durand Company to achieve even greater regional growth and form the basis of what evolved into today's Brigham's Inc.

Soon Brigham's opened an ice cream manufacturing plant, which supplied an additional three stores the company opened. By now, candy consumption in America had declined, and the shops focused on ice cream. Despite the Great Depression of the 1930s, the company continued to prosper, opening another 20 stores during the decade. Primarily as a way to add business during the winter months, Brigham's acquired Dorothy Muriel's bakery in 1940, and the shops began selling baked goods as well as ice cream. It was not until the early 1960s that Brigham's began to move into the dining sector. During the interim, it was acquired by Star Markets, which then opened 40 new colonial-style shops that began offering sandwiches. Next, Brigham's was acquired by the Jewell Companies in 1968, and the business was supplemented by the addition of Buttrick's chain of colonial-style restaurants located in Arlington, Massachusetts, which would become the home of Brigham's headquarters.

Franchising in the 1970s

To supply its chain of retail operations, Brigham's expanded its manufacturing operation during the early 1970s. The company turned to franchising in 1977, a move that greatly expanded the Brigham's presence in New England. The company changed owners again in 1982 when Jewell sold it to New York financier Bennett S. Lebow, who tucked it into Lebow Industries, a privately held company. Under his ownership, Brigham's began pursuing supermarket sales. In 1983, the first quarts of Brigham's ice cream were sold in supermarkets and grocery stores. On the restaurant side, expansion continued, the chain peaking at 105 units in the mid-1980s. Around this time, however, the company began to exhibit some serious problems. According to Tina Cassidy, writing for the *Boston Business Journal* in 1992, ''Under Lebow's stewardship, consumer products were priced irrationally, there were too many restaurants in bad locations, the shops needed a face lift, and little attention had been paid to the increased competitiveness among other ice cream and frozen yogurt makers.'' An attempt to build a dinner clientele at Brigham's restaurants also proved to be ill conceived.

Charged with revitalizing Brigham's was Richard Silva, a 17-year veteran of the company, named president in August 1987. He shared his assessment of the company with *New England Business* a few months later: "One of the problems at Brigham's over the years is that we never knew what we wanted to be when we grew up. . . . We have really not had consistent leadership at the top. We've had talented people at the top, but we haven't had any consistency of direction in the last 30 years." In response to market research that indicated consumers associated Brigham's with ice cream and a quick place for a sandwich, Silva created a five-year plan that would expand supermarket ice cream sales throughout the Northeast in an effort to establish Brigham's as a premium brand in the family category, differentiating itself from the economy brands sold in half-gallon and gallon cartons and the specialty brands sold in pints. The restaurant chain at this stage had declined to 72 units, many of which were franchised to operators who had no equity stake in the business. Instead, they maintained a small security deposit while Brigham's held the restaurant's lease and owned all the equipment. As these franchise agreements began to expire, Silva wanted to convert franchisees to an equity position.

Silva never had the chance to complete his five-year plan, as once again Brigham's underwent yet another change in direction at a time when the company was losing a reported $4.5 million a year. In 1988, Lebow brought in a consultant, Milton Namiot, to determine why Brigham's was losing money. A year later, in April 1989, Naimot replaced Silva as president. He took over a company that was generating about $36 million in annual sales, 70 percent of which came from the restaurant business. Naimot believed that Brigham's had to sell pre-packed pints in order to remain competitive, and in the fall of 1989 the company introduced pints in eight flavors, priced as much as a dollar less than Ben & Jerry's. To accommodate this price point, Brigham's not only took less of a profit, it cut back on the butterfat content and added some air to the product. Naimot also took on the frozen yogurt market, as Brigham's introduced six flavors of frozen yogurt quarts in the fall of 1989. In addition, the company tried its hand at novelty products, bringing out a microwave milkshake called Zapp-A-Frappe and premium sundae cups. Brigham's also became aggressive in its geographic expansion, moving into the New York City market in 1990. It placed an advertisement in the *Miami Herald* to gauge interest in bringing Brigham's ice cream to Florida. The response was encouraging, and in 1992 the company began distributing its products in the Sunshine State. Other markets Naimot considered were Philadelphia, Washington, D.C., and the United Kingdom. Naimot clearly focused on pre-pack sales, and on the restaurant side of the business he closed down struggling operations and opened a handful of new ones located in more promising locations, including scaled-down versions in shopping mall food courts. By mid-1992 the chain was reduced to 55 units. What remained were remodeled with a retro 1930s and 1940s interior look and menus revamped to include such fare as pita pocket sandwiches and entrees that included sirloin steak and fried haddock. In 1992, Naimot reorganized the company into separate restaurant and pre-packed ice cream divisions, appointing senior managers to oversee each operation.

Elan Foods Acquired in the Early 1990s

After stabilizing Brigham's, in July 1991 Namiot bought a controlling interest in the company with funding from Grotech Partners, a Baltimore venture capital firm, and an Italian holding company, Raggio diSole Finanziaria. With his new financial backing, Naimot completed a major acquisition in 1993, buying Elan Foods Inc., makers of Elan Frozen Yogurt, a nine-year-old premium brand that had lost its elite standing, unable to keep pace with more aggressive competitors like Häagen-Dazs, Colombo, and Ben & Jerry's. Elan did not label its products as low-fat and failed to introduce the kind of chunky, mixed-in flavors concocted by its rivals. By acquiring Elan, Brigham's hoped to broaden its demographics, in particular to increase its base among women and 25 to 50-year-olds without cannibalizing sales from the Brigham's brand. Brigham's following, according to market research, was with consumers 50 years and older. Soon after Brigham's took over, Elan dropped some of its low-selling flavors and replaced them with such items as Andres!, Mint Drift, and Carrot Cake Rapture. Most of its traditional flavors were also reformulated and labeled low fat. Packaging also received a design make-over to give the yogurt cartons what the company called an upscale European look, and a new marketing effort was launched. As a result, Elan began winning back distribution as a number of supermarkets elected to once again carry the full Elan line.

Despite the changes Naimot made, Brigham's did little more than hold its own. In 1995, the business was reorganized, and the company experienced yet another change at the top as Roger Theriault was named chief executive officer. He had been with the company since 1989. The structure of having separate divisions was scrapped, and ice cream and restaurants were reunited as part of a brand building strategy. While pre-packed supermarket ice cream was by now the dominant sales generator, accounting for about 65 percent of total revenues, the restaurants remained important as a branding tool and because many consumer's first taste of Brigham's ice cream was in a Brigham's restaurant. Another new look, "cheerier and brighter," according to Theriault, was introduced in the Burlington Mall in 1998. The smaller mall units also proved to be more profitable because of lower staffing needs, easier maintenance, and less overhead in general. Soon afterward, the company introduced a kiosk format, less than 300 square feet, much smaller than the mall units and limited to selling ice cream and beverages. All the while, Brigham's closed down older, less profitable restaurants. All units in Florida and New York were shut down, and the company focused its efforts in these markets entirely on supermarket sales. Under Theriault, Elan enjoyed steady growth. From 1998 through 2001, the brand experienced a 46 percent increase in sales during a period in which the category as a whole had suffered a sizeable decline.

Strategic Changes Continue into the 2000s

As Brigham's entered the 2000s, sales had grown to the $50 million range, and the company had been profitable since

Key Dates:

1914: The Durand Company opens a Boston candy and ice cream shop.
1924: Edward L. Brigham opens "The Little Shop," selling candy and ice cream.
1929: Durand and Brigham merge.
1940: Brigham's shops begin selling baked goods.
1968: Jewell companies acquire the Brigham's.
1983: Brigham's ice cream is first sold to supermarkets.
1993: The company acquires the premium Elan brand.
1991: Brigham's ownership changes in a management-led buyout.
2004: New England Capital acquires Brigham's.

Theriault had taken over. To stay current, the company brought out new product launches such as the Big Dig, which commemorated Boston's long-term Central Artery highway project. Brigham's significantly expanded its geographic reach in 2002 by signing an agreement with Pathmark supermarkets to distribute its products in Pathmarks stores in New York, New Jersey, and parts of Delaware and Pennsylvania. In 2003, Brigham's broadened its product line with the introduction of a line of premium, stickless three-ounce ice cream bars, available in milk chocolate and dark chocolate varieties.

Brigham's celebrated its 90th anniversary in 2004, and although the company had experienced many challenges throughout its history, it was a survivor in a tough category. As was often the case in the company's past, Brigham's now experienced another change in ownership. In 2004, the Newton, Massachusetts-based private equity investment firm of New England Capital Partners acquired Brigham's for an undisclosed price from the previous ownership group, which by this time had been dominated by foreign investors. It was Theriault who played a key role in bringing Brigham's and New England Capital together. He then stepped down and in April 2004 a new chief executive, Charles Green, was installed. He would also become an equity owner in the business. Green was well experienced in the ice cream trade, having served as vice-president of strategy and distribution at Unilever Ice Cream and senior director of North American sales and distribution at Ben & Jerry's, which was owned by Unilever. The new team considered the Brigham brand a "jewel" not fully exploited by previous owners. "At first glance," in the opinion of Chris Reidy, writing for the *Boston Globe*, "the highly competitive ice cream business would seem to be experiencing challenging times. The

cost of many ice cream ingredients are up sharply, and for many health-conscious consumers following low-carbohydrate diets, ice cream is something they've scratched off their grocery store shopping list." Nevertheless, Brigham's new management team believed there were channels of distribution the company had not fully exploited, like food service opportunities at universities and sporting events. The restaurants would still find a place within the new organization, but ice cream would take precedence over other foods. In 2004, the company continued to introduce new products, including a Reverse the Curse ice cream dedicated to the Boston Red Sox baseball team, which had been denied a World Series championship for decades. In the fall of that year, the team won the World Series, and Brigham's claimed a share of the credit, changing the name of the flavor to Curse Reversed.

In 2005, Elan marked its 20th anniversary with a revamped package design, a new size, and several new flavors. Brigham's attempted its first co-branding venture in the same year, teaming up with iParty, a party goods retailer, to market an ice cream flavor called iParty No Bake Cake that tried to emulate the taste of golden cake mix and swirls of chocolate frosting. The alliance between Brigham's and iParty was designed to give the latter company more brand exposure, while Brigham's hoped the iParty name would help its product stand out on already crowded store shelves. It was just one of five new ice cream flavors the company hoped to introduce in 2005.

Principal Competitors

Denny's Corporation; Friendly Ice Cream Corporation; HP Hood LLC.

Further Reading

Carlino, Bill, "Brigham's Chain Sets Sights on Shopping Malls for Growth," *Nation's Restaurant News*, October 7, 1991, p. 70.

Cassidy, Tina, "Brigham's Scoops Out a New Image," *Boston Business Journal*, June 1, 1992, p. 1.

"Elan Shines Again," *Dairy Foods*, June 1994, p. 765.

Goodison, Donna L., "Brigham's Scoops Profits with Willingness to Evolve," *Biston Business Journal*, June 8, 2001, p. 10.

"Growing Up Tastefully: Brigham's Ice Cream Celebrates 90th Anniversary," *Dairy Foods*, March 2004, p. 56.

McLaughlin, Mark, "Adhering to Reality Principle Stands Brigham's in Good Stead," *New England Business*, October 19, 1987, p. 54.

Reidy, Chris, "New Owners of Ice Cream Maker Brigham's Aim to Strengthen Brand," *Boston Globe*, April 21, 2004.

Reiter, Jeff, "Growing a New England Tradition," *Dairy Foods*, August 1989, p. 56.

—Ed Dinger

CACI

CACI International Inc.

1100 North Glebe Road
Arlington, Virginia 22201
U.S.A.
Telephone: (703) 841-7800
Fax: (703) 841-7882
Web site: http://www.caci.com

Public Company
Incorporated: 1962 as California Analysis Center, Inc.
Employees: 9,500
Sales: $1.45 billion (2004)
Stock Exchanges: New York
Ticker Symbol: CAI
NAIC: 336419 Other Guided Missile and Space Vehicle
Parts and Auxiliary Equipment Manufacturing; 54151
Computer Systems Design and Related Services;
541511 Custom Computer Programming Services;
541512 Computer Systems Design Services; 541519
Other Computer Related Services; 541614 Process,
Physical Distribution, and Logistics Consulting
Services

CACI International Inc. is a leading provider of informational technology (IT) services for the intelligence and defense community. The federal government accounts for 95 percent of the company's revenues. CACI is a world leader in technology systems, custom software, integration and operations, imaging and document management, simulation, and proprietary database and software products. Headquartered in the Washington, D.C., area, the company has more than 100 offices in the United States and western Europe. It has been a voracious acquirer, buying 29 companies in one twelve-year period.

CACI is a technological leader in the supply of automated information systems for state government management of vehicle registration, licensing and wheeled-vehicle revenue support, local government management of false emergency alarm billing systems, and housing registration systems. Other representative systems applications include airport and airspace traffic planning, ammunition management information systems, automated document and records management systems, automated procurement, business process re-engineering, business support systems, computer-aided logistics and data information systems, electronic commerce, executive decision support systems, imaging services, information management systems, legal systems and litigation support services, manufacturing requirements planning systems, marketing and customer database management systems, product data management, retail market modeling, simulation languages and derivative products, site location planning and analysis systems, software development and reuse, systems re-engineering, systems integration, and weapons systems and equipment configuration management systems.

CACI products are installed in more than 10,000 locations throughout the world and used in a wide variety of applications. Products include ACORN, a demographic information service that analyzes consumers according to the type of residential area in which they live and is used to identify prime prospects for all types of consumer goods and services; COMNET, a network simulation software product for communications engineers to study wide area networks (WANs) of satellites, land lines, switching systems and protocols; InSite, a marketing and demographics information system providing PC-based geographic information systems combining software, data, and mapping capabilities to enable planners to determine the location of retail outlets, branch networks, sales territories, potential customers, and competitors; MIRACLE, a financial accounting system; MODSIM, a simulation programming language for computer programming and graphics environments that provides an object-oriented approach to structuring software, providing an intuitive development framework for programmers and which allows code to be reused; NETWORK, a computer architecture simulation software program for engineers to study alternative combinations of computers and data storage devices; REenterprise, a technology management solution which combines proprietary methodologies and computer software to analyze and reconfigure an organization's business process; SIMFACTORY, a general factory simulator for factory planners to study alternative plant and equipment configurations; SIMOBJECT, a software framework for the reduction of time and cost in building simulation models; SIMPROCESS, an object-oriented analyti-

---

Company Perspectives:

CACI's mission is to be the world leader in information technology and networld solutions. We deliver in-demand products and services—providing innovative solutions for Homeland Security, Systems integration, Network services, Information assurance, Intelligence services, Knowledge management, Modeling and simulation, Engineering and logistics. Our strength is developing superior IT solutions that evolve over time to ensure exceptional performance and outstanding client success. Through growth we provide opportunity for our people, create solutions for our clients and make good profits for our shareholders.

cal simulation software prototyping tool for business process re-engineering enabling managers to model a current business process and then explore alternative approaches before implementation; and SIMSCRIPT, a simulation programming language designed specifically for analysts to build computer-based representations of complex activities such as airways and airport traffic, maintenance procedures for fleets of ships, warfare studies of military equipment and tactics, and communications networks, among many others.

Formed in 1962

The company that would become CACI International was founded in Santa Monica by Herb Karr and Harry Markowitz as California Analysis Center, Inc. on July 17, 1962. The two men had helped develop the SIMSCRIPT, the first simulation programming language, at RAND Corporation.

After SIMSCRIPT was released to the public domain, Karr and Markowitz started CACI to provide support and training for the new programming language. Years later, the company's future leader, Dr. Jack J.P. London, told the Newcomen Society that CACI's first office consisted of a phone booth and a park bench.

CACI had revenues of $34,000 in its first year. In 1963, the company won a contract to design an inventory control simulation for the Navy's Ships Parts Control Center in Mechanicsburg, Pennsylvania.

The company became one of the first to sell proprietary software with the 1965 release of Simscript 1.5. This was a compiler developed for translating SIMSCRIPT programs into assembly language for IBM's 7090/7094 computers.

The company was renamed Consolidated Analysis Centers Inc. in 1967 as it opened offices in Washington, D.C., and New York City. By this time, CACI had a second proprietary product, called QUICK QWERY, which was based on work for the U.S. Commerce Department. This represented a significant expansion of the company's capabilities into information processing systems.

CACI went public on August 15, 1968. Revenues exceeded $1 million for the year, and the company had grown to employ 40 people. Harry Markowitz left the company while Herb Karr became board chairman.

Expansion in the 1970s and 1980s

CACI released SIMSCRIPT II.5 in 1971. This would remain the leading simulation language for decades. Other key products evolved from the Commerce Department work. These included InSite and ACORN, programs to help businesses mine Census Bureau data.

The corporate headquarters were relocated to a suburb of Washington, D.C., in 1972. By this time, the East Coast was accounting for 80 percent of revenues. The company's official name was abbreviated to CACI, Inc. in 1973. In 1974, CACI set up a European division with headquarters at The Hague and branches in London, Dublin, Milan, and Bermuda. Within three years, Europe was boasting $1 million of revenues.

CACI began contracting for the U.S. Department of Defense in the mid-1970s. Another important long-term relationship began in 1978 when CACI won its first contract with the U.S. Department of Justice.

By 1980, the company had revenues approaching $35 million and a staff of 1,000. Growth was accelerating, and revenues exceeded $100 million in 1983. In 1984, Dr. J.P. ''Jack'' London became the company's president and CEO. London had joined the company 12 years earlier. He would be named chairman following the death of Herb Karr in 1990.

London was credited with helping the company transition from sole source to competitive bidding for federal contracts in the mid-1980s. CACI was also entering new markets with state and provincial governments. It developed an IT system for motor vehicle departments, beginning with that of Alberta, Canada.

In October 1985, CACI was reorganized as a Delaware corporation. Through a merger in June 1986, CACI became the parent company of CACI Inc. and CACI N.V., a Netherlands corporation. It was renamed CACI International Inc. in December 1986.

The late 1980s saw CACI pioneering another IT field, electronic data interchange (EDI). It was also working on the military procurement system called SAACONS (Standard Army Automated Contracting System), later commercialized as SACONS-FEDERAL. Six years after helping the Navy monitor its ammunition inventories with bar codes, CACI introduced its own optical imaging systems for records management in 1988.

Networking in the 1990s

With the falloff in defense work facing contractors at the end of the Cold War, CEO Jack London told *Investor's Business Daily,* ''We faced a traumatic crossroads for the company about where we would go in the future.''

CACI chose to transform itself from a professional services firm to a prime contractor of IT systems, focusing on the emerging field of networking. It grew aggressively by acquisition, buying American Legal Systems Corp. for $2 million in July 1992. In December 1993, CACI purchased certain contracts and assets from the Government Services business of SofTech Inc. for $4.2 million. Pinpoint Analysis Ltd. and Miracle Products Ltd. were also acquired in the early 1990s.

Key Dates:

1962: California Analysis Center, Inc. is founded.
1968: CACI goes public; revenues top $1 million.
1974: A European headquarters is established.
1986: The company is renamed CACI International Inc.
1995: Revenues exceed $200 million.
2002: The company's stock migrates from the NASDAQ to the New York Stock Exchange.
2004: Revenues exceed $1 billion.

In the 1990s, simulations became a powerful tool enabling people to visualize how new systems or processes will work prior to investing large amounts of capital and energy into them. One of the company's simulation clients has been the Office of the Secretary of Defense (OSD). The company provided modeling and simulation support for the Joint Warfare System (JWARS) development. This project simulates military campaigns to develop strategies for the most effective use of military forces and battlefield data. The company also defined and implemented the JWARS system architecture, provided software engineering expertise, and facilitated simulation and analytic interfaces between the services and the OSD.

In process re-engineering, the company analyzed current and proposed processes and systems, focusing on examining and implementing technology and system simulation for prediction and risk reduction. One of the company's clients in process re-engineering was the Arizona State Department of Liquor Licensing and Control. The company looked at all of the processes the department was using, determined the best re-engineering solution and implemented it, accurately predicting a 33 percent cost reduction in some processes and a 66 percent reduction in others. The company also supported the cost justification for implementation, predicted required staffing levels and increases in investigation work, and supported system sizing and technical architecture. In addition, CACI worked with the U.S. Navy to design a computer system to support concurrent, distributed document development such as text, graphics, email, and images in a secure environment. The system developed required geographical distribution over both LANs (local area computer networks) and WANs and logical distribution among storage devices. CACI engineers simulated the design in order to test it prior to development and implementation, identified bottlenecks and determined the number of communication lines needed at the sites.

Systems re-engineering involved modernizing a system by adding some new capabilities while retaining the best parts of the existing system. The company helped clients avoid costly new systems development and protected its current investments in technology. One of the company's clients in the area of systems re-engineering was Blue Cross/Blue Shield of Oregon. For Blue Cross, the company converted and migrated the claims information system to a distributed client/server computer platform with some enhancements. CACI produced the software re-engineering plan with tool and interface selections. During the conversion, the company developed an object-oriented reuse library which facilitated any future enhancements to be made, created a cost-effective solution to Year 2000 conversion, conducted comprehensive training for Blue Cross employees, and won the Innovator of the Year Award for methodology on this project.

Software reuse avoids reinventing the wheel when a government agency installs new technology. The company's software reuse programs have helped the government reuse as much software as possible, saving millions of dollars. One of the company's customers in this field was the U.S. Army's Sustaining Base Information Services. The company developed a reusable software module for budgeting, training, safety, and security across all U.S. Army posts. The module included data warehousing or migrating data from hundreds of existing databases, regardless of the source application or data characteristics, a breakthrough in reusable software that speeds migration and reduces software life-cycle costs while at the same time allowing existing technology to remain transferable to other projects.

The company specialized in processing huge numbers of documents so they can be indexed, sorted, searched, and retrieved. CACI integrated the legal process with the technology tools its commercial and government clients needed to manage their information requirements. CACI's main client in this field was the U.S. Department of Justice (DOJ). The system focused on the DOJ litigation support and records management, and CACI won an award for the integrated document management system it created for the Army's Gulf War Declassification Project, which involved document receipt and logging that included bar-coding, document scanning and conversion to machine-readable format, document image processing, format conversion, classified and declassified electronic file-room storage, workload prioritization/keyword searching to identify health-related documents, document declassification support, and preparation and release of documents for distribution via the Internet. Any military person who served in the Gulf War and had health-related concerns, or anyone curious about investigating such matters, could gain access to the government's entire file of health-related Gulf War documents by accessing the Internet using only a conventional computer and a modem.

CACI had been supplying electronic commerce technologies to its government clients for over ten years. As the 20th century came to a close, the company moved towards the next step of taking its clients to electronic commerce via the Internet. One of the company's clients in this area was the U.S. Department of Veterans Affairs. CACI developed an electronic pharmaceutical catalog purchasing system with an Internet interface. In a strategic alliance with Ingram Micro, the company was also creating an electronic catalog of computer products for all government buyers and sellers.

CACI also developed complex product data management (PDM) systems for clients operating in geographically dispersed, global development environments. Internationally recognized commercial enterprises applied the company's PDM capabilities for both client and internal use. Unisys Corporation used C-GATE, a configuration management repository support for the U.S. Navy's Trident submarine navigational program, and utilized a streamlined client/server architecture to help migrate the navy systems to open environments. Teledyne used the same program, C-GATE, internally to help move mainframe-based processes to a paperless environment which easily tracked blueprints and other engineering documents online, enhancing access to such documents.

A Top Contractor in the Mid-1990s

Annual revenues exceeded $200 million in 1995. A number of publications ranked CACI as one of the top federal IT contractors. September 1995 saw the company purchasing all the outstanding stock of Automated Sciences Group Inc., a provider of information technology for engineering and scientific environmental services to the U.S. Department of Defense and the U.S. Department of Energy, for $4.9 million in cash.

In January 1996, the company's subsidiary CACI Inc. purchased all of the outstanding stock of IMS Technologies Inc., a company which supplied information management for a variety of federal agencies, for $6.5 million. In October of that same year, the company acquired the business and certain net assets of Sunset Resources Inc., a company which provided engineering and information technology services to the U.S. Air Force and specialized in electronic data interchange, for $5.3 million in cash.

The diverse areas in which the company worked in the information technology market have helped it grow. Revenues continually climbed, from $145 million in 1993 to $245 million in 1996, with net income growth rising from $3 million in 1993 to $9.9 million in 1996. In 1997, the company's acquisition strategy included looking for strategic fits in government and commercial sectors and purchasing new and existing products and services, with a growth target of 15 percent through internal expansion as well as acquisitions.

In the 15 years from 1982 to 1997, the information technology industry grew from a $9 billion market to a $26 billion market. While IT spending in the defense market remained relatively stable, the commercial IT market tripled from $5 billion to just over $15 billion. CACI relied on a wide range of partners, vendors, and suppliers, which it considered "teammates." Some of the strategic alliances CACI made were with such companies as AT&T Global Information Solutions, IBM, Litton, Lockheed Martin, Lotus Development Corporation, Microsoft, Oracle, Sun Microsystems, and Unisys. Incorporating a full range of commercial off-the-shelf computer hardware and software products as part of its "customer solution" program, CACI was able to design custom and proprietary IT systems for its clients. The company has continued to expand its portfolio of proprietary software and database products, offering marketing systems software and database products to clients who need systems and analysis for retail sales of consumer products, direct mail campaigns, and franchise or branch site location projects.

As the year 2000 approached with all its potential computer software problems, organizations turned to firms like CACI. In addition, the information technology industry continued to grow with new software and hardware products. With a 1997 backlog of approximately $1 billion, CACI was positioned to continue to grow as an industry leader.

January 1997 saw the company acquire Sales Performance Analysis Limited, a software development company, for $2.6 million. Government Systems, Inc. (GSI), a division of leading

edge communications firm Infonet Services Corporation, was also acquired in 1997, as was Statistica, Inc.'s System Engineering Division, a developer of simulation-based manufacturing task trainers. U.K. database marketing software provider AnaData was acquired as well and renamed CACI Ltd.

CACI entered the intelligence community market in 1998 with the acquisition of QuesTech, Inc., later renamed CACI Technologies. Information Decision System was also acquired in 1998.

MapData was added in 1999. The company made a divestment late in the year, selling its Comnet Products Group to Michigan's Compuware Corp. for $40 million. By this time, according to the *Washington Business Journal,* CACI was the largest software developer in the Washington, D.C., area.

Still Growing in the 2000s

CACI's acquisition binge continued in February 2000, when it bought XEN Corp., another intelligence community specialist. Century Technologies, Inc. (CENTECH), a leading provider of electronic benefits transfer systems, was acquired the next month. The Special Projects division of Radian International, LLC, and network services provider N.E.T. Federal, Inc. were also added during the year. Digital Systems International, Inc. was acquired in 2001.

The Department of Defense accounted for more than half of CACI's revenues. CACI was poised to profit from the intensive IT demands of the homeland defense industry after 9/11. The company posted record revenues in 2001 ($564 million) and 2002 ($682 million) and showed no signs of slowing. In 2002, the company's shares migrated from the NASDAQ to the Big Board on the New York Stock Exchange. CACI then had about 5,000 employees at its 90 offices in the United States and Europe.

In 2002, the company acquired Condor Technology Solutions, Inc.'s Government Solutions Division for $16 million and the IT firm Acton Burnell, Inc. for $29 million. Another intelligence specialist, Premier Technology Group, Inc., was acquired for $49 million in 2003. Also purchased in 2003 were Applied Technology Solutions of Northern VA, Inc. for $13 million, C-Cubed Corporation, a producer of mobile command centers and reconnaissance equipment, for $36 million, and Britain's Rochester Information Systems, Ltd. for $2 million.

The acquisition of Premier brought with it a $500 million blanket U.S. Army contract that included, in addition to IT services, supplying interrogators at Iraq's Abu Ghraib prison. CACI was soon faced with a worldwide media frenzy after an early army report implicated one of its employees in the torture there. (CACI's larger rival Titan Corp. was also embroiled in the scandal.) In July 2004, another U.S. Army report cleared CACI's ten interrogators.

Revenues exceeded $1 billion in the fiscal year ended June 30, 2004. During the year, CACI bought MTL Systems Inc. ($4 million), CMS Information Services, Inc., and the Defense and Intelligence Group of AMS, Inc. (AMS-D&IG). The $413 million AMS-D&IG buy was considered the second-largest "big impact" government IT service deal of the year by *Washington Technology.*

Revenues were expected to be $1.5 billion for fiscal 2005. The company had previously stated the goal of reaching $2 billion in revenues by 2008.

Principal Subsidiaries

Automated Sciences Group, Inc.; CACI Dynamic Systems, Inc.; CACI Enterprise Solutions, Inc.; CACI Ltd. (United Kingdom); CACI Premier Technology, Inc.; CACI Systems and Technology Ltd. (Canada); CACI Technologies, Inc. (dba CACI Productions Group); CACI Inc.

Principal Competitors

Anteon International Corporation; Computer Sciences Corporation; General Dynamics Corporation; Lockheed Martin Corporation; Science Applications International Corporation; Titan Corporation.

Further Reading

Benesh, Peter, ''Bad Publicity Doesn't Slow Military Supplier,'' *Investor's Business Daily*, October 14, 2004, p. A8.

Bonasia, J., ''CACI Goes Great Guns Amid Defense's Growth Plans,'' *Investor's Business Daily*, May 2, 2001, p. A4.

Gerin, Roseanne, ''How Do You Respond? Controversy and Scandal Can Put a Media Bull's-Eye on Government Contractors,'' *Washington Technology*, February 21, 2005, pp. 25ff.

Jones, Jennifer, ''CACI Enhances E-Commerce Image with New Software,'' *Washington Business Journal*, August 27, 1999, p. 6.

Keri, Jonah, ''CACI Int'l on the Offensive; Defense Firm Acquiring Rivals, Winning Contracts,'' *Investor's Business Daily*, May 9, 2005, p. B2.

London, J.P., *CACI: Creation of an Opportunity*, New York: Newcomen Society of the United States, 2001.

McCarthy, Ellen, ''CACI Contract: From Supplies to Interrogation,'' *Technews.com*, May 17, 2004.

Reddy, Anitha, ''CACI Hungers to Reach the Top Tier,'' *Technews.com*, October 20, 2003.

Tsao, Amy, ''CACI: Wiping Off Abu Ghaib's Taint,'' *BusinessWeek Online*, August 18, 2004.

Verton, Dan, ''Army's Use of IT Contract to Hire Interrogators Questioned: Interior Department Audits $500M Blanket Agreement with CACI,'' *Computerworld*, May 31, 2004, pp. 1f.

Wakeman, Nick, ''More Suitors on CACI's Horizon,'' *Washington Technology*, January 10, 2000, p. 14.

—Daryl F. Mallett
—update: Frederick C. Ingram

Camaïeu S.A.

211 av Brame, BP 229
Roubaix
F-59054 Cedex 1
France
Telephone: +33 3 20 99 71 13
Fax: +33 3 20 80 71 70
Web site: http://www.Camaïeu.com

Public Company
Incorporated: 1984
Employees: 3,000
Sales: EUR 393.3 million ($450 million) (2004)
Stock Exchanges: Euronext Paris
Ticker Symbol: 7633
NAIC: 424330 Women's, Children's, and Infants'
    Clothing and Accessories Merchant Wholesalers

Camaïeu S.A. operates one of France's largest chains of women's clothing stores. The company, based in the northern city of Roubais, also has been expanding its network into international markets in the mid-2000s. Camaïeu's store network topped 440 stores at the beginning of 2005—including 69 stores in foreign markets such as Spain, Italy, Belgium, the Czech Republic, Poland and, since 2004, Russia. Camaïeu's stores tend to be small—with an average selling space of just 200 square meters—and focused on the lower mid-range ready-to-wear market. The company has established its reputation as a strong price competitor, rather than as a fashion house. As such the company's stores tend to feature styles inspired by—rather than setting—seasonal trends. Sourcing its goods from low-wage markets including China, Turkey, and the Middle East enables Camaïeu to position itself as a low-cost alternative, while offering reasonable quality. The company owns most of its stores, although a proportion continues to operate as franchises. A public company listed on the Euronext Paris Stock Exchange since 2000, Camaïeu has become the subject of a friendly takeover offer at the beginning of 2005, from private equity firm AXA Private Equity. The offer has enabled the founding Torck and Giraud-Verspieren families to cash out their holdings in the company; however, AXA Private Equity has not yet been able to buy full control of Camaïeu. In 2004, the company's revenues topped EUR 393 million ($450 million).

Retailing Success in the 1980s

Jean-Pierre Torck began his career working for French retailing powerhouse Auchan (Auchan, Decathlon, Kiabi, Boulanger, Leroy Merlin, Flunch, etc.). In 1984, Torck, together with Jean Duforest and another Auchan colleague, decided to go into business for himself. The partners decided to enter the clothing retailing business, targeting the women's ready-to-wear market. From the start, the new company identified itself clearly as a retailing business—rather than as a fashion house—targeting the development of an extended network of stores. Instead of seeking to create its own fashion, the company instead sought to provide low-priced variations of current seasonal trends, with an emphasis on a range of colors in order to stimulate high-volume sales. The company chose the name Camaïeu, playing off its retailing strategy.

Camaïeu opened its first store in Roubais in 1984, which was soon followed by several others as Torck and partners fine-tuned its product offering. By 1987, the network had expanded to a chain of 17 stores, including the first franchised store. By then, too, the company had completed the development of its retail concept and prepared to begin a full-fledged expansion of the chain.

The strong cash flow generated by the retail network became the financial motor for Camaïeu's first growth phase as the company began opening new stores at a brisk pace. By 1991, the company's network had topped 100 stores, and Camaïeu had established a fully national presence. Although many of the stores remained owned directly by Camaïeu, franchising had enabled the company to double its growth, and into the mid-1990s, the number of franchised stores increased to represent more than half of the group's total.

Camaïeu next turned to diversifying its retail offering. In 1991, the company created a second retail format, Camaïeu Homme, meant to replicate the company's success in the men's clothing sector. The effort proved successful, and the company began rolling out a number of Camaïeu Homme stores in the

Company Perspectives:

Allowing the greatest number of women to express their femininity, making them more beautiful, this is the desire of Camaïeu.

Camaïeu has become one of the French woman's favourite brands by providing modern, attractive and affordable collections. You will find you receive a simple, warm welcome in all Camaïeu boutiques. This is what makes our success in France and Internationally.

early 1990s. Nonetheless, the group's women's clothing network remained its flagship.

The group's success at home encouraged it to turn its attention toward developing an international presence. The company opened its first foreign Camaïeu in 1991, and by 1993, Camaïeu stores had been opened in Belgium, The Netherlands, Spain, Switzerland, and Luxembourg. By 1994, there were 20 foreign stores in operation.

In the meantime, Camaïeu's domestic network had taken off, topping 200 stores in 1993. That year marked a dramatic acceleration of the group's expansion, with 59 women's stores opened in just one year. The company kept up this pace in 1994, adding more than 70 stores that year. This expansion also included the company's first acquisition, with the purchase of the 50-store Tandy clothing chain.

With its total network nearing 300 stores, Camaïeu decided to add a third clothing store format to complete its offering. In 1994, the company debuted its Camaïeu Enfant store format with clothing targeting the children's market. That format also proved a success with price-conscious French consumers. As before, the company continued to finance its expansion through the steady cash flow generated by its growing chain. In this way, the company was able to absorb the start-up losses of new stores and its new clothing store formats.

Rebuilding in the New Century

With three retail formats to develop, Camaïeu committed itself to a still more aggressive expansion strategy as it turned toward the mid-decade. Yet a sudden drop-off in consumer spending in 1994 and 1995 caught the company short; with its cash supplies dwindling, Camaïeu was forced to borrow in order to finance its expansion strategy.

Yet the downturn in the French retail sector continued through 1995. By the end of the year, the group's creditors were demanding to be repaid, and Camaïeu found itself on the edge of bankruptcy. Under pressure from its creditors, Camaïeu was forced to split its operations into three separate enterprises, selling off the Camaïeu Homme and Camaïeu Enfant chains as separate businesses. Cofounder Duforest led a buyout of the latter chain, which was rebranded as Okaïdi in 2000 and later grew into one of the country's leading children's clothing chains.

Torck remained with Camaïeu, now reduced to its women's wear stores. Yet in order to lead the company's refocusing,

Key Dates:

1984: Jean-Pierre Torck and Jean Duforest found Camaïeu as a retail women's clothing network.
1988: The company launches aggressive expansion, topping 100 stores by 1991.
1991: The company launches international expansion, with its first foreign stores in Belgium, Spain, Switzerland, and The Netherlands; Camaïeu Homme, a men's clothing retail format, is launched.
1993: The company opens its 200th store in France.
1994: The company acquires 50 Tandy retail stores; Camaïeu Enfant, a children's clothing format, is launched.
1995: A downturn in the retail sector forces the company to sell off Camaïeu Enfant and Camaïeu Homme; Jean-François Duprez is named as company CEO to lead its restructuring; Camaïeu shuts down its foreign operations.
1997: A storewide refitting is launched, and the company begins buying up many of its franchised stores.
2000: Camaïeu goes public on the Euronext Paris Stock Exchange; the company returns to the international market with its first stores in Spain and Poland.
2002: The company opens stores in Italy and the Czech Republic.
2003: The company opens its first stores in Belgium.
2004: Camaïeu enters Russia with the opening of its first three stores there.
2005: AXA Private Equity acquires majority control of Camaïeu and launches a full takeover offer.

Torck called on Jean-François Duprez, a former Auchan colleague. Duprez, who had spent most of his career at Auchan, set to work restructuring the company. One of Duprez's first actions was to shut down the group's international operations, refocusing the company's efforts on its French women's clothing stores. The company also shut down four unprofitable stores in France. In addition, in an effort to solidify its balance sheet, the group brought in a number of outside investors.

Into the mid-1990s, most of the items in Camaïeu stores had been made in France. Under the company's restructuring, however, Camaïeu began turning to lower wage markets in India, North Africa, Turkey, and China, drastically reducing its purchasing costs. Meanwhile, back at home the company launched a complete refurbishment of its company-owned stores; by 1999, this process had, in large part, been completed. Concurrent with the store makeover, Camaïeu also moved to take control over its network, beginning a program of buying out its franchise-holders. By the end of the decade, the company had reduced the proportion of franchise stores to just 25 percent of the group's total. This process continued into the early years of the new decade as the number of franchised shops in France fell to less than 30.

Duprez's efforts paid off, and by the end of the 1990s, Camaïeu was growing again, in a more controlled expansion that nonetheless allowed the company to top 300 stores by the end of 1999. The following year, Camaïeu also relaunched its international effort, opening its first new foreign stores in Spain and in Poland. Also in 2000, Camaïeu went public, in part to enable its financial backers to cash out on their investment. Torck, who continued as company chairman, maintained a significant stake in the company, with 37 percent of shares and 52 percent of voting rights.

The public offering allowed Camaïeu to continue its expansion into the new decade. The company maintained a slow but steady string of store openings in France, and by 2005 the company's total domestic network included 373 stores. At the same time, the company began targeting new foreign markets, opening stores in Italy and the Czech Republic in 2002 and Belgium in 2003, and then opening its first three in Russia in 2004. By the beginning of 2005, the company operated 49 international stores altogether. The company's total number of stores now topped 420. The company's sales also were rising strongly, topping EUR 393 million in 2004.

Camaïeu's return to health was all the more remarkable given the difficulties faced by most of its competitors in the shrinking retail climate of the first half of the 2000s. Buoyed by the success of its retail concept, Camaïeu made plans to shift its expansion strategy to a higher gear, announcing plans to open some 30 to 40 new stores per year in France as well as internationally, with a focus on southern Europe, into the next half of the decade. Meanwhile, the company found itself with a new majority shareholder when Torck and family announced their

decision to sell their holding in the company to investment group AXA Private Equity in January 2005. That company then announced its intention to take full control of Camaïeu—a move that failed, however, as Camaïeu's share price began to rise toward the middle of the year. In the meantime, both Duprez and Torck remained at the helm, guiding Camaïeu toward new successes in the future.

Principal Competitors

Hennes & Mauritz AB; Benetton Group S.p.A.; Vivarte; Gruppo Coin S.p.A.; Kiabi S.A.; NafNaf S.A.; Pimkie S.A.; Promod S.A.

Further Reading

Allienne, Phillippe, ''Camaïeu, société de prêt-à-porter, passe sous le contrôle d'un fonds d'investissement,'' *Le Monde,* January 18, 2005.
''Camaïeu, entreprise citoyenne,'' *Nouvel Observateur,* April 28, 1994.
Ducourtieux, Cécile, ''L'OPA d'Axa Private Equity sur Camaïeu pourrait se solder par un échec,'' *Le Monde,* April 8, 2005.
Mérieux, Alice, ''Camaïeu redonne le ton,'' *Challenges,* September 11, 2003.
——, ''Le rachat de Camaïeu, c'est celui d'une équipe qui gagne,'' *Challenges,* January 20, 2005.
Rousseau, Anna, ''Jean-François Duprez,'' *Challenges,* November 18, 2004.

—M.L. Cohen

Caritas Internationalis

Palazzo San Calisto
00120
Vatican City
Telephone: +39 06 698 797 99
Fax: +39 06 698 87 237
Web site: http://www.caritas.org

Not for Profit Organization
Incorporated: 1928 as Caritas Catholica
NAIC: 624230 Emergency and Other Relief Services

Caritas Internationalis is the central coordinating hub for a confederation of more than 160 relief, humanitarian, and social aid organizations, linked through the Catholic Church and operating throughout the world. Caritas and its members reach more than 150 countries, focusing especially on underdeveloped and disaster-stricken regions. In addition to its members' direct relief and development work, Caritas Internationalis is an active advocacy group, promoting the Vatican's concept of Globalizing Solidarity. As such, Caritas Internationalis supports and coordinates local, national, regional, and international lobbying programs and campaigns to back its selected platform of issues. Based in Vatican City, Caritas Internationalis is structured along parliamentary lines: the General Assembly consists of representatives from each of Caritas's member organizations; the Executive Committee, composed of a president and treasurer, is elected by the General Assembly, in turn supported by the Bureau, composed of the president, treasurer, and a number of vice-presidents. Last, the General Secretariat includes the Secretary General and administrative staff and personnel. Since 2003, the General Assembly also has formed a number of working groups and task forces, which target specific topics and issues under consideration by the full confederation. The member organizations of Caritas Internationalis are further structured into seven regional groups, representing Europe, North America, South America, Africa, Asia, the Middle East, and Oceania.

German Origins at the Turn of the 20th Century

Catholic aid and relief activities remained uncoordinated in large part and locally focused into the late 19th century in Germany. Movement toward a more centralized organization began among socially active priests and politicians toward the dawn of the 20th century. By the early 1890s, that movement had found its leader, in the form of Lorenz Werthmann, a young priest in the town of Freiburg. Werthmann gathered a number of like-minded church members, forming the Charitas Comité in 1895. By 1897, Charitas, as the new organization became known, launched its official operations.

Charitas initially focused on providing charity and other relief and social aid services to Germany's poor, primarily targeting the nation's Christian population. From the outset, Charitas exhibited a strong degree of social advocacy, tackling societal problems such as welfare services, alcoholism, protection of the mentally and physically handicapped, as well as of migrant workers, women's health, and the like.

Less than three years after its founding, Charitas boasted more than 1,500 members. Yet the organization remained relatively informal in structure, financial planning, and operational organization as well. At the same time, Charitas did not enjoy the official sanction of the German Catholic Church. The outbreak of World War I and the resulting pressure on the organization's emergency relief capacity exposed the need for a more formalized operating structure. In 1916, Charitas was recognized as the single official umbrella organization for the German Catholic Church's relief operations.

Over the next decade, Charitas's operations were extended to provide complete coverage of Germany. By 1922, the organization was present in all of the country's dioceses. Charitas also created its own educational network, providing training in various social fields, as well as specific advanced training programs such as nursing, child and youth welfare services, and others. By the time of Werthmann's death that year, Deutsche Caritasverbandes (DCV), the new name of the organization, had developed solid foundations as one of Germany's most important social aid institutions. Growth continued through the decade, and before the end of the 1920s, DCV counted more than 10,000 programs in place throughout Germany.

The DCV in Germany had inspired the creation of similar organizations in other countries. One of the first of the new generation of Catholic relief organizations was created in

---

Company Perspectives:

Guiding Values: The guiding values and principles provide the moral and strategic basis for all the work of the Caritas Confederation. Dignity of the human person: The dignity of the human person is our foundational moral value. We reject the reification of the poor and seek to make them not objects of our pity but subjects of their own development and agents of change. In this way, Caritas makes God's love for creation manifest in the world. Option for the poor: The Caritas Confederation commits itself to combating dehumanising poverty, which robs people of their dignity and humanity, and to promoting the rights of the poor. We commit ourselves to restoring their sense of co-responsibility in building a better world. We also need to underline the position of women, recognising that they have to be given their rightful place in Caritas structures. Universal destination of the Earth's goods: Any economic, social, political or cultural structure which opposes or oppresses and prevents change towards justice is sinful. We seek to encourage our membership to redress the balance by working to transform these structures into graced social structures which favour the poor. Solidarity: The Caritas Confederation seeks to inculcate in its membership and its dealings with other non-governmental organisations and global institutions a genuine sense of solidarity, not as a feeling of sympathy but of empathy, of putting oneself in the shoes of the poor and seeing the world from their perspective. Stewardship: The Caritas Confederation commits itself to being in solidarity not only with people but with the whole of creation and therefore seeks to act in an environmentally sustainable way at all times.

Lucerne, Switzerland in 1901. The United States followed soon after with the establishment of the Catholic Charities in 1910. The Netherlands added the Roman Katholieke Huisvestingscomité in 1914, which later evolved into Mensen in Nood.

In 1924, a first attempt at international coordination of the various Catholic relief societies resulted in the first Catholic charities conference. The conference, held in Lucerne, attracted some 60 delegates from 22 countries in its first year. By 1928, the conference had evolved into Caritas Catholica, which held meetings every two years.

International Mandate in the Postwar Years

World War II cut short the activities of Caritas Catholica, although most of the relief organizations that composed its membership were able to continue operations. The war years also saw the creation of a number of new national organizations, such as the Secretariado Nacional de Caridad, created in Spain in 1942, and Catholic Relief Services, formed in the United States in 1943. The immediate postwar period saw the emergence of a number of new nationally sanctioned relief organizations, such as the Secours Catholique, formed in France in 1946, and Secours Internationale de Caritas Catholica, formed in Belgium in 1948.

Caritas Catholica had to wait until 1947 until the Vatican gave its approval for the reformation of the organization. Caritas organized two conferences in Lucerne that year, to coordinate the massive relief effort needed in the face of the war's devastation. In order to formalize the conference's task of overseeing a now-global relief effort, the Vatican endowed Caritas with its endorsement as its official relief representative in its international capacity. This meant also that Caritas became the Vatican's official relief and development aid organization in contact with the United Nations.

In 1950, the Vatican sponsored a study week under the guidance of Vatican Secretariat of State Msgr Montini, the future Pope Paul VI, to discuss the concerns of coordinating international relief and aid services among Catholic organizations. Once again, the meeting was attended by delegates from 22 countries. The result of the meeting was the decision to establish a central internationally focused organization for the Church's relief efforts.

By the end of 1951, the structure for the new organization was in place, and in December 1951, the new Caritas held its first general assembly. The founding members of Caritas included Germany, Austria, Belgium, the United States, Canada, Switzerland, The Netherlands, France, Italy, Luxembourg, Spain, Denmark, and Portugal.

The creation of a single, centralized coordinating organization launched the start of Caritas's global expansion. Over the next decade, new Caritas member operations were either established or added throughout the world—by the beginning of the 21st century, the conference boasted operations in more than 200 countries and territories throughout the world. To underscore its extensive geographic reach, Caritas adopted the new name of Caritas Internationalis in 1957.

Global Advocate in the New Century

A turning point in Caritas's history came in the early 1960s, with the release in 1965 of Vatican II. In addition to sweeping reforms within the Catholic Church itself, Vatican II also called for Catholic aid efforts—led by Caritas Internationalis—to adopt a new and broader global focus. As a result, Caritas's relief operations no longer targeted especially the world's Catholic and Christian populations, but instead sought to extend its efforts toward the world's poor and needy, regardless of religion or other affiliation.

Vatican II signaled the creation of a new round of Caritas members, as Catholic relief services extended into new areas of the world. An example of this new expansion came in Pakistan, at the signing of Vatican II in 1965, with a first donation from the Vatican toward the establishment of a wing of Caritas in that country. Caritas Pakistan opened its doors in Lahore in 1966 under the leadership of Rev. Marcel Roger.

In other parts of the world, Vatican II inspired existing Catholic aid organizations to expand their range of operations beyond their domestic borders. Such was the case in Australia, which saw the creation of the Catholic Overseas Relief Committee in 1964. Similarly in 1966, Bishop Delargy of New Zealand was placed in charge of forming that country's National Commission on Missions and Overseas Aid. This in turn led to the creation of NZ Catholic Overseas Aid in 1969, which in 1998 changed its name to Caritas Aotearoa New Zealand. By then, too, the Catholic Bishops of England and Wales had established the Catholic Fund for Overseas Development, or CAFOD.

Key Dates:

1895: The Charitas Comité, a Catholic aid and relief organization, is formed under the leadership of priest Lorenz Werthmann in Freiburg, Germany.

1916: Charitas is recognized as the single official umbrella organization for the German Catholic church's relief operations.

1924: The first international Catholic charities conference is held in Lucerne, Switzerland.

1947: The organization, now known as Caritas Catholica, is endorsed by the Vatican as its official relief representative and relief and development aid organization in contact with the United Nations.

1951: The structure for the new centralized international Catholic relief and aid organization is established and the first general assembly is held.

1957: The name Caritas Internationalis is adopted.

1965: Vatican II is released, calling for Catholic aid efforts led by Caritas Internationalis to adopt a new and broader global focus, regardless of religion or other affiliation.

1991: In response to Pope John Paul II's call for "Globalizing Solidarity," Caritas Internationalis begins to extend its efforts beyond the provision of relief aid to emerge as a provider of development programs and as a major advocacy group in the political arena.

2002: Caritas Internationalis launches an effort to reduce corruption among humanitarian assistance operations.

An important step toward the development of Caritas Internationalis's later structure was the creation of Caritas Europe. That organization grouped together the operations of some 48 European members in 44 European countries. The creation of regional organizations, such as Caritas Europe, permitted Caritas Internationalis to respond still more efficiently to issues surrounding local and regional populations. By the end of the century, Caritas Internationalis oversaw the functioning of seven regional organizations.

By the beginning of the 21st century, Caritas Internationalis had become a central player in international relief and development efforts. Caritas also had extended its range of interests beyond the mere provision of relief aid. The organization had become a major provider of development programs. At the same time, Caritas Internationalis put its scope and scale into play, responding to Pope John Paul II's call, in 1991, for what was termed as "Globalizing Solidarity." Since then, Caritas International has emerged as a major advocacy group, applying pressure to affect local, national, and international politics.

In 2002, Caritas Internationalis launched an effort to reduce the level of corruption among humanitarian assistance operations—including its own—estimated to result in the loss of as much as 30 percent of public aid expenses. At the end of 2002, Caritas organized a conference toward the drafting of international guidelines countering corruption among its member operations.

In 2003, Caritas's advocacy interests led it to create a series of working groups and task forces focused on specific issues facing the organization's global operations. In this way, Caritas began to put into place a centrally coordinated lobbying position as well. Caritas Internationalis had evolved from a single organization to a globally operating association representing more than 162 Catholic relief, development, and social aid services throughout the world.

Principal Subsidiaries

CAFOD (United Kingdom); Caritas Aotearoa (New Zealand); Caritas Australia; Caritas Austria; Caritas Belgium; Caritas Ecuador; Caritas Germany; Caritas Italy; Caritas Mauritania; Caritas Norway; Caritas Switzerland; Caritas Turkey; Catholic Relief Services (United States); Mensen in Nood (Netherlands); Secours Catholique (France); Trocaire (Ireland).

Further Reading

"Caritas," *Catholic Insight,* June 2004, p. 29.

"Caritas Examines Curbs on Corruption in Humanitarian Aid," *America,* December 16, 2002.

"Caritas, U.N. AIDS Program Sign Cooperation Agreement," *America,* June 23, 2003, p. 5.

—M.L. Cohen

Carl Allers Etablissement A/S

Vigerslev Alle 18
Valby DK-2500
Denmark
Telephone: (+45) 36 15 20 20
Fax: (+45) 36 44 23 33
Web site: http://www.aller.dk

Private Company
Incorporated: 1873
Employees: 2,001
Sales: DKK 3.59 billion ($632.2 million)(2004)
NAIC: 511120 Periodical Publishers; 511110 Newspaper
    Publishers

Carl Allers Etablissement A/S is one of the Scandinavian region's leading media groups. The company focuses primarily on publishing its wide range of some 70 weekly magazines in Denmark, Sweden, Norway, and Finland. The company claims an impressive market share, with more than 70 percent of the weekly market in Denmark, around 80 percent in Sweden, more than 50 percent in Norway, and, in Finland, its youngest market, 26 percent. Allers' Danish publications include the television listings magazines *Se og Hor* (circulation of 215,000) and *Billed Bladet* (183,000), the women's weekly *Femina* and the family-oriented *Familie Journalen,* as well as a variety of special interest titles, including *Antik og Auktion, Cross Words, Fiction,* and *Mad og Bolig.* In Sweden, the company's top-selling titles include *Hemmets Journal, Allers* (a localized version of *Familie Journalen*), *Hemmets Veckotidning,* and *Aret Runt,* the women's titles *Allas Veckotidning* and *Svensk Damtidning,* as well as the television listings weekly *Se og Hor.* Allers top-selling titles in Norway include localized versions of its flagship publications, including *Allers, KK* (the Norwegian version of *Femina*) and *Se og Hor,* as well as other strong-selling titles such as *MAG* and *Norsk Golf.* Allers entry into the Finnish market came about in 1992. The company's main title in that country is the television listing weekly *7 Päivää.* Allers also operates a range of Web sites supporting its magazine titles in Denmark, Norway, Sweden, and Finland. In addition to its family-oriented titles, Allers has also

established a business-to-business operation, buying up several companies in the early 2000s. Carl Allers Etablissement remains tightly controlled by the founding Aller family. In order to provide a degree of liquidity for its shareholders, the company sold a portion of its B class shares to Rella Holding A/S, a company created and listed on the Copenhagen Stock Exchange in 1991 as a vehicle for this purpose.

19th Century Origins

Carl Allers Etablissement grew from its origins as a small husband-and-wife run publishing house in Copenhagen to become one of the Scandinavian region's leading magazine publishers. The company was founded in 1873 in Denmark by Carl Aller, then 27 years old, and his wife Laura Aller, then 24 years old. By 1874, the Allers had already launched their first magazine, a weekly originally called *Nordisk Monster Tidende.* The magazine, guided by Laura Aller, quickly captured a leading share of the Danish women's market. It was also to become the Aller company's flagship publication in the future, remaining in publication (as *Femina*) into the 21st century.

Laura Aller continued to provide the editorial leadership for the company as it added new titles into the 20th century. The company's next major success came as early as 1877, with the launch of the family-oriented weekly, *Illustreret Familie Journal.* That magazine, which continued its popularity under the name *Familie Journalen,* pioneered this weekly magazine segment in Denmark. The company quickly became Denmark's top magazine publisher, a position it never relinquished.

As the Allers approached the turn of the 20th century, they began to develop an interest in the neighboring Scandinavian markets. In 1894, the company set up a subsidiary in Sweden, Svenska Aller AB, which began operations in Helsingborg. Instead of developing an entirely new format for this market, the Aller company instead created a localized version of its successful Danish titles. As such the company's first Sweden magazine appeared under the title of *Aller's Familie Journal.* *Femina* was also to become a leading Swedish title.

The Allers next turned their attention to the Norwegian market, setting up a subsidiary there in 1897. The *Familie*

Company Perspectives:

From the beginning in 1873, the Aller Group has grown to be the largest publisher of weeklies in the Nordic countries. In Denmark the market share is more than 70%, and Aller publishes the largest family weekly, the largest weekly for women, and the two largest celebrity/TV-Guide weeklies.

In Sweden the market share is above 78%, and the largest celebrity/TV-Guide weekly is published by Aller. In Norway the market share is more than 50%, and Aller publishes the largest weekly in the Nordic countries. In Finland the market share is more than 20% and still growing. Each week, the Aller Group is selling more than 3.1 million weeklies.

Journal format once again provided the company's entry into the new market. Like its Swedish counterpart, the Norwegian family weekly became known simply as *Allers* and grew into the country's leading magazine title.

Laura Aller died in 1917 at the age of 68. Carl Aller remained at the head of the company until his death in 1926 at the age of 80. Yet the company, which incorporated as the limited liability concern Carl Allers Etablissement A/S in 1930, remained firmly under the control of the Aller family as succeeding generations guided the company to further success.

Guided by Television in the 1950s

The emerging radio market inspired the company to launch a new weekly focusing on the country's radio programming. *Det Ny Radioblad,* as the title was called, also provided programming listings, making it a popular publication among the country's eager listening audience.

In the early 1950s, however, Aller recognized the potential of the newly developing television market. In 1953, the company revamped its radio magazine format, converting it to a weekly covering both the radio and television markets. The company once again included television listings, and the new magazine, *Se og Hor,* quickly became the leading broadcast-oriented publication in Norway.

Aller reorganized its operations at the beginning of the 1970s. In 1971, the company restructured Carl Allers Etablissement as a holding company for three primary subsidiaries: Aller Press A/S, in Denmark, and the Svensk Aller and Norsk Aller operations.

Aller's success continued in all three of its markets throughout the 1970s and into the 1980s. In 1978, for example, the company created Oslo-based *Se og Hor Forlaget* in order to launch its television weekly in the Norwegian market. The format proved a hit with Norwegian consumers and quickly established itself as the illustrated weekly including television listings with the largest circulation in the entire Scandinavian market.

Aller marked the 1980s with a series of acquisitions as it continued to expand its range of publications. In 1983, for example, the company acquired TIFA AB, based in Sweden, a

publisher of two prominent women-oriented weeklies, *Hemmets Veckotidning* and *Allas.* Two years later, Aller set up a new publishing subsidiary in Denmark, In A/S, which launched a new monthly magazine, *Madesmagasinet IN.*

Aller took the leading position among weekly magazine publishers in the Danish market in 1987 when it acquired two magazines from Den Berlingske Gruppe. The titles, *Sondags BT* and the television listings magazine *Billed Bladet,* gave the company the largest circulation in the country.

Scandinavian Leader in the 2000s

By the beginning of the 2000s, Aller had successfully claimed the leading share of the entire Scandinavian weekly magazine market, with a total circulation topping 3.2 million. By then, Aller had expanded into the last of the four major Scandinavian markets when it created Allers Julkaisut OY in Finland in 1992. The company launched its first title there, *7 Päivää,* a Finnish-language version of its *Se og Hor,* that year, quickly claiming the top spot in the Finnish television listings segment. Over the next decade, the company rolled out several more titles in Finland, including *Koti ja keittio* in 1996, *MIX* in 1998, and *OHO!* in 2002.

The company also boosted its presence in Sweden through the acquisition of *Aret Runt,* a popular women's title, in 1999. That purchase, from Bonniers Veckotidninger AB, enabled Aller to claim a market share of more than 80 percent in the Swedish weekly magazine market. With market shares of 70 percent in Denmark, 49 percent in Norway, and 26 percent in Finland, its fastest-growing market, Aller could lay claim to a 59 percent share of the total Scandinavian market.

Although Aller remained privately held and controlled by the founding Aller family, the company had made an effort to increase the liquidity of its shares by the turn of the 21st century. The company created a two-tier shareholding system, including class A shares with voting rights and class B shares with no voting rights. In 1981, the family created the Aller Foundation, which took over a major portion of the company's class A shares. In 1991, a new investment vehicle was established, called Rella Holding A/S, which acquired the Aller's class B shares. The investment group behind Rella (Aller spelled backwards) included a number of private investors. Among this group was Codan, an insurance company, that held 20 percent of the class B shares.

At the same time, Aller registered its shares at Denmark's Authorized Market Place. Nonetheless, very little of the group's shareholding came up for sale. This situation prompted a rumor in 2001 that Rella was seeking a buyer for its own shareholding. Rella, however, confirmed its commitment to its shareholding in Aller as a long-term investment. At the end of 2004, Rella's holding of Aller's class B shares stood at 78.5 percent. The shareholding structure of the company's class A shares split at 56 percent held by the Aller Foundation and 27 percent held directly by Suzanne Aller, who also served as the group's deputy chairman.

Aller continued building up its portfolio into the mid-2000s. In 1997, for example, the company created a new Swedish subsidiary, S&H Forlag, which then launched a Swedish-

Key Dates:

1873: Husband-and-wife team Carl and Laura Aller establish a publishing company in Copenhagen.

1874: The company publishes its first magazine title, the weekly *Nordisk Monster Tidende* (later *Femina*), with Laura Aller as chief editor.

1877: Publication begins of a second successful title, *Illustreret Familie Journal.*

1894: The company expands into Sweden with its new subsidiary, Svenska Aller, and the launch of *Aller's Familie Journal.*

1897: Aller enters Norway with the launch of *Aller's Familie Journal* under its subsidiary Norsk Aller.

1930: The company registers as a limited liability concern, Carl Aller Establissement.

1939: A radio program guide, *Det Ny Radioblad,* is established.

1953: *Radioblad* is revamped as a television and radio guide, *Se og Hor.*

1971: Aller is restructured as a holding company.

1978: The company creates a Norwegian subsidiary, *Se og Hor Forlaget,* launching that title in Norway.

1981: Aller Foundation is created to acquire a majority of the company's class A shares.

1983: TIFA AB of Sweden is acquired.

1985: The company creates a new subsidiary, IN A/S, to publish a monthly magazine, *Madesmagasinet IN.*

1987: *Billed Bladet* and *Sondags BT* are acquired from Den Berlingske Grupper, making Carl Allers the leading weekly magazine publisher in Denmark.

1991: Rella Holding is created to acquire a majority of the company's class B shares.

1992: The company enters Finland with the launch of *7 Päivää* under a new subsidiary, Aller Julkaisut OY.

1997: *Se og Hor* is launched in Sweden.

1999: The weekly magazine *Aret Rundt* is acquired from Bonniers Veckotidninger in Sweden.

2001: Aller establishes a business-to-business publishing unit with the acquisitions of Visholm Media, T-Press, and Brorson.

2004: The company's circulation tops 3.2 million with sales of DKK 3.59 billion ($632 million).

language version of *Se og Hor.* The company's expanding portfolio included an increasingly diverse array of titles. In Denmark, the company's list of titles featured *Daadnyt,* a boating enthusiasts title; *Bazarmag,* devoted to celebrity and fashion news and gossip; *Foraeldre og Boern,* covering parenting subjects; and the erotic titles *Tidens Kvinder* and *Tidens Mand.* In Norway, the company published fashion and style-oriented *Henne,* the hunting title *Jeger Hund & Vapen,* and the boating magazine *Baatmagasinet.* In 2000, the company added a new title, *Rapoprt,* when it took over Copenhagen-based A&L.

In the 1990s and early 2000s, Aller adopted a strong Internet presence, establishing sites based on many of its prominent titles. In 2001, the company also added a new area of operations, creating a business-to-business division under subsidiary Aller International A/S. As part of that extension, the company made three acquisitions: Visholm Media, T-Press, and Brorson ApS. As it turned toward mid-decade, Aller appeared interested in extending into a new media, with the suggestion that it might bid for a stake in the state-owned television broadcaster TV 2. Meanwhile, with a circulation topping 3.2 million and sales of DKK 3.59 billion ($632 million) at the end of 2004, Carl Aller Etablissement remained a major force in the Scandinavian media market.

Principal Subsidiaries

Aller Press A/S; Aller Julkaisut Oy (Finland); Aller International A/S; Norsk Aller A/S (Norway); Svenska Aller AB (Sweden).

Principal Competitors

Bertelsmann AG; News Corporation Ltd.; Reed Elsevier N.V.; Pearson plc; Orkla ASA; Wolters Kluwer N.V.; SanomaWSOY Group; Preses Nams; Egmont Magasiner.

Further Reading

"Aller May Bid for TV2," *Boersen*, June 12, 2002.
"Aller's Printing Press Investment Proves Costly," *Boersen*, August 7, 2002.
"Egmont More Profitable Than Aller," *Boersen*, August 28, 2002.
"Norsk Aller Might Acquire Nettavisen," *Dagens Naeringsliv*, September 19, 2002.
"TV2 and Aller to Co-operate," *Boersen*, April 23, 2002.
Williams, Granville, "European Media Ownership: Threats on the Landscape," *European Federation of Journalists*, January 2003.

—M.L. Cohen

CAZENOVE

Cazenove Group plc

20 Moorgate
London EC2R 6DA
United Kingdom
Telephone: (+44) 20 7588 2828
Fax: (+44) 20 7155 9000
Web site: http://www.cazenove.com

Private Company
Incorporated: 1954 as Casenove & Co.
Employees: 1,134
Sales: £292.9 million ($500 million) (2004 prorated)
NAIC: 523110 Investment Banking and Securities
Dealing; 522293 International Trade Financing

Cazenove Group plc is one of the United Kingdom's oldest and most venerable investment bankers, providing capital management and equities and international market investment services to the country's elite. The company counts the Queen of England among its clients, as well as nearly half of the country's largest 100 companies. With a history reaching back to the early decades of the 19th century, Cazenove has been forced to undergo a sea-change at the beginning of the 21st century in order to remain a competitive banking force. Operated as a partnership for most of its more than 180 years, Cazenove converted to a corporation in 2001 and even toyed with the idea of going public. Instead, at the beginning of 2005, the company spun off its investment banking business into a joint venture with JPMorgan of the United States, creating JPMorgan Cazenove Holdings. In this way, JPMorgan achieved an entry into the dynamic London investment banking sector, while Cazenove obtained the deep pockets and career perspective capable of attracting the financial industry's top talents. Nonetheless, soon after the launch of the joint venture, the company announced the defection of three of its senior members. The agreement also gives JPMorgan the right to acquire full control of the joint venture as early as 2010. Cazenove traditionally conducts most of its operations from its London offices, and in the early 2000s the company closed a number of its overseas offices, notably in India and Australia. Cazenove maintains subsidiary offices in the United States, Germany, France, China, Hong Kong, and South Africa. The group posted turnover of £292.9 million ($500 million), prorated for the full year 2004 in order to align itself with JPMorgan's calendar year. Cazenove is led by chairman David Mayhew, who joined as a partner in 1968.

Huguenot Origins in the 18th Century

Cazenove's roots lay in the Huguenot exile, following the revocation of France's Edict of Nantes, which had established guarantees of religious freedom for the country's Protestants in 1685. Many Huguenots moved to Geneva, where they became leading financiers. By the late 18th century, the Huguenot population had begun to emigrate to other parts of Europe and to the United States. England, already the financial center of Europe, attracted many Huguenot banking families, notably the Cazenove family, led by James Casenove.

James Casenove's youngest son, Philip, was born in 1799 and entered the financial world in 1819, joining brother-in-law and fellow Huguenot John Menet at his brokerage. By 1823, Philip Casenove had become a partner in that business, marking the beginning of the late Cazenove Group. Menet died in 1835, and Cazenove then formed a partnership with Joseph Laurence and Charles Pearce.

In 1854, however, Philip Cazenove formed P. Cazenove & Co. in a partnership with his son and nephew. That partnership quickly rose to prominence, in large part because of its involvement in the financial side of the railroad industry. Yet a part of Philip Cazenove's success was also attributed to his relationship with the powerful Rothschild banking family, which served as a patron and later as a financial partner in many of Cazenove's transactions. In 1859, for example, Cazenove joined with the Rothschilds to act as a broker for the raising of capital for the San Paulo Railway Company.

In 1862, the company served another important client, acting as broker for the formation of the Bank of Hindustan. Cazenove's interests in India extended to the construction of the country's railroad industry. In the 1870s, the company served as broker for His Highness the Nizam's State Railway Company. In 1883, the company helped raise funding for the launch of the

63

Key Dates:

1819: Philip Cazenove joins brother-in-law John Menet's brokerage business.
1823: Cazenove becomes a partner in Menet's firm.
1835: After Menet's death, Casenove forms a partnership with Joseph Laurence and Charles Pierce.
1854: Casenove sets up a new partnership, J. Casenove & Co., with his son and nephew.
1889: The company becomes Casenove and Akroyd and later Casenove, Akroyd and Greenwood and Co.
1954: The company changes its name to Casenove & Co.
1986: Casenove & Co. joins a fund alliance with the Bank of Scotland, Norwich Union, Scottish Equitable, and Legal & General, among others.
2001: The company converts from a partnership to a corporation, changing its name to The Casenove Group.
2005: The company spins off its investment management arm into a joint venture with JPMorgan.

Bengal Central Flotilla Company, which operated a steamship service between Khoolna and Burrisaul. Closer to home, Cazenove's helped raise the funding for the Atlantic Telegraph Company, launched in 1863, and the Great Eastern Railway Company in 1868.

Through the end of the 19th century, Cazenove was involved in a number of exotic transactions, such as the issuing of land mortgage bonds in Russia in 1874, as well as the creation of the Metropolitan District Railway Company, which built the London Underground. The partnership's reputation as a preeminent investment banker was solidified when it acquired such prominent clients as the British royal family. Indeed, into the 21st century, the Queen of England remained a steadfast Cazenove client.

Weathering Railway Nationalization in the 1940s

Philip Cazenove died in 1880, leaving behind one of England's most important financial houses. The Cazenove family remained prominent members of the partnership through the 19th and 20th centuries, during which the firm continued to bring in new partners. One of the most important of these was Swainston Howeden Akroyd, who joined the partnership in 1889. Considered one of the "fathers" of the London Stock Exchange, Akroyd brought in his brother, as well as his name, to the partnership, which became known as Cazenove and Akroyd.

By then, Cazenove had already established its rather exclusive recruiting practices. Partners seemed more or less required to have attended elite schools such as Eton or Winchester and to have been members of the Brigade of Guards. The partnership also became famous for its embrace of formality and tradition, enforcing highly restrictive dress codes into the "casual dress" era of the 1990s and 2000s.

Cazenove made a number of acquisitions of other brokerage and private banking firms in the early decades of the 20th century. The partnership later extended its name to Cazenove Akroyds and Greenwood & Co. in order to reflect its expanded

form. Much of Cazenove's financial success had been linked to its longstanding involvement in the British and worldwide railroad industry. Cazenove had played a prominent role in the development of the British railroads, which in turn were a major stimulant to the country's economic and industrial growth through the 19th century and into the 20th century. The British railroad system, like that of the American railroad industry, had been largely built up and controlled by private interests.

Into the 1940s, Cazenove's fortunes remained entwined with the railroad industry, notably with its involvement in the Butler-Henderson Great Western Railway, as well as its dealings in railway shares. Yet the outbreak of World War II, and the nationalization of Britain's railroad system, nearly spelled disaster for the Cazenove partnership. As the London *Times* pointed out in an article in 1968: "Before the war it was said that . . . if the railways disappeared, Cazenove would go bust. In fact, it has adapted itself so well since nationalization that it is more powerful than ever."

A big part of Cazenove's success lay in its ability to shift its operations from a focus on the railroad industry to an embrace of the wider corporate and financial markets. Known more simply as Casenove & Co. since a name change in 1954, the firm had succeeded in winning a number of new clients, such as the merchant bank Brown Shipley Holdings, formed in 1960. Cazenove also expanded into a number of international markets, such as the United States, where its subsidiary, Casenove Inc., became the first foreign company to list on the Pacific Coast Stock Exchange. In 1974, Cazenove opened an office in Hong Kong, its first in the fast-growing Asian markets. The company also added subsidiaries in Australia, India, Singapore, South Africa, and elsewhere into the 1980s.

Independent Survivor in the 21st Century

Cazenove emerged as a prominent partner in the Thatcher government's privatization drive of the early 1980s. That same government proved among the world's most aggressive in liberalizing and deregulating many of the country's industries. The British banking industry's turn came in 1986 with the launch of the so-called "Big Bang" that removed many of the restrictions on the banking sector, especially limitations barring banks from acquiring and operating their own brokerages. As a result, the late 1980s saw a flurry of mergers and acquisitions as the country's banks bought up many of Cazenove's rival brokers and assets managers. Other rivals formed mergers among themselves, then listed their shares on the stock exchange as part of an effort to expand their operations into the private banking sphere.

Cazenove, however, resisted these trends and instead remained steadfast in its tradition as an independent partnership. The firm was greatly aided by the impressive loyalty of its clients: by then the partnership counted nearly half of the country's top 100 firms among its client list. Cazenove nonetheless sought out allies in an effort to remain competitive in such areas requiring large-scale funds as the new issues underwriting market. Toward this end, the company joined an alliance formed in 1986 among such leading financial players as the Bank of Scotland, Norwich Union, Scottish Equitable, and Legal & General.

Cazenove, along with David Mayhew, then the head of the firm's institutional equity division, became embroiled in the Guinness fraud scandal of 1988, in which Cazenove was accused of aiding Guinness in a fraudulent share purchase during its takeover battle for Distillers in 1985. Mayhew never went to trial, however, and Casenove emerged relatively untarnished, benefiting from the continued loyalty of its client base.

While Cazenove remained committed to its independent status, it nonetheless found itself forced to move with the times during the 1990s. The increasing transparency of the London financial sector, accelerated by the arrival of large U.S. and other foreign banks as major players, began to cast Cazenove's traditional secrecy and refusal to speak to the press as, according to the *Sunday Times,* "sinister." The company also remained one of the few in its sector to refuse to publish its company research. However, Cazenove made an effort to modernize its product offering and expand its range of services, including the launch of a wing dedicated to emerging markets.

By the beginning of the 2000s, however, it had become clear that Cazenove would not be able to survive in its present condition, if only because of its increasing difficulty in attracting London's top financial talent to join its partnership. In 2001, therefore, Cazenove announced that it was converting its status from a partnership to a corporation, with its partners becoming its initial shareholders. The firm, now led by Mayhew as chairman, also announced its intention to go public. Cazenove also changed its name, becoming the Cazenove Group.

Nevertheless, by the end of that year, the company was forced to backpedal on the public offering due to weak market conditions. At the same time, Cazenove announced that it was shutting down its office in India and eliminating its emerging markets operation.

Cazenove broke with more than 180 years of tradition when it revealed its financial information with the release of its first annual report in 2002. The company surprised the investment community with its announcement that it intended to seek a listing on London's Alternative Investment Market (AIM). Yet by 2003, the company was forced to call off that listing as well.

Instead, in early 2004 Cazenove announced that it was putting itself up for sale and began accepting offers. The company's position as one of the British financial market's leading investment banks made it highly attractive, especially for foreign companies seeking entry into the United Kingdom. However, Cazenove was not quite ready to give up its independence. In November 2004, the company announced that it had reached an agreement with JPMorgan to form a new joint-venture company, JPMorgan Casenove Holdings. Under terms of the agreement, Casenove spun off its investment management arm into the joint venture, maintaining its equities and international capital markets operations under the still independent Casenove Group.

As part of the joint-venture agreement, JPMorgan was granted the option to acquire full control of JPMorgan Casenove as early as 2010. This arrangement enabled Casenove Group to preserve its independence and its long tradition of financial service to the cream of the United Kingdom's corporate and private community into the new century.

Principal Subsidiaries

Cazenove & Co. (Singapore) PTE. Limited; Cazenove & Co. Ltd ; Cazenove AG (Germany); Cazenove Asia Limited (Hong Kong); Cazenove Capital; Cazenove Fund Management Limited; Cazenove Incorporated (USA); Cazenove International Holdings Limited; Cazenove Investment Fund Management Limited; Cazenove Service Company; Cazenove South Africa (PTY) Limited; JPMorgan Casenove Holdings.

Principal Competitors

3i Group Plc.; Aberdeen Asset Management PLC; AMVESCAP PLC; Barclays Plc; Close Brothers Plc; Singer and Friedlander Plc; Durlacher Corporation PLC; Old Mutual plc; Schroders plc; St. James's Place Capital; UBS Warburg.

Further Reading

Cattell, Brian, "Cazenove Aim: Preserve Name," *Daily Deal,* October 12, 2004.

Cave, Andrew, "Cazenove Breaks Its 180-year Secrecy Rule," *Daily Telegraph,* September 19, 2002, p. 1.

"Cazenove Closes India Operations," *Business Line,* November 30, 2001.

"Cazenove Group Is Changing the Name of Its Wholly-owned Unit Cazenove International Asset Management," *Global Fund News,* February 2005, p. 17.

"Cazenove's Last Act," *Financial Times,* May 26, 2004, p. 22.

Connon, Heather, "End of the affair for Cazenove," *Observer,* December 3, 2000, p. 7.

Davis, John, "Time to Unlock Cazenove's Treasure Chest of Goodies," *Observer,* May 12, 1996, p. 10.

Gapper, John, and Lina Saigol, "Cazenove Attempts to Resolve a Big Dilemma," *Financial Times,* May 29, 2004, p. 3.

Hamilton, Kirstie, "Changing Face of Cazenove," *Sunday Times,* February 13, 1994, p. 7.

Hobday, Nicola, "Cazenove Mulls Flotation on AIM," *Daily Deal,* August 20, 2002.

Kynaston, David, *Cazenove & Co.: A History,* London: B.T. Batsford: 1991.

McCrystal, Damien, "They May Not Have Degrees, But It Would Take a Very Dim-witted Cazenover Not to See That Cosy Would Be Coming to an End," *Observer,* July 7, 2002, p. 7.

Nisse, Jason, "Is Time Running Out for the City Gents?" *Independent on Sunday,* December 3, 2000, p. 5.

Pretzlik, Charles, "An Annual Report Like Anyone Else's," *Financial Times,* September 19, 2002, p. 22.

Saigol, Lina, "Cazenove Abandons Flotation Plan," *Financial Times,* January 29, 2003, p.1.

Wachman, Richard, "Mammon: Cazenove Uncloaked," *Observer,* September 22, 2002, p. 14.

Wendlandt, Astrid, "Cazenove Closes Emerging Arm," *Financial Times,* October 8, 2001, p. 30.

"Will Cazenove Be a Blushing Bride?" *BusinessWeek,* September 20, 2004.

—M.L. Cohen

Cia Hering

Rua Hermann Hering 1790
Blumenau, Santa Catarina 890 10-900
Brazil
Telephone: (+55) 47 321-3544
Toll Free: (+55) (800) 473-114
Fax: (+55) 47 321-3434
Web site: http://www.ciahering.com.br

Public Company
Incorporated: 1880 as Hering Têxtil S.A.
Employees: 3,588
Sales: BRL 336.59 million ($114.88 million) (2003)
Stock Exchanges: Sao Paulo
Ticker Symbols: HGTX3
NAIC: 313210 Broadwoven Fabric Mills; 448140 Family
  Clothing Stores; 551112 Offices of Other Holding
  Companies

Cia Hering is a Brazilian holding company whose units are engaged in the production and sale of textiles and casual-wear clothing. These clothing items consist of intimate apparel, pullovers, and other general textile products, including T-shirts, pajamas, shirts, jackets, jeans, and fashion clothes. Hering subsidiaries are licensed to produce, sell, and export clothing under the Disney trademark. The company also operates and franchises retail clothing stores in Brazil.

A Century of Textile Production

Hermann Hering was a German immigrant to Brazil who settled in the small southern state of Santa Catarina, which was also home to many other migrating Germans. In 1879, he acquired a circular loom, and the following year he and his brother Bruno opened a cotton-textile plant in Blumenau. The products of this family enterprise were well received, and as a result more looms were acquired and installed. The machines were originally driven by steam, later by waterpower, and still later by electrical energy. Hering began doing business outside Santa Catarina in 1900, when its first agent was sent to Porto Alegre in the neighboring state of Rio Grande do Sul. The company began selling systematically in Sao Paulo between 1908 and 1910 and later in Rio de Janeiro. By 1914, the company, now called Hering & Cia., was able to import its first spinning mill, enabling it to become one of the first textile companies in Brazil to make its own cotton yarn. By 1929, it had adopted its present name, Companhia Hering.

In the course of time, Hering established another cotton-textile plant outside Recife, in Brazil's cotton-growing belt, far to the north of Santa Catarina in the state of Pernambuco. Hering's apparel was well-suited to a poor, tropical country. Its simple unadorned T-shirts, worn by generations of Brazilians, were so unremarkable that they later became ''in'' for young people. Hering was among the largest of the textile firms, and in 1929 the company employed more than half of all Brazilian workers engaged in manufacturing. In the late 1960s, textiles were still supporting 300,000 people directly and 600,000 indirectly. By this time, however, the industry was in trouble due to obsolescent machinery, poor management, and inadequately trained labor. For many years, in an inflationary climate, easy credit had been repaid in devalued currency. Customers quickly spent their money before it lost still more value, and the profits were put into real estate and other such outside investments instead of new machinery.

This situation ended in 1964, when a military government assumed power and stabilized the currency, leading to a crisis in the textile industry but also to a restructuring opportunity. By the early 1970s, new equipment had been installed in most of the largest mills, and the quality of finished goods improved. Hering's spinning and weaving operations had sales of $25.4 million in 1973 and were producing such garments as pajamas, underwear, and sports shirts as well as T-shirts. The company also began making Wrangler jeans, under license, in 1983, and selling them in stores.

Hering's annual sales from textiles and clothing came to about $300 million in the late 1980s. In the trade journal *Knitting Technique,* a visiting group of German and Austrian manufacturers called the company ''one of the largest textile manufacturers in the world'' and described the size of the Blumenau plant as ''well above those appertaining in Europe'' and exceeding

Key Dates:

1880:	Hermann and Bruno Hering open a cotton-textile plant in Blumenau.
1914:	Hering imports its first spinning mill, enabling it to make its own cotton yarn.
1972:	Hering enters the agro-industry by establishing a company named Ceval.
1986:	Ceval becomes Brazil's chief processor of soybeans.
1992:	Hering establishes two franchised retail clothing store chains.
1992:	Hering opens a clothing factory in Badajoz, Spain.
1994:	Now a holding company, Hering is publicly traded for the first time.
1995:	Hering becomes the exclusive Disney clothing licensee in Europe and the Middle East.
1997:	Hering sells its remaining share of Ceval for an estimated $550 million to $700 million.
2003:	The company returns to profitability after losing money in three of the previous four years.

''even the most imaginative expectations.'' Of the large numbers of circular knitting machines, almost 500 had been built by the company itself. The group was surprised to find that hundreds of workers were still color-printing fabrics manually—a practice that had ceased to exist in Western Europe—and that the company employed ten doctors and paramedics to tend to workers around the clock. The group continued on to Recife, where they visited the Tecanor circular-knitting plant and described the manufacturing hall of the Hering do Nordeste factory as one of the largest textile-manufacturing buildings in the world.

Food Production Foremost: 1972–97

By this time, however, Hering's fortunes had taken an unusual direction. Soybeans had become a major crop in Santa Catarina, and Hering decided it could make money by crushing the beans into meal and oil and marketing these products abroad. For this purpose, it formed a company named Ceval Agro Industria S.A. in 1972, establishing its headquarters in Gaspar, a town about 25 miles from Blumenau. Two years later, Ivo Hering, president of the Hering group and a great-grandson of one of the founders, appointed Vilmar de Oliveira Schürmann to be Ceval's general manager. Under Schürmann's capable leadership, Ceval Agro Industrial, which later became Ceval Alimentos S.A., grew rapidly, becoming Brazil's chief processor of soybeans and its fifth-largest exporter. However, after a government-imposed freeze on the Brazilian currency's rate of exchange resulted in an unexpected $3-million loss in 1986, Hering decided the company should diversify its activities and exploit the domestic market. During the late 1980s, Ceval became a major producer of foods for the Brazilian retail market by spending more than $200 million to acquire 17 companies in six states. Its annual revenues rose from $149 million to $1.2 billion in the decade, eclipsing the amount that Hering derived from textiles and clothing.

The original impetus for this diversification came in 1980, when the Hering group acquired the Seara meat-packing busi-

ness for the purpose of marketing slaughtered chickens and pigs that had been raised on Ceval's soybean meal. Three years later, it bought another meat-packing plant, a large chicken producer, and a Swift Armour pork slaughterhouse. By 1990, Ceval was processing seven million chickens a month as well as three million hogs, making it the nation's third-largest pork producer. It was also processing four million metric tons of soybeans a year. In 1989, Ceval opened a $24-million margarine plant in Gaspar, and in 1991 a $60-million facility in Rondonópolis, Mato Grosso, for soybean cooking oil.

Companhia Hering, in early 1991, transformed itself into a new holding company consisting of only two units: Ceval Alimentos and Hering Têxtil. All three, the holding company and the two subsidiary units, made an initial public offering of shares on the Sao Paulo Stock Exchange in 1994. Several layers of administration were eliminated, and as many as 2,000 staffers lost their jobs. Some internal tasks were farmed out, such as the manufacture of specialized products and the transport of cargo between affiliates of the company. Others were completely eliminated, as Hering found that in many cases the same work was being duplicated within the organization. Each subsidiary, for example, had its own production planning unit even though there was a central unit for this purpose. The same applied to the recruitment and selection of workers.

Despite these efforts, Companhia Hering lost money in 1992, 1994, and 1996. Even Ceval's burgeoning revenues could not make up for the high costs of expanding its productive capacity. Hering Têxtil was the largest producer of knitwear in Latin America and the second-largest in the world, but it was losing money for a variety of reasons, including the expense of opening a factory in 1992 in Badajoz, Spain, to serve customers such as Euro Disney, major German department stores, and mail-order outlets. The following year, it sold more than half of its 79 percent share of Hering do Nordeste S.A.–Malhas, to Vicunha Têxtil S.A. for BRL 70 million. This diminished Hering Têxtil's annual revenues by one-third but also reduced the parent company's $170 million debt.

By 1995, Hering Têxtil was preferring to describe itself as a maker of brand-name products rather than of textiles and apparel. It was producing clothing under such recognized labels as Hering, Omino, Mafisa, PUC, Public Image, and Wrangler, as well as under license for The Walt Disney Co. (including a Mickey Mouse T-shirt introduced in 1960), The Coca-Cola Co., Warner Bros., and Hanna-Barbera Cartoons Inc. Various products carrying the Hering name were being sold in more than 80 licensed stores in several South American countries. In that year, Hering Têxtil became the exclusive licensee of Disney for all of Europe and the Middle East under a ten-year contract that began in 1996 and gave it the sole right to print Disney images in these markets. This arrangement was estimated to be worth revenue of $50 million in 1996 and $130 million in 2000. The firm also established Lisbon-based Studio Dream to concentrate on further development of products and marketing in Europe. Also in 1995, Hering Têxtil agreed to produce Coca-Cola's entire line of clothing for sale in Europe.

Hering Têxtil was now a smaller, leaner company, with 40 percent fewer employees than a few years earlier and some of its production turned out by contractors. Its next step, taken at the recommendation of the U.S. consulting firm Booz Allen & Hamilton Inc., was to divide its operations into five units, each one with its own team of engineering, production, and sales. A fashion unit, for example, was charged with administering the Omino, PUC, Public Image, and Mafisa brands, while another handled Wrangler jeans. Fabio Hering, a nephew of Ivo, became Hering Têxtil's chief executive. He indicated that the company, until recently regarded as production-oriented, would concentrate its efforts on marketing.

In addition to strategic alliances formed with retail chains, retail franchising within Brazil was now the focus of Hering Têxtil's marketing. The company had established two franchise chains, Wrangler and Family Store, in 1992. By 1996, the 86 Wrangler branches were selling 60 percent of Hering Têxtil's production of Wrangler-label jeans. The 14 Family Store units, located in shopping centers, were scheduled to increase to 35 by the end of 1996. Hering Têxtil was also promoting its products in joint campaigns with such retailers as Wal-Mart Brasil Ltda. and Lojas Americanas S.A.

Hering Têxtil was, however, dwarfed by Ceval Alimentos, whose $2.7 billion in 1996 revenues was ten times that of its senior brother. It was the fifth-largest soybean processor in the world, the largest Brazilian producer of vegetable oil, and the third-largest producer of frozen meat. However, since the early 1990s, Companhia Hering had been raising money by selling Ceval common stock and debentures convertible to common stock. In 1997, it sold its remaining 39 percent share of Ceval to Bunge International Ltd. for a sum estimated at between $550 million and $700 million. Asked why the holding company was selling Ceval instead of the struggling textile firm, Ivo Hering replied, according to Cláudia Vassallo of *Exame,* "Because the textile business is in our genes. It is our true vocation." Nevertheless, there were other persuasive reasons. The sale proceeds not only went into the coffers of family members but also were earmarked for paying down the combined $250 million debt of Companhia Hering and Hering Têxtil. By contrast, Ceval was now so big that it would have been difficult to maintain its impetus without large additional infusions of money.

Redefining Itself in Retail: 1999–2003

By early 1999, Hering was seeking, even more than it previously had, to redefine itself as a company principally devoted to retailing based on brand name. There was little chance that it would ever again enjoy eminence in cheap clothing, a market lost to East Asian producers. Besides selling its Recife plants in 1994, the company now had also disposed of its spinning mill in Blumenau. Less than half of its sales now came from in-house production. However, building on its ubiquitous T-shirts (still 40 percent of its clothing sales) and knit jerseys, the company was seeking to become the Brazilian Gap: a purveyor of a wide array of basic clothing, including trousers and leather articles. In *Exame,* Glandinston Silvestrini quoted Fabio Hering: "Today it isn't by manufacturing that one makes or loses money. Clothing technology is basically the same. What makes the difference is

the brand and the value added by a chain of stores." Accordingly, the former Family Store chain (now Hering Store) had grown to 63 branches, and a new one for children, based on the company's PUC brand, was emerging. (The license for the Wrangler operation had lapsed in 1998, and the Omino label had been dropped.)

After losing money in 1999, 2001, and 2002, Companhia Hering returned to profitability in 2003. During that year, its Hering and PUC chains, which grew to 125 and 30 locations, respectively, accounted for 32 percent of company sales, compared to 21 percent in 2002. All these stores were in middle- or upper-class shopping centers and neighborhoods, allowing Hering to sell more elaborate clothing than its iconic T-shirts. Nevertheless, the company ranked only seventh nationally in revenues from clothing and textiles, with 2.7 percent of the market, and it dropped out of the 500 biggest Brazilian enterprises in terms of annual revenue. Companhia Hering's long-term debt was BRL 494.82 million ($168.88 million) at the end of 2003.

Principal Subsidiaries

Garena Malhas Ltda.; Hering International S.A.-SAFI; Hering Overseas Ltda.; Têxtil Santa Catarina Ltda.; VH Serviços e Construçoes Ltda. (94%).

Principal Competitors

Guararapes Confecçoes S.A.; Santista Têxtil S.A.; Sao Paulo Alpargatas S.A.; Vicunha Têxtil S.A.

Further Reading

Blecher, Nelson, "A criatura sujpera o seu criador," *Exame,* April 12, 1995, pp. 66–67.
——, "Bonito é ser pequena," *Exame,* March 13, 1996, pp. 50–51.
"Brazil Textiles: New Vigor, Big Growth," *Textile World,* August 1974, pp. 79, 86.
Costa, Flávio, "A nova fase da Hering," *Exame,* September 1, 2004, p. 61.
——, "Grife do Mickey," *Exame,* May 10, 1995, pp. 52–53.
"Hering: Latin America's Textile Giant," *Institutional Investor,* October 1995, Santa Catarina supplement, pp. 22–23.
"Knitters Undertake a Journey of Discovery to Brazil," *Knitting Technique,* September 1987, pp. 373–76.
Millman, Joel, "You Think You Got Problems?" *Forbes,* September 13, 1993, p. 123.
"Prato pronto dá mais dinheiro," *Exame,* February 19, 1992, pp. 74–75.
Silvestrini, Gladinston, "Quero ser a Gap," *Exame,* March 24, 1999, pp. 42–44.
Staviski, Norberto, "Comida para lá, roupa para cá," *Exame,* May 1, 1991, pp. 72–73.
——, "Como crescer na rota inversa," *Exame,* February 21, 1990, pp. 62–63.
Vassallo, Cláudia, "Por que o Bunge quer a Ceval," *Exame,* September 10, 1997, pp. 48–50.

—Robert Halasz

Cincinnati Lamb Inc.

5523 East Nine Mile Road
Warren, Michigan 48091
U.S.A.
Telephone: (586) 497-6000
Toll Free: (877) 246-6224
Fax: (586) 497-6216

*Wholly Owned Subsidiary of Unova Manufacturing
  Technologies Inc.*
Incorporated: 1884 as Cincinnati Screw and Tap Company
Employees: 250 (est.)
Sales: $144.8 million (2002)
NAIC: 333512 Machine Tool Manufacturing

With its headquarters located in Warren, Michigan (outside of Detroit), Cincinnati Lamb Inc. is a leading maker of machine tools, with manufacturing operations in the United States and the United Kingdom. Machine tools are used to make precision parts for other machines, the history of which dates to the mid-19th century when gunmakers became the first to make use of interchangeable parts due to military requirements. Machine tools were developed to produce identical parts on a mass scale, creating the so-called American System of manufacturing. As the concept of interchangeable parts spread from industry to industry, the demand for machine tools increased. A subsidiary of Unova Manufacturing Technologies Inc., Cincinnati Lamb combines the assets and heritages of two old-line machine tool companies: Cincinnati Machine and F. Jos Lamb Company.

1870s Origins

Cincinnati Machine is the older of the two companies comprising Cincinnati Lamb. It was founded in Cincinnati in the 1870s by a pair of German immigrants, Fred Holz and George Mueller, who started out in a shop Mueller inherited from his father making fasteners, screws, and sewing machine parts. By the end of the decade, screw-making became the shop's focus, but because the partners could not afford a new milling machine needed to make taps, which would be used to cut threads inside bolts, Holz made his own from scratch, in the process introduc-

ing a number of innovations. Milling machines at the time were difficult to use, due in large part to the multitude of cranks and levers positioned awkwardly around the machine. Holz created a centralized control panel and added micrometer dials to the adjustment levels, allowing the operator to make two adjustments simultaneously. Moreover, he added a spindle that could spin counterclockwise, which allowed the machine also to make use of standard drills, reamers, and boring tools. Holz's machine was such an improvement over other milling machines that word quickly spread among other shops in Cincinnati, a city known during this period as the machine tool capital of the world, boasting some 50 machine tool companies. Holz built a second unit for a nearby brassworks, and soon the shop was turning out milling machines in addition to screws and taps, the business so strong that the partners moved to a larger facility in 1882.

Holz's milling machine won a prestigious award at the 1884 Cincinnati Industrial Exposition. In order to ramp up production of the machines, the partners turned to venture capitalist Jacob Bloom, who invested $2000 to buy a stake in the company, which in 1884 was incorporated as Cincinnati Screw and Tap Company, with Bloom serving as president. Due to unfortunate circumstances, however, the company struggled: A flood and a fire forced it to relocate twice. Ironically, one of the company's creditors, Frederick A. Geier, became the driving force behind the establishment and prosperity of Cincinnati Screw and Tap.

Geier, the child of German immigrants, grew up in Cincinnati, where his father had a number of business interests, including investments in the high-tech sector of the day, electricity. The younger Geier moved to Newton, Kansas, where he was hired by a bank because of his ability to speak German to the area's Mennonite population. With the death of his father, he was called back home to sort out his father's estate, which included a woodworking shop that made bungs for barrels, a business Geier believed offered little hope for the future. He was looking for a new venture when in 1887 he visited Cincinnati Screw and Tap to collect a debt. There he met with Holz, who enthusiastically showed the young man his new milling machine. As keen as his father had been about new technologies, Geier recognized the potential of Holz's invention. He bought out Bloom's interest for $7,000. Holz now took over as

---

Company Perspectives:

Cincinnati Lamb is a leading global manufacturer of integrated machine and precision grinding systems, primarily for the automotive, aerospace and heavy equipment industries.

---

president while Geier became the company's secretary and treasurer. Mueller stayed on as vice-president, although he too sold out by 1891.

Growth in the 1890s

The company began to concentrate on the production of milling machines, and the screw and tap business was sold off, leading to a new name in 1889: Cincinnati Milling Machine Co., or as its employees called it, "The Mill." Although Holz was president, Geier essentially took over the business functions and allowed Holz to concentrate on the technical side. Most of all, Geier was a passionate salesman. He was known to ride the early-morning milk trains in order to greet potential customers at the door when they came into work. He would then have time to return to the office before the close of the day to do the books and take care of other business. In addition to Holz's original milling machine to promote, Geier had a cutter grinder that Holz developed and was ready to sell in 1889. The device resharpened cutting tools, which previously had to be discarded once they became dull. With two products to sell, Cincinnati Milling enjoyed steady growth in the early 1890s, with sales growing to more than $71,000 in 1892.

In 1893, however, the United States suffered through one of its periodic depressions of the time. Having opened a new plant that tied up all of its cash, Cincinnati Milling was on the verge of collapse. One of the few products that was doing well despite the conditions was the new low-wheel bicycle. Geier found an Indianapolis bicycle manufacturer interested in purchasing a dozen milling machines, but lacked the funds to buy them. Geier called a meeting with his employees to outline the situation. He proposed giving the bicycle company nine months forbearance and asked the workers if they would be willing to take three-quarters of their wages in company script, which he promised to redeem once the orders were paid for. Having little choice, given the state of the economy, the workers agreed to the arrangement, but it proved not to be a hardship since area businesses, which were also in desperate straits, accepted company script as if it were cash. The bicycle maker paid off his debts on time, allowing Geier to redeem the script. Cincinnati Milling was now in a position to supply other bicycle companies with milling machines, which drove the company's business for the rest of the decade.

With improved finances Holz and his team resumed the development of innovative products. In 1900 the company introduced a milling machine that featured the first gear-driven power feed system, replacing the hand-crank mechanism to provide an operator with a variable, yet steady, feed rate. This new product won a gold medal at the Paris World's Fair in 1900. In 1902 Holz struck again, as the company introduced the first milling machine that was independently powered by its own electric motor, a vast improvement over the practice of hooking up the devices to a central steam engine. The old arrangement featured a cumbersome and complex collection of shafts, belts, and pulleys, all prone to get out of alignment and cause an entire production line to grind to a halt while technicians sorted out the problem. Also in 1902, Cincinnati Milling came out with a universal dividing head, which clasped a workpiece tightly enough that it could be rotated with precision, allowing the milling machine to make more precise and complicated cuts.

Holz retired in 1905 at the age of 51, selling out to Geier, who assumed the presidency and continued the company's reputation for innovation, but in a different vein. The company had outgrown its plants, but rather than build more of the same on a larger scale, he decided to build a vertically integrated facility, in short an industrial park where other businesses that Cincinnati Milling depended on would be housed and share the costs—and the savings—of having close proximity. Geier found a 102-acre site, serving mostly as an orchard, in nearby Oakley. He relocated his firm there in 1911 and within a year convinced several other companies to build facilities there as well. At his new plant Geier pioneered another concept. In 1914 he enlisted his brother, Dr. Otto Geier, to establish an onsite employee health and fitness center, one of the first industrial-health programs in the world. Its value would become more than apparent five years later when a flu epidemic spread across the globe killing countless people. Cincinnati Milling fared far better than most companies. Geier also made a contribution to education, setting up a cooperative-education program with the University of Cincinnati, in which students supplemented classroom study with on-the-job experience at Cincinnati Milling and other area manufacturers. It was an approach that would be emulated by universities around the world.

Cincinnati Milling prospered during World War I as huge mechanized armies arose, increasing the demand for machine parts and the machine tools needed to make them. After the war ended in 1918 the worldwide economy lapsed into recession, causing Cincinnati Milling's business to slump as well. By now, Geier was joined by his son, Frederick V. Geier, who urged him to diversify, specifically into grinding machines, which were in much demand by the young automotive industry. The company acquired a controlling interest in Cincinnati Grinder Co. in 1921 to enter the field. But key customer Henry Ford was not pleased with its center-type grinding machine and urged Geier to pursue centerless grinding, which reduced the handling of a part and resulted in higher feed rates. Geier acquired the necessary patents and was able to secure Ford's business as well as those of other automakers, important in the company's rising prosperity in the 1920s and ability to weather the Great Depression of the 1930s. It was during this period, in 1934, that Geier died. He was replaced by his son, who had been groomed to succeed him by working in all aspects of the company's business.

As was the case during World War I, Cincinnati Milling's products were in high demand during World War II. Well before the United States entered the war in late 1941, the company was gearing up for production, so that in 1942 it was able to increase production sevenfold over 1939. After the war, the company also launched a diversification effort. It developed synthetic coolants used on both cutting tools and workpieces. Cincinnati Milling also recognized the emergence of plastic as a material that would replace metal in many applications. In 1968

Key Dates:

1884: Cincinnati Screw and Tap Company is formed.
1900: Cincinnati Screw is renamed Cincinnati Milling Machine Company.
1914: F. Jos Lamb Company is founded.
1982: Lamb changes its name to Lamb Technicon.
1987: Lamb is acquired by Litton Industries.
1998: Lamb's parent corporation, Unova, acquires Cincinnati Milling.
2003: Lamb and Cincinnati are consolidated to form Cincinnati Lamb Inc.

it offered its first plastics injection molding machine. In 1970 Frederick V. Geier stepped down as president, replaced by his 45-year-old son, James Geier. The company now changed its name to Cincinnati Milacron, a name more in keeping with the company's changing profile. Under the third generation of Geier leadership, the company over the next 20 years produced a variety of plastics processing machines, employing technologies such as blow molding and extrusion in addition to injection molding, and by the end of the 1980s it offered a wide range of plastic processing equipment and services. In the 1990s Cincinnati Milacron completed a number of acquisitions to supplement its plastics business. In 1998 the company decided to focus all of its resources on plastics technology and industrial products units, and sold the original machine tool business to Unova for $180 million and shortened its name to Milacron Inc. Cincinnati Milling now took on the Cincinnati Machine name.

Lamb Origins in the World War I Era

Unova also owned another company involved in the machine tool industry, Lamb Technicon Corp. It was founded in 1914 as F. Jos. Lamb Company by electrical engineer Francis Joseph Lamb. It started out making electrical products, then in the 1920s began to make metal components and dial index machines, which were used to retool dial machines. The company established itself in the automotive industry in the early 1950s when it won a General Motors contract to rebuild 60 grinders damaged by fire. Lamb enjoyed strong growth in the 1960s and over the next 20 years introduced a number of technologies and products to assist in material handling, machine controls, and computer-based monitoring systems. To better reflect its diversity, the company adopted the Lamb Technicon name in 1982. Lamb's sales reached $370 million in 1981, but with the advent of a recession, sales fell off, dipping to $200 million in 1983. Revenues began to rebound in the mid-1980s and the company took steps to be less dependent on the automotive industry, but privately held Lamb was not immune to the shakeout under way in the machine tool industry. In 1987 the company faced another

sales slump, caused by decreasing demand for equipment by automakers, and it agreed to be acquired by Litton Industries Inc., a Beverly Hills, California-based defense contractor, in a stock-swap valued at $100 million.

In 1994 Lamb became part of Western Atlas, a company spun off by Litton, and four years later, in 1998, Western Atlas spun off Unova, the same year that Cincinnati Machine was acquired. It was also the beginning of a difficult period for the machine tool industry. With softening demand, Cincinnati Machine cut jobs, and in 2000 Unova hired Credit Suisse First Boston to consider strategic alternatives, which included selling off the company. But Cincinnati Machine was a part of Unova's Industrial Automation Systems division and involved in joint projects with Lamb and sister unit Landis Grinding Systems. Some plants were shuttered but the unit was kept intact. The terrorist attacks of September 11, 2001, took their toll, however, as air travel slumped and had a ripple effect on the aerospace industry and Cincinnati Machine, which was very much dependent on the composite manufacturing systems it sold for aircraft production.

In 2002 Unova decided to combine the business operations of Cincinnati Machine and Lamb, a plan that took effect in late 2003. The hope was to cut overhead costs and improve efficiencies. The merged operation took the name of Cincinnati Lamb, with its headquarters relocated to suburban Detroit. The Oakley facility, the longtime home of Cincinnati Mills, was slowly shut down, with operations either moved to Michigan or across the Ohio River to a facility in Hebron, Kentucky. Business in the meantime began to pick up in the aerospace industry, and management was hopeful that with the consolidation of its operation and the investment in new aerospace technologies, Cincinnati Lamb was well positioned to compete in the long run.

Principal Competitors

Giddings & Lewis; Haas Automation.

Further Reading

Frazier, Mya, "Cincinnati Machine Now 'Right Size' for Market," *Cincinnati—Northern Kentucky,* February 18, 2000, p. 8.

Horstman, Barry M., "Frederick A. Geier: His Empire Had Roots in a Debt," *Cincinnati Post,* November 18, 1999.

LaMotte, Kenneth, and Darlyne Case, "Lamb Sought Shelter with Litton," *Crain's Detroit Business,* March 2, 1987, p. 3.

Newberry, Jon, "Vanishing Machine Tools/Cincinnati Machine Moves, Shrinks Operations," *Cincinnati Post,* October 15, 2003, p. C6.

Stammen, Ken, "New Help for Old Industry Firm Competes with Asia Imports," *Cincinnati Post,* April 28, 2000, p. 8B.

Zdrojewski, Ed, "Frederick Geier and the Cincinnati Mill," *Cutting Tool Engineering,* June 1993.

—Ed Dinger

Clougherty Packing Company

3049 East Vernon Avenue
Los Angeles, California 90058
U.S.A.
Telephone: (323) 583-4621
Fax: (323) 584-1699
Web site: http://www.farmerjohn.com

Wholly-Owned Subsidiary of Hormel Foods Corp.
Incorporated: 1945 as Clougherty Packing Company
Employees: 1,200
Sales: $420 million (2004 est.)
NAIC: 112210 Hog and Pig Farming; 311611 Animal
(except Poultry) Slaughtering; 311612 Meat Processed
from Carcasses; 424470 Meat and Meat Product
Merchant Wholesalers

Clougherty Packing Company is the West Coast's leading pork packer, making products sold under the Farmer John brand name. These include bacon, ham, sausage, and wieners. The company sells more than 400 million pounds of pork a year. The extra-long Dodger Dogs the company sells at Dodger Stadium are a baseball legend. Family-owned for generations, in late 2004 the company was sold to Hormel Foods Corp., which was expanding its presence in the Southwest. Clougherty has a 900,000-square-foot plant on a ten-acre site near downtown Los Angeles and hog farming operations outside of California.

Origins

Francis and Bernard Clougherty began by curing pork bellies and smoked hams for sale out of their home. Born in Los Angeles to Irish immigrants, the two entered the meat business working for a meat producer and a railroad shipper.

According to the *Los Angeles Times,* they progressed to leasing space at the Woodward-Bennett Packing facility and entered the crowded Los Angeles meat business in earnest in 1931. They had one employee and no money, Francis's son Bernard told the paper.

Clougherty Brothers Packing Co., as the business was known, bought the plant in 1941. During the war, sheep and cattle products were included in the lineup. Clougherty Packing Company was incorporated in California at the end of 1945.

A New Brand in the 1950s

The company focused on the pork market in the 1950s. In 1953, the Farmer John brand was introduced, said to be more pronounceable than the family's Irish surname. The brothers promoted the new brand by sponsoring a local television show, *Polka Parade.*

The Cloughertys bought the Harry Carey Ranch in California's Santa Clarita Valley around 1953. However, plans to raise pork there did not pan out due to the hot, dry weather. This site was used for a time as a retreat, then sold to a residential developer in 1998.

The pork plant, located south of Los Angeles in Vernon, became a tourist attraction in 1957 when set painter Les Grimes was hired to decorate one of its walls with a farm scene.

Clougherty needed a new local advertising vehicle when *Polka Parade* shifted to national distribution in 1964. It shifted to sponsorship of radio broadcasts of Dodger baseball games. This led to stadium sales of Farmer John's famous "Dodger Dogs." However, the extra-long wieners did not become the Dodgers' official hot dog until around 1990. Dodger Stadium sold about two million of the "eastern grown, western flavored" wieners a year. In 1999, the National Hot Dog and Sausage Council ranked Dodger fans as baseball's top consumers of hot dogs. Famed sportscaster Vin Scully pitched Dodger Dogs to great effect in his broadcasts. Clougherty also supplied other area sports venues, including the Rose Bowl Coliseum.

In 1962, Clougherty's operations expanded into Tucson, Arizona.

For several years the company supplied beef for its West Coast plant and for local supermarkets from this location. The Tucson plant was also decorated with a farm mural, which became a local landmark.

72

Company Perspectives:

Today, twelve Cloughertys spanning three generations work together to insure Farmer John products are in keeping with the past. They closely supervise every detail of the packing process. Quality control is foremost. So, consumers are always assured fresh delivery daily. What's more, the Farmer John family responds to consumer demand with a growing selection of wholesome meat products. They include: a full line of lean, fresh-cut pork, savory sausage, wonderful wieners, franks, Polish sausage, bacon in two thicknesses, boneless smoked fully cooked ham, as well as a full assortment of pre-packed ready-to-eat luncheon meats, liver spreads and more. Hot or cold, for breakfast, lunch or dinner, Farmer John products always reflect high values and low prices. On the holidays, every day, families who know what's best put Farmer John products between their knives and forks.

Key Dates:

1931: Brothers Francis and Bernard Clougherty enter the pork packing business.
1945: Clougherty Packing Company is incorporated in California.
1953: Farmer John brand is introduced.
1957: Set artist Les Grimes paints a historic mural on the company's Vernon, California, plant.
1962: Operations expand to Tucson.
1985: Meat cutters' stage a two-month strike at the company's Los Angeles plant.
1989: Revenues rise to $300 million.
1994: Wiener line is rebuilt after a fire.
2004: Hormel Foods Corp. buys Cloughtery Packing for $186 million.

According to the *Los Angeles Times,* there were a dozen slaughterhouses and more than 60 meat packing plants in Vernon in 1970s. Fewer than 20 percent of these would survive into the 1990s.

Developments in the 1980s and 1990s

Bernard Clougherty died in 1982, followed two years later by his brother Francis. The company was subsequently run by Francis's four surviving children: Bernard, Joe, Anthony, and Kathleen Regan.

Clougherty was well placed to benefit from Southern California's postwar population boom. By the mid-1980s, Clougherty was the last large meat packer remaining in the region after its competitors had all relocated to the Midwest. Revenues were $300 million by 1989.

Clougherty experienced a two-month meat cutters strike in late 1985. The company also had contentious labor relations with the union in the 1990s, when more than 1,000 workers worked for several years without a contract.

There was a significant positive development in the late 1980s. "The best thing we ever did was to secure our own source of hogs," president Joe Clougherty later told the journal *Meat & Poultry.* In 1988, the company formed a partnership with a California hog farmer, then took over the entire operation in 1994. It also started raising pigs in Arizona in 1992. By the late 1990s, Clougherty was supplying 30 percent of its own hogs.

Clougherty was also upgrading its production line. The company brought in a master sausage maker from Germany to oversee the shop. An X-ray system was added to the sausage line in 1988 to scan for bone fragments. Three years later, the company installed a small lab to speed up nutritional analysis of their product.

In the early 1990s, Clougherty was California's largest meat packer and ranked as a top 100 U.S. food company. The value of concessions at Dodger baseball games went beyond sales of the hot dogs themselves. It was a cornerstone of the company's marketing strategy, a reputation lamented to the *Los Angeles Daily News* after the 1994 season was cut short. In April of that year, the hot dog operation experienced another setback when a fire wiped out the production area. State-of-the-art processing and packaging machinery was subsequently installed.

Sales were about $325 million a year in the late 1990s. The company had to contend with consolidation among the area supermarket chains, reducing its major client list from more than two dozen to five. At the same time, distribution had expanded to Washington State, Las Vegas, and Hawaii. Clougherty also paid attention to the smaller retailers and ethnic groceries that placed a high priority on freshness.

To improve its margins, Clougherty was developing value-added products. The company erected a new cooking plant in 1997.

Beyond 2000

Clougherty's revenues rose about 10 percent to $365 million in 2000. The company employed around 1,500 people, including several hundred butchers and 300 farm workers in California, Arizona, and Wyoming. It shut down its ten-year-old Tucson beef-grinding operation, Arizona Meat Products Co., in 2001. The unit had sales of up to $50 million a year but was unable to compete profitably against industry giants.

In late 2003, Clougherty hired Atlanta's AmeriCold Logistics, LLC to build a 120,000-square-foot distribution center next to its Vernon plant. AmeriCold was under contract to manage the warehouse for ten years.

Family-owned for generations, the company was acquired by Hormel Foods Corp. for $186 million in December 2004. Based in Austin, Minnesota, Hormel was the fifth-largest pork packer in the United States. It owned several leading national brands, including SPAM, but was looking to increase its business in the Southwest. The region's Hispanic population consumed higher than average quantities of pork products, an analyst explained in the *Los Angeles Times.*

Company president Joe Clougherty and several other family members remained on board after the sale. According to Hormel officials, Clougherty was expected to reach $420 million in sales in 2004, up from $370 million in 2003. It was processing more than 1.6 million hogs and selling more than 400 million pounds of pork a year. The company then had about 1,200 employees.

Principal Competitors

ConAgra, Inc.; Excel Corporation; Kraft Foods Inc.; Miller Packing Company; Smithfield Foods Inc.; Tyson Fresh Meats, Inc.

Further Reading

Baker, Bob, "Union Goes After Latino Support in Battling Meat Firm," *Los Angeles Times*, June 28, 1990, p. D1.

"Baseball and Hotdogs," *Meat & Poultry*, June 1, 2001.

Boyle, Dan, "Plans Resubmitted for Housing Project on Saugus Ranch," *Los Angeles Daily News*, Santa Clarita Sec., April 8, 1992, p. SC4.

Collins, Glenn, "Hold the Homogeneity; Hot Dogs Stay Local," *New York Times*, July 15, 2001, p. 6.

Dawson, Angela, "DavisElen Wins Farmer John Pork Account," *ADWEEK*, February 2, 1998.

"Farmer John Fires Up F/F/S Hot Dog Packaging Trio," *Packaging Digest*, January 1, 1995, p.28.

Hoffarth, Tom, "The Writing on (And off) the Wall; It's a Dog with a New Bark," *Daily News of Los Angeles*, January 3, 2005, p. S2.

Kiger, Jeff, "Sale to Hormel Proves Roller-Coaster Ride for Los Angeles-Based Meat Packer," *Post-Bulletin* (Rochester, Minnesota), January 1, 2005.

Kish, Rich, "The Silver Lining," *Meat Processing*, May 2005.

Kratz, Gregory P., "Pigs, Pigs, Pigs," *Deseret News*, September 13, 1998, p. B1.

Lee, Patrick, "Dodger Dogs' Maker Dogged by Competition," *Daily News of Los Angeles*, March 26, 1988, p. B1.

"Meat Packing Plants." *Encyclopedia of American Industries*. Online Edition. Gale, 2004. Reproduced in Business and Company Resource Center. Farmington Hills, Mich.: Thomson Gale, 2005.

"Meat Plant to Get $7 Million for Expansion and Jobs," *Los Angeles Times*, January 6, 1994, p. J2.

Neff, Jack, "Making the ERP Link," *Food Processing*, August 1999, pp. 98f.

Nunes, Keith, "Companies to Watch: Clougherty Packing Co.; A Fresh Perspective," *Meat & Poultry*, September 1, 1999.

Petix, Mark, "Loading Up on the Basics and More; The Basics at Southern California Baseball Stadiums Still Include Some Mean Hot Dogs, But Sushi, Tacos and Chowder Have Joined the Lineup," *Press Enterprise* (Riverside, California), April 1, 2005.

Puzo, Daniel P., "Pig Star: A Pork Story—When Brand-Name Meats Came of Age, No One Was Bigger in Southern California Than Farmer John," *Los Angeles Times*, Food Sec., February 8, 1996, p. H8.

Relly, Jeannine, "Farmer John Layoffs Begin," *Arizona Daily Star*, March 20, 2001, p. D1.

——, "Farmer John Meats Shuts Down," *Arizona Daily Star*, August 24, 2001, p. D1.

Robe, Karl, "Better Sausage, and Quick QC Payouts: Analysis of Ground Meat Helps Bring Formula to Standards; X-Rays Show the Way to Bone-Free QA," *Food Processing*, February 1, 1993, p. 78.

Rutherford, Megan, "Preserving Western Art: Change at Famous Wall," *Arizona Daily Star*, September 16, 2003, p. D1.

Smith, Rod, "Hormel Buys Clougherty in Major Pork Expansion," *Feedstuffs*, January 10, 2005, pp. 1f.

Smith, Sharon D., "Homes Planned for Hog-Farm Site," *Daily News of Los Angeles*, October 5, 1992, p. SC1.

Sullivan, Ben, "Fans Wild for Winning Weiner; Dodger Dog Tops Survey of Major League Ballpark Hot Dog Eaters," *Los Angeles Daily News*, April 3, 1999, p. B1.

Tamaki, Julie, "Hormel Buys Maker of Farmer John Meats, Dodger Dogs; The $186-Million Deal for Clougherty Will Let the Acquirer Expand Its Presence in California," *Los Angeles Times*, December 31, 2004, p. C1.

Taub, Daniel, "Union Ends Boycott against Vernon Meat Processing Firm," *Los Angeles Business Journal*, April 6, 1998, p. 4.

Wagner, Karen, "Maintaining Mighty Machines," *National Provisioner*, May 1997, p. 62.

Weinstein, Henry, "Meatpackers Throw 'Dodger Dogs' Producer a Strike," *Los Angeles Times*, October 2, 1985.

Wilcox, Gregory J., "Business Shut Out by End of Baseball Advertisers; Broadcasters Struggle to Cope," *Los Angeles Daily News*, Valley Sec., September 16, 1994, p. B1.

"X-Ray Meat Inspection Scans Up to Nine Tons Per Hour," *Prepared Foods*, March 1, 1991, p. 87.

—Frederick C. Ingram

Colorado Baseball Management, Inc.

2001 Blake Street
Denver, Colorado 80205-2000
U.S.A.
Telephone: (303) 292-0200
Toll Free: (800) 388-7625
Fax: (303) 312-2116
Web site: http://www.coloradorockies.com

Private Company
Founded: 1990
Sales: $124 million (2003)
NAIC: 711211 Professional Sports Teams & Organizations

Colorado Baseball Management, Inc. owns and manages the Colorado Rockies professional baseball franchise. Since its founding as an expansion team in 1993, the team's poor showing has consistently left it out of the pennant race, and it has finished at or near the bottom of its division at the end of each baseball season from the time of its inception as a ball club. The team is controlled by chief executive officer Charlie Monfort and his brother Dick Monfort. FOX Sports Networks and brewer Adolph Coors each own a 14 percent interest in the team.

Beginnings

In 1989, when professional baseball's National League announced it would expand by two teams for the 1993 season, the Colorado state legislature responded by creating the Colorado Baseball Commission to promote Denver as a viable franchise location. The commission's co-chair was Larry Varnell, a Central Bank executive and former minor league ballplayer who had sought to bring big league baseball to Denver since 1977. Varnell had witnessed several failed attempts to recruit professional baseball to Denver, especially in 1980 when oil magnate Marvin Davis came close to getting the Oakland Athletics. This attempt fell short at the last minute, however, dashing the dreams of local baseball enthusiasts.

With another chance to obtain a major league team, Varnell's commission sought to impress the major league's baseball own-ers, who would select the expansion sites, by getting Denver area voters to pass a 0.1 percent sales tax to finance a new baseball stadium, if major league baseball granted the franchise. The new stadium, which would be financed by both the sales tax and contributions from the private sector, was to be ready by the 1995 season. Much was riding on this show of support, but initial polls in the spring of 1990 showed voter sentiment running against the tax proposal by two-to-one. Given these poll numbers, one state representative suggested withdrawing the stadium issue from the ballot. The reasoning for this suggestion was that it would be better to rework the tax proposal to make it more acceptable to the public than to suffer defeat, which would kill Denver's chances for big-league baseball. Nevertheless, the campaign for the stadium moved forward with a fundraising drive to sway voters. Early in 1990, organizers faced difficulty in raising funds until TV-cable magnate Bill Daniels donated $100,000, which immediately sparked a slew of other donations. By election-day on August 14, 1990, the fund raising drive had raised nearly $500,000, enabling organizers to launch an effective advertising campaign. At the same time, Varnell and others warned that failure meant the end of any chance to bring professional baseball to Denver. The stadium tax passed by a comfortable margin of 54 to 46 percent, positioning the city as a serious contender for an expansion team.

On August 23, 1990, Colorado's Baseball Advisory Committee, led by Governor Roy Romer, designated the Colorado Baseball Partnership to recruit an ownership group. With passage of the stadium tax and devoted sports fans, Denver's civic leaders felt they could offer Major League Baseball everything it wanted. They also believed the franchise would have solid financial backing from real estate tycoon John Dikeou until he abruptly withdrew from the city's bid in July, just two months short of the National League's franchise application deadline. In response to this unexpected reversal, city officials launched a frantic two-week, nationwide search for new investors. By mid-August, the search yielded a new investor group, comprising members who were more conversant with professional sports ownership and management. The new investor group, known as the Colorado Baseball Partnership Ltd, received financial commitments between $80 and $100 million to pay the $95 million franchise cost.

Key Dates:

1989: Major League Baseball announces it will expand by two teams.

1990: Colorado Baseball Partnership is designated to recruit a new ownership group.

1991: The National League designates Denver as an expansion team.

1992: Ownership group restructures.

1992: Ownership group acquires the Rockies franchise.

1993: The Rockies play their inaugural season.

1993: The Rockies set fan attendance records.

1995: The Rockies open Coors Field.

2004: Charlie Monfort and Rupert Murdock sign an investment and broadcasting deal.

Nevertheless, despite the new owners' experience with the sports industry, some civic leaders expressed concern over the number of out-of-town investors recruited by Governor Roy Romer's blue-ribbon commission. In searching for viable locations that could support new expansion teams, the National League sought situations that could assure strong local ownership and ties to the community. In an interview with the *Orlando Sentinel* published on October 28, 1990, Don Hinchley, a spokesman for the Colorado and Denver Baseball Commission, said that the city's bid would have failed without the out-of-town investor's involvement. In Hinchley's words, "No one expected the $95-million price tag, no one. The governor's commission looked locally and nationwide. It was clear that they would have to expand the net to get enough money."

The new investor group included six general partners led by businessmen John Antonucci and Michael I. Monus of Youngstown, Ohio, and lawyer and sports entrepreneur Steven E. Ehrhart of Memphis, Tennessee. Antonucci, who operated a wholesale beverage distributor in Youngstown, and Monus, the owner of Phar-Mor Inc., one the nation's leading drugstore chains in Youngstown, in 1986 had together formed the World Basketball League, a professional league for players six feet five or under. Ehrhart, a native of Colorado, was commissioner of the league and former executive director of the United States Football League before it went defunct. Together, the three partners had considerable experience in building and operating franchises, in addition to negotiating player contracts, product sponsorships, stadium leasing, and cable television deals. The other general partners included David G. Elmore, owner of a Colorado class AAA farm club of the Cleveland Indians and four other minor-league teams; Carey S. Teraji, founder of a Denver computer software firm; and New Yorker Michael Nickolus, whose several businesses encompassed television production, construction management, sports marketing companies, and a Class AA Southern League team, the Memphis Chicks.

In addition to some local businessmen, the investor group also comprised nine limited partners, including such Colorado companies as Coors Brewing Company of Golden, Hensel Phelps Construction Company of Greeley, KOA Radio in Denver, NW Transport Service Inc. of Commerce City, and the *Rocky Mountain News* of Denver.

Denver Selected as Expansion Site

On July 5, 1991, the National League's twenty-six club owners unanimously approved Denver and Miami as the sites for the two expansion teams. With league president Bill White in attendance, Denver team officials immediately identified their team as the Colorado Rockies, which would join the Western Division. The long march toward expansion had been initiated by Peter Ueberroth after he became baseball commissioner in 1984. For various reasons, the process stalled until a committee of United States senators, including those from Colorado and Florida, began pressuring baseball officials and owners to expand. The concept of adding teams met initial resistance, however, from some officials and owners who were concerned that it would dilute the level of talent. Nonetheless, in 1990, the National League began the process of selecting two new teams in earnest, selecting six finalists out of applications from eighteen prospective ownership groups from ten cities. Of these, Denver and Miami won over Washington, Buffalo, and two Florida cities, St. Petersburg and Orlando. As part of the arrangement, both teams were to have minor league teams by 1992 and select 36 players each in an expansion draft. At a July 5, 1991 news conference, the Rockies ownership displayed the team logo—a high flying baseball against the backdrop of the Rocky Mountains. The team would play in Mile High Stadium, home of the Denver Broncos of the National Football League, until the new baseball stadium could be built in downtown Denver. The new stadium was to be called Coors Field after local mega-business Coors Brewing Company, which had signed a $30 million deal with the club for equity and major promotional considerations. The new stadium was slated to open for the 1995 season. The Colorado franchise also negotiated an $8.5 million agreement with the *Rocky Mountain News*.

In addition to public and private financing for a new stadium, other factors contributed to Denver's selection for an expansion team, including an ownership group that raised about $140 million for a franchise, the potential appeal to an eight-state area, a large television market, a rapidly growing population, and a rich tradition of major fan support for professional sports.

Ownership in Colorado Rockies Partnership Shifts

In August 1992, the Rockies owners met to reorganize their financial and ownership structure after vice-chairman Michael I. Monus was accused of embezzling funds and falsifying profits at Phar-Mor Inc. The alleged fraud compelled Monus and his father, Nathan, to give up their approximate $12.5 million interest in the team. Monus's long time partner, John Antonucci, the Rockies' chief executive officer, and his father, Jack, also surrendered a portion of their stock. While the elder Antonucci sold all of his shares for $2.5 million, the younger sold the majority of his interest for $5 million. The partnership accepted John Antonucci's word that he was not involved in any criminal activity with Monus, but it nevertheless expressed a readiness to take control of management.

Because of these events, the controlling interest in the team underwent dramatic change with four Colorado limited partnership investors—Jerry McMorris, owner of NW Transport Systems, Inc; Coors Brewing Company; Denver entrepreneur Orel Brenton; and Charles Monfort, chairman of a meat packing company—agreeing to purchase at least $15 million of the $21 million in general-partnership stock. Although John Antonucci remained as general partner and the team's CEO, under the new arrangement both he and club President Steve Ehrhart no longer exercised complete control of the team's policy and management decisions, which now rested with McMorris, Coors, Benton, and Monfort. As a result of this restructuring, the general partnership that began with the predominance of two Youngstown, Ohio, families passed to local ownership.

While these matters were transpiring, the ownership chose Tucson, Arizona, as the Rockies spring training home, signing an agreement with the Pima County Sports Authority for the club to play its spring training games at Hi Corbett Field. The club also announced its 1993 ticket prices, seating locations, and season ticket packages, while signing a five-year deal with local station KWGN-TV to become the Rockies exclusive television broadcaster. Between early June and late October 1992, the Rockies made its first draft pick (pitcher John Burker from the University of Florida), unveiled their traditional uniforms (home, away, and Sunday alternative), broke ground on the future site of Coors field, and signed Don Baylor as their first manager. By early October, the Rockies had sold nearly 25,000 tickets. On November 9, the partnership completed its acquisition of the franchise by paying the $95 million franchise cost.

In January 1993, the partnership restructured the front office, designating Jerry McMorris as chairman, president, and CEO, and Oren Benton and Charles Monfort as vice-chairmen. On April 5, the Rockies played their first regular season game at Shea Stadium, where the New York Mets' Dwight Gooden pitched a three-hit shut out.

Rockies' Owners in Action in the 1990s

Nevertheless, from the beginning the Rockies set attendance records on their home turf, immediately quieting all criticism surrounding Denver's selection for big league baseball. On April 9, 1993, the Rockies hosted their first game against Montreal at Mile High Stadium. Before a record setting crowd of 80,227, Eric Young hit a homerun to lead off the bottom of the first, helping the team to win 11 to 4. By May 9, attendance had already reached one million in just seventeen home dates. By June 20, it cracked two million; by July 28, the Rockies surpassed three million; and by September 17, the club passed the 4 million mark, breaking the single-season attendance record. On concluding their inaugural season on October 3, the Rockies had scored the most wins by a National League expansion team.

Throughout the remainder of the 1990s, the partnership was able to survive Oren Benton's bankruptcy and prospered as a fan-focused baseball club. The team concerned itself with building the franchise, drafting and trading players, playing before sell-out crowds, and competing in the National League's Western Division. On April 26, 1995, the Rockies inaugurated Coors Field with a dramatic win over New York after Dante Bachette hit a three-run homer in the 14th inning. To cater to the fans, the new Coors Field offered an array of upscale items, including an onsite microbrewery, specialty coffees, and local branded foods as well as traditional ballpark fare. The sports venue also provided a playground and food court for children. Also in 1995,

the team won the wild card in their division, their first and, to date, only post-season appearance. They lost, however, in the first round of the playoffs to the Atlanta Braves.

In 1996, the Colorado Rockies and its owners denied charges that they ostracized and defrauded Stephen Kurtz, a Denver accountant who owned a minor interest in the franchise. Kurtz, who helped start the Colorado Rockies at the urging of Governor Roy Romer, claimed in a lawsuit that he was denied the same privileges given to the other owners, that he was owed nearly $25,000, and that the club's general owners misallocated over $2 million. The defendants in the suit included Colorado Rockies Baseball Club Ltd.; Jerry McMorris, club president and principal investor; Colorado Baseball 1993, the team's general partnership; and Colorado Baseball Management Inc. The defendants filed a counterclaim, contending that Kurtz was consistently granted all lawful rights and obligations due to him stemming from his nonvoting economic interest in the team.

In 1999, the Colorado Rockies once again topped the major leagues in attendance, drawing 3,481,065 to Coors Field. The team had won the attendance race every season since the franchise started in 1993.

Rockies Lose Momentum in the 2000s

In 2004, an alliance emerged between Australian born media mogul Rupert Murdock and Charlie Monfort, the majority owner of the Colorado Rockies. In July, the two signed a deal, providing that Murdock's Fox Sports invest $20 million for a 14 percent limited partnership stake in the Rockies. The cash infusion rescued the team's owners from having to cover the team's capital needs for a second year running. At the same time, Murdock's investment represented a sweetheart valuation, indicating a franchise valuation of only $142 million, which was less than half of what investment specialists in the sports industry estimated the team to be worth. *Forbes* magazine, which published annual valuations of major league baseball franchises, valued the Rockies at almost $300 million in 2004. Murdock therefore got about 50 cents on the dollar for a share of the team. As part of the deal, Murdock also agreed to spend $200 million over ten years to broadcast up to 150 Rockies games each season on Fox Sports Net Rocky Mountain, which was battling a rival network, Altitude, for local sports broadcasting rights and revenue.

Despite the Murdock deal, as the summer of 2005 approached, it was questionable whether the owners under the principal control of the Monfort brothers had enough capital to operate a successful major league team. Both Charlie Monfort with a 27 percent stake in the team and his brother Dick, with 19 percent, had emerged in the lead ownership roles after others had either sold their stakes or were ousted or discredited. The ownership had suffered major loses in the previous four years with the team's lackluster performance on the field and declining attendance. Much of the difficulty stemmed from poor personnel decisions and ill-fated signings. In 2005, as the Monforts looked to the club's future, it seemed apparent that they would have to decide whether to elevate their financial ambitions to put the team back on a competitive footing or to sell their majority stake to deep-pocketed investors, who could plow major resources into the franchise.

Principal Competitors

Colorado Avalanche; Colorado Rapids; Denver Broncos; Denver Nuggets.

Further Reading

Algeo, David, "Rockies Reject Claims," *Denver Post*, May 25, 1996.

Baker, Russell, "No Sox, Birds, Beasts?" *New York Times*, July 2, 1991.

Chass, Murray, "The Marlins? The Rockies? Get Used to It. It's Official," *New York Times*, July 6, 1991.

Enders, Debbie, "AMARK's Coors Field Operation Adds Upscale Items to Standard Fare," *Amusement Business*, April 17, 1995.

Frei, Terry, "Monforts in Rocky Situation," *Denver Post*, May 24, 2005.

Freudenheim, Milt, "Phar-Mor Says Profit was Faked," *New York Times*, August 5, 1992.

Gottlieb, Alan, *In the Shadow of the Rockies: An Outsider's Look Inside a New Major League Baseball Team*, Niwot, Colorado: Roberts Rinehart Publishers, 1994.

Johnson, Dirk, "Coors and Partners Give Baseball to Wild West," *New York Times*, June 11, 1991.

Klis, Mike, "Rockies Partners Regroup/Investors Absorb Monus' Interest," *Gazette Telegraph*, August 7, 1992.

Schley, Stewart, "It's a Rupert World; We Just Live in It," *ColoradoBiz*, September 2004.

Thomas, Scott, "Colorado Rockies Continue to Dominate," *Denver Business Journal*, October 15, 1999.

Weber, Bruce, "Warmup Pitches," *New York Times*, October 11, 1992.

Yasuda, Gene, "Group of New Investors Pads Pockets of Bid Series: Race for Expansion," *Orlando Sentinel*, October 28, 1990.

—Bruce Montgomery

Combe Inc.

1101 Westchester Avenue
White Plains, New York 10604
U.S.A.
Telephone: (914) 694-5454
Toll Free: (800) (873)-7400
Fax: (914) 461-4402
Web site: http://www.combe.com

Private Company
Incorporated: 1949 as Eastco Chemical Company
Employees: 240 (est.)
Sales: $351 million (2003 est.)
NAIC: 325412 Pharmaceutical Preparation Manufacturing

Combe Inc. is a White Plains, New York-based family-owned-and-operated company that markets several lines of niche personal care products. Despite being a small company, Combe is able to survive against much larger competition because of its specialist approach, able to focus more resources on products that the likes of Procter & Gamble and Johnson & Johnson, oriented to the marketing of blockbusters, are unwilling to commit. Combe is little known, primarily because it would rather promote its brands than its corporate name. Most of Combe's brands are, in fact, household words. Men's Grooming products include well-known brands Grecian Formula, Just For Men, Brylcreem, Aqua Velva, and Lectric Shave. In the skincare category, Combe markets the Lanacane brand. The Cepacol brand is the core of the sore throat/oral care category. Vagisil is the main brand of the feminine care business. In the footcare category, Combe relies on Odor-Eaters and Johnson's Foot Soap. Sea-Bond adhesive makes up the denture care category. For more than half a century, Combe has been adept at identifying unmet consumer needs, developing a product to meet these needs, then convincing consumers to take action. All told, Combe products are sold in 64 countries on six continents. The company maintains manufacturing facilities in Illinois and Puerto Rico.

Sales Background in the 1930s

The man behind the Combe name was Ivan DeBlois Combe, regarded as the father of the self-medication industry. He was born in Fremont, Iowa, in 1911, the son of a doctor and his wife. After his father died when Combe was three years old, he was raised by his mother, a schoolteacher, in Greenville, Illinois. He was a good student as well as an athlete, becoming a high school tennis champion before playing college tennis at Northwestern University. After earning an undergraduate degree in 1933, he remained at Northwestern for two more years attending law school. He then took a job at Chicago-based National Dairy Products selling Hydrox Ice Cream before moving to New York City to become a division sales manager for Wilbert Products Co., makers of shoe polish. In 1940, he went to work for Raymond Rubicam, cofounder of Young & Rubicam Advertising Agency, where he served as a merchandising account executive. Three years later, he was named vice-president of sales and advertising at Pharmacraft Corporation, at the time a major pharmaceutical company specializing in over-the-counter drugs.

While at Pharmacraft, Combe was dispatched in 1949 to Philadelphia to investigate the 70 brands of the Dill Company to see if there were any products worth acquiring. Only one brand stood out, a laxative named Espotabs, which he greatly liked and wanted to promote. When Pharmacraft's chairman and CEO Chuck Howell passed on the opportunity, believing that the sales potential for Espotabs was too limited, the 38-year-old Combe decided to strike out on his own and buy the rights to Espotabs and promote it himself. Combe was supported in his venture by Howell, who not only encouraged him but became his first investor and lined up two other backers. Combe set up his offices at 110 East 42nd Street in Manhattan, initially adopting the Eastco Chemical name (combining East, the company's location, with ''Co'' for Combe).

Clearasil Soars in the 1950s

Although Combe did fairly well marketing Espotabs, he needed another product to grow the business. He turned to contacts he made at Pharmacraft and investigated the teen market. After interviewing hundreds of young people and pharmacists, he concluded there was a market for an effective acne product. A number of acne medications had come onto the market but none performed especially well. Combe collaborated with chemist Kedzie Teller to produce a flesh-colored cream that could dry up pimples. When they were satisfied with the formula, Combe launched the product in 1951, calling it Clearasil, a name that played to the teenage desire for clear skin. However, having been disappointed in the past on acne products, retailers were reluctant to stock Clearasil. To get the product on the shelves, Combe had to offer free tubes to owners, who promised to order the product if it sold. It did, the stores placed orders, and teens began touting Clearsil's effectiveness to each other. Sales grew steadily over the next several years, and the product was well established enough that in 1957 it was the second product, after Cheerios, to become a sponsor of ABC's popular teenage dance program *American Bandstand,* hosted by Dick Clark. As a charter advertiser of American Bandstand, the product had its commercials delivered by the popular Clark, sales soared, and Clearsil became a household word.

In the meantime, Combe, who had been living in Scarsdale several miles north of Manhattan, grew weary of his commute and saw no real reason to be located in the city. In 1952, he moved his offices to 100 Mamaroneck Avenue in White Plains, New York, sharing a second floor location with a beauty parlor. Eastco soon outgrew this location too, and in 1956 moved to a larger office in White Plains, where Combe operated for the next 16 years.

Even as Combe was growing Clearasil and continuing to promote Espotabs, he remained on the lookout for new products. Acting on a tip from a friend, he acquired a pair of pet products from an Illinois veterinarian, Dr. Andrew Merrick. These products were Dr. Merrick's Scratch Powder, which he renamed Scratchex Powder, and Sulfodene Skin Medication, used to treat hot spots on dogs. While Sulfodene sold well from the start, decades would pass before Scratchex began to see strong growth.

Ivan Combe reached a turning point with Clearasil in 1960. He wanted to take advantage of the product's popularity to market it internationally but lacked the necessary experience and resources. Fortunately, Clearasil did not lack for larger company suitors, led by Colgate-Palmolive, Bristol-Myers, and Vick Chemical. He decided to sell the product to Vick Chemical, which wanted to hire him as a consultant for two years while launching the product overseas. In this way, Combe, who believed in learning with someone else's money, gained valuable international experience as well as the capital he needed to acquire a new product. He wisely took Vick's cash rather than the stock they offered for Clearasil, since a short time later the price of Vick's stock tumbled.

After his consultancy with Vick, Combe started up again as Combe Chemical Company. His next major product actually came looking for him, a hair dye called Grecian Formula 16. The man who discovered it was Colonel Julius Amos, an agent for the predecessor to the CIA who operated in Greece during World War II. Suffering from a dandruff problem, he visited a Greek barber who sold him a clear liquid to apply daily to his scalp. About two weeks later, Amos realized that not only had his dandruff been cured, his hair had turned from gray to its original brown. Amos lined up American partners to form a company called World Wide Rights, which then acquired the product from the Greek barber. Grecian Formula 16, as it was called, struggled to find adequate distribution as a women's product, prompting World Wide Rights to find someone who could do a better job of marketing it. The search led to the door of Ivan Combe, who recognized the potential of Grecian Formula 16. Rather than buy the product, however, he entered into a licensing deal in 1961. By focusing his marketing efforts on male customers, who appreciated the gradual reintroduction of coloring to their hair, Combe was able to grow Grecian Formula 16 to a successful product and one that was years ahead of the market.

Another product Combe picked up in the early 1960s was Lanacane, a West Coast over-the-counter medication used to relieve itching that he discovered in his ceaseless store checks. A third product Combe added to his stable in the 1960s, Johnson's Foot Soap, was a testament to his patience and persistence. Dating as far back as his time at Pharmcraft, Combe had made periodic attempts to acquire the product. Despite being rebuffed, every year Combe wrote to the manufacturer expressing his interest. Finally, when the owner of the company died, the product was auctioned off, Combe was invited to participate, and his cash offer plus royalties won the day.

In 1971, Combe hired a head of a research and development unit, recruiting a man named Dr. Herbert Lapidus, who would play a major role in the creation of new products over the next 30 years. According to the *New York Times,* Lapidus had been employed at Bristol-Myers, where he worked on "everything from furniture polish to nasal spray." He even developed a whipped-cream based medicine called CoughWhip, a product that would never see the drugstore shelves despite its intriguing concept. He would quickly make his mark at Combe by becoming involved in the development of two major products: Odor Eaters Insoles and Vagisil Creme.

It was actually Combe's wife Elizabeth who provided the inspiration for Odor Eaters. While in England, she came across a product called "Fresh Sox," a paper insole that relied on activated charcoal, a substance that had been used to good effect in freshening the air in cramped quarters like submarines and space capsules. Lapidus loved the concept but realized that paper was not a good choice of material because perspiration caused it to deteriorate too quickly and left charcoal stains on socks and shoes. After some trial and error, Lapidus found a way to combine coconut charcoal with a breathable latex foam. Someone else at Combe contributed the idea of printing a shoe size template on the underside of the insoles, allowing Combe to produce just one size that could be cut for a custom fit. Introduced in 1974, Odor-Eaters was sold under the Johnson's banner and became another Combe product that achieved household name status.

Manufacturing Added in 1970s

Another product Combe launched in 1974 was Vagisil. This application grew out of the success of Lanacane, which was

Key Dates:

1949: Ivan Combe founds a company.
1951: Combe introduces Clearasil.
1952: The company's offices move from Manhattan to White Plains, New York.
1960: Clearasil is sold to Vick Chemical.
1974: Combe's first manufacturing plant opens in Illinois.
1987: Just For Men is introduced.
2000: Ivan Combe dies.
2004: J.B. Williams is acquired.

mostly used to treat dry skin and external vaginal itching. Vagisil was developed as a specialty feminine itching product. The company debated the merits of an alternative name, Gynasil, which sounded less evocative, but in the end Ivan Combe signed off on Vagisil because it was more striking and descriptive. For nine years, Combe was unable to advertise Vagisil on television because of its name, and promotion of the product was relegated to print ads that appeared primarily in women's magazines. Nevertheless, the product developed a market and enjoyed even greater growth after the television ban was lifted. In June 1974, Combe opened its first manufacturing plant, located in Rantoul, Illinois. Later in the 1970s, Combe searched for a second plant location and decided on Puerto Rico, which offered a 100 percent tax exemption. To take advantage of this offer, Combe quickly opened a 23,000-square-foot facility in March 1980, to which another 40,000 square feet was added over the years. It was also during the 1970s that Combe made a major push to market its products outside of the United States, an effort headed by Combe's son, Chris, who joined the company in 1975 to head the new International Division. A Northwestern graduate like his father, Chris also earned an MBA at Columbia University and worked in sales and marketing for five years at American Hospital Supply Corporation before joining the family business. Over the next few years, sales offices were opened in such countries as the United Kingdom, Spain, Italy, Germany, Brazil, Japan, and Australia.

In 1978, Combe came under fire because of the active ingredient in Grecian Formula 16, lead acetate. Because of concerns about possible health risks, the FDA was on the verge of banning lead acetate when Combe was able to provide scientific evidence that only traces of lead acetate, less than one-third of one millionth of a gram, was absorbed into the skin. Lead acetate was eventually place on the Food and Drug Administration (FDA) approved list of substances, but the experience led Lapidus to begin developing a gradual hair coloring agent that did not rely on lead acetate. The result was a dye based on peroxide, and although the product, named Gray Fighter, took only five minutes to apply, it was far too complicated for consumers and was never introduced into the market. Lapidus switched gears and transformed the hair dye into a five-minute, single application product. This new product was named Just for Men, and it quickly staked out a strong position in the marketplace. Although it took away some sales from Grecian Formula 16, Just for Men helped to open up a much larger market. As self-conscious baby boomers began to gray, an increasing number opted to color their hair, a trend that competitors attempted to exploit as well, but 20 years of experience in marketing Grecian Formula 16 gave Combe a distinct advantage and it was able to carve out a dominant share of the market. Combe strengthened its hold on the category in 1993 with the addition of a gel to color beards and mustaches. In 1997, it introduced a five-minute permanent hair color for women called Just 5, and in 1999 took advantage of the Grecian Formula 16 brand by bringing out Grecian 5, another five-minute permanent hair-coloring product.

The 1980s and Beyond

During the 1980s and 1990s, Combe extended other brand lines and reworked some products to expand its portfolio. An example of the latter was the Sea Bond denture adhesive, which had been introduced in 1978 but proved a disappointment. Lapidus and his team then essentially reinvented the product, adding greater holding power while increasing comfort. During the 1980s, the product was reintroduced to the marketplace, but rather than rely on television commercials, which could not adequately explain Sea Bond's unique approach, the company gave out free samples through direct mail and senior center giveaways and grew the business brick by brick. Line extensions during this period included Odor-Eaters, which added insoles for work shoes, sneakers, and winter wear. Odor-Eaters for Women was introduced in 1988, followed a year later by Odor-Eaters Foot Powder. Combe even licensed the Odor-Eaters name to a line of socks. In response to the success of Cortaid, a hydrocortisone product, Combe's Lanacane product experienced eroding sales, leading to the development of the company's own hydrocortisone product called Lanacort. A Lanacane Spray was then introduced in 1976 as a first aid spray, repositioned in 1983 as a sunburn pain remedy, then recast again in the 1990s as an anti-itch first aid spray. Also growing out of Combe's research of hydrocortisone was Scalpicin, a scalp itching and flaking product that was introduced in 1991. Combe also built on its pet care product lines during the 1980s and 1990s, launching Scratchex Spray, a Scratchex shampoo, Scratchex Dip, Scratchex Powder, Scratchex Power Guard Repellent, and Scratchex Pump Spray, as well as the first extended life flea color for dogs sold under the Scratchex name. Johnson's Foot Soap added a foot pain product called Podiacin, and Vagisil introduced the first feminine powder while adding a stronger version of the original cream product.

An era came to an end in January 2000, when 88-year-old Ivan Combe died of a stroke at his Greenwich, Connecticut, home. He remained chairman and CEO of the company he founded until the end. His son Chris succeeded him and the company carried on as an exploiter of consumer niche products, still committed to being a privately owned, close-knit company. Combe also continued to grow through acquisitions as well as home-grown products. In 2002, the company acquired J.B. Williams, a deal that brought such well known brands as Aqua Velva, Brylcreem, and Cepacol mouthwash. Combe's manufacturing plants had to invest in new equipment to bring the production of three dozen new items in house, and the marketing people had to learn the intricacies of the mouthwash, fragrance, and cough and cold remedy markets. However, after more than half a century of operating in a number of consumer markets, there was every reason to expect Combe to enjoy continued success with its new product lines.

Principal Competitors

L'Oreal SA; Pfizer Inc; The Procter & Gamble Company.

Further Reading

"Combe, A Pioneer in the H&BA Industry, Dies," *Chain Drug Review*, February 14, 2000, p. 14.

Ravo, Nick, "Ivan D. Combe, 88, Marketer Of Clearasil and Just for Men (Obituary)," *New York Times*, January 17, 2000, p. B7.

Swansburg, John, "A Company That's Found Its Niches," *New York Times*, September 2, 2001, p. 14WC.

There's No Place Like Combe, White Plains, New York: Combe Inc., 2000, 205 p.

—Ed Dinger

Dallah Albaraka Group

PO Box 430
Jeddah
21411
Saudi Arabia
Telephone: (+966) 2 671 0000
Fax: (+966) 2 669 4264
Web site: http://www.dallah.com

Private Company
Incorporated: 1969 as Dallah Works and Maintenance
    Company
Employees: 61,000
Sales: $12 billion (2005)
NAIC: 522298 All Other Non-Depository Credit
    Intermediation; 488510 Freight Transportation
    Arrangement; 515120 Television Broadcasting;
    517910 Other Telecommunications; 531210 Offices of
    Real Estate Agents and Brokers; 541330 Engineering
    Services; 551112 Offices of Other Holding
    Companies; 561510 Travel Agencies; 622110 General
    Medical and Surgical Hospitals

The Dallah Albaraka Group is one of the leading, privately held conglomerates in Saudi Arabia. The Jeddah-based company controls some 300 companies involved in a variety of industries in more than 40 countries worldwide. Dallah Albaraka groups its operations into three primary categories: Finance, which includes the group's internationally operating network of Islamic banks, as well as investment and insurance vehicles; Business, with operations ranging from hospital operation to cleaning and maintenance to food production and restaurants; and Media, including the company's ownership of satellite broadcaster Arab Radio & Television. Other Dallah Albaraka investments include the manufacture of traffic lights and the production of pesticides, road construction materials, and metal pipes. Since 2002, the company has regrouped its international banking operations, including banks in Jordan, Algeria, Sudan, Pakistan, South Africa, Egypt, and Lebanon under a single entity, Albaraka Banking Group, which became

the world's leading Islamic bank. Dallah Albaraka remains controlled by founder Sheik Saleh Abdullah Kamel. In 2005, Kamel and Dallah Albaraka were cleared of suspected support for Al Qaeda and the 9/11 terrorist attacks. Dallah Albaraka's total assets as of 2005 reportedly topped $12 billion.

Building an Islamic Conglomerate in the 1960s

Saleh Abdullah Kamel's business career began at an early age with the launch of a courier service. By the late 1960s, Kamel had laid the foundation for the development of the Dallah Albaraka Group, which was to become one of Saudi Arabia's largest and most diversified conglomerates in the early 21st century.

In 1969, Kamel formed a new company, Dallah Works and Maintenance Company, in Riyadh. That company, which benefited from a series of contracts with the Saudi government, including the concessions for the cleaning and maintenance of the Mecca and Medina holy sites, provided the financial springboard for Kamel's increasingly diversified investments. In the mid-1970s, Dallah expanded its public works investments to include Dallah Avco Trans Arabia Company, which specialized in the construction, operation, and maintenance of airports. That company profited from Kamel's closer relationship with the Saudi government, winning a large number of airport and related concessions in the country, such as the contract to maintain and operate the country's air traffic control system in 1988.

Kamel also founded the company's own health clinic in Jeddah in 1977. Originally created to provide healthcare services to the growing numbers of Albaraka employees, the clinic grew into a full-fledged medical facility. The involvement in healthcare led the company to expand into hospital ownership as well with the opening of the Dallah Hospital in Riyadh in 1987. The company also launched a chain of medical and dental clinics throughout Saudi Arabia, and into North Africa as well, while also developing a new subsidiary, Dallah Health Service Holding Company, which, in addition to the operation of healthcare facilities, provided various medical and pharmaceutical support services to healthcare facilities throughout the Arab world.

Kamel's interests had also turned toward the media, and in 1977 Dallah Albaraka launched the Arab Media Company, one of Saudi Arabia's first television, radio, and film production companies. Kamel's media operations later expanded to include broadcasting, and his company became one of the founding members of the Middle East Broadcasting Center in the 1980s.

Another business in which Dallah Albaraka became involved was real estate and development investment. In 1983, the company participated in the Tunis Lake project, a complex of commercial and residential developments covering some 13,000,000 square meters. In the early 1990s, the company created the Shareek Marketing and Real Estate Development Company as a marketing arm for its various real estate projects, such as a development at Durrat-al-Arrus.

Dallah Albaraka continued to explore a range of investment and business opportunities throughout the 1980s. The company entered food production in the middle of the decade, financing the 1986 launch of Misr Arab Poultry Company, which produced chickens for the local market. In 1988, the company added the Sardine Canning Company in Morocco, with an initial capacity of 13,000 tons per year.

In the 1980s, the company also added transportation services to its range of concerns. In 1986, Dallah Albaraka formed the Dallah Pilgrims Transport Company in order to accommodate the transportation needs of the influx of pilgrims to the country's holy sites each year. The company launched the service with a fleet of 400 vehicles, later tripling its fleet in response to demand. The move into transportation also included freight services, and in 1986 the company established Dallah Transport Co. Ltd., with a specialty in chilled and frozen goods.

Islamic Banking Pioneer in the 1980s

Kamal had extended Dallah Albaraka's business activities into the financial markets with the launch of Islamic Arab Insurance Company in Dubai in 1979. The company's expansion into the financial industry was due in part to Kamel's interest in the development of theories for the creation of a new type of ''Islamic bank,'' that is, a bank that respected the Islamic Sharia, in particular the rejection of Western-style interest rates, which was considered as usury by many Moslems. Islamic banking principles replaced interest rates with ''Musharakah,'' a partnership system in which lender and borrower together shared both the risk of loss and the possibility of profit of a loan or investment.

In 1982, Kamel became one of the first to launch an Islamic bank, incorporating Albaraka Investment and Development Company (ABID) as a vehicle for the creation of banks, insurance companies, and investment firms based on Islamic financial theory. The company opened its first branches in Saudi Arabia but quickly extended its interests to other Arab and Islamic markets. By 1984, Albaraka had opened a bank in Sudan, and by the end of the 1980s Albaraka banks had been established in Algeria, Jordan, Lebanon, Bahrain, Egypt, Malaysia, South Africa, London, and, in 1991, in Pakistan. These banks, while owned by Dallah Albaraka, remained for the most part independent of one another.

The development of the Albaraka bank network encouraged Kamel to explore further aspects of Islamic financial ideas, and in 1987 the company launched Al-Amin Company for Securities and Investment Funds, one of the first to offer investment vehicles according to Islamic principles. That company converted to bank status in order to be able to launch securities products that respected Islamic banking ideals. The bank also became one of the first to obtain authorization to offer a dual-tier shareholder system, creating management and partnership share classes. Also in 1987, the company launched the International Arab Leasing and Finance Company, providing vehicle and equipment lease financing products to the Arab world.

ABID also continued to develop financial services vehicles for the Arab and Islamic markets, launching a series of companies in the late 1980s and early 1990s. In Tunis, for example, the company opened BEST Re-Insurance, while in Dubai, ABID was behind the launch of the Islamic Arab Insurance Company. In Bahrain, the company opened Islamic Insurance & Re-Insurance, while in Jordan, ABID's Jordan Islamic Bank opened the Islamic Mutual Insurance Company in 1994.

As Dallah Albaraka's bank network grew strongly in the Arab and Islamic markets, the group faced difficulty in establishing a presence in the West. In the early 1990s, the bank came under scrutiny from the Bank of England as a result of changes in ownership rules imposed on international banks after the BCCI scandal of the late 1980s. Albaraka also faced criticism for its reportedly ''aggressive'' loan-collection tactics. In the bank's defense, Kamel told *MEED:* ''In the name of Islam, they (the debtors) wanted to eat up depositors' money at the bank. Since we are guarantors of depositors' money and, as mudaribeen, our duty is to protect deposits by reverting to law on different levels and not one level.'' Faced with Bank of England demands that Albaraka bank widen its shareholder base beyond Dallah Albaraka, the company was forced to shut down the London operation in 1993, leaving only a representative office.

Another factor in the shutting down of its London bank and the group's difficulties in expanding its Islamic banking network westward was the lack of a single unifying structure behind its various banking entities. This situation was exacerbated by the group's failure to obtain a banking license in Saudi Arabia in the early 1990s.

Dallah Albaraka began making preparations for uniting its Albaraka bank operations under a single holding company in the late 1990s. In 1999, the company appointed Kuwait's The International Investor (TII) to guide the consolidation of the Albaraka banking network. The relationship quickly led toward merger negotiations between the two groups. By 2002, a deal appeared to have been reached in which nine of the Albaraka bank branches were to have been merged into TII. The new bank would have become the world's third-largest Islamic bank.

<table>
<tr><td colspan="2">

Key Dates:
</td></tr>
<tr><td>1969:</td><td>Saleh Abdullah Kamel founds the Dallah Works and Maintenance Company, which becomes the cornerstone of the Dallah Albaraka empire.</td></tr>
<tr><td>1975:</td><td>Dallah Avco Trans Arabia Company is established in order to build and operate airports.</td></tr>
<tr><td>1977:</td><td>Dallah Albaraka creates the Arab Media Company to provide film, radio, and television production.</td></tr>
<tr><td>1979:</td><td>The group enters financial markets with creation of Islamic Arab Insurance Co.</td></tr>
<tr><td>1982:</td><td>Dallah Albaraka pioneers Islamic banking with the founding of Albaraka Investment and Development Company.</td></tr>
<tr><td>1984:</td><td>The group establishes the Albaraka bank and joins in the launch of Middle East Broadcasting Center (MBC).</td></tr>
<tr><td>1993:</td><td>Dallah Albaraka leaves MBC and launches a pay-television network, Arab Radio and Television (ART).</td></tr>
<tr><td>1999:</td><td>Parts of international Albaraka banking network are consolidated under a single holding company, and the company later reaches an agreement to merge Dallah Albaraka into Kuwait's TII.</td></tr>
<tr><td>2002:</td><td>After the TII merger falls through, the group establishes the Albaraka Banking Group in Bahrain as a holding company for most of the group's financial services operations.</td></tr>
<tr><td>2004:</td><td>The group joins a consortium to establish an international Islamic investors bank in Bahrain.</td></tr>
<tr><td>2005:</td><td>Kamel and the Albaraka banks are cleared of involvement in Al Qaeda and the September 11, 2001 terrorist attacks on the United States.</td></tr>
</table>

At the last moment, however, the merger was mysteriously cancelled. Instead, Albaraka went ahead and founded the Albaraka Banking Group in Bahrain. That bank then took over nearly all of the existing Albaraka banks and began centralizing back office functions. By 2004, Albaraka Banking Group had also become the holding company for most of the Dallah Albaraka's other financial services operations as well.

Triple Focus for the 21st Century

After a falling out with other members of the Middle East Broadcasting Center partnership, Kamel left that group in order to launch his own satellite broadcasting network, joined by another Saudi investor, Walid bin Talal. Arab Radio and Television (ART) began broadcasting in 1993 and quickly extended its coverage to include five channels available to much of the Arab-speaking world.

ART became a perennial money-loser, with annual losses topping some $76 million per year by the end of the 1990s. Nonetheless, the station formed the centerpiece of Kamel's growing media empire, which included First Net, a pay television service including ART and other channels, launched in 1996, and Iqra, an Islamic Arab satellite channel launched in 1998. By then, ART had acquired some 50 percent of the entire Arab film catalog and had also acquired Arab broadcasting rights

to a number of important sporting events, including the World Cup. In 1999, the company extended its media operations to include the Saudi Digital Distribution Company, which provided marketing and distribution services for ART's own channels as well as some 50 other television channels in the area.

Dallah Albaraka's involvement in media operations—the company also acquired stakes in three Saudi daily newspapers, as a well as a 10 percent stake in Ashar Al-Awsat publisher Saudi Resarch—led it to restructure its operations in 1995. The reorganization divided the company into to three primary divisions: Business, Finance, and Media.

Dallah Albaraka continued to develop its wide-ranging interests in the late 1990s and 2000s. The company's real estate projects included the launch of the Durrat Al-Arus Trousitci City on the Red Sea in 1997. The completion of the first phase of the project included some 2.3 million square meters, while the launch of the second phase at the turn of the 21st century added another five million square meters. By 2003, the company had begun preparations for new projects in Algeria, Malaysia, Tunisia, and Dubai, as well as for a new holiday resort complex in Riyadh.

Kamel and the Dallah Albaraka group faced several difficult years following the September 11, 2001 terrorist attacks on the United States. Kamel and Albaraka Bank were suspected to have provided financial backing to Osama Bin Laden and the Al Qaeda terrorist group. It was not until 2005 that both Kamel and Albaraka were cleared of wrongdoing. In the meantime, Kamel continued to seek means for widening the scope of his financial empire. In 2004, he joined a consortium of investors seeking to establish a new international Islamic investors bank to be based in Bahrain. The new entity, intended to help establish a capital market in the Middle East, was expected to begin operations with a capitalization of $2 billion. Saleh Kamel remained at the head of Dallah Albaraka, one of the Arab world's largest and most successful privately held business empires.

Principal Subsidiaries

Albaraka Bancorp (USA); Albaraka Bank Lebanon; Albaraka Bank Ltd. (South Africa); Albaraka Bank Sudan; Albaraka Islamic Investment Bank (Bahrain); Albaraka Turkish Finance House (Turkey); Al-Tawfeek Co. For Investment Funds Ltd. (Cayman Islands); Al-Amin Co. For Securities & Investment Funds (Bahrain); Albaraka Medical Clinic; Algerian Saudi Leasing Holding Co. (France); Al-Towfeek Investment Bank Ltd. (Pakistan); Arab Leasing International Finance (ALIF) Ltd.; Arab Radio & Television (ART); Arab Reach Media (ARM); BEST Re-Insurance (Tunisia); Banque Albaraka D'algeria; Banque Albaraka D'jibouti; Banque Albaraka Mauritanienne Islamique; Beit Et-Tamweel Al-Tunisi Al-Saudi; Dallah Albaraka (U.K.) Limited; Dallah Albarak Holding Co. (Malaysia); Dallah Al-Baraka (Malaysia) Holding SDN. BHD.; Dallah Albaraka Holding Company for Umra Services; Dallah Communications Holding; Dallah Establishment for Contracting and Maintenance; Dallah Health Service Holding Company; Dallah Hotels and Resorts; Dallah Human Skills Development Co.; Dallah Transport Co. Ltd.; Dallah-Dowail Co.; Egyptian-Saudi Finance Bank (Egypt); Emin Sigorts A.S. (Turkey); International Arab Leasing and Finance Company; International Information & Trading Services Company; Iqraa Co. for Printing and Paper Trading; Islamic Arab Insurance Co. (IAIC) (United Arab Emirates); Islamic Insurance & Re-Insurance Co. (IIRCO) (Bahrain); Jordan Islamic Bank; Misr Arab Poultry Co.; National Wood Works Co.; Sardine Canning Co. (Morocco); Saudi Digital Distribution Company; Saudi Real Estate Maintenance Co.

Principal Divisions

Business; Finance; Media.

Principal Competitors

Temasek Holdings Private Ltd; Banque Algerienne de Dévèloppement; Dimon Zimbabwe Private Ltd; Banque Tu-nisienne de Solidarité; Bank Hapoalim B.M.; Abbar and Zainy Group of Cos.; Alghanim Industries.

Further Reading

Dudly, Nigel, "The Merger That Never Was," *Banker*, May 2002, p. 103.

"Gulf Investors Plan Global Islamic Bank," *Gulf News*, April 30, 2004.

"A New Islamic Heavyweight Arrives," *MEED Middle East Economic Digest*, September 22, 2000, p. 9.

"Regional Reach," *MEED Middle East Economic Digest*, February 22, 2002, p. 34.

"The Truth Behind Islamic Finance," *Business Life*, May 15, 2005.

"TII, Dallah Merger Unravels," *MEED Middle East Economic Digest*, May 17, 2002, p. 12.

Wright, C.D., "Saleh Kamel's Secret," *Arabies Trends*, 1999.

—M.L. Cohen

erfahren · sicher · günstig

Debeka Krankenversicherungsverein auf Gegenseitigkeit

Ferdinand-Sauerbruch-Str. 18
D-56073 Koblenz
Germany
Telephone: (+49) (261) 498-1399
Fax: (+49) (261) 498-1199
Web site: http://www.debeka.de

Mutual Insurance Company
Incorporated: 1905 as Krankenunterstützungskasse für
    die Gemeindebeamten der Rheinprovinz a.G.
Employees: 13,800
Total Assets: EUR 8.8 billion ($11.5 billion) (2004)
NAIC: 524114 Direct Health and Medical Insurance
    Carriers; 524113 Direct Life Insurance Carriers;
    524126 Direct Property and Casualty Insurance
    Carriers; 524128 Other Direct Insurance (Except Life,
    Health, and Medical) Carriers

Debeka Krankenversicherungsverein auf Gegenseitigkeit, based in Koblenz, sees itself as Germany's number one private health insurer and as the country's fourth-largest direct insurance company. More than 3.7 million health insurance customers provide 40 percent of Debeka's premium income. Roughly one-quarter of annual revenues originate from three million life insurance contracts of Debeka's life insurance subsidiary, Debeka Lebensversicherungsverein auf Gegenseitigkeit. Debeka health and life insurance are mutual insurance companies which are organized as cooperatives and owned by their members who are represented by elected member representatives. Civil servants make up a large part of Debeka's member base. Through various subsidiaries the group also offers life, property and casualty, legal, and accident insurance, as well as financial services for homeowners and pension plans.

Early 20th-Century Origins

Debeka's history goes back to the turn of the 19th century, a time of fundamental political, social, and economic change in Germany. While industrialization of the country was under way, the chancellor of the German Empire, Prince Otto von Bismarck, initiated a number of social reforms designed to take the wind out of the sails of the swelling socialist movement. In 1883, he introduced obligatory health insurance for the German working class. Employers were required to contribute one-third of the premiums, and workers had to pay the remaining amount. The new health insurance for blue-collar workers spurred a growing number of organizations offering similar health coverage for other occupations. On July 2, 1905, a group of municipal civil servants from the German Rhine province, led by City Secretary Josef Funken of Koblenz, founded a self-help organization to provide health insurance to municipal civil servants in the Rhine region. Organized as a member-based association, members paid their premiums and received benefits in case of sickness or death from the association's collective funds. In September 1905, the new Krankenunterstützungskasse für die Gemeindebeamten der Rheinprovinz was approved as a mutual insurance association. Only one year later, the Krankenunterstützungskasse expanded its operation into Prussia and received the approval to do business in all of Germany in 1910. To reflect the change, the association was renamed Krankenkasse für die Gemeindebeamten und – Angestellten des Deutschen Reiches (Health Fund for Municipal Civil Servants and Employees of the German Empire).

At first, membership was limited to members of the trade association of municipal civil servants up to 45 years of age. Beginning in 1907, the wives of members could also be covered. Monthly premiums were affordable and depended on the member's age. Members who became ill received a fixed daily amount for up to six months. An optional death benefit insurance completed the coverage. Between 1913 and 1916, the Krankenkasse introduced extended coverage plans that included dental treatments, hospitalization, and certain items such as eyeglasses and bandages. Within the first five years of its existence, 599 members joined Krankenkasse für die Gemeindebeamten. In the next five years, the number of members more than doubled, reaching 1,330 by 1915. During World War I, Krankenkasse für die Gemeindebeamten continued its business under difficult circumstances. By the end of the war, the mutual insurer counted about 2,000 members.

Building a Professional Workforce in the 1920s–30s

Until the early 1920s, Krankenkasse für die Gemeindebeamten relied on volunteers to do its business. The association's board of directors took care of most administrative tasks such as general organizational and legal matters as well as investing the collected funds. Volunteer members, so-called *Vertrauensmänner,* collected the premiums, paid out benefits in cash, and were involved in promotional activities to win new members. According to the association's bylaws, every member had to take on its share of administrative work on an as-needed basis. That way of doing business had kept premiums affordable but became impractical as more and more people joined the organization. In the aftermath of World War I, Germany went through a period of hardship caused by economic problems that culminated in the galloping inflation of 1922 and 1923. The country's population suffered severe financial losses. Making a living became a daily struggle for many people and their general health suffered as well. As the salaries of civil servants grew more slowly than their health expenses, and existing nest eggs were eaten up by hyperinflation, they began to join Krankenkasse für die Gemeindebeamten in increasing numbers. In 1921, the mutual insurer counted 6,400 members. Only four years later, the health insurer had acquired 240,000 contracts. By the end of 1925, Krankenkasse für die Gemeindebeamten had become Germany's largest health insurance for civil servants.

This development was partly due to the fact that once again the range of people who were eligible to join the mutual insurer was expanded to include not only municipal civil servants but civil servants in general. Beginning in February 1925, civil servants working for the State of Prussia and for the German Empire became eligible to join Krankenkasse für die Gemeindebeamten. Three years later, this move was reflected in another name change. From 1928 on the organization was called Deutsche Beamten-Krankenversicherung a.G. (German Civil Servants' Mutual Health Insurance). The abbreviation "De-Be-Ka" soon replaced the insurer's long name in everyday business and later became the company name. In addition to Debeka's exploding member roster of civil servants from all over Germany, a number of similar mutual health insurers and self-help organizations for civil servants from other regions merged with Debeka during the 1920s.

The growing number of contracts made it impossible to rely on volunteer work for managing them. In 1923, the company's first full-time employees were hired and began to work out of an old castle in Koblenz. Debeka divided Germany into administrative regions and established additional offices in Munich, Nuremberg, and Berlin. The Koblenz staff soon outgrew its quarters in the castle and moved into brand-new headquarters in 1928. By the end of the decade, Debeka employed over 200 people. In 1932, the company began to build a professional sales force. A growing number of people were hired and trained to bring in new business exclusively for Debeka. During the 1930s, the company's workforce rose swiftly, reaching 1,109 employees by the end of the decade.

Growth and Turmoil in the 1930s–40s

The ripples of the 1929 New York Stock Exchange crash arrived in Germany in the early 1930s, throwing the country's economy into another crisis. Unemployment skyrocketed and German civil servants were confronted with substantial pay cuts of up to 20 percent of their salary. Debeka lowered premiums two times to keep health insurance affordable for its members, but the situation got worse. The mutual insurer introduced a new plan with significantly lower premiums. However, due to their decreasing income, a growing number of civil servants fell below the amount at which they were required by law to give up their private health coverage and join the state-managed public health insurance system, which offered income-adjusted rates but fewer benefits. On the other hand, more civil servants in the upper income levels signed up for private health coverage.

By 1932, the economic situation had gotten so far out of hand that the radical right-wing National Socialist Party gathered more and more followers and finally took over political rule in Germany in 1933. As part of their campaign against Jews, "non-Aryan" civil servants faced severe discrimination. Debeka followed the guidelines of the new political leadership by excluding Jewish doctors from premium refund programs, by canceling the policies of Jewish members, and by hiring only apprentices who belonged to the Nazi youth organization. As the insurance sector was brought under the central command of the Nazi state, the forced consolidation of the industry led to Debeka's takeover of a number of competitors. As a result of the aforementioned developments, Debeka experienced a surge in membership, climbing from 300,000 in 1930 to 800,000 in 1939.

The dynamic changes faced by Debeka were accompanied by a number of modifications in the company's product policies. Due to the takeovers of other private health insurers, whose offers became part of Debeka's product range, the company offered 13 different health insurance plans by the middle of the 1930s. In addition, a number of severe epidemics resulted in a sudden increase in claims. Consequently Debeka introduced five new health coverage plans in 1937 that replaced the old ones. Since 1923, Debeka had paid benefits based on the actual cost that occurred. Under the new rules, younger members paid higher premiums which were then invested to help contain premium growth for older policy holders. On the other hand, beginning in 1935, Debeka members whose benefit claims had been very moderate over the last five years were refunded part of their premium payments. Beginning in 1936, Debeka members could even recover part of their premiums if they did not exceed a certain claim amount within a single year. Initiated to discourage members from filing minor claims which caused an above-average amount of administrative costs, the

```
┌─────────────────────────────────────────────────────────┐
│                     Key Dates:                          │
│                                                         │
│  1905:  A mutual health insurance association for munici-│
│         pal civil servants of the Rhine Province is     │
│         founded.                                        │
│  1910:  The association expands its reach into the      │
│         entire German Empire.                           │
│  1923:  The company's first full-time employees are     │
│         hired.                                          │
│  1928:  The company takes the name Deutsche Beamten-    │
│         Krankenversicherung (Debeka for short).         │
│  1932:  Debeka begins to build its own professional     │
│         sales force.                                    │
│  1947:  Debeka mutual life insurance is founded.        │
│  1974:  The company launches a branch that offers       │
│         savings plans for homebuilders.                 │
│  1981:  Debeka's general insurance subsidiary is estab- │
│         lished.                                         │
│  2002:  Debeka starts offering private pension plans.   │
└─────────────────────────────────────────────────────────┘
```

refund program was soon also used as a marketing vehicle and became a huge and lasting success.

In 1939, Adolf Hitler's troops marched into Poland, thereby initiating World War II. As Germany occupied ever more territories in eastern and western Europe, Debeka expanded its geographic reach as well. At the home front, the Nazis required private health insurers to offer generous benefit packages but denied the necessary premium increases in order to maintain the population's morale. However, as more and more physicians were called to military duty, Germans remaining in the homeland could not see their doctors anymore and consequently could not claim any health costs. Efforts to introduce a national health insurance system that would have made private health insurance obsolete fell victim to the intensifying war. As the Allied forces started bombing German cities, destroying Debeka's headquarters in Koblenz and many regional offices, the company moved important records and information processing machinery to more remote places in the countryside. However, due to a few more takeovers of other mutual health insurers, Debeka's membership grew to roughly 990,000 by 1944.

On April 3, 1945, only a few days after American troops had taken the city of Koblenz, the American military issued a permit for Debeka to continue its business. However, only two of the company's 21 buildings had survived the bombings. After losing the war, Germany was divided into four zones with four different military administrations. As much of Germany's eastern territory was lost, private health insurance was forbidden in the eastern German zone governed by the Soviet Union, and when the Saar was occupied by France, Debeka lost over 360,000 members.

Nevertheless, the company's remaining employees immediately got to work after the war and rebuilt the enterprise, including its headquarters in Koblenz, in just two years. To reduce Debeka's dependence on a health sector that was heavily influenced by politics, the company founded a mutual life insurance subsidiary in 1947. Starting in 1949, Koblenz-based Debeka Sterbegeld- und Lebensversicherungsverein offered life

insurance plans in all of Western Germany. To recover from the financial losses of the war and immediate postwar years, Debeka Health temporarily introduced deductibles for its members and cut back benefits somewhat. In 1951, Debeka introduced a new range of health coverage plans that replaced the old ones. As a result, the mutual insurer finally came out of the red and entered a period of dynamic growth.

New Political Challenges in the 1960s–70s

During the boom years that followed the postwar reconstruction period, Debeka Health membership soared. By 1950, the number of contracts passed the one-million mark. Five years later, when the company celebrated its 50th anniversary, Debeka had compensated the losses of the late 1940s. By 1965, the number of health contracts reached 1.4 million. Part of this growth was caused by measures taken during the 1950s. The maximum age for new members was increased; special introductory offers for trainees were introduced; certain existing health conditions were included in the coverage for an additional fee; and annual premium refunds for healthy members were extended to three monthly premiums. In addition, Debeka experienced a rising demand for supplemental private coverage for individuals with public health coverage.

With the extension of the income level for obligatory public health insurance in 1965, Debeka's growth came to a sudden halt. In a political climate that favored public over private health insurance, the company suffered severe losses in membership during the second half of the 1960s and in the following decade. To make Debeka membership even more attractive for new members, the company extended the maximum age for joining the health insurance to 65 years, waved the waiting period for certain benefits for trainees, and increased premium refunds to low-cost members to four monthly premiums. Debeka boosted the number of sales personnel and established a central sales department that organized their continuous training. In 1969, the income level for obligatory public health insurance was raised again. Two years later, a new law was introduced that increased the maximum income level for public health insurance automatically every year. At the same time, more and more groups within the population were included in the obligatory health insurance system: pensioners in 1968, farmers in 1972, students in 1975, artists and publicists in 1983. Due to these developments, Debeka reported net losses of 7,500 to 9,300 health plan members in 1968 and 1971. However, Debeka's efforts to make its health coverage more attractive paid off, resulting in a high number of new member acquisitions.

While Debeka Health was struggling with unfavorable circumstances in the 1960s and 1970s, its life insurance subsidiary enjoyed a growth spurt during the same period. In 1974, the company launched a new branch that offered savings plans for homebuilders. Despite a sluggish construction market, the new subsidiary made a profit right from the beginning.

A Full-Service Insurer in the 1990s and Beyond

In 1981, 671 Debeka employees moved to brand-new headquarters. It took another decade to finish the whole complex of buildings, which was designed for future growth. By the time the project was finished in 1992, the number of employees working there had already doubled. Several factors contributed to Debeka's continued growth in the 1980s and early 1990s. The political conditions for private health insurers improved. In 1989, civil servants in Germany were excluded from obligatory public health insurance, expanding Debeka's core market. Debeka Life and the company's construction savings arm, Debeka Bausparkasse, grew at healthy rates as well. In 1981, Debeka entered the Direct Property and Casualty Insurance market when the company founded its general insurance subsidiary, Debeka Allgemeine AG. Starting with accident insurance, the new subsidiary soon offered renter's and homeowners' policies. In the 1990s, auto and legal insurance were added as well. Finally, Debeka quickly claimed its stake in the eastern German states after they joined the Federal Republic of Germany in 1990. By the end of that year, the company had set up 25 offices in eastern Germany in addition to some 100 offices in the western part of the country.

Beginning in the second half of the 1990s, the market for private health insurance was again heavily influenced by political decisions that followed a broad public discussion of issues resulting from the population's growing life span. In 1994, a law was passed that required private health insurers to offer elderly customers who were struggling financially a so-called "standard-rate" health plan that provided basic health coverage similar to the public health plans at premiums no higher than the average cost of public health coverage for seniors. To provide basic funding for the growing number of people who needed constant professional care at old age, an obligatory insurance was introduced in 1995 that had to be adopted by private health insurers, thereby boosting Debeka's premium income. In 2000, another law required private health insurers to charge an additional 10 percent on top of their premiums, funds that had to be used to dampen premium growth for customers age 65 and older. Another demographic issue was the decreasing number of workers contributing to the country's public pension system at a time when the population was aging and the number of pensioners was increasing. New legislation was passed to encourage supplementary private pension plans. Debeka reacted by establishing two new subsidiaries, prorente-Debeka Pensions-Management GmbH in 1995 and Debeka Pensionskasse AG in

2002, that offered the management of corporate pension plans as well as coverage for small businesses. By 2005, due to an attractive product range, a powerful sales force of over 6,500, and a consistently conservative investment strategy, Debeka had become one of Germany's leading insurance companies. Looking into the future, Debeka's management still saw sufficient financial strength to keep its legal form as a mutual insurance firm and sufficient market potential in Germany to restrain it from international expansion. However, Germany's pending health insurance reform constituted a major wild card at the beginning of Debeka's second century of existence.

Principal Subsidiaries

Debeka Krankenversicherungsverein auf Gegenseitigkeit; Debeka Lebensversicherungsverein auf Gegenseitigkeit; Debeka Bausparkasse AG; Debeka Allgemeine Versicherung AG; Debeka Pensionskasse AG; prorente-Debeka Pensions-Management GmbH; Debeka Betriebskrankenkasse.

Principal Competitors

ERGO Versicherungsgruppe AG; HUK-COBURG Haftpflicht-Unterstützungs-Kasse kraftfahrender Beamter Deutschlands a.G. in Coburg; Allianz AG; AMB Generali Holding AG; WWK Versicherungsgruppe.

Further Reading

"Debeka steigert ihren Marktanteil," *Frankfurter Allgemeine Zeitung*, May 25, 2005, p. 15.
"Die Debeka-Versicherungsgruppe wächst," *Frankfurter Allgemeine Zeitung*, May 23, 1997, p. 30.
"Debeka will weiter expandieren," *Süddeutsche Zeitung*, June 30, 1993.
"Debeka wird hundert," *Versicherungswirtschaft*, April 1, 2005, p. 553.
100 Jahre Debeka: Geschichte und Geschichten, Koblenz, Germany: Debeka Krankenversicherungsverein auf Gegenseitigkeit, 2005, 69 p.

—Evelyn Hauser

Duron Inc.

10406 Tucker Street
Beltsville, Maryland 20705
U.S.A.
Telephone: (301) 937-4600
Toll Free: (800) 72-DURON
Fax: (301) 595-3919
Web site: http://www.duron.com

Wholly Owned Subsidiary of Sherwin-Williams Co.
Incorporated: 1949 as Duron Paint Manufacturing
    Company
Employees: 1,800
Sales: $350 million (2003)
NAIC: 325510 Paint and Coating Manufacturing; 424950
    Paint, Varnish, and Supplies Merchant Wholesalers;
    444120 Paint and Wallpaper Stores

Duron Inc. is a paint manufacturer and retailer dedicated to the professional user. It is one of the top three dealers in the United States, according to some sources. Dr. Robert Feinberg, son of company founder Harry Feinberg, helped guide the company to more than two decades of double-digit growth before it was acquired by Sherwin-Williams Co. in September 2004. The company focused its expansion east of the Mississippi, with about 231 retail stores. Duron paint has been used on a number of historic edifices, including the White House.

Origins

Duron Inc. dates back to 1949, when Harry Feinberg, formerly a paint chemist with Baltimore's H.B. Davis Company, acquired a 50 percent share of Washington, D.C.'s Norman Paint Manufacturing Co., which supplied three paint stores from a cramped, 4,000-square-foot factory. Feinberg brought with him a way of making a thick, smooth paint.

Feinberg renamed the newly acquired company Duron Paint Manufacturing Co. According to the *Washington Post,* the name was meant to evoke the idea of durability and the then-cutting edge aura of nylon. Feinberg's main marketing technique was giving out free samples. It worked.

From the beginning, the business was oriented toward professional painters and contractors, rather than the do-it-yourself crowd. To woo these tradesmen, who bought paint in large quantities, Duron put considerable resources into customer service, which would include making deliveries to job sites and maintaining early morning hours. It was able to save money by not advertising to attract the retail consumer.

Feinberg quickly lined up a handful of dealers in neighboring states. The first of Duron's own stores, the Metropolitan Paint Co., opened in 1950 to fill a niche in the Washington, D.C. market. Over the years, the paint came to be used in a number of historic area buildings, including the Pentagon, Capitol Building, and White House.

Feinberg moved the company's operations to a new paint factory in Beltsville, Maryland in 1957. (According to the *Washington Post,* the sloped site helped move the paint through its production line.) It was a time of great expansion. Within a few years, Duron acquired its dealers in Baltimore and Richmond and opened new stores in Pennsylvania and North Carolina. Duron had 45 stores and 450 employees by 1974, when sales were $18 million.

Second Generation On Board in 1976

Dr. Robert Feinberg, son of company founder Harry Feinberg, left a promising career as an organic chemistry professor to join Duron as secretary-treasurer in 1976. (He was an alumnus of both Harvard and Oxford.) This started a period of double-digit annual growth of the company that would continue to the end of the century.

By 1979, the company's Beltsville, Maryland plant was producing 20,000 gallons of latex and oil-based paint a day. With 280,000 square feet of warehouse space, the plant also was used to store wallpaper and painting equipment for distribution.

New Reach for the 1990s

Extending its reach in the South, Duron opened a latex paint plant in Atlanta in 1989. It cost $11.5 million to build and had a capacity of 30,000 gallons a day. Duron already had a dozen stores in the Atlanta area and was planning to open a dozen

Key Dates:

1949: Harry Feinberg acquires a 50 percent share of Norman Paint Manufacturing Co.
1950: The first company store, the Metropolitan Paint Co., is opened.
1957: A plant opens in Beltsville, Maryland.
1976: Dr. Robert Feinberg, son of the founder, joins the company.
1989: The Atlanta plant is opened.
1999: On its 50th anniversary, Duron has 265 stores and annual sales of more than $280 million.
2004: Sherwin-Williams Co. acquires Duron.

more within five years, reported the *Atlanta Journal and Constitution,* on the strength of the area's booming real estate market.

The company also broadened its marketing somewhat. Duron introduced paints aimed at the do-it-yourselfer in 1992. These were retailed first by the Hechinger Co. chain for a few years, then by Home Depot.

Duron had 1,400 employees in 1994. It operated 150 of its own stores and supplied another 150 dealers, according to *National Home Center News.*

The company continued to grow by acquisition. It bought 27 M. Buten & Sons Inc. stores in the Philadelphia area in 1994. Buten, a retail chain, was founded by Max Buten in 1897 and had been family owned and operated for four generations. (It sold Benjamin Moore brand paint before the acquisition.) Duron also was opening 19 stores that year and began 1995 with more than 200 stores in all. Sales were around $250 million in 1995.

The chain was expanding through Ohio, Florida, and New Jersey. It was still strongest in the Washington, D.C. area, where perhaps two-thirds of its stores were located. Duron paint also was sold by more than 250 other paint retailers; this channel accounted for 5 percent of sales, according to the *Washington Post.*

Company founder Harry Feinberg passed away in 1996. Thomas K. Schwartzbeck became Duron's president. He had started with the company as a clerk in 1975.

A dozen stores was acquired from Chicago-based Fancy Colours and Co. in 1997. By the late 1990s, the paint industry in the United States was in the midst of a massive consolidation, reducing the number of players from about 1,500 to 800 in ten years. Dr. Feinberg, then president and CEO, stated his ambition for the company to be one of a half dozen or so surviving national players. The value of the overall paint market was estimated at $13 billion.

50 in 1999

Annual sales were more than $300 million during Duron's 50th anniversary year in 1999, when Duron produced 17 million gallons of paint. The company had 265 company-owned stores and was planning to add at least 30 a year through 2005. It had about 1,900 employees and a fleet of 150 trucks.

According to the *Washington Post,* Dr. Feinberg endeavored to make Duron an engaging place to work. The company was known for giving branch stores a high degree of autonomy and was said to be generous in its benefits, such as profit-sharing. While he lamented the difficulty of maintaining a family

atmosphere at the growing company, the *Post* commented on the number of married couples—100 by one count—who had met while working there.

Duron had entered the southern Florida market early in 1999 by buying a single store from Broward Paint and Wallpaper, a nine-store chain in Tampa and Orlando. Broward had sales of $6.5 million and dated back to 1947.

In 2001 Duron struck a deal to have TruServ Corp. manufacture its paint under license for distribution at qualified True Value hardware stores across the country. True Value dealers who wanted to sell the Duron brand were encouraged to undergo training and hire salespeople dedicated to the pro painting business.

In early 2002, Duron joined Professional Paint, Inc. (PPI) of Denver in an alliance to bid on national accounts. Duron was focusing expansion of its own retail stores east of the Mississippi. In 2002, the company acquired a Raleigh, North Carolina dealer, Johnson Paint, and opened stores in Maryland, Georgia, Florida, and Virginia. It abandoned the Midwest market by selling 27 stores in Illinois, Indiana, and Ohio to Pittsburgh-based PPG Industries.

New Ownership in 2004

Revenues were $350 million in 2003. By some reckonings, this made Duron the country's third largest paint dealer. Late in the year, the company announced that it was licensing the right to reproduce colors from Mount Vernon. The Mount Vernon Ladies' Association had years earlier commissioned a study to determine the mansion's original color scheme in George Washington's day. The Estate of Colours collection included 30 hues from the mansion itself and another 90 inspired by the plantation. A few months later, Duron licensed another line from the Historic Charleston Foundation.

Sherwin-Williams Co., the country's largest paint manufacturer with annual sales of more than $5 billion, acquired Duron on September 2004 for $250 million in cash and assumed obligations. Sherwin-Williams was aiming to bolster its business with paint professionals, and Duron CEO Dr. Robert Feinberg was preparing to retire. At the time of the buy, Duron was the 12th leading paint company in the United States.

Principal Competitors

Benjamin Moore and Co.; Home Depot, Inc.; ICI Paints.

Further Reading

Barbaro, Michael, "Paint Giant Agrees to Buy Duron; Sherwin-Williams Aims at Professional Market," *Washington Post,* May 18, 2004, p. E1.

Bell, Thomas, "Paint It 'Ugly'; Looks of Logan Circle Store Irk Neighbors," *Washington Post,* July 12, 1990, p. J1.

Brackey, Harriet Johnson, "Beltsville, Md.-Based Paint Company Buys Broward County, Fla., Store," *Miami Herald,* January 6, 1999.

Caulfield, John, "TruServ Pairs with Duron to Draw Pro Painters to Stores," *National Home Center News,* February 19, 2001, p. 1.

"Duron and Professional Paint Form Alliance," *Journal of Coatings Technology,* March 1, 2002, p. 28.

"Duron Goes Historic Again with Colors of Charleston," *Coatings World,* June 2004, p. 11.

Duron, Inc., "Duron at 50: Still Focused on the Professional Painter," Beltsville, Md.: Duron, Inc., c. 1999.

"Duron to Manufacture Historic Estate Colours Line," *Coatings World,* November 2003, p. 12.

Gebolys, Debbie, "Home-Construction Supplier Is Hoping to Cover the Town," *Columbus Dispatch* (Ohio), July 11, 1995, p. 1E.

Hinmon, Derrick, "Duron Paints Opens New Factory, Distribution Center in DeKalb," *Atlanta Journal and Constitution,* May 11, 1989, p. A5.

Koncius, Jura, "Green, By George," *Washington Post,* November 20, 2003, p. H3.

Lee, Melissa, "Duron's Credo: Aim High, Don't Spread Thin; By Focusing on the Professional Painter, Beltsville Manufacturer Has Grown by Broad Strokes," *Washington Post,* August 15, 1994, p. F5.

Liu, Caitlin M., "Stroking Professional Painters Keeps Duron in Green," *Washington Post,* August 11, 1997, p. F9.

McConnell, Bill, "Duron Buys Penn. Paint Store Chain: Buten Purchase Adds 27 Outlets to 168-Store Chain," *Daily Record,* July 6, 1994, p. 3.

Noguchi, Yuki, "At Duron Inc., Paint with a Personal Touch," *Washington Post,* September 22, 1999, p. M16.

——, "Duron Founder Poured Self into Firm; Owners Try to Keep a Community Feel," *Washington Post,* September 22, 1999, p. M18.

——, "In So Many Ways, It's a Family Firm; Now-Married Couples Met at Duron," *Washington Post,* September 22, 1999, p. M17.

"Painting a Bull's-Eye on Pro Customers," *National Home Center News,* June 18, 2001, p. 38.

Patalon, William, III, "Paint Retailer Sherwin-Williams to Buy Maryland-Based Rival Duron," *Baltimore Sun* (Knight Ridder/Tribune Business News), May 19, 2004.

Purce, Ed, "150-Unit Paint Dealer Gears Up for Growth," *National Home Center News,* July 4, 1994, p. 1.

"TruServ To Manufacture and Distribute Duron Paint," *Coatings World,* March 2001, p. 14.

—Frederick C. Ingram

GENERAL CONTRACTORS / CONSTRUCTION MANAGERS

E.W. Howell Co., Inc.

113 Crossways Park Drive
Woodbury, New York 11797
U.S.A.
Telephone: (516) 921-7100
Fax: (516) 921-0119
Web site: http://www.ewhowell.com

Wholly Owned Subsidiary of Obayashi Corporation
Founded: 1891 as Brown & Howell
Employees: 200
Sales: $142.7 million (2005)
NAIC: 236220 Commercial and Institutional Building
Construction

E.W. Howell Co., Inc., is a Long Island-based midsized general construction and construction management company, mostly doing work in the New York metropolitan and Long Island markets. Known for the luxury homes it once built on Long Island's "Gold Coast," the firm now serves a variety of clients. Cultural/institutional projects include work for the New York Botanical Garden, the Cradle of Aviation Museum, and Brookhaven National Laboratory. E.W. Howell also builds schools as well as projects for institutions of higher learning such as Columbia University, New York Medical College, and Long Island University. Another part of the firm's portfolio is assisted living facilities. Projects in this sector include the Norwegian Christian Home in Brooklyn, the Suffolk County Nursing Facility, and several facilities on Long Island for Sunrise Assisted Living Facilities. E.W. Howell also does work for a number of retailers—such as Target, Lowe's Home Improvement, and Costco Wholesale—and restaurant chains like Olive Garden and Red Lobster. The firm also does interior work, ranging from corporate offices to country clubs. A longtime family-run business, E.W. Howell is now a subsidiary of Japan's Obayashi Corporation, a global contractor that does more than $12.7 billion worth of business each year.

Company's Founding in the Late 19th Century

The firm that became E.W. Howell was founded by Elmer Winfield Howell and his father-in-law in 1891. Howell had been born 30 years earlier in Yaphank, Long Island, where he received six years of education in a one-room school before quitting at the age of 13. When he turned 17 Howell became an apprentice to an area farmer, but after four years of back-breaking labor he forever swore off the agricultural life, and in 1882 he relocated to Southampton, Long Island, to pursue an occupation more to his liking, becoming an apprentice to a carpenter. After two years he became a journeyman carpenter, plying his trade for different Long Island employers. In 1887 he became a plant foreman for a Staten Island narrow gauge railroad, the same year that he was married to Kizzie Brown in Babylon, Long Island. In 1891 he quit his job on the railroad and teamed up with his wife's father, George S. Brown, to launch a Babylon construction company dubbed Brown & Howell.

Initially, Brown & Howell concentrated on the construction of small, well-built houses. The firm quickly established a reputation for quality workmanship, an important factor in the young firm's ability to weather one of the periodic economic crises, the Panic of 1893, that plagued the United States during this period. After ten years the partnership was dissolved when Howell bought out Brown, and the firm became known as E.W. Howell, Builders. The firm survived the Panic of 1907, and a second generation became involved, Howell's 18-year-old son, Elmer B. Howell. A second son, Ralph DeWitt Howell, joined the company in 1918, leading to the 1926 creation of a partnership between the three Howells and a new name: E.W. Howell Co. A cousin, Louis Emerson Lee, came to work for the firm two years later.

While the family partnership was taking shape, the firm moved beyond the construction of small houses and began to make its mark by building many of the fine Long Island estates on what was known as the Gold Coast. Around the turn of the 20th century this area of Long Island's North Shore, stretching from Great Neck to Huntington, became a popular retreat where New York City's wealthy built lavish mansions, held fox hunts, and played polo—an era that F. Scott Fitzgerald captured in his novel *The Great Gatsby*. Until the stock market of October 1929 changed everything, the Gold Coast saw the construction of scores of mansions, most of them built by E.W. Howell. Illustrious clients included Mrs. John D. Rockefeller, Marjorie Merriweather Post of the Post Cereal fortune, E.F. Hutton,

94

Company Perspectives:

At E.W. Howell Co., Inc., our mission is to provide our clients with the highest level of quality and service, accompanied by competitive pricing and timely performance. Our outstanding reputation allows us to serve our customers with unparalleled excellence through our solid teamwork.

Theodore Roosevelt, copper baron Henry Guggenheim, Henry S. Morgan (son of banker J.P. Morgan), Charles Lindbergh, Marshall Field, Vincent Astor, John T. Pratt, Charles Payson, Henry Luce, and Robert Moses, the longtime autocratic czar of New York City-area parks, highways, and bridges. It was Moses who bullied all opposition and forced the construction of the Long Island Expressway and other highway spurs that cut through many of the Gold Coast's palatial estates. Today, only a handful of the mansions remain in private hands. The rest are either museums, open to the public, or have been converted for use by colleges, religious institutions, or parks.

Luxury Residential Market Collapse During the 1930s

As the luxury residential market collapsed during the mid-1930s, the result of the Great Depression set off by the stock market crash, E.W. Howell was forced to shift its focus. With the founder well into his 70s, the second generation took greater control and moved the firm away from residential to commercial construction, opening a second office, located at 101 Park Avenue in Manhattan, in 1935. Given that it had built the homes of many of the country's greatest industrialists, E.W. Howell was well positioned to take on the commercial needs of many of these same individuals. The economy picked up with the advent of World War II, spurred by defense spending. Then during the postwar boom housing developments sprouted up throughout Long Island, as the parents of the baby boom generation fled the New York City boroughs for the new suburbs. Although E.W. Howell elected not to become involved in the construction of housing developments, limiting its residential work to the luxury market, it did take advantage of Long Island's expansion to take on the construction of other projects made necessary by the growing population: schools, hospitals, commercial buildings, and industrial space.

In 1947 several younger family members were named partners: Ralph D. Howell, Jr., Rogers Howell, Elmer B. Howell, Oliver B. Howell, and Louis E. Lee. In February 1954 Elmer B. Howell died, followed several months later by his father and founder of the firm, E.W. Howell, at the age of 94. Over the next 30 years other members of the Howell family sold their share of the business to outsiders, so that by 1984 only Ralph D. Howell, Jr., remained. When he retired in November of that year, he left the firm in the hands of five nonfamily partners.

The Howell name lived on with the firm, which continued to reap the benefits of its reputation for building quality homes. During the 1980s the firm took on a number of renovation projects on older buildings and, in some cases, the restoration of historic buildings. In 1981, for instance, E.W. Howell restored a pair of landmark Manhattan townhouses to create offices for U.S. Trust Co., work for which the firm received the New York Landmarks Conservancy's 1981 Chairman's Award, and in 1985 it restored the Rhinelander mansion on Long Island, allowing the structure to be converted to a retail store. E.W. Howell was able to draw on older workers as well as the offspring of some of the firm's employees who had worked on some of the Gold Coast mansions to provide some forgotten skills needed in these restoration projects. But the firm still had difficulty finding enough skilled workers, since younger people in the construction trade had been trained to work with steel, concrete, and sheetrock. As a result, E.W. Howell began pouring over old work rosters and looking up the progeny to see if little-used skills had been passed on from father to son. The firm also turned to preservation societies and architectural experts to compile a list of craftsmen, which were then compiled into a computer database for future reference.

In January 1986 Norway's largest civil engineering and construction company, Selmer-Sande A/S, acquired an 80 percent interest in E.W. Howell. At the time, the firm ranked 180th among the largest 400 construction firms in the United States, generating annual sales of $120 million. In addition to its Long Island headquarters, E.W. Howell maintained offices in Manhattan; Cherry Hill, New Jersey; Valhalla, New York; and Denver. Less than three years later, however, the Norwegians sold the company to Obayashi for $7 million.

Obayashi possessed a history as deep as E.W. Howell. Its founder, Yoshigoro Obayashi, founded a construction company in Oskaka, Japan, in 1892, a year after Howell and Brown launched their business. Obayashi's first major break came in 1901 when the firm won an important contract to design and build the grounds for the fifth National Industry Fair held in Osaka three years later. In 1920 some of its executives traveled to the United States to study modern construction techniques, which the firm applied to the construction of major projects in Japan, including the Mainichi Newspaper Office, the Sumitomo Building in Osaka, and the Merchant Marine Building in Kobe, Japan. Expertise gained in earthquake-resistant and fireproof construction techniques were then put to use following the Great Kanto Earthquake of 1923 that virtually destroyed Tokyo. After Japan's defeat in World War II, Obayashi spent a decade recovering, not winning its first major postwar contracts until 1956, when it built the Tokyo railroad station annex. Other projects from this era include work for the Japan Broadcasting Corporation and the firm's first hydroelectric power dam. In the mid-1960s Obayashi branched out further, building its first highway.

In the early 1980s the firm anglicized its name, becoming Obayashi Corporation, and began to expand internationally. It began doing work on mainland Asia, such as renovation work on the Shanghai International Airport in the People's Republic of China. In 1985 Obayashi entered the U.S. market, as did other Japanese construction firms around this time. In the beginning the Japanese came to serve as construction managers in the construction of manufacturing plants for Japanese high-tech companies, but it soon became apparent to their American general contractors that they planned to stay and start looking for building work. Obayashi opened a San Francisco office, where it won a contract to install a major sewer system. To expand its range of job opportunities, the firm in 1986 became a member of the U.S. Civil Engineering Society. It was then awarded a $62 million contract by the Army Corps of Engineers to build a dam

```
┌─────────────────────────────────────────────────────────┐
│                      Key Dates:                          │
│                                                          │
│  1891:  The company is founded by Elmer Howell and       │
│         George Brown.                                    │
│  1901:  Howell buys out Brown.                           │
│  1926:  Howell's sons become partners in E.W. Howell Co. │
│  1935:  The Manhattan office opens.                      │
│  1954:  Elmer Howell dies.                               │
│  1984:  The last member of the Howell family retires from│
│         the firm.                                        │
│  1989:  Obayashi Corporation acquires the company.       │
│  1997:  Howard Rowland is named president.               │
└─────────────────────────────────────────────────────────┘
```

on Elk Creek in Oregon, an ill-fated project that would be shut down a year later by the federal government because of environmental concerns. Nevertheless, Obayashi had established a presence in the U.S. market, one that was strengthened in 1988 by forging an alliance with the U.S. construction firm of Fluor Daniel Inc. to combine their efforts in building plants and research facilities in both countries.

Obayashi's acquisition of E.W. Howell was part of an effort to expand beyond the West Coast to take on projects in the Midwest and the eastern parts of the United States. Under Japanese ownership, E.W. Howell opened offices in Atlanta and Chicago, but the company remained very much a New York metropolitan-oriented construction firm. Obayashi took a hands-off approach to the management of E.W. Howell, allowing American managers to serve the market they knew extremely well, while the company expanded its operations to Europe and took on more work in Asia. E.W. Howell's current president, Howard Rowland, was well familiar with the firm and the market, having come to the firm in 1983 as a project manager, at a time when it was still run by the Howell family. He held a number of positions before ascending to the presidency in February 1997.

Marking Its 100th Anniversary in the 1990s

E.W. Howell celebrated its 100th anniversary in 1992. No longer a builder of fine estates, the firm embarked on its second century of business focused on commercial and institutional work. During the 1990s E.W. Howell completed projects such as the Cradle of Aviation Museum in Garden City, New York; a Short Hills, New York Saks Fifth Avenue department store; a Lord & Taylor department store; three Sunrise Assisted Living Facilities projects; the Huntington Hills Health Care Facility in Melville, New York; the Orange County Residential Health Care Facility in Goshen, New York; and a Multi-Purpose Health Technology Building for the Suffolk County Community College. Also during the 1990s, E.W. Howell established a relationship with Target Stores, building four of the big-box retail locations in the final years of the decade.

After maintaining its headquarters in Port Washington, New York, for 15 years E.W. Howell relocated to Woodbury, New York, in February 2000. The firm continued to do business with a wide selection of clients, with about 85 percent of sales the result of repeat business. E.W. Howell built more Target stores and Sunrise Assisted Living Facilities projects, and completed work for Saks Fifth Avenue. Other important clients included Lowe's Home Improvement, Tiffany & Co., Costco Wholesale, LA Fitness, Morton's Steakhouse, Olive Garden, and Red Lobster. With a 100-year-old reputation for quality work and legendary mansions on its list of accomplishments, the firm was well entrenched in the New York City area and likely to enjoy continued success for many years to come.

Principal Operating Units

Pre-Construction; Construction.

Principal Competitors

Skanska USA Building Inc.; Tishman Realty & Construction Co. Inc.; The Turner Corporation.

Further Reading

Barohn, Ellen Sterling, *Long Island: An Environment for Success,* Montgomery, Ala.: Community Communications, 2001.

Greer, Kimberly, ''LI Builder Renovates a Golden Past,'' *Newsday,* November 24, 1986, p. 3.

Manning, Jeff, ''Japanese Cast an Eye on Local Construction Work,'' *Business Journal-Portland,* March 3, 1986, p. 12.

—Ed Dinger

Éditions Gallimard

5, rue Sébastien-Bottin
75328 Paris cedex 07
France
Telephone: (+33) 01 49 54 42 00
Fax: (+33) 01 45 44 94 03
Web site: http://www.gallimard.fr

Private Company
Founded: 1911
Sales: $317 million (2003)
NAIC: 511120 Periodical Publishers; 511130 Book
   Publishers; 422920 Book, Periodical, and Newspaper
   Wholesalers; 451211 Book Stores; 511210 Software
   Publishers.

Éditions Gallimard is the third-largest publishing group in France. It consists of a number of imprints, including Éditions de la Pléiade, NRF, Denoël, Mercure de France, the Du Monde Entier imprint of foreign authors, and its paperback imprint Folio. The company publishes approximately 750 new titles every year. Gallimard's backlist catalogue of 17,000 titles includes most of the great French and international authors of the twentieth century, including Marcel Proust, Jean-Paul Sartre, Simone de Beauvoir, Jean Genet, Louis-Ferdinand Céline, Ernest Hemingway, William Faulkner, Franz Kafka, James Joyce, Jack Kerouac, Philip Roth, Sigmund Freud, Ludwig Wittgenstein, and Michel Foucault. Gallimard's reputation also rests on the Pléiade collection of classic authors and Gallimard-Jeunesse, its renowned children's book division. Gallimard distributes its books through La Sodis, its distribution company. Gallimard also operates a handful of bookstores, including Schoenhof's Foreign Bookstore in Cambridge, Massachusetts.

Birth of a Publisher in the 1910s

Éditions Gallimard emerged from a marriage of convenience of Gaston Gallimard and the *Nouvelle Revue Française* (*NRF*), a leading French avant-garde literary journal. In December 1910, the magazine's editors, comprised largely of modernist writers such as André Gide, decided to found a book-publishing company. Needing a business manager, they turned to thirty-year old Gaston Gallimard, son of a wealthy patron of leading Impressionist painters. Gallimard's father also possessed large collection of rare first editions and used his wealth to finance the printing of deluxe editions, sometimes limited to as few as two or three copies. Gaston inherited his father's interests. By the time he was twenty years old, his life centered on fine art, rare books, the Parisian theater, gourmet restaurants, beautiful women, and his friends.

Gaston was precisely the kind of person the *NRF* was looking for: wealthy enough to make a significant monetary investment in the new firm, with both good business instincts and refined tastes in literature, who would put quality ahead of short-term profits; who could provide leadership but was flexible enough to consider the opinions of *NRF* editors. Moreover, most the *NRF*'s editors already knew him. Growing bored of his shiftless playboy life, Gallimard jumped at the opportunity. With FRF 20,000 borrowed from an uncle, he became a partner in the new publishing house Les Éditions de la NRF. Gallimard had sole responsibility for managing the publishing house. He threw himself into the job, working from pre-dawn until early evening. In June 1911, the publisher's first three books were issued: Gide's *Isabelle*, Paul Claudel's *L'otage*, and Charles-Louis Philippe's *La mere et l'enfant*. Others by Saint-John Perse, Gide, Claudel, and Dostoyevsky expanded the list further in 1912. Off to a healthy start, Les Éditions de la NRF moved from a storefront and Gallimard's bedroom to larger offices where they would remain until 1921.

The house was determined to position itself at the cutting edge of French letters. Despite its intentions, however, it nearly lost one of the greatest writers of the 20th century. In 1913, Gaston Gallimard solicited two 550-page manuscripts by a little-known writer named Marcel Proust. The *NRF* editors, especially Gide, rejected the work as overly long and overly traditional. Proust had to resort to a vanity publisher to print *Du côté du chez Swann*, the first volume of his masterwork *A la recherche du temps perdu*. When the *NRF* editors saw the published book they realized their mistake. Despite its traditional characters, the work was stylistically adventurous and its language beautiful. Gaston visited Proust again and asked if he had other works. The mammoth novel was the only writing that interested the author, and Gallimard could have it—but only if he published it in its entirety. Gallimard agreed and Proust withdrew the work from Bernard Grasset, another Parisian publisher. When Proust died in 1922, NRF had published all six volumes of *A la recherche*. The Proust affair was the beginning of the fierce competition between Gallimard and Grasset that would last until after World War II.

Later in 1913, Les Éditions de la NRF enjoyed its first modest commercial success with *Jean Barois* by Martin du Gard. By 1914, NRF had published approximately 60 titles, with typical print-runs of about 1500 copies. At the same time, problems were brewing in the NRF offices. André Gide worried that Gallimard's publishing program for NRF coupled with his concurrent investments in a Parisian theater were overextending the house's still tenuous finances. Gide tried to have Gallimard removed from the firm. Gallimard responded by establishing a formal NRF editorial board, which threw its support behind the publisher and rejected the successor Gide had proposed. The establishment of the board brought Gallimard an added advantage, given that he had a seat on it. For the first time, he had a voice in editorial decision-making.

Publishing Disrupted by World War I

Éditions de la NRF was not spared the shock of World War I on European life. Paper, electricity, and manpower were in short supply. The front cut the house off from its Belgian printer. Talented young writers such as Alain-Fournier and Charles Péguy, were dying almost daily. The war sent Gaston Gallimard into a depression so serious he had to be hospitalized. Somehow, though, he kept the NRF publishing program going. Manuscripts were the one thing not in short supply. NRF signed Paul Valéry and acquired the French rights to Joseph Conrad's works.

Éditions de la NRF survived the Great War, but its financial situation was far from healthy in 1919. As the underlying impulse of the enterprise shifted subtly from an idealistic literary endeavor to a full blown business, the tensions between Gide and Gallimard reemerged, threatening to destroy the company. Gide deeply resented Gallimard's growing influence at NRF, but he was also aware of the advantages that giving full responsibility to Gallimard, who could provide the house with a single guiding spirit, would bring. In June 1919, the magazine *NRF* resumed publication with Gaston Gallimard the head of its publishing arm. André Gide distanced himself from NRF's day-to-day operations to concentrate on his writing.

Reorganized in the 1920s

In July 1919, the NRF was renamed Librairie Gallimard. It had five principal shareholders: Gallimard, Gide, and Jean Schlumberger, plus a childhood friend of Gaston's and his brother Raymond Gallimard. The additional shareholders guaranteed Gaston's control over the firm. Moreover Raymond, while not particularly interested in literature, was a superb businessman. With Raymond administering finances, Gaston could give his full attention to the publishing program. Gaston and Raymond's de facto partnership lasted nearly fifty years. Meanwhile, Gaston was struggling to get the house on its feet again. In late 1918, it published Proust's *A l'ombre des jeunes filles en fleurs*. When the book won the Prix Goncourt, France's highest literary honor, sales rocketed. The profits enabled Gaston to become a shareholder in the St. Catherine Press, Gallimard's Belgian printer. The agreement guaranteed that Gallimard could produce large print-runs if it had another surprise bestseller. Proust's success gave Librairie Gallimard a higher profile. The house received more submissions than ever before as the 1920s began.

In 1921, Gallimard established an institution that quickly became a mainstay of its publishing business: the Tuesday afternoon meetings of the readers on its editorial board. Comprising literary authorities in all fields, board members met once a week to present recommendations and vote on works to be published, although final authority rested with Gaston. It became one of the great honors of French literary life to serve on the Gallimard editorial board. By the 1930s, Gaston and his board had made the house one of the most respected and competitive in France.

Little advertising or promotion was done in French publishing in the 1920s. Nonetheless, Gaston managed to publicize Gallimard books. In 1922, he invested in *Les Nouvelles Littéraires*, a literary newspaper, and subsequently the paper gave special attention to its co-owner's products. Gaston also put real effort into winning French literary prizes and capitalizing on the attention they brought. Given the high quality of Gallimard's books, and the friends Gaston managed to place on juries, that was easy. Between 1919 and 1935, Gallimard's authors won eight of 17 Goncourt Prizes awarded. The firm added a host of authors to its ranks in the 1920's and 1930s, including Antonin Artaud, Antoine de Saint-Exupéry, Ernest Hemingway, William Faulkner, John Dos Passos, John Steinbeck, Erskine Caldwell, and George Simenon. André Malraux was lured away from another publisher with the promise of a position on Gallimard's editorial board. Malraux's first book for Gallimard, *La condition humaine,* won the Prix Goncourt.

New Imprints and Magazines in the 1930s

Gallimard acquired Éditions de la Pléiade in 1933. Originally founded in 1929, the house published classic authors in the public domain. The finely manufactured complete editions were leather-bound in a uniform pocket size and printed on Bible paper. The Pléiade's first publication in 1931 was Baudelaire's complete works, and others quickly followed. However, the consignment payment system widespread in French publishing slowed Pléiade's cash-flow and put the house in financial difficulties. Despite the efforts of André Gide, no

Key Dates:

1908: *Nouvelle Revue Française (NRF)* is founded.
1910: Les Éditions de la NRF is founded.
1911: First three NRF books are published.
1913: Gaston Gallimard agrees to publish Marcel Proust's *A la recherche du temps perdu;* the company creates an editorial board.
1919: Éditions de la *NRF* is reorganized as Librairie Gallimard under the leadership of Gaston Gallimard.
1920: *La Revue Musicale* is founded.
1921: Tuesday meetings of the editorial board are inaugurated.
1922: Gallimard purchases a share in *Les Nouvelles Littéraires*.
1928: *Détective* and *La Revue du Cinéma* are launched.
1928: ZED Publications is founded.
1931: *Voilà* is launched.
1932: *Marianne* is founded.
1933: Éditions de la Pléiade is purchased.
1937: Claude Gallimard joins the firm.
1942: *L'étranger* by Albert Camus is published.
1946: Série noire is launched.
1948: Gaston Gallimard is exonerated of charges of collaborating with the Nazis during the occupation of France.
1951: The company is renamed Les Éditions Gallimard.
1952: *NRF* is allowed to resume publication as *Nouvelle NRF*.
1952: Publisher Denoël is purchased.
1957: *Mercure de France* is purchased.
1967: ZED Publications merges with Librairie Gallimard.
1970: Gallimard founds its own distribution company.
1975: Gaston Gallimard dies at age 94.
1988: Claude Gallimard is succeeded by Antoine Gallimard as managing director.
1990: Outside investors acquire Gallimard stock.
1999: The Gallimard family wins control of 61 percent of the company's stock.
2003: The Gallimard family increases its company stock holdings to 98 percent.

French publisher, including Gallimard at first, was interested in taking over Pléiade. After Gaston finally gave in, Éditions de la Pléiade soon became the house's most distinguished imprint.

Gallimard also expanded its magazine line during the 1920s and 1930s. *Detéctive,* launched in October 1928, specialized in hard-boiled crime fiction and mysteries. Despite complaints that the magazine was too lowbrow for the publishing house, *Detéctive* became a huge success, in Gaston's mind his most successful commercial venture ever. While it existed, *Detéctive*'s profits financed, to a large degree, Gallimard's serious publishing. However, to distance *Detéctive* somewhat from Gallimard's more highbrow publications and to provide a springboard for other new periodicals, ZED Publications was founded in December 1928. Other Gallimard periodicals founded around 1930 included *La Revue du Cinéma*, the photo-weekly *Voilà*, and *Marianne*, a weekly journal of news and

opinion. The commercial success of Gallimard's magazines peaked around 1936. Serious political developments in Europe, the Spanish Civil War in particular, caused large drops in *Voilà* and *Detéctive*'s readership. Even *Marianne*'s readers slowly deserted it. The magazine reached a circulation peak of about 120,000 in 1936 and was sold a year later.

Gallimard scored a major victory in its 1932 contract negotiations with Hachette, then France's largest distributor of printed matter. Hachette agreed to pay Gallimard 75 percent of sales upon receipt of its books. The concession, unprecedented in French publishing, was made on the strength of Gallimard's backlist, the *NRF* journal, and the publisher's reputation. At a stroke, the deal eliminated three of the Gallimard's major problems: the financial risk involved with publishing unknown authors, returns of unsold copies, and financial dependence on bookstore sales. By the late 1930s, Gallimard had grown significantly in all respects: annual turnover, the number of new titles published annually, new imprints, and the size of advances to authors. Gaston concluded the decade with another brilliant coup, obtaining the French rights to Margaret Mitchell's *Gone With The Wind*, which would eventually sell nearly one million copies.

Occupation and Liberation in the 1940s

France's defeat and occupation by Nazi Germany in June 1940 caused an upheaval in the country even greater than that brought on by World War I. Gaston Gallimard considered selling his business and going into exile in the United States but ultimately remained in France. Gaston Gallimard's policy during the occupation was to push as much as possible without making waves, to placate the Germans without violating his principles. He published classic German authors like Goethe, Meister Eckhard, and Theodor Fontane, while continuing to publish bold new French works. Albert Camus' *L'étranger* appeared in June 1942, at the height of the occupation, and his *Le mythe de Sisyphe* soon afterward. Saint-Exupéry's *Pilote de guerre* was published despite some disparaging references to Hitler that had to be deleted from the manuscript. The war helped sales. With public entertainment greatly limited, French interest in reading was unprecedented, limited only by the usual shortages of ink, paper, and manpower. Despite his efforts at conciliating the Nazis, Gaston was forced to replace the *NRF*'s editor. He agreed, hoping to maintain some control over book publishing. However, the Nazi takeover of *NRF* cast a dark shadow over the magazine until into the 1950s.

After the liberation of France, Gallimard continued to boast an impressive roster of authors. They included the so-called "Resistance writers"—Jean-Paul Sartre, Camus, and Malraux, among others—who were the most influential literary figures of postwar France. Important new writers such as Émile Cioran and Jean Genet were also joining the house. The Série Noire, a series of crime and mystery novels translated from English, was introduced in 1948. The imprint introduced the work of Dashiell Hammett and Raymond Chandler to a French audience. Indeed, Gallimard was not lacking for product at this time. According to his biographer, in 1949 the publisher had a backlist large enough to support the house for twenty years.

The *NRF* had been banned after the war because of the articles its Nazi editor had published. Gallimard's hopes to resume publication were kindled by two special issues that had been permitted. Eventually the publisher won out and the magazine was allowed to appear once again under the modified title *Nouvelle NRF*, or *Nouvelle Nouvelle Revue Française*. After a few years the redundant ''nouvelle'' was dropped.

Growth and Tension in the 1950s

The Gallimard house entered a period of change in the 1950s. The company adopted the name Les Éditions Gallimard in 1951. A year later, when ZED Publications obtained a 90 percent share in the publisher Denoël, it absorbed an influential competitor. In 1957, the company bought *Mercure de France*, a leading literary journal. Under the Gallimard banner, the acquired companies retained full editorial independence. In 1954, Gallimard published a complete edition of the works of Marcel Proust and Saint-Exupéry's *Vol de nuit* became the first Livre du Poche when Gallimard licensed it to Hachette's new paperback imprint.

However, during the 1950s there were also family tensions that nearly destroyed the proud Gallimard empire. Gaston had brought his twenty-three year-old son Claude into the business at the end of the 1930s. In 1940, Michel Gallimard, Raymond Gallimard's son, joined the company. Michel and Claude were as different as their fathers. Michel, like his uncle Gaston, loved literature and art, but he also favored left-wing politics. Claude, like Raymond, was far more interested in administration and business than literature and was a political conservative. Factions formed around the cousins at Gallimard, and the resultant animosity threatened to tear the publishing house apart. The feud reached such a pitch that a separation of the cousins in offices in different sections of Paris was considered. The impasse was resolved in tragic fashion in January 1960 when Michel and his friend Albert Camus were killed in an automobile accident.

Claude Gallimard at the Helm in the 1960s and 1970s

The 1960s were a period of quiet growth for the company. By 1967, it was publishing 15 separate series, all commercially successful. In 1969, Gallimard's assets were valued at FRF 37.54 million. Two years later, the value had risen to FRF 47.05. In the mid-1960s, the day-to-day operations of the company were taken over by Claude Gallimard. In 1967, he oversaw the merger of the subsidiary ZED Publications with Gallimard, which brought ZED's authors and customers directly into the Gallimard sphere. The zenith of Claude's reign was the Hachette Affair. Hachette, Gallimard's exclusive distributor since the early thirties, renewed its contract with Gallimard in 1949 and again in 1956. That contract eliminated all Hachette's sales guarantees and increased Hachette's commission to 48 percent of the retail price. When it expired in 1971, the ensuing negotiations were more hard fought than any before. The companies had new heads—Claude at Gallimard and Bernard de Fallois at Hachette—both eager to prove their mettle. In the end, Hachette's commission demands were too much for Gallimard, and the publisher chose to end its relationship with its longtime distributor.

Within six months, Gallimard had established its own distribution company, La Sodis, and a new paperback line, Folio. The loss

hurt Hachette more than Gallimard, whose titles accounted for a full 13 percent of the distributor's business in 1970. When Gaston Gallimard died in 1975 at the age of 94, the backlist he had built was one of the most honored in world publishing. Its authors had won a total of 18 Nobel Prizes, 27 Goncourt Prizes, and 18 Grand Prizes for the Novel awarded by the French Academy.

Milestones in the 1980s

In the 1980s, Gallimard was stronger than ever before, with an influential backlist, a regular stream of stimulating new titles, and a variety of successful imprints unparalleled in publishing. In spring 1984, it butted heads with another major media distributor, the French firm FNAC. Gallimard refused further sales to the Europe-wide discount book and music retailer on the grounds that it was violating French law by discounting books by as much as 20 percent. FNAC countered that the pertinent French laws were in violation of the free trade rules of the European Economic Community. In June 1984, Gallimard lost the case and had to resume shipments to FNAC. Three years later, Gallimard passed a milestone when the copyright protection on Proust's *A la recherche du temps perdu* expired. In seventy years time, Gallimard had sold more than four million copies of Proust's masterwork in French alone. Subsequently, any publisher could publish its own edition.

Family Feuds in the 1990s

In 1990, new inter-family conflicts emerged at Gallimard. Claude Gallimard had announced In 1988 that he was stepping down as the company's managing director. As his successor, he named his younger son Antoine, passing over his elder son Christian, who for as long as Gaston was alive had been considered the heir apparent to the publishing concern. Claude had removed Christian as Gallimard's head in 1985. In 1990, to strengthen Antoine's position, Claude secretly gave him an extra 21 percent share in the firm. The deadlock broke when Françoise, one of Antoine's two sisters, announced she wanted to sell her interest in the company. She hired a British bank to estimate Gallimard's value, which was appraised at $315 million, about twice the firm's annual revenues. Antoine offered $86 million for a 75 percent interest from his siblings. Françoise rejected the offer. It looked as if an outside publisher, perhaps Hachette or Presses de la Cité, or a media baron such as Rupert Murdoch or Robert Maxwell might attempt to seize control of Gallimard and that the firm's editorial independence could vanish. The deadlock broke later in 1990 when Isabelle, Antoine's other sister, sold her 12 percent share to the Banque Nationale de Paris. By July, both Christian and Françoise had also sold out. Control of 54 percent of the company passed to a group of outside firms. At the same time, Antoine Gallimard engineered a plan which limited the stake of outside shareholders to 12 percent and the publishing house became a subsidiary of a new holding company, Sopared, which was controlled by Antoine. The scheme preserved Gallimard's independence and left Antoine, for the time being at least, in control.

In the mid-1990s, Gallimard entered another growth phase. The company was building its travel book division, as well as negotiating the licensing of the Pléiade series to the Italian publisher Einaudi. A major source of revenue and prestige was twenty-year-old Gallimard Jeunesse, which was one of the most successful and respected lines of children's books in world publishing. The American publisher Scholastic Books, holder of a small share in Gallimard, licensed a number of Jeunesse titles for translation into English. By 1999, Gallimard boasted an annual turnover of over FRF 1.5 billion. With a list running to more than 40,000 titles, the firm published approximately 28 million individual volumes that year. The print runs of the publisher's numerous titles ranged from as low as 400 to nearly half a million.

The Company Regained in the 2000s

At the end of the 1990s, Madrigall, Gallimard's holding company controlled by Antoine Gallimard and his sister Isabelle, managed to take over a majority share in the publishing house. Shares were repurchased from two of Gallimard's three big corporate shareholders, the Italian publisher Einaudo and the French media giant Havas. Havas was compelled to sell its shares after the Gallimard board ruled its merger with Vivendi made it a direct competitor. After the repurchase, Madrigall had a 60 percent majority holding in the publishing house. That was increased to 98 percent in January 2003 when Madrigall repurchased the Gallimard holdings of five other outside shareholders for EUR92 million. The repurchase of the stock was termed "an act of faith" by French newspapers. Nevertheless, Antoine Gallimard expressed confidence that the firm would continue to prosper, and in 2003 it had sales of $317 million. One year later, in spring 2004, however, Antoine Gallimard announced he might be willing to sell a minority interest in Gallimard to Natexis, an investment bank, to purchase parts of the French publisher Editis Lagardere.

Principal Subsidiaries

Éditions Denoël; Les Éditions du Mercure de France; Nouveaux Loisirs; Gallimard Jeunesse; P.O.L. (88%); Les Éditions de la Table Ronde (57.8%); Centre de Diffusion de l'Édition; La Sodis; France Export Diffusion; Schoenhof's Foreign Books (U.S.).

Principal Competitors

Hachette Livre; Édition Presses de la Cité; Éditions Flammarion; Éditions Albin Michel; Éditions du Seuil.

Further Reading

"The Americans Are Coming," *Hindu*, February 1, 1998.

"Antoine Gallimard: Si la distribution impose ses choix de livres, c'est la fin de l'edition," *Tribune*, March 12, 1997.

Assouline, Pierre, *Gaston Gallimard: A Half Century of French Publishing*, Harcourt Brace Jovanovich, New York, 1988.

"As Time Goes By," *Economist*, November 7, 1987, p. 108.

Cadet, Valerie, "Les quatre-vingts ans de Gallimard," *Monde*, May, 31, 1991.

"Claude Gallimard, 77; Led Publishing House," *New York Times*, May 2, 1991, p. B15.

"Control Shift at Gallimard," *New York Times*, July 14, 1990, p. A40.

Dromard, Thiébault, "La maison familiale, premier éditeur indépendant français, contrôle désormais 98% de son capital," *Figaro*, January 7, 2003.

"Gallimard Case in Higher Court," *New York Times*, April 3, 1990, p. D21.

"Gallimard Chief Gains in Feud," *New York Times*, March 12, 1990, p. D7.

"Gallimard Faces Shareholder Changes," *Figaro*, May 10, 1995, p. 41.

"Gallimard Family Members to Give Up Control of Firm," *Wall Street Journal*, July 16, 1990, p. B6.

"A Gallimard Move Disclosed," *New York Times*, February 8, 1990, p. D25.

"A Gallimard Sets Deadline," *New York Times*, February 7, 1990, p. D17.

"Gaston Gallimard, France's Foremost Publisher, Dies in Paris at Age of 94," *New York Times*, December 28, 1975, p. 33.

Lamy, Jean-Claude, Frédéric De Monicault, and Virginie Vetil "Gallimard: l'irréductible," *Figaro*, October 30, 2000.

Le Pape, Pierre, "La mort de Claude Gallimard Le mainteneur du royaume," *Monde*, April 30, 1991.

"MACIF Acquires Stake in Gallimard," *Echos*, March 23, 1993, p. 39.

Marnham, Patrick, "Attempt to Turn the Gallimard Page Draws Blood," *Independent*, 26 January 1990, p. 10.

Noiville, Florence, "Antoine Gallimard: la liberté de prendre des risques," *Monde*, February 12, 1999.

——, "Gallimard et Bayard s'allient pour contrôler 22,3% du marché du livre pour la jeunesse," *Monde*, October 13, 1999.

——, "L'avenir de Gallimard," *Monde*, May 6, 1995.

"Predators Close on in Feuding Gallimard," *Financial Times*, January 30, 1990, p. 30.

Riding, Alan, "French Publishing House Is Torn by Classic Family Feud," *New York Times*, February 26, 1990, p. C11.

——, "Gallimard's President Wins Control," *New York Times*, July 20, 1990, p. D5.

——, "Stake in Gallimard Is Sold; Fear of Takeover Revived," *New York Times*, April 7, 1990, p. A37.

Rosenberg, Claire, "French Family Publishing House Faces Share Feud," *Guardian*, January 26, 1990.

Savigneau, Josyane, "Gallimard entre frères et soeurs," *Monde*, January 30, 1990.

——, "L'affaire Gallimard et la résistance de l'esprit," *Monde*, February 16, 1990.

Salles, Alain, "La holding familiale de Gallimard contrôle maintenant 98% du capital de l'entreprise," *Monde*, January 7, 2003.

Smith, Alex Duval, "Obituary: Simone Gallimard," *Guardian*, October 25, 1995, p. 15.

"A Tale of Two Brothers," *Economist*, February 3, 1990, p. 72.

—Gerald E. Brennan

Electronics Boutique Holdings Corporation

931 South Matlack Street
West Chester, Pennsylvania 19382
U.S.A.
Telephone: (610) 430-8100
Fax: (610) 430-6574
Web site: http://www.ebholdings.com

Public Company
Incorporated: 1998
Employees: 11,800
Sales: $1.98 billion (2005)
Stock Exchanges: NASDAQ
Ticker Symbol: ELBO
NAIC: 443120 Computer and Software Stores

Electronics Boutique Holdings Corporation is the holding company for a chain of video-game stores operating under the names Electronics Boutique and EB Games. The company operates 2,000 stores in North America, Puerto Rico, Australia, New Zealand, and Europe. Each store, averaging 1,200 square feet, carries more than 2,000 software titles. Electronics Boutique is 48 percent owned by the family of its founder, James J. Kim.

Origins

Electronics Boutique, a sprawling retail giant, was created by James Kim, a native of South Korea whose early career was spent learning and teaching the principles of business, not practicing them. Born in Seoul in 1936, Kim began training for a career in law, but he never developed an interest in his studies. After attending the College of Law of Seoul for a year, he dropped out. "I never liked the law," he said years later in a November 17, 1986 interview with the *Philadelphia Business Journal*. A friend of his father suggested he move to the United States and attend the Wharton School at the University of Pennsylvania. Kim heeded the advice, determined to study economics so that he could help his country recover from the war he had witnessed as a teenager.

Although he had demonstrated little perseverance in his approach to law, Kim applied himself fully to the field of economics. He attended Wharton, receiving a bachelor's degree in economics in 1959, and began pursuing a master's degree in economics at the University of Pennsylvania's Graduate School of Arts and Sciences. By 1963, Kim had completed his doctoral studies, which landed him a job teaching courses in economics and finance in Wilmington, Delaware, at what later became Widener University. Next, Kim made the short trip back to Philadelphia to accept a post as a teaching fellow at Wharton, a stint that led to his selection as an assistant professor at Villanova University. Kim remained at Villanova until 1970, but by that time he had already begun to stray from academia and apply his knowledge in the business world.

Kim's entrepreneurial career was triggered by a trip home. In 1968, he returned to South Korea, which had achieved great strides economically since his departure. Kim was impressed by the wealth of business opportunities available, prompting him to start a company of his own with ties to his native country. In 1968, Kim established Amkor Electronics Inc., a Valley Forge, Pennsylvania-based semiconductor assembly company affiliated with the Seoul-based company, Anam Industrial Co. Ltd., run by his father. Amkor enjoyed brisk growth, encouraging Kim to start another venture, one aimed at tapping the market for consumer goods. Electronics Boutique became Kim's second entrepreneurial creation, a company founded in 1977 that grew in the shadows of its larger cousin, Amkor, whose profits provided the retailer's seed money.

Early Changes in Strategy

Electronics Boutique, based near Amkor in Valley Forge, began as a one-store enterprise. The first unit, which operated under the Electronics Boutique banner, was a kiosk located in the King of Prussia Plaza Shopping Mall. The original idea behind Electronics Boutique was to sell digital watches and digital calculators, the first tremors of the digital revolution to come and the rage of the late 1970s. Like all fads, the demand for Electronics Boutique's first merchandise faded, leaving Kim searching for another retail approach. The name of the retail concept was changed to Games and Gadgets, a new name for an expanded mix of merchandise that included a wider selection of electronics products, including video games and hand-held electronic games. The new name did not last, leading to a return to the Electronics Boutique banner in 1985, when Kim started focusing on personal computers with a particular emphasis on computer software. "We struggled for about six to seven years before really realizing the fruit of our labors," Kim explained in his November 17, 1986 interview with the *Philadelphia Business Journal.*

Although it took several years for Kim to discover a suitable merchandise mix, it did not stop him from expanding from the start. Using money generated by Amkor and the profits produced by his growing retail venture, Kim built Electronics Boutique into a chain. In 1980, he relinquished his posts as president and chief executive officer of Amkor so he could spend more time overseeing the development of both his companies, limiting his role to developing long-term plans for both Amkor and Electronics Boutique. In 1984, he hired Joseph F. Firestone to serve as president of Electronics Boutique, the same year Jeffrey W. Griffiths was hired as merchandise manager. Although it would take several years for Griffiths to distinguish himself and earn promotions to more senior positions, the company had its 21st-century management team in place by 1984.

As Electronics Boutique developed into a chain, it used its first store in suburban Philadelphia as a blueprint for expansion, at least in terms of location. The company grew up in shopping malls, using the location of its stores to advertise itself rather than investing in any substantial marketing campaign. A decade after starting out, Electronics Boutique stood as a 77-store chain with annual revenues of roughly $30 million. Stores averaged 1,200 square feet and stocked 4,000 software titles, with hardware and computer accessories supporting the chain's mainstay merchandise line. Amkor, by far, was the bigger of Kim's two enterprises, collecting more than $100 million in annual sales, but the disparity in size would not last long. Kim, with Firestone in charge of the day-to-day management of the chain, intended to add 30 stores each year for the remainder of the decade, aiming to create a 200-store chain by the beginning of the 1990s.

As Electronics Boutique pressed forward into the 1990s, expansion went according to plan. As the company expanded, it did so in an unusual fashion for a retail concern. Kim ordered the establishment of stores outside the United States, adding an

international dimension to the company's business. By 1993, there were 318 stores in operation, seven of which were international units. In the years ahead, the company expanded domestically and internationally, opening stores in Canada, Puerto Rico, Australia, New Zealand, South Korea, and in Europe.

Electronics Boutique broadened its geographic scope during the mid-1990s, and it began developing other retail formats as well, coupling expansion with diversification. The acquisition of a single store in 1995 became the basis of the company's sports division, a business segment that consisted of what became a small chain of stores operating under the banner BC Sports Collectibles. The sports division would be joined by another format later in the decade, but before the company began developing its third retail chain it turned to Wall Street for financial support in backing its growth plans. In March 1998, a holding company, Electronics Boutique Holdings Corporation, was formed in preparation for the company's initial public offering (IPO) of stock. At the time, there were 466 stores in operation in 42 states, Puerto Rico, Australia, and South Korea. The company also managed 37 mall-based Walden Software stores for Borders Group, Inc. The IPO was completed in July 1998, ushering in a period of expansion that eventually allowed Electronics Boutique to claim it was the largest of its kind in the world.

Expansion and Consolidation at the Dawn of the 21st Century

By the end of the 1990s, Electronics Boutique was a 600-store chain, having tripled in size during the decade. In the new decade ahead, the company greatly increased its pace of expansion domestically and abroad, particularly in Europe. It also added a new retail format, testing the concept at the Garden State Plaza shopping center in Paramus, New Jersey. The store was the prototype for EBKids, a computer software and video game store that sold what was described as "violence-free, educational" merchandise. The success of the Paramus store convinced Firestone to move forward with expansion plans for the concept—an example of one of the ways the company was promoting growth internally. Its efforts to achieve growth through external means took center stage at the beginning of the 21st century, however, highlighted by a bold bid to acquire a competitor. In 2000, the company attempted to acquire FuncoLand, a 400-store specialty retailer, but another competitor, Babbage's, a video-game retail chain owned by Barnes & Noble Inc., offered a higher price for the FuncoLand chain, benefiting from the considerable financial resources of its parent company.

The FuncoLand acquisition would have been Firestone's swan song. After 17 years of leading the company, he announced his retirement in mid-2001, paving the way for the appointment of another 17-year company veteran. Griffiths, who was promoted from senior vice-president of merchandising and distribution to the posts of president and chief executive officer, took control of a 790-store chain, one that, after entering Denmark and Norway, was developing a sizable European arm to its retail operations. The failure to acquire FuncoLand left Electronics Boutique firmly attached to pursuing growth organically, and one of the first major initiatives led by Griffith was to sharpen the company's focus on establishing new stores. In February 2002, he announced that Electronics Boutique would

Key Dates:

1977: James Kim opens an electronics store in suburban Philadelphia.

1984: Joseph F. Firestone and Jeffrey W. Griffiths join Electronics Boutique.

1985: After several years of experimenting with merchandise, Electronics Boutique focuses on computer software.

1995: A sports division is started with the acquisition of a single store.

1998: Electronics Boutique completes its initial public offering of stock.

1999: Electronics Boutique begins developing a chain of EBKids stores.

2001: Griffiths replaces Firestone as chief executive officer.

2002: Electronics Boutique divests its sports and kids divisions.

2005: GameStop Corporation announces that it will merge with Electronics Boutique.

eliminate its sports and kids divisions, appending the news of the divestiture program with an announcement of plans to open 200 new stores during the year. The company, which operated 937 stores by this point, planned to close its 29 EBKids stores and find a buyer for its 22-unit BC Sports Collectibles chain by mid-2002. "These transactions will enable Electronics Boutique to focus on our core video game business," Griffiths explained in a February 25, 2002 interview with *DSN Retailing Today*. "In short," he added, "without the distraction of other store formats, we can focus on what we do best."

As Griffiths led Electronics Boutique into the mid-2000s, it became increasingly important for a video-game retailer to exude discipline and focus. At a time when the release of an eagerly awaited video game could match the opening box-office receipts of a blockbuster movie in terms of sales, the stakes in the retailing industry were substantial. Further, the industry itself was consolidating, creating a fiercely competitive race for market share. Griffiths's announcement of the company's divestiture of its sport and kids divisions came at a pivotal moment in the race for market share. Less than two weeks earlier, Barnes & Noble spun off its video-game retailing business as a separate company named GameStop Corporation, presenting Griffiths with a new formidable foe. GameStop, which operated more than 1,000 stores under the names Software Etc., Babbage's, and FuncoLand, began re-branding its stores under the GameStop name following its spin-off, concurrent with a re-branding effort led by Griffiths to rename the company's stores EB Games.

The race between Electronics Boutique and GameStop was exceptionally close. Griffiths opened 383 stores during the company's fiscal 2004, enabling it to lay claim to ranking as the world's largest specialized retailer of electronics-games software. Sales for the year reached a record high of $1.59 billion, a measure higher than the $1.58 billion collected by GameStop. Griffiths announced that he intended to open 400 more stores in 2005, but in the midst of leading the company's newest wave of expansion, the announcement of the biggest deal in Electronic Boutique's 28-year history grabbed the limelight.

In mid-April 2005, GameStop announced that it was acquiring Electronics Boutique, a deal that would combine the two largest retailers focused exclusively on selling video games. The estimated $1.4 billion merger was set to create a company with more than 3,800 stores and $3.8 billion in annual sales, combining GameStop's domestic operations with the international expertise of Electronics Boutique. Although the two companies were essentially the same size, GameStop was the dominant partner in the corporate marriage. The combined company was to be named GameStop and headed by R. Richard Fontaine, the chief executive officer and chairman of the former Barnes & Noble chain. An executive position for Griffiths was not disclosed, but Fontaine expressed an interest in retaining as much talent as possible from the Electronics Boutique side of the merger.

In the wake of the announcement, Griffiths continued on as he had before the announcement, expanding the chain while the merger was being evaluated by shareholders and regulatory agencies. At the end of May 2005, he bolstered the company's European operations by preparing to enter Spain for the first time. Electronics Boutique signed a definitive agreement to acquire Jump Ordenadores S.L.U., a 141-store chain based in Valencia. The company did not disclose whether additional acquisitions would be completed before its merger with GameStop was completed, but whatever part the company would play in the future of the retail industry, its past contributions helped create dominance in a fast-growing market.

Principal Subsidiaries

EB Investment Corporation; Electronics Boutique of America Inc.; Electronics Boutique Canada Inc.; EB Catalog Company; Elbo, Inc.; EB Finance, Inc.; EB International Holdings, Inc.; Electronics Boutique Australia Pty. Ltd.; EB Games Customer Services, Inc.; Electronics Boutique Denmark Holdings ApS; Electronics Boutique Denmark ApS; Electronics Boutique Norway A.S.; EB Italy S.R.L.; EB Games Sweden AB; Electronics Boutique AG (Germany); EB Specialty Services, Inc.; EG Games Management Services AB; FR Sadsbury Second, LLC; FR Sadsbury General Partner, LP; FR Sadsbury Property Holding, LP.

Principal Competitors

Best Buy Co., Inc.; Toys 'R' Us, Inc.; Wal-Mart Stores, Inc.; Target Corporation.

Further Reading

Abelson, Reed, "Native Korean Plugged in to U.S. Electronics Market," *Philadelphia Business Journal,* November 17, 1986, p. 10.

Belden, Tom, "Electronics Boutique Reports Record Revenues, Profits for Fiscal 2004," *Philadelphia Inquirer,* March 16, 2004.

Bennett, Elizabeth, "Courting Lara Croft," *Business Journal-Portland,* August 10, 2001, p. 10.

——, "Retailer's New CEO to Stay the Course," *Philadelphia Business Journal,* July 6, 2001, p. 3.

Desjardins, Doug, "Electronics Boutique Reorganizes, Cuts Kids, Collectibles Divisions," *DSN Retailing Today,* February 25, 2002, p. 6.

''Electronics Boutique,'' *Chain Store Age,* October 1987, p. 29.

Godinez, Victor, ''GameStop Purchase of Electronics Boutique to Focus on Europe,'' *Dallas Morning News,* April 19, 2005, p. B3.

Johnson-Berg, Kate, ''The Name of the Game,'' *In-Store Marketing,* October 2002, p. 18.

Kasrel, Deni, ''Ship Shape,'' *Philadelphia Business Journal,* September 5, 1997, p. B1.

Landy, Heather, ''GameStop to Buy Electronics Boutique for $1.4 Billion,'' *Fort Worth Star-Telegram,* April 19, 2005, p. B1.

Linecker, Adelia Cellini, ''Electronics Boutique Holdings,'' *Investor's Business Daily,* August 3, 2001, p. A8.

Minton, Anna, ''Electronics Boutique Hurt by Game Purchase,'' *Financial Times,* October 20, 1999, p. 31.

Scally, Robert, ''Electronics Boutique Debuts EBKids,'' *Discount Store News,* December 13, 1999, p. 7.

Stafford, Jim, ''GameStop Set to Acquire Rival,'' *Daily Oklahoman,* April 19, 2005, p. B4.

Ward, Andrew, ''UK and Ireland,'' *Financial Times,* May 4, 2000, p. 28.

Wendlandt, Astrid, ''Electronics Boutique in French Acquisition,'' *Financial Times,* October 9, 2001, p. 30.

—Jeffrey L. Covell

Embrex, Inc.

1040 Swabia Court
Durham, North Carolina 27703-3989
U.S.A.
Telephone: (919) 941-5185
Fax: (919) 941-5186
Web site: http://www.embrex.com

Public Company
Incorporated: 1985
Employees: 309
Sales: $48.7 million (2004)
Stock Exchanges: NASDAQ
Ticker Symbol: EMBX
NAIC: 325414 Biological Product (except Diagnostic)
    Manufacturing

Embrex, Inc., is a publicly traded agricultural biotechnology company based in Durham, North Carolina, and dedicated to the development of *in ovo* ("in the egg") solutions for the poultry industry, including chickens and turkeys. The flagship product is the Inovoject System, the first automated way to vaccinate chicks before they hatch, which is capable of inoculating 60,000 eggs per hour. More than 80 percent of all eggs produced in the United States and Canada rely on Inovoject. Other mechanical products developed by Embrex are the Egg Remover System, which sorts out infertile and early-dead eggs before the vaccination process, and the Vaccine Saver Option, an add-on to Inovoject that also prevents the vaccination of infertile and early-dead eggs. In addition, the company is developing an egg-gender sorting machine to eliminate the time-consuming, invasive procedure of sorting chicks manually, an important step in the poultry industry. On the vaccine side of the business, Embrex offers Bursaplex Vaccine, a USDA-approved vaccine that can be delivered *in ovo*. All told, Embrex systems have been installed in more than 30 countries around the world.

Company Origins in the Mid-1980s

Embrex was founded by entrepreneur Harold V. Smith, a principal partner of the Synertech Group, a venture fund in North

Carolina's Research Triangle Park. He had previously been involved in the launch of three biotech firms: Ecogen, Cambridge Bioscience, and Animal Diagnostics Inc. Prior to Synertech, Smith had been the chief executive officer of Novo Labs, a U.S. subsidiary of Denmark's Novo Industria, a major European pharmaceutical Company. It was during the 1970s that Novo Labs was lobbied by North Carolina's Governor Jim Hunt to build a plant in the state, an experience that brought the potential of biotechnology to the governor's attention and to the creation of the North Carolina Biotechnology Center. Synertech Group was one of the outgrowths of the state's interest in biotechnology. In 1985, Smith read news accounts in Raleigh's *News & Observer* and the *New York Times* about the explosive growth of the poultry industry and recognized that no one had yet attempted to apply biotechnology to poultry. "When I examined the industry," Smith told *Business North Carolina* in 1992, "I realized that poultry involved a large-volume, low-cost product to which you couldn't add much value after the birds were hatched. So I began to wonder whether you could add value before they hatched." Next, he learned about Jagdev Sharma, a scientist working with the U.S. Department of Agriculture who proved that chicks could be vaccinated before hatching, contrary to the prevailing belief. The USDA patented the idea and Smith acquired the exclusive rights through 2002 on a royalty basis. He incorporated Embrex in North Carolina in May 1985.

To fund the venture, Smith tapped investors he had previously worked with: United Kingdom-based Biotechnology Investments Ltd and Wayne, New Jersey-based American Cyanamid. All together, he raised $15.3 million in seed money. Smith decided to base Embrex in North Carolina, since poultry was a major industry in the state, and North Carolina State University housed one of the largest and most respected poultry science departments in the United States. Smith drew on that resource liberally, recruiting several of the school's professors and many of its graduates. To foster a good relationship with the school, Smith would funnel hundreds of thousands of dollars into the poultry science department in the form of contract research and grants. Smith also devoted a good bit of time to building an impressive board of directors, which would include the former chairman and CEO of Holly Farms Foods, Kenneth May, and former Governor Hunt, whom Smith had known from his days heading Novo Labs.

Company Perspectives:

The potential of Embrex's technology is significant. The corporate mission is clear: to provide ever increasing value to the global poultry industry via in ovo-*based products.*

Late 1980s Focus on Research and Development

With all the pieces in place, Embrex began its research and development phase in 1986. What followed were four years of disappointment as the company's researchers struggled to design a machine that could commercially inject an egg to vaccinate against Marek's disease, which resulted in skin lesions and tumors of the nervous system and made the broilers unsuitable for human consumption. The first prototype was slow and had contamination problems because of cracking. Embrex eventually found a way to pierce the shell without cracking it by employing a needle that was smaller that a millimeter in diameter and featured a beveled tip. This mechanism, according to *Forbes* in a 2005 company profile, ''creates a flap of eggshell that stays attached to the egg between the shell and membrane, rather than falling into the embryo.'' *Forbes* also offered a description of how the final Embrex system worked: ''Three days before the eggs are due to hatch, workers feed them to Embrex's machine, a row of dangling injection heads equipped with locators. The injection head zeroes in on an egg, punches a hole in the shell with a hollow tube, pushes an inch inside the egg and squirts in the vaccine. Then the tube pulls out, to be sterilized and reused.'' This procedure was a far cry from the traditional method in which ''workers grab the little fluff balls, jab them against stationary hypodermics . . . then dump them into boxes.'' Each worker could only inoculate about 3,500 chicks an hour, and a typical vaccination line handling 30,000 chicks an hour required the services of 12 workers. The early Embrex system, which could handle 30,000 eggs an hour, needed only two workers. Moreover, chicks immunized in the shell proved to be better able to resist infections, and by not undergoing such rough treatment early in life they enjoyed shorter fattening periods, thus saving on production costs. Moreover, immunization by hand invariably resulted in a certain number of chicks being missed.

However, just as research and development took time, so would gaining the trust of the poultry industry. As the research began to result in a viable commercial system, Smith recruited a seasoned executive to lead Embrex into the initial marketing phase, hiring Randall L. Marcuson, who took over as chief executive officer on January 1, 1990. Marcuson came to Embrex from American Cyanamid, where he had been vice-president of Animal Health Products for the previous six years. Prior to that, he spent ten years with Monsanto Agricultural Products Company.

Smith stayed on as chairman and along with Marcuson began the process of tapping into the equity markets for an infusion of much needed cash. From January 1, 1986 through June 1991, the company had lost $14.3 million, burning through all but $1 million of its seed money. With the New York firm of Josephthal Lyon & Ross, Inc. acting as underwriter, Embrex made an initial public offering of stock in November 1991. The timing was excellent, as biotechnology stocks were the darlings of Wall Street at the time and many startups were commanding prices much higher than companies in other industries. Embrex hoped to sell 1.7 million shares in the $7 to $9 range, thus raising about $12 million. In the end, it netted $16.7 million. The company returned to the market two years later, raising another $10.8 million.

Gaining industry acceptance of the Inovoject System was not without some difficulty. In 1992, the first year that it was installed commercially, Embrex recorded revenues of $700,000. The key to gaining customers was the launch of a policy to allow hatcheries to use the system free on a trial basis for several weeks. The benefits of the automated system were so apparent that invariably the hatcheries became Embrex customers. Rather than sell the equipment, the company leased it on a per-injection fee basis. A major early step in landing business for Inovoject came in 1992 when Tyson Foods, the United States top poultry producer, agreed to convert one of its hatcheries to the automated system. Over the next two years, more Tyson hatcheries installed the Embrex machines, followed by the second largest poultry producer, Gold Kist Inc., and Perdue Farms Inc., the fifth-largest producer. As a result of increasing industry acceptance, Embrex enjoyed steadily rising revenues, so that in 1996 the company turned its first profit, $341,000 on revenues of $20.6 million. By now, Smith was no longer part of the company, having sold his stake in 1995 and moved on to other projects.

Embrex Well Established by 2000

While Inovoject was establishing itself in the U.S. broiler market, Embrex researchers were hard at work developing other *in ovo* products using the Inovoject System as a platform. In the meantime, the company continued to grow the balance sheet, as sales improved to $24.8 million in 1997, $28.6 million in 1998, and $33.8 million in 1999. Net income during this period grew from $1.8 million to $2.9 million to $5.7 million. Despite this steady growth, investors lost enthusiasm for Embrex, its stock generally trading between $4 and $6 and few shares changing hands. By 2000, the company had established itself in the poultry industry, inoculating more than 80 percent of all eggs produced by the North American broiler sector. It had been apparent for some time that the company would have to expand internationally if it were to grow beyond its status as a good little company with a dominant market niche. It was estimated that 70 percent of the world's broiler production took place outside of North America. As early as 1994, Embrex looked to Europe, forming a subsidiary, Embrex Europe Ltd., to tap into that market. In 1997, the company began marketing in Asia and a year later turned its attention to Latin America. Thus, by the end of 1999, Embrex had systems either installed or on trial in 29 countries. Because poultry diseases varied around the globe, Inovoject was used differently in each region. While Marek's disease was widespread in the United States, for example, it was less of a problem in Europe. On the other hand, Gumboro disease was a significant problem in northern Europe and Asia and of lesser importance in the United States. Inovoject was effective no matter what the vaccine, but the problem for Embrex was that the global market for Inovoject in the broiler sector was perhaps 900. By the autumn of 2000, Embrex was already approaching the 500 mark. Moreover, the company's original FDA license was set to expire at the end of 2002, which

Key Dates:
1985: The company is founded by Harold V. Smith.
1990: Randall L. Marcuson becomes the company's CEO.
1991: The company is taken public.
1996: Embrex turns its first annual profit.
2003: A lawsuit with pharmaceutical giant Wyeth is settled.

could possibly lead to new competition. Hence, for some time Embrex had invested a great deal of time and money in the development of new products. The most promising of them were a system to deliver multiple vaccines in a single shot; a vaccine for cocidiosis, an avian parasitic disease that attacked the chicken's digestive system; and an automatic gender sorting system. The gender sorting product was important because it could be used by both the breeder, layer, and broiler markets. Some broilers are grouped by sex in order to better distribute feed and enhance growth. The breeder and broiler producers, on the other hand, want to raise only hens for laying. In addition, breeders needed more females than males. As had been the case with the old method of vaccinating chicks, manually determining a chick's sex was a laborious process, accomplished in one of two ways: Either the feather length is measured when the chicks are a day or two old, a labor-intensive effort, or the genital area is opened and inspected, an expensive method that stresses the chick as well as workers' eyes. Embrex's automated approach sampled material in the egg that contained gender enzyme chemicals, which were then applied to a developed material, triggering a reaction that revealed whether the egg was male or female. The gender-determining system held great potential, possibly worth hundreds of millions of dollars in annual sales. However, to develop a commercial automated system required a long-term commitment and the resolution of a number of problems. In 2004, Embrex was still grappling with the system. During that year, the company received three patents alone related to the transferring of selected eggs to flats and the back filling of those flats.

Embrex's researchers worked on other fronts as well, developing the Egg Remover system and Vaccine Saver option. The company also developed a Bursaplex vaccine to prevent the infectious disease IBD, which weakened a bird's immune system, leading to stunted growth or death from other diseases due to a compromised immune system. IBD was widespread in Northern Europe, the Middle East, Asia, Latin America, and, to a lesser extent, the United States. In 2003, Embrex received approval on a vaccine to combat Newcastle Disease, a contagious disease that not only resulted in respiratory problems but lowered egg production and increased flock mortality. It was a serious problem in Asia, Latin America, the Middle East, and South Africa.

On some of its projects Embrex worked with industrial partners, but one relationship, forged with pharmaceutical giant Wyeth and its Fort Dodge animal vaccine maker, soured. According to *Triangle Business Journal,* shortly after Marcuson took the helm at Embrex, he "began courting partners for a European and African vaccine program." He first turned to his ex-employer, American Cyanamid, "but by the time the collaboration got its legs, American Cyanamid had been acquired, and the vaccine project was handed off to Fort Dodge. Embrex says it quickly noticed its new partner's interest fading." The alliance between the two companies was signed in 1995 to develop an *in ovo* vaccine for Bursamune, used to treat Gumboro disease, but in 1997 Wyeth acquired a Belgian company that manufactured post-hatch poultry vaccines. From the point of view of Embrex, Fort Dodge grew indifferent, thus obstructing development of the *in ovo* vaccine. In 2002, Embrex sued Wyeth for breach of contract and a year later the two parties reached a settlement in which Fort Dodge paid $5 million to Embrex.

Business grew steadily for Embrex in the 2000s, as sales topped $40 million in 2002, increased to $43.5 million in 2003, and to $46.2 million in 2004. Net income totaled $7.2 million in 2002 and $7.6 million in 2003 (inflated by the Fort Dodge settlement), before dipping to $3.3 million in 2004. Embrex, which was better versed than anyone about the inner workings of poultry eggs, was well positioned to enjoy even greater growth in the years to come. It would not be surprising if one or more of its development projects, such as the gender-sorting system, became a blockbuster product, transforming the small niche company into a much larger player in the worldwide poultry industry.

Principal Subsidiaries

Embrex Europe Limited; Embrex Sales, Inc.; Embrex BioTech Trade (Shanghai) Co., Ltd; Inovoject do Brasil Ltda.; Embrex France s.a.s.; Embrex Iberica; Embrex Poultry Health, LLC.

Principal Competitors

IDEXX Laboratories, Inc.; Neogen Corporation; Synbiotics Corporation.

Further Reading

Cohen, Jeff, "Should You Scramble to Bet on Embrex's Best-Laid Plan?" *Business North Carolina*, March 1992, p. 46.

Hutheesing, Nikhil, "Robovet," *Forbes*, March 13, 1995, p. 142.

Ranii, David, "Durham, N.C.-Based Poultry Bioscience Group Gets $5 Million in Suit," *News & Observer*, July 1, 2003.

——, "Embrex Loses Money As It Wins," *News & Observer*, April 30, 1994, p. D1.

Smith, Rick, "Sorting Eggs Is Big Business at Embrex," *Business Journal*, April 20, 2001, p. 22.

Zimmer, Jeff, "Egg-Injection System Pays off for Durahm, N.C.-Based Agricultural Biotech Firm," *Herald-Sun*, November 21, 2000.

—Ed Dinger

Empire Resorts, Inc.

Monticello Raceway, Route 17B
Monticello, New York 12701
U.S.A.
Telephone: (845) 794-4100
Fax: (845) 791-1402
Web site: http://www.empireresorts.com

Public Company
Incorporated: 1993 as Alpha Hospitality Corporation
Employees: 380
Sales: $44.9 million (2004)
Stock Exchanges: NASDAQ
Ticker Symbol: NYNY
NAIC: 713990 All Other Amusement and Recreation
Industries

Maintaining its headquarters at the Monticello Raceway in New York State's Catskills region, Empire Resorts, Inc., operates a harness track, which the company has converted into a "racino." In addition to pari-mutuel wagering, Mighty M Gaming at Monticello Raceway offers more than 1,700 video gambling games, live entertainment, and a 350-seat buffet. But the Raceway operation is just part of a much bigger plan for Empire Resorts, which has agreements with two sets of Native American tribes—The Cayuga Nation of New York and the Seneca-Cayuga Tribe of Oklahoma—to develop separate casino resorts in the Catskills, advantageously located just 90 miles northwest of New York City—closer than Atlantic City and Connecticut's Tribal casinos. The potential riches to be realized from tribal gaming in the Catskills is at the heart of the history of Empire Resorts.

Tribal Gaming Emerging in the Late 1980s

In 1988 the U.S. Congress passed The Indian Gaming Regulatory Act granting Native American tribes the exclusive right to regulate gaming on tribal lands if the gaming activity was not specifically prohibited by federal law and the individual state approved. According to a 2002 *Time* magazine article, tribal gaming emerged in the late 1980s: "In a frenzy of cost cutting and privatization, Washington perceived gaming on reservations as a cheap way to wean tribes from government handouts, encourage economic development and promote tribal self-sufficiency."

The Pequot tribe was able to strike a deal in Connecticut and build the highly successful Foxwoods Resort Casino, followed by the Mohegans who would build the Mohegan Sun Casino. Both were located relatively close to New York City, but even nearer was the Catskills of New York, where interested parties were clamoring for legalized gambling in New York's Sullivan County. Once a thriving tourist area known for resorts such as Grossinger's, Kutsher's, and Brown's, the so-called "Borscht Belt" had fallen on hard times. Many of the popular hotels of a bygone era closed down and the racetrack that in 1980 set a single-day attendance record of 17,000 was now lucky to attract 1,000 patrons. Resort owners and others lobbied Albany to bring casino gambling to the Catskills in an effort to revitalize the economy as Atlantic City had done in the 1970s. After the state legislature in 1994 once again voted against casino gambling in the state, one Sullivan County resident thought he saw a way to bring casinos to the Catskills through the use of the tribal gaming laws. His name was Robert A. Berman, Empire Resorts' chief executive officer.

Berman, the son of an area contractor, became involved in the Catskills' tourist industry in the late 1970s when at the age of 19 he opened a nightclub in a former hotel. Then in the early 1980s he hosted a successful rock concert series using another shuttered hotel, and later in the decade helped to reopen an old ski resort. He and his partners also took advantage of second-home construction in the area, supplementing the ski resort with condominiums, townhouses, and single-family homes, as well as a lodge and clubhouse. But when the economy faltered the building boom came to an end. In 1991 Berman cofounded and became managing partner of Watermark Investments Ltd., a Manhattan real estate investment group legally based in the Bahamas. In addition to real estate ventures and hotel renovations, Berman worked with the Coeur d'Arlene tribe in Idaho to create an Internet lottery. He became familiar with The Indian Gaming Regulatory Act and a little known provision that permitted the building of a casino on land donated in trust for a tribe, in effect carving out sovereign tribal territory on nontribal lands.

Berman shared his idea with Cliff Ehrlich, whose family owned a Catskill hotel and had been a major advocate for bringing casinos to Sullivan County. Through Watermark they acquired the struggling Monticello Raceway, then contacted the Oneidas tribe, which had a 32-acre reservation east of Syracuse, and along with the St. Regis Mohawk Tribe of Hogansburg, New York, close to the Canadian border, had signed compacts with New York in 1993 to operate casinos on reservation land. In July of that year the Oneidas opened a casino near Utica, the first legal casino in the state. Berman's group reached a deal with the Oneidas and in March 1995 they announced a plan to establish a casino on the Monticello Raceway property, after the land had been given to the tribe in trust of the federal government. The Oneidas gained the support of community leaders by promising to make $5 million in annual payments to the local governments. But the Oneidas and Berman failed to agree on a purchase price for the raceway, the tribe reportedly offering $50 million to $60 million over ten years, and Watermark insisting on $100 million. By September 1995 the deal was off. The Oneidas did not lack for alternate sites, however, given that much of Sullivan County was up for sale. But approval from New York's governor, George Pataki, also was needed, and at this juncture he opposed the idea of tribal gaming in the state. Instead, he supported legalized gambling in New York.

Berman now turned to the Cayuga Indian Nation of New York, a tribe that had held no land for more than 200 years. But the Cayugas were divided about gambling and rejected the overture. Next, he approached the Mohawks but they already had a development partner, Alpha Hospitality, the corporate entity that later became Empire Resorts. Berman and Alpha Hospitality would now join forces.

Empire Resorts' Corporate Roots in the Early 1990s

Alpha Hospitality was founded in 1993 by Stanley S. Tollman and Monty D. Hundley. Previously the two men formed the Tollman-Hundley Hotel Group in 1979 and during the 1980s assembled a hotel empire, funded by bank loans. Tollman-Hundley became the largest franchisee of the Days Inn chain, then in 1989 it acquired the Days Inn of America company for $87 million, paying $8 million in cash and the rest in junk bonds. It also assumed $620 million in debt. But Tollman-Hundley then withheld at least $36 million in franchise royalties and mortgage payments and Days Inn filed for bankruptcy in September 1991. The two partners then engineered a restructuring plan that called for them to be personally liable for $100 million in deficiency notes. At the same time, they arranged to sell Days Inn to Hospitality Franchise Systems (HFS) for $250 million, as well as landing a $375,000 annual consulting fee for the two men for the next five years and a $10 million loan. Former Days Inn president Michael Leven expressed his out-

rage to *Atlanta Business Chronicle* in November 1991, saying, "How can Tollman-Hundley take the company into bankruptcy and walk away with $375,000 a year each. And the $10 million loan—something's rotten in Denmark." Leven also maintained that "if Tollman-Hundley has paid what it owed, then Days Inns could have paid the junk bond holders." The business dealings of Tollman and Hundley eventually caught the attention of government, but over the next few years, the partners devoted a lot of their attention to the gambling industry through Alpha Hospitality.

During the 1990s Alpha Hospitality failed in its attempt to run riverboat casinos on the Mississippi River as well as "cruises to nowhere" in Florida that operated floating casinos on ships outside of U.S. territorial waters. The company also eyed tribal gaming, in March 1994 creating a joint venture with the Mohawks to develop and operate a gaming facility on tribal lands. After Berman hatched his plan to deed land to a willing tribe to locate a casino in the more desirable Catskills, Alpha Hospitality and the Mohawks dropped their original plans and turned their attention to Sullivan County. In January 1996 they entered into a memorandum of understanding with Berman's Catskill Development, L.L.C., a Watermark subsidiary, regarding the development and management of a casino adjacent to the Monticello Raceway. Catskill then bought the track in June 1996. The plan was for the tribe to own the casino and have a half-interest in running it, while Alpha Hospitality and Catskill Development took the other half and continued to operate the raceway, which would likely become a more valuable enterprise with a casino next door. The Mohawk tribe then submitted the plan to the National Indian Gaming Commission for approval.

The land trust application for Monticello Raceway was approved by the Bureau of Indian Affairs in 1998, and in April 2000 the Interior Department approved the casino plan at the raceway. Only days later, however, the Mohawks dropped Berman and his partners, instead joining forces with Park Place Entertainment, now Caesars Entertainment, a giant gaming concern operating casinos in Las Vegas, Atlantic City, and other locations. Park Place then secured an option to buy Kutsher's Country Club for $65 million, and soon another developer, David Flaum, announced that he intended to open a pair of casinos at the Shawanga Lodge. Berman sued Park Place for $6.3 billion for luring away the Mohawks, a claim eventually dismissed in court, while telling the press that he believed Park Place had no actual intention of building a Catskills casino and was simply protecting its Atlantic City interests. But according to *Times Herald-Record* columnist Barry Lewis, a major reason for the rupture with the Mohawks was "their disdain for Berman, 'Completely disrespectful,' said Mohawk spokeswoman Rowena General, of the man who the Mohawks' lawyer says, screamed at meetings and 'treated us like idiots.' " Berman did not help his reputation in 2000 by failing to pay $1.4 million in back taxes to the county after his second-home development business failed. Berman again turned to the Cayugas, who once more declined to become involved in the gambling business.

In February 2002 Berman became a director of Alpha Hospitality and replaced Tollman as CEO. Just two months later Tollman, Hundley, and three others, including a company lawyer and accountant, were indicted by federal prosecutors for

<table>
<tr><td colspan="2">Key Dates:</td></tr>
<tr><td>1991:</td><td>Robert Berman founds Watermark Investments.</td></tr>
<tr><td>1993:</td><td>Alpha Hospitality Corporation is formed.</td></tr>
<tr><td>1996:</td><td>Berman and Alpha become partners on the Catskill Casino project.</td></tr>
<tr><td>2002:</td><td>Berman is named CEO of Alpha; his predecessor is indicted on bank and tax fraud charges.</td></tr>
<tr><td>2003:</td><td>Alpha changes its name to Empire Resorts.</td></tr>
<tr><td>2004:</td><td>Mighty M Gaming at Monticello Raceway opens.</td></tr>
</table>

bank fraud and tax fraud. At the time, Tollman was in London, where he owned luxury hotels, and when he failed to return to the United States he was designated a fugitive. He fought extradition and although arrested by British authorities in 2004 he was released on bail and remained in the country. Hundley was in Australia but ultimately was extradited and stood trial. Tollman's wife, Beatrice, also became caught up in the investigation and she fled the country in 2003, joining her husband. Their son, Brett G. Tollman, was implicated, and in September 2003 he reached a plea bargain, pleading guilty to tax evasion, a break that prosecutors used to secure the 2004 convictions of Hundley; James Cutler, Alpha Hospitality's chief financial officer; Sanford Freedman, the company's general counsel; and Howard Zukerman, vice-president of finance. Brett Tollman was sentenced to 33 months in prison, while Hundley received eight years and was ordered to pay more than $110 million in restitutions to creditors and the IRA. During the course of the trial the prosecutors demonstrated that Hundley and Tollman lied to their creditors about their assets, which included luxury homes in Manhattan; Bedford, New York; Palm Beach, Florida; and London. "At the same time that Mr. Tollman and Mr. Hundley were pleading poverty with their creditors," according to the *New York Times,* "they duped the banks into selling the distressed debt on the hotels to supposedly unrelated individuals at steep discounts. In reality, the evidence showed, the companies that bought the debt at about 10 cents on the dollar were sham entities controlled by Mr. Tollman and Mr. Hundley." Hundley, who had not filed income tax returns for more than 20 years, also was convicted on tax evasion.

Change in Prospects for Casinos After Events of 2001

Berman distanced himself from the Tollman-Hundley crowd as much as possible. He restructured Alpha Hospitality, selling off its assets and merged into it the various corporate partners in the raceway project, and in April 2003 took on a new name: Empire Resorts, Inc. Berman also continued to woo the Cayugas, who finally agreed to the Monticello Raceway project. There were still many obstacles to overcome before Empire Resorts or any of the other developers would be able to open a tribal casino in the Catskills. But other events had intervened that gave hope to gaming advocates. Following the terrorist attacks of September 11, 2001, the New York economy slumped and in an effort to boost tourism the state legislature authorized Governor Pataki to negotiate with Indian tribes to build three casino resorts in western New York and three in the Catskills. Then, in 2002, the State of New York Lottery Commission granted permission to eight state racetracks, including Monticello Raceway, to install video lottery and gaming machines.

While continuing to work through the regulatory process on the casino plan, Empire Resorts invested some $23 million to add video gaming to the raceway. In the summer of 2004 the old raceway was reopened as Mighty M Gaming at Monticello Raceway. Whether it would be the beginning of a new era of gambling in the Catskills or a last-gasp attempt to keep a faded racetrack open was yet to be determined. The prospect for tribal gaming in Sullivan County, in the meantime, become more crowded as well as more cloudy. One long-term stumbling block had been outstanding land claims between New York and the tribes. It appeared the Cayugas had reached an agreement in June 2004, giving the tribe the inside track on a Catskill casino, but when the deal fell through Empire Resorts hedged its bet by signing an agreement with Oklahoma's Seneca-Cayugas to develop a Catskill casino. The Cayugas claimed to have an exclusive arrangement but their protests were in vain. It appeared that the Cayugas and other tribes would resolve all their land claims in the fall of 2004. The Seneca-Cayuga tribe of Oklahoma agreed to give up its claims in exchange for the right to operate a Catskill casino. The Cayugas reached a similar deal a few days later, as did the Wisconsin-based Oneida Tribe and the Mohicans, the ancestry of both traced to New York. A land claim with the Mohawks also was undertaken. The Cayugas settlement, however, proved problematic as the tribe experienced a split over the agreement within the nine-person Cayuga council.

Regardless of how the Cayugas resolved their internal conflicts, Empire Resort retained the possibility of developing a casino with the Seneca-Cayugas. Whether any tribe would ever open a casino in the Catskills was far from certain, however. The Sullivan County economy was picking up even without casinos, due to the increase of New York City second-home buyers and the strong growth of neighboring Orange County. Local residents once eager for tribal gaming were now having second thoughts, concerned that new casino workers brought into the county would overtax already crowded schools and the influx of tourists would overwhelm Route 17 stretching from New York to the Catskills. With opposition to the casinos emerging from both Native American groups and area residents, the state legislature was in no hurry to act. Whether Empire Resorts would ever move beyond its racino operation and launch a major casino resort was a question that remained very much undecided.

Principal Subsidiaries

Alpha Monticello, Inc.; Alpha Casino Management Inc.; Monticello Casino Management, LLC; Monticello Raceway Development, LLC; Monticello Raceway Management, Inc.

Principal Competitors

Yonkers Racing Corporation.

Further Reading

Applebome, Peter, ''Taste of Tahoe in Borscht Belt: Here's the Tab,'' *New York Times,* June 27, 2004, p. A1.

Bagil, Charles V., ''Against All Odds, a Complicated Casino Proposal Advances,'' *New York Times,* April 17, 200, p. B1.

——, ''Cayuga Tribe Moves Closer to a Casino in the Catskills,'' *New York Times,* May 4, 2004, p. B1.

Lewis, Barry, ''Lots of Slack for Casino Cat with 9 Lives,'' *Times Herald-Record,* April 10, 2003.

Morgenson, Gretchen, ''Former Hotel Executives Convicted of Fraud,'' *New York Times,* February 6, 2004, p. C5.

Peterson, Ivan, ''Reluctantly, a Tribe Starts to See Casinos As Being Imperative,'' *New York Times,* May 9, 2003, p. A1.

Semple, Kirk, ''Catskill Casino Politics: Game of Delicate Balance,'' *New York Times,* January 31, 2005, p. B1.

Sotto, Cindy M., ''Days Inns' Bankruptcy Bonanza: Chain's Troubled Seller to Pocket Hefty 'Consulting' Fee,'' *Atlanta Business Chronicle,* November 11, 1991, p. 1.

West, Debra, ''Casino Dreams Flourish in the Catskills,'' *New York Times,* October 28, 1995, p. A23.

Worth, Robert F., ''5 Men, One with Political Connections, Are Indicted in $42 Million Bank and Tax Fraud,'' *New York Times,* April 18, 2002, p. B3.

—Ed Dinger

ENGELHARD

Engelhard Corporation

101 Wood Avenue
Iselin, New Jersey 08830
U.S.A.
Telephone: (732) 205-5000
Toll Free: (800) 758-9567
Fax: (732) 906-0337
Web site: http://www.engelhard.com

Public Company
Incorporated: 1938 as Porocel Corporation
Employees: 6,500
Sales: $4.17 billion (2004)
Stock Exchanges: New York
Ticker Symbol: EC
NAIC: 212324 Kaolin and Ball Clay Mining; 325131 Inorganic Dye and Pigment Manufacturing; 325132 Synthetic Organic Dye and Pigment Manufacturing; 325188 All Other Basic Inorganic Chemical Manufacturing; 327992 Ground or Treated Mineral and Earth Manufacturing; 336399 All Other Motor Vehicle Parts Manufacturing; 421510 Metals Service Centers and Offices; 421940 Jewelry, Watch, Precious Stone, and Precious Metal Wholesalers

Engelhard Corporation is a leading supplier of catalysts used in the petroleum, chemical, and food industries. An unusually diversified company, Engelhard also produces a variety of industrial products such as paper coating agents, color pigments, temperature sensing devices, and precious metal-coated anodes, as well as materials for consumer goods such as cosmetics and automotive paints. A unifying thread of its many activities is surface and materials science—chemically or mechanically engineering ingredients to give them specific properties. For most of the 20th century, the name Engelhard was been associated with the glamorous, and sometimes notorious, world of precious metals: gold, silver, and those metals in the platinum group. Since pioneering catalytic converters for automobiles in the 1970s, Engelhard has become involved in a very broad range of industries. It has numerous international subsidiaries.

A little more than half of the company's sales come from outside the United States.

Immigrant Roots

The company's roots in the precious-metals industry extend back to 1891, the year in which Charles Engelhard immigrated to the United States from his native Germany to work as a foreign sales agent for his employer, a marketer of platinum. Engelhard decided to remain in the United States and soon was able to secure equity positions in a number of precious metals companies, chief among them Baker & Co., Irvington Smelting, Hanovia Company, and American Platinum Works. Engelhard, who in *Forbes,* August 1, 1965, was described by his son as a "tough businessman" and "very Germanic," united the companies into a comprehensive precious-metals fabricator under the name of Engelhard Industries. The Engelhard interests bought, refined, and sold the full range of precious metals, but, with Baker & Co. taking the lead, soon developed a special expertise in platinum.

Platinum is valuable not only for its beauty but because it exhibits a number of unusual and useful physical properties, among them its virtually complete resistance to corrosion by chemicals or heat and a molecular formation that accommodated various types of catalysis. By the early 1900s, Engelhard had begun to exploit the metal's industrial value as well as its importance to the jewelry and dental trades, helping develop its use as a heat resistant liner for chemical vessels and as filaments in electric light bulbs. As platinum was scarce, however, the metals industry did not much pursue its industrial applications. Engelhard Industries remained a supplier of precious metals primarily for ornamentation and dentistry. It was not until the 1920s that a secure supply of platinum encouraged further study of the metal's engineering value. A Canadian concern, Inco, formerly called International Nickel Company, demonstrated that platinum could be produced as a byproduct of nickel mining, thus temporarily stabilizing the supply of platinum and prompting intensive research into its properties. Charles Engelhard became Inco's exclusive dealer of platinum in the United States, and in the early 1930s created a research-and-development department of his own to pioneer new uses for the metal. In conjunction with Du Pont, Engelhard's Baker & Co. came up with a revolutionary process

113

Company Perspectives:

Diverse markets. Diverse customers. Diverse products. All from a single focus on surface and materials science. No other company in the world possesses Engelhard's unique combination of capabilities. Fundamentally, we manipulate basic materials—typically minerals—to alter their structure and surface characteristics. We manipulate them mechanically and chemically, altering their size, shape, porosity and chemical characteristics to produce a wide range of functionality with important business uses. We enable our customers, for instance, to change the appearance, image and functionality of everything from product packaging to automotive finishes by controlling the way light is absorbed or reflected from the surface of a particle. Manipulating that same particle to absorb or repel water produces an entirely new set of applications. And that's only the half of it. Because we then use surface chemistry to expand the performance profile and functionality of these engineered materials—creating specialized chemical formulations to tailor their acidity, thermal stability, gloss and other characteristics. The formulations are typically metal-based, predominantly platinum group metals. The result may be a catalyst that cleans a car's exhaust or a pigment that gives eye shadow its pearlescent sheen. Either outcome is made possible by the very same capabilities in materials science and surface chemistry. Whether delivering more cost-effective crop protection or helping a petroleum refiner get the most from a barrel of crude oil, we're in the business of making our customers' products and processes more effective, less costly, more productive, more attractive, safer and more environmentally friendly. No wonder customers turn to Engelhard to change the nature of their products. They get results that change their markets and our world.

---

for the manufacture of nitric acid that employed a platinum and rhodium catalyst. The process was soon adopted throughout the chemicals industry. Engelhard Industries began a long evolution that would first transform the company into the world leader in precious-metals fabricating and later encourage its present focus on catalysis in many of its forms.

The 1930s saw the development of the platinum spinnerette, a platinum nozzle perforated by thousands of microscopic holes designed to spin out synthetic fibers for the manufacture of textiles. World War II fostered other uses of platinum, such as the platinum-tipped sparkplug for aircraft engines, which was able to withstand high temperatures for long periods without corroding. In the early 1950s, platinum began to be used in the petroleum industry for the catalysis of high-octane gasoline and to refine heavy crude oils. Engelhard Industries continued to derive the large majority of its sales from nonindustrial markets such as jewelry, but in the 1940s Charles Engelhard added to his growing assortment of companies with the purchase of D.E. Makepeace Company of Massachusetts, makers of gold and silver sheet, tube, and wire; Amersil Company, industrial appliers of fused quartz; and National Electric Instruments Company, a manufacturer of medical instruments. With these and other industrial acquisitions, Engelhard laid the groundwork for

the later expansion of his business carried out by his son, Charles Engelhard, Jr. Born in 1917, Charles served as a pilot in World War II and afterward joined his father in the metals business. Anxious to make his own mark, young Engelhard soon moved to South Africa and began exploring opportunities in that mineral-rich country, source of much of the world's gold, platinum, and diamonds.

The South African Connection

From the time he took over the business until 1971, the history of Engelhard Corporation was largely the story of Charles Engelhard, Jr. The founder's son had the unusual good fortune to succeed in both of the roles available to a wealthy scion. On the one hand, he became an international socialite and, on the other, led his father's company to greater success. Upon settling in South Africa, Engelhard started a gold-exporting business to supply his father's companies with raw material and turn a profit as well. At the time, gold could not be traded except in the form of art objects, so Engelhard shipped his gold in the shape of dishes, jewelry, and even solid gold pulpit tops, much of which was later melted down by the customer. Engelhard incorporated his firm, Precious Metals Development, in London in 1949, using the services of Robert Fleming & Co. At Fleming & Co. Engelhard met Ian Fleming, the creator of James Bond, who is believed to have used the portly, gold-toting Engelhard as the model for his famous villain Auric Goldfinger. When his father died in 1950, the younger Engelhard assumed control of a complex, heterogenous mix of companies headquartered in Newark, New Jersey. He once again made the United States his home, bringing with him connections with many of the leading figures in South African mining.

Charles Engelhard, Jr. found that his autocratic father had run his various metals businesses virtually without administrative help and thus set about centralizing authority while also delegating its daily implementation. In 1953, he brought in Gordon Richdale as president of Engelhard Industries, the main operating company for the family interests. Richdale had experience in mining in the Transvaal region of South Africa and was a good friend of Sir Ernest Oppenheimer, the chairman of that country's dominant mining company, Anglo American Corporation of South Africa. Engelhard had become friends with Oppenheimer's son Harry as well, and when the Oppenheimers needed a partner for a 1957 bailout of Central Mining and Investment Corporation they turned to Engelhard. Central Mining was a large, London-based oil and mining company with extensive South African holdings that was in danger of a hostile takeover, which it hoped to prevent with Engelhard's help. For a relatively small amount of cash, $3.5 million, Engelhard was able to gain a 30 percent share of Rand American Investments Limited, an Oppenheimer creation that then won the proxy fight at Central Mining and took control of its 12 gold mines, timber holdings, lime quarries, and 13 newspapers, with a total estimated value of $500 million. Engelhard was named chairman of Rand American, having parlayed a youthful lark in South Africa into an intimate partnership with one of the most powerful families in international business.

The South African venture was kept separate from Engelhard's stable of U.S. companies, which in 1957 had sales of $173 million, more than one-third of them derived from plati-

---

Key Dates:

1891: Metals trader Charles Engelhard emigrates to the United States from Germany.

1950: Engelhard's son, Charles, Jr., inherits family metals empire.

1957: Engelhard joins Harry Oppenheimer in takeover of Central Mining.

1963: Engelhard acquires 20 percent share of the newly formed Minerals & Chemicals Philipp.

1967: Engelhard Industries merges with MCP to form Engelhard Minerals & Chemicals Corp. (EMCC).

1971: Anglo American trades 70 percent holding in Engelhard's parent company for 30 percent of EMCC.

1973: Engelhard develops its first production catalytic converter.

1981: EMCC's metals-and-minerals and precious-metals divisions spun off as Engelhard Corporation.

1994: Engelhard reorganizes its facilities after several acquisitions.

2000: Volvo and Nissan models incorporate Engelhard's "smog-eating" PremAir radiator technology.

2001: Orin Smith is succeeded as CEO by Barry Perry, the company's president and COO since 1997.

2003: Engelhard sets up an emissions catalysts venture in China.

2004: The company broadens its involvement with the personal care industry by acquiring The Collaborative Group of New Jersey.

2005: Engelhard acquires a controlling interest in Coletica SA, a French producer of cosmetics ingredients.

---

num fabricating. Engelhard Industries also did about $32 million in gold fabricating and $55 million in silver, making it a world leader in all three of the major precious-metals markets. Industrial applications of precious metals were on the rise, and Engelhard Industries was well positioned to profit from their growing importance. Charles Engelhard, Jr. also continued to pursue his valuable South African connections. As part of the 1957 takeover of Central Mining, Engelhard and Harry Oppenheimer had agreed to a stock swap, each of them taking 10 percent of the other's family holding company. Engelhard thus gained a very valuable piece of Ernest Oppenheimer and Sons, the force behind Anglo American Corporation and the De Beers diamond mines, while Harry Oppenheimer took a similar chunk of Engelhard Hanovia, the family-owned corporation that, in turn, controlled 72 percent of Engelhard Industries. The trade would appear to have been one-sided, as Anglo American was a much larger concern than the Engelhard interests. Over the next two decades, however, Harry Oppenheimer continued to buy stock in Engelhard Hanovia and by 1970 came to own 70 percent, at which time his investment proved to have been very wise indeed.

In the meantime, Engelhard upped his investments in South Africa. In 1958, he set up the American-South African Investment Company Ltd., with $34 million in assets. American-South African was an investment trust trading in South African gold stocks and was the first South African company listed on the New York Stock Exchange. As chairman of Rand Mines,

one of the former Central Mining companies, Engelhard greatly expanded the firm's holding into uranium, coal, and copper refining. In 1961, he paid $17 million for two gold mines owned by Kennecott Copper, rolling all of his South African holdings into a new joint investment company with the Oppenheimers called Rand Selection Corporation Limited. Engelhard had by that time become a figure of recognized importance in South African affairs, an honor that brought with it involvement in all of the moral and political difficulties besetting that country. After the Sharpeville massacre of 1960, Engelhard became more open in his criticisms of apartheid and somewhat curtailed his active investment in the country. Engelhard did not seem to bother himself with apologies or explanations of the relation between his fortune and apartheid. As a businessman and as a strong supporter and confidante of Democratic politicians, he appears to have viewed apartheid as inefficient and doomed but did not further concern himself with its injustices.

A Major Deal in 1963

In 1963, Engelhard put together the deal that would determine the future of his company. At the urging of Andre Meyer of the investment-banking house Lazard Freres, Engelhard took a 20 percent interest in Minerals & Chemicals Philipp (MCP), a recently formed partnership between a rather small producer of nonmetallic minerals such as kaolin and fuller's earth, and Philipp Brothers, a powerful trading firm specializing in the buying and selling of ores on the international market. Again, Engelhard made a stock swap an important part of the deal, giving up 8 percent of Engelhard Hanovia as partial payment for his 20 percent interest in MCP, which in 1964 had sales of $447 million, the bulk of it generated by Philipp Brothers's fast-growing ore trading. In fact, Engelhard's purchase of MCP stock soon proved prescient, as worldwide demand for precious and industrial metals began to take off, and Philipp's sales skyrocketed, gaining as much as 45 percent in a single year.

By 1966, MCP sales had reached $709 million, while Engelhard Industries did only about 40 percent of that figure. Engelhard nevertheless worked out a merger of the two companies in September 1967, creating Engelhard Minerals & Chemicals Corporation (EMCC), with the Engelhard family controlling about 40 percent of the new giant's stock. Given the relative size of the partners in this transaction, and Harry Oppenheimer's increasing role in the Engelhard family interests, it is probable that the merger was made possible by the financial power of Oppenheimer's Anglo American Corporation. EMCC was already a large corporation, but its potential was not yet apparent to many observers. Nearly one-half of the company's 1967 net income of $28 million was generated by the Philipp trading division, with the Engelhard metal processing contributing 34 percent and minerals and chemicals about 19 percent. Philipp's trading worked on a small profit margin but was soon to enjoy phenomenal growth as the world turned increasingly to spot traders to move scarce natural resources around the globe quickly and efficiently. By 1972, EMCC's sales hit $2 billion, about 80 percent of it supplied by Philipp, and in 1974 revenue reached the astonishing figure of $5 billion and climbing.

Charles Engelhard, Jr., did not live to see the success of his combination, however. When the "platinum king," as he was called, died in early 1971, his family's Engelhard Hanovia owned 43 percent of the increasingly profitable EMCC. By that time, however, 70 percent of Hanovia was controlled by Anglo American, which promptly exchanged its Hanovia shares for 30 percent of EMCC, leaving the Engelhard family with 10 percent of EMCC and all of its other interests. The friendship of Engelhard and Oppenheimer thus ended with a rough parity of gain. With the help of Oppenheimer, Engelhard had built an enormous metals combination, but when the dust settled it was Oppenheimer who would reap the long-term benefits.

In the absence of an Engelhard heir interested in business, Milton Rosenthal was appointed chairman of EMCC. Rosenthal had been president of EMCC since the 1967 merger, and after Engelhard's death inaugurated a tightening of controls and general overhaul of the company. In part, this was an inevitable concomitant of the executive change, which saw Engelhard's largely blue-blood management give way to a team dominated by Philipp Brothers's trading veterans, chief among them Ludwig Jesselson. Neither side of the merger particularly enjoyed working with the other, and when the MCP men gained control of the company, many of the Engelhard people left or were fired. Afterward, an air of hardworking sobriety settled over the firm. Rosenthal and his advisors cut back on luxuries but expanded mightily their trading business, which, soon after the 1973 oil crisis, began handling oil on the spot market. Commodities traded on the spot market, as opposed to the futures market, are for immediate delivery. From modest beginnings, the oil spot market quickly reached critical importance during the 1970s, a decade in which all natural resources seemed in short supply, and by 1978 Philipp was trading $4.5 billion in oil alone. Its $9 billion in total sales dwarfed the minerals-and-chemicals and precious-metals business of its partners, even as the latter became increasingly successful in the development of fluid catalytic cracking materials and exhaust emission control converters.

Philipp Brothers owed its success primarily to the scarcity of its commodities and the skill of its traders. By keeping tabs on the needs of both producers and consumers of over 100 kinds of raw materials, Philipp was able to buy and sell large quantities of goods for small but almost instant profits and even offered its clients the use of a company bank in Switzerland to help finance the construction of new plants or to make unusually large purchases. As the markets for raw materials became increasingly widespread, Philipp's business continued to grow at a fantastic rate, and from 1978 to 1980 EMCC's sales jumped from $10 billion to $26.5 billion, about 90 percent of which was due to Philipp. So great a disparity between former partners naturally strained corporate relations, as minerals-and-chemicals people along with those in precious metals felt overshadowed by their trading counterparts and had trouble justifying time spent managing assets that grew at so comparatively slow a rate. In the spring of 1981, therefore, the metals-and-minerals and precious-metals divisions of EMCC were transferred to an existing subsidiary, Porocel, an Arkansas bauxite producer which had been founded in 1938 and acquired in 1967. Porocel was renamed Engelhard Corporation and became a public company (the bauxite business itself would continue to operate under the Porocel name and was sold to private investors in 1996). Philipp Brothers went its way as Phibro toward an eventual merger with Salomon Inc. Harry Oppenheimer's Anglo American Corporation maintained a 30 percent stake in both Philbro and Engelhard, a double wild card waiting to be played at any time.

Engelhard Starts Anew in the 1980s

The new Engelhard Corporation set about revising its mix of sales. In 1983, for example, when the company did about $2 billion in sales, 85 percent of the sales were generated by the precious-metals business, but the much smaller minerals and chemicals division produced 60 percent of Engelhard's net income. As a result, in that year the company began referring to itself as a specialty chemicals firm and two years later regrouped its businesses according to function rather than the raw material involved. Thus, all catalytic businesses became part of the specialty-chemicals division, regardless of whether they made use of kaolin or platinum for their catalysis, while the specialty-metals division worked strictly with metals technology and metals management services. This gradual redefinition and housecleaning continued up to the 1990s, with Engelhard announcing that it would sell off some of its remaining gold and silver businesses and begin deep cuts in its salaried staff in anticipation of which the company took a special charge of $160 million in 1989.

At the end of the 1980s, Engelhard Corporation derived the lion's share of its sales from the remaining portion of its precious-metals fabrication business, $1.6 billion, but far more profitable was the catalysts-and-chemicals division, which earned $43 million on sales of $450 million in 1989. Much of that was generated by fluid catalytic cracking materials made for the petroleum industry. Even more promising was the performance of the company's third product grouping, now known as pigments and additives. This group, a descendent of the EMCC merger partner that produced paper coatings and pigments for the plastic and paint industries, along with several businesses purchased in 1988 from the Harshaw/Filtrol Partnership, netted $53 million on only $360 million in sales. It was no surprise, therefore, that despite its heritage as one of the world's premier users of precious metals, Engelhard was steadily moving toward the more lucrative fields of catalysis and specialty chemicals.

Ups and Downs in the 1990s

Throughout the 1990s, Engelhard tried to grow through acquisitions and the introduction of new products. Revenues hit a high in 1990 of $2.93 billion but would not reach that level again until 1996. Under CEO Orin Smith, in 1992 Engelhard acquired the remaining 50 percent of its German auto catalyst subsidiary, Kali-Chemie, and formed Salem Engelhard in a joint partnership with Salem Industries, a maker of pollution-control systems, as well as forming Heraeus Engelhard Electrochemistry with Heraeus Inc. and founding Acreon Catalysts with Procatalyse. In 1993, it sold off its interest in metal plating firm M&T Harshaw and in 1994 struck a deal with ICC Technologies, Inc. to develop and market air conditioning and air-treatment systems based on Engelhard's new desiccant technology, in which the use of ozone-depleting refrigerants could be avoided by drying the air before it is cooled. The same year, it also purchased the assets of Solvay Catalysts GmbH of Germany and of General Plasma, Advanced Plasma, and Jet-Com, manufacturers of thermal spray coatings for emissions-control applications which Engelhard intended to develop into a major line of emission systems technology products for cars, trucks, and buses. As part of a major reorganization plan, in 1994 Engelhard closed, relocated, or consolidated five of its U.S. facilities and two European sites.

In 1995, Engelhard formed a joint venture named Metreon with W.R. Grace to develop advanced metallic-substrate catalytic converters for the auto industry, purchased the rest of its Salem Engelhard joint venture, expanded the production capacity of its Acreon venture, and established a joint venture with CLAL, a French precious metal fabricator. It also expanded from its historical participation in the precious metals brokerage industry by entering base metals dealing and brokering through a new subsidiary, Engelhard International Ltd., and founded Engelhard Power Marketing to resell electric power to U.S. utilities. In 1996, it formed Engelhard-Highland to produce high-performance color pigments in India, entered into a joint venture with its Japanese affiliate N.E. Chemcat to manufacture auto catalysts in Thailand for sale throughout Southeast Asia, and acquired the assets of infrared gas sensor manufacturer Telaire Systems, which it renamed Engelhard Sensor Technologies. In May 1996, it made its largest acquisition ever by acquiring Mearl Corporation, a maker of pearlescent pigments and iridescent film for the automotive and cosmetic industries, for $272.7 million.

Engelhard's major product launches in the 1990s included a "molecular sieve" water filter capable of significantly reducing contamination of household tap water, an auto emissions-control device that traps polluting hydrocarbons during the two minutes after engine startup in which the catalytic converter is ineffective, a new trimetal catalyst technology named Trimax, a new catalyst for the heavy feedstocks demanded by Pacific Rim refineries, and an all-palladium auto catalyst that could be placed closer to the engine and activated more quickly. Perhaps its most promising innovation, however, was Prem-Air, a catalytic filter that when coated on a car's radiator promised to destroy 90 percent of the ozone passing over it. However, after testing the product on 20 of its cars, Ford Motor decided that Prem-Air was not as effective as advertised and decided not to adopt it. Despite this blow, Engelhard continued to refine the product for other uses and positioned itself to become not only a supplier of auto emission catalysts but of "total solutions," including sensors, multi-component packages, and catalyst substrates.

In 1996, Engelhard enjoyed its sixth consecutive year of record earnings and looked hopefully to emerging catalytics and pigments demand in Eastern Europe and the Pacific Rim. By the mid-1990s, 41 percent of Engelhard's sales were outside the United States, and its engineered materials and commodities dealing operation was accounting for 60 percent of its revenues. The manufacture of catalysts/chemicals and pigments/additives together accounted for the remainder.

Engelhard furthered its operations in India in 1997, forming a joint venture to produce catalytic converters for the booming automotive market there. Its partner was UCAL Fuel Systems Ltd.

In 1998, Engelhard paid $210 million to acquire Catalyst Resources from Mallinckrodt Inc. Catalyst Resources was a $100 million a year business producing catalysts used in manufacturing polypropylene. Engelhard sold off its half interest in Paris-based Procatalyse in November of the year.

In 1999, one of Engelhard's main shareholders, Minorco of Luxembourg, divested its 31.8 percent stake in Engelhard. Minorco was seeking to be acquired by Anglo American, which was reportedly not interested in owning shares in an American,

non-mining company such as Engelhard. As a result of this sale, Engelhard bought back 18 million of its shares for $340 million, offering the other 28 million to the public.

Engelhard's "smog-eating" radiator technology was revived for the 2000 model year, when Volvo and Nissan used it in some models. At $50 each, this version of the PremAir system was now one-tenth the cost for which it sold in 1995, thanks to the substitution of a cheaper catalytic agent than platinum, reported the *New York Times*.

New CEO in 2001

In January 2001, longtime CEO Orin Smith was succeeded by Barry Perry, the company's president and COO since 1997. Perry was a 22-year veteran of General Electric Co. His main focus was distributing technologies across the company's four operating groups: Environmental Technologies; Process Technologies; Appearance and Performance Technologies (created from the former Paper Pigments and Specialty Pigments and Additives groups); and Materials Services. Perry also steered the groups into working to further corporate, rather than divisional, aims.

The core of Engelhard's involvement in the dozens of industries it served was its expertise in surface and materials science, chemically or mechanically engineering ingredients to give them new properties. The company also had knowledge in platinum group metals chemistry. The same tools found applications in a range of areas from emissions controls to cosmetics pigments.

Emissions technologies from the automotive industry were beginning to appear in leaf blowers and the like. Engelhard was even researching the environmental impact of hair dryers. Involvement in a wide variety of industries cushioned the company against market cycles. Looking to the future, it was developing several different aspects of fuel cell technology through partnerships with a dozen different companies.

Also in 2001, Engelhard scaled back its kaolin operations in Georgia, cutting about 20 percent of the 1,100-strong workforce. In 2003, it purchased the Chinese kaolin producer Shouzho Anpeak Kaolin Co. Ltd.

Engelhard was also poised to benefit from the progression of automotive air quality standards to developing countries such as China and the Philippines. Anticipating growth in the Asian auto industry, Engelhard set up an emissions catalysts venture in China in late 2003.

The company broadened its involvement with the personal care industry by acquiring The Collaborative Group of New Jersey in July 2004. Collaborative made liposome ingredients for skincare products. Revenues exceeded $4 billion in 2004.

In 2005, Engelhard acquired a controlling interest in Coletica SA, a French producer of cosmetics ingredients. It was also buying a Chinese synthesis catalyst business.

Principal Subsidiaries

Corporacion Engelhard De Venezuela, C.A.; CTN Assurance Company; EC Delaware Incorporated; ECT Environmental Technologies AB (Sweden); Engelhard (BVI) Corporation; Engelhard (Shanghai) Co. Ltd. (China); Engelhard Asia Pacific (China) Ltd.; Engelhard Asia Pacific (Korea) Ltd.; Engelhard Asia Pacific India Private Ltd.; Engelhard Asia Pacific Mauritius Ltd.; Engelhard Belgium BVBA; Engelhard C Cubed Corporation; Engelhard Canada, ULC; Engelhard Catalyst Center-Tarragona, S.L. (Spain); Engelhard Chemcat (Thailand) Ltd.; Engelhard De Meern, B.V. (Netherlands); Engelhard Do Brasil Industria E Commercio LTDA (Brazil); Engelhard DT, Inc.; Engelhard EM Holding Company; Engelhard Energy Corporation; Engelhard Environmental Systems India Ltd; Engelhard Equity Corporation; Engelhard Europe Finance Ltd. (United Kingdom); Engelhard European Holdings Ltd. (United Kingdom); Engelhard Export Corporation (U.S. Virgin Islands); Engelhard Financial Corporation; Engelhard France SARL; Engelhard Hexcore, L.P.; Engelhard Holdings GmbH (Germany); Engelhard International Holdings Company (Cayman Islands); Engelhard International, Ltd. (United Kingdom); Engelhard Investment Europe B.V. (Netherlands); Engelhard Italiana S.P.A. (Italy); Engelhard Limited (United Kingdom); Engelhard Luxembourg Sarl; Engelhard Metals A.G. (Switzerland); Engelhard Metals Holding Corporation; Engelhard Metals Japan, Ltd.; Engelhard Mexicana S.A. de C.V. (Mexico); Engelhard Netherlands, B.V.; Engelhard Pension Trustees Limited (United Kingdom); Engelhard Performance Technologies (Shanxi) Co., Ltd. (China); Engelhard Peru S.A.; Engelhard Pigments and Additives Europe, B.V. (Netherlands); Engelhard Pigments OY (Finland); Engelhard PM, L.P.; Engelhard Pollution Control, Inc.; Engelhard Power Marketing, Inc.; Engelhard Process Chemicals GmbH (Germany); Engelhard S.A. (France); Engelhard Sales, Ltd. (United Kingdom); Engelhard South Africa Proprietary, Ltd.; Engelhard Srl (Italy); Engelhard Strategic Investments Incorporated; Engelhard Supply Corporation; Engelhard Technologies GmbH (Germany); Engelhard Technologies, Ltd. (United Kingdom); Engelhard Terneuzen, B.V. (Netherlands); Engelhard Trustee Co. Ltd. (United Kingdom); Engelhard West, Inc.; H. Drijfhout & Zoon's Edelmetaalbedrijen B.V. (Netherlands); Harshaw Chemical Company; Heesung-Engelhard (South Korea); Mearl, LLC; Mustang Property Corporation; NE Chemcat Corporation; Prodrive-Engelhard, LLC; The Sheffield Smelting Co., Ltd. (United Kingdom).

Principal Divisions

Environmental Technologies; Process Technologies; Appearance and Performance Technologies; Materials Services.

Principal Competitors

BASF AG; Heraeus Holding GmbH; Johnson Matthey Plc; W.R. Grace & Co.

Further Reading

Baldo, Anthony, "Engelhard's Renewed Lease on Life," *Treasury & Risk Management*, April 1999, pp. 28–32.

"Carwash," *Economist*, July 8, 1995, p. 78.

"The Engelhard Touch," *Forbes*, August 1, 1965.

Flannery, William, "Mallinckrodt Says It's Selling Catalyst Business to Engelhard," *St. Louis Post-Dispatch*, February 25, 1998, p. C9.

"Getting Cold Cars to Clean Up Their Act," *BusinessWeek*, November 29, 1993.

Hall, Alan, "A Roving Ambassador for Clean Technology," *BusinessWeek*, May 1, 2000.

Herzlich, Jamie, "New Jersey's Engelhard Corp. Buys Stony Brook, N.Y., Bioscience Firm," *Newsday*, July 31, 2004.

Jusko, Jill and Patrick Hernan, "Looking for Trouble," *Industry Week*, April 2002, pp. 15ff.

Kutler, Jeffrey, "Mettle Detector: This Prosaic-Seeming Chemicals and Metals Maker Is into Some Cutting-Edge Technology. But the CEO Is Not Going to Boast About It Until the Engineering Proves Out. (Barry Perry Of Engelhard Corp.)," *Institutional Investor*, October 2003, pp. 22f.

McKay, David, "Minorco Sheds Engelhard Ahead of Anglo Merger," *Business Day* (South Africa), March 3, 1999, p. 17.

McKay, Martha, "New Jersey Chemical Company Engelhard Stresses Commitment to Stock Buyback," *Home News Tribune* (New Jersey), May 7, 1999.

Marcial, Gene, "A Scorching Play on Cool Air," *BusinessWeek,* July 11, 1994.

Motavalli, Jim, "Carmakers to Put 'Smog-Eating' Radiator in Some Models," *New York Times*, Autos on Friday/Technology Sec., January 14, 2000.

Mullin, Rick, "Perry's Antifederalist Manifesto," *Chemical Specialties*, May 2001, p. 40.

Reisch, Marc S., "Precious Mettle," *Chemical & Engineering News*, November 15, 2004, pp. 24f.

Seewald, Nancy, "Engelhard Sees R&D As Catalyst to Success," *Chemical Week*, November 10, 2004, pp. 27f.

Taninecz, George, "Perry's All Four One: Engelhard Corp.'s Chairman and CEO Is Assembling Four Operating Units into a Seamless, Yet Diversified Organization," *Industry Week*, August 2002, pp. 43ff.

Velshi, Ali, Pat Kiernan, and Greg Clarkin, "Stock of the Day: Engelhard," CNNfn, *CEOWire*, January 14, 2004.

—Jonathan Martin
—updates: Paul S. Bodine; Frederick C. Ingram

Eschelon Telecom, Inc.

730 2nd Avenue South, Suite 1200
Minneapolis, Minnesota 55402
U.S.A.
Telephone: (612) 376-4400
Fax: (612) 376-4411
Web site: http://www.eschelon.com

Private Company
Incorporated: 1996 as Advanced Telecommunications, Inc.
Employees: 890
Sales: $141 million (2003)
NAIC: 517110 Wired Telecommunications Carriers;
517910 Other Telecommunications; 518210 Data
Processing, Hosting and Related Services; 519190 All
Other Information Services; 561420 Telephone Call
Carriers

Eschelon Telecom, Inc., is a rapidly growing provider of integrated voice, data, and Internet services. Headquartered in Minneapolis, Minnesota, the company offers small and medium-sized businesses a comprehensive range of telecommunications and Internet products, including local lines, long distance, business telephone systems, DSL, Dedicated T-1 access, network solutions, and Web hosting. With almost 900 telecommunications and Internet professionals, Eschelon operates more than 210,000 access lines in service throughout its markets in the Midwest and the Western United States.

Origins

The company that would become known as Eschelon Telecom, Inc. was founded in 1996 as Advanced Telecommunications, Inc. by Clifford D. Williams, a long time executive in the cable television and communications industries. From 1971 to 1991, Williams served in various senior executive positions at Rogers Communications Inc., a cable television company. From 1992 to 1995, he was president and chief executive officer of Enhanced Telemanagement Incorporated, an integrated communications company that provided a full range of services and products to small businesses in Minnesota, Washington, Ore-

gon, Illinois, and Ohio. Eager to start his own communications venture and capitalize on the burgeoning telecommunications market, Williams raised enough venture capital to form Advanced Telecommunications, Inc. (ATI) as a holding and management services company for telecommunications-related enterprises. With venture capital funding, he moved quickly to make a series of acquisitions of small telecommunications firms, including Cady Communications of Plymouth, Minnesota, in 1996, and American Telephone Technology, Inc. of Seattle, Washington, and American Telephone Technology, Inc. of Portland, Oregon, and Electro-Tel, Inc. of Denver, Colorado in 1997. Like many small telecommunications firms of the time, Williams believed the acquisitions had tremendous potential but needed infusions of capital and management expertise to maximize growth and enter new industry segments.

Growth Through Acquisitions in the Late 1990s

In 1998, Williams acquired One Call Telecom, Inc., a competitive local exchange carrier serving the Minneapolis/St. Paul market. The company was merged with Cady Communications, ATI's existing local exchange subsidiary serving the Twin Cities to position it as the leading provider of integrated telecommunications services in the Minneapolis/St. Paul market. In the same year, ATI acquired Seattle-based Tele-Contracting Services, Inc., merging it with American Telephone Technology, its subsidiary serving the Seattle and Portland markets. The combined company made it the Pacific Northwest's leading provider of integrated telecommunications services, including key systems, PBX systems, local dial tone, long-distance, WAN/LAN equipment and services, and other data and voice transmission products and services. In 1999, ATI also acquired Infinite Voice Mail of Boulder, Colorado, and Intellecom, Inc of Reno, Nevada. With these acquisitions, ATI was well underway in establishing a national presence in the western United States as a reseller of U.S. West and Sprint local and long-distance lines and a provider of Internet and digital subscriber lines to small to medium-sized businesses. In 1998, ATI had 330 employees and $29 million in sales.

In November 1999, ATI landed $45.6 million in venture capital with a promise of $30 million more to come from a consortium that included Boston-based Bain Capital, J.P. Mor-

---

Company Perspectives:

Our mission is to be a premiere telecommunications enterprise by delivering superior products and services to our customers, valuing and respecting our employees, and providing outstanding returns to our shareholders.

---

gan & Cos. in New York, and Stolberg Equity Partners in Denver. The funding was the largest single venture capital investment in the state of Minnesota in five years. For ATI, the investment was part of $140 million in debt and equity financing raised by the company in the third quarter of 1999. The funds were earmarked for building the company's sales force, installing large switching platforms in existing markets, and gaining ATI a foothold in new markets. With operations in Seattle, Denver, Reno, and Portland, ATI planned on expanding into Salt Lake City and Phoenix the following year. The sizeable investment in ATI mirrored the red hot investment interest in telecommunications firms, which in 1999 received fully 30 percent of all venture dollars nationwide.

A Name Change and Continued Expansion

In April 2000, ATI announced that it was changing its name to Eschelon Telecom, Inc. to unify the growing firm's integrated telecommunications operating units under one name. The rapidly growing and privately held company also said the name change was important to reduce confusion among regulators, vendors, customers, and the financial community. In the same month, the company expanded its full range telecommunications services to small and medium-sized businesses in Phoenix, Arizona with plans to expand into many other cities by the end of 2001. In order to finance its multi-city expansion, in April Eschelon filed for an initial public offering (IPO) of $172.5 million in common shares but delayed the offering due to the shaky stock market. The company's expansion plans nevertheless received a boost by new quality of service guarantees from US West concerning the installation, repair, and billing of the leased US West phone lines used by Eschelon to provide customer service. In return for these guarantees, Eschelon agreed to drop a filing with the Minnesota Public Utilities Commission opposing the pending acquisition of US West by long-distance provider Qwest Communications.

In May 2000, Eschelon completed a $135 million senior secured debt facility to help fund expansion of its integrated voice and data services network in Minnesota, Washington, Oregon, Utah, Arizona, Nevada, Idaho, Colorado, Montana, New Mexico, Nebraska, and North Dakota. The financing was led by GE Capital Corporation, FleetBoston Financial, and Fistar Bank. In August, the company landed another $35 million in venture capital to pay for switching equipment in Albuquerque, New Mexico; Boise, Idaho; and Reno, Nevada. With this venture funding, Eschelon aimed to become more facilities based as an operator of its own telephone switching equipment and some of the lines used to provide service, which was more profitable than leasing and reselling lines from the major telephone carriers.

In August 2001, Eschelon appointed Richard A. Smith, the company's president and chief operating officer, to its Board of Directors. Smith joined the company in 1998 as its executive vice-president and chief financial officer. He was promoted to president and chief operating officer in March 2000, signaling a vote of confidence in his abilities to lead the company's transformation to become a facilities-based telecommunications firm. Under Smith's direction, Eschelon had raised more than $260 million in private equity and debt financing while overseeing a 50 percent growth rate over the previous two years.

Eschelon Weathers the Telecom Bust

Despite this success, in November the company withdrew its $172.5 million IPO due to worsening conditions in the stock market. Until the stock market improved, the company planned to rely on the private financing markets in which it was having success in contrast to the public markets where the stocks of once high-flying telecom companies had collapsed more than 75 percent. In the past few months, Eschelon had raised approximately $50 million in funding from several sources. The most recent investment of $5 million came from Bermuda-based Global Crossing. The investment stemmed from a larger agreement providing for Eschelon to purchase $100 million in long-distance services over ten years from Global Crossing, which was then building an international fiber network. The deal followed other private agreements with Nortel Networks Corp. providing $10 million and another $35 million in equity investments from Windpoint Partners of Chicago and Bain Capital of Boston. Eschelon also signed an agreement in November 2000 with Qwest Communications International providing Qwest $150 million in revenue over five years in exchange for favorable resale rates for using Qwest's network. With the downturn in the markets and the pulling of its IPO, the agreement would allow Eschelon to more profitably sell Qwest's telephone network services at a time when it could not rapidly expand into a facilities-based telecommunications form.

Nevertheless, Eschelon continued to pursue growth through strategic acquisitions. As a result, in February 2001, as part of its multi-city expansion efforts, Eschelon acquired Rocky Mountain Telephone Company of Salt Lake City, a provider and installer of office telecommunications systems with $2 million in annual revenues. The deal came as the company continued its success in raising private capital, boosting its debt financing by $10 million and looking to raise another $50 million in equity investments by the spring. Eschelon's strategy was to have a company in each of the cities in which it was selling business-telephone services. At the same time, with the severe economic downturn that began in spring 2000 forcing Eschelon to curb its expansion plans, the company pursued a conservative build out of facilities that would leave it less vulnerable to capital markets. As a result, the company began focusing on selling to more businesses in the markets in which they had existing voice and data switching facilities. With this strategy, buying local telecom firms with an established customer base was a natural tactic to penetrate new markets.

In April 2002, Eschelon's agreement with Qwest Communications giving it a discount on services in return for dropping opposition to Qwest's purchase of US West, Inc., came under regulatory scrutiny. This was the result of regulators in several states investigating Qwest for striking secret deals with competitors who agreed not to oppose its efforts to expand its long-

Key Dates:

1996: Clifford D. Williams founds Advanced Telecommunications, Inc.; the company acquires Cady Communications of Minneapolis/St. Paul, Minnesota.
1997: The company acquires American Telephone Technology, Inc. of Seattle, Washington, and Electro-Tel, Inc. of Denver, Colorado.
1998: One Call Telecom of Minneapolis/St. Paul, Minnesota, and Tele-Contracting Specialists, Inc. of Seattle, Washington, are acquired.
1999: The company acquires Infinite Voice Mail of Boulder, Colorado.
2000: Fishnet.com of Minneapolis/St. Paul, Minnesota, is acquired.
2001: The company acquires Rocky Mountain Telephone Company of Salt Lake City, Utah.

distance business. The primary thrust of the investigations was whether and to what extent Qwest had tried to buy the silence of competitors in the beleaguered telecommunications industry. Because Qwest did not publicize the contracts, it allegedly prevented rivals from getting equal treatment. Eschelon's attorney said parts of the company's agreement should have been disclosed by Qwest to regulators, but the agreement never worked out as hoped. In addition to favorable resale rates, the agreement provided for a meeting between Eschelon executives and Qwest Chief Executive Officer Joseph P. Nacchio if problems arose with using Qwest's network. When Eschelon ran into difficulties getting Qwest to provide data it needed, the company requested the meeting to resolve the issue but was rebuffed.

In July 2002, in the midst of the brutal telecom downturn, Eschelon successfully raised an additional $35 million in new capital. Despite the grim state of the private and public equity markets, the new deal partnered the company's three largest stakeholders—Bain Capital, Stolberg Partners, and Windpoint Ventures—with un unidentified university pension fund as a first-time investor. The agreement was premised on a major restructuring of the company's debt load. In the restructuring, some of the participating banks had their positions in the company bought out, while others converted their loans into equity. As a result, the banks assumed a 13 percent equity stake in the company and reduced Eschelon's total debt load from approximately $139 million to $59 million. The investment community viewed Eschelon's ability to secure funding as impressive in an industry in which the vast majority of telecom companies, including such major players as NorthPoint communications, Covad Communications Group, Inc., Rhythms NetConnections, and ExciteAtHome all had sought bankruptcy protection. With many telecom companies going out of business, investors held out hope that Eschelon would survive the attrition among competitors, gain market share, and be well positioned to reach profitability in 2004.

Eschelon Positions Itself for Future Growth

In September 2003, Eschelon achieved its first month of free cash flow, one of the few Competitive Local Exchange Carriers

(CLECs) to reach this financial milestone. The achievement meant the company was generating more cash from operations than it was expending to fund operating costs, capital spending, working capital, and debt obligations. At a time when other telecom firms had been filing for bankruptcy, downsizing, or cutting back on their future capital plans, Eschelon had continued to invest in systems and capabilities to expand its services and customer base. The company announced another milestone in December when it crossed the 200,000 mark for access lines in service, a doubling of its capacity in two years. As a result of this expansion, Eschelon became the number one CLEC in terms of market share in the twelve markets it served.

Eschelon moved into 2004 with strong first quarter results, reporting revenues of $38.2 million, an increase of $6.3 million from the first quarter of 2003. With the worst of the telecom downturn behind it, Eschelon's prospects looked increasingly promising. In October 2004, Eschelon announced it was acquiring Advanced Telecom Inc. (ATI), an independent Santa Rosa, California, company born during the telecom boom of the late 1990s, from General Electric Corp. for $45.5 million in cash. Eschelon's offer for ATI came as an unsolicited bid which marked its continuing strategy to grow through acquisitions and would enable it to enter the California market. ATI was founded in 1999 as Advanced TelCom Group in Santa Rosa during the rapid expansion of the telecommunications industry fueled by the deregulation of the telephone industry. The company, which primarily served business and government institutions, went bankrupt in 2002 with debts of $208 million and was purchased by General Electric Capital in bankruptcy court for $9.5 million. Eschelon saw value in acquiring ATI because of its 18,000 customers in California, Nevada, Oregon, and Washington utilizing 116,000 access lines. With the acquisition, Eschelon gained a leading market position among CLECs in the Pacific Northwest with revenues more than $215 million and over 350,000 access lines in service. After completing the acquisition in January 2005, Eschelon president and CEO Richard A. Smith said the combined companies would create the premier super-regional CLEC operating in key states in the western part of the country and would position the company for future growth.

Principal Competitors

Qwest; SBC Communications.

Further Reading

"Advanced Telecommunications, Inc. Announces New Name; Name Change Unites Rapidly-Growing Integrated Communications Provider," *PR Newswire*, April 18, 2000.
"Advanced Telecommunications, Inc. Announces Acquisition of One Call Telecom, Inc.," *PR Newswire*, July 6, 1998.
"Advanced Telecommunications, Inc. Announces Acquisition of Tele-Contracting Specialists, Inc.," *PR Newswire*, July 23, 1998.
Alexander, Steve, "Eschelon Lands $35 million Venture Capital," *Star Tribune*, August 1, 2000.
——, "Eschelon, Qwest Sign Network Deal Worth About $150 Million in Revenue," *Star Tribune*, November 17, 2000.
Carlsen, Clifford, "Eschelon Lands $35 M," *Daily Deal*, July 2, 2002.
"Eschelon Telecom, Inc. Achieves Milestone, Exceeds 200,000 Access Lines," *Business Wire*, December 1, 2003.
"Eschelon Telecom, Inc. Announces Acquisition of Rocky Mountain Telephone Company," *Business Wire*, February 14, 2001.

"Eschelon Telecom, Inc. Announces Completion of $135 million Senior Secured Debt Facility to Accelerate Market Expansion Plans," *PR* Newswire, May 31, 2000.

"Eschelon Telecom, Inc. Announces Expansion into Phoenix, Arizona," *PR Newswire*, April 21, 2000.

"Eschelon Telecom, Inc. Announces First Quarter 2004 Operating Results," *Business Wire*, April 21, 2004.

"Eschelon Telecom, Inc. Board of Directors Announce Appointment of New Board Member," *PR Newswire*, August 21, 2000.

"Eschelon Telecom, Inc. Becomes Free Cash Flow Positive," *Business Wire*, October 6, 2003.

Feyder, Susan, "State Venture Capital Again Reaches Record of $142.7 million Quarterly Total, 30 Percent Is ATI's," *Star Tribune*, November 12, 1999.

Katz-Stone, Adam, "Money Changes Everything," *CityBusiness*, June 9, 2000.

Norberg, Bob, "Eschelon to Buy Advanced Telecom; Minneapolis Firm to Pay $45.5 Million for Company," *Press Democrat*, October 21, 2004.

Reilly, Mark, "Eschelon Pulls $172 M IPO, Cites Market," *CityBusiness*, November 10, 2000.

Soloman, Deborah, "States Probe Qwest Deals to Expand Long-Distance Service," *Wall Street Journal*, April 29, 2002, A 1.

Williams, Cliff, "Advanced Telecommunications Inc. Announces Acquisition," *PR Newswire*, December 30, 1997.

—Bruce Montgomery

Ezaki Glico Company Ltd.

4-6-5 Utajima, Nishi-Yodogawaku
Osaka
555-8502
Japan
Telephone: (+81) 6 6477 8352
Fax: (+81) 6 6477 5670
Web site: http://www.glico.co.jp

Public Company
Incorporated: 1922
Employees: 4,315
Sales: ($2.53 billion) (2004)
Stock Exchanges: Tokyo
Ticker Symbol: 2206
NAIC: 311330 Confectionery Manufacturing from
     Purchased Chocolate; 311320 Chocolate and
     Confectionery Manufacturing from Cacao Beans;
     311423 Dried and Dehydrated Food Manufacturing;
     311520 Ice Cream and Frozen Dessert Manufacturing

Ezaki Glico Company Ltd. is one of Japan's leading manufacturers of confectionery products and other foods. The company's biggest-selling brands are its stick-like Pocky and Pretz lines, which feature chocolate covered cookies and pretzels, respectively, in a variety of flavors. The brands, especially Pocky, are also the group's biggest international sellers. (Pocky is known as Mikado for markets in the West.) Ezaki Glico is also a major producer of ice cream for the Japanese market, as well as other dairy products, including Putching Pudding. The declining Japanese market for candy and sweets in general has led Ezaki Glico to boost its food operations elsewhere. Thus, the company produces toddlers' food and ready-to-eat foods such as Chinese-style dumplings and mild curries. Another area of company development in the early 2000s has been the fast-growing health food and supplement market. The company's products include its Power Production CCD drink, which contains the company-developed and patented ingredient "cluster dextrin." Ezaki Glico has also entered the market for formula, acquiring Icreo Co. Ltd. in 2001. The company has long bene-fited from a knack for innovation and a commitment to research and development. For example, its original candy was derived from oysters, and in 2005 the company unveiled a method for transforming wood cellulose into compounds digestible by human beings and other animals. Listed on the Tokyo Stock Exchange, Ezaki Glico remains guided by the founding Ezaki family, including president and CEO Katsuhisa Ezaki. In 2004, the company posted sales of $2.53 billion.

Oyster-Inspired Treats in the 1920s

Ezaki Glico was founded by Riichi Ezaki in 1922 in order to produce caramels containing glycogen, a substance found in oysters. Ezaki had come across glycogen on a trip to the seashore earlier in the century, following the death of one of his sons. In a fishing village, Ezaki had noticed a group of children playing and had been impressed by how healthy they were. He determined that their diet was a probable contributor to their good health, especially their consumption of oysters containing glycogen.

Ezaki began experimenting with means of extracting glycogen for use in other foods, particularly in confectionery, in order to improve the health of other Japanese children. By 1921, Ezaki had launched initial production of his first sweet, a caramel containing glycogen named "Glico." Ezaki also established a company, originally called Ezaki Shoten, in Osaka, and began construction of its first factory, known as the Horie Plant.

By 1922, Ezaki was ready to go into business with its Glico candy, beginning sales of its product at a department store in Osaka, thereby officially launching the Ezaki Glico company. Glico quickly became popular, and by 1925 the company was forced to expand its production capacity, moving manufacturing to a new facility in Toyosaki.

Ezaki Glico proved itself an innovator on other fronts as well. The company early on adopted a successful publicity campaign, "300 Meters on a Single Piece," featuring the Glico Running Man. The implication was that a single piece of Glico candy provided enough energy to run a 300-meter race.

The company nonetheless faced stiff competition from two other fast-rising confectionery groups, Morinaga, the company

Company Perspectives:

The Philosophy of Glico: A WHOLESOME LIFE IN THE BEST OF TASTE. Be inspired by tastefulness! Provide delight through wholesomeness! Glory in the resplendence of life! At Glico, we are inspired to contribute to a tastefully wholesome delight in the resplendence of human life. The Glico Spirit: Taking full pleasure in innovation. Let us boldly undertake all actions through that which is interesting, that which is fresh, that which is delightful, that which is excellent and that which challenges ingenuity. We will experience the thrill of the positive. Even more, everyone will experience the thrill of the positive.

that had introduced caramels to Japan in 1914, and Meiji. Ezaki sought a means to set itself apart from its competitors. Ezaki came up with a new innovation based on the reasoning that "both nourishment and playtime activity are essential to a wholesome childhood." In 1927, Ezaki Glico became the first Japanese confectionery company to offer free toys (omake) along with its Glico candies. The operations proved an instant success, securing Ezaki Glico a place among Japan's confectionery leaders.

Glico sought other means of attracting customers. In 1931, for example, the company developed a vending machine with a built-in projector that proved highly popular among department store shoppers. In 1933, the company developed a new type of "mini" advertisement, featuring a short, easily retained message. In 1935, the company unveiled a giant 35-meter neon sign that became an Osaka landmark.

The rising sales of Glico caramels caused the company to expand its production again, moving to a new Osaka facility in 1931. Japan's domination of China in the 1930s also led the company to open a plant in Dalian in 1932 and to begin marketing its products in China and elsewhere in Southeast Asia. Continued growth of Glico sales at home led the company to open a second production facility in Tokyo in order to supply that market directly. In the meantime, the company had developed a second popular product line, the Bisco yeast-based cookie, produced using an innovative method developed by Ezaki Glico itself.

Struggles and Successes: 1940s–70s

Both the Osaka and Tokyo plants were destroyed during World War II. The company also lost control of its Chinese operations during this time and was forced to continue production at temporary facilities. It was not able to rebuild its main facilities and return to full-scale production until 1951. The following year, Ezaki Glico received government approval to market both the Glico caramel and the Bisco cookies as nutritional products. The company also continued seeking means of extending its product line, resulting in the launch of a Almond Glico, the first confectionery item in Japan to include almonds as an ingredient.

In 1956, Ezaki Glico created two new subsidiaries, Glico Dairy Products and Glico Foods, in order to extend its operations into the greater food production industry. The company

then began making ice cream, becoming one of Japan's major producers in this sector, particularly following the launch of the Glico Cone in 1963. In the meantime, Glico Foods oversaw the development of a new type of curry, launched in 1960 as "One-touch Curry". This followed the successful launch of another confectionery product, Almond Chocolate, in 1958.

The introduction of what was perhaps the company's greatest success came in the mid-1960s. In 1963, the company launched its first snack product, Butter Pretz, a flavored pretzel stick. This was followed two years later by the launch of the hugely popular Pocky Chocolate, a chocolate-covered, stick-shaped cookie product. The name for the product purportedly came from the Japanese rendering of the sound ("pokki") made when the sticks were broken.

Pocky, followed by Pretz, not only became the company's major products in Japan but also became Ezaki Glico's flagships for international growth. In 1970, the company moved to expand its presence in Southeast Asia, launching a new subsidiary, Thai Glico Co. Ltd. That company began producing and marketing both Pocky and Pretz for the Thai market, as well as supplying neighboring markets.

The success of these products in Southeast Asia led the company to begin testing them in the European market as well. After a series of encouraging trials, the company launched General Biscuit Glico France, a production joint venture located in Bordeaux. Instead of retaining the Pocky name, however, the company adopted a new designation for its flagship product, Mikado, so called because of the product's resemblance to the sticks used in the popular game. Sales of Mikado quickly spread beyond France, becoming the most successful Japanese confectionery ever to be introduced in Europe.

Diversification and Expansion: 1980s to the Mid-2000s

The early 1980s were marred by a series of crimes directed against Ezaki Glico and other Japanese confectioners. The crime wave began in 1984, when a gang calling itself the Phantom with 21 Faces kidnaped then Ezaki Glico president Katsuhisa Ezakia and demanded a ransom of ¥1 billion and 100 kilograms of gold bullion. While Ezaki managed to escape three days later, the crime wave continued, and the company's headquarters were firebombed as the gang continued to press its demands for money.

The country's other confectionery companies also fell victim to the attacks. These included the lacing of a number of chocolates with cyanide, which caused a national panic and forced a number of confectioners, including Morinaga, to withdraw all of their products from store shelves. By 1985, however, the crime wave ended when the gang suddenly declared that it would not engage in further attacks. The perpetrators of the crimes were never caught, and their identity remained a mystery.

Ezaki Glico continued to roll out new products during the 1980s, including the release of a high-quality ice cream, the Excellent brand, in 1985, the rock candy Ice no Mi in 1986, and KissMint Gum in 1987. The company had also begun to take steps to lessen its reliance on the confectionery market. In 1986,

Key Dates:

1922: Riichi Ezaki founds Ezaki Shoten in Osaka in order to produce caramels containing glycogen, extracted from oysters; the candies, and later the company itself, were called Glico.

1932: The company opens a production subsidiary in Dalian, China.

1933: The popular Bisco cookie is launched.

1945: The company's production facilities in Osaka and Tokyo are destroyed by bombing raids during World War II.

1951: Ezaki Glico rebuilds the company's main facilities in Osaka and Tokyo and returns to full-scale production.

1956: Glico Dairy Products and Glico Foods are launched in order to extend the company's interests into dairy products and foods production.

1963: The first stick-type snack food, Butter Pretz, is introduced.

1965: The highly successful Pocky snack is launched.

1970: The company opens a production and sales subsidiary in Thailand to market products to Southeast Asia.

1982: The company enters into a production joint venture in France in order to introduce Pocky—renamed as Mikado—to the European market.

1984: Katsuhisa Ezakia is kidnapped by the Phantom with 21 Faces gang.

1986: The company opens a biotechnology research and development center.

1995: The company reenters China with the creation of Shanghai Glico Foods Co.

2001: The formula producer Icreo Co. is acquired as part of a diversification effort.

2003: The company enters North America with the creation of Ezaki Glico USA Corp. in California.

2005: The development of a process to transform wood cellulose into edible amylose is announced.

Ezaki Glico opened a new Biotechnology Research Laboratory in order to conduct research into the development of new foods and food additives. In addition, the company began developing new pouch foods, including the Lee line of beef curries, launched in 1986, and the Donburi retort pouch rice, introduced in 1989. Another popular company-developed food product came in 1995 with the launch of the Juku line of mild curries.

Ezaki Glico returned to China in 1995, establishing a new production and marketing subsidiary, Shanghai Glico Foods Co., in order to introduce its products into the vast and fast-growing market there. The company also expanded into the North American market. This effort culminated in 2003 with the creation of a dedicated U.S. subsidiary, Ezaki Glico USA Corporation, in California.

The turn of the 21st century presented a new series of challenges for the company, as confectionery consumption in its core Japanese market continued to decline. In response, Ezaki Glico began a drive to diversify its product offerings. As part of that effort, the company acquired Japanese formula producer Icreo Co. in 2001. The company also entered the market for food and cosmetics additives and the growing market for healthful foods.

Ezaki Glico's research and development branch played an important role in this development. In the early 2000s, the company introduced its patented additive "cluster dextrin," an energy-giving substance which it began marketing as an ingredient in its new Power Production CCD drink. The company also debuted Alpha-Arbutin, an agent prove to be effective for skin-whitening applications. Ezaki's tradition for innovation continued into 2005 as the company announced that it had developed a process to transform wood cellulose, which was normally indigestible by human beings and most animals, into amylose, a substance that can be broken down by human and animal digestive tracts. The discovery opened the possibility of one day deriving food from wood, a fitting future for a company that began by transforming oysters into candy.

Principal Subsidiaries

Ezaki Glico USA Corporation; Generale Biscuit Glico France S.A. (France); Glico Dairy Products Co., Ltd.; Glico Foods Co., Ltd; Icreo Co., Ltd.; Shanghai Glico Foods Co., Ltd (China); Thai Glico Co., Ltd. (Thailand).

Principal Competitors

Morinaga & Co., Ltd.; Central Group of Cos.; Meiji Seika Kaisha Ltd.; Taiwan Sugar Corp.; Tiger Brands Ltd.; Ezaki Glico Company Ltd.; Katokichi Company Ltd.

Further Reading

"Ezaki Glico Develops Method to Make Food from Wood," *Jiji*, March 17, 2005.

"Ezaki Glico Turns to Women's Health," *Nutraceuticals International*, July 2003.

"Industry's First Biscuit Type Breakfast Cereals form Ezaki Glico," *Japan Food Products & Service Journal*, June 25, 2004.

"New Confectionery Range from Glico," *New Food Products in Japan*, December 25, 2002.

Pierce, Michael, "Glico Candy," *Pacific Rim Magazine*, December 1999.

Shoichi Inoue, "View from Saturday: Same Word, Quite Different Meaning," *Yumiuri Shimbun*, November 26, 2001.

"Time Limit Expires for Glico-Morinaga Cases," *Yomiuri Shimbun*, February 14, 2000.

—M.L. Cohen

Farmacias Ahumada S.A.

Avenida Vicuna Mackenna 585
Santiago
Chile
Telephone: (+56) 2 222-1122
Fax: (+56) 2 661-9410
Web site: http://www.farmaciasahumada.cl

Public Company
Incorporated: 1977
Employees: 11,762
Sales: CLP 605.67 billion ($1.08 billion) (2004)
Stock Exchanges: Santiago
Ticker Symbol: FASA
NAIC: 325412 Pharmaceutical Preparation
Manufacturing; 325620 Toilet Preparation
Manufacturing; 445120 Convenience Stores; 446110
Pharmacies and Drug Stores; 446120 Cosmetics,
Beauty Supplies and Perfume Stores

Farmacias Ahumada S.A. (Fasa) is the largest drugstore chain in Latin America and one of the largest in the world in number of outlets, with a network of nearly 1,000 pharmacies in Chile, Peru, Brazil, and Mexico. These well-lit stores function like U.S. and British drugstore chains, offering a large variety of merchandise besides their core business of providing the consumer with cosmetics and chemical and pharmaceutical products. They accept a variety of credit cards, including Fasa's own, and most of them stay open all night, aided by highly visible security. Fasa manufactures some of the products that it sells. The company is based in Santiago, the capital of Chile.

Starting Out in Chile: 1968–96

The son of immigrants, José Codner Chijner began working as a boy in his family's pharmacy in Rancagua, Chile. Long before enrolling in the department of chemistry and pharmacy at the University of Chile, he had learned the ins and outs of sales technique and the importance of quality of service. After attending morning classes, he worked in his father's two Santiago pharmacies, Santo Domingo and York. Immediately after re-ceiving his degree in 1966, he became technical director of Farmacia York.

However, Codner was not satisfied with working in the family business. One day in 1968, he called his father and said he was going to strike out on his own. A year after acquiring his first pharmacy, he opened another at the corner of Ahumada y Huérfanos in Santiago, naming it Farmacia Ahumada (Fasa). During the beginnings of the new company, Codner's wife, Perla Dujovne, played an indispensable part in the business.

There were ten Fasa outlets in 1980, when the company introduced what became one of the most modern prescription-filling services in South America. Eventually this led to the first pharmacy-benefits management system in Latin America, with two million members in 2001, allowing customers to discount the part of their medications covered by insurance at the moment of payment. In 1982, the chain introduced its first private-label products. Although Codner hated to contract debts, around this time he borrowed $3 million from the Banco de Santiago for further expansion. Then the overvalued Chilean peso virtually collapsed in the wake of the high interest rates imposed by the U.S. Federal Reserve Board to put an end to double-digit inflation. Codner's debt now came to almost $30 million. Since the company could not make payments on its loan, the bank appointed a receiver who knew nothing about the pharmacy business. Working with him, Codner was able to keep moving his enterprise forward, but he was not able to retire the debt and recover his business until 1992.

Codner had become convinced in the 1980s that Fasa could not grow further unless it imitated the Anglo-American model. He sent his executives abroad to study U.S. chains like Walgreen Co. and British ones like The Boots Company plc. They noted the store layouts and what kinds of merchandise these chains carried, and they interviewed shoppers and employees. The result was not only that Fasa began carrying a much larger array of products but also that it began selling hundreds of products under its own brand name and logo, from dental floss to diapers. Eventually the chain started selling food as well. "At first it seemed strange to see milk and bread for sale in a pharmacy," a Brazilian woman told Leslie Moore of the *New York Times* in 2003. "But then you see how convenient it can be."

Fasa revolutionized retail distribution in the pharmaceutical sector in Chile, which had traditionally been composed of a large number of small family enterprises. The U.S. drugstore model it adopted called for bigger, self-service outlets, many of them open around the clock, and ample space for personal-hygiene products, perfume, pet supplies, snacks, and drinks. By 1992, Fasa had 44 outlets in the Santiago metropolitan area and was ready to move into other parts of Chile, starting with a branch in Viña del Mar, the nation's premier beach resort. There followed stores in Chillán, Rancagua, and other cities. In association with the local subsidiary of Royal Dutch Shell, Fasa opened a pharmacy in each Shell service station. In 1996, it established a corporate distribution center.

By 1998, Fasa was roughly equal in size to its chief rival, Farmacias Salcobrand S.A., another drugstore chain. Much of its growth was coming from its own Fasa brand of generic drugs. Chile's health regulations allowed pharmacies to substitute the drugs specified in doctors' prescriptions with chemically identical alternatives, and Fasa took full advantage to offer its cheaper generic drugs. It also offered its own credit card and, in 1998, established a subsidiary to manage the prescription-drug benefits programs tied to alliances with healthcare providers. Although the dispensation of prescription medications was a money-loser for the chain, and the profit margin for Fasa's own drugs was very small, the company compensated with high earnings on other products, including Fasa's proprietary brands of health-and-beauty aids. The stores even sold calculators, blank CDs, and small portable television sets. Once again, however, Codner perceived that his chain, which along with two others had swallowed a majority of the independent pharmacies in Chile, had reached its limits of growth. The next step was to take it to other countries.

Expanding into Peru and Brazil: 1996–2001

Codner studied the possibility of opening stores in other South American countries, including Argentina, Brazil, Colombia, and Ecuador. Finally, he settled on Peru. Codner later explained to Lorena Medel of the Chilean business magazine *Capital,* ''I'm always asked why we're not in Argentina. You know why? Because the level of corruption is incredibly high. The entire pharmaceutical market is surrendered to something called ''social works,'' which are the unions. . . . Peru, on the other hand, was like Chile 30 years ago. There wasn't anything. The growth potential was enormous, and it was possible to repeat what was done here.'' Fasa opened its first Peruvian outlet, in Lima, in 1996 in association with the Chilean supermarket chain Santa Isabel. It also reproduced its collaboration with Shell in Peru, once again opening a pharmacy by the side

of each Shell gas station. The situation in Peru was not ideal because of what a company executive described as tremendous anti-Chilean sentiment in Peru stemming from a 19th-century war in which the latter lost territory, but by the end of 1999 there were 45 Boticas Fasa pharmacies in Peru, generating sales of about $16 million a year.

Fasa went public in 1997, raising $21 million by selling shares on the Santiago Stock Exchange. In 1999, the company sold another $47 million worth of stock, increasing the stake of outsiders in the company to almost 50 percent. The biggest investor was Falabella, Chile's largest department-store chain, with 20 percent of the stock, purchased for $25 million. The alliance gave Fasa a powerful competitive edge against its rivals, since it was now accessible to holders of Falabella's popular credit card, CMR. After this augmentation of capital, two other large U.S. shareholders, the insurance company American International Group, Inc. and Latin American Healthcare Fund, pressed Fasa to expand into other countries. The logical target (since Argentina, now in recession, remained a poor prospect) was Brazil, which was the sixth-largest pharmaceutical market in the world and at that time was being served by a fragmented system of 46,000 pharmacies. In 2000 and 2001, Fasa, in partnership with AIG, purchased Drogamed, the largest drugstore chain in the state of Paraná, with the former taking 65 percent and the latter the remainder. In 2000, Fasa had also purchased a half-share of the Chilean subsidiary of General Nutrition Co. and become the exclusive distributor of GNC's nutritional supplements in Chile and Peru. It bought an additional 17 percent share the following year and acquired the rest in 2002.

Under the direction of Fasa, Drogamed, by mid 2002, had grown into a chain with 107 pharmacies and $75 million in sales per year. Fasa intended to follow this acquisition with two more in Brazil by the end of 2004, but it came to the conclusion that the Brazilian market was too fragmented to serve as a platform for the company's growth. Enrique Cibié, Fasa's general manager, told Medel that the firm was at the point of closing a deal for another Brazilian chain when it decided that doing business there was too complicated and bureaucratic. Instead, he suggested that Codner take another look at Mexico, which had previously been ruled out because the business was dominated by supermarkets. A company executive dispatched there came back with a favorable report, including the news that with the North American Free Trade Association the price of medications was going to rise.

Moving into Mexico: 2002 and Beyond

The company that Fasa had in mind was Far-Ben S.A. de C.V., the corporate name of the Farmacias Benavides chain. This chain, the largest in Latin America, comprised over 600 drugstores yet held only 4.5 percent of Mexico's pharmaceutical retail sales market, which was dominated by that country's supermarkets. Deeply in debt and falling in annual sales, Far-Ben S.A. de C.V. was being pulled apart by the seven brothers and sisters who owned it. Codner was unwilling to consider buying the company until Jaime Benavides was able to get permission from his siblings to close a deal. Even then, negotiations remained complex because some 30 family members had a stake in the company and restive bondholders, who held $71 million in debt, were threatening to drive it into bankruptcy.

Key Dates:

1969: The first Ahumada pharmacy opens in Santiago, Chile.

1980: Ten Farmacias Ahumada (Fasa) outlets are in operation.

1982: The company begins to market its first private-label products.

1992: With 44 outlets in the Santiago area, the chain begins expanding elsewhere in Chile.

1996: The company opens its first Peruvian pharmacy; by the end of 1999, it has 45.

1997: Fasa becomes a publicly traded company.

1998: Fasa establishes a subsidiary to manage its prescription-drug benefits programs.

2000: The company acquires a majority stake in the Brazilian chain Drogamed.

2002: Fasa buys most of Mexico's Far-Ben S.A. de C.V., the largest drugstore chain in Latin America.

The situation remained so difficult that the Benavides family contracted a New York investment bank to act as its negotiator. A deal was struck in late 2002. The bondholders recovered their money, the Benavides family members kept 20 percent of their company, and Fasa purchased 62 percent of the shares for 510 million Mexican pesos (about $45 million), plus the assumption of $30 million in debt. It paid for the acquisition by issuing seven-year bonds in Chile.

One of the first tasks of the new management was to close about 30 unprofitable Farmacias Benavides stores in unpromising locations. Some $14 million was invested to fund a center of logistic control and to remodel the remaining stores with better lighting, new equipment, and the introduction of Fasa's own identifying logo.

While Fasa's hundreds of locales in Chile received their supplies from a centralized distribution system, Far-Ben was at the mercy of its exclusive distributor for pharmaceuticals, Casa Saba S.A. de C.V., the largest such wholesaler in Mexico. Casa Saba supplied each Far-Ben outlet individually, making supervision a time-consuming chore for the pharmacy chain's managers. By the end of 2003, a new distribution center was in place that received goods from more than 100 suppliers of non-pharmaceutical products such as soap and toothpaste. Despite closing 23 outlets, Far-Ben's revenues rose 5.6 percent in 2003 to $441 million, and for the first time in years it earned a profit, which amounted to $7.4 million. The chain's goal for future growth was to combat its reputation as a pricy retailer and thereby to generate higher profits by greater sales volume rather than by increasing profit margin. Medications still accounted for more than half of the revenues of Farmacias Benevidas, and Casa Saba remained in control of which products would go to

each store. Nevertheless, the chain's general manager, Walter Westphal, was seeking to bypass Saba by convincing medical laboratories such as Pfizer, S.A. de C.V. and Schering Mexicana S.A. to deal directly with him.

In 2004, the 230 Farmacias Ahumada stores in Chile carried about 300 products with the company logo. Some also housed ATM's, Blockbuster video drop-offs, and GNC booths selling high-margin vitamins. There were 507 Farmacias Benevidas outlets in Mexico. Although the sales volume from these stores now surpassed Farmacias Ahumada's operations in Chile, Cibié made it clear that corporate headquarters would remain in Santiago. He indicated, however, that the company could save $30 million a year, partly by streamlining its operations and dismissing hundreds of middle managers. In an interview with *América economía,* Codner had said that investors could expect an annual return of at least 20 percent on their capital, adding that ''If we don't do it, we prefer to return the money.'' Fasa had a net profit of CLP3.73 billion ($6.69 million) in 2004. Its long-term debt was CLP42.52 billion. ($76.28 million).

Principal Subsidiaries

Boticas Fasa S.A. (Peru); Compañía de Nutrición General S.A.; Far-Ben S.A. de C.V. (Mexico, 68%); Fasint Ltd. (Brazil, 65%).

Principal Competitors

Drogaría Sao Paulo S.A.; Drogasil S.A.; Farmacias Cruz Verde S.A.; Farmacias Salcobrand S.A.; Raía & Cia. Ltda.

Further Reading

Díaz, Alicia, ''Toman chilenos el control de Benavides,'' *Reforma,* October 23, 2002, p. 3.

''Farmacias Ahumada 'Thinks, Acts Like a Local,' '' *Chain Drug Review,* December 10, 2001, p. 60.

González, Felipe, ''Prueba de fuego,'' *América economía,* October 21, 1999, pp. 48–49.

Kaffman, Luis, ''Brazilian-Entry Formula,'' *Business Latin America,* May 1, 2000, p. 3.

——, ''Divergent Formulae,'' *Business Latin America,* February 14, 2000, p. 3.

——, ''Lab Brats,'' *Business Latin America,* June 8, 1998, p. 6.

Medel, Lorena, ''La gran receta americana,'' *Capital,* October 24–November 6, 2003, pp. 32–34, 36.

Moore, Leslie, ''A Latin Makeover For Staid Drugstores,'' *New York Times,* March 16, 2003, p. C5.

''New Script,'' *Business Latin America,* September 16, 2002, p. 3.

Ramírez Tamayo, Zacarías, ''Sangre en la farmacia,'' *Capital,* May 7-20, 2004, pp. 38–39, 41.

''Receta magistral,'' *América economía,* September 19, 2002, pp. 46–47, 49.

Suárez, Gabriel, ''Cambia de imagen Farmacias Benevides,'' *Mural,* October 1, 2003, p. 6.

—Robert Halasz

F5 Networks, Inc.

401 Elliott Avenue West
Seattle, Washington 98119
U.S.A.
Telephone: (206) 272-5555
Toll Free: (888) 882-4447
Fax: (206) 272-5556
Web site: http://www.f5.com

Public Company
Incorporated: 1996 as F5 Labs, Inc.
Employees: 613
Sales: $171.19 million (2004)
Stock Exchanges: NASDAQ
Ticker Symbol: FFIV
NAIC: 541512 Computer Systems Design Services;
   511210 Software Publishers

F5 Networks, Inc., develops software-based technology that helps companies manage their Internet traffic. F5's products monitor, analyze, and route network traffic, determining which servers are best suited for handling a client's request. F5 operates in North America, Europe, and the Asia-Pacific, serving *Fortune* 1000 companies.

Origins

When F5 began its business life, the company had nothing to sell and all its hopes for success tied to industry still in its infancy. The company was started by Jeffrey S. Hussey, an investment banker who earned his undergraduate and graduate degrees in Seattle, at Seattle Pacific University and the University of Washington, respectively. Hussey established his company in Seattle, a hotbed of information technology activity during the mid-1990s, creating F5 to feed off the business generated by the Internet. Specifically, he wanted to help companies better manage the traffic on the Internet, a business idea whose viability hinged on the growth of the Internet and the expected, yet theoretical, emergence of what would become known as the "new economy." In short, without a traffic problem, there would be no need for a traffic solution, making Hussey's small, start-up venture a gamble from the beginning.

F5 was incorporated in February 1996 as F5 Labs, commencing operations two months later in April. Hussey served as the company's principal executive, holding the titles of chairman, chief executive officer, and president as he shepherded his venture through its formative months. For more than a year, Hussey worked toward giving F5 a product to sell. Employees were recruited, a corporate infrastructure was created, and capital was raised, all to support the development and expected launch of the company's first product. This preparatory stage in F5's history—the prelude to the story of its development—ended in July 1997, when the company was ready to market its BIG/ip Controller.

The BIG/ip functioned much like an air traffic controller. As the use of the Internet increased, particularly for e-commerce purposes, the network infrastructures maintained by companies became strained. To keep up with increasing traffic to their web sites, companies added servers to their network infrastructure, deploying them in a group, or array, to better contend with the increasing demands of increasing visits to a web site. BIG/ip, situated between a network's routers and server array, automatically and intelligently managed the flow of this traffic through proprietary software and industry-standard hardware. Instead of merely diverting traffic from one server to another, BIG/ip determined which server had the most free space, enabling an Internet site to achieve greater efficiency with its existing servers without adding additional and costly servers.

Hussey was in business once he had the BIG/ip ready to introduce into the Internet traffic and content management market. His business was small at first, generating a paltry $200,000 by the end of 1997. The total paled in comparison with the financial might of F5's competitors, notably Cisco Systems, Inc., a $5 billion-in-sales maker of networking equipment with products that competed against BIG/ip. Cisco, and another major competitor, Nortel Networks Corporation, benefited from distribution and marketing organizations vastly superior to F5's modest abilities, but Hussey prevailed during his first months in business, giving his company a foothold that gave it a fighting chance against its towering competitors. BIG/ip proved to be a worthy product, excelling as load balancer for local area networks. In September 1998, BIG/ip was joined by its counterpart for wide area networks, the 3DNS Controller, which served as a

129

Company Perspectives:

F5 enables organizations to successfully deliver business-critical applications and gives them the greatest level of agility to stay ahead of growing business demands. As the pioneer and global leader in Application Traffic Management, F5 continues to lead the industry by driving more intelligence into the network to deliver advanced application agility. F5 products ensure the secure and optimized delivery of applications to any user—anywhere. Through its flexible and cohesive architecture, F5 delivers unmatched value by dramatically improving the way organizations serve their employees, customers and constituents, while lowering operational costs.

load balancer for companies that had multiple locations. The introduction of 3DNS coincided with the end of F5's fiscal year, when BIG/ip, as the company's sole product, generated $4.7 million in revenue.

With two products to offer, Hussey was ready to shop his company to Wall Street. In April 1999, the company changed its name from F5 Labs to F5 Networks and filed for an initial public offering (IPO) of stock, hoping to raise up to $40 million to pay off debt and to fund expansion. F5 completed its IPO in June 1999, selling 2.86 million shares at $10 per share, netting it $25.5 million. By the time Hussey completed F5's IPO, the pundits who had claimed that the Internet would become a revolutionary economic force had been proven correct. The gamble Hussey made in 1996, betting that the growth of the Internet would require products like BIG/ip and 3DNS, had paid off. The dot.com industry was in full flower, attracting eager investors and myriad start-up ventures, both seeking to make their riches off anything related to the Internet. F5's performance on Wall Street reflected the frenzied optimism of the day, increasing in value at a phenomenal rate. By the end of 1999, F5's stock was trading at $144 per share, representing a 1,040 percent return to F5 stockholders who had invested six months earlier. The company's sales reached $27 million in 1999 as its stock soared in value, reaching an all-time high of $160 per share by January 2000. The new year promised to bring even greater financial gains, but for those who hailed the dawn of the new economy and dismissed the old economy, the beginning of the 21st century delivered a stinging rebuttal.

The Collapse of an Industry at the Dawn of the 21st Century

F5's main problem as it entered the new decade was keeping up with the escalating demand for its products. The company had more than 1,600 customers, serving the companies who were propelling the fantastic growth of the dot.com industry. As 2000 progressed, however, signs of weakness began to show, their cause tied to the beginning of the spectacular collapse of the dot.com industry. At first, the severity of what was to come was masked by encouraging results. In June 2000, F5 celebrated its 11th consecutive quarter of revenue growth, but its stock was trading for $36 per share, down sharply from the $160 per share at the beginning of the year. The dramatic decline in F5's stock value

soon was joined by lackluster revenue performance, as the technology sector, battered as a whole on Wall Street, began to stagger toward collapse. At the beginning of 2000, F5 was struggling to serve its customers, who turned to F5 for help with their own problems of growth. As the months passed, a more profound problem surfaced, one that threatened to destroy Hussey's burgeoning business. F5 was reliant on the types of companies who were suffering the most, deriving 80 percent of its revenue from dot.com start-ups. BIG/ip and 3DNS were quality products, but they were being sold to a dying breed of companies.

Before F5's problems became readily apparent, Hussey turned to a new executive to help his company keep pace with the increasing demand of its products. In July 2000, John McAdam was hired as president and chief executive officer, an appointment profoundly important to F5's future. A former general manager of the Web server sales business at IBM, McAdam immediately realized his biggest challenge was not to expand F5 to meet growing demand but to contend with the crucible presented by the collapse of the dot.com industry. "When I came on board," McAdam reflected in a December 14, 2001 interview with *Puget Sound Business Journal,* "our business model was broken." McAdam witnessed F5's stock value plummet during his first months in office. By the end of 2000, F5's share price had fallen from $36 to $9.43, a fraction of the $160 at the beginning of the year and below the IPO price of $10. Exacerbating the company's situation, its biggest competitors increased their commitment to dominating F5's market niche. In May 2000, Cisco bought a traffic management competitor, ArrowPoint Communications, in a $5 billion deal. Not to be outdone, Nortel fired a salvo of its own at the end of the year, acquiring Altheon WebSystems in a $7 billion deal that portended disaster for F5. In a January 5, 2001 interview with *Puget Sound Business Journal,* an industry analyst offered his assessment of F5's situation at the end of 2000. "Being a niche player," the analyst noted, "they've been fortunate enough to be profitable. They can survive as a supplier of content management solutions for the lower to mid-end market, but if they really want to continue their growth, they will have to partner with someone. They need to seriously consider their options."

Turnaround Beginning in 2001

In the wake of the tumultuous events of 2000, McAdam took action, becoming F5's savior. Faced with announcing a 40 percent decline in revenues and a loss instead of a profit for the first quarter of 2001, he sought to repair F5's reputation on Wall Street. He reduced F5's staff by 15 percent in January 2001, subleased office space in the company's newly built headquarters, and, most important, streamlined F5's product line to make it more appealing to large companies. McAdam knew that he needed to divorce the company's attachment to the Internet start-ups that were in their death throes and instead court large, bricks-and-mortar companies. He brokered distribution partnerships with Nokia Corp. and Dell Computer Corp. that gave F5 access to a broader range of corporate customers, dramatically altering the profile of the company's customer base. As McAdam orchestrated F5's turnaround, the company's share price continued to slide, dipping below $5 by April, but by the end of the year the sweeping changes realized their intent. By December 2001, F5's stock was trading for $27.73, a 52-week high.

Key Dates:

1996: F5 is incorporated.
1997: F5 launches its first product, BIG/ip Controller.
1999: F5 completes its initial public offering of stock.
2000: F5's stock, trading at $160 per share at the beginning of the year, falls to $9.43 per share by December.
2001: John McAdam spearheads sweeping changes focused on targeting large companies as customers.
2003: F5 acquires uRoam.
2004: F5 acquires MagniFire Websystems.

The same analyst who painted a bleak picture of F5's prospects at the end of 2000, offered a different assessment at the end of 2001. In a December 14, 2001 interview with *Puget Sound Business Journal,* the analyst said, "It's a definite turnaround for this company. You have to give credit to McAdam and his team. F5 went from being 80 percent reliant on dot.com customers to 90 percent reliant on large enterprises." Revamped and financially on the mend, F5 was ready to take on Cisco and Nortel, forgetting its size as it sought to improve its ranking in the traffic management market.

By the beginning of 2002, the devastation caused by the collapse of the dot.com industry had winnowed the ranks of the technology sector. F5 had survived and it found itself involved in a three-horse race for control of a $385 million market. Cisco, aided by a strong distribution channel and relationships with many clients, held sway, controlling a commanding 47 percent share of the traffic management market. Nortel ranked second, but not by much, holding a 17 percent share compared with the 16 percent share held by the rejuvenated F5. McAdam set his sights on overtaking Nortel, scoring encouraging success as F5 completed its first decade of business.

McAdam's restorative work culminated in a profitable 2003 for F5, the first annual profit recorded by the company after two years of losses. The months of scaling back operations were over, ushering in a period of expansion that saw F5 develop a more comprehensive collection of services for its customers, particularly in the security software niche of the market. In July 2003, McAdam spent $25 million to buy uRoam, a developer of software that enabled users to securely access their company's private network from any computer. In May 2004, McAdam struck again, paying $30 million to acquire MagniFire Websys-tems, Inc., an acquisition that provided F5 with entry into the application firewall market. MagniFire sold TrafficShield, a security device that enabled customers to protect their applications and data from hackers and other malicious attacks.

As F5 entered the mid-2000s, the company faced a promising future. Financially, the company was performing remarkably well, increasing its revenues from $115 million in 2003 to $171 million in 2004. More impressive was the profit gain recorded in 2004, a 705 percent increase to $33 million. The company was gaining market share as well, slipping into the market's number two position with 20 percent of the traffic management market compared with the 15 percent share held by Nortel. In the years ahead, F5 figured to play a prominent role in helping companies manage their Internet traffic, as the company displayed its skill in making networks work.

Principal Subsidiaries

F5 Networks Australia Pty. Limited; F5 Networks SARL (France); F5 Networks GmbH (Germany); F5 Networks Hong Kong Limited; F5 Networks Japan K.K.; F5 Networks Korea Ltd.; F5 Networks Singapore Pte. Ltd.; F5 Networks Limited (United Kingdom); F5 RO, Inc.; MagniFire Websystems, Inc.

Principal Competitors

Cisco Systems, Inc.; Nortel Networks Corporation; Foundry Networks, Inc.

Further Reading

Angell, Mike, "F5 Networks Inc.," *Investor's Business Daily,* February 5, 2004, p. A8.
——, "Software, Gear Maker F5 Aims to Be No. 2," *Investor's Business Daily,* January 11, 2002, p. A5.
Baker, M. Sharon, "Cutbacks Due at F5 in Wake of Tech Slowdown," *Puget Sound Business Journal,* January 5, 2001, p. 8.
——, "F5 Going Public on Wave of Net Excitement," *Puget Sound Business Journal,* April 16, 1999, p. 7.
——, "Rapid Growth Creates Challenges at F5 Networks," *Puget Sound Business Journal,* June 2, 2000, p. 31.
"Corporate Profile: F5 Networks," *On Wall Street,* July 2001, p. 8.
"F5 Products Act Like Air-Traffic Controllers," *Puget Sound Business Journal,* February 25, 2000, p. 49.
Meisner, Jeff, "Staying Alive at F5," *Puget Sound Business Journal,* December 14, 2001, p. 3.

—Jeffrey L. Covell

Fisk Corporation

4400 Post Oak Parkway
Houston, Texas 77027-3421
U.S.A.
Telephone: (713) 868-6111
Fax: (713) 599-1066
Web site: http://www.fiskcorp.com

Private Company
Founded: 1913
Sales: $250 million (2004 est.)
NAIC: 235310 Electrical Contractors

Houston-based Fisk Corporation is one of the largest specialty contractors in the United States, providing electrical, communications, security, audiovisual, and network services. Fisk's original focus, electrical contracting, remains a major part of the company's business. This unit provides a complete package of services—from pre-construction planning to execution and close-out—serving a wide range of commercial, industrial, and government clients. The Fisk Technologies unit is devoted to the design and installation of structured cabling systems, in addition to electronic security, audiovisual, networking, telephony, wireless LAN/WAN, and management services. Fisk maintains regional electrical division offices in Houston, Dallas, Las Vegas, San Antonio, New Orleans, Miami, and New York. Regional Fisk Technologies offices are located in Houston, Austin, Dallas, San Antonio, Las Vegas, New Orleans, Miami, Phoenix, and New York. Major projects in recent years include the Marathon Oil Building in Houston; the Bridgeport Center in Bridgeport, Connecticut; the M.D. Anderson Cancer Center at the University of Texas; two additions to the Texas Children's Hospital in Houston; and the New Boston Garden arena in Boston.

A Turn-of-the-20th-Century Electrical Pioneer

Fisk Corporation was founded in Houston in 1913 by John R. Fisk, less than 15 years after electricity first arrived in the area. The young man borrowed $25 to start an electrician's business, working out of a shed in his father's backyard in The Heights, a neighborhood northwest of Houston's downtown. Early on he had to rely on the streetcar, hauling a ladder, roll of wire, and tools to his various worksites, as he wired up homes to the city's widening electrical system. To grow the business, known in the early decades as Fisk Electric Company, he successfully advertised his services. At the time, electricity was primarily used as an illuminant, replacing kerosene and gas lighting. But as electricity found additional applications, Fisk expanded his services to keep pace. Because of electricity, office building construction began to change, as the height of a structure was no longer limited to how many flights of stairs tenants were willing to climb. Not only did Fisk begin to install elevators but also did receptacle wiring to service the new household and office appliances that relied on electricity for power. In 1935 he completed the electrical installations—lights, air conditioning, and elevators—for the 570-feet high San Jacinto Monument, dedicated a year later to commemorate the 1836 Battle of San Jacinto, the final encounter in the war that severed Texas from Mexico.

By this time Fisk was a union electrical contractor, having become a signatory to the International Brotherhood of Electrical Workers in the 1920s. During the 1930s Fisk worked on a number of municipal projects in Houston, including the Jefferson Stadium, for which he was the onsite contractor. Funded by the Civilian Conservation Corps, the project was one of many public works projects sponsored by the government during the Great Depression to create jobs for the unemployed. Municipal projects remained a mainstay for Fisk until the economy began to rebound with the entry of the United States into World War II, spurred on by massive amounts of defense spending.

Postwar Change in Leadership

Shortly after the war, in 1946, Fisk took on his nephew, Lloyd K. Davis. With a degree in electrical engineering from Rice University, Davis quickly emerged as the company's heir apparent. During the eight years the two men worked together, the company was involved in a pair of major projects, providing the electrical work for the eight-story Foley's Department store and the 44-story skyscraper Humble Building. In 1954 Fisk, according to family lore, on his deathbed charged his nephew to continue to grow the business he founded.

Company Perspectives:

At Fisk, we take pride in our past, are committed to our present and look forward to our future. During our storied history, we have gained experience on virtually every building type or unusual site condition in every region of the country. We've brought our expertise in electrical and low voltage systems to numerous notable buildings including the Astrodome, Dallas Galleria, Bank of America Building, MGM Grand Hotel and Casino, Minute Maid Park, Dow Chemical and the Chase Tower. In order to maintain industry leadership, we've been expanding our services to such fields as: structured communication cabling, audio/visual, electronic security, wireless LAN/WAN, network services, VoIP Telephony and managed services.

Under Davis's ownership, Fisk Electric began to expand beyond the Houston area. In 1956 it acquired a company to establish a Dallas office, and then in 1969 additional acquisitions led to branches in San Antonio and New Orleans. But the bulk of the company's business remained tied to the growth of Houston. The selection of the city in the early 1960s to serve as the home of the National Aeronautics and Space Administration's center for manned space flight projects led to a great deal of work for Fisk. Over the years, the company worked on about a third of the buildings that comprised the space center campus. The NASA presence also helped to spur the growth of Houston into a major city, leading to additional work for Fisk. In 1962 it won the electrical contracting bid for the Houston Astrodome, which opened in 1965 as the world's first indoor sports stadium.

Business in Houston only accelerated in the 1970s, with the area enjoying a commercial building boom, and Fisk won a large percentage of the electrical contracting jobs. During the 1970s Fisk also grew on other fronts. It became an international contractor, doing work on some hotels in Cairo, Egypt, and completing all of the electrical work for the University of Petroleum Oil in Saudi Arabia. With the deregulation of the telephone industry, Fisk in 1971 formed subsidiary Fisk Telephone Systems to take on Southwestern Bell and AT&T. The business grew rapidly, then in 1980 was acquired by Centel, eventually becoming part of Sprint Corporation.

Ownership of Fisk changed hands in 1982 when Davis sold the business to William Press Group PLC for a base price of nearly $16 million. The plan was to use Fisk as a foundation for other U.S. acquisitions, but in that same year, London-based William Press changed directions somewhat by merging with another U.K. company, Fairclough Group, to form an international construction and engineering giant named AMEC PLC. Davis stayed on as Fisk's president and chairman until 1984, then quit to found a new Houston company, HTS, which installed telephone systems. During the 14 years it was owned by AMEC, Fisk opened a Las Vegas office in 1989, which became involved in the construction of several major casino resorts, including the Luxor, The Venetian, and the MGM Grand. In the early 1990s, to keep pace with changes in the world, Fisk formed Fisk Technologies to help clients with new and quickly changing technology needs. This new unit concentrated on the installation and design of structured cabling systems, which integrated voice, data, video, and other building management systems, such as safety alarms, security access, and energy control.

In 1996 AMEC sold Fisk to a former Fisk employee, Larry Brookshire, and Fisk Perseus L.L.C. The business thrived under his ownership over the next four years. In 1997 the company opened a Miami office. The following year Fisk expanded its Las Vegas business by acquiring Rodan Inc., a telecommunications infrastructure contractor specializing in voice and data communications cabling solutions. The deal not only helped Fisk to forward a long-term goal of expanding into the network communications field, it brought with it an immediate influx of business, because Rodan was already contracted to do telecommunications installations at The Venetian and another new hotel, the Paris Las Vegas. In 1998 Fisk moved into two new areas, electronic security and audiovisual. As a result, by the end of the 1990s Fisk Corp. was generating $240 million in revenues.

Ownership Change in the New Century

Fisk changed hands once again when in November 2000 Tyco Electronics Corporation acquired the company. Tyco Electronics was one of five operating groups of Tyco International Ltd., a company that started out in the early 1960s as a research laboratory, making its mark with the silicon carbide laser, but over time evolved into a multibillion dollar conglomerate, involved in the fire and security industry, healthcare, engineered products, and plastics and adhesives, in addition to electronics. Tyco International enjoyed tremendous growth in the 1990s, led by CEO Dennis Kozlowski, who went on an acquisition binge. He beefed up the electronics group in 1999 by acquiring Alarmguard Holdings, Inc. and Entergy Security Corporation, followed by Tyco's largest acquisition to that point: the $11.3 billion stock swap for AMP Incorporated, the largest manufacturer of electrical, electronic, fiber-optic, and wireless connection devices and interconnective systems in the world. Also in 1999 Tyco paid $3 million for Raychem Corporation, maker of electric and electronic components used in a variety of industries. By the end of the year Tyco emerged as the world's leader in electronic security and fire protection systems. Despite growing concerns about the way Tyco was accounting for its acquisitions, Kozlowski continued to pick up assets at a furious rate. In 2000 Tyco bought the electronic OEM operations of Thomas & Betts and the Power-systems division of Lucent Technologies Inc. A week after the $2.5 billion Lucent deal was announced, Fisk was brought into the Tyco fold with little fanfare. Generating nearly a quarter-million dollars in annual sales, Fisk may have been one of the largest electrical and technology infrastructure companies in the world, but it was overshadowed by Tyco's other higher-profile and costlier purchases.

Nevertheless, Fisk held a significant place in the plans for Tyco Electronics, which was striving to become a one-stop provider of electrical, data, audio/video, sound, lighting, and heating, air conditioning, and ventilation control systems and services. Fisk was tucked into AMP Netconnect, a company that had always been involved in the electrical market but was seeing a rekindling of the business because of a new demand for cabling and systems integrations in buildings. Fisk was one of the missing pieces, a ''portfolio niche,'' in AMP's strategy to offer complete voice, data, and electrical services to its major

Key Dates:	
1913:	John R. Fisk becomes an electrical contractor.
1946:	Fisk's nephew, Lloyd K. Davis, joins company.
1954:	Lloyd assumes ownership after Fisk's death.
1969:	Offices open in San Antonio and New Orleans.
1982:	William Press Group acquires the company.
1989:	A Las Vegas office opens.
1996:	Former employee Larry Brookshire acquires the company.
2000:	Tyco Electronics acquires the company.
2004:	Brookshire reacquires the business.

international accounts. According to a Tyco Electronics' spokesperson, the Fisk acquisition marked ''a major milestone in our strategy to balance revenue generation between product sales and expanded system integration services.'' It was also a good fit because Fisk already installed and serviced a large number of Tyco Electronics products.

Under the control of Tyco Electronics, Fisk enjoyed some initial growth. In 2001 it formed OneSource Building Technologies to provide integration services for the design, installation, and service of structured cabling systems, network services, IP telephony, distributed video, wireless LAN/WAN, audiovisual, sound, and lighting. The unit was then given international scope with the acquisition of United Kingdom-based Pinacl Communications and Australia-based Heyday Group. Domestically the subsidiary opened offices in Texas, New York, Ohio, Georgia, South Carolina, and North Carolina. Another seven offices were maintained in the United Kingdom and Australia. It was also in 2001 that Fisk's current president and CEO, Bruce F. Davis, assumed the helm. A certified public accountant, he entered the construction industry in 1980, serving as an accountant for a sheet metal contractor. He then accumulated 18 years of financial and operational experience in the electrical contracting field as well as mechanical and heavy industrial general contracting before joining Fisk in 1998 as chief financial officer.

Fisk's corporate parent became caught up in the corporate scandals that punctuated the early years of the new century. The controversial Kozlowski put a halt to further acquisitions in early 2002, and to prop up Tyco's sagging stock price floated the possibility of splitting the conglomerate into four separate public companies, an idea that received a cool reception from investors. In June 2002, he resigned, not because of Tyco's declining fortunes but due to a criminal probe regarding New York sales tax he was alleged to have evaded on the purchase of a painting. He and his CFO, Mark H. Swartz, were later indicted on a variety of grand larceny, securities fraud, and enterprise corruption charges, accused of stealing some $170 million from Tyco as well as garnering $430 million in illegal stock sales. A new CEO, Edward D. Breen, swept house and began to shed assets in order to pare down the massive debt Kozlowski had incurred during his acquisition spree.

In September 2004 Larry Brookshire reacquired Fisk. Independent once again, the well-respected company embarked on the next chapter in its history.

Principal Subsidiaries

Fisk Electric Company; Fisk Technologies; OneSource Building Technologies; Pinacl Solutions.

Principal Competitors

MMR Group, Inc.; The Newton Group, Inc.; Red Simpson, Inc.

Further Reading

''Fisk Nets 90 Years of Electrifying Growth,'' *Houston Construction News,* October 2003, p. 1.
Stromberg, Laura A., ''Fisk Electric Enters New Business Line with Las Vegas Buy,'' *Houston Business Journal,* June 8, 1998.
''Tyco Buys Electrical, Technology Infrastructure Co.—Fisk Deal Furthers Company's Push to Become Full-Service System Integrator,'' *Electronic Buyers' News,* November 27, 2000, p. 14.

—Ed Dinger

5 & Diner Franchise Corporation

1140 East Greenway Street, Suite 1
Mesa, Arizona 85203
U.S.A.
Telephone: (480) 962-7104
Fax: (480) 962-0159
Web site: http://www.5anddiner.com

Private Company
Incorporated: 1987
Employees: 600
Sales: $25 million (2004 est.)
NAIC: 722110 Full-Service Restaurants

Mesa, Arizona-based 5 & Diner Franchise Corporation operates some 20 freestanding 1950s style, family-friendly diners located in Arizona, California, Florida, Iowa, Nevada, Tennessee, and Virginia. Only the original 5 & Diner is company owned, while the rest are franchise operations. Each unit features stainless-steel counters and classic red acrylic soda-fountain stools, along with a real soda fountain, and dozens of red-and-white vinyl booths with Formica table tops. The restaurants also offer a handful of patio tables. Each booth or counter station comes with a small juke box playing period songs, while larger reconditioned vintage juke boxes are found on the floor. In keeping with the retrospective appeal of 5 & Diner, waitresses wear poodle skirts, bobby socks, and pony tails, with coin changers clipped to their belts. Retro advertising and black-and-white photos of 1950s celebrities—such as Elvis Presley, James Dean, and Marilyn Monroe—grace the walls. On occasion a store will hold a hula hoop contest. Menu items include malts, shakes, and egg creams, along with a dozen signature burgers, such as the Big Bopper Burger and the Blue Moon Burger. The 24-hour diners also offer a wide variety of comfort foods, including meatloaf, sloppy joes, fish and chips, spaghetti, chicken fried steak, and BBQ Ribs. 5 & Diner is a private company headed by its founder Kenneth E. Higginbotham.

Founder Launches Business Career in Mid-1960s

Ken Higginbotham was born and raised in Southern California, where both his mother and father were motorcycle enthusi-asts. As a result he grew up around motorcycles and also became involved in go-carts. After high school he attended Portland State University but was soon distracted from his studies because of a sideline business, Wheelsport Distributing, which he launched in 1965 to distribute motorcycle accessories, such as helmets, handlebars, and batteries. It was proving so successful that he decided to drop out of school to focus on it and was able to attract investors in the form of a neighbor, a Xerox salesman, and his friend. With their backing Higginbotham was able to move beyond distribution and begin manufacturing motorcycle parts through California-based KC Manufacturing.

Higginbotham and KC Manufacturing prospered, but Higginbotham eventually grew tired of the business and the Pacific Northwest. In 1978 he decided to move his family to the Southwest, settling in Phoenix, Arizona. Here he worked as a consultant, helping a friend to open a wholesale operation, Amwest Distributing, to sell hardware to cabinet manufacturers. Among other tasks, he set up a warehouse and hired the sales staff, but after the business was up and running Higginbotham grew restless and was on the lookout for a new business opportunity. During the previous 15 years his work had entailed a great deal of travel, and as a result he developed something of an infatuation with restaurants. Most of his favorite places were vintage mom-and-pop diners. He had no experience in the food industry, but felt confident that as a customer he had developed a strong sense of what made a restaurant successful. Higginbotham and a friend from his church, Noel Canland, toyed with the idea of starting a restaurant together, but Canland eventually acquired a Mexican restaurant on his own. Canland's broker, however, helped Higginbotham find his own restaurant to buy: a coffee shop in West Phoenix called Ted's Country Kitchen.

In 1980 Higginbotham bought Ted's, changed its name to K's Family Restaurant (the ''K'' standing for Ken), and quickly discovered that he had a lot to learn about the food industry. He was used to running a straightforward business, like parts manufacturing, in which you delivered a quality, functional part at a reasonable price and you could expect to be successful. ''With a restaurant,'' he explained in a 2005 interview, ''you have to deliver your product to the table, making sure its hot and not cold, at the right price and the right portion. A lot of different elements come into play and you have to rely on a lot of people.'' Fortunately he

---

Company Perspectives:

Our concept is more than just a 50's style diner with 12 signature burgers. We are also a family destination, complete with a full menu featuring breakfast, lunch, and dinner.

---

was well funded and could afford to learn on the job. Although the business was turning a profit after a couple of months, he estimated it took him about a year to turn over the coffee shop's staff and make a true success out of K's. During that time he worked seven days a week without taking off a single day.

The Original 5 & Diner is Built in 1987

Higginbotham continued to nurture a dream of running a vintage diner. In 1988 he had drawings done of a prototype diner with a 1950s retro look, which he called the Silver Streak, inspired by the 1976 Gene Wilder film of the same name. Higginbotham was not a particular fan of 1950s music or culture so much as he was of the 1950s diner architecture, but music and memorabilia of the era were a natural extension of the look. One day while visiting a restaurant supply house he learned that an area diner, called the 5 & Diner, was being put up for sale. Higginbotham tracked down the listing agent before a prospectus had even been drawn up and made a preemptive bid on the business, which he bought in January 1989. 5 & Diner had opened in June 1987, established by Mr. and Mrs. Pat McGroder and their managing partner Lenny Rosenberg. The partners soon had a falling out, Rosenberg left, and Mrs. McGroder attempted to run the diner on her own but was unsuccessful.

Higginbotham took over a restaurant that had a good location in central Phoenix but a poor reputation in the community. It was an operation with a confused identity. The original plan was to make it a quick service diner, but the owners changed their minds along the way. As a result, 5 & Diner was not properly set up for full service. It was supposed to affect a 1950s image, but the décor was, at best, uninspired and the wait staff uniforms were out of keeping with the concept. Upon taking over, Higginbotham closed down 5 & Diner temporarily to renovate and redecorate the place. He installed a lunch counter and outfitted the waitresses in poodle skirts from the 1950s. He also upgraded the diner's sparse menu of hamburgers and other sandwiches, essentially transferring the menu from K's to the new operation. In addition, 5 & Diner began serving breakfast for the first time, correcting an obvious misstep of previous ownership, which tried to succeed by serving just lunch and dinner. Higginbotham also inherited a lackadaisical staff with no leadership and as he had done at K's; he began the process of winnowing the chaff from the wheat to build a motivated workforce.

Overcoming a bad reputation with customers took about two years, according to Higginbotham. To bring in business he was not above buttonholing potential customers on the street. Each weekday after the breakfast business began to tail off around 10 o'clock and before the lunch crowd drifted in, he hit the streets, handing out flyers and coupons to drum up business. Better food and better service led to repeat customers, and word of mouth brought in new customers, as 5 & Diner turned around in the early 1990s.

Early on, Higginbotham began to think about franchising 5 & Diner, encouraged in large part by the positive remarks from tourists who visited Phoenix during the winter and asked if a 5 & Diner might be opening in their home towns. Higginbotham hired a franchise attorney and developed a plan, but did not aggressively seek out franchisees. In the early 1990s a local man who had recently sold his Taco Bell restaurants became the first 5 & Diner franchisee, opening a unit in Reno, Nevada. It proved to be a frustrating experience for Higginbotham. The owner failed to take a hands-on approach to the business, showing up late or not at all, spending most of his time, according to Higginbotham, sitting at the lunch counter looking somewhat bored. No matter how much Higginbotham and his staff tried to support the operation, it failed to take root in Reno, and was eventually sold.

Mid-1990s Bring a Return to Franchising

Higginbotham put the franchising effort on hold while the program was refined. Franchising resumed in 1995, but Higginbotham now required franchisees to have at least five years of experience in the restaurant business. The second 5 & Diner franchise opened in Scottsdale, Arizona, with better results than Reno had experienced. Advertising efforts for the 5 & Diner conducted in 1996 led to increased interest from potential franchisees. Around this time 5 & Diner was also the beneficiary of a rebounding economy, which spurred tourism in Arizona and led to strong gains in the foodservice sector. According to *Nation's Restaurant* in a 1994 article, the Southwest along with the Mountain regions were "one of the last great frontiers for anyone looking for investment or career opportunities in foodservice. . . . Whether national chain or regional operator, independent restaurant or contract feeder, all are looking to ride the wave of strong local economics, above-average population growth, low unemployment, established tourism industries and low tax bases that made this region arguable the country's hottest restaurant market." In Arizona, the key market was Phoenix, which accounted for almost two-thirds of the state's population. Over the next decade, 5 & Diner built upon its base in Phoenix to open Arizona units in Tempe, Chandler, Mesa, Peoria, and Tucson. The company also franchised restaurants in Temecula, California; Orlando, Florida; Pleasant Hill and Johnston, Iowa; three units in Las Vegas; and single units in Franklin, Tennessee, and Fredericksburg, Virginia. Four of these restaurants were originally company-owned, but they were eventually all turned over to franchisees, in keeping with Higginbotham's belief that each restaurant needed a hands-on owner.

In the late 1990s Higginbotham prepared to take the 5 & Diner concept international, targeting Southeast Asia, where all things American held an appeal, but the collapse of the economy in the region forced him to shelve the plans. There had also been some thought to taking 5 & Diner public to fuel growth, but Higginbotham backed away from the idea, opting instead to add units domestically at a comfortable pace, typically one each year. While there was no rush to expand the chain, Higginbotham also set no limits in terms of size, his goal simply to open as many 5 & Diner as possible. He was also helped by his son, John, who joined the company and took over training and product research and development.

In the 2000s 5 & Diner made several changes to maintain momentum. From the start the chain had been active in local

Key Dates:

1980: Ken Higginbotham acquires a Phoenix coffee shop, his first restaurant venture.
1987: 5 & Diner opens in Phoenix.
1989: Higginbotham acquires 5 & Diner, turning it into a 50s style diner.
1994: Second company-owned unit opens in Scottsdale.
2000: Chain totals 17 units, one of which is company-owned.
2004: The 5 & Diner menu is revamped.

marketing, but now it hired a dedicated marketing person. The company also reinvented its hamburger, changing every aspect from bun to meat, and developing its line of a dozen signature burgers. As a result, burger sales doubled. Then in 2004 5 & Diner revamped its entire menu, leading to the Phoenix unit winning numerous local awards for its food. After 5 & Diner added no new restaurants in 2003, it geared up for a significant franchising push. The 20th unit opened its doors in 2004, and another four were set to debut in 2005, located in Tulsa, Oklahoma; Sheffield, Ohio; Madison, Wisconsin; and Idaho Falls, Idaho. In a way the Tulsa restaurant brought Higginbotham full circle in his career. Franchisees Larry and Pat Wofford were adding the restaurant to their Harley-Davidson dealership on Route 66, which was being transformed into an entertainment complex selling all things Harley, using the legendary highway as its theme. While Tulsa was experiencing a surge in restaurant starts, the new 5 & Diner was well located, not only adjacent to a growing tourist attraction but well away from Tulsa's 71st Street corridor, home to most of the new restaurants. Close by were more than 2,000 hotel rooms, a number of office complexes, and about 350,000 residents in surrounding neighborhoods, providing plenty of potential customers in addition to out-of-towners drawn to the Route 66 Harley-Davidson dealership.

Higginbotham had several other franchising deals in the works, including a ten-unit agreement in Cleveland, and restaurants in the works in Boston and central New Jersey. He was also looking overseas again, this time exploring the possibility of franchising 5 & Diner in the United Kingdom.

Principal Competitors

The Johnny Rockets Group, Inc.; Shoney's Inc.; The Steak n Shake Company.

Further Reading

Blossum, Debbie, ''Harley Dealership Gears For Expansion,'' *Tulsa World,* March 25, 2005.
''The Country's Hottest Restaurant Market,'' *Nation's Restaurant News,* February 21, 1994, p. 52.
Mitchell, L.A., ''Nostalgia for '50s Feeds Franchise Boom at 5 & Diner,'' *Arizona Business Gazette,* December 12, 1996, p. 5.
Perlik, Allison, ''All in the Family: Traditional Family-Dining Concepts Still Hold a Warm Place in Americans' Hearts,'' *Restaurants & Institutions,* June 1, 2003, p. 61.

—Ed Dinger

FLSmidth & Co. A/S

77 Vigerslev Alle
Valby
DK-2500
Denmark
Telephone: +45 36 18 18 00
Fax: +45 36 30 44 41
Web site: http://www.flsmidth.com

Public Company
Incorporated: 1882
Employees: 10,234
Sales: DKK 14.91 billion ($2.62 billion) (2004)
Stock Exchanges: Copenhagen
Ticker Symbol: FLS
NAIC: 237990 Other Heavy and Civil Engineering
   Construction; 327310 Cement Manufacturing; 327331
   Concrete Block and Brick Manufacturing; 331111 Iron
   and Steel Mills; 333131 Mining Machinery and
   Equipment Manufacturing; 333298 All Other Industrial
   Machinery Manufacturing; 333922 Conveyor and
   Conveying Equipment Manufacturing; 333923
   Overhead Traveling Crane, Hoist and Monorail System
   Manufacturing; 336412 Aircraft Engine and Engine
   Parts Manufacturing; 336413 Other Aircraft Part and
   Auxiliary Equipment Manufacturing; 551112 Offices of
   Other Holding Companies

FLSmidth & Co. A/S (FLS) is a world-leading manufacturer of industrial and civil engineering production equipment and machinery: The company's historical core has been in the cement making industry, and FLS produces a wide range of machinery and equipment, including cement grinding machines, gears, and silos; crushers and raw materials storage systems; fans, conveyors, gates, valves, and dampers; and kilns and firing equipment for cement and concrete production. Since 2002, FLS has been implementing a new strategy, which on the one hand focuses on a core of machinery and systems production and on the other hand narrows the group's target industries to just the cement and minerals industries. As part of the implementation of that strategy, the group sold off its Unicon cement production unit and its Aalborg Portland cement operation in 2004. In that year, also, the company announced its intention to exit production of machinery and systems for power generation and industrial processes. FLS Group remains a geographically diversified group operating through a number of subsidiaries, including FLSmidth Airtech, FLSmidth Materials Handling, FLSmidth Automation, FLS Airloq, and Densit in Denmark. Internationally, the group's companies include Kovako Materials Handling in The Netherlands, MAAG Gear in Switzerland, MVT Materials Handling and Pfister in Germany, and Ventomatic in Italy. Denmark accounts for slightly more than 14 percent of group sales; the rest of Europe adds more than 43 percent of sales. North America adds 20 percent of the group's revenues, and Africa and Asia combine to generate nearly 17 percent of sales. FLS Group is listed on the Copenhagen Stock Exchange. The group has been led by chief executive Jørgen Huno Rasmussen since 2004.

Danish Cement Pioneer in the 19th Century

Frederick L. Smidth launched his engineering career in a single room in a building owned by his family. Smidth's earliest interests went toward developing steam-powered milling machinery and equipment. Before long, however, Smidth began to focus on building machinery for the brick and tile industry, and in 1884 completed his first large-scale contract for the construction of a tile works. Smidth's innovation was to build a works capable of operating year-round, a rarity in the industry.

Smidth began hiring new employees, including Poul Larsen and Alexander Foss, who became partners in the company in 1887. At that time, the company was renamed FLSmidth & Co. By then the company's work for the tile industry had given it contacts with the growing cement industry. This led to Smidth being given a contract to build a complete cement plant in Limhamm, Sweden, finished in 1887. Cement plants and machinery quickly became a core area of operations for the firm. The successful completion of that contract quickly led to others, including the construction of the cement works in Christiania (later known as Oslo), in Norway. That plant was completed in 1888.

The company next joined in constructing the works for the Aalborg Portland Cement Plant. That project helped the company build on its expertise in the cement manufacturing process. This in turn led the company to invent a new type of cement, sand cement. Sand cement, which mixed sand into the typical cement mixture, was more economical to use than traditional cement. Its success allowed FLSmidth to become a major figure in the global cement industry, as well as an important cement producer in its own right.

FLSmidth opened its first foreign office in London in 1890. By the turn of the 20th century, the company had opened additional offices in New York, Berlin, Paris, and elsewhere. Another factor in the company's continued success was its 1893 acquisition of the rights to the newly invented tube mill, which made possible a number of difficult grinding processes, notably in sand cement production. The company's redesign of the tube mill increased its efficiency and quickly found a worldwide market.

By the end of the 19th century, FLSmidth had added yet another machinery specialty, becoming the first in Europe to develop a coal-fired rotary kiln in 1898. The company built its first two 18-meter rotary kilns that year, and went on to sell more than 2,000 rotary kilns over the next century.

Technological Advances in the Early 20th Century

Smidth's technical expertise placed it at the forefront of the rapidly developing cement and concrete industries, not only in the Scandinavian region, but worldwide as well. The early 20th century saw the adoption on a massive scale of cement- and concrete-based building techniques. The need for new and more efficient cement production machinery and factories meant a steady stream of orders for Smidth. By the outbreak of World War I, the company sales had taken it to North and South America, across western and central Europe into Russia, as well as into the United Kingdom. The company opened a number of new sales offices during this period to support its growing geographic reach.

The company's sales branches proved vital to its survival during World War I. With its primary European markets all but shut down during the war, the company relied on its foreign offices, and especially its New York and London branches, to win continuing business. Meanwhile, the company's Copenhagen headquarters turned its engineering expertise toward developing machinery for other industries, marking FLS's first diversification.

The company also continued to develop its technologies, and during the interwar period Smidth remained one of the cement industry's top innovators. Over the next two decades, the company rolled out important industry innovations such as the Tirax mill, Symetro gears, and the Unax cooler. These played an important role in improving the efficiency of the cement-making process. During the 1920s and 1930s, also, FLSmidth developed into a major producer of ready-mix concrete and fiber-cement.

Just prior to the outbreak of World War II, Smidth's management took the precautionary measure of transferring parts of its operations, including many of its technical plans and other documents, to its office in New York: A number of staff members moved to the United States as well. The move proved prescient, as the Nazi occupation of Denmark soon put an end to the group's normal business. The Copenhagen operations remained in business on a reduced scale.

Business boomed for the company again during the postwar era. The reconstruction of Europe, coupled with an extended period of economic prosperity throughout much of the West during the 1950s and 1960s, created a new surge in demand for FLS's machinery and plant engineering skills. By the late 1950s, Smidth was able to claim that its machinery was responsible for some 40 percent of the global cement production of the period.

Yet FLS leadership position came under threat in the 1960s, as a number of new competitors stole its thunder. By the 1970s, the company found itself struggling to keep up, both technologically and commercially. Nonetheless, FLS continued to play a role in the developing industry. In the 1970s, for example, the company developed a new technology it labeled Densified Systems, or DSP, which formed the basis of a new type of extremely durable, synthetic cement. In 1978, the company launched the new material commercially as Densit, marking the company's extension into specialty mortars. In 1983, the Densit operation was restructured as a separate subsidiary.

FLS also had branched out into a number of new businesses areas. One of these was materials handling, especially such difficult-to-load products as cement and related materials. During the 1980s, FLS increased its operations in this area, adding subsidiaries such as Kovako of The Netherlands, MVT Materials Handling of Germany, and H.W. Carlsen of Germany. FLS's expansion and diversification also brought it into a number of other business areas, such as the production of machinery for power generation and industrial processes.

By the end of the 1980s, FLS had grown into a full-fledged conglomerate, overseeing a global empire of more than 125 companies. To gain more efficient control over its operations, the company restructured in 1989, creating a new parent company, FLS Industries, to oversee its diversified operations.

Refocusing in the New Century

In 1990 FLS made a significant acquisition when it purchased the United States' Fuller Company. That business traced its origins to two companies founded in the early part of the century. Traylor Engineering and Manufacturing Company had been founded in 1902 to provide engineering services for the mining industry. The second company, Fuller Company, was founded in Pennsylvania in 1926 by James W. Fuller, and began producing cement production equipment as well as turnkey cement plants. In 1959, Fuller acquired Traylor, and the combined company emerged as one of the United States' largest cement-related groups.

Following the acquisition of Fuller, FLS restructured its operations, placing its own and Fuller's mineral processing business into two separate divisions, Fuller Mineral Processing Inc. in the United States and FLS Minerals A/S in Europe.

Key Dates:

1882: Frederick L. Smidth founds an engineering firm in Denmark.

1887: Poul Larsen and Alexander Foss become partners; the company is renamed as FLSmidth & Co.; the company's first cement plant is constructed in Limhamm, Sweden.

1889: The company enters cement production with the creation of Aalborg Portland Cement Plant.

1890: The company opens its first foreign office in London.

1920s: The company launches production of ready-mixer concrete and fiber cement.

1957: Smidth machinery accounts for 40 percent of global cement production.

1978: Densit synthetic specialty cement is launched.

1989: Operations are restructured under FLS Industries.

1990: The company acquires the Fuller Company of the United States.

1997: The company acquires MAAG Gear of Switzerland.

1998: The company acquires Pfister of Germany.

2002: The company announces a new strategy of refocusing operations around a core of machinery and plant systems for the cement and mining industries.

2004: The company sells off cement production units in Europe and the United States.

2005: FLS Industries is renamed FLSmidth & Co. A/S.

The remainder of the company's business was placed into FLSmidth-Fuller Engineering, or FFE. After incorporating Fuller Mineral Processing and FLS Minerals as independent subsidiaries in 1995, the company merged them into a single entity, placed under the oversight of FFE. In the meantime, FLS expanded its North American presence again in 1994, when Fuller acquired Canada's Technequip, a leading maker of hydrocyclones and knife gate valves.

FLS's expansion also included the acquisition of Switzerland's MAAG Gear Wheel. The manufacturer of mill gear units for cement product plants, as well as high-speed gears and high-power main gears, was originally founded in Zurich in 1913. Soon after its acquisition by FLS, MAAG moved into Poland, buying up ABB's Polish gear operations in 2000.

In 1998, FLS made another significant acquisition, that of Germany's Pfister Group. That company was founded in Augsburg by blacksmith Ludwig Pfister to produce mechanical weighbridges. The company remained in the Pfister family through much of the century, when it was acquired by

Klockner-Humboldt-Deutz in 1970. In that year, also, the company launched its first fully electronic scale. Pfister was later acquired by The Netherlands' Koninglijke Machinefabriek in 1989, before majority control passed to Maximilian Scheugenpflug in 1991.

The purchases of Pfister, MAAG, and Fuller encouraged FLS to launch a new strategy in the early 2000s. In 2002 the company decided to refocus its operations in a two-step process. On the one hand, the company decided to refocus its business around its machinery and plant systems manufacturing operations. On the other, the company decided to restrict its target industries to the cement and mining industries. As such the company began selling off its newly noncore businesses. This process reached its culmination with the sale of the company's cement production operations in 2004. In this way, the company more or less came full circle, returning to its engineering roots in order to turn fully into the new century.

Principal Subsidiaries

Bhagwati Designs (India); Densit; FLSmidth Airtech; FLSmidth Materials Handling; FLS Airloq; FLSmidth Automation; FLSmidth Pneumatic Transport; Kovako Materials Handling B.V. (Netherlands); H.W. Carlsen; LV Technology; MAAG Gear Wheel (Switzerland); MVT Materials Handling GmbH (Germany); Pfister (Germany); Ventomatic (Italy).

Principal Operating Units

Cement; Minerals.

Principal Competitors

Eurovia S.A.; Balfour Beatty plc; Ferrovial Agroman S.A.; NCC AB; Bilfinger Berger AG; Groupe Fabricom S.A.; Bauholding Strabag AG; Technip-Coflexip; Power Group of Cos.; George Wimpey plc.

Further Reading

"FLS Industries A/S Completes Sale of Aalborg Portland and Unicon to Cementir," *Nordic Business Report,* October 29, 2004.

"FLS Industries A/S Divests German Subsidiary Motan Materials Handling GmbH," *Nordic Business Report,* May 4, 2004.

"FLS Industries' Unicon Divests US Operations," *Nordic Business Report,* October 11, 2002.

"F.L. Smidth A/S Merges Subsidiary into Parent Company," *Nordic Business Report,* March 4, 2004.

Penman, Andrew, Michael Greenwood, and Guy Dennis, "Future Looks Shaky for FLS," *Mirror,* September 18, 2003, p. 40.

—M.L. Cohen

Friendly's

Friendly Ice Cream Corporation

1855 Boston Road
Wilbraham, Massachusetts 01095
U.S.A.
Telephone: (413) 543-2400
Fax: (413) 543-3966
Web site: http://www.friendlys.com

Public Company
Incorporated: 1935
Employees: 14,500
Sales: $574.5 million (2004)
Stock Exchanges: American
Ticker Symbol: FRN
NAIC: 722211 Limited-Service Restaurants; 311520 Ice
    Cream & Frozen Dessert Manufacturing

Friendly Ice Cream Corporation is one of the top names in ice cream in the northeastern United States. The company has nearly 530 Friendly's company-owned and franchised restaurants in 16 states and distributes packaged ice cream products to more than 4,500 retail outlets. Friendly was purchased from the Hershey Food Corporation in 1988 by the Tennessee Restaurant Company, headed by fast-food wunderkind Donald N. Smith. Since that time it has often struggled toward profitability, having shouldered a sizable amount of debt in Smith's leveraged buyout. Friendly was taken public in 1997 to help reduce this burden. Cofounder Prestley Blake purchased $2 million in company stock during 2001 and has publicly criticized Smith's leadership abilities and spending habits. Blake filed suit against Smith in 2003, claiming he misused $3.5 million in corporate funds.

Early Years

In the summer of 1935 two brothers, Curtis and Prestley Blake, decided to go into business for themselves in Springfield, Massachusetts, by opening an ice cream shop. The 18- and 20-year-old Blakes borrowed $547 from their parents to finance the venture, naming their shop ''Friendly Ice Cream'' as a pledge to both themselves and their customers that they would offer warm and caring service. The Blakes made their own ice cream in a two-and-a-half-gallon freezer they had purchased with the borrowed

money. The first four days they served the ice cream in cups, but when they decided to offer double-dip cones for a nickel, business began to take off. As the warm weather of that first summer waned, the brothers realized they would need to offer more than just ice cream to keep customers coming in over the winter. After taking a poll of their patrons, they decided to add hamburgers to the menu. By the following summer the Blakes were doing well enough to hire an additional employee, and in 1940 they opened a second shop in West Springfield, Massachusetts.

The United States entered World War II the following year, and in early 1943 the Blakes closed their shops for the duration. Curtis joined the service, while his older brother worked domestically for the war effort. They put signs in the windows of their restaurants announcing that they would be closed ''until we win the war!'' Following the cessation of hostilities, they returned to civilian life and reopened their shops. They expanded again in the late 1940s, with new locations in Longmeadow, Massachusetts, and Thompsonville, Connecticut. By 1951 a total of ten shops were open in the two states. This year saw the introduction of take-home half gallons of ice cream and expansion of the restaurants' menus to include more ice cream products and a variety of sandwiches. The company also built a manufacturing plant in West Springfield to produce ice cream for the growing chain.

Over the next two decades Friendly Ice Cream expanded into other states throughout New England and the Mid-Atlantic region, establishing an especially strong presence on Long Island. The company constructed its corporate headquarters and a new manufacturing plant in Wilbraham, Massachusetts, in 1960. In the late 1960s the Blake brothers took Friendly Ice Cream public with a stock offering. By 1975 the chain had more than 500 restaurants, and that year the company opened a second manufacturing and distribution plant in Troy, Ohio. Restaurant menus had expanded over time to offer breakfasts, chicken, seafood, salads, and more, although ice cream products continued to account for a major share of the company's business.

1979 Purchase by Hershey

Chocolate maker Hershey Food Corporation, seeking to diversify, purchased Friendly Ice Cream for $162 million in 1979. By this time Friendly had more than 600 restaurants in 16 states

---

Company Perspectives:

*Our vision is to be the leading casual full service restaurant/
ice cream shoppe and premium retail ice cream brand in the
Eastern United States—known for operations excellence,
great signature foods, famous ice cream shoppe desserts,
sparkling clean facilities, prompt, friendly service and dedicated, talented people—resulting in outstanding customer
loyalty and consistent profitable growth.*

---

and annual sales of $200 million. Hershey began to aggressively
expand the chain, opening more than 100 restaurants within the
next five years. In 1984 the company opened its first outlet in
Florida, and by the following year, as it celebrated its 50th
anniversary, there were 740 restaurants and 34,000 employees.
Although annual sales figures had more than doubled since the
Hershey buyout, all was not entirely well. Sales growth was
mostly due to newly opened restaurants, not increases in per-
store sales, and the growing legions of fast-food chains such as
McDonald's were cutting into Friendly Ice Cream's business.
To catch up, the company began experimenting with new strategies, one of which was a guaranteed five-minute delivery of
lunch items on a special menu. The new Express Lunch concept
was promoted with a series of television ads.

Despite this and other efforts, Friendly was still not performing as well as Hershey wished, and in September 1988 it sold
the company to Chicago-based Tennessee Restaurant Company
(TRC) for $375 million. TRC had been founded in the mid-
1980s by Donald N. Smith and a group of investors to purchase
and manage restaurant chains. Smith was considered a star in
the restaurant world, having doubled Burger King's profits
while serving as its president from 1977 to 1980 and later
heading PepsiCo's restaurant division where he boosted profits
600 percent in two years. Smith was given credit for the success
of PepsiCo unit Pizza Hut's popular Personal Pan Pizza concept, as well as the introduction of a successful breakfast menu
during an earlier stint at McDonald's. TRC had purchased the
330-unit Perkins Family Restaurants chain in 1985, and the
acquisition of Friendly made it the second largest operator of
family restaurants in the country. Smith took the title of
Friendly CEO and board chairman, in addition to his roles as
chairman and CEO of TRC.

TRC immediately began to take stock of the company's
strengths and weaknesses and scheduled more than 100 under-
performing restaurants for closing within the next year and a
half. These were located mainly in Virginia, Florida, and Ohio,
with the company's New England stronghold remaining un-
touched for the most part. The brand name also was changed,
with a possessive "s" added to the end. Other changes included
layoffs of 60 people at the corporate level, the planned
revamping of all of the stores in the chain over the next several
years, and folding the company's manufacturing and distribution
operations into the newly created Food Service Division.
Friendly also began to distribute its ice cream to supermarkets,
starting in Albany, New York, and expanding throughout New
England. Products ranged from half gallons of ice cream to pies,
sundae cups, and cakes. The desserts were grouped in a display

that highlighted the company name, which served to cross-
promote the restaurants. When frozen yogurt began to take the
country by storm, Friendly also added this to its product mix.
Looking at other income possibilities, the company opened a
firehouse-styled restaurant concept called Company C Rotisserie
and Grille in a closed Friendly's in Wyoming, Ohio. The experiment was only a limited success and was not developed further.

Still Struggling in the 1990s

Despite the optimism engendered by Donald Smith's successful track record, Friendly Ice Cream's turnaround was moving slowly. In 1992 *Consumer Reports* ranked the company's
restaurants last among 14 family food chains, citing surveyed
customers' dissatisfaction with the food quality, service, and
atmosphere. CEO Smith acknowledged the chain's problems,
telling the *Sunday Patriot-News Harrisburg,* "The Blake brothers came up with a concept that evolved into something a notch
above fast food. When we bought the chain, that image had
become blurred." He declared his intention to continue to upgrade the company's reputation. Ongoing renovations to
Friendly's restaurants, a program called "Focus 2000," included removal of booths, adding more family-sized tables,
hiring additional serving staff, expanding carryout windows,
and upgrading dinner menus. In 1994 healthier items such as
roasted chicken and baked codfish were added. Typical entrees
were priced at between $5.70 and $6.40, which included several
side dishes. Sales per restaurant were up, and the company's
annual revenues were growing slightly each year. Efforts to
expand overseas also were being made, with ventures under
way in the United Kingdom and the Far East.

By mid-1997 the company had renovated nearly 90 percent
of its restaurants. It was on track to profitability, but the debt
load and stiff competition in the marketplace had kept the
balance sheet in the red since the purchase by TRC. In July the
company announced a new franchise program, selling 34 of its
restaurants in Delaware, Maryland, Virginia, and Washington,
D.C., to DavCo Restaurants, which agreed to open a total of
100 more locations within ten years. A new limited-service ice
cream shop concept, Friendly's Cafe, also was planned. In November Smith took Friendly public, offering $90 million worth
of stock and floating $200 million in senior bond notes in an
attempt to reduce the debt load. Unfortunately, in early 1998 the
price of fresh cream began to climb steeply, eventually tripling,
and Friendly was forced to raise prices for its ice cream products while absorbing much of the increased expense. At the
same time, stiff competition in the retail market was causing
packaged ice cream sales to flatten out, and the boost in restaurant business that had been seen at renovated outlets also began
to drop off. In the latter case, analysts blamed the problems on
continuing inconsistent service and a plethora of confusing
menu additions. Friendly's stock, which had risen from an
opening price of under $18 to more than $26 per share in six
months, dropped to less than $5 by the fall.

At the end of 1998, the company announced that it would be
closing its Troy, Ohio manufacturing and distribution center,
moving those operations to the Wilbraham plant and a new
facility in York, Pennsylvania. The move was intended to save
shipping costs, as Friendly no longer had restaurants in Ohio
and York was much closer to its East Coast stronghold. Friendly

Key Dates:

1935: Brothers Curtis and Prestley Blake open an ice cream shop.
1943: A second shop opens in Springfield, Massachusetts.
1951: By now, ten shops are open in Massachusetts and Connecticut.
1979: Hershey Food Corporation purchases Friendly Ice Cream for $162 million.
1984: The company opens its first outlet in Florida.
1988: Hershey sells Friendly to Chicago-based Tennessee Restaurant Company (TRC) for $375 million.
1997: Friendly Ice Cream goes public.
2001: Cofounder Prestley Blake becomes the company's largest shareholder.
2003: Blake files suit against Smith claiming he misused corporate funds.

also pulled out of ventures it had launched in China and the United Kingdom. In early 1999 the company announced the appointment of a new president and chief operating officer and a new chief financial officer. The stock price was inching upward again, and analysts were applauding the new moves. Friendly rolled out a new product in the spring, the "Cyclone" soft-serve ice cream cone, which could be purchased with a variety of mixed-in additions such as candy, cookie, and fruit pieces. This was the company's first soft-serve ice cream product ever and was brought out in part in response to the success of McDonald's new McFlurry dessert. Friendly announced that it would be the company's largest new product introduction ever, with advertisements to run on both television and radio. Billboard ads and coupons in Friendly supermarket displays rounded out the campaign. The company also announced that it was stepping up the pace of franchise openings, with 25 scheduled for 1999 and 50 to 70 per year to follow.

Halfway through its seventh decade in business, Friendly Ice Cream Corporation continued to struggle to extricate itself from a period of sluggish sales and management difficulties. It was starting to look like CEO Donald N. Smith's goal of reinvigoration might be closer to fruition, as the debt load had been reduced and new measures to streamline operations were taking hold. Competition from the company's rivals was strong, however, and there was still work to be done before the company's health would be fully restored.

Problems Continuing in the New Millennium

Indeed, problems followed Friendly Ice Cream into the new millennium. In March 2000, the company announced that it was shuttering 80 restaurants. A few months later, NASDAQ threatened to pull its listing after Friendly stock fell below the $5 per share minimum. As such, the company moved to the American Stock Exchange.

Debt continued to plague the company in 2001. Friendly was forced to close more stores and lay off nearly 100 employees. Cofounder Prestley Blake made the decision that year to save what he called "his baby." Blake paid more than $2 million for

892,000 shares of the company, which secured his position as the largest shareholder. Blake immediately set out to discredit CEO and Chairman Donald Smith. In a very public and bitter battle, Blake blamed Smith for the company's debt. In 2003, Blake filed suit against Smith, claiming he misused $3.5 million in corporate funds. The funds in question were expenses related to a Lear Jet shared with The Restaurant Co. The suit remained unsettled in 2005.

Friendly President and COO, John Cutter, took over as CEO in 2003 while Smith remained chairman. Blake's antics continued the following year at Friendly Ice Cream's annual shareholder meeting. He offered the company a low-interest $50 million loan out of his own pocket. In return, Friendly had to force Smith to repay the alleged $3.5 million in misused funds. Blake offered the loan for a second time in 2005, but Friendly management refused to accept.

While Friendly Ice Cream fended off the negative publicity brought on by Blake's claims, it also was hard at work revamping Friendly Ice Cream's operating structure and strategy in order to shore up profits and sales. In 2004, it re-franchised 27 restaurants in Florida, Ohio, and New Jersey. The firm also looked to expand in the Florida market and signed deals with Jax Family Restaurants and Central Florida Restaurants to grow the Friendly brand throughout Florida. It also updated its menu, adding new offerings including the Carb Fabulous and Lighter Choices menu. A line of decorated ice cream cakes was launched in 2004. The cakes were available in supermarkets as well as in its restaurants.

Restructuring efforts began to pay off and comparable store sales were up during the early years of the new millennium. The company hit a snag in 2004, however, when weak restaurant sales, high cream and commodity costs, fierce competition, and cool Northeast weather forced sales and profits to slide. Nevertheless, Friendly Ice Cream remained focused on four key strategies: improve the dining experience in its restaurants; expand through franchising and re-franchising; increase higher margin revenues; and continue to enhance and build shareholder value. The company celebrated its 70th anniversary in July 2005. While it had faced challenges in recent years, management was confident that the Friendly's brand would continue to put a smile on faces for years to come.

Principal Subsidiaries

Friendly's Restaurants Franchise Inc.; Restaurant Insurance Corporation.

Principal Competitors

Carvel Corporation; Denny's Corporation; International Dairy Queen Inc.

Further Reading

Baily, Steve, and Steven Syre, "Sizable Debt Threatens to Cool Down Proposed Offering by Friendly," *Boston Globe,* October 15, 1997, p. E1.

Bohman, Jim, "Friendly Gets New Face—Restaurant Renovations Boost Sales," *Dayton Daily News,* May 25, 1994, p. 5B.

Bramson, Constance, "Ice Cream: Popular Frozen Yogurt Still Plays Second Fiddle," *Harrisburg Patriot,* September 12, 1990, p. C1.

Carlino, Bill, "Friendly's Eyes Consumers' Vote with Specialty Programs," *Nation's Restaurant News,* September 30, 1996, p. 14.

Carpenter, David G., "TQM As a Driver of Change and Profitability at Friendly's," *National Productivity Review,* September 1, 1995, p. 57.

Cebryznski, Gregg, "Friendly's Launches Soft-Serve Treat in Chain's 'Biggest' Product Introduction," *Nation's Restaurant News,* May 10, 1999.

Freebairn, William, "Friendly Pledges Better Results," *Republican,* May 12, 2005.

——, "Friendly Positioned for Upturn," *Republican,* March 5, 2005.

"Friendly Adds Low-Carb, Low-Cal Entrees," *Nation's Restaurant News,* July 26, 2004.

Gatlin, Greg, "Friendly's Savors Taste of Success," *Boston Herald,* June 3, 2002.

Geehern, Christopher, "Customer Friendly: Company Stabilized; Considers Going Public," *Sunday Patriot-News Harrisburg,* June 14, 1992, p. F1.

"Hershey to Sell Ailing Friendly," *Newsday,* August 9, 1988, p. 31.

Mans, Jack, "Friendly Creativity," *Dairy Foods,* September 1, 1991, p. 95.

Merritt, Jennifer, "Friendly's Stock Price Takes a Licking on Wall Street," *Boston Business Journal,* October 16, 1998, p. 5.

——, "Friendly's Takes Several Steps to Regroup," *Boston Business Journal,* February 26, 1999, p. 13.

Port, Susan T., "Friendly's Founder Steps Back into Fray," *Palm Beach Post,* January 22, 2001.

Reidy, Chris, "Friendly's to Try Franchise Route First Deal, with DavCo Restaurants, Aims to Open 100 Stores in Mid-Atlantic States," *Boston Globe,* July 15, 1997, p. E3.

Seligman, Bob, "Friendly's to Sell 100 Units to Help Upgrade Existing Sites," *Nation's Restaurant News,* February 26, 1990, p. 3.

Wishna, Victor, "A Friend in Need," *Restaurant Business,* August 1, 2000.

Yoo, John C., "Hershey Sells Off Friendly Ice Cream," *Boston Globe,* August 9, 1988, p. 46.

—Frank Uhle
—update: Christina M. Stansell

Galardi Group, Inc.

4440 Von Karman Avenue, Suite 222
Newport Beach, California 92660
U.S.A.
Telephone: (949) 752-5800
Toll Free: (800) 764-9353
Fax: (949) 851-2618
Web site: http://www.wienerschnitzel.com

Private Company
Founded: 1961
Sales: $230 million (2002 est.)
NAIC: 722210 Limited-Service Eating Places

Based in Newport Beach, California, Galardi Group, Inc., is a private company that runs the 350-unit Wienerschnitzel restaurant chain, the world's largest hot dog chain. About 10 percent of the units are company owned, while the rest are operated by franchisees. Wienerschnitzel's signature menu item is the chili dog. Other offerings are all-beef hot dogs with a choice of traditional toppings, Healthy Choice dogs, corn dogs, hamburgers, french fries, and chili cheese French fries. The company also owns the Tastee-Freez chain of more than 225 ice cream stands, acquired in 2003, the offerings of which are being incorporated into the Wienerschnitzel stores. In addition, Galardi Group owns The Original Hamburger Stand chain, which takes a no-frills, low-cost approach to the burger business. Galardi Group is headed by its founder, John N. Galardi.

Founder Involved Emergence of Fast Food in the 1960s

John Galardi traces his involvement in the fast food business to the 1950s when at the age of 12 in Missouri he worked as a soda jerk. After high school, he moved with his family to Southern California and enrolled at Pasadena Junior College. As Galardi recounted in a 1987 interview with the *Orange County Business Journal,* "I walked across the street and a guy was hosing the lot. . . . I said, 'Do you need any help?' " The man with the hose turned out to be Glen Bell, Jr., founder of the Taco Bell chain. Bell hired Galardi at 50 cents an hour for part-

time work, which soon led to Galardi managing Bell's commissary. He was only 20 years old when he took over a poor performing Taco Bell under a partnership arrangement. By working double shifts, and his wife taking on three part-time jobs, Galardi was able to save $6,000. He then lent the money to Bell, who was strapped for cash. Unable to pay back the loan, Bell three months later offered to sell the store to Galardi for $12,000. "So my folks borrowed $2,000 from Household Finance on their furniture," Galardi told *Orange County Business Journal,* "I let everybody go and I worked 30 days to get the other thousands and I paid $12,000 for a little taco store in Long Beach. That's how I got into the ownership position."

Galardi was fortunate in his timing in gaining a toehold in the fast food industry in Southern California, an area that saw the emergence of both Ray Kroc's McDonald's and Taco Bell, as well as Harold Butler's Denny's chain. After learning the ropes from Bell, Galardi was ready to carve out his own niche in the fast food sector. A major break occurred when his hard work was recognized by a businessman who offered to build him a restaurant in Wilmington, California. Because the location was next door to one of Glen Bell's stores, Galardi informed his mentor, who advised him to grab the opportunity—as long as he sold something other than tacos. Galardi decided to try his hand at selling hot dogs, since it was an unexploited area in the market. His wife, after looking through a cookbook, then suggested Wienerschnitzel as the name for the store, an idea that he immediately dismissed. However, three days later, unable to come up with anything better than "John's Hot Dogs," Galardi decided to call his new hot dog stand Der Wienerschnitzel.

Opening in 1961, Der Wienerschnitzel proved popular, in some ways too popular with the car clubs of younger customers who tended to get rowdy. "I'd walk out and sometimes find 100 kids drunk and chase them off," he told *Orange County Business Journal.* "I did a little survey and found out they were 100 percent of my problems and only 5 percent of my business." Galardi then came up with a creative answer to the problem: He set up a drive-through pick-up lane, one of the first in the industry, that passed straight through the middle of the store's A-frame structure. In this way, the customers could not get out of their cars and after they bought their food found themselves back on the streets and looking for somewhere else to go. Not only did Galardi get rid of rowdy loiterers, he was able to use a smaller format for his restaurants, lowering his rent.

Overcoming Difficulties in the Late 1960s

Galardi began franchising the Wienerschnitzel concept, which took off in the early and mid-1960s, making him a millionaire when he was still in his twenties. By 1968, the chain was 200 units in size, and Galardi was turning down offers of as much as $20 million to buy the business. Then the fast food sector hit a rut, and Galardi found he had expanded too quickly. Half the units were losing money, and he had $8.5 million in debt. In addition, he was contending with a monthly negative cash flow of $150,000. Moreover, he was besieged with scores of lawsuits. It took about six years, but Galardi succeeded in paying back his creditors. He also fought off every lawsuit and not only rebuilt the business but also doubled the chain's sales volume. This comeback was accomplished despite hot dogs slipping in popularity because consumers were becoming more health conscious. To remain competitive, Wienerschnitzel began offering hamburgers in 1973. In that same year, it quit building its 800-square-foot A-frames, turning instead to larger structures able to accommodate indoor and outdoor seating. Galardi had succeeded so well in turning around Wienerschnitzel that in the early 1970s he considered taking the company public, with the help of Bank of Boston, in order to fuel further expansion. However, fearful of losing control of the business he built, he elected in the end to remain private.

In the mid-1970s, at the age of 35, Galardi had grown weary of his self-imposed grind and decided to move to Aspen, Colorado, to become a ski bum for a year. Reinvigorated, he returned to work, opening another 150 stores before he was 40. The chain reached its peak in 1975 when it totaled 450 company-owned and franchised operations spread across 20 states. Two years later, the chain dropped the "Der," simply becoming known as Wienerschnitzel. Galardi, in the meantime, went through more life changes, including getting divorced at the age of 39. He told *Orange County Business Journal*, "I figured, you know, why be a workaholic, so I took off five years and kicked around the world. I made another guy president and retired. Lived on a boat in the Bahamas, lived in Hawaii and loved it, and found the right gal, got married and decided to come back to work."

While Galardi was on hiatus, Wienerschnitzel underwent some significant changes. The chain's dalliance with the hamburger culminated in the 1979 introduction of the Weldon P. Wienschnitel line of quarter-pound burgers custom cooked and garnished with such toppings as guacamole and pineapple, a concept in many ways ahead of its time. The company hired the man behind Wendy's "Where's the Beef?" advertising cam-

paign and succeeded in driving up hamburger sales. Nevertheless, despite making up 40 percent of all sales, the burgers cost so much to make that they only accounted for about 20 percent of the profits. Moreover, according to market research consumers still associated Wienerschnitzel with hot dogs, so that hamburgers brought in no additional customers. As a result, the chain was stagnant, with annual sales hovering around $300,000 and little promise that with its current approach the chain would realize any growth. Thus, in 1981, Wienerschnitzel decided to focus on what it was best known for, hot dogs, while still pursuing a marketing theme of "We're not just hotdogs" in a campaign headlined by baseball superstar, and noted "hot dog," Reggie Jackson. In 1985, the chain added chicken sandwiches as well as biscuit breakfast sandwiches, but despite a significant increase in consumer awareness, Wienerschnitzel remained firmly associated with hot dogs. The chain began de-emphasizing everything on the menu other than hotdogs, changing its motto in 1986 to "Nobody hot dogs it like we do." Fortunately, hot dogs were also making a comeback with consumers around this time. To attract more business, the chain introduced its "big 'n beefy" lines of $1.99 hot dogs served on sesame seed buns, as well as double-cheese chili dogs and split-link Polish sandwiches with Swiss cheese on rye.

Wienerschnitzel kept hamburgers on the menu but no longer actively promoted them. In 1983, Galardi Group attempted to gain some diversity by launching two separate burger ventures: Weldon's gourmet hamburgers and the Original Hamburger Stand, which was essentially developed to replace poor performing Wienerschnitzel units. The company's initial attempt to underprice the competition with a no-frills approach became a factor in the burger wars of the period. In the 1980s, Galardi also tried to launch a yogurt and muffin shop concept called Chelsea's. The plan was to "cluster" the various concepts, so that Chelsea yogurt shops could be incorporated into Wienerschnitzel, Hamburger Stand, and Weldon stores, a strategy that anticipated co-branding efforts of the 1990s. However, the combination of hot dogs and burgers with yogurt and muffins failed to take hold in the 1980s.

Galardi had put a halt to new store openings in 1983, but by the late 1980s Wienerschnitzel was ready once again to expand. Serving as president, promoted in 1986, was Dennis Tase, who came to Galardi Group from PepsiCo in 1981 to serve as director of marketing. John Galardi, the company's chairman and majority shareholder, remained actively involved, however. The chain at this juncture totaled about 275 units. The average check was $3.25, resulting in average unit volume of $420,000 and total annual sales of $110 million.

Challenges and a Strategic Acquisition: the 1990s and Beyond

As Wienerschnitzel moved into the 1990s, it once again lost momentum. John Galardi was on the verge of selling the business to the New York buyout firm Kelso Group, but he held out for a higher price and the deal was shelved. To get back on track, the company slashed overhead, including sizable cuts in corporate staff, and closed down more than 53 of the old A-frame units that were no longer profitable. The Weldon's chain was also cast off. In addition, Galardi Group refinanced its debt. The company made steady progress during the first half

Key Dates:

1961: John Galardi opens a hot dog stand called Der Wienerschnitzel.
1962: Galardi opens a drive-thru restaurant.
1973: Wienerschnitzel begins offering hamburgers.
1975: The chain peaks at 450 units.
1986: Dennis Tase is named president.
1999: Dual-branding with Tastee-Freez is launched.
2003: Tastee-Freez is acquired.

of the 1990s, with sales reaching $134 million in 1995 and profits improving at a rapid clip for four consecutive years. Partly responsible for the comeback was the 1991 launch of its irreverent "Cop a Wienerdude Attitude" advertising campaign featuring a cartoon superhero. While it won some awards and garnered Wienerschnitzel national attention, it was never overly popular with franchisees and by 1995 had run its course. In 1996, the chain adopted a more folksy approach, launching an ad campaign featuring Roy Clarke, country singer and star of television's *Hee Haw*.

At the end of the 1990s, Wienerschnitzel entered another growth phase. In 1999, sales reached $170 million, and Galardi Group took in 45 deposits for new franchised stores, perhaps the largest number in company history. Management was also excited by a dual-branding effort with Tastee-Freez soft ice cream, which it tested in 11 company-owned stores, inspired by the success of the California chain El Pollo Loco, which had established a successful dual-branding program with the Foster's Freeze chain. By becoming a Tastee-Freez franchisee, Wienerschnitzel added dessert items to its mix and experienced a significant increase in business during the late afternoons and evenings. As the company moved into the 2000s, it launched plans to add another 100 units in the next few years and add Tastee Freez franchised operations to more of its stores, although the 100 older A-frame units were not able to accommodate the necessary refrigeration for the soft-serve equipment. Some of the new Wienerschnitzel stores would be opened in miniature golf sites and entertainment parks, new venues for the chain. Another venture for the company would be the 2003 introduction of a retail Wienerschnitzel chili sauce developed to be sold in grocery stores. While not likely to add much to the balance sheet, the product was expected to improve name recognition and help in the company's efforts at brand building.

By 2003, Tastee-Freez was incorporated into 52 Wienerschnitzel and eight Original Hamburger Stand units, resulting in sales increases at some locations as high as 14 percent, but generally between 5 and 10 percent. Galardi Group was so pleased with its dual-branding experience that in June 2003 it decided to buy the Tastee-Freez chain, a decision influenced by the news that a major chain was considering acquiring the business. The roots of Tastee-Freez dated back to 1950 when inventor Leo Moranz developed a new soft-serve ice cream pump and freezer that was better than anything else on the market at the time, capable of maintaining a quality product while providing speedy production of ice cream cones and dishes. Moranz teamed up with businessman Harry Axene to rent the equipment under the Tastee-Freez name to entrepreneurs who quickly set up walk-up stands across the country. Over the years, Tastee-Freez developed into a chain of 220 franchised stores located in 33 states and Panama, generating more than $115 million in sales in 2002.

After two years, Galardi Group was operating about 300 dual-branded units. The upgrade costs ranged from $23,000 to $40,000 per unit. As a result, franchisees saw little profit from the addition of ice cream to the menu, but it helped significantly in bringing in customers during what were typically slack periods. Once franchisees paid off their equipment, however, they could expect to see greater benefits from the addition of Tastee-Freez. Galardi Group was already satisfied with the Tastee-Freez acquisition, as ice cream promised to be more of a complementary fit with hot dogs than gourmet hamburgers, yogurt, or muffins had been in the 1980s.

Principal Competitors

International Dairy Queen, Inc.; Jack in the Box Inc.; Nathan's Famous, Inc.; Sonic Corp.

Further Reading

Bell, Alexa, "Wienerschnitzel: Hot Dogs with Relish," *Restaurant Business*, November 20, 1988, p. 74.

Blake, Mike, "The Men Behind the Restaurant Chains," *Orange County Business Journal*, October 27, 1986, p. 10.

Fulmer, Melinda, "New Tricks for Old Dog," *Orange County Business Journal*, May 27, 1996, p. 1.

Liddle, Alan J., "Wienerschnitzel, Tastee-Freez Meld in Co-Branding Push," *Nation's Restaurant News*, May 16, 2005, p. 6.

Lingle, Arthur J., "Wienerschnitzel's John Galardi—No Ordinary Hot Dog," *Orange County Business Journal*, March 30, 1987, p. 12.

Martin, Richard, "Wienerschnitzel Sets New Chili Dog Rollout," *Nation's Restaurant News*, May 16, 1988, p. 1.

Schaben, Susan, "Wienerschnitzel Teams with Tastee-Freez, Steps Up Expansion," *Orange County Business Journal*, August 21–August 28, 2000, p. 1.

Spector, Amy, "Wienerschnitzel Parent Galardi Group Gobbles up Tastee-Freez," *Nation's Restaurant News*, June 16, 2003, p. 4.

"Tastee-Freez Acquired by Galardi Group," *Ice Cream Reporter*, June 20, 2003, p. 1.

"Wienerschnitzel's Formula for Success: Putting on the Chili," *Nation's Restaurant News*, July 24, 2000, p. 164.

—Ed Dinger

Gilman & Ciocia, Inc.

11 Raymond Avenue
Poughkeepsie, New York 12602
U.S.A.
Telephone: (845) 485-3300
Fax: (845) 483-9332
Web site: http://www.e1040.com

Public Company
Incorporated: 1981
Employees: 535
Sales: $59.9 million (2004)
Stock Exchanges: Over the Counter
Ticker Symbol: GTAX
NAIC: 541213 Tax Preparation Services

Gilman & Ciocia, Inc. (G&C) is a Poughkeepsie, New York–based public company providing tax preparation and financial planning services from more than 30 offices located in New York, New Jersey, Connecticut, Florida, Maryland, and Colorado. Although it started out as a single tax preparation shop, and continues to handle local, state, and federal tax preparation, G&C now generates nearly 90 percent of its revenues from financial planning services, which include insurance, mortgage services, estate planning, pensions, and securities brokerage services. A large amount of G&C's financial planning business comes from tax return clients who come to realize the need for financial planning services to minimize their tax liability. A high-flying company in the 1990s, G&C expanded too quickly and took on too much debt, leading to retrenchment in the new century.

Company Roots Dating to the Late 1970s

The men behind the Gilman & Ciocia name were Thomas Gilman, a former New York City policeman, and James Ciocia. In 1978, shortly after graduating from St. John's University with an undergraduate accounting degree, Ciocia teamed up with Gilman to launch a small tax preparation shop in Great Neck, New York, on Long Island. They incorporated the business in 1981, and although the business was doing well, growing through client referrals and their direct mail marketing efforts, the part-

ners came to believe that in the course of their tax preparation work they were giving away financial advice. In 1983 they decided to add financial planning services to not only increase their profits but to better serve their clients. Thus G&C acquired licenses to deal in securities and sell life and health insurance policies. To announce its new capabilities and drum up business, the firm invested in a major marketing campaign, which was so successful that G&C was able to open a second office in 1983.

From 1984 to 1989, G&C expanded at a gradual pace, adding another six offices. It was taking steps to make a significant expansion push when in March 1989 Gilman was killed in an automobile accident. To help lead the company through this difficult period, Ciocia leaned heavily on Tom Povinelli, a longtime friend and G&C's chief operating officer. Holding a degree in accounting from Iona College, Povinelli had joined the company in 1983 as an accountant and became an executive officer a year later. After taking off a year, the firm renewed its expansion efforts in 1991, with Povinelli overseeing the opening of all new offices, achieved primarily through acquisitions. The firm targeted practices that were mostly involved in the preparation of 1040s, in keeping with G&C's expertise, and those whose owners were interested in staying on. In this way G&C could bring to bear economies of scale while maintaining relationships with existing customers. To fuel its growth G&C then initiated plans to take the company public by reincorporating in Delaware in September 1983. The business was beefed up with the opening of 15 offices in early 1994, leading to a stock offering at the end of the year, netting the firm more than $3 million.

Following the initial public offering G&C pursued a goal of establishing a nationwide branch office network composed of 200 to 250 offices by the end of 1997. In January 1995 the firm opened 22 offices, in time to do work on 1994 tax returns, bringing the total number of operations to 79, located in 11 states. At the end of the year, G&C opened another 41 offices in ten states. It also acquired some equipment from a liquidated company in 1995 to launch a direct-mail operation called Progressive Mailing, primarily to take care of G&C's direct-mail marketing, the firm's primary advertising effort, but also intended to service outside clients as well. By the end of fiscal

1996, which ended on June 30 of that year, G&C had a total of 118 offices, with 43 located in New York; 16 in New Jersey; nine each in Arizona, Florida, and Ohio; eight in Maryland; seven in both Connecticut and Washington; five in Nevada; two each in California and Pennsylvania; and a single office in Kentucky. In fiscal 1996 revenues approached $21 million and the firm recorded net income of nearly $535,000. G&C's expansion pace fell off slightly in 1997, with eight new offices opening in January of that year. The firm also acquired ten customer lists, helping to spur sales, which improved to $24.6 million in fiscal 1997, while net income grew to $876,000.

Strong Growth in the Late 1990s

The final years of the 1990s saw G&C make advances on a number of fronts. In fiscal 1998 the firm added offices through several acquisitions, at a cost of $4 million, bringing the total number to 127, located in 16 states. As a result, revenues improved to $28.5 million and net income topped the $2 million. Moreover, G&C reached the 100,000 mark in clients. In fiscal 1999 G&C added eight local offices through acquisitions, but, just as important, it added capabilities through acquisitions and joint ventures. In November 1998 it bought North Ridge Securities Corporation, a securities broker-dealer, for $5.25 million. In February 1999 it acquired an online tax preparation business to serve as a foundation for a new Web-based business called e.1040.com. Also in that month G&C forged an alliance with Houston-based InsurMark, whereby InsurMark helped G&C to recruit and train annuity, life, and long-term care representatives. In addition, the G&C reps would market and sell InsurMark's insurance products, while G&C also sought to hook up with some of InsurMark's 3,500 representatives to establish tax preparation offices in their local markets. Next, in the spring of 1999 G&C completed its largest acquisition, buying Prime Capital Services, a Poughkeepsie broker-dealer with $17 million in annual revenues and 28 offices. As a result, the number of offices increased to 156, the client base surpassed 150,000, and the size of the sales force increased to nearly 550. The Prime Capital deal was also significant because its online trading capabilities complemented the new e1040.com business, and more important, in combination with the North Ridge acquisition, G&C was able to terminate its arrangement with Royal Alliance Associates, Inc., a broker-dealer to which G&C had previously referred clients. Now the business would be referred to either a Prime or North Ridge representative and the commission formerly paid to Royal Alliance would now stay in the coffers of G&C. The firm also made inroads in the insurance business in 1999 with the establishment of a joint venture with Garden City, New York-based Career Brokerage called GTAX/Career Brokerage. Career Brokerage now became the exclusive agent of life and long-term care insurance and annuities, a portfolio of products from 40 insurance companies. In return for bringing in new business for Career Brokerage, G&C received half the brokerage commission—without taking on additional staff. Also in 1999 G&C became directly involved in mortgage

banking for the first time, acquiring Mortgage Line Financial Corp., a Ronkonkoma, New York-based company licensed to mortgage online in the states where G&C maintained operations. The firm was growing at such a rapid clip that one of its major problems at this time was in attracting qualified employees. Because it was getting a better response from applicants in Westchester County than from those in Long Island, in the fall of 1999 G&C elected to move its corporate offices from Great Neck to White Plains, the Westchester County seat and home to many major corporations. Far from severing its ties to Long Island, the firm retained its Great Neck facility for tax preparation and financial planning and continued to operate 30 financial services offices on Long Island.

Due to the addition of offices and services, G&C experienced a sharp increase in revenues, which topped the $50 million mark in fiscal 1999 and approached $90 million a year later. The company posted net income of $2.2 million in 1999, but despite the significant increase in sales the next year, G&C suffered a net loss of more than $4 million in fiscal 2000, primarily because of the costs involved in launching e1040.com. Although G&C continued to add offices and increase sales, in some ways it had already reached a high watermark. Nevertheless, the firm continued to project an air of confidence in November 2000 when it made some changes in senior management. Although he retained the chairmanship, Ciocia turned over the chief executive post to Povinelli. In addition, Michael P. Ryan was named Povinelli's replacement as COO. Ryan had cofounded Prime Capital Services and after G&C acquired the business stayed on as president. That management was somewhat concerned about the future, however, was implied in the firm's new acquisition model. Historically, it took about three years for a new G&C practice to become profitable. Going forward, management wanted an acquired office to meet a target level of profitability in the first year, and if it was not met future purchase payments to the principals of the acquired practice would be reduced.

Problems Emerging in the Early 2000s

The early months of 2001 saw G&C add another dozen small accounting firms, including two in its traditional home market of Long Island, a strategy of growing into prosperity adopted by Povinelli and his chief lieutenant, Chief Financial Officer David Puyear. But the company continued to post losing quarters. In addition to overexpansion and the cash-burning propensity of e1040.com, the firm suffered from poor internal controls. As a result of these problems, G&C saw its stock lose 80 percent of its value from the time Povinelli was named CEO until June 2002, when shares were trading around the $1 mark. The firm also was having trouble with the NASDAQ, being forced to restate its fiscal 2001 results and failing to file a report for the quarter that ended March 31, 2002. Moreover, G&C was casting about for a $2.5 million infusion of capital from a private equity group. In April 2002 the company announced a restructuring plan that called for job cuts and the elimination of e1040.com, in the hope of trimming $2 million a year in overhead. Despite these moves, management now split into warring camps, with Ryan resigning in July 2002—his departure not "voluntary," according to press accounts. He subsequently headed a group of dissident stockholders, who then demanded the resignation of Povinelli and

Key Dates:

1978:   Thomas Gilman and James Ciocia start a 1040 shop.
1981:   The business is incorporated.
1989:   Gilman dies in an automobile accident.
1994:   The company is taken public.
1999:   Prime Capital Services is acquired.
2000:   Ciocia turns over the CEO post to Tom Povinelli.
2002:   Povinelli is ousted, replaced by Michael Ryan.

Puyear. Ryan was a proposed replacement for Povinelli as CEO, and the group also wanted to install its own slate of nominees on the G&C board. Curiously enough, Jim Ciocia, the firm's founder and chairman, was a member of the self-named Concerned Stockholders group. The dissenters arranged a meeting with Povinelli to propose a plan to cut costs, including the closing of some 20 offices and the White Plains headquarters. In the first year alone, the group claimed, these steps could save the company $4.2 million.

G&C appeared to be headed for a contentious proxy fight, with the dissidents retaining the services of McKinsey Partners, Inc., a New York City proxy solicitation and consulting firm. After Concerned Stockholders filed its intent to call for a solicitation of written consents in early August, within a week the two sides reached an agreement to settle the matter. Ryan was named president and set to replace Povinelli as CEO when the latter subsequently resigned. In exchange, Povinelli and Puyear were given an option to purchase some of G&C's offices. Several weeks later a company they controlled, Pinnacle Taxx Advisors LLC, paid approximately $4.7 million to acquire 47 offices, representing $17.6 million in revenues. G&C sold another 16 offices to other parties. G&C also closed down its White Plains headquarters and relocated to the company's Poughkeepsie operations center. But none of these moves could prevent the company's stock from being delisted by the NAS-DAQ in August 2002. Shares were now relegated to Pink Sheets status, trading over the counter.

Ryan also had to placate lenders. In September 2002 G&C was notified by Travelers Insurance Company that it was in default because of nonpayment of a $100,000 penalty for failing to meet a stipulated level of sales. G&C also had to deal with Wachovia Bank, and in November the partners agreed to a forbearance agreement. Wachovia allowed G&C to sell agreed-upon offices as long as the proceeds were then used to pay down the firm's scheduled principal payments. Ryan also had to contend with a formal Securities and Exchange Commission (SEC) investigation that was launched in March 2003, concerning the firm's restatement of financial results and other matters. The firm continued to shed offices, and in January 2004 agreed to sell North Ridge Securities and North Shore Capital Management Corp. for $1.1 million. By the end of fiscal 2004, G&C was reduced to just 30 offices in six states, and revenues had dipped below $60 million. The firm's net loss was reduced to $5 million, an improvement over the $14 million lost in fiscal 2003 and $22.3 million a year before that. Whether the firm had yet turned the corner remained very much an unanswered question, however.

Principal Subsidiaries

Asset & Financial Planning, Inc.; G&C Mortgage Line Inc.; GTAX/Career Brokerage Inc. (50%); Prime Financial Services, Inc.; Prime Capital Services, Inc.; GC Capital Corporation.

Principal Competitors

H&R Block, Inc.; H.D. Vest, Inc.; Intuit Inc.

Further Reading

Carlino, Bill, ''Shareholder Group Demands Changes at Gilman & Ciocia,'' *Accounting Today,* August 5, 2002, p. 3.

Corry, Carl, ''G&C to Acquire Prime Capital,'' *Long Island Business News,* March 26, 1999, p. 1A.

——, ''Gilman & Ciocia Bids Island Adieu,'' *Long Island Business News,* October 29, 1999, p. 1A.

Klein, Meliaa, ''Gilman & Ciocia: A Long Way from a Small 1040 Tax Shop,'' *Accounting Today,* May 24, 1999.

—Ed Dinger

Grand Piano & Furniture Company

4235 Electric Road
Roanoke, Virginia 24014-4145
U.S.A.
Telephone: (540) 776-7000
Fax: (540) 776-5528
Web site: http://www.grand-web.com

Private Company
Founded: 1910 as Grand Piano Company
Employees: 640
Sales: $110 million (2004 est.)
NAIC: 442110 Furniture Stores

Grand Piano & Furniture Company is a private company based in Roanoke, Virginia, operating Grand Home Furnishings, one of the largest furniture store chains in the South. In addition to 19 stores located in Virginia and Tennessee, the company maintains five distribution centers. Grand is owned and run by members of the Cartledge family, with a third generation now assuming top-level positions. For the past half-century, Grand has been known for its signature custom of opening the front door for customers—or anyone who wants to visit—and offering them a cold Coca-Cola. Each year the chain serves about 1.25 million sodas.

Early 1900s Roots in the Music Business

The ''Grand Piano'' in Grand's name is an artifact of the company's history. In 1910, Paul Hash launched the Grand Piano Company in downtown Roanoke to sell a range of pianos. In the ensuing years, the store added other musical instruments, sheet music, and musical supplies. As recorded music and radio gained in popularity, cutting into sales of instruments to the general public, Grand Piano adapted by adding phonographs, in particular Victrolas, and radios to the sale mix. In the late 1920s, it went even further afield and began selling furniture, soon adding appliances as well.

The Cartledge family connection to the business came in 1945 when George B. Cartledge, Sr. and partners L.G. Sherman

and M.B. Seltzer bought Grand Piano from the Hash family. Cartledge was born in Georgia about the time Grand Piano was founded. After managing a grocery store, he became involved in the furniture business in 1931, working as a salesman in Atlanta and Knoxville. In 1937, Cartledge, along with Sherman and Seltzer, started Southeast Wholesale Furniture in Atlanta. The Grand Piano purchase expanded their operation to Roanoke, and Cartledge's brother Karl along with Henry Williamson were dispatched to run the store, the name of which was changed to Grand Piano & Furniture Co. The new owners improved the store's furniture offerings while cutting back musical instruments to just pianos, which remained a key factor in the company's business for many years. In fact, the regular truckload piano sales the company conducted in the region led in some cases to the opening of new stores.

George Cartledge bought out his partners in 1950, the same year that the store launched its popular annual warehouse sale. Grand also nurtured a long-term relationship with North Carolina-based Kincaid Furniture Company, which became the chain's largest supplier of wood furniture and largest single supplier overall. Kincaid was started by George and J. Wade Kincaid in 1946 in a small building where a handful of employees produced cedar chests and wardrobes. Cartledge began buying Kincaid's cedar wardrobes, then around 1950 asked the furniture maker if it could add bedroom furniture. Kincaid's first effort was a solid mahogany suite. Through the years, Grand and Kincaid worked hand in glove to build their businesses, with Cartledge regularly conferring with the Kincaids about what furniture the manufacturer would make. The relationship was so close that Kincaid actually named products for the Cartledge and Bennett families (Cartledge's son-in-law Robert Bennett, Jr. played a major role in Grand). For example, Kincaid offered the Cartledge cupboard and the Bennett wardrobe. For a time, the two companies jointly operated a piano factory in Morganton, North Carolina.

Grand Piano Expands in the 1950s

Grand began expanding outside of Roanoke in February 1951 when it opened a store in Radford, Virginia, followed later in the year with a store in Covington, Virginia. The fourth

Company Perspectives:

Despite significant growth over the past fifty years, Grand still retains its reputation as a local employer whose philosophy is to serve the local customer.

Grand store opened in Lynchburg, Virginia in September 1953. It was here that the tradition of serving Coke in the "little bottles" (holding 6.5 ounces) to customers was born as an opening day promotion. The swarm of people who gathered to visit the store was so great that the police were called in to provide control and the street was blocked off. By the end of the day, the Lynchburg store served 12,000 (some sources say 14,000) ice-cold Cokes. As Grand's vice-president of advertising told *Virginia Business* in 1999, "Forty-six years ago it didn't take much to move people's meter."

George Cartledge, Sr. was quick to recognize the potential of the soda giveaway, and soon free Cokes were being served at all of the Grand stores on a daily basis. It became more than gimmick, evolving into a key element of the chain's success. Cartledge took it so seriously that he issued a memo that has become part of company lore on how to properly serve a bottle of Coke. He wrote in part: "Let me emphasize how important it is to give our Cokes with enthusiasm and a smile.... Salespeople and store managers too should watch the door and be ready with a Coke when the customers walk in." It became a tradition with customers as well, as parents who cherished the memory of their first Coke at a Grand Piano store brought their own children to share the experience. Additionally, while they were visiting the store many of them shopped for furniture. Not only was the offer of a drink a neighborly gesture that customers appreciated, it served as an ideal icebreaker for salesmen who could introduce themselves while offering a Coke. Later, when they relieved the customer of the empty bottle, they were afforded another opportunity to chat. The tradition was ingrained that Grand never considered switching to Pepsi or another brand of cola, and the company continued to offer the small bottles as long as Coca-Cola offered them. Grand finally had to switch to the ten-ounce Cokes, and to keep pace with changing tastes the chain added Diet Coke, Caffeine-free Coke, Sprite, and bottled water to what it offered guests. Although damage caused to the merchandise was rare, there were spills on the carpeting that required vigilance and quick cleaning. Nevertheless, Grand considered the one-day promotion that became an ongoing tradition well worth the costs involved.

Grand added three more stores in the second half of the 1950s. The company grew through acquisition for the first time, buying M.C. Thomas Furniture Co. of Charlottesville, Virginia, and converting it into a Grand Piano store in October 1957. In addition, in that same month Grand opened a clearance center in Charlottesville. Another acquisition took place in Lexington, Virginia, in 1959 when Grand picked up Brown Furniture Co. and added it to the chain of Grand Piano stores. Along the way, Grand also picked up Ball Brothers Furniture Co. in Bristol, Virginia, and United Furniture Co. of Kingsport, Tennessee, both of which continued to operate under their old names.

Continued Expansion: 1960s–1980s

The 1960s were marked by further expansion, a change in structure, and tragedy. The latter occurred in May 1963 when a corporate airplane crashed in the mountains of North Carolina, killing the pilot and one executive and injuring three others, including Karl Cartledge. The company would never again own a plane. George Cartledge, Jr. was just graduating from Hampden-Sydney College and due to the accident took on far greater responsibilities with the furniture chain sooner than expected. Two years later, the family business experienced further changes. George Cartledge, Sr. and Karl Cartledge split the family assets, with Karl taking ownership of Ball Brothers Furniture and United Furniture Co., while George kept the Grand Piano stores. All told, Grand Piano added seven stores in the 1960s. Staunton Furniture Co. of Staunton, Virginia, was acquired and converted into a Grand Piano store in February 1961. A month later, the chain also opened a clearance center in Staunton. Two more stores, located in Harrisonburg and Waynesboro, Virginia, were added in 1965. The Harrisonburg store was the first the company built from scratch. Grand Piano closed the decade by opening a store in Pulaski, Virginia, in October 1968, a Roanoke clearance center in June 1968, and a Grand Piano in Martinsville, Virginia, in July 1969. Piano sales remained an important part of the company's business. During the 1960s, to take advantage of a mirror piano fad, Grand ran a Roanoke shop that turned old upright pianos into the popular ornamented instruments.

By this time, George Cartledge, Sr. had begun developing a succession plan, part of which included naming George Cartledge, Jr. company president in 1972. The elder Cartledge was known for his willingness to delegate responsibility and refrain from criticism. As a result, the family-dominated team of executives grew in ability and learned to work together decades before Cartledge passed from the scene. During the 1970s, the chain added just three stores as the company concentrated on the 15 units already in operation. In 1972 a Lynchburg clearance center opened, followed by a Winchester Grand Piano in July 1973. In July 1976, the first Grand Piano store opened outside the state of Virginia, in Hagerstown, Maryland.

Grand was almost visited with tragedy once again in 1980 when 16-year-old George Cartledge III was in a car accident that left him in a coma for more than two weeks. He recovered and later in the 1980s became involved in the family business, alongside another member of the third generation, his cousin Robert George Bennett. During the 1980s, Grand added to its slate of furniture stores. The company launched a new concept, Grand Interiors, which opened near Roanoke's Tanglewood Mall in October 1981. It would be the only Grand store that carried a number of upscale lines from furniture makers Henredon, Hickory Chair, and Thomasville. A Harrisonburg clearance center was added in September 1982. Grand Piano stores were opened in Blacksburg, Virginia, in August 1983, and in downtown Bristol, Virginia, in September 1984. Next, a Winchester clearance center opened in July 1986, followed by a second Grand Piano in Lynchburg in July 1989, as well as a second Charlottesville store in June 1989. Grand Piano closed only one store, at their Pulaski location, during the 1980s.

Store Closings and Openings in the 1990s and Beyond

The mix of Grand Piano stores underwent greater change in the 1990s, as the shopping district in many communities moved from downtown areas to the suburbs. The Harrisonburg clearance center was closed in 1990, while the Roanoke clearance center shut its doors in 1991 and the Lynchburg clearance center in 1992. The Charlottesville clearance center was shuttered the following year and the Winchester clearance center followed in 1995. The downtown Harrisonburg Grand Piano store was also closed in 1992 and the Martinsville store in 1994, along with the Radford and Blacksburg locations in 1996, the Hagerstown store in 1997, and the downtown Roanoke and downtown Kingsport stores in 1999. The downtown Winchester store was lost to fire in May 1996 and subsequently rebuilt outside the city.

In addition to opening suburban stores in existing markets, Grand also expanded into new markets during the 1990s. The chain added stores in Harrisonburg in May 1990, Roanoke's Valley View Mall in May 1991, and Christiansburg, Virginia, in August 1996. Grand also entered markets outside of Virginia, in September 1995 opening a store in Greenville, South Carolina, a unit in Spartanburg, South Carolina, in August 1998, and a suburban Kingsport location in June 1999. The company consciously avoided large metropolitan areas, preferring markets within 300 miles of Roanoke that it could dominate. To support its assortment of stores, Grand built regional warehouses which were intended to serve clusters of stores.

To stay current, Grand instituted a number of changes during the 1990s, such as cutting back on newspaper inserts in favor of increased television buys. With piano sales experiencing a steady decline over the years, the company finally exited the music business in 1998. As a result, the Grand Piano name no longer applied and, although the corporate name remained unchanged, the furniture stores now adopted the Grand Home Furnishings name, although long-time customers would continue to call the stores Grand Piano, much to the confusion of a younger generation. The 1990s were also marked by the death of its chairman, George Cartledge, Sr., in March 1997 at the age of 87. After suffering a number of strokes that led to his being housebound in the fall of 1996, Cartledge continued to attend every store opening and paid regular visits to the stores, delighting in the tradition of handing out Cokes as he greeted customers at the door. Because he had long since implemented a succession plan, Grand carried on without difficulty after his death. Early in 1999, his son, George Cartledge, Jr., assumed the chairmanship, while at the same time George Cartledge III became president and cousin Robert Bennett was named executive vice-president. Both shared the responsibilities of the chief operating officer.

With a third generation of the Cartledge and Bennett families being groomed to one day take full charge of the company, Grand faced some challenges due to significant changes throughout the furniture industry. The demand for high-priced, high-quality furniture, the kind that a family might pass on to succeeding generations, had abated. Instead, consumers were more interested in buying furniture with the idea that they would be changing their decor within a few years. Hence, stores began stocking less expensive furniture. Even Grand Interiors, which had relied on the sales of upscale furniture for a generation, was now adding moderately priced furniture, much of which was casual and contemporary in design as opposed to the traditional styles that had once been popular. In another attempt to remain current, Grand Interiors began selling the artwork of popular painter Thomas Kinkade, known as the "Painter of Light" because of his distinctive use of back light in his work. A second Kinkade gallery opened in the Winchester store in 2001.

Now topping the $100 million level in annual sales, Grand continued to open and close stores in the 2000s. New units included a Roanoke outlet in February 2000 and a Spartanburg outlet in 2004, as well as Grand Home Furnishings stores in Norton, Virginia, in 2001; Culpeper and Warrenton, Virginia, in 2002; and Bristol in 2004. In November 2005, Grand was scheduled to open its first West Virginia store in Lewisburg.

Principal Competitors

Ethan Allen Interiors Inc.; Scandinavian Gallery, Inc.; Sears Roebuck and Co.

Further Reading

Ashley, Mike, "The Real Thing," *Virginia Business*, December 1999.
Kelly, Sandra Brown, "Cartledges Keep Grand Tradition," *Roanoke Times & World News*, January 23, 1994, p. F1.
Stewart, Keisha, "Roanoke, County, Va., Furniture Store Renovates Style, Selling Strategy," *Roanoke Times*, October 26, 2002.
Sturgeon, Jeff, "Grand Home Furnishings to Expand," *Roanoke Times*, July 14, 1999, p. A7.

—Ed Dinger

Greatbatch Inc.

9645 Wehrle Drive
Clarence, New York 14031
U.S.A.
Telephone: (716) 759-5600
Fax: (716) 759-5654
Web site: http://www.greatbatch.com

Public Company
Incorporated: 1970 as Wilson Greatbatch Ltd.
Employees: 1,225
Sales: $200.1 million (2004)
Stock Exchanges: New York
Ticker Symbol: GB
NAIC: 423690 Other Electronic Parts and Equipment
  Merchant Wholesalers

Greatbatch Inc. is a Buffalo, New York-area manufacturer of lithium batteries, capacitors, feedthrough, enclosures, and other components used in implantable medical devices (IMDs) founded by the inventor of the pacemaker, Wilson Greatbatch. The company has also transferred its expertise to non-medical applications, developing industrial batteries used in such areas as oil and gas exploration and the Space Shuttle. However, with a new generation of IMDs on the horizon, Greatbatch remains focused on the medical field, where the company has earned a reputation for producing well built, reliable batteries, all-important qualities when powering a device that has to be surgically removed to repair. Greatbatch is a public company listed on the New York Stock Exchange.

Early 1900s Background

Wilson Greatbatch was born in Buffalo in 1919, the son of an English building contractor. Early on he displayed an inquisitive nature, experimenting with a harmonica and teaching himself how to play when he was just five. At the age of ten he tackled the challenge of perpetual motion, but like countless inventors before and since, he had to admit defeat. A radio hobbyist, he began to work his way through Buffalo State Teachers College as a radio installer, with the idea of teaching industrial arts, at a time when the United States was about to be drawn into World War II. He had already joined the Naval Reserve in 1938, then in 1940 his unit was called up for a year of active duty. The tour would last five years, as he put his amateur radio experience to good use, rising to the rank of Aviation Chief Radioman. During the war, Greatbatch served on Atlantic convoys, and later in the Pacific he flew combat missions in two-man carrier-based planes, sitting back-to-back with the pilot, manning the radio as well as a rear machine gun.

Discharged from the service in 1945, Greatbatch got married, began raising a family, and worked for a year as a telephone repairman before taking advantage of the GI Bill to continue his college education. He talked his way into Cornell University to study engineering, and to support his family he now earned extra money working at a radio station and at the psychology department's animal behavior farm, where he hooked up monitoring instruments to sheep and goats for experiments. It was also on the farm that one day during 1951 he spent a brown-bag lunch chatting with a pair of visiting brain surgeons, who told him about complete heart block, a condition in which the heart's electrical impulses are unable to reach the tissue. According to Greatbatch, he translated the problem in radio terms: the signal was not getting through. As he recalled years later, "When they described it, I knew I could fix it." Unfamiliar with the field, however, he did not realize that others shared the same idea. In fact, a year later Paul Zoll developed the first external pacemaker, only practical in the sense that it worked. Because it relied on the technology of the day, vacuum tubes and an external power supply, the system was the size of a television set, a virtual anchor on the patient, while the external electrodes could grow hot enough to burn the flesh. In contrast, Greatbatch's idea was to build a self-contained, self-powered implanted pacemaker, but he would have to file away the idea until technology caught up with his vision.

After graduating from Cornell, Greatbatch spent two years as a project engineer at the Cornell Aeronautical Lab, where he was involved in the development of amplifiers that NASA would one day use to send monkeys into space. In 1952, he became an assistant professor of electrical engineering at the University of Buffalo while working on his masters degree in engineering. He was doing some work for the Chronic Disease Research Institute in 1956, attempting to use the new silicon transistors to build an oscillator to record fast heart sounds. By mistake, he installed a resistor with the wrong resistance. It started to pulse in a steady "lub-dub" pace, which Greatbatch recognized as a sound similar to that made by a properly beating heart. He instantly realized that this circuit could provide the basis for building a device that could help a diseased heart stay in rhythm by delivering regular shocks to force the muscles to contract and pump blood, and thus serve as a pacemaker.

Key Partners in the Late 1950s

After Greatbatch received his masters at the University of Buffalo in 1957, he took a job with Tabor Instrument Corporation, where he worked on medical instrumentation and continued the development of his pacemaker. In 1958, he found an important champion for his idea, Dr. William Chardack, chief surgeon at the Buffalo Veterans Administration Hospital. While visiting Chardack to troubleshoot a problem with an oximeter, Greatbatch discovered that Dr. Chardack's assistant was an old high school friend, Dr. Andrew Gage. Greatbatch told them about his idea for a pacemaker, and Dr. Chardack was immediately excited by the idea. Three weeks later, Chardack and Gage implanted Greatbatch's first model of a pacemaker, which relied on a pair of Texas Instrument transistors, in a dog at the Veterans Hospital. Greatbatch touched two wires together and the device worked. He later wrote in his lab diary, "I seriously doubt if anything I ever do will ever give me the elation I felt that day when my own two cubic inch piece of electronic design controlled a living heart." However, after four hours the makeshift electrical tape wrapped around it as a seal proved no match for the dog's bodily fluids, which shorted out the circuit. To address this problem, Greatbatch redesigned his pacemaker using epoxy blocks, and within a year the prototype could last four months. Greatbatch and Chardack began looking for their first human subjects, but it was at this point that Taber Instrument bowed out, fearful of the legal liability.

Committed to the development of the pacemaker, Greatbatch quit his job. With $2,000 in savings and enough money to feed his family for the next two years, he set up shop in his barn, where he built 50 pacemakers of varying design, the first 40 implanted in animals. At this point, the development of the first practical implantable pacemaker had become a global technology race, and the odds that Greatbatch would prevail were slim. Then, starting in April 1960, the first of ten Greatbatch-designed pacemakers was implanted in a human patient. Most of the subjects were more than 60 years of age. The first died after 18 months, but a younger patient lived 30 years after receiving a pacemaker. Greatbatch received a patent on the device and formed a company, Wilson Greatbatch Inc., to license it. Early in 1961, Minneapolis-based Medtronic Inc. licensed the pacemaker. Wilson Greatbatch Inc. was reorganized in 1963 as Menned-Greatbatch Electronics, with Greatbatch taking over as vice-president and technical director, heading the effort to develop the "demand" pacemaker, which

did not work continuously. Instead, it only fired when the patient's natural pacemaker failed to function. During the second half of the 1960s, Greatbatch turned his attention to study the electrochemical functioning of the human body, publishing scholarly papers on the subject.

In 1970, Greatbatch resumed his work on the pacemaker, this time focusing on the batteries the device used. They lasted little more than two years, requiring surgery to replace. He formed another company, Wilson Greatbatch Ltd., today's Greatbatch Inc., and set out to create "lifetime" implantable batteries. After dabbling with nuclear power, he achieved a breakthrough using lithium as a power source. His new lithium-based batteries could last over ten years and became the gold standard for pacemaker batteries, making the company the market leader. Greatbatch turned his attention to other areas, eventually receiving more than 200 patents for his inventions, and left the running of the battery business to others. In 1985, he stepped down as chairman, turning over the post to his eldest son, Warren Greatbatch, and founded a company to become involved in genetic engineering, Greatbatch Gen-Aid Ltd. His latest ambition was to find a genetic cure for AIDS.

In 1990, the company's current chairman, president, and chief executive officer, Edward F. Voboril, joined Wilson Greatbatch Ltd. as president and CEO. He was the former president and general manager of the biomedical division of PPG Industries. Vonoril took over a company that had a near monopoly on the pacemaker battery market, directly manufacturing 60 percent of the batteries and another 30 percent under licenses it granted to other companies. However, it was a mature market, growing at a modest rate, around 4 percent a year. In the 1990s, the company began applying its technology to develop batteries for commercial customers, such as the ones used on the Space Shuttle and in the probes sent out to check for leaks or damage inside oil pipelines. Greatbatch also explored new medical applications, developing batteries for use in implantable defibrillators, drug delivery systems, and neurostimulators. The company even explored the idea of developing lithium battery-powered surgical instruments, eliminating cumbersome power cords. By the mid-1990s, the research and development push resulted in annual sales in the $50 million range. Half of the company's 800,000 batteries sold for medical uses and half for commercial devices. In a matter of five years, Greatbatch doubled its business and outgrew its main facility in Clarence, New York. It was wooed by a number of states, in particular Arizona and the Carolinas, but in the end Greatbatch elected to remain in western New York. Its decision sweetened by $1.4 million in incentives from state and local economic development agencies, management launched a $6 million expansion of company headquarters.

Management Buyout in the Late 1990s

The company was still owned by Wilson Greatbatch and his family, but that changed in 1997 when it became apparent that if the company was to remain competitive it needed greater access to financial backing. With the Wall Street firm Donaldson, Lufkin and Jenrette taking a majority interest through its medical industries unit, Global Health Care Partners, Voboril and his senior management team led a buyout effort. When it was completed, the company changed its name to Wilson Greatbatch Technologies, Inc., and Warren Greatbatch stepped down as chairman, replaced by Voboril.

Management planned to build sales to $200 million in three to five years. To achieve that goal, it looked to add new products as well as grow the business through acquisitions. Essentially Voboril wanted the company to produce every component of a pacemaker, with the exception of the microelectronics, to become in effect a one-stop supplier for its customers. In 1998, a new, more efficient capacitor for defibrillators was added to the lineup (capacitors store a battery's energy before it is delivered to the heart) and a new rechargeable lithium ion battery was also nearing production. In addition, Greatbatch completed an acquisition in August 1998, paying $71.8 million for Columbia, Maryland-based Hittman Materials & Medical Components Inc., a family-run business founded in 1962 that produced hermetic seals, electrodes, and other components for implantable devices.

Greatbatch experienced a difficult 1999, as sales grew by just 2 percent, resulting in a net loss of $2.28 million. A major setback was an industry-wide change in the design of defibrillators, which instead of using two batteries now used one. In addition, Medtronic began making its own batteries for its latest internal defibrillator. Greatbatch's management responded by cutting costs, an effort that included a temporary 10 percent cut in salaries. The company rebounded in 2000, as the addition of Hittman Materials and new products offset the loss in business incurred in 1999. Ever since the business was bought from the Greatbatch family, it was expected that sooner or later Donaldson, Lufkin and Jenrette would look to engineer an initial public offering (IPO) of stock to cash out at least part of its investment. The offering, completed in September 2000, proved successful, as Greatbatch received a $16 price, in the middle of its targeted range of $15 to $17. For its part, the company raised $80 million, earmarked to pay down debt.

A month before its IPO, Greatbatch used some of its stock to make another acquisition, picking up Battery Engineering, Inc. from Hitachi-Maxell, Ltd. Battery Engineering had recently developed the world's first fire-safe rechargeable lithium battery system. Next, in June 2001, Greatbatch paid $49 million to add Maxwell Technologies' Sierra-KD Components division, maker of ceramic capacitors. Another significant move to build the components business followed a year later when the company spent $48 million and assumed $9 million in debt for Globe Tool and Manufacturing, Inc., a Minneapolis-based maker of the titanium cases used by pacemakers and defibrillators. Globe was also a good fit because it shared the same three major customers: Guidant, St. Jude Medical, and Medtronic.

In the meantime, Greatbatch did not lose sight of internal development of new products. It launched an expansion of its Clarence facilities, including the addition of a $4.5 million, 12,300-square-foot dedicated research and development center, which opened in June 2002. The facility would be crucial in the company push to develop the batteries that would be needed to power a host of implantable devices in the current pipelines of medical companies. Cybertronics Inc., for instance, gained approval for a device to treat epilepsy and was also working on an implantable device to treat depression. Moreover, other companies were exploring ways of using implantable devices to deal with pain management, drug delivery, urinary incontinence, and, as stimulators, bone growth. Because of its proven ability to provide reliable batteries, Greatbatch was well positioned to take advantage of this new generation of products. To meet the challenge, the company invested more than $26 million in research and development in 2002 and 2003, as it completed the development of its next generation Symphony Battery. Greatbatch also remained on the lookout for opportunities to buy technology. In 2004, it paid $45 million for Fremont, California-based Nano-Gram Devices Corp., a new spin-off company that possessed technology capable of adding 50 percent more capacity to current batteries and the ability to deliver higher rates of energy. Management believed that the potential of NanoGram's technology was profound and would ensure Greatbatch's leadership position in the implantable battery market for years to come.

With the company broadening its range of products, management decided another name change was in order, given the close association of the Wilson Greatbatch name with pacemakers. In May 2005, the company shortened its name from Wilson Greatbatch Technologies to Greatbatch Inc.

Principal Subsidiaries

WGL Intermediate Holdings, Inc.; Wilson Greatbatch Ltd.; Greatbatch-Hittman, Inc.; Battery Engineering, Inc.; Greatbatch-Sierra, Inc,; Greatbatch-Globe Tool, Inc.

Principal Competitors

Eagle-Pitcher Holding, Inc.; HEI, Inc.; Medtronic, Inc.

Further Reading

Drury, Tracey, "Inventor Pursues the Unknown," *Business First of Buffalo*, September 8, 1997, p. 1.
Greatbatch, Wilson, *The Making of the Pacemaker: Celebrating a Life-saving Invention*, Amherst, New York: Prometheus Press, 1999.
Robinson, David, "Greatbatch to Raise Money by Selling Stock to Public," *Buffalo News*, May 28, 2000, p B7.
——, "Wilson Greatbatch Looks Beyond Pacemakers," *Buffalo News*, February 12, 1995, p. A13.
Thompson, Carolyn, "At 78, Pacemaker Inventor Looks Forward, Not Back," *Associate Press Newswires*, December 11, 1997.
Turner, Douglas, "Acclaim to Fame Inventor Wilson Greatbatch's Life Work Honored," *Buffalo News*, February 1, 2001, p. A1.
Woodard, Chris, "Clarence, New York Battery Maker Puts A Lot of Heart into This Market," *Investor's Business Daily*, December 27, 2001, p. A11.

—Ed Dinger

Bergerat Monnoyeur

Groupe Monnoyeur

117 rue Charles Michels, BP 169
F-93200 Saint Denis
France
Telephone: (+33) 1 49 22 60 61
Fax: (+33) 1 42 43 11 26
Web site: http://www.b-m.fr

Private Company
Incorporated: 1906; 1929 as Hy Bergerat, Monnoyeur
    et Cie
Employees: 1,797
Sales: ($837 million) (2003)
NAIC: 423810 Construction and Mining (except
    Petroleum) Machinery and Equipment Merchant
    Wholesalers; 423830 Industrial Machinery and
    Equipment Merchant Wholesalers

Groupe Monnoyeur is a leading retailer, wholesaler, and rental agency for construction and other machinery in France and elsewhere in Europe. Since 1929, the company has held the exclusive distribution contract for Caterpillar machinery in France. The company has since expanded its relationship with Caterpillar to include operations in Belgium, Poland, Luxembourg, Romania, and Algeria. In addition to the sale and rental of construction machinery, Monnoyeur has established a strong network of service centers that provides repairs and spare parts. The company has also created a number of specialized subsidiaries for markets such as power generation equipment (Eneria), materials handling equipment (Aprolis), as well as a subsidiary focused on the public works market (Bergerat Monnoyeur SCA). Monnoyeur also controls 62 percent of the Feu Vert chain of nearly 400 franchised automotive parts and repair shops in France, Spain, and Poland. Groupe Monnoyeur remains a private company controlled by the founding Monnoyeur family, led by Baudouin Monnoyeur.

Getting on Track in the 1920s

Groupe Monnoyeur's origins traced back to the development of French industry at the beginning of the 20th century. The demand for machinery and equipment in the rapidly industri-alizing country led Henry Bergerat to form a company in 1906 in order to import and sell steam-powered machinery and other equipment. Bergerat's client base came especially from the public works and construction sectors, and Bergerat developed something of a specialty in the trade in construction machinery.

Bergerat was joined in business by his cousin Francis Monnoyeur, and by the 1920s Bergerat's company had become a prominent supplier of equipment in France and, later, elsewhere in Europe. The reconstruction of France brought a steady stream of orders into the company, and by 1929 Bergerat and Monnoyeur decided to form a new company together, called Hy. Bergerat, Monnoyeur et Cie. The Monnoyeur family was to remain in control of the company into the next century.

The year 1929 also marked the beginning of the company's relationship with The Caterpillar Tractor Company. The U.S. company had just launched its famed Caterpillar 60, and Francis Monnoyeur quickly recognized its potential to transform the French construction machinery sector. By the end of that year, Monnoyeur had signed a contract with Caterpillar giving Bergerat, Monnoyeur & Cie the exclusive license to sell Caterpillar equipment in France.

Sales of the machines, including bulldozers, pavers, and the like, grew quickly and on a national level. Bergerat Monnoyeur also made an important decision early on, launching an extensive aftermarket service program, including repairs and an extensive stock of spare parts. By the late 1930s, the company had extended its service segment to provide on-site repairs, an innovation at the time, leading the company to open its first branch office in Toulouse in 1938.

Bergerat Monnoyeur's decision to develop a spare parts and repairs service played a crucial role during World War II, when the occupation of the country cut off the supply of new machinery and parts from the United States. By the end of the war, the company had become one of the country's most prominent names in construction equipment and machinery. This placed the group in a strong position to benefit from the French reconstruction market in the postwar years.

The 1950s marked the beginning of a series of vast new public works projects in France, not the least of which was the

---

Key Dates:

1906: Henry Bergerat launches a business importing and distributing construction equipment and machinery in France.

1929: Bergerat founds Hy. Bergerat, Monnoyeur & Cie with cousin Francis Monnoyeur and obtains exclusive French dealership for Caterpillar machinery.

1938: The company opens its first branch office in Toulouse.

1960: Operations are expanded to include materials handling equipment as well as power generators and engines.

1964: A dedicated engine division is set up in Bonneuil-sur-Maine.

1971: Power generator and engine assembly operations are transferred to a new subsidiary, Energie Autonome.

1980: Energie Autonome is merged into the company's engine division.

1981: A Caterpillar dealership in Algeria is acquired.

1984: The company expands into power plant installation.

1989: Feu Vert, a network of auto supply and service stores founded in 1972, is acquired.

1991: A Caterpillar dealership in Rumania is opened; Feu Vert launches Spanish operations.

1994: The company changes its name to Groupe Monnoyeur.

1996: The group buys generator set rental group Solylomat in France.

1997: The group acquires the short-term equipment rental group Slevmi in France and opens a Caterpillar dealership in Poland.

1998: Feu Vert acquires the auto supply and service division of Casino and takes a 38 percent stake in Feu Vert.

2000: Feu Vert acquires Carrefour's Spanish auto supply and service network.

2002: Feu Vert acquires Carrefour's auto supply and service network in France.

2004: The group acquires Treco, an operator of Caterpillar equipment rental stores under The CAT Store brand.

---

development of the country's Autoroute high-speed toll road system. The company responded to the rising demand for its vehicles and equipment by expanding its branch network throughout France. At the same time, the company put into place a secondary network of specialized repair and service facilities.

Diversified in the 1980s

Bergerat Monnoyeur also branched out from its sales of construction vehicles to offer new types of equipment being developed by Caterpillar and others. In 1960, the company launched a new division for the sales of materials handling equipment, such as forklifts and scissorlifts, as well as engine and generator systems and equipment specific to the public works sector. By 1964, these sales had risen sufficiently for the company to create more specialized divisions for its products. In that year the company opened a new engine division in Bonneuil-sur-Marne.

That site also became the location for a new production line for the assembly of generator sets, an operation launched by the company in 1968. This activity led to the creation of a new subsidiary, Energie Autonome, in 1970, which began assembling generator sets and engines.

Bergerat Monnoyeur's investments in its service network enabled the company to weather the difficult years following the Arab oil embargo in the early 1970s. Nevertheless, the construction sector continued its slump into the early 1980s, while the public works sector plunged into an outright crisis. In response, Bergerat Monnoyeur began seeking to diversify its operation further from its reliance on construction equipment. In the early 1980s, the company boosted its position in the materials handling market. The company also took steps to increase its operations in the engine and generator sectors. As part of that process, the company merged its engine division with Energie Autonome in 1980. That subsidiary then branched out with the launch of power plant installation operations in 1984. Bergerat Monnoyeur also made its first move into the international market, acquiring the dealership for Caterpillar in Algeria.

Bergerat Monnoyeur's longstanding service and spare parts operations led the company to expand in another direction in the late 1980s. The company's attention turned to the fast-growing automobile parts market, particularly to Feu Vert, one of the fastest-growing and largest of these businesses. Feu Vert had been founded in Lyon in 1972 and had developed a strong regional network of more than 40 stores by the end of the decade. The company had also been one of the first to add an automotive service center to its auto parts stores. Feu Vert was to grow especially strongly after it inaugurated a franchise system in 1983, a move that helped the company extend to a national level by the end of the decade.

Bergerat Monnoyeur at first acquired 50 percent of Feu Vert; by 1989, however, the company had acquired full control of the auto parts distributor. Feu Vert had meanwhile completed two significant acquisitions of its own, purchasing the 26-store Bertin group and Perf, the auto parts retail network of the Cora supermarket group. Under Bergerat Monnoyeur, Feu Vert launched a still more aggressive expansion. In 1990 alone, the company opened more than 100 new branches.

International Network in the 2000s

As one of Caterpillar's oldest partners in Europe, Bergerat Monnoyeur became the obvious choice as partner in Caterpillar's expansion into the newly opening markets in Eastern Europe. In 1991, for example, Bergerat Monnoyeur acquired the dealership for Caterpillar's equipment in Rumania. This extension was followed the acquisition of the Caterpillar dealership in Poland as well, taking over from a business that had been in place since the mid-1960s. At the same time, Bergerat's Feu Vert subsidiary had launched its own international growth strategy, targeting Spain in 1991 with the creation of Feu Vert Iberica, a joint venture with the Promodes supermarket group.

Bergerat Monnoyeur changed its name to Groupe Monnoyeur in 1994 as part of a restructuring of its operations. At that time, the company created several new subsidiaries, including Bergerat Monnoyeur Manutention (materials handling), Bergerat Monnoyeur Energie (generators and engines), Bergerat Monnoyeur International, and Bergerat Monnoyeur Travaux Publics (public works).

Groupe Monnoyeur also launched a new activity in the mid-1990s as it entered the equipment rental market. In 1996, the company acquired Solylomat, a generator set rental company. The following year, Monnoyeur added Slevmi, a company specialized in short-term rental of construction equipment. Meanwhile, Monnoyeur had also been expanding its power generator operations, securing the franchise for distributing Caterpillar's entire generator range in France in 1999. The following year, the company added energy and engine operations in Rumania, creating the subsidiary Enertrac there.

Feu Vert had also been expanding, notably with the acquisition of the entire network of automotive parts supplies and service centers operated by the Casino supermarket group in 1998. In exchange for its shops, Casino acquired a 38 percent stake in Feu Vert. Two years later, Feu Vert took over the Carrefour group's Spanish auto supply stores. Then, in 2002, the two companies reached an agreement giving Feu Vert control of Carrefour's French auto supply and service network as well.

Monnoyeur reorganized again in 2001, renaming its engine and generators subsidiary as Eneria, its materials handling business as Aprolis, while its public works operators inherited the group's history name of Bergerat Monnoyeur SCA. In 2004, the company extended into a new market, taking over Belgium's Treco, which operated an equipment rental business under The CAT Store brand in Belgium and Luxembourg. As it turned toward the middle of the decade, Groupe Monnoyeur remained one of Caterpillar's most important European partners.

Principal Subsidiaries

Aprolis; Bergerat Monnoyeur SCA; Eneria; Magellan et Bergerat

Principal Competitors

MAN AG (Germany); Multotec Holdings Proprietary Ltd.; Van Neerbos Bouwmarkten B.V.; Atlas Copco AB; Hitachi Construction Machinery Europe N.V.; Barloworld Holdings plc (United Kingdom); Alfairuz Trading and Contracting Company L.L.C; Bilia AB.

Further Reading

"Carrefour Looks to Sell Auto Repair Shops," *DSN Retail Fax*, December 23, 2002, p. 2.
"Commission Clears France's Feu Vert Stake in Spanish Car Repair Firm, Autocenter Delauto," *European Report*, September 13, 2000, p. 346.
"Feu Vert fete ses trenet ans," *Autoactu*, April 5, 2002.

—M.L. Cohen

Hammacher Schlemmer

Hammacher Schlemmer & Company Inc.

9307 North Milwaukee Avenue
Niles, Illinois 60714
U.S.A.
Telephone: (847) 581-8600
Fax: (847) 581-8616
Web site: http://www.hammacher.com

Private Company
Incorporated: 1898
Employees: 250
Sales: $170 million (2001 est.)
NAIC: 454110 Electronic Shopping and Mail-Order Houses

With over 150 years of history under its belt, Hammacher Schlemmer & Company Inc. publishes America's longest-running mail-order catalog. Though it does not rank among the nation's largest catalogers, its clever and unusual offerings have made it one of the most recognized names in the business. The company's varied lines of specialty goods includes housewares, electronics, leisure and sports products, giftware, collectibles, and toys for adults as well as children. The company boasts that it was first to offer a number of innovative gadgets and goods to American consumers over the years, from the electric toaster in 1930 to the robotic lawnmower in 2000. The catalog, which claims a circulation of over 30 million, generates an estimated 70 percent of revenues, with the remainder coming from online sales and a retail location in New York City.

Mid-19th Century Origins

The origin of Hammacher Schlemmer as a company name comes not from its founder but from a pair of early investors. William Tollner founded the business in 1848 as a hardware store in Manhattan's Bowery section. Over the next 11 years, German immigrant Alfred Hammacher invested about $5,000 in the store, accumulating a half-interest in the business along the way. The company name was changed to Tollner and Hammacher in 1859 in honor of his financial contribution. Throughout the early 1860s, Tollner's nephew, William Schlemmer, gradually bought out his uncle's stake in the store. Young

Schlemmer had immigrated to the United States in 1853 at the age of 12 and thereafter worked for his uncle, often hawking tools on the sidewalk in front of the store. By the time Tollner died in 1867, 26-year-old Schlemmer had entered into partnership with Hammacher. The company published its first catalog in 1881 and took its present name two years later. Hammacher Schlemmer & Company was incorporated in 1898, 50 years after its founding.

Though there were only 600 cars in all of New York in 1908, Hammacher Schlemmer diversified into automotive tools and replacement parts at the turn of the 20th century, soon amassing one of the broadest selections available at the time. The company's international renown grew with its product line; at least one budding Communist considered its collection seminal. According to a company publication, "In 1916 a member of the Russian government's staff purchased a sample of every piece of hardware offered in the company's 1,000-page catalog to use as manufacturing masters in preparation for the Bolshevik Revolution."

Hammacher Schlemmer maintained its original location until 1906, then moved into its flagship, 12-story New York store on East 57th in 1926. Though this would be its sole retail outlet for over a half-century, during which retail sales often exceeded catalog revenues. William F. Schlemmer succeeded his father as president of the company upon the latter's death in 1914.

Hammacher Schlemmer launched its first housewares catalog in 1931 and began to earn a reputation for making the newest technologies available to American consumers. Many of the now-mundane items were the first of their kind to appear in the U.S. market. Company publications crow that the Hammacher Schlemmer catalog offered America's first toaster in 1930, the first steam iron and electric dry shaver in 1948, the first answering machine (the "Telephone Valet"), and first microwave oven (Amana's Radarange) in 1968. Though revolutionary at the time they were launched, these and many other "gadgets and gizmos" inaugurated by Hammacher Schlemmer would later become staples of the American household.

Hammacher Schlemmer had its own trademarked elves to promote its wares, and a 1929 Broadway production titled *The*

Little Show gave the company free nationwide publicity. The program included the song "Hammacher Schlemmer, I Love You," which rhapsodized, "Hammacher Schlemmer, I love you / Roebuck and Sears, I adore you / If you want to buy a bassinet or buy a hog / Don't be in a fog, use our catalogue / Hammacher Schlemmer / You're sweet and dear / Hammacher Schlemmer I repeat dear / Macy's and Gimbel's have plenty of thimbles / But I love you."

Postwar Emphasis on Luxuries

Though the company's early housewares probably seemed exotic to catalog recipients, it was not until after World War II that Hammacher Schlemmer shifted its focus to luxury goods. The change came after 1953, when William Schlemmer's widow, Elsie, sold the cataloger to Chester H. Roth's Kayser-Roth investment group. The firm dropped its hardware items two years later and began to emphasize unique, sometimes one-of-a-kind articles targeted to upscale customers.

Dominic Tampone, who had joined the cataloger as a stock boy at the age of 15, worked his way up to president of the company in 1959. He has been credited with leading Hammacher Schlemmer's quest for the unusual and outlandish for its catalogs and store. Tampone described the typical Hammacher Schlemmer item in a September 1968 profile in *Merchandising Week:* "It's brand new . . . it could be too clever in concept and looks. It could be like a Rube Goldberg contraption. But the idea is good and it serves the purpose for which it is intended." Offerings in the catalog soon ran the gamut from electric shavers and massagers to such fantasy gifts as British taxis and spa trips. In 1961, the company proffered regulation-sized bowling alleys for $4,300 a lane, or a $600 "discount" for two. Hammacher Schlemmer also started offering limited edition and collector's items, including signed baseballs and lithographs during this period.

Over the years, Hammacher Schlemmer's unique range of items drew a globe-trotting clientele. Sheiks, princes, Hollywood stars, and U.S. presidents all shopped at the flagship store, buying everything from flashlights to beds to cars. Their shopping sprees often brought Hammacher Schlemmer free publicity, as the press eagerly covered the spending habits of the rich and famous.

Tampone created a wholesale operation in the early 1960s that quickly grew into Hammacher Schlemmer's Invento Products Corporation. Invento soon evolved into a clearinghouse for the new and unusual, sourcing items from around the world and selling them under its own namesake brand. It sold goods not only to Hammacher Schlemmer but also to such major national retailers as Sears and Neiman Marcus. By the end of the decade, Invento was generating annual sales of about $2.5 million.

Changes in Ownership: 1970s and 1980s

Tampone continued to guide Hammacher Schlemmer through two changes in corporate ownership. Conglomerate Gulf + Western Industries, Inc. acquired the company in 1975, then sold it five years later to John Roderick MacArthur's Bradford Exchange Ltd. Inc. After over a half-century with the company, vice-chairman Tampone died in 1982.

Under MacArthur's chairmanship, Hammacher Schlemmer opened two new retail outlets in Chicago (1984) and Beverly Hills (1986). The company's reputation for carrying outlandish, extravagant, and expensive products continued to grow, driven by such products as $139,000 "bionic dolphin" personal submarines, $39,000 home ski slopes, and $34,000 model train sets. Hammacher Schlemmer's unconditional guarantee of satisfaction clearly inspired a great deal of confidence in its customers. However, high-priced, "gee-whiz" articles like these were little more than attention getting devices for Hammacher Schlemmer. Long-running favorites were far more down-to-earth: electric shoe buffers, portable clothing steamers, ultrasonic jewelry cleaners, and air cleaners. Furthermore, while the prices of its most widely publicized items were often sky-high, the cataloger's annual sales totaled less than $35 million at the end of the 1980s.

Though Hammacher Schlemmer did not manufacture any of its products, it stamped many with its own seal of approval. The company started "an associated but independent" testing arm, the Hammacher-Schlemmer Institute, and inaugurated its "Best" rating in 1983. At the Institute, products are graded by both consumers and category experts for ease of use and durability, among other relevant criteria. Instead of touting brand or manufacturer names in its catalogs, Hammacher Schlemmer emphasizes quality by highlighting products that win its "Best" rating. "Bests" and "Firsts" in 1997 catalogs ranged from the "Best Nose Hair Trimmer," at $19.95, and the "First Flat Panel Television" for $25,000.

The 1990s and Beyond

Like many other catalogers, Hammacher Schlemmer rode a cresting wave of mail-order success in the 1980s and early 1990s. As baby-boomers entered their peak earning years, they found themselves with more disposable income and less time to spend it in malls and shopping centers. Many turned to catalogs as a convenient way to shop without leaving the house, and mail-order houses were quick to oblige them. The catalog industry in general benefited tremendously from these trends in the 1980s, as mail-order sales increased more than 300 percent during the decade. Catalog sales constituted about three-fourths of Hammacher Schlemmer's total revenues by 1989, up from 40 percent in 1968. The company's overall sales grew as well, nearly tripling from an estimated $70 million in 1992 to about $190 million in 1996.

To celebrate the company's 150th anniversary, New York City renamed the block on 57th Street between Lexington and

Key Dates:

1848: William Tollner establishes the business as a hardware store in Manhattan's Bowery section.
1881: The company publishes its first catalog.
1898: Hammacher, Schlemmer & Company incorporates.
1926: The company opens its flagship, 12-story New York store on East 57th Street.
1930: The Hammacher Schlemmer catalog offers America's first toaster.
1953: William Schlemmer's widow, Elsie, sells the cataloger to Chester H. Roth's Kayser-Roth investment group.
1975: Conglomerate Gulf Western Industries, Inc. acquires the firm.
1980: The company is sold to John Roderick MacArthur's Bradford Exchange Ltd. Inc.
1998: Hammacher Schlemmer celebrates its 150th anniversary.
2005: The Chicago-based retail location closes its doors, and company headquarters move to the suburbs.

By now, the company's main product categories included electronics, leisure and recreation, travel, home office, automotive, kitchen, garden, patio and pool, children's toys, memorabilia, furniture, decorative accessories, and apparel. New products such as the Folding Strolling Pet Carrier, the Feline Drinking Fountain, and The Three-Step Pet Staircase hit catalog pages in 2004. Another best selling product was the Progression Wake-up Clock. Retailing at $49.95, this alarm-clock gradually wakes up a sleeper with light, aroma, and nature sounds. The company's new garden-related products included the Upside-Down Tomato Garden, the Umbrella Greenhouse, the Effortless Motorized Wheel Barrow, and the Hover Mower.

Hammacher Schlemmer's focus for the future continued to be on providing exciting products that met its customers' needs. If the company adhered to this tradition, the Hammacher Schlemmer catalog and online shopping site would no doubt feature fun, quirky, and creative products for years to come.

Principal Competitors

Cornerstone Brands Inc.; The Neiman Marcus Group Inc.; Sharper Image Corporation.

Further Reading

Berman, Phyllis, and R. Lee Sullivan, "Limousine Liberal," *Forbes*, October 26, 1992, pp. 168–169.
Bird, Laura, "Forget Ties; Catalogs Now Sell Mansions," *Wall Street Journal*, November 7, 1996, pp. B1–B12.
Dubbs, Ed, "Dominic Tampone: New Item 'Discovery Room' Needed At Housewares Show," *Merchandising Week*, September 9, 1968, p. 8.
——, "Dominic Tampone: The Genial, Offbeat Merchant Who Is Hammacher Schlemmer," *Merchandising Week*, September 2, 1968, p. 8.
"Gadget Seller Grows Online," *Crain's Chicago Business*, April 18, 2005, p. 54.
Masello, Robert, "The Original Gizmo Gallery," *Travel & Leisure*, April 1989, pp. 221–226.
Higgins, Amy, and Sherri Koucky, "The Little Patent Went to Market," *Machine Design*, September 5, 2002, p. 30.
Munde, Jeannine, "Making It Year Round with Novelty Gift Items," *Daily News Record*, November 26, 1984, pp. 2–3.
Okell, Bob, "Dominic Tampone, 68, 'Dean of Housewares,'" *Retailing Home Furnishings*, August 30, 1982, pp. 23–24.
Riedel, Ernest C., *Seventy-Five Years of Constant Growth: Hammacher, Schlemmer & Co.*, New York: Robert L. Stillson Co., 1923.
White, George, "Made to Order; Catalog Industry Turns a New Page in Bid for Holiday Sales," *Los Angeles Times*, December 9, 1995, p. D1.

—April Dougal Gasbarre
—update: Christina M. Stansell

3rd Avenue "Hammacher Schlemmer Way." Notwithstanding its global renown, Hammacher Schlemmer was one of the U.S. catalog business's smaller players in the 1990s, constituting far less than 1 percent of the industry's total annual sales. Moreover, though the venerable merchandiser faced competition from upstarts like Richard Thalheimer's The Sharper Image, it seemed highly unlikely that a company with 150 years of experience and the backing of the wealthy MacArthur family would soon relinquish its reputation for "Offering the Best, the Only and the Unexpected."

Hammacher Schlemmer entered the 2000s on solid ground. Determined to maintain its reputation for offering new and cutting edge products, the company teamed up with PatentCafe to create a Fast-Track Product Review program that expedited the concept-to-store process for new inventions. For the first time in its history, the company relied on an outside firm to review new consumer-created products that would possibly end up in the famous Hammacher Schlemmer catalog.

During this time period, intense competition in the retail sector left Hammacher Schlemmer's catalog sales flat. Meanwhile, the company's online sales were growing at a rate of 30 percent per year from 2002 to 2005. By 2005, online sales accounted for one-third of company revenues. That year, the company shuttered its Chicago retail location, leaving the historic New York City store as the single remaining Hammacher Schlemmer outlet in the cataloger's arsenal. Company headquarters were also moved to a Chicago suburb at this time.

Harris Teeter Inc.

701 Crestdale Drive
Matthews, North Carolina 28105
U.S.A.
Telephone: (704) 845-3100
Fax: (704) 432-6111
Web site: http://www.harristeeter.com

Wholly Owned Subsidiary of Ruddick Corporation
Incorporated: 1960 as Harris Teeter Super Markets, Inc.
Employees: 14,500
Sales: $2.43 billion (2003)
NAIC: 44511 Supermarkets and Other Grocery (Except
   Convenience) Stores

Harris Teeter Inc. has grown from a small North Carolina grocer into a chain of almost 140 grocery stores throughout the Carolinas, Tennessee, Virginia, Florida, and Georgia. While the company maintains stores in both urban and rural areas, Harris Teeter's primary focus is on an upscale urban clientele with a taste for quality and variety in food. Harris Teeter is a subsidiary of Ruddick Corporation, a holding company whose other primary interest is in American & Efird, Inc., a manufacturer of sewing thread. In 2004, Harris Teeter ranked as the 37th largest supermarket in the United States.

Harris and Teeter Teaming Up in the 1950s

The chain that became Harris Teeter started as two small North Carolina enterprises in the late 1930s. The first of these was Harris Super Market, opened in Charlotte in 1939 by W.T. Harris, who had borrowed $1,500 to start the business three years earlier. Although nothing like the vast shopping palaces that would eventually characterize the Harris Teeter chain, Harris Super Market had several notable distinctions: It was the first air-conditioned supermarket in its county, and it stayed open until nine o'clock on Friday nights. In 1939, in the town of Mooresville, North Carolina, Paul and Willis L. Teeter opened Teeter's Food Mart with $1,700 in capital.

The two stores grew into small chains, and by 1958, the Harris and Teeter companies had begun to merge their buying efforts and storage facilities. On February 1, 1960, they formally united as

Harris Teeter Super Markets, Inc., with a combined force of 15 stores. Soon thereafter, in Kannapolis, North Carolina, they opened their first new Harris Teeter store, and by 1963, the company had a total of 25 stores. Harris Teeter opened a newer and larger warehouse, with offices, and in the 1960s made the first two of many acquisitions. First the company purchased five Tilman's Grocery stores in the North Carolina town of Shelby, then it added an independent store in Gastonia and another in Charlotte.

Acquisition Followed by Growth: 1970s–80s

In 1969, Harris Teeter itself was purchased, this time by Ruddick Corporation. The latter had begun business in 1919 as R.S. Dickson & Company, an investment banking firm based in Gastonia, North Carolina. Founder Rush Dickson offered a capital planning service to public and private firms, and in 1968 his sons Alan and Stuart made R.S. Dickson a subsidiary of Ruddick Corporation, along with Efird Mills, a textile company. The corporation had provided financial backing to Harris Teeter, and by purchasing all of the chain's assets in 1969, Ruddick—traded on the New York Stock Exchange—made Harris Teeter its third subsidiary.

In the 1980s Harris Teeter began an expansion program, in large part by acquiring other stores and companies. First came Hunter Dairy, a firm older even than Ruddick Corporation. In 1917, bookkeeper Harvey B. Hunter had started Hunter Dairy, and in 1921 he took over the Selwyn Dairy Farm in Charlotte. In its early days, Hunter Dairy serviced only the nearby area and developed a reputation for delivering its product within four hours of the time the cows were milked. Harvey Hunter was an innovator in his cooling system, using brine water, and he took what was then considered extraordinary care to prevent bacteria or spoilage. In 1937, eight years after the company acquired Burchmont Farm in Charlotte, Hunter began pasteurizing its milk—a first in the area—and a decade later it built a new, modern facility near its Burchmont Farm location. From 1956 to 1980, Harvey Hunter's son Charles ran the company, and in 1980 his younger brother James became general manager, continuing in that position after the acquisition of Hunter Dairy by Harris Teeter in the same year.

Harris Teeter's growth by acquisition continued. In 1984, Ruddick purchased Food World, a Greensboro, North Carolina-based supermarket chain founded in 1917 by George E. Hutchens, and merged it with Harris Teeter. Food World had 52 stores in North Carolina and Virginia, giving Harris Teeter (which had expanded into South Carolina and Tennessee) stores in four states. With Food World's 3,000 people, Harris Teeter now had 7,000 employees—or "associates" as it preferred to call them—making it the second largest food chain in the Carolinas. The Food World acquisition also added a distribution center to the company's holdings.

Four years later, in 1988, Harris Teeter again added 52 new stores through an acquisition, this time purchasing the supermarkets of Big Star, as well as a warehouse from the Grand Union Company. In 1990, ten years after acquiring Hunter Dairy, Harris Teeter bought a Borden Dairy plant, and in 1991 it added a 139,000-square-foot freezer facility to Hunter's 550,000-square-foot nonperishable storage and distribution facility in Greensboro.

During the early 1990s, Harris Teeter moved its corporate offices to a 97,000-square-foot building in Matthews, North Carolina. With the purchase of five Bruno stores in South Carolina in 1993, Harris Teeter increased its presence in that state, one of America's most competitive arenas for grocery stores. Perhaps even more competitive, however, was the Atlanta market, and Harris Teeter moved into Georgia in the fall of 1993 with the opening of a new store in Atlanta's upscale Buckhead district.

Coffee Bars and Floral Shops in the 1990s

Atlanta, with a high per capita income and a large population of transplants, represented a potential growth market for a high-end grocery chain. And yet it was a highly competitive area. According to *Progressive Grocer*, in 1994 the city had 4.2 chains competing for every customer, as compared with 2.9 nationally, and though population growth was explosive, supermarket square-foot growth had outpaced it by 7 percent. "Every supermarket operator thinks his market is the most competitive in the country," *Progressive Grocer* announced in 1994, adding, "Right now, Atlanta retailers may be correct." Among high-end chains, Bruno's had not succeeded in that market, but Publix Super Markets was making inroads, and now Harris Teeter moved in, with an appeal to a somewhat higher income level than that of Publix.

One observer called the Buckhead store a "yuppie heaven," and referred to it as "a giant deli with a few groceries thrown in." Some questioned how the facility, with a floral shop, coffee bar, sushi bar, juice bar, deli, and plenty of other attractive amenities, could possibly make money. Yet it apparently did, and Harris Teeter continued to expand in the Atlanta market,

with stores in Dunwoody in 1995, and in the area near Emory University in 1997. Although the company eventually cut back on the features at the Buckhead location, it began to set the tone for Atlanta supermarkets, which started to adapt to a more high-end strategy.

Harris Teeter's activities in Atlanta are noteworthy precisely because of that market's high competition factor. Although conditions may have been marginally less fierce in other areas where Harris Teeter operated, its base was within some of the fastest-growing areas of the United States, including the "research triangle" of Raleigh-Durham-Chapel Hill, North Carolina, and parts of South Carolina.

To an extent, the company did not follow set patterns with its stores, as *Progressive Grocer* explained in a 1995 profile: "The 139-store chain does not believe in prototypes. It prefers something new every time it opens a store. If the new approach works, it will be used in some, but not all, new and remodeled stores." Instead of concerning itself with economies of scale when entering a new market—that is, establishing several stores at once to reduce per-store start-up costs—Harris Teeter, as it demonstrated in Atlanta, was willing to open just one store at a time.

"We worry about the neighborhood, not the entire market," Fred Morganthall, vice-president for operations, told *Progressive Grocer*, adding, "We only need one store in a market to make it viable." In its concern for the economic environment, the company divided its facilities into two types: neighborhood stores and community stores. Neighborhood stores, which comprised approximately two-thirds of all Harris Teeter operations in the mid-1990s, were the so-called "yuppie heavens," which catered to customers who, in Morganthall's words, "want good variety, chef-prepared entrees and . . . every new frozen food entree and ice cream that comes on the market." Community stores, by contrast, appealed to what Morganthall called the "Mayberry RFD" clientele, a reference to a television show in the 1960s set in rural North Carolina. At community stores, the appeal was more broad, with greater emphasis on customers shopping for bulk items such as "25-pound bags of flour and 10-pound bags of sugar."

A Continuing Urban Emphasis in the 1990s

Despite the apparent lack of a prototype, there were certainly key elements common to most Harris Teeter stores, a fact acknowledged by Morganthall in 1994 when he noted that the company was moving from a typical store size of 33,000 square feet to one of 50,000 square feet. He added in an interview with *Progressive Grocer* that the company's primary interest was in 45,000-square-foot urban stores. Thus the "typical" Harris Teeter store was large and urban, with an upper-middle class customer base. Certain other features distinguished the chain as well.

One of these features was the level of service, which *Service Industries Journal* highlighted in an April 1992 article: Harris Teeter employees are encouraged to "take excellent care of customers," an element of the company's mission statement. Another key feature was the size and design of the stores, which were typically very large—as much as 60,000 square feet, slightly larger than a football field—with high ceilings, elegant

Key Dates:

1939: Harris Super Market opens in Charlotte, North Carolina; Paul and Willis L. Teeter open Teeter's Food Mart in Mooresville, North Carolina.
1960: The two companies formally merge to create Harris Teeter Super Markets Inc.
1969: The Ruddick Corporation acquires Harris Teeter.
1980: The company purchases Hunter Farms.
1984: Ruddick buys Food World, a Greensboro, North Carolina-based supermarket chain.
1988: Harris Teeter adds 52 new stores through an acquisition, this time purchasing the supermarkets of Big Star.
1990: Borden Dairy Plant is added to the firm's holdings.
2001: Twenty-six stores are sold; the company exits the Atlanta market.

lighting, and pleasing architectural features that, in the words of *Chain Store Age*, "recall a turn-of-the-century market hall."

At this time, the company placed a high emphasis on selection, with dozens of brands or variations on a certain item—salad dressing, frozen pizza, bagels, or beer. Among meats, for instance, the choices far exceeded the traditional chicken, beef, pork, and lamb. Even customers with a taste for rattlesnake, if they placed a special order, could purchase this delicacy fresh. The company had a number of on-duty chefs, working in the deli, the bakery, and various specialty areas such as a salad bar where customers could have chef salads made to order. On weekends in some stores, Harris Teeter featured omelets with a choice of ingredients, which customers could enjoy with a cup of coffee chosen from a wide selection at the coffee bar.

Although Harris Teeter stores often included plenty of nonfood items, the emphasis was clearly on food. When it opened in 1997, the Emory University-Sage Hill Shopping Center store in Atlanta was remarkable for consisting of two stories, a result of the fact that when the company purchased a run-down Winn Dixie that it converted (in the process sprucing up the shopping center and repaving the parking lot), it underestimated its need for size. Among students at the nearby campus and residents of adjoining neighborhoods, a considerable Jewish population prompted the company to feature a kosher deli run by a rabbi at the store. There was also a large coffee bar, which Emory students kept busy for much of the day. Moreover, in addition to its many food-related features, the store had a large section devoted to greeting cards, which sold briskly with students. Unlike many grocery stores, however, it offered neither a pharmacy nor many general merchandise product lines. Morganthall stated a key company principle when talking to *Progressive Grocer*: "We go after the customer who likes food; we don't have a lot of general merchandise."

Amenities such as those at the Emory University store came with a price, and customers whose primary concern was cost tended to shop at chains other than Harris Teeter. The company, which ironically started as two different small-town grocery store chains, kept its focus on bigger stores in the more

lucrative and upscale urban markets. In 1996, for instance, Harris Teeter sold seven stores in what Ruddick Corporation's annual report called "less urban markets," and closed down three small stores. It also replaced several older facilities, and as a result had 134 stores at the end of the year—five fewer than when it began. Yet sales increased by 5 percent, a fact that the annual report attributed to "customer acceptance of larger, new-format stores, strong feature plans, merchandising and advertising, strong holiday sales, and a 4% increase in store square footage during the year." During the mid-1990s, the company also instituted its VIC ("Very Important Customer") program, which made use of specially coded cards presented at the time of purchase, to assist in tracking its best customers' buying habits.

Harris Teeter was involved in a number of community-oriented activities during this time, and often the opening of new stores was accompanied by donations to charitable associations. When the company opened a new facility in Nashville's Peartree Village Shopping Center in April 1997, for instance, the company announced donations ranging from $2,000 to $3,000 to organizations such as the Special Olympics and the Nashville Symphony. Harris Teeter was also involved in activities such as Child Safety Awareness Day, a scholarship program at UNC-Charlotte, and Metrolina Food Bank. Through such efforts the company pledged to continue fostering a sense of community pride in the locations Harris Teeter stores serviced. Such locations were bound to increase in number, as the company remained focused on an aggressive expansion program into the late 1990s.

Harris Teeter in the New Millennium

Harris Teeter entered the new millennium on solid ground, but the company faced several challenges. Intense competition forced the supermarket chain to rethink its expansion strategy. In 2001, Harris Teeter made the decision to exit the Atlanta market and to sell 12 South Carolina-based stores. Overall, 26 stores were jettisoned. Thomas W. Dickson, president and CEO of Ruddick Corporation during this time, commented on the move in an August 2001 *Progressive Grocer* article: "A sale of our stores in these areas is a prudent business decision that will substantially strengthen the company's overall performance." He went on to explain, "Capital can now be committed to our core markets, which have consistently generated the attractive levels of profitability and, we believe, offer the greatest potential for long-term return on capital and increased shareholder value."

Along with a renewed focus on its core markets, Harris Teeter also relied heavily on its VIC program. In 2001, the company used information from the program to offer its loyal customers incentives to return. New inventory controls also were put in place in order to reduce waste and lower costs. By the end of 2001, it appeared as though Harris Teeter's efforts were paying off. Despite an economic slowdown, both sales and profits had increased over the previous year's figures.

While continuing to face heightened competition amid a period of sluggish consumer spending, Harris Teeter remained successful. The company opened 12 new stores during 2002. In 2003, it finished construction on a new location in downtown

Charlotte, North Carolina. Meanwhile, customer satisfaction remained at the forefront of Harris Teeter's strategy. In 2002, the Harris Teeter Rancher beef program was launched, giving its shoppers high-quality branded beef, selected by a consortium of ranchers.

In 2004, the company secured a 2.97 percent increase in comparable store sales—among the highest increases in the supermarket retail industry. Overall, sales rose by 5.8 percent over the previous year, to $2.6 billion, and profits grew by 11.5 percent. During the year, seven new Harris Teeter stores opened their doors in North Carolina. Fifteen stores were remodeled and nine underperforming locations were shuttered.

In the years to come, Harris Teeter would no doubt remain in fierce competition with other supermarkets as well as supercenters, chain drug stores, and dollar stores. The company's success in recent years proved it was a stronghold in its core markets. By listening to its customers and adapting its strategy to comply with market demands, Harris Teeter appeared poised to serve shoppers well into the future.

Principal Competitors

Food Lion, LLC; Ingles Markets, Inc.; Wal-Mart Stores, Inc.

Further Reading

Bennett, Stephen, "Best in the East," *Progressive Grocer*, March 1993, pp. 36–53.

Lewis, Leonard, "A Little Bit of Country and a Little Bit of City," *Frozen Food Age*, August 1994, p. 20.

——, "Harris Teeter Takes Honors as '94 Master Merchandiser," *Frozen Food Age*, August 1994, pp. 1, 14+.

Radice, Carol, "Destination: Harris Teeter," *Progressive Grocer*, May 1997, pp. 62–70.

Smith, Doug, "The Charlotte, Observer, N.C., Doug Smith Column," *Charlotte Observer*, April 10, 2002.

Sparks, Leigh, "Customer Service in Retailing—The Next Leap Forward?," *Service Industries Journal*, April 1992, pp. 165–84.

Springer, Jon, "Promotion Fuel Profit Gains at Harris Teeter," *Supermarket News*, May 16, 2005, p. 20.

Weinstein, Steve, "Georgia on Their Minds," *Progressive Grocer*, October 1994, pp. 99–104.

——, "Harris Teeter Dares to Be Different," *Progressive Grocer*, April 1995, pp. 43–46.

Wilson, Marianne, "Harris Teeter Celebrates Food Through Design," *Chain Store Age*, December 1996, pp. 168–69.

Zwiebach, Elliot, "Harris Teeter Cuts Costs with In-House Ad Production," *Supermarket News*, April 18, 2005, p. 28.

—Judson Knight
—update: Christina M. Stansell

HDOS Enterprises

5601 Palmer Way
Carlsbad, California 92008
U.S.A.
Telephone: (760) 930-0456
Toll Free: (800) 321-8400
Fax: (760) 930-0420
Web site: http://www.hotdogonastick.com

Private Company
Founded: 1946
Employees: 1,300 (est.)
Sales: $45 million (2003)
NAIC: 722210 Limited-Service Eating Places

HDOS Enterprises operates the Hot Dog on a Stick chain of more than 100 company-owned units, located mostly in regional shopping malls in 15 states, and several international franchised operations. The Carlsbad, California-based company is a quick serve restaurant chain that is completely owned by employees. In addition to its signature batter-dipped turkey hot dog on a stick, the chain sells batter-dipped cheese on a stick, French fries, and freshly made lemonade. A few locations serve all-beef hot dogs on a bun. The chain is known for the brightly colored uniforms and handmade caps worn by its service personnel. This signature outfit has proved so popular that employees are forbidden to lend them out as costumes.

Beginnings

HDOS was founded by Dave Barham, born in Dexter, Missouri, in 1913. During the Depression years of the 1930s, he moved to Detroit with the dream of one day heading General Motors. Instead, he became a window washer, and like many Midwesterners at the time began to dream of moving to California, lying on a beach, and watching palm trees swaying in the ocean breeze. In 1939, he convinced his wife to move to Southern California, where he found work testing radar and radio equipment at Lockheed Aircraft and at every opportunity visited Santa Monica's Muscle Beach. A small concession selling cotton candy, ice cream, and snow cones caught his eye, and he began badgering the owner to sell the business to him, which is

what eventually transpired. Borrowing $400 from his older brother Hugh, Barham bought the business in 1946, renaming it Party Puffs. Instead of selling cotton candy, ice cream, and snow cones, he developed his hot dog on a stick that could be eaten while strolling the beach. For the batter, he modified his mother's cornbread recipe, then fried the batter-covered hot dogs in cooking oil. Always the promoter, Barham claimed the stick performed three functions: it acted as a "handy handle," provided hickory smoke flavoring, and could serve as a toothpick after the hot dog was eaten. Barham also sold lemonade, attempting to make it with honey to eliminate the need for sugar. Ironically, for someone who would become known as the hot dog king, Barham was a bit of a health nut, a runner long before jogging became popular, a man who seldom ate meat and was conscientious about his diet. His honey-sweetened lemonade, however, tended to congeal, forcing him to rely on sugar. Because Muscle Beach was experiencing problems with broken glass in the sand, he served his lemonade in a green paper cup, which also became a signature element of the business. He liked to boast at the time, "We wash our dishes with a match." Barham would always buy his hot dogs from Oscar Mayer (before he turned to all-turkey dogs in the late 1980s) and relied on one grower in Ventura County for his lemons.

With his Muscle Beach concession a success, helped to some extent by a giant slide he built on the beach, Barham turned his attention to the fair business. In 1948, he first began selling hot dogs on a stick and lemonade at the Los Angeles County Fair, establishing a relationship that would last for the rest of his life. For the next 35 years, he operated trailers at a dozen fairs, the profits of which were instrumental in supporting the growth of the Hot Dog on a Stick chain. He also tried to sell his Hot Dog on a Stick idea to other fair concessionaires, traveling the fair circuit around the country with little more than a bowl, some ingredients, and a whip to make the batter. However, vendors were able to concoct their own batters to make "corn dogs," and while the item became a staple around the country Barham failed to profit from the fair business beyond the trailers he ran.

Expansion and Inspiration in the 1950s and 1960s

In the early 1950s, Barham began opening Hot Dog on a Stick stands on other California beaches. Customers never did

Company Perspectives:

An icon since 1946, Hot Dog on a Stick is 100% owned and operated by its employees. What began as an entrepreneurial dream on the beaches of Southern California has flourished into an organization where everyone has a stake in the outcome.

understand why the operations were called Party Puffs, which was perhaps an allusion to the hot dog batter, which Barham always called Party Batter, and so around 1960 he dropped the name in favor of Hot Dog on a Stick. Later in the 1960s, Barham paid a visit to Las Vegas, where he was inspired to develop the chain's classic uniform. He noticed how the Las Vegas show girls wore the same elaborate costumes and headdresses, so that they not only stood out but also appeared interchangeable. More importantly to Barham, they appeared familiar. His idea was to outfit his people in a brightly colored uniform to offer something of a show to his customers, while also creating the impression that the same person was waiting on them, turning each Hot Dog on a Stick stand into a familiar place. He used a sleeveless top with vertical stripes of red, white, blue, and yellow, along with then popular hot pants. The origin of the famous cap worn by employees of Hot Dog on a Stick was a visit Barham made to a horse show, where he admired the caps the riders wore, which he made taller in the fashion of a Las Vegas showgirl headdress. The uniform made its debut at the Indo Fair Grounds near Palm Springs, California. It replaced an earlier polka-dot design uniform and would undergo periodic changes, mostly to the cap, which grew taller with time. To further accentuate the height of the employees, Barham would also install platforms behind the counter so that his gaily colored workers stood out even more.

Moving in Malls in the 1970s

Realizing that beach locations were limited, Barham began looking for other places where potential customers could be found. In the early 1970s, he directed his attention to shopping malls, which were quickly growing in popularity. His first venture in this channel was in a neighborhood mall, the Old Town Mall, where a Hot Dog on a Stick stand opened in October 1972, but already his sights were set on the larger enclosed regional malls. He approached San Diego-based Ernie Hahn, a pioneer mall developer, about opening a Hot Dog on a Stick location in one of his properties. It was a radical idea at a time before the advent of food courts when enclosed malls did not even allow food and drink inside the doors, due primarily to clothing retailers' fears that customers might stain the merchandise. Never a man to take no for an answer, he pestered Hahn until he finally relented. However, Barham was given a location as far away from Hahn as possible—the Fashion Place Mall in Murray, Utah, outside of Salt Lake City. As had been the case on the beach, speedy friendly service, the portability of a hot dog on a stick, and a lemonade in a paper cup proved to be a winning concept. The new outlet, which opened in November 1973, also sold deep-fried cheese on a stick, a new menu item introduced around this time.

Once Barham gained entry into one mall, he found it easier to convince other mall landlords to allow him into their proper-

ties, since they now had a chance to see how the concept worked in practice. Moreover, by keeping his food costs to a minimum, Barham was willing to pay a higher rent than other tenants. The profits from the fair business would now prove instrumental in the chain's expansion drive, as Hot Dog on a Stick became increasingly dedicated to its mall locations. A few units would be franchised operations, but the vast majority were company-owned, which offered a greater payoff. By 1980, the chain had 23 stores doing about $3 million a year in business.

Over the course of the 1980s, Barham added approximately 50 units. In late 1989, he began to develop a succession plan. In order to reward his loyal employees, he decided to set up an Employee Stock Ownership Plan (ESOP) to enable them to take over the chain, choosing this option because he believed it allowed his employees the best opportunity to buy the company with pre-tax dollars. He split off the fair concession business, which was turned over to his children: Dan, Gary, and Diane. (Gary eventually bought out his siblings.) In addition to creating a trust that gave the employees an option to purchase the company, Barham also handpicked a nine-person management committee to run the business.

Employees Buy Company in the 1990s

In March 1991, Dave Barham died from pneumonia and lung complications at the age of 77, just before the chain he founded was about to open its 90th store in a shopping mall. The new management team, in order to exercise the option to purchase HDOS Enterprises, first had to establish the value of the company through an independent valuation firm. The price turned out to be much higher than anyone anticipated, and although the employees had some cash at their disposal and could take advantage of a key man life insurance policy, they fell well short of the amount needed. Because the chain was a leased operation and lacked collateral, management had no choice but to back any loan with their personal assets. Outside consultants recommended that the management committee concentrate ownership of the company in their hands, arguing that younger workers would not be interested in staying long enough to become vested and draw the retirement benefits of gaining an equity stake. The management committee rejected the advise, however, electing instead to remain true to the vision Dave Barham had laid out for the company after his departure.

HDOS started a new chapter in its history $9 million in debt and uncertain of what the future held. Fortunately, the economy was strong during most of the 1990s, malls were expanding, and the chain, supported by an experienced and motivated work force, was able to see its way through a transitional period and continue to grow. In 1997, the company was able to pay off the ESOP loan.

During the six years following the death of Dave Barham, Hot Dog on a Stick essentially followed the path already laid out by its founder, the only real change being the 1994 addition of French fries to the menu. Then, in 1998, management began instituting some significant changes. A design agency was hired to help the company pursue a re-branding effort after 30 years of relying on the same logo and packaging designs. As a result, the company decided to brand its popular lemonade. For decades it was simply called Original Lemonade, but it now

Key Dates:

1946: Dave Barham begins selling hot dogs on a stick on Muscle Beach.
1948: Barham starts working county fairs.
1973: The first Hot Dog on a Stick unit opens in a regional mall.
1991: Barham dies and leaves the company to his employees.
1999: Muscle Breach Lemonade is branded.
2000: Juicy Lucy's hamburger chain is acquired.
2004: Juicy Lucy's is sold.

became Muscle Beach Lemonade. The company even decided to take a fresh look at its iconic uniform, much to the concern of employees who were devoted to it. In the end, the only alteration was the addition of a cap sleeve.

As part of a diversification effort in the late 1990s and early 2000s, HDOS launched a concept built around its popular lemonade called Muscle Beach Lemonade & Hot Dogs. The company also entered into a co-branding arrangement with a pretzel chain. A more ambitious expansion move was the purchase of the Juicy Lucy's hamburger chain in 2000. HDOS also looked to develop frozen corn dogs and frozen lemonade products for sale in grocery stores. However, with the downturn in the economy, and stretched thin by the expenditures of its diversification efforts, HDOS abandoned the Muscle Beach concept and returned to focusing on its core hot dog on a stick business. In addition, the Juicy Lucy's hamburger chain, which had proved difficult to run, was sold to Ultimate Franchise Systems Inc. in 2004.

In 2001, Fredrica Thode took over as president. She had been hired by Barham in 1980 as a receptionist. She took on an increasing amount of responsibility and at various times was involved in every aspect of the company's operations. HDOS began to pay down debt and rebuild value in the company as same store sales climbed and the chain resumed its growth pattern. This was accomplished by following the basic formula established by its founder, who believed in keeping things simple: offer a limited menu but do it well and make it entertaining. It was a formula that worked for more than half a century and promised to succeed for many years to come.

Principal Competitors

Corn Dog 7 Inc.; Galardi Group, Inc.; Nathan's Famous, Inc.

Further Reading

Abbott, Sam, "Hot Dog King Barham Dead at 77," *Amusement Business*, April 1, 1991, p. 17.
Pratte, Bob, "Bold Stripes Proudly Worn," *Press-Enterprise*, October 1, 2003, p. B1.
——, "Proud to Wear Red, White, Blue, Yellow," *Press-Enterprise*, December 20, 1999, p. B1.
Rodrigues, Tanya, "What's More Basic Than Hot Dogs and Lemonade? A Uniform," *San Diego Business Journal*, April 29, 2002, p. 1.

—Ed Dinger

Health Communications, Inc.

3201 Southwest 15th Street
Deerfield Beach, Florida 33442
U.S.A.
Telephone: (954) 360-0909
Fax: (954) 360-0034
Toll free: (800) 441-5569
Web site: http://www.hci-online.com

Private Company
Incorporated: 1977
Employees: 116
Sales: $70 million (2005)
NAIC: 511130 Book Publishers; 511120 Periodical
   Publishers

Health Communications, Inc. (HCI) is a leading publisher of self-help and inspirational books. The company began by publishing books and pamphlets geared towards counselors and therapists involved in rehabilitation from drug and alcohol addiction. The company reached a wider audience in the early 1980s with several best-sellers dealing with life issues and personal growth. The company is best known for its ''Chicken Soup'' series of books. The Chicken Soup books grew to be an international publishing phenomenon in the 1990s. The huge success of these books brought HCI away from the brink of bankruptcy and transformed the small company into the envy of the publishing industry. HCI runs a Spanish-language imprint, offering translations of many of its successful English-language titles; an imprint called HCI Teens; Simcha Press, which publishes books for people searching for ''Jewish enrichment''; and the distribution of trade books published by the Hazeldon Foundation, one of the world's leading centers for addiction recovery. HCI also publishes *Counselor*, a peer-reviewed journal for professionals in the mental health and addiction fields, with a national subscriber base of more than 21,000. Another HCI subsidiary is U.S. Journal Training, Inc., which provides accredited continuing education for mental health professionals. U.S. Journal Training sponsors conferences and workshops and teaches students in distance-learning classes. HCI also operates a creative design business called Reading, Etc. This company specializes in creating reproduction wall art and statuary from primarily ancient civilizations using historically accurate designs. HCI also owns and operates its own printing and binding equipment, producing both hard- and soft-cover books.

Roots in Addiction Recovery

Health Communications was founded in 1977 by Peter Vegso and Gary Seidler, two Canadians with backgrounds in drug abuse counseling. Vegso and Seidler worked in marketing and media relations at a Toronto nonprofit called the Addiction Resource Foundation. They published a newspaper for professionals in the addiction and recovery field, and in 1976 they secured a grant from the U.S. Drug Abuse Council to launch a similar publication in the United States. Vegso and Seidler traveled in a Volkswagen Beetle from Toronto to Florida, where they incorporated Health Communications, Inc. in Pompano Beach. Vegso claimed, in an interview with the *New York Times* (July 3, 1998) that when the pair began the publishing company, ''We didn't know how to do it.'' They knew there was a burgeoning market for publications dealing with addiction, but they did not know that most publishers offered their authors advances, and that few owned and operated their own press and binding machines. Their unconventional approach did not stymie the pair, however. They met many potential authors at conferences and conventions for mental health workers and reached many readers the same way, through personal contacts and word of mouth. With only a handful of employees and no sales staff, the young company managed to keep going by publishing books and pamphlets aimed primarily at a narrow audience of professionals in the drug and alcohol addiction field.

The company achieved its first mass-market success in the early 1980s with the book *Adult Children of Alcoholics*, by Janet Woititz. HCI received Woititz's manuscript in 1982, and Vegso and Seidler decided to publish it, predicting that there was rising interest in the children of alcoholics. Their simple assumption underestimated the book's impact. *Adult Children of Alcoholics* came out in 1983 and slowly garnered a formidable reputation. Woititz's book climbed onto the *New York Times* bestseller list, and it eventually sold close to two million copies. The book is now considered the bible of the Adult Children of Alcoholics movement, bringing broad recognition to the problems of people whose parents drink. The success of

Company Perspectives:

Changing lives . . . one book at a time. Creating personal abundance for readers and customers.

Woititz's book helped propel HCI's sales from $1 million in 1985 to $17 million by 1990.

Ups and Downs in the Late 1980s

The small company's revenue took a steep upward turn with the booming sales of *Adult Children of Alcoholics*. However, one book could not sustain the company, and HCI saw its sales drop again as Woititz's book lost steam. HCI picked another winner in 1988 with a book by psychologist John Bradshaw called *Bradshaw On: The Family*. This book reached the number-one spot on the *New York Times* bestseller list, and it had broad impact on American culture, popularizing the terms ''inner child'' and ''dysfunctional family.'' The company's fortunes whipsawed. It had branched out, offering books meant for a large reading public instead of a narrow professional audience, yet its big hits in self-help publishing did not guarantee HCI a steady income. The year 1990 was a financial high mark for the publisher, but then its revenue fell sharply. Over the fiscal year spanning 1991 and 1992, the company went into the red, losing $2 million. HCI responded by diversifying its list even more, going beyond its recovery and healing niche to put out other titles on inspiration, spirituality, relationships, and women's issues.

HCI's publishing niche became more crowded by the early 1990s as major publishers noticed the popularity and profitability of the self-help category. At the same time, government and private insurers cut back on spending on addiction recovery programs, nipping budgets for professionals who might have been buying HCI's materials. The company scrambled to put out ever more books as its market both dwindled and grew tougher. Facing serious financial trouble by 1992, HCI decided to cut back, both on its staff and its offerings. It concentrated on its back list, which included workhorses like the Woititz and Bradshaw titles, and held back on new ventures. These were darker days than the company had faced since its modest beginnings. Nevertheless, Vegso and Seidler were still willing to take some risks. In 1993, they put out a book that over 30 other publishers had passed on. This decision assured the company's fortune for the next decade and longer.

The Chicken Soup Books in the 1990s

The book that vaulted HCI to the forefront of the publishing industry, making it one of the most envied companies in the business, was a collection of short stories and anecdotes called *Chicken Soup for the Soul*. The tales were written and/or compiled by a pair of professional motivational speakers, Jack Canfield and Mark Victor Hansen. The story of the book's publication and subsequent success reads like one of its own anecdotes of triumph over adversity through hard work and optimism.

Jack Canfield had taken a master's degree in psychology from Harvard and become an inner-city school teacher. His experiences with underprivileged youth led him to write a book for teachers on the importance of ''self-concept,'' later popularized as the term ''self-esteem,'' in the classroom. He eventually went into business for himself giving motivational seminars on self-esteem. Mark Victor Hansen was also a motivational speaker, with a focus on business audiences and sales conventions. The two, though working independently, were colleagues, and each had perfected many audience-grabbing anecdotes: one- or two-minute stories that plucked the heartstrings, so to speak, while delivering a motivational moral. Canfield began writing down some of his stories in the late 1980s, as audience members frequently came up to him after his speeches wondering where they could find published versions of his tales to give to their friends and family members. After a conversation with Hansen, the two decided to do a book together, compiling 101 short stories.

By 1991, the manuscript was completed, and the pair had found a literary agent, Jeffrey Herman. Herman took *Chicken Soup for the Soul* to New York, offering it to various major publishers. He also arranged meetings for the co-authors with industry wheels. However, the project was a flop. Publisher after publisher passed on the manuscript, advising the co-authors that short stories would never sell, that the book was too sentimental, that the title was dumb. Herman showed the book to progressively smaller presses but got no takers. Canfield and Hansen had come up with a detailed marketing plan for the book, which included pledges from readers to buy a certain number of copies of *Chicken Soup* and resell them to their friends. None of this impressed mainstream publishers. When some 33 publishers had said no to the manuscript, Herman resigned, wishing his clients the best of luck elsewhere.

The undaunted authors were still convinced they could sell the book, and they visited the American Booksellers Association meeting in Anaheim, California, flogging the manuscript to countless publishers who had set up booths. At last, the manuscript ended up in the hands of Peter Vegso of Health Communications. Vegso perused *Chicken Soup* while waiting for his plane back to Florida, and he was so overcome by it that he began to cry. So HCI agreed to publish *Chicken Soup for the Soul*, offering the authors no advance. The print run was to be 20,000 copies, and Hansen and Canfield agreed to buy half of that themselves. They would do their own marketing. By the time the book came out in 1993, the co-authors were deeply in debt. They had a lot of merchandise on their hands, and they owed fees left and right for permission to reprint the previously published works in their anthology.

Canfield and Hansen had an unusual marketing strategy that by-passed bookstores altogether. As only a small percentage of the public actually ever entered a bookstore, they decided to sell *Chicken Soup* in all sorts of other venues, including gas stations and nail salons. They sold their book at their motivational seminars as well as at flea markets, and they cajoled owners of many kinds of businesses to place a few books by the cash register. They did radio interviews, and also got an excerpt from the book placed in a Los Angeles parenting magazine. That magazine's editor was so impressed by the piece that he helped the pair reprint it in dozens of similar magazines across the country. Sales grew very gradually, but after 16 months on the market, *Chicken Soup for the Soul* made it onto the *New York Times* bestseller list.

The book had taken a full 16 months to reach bestseller status, but that was only the beginning. HCI's revenues had

```
┌─────────────────────────────────────────────────┐
│                                                   │
│                 Key Dates:                        │
│                                                   │
│  1977:  Vegso and Seidler move to Florida to found a │
│         rehabilitation-oriented press.            │
│  1983:  HCI puts out its first best-seller, Adult Children of │
│         Alcoholics.                               │
│  1992:  Staff and offerings are cut back.         │
│  1993:  HCI publishes Chicken Soup for the Soul.  │
│  1994:  Chicken Soup for the Soul reaches best-seller list │
│         after 16 months on the market.            │
│  1998:  The company reissues A Child Called It.   │
│  2002:  HCI begins distributing books for the Hazeldon │
│         Foundation.                               │
│                                                   │
└─────────────────────────────────────────────────┘
```

climbed and plunged with its previous hit books, but *Chicken Soup for the Soul* had staying power of almost unparalleled proportions. When it made it onto the *New York Times* list, it had sold 1.3 million copies. In mid-1995, the book had been at the top of the list for 39 weeks, and HCI put out the first of many sequels, *A Second Helping of Chicken Soup for the Soul*. Canfield and Hansen followed this up with a slew of new Chicken Soup titles, such as *Chicken Soup for the Country Soul*, which came with its own music CD, *Chicken Soup for the Woman's Soul*, *Chicken Soup for the Teenage Soul*, *Chicken Soup for the Golfer's Soul*, *Chicken Soup for the Cat and Dog Lover's Soul*, and on and on. Some of these popular titles had their own sequels, including four volumes devoted to the woman's soul and two for the golfer. Within five years from the publication of the first volume, the Chicken Soup series had sold some 43 million copies, and the books had been translated into 36 languages. Health Communications made 85 percent of its revenue from the Chicken Soup books. Overall sales at HCI stood at $85 million in 1997 and grew to $95 million in 1998.

On top of the enormous success of the Chicken Soup books, HCI had other strong sellers in its stable as well. In 1997, Peter Vegso bought out his partner Gary Seidler, and the company invested $1.5 million in an improved Web press. The company remained small despite its new wealth, keeping its number of employees to around 100. HCI put out another hit book in 1998, Dave Pelzer's *A Child Called It*. Pelzer had published the book elsewhere in 1993, but his memoir of child abuse had not sold well at all, and he had taken the rights back. Health Communications reissued the book and, promoted with a television talk show appearance, it became another mega-seller, spending more than 300 weeks on the *New York Times* best-seller list. In the late 1990s, HCI had roughly 400 titles on its back list. Its costs were low, as it did its own production and promotion, and its major franchise, the Chicken Soup series, seemed inexhaustible. The chairman of much bigger rival Time Warner Trade Publishing told the *New York Times* (July 3, 1998): "They are the dream not only of small publishers, but large publishers."

Other Ventures in the 2000s

HCI planned to survive beyond Chicken Soup, though by 2000 the series did not seem to be at all lagging. The company varied its offerings, putting out its first work of fiction in 1999.

Health Communications also stepped up the number of books it published annually, increasing from 35 in the late 1990s to around 50. The company also worked tirelessly to sell the Chicken Soup books internationally, where the translations were very popular in countries such as Mexico and Japan. It expanded its physical plant and updated its marketing and distribution plans for better use of the Web.

HCI developed a new imprint in 2000, called Simcha Press. This division specialized in books on spiritual growth and personal enrichment geared towards Jewish readers. The company also diversified into an imprint for its teen books, HCI Teens. Its *Chicken Soup for the Teenage Soul* had grown into a series within a series, with editions for the Christian teen, the pre-teen, and several sequels to the original teenage soul book. HCI also issued a similar book series, *Taste Berries for Teens*, under its HCI Teens imprint. The Taste Berries books were also anthologies of inspirational morsels, authored by Bettie and Jennifer Youngs.

In 2002, Health Communications agreed to take over distribution of trade books produced by the renowned addiction recovery center the Hazelden Foundation. HCI had not distributed other publishers' books before, but the tie with Hazelden was natural, considering HCI's background in materials for rehabilitation professionals. The next year, the company spent a billion dollars on a new binding machine that would for the first time give the publisher the ability to produce its own hardcover books. In 2003, HCI also launched a Spanish-language imprint called HCI Espanol. HCI had put out a Spanish version of *Chicken Soup for the Soul*, *Sopa de Pollo Para el Alma*, as early as 1995, and this volume became one of the best-selling Spanish-language books in the United States. HCI saw potential in the Spanish-language market, not only for the Chicken Soup books but for many other self-help titles on its back list and for new books to come.

Ten years after the first Chicken Soup book came off of HCI's press, the series had sold an estimated 80 million copies in English, and an untold number of copies in 35 different languages. Canfield and Hansen and various other collaborators had put out some 70 Chicken Soup titles, extending the brand into books of cartoons and photographs as well as many variations and follow-ups of earlier titles. However, Health Communications was not entirely defined by the popular non-fiction series. By 2005, its back list had grown to more than 500 separate titles, and it worked with some 150 different authors. It began calling itself the "Life Issues Publisher," meaning it put out diet, women's issues, and business books as well as more traditionally defined self-help tomes. The company had come through a boom-and-bust cycle in the late 1980s and early 1990s, when popular titles had quickly boosted sales and then left HCI struggling. The company handled the much bigger boom of the Chicken Soup books with what seemed to be wisdom and foresight gained from experience. The series had brought HCI unexpected revenue, but the company continued to branch out with new and different books, so that it had other authors to rely on in case the Chicken Soup empire should falter.

Principal Subsidiaries

Reading, Etc.; U.S. Journal Training, Inc.

Principal Competitors

Free Spirit Publishing; Peachtree Publishers, Ltd.; Random House, Inc.

Further Reading

Carvajal, Doreen, ''Breaking the Publishing Mold,'' *New York Times*, July 3, 1998, p. D1.

Farmanfarian, Roxanne, and Katayoon Zandvakili, ''Marketing Blitz for New 'Chicken Soup' Titles,'' *Publishers Weekly*, August 4, 1997, p. 24.

Ferguson, Andrew, ''A River of Chicken Soup,'' *Time*, June 8, 1998, p. 62.

Hughes, Dennis, ''Holistic Writing for Publication,'' *Share Guide*, March-April 2003, p. 16.

Milliot, Jim, ''Health Communications Sales Neared $100 Million in '98,'' *Publishers Weekly*, February 8, 1999, p. 96.

——, ''HCI Makes Distribution Deal with Hazelden,'' *Publishers Weekly*, December 2, 2002, p. 10.

Miracle, Barbara, ''Health Makes Wealth,'' *Florida Trend*, November 1998, p. 106.

Ospina, Carmen, ''HCI Launches Spanish-Language Imprint,'' *School Library Journal*, June 2003, p. SS10.

''Quietly Reaching the Top of the List,'' *Florida Trend*, August 1986, p. 104.

''Spoon Feeding,'' *People Weekly*, July 24, 1995, p. 156.

—A. Woodward

Hensel Phelps Construction Company

420 Sixth Avenue
Greeley, Colorado 80632
U.S.A.
Telephone: (970) 352-6565
Fax: (970) 352-9311
Web site: http://www.henselphelps.com

Private Company
Incorporated: 1937
Employees: 2,600
Sales: $1.83 billion (2004 est.)
NAIC: 236220 Commercial and Institutional Building
   Construction; 237310 Highway, Street, and Bridge
   Construction

Hensel Phelps Construction Company operates as one of the largest private construction companies in the United States. The company, which is employee owned, pursues a broad variety of projects, including the construction and renovation of industrial and residential spaces, commercial offices, airports, sports facilities, healthcare and educational institutions, public assembly areas, and retail space. The company provides a broad range of pre-construction and post-construction services, including scheduling, estimating, budgeting, zoning and code compliance, bid packaging, engineering and status reporting, as well as certificates of occupancy, warranty programs, moving services, and as-built documentation. Hensel Phelps also offers development services, such as land acquisition, feasibility studies, financing, and leasing.

Beginnings

Hensel Phelps Construction Company was founded in 1937 by Hensel Phelps of Greeley, Colorado. The success of Hensel Phelps, however, lay in the extraordinary business odyssey of Hensel Phelps's son, Joseph. Following his graduation from Colorado State University in 1951 with a bachelor's degree in construction management, Joseph Phelps spent four years as a naval reserve officer during the Korean War. Upon his return in 1955, Joseph joined his father as a partner in the Hensel Phelps Construction Company, a modest commercial enterprise that

specialized in supplying remodeling and construction services. Joseph was the company's second full-time employee. When Hensel Phelps retired two years later, the younger Phelps bought his father's share in the business and proceeded to develop it into one of the nation's preeminent construction firms.

After becoming president in 1957, Joseph Hensel introduced the idea of making equity interests available to managers and employees of the company. By doing so, he created a uniquely successful incentive program that he and others later credited with playing a major role in the company's remarkable growth. In 1963, Joseph Phelps hired field engineer Bob Tointon, who was promoted to vice-president one year later and then to president of Hensel Phelps in 1975, with Joseph remaining as chairman of the board. Together, Phelps and Tointon built the company into one of the nation's leading construction firms by opening a series of regional offices around the country and successfully competing for major construction projects.

National Expansion

In 1967, Hensel Phelps opened its first branch office in Burlingame, California, to coordinate and oversee the growing number of construction projects in California. The company then expanded into the Southwest with the opening of an office in Austin, Texas in 1972. The Southwest office focused on construction projects in central and southern Texas and New Mexico. With the real estate boom in the 1980s, the company experience rapid growth and expansion. New offices were opened in both Santa Clara, California, in 1983 and Little Rock, Arkansas, in 1987. The company's national growth was spurred by large projects for such technology companies as IBM, as well as Wal-Mart. Hensel Phelps expanded its presence in Southern California with the opening of its Irvine office in 1990.

By the later 1980s, however, Joseph Phelps and Bob Tointon began to phase out their ownership of Hensel Phelps. Joseph Phelps's day-to-day involvement in the company already began to decline beginning in the late 1970s as he pursued his interests as a wine maker and merchant. In 1973, he bought a ranch in the Napa Valley and launched a second business in the wine industry. By 1982, he was devoting himself full-time to his business interests in the wine industry and had become a resident of California. He later produced one of the top ten red wines of the world, Insignia.

New Ownership and Continued Growth

In 1989, ownership of Hensel Phelps passed to twenty-eight employee stockholders, none of whom held more than a 10 percent stake. The buyout represented the culmination of 25 years of the employee ownership program developed by Joseph Phelps. At the same time, Phelps Inc., the parent company of Hensel Phelps, was reorganized under company president Jerry Morgensen and other long term managers, who assumed control over Phelps Inc.'s general contracting business. After selling his shares in the firm, Joseph Phelps continued his business partnership with Tointon by forming another company, Phelps-Tointon, Inc., which took over the diversified real estate and non-general contracting activities of Phelps Inc. Thereafter, Phelps-Tointon owned and operated several manufacturing companies, including Armor Safe Technologies, Southern Steel Company, and Rocky Mountain Prestress, Inc.

By 1990, Hensel Phelps had become the largest construction firm in Colorado and the thirty-fourth largest in the country. Since 1957, the company's annual sales had grown from $1.6 million to $600 million. The company also succeeded in restoring to life the once venerable Pickens-Bond Construction Company after acquiring it in 1987. Founded in 1947, and once considered Arkansas' premiere construction firm, Pickens-Bond went bankrupt in the summer of 1987 when a number of its real estate ventures turned sour. Hensel Phelps saw the collapsed firm as an entry point in the Southeast market. After untangling its business deals and landing new contracts both within and outside the state, Hensel Phelps turned the firm around, leading it to earn $100 million in 1990. The Southeast was a new market for Hensel Phelps, and it looked to greater Atlanta and other areas for new growth opportunities. At the same time, the firm began to expand into the international arena.

In early 1991, the company could point to numerous and successful major construction projects, such as a 400-room luxury Sheraton Grand Hotel in La Jolla, California, a Ritz

Carleton Hotel in San Diego, the Shamu Stadium at Sea World in Texas, and a terminal at San Antonio International Airport. In 1992, the firm became an equity partner with Elitch Gardens in its planned new and relocated park in Denver. The new park was expected to cost $90 million, with Hensel Phelps serving as both general contractor and long-term investment partner.

Major Projects in the 1990s

In the fall of 1994, United Airlines hired Hensel Phelps to resolve problems with a controversial baggage handling system which repeatedly delayed the opening of the new $5 billion Denver International Airport (DIA). Although the venture came with risks, it also presented opportunities for the company to make a bigger name for itself in airport and terminal construction projects. The company succeeded in resolving the problems to the satisfaction of United Airlines. In 1996, *The Press-Enterprise* of Riverside, California, quoted Gary H. Lantner, director of facilities for United Airlines, as saying that the "successful inauguration of the first phase of the baggage system required to open DIA could not have been achieved without the firm leadership of Hensel Phelps." The successful DIA venture, together with other expansion projects for United Airlines at San Francisco and Los Angeles airports, helped the firm secure a project to build a $250 million, 530,000-square foot, twenty-six gate passenger terminal at Ontario International Airport in 1996. In 1998, the company was also chosen as the overall manager of a massive $1.2 billion expansion at the Dallas/Fort Worth International Airport. The project included plans to expand the airport's existing terminals in addition to the construction of new terminal space and a $650 million passenger transportation system between the terminals.

The company went on to build other major projects, including the National Ignition Facility at Lawrence Livermore National Lab in California, rocket launch facilities at Cape Canaveral in Florida and in California, the Midfield Concourse at Washington Dulles Airport, the Sahara Hotel and Casino in Las Vegas, and the Stealth Fighter Maintenance Docks at Holloman Air Force base in New Mexico. By the late 1990s, the company had a record of building just about anything and had district offices in San Jose and Irvine, California; Phoenix, Arizona; Austin, Texas; Little Rock, Arkansas; Orlando, Florida; and Chantilly, Virginia.

In 1999, Hensel Phelps was in its fourth generation of employee ownership with a net worth exceeding $78 million. In 1973, the company was earning $87 million in business; in 1989, $400 million; and in 1998, business volume had risen to over $1 billion. Despite the company's remarkable success, Hensel Phelps president Jerry L. Morgensen said the company was struggling to recruit workers. He noted that the low-tech construction business now existed in a high-tech world with fewer people looking into the trades to replace a craft base that was aging and retiring.

In 1999, the company also began planning a change in its international focus from foreign clients to pursuing projects for U.S. companies and government agencies that required overseas construction services. Moreover, Hensel Phelps planned on concentrating more on securing project management positions overseas rather than on general contracting work, given the complicated nature of the projects and the constantly changing

Key Dates:

1937: Hensel Phelps Construction Company is founded.
1955: Joseph Phelps, son of founder Hensel Phelps, joins the company.
1957: Joseph Phelps becomes company president after Hensel Phelps retires.
1963: Bob Tointon joins the company, forming a business relationship with Joseph Phelps.
1967: The company opens its first branch office, in Burlingame, California.
1972: The company opens a southwestern branch office in Austin, Texas.
1973: Bob Tointon is appointed company president; Joseph Phelps remains as chairman of the board.
1983: The company opens a branch office in Santa Clara, California.
1985: Jerry L. Morgensen becomes the fourth president of the company.
1987: Hensel Phelps acquires Arkansas firm Pickens-Bond Construction Company.
1989: Ownership of Hensel Phelps passes to twenty-five stockholders.
1990: A Southern California office opens in Irvine.
1994: United Airlines hires Hensel Phelps to resolve its baggage system at Denver International Airport.
1996: A Mid-Atlantic office opens in Chantilly, Virginia.
1998: The company's Southeast district expands to Orlando, Florida.
2001: The company opens a South Central district office in Dallas, Texas.

rules with private foreign clients. Nevertheless, the company saw better returns on international projects with margins in the 10 to 15 percent range as opposed to about 5 percent in the United States. Although Hensel Phelps believed it needed to pursue international business for continued growth, it kept a firm footing in the U.S. market.

Entering the 21st Century

By 2000, Hensel Phelps was consistently ranked among the country's top ten domestic general contractors. The company had a strong financial base, unlimited bonding capacity, and a debt-free portfolio. As Hensel Phelps entered the 21st century, it continued to win prime construction contracts. In 2001, for example, the company won a $125 million building contract from the Smithsonian's National Air and Space Museum at Dulles International Airport, a $285 million expansion contract for the Colorado Convention Center in Denver, and a Pentagon renovation contract worth $758 million. The company had an advantage in obtaining the Pentagon contract because of the more than $1 billion in contract work it had performed around the world for the Army Corps of Engineers. The renovation project began before September 11, 2001 and continued alongside the repairs to the building caused by the terrorist attack.

In 2001, the company expanded its South Central presence with the opening of another office in Dallas, Texas. In suc-

ceeding years, Hensel Phelps's numerous projects included the design and construction of a technical support center for the Federal Bureau of Investigation, a 32-story condominium tower in downtown San Diego, an Electromagnetic Aircraft Launching System facility for the Naval Air Engineering Station at Lakehurst, New Jersey, and a new U.S. consulate Compound in Cape Town, South Africa.

With these and numerous other contracts, Hensel Phelps had firmly established itself as one the nation's leading general contractors. In 2004, the company continued to win significant new contracts, including one with the University of Arizona to expand a chemistry building and to construct concrete frames for a medical research building. Hensel Phelps also secured a project for a new 733-stall parking garage for Denver Health and Hospital Authority. Together these and other projects were expected to provide a continuing stream of revenues for the near future.

Hensel Phelps's strengths relied primarily on its strong relationships with top U.S. corporations, including Kodak, IBM, United Airlines, and Wal-Mart. Nevertheless, while these relationships seemed to assure a stable source of future projects, they also signified a high dependence on the U.S. market. In addition, by 2005, the company still had not pursued significant overseas development projects, leaving it exposed to the risks of fluctuations and downturns of the U.S. economy. Still, the company could look to strong growth in such sectors as new residential development and the life sciences industry, including health care services, which were poised for considerable expansion in the coming decade in the United States.

Principal Competitors

Austin Industries Inc.; Barton Mallow Company; Clark Enterprises, Inc.; Dick Corporation; DPR Construction, Inc.; Hoffman Corporation; McCarthy Building Companies, Inc.; Rooney Brothers Company; Rudolph & Sletten, Inc.; The Sundt Companies, Inc.; The StructureTone Organization; Turner Industries, Ltd.; Walbridge Aldinger Company; Hunt Construction Group.

Further Reading

Allen, Margaret, "Airport Names Five Firms for $1.2 Billion Expansion," *Dallas Business Journal*, October 2, 1998.

Cube, Christine, "National Air and Space Museum," *Washington Business Journal*, April 13, 2001.

Deckard, Linda, "Elitch Gardens' New Chapter Will Speed Relocation Process," *Amusement Business*, September 14, 1992.

"Denver Picks Greeley, Colo.-Based Contractor to Expand Convention Center," *Knight Ridder/Tribune Business News*, August 30, 2001.

Flynn, Larry, "Pentagon Wedges Will Be Rebuilt," *Building Design & Construction*, November 2001.

Graebner, Lynn, "Plenty of Surprises Surround Exporter of the Year Award," *Business Journal*, June 11, 1999.

Hicks, L. Wayne, "AMI Battens Down Hospital Project's Hatches," *Denver Business Journal*, April 23, 1990.

Lorenzen, Rod, "Back from Bankruptcy: Pickens-Bond's New Owner, Hensel Phelps, Has Revved Up Revenues to $100 million in 1990," *Arkansas Business*, October 8, 1990.

McAuliffe, Don, "Ontario, Calif., Airport Terminal Contractor Selected," *Knight Ridder/Tribune Business News*, May 8, 1996.

——, "Ontario Terminal Builder Received High Marks for Its Work at Denver Airport," *Knight Ridder/Tribune Business News*, June 3, 1996.

Moore, Paula, "Hensel Phelps Erects Launch Pad," *Denver Business Journal*, September 4, 1998.

Simpson, Bill, "Hensel Phelps Takes on Big Projects: Construction Company Adds to Colorado's Ocean Journey to Its Growing Resume," *Denver Business Journal*, April 30, 1999.

"$65 Contract Let for NIF Construction," *BMD Monitor*, February 6, 1998.

Tuttle, Al, "Wedged in the Middle: One Distributor's Location at the Pentagon Is the Right Place at the Right Time," *Industrial Distribution*, October 2002.

White, Suzanne, "Pentagon to Award $62M Contract," *Washington Business Journal*, September 14, 2001.

Wood, Christopher, "Developers Submit Downtown Retail, Convention Hotel Ideas," *Denver Business Journal*, January 18, 1991.

——, "Three Teams Likely to Resubmit Denver Dry Building Bids," *Denver Business Journal*, July 30, 1990.

—Bruce P. Montgomery

homasote
COMPANY

Homasote Company

932 Lower Ferry Road
West Trenton, New Jersey 08628-0240
U.S.A.
Telephone: (609) 883-3300
Toll Free: (800) 257-9491
Fax: (609) 883-3497
Web site: http://www.homasote.com

Public Company
Founded: 1909
Employees: 194
Sales: $25.1 million (2002)
Stock Exchanges: Over the Counter
Ticker Symbol: HMTC
NAIC: 321219 Reconstituted Wood Product
    Manufacturing

Homasote Company, based in West Trenton, New Jersey, manufactures insulated wood fiberboard. It is the oldest manufacturer of building products from recycled materials in the United States. Its signature product is homasote, a structural fiberboard made from recycled post-consumer paper and hot water, which are mixed together to create a slurry, then poured into molds, baked to remove the water, and cut to various sizes. Waste materials from this process are returned to the system and also recycled. Homasote is used in construction for structural purposes, paneling, insulation, concrete forming and expansion joint, sound control in floors and walls, and roof decking. Through its Pak-Line Division the company also uses homasote for the packaging and shipping of such industrial items as glass products, stone and metal parts, rolls of paper and film, and metal coils. Homasote estimates that it uses as much as 250 tons of waste paper each day, which translates into the elimination of 65 million pounds of solid waste each year and the saving of 1.4 million trees. The company's products are primarily sold to contractors and building material wholesalers. Publicly traded by way of the Pink Sheets, Homasote is majority owned by the Flicker family.

Homasote's Founder Born in the 1800s

Homasote was founded by Eugenius Harvey Outerbridge, but he is best remembered as the first chairman of the New York-New Jersey Port Authority, which was responsible for a number of projects, including the construction of a bridge linking Staten Island to New Jersey bearing his name. It became familiar to generations of New York City drivers as the Outerbridge Crossing. Outerbridge was born in Philadelphia, Pennsylvania, in 1860. At the age of 16, he gained a practical business education at the venerable Newfoundland mercantile firm of Harvey & Company, one of the last branches of the Bermuda Trading Company, a far-flung enterprise that dissolved in 1767. His mother was a member of the Harvey family, and after her marriage to Alexander Ewing Outerbridge, the Harvey and Outerbridge families established deep-rooted business connections. In 1878, Eugenius Outerbridge moved to New York City to serve as the agent for the family business. He remained in New York for the rest of his life and from there managed his various business enterprises. When he was just 21, Outerbridge established Harvey & Outerbridge, an importing and exporting firm that was heavily reliant on shipping. Thus, Outerbridge took a keen interest in New York's transportation problems, championing the cause while holding top positions in New York State's Chamber of Commerce. For years, the Port of New York, the responsibility of both New York and New Jersey, was intolerably congested. A tangle of railroad lines converged in New Jersey towns that lay across from Manhattan. Here, freight had to be loaded onto ferries to be transported across the Hudson. Rail congestion became so bad at times that trains were backed up as far away as Pittsburgh. Oversea shipments were delayed, a situation that became intolerable when World War I turned New York into the busiest seaport in the world. Outerbridge was one of the men appointed to a bi-state commission to study the problem and led to the creation of the Port Authority of New York and New Jersey in 1921. He was named the Authority's first chairman, a post he held until 1924. Outerbridge died in 1932.

During his business career, Outerbridge also took control and headed the Pantasote Leather Company and served on the board of directors of a number of banks and corporations. In

1891, Panasote began marketing a leather substitute, created by gluing together two fabrics with Pantasote gum. The surface was further treated with Pantasote and embossed to provide a hide leather finish. The Pantasote name was coined using Greek roots, meaning "to serve all purposes." The product lasted longer than leather, was cheaper to make, and more easily cleaned. It was used to make upholstery and curtains and was waterproofed for the manufacture of tents and awnings.

What Pantasote was to leather, homasote would be to wood. In 1909, Outerbridge brought from England what was then the secret manufacturing process to create fiberboard out of newspapers. He built a factory in Trenton Junction, New Jersey, located on the main line of the Reading Railroad. Initially called the Agasote Millboard Company, the business produced sanded "agasote" sheets, a high density material with excellent waterproofing characteristics, primarily used in the roofs of passenger railroad cars.

Due to increasing sales of automobiles and a declining number of rail passengers, coupled with increased competition for agasote, Outerbridge looked to new markets. Automobiles also needed waterproof roofs, and starting in 1915 agasote was used in the making of automobile tops for such manufacturers as Buick, Dodge, Ford, Nash, and Studebaker. The company also entered the truck market, introducing "Vehisote," which was used to make delivery truck panels. It was in 1916 that Agasote Millboard Company turned its attention to building products. In that year, it introduced "Versatile Homasote Board." The unsanded panel was not only strong and lightweight, it was weather resistant, equally suitable for use in blistering hot conditions and sub-zero temperatures, dry conditions and wet. At the time, World War I was raging in Europe and the United States was soon to be drawn into the conflict. The U.S. military became aware of the product, and when the army was deployed in France in 1917 homasote was used in the exterior of military housing units and field hospitals.

The company became more dependent on the construction market after the war due to the fact that in 1925 car manufacturers stopped using agasote for car tops, preferring instead to produce convertibles using canvas roofs. Agasote Millboard Company now began to focus on its Homasote brand, promoting its uses for construction and insulation. One customer put the product to the ultimate test. Arctic explorer Admiral Robert E. Byrd took Homasote boards with him to Antarctica to build his winter headquarters, so-called Little America, for his 1928 to 1930 expedition. He used Homasote for the external walls, while relying on another company product, Thermasote, to insulate the internal walls. When the expedition came to a close, the buildings were disassembled and the sections warehoused in New Zealand under damp conditions. Some of the materials were then brought back to Antarctica to be reassembled to construct a second Little America in 1934. Years later, an Army radio engineer, Amory H. Waite, a member of the expedition,

wrote to the company to express his amazement over how well Homasote withstood the extreme conditions. It was one of the greatest product testimonials a company could ever hope to receive. Not only were the stored sections still strong and easily assembled, he wrote, but the men found buried sections of the original camp in "perfect condition after one year of soaking in melted snow (1929–30) and five years under the terrific pressure of 20 feet of ice." Moreover, Waite returned with the U.S. Navy to the site of the second camp 18 years later, dug down 12 feet to find "the 18-year-old Homasote in the walls and ceilings of the 'Mess Hall' and 'Science Lab' (the only buildings we could reach) absolutely unharmed by time, water, cold. Hundreds of tons of ice had forced up the wood floors and pushed down the ceilings until they met in the center of the room and puddles of ice everywhere evidence the repeated freezing and thawing of the many seasons, but the walls were straight, unbuckled and scarcely stained."

During the Depression years of the 1930s, the company devoted an increasing amount of its energy on the building trade. To counteract a problem of generating repeat sales, which the company suspected was the unintended consequence of manufacturing a product that was too good, a prefabricated housing system was launched in 1935. The first modular housing development to employ the "Precision Built System of Construction" was located in Valejo, California. In just 73 working days, the contractor put up 977 houses.

Company Changes Name in the 1930s

The company became so tied to its signature product that in October 1936 it changed its name to Homasote Company. In the second half of the 1930s, the military remained a valuable customer. The U.S. Navy turned to Homasote because of its proven insulation properties and ability to weather harsh conditions for the construction of barracks and other buildings needed in a major base located near Kodiak, Alaska. Military demand for Homasote increased as World War II erupted in Europe, and it became increasingly apparent that it was only a matter of time before the United States joined the struggle. During the war years, all of Homasote's production was commandeered by the military to construct housing and other base facilities.

Even with the close of the war in 1945, the military need for Homasote did not end. The United States and its allies quickly came into conflict with their wartime partner, the Soviet Union, resulting in what would become known as the Cold War. In order to keep tabs on Soviet aircraft and missiles and thwart any attempted sneak attacks, the military built a line of radar sites, the Distant Early Warning line, spread across the Arctic Circle. Once again, Homasote was the material of choice used in constructing these radar facilities. After World War II ended, the company also returned to serving peacetime needs. Homasote, like all building materials, was in great demand during the postwar housing boom, as returning servicemen married and began moving into the new suburban housing projects that cropped up all over the country. Homasote also looked to expand beyond the construction market, in 1945 establishing the Pak-Line division to create industrial packaging products, custom-made and cut to fit the shape of a product intended for transit.

Relying on recycled newspapers as its primary raw material, Homasote was well ahead of its time as a green company. Then, in the 1950s, it developed a close-loop system to recycle the hundreds of thousands of gallons of water it used each day in the making of fiberboard. Not only did the system save the company money by making use of all its water, it prevented pollution of the local water supply. In 1956, the U.S. Army Corps of Engineers recognized the recycling effort with a special award.

The Flicker family's involvement with Homasote dates to the late 1930s when Irving Flicker supplied the company with its raw material, wastepaper. In 1960, while a partner in an Asbury Park, New Jersey, wastepaper company he was approached by Homasote's head, Basil Outerbridge, who hired him as an executive vice-president. In 1965, Flicker's brother, Shanley Flicker, followed him to Homasote and played a key role in automating the company's production facilities. In the early 1960s, Irving Flicker became Homasote's president and in 1971 was appointed chairman. In 1965, his son, Warren L. Flicker, went to work for the company.

Despite a housing slump in the early 1980s, Homasote, as it had in the past, was able to weather the difficult period with relative ease. However, Oriented Strand Board (OSB) had been introduced in the late 1970s. While this material lacked the properties of Homasote, it was less expensive and along with plywood superseded Homasote as an external sheathing material. The addition of foam products in the early 1980s helped to mitigate somewhat the loss of business. Nevertheless, the conservatively run company held course. It was essentially debt free and consistently paid a dividend, so that during the 1980s Homasote began attracting the attention of investors. Its shares were traded on the Philadelphia Stock Exchange "practically by appointment," in the words of a 1987 *Barron's* profile.

Setbacks in the 1990s and Recovery in the 2000s

In the early 1990s, Homasote had to again contend with the effects of a recession. Sales dropped from $28.1 million in 1990 to $23.5 million in 1991, resulting in a meager profit of just over $7,000. As was typical during the company's history, management shared in the burden of the cost-cutting measures it imposed. Irving Flicker reduced his salary by 25 percent in 1992, while his brother, son, and other officers accepted 15 percent pay cuts. For their part, the ranks of middle management reduced their salaries 10 percent. Further savings were achieved

by eliminating a fleet of trucks and a trucking warehouse and turning to common carriers. The company also switched its health coverage to a health maintenance organization.

Homasote returned to profitability in 1994 when it posted sales of nearly $25.7 million, resulting in net earnings of more than $1.2 million. In 1995, as part of a long-term effort to improve productivity and lower costs, the company invested in a new dryer that relied on a different and less expensive energy source. It was a time-consuming undertaking to make the transition and proved more difficult than expected, adversely impacting the company's balance sheet for the next couple of years. The new dryer was finally put into modified use in September 1997, but even before the company could determine the optimum way to use the new equipment, a fire occurred inside the drier which put it out of service until late December. Another, smaller fire, took place in January 1998, but it was quickly repaired. While the company dealt with its insurance company about either replacing the dryer or bringing it back to its original state, it operated at just a fraction of its anticipated production capability, which was nevertheless equal to double the two units it replaced. The year 1998 was also marked by the retirement of Irving Flicker, who was replaced as CEO and chairman by Warren Flicker. Irving Flicker retained the title of chairman emeritus until his May 2002 death at the age of 87, having served over 55 years as an employee and advisor. Two years earlier, Irving Flicker's brother, Shanley, had passed away shortly after his own retirement at the age of 82.

As a result of its production problems, Homasote experienced a drop in revenues in both 1997 and 1998, resulting in a net loss of nearly $1.2 million for that period. Although a settlement had still not been reached with the insurance company, Homasote saw some improvement in 1999, as well as hope for new business. Over the years, Homasote gained a reputation as a sound controlling material for walls and floors, but it was not until now that the company decided to tap into the growing market for inexpensive sound control in homes, high-rise construction, and commercial buildings. In order for architects to specify the material, however, the company had to commission laboratory tests to provide statistical rather than just anecdotal evidence that Homasote dampened sound and also served as a fire retardant. Tests revealed that Homasote was indeed an excellent sound-attenuating material, opening up a new market for the company, which launched a new line of panels called 440 SoundBarrier. The success of the 440 Sound-Barrier helped Homasote to grow sales by 10.9 percent to $27.7 million in 2000 and record a profit of nearly $314,000. The company was also able to finally reach a settlement with the insurance company over the 1997 dryer fire.

However, just as Homasote was beginning to build momentum, the economy began to slide, a situation made worse by the terrorist attacks on the United States on September 11, 2001. Sales fell by 7.3 percent to $25.7 million in 2001 and difficult conditions continued in 2002, when sales slipped to $25 million, and the company recorded a loss in excess of $500,000. In 2003, the prices of plywood and OSB began to soar, making Homasote once again a viable alternative in exterior sheathing. Builders took a second look at an old material, which was now not only competitively priced but possessed better combined physical qualities than plywood and OSB. The sales of 440

Sound Barrier continued to increase, and the growth of the home theater market held promise for the product line. Moreover, Homasote's long history as a green company was something that could be more fully exploited. Even as it was approaching its 100th anniversary, it would not be surprising that the company's best years were yet to come.

Principal Competitors

Knight-Celotex LLC; Louisiana Pacific Corporation; Georgia-Pacific Corporation; Dennison Inc.; Hacker Industries Inc.; USG Corporation.

Further Reading

Eaton, Leslie, "Humble Homasote—A Gradualist Approach To Going Private," *Barron's*, June 8,1987.

Fitzsimmons, Jim, "Homasote Execs, Managers Tighten Belts in Recession," *Trentonian*, April 17, 1992.

"Homasote Company Marks 85 Years," *Mercer Business*, May 1994, p. 24.

Moniz, Larry, "From World War I to a Marketing Offensive," *Business News New Jersey*, February 8, 2000, p. 8.

"The Trenton Community Lost a Champion When Irving Flicker Passed Away Earlier This Week," *Trentonian*, May 29, 2002.

—Ed Dinger

Howard Johnson International, Inc.

1 Sylvan Way
Parsippany, New Jersey 07054
U.S.A.
Telephone: (973) 428-9700
Fax: (973) 496-7658
Web site: http://www.hojo.com

Wholly Owned Subsidiary of Cendant Corporation
Incorporated: 1961 as Howard Johnson Company
Employees: 340
Sales: $19.5 million (2004)
NAIC: 721110 Hotels (Except Casino Hotels) and Motels

Howard Johnson International, Inc., franchises approximately 465 hotels in the United States, Canada, Mexico, Malta, Romania, Argentina, Columbia, Guatemala, Dominican Republic, Dutch Antilles, Ecuador, Peru, Venezuela, Israel, Jordan, Oman, United Arab Emirates, China, and India. Each year, over 15 million vacationers and business travelers visit a Howard Johnson hotel. The company is a subsidiary of Cendant Corp., which runs Howard Johnson as a franchise operation. Interestingly, Howard Johnson was once the largest restaurant chain in the world, but such fast-food outlets as McDonald's came to replace ''HoJo'' in America's affections, and the 1985 sale of the company essentially divided it into separate lodging and dining operations. By 2005, there were only eight Howard Johnson restaurants left.

Inception and Growth Before World War II

A World War I veteran with only a grammar-school education, Howard Dearing Johnson started out as a salesman for his father, a Boston cigar jobber. As smokers increasingly turned to cigarettes, however, the business fell into debt and, after his father died, Johnson closed it. Looking for a better enterprise, he bought a store selling candy, newspapers, and patent medicines in Wollaston, a Boston suburb, in 1925 for $500 he borrowed, picking up also its debts of at least $28,000. Johnson revived the store's moribund soda fountain and, seeking a quality product that would bear his name, introduced chocolate ice cream with a ''secret'' formula: a butterfat content almost twice the standard. It proved a hit, so he added other flavors and opened a beachfront stand where he sold $60,000 worth of ice-cream cones in a single summer. By 1928, his gross sales of ice cream had risen to $240,000.

When Johnson opened his first restaurant, in neighboring Quincy in 1929, he made fried clams and broiled swordfish the specialties and also included homemade baked beans, brown bread, and pastries. However, he was frustrated in his desire to expand by lack of capital before 1935, when he persuaded an acquaintance to open a restaurant in Orleans, on Cape Cod, and sell his ice cream under a franchise. By the following summer, there were four Howard Johnson franchised restaurants, called ''Howard Johnson's,'' and 13 small Johnson-owned roadside stands being converted into restaurants. By the end of the year, 39 more franchised restaurants had been opened.

Howard Johnson's phenomenal growth was based on the application of two relatively new and untried concepts. Its founder, unable to obtain loans from bankers, was a pioneer in the franchising field. Licensees, rather than the chain, bore the start-up costs. These included an initiation fee paid to the company, which then made more money by selling food and other supplies to the licensees. In addition, Howard Johnson foresaw that the growing popularity of the automobile would send millions of hungry Americans out on the road.

By the end of 1939, there were 107 Howard Johnsons along the eastern seaboard and as far south as Florida, mostly along highways. Gross receipts came to $10.5 million and profit to $207,000. The following year, the company won a contract to locate 24 restaurants on the newly completed Pennsylvania Turnpike, holding a monopoly on the heavily traveled route until 1979. Generally situated along major highways and drafted by Johnson's staff of 27 architects, Howard Johnson's were easily distinguished by porcelain roof tiles of a special orange color, scientifically determined as the best shade for attracting a motorist's attention. A New England-style blue cupola was mounted on the roof. ''Site engineers'' determined the locations, and supervisors hired and trained cooks, waitresses, and counter clerks. Quality control from headquarters assured that the 28 flavors of ice cream, fried clams from the company's own clam bed off Ipswich, Massachusetts, pies baked on the premises according to company recipes, and other items would meet the standards of the Howard D. Johnson Co. The company lured the family trade with children's portions.

The Booming Fifties

With America's entry into World War II, gasoline rationing took such a toll on the Howard Johnson chain that the number of restaurants fell in little more than a year from about 200 (75 of them company-operated) to about 75. By the summer of 1944, only 12 remained in business. The company took up part of the slack by turning some of the restaurants into jam factories and by operating cafeterias for workers in war plants. Once the war ended, Howard Johnson adopted a policy of smaller units in place of big, showy "roadside cathedrals." By the summer of 1947, construction was under way on the first of 200 new branches to stretch across the Southeast and Midwest. Still owned exclusively by its founder, the Howard D. Johnson Co. was providing its restaurants with some 700 items, including the saltwater taffy always found on the counters. Gross sales totaled $115 million in 1951 (25 percent from ice cream), and net income came to $656,000.

By 1954, there were about 400 Howard Johnson restaurants in 32 states, of which about 10 percent were highly profitable company-owned units on turnpike locations. That year, Howard Johnson entered the motel business. In 1959, the company founder, who had accumulated three homes, a 60-foot-long yacht, an art collection, and gone through four marriages, turned the reins over to his son, 26-year-old Howard Brennan Johnson, who succeeded him as president of the company. The junior Howard Johnson, a graduate of Andover, Yale, and Harvard Business School, quipped, "My father felt that I should start at the top and work my way down." Years later, in a more serious vein, he told a *New York Times* reporter, "I knew from the age of five I wanted to join the company. It was all we talked about at home. I saw my father working so hard. He was the kind of person you almost couldn't let down." He established executive offices in New York City's Rockefeller Center, although corporate headquarters remained in Wollaston. The senior Johnson remained chairman and treasurer of the company until 1964. He died in 1972.

Going Public in the 1960s

When Howard Johnson Co. went public in 1961, it consisted of 605 Howard Johnson restaurants (265 operated by the company and 340 by licensees), 10 Red Coach Grill company-owned restaurants (a chain started in 1938 that specialized in steak and lobster), and 88 Howard Johnson's Motor Lodges, all of them franchised, in 33 states and the Bahamas. There were 17 manufacturing and processing plants in 11 states. Net sales came to $95 million in 1960 (compared to $31.8 million in

1951), and net income to $2.3 million. Both annual sales and earnings per share increased every year between 1959 and 1966. Between 1961 and 1967 the company's founder, his son, and his daughter sold nearly two million shares of stock for a sum estimated in the neighborhood of $1 billion.

In 1963, when the firm's profit margin rose to an all-time high for the fourth straight year, the number of company-owned Howard Johnsons exceeded the franchised units for the first time. "It's simple," Howard B. Johnson explained to a *Forbes* reporter in 1962. "Last year our own 279 stores and restaurants had sales of nearly $79 million, on which we got both the wholesale and the retail profit. Naturally, we'd like more of these double-barreled profits." The number of motels reached 130 in 1964, each with a Howard Johnson restaurant on the site or adjacent to it. Popular Howard Johnson staples were now being frozen and distributed through supermarkets in the Northeast. In the mid-1960s, Howard Johnson became a coast-to-coast chain for the first time by opening California outlets. Ground Round, a limited-menu, pub-style suburban chain with banjo-strumming entertainment, was initiated in 1969.

Challenges of the 1970s

Marked by occasional gasoline shortages and frequent gas price hikes, the 1970s were a difficult decade for companies catering to motor traffic, but especially for Howard Johnson, which depended on highway operations for 85 percent of its business. Yet except for 1974, the first full year of the energy crisis, Howard Johnson continued every year to post record sales and earnings per share. It reacted to the challenge by instituting around-the-clock service in more than 80 percent of the company-owned restaurants, installed cocktail lounges in place of soda fountains in about 100 of these locations, increased seating capacity, and stepped up special menu promotions. New HoJos, the company's leader pronounced, would be concentrated in population centers rather than along highways. By the end of 1975, the HoJo empire had grown to 929 Howard Johnson restaurants (649 company-operated), 32 Red Coach Grill restaurants, 63 Ground Round restaurants, and 536 motor lodges (125 company-operated) in 42 states, the District of Columbia, Puerto Rico, the Bahamas, the British West Indies, and Canada.

Nevertheless, in the competitive struggle for the traveler's dollar, Howard Johnson was falling behind fast-food franchisers such as McDonald's and Burger King and growing lodging chains such as Holiday Inns, Ramada Inns, and Marriott. The classic orange-roof Howard Johnsons especially were perceived as past their prime. Customers complained of agonizingly slow service and overpriced, bland, predominantly frozen food that gave rise to the gag, "Howard Johnson's ice cream comes in 28 flavors and its food in one." HoJo outlets accounted for 78 percent of the restaurant group's sales volume in 1977 but only 57 percent of pretax profit. By contrast, the company's motels, although also cited as increasingly behind the times, accounted for only 16 percent of the company sales in 1978 but more than 43 percent of its earnings.

Criticized for choosing to stand pat and hoard company cash, Howard Johnson told a *Forbes* reporter in 1978, "My expansion plans got stalled in the 1974 oil embargo. I overreacted. I stopped all expansion, and once you stop, you know

---

Key Dates:

1929: Howard Dearing Johnson opens his first restaurant.
1961: Howard Johnson Co. goes public.
1979: The company is sold to Imperial Group Ltd. of Great Britain.
1985: Marriott Corp. buys Howard Johnson for $314 million; Marriott keeps the 418 company-owned restaurants but immediately sells the franchise system and the company-owned lodging units to Prime Motor Inns Inc. for $97 million.
1990: Prime sells Howard Johnson to Blackstone Capital Partners L.P.
1992: Hospitality Franchise Systems Inc. goes public; Blackstone retains 65 percent ownership.
1995: Hospitality Franchise Systems changes its name to HFS Inc.
1996: Howard Johnson adopts the Howard Johnson International Inc. moniker.
1997: HFS merges with CUC International to form Cendant Corp.
2005: The company opens its first hotel in Alaska.

---

how hard it is to get the monster going again." Others, however, blamed management's tight-fisted concentration on the balance sheet for the company's lack of dynamism. One of its former executives said, "HoJo always seemed to have ideas to upgrade the restaurants and hotels. But they never wanted to spend the money." By the late 1970s, the future of Howard Johnson Co. was beginning to look better on a balance sheet than its actual operations indicated. It held $90 million in cash and marketable securities and carried no long-term debt aside from $143 million in capital-lease obligations for its company-owned units.

Under British Rule: 1980–85

Although Howard Johnson had professed no interest in selling his namesake company, in September 1979 he accepted, as too lucrative to pass up, an acquisition bid of $28 a share, or $630 million in all, from Imperial Group Ltd. of Great Britain, a tobacco, food, beer, and packaging conglomerate. For its money, Imperial received 1,040 restaurants (75 percent company-owned) and 520 motor lodges (75 percent franchised). Howard Johnson, who had collected $35.2 million for his shares, resigned as chairman, president, and chief executive officer of the company at the end of 1981. He was succeeded by G. Michael Hostage, a manager who had worked his way through business school washing dishes and digging sewers before spending 15 years with the Marriott Corp.

Hostage inherited a declining balance sheet. In 1979, the company had earned $34 million before taxes on sales of $588 million, but earnings dropped to only $14.7 million in 1980 and never fully recovered during the four succeeding years. Sales grew only 22 percent during this period. Hostage vowed to integrate adjacent HoJo restaurants and motels, which were often under different ownership, by unifying their staffs and offering food-and-lodging package deals and to cut costs by allowing restaurant managers to buy food from a variety of sources rather

than exclusively from the company. Some new entrees and a low-cholesterol breakfast were added. The successful Ground Round chain was expanded, growing to 210 units in 1985.

In order to lure business travelers to its motels, which trailed the industry average in occupancy rate and had fallen to sixth place among lodging chains, Howard Johnson initiated corporate discounts and a new reservations system and raised the advertising budget. It gave licensees the choice of accepting low-interest loans to refurbish their properties by mid-1987 or losing their franchises. A new mid-priced Plaza-Hotel chain for the business traveler was opened in 1983, with 90 or more planned over five years at an average cost of $20 million each. These units would include amenities business people expected but were not receiving from the traditionally family-oriented HoJos: restaurants and lounges, banquet and meeting rooms, and executive floors.

Divided between Marriott and Prime

In September 1985, Imperial threw in the towel, selling the Howard Johnson Co. to Marriott Corp. for $314 million. Marriott kept the 418 company-owned restaurants but immediately sold the franchise system and the company-owned lodging units to Prime Motor Inns Inc. for $97 million. Prime also assumed Howard Johnson's $138 million in debt. For its money, Prime received the Howard Johnson trade name and trademark, 125 hotels and motor lodges operated by Howard Johnson, 375 franchised lodges, and 199 franchised restaurants. Imperial kept the Ground Round chain because Marriott was not interested in buying it.

Neither did Marriott have an interest in prolonging the life of a restaurant chain whose name was also held by a lodging operation in competition with its own. The corporation intended to convert these units to Big Boy and Saga restaurants, which would in turn be sold. By the end of 1987, only 90 Marriott-owned Howard Johnson restaurants remained and by mid-1991 only 50. Similarly, Prime wanted to wash its hands of the independently owned units once the franchise agreements expired.

Claiming that their interests were being set aside, about 150 Howard Johnson restaurant franchisees retained former U.S. attorney general Griffin Bell and began threatening a class-action suit against Marriott and Prime. After eight months of negotiations, the parties reached an agreement in May 1986 by which Prime granted to Franchise Associates, Inc., a company established by the franchisees, a perpetual exclusive license to the Howard Johnson name in connection with the operation of Howard Johnson restaurants in the United States, Panama, and the Bahama Islands, and granted Franchise Associates the exclusive right to use the Howard Johnson name or license it to others for Howard Johnson Signature Food Products in these locations. From Marriott, the operators won the free use of HoJo recipes.

Franchise Associates bought 17 of Marriott's HoJos in 1991. It even built a prototype restaurant with a toned-down version of the orange roof and required all new franchisees to use the design. Oat bran muffins, salads, and garden pizzas were among the health-conscious fare added to the familiar standbys in a new menu introduced in 1990. A stockholders' company of 65 franchisees, Franchise Associates owned and operated about 85 of the 110 franchised HoJo restaurants in 1991.

Prime was described by a securities analyst as the fastest-growing company in the lodging industry with the highest profit margins. In 1988, it announced a joint venture to build 20 Howard Johnson suite hotels a year for the next five years at an annual construction cost of about $100 million. A Prime subsidiary was to supply the financing, while AAA Development Corporation would build the hotels. Suite hotels were a fast-growing segment of the lodging industry largely favored by business travelers, and Howard Johnson was planning to charge $55 to $90 a night. The following year, Howard Johnson initiated a $25-million marketing plan to present the chain as "home of the road warrior," the industry name for frequent travelers. Figures showed that 22 percent of U.S. business travelers were responsible for 56 percent of hotel stays.

New Ownership in the 1990s

In order to reduce its $280 million in bank debt, Prime, which had become the nation's second-largest hotel franchiser, sold its Howard Johnson and Ramada systems to Blackstone Capital Partners L.P., an affiliate of Blackstone Group, in 1990 for $170 million. A downturn in the lodging and real-estate industries and problems in the high-yield, high-risk junk-bond market had dried up financing sources for hotels and caused Prime's stock to lose 75 percent of its value in seven months. Blackstone Group, an investment-banking firm, added the Days Inn chain and renamed the operation Hospitality Franchise Systems Inc. The company went public in 1992, but Blackstone retained 65 percent of the shares.

Hospitality Franchise Systems changed its name to HFS Inc. in 1995 and the name of its Howard Johnson Franchise Systems subsidiary to Howard Johnson International, Inc. in 1996. In February 1996, HFS announced that it would require its Howard Johnson franchisees to upgrade their properties, including establishing a rating system designating properties as either full-service hotels or limited-service units and posting a new sign with a bright blue background. It was also considering discontinuing the distinctive orange roofs that still topped about 30 percent of the lodges. While conceding that the orange roof is "an American icon—as American as apple pie and Chevrolet," HoJo President Eric Pfeffer declared, "As we change with the times, we've got to show the newness." Pfeffer, who discontinued the franchises of 37 Howard Johnson properties in 1995 for quality shortfalls, said the company would be expanded worldwide.

At the end of 1995, there were 523 properties with 57,200 rooms in the Howard Johnson lodging system throughout North America and also in Europe, the Middle East, and Central and South America. They were mid-priced, averaged 110 rooms each, and most had a swimming pool, gift shop, and restaurant. HFS received monthly marketing and reservation fees from its Howard Johnson franchisees based on a specified percentage of gross room sales.

Changes in the Late 1990s and Beyond

Howard Johnson experienced changes in its ownership structure once again during the late 1990s. Known for his deal-making prowess, HFS CEO Henry Silverman orchestrated a $14.1 billion merger with CUC International Inc. in 1997. A February 2000 *Business Week* article explained Silverman's motivation for the deal, claiming, "The CUC merger was to have been Silverman's masterstroke. He saw CUC, a direct-marketing outfit that sold memberships in discount buying clubs such as Shoppers Advantage and Travelers Advantage, as the perfect partner. The idea was to feed the names of all the customers HFS channeled through its hotels and real estate brokerages into the CUC direct-marketing machine." The article went on to report, "CUC would then sell them memberships in its discount-buying clubs and, eventually, financial services such as insurance. Silverman also figured CUC's team, viewed as Internet gurus for creating the online shopping site Netmarket, could help extend his brands to the Web."

Silverman's grand scheme fell short in 1998, however, when it was discovered that CUC had inflated its profits and earnings in the years before the merger. The accounting discrepancies eventually led to $13 billion loss in market capitalization and a $2.8 billion shareholder class action lawsuit settlement. In an attempt to rebuild and stabilize Cendant, Silverman sold off 18 non-core assets by 2000, relying on the hotel and real estate operations to bolster sales and earnings.

While Howard Johnson's parent worked to regain credibility with its shareholders, the hotel chain focused on expanding its presence in both international and domestic markets. In 1998, the company secured a master franchise agreement to develop hotels in China. Howard Johnson also set plans in motion to open new properties in eight European countries with U.K.-based Premier Hotels. At the same time, Howard Johnson began to aggressively target business travelers. Known primarily in the hospitality industry as the place to stay for travelers on a budget, the hotel chain wanted to tap into a larger portion of the business traveler segment. As such, a new television marketing campaign with the tagline "We've got a great name to live up to" was launched 1999. The company also introduced SuperMiles, a frequent-stay program designed to entice business travelers.

By the start of the 2000s, Howard Johnson stood on solid ground. While a slowdown in travel after the September 11, 2001 terrorist attacks on the United States plagued the entire industry, the company remained focused on its growth strategy. It had four different formats in its arsenal, including the full-service Howard Johnson Hotels and the Plaza Hotels; Howard Johnson Inns, which had restaurants but not room service; and limited-service Express Inns. Most of the company's international locations were four-star, full-service hotels. In the years to come, Howard Johnson looked to expand further in international markets as well as in center-city markets. It opened a Plaza Hotel, the first Howard Johnson location in downtown Anchorage, Alaska, in March 2005.

Principal Competitors

Accor SA; Hilton Hotels Corporation; InterContinental Hotels Group plc.

Further Reading

Barrett, Amy, "Henry Silverman's Long Road Back," *Business Week*, February 28, 2000.
Casper, Carol, "Howard Johnson's," *Restaurant Business*, January 20, 1991, pp. 78, 80.

"Cendant Signs Pact for China Expansion of Howard Johnson," *Wall Street Journal*, October 21, 1998, p. 19C.

Ettorre, Barbara, "Dry Spell for Howard Johnson," *New York Times*, August 6, 1979, pp. D1, D3.

Hooper, Laurence, "Blackstone Is Planning Public Offering of Shares in Motel-Franchising Business," *Wall Street Journal*, August 31, 1992, p. C9.

"The Howard Johnson Restaurants," *Fortune*, September 1940, pp. 82+.

"Howard Johnson's New Flavor," *Business Week*, October 19, 1963, pp. 109–110, 112.

Howard, Theresa, "Howard Johnson," *Nation's Restaurant News*, February 1996, pp. 85, 88.

Kleinfield, N.R., "Can HoJo's Regain Its Luster?" *New York Times*, April 21, 1985, Sec. 3, p. 4.

Kulkosky, Edward, "Howard Johnson's New Formula," *Financial World*, October 1, 1978, pp. 13–15, 17.

Marcial, Gene G., "Cendant Comes Back," *Business Week*, May 12, 2003.

McLaughlin, Mark, "A Whole Lot of Shakin' Going On Under Orange Roofs of HoJo Franchisers," *New England Business*, October 6, 1986, pp. 41–42.

Preer, Robert, "For Venerable HoJo's Restaurants, a Second Serving," *Boston Globe*, September 5, 1993, South Weekly, pp. 1, 4.

"Prime Motor Inns, Marriott to Acquire Howard Johnson's Motels, Restaurants," *Wall Street Journal*, September 21, 1985, p. 5.

"Putting the HJ Seal on Motels," *Business Week*, October 23, 1954, pp. 126, 130, 132.

Salmans, Sandra, "Remodeling Howard Johnson," *New York Times*, November 12, 1982, pp. D1, D15.

"Tinting Supermarkets with Orange and Blue," *Business Week*, July 2, 1966, pp. 42–43, 46.

"To Be and What to Be—That Is the Question," *Forbes*, May 1, 1978, p. 25.

Webber, Sara Perez, "Updating a Classic," *Travel Agent*, August 9, 1999, p. 46.

Weber, Joseph, "Got My Hojo Workin'," *Business Week*, March 4, 1996, p. 46.

—Robert Halasz
—update: Christina M. Stansell

Intermec Technologies Corporation

6001 36th Avenue West
Everett, Washington 98203-1264
U.S.A.
Telephone: (425) 348-2600
Fax: (425) 355-9551
Toll Free: (800) 934-3163
Web site: http://www.intermec.com

Wholly Owned Subsidiary of Unova Inc.
Incorporated: 1966 as Interface Mechanics Inc.
Employees: 2,700
Sales: $811.3 million (2004)
NAIC: 334119 Other Computer Peripheral Equipment
Manufacturing; 322299 All Other Converted Paper
Product Manufacturing

Based in Everett, Washington, Intermec Technologies Corporation is a leading global supplier of supply chain information products, services, and systems. While the company is recognized for developing the world's most widely used bar code symbology, its offerings have evolved to include the radio frequency identification (RFID) technology that is quickly transforming the world of commerce and logistics. Intermec develops, manufactures, and integrates technology for RFID, mobile computing systems, and both wired and wireless automated data collection (ADC). The company markets a vast array of data capture devices including imagers, laser scanners and wedges, charge coupled devices, wands, scanners, and personal scanning devices. It also offers bar code printers, media and label supplies, as well as local area data management systems that are sold in handheld, vehicle-mounted, and stationary computer terminal form. A division of industrial technologies company UNOVA Inc., Intermec employs more than 2,700 people at six major development and manufacturing facilities. These include the company's world headquarters in Everett, Washington, as well as domestic locations in Cincinnati, Las Vegas, and Cedar Rapids, Iowa. International sites include Gothenburg, Sweden, and Toulouse, France. Intermec's customer base spans several market sectors—government, healthcare, logistics, retail, manu-

facturing, and field service—and includes thousands of organizations throughout the world, including 60 percent of *Fortune* 100 companies and 75 percent of the *Fortune* 500. While Intermec's customers apply its technologies in different ways, they do so for common reasons. As company literature explained: "Supply chain information systems allow companies to compile previously unheard of amounts of information from one end of an enterprise to the other. That's information companies can use to reduce inventory, cut labor costs, speed manufacturing and improve profitability."

Early Technology Pioneer: 1960s–70s

Interface Mechanics Inc. (later known simply as Intermec) was established in 1966 after the The National Association of Food Chains (NAFC) called for equipment manufacturers to develop systems that would speed the checkout process. Comprising a handful of people working from a renovated grocery store in Mountlake Terrace, Washington, the company quickly unveiled a number of "firsts" in a newly emerging technology sector. In the process, Intermec left a lasting mark on the retail industry.

The company's earliest innovations included the first handheld order-entry terminal in 1969, as well as the first portable bar code scanner and the first on-demand bar code label printer in 1971. The following year, Intermec unveiled the first computerized cash register. This development was proceeded by the invention of "Interleaved 2 of 5" symbology, which eventually became the standard that supermarkets use to mark cardboard boxes with barcodes.

In 1973 Dr. David C. Allais, who had joined Intermec in 1968, was named company president. The following year he worked with bar code industry pioneer Raymond L. Stevens to invent Code 39, which became the world's most widely used alphanumeric bar code symbology. In April 1970, Stevens had founded TEMA, a Natick, Massachusetts-based company that ultimately became Intermec's largest and oldest dedicated distributor.

Other pioneering developments occurred at Intermec during the late 1970s, including the invention of Code 11, which was

Company Perspectives:

Intermec invented many of the revolutionary technologies that today make it possible for businesses to track goods and services, known as their supply chains. Intermec also developed key components integral to the current consumer and wireless revolution.

widely adopted by the telecommunications industry. Intermec also developed hand-held computers that wholesale route distributors used to perform accounting functions. By the late 1970s, Intermec employed roughly 50 people.

Explosive Growth in the 1980s

Intermec's role as a technology pioneer continued throughout the 1980s. During the decade, the company emerged as a comprehensive producer of bar code equipment. Led by President David C. Allais, Intermec's products were adopted for use in such industry sectors as government and healthcare.

In 1981 the company unveiled the first on-demand direct thermal bar code printer. The following year, Intermec invented so-called ''smart battery'' technology, which would find widespread adoption in such portable electronic devices as camcorders and laptop computers. A high-density barcode printer capable of printing up to ten lines of regular text was introduced to the grocery industry in mid-1982.

Intermec's sales grew from $14.3 million in 1982 to $20.7 million in 1983. In April of that year, the company acquired Ultra Print Tape & Label Corporation, which produced specialty labels and tags for bar coding and other purposes. Also that year Intermec rolled out a user program development tool called Interactive Reader Language (IRL). According to Intermec, the introduction of IRL was significant because it marked ''the first time local prompting and editing could be done for bar code data entry and allowed a simple PC, rather than a large mainframe, to run an application.'' This milestone was followed by Intermec's 1984 invention of the removable hard drive, which found a sizable market during the 1990s and beyond as the use of servers and laptop computers skyrocketed.

Intermec's sales climbed to $26.9 million in 1984. In April the company loaned $700,000 to the bar code software firm Data Collection Systems Inc. (DCSI) in exchange for a 40-percent ownership stake and an option to acquire the remaining 60 percent in 1988. DCSI specialized in bar code data collection systems for the manufacturing sector. Combined with Intermec's hardware offering, it became possible for Intermec to offer a packaged data collection solution to its customers.

In early 1984 Intermec signed two long-term agreements with Sperry Corporation, valued at $10 million, to provide the U.S. Air Force with bar code equipment. The company also signed a one-year, $2 million deal with IBIS Corporation to provide equipment to the U.S. Army. Intermec then expanded into two additional buildings near its 75,200-square-foot Lynnwood, Washington headquarters. The expansion added some

50,000 square feet of additional space for engineering, manufacturing, and marketing staff. This was followed by physical expansion at Cincinnati-based subsidiary INTERMEC/Ultra Print Inc., which planned to more than double its office and manufacturing facility in Union Township, Ohio.

In October 1984 Intermec announced a public offering of 700,000 shares of common stock. The offering, at $15 per share, raised $10.8 million that Intermec planned to use for future growth. At this time, the company began to forge closer ties with its distributors and original equipment manufacturer suppliers.

In the April 8, 1985, issue of *Business Week*, Norwald, Connecticut-based market researcher International Resource Development Inc. projected 40–60 percent annual growth within the industrial coding market. Industry sales were expected to grow from $170 million in 1984 to $1 billion in 1990, and Intermec was in the prime position to benefit. Dean Witter Reynolds Inc. Analyst Jonathan H. Ziegler commented: ''Intermec has the broadest product line and the strongest distribution network. They're the IBM of the business.''

Indeed, Intermec was having a good year. The company's sales jumped to $40.2 million in 1985, and *Business Week* named it as one of the 100 ''Best Little Growth Companies in America.'' Mid-year, Intermec announced that research and development costs were up 85 percent in the first quarter alone, as were costs related to marketing (63 percent) and fixed manufacturing (44 percent).

Intermec continued to expand its Lynwood, Washington, facility to accommodate growth and ended the year by acquiring Natick, Massachusetts-based TEMA, its largest and oldest dedicated distributor. In addition, the company developed the first radio data network, signifying its entrance into the radio frequency LAN systems market.

Intermec's sales reached $43.1 million in 1986. During the fourth quarter, the company encountered a variety of production problems that affected its performance. To improve profitability, it implemented a company-wide wage freeze and reduced 2 percent of its 490-employee workforce.

In August 1986 David C. Allais, then 53, was named chairman. Retaining his CEO responsibilities, Allais replaced David B. Pivan as chairman. Pivan had been associated with the firm since its inception and had served as its chairman since 1981. John W. Paxton, a 49-year-old executive from the Grimes Division of Springfield, Ohio-based Midland-Ross Corp., was hired as president and chief operating officer (COO).

In 1987 Intermec's sales skyrocketed to $65.6 million. That year, the firm invented Code 49, which it described as ''the first 2D stacked bar code symbology, useful for extremely small-space applications.''

A series of leadership changes began to occur in August 1987. At that time, Phillip W. Arneson, who had served as president of Amphenol Corp., replaced David C. Allais as chairman and CEO. Allais was named chief scientist, and Paxton continued to serve as president and COO. However, in March 1988 Arneson re-

Key Dates:

1966: Interface Mechanics Inc. (Intermec) is established in Mountlake Terrace, Washington.
1971: The company develops the first portable bar code scanner and the first on-demand bar code label printer.
1972: Intermec unveils the first computerized cash register.
1974: President Dr. David C. Allais works with bar code industry pioneer Raymond L. Stevens to invent Code 39, which becomes the world's most widely used alphanumeric bar code symbology.
1983: Sales reach $20.7 million.
1984: Intermec announces a public offering of common stock.
1985: Sales jump to $40.2 million and *Business Week* names Intermec as one of the 100 "Best Little Growth Companies in America."
1988: Sales climb to $85.2 million; construction of a new, headquarters and manufacturing facility in Everett, Washington, is announced.
1991: Intermec is acquired by Litton Industries Inc.
1994: Intermec becomes a subsidiary of Western Atlas Inc.
1997: Western Atlas acquires United Barcode Industries (UBI) and Norand Corporation, creating the industry's largest automatic data collection (ADC) company; the company becomes a subsidiary of UNOVA Inc.
1999: Sales reach $800 million.
2004: Intermec sues Rockville, Maryland-based Matrics Inc. over alleged radio frequency identification (RFID) patent infringement.
2005: Intermec and rival Symbol Technologies engage in a legal battle over intellectual property issues.

signed to lead Hiwood Technologies Inc., a company he had previously founded, and Paxton was named CEO.

Intermec's sales soared again in 1988, reaching $85.2 million. As the company set its sights on surpassing the $100 million mark, Paxton announced a corporate reorganization that put a strategic emphasis on marketing and sales. This strategy was reflected in the firm's acquisition of its distributors, including the 1988 acquisition of Intermec Systems Corporation, its Canadian distributor. It also led to the development of a value-added reseller program and a number of strategic alliances.

Another major development was Intermec's decision to construct a new, 300,000-square-foot headquarters and primary manufacturing facility in Everett, Washington. By late 1988, the company employed 890 people worldwide, including approximately 500 at its headquarters.

Intermec ended the 1980s by inventing the "Pocket RF" product category and winning a string of lucrative contracts. In 1988 these included a $100 million contract to install bar code systems at non-tactical Department of Defense logistics operations installations worldwide; a $6 million deal with the General Services Administration; and a separate $1.4 million contract with the U.S. Defense Logistics Agency. In 1989 the company

secured a $1.4 million deal with Canada Post, as well as a $2 million contract to install bar code access control systems at soccer stadiums throughout Spain.

The 1990s and Beyond

In 1991 Intermec became a wholly owned subsidiary of Litton Industries Inc., a U.S. conglomerate of defense industry businesses that had been on one of history's largest acquisition sprees. Early in the decade the company introduced FCC-approved spread spectrum radio frequency data communication technology, as well as the first high-speed, wide-area scanning technology. In March 1991 Intermec acquired two of its distributors: Reading, England-based Intermec U.K. Ltd. and Melbourne-based Intermec Australia Pty. Ltd. That year the company also introduced its Personal Area Network that enabled wireless communication between body-worn and portable devices.

In 1993 new Intermec products combined PC technology with industrial data collection capabilities. In addition, that year the company claims to have "perfected the first pen-based handheld computer with desktop PC performance." Developments in 1994 included the Janus 2020—a portable data collection computer equipped with a 386 processor, Microsoft ROM DOS, and an integral laser scanner; data collection technology that involved 2.4 GHz wireless local area networking; and what Intermec calls "the first and only product to combine a fully-automatic digital camera for non-contact image capture and decoding with an integrated computer."

In 1994 the beleaguered parent company Litton spun off Western Atlas Inc., and Intermec went with it, becoming a subsidiary of Western Atlas, a $2.5 billion petroleum company whose operations included supplying industrial automation systems and oilfield information services. In recognition of Intermec's quality efforts, ISO 9002 certification was earned in 1994, followed by ISO 9001 certification in 1995.

In 1997, Western Atlas made two acquisitions that would significantly bolster Intermec. First was Cedar Rapids, Iowa-based Norand Corporation, the industry's second largest automatic data collection (ADC) company behind Symbol Technologies. The addition of Norand, which became a subsidiary of Intermec, gave Intermec comprehensive ADC capabilities. Norand had developed mobile computing solutions for the food/beverage, car rental, transportation, and automotive sectors. Following the merger, Intermec's annual revenues reached approximately $600 million.

Intermec's status as the second-leading ADC firm did not last for long. In March 1997 Western Atlas made Intermec the industry leader, based on revenue, following the acquisition of Stockholm, Sweden-based United Barcode Industries (UBI). With roots stretching back to 1985, UBI manufactured bar code decoders, fixed-position laser scanners used in retail settings, hand-held CCD readers, fixed-position data collection terminals, and thermal bar code printers. The deal effectively pushed Intermec's revenues to $700 million, and bolstered the worldwide distribution of both firms.

By the time it acquired UBI, Intermec's sales and service reach extended to some 70 countries. In addition to its Everett,

Washington headquarters, the firm had offices in Australia, Brazil, Germany, Hong Kong, Italy, The Netherlands, Spain, Thailand, and the United Kingdom.

Following the acquisitions, Western Atlas next spun off a new company, UNOVA Inc., with Intermec as a subsidiary of the new $1.5 billion industrial technology company. Intermec adopted a new corporate structure in which UBI, Norand, and Intermec consolidated under the name Intermec Technologies Corporation. The newly organized enterprise had four divisions: Labeling Systems, Government Systems, Norand Mobile Systems, and Local Area Systems.

By the late 1990s, interest was growing in radio frequency identification (RFID) technology, which involves the use of small radio tags that are able to communicate with a networked device known as a reader. These tags, which may contain a variety of data, can be affixed to or embedded within pallets, cartons, merchandise, or parts that companies and retailers need to track. In order to position Intermec as a future RFID systems heavyweight, Unova acquired IBM's RFID division in 1997. By mid-1998 the parent company announced that it also intended to acquire the Transportation Systems Group (TSG) of Dallas-based Amtech Corp., which also focused on RFID.

Intermec's sales reached $800 million in 1999. Among a number of important technology rollouts that took place that year, two were RFID-related. According to the company these included the first scanner that, in addition to reading bar codes, was capable of programming and reading RFID tags. In addition, Intermec unveiled the first Windows-based handheld ADC units that were equipped with RFID capabilities.

In late June, 53-year-old Robert G. O'Malley, formerly the CEO of Pinacor, became Intermec's new CEO. O'Malley's previous experience included a 19-year stint at IBM, where he worked in a variety of roles. Another major development took place when Intermec restructured again, replacing its divisional structure with a global one that included the following units: Strategy and Business Development, Worldwide Sales and Services, Systems and Solutions, and Global Marketing.

In early 2000 O'Malley told *Material Handling Management* that integration was a key strategy for Intermec, as the company sought to build a unified marketing organization. In the publication's February 2000 issue, he explained: "Marketing had been product by product, segment by segment, country by country. We're pulling all these into one marketing organization. . . . What we've done organizationally is put together all the elements that produce hand held and vehicle-mounted products, along with wireless communications and some underlying software, and have created one organization."

Despite these efforts, more than a year later Intermec was still perceived by some observers as a disjointed organization. For example, in its August 2001 issue, *Frontline Solutions* reported that the company's attempt to offer "one-stop shopping" had not been executed flawlessly: "Intermec hasn't yet come to terms with how to integrate its varied technology offerings into a cohesive marketing message and sometimes appears to be operating as four or more different companies."

Intermec's sales totaled $665 million in 2001. A new CEO, Larry Brady, was brought in, and noteworthy developments in 2002 included Intermec's introduction of an RFID tracking system that U.S. tire manufacturers could use to track new car tires through the processes of production, assembly, and distribution. The technology also benefited consumers, in that recalled tires could be identified quickly. By the mid-2000s RFID continued to grow in importance. Subsequently, Intermec joined EPCglobal—a non-profit standards organization founded by the Uniform Code Council and EAN Intl.

With its 40th birthday on the horizon, Intermec found itself embroiled in a legal war with its rival, Symbol Technologies. The dispute, which centered on a number of intellectual property issues, began in June 2004 when Intermec sued Rockville, Maryland-based Matrics Inc. over alleged RFID patent infringements. Symbol acquired the lawsuit in September 2004, when it bought Matrics. Failed attempts to reach a cross-licensing agreement resulted in Symbol suing Intermec in March 2005 over alleged patent infringements related to the wireless communications standard 802.11. Symbol also terminated a supplier agreement with Intermec, under which it provided Intermec with laser scan engines for bar code scanners.

Symbol, which supported a royalty-free RFID interface standard, claimed that Intermec was slowing the industry's adoption of RFID. Other observers have agreed. For example, in the May 13, 2005, issue of the *Long Island Business News*, writer Ken Schachter noted: "Intermec has faced criticism for stifling RFID development because companies feared running afoul of its patent portfolio. Intermec sees its patents yielding a river of income as the RFID industry matures."

Despite this criticism, Intermec called Symbol's suit groundless and reactionary, and claimed to have offered a number of its RFID patents for free or at reasonable rates. A few weeks after Symbol's suit, Intermec sued Symbol over alleged patent infringements related to Wi-Fi, wireless handheld devices, and technology used to electronically capture signatures. Intermec was led during this time by President Tom Miller, who came to Intermec from Norand in 1997. While the outcome of the litigation remained uncertain, Intermec was clearly positioned for continued growth during the second half of the decade.

Principal Competitors

Symbol Technologies Inc.; Fujitsu Ltd.; Zebra Technologies Inc.; Hand Held Products Inc.

Further Reading

Aikman, Rebecca, "Bar Codes: Beyond the Checkout Counter," *Business Week*, April 8, 1985.

Aragon, Lawrence, "O'Malley on Top Again," *VARBusiness*, June 14, 1999.

"Big Becomes Biggest: Intermec Now Largest ADC Vendor," *Automatic I.D. News*, May 1997.

Cane, Alan, "Barcode Printing at Speed," *Financial Times*, June 22, 1982.

"Companies Join, Expand Products and Marketing," *Automatic I.D. News*, January 1995.

"Corporate Restructuring Reflects Global Focus," *Dairy Field*, November 1999.

"Intermec and Norand Merger Creates New #2 in ADC," *Modern Materials Handling*, April 1997.

"Intermec Files RFID Patent Infringement Lawsuit against Matrics," *Control Engineering*, July 2004.

"Intermec on the Move," *Material Handling Management*, February 2000.

"Intermec Rejects Claims in Symbol's Patent Infringement Litigation," *Control Engineering*, April 2005.

"Intermec Releases RFID Tyre-Tracking System," *Frontline Solutions*, April 2002.

"Intermec Restructures," *Material Handling Engineering*, November 1997.

"Intermec, Symbol Start Patent Feud," *Chain Store Age*, May 2005.

Schachter, Ken, "Symbol Technologies, Intermec Technologies Continue Legal Battle Over Intellectual Property," *Long Island Business News*, May 13, 2005.

"Symbol Files Wi-Fi Patent Infringement Suit against Intermec," *Logistics Today*, April 2005.

"Top 100 Frontline Companies," *Frontline Solutions*, August 2001.

"Unova to Acquire Amtech's RF Unit," *Logistics*, June 1998.

—Paul R. Greenland

Ipsen International Inc.

984 Ipsen Road
Cherry Valley, Illinois 61016
U.S.A.
Telephone: (815) 332-4941
Toll Free: (800) 727-7625
Fax: (815) 332-4995
Web site: http://www.ipsen-intl.com

Private Company
Incorporated: 1948
Employees: 145
Sales: $80.1 million (2004 est.)
NAIC: 333994 Industrial Process Furnace and Oven
   Manufacturing

Based in Cherry Valley, Illinois, Ipsen International Inc. is a leading thermal processing equipment and systems manufacturer and is privately owned by investors at Germany's Ruhrgas Industries GmbH. Ipsen has research and development facilities on two continents, as well as four worldwide manufacturing facilities. One segment of Ipsen's business involves atmosphere furnaces, while vacuum furnaces represent another large segment. By drawing from more than 50 years of thermal processing experience, the company has become a market leader in the development of vacuum heat treating equipment, serving a number of end markets including the aerospace and automotive sectors. In addition to standard and custom furnaces, Ipsen markets related software used for advanced process control and automation, as well as various controls and cleaning equipment. The company provides service and support for new furnaces, rebuilds other manufacturers' furnace brands, and performs upgrades, rebuilds, and retrofitting.

The Early Years: 1940–59

Ipsen International's roots stretch back to 1940, when Harold N. Ipsen established Ipsen Industries, a commercial heat treating shop in Loves Park, Illinois. Harold Ipsen was born in 1915 and grew up in Rockford, Illinois. His father, Mogens Ipsen, who was a native of Aarhus, Denmark, worked as an architect and was a nationally known construction expert who later served as director of the Rockford WPA, headed the city's water department, and served as city engineer. Following in Mogens' footsteps, Harold Ipsen pursued a career in engineering and earned a degree from Brown University in 1939. He started his own company the following year.

By 1942 Ipsen Industries was producing shell fuse parts for defense contractors. On June 29 of the following year, Harold Ipsen married Lorraine "Lori" A. Wrobal in Chicago, and the couple opened a decorative pottery business. When the operation's kiln broke, Ipsen designed and built a new one. The young industrialist discovered that the high-performance features of his new pottery kiln could be applied to his heat treating enterprise as well. Inspired by the need to create more uniform shell casings for the defense industry, this led him to build a new furnace for heat treating steel. Ipsen's new design was highly effective, and word of it soon reached other manufacturers, who asked him to produce similar furnaces for them.

An article in the December 19, 1955, *Rockford Morning Star* detailed manufacturers' reaction to Ipsen's invention, explaining: "They were astonished at the bright condition of the finished work after heat treatment. This bright condition was the result of protective atmosphere surrounding the work during the heating cycle as well as during the quenching operation." According to the article, Ipsen would demonstrate how a piece of wood or a newspaper could be placed into the furnace at 1,600 degrees Fahrenheit—a temperature that causes objects to burn bright red—without damage. This was because the absence of oxygen prevented them from burning.

When other furnace manufacturers would not produce a design similar to Ipsen's, he decided to forgo heat treating and concentrate on furnace manufacturing. On July 1, 1948, the company reincorporated and began focusing on this new market niche, relying on investments from outsiders and Ipsen's family.

According to company literature, the business found immediate success during its formative years: "Parts heat treated in Ipsen's new furnace came out uniformly cleaner, brighter and stronger than any furnace before it and demand soared. The consistent performance and dependability of MetalMaster fur-

Company Perspectives:

The vision and creative spirit to design and develop heat treating technology is boundless at Ipsen International, Inc. With a kindled desire to excel in technology, quality and service, the challenges of this feat are unleashed by stepping out of the box as radical thinkers. It is only in this unrestricted environment that ideas can flourish and become product possibilities, and where team members are empowered to make the impossible happen. As a globally synchronized team, product development at Ipsen International occurs through Centers of Excellence that ensure seamless integration of engineering designs and definition of customer requirements. As the largest manufacturer of heat treating equipment in the world, Ipsen is committed to the revolutionary thinking that creates the total solutions modern heat treaters require. This vision remains evident in Ipsen's global structure, which spans the world and includes manufacturing facilities in Rockford, USA; Kleve, Germany; Shanghai, China; and Calcutta, India.

naces became legend, enabling heat treaters to increase production while lowering manufacturing costs.''

With its new focus, Ipsen Industries moved from Loves Park to more suitable quarters in nearby Rockford. A sister operation called Ipsenlab was formed in 1951. Also based in Rockford, it had a combined focus that included commercial heat treating, research and development, and the showcasing of equipment. In August 1953, strong demand prompted the company to form a related subsidiary called Ipsenlab of Canada Ltd. Based in Toronto and headed by Canadian metallurgist Peter B. McCurdy, it mirrored the Rockford Ipsenlab facility, right down to the building's architecture. Each Ipsenlab location was used to test customers' manufacturing problems before solutions were developed.

Ipsen Industries had opened six branch offices by September 1953. Strong demand in the eastern United States led to a new location in Plainfield, New Jersey. The new office joined other sites in Chicago; Cleveland; Detroit; Toronto; Hartford, Connecticut; and Burbank, California. These locations were all staffed with engineers and metallurgists. Around this time, the company also had sales representatives based in Denver and Houston.

Ipsen Industries had achieved pioneer status in its industry by the early 1950s. This was accomplished by turning heat treating furnaces into automated devices. Examples included the Carbotonik and Dewtronic furnaces that controlled steel chemistry during the treatment process. Other innovations included the incorporation of ceramic material that enabled Ipsen furnaces to withstand extreme stress at high temperatures.

By 1955 Ipsen was outgrowing its physical plant once again, and plans were made to construct a new, larger facility. The company even had its own airplane. Similar to President Dwight Eisenhower's personal plane, the aircraft was used to transport customers to and from Rockford. Around this time, end uses for Ipsen's furnaces included the manufacture of washing machines, automobiles, typewriters, and airplanes. The company's client base was highly international, with Paris-based Fours-Cyclops producing Ipsen equipment for European customers. International expansion continued in 1957 with the formation of Ipsen Industries GmbH (Ipsen International) in Kleve, Germany.

In 1957 Ipsen Ceramics, once part of Ipsenlab, began operations in a new, 15,000-square-foot facility in Pecatonica, Illinois. This was followed by the construction of a new factory near Cherry Valley, Illinois, in 1959. Manufacturing operations were relocated to a new, 210-foot-long structure situated on 48 acres. The plant included a 1,200-square-foot utility tunnel that could be used as a defense shelter. In February 1960 Ipsen announced that it would expand the new plant by erecting a new building for engineering, sales, and service personnel.

New Products in the 1960s

During the early 1960s, Ipsen began manufacturing vacuum heat treating equipment, which had applications for metals used in missiles, space probes, aircraft, and rockets. Ipsen produced the first horizontal vacuum furnace in 1960. A refractory metals department opened in Rockford the following year, focusing on ceramic, metallurgical, and electrical research.

By 1962 Ipsen Ceramics was producing materials used by the government for nuclear energy, aviation, and missile production. Plans were made for an addition that would double Ipsen Ceramics' capacity. Developments continued in 1963 as Ipsen introduced the first top load vacuum furnace and Ipsenlab relocated to a larger, 18,000-square-foot facility on the campus near Cherry Valley. That year, the company received a $49,920 contract from NASA to explore the use of foamed metal in spacecraft.

Sadly, Harold Ipsen was killed at age 49 when an airplane he was flying crashed at the Greater Rockford Airport on April 29, 1965.

Harold Ipsen held more than 30 patents during his life and left a permanent mark on both his company and the larger furnace industry. Following his death, Ipsen's widow, who had been first vice-president, was named president and director. In 1965 Ipsen Industries reported sales of $9 million.

A major development occurred in June 1966 when Ipsen Industries and all of its subsidiaries were acquired by Pennsylvania-based Alco Standard Corporation. Lorraine Ipsen was made an honorary director, and Vice President-Treasurer/General Manager Paul Glavin was named president. That year, Ipsen introduced the first bottom load vacuum furnace. By this time the company had opened additional international subsidiaries including Ipsen Industries Ltd. in Surbiton, Surrey, England; and Ipsen Industries SARL in Vincennes, Sein, France.

By 1967 continued expansion of the Ipsen plant had more than doubled its productive capacity. Developments continued the following year with the introduction of the first MetalMaster horizontal vacuum furnace, the MetalMaster bottom-loading vacuum furnace, and the Vacuum Oil Quench Furnace. The Ipsen Ceramics plant ended the decade by installing two roller hearth kilns designed by Harold Ipsen.

Key Dates:

1940: Harold N. Ipsen establishes Ipsen Industries, a commercial heat treating shop in Loves Park, Illinois.

1948: The company reincorporates and focuses on the manufacture of heat treating furnaces.

1951: A sister operation called Ipsenlab is formed.

1953: Ipsenlab of Canada Ltd. is established.

1957: Ipsen Industries GmbH (Ipsen International) is formed in Kleve, Germany.

1959: A new headquarters and factory is erected near Cherry Valley, Illinois.

1961: A refractory metals department opens in Rockford, Illinois.

1962: Ipsenlab relocates to a larger, 18,000-square-foot facility on the campus near Cherry Valley.

1962: The company receives a $49,920 contract from NASA to explore the use of foamed metal in spacecraft.

1965: Harold Ipsen is killed at age 49 in a plane crash.

1966: Ipsen Industries and subsidiaries are acquired by Alco Standard Corporation.

1976: Ipsen develops a kiln that eventually fires glaze on protective tiles for the space shuttle Columbia.

1981: Ipsen acquires manufacturing plants in Bessemer, Alabama, and Nashville, Tennessee.

1985: Ipsen merges with ABAR Corporation, creating Abar Ipsen Industries.

1992: The LOI Group, part of Germany's Ruhrgas Industries GmbH, acquires Abar Ipsen.

1995: Ipsen Industries Furnaces Ltd. is formed in Shanghai, China.

1996: Abar Ipsen becomes part of the Ipsen International Group and all operations move to Illinois.

1998: The company attains ISO 9001 certification and sales reach approximately $175 million.

2004: Ipsen performs major software and hardware upgrades at its Cherry Valley plant.

Expansion in the 1970s

Ipsen started the 1970s with Leslie E. Senet as president and a staff of approximately 500 employees. In 1970 the company expanded its main plant once more with a $300,000, 20,000-square-foot addition. Measuring 250 feet long and 80 feet wide, this was the fourth major expansion since 1961.

In 1973 Louis D. Clay, a civil engineer who had served as general manager of the W.F. and John Barnes Company, was named Ipsen's president. That year Ipsen introduced a batch aluminum brazing furnace, as well as a continuous vacuum diffusion bonding furnace. The company received the largest single order in its history to date when Bochnia, Poland-based Huta Lenia Steel Plant ordered ten horizontal vacuum furnaces for $6 million.

By 1975 the company faced a number of challenges, including high material costs that impacted its competitiveness with foreign players. Nevertheless, Ipsen continued to introduce new products including an automated atmosphere furnace line in

1975, as well as the first ion nitriding furnace in 1976. It also was in 1976 that Ipsen developed a cermaic roller hearth kiln that eventually was used to fire glaze on 34,000 protective ceramic tiles for the space shuttle Columbia.

Ipsen ended the decade by expanding its manufacturing plant in 1978. The expansion provided the company with more office space, as well as expanded and modernized facilities for research and development. That same year, the company unveiled the first continuous vacuum aluminum brazing furnace.

The 1980s–90s

In 1980 Ipsen's business was down 48 percent in the wake of an economic recession. The slowdown led to the layoff of about 40 of the 300 workers at Ipsen's main plant in 1981. Around this time Ipsen's furnaces ranged in price from $50,000 to many millions of dollars. Approximately 20 percent of the company's orders were comprehensive, in which Ipsen handled everything from the units manufacture to installation.

In April 1981 Ipsen acquired manufacturing plants in Bessemer, Alabama, and Nashville, Tennessee, adding to the two Cherry Valley plants, the Pecatonica location, and a facility in Fort Worth, Texas. The company had nine sales offices throughout the United States, as well as five licensees in other countries. Ipsen continued to introduce new products during the early 1980s including a five-bar vacuum furnace in 1982, the I/O 3000 atmosphere furnace in 1983, and the Turbo Treater Vacuum Furnace in 1984.

In 1985 Ipsen merged with Abar Corporation. The resulting Abar Ipsen Industries was a wholly-owned subsidiary of the TI Group. Abar's history dated back to 1960, when Charles Hill established the company to design and manufacture vacuum heat treating equipment. After being acquired by King Fifth Wheel in 1965, Abar moved its manufacturing facilities from Willow Grove, Pennsylvania, to a new facility in Feasterville, Pennsylvania. In 1981 Abar's parent was acquired by Tube Investments Ltd. (TI) of Birmingham, England.

Following its acquisition by Abar, Ipsen continued to roll out new products throughout the decade, including a TurboTreater vacuum furnace in 1986, the Ivadizing furnace in 1987, and the ToolTreater vacuum furnace in 1988.

Abar Ipsen began the 1990s by shuttering its manufacturing site in Feasterville, Pennsylvania, and moving those operations to Illinois. At this time the company also relocated sales, engineering, and marketing personnel to Bensalem, Pennsylvania. An important development occurred in 1992 when the LOI Group, which was part of Germany's Ruhrgas Industries GmbH, acquired Abar Ipsen.

More important developments occurred midway through the decade. In 1995 Ipsen Industries Furnaces Ltd. was formed in Shanghai, China. The following year yet another restructuring occurred as Abar Ipsen became part of the Ipsen International Group and all operations were consolidated at the company's Illinois headquarters.

Many new products were unveiled during the remainder of the 1990s. These included the VUTK 524 TurboHardener in

1996 and a MultiMaster semicontinuous vacuum furnace in 1997, and a redesigned Endothermic Gas Generator in 1998. Two years of hard work paid off for Ipsen in 1998 when it attained ISO 9001 certification after meeting stringent quality control standards.

By the late 1990s Ipsen's annual sales totaled approximately $175 million, and the company counted leading firms such as Boeing, Caterpillar, and DaimlerChrysler among its clients. Mario Ciampini served as the company's president and CEO, overseeing 275 employees at the Cherry Valley plant, including about 50 engineers. The company had a progressive training program for its union workers and paid a very competitive wage. Even so, it had a difficult time finding qualified employees due to its stringent quality standards.

A New Century

Early in the new millennium, Ipsen launched a number of new products. These included the Global VR, a TurboTreater unit with convection, and the AcaV furnace in 2001. In 2002 the company met ISO 9001: 2000 standards. Contributing to the achievement were customer satisfaction efforts such as an online parts store, as well as an online customer satisfaction survey.

In January 2003, Ipsen ratified a contract with the UAW Amalgamated Local 256, which went into effect in February and gave Ipsen's unionized workers a salary increase of 11.8 percent over a period of three years.

Late in the year, the Iowa-based John Deere Waterloo Works chose Ipsen to supply a line of atmosphere furnaces that it would use to heat treat drivetrain shafts and gears for its agricultural equipment manufacturing sites worldwide. According to the November–December 2003 issue of *Furnaces International*, "The key reasons Ipsen was selected were value, technical innovations, ability to make quality parts, equipment reliability and aftermarket support."

By mid-2004 Ipsen had performed software and hardware upgrades at its Cherry Valley plant. New software consolidated controls for its heat treating machines to one user interface instead of two; allowed operators to see displays in foreign languages such as Chinese and German; and enabled Ipsen to connect with its customers via an Ethernet interface. In 2005, Ipsen was on strong footing in a highly specialized industry

that, thanks to the early efforts of Harold Ipsen, it had helped to pioneer more than 60 years before.

Principal Competitors

Carrier Corporation; Linde AG; Robert Bosch GmbH; Thyssen Krupp Stahl Company Inc.

Further Reading

"Alco Standard Buys Ipsen Industries," *Rockford Morning Star*, June 25, 1966.
"Dies Following Heart Attack; Funeral Today (Mogens Ipsen)," *Rockford Register Republic*, October 19, 1939.
"Harold Ipsen and His Vision," Cherry Valley, Ill.: Ipsen International Inc., June 8, 2005.
"Harold N. Ipsen (obituary)," *Rockford Register Republic*, April 30, 1965.
"Ipsen Automatic Heat Treating Units," *Rockford Morning Star*, December 19, 1955.
"Ipsen Builds Design Center," *Rockford Register Republic*, August 9, 1967.
"Ipsen Gets $5.8 Million Contract," *Rockford Register Republic*, May 23, 1973.
"Ipsen Tests Foamed Metal for Use on Space Ships," *Rockford Morning Star*, August 11, 1963.
"Ipsen to Open Canada Branch," *Rockford Morning Star*, August 9, 1953.
"Ipsen Receives Certification," *Industrial Heating*, August 2002.
"Ipsen Receives Order for Atmosphere Heat Treat Line," *Furnaces International*, November-December 2003.
Kleczkowski, Linda, "Ipsen International, Inc. in the Heat of Success," *Business Profile Magazine*, June 1998.
Mraz, Stephen J., "Looks the Same, Works Better: Updated Controls for Heat-Treating Furnaces," *Machine Design*, May 6, 2004.
Rogers, Cathy, "Ipsen Chief Likes to Keep Plant Operations 'Simple,'" *Rockford Register Star*, June 15, 1981.
Rubendall, Ben, "Ipsen, Romania Negotiate Contract Worth $4.6 Million," *Rockford Register Star*, March 18, 1972.
"Solution Started Lab in Business," *Rockford Register Republic*, March 1962.
Stone, Chuck, "Ipsen Oven Glazed Tiles," *Rockford Register Star*, April 15, 1981.
"Wife Succeeds Late Harold Ipsen," *Rockford Register Republic*, May 21, 1965.

—Paul R. Greenland

J.L. Hammett Company

P.O. Box 859057
Braintree, Massachusetts 02185-9057
U.S.A.
Telephone: (781) 848-1000
Toll Free: (800) 955-2200
Fax: (888) 262-1054
Web site: http://www.hammett.com

Private Company
Founded: 1863
Employees: 140
Sales: $165 million (1999)
NAIC: 454111 Web Retailers

J.L. Hammett Company is the oldest and largest independently owned school-supply retailer and distributor in the United States. Once known for its chain of retail outlets—Hammett's Learning World—the company also maintained a popular print catalog for educators. In the 2000s, however, the company was restructured as strictly an Internet retailer of school supplies. As such, Hammett supplies public, private, parochial, and chartered educational institutions with a complete range of core school supplies, including art materials, office and paper goods, furniture, equipment, and products to facilitate early learning and instruction. The company was the first full-line educational distributor to offer electronic commerce capabilities and remains a family-owned operation.

19th-Century Origins

The history of J.L. Hammett can be traced back to 1863. Rhode Islander John L. Hammett was a schoolteacher who had authored grammar books and worked as a representative of a publishing house, all roles that developed his sensitivity to the needs of educators, tapped his potential as an innovator, and developed his business sense. In 1863 he established a small school-supply shop in Rhode Island and, two years later, moved it to a single store location in Boston, Massachusetts. Hammett was an inventor as well, having developed a ''slating paint'' which could be applied to the slates children used in school,

prolonging the life of the boards. The paint could also be used to turn a wall into a chalkboard. Furthermore, Hammett invented the chalkboard eraser: during a presentation, when he could not find a cloth to wipe his slate, he picked up a carpet remnant and discovered that it cleaned the slate much better than the cloths he had been using. With the help of his assistant, Hammett began to nail pieces of carpet to blocks of wood which were then sold as erasers. Invention and manufacture was a concern of the company from its inception until the 1950s, as the company would make ruled paper, mix ink, and manufacture various other school products. By the end of the 19th century, increased production made paper more affordable and accessible for schools and teachers, and the demand for slates and related products diminished. In 1890 Hammett sold his business interests to a new generation of owners composed of Massachusetts investors led by Harry H. Young.

Hammett's merchandise line soon expanded beyond schoolbooks. In 1891 the company formed a partnership with game-producer Milton Bradley of Springfield, Massachusetts, and pioneered the production of kindergarten materials in the United States. Young and his associates brought J.L. Hammett Co. into new fields and product lines: they opened facilities in New York and New Jersey and established a paper-converting and bindery plant in Cambridge, Massachusetts. After spending some time abroad, Hammett attempted to return to the education business but he failed.

New Directions in a New Century

Young's grandson, Richmond Y. Holden, Sr., entered the family business in 1948 as a sales representative in the New Jersey division, became vice-president of the Cambridge, Massachusetts, plant in 1953, and was elected manager/treasurer/clerk of the corporation in 1958. Chosen as president of the company in 1961, with new educational tools he expanded Hammet's services to private, parochial, public, and chartered schools.

In 1967 Holden moved the company's headquarters from Cambridge to Braintree, Massachusetts, and began to explore the concept of retail outlets. In 1974 he opened the first Hammett's

Learning World retail store to sell all kinds of educational supplies and teaching materials. The customers were teachers who used their own money to buy educational supplies and parents who wanted what Holden called "industrial strength" learning products.

In 1978 Richmond Y. Holden, Jr. (Rick) joined J.L. Hammett Co. A modest growth rate and several retail acquisitions expanded the Learning World chain; by 2003 there were more than 62 stores of this kind in the United States. Parents who home-schooled their children came to the stores for text books and teaching supplies. J.L. Hammett was a big player in the school supplies arena and gradually changed the way teachers and schools bought their supplies. Since many of the company's stores were located in shopping malls, even teen-agers went there to evaluate and buy educational products. Teachers and parents were no longer the only ones to search for school supplies.

Rick Holden succeeded his father as president and led J.L. Hammett Co. into a wave of technical change. In addition to its 808-page general catalog, the company created several sub-catalogs for needs related to early childhood and materials for the arts. As his first order of business, Holden chose to update the company's antiquated distribution system in order to cut the costs of writing orders for supplies that had to be tracked through every phase of entry, picking, packing and shipping. He explored the possibilities the Internet offered for improvement of business margins.

As support for the company's mission to recognize excellence in education, the J.L. Hammett Foundation was established in March 1997 to promote educational innovation in the nation's public and private school system. The Foundation focused on teachers and institutions of Pre-K through 12th grades to award cash grants ranging from $1,000 to $5,000 for innovative use of new technology or creative use of simple curriculum materials. The Foundation emphasized the need for discovery and support of projects, people, and schools where bright new ideas were conceived and implemented.

The company's first venture into e-commerce was a modem-based program called EO, for electronic ordering. J.L. Hammet sent disks containing the company's catalog to customers to load onto their school computers for placing orders. In all, about 2,200 schools used EO. Although Internet surfing was still in its infancy, Holden realized that "at least a third of his business . . . had to come through Net marketplaces in the next two years," wrote Richard Karpinski, in *B to B*'s April 2000 issue. In the mid-1990s, Holden had at great expense set up an Internet ordering system for his company's website: (www.Hammett.com).

Net marketplaces quickly multiplied and made life difficult for suppliers who not only had to figure out affordable means of connecting with Internet marketplaces but also had to decide which marketplaces were potential gold mines or possible sink holes. Furthermore, information had to be delivered not only to the Web site but also to aggregators, exchanges, and customers' buying systems. Holden did not want to go through more time and expense to hook up with a marketplace. To obtain a technology solution, he turned to server-vendor Ironside Technologies Inc. of Pleasanton, California. One of the trickiest issues was to bring the back-end of the operation into the electronic age. Additionally, the company had to focus its business plan on ways that would eliminate inefficiencies, cut costs, and operate in real-time. "Let's get a standard here; give us some tools and a methodology to hook up to any exchange we want," said Holden to Ironside, according to the Karpinsky article. Holden had already "teamed up with exchanges 'in stealth mode' for more than a year and was linked with Epylon.com, Simplexis .com, and Eschoolmall.com." Ironside had helped to make these connections and soon released its Ironside Network. With Hammett's former paper-based model, it took three weeks to process orders. The new Ironside-powered automated system reduced this task to a maximum time of three hours.

At the heart of Hammett's e-commerce strategy was eZone, an electronic-sell-side procurement system based on Ironside technology and designed for institutional buying. eZone provided access to the Hammett catalogs and offered procurement tools and services, thereby allowing business managers to see the orders in their company's system, to manage purchase orders, and to control various users' authorizations for purchases. About a year after the installation of eZone, some 26,000 schools placed orders for supplies. Average orders increased from $200 to $510, and shipments were faster. Clients who had formerly placed complicated, paper-based orders could reach the ordering system by means of an easy-to-use browser. For example, according to Julia King's "At the Head of the Class" story in the *Computerworld* issue of September 18, 2000, a purchasing clerk who bought thousands of items for her district of four schools and 325 teachers in Penn Yan, New York, claimed that she could now do in one week all the ordering that had formerly taken her eight weeks to complete.

Hammett invested in several technology ventures, namely Beansprouts.net, an Arlington-based child-welfare network, and PC Build, a company that wired schools for the modern age. From seven partners/advertisers, Holden collected fees that covered about 30 percent of the cost to maintain and update the company website. According to the August 2000 *Heller Report,* another one of Hammett's strategies was to develop "multiple venues for online penetration, primarily agreements with school procurement sites—such as Epylon (Hammett's flagship and first customer)—and alliances that created online stores for other web sites." Holden believed that customers could receive better service via the Internet; and with his brother Jeff as vice-president, he led the company toward a new millennium while safeguarding Hammett's long-held educational traditions. The company sold primarily to preschool and K-12 schools through its catalogs and sales force. "J.L. Hammett is the resource teachers have used and trusted for years," Rick told the *Journal* in a July 1999 interview. Hammett Director of Marketing Dave Merigold commented that "We are in the vernacular now of school supply technology. With an advanced procurement pro-

Key Dates:

1863: John L Hammett opens a small educational-supply shop in Rhode Island.

1865: Hammett moves his J.L. Hammett Company to Boston.

1890: Hammett sells his business interests to an investor group led by Harry H. Young.

1891: J.L. Hammet and Milton Bradley Company partner to offer kindergarten materials in the United States.

1948: Richmond Y. Holden, Sr., enters the family business.

1960s: J.L. Hammett publishes small catalogs of its products.

1967: Company headquarters are moved to Braintree, Massachusetts; Holden, Sr., is elected president of J.L. Hammett Co.

1974: Holden opens the first ''Hammett's Learning World'' retail store.

1978: Richmond Y. Holden, Jr. joins Hammett Co.

1990s: Holden Jr. introduces e-commerce and eZone.

1997: The J.L. Hammett Foundation is established to promote education.

2001: Hammett sells its catalog and wholesale businesses but retains its retail stores.

2005: Company announces sale of retail stores and restructures as an Internet retailer of school supplies.

cess like eZone, dealers of educational products will need to follow Hammett's lead in order to keep pace.''

The company's website gradually became an extension of Hammett's retail stores, thereby enabling teachers and parents from all over the nation to browse and shop in the comfort of their homes, offices, and classrooms. Orders by traditional means—such as phone, fax, and mail order—continued to surpass the company's Website output, but Hammett executives thought that its eZone would soon handle a quarter of the company's bustling summer ordering season. Educators and teachers used eZone as a tool to search and compare products as well as to track purchases and review their accounts.

When an order reached Hammett through the Internet, it was assigned an invoice number on the company's IBM AS/400 and sent to the warehouse where it was received with a radio frequency (RF) scanner, picked, and packed. The warehouse triggered an order to refurnish inventory and sent out an invoice. ''We're not rekeying anything, so our order accuracy is up, and there's no place for orders to get backlogged,'' said Merigold. ''We're also stripping out a lot of costs on our side and on the customers' side'' because schools can generate orders more quickly than formerly, he added. Hammett included its 80-person salesforce, who still made sales visits to school districts, in its online strategy by awarding them bonuses and commissions for migrating customers to online ordering. In the May 1999 *Catalog Age*, Paul Miller commented that RF scanners not only received catalog and online orders electronically but also read the product barcodes and rejected items when their codes didn't match those of the requested merchandise.

1999 and Beyond

Hammett continued to refine its Internet strategies and its online activities rapidly expanded. According to the *Heller Report*, President Holden pursued multiple venues for online penetration, primarily agreements with school procurement sites such as Epylon, and alliances that created online stores for other web sites; he worked with several sites to host more co-branded, online stores ''powered by Hammett.com.'' Many of Hammett's sales came from its Learning World stores. Holden eschewed plans for franchising, and refused to go public. J.L. Hammett Co. was to remain family-owned. ''There's a mentality here about family ownership and full participation in the business,'' he said.

In 1999, Hammett sold school supplies and equipment from three different venues: the Hammett catalog, the Company's website, and a chain of over 62 Hammett's Learning World retail stores. For 1999, Hammett posted annual revenues of $165 million and was the only company that sold school supplies and equipment from three different sources. Business soared. In 2000, two years after J.L. Hammett Co. entered e-commerce as a cost-cutting strategy, e-commerce had yielded a $9.5 milllion increase in sales, a 200 percent increase in average-size orders, and a 46 percent reduction in transaction costs, from about $130 to $70 per order,'' according to the September 18, 2000, issue of *Computerworld*.

In 2000, Hammett sold its catalog and wholesale businesses, as well as its three distribution centers, to School Specialty Inc. (formerly its most aggressive competitor) for $82 million but retained the early education and chartered-schools businesses on which it planned to focus more intensely. Holden had hoped that moving Hammett stores out of enclosed malls into strip malls would increase sales but positive results did not materialize quickly enough. ''We just ran out of time . . . to get that done,'' Holden told Associated Press. To Bill Lane of *Boston Business Journal*, Holden said that over the years teachers had spent much of their own money to buy educational materials from Hammett. However, the economy was bad and tightened school budgets did not allow for reimbursements to these teachers. Furthermore, as Lenny Liebmann commented in his February 5, 2001 article for *NETWORK MAGAZINE*, ''Despite the fact that Hammett opted for premium placement on several B2B shopping portals . . . [Hammett Marketing Director David Merigold said] only 18 percent of our volume comes from new business and, of that, only about 10 percent has come through marketplaces.' ''

In Januray 2005, President Holden announced that the company's retail division ''would fold up and leave only 'a small retail operation.' '' His efforts to sell Hammett's remaining 52 stores did not succeed. ''There wasn't a fit for either the buyer's interests or the company's interests,'' he told *Business Journal's* Bill Lane. ''Since we were the largest [independent provider of school supplies], it was difficult to find someone else in the same business,'' Rick said. J.L. Hammett Co. had to consider ending its brick-and-mortar operations after 141 years in business but opted to remain in Braintree as an online operator under Holden's leadership. About 30 to 40 percent of the Hammett stores were sold to regional and local retailers of school supplies. According to a story in *The Patriot Ledger* of

December 31, 2004, the company had already sold the 42 acres of land it owned in Braintree to a builder of luxury condominiums. ''We'll move to a much smaller office with a smaller staff,'' said Holden.

Principal Competitors

ABC School Supply, Inc.; American Teaching Supply; School Specialty, Inc.: U.S. School Supply, Inc.

Further Reading

Abouzeid, Nehme E., ''Supplying the Future'' *Boston Business Journal*, July 2, 1999.

''Appleton, Wis.-Based School Supply Firm to Buy Unit of Braintree, Mass. Rival,'' *Milwaukee Journal Sentinel*, November 15, 2000.

Bartels, Andrew, ''J.L. Hammett Co. Selects Ironside's E-Commerce Solution,'' *PR Newswire*, February 9, 1998.

Burr, Jeffrey, ''Software Weighs Pros, Cons,'' *eWeek*, October 16, 2000, p. 34.

''Hammett Grows Online Sales Through Multiple Venues:'' *Heller Report,* August 2000.

''J.L. Hammett Co. and Great Source Division of Houghton Mifflin Form Alliances With Chapbooks.com to Enable Classroom Publishing,'' *Boston Business Wire*, September 26, 2000.

Jette, Julie, ''After 141 Years, No More Pens or Erasers,'' *Patriot Ledger* (Quincy, Mass.), December 31, 2004.

Karpinski, Richard, ''Seller Hubs Consolidate E-Markets: Faster, Easier Access to Portals,'' *B to B,* April 24, 2000, pp. 1–2.

King, Julie, ''At the Head of the Class: School Supply Firm Finds Niche Online,'' *Computerworld*, September 18, 2000.

Lane, Bill, ''School Supplier J.L. Hammett to Close Stores,'' *Austin Business Journal*, January 4, 2005.

Liebmann, Lenny, ''Strategies & Issues—Eyes Wide Shut: A Look at B2B Marketplaces,'' *Network Magazine*, February 5, 2001.

Miller, Paul, ''Fine-Tuning Fulfillment,'' *Catalog Age*, May 1, 1999.

''Suppliers Get Help in Hitting the Right Links,'' *Crain's Chicago Business,* May 15, 2000, p. 38.

—Gloria A. Lemieux

JO-ANN
experience the creativity®

Jo-Ann Stores, Inc.

5555 Darrow Road
Hudson, Ohio 44236
U.S.A.
Telephone: (330) 656-2600
Fax: (330) 463-6675
Web site: http://www.joann.com

Public Company
Incorporated: 1951 as Cleveland Fabric Shops, Inc.
Employees: 21,700
Sales: $1.73 billion (2004)
Stock Exchanges: New York
Ticker Symbol: JAS
NAIC: 451130 Sewing, Needlework & Piece Goods Stores

Formerly known as Fabri-Centers of America, Jo-Ann Stores, Inc., is the country's largest fabric retailer, with sales of nearly $2 billion, 851 fabric stores in 48 states, and an estimated 6 percent of the $29 billion retail fabric and craft-supplies market. The company's smaller "traditional" stores and 35,000 square foot superstores carry wide selections of fabric, notions, and craft goods. The chain boasts nearly double the sales and locations of its nearest competitor, Hancock Fabrics. Having survived a dramatic shakeout in the retail fabric industry in the 1990s and growth pains between 1998 and 2002, Jo-Ann made a strong recovery from its unprofitable years and looked to expand to 600 or 700 superstores in the early decades of the 21st century.

Founding and Early Development

The chain was founded in 1943 by two German immigrant families, the Rohrbachs and the Reichs. The Reichs had an importing business dealing in Swiss cheese, anchovy paste and pickles, and they invited their friends to start selling fabric in their suburban Cleveland storefront. When Berthold Rohrbach died that same year, his 30-year-old daughter, Alma Zimmerman, went to work full-time at the store with Hilda Reich. Hilda's daughter, Betty, joined the family business in 1947, and she and Alma opened the chain's second store in Cleveland soon thereafter.

Betty married Martin Rosskamm in 1948, and he quit his upper-level management position at a knitting mill to join the fabric company. Cofounder Hilda Reich continued to supervise a Fabri-Center store until her death at the age of 87 in 1986. Alma, her husband, Freddy, and Betty continued to serve on the board of directors into the mid-1990s, but it was Martin Rosskamm who became a driving force behind the chain's continuous expansion throughout the Midwest. Seeking a less geographically exclusive name to take the chain into the Pittsburgh area, the families created Jo-Ann by merging two of their children's names: Jo from Joan Zimmerman and Ann from Jackie Ann Rosskamm. Fabri-Centers' small specialty stores, which were often located in the regional shopping malls that sprung up in the postwar era, competed well with the fabric departments of larger general merchandise stores. The chain incorporated as Cleveland Fabric Shops, Inc. in February 1951, changing its name to Fabri-Centers of America, Inc. in 1968 and going public the following year. In 1998, the company changed its name to Jo-Ann Stores, Inc.

Facing a Changing Market in the 1970s–80s

The retail fabric market began to decline in the 1970s, as more women went to work outside the home, and home sewing declined. At the same time, however, department stores and mass merchandisers were eliminating their fabric and notions departments, reducing the net number of retail fabric outlets by almost half from 1977 to 1983. This market contraction allowed Fabri-Centers and other leading specialty chains to continue to capture sales and share despite the overall market reduction. Top executives would look back on the 1970s as "glory days," when growth was relatively easy and profitable. By 1983, Fabri-Centers boasted over 600 stores under the Jo-Ann, Showcase of Fine Fabrics, and House of Fine Fabrics names in 33 states. As president and CEO through 1985, Martin Rosskamm guided a doubling of Fabri-Centers' annual sales, from $120.9 million in fiscal 1979 (ended January 31 of that year) to $226.9 million in fiscal 1985. Profits increased robustly during that period as well, from $4 million to $7.2 million, and the chain's share of the national retail fabric market increased to over 5.5 percent as it advanced to the number-two rank.

This period lulled the chain into a false sense of security that would come back to haunt it in the mid- and late-1980s. In a

Company Perspectives:

We will not be satisfied to rest on our accomplishments. Our mission is to provide our customers with the fabric and craft-related products they need to fulfill their creative ambitions. Our goal is to be the leader in our industry.

1995 interview with Financial World's Lore Croghan, Martin's son Alan Rosskamm acknowledged that "We were out-assorted, outpromoted and undersold. . . . There were fundamental industry changes that we had been slow to recognize."

That's when the company found its profit margins squeezed by rising costs and a maturing market. Fabric retailers had historically been recession-resistant—stung by the high cost of retail clothing, many women flocked to fabric stores to make their own clothes during economic downturns—but when the economy went sour in the early 1980s, manufacturers of ready-to-wear apparel slashed their own prices, eradicating any "homemade" savings and taking the wind out of fabric retailers' sails. Rampant price-cutting in the retail fabric industry exacerbated the effects of the early 1980s recession. When Alan Rosskamm succeeded his father as president and CEO of the company in 1985, Fabri-Centers' net profit margin was less than 0.5 percent. While sales continued to rise, from $209.4 million in fiscal 1984 to $239.4 million in fiscal 1987, net income declined from $4.5 million to $1.7 million. The slide culminated in a net loss of $4.9 million on $266.7 million sales in fiscal 1988. It was the first loss in the chain's 45-year history. The new president admitted to Delinda Karle of the Cleveland Plain Dealer in May 1988 that "All of a sudden, our business started shrinking and our expenses started rising."

Transformation and Diversification in the 1990s

Rosskamm launched a multifaceted turnaround plan that year. His was a risky proposition attempted by many of his rivals with varying degrees of success in the late 1980s and early 1990s. A key to the strategy was a wholesale move of its stores from high-rent, relatively small shops in malls to large "superstores" in strip malls. In fiscal 1992 alone, Fabri-Centers opened 121 superstores (with up to 15,000 square feet of space) and closed 108 outmoded locations.

However, Fabri-Centers wasn't the only chain with growth on its mind—its six major competitors were also adding dozens of big stores, leading inexorably to a glut of the mature market. Casualties of these hard-fought "fabric wars" began to mount: by the mid-1990s, only Fabri-Centers and Hancock Fabrics were left standing. Both House of Fabrics and Piece Goods Shops were mired in bankruptcy, and many of the other former leaders were either bought out or liquidated.

Fabri-Centers came out on top but not without its share of bruises and scars. In an effort to diversify from the stagnant fabric market, which stood at about $4 billion throughout the late 1980s and early 1990s, the company launched Cargo Express, a chain of specialty housewares, in 1984. Spearheaded by Alan Rosskamm, this discount chain sold cutlery, stemware, glassware and other tableware in 18 stores by 1988. In spite of its growth, the concept didn't record an annual profit until fiscal 1990, and Rosskamm characterized the business as "a break-even venture" accounting for less than 3 percent of Fabri-Centers' overall sales in 1992. Heavy discounting and intense competition in the category forced Fabri-Centers to put the 41-store operation on the selling block in 1993. Unable to find a buyer, the executives liquidated the inventory and closed the stores in 1994, taking a $5.2 million loss on the transaction.

Cargo Express' protracted failure (combined with the generally poor condition of the retail fabric industry) contributed to a sharp and rapid decline in Fabri-Centers' stock price. The company's stock fell from a high of $47.25 in January 1992, when Fabri-Centers announced record high earnings of $17.5 million, down to less than $13 by that July. Before the year was out, Standard & Poor's had lowered its rating of Fabri-Centers' paper to junk bond status.

CEO Rosskamm reacted quickly, cutting salaries on a sliding scale and eliminating some administrative staffers. Other more fundamental changes that had already been instituted as part of the turnaround program of the late 1980s would be the factors that kept Fabri-Centers at the top of the fabric game in the mid-1990s. Efficiency efforts included construction of a new distribution center and creation of a state-of-the-art computer system that linked operations from the point of sale to the warehouse. From 1987 to 1990, these efforts helped reduce overhead by 20 percent, from 48 percent of sales to 40 percent of sales. The chain also experimented with deep discount Best Fabric Outlets, aired its first television commercials, and launched a custom drapery business.

Fabri-Centers also found a profitable and logical diversification niche in the crafting boom of the 1990s. The craft segment, encompassing everything from seasonal and holiday decorations to home decor, multiplied from $2 billion in 1990 to more than $10 billion by 1995. Along with several other industry observers, CEO Rosskamm attributed the boom to the "cocooning" trend that found families spending more time at home. Craft goods contributed nearly one-third of Fabri-Centers' annual sales by that time.

The Rise to the Top

Fabri-Centers solidified its position at the top of the retail fabric heap with the 1994 acquisition of fourth-ranking Cloth World's 343 stores from Brown Group Inc. The $100 million cash purchase fleshed out Fabri-Centers' presence in the southern United States, bringing it to 48 states. The transaction increased the chain's debt (and brought a revisitation of Standard & Poor's ire), but it also positioned Fabri-Centers to become a "category killer": a destination store whose enormous selection and low prices draws customers. The chain expected to spend 18 months and up to $45 million to convert the Cloth World stores to the Fabri-Centers format (although they kept their well-established name). CEO Rosskamm called the deal "an enormous growth opportunity for Fabri-Centers."

The chain emerged from its industry's shakeout in relatively good health. Over the course of the early 1990s, Fabri-Centers' sales increased 83.3 percent, from $368.6 million in fiscal 1991 to $677.3 million in fiscal 1995. Profits, meanwhile, had not yet

Key Dates:

1943: The business is founded when the Reich family invites the Rohrbach family to sell fabric at their suburban Cleveland import store.
1947: The company opens its second store, in Cleveland.
1951: The company incorporates as Cleveland Fabric Shops, Inc.
1960s: The shops are renamed Jo-Ann Fabrics as the company expands outside of Cleveland.
1968: The company changes its name to Fabri-Centers of America, Inc.
1969: Fabri-Centers goes public.
1984: Jo-Ann launches Cargo Express, a discount housewares chain, in an attempt to diversify.
1988: The chain posts its first loss as the economy and the fabric market stagnate. Jo-Ann's recovery strategy focuses on developing "superstores."
1992: The company's stock is reduced to junk-bond status, and it quickly institutes changes in operations to counter the problem.
1990s: Craft supplies are introduced to the company's merchandise mix.
1993: Cargo Express is put up for sale.
1994: Unable to find a buyer, Jo-Ann liquidates Cargo Express at a loss of $5.2 million.
1998: The company changes its name to Jo-Ann Stores, Inc.
2000: Jo-Ann struggles with heavy debt and inventory system problems, posting the second loss in its history.
2003: The company returns to profitability.

regained the $17.5 million record set in fiscal 1991, slipping to a low of $2.2 million in fiscal 1994 and amounting to $11.7 million in fiscal 1995. While Fabri-Centers was considerably larger than second-ranking Hancock Fabrics, according to a February 1995 article in Barron's, the Cleveland-based chain had a higher debt load, lower market value, and lower profitability, proving that bigger is not always better. Alan Rosskamm, who was in his mid-40s in the mid-1990s, hoped to turn that adage on its ear in the latter years of the decade.

In 1998, Fabri-Centers reached a turning point. The company purchased 250 House of Fabrics stores, its biggest purchase deal to that date, raising its total number of stores to 1,060. More than half of these stores were designated Jo-Ann Fabrics and Crafts, while the rest operated under six different names: Cloth World, Fabri-Centers of America, FabricKing, FabricLand, House of Fabrics, New York Fabrics, and So-Fro Fabrics. The company carried an $180 million debt load, including $106 million stemming from the House of Fabrics purchase, which raised the company's debt-to-total capital ratio to 50%. Consolidation and elimination of redundancies was clearly in order.

In June 1998, shareholders approved a name change to strengthen the company's brand and unify its corporate identity, and the business began operating as Jo-Ann Fabrics. All stores were promptly converted to the new name. Jo-Ann closed the

House of Fabrics administrative offices and 90 Fabri-Centers stores, then consolidated another 90 overlapping former House of Fabrics and Fabri-Centers stores. Realizing that most of their customers sewed as a hobby rather than as a necessity, Jo-Ann decided in 1999 to focus on expanding the superstore concept to be called Jo-Ann etc., gradually replacing traditional fabrics-only stores with 45,000 square foot outlets that presented sewing goods and general craft merchandise.

The superstore plan met with initial success. Whereas 12,000- to 20,000-square-foot traditional stores produced only $99 in sales per square foot, the expanded-inventory superstores generated $150 to $170 in revenues per square foot. Laura Richardson, an analyst for the Winston-Salem, NC, firm BB & T Capital Markets, told Henry Gomez of *Crain's Cleveland Business*, "What I like is that Jo-Ann has a well-known brand name for sewing already. And there's no one else in both the fabrics and crafts business. Jo-Ann is a unique animal in the retail world." Analyst Michael Corelli of the New York investment advisor firm Barry Vogel & Associates told Gomez, "I doubt highly that guys like Michaels would get into the [fabrics] side. I think it's going to be a great high market share for Jo-Ann. On the craft side, Jo-Ann can differentiate itself as a one-stop shop."

The sewing-crafts split and the emphasis on superstores had their downsides, however. The higher-volume done by the superstores severely taxed the company's existing distribution facilities, and the smaller traditional stores found themselves bulging with the additional line of craft products. To handle the flood of new merchandise, a $33 million computer system that combined financial, merchandising, and retail applications into a single platform was put in place in May 2000. Inevitably, problems followed, intensifying the difficulties at store level. Inventory glitches in the new system mixed up store orders; understocked stores were starved of goods while fully-stocked locations received large, unnecessary deliveries. Merchandise counts in orders flip-flopped, causing quantities of lower-performing goods and sparse amounts of higher-performing goods to be sent to stores, bringing stock problems to an unprecedented level of confusion. Brian Carney, Jo-Ann's chief financial officer, remarked to Shannon Mortland of *Crain's Cleveland Business* in February 2002, adding "We really exceeded our capacity for distribution." The bugs in the new system were likely also responsible for a jump in shrinkage, that is, inventory losses due to theft, vendor fraud, damage, and inventory errors. The average rate of shrinkage in the retail industry is about 1.8 percent of sales; in 2001 Jo-Ann's shrinkage rate was 2.5 percent of sales, a level the company's vice president of finance Don Tomoff termed "drastic." As a result of these difficulties, the company posted a loss of $13.6 million.

Jo-Ann immediately set about implementing a recovery plan in January 2001. The company put a moratorium on new store openings and focused on paying down debt and fine-tuning existing stores and its merchandise mix. About 10, 000 redundant or under-performing SKUs (Stock Keeping Units, unique identifying numbers applied to each different type of inventory item) were permanently removed from inventory and placed on clearance sale. Ten thousand square feet were trimmed off of the superstore concept, and the layout of the remaining 35,000 square feet was re-engineered, placing the four chief departments of the store—floral design, home décor, scrapbooking, and quilting—in each corner of the building and the fabric department in the middle. Fabric cutting tables occupying the center of the store were designed to act as a ''community center'' where sales associates and customers could gather and discuss ideas and products. The massive clearancing program and costs associated with closing redundant stores resulted in a $14.9 million loss in 2001. The recovery efforts worked, however; Jo-Ann posted net income of $44.9 million in 2002 and paid down over $100 million of its $203 million debt.

Jo-Ann celebrated its 60th anniversary in 2003 as a profitable company. A total of 892 stores, including 806 traditional stores and 86 superstores, brought in a net income of $41 million. The company's debt-to-total capital ratio reached 24.7 percent, the goal set three years previous in Jo-Ann's recovery plan. By the beginning of 2005, the company operated 851 stores, including 737 traditional outlets and 114 superstores, which brought in a net income $46.2 million in 2004. Steady increases in sales brought about the need for another distribution center. Scheduled to open in 2006 the $45 million, 700,000-square-foot center in Opalika, AL, represented a major investment in cutting-edge distribution technology for Jo-Ann. The center, which was designed move a third of the company's inventory, served developing markets in Texas and other southern states; Jo-Ann was not going to repeat the inventory fiasco that followed its first major push into the superstore concept.

Principal Competitors

A.C. Moore; Hancock Fabrics, Inc.; Michaels Stores, Inc.

Further Reading

Barnes, Jon, ''Fabri-Centers' Turnaround Earns It Spot on Picks List,'' *Crain's Cleveland Business*, December 19, 1988, p. 23.

Brammer, Rhonda, ''A Great Notion?,'' *Barron's*, February 13, 1995, p. 20.

Canedy, Dana, ''Sewing Up the Market,'' *Cleveland Plain Dealer*, February 19, 1995, p. 1H.

Clark, Sandra, ''Fabric Chain Tries New Marketing Strategy,'' *Cleveland Plain Dealer*, September 2, 1992, p. 2H.

——, ''Fabri-Centers,'' *Cleveland Plain Dealer*, June 1, 1992, p. 28F.

——, ''Fabri-Centers to Cut Staff, Salaries,'' *Cleveland Plain Dealer*, July 15, 1992, p. 1E.

——, ''Fabri-Centers to Expand Cargo Express Unit,'' *Cleveland Plain Dealer*, May 22, 1992, p. 2F.

——, ''Superstores Help Boost Net Sales at Fabric Chain,'' *Cleveland Plain Dealer*, May 19, 1992, p. 5G.

Corral, Cecile B., ''Jo-Ann Keeps Plugging Away,'' *Home Textiles Today*, March 14, 2005, p. 4.

''Craft Industry Implemented Strong 1992 Sales Gains,'' *Discount Store News*, July 5, 1993, p. 86.

Croghan, Lore, ''Shakeout at the Strip Mall,'' *Financial World*, May 23, 1995, p. 48.

Gerdel, Thomas W., ''Fabri-Centers Buying Cloth World Chain,'' *Cleveland Plain Dealer*, August 26, 1994, p. 1C.

——, ''Fabri-Centers Cuts 80 Jobs, Closes 8 Stores,'' *Cleveland Plain Dealer,* June 7, 1988, p. 6D.

——, ''Fabri-Centers Led by Rosskamm Son,'' *Cleveland Plain Dealer,* June 4, 1985, p. 1D.

——, ''Fabri-Centers Moving into Tableware Sales,'' *Cleveland Plain Dealer,* December 1, 1984, p. 3B.

——, ''Fabri-Centers to Open Tableware Stores Here,'' *Cleveland Plain Dealer,* April 6, 1984, p. 6E.

——, ''Fabric Firm Adds Sewing Machines,'' *Cleveland Plain Dealer,* June 7, 1983, p. 3C.

——, ''Firms' Chief Downplays Stock Declines,'' *Cleveland Plain Dealer,* June 10, 1992, p. 2F.

——, ''Softer Sales Hit Stock of Fabri-Centers,'' *Cleveland Plain Dealer,* June 4, 1992, p. 1D.

——, ''Store Expansions Aid Fabri-Centers Sales,'' *Cleveland Plain Dealer,* May 21, 1991, p. 2F.

Gomez, Henry, ''Sewing Up a Strong Rebound,'' *Crain's Cleveland Business*, August 9, 2004, p. 1.

Gordon, Mitchell, ''A Special Place: Fabri-Centers Sees Bright Future as Department Stores Leave the Fold,'' *Barron's*, April 18, 1983, p. 59.

Groeber, Janet, ''Sewing Up the Competition,'' *Display & Design Ideas,* August 2004, p. 28.

Hass, Nancy, ''Fabri-Centers: Sewing Up the Market,'' *FW,* March 17, 1992, p. 18.

Hill, Miriam, ''Analysts Applaud Fabri-Centers' Move,'' *Cleveland Plain Dealer*, December 22, 1993, p. 2F.

——, ''Fabri-Centers President Unexpectedly Resigns Post,'' *Cleveland Plain Dealer*, April 6, 1993, p. 1F.

——, ''Fabri-Centers Wants to Unload Money-Losing Cargo Express,'' *Cleveland Plan Dealer*, March 9, 1993, p. 1F.

Karle, Delinda, ''Fabri-Centers Patching Its Financial Quilt,'' *Cleveland Plain Dealer*, May 2, 1988, p. 6C.

Kuhn, Susan E., ''Companies to Watch: Fabri-Centers of America,'' *Fortune,* July 30, 1990, p. 132.

Mortland, Shannon, ''Jo-Ann Stores Crafts Way out of Slump,'' *Crain's Cleveland Business*, February 11, 2002, p. 3.

——, ''Surge in Shrinkage Baffles Jo-Ann,'' *Crain's Cleveland Business,* June 18, 2001, p. 2.

Phillips, Stephen, ''SEC Finds Fault with Fabri-Centers,'' *Cleveland Plain Dealer*, November 16, 1995, p. 1C.

——, ''Store Crafting a Winning Strategy,'' *Cleveland Plain Dealer*, November 17, 1995, p. 1C.

Yerak, Rebecca, ''Fabri-Centers Is Pleased with Cargo Express,'' *Cleveland Plain Dealer*, June 5, 1990, p. 8D.

——, ''Superstores Hike Sales at Fabri-Centers,'' *Cleveland Plain Dealer,* May 17, 1991, p. 1E.

—April Dougal Gasbarre
—update: Jennifer Gariepy

Johnson Publishing Company, Inc.

1820 South Michigan Avenue
Chicago, Illinois 60605
U.S.A.
Telephone: (312) 322-9200
Fax: (312) 322-0918
Web site: http://www.johnsonpublishing.com

Private Company
Incorporated: 1942 as Negro Digest Publishing Co.
Employees: 2,000
Sales: $488.5 million (2003)
NAIC: 511120 Periodical Publishers; 511130 Book
   Publishers; 561510 Travel Agencies

Johnson Publishing Company, Inc., is the world's largest African American-owned publishing company. It is the home of *Ebony* and *Jet* magazines, as well as Fashion Fair Cosmetics, Ebony Fashion Fair, and the Johnson Publishing Company Book Division. Linda Johnson Rice, daughter of founder John H. Johnson, operates as president and CEO of the company.

Humble Beginnings in 1942

Johnson Publishing Company was founded in November 1942 by John H. Johnson—who was working part-time as an office boy for Supreme Life Insurance Company of America, located in Chicago, Illinois—and his wife, Eunice. Johnson's job was to clip magazine and newspaper articles about the African American community. As he clipped, the idea for an African American-oriented magazine came to mind. Using his mother's furniture as collateral, he secured a loan of $500. He then mailed out $2 charter subscription offers to potential subscribers. More than 3,000 replies came in, and the $6,000 was used to print the first issue of *Negro Digest,* a magazine based on the popular *Reader's Digest.*

Negro Digest Publishing Co. was born. Immediately facing obstacles such as finding a landlord willing to rent him office space in a not-yet-desegregated United States, Johnson managed to secure a room in the private law office of Earl B. Dickerson, on the second floor of his employer's building, the Supreme Life Insurance Company. In 1943 Johnson purchased a building at 5619 South State Street, to house the fledgling company. In 1949 the company converted a funeral parlor at 1820 South Michigan Avenue into office space and moved there, a location that would remain the company's headquarters into the new millennium, although it would grow to be 11 stories tall. Along the way, *Negro Digest,* which had a circulation at one time of 100,000 subscribers, was renamed *Black World.* In the 1970s, the readership dwindled, and the magazine was finally canceled in 1975.

By that time, however, the company was going strong with other products. In 1945 Johnson launched *Ebony,* a magazine patterned after *Life,* but focusing on the African American community, culture, and achievements. It was an immediate success and remained the company's flagship publication into the 21st century, with a readership at one point of more than 1.3 million. In 1951 Johnson created another magazine, called *Jet,* a celebrity-oriented magazine focusing on African American entertainers and public figures. For nearly 20 years, these two magazines were the only publications for African Americans in the United States.

Unable to obtain advertising in those years, Johnson created the Beauty Star mail-order company and began advertising its products, such as haircare products, wigs, and vitamins in his own magazines. In 1947 the company picked up its first major advertising account in Zenith Radio and, after sending a salesman to Detroit every week for nearly ten years, finally managed to sign Chrysler Corporation in 1954. The magazine drew the talents of many people, including author Era Bell Thompson (1905–1986), who served as associate editor of *Ebony* from 1948 to 1951, and co-managing editor from 1951 to 1964, before becoming international editor for the company thereafter.

In 1957 Ebony Fashion Fair blazed a trail of fashion excellence that has endured the test of time. Four gorgeous African American models brought fashion excitement to audiences in ten cities—Chicago; Indianapolis; New Orleans; Baltimore; Los Angeles; Dayton, Columbus, and Cleveland, Ohio; Philadelphia; and Washington, D.C.—where they displayed an array of dazzling American designer fashions. The late Freda

Company Perspectives:

Through its brands, which include EBONY and JET magazines, Fashion Fair Cosmetics, EBONY Fashion Fair and JPC Book Division, Johnson Publishing Company has always aimed at increasing African-Americans' pride in themselves by presenting their past and present achievements to America and to the world. This has been done by portraying the Black American experience in all its dynamics through the medium of printed words, images, cosmetics and fashion. Through the years the company has also labored to provide irrefutable proof to millions of Black Americans, young and old, that their dreams can and do come true. The entire Johnson Publishing Company family shares a deep commitment to meet consumer demands by producing quality products. Because of this commitment, JPC brands strive to continually give inspiration and hope to millions.

DeKnight, *Ebony* magazine's home service director and Ebony Fashion Fair's first commentator, paraded fashions in homespun rhetoric weaving imaginary tales about each model and fashion. The 41st annual tour took place in the 1998–99 fashion season, with audiences still experiencing lively commentary, enriched with synthesizer programming, a drummer, a bassist, R&B, jazz, and song and dance routines performed by talented members of the troupe. Thirteen models moved swiftly down the runways and across stages in 1998 and 1999, emphasizing elegance and excitement as they displayed American and European fashions brilliant with color, detail, and pizzazz. At the conclusion of the 40th annual tour, funds raised since inception by sponsors of the show had reached $45 million, all designated for various charities and scholarships. By then the show had given 540 young people and 112 wardrobe assistants the opportunity to visit cities and countries of many cultures, and had been sponsored by more than 180 prestigious social and civic organizations, including the United Negro College Fund, the NAACP, and the Urban League.

Johnson quickly soared to fame. By the early 1960s, he was one of the most prominent African American men in the country. In 1963, he and John F. Kennedy posed together to publicize a special issue of *Ebony,* which was celebrating The Emancipation Proclamation. In 1972, U.S. magazine publishers gave him accolades as Publisher of the Year. He also would go on to become chairman and CEO of Supreme Life Insurance Company, his first employer.

In 1973 the company began publishing *Ebony Jr!* (now defunct), a magazine designed to provide ''positive black images'' for pre-teens. Johnson branched out into new media formats when he began buying radio stations, including WJPC, Chicago's first African American-owned station. The following year, the company purchased WLOU in Louisville, Kentucky, and in the mid-1980s, the company acquired WLNR in Lansing, Illinois, which was merged with WJPC in 1992; the combined station was sold in 1995. Also in 1973, Fashion Fair Cosmetics was founded by the company in answer to the problems that women of color had in finding shades to match their skin tones. The company would go on to compete successfully against such

huge competitors as Revlon and Johnson Products of Chicago, an unrelated company. Fashion Fair would grow to become the world's number one cosmetics company for women of color, with annual sales in 1982 reaching more than $30 million, and the products being sold in more than 2,500 stores throughout the United States, Canada, Europe, Africa, and the Caribbean.

Johnson Publishing in the 1980s

In the early 1980s, Johnson began to groom his daughter Linda, who received her M.B.A. at Northwestern University's J.L. Kellogg School of Management, to take over the business. Linda started working summers for the company at the age of 15, eventually becoming fashion coordinator for both magazines and cosmetics. Linda Johnson Rice would go on to become president and chief executive officer of the company, as well as a director for companies such as Bausch & Lomb. In 1981 Johnson's adopted son, John E., a staff photographer for the company, died of sickle-cell anemia at age 25. That year, the company's total revenues reached $81 million. The following year, the company's revenue grew to $102 million.

In 1985 the company launched a new magazine called *EM* (*Ebony Man*), targeted mainly at the growing ranks of increasingly affluent buppies (black urban professionals). Like an African American version of *GQ* (*Gentlemen's Quarterly*), the inaugural November issue was chock-full of photos of immaculate male models bedecked in the latest fashions of clothing, with a healthy dollop of fashion and grooming tips, and filled with articles on health, fitness, personal finance, and shopping techniques.

In 1988 Johnson was inducted into the Publishing Hall of Fame, along with such other luminaries as Harold K. Guinzburg, founder of Viking Press and The Literary Guild; Maxwell Perkins, editor at Charles Scribners Sons; Richard Leo Simon and Max Lincoln Schuster, founders of Simon & Schuster, Inc.; and William Randolph Hearst, founder of Hearst Publishing Corporation. That year, the company had total revenues of $215 million, making it the second largest African American-owned business in the United States, behind Reginald Lewis's TLC Beatrice International Holdings. By this time, Johnson was also on the boards of Greyhound and two of his first advertisers, Chrysler and Zenith. The following year, Johnson was the recipient of IABC's Excellence in Communication ''EXCEL'' Award. That year, he was also the only African American man on the *Forbes* list of the 400 wealthiest people in the United States. Johnson was also awarded the U.S. Presidential Medal of Freedom in 1996.

Also in 1989, Johnson wrote his autobiography, *Succeeding Against the Odds*, with assistance from longtime *Ebony* editor Lerone Bennett, Jr. In the autobiography, Johnson explained how he got started. ''In organizing the staff [of my first magazine], I reached out to everybody, for I knew nothing about magazine publishing and editing. . . . When all else failed, I looked in the phone book and called an expert. Since I had nothing to lose, I always started at the top. I received valuable advice from Henry Luce of Time-Life and Gardner Cowles of Look. . . . It was hard to get through to Luce, but . . . I used a simple approach that almost always worked. I simply told the secretary or aide that I was the president—I stressed the word president—of my company. 'It is,' I said, 'a small company but I

Key Dates:

1942: John H. Johnson establishes Negro Digest Publishing Co.
1945: *Ebony* is launched.
1951: *Jet* magazine hits store shelves.
1957: The Ebony Fashion Fair is created.
1975: *Black World,* formerly known as *Negro Digest,* is canceled.
1989: Johnson writes his autobiography, *Succeeding Against the Odds,* with assistance from longtime *Ebony* editor Lerone Bennett, Jr.
2002: Linda Johnson Rice is named CEO.

am the president, and I want to talk to your president. . . . If the president of the smallest country in the world comes to Washington, our president, as a matter of public policy and protocol will see him. So it seems to me that your president, in the American tradition, will see me for a few minutes if you pass this request on and tell him that I don't want a donation or a job.' I used that on Henry Luce's secretary, and I got in to see him.''

New Ventures in the 1990s

In 1991 the company sold its controlling interest in the last minority-owned insurance company in Illinois, Supreme Life Insurance, Johnson's first employer, to Chicago-based Unitrin, a life, health, and property insurance company. Total revenues for 1991 climbed to $281 million. Also that year, the company entered into a joint venture with catalog company Spiegel Inc. to develop a fashion line and mail-order catalog aimed at African American women, launching a mail-order catalog called *E Style* to that effect in 1993. An accompanying credit card with the *E Style* imprint appeared in 1994.

In October 1992, the company introduced ''Ebone,'' a new line of cosmetics for women of color, as well as a three-part videotape series called *The Ebony/Jet Guide to Black Excellence,* which profiled African American leaders, entrepreneurs, and entertainers to help provide positive role models for young people.

In November 1995, the company expanded its operations with the launch of *Ebony South Africa,* a counterpart to the U.S. version of the magazine. Because trade tariffs on incoming products to South Africa were taxed at 100 percent of the cost, Johnson Publishing subsidiary EBCO International teamed up with five South African companies, with Johnson holding 51 percent of the joint venture, in order to avoid losing money on the project. The company invested $2 million to $3 million on facilities, equipment, and staffing, opening editorial offices in Sandton, near Johannesburg. In the inaugural November 1995 issue, Bishop Desmond Tutu related the story of when he saw his first issue of *Ebony,* which had Jackie Robinson on the cover, when the cleric was nine years old and living in a ghetto township located some 30 miles outside of Johannesburg.

Total sales for 1997 reached $361.1 million, a 10.9 percent growth over the previous year, in which the company ranked 28th overall in magazine publishing companies by advertising revenue, with $26.8 million for the first half of 1996. Competition in the African American-oriented magazine industry, however, finally began to catch up with Johnson Publishing Company. With a plethora of new titles appearing, such as *Black Enterprise,* and the rise of other African American-oriented entertainment and informational vehicles such as Black Entertainment Television (BET), circulation of *Ebony* dropped 7 percent.

Late 1990s and Beyond

Like many of its competitors, Johnson Publishing faced challenges in the late 1990s and into the new millennium. As competing media companies tapped into the growing number of Internet users, the publisher of *Jet* and *Ebony* was slow to embrace online technology. An August 1999 *Crain's Chicago Business* article provided insight on the company's position claiming, ''The situation Johnson Publishing confronts is shared by many mid-sized private companies as they grapple with the Internet challenge: an aversion to big investments without assurances of a reasonable financial return, and a desire to maintain controlling positions in all of their enterprises—a tenet that can preclude the sort of partnerships that are a centerpiece of the new media economy.''

At the same time, Johnson Publishing faced a decrease in advertising revenues, which were hit even harder after the terrorist attacks of September 11, 2001. As such, the company was forced to make some key changes. It redesigned *Ebony's* look, adding more fashion spreads and lifestyle stories, and focused on younger, up-and-coming African American celebrities. One critic commented on *Ebony's* redesign in a 2004 *Crain's Chicago Business* article: ''It looks a little different, but it's still frozen in the 1970s.'' Despite the company's efforts, circulation remained stagnant at 1.6 million; it had been 11.7 million in the 1970s.

During this time period, Johnson Publishing revamped its holdings. The catalog venture, *E Style,* was shuttered in 1997. *Ebony Man* magazine was canceled in 1998 and *Ebony South Africa* followed suit in 2000. Johnson Rice was named CEO in 2002, and her father remained chairman.

Despite growing competition and a weak advertising market, Johnson Publishing remained the most successful African American-owned publishing firm in the United States. Along with publishing *Ebony* and *Jet* magazines, the company controlled Fashion Fair Cosmetics, which continued to reign as the leading line of makeup and skincare for women of color. Its products were sold in more than 2,500 stores in the United States, Canada, Africa, England, France, Switzerland, the Bahamas, Bermuda, and the Virgin Islands. In 2005, the Ebony Fashion Fair continued as the largest traveling fashion show with more than $51 million donated to charity since its inception. Johnson Publishing's Book Division published works by African American authors, including Lerone Bennett, Jr. With an arsenal of powerful, well-known brands in the company's portfolio, Johnson Publishing's management was confident its products would be found on store shelves for years to come.

Principal Subsidiaries

EBONY Magazine; Jet Magazine; Fashion Fair Cosmetics; EBONY Fashion Fair.

Principal Divisions

Johnson Publishing Company Book Division.

Principal Competitors

Essence Communications Partners Inc.; L'Oreal S.A.; Advance Publications Inc.

Further Reading

Alpert, Mark, "*Jet* Powered," *Fortune,* July 31, 1989, p. 266.

"B.E. Industrial Service 100," *Black Enterprise,* June 1996, p. 117.

Bordon, Jeff, "As Johnson Watches, Others Seizing the Net," *Crain's Chicago Business,* August 23, 1999.

Chaplin, Julia, "A Runway Fair That Still Packs the House," *New York Times,* October 14, 2001.

Cyr, Diane, "Ten Inducted into Publishing Hall of Fame; Scholars, Risk Takers, Writers and Empire Builders Constitute This Year's Honorees," *Folio: The Magazine for Magazine Management,* January 1988, p. 43.

Detar, James, "Publishing for the New Jet Set," *Investor's Business Daily,* June 6, 2005.

Dingle, Derek T., "Doing Business John Johnson's Way," *Black Enterprise,* June 1987, p. 150.

——, "New Directions for Black Business," *Black Enterprise,* August 1985, p. 67.

"Ebony Chief Takes Reins at Father's Publishing Firm," *Times Union Albany,* April 14, 2002.

"EXCEL Award Winner John H. Johnson Communicates Success," *Communication World,* May 1989, p. 18.

Falkof, Lucille, *John H. Johnson, The Man from Ebony,* Ada, Okla.: Garrett Educational Corp., 1991.

Greenberg, Jonathan, "It's a Miracle," *Forbes,* December 20, 1982, p. 104.

Johnson, John H., *Succeeding Against the Odds: The Autobiography of a Great American Businessman,* New York: Amistad Press, 1989.

"Like Father, Like Daughter," *Fortune,* October 3, 1983, p. 180.

Mangelsdorf, Martha E., "Succeeding Against the Odds: The Autobiography of a Great American Business," *Inc.,* October 1993, p. 58.

Mowatt, Raoul, "Jet Magazine Manages to Survive in Hard Times," *Pittsburgh Post-Gazette,* December 10, 2001.

Mullman, Jeremy, "Redo's the Easiest Part for Ebony," *Crain's Chicago Business,* June 7, 2004.

"The Silent Strength of Family Businesses," *U.S. News & World Report,* April 25, 1983, p. 47.

Wellemayer, Marilyn, "A Gym of One's Own," *Fortune,* February 21, 1983, p. 149.

Whigham-Desir, Marjorie, "Forging New Frontiers: Never Ones to Shy Away from New Ventures, B.E. 100s Companies Are Making Their Mark—and Market—Internationally," *Black Enterprise,* May 1996, p. 70.

——, "Marathon Men: 25 Years of Black Entrepreneurial Excellence," *Black Enterprise,* June 1997, p. 104.

—Daryl F. Mallett
—update: Christina M. Stansell

KraftMaid Cabinetry, Inc.

15535 South State Avenue
P.O. Box 1055
Middlefield, Ohio 44062
U.S.A.
Telephone: (440) 632-5333
Fax: (440) 632-5648
Web site: http://www.kraftmaid.com

Wholly Owned Subsidiary of Masco Corporation
Incorporated: 1969
Employees: 4,000
Sales: $511.1 million (2003 est.)
NAIC: 33711 Wood Kitchen Cabinet and Countertop Manufacturing

KraftMaid Cabinetry, Inc., is the leading manufacturer of "semi-custom" cabinets in the United States, which are built to order for each customer. The firm offers close to 100 different styles and finishes of cabinets, primarily for kitchens and bathrooms, and sells them through do-it-yourself chains like Lowe's and Home Depot, as well as via other home design retailers. The company is a subsidiary of Masco Corp., whose combined cabinet-making operations make it the number one cabinetmaker in the world.

Beginnings

The origins of KraftMaid Cabinetry date to 1969, when a one-man cabinetmaking shop was opened in Independence, Ohio. The company's products sold well, and over the next decade KraftMaid grew to serve a five-state area, with revenues hitting an estimated $10 million by 1981. That year, the firm moved its operations to a new, larger plant in the small town of Middlefield Ohio, east of Cleveland in the heart of the state's so-called "Amish Country." KraftMaid also formed an in-house advertising agency whose work helped spur even faster growth. Over the next decade, revenues grew tenfold.

In 1990, the company was acquired by Masco Corporation of Taylor, Michigan. Masco had focused exclusively on manufacturing plumbing products until the mid-1980s, when it started buying cabinet makers. Prior to acquiring Kraftmaid, Masco had purchased Merillat, the second-largest cabinetmaker in the United States, as well as Fieldstone and StarMark. After the Masco purchase, KraftMaid continued its growth, with revenues hitting $130 million in 1992.

The company's specialty was "semi-custom" cabinetry, produced on a mass scale yet built to order for each customer. Its products were typically used in kitchens that were being upgraded, and, given that the dimensions of each were different, every cabinet order was a custom job. The company offered a wide variety of materials, styles, and finishes to customers.

At the firm's plant, parts were cut and finished by its workers for each order. The production process saw each item slowly evolve as different pieces were added to it. The factory was filled with partially completed cabinets and raw materials awaiting batches of different parts for final assembly. Turnaround time was typically three weeks, which was typical for the custom cabinet industry.

"Kaizen" Introduced in 1995

In 1995, the company began working with TBM Consulting Group of North Carolina to help it streamline the manufacturing process. TBM advised the company to implement the Japanese principle of "kaizen," or continuous improvement, which allowed production activities to easily be rearranged to improve workflow and productivity. Kaizen "events" were soon being held regularly in the factory, during which employees helped guide the changes in production based on their own experience. A key element of the philosophy was that no employee would lose his or her job, and when positions were eliminated by workflow improvements, the affected employees were assigned to different departments or the company's new kaizen promotion office.

In 1996, KraftMaid appointed a new senior vice-president of manufacturing, Tom Chieffe, who had previously worked for Masco managing mergers, acquisitions, and divestitures and who also had a background in the auto industry. Under Chieffe the firm added to the kaizen philosophy such manufacturing concepts as the Toyota Production System, just-in-time manufacturing, and total prevention maintenance, which helped further refine the firm's assembly process. New, high-tech equipment was also purchased that allowed greater flexibility and which was positioned to ensure proper workflow and maximum efficiency. A new manufacturing strategy, called "Kitchen at a Time," was developed in which KraftMaid workers would build all the cabinets for a particular order together and then load them onto a truck at the end of the assembly line. Quality was important to the firm, and parts were inspected at numerous points in the process so that effort was not wasted on finishing items with defects.

KraftMaid's suppliers were also given new requirements for deliveries so that materials were on hand just before they were needed, rather than being stockpiled far in advance. This just-in-time strategy significantly cut inventory costs.

The firm invested $10 million in new equipment to make these manufacturing changes, but it proved well spent as production was increased by 250 percent, from 4,000 cabinets per day to 10,000. At the same time, turnaround was reduced from three weeks to five days. Factory floor space also decreased by 36 percent, inventory by 47 percent, and distance traveled by products 69 percent. In addition, the number of operators needed to run equipment fell by 27 percent.

KraftMaid had opened a second finishing plant in Orwell, Ohio, in 1996, and the firm continued to grow rapidly during the decade, with employment increasing from 1,568 in 1995, to 2,078 in 1997, and to 3,062 in 1999. In December 1998, the company appointed Tom Chieffe president of the company.

New Products and Finishes in the Late 1990s

At the same time that it was implementing new manufacturing techniques, KraftMaid was also introducing the largest number of new products and product options in its history. The firm was now seeking to move beyond outfitting kitchens and bathrooms to becoming a supplier of cabinets for family room, bedroom, home office, and home theater applications. New options that were introduced for such uses included a white porcelain glaze and a chocolate glaze that was intentionally "distressed" to mimic antique furniture.

A major innovation from the firm was a line of cabinets called Passport. Designed for older customers as well as those who were handicapped, it featured higher floor heights and other features that made the cabinets easier for people with mobility

problems to use. Passport, which was the first cabinet line certified by an independent testing facility to meet Universal Design standards, was named the year's best product by Today's Homeowner magazine in 1998, while the American Society on Aging gave it an award for Outstanding Design for Mature Consumers. All of the company's products were given "Best Buy" status by *Consumers Digest* during the year as well.

During the 1990s, KraftMaid parent Masco had continued to buy cabinet makers, adding Texwood Industries in the United States as well as firms in the United Kingdom, Germany, and Spain. By 1999, Masco's North American cabinet companies had annual revenues of more than $1 billion, making it the largest cabinetmaker on the continent. Sales of cabinets, along with faucets and plumbing supplies, also made Masco the largest supplier of manufactured goods to Home Depot, the leading retail chain catering to the do-it-yourself home improvement market.

In 1999, KraftMaid began an $11.4 million expansion of its Orwell plant, which would triple in size to 262,000 square feet. That year also saw the firm extend its product warranty from moving parts alone to covering the entire cabinet for as long as it was owned by the original purchaser.

Over the next several years, the company continued to expand its cabinet options, and by 2001 it offered more than 100 cabinet door styles in seven woods and a number of different laminates. There were more than 150 different storage options to choose from along with many molding styles and other decorative enhancements, as well as 21 finishes. Sixty percent of sales were made through home centers such as Home Depot and Lowe's, while 35 percent came from dealers or designers, with the rest of sales made via independent distributors or directly to consumers.

Expansion Continues in the 2000s

While many businesses saw earnings drop as the U.S. economy slumped in 2001 and 2002, KraftMaid's sales surged upward as people began investing in their homes, spurred on by record-low mortgage interest rates. In the fall of 2001, the company hired 100 new workers, then added 300 more early the following year. A new cabinetmaking line, the firm's 15th, was also added. The company's sales had reportedly doubled in the previous five years. Its just-in-time manufacturing was so finely tuned that KraftMaid closed the last of eight warehouses it had been using to store raw materials in December 2001.

The firm had launched its official Web site in the mid-1990s, and it now created a second one called Superkitchens.com to help steer more business its way. The new site offered a wide range of remodeling ideas for kitchens and covered all product categories, not just cabinetry. It was developed in partnership with several other corporations, including General Electric, Armstrong, Andersen Windows, and DuPont Corian. While KraftMaid built and paid for the site, its partners provided links and content. Corporate affiliations were downplayed, and only products made by KraftMaid and its partners were featured.

In early 2003, KraftMaid assigned its advertising account to a new agency, W.B. Doner of Detroit. The company was now spending an estimated $1 million to $2 million on advertising annually. A new campaign launched in the spring included

Key Dates:

1969: A custom cabinet-making shop is founded in Independence, Ohio.

1981: KraftMaid moves to Middlefield, Ohio; the company expands rapidly, and sales reach $100 million by end of the decade.

1990: KraftMaid is acquired by Masco Corporation of Taylor, Michigan; Passport cabinet line for elderly and disabled customers is introduced later in the decade.

1995: The company begins to implement ''kaizen'' and lean manufacturing techniques.

1996: A new plant opens in Orwell, Ohio.

2004: A $25 million expansion program adds 150,000 square feet to the firm's three plants.

2005: Construction of new plant in Utah begins.

advertising in both the print media and on television. The company continued to expand its offerings during the year, adding more than 100 new products including 5 glaze finishes, 9 door designs, and 20 new storage concepts.

The year 2004 saw KraftMaid spend $25 million to add another 150,000 square feet of manufacturing space to its three plants. The firm subsequently hired 500 new workers and announced plans to add as many as 500 more over the next five years. The company's two Middlefield plants employed 2,700, more people than lived in the town itself. Also in 2004, KraftMaid took over some administrative, sales, and marketing tasks from Masco subsidiary Mill's Pride as part of a restructuring of Masco's cabinet business group.

In February 2005, the company announced plans to build its first plant outside of Ohio. After considering locations in five states, KraftMaid officials decided on an 80-acre location in West Jordan, Utah, about 15 miles south of Salt Lake City. Like the firm's Ohio facilities, it would use computerized equipment and laser cutters to perform assembly, milling, and finishing operations under a single roof, with output expected to reach 6,000 cabinets a day. A primary goal of the Utah plant was to decrease turnaround time for orders shipped to the western region of the United States.

To entice KraftMaid to locate there, the state of Utah had pledged a $2.25 million training and recruitment grant to the firm, while the city of West Jordan issued an $11 million bond to buy the land and build needed infrastructure. The bond would

be repaid by KraftMaid's property taxes. The 700,000-square-foot plant was expected to cost $106 million and would employ 1,300 after it opened in mid-2006.

More than 35 years after its founding, KraftMaid Cabinetry, Inc. had become the largest maker of semi-custom cabinets in the United States. Innovative products like the Passport line, as well as the added capacity of its new Utah manufacturing plant, were likely to bring it an even larger share of the U.S. market in the years to come.

Principal Subsidiaries

KraftMaid Trucking, Inc.

Principal Competitors

Masterbrand Cabinets, Inc.; Armstrong Cabinet Products; Elkay Cabinet Group; American Woodmark Corp.; RSI Holding Corp.

Further Reading

Adams, Larry, ''Cabinet Companies Step out of the Kitchen,'' *Wood & Wood Products*, March 1, 1999.

——, ''How KraftMaid Doubled Production,'' *Wood & Wood Products*, November 1, 1999.

——, ''Merger Mania Returns with a Vengeance (Cabinet Industry),'' *Wood & Wood Products*, November 1, 1998.

Bennett, David, ''KraftMaid Pushing West with Plans for $106M Utah Plant,'' *Crain's Cleveland Business*, February 7, 2005, p. 3.

''Cabinet Company Boosts Productivity, Shrinks Lead Time Through Kaizen,'' *Assembly*, October 1, 2000, p. 82.

''Cabinet Maker to Add Hundreds of Jobs in Northeast Ohio,'' *Associated Press Newswires*, May 1, 2004.

Christianson, Rich, ''Masco Amasses an Impressive Collection of Cabinet Companies,'' *Wood & Wood Products*, November 1, 1999, p. 11.

Gerdel, Thomas W., ''KraftMaid Cabinetry to Hire 300 Workers,'' *Plain Dealer* (Cleveland, Ohio), January 5, 2002, p. C1.

Grant, Allison, ''KraftMaid to Add 900 Jobs in NE Ohio,'' *Plain Dealer* (Cleveland Ohio), May 1, 2004, p. A1.

Harrison, Kimberly P., ''KraftMaid In-House Agency Steps Out,'' *Crain's Cleveland Business*, November 9, 1992, p. 24.

Partsch, Bill, ''KraftMaid's Marketing Tag Team,'' *Kitchen & Bath Business*, March 1, 2002, p. 18.

Prizinsky, David, ''KraftMaid Crafting Hike in Output, Jobs,'' *Crain's Cleveland Business*, January 7, 2002, p. 1.

Wallace, Brice, ''Cabinetmaker Picks Utah,'' *Deseret Morning News*, February 3, 2005, p. D12.

Wray, Kimberley, ''Cabinets That Look Like Furniture,'' *HFN*, March 2, 1998, p. 21.

—Frank Uhle

Kumon Institute of Education Co., Ltd.

Osakaekimaedaini Building 9F
1-2-2, Umeda Kita-Ku
Osaka, 530-0001
Japan
Telephone: (+81) 6-4797-8787
Fax: (+81) 6-4797-8785
Web site: http://www.kumon.ne.jp

Private company
Incorporated: 1958
Employees: 2,400
Sales: ¥63.1 billion (2004)
NAIC: 611691 Exam Preparation and Tutoring

Kumon Institute of Education Co., Ltd. is the largest private educational corporation in Japan and one of the world's leading after-school education programs. It offers a unique curriculum of mathematics instruction primarily aimed at elementary school children. Its learning centers also offer instruction in Japanese language for native speakers and English as a second language. The company operates through some 26,200 learning centers in 44 countries worldwide. Kumon claims an overall enrollment of 3.6 million students. The company originated in Osaka, Japan, and spread through franchises, becoming extremely popular all across Japan. Kumon began extending its reach abroad in the 1970s. Kumon has a strong base in Japan, South Korea, and other Asian countries and has become an increasingly felt presence in the North American market in the 2000s.

A Father's Solution: The 1950s

The Kumon Institute of Education is named for its founder, Osaka high school math teacher Toru Kumon. Kumon began investigating a new way of teaching mathematics in 1954 when his son Takeshi, then in second grade, came home with a low grade on a math test. Kumon was not initially concerned with the boy's poor report. He felt that at the age of eight, his son had plenty of time to take care of other aspects of his growth and education, and his grounding in mathematics could come in middle school. But Takeshi's mother was worried, so Kumon

took a look at the boy's math book. At that point, he saw his wife's point of view, and he became worried as well. The textbook Takeshi used seemed disorganized to Kumon, with no clear progression of lessons. To supplement the textbook, he bought his son a drill book. However, nothing he could buy really suited his son's needs. So Kumon began writing his own mathematics drill sheets for Takeshi. He soon devised a system that led to his writing a new drill sheet every day. Kumon's wife supervised her son's work, while Kumon corrected the work sheet every evening and then produced a new sheet with slightly harder problems for the next day's lesson. By the time Takeshi was in sixth grade, he had completed 1,000 of his father's worksheets, and his mathematical skill level had gone from worrisome to exceptional. The 12-year-old had advanced to understanding calculus, and he could tackle math problems from university entrance examinations.

Kumon was surprised and impressed by his son's progress, and he began trying this approach on children outside his family. In 1955, he opened the first Kumon learning center in Osaka, and in 1958 he incorporated the Kumon Institute of Education. The Kumon method revolved around the work sheets, which Kumon revised and improved. The work sheets concentrated strictly on mathematical calculations, as opposed to mathematical concepts that were taught in regular schools. Children were tested to find their level, and then given work sheets set at a much lower level of difficulty. Each work sheet was just a slightly more difficult than the one before it, so progress was slow but steady. Kumon paid careful attention to sequencing, so that children had a thorough understanding of one operation before moving on to a related operation. For example, students might spend months working on addition problems, starting with low numbers such as 5 + 1 and taking it step by step to 99 + 1 before moving on to problems that involved adding 2.

In 1962, Kumon opened his first center in Tokyo, and his method went on to sweep Japan, becoming the most widely used after-school mathematics program in a country where there were many competitors in this sector. Interestingly, the Kumon method was frowned upon by the Japanese Ministry of Education, which supervised the math curriculum in Japanese public schools. The school mathematics curriculum emphasized problem solving and critical thinking skills, while the Kumon method seemed very old fashioned. However, it was perhaps this old-fashioned emphasis on rote learning and memorization that appealed to parents. The Kumon learning centers also found a perfect niche in Japanese society. As Kumon extended his learning centers beyond Osaka, he reproduced his materials and taught his methods to franchisees. These were almost all women with children. It was exceedingly difficult for married women to find employment in Japan, and even those who held advanced degrees dropped out of the workforce to raise children. Women with children could run Kumon centers out of their homes, providing part-time income and a chance to participate in society in a way that was otherwise quite difficult for them. Kumon created a disciplined training program for franchisees that included newsletters, meetings, and workshops.

The Kumon method produced some startlingly skilled children. While most parents enrolled their children in Kumon as a supplement to the regular math curriculum or to help their children catch up, some children, such as Takeshi Kumon, were able to use the worksheets to learn mathematical operations far beyond their years. Children as young as three were doing algebra, having learned the calculations step-by-step through the work sheets. In this way, the Kumon method resembled the famous Suzuki method of violin training, developed around the same time by Shinichi Suzuki. Kumon was friends with Shinichi Suzuki, and both Suzuki violin and Kumon mathematics emphasized repetition, memorization, and step-by-step learning which could be used by any child but also produced extremely precocious performers.

Growth in the 1970s and 1980s

Kumon flourished in Japan as Toru Kumon promulgated the method through a widening network of teacher-franchisees. Despite opposition from some in the educational establishment, Kumon seemed to fill a gap, and so it opened more and more franchised learning centers. Nancy Ukai Russell, in her study ''The Kumon Approach to Teaching and Learning'' (in *Teaching and Learning in Japan*) claims that Kumon did well because of many interlocking cultural factors. She writes, ''Indeed, Kumon's commercial and educational achievements can be attributed in large measure to the company's canny exploitation of many complex elements that characterize the culture of modern Japanese education. Of particular relevance are the nation's competitive exam-driven system, the social aspirations of Japanese parents, and the availability of a large pool of educated women who supervise and carry out the Kumon method.'' These conditions were found more or less throughout Japan.

By the mid-1980s, Kumon learning centers had become highly visible. According to Russell's study, the Kumon method

was familiar to two-thirds of surveyed housewives in Tokyo and Osaka. About half those surveyed whose children attended Kumon learning centers said they chose the program for the good study habits it instilled. A large percentage of those surveyed also said that their children enjoyed the program and that it had a good reputation among their friends and neighbors.

By this time, the company had made some changes, adding a study system for reading the Japanese language. Then, in 1980, it began teaching English as well. The Kumon Institute also began exporting the method. As early as 1974, a Kumon center opened in New York City in the United States, and in 1977 the company had an outpost in Brazil. Kumon first hit Canada in 1980 with a learning center in Toronto. The company's early foreign franchises were primarily aimed at Japanese living abroad. Kumon was also popular in other Asian countries, particularly South Korea, which became the company's second-biggest market after Japan. By the end of the 1980s, there were 41,000 Kumon learning centers in Japan and franchises in 16 foreign markets. At this time, the Kumon Institute claimed about 1.5 million students total. According to 1992 figures, some 8 percent of all Japanese second-graders were enrolled in Kumon. Though Kumon was considered moderately priced in Japan compared to many other after-school programs, the number of students added up to a multi-million dollar enterprise.

Penetrating World Markets in the 1990s

Kumon had enormous success in its domestic market, where social conditions fostered its approach to learning and teaching. Kumon also did well in South Korea, which has an educational system similar to Japan's. Kumon's initial penetration into the North American market was in communities of Japanese and Koreans living abroad. The company began franchising on the East Coast of the United States in the mid-1970s and made a concerted move into California and the western United States in the early 1980s. By the late 1980s, Kumon had broadened its appeal in the United States, but it was still most popular among Asian immigrants. In the Los Angeles area, for example, about two-thirds of Kumon enrollees were children of first-generation Japanese or Korean immigrants, and in New Jersey, Kumon classrooms were filled with a similar percentage of Korean-American and Chinese-American children.

Interest in Kumon began to grow rapidly in the United States after 1988. That year, the vice-principal of an elementary school in Sumiton, Alabama, persuaded the Kumon Institute to let her adopt the method for her school. Kumon had always been an extra after-school program, not a regular part of the math curriculum. However, the company agreed to let the Alabama school try using the Kumon method as an experiment. The students at Sumiton Elementary consistently scored very low on standardized math achievement tests, and it was hoped that Kumon would raise the children's scores. The Sumiton students not only enjoyed the Kumon work sheets, but the school raised its overall test scores, bringing it from one of the lowest-scoring schools in its county to near the middle in only one year.

Sumiton Elementary became a model for Kumon in the schools, and by 1992 some 50,000 American school children in 36 states were using the Kumon method in their regular school classrooms. The Kumon Institute charged a low rate per pupil

Key Dates:

1954: Toru Kumon devises a method for tutoring his son in mathematics.
1958: Kumon Institute of Education incorporates.
1962: The first Kumon learning center opens in Tokyo.
1974: Kumon comes to New York.
1977: The company pushes into the South American market, with its first learning center located in Brazil.
1980: Kumon centers in Japan begin teaching English.
1988: In-school program begins in the United States.
1995: Toru Kumon dies.
2004: The company begins television advertising in the United States.

for the in-school program and operated it at a loss. Initially, the company saw this as a ripe new market and hoped to enroll two million U.S. students by the end of the decade. Kumon later scaled back its expectations for the U.S. market. In 1993, the company restructured its North American market division and stopped encouraging the Kumon method's use in schools. Schools that had already started with Kumon were allowed to continue, but the number of school-based enrollees dropped by more than half by 1994. Nevertheless, North America remained a major emerging market for the Kumon Institute.

Kumon made other overseas moves as well. In 1981, the learning centers came to Germany, and a decade later the company established a presence in the United Kingdom. By the early 1990s, Kumon learning centers were thriving in 27 countries, including Australia, Indonesia, and Brazil. The overall number of students enrolled and the number of learning centers overall increased during the 1990s. The Kumon Institute grew financially as well. Its revenue climbed to approximately $300 million by 1991, and the company seemed to prosper despite increasing competition from other after-school programs and from computer software, as well as in the face of a declining birth rate in Japan.

Competitive Landscape in North America in the 2000s

The Kumon Institute changed its strategy for the U.S. market in the mid-1990s, pulling back its innovative in-school programs to concentrate on its traditional method of supplemental after-school learning. Around the mid-1990s, several factors converged to make after-school tutoring a growth industry. In the United States, several for-profit after-school tutoring chains had been around since at least the 1980s, and these started to expand. Sylvan Learning Systems, Huntington Learning Corporation, and Britannica Learning Centers were the major U.S. tutoring chains. In 1993, Sylvan bought out Britannica and so increased the number of franchises it controlled to close to 500 in the United States and Canada. Huntington ran about 90 learning centers in 20 states in the mid-1990s. Kumon was actually the biggest of the three, with 850 learning centers in North America, plus some 500 schools using the method in 1993. Kumon stood apart from its competitors both because of its Japanese origin and because it was more of a comprehensive method rather than an individualized program of remedial work.

Toru Kumon died in 1995 at the age of 81. By that time, his method had spread to some two million children around the world. The company's overseas growth continued. By 1999, it was considered one of the top five franchise businesses in the world, according to *Entrepreneur International* (March 1999), in terms of its financial strength and stability, growth rate and size. By the year 2000, Kumon had more than a thousand learning centers in the United States, and enrollment was increasing annually at a rate higher than 10 percent. Though the in-school program had slowed, the Kumon method was still used in several schools, reaching approximately 8,000 students. One factor that presumably influenced the growth of Kumon in the United States in the 2000s was the passage of the so-called No Child Left Behind Act in 2001, an educational initiative of the George W. Bush administration that specifically authorized the use of federal tax money for supplemental tutoring programs for children in schools deemed "failing." A profile of Kumon in the United States published in *Education* (Fall 2002) noted that a "senior Bush administration official" specifically singled out the Kumon method as an option for children with poor academic skills. Along with pressure on underperforming schools to improve their students' scores on standardized tests, high-achieving students were also getting more attention in the 2000s. An article in the *New York Times* (October 31, 1999) about suburban New Jersey children tallied the increasing popularity of Kumon with parents' concerns about giving their kids a head start academically. The *Times* article noted the rapidly growing popularity of Kumon classes, along with other supplemental and preparatory programs like "Baby Einstein" videos and the Goddard Schools for Early Childhood Development.

For a mix of reasons, the tutoring industry in the United States saw growth of over 10 percent in the early 2000s. A particular growth segment was the preschool end of the market. Of the biggest tutoring companies in the U.S. market, only Kumon offered academic classes for students from two to six years old. By 2005, Kumon had some 1,210 learning centers in the United States, with over 130,000 students enrolled. The Kumon Institute launched its first advertising campaign in the United States in 2004, spending approximately $10 million on television spots. The company claimed some 3.6 million students worldwide by the mid-2000s. The United Kingdom was another growth area, with 550 centers and an enrollment of 48,000. The company had successfully blanketed a global market by the 2000s, showing that a peculiarly Japanese institution could achieve worldwide popularity.

Principal Subsidiaries

Kumon Service Co., Ltd.; Kumon Publishing Co., Ltd.; Kumon L.I.L. Co., Ltd.; Kumon Learning Therapy Co., Ltd.; Kumon Speech Reading Center Co., Ltd.

Principal Competitors

Educate, Inc.; Huntington Learning Centers, Inc.; Kaplan, Inc.; Sylvan Learning Systems.

Further Reading

Biederman, Marcia, "Japanese Math Program Tallies Success with Discipline," *New York Times*, November 15, 2000, p. B15.

Clayton, Mark, "We're Off to See the Tutor," *Christian Science Monitor*, May 30, 2000, p. 20.

Harris, Sarah, "Japanese Teach Us How to Do Our Sums," *Daily Mail* (London), January 6, 2005, p. 18.

Hwang, Suein, "Parenting: Cram School for Tots," *Asian Wall Street Journal*, October 15, 2004, p. 1.

Lohr, Steve, "Tutoring, the New Growth Industry," *New York Times*, January 10, 1993, p. C24.

Maddocks, Todd, "You Do the Math," *Entrepreneur*, July 1999, p. 152H.

Nussbaum, Debra, "How a Speeded-up Society Trickles Down to Children," *New York Times*, October 31, 1999, p. NJ1.

Phalon, Richard, "Juku," *Forbes*, July 20, 1992, p. 82.

Reingold, Edwin M., "Mathematics Made Easy," *Time*, June 4, 1990, p. 83.

Russell, Nancy Ukai, "The Kumon Approach to Teaching and Learning," in *Teaching and Learning in Japan*, Cambridge, U.K.: Cambridge University Press, 1996.

Thomas, Robert McG., Jr., "Toru Kumon, Innovator, 81, in Math Studies," *New York Times*, July 27, 1995, p. D22.

Van der Pool, Lisa, "TechnoGraphics-Vox Paves Way for Kumon," *Adweek*, March 17, 2004, p. NA.

Weischadle, David E., "Extended Learning Opportunities," *Education*, Fall 2002, p. 73.

Witthaus, Michelle, "It All Adds Up," *Business Franchise*, June 2004, p. 40.

White, George, "Japanese Company Tutors U.S. in Math Education," *Los Angeles Times*, November 19, 1990, p. 1.

—A. Woodward

Malayan Banking Berhad

14th Floor Menara Maybank, 100 Jalan Tun Perak
Kuala Lumpur
50050
Malaysia
Telephone: (+60) 3 2070 8833
Fax: (+60) 3 2070 2611
Web site: http://www.maybank2u.com

Public Company
Incorporated: 1960 as Malayan Banking Berhad
Employees: 20,821
Total Assets: $47.24 billion (2004)
Stock Exchanges: Kuala Lumpur
Ticker Symbol: MAYBANK
NAIC: 522110 Commercial Banking; 522291 Consumer
    Lending; 522292 Real Estate Credit; 522298 All
    Other Non-Depository Credit Intermediation; 523120
    Securities Brokerage; 524113 Direct Life Insurance
    Carriers; 524114 Direct Health and Medical Insurance
    Carriers; 524126 Direct Property and Casualty
    Insurance Carriers

Malayan Banking Berhad is the holding company overseeing Malaysia's largest bank, Maybank and a range of financial sector subsidiaries. Maybank offers a full range of commercials, corporate, and private banking services, with a network of more than 450 branch offices and more than 2,500 ATM machines. Maybank, as the group as a whole is more commonly known, has also built a strong position in the regional market. The company operates more than 20 branches in Singapore and the Philippines and also has a banking presence in most of the other Southeast Asian markets, including Brunei, Papua New Guinea, Indonesia, and Vietnam. The bank also operates branches in New York and London. Maybank was the first Malaysian bank granted the right to establish a branch office in China, a particularly important market given the large and economically powerful ethnic Chinese population in Malaysia. In addition to its commercial banking network, Maybank operates a number of specialized subsidiaries in the insurance, investment banking and assets management, and finance sectors. The group's subsidiaries include Mayban General Assurance, Mayban Life Assurance, and Mayban Takaful, the latter focusing on developing insurance products compatible with Moslem law; the Aseam group, including Aseam Credit, Aseamlease, Aseam Unit Trust, and Aseambankers Malaysia Bhd; Mayban International Trust, Mayban Discount, and Mayban Investment Management; and Maybe Securities. Maybank was founded by Malaysian business tycoon Khoo Tech Puat, who died in 2004. The company has been led, however, for some two decades by President and CEO Amirsham A. Aziz. The largest Malaysian bank, Maybank boasted total assets worth $47 billion in 2004, placing it among the top 120 banks worldwide. Malayan Banking is listed on the Kuala Lumpur Stock Exchange.

1960s Origins

Khoo Teck Puat was born in 1918 into a wealthy Malaysia family of Chinese descent. Khoo's father, Khoo Yang Thin, had founded a trading business and also built up a portfolio of plantations and agricultural properties. The elder Khoo also became an important investor in a number of early Malaysian banking ventures, particularly among Malaysia's Hokkein, or ethnic Chinese community. When a number of Hokkein banks merged to form the Overseas Chinese Banking Corporation (OCBC) in 1933, the elder Khoo became one of its major shareholders.

Khoo Teck Puat went to work for OCBC, starting his career as a simple bank clerk. By the 1950s, Khoo had risen to a position of senior executive. By the end of the decade, however, Khoo recognized that his prospects at OCBC remained limited. Given the lack of further advancement open to him at OCBC, as well as what he considered the company's narrow perspective on its future, Khoo decided to set up his own bank and applied for a banking license. That license was granted to Khoo and a number of other OCBC executives who left the bank to form Malayan Banking Berhad in 1960.

Malayan Banking, which quickly became more commonly known as Maybank, was credited with becoming a founding force in the creation of a consumer banking industry in Malaysia. The country's independence following World War II, along with its swift economic growth into the 1960s, created a small

215

but growing middle class. Maybank recognized the potential for this new market and instituted a rapid growth phase through the 1960s and 1970s. Maybank's growth was such that for an extended period the bank added more than 20 branches per year.

Early on, Maybank had already sought to extend its operations to include a wider array of financial services. The company established Mayban Trustees Bhd (MTB) in 1964 in order to provide a range of trustee products and services. MTB's operations grew to include trustee services for unit trust funds, loan stock and bond, corporate staff retirement and related funds, as well as executor and trust services for individuals and private estates.

In 1973, Maybank extended again, forming its own investment banking subsidiary, Aseambankers Malaysia Berhad, which stood for Asian & Euro-American Merchant Banking (Malaysia) Berhad. Two years later, Aseambankers expanded its own range of business through the establishment of a joint venture, Kota Discount Berhad, in partnership with a group of Kuala Lumpur-based investors. Maybank itself acquired a majority stake in Kota in 1986. Kota's name then changed to Mayban Discount Berhad in 1989.

In the meantime, Maybank's success enabled Khoo himself to emerge as one of Malaysia's wealthiest tycoons, with a fortune estimated at more than $5 billion by the time of his death in 2004. By the early 1980s, Khoo's interests had extended into the hotel market. The company's portfolio included many of Malaysia's most prominent hotels, including the Goodwood Park Hotel and the Ming Court Hotel. As in banking, Khoo's active interest in the hotel sector helped establish Malaysia as a prominent tourist destination.

Surviving into the 21st Century

By the mid-1980s, Khoo's holdings had expanded to an international level. Maybank had also begun to enter other markets, particularly nearby Singapore. Indonesia also formed a strategic market for the bank. At the same time, Maybank began targeting the expatriate Malaysian, focusing on the country's ethnic Chinese population and opening new branches around the world in such financial capitals as New York and London.

Maybank continued seeking new opportunities in the 1980s and 1990s. In 1987, for example, the company set up Mayban Securities Sdn Bhd in order to provide stockbroking and other investment services. Mayban Securities' primary market remained the Malaysian market, including the country's major institutional investors, as well as the growing number of wealthy individuals as Malaysia entered a period of sustained and significant economic growth.

In 1990, Maybank took advantage of the new Malaysian Offshore Banking Act passed that year to set up new operations in the Federal Territory of Labuan. The company established a number of new subsidiaries there, including Maybank International Ltd., offering confidential, personalized banking services, as well as an Offshore Islamic Banking service; Mayban International Trust, which launched a number of services, including the incorporation and registration of offshore companies, as well as tax compliance and administration services; and Mayban International Trust (Labuan) Berhad. Also in 1990, Maybank added Mayban Unit Trust Berhad, a subsidiary focused on the management of unit trust funds.

Maybank also expanded into the insurance market, launching Maybank General Assurance Bhd. In 1993, the company deepened its insurance operations through the acquisition of Safety Life & General insurance Sdn Bhd. That business was then relaunched as Mayban Life Assurance and refocused to provide insurance products exclusively to the large Maybank customer base. Thus, Maybank's life insurance unit remained without an agency network of its own and instead serviced customers through Maybank's own network of branch offices.

In the mid-1990s, Maybank began a new effort to increase its presence in the Southeast Asian region. In 1994, for example, the company set up a subsidiary in Papua New Guinea, which opened two branch offices in Port Moresby and Lae. Two years later, the company entered a joint-venture with PT Bank Nusa Internasional, bringing the Maybank name to the Indonesian market. Maybank later acquired control of the joint venture, PT Maybank Indocorp, holding nearly 94 percent of its shares.

Maybank also entered a number of smaller markets during this time, including Brunei, with three branch offices, and one branch each in Vietnam and Cambodia. The bank also added representative offices in Vietnam, Myanmar, and Uzbekistan.

Maybank next entered the Philippines in 1997, after the Philippine government passed legislation allowing foreign-owned banks to gain majority control of domestic banks. Maybank joined forces with Philippine National Bank, buying 60 percent control of the former Republic Savings Bank. Maybank subsequently renamed its new subsidiary Maybank Philippines Inc. (MPI) and later gained full control of the enterprise. MPI became the first and only foreign-controlled bank in the Philippines to succeed in putting into place a national network of branch offices. By the mid-2000s, MPI's network boasted nearly 60 branches across the Philippines.

These properties were acquired through Philmay Holding Inc., another joint venture with Philippine National Bank. The primary purpose of this venture was the establishment of the real estate and property development vehicle Philmay Property Inc., held at two-thirds by Maybank and one-third by Philmay Holding. These businesses also launched operations in 1997.

The economic crisis that swept through Southeast Asia during the late 1990s exposed the shaky financial foundations of Malaysia's banking sector as well. As the country's largest bank, Maybank was required to participate in a vast consolidation of the country's banking industry. As part of that process, Maybank acquired a number of smaller banks, as well as two larger banks, Pacific Bank and PhileoAllied. The Pacific Bank

<table>
<tr><td colspan="2">Key Dates:</td></tr>
<tr><td>1960:</td><td>Khoo Teck Puat founds Malayan Banking Berhad (Maybank).</td></tr>
<tr><td>1963:</td><td>Maybank establishes a trustee branch, Mayban Trustees Bhd.</td></tr>
<tr><td>1973:</td><td>Aseambankers Malaysia Berhad is founded.</td></tr>
<tr><td>1975:</td><td>Aseambankers launches Kota Discount Berhad joint venture.</td></tr>
<tr><td>1986:</td><td>Maybank acquires a majority share of Kota Discount.</td></tr>
<tr><td>1987:</td><td>Maybank establishes Mayban Securities Sdn Bhd.</td></tr>
<tr><td>1989:</td><td>Kora Discount is renamed Mayban Discount Bhd.</td></tr>
<tr><td>1990:</td><td>Maybank sets up offshore operations in Labuan, including an offshore Islamic banking unit.</td></tr>
<tr><td>1994:</td><td>Maybank establishes a subsidiary in Papua New Guinea.</td></tr>
<tr><td>1995:</td><td>PT Bank Maybank Indocorp joint venture in Indonesia is established.</td></tr>
<tr><td>1997:</td><td>Maybank Philippines Inc. is established; Republic Savings bank is acquired in a joint venture with Philippines National Bank.</td></tr>
<tr><td>2001:</td><td>Maybank opens its first branch office in China, in Shanghai.</td></tr>
<tr><td>2002:</td><td>An Islamic insurance subsidiary is launched.</td></tr>
<tr><td>2005:</td><td>Maybank receives approval to bid for BinaFikir Sdn Bhd.</td></tr>
</table>

merger was completed by mid-2000, while the PhileoAllied merger was finalized by the end of that same year.

The mergers enabled Maybank not only to maintain its position as Malaysia's top banking group, but it also boosted the company significantly in the ranks of the global banking industry. In the early 2000s, Maybank cracked the world top 120 banks for the first time.

Maybank's growing position was enhanced when it received a license to open branch offices in China. At the beginning of 2001, Maybank became the first Malaysian bank to enter the Chinese mainland when it opened a branch office in Shanghai. The move placed Maybank in position to serve as an important liaison between Malaysia's financially powerful Chinese community and China itself.

Into the mid-2000s, Maybank laid out a strategy to establish the bank as a prominent player among the ASEAN market. Yet the bank was prepared to proceed cautiously in its attempt to break into these markets. As one company executive told *Euromoney,* "We have aspirations to be a regional investment bank but it will have to happen slowly because we need to familiarize ourselves with the rules and regulations of those countries, and hopefully, in the not-too-distant future, we will be able to move into that area."

One of Maybank's international expansion efforts came in 2001, when it applied for a license to begin operations in Bahrain. The company, which already ranked as the leading foreign-owned bank in Singapore, also looked to expand in that market by seeking a Qualifying Full Bank license.

Back at home, Maybank entered another area of financial services with the launch of Mayban Takaful Bhd. The new entity enabled Maybank to begin promoting Takaful insurance products, that is, insurance products in compliance with Islamic law. Established in 2002, Mayban Takaful began targeting the individual and personal market with a line of family, education, personal accident, and motor vehicle policies.

Maybank's expansion hit a snag in late 2004 when it failed in a bid to take over Bank Permata of Indonesia. The acquisition would have provided Maybank with a new outlet for growth as the Malaysian market matured. The move to expand its operations in Indonesia was also seen as a way for the company to enhance its competitiveness in the face of a liberalization of the Malaysian market, which reduced restrictions on foreign bank operations there. By early 2005, Maybank appeared to have shrugged off the Permata setback and instead placed its hopes on a new expansion target. In March of that year, Maybank received approval to launch a takeover bid, through its Aseambankers subsidiary, of BinaFikir Sdn Bhd. The proposed acquisition promised to consolidate Maybank's position as a Malaysian and Southeast Asian banking powerhouse.

Principal Subsidiaries

Aseam Credit Sdn Bhd; Aseam Malaysia Nominees (Asing) Sdn Bhd; Aseam Malaysia Nominees (Tempatan) Sdn Bhd; Aseambankers Malaysia Bhd; Aseamlease Bhd; Mayban (Nominees) Sdn Bhd; Mayban Discount Bhd; Mayban General Assurance Bhd; Mayban International Trust; Mayban International Trust (Labuan) Bhd; Mayban Investment Management Sdn Bhd; Mayban Life Assurance Bhd; Mayban Life International (Labuan) Ltd; Mayban Nominees (Asing) Sdn Bhd; Mayban Nominees (Hong Kong) Ltd; Mayban Nominees (Singapore) Pte Ltd; Mayban Nominees (Tempatan) Sdn Bhd; Mayban Offshore Corporate Services (Labuan) Sdn Bhd; Mayban Securities (Holdings) Sdn Bhd; Mayban Securities Nominees (Asing) Sdn Bhd; Mayban Securities Nominees (Tempatan) Sdn Bhd; Mayban Securities Nominees Sdn Bhd; Mayban Securities Sdn Bhd; Mayban Takaful Berhad; Mayban Trustees Bhd; Mayban Unit Trust Berhad; Mayban Venture Capital Co Sdn Bhd; Mayban Ventures Sdn Bhd; Maybank (PNG) Ltd; Maybank International (L) Limited; Maybank International Islamic Banking Operations; Maybank Philippines Inc; Mayfin Nominees (Tempatan) Sdn Bhd; Philmay Holding Inc.; Philmay Property Inc.; PT Bank MayBank Indocorp; RPB Venture Capital Corporation.

Principal Competitors

RHB Bank Bhd; Bumiputra-Commerce Bank Bhd; Rashid Hussain Bhd; RHB Capital Bhd; Public Bank Bhd; AMMB Holdings Bhd; Hong Leong Bank Bhd; AMFB Holdings Bhd; EON Bank Group; HSBC Bank Malaysia Bhd.

Further Reading

"Magazine Names Maybank Best Bank in Malaysia," *Business Times,* March 30, 2001.
"Malayan Banking Bhd—A Profitable Year," *Investor's Digest,* January 4, 2002.

''Malaysia's Banking Industry Searches for Profit,'' *Banker*, November 1, 2004.

''Maybank Applies to Open Branch Office in Bahrain,'' *Business Times*, May 18, 2001.

''Maybank Completes Merger Exercise,'' *Business Times*, May 2, 2001.

''Maybank Gets Not to Talk Ties,'' *Vietnam Investment Review*, March 28, 2005, p. 21.

''Maybank Looking Further Afield,'' *Euromoney*, February 2001, p. 90.

''Maybank Seen Gaining from S'pore Banking Liberalization,'' *Business Times*, July 5, 2001.

Robinson, Karina, ''Ready to Face the Music in Malaysia,'' *Banker*, March 1, 2004.

Yeap, Cindy, ''Maybank Gets Not to Set Up Nation's Third Takaful Firm,'' *Business Times*, December 6, 2001.

—M.L. Cohen

Manutan International S.A.

32 bis Boulevard de Picpus
Paris F-75583 Cedex 12
France
Telephone: (+33) 1 53 33 40 00
Fax: (+33) 1 53 33 40 38
Web site: http://www.manutan.com

Public Company
Incorporated: 1966
Employees: 1,109
Sales: EUR 338 million ($442 million) (2004)
Stock Exchanges: Euronext Paris
Ticker Symbol: MAN
NAIC: 454113 Mail-Order Houses

Manutan International S.A. is a specialist mail-order business providing industrial and office equipment and supplies to the business-to-business, collective, and public sectors. Based in France, Manutan has built up a pan-European network of 23 subsidiaries in 20 countries, as well as through 18 e-commerce Web sites. Manutan's more than 200 catalogs feature over 350,000 items and serve more than 600,000 customers throughout Europe. Manutan operates under its own name as well as a number of other well-known European names, including Overtoom (Netherlands and Belgium), Bott (France and Germany), Plus (Poland, Czech Republic), Key (United Kingdom), and Witre (Sweden, Denmark, Norway, and Finland). In 2004, the company posted total revenues of EUR 338 million ($442 million). The group's Southern division (France, Spain, Portugal, and Italy, as well as Manutan Belgium) accounted for 50 percent of that total. The Central division (Germany, Austria, the Netherlands, Overtoom in Belgium, Switzerland, Hungary, Poland, Czech Republic, Slovenia, and Slovakia) added 35 percent to sales, while the Western division (United Kingdom and Ireland) produced 11 percent of group sales. Manutan's Northern division (Sweden, Norway, Denmark, and Finland) remained its smallest, at just 4 percent of sales. Listed on the Euronext Paris Stock Exchange since 1985, Manutan remains controlled by the founding Guichard family at nearly 76 percent of shares. Founder André Guichard and son Jean-Pierre Guichard continue to lead the company.

Mail Order Pioneer in the 1960s

While mail order houses had been in operation in France for many years, these businesses focused primarily on the consumer market. In 1966, however, André Guichard, joined by son Jean-Pierre, set up a company dedicated to providing mail order services to the business sector. The company's major innovation came with its choice of goods, that of industrial equipment, especially materials handling equipment. The French word for this product segment, *manutention,* provided the basis for the new company's name, Manutan. Guichard set out lining up suppliers and within a year had shipped the company's first 24-page catalog. The company later credited the new catalog with generating some FFr 48,000 in sales.

Manutan grew strongly in France and quickly exerted its dominance of the business-to-business market. The company began expanding its catalog, adding a variety of industrial equipment and later office equipment and supplies. The expanded product offerings enabled the company to begin marketing to municipalities and public and private collectives, such as schools, hospitals, corporations, and the like. Over time, Manutan develop a number of specialized catalogs targeting each of its business segments.

Manutan also quickly recognized the potential of entering other European markets. The company's first choice was the United Kingdom, where, as in France in the 1960s, the market for mail order materials handling, lifting, and storage equipment was more or less nonexistent. In 1973, Manutan became a partner in the creation of a British subsidiary, Key Industrial Equipment Ltd., which, despite the later entry of competitors, was able to maintain its leadership in the U.K. market into the next century. Like its parent, Key later expanded its range of products to include workshop equipment, signage systems, and office equipment and supplies. Manutan gradually built up its stake in Key Industrial, reaching more than 65 percent in the

1980s and over 81 percent at the beginning of the 1990s before acquiring full control.

Manutan's success in the United Kingdom led it to move into a new foreign market in 1974. In that year, the company set up a subsidiary in Belgium, Manutan NV. The company also continued to seek to extend its range of operations, and in 1977 Manutan established Bott SA, which specialized in providing modular technical furnishings and equipment for workshops and utility trucks and vans. Bott itself has been founded in the 1930s in Germany as a small mechanical workshop before growing into one of the European leaders of its category.

By 1984, Manutan sales had topped the FFr 200 million mark, and the company began preparing its second expansion drive. In order to fuel its further expansion, and especially in order to provide a solid foundation for its future European expansion, Manutan went public in 1985, listing its shares on the Paris Stock Exchange's Secondary Market. The Guichard family nonetheless retained tight control of the company, holding some 85 percent of Manutan shares. That holding was later reduced to just under 76 percent by the early 2000s.

European Mail Order Growth in the 1980s

Manutan's success in Belgium led the company to expand its operations there, adding a new warehouse and logistics platform in 1986 that would also provide support for the group's entrance elsewhere in the Benelux and German markets. Also that year, Manutan made a brief attempt to enter the consumer market, establishing a consumer goods mail order house, Temp.L. That experiment proved short-lived, and Manutan once again focused its efforts on its core business-to-business markets.

The year 1987 marked a turning point for Manutan as the company launched a new growth strategy targeting a number of new foreign markets. The first was Italy, where Manutan joined with subsidiary Key Industrial formed a joint venture with a local partner, creating Veico SpA, based in Milan. Manutan and Key both initially held 25 percent of Veico. In 1988, Manutan bought out Key Industrial's stake before taking full control of Veico, which was renamed Manutan Italia in 1990.

By then, Manutan had also expanded into Germany. In January 1988, Ernst Ziegler had founded E. Ziegler Direkt-Marketing GmbH in Leonberg. By May 1988, Manutan had joined Ziegler as a founding partner, again in a joint venture involving Key Industrial. The company then became known as EZ Direkt Marketing, launching its first catalog by September of that year.

Manutan next looked farther north, acquiring the Witre group of companies serving the Scandinavian markets in 1989. Witre

International A/B had been founded in Sweden in 1981 and by 1983 had added a subsidiary in Norway. Under Manutan, Witre continued to develop its Scandinavian operations, launching subsidiaries in Denmark in 1995 and in Finland in 1999. These companies came to form Manutan's North division.

Manutan sold off Temp.L in 1990 as it refocused its efforts on its international business-to-business market. In that year, Manutan also reorganized its shareholding structure. As part of that process, the Guichard family created the shareholding company Manupar, which acquired 55 percent of the family's shares in Manutan. The following year, Manutan began building up a war chest in order to fund its future expansion. The company's efforts in this respect were aided by the continued growth of its annual sales despite the difficult economic climate. By 1992, the company's sales had topped FFr 1 billion (equivalent to EUR 150 million) for the first time.

Jean-Pierre Guichard took over as the company's executive chairman in 1994, while André Guichard remained active with the company as chairman of the board of directors. The following year, Manutan entered a new market, acquiring the Netherlands' Overtoom NV. That company had been one of Europe's pioneering business-to-business mail order houses, set up in 1946 on Amsterdam's Overtoom, a major avenue in that city. The company later moved its operations to Utrecht in 1960, developing into the Dutch leader in its market. In 1974, Overtoom had expanded into Belgium, setting up a subsidiary there. Ten years later, Overtoom was acquired by global trading company Koninklijke Borsumij Wehry. Under Manutan, both the Netherlands and Belgium businesses remained in operation under the Overtoom name.

Pan-European Leader in the 2000s

Manutan boosted its Southern division in 1996 with the opening of an office in Portugal. That operation later became the subsidiary Manutan Unipessoal Lda. Through EZ Direkt, in the meantime, Manutan had expanded its operations to include a number of new offices in Germany, including in Berlin, Rostock, and Hamburg, as well as a new logistics center in Leonberg, opened in 1995. In 1999, EZ Direkt provided Manutan an entrance into the Eastern European market through the acquisition of the Czech Republic's Plus. The following year, EZ Direkt also added operations in Austria, acquiring that country's Dr. Hans Kraus GmbH, which also operated a subsidiary in Slovenia. The company also expanded into Poland in 2000, establishing the Plus brand in that market.

By then, Manutan itself had added operations in Switzerland through the purchase of that country's Fabritec and boosted its presence in the United Kingdom through the purchase of Euroquipment. That purchase was followed by a move into Ireland with the purchase of Metro Storage Equipment in 2000. By then, Manutan had restructured its operations, creating a new holding company, Manutan International, as a reflection of the company's now pan-European presence.

Manutan had focused on its mail-order operations until the early 2000s. In 2001, however, the company expanded established a presence on the Internet, launching its first e-commerce-enabled Web site. That site later provided the platform for the rollout of 18 Web sites targeting each of the company's markets. By 2005, the company had posted more than EUR 1 million in sales through its e-commerce sites.

Into the mid-2000s, Manutan continued to fill in gaps in its geographic coverage while expanding its range. In 2004, the company established Manutan operations in Hungary, Slovakia, and Poland. Then, in 2005, Manutan entered Spain for the first time in an extension of its French operation. The company also expanded its Overtoom operation, establishing a subsidiary of that company in Germany in 2005. Manutan continued seeking growth opportunities with a clear objective of claiming leadership in all of its geographic markets and achieving sales of more than EUR 500 million by the end of the company's 2005 fiscal year.

Principal Subsidiaries

Bott SA; Dr Hans Kraus d.o.o (Slovenia); Dr Hans Kraus GmbH (Austria); Euroquipment Ltd (U.K.); EZ Direkt Marketing GmbH (Germany); Fabritec GmbH (Switzerland); Key (U.K.); Manutan (Spain); Manutan Hungary; Manutan Italia Spa; Manutan NV (Belgium); Manutan Polska; Manutan SA; Manutan Slovakia s.r.o. (Slovakia); Manutan Unipessoal Lda (Portugal); Metro Storage Systems Ltd (Ireland); Overtoom International Belgium; Overtoom International Nederland BV; Plus s.r.o (Czech Republic); WITRE A/S (Norway); WITRE AB (Sweden); WITRE Danmark A/S; WITRE OY (Finland);

Principal Competitors

Bertelsmann AG; Otto GmbH und Company KG; GUS PLC; Littlewoods Ltd; Neckermann Versand AG; Stockmann Oyj Abp; Wenz GmbH.

Further Reading

"Manutan International: scénario positif à court terme," *Cercle Finance*, May 24, 2005.
"Pindar Puts Manutan Online," *Printing World*, May 1, 2000, p. 2.

—M.L. Cohen

MARCHEX

Marchex, Inc.

413 Pine Street, Suite 500
Seattle, Washington 98101
U.S.A.
Telephone: (206) 331-3300
Fax: (206) 331-3695
Web site: http://www.marchex.com

Public Company
Incorporated: 2003
Employees: 211
Sales: $43.8 million (2004)
Stock Exchanges: NASDAQ
Ticker Symbol: MCHX
NAIC: 518111 Internet Service Providers and Web
   Search Portals

Marchex, Inc. provides services that facilitate and promote growth in online transactions, acting as the middleman connecting online merchants and customers. The company offers performance-based advertising and search marketing services to merchants, who pay Marchex for increasing the efficiency and effectiveness their marketing efforts across multiple distribution channels, including search engines, product shopping engines, directories, and other Web properties. The Seattle-based company maintains offices in Provo, Utah; Eugene, Oregon; and Las Vegas.

Origins

In October 2000, a fast-rising, Internet-based company named Go2Net Inc. merged with another Internet-oriented company named InfoSpace Inc. It was a $1.5 billion deal that set the stage for the formation of Marchex, a start-up company whose founders were all former Go2Net executives. John Keister, Ethan Caldwell, and Peter Christothoulou were part of the Go2Net team that founded Marchex, led by a fourth member, Go2Net's founder and the principal executive of Marchex, Russell Horowitz. Marchex was the third company started by entrepreneur Horowitz, whose career provided the background of Marchex's formation.

Horowitz, whom *Forbes* described as "every inch a value investor" in its May 29, 2000, issue, formed his first company when he was in his mid-20s. In 1992, the Seattle-raised Horowitz co-founded Active Apparel Group Inc. with his uncle, establishing the company in New York City. In 1995, while serving as Active Apparel's chief financial officer, he took the company public in a self-underwritten initial public offering (IPO). The success of Active Apparel, which made women's, girl's, and unisex active wear sold under the Everlast, Converse, and MTV's The Grind labels, provided the seed money for Horowitz's next venture. In 1996, he decided to join the technology sector, teaming with John Keister, who previously had founded a Seattle-based software company named ViewCom Technology International, to launch Go2Net, a company whose rapid growth as an Internet-based venture brought national attention to its two young founders.

During the latter half of the 1990s, the dot-com industry was rife with asset-less, money-losing companies that nevertheless attracted hundreds of millions of dollars from excited investors. Although Horowitz pursued growth aggressively, assuming a particularly active stance on the acquisition front, he stressed predictable earnings as his overriding goal for his newest venture, a business approach out of vogue in the Internet frenzy of the late 1990s. "We focus on technology rather than getting involved in marketing and hype," Horowitz commented in a May 1, 1998 interview with *Puget Sound Business Journal*. His new company, Go2Net, launched its Web site in late 1996, the first step in Horowitz's plan to develop an online destination for Internet users, a destination that would link to many other Web sites, all owned by Go2Net. Horowitz's strategy was based on acquisitions, but he acquired with restraint, drawing criticism for his thrift from institutional investors and other Internet executives who were swept up in the hyperbolic craze of the day. "People wanted me to apologize for being profitable," he remarked in a May 29, 2000, interview with *Forbes*. "They said my priorities were all wrong."

At the beginning of 1997, just several months after launching his Web site, Horowitz filed for Go2Net's IPO, hoping to raise more than $10 million to finance the company's development into a popular portal. The public offering of the Seattle-based company was successful, raising $14.7 million. Armed with cash, Horowitz went on a buying spree, but he acquired prudently, buying Web sites with dedicated followings whose content was created by users. He quickly assembled a mishmash of Web properties, purchasing Metacrawler, a search site that simultaneously searches the Internet's leading search engines, and Playsite, an online game area, among other purchases. What resulted was a network of branded Web sites that offered content related to a host of interests, including finance, entertainments, and sports. Sales were collected from a mix of licensing deals and advertising revenue, supporting a company that earned the esteem of investors and industry executives. Perhaps no greater proof of the company's rising stature was offered in 1999, when Paul Allen, Microsoft Corp.'s co-founder, invested in Horowitz's Go2Net. Allen bought a one-third interest in the company, paying $426 million in cash.

With a fresh supply of capital, Horowitz continued his acquisition campaign with vigor. Between the beginning of 1999 and mid-2000, he completed 13 acquisitions or investments. ''Nowadays you're either a buyer or a seller. If you're neither, you're dead,'' he said in his May 29, 2000, interview with *Forbes*. Horowitz proved to be both, agreeing to sell Go2Net in one of the most high-profile mergers in 2000. In July, Go2Net agreed to merge with InfoSpace Inc., a provider of software applications to Web merchants and wireless companies. Headquartered a few miles from Go2Net's Seattle offices, Bellevue-based InfoSpace was led by its founder and chairman Naveen Jain, who was slated to become chairman of the merged company. Infospace's chief executive officer, Arun Sarin, was appointed as the company's vice-chairman and chief executive officer. From the Go2Net side, Horowitz was handed the titles of vice-chairman and president, while Keister, Go2Net's president, was made executive vice-president of InfoSpace's consumer division. The two other Marchex founders, Peter Christothoulou and Ethan Caldwell, moved from Seattle to Bellevue as well. Christothoulou, the senior vice-president of strategic initiatives at Go2Net, was appointed senior vice-president of corporate strategy and development of the combined company. Caldwell, senior vice-president and corporate counsel of Go2Net, assisted with integration of Go2Net into InfoSpace.

The arrangement of Go2Net executives working alongside InfoSpace principals at the new InfoSpace did not last long. The merger was completed in October 2000 and the exodus of Go2Net executives, except for Caldwell, who left in December 2000, occurred in January 2001. The executives not only left the company but also sold nearly all of their InfoSpace stock, including Horowitz, who sold 6.1 million shares at the end of the month.

The Birth of Marchex

Once Horowitz, Keister, Christothoulou, and Caldwell left InfoSpace they immediately began looking for a new business to start. The four-man team began reviewing new business opportunities in the retail, media, finance, and technology industries, devoting 18 months to their careful search. ''We have been working pretty hard to get out there and look under the hood of a lot of companies and really understand what opportunities existed,'' Horowitz explained at the end of the search, as quoted in the March 7, 2003, issue of the *Seattle Post-Intelligencer*. ''Not from the perspective of being an opportunist, but [looking] for the kind of opportunity that could transcend an economic cycle and would be interesting in the longer term,'' he added. The group decided to enter the dot.com world again, choosing to start a company that would facilitate commerce between online merchants and consumers by bringing them together. In January 2003, using their own money and contributions from individual investors, they formed Marchex, Inc. Each member of the founding team assumed executive responsibilities at the new start-up, led by Horowitz, who became the company's chairman and chief executive officer. Keister became president and chief operating officer of Marchex, the identical posts he occupied at Go2Net. Christothoulou became Marchex's chief strategy officer. Caldwell was appointed chief administrative officer and the company's general counsel.

There were similarities between Marchex and Go2Net, a commonality rooted in the business approach used by Horowitz. With Go2Net, Horowitz demonstrated a penchant for being an active acquirer, a trait that would be on display often during Marchex's early development. He also was known for being thrifty in his purchases, buying companies whose performance could be improved with proper marketing and managerial control. ''If you look at it historically with the way we have approached things,'' Horowitz said in a March 7, 2003, interview with the *Seattle Post-Intelligencer*, ''we have focused on what we think are under-commercialized and under-leveraged areas where we can add value.'' The objective with Marchex was to assemble a number of Web properties that would represent a collection of products and services tailored for online merchants. Marchex would be the go-between, enabling merchants to reach their target audiences through Internet search engines and directory results.

Starting out, Marchex was nothing more than a handful of people with no assets. The company would be built through acquisitions, with the first addition arriving five weeks after the company was incorporated. In late February 2003, Horowitz acquired eFamily and its subsidiary Enhance Interactive, paying $15.1 million for the Provo, Utah-based company. The purchase included the Web site ah-ha.com, a profitable asset that specialized in paid online searches, listing Web sites on search engines for a fee. With the addition of Enhance Interactive, Marchex' payroll expanded substantially, jumping from ten employee to 60 employees. A second acquisition followed in October with the purchase of TrafficLeader. A three year-old Eugene, Oregon-based company, TrafficLeader offered search-based tools that enabled merchants to identify customers. Once the TrafficLeader acquisition was completed, Marchex employed 166 workers.

Key Dates:

2001: After merging their company with InfoSpace, former Go2Net executives begin reviewing options for forming another company.
2003: The group of executives, led by Russell Horowitz, incorporates Marchex.
2004: Marchex completes its initial public offering of stock and announces its acquisition of Name Development Ltd.
2005: Marchex completes a secondary offering of stock and acquires Pike Street Industries Inc.

IPO in 2004

After executing his first two moves on the acquisition front, Horowitz was ready to turn to Wall Street for support. He had taken Go2Net public not long after starting the company, and so he would with Marchex, filing for the company's IPO in December 2003. The stock offering was completed in March 2004, when Marchex sold four million shares at $6.50 per share. The company's stock rose 36.6 percent by the end of the first day, raising $27.2 million in what proved to be the most successful IPO in 2004 in the United States.

Marchex's stock value swelled as 2004 progressed, encouraging Horowitz to march forward with his acquisition campaign. In July 2004, the company acquired goClick.com Inc., a Darien, Connecticut, provider of technologies and services for small merchants. Marchex paid $12.5 million for goClick, enhancing its abilities to help its customers advertise through paid listings in search-engine results. The year's most important acquisition followed next, the largest acquisition in the company's brief history. In November 2004, Marchex announced it had agreed to acquire an obscure company based in the British Virgin Islands for $164.2 million. The company was Name Development Ltd., a $19-million-in-sales enterprise that operated in the direct navigation market. Direct navigation referred to the tendency of online searchers to type their search on their browser, typing www.videocamera.com for instance to obtain information about video cameras. According to one research study conducted by WebSideStory, 67 percent of online users arrived at Web sites by using the direct navigation technique in September 2004, up from the 53 percent who used the method in February 2002. Horowitz and his team estimated that 10 percent of the $4.5 billion Internet search market was tied to direct navigation. Name Development, which boasted operating profit margins of more than 80 percent, owned www.videocamera.com, as well as 1,000 other Web sites in categories such as travel, financial services, and electronics. The company owned properties such as Debts.com, LasVegasVacations.com, CareerInfo.com, and RentGuide.com.

Marchex concluded its first year as a publicly traded company as a much-coveted stock. The company's share price increased 223 percent during the year, making the company a darling of Wall Street. The financial community's favorable view of Horowitz's actions enabled the company to turn to the public market to finance its acquisition of Name Development.

In mid-February 2005, the company offered 9.2 million shares at $20 per share and 230,000 shares of preferred stock, raising an estimated $230 million before deducting fees associated with the offering. In addition to paying for the Name Development acquisition, which was completed at the end of February, the company set aside money for future acquisitions. In April 2005, the company completed another acquisition, surely not the last purchase Horowitz would orchestrate as he guided Marchex through its formative years. The company paid $16.5 million for certain assets of Pike Street Industries Inc., a company based east of Seattle that averaged more than two million unique visitors per month to its Web sites. Pike Street operated Web sites such as Yellow.com and Whitepages.net, giving Horowitz several new Web sites to add to his armada of properties. As Marchex pressed forward under his control, future acquisitions promised to bolster the stature of the Wall Street favorite.

Principal Subsidiaries

eFamily; TrafficLeader; goClick; Name Development Ltd.; Pike Street Industries Inc.

Principal Competitors

Google Inc.; Microsoft Corporation; Yahoo! Inc.

Further Reading

Baker, M. Sharon, "Fledgling Go2Net Seeks $10 Million in IPO," *Puget Sound Business Journal*, January 10, 1997, p. 8.
——, "Go2Net Expands, but Competitors Abound," *Puget Sound Business Journal*, May 1, 1998, p. 4.
——, "Go2Net Results: Small but Swift Firm Aims High," *Puget Sound Business Journal*, January 22, 1999, p. 1.
Brown, Erika, "Cautious Hunter," *Forbes*, May 29, 2000, p. 74.
Cook, John, "Happy to Be Back in the Start-Up Game Again; Former Go2Net Executives Reunite to Form Marchex," *Seattle Post-Intelligencer*, March 7, 2003, p. C1.
——, "Marchex Solidifies Its Web Presence," *Seattle Post-Intelligencer*, November 24, 2004, p. C1.
DeSilver, Drew, "IPOs Rebound Locally, Nationally in 2004," *Seattle Times*, p. C1.
"Go2Net Execs Shed Their InfoSpace Stock," *Puget Sound Business Journal*, March 16, 2001, p. 19B.
Meyer, Cheryl, "Marchex Fuels Growth with Additions," *Daily Deal*, November 24, 2004, p. 31.
"Northwest: Marchex to Offer IPO Shares at $20," *Seattle Post-Intelligencer*, February 10, 2005, p. E2.
"Northwest: Pike Street Industries Picked Up by Marchex," *Seattle Post-Intelligencer*, April 28, 2005, p. E2.
Ouchi, Monica Soto, "Marchex Stock Jumps 36.6% in Nasdaq Trading Debut," *Seattle Times*, April 1, 2004, p. E1.
——, "Seattle-Based Online Ad Startup Aims to Raise $26 Million with IPO," *Seattle Times*, March 31, 2004, p. C3.
——, "Seattle-Based Tech Startup Narchex Files to Go Public," *Seattle Times*, December 12, 2003, p. C1.
Peterson, Kim, "Marchex Purchasing Pile of Web Domains," *Seattle Times*, November 24, 2004, p. C1.
——, "Seattle-Based Firm Purchases Pile of Web Domains," *Seattle Times*, November 24, 2004, p. B3.
Yu, Roger, "Seattle-Based Internet Firm InfoSpace to Acquire Local Rival Go2Net," *Seattle Times*, B2.

—Jeffrey L. Covell

Memry Corporation

3 Berkshire Boulevard
Bethel, Connecticut 06801
U.S.A.
Telephone: (203) 739-1100
Toll Free: (866) 466-3679
Fax: (203) 798-6363
Web site: http://www.memry.com

Public Company
Incorporated: 1981 as Memory Metals, Inc.
Employees: 231
Sales: $34.49 million (2004)
Stock Exchanges: American
Ticker Symbol: MRY
NAIC: 541710 Research and Development in the
  Physical Sciences and Engineering Sciences; 332721
  Precision Turned Product Manufacturing; 332911
  Industrial Valve Manufacturing; 332919 Other Metal
  Valve and Pipe Fitting Manufacturing; 333319 Other
  Commercial and Service Industry Machinery
  Manufacturing; 339993 Fastener, Button, Needle and
  Pin Manufacturing

Memry Corporation ranks as the largest independent manufacturer of Nitinol components to the medical device industry and the largest producer of Nitinol tubing, wire, strip, and components. Nitinol is a shape memory alloy able to undergo severe changes in form and return to its original shape. The company offers manufacturers a total solution concept that incorporates design, prototype development, production, and the manufacture of shape memory alloy parts. In the medical device market, Memry's Nitinol and polymer-based components are used in interventional devices such as guide wires, catheters, and delivery systems. Memry owns manufacturing facilities in Bethel, Connecticut, and Menlo Park, California.

Origins

Memry went through several meaningful transitions during its first decades in business, shifting its strategy three times before finding the niche it occupied at the beginning of the 21st century.

The company was incorporated in 1981 in Stamford, Connecticut, a venture started by a group of scientists intent on developing commercial applications for the emerging shape memory alloy business. Shape memory referred to a material's ability to change its shape and return to its original shape, an ability that promised to have many uses in industrial and commercial applications. Initially, the founding scientists concentrated on a family of copper-based shape memory alloys, deriving much of their financial backing from federal research grants. The company spent much of its first decade experimenting with copper-based alloys, experiencing the trial-and-error ups and downs common in any emerging technological field. By the late 1980s, the scientists realized they were on the wrong track, a discovery that prompted Memry's first significant change in strategy.

Memry's lead scientists abandoned further work on copper-based shape memory alloys when they realized the material was not capable of performing well in the long term. Copper-based alloys could not answer the demanding needs of certain applications, but the company's technical crew knew of an alloy that could stand up to the rigors of commercial and industrial demands. During the early 1960s, a new alloy was discovered, a material that drew its name from its birthplace. Nitinol became the answer to Memry's problems with copper-based alloys, a material that was almost equal parts nickel and titanium. Nitinol's name was created from combining the first two letters of nickel and titanium with the acronym for the U.S. Naval Ordnance Laboratory (NOL), where the alloy was discovered in the early 1960s. Nitinol had special, unique properties that allowed it to alter its shape in response to thermal or mechanical changes, but return to its original form, a crystalline phase change known as "thermoelastic martensitic transformation."

Once Memry's engineers found a shape memory alloy that could perform well, the company's commercial activity picked up pace. Beginning around 1989, when the company changed its name from Memory Metals Inc. to Memry Corporation, it began developing products for customers, distributing its goods through its own sales team and through agreements with other agencies. The company also strengthened its metal machining business with the acquisition of a more than century-old Worcester, Massachusetts-based company. In 1990, the company acquired Wright Machine Corp., which increased its manufacturing capacity, particularly for internally developed valve products. Memry's involvement in developing its own shape memory alloy products lasted only briefly, ending in the early 1990s when the company embarked on its second meaningful change in strategy. The first strategic transition had been triggered by a product, the discovery of Nitinol. The impetus for the second change in focus came from an individual, an executive named James G. Binch.

New Leadership in the Early 1990s

Binch received his undergraduate degree from Princeton University before earning a master's degree in business from the Wharton School at the University of Pennsylvania. His career included a stint at Champion Building Products, where he served as vice-president of planning, and a seven-year stay at Combustion Engineering, where he rose to the posts of president and chief operating officer. Binch's introduction to Memry came after he embarked on a new career as a merchant banker. In 1987, he founded Harbour Investment Corporation, which became a major shareholder of Memry, eventually leading to his appointment as chief executive officer of Memry in 1992.

Once at the helm, Binch had the power to make changes as he saw fit. He believed the company lacked focus because, according to the February 19, 2001 issue of the *Fairfield County Business Journal*, "It was going in too many directions." Binch implemented a restructuring program that changed the way the company conducted its business, ushering in a period of development that would see the company realize its first significant growth. For more than its first decade of business, Memry never reached the $1 million-in-sales mark, operating as a very small enterprise with fewer than 20 employees. The company began to develop into a more prominent commercial entity after Binch abandoned the company's strategy of developing proprietary end-user products and recast Memry as a supplier to original equipment manufacturers (OEMs). In the years ahead, Binch focused on offering semi-finished materials and engineered components fabricated from Nitinol, selling such goods to manufacturers involved in industrial, commercial, and defense markets.

The switch from manufacturing finished products to fabricating semi-finished products and components took several years to complete. By 1995, the company still employed fewer than 20 people and it continued to generate less than $1 million in annual revenue, but the spark that ignited the company's growth arrived the following year. In June 1996, Binch bought the electronics division of Raychem Corporation, a purchase that capped the restructuring program begun four years earlier. The acquisition involved Raychem's intellectual property and its manufacturing assets related to its shape memory business, giving Memry a production plant in Menlo Park, California. The purchase also included ties to the medical device market, which Raychem had served before Memry acquired its shape memory assets. A focus on the medical device market represented the company's third

significant change in strategy, one that would propel the Binch-led organization toward unprecedented growth.

Focusing on the Medical Device Market in the Late 1990s

During the second half of the 1990s, the medical device industry began turning increasingly to shape memory alloy-based components to manufacture its products. Shape memory alloys excelled in certain commercial and industrial applications, proving their worth as the underwire for bras, as components of cellular phone antennas, and to make flexible eyeglass frames. The unique behavior of Nitinol—its ability to undergo severe shape changes and fully recover when triggered—found practical use in the medical device market as well. By using shape memory alloy in a medical instrument, the instrument's shape and size could be contorted and returned to its original form once deployed in the patient's body, which aided in the medical community's drive for minimally invasive procedures and instruments. Binch saw a future for Memry in the medical devices market, one in which the demand was strong and the profits were high. For example, one-quarter inch of Nitinol wire cost $30 per pound, the price Memry paid to bring the alloy into its manufacturing facilities. After using the Nitinol to create a component for a medical device, the price of the shape memory alloy increased exponentially, jumping as high as $3,000 per pound.

As the late 1990s progressed, Binch reshaped the company again, focusing his efforts on the medical device market. In 1997, two deals one month apart reflected the decision to move forward in one direction while retreating from another direction. In April, Memry reached a two-year, exclusive purchase order agreement with United States Surgical Corporation for the supply of medical instrument assemblies. The following month, Memry announced it had reached an agreement to sell all of the machinery and equipment belonging to Wright Machine Corp., deeming the subsidiary outside the scope of the company's new focus on becoming a high-technology materials and assembly concern.

The new version of Memry that was taking shape during the late 1990s was a much larger commercial enterprise, one whose growing stature attracted attention from beyond the borders of its home state of Connecticut. Thanks in large part to the Raychem acquisition, the company's annual sales leaped from $1.1 million in 1996 to $11.5 in 1997. Revenues nearly doubled the following year, as Binch pressed forward with his restructuring program. In October 1998, Memry completed another major acquisition, setting its sights on overseas assets to bolster its Nitinol capabilities. The company acquired Advanced Materials and Technologies, N.V. (AMT), a Belgium-based company that ranked as one of the largest providers of shape memory alloys to customers in Europe. The addition of AMT, which owned a 15,000-square-foot manufacturing facility in Herk-de-Stad, coupled with the Raychem purchase made Memry one of the largest producers of Nitinol components in the world—an impressive standing for a company that several years earlier had been unable to generate more than $1 million in revenue.

Memry in the 21st Century

At the dawn of the 21st century, Memry was at a crossroads of sorts, firmly committed to being a supplier of Nitinol-based

Key Dates:

1981: Memry is incorporated.
1992: James G. Binch is appointed chief executive officer.
1996: Memry acquires Raychem Corp.'s shape memory alloy business.
1998: Memry acquires Advanced Materials and Technologies, N.V., a Belgium-based company that becomes Memry Europe.
2001: Memry sells Memry Europe.
2004: Memry acquires Putnam Plastics Corporation.

components, but serving both the medical device market and markets outside the medical industry. The focus on serving medical device manufacturers had grown sharper as the late 1990s progressed, culminating with a small yet symbolic acquisition completed in 1999. In March, Memry purchased Wrentham, Massachusetts-based Wire Solutions, Inc., a maker of specialized micro-coils and guide wire components for the medical device industry. "This acquisition, although small," Binch explained in a statement released March 24, 1999 by *PR Newswire,* "continues Memry's drive into the broader application of its design, engineering, and manufacturing skills for the medical device market." The purchase of Wire Solutions represented one more step toward serving the medical device market, and it was followed by a significant step away from serving OEM manufacturers involved in the automotive, telecommunications, defense, and other, nonmedical, industries. In February 2001, Binch decided to sell Memry Europe, the business formerly known as AMT, shifting the balance between a medical and nonmedical focus strongly toward the medical side.

"Over the past four quarters, we have experienced approximately $750,000 in ordinary operating losses directly attributable to the European operation. With this transaction, we will have eliminated the ongoing financial drain." Binch's statement, taken from a February 19, 2001 interview with the *Fairfield County Business Journal,* explained part of the reason to cut the former AMT free from Memry. "The real reason the European business had not turned the corner in terms of profits," Binch continued, "was with our company-wide emphasis on medical applications. We did not develop the commercial base necessary for other applications." Memry Europe, within three years of its acquisition, had come to represent the company's past. At Memry's headquarters in Brookfield, 85 percent of the components manufactured were designed for medical applications. In Belgium, 90 percent of the Nitinol components were made for commercial and industrial applications not related to medical devices. The focus of the company, sharpened by the divestiture of its European subsidiary, was clearer by this point. In the years ahead, Memry intended to invest nearly all of its efforts in making the laparoscopic surgical assemblies, medical stent materials and components, and catheters and guide wires wanted by medical device manufacturers.

As Binch celebrated his tenth anniversary at Memry, the influence of his reign was easily discernible in both financial and strategic terms. When he joined the company, Memry had discovered the material it would use but not the market for the material. Financially, the gains achieved under his rule were enormous. When Binch joined Memry, the company collected revenues in the hundreds of thousands of dollars. By the mid-2000s, the company was generating roughly $35 million in revenue, earning in profit by a factor of more than ten what it had grossed a decade earlier. Binch made Memry a recognizable player in the business world, and he was committed to further developing the company within the parameters it had taken him nearly a decade to define. The company's acquisition of Putnam Plastics Corporation in 2004 reinforced Binch's strategy for Memry, giving the company a broader platform upon which to build in the future. Putnam, acquired in November, made plastic components for medical devices such as guide wires, catheters, delivery systems, and other interventional devices. Binch, in an interview with the *Fairfield County Business Journal* conducted on November 29, 2004, explained the reasoning behind the purchase, likely not the last acquisition of its type as Memry prepared for the future. "Both of us supply critical products for many of the same device companies, sometimes for the same application," he noted. "For example, we may make a Nitinol self-expanding stent while Putnam may manufacture the shaft for its delivery catheter. Our new combined company gives us greater leveraging in penetrating the market and expanding the customer base."

Principal Subsidiaries

Putnam Plastics Corporation.

Principal Competitors

Special Metals Corporation; Alleghany Technologies; Minitubes S.A.; G. Rau/EuroFlex.

Further Reading

"Memry Announces Agreement to Sell Wright Machine Subsidiary," *Business Wire,* May 13, 1997.
"Memry Corporation Announces Annual Results," *PR Newswire,* September 15, 1998.
"Memry Corporation Announces European Acquisition," *PR Newswire,* October 30, 1998.
"Memry Corporation Announces Supply Agreement with U.S. Surgical Corporation," *Business Wire,* April 17, 1997, p. 04171174.
"Memry Corporation Completes Acquisition," *PR Newswire,* March 24, 1999.
"Memry Nails Agreement with US Surgical," *Performance Materials,* March 17, 2003, p. 4.
"Memry Results Rise But Challenges Lie Ahead," *Performance Materials,* September 29, 2003, p. 5.
"Memry Wrestles with Margins As Sales Rise," *Performance Materials,* March 3, 2003, p. 3.
Strempel, Dan, "Memry Buys Plastics Firm for $26 Million," *Fairfield County Business Journal,* November 29, 2004, p. 20.
——, "Sale of European Unit Reshapes Memry," *Fairfield County Business Journal,* February 19, 2001, p. 2.
Toloken, Steve, "Memry Enters Plastics Realm with the Purchase of Putnam," *Plastics News,* July 19, 2004, p. 5.

—Jeffrey L. Covell

MC SPORTS

Michigan Sporting Goods Distributors, Inc.

3070 Shaffer S.E.
Grand Rapids, Michigan 49512
U.S.A.
Telephone: (616) 942-2600
Toll Free: (800) 626-1762
Fax: (616) 942-2312
Web site: http://www.mcsports.com

Private Company
Incorporated: 1946 as Michigan Clothiers
Employees: 1,300 (est.)
Sales: $148 million (2003 est.)
NAIC: 451110 Sporting Goods Stores

Michigan Sporting Goods Distributors, Inc. operates a chain of nearly 70 MC Sports stores, which are located in seven states in the Midwest. Most of the firm's outlets are about 15,000 square feet in size and carry a full line of sporting goods and clothing, while a handful are twice as large and incorporate an outdoor center that features camping, hunting, and fishing gear. The company is owned by members of senior management.

Early Years

MC Sporting Goods traces its origins to 1946, when Jack Finklestein founded a store in Grand Rapids, Michigan, called Michigan Clothiers. Finklestein had previously managed a local store called Sterling Clothing Company, which had later become known as Fink Clothing. In 1946, he renamed the business Michigan Clothiers and began to focus on selling menswear, war surplus items, and recreational products. Finklestein's wife Genevieve, who had received a business degree from the University of Chicago, also participated in running the business, while helping raise their sons Morton, Edward, and Raleigh.

As sales of sports-related products grew during the 1950s, the company gradually shifted its inventory in this direction. In 1961, now under the control of Morton, Edward, and Raleigh Finklestein, the store was renamed MC Sporting Goods, and its inventory updated to include only sports equipment, clothing, and shoes.

The new concept was a success, and during the next two decades additional stores were opened in western Michigan, and then in other parts of the state and in neighboring Ohio and Illinois. By 1986, the company, which had become known as MC Sporting Goods, was operating a total of 23 stores.

Sporting goods retailers were now seeing a massive consolidation in which a few players sought to create national chains by purchasing strong regional operators. In 1986, the Finklestein brothers decided to sell their firm to Thrifty Corp., a California-based company with $1.6 billion in annual sales that owned several sporting goods and drugstore chains. The brothers would remain in charge of the business following the sale.

Thrifty's other sporting goods chains included Big 5, with 94 West Coast stores; and Gart Brothers, a Denver-based chain of 16. Thrifty itself had recently been acquired by Pacific Lighting Corp., a Los Angeles-based holding company that owned Southern California Gas Co., the largest natural gas utility in the United States.

Expansion in the Late 1980s

Taking advantage of Thrifty's deep pockets, MC Sporting Goods soon began to expand. Shortly after the ownership change was finalized, the company opened three new stores in Ohio, and the following summer it purchased three Chicago-area sporting goods stores owned by Morrie Mages, a well-known local entrepreneur, which were subsequently renamed MC Mages.

Within a year, 20 new stores had been added, including additional ones in Iowa and Illinois. In the fall of 1988, the company also bought Brown's Sporting Goods, which operated a chain of 18 stores in Illinois and Indiana.

By 1990, MC Sporting Goods was ranked the 13th-largest sporting goods chain in the United States by Sports Trend magazine, which estimated its annual sales at $150 million. Late in that year, the Finklestein brothers' four-year contract ended, and they gave up control of the firm their father had founded. They would go on to other business ventures in the Grand Rapids area, including opening several Kenny Rogers Roasters chicken restaurants.

The company soon named B. Chris Schwartz president and CEO. Schwartz had previously headed Bata Shoe Co. and Cevaxs Corp. and served as chief operating officer of BiWay Stores. By this time, the firm was operating 62 outlets in Michigan and four other states. Sales were split evenly between clothing and sports equipment.

In 1991, Thrifty shifted control of 20 Gart Brothers and Casey's Sports stores in Missouri and Kansas to MC Sporting Goods, which reopened them as MC Sports stores. The firm subsequently added a 100,000-square-foot warehouse space in Grand Rapids to handle the larger inventory its new stores required. By the start of 1992, the firm had a total of 77 outlets.

Sale to Leonard Green & Partners in 1992

In the years since its 1986 acquisition by Pacific Lighting, many of Thrifty's divisions had seen revenues decline, and in early 1992 that firm announced that its retail chains, including all 266 of its sporting goods stores, were for sale. In the spring, a deal was reached with buy-out specialists Leonard Green & Partners of Los Angeles to acquire most of Thrifty's operations, with its Pay 'N Save unit to be purchased by Kmart's PayLess Drug Stores subsidiary. The total price of both deals was put at $275 million, about a fourth of the $1.1 billion Pacific Lighting had originally paid.

With competition now fierce in the sporting goods marketplace, MC Sporting Goods began to shift its focus toward improving customer service, rather than emulating big-box chains like The Sports Authority or mass-merchandisers like Wal-Mart and Sears. In July, CEO Schwartz, who had unsuccessfully attempted to buy MC Sporting Goods himself, quit the firm. He was replaced by John Chase on an interim basis until James Minton took the top job in October. Minton had formerly headed Thrifty's Pay 'N Save operation. For 1992, the company's sales were estimated at $155 million.

In October 1993, MC Sporting Goods announced it was closing nine stores in the St. Louis area, all of which had formerly been Casey's Sports outlets. The firm also opened three new stores in Chicago during the year, which left it with a total of 62 by year's end.

In 1994, MC Sporting Goods began a major overhaul of its image. The firm's flagship store in Grand Rapids was remodeled at a cost of $500,000, with video demonstration displays, an in-store workout center, and expanded product lines added. Its name was also changed from MC Sporting Goods to MC Sports. The renovation was a success, and future stores were built in this mold, with existing ones upgraded over time.

The year 1994 also saw the company announce a program called TEAMMATES, through which it would donate goods valued at 5 percent of the total on store receipts collected by various organizations. The program was intended to benefit school athletic programs and charitable sports-related organizations such as the YMCA.

In the fall of 1994, MC Sports announced plans to open 18 new stores over the next year, including several each in Cleveland, Chicago, Detroit, and Kansas City. Sales of sporting goods were again on the upswing, and other chains, including Dick's Sporting Goods, Sports & Recreation, and Sportsmart, were also announcing aggressive new expansion plans. Sales for 1995 were estimated at $175 million, with MC Sports seeing particularly strong growth in sales of camping gear and women's sports apparel.

Senior Management Buys Firm in 1996

In the summer of 1996, a deal was reached for a group of the firm's senior management, including CEO Jim Minton and chief financial officer Bruce Ullery, to buy MC Sports from Leonard Green & Partners. The company was now operating a total of 78 stores.

The year 1996 also saw MC Sports sign on as a primary sponsor of the Great Lakes State Games, an Olympics-style event for Michigan athletes held in the state capital of Lansing. In addition to this and the TEAMMATES program, MC Sporting Goods participated in Miracle May, during which month a portion of sales was given to the Children's Miracle Network.

In the summer of 1997, the company acquired Traverse Bay Tackle Co. of Traverse City, Michigan, a large fishing-goods store, and merged it into a new MC Sports store opening in the area. Their combined operations would offer 44,000 square feet of retail space. It was one of the first examples of a new prototype, dubbed an Outdoor Center, which MC Sports would later begin to build in select markets. Most of its stores, which were typically located in strip and shopping malls, averaged 15,000 square feet.

The firm was also now looking at expanding to smaller markets where the competition was less intense. In 1998, MC Sports opened 20,000 square foot stores in Decatur, Illinois, and Toledo, Ohio, and announced ambitious plans to open 12 to 15 other outlets in Alabama, Georgia, Tennessee, and North Carolina, though this idea was soon scrapped. In September 1998, Jim Minton stepped down and Bruce Ullery was appointed president and CEO.

Fierce competition was just one source of difficulty for sporting goods retailers, who also faced a continuing decline in sports participation among young people. This was attributed in part to financially strapped school districts cutting athletics programs, as well as the growing popularity of stay-at-home activities like video games. Some chains, including one-time industry leader Herman's, had already gone belly-up, while others, like Jumbo Sports/Sports & Recreation, were in serious trouble.

MC Sports itself began to close more underperforming outlets and by the spring of 1999 had slimmed down to a total of 65 stores. The company was also looking at the retail possibilities offered by the Internet, and in May announced an "e-tailing" partnership with Global Sports Interactive (GSI),

Key Dates:

1946: Jack Finklestein founds Michigan Clothiers in Grand Rapids, Michigan.
1961: Finklestein's three sons take charge and rename the store MC Sporting Goods; 20 additional stores are opened in the 1960s, 1970s, and 1980s.
1986: The company is sold to Thrifty Corp. of California.
1987: Three Morrie Mages stores are bought in Chicago and renamed MC Mages.
1988: Brown's Sporting Goods chain of 18 stores is acquired.
1990: Finklestein family members exit the company.
1991: The firm takes control of 20 Gart Brothers/Casey's stores in Missouri and Kansas.
1992: Thrifty Corp. sells the company to Leonard Green & Partners of Los Angeles.
1996: Senior management, led by CEO Jim Minton, buys the firm from Leonard Green.
1998: Minton steps down; Bruce Ullery is named CEO.
1999: Online sales begin through Global Sports Interactive.

which would operate the firm's online business, along with those of competitors like Sports Chalet, The Athlete's Foot, and Sports & Recreation. The plan called for GSI to design and operate each company's Web site and handle ordering, fulfillment, and customer service. MC Sports would receive 10 percent of revenues in exchange for putting the Web address in all of its marketing. The Web site began operating in November, in time for the holiday shopping season.

November 1999 also saw the firm open new stores in Bloomington, Indiana; Joplin, Missouri; and West Bend, Wisconsin. The first was a 30,000-square-foot Outdoor Center, while the Wisconsin and Missouri stores were the more typical 15,000 square foot size.

In 2000, MC Sports added new stores in Grandville, Michigan; Rockford, Illinois; and Madison, Wisconsin. All were Outdoor Centers. The firm expanded its warehouse capacity during the year by leasing part of a vacant Sam's Club store south of Grand Rapids, where it would also sell clearance items.

In 2001, MC Sports closed several stores and shrank to 64 outlets, with sales hitting an estimated $210 million. The year 2002 saw the firm receive a $40 million line of credit from LaSalle Retail Finance to help fund growth. Four more stores were added during the year, bringing the total up to 68. This number held steady for the next two years, even as estimated

sales, according to industry newspaper *Sporting Goods Business,* declined to $148 million.

The nearly 60-year old MC Sports was working to adapt to a tough retail environment by building large Outdoor Centers in some markets and targeting smaller cities in others. Its continued survival was evidence of the skill and tenacity of its management.

Principal Competitors

The Sports Authority, Inc.; Dick's Sporting Goods, Inc.; Dunham's Sports; Winmark Corp.; Wal-Mart Stores, Inc.; Kmart Corp.; Target Corp.

Further Reading

Becker, Bob, "Business Joins Team to Help Prep Sports," *Grand Rapids Press*, May 5, 1994, p. C1.
"Former Gart Stores to Reopen as MC," *St. Louis Post-Dispatch*, August 8, 1991, p. 8D.
Goodman, Adam, "MC Sporting Goods Calling It Quits Here," *St. Louis Post-Dispatch*, October 21, 1993, p. 1C.
Hahn, Cindy, "Sale Puts Morrie Mages on Fast Track," *Crain's Chicago Business*, June 22, 1987, p. 3.
Kaufman, Martin, "MC: Management in Charge," *SportStyle*, August 1, 1996, p. 10.
McCarthy, Tom, "Thrifty Sale Won't Affect MC," *Grand Rapids Press*, October 3, 1992, p. D7.
"MC Sports Out to Give Its Game a Brand-New Look," *Grand Rapids Press*, April 18, 1994, p. A8.
Radigan, Mary, "MC Sporting Goods Chief Tuned to Customers," *Grand Rapids Press*, May 26, 1991, p. E1.
Radigan, Mary, "Gear to Go: MC Sports Outdoor Center Opens," *Grand Rapids Press*, November 18, 2000, p. D4.
——, "Investment Firm Is Buying Parent of MC Sporting Goods," *Grand Rapids Press*, May 29, 1992, p. A8.
——, "MC Sporting Goods Ready for Competition Under New Team," *Grand Rapids Press*, October 7, 1993, p. B5.
——, "On the Grow—MC Sports Chief Keeps Retailer on Course for Future," *Grand Rapids Press*, April 3, 2000, p. B7.
Snow, Amy, "Family Was Key to Clothing Store Owner," *Grand Rapids Press*, June 11, 1997, p. B3.
"Top Sporting Goods Chains Restructure, Change Hands," *Discount Store News*, July 5, 1993, p. 78.
Troy, Mike, "MC Sports Seeks Southern Exposure," *Discount Store News*, September 15, 1997, p. 7.
"Two Founders Leave MC Sporting Goods," *Grand Rapids Press*, November 7, 1990, p. D6.
VanderVeen, Don, "MC Files Lawsuit to Clear Expansion Plan," *Grand Rapids Business Journal*, July 25, 1994, p. 1.
Wells, Garrison, "MC Sports Adds .com for the Net," *Grand Rapids Press*, November 17, 1999, p. A17.

—Frank Uhle

The Monarch Cement Company

449 1200 Street
Humboldt, Kansas 66748
U.S.A.
Telephone: (620) 473-2222
Fax: (620) 473-2447
Web site: http://www.monarchcement.com

Public Company
Incorporated: 1907 as The Monarch Portland Cement
    Company
Employees: 650
Sales: $145.1 million
Stock Exchanges: Over the Counter
Ticker Symbol: MCEM
NAIC: 327320 Ready-Mix Concrete Manufacturing

Based in Humboldt, Kansas, The Monarch Cement Company manufactures two products: Portland Cement, which is used in the production of ready-mixed concrete for the construction of buildings, highways, and bridges, and masonry cement, which is mixed with sand and water to make a masonry mortar suitable for use in bricks, block, and stone construction. The company's service area includes Arkansas, Iowa, Kansas, Missouri, Nebraska, and Oklahoma. Monarch is a public company, its shares trading on an over-the-counter basis. It is run by the third generation of the Wulf family.

Portland Cement Developed in 1820s

Cement is a material that dates back at least to the ancient Greeks and Romans, who used volcanic ash and clay to make cement for building roads, aqueducts, and buildings. The Roman Coliseum, for instance, relied on a cement made from lime and volcanic ash. As was the case with much of the knowledge the Greek and Roman civilizations possessed, however, the art of cement making was lost during the Middle Ages. It was not rediscovered until 1756, when John Smeaton in England developed a durable mortar used to build a lighthouse. Because this type of natural cement relied on local materials, its properties

varied. Then, in 1824, an English bricklayer, Joseph Aspdin, developed a new cement that was not only less expensive and stronger, it was made from a combination of calcium, silicon, iron, and aluminum that could be produced anywhere, thus providing builders with a consistent product. In brief, these materials are combined in a kiln at a temperature approaching 3000 degrees F. Requiring vigilant supervision, the resulting product is called "clinker," and it is then ground to make cement. Aspdin named it Portland Cement, because it resembled a type of stone quarried from the British Isle of Portland. The new cement crossed the Atlantic to the United States in 1868, and in the 1870s David Oliver Saylor developed a Portland Cement from native materials found in Pennsylvania's Lehigh Valley. By 1897, domestic-made Portland Cement exceeded imports, after which the production of American Portland Cement expanded rapidly.

The first cement company, the Iola Portland Cement Company, was formed in Kansas in 1898. The Monarch Portland Cement Company was the third, organized in January 1907. Its founders were O.M. Connet, the president of the company, and William Keith, secretary-treasurer. According to press accounts from the time, the company's headquarters was originally in Wichita, but Connet and Keith settled on Humboldt as the site of their plant because it was served by two railroads and was a well-established town. According to an account in the *Allen County Herald*, Humboldt was "not a boom town with the precarious values of all boom towns, but a town which has withstood all the difficulties which have beset all Kansas towns and come forth victorious. The banks of Humboldt are solid and prosperous institutions. The stores in Humboldt are well stocked with the latest and best of everything and the merchants are progressive business men who do not let old stock accumulate on their hands, but keep up with the times in everything."

Panic of 1907 Fails to Deter New Company

Monarch began building its plant in 1907, and as work proceeded Connet and Keith relocated to Humboldt from Wichita. The timing for a new venture was not fortuitous, however, because in October of that year, shortly after construction began, the United States suffered from one of its periodic financial crises, the Panic of 1907, which led to the failure of banks and other businesses and resulted in some cement plants shutting down their operations. Nevertheless, according to the *Allen County Herald,* ''the Monarch Portland Cement Company began a forward march towards completion which has not stopped a day.'' While construction of the plant proceeded, the company continued to drum up funding, bringing potential investors to Humboldt to see for themselves the progress that was being made. Construction would continue for more than a year, and in the meantime the company procured rooms above the old Humboldt National Bank for ''up-town offices and sleeping rooms.'' In March 1908, the local newspaper reported, ''The demand for stock is growing. The fact that stock holders in Kansas corporations do not have to pay taxes as individuals is an inducement to many to buy stock in a home company. The plant of the company is assessed and thus pays the taxes as a company.'' Keith was also scouting for investors outside of Kansas as well. A month later, the *Allen County Herald* reported that Keith was in Wisconsin, ''where there is a large demand for the stock of the company.''

The Monarch plant was expected to be operational early in 1909 but it was not until July 21 that the company made its first shipment of cement. While Connet and Keith were due credit for having the wherewithal to launch the business, they proved less adroit at actually running it. Yet Monarch continued to pay a dividend to its investors, a fact that persuaded many others to buy stock. One these latecomers was Henry F.G. Wulf, who came to the Wichita area with his parents from Germany in 1885 when he was 14 years old. A man of little education or financial resources, he was nonetheless able to succeed in business. When he was 20 years old, he found work at a hardware and implement company in Garden Plain, west of Wichita. The owners decided after the Panic of 1891 to get out of the business and turned it over to young Wulf and his brother Otto, telling them they could paid them back when they were able. Wulf was able to turn around the company, and he built a solid reputation in the area.

In 1911, some of Wulf's friends bought Monarch stock and induced him to invest in the company as well, claiming it was a ''veritable gold mine.'' Wulf bought 20 shares at $100 a share. He was soon surprised to discover that he had been elected to Monarch's Board of Directors, and to fulfill his duties he attended the company's next board meeting. He quickly uncovered the truth about the Humboldt ''gold mine'': it was broke. The dividends were coming from the sale of stock. His friends refused to believe him, pointing to the solid dividends Monarch was paying. Wulf predicted that within two months the company's creditors would call for receivership. He was proved right, and Monarch was taken to court. His friends now persuaded the judge in charge of the matter to appoint Wulf as receiver, which was accomplished in March 1912. On July 21,

1913, the company was reorganized and incorporated as The Monarch Cement Company. Wulf was named president in September and August C. Kreotzer vice-president. According to recollections of Wulf's son, Walter H. Wulf, ''They had rough going. The new company had no credit. Suppliers would ship only C.O.D. with the guarantee of Dad's firm of Wulf Brothers of Garden Plain. He often wondered how his friends got him into such a mess.''

Developments from the 1910s to the Mid-1940s

In the spring of 1914, Wulf moved his family to Humboldt, and despite difficulties he managed to build up Monarch's business. In those early days, much of the work was done by hand. Raw materials mined from the company quarry were hand-loaded into carts and drawn by mules over narrow gauge rail to a crusher. In this way, Monarch was able to produced 282,000 tons of cement, or 1.5 million barrels, in 1913. A year later, the quarry operation was improved with the introduction of a used Vulcan steam-shovel that moved on railroad tracks and eliminated the need for hand-loading the quarry cars. These cars would soon be replaced by larger side dump cars, and the mules were replaced by a small steam locomotive. Under Wulf, Monarch's power plant was also upgraded. In 1914 and 1915, six of eight boilers were connected to rotary kilns, thus allowing them to make use of waste heat and making them more efficient and economical to run. In the second half of the 1910s, Monarch replaced its original nine mills with newer equipment and open cement bins were replaced by six 70-foot high cement storage silos.

As sales grew in the 1920s, improvements to the physical plant continued. The company had been relying on direct current provided by four steam engines. In 1920, they were superseded by a 1,500 kilowatt General Electric-built turbine-powered generator producing alternating current. The conversion to alternating current would not be completed until 1923, and by the end of the decade, as the demand for power increased, the company installed a 4,000 kilowatt turbine and generator. Also in 1920, a pair of small crushers were replaced with a 42-inch Allis-Chalmers gyrator and a Williams hammermill. Throughout the decade, Monarch added more cement storage silos, six that were 70-feet high and another ten that were 90-feet high. In addition, the company erected six rock and shale storage silos in the milling department.

With the advent of the Depression of the 1930s, expansion at the Monarch plant was brought to a halt. The company also underwent a change in leadership. In October 1934, Henry Wulf died, and a few months later, in January 1935, Kreitzer died as well. Succeeding Wulf as president was Fred H. Rhodes, who had been corporate secretary since the 1913 reincorporation and was named treasurer as well in 1917. Replacing Kreitzer as vice-president was Wulf's son, Walter H. Wulf, who was also Kreitzer's son-in-law. The younger Wulf had been involved in the Monarch operation since moving to Humboldt when he was 14. During the summers while he attended college, he learned the business from the marketing side, going from town to town by train to sell the company's cement, and he also did his best to collect on past due accounts. After college, he joined Monarch, serving as a foreman and then working his way up through the management ranks. He replaced Rhodes as president of the company in March 1945.

Key Dates:

1907: The Monarch Portland Cement Company is formed.
1913: Monarch Portland is reorganized as The Monarch Cement Company by Henry Wulf.
1934: Wulf dies.
1935: Wulf's son, Walter Wulf, becomes the company's president.
1969: Walter Wulf gives up his position as president and remains as chairman for another 30 years.
1997: Walter Wulf, Jr., represents the third generation to lead Monarch.
2001: Walter Wulf dies at age of 101.

Prosperity and Improvements: Postwar Era to the 21st Century

World War II stimulated the U.S. economy and led to a postwar boom, especially in housing, that greatly benefited Monarch. Demand for cement soon outstripped the company's capacity, leading to eight years of upgrades, the first improvements in the physical plant in nearly 20 years. In 1948, a massive kiln, measuring 11 feet by 230 feet, was erected, and two new large boilers were installed. Another kiln of the same design was added in 1951, and new waste heat boilers were placed into service. In 1954, Monarch added a new shale crushing and drying plant, and a year later a new 9,375 kilowatt GE turbine and generator, along with the old 5,000 kilowatt generator, was installed in a new power plant building. All told, the company spent more than $4 million on improvements during this period, and the plant capacity increased to 2.25 million barrels per year. Over the course of the next dozen years, Monarch spent another $12 million on capital upgrades, which included the installation of a third kiln and waste heat boiler combination, new mills, and another dozen storage silos. As a result, annual plant capacity increased to three million barrels.

In April 1969, Walter Wulf turned over the presidency of the company to Charles L. Fussman, who oversaw further improvements to the operation during the 1970s. Wulf stayed on as chairman of the board. The company constructed three new 100-foot high cement storage silos in 1970. Over the next two years, two of the kilns were replaced by a 12-foot-by-165 foot kiln with a four-stage preheater. The third kiln was now operated on a standby basis. An F.L. Smidth single pass Ball mill with a 1250 horsepower motor and symetro drive was also installed. A second kiln equipment with a four-stage preheater was installed in 1974. The result was a much more efficient operation, as raw materials were now preheated before entering the kiln using the kiln's waste heat, which was further utilized by the roller mill. In this way, the company was able to make use of all but 200 degrees of the operation's available heat. These improvements in the 1970s came at a price of $16.4 million.

A new president, Jack R. Callahan, was installed in August 1980. Like his predecessors, he oversaw continued growth in Monarch's business and added to the plant's capabilities. During the early 1980s, the company introduced a new economical roller mill, which was able to turn raw materials into powder, grind them together, and then dry them with waste heat from the

kilns. The next step in the evolution of the physical plant came in the 1990s as the company sought to automate as much of the work as possible. Computer-controlled process control technology were applied to the preheater kilns, roller mill, and all finish mills. The preheater kilns were also set up to dispose of used tires, thus improving Monarch's reputation as a good corporate citizenship by serving as a state-approved tire disposal site while also taking advantage of the fuel potential of a material that was previously thrown away. As a result of improvements over the course of several decades, Monarch increased its cement capacity from 282,000 tons in 1913 to more than 850,000 at the end of the 20th century.

Monarch enjoyed strong growth during the 1990s, starting the decade around $50 million in annual sales and in 1997 realizing $91.8 million. In 1997, Callahan stepped down as president and was succeeded by a third generation of the Wulf family, Walter H. Wulf, Jr. His father, well into his nineties, remained as chairman of the board for a couple more years. He would die in 2001 at the age of 101. Demand was so strong for cement that the company was forced to supplement its production in 1998 by purchasing clinker from overseas. Sales topped the $100 million mark for the first time in company history, but higher sales costs caused Monarch's net income, which had exceeded $10 million in 1996 and 1997, to slip to $9.7 million in 1998. Sales continue to trend upward through 2002, when the company recorded $134.6 million in revenues, but net income dipped below $6 million. A downturn in the economy caught up to Monarch in 2003, when sales fell to $122 million and net income to $3.8 million. The economy began to recover in the Midwest in 2004, resulting in a rebound on the sales side of the ledger, $145.1 million on the year, but net income was a disappointing $2.6 million. Nevertheless, the future demand held promise for Monarch, prompting the company to install a new coal firing system to save money on fuel. Approaching its 100th anniversary, Monarch was well positioned to continue its history of prosperity.

Principal Subsidiaries

Beaver Lake Concrete, Inc.; Concrete Enterprises, Inc.; Concrete Materials, Inc.; Kansas Sand and Concrete, Inc.; Monarch Cement of Iowa, Inc.

Principal Competitors

Buzzi Unicem USA Inc.; Holcim Ltd.; Lafarge North America Inc.

Further Reading

Couch, Mark, "Star 50 Profile: Monarch Cement Co.," *Kansas City Star*, May 14, 2001.
"Fifty Men at Work; Monarch Portland Cement Company a Busy Place," *Allen County Herald*, March 9, 1908, p. 1.
"The Monarch Plant; What Has Been Accomplished in a Year's Work," *Humboldt Daily Herald*, June 14, 1909, p. 1.
"Monarch Progress; Buildings Are Assuming Definite Proportions," *Allen County Herald*, August 24, 1908, p. 1.
"More Men at Work; Monarch Portland Increasing Its Force," *Allen County Herald*, March 16, 1908, p. 1.
"100 Men Employed; Monarch Portland Cement Company Increases Force," *Allen County Herald*, April 13, 1908, p. 1.

—Ed Dinger

Natural Ovens Bakery, Inc.

P.O. Box 730
Manitowoc, Wisconsin 54221-0730
U.S.A.
Telephone: (920) 758-2500
Toll Free: (800) 558-3535
Fax: (920) 758-2671
Web site: http://www.naturalovens.com

Private Company
Incorporated: 1977 as Natural Ovens of Manitowoc, Inc.
Employees: 307
Sales: $30 million (2003 est.)
NAIC: 311810 Bread and Bakery Product Manufacturing;
311812 Commercial Bakeries; 722310 Food Service
Contractors

Natural Ovens Bakery, Inc. produces nutrient-rich baked goods. Its products are full of whole grains and free of preservatives and are fortified with ingredients like flaxseed oil. The company maintains a Farm and Food Museum at its Manitowoc, Wisconsin headquarters.

Origins

Paul A. Stitt began his career with New Jersey's Tenneco Chemicals after earning a master's degree in biochemistry from the University of Wisconsin in 1969. Thus commenced a period of frustration and disillusionment with the food industry.

Stitt opposed the use of ''appetite enhancers''—additives such as fat, salt, caffeine, and sugar, all intended to increase consumption rather than impart nutrients. ''If you make it nutritional, then people eat less,'' he later lamented to the *Christian Science Monitor.* ''And to a food company, that's harmful.'' After a subsequent stint at a Quaker Oats lab in Manitowoc, Wisconsin, Stitt set out on his own.

Author Michelle Stacey features Natural Ovens in a chapter on ''designer foods'' in her 1994 book, *Consumed: Why Americans Love, Hate, and Fear Food.* Paul Stitt told her he bought a 5,000-square-foot bakery in 1976 to complement a cheese store

he had acquired the previous year. He later told the *Milwaukee Journal Sentinel* he started the business with just $5,000 and no recipes; the store began with five employees. Natural Ovens of Manitowoc, Inc. was registered on March 21, 1977.

The health-conscious Stitt soon cut the sugar-laden cinnamon rolls from the menu at the bakery. This proved unpopular with the citizenry and with Stitt's original bankers, who canceled his loan, he told Stacey.

The bakery stayed well ahead of nutritional trends, eschewing partially hydrogenated fats or trans-fatty acids from the beginning. Stitt also began fortifying the breads with more than a dozen vitamins and minerals. He was chiefly concerned with obesity and heart problems.

Stitt's wife Barbara (née Reed) later came on board as vice-president. A former probation officer, she developed a specialty researching the effect of different foods on behavior. (The *Wall Street Journal* ran a story on her work in June 1977.) The two met at a natural foods conference in 1980 and were married two years later.

Flaxseed Oil Added in the Mid-1980s

Stitt became an early proponent of flaxseed oil, which was rich in omega-3 fatty acids and other health-promoting components. Before it could be made suitable for baking, it had to be treated with zinc to keep it from decomposing too rapidly. In 1989 Stitt patented a method of stabilizing flaxseed oil. (This led to the formation of another business, Natural Enterprises, Inc., later called Essential Nutrient Research Corporation, or ENRECO, and Natural Ovens Holdings, Inc.). Large food companies soon began buying Stitt's flaxseed oil for research purposes.

A new 28,000-square-foot plant was constructed outside of town in 1988. Its front entrance featured a 15-foot-high stained glass window depicting agricultural scenes. A small farm next door dated back to 1910 and housed Stitt's collection of vintage farm machinery as well as livestock.

Natural Ovens ended the decade with sales of about $6.5 million a year, according to *Forbes,* which reported that its profit

Company Perspectives:

Our mission is to make the best tasting and most nutritious whole grain breads. We use only the highest quality ingredients including natural wheat and fortified flax, which is high in Omega-3. All our products are certified Kosher, Pareve by the Chicago Rabbinical Council-Pas Yisroel. Our goal is to help you live a long, healthy life by eating our healthy breads. From our ovens in Manitowoc, here's to a healthier you.

Key Dates:

1976: Paul Stitt buys a Manitowoc, Wisconsin bakery.
1986: Stitt begins baking with flaxseed oil.
1988: A new plant opens outside Manitowoc.
1989: Stitt patents a method of stabilizing flaxseed oil.
1997: The company begins outreach in public school cafeterias.
2003: The low-carb trend forces closure of the new Valparaiso, Indiana plant.

margins were unimpressive at the time—just 1 percent—in spite of the premium retail prices (then up to $3) the loaves commanded.

Functional Foods in the 1990s

In the early 1990s, reported Stacey, Natural Ovens had 130 employees and annual sales of $7 million. By 1993, it was baking 20,000 loaves a day, with sales of $9 million a year. Paul Stitt drew a modest salary and helped others break into the bread business.

The National Cancer Institute was undergoing a five-year, $21 million study of phytochemicals, or cancer-fighting compounds, including flaxseed oil. Stitt was developing "functional foods" geared toward preventing specific illnesses, such as cancer. The Food and Drug Administration (FDA), however, prevented him from making such claims on product packaging.

The company had a line of 15 different breads. New products included Seven Grain Herb Bread, which included, according to product literature, almost 200 cancer-fighting compounds. Other items also were packed with goodness. Garden Bread included carrots and sunflower meal. Blueberries made up more than one-quarter of the Blueberry-Oat muffins. Stitt also had formulated drink mixes and energy bars.

School lunch programs were the Stitts' next target for reform. Fat- and sugar-laced junk food had displaced fruits and vegetables. Natural Ovens started with Wisconsin's Appleton Central Alternative High School, donating bagels and underwriting the healthy eating program at a cost of $30,000 a year for the first five years. This program was later featured in the film, *Super Size Me.*

Natural Ovens practiced nutrition in its own cafeteria, which was stocked with fresh fruits and baked items. The healthy food helped employees work together productively, Paul Stitt told the *Washington Post.* "We have a very low sickness rate, very low absenteeism, very low turnover."

Counting Carbs After 2000

By the end of the 1990s, Natural Ovens was supplying 1,300 supermarkets in the Midwest. It had more than 200 employees. In 2001, the company was renamed Natural Ovens Bakery, Inc. Every day it was baking about 25,000 loaves of bread, 15 varieties in all, plus 50,000 bagels and thousands of rolls, muffins, and cookies, noted *Snack Food & Wholesale Bakery.* Its annual shopping list included 500,000 pounds of flaxseed. Sales were $22 million a year.

In September 2002, the company opened its second plant, a $9.4 million, 60,000-square-foot bakery in Valparaiso, Indiana. This facilitated expansion to the east and south. It was entering the East Coast retail market with frozen bread. At the same time, the fresh bread market in the Midwest was becoming more competitive as it attracted the attention of big players such as Sara Lee Corp.

By putting a domed roof on the Valparaiso facility, Natural Ovens created a plant unique to U.S. baking and manufacturing. The two-story building did not have internal columns or walls, to promote open communication among employees.

Natural Ovens began rolling out low-carb breads in 2003 to meet the challenge of the popular Atkins diet. These were soon accounting for 30 percent of sales. The higher margins on the low-carb bread allowed them to be shipped further across the country, Stitt told the *Chicago Tribune.*

Unfortunately, the low-carb trend managed to derail two dozen years of double-digit growth. The new plant at Valparaiso closed after little more than a year, a victim of slow sales.

The company's focus on innovation and wellness was reflected in a new health insurance program that rewarded employees with annual stipends for meeting preset health goals. In late 2003 Natural Ovens became the launch customer for Healthy X Change, a new medical insurance program that emphasized fitness, nutrition, and alternative medicine.

In spite of the low-carb setback, the company was planning to expand distribution of frozen bread to the East Coast and West Coast. At the time, Natural Ovens was supplying 1,200 grocery stores in 18 states, and shipped a small amount of product via UPS.

Principal Subsidiaries

Essential Nutrient Research Corporation (ENRECO).

Principal Competitors

Breadsmith Franchising, Inc.; George Weston Bakeries Inc.; Great Harvest Bread Company; Rudi's Organic Bakery, Inc.; Sara Lee Corporation.

Further Reading

Alexander, Delroy, "Bread Industry Struggles Amid Low-Carb Diets, Changing Tastes," *Chicago Tribune,* December 30, 2003.

Andrews, Edmund L., "Patents: Using Flax to Get Benefit of Fish Oils," *New York Times,* August 19, 1989, p. 1.

"Coming Full Circle: A Domed Roof Is Just One of the Many Innovations Natural Ovens Introduced at Its New Bakery in Valparaiso, Ind.," *Snack Food & Wholesale Bakery,* July 2003, p. 25.

Daykin, Tom, "How Low Can You Go on Carbs? Bakers, Brewers Contend with Latest Diets," *Milwaukee Journal Sentinel,* March 30, 2004, p. 1D.

——, "Natural Ovens Cited for Using Misleading Labels," *Milwaukee Journal Sentinel,* April 23, 2003, p. 2D.

Dillin, John, "Crusader with a Wooden Spoon," *Christian Science Monitor,* January 20, 1994.

——, "Quality Breads on the Rise," *Christian Science Monitor,* January 21, 1994.

Dudek, Duane, "Weighing In on Eating and Obesity; Two New Films and a Book Dig In to America's Love/Hate Affair With Food," *Milwaukee Journal Sentinel,* May 23, 2004, p. 1L.

Erler, Susan, "New Valparaiso, Ind., Bakery Plant to Feature Preservative-Free Products," *Times* (Munster, Ind.), April 15, 2003.

——, "Valparaiso, Ind., Bakery Offers New Approach to Health Insurance," *Times* (Munster, Ind.), November 4, 2003.

Harris, John, "You Are What You Eat," *Forbes,* December 25, 1989, pp. 112ff.

Johnson, Mark, and John Fauber, "Lessons of Poor Eating Learned Early; Mixed Messages from Adults Fuel Explosion in Child Obesity," *Milwaukee Journal Sentinel,* July 7, 2003, p. 1A.

Lindner, Lawrence, "What's Cookin' at Work? Some Employers Find That the Road to Better Productivity Runs Through the Cafeteria," *Washington Post,* March 30, 1999, p. Z16.

"Natural Ovens to Build Plant in Indiana," *Milwaukee Journal Sentinel,* September 28, 2000, p. 2D.

"Natural Ovens Rolls Out Last Batch of Bread," *Times* (Munster, Ind.), March 11, 2005.

O'Neill, Molly, "Eating to Heal: Mapping Out New Frontiers," *New York Times,* February 7, 1990, p. C1.

Schellhardt, Timothy D., "Can Chocolate Turn You into a Criminal? Some Experts Say So! Food Allergies, Malnutrition Are Tied to Violent Acts; A Banana Leads to Blows!," *Wall Street Journal,* June 2, 1977.

Schultz, Martin, "Natural Feast," *Snack Food & Wholesale Bakery,* July 2002, pp. 18–21.

Stacey, Michelle, "Designer Foods: Making Breads with a Blueprint," *Consumed: Why Americans Love, Hate, and Fear Food,* New York: Simon & Schuster, 1994.

Stitt, Paul A., *Beating the Food Giants,* Natural Press, 1993.

——, *Fighting the Food Giants,* rev. ed., Natural Press, 1983.

——, *The Real Cause of Heart Disease Is Not Cholesterol,* Natural Press, 2003.

——, *The Secret Recipes of Natural Ovens,* Natural Press, 1983.

——, *Why Calories Don't Count,* 2nd ed., Contemporary Books, 1982.

——, *Why George Should Eat Broccoli,* Dougherty Co., 1990.

Turner, Stephanie, "Low-Carb Diets Mean More Dough," *Wisconsin State Journal* (Madison), January 31, 2004, p. A1.

—Frederick C. Ingram

New York Health Care, Inc.

1850 McDonald Avenue
Brooklyn, New York 11223
U.S.A.
Telephone: (718) 375-6700
Fax: (718) 375-1555
Web site: http://www.nyhc.com

Public Company
Incorporated: 1983
Employees: 1,929
Sales: $48.9 million (2004)
Stock Exchanges: Over the Counter
Ticker Symbol: BBAL
NAIC: 621610 Home Health Care Services

New York Health Care, Inc. derives all of its income by providing home healthcare services to New York City and surrounding counties in New York State and New Jersey. Since 2004, however, the company has embarked on a course that would divest this business in favor of concentrating on the activities of a wholly owned subsidiary, Bio Balance, developer of treatments for chronic gastrointestinal disorders in an effort to create a pure-play pharmaceutical company. New York Health Care is a public company, trading on a Pink Sheet basis since being delisted by the NASDAQ in 2004.

Company Founding in 1983

New York Health Care was founded in Brooklyn, New York, in 1983 by Jerry Braun. He was originally employed in the garment industry but turned his attention to the healthcare field where he believed there were greater opportunities. He launched the company as a staffing agency, providing nursing staff to area nursing homes. It proved to be a prosperous line of work, as the demand for nurses, especially quality ones, grew, and hospitals were forced to pay increasingly higher salaries. Later in the 1980s, however, the healthcare model began to change, with patient stays curtailed, resulting in the reduction of hospital staffs. In 1988 Braun transformed his business by acquiring National Medical Home Care, Inc., provider of home healthcare support services, with offices in Brooklyn, Queens Village, Rockville Centre, and Mount Vernon, New York. Braun bought the fixtures and equipment, but more important, he picked up National Medical's paraprofessional aide lists and roster of clients. New York Health Care was now in the home nursing business, operating out of three offices: Brooklyn, Hempstead in Westchester County, and Mount Vernon on Long Island.

By the early 1990s, after achieving steady growth, Braun was ready to expand the company. In 1992 New York Health Care opened a fourth office in Spring Valley, located in New York's Rockland County. A year later an office was opened in New York's Orange County in the town of Newburgh. Each of New York Health Care's five offices operated essentially as separate entities, with each responsible for its own recruitment, training, scheduling, and quality assurance programs. Also in 1993 New York Health Care broadened its business by adding a specialty division called "Special Deliveries," which provided home nursing services to women during pregnancy and after childbirth to both mother and newborn. For this unit the company recruited Neonatal Intensive Care Unit Nurses, Maternal/Newborn Registered Nurses, and Registered Nurses with at least two years of experience in maternal childcare. In other ways, New York Health Care adapted to the needs of the communities it served. For instance, it recruited Russian-speaking staff to serve Brooklyn's growing Russian neighborhoods, where many patients spoke little or no English. The company also recruited nurses and paraprofessionals fluent in Spanish and Yiddish and who were knowledgeable about the practices and requirements of keeping a Kosher home. Revenues approached $9 million in 1994 and reached $11.8 million in 1995, while net income during this period improved from $771,000 to more than $1.1 million.

In 1995 Braun and four other directors of New York Health Care formed and became the sole stockholders of a new company, Heart to Heart Health Care Services, Inc., to provide home healthcare services to northern New Jersey. Although technically a separate company, Heart to Heart relied on New York Health Care's personnel to provide payroll, data processing, and benefits management services, for which the start-up paid about $15,000 a year.

Company Perspectives:

Our mission is to provide comprehensive, cost-effective and competitively-priced quality home care services, that can allow patients to remain at home, in their communities.

Going Public in the Mid-1990s

Braun took New York Health Care public in 1996 to raise money to fuel further growth. With H.J. Meyers & Co. Inc. serving as underwriter, the company completed the offering in December 1996, raising $5 million. According to the company's prospectus, the money was earmarked for acquisitions, the opening of additional offices, expansion and upgrading of computer systems, and expansion of the pediatric services division, as well as for marketing and working capital. Revenues grew to $11.9 million in 1996, and the company recorded net income of $571,000.

The Special Deliveries Division added services in 1997 following the renewal and expansion of its contract with a major area HMO. Special Deliveries now offered home uterine monitoring and terbutaline pump therapy. Moveover, the division now packaged its perinatal support program for hypertension, diabetes, and preterm self-palpation, charging per episode rather than on an individual cost basis. This bundling approach saved money for the HMO and served to attract the business of other managed care companies, healthcare institutions, as well as traditional insurance companies. In 1997 Special Deliveries also reached an agreement with Biomedical Systems Corporation (BMS), a St. Louis-based medical monitoring and telecommunications company. Special Deliveries would supply the personnel trained to use the BMS equipment for managed care organizations and other providers who contracted with BMS. On another front, New York Health Care expanded its Westchester business, landing a contract with Hospice of Westchester to work jointly with White Plains Hospital Center and Visiting Nurse in Westchester to provide healthcare services to terminally ill hospice clients at home or in nursing homes.

New York Health Care flirted with expansion outside of the New York City metropolitan area in 1997. It announced in May that it had signed a letter of intent to acquire a Florida home health agency to gain a toehold in the growing market of the Southeast. But two months later, following the completion of due diligence, management scuttled the deal, electing instead to focus on the New York market. In keeping with this approach, New York Health Care formed another subsidiary in December 1997, NYHC Newco Paxxon, Inc., to purchase New Jersey-based Metro Healthcare Services, Inc., operator of paraprofessional home healthcare services in West Orange, Budd Lake, and Jersey City, New Jersey. Two months later, in February 1998, NYHC Newco acquired three additional Metro Health Care offices, located in Edison, Toms River, and Shrewsbury, New Jersey. At this point, New York Health Care elected to bring Heart to Heart into the fold to combine all of the New Jersey assets within the NYHC Newco subsidiary. One March 26, 1998, Heart to Heart was acquired from Braun and the other stockholders for $1.15 million in the form of a promissory note, to be paid off in installments over the next two years. Primarily

due to the addition of the New Jersey operations, New York Health Care's revenues grew from $13.2 million in 1997 to $20.2 million in 1998. Net income totaled $184,000 in 1997 and $341,000 in 1998.

During 1999 New York Health Care continued to add offices. In February NYHC Newco acquired the Shrewsbury, New Jersey, office of Staff Builders Services, Inc., primarily providing home healthcare services in central New Jersey. Then, in June 1999, NYHC Newco bought another Staff Builder office, this one located in Hackensack, serving Northern New Jersey. Finally, in October 1999, New York Health Care bought the Staff Builder operation in Manhattan, and the business was transferred to the established New York Health Care offices in the city.

Turning to Pharmaceuticals in the 2000s

Revenues totaled $23.8 million in 1999 and grew to $29.4 million in 2000. It was at this point that New York Health Care began to look in an entirely different direction, from home healthcare to dabbling in the pharmaceutical industry. In October 2001, it agreed to acquire a start-up company, The Bio Balance Corporation. It was incorporated as ''The Zig Zag Corp.'' in May 2001 and changed its name to Bio Balance shortly before the acquisition overture from New York Health Care. The company was engaged in research in Israel to develop ''probiotic'' technology for use in treating gastrointestinal diseases such as irritable bowel syndrome and forms of chronic diarrhea and inflammatory bowel disease in both animals and humans. Probiotics are live microorganisms or microbial mixtures that have the potential of stimulating the growth of healthy bacteria inside a host and restoring the microbial balance to address gastrointestinal disorders. Bio Balance was already working on its first product in Israel, an oral liquid called Bactrix, later renamed Probactrix. It consisted of a nontoxic strain of E.coli preserved in a vegetable extract formulation. The plan was to market it as a medical food, rather than a drug. In this way, the company avoided the more stringent requirements facing a drug. Classifying the product as a food ingredient, Bio Balance could self-determine that Probactrix was ''generally recognized as safe.'' A potential major use for the product was in treating AIDS-related diarrhea caused by a reaction to antibiotics and irritable bowel syndrome suffered by AIDS patients. Company researchers also would pursue the development of a prescription drug for AIDS-related diarrhea. The upside for the technology was tremendous, with the company estimating that the market for an effective irritable bowel syndrome treatment could top $1 billion a year. For a small company like New York Health Care, which posted sales of $34.3 million in 2001, the allure proved irresistible.

The Bio Balance transaction was not consummated until January 2003, in what became a reverse merger. Technically, although New York Health Care acquired Bio Balance, it was the start-up business that was the key player in the deal, as revealed by the company's new ticker symbol, BBAL. Following a reverse stock split the pre-merger shareholders of Bio Balance owned about 90 percent of the company. In conjunction with the merger, Bio Balance privately placed more than $6 million in stock, the proceeds of which were earmarked for its operations. In essence, New York Health Care's function was to

Key Dates:

1983:   Jerry Braun forms the company as a nursing staffing agency.
1988:   The company switches to the home healthcare business.
1996:   An initial public offering of stock is made.
2001:   Bio Balance is incorporated.
2003:   Bio Balance and the company merge.
2005:   New Jersey Health Care assets are sold.

provide cash flow to support Bio Balance while it developed a revenue-generating business.

Although it had been in operation for 20 years, New York Health Care was little known on Wall Street until the summer of 2003. Priced at $2 in early July, the company's stock topped $3.25 a month later, prompting a notice in *Business Week*. The company attributed investor interest to excellent trial results on AIDS patients at The Moscow Center of HIV. That reasoning was thrown into doubt a few months later when a former Bio Balance director, Paul Stark, and a company consultant were indicted by the U.S. Attorney's Office, accused of trying to inflate the price of New York Health Care stock by bribing a hedge fund manager to buy 500,000 shares. In reality the manager was an undercover FBI agent. The company emphasized that the indictment made no mention that the price of the stock had actually been manipulated and following an internal investigation concluded that none of its current officers, directors, or employees were involved in or knew about the scheme.

In 2003 New York Health Care recorded revenues of more than $45 million, but because of the cash requirements of Bio Balance, the company lost $22 million. The company took the next step in its transition from healthcare provider to biotech in August 2004 when Jerry Braun stepped down as CEO, replaced by Bio Balance's president Dennis O'Donnell, a 20-year veteran of the pharmaceutical industry. At the same time, the company announced that it would sell off its home healthcare business in order to become a dedicated pharmaceutical company, and it intended to change its name to Bio Balance Holdings Inc. Three weeks later, the company reached an agreement with Braun and Jacob Rosenberg, a New York Health Care director since 1983, to acquire the healthcare business for $4 million. Yet, several months later the pair had still not raised the necessary money. Instead, in April 2005, New York Health Care divested its New Jersey healthcare business to Accredited Health Services, Inc. It was a significant step in restructuring the company as a dedicated pharmaceutical company. When New York Health Care would sell off its remaining home healthcare assets and whether Bio Balance would ever achieve the kind of growth and profitability management envisioned remained open questions.

Principal Subsidiaries

Bio Balance Corporation.

Principal Competitors

Apria Healthcare Group Inc.; Gentiva Health Service, Inc.; North Shore-Long Island Jewish Health System.

Further Reading

Citrano, Virginia, ''Facing Pataki Budget Cuts, Home-Health Firm Checks Vital Sings,'' *Crain's New York Business,* May 8, 1995, p. 28.
Marcial, Gene G., ''Good Test Results at New York Health Care,'' *Business Week,* August 25, 2003, p. 154.
''New York Health Care Divest Home Heathcare Business,'' *Health & Medicine Week,* August 9, 2004, p. 168.

—Ed Dinger

Nigerian National Petroleum Corporation

NNPC Towers
Herbert Macaulay Way, Central Business District
Garki Abuja
Nigeria
Telephone: (234) 9 523-9141
Fax: (234) 9 234-0029
Web site: http://www.nnpc-nigeria.com

State-Owned Company
Incorporated: 1971 as Nigerian National Oil Corporation
Employees: 15,000
Sales: $2.6 billion (2005)
NAIC: 211111 Crude Petroleum and Natural Gas
    Extraction; 211112 Natural Gas Liquid Extraction;
    213111 Drilling Oil and Gas Wells

The Nigerian National Petroleum Corporation (NNPC) is the holding company that oversees the Nigerian state's interests in the country's oil industry. The company is composed of four main operating units: Refineries and Petrochemicals; Exploration and Production; Finance and Accounts; and Corporate Services. Oil production is the cornerstone of Nigeria's economy—the country ranks as the largest oil producer in Africa. A total of 95 percent of the country's foreign exchange revenue stems from NNPC's operations. Oil operations account for 20 percent of the country's gross domestic product and NNPC is responsible for nearly 65 percent of the government's budgetary revenues. After 16 years of military rule, democratically elected Olusegun Obasanjo took office in 1999. Since that time he has worked to reform the oil and gas industry in the country.

Early History of Oil Industry in Nigeria

Oil was first discovered in Nigeria in 1908, and exploration proceeded during the 1930s in the form of the Shell-BP Petroleum Development Company of Nigeria Ltd. (Shell-BP), under the control of Shell and British Petroleum (BP). Commercial exploitation of the country's reserves, however, did not begin until the late 1950s. The Nigerian government introduced its first regulations governing the taxation of oil industry profits in 1959 whereby profits would be split 50–50 between the government and the oil company in question, and the industry grew during the 1960s as export markets were developed, predominantly in the United Kingdom and Europe. By the mid-1960s, Nigeria began to consider ways in which the resources being exploited by Western oil companies could better be harnessed to the country's development, and formulated its first agreement for taking an equity stake in one of the companies producing there, the Nigerian Agip Oil Company, jointly owned by Agip of Italy and Phillips of the United States. The option to take up an equity stake—in effect the first step toward the creation of the NNPC—was not, however, exercised until April 1971.

By 1971, other factors were pushing the Nigerian government toward taking the stakes in the Western companies that would constitute the basis of the NNPC's holdings. One was the Biafran war of secession, which began in 1967. The support given by one French oil company to Biafra, within whose territory some two-thirds of the country's then-known oil reserves were located, led the federal government to question the contribution of the foreign oil companies to the country's development. So, too, did the companies' unimpressive record in assisting transfer of technology, in social development, and in the employment of indigenous staff. The overriding factor was probably Nigeria's decision to join OPEC in July 1971, obliging the government to take significant stakes in the companies producing in the country.

Formation of Nigerian National Oil Corporation in 1971

This combination of pressures led to the formation of the Nigerian National Oil Corporation (NNOC) on April 1, 1971. The NNOC acquired a 33.33 percent stake in the Nigerian Agip Oil Company and 35 percent in Safrap, the Nigerian arm of the French company Elf. After Nigeria joined OPEC, NNOC acquired 35 percent stakes in Shell-BP, Gulf, and Mobil, on April 1, 1973. Also in 1973 it entered into a production-sharing agreement with Ashland Oil. On April 1, 1974, stakes in Elf, Agip/Phillips, Shell-BP, Gulf, and Mobil were increased to 55 percent and, on May 1, 1975, the NNOC acquired 55 percent of Texaco's operations in Nigeria.

Company Perspectives:

The Nigerian National Petroleum Corporation (NNPC) is the driving force behind the economic development of Nigeria, providing fuel and feedstock for the nation's industrial facilities and meeting the energy needs of individual customers and commercial enterprises. NNPC is the major revenue earner for the nation. NNPC's operations span the length and breadth of Nigeria and involve the entire spectrum of the petroleum industry.

The NNOC had been established under the terms of the government's Decree no. 18 of 1971. Its brief was to "participate in all aspects of petroleum including exploration, production, refining, marketing, transportation, and distribution." More specifically, the corporation was given the task of training indigenous workers; managing oil leases over large areas of the country; encouraging indigenous participation in the development of infrastructure for the industry; managing refineries, only one of which was operational at this time; participating in marketing and ensuring price uniformity across the domestic market; developing a national tanker fleet; constructing pipelines; and investigating allied industries, such as fertilizers.

This was an ambitious set of objectives, several of which were only just beginning to be realized in the 1990s. The problem that the NNOC faced from its inception was that of attempting to manage a highly complex industry without adequate technical and financial resources, problems that were to be dramatically illustrated several times during its subsequent history.

The NNOC had limited powers as a public corporation. It could sue and be sued, hold or purchase assets, and enter into partnerships. It could not borrow funds or dispose of assets without the specific approval of the commissioner of mines and power, and any surplus funds had to be disposed of at the commissioner's discretion, subject to the approval of the ruling Federal Executive Council. Any activities beyond the scope of Decree no. 18 required government approval, and the government was well represented on the NNOC's board, which was chaired by the permanent secretary of the Ministry of Mines and Power. Other board members included representatives from the ministries of Finance and of Economic Development and Planning, the director of Petroleum Resources in the Ministry of Mines and Power, the general manager of NNOC, and three other representatives with special knowledge of the industry. Thus, from the very start, a body that was seen as crucial to the future prosperity of the nation was subject to close government control, a feature of its operation that has remained throughout its history.

The NNOC operated a number of subsidiaries during the 1970s, including those in exploration and production, refining and petrochemicals, distribution and marketing, transportation, and equipment and supplies. Its success was perhaps most marked in the export field. Boosted by the sharp price rises that followed the first oil shock of 1973, Nigeria saw its oil export earnings rise from NGN 219 million in 1970 to NGN 10.6 billion in 1979, thereby achieving an enviable status as the first tropical African country successfully to exploit its oil reserves.

Becoming a Corporation in 1977

The NNOC was reconstituted as the Nigerian National Petroleum Corporation (NNPC) on April 1, 1977, just six years after it had been set up. One reason for the change may have been the operating failures of the 1970s, which became publicly known at the time of the 1980 Crude Oil Sales Tribunal. This investigation revealed that, for instance, from 1975 to 1978 the NNOC and NNPC had failed to collect some 182.95 million barrels of their equity share of oil being produced by Shell, Mobil, and Gulf—with potential revenue estimated to be in excess of $2 billion. This situation had arisen because NNOC was unable to find buyers for its oil at the price it wanted. It had, however, paid the full share of operating costs to the producers during the period of deemed operation. An additional revelation was that, until forced to do so by the Tribunal, NNOC had not produced audited accounts from 1975 onward.

The NNPC felt the brunt of the Oil Sales Tribunal investigations only three years after it was set up. While some of the criticisms related to events that had occurred before the change in name, the NNPC's practices undoubtedly bore more than a passing resemblance to those of its predecessor. Like the NNOC, the NNPC began life essentially as a holding company. Decree no. 33 vested the assets and liabilities of the NNOC in the NNPC, and conferred on the new body responsibility for some functions of the Ministry of Mines and Power. NNPC also had some additional commercial freedom as the ceiling on contracts that it could award rose 50-fold and it was granted limited borrowing powers. Its board structure was similar to the NNOC's, although the federal commissioner for petroleum replaced the permanent secretary of mines and power as chairman. Judging by the inefficiencies in its record-keeping and its error in overstocking in 1978 in anticipation of oil price rises, greater freedom did not bring with it a greater commercial astuteness.

Also established by Decree no. 33 as part of the NNPC was the Petroleum Inspectorate, which was given responsibility for issuing licenses for various activities, for enforcing the Oil Pipelines Act and the Petroleum Decrees, and for other duties. The chief executive of the division was nevertheless free from control by the NNPC board and reported to the commissioner for petroleum.

In line with the objectives of the government's 1977 Indigenization Decree, the NNPC's holdings in the oil industry operations in Nigeria increased significantly on July 1, 1979, when its stakes in the Nigerian businesses of the following companies were raised to 60 percent: Elf, Agip, Gulf, Mobil, Texaco, and Pan Ocean. NNPC's stake in the Shell venture was raised to 80 percent on August 1, 1979, after BP lost its 20 percent stake following disagreements with the Nigerian government over South Africa. Later that same year a number of accusations originating in the magazine *Punch*, alleging various forms of misappropriation, broke over the corporation, prompting the newly installed civilian President Alhaji Shagari to broadcast to the nation and establish the tribunal that uncovered the lax management practices referred to previously.

Problems Leading to Reforms in the 1980s

A further setback to the reputation of the Nigerian oil industry occurred at the start of 1980 with the Funiwa-5 incident. A

Key Dates:

1908: Oil is discovered in Nigeria.

1971: Nigeria decides to join OPEC; Nigerian National Oil Corp. (NNOC) is created.

1977: NNOC becomes Nigerian National Petroleum Corp. (NNPC).

1981: NNPC decentralizes into nine subsidiaries.

1999: Nigeria adopts a new constitution; democratically elected president Olusegun Obasanjo is inaugurated.

2003: The government begins to deregulate fuel prices and announces that its four major oil refineries will eventually be privatized.

2005: The company signs a $1 billion contract with Chevron Texaco Nigeria to construct the Floating, Production, Storage, and Offloading Vessel (FPSO) for the Agbami deep offshore oil field.

14-day blowout at an offshore well 60 percent owned by NNPC, but operated by Texaco, spilled 146,000 barrels and may have been responsible for the deaths of 180 people and illnesses among a further 3,000.

The outcome of the Oil Sales Tribunal was a series of reforms designed to decentralize the NNPC. Nine subsidiaries were established in 1981: the Nigerian Petroleum Exploration and Exploitation Company; the Nigerian Petroleum Refining Company, Kaduna Ltd.; the Nigerian Petroleum Refining, Company, Warri Ltd.; the Nigerian Petroleum Refining Company, Port Harcourt Ltd.; the Nigerian Petroleum Products Pipelines and Depots Company Ltd.; the Nigerian Petro Chemicals Company; the Nigerian Gas Company Ltd.; the Nigerian Petroleum Marine Transportation Company Ltd.; and the Petroleum Research and Engineering Company Ltd. The decentralization of Nigeria's three refineries, two of which had been built in the late 1970s and early 1980s, was intended to promote competition and the establishment of this number of subsidiaries was designed to instill a more commercial approach in a more diversified corporation. The goal of diversification was, however, one that the NNPC was slow to realize.

The 1980s did not see an end to close government control and to controversy over the performance of the NNPC. The oil sector took a beating in the 1982 oil glut, when the oil companies' offensive against OPEC targeted Nigeria as the weakest of the producing nations. There were self-inflicted problems as well. Once again, management of the corporation was tainted by scandal, this time involving the former Petroleum Resources Minister Tam David-West, who was jailed at the end of 1990 for his part in another dispute over foreign oil companies. David-West's bad relations with the government were partly responsible for the imposition of direct control of the NNPC by the Ministry of Petroleum Resources between 1986 and 1989. Relations with the foreign oil companies were marked by the 1986 Memorandum of Understanding, which set a profit limit of $2 per barrel.

The end of the 1980s saw a number of initiatives that had the potential to see the NNPC established on a more commercially oriented footing. In March 1988, another new structure was

unveiled for the corporation, described by Nigerian President General Ibrahim Babangida as establishing the NNPC as a "financially autonomous" and "commercially integrated" oil company. Petroleum Resources Minister Rilwanu Lukman defined three areas of responsibility for the corporation—corporate services, operations, and petroleum investment management services—and 11 subsidiary companies: the Nigerian Petroleum Development Company, the Warri Refining and Petrochemicals Company, the Kaduna Refining and Petrochemicals Company, the Pipeline and Products Marketing Company, the Hydrocarbon Services of Nigeria Company, the Engineering Company of Nigeria, the Nigerian Gas Development Company, the LNG Company, the Port Harcourt Refining Company, the Eleme Petrochemicals Company, and the Integrated Data Services Company. At the same time, a new sales policy was introduced, eliminating middlemen and setting out three types of purchasers to which the NNPC could sell its products: joint venture producing companies, foreign refineries in which Nigeria has a holding, and indigenous and foreign firms exploring in Nigeria. Aret Adams was appointed as the group managing director and, in February 1989, a new board was constituted, headed by Lukman.

The determination to eradicate subsidies to NNPC and to have it function commercially, rather than as a revenue-raising and development corporation, was apparent in the decision in June 1989 to sell 20 percent of its holding in the Shell joint venture. NNPC reduced its holding to 60 percent, selling 10 percent to Shell and 5 percent apiece to Elf and Agip, in a deal that may have netted the corporation as much as $2 billion. The money raised from the equity sale was to underpin the expansion in reserves (to 20 billion barrels a day) and in output (to 2.5 million barrels a day), to which Nigeria was committed up to 1995. These targets, however, were likely to require the divestment of further holdings to raise cash, and such divestments could not be assured in the uncertain political future faced by Nigeria. As a 60 percent stakeholder, NNPC had persistent problems in raising its share of any development costs.

One positive development was the increasing involvement of the corporation in the development of Nigeria's gas resources. Having been granted a monopoly over gas transmission, the NNPC was well placed to participate in the gas industry. Its 60 percent holding in the LNG Company (Shell owned 20 percent, and Agip and Elf each owned 10 percent) was the springboard for an ambitious $2.5 billion liquefaction project. In addition, Nigeria's fourth refinery, at Eleme, was commissioned early in 1989 and provided the basis for the expansion of a petrochemicals and plastics industry during the 1990s. In its core activity of oil production, NNPC's partner Mobil was developing the large 500-million-barrel Oso oil field, and Nigeria stood to benefit from the environmental attractions of its low-sulfur oil product.

The period since 1988 was not entirely positive for the NNPC. The plan to market oil products through co-owned refineries overseas did not fully mature. Only one joint venture deal was signed in 1989, with Farmland Industries of the United States, enabling NNPC to make use of a 60,000-barrels-per-day refinery at Coffeyville in Kansas. This was a landlocked site, however, that was not entirely suitable for operations. Of greater concern was the strong possibility that the state did not relinquish its desire to exercise control over NNPC's operations. Managing director Adams and his counterpart at the LNG Company were suspended late in 1989, apparently for refusing to accept government appointees to the LNG Company. In April 1990, Thomas John took over as managing director.

Thus the NNPC entered the last decade of the century as a young company still trying to carve out an identity for itself, independent of political control, and still learning how to master the technological and commercial complexities of the oil industry. It did have a more developed diversification strategy than ever before in its history, however, and, for the moment, a government that was willing to dilute its holdings in the industry as the price for supporting the corporation's growth.

The Late 1990s and Beyond

Throughout most of the 1990s, Nigeria and NNPC dealt with civil unrest, political instability, border disputes, corruption at the highest levels, and poor governance. Even so, international oil companies looked to Nigeria as a lucrative investment opportunity related to upstream oil exploration. Especially attractive was the sedimentary basin of the Niger Delta, as well as the Anambra Basin, the Benue Trough, the Chad Basin, and the Benin Basin.

Although NNPC management had been promising changes for years, company efforts had been slow at best and many Nigerians looked at NNPC with disdain. New reforms, however, were on the horizon for the new millennium. After 16 years of military rule, Nigeria held democratic elections in 1999. Olusegun Obasanjo was elected president and immediately set out to reorganize the country's oil and gas sector. As part of his restructuring efforts, President Obasanjo placed a strong emphasis on natural gas development. At the time, most of the country's natural gas was being flared, a very wasteful and environmentally unfriendly process. As such, a mandate was set forth that called for the termination of gas flare, a focus on environmental cleanup, and the realization of economic gains from natural gas in both the import and export market so that gas revenues equaled oil revenues by 2010. Nigeria had secured a position as a significant exporter of natural gas through the Nigeria liquefied natural gas (LNG) Plant in Bonny by 2005. In December 2004, NNPC management set plans in motion to launch the West African Gas Pipeline, which would supply gas from Nigeria to West Africa including Ghana, Benin, and Togo.

In February 2005, the government set plans in motion to host a three-day public hearing in the capital city of Abuja. The hearing was designed to create changes in the oil industry that would bring about higher revenues and new jobs. In March of that year, the Hart Group was appointed to conduct a five-year audit of Nigeria's oil and gas operations. Another reform set forth was the hotly contested privatization of certain segments of the oil and gas industry. In 2003, the government began to deregulate fuel prices and announced that its four major oil refineries would be privatized. NNPC was slow to respond to this mandate, unsure of how privatization would affect its business.

Led by managing director Funsho Kupolokun, NNPC launched a series of job cuts in the early years of the new millennium. Massive layoffs began in 2003 and approximately 2,355 employees were let go in 2005. The company also made several key partnerships at this time. Working with Chevron Texaco and British Gas, NNPC developed a LNG project in the border town of Olokola. It was expected that the project would gross $57.4 billion in its lifetime. In February 2005, NNPC signed a $1 billion contract with Chevron Texaco Nigeria to construct the Floating, Production, Storage, and Offloading Vessel (FPSO) for the Agbami deep offshore oil field. The FPSO was expected to process 250,000 barrels per day of crude oil and 450 million standard cubic feet of gas per day.

Although NNPC looked to be on a positive path for the future, it continued to face issues related to civil unrest and corruption. Kupolokun faced a tough road ahead, but there were no doubts that NNPC would remain a fixture in Nigeria's oil and gas sector for years to come.

Principal Subsidiaries

Duke Oil Ltd.; Eleme Petrochemicals Company Ltd. (EPCL); Integrated Data Services Ltd. (IDSL); Kaduna Refining and Petrochemicals Company Ltd. (KRPC); National Engineering and Technical Company (NETCO); Nigerian Gas Company (NGC); Nigerian Petroleum Development Company Ltd. (NPDC); Pipelines and Products Marketing Company Ltd. (PPMC); Port Harcourt Refining and Petrochemicals Company Ltd. (PHRC); Warri Refining and Petrochemicals Company Ltd. (WRPC).

Principal Competitors

National Iranian Oil Company; Petróleos de Venezuela S.A.; Saudi Arabian Oil Company.

Further Reading

Ake, Claude, *The Political Economy of Nigeria,* London: Longman, 1985.
Mahtani, Dino, ''Hopes Pinned on Offshore Development,'' *Financial Times London,* April 26, 2005.
''Nigerian Economy Is Expected to Gross US$57.4 Billion,'' *Liquid Africa,* January 18, 2005.
''Nigeria's Oil and Gas Sector Faces Overhaul,'' *LPG World,* May 18, 2005.
''NNPC Sacks Over 2,000 Employees,'' *Weekly Petroleum Argus,* January 3, 2005.
Oduniyi, Mike, ''NNPC: Helping to Sustain Democracy,'' *All Africa,* June 1, 2005.
Onoh, J.K., *The Nigerian Oil Economy,* Beckenham: Croom Helm, 1983.
Pearson, Scott R., *Petroleum and the Nigerian Economy,* Stanford, Calif.: Stanford University Press, 1970.

—Graham Field
—update: Christina M. Stansell

Nippon Yusen Kabushiki Kaisha (NYK)

Yusen Building
3-2 Marunouchi 2-chome
Chiyoda-ku, Tokyo 100-0005
Japan
Telephone: (3) 3284-5151
Fax: (3) 3284-6361
Web site: http://www.nykline.com

Public Company
Incorporated: 1885 as Nippon Yusen Kaisha
Employees: 1,739
Sales: ¥1.6 trillion ($14.95 billion) (2005)
Stock Exchanges: Tokyo Osaka Nagoya
Ticker Symbol: 9101
NAIC: 483111 Deep Sea Freight Transportation; 488320
    Marine Cargo Handling; 488510 Freight
    Transportation Arrangement

Nippon Yusen Kabushiki Kaisha (NYK) is the largest marine transporter in Japan. The company has 615 vessels in its arsenal and provides liner service, tramps, specialized carriers, and tankers. Through nearly 500 subsidiaries, NYK also offers services related to terminal and harbor transport, cruise lines and travel, logistics services, tugboat operations, and air transport. Shipping accounts for just over 60 percent of company revenues while logistics brings in 20 percent. NYK's terminal and harbor transport, shipping-related services, cruise, and real estate operations are responsible for the remaining portion of revenues. The history of NYK's business operations can be divided into four periods. The first marks the company's establishment in 1885 and consolidation over the next decade. In the second, from the mid-1890s to around 1908, the company carried out an initial and rapid expansion of overseas lines. In the third, after the Russo-Japanese War of 1904 to 1905, NYK began to concentrate more exclusively on regular lines within conferences. This was a conservative strategy that lasted until the late 1950s, when the company started a comprehensive series of services, a move which led to the fourth period, one of diversification and expansion, that continued into the new millennium.

Early History

NYK was formed in 1885 through a merger between the shipping assets of Mitsubishi and the Kyodo Unyu Kaisha (KUK) or Union Transport Company. The Mitsubishi firm had been subsidized by the new Meiji government since 1875, while KUK was an amalgam of trading firms, local shipping enterprises, and government investment that had been motivated by Mitsubishi's increasing neglect of shipping in favor of outside investments, mostly in mining. NYK was initially a joint-stock company, with more than three-quarters of the steamships in Japan. It spent its first decade consolidating its finances and fleet under government subsidization and regulation. At first most of its routes were domestic. These became less profitable by the early 1890s because of competition from railways and another shipping firm with regional strength in western Japan, the Osaka Shosen Kaisha (OSK).

There were two main forces behind NYK's expansion in the 1890s. One was the support of the cotton-spinning industry, which enabled NYK to start a line to Bombay in 1893 to import raw cotton. This trade entailed a series of mutual guarantees among the cotton spinners, NYK, and trading firms such as Mitsui Bussan Kaisha, as well as credit to shippers from government-affiliated banks. The second impetus came from greatly increased subsidization made possible by the indemnity Japan received from China after the Sino-Japanese War. This encouraged NYK to establish lines to Australia and Europe, and to Seattle in the United States in 1896. The subsidies were particularly efficacious on the European line, where they gave the company bargaining power to overcome initial opposition from British firms to NYK's entrance into the Far Eastern Freight Conference, which operated between Europe and East Asia. Generally, lines to India could operate with little or no subsidization, whereas the Seattle line was more dependent. In contrast to the plentiful cargo of the outward-bound silk trade, the inward-bound trans-Pacific route was much less profitable because many manufactured goods from the eastern and southern United States went to Japan via the Suez Canal before the Panama Canal was opened. The European line generated about 40 percent of the company's revenue, and was strong on its eastward run because Japan imported much of its machinery. On the westward run, however, Japanese export freight was

Company Perspectives:

Through safe and dependable monohakobi *(transport), we contribute to the betterment of societies throughout the world as a comprehensive global logistics enterprise offering ocean, land, and air transportation.*

insufficient, and NYK came to depend on Chinese goods, which it loaded through feeder services in China, with trans-shipment at Shanghai.

This pattern of expansion changed after the Russo-Japanese War. Domestic business was hurt by recession and the emergence of many new shipowners that had sprung up with the government's wartime ship purchasing policy. Also, government colonial policy overseas, and hence closer supervision, made feeder lines more problematic, and stricter subsidy legislation encouraged withdrawal from many domestic services and concentration on regular transoceanic lines. This change in strategy occurred in the third period of NYK business. In the years prior to World War I, the company was reluctant to initiate new lines without subsidization unless it had a strong shippers' network. This was available on the Calcutta line, opened in 1911, but it lacked one on a proposed line through Panama, and the silk export trade remained on the northern route through Seattle. For this reason it held back until subsidies were received early in World War I.

Although NYK earned huge profits during World War I, with government controls over freight rates on subsidized lines, the company exploited the war less effectively than many independent Japanese operators, who carried on tramp services outside of government restrictions. The war and its aftermath opened up new lines for the company, to New York via Panama, to Liverpool, and to Hamburg. The central problem of the interwar years was how to operate this more geographically extensive network with steady growth in the face of increased competition from Japanese firms and the emergence of a much larger U.S. fleet.

The most famous strategic response of NYK during these years was its substantial investment in passenger services. In 1926 it purchased the Pacific operations of the Toyo Kisen Kaisha, which ran mostly to San Francisco, and proceeded to build a series of world-class passenger ships. Decades later, long after NYK had withdrawn from the passenger business, the company's popular identity was still associated with these vessels. Despite their popularity, the passenger business did represent a specialized version of the already cautious liner strategy and NYK fell behind OSK in introducing express ships on the New York line in the late 1920s. These ships were fast enough to effect a change in the silk trade, from the rail route via northern Pacific ports to the Panama route. NYK was slow to enter the tramp business also, remaining instead primarily within the conference systems. This presented two additional problems linked to the United States. One was U.S. antitrust law, which forbids exclusionary practices of cartels like the Far Eastern Freight Conference. The second was economic, and emerged through the restructuring of many shipping routes in response to

changing demand from U.S. trade and industry. With its cautious strategy NYK had difficulty responding to these changes, and by the eve of World War II it was being seriously challenged by OSK for pre-eminence among Japanese shipping firms.

Surviving the Postwar Era

During World War II NYK lost virtually all of its large oceangoing vessels, and its fleet fell from a peak of 866,000 gross tons in 1941 to 155,000 at the end of the war. Under the restrictive economic policies of the early U.S. occupation of Japan, large shipping firms like NYK had three strikes against them: severe limits on the size of ships to 6,000 tons, threats of dissolution under corporate deconcentration programs, and prohibitions against private trade. Nevertheless, in the most general sense, the war and occupation had a leveling effect on all shipping firms, and in the long run allowed NYK to recapture the strategic initiative that had been passing to OSK and others, like Mitsui Bussan's shipping division, before the war.

In the late occupation, the United States began some subsidization through its aid programs, the Korean War affected shipping recovery, and occupation authorities helped Japanese firms re-enter overseas lines and conferences. The event that triggered a transformation in NYK strategy, leading to the fourth period, was known as the "Mitsui Fight." This was an unsuccessful three-year attempt in the mid-1950s by NYK and OSK, in cooperation with European firms, to keep Mitsui Senpaku KK—Mitsui Bussan's former division—out of the Far Eastern Freight Conference. All firms suffered in this struggle, but Mitsui survived because of its strength in the tanker business which had supported it during the competition. This realization led NYK to undertake its strategy of diversification, a move accompanied by a restructuring of its business division into three major services—liners, trampers, and tankers.

It was some time, however, before NYK enjoyed the fruits of this strategic change. The 1950s were a difficult time for all Japanese shipping companies, and NYK operated without profit from 1956 to 1965. Two forms of financial consolidation emerged in the 1960s. First, the government encouraged consolidation in the industry, linking a policy of merger with a commitment to increased subsidization. Under this process, six groups emerged to constitute the core of the industry. NYK merged with Mitsubishi Kaiun KK, a former division within Mitsubishi Corporation, while rivals OSK and Mitsui Senpaku joined to form Mitsui O.S.K. Lines, Ltd. The second form of consolidation was technological. The government aided the shift to containerization by aiding firms that formed cooperative container groupings known as the space charter system. This was particularly effective on the Pacific. Earlier, NYK had worked with the Matson Navigation Company of San Francisco to introduce containers, and on the European line, along with Mitsui O.S.K., it established a container consortium with British and German firms called the Trio Group.

NYK also pursued its diversification by building tankers for both oil and ores and developing a fleet of car carriers. These promising beginnings, however, were partially offset by a series of shocks in the early 1970s. These included a revaluation of the Japanese yen and a major strike, both of which increased the cost of Japanese shipping. In addition, the oil crisis entailed

Key Dates:

1885: Nippon Yusen Kaisha (NYK) is formed through a merger between the shipping assets of Mitsubishi and the Kyodo Unyu Kaisha (KUK) or Union Transport Company.
1926: The company purchases the Pacific operations of the Toyo Kisen Kaisha, which runs mostly to San Francisco, California.
1975: NYK partial withdrawals from the tanker business.
1987: By now, the value of the yen has doubled against the U.S. dollar leading to major losses in income.
1998: NYK merges with Showa Line Ltd.
2003: A new management plan, NYK 21 "Forward 120," is launched.
2005: The company posts record profits and earnings.

both a short-term boom and long-term risk. Freight conferences were threatened by flag-preference policies of developing countries—the latter shipped goods on the ships of their own countries wherever possible—supported by the United Nations Conference on Trade and Development (UNCTAD), and rate-cutting wars on the Pacific undermined profitability there. During this era of crisis for the shipping industry, NYK displayed remarkable strategic adaptability. Its most decisive move was a partial withdrawal in 1975 from the tanker business, to the point of canceling contracts on some ships already under construction, even though this business was still very profitable. The wisdom of this decision was borne out in the 1980s when several Japanese firms that had continued to pursue the oil tanker boom went bankrupt. Meanwhile, NYK continued to diversify, ordering liquefied natural gas (LNG) tankers and a larger fleet of car carriers to service the growing exports of automobiles to North America. With its still profitable base in conferences systems, these moves gave NYK a balanced business profile that enabled it to remain the largest and generally most profitable Japanese shipping firm into the early 1990s.

During its first half-century, NYK's largest stockholders were the Mitsubishi *zaibatsu* (family-owned enterprise group) and the Imperial Household Ministry, whose shares had been transferred from the Finance Ministry in the late 1880s. Most of the leading managers in the early NYK came from Mitsubishi. During its era of expansion, however, because most of its shippers were outside the Mitsubishi *zaibatsu*, NYK was able to conduct a relatively autonomous management. As a ship purchaser, it also played an important role in the development of Mitsubishi Heavy Industries, Ltd. During the occupation, all *zaibatsu*-related shareholding was broken up and NYK stock became widely dispersed for the next decade. Following the reorganization of the industry in 1964, Mitsubishi firms quickly began to purchase NYK shares so that by the 1970s they controlled about 30 percent. Likewise, NYK held substantial shares in numerous Mitsubishi companies and was a full member of the present Mitsubishi Group.

Through its earlier era of expansion NYK had been led by its president, Rempei Kondo. During World War I, however, he began to lose control of the firm as internal disputes arose over capital stock increases and dividend policy, and several execu-

tives resigned. After his death in 1921 the company suffered labor problems involving a split between shore and sea employees, and many more executives left. Consequently, over the next decade NYK presidents came from outside the company to restore order. The most important of these was Kenkichi Kagami, the chairman of The Tokio Marine and Fire Insurance Company, another member of the Mitsubishi *zaibatsu*. Serving from 1929 to 1935, Kagami was known as an economizer and was reluctant to invest in the new express ships for the New York line. Managerially, his key contribution was to promote NYK career managers from within. Since then, all NYK presidents have risen from within the company.

In the postwar period, perhaps the most effective of these presidents was Shojiro Kikuchi who was president from 1971 to 1978 and chairman from 1978 to 1984. As a junior executive in the 1950s he played a key role in company strategy, particularly in the era of changes that followed the Mitsui Fight and in the container arrangement with the Matson Line. Something of an intellectual, Kikuchi worked closely with the company's Research Chamber in anticipating long-term changes in the country's industrial structure. This vision gave him the courage in 1975 to override the almost unanimous opposition of his executives and cut back on tanker operations.

NYK was able to finance some of its new investments from its own capital. This marked a shift from its heavy reliance on subsidies and loans in the 25 years after the occupation. In the early years of its expansion, up to about 1910, NYK's main source of financing was subsidies. Thereafter reserves grew rapidly and they became a key source of funds until the 1920s. After World War I, however, the company allowed money to flow out of the firm in excessive dividends. For the remainder of the interwar years it relied on bonds and loans.

Overcoming Challenges in the 1980s

Financially, the major shock to the Japanese shipping industry in the 1980s was the doubling of the value of the yen against the U.S. dollar between 1985 and 1987. Since so much freight is denominated in dollars, this meant a substantial reduction in income. NYK responded to this crisis in three ways: retrenchment, diversification, and broadening of its base in shipping, in which it held a comparative advantage. Perhaps the key measure under the retrenchment strategy was to spin off internal functions such as accounting and information systems as new subsidiaries. Between 1987 and 1991 this helped to reduce the number of company employees by 30 percent. The wide range of the company's diversification was best typified by two firms that began operations in the 1980s. One, Nippon Cargo Airlines, was a joint venture of NYK, several shipping firms, and an airline, and was established to preserve market share in what was increasingly miniaturized cargo. The other, Crystal Cruises, Inc. a wholly owned subsidiary registered in Los Angeles, was NYK's entry into the luxury cruise market.

What profits NYK earned in the first few years after the 1985 to 1987 yen shock came from another form of diversification, financial subsidiaries and other financial investments, not from shipping operations themselves. In the late 1980s, however, increases in freight rates sparked a business recovery in the shipping industry, a trend that NYK itself was well prepared for with its expanded investments in transportation infrastructure. Since its 100th anniversary in 1985, the company took to calling itself a "mega-carrier," a term that symbolized its global network of multi-modal transport and the broad logistical capability to integrate shippers and cargo movement. Much of this effort concentrated on new computerized information systems. Business of this sort also was being spun off in the form of new subsidiaries.

One trend that emerged in 1991 was that the presidents of some of these new subsidiaries, who were themselves former NYK career employees, were appointed to the company's board of directors. This was a departure from the pattern of most of the postwar period, when the board was composed almost exclusively of executives from within NYK itself. These strategies, therefore, had the potential to change the company's structure to reflect the broadening base of company operations. Most of these subsidiaries, however, supported shipping itself. This suggested that, in contrast to the pattern of diversification followed by British shipping firms, where shipping operations have shrunk to a small portion of their overall business, NYK was not moving far from its core business of shipping.

NYK in the 1990s and Beyond

NYK battled intense competition, a slowdown in international trade, a weak domestic economy, and a strong yen throughout much of the 1990s. During this time period, the Japanese shipping industry was changing dramatically. Competitors from Taiwan, South Korea, China, and Hong Kong began to secure large portions of the shipping market. High costs in Japan were forcing NYK and its competitors to reflag their ships and hire foreign seamen. In fact, the Japanese Shipowners Association predicted that the number of Japanese-flagged ships would decline to less than 100 by 2000—there were 1,028 in 1985. At the same time, Japanese exporters began building their factories overseas, thus eliminating a major source of business for Japanese shipping companies.

In 1997 NYK's tanker, the Diamond Grace, ran aground and ruptured three of its tanks. The accident spilled 10,000 bbl of crude oil into Tokyo Bay. Determined to remain Japan's largest marine transporter, NYK forged ahead despite the harsh operating conditions. In 1998, NYK merged with Showa Line Ltd., leaving Japan with four major shipping companies—NYK, Mitsui OSK Lines, Kawasaki Kisen Kaisha, and Navix. As a result of the merger, NYK operated 535 ships. The company established a handful of new subsidiaries over the next several years including e-JAN Co. Ltd., NYK Logistics China, NYK Logistics Europe, and Singapore-based NYK Ship Management Co. Ltd.

During the early years of the 21st century, NYK positioned itself as a megacarrier offering global logistics over sea, land, and air. In 2001, the company adopted a new corporate logo. Two years later it launched a new strategic plan entitled, NYK 21 "Forward 120." As part of its revamped vision, the company focused on expanding its shipping segment, which accounted for nearly 60 percent of its annual revenues. It looked to increase its fleet of vessels for the bulk/energy resources transportation market. NYK also eyed service development in logistics as crucial for future growth. That segment accounted for approximately 20 percent of total revenues in 2004, and NYK hoped to tap into a greater share of the logistics market. Its strategy included providing logistics services to the automobile industry, to electronics and other manufacturers, and to and retailers. By expanding its reach in China, Asia, and Europe, NYK aimed to increase its profits in this business segment. "Forward 120" was also heavily focused on corporate social responsibility (CSR). NYK pledged to promote environmentally-friendly activities while providing safe and reliable transportation.

NYK's responses to the changes in Japan's shipping industry left it in an enviable position among its competitors. In 2004 and 2005, the company posted record profits and revenues, as demand for its shipping services increased. NYK expected its good fortunes to continue in the years to come due to its cost cutting efforts as well as its ability to secure lucrative international contracts. In 2004, the company signed a three-year shipping contract with International Paper Company to transport wood chips from Brazil to the United States.

Principal Subsidiaries

NYK Global Bulk Corporation; Tokyo Senpaku Kaisha Ltd.; NKY-Hinode Line Ltd.; Kinkai Yusen Logistics Co. Ltd.; Hachiuma Steamship Co. Ltd.; Asahi Shipping Co. Ltd.; NYK Bulkship Europe Ltd.; Albireo Maritima S.A.; NYK Line North America Ltd.; NYK Line Europe Ltd.; UNI-Z Corp.; Geneq Corporation; Nippon Container Terminals Co. Ltd.; Nippon Container Yuso Co. Ltd.; Asahi Shipping Co. Ltd.; Yusen Terminals Inc.; NYK Terminals North America Inc.; NYK Cruise Co. Ltd.; Crystal Cruises Inc.; Yusen Air & Sea Service Co. Ltd.; JIT Corp.; Yusen Koun Co. Ltd.; Asahi Shipping Co. Ltd.; GST Corporation; NKY Logistics UK Manufacturing & Retail Ltd.; Yusen Air & Sea Service USA Inc.; Nippon Kaiyosha Ltd.; NKY Trading Corp.; Sanyo Trading Co. Ltd.; Yusen Real Estate Corporation; NYK Systems Research Institute; Yusen Travel Co. Ltd.; NYK Trading Corp.; Nippon Cargo Airlines Co. Ltd.

Principal Competitors

Kawasaki Kisen Kaisha, Ltd.; Mitsui O.S.K. Lines, Ltd.; Neptune Orient Lines Ltd.

Further Reading

Cyphers, Luke, "Southeast Asia's Shipping Services Grow," *Asian Wall Street Journal*, November 25, 1991.
Essays in International Maritime Economic History, Pontefract: Lofthouse Publications, 1990.
Hand, Marcus, "MYK to Take Over Ailing Showa Line in Share Swap," *Business Times Singapore*, March 31, 1998.
Kanabayashi, Masayoshi, "Treading Water: Japan's Ship Operators Sail Abroad as Local Costs Rise," *Asian Wall Street Journal*, March 20, 1996.
"Mitsui O.S.K. and Nippon Yusen to End U.S. Shipping Agreement," *Asian Wall Street Journal*, December 28, 1992.
Nippon Yusen Kabushiki Kaisha Hyakunen Shi, Tokyo: NYK, 1988.
"Pretax Earnings at Japan Shippers are Flat to Lower," *Asian Wall Street Journal*, May 24, 1993.
Takahashi, Yoshio, "Japan's Top Shipping Concerns Post Record Earnings for Year," *Asian Wall Street Journal*, May 13, 2005.
Takita, Kazuo, "NYK Completes Showa Link," *Lloyd's List International*, October 2, 1998.

Tomohei, Chida, and Peter N. Davies, *The Japanese Shipping and Shipbuilding Industries: A History of Their Modern Growth,* London: Athlone Press, 1990.

Wray, William D., *Mitsubishi and the N.Y.K., 1870–1914: Business Strategy in the Japanese Shipping Industry,* Cambridge: Harvard University Press, 1984.

——, "NYK and the Commercial Diplomacy of the Far Eastern Freight Conference, 1896–1956," in *Business History of Shipping: Strategy and Structure,* edited by Tsunehiko Yui and Keiichiro Nakagawa, Tokyo: Tokyo University Press, 1985.

——, "Kagami Kenkichi and the N.Y.K., 1929–1935: Vertical Control, Horizontal Strategy, and Company Autonomy," in *Managing Industrial Enterprise: Cases From Japan's Prewar Experience,* Cambridge: Harvard University Press, 1989.

——, " 'The Mitsui Fight,' 1953–1956: Japan and the Far Eastern Freight Conference," in *Shipping and Trade, 1750–1950: Essays in International Maritime Economic History,* edited by Lewis Fischer and Helge Nordvik, Pontefract: Lofthouse Publications, 1990.

—William D. Wray
—update: Christina M. Stansell

NOF Corporation

Yebisu Garden Place Tower, 4-20-3 E
Tokyo
150-6019
Japan
Telephone: +81 3 5424 6600
Fax: +81 3 5424 6800
Web site: http://www.nof.co.jp

Public Company
Incorporated: 1937 as Nippon Oil & Fats Co. Ltd.
Employees: 3,695
Sales: ¥137.47 billion ($1.34 billion) (2004)
Stock Exchanges: Tokyo
Ticker Symbol: 4403
NAIC: 325998 All Other Miscellaneous Chemical
    Product Manufacturing; 311225 Fats and Oils
    Refining and Blending; 324199 All Other Petroleum
    and Coal Products Manufacturing; 325131 Inorganic
    Dye and Pigment Manufacturing; 325188 All Other
    Inorganic Chemical Manufacturing; 325211 Plastics
    Material and Resin Manufacturing; 325412
    Pharmaceutical Preparation Manufacturing; 325510
    Paint and Coating Manufacturing; 325613 Surface
    Active Agent Manufacturing; 333992 Welding and
    Soldering Equipment Manufacturing; 339112 Surgical
    and Medical Instrument Manufacturing

NOF Corporation is Japan's leading oleochemicals group, producing a highly diversified range of products derived from oilseeds and petrochemicals. NOF—formerly known as Nippon Oil & Fats—produces fatty acids and derivatives, surfactants, and related products, which are used in preparations such as soap, detergent, cosmetic bases, and foods, including margarine and vegetable oils, as well as rubber and plastics. The company's petrochemicals production includes polyethylene glycol, polypropylene glycol, and polyalkylene glycol, as well as fire retardant and defoaming agents, among others. The company's production also includes chemicals for the papermaking, fermentation, and other industries, as well as additives for construction and other materials. NOF's Oleochemicals & Foods division accounts for approximately 39 percent of the group's sales, which topped ¥137 billion ($1.34 billion) in 2004. The company's Chemicals division includes petrochemicals, organic peroxides, automotive coatings, and drug delivery systems (and specifically the company's polyethylene glycol modifiers launched in the mid-2000s). That division accounted for approximately 35 percent of NOF's 2004 sales. In addition to its focus on oleochemicals, NOF has long played a leading role in Japan's explosives industry. The company's Explosives and Propulsion division produces dynamite, powdered and emulsion explosives, aluminum nitrate-based explosives, and detonators, as well as rocket propellants. In addition, the company is a major producer of inflators for automotive airbags. This division produced approximately 25 percent of NOF's 2004 revenues. NOF Corporation is listed on the Tokyo Stock Exchange. The company is led by CEO and President Youhei Nakajima and is affiliated with Japan's Fuyo Group.

Mixing Oils and Fats in the 1930s

NOF Corporation was founded as Nippon Oil & Fats Co. Ltd. in 1937, merging the operations of four companies. The first of these was the Japanese branch of fast-growing Lever Brothers, the soap and detergent group that later became global agro-industrial giant Unilever. That company founded its own production facility in Japan, in Amagasaki, in 1910.

Another part of the later NOF originated in 1917, when the Suzuki Shoten company opened an oil refinery in Oji. Suzuki Shoten was then in the process of transforming itself from a small sugar trader to become one of the largest and most diversified conglomerates of World War I-era Japan.

Formally established in 1937, Nippon Oil & Fats added other product operations. One of these was coatings for the paint industry, added through the merger of Kokusan Industry Co. in its Fuji Paint Works. That company originally had been set up in 1924.

Nippon Oil & Fats added new production facilities into the 1940s, including a factory in Mikuni in 1939 and another in

---

Shinmei, in 1943. In 1945, the company was merged into the chemical department of Nippon Mining Co. Ltd., which then became known as Nippon Chemical Industries Ltd.

The merger did not last long, however. By 1949, Nippon Chemical had split up again, spinning off Nippon Oil & Fats Co. in order to focus its own efforts on developing its petroleum operations. Nippon Oil & Fats (NOF) in the meantime had been expanded, with the inclusion of Hokkaido Oil and Fats, a company established in 1938 through the merger of 14 oilseed producers on Hokkaido island. In support of its Hokkaido operations, NOF built a new production plant, in Bibai in 1954.

The ''new'' NOF by then had already taken on the form that was to lead it into the next century, with operations concentrated around its core of oil and fats on the one hand, and explosives on the other. In the 1950s NOF continued to add new areas of operations. Organic peroxides became a major area of activity for the company, with production launched in 1957. This activity led the company into the larger petrochemicals sector, with production including polybutene and others.

Through the 1960s, NOF added a number of new production facilities. In 1961, the company opened its Chidori factory, which was joined by a new plant in Totsuka in 1964. The company opened two more plants before the end of the decade, in Kimitsu in 1968, and Oita in 1969. The latter marked the company's expansion into a new area of the petrochemicals market, with the launch of the production of C4 (butane and butene) derivatives.

NOF added another major product area in 1970 when it merged with Tekioku Polytechnics Co. Ltd. That company had been founded in 1919, when it established a factory for producing smokeless gunpowder, Teikoku Explosives Ind. After becoming a major producer of gunpowder and explosives, Teikoku expanded in the 1950s. A major part of that expansion was the company's extension into the production of rocket propellant in 1954. Production of propellants was at first limited to defense applications. Later, however, the company, and then NOF, began developing a range of civilian applications for its explosives and propellants expertise, such as the propellants for automotive airbags and other safety features. Another important

product area was the production of nitroglycerin for medical and pharmaceutical purposes.

Refocusing on the New Century

NOF's expansion, on the one hand into explosives and propellants and on the other into petrochemicals, led it to reorganize its operations in the early 1970s. An important feature of the reorganization was the decision to regroup the production of household products, including soaps, detergents, and related products, into a dedicated subsidiary, Nissan Soap Co. Ltd. In 1973, the company expanded its coatings business with the creation of Nippon Dacro Shamrock Co, a 50–50 joint venture partnership with Metal Coatings International. In 1980, the company split off production of fatty acids and related oleochemicals into a dedicated unit as well, called Nichiyu Giken Kogyo Co.

The establishment of a research and development department, Tusukuba Research Lab, in 1984, provided a launching pad for further expansion into the 1990s for the company. NOF developed a number of technologies supporting applications ranging from new detergents and cleansers, to new food additives, and even to the development of a new flooring system, based on the company's methacrylic resin. NOF also began expanding beyond Japan, notably acquiring the United States' US Paint, specialized in coatings for the automotive, marine, and aerospace markets. Acquired in 1989, US Paint had been founded in 1931.

Nippon Oil & Fats Co. officially changed its name to NOF Corporation in 1992. At the same time the company launched a reorganization effort to meet the challenges of the global recession at the beginning of the 1990s. In 1994, the company continued restructuring, splitting off its Bibai production facility into a new subsidiary, Hokkaido NOF Corporation. In that year, NOF moved its headquarters to a new building complex, Yebisu Garden Place Tower.

NOF's expansion continued into the dawn of the 21st century. The company stepped up its propellants operations through a joint venture agreement with Autoliv Inc., a major supplier of airbag inflators to the Japanese market. Under the joint venture the companies set up a new production plant in Taketoyo. In 1999, the company boosted its explosives and propellants division again with the acquisition of Nippon Koki Co. Founded in 1970, Nippon Koki had become one of Japan's leading manufacturers of industrial-grade gunpowder.

In the early 2000s, NOF began a refocusing effort, narrowing its range of operations to a dual core of oleochemicals and explosives/propellants. As part of that restructuring the company shed a number of nonrelated businesses, such as a welding materials business, which was sold to Taseto Co. in 2000. That year, NOF began spinning off its automotive coatings business, too, transferring those operations to a joint venture set up in partnership with BASF. In 2002, the company sold its U.S. and European marine and aerospace coatings operations to Akzo Nmobel.

The restructuring paved the way for the company to explore the widening of its oleochemicals operations to include medical applications. In 1998, for example, the company launched a cooperation agreement with Bio Compatible of the United

Key Dates:

1910: Lever Brothers is founded in Japan.
1917: Suzuki Shoten establishes an oil refinery in Oji.
1919: Teikoku Explosives is founded.
1924: Kojusan Industry, a paint and coatings business, is founded.
1937: Nippon Oil & Fats Co. (NOF) is founded, regrouping Lever Brothers and three other businesses.
1945: The company merges into Nippon Mining Co., which becomes Nippon Chemical Industries.
1949: NOF splits off from Nippon Chemical.
1957: NOF launches production of organic peroxide.
1970: Teikoku Pyrotechnics is acquired.
1974: Nissan Soap Co. is created as a dedicated soap and detergents business.
1984: The company establishes a research and development laboratory.
1989: NOF acquires US Paint.
1992: The company restructures and changes its name to NOF Corporation; a bio-affinity materials development cooperation agreement is launched with Bio Compatible of the United Kingdom.
1999: The company acquires Nippon Koki Co., a leading industrial grade gunpowder producer.
2000: The company spins off its automotive coatings business to a joint venture with BASF.
2002: The company sells its marine and aerospace coatings business to Akzo Nobel.
2003: Plans are announced to build a ¥1 billion PEG modifier production facility.

Kingdom to produce biologically compatible polymer applied products. By 1999, NOF had successed in developing a means of mass-producing its MPC Polymer, which boasted a high level of "bio-affinity," making it an important material for use in the development of artificial blood vessels and organs.

In 2001, NOF moved into a new business area with the launch of a new division, Drug Delivery Systems. This operation included the group's development of new materials for the controlled delivery of medications. By 2004, the company had developed a polyethylene glycol (PEG) derivative capable of transporting protein drugs into the bloodstream. The material, known as a PEG modifier, proved so promising that by the end of 2004, NOF announced that it was building a new, ¥1 billion production facility. At 20,000 square feet, the new plant was expected to become one of the world's largest, and enable NOF to quintuple its PEG production. As it moved into the second half of the 2000s, NOF remained one of Japan's leading specialty chemicals groups.

Principal Subsidiaries

Cactus Co., Ltd. (66.7%); Hokkaido NOF Corporation; Japex Corporation (70%); Nichibu Sangyo Co., Ltd.; Nichiyu Estate Co., Ltd.; Nichiyu Giken Kogyo Co., Ltd. (66.7%); Nichiyu Kogyo Co., Ltd.; Nichiyu Service Corporation; Nichiyu Solution Inc.; Nichiyu Trading Co., Ltd; Nippon Kogyo Co., Ltd. (89.3%); Nippon Dacro Shamrock Co., Ltd.; Nippon Koki Co., Ltd. (95.0%); Pyro Safety Device Co., Ltd.; Showa Kinzoku Kogyo Co., Ltd. (74.7%); Taseto Co., Ltd.; Yuka Sangyo Co., Ltd.

Principal Competitors

Itochu Corporation; Kaneka Corporation; Nisshin Oillio Group; Showa Sangyo Company Ltd.; J-Oil Mills Inc.; Fuji Oil Company Ltd.; Asahi Denka Kogyo KKNOF Corporation.

Further Reading

"Akzo Nobel Gets Bigger in Japan," *PPCJ Polymers Paint Colour Journal,* May 2002, p. 4.
Chew, Edmund, "BASF Forms Venture in Japan," *Automotive News,* January 31, 2000.
"Japan's NOF Develops Cosmetics Base That Spreads Evenly on Skin," *Asia Pulse,* July 14, 2004.
"Japan's NOF Redoubles R&D for Drug Delivery System Materials," *Asia Pulse,* January 28, 2004.
"Japan's NOF to Quintuple Output Capacity for PEG Derivative," *Asia Pulse,* December 15, 2004.
"NOF to Invest 1b Yen in Biotech Plant," *Jiji,* December 15, 2004.
"NOF to Take Over Nippon Koki to Expand Powder Business," *Japan Weekly Monitor,* September 20, 1999.

—M.L. Cohen

NSF International

P.O. Box 130140
789 North Dixboro Road
Ann Arbor, Michigan 48113-0140
U.S.A.
Telephone: (734) 769-8010
Toll Free: (800)-673-6275
Fax: (734) 769-0109
Web site: http://www.nsf.org

Nonprofit Corporation
Incorporated: 1944 as the National Sanitation Foundation
Employees: 473
Sales: $80 million (2005 est.)
NAIC: 541380 Testing Laboratories

NSF International is a world leader in the testing and certification of products that affect the safety of water, food, and air. NSF develops standards, tests products, certifies compliance, educates the public, and provides risk-management services for business. Fees charged for testing comprise its main source of income. The company's clients include the makers of Evian spring water, nutritional supplement chain GNC, and the National Football League. Its educational efforts include "Scrub Club," a print and Web-based program that promotes better hand-washing among children. The NSF is a designated World Health Organization Collaborating Center for water quality, food safety, and indoor environment health standards. Headquartered in Ann Arbor, Michigan, NSF International and its subsidiaries have offices in several American cities and in Belgium, Brazil, and Japan.

Beginnings

NSF International was founded in 1944 as the National Sanitation Foundation (NSF) at the University of Michigan's School of Public Health in Ann Arbor, Michigan. Its three founders, Walter Snyder, Henry Vaughn, and Nathan Sinai, were two professors and a health department official from nearby Toledo, Ohio.

The NSF was created to make advances in the field of sanitation through the promotion of research and collaboration.

Its bylaws stated that the organization would "be operated exclusively for charitable, educational, and scientific purposes and for the purpose of testing for public safety ... as a nonprofit corporation." Funding would come from foundation grants and businesses.

At this time, the United States had no national sanitation standards, with each municipality developing its own, often conflicting, set of regulations. This lack of consistency was particularly troublesome for manufacturers, whose products might be salable in one area but not in another. Executive director Walter Snyder and his colleagues sought to develop standards for sanitation by reaching a consensus of the parties that had a stake in the outcome, namely the public, the business community, and government agencies. By involving all three, each could feel invested in the process and would work to achieve a common goal.

In 1948, the NSF sponsored its first clinics to discuss sanitation education, supervision, and administration, as well as ordinances for eating and drinking establishments, dishwashing, installation of food-service equipment, vending machines, rodent and insect control, and other topics. In 1952, the organization published its first consensus sanitation standards and introduced its official mark of recognition. The same year saw the launch of the Food Equipment Program, in which the organization would certify products for manufacturers. Testing would be performed in the former Federal Mogul Corp. laboratory on the west side of Ann Arbor.

During the 1950s, NSF executive director Walter Snyder spent much of his time on the road promoting the organization's standards around the United States. As they were adopted, more product testing work was generated. In 1959, an agreement was reached with the Society of the Plastics Industry to establish health effects testing and certification standards for plastics, and in 1963 the organization opened its first regional offices.

Expansion in the 1960s

In 1965, the NSF launched new plastic piping and wastewater treatment programs, which brought the organization additional testing work. That year, Walter Snyder died of a heart

Company Perspectives:

NSF International, an independent, not-for-profit, non-governmental organization, is dedicated to being the leading global provider of public health and safety-based risk management solutions while serving the interests of all stakeholders.

attack, and the job of leading the organization was given to Dr. Robert M. Brown.

In 1966, the growing NSF built a two-story addition to its Ann Arbor testing facility, and in 1971 the organization spent $1.5 million to buy part of the former home of McDonnell-Douglas subsidiary Conductron. The 65,000-square-foot building was located on 20 acres of land on the east side of Ann Arbor. At this time, some of the organization's research was still being conducted at the School of Public Health, but it was moved to the new building, along with most other NSF operations, a few months later. A wastewater test site was maintained on the nearby Huron River, with another small office and testing facility in Grand Rapids, Michigan.

In 1975, a national survey of public health departments found that 90 percent of responding agencies had adopted the organization's standards for food-service equipment. NSF was now responsible for evaluating the food service products of more than 1,000 manufacturers in the United States. A range of different tests were performed, including measurements of the effectiveness of dishwashing equipment in removing bacteria and the cleanability of various materials used in dispensing food.

Other NSF programs at this time tested water quality in rivers where wastewater was present; sewage treatment plants; swimming pool equipment such as pumps, valves, chemical feeders and test kits; and plastic water pipes. In the latter category, more than 240 firms in the United States, the United Kingdom, Germany, and Japan were using NSF standards. The organization was also sponsoring educational programs that taught food sanitation through seminars and via audio/visual training materials. They were used by managers of food service establishments throughout the United States.

In 1976, the NSF received an award from the National Institutes of Health to set standards for hospital cabinets. The organization employed 65 and had annual revenues of more than $2.5 million.

The year 1980 saw the NSF initiate a program to set standards for the purity of drinking water as well as name a new president, Nina McClelland. She had joined the organization in 1968 as the head of its water resource program. That year also brought victory in a ten-year court battle that had made its way to the U.S. Supreme Court. It involved a lawsuit filed by a Kalamazoo, Michigan, company whose refrigeration unit had been tested, but not approved, by the NSF. When a store refused to buy one of its coolers because it did not bear the NSF mark, the manufacturer sued the organization, several of its officers, four public health officials, six other manufacturers, and the National Restaurant Association, alleging restraint of free trade. The Supreme Court refused to hear the case, letting a Federal Appellate Court ruling stand.

Work for EPA Begins in 1985

In 1984, the NSF started a bottled drinking water program and established a body called the Health Advisory Board. The organization scored a major coup a year later when the United States Environmental Protection Agency (EPA) gave it the task of developing national health standards for products that came in contact with drinking water. The assignment involved a wide range of items including pumps, pipes, gaskets, faucets, and paints. The historic move of delegating regulatory work to a private agency had come as the EPA was seeing a growing backlog of products to be tested and as its funding was being cut by the Reagan administration.

The EPA would supervise the NSF's work, which would be performed in cooperation with other bodies, including the American Waterworks Association Research Foundation and the Conference of State Health and Environmental Managers. Funding would largely be provided by the companies whose products were being tested, with the EPA itself paying just $85,000. This assignment would become one of the NSF's leading sources of income. At the time, the agreement was reached, the NSF had 100 employees and annual revenues of $5 million per year.

The organization's first foreign office was established in 1985 in Brussels, Belgium, and the following year the NSF began a testing program for household water filters, which, like drinking water product certification, would become a major revenue source for the firm. The year 1986 also saw the organization begin inspecting cruise ships that docked in the United States for sanitation after the Centers for Disease Control stopped performing the work. The NSF would perform work for 15 cruise lines that operated 48 ships.

In 1987, a new testing laboratory was opened in Sacramento, California. Regional offices had been established in Pennsylvania and Georgia by this time as well. Projects the firm was now involved with included testing materials for Kimberly-Clark to develop a way of making compostable disposable diapers.

In 1990, the National Sanitation Foundation and the National Sanitation Foundation Testing Laboratory were merged and the organization renamed NSF International. In 1991, the firm was accredited by the American National Standards Institute (ANSI) for its product certification programs, and NSF established agreements with organizations in the Netherlands, Japan, and Taiwan to cooperate on performing plant inspections in each country. Similar agreements would later be signed in Canada and Mexico.

In 1995, the NSF's board appointed Dennis Mangino to head the organization. The first NSF president who had not come up through the ranks, Mangino had a degree in ceramics sciences and had worked as an executive at several companies, most recently as vice-president in charge of research and development at Weirton Steel in West Virginia.

NSF-ISR is Founded in 1996

In 1996, a new, for-profit subsidiary of the NSF was formed. NSF International Strategic Registrations, Ltd. (NSF-ISR) would audit automotive suppliers to assure that they met International Organization for Standardization (ISO) environmental

Key Dates:

1944: National Sanitation Foundation (NSF) is formed in Ann Arbor, Michigan.

1952: NSF Testing Laboratory is chartered; Food Equipment Program starts.

1965: Plastic piping and wastewater treatment programs begin.

1971: NSF buys a 65,000-square-foot building for its laboratories and headquarters.

1985: The Environmental Protection Agency (EPA) asks NSF to help set drinking water standards; a Belgian office is opened.

1990: The organization changes its name to NSF International.

1996: NSF International Strategic Registrations, Ltd. subsidiary is formed.

1996: NSF begins working with the World Health Organization.

1999: The Toxicology Group LLC and Center for Public Health Education is founded; a new headquarters building opens in Ann Arbor.

2001: Cook & Thurber and Institute for Nutritional Advancement are purchased.

2002: FreshCheck is acquired.

2004: Organic certification firm Quality Assurance International, Inc. is acquired.

and quality standards. The year 1996 also saw the NSF chosen to be a Collaborating Center by the World Health Organization (WHO) to develop drinking water standards. The following year, this relationship was expanded to include food safety.

The NSF's payroll was now expanding rapidly, reaching 260 in 1997. The fall of that year saw ground broken on a new 150,000-square-foot headquarters and laboratory and the opening of a new office in Nairobi, Kenya. Offices were added the following year in Sydney, Australia, and Tokyo, Japan. The organization had also opened an office in Washington, D.C., by this time. The year 1998 also saw the NSF recognized by the U.S. Occupational Safety and Health Administration (OSHA) as a Nationally Accredited Testing Laboratory for electrical certification.

In March 1999, a joint venture was formed in the United Kingdom called WRc-NSF with the British research and consulting firm WRc, plc. It would offer testing and certification services to a variety of international clients. In April, the NSF's new headquarters opened, and the organization sponsored its first conference on indoor air quality, in Denver. A new trademark, "The Public Health and Safety Company," was introduced at this time as well. The organization also formed a new division during the year called The Center for Public Health Education and a subsidiary called The Toxicology Group, LLC. NSF was now working on its first standard for safety of a food product, involving baked goods containing soft cheese or vegetables that could be stored at room temperature.

New CEO Mangino was guiding the NSF through a period of rapid growth, but it was not without controversy. Six months

after taking the top job, he had fired two vice-presidents and an assistant vice-president, and in the following months a number of other top personnel left or were fired. Mangino was also accused of sexually harassing several women in the organization. One alleged victim later sued him and the NSF, while a fired vice-president sued for age discrimination and received an undisclosed settlement.

Mangino's reported focus on increasing revenues led to additional controversy, as allegations surfaced that a program manager on the firm's staff had directed that a relatively high level of a probable carcinogen be allowed in a well-drilling equipment standard. Later, complaints were made by rival testing firm Underwriters Laboratories over the NSF's lack of cooperation in sharing information. Standards coordinating body the ANSI audited the organization and put it on probation in 2000, nearly costing the NSF its lucrative drinking water work. The company soon implemented changes recommended by the ANSI, including allowing greater access to outsiders during the standards-setting process, and the NSF retained the contract.

Round of Acquisitions Starts in 2001

In June 2001, the organization acquired Cook & Thurber, LLC, a six-year-old auditor of product safety and quality for the food, beverage, animal feed, and packaging industries. It would operate as a division of NSF and remain headquartered in Madison, Wisconsin. In the fall of the same year, NSF bought the Institute for Nutraceutical Advancement (INA), which developed and validated analytical methods for testing botanical ingredients, and formed a strategic partnership with the National Nutritional Foods Association (NNFA), the largest trade association in the United States for manufacturers, retailers, and suppliers of natural products, to provide a certification program for dietary supplements. NSF would verify that ingredients were as listed on labels and test for contaminants. Several other organizations, including U.S. Pharmacopeia (USP) and the Good Housekeeping Institute, were offering similar programs, but NSF was the only one to be accepted by the ANSI and the Standards Council of Canada. In 2001, the NSF also reached an agreement with the government of Taiwan for that country to adopt the agency's standard for drinking water purity. The company was now expanding its efforts in a number of areas, including mechanical plumbing, mobile food truck, and plastic conduit certification.

In the wake of the September 11, 2001 terrorist attacks on the United States, the NSF sponsored a conference on bio-terrorism in early 2002 in Ann Arbor. This was done in partnership with the Water Quality Association. The two organizations had begun working jointly to develop standards that assured the nation's water supply would be guarded against bio-terrorist attacks.

In 2002, the company acquired FreshCheck, which provided microbiological testing and sanitation audits for the supermarket industry, focusing on perishable foods made on-premises. The NSF also realigned its operations during the year to focus on its two major markets of food and water. The firm employed 350 and had revenues of $52 million.

In 2003, CEO Mangino retired and was replaced by Kevan Lawlor, an 18-year veteran of the firm who had served as chief financial officer and head of the NSF-ISR subsidiary. During the eight years of Mangino's leadership, the organization had quadrupled in size. The year 2003 also saw the NSF's work with the WHO expanded to include indoor air standards.

In October 2003, the NSF launched its first-ever advertising campaign, which was budgeted at $2 million. Print advertisements using the tagline "Live Safer" appeared in national publications including *People* magazine, *Time, The Wall Street Journal,* and *USA Today.* These were intended to raise awareness of the organization among consumers. Several months later, the NSF also launched a national educational campaign called Clean Hands Across America, which utilized cartoon characters of the "Scrub Club" to encourage children to wash their hands properly and regularly. A Scrub Club Web site was launched as well. The NSF's own Web site offered information about the standards it had developed and the products that it tested, as well as serving as a client interface.

In December 2003, General Nutrition Companies (GNC), the largest supplier of nutritional supplements in the United States, signed an agreement with NSF for the organization to certify its products. This agreement was followed in January 2004 by one with the National Football League. NSF would certify that nutritional supplements adhered to the football league's standards, which banned products containing steroids and related substances.

March 2004 saw the firm acquire Quality Assurance International, Inc. (QAI), a leading international provider of organic certification that was operated on a for-profit basis. QAI had been founded in California in 1989 and provided certification services to growers, manufacturers, and retailers. An estimated two-thirds of organic products sold in stores were QAI certified. In 2005, NSF began preparations to enlarge its headquarters facility by 82,000 square feet, a project that would largely be funded by an issuance of $10 million in bonds. The organization was now serving clients in nearly 80 countries.

After more than 60 years, NSF International had grown into the world's leading non-governmental organization dedicated to testing and certification of products that affected the safety of water, food, and air. It was working to cement its position as the leader in its field through strategic acquisitions and new marketing efforts.

Principal Subsidiaries

NSF International Strategic Registrations, Ltd.; Quality Assurance International; The Toxicology Group, LLC; NSF International Strategic Registrations Canada Co.; NSF do Brasil.

Principal Competitors

Underwriters Laboratories, Inc.; Intertek Group Plc; SGS SA; The United States Pharmacopeial Convention, Inc.; ConsumerLab.com, LLC; The Canadian Standards Association; The Good Housekeeping Institute.

Further Reading

Anderson, Scott, "Known in Business, NSF Courts Public," *Ann Arbor News,* October 3, 2003, p. C1.

——, "NSF International CEO Stepping Down," *Ann Arbor News,* September 16, 2003, p. C1.

"At Ann Arbor's NSF, Water's the Next Wave," *Ann Arbor News,* July 10, 1988, p. F1.

Begin, Sherri, "NSF International Adds Organic-Certification Biz," *Crain's Detroit Business,* March 8, 2004, p. 28.

——, "Testing the Waters; NSF International Tries to Build Recognition Among Consumers for Testing Certification," *Crain's Detroit Business,* October 4, 2004, p. 48.

Bush, Larry, "Foundation Helps You More than You Know," *Ann Arbor News,* November 14, 1976.

Freeman, Laurie, "NSF: Greener Than Thou?," *Crain's Detroit Business,* April 1, 1991, p. 3.

Garber, Ken, "The Shake-up at NSF," *Ann Arbor Observer,* November, 1997, pp. 27–30.

Haglund, Rick, "Sanitation Foundation Wins 'Historic' EPA Contract," *Ann Arbor News,* October 24, 1985, p. E1.

Klein, Pamela, "NSF Wins Court Fight," *Ann Arbor News,* October 24, 1980, p. C1.

"Making the Grade: Battle Over Certification, Standardization Heating Up," *HFN,* March 10, 1997, p. 26S.

"Merger Announced by Food Safety Auditors," *Feedstuffs,* May 21, 2001, p. 6.

Murphy, Joan, "Baking Industry Questions NSF's Role in Setting Third-Party Testing Standards," *Food Chemical News,* March 15, 1999.

"New Supplement Certification Option from NSF International," *Nutraceuticals International,* March 1, 2001.

"NFL/NFLPA Supplement Certification Program Launched," *Nutraceuticals World,* March 1, 2004, p. 9.

"Regulatory News—Supplements: Debate Over Certification Marks Examined," *American Health Line,* November 20, 2002.

Serwach, Joseph, "Food-Safety Agency NSF Gets New Headquarters," *Crain's Detroit Business,* October 14, 1997, p. 45.

Wiant, Chris J., "Walter F. Snyder—The Legacy of a Leader in Environmental Health," *Journal of Environmental Health,* October 1, 1998, p. 58.

—Frank Uhle

Orion Oyj

Espoo
FIN-02101
Finland
Telephone: (+358) 10 42 91
Fax: (+358) 10 429 2801
Web site: http://www.orion.fi

Public Company
Incorporated: 1917
Employees: 4,549
Sales: EUR 1.94 billion ($2.54 billion) (2004)
Stock Exchanges: Helsinki
Ticker Symbol: Orion
NAIC: 325412 Pharmaceutical Preparation
Manufacturing; 325413 In-Vitro Diagnostic Substance
Manufacturing; 325620 Toilet Preparation Manufac-
turing; 334517 Irradiation Apparatus Manufacturing;
339114 Dental Equipment and Supplies Manufacturing;
424210 Drugs and Druggists' Sundries Merchant
Wholesalers

Orion Oyj is one Finland's leading pharmaceutical companies, marketing some 250 products in Finland and claiming about
a one-third share of the domestic market. Orion also develops and
markets drugs for the global market, notably in the fields of
Parkinson's Disease and heart disease treatment. Among the
company's top-selling drugs are Comtess/Comtan and Stalevo
(Parkinson's); Divina (menopausal symptoms); Burana (inflammatory pain); Enanton (prostate cancer); Easyhaler (asthma);
Calcimago (osteoporosis), Fareston (breast cancer), and Simdax.
This last drug, a treatment for severe heart failure, began undergoing Phase III Clinical trial testing in partnership with Abbott
Laboratories in 2004. Orion operates through three primary divisions. Orion Pharma forms the core of the group's operations,
representing the group's drug development wing, focusing on
Proprietary Products, Specialty Products, Active Ingredients
(through its Fermion unit), and Animal Health products. Forty
percent of the drug technologies sold by Orion Pharma have been
developed in-house, and in 2003 the company inaugurated a new

research and development facility. Orion Pharma generates 26
percent of Orion's annual sales, and 78 percent of its net profits.
The company's Wholesale and Distribution division is represented by Oriola in Finland and Kronans Drughandel (KD) in
Sweden, which together account for 72 percent of the company's
total revenues. Both companies focus on the Scandinavian and
greater Nordic market, distributing Orion Pharma and other companies' products. Orion Diagnostica, the group's smallest unit at
just 2 percent of sales, distributes diagnostic and imaging equipment to healthcare professionals in the Scandinavian market.
Together, Orion's operations combined to produce EUR 1.94
billion ($2.54 billion) in sales in 2004. The company is listed on
the Helsinki Stock Exchange.

Origins in the Early 20th Century

When Finland gained its independence from Russia following
World War I, the country's new government put in place a policy
of stimulating domestic infrastructure initiatives in order to enable the country to gain a degree of self-sufficiency. The period
also marked one of opportunity for a number of Finnish entrepreneurs who were eager to be domestic players in a number of
industries. The Finnish government's interest in developing a
domestic chemicals industry, as well as the growing demand for
new classes of medications and pharmaceutical compounds, inspired the creation of Osakaeyhtiö Orion in Helsinki in 1917.
Production began in a former margarine factory that year.

The new company was led by Dr. Onni Turpeinen, pharma-
cist Emil Tuurala, and Wikki Walkama, who also held a degree
in pharmacy. The partners' initial ambition for Orion was to
develop a business producing and distributing chemicals, as well
as medicines and other substances, such as cleaners. As such,
Orion's initial production was somewhat eclectic, including rifle
oil, artificial sugar, ammonia, and Lysol-branded cleaner.

Orion launched production of pharmaceuticals at the beginning of the 1920s. The company's early drug products included
aspirin, eye ointments, and morphine. An early success was the
group's iodine product, known as Jodlysin. Nonetheless, the
early years proved extremely difficult for the company which
struggled to maintain profitability. The company's difficulties
were due in part to the fact that Finland's independence had also

Company Perspectives:

Values: mutual trust and respect customer focus, innovation, achievement, and quality, reliability and safety. Our values express how we can and want to commit ourselves to the things we do. With these values we have jointly defined what we desire from Orion as a working community. They are also very personal in respect of our individual relation to work and the colleagues. Although Orion's values are equally important, we emphasise Mutual Trust and Respect. This value is the cornerstone of our attitudes, whatever we are engaged in. Our values are meant to be part of our daily life, and we are doing our best to work and live up to them.

opened the market to foreign products. Orion now found itself forced to compete against well-established foreign brands. The company responded by boosting its marketing initiatives and succeeded in establishing Orion as the country's leading pharmaceuticals brand.

By the early 1930s, Orion's production facilities, originally contained in the 180-meter-square margarine plant, had grown too small. The company built a new plant for itself, in Vallila, Helsinki, launching production there in 1934. That move was also the impetus for the group to specialize in pharmaceuticals. In keeping with its new focus, the company changed its name, becoming Lääketehdas Orion Oy (Orion Pharmaceuticals). A major impetus behind the group's refocus was the naming of Erkki Leikola as managing director. Leikola remained as managing director until 1951 and continued to lead the company as chairman in the 1970s. Under Leikola, Orion grew steadily through the 1930s. The success of the group's pharmaceutical preparations led it to expand its production facilities several times.

Diversification in the Post-World War II Era

Orion's growing market position opened new opportunities for importing and marketing foreign products to its Finnish customers. In 1934, the company reached an agreement with Denmark's Novo Terapeutisk Laboratorium to act as an importer and distributor for its insulin and blood serum products. World War II interrupted imports of Novo's products. In 1947, however, Orion once again began distributing Novo's insulin and blood serum. The company quickly extended its import operation to include other drugs and medicines that it did not manufacture itself and which were considered important to the Finnish healthcare market in the postwar years.

Yet Orion, which already distributed its own products directly to the country's pharmacies, hospitals, and other healthcare facilities, soon ran into a potential conflict of interests. In 1948, therefore, Orion established a dedicated wholesale and distribution subsidiary, Apteekkitavarakauppa Oriola Oy (simplified to Oriola Oy in 1954). In addition to direct distribution operations, Oriola also launched a wholesale business. This was based in part on Orion's support of the Finnish defense effort during World War II, when the company received a contract to supply field medical supplies to the army. Part of that contract stipulated that Orion repurchase any surplus following the war. This stockpile served as the basis for the launch of Oriola's wholesale business.

Oriola at first operated at a loss. By the mid-1950s, however, the subsidiary had become profitable, and by 1956 had become a full-fledged pharmaceutical wholesaler. As part of this effort, Oriola began opening local branch offices, with the first opened in Seinäjoki in 1956. A second office opened in Joensu in 1960, with offices opening in Oulu and Pori in 1962. By then, Oriola had also launched an international division in order to build its business acting as a Finnish partner for foreign pharmaceutical companies.

Orion acquired laboratory supplies business Lyrra Oy in 1961, placing this new operation under Oriola. The following year, Orion itself exited the distribution business, transferring its activities in this area to Oriola, which in the same year also took over the distribution operations of another pharmaceutical business, Albin Koponen.

Meanwhile, Orion had also been expanding, particularly following its decision to establish a committee for scientific research in 1956. Nonetheless, the company sales remained based on third-party formulations and molecules for some time. Sales of the company's product continued to grow strongly through the 1950s, and by the end of the decade the company was forced to expand its production capacity again. In 1962, Orion inaugurated the first phase of a new, modern facility in Mankkaa, Espoo. The company then began transferring its production operations, a process completed before the end of the decade, with the transfer of Oriola to Mankkaa in 1968. In 1970, the company changed its name to Orion-yhtymä (Orion Corporation).

Orion continued to seek new areas for expansion. In 1970, this search took the company into two directions. The first was the creation of a joint venture for the production of bulk active ingredients, launched as Fermion in 1970. Kemira, the top Finnish chemicals group, was Orion's partner in the Fermion joint venture. In 1980, however, Orion bought out Kemira and took full control of Fermion. The other direction brought Orion into the manufacture of cosmetics and other beauty products when it took over the operations of Noira, founded in 1948. Noira also added its production of detergents and cleansers to the Orion's business.

At the same time that Orion was expanding, Oriola had been adding to its range of operations. In 1970, the company launched a medical products distribution business, followed by the addition of laboratory supplies in 1972. In 1974, Oriola had also added a dental care division as well. Oriola made a number of acquisitions later in the decade in order to boost these operations. In 1978, for example, the company acquired laboratory supplies specialist Prolab Oy. That purchase was followed in 1979 by an entry into X-ray supplies with the acquisition of a 50 percent stake in Medivalmet Oy. In 1980, Orion acquired dental care business Soredex Oy, while Oriola acquired another dental supplies business that year, Finndent Oy. Oriola also added a new optical supplies business in 1982. A year earlier, the company had created a new division focused on the export market, Oriola SLG. In the meantime, Oriola had established a new wholesale agency for its pharmaceutical imports, Panfarma Oy.

This move was made in part to counter Orion's poor reputation in the international pharmaceutical market. As Paavp Ruttu, who had served as Oriola's managing director since 1952, re-

Key Dates:

1917: Orion is founded as a company manufacturing a diverse range of chemicals and cleaners.

1920: The company launches its first pharmaceutical products, including aspirin, morphine, and eye ointments.

1934: Orion moves to a larger production site in Helsinki, Vallila and begins importing insulin and blood serum from Denmark.

1948: A dedicated wholesale and distribution business, Oriola, is created.

1962: The company moves to a new modern production facility in Mankkaa, Espoo.

1970: The company enters into Fermion joint venture with Kemira; full control is acquired in 1981.

1983: The company releases Domosedan, part of an effort to develop proprietary pharmaceutical molecules and preparations.

1988: Farmos Corporation is acquired and merged into Orion in 1990.

1995: Orion goes public on the Helsinki Stock Exchange.

2002: Konans Droghandel in Sweden is acquired.

2005: Rusch Danmark, a healthcare supplies marketer, is acquired.

ported in Oriola's own corporate history: "Oriola started to have problems with many foreign manufacturers, as we always had to explain who is the owner of Oriola. This raised suspicion; the drug manufacturer Orion was a terrible monster abroad, because 'they will steal all the ideas and products and no one wants to be involved with them.' I started to push the idea of transforming Oriola's pharmaceutical agency department into a separate company. We had to find a name that does not directly resemble Orion. We arranged a name competition. The name Panfarma was invented by the doctor Samuli Sarajas."

Research Driven for the 21st Century

In the 1980s, Orion began to take steps to reinvent itself as an internationally focused, research-driven pharmaceutical company. In 1977, the company acquired its first foreign business, Ercopharm A/S, in Denmark. The acquisition of full control of Fermion also gave the company its own bulk actives unit, supporting both its own production as well as that of the international pharmaceutical industry.

Orion had also launched a fully fledged research and development program, resulting in the release of its first proprietary molecule in 1983, Domosedan, an animal sedative destined for the veterinary care industry. Orion remained focused on the animal care market through the 1980s, releasing Domitor in 1987 and its antagonist Antisedan in 1989. The success of these formulations also enabled Orion to begin building an international market for these drugs by the beginning of the 1990s.

Despite its success in the veterinary field, Orion's research program had also begun developing drugs for human application. The company's first successful drug formulation for human use was approved by the Finnish government in 1988. The drug, antiestrogen toremifen, a treatment for advanced hormonal breast cancer marketed under the Fareston brand, became the company's first drug to receive approval by the European Union, which came about in 1996. Japan also permitted sale of the drug in 1996, followed by the United States in 1997.

Orion boosted its pharmaceutical operations through the acquisition of another major pharmaceuticals group, Farmos Corporation, in 1988. That company was merged into Orion in 1990. During the ensuing decade, Orion continued to build its international focus, a move aided by its decision to go public in 1995 with a listing on the Helsinki Stock Exchange. This coincided with Orion's decision to become a focused research-driven pharmaceuticals group. The company began divesting a number of operations, including an engineering business, originally acquired in the 1970s, in 1999, followed by the sale of the Soredex medical supplies operation that same year. In 2003, the company completed its streamlining, selling off its Noiro cosmetics business.

These moves came amidst the launch of a number of successful proprietary pharmaceutical molecules and preparations, including 1998's entacapone, marketed as Comtess, as a treatment for Parkinson's Disease symptoms. That drug rapidly received international approval. Orion continued to release new proprietary molecules into the 2000s, including the heart failure drug levosimendan, and Stalevo, a new Parkinson's Disease therapy. By the mid-2000s, Orion boasted seven proprietary drugs on the international market.

The company's transformation into a research-driven group had also enabled it to establish a new reputation for itself in the international drug industry. Orion began a series of drug-development and marketing partnerships and alliances, such as its 2002 agreement with Quintiles Transnational Corp to form a joint venture into order to develop certain new Orion molecules through Phase III clinical trials. This followed a collaboration agreement with Pharmacia Corp. in 2001 and a marketing alliance with Abbott Laboratories, later strengthened in 2004.

Orion continued to strengthen its wholesale and distribution wing as well. In 2002, that operation became Scandinavia's largest when Orion acquired Sweden's Kronans Droghandel (KD). That company remained separate from Oriola. However, in 2003 Oriola acquired KD's Finnish operation, KD Tukku Oy. The addition of KD helped boost the company's distribution wing to represent some 72 percent of Orion's total revenues. Oriola grew again, buying up Rusch Danmark A/S, a healthcare supplies marketer, from the U.S.-based company Teleflex Medical.

Nonetheless, Orion Pharma remained the company's core operation, despite accounting for just 26 percent of the group's total sales of EUR 1.9 billion ($2.5 billion) in 2004, while the company's pharmaceutical operation represented some 78 percent of its net profits. Orion, which formally simplified its name to Orion Oyj in 2004, had successfully established itself as a Finland's leading research-driven pharmaceuticals group in the new century.

Principal Subsidiaries

Kronans Droghandel; Orioala; Orion Diagnostica; Orion Pharma.

Principal Competitors

Abbott Laboratories; Bristol-Myers Squibb Company; Dow Europe GmbH; AstraZeneca plc; L'Oreal SA; Mitsubishi Chemical Corporation; Wyeth; GlaxoSmithKline; Degussa AG; Eli Lilly and Co.

Further Reading

"Abbott Laboratories and Orion Corp," *Chemical Market Reporter*, April 26, 2004, p. 8.

Boersig, Charles, "Longer-lasting Parkinson Relief," *Med Ad News*, November 2003, p. 10.

"Oriola Oy Acquires Business Operations of Rusch Danmark ApS," *Nordic Business Report*, February 2, 2005.

"Orion Centralises Pharmaceutical Manufacturing in Finland," *Hugin*, July 3, 2003.

"Orion Hopes for Heart Drug Approval in 8 European Countries in Coming Months," *M2 Europharma*, April 23, 2001.

"Orion Pharma Is Focusing R&D," *Hugin*, June 5, 2003.

"Orion Pharma's New R&D Facility Close to Completion," *M2 Europharma*, January 31, 2002.

"Orion Reduces Workforce," *R&D Directions*, July-August 2003, p. 13.

"Orion Sells Noiro Cosmetics to CapMan," *Chemical Market Reporter*, September 8, 2003, p. 3.

"Orion's New Corporate Name," *Europe Intelligence Wire*, April 1, 2004.

"The European Investment Bank Government Subsidy to Orion Corp.," *Manufacturing Chemist*, March 2005, p. 10.

"Company History," Orion Corporation Annual Report, 2004.

"Company History," Available from http:/www.oriola.fi, 2005.

—M.L. Cohen

⊕ORTHOFIX®

Orthofix International NV

7 Abraham de Veerstraat
Curaçao
Netherlands Antilles
Telephone: (+599) 94658525
Fax: (+599) 94616978
Web site: http://www.orthofix.com

Public Company
Incorporated: 1979
Employees: 988
Sales: $286.63 million (2004)
Stock Exchanges: NASDAQ
Ticker Symbol: OFIX
NAIC: 339112 Surgical and Medical Instrument
   Manufacturing

Orthofix International NV is a leading manufacturer of orthopedic and other medical products focused on three primary areas: Spine, which accounts for 28 percent of group sales; Reconstruction (42 percent); and Trauma (22 percent). The company major products feature external and internal fixation devices, which can be used to treat fractures, promote bone growth and reconstruction, and lengthen limbs. The company also develops stimulant devices, such its non-invasive Physio-Stim and Spinal-Stim devices, used for enhancing bone and other post-injury and post-surgical repair. Other products developed by Orthofix include its Oasis system for aiding osteo-arthritis suffering from knee pain; the Xcaliber line of fracture fixators; VacoSplint and Storm, both used for tendon and other soft tissue injuries; AV Impulse, a vascular therapy device used to promote circulation in post-operative patients; limb lengthening and limb reconstruction devices, including the Sheffield Ring Fixator, and an internal bone lengthening system, ISKD; and pneumatic bracing devices, such as its Orthotrac Pneumatic Vest, used for relieve pain and promoting recovery from spinal injuries. Orthofix's product line also includes a limited range of non-orthopedic devices, including women's care and respiratory assistance products. Non-medical sales accounted for just 8 percent of group sales of $287 million in 2004. Founded in

Verona, Italy, but registered in Curaçao, in the Dutch Antilles, Orthofix operates primary manufacturing facilities in the United States, Mexico, and Italy, as well as sales and marketing subsidiaries in France, Germany, Switzerland, the United Kingdom, Belgium, and elsewhere. At the end of 2004, Orthofix strengthened its U.S. presence as well as its position in the American market with the acquisition of California-based BREG Inc. Orthofix is listed on the NASDAQ and is led by president and CEO Charles W. Federico.

Italian Origins in the 1980s

Orthofix International stemmed from the work of orthopedic researcher Giovanni de Bastiani of the University of Verona in Italy. Toward the end of the 1970s, Bastiania proposed the concept of "dynamization," based on the natural ability of bone to repair itself. Bastiani developed an external axial frame device that could be fitted to a fracture in order to stimulate and assist the reconstruction of the bone. In 1979, Bastiani presented the device at an orthopedic conference. The following year, he founded Orthofix Srl in order to continue the development of the device and launch it as a commercially available product. The company grew slowly, reaching sales of about $7 million by the mid-1980s.

Orthofix's fortunes changed with the arrival of investment and management team Robert Gaines-Cooper and Edgar Wallner. Backed by pension fund investors, Gaines-Cooper and Wallner acquired Orthofix and reoriented it toward an international market. The company was reincorporated in Curaçao, in the Netherlands Antilles, becoming Orthofix International. Nonetheless, Orthofix remained closely connected to the university at Verona and maintained a research and development and manufacturing base in that city. Soon after the takeover, Orthofix completed its Modulsystem, an external fixation system, which became the group's first major success on the international orthopedic market.

Orthofix continued to focus on developing minimally invasive orthopedic devices, growing steadily into the early 1990s, as sales topped $20 million in 1991 and then $30 million by the end of 1993. By then, Orthofix had developed relationships with a network of distributors, bringing its products to more than 70

Company Perspectives:

The company's mission is to offer highly valued minimally invasive medical devices for the orthopedic and trauma markets and to achieve market leadership in each of our chosen segments by focusing on continuous innovation in the products and services we offer. We will ask ourselves every day what we have done to delight our customers.

Key Dates:

1979: Giovanni de Bastiani of the University of Verona in Italy introduces an axial frame device for the stimulation of bone growth.
1980: Orthofix Srl is created to market the axial frame device.
1987: Orthofix is acquired in a buyout led by Robert Gaines-Cooper and Edgar Wallner.
1992: Orthofix goes public on the NASDAQ and acquires Novamedix in England.
1993: Orthofix acquires Orthosonics in England and distributor Colgate Medical (renamed as Intavent Orthofix) in a joint venture with Intavent.
1995: American Medical Electronics is acquired and renamed Orthofix Inc.
1999: New Jersey-based Neomedics Inc. is acquired.
2000: Minnesota-based Kinesis Medical Products is acquired.
2002: OrthoRX is formed in a joint venture with Health-South Corporation.
2003: Full control of Intavent Orthofix is acquired.
2004: California-based BREG Inc. is acquired.
2005: The company becomes the distributor for Berkeley Advanced Biomaterials' OsteoMax synthetic bone-graft products.

countries. The United States represented the company's single largest market. A new milestone for the company came in 1992, when Orthofix listed its stock on the NASDAQ. The public offering enabled Orthofix to begin plotting its next expansion phase.

Acquisition played a prominent role in Orthofix's growth throughout the 1990s and into the 2000s. The company's first purchase came soon after its public offering, when Orthofix acquired a 20 percent stake in the United Kingdom's Novamedix Ltd. By the end of 1992, the company had boosted its stake in Novamedics to 40 percent, while also acquiring a 60 percent stake in NMX Distribution Ltd., which handled distribution for Novamedix in the Americas and elsewhere. The eventual purchase of the whole of Novamedix by Orthofix allowed the latter company to extend its product offering into a new category, adding its subsidiary's A-V Impulse System Foot Pump. This non-invasive device attached to a bedridden patient's foot in order to stimulate the return of blood from the legs, enhancing circulation in order to maintain muscular and circulatory function. The product exemplified Orthofix's focus on innovative yet minimally invasive orthopedic devices.

Orthofix continued to target the United Kingdom for its next acquisitions. In 1993, the company acquired two more British companies, Orthosonics and Colgate Medical. Orthosonics brought Orthofix an important extension to its product categories, adding the development and manufacture of orthopedic devices utilizing ultrasound technology. Colgate Medical had been established in the mid-1970s as a distributor of breast pumps and breast shields before adding medical products such as respiratory devices. Colgate Medical also became the U.K. distributor for the A-V Impulse. Its acquisition by Orthofix came as a joint venture with Intavent Ltd., and initially the distribution group took on the name of Intavent Orthofix Ltd. Orthofix acquired 100 percent control of Intavent Orthofix in the early 2000s.

Building a U.S. Presence in the 1990s and 2000s

Although the United States represented Orthofix's most important market, the company had not yet established a presence there. That move came in 1995, when Orthofix acquired American Medical Electronics Inc. (AME). The acquisition brought Orthofix a new specialty, that of bone growth stimulators and bone substitutes. AME also gave Orthofix an extensive sales and distribution network in the United States, as well as a manufacturing complex in Richardson, Texas. Following its acquisition, the subsidiary was renamed Orthofix Inc.

The addition of Orthofix Inc. helped boost the company's total sales past $77 million by the end of 1996. Nonetheless, the company's extension into the United States was not immediately successful, and losses were posted in the U.S. subsidiary's first years with the company. In 1996, however, Orthofix brought in Charles Federico to take over as CEO of the U.S. subsidiary and turn it around. Federico's success later led him to take over as president and CEO of Orthofix International.

In the meantime, Orthofix continued to extend its range of offerings, adding products including Radiolucent Wrist Fixator, the Spinal Stim and Physio-Stim Lite Bone Growth Stimulator, and the OSCAR ultrasonic bone cement removal system for the hip. In 1997, the company introduced another new product, a synthetic bone replacement material called Intramedullary Nail and Osteogenics BoneSource. Also in 1997, the company shifted its U.S. headquarters to North Carolina, where it launched a joint research initiative with Wake Forest University.

Orthofix continued to expand in the United States at the end of the 1990s. The company acquired a 30 percent stake in Neomedics Inc., based in New Jersey, which specialized in the development of implantable tissue growth stimulation devices. Orthofix acquired full control of Neomedics in 1999. The addition of Neomedics expanded Orthofix's product offering, particularly in the area of spinal care, to include both non-invasive and invasive devices.

The following year, Orthofix boosted its range of spinal care products again when it acquired Kinesis Medical Inc., based in Bloomington, Minnesota. That company specialized in support devices providing ambulatory unloading in order to diminish pain from spinal and back injuries. Kinesis' core product was its patented pneumatic vest system, Orthotrac, proven to reduce lower back pain in patients with herniated discs and related injuries. Sales at the end of 2000 topped $131 million.

In 2002, Orthofix stepped up its distribution reach with the formation of a 50–50 joint venture, OrthoRX Inc., with Health-South Corporation. The joint venture provided orthopedic inventory, insurance authorization, and billing services for HealthSouth's more than 1,900 health centers. The following year, the company strengthened its U.K. distribution arm as well, buying up full control of Intavent Orthofix Ltd. By 2004, the company's distribution network had extended its product reach into more than 85 countries worldwide, with direct sales operations in the United States, the United Kingdom, Italy, France, Germany, Mexico, Switzerland, and Brazil, as well as its stake in OrthoRX.

Orthofix's expansion in the United States took a major step forward in 2004. In that year, the company completed its acquisition of privately-held BREG Inc. for a purchase price of $150 million. The California-based company complemented Orthofix's own focus on the spine, bone reconstruction, and trauma sectors, and added nearly $60 million in annual revenues. By the end of 2004, Orthofix's sales had jumped to nearly $287 million.

Orthofix continued to seek out new expansion opportunities in 2004 and into 2005. In April 2005, for example, the company announced its agreement to handle marketing and distribution for Berkeley Advanced BioMaterials Inc.'s bone-repair products. Orthofix itself unveiled extensions of its own product line, notably with the launch of updated versions of the Physio-Stim and Spinal-Stim bone-growth generation systems. Orthofix had established itself a leader and major innovator in the field of non-invasive osteopedic devices.

Principal Subsidiaries

Breg, Inc. (United States); Colgate Medical Ltd. (United Kingdom); Implantes Y Sistemas Medicos, Inc. (Puerto Rico); Intavent Orthofix Ltd. (United Kingdom); Inter Medical Supplies Limited (Cyprus); Inter Medical Supplies Ltd. (Seychelles); Novamedix Distribution Limited (Cyprus); Novamedix Services Ltd. (United Kingdom); Orthofix AG (Switzerland); Orthofix do Brasil (Brazil; 89.5%); Orthofix GmbH (Germany); Orthofix Holdings Inc. (United States); Orthofix II B.V. (Holland); Orthofix Inc. (United States); Orthofix International B.V. (Holland); Orthofix Ltd. (United Kingdom); Orthofix S.A. (France); Orthofix S.r.l. (Italy); Orthofix UK Ltd. (United Kingdom); Orthofix US LLC (United States); Orthosonics Ltd. (United Kingdom); Promeca S.A. de C.V. (Mexico; 61.25%)

Principal Competitors

Merial Ltd.; McKesson Medical-Surgical; Medline Industries Inc; Siemens AB; Cadwell Laboratories Inc; Agilent Technologies Deutschland GmbH; Instrumentarium Corporation; NOF Corporation; 3M United Kingdom plc; Centerpulse Orthopedics AG.

Further Reading

"Change at the Helm of Orthopedics Company Announced," *Medical Devices & Surgical Technology Week*, April 25, 2004, p. 129.

Edwards, Anthony R., "With Breg Acquisition, Orthofix Broadens Orthopedic Holdings," *Biomechanics*, January 1, 2004, p. 62.

"Orthofix Acquires Firm Focused on Tissue Growth Stimulation," *Biotech Equipment Update*, July 1999.

"Orthofix Inks Distribution Pact," *Charlotte Business Journal*, April 26, 2005.

"Orthofix Acquires 100% of Its UK Distributor," *Medical Devices & Surgical Technology Week*, April 6, 2003, p. 69.

"Orthopedics Products Company Bought for $150 Million," *Medical Devices & Surgical Technology Week*, December 21, 2003, p. 112.

Tanner, Lisa, "More Changes Ahead for Orthofix Inc.," *Dallas Business Journal*, March 28, 1997, p. 11.

—M.L. Cohen

Pall Corporation

2200 Northern Boulevard
East Hills, New York 11548
U.S.A.
Telephone: (516) 484-5400
Fax: (516) 484-5228
Web site: http://www.pall.com

Public Company
Incorporated: 1946 as Micro Metallic Corporation
Employees: 10,300
Sales: $1.77 billion (2004)
Stock Exchanges: New York
Ticker Symbol: PLL
NAIC: 333999 All Other Miscellaneous General Purpose
    Machinery Manufacturing

Pall Corporation is the largest manufacturer of filtration, separation, and purification products in the world. The company markets its products in four major industries: healthcare, pharmaceutical, fluid processing, and aerospace. According to the company, fluids are processed by a Pall product over 60 million times each day across the globe. Approximately 40 percent of company sales stem from operations in Europe.

Early History

Pall Corporation traces its origins to the formation of the Micro Metallic Corporation by David Pall in 1946. During World War II, Pall, a Canadian-born chemist, worked on the Manhattan Project, a covert operation in which the American government sought to develop the first atomic bomb. Pall, then 27 years old, helped design a filter to separate uranium 235 from uranium 238. He and his colleagues developed the filter to separate the raw uranium material from the heavier, less stable uranium by sintering—heating to just below melting point—powdered stainless steel and producing a very fine screen. Pall and his company, renamed the Pall Corporation in 1957, remained focused on developing filters for special tasks, and, as technology in other fields emerged, new markets opened up for the company's filters.

In 1950, Pall brought his neighbor, a certified public accountant named Abraham Krasnoff, into the company to help with administration and finance. Krasnoff's organizational skills along with Pall's scientific genius resulted in a successful organization.

In 1958, Pall began developing filters for the aircraft industry. Its first filters were for the American Airlines fleet of Boeing 707s, the technicians for which had resorted to operating their landing gear manually after finding that impurities were causing the hydraulic landing gear system to malfunction. Next, Pall developed a filter for purifying jet fuel. The company soon became the leading supplier of aircraft filters, and in the 1960s and 1970s Pall filters were used on most major military aircraft, including helicopters and fighter jets.

In fact, by the late 1970s Pall had become overly dependent on military and defense industries, and the company sought new markets for its fine filter technology. During this time, Pall was able to provide the emerging semiconductor and biotechnical industries with the finer filters needed in their manufacturing processes.

According to Abraham Krasnoff, who became the company chairperson in 1989, Pall preferred to service niche markets, where manufacturing needs were very specialized and challenging. Accordingly, Pall eschewed the production of filters widely used by individual consumers, such as gasoline or oil filters for cars. Furthermore, once Pall's development of a certain technology was complete, the company usually jettisoned its business in that area. For example, in 1988, Pall sold its compressed air dryer business as well as its facility that produced gas mask filters, as they both became technologically and financially mature units.

Recognizing that Pall Corporation could not rely solely on the genius of one person, David Pall, the company focused on building a research and development department. Referring to David Pall, Krasnoff told *Industry Week,* "You can always succeed a good manager, but you can never succeed a genius." Therefore, Krasnoff and Pall set about assembling an impressive array of scientists who would help develop fluid clarification products. Pall spent only about 4 percent of its sales on research and development, compared to the budgets of some of its chief competitors, such as Millipore, which allotted more than 7 percent of sales. The company was able to keep its costs down by focusing solely on fluid clarification, unlike Millipore and other companies, which had diversified their interests and therefore required a wider array of researchers.

Another of Krasnoff's organizational strategies was to assemble a team of scientists known collectively as the company's Scientific Laboratory Services, or SLS, to help test, advise, and communicate with researchers. Krasnoff told *Financial World* that SLS was "a bridge between the leading edge customer and our own marketing and research people."

In order to ensure that supplies and prices remained steady worldwide, manufacturing for each of Pall's product lines took place in at least two Pall facilities. The size of each facility was limited to no more than 450 employees, fostering a sense of team spirit and familiarity.

Pall in the 1980s and Early 1990s

Much of the steady growth Pall experienced, measuring about 17 percent annually through the 1980s and into the 1990s, was accomplished through internal growth rather than through acquisitions. Pall focused on building new factories and creating subsidiaries throughout the world. Pall faced international competition but maintained its edge in several markets and managed to dominate almost every niche it carved out for its subsidiaries.

In the early 1990s, Pall's healthcare products division was the fastest growing segment of the company. In 1992, with sales of $331.6 million, the division represented almost half of Pall's sales and 60 percent of its operating expenses. It included filters for direct use with hospital patients to provide protection against contamination and infection through blood, breathing, or IVs. Blood filters in particular were a high growth area in the first part of the decade, with sales estimated to reach $260 million, or 26 percent of total sales, by 1995.

Pall's leukocyte filters treated with gamma rays were used to filter out white blood cells, which caused the rejection of platelets during the multiple transfusions necessary for organ donors and recipients, AIDs patients, and those undergoing chemotherapy. David Pall led the team that developed the blood filter, which proved a vital part of the system used for processing whole blood at blood collection sites.

Other Pall healthcare products included filters to use in diagnostic devices and filters for the manufacture of contamination-free pharmaceuticals, biopharmaceuticals, and biologicals. Moreover, Pall produced electronic instruments for use in testing the filters before and after use. Pall's operations also included food, beverage, and household water filters in its healthcare segment. Products in this market included filters for the final filtration process of beer, wine, and bottled water and filters used in the production of high fructose corn syrup. Pall entered into an agreement to apply its dynamic microfiltration systems to a series of dairy product applications of Ault Foods of Toronto, Canada.

The company's Aeropower division accounted for sales of $204.7 million in 1992. This division produced fluid clarification filters used to clean hydraulic, lubricating, and transmission fluids for both military and commercial aircraft. Other industrial customers included manufacturers and end users of fluid power equipment and bearing lubrication systems for steel, aluminum, and paper mills and the automobile and aerospace industries. Furthermore, Pall's filters were used by manufacturers of on- and off-road vehicles and construction equipment and machinery for moving earth, as well as having applications in agriculture machinery, oil drilling and exploration, mining, metal cutting, and electric power generation.

Military sales accounted for only 10 percent of Pall's sales in 1990, down from 25 percent ten years earlier. During the Persian Gulf crisis involving Operation Desert Shield and Operation Desert Storm, however, military sales went up when Pall supplied $26 million worth of filters to keep sand out of helicopter engines. Furthermore, Pall entered into an agreement with FMC Corporation, a defense and military systems contractor, to provide an industrial air purification method (called Pressure Swing Absorption or PSA) to FMC for most military applications in North America, including foreign military sales. Pall anticipated that this would build a strong base for military sales, which the company expected to slowly increase despite the downsizing of the military occurring in the early 1990s.

The fluid processing market, with sales of $148.8 million in 1992, included service to manufacturers of electronic components, liquid crystal displays, magnetic tape, electric power, film, fiber, chemicals, petrochemicals, oil, gas, paper, steel, and other products in which filters are needed for removing contaminants or particles. Pall worked with several world-renowned scientists to develop new products in this market segment, especially the area of semiconductor technology. Although this was a mature market, research and development was opening new applications for Pall.

International Operations in the Early 1990s

Pall's international operations provided about two-thirds of its revenues in the early 1990s. In the mid-1960s Pall had acquired a small English metalworking company run by Maurice Hardy. This initial investment in Hardy's company was Pall's jumping-off point for further overseas expansion. By the time England became a full member of the European Common Market more than a decade later, Pall Europe was generating

Key Dates:

1946: David Pall establishes the Micro Metallic Corporation.
1950: Abraham Krasnoff joins the company.
1957: Micro Metallic is renamed Pall Corp.
1958: Pall begins to develop filters for the aircraft industry.
1991: By now, Pall's sales growth in Europe is at 18 percent and its growth in Asia reaches 31 percent.
1994: Eric Krasnoff is named chairman and CEO.
2004: Pall begins to restructure into three operating companies: Pall Life Sciences, Pall Process Technologies, and Pall Aeropower.

sales revenues of $9 million. Despite duties imposed by the European Economic Community, 40 percent of Pall's sales were in West Germany, Italy, and Holland, while 10 percent were in Scandinavia.

In each country Pall entered, it used roughly the same strategy, setting up a small sales unit, then expanding to include technological and engineering support. It then added distribution to its services. Krasnoff maintained that Pall did not establish foreign facilities to take advantage of lower labor costs, telling *U.S. News & World Report* in 1988 that the three most important rules he had learned about operating overseas were, "Hire competent locals, use competent locals, and listen to competent locals."

In 1991, Pall's sales growth in Europe was at 18 percent, and its growth in Asia reached 31 percent, while its growth in the United States that year was only 8 percent. By 1993, Pall was generating about two-thirds of its revenues from foreign markets and had subsidiaries in Brazil, Spain, Germany, France, Singapore, Canada, Japan, Korea, and other nations and was considering further expansion in Japan and the rest of the Pacific Rim. Pall projected that by 1995, as much as 75 percent of its sales could be generated abroad.

In the early 1990s, Pall faced intense competition from the Japanese, particularly in the blood filtering market. While Pall controlled about 50 percent of that market, its share was threatened by Asahi, a Japanese chemistry conglomerate worth billions of dollars, and Terumo, a medical equipment manufacturer. Nevertheless, Pall was able to beat these Japanese firms to market with its improved leukocyte filter.

In 1993, Pall looked forward to international growth, particularly in the high-tech areas of ultrafiltration (molecular separation) and dynamic microfiltration. To this end, the company sought to form alliances with global operations rather than to acquire them. According to CEO Maurice Hardy, who replaced Krasnoff, a company must have "a multinational and, later, a global operating strategy." Hardy died of cancer in July 1994, leaving Eric Krasnoff at the helm as chairman and CEO.

Mid-1990s and Beyond

Under the continued leadership of Krasnoff, Pall focused on expansion and diversification in the mid-1990s. The company relied on high-end separations to fuel its growth well into the 2000s. It also made several key acquisitions and launched several new products as part of its growth strategy. In 1995, Pall announced the development of a filter used in HIV-related blood filtration. Two years later, the firm acquired Gelman Sciences. In 1998, Rochem, a German filtration systems manufacturer, was added to the company's arsenal. In 1999, Pall secured a $6 million water purification contract with the Pittsburgh Water and Sewer Authority. During that year, the United Kingdom began to require the removal of white blood cells—leukocytes—from all blood and blood products after nearly 30 people died from Mad Cow disease. Shortly thereafter, Austria, France, Ireland, Malta, Norway, Poland, and Canada adopted the requirement that blood products go through the process called leukocyte reduction. In 2000, Germany followed suit. As a result, Pall landed a $6 million blood filtration contract from the German Red Cross Transfusion Center.

Pall entered the 21st century on solid ground. Strategic alliances, acquisitions, and research and development were cornerstones in the firm's long-term strategy. The company partnered with QIAGEN NV and Stedim SA in 2001. During 2002, Pall purchased the Filtration and Separations Group of U.S. Filter Corp. Whatman HemaSure, the blood filtration arm of Whatman plc, and the BioSepra Process Division of Ciphergen Biosystems Inc., were added to Pall's coffers in 2003 and 2004, respectively.

During this time period, Pall began to make some internal changes. The company adopted the CoRe Cost Reduction program, which was expected to generate savings of nearly $20 million in 2005. Pall also began to realign its business segments in 2004. It restructured into three operating companies: Pall Life Sciences, which included the medical and biopharmaceuticals business; Pall Process Technologies, the combination of microelectronics and general industrial interests; and Pall Aeropower, which integrated the company's aerospace and machinery and equipment holdings.

By 2005, it was evident that Pall's efforts over the past several years were paying off. Both revenue and income were on the rise, and the company appeared to be on solid financial ground. Founder David Pall—a holder of 181 U.S. patents—died in 2004, leaving behind a company that was far different from the small firm he founded in a New York garage in the 1940s. Indeed, with nearly 60 years of history under its belt, Pall had grown into a formidable competitor in the purification, filtration, and separations industries. Its good fortune in the recent decade left it well positioned for success in the years to come.

Principal Subsidiaries

Medsep Corporation; Pall Acquisition LLC; Pall Aeropower Corporation; Pall Biomedical, Inc.; Pall International Corporation; Pall Puerto Rico, Inc.; Pall PASS US, Inc.; Russell Associates Inc.; Gelman Sciences, Inc.; Pall Austria Filter GmbH; Pall (Canada) Ltd.; Pall Europe Ltd. (United Kingdom); Pall France S.A.; Pall Deutschland Beteiligungs GmbH (Germany); Pall Deutschland Holding GmbH & Co. KG Partnership (Germany); Pall Italia S.R.L.; Gelman Ireland Ltd.; Pall Netherlands B.V.; PLLN C.V. Partnership (Netherlands); Pall Norge AS (Norway); Pall Espana S.A. (Spain); Pall Norden AB (Sweden); Pall (Schweiz) A.G. (Switzerland); Argentaurum A.G. (Switzerland); Pall Filter (Beijing) Co., Ltd. (China); Pall Asia International Ltd. (Hong Kong); Nihon Pall Ltd. (Japan); Pall Filtration Pte. Ltd. (Singapore); Pall Korea Ltd. (South Korea); Pall India Private Ltd.; Pall New Zealand; Pall Corporation Filtration and Separations Thailand Ltd.

Principal Competitors

CUNO Inc.; Millipore Corp.; USFilter Corp.

Further Reading

''Filtration, Separations and Purification Company Acquires Division of Ciphergen,'' *Biotech Business Week*, December 27, 2004.

''Filtration, Separations and Purification Company Acquires Euroflow,'' *Drug Week*, February 25, 2005.

''Germany Mandates Blood Filtration,'' *Membrane & Separation Technology News*, October 1, 2000.

Hardy, Maurice, ''Going Global: One Company's Road to International Markets,'' *Journal of Business Strategy*, November–December, pp. 24–27.

''His Business Knows No Borders,'' *U.S. News & World Report*, March 7, 1988, p. 52.

Hord, Christopher, ''Pall's Krasnoff Heads Quiet Diversification,'' *Long Island Business News*, May 30, 1994, p. 15.

Kanner, Bernice, ''Blood Simple,'' *Chief Executive*, April 1999, p. 30.

''Pall Names Krasnoff Chairman and Chief,'' *Wall Street Journal*, July 12, 1994, p. B10.

''Purely by Chance,'' *Long Island Business News*, June 30, 2000, p. 5A.

Slutsker, Gary, ''To Catch a Particle,'' *Forbes*, January 23, 1989, pp. 88–89.

Teitelman, Robert, ''Focused Functions,'' *Financial World*, July 11, 1989, pp. 54–55.

Tillier, Alan, and Claire Poole, ''U.S. Filter Sells FSG to Pall,'' *Daily Deal*, February 15, 2002.

—Wendy J. Stein
—update: Christina M. Stansell

Parque Arauco S.A.

Avenida Kennedy 5413
Las Condes, Santiago
Chile
Telephone: (+56) 2 299-0500
Fax: (+56) 2 211-4077, 211-4131
Web site: http://www.parquearauco.cl

Public Company
Incorporated: 1981
Employees: 300
Sales: CLP 24.89 billion ($44.65 million) (2004)
Stock Exchanges: Santiago
Ticker Symbol: PARAUCO
NAIC: 531120 Lessors of Nonresidential Buildings;
    531312 Nonresidential Property Managers

Parque Arauco S.A. is the one of the largest operators of shopping malls in Chile and Argentina. It manages two commercial centers in Santiago, the capital of Chile, and a third in Viña del Mar, the nation's chief beach resort. Through its holding in a similar Argentine company, Alto Palermo S.A., Parque Arauco has a stake in several shopping centers in Buenos Aires and provincial Argentine cities. The company receives revenues both in the form of rent and a percentage of the net sales of its retail tenants.

Parque Arauco in Chile: 1982–99

The powerful Said clan in South America was founded by Isa Said, who came to Peru from Jerusalem and made a fortune in commerce. His five sons did much to develop the textile industry in Peru and Bolivia, managing extensive cotton plantations and cotton-yarn factories. One of the five was Salvador, the father of nine children, among whom only one, José Said Saffie, was male. Because Salvador was an invalid, José was enrolled early into the extended family's operations. During the 1940s, the Said clan moved to Chile to develop a textile industry there, and José Said took an active part in their first business, Industrias Químicas Generales. In the 1960s, José Said and his uncle Jacobo founded Banco del Trabajo, which grew to be one

of the five largest in Chile. In the 1980s, he, along with partners, bought another bank, BHIF, and a big industrial company, Envases del Pacífico S.A., as well as founding one of the nation's largest beverage companies, Embotelledora Andina S.A. In addition, José Said entered the field of computers.

Among José Said's ventures in the early 1980s was Parque Arauco, a real estate development firm founded in 1979 and incorporated in 1981. The following year, he and his associates, who included Tomás Fürst Freiwirth and the Martínez Perales brothers, opened Parque Arauco Shopping Center in the Alto las Condes neighborhood of Santiago. The choice of location, on the outskirts of the city, was based on the availability there of cheap land. This large mall came to include 200 shops, branches of Chile's largest department stores, a branch of the nation's largest supermarket chain, a food court, a clinic, and a 14-screen cinema. Because its adjoins Avenida Kennedy, this mall is often called Parque Arauco Kennedy to distinguish it from the corporation.

Aided by an overvalued peso and an economic free-trade policy, Chile was awash with cheap foreign goods at the time of the opening of Parque Arauco Kennedy, and those who could afford to buy filled the new mall. However, the economy was falling into deep recession. Parque Arauco did not establish another shopping mall until 1988, when it opened Shopping Center La Florida, also on the outskirts of Santiago. This commercial center was later renamed Plaza Vespucio. About the same time, the company introduced Mall Arauco Maipú on a 165,500-square-meter tract of land in Santiago's Maipú neighborhood. This commercial center did not fare well and was eventually converted into a mall for outlet stores.

The partners in Parque Arauco decided to divide their Chilean holdings in 1997. The Said group acquired Fürst's 12 percent holding and turned over to Fürst its 14 percent share of Plaza Vespucio, which became the core property of Fürst's rival venture, Grupo Plaza (or Mall Plaza). The Said group now held 38 percent of Parque Arauco's shares. The Abumohr family, also active in textiles and, like the Saids, of Arab origin, held 10 percent. Two pension funds held a combined 24 percent. Parque Arauco Kennedy was Chile's largest shopping mall at the time, with annual sales of $500 million, while Plaza Vespucio ranked third, at $380 million. A medical tower and 1,000 new parking

Key Dates:

1979: Parque Arauco is founded.
1982: Parque Arauco Kennedy is opened on the outskirts of Santiago, Chile.
1988: La Florida (later Plaza Vespucio) is opened on the outskirts of Santiago; Mall Arauco Maipú opens in Santiago.
1992: Parque Arauco enters Argentina with a one-fourth share in a Mendoza shopping center.
1994: The company takes a stake in an Argentine mall-development firm.
1997: The firm acquires Alto Palermo S.A., owner of three malls, and takes its name; partners divide their Chilean holdings.
1998: Alto Palermo completes one Buenos Aires mall, Abasto, and buys another, Patio Bullrich.
1999: Mall Arauco Marina is completed in Chile's premier beach resort, Viña del Mar.
2003: A food and entertainment center within Parque Arauco Kennedy opens.
2004: Alto Rosario Shopping, an Argentine mall in which Parque Arauco is a partner, is opened.

spaces were being constructed at Parque Arauco Kennedy, and a 42-story office building was being contemplated at a cost of $100 million. For Mall Arauco Maipú, Parque Arauco was considering building another medical tower and a high-rise apartment building. In 1999, Parque Arauco, in partnership with the Almacenes Paris and Ripley department-store chains, completed Marina Arauco Mall, a shopping center in Viña del Mar, Chile's main beach resort, at a cost of $120 million. Parque Arauco malls accounted for 24 percent of Chile's shopping-center revenues in that year.

Parque Arauco found itself in conflict with its tenants, who through their retailers' association began legal action against the company. According to the association, while commercial-center tenants in North America paid no more than 10 percent of their sales revenue to the operators, the ones in Parque Arauco malls had seen their payments for rent, common charges, and promotion increase from 16.93 percent in 1996 to 22.98 percent of sales in the first semester of 1999.

Parque Arauco in Argentina: 1992–99

Parque Arauco entered Argentina at the beginning of the 1990s, when the nation was emerging from a decade of economic crisis. In 1992, the company acquired a 25 percent share of Centro Comercial Mendoza Plaza Shopping, located in one of Argentina's main provincial cities. Then Parque Arauco became a major investor in Argentine real estate in association with Inversiones y Representaciones S.A. (IRSA), an enterprise which had the participation of New York-based hedge-fund operator George Soros's Soros Fund Management LLC. In 1994, IRSA and Parque Arauco became partners in Sociedad Anónimo del Mercado de Abasto Provedor (Samap), a joint venture to convert the former main produce market in Buenos Aires to a modern shopping mall. Parque Arauco donated its share of the Mendoza shopping center to Samap, while IRSA turned over its holding in Nuevo Noa Shopping, a mall located in the northern city of Salta. In 1997, when Samap was renamed Alto Palermo S.A., IRSA held 51 percent, while Parque Arauco held 35 percent.

Nueva Noa, later renamed Alto Noa, was a 94-store shopping center that opened in 1994 and included a food court, a large entertainment center, a supermarket, and a multiplex cinema. Mendoza Plaza, opened in 1992, was a 144-store shopping center with a department store, a supermarket, a food court, a multiplex cinema, and an entertainment center. Acting on its own, Parque Arauco developed high-rise apartment towers in Mendoza and Salta.

In 1997, Samap acquired Alto Palermo S.A. from the Pérez Company S.A. holding company. This real estate development firm held three Buenos Aires shopping centers: Alto Palermo, Alto Avellaneda, and Paseo Alcorta, plus 50.5 percent of a fourth, Buenos Aires Design. Developed by Pérez Company, Alto Palermo Shopping Center was a 152-store mall in the upper-middle-class neighborhood of Palermo in Buenos Aires. A $45-million structure clad in glass, marble, granite, and chrome, it was spread out over four levels and included an entertainment center, a food court with 20 restaurants, and a 647-car pay parking lot. A novelty when it opened in late 1990, Alto Palermo was visited by one million people in its first two weeks. Alto Avellaneda, opened in 1995, was a 156-store shopping center just south of Buenos Aires and included the first Wal-Mart in Argentina, a multiplex cinema, an entertainment center, a bowling alley, a food court, and 2,700 free parking spaces. Paseo Alcorta, opened in 1992 in Palermo Chico, one of Buenos Aires's finest neighborhoods, was the largest in Argentina: a three-level balconied shopping center with transparent walls and glass roofs, covering 105,000 square meters, with 122 stores, a Carrefour hypermarket, a multiplex cinema, a food court, and a view of the Río de la Plata. Opened in 1993 in Centro Cultural Recoleta, Buenos Aires Design was a shopping center with 59 stores specialized in interior and home decoration.

Abasto Shopping Center was completed in 1998 at a cost of about $112 million. Located in the heart of Once, a formerly Jewish neighborhood that was also the stamping grounds of Carlos Gardel, Argentina's legendary tango dancer and singer, it occupied five levels, with 189 stores, a food court, a multiplex cinema, entertainment facilities, and a children's museum. Alto Palermo built a residential apartment complex nearby. In 1998, it purchased Patio Bullrich, a shopping mall located in an elegant neighborhood, for $72.3 million. Once a livestock auction house, Patio Bullrich reopened in 1988 as the first shopping center in Argentina. It was located in the prosperous Recoleta neighborhood, facing, on one side, the wide Avenida del Libertador. It preserved intact the metal structure of its 19th-century predecessor and had four levels, 93 stores, a movie complex, an entertainment area, and a food court.

Parque Arauco in the 21st Century

The Argentine recession that began in 1998 culminated in the government's default on its debt and the devaluation of the Argentine peso at the end of 2001. Alto Palermo's market value dropped from $390 million to as low as $40 million. The damage to Parque Arauco's own fortunes led to a shakeup of the company's management. In an interview with the new general manager, Andrés Olivos, for the Chilean business magazine *Capital* in 2003, Lorena Medel contended that "it was greatly rumored that Parque Arauco had had a grade-10 earthquake. That its finances were delicate, that the shareholders couldn't believe the level of debt that had been permitted to arise with respect to Arauco Salud" (the medical tower). Olivos denied that the situation had ever been grave. He revealed that for Parque Arauco Kennedy the company was opening a "gastronomical boulevard" of 16,000 square meters that would unite in one place restaurants, bookstores, cafés, theater halls, a bowling alley, and outdoor live performances as a one-stop resource for an entire family. Arauco Maipú, he conceded, had failed as a center for outlet stores and had returned to its role as a traditional mall, with key stores, cinemas, and, coming soon, a medical center.

Olivos acknowledged that Parque Arauco had fallen behind Grupo Plaza and Cencosud S.A. in the development of commercial real estate in Chile. "Our strategy," he maintained, "is distinct, and we believe that to enter this headlong race by adding square meters doesn't necessarily add value. A good part of this growth only generates cannibalization, and many of the new investments won't pay off in any foreseeable amount of time." Olivos said that Parque Arauco had a 32 percent share of the market in Santiago, with sales of about $200 million a year, and 20 million customers a year for Arauco Kennedy, 15 million for Arauco Maipú, and 17 million for Marina Arauco in Viña del Mar. He added that the company had 45 percent of the mall market in Buenos Aires.

Olivos revealed that Parque Arauco had signed a contract with the new owners of Arauco Salud that would permit it to recover the $2.5 million debt that had been sustained in constructing the 13-story tower. The company was also contemplating the construction of a dental-office building in Arauco Kennedy. In addition, in late 2003 Parque Arauco completed its gastronomical boulevard.

With the revival of the Argentine economy well underway, Parque Arauco was planning new shopping malls in Rosario, Neuquén, and the Buenos Aires neighborhood of Caballito, the latter two in collaboration with IRSA by means of Alto Palermo. Alto Rosario Shopping, completed in late 2004 in partnership with Coto Centro Integral de Comercialización S.A., was a conversion of an old railroad station within the original structure. It included 123 retail stores, market stands, fast-food stores, restaurants and cafés, a Coto hypermarket, a multiplex cinema, and a children's museum. Alto Palermo also had a plan to enter Córdoba by purchasing land or acquiring one of three existing shopping centers. The sales in Parque Arauco properties were expected to reach $1.1 billion in 2004, with Argentina providing 38 percent of the total. All of Alto Palermo's properties were at least 96 percent leased. Parque Arauco's debt in Argentina had been reduced from more than $200 million in 2002 to about $28 million in 2003.

In a 2005 article, *Capital* proclaimed that Parque Arauco had "woken up," with its three Chilean malls fully occupied, the success of Boulevard Gastronómico, an enviable financial structure, many new projects for the next two years, and an intention to enter the retail market. The company was planning to construct 40 new Boulevard sites, including areas for fashion, home decoration and supplies, sports, restaurants, and even a skating rink. Olivos said the company intended to begin a $20 million office real-estate project, remodel Arauco Maipú, build, in alliance with the Almacenes Paris and Ripley department-store chains, a new 60,000-square-meter commercial center in Curicó, and even possibly participate in financing retail businesses. He told the magazine, however, that the market was saturated in Santiago for big shopping malls and that Parque Arauco was not interested in entering "the war for square meters." Indeed, he voiced his belief that only three or four malls in Chile were generating enough business to justify the level of investment that had been made in them.

In Argentina, Parque Arauco, besides participating in the construction and opening of Alto Rosario, was about to raise its stake in Alto Palmero from 27 percent to 32 percent with the impending conversion of $200 million in convertible bonds to common stock. Parque Arauco reported net profit of CLP 7.56 billion ($13.56 million) on revenues of CLP 24.89 billion pesos ($44.65 million) in 2004. The company's long-term debt was CLP 101.92 billion ($182.85 million) at the end of 2004.

Principal Subsidiaries

Comercial Arauco Ltda. (95%); Constructora y Administradora Uno S.A.; Parque Arauco Argentina S.A. (Argentina); Sociedad de Inversiones Internacionales Parque Arauco S.A.

Principal Competitors

Cencosud S.A.; Mall Plaza.

Further Reading

"Los amos del retail chileno," *Gestión*, December 2004, p. 78.

"De compras en el cono sur," *Capital*, December 1997, Anuario '97, p. 29.

"El despertar de Parque Arauco," *Capital*, April 8–21, 2005, pp. 68–69.

Fazio, Hugo, *La transnacionalización de la economía chilena*, Santiago: LOM Ediciones, 2000, pp. 94–95.

——, *Mapa de la extrema riqueza en Chile*, Santiago: LOM-ARCIS, 1997, pp. 254–56.

"La guerra de los malls," *Gestión*, January–February 2005, pp. 22, 24–25.

Kamm, Thomas, "Argentines Escape to Shopping Malls, Spending Away Their Recession Blues," *Wall Street Journal*, December 24, 1990, p. A4.

Malatesta, Parisina, "Megashoppings, Playgrounds for Today's Porteños," *Américas*, July–August, 1993, pp. 14–19.

Medel, Lorena, "El Parque de Olivos," *Capital*, October 10–23, 2003, pp. 30–32, 34.

Sullivan, Tara, "En buena compañía," *América economía*, October 8, 1998, p. 68.

Vega, Francisca, "El comprador silencioso," *América economía*, December 10, 2004, pp. 48–49.

Villamil, Ximena, "El cuartito andina," *Capital*, July 1997, p. 16.

—Robert Halasz

Perfetti Van Melle S.p.A.

Via XXV Aprile 7
Lainate I-20020 MI
Italy
Telephone: (+39) 02 935351
Fax: (+39) 02 9374465
Web site: http://www.perfetti.it

Private Company
Incorporated: 1900 as Van Melle; 1946 as Dolcifico
Lombardo; 2001 as Perfetti Van Melle
Employees: 700
Sales: EUR 1.3 billion ($1.6 billion) (2004 est.)
NAIC: 311330 Confectionery Manufacturing from
Purchased Chocolate; 311340 Non-Chocolate
Confectionery Manufacturing

Perfetti Van Melle S.p.A. is the world's sixth-largest candy and confectionery producer and number two in Europe. Representing the combination of Italy's Perfetti with the Netherlands' Van Melle, Perfetti Van Melle produces and markets a host of top-selling candy brands, including Mentos, Fruittella, Brooklyn, Alpenlieve, Golia, and Frisk. Perfetti Van Melle has a worldwide presence, with factories in Italy, the Netherlands, Germany, Spain, and elsewhere in Europe, as well as manufacturing sites in the United States, Brazil, Turkey, India, China, Indonesia, and Vietnam. The company has also announced its intention to begin manufacturing in Russia in 2005. Sales of the privately held company's products reach more than 130 countries. Perfetti Van Melle operates dual headquarters in Lainate, Italy, and Breda, the Netherlands. The company's sales were estimated to top EUR 1.3 billion ($1.6 billion) in the mid-2000s.

Van Melle's Origins in the 19th Century

The merger between Italy's Perfetti and Van Melle of the Netherlands in 2001 created one of the world's top confectionery companies, with a rank of number two in Europe and a global ranking of number six. The merger cemented the friendly relationship that existed between the companies for some two

decades and had led Perfetti to become a major shareholder in Van Melle by the early 1990s.

Van Melle was the older of the two companies, tracing its origins to a bakery founded by Izaak van Melle in Breskens, the Netherlands, in 1841. The bakery was taken over by one of van Melle's sons, Abraham van Melle, in 1882. It was under this generation that the family made its first entry into the confectionery business. One of the bakeries employees came from Belgium and knew how to prepare sugar in order to make candy. Van Melle decided to begin cooking up candies besides its usual bakery goods. The shop's "suikerballetjes" (sugar balls) quickly became a popular local favorite. Production remained on a small, homemade scale, however.

Abraham van Melle's son Izaak joined the family business by the turn of the 20th century. Recognizing the popularity of the bakery's candies, the younger Van Melle decided to launch large-scale production of the confectionery and invested in machinery and equipment to establish a full-fledged candy factory in 1900. Izaak van Melle also continued to seek to improve the company's products, establishing high-quality standards and expanding and modernizing its production facilities.

The company also rapidly turned to the international market for sales. By the 1920s, the company's products had found their way across the world, reaching the Dutch Indies, South Africa, Morocco, Tunisia, and Algeria, many Asian markets, and, closer to home, markets in Europe, such as Greece. Izaak van Melle himself traveled extensively, seeking out new clients and markets.

Van Melle's many travels had led him to discover many new candy and confectionery varieties, which he brought back to the company. In this way, in 1926, the company launched production of toffee candies, an English favorite. Van Melle soon made the recipe its own, and, working in its own test kitchen, extended its range of toffee to include a variety of flavors, including licorice. The company's recipe proved so successful that Van Melle toffees became popular even in the United Kingdom.

A trip to Poland in the early 1930s gave the company two new recipes. The first was for a soft caramel-like candy containing real fruit flavors. The second was a candy-coated peppermint-flavored

Company Perspectives:

OUR VISION—We will enhance our world leadership in confectionery by creating value for people through delightful and imaginative high-quality products. OUR MISSION—We at Perfetti Van Melle: develop, manufacture and market high-quality and innovative products for our consumers through efficient use of our resources and in partnership with our customers; create a fulfilling workplace for our employees built on trust, mutual respect and appreciation of their diversity; value the role we play in our communities, as a socially and environmentally committed organization; generate economic value through superior growth and profitability.

caramel. These candies later became known as Fruittella and Mentos, respectively, and helped launch Van Melle into the ranks of the world's leading confectionery companies.

By the 1930s, however, Van Melle was already a prominent confectioner, and by 1935 the company had even purchased its own airplane, a rarity at the time. However, the German occupation of the Netherlands during World War II brought hard times to the company. Wartime restrictions on sugar consumption severely cut into production. By the end of the war, bombing raids had destroyed the Van Melle factory.

Expansion and Innovation: Mid-1940s to the 1970s

Instead of rebuilding in Breskens, Van Melle decided to relaunch the company with a new purpose-built facility in Rotterdam in 1946. The new facility therefore gained access to Rotterdam's busy port, facilitating its international sales. By 1950, Van Melle had reached full production capacity at the new site. During this period, however, the company decided to narrow its range of confectionery in order to target its efforts on a smaller group of core candy brands. The period also marked the beginning of Van Melle's true internationalization.

The company launched initiatives in a number of new markets through the 1950s and into the 1960s and 1970s. Among these was the introduction of a new packaging form for its Fruittella and Mentos candies, which were quickly becoming company flagships. Both candy types had previously been packaged as loose, bagged candies. In the 1950s, however, Van Melle developed a new roll-type packaging, easier to stock for grocers and easier to carry for consumers. The new packaging helped turn both candies into top-selling international brands.

Van Melle backed up its international expansion with the opening of a series of foreign subsidiaries. In 1956, the company established its first foreign manufacturing plant, opening a facility in Brazil. The company also began opening sales and marketing subsidiaries in order to be closer to local markets, setting up in Belgium in 1950, Germany in 1953, and France in 1960, before expanding elsewhere. The company entered the United States in 1972, establishing a manufacturing and marketing subsidiary in Erlanger, Kentucky, that year. Later in the 1970s, Van Melle expanded into Asia as well, ultimately setting up subsidiaries in India, Singapore, and Vietnam. In addition to producing and promoting Van Melle's core brands, the new

subsidiaries also helped the company adapt its recipes and product offering for these local markets.

Building Relationships in the 1980s

Van Melle launched a new expansion phase in the 1980s, seeking to build up its range of brands and expand its production capacity. In 1982, the company made its first acquisition, buying up a small candy producer, PPW, based in Gilda, and acquiring that company's Mintina and Dropmintina brands as well. By then, the company had reached the limits of its production capacity at its Rotterdam site. The company went looking for a new site, buying up a large factory site in Breda. Fueling this expansion, Van Melle listed its shares of the Amsterdam Stock Exchange's Parallelmarkt in 1983.

At the same time, the company retained its interest in new growth opportunities. One of these came in the early 1980s when the company formed a relationship with Italian confectionery company Perfetti, and the two companies began developing joint-marketing efforts. Van Melle also added a number of acquisitions through the 1980s and into the 1990s, including a candy factory from Gebr. Verduijn, which marked the company's return to Breskens as well. The company then purchased Peco Suikerwerken, based in Den Haag, followed by the acquisition of Look-O-Look, a maker of lollipops and bagged candies, based in Ridderkerk, in 1987. Meanwhile, Van Melle also worked on the in-house development of new candy types and brands, leading to the launch of Airheads candies in the United States in 1986.

Merging Market Leaders in the 1990s and 2000s

Van Melle's expansion continued through the 1990s, notably with an entry into the Eastern European markets. After establishing local sales and marketing subsidiaries in these countries, Van Melle sought to acquire production capacity as well, and in 1998 the company acquired VDG, which operated in the Czech Republic, Slovakia, and Hungary. The company opened a production facility in Poland, and a packaging plant in Russia, then established a factory in Indonesia. The company also entered India and China, establishing sales and production subsidiaries in those markets in the late 1990s. The company built its first Chinese factory in Shenzen in 1997, launching production in 2000. At the end of the 1990s, Van Melle's expansion program led it to acquire a number of new businesses, including Klene in the Netherlands, Candy Tech in the United States, and Fundy in Hungary and Romania, all in 1999. Also in that year, Van Melle acquired the Wybert brand of throat lozenges, including a production site in the Netherlands, from GABA International of Switzerland.

Van Melle moved its stock listing to the Euronext Amsterdam Stock Exchange's Officiële Markt in 2000. By then, Perfetti was already a major shareholder in the company, having bought a 36 percent stake in Van Melle in the early 1990s. Soon after Van Melle's listing, the two companies, which had continued strengthening their marketing partnerships over the last decade, agreed to a full-fledged merger. In 2001, Perfetti acquired 100 percent control of the company and removed its public listing. The newly enlarged company then adopted the name Perfetti Van Melle.

Key Dates:

1841: Izaak Van Melle opens a bakery in Breskens, the Netherlands.

1882: Abraham Van Melle takes over the bakery and begins producing candies.

1900: Izaak van Melle, the founder's grandson, takes over the bakery and builds a new factory for large-scale production of candy and confectionery.

1926: Van Melle begins production of English-style toffee.

1946: After its production site destroyed during war, Van Melle builds a new factory in Rotterdam; Perfetti brothers launch Dolcifico Lombardo, later Perfetti, in Lainate, Italy, in order to produce chewing gum and other candies.

1950: Van Melle opens its first foreign sales and distribution subsidiary in Belgium.

1966: Perfetti launches a subsidiary, Gum Base Company, for production of natural and artificial gum bases.

1972: Van Melle starts U.S. operations in Kentucky.

1982: Van Melle moves to a new production site in Breda and makes its first acquisition, of PPW in Gilda; Perfetti sets up its first foreign production site in Greece.

1983: Van Melle lists shares on Amsterdam Beurs' Parallel Markt and begins a marketing relationship with Perfetti.

1991: Perfetti buys a 37 percent stake in Van Melle.

1995: Van Melle enters India.

1997: Van Melle enters China, building a production site in Shenzen.

2000: Van Melle switches its listing to Amsterdam exchange's primary board.

2001: Perfetti acquires 100 percent control of Van Melle for EUR 966 million.

Perfetti: Postwar Beginnings to Merger with Van Melle

Perfetti had been founded in the town of Lainate, Italy, in 1946, by brothers Ambrogio and Egidio Perfetti. The brothers initially called their company Docificio Lombardo, and the small company began producing candies and confectionery for the nearby market in Milan. The Perfettis grew quickly, expanding their factory into the 1950s.

The product that put the Perfetti name on the international candy map was launched soon after the company's founding. The arrival of the American army in Italy during World War II had introduced Italians to a novel new confectionery—chewing gum. The Perfettis became the first in Italy to begin producing chewing gum, adopting the name "Brooklyn" for their product. The brand became an instant success across the country and was to remain Italy's top-selling chewing gum into the 21st century. The company later changed its name to Perfetti. In the 1960s, the company expanded its production, notably through the founding of Gum Base Company SpA, which specialized in developing bases for Perfetti's and other companies' chewing gum.

By the end of the 1970s, Perfetti boasted a strong portfolio of confectionery brands, including Alpenliebe, Babol, Morositas, Vigorsol, and Happydent. The company backed up its products with innovative advertising campaigns that enabled its brands to become leaders in their categories. Perfetti also expanded into international markets, achieving strength particularly in southern Europe. This position made the company an attractive partner for Van Melle, which focused more strongly on northern Europe, leading the companies to develop their first cross-marketing efforts in the early 1980s.

Perfetti launched its own acquisition drive in the 1980s, acquiring Caremoli and its Golia brand; lollipop and candy maker La Giulia; and Gelco, which specialized in jelly candies and licorice. Perfetti also developed its presence in the international markets, acquiring Belgium's Frisk in the mid-1980s and opening its first foreign factory in Greece in 1982. Through the end of the 1980s and into the 1990s, Perfetti added production sites in Turkey, India, and China, an expansion that culminated in the opening of a modern production site in Brazil in 1999.

The merger with Van Melle, which cost Perfetti EUR 966 million, provided the new company with total sales of more than EUR 1 billion. The combined operations of Perfetti and Van Melle also gave the company a particularly strong position in many of the markets in the Asian region, such as China and India, where the company held number one or two positions in several categories.

Perfetti Van Melle continued enhancing its market position, notably through the creation of new marketing alliances, such as the creation of a joint-venture distribution business with Spain's Chupa Chups for the U.K. market in 2005. Also in 2005, Perfetti Van Melle announced its plans to build a factory in Russia. By then, too, the company's continued success in the United States had led it to announce plans to nearly double the size of its Erlanger, Kentucky, site. Perfetti Van Melle looked forward to a sweet future in the 21st century.

Principal Subsidiaries

Dimpex S.A. (Switzerland); Frisk Int. Nv (Belgium); Gelco S.R.L.; Gum Base Asia Ltd. (Hong Kong); Gum Base Co. S.P.A.; Gum Base Shanghai (China); La Giulia Ind. S.P.A.; Perfetti Confectionery Co. Ltd (China); Perfetti Confectionery Vietnam Ltd; Perfetti Cr S.R.O. (Czech Republic); Perfetti Do Brasil; Perfetti Gida San. Ve Tic. A.S. (Turkey); Perfetti Hellas S.A. (Greece); Perfetti India Ltd.; Perfetti S.A. (Spain); Perfetti S.P.A.; Perfetti South Africa Pty Ltd (South Africa); Perfetti Van Melle Benelux BV (Netherlands); Pt. Perfetti Indonesia; Sulá Gmbh & Co. Kg (Germany); Van Melle Export B.V. (Holland).

Principal Competitors

Nestlé S.A.; Kraft Foods North America Inc.; Mars Inc.; Cadbury Schweppes PLC; Hershey Foods Corp; HARIBO GmbH und Company KG; Ferrero S.p.A.; Chupa Chups SA; Oy Karl Fazer Ab; Masterfoods Veghel B.V.; August Storck KG.

Further Reading

"Admiraal, Karin, "A Sugary, Fruity Smell Fills the Air at the Perfetti van Melle Plant in Erlanger, Ky, Where Each Day 20 Tons of Sugar,

Are Mixed, Melted and Molded into 3 Million Airheads Chewy Candies,'' *Cincinatti Post*, March 30, 2002, p. 10A.

Bhattacharya, Sindhu J., ''Perfetti's Sweet Success,'' *Business Line*, October 7, 2004, p. 19.

Bickerton, Ian, ''Van Melle Gives Consent for Takeover by Perfetti,'' *Financial Times*, January 16, 2001, p. 32.

''Chups Links to Fruittella,'' *Grocer*, March 19, 2005, p. 8.

''Foreign Principals Growing in Russian Candy Market,'' *Candy Industry*, January 2005, p. 11.

Newberry, Jon, ''Candy Plant Will Add Jobs,'' *Kentucky Post*, February 18, 2005, p. K1.

''Perfetti Aims at Larger Slice of Confectionery Market,'' *Business Line*, November 21, 2004.

''Perfetti van Melle Sets Out to Prove Itself,'' *Duty Free News International*, March 15, 2003, p. 30.

''Perfetti Van Melle Thinks Outside the Roll,'' *Confectioner*, June 2003, p. 48.

—M.L. Cohen

Pernod Ricard S.A.

12, place des Etats-Unis
75783 Paris cedex 16
France
Telephone: (+33) 01 41 00 41 00
Fax: (+33) 01 41 00 40 85
Web site: http://www.pernod-ricard.com

Public Company
Incorporated: 1974
Employees: 12,130
Sales: EUR 3.57 billion ($4.87 billion) (2004)
Stock Exchanges: Euronext Paris New York
Ticker Symbol: 120693
NAIC: 312130 Wineries; 312140 Distilleries; 422820
    Wine and Distilled Alcoholic Beverage Wholesalers

Pernod Ricard S.A. is a top global producer of wine and spirits. At the time of the company's 30th anniversary in 2004, Pernod Ricard had become the world's third-largest producer of wines and spirits. Eighty percent of revenues come from outside France. In its first three decades, Pernod Ricard skillfully effected its transformation from a France-focused, pastis-based concern to a global leader.

If it were not for the French tradition of gathering for a predinner aperitif, Pernod Ricard might not be the largest alcoholic beverage company in Continental Europe. As it is, the customary French toast "to health" (*à santé*) has helped to keep Pernod Ricard in excellent condition. The company is the world's largest producer and distributor of anise-flavored alcohol beverages, popularly known as "pastis" in France and that country's single largest selling variety of spirits under the venerable Pernod, Ricard, Pastis 51, and other brand names. The company also produces, markets, and/or distributes other types of anise-flavored spirits, including Italy's Sambucco and Greece's Mini Ouzo, acquired in 1997.

In addition to the company's, and France's, penchant for pastis, Pernod Ricard has built up a strong portfolio of subsidiary brand names spanning virtually every spirits category.

Among the company's products are Jameson, Bushmills, and other Irish whiskeys; Clan Campbell and Aberlour Scotch whiskeys, rum, cognac, vodka, and gin; bitters, including the topselling Suze brand; a range of wine-based and sweet wine aperitifs; wine, including Australia's Jacob's Creek brand; and a variety of light-alcohol beverages. After building up its portfolio with local brands, in 2001 Pernod Ricard acquired a number of international market leaders from Vivendi Universal.

Merging Two Pastis Dynasties

Pernod Ricard was formed in 1974 through the merger of the Pernod and Ricard companies, two of France's largest suppliers and distributors of aniseed beverages. Anise, a distinctively flavored aromatic seed, gained popularity during the 18th century as a substitute for absinthe. Absinthe, discovered some years earlier by a Swiss doctor, was mixed with wormwood and other herbs and used as a medical elixir. The drink became popular, and in 1797 an aspiring businessman named Pernod purchased the recipe. However, absinthe was later determined to cause nerve damage and was banned from France, Switzerland, and the United States. Pernod altered the recipe by substituting anise or pastis for absinthe, and thereby created two new beverages which were found to stimulate the palate.

Pernod founded a company in 1805, and though it was the first to produce anise-flavored aperitifs, it remained small. Nevertheless, the company produced introduced a variety of brands, including Pernod, Pastis 51, Byrrh, and Cinzano, as inexpensive alternatives to wine aperitifs. After over 100 years as a modest family-run company, Pernod acquired the Suze company, a firm which made bitters from the distilled roots of the gentian plant.

The expansion of Pernod encouraged imitators to establish competing firms in the early 1930s. Once such imitator, Paul Ricard, introduced his own aniseed aperitif in 1932. Ricard's extensive and often innovative marketing methods maintained the popularity of anise, despite growing demand for whiskey and wine aperitifs. Ricard established foundations to sponsor art and cultural activities (an unheard of practice for French business at that time), a world yacht race, and to build an auto race track. Additionally, Ricard donated several Mediterranean islands to the French government to promote tourism. In recognition of

Ricard's support for auto racing, an annual contest, the Circuit
Paul Ricard, was named in his honor. Ricard's publicity stunts
paid off handsomely, and by the time of his retirement in 1968
his 15 percent stake in the company was worth $104 million.

The merger of Pernod and Ricard, termed ''the equivalent of
a merger between General Motors and Ford,'' enabled the new
company to solidify its base as a major French beverage company in order to launch an export business. Since the merger,
the Pernod Ricard group has embarked on a massive reorganization and diversification campaign. Paul Ricard's son Patrick
became a major force within the company after being named
general manager in 1967. Patrick was an astute businessman,
was well-trained by his father, and had gained considerable
experience outside the company.

In 1976, Pernod Ricard purchased Cusenier of Argentina,
which made liqueurs from the extracted essences of plants,
fruits, and grains. Cusenier was also the Argentine distributor of
Cutty Sark, Gilbey's gin, and Ambassadeur aperitifs, in addition
to champagnes, fruit juices, and syrups. At this time, Pernod
Ricard purchased Campbell, a whisky distiller whose brands
included White Heather and Aberlour scotch and Dubonnet and
Clan Campbell liqueurs.

By 1979, it was clear that Pernod Ricard had to continue to
look outside of France to maintain its sales growth. Even though
the group recorded a 3.2 percent increase (by volume) in sales
of anise aperitifs, liquor sales domestically had only increased
1.3 percent. While other Pernod Ricard brands fared slightly
better, the company recognized that its French earning growth
would be limited.

Expanding the Company Portfolio in the 1980s

During 1980, Pernod Ricard spent $48 million on a market-
ing campaign in England, Spain, and Germany. Much of this
money was spent in sales promotion, including posters, taste
tests, and product giveaways at discos (intended to introduce
young adults to the taste of anise and pastis liqueurs). ''It's the
third glass that makes a convert,'' Patrick Ricard said at the
time, ''so we have to put glasses of Pernod in people's hands.''
In England, where Pernod had a small following, the campaign
succeeded brilliantly and sales increased by 34 percent. So that
it might solve a distribution problem caused by the increased
demand, Pernod Ricard purchased its English distributor, the
J.R. Parkington Company.

Continuing its expansion program, Pernod Ricard bought its
American sales agent, Austin Nichols, a well-known wine and
spirits firm whose best-selling brand was Wild Turkey bourbon.
This acquisition increased Pernod Ricard's revenue in 1980 to
about FRF 280 million.

In a 1980 interview with *Management Today,* Patrick Ricard
said, ''Ours is a young export country, and for too long we were
held back by an official attitude that it was unpatriotic to invest
abroad, though that is now changing. That's why we're following a policy of buying companies in prime markets, such as
Austin Nichols. It would take too long to start from scratch,
building up our own distribution and sales organization.''

Another reason behind the Austin Nichols purchase was the
fact that Americans simply were not excited about anise beverages, which Patrick Picard himself once termed ''a strange
drink with a funny taste.'' While the popularity of anise-
flavored drinks remained largely limited to France and the
Mediterranean region, Pernod Ricard's launch into England met
with a fair amount of success. Nonetheless, an overall trend of
declining alcohol consumption compelled Pernod Ricard to
seek opportunities in the soft drinks business.

The company's most important acquisition occurred in 1983,
with Française des Produits d'Orangina, makers of Orangina
soda, which contained 12 percent real fruit juice, which was more
than the 10 percent in Slice and the 3 percent in Minute Maid
orange soda. Orangina was first introduced in the United States in
1984 as the ''French quench'' and the ''soft drink with juice you
can taste.'' Patrick Ricard intended to make Orangina a worldwide brand name by the year 2000. Pernod Ricard officials told
Business Week in 1984 that the company had planned for
Orangina to take a 1 percent market share (all orange drinks
together constituted only 6 percent of the soda market). Other
companies, such as PepsiCo and Canada Dry, followed suit by
test marketing their own brands of natural soft drinks.

Besides Orangina, Pernod Ricard also began marketing fruit
juices (Fruidam, Banga, Pampryl, and Pam Pam) through its
JAF-Pampryl subsidiary. Pernod Ricard ventured into the fruit
preparation business in 1982 with the purchase of a 66 percent
interest in SIAS-MPA, the world's leading producer of fruit
preparations for dairy products. Despite poor economic conditions during the early 1980s, Pernod Ricard's sales grew an
average of 20 percent per year. Altogether, the company would
spend some $250 million on its acquisition strategy in an attempt
to establish its products in every French soft drink category.

In order to increase liquor sales, the company arranged an
agreement in 1985 with Heublein, an American alcoholic beverage company, which would give Pernod Ricard access to Japa-

Key Dates:

1805: Société Pernod Fils is formed in Pontarlier.
1915: Pernod's absinthe-based elixir is banned.
1951: Pernod launches its first pastis.
1980: Pernod Ricard launches a $50 million European marketing campaign.
1983: Orangina fruit drinks is acquired.
1988: Yoo Hoo Industries is acquired.
1995: Non-alcohol drinks account for half of the company's sales.
1997: Pernod Ricard acquires the continent's top gin, Larios of Spain.
2001: Poland's Polmos distillery is acquired; a share of Seagram's wine and spirits business acquired; the company divests its soft drinks products.
2005: Pernod Ricard launches a friendly takeover bid for Allied Domecq PLC.

nese and Brazilian markets and better exposure in the United States. Through a 15 percent interest in Heublein's Japanese subsidiary, Pernod Ricard sold Wild Turkey and Bisquit brandy in Japan. In Brazil, Pernod Ricard purchased a 30 percent interest in Heublein Industria e Commercia, Brazil's leading spirits distributor. Pernod Ricard officials said they joined Heublein in international markets to increase the company's foreign sales by 5 to 10 percent, despite the fact that the market was growing smaller. Foreign liquor sales accounted for 19 percent of group turnover, compared to 13 percent when Pernod and Ricard merged in 1974.

Pernod Ricard's export subsidiary SEGM (Société pour l'Exportation de Grandes Marques) acquired Ramazotti, an Italian aperitif producer, and established a joint venture with Deinhard of West Germany to sell Dubonnet, Pernod, Bisquit, and Ricard brands. SEGM also orchestrated the acquisition of Perisem in Switzerland and Prac in Spain. In addition, Pernod Ricard purchased an additional 45 percent interest in the Société des Vins de France (SVF), France's leading table wine group, which was Pernod Ricard's largest subsidiary in terms of sales. In February 1987, Pernod Ricard began negotiating the purchase of yet another European group, Cooymans. A Dutch firm founded in 1829, Cooymans had three plants and control of half of the Dutch liquor market, with sales of $37 million in 1986.

Company officials expected a strong increase in earnings during the late 1980s, primarily from its expanding line of non-alcoholic drinks, which in 1986 represented 36 percent of group activities. Foreign sales of soft drinks accounted for 25 percent of the company's sales. In France, the group introduced Pacific, the first non-alcoholic aniseed drink. It was an immediate success. In the late 1980s, the company also added Brut de Pomme a low-calorie apple-based soft drink. Further strengthening the company's non-alcoholic beverage arm was its acquisition of Yoo Hoo Industries and that company's perennially popular chocolate drink in 1988. In 1989, however, the success of Orangina came to haunt the company when Pernod Ricard lost its France concession of Coca-Cola, as that company geared up its Minute Maid division, resulting in a cut in the company's total revenues of

some 20 percent. This would be only one of the difficulties the company faced as it moved into the next decade.

Taking on the Giants in the 1990s

While Pernod Ricard's sales, spurred by its emphasis on international growth, had nearly doubled from FRF 8.5 billion in 1985 to FRF 14.5 billion in 1992, the company's growth would slow significantly in the 1990s. At home in France, where Pernod Ricard had previously enjoyed some 70 percent of the French pastis market, the company was suddenly confronted by the introduction of less-expensive private label brands from the country's hypermarket chains and other distribution groups. Pernod Ricard's share of the pastis market would soon drop to less than 55 percent of the total market. Equally troubling, however, was the dwindling popularity of the French favorite among consumers, especially younger consumers, who were turning toward whiskeys and "long drinks" based on vodka, gin, and other white alcohol varieties. Pernod Ricard's portfolio lacked a strong white alcohol complement. In 1993, the company added the distribution of Havana Club Cuban rums, and in 1994 the company acquired Russia's Altai brand of vodka.

Yet none of the company's white alcohol labels could hope to top the popularity of such brands as Smirnoff and Gibson. Although established as one of the top beverage distributors in the world, Pernod Ricard remained nonetheless small in comparison to alcohol giants Grand Metropolitan and Seagram and soft drink giants Coca Cola and Pepsi. The company needed to acquire a strong brand name, but these had become much too expensive. Furthermore, as Pernod Ricard moved to expand the relatively expensive (because of its high real fruit content) Orangina brand into new markets, particularly Asia, it found itself going head-to-head with the massive marketing power of Coca Cola and Pepsi. In Vietnam, for example, the company arrived first. However, Coca Cola arrived soon after, and, with a massive promotional campaign, including the giveaway of millions of free soft drinks, quickly captured 99 percent of that market. Even in Europe, Orangina found itself losing market share to the larger companies' new arrivals.

Meanwhile, Pernod Ricard faced an increase in the tax on alcoholic beverages in 1993. Sales of aniseed drinks plunged 8.5 percent in a single year. By the end of the year, Pernod Ricard saw its sales slip for the first time in a decade. By 1994, the company was forced to close down some of its French operations, including its Marseilles plant, the first home of Ricard.

Despite these difficulties, Pernod Ricard remained a major player in the beverage world. Its non-alcoholic beverage sales had grown strongly, equaling the contribution of alcoholic beverages for the first time in 1995. Unable to compete on the grand scale with the industry's true giants, Pernod Ricard turned instead to expanding its portfolio of "niche" alcohols, embarking on a series of acquisitions that included Somagnum of Portugal in 1995, Venezuela's El Muco Bebidas in 1996, and the 1997 acquisitions of Riqules, from the Perrier Vittel division of Nestlé; Greece's EPOM, the number two producer of ouzo in that country with its Mini brand; and Spain's Larios, with the leading gin brand in that country. Pernod Ricard also invested in the Czech Republic's newly privatized Jan Becher, maker of Becherovka bitters.

Pernod Ricard remained consistently profitable, posting nearly FRF 1.2 billion in net income in 1996, after a light drop in net income the previous year. However, the obstacle to the company's future growth remained in place: in order to compete against the industry's heavyweights, the company needed to generate a heavy capital investment to finance any future large-scale expansion. Nevertheless, under Patrick Ricard, the company steadfastly refused to turn to the market for that capital. There was good reason for this: any further dilution of the company's shares (approximately 60 percent of the company was already owned by the public) could introduce the family-controlled company to the risk of a hostile takeover. With the heritage of France's favorite aperitif at stake, Pernod Ricard remained committed to the slow-but-steady approach to growth.

Pernod Ricard continued to build its portfolio by buying local brands in the late 1990s and beyond, while divesting its non-alcohol portfolio and eventually acquiring a slew of market-leading international brands through the 2001 purchase of Seagram's. In 1999, the group obtained international distribution rights to Wyborowa (''exquisite'') brand rye vodka by buying a majority share of the Polish food business Agros. Two years later, Pernod Ricard paid 300 million zlotys (EUR 82 million) for an 80 percent stake in the vodka's producer, Polmos Poznan, Poland's second-largest distillery. Armenia's Yerevan Brandy Company had also been acquired in 1999, followed the next year by the purchase of Mexico's Viuda de Romero tequila.

Selling Soft Drinks, Buying Spirits in the 2000s

Pernod Ricard was also selling off its non-alcohol assets. A majority interest in the company's soft drinks businesses in Continental Europe, North America, and Australia was acquired by Cadbury Schweppes plc in 2001 for EUR 700 million. These activities had sales of EUR 466 million a year, half from Orangina. Cadbury bought the remaining interest in the soft drinks business three years later. Coca-Cola Co. had tried to buy Orangina for FRF 5 billion ($840 million) but the deal was blocked by the French government in 1999.

The Italian flavorings subsidiary San Giorgio Flavours was sold to the Irish Kerry Group and fruit preparation producer SIAS-MPA was also divested. BWG, a distributor in the British Isles, was disposed of the next year.

The proceeds from these divestments helped fund acquisition of 39.1 percent of Seagram's wine and spirits business from French media conglomerate Vivendi Universal SA for $3.2 billion in March 2001. (Pernod Ricard's partner in the buy was Britain's Diageo PLC.) Pernod Ricard acquired four brands (Chivas Regal and Glenlivet whiskey, Martell cognac, and Seagram's gin) which together had combined sales of more than $1 billion a year. The Seagram's deal doubled Pernod Ricard's size and made it the world's third-largest producer of wines and spirits.

At the time of the company's 30th anniversary in 2004, Pernod Ricard had become the leading wine and spirits supplier in Continental Europe and South America, second in Asia and the Pacific, and sixth in North America. Annual sales were EUR 3.6 billion, producing a net profit of EUR 487 million, and the group had more than 12,000 employees at 68 production facilities. The Ricard family remained the largest shareholder, own-

ing 12 percent of the capital and controlling 19 percent of voting rights through SA Paul Ricard.

New Zealand's Framingham Winery was acquired in 2004. At the same time, Pernod Ricard was attempting to boost the large but lagging market for aniseed pastis in France by introducing ready-mixed versions of the drinks. Pernod Ricard was also looking for growth in China, particularly in the fast-growing wine market.

Pernod Ricard, then the world's third largest wine and spirits producer, made another play for a portfolio of leading international brands. It launched a friendly takeover bid of British rival Allied Domecq plc in 2005, offering EUR 10.7 billion ($13.9 billion) for the company. If the offer were successful, the combination of Pernod Ricard and Allied Domecq would be second only to Diageo plc in the global wine and spirits market. Allied Domecq was then ranked second in the world; its brands included Beefeater gin, Stolichnaya vodka, and Perrier Jouet champagne. To avoid antitrust issues, Pernod Ricard intended to sell off assets worth EUR 4 billion to Fortune Brands, Inc. of the United States.

Principal Subsidiaries

Chivas Brothers Ltd (Scotland); Havana Club International S.A. (50%; Cuba); Irish Distillers Ltd. (Ireland); Martell & Co; Pernod SA; Pernod Ricard Australia; Pernod Ricard Europe; Pernod Ricard USA; Ricard SA.

Principal Divisions

Pernod Ricard Europe; Pernod Ricard North America; Pernod Ricard World Trade; Pernod Ricard Asia; Pernod Ricard Central & South America; Pernod Ricard South Asia.

Principal Competitors

Allied Domecq plc; Bacardi-Martini; Diageo plc.

Further Reading

''30 Years of Uninterrupted Success,'' *Entreprendre: The Magazine for Pernod Ricard Shareholders*, No. 46, Special ''30th Anniversary'': 1975–2005, pp. 12–23.

''Allied Domecq Confirms Takeover Talks with Drinks Peers,'' *Agence France Presse*, April 5, 2005.

Branch, Shelly, ''Diageo, Pernod Sort Out Seagram Terms with Deal to Pay $8.15 Billion for Unit,'' *Wall Street Journal*, December 20, 2000, p. B10.

''Hangover Clears on Polish Vodka Trademark Rights,'' *European Report*, July 21, 2001.

''Pernod Ricard Aims for Mass Sale of Ready-Mixed Pastis (Le 'petit Ricard' veut reveiller le marche de l'anise), *Echos*, June 3, 2004, p. 21.

''Pernod Ricard Bids 10.7 Bln Euros for Allied Domecq in Drinks Shake-Up,'' *Agence France Presse*, April 21, 2005.

''Pernod Ricard Falls as Orangina Sale Plan Blocked,'' *Echos*, November 25, 1999, p. 12.

''Pernod Ricard Pursues Growth in China (Pernod Ricard poursuit son offensive en Chine),'' *Echos*, May 27, 2005, p. 19.

''Pernod Ricard Signs Formal Agreement on Sale of Orangina to Cadbury Schweppes,'' *Agri-Industry Europe*, October 19, 2001.

—updates: M.L. Cohen; Frederick C. Ingram

Petrobras Energia Participaciones S.A.

Maipu 1
Buenos Aires, C.F. C1084ABA
Argentina
Telephone: (54) (11) 4344-6000
Fax: (54) (11) 4344-6315
Web site: http://www.petrobrasenergia.com

Public Company
Incorporated: 1947 as Compania Naviera Perez Companc
S.A.C.F.I.M.F.A.
Employees: 3,334
Sales: ARS 6.97 billion ($2.39 billion) (2004)
Stock Exchanges: Buenos Aires New York
Ticker Symbol: PC
NAIC: 211111 Crude Petroleum and Natural Gas
Extraction; 221111 Hydroelectric Power Generation;
221112 Fossil Fuel Electric Power Generation;
221122 Electric Power Distribution; 221210 Natural
Gas Distribution; 324110 Petroleum Refineries;
325110 Petrochemical Manufacturing; 325212
Synthetic Rubber Manufacturing; 325311 Nitrogenous
Fertilizer Manufacturing; 447190 Other Gasoline
Stations; 551112 Offices of Other Holding Companies

Petrobras Energia Participaciones S.A. is the holding company for Petrobras Energia S.A., an integrated energy company that is the second largest petroleum and natural gas producer in Argentina and also maintains facilities for the exploration and production of oil and natural gas in Bolivia, Ecuador, Peru, and Venezuela. It also is engaged in refining crude oil, producing petrochemicals, and—by holding minority stakes in other Argentine enterprises—in generating, transmitting, and distributing electricity and in transporting and distributing natural gas. In addition, the company owns a network of gasoline service stations in Argentina. Based in Buenos Aires, Petrobras Energia Participaciones is majority-owned by Petroleo Brasileira S.A. (Petrobras), Brazil's largest company.

Emerging Conglomerate: 1946–89

Jorge Perez Companc was a doctor and his brother Carlos was a lawyer when they began their business careers in 1946 by purchasing four surplus U.S. merchant vessels that had been used in World War II and founding the Argentine shipping company Compania Naviera Perez Companc to haul equipment and supplies for Yacimientos Petroliferos Fiscales (later YPF S.A.), the giant state-owned petroleum company. These shallow-draft 100-meter-long barges were well suited for duty in the brothers' native Patagonia, with its lack of developed harbors. They also had inherited thousands of acres of land in southern Argentina and began ranching and farming activities in 1952, a year after establishing the insurance company La Patagonia. Two years later they founded a travel agency, Turismo Pecom. In 1956 they also acquired forest land in northeastern Argentina for timber exploitation and in that year began selling shares in their budding conglomerate on the Bolsa de Comercio de Buenos Aires. Perez Companc, or Pecom for short, had about 60 employees and annual revenue of perhaps $10 million in 1958, the year before Jorge died.

Perez Companc entered the energy business in 1960, when it began servicing oil wells. It expanded its scope during the decade to include drilling oil and gas wells as a subcontractor for YPF and won its first production contract in 1964. Four years later YPF awarded it a 15-year contract to explore and develop what proved its first significant oilfield, Entre Lomas. The company's maritime operations were gradually discontinued and replaced by oil-related activities. In 1968 Pecom had about $30 million in annual sales, but the Entre Lomas field soon tripled its revenue.

Perez Companc established, in 1971, a company to process lead and tin. The following year it won its first oil production contract without partners. But its biggest coup of the decade was its purchase, in 1976, of the majority holding in the big public works contractor Sociedad Anonimo de Electricidad (SADE) for only $15 million from General Electric Co., which was anxious to leave violence-wracked Argentina, where urban guerrillas were kidnapping business executives for ransom. Here, as in the case of YPF, Perez Companc's ties to the government served it well, for SADE won many contracts to

278

build power plants and roads. SADE also allied itself with the Japanese firm NEC in Pecom Nec S.A., a joint venture producing electrical machinery and communications equipment.

Energy-Oriented Powerhouse in the 1990s

In spite of its far-flung activities, Perez Companc was not yet big enough to attract major attention in Argentina. In 1975 it ranked only 109th in sales. By 1980, however, it ranked 50th, and in 1985 it rose to 33rd. By 1983 Pecom had 48 enterprises under its banner, and during the latter years of the decade, when company valuations were low, it had the funds to buy, on average, an enterprise per month. With the election of Carlos Menem to the presidency in 1989, an era of privatizing state enterprises began, and Perez Companc was one of the chief beneficiaries, investing $980 million between 1990 and 1992 for stakes in Argentina's two major telephone companies, road and rail concessions, oil and gas fields and oil refineries, a gas pipeline, an electricity generating station, and electricity and gas distributors. In 1991, when the conglomerate had divisions for petroleum, petrochemicals, agroindustry, energy, communications and services, and mining, it employed about 10,000 people and had sales of $705 million and profits of $72 million.

These sums included only the public company, however, and counting nonconsolidated enterprises such as La Patagonia, Banco Rio de la Plata S.A. (a private bank acquired in 1968), and large agroindustrial enterprises, all managed directly by the Perez Companc family, it was probable that sales came to $1.5 billion a year. Banco Rio, which had grown to be Argentina's largest private bank, had raised $225 million in New York and had used some of these funds to buy parts of privatized enterprises for Perez Companc, such as the giant telephone companies Telecom Argentina S.A. and Telefonica de Argentina S.A., in which it held minority stakes in the controlling consortiums.

But Pecom's oil and gas holdings constituted its chief activity, accounting for more than half of the company's sales. Pecom had ranked only sixth among oil companies in sales in 1990, but in that year it was awarded part of concessions to operate Puerto Hernandez, the second-ranking oilfield in Argentina, and the Faro Virgenes and Santa Cruz II areas in the Austral basin, Argentina's most important area of oil and gas production. By 1992 Pecom was second only to YPF in national crude oil production.

With headquarters in a Buenos Aires high-rise office building close to the seat of government, the Perez Companc interests, although far-ranging, were closely supervised by an experienced management team of no more than 15 people. "We were working until 10 at night every weekday and 40 percent on weekends," the principal manager of the international division told Maria Eugenia Estenssoro of the business magazine *Mercado* in 1992. Jorge Fernandez, administrative director of Banco Rio, was in the habit of working until three in the morning and was said to have married his secretary "because she was the only woman that he had occasion to meet." There were two general managers: Ernesto Casabal for finance, and Oscar Vicente for other matters, but especially petroleum.

These two had been appointed by Carlos Perez Companc. Neither he nor the deceased Jorge left children. After Carlos' death in 1977, the presidency of the group passed to his much-younger adopted brother, Jorge Gregorio (Goyo) Perez Companc. A poll of influential Argentines in 1992 rated him the second most powerful person in the nation, surpassed only by Menem himself. Wealthy but austere, he could be seen until the 1990s driving a Ford Falcon. His piety was reflected in an enormous image of the Virgin Mary in the company's reception room and a stained-glass window image of Our Lady of Patagonia on the floor that housed the chief officers. The company was noted for its Japanese-style human resources management, valuing loyalty above all else and in return offering an unwritten promise of secure employment for life.

By mid-1993 Perez Companc had annual sales of $925 million and total assets, counting nonconsolidated holdings, of more than $2 billion. These holdings, direct or indirect, included, aside from all of SADE, half of Pecom Nec, and parts of Telecom and Telefonica; 74 percent of Quitral-Co S.A.I.C., its oil services subsidiary; 17.5 percent of Transportadora de Gas del Sur S.A and MetroGas S.A., privatized gas pipelines and distributors; one-third of Petroquimicas Argentinas S.A. (PASA) and 40 percent of Petroquimica Cuyo S.A., both big petrochemical producers; one-sixth of the large privatized electricity-generating company Empresa Distribuidora Sur S.A. (Edesur); 28 percent of Refineria del Norte S.A., a privatized oil refinery; 57.5 percent of newly established Refineria San Lorenzo; and all of Alto Palermo S.A., a big real estate development firm that included half-ownership of one of Buenos Aires' main shopping centers. Perez Companc had also acquired in 1990 a 3 percent stake in YPF, making it for a time the privatized oil giant's principal shareholder. The company purchased the rest of PASA in 1994. In 1995 *Forbes* ranked the Perez Companc family as the richest in Argentina, holding about 55 percent of Perez Companc S.A. ("Compania Naviera" was dropped from the company name that year). At the same time, however, Pecom was divesting itself of enterprises outside its core businesses of energy, communications, and construction.

Perez Companc celebrated its 50th anniversary in 1996 with annual consolidated sales of $1.41 billion and an estimated market value of $4.68 billion. Its net income had grown from $50 million in 1990 to $328 million in 1996. Petroleum and gas sales accounted for 69 percent of the total, with the company still the second largest oil producer and third largest in natural gas. By now operations in this field had spread to Bolivia (1989), Venezuela (1994), and Peru (1996). Its policy of vertical integration in energy extended to pipelines, power plants, and the transmission of electricity along its own high-capacity lines. Communications was now being downgraded, with the company having divested itself of its interest in Telefonica and being on the way to do the same with its Telecom holding, a

Key Dates:

1946: The Argentine shipping firm Compania Naviera Perez Companc is founded.

1960: Perez Companc enters the energy business by servicing oil wells.

1972: The company wins its first contract to extract petroleum without partners.

1983: Perez Companc (Pecom) is a conglomerate composed of 48 enterprises.

1990–92: Perez Companc invests nearly $1 billion for stakes in privatized state-owned enterprises.

1996: In its 50th year, Perez Companc has consolidated sales of $1.41 billion.

1999: Concentrating on energy, Perez Companc has sold $1.1 billion worth of other enterprises.

2003: The Perez Companc family sells its stock to Petroleo Brasileira (Petrobras).

process completed in 1999. Also sold were Quitral (1996), Banco Rio (1997 to 2000), Pecom Nec (1997), Alto Palermo (1997), SADE (1999), and the holdings in YPF (1999). These sales raised $1.1 billion. The number of divisions was reduced from eight to five.

There were a number of other developments. Casabal was removed from his post in early 1997. Near the end of that year Gregorio Perez Companc, flanked by his wife and eight children—rather than, as traditional, high company executives—told the 3,000 employees assembled that "the next 50 years of the company will be in the hands of my family." In 1999 he indicated that the family's future might lie outside the company when one of Argentina's largest food companies, Molinas de la Plata S.A., was purchased for $377 million—not by Perez Companc S.A. but by a family group based in the Cayman Islands.

Shares of Perez Companc had increased one hundredfold in value between 1982 and 1997. On the other hand profits had stagnated since 1996, the level of company debt was beginning to raise attention, and the increasing size of the main enterprises in the world energy field meant it would be difficult for Pecom to continue competing. Moreover, oil production in Argentina was diminishing with the slow exhaustion of exploitable deposits of hydrocarbons, and the cost of financing expansion to other South American countries had raised Pecom's debt to $1.5 billion.

Transition to the 21st Century

Perez Companc was reorganized in 2000 to give the family's 58 percent holding a greater share—80 percent—of the voting power and hence fend off any hostile bid for control that might occur after selling more shares of stock. Perez Companc became the controlling company of Pecom Energia, S.A., which had 35 subsidiaries and minority interests in 25 other companies. Of Perez Companc's $1.34 billion in 1999 revenue, exploration and production of oil and gas, commercialization and transport of hydrocarbons, refining and petrochemicals, and electricity accounted for all but $60 million. In 2000 the company acquired the remainder of Refineria San Lorenzo, and with

it full control of a network of 75 service stations. It also had begun exploratory drilling in Ecuador and had begun work on styrene and polystyrene plants in Brazil. The nonenergy assets represented Perez Companc's remaining company holdings in agriculture, livestock raising, forestry, and mining. The latter included a Patagonian venture with U.S. partners that, in 1998, after ten years and $60 million in investment, uncovered a medium-sized gold-and-silver deposit.

By the end of 2001 the economic recession in Argentina that had begun in 1998 had so deepened that the government was unable to make payments on its debts and thereby maintain the peso at parity with the U.S. dollar. The subsequent devaluation left Perez Companc in a difficult position; more than half of its revenue was in the form of pesos that were worth only about one-third their former value, but it had to make payments on about $1.6 billion in dollar-denominated long-term debt. In October 2002 the Perez Companc family sold its stock in the company to Petroleo Brasileira S.A. (Petrobras) for $1.03 billion in cash and bonds. Perez Companc's agricultural, livestock-raising, forestry, and mining interests were sold to companies representing the Perez Companc family for about $190 million.

Petrobras, the world's 12th largest oil and gas producer, had entered Argentina in 1993 and was active in the exploration, production, transport, industrialization, and commercialization of petroleum. In 2001 it acquired control of the Argentine oil refining and distribution company Eg3 S.A., including a network of almost 700 service stations and, in 2002, the oil and gas producer Petrolera Santa Fe S.R.L. Perez Companc S.A. was renamed Petrobras Energia Participaciones S.A. in 2003, and its subsidiary Pecom Energia S.A. was renamed Petrobras Energia S.A. Petrobras Energia absorbed Eg3 and Petrolera Santa Fe, as well as the parent Brazilian company's prior Argentine subsidiary, Petrobras Argentina S.A., in 2004.

Petrobras Energia, in 2003, had interests in 24 oilfields, of which 17 were producing oil and gas fields. The ten producing fields in Argentina were concentrated in the Neuquen and Austral basins of Patagonia and accounted for 4.6 and 3.9 percent, respectively, of national production. About 60 percent of the company's reserves were now outside Argentina. Of the seven producing oil and gas fields outside the country, four were in Venezuela and one each was in Bolivia, Ecuador, and Peru. The company had an Argentine refinery in San Lorenzo, Santa Fe, and shared with parent Petrobras two refineries in Bolivia. It maintained, in Argentina and Brazil, petrochemical plants producing styrene, polystyrene, polypropylene, fertilizers, and synthetic rubber. Innova S.A., the company's Brazilian subsidiary for petrochemicals, was the nation's largest producer of styrene. Petrobras Energia also owned two Argentine power plants, held 70 percent of Enecor S.A., a transmission company, and had minority interests in others, including Edesur S.A., Transener S.A., and Yacylec S.A. Other minority holdings included Petroquimica Cuyo S.A., Refineria del Norte, and Transportadora de Gas del Sur S.A. When Petrobras Energia absorbed Eg3 in 2004, it added Eg3's Bahia Blanca, Buenos Aires, refinery to its holdings. It also opened an ethylene plant in San Lorenzo in 2004.

Petrobras Energia had net sales of ARS 6.97 billion ($2.39 billion) in 2004, of which (excluding minority interests) oil and gas accounted for about half and refining and petrochemicals for about one-quarter each. Oil and gas accounted for 71 percent of gross profits in 2003, excluding minority interests. The company's dollar-denominated debt came to ARS 8.3 billion ($2.62 billion) at the end of 2003.

Principal Subsidiaries

Enecor S.A. (70%); Innova S.A. (Brazil); Petrobras Bolivia International S.A. (Bolivia); Petrobras Energia S.A.; Petrobras Energia Ecuador S.A. (Cayman Islands); Petrobras Energia Peru S.A. (Peru); Petrobras Energia Venezuela S.A. (Venezuela).

Principal Divisions

Electricity; Hydrocarbon Marketing and Transport; Oil and Gas; Petrochemicals; Refining.

Principal Competitors

BHP Petroleum (Argentina) Inc.; Dow Brasil S.A. (Brazil); Dow Quimica Argentina S.A.; Esso Petrolera Argentina S.R.L.; Petrokea S.A.; Profertil S.A.; Shell Argentina; Sol Petroleo; YPF S.A.

Further Reading

Bachelet, Pablo, ''Concentracion con matices,'' *America economia,* July 29, 1999, pp. 26–28, 30.

''Development Set for Argentine Prospect,'' *Oil and Gas Journal,* July 15, 1968, p. 87.

Esquivel, Natacha, ''De compras, fuera de la region,'' *Mercado,* October 2000, pp. 60–62, 64.

Estenssoro, Maria Eugenia, ''El Nuevo Numero 1,'' *Mercado,* March 1992, pp. 22–24, 26, 28–29.

Friedland, Jonathan, ''Argentine Clan Sees a Bonanza in Privatization,'' *Wall Street Journal,* December 12, 1995, p. A17.

''Los herederos,'' *Mercado,* December 1999, p. 32.

Kamm, Thomas, ''Four Big Argentine Firms Stake Future on Role in Nation's Privatization Push,'' *Wall Street Journal,* March 10, 1993, p. A10.

Majul, Luis, *Los duenos de la Argentina,* Buenos Aires: Editorial Sudamerica, 1994, Vol. 2, pp. 15–109.

Moffett, Matt, ''Argentine Conglomerate Slims Down,'' *Wall Street Journal,* October 25, 1994, p. A13.

Nash, Nathaniel C., ''The Big Push Toward Privatization in Argentina,'' *New York Times,* September 6, 1992, Sec. 3, p. 12.

''Petrobras, un simple cambio de manos?,'' *Mercado,* October 2003, p. 30.

''Los proximos 50 anos,'' *Mercado,* December 1996, pp. 112–14, 116, 118.

Remeseira, Carlos Ivan, ''Obras son amores,'' *Apertura,* January 1994, pp. 79–81.

Salles, Flavio, and Andrew Wood, ''Argentine Groups Shape Up,'' *Chemical Week,* November 16, 1994, p. s12.

Sguiglia, Eduardo, *El club de los poderosos,* Buenos Aires: Editorial Planeta, 1991, pp. 62–67.

Stok, Gustavo, ''Que tan grande sos?,'' *America economia,* May 1997, pp. 36–37.

''Techint y Perez Companc vuelven a las raices,'' *Mercado,* October 1997, pp. 56–58, 60.

Torres, Craig, ''Argentine Oil Firm Bucks Merger Trend,'' *Wall Street Journal,* November 22, 1999, p. A19.

—Robert Halasz

PMP Ltd.

Level 13, 67 Albert Avenue
Chatswood
NSW 2067
Australia
Telephone: +61 2 9412 6000
Fax: +61 2 9413 3939
Web site: http://www.pmplimited.com.au

Public Company
Incorporated: 1991 as Pacific Magazines and Printing
Employees: 3,981
Sales: AUD 1.21 billion ($900 million) (2004)
Stock Exchanges: Australian
Ticker Symbol: PMP
NAIC: 511120 Periodical Publishers; 323110 Commercial Lithographic Printing; 323117 Book Printing; 511130 Book Publishers; 511140 Database and Directory Publishers

PMP Ltd. is Australia's leading media services company. PMP's primary business is commercial printing, and the company's PMP Print division is the leading commercial printer in Australia and New Zealand. The company's range of products include magazines—PMP formerly owned the Pacific Magazines group of titles—books, catalogs, directories, newspapers, government publications, direct-mail and other promotional printing, as well as printing for corporations. PMP's range of media production services also includes micromarketing, through subsidiary Pacific Micromarketing; digital premedia, through digital publishing subsidiary PMP dbooks; and distribution services, including addressing and plastic wrapping. PMP Distribution handles the company's market-leading distribution operations, providing door-to-door delivery services for printed matter. The company's distribution wing covers more than 96 percent of Australia's and New Zealand's homes. PMP also operates Australia and New Zealand's oldest and largest magazine distribution business, through subsidiary Gordon & Gotch, supplying more than 3,300 newspapers and magazines throughout Australia. Since adopting a new strategic focus in 2002, PMP has been phasing out its publishing operations, including the sale of its U.K. publishing house, Attic Futura, to France's Hachette Filipacchi Medias, and its magazine division to Seven Network, in 2002. PMP continues to operate its Australian book publishing business, Griffin Press. Listed on the Australian Stock Exchange, PMP posted revenues of AUD 1.21 billion ($900 million) in 2004. The company is led by former All Blacks—the Australian rugby team—captain David Kirk.

News Corporation Offshoot in the 1990s

PMP originated as part of the global media empire constructed by Rupert Murdoch through the 1970s and 1980s. While Murdoch's News Corporation gained leading positions in the print and broadcasting markets in the United Kingdom and the United States, the company also built up extensive interests across most of Australia's media landscape as well. Murdoch's interests in magazines began with his father, Keith Murdoch, who founded News Ltd. and gained control of Southdown Press soon after World War II. Southdown had by then acquired one of Australia's oldest and most popular magazine titles, *New Idea—A Women's Home Journal for Australia,* originally launched in 1902 by T. Shaw Fitchett.

New Idea remained a cornerstone of Southdown's growth into one of Australia's major magazine and newspaper publishers. Rupert Murdoch took over News Ltd. after his father's death in 1952 and, backed by *New Idea*'s strong revenues, sought to expand the group's magazine portfolio. In 1957, the company launched a new magazine format for Australia, *TV Week.* Using the United States' *TV Guide* as a model, *TV Week* became Australia's first television-oriented magazine, at a time when the country had just two television stations, reaching no farther than Melbourne and Sydney. *TV Week* became the best-selling magazine in Australia and over the next decades provided a solid cornerstone for Murdoch's empire building.

Into the 1980s, News Ltd. built up a substantial magazine portfolio, which, together with the group's strong array of Australian newspapers, was placed under subsidiary Southdown Press. At the same time, News Ltd. expanded its printing capacity in Australia. By the end of the decade, the company was one of Australia's leading printers as well.

Company Perspectives:

Increasing the return on your marketing investment—in today's fast-moving market. PMP provides innovative and tailored solutions. Our technology and deep expertise can improve the way you create and deliver your message, and it can help you target that message to the right people in the right way. PMP's integrated media production solutions help our clients to exploit new opportunities rapidly. By adopting a digital approach to communication workflows, your information (data, text, documents and images) can be captured and managed in a digital environment, streamlining your communications and creating efficiency gains. PMP's products, services and expertise can help you exploit the digital era—reducing costs, improving processes, controlling inventory, and developing new products all through a digital environment and workflow. The PMP approach is to leverage the finest technology, the best people and the most carefully-chosen solutions to your advantage. It's an approach that gets results.

Rupert Murdoch's massive spending spree during the 1980s—which included the acquisitions of the *Chicago Sun Times,* the *Herald and Weekly Times, South China Morning Post,* and publishers Harper & Row and William Collins and Sons—had transformed News Ltd. into the world's largest English-language publisher. News Ltd. also added U.K.-based Attic Futura, a specialist publisher of teen-oriented magazines active in the United Kingdom and in Germany. Meanwhile, News Ltd. had continued adding to its stable of magazines, including titles such as *Listener In-TV,* based in Victoria, renamed as *TV Scene.*

Another operation added during this time was Griffin Press. That company originally had been founded as the book printing subsidiary of Advertiser Newspapers Ltd., based in Adelaide, in 1858. Over the next century, Griffin grew into a respected printer and publisher. In 1931, the operation gained further scale when it acquired a new printing plant, called The Register. Following World War II, Griffin began investing in new printing technologies, including offset lithography and die stamping, as well as adding automatic bookbinding facilities. In the 1950s and early 1960s, Griffin also acquired a number of additional printing plants. These were then consolidated into a single state-of-the-art facility in Netley, near Adelaide, in 1964. Into the 1980s, Griffin branched out from book publishing, adding a range of general printing services, such as labels for bottles, cartons, and other graphic materials. Griffin also later added digital graphics and printing capabilities and micro-marketing capacity. By the early 1990s, Griffin claimed the leadership in Australia's print media production sector.

In the meantime, Murdoch's spending spree had placed the group heavily in debt. By 1990, News Ltd. was buckling under a debt topping $8 billion, with more than $1.2 billion due by 1992. In response, Murdoch launched a dramatic restructuring of News Corp. In exchange for a refinancing package from his more than 146 creditor banks, Murdoch agreed to sell a number of News Ltd. holdings.

In 1991, News Ltd. bundled the Australian magazine operations of Southdown Press and Attic Futura together with the company's Australian printing division and spun them off as a new company, Pacific Magazines and Printing. A total of 55 percent of the new company was then listed on the Australian Stock Exchange, with News Ltd. retaining a 45 percent stake. Included in the creation of PMP was the Griffin Press business, which formed the heart of its printing operations. Other PMP printing interests included Progress Press, Wilke Color, and Wilke Directories. PMP activities also included the largest combined door-to-door distribution business in Australia.

Refocused in the New Century

PMP remained dominated by News Ltd. into the second half of the 1990s. One result of this was the extension of the company into still more areas of operations, such as a $175 million bid in 1996 to enter the CD and video printing business through a takeover of Shomega, itself formed through a merger with digital media group Show-Ads. Founded in 1928, Show-Ads not only gave PMP a boost in the digital media market, but also in the market for direct-mail and related publications and distribution. The acquisition was also part of the decision by the company to take on a new name, PMP Communications, that year.

News Ltd. sold off its 45 percent stake in PMP in 1997, saying that PMP no longer fit within its core operations. Yet by the beginning of the next decade, PMP also was forced to re-examine its own operational core. Profits were proving harder to come by for the company, especially as its flagship *TV Week,* battered both by the appearance of free television supplements in many Australian newspapers, and by the availability of television listings on the Internet, saw a steady circulation decline through the 1990s and into the 2000s. The rise of Internet usage also had led to an erosion in the group's other titles. As it entered the new century, PMP found itself burdened with debt and slipping profits.

PMP attempted to launch its own Internet strategy in 2000. In that year, the company teamed up with ''convergent media expert'' Imagination Entertainment, forming the joint venture Pacific Imagination Online. The two companies hoped to unlock the potential Internet value of subsidiary Pacific Publications' magazine portfolio. Yet PMP already had been outpaced to the Internet by its competitors, and its online efforts failed to take hold. By the end of that year, the company had slipped into the red. The company then announced that it would conduct a review of its publishing operations.

In 2001, PMP appeared to have found a solution for its magazine publishing woes when it reached an agreement with its chief Australian rival, Independent Print Media Group (IPMG), to merge their operations. The resulting company might have become a true magazine powerhouse in the Australia and New Zealand market. The deal was quickly quashed, however, by the Australian Competition and Consumer Commission. PMP and IPMG continued to hold talks through the end of that year in an attempt to come up with concessions that would appease the competition commission. Those talks ended bitterly in December 2001.

Instead, PMP found a different partner, turning to Seven Network in July 2001 in an effort to raise cash to pay down its debt. The two sides agreed for Seven to pay AUD 85 million ($43

Key Dates:

1991: News Ltd. spins off magazine divisions Southdown Press and Attic Futura, as well as Griffin Press and printing operations into a new company, Pacific Magazines and Printing (PMP), which is listed on the Australian Stock Exchange.
1996: PMP acquires Show-Ads and changes its name to PMP Communications.
1997: News Ltd. sell off its 45 percent stake in PMP.
2000: PMP acquires the Australian operations of Gordon & Gotch.
2001: After a failed merger with IPMG, PMP merges Pacific Publications into a joint venture with Seven Network.
2002: PMP announces its decision to exit magazine publishing, selling off its share of the joint venture; Attic Futura is sold to Hachette Filipacchi Medias.
2004: PMP acquires Gordon & Gotch's New Zealand operations; the company launches construction of four new presses, expected to be completed in 2005.

million) to acquire 50 percent of Pacific Publications. The deal also called for the two parties to share PMP's Gordon & Gotch Australia magazine distribution business. Gordon & Gotch was originally founded in the early 1850s, and had grown into Australia and New Zealand's largest magazine and newspaper distributor. PMP had acquired Gordon & Gotch's Australian operations in 2000, from INL, based in New Zealand. PMP acquired Gordon & Gotch's New Zealand operations as well in 2004.

By then, however, PMP's magazines had slumped in value, sending the group's share price plummeting into the penny stocks region. By June 2002, the company decided to exercise its option to sell Seven Network its stake in their joint venture. In exchange for AUD 65 million, PMP sold Seven Network full control of Pacific Publications. PMP kept, however, the Gordon & Gotch distribution operation.

Following the sale of Pacific Publications, PMP announced a strategic refocus of its operations in general, which included its decision to exit the magazine publishing business altogether. Soon after, PMP announced that it had found a buyer for its U.K. publishing operation, when France's Hachette Fillipacchi Medias agreed to buy Attic Futura for AUD 115 million.

PMP's stock remained in the basement, however. By the beginning of 2003, the company's shares were worth less than 50 cents (Australian) each. In March 2003, the company brought in a new CEO, David Kirk, to help turn the company around. Kirk, formerly a captain of the country's All Blacks rugby team, had experience in the Australian media market and was president of Norske Skog Australia at the time of his appointment.

Kirk led the company on a new strategic review. As part of that review, the company moved to reduce its debt, in large part through the sale of a number of noncore subsidiaries. At the same time, the company began restructuring its focus around a new core of printing, launching an investment program to step up its print division's efficiency. To this end, the company pledged AUD 124 million in May 2004 to upgrade its equipment and install four new heat-set presses at its main plant. The company expected the new presses to come online in 2005.

PMP's refocusing effort appeared to be paying off by then. At the beginning of 2005, the company announced rising profits, up nearly 54 percent over the previous year. The company expected to reap the benefits of its printing press expansion as well in the coming year, especially by 2006. In the meantime, PMP continued in its efforts to pay down debt in order to release the group's full profit value. Although its legacy lay in magazines, PMP turned into the new century as one of Australia's leading printing and distribution companies.

Principal Subsidiaries

Canberra Press (Melb) Pty.; Canberra Press (Plant) Pty.; Canberra Press Holdings Pty.; Gordon and Gotch Australia Pty.; Griffin Press Pty.; Keppell Printing Pty.; Marketspace Pty.; Mercury Walch Pty.; Pacific Intermedia (NZ) Limited; Pacific Intermedia Pty.; Pacific Micromarketing Pty.; Pac-Rim Printing Pty.; PMP (NZ) Limited; PMP Digital Pty.; PMP Distribution Limited (New Zealand); PMP Print Pty.; PMP Property Pty.; PMP Publishing Pty.; PMP Wholesale Pty.; Prestige Litho Pty.; Shomega Limited; Show-Ads Pty.; The Argus & Australasian Pty.

Principal Competitors

Publishing and Broadcasting Ltd.; Independent Print Media Group Proprietary Ltd.; Rural Press Ltd.; R.M. Williams Holdings Ltd.; Consolidated Press Holdings Ltd.; Reader's Digest Australia Proprietary Ltd.; Retail Technology and Services Ltd.; General Publishers Ltd.; Enterprise Information Management Proprietary Ltd.

Further Reading

"Australia's PMP Communications to Review Publications Sector," *AsiaPulse News,* August 16, 2000.
"Australia's PMP Expects Review to Deliver US$18 mln," *AsiaPulse News,* April 7, 2003.
"Australia's Seven Network, PMP in US$43 mln JV," *AsiaPulse News,* July 10, 2001.
Charlesworth, Eric, "News Corp. Pulls Out Stake (Unit News Ltd. Sells Its Shares in PMP Communications," *Folio: The Magazine for Magazine Management,* September 1, 1997, p. 17.
"Former All Blacks Captain to Lead the Charge at PMP," *Sydney Morning Herald,* February 11, 2003.
"Kirk Steers PMP from Red to All Black," *Australian Financial Review,* January 9, 2005.
"New Business for PMP," *New Zealand Printer Magazine,* October 20, 2004.
"PMP Gets Gordon & Gotch," *New Zealand Printer Magazine,* October 21, 2004.
"PMP Quits UK Publisher for $115m," *Sydney Morning Herald,* August 13, 2002.
"PMP Spends $124 Million to Become Lowest Cost Heat-Set Printer," *Print 21,* May 2004.
Schulze, Jane, "Printer PMP Swaps Unit for Rival Promentum's Stock in $24m Deal," *Australasian Business Intelligence,* December 13, 2004.
" 'We're No Patsy,' PMP Warns Intended Partner," *Sydney Morning Herald,* November 29, 2001.

—M.L. Cohen

Pure World, Inc.

<table>
<tr><td>

376 Main Street
Bedminster, New Jersey 07921
U.S.A.
Telephone: (908) 234-9220
Fax: (908) 234-9355
Web site: http://www.pureworld.com

Public Company
Incorporated: 1983 as Computer Memories (Far East) Ltd.
Employees: 109
Sales: $37.1 million (2004)
Stock Exchanges: NASDAQ
Ticker Symbol: PURW
NAIC: 325414 Biological Product (Except Diagnostic
    Manufacturing)

</td></tr>
</table>

Pure World, Inc., is a Bedminster, New Jersey-based company that operates through subsidiary Pure World Botanicals, Inc. producing natural ingredients from plants, which are then sold to cosmetic, food and flavor, nutraceutical, and pharmaceutical customers to be manufactured into consumer products. The company employs three different proprietary technologies to derive its natural ingredients: extraction, which uses a solution of water or water mixed with alcohol to produce an extract that can be converted to a fluid, paste, or powder; purification, a value-added process that isolates desirable plant compounds; and granulation, an enhancing process for powdered substances. Pure World maintains a New Jersey manufacturing plant that it claims is the largest botanical extraction facility in North America, producing dozens of products, including Cascara Sagrada Bark, Wild Cherry Bark, Devil's Claw, Ginger Root, Ginseng, St. John's Wort, Ginko Biloba, Kava, and powdered Vitamin E. Pure World is a public company listed on the NASDAQ SmallCap Market.

The Founders Wed in the 1970s

Pure World was rescued from bankruptcy in 1995 by investors Paul and Natalie Koether, with Paul assuming the chairmanship and Natalie handling day-to-day responsibilities as president. Both of them, especially Natalie, had earned reputa-

tions as corporate raiders. She earned a law degree from the University of Pennsylvania in 1965, then after clerking for a judge became the only woman lawyer at a 145-person Philadelphia law firm, Morgan Lewis and Bockius. Her area of expertise was corporate law and she met Paul Koether, a New York stockbroker, while working on a stock deal. Their working relationship turned romantic and they were married in 1971.

In 1978 the Koethers launched their careers as corporate raiders, creating a limited partnership called Shamrock Associates, attracting scores of investors who each chipped in $100,000 and engaging in a practice known as greenmailing. In essence, greenmailers bought stock in what they considered were undervalued companies. They then approached management to inform them that they or a third party might seek to gain control of the company. When the price of the stock rose, due to the prospect of a hostile takeover, they sold their shares on the open market, but in many cases the company simply bought back the shares at a premium to eliminate the threat. With Natalie Koether the most visible partner, Shamrock started out by attempting to take over a real estate investment trust (REIT) called CL Assets. When the dust settled Shamrock sold back the shares to the REIT, realizing a 60 percent profit.

Shamrock focused its efforts on investments of $100 million and less. Over the course of a decade it targeted 40 companies, 12 of which paid the partnership to go away; the investment in many others paid off with a bump in the company's stock price. The amount of money under Shamrock's management increased from $1.2 million to $20 million. Notable successes included Dorsey Company, Tennessee maker of plastic containers and cargo trailers that paid a $1 premium over its stock's top price to retire more than 1 million shares; Scientific Computers, a Minnesota computer service company that bought back a third of its shares from Shamrock at a $2 premium; and Seaway Food Town Inc., an Ohio supermarket operator that paid $16.625 a share for 9 percent of its stock, which Shamrock had bought for less than $14 a share.

Corporate Lineage Dating to the Early 1990s

The Koethers made a run at Computer Memories, a California hard disk manufacturer, and unlike their other greenmail ventures they succeeded in taking over the company in 1988. It was Computer Memories, originally incorporated in 1983, that would one day become Pure World. After the Koethers took over, Computer Memories exited the manufacturing business, leaving a shell of a public company to serve as another investment vehicle for the couple. In June 1992 they paid $1 million in cash and another $500,000 in stock to acquire NorthCorp Realty Advisors, Inc., a Dallas-based firm providing asset management services to the commercial real estate industry. A month later Computer Memories changed its name to American Holdings Inc. In September 1993 American Holdings distributed about half of NorthCorp to stockholders and a year later sold its remaining interest for $1.5 million.

American Holdings invested in a Dallas REIT, American Industrial Properties (AIP), acquiring a 5 percent stake in 1993. Specializing in industrial properties and office buildings, AIP had gone public in 1985, enjoyed initial success, and then had begun to falter. According to *Business News New Jersey,* "Newspaper reports have called the REIT 'one of the worst performing of the breed.' " In 1993 AIP planned to reincorporate in Maryland, a move that the Koethers opposed, believing it would "entrench management and give the trust managers a blank check to recapitalize the trust." After this bid was rejected by shareholders, American Holdings increased its holdings and initiated a proxy fight to gain control of the REIT. In November 1994 at the company's annual meeting, the Koethers' slate of directors failed to receive the required two-thirds majority required for the election of non-incumbents. However, AIP's slate also failed to garner enough votes to win re-election. As a result, management remained in office and the matter was carried over to the next annual meeting, when again American Holdings was unable to secure enough votes to oust current management. Then in January 1996 the REIT filed a suit that accused Paul Koether of attempting to cut a deal with its lender, Manufacturers Life Insurance, a charge that Koether called ridiculous. The Koethers countersued, accusing AIP's management of illegally entrenching themselves and wasting the REIT's assets. Finally in November 1996 the two sides reached a settlement, with the agreement calling for AIP to pay $825,000 to Pure World as a reimbursement for costs incurred during the squabble and the Koethers agreeing to sell its stake in AIP.

While the AIP matter was playing out, American Holdings turned its attention to a new field: natural products. In November 1994 a bankruptcy court approved American Holdings' bid to acquire 80 percent of Dr. Madis Laboratories (DML), a South Hackensack, New Jersey-based manufacturer of botanical extracts. American Holdings outbid two European and three other American suitors. It would acquire the rest of DML in 1997. Founded as a family business in 1959, DML fell on hard times during the 1980s, due in part to a plant explosion that led to an expensive reconstruction. But the company also was unfocused, unable to tap into a specific customer base for its health and beauty products. DML filed for bankruptcy in 1988. A court-appointed trustee, Edward Bond, took over the running of the company in 1991. After four years he succeeded in getting the company back on its feet, paying off back taxes while coming to terms with creditors and paying them off. The next step was to find new owners who would not only bring new capital to the business but also supply it with purpose and vision. The Koethers' business plan, which won court approval, called for DML to move away from a commodity approach that simply produced botanical extracts and instead to make proprietary health and nutritional supplements.

American Holdings gained majority control of DML in January 1995 and several months later, in September, changed its name to something more suitable: Pure World, Inc. In was also in 1995 that the company found its first major herbal supplement, kava, produced from the root and stem of a South Pacific plant that was used to alleviate stress and anxiety. It was brought to the attention of Pure World by Chris Kilham, who first tried kava in a Massachusetts natural-food store in 1980 and became an untiring advocate of the supplement. According to the *Wall Street Journal,* he persuaded the Koethers "to send him to the republic of Vanatu in the South Pacific to line up a source of kava. Things must have gone well: He later became an honorary tribal chief there." As a result of Kilham's efforts, Pure World became one of the largest kava suppliers in the United States.

Pure World quickly introduced new products to spur growth. Sales grew from $6.2 million in 1995 to $6.6 million in 1996, while net income improved from $41,000 to $229,000. The company now began to add to its capabilities, in 1997 opening a laboratory to develop purified products such as ginko biloba and milk thistle, and to serve the needs of customers such as cosmetic companies, which needed purified botanicals to eliminate unwanted odor and color. Although it would take another couple of years before Pure World would see any significant sales from purified products, the company continued to experience a strong climb in sales, which soared to $10.8 million in 1997. Net income topped $2.3 million.

Pure World continued to invest in its facilities in 1998, upgrading the plant facilities and constructing a new 13,000-square-foot warehouse. The old warehouse located in Teterboro, New Jersey, was then renovated, and in March opened as a botanical powdering facility. The demand for nutraceuticals continued to grow in 1998, resulting in revenues of $23 million for the year and net income of nearly $5.7 million. But 1998 also would prove to be the high watermark for the company and the industry in general, as sales began to tail off in the first quarter of 1999.

Declining Demand in the Late 1990s

Despite the addition of new products and powdering capabilities in 1999, Pure World experienced a dip in sales to $15 million. The company also wrote down some long-term investments, accounting for more than half of a $2.1 million loss. Demand for botanical extracts remained weak in 2000, but due to a large processing contract, Pure World was able to post revenues of $24.2 million. It still incurred a net loss of $1.6 million, and the processing order was a one-time sale, providing no momentum for 2001. The adverse impact on the economy of

Key Dates:

1983: Computer Memories is incorporated.
1988: Paul and Natalie Koether acquire the company.
1992: The company name is changed to American Holdings Inc.
1995: Dr. Madis Laboratories, Inc. is acquired and the name is changed to Pure World, Inc.
2003: Natalie Koether dies.
2004: Dr. Qun Yi Zheng is named president.

the terrorist attacks of September 11, 2001 placed a further damper on Pure World's business. At the end of the year, Pure World recorded sales of $18.4 million, and its net loss continued to grow to $2.9 million.

Pure World had been trading on the NASDAQ, but it was no longer able to meet minimum listing requirements, and in 2002 it received a delisting notice. The company then transferred its listing to the NASDAQ SmallCap Market. But Pure World continued to flounder in 2002, with sales slipping to $18.2 million and the company losing another $1.8 million. Business picked up in 2003, as sales improved to nearly $21.9 million and the company trimmed its net loss to $245,000. But 2003 also was marked by misfortune. Natalie Koether was forced to take a leave of absence due to an ongoing fight with heart disease. A few weeks later, in October 2003, she died at Columbia Presbyterian Hospital in New York City.

Paul Koether took over as Pure World's acting president, then in January 2004 he turned over the reins to Dr. Qun Yi Zheng, the company's chief operating officer. Zheng had come to Pure World in 1996 from Hauser Nutraceuticals, where as technical manager he developed innovative extraction and purification technologies. He became Pure World director of research and development and over the years assumed increasing administrative responsibilities, working closely with Natalie Koether. At the same time, the company announced that it had hired the Boston-based investment banking firm of Adam, Harkness & Hill to explore a possible merger or sale of the company.

Pure World received a number of feelers from potential buyers, but in the end the company allowed the engagement of Adams, Harkness & Hill to expire, electing instead to make a further attempt at growing the business in the belief that Pure World still held a great deal of potential. Paul Koether told the Newark *Star-Ledger,* "We're operating at a fraction of our capacity. It's like an airplane. At 50 percent capacity, it's operating at a loss. At 65 capacity, it's a different story. We're not realizing the full potential of what we have, given our marketing situation." In 2004 the company's commitment to research and development began to pay major dividends. One new product created sales of $18.2 million during the year, resulting in an increase in sales to $37 million and a return to profitability after six years, as the company recorded net income of $635,000. Strong numbers continued in 2005. Although it remained uncertain whether or not Pure World had turned a corner, there was no doubt that given its technical capabilities and strong research and development program it was well positioned to take advantage of any future opportunities.

Principal Subsidiaries

American Holdings, Inc.; Eco-Pure, Inc.; Pure World Botanicals, Inc.; Pure World Botanicals Powders, Inc.

Principal Competitors

GNC Corporation; Nature's Sunshine Products, Inc.; Triarco Industries, Inc.

Further Reading

Fiorilla, Paul, and Mukul Pandya, "The Koethers Aim at a New Target," *Business News New Jersey,* July 10, 1996, p. 4.

Martin, Josh, "Down But Not Out," *Management Review,* December 1999, p. 57.

"Natalie Koether, 63, a Giver and a Taker," *Star Ledger* (Newark, N.J.), October 8, 2003, p. 51.

Petersen, Andrea, "The Making of an Herbal Superstar," *Wall Street Journal,* February 26, 1998, p. B1.

"PureWorld Botanicals, Inc.: Unlocking the Secrets of Nature," *Nutraceuticals World,* September 2004, p. 94.

Todd, Susan, "Pure World Mulls Merger or Sale," *Star Ledger* (Newark, N.J.), January 15, 2004, p. 44.

Tracy, Elanor Johnson, "A New Greenmailer Swings into Action," *Fortune,* August 5, 1985, p. 71.

—Ed Dinger

Cussons

PZ Cussons plc

PZ Cussons House, Bird Hall Lane
Stockport
SK3 0XN
United Kingdom
Telephone: +44 161 491 8000
Fax: +44 161 491 8191
Web site: http://www.cussons.com

Public Company
Incorporated: 1879
Employees: 11,659
Sales: £488 million ($935.5 million) (2004)
Stock Exchanges: London
Ticker Symbol: PZC
NAIC: 325611 Soap and Other Detergent Manufacturing;
    311225 Fats and Oils Refining and Blending; 325412
    Pharmaceutical Preparation Manufacturing; 325612
    Polish and Other Sanitation Good Manufacturing;
    325620 Toilet Preparation Manufacturing; 335222
    Household Refrigerator and Home and Farm Freezer
    Manufacturing

PZ Cussons plc is a leading manufacturer and distributor of a variety of products, especially soaps and other personal care items, including shampoo, baby powder, and the like. These are marketed under PZ Cussons's flagship Imperial Leather brand and others, including Original Source and Carex. The company also manufactures refrigerators and other white goods, including freezers and air conditioners; detergents and cleansers; feminine hygiene products; olive oil; packaging materials; and even pharmaceuticals. In 2003, PZ Cussons formed a joint venture with Ireland's Glanbia to supply evaporated milk and milk powder in Nigeria. The company also acquired U.K. hair care brand Charles Worthington in 2005. Although based in Manchester, PZ Cussons has long been controlled by the founding Zochonis family, from Greece, and has carved a niche for itself by focusing on various markets in Africa, especially Nigeria, Ghana, Cameroon, and East Africa. The company's African operations continued to represent some 26 percent of its annual sales. Europe, especially the United Kingdom, is the group's largest market, at 43 percent, while the Asia Pacific region, including Australia, accounts for 26 percent of sales. In addition to its African manufacturing sites, the company operates manufacturing plants in Thailand, Poland, Australia, and Athens. In 2005, the company announced that it would shut down its U.K. soap producing facility by 2007. Listed on the London Stock Exchange, the Zochonis family, which includes Chairman A.J. Green, controls as much as 80 percent of the company's stock. The family also is highly active in the company's operations, filling most of the group's primary management positions around the world. In 2004, PZ Cussons posted revenues of £488 million ($935 million).

Trading Origins in the 19th Century

Known as Paterson Zochonis until its name change in 2002, the company's history reached all the way back to the late 19th century, when it was founded as a trading post, called West African Merchants, in Sierra Leone by two partners, George Paterson, originally from England, and George Zochonis, from Greece. Paterson and Zochonis started out by shipping palm oil and other produce, such as palm kernels, cocoa, groundnuts, and seed cottons, as well as animal hides and skins, to the United Kingdom, and bringing back goods from England, such as cloth from Manchester. The business proved strong, and in 1884 Paterson and Zochonis incorporated the company as Paterson Zochonis (PZ).

PZ gradually expanded its range of goods, establishing a degree of expertise in what was considered a difficult trading market. This expertise enabled the company to begin expanding into other African markets and, most important, into Nigeria. PZ set up its Nigerian subsidiary in Lagos in 1899. Like its Sierra Leone brand, the Nigerian subsidiary at first operated as a trading merchant.

George Paterson died in 1934, leaving George Zochonis in control of the company. The Zochonis family was by then already highly involved in the company's expansion, and a company tradition became the placing of members of the extended Zochonis family in key management positions. Indeed, by the beginning of the 21st century, the Zochonis family was said to represent about half of the group's total payroll.

PZ expanded into Ghana in 1934, setting up a trading office in Tema that year. Over its first 50 years, PZ grew from a simple trading house into a major wholesale and retailer of general merchandise for the West African region. The company operated its own shops—often simple stalls in local markets—selling a wide variety of goods. By the early 1950s, PZ's zone of operations covered Liberia, French Guinea, Cameroon, and the Gold Coast.

Public Offering in the 1950s

Yet PZ's interest began to turn toward manufacturing in the late 1940s. In 1948, the company purchased a small soap factory owned by PB Nicholls & Co in Nigeria. The company changed its subsidiary's name to Alagbon Industries Ltd. in 1953. In that year, PZ itself went public, listing its shares on the London Stock Exchange as Paterson, Zochonis & Company.

The rapid growth of the population in Africa, coupled with the development of a consumer market, encouraged PZ to begin seeking to expand its manufacturing operations in the late 1960s. The company turned to Ghana, launching a manufacturing facility there in 1969. White goods, including refrigerators, freezers, and air conditioners, were among the company's first products. In Nigeria, meanwhile, the company had expanded its soap production to include other personal care items. By 1973, the company had decided to launch the production of detergents and refrigerators in Nigeria as well.

The year 1975 marked a major milestone in PZ's history. In that year the company acquired Cussons Group Ltd. Based in Manchester, England, Cussons had originated in 1869 as a chemist's shop founded by Thomas Cussons. By 1909, the business, now under Alex Cussons, had begun to specialize in detergents, acquiring a bleach mill in Salford. The company then entered the production of soap in 1920.

Yet Cussons's fortunes were assured in the 1930s, when the company bought up perfumers Bayley's of Bond Street. That purchase brought Cussons among other things, a popular fragrance known as Imperial Russian Leather. Bayley's had created the fragrance in 1760, at the request of Russia's Count Orloff, a member of the Tsarist court, who wanted a fragrance with a leathery scent. In addition to the distinctive fragrance, Cussons's new soap featured novel packaging, as well as other features, such as a badge that remained visible to the end of the bar's use. These features helped Imperial Leather become England's best-selling bar soap brand, a position held into the next century.

Cussons's growing sales led it to complete a new acquisition, of Gerard Bros Ltd. in Nottingham, which became the focus of the company's soap production in the United Kingdom.

Imperial became Cussons's flagship brand as the company established a strong export business, shipping to other parts of the British Empire, notably to Australia and New Zealand. The company also set up a subsidiary in Malaysia in order to market its brands, primarily through other distributors. In the 1960s, Cussons entered Africa, renting facilities to produce soaps and other toiletries and hair care products.

PZ acquired the Preservene Soap Company, based in Richmond, Victoria in Australia in 1976. The purchase allowed Cussons to establish its own manufacturing business in that country and take over its own marketing for Australia and New Zealand for the first time. The Australian business later expanded, adding a detergent factory in Dadenong, Victoria, in 1987.

International Growth in the 1990s

In the meantime, PZ continued its own expansion. In 1977, the company moved into a new direction though the acquisition of Minerva, a company founded in Athens in 1902 for the manufacture and marketing of olive oils, as well as margarine and cooking fats. That company had begun exporting to the North American, African, and Australian markets, as well as to the rest of Europe, in the 1950s. In 1957, Minerva expanded its production capacity with the construction of a new plant in Moschato, in Piraeus.

Yet the personal care market held the most interest for the company. Through the 1980s, PZ made a number of expansion moves, adding to its production capacity as well as extending its reach into new markets. In 1983, for example, the company acquired a soap factory in Kenya. This was followed in 1986 by the acquisition of the Lervia Soap Factory in Thailand. The company's Australian detergent plant launched production in 1987. The following year, PZ entered the Indonesian market as well through the acquisition of PT Jaya Makmur Raya, a manufacturer of soaps, toiletries, and baby powder and other baby products.

PZ's interest shifted to the European market in the early 1990s, especially to the Eastern Europe bloc, newly emerging from decades of Soviet dominance. In 1990, PZ entered Poland, launching exports to that country. By 1993, the company decided to install its own production capacity in Poland, buying up the former state-owned soap plant Pollena Wroclaw. Two years later, PZ acquired a second state-owned company in Poland, Pollena Uroda.

PZ expanded its distribution operations in the second half of the 1990s, starting with the creation of PZ Cussons India in 1995. That subsidiary supplied soaps and talcs to the Indian, Sri Lankan, Nepalese, and Bangladeshi markets. In 1997, PZ established a new subsidiary for its Middle East distribution, in Dubai. Then, in 1988, PZ launched a dedicated marketing subsidiary in Malaysia, which then took over the company's distribution needs for both Malaysia and Singapore. PZ also expanded its manufacturing base, transferring its olive oil production to a newly completed facility in Schimatari.

Key Dates:

1760: Bayley's of Bond Street creates Imperial Russian Leather fragrance at the request of Count Orloff.
1869: Thomas Cussons founds a chemist shop in Manchester.
1879: George Paterson and George Zochonis open a trading office in Sierra Leone, Western Africa Merchants.
1884: Paterson and Zochonis incorporate their business.
1899: Paterson and Zochonis open an office in Nigeria.
1909: Cussons enters bleach production.
1934: Paterson Zochonis opens an office in Ghana; Cussons acquires Bayley's and launches Imperial Leather as a bar soap.
1948: Paterson Zochonis acquires a soap manufacturing business in Nigeria.
1953: Paterson, Zochonis & Company lists on the London Stock Exchange.
1969: PZ launches manufacturing in Ghana.
1975: PZ acquires Cussons.
1977: PZ acquires Greek olive oil producer Minerva.
1983: PZ acquires a soap factory in Kenya.
1986: The company begins manufacturing in Thailand.
1988: A subsidiary is launched in Indonesia.
1993: Pollena Wroclaw, in Poland, is acquired.
1995: The company acquires Pollena Uroda in Poland; a marketing subsidiary is established in India.
1998: Minerva moves production to a new facility.
2002: The company name is changed to PZ Cussons.
2003: The company acquires the Original Source personal care brand.
2004: The company acquires the Charles Worthington hair care brand.

Personal Care Focus for the New Century

Into the 2000s, PZ adopted a new strategy focusing more strongly on its personal care products operations. As part of that effort, the company changed its name to PZ Cussons in 2002 in order to underline its core business. PZ then began seeking new acquisition opportunities to boost its range of personal care brands. The first of these came in 2003, when the company paid more than £11 million to acquire the Original Source brand. That business had been started only in 1997 with an investment of just £45,000.

PZ added to its personal care line with the purchase of hair care specialist Charles Worthington, for £25 million, in 2004. That acquisition not only gave the company an entry into the U.K. hair care market, it also provided a foothold into the U.S. market.

Difficulties in Russia led PZ to pull out of that country in 2005, representing an end to Imperial Leather's reign of nearly 250 years there. In 2005, also, PZ completed construction of a new production facility in Thailand. At the same time, the company announced that it intended to close its Nottingham, England plant and transfer that production to the Thai plant by 2007. PZ Cussons expected to remain an important name in the international personal care market.

Principal Subsidiaries

Minerva; PT PZ Cussons Indonesia; PZ Cussons Australia; PZ Cussons East Africa Ltd. (Nairobi); PZ Cussons Ghana Industries Limited; PZ Cussons India Private Limited; PZ Cussons Malaysia Sdn. Bhd.; PZ Cussons Middle East and South Asia FZE; PZ Cussons Poland; PZ Cussons Thailand; PZ Cussons UK; PZ Industries PLC (Nigeria); SIPCA S.A. (Cameroon).

Principal Competitors

Doyin Group of Cos.; Madhvani Group; Lever Brothers Private Ltd.; DiverseyLever Marsavco Congo; Procter and Gamble S.A. Proprietary Ltd.; Sinopec Jinling Co.; Unilever PLC; Colgate Palmolive Proprietary Ltd.; Procter and Gamble Co.; Johnson & Johnson.

Further Reading

Aldrick, Philip, "Stay in Touch with Colonial Cussons," *Daily Telegraph,* February 16, 2005.

Burgess, Kate, "Setback As Cussons Five-Year Plan Stalls with Detergent Loss," *Financial Times,* February 9,. 2005, p. 22.

"Cleaning Up on the Quiet," *Manchester Evening News,* January 9, 2004.

"Cussons to Relocate Main Plant from UK to Thailand," *Bangkok Post,* February 11, 2005.

Feddy, Kevin, "Imperial Year at PZC," *Manchester Evening News,* September 9, 2003.

Goodway, Nick, "Cussons Washes Its Hands of Russia After 250 Years," *Evening Standard,* February 8, 2005, p. 34.

Jones, Sheila, "Bubbly PZ Washes Hands of Some of Its Imperial Past," *Financial Times,* November 17, 2001, p. 2.

Keers, Helena, "Personal Touch Adds to Appeal," *Daily Telegraph,* August 28, 2004.

Pandya, Nick, "Rise: Cool Companies: No. 71 Paterson Zochonis," *Guardian,* January 19, 2002, p. 5.

"PZ's Keeping Up Appearances," *Manchester Evening News,* September 7, 2004.

"U.K.'s PZ Cussons to Set Up Soap Factory in Thailand," *Thai Press Reports,* February 15, 2005.

Urquhart, Lisa, "Cussons Expands into UK Haircare," *Financial Times,* July 2, 2004, p. 26.

—M.L. Cohen

One Place, So Many Possibilities.

R.C. Willey Home Furnishings

2301 South 300 West
Salt Lake City, Utah 84115
U.S.A.
Telephone: (801) 461-3900
Fax: (801) 461-3990
Web site: http://www.rcwilley.com

Wholly Owned Subsidiary of Berkshire Hathaway, Inc.
Incorporated: 1959
Employees: 2,500
Sales: $600 million (2004 est.)
NAIC: 442110 Furniture Stores; 442299 All Other Home
    Furnishings Stores; 443111 Household Appliance
    Stores; 443112 Radio, Television, and Other
    Electronics Stores; 522220 Sales Financing

R.C. Willey Home Furnishings is a leading home furnishings and electronics chain based in Salt Lake City, Utah. The company has grown into the biggest furniture dealer west of the Mississippi by offering a huge selection, convenient credit, and prompt delivery. R.C. Willey stocks its dozen stores from a nearly 900,000-square-foot distribution center, said to be the largest of its kind in the country. The company was acquired by Berkshire Hathaway, Inc. in 1995.

Origins

Like many businesses, R.C. Willey Home Furnishings started as a sideline. Rufus Call Willey, an employee of the local electric company in Syracuse, Utah, began selling Hotpoint brand appliances door-to-door in 1932.

To get people using refrigerators or electric ranges when electricity was brand new to the area, he would let them try out the appliances for a week. He also let them finance the purchases in installments over a three-year period, payable at harvest time.

Willey resorted to refurbishing ranges and refrigerators from salvage yards during World War II. However, sales of new appliances boomed after the war.

Until this time, Willey had conducted business out of the back of a red pickup truck. In 1950, he built his first small store next door to his house in Syracuse, Utah, a small town northwest of Salt Lake City.

Leadership Change in 1954

Willey left the business in June 1954 due to terminal cancer. William H. Child, who had married Willey's daughter Pat two years earlier, took over the business. Child's brother Sheldon joined him in 1956. At the time, sales were about $200,000 a year, according to one source. William Child is credited with adding furniture to the company's appliance offerings.

The original 600-square-foot store in Syracuse was remodeled for the first time in 1956. It would eventually grow to 100,000 square feet.

Growing from the 1970s through the 1990s

The company built its second store in 1969. It was located in Murray, a suburb to the south of Salt Lake City. West Valley City, to the west, got a store in 1986. Both of these would be expanded repeatedly as the business grew.

R.C. Willey began an important marketing tactic in the early 1980s: giving out free hot dogs to increase traffic. In *HFD—The Weekly Home Furnishings Newspaper,* company executives credited the chain's success to three factors: an eye for expansion, focus on the middle segment of the market, and dedication to customer satisfaction.

A 73,000-square-foot store was opened in Orem, a community just north of Provo in Utah County, in November 1990. It cost $5 million to open, reported *HFD*. By this time, R.C. Willey had six stores (one a clearance outlet) and employed 700 people. Sales were $100 million in 1990, reported *HFD*.

The company opened its Central Distribution Center in the middle of the Salt Lake Valley in 1991. This included an 80,000-square-foot store adjacent to a 400,000-square-foot warehouse. The combined project cost $13.5 million, according to *HFD*.

Key Dates:

1932: Rufus Call Willey begins selling appliances door-to-door.
1950: R.C. Willey opens its first store in Syracuse, Utah.
1954: William Child takes over the business.
1969: A second store opens in Murray, Utah.
1990: Six stores have sales of $100 million.
1995: Berkshire Hathaway, Inc. acquires the company.
1999: The company expands outside Utah with Meridian, Idaho, store.
2001: The company's first Las Vegas store opens.
2005: Expansion continues in Nevada and California.

A smaller furniture outlet and a carpet outlet opened nearby in the mid-1990s. A 100,000-square-foot store opened in a suburb of Ogden, north of Salt Lake City, in 1996.

The chain's range of offerings continued to expand with the addition of fitness equipment, personal computers, and snow blowers. Some stores were being fitted with garages for installing car stereos. The company began selling futons in late 1994 and by 1996, they were a million-dollar business.

Berkshire Hathaway Buys Company in 1995

By 1995, R.C. Willey's seven furniture stores were claiming annual sales of about $300 million, and the company had 1,300 employees. By this time, electronics were an important part of the product mix, and the company was holding its own against competition from big box retailers. A study done for R.C. Willey estimated it led the Utah home electronics market with a 28 percent share, while it commanded more than half of the furniture market. Its personal computer sales were worth about $20 million a year, according to *Computer Retail Week*.

Berkshire Hathaway, Inc., the holding company led by billionaire investment guru Warren Buffet, acquired R.C. Willey on May 24, 1995. The price was a reported $150 million in stock. For a dozen years, Berkshire owned another furniture retailer, Nebraska Furniture Mart, which operated what was considered to be the industry's largest single store. R.C. Willey CEO Bill Child credited Nebraska Furniture Mart president with suggesting the deal to Buffet, reported the *Omaha World Herald*.

With the backing of Berkshire Hathaway, R.C. Willey continued to build. Its Intermountain Distribution Center, erected next to Salt Lake International Airport in 1997, was the largest of its kind in the United States at 860,000 square feet. It cost $30 million and replaced three existing warehouses.

An outlet opened in Provo in 1998. The same year, R.C. Willey's store in South Salt Lake City became the site of a ''Whaling Wall'' mural by the famous marine artist Wyland. The company was also testing an interactive kiosk system inside three of its stores.

Beyond Utah in 1999

R.C. Willey expanded outside Utah for the first time in August 1999, when it opened a store in Meridian, Idaho (near Boise). It instantly claimed the leading spot in that market.

A 162,500-square-foot store opened in Henderson, Nevada, two years later. According to *HFN*, the Las Vegas metro area was the fastest growing in the United States, attracting 8,000 new residents a month. R.C. Willey was unique in the range of products it offered under one roof, allowing shoppers to buy home electronics and cabinets on the same trip. Another distinct practice was the company's policy of closing stores on Sundays.

Revenues were about $400 million in 2000, when the company had about 2,000 employees. Furniture accounted for about 60 percent of sales. Its credit operations had more than $185 million in loans, making it one of Utah's largest finance companies, noted the *Salt Lake Tribune*. Bedding sales alone were worth $25 million, according to *HFN*.

To keep volume up, the company spent heavily on advertising and promotions such as giving away 600,000 hot dogs a year. For special occasions, the company teamed up with pizza restaurants like Domino's in the giveaways.

Chief financial officer Scott L. Hymas, who had been with the company since 1987, succeeded Bill Child as CEO in February 2001. Child remained chairman. At the same time, Bill Child's nephew, Jeffrey S. Child, became the company's president.

A second Las Vegas area store opened in May 2003. Stores were averaging sales between $35 million and $90 million a year, according to the *Las Vegas Review-Journal*. *Furniture Today* reported the second Las Vegas store as having sales between $85 million and $100 million. By 2004, 41 percent of sales were coming from outside Utah, according to Warren Buffet's yearly letter to Berkshire Hathaway shareholders.

R.C. Willey was opening a new store in Reno, Nevada, in 2005. A 150,000-square-foot site was planned for Sacramento, California, the following year. The pro-business atmosphere of Governor Arnold Schwarzenegger encouraged the entry into California, Hymas told *Furniture Today*. A third store was under consideration for Las Vegas. The company had also been scouting locations in the Pacific Northwest.

Parent company Berkshire Hathaway applied to open an industrial bank in Utah in 2005 in order to consolidate R.C. Willey's extensive credit operations. The company's finance department then employed about five dozen people, and more than 130,000 customers had charge cards with the company. R.C. Willey also provided financing for about 50 Big-O Tires stores. Its consumer loans were worth $185 million, according to the *Salt Lake Tribune.*

Principal Operating Units

R.C. Willey Finance.

Principal Competitors

Best Buy; Circuit City; Costco Wholesale; Granite Furniture; Ultimate Electronics; Walker Furniture.

Further Reading

Allegrezza, Ray, "A Child's Success Story," *Furniture Today*, October 11, 2004, p. 4.
——, "Flat-Packed Bandwagon," *HFN*, April 7, 1997, p. 1.
Arave, Lynn, "R.C. Willey Has Hot Dog of a Slogan," *Deseret News* (Salt Lake City), January 15, 2002, p. E3.
"A Better Way to Sleep: Upscale Bedding Departments Are Gaining Prominence on the Sales Floor," *HFN*, May 5, 2003, p. 36.
Engel, Clint, "Buffett Heralds R.C. Willey in Shareholders Letter," *Furniture Today*, March 21, 2005, p. 25.
——, "R.C. Willey to Build Sacramento Store," *Furniture Today*, January 10, 2005, p. 1.
Friesen, Wendy, "R.C. Willey Cites Success Factors: Of Three Components, Company Most Heavily into Corporate Expansion," *HFD—The Weekly Home Furnishings Newspaper*, July 15, 1991, p. 10.
Georgianis, Maria V., "Computer Business in Guise of Furniture Store," *Computer Retail Week*, November 6, 1995, p. 35.
Gibson, Stephen W., "R.C. Willey Got Its Humble Start Selling Refrigerators to Farmers," *Deseret News* (Salt Lake City), April 11, 1999, p. M8.
Ginos, Becky, "A Whale of an Art Project in S.L.," *Deseret News*, September 8, 1998, p. B1.
Hicken, Robb, "Honesty, Integrity Needed in Business," *Daily Herald* (Provo, Utah), March 27, 1993.
Historical Highlights, Salt Lake City: R.C. Willey Home Furnishings, 2005.
Jones, Chris, "Berkshire Hathaway Chief Attends Opening of Las Vegas Furnishings Store," *Las Vegas Review-Journal*, June 21, 2003.
Jordon, Steve, "Berkshire Hathaway to Buy Utah Retailer," *Omaha World Herald*, Bus. Sec., May 25, 1995, p. 21.
Kunkel, Karl, "Creative Promotions Drive Bedding Business," *HFN*, January 31, 2000, p. 20.
——, "Place Your Bets, Ladies and Gentlemen," *High Points*, July 2000, p. 14.
Meyers, Donald W., "Business Booms for R.C. Willey Store," *Daily Herald*, March 12, 1995, p. 34.
Mitchell, Lesley, "Better Business Bureau of Utah Loses Important Member," *Salt Lake Tribune*, October 10, 1998.
——, "Salt Lake City-Based Furniture Store to Gamble in Vegas, But Not on Sundays," *Salt Lake Tribune*, October 22, 2001.
Nii, Jenifer K., "R.C. Willey Chief Is Named to the Furniture Hall of Fame," *Deseret News* (Salt Lake City), October 22, 2002, p. E1.
——, "R.C. Willey to Start Bank," *Deseret Morning News*, May 24, 2005, p. E1.
Oberbeck, Steven, "Buffett to Open Bank in Utah," *Salt Lake Tribune*, May 24, 2005, p. E1.
——, "R.C. Willey Sees Room to Grow—In Idaho; R.C. Willey to Build Store in Boise," *Salt Lake Tribune*, July 25, 1997, p. D1.
Pusey, Roger, "R.C. Willey to Keep Its Name and Management But Tap into Berkshire Hathaway Connections," *Deseret News*, May 25, 1995, p. B14.
"R.C. Willey CEO Gives $1 Million in Stock to WSU," *Salt Lake Tribune*, October 11, 1995, p. B2.
"R.C. Willey Constructing New Distribution Center," *Enterprise* (Salt Lake City), November 4, 1996, p. 1.
"R.C. Willey Depot Nears Completion," *HFN*, August 11, 1997, p. 36.
"R.C. Willey Looks at Pacific Northwest," *HFN*, December 16, 2002, p. 4.
"R.C. Willey Under New Direction for First Time in Over 46 Years," *Deseret News* (Salt Lake City), February 8, 2001, p. E1.
Silberg, Lurie, "R.C. Willey to Test Interactive Kiosk," *HFN*, February 23, 1998, p. 6.
Sorcher, Jamie, "R.C. Willey Futons Strong from Middle to Upper End at Utah Chain," *HFN*, April 15, 1996.
Sorcher, Jamie, and Doug Olenick, "R.C. Willey Sold," *HFN*, May 29, 1995, p. 1.
Taylor, John, "Furniture Mart President Steered Berkshire Toward Utah Deal," *Omaha World Herald*, Bus. Sec., May 26, 1996, p. 18.
Wolf, Alan, "R.C. Willey's Steve Child to Retire," *TWICE*, December 17, 2001, p. 8.
"Work to Start on R.C. Willey Store," *Idaho Business Review*, November 16, 1998, p. 7A.

—Frederick C. Ingram

Ratner Companies

2815 Hartland Road
Falls Church, Virginia 22043
U.S.A.
Telephone: (703) 698-7090
Toll Free: (800) 874-6288
Fax: (703) 876-2897
Web site: http://www.ratnerco.com

Private Company
Incorporated: 1974 as Creative Hairdressers Inc.
Employees: 10,000
Sales: $204 million (2004 est.)
NAIC: 812112 Beauty Salons

Ratner Companies is the Falls Church, Virginia-based parent company of six hair salon subsidiaries. The main enterprise is Hair Cuttery, a 800-unit value-priced salon chain found on the East Coast and the Chicago area, comprised of both company-owned and franchised operations. Although Hair Cuttery offers a full complement of hair care services, no appointment is necessary. A similar concept is employed by Hair Cuttery United Kingdom, a chain located in northwest England. With 23 locations, Bubbles Salons is a more fashion-conscious full-service salon that also offers spa services. A fourth member of the Ratner Companies, Salon Cielo and Spa is an upscale offshoot of Bubbles. Of the ten Cielo locations, eight offer spa services. Another upscale format is ColorWorks Salon, a six-unit chain that specializes in a full range of hair color services. Finally, Ratner Companies is home to Salon Plaza, styled by the company as "beauty malls." Ratner Companies is privately owned by chief executive officer Dennis Ratner, his family, and ex-wife.

Getting into the Beauty Industry in the 1930s

Dennis Ratner learned the hair styling trade from his father Louis Ratner, who was born in Washington, D.C., in 1912. A high school dropout who went to work to help support his family, he became a professional piano player, then in the 1930s established himself as a Washington hairdresser. Soon he was running one of the largest salons in the country. He struck out on his own in 1936, establishing Louis Ratner Creative Hair Designs in Washington, D.C., which became a pioneer beauty parlor chain. An astute marketer, he conceived of the $5 permanent wave, thus becoming "$5 Louis," the king of permanents. He then built an empire of 25 District of Columbia-area beauty salons before retiring in 1971. At the age of 18, Dennis Ratner took up the scissors and went "behind the chair" full-time in one of his father's salons and learned the business from him. Years later, Ratner told *Washington Business Journal* in a 1991 company profile, "Dad was brilliant, a visionary. He related to me everything he knew. He's 80 now, lives in Florida, and we talk four or five times a week. . . . There's nothing better than a family in business." Dennis Ratner married a British-born stylist, Ann, and one night they conceived of a new kind of salon, using a cocktail napkin to sketch out their idea for a unisex shop that catered to the family trade, offering inexpensive haircuts with no appointment necessary. Ratner was 29 years old when he and Ann invested $5,000 to open the first Hair Cuttery in West Springfield, Virginia. He did not even have a logo for the business when he approached the *Washington Star* to place the salon's first advertisement. For $50 the newspaper's display ad department offered to provide him with ten different logo ideas. He selected one that featured a pair of shears cutting through the Hair Cuttery name, a logo that would become well known in the Washington, D.C., metropolitan market. The first Hair Cuttery salon caught on quickly, and Ratner opened two more stores in Virginia later in 1974, laying the foundation for the Hair Cuttery chain.

Because Ratner was brimming with other business ideas, he elected to create a parent company to house them, along with the remaining salons of his father that he continued to manage, choosing the name Creative Hairdressers Inc. He and Ann eventually divorced but remained business partners. In 1978, she branched out on her own, adding an element to Creative Hairdressers with the founding of a more up-market salon, which she called Bubbles. It too grew into an area chain, albeit on a much smaller scale than Hair Cuttery, numbering only seven salons by 1991. In contrast, Hair Cuttery added about 350 units, picking up the pace of openings as the years went on, adding nearly 100 units in the Washington, D.C., area and another 50 or so in the Baltimore–Annapolis, Maryland corridor; 60 in southern Virginia; 50 in Pennsylvania, New Jersey, and Delaware; 50 in Florida; and another two dozen stores in Atlanta and other locations in Georgia. To find enough qualified stylists, the chain sometimes took unusual steps. Once it mailed surveys to every licensed hair dresser in the Washington, D.C., area, listing Creative Hairdressers' offices as the return address but making no mention of Hair Cuttery. The survey asked where the people worked and whether or not they had any interest in changing jobs. Hair Cutters contacted everyone who indicated they would entertain an offer to switch salons and successfully convinced a number of them to join Hair Cuttery. As the chain grew, it added its own line of hair care products and used its size to align itself with such hair care giants as Clairol, Redken, and Paul Mitchell, promoting their products and in turn receiving steep discounts.

Wide-ranging Ventures Launched in 1980s

Along the way, Ratner launched other enterprises under the Creative Hairdressers umbrella. He started a beauty school called Image Makers, which he sold in the mid-1980s, and earlier in the decade he tried to establish a vitamin store chain and made a stab at a nail care salon, which he told *Washington Business Journal* had "a cute name, but I can't remember what it was." By the early 1990s, with the U.S. economy lapsing into recession, Ratner took a step back and concentrated his efforts on the salon business. Hair Cuttery, which on average had been opening a new salon each week, now cut back to about 35 new units a year, and instead of breaking into new markets, Ratner elected to fill in the markets where the chain was already represented.

The 1990s brought the death of Louis Ratner, who succumbed to leukemia at the age of 82 in late 1994. His son continued to build the family empire founded on the legacy of the king of permanents. By the end of the 1990s, after a quarter-century, Hair Cuttery grew to 800 salons in size. In addition to entering nearby markets in North Carolina and South Carolina, the chain also entered the Chicago area in 1999 through the acquisition of 30 salons owned by hairstylist Peter Poggi and Poggi Enterprises, Inc. The Salons—operating as Chicago Hair Cutting Co., Chicago Hair and Tans, and Hair America—were gradually converted to the Hair Cuttery name.

New Directions and a New Name: Late 1990s and Beyond

In the late 1990s, Hair Cuttery went international. A United Kingdom couple, Gary and Michele Levy, who owned a salon chain in Altrincham and Stockport in Great Britain, came across an article in the *Manchester Evening News* which profiled the career of Ann Ratner, a Manchester native. Interested in what they learned about the Hair Cuttery concept, the couple faxed Ratner, who promptly telephoned them. Weeks later, the Levys traveled to the United States to meet with Dennis and Ann Ratner and forged a franchising agreement to bring Hair Cuttery to the United Kingdom. The first U.K. salon opened in 1998 and within a year five more shops followed, including a Manchester flagship salon that featured a state-of-the-art training facility. The goal was to launch 300 Hair Cuttery salons by 2010, although by 2005 the chain had only reached 30 units.

Meanwhile, Creative Hairdressers launched Salon Plaza. Billed as a "beauty mall," this operation is in essence a booth rental business in which independent operators lease individual private salon suites sharing a common lobby. Maintenance, utilities, styling chairs, shampoo bowls, and professional liability insurance are also provided. By the end of the 1990s, the company was operating three of the beauty malls in Maryland and Virginia. In 1999, Creative Hairdressers celebrated its 25th anniversary with a number of changes. A new corporate name was adopted, Ratner Companies, which both reflected the Ratner family connection and the holding company nature of the business. The company also tightened controls, for the first time bringing together all the subsidiaries' back-of-the-house functions to be run out of the corporate headquarters in Virginia. Furthermore, there was as a change in attitude at the top. "The first 25 years was about building a business," Dennis Ratner told Chantal Tode of *Salon News* in March 2000. "For the next 25 years, giving back to our people is the sole reason this company is going to survive. We have the luxury of being a large company now and of being able to do something significant."

A major element in helping associates to "earn a better living and live a better life," as well as to retain talented people, was education. According to *Salon News,* it "quickly dawned on [Ratner] that he would need to partner with a manufacturer to provide the necessary educational support. But, rather than pick a company himself, he let the employees make the choice. The stylists chose Redken [Fifth Avenue], says Ratner, because the two companies seemed the most aligned on the idea of helping stylists to earn a better living." In exchange for becoming the exclusive provider of products at the "back bar" at Hair Cuttery, Redken set up an educational program that dealt with both technical and non-technical subjects. Unlike previous training, the stylists helped to choose the subject matter, from new styling techniques to how to handle finances. Although it was expensive to do so, the technical classes took place in the salons for the sake of convenience.

The alliance with Redken also provided focus, since stylists now had to be educated only on one product line. However, they would not be required to promoted Redken products. Hair Cuttery continued to take a multi-line approach to its retail area, running product-based promotions about once a month, a number of which were done on an exclusive basis. Some non-technical aspects of being a stylist were conducted offsite at local beauty schools, where students learned what Ratner called the "softer side" of the business. Among the principles Ratner believed successful stylists should practice every day were communication, making sure they truly listened to what customers wanted; doing something for customers that was unex-

Key Dates:

1936: Hairdresser Louis Ratner opens his first salon in Washington, D.C.
1974: Hair Cuttery opens its first salon.
1978: First Bubbles salon opens.
1994: Louis Ratner dies.
1998: Hair Cuttery is launched in the United Kingdom.
1999: Parent company Creative Hairdressers Inc. changes its name to Ratner Companies.
2002: ColorWorks is launched.

pected but appreciated, such as his favorite, a quick shoulder rub; and teaching customers how to take care of their hair at home. By doing these things, stylists could build relationships and keep customers. He urged stylists to not be afraid to hand out business cards to build a customer base. On the personal side, Ratner urged stylists to take good care of themselves, to make sure to wear comfortable shoes and clothes. Another facet of the softer side of the business was for stylists to view tips as part of their income, not throwaway money. As a young stylist, for instance, Ratner lived on his tips and saved his salary.

As Ratner Companies expanded the Hair Cuttery chain in both the United States and the United Kingdom, as well as grow the other brands, it continued to look for new opportunities in the 2000s. Dennis Ratner even talked about the possibility of again becoming involved in the beauty school business. Out of Bubbles emerged the Salon Cielo and Spa minispa concept. Ratner companies also found niche opportunities in coloring, launching a salon concept called ColorWorks. Although Color-Works salons offered hair cuts, the primary focus was on hair

coloring. Ratner Companies attempted to launch a down-market version called Easycolor, but it failed to take hold. By the summer of 2005, Colorworks could be found in six Maryland and Virginia locations, with two more salons set to open in Maryland and Jacksonville, Florida.

With a number of its brands prospering, Ratner Companies appeared well positioned to grow for some years to come. As for selling the business or taking it public, Dennis Ratner showed no interest, telling *Salon News,* "We will stay private—selling the company is just not appealing to me."

Principal Subsidiaries

ColorWorks Salon; Hair Cuttery; Hair Cuttery United Kingdom; Bubbles; Salon Cielo and Spa; Salon Plaza.

Principal Competitors

Mascolo Ltd.; Regis Corporation.

Further Reading

Kretikos, Eleni, "Falls Church Salon Streaks Color Shops Across Region," *Washington Business Journal*, September 5, 2003, p. 6.

"Louis Ratner, 82, Founded Salon Chain," *Washington Times*, January 2, 1995, p. C9.

"Redken and HairCuttery—A Unique Relationship," *Salon News*, November 2000, p. S4.

Toda, Chantal, "Hair Cuttery Cuts A New Swath," *Salon News*, March 2000, p. 48.

Wells, Melanie, "Cuttery Clips Away During Recession," *Washington Business Journal*, June 10, 1992, p. 1.

—Ed Dinger

Renal Care Group, Inc.

2525 West End Avenue, Suite 600
Nashville, Tennessee 37203
U.S.A.
Telephone: (615) 345-5500
Fax: (615) 345-5505
Web site: http://www.renalcaregroup.com

Public Company
Incorporated: 1995
Employees: 7,352
Sales: $1.34 billion (2004)
Stock Exchanges: New York
Ticker Symbol: RCI
NAIC: 621492 Kidney Dialysis Centers

Renal Care Group, Inc., provides dialysis services to individuals with chronic kidney failure. The company serves the majority of its patients through its own dialysis centers and a lesser number though contractual relationships with hospitals. Renal Care operates 425 outpatient dialysis facilities in 33 states, performing more than four million dialysis treatments annually. Through contracts, the company provides acute dialysis services to more than 200 hospitals. Renal Care also provides practice management and administrative services to groups of physicians. Roughly 50 percent of the company's annual revenue is derived from Medicare reimbursement payments. In mid-2005, Renal Care agreed to be acquired by Fresenius Medical Care AG, the largest integrated provider of products and services for individuals with chronic kidney failure.

Origins

Renal Care was formed to provide a specific service: to help those with chronic kidney failure. Individuals with chronic kidney failure, also known as end-stage renal disease (ESRD), faced three treatment options for their affliction. A kidney transplant offered the only cure for ESRD; without a successful transplant, the disease was irreversible and ultimately fatal. A shortage of kidney donors severely limited the number of transplants, however. Only 5 percent of ESRD patients in the United

States could hope for a transplant, leaving dialysis (the removal of waste and toxins from the blood) as the only treatment option for a vast majority of ESRD patients. With dialysis, there were two treatment options: peritoneal dialysis and hemodialysis. Peritoneal dialysis usually was performed in the patient's home, and hemodialysis, the most common form of ESRD treatment, typically was performed in a hospital or an outpatient facility. Of those on dialysis in the United States, an estimated 92 percent received hemodialysis, a treatment that used a dialyzer to remove toxins, fluid, and chemicals from the patient's blood and another device that controlled external blood flow and monitored the patient's vital signs. Hemodialysis typically was administered three times a week to an individual patient. Renal Care intended to focus on providing hemodialysis at its facilities, targeting the vast majority of all ESRD patients.

From a business standpoint, Renal Care courted a large customer base. As the company set out, it also benefited from two other qualities of the market it served. In macabre terms, ESRD was a growth industry. According to the Centers for Medicare and Medicaid Services, the number of ESRD patients in the United States who needed dialysis increased exponentially between 1982 and 2002, jumping from 66,000 to 309,000. These patients were treated by nephrologists in either a hospital setting or in a freestanding outpatient facility. Historically, outpatient dialysis facilities composed a loosely-knit, fragmented industry, with ownership of the centers held by groups of nephrologists. During the 1990s, however, the industry began to consolidate, giving rise to multi-center dialysis companies like Renal Care. In a consolidating industry, Renal Care presented itself as a consolidator, focusing on capturing market share and achieving the economies of scale realized by size. In Renal Care's case, increased size gave the company more leverage with local health payers in local markets.

Renal Care entered the race for national dominance in the dialysis services industry as the demand for such treatment was increasing with each passing year. The company's role as a consolidator began with an act of consolidation in June 1995, when a group of leading nephrologists decided to create a company with the clinical and financial capability to offer comprehensive care for ESRD patients on a cost-effective basis.

The nephrologists represented six companies, the six founding companies of Renal Care. In a single transaction, Kidney Care, Inc., Medical Enterprises Ltd., D.M.N. Professional Corporation, Tyler Nephrology Associates, Kansas Nephrology Association, and a Tennessee-based company, Renal Care Group, Inc., joined together. The transaction was paid for with an initial public offering (IPO) of stock in February 1996 that marked the official start date of the combined company. In the IPO, 3.9 million shares were sold to the public at $18 per share, yielding net proceeds of $64 million that paid for the foundation upon which the company would build.

Renal Care's growth was achieved through acquisitions, which occurred on an almost monthly basis during the company's formative years. When the company started out, it provided dialysis services to 2,700 patients at 41 outpatient facilities located in eight states. The company also had contractual relationships with 21 hospitals, offering acute dialysis services in a hospital setting. These were the primary markers used to chart Renal Care's growth, the starting point of the company's attempt to build itself into a national dialysis-services provider. Although the company operated an ancillary business offering wound and diabetic care services and a practice management and administrative services business for physicians, the basic indicators of its expansion were patients served, facilities owned, markets penetrated, and hospital contracts signed. Renal Care was a company formed to provide medical services, but to be successful, a business perspective had to be maintained. The company was involved in a growth industry populated by small, independent operators that offered a consolidator the opportunity to provide dialysis services to the bulk of the nation's ESRD patients.

Acquisitions in the Late 1990s

Renal Care was not alone in the pursuit of nationwide dominance. Joining Renal Care as industry consolidators were DaVita Inc., Gambro Healthcare, and a German company named Fresenius Medical Care, the band of big, publicly traded, dialysis companies with national, if not global, aspirations. The industry was in the midst of consolidating as Renal Care completed its IPO, creating a sense of urgency for the Nashville-based company to begin its drive for growth. The acquisition campaign began in earnest in early 1997. By the beginning of April, Renal Care had acquired seven federated dialysis facilities in Indiana, adding 600 patients to its customer rolls and contracts with four hospitals. The acquisition, which gave the company offices in Indianapolis, Richmond, Greensburg, and

Kokomo, also included an agreement to manage the practice of 17 physicians, 12 of whom were nephrologists. One week later, the company signed acquisition agreements that provided it with entry into New Jersey. The company agreed to acquire dialysis operations in Toms River, New Jersey, and to jointly develop a new dialysis center capable of serving 260 patients. At the same time, Renal Care reached an agreement with Southern Ocean County Hospital in Manahawkin, New Jersey, to jointly develop a new dialysis center capable of serving 40 patients. In May 1997, the company strengthened its presence in Texas, acquiring Bay Area Dialysis Services of Corpus Christi. The purchase added 330 patients, six dialysis centers, and contracts with two hospitals. By the time the transaction was concluded, Renal Care served 6,300 patients in 103 centers spread across 17 states and through contractual relationships with 51 hospitals.

Renal Care's pace of expansion continued at the rate established in 1997. By the end of the 1990s, the company represented a formidable national force, having taken hold of a sizable portion of the nation's dialysis business. In early 1999, Renal Care entered Illinois for the first time, completing the acquisition of Dialysis Centers of America, a Chicago-based operator of 12 centers that served 1,700 patients and provided acute dialysis services to six hospitals. The acquisition gave Renal Care a total of 172 centers in 21 states serving 13,200 patients. The addition of six hospitals served by Dialysis Centers of America gave Renal Care contractual relationships with 102 hospitals. The company's stature by this point was large enough to attract attention from the mainstream business press. In the fall of 1999, Renal Care was on *Fortune* magazine's list of the "One Hundred Fastest-Growing Companies" in the United States, earning the recognition the first year it was eligible for consideration. To make the list, companies were required to post a minimum 30 percent growth rate in both revenues and earnings per share for three years, a record Renal Care exceeded during its first three years in business. By the end of the year, the company provided dialysis and related service to 14,200 patients, nearly 12,000 more than it served three years earlier. During the same time span, Renal Care's network of company-owned facilities leaped from 41 to 181, driving geographic expansion that fanned out from a territory of eight states to 23 states. The growth of the company's annual sales totals reflected the robust expansion, jumping exponentially from $163 million in 1996 to $520 million by 1999.

Renal Care established an impressive rate of growth during its first years in business, one that would be shattered during the first years of the 21st century. The race to seize control of the estimated $13 billion U.S. dialysis center industry picked up pace in the new decade, but only after a lull in activity on the acquisition front. In 2000 and 2001, the national competitors made relatively few purchases, focusing on internal challenges instead—a pause to refresh and to reorganize before resuming the chase for market share.

As Renal Care entered the mid-2000s, fast-paced expansion propelled the company's financial growth. Acquisitions in 2003, particularly in Ohio, Illinois, Arizona, Mississippi, and Texas (Renal Care's five biggest markets), pushed sales beyond the $1 billion mark and net income beyond the $100 million mark for the first time. In 2004, the company continued to press

Key Dates:

1995: Renal Care is formed.
1996: Renal Care completes its initial public offering of stock.
2004: Renal Care acquires National Nephrology Associates.
2005: Renal Care agrees to be acquired by Fresenius Medical Care.

forward, completing the massive acquisition of a Nashville neighbor. After acquiring the 14-center Midwest Kidney Centers in January, which added 850 patients, the company agreed to acquire Nashville-based National Nephrology Associates, a company with a solid presence in Phoenix, Chicago, Portland, Oregon, and in Mississippi. The National Nephrology acquisition was a $345 million deal, adding 87 dialysis centers and 5,600 patients to Renal Care's 22,300-patient base.

During the first years of the new century, Renal Care greatly increased the number of centers it operated. By 2004, the company maintained a presence in 33 states through 418 outpatient facilities. Sales stood at $1.34 billion. The growth during the previous four years was substantial, increasing the number of company-operated facilities from 181 to 418, but the company still trailed in the race for national dominance. Fresenius Medical Care led the pack with a more than 25 percent share of the U.S. market, followed by Gambro Healthcare and DaVita, who each controlled 15 percent of the domestic market. Renal Care, despite the intensity of its acquisition campaign, ranked fourth, holding a 9 percent share of the market. There was a substantial gap separating Renal Care from Fresenius Medical Care, but at the end of 2004, the most threatening challenge was posed by Renal Care's closest rivals. In December, in a move that typified the pervasive trend toward industry consolidation, DaVita and Gambro Healthcare announced a definitive agreement to merge. Under the terms of the agreement, DaVita was slated to acquire Gambro Healthcare's U.S. dialysis business, which would make Renal Care a distant third behind Fresenius Medical Care and DaVita.

The End of Independence in 2005

As Renal Care entered 2005, its bid to achieve national leadership was all but over. The presence of a greatly enlarged DaVita coupled with an already towering Fresenius Medical Care (the largest integrated dialysis services company in the world) gave Renal Care's management little hope of seriously competing with its two rivals. Combined, DaVita and Fresenius Medical Care controlled an estimated 55 percent of the U.S. market, while Renal Care held a 9 percent share. In an industry that was consolidating, however, there was one way for Renal Care to fight back, and its management seized the opportunity. In May 2005, Renal Care announced that it had agreed to be acquired by Fresenius Medical Care in a $3.5 billion deal that

offered a riposte to the DaVita-Gambro Healthcare merger. The deal promised to end Renal Care's nine-year history as an independent company, adding its 425 dialysis facilities to the 1,630 centers operated by Fresenius Medical Care in North America, Europe, Latin America, and Asia. In announcing the deal in a company press release, Renal Care's chief executive officer, Dr. Ben Lipps, offered what was likely the last independent statement to be issued from Renal Care. ''This transaction demonstrates the value that Renal Care Group has built in the marketplace,'' he wrote. ''It is a testament to the vision of our founders and the dedication and hard work of our associates and affiliated physicians during Renal Care Group's nine-year history that we have created this value and can now return it to our shareholders. By joining with Fresenius Medical Care, we will give our associates and affiliated physicians the opportunity to work with the world's leading dialysis therapy company, and our shareholder will receive an excellent return on their investment. We are convinced that our patients will be well served and will continue to receive high-quality dialysis care.''

Principal Subsidiaries

RCG Mississippi, Inc.; Renal Care Group of the Southeast, Inc.; Renal Care Group East, Inc.; Renal Care Group Arizona, Inc.; Dialysis Management Corporation; Four State Regional Dialysis Center, Inc.; Renal Care Group Michigan, Inc.; Renal Care Group Northwest, Inc.; Renal Care Group Alaska, Inc.; Renal Care Group Southwest Holdings, Inc.; Physicians Dialysis Company, Inc.; Renal Care Group of the South, Inc.; Wound Care Group, Inc.; Renex Corporation.

Principal Competitors

DaVita Inc.; Gambro AB; Fresenius Medical Care AG.

Further Reading

Barker, Robert, ''Bargain-Hunting in the Small-Cap Patch,'' *Business Week,* July 15, 2002, p. 142.

Barton, Christopher, ''Healthcare Company Sells Memphis, Tenn., Unit to Nashville, Tenn.-Based Firm,'' *Commercial Appeal,* March 14, 2001, p. B2.

''Dialysis Services Co. Targets Up to 10 Buys,'' *Corporate Financing Week,* December 23, 2002, p. 7.

Lunday, Sarah, ''Two Dialysis Centers to Open in Newton, Kansas,'' *Knight Ridder/Tribune Business News,* March 5, 1997, p. 305B1067.

Manning, Joe, ''Bone Care International Questioned in Broader Probe of Dialysis Testing,'' *Milwaukee Journal Sentinel,* October 29, 2004, p. B3.

Reeves, Amy, ''Renal Care Group Inc.,'' *Investor's Business Daily,* May 24, 2001, p. A9.

Roberts, Ricardo, ''Renal Care M&A: Coming Back to Life,'' *Mergers & Acquisitions,* March 1, 2004.

Santiago, Racquel, ''Renal Care Venture Opens Dialysis Centers,'' *Crain's Cleveland Business,* October 20, 1997, p. 4.

Shinkle, Kirk, ''Renal Care Group Inc.,'' *Investor's Business Daily,* May 25, 2004, p. A6.

—Jeffrey L. Covell

Ryoshoku Ltd.

6-1-1 Heiwajima, Ota-ku
Tokyo 143-6556
Japan
Telephone: +81 3 3767 5111
Fax: +81 3 3767 0422
Web site: http://www.ryoshoku.co.jp

Public Subsidiary of the Mitsubishi Corporation
Incorporated: 1979
Employees: 4,310
Sales: ¥1.3 trillion ($12.09 billion) (2004)
Stock Exchanges: Tokyo
Ticker Symbol: RYHKF
NAIC: 424410 General Line Grocery Merchant
     Wholesalers; 424490 Other Grocery and Related
     Product Merchant Wholesalers

Ryoshoku Ltd. is Japan's second largest wholesale distribution group. A subsidiary of the Mitsubishi Corporation, which holds more than 50 percent of the company, Ryoshoku operates more than 150 distribution and logistics centers throughout Japan, as well as a number of RKG branded cash-and-carry stores. Ryoshoku has traditionally focused the majority of its business on the processed foods sector, which continues to account for more than half of the group's revenues each year. In the 2000s, however, Ryoshoku had made an effort to step up its business in the beverage distribution sector, including beer and other alcohol. By the mid-2000s, this sector accounted for some 25 percent of Ryoshoku's business. The company also has begun to carry over-the-counter drugs in a partnership with pharmaceutical group Kobayashi. In another expansion move into the middle of the decade, Ryoshoku has been solidifying its presence in western Japan, notably through the acquisition of Saihara, a food wholesaler that also has a strong business in beverage distribution. Listed on the Tokyo Stock Exchange, Ryoshoku posts annual sales of more than ¥1.3 trillion ($12 billion). The company is led by Masaharu Goto, chairman of the board, and Tadashi Hirota, president and CEO.

Merger Origins in the 1970s

From the start, Ryoshoku was closely associated with Japan's highly diversified Mitsubishi Corporation, which launched its own food processing operations in the early part of the 20th century. In support of this business, Mitsubishi also entered the food wholesaling market, establishing four regional wholesaling companies, Hokuyo Shoji, Nodaki Shoji, and Shinbushi Shoji in Tokyo and Osaka, in 1925. The Mitsubishi companies focused especially on the distribution of canned seafood and water chestnuts products; the market for other processed foods remained relatively limited in Japan until as late as the 1970s.

Changing food consumption patterns and shifts in consumer shopping trends led Mitsubishi to begin integrating its wholesaling operations at the end of the 1970s. Japan's retail food market traditionally had been dominated by many thousands of small grocery shops. The multitude of these stores, which required a high degree of personalized contact for suppliers, led to the development of a complex and highly inefficient multi-tiered wholesaler model, with a number of large-scale wholesalers, served by an army of small-scale wholesalers, placed several layers between supplier and consumer. The rise of the supermarket in Japan in the 1960s and 1970s, however, brought about a shift not only in consumer shopping habits, but also in the wholesale market. A number of larger regionally and nationally operating retail chains emerged, creating a need for a more limited number of larger and more diversified wholesalers.

In 1979, Mitsubishi decided to merge its four regional wholesalers into a single company, called Ryoshoku Ltd. Integrating the four companies, which each had developed its own corporate culture during the previous decades, proved difficult, and required some years before a single, unified Ryoshoku truly emerged. A major step in that direction came, however, with the company's implementation of its first computer-controlled logistics network, dubbed Tomas, for Total Management System, launched in 1982. In the meantime, Ryoshoku also was faced with difficult market conditions stemming from the economic downturn provoked by the oil crisis in the 1970s.

From the start, Ryoshoku was set up as an independently operating company. On the one hand, Ryoshoku benefited from the confidence inspired in customers by the Mitsubishi name; on the other hand, acting as an independent entity under its own name allowed Ryoshoku to build a closer relationship with its customers. At the outset, the company's own distribution remained rather limited, focusing on canned water chestnuts and canned seafood. Yet Ryoshoku soon began to add other products to its line.

Ryoshoku continued seeking to integrate its operations on a national level. In 1981, the company established RKG, regrouping its regional wholesale operations into a network of large-scale wholesale outlets. The strength of the RKG chain, which also helped to reduce cultural differences among the original Ryoshoku players, enabled Ryoshoku to build its streamlined distribution network into a national operation by the end of the 1980s.

Ryoshoku began expanding its range of goods through the 1980s as well. In 1986, for example, the company received a license to import and distribute alcoholic beverages. The shifting pattern of Japanese food consumption behavior, from a traditional diet based on fresh foods to a diet heavily favoring processed foods, also encouraged Ryoshoku to add more product categories to its distribution operations. In addition, during the 1980s, Ryoshoku continued integrating its business, rolling out the Tomas system on a companywide level by 1988. In that year, the company also added new branch offices in Sapporo, Sendai, and Hiroshima, bringing its total to seven.

''DREAMing'' in the 1990s

Through the 1980s, Ryoshoku's distribution operations remained focused on a centralized model based on the traditional so-called front distribution center (FDC). Yet distributing from a central facility proved inefficient as Japan's retail market changed. The emergence of large-scale supermarket groups had created a demand for shipments of cases and even pallets of processed foods, while the country's large number of small mom-and-pop groceries continued to require the supply of single products. The reliance on FDCs also meant that the company was required to invest in and maintain a number of large-scale, but underutilized facilities.

In 1990, Ryoshoku became one of the first in the wholesale sector to recognize this situation and act accordingly, setting up the first of its network of regional distribution centers (RDCs) in Okayama that year. The company's RDCs then took over the work of organizing shipments in cases or as single products, as required. In this way, Ryoshoku achieved far greater productivity, and at the same time reduced the need to invest in additional RDCs.

The creation of the RDC network marked a turning point for Ryoshoku and became a central component for the launch of the company's new long-term strategy, dubbed DREAMS. This new strategy provided a significant departure for the group and the wholesale distribution sector in general. Previously, wholesalers focused their attention on food producers, and the wholesale distribution model was oriented toward serving the needs of the suppliers. Yet under the DREAMS plan, Ryoshoku began a shift in focus that targeted its retailer, and ultimately the consumer, as its primary clientele. In this way, Ryoshoku began transforming its business from that of wholesaling to that of direct sales.

The DREAMS strategy was more specifically developed to enable Ryoshoku to respond more immediately to the requirements of the rapidly growing large- and medium-scale supermarket groups. In particular, the company sought to establish itself as a primary partner with these groups, if only to head off an increasing trend among the supermarket sector of dealing directly with producers. Ryoshoku positioned itself as a cost-efficient alternative, enabling the supermarket groups to avoid the high costs of establishing their own logistics and supply systems.

Ryoshoku scored a major advance in 1993 when it reached an agreement with midsized supermarket group Sotetsu Rosen to supply some 75 percent of the Kanagawa-based retailer's nonfrozen processed foods needs. The contract marked a first in the wholesaling market, and helped establish Ryoshoku as one of the sector's leaders. By 1994, Sotetsu Rosen and Ryoshoku had expanded their relationship to include frozen processed foods as well as candy and pastry.

Ryoshoku's success with Sotetsu Rosen enabled it to attract other customers, such as Daimaru Peacock. In 1993, that retailing group turned to Ryoshoku for its processed and frozen foods supply needs. The following year, Ryoshoku signed on another important client, when Sun-net Tohoku Consumers' Co-operative Union contracted the company for its processed foods, candy, and pastry products. The increase in these latter categories encouraged the company to set up dedicated distribution subsidiaries, such as Ryoku Japan, set up in 1995 to handle the group's confectionery distribution.

National Focus in the 2000s

To serve its growing client list, Ryoshoku expanded its RDC network, establishing new facilities in Kyushu, Tokai, and Hokuriku in 1994, followed by the opening of a site in Hokkaido in 1995. In that year, as well, the company went public, listing its stock on the Tokyo Stock Exchange's secondary board. Mitsubishi nonetheless remained the company's controlling shareholder, with more than 50 percent of its shares.

Ryoshoku deepened its interests in the distribution of alcoholic beverages with the purchase of a major stake in Saitama-ken Shurui Hanbai in 1996. The company achieved a new success in 1997, when York-Benimaru contracted with the company for its processed foods distribution needs. That contract marked Ryoshoku's entry into the wholesale toiletries distribution sector as well. Also in 1997, Ryoshoku rolled out its new total management IT system, called New Tomas, in development since 1995.

The launch of New Tomas coincided with the début of a new type of Ryoshoku distribution facility. As the number of its

Key Dates:

1925: Mitsubishi launches wholesale distribution of canned fish and related goods.
1979: Mitsubishi merges its four regional wholesale food distribution companies into a single unit, Ryoshoku.
1981: Ryoshoku reorganizes its operations into a new RKG regional distribution network.
1982: The Tomas total management IT system is launched.
1986: Distribution of alcoholic beverages begins.
1988: Branch offices are opened in Sapporo, Sendai, and Hiroshima.
1990: The company launches the DREAMS long-term strategy, shifting focus from food producers to food retailers; the first RDC opens.
1993: The company wins the distribution contract for Sotetsu Rosen.
1995: The company is listed on the Tokyo Stock Exchange secondary board; dedicated confectionery distribution subsidiary Ryoka Japan is launched; a stake in alcoholic beverage distributor Saitama-ken is acquired.
1997: The New Tomas IT system is launched.
2000: A stake in alcoholic beverages distributor Nakaizumi is acquired.
2001: Full control of Saitama-ken, renamed as Ryoshoku Liquor, is acquired.
2002: Saihara, based in western Japan, is acquired.
2004: The company announces an OTC distribution agreement with Kobayashi Pharmaceutical.

large-scale supermarket clients grew, the company had recognized the need to develop dedicated facilities. In 1997, Ryoshoku opened the first of its specialized distribution centers (SDCs) in order to provide dedicated facilities for individual large-scale retailer clients. By the early 2000s, Ryoshoku had opened some 45 SDCs around Japan.

Ryoshoku continued its push into the alcoholic beverage sector in the early 2000s. In order to overcome a number of restrictions in that market, notably the need for regional licenses, and the specific complexities of the country's alcoholic beverage market, Ryoshoku continued to seek out new acquisitions. In 2000, the company acquired a stake in Nakaizumi, based in Tokyo, the fifth largest alcoholic beverage wholesaler in the Tokyo and Shizuoka prefectures. The following year, Ryoshoku acquired full control of Saitama-ken Shurui Hanbai, which was renamed as Ryoshoku Liquor. By the middle of the decade, alcoholic beverage distribution accounted for nearly one-third of Ryoshoku's sales, and the company had emerged as the number two in the country in that area.

Ryoshoku finally achieved its ambition to transform itself into a major Japanese wholesaler group operating on a national level in 2002, when it acquired Saihara. Based in west Japan, Saihara not only boosted Ryoshoku's alcoholic beverage distribution division, it also established the company as a major distributor of a full range of goods to that region.

Ryoshoku adopted a new long-term strategy, Evolution21, to guide the company into the new century. Under the new strategy, the company continued to seek out new business opportunities. In the early 2000s, for example, the company began targeting the fast-growing convenience store market, signing up major clients such as 7-11. The company's position in this sector was strengthened when Mitsubishi became a major investor in rival convenience store group, Lawsons. Ryoshoku also had begun providing services to the restaurant industry, and in 2002 the company received a major contract to supply the Royal Co. restaurant chain. In another direction, Ryoshoku reached a cooperation agreement with chief rival Kokubu to set up a joint distribution company, Food Logistics Networks, serving as a link between food producers and food wholesalers.

The company also sought to expand its range of goods. In 2004, for example, Ryoshoku joined with parent Mitsubishi, reaching an agreement with Kobayashi Pharmaceutical to begin distributing the over-the-counter (OTC) products of its Kobashou subsidiaries. The agreement gave the company an entry into OTC drug distribution in the Tokyo, Kobe, Osaka, and Kyoto markets. With sales of more than ¥1.3 trillion ($12 billion) at the end of 2004, Ryoshoku claimed the number two position among Japan's wholesale market.

Principal Competitors

Kokubu & Co., Ltd.; Itochu-Shokuhin Company Ltd.; Kato Sangyo Company Ltd.; Arata Corporation; Yuasa Trading Company Ltd.; Meiji Seika Kaisha Ltd.; Kikkoman Corporation.

Further Reading

"Japan's Ryoshoku Buys into Osaka Liquor Company," *AsiaPulse News,* December 26, 2000.
"Japan's Ryoshoku Interim Group Pretax Profit Seen Beating Projection," *AsiaPulse,* August 14, 2002.
"Mitsubishi to Enter Wholesale Operations for Drug Products," *Asia Pulse,* March 23, 2004.
"Royal, Ryoshoku Tie Up," *Jiji,* February 25, 2002.
"Ryoshoku, Kokubu to Set Up Joint Distribution Venture," *Japan Weekly Monitor,* July 22, 2002.
"Ryoshoku Planning Take-Out Salad Shops," *Japan Food Service Journal,* April 10, 2002.

—M.L. Cohen

Schreiber Foods, Inc.

425 Pine Street
Green Bay, Wisconsin 54301
U.S.A.
Telephone: (920) 437-7601
Web site: http://www.sficorp.com

Private Company
Incorporated: 1945 as L.D. Schreiber Cheese Co.
Employees: 4,500
Sales: $2.2 billion (2004)
NAIC: 311513 Cheese Manufacturing

Schreiber Foods, Inc., is the largest privately held cheese company in the world. Schreiber manufactures primarily private-label cheeses. That is, it mostly does not sell its own brands, but produces cheese for others. Its products include natural cheeses, processed cheese products, and cream cheese. It is one of the leading suppliers of cheese to fast-food restaurant chains, supplying the cheese slices that go on cheeseburgers to 17 of the top 20 hamburger chains. Some 90 percent of cheeseburgers in the United States are made with Schreiber products. It is the second largest producer of cream cheese in the United States, behind giant industry leader Kraft. Schreiber also sells private-label cheese and dairy products to grocery stores, to club and warehouse stores, to the military, to school foodservice programs, and to drugstores and discount stores. The company's own brands include Raskas cream cheese, Clearfield processed and natural cheeses, and Ready-Cut cheese products. Schreiber maintains 22 production facilities spread across Wisconsin, Arizona, Georgia, Missouri, Pennsylvania, Texas, and Utah, as well as in Germany, Mexico, and Brazil, and it runs four distribution centers in the United States. Schreiber also participates in joint ventures with companies in Brazil, France, Germany, India, and Mexico and operates overseas subsidiaries in Europe and the Middle East. The company started small and then expanded as it gained prominent nationwide customers such as McDonald's. The privately owned company was bought out by its employees in 1999.

Fighting for a Market in the 1940s and 1950s

Three men are credited with founding Schreiber in 1945, but the name, idea, and capital came from Chicago businessman L.D. "Barney" Schreiber. Schreiber was a trader on the Chicago Mercantile Exchange, well versed in the dairy industry. He had written the quality standards for butter for the U.S. Department of Agriculture in 1935 and had made a fortune through various farm ventures and his L.D. Schreiber Co. In the early part of the 20th century, one company, the Kraft Cheese Company, dominated the market for processed cheese. Processed cheese is made by blending different cheeses under heat. Kraft's founder, James L. Kraft, held patents for most of the technology needed to make this type of cheese, and competitors could not get a foot in the door. But Kraft's patents expired in 1938. This evidently was the inspiration for Barney Schreiber. He contacted an experienced cheese production manager, Merlin Bush, in 1945 and asked him to set up a new division of Schreiber's existing company, to be called the L.D. Schreiber Cheese Co. The new company would make processed cheese, getting in on this previously closed market. Bush accepted Schreiber's offer, and then hired Daniel David Nusbaum as plant manager. Bush, Nusbaum, and Schreiber put the new company together.

The first Schreiber plant was located in an old brewery building in Green Bay, Wisconsin. Wisconsin was one of the largest dairy producers in the United States, and centrally located Green Bay was the capital of the state's industry. Green Bay was also the home of the dairy cooperative Marketing Association of America (MAA). MAA bought cheese from hundreds of small farms and factories throughout Wisconsin and distributed it to larger vendors. Schreiber formed a close relationship with MAA that lasted until 1994, buying almost all its cheese through the group.

Schreiber's location was good. Its timing, however, was not so great. Although World War II ended in 1945, for several more years, the country was still governed by wartime regulations that had a profound impact on what a business could or could not do. Raw materials, such as metals for machine parts, were tightly restricted, making it doubtful that Schreiber could get a new plant going. Hiring was also difficult, and production of cheese was rationed. Rationed products were apportioned by

---

Company Perspectives:

Today, Schreiber still uses "16 ounces to the pound" as shorthand for two cornerstones of its character: unquestionable integrity and an ongoing commitment to quality. Schreiber has come a long way from its modest beginnings, but honesty and integrity are values the company will never leave behind.

---

a points system that could change without notice, making profit projections perilous. Nevertheless, the company plunged into the cheese business. As it happened, its first major customer was the U.S. government. The catch was that the order was for processed cheese in seven-pound cans. Merlin Bush bid on and won the contract even though his company had no can production line. Schreiber hurriedly put together a system for canning cheese. Making cheese for the government provided the company with steady business for the next several years. Schreiber's other early large customer was the grocery chain Safeway. Safeway had recently ended its relationship with another Green Bay cheese company, and Schreiber stepped in. It made private-label cheese products for Safeway's vast chain of groceries.

Schreiber bought its first production plant outside of Wisconsin in 1950, in order to keep up with growing demand from Safeway. This was in Carthage, Missouri. Schreiber poured money into technology as it built and renovated, trying to keep up with industry leader Kraft. Kraft brought out a landmark product, sliced cheese, in 1948. Schreiber needed to offer a private-label alternative to Kraft. But it could not use Kraft's patented process or equipment. Schreiber's production manager Nusbaum experimented with a blowtorch, heating the surface of cheese slices so that they dried and did not stick together. This may not have been how Kraft did it, but it worked, and allowed Schreiber to put out its own private-label sliced cheese line. Schreiber also applied its engineering know-how to packaging. In the late 1950s, the company came out with a new plastic packaging system that gave its cheeses significantly longer shelf life than its competitors. With several steady customers and nimble innovation, Schreiber grew solidly through the early 1960s.

New Ownership and New Challenges in the 1960s

The small company was modestly profitable in its early years, and by the early 1960s, it had established a wider range of customers. In 1962, Barney Schreiber decided to sell the company to cofounders Bush and Nusbaum, Bush's sons, who were very active in the business, and several other employees. This core group of 13 managers borrowed close to $500,000 to buy 49 percent of L.D. Schreiber Cheese Co. Then the company incorporated as a stand-alone company, no longer a division of L.D. Schreiber Co. The new owners had taken a substantial financial risk, borrowing against their homes to raise the cash to pay off Schreiber. Within a few years, the company faced a grave crisis that could have led to bankruptcy. And the company ran into a similar catastrophe again a few years later.

In 1965, Safeway notified L.D. Schreiber Cheese that one of its customers had gotten seriously ill from eating contaminated

cheese made under Schreiber's aegis. The cheese actually was manufactured by a Missouri company, Standard Milk, but Schreiber acted as a middleman between Standard and Safeway, and it had guaranteed the quality of Standard's product. The contaminant turned out to be a toxin derived from the staphylococcus bacteria, and a court ordered four million pounds of Standard's cheese impounded until it could be proved safe. Unable to sell this huge inventory, it seemed likely that Schreiber would go out of business. Schreiber's own testing had shown that only a small portion of the embargoed cheese was contaminated, but it needed to prove this to the government in order to be able to sell the product. Schreiber's leaders met fruitlessly with the Food and Drug Administration (FDA) in Washington, D.C., and after the first day's meeting, concluded that their company would have to fold. As a last hope, the executives returned to the FDA the next day and met with a microbiologist. This scientist advised the men to work with another government agency, the Communicable Disease Center (CDC) in Atlanta, Georgia, to come up with a reliable test for the suspect cheese. In a collaborative effort, Schreiber's scientists and government researchers found a way to test the cheese for the toxin. Schreiber worked for many months to test the entire four million pounds. A year after the first case of food poisoning surfaced, the government lifted the ban on Schreiber's inventory. The company sold almost all the embargoed cheese, and actually turned a profit, as the cheese had become more valuable with age.

Then in 1968, the company faced another major problem with its inventory. In this case, cheese manufactured for a government contract was rejected because of unsightly brown lumps. The lumps were not contaminants but a phosphate emulsifier that had caked instead of blending. The emulsifier was manufactured by the chemical company Monsanto. Schreiber had alerted Monsanto that their emulsifier sometimes caused the lumping problem, and Monsanto pledged to do something about it. But somehow the lumpy cheese got produced anyway, and the government eventually turned back to Schreiber some 5.5 million pounds of unacceptable product. Schreiber was again in danger of bankruptcy, as the value of the unsellable cheese was more than the company's net worth. So it did two things. The company sued Monsanto, and it devised a way to salvage the lumpy cheese. The only hope was to filter out the unsightly lumps. No cheese filtering technology existed at the time that would do this specific job. So Schreiber engineers took it on themselves to invent a filtering machine. The company was able to rescue the rejected cheese and sell it at a profit. Schreiber settled its suit against Monsanto in 1974.

Developing Bigger Markets in the 1970s

Schreiber began marketing its cheese products to fast-food restaurant chains in the late 1960s. This added significantly to the company's production volume. But Schreiber was still a small player in the fast-food market, which was dominated by Kraft, Borden, and Pauly. In the early 1970s, Schreiber increased its sales to the leading hamburger chain McDonald's year by year. McDonald's was just one of many companies with which Schreiber did business in 1970, but by 1974, the restaurant chain had become Schreiber's largest customer. Over the next few years, sales to McDonald's and other fast-food chains became half of all Schreiber's business.

Key Dates:

1945: The company is founded in Green Bay.
1950: The company opens its first plant outside Wisconsin.
1962: Managers buy the company from L.D. Schreiber.
1965: Much of the company's inventory is recalled because of contamination.
1970: Fast-food chain McDonald's is gained as a customer.
1977: The company moves to larger headquarters.
1985: The company picks a new president from outside the families of the founders.
1992: Schreiber acquires Wal-Mart as a customer.
2002: Private-label cream cheese maker Raskas is acquired.

The company had to build more plants in order to keep up with this growing demand. Schreiber did very well in the 1970s, with the number of pounds of cheese produced rising by more than 200 percent, and total sales rising by more than 600 percent. Schreiber opened plants in Utah and Missouri, and in 1977 moved to much larger corporate headquarters in Green Bay. The company had become a major player in the fast-food industry, and it made many changes to adapt to its new circumstances. Schreiber invested heavily in innovative technology, first at its newest plant and then at its existing facilities. Schreiber also hired a management consultant to look at communication within the organization. Many patterns that had worked when the company was small no longer served, and it took outside help to find ways to change. Founder Merlin Bush's son Robert became president of Schreiber in 1978. He had worked for the company since graduating from college. Yet he realized that the company needed someone with different expertise. When he stepped aside in 1985, the new president, Jack Meng, was the first Schreiber top executive not related to the three company founders. (An earlier president had been the son-in-law of Barney Schreiber.)

Acquisitions in the 1980s and 1990s

In 1980, the company changed its name from the L.D. Schreiber Cheese Co. to Schreiber Foods, Inc. The name change signified that the company was ready to move beyond just cheese, yet it became even more of a force in the cheese market in the 1980s. Schreiber began growing through acquisitions in the 1980s, giving it greater presence on the East and West Coasts. By the middle of the decade, Schreiber had drawn nearer to the dominant U.S. cheese manufacturer, Kraft. In 1983, Schreiber decided to build a production facility in Maryland, getting it closer to eastern markets. The announcement came just weeks after Pennsylvania-based Clearfield Cheese Co. revealed that it was relocating to Baltimore. After some consideration, Schreiber thought better of building the Maryland facility. Instead, it acquired rival Clearfield Cheese. Clearfield had been considered the second leading retail cheese processor behind Kraft, though some analysts gave Schreiber the number-two title. By purchasing Clearfield in 1985, Schreiber clearly claimed the number-two ranking for itself, and drew closer to Kraft. The acquisition gave Schreiber its needed East Coast distribution center, plus production facilities in Missouri, Utah, and Pennsylvania.

Schreiber made another acquisition in 1985, within a week of purchasing Clearfield. The company bought California-based Westland Foods Corporation, a manufacturer of pre-cooked bacon. Westland had sales of around $7 million annually, and its principal customers overlapped with Schreiber's, as it sold mostly to fast-food restaurant chains. Schreiber also opened a new production facility in 1985, ramping up a plant in Tempe, Arizona to manufacture cheddar cheese.

Schreiber continued to make acquisitions in the 1990s. The company had a strong relationship with the fast-food chain McDonald's, which gave Schreiber the designation "World Standard" in 1990. Schreiber gained another huge customer in the early 1990s, the discount store chain Wal-Mart. Schreiber began selling to Wal-Mart in 1992, and that company soon became one of Schreiber's largest accounts. Schreiber introduced profit-sharing to its employees as it continued to do well. Schreiber modernized its plant equipment in the 1990s and also refined its sales and marketing. The company one-upped its competitors by promising to deliver to customers the exact amount ordered, at a time when the industry standard was for delivery of the promised amount plus or minus 10 percent. In many ways Schreiber had left its small-town roots behind by the 1990s, becoming a truly national business with ties to some of the biggest corporations in the United States.

Schreiber also began moving into international markets, following many of its large customers into the global arena. The company had made some international joint ventures in the 1980s, but these were short-lived. It opened a plant in Mexico City in 1980, but withdrew in 1982. Another joint venture in Northern Ireland lasted from 1980 to 1985. Schreiber Foods started over in the 1990s, going into overseas joint ventures only where it already had a clear market demand. Its multinational customers, such as McDonald's, were deriving an ever-increasing percentage of sales from markets outside the United States, so Schreiber needed to follow along. It started European operations in 1992, with a German joint venture, and that same year began operating in Saudi Arabia. The company began operating in India in 1996, finding a large, low-cost dairy market, though with little distribution infrastructure. Schreiber moved into Brazil in 1999. Over the next few years, Schreiber developed another European joint venture, opened a production facility in Mexico, and eventually had sales offices around the world.

Filling the Number-Two Slot in the 2000s

Schreiber Foods continued to acquire smaller companies in the 2000s, cementing its position as the second-place company in an industry long dominated by Kraft. By 2000, Schreiber's sales had passed the $1 billion mark and were on their way to $2 billion. The company had achieved a formidable presence in the fast-food market by the beginning of the decade. Its processed cheese slices were found on 90 percent of the nation's cheeseburgers. New acquisitions helped it keep up with its growing production needs. The company bought several Wisconsin cheese factories from ConAgra in 2000, and later that year also acquired a Pittsburgh, Pennsylvania manufacturer, Pinnacle Cheese Company.

In 2002, Schreiber made a key acquisition in the Southeast, buying Deep South Products, Inc. from Winn Dixie Stores. The purchase included a warehouse and production facility in Gainesville, Georgia. Schreiber increased its penetration into southeastern markets with the Deep South acquisition, and also gained a gateway into markets in the Caribbean. Also that year, Schreiber made a purchase that greatly increased its production of private-label cream cheese. Schreiber bought a venerable, family-owned cream cheese maker based in St. Louis, called Raskas Foods, Inc. Raskas was a medium-sized company, with sales of $185 million, yet it had a huge market share, making as much as 80 percent of the private label cream cheese in the United States. Raskas determined that it was not a big enough player to remain profitable in the 2000s, faced with competition from the much bigger Kraft as well as volatility in the markets for raw materials. Schreiber stepped in, buying Raskas for an undisclosed amount and gaining a St. Louis manufacturing plant, research facility, and distribution center, and Raskas factories in Texas and Pennsylvania.

The Raskas acquisition gave Schreiber even more of a leg up on Kraft. The industry leader saw its market share fall in the 2000s, while Schreiber and other private-label makers gained. Schreiber continued to build its cream cheese assets, buying another manufacturing plant in 2003. This was a cream cheese and sour cream facility in Fredericksburg, Iowa owned by ConAgra Foods. By that year, Schreiber's sales had passed $2 billion, and with its growth in cream cheese, it was becoming more of a full-line dairy product maker. The company followed the ConAgra purchase with an announcement that it was spending $24 million on a distribution plant in Utah so it could more easily serve West Coast cream cheese markets. In 2004, Schreiber bought Level Valley Creamery, a Wisconsin manufacturer of cream cheese, sweetened condensed milk, and butter and milk powders. Level Valley had sales of around $125 million annually. It had been a major competitor of Raskas before Schreiber absorbed the St. Louis company. Over just a few years in the early 2000s, Schreiber had done much to consolidate the private label cream cheese market in the United States.

Principal Competitors

Kraft Foods, Inc.; ConAgra Foods, Inc.; Great Lakes Cheese Co., Inc.

Further Reading

"Arden Agrees to Be Acquired," *Wall Street Journal,* April 21, 1994, p. A8.

Cancelada, Gregory, "Schreiber Will Close Former Raskas Foods Plant," *St. Louis Post-Dispatch,* March 3, 2005.

Delroy, Alexander, "Private Labels Milking Sales from Kraft Cheese Business," *Knight Ridder Tribune News Service,* June 19, 2003, p. 1.

Schreiber Foods, Inc., *Sixteen Ounces to the Pound,* Green Bay: Schreiber Foods, 2003.

"Schreiber Foods Near Top in Making Processed Cheese," *Capital Times* (Madison, Wis.), April 2, 1995.

"Schreiber Foods to Build $24 Million Plant in Logan," *Enterprise* (Salt Lake City), November 17–23, 2003, p. 9.

"Schreiber Seeks More Acquisitions," *Dairy Foods,* June 2003, p. 10.

Steele, Laura, "Green Bay, Wis.-Based Food Company Acquires Creamery," *Milwaukee Journal Sentinel,* August 8, 2004.

"Wisconsin Cheese Firm to Open Plant in Westminster, Md.," *Washington Post,* September 19, 1983, p. 35.

—A. Woodward

Schwebel Baking Company

P.O. Box 6018
965 East Midlothian Boulevard
Youngstown, Ohio 44502
U.S.A.
Telephone: (330) 783-2860
Toll Free: (800) 860-2867
Fax: (330) 782-1774
Web site: http://www.schwebels.com

Private Company
Incorporated: 1906
Employees: 1,400
Sales: $130 million (2004 est.)
NAIC: 311812 Commercial Bakeries

Schwebel Baking Company is a large regional bakery based in Youngstown, Ohio. The firm produces 700,000 loaves of bread and packages of buns a day, along with bagels, English muffins, pita bread, and tortillas. Its products are distributed throughout Ohio and in parts of New York, Pennsylvania, and West Virginia. Schwebel's brands include Country Hearth, Roman Meal, Cinnabon, 'taliano, Millbrook, Vogel's, Fit for Life, Aladdin's, and Sun-Maid Raisin. Frozen bread products also are produced for sale to wholesale and foodservice accounts around the United States. The 100-year-old company is owned and run by members of the Schwebel family.

Early Years

The beginnings of Schwebel Baking Company date to 1906, when Dora and Joseph Schwebel began baking bread and selling it in and around the small town of Campbell, Ohio. Their first offering was Jewish Rye, which was delivered on foot in wicker laundry baskets. After several years the Schwebels started using a horse and wagon and expanded their delivery area to nearby Youngstown.

In 1914 the Schwebels began selling their bread through several local grocery stores. To keep up with the increased demand, they hired additional bakers and a delivery driver/ salesman. In 1923 they invested $25,000 in building a new bakery, which also featured a retail sales counter. The small company now had six delivery trucks and 15 employees and was delivering 1,000 loaves of bread per day.

In 1928 tragedy struck when Joseph Schwebel died suddenly at the age of 46. Although friends advised Dora to sell the bakery and stay at home with her six children, she decided to keep running the business. The stock market crashed the following year, but she was able to negotiate several critical agreements that enabled the firm to keep operating.

In 1932, in the depths of the Great Depression, Dora Schwebel created "Happy the Clown," a character whose face was placed on the company's bread wrappers as a symbol of hope for the future. The company was growing despite the hard times, and in 1936 a new $100,000 bakery was built that doubled production capacity and improved efficiency. It was expanded in 1938 and again in 1941.

Opening of "Million Dollar Bakery" in 1951

Following World War II Schwebel Baking continued to grow, and in 1951 the company built a new $1 million bakery in Youngstown that featured state-of-the-art equipment, enabling it to create new product lines like Toasti-Taste Bread. By 1960, the company's annual revenues had grown to approximately $2 million.

Over the years a number of Schwebel family members had taken jobs with the company, which continued to be family owned. They were not given a quick and easy path to the top, however. After Dora's grandson Joseph graduated from the University of Pennsylvania's prestigious Wharton School of Business in 1960, he asked her where his office would be. As he told *Inside Business* years later, "She told me the next day I would ride route No. 1, which left at 4:30 in the morning. She told me that I was going to ride every route and then we were going to talk about what I was going to do after that." At that time, the company had 39 delivery routes. He soon came to realize the wisdom of her approach, however. "All the action, in stores, with customers, in restaurants, that's where you learn. So that was my real education."

Company Perspectives:

Our Pledge To You: Many things change over time, but for nearly a century, the quality, freshness and great taste of Schwebel's breads and buns has been something that consumers have come to expect. Guaranteed Quality. At Schwebel's, our master bakers make use of some of the most innovative, state-of-the-art baking equipment available today to keep quality its highest. Guaranteed Freshness. Four strategically located bakeries and a comprehensive direct store delivery system guarantee product freshness. Guaranteed Product Variety. Schwebel's caters to the many tastes and lifestyles of today's consumers, with a large selection of mainstream and specialty breads, buns and rolls to please any palate. Guaranteed Nutrition. Rich in complex carbohydrates, a vital energy source, Schwebel's bakery products are vitamin enriched, low in fat, and cholesterol free. Guaranteed Food Safety. Schwebel's is continually awarded for excellence in quality, cleanliness and food safety by the American Institute of Baking (AIB) and Quality Bakers of America (QBA).

In 1964 Dora Schwebel died at age 76, and her son Irving was named president of the firm. In 1967 the company began licensing its popular Golden Rich Bread nationwide, and in 1972 the company opened a distribution center in Canton, Ohio, its first facility outside of Youngstown.

In 1974 Schwebel's entered the Cleveland market, and two years later the firm purchased the Vienna Baking Company in McKeesport, Pennsylvania, and began selling bread in Pittsburgh. The year 1977 saw the Youngstown plant expanded and fully automated, allowing it to produce more than 100 loaves of bread per minute. This and other expansion efforts would allow the firm to double its output.

Growth continued in the early 1980s with the acquisition of the Lawson Bakery of Cuyahoga Falls, Ohio in 1981 and the opening of a new distribution center in Columbus, Ohio in 1983. That same year the firm signed a contract to supply bread to the Epcot Center at Florida's Walt Disney World, and also began broadcasting radio commercials using the catchy "We Want Schwebel's" jingle.

Naming Joseph Schwebel President in 1984

In 1984 Irving Schwebel's eldest son Joseph was named president of the company. He had worked for a number of years as restaurant and institutional sales manager for the firm and as vice-president of sales since 1981.

In 1987 Schwebel's acquired Millbrook Bread of Cleveland from Interstate Brands Corp. and also expanded to western New York by opening a distribution center in Buffalo. The growth of the company's wholesale baking business was recognized in 1989 by the Quality Bakers of America President's Cup, which was given to the country's premier wholesale baker.

Members of the Schwebel family had often given generously to others, and in 1988 they formed the Schwebel Family

Foundation to oversee their philanthropic efforts. They had been particularly supportive of local educational organizations, including Kent State University and Youngstown State University. At Kent State the Schwebels established a scholarship fund for employees, endowed a Hospitality Management lecture series, supported the school's Jewish Studies and athletic departments, and helped create a restaurant in the Kent State Student Center, the Schwebel Garden Room.

The 1990s saw expansion continue with the 1990 purchase of the Kroger Company's Northcoast Bakery in Solon, Ohio, and the 1995 acquisition of a similar facility in Hebron, Ohio from Kaufman's Bakery. By now, annual revenues had grown to nearly $100 million.

In the mid-1990s a licensing deal was signed that enabled Schwebel's to bake bread using ingredients from cereal maker Kellogg's and use that firm's logo on its packaging. Several different varieties were produced, including All-Bran, Low-Fat Granola, and Nutri-Grain. By this time the firm also had signed agreements to produce baked goods for Stouffer's and Pillsbury.

Formation of a Trucking Subsidiary in 1996

The year 1996 saw the formation of a separate trucking subsidiary, SBC Transportation, Inc. Delivering the firm's fresh baked goods in a timely fashion required more than 600 vehicles. The year 1996 also saw Schwebel's switch advertising agencies to Pittsburgh-based MARC. The company was spending an estimated $2 million per year on advertising at this time.

In 1997 Schwebel's acquired several sales routes from Flowers Industries, Inc. of West Virginia. The company would supply bread, buns, and rolls to Flowers customers in central Ohio and Pittsburgh, and gained exclusive distribution rights to Flowers' BlueBird snack cakes and pastries in central Ohio. In September, 100 teamsters briefly struck the firm, stopping its deliveries to Pittsburgh, before they agreed to a new three-year contract.

The year 1997 also saw Schwebel Baking Company inducted into the Family Business Hall of Fame, located at Case Western Reserve University's Weatherhead School of Management in Cleveland. Numerous Schwebel family members continued to be involved in the firm, ranging from board chairman Frances Solomon, the 84-year-old daughter of Dora and Joseph Schwebel, to a recently hired fourth-generation family member. The firm was still entirely family owned.

In 1999 annual sales reached a new height of $125 million. The firm was now using the Internet to communicate with supermarket chains and take payments, and it expanded this capability over the next several years.

In early 2000 Schwebel's began running advertisements on radio stations in Cleveland, Columbus, and Pittsburgh that revived the catchy "We Want Schwebel's" jingle that first had been used almost two decades earlier. At this time the company was selling 52 percent white bread, 18 percent whole wheat, and 18 percent Italian and potato bread. The firm was the top maker of premium white bread in central Ohio, Pittsburgh, and Erie, Pennsylvania. In addition to its own brands, the company had contracts to produce Roman Meal, Country Hearth, and Sun-Maid Raisin bread.

Key Dates:

1906: Dora and Joseph Schwebel begin selling home-baked bread in Campbell, Ohio.
1914: Sales through retail outlets begin.
1923: The company builds a new bakery/store.
1928: Joseph Schwebel dies; Dora Schwebel takes control of the firm.
1936: A new, larger bakery is built, doubling output.
1951: A modern $1 million bakery is opened in Youngstown, Ohio.
1964: Dora Schwebel dies; Irving Schwebel takes over the presidency of the firm.
1967: National licensing of Schwebel's Golden Rich Bread begins.
1976: Vienna Baking Co. is acquired.
1981: Lawson Bakery is purchased.
1984: Joseph Schwebel is named president of the firm.
1987: Millbrook Bread of Cleveland is acquired.
1990: The company purchases Kroger Company's Northcoast Bakery in Solon, Ohio.
1995: Additional baking facilities in Hebron, Ohio are acquired from Kaufman's Bakery.
1996: SBC Transportation is formed.
1997: Schwebel Baking Company is inducted into the Family Business Hall of Fame, located at Case Western Reserve University's Weatherhead School of Management in Cleveland.

In 2002 Schwebel's partnered with children's cable television network Nickelodeon for a three-month promotional campaign. Purchasers of loaves of Giant White Bread would receive a free trial issue of *Nickelodeon Magazine.*

During this period the bread industry was seeing a steady decline in the sales of many of its products. A national consumer trend away from white bread and toward more whole grain products caused white bread sales to fall by approximately 10 percent beginning in the late 1990s. Bagel sales had dropped 15 percent, while sales of hamburger and hot dog buns to fast-food restaurants had declined even more, by 20 percent, over a five-year span. Only more expensive premium bread and artisan bakery bread had increased in popularity.

When the craze for low-carbohydrate diets like Atkins and South Beach reached a fever pitch in 2003, millions of Americans began cutting back even further on carbohydrate-rich bread products. As sales at many baking firms plunged, the industry entered full crisis mode. Schwebel's fought back by creating a low-carbohydrate bread that used wheat gluten or proteins derived from beans instead of flour, while also taking a pro-carbohydrate stance and promoting the nutritional value of its products, which until only recently had been taken for granted.

Company president Joseph Schwebel, a former chairman of the American Institute of Baking, also helped form a new lobbying group, the Foundation for the Advancement of Grain-Based Foods, which would perform research into the health benefits of bread and other grain foods. By November of 2004 the number of American adults on low-carbohydrate diets was fading, dropping to 3.6 percent from 9.1 percent in February, according to research firm NPD Group.

After nearly 100 years, Schwebel Baking Company had grown into the leading baking firm in Ohio and parts of New York, Pennsylvania, and West Virginia. Still family owned and managed, the firm anticipated producing tasty, healthful baked goods for many more years to come.

Principal Subsidiaries

SBC Transportation, Inc.

Principal Competitors

Interstate Bakeries Corporation; Sara Lee Bakery Group; Pepperidge Farm, Inc.; Alfred Nickles Bakery, Inc.

Further Reading

Laurence, Charles, "US Bakers Take Fight to Atkins at 'Bread Summit'," *Sunday Telegraph,* November 23, 2003, p. 33.
Lepro, Sara, "Rising to the Challenge: At the Head of the Table for Two Decades, Joseph Schwebel Has Steered Schwebel Baking Co. to the Forefront of the Industry," *Inside Business,* October 1, 2004.
Pledger, Marcia, "Schwebel to Return Its Venerable Jingle to Area's Airwaves," *Cleveland Plain Dealer,* February 6, 2000, p. 1I.

—Frank Uhle

Screen Actors Guild

5757 Wilshire Boulevard
Los Angeles, California 90036-3600
U.S.A.
Telephone: (323) 954-1600
Fax: (323) 549-6603
Web site: http://www.sag.org

Private Company
Founded: 1933
Employees: 294
Operating Revenues: $13.6 million (2004 est.)
NAIC: 813930 Labor Unions and Similar Labor
   Organizations

The Screen Actors Guild (SAG) is a labor union based in Los Angeles with 20 branches spread across the United States, representing about 120,000 actors in film, television, commercials, music videos, and industrial films. The guild represents its members in contract negotiations, establishing compensation, working conditions, and benefits. In addition, SAG offers members a pension and health plan, authorizes showcase productions, and sponsors acting workshops and seminars. Although most of the administrative duties are handled by a chief executive officer hired outside of guild membership, the presidency is filled by an active member. Ronald Regan used this high-profile position as a springboard for his political career.

Actors Attempt to Organize in 1800s

Decades before the rise of motion pictures and a century before the advent of television, American performance arts were limited to the stage. Hundreds of cities and towns maintained theaters housing stock companies of actors that mounted a variety of plays to entertain their patrons. The stock theater tradition was undercut by the advent of touring stars who used a company's actors in supporting roles. Because this arrangement led to uneven performances, the stars began to take along key supporting actors and eventually toured with complete ensembles. Theater owners became landlords and stock companies began to fade from the scene. New York City became the center

of the theater world during the latter half of the 1800s, serving as a clearinghouse for productions that originated there but played only brief runs before the show was taken on the road. It was a time when playwrights received no royalties and actors were often at the mercy of unscrupulous managers and producers. The first attempt to organize actors was made in the 1860s with the Actor's Protective Union. In the 1890s, the American Federation of Labor granted the first actors' union charter to the Actors National Protective Union. The first modern actors' union was Actors' Equity Association (Equity), founded in 1913. It was accepted into organized labor in 1919 and launched a major Broadway strike in that same year, establishing itself as a force to be reckoned with in the theater.

While Equity was establishing itself, the motion picture industry was growing rapidly and employing an increasing number of stage actors. In the early days, screen actors were not even named, a practice that eliminated the costly star system that had evolved in the theater, but the audience soon demanded to know the names of their screen favorites, and the star system took hold in the movies as well. After the film industry settled in Hollywood, screen actors looked to band together as had their stage brethren, forming an organization called the Screen Actors of America as well as the Motion Picture Players Union, which represented extra players. In 1920, Equity superseded these organizations and was granted jurisdiction by the American Federation of Labor to represent both principal and extra motion picture performers. Hollywood did not recognize the union, however. In 1929, Equity launched a strike to gain recognition in motion pictures, but the strike was broken and recognition denied.

While Equity may have failed to establish itself in California, an increasing number of its members were taking the train to the West Coast to work in the movies. Following the success of *The Jazz Singer,* which launched the era of "talking pictures," there was a major shift in Hollywood's acting pool. Many stars of the silent movie era were unable to make the transition because their voices did not translate to the screen. As a result, stage actors were in high demand. However, talking pictures were also more difficult to make, requiring longer hours and leading to abuse of performers, who had no required meal breaks and worked 12- to 14-hours stretches for days on end. Moreover, under the Hollywood studio system, they were bound to seven-year contracts that because of a gentleman's agreement between studio moguls not to poach one other's talent, could essentially be renewed at the whim of the studios. Nor were they reluctant to dictate to actors about how to conduct their personal lives. The only recourse to actors was to quit their chosen profession.

Stage actors, having gotten a taste of power through Equity, were willing to be more confrontational with the studios, but former silent actors were disgruntled as well, especially after the studios announced massive pay cuts. The Masquers Club in Los Angeles, founded by silent actor Antonio Moreno, had become a place where actors voiced their complaints about the studio system. Late in 1932, about two dozen of these actors began to meet weekly at each other's homes and following the announced pay cuts they were ready to form a new union, one primarily focused on supporting players. Over the years, Hollywood had established its own caste system within which stars, supporting actors, bit players, and extras had little to do with one another. The need to attract stars to the union cause for the sake of publicity would begin to break down these barriers.

SAG Takes Shape in the Early 1930s

The studios were well aware of the actors secret meetings held in the spring of 1933. The malcontents hired attorney Laurence Beilenson, recommended by the newly established Screen Writers Guild. During a June 1933 meeting at the home of Equity's West Coast representative, Kenneth Thomson, 18 actors gathered, with Beilenson in attendance, and decided to make a legal organization out of their informal meetings. They decided to incorporate to insulate members from financial liability, an important factor in attracting stars, and opted to use ''guild'' in the name, lest ''union'' scare off the more conservative members. Hence, the Screen Actors Guild was incorporated by Beilenson on June 30, 1933. At the first corporate meeting, held two weeks later, the first union cards were issued and Ralph Morgan was named president. According to SAG's bylaws, it was a nonpaying post, because unlike other unions SAG officers volunteered their time and did not make union work their livelihood.

Slowly, SAG attracted stars to its ranks, but gaining recognition from the studios proved more difficult. Starting in 1936, the Guild began building support among its membership for a showdown with management. Finally, members voted to go on strike at midnight May 10, 1937 if the Guild was not recognized. The studios were further pressured by the International Alliance of Theatrical Stage Employees and a coalition of rival unions called the Federation of Motion Picture Crafts. Following a negotiation session on the morning of May 9, studio producers finally agreed to accept SAG as the bargaining representative for the actors. A few days later, the Guild signed a contract with 13 producers stipulating minimum salaries and establishing rules on such matters as overtime and location shooting. The main work for SAG now became the enforcement of that contract. Many of the problems involved extra players, and since their numbers were far greater than actors they had the potential to control the union and were thus denied the right to vote. Unhappy with both the producers and SAG, some extras defected to a new union in 1944, the Screen Players Union. A SAG-backed union for extras, Screen Extras Guild was also formed and was able to receive recognition from the Associated Actors and Artistes of America, the American Federation of Labor's holding corporation for performers' unions.

The post-World War II years were a contentious period for SAG as the House of Representatives launched a far-reaching investigation of Communist infiltration in American institutions, including the film industry. Many film people were summoned to Washington, D.C., to testify before the House Committee on Un-American Activities (HUAC). Some SAG members, including the Guild's newly elected president, Ronald Reagan, and Gary Cooper were ''friendly witnesses'' and willingly cooperated, telling what they knew about the impact of Communism on Hollywood. Other SAG members flew to Washington to support the ''Hollywood Ten,'' nine screenwriters and one director who refused to answered the committee's questions. All would be held in contempt of the U.S. Congress and imprisoned, and nine of them would be blacklisted by the studios. Although far from alone, SAG caved to political pressure during the Communist witch hunt years. In 1948, members voted overwhelmingly to require officers, directors, and committee members to sign affidavits swearing that they were not members of the Communist Party. Then, in 1953, they approved a bylaw that required new members to swear they were not party members and pledged that they would not join the Communist Party. As HUAC continued its work well into the 1950s, many more film people would be called before the committee. Either they refused to testify and were blacklisted, or they named names, which led to the graylisting of colleagues. Because such bans were semi-secret, the exact number of actors affected was uncertain. According to David F. Prindle in *The Politics of Glamour,* ''Perhaps a hundred SAG members discovered at one time or another that they could not get work for political reasons. Some of those talked to a 'clearance officer' and were reestablished; some waited out the 1950s on Broadway or elsewhere and eventually returned to the screen; some dropped into obscurity; a few died of stress or committed suicide.''

A significant tool employed by HUAC was the growing medium of television, which during the postwar years went national and broadcast the hearings. The movies were already undergoing a major upheaval when the Hollywood studio system was ruled monopolistic and illegal in 1948, leading to a major restructuring of the industry. Television became a significant threat to the financial health of the film industry and in turn to the existence of SAG. The era of studio contract players was essentially over, turning the vast majority of actors into freelancers whose lives were fraught with uncertainty. Fewer films were now produced, resulting in fewer acting jobs and making unemployment among SAG members an even greater problem. Television would of course need the services of actors, but there

Key Dates:

1933: Screen Actors Guild (SAG) is incorporated.
1937: SAG is recognized by major film studios.
1948: The Hollywood studio system is ruled to be monopolistic.
1960: A pension plan is established.
1975: Kathleen Nolan becomes SAG's first woman president.
1981: A merger attempt with the American Federation of Radio and Television Artists (AFTRA) fails.
2000: SAG launches a six-month strike over commercials.
2003: A merger with AFTRA is again rejected by SAG members.

was an open question about who would represent them: SAG or the American Federation of Radio Artists (AFRA). Because television could be a live broadcast medium comparable in some ways to radio, and also broadcast filmed material, tensions began to develop between SAG and AFRA about which union should represent television performers. In 1934, Actors Equity, Chorus Equity, the American Guild of Variety Artists, and the American Guild of Musical Artists created the Television Authority (TVA) to coordinate a response to the new medium. Then, in the 1940s, these four unions joined with AFRA in supporting the idea of granting jurisdiction over television acting to TVA. For California-based SAG, such a proposal smacked of New York collusion. According to Prindle, "If, as appeared possible in the late forties, television killed the movies altogether, then the only way the guild would survive would be by representing actors making films for the new medium. To give that jurisdiction to AFRA in the guise of TVA would be to commit slow suicide, for as television suffocated the motion-picture industry AFRA would inherit the right to represent screen actors." The dispute between the two sides was eventually put before the National Labor Relations Board, leading to certification elections that were won overwhelmingly by SAG, whose members preferred to stick with a successful union located where they worked rather than throwing in with an upstart headquartered 3,000 miles away. TVA disbanded, leaving AFRA with jurisdiction over live television and SAG over filmed work. AFRA then added "Television" to its name, becoming AFTRA. Nevertheless, the lines of jurisdiction between the two unions would only grow more blurry with time and remain an important issue for SAG over the next half century.

Rise of Television Leads to 1950s Setback

A drop in film production led to a decline in SAG membership in the early 1950s, but the Guild was able to strike a deal with talent agency Music Corporation of America (MCA), to bring the filming of television programs to Hollywood. In exchange for issuing a waiver allowing a talent agency to act as producer, SAG won residual payments for its members on any television programs that were rerun. The other Hollywood producers followed suit, and the filming of television series in Hollywood increased dramatically during the 1950s, so that by the early 1960s about 75 percent of all work in Hollywood was television related. As a result, SAG's membership grew, and

any thought that Hollywood would turn into a ghost town or the Guild would be disbanded were quickly forgotten.

In addition to steadily increasing residual payments on television reruns for its members, SAG negotiated payments from producers for films sold to television. In March 1960, SAG went on strike over the issue and members stayed out until April 18, bringing to a halt several major productions. A settlement was reached resulting in a lump sum payment of $2.65 million, which was then used to establish a pension and welfare plan.

The way SAG elected its leaders changed in the 1970s, as independent candidates began to challenge the slate of seven officer positions put forward by the Guild's nominating committee. The first incumbent to be defeated by an independent was John Gavin, replaced in 1973 by Dennis Weaver, joined by six other independent candidates. As a result, SAG's longtime conservative leadership was replaced by a decidedly more liberal and activist officers. The Guild's first woman president, Kathleen Nolan, was elected two years later. She would lead the SAG strike of 1978 to 1979 over increased residuals for actors appearing in television commercials. A year later, a new president, William Schallert, would be in charge when SAG once again walked out, this time striking from July 21 to October 1980 in support of negotiations over Pay-TV and video-cassette productions.

During the late 1970s and early 1980s, SAG and AFTRA began launched talks to merge the two unions. However, despite a recommendation for a merger from its leadership, SAG members voted down the measure in 1981. The idea of joining forces with AFTRA would be shelved for the time being and would not be revisited until the 1990s. The Guild also took steps to merge with Screen Extras Guild, but this proposal was also rejected, once in 1982 and again in 1984.

In the meantime, SAG continued to adapt to changes in the media landscape. The increasing importance of cable television networks was a major issue. In 1991, the Guild won increased payments for commercials appearing on cable television. SAG also recognized the rise of new media, signing its first Interactive contract covering multimedia productions in 1993. The following year, SAG also added stunt players to the fold and negotiated contracts for the growing Spanish television market. The Guild ended the decade by once again taking on the question of merging with AFTRA. While 67.6 percent of AFTRA members approved the idea, only 46.5 percent of SAG members voted yes, and once again the merger was defeated.

As the 21st century dawned, SAG's new, aggressive leadership, headed by president William Daniels, launched a strike over commercials. Again, the changing balance between the broadcast television networks and cable television was at the heart of the matter. While actors received a payment for each time a commercial aired on broadcast television, they received only a flat fee for 13 weeks for commercials playing on cable. The strike lasted from May through October 2000. Many members were displeased with the outcome, contending that whatever gains the union may have realized were offset by the loss of income actors suffered during the six-month strike. When it came time to negotiate a new contract with the major studios a year later, SAG, in conjunction with AFTRA, took a more conciliatory approach, brokered a deal, and averted a strike many assumed was inevitable. Left unresolved, however, was how to compensate actors when their work appeared on the Internet, an issue that was likely to become a matter of contention when Web-based, video-on-demand services became commercial. Since no one knew how that market might develop, it was a fight neither side was willing to join at the moment.

In 2003, SAG leadership once again put forward a proposal to merge with AFTRA, only to see members vote down the idea. The Guild's CEO, Bob Pisano, also came under fire because he sat on the board of directors of the DVD rental company Netflix at a time when the Guild was attempting to negotiate higher DVD residuals for actors. Moreover, SAG was divided on other issues, as members defeated an attempt to raise dues and rejected a proposed franchise agreement between the Guild and talent agents. There was genuine concern that SAG had become so fractured that its ability to negotiate new contracts was mitigated, since there were major concerns about the Guild's ability to convince its members to ratify what was agreed to at the bargaining table. In March 2005, Pisano was replaced by a new CEO, but it was thought that his replacement, Greg Hessinger, might very well open up old wounds. Hessinger was the current CEO of AFTRA.

Principal Competitors

American Federation of Radio and Television Artists.

Further Reading

Hernandez, Greg, "Actors Derail Campaign to Merge Unions," *Los Angeles Daily News*, July 3, 2003.

Lippman, John, "Fil, TV Actors Agree on 3-Year Contract with the Major Studios, Averting a Strike," *Wall Street Journal*, July 5, 2001, p. A2.

Moldea, Dan E., *Dark Victory*, New York: Viking Penguin Inc., 1986, 382 p.

Prindle, David F., *The Politics of Glamour*, Madison, Wisconsin: University of Wisconsin Press, 1988, 274 p.

Sharp, Kathleen, Kathleen, "Actors to SAG Boss: It's Netflix or Us," *Fortune*, June 28, 2004, p. 32.

—Ed Dinger

SEIKO CORPORATION

Seiko Corporation

1-2-1, Shibaura
Minato-ku
Tokyo 105-8459
Japan
Telephone: (03) 6401-2111
Fax: (03) 6401-2216
Web site: http://www.seiko.co.jp

Public Company
Incorporated: 1881 as K. Hattori & Co., Ltd.
Employees: 9,245
Sales: $1.98 billion (2004)
Stock Exchanges: Tokyo
Ticker Symbol: 8050
NAIC: 334518 Watch, Clock, and Part Manufacturing;
    42194 Jewelry, Watch, Precious Stone, and Precious
    Metal Wholesalers

Seiko Corporation acts as a holding company for subsidiaries that develop and manufacture watches, clocks, camera components, electronic devices, eyeglasses, jewelry, and sports products. Some of its popular watch brands include Sportura, Rivoli, Vivace, and Arctura. Watches and clocks secured 70 percent of company revenues in 2005, while optical, sports, and other products were responsible for the remainder of sales. Over 60 percent of sales stem from operations in Japan. Seiko products are also found in the Americas, Asia, and Europe.

Late 19th and Early 20th Centuries

In 1881, in Uneme-cho, Kyobashi, part of Tokyo's Ginza district, Kintaro Hattori, a jeweler, established K. Hattori & Co., Ltd. Although 21 years old, Hattori was already an eight-year veteran of the business world. According to the company typescript, ''A Brief History of Hattori Seiko Co. Ltd.,'' it was enough experience to lead him to observe, ''On a rainy day, every retail shop will have less customers. However, jewelers can make good use of these slack days by repairing timepieces and thus not waste precious time.''

Near the end of the 19th century, increasing railroad traffic produced growing demand for accurate timepieces. In 1884 the adoption of the worldwide 24-hour time zone system, with its reference meridian at Greenwich near London, produced a standardization of time that further increased that demand. In 1892 Hattori established the Seikosha clock manufacturing plant in Ishiwara-cho, Tokyo. Initially employing ten workers, the firm made primarily wall clocks, which, at that time, was the most popular type of timepiece. In October 1893 the plant was moved to its present site in Taihei-cho, Tokyo. Two years later, the main office was moved to new facilities at Ginza that included a clock tower that stood more than 50 feet high. As tall buildings were a rare sight in Tokyo at the time, the tower garnered much attention.

The firm added pocket watches to its product line in 1895. Alarm clocks were added in 1899 and table clocks in 1902. As the market expanded, the company began exporting clocks to China, and by 1912 China received 70 percent of Japan's total export of timepieces. In 1913, Hattori opened its first overseas branch, in Shanghai.

To satisfy in part the growing demand for pocket watches Hattori introduced its first line of wristwatches, which were sold under the Laurel brand name. The wristwatch gained in popularity worldwide and, by the end of the World War I, had replaced the pocket watch as the standard portable timepiece.

In 1917, K. Hattori & Co., Ltd. became a public company. In September 1923, an earthquake hit Tokyo, destroying the Seikosha plant. Hattori tried to compensate hundreds of customers, who had lost a total of 1,500 timepieces left for repair, with replacement clocks and watches. In 1924, annual production was less than 10 percent of the 1922 output. In 1924, also, the Seikosha plant introduced the first Seiko brand wristwatch.

In 1927, Kintaro Hattori, at age 69, was honored as the imperial nominee to the House of Peers. Also at this time, Hattori launched its first ladies' wristwatch, the smallest ever produced in Japan.

Using the microengineering expertise acquired in its clock and watch production, the Seikosha plant began producing camera shutters in 1930. Eventually, Hattori became one of the world's largest suppliers of camera products, although its brand names do not appear on the products.

Marketing Other Companies' Products in the 1930s

In 1934, Kintaro Hattori died, and his eldest son, Genzo Hattori, became president. Genzo Hattori chose to satisfy market needs by adopting a unique corporate structure. It allowed private plants to develop products to be marketed by K. Hattori. In 1936 K. Hattori & Co., Ltd. marketed a total of 2.06 million clocks and watches, the highest figure since the opening of the Seikosha plant. Japan's total watch and clock production came to 3.54 million. In 1939 the company started marketing Braille pocket watches.

As Japan entered World War II, K. Hattori's normal marketing activities were hindered, as reflected in the Seiko group's 1945 production figures. Only 6,260 clocks and 13,318 watches were produced by K. Hattori's affiliates for marketing by K. Hattori. Production was slowed in part because members of the Seiko group, like many other Japanese companies, were ordered to produce military items, such as time fuses and ammunition.

By 1953, however, K. Hattori & Co., Ltd. had recovered to its prewar sales level. In that year, the company purchased a total of 2.46 million watches and clocks from group plants, representing 54.3 percent of Japan's total production, and exported 101,000 watches and clocks. By the late 1950s, the firm's watches were gaining international attention, and Hattori had begun marketing watches in the United States and other countries. The company marketed its first self-winding wristwatch in 1955. Utilizing conveyor-belt production technology, by 1959, production of watches reached three million per year.

Expanding Overseas in the 1960s

In 1964, Chairman Genzo Hattori died. Shoji Hattori, president since 1946, recognized the need for the company to strengthen its global marketing after a visit to Europe in 1962, during which he was asked if there was a watch industry in Japan. Seiko, with the reputation earned by its quartz clock, became the official timer of the Olympic Games in Tokyo, an honor previously held by the Swiss. The company supplied the games with 1,278 stopwatches, made up of 36 different styles plus the world's first portable quartz chronometers. The sponsorship of various events, including tennis, golf, soccer, track, and other sports, resulted in increased international recognition. Its quartz technology allowed production of a full range of precision timing equipment, designed to meet the needs of sports competitions under varied conditions. This expertise has

since helped the firm to become the sponsor or official timer of more than 150 international sports events annually.

Like other Japanese companies, K. Hattori employed a global marketing strategy and looked to overseas expansion. With advertising of new styles and substantially lower prices, it successfully challenged the Swiss in Asian markets, in Hong Kong, Bangkok, and Singapore. Hattori (Hong Kong) Ltd., a new subsidiary, was established in 1968. Marketing was then directed to Britain, West Germany, France, Spain, Italy, and Greece. In the mid-1960s the United States, initially a difficult market for the Japanese to penetrate, presented an additional challenge. Rather than competing with cheap American brands or with high-priced Swiss watches, K. Hattori entered the mid-range of the market, offering jewel-lever watches with an average price tag of $50.

In 1969 K. Hattori began marketing the world's first quartz watch, under the Seiko name. The watch resulted from a "technology contest" between Suwa Seikosha and Daina Seikosha, two K. Hattori affiliates. The new watch, Seiko Astron 35SQ, was encased in 18-karat gold and featured an accuracy within five seconds per month. Developed and manufactured at the Suwa Seikosha plant, it was launched to the Japanese market with a retail price of ¥450.000.

Seiko Brand Soars in Popularity in the 1970s

By the early 1970s, a few years after the introduction of the world's first quartz wristwatch, the Seiko brand soared in popularity, and Seiko adopted the slogan, "Someday all watches will be made this way." About that same time, the company scored a publicity coup when it once again served as official timer of an Olympics, this time the 1972 winter games in Sapporo. Also in 1972, Hattori marketed the world's first ladies' quartz watch, also made at Suwa Seikosha. A year later, it introduced the first Seiko liquid-crystal display (LCD) digital quartz watch. Also manufactured at Suwa Seikosha, the product included built-in illumination and six-digit numerical readout that displayed the time in hours, minutes, and seconds.

In 1970, the firm established Seiko Service Centre (Australia) Pty. Ltd. and Seiko Time Corporation in the United States, the latter adding a Canadian office in the following year. In 1971, the firm expanded into the United Kingdom with Seiko Time (U.K.) Ltd. Seiko Time GmbH was established in West Germany in 1972. Global expansion of the sales effort continued with the opening of Seiko Time Ltda., Brazil, in 1974; Seiko Time (Panama) S.A. in 1977; Seiko Time S.A., Switzerland, in 1978; Seiko Time AB, Sweden, in 1979; and Hattori Overseas (Hong Kong) Ltd. in 1979.

In 1975 the company introduced its plastic ophthalmic lenses. Initially, in 1977, the lenses were exported to a U.S. supplier but since 1986 have been marketed in the United States under the Seiko name. Also in 1975, the firm began marketing digital quartz chronographs.

In 1974, Shoji Hattori died, and Kentaro Hattori, Shoji's nephew and Genzo's oldest son, took over as president. The year 1977 saw record earnings and new products for Hattori Seiko, many of which appeared under brand names other than Seiko. The firm developed Lorus clocks for the export market in 1977.

Key Dates:

1881: Kintaro Hattori, a jeweler, establishes K. Hattori & Co., Ltd.
1913: Hattori opens the company's first overseas branch in Shanghai.
1924: The Seikosha plant introduces the first Seiko brand wristwatch.
1955: The company markets its first self-winding wristwatch.
1969: Hattori markets the world's first quartz watch under the Seiko name.
1973: The firm introduces the first Seiko liquid-crystal display (LCD) digital quartz watch.
1983: K. Hattori & Co. Ltd. changes its name to Hattori Seiko Co., Ltd.
1990: The company adopts the Seiko Corporation moniker.
1996: Seiko restructures to create a vertically-integrated company.
2001: Watch operations are spun off as Seiko Watch Corporation; Seiko Corporation becomes a holding company.

The clock line, which included a pendulum wall clock, a battery transistor wall clock, and alarm clocks, was first sold to countries in Southeast Asia. In the same year, the firm began marketing the digital quartz calculator, a digital quartz world timer, digital quartz alarm chronograph, quartz watches with 100-meter-depth water resistance, and quartz watches with five-year batteries.

In 1978, Seiko introduced twin quartz watches, with two crystals, which offered accuracy within five seconds per year, and quartz divers' watches with 600-meter-depth water resistance, followed in 1979 by the ultra-thin quartz watch with 0.9 millimeter movement, along with the analog alarm quartz watch. In addition, K. Hattori introduced the Alba brand in Japan, which included digital quartz, and began exporting the Alba analog and digital quartz to Southeast Asia. On the other side of the globe, it began marketing the Pulsar brand watches in the United States. The United States also saw the first Lorus quartz watches in 1983.

Difficult Times in the 1980s

Despite the busy production years of the 1970s, success came to a sudden halt in the 1980s. During the decade's first few years, profits were far less than those of the late 1970s. "In a boom that has sent prices of many high-technology companies to record levels, Hattori's shares have fallen to the mid-700-yen range (about $3.50), barely half their top price in 1978," reported *Business Week* in 1981.

The firm acquired Jean Lassale, a Swiss subsidiary, and developed a product that combined Seiko's quartz movements with a very thin Swiss-style case. By seeking higher profit margins from luxury products, the company expected to make up for declining profit margins on its less expensive products. The Jean Lassale purchase was part of a pricing strategy to offer a more expensive line to complement lower- and medium-priced watches and appeal to a wider range of customers.

As the yen began to rise in the mid-1980s, competition tightened and the company faced difficult times. New competitors entered watchmaking, from fashion designers to companies who bought watch parts from other watchmakers. With marketing and manufacturing handled by separate companies, trying to compete was difficult.

In 1983, the company changed its name from K. Hattori & Co. Ltd. to Hattori Seiko Co., Ltd., partly to further promote the Seiko name. Watches that featured a black-and-white liquid crystal display TV screen entered the market in 1982. The intention, according to Ichiro Hattori, was not to fill a niche for a frivolous product but to promote the company's name and image. The success of the Seiko TV watches proved that some people liked their watches to do more than tell time. Consequently, in 1984, Hattori Seiko introduced the world's first computer wristwatches, manufactured at Seiko Instruments & Electronics Company. At the same time, Hattori Seiko launched the world's first LCD battery-operated, pocket color television.

Reijiro Hattori, Kentaro's brother, became president of Hattori Seiko in 1983. Kentaro remained as chairman. Four years later, Reijiro stepped up to chairman when Kentaro died. Ichiro Hattori, president of Seiko affiliates Seiko Instruments Inc. and Seiko Epson Corporation, also died that year. Hattori Seiko then appointed for the first time a non-Hattori family person to the top. Shiro Yoshimura became president. In 1989 Hattori Seiko introduced a new subsidiary, Hattori (Thailand) Ltd. In an effort to prepare for a new global economy, the Seiko name was brought into heavy use throughout the world. In June 1990, the parent firm changed its name from Hattori Seiko Co., Ltd. to Seiko Corporation.

Posting Losses in the 1990s

Seiko continued to introduce innovative products in the 1990s. In 1990 the Seiko Scubamaster hit the market, incorporating a dive table into a computerized diver's watch. In the following year came the Seiko "Perpetual Calendar," the world's first quartz watch with a full automatic 1,100-year calendar. Also introduced in the early 1990s were the Seiko Kinetic series of battery-free quartz watches and the Seiko MessageWatch.

The Kinetic watches used wrist motion to power what Seiko called the world's smallest and most powerful microgenerator. Prices started at $495 retail. The MessageWatch was more than a decade in the making and was originated by a small San Francisco firm, AT&E Corp. When this company ran into financial difficulties in 1991, Seiko and Seiko Epson (both of which were already backers of AT&E) bought the start-up's assets for $19 million. Seiko then developed a new version of the watch, which it test-marketed in Los Angeles in 1994. The MessageWatch was a digital watch designed to receive messages through FM radio waves. The customer had to buy the watch for $80, plus sign on for additional services at monthly rates. The services included paging, weather reports, voice mail alerts, stock market prices, lottery numbers, ski conditions, and sports scores. Under development were enhanced offerings such as traffic information and vehicle navigation systems.

Seiko also kept its name in the international spotlight with frequent participation in major sporting events as official timer. Most significant of these were the 1992 Barcelona and 1994

Lillehammer Olympics. Although the company lost out in the bidding for the 1996 Atlanta games to rival SMH, maker of Swatch watches, Seiko returned as the official Olympic timer for the 1998 Nagano Olympics. Other major sporting events timed by Seiko during this period included the 1990 FIFA World Cup (of soccer) held in Italy; the 1990 and 1994 Commonwealth Games in New Zealand and Canada, respectively; and the 1994 Asian Games in Japan.

While the company garnered those achievements, it was simultaneously hit extremely hard by the deep Japanese recession that started in late 1991 and by economic difficulties in its export markets, notably Europe. Sales stagnated early in the decade (¥422 billion in 1990, ¥428 billion in both 1991 and 1992) and then fell to a lower plateau (¥378 billion in 1993, ¥335 billion in 1994, ¥331 billion in 1995, and ¥342 billion in 1996). Profitability disappeared as Seiko posted five consecutive full-year net losses, culminating in a ¥11.15 billion loss in 1996. The losses stemmed in part from restructuring efforts and other adjustments made by Seiko's subsidiaries, which resulted in extraordinary losses, such as the ¥5.6 billion loss in 1996.

The most important restructuring move, and a possible harbinger of future restructurings, came in 1996 when Seiko and the affiliated Seikosha Co. Ltd. created a vertically integrated company, Seiko Clock Inc., that would manufacture and market Seiko clocks. At the same time, another vertically integrated subsidiary, Seiko Precision, Inc., was created to manufacture and market such products as camera shutters, printers, and system equipment, all previously made by Seikosha. As a result of these changes, Seikosha was dissolved. More important, Seiko would now be able to exercise greater control over all aspects of these business lines, a development of critical importance in such a difficult operating environment.

Through the difficult early and mid-1990s, Seiko had continued its history of innovation; there was no reason to believe the future would be any different. The company looked forward to more prosperous times ahead as economies recovered from their downturns and people once again clamored for the unique products Seiko offered. The 1998 Nagano Olympics provided an ideal platform for Seiko to reestablish its preeminent position in the timekeeping industry.

Changes in the Late 1990s and Beyond

Seiko continued to look for ways to remain competitive in the late 1990s and into the new millennium. In 1999, the company teamed up with Fossil to create SII Marketing International. The venture was designed to sell inexpensive watches in discount department stores including Wal-Mart. In 2000, Seiko launched a new line of titanium wristwatches suitable for outdoor use. That year it also established Seiko S-Yard Co. Ltd. to oversee its sports and electronics business.

Seiko's most significant change of this time period came in 2001, when it spun off its watch operations as Seiko Watch Corporation. This final move in its restructuring plan positioned Seiko Corporation as a holding company with wholly-owned subsidiaries overseeing watch, clock, electronic device, lens, and sport operations. The restructuring proved costly however, and lead to a loss of approximately $132.9 million in 2001.

Competition remained fierce at this time and watch makers from China and Switzerland were cutting into Seiko's market share. Domestic demand was declining and Japan-based companies saw sales slide by as much as 20 percent in 2000. In response to market conditions, Seiko and Citizen Watch agreed to combine their sales and distribution efforts in order to cut costs. The company also began to license the Seiko brand name in an attempt to shore up watch sales. In 2002, Seiko acted as the official timer for the Salt Lake City Winter Olympic Games. It served as the official timer for the IAAF World Championships in Athletics in Paris, France, the following year.

Sales fell slightly in 2003, down 1.9 percent from the previous year, however the company returned to profitability. While personal consumption in Japan remained weak through 2005, sales of Seiko watches in Europe and Southeast Asia were growing at a steady clip. At this time, Seiko launched a campaign entitled, ''Innovation & Refinement'' in an attempt to strengthen Seiko's brand image. The feature product, a kinetic chronograph watch called the Sportura, experienced success in Europe, the United States, and Southeast Asia. The company's Spring Drive, a combination of a mechanical watch and a quartz, was in high demand as well. Seiko's Brightz and Spirit watches, each with a solar radio wave function, were also popular.

Seiko responded to fluctuating market conditions by focusing on a three-year business strategy that promoted new product and new technology development while at the same time reducing costs. Having undergone a major restructuring effort from 1996 to 2001, Seiko Corp. stood well positioned for success. The company's divisions—watches, clocks, precision products, and optical products—were able to respond to market changes and update their business plans accordingly. While only time would tell how Seiko would fare in the years to come, its long-standing history and solid strategy left chairman Katsumi Yamamura and president Koichi Murano confident that Seiko's products would remain around the wrists of consumers well into future.

Principal Subsidiaries

Wako Co. Ltd.; Seiko Watch Corporation; Seiko Clock Inc.; Seiko Precision Inc.; Seiko Precision Inc.; Seiko Optical Products Inc.; Seiko S-Yard Co. Ltd.; Seiko Jewelry Co. Ltd.; Seiko Time Systems Inc.; Seiko Service Co. Ltd.; Seiko Business Services Inc.; Ohara Inc.

Principal Competitors

Casio Computer Co. Ltd.; Citizen Watch Co. Ltd.; The Swatch Group Ltd.

Further Reading

Armstrong, Larry, ''It's 10 PM. Do You Know What Your Bank Balance Is?,'' *Business Week*, December 26, 1994.

Boyer, Edward, ''A Family Rift Roils Seiko,'' *Fortune*, November 12, 1984.

Kachi, Hiroyuki, and Kanji Ishibashi, ''Seiko Group Net Profit Drops as Watch Sales in Japan Slump,'' *Asian Wall Street Journal*, May 11, 2005.

Karimzadeh, Marc, "Sieko's Five-Year Planned Crowned by Spinoff," *Women's Wear Daily*, May 18, 2001.

Minard, Lawrence, and Willoughby, Jack, "Japan's Dark Horse Computer Company," *Forbes*, October 22, 1984.

"Seiko to Become Holding Company," *Japan Weekly Monitor*, March 19, 2001.

"Seiko, Citizen Link Up Distribution, Sales," *Reuters News*, July 9, 2001.

"Seiko Profit Recovers on Group-Wide Changes," *Asian Wall Street Journal*, May 14, 2003.

Shuster, William George, "Seiko Corp. Sets Record with "Olympic' Campaign," *Jewelers Circular Keystone*, November 1991, p. 112.

——, "Seiko Works To Improve Image, Gain Market Share," *Jewelers Circular Keystone*, February 1991, p. 170.

Takahashi, Yoshio, "Seiko Forecasts Wider Loss for Year," *Asian Wall Street Journal*, March 14, 2001.

—Kim M. Magon
—updates: David E. Salamie; Christina M. Stansell

Achieving the cutting-edge ——————

SEKISUI
Sekisui Chemical, Full of Surprises

Sekisui Chemical Co., Ltd.

4-4, Nishitenma 2-chome
Kita-ku, Osaka 530-8565
Japan
Telephone: (+06) 365-4122
Fax: (+06) 365-4370
Web site: http://www.sekisui.co.jp

Public Company
Incorporated: 1947 as Sekisui Sangyo
Employees: 15,782
Sales: ¥814.8 billion ($7.7 billion)
Stock Exchanges: Tokyo Osaka
Ticker Symbol: 4204
NAIC: 327390 Other Concrete Product Manufacturing; 325211 Plastics Material and Resin Manufacturing; 325991 Custom Compounding of Purchased Resin; 325998 All Other Miscellaneous Chemical Product Manufacturing; 326122 Plastics Pipe and Pipe Fitting Manufacturing; 332919 Other Metal Valve and Pipe Fitting Manufacturing

Sekisui Chemical Co., Ltd., a member of the Sekisui *keiretsu* group of companies, operates three main business divisions, including Housing Company, Urban Infrastructure and Environmental Products Company, and High Performance Plastics Company. Prefabricated housing accounts for over half of Sekisui's sales. Its other products include plastic pipes, rain gutters, roofing materials, foams, packaging and industrial tapes, films, adhesives, high-functional resin, and transdermal and diagnostic drugs.

Early History

A glimpse at post-World War II Japan revealed only devastation. The war left millions homeless and many others, including six million soldiers, looking for jobs. Reconstruction efforts in the economic, industrial, and political sectors, however, were effective. The reform program, led by General Douglas MacArthur through the Allied occupation of Japan, transformed the country's economy by breaking up the largest *zaibatsu* (conglomerates), providing a new sense of freedom for workers, and increasing the number of business owners and managers. Recovery took hold. In this era, Sekisui Chemical Company was established as Sekisui Sangyo in Osaka, in 1947.

The company's initial products were chemicals and plastic products for home and industry. In 1948, it set up plants in Nara and Osaka. The company became the first to install an automatic plastic injection molding machine in the Nara plant. Nevertheless, production demands on Sekisui were such that the company established a new plant in Kyoto in 1952. This was followed by two additional facilities, in Amagasaki and Tokyo, in 1953. That same year, the company listed on the Tokyo Stock Exchange.

International expansion was its next logical direction for Sekisui. In 1962, a new subsidiary, Sekisui Chemical GmbH, in Düsseldorf, was formed. In New Jersey, Sekisui Products, Inc., was established in 1963. That same year, the firm also opened Sekisui Malaysia Company. Eventually, the name of this subsidiary would be changed to Sekisui Singapore (Private) Ltd.

Prefab Housing: Late 1950s and 1960s

As the company continued to develop products for the housing, industrial, and construction industries, a new market developed: prefabricated housing. Prefabricated houses allowed components to be made in a factory before being assembled at the home site. By the close of the 1950s, the practice had caught on in Japan. Prefab housing offered a new approach to the traditional Japanese method of tediously cutting wood for a home, piece by piece, according to a carpenter's specifications; in prefab units, standard lumber sizes were provided.

In the early 1960s, a Sekisui engineer visited Disneyland in California, in part to see the plastic "house of the future" designed by Monsanto Company. He returned to Japan with hopes of creating a similar home, although his efforts were not successful. Like many of the first prefab houses, the new model lacked the style and comfort of conventional homes. Explained a company spokesperson in *Fortune* (October 17, 1983), "The houses were cheap looking, and people weren't interested."

After improving initial designs to include fiberboard and aluminum panels set in steel frames, Sekisui's prefab homes were better received. In 1960, the firm set up Sekisui House Industry as

Company Perspectives:

The Sekisui Chemical Group defines a "good company" as one that has a favorable image and continuing growth. We intend to maximize business growth and corporate value with customer satisfaction to respond to the expectations of our shareholders. In addition, through our business, products and contribution to society, we aim to contribute to the community and the global environment. We actively support the self-actualization of the employees who are the driving force of our corporate activities. The Sekisui Chemical Group will pursue a prominent position in the marketplace and high profitability. We will continue to grow as a "good company," thereby fulfilling our corporate responsibilities and responding to the expectations of our customers, shareholders, employees, community, and environment.

an independent company. It would be active primarily in building steel-frame houses. In 1961, Sekisui House opened a plant in Shiga and began marketing its Type B, one-story prefab home. In 1962, Sekisui then introduced a new model, the two-story Type 2B. The following year, the firm changed its name to Sekisui House. The remainder of the decade saw a flurry of activity from the young company, including several new models. Among them were the Sekisui House Type E, a one-story home developed in 1965; Type F, a two-story home, also developed in 1965; Type G, a five-story house designed in 1968; and Type H, a two-story model designed in 1969.

By the early 1970s, the "unit house" entered the market as a new form of prefab housing. It differed from previous wood-frame prefabs in that it was enclosed in a steel frame and it utilized concrete and metal in its walls and ceilings. In addition, the home could be built on an assembly line in room-size segments. In 1971, Sekisui erected 260 such homes, which were termed Sekisui Heim. Each could be built in a matter of hours. While the majority of Japanese homes continued to be built by conventional methods, prefab houses gained a good market share. In 1972, the total housing market in Japan reached a record high: two million new homes. By 1973, the company's Musashi and Nara plants were each producing 2,000 unit homes per month.

Problems in Germany in the 1970s

In 1970, Sekisui House built a new plant, in Kanto. The following year, the firm was listed on the Osaka and Tokyo Stock Exchanges and unveiled the Terrace House and Type K House, which featured a hip roof. The firm's success in the Japanese market sparked ambitious hopes of exporting its prefab homes. In 1973, Sekisui invested in a West German plant, with plans to build 500 homes there annually. Because the houses cost more than expected, however, actual sales were closer to 120. Masaru Tanabe, president of Sekisui House, told *Fortune* (October 17, 1983) that expectations were not met because "the Germans didn't work hard enough, so our productivity went down." After investing $7 million in the German facility, Sekisui finally gave up in 1982, and the plant was closed.

While the unsuccessful venture in West Germany may have left the company apprehensive about exporting its housing products, it did manage to build a hotel and group of college classrooms and dormitories in Nigeria in the early 1980s. It continued to make capital investments in major rural construction, setting up specialized firms along the way. The company engaged in other real estate activities, including developing and selling housing lots.

In 1972, Sekisui House listed its stock on the Amsterdam and Nagoya Stock Exchanges. The following year, it built a new plant in Yamaguchi. In 1977, its stock was also listed on the Frankfurt Stock Exchange. For its quality-control efforts, Sekisui Chemical was awarded Japan's prestigious Deming Prize in 1979.

In the 1980s, the use of computer-aided design helped Sekisui offer more customized homes. Seated before a computer terminal with a Sekisui sales representative, customers could then view a standard model and add extra rooms or increase the size of present rooms, all with the touch of a few buttons. After sending the order to a regional factory, the finished components could be assembled in a few hours thanks to the company's highly automated facilities. Similar to automobile factories, the plants featured assembly lines that moved housing modules into an assembly area. Robots helped to collect various components that were to be shipped to a building site. At the site, the structure was assembled in less than a day, although plumbing and electrical work required another one or two weeks.

With a population of 119 million people living in a comparatively small area, about the size of California, prefab housing continued to be a viable solution for the nation's housing problem. For Sekisui, the homes' success seemed undaunted by the slowing real estate market of the 1980s. By 1982, total housing construction dropped to 1.2 million homes, yet prefab sales continued to climb. Overall prefabs dominated 12 percent of the housing market, surpassing industry expectations. The five manufacturing plants of Sekisui House, by then the largest housing firm in Japan, built more than 40,000 houses in 1983.

Recession Leads to Diversification in the 1980s

At Sekisui Chemical, the recession of the early 1980s sparked a move toward diversification. Chemical companies throughout the world looked to higher-priced specialty products for their profits. Sekisui Chemical, whose sales dropped from $1.34 billion in 1981 to $1.29 billion in 1982, was no exception. By the end of the decade, its diverse product line would include not only home products and housing materials but agricultural and fishing products, packaging products, and automotive products. By 1984, Japanese plastic and chemical companies saw a return to higher production and profit levels; annual sales at Sekisui climbed to $1.43 billion. An agreement in 1986 with Meisei Electric helped the firm expand its home product line to include home security equipment. Throughout the mid-1980s, chemical companies that had diversified, rather than relying on basic petrochemicals, earned higher profits. Despite the declining yen, the company saw increased sales because of higher domestic demand. By 1987, sales amounted to $3 billion, more than double the figures of five years earlier.

Key Dates:

1947: Sekisui Sangyo is established in Osaka.
1953: The company lists on the Tokyo Stock Exchange.
1960: The firm sets up Sekisui House Industry as an independent company.
1983: The five manufacturing plants of Sekisui House, by now the largest housing firm in Japan, build more than 40,000 houses.
1998: A weak housing market forces Sekisui to post a loss.
2002: Sekisui continues to restructure; the company reports a net loss of ¥52.11 billion.

Sekisui continued its diversification efforts in 1989, when it formed a joint venture with Union Carbide Chemicals & Plastics Company. The venture, Hexatec Polymers, was developed to make resins for toners used in copying machines and laser printers. The venture relied on Sekisui's technology, as well as the marketing expertise of both firms, to make the new start-up successful.

Automotive products, including parts, anticorrosive materials, and foam products, also held new promise for Sekisui. In 1989, Voltek, a division of Sekisui America Corporation, developed an extrusion coating process for use as an automotive headliner. The new method, which combined polyolefin foam and thermoplastic elastomer, was developed as an alternative to PVC material to resist cracking, heat, and fading. It was first installed on 1990 Toyota Camry and Nissan Sentra models. In addition, the company's polyvinyl butyral film, used in automotive safety glass, had gained more than half of market share.

By the end of the 1980s, Sekisui's new ventures were clearly paying off. The company began producing medical instruments and electronic equipment, such as photoelectromagnetic discs. To prepare for the coming unification of the European Economic Community, it added a new subsidiary, Sekisui International Finance, in 1989. In addition to supplying data on Europe's financial markets, the new venture was developed to handle such financial activities as loans, foreign exchanges, mergers and acquisitions, and technology transfer agreements. In the meantime, Sekisui House expanded its product line to include wooden and concrete houses, as well as apartments. The firm also began work on a research institute in Kyoto in the late 1980s.

The 1990s and Beyond

Sekisui Chemical entered the 1990s with a product line that encompassed flooring and furniture for office automation; pipes, gutters, and other construction products; industrial and automotive products; packaging materials; medical and electronic equipment; and agricultural and fishing products. Products for the home ranged from furniture to household chemicals.

During this time period, Sekisui Chemical operated as Japan's largest synthetic resin processing company and the largest prefabricated home builder. While the company experienced success in the early to mid-1990s, however, it began to struggle during the latter half of the decade. A slowdown in the housing

sector forced Sekisui to rethink its strategy for its prefabricated division. As such, the firm executed a restructuring plan that refocused the division's core business. As a result of the reorganization, the company shuttered some of its steel and wood-based operations.

Weak consumer spending and the continued slowdown in housing development wreaked havoc on the company's bottom line. From 1998 to 2002, Sekisui reported losses. In order to combat turbulent market conditions, Sekisui embarked on an aggressive restructuring of its entire business line. The plan included the sale of unprofitable subsidiaries, including its U.S.-based PVC pipe manufacturer. Overall, the company laid off over 2,000 employees and discontinued two prefabricated housing product lines. Poor demand for its office equipment plastic parts forced the closure of its plasticizers plant in Sakai and its plastics part facility in Fujieda. Sekisui's net loss for fiscal 2002 grew to ¥52.11 billion.

In order to shore up sales and profits, Sekisui's management team launched a new strategy that focused the company's efforts on products related to the environment and cutting-edge chemistry. The firm's 2004 annual report outlined the new Sekisui vision: "We aim to build a highly profitable group of businesses by providing strikingly original products and services. We will achieve this by developing the cutting-edge chemistry and environmental technologies that are our unique strengths to a level of prominence that cannot be paralleled by competitors."

As part of this strategy, Sekisui entered into several key partnerships and acquisitions. In 2002, it formed a joint venture with Qingdao Construction Group to manufacture and sell water pipes in Qingdao, China. It also landed a contract to provide thermal barrier films for auto glass to Euyao Glass Industry Group Co. In 2003, the company purchased a 51 percent interest in Shanghai Redflag Plastic Co. Ltd. As a result of the deal, Sekisui secured a 30 percent share of the foaming polyolefin market in China.

By now, Sekisui was organized into three main business divisions: Housing Company, Urban Infrastructure and Environmental Products Company (UIEP), and High Performance Plastics Company (HPP). Each division focused on increasing its competitive stance by offering products and solutions based on the company's new vision. For example, the Housing Company focused on the environment by offering customers "zero utility expense" houses. These homes were equipped with photovoltaic generators. UIEP targeted environmental solutions in pipe systems while HPP focused on information technology, automotive parts, medical products, and functional building materials.

The company's efforts appeared to pay off. During 2003 and 2004, both sales and net income grew. In fact, during 2004 net income climbed by 61.5 percent over the previous year to ¥15 billion. While weak economic conditions had forced Sekisui to undergo significant change during the early 2000s, its management was confident that their actions had left the company well positioned to experience success in the years to come.

Principal Divisions

Housing Company; Urban Infrastructureand Environmental Products Company; High Performance Plastics Company.

Principal Competitors

Asahi Kasei Corporation; Kubota Corporation; Taisei Corporation.

Further Reading

"Dire Straits—Komatsu Is the Latest Japanese Vinyls Player to Embark on Restructuring," *Asian Chemical News*, September 26, 1997.

"Japan's Sekisui Chem to Exit Office Equipment Plastics Parts Business," *Asia Pulse*, December 3, 2001.

Levy, Emanual, "P/A Technics Industrialized Housing," *Progressive Architecture*, February 1987.

Onosko, Tim, "Digitized Dream Dwelling," *Omni*, June 1985.

"Sekisui Chem Aims to Raise Profitability," *Reuters News*, March 23, 2001.

"Sekisui Chemical Expects This FY Group Net Profit Y22B," *Dow Jones International News*, April 27, 2004.

"Sekisui Chemical Posts Wider Loss for Its Fiscal Year," *Asian Wall Street Journal*, May 17, 2002, p. M3.

"Sekisui Chemical to Restructure Prefab Housing Business," *Dow Jones International News*, September 25, 1998.

"Sekisui Chemical to Top Group Profit Growth Rankings," *Japan Economic Newswire*, July 10, 1995.

Smith, Lee, "Now Japan Moves Ahead in Prefabs," *Fortune*, October 17, 1983.

Ushio, Shota, and Paula Block, "Japanese Specialty Chemicals: The Coming Wave," *Chemical Week*, July 9, 1986.

—Kim M. Magon
—update: Christina M. Stansell

Shearer's Foods, Inc.

692 Wabash Avenue North
Brewster, Ohio 44613
U.S.A.
Telephone: (330) 767-3426
Toll Free: (888) GREAT-CHIPS
Fax: (330) 767-3393
Web site: http://www.shearers.com

Private Company
Incorporated: 1974
Employees: 482
Sales: $60 million (2005 est.)
NAIC: 311919 Other Snack Food Manufacturing

Shearer's Foods, Inc., is northeast Ohio's leading maker of potato chips and tortilla chips. Other major markets include Columbus, Cincinnati, and Pittsburgh, and the company produces a significant amount of snacks on a private-label or co-pack basis. Shearer's makes 130,000 pounds a day of more than 20 different kinds of potato chips. It also prepares 30,000 pounds of tortilla chips daily. Cheese curls, popcorn, pretzels, and pork rinds are also on the menu, each with the promise of "Perfection in Every Bag." The company has extended its expertise with its legendary kettle chips into a regional snack food empire. It has grown steadily and tends to weather recessions well due to the perennial appeal of its snacks. Shearer's has addressed healthy eating concerns by making most of its products without trans fats and by encouraging customers to choose its high quality snacks when they do indulge.

Origins

The origins of Shearer's Foods, Inc. date back to the early 20th century, when William Shearer opened Shearer's Market on the corner of 9th and Dartmouth in Canton, Ohio. It was operated by his sons, Nelson and Howard, after his retirement.

Nelson's son Jack and his wife Rosemary took over the business in the 1950s and eventually acquired ownership of it. They later sold the store after beginning their snack food venture.

The pair acquired a small snack distributor in 1974 and renamed it Brookside Distributing. Five years later, convinced they could produce a superior product themselves, the Shearers began making their own potato chips, by hand, under the "Kettle-Cook'd" brand. The original facility was just 3,000 square feet in size, Rosemary Shearer later told *Snack Food & Wholesale Bakery.*

The kettle chips were successful and in 1982 prompted a move to a 20,000-square-foot plant in rural Brewster, Ohio. The company then had about 30 employees. Roasted peanuts were added to the lineup. The next year saw the introduction of the Grandma Shearer's logo. The name referred to Rosemary Shearer, who developed the potato chip recipe. By this time, the company was going through nearly two tons of potatoes every day. Annual sales were about $4 million, according to one source.

The production line was upgraded with a continuous fryer in 1986, allowing the plant to produce one ton of potato chips every two hours. The company also began making popcorn. A second continuous fryer was added in 1988, when the facility was expanded to 52,000 square feet. After a two-month, industry-wide potato shortage in 1987, Shearer's began contracting farmers for potatoes from six months to a year in advance. Other agricultural disruptions included flooding in Florida in 1997 and a drought in 1999.

Sizzling in the 1990s

Demand prompted Shearer's to continue to upgrade its facilities in the 1990s. Two unique hand-kettle fryers with automated stirring systems were added in 1990, along with a garage for maintaining the company's vehicles.

The company opened a factory outlet at the plant in 1996. There was another major expansion in the late 1990s, when nearly 80,000 square feet were added for production, storage, and offices. The project cost about $14 million. Among the new technology was an optical chip sorter ("Opti-Sort") for detecting defective chips.

Around this time, Shearer's began making tortilla chips and cheese curls. The company also sold dozens of other products,

Key Dates:

1974: Jack and Rosemary Shearer acquire a small snack food distributor.
1979: The Shearers begin making their own potato chips.
1982: The company moves from Canton, Ohio, to a new plant in Brewster.
1983: Grandma Shearer's logo debuts; sales are about $4 million a year.
1986: The first continuous fryer is installed.
1998: Production capacity is doubled after a $14 million expansion.
2002: Shearer's is named ''Snack Food Manufacturer of the Year.''
2004: ''Grandma'' and ''Grandpa'' brands dropped in packaging redesign.

including salsa and pretzels. Chips accounted for 60 percent of sales, according to the *Akron Beacon Journal.*

About 15 to 30 percent of revenues came from private label sales. Private label chips were fried in cottonseed oil, noted *Snack Food & Wholesale Bakery,* while peanut oil was used for the kettle chips and soybean for others. Private label customers included Buehler's, Giant Eagle, and Super Kmart, reported *Inside Business.*

Shearer's was primarily a regional producer, though distribution extended into New England in early 1997. Major markets included Akron, Cleveland, Cincinnati, Columbus, Toledo, and Pittsburgh. Shearer's snacks were also distributed in parts of Kentucky, Tennessee, Michigan, and Canada.

Annual revenues were estimated at $28 million in 1998, when Shearer's began sponsoring the Cleveland Indians baseball team, and were growing more than 20 percent a year. In addition to sponsoring the Cleveland Indians, the company also supported arts groups.

Still Growing in the 2000s

Employment at Shearer's grew to about 280 people in 1999. In 2001, the company began raffling off a Caribbean cruise to reward employees with perfect attendance. Weekly cash giveaways also helped discourage absenteeism. Shearer's had about 400 employees at the time. ''Happy people produce happy results,'' CEO Bob Shearer told *Snack Food & Wholesale Bakery.*

Shearer's continued to grow, installing still more new equipment in a 2001 expansion that added six hand-kettle fryers and a new potato peeling system. The plant had eight production lines in all. The company also boosted its customer service staff with new hires and new technology.

The growth seemed to be fueled by quality. Shearer's was picking up industry awards for both taste and manufacturing processes. The company was picked as *Snack Food and Wholesale Bakery's* ''Snack Manufacturer of the Year'' for 2002.

In 2003, Shearer's joined a few other snack manufacturers to produce the world's largest bag of potato chips. Created to help celebrate the potato chip's 150th anniversary, the sack weighed 1,082.5 pounds.

Part of the company's warehousing was moved off site in 2003. The factory outlet was upgraded in 2004.

The Associated Press chronicled Shearer's strategy to thrive in the face of low-carb and low-fat dietary trends. Though it had developed baked and low-carb variations of corn and potato chips before, Shearer's took to highlighting the quality their snacks offered. ''If you're going to indulge, you want it to be the best,'' said CEO Robert Shearer. The company added slogans to its packaging recommending moderate portions and exercise.

Gourmet chips made up one of the few growth segments of the otherwise flat, $23 billion potato chip industry. A number of strong regional competitors fought for market share with national giants, particularly Frito-Lay, Inc.

Shearer's was introducing new flavors, such as Margarita Lime Tortilla Chips and Butter Corn Puffs, as well as some organic products. Most of the chips were being cooked with trans fat free oils.

Sales for the privately owned company were reported in the press as being between $38 million and $65 million. A company source told the Associated Press that revenues had quadrupled since 2000.

The company restyled its packaging in early 2004 in order to stay competitive on the shelves. The ''Grandma Shearer'' icon was removed from the logo, while product photos were added to the bags. ''Snack foods are a high impulse item, so it's important for us to offer high quality packages and display pieces,'' a company official told the *Dayton Business Journal.*

Shearer's was also making changes in its manufacturing processes. The company began extracting potato chip waste from wastewater for use as cattle feed. Forty tons of the material was extracted from 12,000 gallons of water every day, according to *Inside Business.* A half-dozen more hand kettles and new packaging machines were added to the plant in 2004.

By 2005, Shearer's had phased out the truck maintenance garage it had opened in 1990s. Instead, the company turned to Penske for leased equipment. In 2005, its fleet numbered 65 vans, ten semis, and 35 trailers, according to *Light & Medium Truck Magazine.* Some of the older trucks were company owned. Shearer's was getting rid of these in favor of newer, more fuel efficient models.

Principal Competitors

Birds Eye Inc.; Frito-Lay Inc.; Herr Foods Inc.; Mike-Sell's Potato Chip Co.; Procter & Gamble; Utz Quality Foods.

Further Reading

Adams, Bret, "A Taste for Growth," *Small Business News—Stark County* (Ohio), December 1, 1999.

Demetrakakes, Pan, "Chips Off the Old Block," *Food Processing*, December 1, 1999, p. 57.

——, "Snack Makers Crunched on Brand Identity: For Those Up Against Frito-Lay, Packaging Is an Important Way to Break Into Consumers' Consciousness," *Food & Drug Packaging*, February 1, 2004, p. 40.

Ethridge, Mary, "Shearer Foods Inc. Expanding Brewster, Ohio, Snack Food Plant," *Akron Beacon Journal*, October 8, 1997.

Hanacek, Andy, "Culture Club," *Snack Food and Wholesale Bakery*, March 2005, pp. 30, 32, 34, 36.

Koff, Stephen, "Snacks PAC Is Ohio Chip Off Old Block," *Plain Dealer* (Cleveland), March 11, 2001, p. 1A.

Irwin, Gloria, "Ohio Potato Farmers, Restaurateur Form Potato-Chip Partnership," *Akron Beacon Journal*, May 2, 2002.

Lepro, Sara, "At Home with Bob Shearer: The President and CEO of Shearer's Foods Inc. May Live Off the Beaten Track, But He's No Country Bumpkin," *Inside Business*, March 1, 2005, p. 121.

Mabin, Conie, "Company Finds Success with Kettle Fried Chips in Low-Carb, Low-Fat Age," *Associated Press State & Local Wire*, March 25, 2005.

"A More Appealing Image," *Snack Food & Wholesale Bakery*, February 2004, p. 74.

"No Sacrifice on Taste," *Snack Food & Wholesale Bakery*, May 2004.

Pacyniak, Bernard, "Sheer Growth," *Snack Food & Wholesale Bakery*, November 1998, p. 24.

Schultz, Martin, "True Grit: How Shearer's Foods Started Out As a Corner Store and Became One of the U.S.'s Fastest-Growing Snack Food Manufacturers and Most Progressive Companies," *Snack Food & Wholesale Bakery*, March 2002, pp. 28ff.

Semmler, Edward R., "Shearer's Foods Really in the Chips," *Repository*, April 29, 1996, p. B1.

"SFA Members Create World's Largest Bag of Potato Chips," *Snack Food & Wholesale Bakery*, August 2003, p. 30.

Shryock, Todd, "Bob Shearer, Shearer Success," *SBN Cleveland*, July 2002.

——, "2004 Pillar Award for Community Service: Shearer's Foods, Sharing and Caring," *Smart Business Cleveland*, December 1, 2004, p. 50.

Skipper, G.C., "A Fleet in Transition," *Light & Medium Truck Magazine*, March 2005.

Stephans, Caleb, "Tough Market: National Chip Maker Taking a Bit Out of Regional Potato Chip Makers' Business," *Dayton Business Journal*, May 21, 2004.

Stewart, Fran A., "Hot Potato," *Inside Business*, May 1999, p. 49.

Swenson, Kyle, "Cow Chips: Shearer's Is Entering the Bovine Snack Market," *Inside Business*, August 1, 2004, p. 8.

Truman, Dave, "Ohio Companies Try to Encourage Employees Not to Take Sick Days," *News-Herald* (Willoughby, Ohio), November 15, 2003.

Turcsik, Richard, "Reprogrammed Chips," *Progressive Grocer*, December 1, 2002, pp. 44ff.

"Waving a Wand Over the Kettle," *Snack Food & Wholesale Bakery*, June 2003.

Zawacki, Michael, "Five Habits of Success," *Inside Business*, January 2003, pp. 34ff.

—Frederick C. Ingram

SHOE CARNIVAL, INC.

Shoe Carnival Inc.

8233 Baumgart Road
Evansville, Indiana 47725
U.S.A.
Telephone: (812) 867-6471
Fax: (812) 867-4261
Web site: http://www.shoecarnival.com

Public Company
Incorporated: 1978 as Russell Shoe Biz Inc.
Employees: 3,770
Sales: $590.2 million (2004)
Stock Exchanges: NASDAQ
Ticker Symbol: SCVL
NAIC: 44821 Shoe Stores

Shoe Carnival Inc. is one of the leading retailers of family footwear in the United States. The company differentiates its shoe stores with value pricing, its large selection of brand names, and a carnival-like shopping atmosphere. Following rapid growth during the late 1990s and into the 21st century, Shoe Carnival was operating 255 stores in 24 states in the Midwest, South, and southeastern regions of the United States.

Russell's Creative Ideas Lead to Success

Shoe Carnival was inspired by shoe salesman David Russell of Evansville, Indiana. Russell worked for 20 years selling shoes in the traditional fashion. He knelt in front of customers to measure their feet, carried boxes from the back room, and earned a commission from every pair of shoes he sold. Throughout his career, however, he had the feeling that there had to be a better way to sell shoes. Finally, in 1978, the 34-year-old Russell quit his job at Kinney Shoe Corp. to open his own shop. He combined his savings with money from his in-laws and opened a small shoe store that he dubbed "Shoe Biz." His idea was to create a selling environment completely different from the traditional, staid shoe store that was so common at the time. He wanted to create a shoe store that was fun. Thus, Shoe Biz offered thousands of boxes of shoes on self-

service racks. Jukebox music that featured tunes from the 1950s blared away, though the music was often interrupted by announcements by the store manager, who was authorized to hawk footwear and cut deals with customers on the spot.

Russell's idea was a hit. Sales were so strong that he was able to open a second store in Evansville, called Shoe Shower, which, along with Shoe Biz and the other stores to follow, would come to operate under the Shoe Carnival name. Russell also opened a third Shoe Carnival across the river from Evansville in Owensboro, Kentucky, in the early 1980s. Like the original store, the new stores enticed shoppers with low-cost shoes and self-service shopping, a chaotic and entertaining shopping environment, and a sort of let's-make-a-deal atmosphere. Only "Elvis music or older" was allowed on the jukebox, and customers were encouraged to haggle over the price of the shoes. Managers were instructed to beat any price in town, and the stores featured an elevated stage where a store employee hawked specials on the store public address system every few minutes. The deals occasionally involved spectacular giveaways that generated valuable press for the stores. The shop in Owensboro, for example, once gave away a cow, and one of the Evansville stores awarded $25,000 in cash to a customer.

Russell also grabbed attention with screaming advertisements. On one occasion, he had to prove to the Better Business Bureau the validity of an advertising claim that he literally had "miles of boots" in stock. He measured a boot and multiplied the length by his inventory to discover that he was stocking exactly 5.7 miles of boots. Once the promotions got the customers into the stores, the carnival atmosphere was honed to get them into a buying mood. A free pair of tennis shoes might be offered to anyone who could hula-hoop for a minute or to the first person who could bring an aspirin to the manager. Customers were also enticed by the sheer size of, and selection at, the stores. The shops eventually offered an average of more than 10,000 square feet of floor space, upon which name-brand stock was displayed on tall, self-service racks. By using a smaller number of salespeople, the company was able to keep prices low and generate profits through high-volume sales of name-brand shoes.

Expansion Begins in the Mid-1980s

By 1984, Shoe Carnival was generating a lofty $8 million in annual sales from its three stores. Sales at the private company continued to grow and to catch the attention of other shoe industry players. In 1986, in fact, Russell sold a controlling interest in his company to Fisher-Camuto Corporation, although he remained as chief executive in charge of the company's operation. Based in Stamford, Connecticut, Fisher-Camuto was the manufacturer of shoes under designer labels, including Gloria Vanderbilt, Enzo, Esties, and Nine West. Fisher-Camuto bought into the chain because it believed that it had access to the financing needed to expand Russell's proven concept outside of Evansville. To that end, in October and November of 1986 Fisher-Camuto financed the construction of three Shoe Carnival outlets in Indianapolis. The success of those new stores mimicked that of the Evansville-area outlets. Enthusiastic at this outcome, the Shoe Carnival organization opened a total of 15 additional outlets in major Midwest markets in under two years.

Realizing the potential of the Shoe Carnival concept, J. Wayne Weaver, with Russell's help, purchased Shoe Carnival from Fisher-Camuto in 1989 for a lowly $17 million. Weaver was serving as president and chief executive of Nine West at the time. After the buyout, Weaver became chairman of the again independent Shoe Carnival as well as chief executive of Nine West, and Russell retained his chief executive slot. Shoe Carnival continued to expand at a rapid clip under their leadership. By the end of 1989, Shoe Carnival was sporting 30 stores spread throughout nine states in the Midwest and South, including Kentucky, Indiana, Illinois, Iowa, Michigan, Tennessee, Ohio, and Alabama. To support this growth, the chain employed a total of 1,500 part-time and full-time workers. At one point, Shoe Carnival was opening an average of one store per week. Russell and Weaver planned to open only six or seven additional outlets in 1990, however.

Russell managed the expansion of Shoe Carnival during the late 1980s and early 1990s with the help of a close-knit management team that consisted of longtime friends and executives lured from competing shoe companies. The executives stayed close to the day-to-day operation of the stores, and Russell himself was occasionally seen packing merchandise in the company's Evansville distribution center, manning the microphone at Shoe Carnival outlets, and even handing out dollar bills to customers waiting in the check-out lines. Although his retail management experience was limited prior to the start-up of Shoe Carnival, few could argue with his success. Nevertheless, the rapid expansion had not been without minor setbacks. "Initially, we expected to have the success of the Evansville store in every city," said Laura Ray, vice-president of marketing, in the November 1989 issue of *Indiana Business.* "But after the opening it tended to slow down a little. So it has been an education for us, getting customers used to the Carnival and our way of doing things. But overall we're pleased as punch with everything."

Shoe Carnival Goes Public in 1993

Shoe Carnival slowed its expansion during the early 1990s and concentrated on whipping its existing operations into shape. About ten new stores were added between 1990 and mid-1993. That grew the chain to a total of 41 outlets, most of which were in the Midwest. Throughout this period, Shoe Carnival was effectively a private company and was not required to release sales and earnings information. Early in 1993, though, the company converted from a Chapter S corporation to a public company. The change was made because Weaver and Russell wanted to generate expansion capital by way of a public stock offering. To that end, Shoe Carnival conducted an initial public offering that brought about $28 million into its coffers. That left Russell with about 7 percent ownership in the company. Weaver, who was also a significant owner of Nine West shares and several other interests, retained a 54 percent stake in the company. Subsequent stock offerings shortly thereafter brought additional funds into Shoe Carnival's war chest.

Shoe Carnival generated sales of about $127 million in 1992. Rapid growth following the initial public offering would nearly double that figure within a few years. This revenue gain was primarily the result of new store openings. By the end of 1993, Shoe Carnival had opened a total of 57 stores in 15 states. Sales in that year climbed to $157 million, about $6 million of which was netted as income. Importantly, Shoe Carnival also realized improvements in its net profit margins and sales-per-square-foot of floor space, which were among the highest in the industry.

Going into 1994, Shoe Carnival was an emerging power in the U.S. family footwear industry. Athletic and women's shoes represented 33 percent and 29 percent, respectively, of company sales, while children's and men's shoes accounted for a combined 33 percent. Accessories such as belts and purses made up the remainder of the company's revenues. Popular name brands sold at Shoe Carnival outlets included Nike, Reebok, Hush Puppies, Dexter, Florsheim, and Rockport.

Shoe Carnival continued to add new stores to its chain during 1994. By the end of the year, there were 87 Shoe Carnival stores operating in 15 states. Besides increasing the store number, the company upgraded its Evansville distribution center to 108,000 square feet and installed a mechanized merchandise handling system. The new system allowed Shoe Carnival to reduce its store inventories and to deliver shoe styles that were hot sellers more quickly. That system was augmented by a new computerized point-of-sale system that connected all of the store's cash registers into the company's headquarters computer system. This arrangement enabled managers at both the store and headquarters levels to make decisions based on up-to-the-minute sales, inventory, and payroll data.

Meanwhile, store shenanigans and promotions continued to draw customers. For example, one long-time practice was for Shoe Carnival stores to offer deals at selected times by having an employee spin a big roulette wheel that was part of a Spin-

Key Dates:

1978: David Russell opens his first small shoe store, Shoe Biz.
1984: Shoe Carnival generates $8 million in annual sales from its three stores.
1986: Russell sells a controlling interest in his company to Fisher-Camuto Corporation but remains chief executive in charge of the company's operation.
1989: J. Wayne Weaver, with Russell's help, purchases Shoe Carnival from Fisher-Camuto for $17 million.
1993: Shoe Carnival goes public.
1996: Mark L. Lemond is named president and CEO.
2004: Sales reach $590.2 million and store count exceeds 240 locations.

'n-Win game. The wheel was divided into specials such as "$1 off," "$2 off," or "free prize." The deal that came up on the wheel was the one offered to people that were in the store at the time. Another example of Shoe Carnival's unique promotional efforts was its kick-off of the sale of the popular Fila brand of shoes. Shoe Carnival brought in Pop-A-Shot electronic basketball games and invited customers to come in and shoot to win prizes and in some cases to engage in shooting contests with well-known basketball players. Rounding out the carnival-like atmosphere in all of Shoe Carnival's stores were neon signs, colored lights, colorful displays, large mirrors, and 1950s jukebox music similar to what David Russell played in the first Shoe Biz outlet in 1978.

Shoe Carnival's revenues rose 37 percent in 1994 to $214 million. At the same time, the company's sales-per-square-foot figure declined slightly and net income fell to just $1.2 million. The slide in net income was attributed to a number of factors. Several of the new stores that had been opened in Detroit, Alabama, and Georgia failed to live up to management's expectations. Additionally, Shoe Carnival's attempt to market private-label shoes was a flop. The company had hoped that they could boost profit margins by offering private-label women's shoes. However, the shoes consumed valuable shelf space previously occupied by name brands, and Shoe Carnival lost money on the project. "We got a little bit out of our element," Russell said of the experiment in *Forbes* in 1994. Another part of the problem, according to some analysts, was that the shoe market was become increasingly crowded with other discount retailers that were eating into Shoe Carnival's piece of the pie.

To boost the profitability of existing stores, Shoe Carnival reduced its expansion plans for 1995, although it still expected to open up to 15 new outlets. Executives were also planning to further reduce sales of private-label shoes and to trim the organization's inventory and overall operating costs. By mid-1995 management had made significant progress toward those goals. Despite management's efforts, the company reported a $7.2 million loss for the year, the largest loss in its history.

Lemond Takes Over as President and CEO

Founder Russell resigned in 1996 due to health problems. Thereafter, Mark L. Lemond, Shoe Carnival's chief operating officer and chief financial officer, took over as president and CEO in September. Under new leadership, Shoe Carnival launched an aggressive strategy to upgrade its image and increase earnings. It closed eight of its unprofitable stores, began remodeling existing locations, and cut 10 percent of its administrative staff. The company also started to bolster its product line by adding more brand names, including Etienne Aigner, to its arsenal. In-store displays were also revamped, giving the stores a cleaner, easier-to-shop look.

Lemond's bold moves paid off in the late 1990s and into the 2000s. Sales and profits rebounded, and in 1999 the company received a line of credit that would allow it to expand by up to 30 stores per year. The firm also restructured its buying organization, upgraded its information systems, and trimmed its selling, general, and administrative expenses. By 2001, Shoe Carnival's sales had nearly doubled since 1996. In 2002, sales climbed to $519.7 million while net income grew to $15.6 million.

In August 2002, the company introduced a new store design. Over the next two years, 80 of its stores were showcasing the new look. Twenty-two new stores opened their doors in 2004, and 12 to 14 new stores were slated to begin operations the following year. Shoe Carnival also revamped its advertising strategy and hired a new advertising firm in November 2004. An advertising blitz entitled the "Red Nose" campaign focused on the store's fun atmosphere and popular new fashions.

With president and CEO Lemond at the helm, Shoe Carnival had overcome its financial troubles of the mid-1990s. While intense competition and fluctuating sales remained everyday challenges, the company appeared to be on the right track for continued success in the years to come. When asked what his top priority was in a 2005 *Evansville Courier* interview, Lemond replied, "Continued growth. The growth of our company in terms of the number of stores, in terms of sales and earning growth and the economic growth of our shareholders and employees."

Principal Subsidiaries

SCHC, Inc.; SCLC, Inc.; Shoe Carnival Ventures, LLC.

Principal Competitors

Brown Shoe Company Inc.; Foot Locker Inc.; Payless ShoeSource Inc.

Further Reading

Basch, Mark, "Weaver to Sell $11 Million of Shoe Stock," *Florida Times Union*, October 20, 1993.
Darlin, Damon, "Send in the Clowns," *Forbes*, August 1, 1994, p. 89.
Derk, James S., "The Shoe Carnival," *Indiana Business*, November 1989, p. 28.
"Executive Exchange Common Sense," *Evansville Courier*, February 1, 2003, p. J10.
"Glitz, Glitter, and, of Course, Shoes Galore," *Tribune Business Weekly*, August 11, 1993, p. 3.
Julian, Alan, "Shoe Store Tries to Kick Sales Slump," *Evansville Courier & Press*, September 15, 2002, p. E1.
Kent, Jennifer, "Shoe Carnival Coming," *Cincinnati Post*, May 26, 1993.

Massa, Sherri, ''Shoe Carnival Swings into Town with Low Prices, Crazy Gimmicks,'' *Indianapolis Business Journal*, January 19, 1987, p. 12.

Miller, Laura Novello, ''Shoe Carnival Spins IPO Wheel to Finance Expansion,'' *Indianapolis Business Journal*, May 23, 1994, p. 9B.

Raithel, Tom, ''Stepping up Shoe Carnival Takes on a New Look and New Ideas as It Treads toward Better Profitability,'' *Evansville Courier*, March 30, 1997, p. E1.

''Retail Entrepreneurs of the Year: Mark Lemond,'' *Chain Store Age*, December 2001, p. 74.

''Shoe Carnival Inc.,'' *The Wall Street Journal*, September 20, 1996.

''Shoe Carnival Reports Second Quarter Results,'' *PR Newswire*, August 24, 1995.

''Shoe Carnival's Wheel of Fortune,'' *Chain Store Age*, November 2002, p. 46.

Wilson, Melinda, ''The Shoe Carnival Is Coming to Town,'' *Detroit News*, February 25, 1994, p. 1E.

—Dave Mote

—update: Christina M. Stansell

SNC·LAVALIN

SNC-Lavalin Group Inc.

455 René-Lévesque Boulevard West
Montreal, Quebec
H2Z 1Z3
Canada
Telephone: (514) 393-1000
Fax: (514) 866-0795
Web site: http://www.snclavalin.com

Public Company
Incorporated: 1967
Employees: 11,098
Sales: $2.87 billion (2004)
Stock Exchanges: Toronto
Ticker Symbol: SNC
NAIC: 235990 All Other Special Trade Contractors;
236210 Industrial Building Construction; 237110 Water
and Sewer Line and Related Structures Construction;
237120 Oil and Gas Pipeline and Related Structures
Construction; 237130 Power and Communication Line
and Related Structures Construction; 237310 Highway,
Street, and Bridge Construction; 237990 Other Heavy
and Civil Engineering Construction; 332992 Small
Arms Ammunition Manufacturing; 332993 Ammunition
(Except Small Arms) Manufacturing; 541330
Engineering Services

SNC-Lavalin Group Inc. is a leading international engineering and construction firm with offices in more than 30 countries. Services offered include engineering, construction, project management, procurement, and financing. In 1991, SNC Group acquired its main rival, Lavalin Inc., which had collapsed after an overambitious diversification plan. The combined company has continued to grow ever since. It has focused its growth-by-acquisition strategy on international companies since the mid-1990s. More than half of revenues come from outside Canada.

SNC Is Formed in 1911

SNC-Lavalin Group Inc.'s origins date back to 1911, when Dr. Arthur Surveyer opened an engineering office in Montreal.

Surveyer specialized in civil engineering and later diversified into industrial plant design.

In 1937, Emil Nenniger and Georges Chênevert became Surveyer's partners. The partnership was renamed Surveyer, Nenniger & Chênevert (SNC) in 1947.

Engineer Camille Dagenais joined Surveyer, Nenniger & Chênevert in 1953, when it had 130 employees, and became partner six years later. In 1965, he was named chairman and general manager. SNC was incorporated as a limited company in 1966.

SNC worked on a number of noteworthy projects in the early 1960s, including Manic 5 Dam in northern Quebec. According to company literature, its first international job was building the Idukki power station in Kerala, India, in 1963.

The policy of Quebec's government of relying on private sector engineers helped foster the development of the province's engineering firms, noted Britain's *Financial Times*. In the late 1960s, Dagenais later told the *Canadian Business Review*, Canada's engineering firms such as SNC began incorporating procurement and construction services to better serve their overseas customers. They also became proficient at arranging financing for major infrastructure projects.

SNC Group grew aggressively by acquisition in the 1970s. It had revenues of C$180 million in 1981. The company had ventured into the defense segment the previous year by acquiring IVI Inc., which made smaller caliber ammunition.

SNC Goes Public in 1986

SNC became a public company in 1986. By this time, the group's defense business (made up of IVI, Canadian Arsenals, and Securiplex Systems Inc.) was rivaling the traditional engineering and construction activities in importance.

Half of SNC's revenues were now coming from abroad. Both SNC and Lavalin thrived in francophone Africa (particularly Algeria in the case of Lavalin). These projects were generally funded by international development agencies.

To cope with the early 1980s slowdown in engineering services, SNC Group pursued growth in the defense market. It

Company Perspectives:

Founded in 1911, SNC-Lavalin has been active internationally for nearly 40 years, establishing a multicultural network that spans every continent. The SNC-Lavalin companies have offices across Canada and in 30 other countries around the world and are currently working in some 100 countries.

SNC-Lavalin maintains exceptionally high standards for quality, health and safety, and environmental protection, and is committed to delivering projects on budget and on schedule to the complete satisfaction of its clients. SNC-Lavalin's business strategy rests on four strong pillars: Build on its recognized expertise in its core sectors and develop new expertise in technical fields with promising growth opportunities . . . Use its financing capabilities to enhance its competitiveness in major projects . . . Use its technical expertise and financial capabilities to develop and acquire infrastructure concessions with solid fundamentals and potential . . . Continue to leverage the international network it has built up over nearly 40 years.

acquired artillery ammunition producer Canadian Arsenals Ltd. for C$92 million in 1986. This added more than C$100 million to SNC's annual revenues. SNC also invested in diverse joint ventures, including a compact disc plant (Americ Disc) and a natural gas supplier.

Lavalin Formed in 1936

Jean-Paul Lalonde and Romeo Valois of Montreal formed the Lavalin civil engineering firm in 1936. This would become SNC's chief rival under the direction of Bernard Lamarre, who joined Lavalin in 1952 after marrying Louise Lalonde, daughter of one of the company's founders. He had first learned the construction business while working for his father, a contractor in rural Quebec. Lamarre became head of Lavalin in 1962. Under Lamarre, Lavalin extended its global reach, then greatly diversified its range of activities.

The firm started by Lalonde and Valois became known as Lavalin Inc. by the early 1970s. Major projects for Lavalin during the decade included the James Bay hydroelectric plant (in collaboration with Bechtel of the United States) and the roof of Montreal's Olympic Stadium.

Lavalin took over a number of firms, including Canada's Shawinigan Engineering and Warnock Hersey and Europe's Lafarge Coppee. Lavalin was the largest engineering firm in Canada by the mid-1980s, with revenues of C$500 million in 1983. It had 5,700 employees at this point.

Lavalin Overreaches in the 1980s

However, as the international business became more competitive, Lavalin looked to build petrochemical and manufacturing segments. In 1986, it acquired an 85 percent interest in Urban Transportation Development Corp. (UTDC) from the government of Ontario for C$50 million. UTDC was eventually sold to Bombardier Inc. The group also bought a money-losing petrochemical plant called Kemtec that was sold off as well.

Lavalin was already exporting C$300 million worth of manufactured goods a year, according to Toronto's *Financial Post.* Lavalin even acquired Montreal's Bellechasse hospital and attempted to enter the aircraft leasing business. Other disparate new purchases included Quebec's MeteoMedia television weather channel, the book publisher Mondia, and real estate, including a new 55-floor headquarters building. At the dawn of the 1990s, Lavalin was a C$1.2 billion conglomerate of more than 70 companies, but it was on the verge of collapse due to its overly ambitious expansion into loss-making side ventures. In 1991, Lavalin's bankers put it under pressure to be acquired by its chief rival, SNC.

SNC Acquires Lavalin in 1991

SNC Group Inc. bought Lavalin Inc., the Lavalin Group's C$400 million ($348 million) engineering business, in August 1991. The combined group, dubbed SNC-Lavalin Group Inc., was led by SNC chairman Guy Saint-Pierre, who had steered the group through a turnaround in the previous two years. (SNC posted a profit of C$23 million on revenues of C$447 million in 1990.)

SNC-Lavalin was the fifth-largest engineering firm in the world, according to one estimate. It had more than 7,000 employees after the merger but cut 2,000 jobs in the next two years. The two had markedly different cultures, with Lalonde's autocratic style contrasting with the publicly traded and largely employee-owned SNC.

In the mid-1990s, Saint-Pierre pursued growth abroad via acquisitions, hiring more local talent than had traditionally been the case among Canada's international engineering firms, noted the *Financial Post.* Saint-Pierre stepped down as CEO of SNC-Lavalin Group in 1996, a couple of years after being named CEO of the Year by Toronto's *Financial Post.* He continued to work part-time as chairman. His successor as CEO was Jacques Lamarre, brother of former Lavalin CEO Bernard Lamarre.

SNC-Lavalin acquired Kilborn Holdings Inc. in 1996. Based in Toronto, Kilborn dated back to 1947 and specialized in engineering for uranium and potash mining projects. It employed 1,200 people and had annual sales of C$125 million.

In the 1990s, SNC-Lavalin partnered with Bombardier, Inc., the new owner of the UTDC division, to develop transportation projects in Mayalsia (Kuala Lumpur) and Turkey (Ankara) based on the automated SkyTrain system that had proven successful in Vancouver.

The company bought a 27 percent share in Ontario's Highway 407 toll road in 1999 for C$175 million. Part of this was sold off in 2002 at a substantial profit. Other bright spots for 2002 included signing C$1 billion in thermal power-related contracts in the United States.

Still Acquisitive After 2000

SNC-Lavalin bought GDS Engineers, Inc., of Texas, a petrochemical industry specialist, in early 2003. In 2003 and 2004, the group bolstered its operations in France through a number of diversified acquisitions (Trouvin S.A.S., Fimatec, Chovet Engineering S.A., Sogequip Groupe S.A.S.).

Key Dates:

1911: Arthur Surveyer forms a precursor to SNC-Lavalin Group.

1936: Jean-Paul Lalonde and Romeo Valois of Montreal form Lavalin.

1937: Emil Nenniger and Georges Chênevert become Surveyer's partners.

1963: SNC completes its first international project, India's Idukki power station.

1967: SNC becomes part of a new Canatom nuclear engineering consortium.

1986: SNC goes public.

1991: SNC Group Inc. acquires Lavalin Inc.

2004: SNC takes full ownership of Canatom.

In 2003, SNC-Lavalin's revenues were more than C$3.3 billion ($2.5 billion); two-thirds was from outside Canada. Net income was C$86.5 million ($66.8 million). The company had 10,500 employees. In 2004, sales rose to C$3.5 billion ($2.9 billion), 56 percent from outside Canada, as net income reached C$104 million ($87.8 million).

In 2004, SNC-Lavalin bought out its partner in the Canatom NPM Inc. nuclear engineering venture, which dated back to 1967. SNC-Lavalin continued to look abroad for growth opportunities. In 2005, the company acquired engineering and construction firm RJ Associates (Engineers) Pvt. Ltd. of Mumbai, India.

Principal Subsidiaries

BAE-Newplan Group Ltd.; Boplan Ingénierie S.A.S. (France); Canatom NPM Inc.; Chovet Engineering S.A. (France); The Equinox Indemnity Co. Ltd. (Bermuda); Eurotec S.A.S. (France); EXPRO Technologies Inc.; International Cleanroom Control and Engineering (ICCE) s.a./n.v. (Belgium); Lalonde, Girouard, Letendre & Associates Inc.; Nexacor Realty Management Inc.; Pacific Liaicon and Associates Inc.; Pellemon Inc.; Piette, Audy, Bertrand, Lemieux & Associates Inc.; Pingat Ingénierie S.A.S. (France); Polygec Inc.; Procean Environment Inc.; SNC Italia S.p.A.; P.T. SNC-Lavalin TPS (Indonesia); S.A. Coppée-Courtoy N.V. (Belgium); S.A. SNC-Lavalin Europe N.V. (Belgium); SLIVIA Inc. (60%); SNC-Lavalin America Inc. (United States); SNC-Lavalin ATP Inc.; SNC-Lavalin Australia Pty. Ltd.; SNC-Lavalin do Brasil Ltda; SNC-Lavalin Capital Inc.; SNC-Lavalin Chile S.A.; SNC-Lavalin Constructors Inc. (United States); SNC-Lavalin Defence Programs Inc.; SNC-Lavalin Dominican Republic S.A.; SNC-Lavalin Energy Control Systems Inc.; SNC-Lavalin Engineers & Constructors Inc.; SNC-Lavalin Environment Inc.; SNC-Lavalin Europe B.V. (Netherlands); SNC-Lavalin France S.A.S.; SNC-Lavalin GDS, Inc. (United States); SNC-Lavalin Inc.; SNC-Lavalin (S.A.) Inc.; SNC-Lavalin International Inc.; SNC-Lavalin International (Tunisia) Inc.; SNC-Lavalin Maghreb EURL (Algeria); SNC-Lavalin (Malaysia) Sdn. Bhd.; SNC-Lavalin Mühendislik VE Taahhüt Limited Sirketi (Turkey); SNC-Lavalin Peru S.A.; SNC-Lavalin Pharma Inc.; SNC-Lavalin Polska Sp. z.o.o. (Poland); SNC-Lavalin Power Ontario Inc.;

SNC-Lavalin Profac Inc.; SNC-Lavalin Services Ltd.; SNC-Lavalin South Africa (Proprietary) Limited; SNC-Lavalin UK Ltd.; SNC Technologies Corporation (United States); SNC Technologies Inc.; Socodec Inc.; Socodec Venezuela C.A.; Sogequip Groupe S.A.S. (France); Trouvin S.A.S. (France).

Principal Divisions

Infrastructure; Mining and Metallurgy; Power; Defense; Facilities and Operations Management; Investments; Other Segments; International Network.

Principal Competitors

Bechtel Group Inc.; Fluor Corporation; Jacobs Engineering Group; Technip.

Further Reading

Allard, Carole-Marie, *Lavalin: Les Ficelles du Pouvoir* (The Strings of Power), Saguenay, Quebec, Canada: Editions JCL, 1990.

Crocker, Janet, ''The Stuff That Dreams Are Made Of: Dagenais Engineered Small Partnership Into International Corporation,'' *Financial Post* (Toronto), March 21, 1988, Sec. 4, p. 46.

Dougherty, Kevin, ''A CEO with a Vision,'' *Financial Post* (Toronto), July 2, 1994, pp. S12f.

——, ''Canada's No. 1 Engineer: Guy Saint-Pierre Must Meld the Two Cultures Of Giant SNC-Lavalin,'' *Financial Post* (Toronto), August 19, 1991, Sec. 2, p. 16.

——, ''Lavalin's Powerful Friends: Troubled Firm Still Using Its Connections,'' *Financial Post* (Toronto), August 12, 1991, p. 2.

——, ''Network Pays for Giant Engineer: Lavalin Out to Build Global Power Base,'' *Financial Post* (Toronto), August 8, 1988, p. 1.

——, ''SNC-Lavalin Eyes Growth in Europe,'' *Financial Post* (Toronto), August 14, 1991, p. 3.

''Engineering Giant Buys Mining Specialist,'' *Plant*, February 12, 1996, p. 5.

Fraser, Matthew, ''Homme qui a créé Lavalin: à la tête d'une des plus importantes firmes d'ingénierie au monde, Bernard Lamarre est le symbole même de la réussite,'' *Sélection Du Reader's Digest*, August 1988, pp. 79–82.

French, Carey, ''Diversification Makes SNC More Attractive,'' *Globe and Mail*, January 5, 1987, p. B8.

Grant, Michael, ''Building Bridges at Home and Abroad (SNC Group Ex-Chairman Camille A. Dagenais),'' *Canadian Business Review*, Winter 1991, pp. 5ff.

Horsman, Mathew, ''Manufacturing Thrust to Boost Lavalin Exports,'' *Financial Post* (Toronto), October 4, 1986, Sec. 4, p. 32.

''Lavalin's Long March to Greatness,'' *Maclean's*, October 20, 1986, p. 49.

Leger, Kathryn, ''Saint-Pierre Bows Out at SNC,'' *Financial Post* (Toronto), March 12, 1996, p. 7.

Mollins, Carl, ''Bernard Lamarre: Persistence in Pursuit of Success,'' *Maclean's*, December 29, 1986, pp. 46f.

Newman, Peter C., ''Requiem for a Corporate Heavyweight,'' *Maclean's*, August 26, 1991, p. 38.

Pepin, Laurent, ''Retour de Bernard Lamarre: l'ancien president de Lavalin refait lentement surface apres une eclipse de presque deux ans,'' *Revue Commerce*, April 1993, pp. 75–76.

Simon, Bernard, ''Lavalin Builds on Francophone Base; Quebec's Engineering Consultants Are Expanding Abroad,'' *Financial Times* (London), June 19, 1984, p. 30.

Steed, Judy, ''Moving the World: Canada's Cities Lag Behind in Deploying Transit Technologies Developed Here; Yet Canadian Firms Are Top Global Players in a Growing, Fiercely Competitive Field,'' *Toronto Star*, March 24, 2003, p. D1.

Tomesco, Frédéric, "SNC après Lavalin," *Revue Commerce*, December 1991, pp. 60–62.

"The Total Solution Approach," *Infrastructure Finance*, September 1, 1997, p. 8.

Wallace, Bruce, " 'On Their Knees': Lavalin Succumbs to a Longtime Rival," *Maclean's*, August 26, 1991, pp. 36f.

Watson, Thomas, "All-Star Execs: Jacque Lamarre," *Canadian Business*, April 28, 2003, p. 28ff.

Weinberg, Stuart, "SNC-Lavalin Stands Firm On Munition Sales: U.S. Army Contract: Protesters Outside Annual Meeting Demand Changes," *National Post's Financial Post & FP Investing*, May 6, 2005, p. FP7.

Wilson-Smith, Anthony, "Conquering the Big-Steel World," *Maclean's*, June 30, 1986, p.32.

—Frederick C. Ingram

Spinnaker Exploration Company

1200 Smith Street, Suite 800
Houston, Texas 77002
U.S.A.
Telephone: (713) 759-1770
Fax: (713) 759-1773
Web site: http://www.spinnakerexploration.com

Public Company
Incorporated: 1996 as Spinnaker Exploration Company, L.L.C.
Employees: 78
Sales: $272.9 million (2004)
Stock Exchanges: New York
Ticker Symbol: SKE
NAIC: 211111 Crude Petroleum and Natural Gas Extraction

Spinnaker Exploration Company is a Houston, Texas-based natural gas and oil exploration company operating in the Gulf of Mexico. Although most of its success has come from drilling in shallow waters, the company has become increasingly involved in riskier, but potentially more rewarding, deepwater plays. Unlike most of its competition, Spinnaker eschews growth through acquisitions, preferring instead to keep a clean balance sheet and rely on its technical expertise to grow through the drill bit. The company has a massive 3-D seismic database of the Gulf of Mexico, one suitable for a business far larger in size, which has created a competitive advantage for Spinnaker. With a large-scale view of the region, Spinnaker's researchers are able to detect geographic trends that allow them to pinpoint likely deposits of natural gas and oil. Armed with this knowledge, the company is able to intelligently bid on available leases and then drill successful wells. From its start in late 1996 until early March 2005, the company has drilled 104 successful wells out of 176 attempts. As a result, Spinnaker boasts proved reserves of 332.6 billion cubic feet equivalent (Bcfe) of natural gas. The company is publicly traded on the New York Stock Exchange.

Exploration Company Turned Around in the 1980s

After earning a petroleum engineering degree, Spinnaker's future chairman, president, and CEO, Roger L. Jarvis, gained chief executive officer experience at King Ranch Inc., the famous cattle ranch that over the years became involved in a number of businesses, including oil. Jarvis was hired in 1987 to head King Ranch Oil & Gas Co. but was soon tapped to head the parent company as president and CEO, posts he held until 1995 when King Ranch underwent another management upheaval. Jarvis was responsible for expanding King Ranch's activities in the Gulf of Mexico. After taking off a year, Jarvis decided to return to the oil and gas business and once again he looked to the Gulf, a play that many in the exploration business had dismissed. "Not long ago it was known as the 'Dead Sea'—the continental shelf in the Gulf of Mexico that juts out 200 nautical miles," explained *Forbes* in a 2001 company profile. "The Department of Energy had predicted the Gulf would be drilled dry of natural gas by 1985. Didn't happen: The region still supplies 24% of U.S. natural gas production. Then, in the mid-1990s, Exxon, Mobil, Royal Dutch/Shell and BP all pulled up their shallow-water stakes and paddled out to the oil-rich deep end."

It was this opening in the shallow waters of the Gulf that Jarvis targeted for his new company. For a name he wanted something nautical, latching onto "spinnaker," the large billowing sail used by a ship running ahead of the wind. "A spinnaker creates great speed, is colorful and easily recognized, and all of these aspects are consistent with our company," Jarvis explained in 2002 to *Rigamarole,* a magazine published by vendor Diamond Offshore Drilling, Inc. "We have the ability to move fast when necessary, we have a niche and we are unique." After incorporating Spinnaker as a limited liability partnership in December 1996, Jarvis lined up funding and, more importantly, the data he would need to successfully compete in the mature Gulf of Mexico. First, he arranged for $60 million in private equity funds from New York's giant venture capital firm, Warburg, Pincus & Co. LLC. Another investor was Petroleum GeoServices ASA (PGS), a $1 billion Norwegian global oilfield service company. In addition, through Diamond Geophysical Service Corp., PGS licensed to Spinnaker 3D seismic data on 1,400 blocks in the Gulf of Mexico blocks, giving the company one of the largest databases of anyone operating in the Gulf and providing the kind of advantage Jarvis felt was necessary before embarking on a drilling program. PGS also promised to provide Spinnaker with all new data it gathered for the next five years on a nonexclusive basis.

Company Perspectives:

Spinnaker's goals are to expand its reserve base, increase cash flow and net income and to generate an attractive return on capital.

Jarvis told *Oil & Gas Investor* in 2000 that central to Spinnaker's strategy was "the belief that an exploration company must have a very large pool of prospect opportunities on its plate relative to its projected activity. . . . Put more bluntly, it's been shown time and time again that when too much money chases too few good ideas, the outcome isn't favorable." Using the PGS seismic data, Spinnaker began creating a large pool of drilling prospects, which were then graded to select the best possible candidates. *Forbes* detailed the work of the company's geoscientists in a 2001 article: "They're looking at seismic data illuminating the porous gas-trapping geologic formations under the seabed. Deciding where to drill is a constant tradeoff between anticipated reserves and risk factors—from sand quality to vertical stresses on the rock. Those risks are assigned numerical values and measured against the probability of finding natural gas deposits."

First Successful Well Dug in 1997

Starting in March 1997, Spinnaker began participating in federal offshore lease sales, and also landed partnership and farm-in arrangements, to gain interests in targeted Gulf of Mexico blocks. The company drilled its first successful well later in 1997 and began generating revenues, more than $200,000 for the year. The focus at first was on the shallow waters, but even at this stage management was beginning to look at the deep water plays of the Gulf and developing a long-term goal of creating a balance between shallow and deep water properties, a combination that promised both stable growth and a high rate of return. The shallow water wells quickly generated cash flow, while the deep water projects, though more costly and time-consuming to develop, offered a greater potential return. Whether deep water or shallow, however, Spinnaker pursued big fields, an approach that avoided the problematic combination of high start-up costs and a quickly depleted field. Although not part of the plan, the big field focus would make Spinnaker the lowest-cost operator in the Gulf. By taking a portfolio approach, the company was also able to avoid the pitfall of many an independent who hyped a particular well and became perceived in the market as a one-trick pony. Furthermore, Spinnaker developed a sophisticated hedging program to make sure of steady, predictable cash flow.

In 1998 and 1999, Spinnaker continued to build on its early success. Sales increased to $3.3 million in 1998 and the company started out strong in 1999, on its way to recording $34.3 million in revenues (90 percent derived from gas sales), and its first profitable year, netting $1.4 million, this despite drilling five dry holes in a row. Nevertheless, successes far outweighed failures as the company hit on 21 of 30 attempts, an enviable 70 percent success rate. As a result, from the beginning of 1998 to the close of 1999 Spinnaker was able to increase its proved reserves from 13.4 billion Bcfe to 84 Bcfe and increase daily production nine-fold. It also added significantly to its seismic database, procured mostly from PGS.

The company sought to take advantage of its strong growth to tap the public equity market for funds. The company had already reincorporated in Delaware in 1998 as Spinnakers Exploration Corp. and four months later changed its name to Spinnaker Exploration Company in anticipation of going public. However, due to depressed oil and gas prices during this period, market conditions were not suited to energy exploration and production companies attempting to make an initial public offering (IPO). After a 20-month drought for energy IPOs, Spinnaker saw an opportunity when commodity prices rebounded in 1999 and launched its offering in late September of that year, with Credit Suisse First Boston acting as lead underwriter, joined by co-underwriters Donaldson, Lufkin & Jenrette; Nesbitt Burns Securities Inc.; Prudential Securities; and Bank of America Securities LLC. The company hoped to price its shares between $16 and $18 per share, but in the end settled for $14.50, resulting in a net of $108 million. This cash, along with Spinnaker's $85 million bank credit facility, would fund a $115 million drilling budget for 2000. Drawing on its large seismic database, the company did not lack for drilling candidates.

Continued Success and Expansion in the 2000s

In 2000, Spinnaker remained focused on shallow water wells, although it was involved in a supporting role in a pair of deep water plays, including one with Shell Oil Company. However, Jarvis made it clear that the company intended to become a deepwater operator. In the near term, Spinnaker took advantage of market conditions—rising oil and gas prices, coupled with low oil inventories and a natural gas shortage—to enjoy a strong year. The company increased its drilling activity and grew its oil and gas reserves by 75 percent despite increased production. For the year, Spinnaker posted revenues of $121.4 million and net income of $38.6 million. It was also well positioned for even greater growth. Its seismic database now covered 1,400 blocks in the Gulf of Mexico, a 50 percent increase over the previous year, and the company also held interests in 207 Gulf leases, an 80 percent increase over the previous year. As a result, Spinnaker possessed an abundance of solid drilling prospects at a time when such leads were in short supply.

Strong growth continued in 2001 as the company made 19 new discoveries in the Gulf, including four fields in deep water: Front Runner, Front Runner South, Seventeen Hands, and Callisto. Front Runner and Front Runner South looked especially promising, possibly containing 120 million barrels of oil, making them world-class fields. Spinnaker owned a 25 percent interest in the fields, meaning that it might own about 30 million barrels of oil, an especially high number when compared to the 26 million barrels the company possessed in total reserves at the end of 2000. The company also held interests in untested acreage in the area, as well as interests in five other deep water discoveries and a slate of other deep water prospects. It also improved its long-term prospects by submitting winning bids in a pair of auctions of federal offshore and gas drilling leases. In the second auction, covering the Eastern Gulf, held in December 2001, Spinnaker and its partners landed two of the top three prospects.

Natural gas prices were soft in 2001, prompting some independents to step back on production, but debt-free, cash flow-strong Spinnaker viewed the same conditions as an opportunity. A lack of demand for drilling rigs in the Gulf meant that day rates for jack-up drill rigs dropped from $50,000 a day to $15,000. The competition's cutting back on production meant that gas supplies would begin to diminish, leading to a rebound in prices. At the end of 2001, Spinnaker's balance sheet revealed significant improvement over the previous year, with revenues increasing to $210.4 million and net income to $66.3 million.

To all appearances, Spinnaker took a step back in 2002. Its drilling success rate took a hit and the company was unable to locate the major finds that had marked the company's brief existence. Sales dipped to $188.4 million for the year, and net income fell to $31.6 million. On the positive side, however, 2002 demonstrated that Spinnaker's business model was sound, as the company continued to generate a strong return. Moreover, it was making significant progress in building a balanced portfolio between shallow and deepwater projects and gaining greater expertise in deepwater drilling.

High commodity prices were a significant factor in Spinnaker's improved balance sheet in 2003, as revenues rebounded to $226.9 million while net income improved to $36.6 million. Much of the company's money, and management's attention, was devoted to Front Runner and another deepwater play, Zia. The latter commenced production in 2003, and in 2004 the Front Runner field complex began producing as well. High commodity prices continued in 2004, leading to an increase in revenues to $272.9 million and net income to $53.9 million. During 2004, Spinnaker discovered another potentially large field, the Thunder Hawk Field, in which the company held a 25 percent interest. It also looked beyond the Gulf of Mexico for the first time, announcing in early 2005 that it would participate with Devon Energy Corporation to take a 12.5 percent stake in a deepwater play in Nigeria. The deal was the culmination of years of searching around the world for investment opportunities. Spinnaker hoped to transfer the expertise it gained in the Gulf of Mexico to West Africa where it hoped to build a significant business. The year 2005 started out strong, as Spinnaker posted revenues well above the same period the previous year. The company, with its balanced approach, appeared to be well situated to enjoy sustained, long-term growth.

Principal Subsidiaries

WP Spinnaker Holdings, Inc.; Spinnaker Exploration Company, L.L.C.

Principal Competitors

Devon Energy Corporation; The Houston Exploration Company; Pioneer Natural Resources Company.

Further Reading

Antosh, Nelson, "Spinnaker Races Ahead in Gulf in High-Tech Search for Oil, Gas," *Houston Chronicle*, May 20, 2001, p. 16.

Cook, Lynn J., "Rigging the System," *Forbes*, November 26, 2001, p. 205.

——, "Top Shelf," *Forbes*, November 26, 2001, p. 204.

Haines, Leslie, and Rhonda Duey, "The Deep Shelf," *Oil & Gas Investor*, May 2003, p. 24.

Much, Marilyn, "Houston, Texas Oil Company Prepares for Demand Onslaught," *Investor's Business Daily*, August 28, 2000, p. A12.

Perin, Monica, "Spinnaker Exploration Launches $115 Million Public Offering Bid," *Houston Business Journal*, July 23, 1999, p. 7.

Toal, Brian A., "Setting Sail," *Oil & Gas Investor*, February 2000, p. 40.

Wetuski, Jodi, "Small Companies. Big Plans," *Oil & Gas Investor*, December 2000, p. 70.

—Ed Dinger

Stein Mart Inc.

1200 Riverplace Boulevard
Jacksonville, Florida 32207
U.S.A.
Telephone: (904) 346-1500
Fax: (904) 398-4341
Web site: http://www.steinmart.com

Public Company
Incorporated: 1968
Employees: 14,000
Sales: $1.45 billion (2004)
Stock Exchanges: NASDAQ
Ticker Symbol: SMRT
NAIC: 448140 Family Clothing Stores; 448150 Clothing
    Accessories Stores; 442299 All Other Home
    Furnishings Stores

Stein Mart Inc. is an ''off-pricer,'' a leading retail chain which sells upscale merchandise at 25 to 60 percent off of department store prices. Founded in 1902 in Greenville, Mississippi, as a general merchandise department store, it later developed into a discount store which purchased cancellations and overproductions from clothing mills. Stein Mart found increased success beginning in 1977 after opening up branches in Memphis and Nashville and rapidly increased its number of branches since 1984 to a current total of 261 stores, which garnered sales in 2004 of $1.45 billion. Stein Mart stores offer quality merchandise at discounted prices in a department store atmosphere in 30 states across the United States.

Origins

Stein Mart was founded by Sam Stein, a Russian immigrant who opened his first store in Greenville, Mississippi, in 1902. Under Stein, the store remained a general merchandise department store, providing basic goods to the residents of Greenville. Upon his death in 1932, Stein's son Jake took over the store and redirected its focus toward discounted clothing. Jay Stein (Jake's son and chairman of the company in 2005) later recalled that his father ''thought that to be a successful merchant, you had to do something special—either have a wider selection, or the prettiest store, or the cheapest price.'' Jake Stein's specialty would become men's and women's apparel at low prices.

A focus on discounted clothing was certainly timely as the country was at the height of the Great Depression of the 1930s. The original Stein Mart department store withstood the Depression and enjoyed moderate success during the postwar period, when a return to full employment increased the purchasing power of consumers.

In fact, the period from 1948 to 1962 has been called the ''retail revolution.'' During this time, retail rapidly expanded due to technological innovations and the growth of the middle class. The resulting marketplace was highly competitive, forcing institutions to innovate or fade away. A key development during this time was the growth of discount merchandising, such as that practiced by Stein Mart. The concept had been established in the 1930s with the advent of supermarkets whose inexpensive locations, increased hours of operation, and advertising resulted in low margins. In the late 1940s, discounting increased in popularity as consumers' distress over rising prices caused them to seek out bargains. In addition, consumer confidence in the quality of goods had increased thanks to advertising. Also, while incomes rose in the postwar boom, consumers resisted paying higher prices caused by inflation.

By purchasing cancellations and overproductions from clothing manufacturers, many of which were also located in the South, Jake Stein was able to offer quality merchandise to his customers at a price they were able to afford. Stein achieved moderate success with this somewhat revolutionary concept, which rose in popularity throughout the country. However, the company remained a one-store operation in Greenville until Jay Stein took over operations in 1977 and began to pursue a plan of expansion.

Expansion Begins in the Late 1970s

While traditional department stores serve as anchors in shopping malls and offer moderate to upscale merchandise at full price, discount clothiers generally offer brand-name merchandise in an informal atmosphere. Following the end of the Korean War, the production of retail goods began to meet or

---

exceed consumer demand, resulting in a buyer's market. While yielding lower margins per item than department stores, discount retailers made up the difference by selling large quantities of merchandise rapidly.

Stein Mart straddled both concepts by offering customers the same ambience as a regular department store with discounted prices. In doing so, it helped to define "off-pricers" as a new category in retail. Stein Mart targeted customers who shopped department stores on a regular basis, inducing them to purchase Stein Mart goods by offering discounts of 25 to 60 percent off of department store prices. By the late 1970s, Stein Mart was the leading retailer of clothing for the family in the Mississippi Delta.

When Stein Mart expanded its original Greenville store during this time, several affluent women from the Greenville area offered to act as sales assistants during the store's liquidation sale of some designer clothing. At that time, Jay Stein noticed the women, "boutique ladies" as they came to be known, were able to provide an extraordinary level of service; they were knowledgeable on these more expensive brands given their own purchasing power and sophisticated taste.

Thus, when Stein Mart expanded into Memphis in 1977, Stein and his wife developed a designer boutique within the store and sought out local shopping mavens to operate it. Stein was quoted in American Demographics as saying, "The boutique ladies are our secret weapon." This practice would continue as a unique part of Stein Mart's strategy. Boutique ladies would consult with in-store clothing buyers to stock stores and ensure that Stein Mart kept abreast of trends. These women also tipped off friends and acquaintances when key new shipments arrived, ensuring that the merchandise would sell quickly.

Furthermore, when entering a new location, Stein Mart sought references for possible "boutique ladies" from its ranks in other areas. The position became a status symbol in some Stein Mart locations, placing interested local women on waiting lists. In addition to the boutique ladies, Stein Mart stores also employed personal shoppers, referred to by the company as "agenda consultants."

Under Jay Stein, Stein Mart pursued a steady expansion program, growing from three stores in 1977 to 40 stores in 1990

and to 123 stores by the end of 1996. The chain first tackled new markets in the Southeast, establishing stores in Alabama, Georgia, Louisiana, and Texas. Later, Stein Marts began cropping up in the Midwest, with stores in Indiana, Ohio, and Missouri. In determining the prime locations for new Stein Mart stores, management targeted cities with populations of 125,000 or more and relied on demographic research regarding income, education, and occupation to help predict whether a community might support a discounter of designer merchandise.

In the 1990s, Stein Marts generally served as anchor stores in neighborhood shopping centers. To enhance its image as an upscale clothier, Stein Mart initiated several marketing concepts, including store ambience, quality merchandise, and its "boutique ladies." A typical Stein Mart store averaged approximately 38,000 square feet in size. Plush carpeting, marble flooring, soft lighting, and handsome furnishings all contributed to its department store ambience. Stein Mart also limited in-store "sale" signage and used discreet price tags to reduce any trace of the "discount store" appearance. Similarly, while Stein Mart kept costs in check through a centralized checkout system, it did not provide shopping carts. Another marketing tactic of Stein Mart was that their stores displayed merchandise in "lifestyle groupings," such as activewear and career apparel, rather than the traditional size/age departments, believing this encouraged customers to make multiple purchases.

The Stein Mart store of the 1990s carried brand name merchandise, including apparel, accessories, hosiery, costume jewelry, glassware, dishes, and cookware. While stores did carry private label merchandise to ensure selection, inventory was focused on designer apparel at discounted prices. Beginning in 1995, Stein Mart leased its shoe and fragrance departments to independent operators in order to provide customers with full-service without taking on additional stock.

The company relied on the efficient handling of inventory through drop shipments to each store rather than incurring the expenses of maintaining a distribution or warehouse center. Moreover, Stein Mart kept advertising costs low by relying primarily on limited print media ads and word-of-mouth to build a customer base. Unlike traditional discounters, who generally responded to unplanned buying opportunities of overstocked or returned merchandise, Stein Mart buyers simply waited about one month later than traditional department stores in order to negotiate lower prices from manufacturers, while still retaining access to a majority of that manufacturer's product line, ensuring that their selections would be timely and fashionable.

Stein Mart went public on NASDAQ in April 1992, and the company's stock doubled in value within 16 months. In the 1990s, Stein Mart stock proved to be a good investment, with some fluctuations reflecting general trends in the retail industry. Stein Mart appeared to have been successful in pursuing investors. As of early 1997, company stock was cited as a good purchase by several brokers and received flattering coverage in a number of investor publications.

Stein Mart's Future

According to Stein Mart's early 1997 10K report, the company planned to open between 26 and 28 stores in 1997, some in

Key Dates:

1902: Stein Mart is founded by Sam Stein, a Russian immigrant who opens his first store in Greenville, Mississippi.
1977: Jay Stein takes over operations and begins to pursue a plan of expansion; the ''boutique lady'' concept is born.
1990: The company's store count grows to 40 locations.
1992: Stein Mart goes public.
2003: Michael D. Fisher is named president and CEO.
2005: Stein Mart operates over 260 stores.

states new to the company, such as California, Nevada, Iowa, and Wisconsin. After 75 years of existence as a single store, Stein Mart's accelerated growth between 1977 and the 1997 could only be regarded as phenomenal. By creating a new niche between discount and department stores while funding growth internally and keeping costs down, Stein Mart was extremely successful. With its concept of upscale discounting, Stein Mart hoped to meet an internal goal of 600 stores by the end of the decade according to an article in the *Milwaukee Journal Sentinel*. Given the intense competition and fragmentation in the retail industry, reaching this goal would present a challenge.

Indeed, the company was forced to curtail its aggressive growth strategy during the latter half of the 1990s due to sluggish sales and earnings. Poor merchandising decisions and a slowdown in the retail industry continued to plague the company into the 2000s, forcing Stein Mart to make several strategic changes. Retail executive Gwen Manto was brought in as an executive vice-president in 2000 to revamp the company's merchandising strategy. In 2003, Michael D. Fisher took over as CEO while Manto was named vice-chairman.

A November 2003 *Florida Trend* article commented on activity in the retail industry claiming, ''Before the economic slump began in 2000, Stein Mart did well competing against department stores and pure discounters. But as department stores responded to the slump by slashing their prices, Stein Mart lost some of its pricing edge.'' As a result, Stein Mart faced an incredible amount of competition as shoppers sought out even lower prices. ''The slump drove many shoppers into the arms of pure discounters such as TJ Maxx and Ross Dress for Less,'' the aforementioned article reported, adding that ''even Target, a discounter without the fashion depth of a Stein Mart but with its own sense of flair, is successfully wooing Stein Mart shoppers.''

As a consequence of these factors, Stein Mart's new leadership team faced a tough road ahead. The company thus set out to increase store productivity and profitability. In 2003, Stein Mart shuttered 16 unprofitable locations. It also refocused its advertising and marketing efforts and launched a new television campaign aimed at its target shoppers, women between the ages of 35 and 60 with higher incomes and education levels than average Americans. Stein Mart also put an end to its coupon promotion strategy.

The company's efforts slowly began to pay off. In 2004, sales increased by 8 percent over the previous year while net income reached $38 million, the second-highest amount in company history. Seven new stores opened their doors that year, while seven under-performing stores closed. Plans were in the works to open 15 new stores in 2005.

Stein Mart's strategy for the future included focusing on increasing store productivity while offering new and exciting products. The company would also rely heavily on its marketing program to draw in new and existing customers. With approximately 261 stores in its arsenal, Stein Mart appeared to have overcome the problems it had faced in the early years 2000s. With over 100 years of history under its belt, the company seemed likely to remain a popular name in the retailing industry.

Principal Competitors

Federated Department Stores Inc.; JC Penney Corporation Inc.; The TJX Companies Inc.

Further Reading

Basch, Mark, ''Jacksonville, Fla.-Based Discount Clothing Chain Chooses 'Non-Family CEO,' '' *Florida Times-Union*, July 22, 2002.
——, ''Stein Mart Expects to Keep Growing,'' *Florida Times-Union*, May 19, 1998, p. B4.
——, ''Stein's Goal Is Return to '97 Profits in 2000,'' *Florida Times-Union*, May 18, 1999, p. F6.
Carey, Bill, ''Stein Mart's Growth Impressive,'' *Gannett News Service*, February 10, 1994.
Finotti, John, ''A Tale of Two Retailers,'' *Florida Trend*, November 1, 2003, p. 50.
Griffith, Jill, ''Talk of the Town; Marketing Tools,'' *American Demographics*, October 1, 1995, p. 76.
Hajewski, Doris, ''Stein Mart's Lowbrow Name Misleading,'' *Milwaukee Journal Sentinel*, March 18, 1997, p. 1.
Harrington, Jeff, ''The Stein Mart Saga: A Personal Perspective,'' *St. Petersburg Times*, October 16, 2004, p. 1D.
Lloyd, Brenda ''Stein Mart Takes Fashion/Value Formula on the Road; Florida-Based Retailer Builds 133-Unit Chain in 23 States,'' *Daily News Record*, April 21, 1997, p. 16.
Price, Joliene, '' 'Bou Ladies' Coming to Peachtree City,'' *Atlanta Journal and Constitution*, February 15, 1996, p. 3.

—Karen Troshynski-Thomas
—update: Christina M. Stansell

Stoddard International plc

Riverside Mill
Barbadoes Road
Kilmarnock, East Ayrshire KA1 1SX
United Kingdom
Telephone: (+44) 1563-578-000
Fax: (+44) 1563-578-011
Web site: http://www.stoddard.co.uk

Private Company
Incorporated: 1862; 1895 as A.F. Stoddard & Co.; 1998
　 as Stoddard International
Employees: 585
Sales: £32 million ($56 million) (2003)
NAIC: 314110 Carpet and Rug Mills; 313311 Broad-
　 woven Fabric Finishing Mills; 313312 Textile and
　 Fabric Finishing (except Broadwoven Fabric) Mills

Perhaps more than any other company, Stoddard International plc represents the glory as well as the devastation of the United Kingdom's textiles industry. The country's oldest, and once one of its largest carpet makers, the Elderslie, Scotland-based company entered 2005 with little hope of surviving as a going concern. Founded in 1862, Stoddard has become nearly synonymous with fine British carpets, producing both tufted and axminster carpets for some of the world's most prestigious floors: Stoddard provided the carpets for HRH Princess Elizabeth's wedding in 1947, and the company has produced carpets for the White House, the Scottish Parliament, and, more recently, for the set of the blockbuster movie Titanic. Yet after battling competition for more than 40 years from lower-priced imports, Stoddard has succumbed to the sustained consumer preference for bare and wooden floors at the turn of the 21st century. Despite restructuring its production base—closing two factories, including its former headquarters, and consolidating its manufacturing at a single location in Kilmarnock—Stoddard continued to suffer mounting debt and dwindling sales. By the beginning of 2005, with annual sales dropping to just £30 million (approximately $55 million), Stoddard's debt had climbed to £9 million, while losses reached £100,000 per day.

Placed in receivership in February 2005, the company has entered negotiations with a prospective buyer, although Stoddard was not expected to continue operations as an autonomous company.

Founding the Scottish Carpet Industry in the 1860s

The glory years of the British carpet industry, and its textiles industry in general, began in the early 19th century as the United Kingdom took the lead in the industrial revolution. The invention of the steam engine, which was then linked to the newly invented mechanical looms, permitted the industrial production of carpets for the first time. Previously a luxury affordable only by royalty and the very wealthy, carpets gradually became available to the growing middle class as well.

The 1830s marked an era of accelerated innovation in the British carpet industry. In 1832, for example, a new method for printing and weaving yarn with incorporated designs was invented. That machine was known as the Tapestry Carpet Loom. Scotland, with its access to large quantities of wool, became an important center for the United Kingdom's carpet industry and boasted a number of prominent names in carpet weaving, such as Henry Widnell & Stewart, based in Edinburgh; Templetons, in Kilmarnock; and J&R Ronald, operating a tapestry factory in Elderslie.

Another important U.K. carpet maker, Chenille Axminster, was founded in 1837 by William Quigley and grew into one of the major manufacturers of axminster type carpet in the United Kingdom. Invented in the early 19th century, Axminster—named after the town, which was another major U.K. carpet-making center—automated the process for creating pattern designs during weaving. Quigley's addition to carpet-making technology came through his discovery that he one could steam and press the tufted chenille fabric to make a smooth surface.

A talent for innovation, in conjunction with a need to cut production costs, enabled Great Britain's carpet makers to dominate the industry by the middle of the century. British carpet makers also enjoyed ready and cheap access to raw materials, especially jute, cotton, and wool, which were brought in from the United Kingdom's rapidly expanding colonial empire. Great

Company Perspectives:

In the carpet world, the name Stoddard reigns supreme. With a history and experience stretching back over 160 years, we are now Scotland's oldest and largest carpet company.

Britain emerged as the world center for textile production, particularly in the sector of high-quality carpets. Within the United Kingdom itself, competition among carpet makers was often quite fierce, especially during the many downturns that marked the industry's history.

The reputation of Scottish-made carpets in particular received a boost in the early 1860s with the arrival of Alfred Stoddard. A retired commissions agent, Stoddard arrived in Scotland in 1862 and bought J&R Ronald in Elderslie, which by then had gone bankrupt. Stoddard relaunched the Elderslie plant and reoriented its focus. Using his American connections, Stoddard steered the company toward supplying the export market, especially the fast-growing market in the United States.

By 1875, Stoddard was exporting more than 75 percent of the carpets it made, for the most part to the United States. Joining Stoddard at the company was son-in-law Charles Renshaw, who later took over as head of the company. Under Renshaw, the company began supplying other export markets, especially Australia, New Zealand, and South Africa. In 1895, Renshaw incorporated the company as A.F. Stoddard & Sons, listing it on the London Stock Exchange.

Expansion in the 1960s

In the mid-20th century, Stoddard had gained a reputation as one of the United Kingdom's top producers of high-quality carpets. The company's reputation was cemented in 1947 when it was selected to provide the carpets for HRH Princess Elizabeth's marriage at Westminster Abbey. Stoddard's carpets also became featured in such prominent locations as the White House, Balmoral Hall, and Scottish Parliament.

The development of new carpet-making techniques, such as those that enabled the creation of tufted carpets and broadloom carpets, as well as continuing improvements in mass production techniques, had made carpets more affordable. In the United Kingdom, consumer tastes embraced the comfort of carpeting for the home, and Stoddard's domestic sales grew in consequence. By the end of the 1940s, domestic sales represented more than 40 percent of the group's total sales.

The 1950s, however, marked a challenging period for the company. By then, Stoddard's export focus had shifted to Australia, which became the group's largest market into the early 1950s. However, when Australia implemented new import restrictions in 1952, Stoddard found itself more or less cut off from its primary foreign market.

Into the late 1950s, Stoddard recognized the need to brace itself for the changes associated with Britain's joining the European Common Market. With the lowering of trade barriers among European nations, Britain's carpet industry faced a new round of intensified competition. Stoddard saw expansion as a means of countering the threat. In 1959, the company acquired rival Scottish carpet maker Henry Widnell & Stewart Ltd. The following year, the company built a new tufted mill in order to expand its capacity. That mill was operated as subsidiary Glenvale Carpets Ltd. Through the 1960s, the company acquired a number of other Scottish carpet markets. In 1966, Stoddard received the Royal Warrant.

Stoddard also took advantage of the Common Market to make a move onto the European continent. In 1961, the company formed Bergoss/Stoddard BV., a 50–50 joint venture with the Netherlands' Bergoss Gerbre van der Bergh Koninklijke Fabrieken. The joint venture launched construction of a new tufted mill, and production began in 1962. This continental presence encouraged Stoddard to begin exploring further expansion into the European market.

Struggles in the 1980s

By then, the British textile sector was already beginning its long decline. For more than 100 years, the textile industry had been the country's single largest employer. Even as late as the 1960s, the carpet manufacturing continued to employ more than 1.5 million people. Yet that number was to shrink dramatically over the next decades as cheaper textile products, including carpets, began to flood the United Kingdom from Asian countries and elsewhere.

Stoddard, given its focus on the high-end market, was able to resist the trend toward cheaper imports longer than many of its peers. Indeed, in the 1970s, the company appeared buoyant, instituting a policy of expanding its foreign sales, in part by creating new international subsidiaries in France, Germany, and Australia, among other countries. The difficulties in the textile sector forced the closure of a number of prominent carpet makers, including Chenille Axminister, which failed in 1968 before being bought by Stoddard.

Yet the sluggish economy of that decade, and new rounds of protective tariffs and subsidies in such countries as Australia and the United States, made it difficult for Stoddard to break out. By the beginning of the 1980s, the company had begun cutting back on its foreign operations, shutting down its subsidiaries in France and Germany and restructuring its U.S. operations.

Stoddard's difficulties imposing itself overseas led it to focus its efforts back home. In 1980, the company reached an agreement with Guthrie Corporation to merge their carpet manufacturing operations. The deal involved Stoddard's acquisition of Guthrie's Templeton and Kingmead Carpets subsidiaries in exchange for a 39.4 percent stake in Stoddard.

The newly enlarged company now took its place as the United Kingdom's number two carpet manufacturer, trailing only Carpets International. Yet the merger of the two companies tipped Stoddard into the red by 1981. In response, Stoddard underwent a restructuring, shutting down a spinning mill in Cumnock, a dye house in Glasgow, and consolidating production from the Templeton and Kingsmead sites into its main Elderslie facility.

Continued pressure on the U.K. carpet industry through the 1980s led Stoddard to attempt to diversify its operations in the

Key Dates:

1862: Alfred Stoddard acquires a Scottish tapestry maker, J&R Ronald, and begins producing carpets at Elderslie, primarily for American market.

1895: Son-in-law Charles Renshaw incorporates the company as A.F. Stoddard & Co. and lists it on the London Stock Exchange.

1947: Stoddard provides the carpet for Princess Elizabeth's marriage at Westminster Abbey.

1959: Stoddard acquires Henry Windnell & Stewart.

1966: The company receives the Queen's Royal Warrant.

1970: Chenille Axminster is acquired.

1980: Stoddard acquires Templeton and Kingsmead Carpets from Guthrie Corporation.

1988: Stoddard acquires fabrics and silks maker Sekers and changes its name to Stoddard Sekers International.

1989: The silk operation of Sekers Silks is sold off in a management buyout.

1991: Stoddard acquires the U.K. sales operations of Belgium's Louis de Poortere.

1998: The company sells off Sekers and refocuses on carpets as Stoddard International.

2002: Soddard announces plans to consolidate its manufacturing at its Kilmarnock plant.

2003: The company sells off its Elderslie site.

2005: Stoddard is placed in receivership.

late 1980s. In 1988, the company acquired Sekers, a textiles manufacturer specialized in the production of curtain fabrics and silks, paying £17 million. Following the acquisition, Stoddard changed its name to Stoddard Sekers International.

However, the Sekers deal quickly turned sour for Stoddard, in part because accounting discrepancies had overvalued the company. Hard hit by a rise in silk prices, the company decided to sell off the silk operation in 1989, which was spun off in a management buyout worth £8 million. Instead, the company attempted to shore up its carpeting operations, acquiring the U.K. operations of Belgian carpet producer Louis de Poortere for £950,000 in 1991.

Collapsing in the 2000s

The 1990s spelled the beginning of the end for the British textiles industry. The rapid globalization of production techniques, which saw the development of a new manufacturing model based on outsourcing to third-party producers in low-wage developing markets, made it all but impossible for British textiles manufacturers to compete. In Scotland, the loss of jobs was dramatic. By 1993, just 57,000 textile jobs remained.

The carpet industry faced a still more fundamental concern. The 1990s and early 2000s saw a massive consumer disaffection with carpeting in favor of bare and wooden flooring styles. The rise in popularity in do-it-yourself television programs, which often presented carpets as old fashioned, only made matters worse for the carpeting industry.

Stoddard now found itself doubly vulnerable. As it struggled to maintain carpet sales and profits, its Sekers textiles business slipped into losses. By 1998, with Sekers' losses mounting to £1.5 million, Stoddard decided to exit the fabrics business and refocus on its core carpets production. In that year, the company sold Sekers to Wemyss Fabrics for just £600,000. Stoddard then changed its name to Stoddard International.

The refocusing effort was accompanied by a change in management, with Alan Lawson named CEO in 1998. Lawson and his new management team then launched a restructuring effort, which included streamlining the company's lineup of brands and cutting down on its range of carpets. Lawson also attempted to convince the United Kingdom's 16 remaining carpet manufacturers to group together to create a unified marketing front, similar to that used to boost the Scottish whisky industry. That effort resulted in a controversial advertising campaign featuring model Helle Maested naked on a carpet. The campaign proved successful, however, briefly boosting carpet sales and enabling Stoddard to post a profit in 2001 for the first time in several years. The company also received a boost when it provided the carpets for the blockbuster film *Titanic*.

Nevertheless, the recovery proved short-lived. By 2002, Stoddard's sales were once again sagging. In that year, in an effort to pay down debt and streamline its production, the company announced its intention to shut down two of its production sites, including its Elderslie headquarters, and consolidate production solely at the Kilmarnock site. The sell off of its property was completed in 2003. However, the company, which had hoped to raise as much as £17 million from the sale, was finally forced to settle for just £7 million. With its debt at more than £12 million, the company's finances remained in crisis.

Stoddard losses, which doubled to £6 million at the end of its 2003 year, continued to mount throughout 2004. By the beginning of 2005, the company was reeling under a debt load of £9 million, while its losses were increasing by as much as £100,000 per day. Finally, in January 2005, the company was forced into receivership. The company's receivers, accounting firm Ernst & Young, announced that it intended to find a buyer for the company, and as late as the end of February remained in negotiations with a potential unnamed buyer. By the beginning of March, however, Stoddard's rescue appeared increasingly unlikely. At that point, the Scottish textile industry as a whole had nearly vanished. By 2005, fewer than 20,000 textile workers remained. Stoddard International, after nearly 150 years, remained a symbol of the once-great British textiles industry.

Principal Competitors

Coats Holdings Ltd.; Howrah Mills Company Ltd.; Allied Textile Companies Ltd.; Chapelthorpe plc; Gaskell plc; Sirdar plc; Victoria plc.

Further Reading

Black, David, "Stoddard Future Threadbare," *Scotsman*, January 7, 2005, p. 45.

"Carpet Maker Stoddard International Waiting for Buyer to Muster Finances," *Fibre & Fashion*, February 18, 2005.

Dixon, Guy, "Carpet Maker Lays Down a Survival Plan," *Scotland on Sunday*, May 26, 2002, p. 2.

Dorsey, Kristy, "Stoddard Lays out Strategy for Recovery," *Herald*, August 29, 2003, p. 28.

Koster, Olinka, "End of an Era as Trendy Floors Pull Rug from under Royal Carpet Firm," *Daily Mail*, January 7, 2005, p. 29.

Laing, Allan, "Can a Fitting Future Be Found for Firm That Gave Us the Slab Boys?," *Herald*, January 7, 2005, p. 3.

McConnell, Ian, "Carpet Maker Stoddard's Losses Double," *Herald*, April 30, 2004, p. 31.

Paisley, Jonathan, "Mystery Buyer Bids for Carpet Makers," *Evening Times*, February 1, 2005.

Powell, Robert, "Stoddard Recovers against All the Odds," *Herald*, March 31, 2001, p. 19.

Simpson, Cameron, "Final Collapse for Famous Carpet Firm," *Herald*, February 22, 2005.

Smith, Mark, "Life-Saving Deal Imminent for Carpetmaker," *Herald*, February 1, 2005.

——, "Receiver Has Doubts About Sale of Stoddard as a Going Concern," *Herald*, January 7, 2005, p. 27.

West, Karl, "Troubled Carpet Manufacturer Teeters on the Brink of Collapse," *Herald*, December 24, 2004, p. 18.

Williamson, Mark, "Lifeline for Stoddard as Bank Rolls out Crisis Loan," *Herald*, January 14, 2005.

—M.L. Cohen

Taco Cabana, Inc.

8918 Tesoro Drive, Suite 200
San Antonio, Texas 78217
U.S.A.
Telephone: (210) 804-0990
Fax: (210) 804-1970
Web site: http://www.tacocabana.com

Wholly Owned Subsidiary of Carrols Holdings
Corporation
Incorporated: 1978
Employees: 4,000
Sales: $159.6 million (2000)
NAIC: 722211 Limited-Service Restaurants

Taco Cabana, Inc., operates and franchises 123 restaurants that serve Mexican and Tex-Mex food in Texas, Oklahoma, and New Mexico. Started as a taco stand in 1978, the company pioneered the concept of "patio cafes," which are semi-enclosed patio dining areas decorated in festive Mexican themes. Taco Cabana restaurants serve such items as quesa-dillas, salad entrees, marinated rotisserie chicken (otherwise known as "Chicken Flameante"), traditionally prepared Mexican breakfasts, enchiladas, margaritas, and flame-grilled chicken, beef, pork, or shrimp fajitas served on hot iron skillets. Each year, over 46 million guests in Texas, Oklahoma, and New Mexico are patrons of a Taco Cabana restaurant. Carrols Corporation purchased the chain in January 2001.

Early History

Taco Cabana was founded by Felix Stehling, a businessman who figured prominently in the San Antonio area and owned numerous restaurants and taverns throughout the city. One of his most popular establishments was the Crystal Pistol Bar situated on the corner of Hildebrand and San Pedro avenues. Students from Trinity University frequented the Crystal Pistol Bar on a regular basis; every weekend, and some weekday evenings as well, the place was crowded with people. In fact, the bar was so crowded on certain nights that parking became a major problem. With the convenience and comfort of his cus-tomers in mind, not to mention the growing profits from the bar, Stehling decided to purchase the lot across the street on which sat an abandoned Dairy Queen and turn it into a parking lot.

After he purchased the lot, Stehling took the next natural step. Since the property had previously been used for a restaurant, he would transform part of lot and use it to open a taco stand to feed ravenous students as they left the bar. Anticipating success with his new taco stand, Stehling was overwhelmingly disappointed when he woke up after the first night's business only to find all of the patio furniture stolen. Not knowing what to do, Stehling's first thought was to close the operation and go back to what he knew would work. However, the entrepreneur in him refused to let go of the idea for a taco stand in the parking lot, and soon Stehling came up with a solution to the problem, namely, keeping the place open through the night. This decision would ultimately give rise to Taco Cabana becoming a round-the-clock operation.

Not surprisingly, with Stehling's organizational ability and his talent for implementing all the appropriate operating systems and accounting mechanisms, in addition to his experience in hiring the right personnel and extensive background in restaurant design, Taco Cabana was a rapid success. From its inception, Stehling was committed to purchasing and selling the highest quality food for his customers. Made from fresh meat and produce delivered by vendors to the small restaurant three times per week, the menu was prepared fresh every day. Stehling was convinced that this would significantly set his restaurant apart from other traditional Mexican restaurants and fast food establishments that heavily depended on serving pre-prepared, pre-packaged, and frozen food to maintain their large customer base.

One of the most attractive features of his taco stand was the inexpensive price for every item on the menu. This policy of Stehling's was intentional, since he thought that Taco Cabana could garner a loyal following by pricing its menu lower than for comparable fare sold in sit-down Mexican restaurants where traditionally prepared food was the primary attraction. Home-tested recipes and authentic Mexican cuisine, along with alcoholic beverages such as beer and margaritas, were a hit at their low-selling price.

Soon Stehling came to realize that he was sitting on top of a potential gold mine. He decided therefore to open up a chain of the Taco Cabana restaurants throughout the city of San Antonio. However, Stehling knew that he could not expand without additional help. As a result, he asked two of his brothers to assist him in expanding the business. Brought in as equal partners, the two brothers worked hard to make the Taco Cabana concept successful. Within a short period of time, the brothers' hard work paid off handsomely. Under the direction of the family partnership, Taco Cabana grew to include nine restaurants in and around San Antonio. Just as important, revenues were increasing at a dramatic rate.

Growth and Expansion in the 1980s

Throughout the early 1980s, Taco Cabana continued to provide its customers with fresh food and efficient service. At first, Stehling and his brothers had an informal and close-working relationship, with each of the siblings assuming certain responsibilities related to the business. From one small taco stand, the brothers had built up what was regarded across the city as a highly successful restaurant business. However, as the company grew larger and its revenues increased, the brothers began to express significant differences in their vision for the expanding firm. Most of these disagreements centered on management issues, but as time went on they encompassed other areas of the business. Finally, in 1986, Felix Stehling's two brothers left the company, and the founder of Taco Cabana was once again solely in charge.

The disagreements among the brothers had not hurt Taco Cabana's revenues at all, and Stehling decided that he did not want to wait any longer to expand the firm's operations in a dramatic way. The first step in his expansion plan was to hire a right-hand man who would help him in the endeavor. Stehling found the perfect candidate in Richard Cervera. Cervera had been working as a middle management executive at Fuddruckers, a national restaurant chain based in San Antonio. More importantly, Cervera was a regular customer at Taco Cabana, sometimes eating there six times a week, and had inquired about franchise opportunities at the company. Intrigued with Cervera's passion for Taco Cabana food, as well as impressed with his executive management capabilities, Stehling decided to bring him on board.

Taco Cabana prospered under the dual leadership of Stehling and Cervera. Hired as the executive vice-president in 1987, Cervera was responsible not only for implementing a strategic expansion plan that he and Stehling conceived, but the new manager also had oversight of many of the day-to-day opera-

tions at the firm. By 1990, the company had added a number of new restaurants to its chain and began expanding into neighboring states. For his effort and accomplishments, Cervera was appointed president of the company in 1990 and in this capacity continued to pursue an aggressive expansion policy. A strong supporter of franchising, he made a comprehensive support system available to people who arranged franchise agreements with Taco Cabana. The company was now experiencing explosive growth with a private placement in 1991 and the purchase of four restaurants owned and operated by Sombrero Rosa. Another private placement was made the following year, with the acquisition occurring during the early part of 1992. By the end of that year, the company had gone public with its first stock offering and counted 17 restaurants that were managed and operating under the name Taco Cabana.

Growth and Transition in the 1990s

Taco Cabana's quick growth and success had inspired many imitators, and some of these decorated their restaurants and patio cafes in the same bright pastels as those of Taco Cabana. Stehling and Cervera brought a lawsuit against the most flagrant of the imitators, a restaurant chain based in San Antonio named Two Pesos. In 1992, the Supreme Court decided the case in favor of Taco Cabana and awarded the firm $3.7 million in damages. The lawsuit had severely damaged the financial viability of Two Pesos, and Taco Cabana acquired the firm that had grown to include 30 restaurants in the city of San Antonio and its suburbs.

Having succeeded in protecting its niche in the local restaurant market, Taco Cabana flourished. The acquisitions made during the early 1990s began to pay off enormous dividends in sales and an ever-larger customer base. From 1989 to 1993, sales for the company rose from $29.1 million to $96.9 million. In 1994, sales skyrocketed to $127 million. There was no doubt that Cervera had done his job well, and, assured that the company was in good hands, Stehling resigned as chairman of the company in 1994. Succeeded by Cervera, there was no interruption in the operations of the firm.

In spite of increasing revenues and expanding operations, however, Taco Cabana's stock price had dropped rather precipitously. Stockholders blamed Cervera for the nose-dive in stock prices, and there was mounting pressure for him to be replaced. In 1995, Cervera resigned from his position at Taco Cabana and became the new president of the House of Blues restaurant chain. He was replaced by Stephen Clark, who was appointed both chief operating officer and president in the same year.

Prior to his work with Taco Cabana, Clark had worked over 18 years for Church's Fried Chicken, Inc., rising in the company to senior vice-president and concept general manager. His responsibilities included oversight of the company's day-to-day operations for nearly 1,100 firm-owned and franchised restaurants with a sales volume of $600 million. Upon his appointment, Clark immediately began a comprehensive review of the firm's operations, scrutinizing its expansion strategy, marketing plans, and relations with franchisees, as well as analyzing in detail the sales and profitability trends within its network of restaurants.

The review did not take much time, and the consequences for Taco Cabana's operations were far-reaching. Clark decided

Key Dates:

1978: Felix Stehling opens the first Taco Cabana.
1987: Richard Cervera joins the company.
1992: Taco Cabana goes public.
1994: Sales skyrocket to $127 million.
1995: Stephen Clark is named president and chief operating officer.
2001: Carrols Corporation purchases Taco Cabana.

to close a number of the company's restaurants, restructure some of the franchisee debts, bring in his own management team, get rid of many non-restaurant related assets, revamp the firm's marketing strategy, and, most importantly, slow down all current plans for expansion, including the opening of new restaurants and the extension of any further franchise agreements. The overall plan was to streamline the company's operations, introduce economies of scale, and implement accounting systems and management standards which would enable Taco Cabana to continue growing in the most cost-efficient way.

Perhaps the best example of Clark's strategy to improve Taco Cabana's position within its market was his concern with the layout of the company's restaurants. Near the end of 1996, under Clark's direction, Taco Cabana opened up a new type of restaurant in Dallas to test non-traditional market locations and prototypes for smaller, community-based units. Incorporating new designs and features that set it apart from the usual design of a Taco Cabana restaurant, the prototype unit in Dallas featured a rounded front, clay tile roof, a trellis shading the patio area, and aged wood paneling and distressed stainless steel counter tops that gave the customer the impression of walking into an old Mexican café. One of the most important additions to this prototype design was a neon sign on the exterior of the building to advertise the Taco Cabana menu. Designs kept from the original Taco Cabana restaurants included the bright pink signature paint used generously throughout the restaurant, an open cooking area where patrons could see their food being prepared, and retractable garage doors so that the dining area could be opened to the outside during good weather.

Clark's strategy worked well. The newly designed prototype attracted more customers than expected, and plans for a series of these new designs to be built in Texas were underway in the late 1990s. The implementation of a new vision and mission statement, the writing of the company's first business plan, and the installation of new operating principles for managers and employees at all the company's restaurants had tangible results. While growth slowed, more cost-effective financial systems improved employee accountability and profit margins, and a more streamlined administrative and management system garnered a more effective operating structure.

With the dramatic growth of Taco Cabana brought under control by Clark's leadership, the restaurant appeared to be poised for steady growth and increased profits. The company planned for such growth to be measured and calculated, so that construction costs were minimized, customer service was enhanced, operational efficiency was improved, and the image of Taco Cabana as a unique type of Mexican restaurant would be assured.

Changes in the Late 1990s and Beyond

Clark's strategy continued to pay off in the late 1990s. With sales and income back on track, Taco Cabana once again began to expand outside of Texas. New restaurants were opened in Tulsa and Oklahoma City, Oklahoma, as well as in Phoenix, Arizona. These stores were 500 square feet smaller than most Taco Cabana locations and included a covered patio instead of the trademark open air concept. Clark commented on the new store design and expansion strategy in an April 1999 *Nation's Restaurant News* article. "Going outside of Texas with the new units, we realized we were going to have to drive more business in the lunch and dinner dayparts. We don't know if we'll have has much success with the Mexican-style breakfast, which is a big part of our sales in Texas." He went on to state, "We wanted to increase the capacity in the lunch and dinner dayparts, so we've gone to the covered patio with a lot of fans and heaters. It gives us a lot more use of those 45 seats in either cold or hot weather."

By 2000, Taco Cabana had spent nearly $30 million upgrading and revamping its image. While the company recorded its 11th consecutive quarter of positive comparable sales, its stock price nevertheless remained stagnant. Consequently, Clark and his management team began to consider Taco Cabana's options. Carrols Corp., one of the largest Burger King franchisees and owner of Pollo Tropical, agreed to acquire the company for just over $152 million in late 2000. At the time of the deal, Carrols was eager to expand geographically as well as enter into new market segments. Taco Cabana was a good fit, and Carrols expected the chain to fuel its growth over the next several years. The acquisition was completed in early 2001. Clark left the company shortly thereafter.

Under new ownership, Taco Cabana continued to thrive. It introduced a new Mexican Grill concept in 2001 that included made-to-order, fresh-grilled chicken, pork, beef, and shrimp. While the chain was forced to close seven stores in the Phoenix area in 2002, its sales contributed to a 41 percent revenue gain for its parent company. In order to remain competitive in the fast casual segment of the restaurant industry, Taco Cabana began to develop a new store prototype in 2003 that would feature eight-foot char-grills in the restaurants. The company also began to place a stronger emphasis on its premium menu items.

During 2005, Taco Cabana operated over 120 locations. Indeed, the company had come a long way from its roots as a taco stand in San Antonio. Its success in the 1990s and the early 2000s left it well positioned for future growth. With the backing of its parent company, Taco Cabana would no doubt continue to serve its guests Mexican fare for years to come.

Principal Competitors

Consolidated Restaurant Operations Inc.; Taco Bell Corp.; Taco Bueno Restaurants L.P.

Further Reading

"Carrols Finishes $153M Taco Cabana Buyout," *Nation's Restaurant News*, January 8, 2001.
"Carrols Posts '01 Loss After Unit-Closing Charges Slices Net," *Nation's Restaurant News*, March 18, 2002.

Frumpkin, Paul, and Richard L. Papieruik, "Carrols Corp. Spices Up Holdings with $152M Taco Cabana Buy," *Nation's Restaurant News*, October 16, 2000.

Liddle, Alan, "Chains Traveling Different Roads to Interactive Nirvana," *Nation's Restaurant News*, January 13, 1997, p. 21.

"Marketing Miscellaneous," *Nation's Restaurant News*, November 27, 1995, p. 14.

McLaughlin, John, "Growth Chains Are Missing the Mark on Expansion," *Restaurant Business*, March 20, 1995, p. 14.

Opdyke, Jeff D., "Taco Cabana Has New Hope for Old Ideas," *Wall Street Journal*, May 6, 1998.

Robertiello, Jack, "H-E-B to Test Whether In-Store Taco Cabanas Will Be Hot," *Supermarket News*, November 18, 1996, p. 21.

Ruggless, Ron, "Taco Cabana Expands, Opens Prototype Unit in Dallas Suburb," *Nation's Restaurant News*, January 6, 1997, p. 7.

——, "Taco Cabana Unveils New Look, Eyes Expansion," *Nation's Restaurant News*, April 19, 1999.

——, "Taco Closes Doors in Colorado, Turns Focus to Core Markets," *Nation's Restaurant News*, December 1, 1997, p. 3.

"Taco Cabana Eyes New Design," *Restaurant Business*, May 1, 2003, p. 16.

"Taco Cabana, Inc.," *Wall Street Journal*, August 19, 1997, p. B9(E).

"Taco Cabana Sets Buyback," *Wall Street Journal*, April 17, 1997, p. A10(E).

"Taco Cabana Opens New Test Concept," *Journal Record*, September 13, 2001.

—Thomas Derdak
—update: Christina M. Stansell

Tiger Aspect Productions Ltd.

7 Soho Street
London W1D 3DQ
United Kingdom
Telephone: +44 20 7434 6700
Fax: +44 20 7434 1798
Web site: http://www.tigeraspect.co.uk

Private Company
Incorporated: 1988 as Tiger Productions
Employees: 79
Sales: $59.7 million (2003)
NAIC: 512110 Motion Picture, Video Tape Production

Tiger Aspect Productions Ltd. is one of the United Kingdom's most successful independent television and film production houses. The company is notably behind such international successes as *Mr. Bean,* the hit television series starring actor and company shareholder Rowan Atkinson, and *Billy Elliot,* which claims the number two spot in international box office sales among all British-produced films. Other Tiger Aspect television productions include the highly popular *Lenny Henry Show,* drama series *Teachers, Gimme Gimme Gimme, A Place in France,* and *DoubleTake.* The company has capitalized on the success of *Mr. Bean* with a full-length feature film, *Bean— The Ultimate Disaster Movie,* and through the creation of a hit animated series featuring the otherworldly character. Tiger Aspect's operations include a dedicated film-making unit, Tiger Pictures, created in 1999, which, in addition to *Billy Elliot* has produced British film hits such as *Kevin & Perry Go Large* and *Dog Eat Dog.* The company's Tigress Productions unit is a producer of nature, wildlife, scientific, and adventure documentaries, including the hit celebrity vehicle *In the Wild* and the *Africa* series produced in conjunction with National Geographic and PBS. Tiger Aspect also has produced a number of award-winning television commercials, including a long-running series of spots for Barclaycard. The company's international success had led it to enter the United States. In 2005, for example, the company's projects included production partnerships with NBC Universal, MTV, and Disney Playhouse. Tiger Aspect is led by founder and Chairman Peter Bennett-Jones, who also operates two talent agencies (many of Bennett-Jones's clients appear regularly in Tiger Aspect's productions). A private company, Tiger Aspect generates revenues of more than £59 million ($110 million).

Productive Friendship in the 1980s

Peter Bennett-Jones began his relationship with theatrical production while studying law at Cambridge University in the mid-1970s. Bennett-Jones's interest in theater led him to become the president of both of the university's primary drama groups. While still in school Bennett-Jones began touring with Footlights, and acted at the prestigious Edinburgh Festival as well. It was during this time that Bennett-Jones began forming relationships with many of the country's up-and-coming British performers, especially Rowan Atkinson.

Upon graduation, Bennett-Jones launched an active career, managing theater productions in the United Kingdom, but also in North America and Asia. Returning to England in 1982, Bennett-Jones became managing director of Talkback Productions, and also worked as a director for Pola Jones Associates, a theatrical producer. Bennett-Jones decided to launch his own business in 1987, creating a talent agency, PBJ Management.

By then, Bennett-Jones's friend Rowan Atkinson had established himself as one of the United Kingdom's fast-rising television personalities, having had particular success with his Blackadder character for the BBC in the early and mid-1980s. In 1987, the pair decided to team up, together with another friend, writer Robin Driscoll, to create a new television series based on Atkinson's "otherworldly" Mr. Bean character. In 1988, Bennett-Jones launched a new company to provide a vehicle for the new production. Bennett-Jones named his company Tiger Productions.

Mr. Bean became a major hit in the United Kingdom in 1990. Of importance, because the character was mostly silent, the series was easily exportable—and in the early 1990s Tiger Productions found itself the owner of an international hit, becoming one of the largest-selling British television programs on the foreign market. By the middle of the decade, *Mr. Bean* had been shown in more than 80 countries. Aiding *Mr. Bean*'s success was its 1991 International Emmy award. Another successful early comedy series for the company was *The Vicar of Dibley.*

King of British Comedy in the 1990s

Tiger Productions quickly branched out into other areas of television production. In 1991, for example, the company joined in the launch of Tigress Productions, which specialized in the production of wildlife, scientific, and other documentaries. The company also began producing television advertising. As part of Tiger's expansion, the company joined forces with another rising London-based production company, Aspect Film & Television. The two companies merged in 1993, forming Tiger Aspect Productions, with Bennett-Jones as its head.

Tiger Aspect established a reputation as the United Kingdom's leading independent producer of television comedy programming. The company was helped in part by Bennett-Jones's relationship with a large portion of the country's leading comedians, including Lenny Henry, Barry Humphries, Dawn French, and Harry Enfield, among others. Bennett-Jones also had been a major force behind the country's popular Comic Relief charity.

In 1995, Tiger Aspect had a new hit with the television series, *The Thin Blue Line,* also starring Rowan Atkinson. By then, the addition of Aspect's production team also had been paying off for the company, particularly in allowing it to expand into dramatic productions as well. In 1996, the company set up a dedicated unit for its drama productions, which were to include popular programs such as *Teachers* and *A Place in France.*

Tiger Aspect made its first foray into film production in 1997. The Mr. Bean franchise proved the stepping stone for the company's entry into the film world, when the company entered a co-production agreement with Working Title to develop *Bean—The Ultimate Disaster Movie.* Released in 1997, the film was a huge international hit.

The success of the Bean film encouraged Tiger Aspect to expand its interest in film production. In 1999, the company set up a dedicated subsidiary, Tiger Aspect Pictures. That company began work on a number of titles, especially a film about a ballet-dancing miner's son, *Billy Elliot.* Co-produced with Working Title, *Billy Elliot* became one of the largest grossing British films of all time, trailing only the earlier hits *Four Weddings and a Funeral* and *Notting Hill.* While *Billy Elliot* was conquering international box offices, Tiger Pictures had a second hit back home, *Kevin & Perry Go Large,* which became one of the top-selling films in England in 2000.

Targeting International Markets in the 2000s

Tiger Aspect's interests increasingly turned international by the dawn of the 21st century. Tigress Productions, for example,

opened an office in Washington, D.C., a move that helped the company win the production contract for the award-winning documentary series *Africa,* produced in cooperation with National Geographic and WNET, part of the PBS network in the United States. Tigress also produced the hit "celebrity wildlife" series, *In the Wild,* which featured a variety of international celebrities, including Julia Roberts, John Cleese, and Robin Williams, among others.

Tiger Aspect returned to the Mr. Bean franchise at the beginning of the 2000s, now launching an animated television series based on the character. The hit series led the company to launch a dedicated animation division in 2002. In that year, Tiger Aspect branched out again, this time entering the musicals market with *That's Our House,* a show based on the music of the group Madness. *That's Our House* went on to win the Olivier Award for Best Musical in 2003.

Whereas Tiger Aspect remained an active producer for the British television market, with such mid-2000s hits as the *Lenny Henry Show* and the *Teachers* television drama, the company also sought to expand its reach in the international market, especially the United States. In 2004, the company received a number of commissions to create programming for the U.S. market, notably two shows for MTV in 2004, and a deal with NBC Universal to adapt *Teachers* for a U.S. audience in 2005. The company also was preparing the release of a new and highly awaited animation series, *Charlie and Lola,* based on a popular children's book. In 2005, the company signed a broadcast deal with Disney Playhouse for that series.

Tiger Aspect, which reportedly had been up for sale in the early 2000s, continued to seek partners in order to broaden the range of its expansion interests. In May 2005, for example, the company announced that it had signed a deal to form a joint venture, called The Wildlife Unit, with Sky One to produce wildlife programming. Tiger Aspect remained one of the United Kingdom's top independent film and television producers, while claiming increasing prominence in the international market.

Principal Subsidiaries

Tiger Aspect Pictures; Tigress Productions.

Principal Competitors

InvestinMedia PLC; Endemol UK PLC; Avesco PLC; Complete Communications Corporation Ltd.; RDF Media Ltd.; Entertainment Rights PLC; Aardman Animations PLC; Medal Entertainment and Media PLC; Ascent Media Group Ltd.

Further Reading

"An Eloquent Mime," *Televisual,* April 2001, p. 22.

Bennet, Ray, and Peter Pryor, "Tiger Aspect Opts Out of Deal at Working Title," *Hollywood Reporter,* October 1, 2002, p. 81.

Creamer, Jonathan, "Tiger Expands and Bags MTV Job," *Televisual,* June 2004, p. 7.

Dawtrey, Adam, "Tiger Chasing Tales," *Variety,* December 13, 1999, p. 28.

——, "Tigress Goes on the Prowl for US Ops," *Variety,* June 25, 2001, p. 16.

Hamilton, James, "Tiger Aspect Wins First US Orders," *Televisual,* July 2003, p. 5.

Johnson, Debra, "Zein Grabs Reins at Tiger," *Daily Variety,* August 7, 2002, p. 5.

"New Commissions for Tiger Aspect," *Televisual,* February 7, 2005, p. 9.

"Peter Bennett-Jones and Tiger Aspect," *Marlowe,* February 19, 2003.

"Sky and Tiger Team on New Unit," *Televisual,* May 11, 2005, p. 11.

"Tiger Aspect Creates Animation Arm," *Television Europe,* February 2002, p. 6.

"Tiger Aspect Taps Trio," *Hollywood Reporter,* May 28, 2004, p. 16.

Tomlinson, Heather, "Tiger Aspect Primed to Have Last Laugh After the Thin Bottom Line," *Independent on Sunday,* June 1, 2003, p. 6.

—M.L. Cohen

TURKISH AIRLINES ⬤

Turkish Airlines Inc. (Türk Hava Yollari A.O.)

General Management Building
Ataturk Airport
Yesilkoy 34830
Istanbul
Turkey
Telephone: (+90) 212-663-6300
Toll Free: (800) 874-8875
Fax: (+90) 212-663-4744
Web site: http://www.turkishairlines.com

Public Company
Incorporated: 1933 as Devlet Hava Yollari (State
   Airlines Administration)
Employees: 10,956
Sales: TRL 2.79 billion ($2.08 billion) (2004)
Stock Exchanges: Istanbul
Ticker Symbol: THYAO
NAIC: 481111 Scheduled Passenger Air Transportation;
   481112 Scheduled Freight Air Transportation; 488190
   Other Support Activities for Air Transportation

Turkish Airlines Inc., or Türk Hava Yollari A.O. (THY), is the flag carrier of Turkish air transportation. Its 70 aircraft comprise one of the youngest fleets in Europe. More than ten million passengers a year fly THY's network of 100 destinations, three-quarters of them international.

THY was formed in 1933 as a domestic carrier. It built up an international network after World War II but eventually was hindered by mishaps and poor customer relations. The airline began a turnaround in the mid-1980s. It slowly began a privatization process in 1990, when 2 percent of stock was floated. This was accelerated in late 2004 with the offering of an additional 20 percent of shares.

Origins

Turkish Airlines was established on May 20, 1933 as Devlet Hava Yollari (DHY) (State Airlines Administration), a department of Turkey's Ministry of Defense. Its fleet was made up of a handful of four- to ten-seat aircraft.

In 1935, the administration was placed under the Ministry of Public Works. Three years later, it was renamed the "General Directorate of State Airlines" and became part of the Ministry of Transportation.

Postwar Growth

The airline benefited from the postwar U.S. assistance program to Turkey. With the help of Pan American, the fleet was upgraded with Douglas DC-3s, and THY became the largest airline in the Middle East, according to one source.

THY made its first international flight in 1947, connecting Ankara with Athens, Greece, via Istanbul. Soon added to the route network were Nicosia, Cyprus; Beirut, Lebanon; and Cairo, Egypt. Domestic service remained the airline's focus until the 1960s, however.

The Turkish government reorganized the airline in 1956 under the name Türk Hava Yollari A.O. (THY). It was capitalized at TRL 60 million. British Overseas Airways Corporation (BOAC) began supplying technical support after acquiring a 6 percent shareholding, which it held for about 20 years.

The fleet was upgraded with Viscounts and Fokker F27s in the late 1950s. The company began operating its first jet, a DC-9, in 1967. This was followed by the addition of a leased Boeing 707 in 1971. Other jets operated in the early 1970s included the DC-10 and Boeing 727.

Turning Around in the 1980s

THY lost TRL 2 billion in 1980. However, it was soon profitable again, as flights to West Germany made up for loss-making internal operations. Fares were kept low on domestic routes, £30 for the 40-minute hop between Istanbul and Ankara, noted Britain's *Financial Times*. This compared to a £20 (first-class), 12-hour train ride. West Germany and the Middle East attracted a number of workers from Turkey.

Unfortunately, the airline was plagued by a several difficult issues. It developed a reputation for poor customer service and delays. It also endured hijackings and suffered seven accidents between 1974 and 1983, noted *Air Transport World*.

351

However, a new government came to power in 1983 which recognized THY's importance as Turkey's ambassador to the world, beginning the airline's make-over into a modern operation. It would maintain one of the youngest fleets in the world. Security was intensified, causing one shipper to compare it to Israel's El Al, at least in terms of delays.

THY built a new, state-of-the-art technical center at Yesilkoy Airport in 1984. It was capable of both light and heavy maintenance on a number of different aircraft type. Technical staff then made up one-quarter of the airline's 6,000 employees, according to *Air Transport World.*

In 1984, the company's capital was raised to TRL 60 billion as it was classified as a state economic enterprise. Three years later, the capital was raised again, to TL150 billion.

By the mid-1980s, THY had a fleet of 30 aircraft. It was flying about three million passengers a year to 16 domestic destinations and three dozen international ones. The airline was Turkey's largest source of foreign currency, according to *Air Transport World.* Turkish Airlines operating Airbus 310s in 1985, allowing the addition of flights to Singapore in 1986. A route to Brussels and New York was added in 1988.

The company posted losses in 1987 and 1988, largely due to high payments on its dozen new Airbus A310s, according to *Air Transport World.* The fleet also included 11 Boeing 727s and nine DC-9s. THY ended the decade with 8,500 employees.

Partially Privatized in 1990

Private investors took 1.8 percent of shares in a small public offering in November 1990. However, the process leading to the greater privatization was delayed by several years of economic and political setbacks.

By the end of 1992, the company was capitalized at TRL 2.5 trillion. This allowed it to maintain a current fleet, operating Boeing 737s, Airbus A340s, and RJ-100s in the early 1990s. In fact, the airline's fleet would double in size during the decade. Staffing levels would be kept around 8,000 employees, greatly increasing productivity.

Looking to acquire 40 percent of a new charter airline, Sun Express, along with Lufthansa and German tour operators, THY now held a 50 percent interest in Cyprus Turkish Airlines (Kibris Turk Hava Yollari). Turkish Airlines merged with its partially owned domestic subsidiary THT Inc. (Turkish Air Transportation) in September 1993.

The company suffered in the global aviation crisis following the Persian Gulf War and would not break even again until 1994. However, business was again booming in the mid-1990s, with the greatest growth coming from North American destinations. THY launched a nonstop to New York in July 1994.

The company's capital continued to be raised, reaching TRL 10 trillion in 1995. During that year, the airline also converted three of its Boeing 727s to dedicated freighters. (The old DC-9s had been sold off.) The company posted a $6 million profit on revenues of $1 billion for the year. While profitable, THY had to contend with Turkey's exorbitant inflation, making capital improvements difficult.

The domestic market was deregulated in 1996, allowing new scheduled competition from charter airlines. At the same time, larger international carriers were providing stiff competition on routes to Western Europe. THY entered into marketing agreements with other international airlines to enhance its competitiveness. The company teamed with Japan Airlines to offer service to Osaka and Tokyo in 1997 and 1998. Other jointly operated flights soon followed with Austrian Airlines, Swissair, and Croatian Airlines.

Cargo operations were growing as Turkey's manufacturing sector took off. Situated at an ancient crossroads, the country had strong ethnic links with several former Soviet republics, although trade with Russia collapsed during that country's economic crisis in 1998. According to *Air Cargo World,* THY had a 40 percent share of Turkey's international cargo market, with most business coming from Germany, where there was a large expatriate Turkish population. Cargo was then accounting for about $5 million of THY's annual revenues.

By the end of the 1990s, the company had TRL 175 trillion in registered capital. Its fleet consisted primarily of Airbus A310s and A340s and the latest generation Boeing 737s. Unfortunately, it posted a $167 million loss in 1999 in the face of terrorist threats and an earthquake.

Challenges in 2000 and Beyond

A new terminal opened for the airline in January 2000 at Istanbul's Atatürk International Airport. Turkish Airlines continued to extend its international reach, forging marketing agreements with Asiana Airlines (Seoul, Korea), American Airlines, Malaysian Airlines, LOT Polish Airlines, Czech Airlines, and Cathay Pacific Airlines (Hong Kong) in 2000. An Antalya-Frankfurt route was added in 2001 through a code sharing agreement with Sun Express. However, THY withdrew from the Swissair-led Qualiflyer Alliance in order to help attract a strategic investor in its privatization.

Turkey underwent an economic crisis throughout most of 2001, cutting traffic on domestic routes in particular. THY managed to survive after the September 11, 2001 terrorist attacks on the United States without a government bailout or mass layoffs, although 300 middle management positions were eliminated, 400 part-timers were laid off, and wages were cut 10 percent. *Turkish Daily News* credited the airline's survival to entrepreneurial management, which was quick to cancel loss-making routes at home and abroad.

Key Dates:

1933: Airline is founded.
1947: The airline's first international flights connect Ankara and Istanbul to Athens.
1967: The airline begins flying jets.
1984: A new technical facility is constructed as the airline begins a turnaround.
1990: Türk Hava Yollari A.O. (THY), is earmarked for privatization; 2 percent of the company's shares is floated.
2004: An additional 20 percent of shares is floated.

In 2003, the war in Iraq prompted Turkish Airlines to close some routes in the Persian Gulf, while flights to Asia were suspended during the SARS epidemic. However, the airline soon recovered, increasing frequencies on existing routes and adding service to India (New Delhi) after an 11-year lapse.

Another fleet expansion program kicked off in 2004, helping THY maintain one of the youngest fleets in Europe. In July, the airline announced the massive order of 36 jets from Airbus, worth $2.8 billion, plus another 15 Boeing 737s.

THY was not just ordering new planes. It was planning to spend $350 million on a new technical and training facility at Istanbul's underutilized Sabiha Gokcen International Airport, reported *Air Transport World*. The airline had built up a significant technical services operation, maintaining not just its own aircraft but those of third parties. Turkish Technic employed 2,700 and was planning to hire another 2,000 by 2010. THY also had three flight simulators and offered flight training services.

Floating in 2004

Although the company was publicly traded, the government owned 98 percent of shares. The privatization program was revived in 2004 with a public offering of 20 percent of shares on the Istanbul Stock Exchange. The Turkish government owned 75 percent of shares after the offering, which raised $170 million. THY was divesting its 50 percent holding in Cyprus Turkish Airlines (Kibris Turk Hava Yollari) in 2005.

THY faced the entry of new competitors into the liberalizing Turkish aviation market. However, tourism was booming, with 20 million people expected to visit the country in 2005 versus 12 million in 2003.

THY's financial statements should be read in light of a new currency created in January 2005. One New Turkish Lira (YTL) is equivalent to one million of the former Turkish Lira (TRL).

Principal Divisions

Turkish Technic.

Principal Competitors

Azerbaijan Airlines; Cyprus Air; Fly Air; Lufthansa A.G.; Onur Air.

Further Reading

"Airbus, THY Deal for 36 Planes Worth $2.8 Bln," *Turkish Daily News*, October 23, 2004.

Barchard, David, "Turkey to Privatise Its National Airline," *Financial Times* (London), Sec. I, September 19, 1984, p. 3.

Blacklock, Mark, "Turkish Transitions: After Three Successive Years of Losses, THY Turkish Airlines Is Changing Its Marketing Priorities Before Another Attempt at Partial Privatisation," *Airline Business*, July 1993, p. 42.

Bodgener, Jim, "Old Airline Finds a Very Young Fleet," *MEED Middle East Economic Digest*, June 7, 1996, pp. 8ff.

——, "THY Plans to Privatise and Modernise," *MEED Middle East Economic Digest*, January 18, 1991.

Boland, Vincent, and Metin Munir, "Hopes Are High for the Future of THY: With Plans to Buy 51 New Aircraft, the Turkish Airline Is Confident Its Expansion Plans Will Take Off," *Financial Times* (London), August 17, 2004, p. 27.

Boulton, Leyla, "Ambition Lies Behind Turkish Airlines' New Friendly Smile; Privatisation Will Help the Group Complete Its Transformation," *Financial Times* (London), Companies & Finance Europe, October 17, 2000, p. 26.

Daeb, Stewart, "Overseas Routes Bring in Profits," *Financial Times* (London), Sec. III, Survey: Turkey, May 20, 1985.

Daly, Kieran, "Turkish Turnaround," *Flight International*, June 16, 1993, pp. 44ff.

Demir, Gul, "Turkish Airlines—Full of New Surprises," *Turkish Daily News*, November 6, 2003.

Hill, Leonard, "THY in Transition: Major Aircraft Order Propels Turkish Airlines' Vision to Become a Global Carrier," *Air Transport World*, October 2004, pp. 37ff.

Nesmith, Susannah A., "Turkish Straits," *Air Cargo World*, December 1999, p. 43.

Odell, Mark, "Turkish Blend," *Airline Business*, September 1997, pp. 88ff.

"Out from Under: Though Turkish Airlines Has Benefitted from Its Close Link to the Turkish Government, Cutting Loose from State Oversight Will Make Running the Airline Much Easier, Says the Airline's VP Finance Rengin Akillioglu," *Aircraft Economics*, January-February 2005, pp. 32f.

Putzger, Ian, "Two Carriers Still Offer Direct Service to Istanbul," *Journal of Commerce*, August 3, 1999, p. 11.

"Turkey to Offer 20 Pct Stake in THY to Public," *Turkish Daily News*, October 16, 2004.

"Turkish Airlines Again Opt for Leasing," *International Trade Finance*, November 17, 1988.

"Turkish Airlines—A Success Story," *Turkish Daily News*, February 1, 2002.

Vandyk, Anthony, "The Revitalization of THY," *Air Transport World*, January 1990, pp. 91ff.

——, "Turkish Airlines Prepares for Big Changes," *Air Transport World*, April 1985, pp. 49ff.

—Frederick C. Ingram

UAW (International Union, United Automobile, Aerospace and Agricultural Implement Workers of America)

8000 East Jefferson
Detroit, Michigan 48214
U.S.A.
Telephone: (313) 926-5000
Fax: (313) 926-5009
Web site: http://www.uaw.org

Private Company—Labor Union
Founded: 1935
Employees: 200 (est.)
Operating Revenues: $325 million (2003)
NAIC: 813930 Labor Unions and Similar Labor
Organizations

The UAW (International Union, United Automobile, Aerospace and Agricultural Implement Workers of America) remains one of the most influential labor union in the United States, although its power has waned since its peak in the 1970s. The union now has about 700,000 active members belonging to more than 950 local unions, as well as over 500,000 retired members. The Detroit, Michigan-based organization negotiates contracts for its members and also offers them education and training programs. Over the course of its history, the UAW has won a number of contract concessions now taken for granted, such as employer-paid health insurance and cost-of-living allowances. In more recent years, however, as economic conditions have changed, the UAW has devoted much of it energy fighting a rearguard action to hold onto the gains achieved in previous decades, while learning how to adapt to life in a global economy. Long allied with the Democratic party, the UAW has always been a politically active organization, not just relating to economic issues but social issues as well, such as civil rights legislation, the Fair Housing act, Medicare and Medicaid legislation, the Occupational Safety and Health Act, and the Family and Medical Leave Act.

Rise of the Auto Industry in the Early 1900s

When the automobile industry began to establish itself in the early years of the 20th century, it relied mostly on craftsmen: cabinetmakers, upholsterers, molders, foundrymen, and others skilled in the metal and woodworking trades. Even as late as 1910, three out of every four autoworkers were skilled. However, as demand for cars increased, automakers were hard pressed to find skilled workers, resulting in escalating wages. In response, the manufacturers turned to labor-saving machinery that could be operated by semi-skilled or unskilled workers, who would accept lower wages than skilled employees. It was because of its location on the Great Lakes and accessibility by rail and road that Detroit became a magnet for automakers and workers alike. The city's skilled workers had long been members of strong craft unions, but automakers fought hard to make Detroit an open shop city, where unions had a difficult time taking root and collective bargaining was rare. Automation in car manufacturing reached a new level in 1913 when the Ford Motor Company introduced the continuously moving assembly line. As a result, an increasing number of autoworkers simply tended machines and could be trained to do their job within a week, sometimes in mere hours. By the mid-1920s, 85 percent of autoworkers were unskilled and easily replaced. Younger workers, many earning probationary rates, were preferred, since the assembly line could be speeded up as needed and what was now valued was strength and stamina not skill. Led by Henry Ford, automakers paid their workers more than other manufacturers, but this was mitigated by seasonal layoffs, so that during the 1920s autoworkers earned only slightly higher incomes than manual workers. Moreover, many were victimized by unscrupulous foremen, who had the power to hire and fire, resulting in a building resentment among workers that was to fuel militancy during the 1930s.

AFL Forms Autoworkers Union in the Mid-1930s

There were occasional attempts to form unions in the auto industry but they failed, solidifying Detroit's reputation as the "graveyard of organizers." The American Federation of Labor

(AFL) tried twice during the 1920s to unionize autoworkers along craft lines rather than as a industrial union. The auto industry thrived in the late 1920s, but after the 1929 stock crash ushered in the Great Depression of the 1930s, demand for new cars plummeted leading to mass layoffs and creating fertile ground for labor unrest. A number of strikes broke out in Detroit in 1933, achieving little, but in June of that year the new Roosevelt administration passed the National Recovery Act, which included a provision that guaranteed workers the right to organize and bargain collectively, leading to increased efforts to organize autoworkers. The AFL continued to take a craft union approach to the auto industry, although unskilled production workers clearly had no trade. The AFL began signing up workers but it was not until August 1935 that it formed the United Automobile Workers union under its auspices. The organization was poorly led and ineffective, but that would change with the rising influence of one of its members, Walter Phillip Reuther, who would build and lead the UAW for decades and rise to the highest ranks in the labor movement.

Reuther was born in Wheeling, West Virginia, in 1906, the son of a German-born brewery-wagon driver who was a staunch trade unionist and Socialist. A high school dropout, Reuther, along with his brothers Roy and Victor, moved to Detroit in 1927, took a job at the Ford plant and became a supervising die maker. During the early 1930s, he became more of an activist, joining the Auto Workers Union, formed years earlier by the AFL and taken over by Communists in 1925 as part of their effort to organize Detroit. Reuther was laid off at Ford—in his mind, at least, because of his union activities—then in 1933 traveled to the Soviet Union, where he and Victor worked in the Gorki auto works, which needed workers experienced with the Ford equipment it had acquired. Reuther returned to the United States at a pivotal time in the labor movement: in 1935 Congress passed the Wagner Act which stated that if a majority of employees at a company voted to be represented by a union, then it became the bargaining agent for all. Although it would be another two years before the United States Supreme Court confirmed the Wagner Acts' constitutionality, labor organizers were given a shot in the arm. Later in 1935, Reuther attended the AFL convention in Atlantic City, where the organization remained conflicted over the industrial union issue. Reuther returned to New York, and despite having no job he procured a union card and in early 1936 became a member of small UAW Local 86, soon becoming its president. In April, he was a delegate at the UAW convention, where not only would the organization elect its first president, it would essentially declare its independence from the AFL. Reuther quickly established himself in the union and was elected to the general executive board.

As the president of the amalgamated Local 174, covering all of Detroit's west side, Reuther, aided by his brothers, began launching strikes against parts factories and assembly plants. Although he was not a major factor in the 1937 sit-down strike at Flint, Michigan, resulting in General Motors recognizing the UAW, his brothers were involved, and the Reuther name benefited from the victory and solidified his reputation. Of more importance to the building of his image was the "Battle of the Overpass" that took place on May 26, 1937. In front of the Ford River Rouge plant, Reuther and other UAW organizers, who had permits to distribute leaflets, were surrounded and severely beaten by a group of 40 Ford hirelings. A *Detroit News* photographer won a Pulitzer Prize for the pictures he took of the encounter, and the image of the bloodied Reuther only served to elevate his status. Although the UAW failed to organize Ford on this attempt, with the help of the surrounding controversy it succeeded in swelling its membership ranks to about 300,000 by the end of 1937.

However, even as the UAW was taking on the auto industry, it had to contend with internal conflict over who was going to control the union. In 1938, an uneasy coalition fell apart, resulting in a split, with UAW president Homer Martin a year later taking a splinter group into the AFL, leaving the rest of the union under the auspices of the Congress of Industrial Organizations (CIO). R.J. Thomas was installed as president, and he quickly appointed Reuther director of the General Motors Department, essentially a paper organization at the time.

Reuther took on GM at a weak point, concentrating on its tool and die makers, building on the successful strikes of more militant shops to build a walkout against all of GM's tool and die makers. Unable to retool for 1940 models, the company had no choice but to recognize the UAW as the bargaining agent for GM's tool and die makers, the first in a series of dominoes that were to fall. Next, GM production workers were brought into the fold, leading to other industry victories, with Ford finally capitulating in 1941. It was also during this period that the UAW began organizing aircraft workers, competing against the AFL's machinist union. Later, in the 1950s, the Farm Equipment Workers union would be brought into the fold, resulting in the present-day combination and the union's official name: The International Union, United Automobile, Aerospace and Agricultural Implement Workers of America.

At the same time that he was becoming the automakers chief antagonist, Reuther was solidifying his power in the UAW. Finally, in 1946, he defeated Thomas in a tight election, then over the course of the next year gained control of the other national offices. He purged the organization of all opposition and entrenched himself in power, no doubt making enemies along the way. In April 1948, he survived an assassination attempt, suffering a shotgun wound that crippled his right arm. The crime was never solved.

Despite his sympathy with socialism, Reuther quit the Socialist Party in 1939, then in the 1940s became a leading member of the anti-Communist Left, purging Communists from the ranks of the UAW as well as the CIO. He supported Roosevelt's New Deal legislation, but it was not until Harry Truman's victory in 1948 that he finally embraced the Democratic party as labor's only viable champion in government. He and the UAW became a force in Democratic politics, leading to the union's pivotal role

Key Dates:

1935: The United Automobile Workers (UAW) is formed by American Federation of Labor.
1937: General Motors recognizes the UAW.
1946: Walter Reuther is named president of the union.
1950: The UAW wins pension and medical insurance benefits.
1968: The UAW leaves the AFL-CIO.
1970: Reuther dies in an airplane accident.
1979: Membership peaks around 1.5 million.
1985: Canadian autoworkers secede from the UAW.
1995: Stephen P. Yokich is named president.
1999: Membership increases for first time in ten years.
2001: Ronald A. Gettelfinger is named president.

in electing John F. Kennedy to the presidency in 1960s and influencing civil rights and welfare legislation during Lyndon Johnson's ''Great Society'' initiative.

Post-World War II Victories

Pre-eminent among his abilities as a labor leader was Reuther's keen aptitude for collective bargaining. He developed the concept of ''Pattern Bargaining,'' targeting one of the ''Big Three'' automakers for a strike and relying on the zeal of its competitors to take advantage of the situation to drive the company to the bargaining table. Once a deal was struck, it established a pattern and the other automakers fell in line. As a result, the UAW won a string of significant victories, resulting in higher wages and improved benefits. In 1948, a settlement with GM established the concept of an annual wage increase tied to a cost-of-living adjustment. A deal with Chrysler in 1950 brought with it employer-funded pensions, and in that same year medical insurance was granted by GM.

In addition to his role at the UAW, Reuther became president of the CIO in 1952 and was instrumental in finding common ground with the AFL, leading to the 1955 merger that resulted in the AFL-CIO. But the more progressive Reuther and conservative AFL-CIO president George Meany would eventually fall out during the 1960s. Reuther became disenchanted with the war in Vietnam, while Meany maintained loyal to the administration. Moreover, Reuther believed the labor movement was failing to stay current and not connecting with new reform moments, such as peace, minority rights, and the environment. The rupture between the two men culminated in 1968 when the UAW left the AFL-CIO, but no other unions followed its lead. The UAW would not return to the AFL-CIO until 1981.

Reuther and his wife were killed in a plane crash in 1970. He left his successor, Leonard Woodcock, in charge of one of America's strongest labor unions (along with the United Steelworkers of America). Woodcock remained loyal to Reuther's vision during the seven years he headed the UAW, and during his tenure the union reached its high water mark in a number of ways. Its last national strike, against Ford, took place in 1976, and membership peaked in 1979 around 1.5 million. Woodcock was replaced in 1977 by Douglas A. Fraser, considered the last

of the 1930s firebrands that established the UAW. In addition to his challenges as a union leader, Fraser had to contend with issues beyond the control of the automakers. Earlier in the decade, the OPEC oil cartel rocked the United States economy with price increases. A second round of increases was launched in 1978, leading to a greater demand on the part of auto buyers for Japanese imports and a significant drop-off in the sale of U.S.-made cars. The UAW joined forces with the Big Three to fend off the Japanese threat and offered wage concessions to improve competitiveness. Fraser even took a set on Chrysler's board of directors, ostensibly to serve as a watchdog, but when Chrysler cut employment by 57,000, closing ten plants, the UAW was complicit in the decisions, and the locals had no choice but to capitulate. The UAW was not alone in experiencing a decline in power. The steel industry and its workers were devastated by cheap steel imported or produced by the new domestic mini-mills. Arguably, the recession of 1981 to 1982 brought a close to the golden era of the U.S. labor movement. After President Ronald Reagan hired replacement air traffic controllers, all unions became hard pressed to keep the gains they had made during the previous decades, let alone attempt to secure better terms from employers.

Fraser, who retired, was replaced as the UAW's president in 1983 by Owen F. Bieber, more an administrator than a visionary. He maintained that because the Big Three were rebounding, the union would no longer agree to givebacks. He was also committed to organizing the Japanese auto plants cropping up in the Southeast, but these efforts ended in failure. In addition, under his watch the Canadian section of the union, angry over concessions made to the Big Three, seceded from the UAW in 1985. As a result of the split, automakers would now be able to threaten the union with moving jobs to Canada, where labor costs were cheaper. Many U.S. members were also displeased with their leadership's non-adversarial approach, resulting in the rise of a dissident faction under the New Directions banner. Nevertheless, Bieber retained his post until his retirement in 1995. He was replaced by a more truculent president, Stephen P. Yokich, a third generation UAW member, who first ''walked'' a picket line at the age of 22 months in a stroller pushed by his mother, a GM worker. In 1989, he was put in charge of relations with GM and was successful in launching strikes against parts-making and car assembly plants that resulted in GM meeting the union's demands. At the same time, he proved to automakers that behind the scenes he was willing to cooperate to help employers become more efficient and thus more competitive. One of his greatest challenges was in the auto-parts sector, where the union had experienced its greatest loss of membership in recent years. During the late 1970s, close to 70 percent of auto parts workers were UAW members, but that number had fallen to less than 25 percent. The independent auto-parts makers paid well below UAW scale, putting Big Three operations at a competitive disadvantage. In order to maintain wages and benefits with the Big Three, Yokich had to organize the suppliers, lest the Big Three simply opt to outsource the supply of auto parts. Under Yokich, the UAW also looked to restore some of its clout in the labor movement by merging with the International Association of Machinists and the United Steelworkers. The idea was floated in 1995 but in 1999 the Machinists dropped out and the merger with the Steelworkers, scheduled to occur in 2000, petered out as well.

Yokich enjoyed some success launching sudden local strikes, but again it was on ground determined by the automakers, as the union fought to hang onto earlier gains and stem the erosion of its membership. Although it enjoyed a bump in membership in 1999, the first increase in a decade, the ranks continued to thin. Moreover, younger members were less active in the union. Unlike previous generations that were determined to hold onto a good-paying job for life, new blue collar workers shared a similar attitude of many white collar workers, who periodically changed jobs to advance their careers. The new generation of autoworkers all but assumed that high-paying jobs would eventually go overseas and took steps, or at least expected, to eventually move into a new career.

Following Yokich's retirement in 2002, Ronald A. Gettelfinger was elected the UAW's president. Not only did he have to contend with outsourcing and technological efficiencies that eliminated jobs, but he was also confronted with the UAW's continued inability to organize foreign-operated auto plants. Gettelfinger soon proved, however, that he was a worthy adversary for automakers. Like Reuther before him, he zeroed in on a weakness, in this case automaker's increasing dependence on just-in-time ordering of parts. He launched sudden two-day strikes against factories that made interior parts for some of General Motors and Chrysler's most popular vehicles. The workers lost little in the way of income, while the automakers were forced to shut down production on bestselling SUVs Chevy Trailblazer and Jeep Liberty. The automakers then applied pressure on their suppliers to come to terms with the UAW. The master plan was to reunionize the parts sector. At the same time, Gettelfinger proved willing to adapt to changing times and eschew traditional bargaining techniques. In 2003, rather than singling out one of the Big Three in an attempt at pattern bargaining, he worked out an agreement with all three automakers simultaneously. This move was indicative that both management and labor were feeling competitive pressures. From the union's point of view, a quick and peaceful settlement might give it a better chance at finally organizing the U.S. operations of foreign auto makers.

The effort to revitalize the UAW was complicated by the George W. Bush administration, and the Republican-majority National Labor Relations Board was far from sympathetic to its cause, especially after the UAW backed Senator John Kerry during the 2004 presidential election. The union's difficult situation was highlighted in 2004 by the adoption of cost-cutting measures, which included the cutting of its work force at headquarters and in regional offices by 15 percent, to be achieved by attrition. Although still a force not to be taken lightly in the U.S. auto industry, the UAW faced a challenging future succeeding in a global economy. For years the union had talked about operating transnationally, and now more than ever it appeared that the UAW would have to find a way to take its place on the world stage or face the prospect of receding into irrelevance.

Further Reading

Ball, Jeffrey, Lee Hawkins, Jr., and Sholnn Freeman, ''Big Three, UAW Show Rare Unity,'' *Wall Street Journal*, September 8, 2003, p. A2.

Barnard, John, *Walter Reuther and the Rise of the Auto Workers*, Boston: Little, Brown and Company, 1983, 236 p.

Bluestone, Irving, ''Working-Class Hero—Walter Reuther,'' *Time*, December 7, 1998, p. 157.

Bradsher, Keith, ''U.A.W. Is Just Trying to Hold Its Ground with Detroit,'' *New York Times*, September 13, 1996, p. D1.

Burkins, Glenn, ''Picket Line's Next Generation Shows UAW Weakness, Problems,'' *Wall Street Journal*, June 26, 1998, p. B1.

Davis, Bob, Neal Templin, and Brandon Mitchener, *Wall Street Journal*, March 25, 1996, p. A11.

Lichtenstein, Nelson, *The Most Dangerous Man in Detroit: Walter Reuther and the Fate of American Labor*, New York: BasicBooks, 1995, 575 p.

Lowell, Jon, ''Hard Times for the UAW,'' *Ward's Auto World*, September 1985, p. 67.

Muller, Joann, ''Has the UAW Found a Better Road?,'' *BusinessWeek*, July 15, 2002, p. 108.

—Ed Dinger

Utz Quality Foods, Inc.

900 High Street
Hanover, Pennsylvania 17331
U.S.A.
Telephone: (717) 637-6644
Toll Free: (800) 367-7629
Fax: (717) 633-5102
Web site: http://www.utzsnacks.com

Private Company
Incorporated: 1921
Employees: 1,800 (2004)
Sales: $235 million (2003 est.)
NAIC: 311919 Other Snack Food Manufacturing

Utz Quality Foods, Inc., is one of the leading makers of potato chips in the United States and also produces other salty snacks such as corn chips, pretzels, popcorn, and cheese curls. Utz products are distributed to more than a dozen states on the East Coast and via the firm's Web site. The company is owned and managed by descendants of founders Bill and Salie Utz.

Early Years

The beginnings of Utz Quality Foods date to 1921, when William Utz of Hanover, Pennsylvania, decided to quit his shoe factory job and go into the potato chip business. Utz and his wife Salie, a skilled cook in the "Pennsylvania Dutch" style, felt they could make a better-tasting chip than other producers in their area, and they invested $300 to buy the necessary equipment. Working at first from a small outbuilding behind their home, the Utzes were able to produce about 50 pounds of chips per hour, which they began selling under the name Hanover Home Brand Potato Chips.

With Salie doing the cooking, Bill Utz delivered the chips to stores and farmer's markets in the Hanover and Baltimore, Maryland areas. As sales grew, production was moved into a room in their house, and then to a new cement block building in their backyard. In 1936, the Utzes dramatically boosted production by buying an automatic fryer that could produce 300 pounds of chips per hour. Their small plant's capacity was soon outpaced by growing sales, and over the next five years it was expanded until it had nearly doubled in size.

After World War II, sales continued to grow, and in 1949 a larger plant was built on ten acres in Hanover. Like its predecessor, it would see numerous expansions over the ensuing years. Management of the firm was now being handled by Francis Xavier "F.X." Rice, a business school graduate who had married the Utzes' daughter Arlene. After the deaths of Salie Utz in 1965 and Bill Utz in 1968, F.X. Rice became president of the firm.

The early 1970s saw Utz purchase another plant in Hanover, which was soon renovated. The firm began making pretzels in 1971 and several years later added popcorn. In 1976, the company built a third plant in Hanover, which boosted potato chip production to 7,000 pounds per hour.

Utz now had the best-selling chip in south central Pennsylvania and Baltimore, Maryland, and during the 1970s the firm's territory was expanded to include the rest of Maryland, Washington, D.C., Delaware, Virginia, and West Virginia. In 1978, F.X. Rice retired, and his son Michael took over the job of president, with Arlene Utz Rice serving as board chairman.

Major Expansion Completed in 1983

In 1980, the firm broke ground on its largest building project to date, the expansion of its newest plant into one of the most modern snack food manufacturing facilities in the United States. Completed in 1983, it would house the firm's administrative offices as well as most manufacturing and distribution operations. By this time, Utz route salesmen had begun using handheld computers to record daily sales for transmission to headquarters, and the firm's potato chips had been rated the best-tasting in the United States by *Food & Wine* magazine.

In 1983, the company also bought equipment to produce a new line of "hand-cooked" potato chips, whose crunchier texture and stronger taste had begun to find favor with the public. Over the next few years, the firm's plants were expanded yet again to house more chip fryers. In 1986, production of cheese curls began, to be followed by corn and tortilla chips. With annual sales growth averaging 13 percent, by 1989 the firm's output had increased to 500,000 pounds of chips per week.

Production of potato chips was a straightforward process. Potatoes, largely sourced from farms in the region, were either used fresh or stored until needed in underground cellars with a capacity of 40 million pounds. After being run through peeling and washing machines, workers cut off bad parts as they passed along a conveyor belt to a high-speed centrifugal slicer. There, they were cut into slices (.055 inches thick for plain chips or .062 inches thick for rippled ones) before being fried at 390 degrees in cottonseed oil. They were then conveyed past a salter or machines which dispensed flavorings like Bar-B-Q or Sour Cream and Onion before being sealed in flexible bags and boxed for shipment. The public was allowed to view the production process on a factory tour that was offered each weekday.

The firm used different methods for each type of snack it produced. Grandma Utz's Handcooked Potato Chips, for example, were cooked in three bathtub-size fryers in boiling lard that was agitated by an employee with a sanitized garden rake to keep the chips from sticking together. After six minutes they were removed, hand-salted, and packaged.

The firm had worked over the years with horticulturists to develop strains of potatoes that were ideal for chip-making. Round, rather than oval, ones were preferred, as less was wasted in peeling. Moisture and sugar content were also important, and these too had been optimized.

Byproducts of Utz's manufacturing process included potato peelings, which were sold to animal food producers, and starch, which was converted to a slurry and sold to paper manufacturers. The firm had also recently begun to recycle its unsold past-date chips by turning them into animal feed.

Pretzel Sales Surge in the Early 1990s

Utz was now seeing a dramatic increase in pretzel sales, which by 1991 had come to comprise nearly 10 percent of total revenues, following several years of growth by 20 percent annually. Factors boosting demand included low fat content and price, which was roughly one-third less than other salted snacks. To keep up, by the summer of 1992 Utz was baking pretzels around the clock. In August, the firm added a third pretzel oven, which doubled production, but sales continued to rise, and additional ones came online over the next several years.

By the mid-1990s, Utz employed over 1,000 and had annual sales estimated at more than $100 million. In 1996, the company added a new distribution warehouse, which it would subsequently expand.

Utz products were now being sold in seven Mid-Atlantic states and were especially popular in Baltimore and Washington, D.C., where the firm's potato chips had a 40 percent market share. The company used a variety of promotional techniques, including advertising, giveaways, and in-store displays, and in early 1996 a billboard in New York's Yankee Stadium began to feature the Utz logo, replacing that of rival chipmaker Bon Ton Foods. The move was made by a regional distributor which controlled the sign and had recently dropped the Bon Ton account in favor of Utz. To keep up with its steady growth, the firm was once again in the process of modernizing all three of its plants.

In January 1998, Utz sued the University of Maryland after that institution barred its products from campus and removed its advertising signs from sports arenas. The school had recently signed an exclusive contract with Pepsico, Inc., whose Frito-Lay unit's brands would replace Utz products on campus. Utz was in an ongoing struggle with the dominant Frito-Lay, and worked to distinguish itself with moves such as creating regionally popular varieties like Crab Chips or by gaining Kosher certification for all of its regular potato chips, which helped boost sales in cities like New York, which had a large Jewish population.

Beginning in 1996, Frito-Lay had begun marketing potato chips fried in Procter & Gamble's olestra, an oil that was not absorbed by the body and thus resulted in a lower calorie count. Though the Wow! line did not prove as big a hit as anticipated, in large part because of a government-required label warning about potential digestion problems, in 1999 Utz introduced an olestra chip of its own. Yes! chips, with half the calories of traditional ones, were offered in regular, ripple, and Bar-B-Q varieties.

The year 1999 also saw the firm begin using UtzFocus, a Web-based data tracking system that allowed it to analyze sales down to the single store, which helped boost the efficiency of its distribution force. The company had recently created a public Web site as well, which offered information about its products and allowed visitors to buy them through the mail. Utz now employed more than 1,300 and had annual revenues of approximately $150 million.

In March 2000, Bill and Salie Utz's daughter Arlene Utz Hollinger died. She had served as board chairman until 1992. Family involvement remained strong, and several fourth-generation Utzes had begun working for the firm.

Utz Sponsors NASCAR's Rusty Wallace in 2001

The firm got a promotional boost in January 2001 when popular NASCAR driver Rusty Wallace began sporting the Utz logo on his car and uniform. Wallace was a fan of Utz chips and had approached the company about working on its behalf. He subsequently agreed to perform a variety of promotional duties for the firm. Chip varieties available at this time included Crab, Bar-B-Q, Carolina Bar-B-Q, Salt & Pepper, Onion & Garlic, Red Hot, Salt & Vinegar, Sour Cream & Onion, Grandma Utz's, Homestyle, and Kettle Classics. Annual sales were now estimated at $200 million.

Early 2001 saw introduction of russet potato chips. This potato variety produced a darker chip due to the caramelization of its higher sugar content. The firm was seeing strong growth in its old-fashioned kettle chips at this time, as increasing

Key Dates:

1921: William and Salie Utz begin making and selling potato chips from their home.
1936: A new automatic chip fryer boosts production six-fold.
1949: A larger plant is built in the firm's hometown of Hanover, Pennsylvania.
1968: F.X. Rice is named president of the company after father-in-law William Utz's death.
1970s: The firm begins making pretzels and popcorn at a second Hanover plant.
1976: A new, larger plant is built to house most of the company's potato chip production.
1978: Michael Rice takes over as president from his father.
1983: An extensive upgrade of the main plant is completed.
1980s: Production of "hand-cooked" chips, cheese curls, and corn chips begun.
1990s: Pretzel sales grow rapidly.
2001: A new Hanover facility purchased; the firm sponsors NASCAR's Ricky Wallace.
2004: Distribution is expanded to New England.

numbers of consumers sought a crispier, more flavorful chip. Utz was also selling more chips with spicy flavorings, while the low-fat product lines, including pretzels, were in decline. Sales climbed to $218 million during the year, boosted in part by a *Consumer Reports* magazine taste test that ranked Utz the best-tasting chip in the United States. The year had also seen Utz purchase a manufacturing facility and warehouse from Hanover Direct, Inc. for $4.7 million.

Moving to further increase sales in the New York metro area, in 2002 the firm hired Dircks Associates to design outdoor advertising that would be placed on 200 billboards in the city's five boroughs. Utz chips were now available in a total of ten states via 20 distribution centers. Its products were sold in a wide range of outlets, ranging from gas stations and small convenience stores to mass merchandisers like Wal-Mart and Costco.

In the summer of 2003, Utz was named the "Official Salty Snack" of the Philadelphia Eagles football team, and the firm introduced a special one-pound bag of chips bearing the Eagles' logo. The company's "Utz girl" logo would be displayed in the Eagles' ballpark, where its products would be sold by food vendors. Though only available on the East Coast, Utz was now the number three potato chip in the United States, behind only Frito Lay and store brands. Procter & Gamble's Pringles, while not a true potato chip, also had greater market share than Utz. For 2003, earnings hit an estimated $235 million, up 4 percent from the year before.

In February 2004, Utz acquired the New England distribution rights of Bachman Co., whose products would be distrib-

uted with Utz's all the way to Maine. The firm also began to make sweet potato kettle chips and reduced-carbohydrate baked crisps from soy flour. The latter product was introduced in response to the Atkins and South Beach diet crazes that were then sweeping the country. Followers of the low-carbohydrate diets shunned both potato chips and pretzels, each of which was high in carbohydrates. Development of a low-carbohydrate potato variety was in the works, but the public soon tired of the fad and many dieters began to return to carbohydrate-rich potato and grain-based foods by year's end.

For over 80 years, Utz Quality Foods, Inc. had experienced almost continuous growth. The firm's commitment to quality and its unbroken line of family management were both key factors in its success. Though operating in a highly competitive field, Utz's products commanded strong consumer loyalty, and the company's future growth looked to be a given.

Principal Competitors

Frito-Lay, Inc.; The Procter & Gamble Company; Snyders of Hanover; Herr Foods, Inc.; Wise Foods, Inc.; Bickel's Snack Foods, Inc.

Further Reading

Adkins, Sean, "Hanover, Pa. Snack Makers Respond to Low-Carb Craze," *York Daily Record*, August 8, 2004.

Berselli, Beth, "Utz Takes on the Terps Over Snack Food Contract—Pa. Firm Challenges University-PepsiCo Pact," *Washington Post*, January 30, 1998, p. G3.

Clarke, Caryl, Pretzels Bite into Snack Market—Sales Jumps Allow Utz to Expand," *York Daily Record*, April 6, 1993, p. 4.

"Conveyors/Scales Chip Away at Snackfood Breakage," *Packaging Digest*, January 1, 1998, p. 82.

"Flexibility Fuels Snack Food Production," *Chilton's Food Engineering*, January 1, 1998, p. 25.

Goulet, Neal G., "Utz Makes It Big in the Bronx," *York Daily Record*, May 9, 1996, p. 1.

Grove, Lloyd, "Memorial Day by the Mouthful; Raking the Chips at the Utz Factory," *Washington Post*, May 29, 1989, p. D1.

Hughes, Mike, "Pennsylvania Is King of the Snack Food Universe," *Delaware Valley Business Digest*, January 1, 1985, p. 22.

Mullaney, Timothy J., "Using the Net to Stay Crisp," *Business Week*, April 16, 2001, p. EB34.

Olenchek, Christina, "Snack Attack," *Central Penn Business Journal*, August 6, 2004. p. 35.

"Snack Food Maker Acquires Firm's Rights to Distribute in New England," *Reading Eagle*, February 12, 2004.

The Story of Utz Quality Foods (video narration script), Utz Quality Foods, Inc., 2004.

"Utz Quality Foods Inc.—SWOT Analysis," *Datamonitor Company Profiles*, January 23, 2004.

Walker, Elizabeth, "Top 50 Fastest-Growing Companies: Utz Quality Foods, Inc.," *Central Penn Business Journal*, October 4, 2002, p. S13.

Warner, Mary, "All In the Family," *Sunday Patriot-News Harrisburg*, January 10, 1999, p. D1.

—Frank Uhle

Velcro Industries N.V.

15 Pietermaai
Willemstad, Curaçao
Netherlands Antilles
Telephone: (599) 9 433 5000
Fax: (599) 800 235 6640
Web site: http://www.velcro.com

Public Company
Incorporated: 1957 as Velok Ltd.
Employees: 2,858
Sales: $261.2 million (2003)
Stock Exchanges: NASDAQ
Ticker Symbol: VELCF
NAIC: 313221 Narrow Fabric Mills; 339993 Fastener,
   Button, Needle and Pin Manufacturing; 551112
   Offices of Other Holding Companies

Velcro Industries N.V. was created to market one of the 20th century's handiest inventions: hook and loop tape. The ubiquitous fastener is used in innumerable applications: fastening blood pressure cuffs, sneakers, wallets, industrial lift belts, prisoner leg restraints, and ready-to-assemble furniture. VELCRO brand hook and loop fasteners can be found around the world on all manner of products. The company also manufactures more conventional belts and fasteners. Ultra-Mate, One-Wrap, and Texacro are three of the company's other brands. The family of Chairman Robert Cripps has been the chief shareholder since the 1970s, and there has been speculation of plans to take the company private.

A 1940s Discovery

Walking is said by some to promote creativity, and this was literally true in the invention of the VELCRO brand hook and loop fastener. As George de Mestral hiked with his dog along some alpine countryside one day in 1941, cockleburs continually fastened themselves to his trousers. Wondering what made the spiny seeds so tacky, he examined them under a microscope, revealing thousands of tiny hooks on the surface of each one. His trousers, which he also examined, were essentially covered with loops of fabric. Although he appreciated the engineering implications of the discovery right away, it took eight years of tinkering for de Mestral to develop a usable product made out of nylon hooks and loops. The main challenge was perfecting the manufacturing process to ensure consistent results.

By the 1950s the inventor had created a company to market his novel product. The trademark ''VELCRO'' was appropriately derived from the French words for velvet and hook: ''velour'' and ''crochet.'' Although he earned less than $60 per week in his first years in business, de Mestral earned millions after he sold rights to the invention to a new company created by Jean Revaud, an American national.

Velcro S.A. was established in Switzerland in 1952. In the mid-1950s it licensed the British rights to the hook and loop technology to a subsidiary of Senn & Co., a Swiss ribbon manufacturer. Velcro S.A. also entered a licensing agreement with Velok Ltd. of Canada in 1957. The agreement allowed Velok to produce Velcro tape in the western hemisphere as well as Asia and the Pacific. Velok agreed to give the Swiss company the rights to all patents it subsequently developed.

Velok eclipsed Velcro S.A. in innovations and growth and changed its name to Velcro Industries Ltd. in 1967. Velcro USA Inc. (originally American Velcro Inc.) and Velcro Canada Ltd. (Canadian Velcro Ltd.) were subsidiaries of Velcro Industries Ltd., which acquired the rights to the patent in the late 1960s.

Cripps Acquiring Control in the Early 1970s

In 1967, its sales were worth about $10 million a year and its stock $81 per share. C. Humphrey Cripps began acquiring shares of the company (through a Channel Islands holding company, Cohere Ltd.) when their price fell to around $5 each in the early 1970s. Cripps also took the post of company chairman and later installed two sons on the board. Velcro Industries N.V. was incorporated in the Netherlands Antilles on June 7, 1972, and soon acquired the assets of the Canadian operation, Velcro Industries, Ltd.

Velcro was not the Cripps family's first foray into entrepreneurship. Humphrey's father, Cyril, established a factory to make piano frames in 1919; it later was a supplier for the automotive industry. Other holdings included private livestock and tourism investments. Known for its philanthropy (the Cripps Foundation gave Cambridge University £1 million in the 1960s), the family drew some scrutiny in the late 1980s after the company failed to offer a dividend in spite of healthy sales and cash reserves, prompting speculation about the family taking the company private. A minority shareholder, Alan Kahn, sued to prevent the transaction, and a U.S. judge ruled that the United States had jurisdiction in the case. Cripps then canceled his plans. Within five years, however, rumors of the chairman entertaining takeover offers were reported.

The company maintained a reputation for secrecy in financial matters and product development. The *New York Times* likened it to a private company. It held its annual meetings on the isolated Caribbean island of St. Maarten, meetings that, as reported in *Forbes* magazine, were not even attended by the board, who instead met with Cripps privately.

Competition in the 1980s

By the time the patent for the original Velcro tape expired in 1978, the word ''Velcro'' had become a synonym for hook and loop tape. The company launched a campaign to protect the brand name from falling into general use. A subsequent advertising campaign touted the product as ''the first, the best.''

The expiration of the patent opened the market to a slew of low-cost competitors. The French company Aplix (the leading European fastener supplier) and Japanese-owned YKK (a leading manufacturer of zippers for clothing) capitalized on the opportunity, particularly in the apparel and footwear industries. The demand for the fastener among shoemakers was so great that Velcro could not meet it alone, and it lost some business to foreign suppliers, some of whom had licensed the Velcro technology and name until 1978. When the fashion buzz wore off, however, excess capacity among hook and loop tape suppliers forced prices down.

Fashion designers, courted by the company since the 1960s, had finally begun to appreciate the possibilities. Like the first Ford automobiles, however, Velcro tape was originally only available in black. Eventually the tape was formulated in 16 different colors. An elastic version also was developed.

The company concentrated on supplying more stable, industrial markets after the shoe fad declined. Velcro products, the company explained, helped lower assembly costs in the automotive industry. The fastening devices were used to attach door

panels, among other things. The aerospace industry also appreciated the lightweight, rustproof fasteners that would not rattle. A standard component in jet planes since the 1960s, VELCRO® brand hook and loop fasteners were used on aircraft ranging from small Pipers to the space shuttle. Medical supplies provided a field in which Velcro could sell higher quality, more costly products, including the fasteners used on the Symbion Total artificial heart. Not only did the fasteners have to work perfectly, but they had to be immaculately clean as well, and, as in the fashion industry, the appearance of the products was often important.

The tape was enhanced to perform in different conditions. Flame resistant (Hi-Air), silver-coated, electrically conductive (Hi-Meg), heat and corrosion resistant (Hi-Garde), fire retardant, and weather resistant polyester were among the formulations developed.

The hook side of the tape was available in differing densities and levels of durability, as was the loop side. The orientation of the loops made a difference, however, in ''peel strength.'' Randomly oriented loops held more firmly, whereas orderly rows of loops had a somewhat more attractive appearance. The final, unsung layer, the adhesive, was also available in different formulations. Standard backed tape, meant to be sewn, had no adhesive at all. Most had peel-off backing and pressure-sensitive adhesives of different formulations for use in different applications and environments. The most durable involved a separate adhesive to be applied and activated by the user.

One-Wrap fasteners had a hook layer on one side and loops on the other and were used for wrapping purposes. Half and Half Tape featured hook tape with an adhesive backing and the opposite, with the loops, with a fabric backing that could be sewn onto other fabrics. Texacro, a less expensive brand of standard backed tape, was manufactured in Mexico. Velstick fasteners had a rigid plastic backing. The WrapStrap, an offering of Canada's WrapStrap Industries Inc., anchored two pieces of Velcro tape with an aluminum plate for securing cables and automotive and marine applications. Velcro tapes were available in a variety of widths, from ⅝ to 12 inches, and were available cut into small circles, called ''Velcoin'' fasteners.

The fastener also proved handy for hanging displays at conventions and in retail stores. Inevitably, more whimsical applications for Velcro tape had to surface. At some bars, customers could don a suit covered with Velcro tape and fasten themselves to a wall covered with the complementary layer. Late-night talk show host David Letterman popularized this stunt. The more adventuresome could attempt to navigate a similarly fashioned inflatable obstacle course.

Expansion in the 1990s

Annual sales in fiscal year 1988 were $93 million. They had reached $115 million by 1992. In the mid-1990s, several factors sent the company's earnings and stock price downward. Velcro was forced to make a large tax payment to the Dutch government. Overseas expansion had to be funded, and the United States—where the company ran its operations from Manchester, New Hampshire—required an increase in tax payments as well.

Velcro included hundreds of types of fasteners in its product offerings in the 1990s. It diversified into conventional fasteners

Key Dates:

1957: George de Mestral forms the company to market a novel hook and loop tape fastener.
1967: Velcro Industries Ltd. logs annual sales of $10 million.
1978: Expiration of the original patent opens the company to competition.
1995: Sales are more than $150 million.
1998: Velcro Industries acquires British rights to the VELCRO® brand.
2001: The Velcro Direct Online business-to-business site is launched.

such as screws and clips, which were usually custom engineered. Velcro began using stainless steel in manufacturing some of these new products, although nylon remained a component of some.

The company also developed variations of its original nylon hook and loop tape using less expensive materials. The Ultra-Mate brand HTH ("High Technology Hook") line was the pinnacle of this technology.

Ultra-Mate figured significantly in a potentially lucrative cobranding exercise with Kimberly-Clark Corporation, which used the fastener on its premium line of diapers, Huggies Supreme. Ultra-Mate's injection molding process made it more cost-effective for this application than the traditional Velcro loop tape. The Velcro brand name, however, was featured on Huggies Supreme packaging because it was so valued by consumers. The venture was expected to increase Velcro USA's sales by $5 to $10 million per year.

New uses for traditional nylon-based Velcro tape continued to be developed. TacFast Systems Canada Limited developed the TacFast carpet fastening system based on Velcro tape. The system secured carpet effectively while allowing it to be easily moved if need arose. Velcro tape also anchored the artificial turf at the Toronto SkyDome and was employed to hold down toupees.

In 1996, earnings jumped nearly 20 percent to $16.3 million, while sales increased more than 10 percent to $177.1 million. Although sales lagged in North America, Velcro Industries expected to benefit from the growth of markets in Asia and Latin America. A strong European presence remained a priority for the company, as evidenced by its acquisition of Ausonia S.R.L., the leading hook and loop producer in Italy.

Consolidating for the New Millennium

Velcro was enjoying renewed popularity in the shoe industry in the late 1990s. Well known for its contributions to the athletic sneakers of the 1980s, hook and loop closures were catching on with more high-fashion shoes, such as sandals.

Velcro Industries posted a pretax profit of $41 million on sales of $235 million in 1998. It had 1,200 employees at the time. About 240 people worked for its British licensee, Selectus Ltd. In 1999, Selectus sold the British rights to the VELCRO®

trademark to Velcro's U.K. subsidiary, Addey Milner Ltd. Velcro Industries also bought its Argentine importer, Gavest, during the year.

After 50 years of development, there were still new industries to exploit, such as packaging. Outsiders also were coming up with new ways to have fun with VELCRO® hook and tape fastener, such as the fad of wearing clothing covered with the fabric and jumping onto a wall covered with matching strips, as popularized by David Letterman's late night TV show. Company officials frowned on the practice, calling it "dangerous and inappropriate."

Velcro Group officials were also vigorously defending the brand name to keep it from falling into common usage. "VELCRO® brand hook and loop fastener," as it was properly known, was considered one of the top inventions of the 20th century, and in spite of competitors, appeared to have a promising future in the new millennium.

Two of Velcro's chief competitors were former subsidiaries: APLIX S.A. (established as Velcro France in 1958), which claimed to be Europe's leading hook and loop manufacturer, and Kuraray Co., Ltd. (formerly Velcro's Japanese unit).

Velcro USA was expanding its existing facilities and building a 225,000-square-foot plant in Somersworth, New Hampshire. Velcro's U.S. subsidiary paid $700,000 to settle an air pollution lawsuit from the state of New Hampshire. The company was not required to admit guilt. In late 2001 Velcro USA introduced a business-to-business e-commerce site, Velcro Direct Online.

Another new application for Velcro closures was to help fasten ceramic armor plates to military vehicles. This system was developed with LAST Armor. LAST was a division of Waltham, Massachusetts-based Foster-Miller Inc., which had helped Velcro develop an injection-molding process in the 1970s.

Velcro USA had 650 employees and sales of around $50 million a year. About 50 of them worked in Arizona, where the sales and marketing was being expanded in 2002. Velcro also had a couple of factories in the state. One was closed in 2003 and its equipment moved to Lancaster, South Carolina. The Lancaster operation was relocated to Mexico two years later to compete with imports from Asia.

Velcro Industries employed more than 2,800 people overall. Velcro Industries posted revenues of $261.20 million for the fiscal year ended September 2003. The Americas accounted for 73 percent of sales, with Europe making up 22 percent.

Income slipped in 2004 due to increased competition and unfavorable exchange rates, reported *Business Week*. There was new speculation of Velcro Industries going private. The family of Chairman Robert W.H. Cripps, son of Sir Humphrey Cripps, then owned 82 percent of the company.

Principal Subsidiaries

Velcro Hong Kong Ltd.; Velcro Australia Pty. Ltd.; Zhangjiagang Velcro Fastening Systems Co., Ltd. (China; 90%); Velcro Europe S.A. (Spain); Velcro GmbH (Germany); Velcro

Industries France S.A.; Velcro Italia, S.R.L.; Velcro Limited (United Kingdom); Addey Milner Limited (Great Britain); Velcro Holdings B.V. (Netherlands); Velcro USA Inc.; Velcro Canada Inc.; Velcro Group Corporation (United States); Velcro de Mexico, S.A. de C.V.; Velcro do Brasil LTDA.; Velcro Industries B.V. (Netherlands Antilles).

Principal Competitors

APLIX S.A.; Kuraray Co., Ltd.; YKK Corporation.

Further Reading

Bannister, Nicholas, ''Hooked on a Piece of Tape,'' *Guardian* (London), May 29, 1999, p. 30.

Berss, Marcia, '' 'A Wacko Situation,' '' *Forbes,* May 23, 1994, p. 82.

Brush, Michael, ''It Keeps Your Pants On, But Can It Fatten Your Wallet?,'' *New York Times,* April 14, 1996, p. F3.

''Company Announces Plans for Somersworth Facility,'' *New Hampshire Business Review,* February 25, 2000, pp. 1ff.

Giges, Nancy, ''Velcro Faces Patent Problems by Diversifying Line,'' *Advertising Age,* November 7, 1977, p. 24.

Hartley, Jenny, ''Velcro Plant to Close in September,'' *Lancaster News* (South Carolina), May 5, 2005.

Hegarty, Liam, ''VELCRO Sticks It to a Reporter,'' *Westchester County Business Journal,* February 15, 1999, p. 4.

Infantino, Vivian, ''The Sound of Money,'' *Footwear News,* September 14, 1998, p. 14.

Jancsurak, Joe, ''Getting Hooked,'' *Appliance Manufacturer,* February 1994.

''Kimberly-Clark Revamps Huggies to Steal March on P&G's Pampers,'' *Marketing Week,* August 9, 1996, p. 10.

Krantz, K. Theodor, ''How Velcro Got Hooked on Quality,'' *Harvard Business Review,* September/October 1989, pp. 34–40.

Marcial, Gene G., ''Sticking with Velcro,'' *Business Week,* January 18, 1993, p. 74.

Meeks, Fleming, ''Some Call It Greed,'' *Forbes,* October 3, 1988.

Pugh, Clifford, ''We've Become Attached; VELCRO and Its Imitators Have Us Hooked,'' *Houston Chronicle,* Houston Sec., September 24, 1998, p. 1.

Stanistreet, Andy, ''Jobs Will Stay in Place Says Firm Which Sold Off Its Velcro Brand,'' *Sentinel* (Stoke, U.K.), Bus. Sec., July 14, 1999, p. 5.

''Strategic Partners Produce Better Fasteners,'' *Advanced Materials & Processes,* January 2005, p. 7.

Streit, Jim, ''Up Against the Wall,'' *Newark Post,* July 30, 2004.

''There's No Such Thing as 'Velcro,' '' Manchester, N.H.: Velcro USA Inc., n.d.

''Touch-and-Close Fabric,'' *Advances in Textiles Technology,* June 2002, p. 5.

Tsuruoka, Doug, ''Stick to the Fine Points,'' *Investor's Business Daily,* July 14, 2003, p. A4.

''Velcro Buys Argentinian Importer and Grows (Velcro Compro A Su Importador y Crece),'' *Buenos Aires Economico,* August 24, 1999, p. 6.

''Velcro Comes Unstuck,'' *Management Today,* March 1991, pp. 11f.

''Velcro: A Success Story,'' *Magazine of Wall Street,* June 10, 1967, pp. 31–32, 40.

''Velcro's Stuck on Flying Disk Game,'' *Playthings,* April 1994.

''Velcro USA Inc.,'' *Automotive Industries,* June 1995.

''Velcro U.S.A. Customers Now Can Order Online,'' *Outdoor Retailer,* January 2002.

Wahlgren, Eric, ''Worth Sticking with Velcro? Some Pros See the Famous-Named Fastener Outfit As a 'Classic Value Play' That May Be on the Verge of Being Taken Private,'' *BusinessWeek Online,* July 30, 2004.

—Frederick C. Ingram

ViewSonic

ViewSonic Corporation

381 Brea Canyon Road
Walnut, California 91789
U.S.A.
Telephone: (909) 444-8888
Toll Free: (800) 888-8583
Fax: (909) 468-1202
Web site: http://www.viewsonic.com

Private Company
Incorporated: 1987 as Keypoint Technology Corporation
Employees: 743
Sales: $1.1 billion (2003)
NAIC: 334110 Computer and Peripheral Equipment
Manufacturing; 334111 Electronic Computer
Manufacturing; 334119 Other Computer Peripheral
Equipment Manufacturing; 334310 Audio and Video
Equipment Manufacturing

ViewSonic Corporation is a leading provider of cathode ray tube (CRT) and liquid crystal display (LCD) computer monitors, including those for high-end, computer-aided design, desktop publishing, and graphic design, and those offering state-of-the art technology at affordable prices. ViewSonic has six distinct product lines: desktop displays; television/entertainment displays; plasma displays; projectors; mobile and wireless displays; and peripherals, such as speakers, keyboards, and mice.

Specialist to International Presence: 1987 to the Early 1990s

In 1987, James Chu launched Keypoint Technology Corporation, a distribution company that specialized in computer peripherals, such as power supplies, keyboards, and computer monitors. Chu, a native of Taiwan, had held a variety of sales positions before immigrating to the United States in 1986 to become president of United States operations for a Taiwanese keyboard manufacturer.

The early 1990s saw a decrease in personal computer prices, a proliferation of high-end workstations, the growing use of graphical interfaces, and increased corporate demand for monitors with lower radiation emissions, higher refresh rates, and better ergonomics. In keeping with the times, in 1990 Keypoint Technologies introduced the ViewSonic brand of color computer monitors in two series, professional and graphics. The monitors were especially suited for Windows, graphical user interfaces, and desktop publishing environments. ViewSonic also introduced its "green" monitor, which conformed to the energy conservation guidelines of the Environmental Protection Agency's Star Program. The company adopted the mission and focus of developing and delivering affordable advanced visual display products and changed its name to ViewSonic. Its new logo, three colorful finches, was intended to symbolize innovation, quality, and value.

ViewSonic experienced a steady demand for its monitors, and in 1992 *Inc.* magazine included the firm in its fastest-growing companies list. A year later, with revenues of just over $100 million, the company began to branch out internationally, joining with Al Ghurair Enterprises for Computers to distribute ViewSonic products in the United Arab Emirates. Further expansion occurred in 1994 both domestically and internationally with the addition of two new regional sales offices in Tampa Bay, Florida, and Chicago, Illinois, and two new European offices, one in Paris and the other in Dusseldorf.

Diversification: The Mid-1990s

During the second half of the 1990s, View Sonic turned its attention to strengthening its European operations in response to increased demand for its color monitors. As part of its bid to become a major player in the European display technology market, it improved its customer, technical, and coordination services throughout Europe, including free, life-time technical support. By 1996, ViewSonic offered the widest range of monitors available from a single manufacturer in the European market, and by 1998 it was undisputedly a European leader in the color monitor market.

At the same time, ViewSonic was expanding its product lines. It entered the multimedia market in 1994 with the introduction of speakers and its first in a line of multimedia monitors.

Company Perspectives:

*ViewSonic is committed to meeting and exceeding its cus-
tomers' expectations in quality, value and innovation. Its
ability and dedication to deliver products to the market
ahead of its competition remains a primary focus of the
company. Unlike some of its competitors, ViewSonic is exclusively devoted to the visual display products business,
which enables the company to better focus its resources.*

The company also formed a strategic alliance with Optiquest, a
major supplier of monitors and uninterruptible power supplies
in 1995. Under the terms of the alliance, Optiquest's monitors
became ViewSonic's value line, and the two companies united
their sales and marketing efforts. The alliance meant that
ViewSonic now offered four lines of monitors: professional,
multimedia, graphics, and economy.

Growth in ViewSonic's range of products and global distribution was paralleled by increases in its annual revenues and
number of employees. Between 1993 and 1997, the company's
workforce grew from 84 to more than 600 in number, while
revenues increased 716 percent to $830 million. In fact, the
increase in revenues from 1996 to 1997 alone totaled 48 percent
as ViewSonic became the nation's top producer of branded
computer monitors, displacing NEC, the former market leader
in 1997. The company's increased sales also reflected its entrance into the projector market in 1997. By 1998, ViewSonic's
range of liquid crystal display and cathode ray tube monitors
exceeded 20 in number.

In 1998, *Inc., Forbes*, Deloitte & Touche, and the *Los
Angeles Business Journal* all recognized ViewSonic as one of
the fastest growing private companies in the United States. *VAR
Business* attributed its ongoing success to several factors. While
still known for its competitive pricing and extensive low- to
high-end product line, the company's products received highest
rankings for image quality, reliability, cross-platform capability, ease of screen control and nonstandard features, and vendor
support. It had also established a distribution sales model that
involved creating regional service centers. In 1998, it added to
this system with a center in Duluth, Minnesota, to serve re-
sellers and end-users throughout the eastern United States and
signed up Midwich Thame as its European distributor specializing in its higher end products. By the end of the decade,
despite some complaints that the company had not kept pace
with other companies in lowering its prices on monitors and
other equipment and that it was experiencing some slip-ups in
quality, ViewSonic was one of the top three monitor providers
in the branded LCD market in Europe.

Continued Expansion and Success
in the Late 1990s and Beyond

ViewSonic's focus on continued expansion both domestically and internationally paid off. In 1999, revenues reached $1
billion, and ViewSonic joined with Dell in a marketing campaign to promote its monitors coupled with Dell systems. It also
attempted to capture market share in the ultralight category of

presentation products with its full-size projection screen with
self-contained LCD projector. The introduction coincided with
a precipitous increase in sales of ultralight projectors. While
projectors in general increase by a third in 1998, they simultaneously tripled in the ultralight category.

By 2000, ViewSonic had achieved 15 percent share of the
LCD monitor market and 13.5 percent share of the CRT monitor market in the United States with $1.3 billion in annual sales.
It was the fifth-largest seller of computer monitors in the country behind Dell, Compaq, Gateway, and Hewlett-Packard. The
trend in the computer display market in the early years of the
new century was a move from CRT to LCD, according to James
Chu in a 2001 *VAR Business* article, a move for which his
company was prepared. "ViewSonic is the market leader in
North America for the CRT, and we want to be the leader for
LCDs in North America, too." Worldwide, ViewSonic delivered more than one million LCD monitors in 2002 and that
number more or less doubled in 2003.

The company began reaching for the high-end monitor market with the 2001 acquisition of the display products unit of
Finland's Nokia, Europe's display specialist, and also moved
into the market for hand-held Internet access devices with ten
versions of wireless handhelds. In so doing, ViewSonic hoped
to leverage its strong position in displays since a handheld's
screen accounted for as much as 75 percent of its value.

ViewSonic moved forward in the field of projectors as well.
In 2001, it purchased Advanced Optical Engineering Inc. of
California, a company that made optical equipment and light
engines for use in digital projection displays. The new subsidiary, renamed Advanced Digital Optics Inc., continued to develop equipment for IMAX, JVC, and Prokia, while also developing light engines for digital projections displays for its parent
company. The acquisition also put ViewSonic in a position to
partner with Cogent Technologies, a company with a broad
array of patented, energy efficient methods for light delivery,
including novel uses of plastic fiber optics, to produce brighter,
higher-resolution, lower-cost displays for computer monitors
and high-definition and smart televisions.

Other product developments included the 2000 introduction
of a phone with touch sensitive screen and Web browsing
capabilities and the 2002 introduction of high-definition monitors using rear projection technology for computers or high-
definition televisions. ViewSonic also collaborated with Mesh-
Networks Inc., a developer of mobile broadband networking
technology to develop and market PDAs and tablet PCs with
high-speed Internet access. In 2003, ViewSonic introduced its
portable video player, which combined an MP3 player, digital
photo album, and portable DVD player.

ViewSonic also continued its penetration into the global marketplace. Having entered the Chinese mainland in the late 1990s,
it formed several alliances with partners in Taiwan to expand its
presence in the information appliance market there in 2000.
"About a decade ago, we promised to surpass NEC Corp. as the
No. 1 monitor brand in the U.S., and we did it," chairman and
chief executive Chu recalled in a *Taiwan Economic News* article
in 2000. "By forming strategic alliances with firms in Taiwan
[to manufacture LCD modules], we will be well-positioned to

Key Dates:

1987: James Chu founds Keypoint Technology Corporation.
1990: Keypoint Technologies introduces the ViewSonic brand of color computer monitors.
1994: Viewsonic forms a strategic alliance with Optiquest.
1998: Midwich Thame becomes the company's European distributor.
2000: Viewsonic partners with Microgobal Argentina SA to distribute its products in South America and acquires the display products unit of Finland's Nokia.
2001: The company purchases Advanced Optical Engineering Inc. of California; the new subsidiary is renamed Advanced Digital Optics Inc.
2002: ViewSonic collaborates with MeshNetworks Inc.
2004: The company sells Advanced Digital Optics, Inc. to JDS Uniphase.

out-gun Sony, Panasonic, and other top monitor makers in the global market.'' Aiming to enhance its presence in South America as well, it joined with Microgobal Argentina SA as the official distributor of its products in Argentina, Uruguay, Brazil, Colombia, and Venezuela in 2003.

As ViewSonic's leadership looked to the future, it foresaw a shift toward wireless and mobile capability for the personal computer accompanied by the use of multiple smart displays. It set itself the goal of continuing to lead the ''visual revolution'' as the ''world moved from analog to digital and from PC-centric to display-centric,'' where the display, as the focal point for access to and control of information or entertainment, might be on the desk, on the wall, or in hand. ViewSonic sold Advanced Digital Optics, Inc. to JDS Uniphase in 2004. It entered the home networking market in 2004 with the release of wireless equipment that included media gateways and adapters.

Principal Subsidiaries

ViewSonic Europe Ltd.; ViewSonic Canada.

Principal Competitors

Acer; ADI Systems; Apple Computer; BenQ; Daewoo International; Dell; Fujitsu; Gateway; Hewlett-Packard; InFocus; LG Electronics; LG Philips LCD; Matsushita; Mitsubishi Corporation; NEC; NEC-Mistubishi Electrical Visual Systems; palmOne; Philips North America; Philips Electronics; Planar Systems; Princeton Digital; Samsung Electronics; Sharp; Sony.

Further Reading

Kaplan, Karen, ''Computing's Next Big Thing: For James Chu, the Next Step Is to Transform Monitors into Net Appliances,'' *Financial Post*, March 30, 2000.

Pepe, Michelle, ''ViewSonic Strong in All Areas,'' *Computer Reseller News*, June 21, 1999, p. C 51.

Schick, Shane, ''ViewSonic Projects Big Market for Office Theater Portables, *Computer Dealer News*, July 23, 1999, p. 18.

Stafford, Jane, ''ViewSonic Monitors Paint a Winning Picture: Tops in Products/Pricing and Support,'' *VAR Business*, November 15, 1997, p. 128.

''ViewSonic Builds Ties with Taiwan Firms,'' *Taiwan Economic News*, September 22, 2000.

Walker, Meg, ''Q & A with President and CEO James Chu,'' *VAR Business*, October 1, 2001, p. 115.

—Carrie Rothburd

Walter Industries, Inc.

Walter Industries, Inc.

4211 West Boy Scout Boulevard
Tampa, Florida 33607-2551
U.S.A.
Telephone: (813) 871-4811
Fax: (813) 871-4399
Web site: http://www.walterind.com

Public Company
Incorporated: 1955 as Jim Walter Corporation
Employees: 4,953
Sales: $1.5 billion (2004)
Stock Exchanges: New York
Ticker Symbol: WLT
NAIC: 332996 Fabricated Pipe and Fittings; 522310
   Mortgage and Nonmortgage Loan Brokers; 531110
   Lessors of Residential Buildings and Dwellings

Walter Industries, Inc., is a holding company that owns home building, natural resources development, and industrial manufacturing companies. Subsidiary Jim Walter Homes, Inc., builds and sells detached, single-family residential homes, mainly in the southern United States; other company subsidiaries offer home mortgages and homeowner's insurance. Jim Walter Resources, Inc. mines coal and extracts methane gas from coal seams in Alabama. The company's primary industrial operations include Sloss Industries Corporation, which manufactures coke, slag wool, and specialty chemicals, and United States Pipe and Foundry Company Inc., the leading maker of ductile iron pressure pipe in the nation.

Origins as Marketer of Shell Homes in 1940s

In 1946 James W. Walter borrowed $400 from his father, a citrus grower, and purchased a "shell," or unfinished home, for $895 from Tampa, Florida, builder, O.L. Davenport. When just three days later, the 23-year-old, newly married Walter sold the home to a passerby for a profit, he saw a way out of his $50-a-week truck-driving job and $50-a-month apartment. Walter convinced Davenport, also in his 20s, to take him on as a partner. As Walter remembered in *Nation's Business* in 1970, "we made out

all right, but I thought we could move faster." Walter encouraged Davenport to run bigger advertisements featuring photographs of the homes; they sold more houses. Walter was enthusiastic about building the business even faster. Davenport was reluctant, and after two years, they dissolved the partnership of Davenport & Walter. The men decided to divide the business: one of them would take the assets of about $50,000, the other the business. Since Davenport was the founder, he first opted to take the business. A day after he made his decision, he told his partner he had changed his mind and chose the assets instead. Davenport took his share and bought a motel and small construction firm in Troy, Alabama. Jim Walter continued the business, now called the Walter Construction Company.

In the post-World War II era, housing was scarce. Jim Walter sold unfinished, traditionally constructed homes as affordable, alternative housing. The wood homes were built on concrete foundations or wood pilings. Each home was completely finished on the outside with an unfinished interior. Buyers installed plumbing, electrical systems, insulation, walls, and doors themselves. Homes were sold directly to owners prior to construction, through one of Jim Walter Homes Division sales offices.

In 1955 Jim Walter incorporated the Walter Construction Company as the Jim Walter Corporation. Three men who would be pivotal to the company's success through the coming decades had already joined the firm. James O. Alston came to the company in 1947 and was instrumental in its early growth. Alston was president of the corporation from 1963 to 1970, chairman of the homebuilding operation, and vice-chairman of the corporation by 1970. Arnold F. Saraw, a partner in Walter Construction, was secretary-treasurer of the corporation from 1955 to 1970. In 1970 he was promoted to senior vice-president, heading the corporate mortgage division. The third man, Joe B. Cordell, an accountant who joined the company in 1958 was vice-president and chief financial officer, becoming president in 1974 and chief executive officer in 1983.

Expansion into Mortgages in the 1950s

During the 1950s the company expanded and entered the mortgage business. Initially, financing was difficult. The turning point for the fledgling company came in 1956 when Chicago creditors Walter E. Heller & Company approved a $1 million line of credit. Jim Walter's mortgages, like his homes, were attractive to buyers who found more conventional sources too costly. Jim Walter Corporation's innovative financing plan was outlined in the May 19, 1987, edition of *Financial World:* "most of the houses . . . are financed on the basis of ten percent fixed mortgages or installment notes maturing in up to 20 years. Unlike a conventional mortgage, . . . Jim Walter's buyers spread the interest and principal payments evenly across the term to lessen its risk of defaults." Such mortgages were possible because the company required the purchaser to own the land on which the house was to be built. The equity in the land substituted for the traditional cash down payment. The company's mortgage portfolio was traditionally one of its strongest assets. The mortgage finance division maintained more than $1 billion in installment notes in the 1970s. By 1987 Jim Walter's $1.6 billion mortgage portfolio was larger than those of most Florida savings and loans. An evaluation performed in 1988 by Financial Security Assurance, in a maneuver designed to help Kohlberg Kravis Roberts (KKR) and Walter Industries refinance $1.2 billion in bank debt, put the value of Walter's mortgage portfolio at $1.75 billion.

Sales of Walter homes historically ran counter to other builders' sales due to the availability of low-cost financing. Low, fixed interest rates, combined with an affordable product, ensured that when housing starts were generally down and money was tight, buyers looked for alternatives such as those offered by Jim Walter. During 1982 Jim Walter built 10,000 of the 300,000 homes constructed that year. In 1986 Walter homes accounted for just 6,500 of the 500,000 homes built. The company tallied some of its best years during recessions in the housing industry.

From 1955 to 1962, Jim Walter Corporation was primarily involved in the building industry. Walter's only notable acquisition during the 1950s was the First National Bank in St. Petersburg, Florida, later sold. This foray was the start of a policy of diversification.

Diversification in the 1960s and 1970s

During the 1960s and 1970s, the company made a large number of acquisitions and mergers. Walter acquired no less than 15 different subsidiaries in the 1960s, ranging from building-materials and industrial-products manufacturers to a California savings and loan. The Celotex Corporation merger was initiated in 1962 and completed in 1964. A pioneer in sound insulation and a leading manufacturer of building products, Celotex also made a spray-on asbestos insulation. The company

also acquired a sugar firm and an oil exploration company. Two paper companies acquired in 1968, Marquette Paper Corporation and Knight Paper Company, rounded out Jim Walter's early acquisitions.

On March 9, 1964, Jim Walter Corporation was first listed on the New York Stock Exchange. Shares initially sold for $.50. From 1969 until 1979, stockholders enjoyed positive results: dividends increased from $.40 to $1.80 per share; book value increased from $6.46 to $34 per share. By 1970, the shares had twice split three ways.

Over the course of the 1960s, over 200 competitors tried to emulate the company's success in the production of shell homes. By the end of the 1970s, Jim Walter, the originator of the concept, was the only one left and his "rags-to-riches" saga had become a part of Florida folklore. A Tampa cab driver, who did not recognize his passenger, regaled Jim Walter with the story of Jim's life. In 1968, on the 20th anniversary of the founding of the company, Jim Walter commemorated his beginnings by buying back the original shell house he had first owned for just three days in 1946.

In 1969 the company bought United States Pipe and Foundry Company of Birmingham, Alabama, for $135 million in stock and cash. By 1979, U.S. Pipe had increased profits five times over. In the July 13, 1979, issue of *Forbes*, Walter called the purchase "the quickest deal I ever made."

At the time of the acquisition, U.S. Pipe's modest coke operation and unmined coal reserves attracted little attention. By 1973, however, the Arab oil embargo made coal mining a potential bonanza. In 1976 the company created a subsidiary, Jim Walter Resources, Inc., to direct the company's mine-development program. Since Jim Walter knew home building but not mining, he hired experienced people to guide the mining division. The magnitude of the task, faced by a company with no experience in the difficult longwall mining that was required due to the depth of the coal, was daunting. The company's robust cash flow was able to absorb the crush of capital expenditures during the nearly ten years it took to make the mines operational.

During the 1970s Jim Walter continued to diversify the company, adding another dozen subsidiaries. By the end of the decade Jim Walter was involved in coal mining; marble, limestone, and granite quarrying; oil and gas production; gypsum and asbestos mining; a savings and loan association; an insurance company; a paper-marketing firm; water and waste-water pipe manufacturing; and retail jewelry. While the various mergers and acquisitions broadened Jim Walter's base of operations, the bulk of its revenues remained in the building industry, with more than 200,000 shell homes completed by 1979. Sales in 1979 exceeded $2 billion a year.

Asbestos Litigation and KKR Takeover in the 1980s

In 1972 Panacon Corporation, the third-largest Canadian producer of asbestos, was merged into Celotex Corporation. As the link between asbestos and cancer became clear, lawsuits from workers began to accumulate. Jim Walter's 1986 10-K form reported that two subsidiaries, Celotex and Carey Canada Inc., were co-defendants with a number of other miners, manufacturers, and distributors of asbestos products in a "substantial num-

Key Dates:

1946: James W. Walter and O.L. Davenport go into business selling shell houses.

1948: Walter and Davenport divide their business and assets; Walter takes the business, renaming it Walter Construction Company.

1955: The business is incorporated as the Jim Walter Corporation.

1956: Walter enters the mortgage business.

1964: The company acquires Celotex and goes public.

1969: Walter acquires U.S. Pipe and Foundry Company.

1972: Panacon Corporation, Canada's number three asbestos producer, merges with Celotex.

1976: Jim Walter Resources is founded.

1985: Celotex struggles under the load of asbestos lawsuits.

1987: Kohlberg Kravis Roberts acquires the Jim Walter Corporation and takes the company private.

1988: Celotex is sold off, and Walter's other subsidiaries are organized under the name Hillsborough Holdings Corporation and and renamed Walter Industries.

1989: Company is forced into Chapter 11 bankruptcy proceedings.

1991: The company's long-time CEO Joe Cordell steps down, and Robert "Bull" Durham takes over.

1994: The courts find Walter not liable for Celotex asbestos claims.

1995: Walter emerges from Chapter 11 and is taken public the following year.

1997: KKR increases its stake in Walter to 26 percent; Walter returns to profitability.

1998: The company identifies core business components and begins efforts to sell off the rest.

2000: Walter begins a three-year stretch in the red with a loss of $104.7 million. A proposal to liquidate Walter is voted down at the shareholders' meeting.

2001: Amid continuing struggles, Don DeFosset takes over as CEO in November.

2004: Coal prices rise, bringing Walter Industries back to profitability.

ber" of lawsuits alleging work-related injuries. Many of the suits requested punitive as well as compensatory damages. According to the company, "the aggregate damages sought in these cases is substantial." What followed was a series of convoluted suits, and counter suits, on behalf of both defendants and plaintiffs, with mixed results. The company thought its insurance carriers would handle the claims, but coverage after 1977 disallowed asbestos-related claims. In 1985 the subsidiaries and codefendants entered into an agreement to resolve the claims. All claims filed after June 19, 1985, were to be referred to the Asbestos Claim Facility, set up by the agreement, with the cost of litigation or mediation to be shared by all the defendants according to a formula based on their asbestos litigation experiences.

Jim Walter's home-building division continued to produce strong results through the 1980s. In 1986 the company maintained 103 sales offices scattered through 29 states, most of them in the South. The homes were constructed by local construction firms who were subcontracted to do the work. Shell homes accounted for only 28 percent of units sold while sales of 90 percent-completed homes totaled nearly 60 percent. In the same year, homebuilding and related financing accounted for 14 percent of total revenues for the company, contributing $108.4 million.

By the mid-1980s Celotex found itself staggering under an ever mounting litigation load. In 1984 approximately 21,100 lawsuits representing 25,600 persons were pending against one or more of the subscribers of the Asbestos Claim Facility, including Celotex. By the following year this figure had climbed to 28,800 lawsuits representing 34,900 persons, and a year later there were approximately 43,900 bodily injury claims pending. By the time Kohlberg Kravis Roberts moved to acquire the company in 1987, pending lawsuits exceeded 50,000, only to climb again, to 58,000, in the following year. The actions taken by the subsidiaries, however, allowed KKR to proclaim the company's litigation risk "manageable." Under corporate law, the parent company could not be held liable for claims against its subsidiaries.

Kohlberg Kravis Roberts proceeded with its purchase of Jim Walter Corporation for $2.4 billion—including $1.1 billion in junk bonds—in August 1987. The company was a perfect takeover target; it had healthy profits, strong cash flow, and a raft of subsidiaries that could be sold to reduce debt. Share price for the takeover jumped to $60, with bidding at one point reaching the heady level of $67 per share. At KKR's request, Jim Walter joined the group of investors who bought the company. He became a chairman of Hillsborough Holdings Corporation and Walter Industries, Inc.—two companies organized to acquire Jim Walter Corporation—and retained his existing management team.

The company was split into two holding companies following the sale. Jim Walter Corporation retained ownership of Celotex, and Hillsborough Holdings Corporation became the parent of the other subsidiaries. Jim Walter Corporation was sold to Jasper Corporation in April 1988. The other subsidiaries merged into HHC, all under the name of Walter Industries, Inc., which was the main subsidiary of HHC. Several of the company's businesses, including the marble quarrying and paper operations, were quickly sold to pay down debt.

Chapter 11 Protection: 1989–95

In 1989 Houston attorney Stephen D. Sussman, of Sussman Godfrey, filed a suit on behalf of asbestos victims in Beaumont, Texas, an industrial area where many of the plaintiffs lived. The new lawsuit named KKR, Hillsborough Holdings, and Walter Industries as principal defendants. The suit put an end to KKR's plan to restructure the debt assumed by Hillsborough Holdings Corporation. Further asset sales were blocked, and the price of HHC's junk bonds plummeted. HHC was unable to meet the obligations imposed by the sale of the junk bonds that funded the buyout. On December 27, 1989, Hillsborough Holdings Corporation and 31 of its subsidiaries each filed for Chapter 11 bankruptcy in Tampa. Only two subsidiaries, Cardem Insurance Co. and Jefferson Warrior Railroad Company, did not file petitions for court-protected reorganization.

In April 1990 Judge Alexander L. Paskay, chief bankruptcy judge for the U.S. Bankruptcy Court in the Middle District of Florida, recommended that the asbestos suit filed in Texas be heard in his court. In July the U.S. District Court for the same district adopted his recommendation, and the case was moved to the Tampa federal bankruptcy court.

While the legal wrangling continued, in early 1991 the CEO of Walter Industries, Joe Cordell, announced his retirement because of his battle with cancer. Lacking solid leadership from within the company, Walter Industries conducted an executive search that led to the hiring of G. Robert (Bull) Durham, who had retired two years earlier after turning around Phelps Dodge Corporation. When asked by *Financial World* in 1991 why he would come out of retirement to take over such a troubled company, Durham replied, ''There is not a whole lot of fun to running a company that is doing well.'' Jim Walter continued as chairman of Walter Industries.

Despite the new leadership, the company would be unable to reorganize until the asbestos litigation was resolved. Judge Paskay finally issued a ruling in April 1994, stating that Walter Industries could not be held liable for the Celotex asbestos claims. Appeals ensued, with the company initially proposing a reorganization plan that set aside no funds to settle the continuing claims. Under pressure from its creditors, however, on March 17, 1995, Walter Industries emerged from Chapter 11 through a plan that settled the more than $2.6 billion in claims by having the company contribute $375 million to the Celotex Settlement Fund, which had been set up by Celotex and included the asbestos claimants. Part of the payment was in the form of Walter Industries stock; by early 1997 the fund claimed a 10.9 percent stake in the company.

Postbankruptcy: The Late 1990s

Upon the company's emergence from bankruptcy, KKR held just 12 percent of Walter Industries. KKR remained committed to its investment, however, and by January 1997 had increased its stake to 26 percent. In January 1996 Walter Industries became a public company listed on the NASDAQ. Jim Walter, meanwhile, retired in October 1995 and was succeeded as chairman by Durham, with Kenneth E. Hyatt, who had been president of Celotex, taking over as president. The company's troubles seemingly over, Durham himself then retired in June 1996, with Hyatt becoming chairman, CEO, and president. At the same time, Richard E. Almy was named executive vice-president and chief operating officer, having previously served as president and COO of JW Aluminum and JW Window Components.

Walter Industries recovered quickly from its dark days of bankruptcy, surging in the strong market for new homes of the mid-1990s. The financial picture was strong enough by December 1995 for the company to be able to retire the $490 million in junk bonds that it had used to finance the reorganization plan just nine months earlier. More evidence of a recovery came in the form of a return to acquisitions. In June 1997 Walter Industries acquired Neatherlin Homes Inc., a builder of low-priced homes based in Texas. In September of that same year, the company announced that it would pay about $400 million for Applied Industrial Materials Corporation (AIMCOR), a private

company based in Stamford, Connecticut, with about $450 million in revenues and $50 million in operating income annually. AIMCOR, through its Carbon Products Group, was the world leader in the production of petroleum coke, which is used in numerous industrial processes, including the manufacture of steel and cement. Its Metals Group manufactured and sold a variety of ferroalloys, metals, and specialty materials used in the steelmaking and metal-casting industries. AIMCOR fit in nicely with Walter Industries' other industrial subsidiaries, such as U.S. Pipe, Sloss Industries, and JW Aluminum.

After posting a heavy loss in fiscal 1995, a net loss of just $84.7 million was posted for 1996, and the company was back in the black in 1997 with net income of $37.1 million. Well on the road to recovery, Walter Industries had the same solid core of businesses that had made it an attractive takeover target in the mid-1980s. By aggressively building on this core through acquisitions, Walter Industries seemed capable of exceeding the glory days of the original Jim Walter Corporation.

Rocky times were still to come for the company, however. In 1998 and 1999, Walter Industries identified and began the process of selling off its non-core businesses. Jim Walter Homes and United States Pipe and Foundry, the company's most profitable businesses, led the list of core properties. J.W. Window Components was sold off in 1998, and the coal-mining subsidiary Jim Walter Resources, building product manufacturer Vestal Industries, industrial materials and tool provider Southern Precision Corporation, and coke and slag wool company Sloss Industries were targeted for divestiture.

2000 and Beyond

By August 2000, Walter Industries' success was reversed. Revenues remained at $1.91 billion, with no change over the previous year, and the 1999 net earnings of $35.6 million were gobbled up by a $104.7 million loss posted at the end of 2000. A $167 million write-down on the value of Jim Walter Resources, for which Walter Industries was unable to find a buyer, contributed to the loss. In March, as the company's fortunes began to slip, CEO Ken Hyatt was fired. After a period under the guidance of an interim CEO, majority shareholder Kohlberg Kravis Roberts hand-picked a turnaround expert for the top office: Robert G. Burton, formerly of the printing giant World Color. He remained on the job only 14 weeks before quitting. According to the *Tampa Tribune* in February 2001, ''Burton's brusque management style'' and his elimination of 375 jobs—about five percent of Walter's workforce—created a great deal of ill will among employees and did little to reverse the company's losses. After another stretch with an interim CEO, the company hired Don DeFosset, who was previously CEO of an auto parts supplier in Rochester Hills, Michigan, in November. Commenting that he took the job at Walter because of, not despite, the company's problems, DeFosset remarked to the *Tampa Tribune* in February 2001, ''Walter Industries has already taken the traditional kind of approaches to improving its bottom line. . . . Now it's time to change the nature of the work.''

DeFosset had his work cut out for him. At the October 2000 shareholders' meeting, Tom McKay, manager of an investment fund that controlled two percent of the company's stock, raised a vote on the question of liquidating Walter. McKay argued that liquidation could bring shareholders between $20.50 and $25 per share at a time when Walter's stock hovered between $7 and $9 per share. Although the proposal was voted down, three voters, including McKay, who represented 20 percent of the company's shares lent their approval to the idea. DeFosset responded to the challenge by changing the culture at Walter. He introduced Six Sigma, a work analysis model made popular by General Electric CEO Jack Welch, which focused on reducing variations and defects in processes. DeFosset also emphasized openness and candid communications with employees. When McKay renewed his liquidation proposal at the April 2001 shareholders' meeting, not only was the idea voted down, but it met with the approval of less—only 16 percent—of the ownership of the company.

There was good reason for such hopefulness. In July 2001 Walter Mortgage Co. began business issuing loans to people who needed assistance securing lots—whether buying, buying out a partner's share, or removing liens on land—on which to build a Jim Walter home. The new company opened up previously untapped avenues of business for Walter Homes and complemented progress in creating efficiencies at the company, which was scaling back its operations in places where it had less visible market presence, reducing the number of its model home parks and the number of models in them, and introducing new models to attract buyers who could afford more expensive houses due to low interest rates. Walter Homes also ventured into building subdivisions on unused company property. Avoiding major metropolitan markets, where competition from other builders would be stiff, the company sited developments in such smaller communities in the South as Houma, Louisiana.

In September 2001, however, high hopes were put aside when methane explosions killed 13 miners 2,140 feet below Brookwood, Alabama, in Jim Walter Resources (JWR) Mine No. 5. The accident was the worst mine disaster in the United States since 1984 and the worst in Alabama since 1943. The miners' bodies were not recovered until November, after the damaged part of the mine was made safe for rescuers to enter by such measures as pumping 33.5 million gallons of water into the pit to drive off unvented methane. Families of the miners filed wrongful death suits, and the United Mine Workers of America pointed out a number of serious violations at the facility, which was America's deepest vertical-shaft coal mine; the federal government levied a $435,000 fine on JWR, citing the company for seven "high negligence" safety violations. Shortly thereafter, the mine was closed for a brief period. JWR reached a confidential settlement with the miners' families in January 2005.

Unable to find a buyer for the coal mining operation, Walter withdrew the company from the market in 2001, along with JW Aluminum, both of which had been put up for sale in 1999. In 2002, Walter posted a $52.5 million loss on sales of $1.4 billion; in 2001 sales had been $1.3 billion. In 2003 sales dropped again to $1.3 billion, and Walter lost $29 million. A price war in the pipe industry, falling coal prices, and difficulties rolling out a new data management and sales computer system at Walter Homes contributed to the 2003 loss. In addition, although mining operations had resumed at Mine No. 5, geological faults in the mine drove up the cost of extracting coal, and JWR closed the mine again, losing $16.1 million for the year. The year was not without some success, however; Walter managed to sell Applied Industrial Materials Corp. (AIMCOR), a manufacturer of petroleum coke Walter had acquired in 1997, to Oxbow Carbon & Minerals for $127.7 million. JW Aluminum, which had been withdrawn from sale due to lack of suitable bids, managed to fetch $125 million from Wellspring Capital.

In 2004, the company's fortunes turned once again. Coal prices began to rise due to an increased demand for steel worldwide. Walter took JWR off the market and re-opened Mine No. 5 as old customers increased their orders, onetime customers resumed buying, and new customers importuned JWR for coal. Walter's majority owner Kohlberg Kravis Roberts began slowly divesting its holdings, reducing its stake from 33.3 percent ownership to 27 percent by selling stock back to the company. Analysts considered the divestiture a sign of renewed health at Walter, since KKR specialized in bringing ailing companies back to health and then selling them at a profit. KKR had controlled Walter for 17 years, whereas it usually owned companies for an average of eight years. By the beginning of 2005, Walter Industries stock jumped from an average price between $10 and $15 per share to an average price around $30 per share. Janet Gellici, executive director of the American Coal Council in Phoenix, Arizona, and a 25-year veteran in the coal industry, told Dave Simanoff of the *Tampa Tribune* (January 9, 2005) that building booms in such countries as India and China and reduced exports from some coal-producing countries drove up demand for and prices of U.S. coal. Increased U.S. exports of the mineral would likely increase demand for coal and steel at home as the U.S. economy rebounded. Walter's return to profitability was directly linked to the rising coal market. "I think it's a longer-term trend," said Gellici, adding "I don't see that going away anytime soon."

Principal Subsidiaries

Best Insurors,Inc.; Cardem Insurance Company, Ltd.; Crestline Homes, Inc.; Jim Walter Homes, Inc.; Jim Walter Resources, Inc.; Mid-State Homes, Inc.; Neatherlin Homes; Sloss Industries; United States Pipe and Foundry Company, Inc.; Walter Mortgage Company.

Principal Operating Units

Homebuilding; Financing; Industrial Products.

Principal Competitors

American Cast Iron Pipe Company, Centex Corporation, Drummond Company Inc.

Further Reading

Barrett, Amy, "Bad-Time Bull," *Financial World,* July 23, 1991, pp. 28–29.

Barancik, Scott, "A New Tract for Walter," *St. Petersburg Times,* February 8, 2002, p. 1E.

——, "Asbestos Specter Haunts Walter," *St. Petersburg Times,* May 1, 2003, p. 1E.

——, "Coal's So Hot, It Warms Walter," *St. Petersburg Times,* November 25, 2004, p. 1D.

——, "Walter Enters Lending Business," *St. Petersburg Times,* July 27, 2001, p. 1E.

——, "Walter Industries Says It Will Trim Its Board," *St. Petersburg Times,* March 23, 2005, p. 1D.

——, "Walter's Stock Rise Good for Its Bonds," *St. Petersburg Times,* January 5, 2005, p. 5D.

Canning, Michael, "Known Both for Gifts and No Nonsense," *St. Petersburg Times,* August 6, 2004, p. 4.

de Lisser, Eleena, "Walter Industries Ends Proceedings Under Chapter 11," *Wall Street Journal,* March 20, 1995, p. B4.

"Diversified Co. Eyes Water Transmission Buys," *Corporate Financing Week,* November 15, 2004, p. 4.

"Firm Closes Two Buys, Has $500 Million more to Spend," *Corporate Financing Week,* December 15, 2003, p. B1.

Heller, Emily, "Walter Inds. Faces Legal Crossroads," *Tampa Bay Business Journal,* October 9, 1992, p. 1.

Hundley, Kris, "Walter to Trim up to 375 Jobs," *St. Petersburg Times,* August 3, 2000, p. 1E.

Kelly, Bruce, "Ferrosilicon Maker Set for Purchase, Expansion," *American Metal Market,* October 14, 1997, p. 16.

Lambert, Wade, and Greg Steinmetz, "Walter Industries Is Found Not Liable for Asbestos Claims at a Former Unit," *Wall Street Journal,* April 19, 1994, p. A4.

Lesly, Elizabeth, and Gail DeGeorge, "Another Embarrassment for KKR?," *Business Week,* August 1, 1994, pp. 56–57.

Marcial, Gene G., "Walter's Firm New Foundation," *Business Week,* January 13, 1997, p. 55.

Meinhardt, Jane, "DeFossett Sees New Market, Costs Cutting at Walter," *Business Journal* (Tampa, Fla.), June 29, 2001, p. 25.

Moscow, Alvin, *Building a Business: The Jim Walter Story,* Sarasota, Fla.: Pineapple Press, 1995.

"Oxbow Carbon & Minerals Has Agreed to Acquire Applied Industrial Materials (AIMCOR) from Walter Industries for $127.7m," *Petroleum Economist,* December 2003, p. 44.

Parks, Kyle, "Critics Fire Away at Walter Meeting," *St. Petersburg Times,* October 20, 2000, p. 1E.

Regan, Bob, "Durham Gets Back into Driver's Seat: Ex-PD Chief Steers Walter Industries," *American Metal Market,* June 13, 1991, p. 4.

Sachar, Laura, "Building the Blue-Collar Dreams," *Financial World,* May 19, 1987.

Simanoff, Dave, "Company Working to Renew Fortunes," *Tampa Tribune,* April 21, 2004, p. 1.

——, "King Coal," *Tampa Tribune,* January 9, 2005, p. 1.

——, "Walter Industries CEO Says He's Confident of Future Profit Despite Loss," *Tampa Tribune,* April 30, 2004.

——, "Walter Industries Hits Market," *Tampa Tribune,* April 25, 2003, p. 1.

——, "Walter Industries Rebuilds," *Tampa Tribune,* October 31, 2003, p. 1.

"Under Construction," *Tampa Tribune,* October 22, 2001, p. 1.

"Vote Nixes Liquidation of Walter Holdings," *Tampa Tribune,* October 20, 2000, p. 1.

"Walter Industries Keeps Formula for Success Simple," *Tampa Tribune,* June 6, 1999, p. 26.

"Walter Industries to Offer Bonds to Help Pay Off Debt," *St. Petersburg Times,* April 14, 2004, p. 6D.

"Walter Industries: The Sum of Its Parts," *Tampa Tribune,* October 9, 2000.

"Walter's New Chief Aims for Turnabout," *Tampa Tribune,* February 13, 2001, p. 1.

"Walter Starts Lending Unit to Fund Homes," *Origination News,* September 2001, p. 17.

White, George, "KKR's Sells off Portfolio Companies," *Daily Deal,* April 29, 2004.

—Lynn M. Kalanik
—updates: David E. Salamie; Jennifer Gariepy

Wirtz Corporation

680 North Lakeshore Drive, 19th Floor
Chicago, Illinois 60611
U.S.A.
Telephone: (312) 943-7000
Fax: (312) 943-9017

Private Company
Founded: 1922
Employees: 2,200
Sales: $1 billion (2004 est.)
NAIC: 711211 Sports Teams and Clubs; 531210 Offices of Real Estate Agents and Brokers; 424819 Beer and Ale Merchant Wholesalers; 424820 Wine and Distilled Alcoholic Beverage Merchant Wholesalers

Wirtz Corporation houses the varied business interests of Chicago's influential Wirtz family, best known as the owners of the Chicago Blackhawks National Hockey League team. The company is also part owner of the United Center, where the Blackhawks and the Chicago Bulls basketball team play. The privately held Wirtz Corporation is highly discreet about its holdings, which at the very least include insurance, liquor distributorships in Illinois and Nevada, banks in suburban Chicago and Miami, apartment buildings on Chicago's North Side, and real estate interests in Florida, Mississippi, Nevada, Texas, and Wisconsin. The company is headed by William W. Wirtz, son of its founder. Next in line to inherit control of the corporation's voting stock is William Wirtz' son, William Rockwell "Rocky" Wirtz. Generating approximately $1 billion in annual revenues, Wirtz Corporation is one of the largest private companies in the United States.

Company Founded in the 1920s

The founder of the Wirtz empire was Arthur Michael Wirtz, who was born in Chicago in 1901 to a policeman and his wife. After graduating from the University of Michigan, he returned to Chicago to become a real estate salesman in 1922, which represents the start of the Wirtz Corporation. He was a gruff, imposing man, standing six-foot five-inches and eventually weighing 340 pounds. He was also driven to succeed, working all hours of the day. Wags suggested that his initials (A. M.) stood for "after midnight." After the stock market crash of 1929 ushered in the Great Depression, while other businessmen retrenched or failed, Wirtz hit his stride, picking up distressed properties for nickels on the dollar. He also became involved in sports during the early 1930s, joining forces with grain speculator James Norris and his sons. More than 20 years older than Wirtz, Norris was a Canadian-born businessman who had set up his grain brokerage in Chicago. Growing up, he was an excellent athlete, a standout at squash and tennis and an amateur hockey player as well. Norris attempted to land a National Hockey League franchise in Chicago, and when that effort failed he set his sites on a struggling Detroit franchise. In 1933, Wirtz and Norris formed a partnership to purchase the team and the Olympia Stadium where the Falcons, as they were then called, played their home games. Two years later, Wirtz and Norris acquired Chicago Stadium, home of the Chicago Blackhawks, but they would not gain control of the team until much later. During the intervening years, the partners acquired interests in other arenas and convention centers around the country, including New York's Madison Square Garden and facilities in St, Louis, Omaha, and Indianapolis.

Although not yet a hockey mogul, Wirtz became involved in a different ice skating business. In December 1935, he produced one of the first ice shows, which played for two nights at Chicago Stadium. Encouraged by the results, in 1936 he signed Norwegian figure skater Sonja Henie after she won her third consecutive Olympic gold medal to star in a touring ice show, "Hollywood Ice Revue." It played 17 performances in nine U.S. cities, primarily in the arenas that Wirtz owned or held an interest in. Henie then launched a movie career, starring in musical comedies that showed off her skating skills and to Wirtz's delight promoted her ice shows. From 1937 to 1951, Wirtz and Henie co-produced an annual Hollywood Ice Revue that toured the United States and Europe. Wirzt focused on New York City in 1940, producing "It Happens On Ice" at the Radio City Music Hall and drawing 1.5 million people. Later in 1940, he and Henie took on Broadway, co-producing the Rockefeller Center Ice Revue. Although Henie did not skate in the show, it would draw 12 million customers during its ten-year run at Broadway's Center Theatre. Henie broke away from Wirtz in 1950 and tried

1922: Company founded by Arthur M. Wirtz.
1935: Wirtz and a partner acquire a Chicago Stadium.
1936: Wirtz signs Sonja Henie for ice shows.
1941: Wirtz acquires its first liquor distributorship.
1954: Wirtz Corporation acquires controlling interest in Blackhawks hockey team.
1957: A Wirtz boxing venture is ruled a monopoly and broken up.
1970: A controlling interest the in Chicago Bulls is acquired.
1983: Wirtz dies and is succeeded by his son, William W. Wirtz.
1994: Wirtz and Bulls' owner Jerry Reinsdorf build United Center.
2004: National Hockey League (NHL) season is cancelled.

competing against him. Wirtz replaced her with a younger Olympic champion, Canadian Barbara Ann Scott. Henie's review soon hit financial difficulties, exacerbated by a bleacher collapse at one of her performances, and in 1953 she was forced to terminate her show. Wirtz, meanwhile, continued to solidify his reputation as the king of the ice show format, going on to promote more Olympic skating champions: Jo Jo Starbuck, Dorothy Hamill, and Janet Lynn. He finally exited the show business in 1979 when he sold "Holiday on Ice" and another show to the owners of Ringling Brothers and Barnum & Bailey Circus.

A Basketball Pioneer in the 1940s

Wirtz's evolution into a sports promoter was a function of his real estate business, essentially an attempt to find a way to make money out of his arena properties. After his success with Sonja Henie, Wirtz looked to professional basketball in the 1940s as a way to fill more open dates. College basketball had become quite popular in the 1930s, and many college players, to continue playing, joined industrial leagues or nascent professional leagues. In 1937, the National Basketball league was launched but struggled to survive until the end of World War II. In 1946, Wirtz, who was credited with creating the popular concept of the college basketball doubleheader, became the key figure in the creation of a rival professional league. He convinced arena owners who owned hockey teams to create the Arena Managers Association of America in order to establish the Basketball Association of America. For his part, Wirtz became part owner of the Chicago Stags franchise. The two leagues attempted to coexist, but the market for professional basketball proved too small. On the verge of collapse, in 1949 the NBL's six remaining teams joined the BAA, which then modified its name, becoming the National Basketball Association. The Stags played in the NBA's inaugural season, but the team never caught on with Chicago fans and ultimately folded. The NBA tried Chicago again in 1961 with a franchise called the Packers, but it soon moved to Baltimore to become the Bullets, later relocating to Washington, D.C., to become the Wizards. In 1966, Chicago received an NBA expansion franchise called the Bulls, but ownership was uncertain, leading Wirtz to once again become involved in professional basketball. He put together an investment

group in 1970 to purchase a controlling interest in the Bulls, which he would head until his death.

Boxing was another sport Wirtz promoted as a way to fill Chicago Stadium and his other arenas. In 1949, he and Norris formed the International Boxing Club, which would go on to produce twice-weekly nationally televised prizefights and gain a stranglehold on championship fights. From 1949 to 1955, IBC promoted 47 out of 51 championship bouts held in the United States. The venture's control of the sport was so great that it attracted the attention of the government, and in 1957 IBC was broken up as a monopoly.

As a sportsman, Wirtz was best remembered as the owner of the Chicago Blackhawks. In September 1952, he and the Norris family gained control of the franchise. Three months later, James Norris died, leaving his interest to his sons. By 1954, Wirtz, along with his brother Michael, gained a controlling interest in the team. His son, William Wadsworth Wirtz, would play an increasing role in the running of the club and was named president of the Blackhawks and Chicago Stadium Corporation in 1966. The team enjoyed a golden era during the 1960s and early 1970s, winning the Stanley Cup in 1961 and fielding such players as high-scoring Bobby Hull and goalie Tony Esposito.

Real estate ventures and sporting interests were not enough to keep the inexhaustible Arthur Wirtz fully occupied, however. In 1941, eight years after the repeal of Prohibition, he acquired his first liquor distributorship, Milwaukee-based Edison Liquor Company. Over the ensuing years other distributorships would be brought into the fold, such as Judge & Dolph, Ltd., which he purchased from the Walgreen Drug Company in 1945. Judge & Dolph had started out in St. Louis in 1890 as a pharmaceutical company, then in 1933 was incorporated in Illinois as a Chicago wine and spirits wholesaler. The company added smaller operations so that by the mid-1990s it was selling more then half of the liquor and wine sold in Illinois. In addition, Wirtz Corporation became involved in the selling of liquor in other markets, such as Nevada, Minnesota, and Texas. Wirtz also entered the insurance field in 1960, when it launched the Wirtz Insurance Agency, offering property, casualty, and health insurance. Although it is difficult to determine when Wirtz Corporation became involved in the banking business, its holdings in this area eventually included Elmwood Park, Illinois-based First Security Trust & Savings Bank, First National Bank of South Miami, as well as a holding company which acquired interests in another 15 banks, including Charlotte, North Carolina-based NationsBank Corp. and First Union Corp; Columbus, Ohio-based Banc One Corp.; and Jacksonville, Florida-based Barnett Banks Inc.

A New Generation Takes the Reins in the 1980s

In August 1983, Arthur Wirtz died of cancer. Control of Wirtz Corporation passed to his eldest son, William, who inherited the voting stock. William Wirtz nonetheless work closely with brother Arthur Michael Wirtz, Jr. After graduating from Brown University in 1950, William Wirtz considered a career in the Central Intelligence Agency as well as archaeology before taking a job as a certified public accountant with Peat Marwick. Three years later, he joined his father in managing the family's myriad business affairs. When his father died, William was in his early 50s. He was politically and socially connected and had forged his own reputation as a hard-nosed businessman. Essentially, he carried on where his father left off, buying smart, holding onto assets, and looking to operate them efficiently. The Blackhawks remained a prized asset, the Bulls basketball team less so. In 1984, the owner of the Chicago White Sox, Jerry Reinsdorf, assembled a group of investors and purchased a controlling interest in the team. That was also the rookie season of Michael Jordan, who would lead the Bulls to six NBA championships and eclipse the Blackhawks, which became mired in mediocrity, a situation many fans laid at the door of William Wirtz, whom they regarded as cheap and derisively called "Dollar Bill."

Like his father, Wirtz was not a man to cross. In the late 1980s, he became interested in building a West Side stadium for the Bears football team and invited Bears' president Michael McCaskey to explore the idea with him. According to the *Chicago Sun-Times*, McCaskey joined forces with Mayor Eurgene Sawyer "in an attempted end-run around Wirtz in Springfield." The means for this action was a bill requesting state funds for street and sewer repairs that "included a clause that would have ceded control of 40 acres of Wirtz-owned parking lots to the Bears upon the death of Bill Wirtz or the sale of Chicago Stadium. In a flash, Wirtz assembled a clout-heavy lobbying team and snuffed out the move. It never even came to a vote. 'It's embarrassing. They should have known better.' Wirtz said of the episode."

United Center Built in the Early 1990s

The Bears remained in their longtime home of Soldier's Field, which was eventually renovated, but Wirtz and Reinsdorf joined forces in the early 1994 to build a new arena for the Bulls and the Blackhawks, the United Center. The project required the demolition of numerous homes, resulting in outcries from the community and the politicians that represented them. At the insistence of the mayor, Wirtz and Reinsdorf entered into talks with West Side residents and eventually agreed to invest millions in replacement housing, small business loans, and community projects.

The added revenues derived from the United Center helped to bolster the balance sheet of Wirtz Corporation, but Blackhawk fans continued to complain that the extra money did not trickle down to the players the team put on the ice. Wirtz also failed to keep up with the changing nature of the game. During the 1990s, the National Hockey League added four teams that played in the Western and Mountain time zones. Wirtz refused to televise home games in the belief that attendance would suffer, a policy long abandoned by other clubs. Because Chicago was in the NHL's Western Conference, a large percentage of its televised away games had late start times. In essence, the Blackhawks began to slip from the city's sports consciousness, and fans found it increasingly difficult to follow the team. The situation became so bad that the Blackhawks had to pay a local radio station to broadcast its games. The game itself was in trouble, due in large part to the owners' inability to rein in escalating player salaries. The league wanted the players to accept a salary cap that, in effect, would save the owners from themselves, but the players refused the proposal when a new collective bargaining agreement was negotiated in 2003 and 2004. In truth, because of Wirtz, the Blackhawks already oper-

ated with a self-imposed salary cap. Chicago fans took cold comfort in having an owner who, for the sake of fiscal responsibility, was willing to dump high-priced stars and put on the ice a collection of young players and lower caliber veterans. They gave Wirtz no credit for taking a principled stand. Instead, they thought he was finding a way to make money on a losing team. Consequently, Blackhawks' fans retained interest in the team only to the extent that they became embittered about how it was being run. When negotiations broke down between the players and league in 2004, the owners locked out the players, resulting in the cancellation of the 2004–05 season, the first time that a professional sports league had been forced to cancel an entire season because of a labor impasse. Players and owners finally reached an agreement in the summer of 2005. Moreover, with the Bulls enjoying a resurgence, there was a question regarding how much Chicago fans would care about the Blackhawks if and when the team returned to the ice. The Wirtz Corporation, because of its stake in the United Center, was better off than most hockey owners, and, given the company's many other business interests, the plight of the Blackhawks meant more to the Wirtz family's pride than its balance sheet.

William Wirtz suffered a heart attack in 1995, prompting him to quit drinking and give up a five-pack-a-day cigarette habit. A year later, he suffered a major loss when his brother, whom he regarded as his right-hand man, died. He continued to head Wirtz Corporation in 2005, but succession plans were already in place. William Wirtz's eldest son, William "Rocky" Wirtz, was to inherit the voting stock, so that one of the Wirtz children would have final say, thus emulating what his father had done when passing the mantle to him. There was also every reason to believe that the Wirtz Corporation would continue to be run in much the same way it had for decades: close to the vest. There was certainly no thought about taking the company public. As William Wirtz told *Crain's Chicago Business*, "I don't know anyone who has taken their family business public who doesn't regret it."

Principal Subsidiaries

Chicago Blackhawk Hockey Team, Inc.; The United Center (50%); Judge & Dolph, Ltd.; First Miami Bancorp, Inc.

Principal Competitors

Detroit Red Wings; St. Louis Blues Hockey Club L.L.C.; Johnson Brothers Liquor Company; Southern Wine & Spirits of America, Inc.

Further Reading

"Arthur M. Wirtz," *Amusement Business*, December 27, 1999, p. 11.
"Arthur M. Wirtz, Team Owner, Dies," *New York Times*, July 22, 1983.
Borden, Jeff, "Banks, Booze, Buildings," *Crain's Chicago Business*, April 14, 1997, p. 1.
Mullman, Jeremy, "Blackhawks Down," *Crain's Chicago Business*, November 2, 2003, p. 1.
Spielman, Fran, "The Puck Stops Here," *Chicago Sun-Times*, August 28, 1994.

—Ed Dinger

ZiLOG, Inc.

523 Race Street
San Jose, California 95126
U.S.A.
Telephone: (408) 558-8500
Fax: (408) 558-8300
Web site: http://www.zilog.com

Public Company
Incorporated: 1974
Employees: 509
Sales: $95.6 million (2004)
Stock Exchanges: NASDAQ
Ticker Symbol: ZILG
NAIC: 334413 Semiconductor and Related Device
    Manufacturing

ZiLOG, Inc., designs, develops, and manufactures 8-bit micrologic semiconductor devices, also known as embedded control devices, used in consumer electronics, home appliances, security systems, point-of-sale terminals, personal computer peripherals, personal health and medical products, and industrial and automotive applications. The company was a pioneer of the computer chip industry in the mid-1970s. Weak demand for its products and lack of a stable business strategy left it stumbling for many years during the 1980s and 1990s. ZiLOG filed for Chapter 11 bankruptcy protection in 2001. It emerged the following year with plans to focus solely on embedded control devices.

Establishing ZiLOG in the 1970s

Formed in the mid-1970s, ZiLOG was a trailblazer in the semiconductor industry and a pioneer of the California high-tech hotbed known as Silicon Valley. The company was founded by electrical engineer and entrepreneur Ralph Ungermann. Ungermann grew up in California. His parents, both educators, encouraged active learning, and Ralph proved to be a quick study and hard worker. In high school, Ungermann was fascinated by an event that would change the course of his life: The Soviet Union launched Sputnik, the world's first satellite. "I was leaning toward a career in law or medicine when the Russians launched the space race," Ungermann recalled in the December 17, 1990 *Business Journal-San Jose.* "I was absolutely enthralled. I would be an engineer."

Ungermann won a Navy scholarship that allowed him to eventually complete his electrical engineering degree at the University of California at Berkeley, and then a master's degree in computer architecture from the University of California at Irvine. After college, Ungermann took a job with Collins Radio, which was one of the leading technology firms of its day. During his stint at Collins, Ungermann became fascinated with semiconductors. Semiconductor breakthroughs during the 1960s by Bell Labs and other companies were just beginning to open the door to a commercial chip industry. When Rockwell International purchased Collins in 1969, Ungermann decided to leave the company for Silicon Valley pioneer Intel.

Ungermann gained valuable experience working for Intel between 1971 and 1974. He also invested heavily in Intel stock options and learned a tough lesson in personal debt accumulation. While looking for a better-paying job to help him pay off some of his debts, he developed a plan to start his own company. Ungermann teamed up with another Intel engineer, Federico Faggin, to cofound ZiLOG. They planned to develop an 8-bit microprocessor (a computer's central processing unit on a silicon chip) that could drive desktop computers, which were a relatively new concept at the time. Shortly after starting the company, the two engineers scored a major victory when they managed to convince the giant Exxon Corporation to write a $1.5 million check to launch their research and development effort.

In less than a year Ungermann's team had created a breakthrough 8-bit microprocessor, beating the well-heeled Intel and Motorola to the punch. Dubbed the Z80, ZiLOG's chip was an immediate hit. The Z80 became the heart of many of the earliest personal computers and the processor of choice for electronic game manufacturers like Coleco in the emerging video game industry. Within a few years ZiLOG was generating $50 million in sales annually. Exxon, delighted with ZiLOG's success, began investing heavily in the company. With Exxon's financial backing, ZiLOG began drafting plans to start manufacturing computer systems and semiconductor components to complement its cutting-edge chips.

Company Perspectives:

Our strategy is to be a key provider of micrologic devices. To implement our business strategy, we intend to focus on our core 8-bit micrologic business, expand our addressable portion of 8-bit market, introduce devices targeted at key vertical markets, deliver complete solutions to our customers, and utilize efficient manufacturing.

Overcoming Problems in the Late 1970s and Early 1980s

At the same time, ZiLOG tried to maintain its lead in the race to build faster, more powerful microprocessor chips. To that end, in 1979 ZiLOG introduced its second-generation, 16-bit chip, called the Z8000. The chip was a dynamo, but it appeared about a year after Intel's 16-bit chip, the 8086. ZiLOG was also slow to bring out the complementary software that potential users of the chip needed to incorporate the microprocessors into their electronics products, and as a result the company was unable to capitalize on its established market presence to counter its late start. The result was a pounding by the competition.

The hardest blow to ZiLOG was delivered by IBM, which selected Intel's easier-to-program 8086 to drive its first personal computer, and Intel went on to become the multibillion-dollar leader of the global chip industry. Aside from losing its command of the chip industry, ZiLOG was forced to deal with the displeasure of Exxon. After investing millions of dollars into research and development at ZiLOG, Exxon began to lose patience.

Throughout the late 1970s Exxon had allowed ZiLOG to operate autonomously. Critics charged that ZiLOG, free from constraints placed on other companies by financial markets, wasted millions of dollars developing technologies without a solid business plan. When it became clear that ZiLOG was losing the chip race, Exxon began to assert more control and started to steer ZiLOG toward the field of computerized manufacturing. ZiLOG's management resisted Exxon's direction, and in 1979 Ungermann left to start a new company. Faggin remained for another year in a diminished managerial role before leaving to start his own venture.

After peaking at more than $100 million in annual sales, ZiLOG's revenues started to slip and the company began to lose money, posting an embarrassing deficit of more than $30 million in 1981 and 1982, combined, as Exxon scrambled to fill the leadership void left by Ungermann. Manny Fernandez, a rising star who Exxon lured away from Fairchild, filled in as chief executive for several months. He, too, fled to start his own computer company, however, after becoming disillusioned with ZiLOG.

In May 1982 Exxon hired Franc deWeeger to head the limping ZiLOG. The 50-year-old deWeeger was a seasoned semiconductor manager with more than 15 years at Motorola and two years with a small technology company called Signetics. DeWeeger moved quickly to change the situation at ZiLOG. "When I joined the company," he said in the June 20, 1983 *Forbes,* "everybody was moaning and groaning about Exxon. I said, stop pointing the finger at Exxon . . . the responsibility lies

with the management team." Aside from shaking up management, deWeeger scored a few encouraging victories. Significantly, he succeeded in getting Commodore to adopt ZiLOG's Z8000 chip as the microprocessor for its next-generation home and business computers. He also won an $18 million contract to supply the Internal Revenue Service with computers from ZiLOG's struggling systems division.

Turnaround in the Late 1980s

Despite deWeeger's best efforts, ZiLOG posted successive losses throughout the early 1980s and into the mid-1980s and, were it not for the deep-pocketed Exxon, would likely have gone out of business. By 1985 the end seemed near. "It did not seem as if there were any way to recover," William Walker, senior vice-president and chief financial officer of Exxon Corporation, recalled in the June 1989 *Electronics*. As a last-ditch effort, Walker brought in 55-year-old E.A. Sack to try his hand at revitalizing the chip company. "Turn it around or shut it down," was the mandate given to Sack.

Sack was born and raised in Pittsburgh and had worked as an underaged employee in the local steel mills during World War II. Older G.I.s got him interested in the field of electronics at Carnegie Mellon University, where Sack was a top student. One of his professors was Gaylord Penney, the inventor of many early cutting-edge electronics products. Sack and Penney struck up a relationship and continued to talk regularly on the telephone into the early 1990s, by which time Penney was 95 years old. Sack graduated at the top of his class and went on to get master's and doctoral degrees in electrical engineering. He worked at various technology leaders including Bell Labs, General Electric Co., and Westinghouse, where he was a rising star in research and development. Sack also had a knack for sales, which allowed him to work his way into the executive ranks first at Westinghouse and then at General Instruments Corp. He boosted sales from $10 million to $180 million over a 10-year period at General Instruments before accepting Exxon's ZiLOG challenge.

By the time Sack took over, sales had fallen to $50 million, the organization was losing $5 million per month, employee morale was at an all-time low, and the company's prospects were dismal. In Sack's estimation, ZiLOG was still trying to be a contender in an industry niche that it had long ago forfeited. Sack quickly took drastic steps, laying off most of the 1,000 employees at ZiLOG's Campbell, California headquarters and moving manufacturing activities to lower-cost regions in the United States and overseas. He jettisoned unremarkable managers and junked many of ZiLOG's poorly performing operations. His actions earned him little favor within the ranks of ZiLOG's workforce. One disgruntled former employee, in fact, returned with a rifle and fired shots into windows at the headquarters building.

ZiLOG's financial performance quickly began to improve, with the company posting its first profit in 1986 after several years of consecutive losses and continuing to record surpluses throughout the late 1980s and early 1990s. Much of the key to ZiLOG's turnaround was Sack's innovative product strategy. Rather than chase the hyper-competitive market for cutting-edge microprocessors, he decided to tailor ZiLOG's existing and proven technologies for specific niche markets that were less competitive, but also less risky. "The whole company was trying to relive the Z80 thing,'' Walker explained in the October 12, 1992 *Business Journal-San Jose*. ''He was quick and decisive in making the fundamental changes that clearly saved the company.''

Recognizing ZiLOG's limited ability to compete in 16-bit and emerging 32-bit technologies, Sack decided to draw on ZiLOG's old Z80 8-bit chip to manufacture new application-specific standard circuits (ASSCs), which are essentially chips tailored for specific applications. For example, ZiLOG was able to create special versions of its Z80 chip for use in telephone answering machines and to control closed-caption television systems. The strategy was effective, as evidenced by sales and profit gains beginning in 1986. To augment its 8-bit ASSCs, Sack initiated the development of a new family of 8-bit microcontroller chips called the Z8. Sales of those controllers, combined with demand growth for Z80 processors, allowed ZiLOG to double its revenues between 1985 and 1989 to more than $100 million annually. Furthermore, ZiLOG was aggressively developing technology for cell-based application-specific integrated circuits, or circuits designed for a specific customer, rather than a standard application.

In addition to his savvy product strategy, Sack was able to realize impressive gains at ZiLOG with a management strategy he had created at General Instrument Corp. called ''forward controllership.'' Forward controllership was a closed-loop system used to manage revenue, variable costs, fixed costs, and cash. The advantage of the system was that it helped managers to focus on current and future growth and costs, rather than on past performance. The system involved relatively advanced computer modeling techniques and information management systems. Sack had found it extremely helpful in minimizing expenses and maximizing the return from limited resources.

Going Public in 1991

Having achieved profitability with the subsidiary, Exxon decided early in 1989 that it was time to sell off ZiLOG and get out of the semiconductor business. With the backing of venture capital firm Warburg Pincus, Sack and a group of executives spearheaded a leveraged buyout that included ZiLOG's employees. The purchase made ZiLOG independent, but it also saddled the company with $33 million in debt. Fortunately for ZiLOG, Sack's new operating strategy proved more successful than most observers had suspected it would. The company was soon generating more than enough cash to cover its debt service and was even able to begin reducing its liabilities. ZiLOG capitalized on its success in 1991 by taking the company public. The initial

public offering virtually eliminated ZiLOG's long-term debt and positioned it to capitalize on overall semiconductor market growth throughout the early 1990s and into the mid-1990s.

ZiLOG topped its remarkable late 1980s recovery with impressive revenue and profit gains in the 1990s. Sales grew 10 percent to $110 million in 1991 before jumping to $146 million in 1992, $203 million in 1993, and $223 million in 1994. Likewise, net income grew from $6.8 million in 1990 to $15.8 million in 1992, and $34.9 million in 1994. ZiLOG managed to achieve that growth without assuming any long-term debt, and invested heavily to continually upgrade its state-of-the-art production facilities and to sustain its research and development pipeline of new circuits. By the mid-1990s, ZiLOG was manufacturing and marketing circuits for a wide range of applications, including interactive television controllers, computer modems, electronic musical instruments, garage door openers, and a digital video-image enhancement system that converted standard television pictures to much sharper images.

ZiLOG entered the mid-1990s with its sights set on the sprawling information highway. Still drawing on Z80 and Z8 ASSP technology, as well as other proprietary technologies, it was manufacturing and developing a wide range of semiconductor products aimed at computer networks, interactive multimedia, and wireless communications. In 1995 ZiLOG employed about 1,500 workers, operated manufacturing facilities in the United States and the Philippines, and supported 26 direct sales offices and 120 distributors throughout the world.

Changes in the Late 1990s and Beyond

ZiLOG faced falling profits once again in 1996 and 1997 as demand for its products began to weaken. When Lucent Technologies Inc.—its largest customer—failed to renew a contract, ZiLOG found itself facing a major financial setback. To make matters worse, a new fabrication facility that opened in Idaho remained underutilized due to the falling demand.

In 1997, private investment firm Texas Pacific Group (TPG) agreed to acquire ZiLOG. The $396 million transaction was completed early the following year. Curtis Crawford, a seasoned executive who had worked for IBM, AT&T, and Lucent Technologies, was tapped to orchestrate a turnaround. ''I did not come here to be part of a small company,'' Crawford claimed in a June 1998 *Electronics Times* article. ''I came to ZiLOG to change its direction, and make it an even larger, more successful microconductor company.'' Indeed, Crawford quickly launched a realignment that turned ZiLOG's focus to supplying embedded chips to the home entertainment industry, to the standard products and integrated devices market, and to the transaction-style communications devices market.

As part of this strategy, ZiLOG acquired chip designer Production Languages in 1999 and bought a 20 percent interest in Qualcore Inc. The company also set plans in motion to team up with Sunbeam Corp. to develop chips that would enable household appliances to communicate, or be connected, with each other. With ZiLOG's fortunes back on the rise, TPG planned to take the company public in 2000.

Those plans were scrapped, however, when problems began once again to plague the company. As demand for the company's products waned, the firm found itself buried in debt as costs continued to climb. Crawford stepped down in early 2001, leaving former chief financial officer Jim Thorburn at the helm. Knowing the company needed some drastic measures to keep it afloat, Thorburn immediately set out to restructure the company's finances. ZiLOG filed for Chapter 11 bankruptcy protection while its creditors swapped more than $300 million in debt for equity. By the time ZiLOG emerged from bankruptcy in 2002, TPG had sold off its ownership stake.

Under Thorburn's leadership, ZiLOG went back to its roots and focused heavily on 8-bit micrologic semiconductor devices—also known as embedded control devices. The company defined micrologic device in its 2004 Securities and Exchange filing. "Micrologic devices," ZiLOG reported, "typically combine a microprocessor, memory, and peripheral functions on a single device. Our embedded control devices enable customers in our target markets to control the functions and performance of their products. By embedding their application software on our devices, customers can control a wide variety of products such as consumer appliances, infrared remote controls, security systems and battery chargers."

As part of its new strategy, ZiLOG shuttered its communications business while producing 60 new products including the eZ80 Acclaim! 8-bit microcontroller that was used in products such as USA Technologies' cashless vending machines. In 2004, it launched its Z8 Encore! XP flash microcontroller product line. By that time, ZiLOG was once again trading on the NASDAQ and its financial position appeared to be stable. The company's management team was confident ZiLOG was finally on the right track for success in the years to come.

Principal Subsidiaries

ZiLOG Philippines, Inc.; ZiLOG Electronic Philippines, Inc.; ZiLOG Asia Ltd.; ZiLOG Japan K.K.; ZiLOG International Ltd.; ZiLOG International Pte. Ltd.; ZiLOG UK, Ltd.; ZiLOG India Electronics Private Ltd.; ZiLOG MOD III, Inc.

Principal Competitors

Atmel Corporation; Freescale Semiconductor Inc.; Microchip Technology Inc.

Further Reading

Bursky, Dave, "The Secret's Out: ZiLOG's in the Black," *Electronics,* January 1989, p. 159.

Carlson, Brad, "After Reorganization, Zilog Sees Growth in Core 8-bit Business," *Idaho Business Review,* June 14, 2002, p. A1.

Cole, Bernard C., "How ZiLOG Managed to Turn Itself Around: The Key Is a Concept Called Forward Controllership," *Electronics,* June 1989, p. 117.

"Flying Start," *Electronic Times,* June 8, 1998.

Krey, Michael, "Edgar Stack: Strong Leadership Helped Save ZiLOG from Total Failure," *Business Journal-San Jose,* October 12, 1992, p. 12.

——, "Ralph Ungermann: Former Dean of ZiLOG U. Now in Networking," *Business Journal-San Jose,* December 17, 1990, p. 12.

Lapedus, Mark, and Mike Clendenin, "Zilog Turns Toward China to Pump 8-bit MCU Sales," *Electronic Engineering Times,* April 5, 2004, p. 34.

Pitta, Julie, "Back to Basics," *Forbes,* July 8, 1991, p. 95.

Poletti, Therese, "Manny Fernandez: Resilient Entrepreneur, Thoughtful Leader Rides Career Roller Coaster to Sweeping Heights," *Business Journal-San Jose,* December 12, 1988, p. 12.

Ristelhueber, Robert, "As Crawford Surrenders CEO Post, His Vision Remains Unfulfilled," *Electronic Business,* February 5, 2001.

——, "Silicon Valley Standout," *Electronic Business,* May 1, 1998, p. 36.

Sperling, Ed, and Peter Brown, "Zilog Writes New Chapter in Tax Code," *Chilton's Electronic News,* December 3, 2001.

Weigner, Kathleen, "Remember 'Spare the Rod' . . . ? (ZiLOG and Exxon)," *Forbes,* June 20, 1983, p. 36.

—Dave Mote
—update: Christina Stansell Weaver

INDEX TO COMPANIES

Index to Companies

Listings in this index are arranged in alphabetical order under the company name. Company names beginning with a letter or proper name such as Eli Lilly & Co. will be found under the first letter of the company name. Definite articles (The, Le, La) are ignored for alphabetical purposes as are forms of incorporation that precede the company name (AB, NV). Company names printed in bold type have full, historical essays on the page numbers appearing in bold. Updates to entries that appeared in earlier volumes are signified by the notation (**upd.**). Company names in light type are references within an essay to that company, not full historical essays. This index is cumulative with volume numbers printed in bold type.

A & A Die Casting Company, **25** 312
A and A Limousine Renting, Inc., **26** 62
A & A Medical Supply, **61** 206
A & C Black Ltd., **7** 165
A&E Plastics, **12** 377
A&E Television Networks, 32 3–7
A. & J. McKenna, **13** 295
A&K Petroleum Company. *See* Kerr-McGee Corporation.
A & M Instrument Co., **9** 323
A&M Records, **23** 389
A&N Foods Co., **II** 553
A&P. *See* The Great Atlantic & Pacific Tea Company, Inc.
A. and T. McKenna Brass and Copper Works, **13** 295
A & W Brands, Inc., 25 3–5; **57** 227; **58** 384
A-dec, Inc., 53 3–5
á la Zing, **62** 259
A-Mark Financial Corporation, 71 3–6
A-1 Supply. *See* International Game Technology.
A-R Technologies, **48** 275
A.A. Mathews. *See* CRSS Inc.
A. Ahlström Oy. *See* Ahlstrom Corporation.
A.B. Chance Industries Co., Inc., **31** 259
A.B.Dick Company, 28 6–8
A.B. Hemmings, Ltd., **13** 51
A.B. Leasing Corp., **13** 111–12
A-B Nippondenso, **III** 593
A.B. Watley Group Inc., 45 3–5
A-BEC Mobility, **11** 487
A.C. Delco, **26** 347, 349
A.C. Moore Arts & Crafts, Inc., 30 3–5
A.C. Nielsen Company, 13 3–5. *See also* ACNielsen Corporation.
A.C. Wickman, **13** 296
A.D. International (Australia) Pty. Ltd., **10** 272
A/E/C/ Systems International, **27** 362
A.E. Fitkin & Company, **6** 592–93; **50** 37
A.E. Gutman, **16** 486
A.E. Lottes, **29** 86

A.G. Becker, **11** 318; **20** 260
A.G. Edwards, Inc., 8 3–5; **19** 502; **32** 17–21 (**upd.**)
A.G. Industries, Inc., **7** 24
A.G. Morris, **12** 427
A.G. Spalding & Bros., Inc., **24** 402–03
A.G. Stanley Ltd. *See* The Boots Company PLC.
A.H. Belo Corporation, 10 3–5; **28** 367, 369; **30** 13–17 (**upd.**)
A.H. Robins Co., **10** 70; **12** 188; **16** 438; **50** 538
A. Hirsch & Son, **30** 408
A. Hölscher GmbH, **53** 195
A. Johnson & Co. *See* Axel Johnson Group.
A.L. Laboratories Inc., **12** 3
A.L. Pharma Inc., 12 3–5. *See also* Alpharma Inc.
A.L. Van Houtte Inc. *See* Van Houtte Inc.
A. Lambert International Inc., **16** 80
A. Leon Capel and Sons, Inc. *See* Capel Incorporated.
A.M. Castle & Co., 25 6–8
A. Michel et Cie., **49** 84
A. Moksel AG, 59 3–6
A.O. Smith Corporation, 7 139; **22** 181, **11** 3–6; **24** 499; **40** 3–8 (**upd.**)
A.P. Green Refractories, **22** 285
A.P. Møller - Maersk A/S, 57 3–6
A.P. Orleans, Inc. of New Jersey, **62** 262
A.S. Abell Co., **IV** 678
A.S. Watson & Company, **18** 254
A.S. Yakovlev Design Bureau, 15 3–6
A. Schilling & Company. *See* McCormick & Company, Incorporated.
A. Schulman, Inc., 8 6–8; **49** 3–7 (**upd.**)
A. Sulka & Co., **29** 457
A.T. Cross Company, 17 3–5; **49** 8–12 (**upd.**)
A.T. Massey Coal Company, Inc., **34** 164; **57** 236
A.T. Mays, **55** 90
A-T-O Inc. *See* Figgie International, Inc.

A.W. Baulderstone Holdings Pty. Ltd., **55** 62
A.W. Faber-Castell Unternehmensverwaltung GmbH & Co., 51 3–6
A.W. Sijthoff, **14** 555
A-Z International Companies, **III** 569; **20** 361
AA Distributors, **22** 14
AA Energy Corp., **I** 91
AAA Development Corp., **17** 238
AADC Holding Company, Inc., **62** 347
AAE Ahaus Alstatter Eisenbahn Holding AG, **25** 171
AAF-McQuay Incorporated, 26 3–5
AAI Corporation, **37** 399
Aai.FosterGrant, Inc., **60** 131, 133
Aansworth Shirt Makers, **8** 406
AAON, Inc., 22 3–6
AAPT, **54** 355–57
AAR Corp., 28 3–5
Aardman Animations Ltd., 43 143; **61** 3–5
Aareal Bank AG. *See* DEPFA BANK PLC.
Aarhus United A/S, 68 3–5
Aaron Brothers Holdings, Inc. *See* Michaels Stores, Inc.
Aaron Rents, Inc., 14 3–5; **33** 368; **35** 3–6 (**upd.**)
AARP, 27 3–5
Aasche Transportation, **27** 404
AASE SARL, **53** 32
Aastrom Biosciences, Inc., **13** 161
AAV Cos., **13** 48; **41** 22
Aavant Health Management Group, Inc., **11** 394
Aavid Thermal Technologies, Inc., 29 3–6
Aavid Thermalloy, LLC, **69** 337
AB Capital & Investment Corporation, **23** 381
AB Ingredients Limited, **41** 32
AB Metal Pty Ltd, **62** 331
AB-PT. *See* American Broadcasting-Paramount Theatres, Inc.

ABA. *See* Aktiebolaget Aerotransport.
Abacus Direct Corporation, **46** 156
ABACUS International Holdings Ltd., **26** 429
Abana Pharmaceuticals, **24** 257
Abar Corporation. *See* Ipsen International Inc.
Abar Staffing, **25** 434
Abatix Corp., 57 7–9
ABB Asea Brown Boveri Ltd., II 1–4, 13; **III** 427, 466, 631–32; **IV** 109, 204, 300; **15** 483; **22** 7–12 (upd.), 64, 288; **28** 39; **34** 132. *See also* ABB Ltd.
ABB Hafo AB. *See* Mitel Corp.
ABB Ltd., 65 3–10 (upd.)
ABB RDM Service, **41** 326
Abba Seafood AB, **18** 396
Abbatoir St.-Valerien Inc., **II** 652
Abbey Business Consultants, **14** 36
Abbey Home Entertainment, **23** 391
Abbey Life Group PLC, **II** 309
Abbey Medical, Inc., **11** 486; **13** 366–67
Abbey National plc, 10 6–8; **39** 3–6 (upd.)
Abbey Road Building Society, **10** 6–7
Abbott Laboratories, I 619–21; **11** 7–9 (upd.); **40** 9–13 (upd.); **46** 394–95; **50** 538; **63** 206–07
ABC Appliance, Inc., 10 9–11
ABC Carpet & Home Co. Inc., 26 6–8
ABC Family Worldwide, Inc., 52 3–6, 84
ABC, Inc., **II** 129–33; **III** 214, 251–52; **17** 150; **XVIII** 65; **19** 201; **21** 25; **24** 516–17; **32** 3; **51** 218–19. *See also* Capital Cities/ABC Inc.
ABC Markets, **17** 558
ABC Rail Products Corporation, 18 3–5
ABC Stores. *See* MNS, Ltd.
ABC Supply Co., Inc., 22 13–16
ABC Treadco, **19** 455
ABECOR. *See* Associated Banks of Europe Corp.
Abeille Vie. *See* Aviva.
Les Abeilles International SA, **60** 149
Abell-Howe Construction Inc., **42** 434
Abelle Limited, **63** 182, 184
Abercrombie & Fitch Co., 15 7–9; **17** 369; **25** 90; **35** 7–10 (upd.)
Abertis Infraestructuras, S.A., 65 11–13
ABF. *See* Associated British Foods PLC.
ABF Freight System, Inc., **16** 39–41
ABI. *See* American Furniture Company, Inc.
Abigail Adams National Bancorp, Inc., 23 3–5
Abilis, **49** 222
Abington Shoe Company. *See* The Timberland Company.
Abiomed, Inc., 47 3–6
Abita Springs Water Co., **58** 373
Abitec Corporation, **41** 32–33
Abitibi-Consolidated, Inc., 25 9–13 (upd.); **26** 445; **63** 314–15
Abitibi-Price Inc., IV 245–47, 721; **9** 391
ABM Industries Incorporated, 25 14–16 (upd.); **51** 295
ABN. *See* Algemene Bank Nederland N.V.
ABN AMRO Holding, N.V., 39 295; **50** 3–7
Above The Belt, Inc., **16** 37
AboveNet, Inc., **61** 210, 213
ABR Foods, **II** 466
Abrafract Abrasives. *See* Carbo PLC.
Abraham & Straus, **9** 209; **31** 192

Abrams Industries Inc., 23 6–8
ABRY Partners LLC, **72** 36, 39
ABS Pump AB, **53** 85
Absolut Company, **31** 458, 460
Abu Dhabi National Oil Company, IV 363–64, 476; **45** 6–9 (upd.)
AC Design Inc., **22** 196
AC Humko Corporation, **41** 32–33
AC Roma SpA, **44** 388
ACA Corporation, **25** 368
Academic Press. *See* Reed Elsevier.
Academy of Television Arts & Sciences, Inc., 55 3–5
Academy Sports & Outdoors, 27 6–8
Acadia Entities, **24** 456
Acadia Investors, **23** 99
Acadia Partners, **21** 92
Acadian Ambulance & Air Med Services, Inc., 39 7–10
ACC Corporation. *See* AT&T Corporation.
Accel, S.A. de C.V., **51** 115–17
Accenture Ltd., **59** 130; **68** 26
Access Business Group. *See* Alticor Inc.
Access Dynamics Inc., **17** 255
Access Graphics Technology Inc., **13** 128
Accessory Network Group, Inc., **8** 219
Acclaim Entertainment Inc., 13 115; **24** 3–8, 538
ACCO World Corporation, 7 3–5; **12** 264; **51** 7–10 (upd.)
Accolade Inc., **35** 227
Accor S.A., 10 12–14; **13** 364; **27** 9–12 (upd.); **48** 199; **49** 126; **53** 301; **56** 248; **59** 361; **69** 3–8 (upd.)
Accord Energy, **18** 367; **49** 120
Accres Uitgevers B.V., **51** 328
Acctex Information Systems, **17** 468
Accudata Inc., **64** 237
Accuralite Company, **10** 492
AccuRead Limited, **42** 165, 167
Accuscan, Inc., **14** 380
AccuStaff Inc. *See* MPS Group, Inc.
Ace Bag Company Limited, **70** 43
ACE Cash Express, Inc., 33 3–6
Ace Comb Company, **12** 216
Ace Hardware Corporation, 12 6–8; **35** 11–14 (upd.)
Ace Medical Company, **30** 164
Ace Novelty Company, **26** 374
Acer Inc., 10 257; **16** 3–6; **47** 385
Acer Sertek, **24** 31
Aceralia, **42** 414
Acerinox, **59** 226
Aceros Fortuna S.A. de C.V., **13** 141
Acesa. *See* Abertis Infraestructuras, S.A.
Aceto Corp., 38 3–5
ACF Industries, **30** 282
ACG. *See* American Cotton Growers Association.
Achatz GmbH Bauunternehmung, **55** 62
Achiever Computers Pty Ltd, **56** 155
ACI. *See* Advance Circuits Inc.
ACI Billing Services, Inc., **72** 36, 39
ACI Holdings Inc., **I** 91; **28** 24
ACI Ltd., **29** 478
Aciéries de Ploërmel, **16** 514
Aciéries Réunies de Burbach-Eich-Dudelange S.A. *See* ARBED S.A.
Acker Drill Company, **26** 70
Ackerley Communications, Inc., 9 3–5; **50** 95
Acklin Stamping Company, **8** 515
ACL. *See* Automotive Components Limited.

ACLC. *See* Allegheny County Light Company.
ACLU. *See* American Civil Liberties Union (ACLU).
ACM. *See* Advanced Custom Molders, Inc.
Acme Brick Company, **19** 231–32
Acme Can Co., **13** 188
Acme-Cleveland Corp., 13 6–8
Acme Cotton Products, **13** 366
Acme-Delta Company, **11** 411
Acme Fast Freight Inc., **27** 473
Acme Market. *See* American Stores Company.
Acme Newspictures, **25** 507
Acme Quilting Co., Inc., **19** 304
Acme Screw Products, **14** 181
Acme United Corporation, 70 3–6
ACMI, **21** 118–19
ACNielsen Corporation, 38 6–9 (upd.); **61** 81
Acordis, **41** 10
Acorn Financial Corp., **15** 328
Acorn Products, Inc., 55 6–9
Acova S.A., **26** 4
Acquired Systems Enhancement Corporation, **24** 31
ACR. *See* American Capital and Research Corp.
AcroMed Corporation, **30** 164
ACS. *See* Affiliated Computer Services, Inc.
Acsys, Inc., 44 3–5
ACT Group, **45** 280
ACT Inc, **50** 48
ACT Research Center Inc., **56** 238
Act III Theatres, **25** 453
Actava Group, **14** 332
Action, **6** 393
Action Furniture by Lane, **17** 183
Action Gaming Inc., **44** 337
Action Labs Inc., **37** 285
Action Performance Companies, Inc., 27 13–15; **32** 344; **37** 319
Action Temporary Services, **29** 273
Active Apparel Group. *See* Everlast Worldwide Inc.
Activenture Corporation, **16** 253; **43** 209
Actividades de Construcción y Servicios S.A. (ACS), **55** 179
Activision, Inc., 24 3; **32** 8–11
Acuity Brands, Inc., **54** 255
Acumos, **11** 57
Acushnet Company, 64 3–5
Acuson Corporation, 10 15–17; **36** 3–6 (upd.)
ACX Technologies, **13** 11; **36** 15
Acxiom Corporation, 35 15–18
AD-AM Gas Company, **11** 28
AD South Africa, Inc., **60** 34
Ad Vantage Computer Systems Inc., **58** 273
Adaco, **70** 58
Adage Systems International, Inc., **19** 438
Adam, Meldrum & Anderson Company (AM&A), **16** 61–62; **50** 107
Adam Opel AG, 7 6–8; **21** 3–7 (upd.); **61** 6–11 (upd.)
Adams/Cates Company, **21** 257
Adams Childrenswear. *See* Sears plc.
Adams Golf, Inc., 37 3–5; **45** 76
Adams Industries, **19** 414
Adams Media Corporation. *See* F&W Publications, Inc.
Adanac General Insurance Company, **13** 63

Adaptec, Inc., **11** 56; **31 3–6**
Adaptive Data Systems, **25** 531
Adar Associates, Inc. *See* Scientific-
   Atlanta, Inc.
ADC of Greater Kansas City, Inc., **22** 443
ADC Telecommunications, Inc., 10
   18–21; 30 6–9 (upd.); 44 69
Addison Communications Plc, **45** 272
Addison Corporation, **31** 399
Addison Structural Services, Inc., **26** 433
Addison Wesley, **IV** 659
Addressograph-Multigraph, **11** 494
Adecco S.A., 26 240; **35** 441–42; **36 7–11**
   (upd.)
Adeletom Aviation L.L.C., **61** 100
Adelphia Communications Corporation,
   17 6–8; 52 7–10 (upd.)
Ademco. *See* Alarm Device Manufacturing
   Company.
Adero Inc., **45** 202
ADESA, Inc., 71 7–10
Adesso-Madden, Inc., **37** 372
ADI Group Limited. *See* AHL Services,
   Inc.
Adia S.A., 6 9–11; 9 327. *See also*
   Adecco S.A.
Adiainvest S.A. *See* Adecco S.A.
adidas AG, 8 392–93; **13** 513; **14 6–9; 17**
   244; **22** 202; **23** 472, 474; **25** 205, 207;
   36 344, 346
adidas-Salomon AG, 33 7–11 (upd.)
Adirondack Industries, **24** 403
Adjusters Auto Rental Inc. **16** 380
Adler, **23** 219
Adler and Shaykin, **11** 556–57
Adler Line. *See* Transatlantische
   Dampfschiffahrts Gesellschaft.
Adley Express, **14** 567
ADM. *See* Archer-Daniels-Midland Co.
ADME Bioanalyses SAS. *See* Eurofins
   Scientific S.A.
Administaff, Inc., 52 11–13
Administracion Corporativa y Mercantil,
   S.A. de C.V., **37** 178
Admiral Co. *See* Maytag Corporation.
ADNOC. *See* Abu Dhabi National Oil
   Company.
Adobe Systems Incorporated, 10 22–24;
   15 149; **20** 46, 237; **33 12–16 (upd.); 43**
   151
Adolf Würth GmbH & Co. KG, 49
   13–15
Adolfo Dominguez S.A., 72 3–5
Adolph Coors Company, I 236–38, 273;
   13 9–11 (upd.); 18 72; **26** 303, 306; **34**
   37; **36 12–16 (upd.); 44** 198; **59** 68
Adolphe Lafont, **17** 210
Adonis Radio Corp., **9** 320
Adorence, **16** 482
ADP. *See* Automatic Data Processing, Inc.
Adria Produtos Alimenticios, Ltd., **12** 411
Adrian Hope and Company, **14** 46
Adrienne Vittadini, **15** 291
ADS. *See* Aerospace Display Systems.
Adsega, **II** 677
Adstaff Associates, Ltd., **26** 240
Adsteam, **60** 101
ADT Automotive, **71 8–9**
ADT Ltd., **26** 410; **28** 486; **63** 403
ADT Security Services, Inc., 44 6–9
   (upd.)
ADT Security Systems, Inc., 12 9–11
Adtel, Inc., **10** 358
Adtran Inc., 22 17–20

Adtranz **34** 128, 132–33, 136; **42** 45. *See*
   also ABB Ltd.
Advacel, **18** 20; **43** 17
Advance Auto Parts, Inc., 57 10–12
Advance Chemical Company, **25** 15
Advance Circuits Inc., **49** 234
Advance Foundry, **14** 42
Advance Gems & Jewelry Co., Ltd., **62**
   371
Advance/Newhouse Communications, **42**
   114
Advance Publications Inc., IV 581–84;
   13 178, 180, 429; **19 3–7 (upd.); 31**
   376, 378; **59** 132–33
Advance-Rumely Thresher Co., **13** 16
Advance Transformer Co., **13** 397
Advanced Aerodynamics & Structures Inc.
   See Mooney Aerospace Group Ltd.
Advanced Broadband, L.P., **70** 325
Advanced Casino Systems Corporation, **21**
   277
Advanced Circuits Inc., 67 3–5
Advanced Colortech Inc., **56** 238
Advanced Communications Engineering.
   See Scientific-Atlanta, Inc.
Advanced Communications Inc. *See*
   Metrocall, Inc.
Advanced Custom Molders, Inc., **17** 533
Advanced Data Management Group S.A.,
   23 212
Advanced Entertainment Group, **10** 286
Advanced Fiberoptic Technologies, **30** 267
Advanced Fibre Communications, Inc.,
   63 3–5
Advanced Gravis, **28** 244; **69** 243
Advanced Logic Research, Inc., **27** 169
Advanced Marine Enterprises, Inc., **18** 370
Advanced Marketing Services, Inc., 24
   354; **34 3–6**
Advanced Medical Technologies, **III** 512
Advanced Metal Technologies Inc., **17** 234
Advanced Metallurgy, Inc., **29** 460
Advanced Micro Devices, Inc., 6 215–17;
   9 115; **10** 367; **11** 308; **16** 316; **18**
   18–19, 382; **19** 312; **20** 175; **30 10–12**
   (upd.); 32 498; **43** 15–16; **47** 384
Advanced MobilComm, **10** 432
Advanced Parking Systems Ltd., **58** 184
Advanced Plasma Systems, Inc., **48** 299
Advanced Pollution Instrumentation Inc.,
   62 362
Advanced Structures, Inc., **18** 163
Advanced System Applications, **11** 395
Advanced Technology Laboratories, Inc.,
   9 6–8
Advanced Telecommunications, Inc. *See*
   Eschelon Telecom, Inc.
Advanced Tissue Sciences Inc., **41** 377
Advanced Web Technologies, **22** 357
AdvanceMed LLC, **45** 146
AdvancePCS, Inc., **63** 336
Advanstar Communications, Inc., 27
   361; **57 13–17**
Advanta Corporation, 8 9–11; 11 123; **38**
   10–14 (upd.)
Advanta Partners, LP, **42** 322
Advantage Company, **8** 311; **27** 306
The Advantage Group, Inc., **25** 185–86
Advantage Health Plans, Inc., **11** 379
Advantage Health Systems, Inc., **25** 383
Advantage Insurers, Inc., **25** 185, 187
Advantage Publishers Group, **34** 5
Advantest Corporation, **39** 350, 353

Advantica Restaurant Group, Inc., 27
   16–19 (upd.); 29 150
Advantra International NV. *See* Punch
   International N.V.
Advent Corporation, **22** 97
Adventist Health, 53 6–8
Advertising Unlimited, Inc., **10** 461
Advo, Inc., 6 12–14; 53 9–13 (upd.)
Advocat Inc., 46 3–5
AEA. *See* United Kingdom Atomic Energy
   Authority.
AEA Investors Inc., **II** 628; **13** 97; **22** 169,
   171; **28** 380; **30** 328
AEG A.G., I 151, 193, **409–11; IX** 11; **14**
   169; **15** 142; **23** 495; **34** 131–32
AEG Hausgeräte, **53** 128
Aegek S.A., 64 6–8
Aegis Group plc, 6 15–16
Aegis Insurance Co., **III** 273
AEGON N.V., III 177–79, 201, 273; **33**
   418–20; **50 8–12 (upd.); 52** 288; **63**
   166; **64** 171. *See also* Transamerica–An
   AEGON Company
AEI Music Network Inc., 35 19–21
AEL Ventures Ltd., **9** 512
Aeneas Venture Corp., **26** 502
AEON Co., Ltd., V 96–99; 11 498–99;
   31 430–31; **37** 227; **56** 202; **68 6–10**
   (upd.)
AEP. *See* American Electric Power
   Company.
AEP Industries, Inc., 36 17–19
AEP-Span, **8** 546
Aer Lingus Group plc, 6 59; **12** 367–68;
   34 7–10; 35 382–84; **36** 230–31
Aera Energy LLC, **41** 359
Aérazur, **36** 529
Aereos Del Mercosur, **68** 365
Aerial Communications Inc., **31** 452
Aeries Health Care Corporation, **68** 299
Aeritalia, **I** 467
Aero Engines, **9** 418
Aero International (Regional) SAS, **24** 88
Aero International Inc., **14** 43
Aero Mayflower Transit Company. *See*
   Mayflower Group Inc.
Aero O/Y. *See* Finnair Oy.
Aeroflot—Russian International Airlines,
   I 118; **6 57–59; 14** 73; **27** 475; **29 7–10**
   (upd.)
Aerojet, **8** 206, 208
Aerojet-General Corp., 9 266; **63 6–9**
Aerolíneas Argentinas S.A., 33 17–19; 69
   9–12 (upd.)
Aeroméxico, **20** 168
Aeromotive Systems Co., **55** 31
Aeronautics Leasing, Inc., **39** 33
Aeronca Inc., 46 6–8; 48 274
Aeropharm Technology, Inc., **63** 233–34
Aéroports de Paris, 33 20–22
Aeroquip Corporation, III 640–42; 16
   7–9. *See also* Eaton Corporation.
Aerosance Inc., **62** 362
Aerosonic Corporation, 69 13–15
Aerospace Display Systems, **36** 158
Aerospace International Services, **41** 38
Aerospace Products International, Inc., **49**
   141
The Aérospatiale Group, I 46, 50, 74, 94;
   7 9–12; 12 190–91; **14** 72; **21 8–11**
   (upd.); 24 84–86, 88–89; **26** 179. *See*
   also European Aeronautic Defence and
   Space Company EADS N.V.
Aerostar, **33** 359–61

The AES Corporation, 10 25–27; **13** 12–15 (upd.); **24** 359; **53** 14–18 (upd.); **65** 119

Aetna, Inc., 20 59; **21** 12–16 (upd.), 95; **22** 139, 142–43; **30** 364; **63** 10–16 (upd.)

Aetna Insulated Wire. See The Marmon Group, Inc.

Aetna Life and Casualty Company, III 180–82, 209, 223, 226, 236, 254, 296, 298, 305, 313, 329; **10** 75–76; **12** 367; **15** 26; **23** 135; **40** 199

Aetna National Bank, **13** 466

AF Insurance Agency, **44** 33

AFC. See Advanced Fibre Communications, Inc.

AFC Enterprises, Inc., 32 12–16 (upd.); **36** 517, 520; **54** 373

AFE Ltd., **IV** 241

Affiliated Computer Services, Inc., 61 12–16

Affiliated Foods Inc., 53 19–21

Affiliated Hospital Products Inc., **37** 400

Affiliated Music Publishing, **22** 193

Affiliated Paper Companies, Inc., **31** 359, 361

Affiliated Physicians Network, Inc., **45** 194

Affiliated Publications, Inc., 7 13–16; **19** 285; **61** 241

Affinity Group Holding Inc., 56 3–6

Affordable Inns, **13** 364

AFG Industries Inc., **I** 483; **9** 248; **48** 42

AFIA, **22** 143; **45** 104, 108

Afianzadora Insurgentes Serfin, **19** 190

AFK Sistema, **59** 300

AFL. See American Football League.

AFLAC Incorporated, 10 28–30 (upd.); **38** 15–19 (upd.)

AFP. See Australian Forest Products.

AFRA Enterprises Inc., **26** 102

AFRAM Carriers, Inc. See Kirby Corporation.

African Rainbow Minerals, **63** 185

Africare, 59 7–10

AFT. See Advanced Fiberoptic Technologies.

After Hours Formalwear Inc., 60 3–5

AFW Fabric Corp., **16** 124

AG&E. See American Electric Power Company.

AG Barr plc, 64 9–12

Ag-Chem Equipment Company, Inc., 17 9–11. See also AGCO Corporation.

AG Communication Systems Corporation, **15** 194; **43** 446

Ag Services of America, Inc., 59 11–13

Agan Chemical Manufacturers Ltd., **25** 266–67

Agape S.p.A., **57** 82–83

Agar Manufacturing Company, **8** 2

Agasote Millboard Company. See Homasote Company.

Agatha Christie Ltd., **31** 63 67

AGCO Corp., 13 16–18; **67** 6–10 (upd.)

Age International, Inc., **62** 347

Agefi, **34** 13

AGEL&P. See Albuquerque Gas, Electric Light and Power Company.

Agema Infrared Systems AB, **69** 171

Agence France-Presse, 34 11–14

Agency, **6** 393

Agency Rent-A-Car, **16** 379

Agere Systems Inc., 61 17–19

AGF. See Assurances Generales de France.

Agfa Gevaert Group N.V., III 487; **18** 50, 184–86; **26** 540–41; **50** 90; **59** 14–16

Aggregate Industries plc, 36 20–22

Aggreko Plc, 45 10–13

AGI Industries, **57** 208–09

Agiba Petroleum, **IV** 414

Agie Charmilles, **61** 106, 108

Agilent Technologies Inc., 38 20–23; **63** 33–34

Agip SpA. See ENI S.p.A.

Agiv AG, **39** 40–41; **51** 25

Agnew Gold Mining Company (Pty) Ltd., **62** 164

Agnico-Eagle Mines Limited, 71 11–14

Agouron Pharmaceuticals, Inc., **38** 365

Agr. See Artes Grafica Rioplatense S.A.

Agra Europe Limited, **58** 191

AGRANA, **27** 436, 439

Agri-Foods, Inc., **60** 256

Agri-Insurance Company, Ltd., **63** 23

AgriBank FCB, **8** 489

Agribrands International, Inc., **40** 89

Agrico Chemical Company. See The Williams Companies.

Agricole de Roquefort et Maria Grimal, **23** 219

Agricultural Minerals and Chemicals Inc., **13** 504

Agrifull, **22** 380

Agrigenetics, Inc. See Mycogen Corporation.

Agrilusa, Agro-Industria, **51** 54

Agrobios S.A., **23** 172

Agroferm Hungarian Japanese Fermentation Industry, **III** 43

Agrologica, **51** 54

Agromán S.A., **40** 218

AGTL. See Alberta Gas Trunk Line Company, Ltd.

Agua de la Falda S.A., **38** 231

Agua Pura Water Company, **24** 467

Agusta S.p.A., **46** 66

Agway, Inc., 7 17–18; **21** 17–19 (upd.); **36** 440

Aherns Holding, **60** 100

AHI Building Products. See Carter Holt Harvey Ltd.

AHL Services, Inc., 26 149; **27** 20–23; **45** 379

Ahlstrom Corporation, 53 22–25

Ahmanson. See H.F. Ahmanson & Company.

AHMSA. See Altos Hornos de México, S.A. de C.V.

Ahold. See Koninklijke Ahold NV.

AHP. See American Home Products Corporation.

AHS. See American Hospital Supply Corporation.

AHSC Holdings Corp. See Alco Health Services Corporation.

Ahtna AGA Security, Inc., **14** 541

AI Automotive, **24** 204

AIC. See Allied Import Company.

AICA, **16** 421; **43** 308

AICPA. See The American Institute of Certified Public Accountants.

Aid Auto, **18** 144

Aida Corporation, **11** 504

AIG. See American International Group, Inc.

AIG Global Real Estate Investment Corp., **54** 225

AIG/Lincoln International L.L.C., **54** 225

Aigner. See Etienne Aigner AG.

Aiken Stores, Inc., **14** 92

Aikenhead's Home Improvement Warehouse, **18** 240; **26** 306

AIL Technologies, **46** 160

AIM Create Co., Ltd. See Marui Co., Ltd.

AIM Management Group Inc., **65** 43–45

AIMCO. See Apartment Investment and Management Company.

Ainsworth Gaming Technologies, **54** 15

Ainsworth National, **14** 528

AIP. See American Industrial Properties; Amorim Investimentos e Participaço.

Air & Water Technologies Corporation, 6 441–42. See also Aqua Alliance Inc.

Air Berlin GmbH & Co. Luftverkehrs KG, 71 15–17

Air BP, **7** 141

Air By Pleasant, **62** 276

Air Canada, 6 60–62; **23** 9–12 (upd.); **29** 302; **36** 230; **59** 17–22 (upd.)

Air China, 46 9–11

Air Compak, **12** 182

Air de Cologne, **27** 474

Air Express International Corporation, 13 19–20; **40** 138; **46** 71

Air France. See Groupe Air France; Societe Air France.

Air Global International, **55** 30

Air-India Limited, 6 63–64; **27** 24–26 (upd.); **41** 336–37; **63** 17–18; **65** 14

Air Inter. See Groupe Air France.

Air Inuit, **56** 38–39

Air Jamaica Limited, 54 3–6

Air La Carte Inc., **13** 48

Air Lanka Catering Services Ltd. See Thai Airways International.

Air Liberté, **6** 208

Air Liquide. See L'Air Liquide SA.

Air London International, **36** 190

Air Mauritius Ltd., 63 17–19

Air Methods Corporation, 53 26–29

Air Midwest, Inc., **11** 299

Air New Zealand Limited, 14 10–12; **24** 399–400; **27** 475; **38** 24–27 (upd.)

Air NorTerra Inc., **56** 39

Air Pacific Ltd., 70 7–9

Air Products and Chemicals, Inc., I 297–99, 315, 358, 674; **10** 31–33 (upd.); **11** 403; **14** 125; **54** 10

Air Pub S.à.r.l., **64** 359

Air Russia, **24** 400

Air Sahara Limited, 65 14–16

Air Sea Broker AG, **47** 286–87

Air Southwest Co. See Southwest Airlines Co.

Air Taser, Inc. See Taser International, Inc.

Air Transport International LLC, **58** 43

Air Wisconsin Airlines Corporation, 55 10–12

Airborne Freight Corporation, 6 345–47 345; **13** 19; **14** 517; **18** 177; **34** 15–18 (upd.); **46** 72

Airbus Industrie, **7** 9–11, 504; **9** 418; **10** 164; **13** 356; **21** 8; **24** 84–89; **34** 128, 135; **48** 219. See also G.I.E. Airbus Industrie.

AirCal, **I** 91

Airco, **25** 81–82; **26** 94

Aircraft Modular Products, **30** 73

Aircraft Turbine Center, Inc., **28** 3

Airex Corporation, **16** 337

AirFoyle Ltd., **53** 50

Airgas, Inc., 54 7–10
Airguard Industries, Inc., **17** 104, 106; **61** 66
AirLib. *See* Société d'Exploitation AOM.
Airline Interiors Inc., **41** 368–69
Airlines of Britain Holdings, **34** 398; **38** 105–06
Airlink Pty Ltd. *See* Qantas Airways Ltd.
Airmark Plastics Corp., **18** 497–98
Airopak Corporation. *See* PVC Container Corporation.
Airpax Electronics, Inc., **13** 398
Airport Leather Concessions LLC, **58** 369
Airrest S.A., **64** 359
Airshop Ltd., **25** 246
Airstream. *See* Thor Industries, Inc.
AirTouch Communications, 11 10–12. *See also* Vodafone Group PLC.
Airtours Plc, 27 27–29, 90, 92
AirTran Holdings, Inc., 22 21–23; **28** 266; **33** 302; **34** 32; **55** 10–11
AirWair Ltd., **23** 399, 401–02
AirWays Corporation. *See* AirTran Holdings, Inc.
Aisin Seiki Co., Ltd., III 415–16; **14** 64; **48** 3–5 (upd.)
AIT Worldwide, **47** 286–87
Aitchison & Colegrave. *See* Bradford & Bingley PLC.
Aitken, Inc., **26** 433
AITS. *See* American International Travel Service.
Aiuruoca, **25** 85
Aiwa Co., Ltd., 28 360; **30** 18–20
Ajax Iron Works, **II** 16
Ajax Repair & Supply, **58** 75
Ajinomoto Co., Inc., II 463–64, 475; **III** 705; **28** 9–11 (upd.)
AJS Auto Parts Inc., **15** 246
AK Steel Holding Corporation, 19 8–9; **41** 3–6 (upd.)
Akamai Technologies, Inc., 71 18–21
Akane Securities Co. Ltd., **II** 443
AKAY Flavours & Aromatics Ltd., **70** 56
Akemi, **17** 310; **24** 160
Aker RGI, **32** 99
AKG Acoustics GmbH, 62 3–6
AKH Co. Inc., **20** 63
Akin, Gump, Strauss, Hauer & Feld, L.L.P., 18 366; **33** 23–25; **47** 140
Akorn, Inc., 32 22–24
Akro-Mills Inc., **19** 277–78
Akron Brass Manufacturing Co., **9** 419
Akron Extruders Inc., **53** 230
Akroyd & Smithers, **14** 419
Aktia Sparbank Abp, **69** 177, 179
Aktiebolaget Electrolux, 22 24–28 (upd.). *See also* Electrolux A.B.
Aktiebolaget SKF, III 622–25; **38** 28–33 (upd.)
Aktieselskabet Dampskibsselskabet Svendborg, **57** 3, 5
Akzo Nobel N.V., 13 21–23, 545; **14** 27; **16** 69, 462; **21** 466; **41** 7–10 (upd.); **52** 410
Al-Amin Co. For Securities & Investment Funds. *See* Dallah Albaraka Group.
Al Copeland Enterprises, Inc., **7** 26–28; **32** 13–15
Al-Tawfeek Co. For Investment Funds Ltd. *See* Dallah Albaraka Group.
Alaadin Middle East-Ersan, **IV** 564
Alabama Bancorp., **17** 152

Alabama Farmers Cooperative, Inc., 63 20–22
Alabama Gas Corporation, **21** 207–08
Alabama Power Company, **38** 445, 447–48
Alabama Shipyards Inc., **21** 39–40
Aladdin Industries, **16** 487
Aladdin Mills Inc., **19** 276; **63** 300
Alagasco, **21** 207–08
Alagroup, **45** 337
Alain Afflelou SA, 53 30–32
Alain Manoukian. *See* Groupe Alain Manoukian.
Alamac Knit Fabrics, Inc., **16** 533–34; **21** 192
Alamito Company, **6** 590
Alamo Engine Company, **8** 514
Alamo Group Inc., 32 25–28
Alamo Rent A Car, Inc., 6 348–50; **24** 9–12 (upd.); **25** 93; **26** 409
Alamo Water Refiners, Inc. *See* The Marmon Group, Inc.
Alania, **24** 88
ALANTEC Corporation, **25** 162
ALARIS Medical Systems, Inc., 65 17–20
Alarm Device Manufacturing Company, **9** 413–15
Alaron Inc., **16** 357
Alascom, Inc. *See* AT&T Corporation.
Alaska Air Group, Inc., 6 65–67; **11** 50; **29** 11–14 (upd.); **48** 219
Alaska Commercial Company, **12** 363
Alaska Junk Co., **19** 380
Alaska Native Wireless LLC, **60** 264
Alaska Railroad Corporation, 60 6–9
Alaska Steel Co., **19** 381
Alatas Mammoet, **26** 279
Alba Foods, **27** 197; **43** 218
Alba-Waldensian, Inc., 30 21–23
Albany Cheese, **23** 219
Albany International Corporation, 8 12–14; **51** 11–14 (upd.)
Albaugh Inc., **62** 19
Albemarle Corporation, 59 23–25
Albert E. Reed & Co. Ltd. *See* Reed International PLC.
The Albert Fisher Group plc, 41 11–13
Albert Heijn NV, **II** 641–42; **38** 200, 202
Albert Nipon, Inc., **8** 323
Albert Willcox & Co., **14** 278
Alberta Energy Company Ltd., 16 10–12; **43** 3–6 (upd.)
Alberta Gas Trunk Line Company, Ltd. *See* Nova Corporation of Alberta.
Alberto-Culver Company, II 641–42; **8** 15–17; **36** 23–27 (upd.); **60** 258
Albertson's, Inc., II 601–03, 604–05, 637; **7** 19–22 (upd.); **8** 474; **15** 178, 480; **16** 249; **18** 8; **22** 38; **27** 247, 290, 292; **30** 24–28 (upd.); **33** 306; **40** 366; **65** 21–26 (upd.)
Albion Industries, Inc., **16** 357
Albright & Wilson Ltd., **12** 351; **16** 461; **38** 378, 380; **50** 282; **59** 25
Albuquerque Gas & Electric Company. *See* Public Service Company of New Mexico.
Albuquerque Gas, Electric Light and Power Company, **6** 561–62
Alcan Aluminium Limited, IV 9–13, 14, 59, 154–55; **9** 512; **14** 35; **31** 7–12 (upd.); **45** 337
Alcan Inc., **60** 338

Alcatel Alsthom Compagnie Générale d'Electricité, 6 304; **7** 9; **9** 9–11, 32; **11** 59, 198; **15** 125; **17** 353; **18** 155; **19** 164, 166; **21** 233
Alcatel S.A., 36 28–31 (upd.); **42** 375–76; **52** 332, 334; **53** 237; **54** 264; **57** 409
Alchem Capital Corp., **8** 141, 143
Alchem Plastics, **19** 414
Alco Capital Group, Inc., **27** 288
Alco Health Services Corporation, III 9–10. *See also* AmeriSource Health Corporation.
Alco Office Products Inc., **24** 362
Alco Standard Corporation, I 412–13; **9** 261; **16** 473–74
ALCO Trade Show Services, **26** 102
Alcoa Inc., 56 7–11 (upd.)
Alcon Laboratories, **10** 46, 48; **30** 30–31
Alden Merrell Corporation, **23** 169
Alderwoods Group, Inc., 68 11–15 (upd.)
Aldi Group, 11 240; **13** 24–26; **17** 125
Aldila Inc., 46 12–14
Aldine Press, **10** 34
Aldiscon, **37** 232
Aldus Corporation, 10 34–36
Alenia, **7** 9, 11
Alert Centre Inc., **32** 373
Alert Management Systems Inc., **12** 380
Alessio Tubi, **IV** 228
Alestra, **19** 12
Alex & Ivy, **10** 166–68
Alex Lee Inc., 18 6–9; **44** 10–14 (upd.)
Alexander & Alexander Services Inc., 10 37–39; **13** 476
Alexander & Baldwin, Inc., 10 40–42; **29** 307; **40** 14–19 (upd.)
Alexander and Lord, **13** 482
Alexander Hamilton Life Insurance Co., **II** 420; **29** 256
Alexander Howden Group, **10** 38–39
Alexander-Schroder Lumber Company, **18** 514
Alexander Smith, Inc., **19** 275
Alexander's, Inc., 10 282; **12** 221; **26** 111; **45** 14–16
Alexandria Petroleum Co., **51** 113
Alexis Lichine, **III** 43
Alfa Corporation, 59 210; **60** 10–12
Alfa-Laval AB, III 417–21; **8** 376; **53** 328; **64** 13–18 (upd.)
Alfa Romeo, **I** 163, 167; **11** 102, 104, 139, 205; **13** 27–29, 218–19; **36** 32–35 (upd.), 196–97
Alfa, S.A. de C.V., 11 386; **19** 10–12; **37** 176
Alfa Trading Company, **23** 358
Alfalfa's Markets, **19** 500–02
alfi Zitzmann, **60** 364
Alfred A. Knopf, Inc., 13 428, 429; **31** 376–79
Alfred Bullows & Sons, Ltd., **21** 64
Alfred Dunhill Limited, **19** 369; **27** 487–89
Alfred Marks Bureau, Ltd. *See* Adia S.A.
Alfred McAlpine plc, **51** 138
Alfred Ritter GmbH & Co. KG, 58 3–7
Alfried Krupp von Bohlen und Halbach Foundation, **IV** 89
ALG. *See* Arkla, Inc.
Alga, **24** 83
Algamar, S.A., **64** 91
Algemeen Burgerlijk Pensioenfonds, **26** 421
Algemeen Dagblad BV, **53** 273

**Algemene Bank Nederland N.V., II
183–84**, 185, 239, 527
Algerian Saudi Leasing Holding Co. *See*
Dallah Albaraka Group.
Algo Group Inc., 24 13–15
Algoma Steel Corp., **8** 544–45
Algonquin Gas Transmission Company, **14**
124–26
ALI. *See* Aeronautics Leasing, Inc.
Aliança Florestal-Sociedade para o
Desenvolvimento Agro-Florestal, S.A.,
60 156
Alicia S.A. *See* Arcor S.A.I.C.
Alico, Inc., 63 23–25
Alidata SpA. *See* Alitalia—Linee Aeree
Italiana, S.P.A.
Aligro Inc., **II** 664
Alimenta (USA), Inc., **17** 207
Alimentos Indal S.A., **66** 9
Alimondo, **17** 505
**Alitalia–Linee Aeree Italiana, S.p.A., 6
68–69; 24** 311; **29 15–17 (upd.)**
Alkor-Oerlikon Plastic GmbH, **7** 141
All American Airways. *See* USAir Group,
Inc.
**All American Communications Inc., 20
3–7; 25** 138
All American Gourmet Co., **12** 178, 199
All American Sports Co., **22** 458–59
All British Escarpment Company LTD, **25**
430
All-Clad Metalcrafters Inc., **34** 493,
496–97
**The All England Lawn Tennis &
Croquet Club, 54 11–13**
All-Glass Aquarium Co., Inc., **58** 60
All Nippon Airways Co., Ltd., I 106; **6
70–71** 118, 427; **16** 168; **24** 326; **33**
50–51; **38 34–37 (upd.)**
All Seasons Vehicles, Inc. *See* ASV, Inc.
All Woods, Inc., **18** 514
Allami Biztosito, **III** 209; **15** 30
Allcom, **16** 392
Alldays plc, 49 16–19
Allders plc, 37 6–8
Alleanza Assicurazioni S.p.A., 65 27–29
Alleghany Corporation, 10 43–45; 19
319; **22** 494; **60 13–16 (upd.)**
Allegheny Airlines. *See* USAir Group, Inc.;
US Airways Group, Inc.
Allegheny Beverage Corp., **7** 472–73
Allegheny Energy, Inc., 38 38–41 (upd.)
Allegheny International, Inc., **8** 545; **9** 484;
22 3, 436
**Allegheny Ludlum Corporation, 8
18–20; 9** 484; **21** 489
Allegheny Power System, Inc., V 543–45.
See also Allegheny Energy, Inc.
Allegheny Steel and Iron Company, **9** 484
Allegheny Steel Distributors, Inc. *See*
Reliance Steel & Aluminum Company.
Allegiance Life Insurance Company, **22**
268; **50** 122
Allegis, Inc. *See* United Airlines.
Allegretti & Co., **22** 26
Allen & Co., **12** 496; **13** 366; **25** 270
Allen & Ginter, **12** 108
Allen-Bradley Co., **I** 80; **III** 593; **11**
429–30; **17** 478; **22** 373; **23** 211
**Allen-Edmonds Shoe Corporation, 61
20–23**
Allen Foods, Inc., 60 17–19
Allen Group Inc. *See* TransPro, Inc.
Allen Organ Company, 33 26–29

Allen-Stuart Equipment Company, **49** 160
Allen Systems Group, Inc., 59 26–28
Allen Tank Ltd., **21** 499
Allen's Convenience Stores, Inc., **17** 170
Allergan, Inc., 10 46–49; 23 196; **30
29–33 (upd.)**
ALLETE, Inc., **71** 9
Allforms Packaging Corp., **13** 442
Allgemeine Elektricitäts-Gesellschaft. *See*
AEG A.G.
Allgemeine Handelsgesellschaft der
Verbraucher AG. *See* AVA AG.
Allgemeine Schweizerische Uhrenindustrie,
26 480
Allhabo AB, **53** 85
Allia S.A., **51** 324
Alliance Amusement Company, **10** 319
Alliance Assurance Company, **III** 369–73;
55 333
**Alliance Atlantis Communications Inc.,
35** 69; **39 11–14**
**Alliance Capital Management Holding
L.P., 22** 189; **63 26–28**
Alliance de Sud, **53** 301
**Alliance Entertainment Corp., 17 12–14;
35** 430
Alliance Gaming Corp., **15** 539; **24** 36
Alliance Manufacturing Co., **13** 397
Alliance Packaging, **13** 443
Alliance Paper Group, **IV** 316
AllianceWare, Inc., **16** 321
Alliant Energy Corp., **39** 261
**Alliant Techsystems Inc., 8 21–23; 30
34–37 (upd.)**
Allianz AG, 57 18–24 (upd.), 112–13; **60**
110; **63** 45, 47
Allianz AG Holding, I 426; **III 183–86**,
200, 250, 252, 299–301, 347–48, 373,
377, 393; **14** 169–70; **15 10–14 (upd.)**;
51 23
Allied Bakeries Limited. *See* Greggs PLC.
Allied Chemical. *See* General Chemical
Corp.
Allied Chemical & Dye Corp., **7** 262; **9**
154; **22** 29
Allied Color Industries, **8** 347
Allied Communications Group, **18** 77; **22**
297
Allied Construction Products, **17** 384
Allied Corporation. *See* AlliedSignal Inc.
**The Allied Defense Group, Inc., 65
30–33**
Allied Department Stores, **50** 106
Allied Distributing Co., **12** 106
Allied Domecq PLC, 24 220; **29 18–20;
52** 416; **54** 229; **59** 256; **71** 69
Allied Drink Distributors Ltd., **68** 99
Allied Dunbar, **I** 427
Allied Engineering Co., **8** 177
Allied Fibers, **19** 275
Allied Food Markets, **II** 662
Allied Gas Company, **6** 529
Allied Grape Growers, **I** 261
Allied Health and Scientific Products
Company, **8** 215
**Allied Healthcare Products, Inc., 24
16–19**
Allied Holdings, Inc., **24** 411
**Allied Irish Banks, plc, 16 13–15; 43
7–10 (upd.)**
Allied Leisure, **40** 296–98
Allied-Lyons plc, I 215–16, 438; **9** 100;
10 170; **13** 258; **21** 228, 323; **29** 18, 84;
50 200. *See also* Carlsberg A/S.

Allied Maintenance Corp., **I** 514
Allied Mills, Inc., **10** 249; **13** 186; **43** 121
Allied Pipe & Tube Corporation, **63** 403
Allied Plywood Corporation, **12** 397
Allied Products Corporation, 21 20–22
Allied Radio, **19** 310
Allied Safety, Inc. *See* W.W. Grainger, Inc.
Allied Shoe Corp., **22** 213
Allied-Signal Corp., I 414–16; 6
599–600; **9** 519; **11** 435, 444; **13** 227;
16 436; **17** 20; **21** 200, 396–97; **40** 35;
43 320. *See also* AlliedSignal, Inc.
Allied Signal Engines, 9 12–15
Allied Steel and Conveyors, **18** 493
Allied Stores Corporation, **II** 611–12; **9**
211; **10** 282; **13** 43; **15** 94, 274; **16** 60;
22 110; **23** 59–60; **25** 249; **31** 192; **37**
Allied Structural Steel Company, **10** 44
Allied Supermarkets, Inc., **7** 570; **28** 511
Allied Suppliers, **II** 609; **50** 401
Allied Telephone Company. *See* Alltel
Corporation.
Allied Towers Merchants Ltd., **II** 649
Allied Van Lines Inc. *See* Allied
Worldwide, Inc.
Allied Waste Industries, Inc., 50 13–16
Allied Worldwide, Inc., 49 20–23
AlliedSignal Inc., 22 29–32 (upd.); 29
408; **31** 154; **37** 158; **50** 234
Allis Chalmers Corporation, **I** 163; **III**
543–44; **9** 17; **11** 104; **13** 16–17, 563;
21 502–03; **22** 380; **50** 196
Allis-Gleaner Corp. *See* AGCO Corp.
Allison Engine Company, **21** 436
Allison Engineering Company. *See* Rolls-
Royce Allison.
Allison Gas Turbine Division, 9 16–19,
417; **10** 537; **11** 473
Allmanna Svenska Elektriska Aktiebolaget.
See ABB Ltd.
Allmänna Telefonaktiebolaget L.M.
Ericsson. *See* Telefonaktiebolaget L.M.
Ericsson.
**Allmerica Financial Corporation, 63
29–31**
Allnet, **10** 19
Allo Pro, **III** 633
Allor Leasing Corp., **9** 323
**Allou Health & Beauty Care, Inc., 28
12–14**
Alloy & Stainless, Inc., **IV** 228
Alloy, Inc., 55 13–15
Allparts, Inc., **51** 307
Allserve Inc., **25** 367
Allsport plc., **31** 216, 218
The Allstate Corporation, III 259, 294;
10 50–52; 13 539; **21** 96–97; **22** 495;
23 286–87; **25** 155; **27 30–33 (upd.)**;
29 397; **49** 332
ALLTEL Corporation, 6 299–301; 16
318; **20** 440; **46 15–19 (upd.); 54** 63,
108
Alltrans Group, **27** 472
Alltrista Corporation, 30 38–41
Allwaste, Inc., 18 10–13
Allweiler, **58** 67
Alma Media Group, **52** 51
Almac Electronics Corporation, **10** 113; **50**
42
Almac's Inc., **17** 558–59
Almacenes de Baja y Media, **39** 201, 204
Almaden Vineyards, **13** 134; **34** 89
Almanacksförlaget AB, **51** 328

Almanij NV, 44 15–18. *See also* Algemeene Maatschappij voor Nijverheidskrediet.

Almay, Inc. *See* Revlon Inc.

Almeida Banking House. *See* Banco Bradesco S.A.

Almys, **24** 461

ALNM. *See* Ayres, Lewis, Norris & May.

Aloe Vera of America, **17** 187

Aloha Airlines, Incorporated, 9 271–72; **21** 142; **24** 20–22

ALP. *See* Associated London Properties.

Alp Sport Sandals, **22** 173

Alpex, S.A. de C.V., **19** 12

Alpha Beta Co., **II** 605, 625, 653; **17** 559

Alpha Engineering Group, Inc., **16** 259–60

Alpha Healthcare Ltd., **25** 455

Alpha Processor Inc., **41** 349

Alpha Technical Systems, **19** 279

Alphaform, **40** 214–15

Alphanumeric Publication Systems, Inc., **26** 518

Alpharma Inc., 35 22–26 (upd.)

Alphonse Allard Inc., **II** 652; **51** 303

Alpine Confections, Inc., 71 22–24

Alpine Electronics, Inc., 13 30–31

Alpine Gaming. *See* Century Casinos, Inc.

Alpine Lace Brands, Inc., 18 14–16

Alpine Securities Corporation, **22** 5

Alpnet Inc. *See* SDL PLC.

Alpre, **19** 192

Alps Electric Co., Ltd., II 5–6; **13** 30; **44** 19–21 (upd.)

Alric Packing, **II** 466

Alrosa Company Ltd., 62 7–11

Alsco. *See* Steiner Corporation.

Alsen-Breitenbury, **III** 702

ALSO Holding AG, **29** 419, 422

Alsons Corp., **III** 571; **20** 362

Alsthom, **II** 12

Alsthom-Atlantique, **9** 9

Alta Dena, **25** 83, 85

Alta Electric Company, **25** 15

ALTA Health Strategies, Inc., **11** 113

Alta Vista Company, **50** 228

Altadis S.A., 72 6–13 (upd.)

Altamil Corp., **IV** 137

Altana AG, **23** 498

AltaSteel Ltd., **51** 352

AltaVista Company, 43 11–13

ALTEC International, **21** 107–09

Altenburg & Gooding, **22** 428

Altera Corporation, 18 17–20; **43** 14–18 (upd.); **47** 384

Alternative Living Services. *See* Alterra Healthcare Corporation.

Alternative Tentacles Records, 66 3–6

Alternative Youth Services, Inc., **29** 399–400

Alterra Healthcare Corporation, 42 3–5

Altex, **19** 192–93

Althouse Chemical Company, **9** 153

Alticor Inc., 71 25–30 (upd.)

Altiris, Inc., 65 34–36

Altman Weil Pensa, **29** 237

Alton Towers, **55** 378

Altos Computer Systems, **10** 362

Altos Hornos de México, S.A. de C.V., 13 144; **19** 220; **39** 188; **42** 6–8

Altra Broadband Inc., **63** 34

Altran Technologies, 51 15–18

Altron Incorporated, 20 8–10

Altura Energy Ltd. *See* Occidental Petroleum Corporation.

Aluar. *See* Aluminios Argentinos.

Aluma Systems Corp., **9** 512; **22** 14

Alumalsa. *See* Aluminoy y Aleaciones S.A.

Alumax Inc., **I** 508; **III** 758; **8** 505–06; **22** 286; **56** 11

Aluminios Argentinos, **26** 433

Aluminoy y Aleaciones S.A., **63** 303

Aluminum and Stainless, Inc. *See* Reliance Steel & Aluminum Company.

Aluminum Company of America, IV 14–16, 56, 59, 121–22, 131, 173, 703; **19** 240, 292; **20** 11–14 (upd.); **22** 455; **42** 438; **52** 71. *See also* Alcoa Inc.

Aluminum Forge Co., **IV** 137

Aluminum Rolling Mills, **17** 280

Aluminum Sales Corporation, **12** 346

Alupak, A.G., **12** 377

Alvic Group, **20** 363

Alvin Ailey Dance Foundation, Inc., 52 14–17

Alvis Plc, 47 7–9

Alyeska Pipeline Service Co., **IV** 571; **14** 542; **24** 521

ALZA Corporation, 10 53–55; **36** 36–39 (upd.); **40** 11; **41** 200–01

Alzouman Aviation, **56** 148

AM Acquisition Inc., **8** 559–60

AM Cosmetics, Inc., **31** 89

Am-Safe, Inc., **16** 357

AM-TEX Corp., Inc., **12** 443

Amagasaki Spinners Ltd. *See* Unitika Ltd.

Amalgamaize Co., **14** 18

Amalgamated Bank, 60 20–22

Amalgamated Dental International, **10** 271–72

Amalgamated Distilled Products, **II** 609

Amalgamated Press, **7** 244, 342

Amalgamated Sugar Co., **14** 18; **19** 467–68

Amana Refrigeration Company, **18** 226; **38** 374; **42** 159

Amaray International Corporation, **12** 264

Amarillo Gas Company. *See* Atmos Energy Corporation.

Amarillo Railcar Services, **6** 580

Amati Communications Corporation, **57** 409

Amax Gold, **36** 316

AMAX Inc., I 508; **IV** 17–19, 46, 139, 171, 239, 387; **12** 244; **22** 106, 286. *See also* Cyprus Amex.

Amazon.com, Inc., 25 17–19; **56** 12–15 (upd.)

AMB Generali Holding AG, 51 19–23

AMB Property Corporation, 57 25–27

Ambac Financial Group, Inc., 65 37–39

AmBase Corp., **III** 264

Ambassadors International, Inc., 68 16–18 (upd.)

Amber's Stores, Inc., **17** 360

Amberg Hospach AG, **49** 436

AmBev. *See* Companhia de Bebidas das Américas.

Amblin Entertainment, 21 23–27; **33** 431

AMBRA, Inc., **48** 209

AMC Entertainment Inc., 12 12–14; **14** 87; **21** 362; **23** 126; **35** 27–29 (upd.); **59** 342

AMCA International Corporation, **7** 513; **8** 545; **10** 329; **23** 299

AMCC. *See* Applied Micro Circuits Corporation.

Amcell. *See* American Cellular Network.

AMCO, Inc., **13** 159

AMCOL International Corporation, 59 29–33 (upd.)

Amcor Limited, IV 248–50; **19** 13–16 (upd.)

AMCORE Financial Inc., 44 22–26

Amcraft Building Products Co., Inc., **22** 15

AMD. *See* Advanced Micro Devices, Inc.

Amdahl Corporation, III 109–11, 140; **12** 238; **13** 202; **14** 13–16 (upd.); **16** 194, 225–26; **22** 293; **25** 87; **40** 20–25 (upd.); **42** 147. *See also* Fujitsu Limited.

Amdocs Ltd., 47 10–12

AME Finanziaria, **IV** 587; **19** 19; **54** 20

Amec Spie S.A., I 568; **36** 322; **49** 65; **57** 28–31

Amedysis, Inc., 53 33–36

Amer Group plc, 24 530; **41** 14–16

Amer Sport, **22** 202; **68** 245

Amerace Corporation, **54** 373

Amerada Hess Corporation, IV 365–67, 400, 454, 522, 571, 658; **11** 353; **21** 28–31 (upd.); **24** 521; **55** 16–20 (upd.)

AMERCO, 6 351–52; **67** 11–14 (upd.)

Ameren Corporation, 60 23–27 (upd.)

AmerGen Energy LLC, **49** 65, 67

Ameri-Kart Corp., **19** 277, 279

America Latina Companhia de Seguros, **III** 289

America Online, Inc., 10 56–58, 237; **13** 147; **15** 54, 265, 321; **18** 24; **19** 41; **22** 52, 519, 522; **26** 16–20 (upd.); **27** 20, 106, 301, 430, 517–18; **29** 143, 227; **32** 163; **33** 254; **34** 361; **35** 304, 306; **38** 269–71; **49** 311–12; **54** 74; **63** 393. *See also* CompuServe Interactive Services, Inc.; AOL Time Warner Inc.

America Publishing Company, **18** 213

America Today, **13** 545

America Unplugged, **18** 77

America West Airlines, 6 72–74, 121

America West Express, **32** 334

America West Holdings Corporation, 34 22–26 (upd.)

America's Car-Mart, Inc., 64 19–21

America's Favorite Chicken Company, Inc., 7 26–28. *See also* AFC Enterprises, Inc.

American & Efird, Inc., **12** 501; **23** 260

American Acquisitions, Inc., **49** 279

American Air Conditioning, **25** 15

American Air Filter, **26** 3–4

American Airlines, I 89–91, 97, 106, 115, 118, 124–26, 130, 132, 530; **6** 75–77 (upd.); **9** 271–72; **11** 279; **12** 190, 192, 379, 381, 487, 513; **13** 173; **14** 73; **16** 146; **18** 73; **21** 141, 143; **24** 21, 399–400; **25** 90–91, 403, 421–22; **26** 427–28, 441; **31** 103, 306; **33** 270, 302; **34** 118; **38** 105; **55** 10–11. *See also* AMR Corporation.

American Allsafe Co., **8** 386

American Association of Retired Persons. *See* AARP.

American Austin Quality Foods Inc., **44** 40

American Automar Inc., **12** 29

American Automated, **11** 111

American Aviation Manufacturing Corp., **15** 246

American Axle & Manufacturing Holdings, Inc., 67 15–17

American Bakeries Company, **12** 275–76

American Bancorp, **11** 295

American Bancshares, Inc., **11** 457

American Bank, **9** 474–75

American Bank of Vicksburg, **14** 41

American Bankcorp, Inc., **8** 188

American Banker/Bond Buyer, **8** 526

American Banknote Corporation, 30 42–45

American Bar Association, 35 30–33

American Barge and Towing Company, **11** 194

American Beauty Cover Company, **12** 472

American Beef Packers, Inc., **16** 473

American Beet Sugar Company, **11** 13–14

American Beryllium Co., Inc., **9** 323

American Biltrite Inc., 16 16–18; **18** 116, 118; **43** 19–22 (upd.)

American Bio Corporation Inc., **70** 346

American Biodyne Inc., **9** 348

American Biomedical Corporation, **11** 333

American BioScience, **69** 20–21

American Bottling, **49** 78

American Box Board Company, **12** 376

American Box Co., **IV** 137

American Brands, Inc., V 395–97; **7** 3–4; **9** 408; **12** 87, 344; **14** 95, 271–72; **16** 108, 110, 242; **19** 168–69; **38** 169; **49** 150–51, 153. *See also* Fortune Brands, Inc.

American Broadcasting Co. *See* ABC, Inc.; Capital Cities/ABC Inc.

American Builders & Contractors Supply Co. *See* ABC Supply Co., Inc.

American Builders, Inc., **8** 436

American Building Maintenance Industries, Inc., 6 17–19. *See also* ABM Industries Incorporated.

American Bus Lines Inc., **24** 118

American Business Information, Inc., 18 21–25

American Business Interiors. *See* American Furniture Company, Inc.

American Business Products, Inc., 20 15–17

American Cabinet Hardware Corp. *See* Amerock Corporation.

American Cable Systems, Inc. *See* Comcast Corporation.

American Cablesystems, **7** 99

American Can Co., **8** 476; **10** 130; **11** 29; **12** 408; **13** 255; **15** 127–28; **17** 106; **23** 98; **49** 293. *See also* Primerica Corp.

The American Cancer Society, 24 23–25

American Capital and Research Corp., **28** 201

American Carbide Corporation, **7** 584

American Cast Iron Pipe Company, 50 17–20

American Cellular Corporation, **63** 131–32

American Cellular Network, **7** 91; **24** 122

American Cement Co. *See* Giant Cement Holding, Inc.

American Chrome, **III** 699

American Civil Liberties Union (ACLU), 60 28–31

American Classic Voyages Company, 22 340, **27** 34–37

American Clay Forming Company, **8** 178

American Clip Company, **7** 3

American Coin Merchandising, Inc., 28 15–17

American Colloid Co., 13 32–35. *See* AMCOL International Corporation.

American Colonial Insurance Company, **44** 356

American Commercial Lines Inc., **22** 164, 166–67

American Commonwealths Power Corporation, **6** 579

American Community Grocers, **II** 670

American Computer Systems. *See* American Software Inc.

American Construction Lending Services, Inc., **39** 380, 382

American Cotton Cooperative Association, **17** 207; **33** 85

American Cotton Growers Association, **57** 283

American Council on Education, **12** 141

American Courier Express, Inc., **24** 126

American Crayon Company, **12** 115

American Crystal Sugar Company, 7 377; **11** 13–15; **32** 29–33 (upd.)

American Cyanamid, I 300–02; **8** 24–26 (upd.); **10** 269; **11** 494; **13** 231–32; **14** 254, 256; **16** 68; **22** 147; **27** 115–16; **50** 248, 250

American Dairy Queen Corporation, **10** 373

American Data Technology, Inc., **11** 111

American Digital Communications, Inc., **33** 329

American Diversified Foods, Inc., **14** 351

American Drew, Inc., **12** 301

American Drug Company, **13** 367

American Eagle Airlines, Inc., **28** 22

American Eagle Outfitters, Inc., 14 427; **24** 26–28; **25** 121; **55** 21–24 (upd.)

American Education Press, **10** 479

American Electric Company, **12** 193; **22** 10; **54** 371–73

American Electric Power Company, V 546–49; **6** 524; **11** 516; **45** 17–21 (upd.)

American Emulsions Co., **8** 455

American Encaustic Tiling Co., **22** 170

American Energy Management Inc., **39** 261

American Envelope Co., **28** 251

American Equipment Co., **I** 571

American Express Company, I 480, 614; **II** 108, 176, 309, 380–82, **395–99**, 450–52, 544; **III** 319, 340, 389; **8** 118; **9** 335, 343, 468–69, 538; **10** 44–45, **59–64** (upd.); **11** 41, 416–17, 532; **12** 533; **14** 106; **15** 50; **18** 60, 112, 516, 543; **21** 97; **23** 229; **26** 516; **33** 394–96; **38** 42–48 (upd.); **52** 13

American Factors, Ltd. *See* Amfac/JMB Hawaii L.L.C.

American Family Corporation, III 187–89. *See also* AFLAC Inc.

American Family Publishers, **23** 393–94

American Feldmühle Corp., **II** 51; **21** 330

American Financial Corporation, III 190–92, 221; **8** 537; **9** 452; **18** 549

American Financial Group Inc., 48 6–10 (upd.)

American Fine Wire, Inc., **33** 248

American First National Supermarkets, **16** 313

American Fitness Centers, **25** 40

American Fitness Products, Inc., **47** 128

American Flange, **30** 397

American Flavor & Fragrance Company, **9** 154

American Flyer Trains, **16** 336–37

American Foods Group, 43 23–27

American Football League, **29** 346

American Foreign Insurance Association. *See* AFIA.

American Freightways Corporation, **42** 141

American Fructose Corp., **14** 18–19

American Fur Company, **25** 220

American Furniture Company, Inc., 12 300; **21** 32–34

American Gaming and Electronics, Inc., **43** 461

American Gas & Electric. *See* American Electric Power Company.

American General Capital Corp., **I** 614

American General Corporation, III 193–94; **10** 65–67 (upd.); **11** 16; **46** 20–23 (upd.); **47** 15

American General Finance Corp., 11 16–17

American Girl, Inc., 69 16–19 (upd)

American Golf Corporation, 45 22–24

American Gramaphone LLC, 52 18–20

American Graphics, **23** 100

American Greetings Corporation, 7 23–25; **12** 207–08; **15** 507; **16** 256; **21** 426–28; **22** 33–36 (upd.); **59** 34–39 (upd.); **61** 336

American Grinder and Manufacturing Company, **9** 26

American Hardware & Supply Company. *See* TruServ Corporation.

American Hawaii Cruises, **27** 34

American Health & Life Insurance Company, **27** 47

American Healthcorp Inc., **48** 25

American Healthways, Inc., 65 40–42

American Heritage Savings, **II** 420

American Hoechst Corporation. *See* Hoechst Celanese Corporation.

American Hoist & Derrick Co., **8** 544

American Home Mortgage Holdings, Inc., 46 24–26

American Home Patients Centers Inc., **46** 4

American Home Products, I 622–24; **10** **68–70** (upd.), 528; **11** 35; **15** 64–65; **16** 191, 438; **21** 466; **24** 288; **25** 477; **36** 87; **38** 365; **49** 349–50. *See also* Wyeth.

American Home Publishing Co., Inc., **14** 460

American Home Shield. *See* ServiceMaster Inc.

American Home Video, **9** 186

American Homestar Corporation, 18 26–29; **41** 17–20 (upd.)

American Homeware Inc., **15** 501

American Hospital Association, **10** 159

American Hospital Supply Co., **III** 80; **11** 459, 486; **19** 103; **21** 118; **30** 496; **53** 345

American Hydron, **13** 366; **25** 55

American I.G. Chemical Corporation. *See* GAF Corporation.

American Impacts Corporation, **8** 464

American Improved Cements. *See* Giant Cement Holding, Inc.

American Independent Oil Co. *See* Aminoil, Inc.

American Industrial Properties. *See* Developers Diversified Realty Corporation.

American Information Services, Inc., **11** 111

American Institute of Certified Public Accountants (AICPA), 44 27–30

American Institutional Products, Inc., **18** 246

American Instrument Co., **13** 233

American International Airways, Inc., **17** 318; **22** 311

American International Group, Inc., III 195–98, 200; **10** 39; **11** 532–33; **15** 15–19 (upd.); **18** 159; **45** 109; **46** 20; **47** 13–19 (upd.); **48** 219; **63** 175

American Isuzu Motors, Inc. *See* Isuzu Motors, Ltd.

American Italian Pasta Company, 27 38–40

American Janitor Service, **25** 15

American Jet Industries, **7** 205

American Ka-Ro, **8** 476

American Knitting Mills of Miami, Inc., **22** 213

American La-France, **10** 296

American Land Cruiser Company. *See* Cruise America Inc.

American Lawyer Media Holdings, Inc., 32 34–37

American Learning Corporation, **7** 168

American Light and Traction. *See* MCN Corporation.

American Lightwave Systems, Inc., **10** 19

American Limousine Corp., **26** 62

American Linen Supply Company. *See* Steiner Corporation.

American Locker Group Incorporated, 34 19–21

American Lung Association, 48 11–14

American Machine and Foundry Co., **7** 211–13; **11** 397; **25** 197

American Machine and Metals, **9** 23

American Machine and Tool Co., Inc., **57** 160

American Machinery and Foundry, Inc., **57** 85

American Maize-Products Co., 14 17–20; **23** 464

American Management Systems, Inc., 11 18–20

American Materials & Technologies Corporation, **27** 117

American Media, Inc., 27 41–44

American Medical Association, 39 15–18

American Medical Holdings, **55** 370

American Medical International, Inc., III 73–75, 79; **14** 232

American Medical Optics, **25** 55

American Medical Response, Inc., 39 19–22

American Medical Services, **II** 679–80; **14** 209

American Medicorp, Inc., **14** 432; **24** 230

American Melamine, **27** 317

American Merchandising Associates Inc., **14** 411

American Metal Climax, Inc. *See* AMAX.

American Metals and Alloys, Inc., **19** 432

American Metals Corporation. *See* Reliance Steel & Aluminum Company.

American Micro Devices, Inc., **16** 549

The American Mineral Spirits Company, **8** 99–100

American Modern Insurance Group. *See* The Midland Company.

American Motors Corp., I 135–37; **8** 373; **10** 262, 264; **18** 493; **26** 403

American Multi-Cinema. *See* AMC Entertainment Inc.

American National Bank, **13** 221–22

American National Can Co., **IV** 175

American National General Agencies Inc., **III** 221; **14** 109; **37** 85

American National Insurance Company, 8 27–29; **27** 45–48 (upd.); **39** 158

American Natural Resources Co., **13** 416

American Natural Snacks Inc., **29** 480

American Oil Co., **7** 101; **14** 22

American Olean Tile Company, **III** 424; **22** 48, 170

American Optical Co., **7** 436; **38** 363–64

American Overseas Airlines, **12** 380

American Pad & Paper Company, 20 18–21

American Paging, **9** 494–96

American Paper Box Company, **12** 376

American Patriot Insurance, **22** 15

American Payment Systems, Inc., **21** 514

American Petrofina, Inc., **7** 179–80; **19** 11

American Pfauter, **24** 186

American Pharmaceutical Partners, Inc., 69 20–22

American Phone Centers, Inc., **21** 135

American Pop Corn Company, 59 40–43

American Port Services (Amports), **45** 29

American Power & Light Co., **6** 545, 596–97; **12** 542; **49** 143

American Power Conversion Corporation, 24 29–31; **67** 18–20 (upd.)

American Premier Underwriters, Inc., 10 71–74; **48** 9

American Prepaid Professional Services, Inc. *See* CompDent Corporation.

American President Companies Ltd., 6 353–55; **54** 274. *See also* APL Limited.

American Printing House for the Blind, 26 13–15

American Prospecting Equipment Co., **49** 174

American Public Automotive Group, **37** 115

American Publishing Co., **24** 222; **62** 188

American Re Corporation, 10 75–77; **35** 34–37 (upd.); **46** 303; **63** 13–14, 411–12

American Recreation Company Holdings, Inc., **16** 53; **44** 53–54

American Red Cross, 40 26–29

American Refrigeration Products S.A, **7** 429

American Research and Development Corp., **19** 103

American Residential Mortgage Corporation, 8 30–31

American Residential Services, **33** 141

American Retirement Corporation, 42 9–12; **43** 46

American Rice, Inc., 17 161–62; **33** 30–33

American Rug Craftsmen, **19** 275

American Safety Razor Company, 20 22–24

American Salt Co., **12** 199

American Satellite Co., **15** 195

American Savings & Loan, **10** 117

American Savings Bank, **9** 276; **17** 528, 531

American Sealants Company. *See* Loctite Corporation.

American Seating Co., **I** 447; **21** 33

American Seaway Foods, Inc, **9** 451

American Securities Capital Partners, L.P., **59** 13; **69** 138–39

American Service Corporation, **19** 223

American Shipbuilding, **18** 318

American Ships Ltd., **50** 209

American Skiing Company, 28 18–21; **31** 67, 229

American Sky Broadcasting, **27** 305; **35** 156

American Smelting and Refining Co. *See* ASARCO.

American Society for the Prevention of Cruelty to Animals (ASPCA), 68 19–22

The American Society of Composers, Authors and Publishers (ASCAP), 29 21–24

American Software Inc., 22 214; **25** 20–22

American Southern Insurance Co., **17** 196

American Standard Companies Inc., III 663–65; **19** 455; **22** 4, 6; **28** 486; **30** 46–50 (upd.); **40** 452

American States Water Company, 46 27–30

American Steamship Company. *See* GATX.

American Steel & Wire Co., **13** 97–98; **40** 70, 72

American Steel Foundries, **7** 29–30

American Stock Exchange, **10** 416–17; **54** 242

American Stores Company, II 604–06; **12** 63, 333; **13** 395; **17** 559; **18** 89; **22** 37–40 (upd.); **25** 297; **27** 290–92; **30** 24, 26–27. *See also* Albertson's, Inc.

American Sugar Refining Company. *See* Domino Sugar Corporation.

American Sumatra Tobacco Corp., **15** 138

American Superconductor Corporation, **41** 141

American Surety Co., **26** 486

American Systems Technologies, Inc., **18** 5

American Teaching Aids Inc., **19** 405

American Technical Ceramics Corp., 67 21–23

American Technical Services Company. *See* American Building Maintenance Industries, Inc.; ABM Industries Incorporated.

American Telephone and Telegraph Company. *See* AT&T.

American Television and Communications Corp., **IV** 675; **7** 528–30; **18** 65

American Textile Co., **III** 571; **20** 362

American Thermos Bottle Company. *See* Thermos Company.

American Threshold, **50** 123

American Tile Supply Company, **19** 233

American Tissue Company, **29** 136

American Tobacco Co., **14** 77, 79; **15** 137–38; **16** 242; **18** 416; **27** 128–29; **33** 82; **43** 126; **50** 116–17, 119, 259–60. *See also* American Brands Inc., B.A.T. Industries PLC.; Fortune Brands, Inc.

American Tool Companies, Inc., **52** 270

American Tool Company, **13** 563

American Totalisator Corporation, **10** 319–20

American Tourister, Inc., 10 350; **13** 451, 453; **16** 19–21. *See also* Samsonite Corporation.

American Tower Corporation, 33 34–38

American Tractor Corporation, **10** 379

American Trading and Production Corporation, **7** 101

American Trans Air, **34** 31

American Transitional Hospitals, Ltd., **65** 307

American Transport Lines, **6** 384
American Twist Drill Co., **23** 82
American Vanguard Corporation, **47** 20–22
American VIP Limousine, Inc., **26** 62
American Water Works Company, Inc., **6** 443–45; **26** 451; **38** 49–52 (upd.)
American Wood Reduction Company, **14** 174
American Woodmark Corporation, **31** 13–16
American Yard Products, **22** 26, 28
American Yearbook Company, **7** 255; **25** 252
American-Strevell Inc., **II** 625
Americana Entertainment Group, Inc., **19** 435
Americana Foods, Inc., **17** 474–75
Americana Healthcare Corp., **15** 522
Americana Ships Ltd., **50** 210
Americom, **61** 272
Ameridrive, **58** 67
AmeriFirst Bank, **11** 258
Amerifirst Federal Savings, **10** 340
AmeriGas Partners, L.P., **12** 498, 500; **56** 36
AMERIGROUP Corporation, **69** 23–26
Amerihost Properties, Inc., **30** 51–53
AmeriKing Corp., **36** 309
Amerimark Inc., **II** 682
Amerin Corporation. *See* Radian Group Inc.
AmeriServe Food Distribution. *See* Holberg Industries, Inc.
Amerisex, **64** 198
AmeriSource Health Corporation, **37** 9–11 (upd.)
AmerisourceBergen Corporation, **64** 22–28 (upd.)
Ameristar Casinos, Inc., **33** 39–42; **69** 27–31 (upd.)
AmeriSteel Corp., **59** 202
AmeriSuites, **52** 281
Amerisystems, **8** 328
Ameritech Corporation, **V** 265–68; **6** 248; **7** 118; **10** 431; **11** 382; **12** 137; **14** 252–53, 257, 259–61, 364; **15** 197; **18** 30–34 (upd.); **25** 499; **41** 288–90; **43** 447; **44** 49
Ameritech Illinois. *See* Illinois Bell Telephone Company.
Ameritrade Holding Corporation, **34** 27–30
Ameritrust Corporation, **9** 476
Ameriwood Industries International Corp., **17** 15–17; **59** 164
Amerock Corporation, **13** 41; **53** 37–40
Ameron International Corporation, **67** 24–26
Amerop Sugar Corporation, **60** 96
Amersham PLC, **50** 21–25; **63** 166
Ames Department Stores, Inc., **9** 20–22; **10** 497; **15** 88; **30** 54–57 (upd.)
Ametek Inc., **9** 23–25; **12** 88; **38** 169
N.V. Amev, **III** 199–202
AMEX. *See* American Stock Exchange.
Amey Plc, **47** 23–25; **49** 320
AMF. *See* American Machinery and Foundry, Inc.
AMF Bowling, Inc., **19** 312; **23** 450; **40** 30–33
Amfac Inc., **I** 417–18, 566; **10** 42; **23** 320
Amfac/JMB Hawaii L.L.C., **24** 32–35 (upd.)

AMFM Inc., **35** 221, 245, 248; **37** 104; **41** 384
Amgen, Inc., **8** 216–17; **10** 78–81; **13** 240; **14** 255; **21** 320; **30** 58–61 (upd.); **38** 204; **50** 248, 250, 538; **54** 111
Amherst Coal Co., **7** 309
AMI. *See* Advanced Metallurgy, Inc.
AMI Metals, Inc. *See* Reliance Steel & Aluminum Company.
AMICAS, Inc., **69** 32–34
Amiga Corporation, **7** 96
Aminoil, Inc. *See* American Independent Oil Co.
Amisys Managed Care Information Systems, **16** 94
Amitron S.A., **10** 113; **50** 43
Amity Leather Products Company. *See* AR Accessories Group, Inc.
AMK Corporation, **7** 85; **21** 111
Amkor Technology, Inc., **69** 35–37
AMLI Realty Company, **33** 418, 420
Amling Co., **25** 89
Amnesty International, **50** 26–29
Amoco Corporation, **IV** 368–71, 412, 424–25, 453, 525; **7** 107, 443; **10** 83–84; **11** 441; **12** 18; **14** 21–25 (upd.), 494; **18** 365; **19** 297; **26** 369. *See also* BP p.l.c.
AMOR 14 Corporation, **64** 95
Amorim Investimentos e Participaço, **48** 117, 119
Amorim Revestimentos, **48** 118
Amoskeag Company, **8** 32–33; **9** 213–14, 217; **31** 199
Amot Controls Corporation, **15** 404; **50** 394
AMP, Inc., **II** 7–8; **11** 319; **13** 344; **14** 26–28 (upd.); **17** 274; **22** 542; **28** 486; **36** 158; **54** 239; **63** 404
Ampacet Corporation, **67** 27–29
Ampad Holding Corporation. *See* American Pad & Paper Company.
AMPAL. *See* American-Palestine Trading Corp.
AMPCO Auto Parks, Inc. *See* American Building Maintenance Industries, Inc.; ABM Industries Incorporated.
Ampeg Company, **48** 353
AMPEP, **III** 625
Ampex Corporation, **17** 18–20
Amphenol Corporation, **40** 34–37
Ampol Petroleum Ltd., **III** 729; **27** 473
Ampro, **25** 504–05
AMR. *See* American Medical Response, Inc.
AMR Combs Inc., **36** 190
AMR Corporation, **8** 315; **22** 252; **26** 427–28; **28** 22–26 (upd.); **29** 409; **33** 19; **34** 119; **52** 21–26 (upd.); **54** 4
AMR Information Services, **9** 95
Amram's Distributing Limited, **12** 425
AMRE, **III** 211
AMREP Corporation, **21** 35–37; **24** 78
Amro. *See* Amsterdam-Rotterdam Bank N.V.
Amrop International Australasia, **34** 249
AMS. *See* Advanced Marketing Services, Inc.
Amsbra Limited, **62** 48
Amscan Holdings, Inc., **61** 24–26
Amsco International, **29** 450
Amserve Ltd., **48** 23

AmSouth Bancorporation, **12** 15–17; **48** 15–18 (upd.)
Amstar Corp., **14** 18
Amstar Sugar Corporation, **7** 466–67; **26** 122
Amsted Industries Incorporated, **7** 29–31; **66** 27
Amsterdam-Rotterdam Bank N.V., **II** 185–86; **14** 169; **17** 324
Amstrad plc, **III** 112–14; **48** 19–23 (upd.)
AmSurg Corporation, **48** 24–27
AMT. *See* American Machine and Tool Co., Inc.; American Materials & Technologies Corporation.
Amtech. *See* American Building Maintenance Industries, Inc.; ABM Industries Incorporated.
Amtech Systems Corporation, **11** 65; **27** 405
Amtel, Inc., **8** 545; **10** 136
Amtorg, **13** 365
Amtrak. *See* The National Railroad Passenger Corporation.
Amtran, Inc., **34** 31–33
AmTrans. *See* American Transport Lines.
Amurol Confections Company, **58** 378
Amvac Chemical Corporation, **47** 20
Amvent, Inc., **25** 120
AMVESCAP PLC, **65** 43–45
Amway Corporation, **III** 11–14; **13** 36–39 (upd.); **30** 62–66 (upd.). *See also* Alticor Inc.
Amylin Pharmaceuticals, Inc., **67** 30–32
ANA. *See* All Nippon Airways Co., Ltd.
Anacomp, Inc., **11** 19
Anaconda Aluminum, **11** 38
Anaconda Co., **7** 261–63
Anaconda-Jurden Associates, **8** 415
Anadarko Petroleum Corporation, **10** 82–84; **52** 27–30 (upd.); **65** 316–17
Anadex, Inc., **18** 435–36
Anaheim Angels Baseball Club, Inc., **53** 41–44
Anaheim Imaging, **19** 336
Analog Devices, Inc., **10** 85–87; **18** 20; **19** 67; **38** 54; **43** 17, 311; **47** 384
Analogic Corporation, **23** 13–16
Analysts International Corporation, **36** 40–42
Analytic Sciences Corporation, **10** 88–90; **13** 417
Analytical Nursing Management Corporation (ANMC). *See* Amedisys, Inc.
Analytical Science Laboratories Inc., **58** 134
Analytical Surveys, Inc., **33** 43–45
Analytico Food BV. *See* Eurofins Scientific S.A.
Anam Group, **21** 239; **23** 17–19
Anarad, Inc., **18** 515
Anaren Microwave, Inc., **33** 46–48
Anchor Bancorp, Inc., **10** 91–93
Anchor Brake Shoe, **18** 5
Anchor Brewing Company, **47** 26–28
Anchor Corporation, **12** 525
Anchor Gaming, **24** 36–39; **41** 216
Anchor Hocking Glassware, **13** 40–42; **14** 483; **26** 353; **49** 253; **53** 39
Anchor Motor Freight, Inc., **12** 309–10
Anchor National Financial Services, Inc., **11** 482

Anchor National Life Insurance Company, **11** 482

Andenne Bricolage BVBA, **68** 64

Anders Wilhelmsen & Co., **22** 471

Andersen, 68 23–27 **(upd.)**

Andersen Consulting. *See* Accenture Ltd

Andersen Corporation, 9 344; **10** 94–95; **11** 305; **22** 346; **39** 324

Andersen Worldwide, 29 25–28 **(upd.)**; **57** 165

Anderson Animal Hospital, Inc., **58** 354

Anderson Box Co., **8** 267

The Anderson-DuBose Company, 60 32–34

Anderson Exploration Ltd., **61** 75

Anderson, Greenwood & Co., **11** 225–26

Anderson Packaging, Inc., **64** 27

Anderson Testing Company, Inc., **6** 441

The Andersons, Inc., 31 17–21

Andlinger & Co., **60** 132

Andreas Christ, **26** 243

Andreas Stihl AG & Co. KG, 16 22–24; **59** 44–47 **(upd.)**

Andrew Corporation, 10 96–98; **32** 38–41 **(upd.)**

Andrew Jergens Co., **25** 56

Andrews Group, Inc., **10** 402

Andrews Kurth, LLP, 71 31–34

Andrews McMeel Universal, 40 38–41

Andrews Office Supply and Equipment Co., **25** 500

Andritz AG, 27 269; **51** 24–26

Andronico's Market, 70 10–13

Andrx Corporation, 55 25–27

Anfor, **IV** 249–50

Angele Ghigi, **II** 475

Angelica Corporation, 15 20–22; **43** 28–31 **(upd.)**; **61** 206

Angelo's Supermarkets, Inc., **II** 674

ANGI Ltd., **11** 28

Angle Steel, **25** 261

Anglian Water Plc, **38** 51

Anglo-Abrasives Ltd. *See* Carbo PLC.

Anglo-American Clays Corp., **IV** 346

Anglo American Corporation of South Africa Limited, IV 20–23, 56–57, 64–68, 79–80, 90, 92, 94–96, 118–20, 191, 239–40; **7** 121–23, 125; **16** 25–30 **(upd.)**, 292; **21** 211, 354; **22** 233; **28** 88, 93; **49** 232–34

Anglo American Industrial Corporation, **59** 224–25

Anglo American PLC, 50 30–36 **(upd.)**

Anglo-American Telegraph Company Ltd., **25** 98

Anglo-Canadian Telephone Company of Montreal. *See* British Columbia Telephone Company.

Anglo-Celtic Watch Company, **25** 430

Anglo Company, Ltd., **9** 363

Anglo-Dutch Unilever group, **9** 317

Anglo Energy, Ltd., **9** 364

Anglo-Iranian Oil Co., **7** 141

Anglo-Lautaro Nitrate Corporation, **9** 363

Anglo-Persian Oil Co., **7** 140

Anglovaal Industries Ltd., **20** 263

Anheuser-Busch Companies, Inc., I 217–19; **10** 99–101 **(upd.)**; **34** 34–37 **(upd.)**; **36** 12–15, 163; **59** 97, 352; **63** 229

ANI America Inc., **62** 331

Anker BV, 53 45–47

ANMC. *See* Amedisys, Inc.

Ann Street Group Ltd., **61** 44–46

Anne Klein & Co., **15** 145–46; **24** 299; **40** 277–78; **56** 90

Annecy Béton Carrières, **70** 343

Anneplas, **25** 464

Annie's Homegrown, Inc., 59 48–50

AnnTaylor Stores Corporation, 13 43–45; **15** 9; **25** 120–22; **37** 12–15 **(upd.)**; **67** 33–37 **(upd.)**

Annuaries Marcotte Ltd., **10** 461

Anocout Engineering Co., **23** 82

ANR Pipeline Co., 17 21–23; **31** 119

Anritsu Corporation, 68 28–30

Ansa Software, **9** 81

Ansbacher-Siegle Corp., **13** 460

The Anschutz Corporation, 12 18–20; **36** 43–47 **(upd.)**; **37** 312

Ansco & Associates, LLC, **57** 119

Ansell Ltd., 60 35–38 **(upd.)**

Ansell Ltd., 60 35–38 **(upd.)**

Ansell Rubber Company, **10** 445

Anselmo L. Morvillo S.A., **19** 336

Ansett Airlines, **6** 73; **14** 11; **27** 475

Ansett Australia, **24** 398, 400; **26** 113

Ansett Transport Industries Limited, **V** 523–25; **27** 473

Ansoft Corporation, 63 32–34

ANSYS Technologies Inc., **48** 410

Antalis, **34** 38, 40

AntarChile S.A., **69** 141, 143

Antares Alliance Group, **14** 15

Antares Capital Corp., **53** 213

Antares Electronics, Inc., **10** 257

Ante Corp., **22** 222

Antenna Company, **32** 40

Anteon Corporation, 57 32–34

ANTEX. *See* American National Life Insurance Company of Texas.

Anthem Electronics, Inc., 13 46–47; **17** 276

Anthem P&C Holdings, **15** 257

Anthes Industries Inc., **9** 512

Anthony & Sylvan Pools Corporation, 56 16–18

Anthony Industries Inc. *See* K2 Inc.

Anthony Stumpf Publishing Company, **10** 460

Anthracite Industries, Inc. *See* Asbury Carbons, Inc.

Anthropologie, **14** 524–25

Antinori. *See* Marchesi Antinori SRL.

The Antioch Company, 40 42–45

Antique Street Lamps, **19** 212

ANTK Tupolev. *See* Aviacionny Nauchno-Tehnicheskii Komplex im. A.N. Tupoleva.

Antofagasta plc, 65 46–49

Antonio Puig, S.A. *See* Puig Beauty and Fashion Group S.L.

Antonov Design Bureau, 53 48–51

ANZ. *See* Australia and New Zealand Banking Group Limited.

ANZ Securities, **24** 400

AO Sidanco, **45** 50

AO VimpelCom, **59** 300

AOE Plastic GmbH, **7** 141

Aohata Corporation, **57** 202, 204

Aoki Corporation, **9** 547, 549; **29** 508

AOL Time Warner Inc., 45 201; **47** 271; **57** 35–44 **(upd.)**

Aon Corporation, III 203–05; **22** 495; **45** 25–28 **(upd.)**; **50** 267, 433

AP. *See* The Associated Press.

AP&L. *See* American Power & Light Co.

AP Bank, Ltd., **13** 439

AP-Dow Jones/Telerate Company, **10** 277

AP Support Services, **25** 13

Apache Corporation, 10 102–04; **11** 28; **18** 366; **32** 42–46 **(upd.)**

Apache Energy Ltd., **25** 471

APACHE Medical Systems, Inc., **16** 94

Apanage GmbH & Co. KG, **53** 195

Apartment Furniture Rental, **26** 102

Apartment Investment and Management Company, 49 24–26

Apasco S.A. de C.V., 51 27–29

APB. *See* Atlantic Premium Brands, Ltd.

APCOA/Standard Parking. *See* Holberg Industries, Inc.

Apex, **17** 363

Apex Digital, Inc., 63 35–37

Apex Financial Corp., **8** 10

Apex Oil, **37** 310–11

Apex One Inc., **31** 137

APH. *See* American Printing House for the Blind.

APi Group, Inc., 56 238; **64** 29–32

APL Corporation, **9** 346

APL Limited, 41 399; **61** 27–30 **(upd.)**

Aplex Industries, Inc., **26** 363

Apline Guild, **12** 173

APLIX S.A. *See* Velcro Industries N.V.

APM Ltd. *See* Amcor Limited

APN. *See* Affiliated Physicians Network, Inc.

Apogee Enterprises, Inc., 8 34–36; **22** 347

Apogee Sound International LLC, **62** 39

Apollo Advisors L.P., **16** 37; **26** 500, 502; **43** 438

Apollo Apparel Partners, L.P., **12** 431

Apollo Computer, **9** 471; **11** 284

Apollo Group, Inc., 24 40–42

Apollo Heating & Air Conditioning Inc., **15** 411

Apollo Investment Fund Ltd., **31** 211; **39** 174

Apollo Ski Partners LP of New York, **11** 543, 545

Apothekernes Laboratorium A.S., **12** 3–5

Appalachian Computer Services, **11** 112

Appalachian Travel Services, Inc., **25** 185, 187

Apparel Ventures, Inc. *See* The Jordan Company, LP.

Appetifrais S.A., **51** 54

Applause Inc., 17 461; **24** 43–46

Apple Bank for Savings, 59 51–53

Apple Computer, Inc., III 115–16; **6** 218–20 **(upd.)**; **36** 48–51 **(upd.)**; **38** 69; **71** 19

Apple Orthodontix, Inc., **35** 325

Apple South, Inc. *See* Avado Brands, Inc.

Applebee's International Inc., 14 29–31; **19** 258; **20** 159; **21** 362; **31** 40; **35** 38–41 **(upd.)**

Appleton Papers, **I** 426

Appleton Wire Works Corp., **8** 13

Appliance Recycling Centers of America, Inc., 42 13–16

Applica Incorporated, 43 32–36 **(upd.)**

Applied Beverage Systems Ltd., **21** 339

Applied Biomedical Corp., **47** 4

Applied Bioscience International, Inc., 10 105–07

Applied Color Systems, **III** 424

Applied Communications, Inc., **6** 280; **11** 151; **25** 496; **29** 477–79

Applied Data Research, Inc., **18** 31–32

Applied Digital Data Systems Inc., **9** 514
Applied Engineering Services, Inc. *See* The AES Corporation.
Applied Films Corporation, 12 121; **35** 148; **48 28–31**
Applied Industrial Materials Corporation, **22** 544, 547
Applied Komatsu Technology, Inc., **10** 109
Applied Laser Systems, **31** 124
Applied Learning International, **IV** 680
Applied Materials, Inc., 10 108–09; 18 382–84; **46 31–34 (upd.)**
Applied Micro Circuits Corporation, 38 53–55
Applied Network Technology, Inc., **25** 162
Applied Power Inc., 9 26–28; 32 47–51 (upd.)
Applied Programming Technologies, Inc., **12** 61
Applied Solar Energy, **8** 26
Applied Technology Corp., **11** 87
Applied Thermal Technologies, Inc., **29** 5
Approvisionnement Atlantique, **II** 652; **51** 303
Apria Healthcare Inc., **43** 266
Aprilia SpA, 17 24–26
Aprolis, **72** 159
APS. *See* Arizona Public Service Company.
APS Healthcare, **17** 166, 168
APSA, **63** 214
AptarGroup, Inc., 69 38–41
Apura GmbH, **IV** 325
Aqua Alliance Inc., 32 52–54 (upd.)
Aqua Cool Pure Bottled Water, **52** 188
Aqua de Oro Venture, **58** 23
Aquafin N.V., **12** 443; **38** 427
Aquarium Supply Co., **12** 230
Aquarius Group. *See* Club Mediterranee SA.
Aquarius Platinum Ltd., 63 38–40
Aquatech, **53** 232
Aquila Energy Corp., **6** 593
Aquila, Inc., 50 37–40 (upd.)
Aquitaine. *See* Société Nationale des Petroles d'Aquitaine.
AR Accessories Group, Inc., 23 20–22
AR-TIK Systems, Inc., **10** 372
ARA Services, II 607–08; 21 507; **25** 181. *See also* Aramark.
Arab-Israel Bank Ltd., **60** 50
Arab Japanese Insurance Co., **III** 296
Arab Leasing International Finance, **72** 85
Arab Radio & Television, **72** 85
Arabian American Oil Co. *See* Saudi Arabian Oil Co.
Arabian Gulf Oil Company. *See* Natinal Oil Corporation.
Arabian Investment Banking Corp., **15** 94; **26** 53; **47** 361
Aracruz Celulose S.A., 57 45–47
Aral AG, 62 12–15
ARAMARK Corporation, 13 48–50; 16 228; **21** 114–15; **35** 415; **41 21–24**
Aramco. *See* Arabian American Oil Co.; Saudi Arabian Oil Company.
Aramis Inc., **30** 191
Arandell Corporation, 37 16–18
Arapuã. *See* Lojas Arapuã S.A.
Aratex Inc., **13** 49
ARBED S.A., IV 24–27, 53; **22 41–45 (upd.); 26** 83; **42** 414

Arbeitsgemeinschaft der öffentlich-rechtlichen Rundfunkanstalten der Bundesrepublick. *See* ARD.
The Arbitron Company, 10 255, 359; **13** 5; **38 56–61**
Arbor Acres, **13** 103
Arbor Drugs Inc., 12 21–23. *See also* CVS Corporation.
Arbor International, **18** 542
Arbor Living Centers Inc., **6** 478
Arby's Inc., II 614; **8** 536–37; **14 32–34,** 351; **58** 323
ARC. *See* American Rug Craftsmen.
ARC International Corporation, **27** 57
ARC Materials Corp., **III** 688
ARC Propulsion, **13** 462
ARCA. *See* Appliance Recycling Centers of America, Inc.
Arcadia Company, **14** 138
Arcadia Group plc, 28 27–30 (upd.), 95–96
Arcadia Partners, **17** 321
Arcadian Corporation, **18** 433; **27** 317–18
Arcadian Marine Service, Inc., **6** 530
Arcadis NV, 26 21–24
Arcata Corporation, **12** 413
Arcata National Corp., **9** 305
Arcelor S.A., **65** 311
ARCH Air Medical Service, Inc., **53** 29
Arch Mineral Corporation, 7 32–34
Arch Petroleum Inc., **39** 331
Arch Wireless, Inc., 39 23–26; 41 265, 267
Archbold Container Co., **35** 390
Archbold Ladder Co., **12** 433
Archer-Daniels-Midland Co., I 419–21; 7 432–33, 241 **8** 53; **11 21–23 (upd.); 17** 207; **22** 85, 426; **23** 384; **25** 241; **31** 234; **32 55–59 (upd.)**
Archer Management Services Inc., **24** 360
Archibald Candy Corporation, **36** 309; **71** 22
Archie Comics Publications, Inc., 63 41–44
Archipelago RediBook, **48** 226, 228
Archstone-Smith Trust, 49 27–30
Archway Cookies, Inc., 29 29–31
ArcLight, LLC, **50** 123
ARCO. *See* Atlantic Richfield Company.
ARCO Chemical Company, 10 110–11
ARCO Comfort Products Co., **26** 4
Arco Electronics, **9** 323
Arco Pharmaceuticals, Inc., **31** 346
Arcon Corporation, **26** 287
Arcor S.A.I.C., 66 7–9
Arcorp Properties, **70** 226
Arctco, Inc., 12 400–01; 16 31–34; 35 349, 351
Arctic Alaska Fisheries Corporation, **14** 515; **50** 493–94
Arctic Cat Inc., 40 46–50 (upd.)
Arctic Enterprises, **34** 44
Arctic Slope Regional Corporation, 38 62–65
ARD, 41 25–29
Ardal og Sunndal Verk AS, **10** 439
Arden Group, Inc., 29 32–35
Ardent Risk Services, Inc. *See* General Re Corporation.
Ardent Software Inc., **59** 54–55
Argenbright Security Inc. *See* Securicor Plc.

Argentaria Caja Postal y Banco Hipotecario S.A. *See* Banco Bilbao Vizcaya Argentaria S.A.
Argentaurum A.G. *See* Pall Corporation.
Argentine National Bank, **14** 46
Argon Medical, **12** 327
Argonaut, **10** 520–22
Argos, **I** 426; **22** 72; **50** 117
Argos Retail Group, **47** 165, 169
Argos Soditic, **43** 147, 149
Argosy Gaming Company, 21 38–41
Argosy Group LP, **27** 197
Argus Corp., **IV** 611
Argus Energy, **7** 538
Argus Motor Company, **16** 7
Arguss Communications, Inc., **57** 120
Argyle Television Inc., **19** 204
Argyll Group PLC, I 241; **II 609–10,** 656; **12** 152–53; **24** 418. *See also* Safeway PLC.
Aria Communications, Inc. *See* Ascend Communications, Inc.
Ariba, Inc., 38 432; **57 48–51**
Ariel Capital Management, **28** 421
Ariens Company, 48 32–34
Aries Technology, **25** 305
Ariete S.P.A. *See* De'Longhi S.p.A.
Aris Industries, Inc., 15 275; **16 35–38**
Arista Laboratories Inc., **51** 249, 251
Aristech Chemical Corp., **12** 342
Aristocrat Leisure Limited, 54 14–16
Aristokraft Inc. *See* MasterBrand Cabinets, Inc.
The Aristotle Corporation, 62 16–18
Arizona Airways, **22** 219
Arizona Daily Star, **58** 282
Arizona Edison Co., **6** 545
Arizona Growth Capital, Inc., **18** 513
AriZona Iced Tea. *See* Ferolito, Vultaggio & Sons.
Arizona One, **24** 455
Arizona Public Service Company, **6** 545–47; **19** 376, 412; **26** 359; **28** 425–26; **54** 290
Arizona Refrigeration Supplies, **14** 297–98
Arjo Wiggins Appleton p.l.c., 13 458; **27** 513; **34 38–40**
Ark Restaurants Corp., 20 25–27
Arkansas Best Corporation, 16 39–41; 19 455; **42** 410
Arkansas Louisiana Gas Company. *See* Arkla, Inc.
Arkia, **23** 184, 186–87
Arkla, Inc., V 550–51; 11 441
Arla Foods amba, 48 35–38
Arlington Securities plc, **24** 84, 87–89
Arlon, Inc., **28** 42, 45
Armani. *See* Giorgio Armani S.p.A.
Armaturindistri, **III** 569
Armco Inc., IV 28–30; 10 448; **11** 5, 255; **12** 353; **19** 8; **26** 407; **30** 282–83; **41** 3, 5; **54** 247–48. *See also* AK Steel.
Armement Sapmer Distribution, **60** 149
Armin Corporation. *See* Tyco International Ltd.
Armor All Products Corp., 12 333; **15** 507; **16 42–44; 22** 148; **26** 349; **47** 235
Armor Elevator, **11** 5
Armor Holdings, Inc., 27 49–51
Armour. *See* Tommy Armour Golf Co.
Armour & Company, **8** 144; **12** 198; **13** 21, 506; **23** 173; **55** 365
Armour-Dial, **8** 144; **23** 173–74
Armour Food Co., **12** 370; **13** 270

Armstrong Air Conditioning Inc. *See* Lennox International Inc.

Armstrong Tire Co., **15** 355

Armstrong World Industries, Inc., III 422–24; 9 466; **12** 474–75; **22 46–50 (upd.)**, 170–71; **26** 507; **53** 175–76; **59** 381–82

Armtek, **7** 297

Army and Air Force Exchange Service, 39 27–29

Army Cooperative Fire Insurance Company, **10** 541

Army Ordnance, **19** 430

Army Signal Corps Laboratories, **10** 96

Arnold & Porter, 35 42–44

Arnold Clark Automobiles Ltd., 60 39–41

Arnold Communications, **25** 381

Arnold Electric Company, **17** 213

Arnold Industries Inc., **35** 297

Arnold, Schwinn & Company. *See* Schwinn Cycle and Fitness L.P.

Arnold Thomas Co., **9** 411

Arnoldo Mondadori Editore S.p.A., IV 585–88; **19 17–21 (upd.)**; **54 17–23 (upd.)**

Arnott's Ltd., 66 10–12

Aro Corp., **III** 527; **14** 477, 508; **15** 225

Aromat Corporation, **III** 710; **7** 303

Aromatic Industries, **18** 69

ArQule, Inc., 68 31–34

Arrendadora del Norte, S.A. de C.V., **51** 150

Arriva PLC, 69 42–44

Arrosto Coffee Company, **25** 263

Arrow Air Holdings Corporation, 55 28–30

Arrow Electronics, Inc., 10 112–14; **13** 47; **19** 310–11, 313; **29** 414; **30** 175; **50 41–44 (upd.)**

Arrow Freight Corporation, **58** 23

Arrow Furniture Co., **21** 32

Arrow Pacific Plastics, **48** 334

Arrow Shirt Co., **24** 384

Arrowhead Mills Inc., **27** 197–98; **43** 218–19

Arsam Investment Co., **26** 261

Arsynco, Inc., **38** 4

The Art Institute of Chicago, 29 36–38

Art Van Furniture, Inc., 28 31–33

Artal Luxembourg SA, **33** 446, 449

Artal NV, **40** 51

Artear S.A. *See* Grupo Clarín S.A.

Artec, **12** 297

Artech Digital Entertainments, Inc., **15** 133

Artek Systems Corporation, **13** 194

Artémis Group, **27** 513

Artes Grafica Rioplatense S.A., **67** 202

Artesian Manufacturing and Bottling Company, **9** 177

Artesian Resources Corporation, **45** 277

Artesyn Solutions Inc., **48** 369

Artesyn Technologies Inc., 46 35–38 (upd.)

Artex Enterprises, **7** 256; **25** 167, 253

Arthur Andersen & Company, Société Coopérative, 10 115–17, 174; **16** 92; **25** 358; **29** 392; **46** 186. *See also* Andersen.

Arthur D. Little, Inc., 35 45–48

Arthur H. Fulton, Inc., **42** 363

Arthur Murray International, Inc., 32 60–62

Arthur Rank Organisation, **25** 328

Arthur Young & Company. *See* Ernst & Young.

Artigiancassa SpA, **72** 21

Artisan Entertainment Inc., 32 63–66 (upd.)

Artisan Life Insurance Cooperative, **24** 104

Artisoft, Inc., **18** 143

Artistic Direct, Inc., **37** 108

Artists & Writers Press, Inc., **13** 560

Artists Management Group, **38** 164

ArtMold Products Corporation, **26** 342

Artra Group Inc., **40** 119–20

Arts and Entertainment Network. *See* A&E Television Networks.

Arundel Corp., **46** 196

Arval. *See* PHH Arval.

Arvin Industries, Inc., 8 37–40. *See also* ArvinMeritor, Inc.

ArvinMeritor, Inc., 54 24–28 (upd.)

A/S Air Baltic Corporation, 71 35–37

AS Estonian Air, 71 38–40

ASA Holdings, **47** 30

Asahi Breweries, Ltd., I 220–21, 282, 520; **13** 454; **20 28–30 (upd.)**; **21** 230, 319–20; **26** 456; **36** 404–05; **50** 201–02; **52 31–34 (upd.)**; **63** 229

Asahi Chemical Industry Co., **I** 221

Asahi Corporation, **16** 84; **40** 93

Asahi Denka Kogyo KK, 64 33–35

Asahi Glass Company, Ltd., III 666–68; **11** 234–35; **48 39–42 (upd.)**

Asahi Komag Co., Ltd., **11** 234

Asahi Kyoei Co., **I** 221

Asahi Medix Co., Ltd., **36** 420

Asahi National Broadcasting Company, Ltd., 9 29–31

Asahi Real Estate Facilities Co., Ltd. *See* Seino Transportation Company, Ltd.

Asahi Shimbun, **9** 29–30

Asanté Technologies, Inc., 20 31–33

ASARCO Incorporated, IV 31–34; **40** 220–22, 411

ASB Agency, Inc., **10** 92

ASB Air, **47** 286–87

Asbury Associates Inc., **22** 354–55

Asbury Automotive Group Inc., 26 501; **60 42–44**

Asbury Carbons, Inc., 68 35–37

ASC, Inc., 55 31–34

ASCAP. *See* The American Society of Composers, Authors and Publishers.

Ascend Communications, Inc., 24 47–51; **34** 258

Ascension Health, **61** 206

Ascential Software Corporation, 59 54–57

ASCO Healthcare, Inc., **18** 195–97

Asco Products, Inc., **22** 413

Ascom AG, 9 32–34; **15** 125

Ascotts, **19** 122

ASCP. *See* American Securities Capital Partners.

ASD, **IV** 228

ASD Specialty Healthcare, Inc., **64** 27

ASDA Group Ltd., II 611–12, 513, 629; **11** 240; **28 34–36 (upd.)**; **63** 431; **64 36–38 (upd.)**

ASEA AB. *See* ABB Ltd.

Aseam Credit Sdn Bhd, **72** 217

Asepak Corp., **16** 339

A.B. Asesores Bursatiles, **III** 197–98; **15** 18

ASF. *See* American Steel Foundries.

ASG. *See* Allen Systems Group, Inc.

Asgrow Florida Company, **13** 503

Asgrow Seed Co., **29** 435; **41** 306

Ash Company, **10** 271

Ash Resources Ltd., **31** 398–99

Ashanti Goldfields Company Limited, 43 37–40

Ashbourne PLC, **25** 455

Ashland Inc., 19 22–25; **27** 316, 318; **50 45–50 (upd.)**

Ashland Oil, Inc., IV 71, 198, 366, **372–74**, 472, 658; **7** 32–33; **8** 99; **9** 108; **18** 279. *See also* Marathon.

Ashley Furniture Industries, Inc., 35 49–51

Ashtead Group plc, 34 41–43

Ashton-Tate Corporation, **9** 81–82; **10** 504–05

Ashworth, Inc., 26 25–28

ASIA & PACIFIC Business Description Paid-in Capital Voting Rights, **68** 30

Asia Oil Co., Ltd., **IV** 404, 476; **53** 115

Asia Pacific Breweries Limited, 59 58–60

Asia Pulp & Paper, **38** 227

Asia Shuang He Sheng Five Star Beer Co., Ltd., **49** 418

Asia Television, **IV** 718; **38** 320

Asia Terminals Ltd., **IV** 718; **38** 319

AsiaInfo Holdings, Inc., 43 41–44

Asiamerica Equities Ltd. *See* Mercer International.

Asian Football Confederation, **27** 150

Asiana Airlines, Inc., 24 400; **46 39–42**

ASICS Corporation, 24 404; **57 52–55**

ASK Group, Inc., 9 35–37; **25** 34

Ask Jeeves, Inc., 65 50–52

Ask Mr. Foster Agency, **22** 127; **26** 308; **55** 90

Asland SA, **III** 705, 740

ASMI. *See* Acer Semiconductor Manufacturing Inc.

ASML Holding N.V., 50 51–54

Aso Cement, **III** 705

ASPCA. *See* American Society for the Prevention of Cruelty to Animals (ASPCA).

Aspect Telecommunications Corporation, 16 392–93; **22 51–53**

ASPECTA Global Group AG, **53** 162

Aspen Imaging International, Inc., **17** 384

Aspen Mountain Gas Co., **6** 568

Aspen Skiing Company, 15 23–26, 234; **43** 438

Aspen Systems, **14** 555

Asplundh Tree Expert Co., 20 34–36; **59 61–65 (upd.)**

Asprofos S.A., **64** 177

Asset Management Company, **25** 86

Asset Marketing Inc. *See* Commercial Financial Services, Inc.

Assicurazioni Generali SpA, III 206–09, 211, 296, 298; **14** 85; **15 27–31 (upd.)**; **51** 19, 23; **65** 27–28

Assisted Living Concepts, Inc., 43 45–47

Associate Venture Investors, **16** 418

Associated Book Publishers, **8** 527

Associated British Foods plc, II 465–66, 565, 609; **11** 526; **13 51–53 (upd.)**; **24** 475; **41 30–33 (upd.)**

Associated British Ports Holdings Plc, 45 29–32

Associated Bulk Carriers Ltd., **38** 345

Associated Communications Companies, **7** 78; **23** 479

Associated Container Transportation, **23** 161

Associated Cooperative Investment Trust Ltd. *See* Hammerson plc.

Associated Dry Goods Corp., **V** 134; **12** 54–55; **24** 298; **63** 259

Associated Estates Realty Corporation, 25 23–25

Associated Fire Marine Insurance Co., **26** 486

Associated Food Holdings Ltd., **II** 628

Associated Fresh Foods, **II** 611–12; **48** 37

Associated Gas & Electric Company. *See* General Public Utilities Corporation.

Associated Gas Services, Inc., **11** 28

Associated Grocers, Incorporated, 9 38–40; **19** 301; **31** 22–26 **(upd.)**

Associated Grocers of Arizona, **II** 625

Associated Grocers of Colorado, **II** 670

The Associated Group, **10** 45

Associated Hospital Service of New York. *See* Empire Blue Cross and Blue Shield.

Associated Inns and Restaurants Company of America, **14** 106; **25** 309; **26** 459

Associated International Insurance Co. *See* Gryphon Holdings, Inc.

Associated Lead Manufacturers Ltd. *See* Cookson Group plc.

Associated London Properties. *See* Land Securities PLC.

Associated Madison Insurance, **I** 614

Associated Merchandisers, Inc., **27** 246

Associated Merchandising Corp., **16** 215

Associated Milk Producers, Inc., 11 24–26; **48** 43–46 **(upd.)**

Associated Natural Gas Corporation, 11 27–28

Associated Newspapers Holdings P.L.C., **19** 118, 120; **37** 121

Associated Octel Company Limited, **10** 290

The Associated Press, 7 158; **10** 277; **13** 54–56; **25** 506; **31** 27–30 **(upd.)**; **34** 11

Associated Publishing Company, **19** 201

Associated Pulp & Paper Mills, **IV** 328

Associated Sales Agency, **16** 389

Associated Spring Co., **13** 73

Associated Stationers, **14** 521, 523

Associated Television, **7** 78

Associates First Capital Corporation, **22** 207; **59** 126

Association des Centres Distributeurs E. Leclerc, 37 19–21

Association of Junior Leagues International Inc., 60 45–47

Assurances du Groupe de Paris, **III** 211

Assurances Générales de France, III 351; **27** 513; **42** 151; **51** 23; **57** 23; **63** 45–48

AST Holding Corp. *See* American Standard Companies, Inc.

AST Research, Inc., 9 41–43; **10** 459, 518–19; **12** 470; **18** 260

Astakos Terminal S.A., **64** 8

Astech, **18** 370

Asteroid, **IV** 97

Astley & Pearce, **10** 277

Aston Brooke Software, **14** 392

Aston Villa plc, 41 34–36

Astor Holdings Inc., **22** 32

Astoria Financial Corporation, 44 31–34; **46** 316

Astra. *See* PT Astra International Tbk.

Astra AB, I 625–26, 635, 651; **11** 290; **20** 37–40 **(upd.)**; **34** 282, 284

Astra Resources, **12** 543

AstraZeneca PLC, 50 55–60 **(upd.)**; **53** 290; **55** 27

Astrium N.V., **52** 113

Astrolink International LLC, **54** 406–07

Astronics Corporation, 35 52–54

Astrotech Space Operations, L.P., **11** 429; **37** 365

Astrum International Corp., **12** 88; **13** 453; **16** 20–21; **43** 355

Asur. *See* Grupo Aeropuerto del Sureste, S.A. de C.V.

ASV, Inc., 34 44–47; **66** 13–15 **(upd.)**

ASW. *See* American Steel & Wire Corp.

Asylum Records, **23** 33; **26** 150

AT&E Corp., **17** 430

AT&T Bell Laboratories, Inc., 13 57–59; **22** 17

AT&T Istel Ltd., 14 35–36

AT&T Microelectronics, **63** 397

AT&T Wireless Services, Inc., 54 29–32 **(upd.)**, 313; **63** 131–32

At Home Corporation, **43** 48–51

AT&T Corporation, V 259–64; **29** 39–45 **(upd.)**; **61 68** 38–45 **(upd.)**

Atanor S.A., 62 19–22

Atari Corporation, 9 44–47; **10** 284, 482, 485; **13** 472; **23** 23–26 **(upd.)**; **32** 8; **66** 16–20 **(upd.)**

ATAS International, **26** 527, 530

ATC, **13** 280

ATC Healthcare Inc., 64 39–42

Atchison Casting Corporation, 24 144; **39** 30–32

ATCO Ltd., **13** 132

ATD Group, **10** 113; **50** 43

ATE Investment. *See* Atlantic Energy, Inc.

Atelier de Construction Electrique de Delle, **9** 9

ATEQ Corp., **III** 533

Atex, Inc., **10** 34

Athalon Products, Ltd., **10** 181; **12** 313

Athena Assurances, **27** 513, 515

Athena Neuroscience, **63** 142

Athenia Steel Co., **13** 369

Athern, **16** 337

Athlete's Foot Inc., **29** 186; **54** 306, 308; **67** 204–05

Athletic Attic, **19** 230

Athletic Shoe Company, **17** 243

Athletic Textile Company, Inc., **13** 532

Athletic X-Press, **14** 293

The Athletics Investment Group, 62 23–26

Athleticum Sportmarket, **48** 279

Athol Machine Co., **13** 301

ATI Technologies Inc., **54** 269–71

Atkins Nutritionals, Inc., 58 8–10

ATL Group, **65** 304

Atlalait, **19** 50

Atlanta Bread Company International, Inc., 70 14–16

Atlanta Gas Light Company, 6 446–48; **23** 27–30 **(upd.)**

Atlanta-LaSalle Corporation, **43** 54

Atlanta National Bank, **16** 521

Atlanta National League Baseball Club, Inc., 43 52–55

Atlantia Offshore Limited. *See* IHC Caland N.V.

Atlantic & Pacific Tea Company (A&P). *See* Great Atlantic & Pacific Tea Company, Inc.

Atlantic Acceptance Corporation, **7** 95

Atlantic Airways, **52** 167

Atlantic American Corporation, 23 413; **44** 35–37

Atlantic Auto Finance Corp. *See* United Auto Group, Inc.

Atlantic Cellular, **43** 341

Atlantic Coast Airlines Holdings, Inc., 55 35–37

Atlantic Coast Carton Company, **19** 77

Atlantic Coast Line Railroad Company. *See* CSX Corporation.

Atlantic Computers, **14** 35

Atlantic Container Lines Ltd., **23** 161

Atlantic Energy, Inc., 6 449–50

Atlantic Envelope Company, **54** 251–52, 255

The Atlantic Group, 23 31–33

Atlantic Mills, **27** 188

Atlantic Mutual, **41** 65

Atlantic Precision Instrument Company, **13** 234

Atlantic Precision Works, **9** 72

Atlantic Premium Brands, Ltd., 57 56–58

Atlantic Records Group, **18** 458; **26** 150; **64** 115

Atlantic Refining Co. *See* Atlantic Richfield Company.

Atlantic Research Corporation, **13** 462; **54** 330–31

Atlantic Richfield Company, IV 375–77; **31** 31–34 **(upd.)**; **40** 358; **45** 49, 55, 252; **63** 113

Atlantic Sea Products, **13** 103

The Atlantic Seaboard Dispatch. *See* GATX.

Atlantic Securities Ltd., **II** 223

Atlantic Southeast Airlines, Inc., 26 439; **47** 29–31

Atlantic Southern Properties, Inc. *See* Atlantic Energy, Inc.

Atlantic Transport Company, **19** 198

Atlantic Wholesalers, **II** 631

Atlantis Energy Inc., **44** 182

Atlantis Group, Inc., **17** 16; **19** 50, 390

Atlantis Resort and Casino. *See* Sun International Hotels Limited.

Atlas Air, Inc., 39 33–35

Atlas Air Worldwide Holdings, Inc., **60** 238

Atlas America, Inc., **42** 311

Atlas Bolt & Screw Company. *See* The Marmon Group, Inc.

Atlas Cement Company, **31** 252

Atlas Copco AB, III 425–27, 480; **28** 37–41 **(upd.)**; **63** 211

Atlas Eléctrica S.A., **22** 27

Atlas Hotels, Inc., **V** 164

Atlas Plastics, **19** 414

Atlas Securities, **47** 160

Atlas Tag & Label, **9** 72

Atlas Van Lines, Inc., 14 37–39

Atlas Ventures, **25** 96

Atlatec SA de CV, **39** 192

Atle Byrnestad, **6** 368; **27** 92

Atmel Corporation, 17 32–34; **19** 313

Atmos Energy Corporation, 43 56–58

Atmospherix Ltd. *See* Blyth Industries, Inc.

Atochem S.A., I 303–04, 676. *See also* Total-Fina-Elf.

AtoHaas Americas, **26** 425

Atoll Soft Nederland BV, **72** 35

Atomic Austria GmbH, **41** 14–16

Atos Origin S.A., 69 45–47

ATR, **7** 9, 11
Atrix Laboratories, Inc. *See* QLT Inc.
ATS. *See* Magasins Armand Thiéry et Sigrand.
ATT Microelectrica España, **V** 339
Attachmate Corporation, 11 520; **56 19–21**
ATTC Manufacturing Inc., **48** 5
Attic Futura. *See* PMP Ltd.
Attica Enterprises S.A., 64 43–45
Atvidabergs Industrier, **25** 463
Atwater McMillian. *See* St. Paul Companies, Inc.
Atwood Mobil Products, 53 52–55
Atwood Resources Inc., **17** 372
ATX Technologies, Inc., **32** 374
ATx Telecom Systems Inc., **31** 124
Au Bon Marché, **26** 160
Au Bon Pain Co., Inc., 18 35–38; 44 327
AU Optronics Corporation, 67 38–40, 53
Au Printemps S.A., V 9–11; 17 124; **41** 114. *See also* Pinault-Printemps-Redoute S.A.
Auchan, 10 205; **23** 230; **27** 94; **37 22–24; 39** 183–85; **54** 219–20
Auctentia Subastas S.L., **60** 146
Audifon U.K. Ltd., **56** 338
Audio Accessories, Inc., **37** 301
Audio Development Company, **10** 18
Audio International Inc., **36** 159
Audio King Corporation, 24 52–54
Audio/Video Affiliates, Inc., **10** 468–69
Audiofina, **44** 377
Audiovox Corporation, 34 48–50
Audits & Surveys Worldwide Inc., **28** 501, 504
Auerhahn, **60** 364
Augat Inc., **54** 373
Aughton Group, **II** 466
August Max Woman. *See* The United States Shoe Corporation.
August Schell Brewing Company Inc., 22 421; **59 66–69**
August Storck KG, 66 21–23
Ault Incorporated, 34 51–54
Aunt Fanny's Bakery, **7** 429
Auntie Anne's, Inc., 35 55–57
Aura Books plc, **34** 5
Aurea Concesiones de Infraestructuras SA. *See* Abertis Infraestructuras, S.A.
Aurec Information and Directory Systems. *See* Amdocs Ltd.
Aurigene Discovery Technologies Limited, **59** 168
AurionGold Limited, **61** 293
Aurora Casket Company, Inc., 56 22–24
Aurora Dairy Corporation, **37** 195, 198
Aurora Foods Inc., 26 384; **32 67–69**
Aurora Systems, Inc., **21** 135
Aurrera S.A., **35** 459
Aurum Corp., **38** 431
Ausimont S.p.A., **8** 271; **61** 333
Ausplay, **13** 319
Aussedat-Rey, **IV** 288; **23** 366, 368
The Austin Company, 8 41–44; 72 14–18 (upd.)
Austin Industries, **25** 402
Austin Nichols, **I** 261, 280–81
Austin Quality Foods, **36** 313
Austin Rover, **14** 321
Austins Steaks & Saloon, Inc. *See* WesterN SizzliN Corporation.

Australia and New Zealand Banking Group Limited, II 187–90; **52 35–40 (upd.)**
Australia National Bank, Limited, **10** 170
Australian Airlines. *See* Qantas Airways Limited.
Australian and Overseas Telecommunications Corporation. *See* Telecom Australia.
Australian Automotive Air, Pty. Ltd., **III** 593
Australian Consolidated Investments, Limited, **10** 170
Australian Consolidated Press, **27** 42; **54** 299
Australian Mutual Provident Society, **IV** 61, 697
Australian Petroleum Pty. Ltd., **25** 471
Australian Tankerships Pty. Ltd., **25** 471
Australian Telecommunications Corporation, **6** 342
Australian Wheat Board. *See* AWB Ltd.
Austria Tabak, **55** 200
Austrian Airlines AG (Österreichische Luftverkehrs AG), 27 26; **33 49–52; 34** 398; **48** 258, 259
Austrian Star Gastronomie GmbH, **48** 63
Authentic Fitness Corp., 16 511; **20 41–43; 46** 450; **51 30–33 (upd.)**
Auto Avio Costruzione, **13** 219
Auto Ordnance Corporation, **19** 430–31
Auto Parts Wholesale, **26** 348
Auto Shack. *See* AutoZone, Inc.
Auto Value Associates, Inc., 25 26–28
Autobytel Inc., 47 32–34
Autocam Corporation, 51 34–36
Autodesk, Inc., 10 118–20
Autogrill SpA, 24 195; **49 31–33**
Autoliv, Inc., 41 369; **65 53–55**
Autologic Information International, Inc., 20 44–46; 26 518–20
Automat, **II** 614
Automated Communications, Inc., **8** 311
Automated Design Systems, **25** 348
Automated Loss Prevention Systems, **11** 445
Automated Sciences Group, Inc. *See* CACI International Inc.
Automated Security (Holdings) PLC, **11** 444
Automatic Coil Corp., **33** 359, 361
Automatic Data Processing, Inc., III 117–19; 9 48–51 (upd.), 125, 173; **21** 69; **46** 333; **47 35–39 (upd.)**
Automatic Liquid Packaging, **50** 122
Automatic Manufacturing Corporation, **10** 319
Automatic Payrolls, Inc. *See* Automatic Data Processing, Inc.
Automatic Retailers of America, Inc., **II** 607; **13** 48
Automatic Sprinkler Corp. of America. *See* Figgie International, Inc.
Automatic Toll Systems, **19** 111
Automatic Voting Machine Corporation. *See* American Locker Group Incorporated.
AutoMed Technologies, Inc., **64** 27
Automobiles Citroen, 7 35–38; 16 420
Automobili Lamborghini Holding S.p.A., 34 55–58 (upd.)
Automobili Lamborghini S.p.A., 13 60–62, 219

Automotive Components Limited, **10** 325; **56** 158
Automotive Diagnostics, **10** 492
Automotive Group. *See* Lear Seating Corporation.
Automotive Industries Holding Inc., **16** 323
AutoNation, Inc., 41 239; **50 61–64**
Autonet, **6** 435
Autonom Computer, **47** 36
Autophon AG, **9** 32
Autoroutes du Sud de la France SA, 55 38–40
Autosite.com, **47** 34
Autotote Corporation, 20 47–49. *See also* Scientific Games Corporation.
Autoweb.com, **47** 34
AUTOWORKS Holdings, Inc., **24** 205
AutoZone, Inc., 9 52–54; 26 348; **31 35–38 (upd.); 36** 364; **57 10–12**
AVA AG (Allgemeine Handelsgesellschaft der Verbraucher AG), 33 53–56
Avado Brands, Inc., 31 39–42; 46 234
Avalon Publishing Group. *See* Publishers Group, Inc.
AvalonBay Communities, Inc., 58 11–13
Avantel, **27** 304
Avaya Inc., **41** 287, 289–90
Avco. *See* Aviation Corp. of the Americas.
Avco Corp., **34** 433
Avco Financial Services Inc., 13 63–65
Avco National Bank, **II** 420
Avdel, **34** 433
Avecia Group PLC, 63 49–51
Avecor Cardiovascular Inc., **8** 347; **22** 360
Aveda Corporation, 24 55–57
Avedis Zildjian Co., 38 66–68
Avendt Group, Inc., **IV** 137
Avenor Inc., **25** 13
Aventis Pharmaceuticals, **34** 280, 283–84; **38** 378, 380; **63** 232, 235
Avery Communications, Inc., **72** 39
Avery Dennison Corporation, IV 251–54; 15 229, 401; **17 27–31 (upd.),** 445; **49 34–40 (upd.)**
AvestaPolarit, **49** 104
Avex Electronics Inc., **40** 68
Avfuel, **11** 538
Avgain Marine A/S, **7** 40; **41** 42
Avia Group International, Inc. *See* Reebok International Ltd.
Aviacionny Nauchno-Tehnicheskii Komplek im. A.N. Tupoleva, 24 58–60
AVIACO. *See* Aviacion y Comercio.
Avianca Aerovías Nacionales de Colombia SA, 36 52–55
Aviation Corp. of the Americas, **9** 497–99; **11** 261, 427; **12** 379, 383; **13** 64
Aviation Inventory Management Co., **28** 5
Aviation Power Supply, **II** 16
Aviation Sales Company, 41 37–39
Aviation Services West, Inc. *See* Scenic Airlines, Inc.
Avid Technology Inc., 38 69–73
Avimo, **47** 7–8
Avion Coach Corporation, **11** 363
Avionics Specialties Inc. *See* Aerosonic Corporation.
Avions Marcel Dassault-Breguet Aviation, I 44–46; 7 11; **7** 205; **8** 314. *See also* Groupe Dassault Aviation SA.
Avis Rent A Car, Inc., 6 356–58; 8 33; **9** 284; **10** 419; **16** 379–80; **22 54–57 (upd.),** 524; **25** 93, 143, 420–22

Avista Corporation, **69** 48–50 (upd.)
Avisun Corp., **IV** 371
Aviva PLC, **50** 65–68 (upd.)
Avnet Electronics Supply Co., **19** 311, 313
Avnet Inc., **9** 55–57; **10** 112–13; **13** 47; **50** 41
Avocent Corporation, **65** 56–58
Avon Products, Inc., **III** 15–16; **19** 26–29 (upd.); **46** 43–46 (upd.)
Avon Rubber plc, **23** 146
Avondale Industries, Inc., **7** 39–41; **41** 40–43 (upd.)
Avondale Mills, Inc., **8** 558–60; **9** 466
Avonmore Foods Plc, **59** 205
Avril Alimentaire SNC, **51** 54
Avro. *See* A.V. Roe & Company.
Avstar, **38** 72
Avtech Corp., **36** 159
AVTOVAZ Joint Stock Company, **65** 59–62
AVX Corporation, **21** 329, 331; **67** 21–22; **41–43**
AW Bruna Uitgevers BV, **53** 273
AW North Carolina Inc., **48** 5
AWA. *See* America West Holdings Corporation.
AWA Defence Industries (AWADI). *See* British Aerospace Defence Industries.
AwardTrack, Inc., **49** 423
AWB Ltd., **56** 25–27
Awesome Transportation, Inc., **22** 549
Awrey Bakeries, Inc., **56** 28–30
AXA Colonia Konzern AG, **III** 210–12; **15** 30; **21** 147; **27** 52–55; **49** 41–45 (upd.)
AXA Financial, Inc., **63** 26–27
AXA Private Equity. *See* Camaïeu S.A.
AXA UK plc, **64** 173
Axe-Houghton Associates Inc., **41** 208
Axel Johnson Group, **I** 553–55
Axel Springer Verlag AG, **IV** 589–91; **20** 50–53 (upd.); **23** 86; **35** 452; **54** 295
Axon Systems Inc., **7** 336
Ayala Corporation, **70** 182
Ayala Plans, Inc., **58** 20
Aydin Corp., **19** 30–32
Aynsley China Ltd. *See* Belleek Pottery Ltd.
Ayr-Way Stores, **27** 452
Ayres, Lewis, Norris & May, Inc., **54** 184
AYS. *See* Alternative Youth Services, Inc.
AZA Immobilien AG, **51** 196
Azcon Corporation, **23** 34–36
Azerty, **25** 13
Azienda Generale Italiana Petroli. *See* ENI S.p.A.
AZL Resources, **7** 538
Aznar International, **14** 225
Azon Limited, **22** 282
AZP Group Inc., **6** 546
Aztar Corporation, **13** 66–68; **71** 41–45 (upd.)
Azteca, **18** 211, 213

B&D. *See* Barker & Dobson.
B&G Foods, Inc., **40** 51–54
B&J Music Ltd. *See* Kaman Music Corporation.
B & K Steel Fabrications, Inc., **26** 432
B & L Insurance, Ltd., **51** 38
B&M Baked Beans, **40** 53
B & O. *See* Baltimore and Ohio Railroad.
B&Q plc. *See* Kingfisher plc.
B&S. *See* Binney & Smith Inc.

B.A.T. Industries PLC, **14** 77; **16** 242; **22** 70–73 (upd.); **25** 154–56; **29** 196; **63** 260–61. *See also* Brown & Williamson Tobacco Corporation
B. B. & R. Knight Brothers, **8** 200; **25** 164
B.B. Foods, **13** 244
B-Bar-B Corp., **16** 340
B.C. Rail Telecommunications, **6** 311
B.C. Sugar, **II** 664
B.C. Ziegler and Co. *See* The Ziegler Companies, Inc.
B. Dalton Bookseller Inc., **10** 136; **13** 545; **16** 160; **18** 136; **25** 29–31; **30** 68
B-E Holdings, **17** 60
B/E Aerospace, Inc., **30** 72–74
B.F. Goodrich Co. *See* The BFGoodrich Company.
B.F. Walker, Inc., **11** 354
B.I.C. America, **17** 15, 17
B.J.'s Wholesale, **12** 335
B.J. Alan Co., Inc., **67** 44–46
The B. Manischewitz Company, LLC, **31** 43–46
B. Perini & Sons, Inc., **8** 418
B Ticino, **21** 350
B.V. Tabak Export & Import Compagnie, **12** 109
BA. *See* British Airways.
BAA plc, **10** 121–23; **29** 509, 511; **33** 57–61 (upd.); **37** 8
Bålforsens Kraft AB, **28** 444
Baan Company, **25** 32–34; **26** 496, 498
Babbage's, Inc., **10** 124–25. *See also* GameStop Corp.
Babcock International Group PLC, **37** 242–45; **57** 142; **69** 51–54
BABE. *See* British Aerospace plc.
Baby Dairy Products, **48** 438
Baby Lock USA. *See* Tacony Corporation.
Baby Phat. *See* Phat Fashions LLC.
Baby Superstore, Inc., **15** 32–34; **57** 372
Babybird Co., Ltd. *See* Nagasakiya Co., Ltd.
BabyCenter.com, **37** 130
Babyliss, S.A. *See* Conair Corporation.
BAC. *See* Barclays American Corp.; Beverage Associates Corp.; British Aircraft Corporation.
Bacardi Limited, **18** 39–42; **63** 264, 266
Baccarat, **23** 241; **24** 61–63; **27** 421, 423
Bache & Company, **III** 340; **8** 349
Bachman Foods, **15** 139
Bachman Holdings, Inc., **14** 165; **34** 144–45
Bachman's Inc., **22** 58–60; **24** 513
Bachoco. *See* Industrias Bacholo, S.A. de C.V.
Back Bay Investments Ltd., **64** 217
Back Bay Restaurant Group, Inc., **20** 54–56
Back Yard Burgers, Inc., **45** 33–36
Backer & Spielvogel, **12** 168; **14** 48–49; **22** 296
Backer Spielvogel Bates Worldwide. *See* Bates Worldwide, Inc.
Bacon's Information, Inc., **55** 289
Bacova Guild, Ltd., **17** 76
Bad Boy Worldwide Entertainment Group, **31** 269; **58** 14–17
Badak LNG Transport Inc., **56** 181
Baddour, Inc. *See* Fred's, Inc.
Badger Illuminating Company, **6** 601
Badger Meter, Inc., **22** 61–65
Badger Paper Mills, Inc., **15** 35–37

Badin-Defforey, **27** 93
BAe. *See* British Aerospace plc.
BAE-Newplan Group Ltd. *See* SNC-Lavalin Group Inc.
BAE Systems, **41** 412; **52** 114
BAFS. *See* Bangkok Aviation Fuel Services Ltd.
Bahamas Air Holdings Ltd., **66** 24–26
Bahlsen GmbH & Co. KG, **44** 38–41
Bailey, Banks & Biddle, **16** 559
Bailey Nurseries, Inc., **57** 59–61
Bailey Street Trading Company, **71** 60
Bailey's Pub and Grille. *See* Total Entertainment Restaurant Corporation.
Bain & Company, **9** 343; **21** 143; **55** 41–43
Bain Capital, Inc., **14** 244–45; **16** 466; **20** 18; **24** 456, 482; **25** 254; **26** 184; **38** 107–09; **63** 133, 137–38
Baird, **7** 235, 237
Bairnco Corporation, **28** 42–45
Bajaj Auto Limited, **39** 36–38
BÅKAB. *See* Bålforsens Kraft AB.
Bakelite Corp., **13** 231
Baker. *See* Michael Baker Corporation.
Baker and Botts, L.L.P., **28** 46–49
Baker & Hostetler LLP, **40** 55–58
Baker & McKenzie, **10** 126–28; **42** 17–20 (upd.)
Baker & Taylor Corporation, **16** 45–47; **43** 59–62 (upd.)
Baker Cummins Pharmaceuticals Inc., **11** 208
Baker Extract Co., **27** 299
Baker Hughes Incorporated, **III** 428–29; **11** 62–66 (upd.); **22** 66–69 (upd.); **25** 74; **57** 62–66 (upd.); **59** 366; **63** 306
Baker Industries, Inc., **8** 476; **13** 124
Baker Oil Tools. *See* Baker Hughes Incorporated.
Baker-Raulang Co., **13** 385
Bakers Best Snack Food Corporation, **24** 241
Bakers Square. *See* VICORP Restaurants, Inc.
Bakersfield Savings and Loan, **10** 339
Bakery Feeds Inc. *See* Griffin Industries, Inc.
Bal-Sam India Holdings Ltd., **64** 95
Balance Bar Company, **32** 70–72
Balchem Corporation, **42** 21–23
Balatongáz Kft. (Ltd), **70** 195
Balco, Inc., **7** 479–80; **27** 415
Balcor, Inc., **10** 62
Bald Eagle Corporation, **45** 126
Baldor Electric Company, **21** 42–44
Baldwin & Lyons, Inc., **51** 37–39
Baldwin-Ehret-Hill Inc., **28** 42
Baldwin Filters, Inc., **17** 104
Baldwin Hardware Manufacturing Co. *See* Masco Corporation.
Baldwin-Montrose Chemical Co., Inc., **31** 110
Baldwin Piano & Organ Company, **16** 201; **18** 43–46
Baldwin Rubber Industries, **13** 79
Baldwin Technology Company, Inc., **25** 35–39
Baldwin-United Corp., **III** 254, 293; **52** 243–44
Balfour Beatty Construction Ltd., **III** 433–34; **36** 56–60 (upd.); **58** 156–57
Balfour Company, L.G., **19** 451–52
Ball & Young Adhesives, **9** 92

Ball Corporation, **I** 597–98; **10** 129–31 (**upd.**); **13** 254, 256; **15** 129; **16** 123; **30** 38; **64** 86
The Ball Ground Reps, Inc., **26** 257
Ball Industries, Inc., **26** 539
Ball Stalker Inc., **14** 4
Ballantine Books, **13** 429; **31** 376–77, 379
Ballantyne of Omaha, Inc., **27** 56–58
Ballard Medical Products, **21** 45–48
Ballast Nedam Group, **24** 87–88
Ballet Makers-Europe, Ltd., **62** 59
Balli Group plc, **26** 527, 530
Bally Entertainment Corp., **19** 205, 207
Bally Gaming International, **15** 539
Bally Manufacturing Corporation, **III** 430–32; **10** 375, 482; **12** 107; **15** 538–39; **17** 316–17, 443; **41** 214–15; **53** 364–65
Bally Total Fitness Holding Corp., **25** 40–42
Bâloise-Holding, **40** 59–62
Baltek Corporation, **34** 59–61
Baltic Cable, **15** 521
Baltic International USA, **71** 35
Baltica, **27** 54
Baltika Brewery Joint Stock Company, **65** 63–66
Baltimar Overseas Limited, **25** 469
Baltimore & Ohio Railroad. *See* CSX Corporation.
Baltimore Aircoil Company, Inc., **7** 30–31; **66** 27–29
Baltimore Gas and Electric Company, **V** 552–54; **11** 388; **25** 43–46 (**upd.**)
Baltimore Orioles L.P., **66** 30–33
Baltimore Paper Box Company, **8** 102
Baltimore Technologies Plc, **42** 24–26
Baltino Foods, **13** 383
Balzers Process Systems GmbH, **48** 30
Banamex. *See* Banco Nacional de Mexico; Grupo Financiero Banamex S.A.
Banana Boat Holding Corp., **15** 359
Banana Brothers, **31** 229
Banana Importers of Ireland, **38** 197
Banana Republic Inc., **25** 47–49; **31** 51–52
Banc Internacional d'Andorra-Banca Mora, **48** 51
Banc One Corporation, **9** 475; **10** 132–34; **11** 181. *See also* Bank One Corporation.
Banca Commerciale Italiana SpA, **II** 191–93, 242, 271, 278, 295, 319; **17** 324; **50** 410
BancA Corp., **11** 305
Banca del Salento, **65** 73
Banca di Roma S.p.A., **65** 86, 88
Banca Esperia, **65** 230–31
Banca Fideuram SpA, **63** 52–54
Banca Intesa SpA, **65** 27, 29, 67–70
Banca Monte dei Paschi di Siena SpA, **65** 71–73
Banca Nazionale del Lavoro SpA, **72** 19–21
Banca Nazionale dell'Agricoltura, **II** 272
Banca Serfin. *See* Grupo Financiero Serfin, S.A.
Bancard Systems, **24** 395
BancBoston Capital, **48** 412
Bancen. *See* Banco del Centro S.A.
BancFinancial Services Corporation, **25** 187
BancMortgage Financial Corp., **25** 185, 187

Banco Aliança S.A., **19** 34
Banco Azteca, **19** 189
Banco Bilbao Vizcaya Argentaria S.A., **48** 47–51 (**upd.**)
Banco Bilbao Vizcaya, S.A., **II** 194–96
Banco Bradesco S.A., **13** 69–71; **19** 33
Banco Capitalizador de Monterrey, **19** 189
Banco Central, **II** 197–98; **56** 65. *See also* Banco Santander Central Hispano S.A.
Banco Central de Crédito. *See* Banco Itaú.
Banco Chemical (Portugal) S.A. *See* Chemical Banking Corp.
Banco Comercial, **19** 188
Banco Comercial de Puerto Rico, **41** 311
Banco Comercial Português, SA, **50** 69–72
Banco Credito y Ahorro Ponceno, **41** 312
Banco da América, **19** 34
Banco de Chile, **69** 55–57
Banco de Comercio, S.A. *See* Grupo Financiero BBVA Bancomer S.A.
Banco de Credito Local, **48** 51
Banco de Credito y Servicio, **51** 151
Banco de Galicia y Buenos Aires, S.A., **63** 178–80
Banco de Londres, Mexico y Sudamerica. *See* Grupo Financiero Serfin, S.A.
Banco de Madrid, **40** 147
Banco de Mexico, **19** 189
Banco de Ponce, **41** 313
Banco del Centro S.A., **51** 150
Banco del Norte, **19** 189
Banco di Roma, **II**, 257, 271
Banco di Santo Spirito, **I** 467
Banco di Sicilia S.p.A., **65** 86, 88
Banco do Brasil S.A., **II** 199–200
Banco Español de Credito, **II** 198
Banco Espírito Santo e Comercial de Lisboa S.A., **15** 38–40
Banco Federal de Crédito. *See* Banco Itaú.
Banco Frances y Brasiliero, **19** 34
Banco Industrial de Monterrey, **19** 189
Banco Itaú S.A., **19** 33–35
Banco Mercantil del Norte, S.A., **51** 149
Banco Nacional de Mexico, **9** 333; **19** 188, 193
Banco Opportunity, **57** 67, 69
Banco Pinto de Mahalhãhes, **19** 34
Banco Popolar. *See* Popular, Inc.
Banco Português do Brasil S.A., **19** 34
Banco Santander Central Hispano S.A., **36** 61–64 (**upd.**); **42** 349; **63** 179
Banco Santander-Chile, **71** 143
Banco Serfin, **34** 82
Banco Sul Americano S.A., **19** 34
Banco União Comercial, **19** 34
BancOhio National Bank in Columbus, **9** 475
Bancomer S.A. *See* Grupo Financiero BBVA Bancomer S.A.
Bancorp Leasing, Inc., **14** 529
BancorpSouth, Inc., **14** 40–41
Bancrecer. *See* Banco de Credito y Servicio.
BancSystems Association Inc., **9** 475, 476
Bandag, Inc., **19** 36–38, 454–56
Bandai Co., Ltd., **23** 388; **25** 488; **38** 415; **55** 44–48; **61** 202; **67** 274
Bando McGlocklin Small Business Lending Corporation, **53** 222–24
Banesto. *See* Banco Español de Credito.
Banfi Products Corp., **36** 65–67

Banfield, The Pet Hospital. *See* Medical Management International, Inc.
Bang & Olufsen Holding A/S, **37** 25–28
Bangkok Airport Hotel. *See* Thai Airways International.
Bangkok Aviation Fuel Services Ltd. *See* Thai Airways International.
Bangladesh Krishi Bank, **31** 220
Bangor and Aroostook Railroad Company, **8** 33
Bangor Mills, **13** 169
Bangor Punta Alegre Sugar Corp., **30** 425
Banister Continental Corp. *See* BFC Construction Corporation.
Bank Austria AG, **23** 37–39; **59** 239
Bank Brussels Lambert, **II** 201–03, 295, 407
Bank Central Asia, **18** 181; **62** 96, 98
Bank du Louvre, **27** 423
Bank für Elektrische Unternehmungen. *See* Elektrowatt AG.
Bank Hapoalim B.M., **II** 204–06; **25** 266, 268; **54** 33–37 (**upd.**)
Bank Hofmann, **21** 146–47
Bank Leumi le-Israel B.M., **25** 268; **60** 48–51
Bank of America Corporation, **9** 50, 123–24, 333, 536; **12** 106, 466; **14** 170; **18** 516; **22** 542; **25** 432; **26** 486; **46** 47–54 (**upd.**); **47** 37
The Bank of Bishop and Co., Ltd., **11** 114
Bank of Boston Corporation, **II** 207–09; **7** 114; **12** 31; **13** 467; **14** 90. *See also* FleetBoston Financial Corporation.
Bank of Brandywine Valley, **25** 542
Bank of Britain, **14** 46–47
Bank of China, **63** 55–57
Bank of Delaware, **25** 542
Bank of East Asia Ltd., **63** 58–60
Bank of England, **10** 8, 336; **14** 45–46; **47** 227
Bank of Ireland, **16** 13–14; **19** 198; **50** 73–76
Bank of Italy, **III** 209, 347; **8** 45
The Bank of Jacksonville, **9** 58
Bank of Lee County, **14** 40
Bank of Mexico Ltd., **19** 188
The Bank of Milwaukee, **14** 529
Bank of Mississippi, Inc., **14** 40–41
Bank of Montreal, **II** 210–12, 231, 375; **26** 304; **46** 55–58 (**upd.**)
Bank of Nettleton, **14** 40
Bank of New England Corporation, **II** 213–15; **9** 229
Bank of New Orleans, **11** 106
Bank of New South Wales. *See* Westpac Banking Corporation.
Bank of New York Company, Inc., **II** 216–19, 247; **34** 82; **46** 59–63 (**upd.**)
Bank of North Mississippi, **14** 41
The Bank of Nova Scotia, **II** 220–23, 345; **59** 70–76 (**upd.**)
Bank of Oklahoma, **22** 4
The Bank of Scotland. *See* The Governor and Company of the Bank of Scotland.
Bank of Sherman, **14** 40
Bank of the Ohio Valley, **13** 221
Bank of the Philippine Islands, **58** 18–20
Bank of Tokyo, Ltd., **II** 224–25, 276, 301, 341, 358; **12** 138; **16** 496, 498; **50** 498
Bank of Tokyo-Mitsubishi Ltd., **15** 41–43 (**upd.**), 431; **26** 454, 457; **38** 387
Bank of Tupelo, **14** 40

Bank of Wales, **10** 336, 338
Bank One Corporation, 36 68–75 (upd.)
Bank-R Systems Inc., **18** 517
BankAmerica Corporation, II 226–28, 436; **8 45–48 (upd.)**, 295, 469, 471; **13** 69; **17** 546; **18** 518; **25** 187; **26** 65; **47** 401; **61** 249. *See also* Bank of America.
BankAtlantic Bancorp., Inc., **66** 273
BankBoston. *See* FleetBoston Financial Corporation.
BankCard America, Inc., **24** 394
Bankers and Shippers Insurance Co., **III** 389
Bankers Corporation, **14** 473
Bankers Life and Casualty Co., **10** 247; **16** 207; **33** 110
Bankers Life Association. *See* Principal Mutual Life Insurance Company.
Bankers National Life Insurance Co., **10** 246
Bankers Trust Co., **38** 411
Bankers Trust New York Corporation, II 229–31; **10** 425; **11** 416; **12** 165, 209; **13** 188, 466; **17** 559; **19** 34; **22** 102; **25** 268
Bankhaus August Lenz AG, **65** 230, 232
Banknorth Group, Inc., 55 49–53
Bankruptcy Services LLC, **56** 112
Banksia Wines Ltd., **54** 227, 229
BankWatch, **37** 143, 145
Banner Aerospace, Inc., 14 42–44; 37 29–32 (upd.)
Banner International, **13** 20
Banner Life Insurance Company, **III** 273; **24** 284
Banorte. *See* Grupo Financiero Banorte, S.A. de C.V.
Banpais. *See* Grupo Financiero Asemex-Banpais S.A.
BanPonce Corporation, **41** 312
Banque Bruxelles Lambert. *See* Bank Brussels Lambert.
Banque de Bruxelles. *See* Bank Brussels Lambert.
Banque de France, **14** 45–46
Banque de la Société Générale de Belgique. *See* Generale Bank.
Banque de Paris et des Pays-Bas, **10** 346; **19** 188–89; **33** 179
Banque Indosuez, **II** 429; **52** 361–62
Banque Internationale de Luxembourg, **42** 111
Banque Lambert. *See* Bank Brussels Lambert.
Banque Nationale de Paris S.A., II 232–34, 239; **III** 201, 392–94; **9** 148; **13** 203; **15** 309; **19** 51; **33** 119; **49** 382. *See also* BNP Paribas Group.
Banque Paribas. *See* BNP Paribas Group.
Banque Sanpaolo of France, **50** 410
La Banque Suisse et Française. *See* Crédit Commercial de France.
Banque Worms, **27** 514
Banta Corporation, 12 24–26; 19 333; 32 73–77 (upd.)
Bantam Ball Bearing Company, **13** 522
Bantam Doubleday Dell Publishing Group, **IV** 594; **13** 429; **15** 51; **27** 222; **31** 375–76, 378
Banyan Systems Inc., 25 50–52
Banyu Pharmaceutical Co., **11** 290; **34** 283
Baoshan Iron and Steel, **19** 220

Baosteel Group International Trade Corporation. *See* Baosteel Group International Trade Corporation.
BAP of New York, Inc., **15** 246
Bar Technologies, Inc., **26** 408
Barastoc Stockfeeds Pty Ltd., **62** 307
Barat. *See* Barclays PLC.
Barber Dental Supply Inc., **19** 291
Barberet & Blanc, **I** 677; **49** 350
Barcel, **19** 192
Barclay Furniture Co., **12** 300
Barclay White Inc., **38** 436
Barclays Business Credit, **13** 468
Barclays PLC, II 235–37; 20 57–60 (upd.); 64 46–50 (upd.)
BarclaysAmerican Mortgage Corporation, 11 29–30
Barco Manufacturing Co., **16** 8; **26** 541
Barco NV, 44 42–45
Barcolo Manufacturing, **15** 103; **26** 100
Barden Cablevision, **IV** 640; **26** 273
Bardon Group. *See* Aggregate Industries plc.
Bareco Products, **15** 352
Barefoot Inc., **23** 428, 431
Bari Shoes, Inc., **22** 213
Barilla G. e R. Fratelli S.p.A., 17 35–37; 50 77–80 (upd.); 53 243
Baring Brothers & Co., Ltd., **39** 5
Barings PLC, 14 45–47
Barker & Dobson, **II** 629; **47** 367
Barker and Company, Ltd., **13** 286
Barlow Rand Ltd., I 422–24
Barlow Specialty Advertising, Inc., **26** 341
Barmag AG, 39 39–42
Barneda Carton SA, **41** 326
Barnes & Noble, Inc., 10 135–37; 12 172; **13** 494, 545; **14** 61–62; **15** 62; **16** 160; **17** 524; **23** 370; **25** 17, 29–30; **30** 67–71 (upd.); **41** 61; **43** 78, 408
Barnes Group, Inc., 13 72–74; 69 58–62 (upd.)
Barnett Banks, Inc., 9 58–60
Barnett Brass & Copper Inc., **9** 543
Barnett Inc., 28 50–52
Barney's, Inc., 28 53–55; 36 290, 292
Barnstead/Thermolyne Corporation, **14** 479–80
Baroid, **19** 467–68
Baron Industries Corporation, **53** 298
Baron Philippe de Rothschild S.A., 39 43–46
Barr. *See* AG Barr plc.
Barr & Stroud Ltd., **III** 727
Barr Laboratories, Inc., 26 29–31
Barr Pharmaceuticals, Inc., 68 46–49 (upd.)
Barracuda Technologies, **47** 7, 9
Barratt Developments plc, I 556–57; 56 31–33 (upd.)
Barrett Business Services, Inc., 16 48–50
Barricini Foods Inc., **27** 197
Barrick Gold Corporation, 34 62–65; 38 232
Barris Industries, Inc., **23** 225
Barry Callebaut AG, 29 46–48; 71 46–49 (upd.)
Barry Wright Corporation, **9** 27; **32** 49
Barry's Jewelers. *See* Samuels Jewelers Incorporated.
Barsab Investment Trust. *See* South African Breweries Ltd.
Barsotti's, Inc. *See* Foster Wheeler Corp.
Bart Starr, **12** 284

Bartlett & Co., **33** 261
Barton & Ludwig, Inc., **21** 96
Barton Beers, Ltd., **29** 219
Barton Brands, **II** 609
Barton Incorporated, **13** 134; **24** 140; **34** 89; **68** 99
Barton Malow Company, 51 40–43
Barton Protective Services Inc., 53 56–58
Bartow Food Company, **25** 332
Barwig Medizinische Systeme. *See* OEC Medical Systems, Inc.
The Baseball Club of Seattle, LP, 50 81–85
Baseline, **58** 167
BASF Aktiengesellschaft, I 305–08, 309, 319, 346–47, 632, 638; **13** 75; **14** 308; **16** 462; **18 47–51 (upd.)**, 186, 234; **21** 544; **24** 75; **26** 305, 368; **27** 22; **28** 194; **41** 45; **50 86–92 (upd.)**; **59** 31
Bashas' Inc., 33 62–64
Basic Resources, Inc. *See* Texas Utilities Company.
Basics, **14** 295
BASIS Information Technologies, Inc., **11** 112–13, 132
The Basketball Club of Seattle, LLC, 50 93–97
Basketball Properties Ltd, **53** 166
Baskin-Robbins Ice Cream Co., **7** 128, 372; **17** 474–75; **25** 366; **29** 18
Basle A.G., **8** 108–09
Bass Anglers Sportsman Society Inc., **52** 192
Bass Brewers Ltd., **15** 441; **29** 85
Bass Brothers Enterprises Inc., **28** 107; **36** 472
Bass Charington, **29** 84
Bass PLC, I 222–24; III 94–95; 9 99, 425–26; **15 44–47 (upd.)**; **16** 263; **23** 482; **24** 194; **33** 127; **35** 396; **38 74–78 (upd.)**; **43** 226
Bass Pro Shops, Inc., 42 27–30
Bassett Boat Company, **30** 303
Bassett Furniture Industries, Inc., 18 52–55; 19 275
Bassett Lowke Ltd., **60** 372
Bassett-Walker Inc. *See* VF Corporation.
Bassins Food Chain, **II** 649
BAT Industries plc, I 425–27, 605; **II** 628; **III** 185, 522; **9** 312; **23** 427; **30** 273. *See also* British American Tobacco PLC.
Bata Ltd., 62 27–30
Batavia Wine Company, **13** 134
Bateaux Parisiens, **29** 442
Bates, **16** 545
Bates Chemical Company, **9** 154
Bates Manufacturing Company, **10** 314
Bates Worldwide, Inc., 14 48–51; 26 500; **33 65–69 (upd.)**
Batesville Casket Company, **10** 349–50
Bath & Body Works, **11** 41; **24** 237
Bath Industries Inc., **18** 117–18
Bath Iron Works Corporation, 12 27–29; 36 76–79 (upd.)
Bath Plus Inc., **51** 196
Batkor Finances BV, **68** 64
Baton Rouge Gas Light Company. *See* Gulf States Utilities Company.
Battelle Memorial Institute, Inc., 10 138–40
Batten Barton Durstine & Osborn. *See* Omnicom Group Inc.

Battery Engineering, Inc. *See* Greatbatch Inc.
Battle Creek Food Company, **14** 557–58
Battle Mountain Gold Company, 23 40–42
Battlefield Equipment Rentals, **21** 499, 501
BATUS Inc., **9** 312; **18** 136; **30** 273; **63** 260
Baublys-Control Laser Corporation. *See* Excel Technology, Inc.
Baudhuin-Anderson Company, **8** 553
Bauer + Kunzi, **64** 226
Bauer Audio Visual, Inc., **24** 96
Bauer Nike Hockey Inc., **36** 347
Bauer Publishing Group, 7 42–43; 20 53
Bauerly Companies, 61 31–33
Baume & Mercier, **27** 487, 489
Bausch & Lomb Inc., 7 44–47; 10 46–47; **13** 365–66; **25** 22, **53–57 (upd.)**, 183; **30** 30; **42** 66; **65** 273–74
Bavaria SA, **36** 52
Bavarian Brewing Limited, **25** 280
Bavarian Specialty Foods, **13** 383
BAX Global, **58** 43
Baxter Healthcare, **36** 497–98
Baxter International Inc., I 627–29; 9 346; **10 141–43 (upd.)**, 198–99; **11** 459–60; **12** 325; **18** 469; **22** 361; **25** 82; **26** 433; **36** 92; **54** 42
Baxter Travenol, **21** 119; **24** 75
The Bay, **16** 216
Bay Area Review Course, Inc., **IV** 623
Bay Colony Life Insurance Co., **III** 254
Bay Frontier Onoda Co. Ltd., **60** 301
Bay Harbour Management L.C., **28** 55
Bay Networks, Inc., **20** 33, 69; **26** 276; **36** 352
Bay Ridge Savings Bank, **10** 91
Bay Shipbuilding Corporation, **18** 320; **59** 274, 277
Bay State Gas Company, 38 79–82
Bay State Iron Manufacturing Co., **13** 16
Bay State Tap and Die Company, **13** 7
Bay West Paper Corporation. *See* Mosinee Paper Corporation.
Bayard SA, 49 46–49
BayBanks, Inc., 12 30–32
Bayer A.G., I 309–11, 319, 346–47, 350; **12** 364; **13 75–77 (upd.)**; **14** 169; **16** 439; **18** 234; **21** 544; **22** 225; **41 44–48 (upd.)**; **45** 255; **59** 15; **63** 352
Bayer S.p.A., **8** 179
Bayerische Hypotheken- und Wechsel-Bank AG, II 238–40. *See also* HVB Group.
Bayerische Landesbank, **14** 170; **47** 83
Bayerische Motoren Werke A.G., I 75, 138–40, 198; **11 31–33 (upd.)**; **13** 30; **17** 25; **21** 441; **27** 20, 203; **38 83–87 (upd.)**
Bayerische Vereinsbank A.G., II 241–43; III 401. *See also* HVB Group.
Bayerische Wagnisbeteiligung GmbH, **27** 192
Bayerische Zellstoff, **IV** 325
Bayernwerk AG, V 555–58, 698–700; **23 43–47 (upd.)**; **39** 57
Bayliner Marine Corporation, **22** 116
Bayou Steel Corporation, 31 47–49
Baystate Corporation, **12** 30
Baytree Investors Inc., **15** 87
Bayview Water Company, **45** 277
Bazaar & Novelty. *See* Stuart Entertainment Inc.

Bazar de l'Hotel de Ville, **19** 308
BBA. *See* Bush Boake Allen Inc.
BBAG Osterreichische Brau-Beteiligungs-AG, 38 88–90
BBC. *See* British Broadcasting Corp.
BBC Brown, Boveri Ltd. *See* ABB Ltd.
BBDO. *See* Batten Barton Durstine & Osborn.
BBDO Worldwide Network, **22** 394
BBGI. *See* Beasley Broadcast Group, Inc.
BBME. *See* British Bank of the Middle East.
BBN Corp., 19 39–42
BBO & Co., **14** 433
BBVA. *See* Banco Bilbao Vizcaya Argentaria S.A.
BC Development, **16** 481
BC Natural Foods, Inc., **68** 91
BC Partners, **51** 322; **53** 138
BC Property Management Inc., **58** 23
BC Rail Ltd., **71** 82, 88
BC TEL. *See* British Columbia Telephone Company.
BCal. *See* British Caledonian Airways.
BCC, **24** 266, 270
BCE, Inc., V 269–71; 7 333; **12** 413; **18** 32; **36** 351; **44 46–50 (upd.)**
BCI. *See* Banca Commerciale Italiana SpA.
Bcom3 Group, Inc., **40** 142
BCOP. *See* Boise Cascade Office Products.
BCP Corporation, **16** 228–29
BCPA. *See* British Commonwealth Pacific Airways.
BDB. *See* British Digital Broadcasting plc.
BDB Corp., **10** 136
BDDP. *See* Wells Rich Greene BDDP.
Be Free Inc., **49** 434
BEA. *See* Bank of East Asia Ltd.
BEA Systems, Inc., 36 80–83
Beach Hill Investments Pty Ltd., **48** 427
Beach Patrol Inc., **29** 181
Beacon Communications Group, **23** 135
Beacon Education Management LLC. *See* Chancellor Beacon Academies, Inc.
Beacon Manufacturing Company, **19** 304–05
Beall-Ladymon, Inc., **24** 458
Bealls, **24** 456
Beamach Group Ltd., **17** 182–83
Beaman Corporation, **16** 96; **25** 390
Bean Fiberglass Inc., **15** 247
Bear Automotive Service Equipment Company, **10** 494
Bear Creek Corporation, 12 444–45; 38 91–94; 39 361
Bear Instruments Inc., **48** 410
Bear Stearns Companies, Inc., II 400–01, 450; **10 144–45 (upd.)**, 382; **20** 313; **24** 272; **52 41–44 (upd.)**
Bearings, Inc., 13 78–80
Beasley Broadcast Group, Inc., 51 44–46
Beasley Industries, Inc., **19** 125–26
Beatrice Company, **II 467–69**, 475; **9** 318; **12** 82, 87, 93; **13** 162–63, 452; **14** 149–50; **15** 213–14, 358; **16** 160, 396; **19** 290; **24** 273; **26** 476, 494; **28** 475; **42** 92; **62** 89–90. *See also* TLC Beatrice International Holdings, Inc.
Beatrice Foods, **21** 322–24, 507, 545; **25** 277–78; **38** 169; **43** 355
Beatrix Mines Ltd., **62** 164
Beaulieu of America, **19** 276
Beauté Prestige International S.A. *See* Shiseido Company Limited.

BeautiControl Cosmetics, Inc., 21 49–52
Beauty Biz Inc., **18** 230
Beauty Systems Group, Inc., **60** 260
Beaver Lake Concrete, Inc. *See* The Monarch Cement Company.
Beazer Homes USA, Inc., 17 38–41
Beazer Plc., **7** 209
bebe stores, inc., 31 50–52
BEC Group Inc., **22** 35; **60** 133
BEC Ventures, **57** 124–25
Bechstein, **56** 299
Bechtel Group, Inc., I 558–59, 563; **6** 556; **13** 13; **24 64–67 (upd.)**; **25** 402; **52** 374
Beck & Gregg Hardware Co., **9** 253
Beck's North America, Inc. *See* Brauerei Beck & Co.
Becker Drill, Inc., **19** 247
Becker Group of Germany, **26** 231
Beckett Papers, 23 48–50
Beckley-Cardy Group. *See* School Specialty, Inc.
Beckman Coulter, Inc., 22 74–77
Beckman Instruments, Inc., 14 52–54; 16 94
BECOL. *See* Belize Electric Company Limited.
Becton, Dickinson & Company, I 630–31; 11 34–36 (upd.); 36 84–89 (upd.); 42 182–83; **52** 171
Bed Bath & Beyond Inc., 13 81–83; 14 61; **18** 239; **24** 292; **33** 384; **41 49–52 (upd.)**
Bedcovers, Inc., **19** 304
Beddor Companies, **12** 25
Bedford Chemical, **8** 177
Bedford-Stuyvesant Restoration Corp., **II** 673
Bee Chemicals, **I** 372
Bee Discount, **26** 476
Bee Gee Shoe Corporation, **10** 281
Beech Aircraft Corporation, II 87; 8 49–52, 313; **11** 411, 413; **27** 98; **38** 375; **46** 354
Beech Holdings Corp., **9** 94
Beech-Nut Nutrition Corporation, 21 53–56; 46 290; **51 47–51 (upd.)**
Beecham Group PLC, **I** 668; **9** 264; **14** 53; **16** 438
Beechcroft Developments Ltd., **51** 173
Beechwood Insurance Agency, Inc., **14** 472
Beeck-Feinkost GmbH, **26** 59
ZAO BeeOnLine-Portal, **48** 419
Beerman Stores, Inc., **10** 281
Beers Construction Company, **38** 437
Behr GmbH & Co. KG, 72 22–25
Behr-Manning Company, **8** 396
Behring Diagnostics. *See* Dade Behring Holdings Inc.
Behringwerke AG, **14** 255; **50** 249
BEI Technologies, Inc., 65 74–76
Beiersdorf AG, 29 49–53; 41 374–77
Beijing Contact Lens Ltd., **25** 56
Beijing Dentsu, **16** 168
Beijing-Landauer, Ltd., **51** 210
Beijing Liyuan Co., **22** 487
Beijing Yanshan Petrochemical Company, **22** 263
Beijing ZF North Drive Systems Technical Co. Ltd., **48** 450
Beirao, Pinto, Silva and Co. *See* Banco Espírito Santo e Comercial de Lisboa S.A.

Bejam Group PLC. *See* The Big Food Group plc.
Bekins Company, 15 48–50; **26** 197
Bel. *See* Fromageries Bel.
Bel Air Markets, **14** 397; **58** 290
Bel Fuse, Inc., 53 59–62
Belco Oil & Gas Corp., 23 219; **40** 63–65; **63** 440
Belcom Holding AG, **53** 323, 325
Belden Inc., 19 43–45
Beldis, **23** 219
Beldoch Industries Corp., **17** 137–38
Belgacom, 6 302–04; **63** 371–72
Belgian Rapid Access to Information Network Services, **6** 304
Belglas, **16** 420; **43** 307
Belgo Group plc, **31** 41
Belize Electric Company Limited, **47** 137
Belk, Inc., V 12–13; **19** 46–48 **(upd.); 72** 26–29 **(upd.)**
Bell and Howell Company, 9 33, 61–64; **11** 197; **14** 569; **15** 71; **29** 54–58 **(upd.),** 159
Bell Aerospace, **24** 442
Bell Aircraft Company, **11** 267; **13** 267
Bell Atlantic Corporation, V 272–74; **9** 171; **10** 232, 456; **11** 59, 87, 274; **12** 137; **13** 399; **18** 33; **25** 58–62 **(upd.),** 91, 497; **27** 22, 365. *See also* Verizon Communications.
Bell Canada Enterprises Inc. *See* BCE, Inc.
Bell Canada International, Inc., 6 305–08; **12** 413; **21** 308; **25** 102
Bell Communications Research. *See* Telcordia Technologies, Inc.
Bell Fibre Products, **12** 377
Bell Helicopter Textron Inc., 46 64–67
Bell Helmets Inc., **22** 458
Bell Industries, Inc., 13 47; **18** 498; **19** 311; **47** 40–43
Bell Laboratories, 8 157; **9** 171; **10** 108; **11** 327; **12** 61; **14** 52, 281–82; **23** 181; **34** 257–58. *See also* AT&T Bell Laboratories, Inc.
Bell Microproducts Inc., 69 63–65
Bell Mountain Partnership, Ltd., **15** 26
Bell-Northern Research, Ltd. *See* BCE Inc.
Bell Pharmacal Labs, **12** 387
Bell Resources, **III** 729; **10** 170; **27** 473
Bell Sports Corporation, 16 51–53; **44** 51–54 **(upd.)**
Bell System, **7** 99, 333; **11** 500; **16** 392–93
Bell Telephone Manufacturing, **II** 13
Bellcore. *See* Telcordia Technologies, Inc.
Belle Alkali Co., **7** 308
Belleek Pottery Ltd., 71 50–53
Bellofram Corp., **14** 43
BellSouth Corporation, V 276–78; **9** 171, 321; **10** 431, 501; **15** 197; **18** 23, 74, 76; **19** 254–55; **22** 19; **27** 20; **29** 59–62 **(upd.); 43** 447; **45** 390
Bellway Plc, 45 37–39
Belmin Systems, **14** 36
Belmont Savings and Loan, **10** 339
Belo Corporation. *See* A.H. Belo Corporation.
Beloit Corporation, 8 243; **14** 55–57; **34** 358; **38** 224, 226–28
Beloit Tool Company. *See* Regal-Beloit Corporation.
Beloit Woodlands, **10** 380
Bemis Company, Inc., 8 53–55; **26** 43
Ben & Jerry's Homemade, Inc., 10 146–48; **35** 58–62

Ben Bridge Jeweler, Inc., 60 52–54
Ben Franklin Retail Stores, Inc. *See* FoxMeyer Health Corporation.
Ben Franklin Savings & Trust, **10** 117
Ben Hill Griffin, **III** 53
Ben Myerson Candy Co., Inc., **26** 468
Ben Venue Laboratories Inc., **16** 439; **39** 73
Benchmark Capital, 49 50–52; **57** 49
Benchmark Electronics, Inc., 40 66–69
Benchmark Tape Systems Ltd, **62** 293
Benckiser Group, **37** 269
Benckiser N.V. *See* Reckitt Benckiser plc.
Benderson Development Company, **69** 120
Bendick's of Mayfair. *See* August Storck KG.
Bendix Corporation, I 141–43; **7** 356; **8** 545; **9** 16–17; **10** 260, 279; **11** 138; **13** 356–57; **15** 284; **17** 564; **21** 416; **22** 31
Beneficial Corporation, 8 56–58, 117; **10** 490
Beneficial Finance Company, **27** 428–29
Beneficial Standard Life, **10** 247
Benefit Consultants, Inc., **16** 145
Benefits Technologies, Inc., **52** 382
Benelli Arms S.p.A., **39** 151
Benesse Corporation, **13** 91, 93; **39** 49
Bénéteau SA, 55 54–56
Benetton Group S.p.A., 8 171; **10** 149–52; **15** 369; **18** 193; **25** 56; **49** 31; **63** 361–62; **67** 47–51 **(upd.)**
Benfield Greig Group plc, 53 63–65
Benguet Corporation, 58 21–24
Benihana, Inc., 18 56–59
Benjamin Moore and Co., 13 84–87; **38** 95–99 **(upd.)**
Benjamin Sheridan Corporation, **62** 82
Benlee, Inc., **51** 237
Benlox Holdings PLC, **16** 465
Benn Bros. plc, **IV** 687
Bennett Industries, Inc., **17** 371–73
Bennett's Smokehouse and Saloon, **19** 122; **29** 201
Bennigan's, **7** 336; **12** 373; **19** 286; **25** 181
Benpres Holdings, **56** 214
BenQ Corporation, 67 52–54
Bensdorp, **29** 47
Benson & Hedges, Ltd. *See* Gallaher Limited.
Benson Wholesale Co., **II** 624
Bentalls, **37** 6, 8
Bentex Holding S.A., **48** 209
Bentley Laboratories, **22** 360
Bentley Mills, Inc., **8** 272
Bentley Motor Ltd., **21** 435
Bentley's Luggage Corp., **58** 370
Bentoel, PT, **62** 97
Benton International, Inc., **29** 376
Benton Oil and Gas Company, 47 44–46
Bentwood Ltd., **62** 342
Benwood Iron Works, **17** 355
Bercy Management. *See* Elior SA.
Beresford International plc, **24** 335; **27** 159
Beretta. *See* Fabbrica D' Armi Pietro Beretta S.p.A.
Bergdorf Goodman Inc., 25 177; **52** 45–48
Bergen Brunswig Corporation, V 14–16, 152; **13** 88–90 **(upd.); 18** 97. *See also* AmerisourceBergen Corporation.
Berger Associates, Inc., **26** 233
Berger Bros Company, 62 31–33
Berger Manufacturing Company, **26** 405

Bergerat Monnoyeur. *See* Groupe Monnoyeur.
Berges electronic GmbH, **56** 357
Bergstrom Paper Company, **8** 413
Beringer Blass Wine Estates Ltd., 66 34–37 **(upd.)**
Beringer Wine Estates Holdings, Inc., 22 78–81; **36** 472. *See also* Beringer Blass Wine Estates Ltd.
Berisford International plc. *See* Enodis plc.
Berjaya Group Bhd., 22 464–65; **57** 84; **67** 55–57
Berk Corp., **52** 193
Berkeley Farms, Inc., 46 68–70
Berkey Photo Inc., **I** 447
Berkley Dean & Co., **15** 525
Berkley Petroleum Corporation, **52** 30
Berkline Corp., **17** 183; **20** 363; **39** 267
Berkshire Hathaway Inc., III 213–15; **18** 60–63 **(upd.); 29** 191; **30** 411; **36** 191; **38** 98; **40** 196, 199, 398; **39** 232, 235; **42** 31–36 **(upd.); 60** 52; **64** 140, 209
Berkshire Partners, **10** 393
Berkshire Realty Holdings, L.P., 49 53–55
Berleca Ltd., **9** 395; **42** 269
Berlex Laboratories, Inc., 10 214; **66** 38–40
Berli Jucker, **18** 180–82
BerlinDat Gesellschaft für Informationsverarbeitung und Systemtechnik GmbH, **39** 57
Berliner Stadtreinigungsbetriebe, 58 25–28
Berliner Verkehrsbetriebe (BVG), 58 29–31
Berlitz International, Inc., IV 643; **7** 286, 312; **13** 91–93; **39** 47–50 **(upd.)**
Berman Brothers Fur Co., **21** 525
Berman Buckskin, **21** 525
Bernard C. Harris Publishing Company, Inc., 39 51–53
Bernard Chaus, Inc., 27 59–61
Bernard Warschaw Insurance Sales Agency, Inc., **55** 128
Bernardin Ltd., **30** 39
Berndorf Austria, **44** 206
Berndorf Switzerland, **44** 206
Berner Nut Company, **64** 110
Bernheim-Meyer: A l'Innovation. *See* GIB Group.
Bernie Schulman's, **12** 132
Bernina Holding AG, 47 47–50
Berrios Enterprises, **14** 236
Berry Bearing Company, **9** 254
Berry Petroleum Company, 47 51–53
Berry Plastics Corporation, 21 57–59
Berryhill Nursery. *See* Monrovia Nursery Company.
Bert L. Smokler & Company, **11** 257
Bertelsmann A.G., IV 592–94, 614–15; **10** 196; **15** 51–54 **(upd.); 17** 399; **19** 285; **22** 194; **26** 19, 43; **30** 67, 70; **31** 375, 378; **43** 63–67 **(upd.),** 422; **44** 377; **54** 17, 21–22; **61** 88, 241
Bertelsmann Music Group, **52** 428
Bertolini's Authentic Trattorias, **30** 329
Bertram & Graf Gmbh, **28** 45
Bertucci's Corporation, 16 54–56, 447; **64** 51–54 **(upd.)**
Berwick Offray, LLC, 35 130–31; **70** 17–19
Berwind Corp., **14** 18
Beryl Corp., **26** 149

Beryllium Resources, **14** 80
Berzelius Umwelt-Service, **IV** 141
Besi, **26** 498
Besnier SA, 19 49–51; 23 217, 219; **24** 444–45; **25** 83, 85
Bess Mfg., **8** 510
Bessemer Capital Partners L.P., **15** 505
Best Buy Co., Inc., 9 65–66; 10 305; **17** 489; **18** 532–33; **19** 362; **23 51–53** **(upd.); 24** 52, 502; **29** 120, 123; **30** 464, 466; **38** 315; **62** 152; **63 61–66 (upd.)**
best energy GmbH, **39** 54, 57
Best Fabric Outlets, **16** 198
Best Holding Corporation. *See* Arkansas Best Corporation.
Best Manufacturing, **15** 490
Best Power, **24** 29
Best Products Inc., **19** 396–97
Best Read Guides Franchise Corp., **36** 341
Best Western, **14** 106; **25** 308
BestChoice Administrators, Inc., **51** 276–77
Bestfoods, II 496–97; **22 82–86 (upd.)**
Bestform Group Inc., **54** 403
Bestline Products, **17** 227
Bestmeat Company, **59** 3, 5
Bestop Inc., **16** 184
Bestway Distribution Services, Inc., **24** 126
Bestway Transportation, **14** 505
Beswick, **II** 17
BET Holdings, Inc., 18 64–66; 22 224; **25** 213; **34** 43
BETA AIR CJSC, **68** 204
Beta West Properties, **25** 496–97
Beth Israel Medical Center. *See* Continuum Health Partners, Inc.
Bethesda Research Laboratories, Inc., **17** 287, 289
Bethlehem Steel Corporation, IV 35–37, 228, 572–73; **6** 540; **7 48–51 (upd.)**, 447, 549–50; **11** 65; **12** 354; **13** 97, 157; **18** 378; **22** 285; **23** 305; **25** 45; **26** 405; **27 62–66 (upd.); 50** 501–02
Betriebs- und Baugesellschaft GmbH, **53** 285
Better Brands Ltd., **32** 518–19
Bettys & Taylors of Harrogate Ltd., 72 30–32
Betz Laboratories, Inc., I 312–13; **10 153–55 (upd.); 15** 536
Beverage Associates Corp., **67** 317
Beveridge-Marvellum Company, **8** 483
Beverly Enterprises, Inc., III 76–77; **14** 242; **16 57–59 (upd.); 25** 309
Beverly Hills Savings, **II** 420
Beverly Pest Control, **25** 15
Bevis Custom Furniture, Inc., **12** 263
Bevrachtingskantoor, **26** 280
Bewag AG, 38 449; **39 54–57; 57** 395, 397
Bezeq, **25** 266
BFC Construction Corporation, 25 63–65
The BFGoodrich Company, V 231–33; **8** 80–81, 290; **9** 12, 96, 133; **10** 438; **11** 158; **19 52–55 (upd.); 20** 260, 262; **21** 260; **23** 170; **25** 70; **30** 158; **31** 135; **61** 196. *See also* Goodrich Corporation.
BFI. *See* Browning-Ferris Industries, Inc.
BFP Holdings Corp. *See* Big Flower Press Holdings, Inc.
BG Freight Line Holding B.V., **30** 318
BG plc, **29** 104

BG&E. *See* Baltimore Gas and Electric Company.
BGC Finance, **II** 420
BGITC. *See* Baosteel Group International Trade Corporation.
BGJ Enterprises, Inc. *See* Brown Printing Company.
BH Acquisition Corporation, **22** 439
Bharti Telecom, **16** 84
BHC Communications, Inc., 9 119; **26 32–34; 31** 109
BHP Billiton, 67 58–64 (upd.)
BHP Steel of Australia, **18** 380
BHPC Marketing, Inc., **45** 41
Bhs plc, 16 466; **17 42–44**, 334–35
BHV. *See* Bazar de l'Hotel de Ville.
Bi-Lo Inc., **II** 641; **V** 35; **16** 313
Biacore International AB, **25** 377
Bianchi, **13** 27
Bibb Co., **31** 199
Bibop-Carire S.p.A., **65** 86, 88
BIC Corporation, 8 59–61; 20 23; **23 54–57 (upd.)**
BICC PLC, III 433–34; **11** 520. *See also* Balfour Beatty plc.
BICE Med Grille, **16** 447
Bicoastal Corporation, II 9–11
Bicycle Holding, Inc. *See* United States Playing Card Company.
Bidermann Industries, **22** 122; **41** 129
Biederman & Company, **14** 160
Biedermann Motech, **37** 112
Bieffe, **16** 52
Bierbrauerei Wilhelm Remmer, **9** 86
Biesemeyer Manufacturing Corporation, **26** 363
Biffa Waste Services Ltd. *See* Severn Trent PLC.
Big B, Inc., 17 45–47
Big Bear Stores Co., 13 94–96
Big D Construction Corporation, **42** 432
Big Dog Holdings, Inc., 45 40–42
Big Entertainment, Inc., **58** 164
Big 5 Sporting Goods Corporation, 12 477; **55 57–59**
Big Flower Press Holdings, Inc., 21 60–62; 32 465–66
Big Fluke Wine Co. *See* Click Wine Group.
The Big Food Group plc, 68 50–53 (upd.), 57, 60
Big Foot Cattle Co., **14** 537
Big Guns, Inc., **51** 229
Big Horn Mining Co., **8** 423
Big Idea Productions, Inc., 49 56–59
Big Lots, Inc., 50 98–101
Big M, **8** 409–10
Big O Tires, Inc., 20 61–63
Big Rivers Electric Corporation, 11 37–39
Big Sky Resort. *See* Boyne USA Resorts.
Big Sky Western Bank, **35** 197, 199
Big V Supermarkets, Inc., 25 66–68
Big Y Foods, Inc., 23 169; **53 66–68**
BigBen Interactive S.A., 72 33–35
Bigelow-Sanford, Inc., **31** 199
BII. *See* Banana Importers of Ireland.
Bike Athletics, **23** 449
BIL. *See* Brierley Investments.
Bilfinger & Berger AG, I 560–61; **55 60–63 (upd.)**
Bill & Melinda Gates Foundation, 41 53–55, 119
Bill Acceptance Corporation Ltd., **48** 427

Bill Barrett Corporation, 71 54–56
Bill Blass Ltd., 32 78–80
Bill France Racing, **19** 222
Billabong International Ltd., 44 55–58
Billboard Publications, Inc., **7** 15
Billing Concepts, Inc., 26 35–38; 72 36–39 (upd.)
Billiton International, **IV** 532; **22** 237
BillPoint Inc., **58** 266
Bilsom, **40** 96–97
Bilt-Rite Chase-Pitkin, Inc., **41** 416
Biltwell Company, **8** 249
Bimar Foods Inc., **19** 192
Bimbo Bakeries USA, **29** 341
Bimbo, S.A., **36** 162, 164
Bin Zayed Group, **55** 54, 56
Binderline Development, Inc., **22** 175
Bindley Western Industries, Inc., 9 67–69; 50 123
The Bing Group, 60 55–58
Bingham Dana LLP, 43 68–71
Binghamton Container Company, **8** 102
Bingo Express Co., Ltd., **64** 290
Bingo King. *See* Stuart Entertainment Inc.
Binks Sames Corporation, 21 63–66
Binney & Smith Inc., 25 69–72; 58 313
Binnie & Partners, **22** 89
Binter Canarias. *See* Iberia.
Bio Balance Corporation. *See* New York Health Care, Inc.
Bio-Clinic, **11** 486–87
Bio-Dental Technologies Corporation, **46** 466
Bio-Dynamics, Inc., **10** 105, 107; **37** 111
Bio Foods Inc. *See* Balance Bar Company.
Bio Synthetics, Inc., **21** 386
Biodevelopment Laboratories, Inc., **35** 47
Biogen Idec Inc., 14 58–60; 36 90–93 (upd.); 71 57–59 (upd.)
Bioindustrias, **19** 475
bioKinetics, **64** 18
Biokyowa, **III** 43; **48** 250
Biomedical Reference Laboratories of North Carolina, **11** 424
Biomega Corp., **18** 422
Biomet, Inc., 10 156–58
Bionaire, Inc., **19** 360
BioScience Communications, **62** 115
Bioscot, Ltd., **63** 351
Biovail Corporation, 47 54–56
Biralo Pty Ltd., **48** 427
Bird & Sons, **22** 14
Bird Corporation, 19 56–58
Birdair, Inc., **35** 99–100
Birds Eye Foods, Inc., 69 66–72 (upd.)
Birdsall, Inc., **6** 529, 531
Bireley's, **22** 515
Birkbeck, **10** 6
Birkenstock Footprint Sandals, Inc., 12 33–35; 42 37–40 (upd.)
Birmingham & Midland Bank. *See* Midland Bank plc.
Birmingham Slag Company, **7** 572–73, 575
Birmingham Steel Corporation, 13 97–98; 18 379–80; **19** 380; **40 70–73 (upd.)**
Birra Moretti, **25** 281–82
Birra Peroni S.p.A., **59** 357
Birthdays Ltd., 70 20–22
Biscayne Bank. *See* Banco Espírito Santo e Comercial de Lisboa S.A.

Biscayne Federal Savings and Loan Association, **11** 481
Bishop & Co. Savings Bank, **11** 114
Bishop National Bank of Hawaii, **11** 114
BISSELL, Inc., 9 70–72; **30** 75–78 (upd.)
Bisset Gold Mining Company, **63** 182–83
Bit LLC, **59** 303
Bit Software, Inc., **12** 62
Bitco Corporation, **58** 258
Bits & Pieces, **26** 439
Bitumen & Oil Refineries (Australia) Ltd. *See* Boral Limited.
Bituminous Casualty Corporation, **58** 258–59
Bivac International, **55** 79
BIW. *See* Bath Iron Works.
BIZ Enterprises, **23** 390
Bizarro e Milho, Lda., **64** 91
BizBuyer.com, **39** 25
Bizimgaz Ticaret Ve Sanayi A.S., **55** 346
Bizmark, **13** 176
BizMart, **6** 244–45; **8** 404–05
BJ Services Company, 15 534, 536; **25** 73–75
BJ's Pizza & Grill, **44** 85
BJ's Restaurant & Brewhouse, **44** 85
BJ's Wholesale Club, **12** 221; **13** 547–49; **33** 198
BJK&E. *See* Bozell Worldwide Inc.
BK Tag, **28** 157
BK Vision AG, **52** 357
BL Systems. *See* AT&T Istel Ltd.
BL Universal PLC, **47** 168
The Black & Decker Corporation, III 435–37, 628, 665; **8** 332, 349; **15** 417–18; **16** 384; **17** 215; **20** 64–68 (upd.); **22** 334; **43** 101, 289; **59** 271; **67** 65–70 (upd.)
Black & Veatch LLP, 22 87–90
Black Box Corporation, 20 69–71
Black Clawson Company, **24** 478
Black Diamond Equipment, Ltd., 62 34–37
Black Entertainment Television. *See* BET Holdings, Inc.
Black Hawk Broadcasting Group, **10** 29; **38** 17
Black Hills Corporation, 20 72–74
Black Pearl Software, Inc., **39** 396
BlackBerry. *See* Research in Motion Ltd.
Blackfoot Telecommunications Group, 60 59–62
Blackhawk Holdings, Inc. *See* PW Eagle Inc.
Blackhorse Agencies, **II** 309; **47** 227
Blacks Leisure Group plc, 39 58–60
Blackstone Dredging Partners LP, **69** 197
The Blackstone Group, **II** 434, 444; **IV** 718; **11** 177, 179; **13** 170; **17** 238, 443; **22** 404, 416; **26** 408; **37** 309, 311; **61** 208; **69** 101, 103
Blackstone Hotel Acquisition Co., **24** 195
Blaine Construction Company. *See* The Yates Companies, Inc.
Blair Corporation, 25 76–78; **31** 53–55
Blakeman's Floor Care Parts & Equipment. *See* Tacony Corporation.
Blandburgh Ltd., **63** 77
Blanes, S.A. de C.V., **34** 197
BLC Insurance Co., **III** 330
BLD Europe, **16** 168
Blendax, **III** 53; **8** 434; **26** 384
Blessings Corp., 14 550; **19** 59–61

Blimpie International, Inc., 15 55–57; **17** 501; **32** 444; **49** 60–64 (upd.)
Bliss Manufacturing Co., **17** 234–35
Blitz-Weinhart Brewing, **18** 71–72; **50** 112, 114
Bloch & Guggenheimer, Inc., **40** 51–52
Block Drug Company, Inc., 8 62–64; **27** 67–70 (upd.)
Block Financial Corporation, **17** 265; **29** 227
Block Management, **29** 226
Block Medical, Inc., **10** 351
Blockbuster Inc., 9 73–75; **361; 11** 556–58; **12** 43, 515; **13** 494; **18** 64, 66; **19** 417; **23** 88, 503; **25** 208–10, 222; **26** 409; **28** 296; **29** 504; **31** 56–60 (upd.), 339–40; **50** 61. *See also* Viacom Inc.
Blockson Chemical, **I** 380; **13** 379
Blodgett Holdings, Inc., 61 34–37 (upd.)
Blohm Maschinenbau GmbH, **60** 193
Blonder Tongue Laboratories, Inc., 48 52–55
Bloomberg L.P., 18 24; **21** 67–71; **63** 326
Bloomingdale's Inc., 9 209, 393; **10** 487; **12** 36–38, 307, 403–04; **16** 328; **23** 210; **25** 257; **31** 190
Blount International, Inc., 12 39–41; **24** 78; **26** 117, 119, 363; **48** 56–60 (upd.)
Blow-ko Ltd., **60** 372
BLP Group Companies. *See* Boron, LePore & Associates, Inc.
BLT Ventures, **25** 270
Blue, **62** 115
Blue Arrow PLC, **9** 327; **30** 300
Blue Bell Creameries L.P., 30 79–81
Blue Bell, Inc., **V** 390–91; **12** 205; **17** 512
Blue Bell Mattress Company, **58** 63
Blue Bird Corporation, 35 63–66
Blue Bunny Ice Cream. *See* Wells' Dairy, Inc.
Blue Byte, **41** 409
Blue Chip Stamps, **30** 412
Blue Circle Industries PLC, III 669–71, 702. *See also* Lafarge Cement UK.
Blue Cross and Blue Shield Association, 10 159–61; **14** 84
Blue Cross and Blue Shield Mutual of Northern Ohio, **12** 176
Blue Cross and Blue Shield of Colorado, **11** 175
Blue Cross and Blue Shield of Greater New York, **III** 245–46
Blue Cross and Blue Shield of Minnesota, **65** 41–42
Blue Cross and Blue Shield of Ohio, **15** 114
Blue Cross Blue Shield of Michigan, **12** 22
Blue Cross of California, **25** 525
Blue Cross of Northeastern New York, **III** 245–46
Blue Diamond Growers, 28 56–58
Blue Dot Services, **37** 280, 283
Blue Line Distributing, **7** 278–79
Blue Martini Software, Inc., 59 77–80
Blue Mountain Arts, Inc., 29 63–66
Blue Mountain Springs Ltd., **48** 97
Blue Nile Inc., 61 38–40
Blue Rhino Corporation, 56 34–37
Blue Ribbon Packing Company, **57** 57
Blue Ribbon Sports. *See* Nike, Inc.
Blue Ridge Lumber Ltd., **16** 11
Blue Shield of California, **25** 527
Blue Square Israel Ltd., 41 56–58
Blue Tee Corporation, **23** 34, 36

Blue Water Food Service, **13** 244
Bluebird Inc., **10** 443
Bluefly, Inc., 60 63–65
BlueScope Steel Limited, **62** 55
Bluewin AG, **58** 337
Blumberg Communications Inc., **24** 96
Blyth and Co., **13** 448, 529
Blyth Industries, Inc., 18 67–69
BM-Telecom, **59** 303
BMC Forestry Corporation, **58** 23
BMC Industries, Inc., 17 48–51; **59** 81–86 (upd.)
BMC Real Estate, Inc., **62** 55
BMC Software, Inc., 14 391; **55** 64–67; **58** 295
bmd wireless AG, **63** 204
BMG/Music. *See* Bertelsmann AG.
BMHC. *See* Building Materials Holding Corporation.
BMI. *See* Broadcast Music Inc.
BMI Systems Inc., **12** 174
BMML, Confecçoes, Lda., **64** 91
BMO Corp., **III** 209
BMO Nesbitt Burns, **46** 55
BMS Laboratories Ltd., **59** 168
BMW. *See* Bayerische Motoren Werke.
BNA. *See* Banca Nazionale dell'Agricoltura; Bureau of National Affairs, Inc.
BNCI. *See* Banque Nationale Pour le Commerce et l'Industrie.
BNE. *See* Bank of New England Corp.
BNE Land & Development, **68** 54, 56
BNG, Inc., **19** 487
BNL. *See* Banca Nazionale del Lavoro S.p.A.
BNP Paribas Group, 36 94–97 (upd.); **42** 349
BNS Acquisitions, **26** 247
Boa Shoe Company, **42** 325
Oy Board International AB, **56** 255
Boart Longyear Company, 26 39–42, 69
Boatmen's Bancshares Inc., 15 58–60
BoatsDirect.com, **37** 398
Bob Evans Farms, Inc., 9 76–79; **10** 259; **35** 83–84; **63** 67–72 (upd.)
Bob's Red Mill Natural Foods, Inc., 63 73–75
Bobbie Brooks Inc., **17** 384
Bobbs-Merrill, **11** 198
Bobit Publishing Company, 55 68–70
Bobro Products. *See* BWP Distributors.
Bobs Candies, Inc., 70 23–25
BOC Group plc, I 314–16, 358; **11** 402; **12** 500; **25** 79–82 (upd.); **63** 56
Boca Resorts, Inc., 37 33–36
BOCAP Corp., **37** 372
Bock Bearing Co., **8** 530
BOCM Fish Feed Group, **56** 257
BOCOM International, **71** 366, 368
Boddie-Noell Enterprises, Inc., 68 54–56
Boddington, **21** 247
Bodegas y Vinedos Penaflor S.A. *See* Penaflor S.A.
Bodeker Drug Company, **16** 399
Bodum Design Group AG, 47 57–59
The Body Shop International plc, 11 40–42; **53** 69–72 (upd.)
Bodycote International PLC, **63** 76–78
Boehringer Gastro Profi, **60** 364
Boehringer Ingelheim GmbH. *See* C.H. Boehringer Sohn.
Boehringer Mannheim Companies, **37** 111–12

The Boeing Company, I 47–49; **10** 162–65 (upd.); **32** 81–87 (upd.); **36** 122, 190; **38** 372; **48** 218–20; **50** 367

Bofors Nobel Inc., **9** 380–81; **13** 22

Bogen Communications International, Inc., 62 38–41

Bohemia, Inc., 13 99–101; **31** 467

Bohm-Allen Jewelry, **12** 112

Bohn Aluminum & Brass, **10** 439

Boise Cascade Corporation, IV 255–56, 333; **6** 577; **7** 356; **8** 65–67 (upd.), 477; **15** 229; **16** 510; **19** 269, 445–46; **22** 154; **31** 13; **32** 88–92 (upd.); **36** 509; **37** 140; **52** 55

Bolands Ltd., **II** 649

Bolar Pharmaceutical Co., **16** 529

Boley G.m.b.H., **21** 123

Bolles & Houghton, **10** 355

Bollinger Shipyards, Inc., 61 41–43

Bollore, S.A., **65** 266–67

The Bolsa Chica Company, **8** 300

BolsWessanen N.V. *See* Koninklijke Wessanen nv.

Bolt, Beranek & Newman Inc., **26** 520

Bolt Security, **32** 373

Bolthouse Farms, Inc., **54** 257

BOMAG, **8** 544, 546

Bombadier Defence Services UK, **41** 412

Bombardier Aerospace Group, **36** 190–91

Bombardier, Inc., 12 400–01; **16** 78; **25** 423; **27** 281, 284; **34** 118–19; **35** 350–51; **42** 41–46 (upd.)

The Bombay Company, Inc., 10 166–68; **71** 60–64 (upd.)

Bon Appetit Holding AG, II 656; **48** 61–63

Bon Dente International Inc., **39** 320

The Bon Marché, Inc., 9 209; **19** 88, 306, 309; **23** 58–60; **26** 158, 160

Bon Secours Health System, Inc., 24 68–71

The Bon-Ton Stores, Inc., 16 60–62; **50** 106–10 (upd.); **63** 144, 148

Bonanza, **7** 336; **10** 331; **15** 361–63

Bonanza Steakhouse, **17** 320

Bonaventura, **IV** 611

Bond Brewing International, **23** 405

Bond Corporation Holdings Limited, 10 169–71; **54** 228

Bondex International, **8** 456

Bonduel Pickling Co. Inc., **25** 517

Bonduelle SA, 51 52–54

Bongrain SA, 19 50; **23** 217, 219; **25** 83–85

Bonhams 1793 Ltd., 72 40–42

Boni & Liveright, **13** 428

Bonifiche Siele, **II** 272

Bonimart, **II** 649

Bonneville International Corporation, 29 67–70; **30** 15

Bonneville Power Administration, 50 102–05

Bonnie Plant Farm, **63** 21

Bonnier AB, 52 49–52

Bontrager Bicycles, **16** 495

Bonwit Teller, **13** 43; **17** 43; **54** 304–05

Book-Mart Press, Inc., **41** 111

Book-of-the-Month Club, Inc., 13 105–07

Booker Cash & Carry Ltd., 68 57–61 (upd.)

Booker plc, 13 102–04; **31** 61–64 (upd.)

Booker Tate, **13** 102

Booklink Technologies, **26** 19

Bookmasters, **10** 136

Books-A-Million, Inc., 14 61–62; **16** 161; **41** 59–62 (upd.)

Books Are Fun, Ltd. *See* The Reader's Digest Association, Inc.

Bookstop, **10** 136

Boole & Babbage, Inc., 25 86–88

Booth Bay, Ltd., **16** 37

Booth Creek Ski Holdings, Inc., 31 65–67

Booth, Inc., **II** 420

Bootprint Entertainment, **31** 240

The Boots Company PLC, I 668, 708; **II** 650; **V** 17–19; **8** 548; **18** 51; **19** 122; **24** 72–76 (upd.)

Booz Allen & Hamilton Inc., 10 172–75

Boplan Ingénierie S.A.S. *See* SNC-Lavalin Group Inc.[

Boral Limited, III 672–74; **43** 72–76 (upd.)

Borden Cabinet Corporation, **12** 296

Borden, Inc., II 470–73, 486, 498, 538, 545; **7** 127, 129, 380; **11** 173; **15** 490; **16** 43; **17** 56; **22** 84, 91–96 (upd.); **24** 273, 288; **27** 38, 40, 316, 318

Border Fine Arts, **11** 95

Border Television, **41** 352

Borders Group, Inc., 9 361; **10** 137; **15** 61–62; **17** 522; **18** 286; **25** 17; **30** 69; **43** 77–79 (upd.), 408; **47** 211

Borders, Perrin and Norrander, **23** 480

Borealis A/S, **30** 205; **45** 8; **61** 346

Borealis Industrier, A.B., **71** 193

Borg Instruments, **23** 494

Borg-Warner Australia, **47** 280

Borg-Warner Automotive, Inc., 14 63–66; **23** 171; **32** 93–97 (upd.)

Borg-Warner Corporation, III 438–41; **13** 123–25; **14** 63, 65, 357, 541; **25** 74, 253; **41** 79. *See also* Burns International.

Borland International, Inc., 9 80–82; **10** 237, 509, 519, 558; **15** 492; **25** 349; **38** 417

Borman's, Inc., **II** 638; **16** 249

Borneo Airways. *See* Malaysian Airlines System BHD.

Boron, LePore & Associates, Inc., 45 43–45

Borregaard Osterreich AG, **18** 395

Borror Corporation. *See* Dominion Homes, Inc.

Borsheim's, **III** 215; **18** 60

Borun Bros., **12** 477

Bosch. *See* Robert Bosch GmbH.

Boscov's Department Store, Inc., 31 68–70

Bose Corporation, 13 108–10; **36** 98–101 (upd.)

Bosendorfer, L., Klavierfabrik, A.G., **12** 297

Bosert Industrial Supply. *See* W.W. Grainger, Inc.

Bossa, **55** 188

Bost Sports Clubs. *See* Town Sports International, Inc.

Boston Acoustics, Inc., 22 97–99

Boston and Maine Corporation, **16** 350

The Boston Beer Company, Inc., 18 70–73, 502; **22** 422; **31** 383; **50** 111–15 (upd.)

Boston Celtics Limited Partnership, 14 67–69

Boston Chicken, Inc., 12 42–44; **23** 266; **29** 170, 172. *See also* Boston Market Corporation.

The Boston Consulting Group, 9 343; **18** 70; **22** 193; **58** 32–35

Boston Corp., **25** 66

Boston Distributors, **9** 453

Boston Edison Company, 12 45–47

Boston Educational Research, **27** 373

Boston Garden Arena Corporation, **14** 67

Boston Gas Company. *See* Eastern Enterprises.

Boston Globe, **7** 13–16

Boston Herald, **7** 15

Boston Market Corporation, 48 64–67 (upd.); **63** 280, 284–85

Boston National Bank, **13** 465

Boston Popcorn Co., **27** 197–98; **43** 218

Boston Professional Hockey Association Inc., 39 61–63

Boston Properties, Inc., 22 100–02

Boston Scientific Corporation, 37 37–40

Boston Technology, **43** 117

Boston Ventures Management, Inc., **17** 444; **27** 41, 393; **54** 334, 337; **65** 374

Boston Whaler, Inc. *See* Reebok International Ltd.

Bostrom Seating, Inc., **23** 306

BOTAS. *See* Türkiye Petrolleri Anonim Ortakliği.

Boticas Fasa S.A., **72** 128

Botswana General Insurance Company, **22** 495

Bott SA, **72** 221

Bottu, **II** 475

BOTWEB, Inc., **39** 95

Bou-Matic, 62 42–44

Bougainville Copper Pty., **IV** 60–61

Boulanger, **37** 22

Boulder Creek Steaks & Saloon, **16** 447

Boulder Natural Gas Company, **19** 411

Boulet Dru DuPuy Petit Group. *See* Wells Rich Greene BDDP.

Boulevard Bancorp, **12** 165

Boulton & Paul Ltd., **31** 398–400

Boundary Gas Inc., **6** 457; **54** 260

Boundary Healthcare, **12** 327

Bountiful Psychiatric Hospital, Inc., **68** 299

Bourbon. *See* Groupe Bourbon S.A.

Bourdon, **19** 49

Bourjois, **12** 57

Bouverat Industries, **51** 36

Bouwmar N.V., **68** 64

Bouygues S.A., I 562–64; **13** 206; **23** 475–76; **24** 77–80 (upd.); **31** 126, 128; **48** 204

Bovis Construction, **38** 344–45

Bovis Lend Lease, **52** 222

Bovis Ltd., **I** 588

Bow Bangles, **17** 101, 103

Bow Flex of America, Inc. *See* Direct Focus, Inc.

Bow Valley Energy Inc., **47** 397

Bowater PLC, IV 257–59; **8** 483–84; **25** 13

Bowdens Media Monitoring Ltd., **55** 289

Bowers and Merena Galleries Inc., **48** 99

Bowery Savings Bank, **9** 173

Bowes Co., **II** 631

Bowling Green Wholesale, Inc. *See* Houchens Industries Inc.

Bowman Gum, Inc., **13** 520

Bowne & Co., Inc., 18 331–32; **23** 61–64

Bowthorpe plc, 33 70–72

Box Innards Inc., **13** 442
BoxCrow Cement Company, **8** 259
The Boy Scouts of America, 34 66–69
Boyd Bros. Transportation Inc., 39
64–66
Boyd Coffee Company, 53 73–75
Boyd Gaming Corporation, 43 80–82
The Boyds Collection, Ltd., 29 71–73
Boyer Brothers, Inc., **14** 17–18
Boyer's International, Inc., **20** 83
Boyles Bros. Drilling Company. *See*
Christensen Boyles Corporation.
Boyne USA Resorts, 71 65–68
Boys & Girls Clubs of America, 69
73–75
Boys Market, **17** 558–59
Bozell, Jacobs, Kenyon, and Eckhardt Inc.
See True North Communications Inc.
Bozell Worldwide Inc., 25 89–91
Bozkurt, **27** 188
Bozzuto's, Inc., 13 111–12
BP Amoco plc, **31** 31, 34; **40** 358; **63** 113
BP Canada. *See* Talisman Energy Inc.
BP p.l.c., 45 46–56 (upd.), 409, 412; **61**
117, 346–47; **62** 12
BPB, **III** 736
BPD, **13** 356
BPI Communications, Inc., **7** 15; **19** 285;
27 500; **61** 241
BR. *See* British Rail.
Braathens ASA, 47 60–62
Brabants Dagblad BV, **III** 199, 201; **53**
362
Brach and Brock Confections, Inc., 15
63–65; **29** 47
Brad Foote Gear Works, **18** 453
Braden Manufacturing, **23** 299–301
Bradford & Bingley PLC, 65 77–80
Bradford Exchange Ltd. Inc., **21** 269
Bradlees Discount Department Store
Company, II 666–67; **12** 48–50; **24**
461
Bradley Air Services Ltd., 56 38–40
Bradley Lumber Company, **8** 430
Bradstreet Co. *See* The Dun & Bradstreet
Corp.
Braegen Corp., **13** 127
Bragussa, **IV** 71
Braine L'Alleud Bricolage BV, **68** 64
BRAINS. *See* Belgian Rapid Access to
Information Network Services.
Brake Bros plc, 45 57–59
BRAL Reststoff-Bearbeitungs-GmbH, **58**
28
Bramac Dachsysteme International GmbH,
70 363
Bramalea Ltd., 9 83–85; **10** 530–31
Brambles Industries Limited, 24 400; **42**
47–50; **57** 258, 260
Bramco, **III** 600
The Branch Group, Inc., 72 43–45
Brand Companies, Inc., **9** 110; **11** 436
Branded Restaurant Group, Inc., **12** 372
Brandeis & Sons, **19** 511
BrandPartners Group, Inc., 58 36–38
Brandt Zwieback-Biskuits GmbH, **44** 40
Brandywine Asset Management, Inc., **33**
261
Brandywine Holdings Ltd., **45** 109
Brandywine Insurance Agency, Inc., **25**
540
Brandywine Iron Works and Nail Factory,
14 323
Brandywine Valley Railroad Co., **14** 324

Braniff Airlines, **16** 274; **17** 504; **36** 231
Brannock Device Company, 48 68–70
Brascan Corporation, 25 281; **67** 71–73
Brasil Telecom Participaçoes S.A., 57
67–70; **63** 378
Brass-Craft Manufacturing Co. *See* Masco
Corporation.
Brass Eagle Inc., 34 70–72; **58** 87–88
Braswell Motor Freight, **14** 567
Braud & Faucheux. *See* Manitou BF S.A.
Brauerei Beck & Co., 9 86–87; **33** 73–76
(upd.)
Braun GmbH, 17 214–15; **26** 335; **51**
55–58
Brauns Fashions Corporation. *See*
Christopher & Banks Corporation.
Brazcot Limitada, **53** 344
Brazos Gas Compressing, **7** 345
Brazos Sportswear, Inc., 23 65–67
Breakthrough Software, **10** 507
Breckenridge-Remy, **18** 216
Breco Holding Company, **17** 558, 561
Bredel Exploitatie B.V., **8** 546
Breed Corp., **63** 224
BREED Technologies, Inc., **22** 31
Breg, Inc. *See* Orthofix International NV.
Bremer Financial Corp., 45 60–63
Brenco Inc., **16** 514
Brenda Mines Ltd., **7** 399
Brennan College Services, **12** 173
Brenntag AG, 8 68–69, 496; **23** 68–70
(upd.), **23** 453–54; **59** 387, 389–91
Brent Walker Ltd., **49** 450–51
Brentwood Acquisition, Inc., **68** 299
Brentwood Associates Buyout Fund II LP,
44 54
Brentwood Corporation, **61** 398
Bresler's Industries, Inc., **35** 121
Breslube Enterprises, **8** 464
Bresser Optik, **41** 264
Brewster Lines, **6** 410
Breyers Ice Cream Co. *See* Good Humor-
Breyers.
BRI Bar Review Institute, Inc., **IV** 623; **12**
224
BRI International. *See* Quintiles
Transnational Corporation
Briarpatch, Inc., **12** 109
Briazz, Inc., 53 76–79
Bricorama S.A., 23 231; **68** 62–64
Bricotruc, **37** 259
Bridas S.A., **24** 522
Bridel, **19** 49–50; **25** 85
Bridge Communications Inc., **34** 442–43
The Bridge Group, **55** 41
Bridge Technology, Inc., **10** 395
Bridgeport Machines, Inc., 17 52–54
Bridgestone Americas Holding Inc., **64** 133
Bridgestone Corporation, V 234–35; **15**
355; **20** 262; **21** 72–75 (upd.); **59**
87–92 (upd.)
Bridgestone/Firestone, **19** 454, 456
BridgeStreet Corporate Housing Worldwide
Inc., **58** 194
Bridgewater Properties, Inc., **51** 229
Bridgeway Plan for Health, **6** 186
Bridgford Company, **13** 382
Bridgford Foods Corporation, 27 71–73
Brierly Investment Limited, **19** 156; **24** 399
Briggs and Lundy Lumber Cos., **14** 18
Briggs & Stratton Corporation, 8 70–73;
27 74–78 (upd.); **64** 353, 355
Brigham's Inc., 72 46–48

Bright Horizons Family Solutions, Inc.,
31 71–73
Bright of America Inc., **12** 426
Bright Star Technologies, **13** 92; **15** 455;
41 362
Brighter Vision Learning Adventures, **29**
470, 472
Brighton & Hove Bus and Coach
Company, **28** 155–56
Brighton Federal Savings and Loan Assoc.,
II 420
Brightpoint, Inc., 18 74–77
Brightwork Development Inc., **25** 348
Briker, **23** 231
Brilianty Alrosa, **62** 9
Brillion Iron Works Inc., **23** 306
Brin's Oxygen Company Limited. *See*
BOC Group plc.
The Brink's Company, IV 180–82; **19**
319; **58** 39–43 (upd.)
Brinker International, Inc., **10** 176–78;
18 438; **38** 100–03 (upd.)
Brinson Partners Inc., **41** 198
BRIO AB, 24 81–83
Brio Technology, **25** 97
Brioche Pasquier S.A., 58 44–46
Briones Alonso y Martin, **42** 19
Brioni Roman Style S.p.A., 67 74–76
BRISA Auto-estradas de Portugal S.A.,
64 55–58
Brisco Engineering, **41** 412
Bristol-Erickson, **13** 297
Bristol Gaming Corporation, **21** 298
Bristol Hotel Company, **23** 71–73; **38** 77
Bristol-Myers Squibb Company, III
17–19; **7** 255; **8** 210, 282–83; **9** 88–91
(upd.); **10** 70; **11** 289; **12** 126–27; **16**
438; **21** 546; **25** 91, 253, 365; **32** 213;
34 280, 282, 284; **37** 41–45 (upd.); **50**
538; **51** 223, 225; **58** 180; **59** 307; **63**
234
Bristow Helicopters Ltd., 67 101; **70**
26–28
Britannia Airways, **8** 525–26
Britannia Security Group PLC, **12** 10
Britannia Soft Drinks Ltd. (Britvic), 71
69–71
Britannica Software, **7** 168
Britannica.com, **39** 140, 144
Britches of Georgetowne, **10** 215–16
BRITE. *See* Granada Group PLC.
Brite Voice Systems, Inc., 20 75–78
BriteSmile, Inc., **35** 325
British & Commonwealth Shipping
Company, **10** 277
British Aerospace plc, I 46, 50–53, 55,
74, 83, 132, 532; **7** 9, 11, 458–59; **8**
315; **9** 499; **11** 413; **12** 191; **14** 36; **21**
8, 443; **24** 84–90 (upd.); **27** 474; **48** 81,
274
British Airways plc, I 83, 92–95; **14**
70–74 (upd.); **18** 80; **22** 52; **24** 86, 311,
396, 399–400; **26** 115; **27** 20–21, 466;
28 25; **31** 103; **33** 270; **34** 398; **37** 232;
38 104–05; **39** 137–38; **43** 83–88
(upd.); **52** 24–25; **63** 17–18
British American Cosmetics, **I** 427
British American Financial Services, **42**
450
British American Tobacco PLC, 9 312;
29 194–95; **34** 39; **49** 367, 369; **50**
116–19 (upd.); **64** 291
British and Foreign Steam Navigation
Company, **23** 160

British and North American Royal Mail Steam Packet Company. *See* Cunard Line Ltd.

British-Borneo Oil & Gas PLC, 34 73–75

British Broadcasting Corporation Ltd., 7 52–55; **21 76–79 (upd.); 24** 192; **39** 198; **42** 114, 116

British Bus Group Limited, **69** 43

British Car Auctions, **14** 321

British Chrome, **III** 699

British Coal Corporation, IV 38–40; 50 282

British Columbia Packers, **II** 631–32

British Columbia Telephone Company, 6 309–11

British Commonwealth Insurance, **III** 273

British Credit Trust, **10** 443

British Data Management, Ltd., **33** 212, 214

British Digital Broadcasting plc, **24** 192, 194

British Electric Traction Company. *See* Rentokil Initial Plc.

British Energy Plc, 19 391; **49 65–68.** *See also* British Nuclear Fuels PLC.

British European Airways. *See* Jersey European Airways (UK) Ltd.

British Gas plc, V 559–63; 6 478–79; 11 97; **18** 365–67; **38** 408; **49** 120–21; **50** 178. *See also* Centrica plc.

British Gauge and Instrument Company, **13** 234

British General Post Office, **25** 99–100

British Home Stores PLC. *See* Storehouse PLC.

British Independent Television Enterprises Ltd. *See* Granada Group PLC.

British Insulated Callender's Cables Limited. *See* BICC PLC

British Interactive Broadcasting Ltd., **20** 79

British Land Plc, 10 6; **47** 168; **54 38–41**

British Leyland Motor Corporation, **13** 286–87; **14** 35–36; **47** 8

British Linen Bank, **10** 336

British Midland plc, 34 398; **38 104–06**

British Motor Corporation, **7** 459; **13** 286

British Motor Holdings, **7** 459

The British Museum, 71 72–74

British Nuclear Fuels PLC, 6 451–54; 13 458; **50** 281

British Nylon Spinners (BNS), **17** 118

British Oxygen Co. *See* BOC Group.

The British Petroleum Company plc, I 241, 303; **II** 563; **IV** 61, 280, 363–64, **378–80,** 381–82, 412–13, 450–54, 456, 466, 472, 486, 497–99, 505, 515, 524–25, 531–32, 557; **6** 304; **7 56–59 (upd.),** 140–41, 332–33, 516, 559; **9** 490, 519; **11** 538; **14** 317; **16** 394, 461–62; **19** 155, 391; **21 80–84 (upd.),** 352; **25** 101; **26** 366, 369; **30** 86, 88; **47** 393. *See also* BP p.l.c.

British Printing and Communications Corp., **IV** 623–24, 642; **7** 312; **12** 224

British Railways Board, V 421–24

British Satellite Broadcasting, **10** 170

British Shoe Corporation. *See* Sears plc.

British Sky Broadcasting Group plc, 20 79–81; 24 192, 194; **60 66–69 (upd.)**

British Steel plc, IV 41–43, 128; **17** 481; **19 62–65 (upd.),** 391; **24** 302; **49** 98, 101, 104; **59** 225

British Sugar plc, **13** 53; **41** 30, 32–33

British Telecommunications plc, I 83, 330; **V 279–82; 7** 332–33; **8** 153; **9** 32; **11** 59, 185, 547; **15 66–70 (upd.),** 131; **16** 468; **18** 155, 345; **20** 81; **21** 233; **24** 370; **25** 101–02, 301; **27** 304; **29** 44. *See also* BT Group plc.

British Thermoplastics and Rubber. *See* BTR plc.

British Timken Ltd., **8** 530

British Trimmings Ltd., **29** 133

British Twin Disc Ltd., **21** 504

British Vita plc, 9 92–93; 19 413–15; **33 77–79 (upd.)**

British World Airlines Ltd., 18 78–80

Britoil, **IV** 380; **21** 82

Britt Airways, **I** 118

Britt Lumber Co., Inc., **8** 348

Brittania Sportswear, **16** 509

Britvic Soft Drinks Limited. *See* Britannia Soft Drinks Ltd. (Britvic)

BritWill Healthcare Corp., **25** 504

BRK Brands, Inc., **28** 134

BRK Electronics, **9** 414

Bro-Well, **17** 56

Broad, Inc., **11** 482

Broad River Power Company, **6** 575

Broadband Networks Inc., **36** 352

Broadbandtalentneet.com, **44** 164

Broadbase Software, Inc., **51** 181

Broadcast Music Inc., 23 74–77; 29 22–23

Broadcast Technology Systems, Inc., **13** 398

Broadcaster Press, **36** 341

Broadcom Corporation, 34 76–79; 36 123

Broadcom Eireann Research, **7** 510

Broadcort Capital Corp., **13** 342

Broadgate Property Holdings Limited, **54** 40

The Broadmoor Hotel, 30 82–85

BroadVision Inc., **18** 543; **38** 432

Broadway & Seymour Inc., **17** 264; **18** 112

Broadway.com, **58** 167

Broadway-Hale Stores, Inc., **12** 356

Broadway Stores, Inc., **31** 193

Broadwing Corporation, 70 29–32

Brobeck, Phleger & Harrison, LLP, 31 74–76

Brock Candy Company. *See* Brach and Brock Confections, Inc.

Brock Hotel Corp., **13** 472–73; **31** 94

Brock Residence Inn, **9** 426

Brockway Glass Co., **15** 128

Brockway Standard Holdings Corporation. *See* BWAY Corporation.

Broder Bros. Co., 38 107–09

Broderbund Software, Inc., 10 285; **13** 113–16; **25** 118; **29 74–78 (upd.)**

Les broderies Lesage, **49** 83

Brok SA, **54** 315, 317

Broken Hill Proprietary Company Ltd., IV 44–47, 58, 61, 171, 484; **10** 170; **21** 227; **22 103–08 (upd.); 26** 248; **50** 199–202. *See also* BHP Billiton.

Bronson Laboratories, Inc., **34** 460

Bronson Pharmaceuticals, **24** 257

Brooke Bond, **32** 475

Brooke Group Ltd., 15 71–73. *See also* Vector Group Ltd.

Brooke Partners L.P., **11** 275

Brookfield Athletic Shoe Company, **17** 244

Brookfield International Inc., **35** 388

Brookfield Properties Inc., **67** 72

Brooklyn Union Gas, **6** 455–57; **27** 264–66

Brooks Brothers Inc., 13 43; **22 109–12; 24** 313, 316

Brooks Fashion, **29** 164

Brooks Fiber Communications, **41** 289–90

Brooks Fiber Properties, Inc., **27** 301, 307

Brooks, Harvey & Company, Inc., **16** 376

Brooks Shoe Manufacturing Co., **16** 546

Brooks Sports Inc., 32 98–101

Brookshire Grocery Company, 16 63–66

Brookstone, Inc., II 560; **12** 411; **18 81–83**

Brother Industries, Ltd., 13 478; **14 75–76**

Brother International, **23** 212

Brothers Foods, **18** 7

Brothers Gourmet Coffees, Inc., 20 82–85

Brotherton Chemicals, **29** 113

Brotherton Speciality Products Ltd., **68** 81

Broughton Foods Co., 17 55–57

Brown & Bigelow, **27** 193

Brown & Brown, Inc., 41 63–66

Brown & Haley, 23 78–80

Brown & Root, Inc., 13 117–19; 38 481. *See also* Kellogg Brown & Root Inc.

Brown & Sharpe Manufacturing Co., 23 81–84

Brown and Williamson Tobacco Corporation, I 426; **14 77–79; 15** 72; **22** 72–73; **33 80–83 (upd.)**

Brown Boveri. *See* BBC Brown Boveri.

Brown Brothers Harriman & Co., 45 64–67

Brown Cow West Corporation, **55** 360

Brown-Forman Corporation, I 225–27; 10 179–82 (upd.); 12 313; **18** 69; **38 110–14 (upd.)**

Brown Group, Inc., V 351–53; 9 192; **10** 282; **16** 198; **20 86–89 (upd.).** *See also* Brown Shoe Company, Inc.

Brown Institute, **45** 87

Brown Jordan Co., **12** 301

Brown Printing Company, 26 43–45

Brown-Service Insurance Company, **9** 507

Brown Shipbuilding Company. *See* Brown & Root, Inc.

Brown, Shipley & Co., Limited, **45** 65

Brown Shoe Company, Inc., 68 65–69 (upd.)

Browning-Ferris Industries, Inc., V 749–53; 8 562; **10** 33; **17** 552; **18** 10; **20 90–93 (upd.); 23** 491; **33** 382; **46** 456; **50** 13–14

Browning International, **58** 147

Browning Manufacturing, **II** 19

Browning Telephone Corp., **14** 258

Broyhill Furniture Industries, Inc., 10 183–85; 12 308

BRS Ltd. *See* Ecel plc.

Bruce Foods Corporation, 39 67–69

Bruce Power LP, **49** 65, 67

Bruce's Furniture Stores, **14** 235

Bruckmann, Rosser, Sherill & Co., **27** 247; **40** 51. *See also* Lazy Days RV Center, Inc.

Bruegger's Corporation, 29 171; **63 79–82**

Brugman, **27** 502

Brummer Seal Company, **14** 64

Bruno's Supermarkets, Inc., 7 60–62; 13 404, 406; **23** 261; **26 46–48 (upd.); 68 70–73 (upd.)**

Brunswick Corporation, III **442–44**, 599; **9** 67, 119; **10** 262; **17** 453; **21** 291; **22** **113–17 (upd.)**, 118; **30** 303; **40** 30; **45** 175

Brunswick Mining, **64** 297

The Brush Electric Light Company, **11** 387; **25** 44

Brush Electrical Machines, III 507–09

Brush Engineered Materials Inc., **67** **77–79**

Brush Moore Newspaper, Inc., **8** 527

Brush Wellman Inc., **14 80–82**

Bruxeland S.P.R.L., **64** 91

Bryce Brothers, **12** 313

Brylane Inc., **29** 106–07; **64** 232

Bryn Mawr Stereo & Video, **30** 465

Brynwood Partners, **13** 19

BSA. See The Boy Scouts of America.

BSB, IV 653; **7** 392

BSC. See Birmingham Steel Corporation; British Steel Corporation.

BSH Bosch und Siemens Hausgeräte GmbH, **67 80–84**

BSkyB, IV 653; **7** 392; **29** 369, 371; **34** 85

BSN Groupe S.A., II **474–75**, 544; **22** 458; **23** 448. See also Groupe Danone

BSN Medical, **41** 374, 377

BT Group plc, **49 69–74 (upd.)**

BTG, Inc., **45 68–70**; **57** 173

BTI Services, **9** 59

BTM. See British Tabulating Machine Company.

BTR Dunlop Holdings, Inc., **21** 432

BTR plc, I **428–30**; **8** 397; **24** 88

BTR Siebe plc, **27 79–81**. See also Invensys PLC.

B2B Initiatives Ltd. See O.C. Tanner Co.

Bubbles Salon. See Ratner Companies.

Bublitz Case Company, **55** 151

Buca, Inc., **38 115–17**

Buchanan Electric Steel Company, **8** 114

Buck Consultants, Inc., **32** 459; **55 71–73**

Buck Knives Inc., **48 71–74**

Buckaroo International. See Bugle Boy Industries, Inc.

Buckbee-Mears Company. See BMC Industries, Inc.

Buckeye Business Products Inc., **17** 384

Buckeye Partners, L.P., **70 33–36**

Buckeye Technologies, Inc., **42 51–54**

Buckhorn, Inc., **19** 277–78

The Buckle, Inc., **18 84–86**

Buckley/DeCerchio New York, **25** 180

BUCON, Inc., **62** 55

Bucyrus Blades, Inc., **14** 81

Bucyrus-Erie Company, **7** 513

Bucyrus International, Inc., **17 58–61**

Bud Bailey Construction, **43** 400

Budapest Bank, **16** 14

The Budd Company, **8 74–76**; **20** 359

Buderus AG, III **694–95**; **37 46–49**

Budgens Ltd., **57** 257; **59 93–96**

Budget Group, Inc., **25 92–94**

Budget Rent a Car Corporation, **6** 393; **9 94–95**; **22** 524; **24** 409; **25** 143; **39** 370; **41** 402

Budgetel Inn. See Marcus Corporation.

Budweiser, **18** 70

Budweiser Budvar, National Corporation, **59 97–100**

Budweiser Japan Co., **21** 320

Buena Vista Home Video. See The Walt Disney Company.

Buena Vista Music Group, **44** 164

Bufete Industrial, S.A. de C.V., **34 80–82**

Buffalo Forge Company, **7** 70–71

Buffalo News, **18** 60

Buffalo Paperboard, **19** 78

Buffalo Wild Wings, Inc., **56 41–43**

Buffets, Inc., **10 186–87**; **22** 465; **32** **102–04 (upd.)**

Bugaboo Creek Steak House Inc., **19** 342

Bugatti Industries, **14** 321

Bugle Boy Industries, Inc., **18 87–88**

Buhrmann NV, **41 67–69**; **47** 90–91; **49** 440

Buick Motor Co. See General Motors Corporation.

Build-A-Bear Workshop Inc., **62 45–48**

Builders Concrete. See Vicat S.A.

Builders Emporium, **13** 169; **25** 535

Builders Square. See Kmart Corporation.

Building Materials Holding Corporation, **52 53–55**

Building One Services Corporation. See Encompass Services Corporation.

Building Products of Canada Limited, **25** 232

Buitoni SpA, II 548; **17** 36; **50** 78

Bulgari S.p.A., **20 94–97**

Bulgheroni SpA, **27** 105

Bulkships, **27** 473

Bull. See Compagnie des Machines Bull S.A.

Bull Motors, **11** 5

Bull Run Corp., **24** 404

Bull S.A., III **122–23**; **43 89–91 (upd.)**

Bull Tractor Company, **7** 534; **16** 178; **26** 492

Bull-Zenith, **25** 531

Bulldog Computer Products, **10** 519

Bulletin Broadfaxing Network Inc., **67** 257

Bulley & Andrews, LLC, **55 74–76**

Bullock's, **31** 191

Bulova Corporation, **12** 316–17, 453; **13** **120–22**; **14** 501; **36** 325; **41 70–73** **(upd.)**

Bumble Bee Seafoods L.L.C., **24** 114; **64** **59–61**

Bundall Computers Pty Limited, **56** 155

Bundy Corporation, **17 62–65**, 480

Bunge Ltd., **62 49–51**

Bunte Candy, **12** 427

Bunzl plc, IV **260–62**; **12** 264; **31 77–80** **(upd.)**

Buquet, **19** 49

Burbank Aircraft Supply, Inc., **14** 42–43; **37** 29, 31

Burberry Ltd., **10** 122; **17 66–68**; **19** 181; **41 74–76 (upd.)**; **47** 167, 169

Burda Holding GmbH. & Co., **20** 53; **23** **85–89**

Burdines, Inc., **9** 209; **31** 192; **60 70–73**

Bureau de Recherches de Pétrole, **7** 481–83; **21** 203–04

The Bureau of National Affairs, Inc., **23** **90–93**

Bureau Veritas SA, **55 77–79**

Burelle S.A., **23 94–96**

Burger and Aschenbrenner, **16** 486

Burger Boy Food-A-Rama, **8** 564

Burger King Corporation, II **613–15**, 647; **7** 316; **8** 564; **9** 178; **10** 122; **12** 43, 553; **14** 25, 32, 212, 214, 452; **16** 95–97, 396; **17 69–72 (upd.)**, 501; **18** 437; **21** 25, 362; **23** 505; **24** 140–41; **25** 228; **26** 284; **33** 240–41; **36** 517, 519; **56 44–48 (upd.)**; **63** 282–84

Burgess, Anderson & Tate Inc., **25** 500

Burgundy Ltd., **68** 53

Bürhle, **17** 36; **50** 78

Burhmann-Tetterode, **22** 154

Buriot International, Inc., **53** 236

Burke Mills, Inc., **66 41–43**

Burke Scaffolding Co., **9** 512

BURLE Industries Inc., **11** 444

Burlington Coat Factory Warehouse Corporation, **10 188–89**; **60 74–76** **(upd.)**

Burlington Homes of New England, **14** 138

Burlington Industries, Inc., V **354–55**; **8** 234; **9** 231; **12** 501; **17 73–76 (upd.)**, 304–05; **19** 275

Burlington Mills Corporation, **12** 117–18

Burlington Motor Holdings, **30** 114

Burlington Northern Santa Fe Corporation, V **425–28**; **10 190–91**; **11** 315; **12** 145, 278; **27 82–89 (upd.)**; **28** 495

Burlington Resources Inc., **10 190–92**; **11** 135; **12** 144; **47** 238

Burmah Castrol PLC, IV **381–84**; **15** 246; **30 86–91 (upd.)**

Burnards, II 677

Burndy, **19** 166

Burney Mountain Power, **64** 95

Burns & Ricker, Inc., **40** 51, 53

Burns & Wilcox Ltd., **6** 290

Burns-Alton Corp., **21** 154–55

Burns Companies, III 569; **20** 360

Burns International Security Services, III **440**; **13 123–25**; **42** 338. See also Securitas AB.

Burns International Services Corporation, **41 77–80 (upd.)**

Burns Lumber Company, Inc., **61** 254, 256

Burns, Philp & Company Ltd., **21** **496–98**; **63 83–86**

Burnup & Sims, Inc., **19** 254; **26** 324

Burpee & Co. See W. Atlee Burpee & Co.

Burr-Brown Corporation, **19 66–68**

Burris Industries, **14** 303; **50** 311

Burroughs Corp. See Unisys Corporation.

Burroughs Mfg. Co., **16** 321

Burrups Ltd., **18** 331, 333; **47** 243

Burry, II 560; **12** 410

Burt's Bees, Inc., **58 47–50**

The Burton Group plc, V **20–22**. See also Arcadia Group plc.

Burton Rubber Processing, **8** 347

Burton Snowboards Inc., **22 118–20**, 460

Burtons Gold Medal Biscuits Limited, II 466; **13** 53

Burwell Brick, **14** 248

Busch Entertainment Corporation, **34** 36

Bush Boake Allen Inc., **30 92–94**; **38** 247

Bush Brothers & Company, **45 71–73**

Bush Hog, **21** 20–22

Bush Industries, Inc., **20 98–100**

Bush Terminal Company, **15** 138

Business Communications Group, Inc. See Caribiner International, Inc.

The Business Depot, Ltd., **10** 498; **55** 353

Business Expansion Capital Corp., **12** 42

Business Express Airlines, Inc., **28** 22

Business Information Technology, Inc., **18** 112

Business Men's Assurance Company of America, III 209; **13** 476; **14 83–85**; **15** 30

Business Objects S.A., **25 95–97**

Business Post Group plc, **46 71–73**

Business Resources Corp., **23** 489, 491
Business Science Computing, **14** 36
Business Software Association, **10** 35
Business Software Technology, **10** 394
Business Wire, **25** 240
Businessland Inc., **III** 153; **6** 267; **10** 235; **13** 175–76, 277, 482
Busse Broadcasting Corporation, **7** 200; **24** 199
Buster Brown & Company. *See* Brown Shoe Company, Inc.
BUT S.A., **24** 266, 270
Butler Bros., **21** 96
Butler Cox PLC, **6** 229
Butler Group, Inc., **30** 310–11
Butler Manufacturing Company, 12 51–53; 43 130; **62 52–56 (upd.)**
Butler Shoes, **16** 560
Butterfield & Butterfield. *See* eBay Inc.
Butterfield & Swire. *See* Swire Pacific Ltd.
Butterick Co., Inc., 23 97–99
Buttrey Food & Drug Stores Co., 18 89–91
Butzbacher Weichenbau GmbH & Co. KG, **53** 352
Buxton, **23** 21
buy.com, Inc., 46 74–77
Buzzard Electrical & Plumbing Supply, **9** 399; **16** 186
BVA Investment Corp., **11** 446–47
BWAY Corporation, 24 91–93
BWP Distributors, **29** 86, 88
Byerly's, Inc. *See* Lund Food Holdings, Inc.
Byron Weston Company, **26** 105

C&A, 40 74–77 (upd.)
C&A Brenninkmeyer KG, V 23–24
C&D. *See* Church & Dwight Co., Inc.
C&E Software, **10** 507
C&G. *See* Cheltenham & Gloucester PLC.
C & G Systems, **19** 442
C & H Distributors, Inc., **27** 177
C&J Clark International Ltd., 52 56–59
C & O. *See* Chesapeake and Ohio Railway.
C&R Clothiers, **17** 313
C&S Bank, **10** 425–26
C&S Co., Ltd., **49** 425, 427
C&S/Sovran Corporation, **10** 425–27; **18** 518; **26** 453; **46** 52
C & S Wholesale Grocers, Inc., 55 80–83
C&W. *See* Cable and Wireless plc.
C-COR.net Corp., 38 118–21
C-Cube Microsystems, Inc., 37 50–54; 43 221–22
C.A. Delaney Capital Management Ltd., **32** 437
C.A. La Electricidad de Caracas, **53** 18
C.A. Muer Corporation, **65** 205
C.A.S. Sports Agency Inc., **22** 460, 462
C.A. Swanson & Sons. *See* Vlasic Foods International Inc.
C.D. Haupt, **IV** 296; **19** 226
C.E. Chappell & Sons, Inc., **16** 61–62; **50** 107
C.E.T. *See* Club Européen du Tourisme.
C.F. Burns and Son, Inc., **21** 154
C.F. Hathaway Company, **12** 522
C.F. Martin & Co., Inc., 42 55–58; 48 231
C.F. Mueller Co., **12** 332; **47** 234
C.F. Orvis Company. *See* The Orvis Company, Inc.

C.G. Conn, **7** 286
C.H. Boehringer Sohn, 39 70–73
C.H. Heist Corporation, 24 111–13
C.H. Masland & Sons. *See* Masland Corporation.
C.H. Musselman Co., **7** 429
C.H. Robinson, Inc., 8 379–80; 11 43–44; 23 357
C.H. Robinson Worldwide, Inc., 40 78–81 (upd.)
C.I. Traders Limited, 61 44–46
C. Itoh & Co., **I 431–33; II** 679; **7** 529; **10** 500; **17** 124; **26** 456. *See also* ITOCHU Corporation.
C.J. Lawrence, Morgan Grenfell Inc., **II** 429
C.J. Smith and Sons, **11** 3
C.M. Aikman & Co., **13** 168
C.M. Armstrong, Inc., **14** 17
C.M. Barnes Company, **10** 135
C.M. Life Insurance Company, **53** 213
C.M. Page, **14** 112
C-MAC Industries Inc., **48** 369
C.O.M.B. Company, **18** 131–33
C. Of Eko-Elda A.B.E.E., **64** 177
C/P Utility Services Company, **14** 138
C.P.T. Holding B.V., **56** 152
C.P.U., Inc., **18** 111–12
C.R. Anthony Company, **24** 458
C.R. Bard, Inc., 9 96–98; 22 360–61; **65 81–85 (upd.)**
C.R. Eggs, Inc., **25** 332
C-Tec Corp. *See* Commonwealth Telephone Enterprises, Inc.
C.V. Gebroeders Pel, **7** 429
C.W. Acquisitions, **27** 288
C.W. Costello & Associates Inc., **31** 131
C.W. Zumbiel Company, **11** 422
C. Wuppesahl & Co. Assekuranzmakler, **25** 538
CAA. *See* Creative Artists Agency LLC.
Cabana (Holdings) Ltd., **44** 318
Cabela's Inc., 26 49–51; 68 74–77 (upd.)
Cable & Wireless HKT, 30 95–98 (upd.)
Cable and Wireless plc, **IV** 695; **V 283–86; 7** 332–33; **11** 547; **15** 69, 521; **17** 419; **18** 253; **25 98–102 (upd.); 26** 332; **27** 307; **49** 70, 73
Cable London, **25** 497
Cable Management Advertising Control System, **25** 497
Cable News Network, **9** 30; **12** 546
Cabletron Systems, Inc., 10 193–94; 10 511; **20** 8; **24** 183; **26** 276
Cablevision Electronic Instruments, Inc., 32 105–07
Cablevision Systems Corporation, 7 63–65; 18 211; **30 99–103 (upd.)**, 106; **47** 421; **67** 369. *See also* Cablevision Electronic Instruments, Inc.
Cablex AG, **58** 337
CABLO Metall-Recycling & Handel GmbH, **62** 253
Cabot, Cabot & Forbes, **22** 100
Cabot Corporation, 8 77–79; 29 79–82 (upd.)
Cabot Medical Corporation, **21** 117, 119
Cabot-Morgan Real Estate Co., **16** 159
Cabot Noble Inc., **18** 503, 507; **50** 457
Cabrera Vulcan Shoe Corp., **22** 213
Cache Incorporated, 30 104–06
CACI International Inc., 21 85–87; 72 49–53 (upd.)
Cacique, **24** 237

Cactus Feeders, Inc., **63** 120
Cadadia, **II** 641–42
Cadbury Schweppes PLC, II 476–78, 510, 512, 592; **9** 178; **15** 221; **22** 513; **25** 3, 5; **39** 383, 385; **49 75–79 (upd.); 52** 95; **57** 250
CADCAM Technology Inc., **22** 196
Caddell Construction Company, **12** 41
Cademartori, **23** 219
Cadence Design Systems, Inc., 10 118; **11 45–48,** 285, 490–91; **35** 346; **38** 188; **48 75–79 (upd.); 69** 340–42
Cadence Industries Corporation, **10** 401–02
Cadet Uniform Services Ltd., **21** 116
Cadillac Fairview Corporation Ltd., **61** 273, 275
Cadillac Plastic, **8** 347
Cadisys Corporation, **10** 119
Cadmus Communications Corporation, 16 531; **23 100–03**
CAE USA Inc., **8** 519; **48 80–82**
Caere Corporation, 20 101–03
Caesar's Entertainment Inc., **62** 179
Caesars World, Inc., 6 199–202; 17 318
Caf'Casino, **12** 152
Café Express, **47** 443
Caffarel, **27** 105
Caffè Nero Group PLC, 63 87–89
Cagiva Group, **17** 24; **30** 172; **39** 37
Cagle's, Inc., 20 104–07
Cahners Business Information, 43 92–95
Cahners Publishing, **IV** 667; **12** 561; **17** 398; **22** 442
CAI Corp., **12** 79
Cain Chemical. *See* Occidental Petroleum Corporation.
Cain Sloan, Inc., **68** 114
Cains Marcelle Potato Chips Inc., **15** 139
Cains Pickles, Inc., **51** 232
Cairncom Pty Limited, **56** 155
Cairo Petroleum Refining Co., **51** 113
Caisse de dépôt et placement du Quebec, **II** 664
Caisse des Dépôts—Développement (C3D), **48** 107
Caisse Nationale de Crédit Agricole, **15** 38–39
Caithness Glass Limited, **38** 402; **69** 301, 303
Cajun Bayou Distributors and Management, Inc., **19** 301
Cajun Electric Power Cooperative, Inc., **21** 470
CAK Universal Credit Corp., **32** 80
CAL. *See* China Airlines.
Cal Circuit Abco Inc., **13** 387
CAL Corporation, **21** 199, 201
Cal-Dive International Inc., **25** 104–05
Cal/Ink, **13** 228
Cal-Maine Foods, Inc., 69 76–78
Cal-Van Tools. *See* Chemi-Trol Chemical Co.
Cala, **17** 558
Calais Railroad Company, **16** 348
Calardu Pty Limited, **56** 155
Calavo Growers, Inc., **47 63–66**
Calcast Ltd., **63** 304
Calcined Coke Corp., **IV** 402
Calcitherm Group, **24** 144
CalComp Inc., 13 126–29
Calcot Ltd., 33 84–87
Calder Race Course, Inc., **29** 118
Caldera Systems Inc., **38** 416, 420
Caldor Inc., 12 54–56, 508; **30** 57

Caledonian Airways. *See* British Caledonian Airways.
Caledonian Bank, **10** 337
Calgary Power Company. *See* TransAlta Utilities Corporation.
Calgene, Inc., **29** 330; **41** 155
Calgon Corporation, **16** 387; **34** 281
Calgon Vestal Laboratories, **37** 44
Calgon Water Management, **15** 154; **40** 176
Cali Realty. *See* Mack-Cali Realty Corporation.
California Automated Design, Inc., **11** 284
California Bank & Trust, **53** 378
California Cedar Products Company, 58 51–53
California Charter Inc., **24** 118
California Cheese, **24** 444
California Computer Products, Inc. *See* CalComp Inc.
California Dental Supply Co., **19** 289
California Design Studio, **31** 52
California Federal Bank, **22** 275
California Fruit Growers Exchange. *See* Sunkist Growers, Inc.
California Ink Company, **13** 227
California Institute of Technology, **9** 367
California Pacific, **22** 172
California Pizza Kitchen Inc., 15 74–76
California Plant Protection, **9** 408
California Portland Cement Co., **III** 718; **19** 69
California Pro Sports Inc., **24** 404
California Slim, **27** 197
California Sports, Inc., 56 49–52
California Steel Industries, Inc., IV 125; **67 85–87**
Caligen, **9** 92
Caligor. *See* Henry Schein Medical.
Caliper Life Sciences, Inc., 70 37–40
CALipso Sales Company, **62** 74
Call-Chronicle Newspapers, Inc., **IV** 678
Callaghan & Company, **8** 526
Callanan Industries, Inc., 60 77–79
Callaway Golf Company, 15 77–79; **16** 109; **19** 430, 432; **23** 267, 474; **37** 4; **45** 74–77 (upd.); **46** 13
Callaway Wines, **I** 264
Callon Petroleum Company, 47 67–69
Calloway's Nursery, Inc., **12** 200; **51** 59–61
Calmar Co., **12** 127
CalMat Co., 19 69–72
Calor Gas Ltd., **55** 346
Calor Group, **53** 166
Calpine Corporation, 36 102–04
Calspan SRL Corporation, **54** 395
Caltex Petroleum Corporation, IV 560, 562, 718; **7** 483; **19** 73–75; **21** 204; **25** 471; **38** 320
Calumatic Group, **25** 82
Calumet Electric Company, **6** 532
Calvert Insurance Co. *See* Gryphon Holdings, Inc.
Calvin Klein, Inc., 9 203; **22** 121–24; **25** 258; **27** 329; **32** 476; **55 84–88 (upd.)**
Calyx & Corolla Inc., **37** 162–63
Camaïeu S.A., 72 54–56
Camargo Foods, **12** 531
Camas. *See* Aggregate Industries plc.
CamBar. *See* Cameron & Barkley Company.
Camber Corporation, **25** 405
Camberley Enterprises Limited, **59** 261

Cambex, **46** 164
Cambrex Corporation, 12 147–48; **16** 67–69; **44 59–62 (upd.)**
Cambrian Wagon Works Ltd., **31** 369
Cambridge Applied Nutrition Toxicology and Biosciences Ltd., **10** 105
Cambridge Biotech Corp., **13** 241
Cambridge Electric Co., **14** 124, 126
Cambridge Gas Co., **14** 124
The Cambridge Instrument Company, **35** 272
Cambridge Interactive Systems Ltd., **10** 241
Cambridge SoundWorks, 36 101; Inc., **48** 83–86
Cambridge Steam Corp., **14** 124
Cambridge Technology Partners, Inc., 36 105–08
Cambridge Tool & Mfg. Co. Inc., **48** 268
Cambridge Water, **51** 389
Camden Wire Co., Inc., **7** 408; **31** 354–55
CAMECO, **IV** 436
Camelot Barthropp Ltd., **26** 62
Camelot Community Care, Inc., **64** 311
Camelot Group plc, **34** 140
Camelot Music, Inc., 26 52–54
Cameron & Barkley Company, 13 79; **28** 59–61; **63** 288–89
Cameron Ashley Inc., **19** 57
Cameron-Brown Company, **10** 298
Cameron Iron Works, **II** 17
Camintonn, **9** 41–42
Campagnia della Fede Cattolica sotto l'Invocazione di San Paolo, **50** 407
Campbell Cereal Company. *See* Malt-O-Meal Company.
Campbell, Cowperthwait & Co., **17** 498
Campbell Hausfeld. *See* Scott Fetzer Company.
Campbell Industries, Inc., **11** 534
Campbell-Mithun-Esty, Inc., 13 516; **16** 70–72
Campbell Scientific, Inc., 51 62–65
Campbell Soup Company, II 479–81; **7** 66–69 (upd.); **26** 55–59 (upd.); **71** 75–81 (upd.)
Campeau Corporation, V 25–28; **9** 209, 211; **12** 36–37; **13** 43; **15** 94; **17** 560; **22** 110; **23** 60; **31** 192; **37** 13; **60** 72; **67** 34
Camping World, Inc., **56** 5
Campo Electronics, Appliances & Computers, Inc., 16 73–75
Campo Lindo, **25** 85
Campofrío Alimentación S.A., 18 247; **59** 101–03
CAMPSA. *See* Compañia Arrendataria del Monopolio de Petróleos Sociedad Anónima.
Campus Services, Inc., **12** 173
Canada Cable & Wire Company, **9** 11
Canada, Limited, **24** 143
Canada Packers Inc., II 482–85; 41 249
Canada Safeway Ltd., **II** 650, 654
Canada Surety Co., **26** 486
Canada Trust. *See* CT Financial Services Inc.
Canadair, Inc., 7 205; **13** 358; **16 76–78**
Canadian Ad-Check Services Inc., **26** 270
Canadian Airlines International Ltd., **6** 61–62, 101; **12** 192; **23** 10; **24** 400; **59** 20
The Canadian Broadcasting Corporation (CBC), 37 55–58

Canadian Electrolytic Zinc Ltd., **64** 297
Canadian Football League, **12** 457
Canadian Forest Products. *See* Canfor Corporation.
Canadian Freightways, Ltd., **48** 113
Canadian General Electric Co., **8** 544–45
Canadian Imperial Bank of Commerce, II 244–46; **7** 26–28; **10** 8; **32** 12, 14; **61** 47–51 (upd.)
Canadian Industrial Alcohol Company Limited, **14** 141
Canadian Keyes Fibre Company, Limited of Nova Scotia, **9** 305
Canadian National Railway Company, 6 359–62; **71 82–88 (upd.)**
Canadian Niagara Power Company, **47** 137
Canadian Odeon Theatres. *See* Cineplex Odeon Corporation.
Canadian Overseas Telecommunications Corporation, **25** 100
Canadian Pacific Limited, V 429–31; 8 544–46
Canadian Pacific Railway Limited, 45 78–83 (upd.)
Canadian Steel Foundries, Ltd., **39** 31
Canadian Telephones and Supplies. *See* British Columbia Telephone Company.
Canadian Tire Corporation, Limited, 71 89–93 (upd.)
Canadian Utilities Limited, 13 130–32; **56 53–56 (upd.)**
Canadian Vickers, **16** 76
Canal Bank, **11** 105
Canal Digital, **69** 344–46
Canal Electric Co., **14** 125–26
Canal Plus, III 48; **7** 392; **10** 195–97, 345, 347; **23** 476; **29** 369, 371; **31** 330; **33** 181; **34 83–86 (upd.)**
CanalSatellite, **29** 369, 371
CanAmera Foods, **7** 82
Canandaigua Brands, Inc., 34 87–91 (upd.). *See also* Constellation Brands, Inc.
Canandaigua Wine Company, Inc., 13 133–35
Cananwill, **III** 344
Canary Wharf Group Plc, 30 107–09
Canatom NPM Inc. *See* SNC-Lavalin Group Inc.
Candela Corporation, 48 87–89
Candie's, Inc., 31 81–84
Candle Corporation, 64 62–65
Candle Corporation of America. *See* Blyth Industries, Inc.
Candle-Lite Inc., **61** 172
Candlewood Hotel Company, Inc., 41 81–83
Candover Partners Limited, **70** 310
Candy SpA. *See* Arcor S.A.I.C.
Canfor Corporation, 17 540; **42 59–61**
Cannapp Pty Limited, **56** 155
Cannell Communications, **25** 418
Cannon Design, 63 90–92
Cannon Express, Inc., 53 80–82
Cannon Mills, Co., **9** 214–16
Cannondale Corporation, 16 494; **21** 88–90; **26** 183, 412
Canon Inc., III 120–21; **9** 251; **10** 23; **13** 482; **15** 150; **18 92–95 (upd.)**, 186, 341–42, 383, 386–87; **24** 324; **26** 213; **33** 13; **43** 152, 283–84
Canpotex Ltd., **18** 432
Canrad-Hanovia, **27** 57

Canstar Sports Inc., 15 396–97; **16** 79–81

Canteen Corp., **II** 679–80; **13** 321

Cantel Corp., **11** 184; **18** 32; **20** 76; **30** 388

Canterbury Park Holding Corporation, 42 62–65

Canterra Energy Ltd., **47** 180

Cantine Giorgio Lungarotti S.R.L., 67 88–90

Canton Railway Corp., **IV** 718; **38** 320

Cantor Fitzgerald Securities Corporation, **10** 276–78

CanWest Global Communications Corporation, 35 67–70; **39** 13

Canyon Cafes, **31** 41

Cap Gemini Ernst & Young, 37 59–61

Cap Rock Energy Corporation, 6 580; **46** 78–81

Capacity of Texas, Inc., **33** 105–06

CAPCO. See Central Area Power Coordination Group; Custom Academic Publishing Company.

Capco Energy, Inc., **33** 296

Capcom Co., **7** 396

Cape and Vineyard Electric Co., **14** 124–25

Cape Cod-Cricket Lane, Inc., **8** 289

Cape Cod Potato Chip Company, Inc., **41** 233

Cape PLC, **22** 49

Capel Incorporated, 45 84–86

Capezio/Ballet Makers Inc., 62 57–59

Capita Group PLC, 69 79–81

AB Capital & Investment Corporation, **6** 108; **23** 381

Capital Advisors, Inc., **22** 4

Capital Bank N.A., **16** 162

Capital Cities/ABC Inc., II 129–31; **III** 214; **11** 331; **15** 464; **18** 60, 62–63, 329; **30** 490; **42** 31, 33–34; **56** 119; **63** 433, 436. See also ABC, Inc.

Capital Concrete Pipe Company, **14** 250

Capital Controls Co., Inc. See Severn Trent PLC.

Capital Distributing Co., **21** 37

Capital Factors, Inc., **54** 387

Capital-Gazette Communications, Inc., **12** 302

Capital Grille, **19** 342

Capital Group, **26** 187

Capital Holding Corporation, III 216–19. See also Providian Financial Corporation.

Capital Life Insurance Company, **11** 482–83

Capital Management Services. See CB Commercial Real Estate Services Group, Inc.

Capital One Financial Corporation, 18 535; **52** 60–63

Capital Radio plc, 35 71–73; **39** 199

Capital Trust Corp., **17** 498

Capitalia S.p.A., 65 86–89

Capitol-EMI, **11** 557

Capitol Film + TV International, **IV** 591

Capitol Films, **25** 270

Capitol Pack, Inc., **13** 350

Capitol Printing Ink Company, **13** 227–28

Capitol Publishing, **13** 560

Capitol Transamerica Corporation, **60** 16

Capseals, Ltd., **8** 476

Capstar, **62** 119

CapStar Hotel Company, 21 91–93

Capstone Pharmacy of Delaware, Inc., **64** 27

Captain D's, LLC, 59 104–06

Car-lac Electronic Industrial Sales Inc., **9** 420

Car Toys, Inc., 67 91–93

Car-X, **10** 415

Caraco Pharmaceutical Laboratories Inc., **57** 345–46

Caradco, Inc., **45** 216

Caradon plc, 18 561; **20** 108–12 (upd.). See also Novar plc.

Carando Foods, **7** 174–75

Carat Group. See Aegis Group plc.

Caratti Sports, Ltd., **26** 184

Caraustar Industries, Inc., 19 76–78; **44** 63–67 (upd.)

Caravali, **13** 493–94

Caravelle Foods, **21** 500

The Carbide/Graphite Group, Inc., 40 82–84

Carbo PLC, 67 94–96 (upd.)

Carbocol, **IV** 417

Carboline Co., **8** 455

CarboMedics, **11** 458–60

Carbon Research Laboratories, **9** 517

Carbone Lorraine S.A., 33 88–90

La Carbonique, **23** 217, 219

Carborundum Company, 15 80–82. See also Carbo PLC.

Cardàpio, **29** 444

Cardell Corporation, **54** 239

Cardem Insurance Co., **III** 767; **22** 546

Cardiac Pacemakers, Inc., **11** 90; **11** 458; **22** 361

Cardinal Distributors Ltd., **II** 663

Cardinal Freight Carriers, Inc., **42** 365

Cardinal Health, Inc., 18 96–98; **50** 120–23 (upd.)

Cardinal Holdings Corporation, **65** 334

Cardiotronics Systems, Inc., **21** 47

Cardo AB, 49 156; **53** 83–85

Cardon-Phonocraft Company, **18** 492

Care Advantage, Inc., **25** 383

Care Group, **22** 276

Career Education Corporation, 45 87–89

Career Horizons Inc., **49** 265

CareerCom Corp., **25** 253

CareerStaff Unlimited Inc., **25** 455

Caremark International Inc., 10 143, 198–200; **33** 185

Caremark Rx, Inc., 54 42–45 (upd.)

Carenes, SA, **12** 377

CareScience, Inc. See Quovadx Inc.

CareTel, Inc., **53** 209

CareUnit, Inc., **15** 123

CareWise, Inc., **36** 365, 367–68

Carey Diversified LLC. See W.P. Carey & Co. LLC.

Carey International, Inc., 26 60–63

Carey-McFall Corp. See Springs Industries, Inc.

Carey Straw Mill, **12** 376

S.A. CARFUEL, **12** 152

Cargill, Incorporated, II 517, 616–18; **13** 136–38 (upd.), 186, 351; **18** 378, 380; **21** 290, 500; **22** 85, 426; **25** 332; **31** 17, 20; **40** 85–90 (upd.); **41** 306

Cargill Trust Co., **13** 467

Cargo Express, **16** 198

Cargo Furniture, **31** 436

Cargolux Airlines International S.A., 47 287; **49** 80–82

CARGOSUR. See Iberia.

Carhartt, Inc., 30 110–12

Caribiner International, Inc., 24 94–97

Caribou Coffee Company, Inc., 28 62–65

Carintusa Inc., **8** 271

Carisam International Corp., **29** 511

Caritas Internationalis, 72 57–59

Carl Allers Etablissement A/S, 72 60–62

Carl Ed. Meyer GmbH, **48** 119

Carl I. Brown and Company, **48** 178

Carl Karcher Enterprises, Inc., **19** 435; **46** 94

Carl Marks & Co., **11** 260–61

Carl-Zeiss-Stiftung, III 445–47, 583; **33** 218; **34** 92–97 (upd.)

Carl's Jr. See CKE Restaurants, Inc.

Carl's Superstores, **9** 452

Carlin Foods Corporation, **62** 50

Carlin Gold Mining Company, **7** 386–87

Carling O'Keefe Ltd., **I** 229, 254, 269, 438–39; **7** 183; **12** 337; **26** 305

Carlisa S.A. See Arcor S.A.I.C.

Carlisle Companies Incorporated, 8 80–82

Carlisle Memory Products, **14** 535

Carlon, **13** 304–06

Carlova, Inc., **21** 54

Carlsberg A/S, 9 99–101; **29** 83–85 (upd.)

Carlson Companies, Inc., 6 363–66; **22** 125–29 (upd.); **26** 147, 439–40; **27** 9, 11; **29** 200; **38** 387

Carlson Restaurants Worldwide, 69 82–85

Carlson Wagonlit Travel, 55 89–92

Carlton and United Breweries Ltd., I 228–29, 437–39; **7** 182–83. See also Foster's Group Limited

Carlton Cards Retail, Inc., **39** 87; **59** 34–35

Carlton Communications plc, 15 83–85; **50** 124–27 (upd.)

Carlton Foods Corporation, **57** 56–57

Carlton Investments L.P., **22** 514

The Carlyle Group, **11** 364; **14** 43; **16** 47; **21** 97; **30** 472; **43** 60; **49** 444

Carlyle Management Group, **63** 226

Carma Laboratories, Inc., 60 80–82

CarMax, Inc., **26** 410; **29** 120, 123; **55** 93–95; **65** 113

Carmeda AB, **10** 439

Carmichael Lynch Inc., 28 66–68

Carmike Cinemas, Inc., 14 86–88; **21** 362; **37** 62–65 (upd.)

Carmine's Prime Meats, Inc., **35** 84

Carnation Company, II 486–89, 518, 548; **7** 339, 383, 429; **10** 382; **28** 311; **61** 138

Carnaud Basse-Indre, **IV** 228

Carnaud MetalBox, **13** 190; **20** 111; **32** 125–26; **49** 295

Carnegie Brothers & Co., Ltd., **9** 407

Carnegie Corporation of New York, 35 74–77; **45** 403–05

Carnegie Foundation for the Advancement of Teaching, **12** 141

Carnegie Group, **41** 371–72

Carnival Corporation, 27 90–92 (upd.); **36** 194

Carnival Cruise Lines, Inc., 6 367–68; **21** 106; **22** 444–46, 470; **27** 27; **52** 297–98

Caro Produce and Institutional Foods, **31** 359–61

Carol's Shoe Corp., **22** 213

Carolco Pictures Inc., **III** 48; **10** 196

Carolina Biological Supply, **11** 424

Carolina Coach Co., **13** 397–98

Carolina Coin Caterers Corporation, **10** 222

Carolina Energies, Inc., **6** 576

Carolina First Corporation, 31 85–87

Carolina Freight Corporation, 6 369–72

Carolina Paper Board Corporation. *See* Caraustar Industries, Inc.

Carolina Power & Light Company, V 564–66; 23 104–07 (upd.)

Carolina Telephone and Telegraph Company, 10 201–03

Carolinas Capital Funds Group, **29** 132

Carolinas-Virginia Nuclear Power Association, **27** 130

Carpenter Investment and Development Corporation, **31** 279

Carpenter Technology Corporation, 13 139–41

CarpetMAX, **25** 320

Carpets International Plc., **8** 270–71

Carpro, Inc., **65** 127

CARQUEST Corporation, 26 348; **29 86–89**

Carr-Gottstein Foods Co., 17 77–80

Carr-Lowrey Glass Co., **13** 40

Carrabba's Italian Grill, **12** 373–75

CarrAmerica Realty Corporation, 56 57–59

Carre Orban International, **34** 248

Carrefour SA, 10 204–06; 27 93–96 (upd.); **64 66–69** (upd.)

Carrera-Optyl Group, **54** 319–20

Carrera y Carrera, **52** 147, 149

The Carriage House Companies, Inc., 55 96–98

Carriage Services, Inc., 37 66–68

Carrier Access Corporation, 44 68–73

Carrier Corporation, 7 70–73; 13 507; **22** 6; **26** 4; **29** 216; **67** 239; **69 86–91** (upd.)

Carrington Laboratories, **33** 282

Carrington Viyella, **44** 105

Carroll County Electric Company, **6** 511

Carroll Reed Ski Shops, Inc., **10** 215

Carroll's Foods, Inc., 7 477; **22** 368; **43** 382; **46 82–85**

Carrols Corporation, **72** 344

Carrows, **27** 16, 19

Carry Machine Supply, Inc., **18** 513

The Carsey-Werner Company, L.L.C., 37 69–72

Carsmart.com, **47** 34

Carso Global Telecom S.A. de C.V., 34 362

Carson, Inc., 31 88–90; 46 278

Carson Pirie Scott & Company, II 669; **9** 142; **15** 86–88; **19** 324, 511–12; **41** 343–44; **63** 147

Carson Water Company, **19** 411

Carswell Insurance Group. *See* Plamer & Cay, Inc.

CART. *See* Championship Auto Racing Teams, Inc.

Carte Blanche, **9** 335

Cartem Wilco Group Inc., **59** 350

CarTemps USA. *See* Republic Industries, Inc.

Carter & Sons Freightways, Inc., **57** 278

Carter Hawley Hale Stores, V 29–32; 8 160; **12** 356; **15** 88; **16** 466; **17** 43, 523; **18** 488; **25** 177; **63** 259–60

Carter Holt Harvey Ltd., IV 280; **15** 229; **19** 155; **69** 142–43; **70 41–44**

Carter Lumber Company, 45 90–92

Carter Oil Company, **11** 353

Carter-Wallace, Inc., 8 83–86; 38 122–26 (upd.)

Carteret Savings Bank, **III** 263–64; **10** 340

Carterphone, **22** 17

Cartier, **27** 329, 487–89

Cartier Monde, IV 93; **29 90–92**

Cartier Refined Sugars Ltd., **II** 662–63

Cartiera F.A. Marsoni, **IV** 587

Cartiers Superfoods, **II** 678

Cartocor S.A. *See* Arcor S.A.I.C.

Carton Titan S.A. de C.V., **37** 176–77

Cartotech, Inc., **33** 44

Carvel Corporation, 35 78–81

Carver Pump Co., **19** 36

Cary-Davis Tug and Barge Company. *See* Puget Sound Tug and Barge Company.

CASA. *See* Construcciones Aeronautics S.A.

Casa Bancária Almeida e Companhia. *See* Banco Bradesco S.A.

Casa Cuervo, S.A. de C.V., 31 91–93

Casa Ley, S.A. de C.V., **24** 416

Casa Saba. *See* Grupo Casa Saba, S.A. de C.V.

Casablanca Records, **23** 390

Casalee, Inc., **48** 406

Casarotto Security, **24** 510

Cascade Communications Corp., **16** 468; **20** 8; **24** 50

Cascade Corporation, 65 90–92

Cascade Fertilizers Ltd., **25** 232

Cascade General, Inc., 65 93–95

Cascade Natural Gas Corporation, 6 568; **9 102–04**

Cascade Steel Rolling Mills, Inc., **19** 380–81

Cascades Inc., 71 94–96

CasChem, Inc. *See* Cambrex Corporation.

Casco Northern Bank, 14 89–91

Casden Properties, **49** 26

Case Corporation. *See* CNH Global N.V.

Case Technologies, Inc., **11** 504

Casey's General Stores, Inc., 19 79–81

Cash & Go, Inc., **57** 139

Cash America International, Inc., 20 113–15; 33 4; **61 52–55** (upd.)

Cash Wise Foods and Liquor, **30** 133

Casino, **10** 205; **23** 231; **26** 160; **27** 93–94

Casino America, Inc. *See* Isle of Capri Casinos, Inc.

Casino Frozen Foods, Inc., **16** 453

Casino Guichard-Perrachon S.A., 22 515; **37** 23; **54** 306–07; **59 107–10** (upd.)

Casino USA, **16** 452

Casinos International Inc., **21** 300

CASIO Computer Co., Ltd., III 448–49, 455; **10** 57; **16 82–84** (upd.); **21** 123; **26** 18; **40 91–95** (upd.)

Casite Intraco LLC, **56** 156–57

Caspian Pipeline Consortium, **47** 75

Cassa Risparmio Firenze, **50** 410

Cassandra Group, **42** 272

Cassco Ice & Cold Storage, Inc., **21** 534–35

CAST Inc., **18** 20; **43** 17

Cast-Matic Corporation, **16** 475

Castel MAC S.p.A., **68** 136

Castex, **13** 501

Castings, Inc., **29** 98

Castle & Cooke, Inc., II 490–92; 9 175–76; **10** 40; **20 116–19** (upd.); **24** 115. *See also* Dole Food Company, Inc.

Castle Cement, **31** 400

Castle Communications plc, **17** 13

Castle Harlan Investment Partners III, **36** 468, 471

Castle Rock Entertainment, **57** 35

Castle Rock Pictures, **23** 392

Castle Rubber Co., **17** 371

Castlemaine Tooheys, **10** 169–70

Castleton Thermostats. *See* Strix Ltd.

Castorama S.A. *See* Groupe Castorama-Dubois Investissements.

Castro Convertibles. *See* Krause's Furniture, Inc.

Castrorama, **10** 205; **27** 95

Casual Corner Group, Inc., 25 121; **43 96–98; 52** 229

Casual Male Retail Group, Inc., 52 64–66

Casual Wear Española, S.A., **64** 91

Caswell-Massey Co. Ltd., 51 66–69

CAT Scale Company, **49** 329–30

Catalina Lighting, Inc., 43 99–102 (upd.)

Catalina Marketing Corporation, 18 99–102

Catalogue Marketing, Inc., **17** 232

Catalyst Telecom, **29** 414–15

Catalytica Energy Systems, Inc., 44 74–77

Catalytica Pharmaceuticals Inc., **56** 95

Catamaran Cruisers, **29** 442

Catamount Petroleum Corp., **17** 121

Cataract, Inc., **34** 373

CATCO. *See* Crowley All Terrain Corporation.

Catellus Development Corporation, 24 98–101; 27 88

Caterair International Corporation, **16** 396

Caterpillar Inc., III 450–53; 15 89–93 (upd.); **63 93–99** (upd.); **69** 167, 169

Cathay Insurance Co., **III** 221; **14** 109

Cathay Pacific Airways Limited, 6 78–80; 18 114–15; **34 98–102** (upd.)

Catherines Stores Corporation, 15 94–97; 38 129

Cathodic Protection Services Co., **14** 325

Catholic Digest, **49** 48

Catholic Order of Foresters, 24 102–05

CatiCentre Ltd. Co, **48** 224

Cato Corporation, 14 92–94

Catteau S.A., **24** 475

Catterton Partners, **62** 137

Cattleman's, Inc., 20 120–22

Cattles plc, 58 54–56

Cattybrook Brick Company, **14** 249

CATV, **10** 319

Caudill Rowlett Scott. *See* CRSS Inc.

Caudle Engraving, **12** 471

Cavalcade Holdings, Inc., **53** 146

Cavallo Pipeline Company, **11** 441

Cavco Industries, Inc., 65 96–99

Cavendish International Holdings, **IV** 695

Cavenham Ltd., **7** 202–03; **28** 163

Caves Altovisto, **22** 344

Caves de Roquefort, **19** 51; **24** 445

Caviton Ltd. *See* Harvey Norman.

Caxton Superannuation Fund Trustee Limited, **70** 43

Cazenove Group plc, 72 63–65

CB&I, **7** 76–77
CB&Q. *See* Chicago, Burlington and Quincy Railroad Company.
CB&T. *See* Synovus Financial Corp.
CB Commercial Real Estate Services Group, Inc., 21 94–98
CB International Finance S.A.R.L. *See* Constellation Brands, Inc.
CB Richard Ellis Group, Inc., 70 45–50 (upd.)
CBE Technologies Inc., **39** 346
CBI Industries, Inc., 7 74–77; 22 228; 48 323
CBN. *See* The Christian Broadcasting Network, Inc.
CBN Cable Network, **13** 279–81
CBN Satellite Services, **13** 279
CBOT. *See* Chicago Board of Trade.
CBPI. *See* Companhia Brasileira de Petróleo Ipiranga.
CBR-HCI Construction Materials Corp., **31** 253
CBRL Group, Inc., 35 82–85 (upd.)
CBS Corporation, II 132–34; III 188; IV 623, 652, 675, 703; 6 157–60 (upd.); 11 327; 12 75, 561; 16 201–02; 17 150, 182; 19 210, 426, 428; 21 24; 24 516–17; 25 330, 418; 26 102; 28 69–73 (upd.); 30 269, 272; 36 326; 43 170–71. *See also* CBS Television Network.
CBS.MarketWatch.com, **49** 290
CBS Musical Instruments, **16** 201–02; **43** 170–71
CBS Radio Group, **37** 192; **48** 217
CBS Records, **22** 194; **23** 33; **28** 419
CBS Television Network, 66 44–48 (upd.)
CBSI. *See* Complete Business Solutions, Inc.
CBW Inc., **42** 129
CC Beverage Corporation, **48** 97
cc:Mail, Inc., **25** 300
CCA. *See* Container Corporation of America; Corrections Corporation of America.
CCA Industries, Inc., 53 86–89
CCAir Inc., **11** 300
CCB Financial Corp., **33** 293
CCC Franchising Corporation. *See* Primedex Health Systems, Inc.
CCG. *See* The Clark Construction Group, Inc.
CCH Computax, **7** 93–94
CCH Inc., 7 93; 14 95–97; 33 461
CCI Asia-Pacific Ltd., **27** 362
CCI Electronique, **10** 113; **50** 43
CCL Industries, Ltd., **15** 129
CCM Inc. *See* The Hockey Company.
CCM Sport Maska, Inc., **15** 396
CCN Group Ltd., **45** 154
CCP Insurance, Inc., **10** 248
CCR, Inc. *See* Rica Foods, Inc.
CCS Automation Systems Inc., **I** 124
CCT. *See* Crowley Caribbean Transport.
CD Titles, Inc., **22** 409
CDB Infotek Inc. *See* ChoicePoint Inc.
CDC. *See* Canada Development Corporation; Control Data Corporation.
CDC Corporation, 71 97–99
CDG Books Canada Inc., **27** 224
CDI. *See* Centre de Dechets Industriels Group.
CDI Corporation, 6 139–41; 54 46–49 (upd.)

CDL. *See* City Developments Limited.
CDMS. *See* Credit and Data Marketing Services.
CDR. *See* Consortium de Realisation.
CDR International, **13** 228
CDS Holding Corp., **22** 475
CDW Computer Centers, Inc., 16 85–87; 52 67–70 (upd.)
CDX Audio Development, Inc., **18** 208
CE Consulting, **51** 17
CE-Minerals, **IV** 109
CEAG AG, **23** 498
CEAT, **20** 263; **71** 210–11
Ceatech Engineering, **68** 143
Cébé, **61** 191–92
CEC Entertainment, Inc., 31 94–98 (upd.)
Cecil Gee, **51** 253
Ceco Doors, **8** 544–46
Ceco Industries, Inc. *See* Robertson-Ceco Corporation.
CeCorr Inc., **47** 149
CECOS International, Inc. *See* Browning-Ferris Industries, Inc.
Cedar Fair, L.P., 22 130–32
Cedarapids, Inc., **11** 413; **38** 374, 376; **40** 432
Cedec S.A., **14** 43
Cederroth International AB, **8** 17; **36** 25–26
CEDIS, **12** 153
Cedric Chivers, **35** 243–44
Cegedim S.A., **70** 72
Cegetel SA, **38** 300
CEIR, **10** 255
Celadon Group Inc., 30 113–16
Celanese Corp., I 317–19, 347; 19 192; 54 50, 52. *See also* Hoechst Celanese Corporation.
Celanese Mexicana, S.A. de C.V., 54 50–52
Celebrate Express, Inc., 70 51–53
Celebrity Entertainment, Inc., **27** 43
Celebrity, Inc., 22 133–35, 472
Celeron Corporation, **20** 258, 262–63
Celestial Farms, **13** 383
Celestial Seasonings, Inc., 16 88–91; 49 336. *See also* The Hain Celestial Group, Inc.
Celestica Inc., **65** 283–84
Celestron International, **41** 262–63
Celfor Tool Company. *See* Clark Equipment Company.
Celgene Corporation, 67 97–100
Celite Corporation, **7** 291; **10** 43, 45; **60** 16
Celite Mineracao do Nordeste Ltda, **51** 196
Cell Technology, Inc. *See* Air Methods Corporation.
Cell-Tel Monitoring, Inc., **46** 386
Cella Italian Wines, **10** 181
CellAccess Technology, Inc., **25** 162
CellLife International, **49** 369
Cellnet Data Systems, **11** 547; **22** 65
Cellstar Corporation, **18** 74
Cellu-Products Co., **14** 430
CellularOne. *See* Rural Cellular Corporation.
CellularVision, **13** 399
Celluloid Studios, **63** 422
Cellulose & Specialties, **8** 434
Cellulose du Pin, **19** 226–27
Celotex Corporation, **III** 766–67; **22** 545
Celsius Energy Company, **6** 569
Celtrion, **62** 221

Celulosa Arauco y Constitución S.A., **69** 142
Celulosa de Levante, S.A., **68** 258
Cement Products, **46** 196
Cement Roadstone Holdings. *See* CRH PLC.
Cementhai Chemicals Co., **56** 322
Cementi Centro Sud Spa, **70** 343
Cementia, **III** 705
Cementos Apasco, S.A. de C.V., **51** 29
Cementos de Acapulco, S.A. de C.V., **51** 28
Cementos Portland Moctezuma, **21** 261
Cementos Veracruz, S.A. de C.V., **51** 27, 29
Cementownia Chelm, **31** 398, 400
CEMEX S.A. de C.V., 20 123–26; 51 27–28; 59 111–16 (upd.)
CEMIG. *See* Companhia Energética De Minas Gerais S.A.
Cemp Investments Ltd., **16** 79–80
Cemsto, **13** 545
CenCall Communications, **10** 433
Cenco, Inc., **10** 262–63; **35** 135
Cencor, **25** 432
Cencosud S.A., **71** 144
Cencosud S.A., 69 92–94
Cendant Corporation, 41 363; 44 78–84 (upd.); 48 234–35; 53 274–75; 57 380; 58 77; 61 267
Cenex Cooperative, **21** 342
Cenex Harvest States Cooperative. *See* CHS Inc.
Cenex Inc., **19** 160
Centaur Communications, **43** 204, 206
Centel Corporation, 6 312–15, 593; 9 106, 480; 10 203; 14 258; 16 318; 17 7; 50 39
Centennial Communications Corporation, 39 74–76
Centennial Technologies Inc., **48** 369
Center Co., Ltd., **48** 182
Center of Insurance, **51** 170
Center Rental & Sales Inc., **28** 387
Centerior Energy Corporation, V 567–68
CenterMark Properties, **57** 156
Centerpulse AG, **68** 362
Centerra Corporation, **24** 79
Centertel, **18** 33
Centex Corporation, 8 87–89, 461; 11 302; 23 327; 29 93–96 (upd.)
Centocor Inc., 14 98–100; 36 306
CenTrade, a.s., **64** 73
Central Alloy Steel Corporation. *See* Republic Engineered Steels, Inc.
Central and South West Corporation, V 569–70; 21 197–98; 45 21
Central Arizona Light & Power Company, **6** 545
Central Asia Gas Pipeline Ltd, **24** 522
Central Bank of Scotland, **10** 337
Central Computer Systems Inc., **11** 65
Central Detallista, S.A. de C.V., **12** 154; **16** 453
Central Electric & Gas Company. *See* Centel Corporation.
Central Electric and Telephone Company, Inc. *See* Centel Corporation.
Central Elevator Co., **19** 111
Central European Media Enterprises Ltd., 61 56–59
Central Fiber Products Company, **12** 376
Central Florida Press, **23** 101

Central Freight Lines, Inc., **53** 249
Central Garden & Pet Company, 23
    108–10; **58** 57–60 (upd.)
Central Hudson Gas And Electricity
    Corporation, 6 458–60
Central Illinois Public Service Company.
    See CIPSCO Inc.
Central Independent Television, 7
    78–80; **15** 84; **23** 111–14 (upd.); **50**
    125
Central Indiana Power Company, **6** 556
Central Investment Corp., **12** 184
Central Japan Railway Company, 43
    103–06
Central Maine Power, 6 461–64; **14** 126
Central Mining and Investment Corp., **IV**
    23, 79, 95–96, 524, 565
Central National Bank, **9** 475
Central National Bank & Trust Co., **13** 467
Central Nebraska Packing, **10** 250
Central Newspapers, Inc., 10 207–09
Central Ohio Mobile Power Wash. *See*
    MPW Industrial Services, Inc.
Central Pacific Railroad, **13** 372
Central Park Bank of Buffalo, **11** 108
Central Parking Corporation, 18 103–05
Central Penn National Corp., **11** 295
Central Plains Steel Company. *See*
    Reliance Steel & Aluminum Company.
Central Point Software, **10** 509
Central Public Utility Corp., **13** 397
Central Research Laboratories, **22** 194
Central Savings and Loan, **10** 339
Central Solvents & Chemicals Company, **8**
    100
Central Songs, **22** 193
Central Soya Company, Inc., 7 81–83;
    31 20; **36** 185, 187
Central Sprinkler Corporation, 29
    97–99
Central States Indemnity, **18** 62
Central Supply Company. *See* Granite
    Rock Company.
Central Telephone & Utilities Corporation.
    See Centel Corporation.
Central Textile, **16** 36
Central Trust Co., **11** 110
Central Union Telephone Company, **14**
    251, 257
Central Vermont Public Service
    Corporation, 54 53–56
Central West Public Service Company. *See*
    Centel Corporation.
Centralab Inc., **13** 398
Centrale Verzorgingsdienst Cotrans N.V.,
    12 443
Centran Corp., **9** 475
Centre de Dechets Industriels Group, **IV**
    296; **19** 226
Centre de Diffusion de l'Édition. *See*
    Éditions Gallimard.
Centre Investissements et Loisirs, **48** 107
Centre Partners Management LLC, **18** 355;
    24 482; **70** 337
Centrepoint Properties Ltd., **54** 116–17
Centric Group, **69** 153
Centrica plc, 29 100–05 (upd.)
Centron DPL Company, Inc., **25** 171
Centronics Corp., **16** 192
Centros Commerciales Pryca, **23** 246, 248
Centrum Communications Inc., **11** 520
CenTrust Federal Savings, **10** 340
Centura Software, **10** 244
Centuri Corporation, 54 57–59

Centurion Brick, **14** 250
Century Aluminum Company, 52 71–74
Century Bakery. *See* Dawn Food Products,
    Inc.
Century Brewing Company. *See* Rainier
    Brewing Company.
Century Business Services, Inc., 52
    75–78
Century Casinos, Inc., 53 90–93
Century Cellular Network, Inc., **18** 74
Century Communications Corp., 10
    210–12; **52** 9
Century Data Systems, Inc., **13** 127
Century Electric Company, **13** 273
Century Finance, **25** 432
Century Hutchinson, Ltd., **13** 429
Century Manufacturing Company, **26** 363
Century Papers, Inc., **16** 387
Century Savings Assoc. of Kansas, **II** 420
Century Supply Corporation, **39** 346
Century Telephone Enterprises, Inc., 9
    105–07; **54** 60–63 (upd.)
Century Theatres, Inc., 31 99–101
Century Tool Co., **III** 569; **20** 360
Century 21 Real Estate, **II** 679; **11** 292; **21**
    97; **25** 444; **59** 345; **61** 267
Century Wood Door Ltd., **63** 268
CenturyTel. *See* Century Telephone
    Enterprises, Inc.
Cenveo Inc., 71 100–104 (upd.)
CEP Industrie, **55** 79
CEPA. *See* Consolidated Electric Power
    Asia.
CEPAM, **21** 438
CEPCO. *See* Chugoku Electric Power
    Company Inc.
Cephalon, Inc., 45 93–96
CEPSA. *See* Compañía Española de
    Petroleos S.A.
Cera Trading Co. *See* Toto Ltd.
Ceradyne, Inc., 65 100–02
Ceramconsult AG, **51** 196
Ceramesh, **11** 361
Ceramic Art Company, **12** 312
Ceramic Supply Company, **8** 177
Ceramic Tile International, Inc., **53** 176
Cerberus Group, **69** 261
Cerberus Limited. *See* Elektrowatt AG.
Cerco S.A., **62** 51
Cereal and Fruit Products, **32** 519
Cereal Industries, **II** 466
Cereal Packaging, Ltd., **13** 294; **50** 294
Cereal Partners Worldwide, **10** 324; **13**
    294; **36** 234, 237; **50** 295
Cereol SA, **36** 185; **62** 51
CERES, **55** 178
Cerestar, **36** 185, 187
Ceresucre, **36** 185
Ceridian Corporation, **10** 257; **38** 58; **71**
    262
Cerner Corporation, **16** 92–94
Cerro de Pasco Corp., **40** 411
Cerro E.M.S. Limited. *See* The Marmon
    Group, Inc.
CertainTeed Corporation, 16 8; **19** 58;
    35 86–89
Certanium Alloys and Research Co., **9** 419
Certegy, Inc., 63 100–03
Certified Grocers of Florida, Inc., **15** 139
Certified Laboratories, **8** 385
Certified TV and Appliance Company, **9**
    120
Certus International Corp., **10** 509
Cerulean, **51** 249, 251

Cerus, **23** 492
Cerveceria Cuahtémoc Moctezuma, **25** 281
Cerveceria Cuauhtemoc, **19** 10
Cerveceria Moctezuma, **23** 170
Cerveceria Polar, I 230–31. *See also*
    Empresas Polar SA.
Cerveceria y Malteria Quilmes S.A.I.C.A.
    y G., **70** 62
Ceska Nezavisla Televizni Spolecnost, **61**
    56
Ceská Sporitelna a.s. *See* Erste Bank der
    Osterreichischen Sparkassen AG
Ceské aerolinie, a.s., 66 49–51
Cesky Telecom, a.s., 64 70–73
Cessna Aircraft Company, 8 49–51,
    90–93, 313–14; **26** 117; **27** 97–101
    (upd.); **34** 431, 433; **36** 190; **44** 309
CET. *See* Compagnie Européenne de
    Télésecurité.
CET 21, **61** 56, 58
Cetelem S.A., 21 99–102
Cetus Corp., **III** 53; **7** 427; **10** 78, 214; **41**
    201; **50** 193
CF&I Steel Corporation, **8** 135
CF AirFreight, **6** 390; **25** 149
CF Braun, **13** 119
CF Holding Corporation, **12** 71
CFC Investment Company, **16** 104
CFM. *See* Compagnie Française du
    Méthane.
CFP. *See* Compagnie Française des
    Pétroles.
CFR Corporation. *See* Tacony Corporation.
CFS Continental, Inc., **II** 675; **26** 504
CG&E. *See* Cincinnati Gas & Electric
    Company.
CGE. *See* Alcatel Alsthom.
CGIP, **57** 380
CGM. *See* Compagnie Générale Maritime.
CGR Management Corporation, **51** 85
CH Mortgage Company I Ltd., **58** 84
Chace Precision Metals, Inc., **29** 460–61
Chaco Energy Corporation. *See* Texas
    Utilities Company.
Chadbourne & Parke, 36 109–12
Chadwick's of Boston, Ltd., 27 348; **29**
    106–08
Chalet Suisse International, Inc., **13** 362
Chalk Line Productions, Inc., **58** 124
Chalk's Ocean Airways. *See* Flying Boat,
    Inc.
Challenge Corp. Ltd. *See* Fletcher
    Challenge Ltd.
Challenger Airlines, **22** 219
Challenger Minerals Inc., **9** 267
Challenger Series, **55** 312
Challice, **71** 238
The Chalone Wine Group, Ltd., 36
    113–16
Chamberlain Group, Ltd., **23** 82
Chambers Corporation, **8** 298; **17** 548–49
Chambon Offshore International, **60** 149
Chambosse Brokerage Co., **29** 33
Champ Industries, Inc., **22** 15
Champalimaud, **36** 63
Champcork–Rolhas de Champanhe SA, **48**
    118
Champion Engineering Co., **III** 582
Champion Enterprises, Inc., 17 81–84;
    22 207
Champion Forge Co., **41** 366
Champion, Inc., **8** 459; **12** 457
Champion Industries, Inc., 28 74–76

Champion International Corporation,
III 215; IV 263–65, 334; **12** 130; **15**
229; **18** 62; **20** 127–30 (upd.); **22** 352;
26 444; **47** 189, 191
Champion Modular Restaurant Company,
Inc. *See* Checkers Drive-Up Restaurants
Inc.
Champion Productions, **56** 74
Champion Products Inc., **27** 194
Champion Spark Plug Co., **II** 17; **III** 593
Championship Auto Racing Teams, Inc.,
37 73–75
Champlin Petroleum Company, **10** 83
Champps Americana, **27** 480–82
Champs Sports. *See* Venator Group Inc.
Chancellor Beacon Academies, Inc., 53
94–97
Chancellor Media Corporation, 24
106–10; 35 247
Chancery Law Publishing Ltd., **17** 272
Chandeleur Homes, Inc., **17** 83
The Chandris Group, **11** 377
Chanel SA, 12 57–59; **23** 241; **49** 83–86
(upd.)
Changchun Terumo Medical Products Co.
Ltd., **48** 395
Channel Master Corporation, **15** 134
Channel One Communications Corp., **22**
442
Channel Tunnel Group, **13** 206
Chansam Investments, **23** 388
Chantex Inc., **18** 519
Chantiers de l'Atlantique, **9** 9
Chaparral Steel Co., 8 522–24; **13**
142–44; **18** 379; **19** 380
Chapman Printing Company. *See*
Champion Industries, Inc.
Chapman Valve Manufacturing Company,
8 135
Chappel Music, **23** 389
Chapters Campus Bookstores Company, **58**
187
Chapters Inc., **62** 153
Charan Industries Inc., **18** 519
Charan Toy Co., Inc., **18** 519
Chargeurs International, 6 373–75, 379;
20 79; **21** 103–06 (upd.); **29** 369, 371
Charise Charles Ltd., **9** 68
Charles B. Perkins Co., **II** 667; **24** 461
Charles Barker, plc, **25** 91
Charles D. Burnes Co., Inc. *See* The
Holson Burnes Group, Inc.
Charles E. Smith Residential Realty Inc.,
49 29
Charles Huston & Sons, **14** 323
Charles Krug Winery, **50** 387
Charles M. Schulz Creative Associates, **39**
95
The Charles Machine Works, Inc., 64
74–76
Charles of the Ritz Group Ltd., **64** 334
Charles Phillips & Co. Ltd., **II** 677
Charles R. McCormick Lumber Company,
12 407
Charles Revson Inc. *See* Revlon Inc.
Charles River Laboratories
International, Inc., 25 55; **42** 66–69
The Charles Schwab Corporation, II
228; **8** 94–96; **18** 552; **22** 52; **26** 64–67
(upd.); 34 407; **38** 430; **59** 75
Charles Scribner's Sons, **7** 166
The Charles Stark Draper Laboratory,
Inc., 35 90–92
Charlesbank Capital Partners LLC, **44** 54

Charleston Consolidated Railway, Gas and
Electric Company, **6** 574
Charley Brothers, **II** 669
Charley's Eating & Drinking Saloon, **20** 54
Charlie Browns, **24** 269–70
Charlotte Russe Holding, Inc., 35 93–96
Charming Shoppes, Inc., 8 97–98; **38**
127–29; **39** 287, 289; **64** 232
Charoen Pokphand Group, 62 60–63
Charrington United Breweries, **38** 76
Chart House Enterprises, Inc., II
613–14; **17** 70, 71, 85–88; **56** 46
Chart Industries, Inc., 21 107–09
Charter Club, **9** 315
Charter Communications, Inc., 33 91–94
Charter Consolidated, **IV** 23, 119–20; **16**
293; **49** 234
Charter Corp., **III** 254; **14** 460
Charter Golf, Inc. *See* Ashworth, Inc.
Charter Medical Corporation, **31** 356
Charter National Life Insurance Company,
11 261
Charter Oak Capital Partners, **58** 88
Charter Oil Co., **II** 620; **12** 240
Charterhouse Japhet, **24** 269
ChartHouse International Learning
Corporation, 49 87–89
Chartwell Associates, **9** 331
Chartwell Investments, **44** 54
Chartwell Land plc, **V** 106; **24** 266, 269
Chas. H. Tompkins Co., **16** 285–86
Chas. Levy Company LLC, 60 83–85
Chase Drier & Chemical Co., **8** 177
The Chase Manhattan Corporation, II
247–49; III 248; **9** 124; **10** 61; **13**
145–48 (upd.), 476; **14** 48, 103; **15**
38–39; **16** 460; **17** 498; **23** 482; **36** 358;
46 316. *See* J.P. Morgan Chase & Co.
Chase National Bank, **25** 114
Chaston Medical & Surgical Products, **13**
366
Chateau Communities, Inc., 37 76–79
Chateau St. Jean, **22** 80
Chateau Souverain, **22** 80
Chateau Ste. Michelle Winery, **42** 245, 247
Chateaux St. Jacques, **24** 307
Chatham Steel Corporation. *See* Reliance
Steel & Aluminum Company.
Chatham Technologies Inc., **38** 189
Chatillon. *See* John Chatillon & Sons Inc.
Chattanooga Gas Company, Inc., **6** 577
Chattanooga Gas Light Company, **6** 448;
23 30
Chattanooga Medicine Company. *See*
Chattem, Inc.
Chattem, Inc., 17 89–92
Chatto, Virago, Bodley Head & Jonathan
Cape, Ltd., **13** 429; **31** 376
Chautauqua Airlines, Inc., 38 130–32
CHC Helicopter Corporation, 67 101–03
Check Express, **33** 4–5
Check Point Software Technologies Ltd.,
20 238
Checker Auto Parts. *See* CSK Auto
Corporation.
Checker Holding, **10** 370
Checker Motors Corp., **10** 369
Checkers Drive-Up Restaurants Inc., 14
452; **16** 95–98; **46** 98
CheckFree Corporation, **22** 522
Checkpoint Systems, Inc., 39 77–80
Checkport Schweiz AG. *See* Swissport
International Ltd.
The Cheesecake Factory Inc., 17 93–96

Cheetham Salt Ltd., **62** 307
Chef Boyardee, **10** 70; **50** 538
Chef Francisco, **13** 383
Chelan Power Company, **6** 596
Chelsea GCA Realty, Inc., **27** 401
Chelsea Milling Company, 29 109–11
Chelsfield PLC, 67 104–06
Cheltenham & Gloucester PLC, 61
60–62
Chem-Nuclear Systems, Inc., **9** 109–10
Chemcentral Corporation, 8 99–101
Chemdal Corp., **13** 34; **59** 31
Chemed Corporation, 13 149–50; **15**
409–11; **16** 386–87; **49** 307–08; **61** 314
Chemetron Process Equipment, Inc., **8** 545
Chemex Pharmaceuticals, Inc., **8** 63; **27** 69
Chemfab Corporation, 35 97–101
ChemFirst, Inc., **27** 316
Chemgas Holding BV, **41** 340
Chemgrout, **26** 42
Chemi-Trol Chemical Co., 16 99–101
Chemical Banking Corporation, II 234,
250–52, 254; **9** 124, 361; **12** 15, 31; **13**
49, 147, 411; **14** 101–04 (upd.); **15** 39;
21 138; **26** 453; **38** 253
Chemical Grouting Co. Ltd., **51** 179
Chemical Process Co., **7** 308
Chemical Products Company, **13** 295
Chemical Waste Management, Inc., 9
108–10; 11 435–36
Chemicon International, Inc., **63** 353
Chemie Linz, **16** 439
Cheminor Drugs Limited, **59** 168
Chemische Werke Hüls GmbH. *See* Hüls
A.G.
Chemise Lacoste, **9** 157
ChemLawn, **13** 199; **23** 428, 431; **34** 153
Chemmar Associates, Inc., **8** 271
Chemonics Industries–Fire-Trol, **17**
161–62
Chemonics International–Consulting, **17**
161–62
Chempump, **8** 135
Chemquest Sdn Bhd, **57** 292, 294–95
Cheney Bigelow Wire Works, **13** 370
CHEP Pty Ltd., **42** 50
Cherokee Inc., 18 106–09
Cherry-Burrell Process Equipment, **8**
544–45
Cherry Hill Cheese, **7** 429
Cherry Lane Music Publishing
Company, Inc., 62 64–67
Cherry-Levis Co., **26** 172
Chesapeake and Ohio Railroad. *See* CSX
Corporation.
Chesapeake Corporation, 8 102–04; **10**
540; **25** 44; **30** 117–20 (upd.)
Chesapeake Microwave Technologies, Inc.,
32 41
Chesapeake Paperboard Company, **44** 66
Chesapeake Utilities Corporation, 56
60–62
Chesebrough-Pond's USA, Inc., 8
105–07; **9** 319; **17** 224–25; **22** 123
Chessington World of Adventures, **55** 378
Chester Engineers, **10** 412
Cheung Kong (Holdings) Limited, IV
693–95; **18** 252; **20** 131–34 (upd.); **23**
278, 280; **49** 199. *See also* Hutchison
Whampoa Ltd.
Chevignon, **44** 296
Chevrolet, **9** 17; **19** 221, 223; **21** 153; **26**
500
Chevron U.K. Ltd., **15** 352

ChevronTexaco Corporation, IV 385–87;19 82–85 (upd.); 47 70–76 (upd.), 343; 63 104, 113

Chevy Chase Savings Bank, 13 439

Chevy's, Inc., 33 140

Chevy's Mexican Restaurants, 27 226

ChexSystems, 22 181

Cheyenne Software, Inc., 12 60–62; 25 348–49

CHF. See Chase, Harris, Forbes.

Chi-Chi's Inc., 13 151–53; 14 195; 25 181; 51 70–73 (upd.)

CHI Construction Company, 58 84

Chiasso Inc., 53 98–100

Chiat/Day Inc. Advertising, 9 438; 11 49–52. See also TBWA/Chiat/Day.

Chiba Gas Co. Ltd., 55 375

Chiba Mitsukoshi Ltd., 56 242

Chibu Electric Power Company, **Incorporated, V 571–73**

Chic by H.I.S, Inc., 20 135–37; 54 403

Chicago and North Western Holdings **Corporation, 6 376–78**

Chicago and Southern Airlines Inc. See Delta Air Lines, Inc.

Chicago Bears Football Club, Inc., 33 95–97

Chicago Blackhawk Hockey Team, Inc. See Wirtz Corporation.

Chicago Board of Trade, 41 84–87

Chicago Bridge & Iron Company, 7 74–77

Chicago Cutlery, 16 234

Chicago Faucet Company, 49 161, 163

Chicago Flexible Shaft Company, 9 484

Chicago Heater Company, Inc., 8 135

Chicago Magnet Wire Corp., 13 397

Chicago Medical Equipment Co., 31 255

Chicago Motor Club, 10 126

Chicago Musical Instrument Company, 16 238

Chicago National League Ball Club, **Inc., 66 52–55**

Chicago O'Hare Leather Concessions Joint Venture Inc., 58 369

Chicago Pacific Corp., III 573; 12 251; 22 349; 23 244; 34 432

Chicago Pizza & Brewery, Inc., 44 85–88

Chicago Pneumatic Tool Co., III 427, 452; 7 480; 26 41; 28 40

Chicago Rawhide Manufacturing Company, 8 462–63

Chicago Rollerskate, 15 395

Chicago Screw Co., 12 344

Chicago Shipbuilding Company, 18 318

Chicago Sun-Times, Inc., 62 188

Chicago Times, 11 251

Chicago Title and Trust Co., 10 43–45

Chicago Title Corp., 54 107

Chicago Tribune. See Tribune Company.

Chichibu Concrete Industry Co. Ltd., 60 301

Chick-fil-A Inc., 23 115–18

Chicken of the Sea International, 24 **114–16 (upd.)**

Chico's FAS, Inc., 45 97–99; 60 348

Chicobel S.A. Belgique. See Leroux S.A.S.

Chief Auto Parts, II 661; 32 416

Chieftain Development Company, Ltd., 16 11

Child World Inc., 13 166; 18 524

Childers Products Co., 21 108

Children's Book-of-the-Month Club, 13 105

Children's Comprehensive Services, Inc., **42 70–72**

Children's Discovery Centers of America. See Knowledge Learning Corporation.

Children's Hospitals and Clinics, Inc., **54 64–67**

The Children's Place Retail Stores, Inc., **37 80–82**

Children's Record Guild, 13 105

Children's Television Workshop, 12 495; 13 560; 35 75

Children's World Learning Centers, II 608; 13 48

Children's World Ltd. See The Boots Company PLC.

ChildrenFirst, Inc., 59 117–20

Childtime Learning Centers, Inc., 34 **103–06**

Chiles Offshore Corporation, 9 111–13; 57 126; 59 322

Chili's Grill & Bar, 10 331; 12 373–74; 19 258; 20 159

Chilton Corp., 25 239; 27 361

Chilton Publications. See Cahners Business Information.

Chimney Rock Winery, 48 392

China Airlines, 34 107–10; 39 33–34

China Coast, 10 322, 324; 16 156, 158

China.com Corp., 49 422

China Communications System Company, Inc. (Chinacom), 18 34

China Development Corporation, 16 4

China Eastern Airlines Co. Ltd., 31 **102–04; 46 10**

China International Capital Corp., 16 377

China International Trade and Investment Corporation. See CITIC Pacific Ltd.

China Life Insurance Company Limited, **65 103–05**

China Merchants International Holdings **Co., Ltd., 52 79–82**

China National Aviation Company Ltd., 18 115; 21 140; 66 192

China National Cereals, Oils & Foodstuffs Import and Export Corporation, 24 359

China National Heavy Duty Truck Corporation, 21 274

China National Machinery Import and Export Corporation, 8 279

China National Offshore Oil Corporation, 71 383

China National Petroleum Corporation, **18 483; 46 86–89**

China OceanShipping Company, 50 187

China Resources (Shenyang) Snowflake Brewery Co., 21 320

China Southern Airlines Company Ltd., **31 102; 33 98–100; 46 10**

China Telecom, 50 128–32

China Unicom, 47 320–21

chinadotcom Corporation. See CDC Corporation.

Chinese Electronics Import and Export Corp., I 535

Chinese Metallurgical Import and Export Corp., IV 61

Chinese Petroleum Corporation, IV **388–90, 493, 519; 31 105–108 (upd.)**

The Chinet Company, 30 397

Chipcom, 16 392

Chipotle Mexican Grill, Inc., 63 280, 284–85; 67 107–10, 268

Chippewa Shoe, 19 232

CHIPS and Technologies, Inc., 6 217; 9 114–17

Chiquita Brands International, Inc., 7 **84–86; 21 110–13 (upd.); 38 197; 60** 268

ChiRex, 38 380

Chiro Tool Manufacturing Corp., III 629

Chiron Corporation, 7 427; 10 213–14; **36 117–20 (upd.); 45 94**

Chisholm Coal Company, 51 352

Chisholm-Mingo Group, Inc., 41 88–90

Chitaka Foods International, 24 365

Chittenden & Eastman Company, 58 **61–64**

Chiyoda Fire and Marine, III 404

Chock Full o'Nuts Corp., 17 97–100; 20 83

Chocoladefabriken Lindt & Sprüngli **AG, 27 102–05; 30 220**

Choice Hotels International Inc., 14 **105–07; 26 460**

ChoiceCare Corporation, 24 231

ChoicePoint Inc., 31 358; 65 106–08

Chorus Line Corporation, 25 247; 30 **121–23**

Chouinard Equipment. See Lost Arrow Inc.

Chovet Engineering S.A. See SNC-Lavalin Group Inc.

Chr. Hansen Group A/S, 70 54–57

Chris-Craft Industries, Inc., 9 118–19; **26 32; 31 109–12 (upd.); 46 313**

Christensen Boyles Corporation, 19 247; **26 68–71**

Christensen Company, 8 397

Christiaensen, 26 160

The Christian Broadcasting Network, **Inc., 13 279; 52 83–85; 57 392**

Christian Dalloz SA, 40 96–98

Christian Dior S.A., 19 86–88; 23 237, 242; 49 90–93 (upd.)

Christian Salvesen Plc, 45 10, 100–03

The Christian Science Publishing **Society, 55 99–102**

Christian Supply Centers, Inc., 45 352

Christiana Bank og Kreditklasse, 40 336

Christie, Mitchell & Mitchell, 7 344

Christie's International plc, 15 98–101; **39 81–85 (upd.); 49 325**

Christofle Orfevrerie, 44 206

Christofle SA, 40 99–102

Christopher & Banks Corporation, 42 **73–75**

Christopher Charters, Inc. See Kitty Hawk, Inc.

Chromalloy American Corp., 13 461; 54 330

Chromalloy Gas Turbine Corp., 13 462; 54 331

Chromatic Color, 13 227–28

Chromcraft Revington, Inc., 15 102–05; **26 100**

Chromium Corporation, 52 103–05

Chrompack, Inc., 48 410

The Chronicle Publishing Company, **Inc., 23 119–22**

Chronimed Inc., 26 72–75

Chronoservice, 27 475

Chrysalis Group plc, 22 194; 40 103–06

Chrysler Corporation, I 144–45; 11 **53–55 (upd.).** See also DaimlerChrysler AG

Chrysler Financial Company, LLC, 45 262

CHS Inc., 60 86–89

CHT Steel Company Ltd., 51 352

CH2M Hill Ltd., 22 136–38
Chubb Corporation, III 220–22, 368; 11 481; 14 108–10 (upd.); 29 256; 37 83–87 (upd.); 45 109
Chubb, PLC, 50 133–36
Chubb Security plc, 44 258
Chubu Electric Power Company, Inc., V 571–73; 46 90–93 (upd.)
Chuck E. Cheese, 13 472–74; 31 94
Chugach Alaska Corporation, 60 90–93
Chugai Boyeki Co. Ltd., 44 441
Chugai Pharmaceutical Co., Ltd., 8 215–16; 10 79; 50 137–40
Chugai Shogyo Shimposha. See Nihon Keizai Shimbun, Inc.
Chugoku Electric Power Company Inc., V 574–76; 53 101–04 (upd.)
Chugoku Funai Electric Company Ltd., 62 150
Chunghwa Picture Tubes, 23 469
Chuo Rika Kogyo Corp., 56 238
Chuo Trust & Banking Co. See Yasuda Trust and Banking Company, Limited.
Chupa Chups S.A., 38 133–35
Church & Company, 45 342, 344
Church & Dwight Co., Inc., 29 112–15; 68 78–82 (upd.)
Church and Tower Group, 19 254
Church's Chicken, 7 26–28; 15 345; 23 468; 32 13–14; 66 56–59
Churchill Downs Incorporated, 29 116–19
Churchill Insurance Co. Ltd., III 404
CI Holdings, Limited, 53 120
Cia Hering, 72 66–68
Cianbro Corporation, 14 111–13
Cianchette Brothers, Inc. See Cianbro Corporation.
Ciba-Geigy Ltd., I 632–34; IV 288; 8 63, 108–11 (upd.), 376–77; 9 153, 441; 10 53–54, 213; 15 229; 18 51; 21 386; 23 195–96; 25 55; 27 69; 28 193, 195; 30 327; 36 36, 119; 50 90; 61 226–27. See also Novartis AG.
CIBC. See Canadian Imperial Bank of Commerce.
CIBC Wood Gundy Securities Corp., 24 482
Ciber, Inc., 18 110–12
Ciby 2000, 24 79
CIC. See Commercial Intertech Corporation.
CIC Investors #13 LP, 60 130
CICI, 11 184
Cie Continental d'Importation, 10 249
Cie des Lampes, 9 9
Cie Générale d'Electro-Ceramique, 9 9
Cie.Generale des Eaux S.A., 24 327
CIENA Corporation, 54 68–71
Cifra, S.A. de C.V., 8 556; 12 63–65; 26 524; 34 197–98; 35 320; 63 430. See also Wal-Mart de Mexico, S.A. de C.V.
Cifunsa. See Compania Fundidora del Norte, S.A.
Ciga Group, 54 345, 347
Cigarrera La Moderna, 21 260; 22 73
Cigarros la Tabacelera Mexicana (Cigatam), 21 259
CIGNA Corporation, III 223–27; 10 30; 11 243; 22 139–44 (upd.), 269; 38 18; 45 104–10 (upd.)
CIGWELD, 19 442
Cii-HB, III 678; 16 122
Cilbarco, II 25

CILCORP Energy Services Inc., 60 27
Cilva Holdings PLC, 6 358
Cima, 14 224–25
CIMA Precision Spring Europa, 55 305–06
Cimarron Communications Corp., 38 54
Cimarron Utilities Company, 6 580
CIMCO Ltd., 21 499–501
Cimeco S.A. See Grupo Clarín S.A.
Cimenteries CBR S.A., 23 325, 327
Ciments Français, 40 107–10
Ciments Lafarge France/Quebec. See Lafarge Cement
Cimos, 7 37
Cinar Corporation, 40 111–14
Cincinnati Bell, Inc., 6 316–18; 29 250, 252
Cincinnati Electronics Corp., II 25
Cincinnati Financial Corporation, 16 102–04; 44 89–92 (upd.)
Cincinnati Gas & Electric Company, 6 465–68, 481–82
Cincinnati Lamb Inc., 72 69–71
Cincinnati Milacron Inc., 12 66–69. See also Milacron, Inc.
Cincom Systems Inc., 15 106–08
Cine-Groupe, 35 279
Cinecentrum, IV 591
Cinemark, 21 362; 23 125
CinemaSource, 58 167
Cinemax, IV 675; 7 222–24, 528–29; 23 276
Cinemex, 71 256
Cineplex Odeon Corporation, II 145, 6 161–63; 14 87; 23 123–26 (upd.); 33 432
Cinerama Group, 67 291
Cinnabon Inc., 13 435–37; 23 127–29; 32 12, 15
Cinquième Saison, 38 200, 202
Cinram International, Inc., 43 107–10
Cinsa. See Compania Industrial del Norte, S.A.
Cintas Corporation, 16 228; 21 114–16, 507; 30 455; 51 74–77 (upd.)
Cintra. See Concesiones de Infraestructuras de Transportes, S.A.; Corporacion Internacional de Aviacion, S.A. de C.V.
Cinven, 49 451; 63 49–50
Cipal-Parc Astérix, 27 10
Ciprial S.A., 27 260
CIPSCO Inc., 6 469–72, 505–06. See also Ameren Corporation.
CIR. See Compagnie Industriali Riunite S.p.A.
Circa Pharmaceuticals, 16 529; 56 375
Circle A Ginger Ale Company, 9 177
Circle International Group Inc., 17 216; 59 171
The Circle K Company, II 619–20; 7 113–14, 372, 374; 20 138–40 (upd.); 25 125; 26 447; 49 17
Circle Plastics, 9 323
Circon Corporation, 21 117–20
Circuit City Stores, Inc., 9 65–66, 120–22; 10 235, 305–06, 334–35, 468–69; 12 335; 14 61; 15 215; 16 73, 75; 17 489; 18 533; 19 362; 23 51–53, 363; 24 52, 502; 26 410; 29 120–24 (upd.); 30 464–65; 55 93, 107; 63 61; 65 109–14 (upd.)
Circus Circus Enterprises, Inc., 6 203–05; 19 377, 379
Circus Distribution, Inc. See DC Shoes, Inc.

Circus Knie, 29 126
Circus World, 16 389–90
Cirque du Soleil Inc., 29 125–28
Cirrus Design Corporation, 44 93–95
Cirrus Logic, Inc., 9 334; 11 56–57; 25 117; 48 90–93 (upd.)
CIS Acquisition Corporation, 56 134
CIS Mortgage Maker Ltd., 51 89
Cisco Systems, Inc., 11 58–60; 34 111–15 (upd.); 36 300; 38 430; 43 251
Cise, 24 79
Cisneros Group of Companies, 47 312; 54 72–75
CIT Alcatel, 9 9–10
CIT Financial Corp., 8 117; 12 207
CIT Group, Inc., 13 446, 536; 63 404
Citadel Communications Corporation, 35 102–05
Citadel General, III 404
Citadel, Inc., 27 46
CitFed Bancorp, Inc., 16 105–07
CITGO Petroleum Corporation, II 660–61; IV 391–93, 508; 7 491; 31 113–17 (upd.); 32 414, 416–17; 45 252, 254
Citibanc Group, Inc., 11 456
Citibank, III 243, 340; 9 124; 10 150; 11 418; 13 146; 14 101; 23 3–4, 482; 25 180, 542; 50 6; 59 121, 124–25. See also Citigroup Inc
Citibank of Mexico, 34 82
CITIC Pacific Ltd., 16 481; 18 113–15; 20 134
Citicasters Inc., 23 293–94
Citicorp, II 253–55; III 397; 7 212–13; 8 196; 9 123–26 (upd.), 441; 10 463, 469; 11 140; 12 30, 310, 334; 13 535; 14 103, 108, 235; 15 94, 146, 281; 17 324, 559; 21 69, 145; 22 169, 406; 25 198, 542. See also Citigroup Inc.
Cities Service Company, 12 542; 22 172; 71 258
CitiFinancial, 59 121, 125
Citifor, 19 156
Citigroup Inc., 30 124–28 (upd.); 42 332; 46 316; 54 143; 59 121–27 (upd.)
Citivision PLC, 9 75
Citizen Watch Co., Ltd., III 454–56, 549; 13 121–22; 21 121–24 (upd.); 23 212; 41 71–82
Citizen's Federal Savings Bank, 10 93
Citizen's Industrial Bank, 14 529
Citizens Bank, 11 105
Citizens Bank of Hamilton, 9 475
Citizens Bank of Savannah, 10 426
Citizens Building & Loan Association, 14 191
Citizens Federal Savings and Loan Association, 9 476
Citizens Financial Group, Inc., 12 422; 42 76–80
Citizens Gas Co., 6 529
Citizens Gas Fuel Company. See MCN Corporation.
Citizens Gas Supply Corporation, 6 527
Citizens Insurance Company of America, 63 29
Citizens Mutual Savings Bank, 17 529–30
Citizens National Bank, 13 466; 25 114; 41 312
Citizens National Gas Company, 6 527
Citizens Saving and Trust Company, 17 356

Citizens Savings & Loan Association, **9** 173

Citizens Savings and Loan Society. *See* Citizens Mutual Savings Bank.

Citizens State Bank, **41** 178, 180

Citizens Telephone Company, **14** 257–58

Citizens Utilities Company, 7 87–89; 37 124–27

Citizens' Savings and Loan, **10** 339

Citrix Systems, Inc., 44 96–99

Citroën. *See* Automobiles Citroen; PSA Peugeot Citroen S.A.

City and Suburban Telegraph Association. *See* Cincinnati Bell Inc.

City Capital Associates, **31** 211

City Centre Properties Ltd. *See* Land Securities PLC.

City Collection Company, Inc., **58** 184

City Developments Limited, **71** 231

City Finance Company, **10** 340; **11** 261

City Investing Co., **13** 363

City Light and Traction Company, **6** 593

City Light and Water Company, **6** 579

City Market Inc., **12** 112

City National Bank of Baton Rouge, **11** 107

City of Seattle Water Department, **12** 443

City of Westminster Assurance Company Ltd., **59** 246

The City Post Publishing Corp., **12** 359

City Public Service, 6 473–75

City Savings, **10** 340

City Stores Company, **16** 207

Civic Drugs, **12** 21

Civic Parking LLC, **18** 105

Civil & Civic Contractors. *See* Lend Lease Corporation Ltd.

Civil Aviation Administration of China, **31** 102; **33** 98

Civil Service Employees Insurance Co., **III** 214

CJ Banks. *See* Christopher & Banks Corporation.

CJ Corporation, 62 68–70

CKE Restaurants, Inc., 19 89–93, 433, 435; **25** 389; **27** 19; **29** 203; **37** 349–51; **46 94–99 (upd.)**

CKS Group Inc. *See* marchFIRST, Inc.

CKS Inc., **23** 479

Clabir Corp., **12** 199

Claeys, **22** 379–80

Claire's Stores, Inc., 17 101–03; 18 411

Clairol, **III** 17–18; **17** 110

Clal Electronic Industries Ltd., **24** 429

Clal Group, **18** 154

CLAM Petroleum, **7** 282

Clancy Paul Inc., **13** 276

Clapp-Eastham Company. *See* GenRad, Inc.

Clara Candy, **15** 65

CLARCOR Inc., 17 104–07; 56 157; **61 63–67 (upd.)**

Clare Rose Inc., 68 83–85

Claremont Technology Group Inc., **31** 131

Clariden Bank, **21** 146–47; **59** 142, 144

Claridge Group, **25** 266, 268; **68** 222, 224

Clarify Corp., **38** 431

Clarion Company Ltd., 64 77–79

Clarion Hotels and Resorts, **25** 309

Clark & McKenney Hardware Co. *See* Clarcor Inc.

Clark Bar Candy Company, **53** 304

The Clark Construction Group, Inc., 8 112–13

Clark, Dietz & Associates-Engineers. *See* CRSS Inc.

Clark Equipment Company, 7 513–14; 8 114–16; **10** 265; **13** 500; **15** 226; **55** 221

Clark Estates Inc., **8** 13

Clark Filter, Inc., **17** 104

Clark Materials Handling Company, **7** 514

Clark Retail Enterprises Inc., **37** 311

Clark-Schwebel, Inc., **28** 195

Clarkins, Inc., **16** 35–36

Clarksburg Casket Co., **56** 23

CLASSA. *See* Compañia de Líneas Aéreas Subvencionadas S.A.

Classic FM plc, **39** 198–200

Classic Vacation Group, Inc., 46 100–03

Claudel Roustand Galac, **19** 50

Clause Tezier, **70** 346

Claussen Pickle Co., **12** 371

Claxson Interactive Group, **54** 74

Clayco Construction Company, **41** 225–26

Clayton Brown Holding Company, **15** 232

Clayton Dubilier & Rice Inc., **25** 501; **29** 408; **40** 370; **49** 22

Clayton Homes Incorporated, 13 154–55; **37** 77; **54 76–79 (upd.)**

Clayton-Marcus Co., **12** 300

Clayton/National Courier Systems, Inc., **24** 126

CLE. *See* Compagnie Laitière Européenne.

Cleancoal Terminal, **7** 582, 584

Clear Channel Communications, Inc., 23 130–32, 294; **25** 418; **27** 278; **33** 322, 324; **35** 219–21, 233; **36** 422, 424; **37** 104–05

Clear Shield Inc., **17** 157, 159

Clearly Canadian Beverage Corporation, 48 94–97

Clearwater Tissue Mills, Inc., **8** 430

Clearwire, Inc., 69 95–97

Cleary, Gottlieb, Steen & Hamilton, 35 106–09

Cleco Corporation, 37 88–91

Clef, **IV** 125

Clemente Capital Inc., **25** 542

Clements Energy, Inc., **7** 376

Cleo Inc., **12** 207–09; **35** 131

Le Clerc, **21** 225–26

Cleve-Co Jig Boring Co., **23** 82

Cleveland and Western Coal Company, **7** 369

Cleveland-Cliffs Inc., 13 156–58; 17 355; **62 71–75 (upd.)**

Cleveland Cotton Products Co., **37** 393

Cleveland Electric Illuminating Company. *See* Centerior Energy Theodor.

Cleveland Fabric Centers, Inc. *See* Fabri-Centers of America Inc.

Cleveland Grinding Machine Co., **23** 82

Cleveland Indians Baseball Company, Inc., 37 92–94

Cleveland Iron Mining Company. *See* Cleveland-Cliffs Inc.

Cleveland Pneumatic Co., **III** 512

Cleveland Precision Instruments, Inc., **23** 82

Cleveland Range Ltd. *See* Enodis plc.

Cleveland Twist Drill Company. *See* Acme-Cleveland Corp.

Clevepak Corporation, **8** 229; **13** 442; **59** 349

Clevite Corporation, **14** 207

CLF Research, **16** 202; **43** 170

Click Messenger Service, Inc., **24** 126

Click Wine Group, 68 86–88

ClickAgents.com, Inc., **49** 433

ClientLogic Corporation. *See* Onex Corporation.

Clif Bar Inc., 50 141–43

Clifford & Wills, **12** 280–81

Clifford Chance LLP, 38 136–39

Cliffs Corporation, **13** 157; **27** 224

Climaveneta Deutschland GmbH. *See* De'Longhi S.p.A.

Clinical Partners, Inc., **26** 74

Clinical Pathology Facility, Inc., **26** 391

Clinical Science Research Ltd., **10** 106

Clinique Laboratories, Inc., **30** 191

Clinton Cards plc, 39 86–88; 70 20–21

Clipper Group, **12** 439

Clipper, Inc., **IV** 597

Clipper Manufacturing Company, **7** 3

La Cloche d'Or, **25** 85

Cloetta Fazer AB, 70 58–60

Clopay Corporation, **34** 195

The Clorox Company, III 20–22, 52; 8 433; **22 145–48 (upd.)**, 436; **26** 383

Close Brothers Group plc, 39 89–92

Clothesline Corporation, **60** 65

The Clothestime, Inc., 20 141–44

Clougherty Packing Company, 72 72–74

Clouterie et Tréfilerie des Flandres, **IV** 25–26

Clover Club, **44** 348

Clovis Water Co., **6** 580

Clow Water Systems Co., **55** 266

CLRP. *See* City of London Real Property Company Ltd.

CLSI Inc., **15** 372; **43** 182

Club Aurrera, **8** 556

Club Corporation of America, **26** 27

Club de Hockey Canadien Inc., **26** 305

Club Méditerranée S.A., 6 206–08; 21 125–28 (upd.); **27** 10

Club Monaco Inc., **62** 284

ClubCorp, Inc., 33 101–04

Cluett Corporation, **22** 133

Cluett, Peabody & Co., Inc., **8** 567–68

Cluster Consulting, **51** 98

Clyde Iron Works, **8** 545

Clydesdale Group, **19** 390

CM&M Equilease, **7** 344

CM&P. *See* Cresap, McCormick and Paget.

CMAC Investment Corporation. *See* Radian Group Inc.

CMB Acier, **IV** 228

CMB Packaging SA, **8** 477; **49** 295

CMC. *See* Commercial Metals Company.

CME. *See* Campbell-Mithun-Esty, Inc.; Central European Media Enterprises Ltd.

CMGI, Inc., **43** 11, 13, 420, 422

CMI International, Inc., **27** 202, 204

CMIH. *See* China Merchants International Holdings Co., Ltd.

CML Group, Inc., 10 215–18; 22 382, 536; **38** 238

CMP Media Inc., 26 76–80; 28 504

CMP Properties Inc., **15** 122

CMS Energy Corporation, IV 23; V 577–79; **8** 466; **14 114–16 (upd.)**

CMS Healthcare, **29** 412

CMT Enterprises, Inc., **22** 249

CN. *See* Canadian National Railway Company.

CNA Financial Corporation, III 228–32, 339; **38 140–46 (upd.)**; **63** 174

CNB Bancshares Inc., **31** 207

CNBC, Inc., **28** 298

CNC Holding Corp., **13** 166

CNCA. *See* Caisse National de Crédit Agricole.
CNEP. *See* Comptoir National d'Escompte de Paris.
CNET Networks, Inc., 47 77–80
CNF Transportation. *See* Consolidated Freightways, Inc.
CNG. *See* Consolidated Natural Gas Company.
CNH Global N.V., 38 147–56 (upd.); 67 9
CNI. *See* Community Networks Inc.
CNN. *See* Cable News Network.
CNP. *See* Compagnie Nationale à Portefeuille.
CNPC. *See* China National Petroleum Corporation.
CNS, Inc., 20 145–47
CNTS. *See* Ceska Nezavisla Televizni Spolecnost.
Co-Counsel, Inc., 29 364
Co-Op Blue Square Consumer Cooperative Society, 41 56–58
Co-operative Group (CWS) Ltd., 51 86–89
Co-operative Insurance Society Ltd., 51 89
Co-Steel International Ltd., 8 523–24; 13 142–43; 24 144
Coach and Car Equipment Corp., 41 369
Coach, Inc., 45 111–15 (upd.); 54 325–26
Coach Leatherware, 10 219–21; 12 559
Coach Specialties Co. *See* Fleetwood Enterprises, Inc.
Coach USA, Inc., 24 117–19; 30 431, 433; 55 103–06 (upd.)
Coachmen Industries Inc., 21 153; 39 393
Coal India Ltd., IV 48–50; 44 100–03 (upd.)
Coalport, 12 528
Coast American Corporation, 13 216
Coast Consolidators, Inc., 14 505
Coast to Coast Hardware. *See* TruServ Corporation.
Coast-to-Coast Stores, 12 8
Coastal Coca-Cola Bottling Co., 10 223
Coastal Container Line Inc., 30 318
Coastal Corporation, IV 394–95; 7 553–54; 31 118–21 (upd.)
Coastal Lumber, S.A., 18 514
Coastal States Corporation, 11 481
Coastal States Life Insurance Company, 11 482
CoastAmerica Corp., 13 176
Coastline Distribution, Inc., 52 399
Coates/Lorilleux, 14 308
Coats plc, V 356–58; 44 104–07 (upd.)
CoBank. *See* National Bank for Cooperatives.
Cobb & Branham, 14 257
COBE Cardiovascular, Inc., 61 68–72
COBE Laboratories, Inc., 13 159–61; 22 360; 49 156; 61 70
Coberco. *See* Friesland Coberco Dairy Foods Holding N.V.
Cobham plc, 30 129–32
Coborn's, Inc., 30 133–35
Cobra Electronics Corporation, 14 117–19; 60 137
Cobra Golf Inc., 16 108–10; 23 474; 64 5
Cobra Ventilation Products, 22 229
Coburn Vision Care, III 727
Coca-Cola Bottling Co. Consolidated, 10 222–24; 15 299

Coca-Cola Bottling Company of Northern New England, Inc., 21 319
The Coca-Cola Company, I 232–35; 10 225–28 (upd.); 32 111–16 (upd.); 67 111–17 (upd.)
Coca-Cola Enterprises, Inc., 10 223; 13 162–64; 23 455–57; 32 115
Cochrane Corporation, 8 135
Cochrane Foil Co., 15 128
Cockburn & Campbell Ltd., 38 501
Cockburn-Adelaide Cement, 31 398, 400
Cockerill Sambre Group, IV 51–53; 22 44; 26 81–84 (upd.); 42 416
Coco's, 27 16, 19
Code Hennessey & Simmons Limited, 39 358
Codec, 19 328
Codelco. *See* Corporacion Nacional del Cobre de Chile.
Coelba. *See* Companhia de Electricidade da Bahia.
Coeur d'Alene Mines Corporation, 20 148–51
COFAL. *See* Compagnie financiere pour l'Amerique Latine.
Coffee Club Franchise B.V., 53 221
Coffee People, Inc., 40 152–54
Cofica, 21 99
Cofitel SA, 25 466
Coflexip S.A., 25 103–05
Cofresco Frischhalteprodukte GmbH & Co. KG, 53 221
Cofroma, 23 219
COGEMA Canada, IV 436
Cogeneracion Prat SA, 41 325, 327
Cogeneration Development Corp., 42 387–88
Cogent Communications Group, Inc., 55 107–10
Cogent Data Technologies, Inc., 31 5
Cogentrix Energy, Inc., 10 229–31
Cogetex, 14 225
Cogifer, S.A., 18 4; 31 156, 158
Cognex Corp., 22 373
CogniSeis Development, Inc., 18 513, 515
Cognitive Solutions, Inc., 18 140
Cognizant Technology Solutions Corporation, 57 176–77; 59 128–30; 61 82
Cognos Inc., 11 78; 25 97; 44 108–11
Cohasset Savings Bank, 13 468
Coherent, Inc., 31 122–24
Coherix Corporation, 48 446
Cohn-Hall-Marx Co. *See* United Merchants & Manufacturers, Inc.
Cohoes Bancorp Inc., 41 212
Cohu, Inc., 32 117–19
Coils Plus, Inc., 22 4
Coinamatic Laundry Equipment, II 650
Coinmach Laundry Corporation, 20 152–54
Coinstar, Inc., 44 112–14
Coktel Vision, 15 455
Colas S.A., 31 126–29
Colbert Television Sales, 9 306
Colby Group Holdings Limited, 59 261
Cold Spring Granite Company, 16 111–14; 67 118–22 (upd.)
Cold Stone Creamery, 69 98–100
Coldwater Creek Inc., 21 129–31
Coldwell Banker Co. *See* CB Richard Ellis Group, Inc.
Cole Haan Holdings Incorporated, 36 346

Cole National Corporation, 13 165–67, 391
Cole Sewell Corporation, 39 322, 324
Cole's Craft Showcase, 13 166
Cole's Quality Foods, Inc., 68 92–94
Coleco Industries, Inc., 18 520; 21 375
The Coleman Company, Inc., 9 127–29; 26 119; 28 135, 247; 30 136–39 (upd.)
Coleman Natural Products, Inc., 68 89–91
Coleman Outdoor Products Inc., 21 293
Colemans Ltd., 11 241
Coles Book Stores Ltd., 7 486, 488–89; 58 185
Coles Express Inc., 15 109–11
Coles Myer Ltd., V 33–35; 18 286; 20 155–58 (upd.)
Colex Data, 14 556
Colfax Corporation, 58 65–67
Colgate Medical Ltd. *See* Orthofix International NV.
Colgate-Palmolive Company, III 23–26; 14 120–23 (upd.); 35 110–15 (upd.); 71 105–10 (upd.)
Colgens, 22 193
Collaborative Care Corporation, 68 299
Collabra Software Inc., 15 322
Collect-a-Can (Pty) Ltd., 57 183
Collectors Universe, Inc., 48 98–100
College Construction Loan Insurance Assoc., II 455; 25 427
College Entrance Examination Board, 12 141
College Survival, Inc., 10 357
Collegiate Arlington Sports Inc., II 652
Collins & Aikman Corporation, I 483; 13 168–70; 25 535; 41 91–95 (upd.)
Collins Industries, Inc., 33 105–07
Collins Stewart, 41 371–72
Colo-Macco. *See* CRSS Inc.
Cologne Re. *See* General Re Corporation; Kölnische Rückversicherungs-Gesellschaft AG.
Colombia Graphophone Company, 22 192
Colombo, 25 84
Colonia Insurance Company (UK) Ltd., III 273, 394; 49 43
Colonia Versicherung Aktiengesellschaft. *See* AXA Colonia Konzern AG.
Colonial Candle of Cape Cod, 18 69
Colonial Companies Inc., 52 381
Colonial Container, 8 359
Colonial Food Stores, 7 373
Colonial Healthcare Supply Co., 13 90
Colonial Life Insurance Company, 11 481
Colonial National Bank, 8 9; 38 10–12
Colonial National Leasing, Inc., 8 9
Colonial Packaging Corporation, 12 150
Colonial Penn Group Insurance Co., 11 262; 27 4
Colonial Properties Trust, 65 115–17
Colonial Rubber Works, 8 347
Colonial Sugar Refining Co. Ltd. *See* CSR Limited.
Colonial Williamsburg Foundation, 53 105–07
Colony Capital, Inc., 27 201
Colony Communications, 7 99
Colony Gift Corporation, Ltd., 18 67, 69
Color-Box, Inc., 8 103
Color Corporation of America, 8 553
Color Me Mine, 25 263
Color Tile, 31 435

Colorado Baseball Management, Inc., 72 75–78
Colorado Belle Casino. *See* Circus Circus Enterprises, Inc.
Colorado Electric Company. *See* Public Service Company of Colorado.
Colorado Fuel & Iron (CF&I), **14** 369
Colorado Gaming & Entertainment Co., **21** 335
Colorado Gathering & Processing Corporation, **11** 27
Colorado MEDtech, Inc., 48 101–05
Colorado National Bank, **12** 165
Colorado Technical University, Inc., **41** 419
Colorfoto Inc., **I** 447
Coloroll, **44** 148
Colorstrip, Inc., **63** 272
Colortree. *See* National Envelope Corporation.
ColorTyme, Inc., **45** 367
ColorWorks Salon. *See* Ratner Companies.
Colossal Pictures, **10** 286
Colt, **19** 430–31
Colt Industries Inc., I 434–36
Colt Pistol Factory, **9** 416
COLT Telecom Group plc, 41 96–99
Colt's Manufacturing Company, Inc., 12 70–72
Coltec Industries Inc., **30** 158; **32** 96; **46** 213; **52** 158–59
Columbia Administration Software Publishing Corporation, **51** 244
Columbia Artists Management, Inc., **52** 199–200
Columbia Brewery, **25** 281
Columbia Broadcasting System. *See* CBS Corporation.
Columbia Chemical Co. *See* PPG Industries, Inc.
Columbia Electric Street Railway, Light and Power Company, **6** 575
Columbia Gas & Electric Company. *See* Columbia Gas System, Inc.
Columbia Gas Light Company, **6** 574
Columbia Gas of New York, Inc., **6** 536
The Columbia Gas System, Inc., V 580–82; 16 115–18 (upd.)
Columbia Gas Transmission Corporation, **6** 467
Columbia General Life Insurance Company of Indiana, **11** 378
Columbia Hat Company. *See* Columbia Sportswear Company.
Columbia/HCA Healthcare Corporation, 13 90; **15 112–14; 22** 409–10; **27** 356;
Columbia House Company, 69 101–03
Columbia Insurance Co., **III** 214
Columbia Pictures Entertainment, Inc., II 135–37, 170, 234, 619; **10** 227; **12** 73; **21** 360; **22** 193; **25** 139; **28** 71. *See also* Columbia TriStar Motion Pictures Companies.
Columbia Railroad, Gas and Electric Company, **6** 575
Columbia Records, **16** 201; **26** 150
Columbia Records Distribution Corp., **43** 170
Columbia Sportswear Company, 19 94–96; 41 100–03 (upd.)
Columbia Steamship Company, **17** 356
Columbia Transportation Co., **17** 357
Columbia TriStar Motion Pictures Companies, 12 73–76 (upd.); 28 71

Columbia TriStar Television Distribution, **17** 149
Columbian Carbon Company, **25** 70–71
Columbian Chemicals Co., **IV** 179; **28** 352, 356
Columbus & Southern Ohio Electric Company (CSO), **6** 467, 481–82
Columbus Bank & Trust. *See* Synovus Financial Corp.
Columbus McKinnon Corporation, 37 95–98
Columbus Realty Trust, **26** 378
Columbus Stainless, **59** 226
Colwell Systems, **19** 291; **22** 181
Com Dev, Inc., **32** 435
Com Ed. *See* Commonwealth Edison.
Com-Link 21, Inc., **8** 310
Com Tech Communications Ltd. *See* Dimension Data Holdings PLC.
Comair Holdings Inc., 13 171–73; 31 420; **34 116–20 (upd.)**
Comalco Fabricators (Hong Kong) Ltd., **III** 758
Comalco Ltd., **IV** 59–61, 122, 191
Comark, **24** 316; **25** 417–18
Comat Services Pte. Ltd., **10** 514
Combe Inc., 72 79–82
Combibloc Inc., **16** 339
Combined International Corporation. *See* Aon Corporation
Combined Properties, Inc., **16** 160
Combustion Engineering Group, **22** 11; **25** 534
Combustiveis Industriais e Domésticos. *See* CIDLA.
Comcast Corporation, 7 90–92; 9 428; **10** 432–33; **17** 148; **22** 162; **24 120–24 (upd.); 27** 342, 344; **49** 175; **63** 437
ComCore Semiconductor, Inc., **26** 330
Comdata, **19** 160
Comdial Corporation, 21 132–35
Comdisco, Inc., 9 130–32; 11 47, 86, 484, 490
Comerci. *See* Controladora Comercial Mexicana, S.A. de C.V.
Comercial Arauco Ltda., **72** 269
Comercial Mexicana, S.A. *See* Controladora Comercial Mexicana, S.A. de C.V.
Comerica Incorporated, 40 115–17
Comesi San Luis S.A.I.C. *See* Siderar S.A.I.C.
Comet. *See* Kingfisher plc.
Comet American Marketing, **33** 31
Comet Rice, Inc., **33** 31
ComFed Bancorp, **11** 29
Comfin, **60** 96
COMFORCE Corporation, 40 118–20
Comfort Inns, **21** 362
Comforto GmbH, **8** 252; **39** 206
Cominco Ltd., 37 99–102 55
Comision Federal de Electricidad de Mexico (CFE), **21** 196–97
CommAir. *See* American Building Maintenance Industries, Inc.
Command Security Corporation, 57 71–73
Commander Foods, **8** 409
Commander-Larabee Co., **25** 242
Commemorative Brands Inc., **19** 453
Commerce Clearing House, Inc., 7 93–94. *See also* CCH Inc.
Commerce.TV, **42** 323
Commerce Union, **10** 426

The CommerceBank of Washington, **53** 378
CommerceConnect LLC, **56** 73
Commercial Air Conditioning of Northern California, **25** 15
Commercial Air Lines, Inc., **23** 380
Commercial Aseguradora Suizo Americana, S.A., **III** 243
Commercial Chemical Company, **16** 99
Commercial Credit Company, 8 117–19; 10 255–56; **15** 464
Commercial Federal Corporation, 12 77–79; 62 76–80 (upd.)
Commercial Financial Services, Inc., 26 85–89
Commercial Intertech Corporation, **57** 86
Commercial Life, **III** 243
Commercial Metals Company, 15 115–17; 42 81–84(upd.)
Commercial Motor Freight, Inc., **14** 42
Commercial Realty Services Group, **21** 257
Commercial Union plc, II 272, 308; **III 233–35**
Commerzbank A.G., II 256–58; 9 283; **14** 170; **47 81–84 (upd.); 51** 19, 23
Commerzbank AG, **57** 113
Commerzfilm, **IV** 591
CommLink Corp., **17** 264
Commodity Credit Corp., **11** 24
Commodore Corporation, **8** 229
Commodore International, Ltd., II 6; **7 95–97,** 532; **9** 46; **10** 56, 284; **23** 25; **26** 16
Commonwealth Aluminium Corp., Ltd. *See* Comalco Ltd.
Commonwealth Brands, Inc., **51** 170
Commonwealth Edison, V 583–85; 6 529, 531; **12** 548; **15** 422; **48** 163
Commonwealth Energy System, 14 124–26
Commonwealth Industrial Gases, **25** 82
Commonwealth Industries, **III** 569; **11** 536; **20** 360
Commonwealth Insurance Co., **III** 264
Commonwealth Life and Accident Insurance Company, **27** 46–47
Commonwealth Life Insurance Co. *See* Providian Financial Corporation
Commonwealth Limousine Services, Ltd., **26** 62
Commonwealth Mortgage Assurance Co., **III** 344
Commonwealth Oil Refining Company, **7** 517; **45** 410
Commonwealth Power Railway and Light Company, **14** 134
Commonwealth Southern Corporation, **14** 134
Commonwealth Steel Company Ltd, **62** 331
Commonwealth Telephone Enterprises, Inc., 25 106–08
Commonwealth United Corp., **53** 364
CommQuest Technologies, **63** 199
Commtron, Inc. *See* AmerisourceBergen Corporation.
Communications and Systems Specialists, **18** 370
Communications Consultants, Inc., **16** 393
Communications Corp. of America, **25** 418
Communications Industries Inc., **25** 496
Communications Network Consultants, **29** 400
Communications Solutions Inc., **11** 520

Communications Technology Corp. (CTC),
13 7–8
**Community Coffee Co. L.L.C., 53
108–10**
Community Direct, Inc., 7 16
**Community Health Systems, Inc., 71
111–13**
Community HealthCare Services, 6 182
Community National Bank, 9 474
Community Networks Inc., 45 69
Community Newspapers, Inc., 45 352
Community Power & Light Company, 6
579–80
**Community Psychiatric Centers, 15
118–20**
Community Public Service Company, 6
514
Comnet Corporation, 9 347
Comp-U-Card of America, Inc. See CUC
International Inc.
Compac Corp., 11 535
Compagnia di Participazioni Assicurative
ed Industriali S.p.A., 24 341
**Compagnia Italiana dei Jolly Hotels
S.p.A., 71 114–16**
Compagnie Bancaire, 21 99–100
Compagnie d'Assurances Générales, III
391
Compagnie de Recherche et d'Exploitation
du Pétrole du Sahara, 21 203
Compagnie de Saint-Gobain, III 675–78,
704; 8 395, 397; 15 80; 16 119–23
(upd.); 19 58, 226; 21 222; 26 446; 33
338, 340; 35 86, 88; 64 80–84 (upd.)
Compagnie des Alpes, 48 106–08; 56
143, 145
Compagnie des Cristalleries de Baccarat.
See Baccarat.
**Compagnie des Machines Bull S.A., III
122–23,** 154; IV 600; 12 139; 25 33.
See also Bull S.A.; Groupe Bull.
Compagnie du Midi, III 209, 211
Compagnie Européenne de Publication, IV
614–16
Compagnie Européenne de Télésecurité, 32
374
Compagnie Financier Richemont AG, 19
367, 369–70
Compagnie Financiere Alcatel, 9 10
Compagnie Financière Belge des Pétroles.
See PetroFina S.A.
Compagnie Financiere De Bourbon, 60 149
Compagnie Financière de Paribas, II
259–60; 21 99; 27 138; 33 339. See also
BNP Paribas Group.
Compagnie Financière de Richemont AG,
29 90
Compagnie Financière de Suez. See Suez
Lyonnaise des Eaux.
Compagnie Financière du Groupe Victoire,
27 54; 49 44
Compagnie Financiere pour l'Amerique
Latine, 67 326
Compagnie Financière Richemont AG,
27 487; 29 91–92; 50 144–47
**Compagnie Financière Sucres et Denrées
S.A., 60 94–96**
Compagnie Française Chaufour
Investissement, 27 100
Compagnie Française de Manutention, 27
295
Compagnie Française des Pétroles. See
TOTAL S.A.

Compagnie Fromagère de la Vallée de
l'Ance, 25 84
**Compagnie Générale d'Électricité, II
12–13;** 9 9–10
Compagnie Generale de Cartons Ondules,
IV 296; 19 226
Compagnie Générale des Eaux. See
Vivendi SA.
**Compagnie Générale des Établissements
Michelin, V 236–39;** 19 508; 42 85–89
(upd.); 59 87
**Compagnie Générale Maritime et
Financière, 6 379–81**
Compagnie Industriali Riunite S.p.A., IV
587–88; 54 21
Compagnie Industrielle de Matérials de
Manutention, 27 296
Compagnie Industrielle des Fillers. See
L'Entreprise Jean Lefebvre.
Compagnie Internationale Express, 25 120
Compagnie Laitière Européenne, 25 83, 85
Compagnie Luxembourgeoise de
Télédiffusion, 15 54
Compagnie Monegasque du Banque, 65
230, 232
Compagnie Nationale à Portefeuille, 29 48
Compagnie Nationale de Navigation, 27
515
Compagnie Parisienne de Garantie, III 211
Compagnie Transcontinentale de
Reassurance, 57 136
Compagnie Union des Assurances de Paris
(UAP), 49 44
Compal, 47 152–53
Companhia Brasileira de Petróleo Ipiranga,
67 216
**Companhia de Bebidas das Américas, 57
74–77;** 67 316
Companhia de Celulose do Caima, 14 250
Companhia de Electricidade da Bahia, 49
211
Companhia de Seguros Argos Fluminense,
III 221
Companhia de Seguros Tranquilidade Vida,
S.A. See Banco Espírito Santo e
Comercial de Lisboa S.A.
**Companhia Energética de Minas Gerais
S.A., 53 18; 65 118–20**
Companhia Industrial de Papel Pirahy, 52
301
Companhia Siderúrgica de Tubarao, IV
125
Companhia Siderúrgica Mannesmann S.A.
See Mannesmann AG.
**Companhia Vale do Rio Doce, IV 54–57;
43 111–14 (upd.);** 67 85–86
**Compania Cervecerias Unidas S.A., 70
61–63**
Compañía de Nutrición General S.A., 72
128
Compania Electro Metaluurgica, 67 13
**Compañia Española de Petróleos S.A.
(Cepsa), IV 396–98; 56 63–66 (upd.)**
Compania Fresnillo, 22 286
Compania Fundidora del Norte, S.A., 54
152
Compania General de Aceptaciones. See
Financiera Aceptaciones.
Compania Hulera Euzkadi, 21 260; 23 170
Compania Industrial de San Cristobal, S.A.
de C.V., 54 186
Compania Industrial del Norte, S.A., 54
152

Compañia Mexicana de Transportación
Aérea, 20 167
Compania Minera de Penoles. See
Industrias Penoles, S.A. de C.V.
Compania Minera Las Torres, 22 286
Compania Siderurgica Huachipato, 24 209
Compañía Telefónica Nacional de España
S.A. See Telefónica Nacional de España
S.A.
**Compaq Computer Corporation, III
124–25; 6 217, 221–23 (upd.);** 9
42–43, 166, 170–71, 472; 10 87,
232–33, 366, 459, 518–19; 12 61, 183,
335, 470; 13 388, 483; 16 4, 196,
367–68; 17 274; 21 123, 391; 22 288;
25 184, 239, 498, 531; 26 90–93 (upd.);
27 365; 28 191; 29 439; 30 12; 36 384;
43 13; 47 153; 63 123, 125. See also
Hewlett-Packard Company.
Comparex Holdings, 69 127
Compart, 24 341
Compass Airlines, 27 475
Compass Design Automation, 16 520
Compass Group PLC, 6 193; 24 194; 27
482; 34 121–24
CompDent Corporation, 22 149–51
Compeda, Ltd., 10 240
Competence ApS, 26 240
Competrol Ltd., 22 189
CompHealth Inc., 25 109–12
**Complete Business Solutions, Inc., 31
130–33**
Complete Post, 50 126
Completion Bond Co., 26 487
Components Agents Ltd., 10 113; 50 43
Composite Craft Inc., I 387
Composite Research & Management Co.,
17 528, 530
**Comprehensive Care Corporation, 15
121–23**
Compression Labs Inc., 10 456; 16 392,
394; 27 365
Compressor Controls Corporation, 15 404;
50 394
Comptoir Général de la Photographie. See
Gaumont SA.
Comptoir Métallurgique Luxembourgeois,
IV 25
Comptoirs Modernes S.A., 19 97–99
Compton Foods, II 675
Compton's MultiMedia Publishing Group,
Inc., 7 165
Compton's New Media, Inc., 7 168
Compu-Notes, Inc., 22 413
**CompuAdd Computer Corporation, 11
61–63**
CompuChem Corporation, 11 425
CompuCom Systems, Inc., 10 232–34,
474; 13 176
CompuDyne Corporation, 51 78–81
Compumech Technologies, 19 312
CompuPharm, Inc., 14 210
**CompUSA, Inc., 10 235–36; 35 116–18
(upd.)**
Compuscript, Inc., 64 27
**CompuServe Incorporated, 9 268–70; 10
237–39;** 12 562; 13 147; 15 265; 16
467, 508; 26 16; 29 224, 226–27; 34
361; 50 329. See also America Online,
Inc.
**CompuServe Interactive Services, Inc.,
27 106, 106–08 (upd.),** 301, 307; 57 42.
See also AOL Time Warner Inc.

**Computer Associates International, Inc.,
6** 224–26; **10** 394; **12** 62; **14** 392; **27**
492; **49 94–97 (upd.)**
Computer City, **12** 470; **36** 387
The Computer Company, **11** 112
Computer Consoles Inc., **III** 164
Computer Data Systems, Inc., 14 127–29
The Computer Department, Ltd., **10** 89
Computer Discount Corporation. *See*
Comdisco, Inc.
Computer Discount Warehouse. *See* CDW
Computer Centers, Inc.
Computer Engineering Associates, **25** 303
Computer Factory, Inc., **13** 176
**Computer Learning Centers, Inc., 26
94–96**
Computer Network, **20** 237
Computer Peripheral Manufacturers
Association, **13** 127
Computer Power, **6** 301
Computer Renaissance, Inc., **18** 207–8
Computer Resources Management, Inc., **26**
36
Computer Sciences Corporation, 6 25,
227–29; 13 462; **15** 474; **18** 370
Computer Systems and Applications, **12**
442
Computer Systems Division (CDS), **13** 201
Computer Terminal Corporation, **11** 67–68
ComputerCity, **10** 235
ComputerCraft, **27** 163
Computerized Lodging Systems, Inc., **11**
275
Computerized Waste Systems, **46** 248
ComputerLand Corp., 9 116; **10** 233,
563; **12** 335; **13 174–76,** 277; **33**
341–42
Computervision Corporation, 7 498; **10**
240–42; 11 275; **13** 201
**Compuware Corporation, 10 243–45; 30
140–43 (upd.); 38** 482; **66 60–64 (upd.)**
CompX International, Inc., **19** 466, 468
Comsat Corporation, 13 341; **23 133–36;**
28 241; **29** 42
Comshare Inc., 23 137–39
Comstock Canada, **9** 301
Comstock Resources, Inc., 47 85–87
Comtec Information Systems Inc., **53** 374
Comtel Electronics, Inc., **22** 409
Comunicaciones Avanzados, S.A. de C.V.,
39 195
Comverse Technology, Inc., 15 124–26;
43 115–18 (upd.)
Comviq GSM AB, **26** 331–33
Con Ed. *See* Consolidated Edison, Inc.
Con-Ferro Paint and Varnish Company, **8**
553
ConAgra, Inc., II 493–95, 517, 585; **7**
432, 525; **8** 53, 499–500; **12 80–82
(upd.); 13** 138, 294, 350, 352; **14** 515;
17 56, 240–41; **18** 247, 290; **21** 290; **23**
320; **25** 243, 278; **26** 172, 174; **36** 416;
42 90–94 (upd.); 50 275, 295, 493; **55**
364–65; **64** 61
Conair Corporation, 16 539; **17 108–10;**
24 131; **25** 56; **69 104–08 (upd.)**
Concentra Inc., 71 117–19
Concept, Inc., **23** 154
Concepts Direct, Inc., 39 93–96
Concepts in Community Living, Inc., **43** 46
Concert Communications Company, **15** 69;
27 304–05; **49** 72
Concesiones de Infraestructuras de
Transportes, S.A., **40** 217

Concession Air, **16** 446
Concha y Toro. *See* Viña Concha y Toro
S.A.
**Concord Camera Corporation, 41
104–07**
Concord EFS, Inc., 52 86–88
Concord Fabrics, Inc., 16 124–26
Concord Leasing, Inc., **51** 108
Concord Watch Company, S.A., **28** 291
Concorde Acceptance Corporation, **64**
20–21
Concorde Hotels & Resorts, **27** 421; **71**
176
Concrete Enterprises, Inc., **72** 233
Concrete Safety Systems, Inc., **56** 332
Concretos Apasco, S.A. de C.V., **51** 28–29
Concurrent Logic, **17** 34
**Condé Nast Publications, Inc., 13
177–81; 23** 98; **59 131–34 (upd.)**
CONDEA Vista Company, **61** 113
Condor Systems Inc., **15** 530
Cone Communications, **25** 258
**Cone Mills LLC, 8 120–22; 67 123–27
(upd.)**
Conelectron, **13** 398
Conexant Systems, Inc., 36 121–25; 43
328
Confecciones Cuscatlecas, S.A. de C.V., **64**
142
Confectionaire, **25** 283
Confederacion Norte-Centromericana y del
Caribe de Futbol, **27** 150
Confederacion Sudamericana de Futbol, **27**
150
Confederation Africaine de Football, **27**
150
Confederation Freezers, **21** 501
ConferencePlus, Inc., **57** 408–09
Confidata Corporation, **11** 111
Confiserie-Group Hofbauer, **27** 105
Confiseriefabrik Richterich & Co. Laufen.
See Ricola Ltd.
Congas Engineering Canada Ltd., **6** 478
Congoleum Corp., 12 28; **16** 18; **18
116–19; 36** 77–78; **43** 19, 21; **63** 300
Congress Financial Corp., **13** 305–06; **19**
108; **27** 276
Congressional Information Services. *See*
Reed Elsevier.
Conic, **9** 324
Conifer Records Ltd., **52** 429
Coniston Partners, **I** 130; **II** 680; **6** 130; **10**
302
Conn-Selmer, Inc., 55 111–14
Conn's, Inc., 67 128–30
CONNA Corp., **7** 113; **25** 125
Connect Group Corporation, **28** 242
Connecticut General Corporation. *See*
CIGNA Corporation.
Connecticut Health Enterprises Network,
22 425
**Connecticut Light and Power Co., 13
182–84; 21** 514; **48** 305
**Connecticut Mutual Life Insurance
Company, III 236–38,** 254, 285
Connecticut National Bank, **13** 467
Connecticut River Banking Company, **13**
467
Connecticut Telephone Company. *See*
Southern New England
Telecommunications Corporation.
Connecticut Yankee Atomic Power
Company, **21** 513
The Connection Group, Inc., **26** 257

Connective Therapeutics, Inc. *See*
Connetics Corporation.
Connectix Corporation, **28** 245
The Connell Company, 29 129–31
Conner Corp., **15** 327
Conner Peripherals, Inc., 6 230–32; 10
403, 459, 463–64, 519; **11** 56, 234; **18**
260
Connetics Corporation, 70 64–66
Connie Lee. *See* College Construction
Loan Insurance Assoc.
Connoisseur Communications, **37** 104
Connolly Data Systems, **11** 66
Connolly Tool and Machine Company, **21**
215
Connors Bros. Income Fund, **II** 631–32;
64 61
Connors Steel Co., **15** 116
Conoco Inc., IV 399–402; 6 539; **7** 346,
559; **8** 556; **11** 97, 400; **16 127–32
(upd.); 18** 366; **21** 29; **50** 178, 363; **63**
439
ConocoPhillips, 61 114; **63 104–15 (upd.)**
Conover Furniture Company, **10** 183
ConQuest Telecommunication Services
Inc., **16** 319
Conquistador Films, **25** 270
Conrad Industries, Inc., 58 68–70
Conrad International Corporation, **62** 179
Conrail Inc. *See* Consolidated Rail
Corporation.
Conran Associates, **17** 43
Conrock Co., **19** 70
Conseco Inc., 10 246–48; 15 257; **33
108–12 (upd.); 64** 396
Conseo GmbH, **68** 289
Conshu Holdings, **24** 450
**Conso International Corporation, 29
132–34**
Consodata S.A., **47** 345, 347
CONSOL Energy Inc., 59 135–37
Consolidated Aircraft Corporation, **9** 16,
497
Consolidated Analysis Centers, Inc. *See*
CACI International Inc.
Consolidated Asset Management Company,
Inc., **25** 204
Consolidated-Bathurst Inc., **26** 445
Consolidated Brands Inc., **14** 18
Consolidated Cigar Holdings, Inc., **15**
137–38; **27** 139–40; **28** 247
Consolidated Citrus Limited Partnership,
60 189
Consolidated Coin Caterers Corporation, **10**
222
Consolidated Converting Co., **19** 109
Consolidated Copper Corp., **13** 503
**Consolidated Delivery & Logistics, Inc.,
24 125–28**
Consolidated Denison Mines Ltd., **8** 418
Consolidated Edison, Inc., V 586–89; 35
479; **45 116–20 (upd.)**
Consolidated Electric Power Asia, **38** 448
Consolidated Electric Supply Inc., **15** 385
Consolidated Electronics Industries Corp.
(Conelco), **13** 397–98
Consolidated Foods Corp., **12** 159, 494; **29**
132
**Consolidated Freightways Corporation,
V 432–34; 6** 280, 388; **12** 278, 309; **13**
19; **14** 567; **21 136–39 (upd.); 25**
148–50; **48 109–13 (upd.)**
Consolidated Gas Company. *See* Baltimore
Gas and Electric Company.

Consolidated Graphics, Inc., 70 67–69
Consolidated International, **50** 98
Consolidated National Life Insurance Co., **10** 246
Consolidated Natural Gas Company, V 590–91; **19** 100–02 (upd.); **54** 83
Consolidated Papers, Inc., 8 123–25; **36** 126–30 (upd.)
Consolidated Plantations Berhad, **36** 434–35
Consolidated Power & Light Company, **6** 580
Consolidated Power & Telephone Company, **11** 342
Consolidated Press Holdings, **8** 551; **37** 408–09
Consolidated Products, Inc., 14 130–32, 352
Consolidated Rail Corporation, V 435–37, 485; **10** 44; **12** 278; **14** 324; **29** 360; **35** 291
Consolidated Restaurant Cos. *See* Landry's Restaurants, Inc.
Consolidated Rock Products Co., **19** 69
Consolidated Specialty Restaurants, Inc., **14** 131–32
Consolidated Stores Corp., **13** 543; **29** 311; **35** 254; **50** 98
Consolidated Theaters, Inc., **14** 87
Consolidated Tire Company, **20** 258
Consolidated Trust Inc., **22** 540
Consolidated TVX Mining Corporation, **61** 290
Consolidated Tyre Services Ltd., **IV** 241
Consolidated Vultee, **II** 32
Consolidation Coal Co., **8** 154, 346–47
Consolidation Services, **44** 10, 13
Consorcio G Grupo Dina, S.A. de C.V., 36 131–33
Consorcio Siderurgica Amazonia Ltd. *See* Siderar S.A.I.C.
Consortium, **34** 373
Consortium de Realisation, **25** 329
Consortium De Realization SAS, **23** 392
Consoweld Corporation, **8** 124
Constar International Inc., 8 562; **13** 190; **32** 125; **64 85–88**
Constellation Brands, Inc., 68 95–100 (upd.)
Constellation Energy Corporation, **24** 29
Constellation Enterprises Inc., **25** 46
Constinsouza, **25** 174
Constitution Insurance Company, **51** 143
Construcciones Aeronáuticas SA, **7** 9; **12** 190; **24** 88. *See also* European Aeronautic Defence and Space Company EADS N.V.
Construction Developers Inc., **68** 114
Construction DJL Inc., **23** 332–33
Constructora CAMSA, C.A., **56** 383
Constructora y Administradora Uno S.A., **72** 269
Consul GmbH, **51** 58
Consul Restaurant Corp., **13** 152
Consumer Access Limited, **24** 95
Consumer Products Company, **30** 39
Consumer Value Stores. *See* CVS Corporation.
Consumer's Gas Co., **I** 264
ConsumerNet, **49** 422
Consumers Cooperative Association. *See* Farmland Industries, Inc.
Consumers Distributing Co. Ltd., **II** 649, 652–53

Consumers Electric Light and Power, **6** 582
The Consumers Gas Company Ltd., 6 476–79; **43** 154. *See also* Enbridge Inc.
Consumers Mutual Gas Light Company. *See* Baltimore and Electric Company.
Consumers Power Co., 14 133–36
Consumers Public Power District, **29** 352
Consumers Union, 26 97–99
Consumers Water Company, 14 137–39; **39** 329
Contact Software International Inc., **10** 509
Container Corporation of America, **V** 147; **8** 476; **26** 446
The Container Store, 36 134–36
Container Transport International, **III** 344
Contaminant Recovery Systems, Inc., **18** 162
CONTAQ Microsystems Inc., **48** 127
Conte S.A., **12** 262
Contech, **10** 493
Contel Corporation, **V** 296–98; **13** 212; **14** 259; **15** 192; **43** 447
Contempo Associates, **14** 105; **25** 307
Contempo Casuals, Inc. *See* The Wet Seal, Inc.
Contemporary Books, **22** 522
Content Technologies Inc., **42** 24–25
Contex Graphics Systems Inc., **24** 428
Conti-Carriers & Terminals Inc., **22** 167
Contico International, L.L.C., **51** 190
ContiCommodity Services, Inc., **10** 250–51
ContiGroup Companies, Inc., 43 119–22 (upd.)
Continental AG, V 240–43, 250–51, 256; **8** 212–14; **9** 248; **15** 355; **19** 508; **56** 67–72 (upd.)
Continental Airlines, Inc., I 96–98, 103, 118, 123–24, 129–30; **6** 105, 120–21, 129–30; **12** 381; **20** 84, 262; **21** 140–43 (upd.); **22** 80, 220; **25** 420, 423; **26** 439–40; **34** 398; **52 89–94 (upd.)**
Continental American Life Insurance Company, **7** 102
Continental Baking Co., **7** 320–21; **12** 276; **13** 427; **27** 309–10; **38** 252
Continental Bank Corporation, II 261–63, 285, 289, 348; **47** 231. *See also* Bank of America.
Continental Bio-Clinical Laboratories, **26** 391
Continental Cablevision, Inc., 7 98–100; **17** 148; **19** 201
Continental Can Co., Inc., 10 130; **13** 255; **15 127–30; 24** 428; **26** 117, 449; **32** 125; **49** 293–94
Continental-Caoutchouc und Gutta-Percha Compagnie. *See* Continental AG.
Continental Carbon Co., **36** 146–48
Continental Care Group, **10** 252–53
Continental Casualty Co., **III** 228–32; **16** 204
Continental Cities Corp., **III** 344
Continental Corporation, III 239–44, 273; **10** 561; **12** 318; **15** 30; **38** 142
Continental Design, **58** 194
Continental Divide Insurance Co., **III** 214
Continental Electronics Corporation, **18** 513–14
Continental Emsco, **24** 305
Continental Equipment Company, **13** 225
Continental Express, **11** 299
Continental Fiber Drum, **8** 476

Continental Gas & Electric Corporation, **6** 511
Continental General Tire Corp., 23 140–42
Continental Grain Company, 10 249–51; **13 185–87 (upd.); 30** 353, 355; **40** 87. *See also* ContiGroup Companies, Inc.
Continental Group Co., I 599–600; 8 175, 424; **17** 106
Continental Hair Products, Inc. *See* Conair Corp.
Continental Health Affiliates, **17** 307
Continental Homes Inc., **26** 291; **58** 84
Continental Illinois Corp. *See* Continental Bank Corporation.
Continental Investment Corporation, **9** 507; **12** 463; **22** 541; **33** 407
Continental Medical Systems, Inc., 10 252–54; **11** 282; **14** 233; **25** 111; **33** 185
Continental Milling Company, **10** 250
Continental Modules, Inc., **45** 328
Continental Motors Corp., **10** 521–22
Continental Mutual Savings Bank, **17** 529
Continental Oil Co. *See* ConocoPhillips.
Continental Packaging Inc., **13** 255
Continental Plastic Containers, Inc., **25** 512
Continental Reinsurance, **11** 533
Continental Research Corporation, **22** 541
Continental Restaurant Systems, **12** 510
Continental Risk Services, **III** 243
Continental Scale Works, **14** 229–30
Continental Telephone Company. *See* GTE Corporation.
Continental Wood Preservers, Inc., **12** 397
ContinueCare Corporation, **25** 41
Continuum Electro-Optics, Inc. *See* Excel Technology, Inc.
Continuum Health Partners, Inc., 60 97–99
Contran Corporation, **19** 467
Contrans Acquisitions, Inc., **14** 38
Contred Ltd., **20** 263
Control Data Corporation, III 126–28; **17** 49; **19** 110, 513–15; **25** 496; **30** 338; **38** 58; **46** 35
Control Data Systems, Inc., 8 117–18, 467; **10 255–57,** 359, 458–59; **11** 469; **16** 137
Control Systemation, Inc. *See* Excel Technology, Inc.
Controladora Comercial Mexicana, S.A. de C.V., 36 137–39
Controladora PROSA, **18** 516, 518
Controlled Materials and Equipment Transportation, **29** 354
Controlonics Corporation, **13** 195
Controls Company of America, **9** 67
Controlware GmbH, **22** 53
Convair, **9** 18, 498; **13** 357
Convenient Food Mart Inc., **7** 114; **25** 125
Convergent Technologies, **11** 519
Converse Inc., 9 133–36, 234; **12** 308; **31** 134–38 (upd.), 211
Convotherm Ltd. *See* Enodis plc.
Conway Computer Group, **18** 370
Conwest Exploration Company Ltd., **16** 10, 12; **43** 3
Conycon. *See* Construcciones y Contratas.
Conzinc Riotinto of Australia. *See* CRA Limited.
Cook Bates Inc., **40** 347–48
Cook Data Services, Inc., **9** 73
Cook Standard Tool Co., **13** 369
Cooke Engineering Company, **13** 194

Cooker Restaurant Corporation, 20 159–61; **51** 82–85 **(upd.)**
Cooking and Crafts Club, **13** 106
Cookson Group plc, III 679–82; **16** 290; **44** 115–20 **(upd.); 49** 234–35
CoolBrands International Inc., 35 119–22
Coolidge Mutual Savings Bank, **17** 529
Coop Schweiz Genossenschaftsverband, 48 114–16
Cooper Cameron Corporation, 20 162–66 **(upd.); 58** 71–75 **(upd.)**
Cooper Canada Ltd., **16** 80
The Cooper Companies, Inc., 39 97–100
Cooper Industries, Inc., II 14–17; **14** 564; **19** 43, 45, 140; **30** 266; **44** 121–25 **(upd.); 49** 159
Cooper Tire & Rubber Company, 8 126–28; **23** 143–46 **(upd.)**
Cooper-Weymouth, **10** 412
Cooper's, Inc., **12** 283
Cooperative Business International, Inc., **60** 88
Cooperative Grange League Federation Exchange, **7** 17
Coopercredito SpA, **72** 21
Coopers & Lybrand, 9 137–38; **12** 391; **25** 383. See also PricewaterhouseCoopers.
CooperVision, **7** 46; **25** 55
Coordinados Elite, S.A. de United Apparel Ventures, **62** 353
Coordinated Caribbean Transport. See Crowley Caribbean Transport.
Coors Company. See Adolph Coors Company.
Coorsh and Bittner, **7** 430
Coote & Jurgenson, **14** 64
Copart Inc., 23 147–49, 285, 287
Copec. See Empresas Copec S.A.
Copeman Ridley, **13** 103
Coperion Holding GmbH, **61** 108
Copico, **44** 273
Copley Pharmaceuticals Inc., **13** 264
The Copley Press, Inc., 23 150–52
Copolymer Corporation, **9** 242
Copper Range Company, **7** 281–82
The Copps Corporation, 32 120–22; **58** 320
Copycat Ltd., **8** 383
Cor Therapeutics, **47** 251
Coral Energy, **41** 359
Corange, Ltd., **37** 111–13
Corbett Canyon. See The Wine Group, Inc.
Corbett Enterprises Inc., **13** 270
Corbis Corporation, 31 139–42
Corby Distilleries Limited, 14 140–42
Corchos de Mérida S.A., **48** 349
Corco. See Commonwealth Oil Refining Company.
Corco, Inc. See Liqui-Box Corporation.
Corcoran & Riggs. See Riggs National Corporation.
The Corcoran Group, Inc., 58 76–78; **61** 267
Cordant Technologies, **56** 11
Cordes, **56** 234
Cordiant plc. See Saatchi & Saatchi plc.
Cordis Corporation, 19 103–05; **36** 306; **46** 104–07 **(upd.)**
Cordon & Gotch, **IV** 619
Cordon Bleu. See Le Cordon Bleu S.A.
Core Laboratories Inc., **I** 486; **11** 265

Corel Corporation, 15 131–33; **33** 113–16 **(upd.)**
CoreStates Financial Corp, 17 111–15
CoreTek, Inc., **36** 353
Corfo. See Corporación de Fomento de la Producción.
Corfuerte S.A. de C.V., **23** 171
Corimon, **12** 218
Corin Othopedic Products, **68** 379
Corinthian Broadcast Corporation, **10** 4
Corinthian Colleges, Inc., 39 101–04
Corio Inc., **38** 188, 432
Cork Asia Pacific. See McPherson's Ltd.
Cormetech. See Corning Inc.
Cornelia Insurance Agency. See Advantage Insurers, Inc.
Cornelius Nurseries, Inc., **51** 61
Cornell Corrections, **28** 255
Cornerstone Direct Marketing, **8** 385–86
Cornerstone Propane Partners, L.P., **37** 280, 283
Cornerstone Real Estate Advisors Inc., **53** 213
Cornerstone Title Company, **8** 461
Corning Clinical Laboratories, **26** 390–92
Corning Consumer Products Company, **27** 288
Corning Inc., III 683–85; **8** 468; **11** 334; **13** 398; **22** 454; **25** 254; **30** 151–52; **44** 126–30 **(upd.)**
Coro International A.V.V., **39** 346
Coronet Industries, Inc., **14** 436
Corporación de Fomento de la Producción, **71** 210
Corporacion Durango, S.A. de C.V., **37** 178
Corporacion Engelhard De Venezuela, C.A. See Engelhard Corporation.
Corporacion Financiera Hipotecaria, **63** 213
Corporación Internacional de Aviación, S.A. de C.V. (Cintra), 20 167–69
Corporación Moctezuma, **21** 261
Corporacion Nacional del Cobre de Chile, 38 231; **40** 121–23
Corporacion Siderurgica Integral, **22** 44
Corporate Childcare Development, Inc. See Bright Horizons Family Solutions, Inc.
Corporate Express, Inc., 22 152–55, 531; **41** 67–69; **47** 88–92 **(upd.); 49** 440
Corporate Intelligence, **55** 251
Corporate Microsystems, Inc., **10** 395
Corporate Partners, **12** 391
Corporate Software Inc., 9 139–41
CorporateFamily Solutions. See Bright Horizons Family Solutions, Inc.
Corporation for Public Broadcasting, 14 143–45; **47** 259
Corporation Trust Co. See CCH Inc.
Corrado Passera, **IV** 588
Corral Midwest, Inc., **10** 333
CorrChoice, Inc. See Greif Inc.
Correctional Services Corporation, 30 144–46
Corrections Corporation of America, 23 153–55; **28** 255; **63** 425
Correo Argentina S.A., **63** 179; **67** 348
Corrigan-McKinney Steel Company, **13** 157
Corrigan's, **16** 559
CorrLogic, Inc., **51** 81
Corroon & Black. See Willis Corroon Group Plc.
Corrosion Technologies de México SA de C V, **53** 285

Corrpro Companies, Inc., 20 170–73
CORT Business Services Corporation, 26 100–02
El Corte Inglés Group, 26 128–31 **(upd.)**
Cortec Corporation, **14** 430
Cortefiel S.A., 64 89–91
Corticeira Amorim, Sociedade Gestora de Participaço es Sociais, S.A., 48 117–20, 349
Corus Group plc, 49 98–105 **(upd.)**
Corvis Corporation. See Broadwing Corporation.
Cory Bros & Co. Ltd., **31** 367, 369
Cory Components, **36** 158
Cory Environmental Ltd., **51** 130
Cory Food Services, Inc., **II** 608
Cory Orchard and Turf. See Chemi-Trol Chemical Co.
Cosco, Inc., **59** 164
Cosco Pacific, **20** 313
Cosi, Inc., 53 111–13
Cosmair Inc., 8 129–32; **12** 404; **31** 418; **62** 282
Cosmar Corp., **37** 269–71
The Cosmetic Center, Inc., 22 156–58
Cosmetic Technology International, Inc., **22** 409
Cosmetics & More Inc., **64** 334
Cosmo Oil Co., Ltd., IV 403–04; **53** 114–16 **(upd.); 63** 308, 311
Cosmopolitan Cosmetics GmbH, **48** 420, 422
Cosmopolitan Productions, **IV** 626; **19** 203
Cosmos International, Inc., **51** 307
Cosmotel, **46** 401
Cosorzio Interprovinciale Vini, **10** 181
Cost Plus, Inc., 12 393; **27** 109–11; **34** 337, 340
Cost-U-Less, Inc., 51 90–93
Costa Coffee, **63** 88
Costa Cruise Lines, **27** 29, 90, 92
Costa Rica International, Inc., **41** 329
Costain Civil Engineering Ltd., **13** 206
Costain Homes, **31** 386
Costco Wholesale Corporation, V 36; **10** 206; **11** 240; **14** 393–95; **15** 470; **25** 235; **27** 95; **43** 123–25 **(upd.); 63** 427, 430; **64** 68
Costruzioni Meccaniche Nazionalia, **13** 218
Cosway Corporation Berhad. See Berjaya Group Bhd.
Coto Centro Integral de Comercializacion S.A., 66 65–67
Cott Corporation, 9 291; **52** 95–98
Cotter & Company, V 37–38; **12** 8. See also TruServ Corporation.
Cotter Corporation, **29** 488
Cotton Incorporated, 46 108–11
Cotton Producers Association. See Gold Kist Inc.
Coty, Inc., 36 140–42; **37** 270
Coudert Brothers, 30 147–50
Coulee Region Organic Produce Pool. See Organic Valley.
Coulter Corporation. See Beckman Coulter, Inc.
Counsel Corp., **46** 3
Counselor Co., **14** 230
Country Fresh, Inc., **26** 449
Country Hedging, Inc., **60** 88
Country Kitchen International, **22** 127
Country Music Television, **11** 153
Country Seat Stores, Inc., **15** 87
Country Store of Concord, Inc., **10** 216

Countrywide Credit Industries, Inc., 16 133–36
County Catering Co., **13** 103
County Data Corporation, **18** 24
County Market, **II** 670
County Seat Stores Inc., II 669; **9** 142–43; **50** 455
Courage Brewing Group., **I** 229, 438–39
Courier Corporation, 41 108–12
Courir S.A., **39** 183–85
Courrèges Parfums, **III** 48; **8** 343
The Courseware Developers, **11** 19
Court Courier Systems, Inc., **24** 126
Court House Square, **10** 44
Courtaulds plc, V 359–61; **17** 116–19 (upd.); **33** 134; **41** 9; **52** 99, 101; **54** 326
Courts Plc, 45 121–24
Courtyard by Marriott, **9** 427
Cousins Mortgage and Equity Investments, **12** 393
Cousins Properties Incorporated, 65 121–23
Covance Inc., 30 151–53
Covanta Energy Corporation, 64 92–95 (upd.)
Covantage, **11** 379
Covenant Life Insurance, **III** 314
Coventry Climax Engines, Ltd., **13** 286
Coventry Corporation, **17** 166, 168
Coventry Health Care, Inc., 59 138–40
Coventry Machinists Company, **7** 458
Coville Inc., **16** 353
Covington & Burling, 40 124–27
Covisint LLC. *See* Compuware Corporation.
Covol Technologies Inc. *See* Headwaters Incorporated.
Cowles Media Company, 23 156–58
Cox Cable Communications, Inc., **42** 114
Cox Enterprises, Inc., IV 595–97; **7** 327; **9** 74; **17** 148; **22** 159–63 (upd.); **24** 120; **30** 217; **38** 307–08; **67** 131–35 (upd.)
Cox Medical Enterprises, Inc., **21** 47
Cox Newsprint, Inc., **25** 11
Cox Pharmaceuticals, **35** 25
Cox Woodlands Company, **25** 11
Coz Chemical Co., **21** 20, 22
CP. *See* Canadian Pacific Limited.
CP/AAON. *See* AAON, Inc.
CP National, **19** 412
CP Ships Holding, Inc., **45** 80; **50** 209–10
CPC International Inc., II 496–98; **27** 40. *See also* Bestfoods.
CP8, **43** 89
CPI Corp., 38 157–60
CPL. *See* Carolina Power & Light Company.
CR England, Inc., 63 116–18
CR2A Holding, **48** 402
CRA Limited, IV 58–61, 67, 192; **7** 124. *See also* Rio Tinto plc.
Crabtree & Evelyn Ltd., **51** 67
Crabtree Electricals, **III** 503; **7** 210
Cracker Barrel Old Country Store, Inc., 10 258–59. *See also* CBRL Group, Inc.
Craft House Corp., **8** 456
Craftique, **33** 350–51
Craftmade International, Inc., 44 131–33
Craftopia.com, **64** 185
Craig Bit Company, **13** 297
Crain Communications, Inc., 12 83–86; **35** 123–27 (upd.)

Cram Company. *See* The George F. Cram Company, Inc.
Cramer, Berkowitz & Co., 34 125–27
Cramer Electronics, **10** 112; **50** 41
Cranberry Canners, Inc. *See* Ocean Spray Cranberries, Inc.
Crane & Co., Inc., 26 103–06; **30** 42
Crane Carton Co., **44** 66
Crane Co., 8 133–36, 179; **24** 332; **30** 154–58 (upd.)
Crane Packing Company, **19** 311
Crane Supply Company, **8** 135
Cranium, Inc., 69 109–11
Cranston Mills, **13** 168
Cranswick plc, 40 128–30
Crate and Barrel, 9 144–46; **27** 429; **36** 135. *See also* Euromarket Designs Inc.
Cravath, Swaine & Moore, 27 325; **43** 126–28
Crawford Door Försäljnings AB, **53** 85
Crawford Group, Inc., **17** 372
Cray Research, Inc., III 129–31; **10** 256; **16** 137–40 (upd.); **21** 391; **22** 428; **29** 440
Crayfish Company, Ltd., **36** 153
Crazy Eddie Inc., **23** 373
Crazy Shirts, Inc., **45** 42
CRC Holdings Corp., **51** 217
CRD Total France, **IV** 560
Creaciones Victorio & Lucchino, **60** 246
Cream City Railway Company, **6** 601
Cream Wine Company, **48** 392
Creasy Co., **II** 682
Creative Artists Agency LLC, 10 228; **22** 297; **23** 512, 514; **32** 115; **38** 161–64
Creative Artists Associates, **43** 235
Creative BioMolecules, Inc., **29** 454
Creative Business Concepts, Inc., **39** 346
Creative Concepts in Advertising, **27** 194
Creative Displays, Inc., **27** 279
Creative Engineering Inc., **13** 472
Creative Food 'N Fun Co., **14** 29
Creative Forming, Inc., **8** 562
Creative Gems & Jewelry, Ltd., **62** 371
Creative Hairdressers Inc. *See* Ratner Companies.
Creative Integration and Design Inc., **20** 146
Creative Memories, **40** 44
Creative Optics Inc., **61** 193
Creative Technologies Corp., **15** 401
Creative Technology Ltd., 48 83; **57** 78–81
Credit & Risk Management Associates, Inc., **18** 170
Credit Acceptance Corporation, 18 120–22
Crédit Agricole, II 264–66, 355; **19** 51; **59** 190, 193
Crédit Commercial de France, **25** 173
Crédit Communal de Belgique, **42** 111
Credit Immobilier, **7** 538
Crédit Local de France, **42** 111
Crédit Lyonnais, 6 396; **7** 12; **9** 147–49; **19** 34, 51, 166; **21** 226; **25** 170, 329; **33** 117–21 (upd.)
Crédit National S.A., 9 150–52
Crédit Suisse Group, II 267–69, 369–70, 378–79, 402–04; **21** 144–47 (upd.); **52** 354, 356–358; **59** 141–47 (upd.). *See also* Schweizerische Kreditanstalt.
Credit Union Federation, **48** 290
CrediThrift Financial, **11** 16
Credito Agrario, **65** 72

Credito Italiano, II 270–72
Credito Minero y Mercantil, S.A., **22** 285
Credito Provincial Hipotecario, **19** 189
Creditrust Corp., **42** 259
Cree Inc., 13 399; **53** 117–20
Crellin Holding, Inc., **8** 477
Crellin Plastics, **8** 13
Cremascoli Ortho Group, **61** 403
Cremonini S.p.A., 57 82–84
Creo Inc., 48 121–24
Cresap, McCormick and Paget, **32** 458
Crescent Box & Printing Co., **13** 442
Crescent Capital, **44** 95
Crescent Niagara Corp., **II** 16
Crescent Real Estate Equities Company, **25** 454
Crescent Software Inc., **15** 373
Crescent Vert Company, Ltd., **II** 51; **21** 330
Crescent Washing Machine Company, **8** 298
Crescott, Inc., **15** 501
Crest Fruit Co., **17** 458
Crest Ridge Homes, Inc., **17** 83
Crest Service Company, **9** 364
Crestbrook Forest Industries Ltd., **IV** 285
Crestline, **60** 140
Crestmont Financial Corporation, **14** 472
Cresud S.A.C.I.F. y A., 63 119–21, 214
Creusot-Loire, **19** 166
Crevettes du Cameroun, **13** 244
CRH plc, 37 203, 206; **60** 77; **64** 96–99
Cricket Communications, Inc. *See* Leap Wireless International, Inc.
Crimson Associates L.P., **26** 48
Crisnova S.A. *See* Vidrala S.A.
Crisoba. *See* Compania Industrial de San Cristobal, S.A. de C.V.
Crist Partners, **34** 249
Cristalerias de Chile S.A., 67 136–38
Criterion Casualty Company, **10** 312
Criterion Life Insurance Company, **10** 311
Critical Care Concepts, **50** 123
Crocker National Bank, **13** 535
Crocker National Corporation, **12** 536
Crockett Container Corporation, **8** 268
Croda International Plc, 45 125–28
Croitex S.A., **26** 374
Crompton & Knowles Corp., I 633; **9** 153–55
Crompton Corporation, 36 143–50 (upd.); **52** 305
CROPP. *See* Organic Valley.
Crosby Enterprises, **17** 19
Croscill Home Fashions, **8** 510
Croscill, Inc., 42 95–97
Crosman Corporation, 62 81–83
Cross & Trecker Corporation, **10** 330
Cross Company. *See* A.T. Cross Company.
Cross-Continent Auto Retailers, **26** 501
Cross Country Group, **25** 358
Cross Creek Apparel, Inc., **30** 400
Cross Pointe Paper Corporation, **26** 363
Cross/Tessitore & Associates, **16** 259
Cross Timbers Oil Company. *See* XTO Energy, Inc.
Crossair AG. *See* Swiss International Air Lines Ltd.
Crossfield Foods, **61** 133
Crossley Motors, Ltd., **13** 285
Crosspoint Venture Partners, **57** 49
Crothers Properties, Ltd., **21** 500
Crouse-Hinds Co., **19** 45

Crowell-Collier Publishing Company, **7** 286

Crowell Publishing Company, **19** 266

Crowley Maritime Corporation, 6 382–84; 9 510–11; **28 77–80 (upd.)**

Crowley, Milner & Company, 19 106–08

Crown Advertising Agency. *See* King Kullen Grocery Co., Inc.

Crown America Corp., **13** 393

Crown Books Corporation, 14 61; **16** 159–61; **21 148–50; 41** 61

Crown Casino, **54** 299

Crown Central Petroleum Corporation, 7 101–03

Crown, Cork & Seal Company, Inc., I 601–03; **13** 188–90 (upd.); **15** 129; **17** 106; **24** 264; **30** 475; **32** 123–27 (upd.); **64** 86–87

Crown Courier Systems, Inc., **24** 126

Crown Crafts, Inc., 16 141–43

Crown Drugs, **II** 673

Crown Equipment Corporation, 15 134–36

Crown House Engineering, **44** 148

Crown Media Holdings, Inc., 45 129–32

Crown Oil and Refining Company, **7** 101

Crown Packaging, **19** 155

Crown Pet Foods Ltd., **39** 356

Crown Point Ventures, **49** 316

Crown Publishing Group, **IV** 584; **13** 429; **31** 376, 379

Crown Radio, **17** 123–24; **41** 114

Crown Steel Products Co. *See* TransPro, Inc.

Crown Technical Systems, Inc., **37** 215

Crown Vantage Inc., 29 135–37

Crown Zellerbach Corporation, **8** 261; **24** 247

Crownx Inc. *See* Extendicare Health Services, Inc.

Crowson and Son Ltd., **23** 219

CRSS Inc., 6 142–44; 23 491

CRT, **51** 199

CRTC. *See* Canadian Radio-Television and Telecommunications Commission.

Cruise America Inc., 21 151–53

Cruise Associates, **22** 471

Crum & Forster Holdings, Inc., **III** 172; **6** 290; **26** 546; **57** 136; **69** 377

Crump E & S, **6** 290

Crupo Camino Real. *See* Real Turismo, S.A. de C.V.

Cruse Bekleidung GmbH & Co. KG, **53** 195

Crush International, **III** 53

Crushed Stone Sales Ltd., **IV** 241

Cruzan Rum Distillery, Ltd., **27** 478

Cruzcampo, **18** 501

Cruzeiro do Sul Airlines. *See* Varig, SA.

Cryenco Sciences Inc., **21** 109

CryoLife, Inc., 46 112–14

Crystal Brands, Inc., 9 156–58; 12 431

Crystal Choice Water Service LLC. *See* SJW Corporation.

Crystal Market, **41** 174

Crystal Rock Water Co., **51** 396

Crystal SA. *See* Dalkia Holding.

Crystaline Company Limited, **70** 234

Crystallex International Corporation, **61** 291

CS Crable Sportswear Inc., **23** 66

CS First Boston Inc., II 269, 402–04; **12** 209; **21** 146. *See also* Credit Suisse Group.

CS Holding. *See* Credit Suisse Group.

CS Life, **21** 146–47

CSA. *See* China Southern Airlines Company Ltd.

CSC. *See* Computer Sciences Corporation.

CSC Holdings, Inc., **32** 105

CSC Service Co Ltd., **62** 245

CSE Corp., **III** 214

Csemege, **53** 178

CSFB. *See* Financière Crédit Suisse-First Boston; Credit Suisse Group.

CSFBdirect Inc., **46** 55

CSG Information Services, **55** 250–51

CSI Computer Systems, **47** 36

CSK, **10** 482

CSK Auto Corporation, 38 165–67

CSM N.V., 65 124–27

CSO. *See* Columbus & Southern Ohio Electric Company.

CSR Limited, III 686–88; **28 81–84 (upd.)**

CSR Rinker Materials Corp., **46** 197

CSS Industries, Inc., 35 128–31

CST Office Products, **15** 36; **42** 416

CSX Corporation, V 438–40, 485; **6** 340; **9** 59; **13** 462; **22** 164–68 (upd.); **29** 360–61

CSY Agri-Processing, **7** 81–82

CT Financial Services Inc., **49** 397

CT&T. *See* Carolina Telephone and Telegraph Company.

CTA. *See* Comptoir des Textiles Artificielles.

CTA Makro Commercial Co., Ltd., **55** 347

CTB International Corporation, 43 129–31 (upd.)

CTG, Inc., 11 64–66

CTI. *See* Cosmetic Technology International, Inc.

CTN Assurance Company, **72** 117

CTR. *See* Compagnie Transcontinentale de Reassurance.

CTS Corporation, 19 104; **39 105–08**

CTV Network, **35** 69

C2B Technologies, **45** 201

CTX Mortgage Company, **8** 88

Cub Foods, **II** 669–70; **14** 411; **17** 302; **18** 505; **22** 327; **50** 455

Cuban American Oil Company, **8** 348

Cubic Corporation, 19 109–11

CUC International Inc., 16 144–46. *See also* Cendant Corporation.

Cudahy Corp., **12** 199

Cuisinart Corporation, 17 110; **24 129–32**

Culbro Corporation, 14 19; **15 137–39.** *See also* General Cigar Holdings, Inc.

Culinar Inc., **59** 364

Culinary Foods, Inc., **14** 516; **50** 493

Cullen/Frost Bankers, Inc., 25 113–16

Culligan International Company, 12 87–88, 346; **16** 20

Culligan Water Technologies, Inc., 38 168–70 (upd.)

Cullinet Software Corporation, **14** 390; **15** 108

Cullman Bros. *See* Culbro Corporation.

Culp, Inc., 29 138–40

Culter Industries, Inc., **22** 353

Culver Franchising System, Inc., 58 79–81

Cumberland Farms, Inc., 17 120–22; 26 450

Cumberland Federal Bancorporation, **13** 223; **31** 206

Cumberland Newspapers, **7** 389

Cumberland Packing Corporation, 26 107–09

Cummings-Moore Graphite Company. *See* Asbury Carbons, Inc.

Cummins Cogeneration Co. *See* Cogeneration Development Corp.

Cummins Engine Co., Inc., I 146–48, 186; **10** 273–74; **12 89–92 (upd.);** **16** 297; **19** 293; **21** 503; **26** 256; **40 131–35 (upd.); 42** 387

Cummins Utility Supply, **58** 334

Cumo Sports, **16** 109

Cumulus Media Inc., 37 103–05

CUNA Mutual Group, 11 495; **62 84–87**

Cunard Line Ltd., 23 159–62; 27 90, 92; **36** 323; **38** 341, 344

CUNO Incorporated, 57 85–89

CurranCare, LLC, **50** 122

Current, Inc., 37 106–09

Currys Group PLC. *See* Dixons Group PLC.

Curtas Technologie SA, **58** 221

Curtice-Burns Foods, Inc., 7 17–18, 104–06; **21** 18, 154–57 (upd.). *See also* Birds Eye Foods, Inc.

Curtin & Pease/Peneco, **27** 361

Curtis Circulation Co., **IV** 619

Curtis Homes, **22** 127

Curtis Industries, **13** 165

Curtis 1000 Inc. *See* American Business Products, Inc.

Curtis Restaurant Supply, **60** 160

Curtis Squire Inc., **18** 455; **70** 262

Curtiss-Wright Corporation, 7 263; **8** 49; **9** 14, 244, 341, 417; **10 260–63; 11** 427; **23** 340; **35 132–37 (upd.)**

Curver-Rubbermaid. *See* Newell Rubbermaid.

Curves International, Inc., 54 80–82

Cushman & Wakefield Inc., **58** 303

Cussons. *See* PZ Cussons plc.

Custom Academic Publishing Company, **12** 174

Custom Building Products of California, Inc., **53** 176

Custom Chrome, Inc., 16 147–49

Custom Electronics, Inc., **9** 120

Custom Expressions, Inc., **7** 24; **22** 35

Custom Hoists, Inc., **17** 458

Custom, Ltd, **46** 197

Custom Organics, **8** 464

Custom Primers, **17** 288

Custom Publishing Group, **27** 361

Custom Technologies Corp., **19** 152

Custom Thermoform, **24** 512

Custom Tool and Manufacturing Company, **41** 366

Custom Transportation Services, Inc., **26** 62

Custom Woodwork & Plastics Inc., **36** 159

Customized Transportation Inc., **22** 164, 167

AB Custos, **25** 464

Cutisin, **55** 123

Cutler-Hammer Inc., **63** 401

Cutter & Buck Inc., 27 112–14

Cutter Precision Metals, Inc., **25** 7

CVC Capital Partners Limited, **49** 451; **54** 207

CVE Corporation, Inc., **24** 395

CVG Aviation, **34** 118

CVI Incorporated, **21** 108

CVN Companies, **9** 218

CVPS. *See* Central Vermont Public Service Corporation.

CVRD. *See* Companhia Vale do Rio Doce Ltd.

CVS Corporation, 32 166, 170; **34** 285; **45 133–38 (upd.); 63** 335–36

CWA. *See* City of Westminster Assurance Company Ltd.

CWM. *See* Chemical Waste Management, Inc.

CWP. *See* Custom Woodwork & Plastics Inc.

CWT Farms International Inc., **13** 103

CXT Inc., **33** 257

Cyber Communications Inc., **16** 168

CyberCash Inc., **18** 541, 543

Cybermedia, Inc., 25 117–19, 349

Cybernet Electronics Corp., **II** 51; **21** 330

Cybernex, **10** 463

Cybershield, Inc., **52** 103, 105

CyberSource Corp., **26** 441

CYBERTEK Corporation, **11** 395

CyberTrust Solutions Inc., **42** 24–25

Cybex International, Inc., 49 106–09

Cycle & Carriage Ltd., **20** 313; **56** 285

Cycle Video Inc., **7** 590

Cyclops Corporation, **10** 45; **13** 157

Cydsa. *See* Grupo Cydsa, S.A. de C.V.

Cygna Energy Services, **13** 367

Cygne Designs, Inc., 25 120–23; **37** 14

Cygnus Business Media, Inc., 56 73–77

Cymbal Co., Ltd. *See* Nagasakiya Co., Ltd.

Cynosure Inc., **11** 88

Cypress Amax Minerals Co., **13** 158; **22** 285–86

Cypress Insurance Co., **III** 214

Cypress Management Services, Inc., **64** 311

Cypress Semiconductor Corporation, 18 17, 383; **20 174–76; 43** 14; **48 125–29 (upd.)**

Cyprus Amax Coal Company, **35** 367

Cyprus Amax Minerals Company, 21 158–61

Cyprus Minerals Company, 7 107–09

Cyrix Corporation. *See* National Semiconductor Corporation.

Cyrk Inc., 19 112–14; 21 516; **33** 416

Cytec Industries Inc., 27 115–17

Cytyc Corporation, 69 112–14

Czarnikow-Rionda Company, Inc., 32 128–30

D&B. *See* Dun & Bradstreet Corporation.

D&D Enterprises, Inc., **24** 96

D&F Industries, Inc., **17** 227; **41** 204

D&K Wholesale Drug, Inc., 14 146–48

D&N Systems, Inc., **10** 505

D&O Inc., **17** 363

D&W Computer Stores, **13** 176

D & W Food Stores, Inc., **8** 482; **27** 314

D Green (Electronics) Limited, **65** 141

D.B. Kaplan's, **26** 263

D.C. Heath & Co., **36** 273; **38** 374

D.C. National Bancorp, **10** 426

D. de Ricci-G. Selnet et Associes, **28** 141

d.e.m.o., **28** 345

D.E. Shaw & Co., **25** 17; **38** 269

D.E. Winebrenner Co., **7** 429

D.G. Calhoun, **12** 112

D.G. Yuengling & Son, Inc., 38 171–73

D.H. Holmes Company, Limited. *See* Dillard's Inc.

D.I. Manufacturing Inc., **37** 351

D.K. Gold, **17** 138

D.L. Rogers Group, **37** 363

D.L. Saslow Co., **19** 290

D.M. Nacional, **23** 170

D.R. Horton, Inc., 25 217; **26** 291; **58 82–84**

D.W. Mikesell Co. *See* Mike-Sell's Inc.

Da Gama Textiles Company, **24** 450

D'Addario & Company, Inc. *See* J. D'Addario & Company, Inc.

Dade Behring Holdings Inc., 71 120–22

Dade Reagents Inc., **19** 103

DADG. *See* Deutsch-Australische Dampfschiffs-Gesellschaft.

DAEDUK Techno Valley Company Ltd., **62** 174

Daewoo Group, III 457–59, 749; **18 123–27 (upd.); 30** 185; **57 90–94 (upd.)**

DAF, **7** 566–67

Daffy's Inc., 26 110–12

NV Dagblad De Telegraaf. *See* N.V. Holdingmaatschappij De Telegraaf.

D'Agostino Supermarkets Inc., 19 115–17

Dagsbladunie, **IV** 611

DAH. *See* DeCrane Aircraft Holdings Inc.

Dahl Manufacturing, Inc., **17** 106

Dahlberg, Inc., **18** 207–08

Dahlonega Equipment and Supply Company, **12** 377

Dai-Ichi. *See also listings under* Daiichi.

Dai-Ichi Bank, **I** 511

Dai-Ichi Kangyo Asset Management Co. Ltd., **58** 235

Dai-Ichi Kangyo Bank Ltd., II 273–75, 325–26, 360–61, 374; **58** 228

Dai-Ichi Mokko Co., **III** 758

Dai-Ichi Mutual Life Insurance Co., **III** 277, 401; **25** 289; **26** 511; **38** 18

Dai Nippon. *See also listings under* Dainippon.

Dai Nippon Brewery Co., **I**, 282; **21** 319

Dai Nippon Ink and Chemicals, Inc., **54** 330

Dai Nippon Printing Co., Ltd., IV 598–600; 57 95–99 (upd.)

Dai Nippon Yuben Kai Kodansha. *See* Kodansha Ltd.

Daido Boeki, **24** 325

Daido Steel Co., Ltd., IV 62–63

The Daiei, Inc., V 39–40; **17 123–25 (upd.); 18** 186, 285; **36** 418–19; **41 113–16 (upd.)**

Daig Corporation, **43** 349–50

Daignault Rolland, **24** 404

Daihatsu Motor Company, Ltd., 7 110–11; **21 162–64 (upd.); 38** 415

Daiichi. *See also listings under* Dai-Ichi.

Daiichi Atomic Power Industry Group, **II** 22

Daikin Industries, Ltd., III 460–61

Daikyo Oil Co., Ltd., **IV** 403–04, 476; **53** 114

Daily Mail and General Trust plc, 19 118–20; 39 198–99

Daily Press Inc., **IV** 684; **22** 522

The Daimaru, Inc., V 41–42, 130; **42 98–100 (upd.)**

Daimler-Benz Aerospace AG, 16 150–52; 24 84

Daimler-Benz AG, I 149–51, 186–87, 411, 549; **III** 750; **7** 219; **10** 261, 274; **11** 31; **12** 192, 342; **13** 30, 286, 414; **14** 169; **15 140–44 (upd.); 20** 312–13; **22** 11; **26** 481, 498

DaimlerChrysler Aerospace AG. *See* European Aeronautic Defence and Space Company EADS N.V.

DaimlerChrysler AG, 34 128–37 (upd.), 306; **57** 247; **64 100–07 (upd.)**

Dain Bosworth Inc., **15** 231–33, 486

Dain Rauscher Corporation, 35 138–41 (upd.)

Daini-Denden Incorporated, **12** 136–37

Daini-Denden Kikaku Company, Ltd. *See* DDI Corporation.

Dainippon. *See also listings under* Dai-Nippon.

Dainippon Ink & Chemicals, Inc., **10** 466–67; **13** 308, 461; **17** 363; **28** 194

Daio Paper Corporation, IV 266–67

Dairy Crest Group plc, 32 131–33

Dairy Equipment Company, **62** 43

Dairy Farm Ice and Cold Storage Co., **IV** 700; **47** 176

Dairy Farm Management Services Ltd., **I** 471; **20** 312

Dairy Farmers of America Inc., **48** 45

Dairy Fresh, Inc., **26** 449

Dairy Mart Convenience Stores, Inc., 7 113–15; 17 501; **25 124–27 (upd.)**

Dairy Queen. *See* International Dairy Queen, Inc.

Dairymen, Inc., **11** 24

Dairyworld Foods, **59** 364

Daishowa Paper Manufacturing Co., Ltd. IV 268–70, 326, 667; **17** 398; **57 100–03 (upd.)**

Daisy/Cadnetix Inc., **6** 248; **24** 235

Daisy Manufacturing Company, Inc., **34** 72; **60** 291

Daisy Outdoor Products Inc., 58 85–88

Daisy Systems Corp., **11** 46, 284–85, 489

Daisytek International Corporation, 18 128–30

Daiwa Bank, Ltd., II 276–77, 347, 438; **26** 457; **39 109–11 (upd.)**

Daiwa Securities Company, Limited, II 405–06; 9 377

Daiwa Securities Group Inc., 55 115–18 (upd.)

Daka, Inc. *See* Unique Casual Restaurants, Inc.

Dakin Inc., **24** 44; **33** 415

Dakota Power Company, **6** 580; **20** 73

Dakotah Mills, **8** 558–59; **16** 353

Daksoft, Inc., **20** 74

Daktronics, Inc., 32 134–37

Dal-Tile International Inc., 22 46, 49, **169–71; 53** 175–76

Dale Carnegie Training, Inc., 28 85–87

Dale Electronics, **21** 519

Daleville & Middletown Telephone Company, **14** 258

Dalfort Corp., **15** 281

Dalgety PLC, II 499–500; 12 411; **22** 147; **27** 258, 260. *See also* PIC International Group PLC

Dalian, **14** 556

Dalian Cement Factory, **III** 718

Dalian Dali Steel Works Co. Ltd., **53** 173

Dalian International Nordic Tire Co., **20** 263

Dalkia Holding, 66 68–70

Dallah Albaraka Group, 72 83–86
D'Allaird's, **24** 315–16
Dallas Airmotive, **II** 16
Dallas Ceramic Co. *See* Dal-Tile
International Inc.
Dallas Cowboys Football Club, Ltd., 33
122–25
Dallas-Fort Worth Suburban Newspapers,
Inc., **10** 3
Dallas Semiconductor Corporation, 13
191–93; 31 143–46 (upd.)
Daltex General Agency, Inc., **25** 115
Damark International, Inc., 18 131–34.
See also Provell Inc.
Damart, **25** 523
Dameron-Pierson Co., **25** 500
Dames & Moore, Inc., 25 128–31. *See*
also URS Corporation.
Damon, **21** 153
Damon Clinical Laboratories Inc., **26** 392
Damon Corp., **11** 334; **54** 57
Dan River Inc., 35 142–46
Dan's Supreme, **24** 528
Dana Alexander Inc., **27** 197; **43** 218
Dana Corporation, I 152–53; 10 264–66
(upd.); 23 170–71; 47 376
Dana Design Ltd., **16** 297
Danaher Corporation, 7 116–17; 58 65
Danapak Holding Ltd., **11** 422
Danapak Riverwood Multipack A/S, **48**
344
Danbury Mint, **34** 370
Danbury Phamacal Inc., **31** 254
Dancing Sandwiches, Inc. *See* Zingerman's
Community of Businesses.
Danfoss A/S, **61** 322
Daniel Industries, Inc., 16 153–55
Daniel International Corp., **I** 570–71; **8**
192
Daniel James Insurance Group, **41** 64
Daniel P. Creed Co., Inc., **8** 386
Daniel's Jewelers, **16** 559
Danieli & C. Officine Meccaniche, **13** 98
Daniels Packaging, **12** 25
Daniels Pharmaceuticals, Inc., **24** 257
Danielson Holding Corporation, **64** 92
Danisco A/S, 44 134–37
Danish Aalborg, **27** 91
Danley Machine Corp., **I** 514
Danner Shoe Manufacturing Company, **18**
300; **61** 164
Dannon Co., Inc., 14 149–51
Danone Group, **25** 85; **35** 394, 397
Danray, **12** 135
Dansk Bioprotein, **IV** 406–07
Dansk International Designs Ltd., **10** 179,
181; **12** 313
Dansk Metal and Armaturindistri, **III** 569;
20 361
Danske Bank Aktieselskab, 50 148–51
Danskin, Inc., 12 93–95; 15 358; 62
88–92 (upd.)
Danville Resources, Inc., **13** 502
Danzas Group, V 441–43; 40 136–39
(upd.)
DAP, Inc., **12** 7; **18** 549
DAP Products Inc., **36** 396
Daphne's Greek Café. *See* Fili Enterprises,
Inc.
Dara Michelle, **17** 101–03
D'Arcy Masius Benton & Bowles, Inc., 6
20–22; 26 187; 28 137; 32 138–43
(upd.)

Darden Restaurants, Inc., 16 156–58; 36
238; **44 138–42 (upd.)**
Darigold, Inc., 9 159–61
Darius International, Inc., **62** 296
Darling, Brown & Sharpe. *See* Brown &
Sharpe Manufacturing Co.
Darracq, **7** 6
Darrell J. Sekin Transport Co., **17** 218
Dart & Kraft Financial Corp., **III** 610–11;
12 310; **14** 547
Dart Group Corporation, II 645, 656,
667, 674; **12** 49; **15** 270; **16 159–62; 21**
148; **23** 370; **24** 418; **27** 158; **32** 168
Dart Industries. *See* Premark International
Inc.
Dart Transit Co., **13** 550
Dartex, **18** 434
Darty S.A., 27 118–20
Darvel Realty Trust, **14** 126
Darya-Varia Laboratoria, **18** 182
DASA. *See* Daimler-Benz Aerospace AG;
Deutsche Aerospace Airbus.
Dashwood Industries, **19** 446
DASS Die andere
SystementsorgungsGesellschaft mbH, **58**
28
Dassault Aviation SA, **21** 11
Dassault-Breguet. *See* Avions Marcel
Dassault-Breguet Aviation.
Dassault Systèmes S.A., 25 132–34; 26
179. *See also* Groupe Dassault Aviation
SA.
Dassler, **14** 6
Dastek Inc., **10** 464; **11** 234–35
DAT GmbH, **10** 514
Data Acquisition Systems, Inc., **16** 300
Data Architects, **14** 318
Data Base Management Inc., **11** 19
Data-Beam Corp., **25** 301
Data Broadcasting Corporation, 31
147–50
Data Card Corporation, **IV** 680; **58** 340
Data Force Inc., **11** 65
Data General Corporation, 8 137–40; 9
297; **10** 499; **12** 162; **13** 201; **16** 418; **20**
8
Data One Corporation, **11** 111
Data Preparation, Inc., **11** 112
Data Printer, Inc., **18** 435
Data Specialties Inc. *See* Zebra
Technologies Corporation.
Data Structures Inc., **11** 65
Data Systems Technology, **11** 57; **38** 375
Data Technology Corp., **18** 510
Data 3 Systems, **9** 36
Datac plc, **18** 140
Datachecker Systems, **III** 164; **11** 150
Datacraft Asia Limited, **69** 127
Datacraft Corp., **II** 38
DataFocus, Inc., **18** 112
DataPath Systems, **64** 246
Datapoint Corporation, 11 67–70
Dataquest Inc., **10** 558; **21** 235, 237; **22**
51; **25** 347
Datas Incorporated. *See* Delta Air Lines,
Inc.
Datascope Corporation, 39 112–14
Dataset Communications Inc., **23** 100
Datastream International Ltd., **10** 89; **13**
417
Datatec Ltd., **67** 392–94
DataTimes Corporation, **29** 58
Datavision Inc., **11** 444
Datec, **22** 17

Datek Online Holdings Corp., 32
144–46; 48 225–27
Datran, **11** 468
Datsun. *See* Nissan Motor Company, Ltd.
Datura Corp., **14** 391
Dauphin Deposit Corporation, 14
152–54
Dauphin Distribution Services. *See* Exel
Logistics Ltd.
Daut + Rietz and Connectors Pontarlier,
19 166
Dave & Buster's, Inc., 33 126–29
Davenport Mammoet Heavy Transport Inc.,
26 280
The Davey Tree Expert Company, 11
71–73
David & Charles Group. *See* F&W
Publications, Inc.
The David and Lucile Packard
Foundation, 41 117–19
David B. Smith & Company, **13** 243
David Berg & Co., **14** 537
David Brown & Son. *See* Brown & Sharpe
Manufacturing Co.
David Brown, Ltd., **10** 380
David Clark, **30** 357
David Crystal, Inc., **9** 156
David Hafler Company, **43** 323
The David J. Joseph Company, 14
155–56; 19 380; 55 347
David Jones Ltd., 60 100–02
David Kelley Design. *See* IDEO Inc.
David L. Babson & Company Inc., **53** 213
David Lloyd Leisure Ltd., **52** 412, 415–16
David S. Smith Ltd. *See* DS Smith Plc.
David Wilson Homes Ltd., **45** 442–43
David's Bridal, Inc., 33 130–32; 46 288
David's Supermarkets, **17** 180
Davide Campari-Milano S.p.A., 57
104–06
Davids. *See* Metcash Trading Ltd.
Davidson & Associates, **16** 146
Davidson & Leigh, **21** 94
Davidson Brothers Co., **19** 510
Davis & Geck, **27** 115
Davis Manufacturing Company, **10** 380
Davis Polk & Wardwell, 36 151–54
Davis Service Group PLC, 45 139–41;
49 374, 377
Davis-Standard Company, **9** 154; **36** 144
Davis Vision, Inc., **27** 209
Davis Wholesale Company, **9** 20
Davlyn Industries, Inc., **22** 487
Davox Corporation, **18** 31
Davy Bamag GmbH, **IV** 142
Davy McKee AG, **IV** 142
DAW Technologies, Inc., 25 135–37
Dawe's Laboratories, Inc., **12** 3
Dawn Food Products, Inc., 17 126–28
Dawson Holdings PLC, 43 132–34
Day & Zimmermann Inc., 6 579; **9**
162–64; **31 151–55 (upd.)**
Day Brite Lighting, **II** 19
Day-Glo Color Corp., **8** 456
Day International, **8** 347
Day-N-Nite, **II** 620
Day Runner, Inc., 14 157–58; 41 120–23
(upd.)
Day-Timers, Inc., **51** 9
Daybridge Learning Centers, **13** 49, 299
Dayco Products, **7** 297
Daylin Corporation, **46** 271
Days Inns of America, Inc., **III** 344; **11**
178; **13** 362, 364; **21** 362

Daystar International Inc., **11** 44
Daytex, Inc., **II** 669; **18** 505; **50** 455
Dayton Engineering Laboratories, **9** 416
Dayton Hudson Corporation, **V** 43–44; **8** 35; **9** 360; **10** 136, 391–93, 409–10, 515–16; **13** 330; **14** 376; **16** 176, 559; **18** 108, 135–37 **(upd.)**; **22** 59. *See also* Target Corporation.
Dayton Power & Light Company, **6** 467, 480–82
Daytron Mortgage Systems, **11** 485
Dazey Corp., **16** 384; **43** 289
DB. *See* Deutsche Bundesbahn.
DB Group, **59** 59–60
DB Reise & Touristik AG, **37** 250
DBA Holdings, Inc., **18** 24
DBMS Inc., **14** 390
DBS, **56** 363
DBT Online Inc. *See* ChoicePoint Inc.
DC Comics Inc., **25** 138–41
DC Shoes, Inc., **60** 103–05
DCA Advertising, **16** 168
DCA Food Industries, **27** 258–60, 299
DCE Consultants, **51** 17
DCL BioMedical, Inc., **11** 333
DCMS Holdings Inc., **7** 114; **25** 125
DDB Needham Worldwide, **14** 159–61; **22** 394
DDD Energy, Inc., **47** 348, 350
DDI Corporation, **7** 118–20; **13** 482; **21** 330–31
DDJ Capital, **68** 345
NV De Beer and Partners, **45** 386
De Beers Consolidated Mines Limited / De Beers Centenary AG, **IV** 64–68, 79, 94; **7** 121–26 **(upd.)**; **16** 25–26, 29; **21** 345–46; **28** 88–94 **(upd.)**; **50** 31, 34; **62** 7, 9–10
De Bono Industries, **24** 443
De Dietrich & Cie., **31** 156–59
De Grenswisselkantoren NV, **III** 201
de Havilland Aircraft Co. *See* Bombardier Inc.
de Havilland Holdings, Ltd., **24** 85–86
De La Rue plc, **10** 267–69; **34** 138–43 **(upd.)**; **46** 251
De Leuw, Cather & Company, **8** 416
De Paepe, **45** 386
De Streekkrant-De Weekkrantgroep NV, **48** 347
De Tomaso Industries, **11** 104; **50** 197
De Trey Gesellschaft, **10** 271
De Vito/Verdi, **26** 111
DEA Group, **23** 83
Dead Sea Works Ltd., **55** 229
Dealer Equipment and Services, **10** 492
Dealers Wholesale Inc., **56** 230
Dean & Barry Co., **8** 455
Dean & DeLuca, Inc., **36** 155–57
Dean Foods Company, **7** 127–29; **17** 56; **21** 157, 165–68 **(upd.)**; **26** 447; **29** 434; **46** 70
Dean Witter, Discover & Co., **7** 213; **12** 96–98; **21** 97; **22** 405–07. *See also* Morgan Stanley Dean Witter & Company.
Dearborn Mid-West Conveyor Company, **56** 78–80
Dearborn Publishing Group, **42** 211
Death Row Records, **27** 121–23. *See also* Tha Row Records.
Deb Shops, Inc., **16** 163–65
DeBartolo Realty Corp., **27** 401

Debeka Krankenversicherungsverein auf Gegenseitigkeit, **72** 87–90
Debenhams Plc, **28** 95–97; **39** 88
Debevoise & Plimpton, **39** 115–17
Debis, **26** 498
DeBoles Nutritional Foods Inc., **27** 197–98; **43** 218–19
Debron Investments Plc., **8** 271
DEC. *See* Digital Equipment Corp.
Decafin SpA, **26** 278, 280
Decathlon S.A., **39** 183–84
Decca Record Company Ltd., **23** 389
Dechert, **43** 135–38
Decision Systems Israel Ltd. (DSI), **21** 239
DecisionQuest, Inc., **25** 130
Decker, Howell & Co., **26** 451
Decker-Indelqui S.A., **71** 211
Deckers Outdoor Corporation, **22** 172–74
Deco Industries, Inc., **18** 5
Deco Purchasing Company, **39** 211
Decolletage S.A. St.-Maurice, **14** 27
Decora Industries, Inc., **31** 160–62
Decorator Industries Inc., **68** 101–04
DeCrane Aircraft Holdings Inc., **36** 158–60
Dee and Cee Toy Co., **25** 312
Dee Corporation plc, **II** 628–29, 642; **24** 269
Dee Zee Inc., **61** 173
Deep Ocean Services, L.L.C., **44** 203
Deep Rock Oil Company. *See* Kerr-McGee Corporation.
DeepFlex Production Partners, L.P., **21** 171
Deepsea Ventures, Inc., **IV** 152; **24** 358
DeepTech International Inc., **21** 169–71
Deere & Company, **III** 462–64; **10** 377–78, 380; **11** 472; **13** 16–17, 267; **16** 179; **17** 533; **21** 172–76 **(upd.)**; **22** 542; **26** 492; **42** 101–06 **(upd.)**
Deering Harvesting Machinery Company. *See* Navistar.
Deering Milliken & Co. *See* Milliken & Co.
Def Jam Records, Inc., **23** 389, 391; **31** 269; **33** 373–75
Defense Technology Corporation of America, **27** 50
Defiance, Inc., **22** 175–78
Deflecta-Shield Corporation, **40** 299–300
Deft Software, Inc., **10** 505
Degussa Group, **IV** 69–72, 118
Degussa-Hüls AG, **32** 147–53 **(upd.)**; **34** 209
Degussa-Metais, Catalisadores e Ceramica, Lda, **56** 127
DEKA Research & Development Corporation. *See* Segway LLC.
DeKalb AgResearch Inc., **9** 411; **41** 304–06
Dekalb Energy Company, **18** 366
DeKalb Farmers Market, **23** 263–64
DeKalb Genetics Corporation, **17** 129–31; **29** 330
DeKalb Office Supply, **25** 500
DeKuyper, **58** 194
Del Laboratories, Inc., **28** 98–100
Del Mar Avionics, **26** 491
Del Monte Corporation, **7** 130–32; **12** 439; **14** 287; **25** 234
Del Monte Foods Company, **23** 163–66 **(upd.)**; **36** 472; **38** 198
Del Taco, Inc., **58** 89–92

Del Webb Corporation, **14** 162–64; **17** 186–87; **19** 377–78; **26** 291
Delafield, Harvey, Tabrell, Inc., **17** 498
Delafield Industries, **12** 418
Delamine B.V., **70** 329
Delaware and Hudson Railway Company, Inc., **16** 350; **45** 78
Delaware Charter Guarantee & Trust Co., **III** 330
Delaware Guarantee and Trust Co. *See* Wilmington Trust Company.
Delaware Management Holdings, **III** 386
Delaware North Companies Incorporated, **7** 133–36
Delchamps, Inc., **II** 638; **27** 247
Delco Electronics Corporation, **II** 32–35; **25** 223–24; **45** 142–43
Delek Investment & Properties Ltd., **45** 170
Delhaize "Le Lion" S.A., **II** 626; **15** 176; **27** 94; **44** 143–46
Delhi Gas Pipeline Corporation, **7** 551
Deli Unique. *See* Matt Prentice Restaurant Group.
Deli Universal NV, **13** 545; **66** 71–74
dELiA*s Inc., **29** 141–44
Delicato Vineyards, Inc., **50** 152–55
Delicious Foods, **13** 383
Delimaatschappij, **13** 545
Dell Computer Corporation, **9** 165–66; **10** 309, 459; **11** 62; **16** 5, 196; **24** 31; **25** 254; **27** 168; **31** 163–66 **(upd.)**; **47** 323; **50** 92; **63** 122–26 **(upd.)**, 153
Dell Distributing, **25** 483
Dell Publishing Co., **13** 560
Delmarva Properties, Inc., **8** 103; **30** 118
Delmas-Vieljeux. *See* Groupe Bolloré.
Deloitte Touche Tohmatsu International, **9** 167–69, 423; **24** 29; **29** 145–48 **(upd.)**
De'Longhi S.p.A., **66** 75–77
DeLorean Motor Co., **10** 117; **14** 321
DeLorme Publishing Company, Inc., **53** 121–23
Delphi Automotive Systems Corporation, **22** 52; **36** 243; **25** 223; **37** 429; **45** 142–44
Delphy Industries S.A.S., **53** 221
Delta and Pine Land Company, **21** 386; **33** 133–37; **59** 148–50
Delta Acceptance Corporation Limited, **13** 63
Delta Air Lines, Inc., **I** 99–100; **6** 81–83 **(upd.)**; **39** 118–21 **(upd.)**; **47** 29; **52** 90, 92–93
Delta Biologicals S.r.l., **11** 208
Delta Biotechnology Ltd., **25** 82
Delta Campground Management Corp., **33** 399
Delta Communications. *See* Reed Elsevier.
Delta Education, **29** 470, 472
Delta Faucet Co. *See* Masco Corporation.
Delta Health, Inc. *See* DVI, Inc.
Delta International Machinery Corp., **26** 361–63
Delta Lloyd, **III** 235
Delta Play, Ltd., **44** 261
Delta Pride Catfish Inc., **18** 247
Delta Queen Steamboat Company, **27** 34–35
Delta Resources Inc., **26** 519
Delta Savings Assoc. of Texas, **IV** 343
Delta Steamship Lines, **9** 425–26
Delta V Technologies, Inc., **33** 348

Delta Woodside Industries, Inc., 8
  141–43; 17 329; **30 159–61 (upd.); 42**
  118
Deltak, L.L.C., **23** 300; **52** 139
Deltec, Inc., 56 81–83
Deltic Timber Corporation, 32 339, 341;
  46 115–17
Deluxe Corporation, 7 137–39; 19 291;
  22 179–82 (upd.); 37 107–08
Deluxe Data, **18** 518
Deluxe Media Services Inc., **64** 320
Deluxe Upholstering Ltd., **14** 303
DEMCO, Inc., 60 106–09
Demerara Company, **13** 102
Deming Company, **8** 135
Demko, **30** 469
DeMoulas / Market Basket Inc., 23
  167–69
Den Fujita, **9** 74
Den Norske Bank, **22** 275
Den Norske Stats Oljeselskap AS, IV
  405–07, 486. *See also* Statoil ASA.
DenAmerica Corporation, 29 149–51
Denault Ltd., **II** 651
Denbury Resources, Inc., 67 139–41
Denby Group plc, 44 147–50
Dendrite International, Inc., 70 70–73
Denison International plc, 46 118–20
Denison Mines, Ltd., **12** 198
Denker & Goodwin, **17** 498
Denmark Tiscali A/S, **48** 398
Denney-Reyburn, **8** 360
Dennis Publishing Ltd., 62 93–95
Dennison Manufacturing Company. *See*
  Avery Dennison Corporation.
Denny's Restaurants Inc., **II** 680; **12** 511;
  13 526; **27** 16–18; **50** 489
Denshi Media Services, **IV** 680
DENSO Corporation, 46 121–26 (upd.)
Dental Benefits Insurance Company, **51**
  276, 278
Dental Capital Corp., **19** 290
Dental Research, **25** 56
DentiCare, Inc., **22** 149
Dentists Management Corporation, **51**
  276–78
Dentons Green Brewery, **21** 246
Dentsply International Inc., 10 270–72
Dentsu Inc., I 9–11, 36, 38; **9** 30; **13** 204;
  16 166–69 (upd.); 25 91; **40 140–44**
  (upd.)
Denver & Rio Grande Railroad, **12** 18–19
Denver Chemical Company, **8** 84; **38** 124
Denver Gas & Electric Company. *See*
  Public Service Company of Colorado.
Denver Nuggets, 51 94–97
Deocsa, **51** 389
DEP. *See* Hellenic Petroleum SA.
DEP Corporation, 20 177–80; 34 209
Depa, **69** 190, 192
Department 56, Inc., 14 165–67; 22 59;
  34 144–47 (upd.)
Department of Currency and Coinage, **62**
  248
Department Stores International, **I** 426; **22**
  72; **50** 117
DEPFA BANK PLC, 69 115–17
Deposit Guaranty Corporation, 17
  132–35
DePree Company, **17** 90–91
DePuy, Inc., 10 156–57; 30 162–65; 36
  306; **37 110–13 (upd.)**
Derby Cycle Corporation, **65** 297
Derby International, **69** 303

Derby Outdoor, **27** 280
Deritend Computers, **14** 36
Dermablend, Inc., **31** 89
Derwent Publications, **8** 526
DESA Industries, **8** 545
Desc, S.A. de C.V., 23 170–72
Deschutes Brewery, Inc., 57 107–09
Desco, **51** 120
Deseret Management Corporation, **29** 67
Deseret National Bank, **11** 118
Deseret Pharmaceutical Company, **21** 45
Design-Center Southwest, **19** 411
Design Trend, Inc., **37** 394
Designcraft Inc. *See* Sloan's Supermarkets
  Inc.
Designer Holdings Ltd., 20 181–84; 22
  123
Designs, Inc. *See* Casual Male Retail
  Group, Inc.
Designtroupe, **60** 143–44
Desmonds Formalwear, **60** 5
DeSoto, Inc., **8** 553; **13** 471
Desoutter Brothers plc, **III** 427; **28** 40
Destec Energy, Inc., 12 99–101; 49 121
Desvi, S.A., **68** 258
Det Danske Rengorings Selskab A/S, **49**
  221
Detroit Ball Bearing Co., **13** 78
Detroit Chemical Coatings, **8** 553
Detroit City Gas Company. *See* MCN
  Corporation.
Detroit Diesel Corporation, V 494–95; 9
  18; **10 273–75; 11** 471; **12** 90–91; **18**
  308; **19** 292–94; **21** 503
The Detroit Edison Company, V 592–95;
  7 377–78; **14** 135; **18** 320. *See also*
  DTE Energy Co.
Detroit-Graphite Company, **8** 553
The Detroit Lions, Inc., 55 119–21
The Detroit Pistons Basketball
  Company, 41 124–27
Detroit Red Wings, **7** 278–79; **24** 293; **37**
  207; **46** 127
Detroit Steel Products Co., Inc. *See* The
  Marmon Group, Inc.
Detroit Stoker Company, **37** 399–401
Detroit Tigers Baseball Club, Inc., 24
  293; **37** 207; **46** 127–30
Dettmers Industries Inc., **36** 159–60
Deutsch, Inc., 42 107–10
Deutsche Aerospace Airbus, **7** 9, 11; **12**
  190–91; **21** 8; **52** 113–14
Deutsche BA, **14** 73; **24** 400; **26** 115
Deutsche Babcock AG, III 465–66
Deutsche Bahn AG, 37 250, 253; **46**
  131–35 (upd.); 59 387, 390–91
Deutsche Bank AG, I 151, 549; **II**
  278–80; 14 168–71 (upd.); 15 13; **16**
  364–65; **17** 324; **21** 147, **34** 29; **40**
  145–51 (upd.); 47 81–84; **49** 44
Deutsche Börse AG, 37 131–32; 59
  151–55
Deutsche BP Aktiengesellschaft, 7
  140–43; 62 12, 14
Deutsche Bundepost Telekom, V 287–90;
  18 155. *See also* Deutsche Telekom AG
Deutsche Bundesbahn, V 444–47
Deutsche Erdol Aktiengesellschaft, **7** 140
Deutsche Grammophon Gesellschaft, **23**
  389
Deutsche Herold, **49** 44
Deutsche Lufthansa AG, I 110–11, 120;
  6 59–60, 69, 95–96, 386; **12** 191; **25**

  159; **26 113–16 (upd.); 27** 465; **33** 49;
  36 426; **48** 258; **68 105–09 (upd.)**
Deutsche Petroleum-Verkaufsgesellschaft
  mbH, **7** 140
Deutsche Post AG, 29 152–58; 40 138;
  63 418
Deutsche Reichsbahn. *See* Deutsche
  Bundesbahn.
Deutsche Shell, **7** 140
Deutsche Steinkohle AG, **60** 250
Deutsche Telekom AG, 18 155; **25** 102;
  38 296; **48 130–35 (upd.)**
Deutsche Verlags-Anstalt GmbH, **66** 123
Deutsche Vermögensberatung AG, **51** 19,
  23
Deutsche Wagnisfinanzierung, **47** 83
Deutscher Kommunal-Verlag Dr. Naujoks
  & Behrendt, **14** 556
Deutscher Ring, **40** 61
Deutz AG, 39 122–26
Deutz-Allis. *See* AGCO Corp.
Deutz Farm Equipment, **13** 17
Devanlay SA, **48** 279
Devcon Corporation, **III** 519; **22** 282
Deveaux S.A., 41 128–30
Developer's Mortgage Corp., **16** 347
Developers Diversified Realty
  Corporation, 69 118–20
Devenish, **21** 247
DeVilbiss Company, **8** 230
DeVilbiss Health Care, Inc., **11** 488
Deville, **27** 421
Devoe & Raynolds Co., **12** 217
Devoke Company, **18** 362
Devon Energy Corporation, 22 304; **61**
  73–75
Devro plc, 55 122–24
DeVry Incorporated, 9 63; **29** 56, **159–61**
Devtek Corporation. *See* Héroux-Devtek
  Inc.
Dewey Ballantine LLP, 48 136–39
Dex Media, Inc., 65 128–30
Dexer Corporation, **41** 10
Dexia Group, 42 111–13
The Dexter Corporation, I 320–22; 12
  102–04 (upd.); 17 287; **52** 183. *See also*
  Invitrogen Corporation.
Dexter Lock Company, **45** 269
Dexter Shoe, **18** 60, 63
DFS Group Ltd., I 35; **33** 276; **66 78–80**
DFW Printing Company, **10** 3
DG&E. *See* Denver Gas & Electric
  Company.
DG Bank, **33** 358
DGS SpA, **62** 100
DH Compounding, **8** 347
DH Technology, Inc., 18 138–40
Dharma Juice, **31** 350
DHI Corp., **II** 680
DHJ Industries, Inc., **12** 118
DHL Worldwide Network S.A./N.V., 6
  385–87; 18 177, 316; **24 133–36 (upd.);**
  26 441; **27** 471, 475; **29** 152; **69 121–25**
  (upd.)
Di Giorgio Corp., II 602; **12 105–07; 24**
  528–29
Di-Rite Company, **11** 534
Diageo plc, 24 137–41 (upd.); 25 411; **29**
  19; **31** 92; **34** 89; **36** 404; **42** 223; **56**
  46, 48; **61** 323, 325
Diagnostic Health Corporation, **14** 233
Diagnostic Imaging Services, Inc., **25** 384
Diagnostic/Retrieval Systems Inc. *See* DRS
  Technologies Inc.

Diagnostic Ventures Inc. *See* DVI, Inc.
Dial-A-Mattress Operating Corporation, **32** 427; **46 136–39**
The Dial Corporation, **8 144–46**; **23 173–75 (upd.)**; **29** 114; **32** 230; **34** 209
Dial Home Shopping Ltd., **28** 30
Dial-Net Inc., **27** 306
Dialight Corp., **13** 397–98
Dialog Information Services, Inc., **IV** 630
Dialogic Corporation, **18 141–43**
Diamandis Communications Inc., **IV** 619, 678
Diamedix, **11** 207
Diamond Animal Health, Inc., **39** 216
Diamond Communications, **10** 288
Diamond Crystal Brands, Inc., **32** 274, 277
Diamond Electronics, **24** 510
Diamond Fields Resources Inc., **27** 457
Diamond Head Resources, Inc. *See* AAON, Inc.
Diamond International Corp., **13** 254–55; **26** 446
Diamond M Offshore Inc., **12** 318
Diamond Match Company, **14** 163
Diamond of California, **64 108–11 (upd.)**
Diamond Offshore Drilling, Inc., **36** 325; **43** 202
Diamond Park Fine Jewelers, **16** 559
Diamond Rug & Carpet Mills, **19** 276
Diamond Savings & Loan, **II** 420
Diamond Shamrock Corporation, **IV 408–11**, 481; **7** 34, 308–099, 345; **13** 118; **19** 177; **45** 411. *See also* Ultramar Diamond Shamrock Corporation.
Diamond Sparkler Manufacturing Co. Inc. *See* B.J. Alan Co., Inc.
Diamond-Star Motors Corporation, **9** 349–51
Diamond State Insurance Company, **63** 410–12
Diamond Walnut Growers, **7** 496–97
DiamondCluster International, Inc., **51 98–101**
Dianatel, **18** 143
Diapositive, **44** 296
Diasonics Ultrasound, Inc., **27** 355
Diaxon A.B.E.E., **64** 177
Dibrell Brothers, Incorporated, **12 108–10**; **13** 492
dick clark productions, inc., **16 170–73**
Dick Corporation, **64 112–14**
Dick Simon Trucking, Inc. *See* Simon Transporation Services Inc.
Dick's Sporting Goods, Inc., **59 156–59**
Dickerman, **8** 366
Dickson Forest Products, Inc., **15** 305
Dickstein Partners, L.P., **13** 261
Didier Lamarthe, **17** 210
Didier-Werke AG, **IV** 232; **53** 285
Diebold, Incorporated, **7 144–46**; **22 183–87 (upd.)**
Diedrich Coffee, Inc., **40 152–54**
Diehl Manufacturing Co., **II** 9
Dierbergs Markets Inc., **63 127–29**
Diesel Nacional, S.A. *See* Consorcio G Grupo Dina, S.A. de C.V.
Diesel SpA, **40 155–57**; **63** 361–62
Diesel United Co., **III** 533
Diet Center, **10** 383
Dieter Hein Co., **14** 537
Dietrich & Cie. *See* De Dietrich & Cie.
Dietrich Corp., **II** 512; **15** 221; **51** 158
DiFeo Automotive Group, **26** 500–01

Diffusion Immobilier. *See* Union Financière de France Banque.
DiFranza Williamson, **6** 40
DIG Acquisition Corp., **12** 107
Digex, Inc., **45** 201; **46 140–43**
Digi International Inc., **9 170–72**; **20** 237; **67** 55–56
Digicom, **22** 17
Digidesign Inc., **38** 70, 72
DiGiorgio Corporation, **25** 421
Digital City, Inc., **22** 522; **63** 393
Digital Data Systems Company, **11** 408
Digital Directory Assistance, **18** 24
Digital Entertainment Network, **42** 272
Digital Equipment Corporation, **II** 62, 108; **III 132–35**, 142, 149, 166; **6 233–36 (upd.)**; **8** 137–39, 519; **9** 35, 43, 57, 166, 170–71, 514; **10** 22–23, 34, 86, 242, 361, 463, 477; **11** 46, 86–88, 274, 491, 518–19; **12** 147, 162, 470; **13** 127, 202, 482; **14** 318; **15** 108; **16** 394, 418; **18** 143, 345; **19** 310; **21** 123; **25** 499; **26** 90, 93; **34 441–43**; **36** 81, 287; **43** 13; **45** 201; **50** 227
Digital Marketing, Inc., **22** 357
Digital Research in Electronic Acoustics and Music S.A., **17** 34
Digital River, Inc., **50 156–59**
Digitech, **19** 414
Digitel, **63** 380
Dii Group Inc., **38** 188–89
Dill Enterprises, Inc., **14** 18
Dillard Paper Company, **11 74–76**
Dillard's Inc., **V 45–47**; **10** 488; **11** 349; **12** 64; **13** 544–45; **16 174–77 (upd.)**, 559; **19** 48, 324; **27** 61; **63** 261; **68 110–14 (upd.)**
Dillingham Construction Corporation, **44 151–54 (upd.)**
Dillingham Corp., **I 565–66**
Dillingham Holdings Inc., **9** 511
Dillon Companies Inc., **II** 645; **12 111–13**; **15** 267; **22** 194
Dillon Paper, **IV** 288
Dillon, Read, and Co., Inc., **11** 53; **20** 259; **24** 66
Dillons, **59** 230
DiMark, Inc., **63** 189
Dime Bancorp, **44** 32–33; **46** 316
Dime Savings Bank of New York, F.S.B., **9 173–74**
Dimeling, Schrieber & Park, **11** 63; **44** 309
Dimension Data Holdings PLC, **69 126–28**
Dimension Films, **64** 285
Dimensions in Sport, Ltd., **37** 5
Dimeric Development Corporation, **14** 392
DIMON Inc., **12** 110; **27 124–27**
Dimpex S.A., **72** 272
Dina. *See* Consorcio G Grupo Dina, S.A. de C.V.
Dinamica, S.A., **19** 12
Dine S.A., **23** 170–72
Dineen Mechanical Contractors, Inc., **48** 238
Diners Club, **6** 62; **9** 335
Dinner Bell Foods, Inc., **11** 93
Dionex Corporation, **46 144–46**
Dior. *See* Christian Dior S.A.
Dippin' Dots, Inc., **56 84–86**
Dirección General de Correos y Telecomunicaciónes. *See* Telefónica Nacional de España S.A.
Direct Container Lines, **14** 505

Direct Focus, Inc., **47 93–95**
Direct Friends, **25** 91
Direct Line, **12** 422
Direct Mail Services Pty. Ltd., **10** 461
Direct Marketing Technology Inc., **19** 184
Direct Merchants Credit Card Bank, N.A., **56** 224
Direct Transit, Inc., **42** 364
Direction of Coins and Medals, **62** 248
DirectLine Insurance, **22** 52
Directorate General of Telecommunications, **7 147–49**
DIRECTV, Inc., **21** 70; **35** 156, 158–59; **38 174–77**
Dirki S.A., **64** 8
Disc Go Round, **18** 207, 209
Disc Manufacturing, Inc., **15** 378
Disclosure, Inc., **18** 24
Disco SA, **V** 11; **19** 308–09; **69** 94
Discount Auto Parts, Inc., **18 144–46**; **26** 348; **57** 12
Discount Corporation, **12** 565
Discount Drug Mart, Inc., **14 172–73**
Discount Investment Corporation Ltd., **24** 429
Discount Labels, Inc., **20** 15
Discount Tire Co., **19** 294; **20** 263
Discover, **9** 335; **12** 97
Discovery Communications, Inc., **42 114–17**
Discovery Partners International, Inc., **58 93–95**
Discovery Toys, Inc., **19** 28
Discovery Zone, **31** 97
Discreet Logic Inc., **20 185–87**
Disctronics, Ltd., **15** 380
Disney. *See* The Walt Disney Company.
Disneyland Paris. *See* Euro Disney S.C.A.
Disnorte, **51** 389
Dispatch Communications, **10** 432
Displayco Midwest Inc., **8** 103
Distillers Co. plc, **I 239–41**, 252, 263, 284–85; **II** 609–10; **43** 214. *See also* Diageo PLC.
Distinctive Printing and Packaging Co., **8** 103
Distinctive Software Inc., **10** 285
Distribución y Servicio D&S S.A., **71 123–26**
Distribuidora Bega, S.A. de C.V., **31** 92
Distribuidora de Produtos de Petróleo Ipiranga, **67** 216–17
Distribution Centers Incorporated. *See* Exel Logistics Ltd.
Distribution Centre Sdn. Bhd., **62** 268
Distribution Services, Inc., **10** 287
Distribution Solutions International, Inc., **24** 126
District News Co., **II** 607
Distrigas, **IV** 425
DITAS. *See* Türkiye Petrolleri Anonim Ortakliği.
Divani & Divani. *See* Industrie Natuzzi S.p.A.
Divco-Wayne Corp., **17** 82
DIVE!, **26** 264
Diversey Corp., **I** 275, 333; **13** 150, 199; **26** 305–06; **32** 476
Diversified Agency Services, **I** 32
Diversified Foods Inc., **25** 179
Diversified Retailing Co., **III** 214
Diversified Services, **9** 95
Diversion Entertainment, Inc., **58** 124
Diversity Consultants Inc., **32** 459

Divesco Inc., **58** 333
DiviCom, **43** 221–22
Dixie Airline, **25** 420
Dixie Bearings, Inc., **13** 78
Dixie Carriers, Inc., **18** 277
Dixie Container Corporation, **12** 377
Dixie Crystals Brands, Inc., **32** 277
The Dixie Group, Inc., 20 188–90
Dixie Hi-Fi, **9** 120–21
Dixie-Narco Inc., **III** 573; **22** 349
Dixie Offshore Transportation Company.
   See Kirby Corporation.
Dixie Power & Light Company, **6** 514
Dixie Yarns, Inc., **9** 466; **19** 305
Dixieland Food Stores, **II** 624
Dixieline. *See* Lanoga Corporation.
Dixon Industries, Inc., 26 117–19; 48 59
**Dixon Ticonderoga Company, 12
   114–16; 69 129–33 (upd.)**
Dixons Group plc, **V** 48–50; **9** 65; **10** 45,
   306; **19** 121–24 (upd.); **23** 52; **24**
   269–70; **49** 110–13 (upd.)
DIY Home Warehouse, **16** 210
DJ Moldings Corp., **18** 276
DJ Pharma, Inc., **47** 56
Djarum PT, 62 96–98
Djedi Holding SA, **23** 242
DKB. *See* Dai-Ichi Kangyo Bank Ltd.
DKNY. *See* Donna Karan International Inc.
Dl Radiators France S.A.R.L. *See*
   De'Longhi S.p.A.
DLC. *See* Duquesne Light Company.
DLJ. *See* Donaldson, Lufkin & Jenrette.
DLJ Merchant Banking Partners II, **21** 188;
   36 158–59
DLL. *See* David Lloyd Leisure Ltd.
DM Associates Limited Partnership, **25**
   127
DMA, **18** 510
DMAX-Ltd., **57** 190
DMB&B. *See* D'Arcy Masius Benton &
   Bowles.
dmc2 Italia SrL, **56** 127
DMGT. *See* Daily Mail and General Trust.
DMI Furniture, Inc., 44 132; 46 147–50
DMP Mineralöl Petrochemie GmbH, **IV**
   487
DMV Stainless, **54** 393
DNATA, **39** 137, 139
DNN Galvanizing Limited Partnership, **24**
   144
DNP DENMARK A/S, **IV** 600
Do It All, **24** 75
Do it Best Corporation, 30 166–70
Dobbs House, **21** 54
Dobbs Houses Inc., **15** 87
Dobrolet. *See* Aeroflot.
**Dobson Communications Corporation,
   63 130–32**
Dobson Park Industries, **38** 227
Doc Green's Gourmet Salads Inc., **64** 327,
   329
Doc Holliday's Pawnbrokers and Jewelers,
   Inc., **61** 55
Docks de France, **37** 23; **39** 183–84
**Doctor's Associates Inc., 67 142–45
   (upd.)**
The Doctors' Company, 55 125–28
Documentation Resources, **11** 65
Documentum, Inc., 46 151–53
DOD Electronics Corp., **15** 215
Dodd, Mead & Co., **14** 498
Dodge & Day. *See* Day & Zimmermann,
   Inc.

The Dodge Group, **11** 78
Dodge Manufacturing Company, **9** 440
Dodge Motor Company, **20** 259
Doduco Corporation, **29** 460–61
Doe Run Company, **12** 244
Doeflex PLC, **33** 79
**Dofasco Inc., IV 73–74; 24 142–44
   (upd.)**
**Dogi International Fabrics S.A., 52
   99–102**
Doherty, Mann & Olshan. *See* Wells Rich
   Greene BDDP.
Dolan Design, Inc., **44** 133
Dolby Laboratories Inc., 20 191–93
**Dolce & Gabbana SpA, 61 192–93; 62
   99–101**
Dole Corporation, **44** 152
Dole Food Company, Inc., II 491–92; **9**
   175–76; **20** 116; **31** 167–70 (upd.); **68**
   115–19 (upd.)
Dollar Bills, Inc. *See* Dollar Tree Stores,
   Inc.
Dollar Express Inc., **62** 104
Dollar General, **26** 533
**Dollar Thrifty Automotive Group, Inc.,
   25** 92, 142–45
Dollar Tree Stores, Inc., 16 161; **23**
   176–78; **62** 102–05 (upd.)
Dollfus Mieg & Cie. *See* Groupe DMC.
Dollond & Aitchison Group, **49** 151–52
Dolmar GmbH, **59** 272
Dolomite Franchi SpA, **53** 285
Dolphin Book Club, **13** 106
Dolphin Services, Inc., **44** 203
Dom Perignon, **25** 258
Domaine Carneros, **43** 401
Domaines Barons de Rothschild, **36** 113,
   115
Doman Industries Limited, 59 160–62
Dombrico, Inc., **8** 545
Domco Industries, **19** 407
Dome Petroleum, Ltd., **IV** 371, 401, 494;
   12 364
Dominick International Corp., **12** 131
Dominick's Finer Foods, Inc., 9 451; **13**
   25, 516; **17** 558, 560–61; **56** 87–89
Dominion Bond Rating Service Ltd., **65**
   244
Dominion Bridge Company, Limited, **8**
   544
Dominion Dairies, **7** 429
Dominion Engineering Works Ltd., **8** 544
Dominion Foils Ltd., **17** 280
Dominion Hoist & Shovel Co., **8** 544
Dominion Homes, Inc., 19 125–27
Dominion Industries Ltd., **15** 229
Dominion Mushroom Co., **II** 649–50
Dominion Resources, Inc., V 596–99; **54**
   83–87 (upd.); **60** 152
Dominion Salt Ltd., **62** 307
Dominion Stores Ltd., **II** 650, 652
Dominion Terminal Associates, **IV** 171; **7**
   582, 584
Dominion Textile Inc., 8 559–60; **12**
   117–19
Domino S.p.A., **51** 324
**Domino Sugar Corporation, 26 120–22;
   42** 370
Domino Supermarkets, **24** 528
Domino's, Inc., 7 150–53; **9** 74; **12** 123;
   15 344, 346; **16** 447; **21** 177–81 (upd.);
   22 353; **24** 295; **25** 179–80, 227–28; **26**
   177; **33** 388; **37** 208; **63** 133–39 (upd.)
Domtar Inc., IV 271–73

Don Canham Enterprises. *See* School-Tech,
   Inc.
Don Massey Cadillac, Inc., 37 114–16
Don's Foods, Inc., **26** 164
**Donaldson Company, Inc., 16 178–81; 49
   114–18 (upd.)**
Donaldson, Lufkin & Jenrette, Inc., 9
   115, 142, 360–61; **18** 68; **22** 188–91; **26**
   348; **35** 247; **41** 197; **57** 16; **59** 143; **63**
   26
Donaldson's Department Stores, **15** 274
**Donatos Pizzeria Corporation, 58 96–98;
   63** 284–85
Donegal Parian China Ltd. *See* Belleek
   Pottery Ltd.
Dong Guan Highsonic Electronic Products
   Company, **62** 150
Dong Yang Department Store Company,
   62 174
Dong-Myung Industrial Company Ltd., **64**
   270
DongGuan Leeway Footwear Company
   Ltd., **68** 69
Dongguan Shilong Kyocera Optics Co.,
   Ltd., **21** 331
Dongguan Xinda Giftware Co. Ltd., **60** 372
Dongil Frozen Foods Co., **II** 553
Dönkasan, **55** 188
Donn, Inc., **18** 162
**Donna Karan International Inc., 15
   145–47; 56 90–93 (upd.)**
Donnellon McCarthy Inc., **12** 184
Donnelly Coated Corporation, **48** 28
**Donnelly Corporation, 12 120–22; 35
   147–50 (upd.)**
Donnkenny, Inc., 17 136–38
Donohue Inc., **12** 412
Donohue Meehan Publishing Co., **27** 362
Donruss Leaf Inc., **19** 386
Donruss Playoff L.P., 66 81–84
Donzi Marine Corp., **III** 600
Dorel Industries Inc., 59 163–65
Dorenbecher Properties, **19** 381
Doric Corp., **19** 290
**Dorling Kindersley Holdings plc, 20
   194–96**
Dorman Products of America, Ltd., **51** 307
Dorman's, Inc., **27** 291
Dorney Park, **22** 130
Dornier GmbH, **I** 151; **15** 142; **34** 131; **52**
   113
Dorothy Hamill International, **13** 279, 281
Dorr-Oliver Inc., **35** 134–35
Dorset Capital, **49** 189
Dorsey & Whitney LLP, 47 96–99
Doskocil Companies, Inc., 12 123–25.
   See also Foodbrands America, Inc.
Dot Foods, Inc., 69 134–37
Dot Wireless Inc., **46** 422
Doty Agency, Inc., **41** 178, 180
Double A Products Co., **23** 82–83
Double-Cola Co.-USA, 70 74–76
DoubleClick Inc., 46 154–57; 49 423, 432
Doubleday Book Shops, Inc., **10** 136; **25**
   31; **30** 68
Doubleday-Dell, **IV** 594, 636
Doubletree Corporation, 21 182–85; 41
   81–82; **62** 179
Doughty Handson, **49** 163
**Douglas & Lomason Company, 16
   182–85**
Douglas Aircraft Co., **I** 195; **9** 12, 18, 206;
   13 48; **16** 77; **21** 141; **24** 375
Douglas Dynamics L.L.C., **41** 3

Doulton Glass Industries Ltd., **IV** 659
Douwe Egberts, **II** 572; **54** 324–25
Dove International, **7** 299–300
Dover Corporation, **III** 467–69; **28** 101–05 (upd.)
Dover Downs Entertainment, Inc., **43** 139–41
Dover Publications Inc., **34** 148–50; **41** 111
Dovrat Shrem, **15** 470
The Dow Chemical Company, **I** 323–25, 334, 341–42, 360, 370–71, 708; **8** 147–50 (upd.), 153, 261–62, 548; **9** 500–1; **10** 289; **11** 271; **12** 99–100, 254, 364; **14** 114, 217; **16** 99; **18** 279; **21** 387; **28** 411; **38** 187; **50** 160–64 (upd.)
Dow Corning. *See* Corning Inc.; Dow Chemical Co.; Wright Medical Group, Inc.
Dow Jones & Company, Inc., **IV** 601–03, 654, 656, 670, 678; **7** 99; **10** 276–78, 407; **13** 55; **15** 335–36; **19** 128–31 (upd.), 204; **21** 68–70; **23** 157; **47** 100–04 (upd.)
Dow Jones Telerate, **10** 276–78
DOW Stereo/Video Inc., **30** 466
DowElanco, **21** 385, 387
Dowell Schlumberger. *See* Schlumberger Limited.
Down River International, Inc., **15** 188
Downe Communications, Inc., **14** 460
Downingtown Paper Company, **8** 476
Downyflake Foods, **7** 429
Dowty Aerospace, **17** 480
Dowty Group plc, **58** 345
Doyle Dane Bernbach. *See* Omnicom Group Inc.
Doyle Hotel Group, **64** 216
DP&L. *See* Dayton Power & Light Company.
DPF, Inc., **12** 275; **38** 250–51
DPL Inc., **6** 480–82
DPPI. *See* Distribuidora de Produtos de Petróleo Ipiranga.
DQE, **6** 483–85; **38** 40
Dr. August Oetker KG, **51** 102–06
Dr. E. Fresenius KG. *See* Fresenius Aktiengesellschaft.
Dr. Gerhard Mann Pharma, **25** 56
Dr Hans Kraus d.o.o, **72** 221
DR Holdings, Inc., **10** 242
Dr. Ing he F. Porsche GmbH, **13** 413–14
Dr. Karl Thomae GmbH, **39** 72–73
Dr. Martens, **23** 399, 401
Dr Pepper/Seven Up, Inc., **9** 177–78; **32** 154–57 (upd.); **57** 252
Dr. Reddy's Laboratories Ltd., **59** 166–69
The Dr. Robert C. Atkins Foundation, **58** 8–9
Dr. Solomon's Software Ltd., **25** 349
Dr Specht & Partner GmbH, **70** 90
Drackett Professional Products, **12** 126–28
DraftDirect Worldwide, **22** 297
Draftline Engineering Co., **22** 175
Dragados y Construcciones. *See* Grupo Dragados SA.
Dragon Genomics Co. Ltd., **62** 347
Dragon International, **18** 87
Dragonair. *See* Hong Kong Dragon Airlines Ltd.
Drake Beam Morin, Inc., **IV** 623; **44** 155–57

Drake Steel Supply Co., **19** 343
Drallos Potato Company, **25** 332
Draper Corporation, **14** 219; **15** 384
Draw-Tite, Inc., **11** 535
DreamLand. *See* Etablissements Franz Colruyt N.V.
DreamWorks SKG, **17** 72; **21** 23, 26; **26** 150, 188; **43** 142–46; **61** 3; **62** 68–69
The Drees Company, Inc., **41** 131–33
Dreher Breweries, **24** 450
Drescher Corporation. *See* Dor Foods, Inc.
Dresden Papier GmbH, **64** 275
Dresdner Bank A.G., **II** 281–83; **III** 201, 289, 401; **14** 169–70; **15** 13; **47** 81–84; **57** 20, 110–14 (upd.); **60** 110
Dresdner Kleinwort Wasserstein, **60** 110–13 (upd.)
Dresdner RCM Global Investors, **33** 128
The Dress Barn, Inc., **24** 145–46
Dresser Industries, Inc., **I** 486; **III** 470–73; **12** 539; **14** 325; **15** 225–26, 468; **16** 310; **18** 219; **24** 208; **25** 188, 191; **52** 214–216; **55** 129–31 (upd.), 194, 221; **62** 204
Dresser Power, **6** 555
Dressmaster GmbH, **53** 195
Drew Graphics, Inc., **13** 227–28
Drew Industries Inc., **28** 106–08
Drewry Photocolor, **I** 447
Drexel Burnham Lambert Incorporated, **II** 407–09; **III** 254–55, 531; **7** 305; **8** 327, 349, 388–90, 568; **9** 346; **12** 229; **13** 169, 299, 449; **14** 43; **15** 71, 281, 464; **16** 535, 561; **20** 415; **22** 55, 189; **24** 273; **25** 313; **33** 253. *See also* New Street Capital Inc.
Drexel Heritage Furnishings Inc., **III** 571; **11** 534; **12** 129–31; **20** 362; **39** 266
Dreyer's Grand Ice Cream, Inc., **10** 147–48; **17** 139–41; **30** 81; **35** 59–61
The Dreyfus Corporation, **70** 77–80
DRH Cambridge Homes, Inc., **58** 84
DRI. *See* Dominion Resources, Inc.
Dribeck Importers Inc., **9** 87
Driefontein Consolidated (Pty.) Ltd., **62** 164
Drip In Irrigation, **26** 494
DriveTime Automotive Group Inc., **68** 120–24 (upd.)
Drogueros S.A., **39** 188
Drott Manufacturing Company, **10** 379
Drouot Group, **III** 211
Drs. Foster & Smith, Inc., **62** 106–08
DRS Investment Group, **27** 370
DRS Technologies, Inc., **58** 99–101
Drug Emporium, Inc., **12** 132–34, 477
Drummond Lighterage. *See* Puget Sound Tug and Barge Company.
Drummonds' Bank, **12** 422
Druout, **I** 563; **24** 78
DryClean U.S.A., **14** 25
Dryden and Co., **III** 340
Drypers Corporation, **18** 147–49
Drysdale Government Securities, **10** 117
DS Smith Plc, **61** 76–79
DSC Communications Corporation, **9** 170; **12** 135–37; **63** 3–4
DSIC. *See* Diamond State Insurance Company.
DSL Group Ltd., **27** 49
DSM Melamine America, **27** 316–18
DSM N.V., **I** 326–27; **15** 229; **56** 94–96 (upd.); **58** 324, 326
DST Alliance, **63** 386

DTAG. *See* Dollar Thrifty Automotive Group, Inc.
DTE Energy Company, **20** 197–201 (upd.)
Du Mont Company, **8** 517
Du Pareil au Même, **43** 147–49
Du Pont. *See* E.I. du Pont de Nemours & Co.
Du Pont Photomask, **IV** 600
Duane Reade Holding Corp., **21** 186–88
Dublin Corporation, **50** 74
DuBois Chemicals Division, **13** 149–50; **22** 188; **26** 306
Ducati Motor Holding S.p.A., **17** 24; **30** 171–73; **36** 472
Duck Head Apparel Company, Inc., **8** 141–43; **30** 159; **42** 118–21
Duckback Products, Inc., **51** 190
Ducks Unlimited, **28** 306
Duckwall-ALCO Stores, Inc., **24** 147–49
Duco Ltd., **25** 104–05
Ducommun Incorporated, **30** 174–76
Ducros, **36** 185, 187–88
Dudley Jenkins Group Plc, **53** 362
Dudley Stationery Ltd., **25** 501
Duff & Phelps Credit Rating, **37** 143, 145
Duffy Meats, **27** 259
Duke Energy Corporation, **V** 600–02; **27** 128–31 (upd.); **40** 354, 358; **63** 104, 113
Duke Energy Field Services, Inc., **24** 379; **40** 354, 358
Duke Realty Corporation, **57** 115–17
Dumes SA, **13** 206
Dumont Broadcasting Corporation, **7** 335
The Dun & Bradstreet Corporation, **IV** 604–05, 643, 661; **8** 526; **9** 505; **10** 4, 358; **13** 3–4; **19** 132–34 (upd.); **38** 6; **57** 175; **59** 128; **61** 80–84 (upd.)
Dun & Bradstreet Software Services Inc., **11** 77–79; **43** 183
Dunavant Enterprises, Inc., **54** 88–90
Dunbar-Stark Drillings, Inc., **19** 247
Duncan Toys Company, **55** 132–35
Duncanson & Holt, Inc., **13** 539
Dundee Acquisition Corp., **19** 421
Dundee Bancorp, **36** 314
Dundee Cement Co., **III** 702; **8** 258–59
Dunfey Brothers Capital Group, **12** 368
Dunfey Hotels Corporation, **12** 367
Dunhill Staffing Systems, Inc., **52** 397–98
Dunkin' Donuts, **II** 619; **21** 323; **29** 18–19
Dunlop Coflexip Umbilicals Ltd. *See* Duco Ltd.
Dunlop Ltd., **25** 104
Dunlop Tire Corporation. *See* Sumitomo Rubber Industries, Ltd.
Dunn Bennett, **38** 401
Dunn Bros., **28** 63
Dunn-Edwards Corporation, **56** 97–99
Dunn Manufacturing Company, **25** 74
Dunnes Stores Ltd., **58** 102–04
Dunning Industries, **12** 109
Dunphy Holding Pty. Ltd., **64** 349
Dunwoodie Manufacturing Co., **17** 136
Duo-Bed Corp., **14** 435
Dupey Enterprises, Inc., **17** 320
Duplainville Transport, **19** 333–34
Duplex Products, Inc., **17** 142–44, 445
Dupont. *See* E.I. du Pont de Nemours & Company.
Duquesne Light Company. *See* DQE.
Duquesne Systems, **10** 394

Dura Automotive Systems Inc., **53** 55; **65** 282, 284

Dura Convertible Systems, **13** 170

Duracell International Inc., 9 179–81; **71** 127–31 **(upd.)**

Durachemie. *See* Hexal AG.

Duraflame Inc., **58** 52

Duramed Research Inc. *See* Barr Pharmaceuticals, Inc.

Durametallic, 17 147; **21 189–91**

Durango-Mapimi Mining Co., **22** 284

Duravit AG, **51** 196

Duray, Inc., **12** 215

D'Urban, Inc., **41** 169

Duriron Company Inc., 17 145–47; **21** 189, 191

Durkee Famous Foods, **7** 314; **8** 222; **17** 106; **27** 297

Dürkopp Adler AG, 65 131–34

Duro-Matic Products Co., **51** 368

Duron Inc., 72 91–93

Dürr AG, 44 158–61

Durr-Fillauer Medical Inc., **13** 90; **18** 97; **50** 121

Dürrkopp Adler AG, **62** 132

Dutch Boy, **II** 649; **10** 434–35

Dutch Crude Oil Company. *See* Nederlandse Aardolie Maatschappij.

Dutch State Mines. *See* DSM N.V.

Dutchland Farms, **25** 124

Duttons Ltd., **24** 267

Duty Free International, Inc., 11 80–82. *See also* World Duty Free Americas, Inc.

Duval Corp., **7** 280; **25** 461

DVI, Inc., 51 107–09

DVM Pharmaceuticals Inc., **55** 233

DWG Corporation. *See* Triarc Companies, Inc.

Dyas B.V., **55** 347

Dyckerhoff AG, 35 151–54

Dycom Industries, Inc., 57 118–20

Dyersburg Corporation, 21 192–95

Dyke and Dryden, Ltd., **31** 417

Dylex Limited, 29 162–65

Dymed Corporation. *See* Palomar Medical Technologies, Inc.

DYMO. *See* Esselte Worldwide.

Dynaction S.A., 67 146–48

Dynalectric Co., **45** 146

DynaMark, Inc., **18** 168, 170, 516, 518

Dynamem Corporation, **22** 409

Dynamic Capital Corp., **16** 80

Dynamic Controls, **11** 202

Dynamic Foods, **53** 148

Dynamic Health Products Inc., **62** 296

Dynamic Homes, **61** 125–27

Dynamic Microprocessor Associated Inc., **10** 508

Dynamics Corporation of America, **39** 106

Dynamit Nobel AG, **III** 692–95; **16** 364; **18** 559

Dynamix, **15** 455

Dynapar, **7** 116–17

Dynaplast, **40** 214–15

Dynascan AK, **14** 118

Dynasty Footwear, Ltd., **18** 88

Dynatech Corporation, 13 194–96

Dynatron/Bondo Corporation, **8** 456

DynCorp, 45 145–47

Dynea, 68 125–27

Dynegy Inc., 47 70; **49 119–22 (upd.)**

Dyno Industrier AS, **13** 555

Dyson Group PLC, 71 132–34

Dystrybucja, **41** 340

E&B Company, **9** 72

E&B Marine, Inc., **17** 542–43

E. & J. Gallo Winery, I 242–44, 260; **7** 154–56 **(upd.)**; **15** 391; **28 109–11 (upd.)**, 223

E&M Laboratories, **18** 514

E & S Retail Ltd. *See* Powerhouse.

E! Entertainment Television Inc., 17 148–50; **24** 120, 123; **47** 78

E-mu Systems, Inc., **57** 78–79

E-Stamp Corporation, **34** 474

E-Systems, Inc., 9 182–85

E*Trade Financial Corporation, 20 206–08; **60 114–17 (upd.)**

E-II Holdings Inc. *See* Astrum International Corp.

E-Z Haul, **24** 409

E-Z Serve Corporation, 15 270; **17 169–71**

E A Rosengrens AB, **53** 158

E.B. Badger Co., **11** 413

E.B. Eddy Forest Products, **II** 631

E.C. Snodgrass Company, **14** 112

E.C. Steed, **13** 103

E. de Trey & Sons, **10** 270–71

E.F. Hutton Group, **II** 399, 450–51; **8** 139; **9** 469; **10** 63

E.F. Hutton LBO, **24** 148

E.H. Bindley & Company, **9** 67

E.I. du Pont de Nemours & Company, I 328–30; **8** 151–54 **(upd.)**; **26** 123–27 **(upd.)**; **34** 80, 283–84; **37** 111; **40** 370; **45** 246; **59** 135; **63** 108

E.J. Brach & Sons. *See* Brach and Brock Confections, Inc.

E.J. Longyear Company. *See* Boart Longyear Company.

E. Katz Special Advertising Agency. *See* Katz Communications, Inc.

E.M. Warburg Pincus & Co., **7** 305; **13** 176; **16** 319; **25** 313; **29** 262

E. Missel GmbH, **20** 363

E.On AG, 50 165–73 (upd.); **51** 217; **59** 391; **62** 14

E.piphany, Inc., 49 123–25

E.R.R. Enterprises, **44** 227

E. Rabinowe & Co., Inc., **13** 367

E. Rosen Co., **53** 303–04

E.S. International Holding S.A. *See* Banco Espírito Santo e Comercial de Lisboa S.A.

E.V. Williams Inc. *See* The Branch Group, Inc.

E.W. Howell Co., Inc., 72 94–96

The E.W. Scripps Company, IV 606–09; **7** 157–59 **(upd.)**; **28** 122–26 **(upd.)**; **66** 85–89 **(upd.)**

EADS N.V. *See* European Aeronautic Defence and Space Company EADS N.V.

EADS SOCATA, 54 91–94

Eagel One Industries, **50** 49

Eagle Airways Ltd., **23** 161

Eagle Credit Corp., **10** 248

Eagle Distributing Co., **37** 351

Eagle Family Foods, Inc., **22** 95

Eagle Floor Care, Inc., **13** 501; **33** 392

Eagle Gaming, L.P., **16** 263; **43** 226

Eagle Global Logistics. *See* EGL, Inc.

Eagle Hardware & Garden, Inc., 9 399; **16 186–89**; **17** 539–40

Eagle Industries Inc., **8** 230; **22** 282; **25** 536

Eagle Managed Care Corp., **19** 354, 357; **63** 334

Eagle-Picher Industries, Inc., 8 155–58; **23 179–83 (upd.)**

Eagle Plastics, **19** 414

Eagle Sentry Inc., **32** 373

Eagle Star Insurance Co., **I** 426–27; **III** 185, 200

Eagle Thrifty Drug, **14** 397

Eagle Trading, **55** 24

Eagle Travel Ltd., **IV** 241

Earl Scheib, Inc., 32 158–61

Early American Insurance Co., **22** 230

Early Learning Centre, **39** 240, 242

Earth Resources Company, **17** 320

Earth Wise, Inc., **16** 90

Earth's Best, Inc., **21** 56; **36** 256

The Earthgrains Company, 36 161–65; **54** 326

EarthLink, Inc., 33 92; **36 166–68**; **38** 269

EAS. *See* Engineered Air Systems, Inc.; Executive Aircraft Services.

Easco Hand Tools, Inc., **7** 117

Easi-Set Industries, Inc., **56** 332

Eason Oil Company, **6** 578; **11** 198

East African External Communications Limited, **25** 100

East African Gold Mines Limited, **61** 293

East Hartford Trust Co., **13** 467

East Japan Railway Company, V 448–50; **66 90–94 (upd.)**

The East New York Savings Bank, **11** 108–09

East Tennessee Steel Supply Inc. *See* Siskin Steel & Supply Company.

East-West Airlines, **27** 475

East-West Federal Bank, **16** 484

East West Motor Express, Inc., **39** 377

Easter Enterprises. *See* Nash Finch Company.

Easter Seals, Inc., 58 105–07

Easterday Supply Company, **25** 15

Eastern Air Group Co., **31** 102

Eastern Airlines, I 66, 78, 90, 98–99, **101–03**, 116, 118, 123–25; **6** , 104–05; **8** 416; **9** 17–18, 80; **11** 268, 427; **12** 191, 487; **21** 142, 143; **23** 483; **26** 339, 439

Eastern Australia Airlines Pty Ltd., **24** 396; **68** 306

Eastern Aviation Group, **23** 408

Eastern Carolina Bottling Company, **10** 223

The Eastern Company, 48 140–43

Eastern Electricity, **13** 485

Eastern Enterprises, 6 486–88

Eastern Kansas Utilities, **6** 511

Eastern Machine Screw Products Co., **13** 7

Eastern Market Beef Processing Corp., **20** 120

Eastern Pine Sales Corporation, **13** 249

Eastern Platinum Ltd. *See* Lonmin plc.

Eastern Shore Natural Gas Company, **56** 62

Eastern Software Distributors, Inc., **16** 125

Eastern States Farmers Exchange, **7** 17

Eastern Texas Electric. *See* Gulf States Utilities Company.

Eastern Torpedo Company, **25** 74

Eastern Wisconsin Power, **6** 604

Eastern Wisconsin Railway and Light Company, **6** 601
EastGroup Properties, Inc., 67 149–51
Eastman Chemical Company, 14 174–75; 25 22; **38 178–81 (upd.)**
Eastman Christensen Company, **22** 68
Eastman House. *See* Chittenden & Eastman Company.
Eastman Kodak Company, III 474–77; 7 160–64 (upd.); 36 169–76 (upd.); 38 178–79; **41** 104, 106; **43** 284; **45** 284; **61** 226–27
Eastmaque Gold Mines, Ltd., **7** 356
Easton Sports, Inc., 51 163; **66 95–97**
Eastover Mining, **27** 130
Eastpak, Inc., **30** 138; **70** 136
Eastport International Inc., **63** 318
Eastwynn Theatres, Inc., **37** 63
easyJet Airline Company Limited, 39 127–29; 52 330
Eatco, Inc., **15** 246
Eateries, Inc., 33 138–40
Eaton, Cole & Burnham Company, **8** 134
Eaton Corporation, I 154–55, 186; **10 279–80 (upd.); 12** 547; **27** 100; **67 152–56 (upd.)**
Eaton Vance Corporation, 18 150–53
EAudio, Inc., **48** 92
EBA Holding S.A., **63** 180
EBASCO. *See* Electric Bond and Share Company.
eBay Inc., 32 162–65; 49 51; **67 157–61 (upd.)**
EBCO, **55** 302
Eberhard Faber, **12** 115
Eberhard Foods, **8** 482
Eberhard Manufacturing Company, **48** 141
EBIC. *See* European Banks' International Co.
Ebiex S.A., **25** 312
EBS. *See* Electric Bond & Share Company; Electronic Bookshelf.
EBSCO Industries, Inc., 17 151–53; 40 158–61 (upd.)
EC Delaware Incorporated, **72** 117
EC Erdolchemie GmbH, **7** 141
ECAD Inc., **48** 75
ECC. *See* Educational Credit Corporation.
ECC Group plc, III 689–91. *See also* English China Clays plc.
ECC International Corp., 42 122–24
Ecce, **41** 129
ECCO. *See* Adecco S.A.
Ecco Sko A/S, 62 109–11
Echlin Inc., I 156–57; 11 83–85 (upd.); 15 310
Echo Bay Mines Ltd., IV 75–77; 23 40; **38 182–85 (upd.)**
The Echo Design Group, Inc., 68 128–30
Les Echos, **IV** 659
EchoStar Communications Corporation, 35 155–59
EchoStar Satellite Corp., **39** 400
ECI Telecom Ltd., 18 154–56
Eckerd Corporation, 9 186–87; 18 272; **24** 263; **43** 247; **63** 335–36. *See also* J.C. Penney Company, Inc.
Eckes AG, 56 100–03
ECL, **16** 238
Eclipse Candles, Ltd., **18** 67, 69
Eclipse Telecommunications, Inc., **29** 252
Eco Hotels, **14** 107
Eco SA, **48** 224
Eco-Tech Company Inc., **60** 272

Ecoiffier, **56** 335
Ecolab Inc., I 331–33; 13 197–200 (upd.); 26 306; **34 151–56 (upd.),** 205, 208
Ecology and Environment, Inc., 39 130–33
Econo Lodges of America, **25** 309
Econo-Travel Corporation, **13** 362
Economist Group, **15** 265
The Economist Group Ltd., 67 162–65
Economy Book Store, **10** 135
Economy Fire & Casualty, **22** 495
Ecopetrol. *See* Empresa Colombiana de Petróleos.
EcoSystems Software, Inc., **10** 245; **30** 142
EcoWater Systems, Inc., **16** 357
ECS S.A, 12 138–40
ECT Environmental Technologies AB, **72** 117
Ecton, Inc., **36** 5
Ecusta Corporation, **8** 414
ed bazinet international, inc., **34** 144–45
Edah, **13** 544–45
Edasa. *See* Embotelladoras del Atlántico, S.A.
Eddelbüttel & Schneider GmbH, **68** 289
Eddie Bauer, Inc., 9 188–90; 36 177–81 (upd.)
Edeka Zentrale A.G., II 621–23; 33 56; **47 105–07 (upd.)**
edel music AG, 44 162–65
Edelbrock Corporation, 37 117–19
Edelhoff AG & Co., **39** 415
Edelman, 62 112–15
Edenton Cotton Mills, **12** 503
EDF. *See* Electricité de France.
Edgars Consolidated Stores Ltd., 66 98–100
Edge Petroleum Corporation, 67 166–68
Edge Research, **25** 301
Edgell Communications Inc., **IV** 624
Edgewater Hotel and Casino. *See* Circus Circus Enterprises, Inc.
EDI, **26** 441
Edina Realty Inc., **13** 348
Edison Brothers Stores, Inc., 9 191–93; 17 369, 409; **33 126–28**
Edison Electric Co., **6** 572
Edison Electric Illuminating Co., **6** 595, 601; **14** 124
Edison Electric Illuminating Company of Boston, **12** 45
Edison Electric Light & Power, **6** 510
Edison Electric Light Co., **6** 565, 595; **11** 387; **12** 193; **50** 365
Edison General Electric Co., **12** 193; **14** 168; **26** 451
Edison International, 56 104–07 (upd.)
Edison Schools Inc., 37 120–23
Éditions Dalloz, **IV** 615
Éditions Gallimard, 72 97–101
Editions Jean-Baptiste Baillière, **25** 285
Editions Ramsay, **25** 174
Editorial Centro de Estudios Ramón Areces, S.A., **V** 52; **26** 130
Editorial Television, S.A. de C.V., 18 211, 213; **23** 417; **57 121–23**
Editoriale L'Espresso, **IV** 586–87
Editoriale Le Gazzette, **IV** 587
Edivisa. *See* Editorial Television, S.A. de C.V.
EDiX Corporation, **64** 191
EdK. *See* Edeka Zentrale A.G.

Edmark Corporation, 14 176–78; 41 134–37 (upd.)
EDO Corporation, 46 158–61
EdoWater Systems, Inc., **IV** 137
EDP Group. *See* Electricidade de Portugal, S.A.
Edrington Group, **63** 246
EDS. *See* Electronic Data Systems Corporation.
Education Association Mutual Assurance Company. *See* Horace Mann Educators Corporation.
The Education Finance Group, **33** 418, 420
Education Loan Processing, **53** 319
Education Management Corporation, 35 160–63
Education Systems Corporation, **7** 256; **25** 253
Educational & Recreational Services, Inc., **II** 607
Educational Broadcasting Corporation, 48 144–47
Educational Computer International, Inc. *See* ECC International Corp.
Educational Credit Corporation, **8** 10; **38** 12
Educational Development Corporation. *See* National Heritage Academies, Inc.
Educational Loan Administration Group, Inc., **33** 420
Educational Publishing Corporation, **22** 519, 522
Educational Supply Company, **7** 255; **25** 252
Educational Testing Service, 12 141–43; 42 209–10, 290; **62 116–20 (upd.)**
Educor. *See* Naspers Ltd.
Educorp, Inc., **39** 103
Edumond Le Monnier S.p.A., **54** 22
EduServ Technologies, Inc., **33** 420
Edusoft Ltd., **40** 113
EduTrek International, Inc., **45** 88
Edw. C. Levy Co., 42 125–27
Edward D. Jones & Company L.P., 30 177–79; 66 101–04 (upd.)
Edward Hines Lumber Company, 68 131–33
Edward J. DeBartolo Corporation, 8 159–62
Edward P. Allis Company, **13** 16
Edward Smith & Company, **8** 553
Edwards & Jones, **11** 360
Edwards and Kelcey, 70 81–83
Edwards Food Warehouse, **II** 642
Edwards George and Co., **III** 283
Edwards Theatres Circuit, Inc., 31 171–73; 59 341–42
Edwardstone Partners, **14** 377
EEC Environmental, Inc., **16** 259
EEGSA. *See* Empresa Eléctrica de Guatemala S.A.
EEX Corporation, **65** 262
eFamily. *See* Marchex, Inc.
EFM Media Management, **23** 294
Efnadruck GmbH, **IV** 325
Efrat Future Technology Ltd. *See* Comverse Technology, Inc.
EFS National Bank, **52** 87
EFTEC, 32 257
EG&G Incorporated, 8 163–65; 18 219; **22** 410; **29 166–69 (upd.)**
EGAM, **IV** 422

EGAT. *See* Electricity Generating Authority of Thailand (EGAT).
Egg plc, **48** 328
Egghead Inc., 9 194–95; 10 284
Egghead.com, Inc., 31 174–77 (upd.)
EGL, Inc., 59 170–73
EGPC. *See* Egyptian General Petroleum Corporation.
eGrail Inc., **62** 142
EgyptAir, 6 84–86; 27 132–35 (upd.)
Egyptian General Petroleum Corporation, IV 412–14; 32 45; **51 110–14 (upd.)**
EHAPE Einheitspreis Handels Gesellschaft mbH. *See* Kaufhalle AG.
eHarmony.com Inc., 71 135–38
eHow.com, **49** 290
Ehrlich-Rominger, **48** 204
Eiffage, 27 136–38
Eiffel Construction Metallique, **27** 138
800-JR Cigar, Inc., 27 139–41
84 Lumber Company, 9 196–97; 39 134–36 (upd.)
Eildon Electronics Ltd., **15** 385
Eileen Fisher Inc., 61 85–87
Einstein/Noah Bagel Corporation, 29 170–73; 44 313; **63** 81
eircom plc, 31 178–81 (upd.)
EIS, Inc., **45** 176, 179; **62** 115
Eisai Company, **13** 77
EJ Financial Enterprises Inc., **48** 308–09
Ek Chor China Motorcycle, **62** 63
Eka Nobel AB, **9** 380
Ekco Group, Inc., 12 377; **16 190–93**
Eko-Elda A.B.E.E., **64** 177
Ekoterm CR. *See* Dalkia Holding.
EKT, Inc., **44** 4
El Al Israel Airlines Ltd., 23 184–87
El Camino Resources International, Inc., 11 86–88
El Chico Restaurants, Inc., 19 135–38; 36 162–63
El Corte Inglés, S.A., V 51–53; 26 128–31 (upd.)
El Dorado Investment Company, **6** 546–47
El-Mel-Parts Ltd., **21** 499
El Nasr Petroleum Co., **51** 113
El Paso Corporation, 66 105–08 (upd.)
El Paso Electric Company, 21 196–98
El Paso Healthcare System, Ltd., **15** 112; **35** 215
El Paso Natural Gas Company, 10 190; **11** 28; **12 144–46; 19** 411; **27** 86. *See also* El Paso Corporation.
El Pollo Loco, Inc., 69 138–40
El Portal Group, Inc., **58** 370
El Taco, **7** 505
Elamex, S.A. de C.V., 51 115–17
Elan Corporation PLC, 10 54; **63 140–43**
Elan Ski Company, **22** 483
Elanco Animal Health, **47** 112
Elano Corporation, 14 179–81
Elantis, **48** 290
Elastic Reality Inc., **38** 70
Elcat Company, **17** 91
Elco Corporation, **21** 329, 331
Elco Industries Inc., **22** 282
The Elder-Beerman Stores Corp., 10 281–83; 19 362; **63 144–48 (upd.)**
Elders IXL Ltd., I 264, **437–39**, 592–93; **7** 182–83; **21** 227; **26** 305; **28** 201; **50** 199
Elders Keep, **13** 440

Eldorado Gold Corporation, **22** 237
ele Corporation, **23** 251
Electra Corp., **III** 569; **20** 361–62
Electra/Midland Corp., **13** 398
Electrabel N.V., 67 169–71
Electric Boat Co. *See* General Dynamics Corporation.
Electric Bond & Share Company, **6** 596
Electric Clearinghouse, Inc., **18** 365, 367
Electric Fuels Corp. *See* Florida Progress Corporation.
Electric Light Company of Atlantic City. *See* Atlantic Energy, Inc.
Electric Lightwave, Inc., 37 124–27
Electric Storage Battery Co., **39** 338
Electric Transit, Inc., **37** 399–400
Electricidade de Portugal, S.A., 47 108–11; 49 211
Electricité de France, V 603–05, 626–28; **41 138–41 (upd.)**
Electricity Generating Authority of Thailand (EGAT), 56 108–10
Electricity Metering Distribucion, S.A. DE C.V., **64** 205
Electro-Flo, Inc., **9** 27
Electro Metallurgical Co., **11** 402
Electro-Motive Engineering Company, **10** 273
Electro Refractories and Abrasives Company, **8** 178
Electro Rent Corporation, 58 108–10
Electro String Instrument Corporation, **16** 201; **43** 169
Electrocomponents PLC, 50 174–77
Electrolux AB, 53 124–29 (upd.); 63 211
Electrolux Group, III 478–81; 11 439; **12** 158–59, 250; **13** 562, 564; **17** 353; **21** 383
Electromagnetic Sciences Inc., 21 199–201
Electromedics, **11** 460
Electronic Arts Inc., 10 284–86; 13 115; **29** 76; **35** 227
Electronic Banking Systems, **9** 173
Electronic Book Technologies, Inc., **26** 216 **29** 427
Electronic Data Systems Corporation, III 136–38; 28 112–16 (upd.). *See also* Perot Systems Corporation.
Electronic Engineering Co., **16** 393
Electronic Hair Styling, Inc., **41** 228
Electronic Processing Inc. *See* EPIQ Systems, Inc.
Electronics Boutique Holdings Corporation, 72 102–05
Electronics Corp. of Israel Ltd. *See* ECI Telecom Ltd.
Electronics for Imaging, Inc., 15 148–50; 43 150–53 (upd.)
Electrowatt Ltd., **21** 146–47
Elekom, **31** 176
Elektra. *See* Grupo Elektra, S.A. de C.V.
Elektra Entertainment Group, 64 115–18
Elektra Records, **III** 480; **23** 33
Elektriska Aktiebolaget. *See* ABB Asea Brown Boveri Ltd.
Elektrizitäts-Gesellschaft Laufenburg. *See* Elektrowatt AG.
Elektrizitätswerk Wesertal GmbH, **30** 206
Elektrocieplownie Warszawskie S.A., **57** 395, 397
Elektrowatt AG, 6 489–91
Elementis plc, 40 162–68 (upd.)

Eletropaulo Metropolitana, **53** 18
Eletson Corp., **13** 374
Elettra Broadcasting Corporation, **14** 509
Elettrofinanziaria Spa, **9** 152
Elf Aquitaine SA, 21 202–06 (upd.); 23 236, 238; **24** 494; **25** 104; **26** 369, 425; **49** 349–51; **50** 179–80, 479, 484; **61** 238. *See also* Société Nationale Elf Aquitaine.
Elfa International, **36** 134–35
Elgin Blenders, Inc., **7** 128
Elgin Exploration, Inc., **19** 247; **26** 70
Eli Lilly and Company, I 645–47; 11 89–91 (upd.); 47 112–16 (upd.); 50 139
Eli Witt Company, **15** 137, 139; **43** 205
Elior SA, 49 126–28
Elisra Defense Group, **68** 222, 224
Elite Acquisitions, Inc., **65** 150
Elite Microelectronics, **9** 116
Elizabeth Arden, Inc., III 48; **8 166–68**, 344; **9** 201–02, 428, 449; **11** 90; **12** 314; **30** 188; **32** 476; **40 169–72 (upd.); 47** 113
Eljer Industries, Inc., II 420; **24 150–52**
ElkCorp, 52 103–05
Elke Corporation, **10** 514
Elkjop ASA, **49** 113
Elko-Lamoille Power Company, **11** 343
Ellanef Manufacturing Corp., **48** 274
Ellen Tracy, Inc., 55 136–38
Ellerbe Becket, 41 142–45
Ellesse International S.p.A. *See* Reebok International Ltd.
Ellett Brothers, Inc., 17 154–56
Ellington Recycling Center, **12** 377
Elliot Group Limited, **45** 139–40
Elliott Automation, **13** 225
Elliott Bay Design Group, **22** 276
Elliott Paint and Varnish, **8** 553
Ellipse Programmes, **48** 164–65
Ellis & Everard, **41** 341
Ellis-Don Ltd., **38** 481
Ellis Paperboard Products Inc., **13** 442
Ellis Park Race Course, **29** 118
Ellisco Co., **35** 130
Ellos A.B., **II** 640
Elmendorf Board, **IV** 343
Elmer's Products, Inc. *See* Borden, Inc.
Elmer's Restaurants, Inc., 42 128–30
Elmo Semiconductor Corp., **48** 246
Elna USA. *See* Tacony Corporation.
Elphinstone, **21** 501
Elrick Industries, Inc., **19** 278
Elscint Ltd., 20 202–05
Elsevier NV, IV 610–11, 643, 659; **7** 244; **14** 555–56; **17** 396, 399. *See also* Reed Elsevier.
Elsinore Corporation, 36 158; **48 148–51**
Eltra Corporation, **I** 416; **22** 31; **31** 135
Eltron International Inc., **53** 374
Elvirasminde A/S. *See* August Storck KG.
Elvis Presley Enterprises, Inc., 61 88–90
ELYO, **42** 387–88
eMachines, Inc., **63** 155
Email Ltd., **62** 331
EMAP plc, 35 71–72, **164–66**, 242–44
Embankment Trust Ltd., **IV** 659
Embassy Suites, **9** 425; **24** 253
Embedded Support Tools Corporation, **37** 419, 421
Embers America Restaurants, 30 180–82
Embotelladora Andina S.A., 71 139–41
Embotelladora Central, S.A., **47** 291

Embraer. *See* Empresa Brasileira de Aeronáutica S.A.

Embraer-Liebherr Equipamentos do Brasil S.A., **64** 241

Embrex, Inc., 72 106–08

EMC Corporation, 12 147–49; 20 8; **46 162–66 (upd.)**

EMC Technology Services, Inc., **30** 469

Emco, **III** 569; **20** 361

EMCOR Group Inc., 60 118–21

EMD Holding, Inc., **64** 205

EMD Technologies, **27** 21; **40** 67

Emerald Technology, Inc., **10** 97

Emerson, 46 167–71 (upd.)

Emerson-Brantingham Company, **10** 378

Emerson Electric Co., II 18–21, 92; **8** 298; **12** 248; **13** 225; **14** 357; **15** 405–06; **21** 43; **22** 64; **25** 530; **36** 400; **61** 96, 98

Emerson Foote, Inc., **25** 90

Emerson Radio Corp., 30 183–86

Emery Worldwide Airlines, Inc., 6 388–91; 18 177; **21** 139; **25 146–50 (upd.)**

Emge Packing Co., Inc., 11 92–93

Emhart Corp., **III** 437; **8** 332; **20** 67; **67** 67

EMI Group plc, 22 192–95 (upd.); 24 485; **26** 188, 314; **52** 428

Emigrant Savings Bank, 59 174–76

Emil Moestue as, **51** 328

Emil Schlemper GmbH. *See* Acme United Corporation.

The Emirates Group, 24 400; **39 137–39**

Emmis Communications Corporation, 47 117–21

Empain, **18** 472; **19** 165

Empaques de Carton Titan, **19** 10–11

Empex Hose, **19** 37

Empi, Inc., 27 132–35

Empire Blue Cross and Blue Shield, III 245–46. *See also* WellChoice, Inc.

Empire-Cliffs Partnership, **62** 74

Empire Family Restaurants Inc., **15** 362

Empire Hanna Coal Co., Ltd., **8** 346

Empire Iron Mining Partnership, **62** 74

Empire of America, **11** 110

Empire of Carolina Inc., **66** 370

Empire Resorts, Inc., 72 109–12

Empire State Pickling Company, **21** 155

Empire Steel Castings, Inc., **39** 31–32

Empire Stores, **19** 309

Employee Solutions, Inc., 18 157–60

employeesavings.com, **39** 25

Employers General Insurance Group, **58** 259

Employers Insurance of Wausau, **59** 264

Employers' Liability Assurance, **III** 235

Employer's Overload, **25** 432

Employers Reinsurance Corp., **II** 31; **12** 197

Emporsil-Empresa Portuguesa de Silvicultura, Lda, **60** 156

Empresa Brasileira de Aeronáutica S.A. (Embraer), 36 182–84

Empresa Colombiana de Petróleos, IV 415–18

Empresa Constructora SA, **55** 182

Empresa de Obras y Montajes Ovalle Moore, S.A., **34** 81

Empresa Eléctrica de Guatemala S.A., **49** 211

Empresa Nacional de Telecomunicaciones, **63** 375

Empresas Almacenes Paris S.A., 71 142–44

Empresas CMPC S.A., 70 84–87

Empresas Copec S.A., 69 141–44

Empresas Emel S.A., **41** 316

Empresas Frisco, **21** 259

Empresas ICA Sociedad Controladora, S.A. de C.V., 34 82; **41 146–49**

Empresas La Moderna, **21** 413; **29** 435

Empresas Penta S.A., **69** 56

Empresas Polar SA, 55 139–41 (upd.)

Empresas Tolteca, **20** 123

Emprise Corporation, **7** 134–35

EMS-Chemie Holding AG, **III** 760; **32** 257

EMS Technologies, Inc., **21** 199, 201; **22** 173

Enbridge Inc., 43 154–58

ENCAD, Incorporated, 25 151–53

Encompass Services Corporation, 33 141–44

Encon Safety Products, Inc., **45** 424

Encor Inc., **47** 396

Encore Computer Corporation, 13 201–02

Encore Distributors Inc., **17** 12–13

Encryption Technology Corporation, **23** 102

Encyclopedia Britannica, Inc., 7 165–68; 12 435, 554–55; **16** 252; **39 140–44 (upd.); 43** 208

Endata, Inc., **11** 112

Endeavor Pharmaceuticals Inc. *See* Barr Pharmaceuticals, Inc.

Endemol Entertainment Holding NV, 46 172–74; 53 154

ENDESA S.A., V 606–08; 46 175–79 (upd.); 49 210–11

Endevco Inc., **11** 28

Endicott Trust Company, **11** 110

Endo Pharmaceuticals Holdings Inc., 71 145–47

Endo Vascular Technologies, Inc., **11** 460

ENDOlap, Inc., **50** 122

Endovations, Inc., **21** 47

ENECO. *See* Empresa Nacional Electrica de Cordoba.

Enerchange LLC, **18** 366

Enercon, Inc., **6** 25

Energas Company, **43** 56–57

Energen Corporation, 6 583; **21 207–09**

Energieversorgung Ostbayern AG, **23** 47

Energis plc, 44 363; **47 122–25**

Energizer Holdings, Inc., 9 180; **32 171–74; 39** 336, 339; **60** 349, 352

Energy & Minerals, Inc., **42** 354

Energy Absorption Systems, Inc., **15** 378

Energy Atlantic, LLC. *See* Maine & Maritimes Corporation.

Energy Biosystems Corp., **15** 352

Energy Coatings Co., **14** 325

Energy Electromechanical Projects S.A., **64** 8

Energy Film Library, **31** 216, 218

Energy Foundation, **34** 386

The Energy Group, **26** 359

Energy Increments Inc., **19** 411

Energy National, Inc., **27** 485

Energy Resources, **27** 216

Energy Steel Corporation, **19** 472

Energy Systems Group, Inc., **13** 489

Energy Transportation Systems, Inc., **27** 88

Energy Ventures, Inc., **49** 181

Energyline Systems, **26** 5

EnergyOne, **19** 487

Eneria. *See* Groupe Monnoyeur.

Enerplus Resources, **21** 500

Enesco Corporation, 11 94–96; 15 475, 477–78

Enet S.A., **64** 8

Enforcer Products, Inc., **54** 254

Engelhard Corporation, IV 78–80; 21 210–14 (upd.); 72 113–18 (upd.)

Engen, **IV** 93; **22** 236

Engenio Information Technologies, Inc., **64** 246

Engineered Support Systems, Inc., 59 177–80

Engineering Company, **9** 16

Engineering for the Petroleum and Process Industries, **IV** 414

Engineering Plastics, Ltd., **8** 377

Engineering Systems, Inc., **54** 182

Engineers & Fabricators, Inc., **18** 513

England Corsair Furniture, **14** 302

Engle Homes, Inc., 46 180–82

Engles Management Corp., **26** 448

English China Clays Ltd., III 689–91; **15 151–54 (upd.); 36** 20; **40 173–77 (upd.)**

English Electric Co., **24** 85

Engraph, Inc., 12 150–51

Enhanced Derm Technologies, **50** 122

Enhanced Services Billing, Inc. *See* Billing Concepts Corp.

ENI S.p.A., 34 75; **61** 236, 238; **69 145–50 (upd.)**

Enimont, **IV** 422, 525

Ennis Business Forms, Inc., 21 215–17

Enocell Oy, **IV** 277

The Enoch F. Bills Co., **25** 365

Enodis plc, 68 134–37

Enogex, Inc., **6** 539–40

Enova Corporation. *See* Sempra Energy.

ENPAC Corporation, **18** 162

Enquirer/Star Group, Inc., 10 287–88; 12 358. *See also* American Media, Inc.

ENRECO. *See* Essential Nutrient Research Corporation.

Enrich International, Inc., 33 145–48; 37 340, 342

Enron Corporation, V 609–10; 6 457, 593; **18** 365; **19 139–41**, 162, 487; **27** 266; **34** 82; **46 183–86 (upd.); 49** 121–22; **54** 86; **59** 217

ENSCO International Incorporated, 57 124–26

Enserch Corp., V 611–13. *See also* Texas Utilities.

Ensign Oil Company, **9** 490

Enskilda S.A., **II** 352–53

Enso-Gutzeit Oy, IV 274–77; 17 539. *See also* Stora Enso Oyj

ENSTAR Corporation, **11** 441

Enstar Group Inc., **13** 299

Ensys Environmental Products, Inc., **10** 107

Ente Nazionale Idrocarburi, IV 419–22. *See also* ENI S.p.A.

Ente Nazionale per l'Energia Elettrica, V 614–17

Entenmann's Bakery, **35** 415; **38** 364

Entercom Communications Corporation, 48 272; **58 111–12**

Entergy Corporation, V 618–20; 6 496–97; **45 148–51 (upd.)**

Enterprise Development Company, **15** 413

Enterprise Electronics Corporation, **18** 513–15

Enterprise Federal Savings & Loan, **21** 524

Enterprise Inns plc, 59 181–83
Enterprise Integration Technologies, **18** 541
Enterprise Metals Pty. Ltd., **IV** 61
Enterprise Oil plc, 11 97–99; 50 178–82 (upd.)
Enterprise Rent-A-Car Company, 6 392–93; 16 380; **33** 192; **69 151–54 (upd.)**
Enterra Corp., **25** 546
Entertainment Publications, **16** 146
Entertainment UK, **24** 266, 269
Entertainment Zone, Inc., **15** 212
Entex Information Services, **24** 29
Entity Software, **11** 469
Entrada Industries Incorporated, **6** 568–69; **26** 387
Entravision Communications Corporation, 41 150–52
Entré Computer Centers, **13** 175
Entreprise Nationale Sonatrach, IV 423–25; 10 83–84; **12** 145. See also Sonatrach.
Entrust Financial Corp., **16** 347
Envergure, **27** 421
Envirex, **11** 361
Envirocal Inc., **60** 223
Envirodrill Services, Inc., **19** 247
Envirodyne Industries, Inc., 17 157–60
EnviroLease, Inc., **25** 171
ENVIRON International Corporation, **10** 106
Environmental Defense Fund, **9** 305
Environmental Industries, Inc., 31 182–85
Environmental Mediation, Inc., **47** 20
Environmental Planning & Research. See CRSS Inc.
Environmental Power Corporation, 68 138–40
Environmental Research and Technology, Inc., **23** 135
Environmental Systems Corporation, **9** 109
Environmental Systems Research Institute Inc. (ESRI), 62 121–24
Environmental Technologies Group, LLC, **56** 161
Environmental Testing and Certification Corporation, **10** 106–07
Environmentals Incorporated. See Angelica Corporation.
Envirosciences Pty. Ltd., **16** 260
EnviroSource Inc., **63** 237
Envision Corporation, **24** 96
Enwright Environmental Consulting Laboratories, **9** 110
Enzafruit Worldwide, **38** 202
Enzo Biochem, Inc., 41 153–55
Enzyme Bio-Systems, Ltd., **21** 386
Eon Labs, Inc., 67 172–74
Eon Systems, **38** 409
l'Epargne, **12** 152
EPE Technologies, **18** 473
EPI. See Essentially Pure Ingredients.
EPI Group Limited, **26** 137
Epic Express, **48** 113
Epic Systems Corporation, 62 125–28
Les Epiceries Presto Limitée, **II** 651
Epiphone, **16** 238–39
EPIQ Systems, Inc., 56 111–13
Epoch Software, Plc, **49** 290
Epoch Systems Inc., **9** 140; **12** 149
ePOWER International, **33** 3, 6
Eppler, Guerin & Turner, Inc., **III** 330
Epson, **18** 386–87, 435

EQT Partners AB, **71** 342
Equant N.V., 52 106–08
EQUICOR-Equitable HCA Corp., **III** 80, 226; **45** 104, 109
Equicor Group Ltd., **29** 343
Equifax, Inc., 6 23–25; 25 182, 358; **28 117–21 (upd.); 63** 100, 102; **65 106–08**
Equilink Licensing Group, **22** 458
Equilon Enterprises LLC, **41** 359, 395
The Equinox Indemnity Co. Ltd. See SNC-Lavalin Group Inc.
Equinox Systems. See Avocent Corporation.
Equistar Chemicals, LP, 71 148–50
EquiStar Hotel Investors L.P. See CapStar Hotel Co.
Equitable Bancorporation, **12** 329
Equitable Equipment Company, **7** 540
Equitable Life Assurance Society of the United States, III 80, 229, 237, **247–49**, 274, 289, 291, 305–06, 316, 329, 359; **13** 539; **19** 324, 511; **22** 188–90; **23** 370, 482; **27** 46; **61** 249
Equitable Resources, Inc., 6 492–94; 54 95–98 (upd.); 63 440
Equitas, **22** 315
Equitec Financial Group, **11** 483
Equitex Inc., **16** 431
Equity & Law, **III** 211
Equity Corp. International, **51** 332
Equity Corporation, **6** 599; **37** 67–68
Equity Group Investment, Inc., **22** 339
Equity Marketing, Inc., 26 136–38
Equity Office Properties Trust, 54 99–102
Equity Residential, 49 55, **129–32; 54** 100
Equity Title Services Company, **13** 348
Equivalent Company, **12** 421
Equus Capital Corp., **23** 65
Equus Computer Systems, Inc., 49 133–35
Equus II Inc., **18** 11
ERA, **61** 267
Eram SA, 51 118–20
ERAP. See Entreprise de Recherches et d'Activités Pétrolières.
EraSoft Technologies, **27** 492
Ercea, **41** 128–29
ERCO Systems Group, **16** 461–63
Ercon Corp., **49** 181
ERDA Inc., **36** 160
ERE Yarmouth, **57** 234
ERGO Versicherungsgruppe AG, 44 166–69, 443
Erickson Retirement Communities, 57 127–30
Ericson Yachts, **10** 215
Ericsson, **9** 32–33; **11** 196, 501; **17** 33, 353; **18** 74; **47** 321; **53** 126–28; **61** 137; **63** 211. See also Telefonaktiebolaget LM Ericsson.
Eridania Béghin-Say S.A., 14 17, 19; **36 185–88**
Erie County Bank, **9** 474
Erie Indemnity Company, 35 167–69
Erie Scientific Company, **14** 479–80
ERIM International Inc., **54** 396
Erisco Managed Care Technologies, **57** 176
ERKA. See Reichs Kredit-Gesellschaft mbH.
ERLY Industries Inc., 17 161–62; 33 30–31
Ermenegildo Zegna SpA, 63 149–52

Ernest Jones (Jewelers) Plc, **61** 326
Ernie Ball, Inc., 56 114–16
Ernst & Young, 9 198–200, 309, 311; **10** 115; **25** 358; **29 174–77 (upd.)**, 236, 392
Ernst Göhner Foundation, **47** 286–87
Ernst, Homans, Ware & Keelips, **37** 224
Erol's, **9** 74; **11** 556
Eroski. See Grupo Eroski
ERPI, **7** 167
Ersco Corporation, **17** 310; **24** 160
Erste Bank der Osterreichischen Sparkassen AG, 69 155–57
The Ertl Company, **37** 318
Erving Healthcare, **13** 150
ES&A. See English, Scottish and Australian Bank Ltd.
ES Développement SAS, **70** 90
Esaote Biomedica, **29** 298
ESB Inc., **IV** 112; **18** 488
Esbjerg Thermoplast, **9** 92
ESCADA AG, 71 151–53
Escalade, Incorporated, 19 142–44
Escan, **22** 354
Eschelon Telecom, Inc., 72 119–22
Eschweiler Bergwerks-Verein AG, **IV** 25–26, 193
ESCO Electronics Corporation, **17** 246, 248; **24** 425
Esco Trading, **10** 482
Escota SA, **55** 40
Escotel Mobile Communications, **18** 180
Esdon de Castro, **8** 137
ESGO B.V., **49** 222
ESI Energy, Inc. See FPL Group Inc.
Eskay Screw Corporation, **11** 536
Eskimo Pie Corporation, 21 218–20; 35 119, 121
Esmark, Inc., **12** 93; **15** 357; **19** 290; **62** 89, 91
Esmerk Group, **51** 328
Espaces Gamm Vert, **70** 322
Espírito Santo. See Banco Espírito Santo e Comercial de Lisboa S.A.
ESPN, Inc., 24 516; **56 117–22; 63** 437
Esporta plc, 35 170–72
Esprit de Corp., 8 169–72; 29 178–82 (upd.)
Esquire Education Group, **12** 173
Esquire Inc., **I** 453; **IV** 672; **13** 178; **19** 405
ESS Technology, Inc., 22 196–98
Essanelle Salon Co., **18** 455
Essantee Theatres, Inc., **14** 86
Essef Corporation, 18 161–63; 56 17
Esselte, 64 119–21
Esselte Leitz GmbH & Co. KG, 48 152–55
Esselte Pendaflex Corporation, 11 100–01
Essence Communications, Inc., 24 153–55
Essential Nutrient Research Corporation, **72** 234
Essentially Pure Ingredients, **49** 275–76
Essex International Ltd., **19** 452
Essex Outfitters Inc., **9** 394; **42** 268–69
Essilor International, 18 392; **21 221–23; 40** 96–98
Esso Petroleum. See Exxon Corporation; Imperial Oil Limited; Standard Oil Company of New Jersey.
Essroc Corporation, **40** 108
Estat Telecom Group plc, **31** 180

Estech, Inc., **19** 290

Estee Corp., **27** 197; **43** 218

The Estée Lauder Companies Inc., 8 131; **9 201–04; 11** 41; **24** 55; **30** **187–91 (upd.)**

Esterline Technologies Corp., 15 155–57; **53** 353

Estes Industries Inc. *See* Centuri Corporation.

Estronicks, Inc., **19** 290

ETA Systems, Inc., **10** 256–57

Etablissement Mesnel, **I** 202

Etablissements Badin-Defforey, **19** 98

Etablissements Bourgogne et Grasset, **66** 251

Etablissements Braud. *See* Manitou BF S.A.

Etablissements Economiques du Casino **Guichard, Perrachon et ie, S.C.A., 12** 152–54; **16** 452. *See also* Casino Guichard-Perrachon S.A.

Etablissements Franz Colruyt N.V., 68 **141–43**

Etablissements Robert Ouvrie S.A., **22** 436

Etam Developpement SA, 35 308; **44** **170–72**

ETBD. *See* Europe Through the Back Door.

Eteq Microsystems, **9** 116

Eternal Word Television Network, Inc., **57 131–34**

Ethan Allen Interiors, Inc., 10 184; **12** 307; **12 155–57; 39 145–48 (upd.)**

Ethical Personal Care Products, Ltd., **17** 108

Ethicon, Inc., 10 213; **23 188–90**

Ethyl Corp., I 334–36, 342; **10 289–91** **(upd.); 14** 217; **52** 349; **59** 23–24

Etienne Aigner AG, 14 224; **52 109–12**

Etimex Kunstoffwerke GmbH, **7** 141

Etkin Skanska, **38** 437

Étoile Commerciale S.A., **51** 143

Etos, **II** 641

EToys, Inc., 37 128–30

ETPM Entrêpose, **IV** 468

ETS. *See* Educational Testing Service.

Eu-retec, **71** 393

Euclid Chemical Co., **8** 455–56

Euclid Crane & Hoist Co., **13** 385

Euralux, **III** 209

The Eureka Company, 12 158–60; 15 416. *See also* White Consolidated Industries Inc.

Eureka Technology, **18** 20; **43** 17

Eureka X-Ray Tube, Inc., **10** 272

Eurex, **41** 84, 87

Euris, **22** 365; **54** 306–07

Euro Disney S.C.A., 58 113–16 (upd.); **63** 435

Euro Disneyland SCA, 20 209–12

Euro Exhausts, **54** 206

Euro RSCG Worldwide S.A., 10 345, 347; **13 203–05; 16** 168; **33** 181

Eurobase, **50** 48

Eurocom S.A. *See* Euro RSCG Worldwide S.A.

Eurocopter SA, **7** 9, 11; **21** 8

EuroCross, **48** 381

Eurodis, **46** 71

EuroDollar Rent A Car. *See* Republic Industries, Inc.

Eurofighter Jagdflugzeug GmbH, **24** 84

Eurofilter Airfilters Ltd., **17** 106

Eurofind, **71** 308–09

Eurofins Scientific S.A., 70 88–90

Euroforum BV, **58** 191

Eurogroup, **V** 65

Euroimpex, **18** 163

Euromarché SA, **10** 205; **19** 308–09; **23** 231; **27** 94–95

Euromarket Designs Inc., 9 144; **31** **186–89 (upd.); 34** 324, 327

Euromissile Dynamics Group, **7** 9; **24** 84

Euromoney Publications, **19** 118, 120

Euronda, **IV** 296; **19** 226

Euronext Paris S.A., 37 131–33

Euronova S.R.L., **15** 340

Europa Discount Sud-Ouest, **23** 248

Europaischen Tanklager- und Transport AG, **7** 141

Europate, S.A., **36** 162–63

Europcar Chauffeur Drive U.K. International, **26** 62

Europcar International Corporation, Limited, **25** 142, 144, **27** 9, 11

Europcar Interrent International, **10** 419; **69** 5, 6

Europe Computer Systems. *See* ECS S.A.

Europe Craft Imports, Inc., **16** 37

Europe Publications, **44** 416

Europe Through the Back Door Inc., 65 **135–38**

European Acquisition Capital, **53** 46

European Aeronautic Defence and Space **Company EADS N.V., 34** 128, 135; **52** **113–16 (upd.); 54** 91

European-American Bank & Trust Company, **14** 169

European Gas Turbines, **13** 356

European Health Spa, **46** 431

European Investment Bank, 66 109–11

European Retail Alliance (ERA), **12** 152–53

European Silicon Structures, **17** 34

European Software Company, **25** 87

Europene du Zirconium (Cezus), **21** 491

Europensiones, **III** 348

Europoligrafico SpA, **41** 326

Europspace Technische Entwicklungen, **51** 17

Euroquipment Ltd, **72** 221

Eurosar S.A., **25** 455

Eurotec S.A.S., **72** 332

Eurotech BV, **25** 101

Eurotechnique, **III** 678; **16** 122

Eurotel Praha, spol. s.r.o., **64** 73

Eurotunnel Group, 37 134–38 (upd.)

Eurotunnel PLC, 13 206–08

Eurovida, **III** 348

Euthenics Systems Corp. *See* Michael Baker Corporation.

Euvia Media AG & Co., **54** 295, 297

EVA Airways Corporation, 13 211; **51** **121–23**

Evac International Ltd, **51** 324

Evaluation Associates, LLC. *See* Milliman USA.

Evans & Sutherland Computer **Corporation, 19 145–49**

Evans Drumhead Company, **48** 232

Evans, Inc., 30 192–94

Evans Products Co., **13** 249–50, 550

Evans Rents, **26** 101

Evansville Paint & Varnish Co. *See* Red Spot Paint & Varnish Co.

Evansville Veneer and Lumber Co., **12** 296

Evelyn Wood, Inc., **7** 165, 168

Evence Coppée, **III** 704–05

Evenflo Companies, Inc., **19** 144; **54** 73

Ever Ready Ltd., **7** 209; **9** 179–80; **30** 231

Everan Capital Corp., **15** 257

Evercore Capital Partners, **59** 383

Everdream Corporation, **59** 12

Everest & Jennings, **11** 200

Everett Pulp & Paper Company, **17** 440

Everex Systems, Inc., 12 162; **16 194–96**

Everfresh Beverages Inc., **26** 326

Evergenius, **13** 210

Evergreen Air Cargo Service Co., **51** 123

Evergreen Healthcare, Inc., **14** 210

Evergreen International Aviation, Inc., **53 130–33**

Evergreen Marine Corporation (Taiwan) **Ltd., 13 209–11; 50 183–89 (upd.)**

Evergreen Media Corporation, **24** 106

Evergreen Resources, Inc., **11** 28

Everlast Worldwide Inc., 47 126–29

Everlaurel, **13** 210

Everready Battery Co., **13** 433; **39** 338

Everyday Learning Corporation, **22** 519, 522

Everything for the Office, **22** 154

Everything Yogurt, **25** 180

Everything's A Dollar Inc. (EAD), **13** 541–43

EVI, Inc., **39** 416

Evinrude Outboard Motor Company, **27** 75

Evity, Inc., **55** 67

EWTN. *See* Eternal Word Television Network, Inc.

Ex-Lax Inc., **15** 138–39

Exabyte Corporation, 12 161–63; 26 256; **40 178–81 (upd.)**

Exactis.com Inc., **49** 423

ExamOne World Wide, **48** 256

Exar Corp., 14 182–84

Exatec A/S, **10** 113; **50** 43

Exbud, **38** 437

Excaliber, **6** 205

EXCEL Communications Inc., 18 **164–67**

Excel Corporation, **11** 92–93; **13** 138, 351; **54** 168

Excel Industries Inc., **53** 55

Excel Mining Systems, Inc., **13** 98

Excel Technology, Inc., 65 139–42

Excelsior Life Insurance Co., **21** 14

Excelsior Printing Company, **26** 105

Excerpta Medica International. *See* Reed Elsevier

Excite, Inc. *See* At Home Corporation.

Exco International, **10** 277

Execu-Fit Health Programs, **11** 379

Executive Aircraft Services, **27** 21

Executive Airlines, Inc., **28** 22

Executive Fund Life Insurance Company, **27** 47

Executive Gallery, Inc., **12** 264

Executive Income Life Insurance Co., **10** 246

Executive Jet, Inc., 36 189–91; 42 35; **69** 217

Executive Life Insurance Co., **III** 253–55; **11** 483

Executive Money Management, **57** 269

Executive Risk Inc., **37** 86

Executive Systems, Inc., **11** 18

Executone Information Systems, Inc., 13 **212–14; 15** 195

ExecuTrain. *See* International Data Group, Inc.

Executrans, Inc., **21** 96

Exel Ltd., **13** 150
Exel plc, 6 412, 414; **51 124–30 (upd.)**
Exelon Corporation, 48 156–63 (upd.);
49 65
Exeter & Hampton Electric Company, **37**
406
Exide Electronics Group, Inc., 9 10; **20
213–15; 24** 29
Exmark Manufacturing Company, Inc., **26**
494
Exp@nets, **37** 280, 283
Expand SA, 48 164–66
Expedia, Inc., 46 101, 103; **47** 421; **58
117–21**
**Expeditors International of Washington
Inc., 17 163–65**
Experian Information Solutions Inc., 28
120; **45 152–55**
Experian Ltd., **47** 165, 168–69
Explorer Motor Home Corp., **16** 296
Export & Domestic Can Co., **15** 127
Express Airlines, Inc., **28** 266
Express Baggage Reclaim Services
Limited, **27** 21
Express Gifts Ltd., **60** 122
Express Newspapers plc, **IV** 687; **28** 503
Express Rent-a-Tire, Ltd., **20** 113
**Express Scripts Inc., 17 166–68; 44
173–76 (upd.)**
Expression Homes, **22** 205, 207
ExpressJet Holdings Inc., **52** 89, 93
Exsa, **55** 188
ExSample Media BV, **53** 362
Extel Financial Ltd., **IV** 687
Extended Stay America, Inc., 41 156–58
**Extendicare Health Services, Inc., 6
181–83**
Extron International Inc., **16** 538; **43** 33
EXX Inc., 40 334; **65 143–45**
Exxon Mobil Corporation, IV 426–30; **7
169–73 (upd.)**; **32 175–82 (upd.)**; **67
175–86 (upd.)**
Eyckeler & Malt AG, **59** 4–5
**Eye Care Centers of America, Inc., 69
158–60**
Eye Masters Ltd., **23** 329
Eyeful Home Co., **III** 758
Eyes Multimedia Productions Inc., **51**
286–87
EZ Direkt Marketing GmbH. *See* Manutan
International S.A.
EZ Paintr Corporation, **9** 374
Ezaki Glico Company Ltd., 72 123–25
EZCORP Inc., 43 159–61; 61 53, 55
EZPor Corporation, **12** 377

F. & F. Koenigkramer Company, **10** 272
F&G International Insurance, **III** 397
F & J Meat Packers, Inc., **22** 548–49
F & M Distributors, **12** 132
F&N Foods Ltd., **54** 116–17
F & R Builders, Inc., **11** 257
F&W Publications, Inc., 71 154–56
F.A. Computer Technologies, Inc., **12** 60
F.A.O. Schwarz. *See* FAO Schwarz
F.B. McFarren, Ltd., **21** 499–500
F.C. Internazionale Milano SpA, **44** 387
F.E. Compton Company, **7** 167
F. Egger Co., **22** 49
F.H. Tomkins Buckle Company Ltd., **11**
525
**F. Hoffmann-La Roche & Co. A.G., I
642–44**, 657, 685, 693, 710; **7** 427; **9**

264; **10** 80, 549; **11** 424–25; **14** 406; **32**
211–12; **50 190–93 (upd.)**
F.K.I. Babcock, **III** 466
F. Kanematsu & Co., Ltd. *See* Kanematsu
Corporation.
F. Korbel & Bros. Inc., 68 144–46
F.N. Herstal. *See* Groupe Herstal S.A.
F.W. Means & Company, **11** 337
F.W. Sickles Company, **10** 319
F.W. Woolworth & Co. Ltd. *See*
Kingfisher plc.
F.W. Woolworth Co. *See* Woolworth
Corporation.
F.X. Matt Brewing Co., **18** 72; **50** 114
F.X. Schmid Vereinigte Münchener
Spielkartenfabriken GmbH & Co. KG,
64 325
Fab-Asia, Inc., **22** 354–55
Fab Industries, Inc., 27 142–44
Fab 9, **26** 431
**Fabbrica D' Armi Pietro Beretta S.p.A.,
39 149–51**
Fabco Automotive Corp., **23** 306; **27** 203
Faber-Castell. *See* A.W. Faber-Castell
Unternehmensverwaltung GmbH & Co.
Fabergé, Inc., **III** 48; **8** 168, 344; **11** 90;
47 114
Fabio Perini S.p.A., **60** 193
**Fabri-Centers of America Inc., 16
197–99**. *See also* Jo-Ann Stores, Inc.
Fabritec GmbH, **72** 221
Fabtek Inc., **48** 59
Facet International, **61** 66
Facom S.A., 32 183–85; 37 143, 145
Façonnable S.A., **67** 279–80
Facts on File, Inc., **14** 96–97; **22** 443
FAE Fluid Air Energy SA, **49** 162–63
Fafnir Bearing Company, **13** 523
**FAG—Kugelfischer Georg Schäfer AG,
11** 84; **47** 280; **62 129–32; 65** 134
Fagerdala World Foams, **54** 360–61
FAI, **III** 545–46
Failsafe, **14** 35
Fair Grounds Corporation, 44 177–80
Fair, Isaac and Company, 18 168–71,
516, 518
Fairbanks Morse Co., **12** 71
Fairchild Aircraft, Inc., 9 205–08, 460;
11 278
Fairchild Camera and Instrument Corp., **III**
141, 455, 618; **7** 531; **10** 108; **11** 503;
13 323–24; **17** 418; **21** 122
Fairchild Communications Service, **8** 328
The Fairchild Corporation, **37** 30
**Fairchild Dornier GmbH, 48 167–71
(upd.)**
Fairchild Industries, **14** 43; **15** 195; **34** 117
Fairchild Publications, **59** 133–34
Fairchild Semiconductor Corporation, **II**
63–65; **10** 365–66; **16** 332; **41** 201
**Fairclough Construction Group plc, I
567–68**
Fairey Industries Ltd., **IV** 659
**Fairfax Financial Holdings Limited, 57
135–37**
Fairfield Communities, Inc., 36 192–95
The Fairfield Group, **33** 259–60
Fairfield Manufacturing Co., **14** 43
Fairfield Publishing, **13** 165
Fairfield Resorts. *See* Outrigger
Enterprises, Inc.
Fairmont Foods Co., **7** 430; **15** 139
Fairmont Hotels & Resorts Inc., 45 80;
69 161–63

Fairmont Insurance Co., **26** 487
Fairmount Glass Company, **8** 267
Fairport Machine Shop, Inc., **17** 357
Fairway Marketing Group, Inc., **24** 394
Fairway Outdoor Advertising, Inc., **36** 340,
342
Faiveley S.A., 39 152–54
Falcon Drilling Co. *See* Transocean Sedco
Forex Inc.
Falcon Microsystems, Inc., **57** 172–73
Falcon Products, Inc., 33 149–51
Falcon Seaboard Inc., **7** 309
Falconbridge Limited, 49 136–39
Falley's, Inc., **17** 558, 560–61
**Fallon Worldwide, 22 199–201; 71
157–61 (upd.)**
Falls Financial Inc., **13** 223; **31** 206
Falls National Bank of Niagara Falls, **11**
108
Falls Rubber Company, **8** 126
Falmouth Fertilizer Company. *See* Griffin
Industries, Inc.
FAME Plastics, Inc., **18** 162
Family Bookstores. *See* Family Christian
Stores, Inc.
Family Channel. *See* International Family
Entertainment Inc.
Family Christian Stores, Inc., 51 131–34
**Family Dollar Stores, Inc., 13 215–17; 62
133–36 (upd.)**
Family Golf Centers, Inc., 29 183–85
Family Mart Group, **V** 188; **36** 418, 420
Family Preservation Services, Inc., **64** 311
Family Restaurants, Inc., **14** 194
Family Steak Houses of Florida, Inc. *See*
Ryan's Restaurant Group, Inc.
Famous Amos Chocolate Chip Cookie
Corporation, **27** 332
Famous Atlantic Fish Company, **20** 5
Famous-Barr, **46** 288
**Famous Dave's of America, Inc., 40
182–84** 4
Famous Footwear. *See* Brown Shoe
Company, Inc.
Famous Restaurants Inc., **33** 139–40
FAN, **13** 370
Fanafel Ltda., **62** 348, 350
Fancom Holding B.V., **43** 130
Fannie Mae, 45 156–59 (upd.); 54
122–24
Fannie May Candy Shops Inc. *See* Alpine
Confections, Inc.
Fansteel Inc., 19 150–52
Fantastic Sam's, **26** 476
Fanthing Electrical Corp., **44** 132
Fantle's Drug Stores, **16** 160
**Fanuc Ltd., III 482–83; 17 172–74
(upd.)**
Fanzz, **29** 282
FAO Schwarz, 46 187–90; 62 208
Faprena, **25** 85
Far-Ben S.A. de C.V., **72** 128
Far Eastern Air Transport, Inc., **23** 380
Far Eastern Bank, **56** 363
Faraday National Corporation, **10** 269
Farah Incorporated, 24 156–58
Farben. *See* I.G. Farbenindustrie AG.
Farberware, Inc., **27** 287–88
Farbro Corp., **45** 15
Farbwerke Hoechst A.G., **13** 262
FAREC Fahrzeugrecycling GmbH, **58** 28
Farley Industries, **25** 166
**Farley Northwest Industries Inc., I
440–41**

Farley's & Sathers Candy Company, Inc., 15 190; **62 137–39**
Farm Credit Bank of St. Louis/St. Paul, **8** 489–90
Farm Electric Services Ltd., **6** 586
Farm Family Holdings, Inc., 39 155–58
Farm Fresh Catfish Company, **54** 167
Farm Fresh Foods, **25** 332
Farm Journal Corporation, 42 131–34
Farm Power Laboratory, **6** 565; **50** 366
Farmacias Ahumada S.A., 72 126–28
Farmacias Ahumada S.A., **69** 312
Farmcare Ltd., **51** 89
Farmer Bros. Co., 52 117–19
Farmer Jack, **16** 247; **44** 145
Farmers and Mechanics Bank of Georgetown, **13** 439
Farmers Insurance Group of Companies, 23 286; **25 154–56**; **29** 397
Farmers National Bank & Trust Co., **9** 474
Farmers Petroleum, **48** 175
Farmland Foods, Inc., IV 474; **7** 17, **7 174–75**
Farmland Industries, Inc., 39 282; **48 172–75**
Farmstock Pty Ltd., **62** 307
Farrar, Straus and Giroux Inc., 15 158–60; **35** 451
FAS Acquisition Co., **53** 142
FASC. *See* First Analysis Securities Corporation.
Fasco Consumer Products, **19** 360
FASCO Motors. *See* Tecumseh Products Company.
Fashion Bar, Inc., **24** 457
Fashion Bug, **8** 97
Fashion Fair Cosmetics. *See* Johnson Publishing Company, Inc.
Fashion Resource, Inc. *See* Tarrant Apparel Group.
Fasint Ltd., **72** 128
Fasson. *See* Avery Dennison Corporation.
Fast Air, **31** 305
Fast Fare, **7** 102
Fast Trak Inc. *See* Ultimate Electronics, Inc.
Fastenal Company, 14 185–87; **42 135–38 (upd.)**
Fat Bastard Wine Co., **68** 86
Fat Face Ltd., 68 147–49
FAT KAT, Inc., **51** 200, 203
Fata European Group, **IV** 187; **19** 348
Fatburger Corporation, 64 122–24
Fateco Förlag, **14** 556
FATS, Inc., **27** 156, 158
Faugere et Jutheau, **III** 283
Faultless Starch/Bon Ami Company, 55 142–45
Fauquet, **25** 85
Faurecia S.A., 70 91–93
Favorite Plastics, **19** 414
FAvS. *See* First Aviation Services Inc.
Fawcett Books, **13** 429
Fay's Inc., 17 175–77
Faydler Company, **60** 160
Fayette Tubular Products, **7** 116–17
Faygo Beverages Inc., 55 146–48
Fayva, **13** 359–61
Fazoli's Systems, Inc., 13 321; **27 145–47**
FB&T Corporation, **14** 154
FBC. *See* First Boston Corp.
FBO. *See* Film Booking Office of America.
FBR. *See* Friedman, Billings, Ramsey Group, Inc.

FBS Fuhrpark Business Service GmbH, **58** 28
FC Holdings, Inc., **26** 363
FCA Ltd. *See* Life Time Fitness, Inc.
FCC. *See* Federal Communications Commission.
FCI. *See* Framatome SA.
FDIC. *See* Federal Deposit Insurance Corp.
Feather Fine, **27** 361
Featherlite Inc., 28 127–29
Feature Enterprises Inc., **19** 452
FECR. *See* Florida East Coast Railway, L.L.C.
Fedders Corporation, 18 172–75; **43 162–67 (upd.)**
Federal Bicycle Corporation of America, **11** 3
Federal Cartridge, **26** 363
Federal Coca-Cola Bottling Co., **10** 222
Federal Deposit Insurance Corp., **12** 30, 79
Federal Express Corporation, II 620; **V 451–53**; **12** 180, 192; **13** 19; **14** 517; **17** 504–05; **18** 315–17, 368, 370; **24** 22; **25** 148; **26** 441; **27** 20, 22, 471, 475; **39** 33, 35; **41** 245–47; **63** 415. *See also* FedEx Corporation.
Federal Home Life Insurance Co., **IV** 623
Federal Home Loan Mortgage Corp. *See* Freddie Mac.
Federal Insurance Co., **III** 220–21; **14** 108–109; **37** 83–85
Federal Laboratories, **57** 230
Federal Light and Traction Company, **6** 561–62
Federal-Mogul Corporation, I 158–60; **10 292–94 (upd.)**; **26 139–43 (upd.)**
Federal National Mortgage Association, II 410–11; **18** 168; **25** 427. *See also* Fannie Mae.
Federal Pacific Electric, **9** 440
Federal Packaging and Partition Co., **8** 476
Federal Packaging Corp., **19** 78
Federal Paper Board Company, Inc., 8 173–75; **15** 229; **47** 189
Federal Power, **18** 473
Federal Prison Industries, Inc., 34 157–60
Federal Reserve Bank of New York, **21** 68
Federal Savings and Loan Insurance Corp., **16** 346
Federal Signal Corp., 10 295–97
Federal Trade Commission, **6** 260; **9** 370
Federated Department Stores Inc., 9 209–12; **31 190–94 (upd.)**; **35** 368; **36** 201, 204; **37** 13; **50** 107; **60** 70; **63** 145, 259, 263
Federated Development Company, **8** 349
Federated Livestock Corporation, **64** 306
Fédération Internationale de Football Association, 27 148–51
Federation Nationale d'Achats des Cadres. *See* FNAC.
Federation of Migro Cooperatives. *See* Migros-Genossenschafts-Bund.
Federico Paternina S.A., 69 164–66
FedEx Corporation, 18 128, **176–79 (upd.)**, 535; **33** 20, 22; **34** 474; **42 139–44 (upd.)**; **46** 71
FEE Technology, **29** 461–62
Feed-Rite Controls, Inc., **16** 270
Feed-Rite, Inc., **62** 307
Feed The Children, Inc., 68 150–52
Feffer & Simons, **16** 46
Feikes & Sohn KG, **IV** 325

Felco. *See* Farmers Regional Cooperative.
Feld Entertainment, Inc., 32 186–89 (upd.)
Feldmühle Nobel AG, III 692–95; **IV** 142, 325, 337; **36** 449. *See also* Metallgesellschaft.
Felixstowe Ltd., **18** 254
Fellowes Manufacturing Company, 28 130–32
Felten & Guilleaume, **IV** 25
Femsa. *See* Formento Económico Mexicano, S.A. de C.V.
Femtech, **8** 513
Fendall Company, **40** 96, 98
Fendel Schiffahrts-Aktiengesellschaft, **6** 426
Fender Musical Instruments Company, 16 200–02; **43 168–72 (upd.)**
Fendi S.p.A., **45** 344
Fenicia S.A., **22** 320; **61** 175
Fenn, Wright & Manson, **25** 121–22
Fenton Hill American Limited, **29** 510
Fenway Partners, **47** 361
Fenwick & West LLP, 34 161–63, 512
Ferembal S.A., **25** 512
Ferfin, **24** 341
Fergus Brush Electric Company, **18** 402
Ferguson Enterprises, **64** 409, 411
Ferguson Machine Co., **8** 135
Ferguson Manufacturing Company, **25** 164
Fermec Manufacturing Limited, **40** 432
Fermentaciones Mexicanas S.A. de C.V., **III** 43; **48** 250
Fernando Roqué, **6** 404; **26** 243
Ferolito, Vultaggio & Sons, 27 152–55
Ferragamo, **63** 151
Ferranti Business Communications, **20** 75
Ferrari S.p.A., **13** 218–20; **36 196–200 (upd.)**
Ferrellgas Partners, L.P., 35 173–75
Ferrero SpA, **54 103–05**
Ferrier Hodgson, **10** 170
Ferris Industries, **64** 355
Ferro Corporation, 8 176–79; **9** 10; **56 123–28 (upd.)**
Ferro Engineering Co., **17** 357
Ferrocarril del Noreste, S.A. de C.V. *See* Grupo Transportación Ferroviaria Mexicana, S.A. de C.V.
Ferrolux Metals Co., **63** 360
Ferrovial. *See* Grupo Ferrovail
Ferroxcube Corp. of America, **13** 397
Ferrum Inc., **24** 144
Ferruzzi Agricola Finanziario, **7** 81–83
Ferruzzi Finanziaria S.p.A., **24** 341; **36** 186
Fertisere SAS, **58** 221
Fetzer Vineyards, **10** 182
FFI Fragrances. *See* Elizabeth Arden, Inc.
F5 Networks, Inc., 72 129–31
FFM Bhd, **57** 292–95
FHP International Corporation, 6 184–86; **17** 166, 168; **44** 174
Fiamm Technologies. *See* Valeo.
Fianzas Monterrey, **19** 189
Fiat SpA, I 161–63; **11 102–04 (upd.)**; **50 194–98 (upd.)**
Fibamex, **17** 106
Fibanc SA, **65** 230, 232
Fibar, **44** 261
Fiber Chemical Corporation, **7** 308
Fiberglas Canada, **III** 722
Fiberite, Inc., **27** 117; **28** 195
FiberMark, Inc., 37 139–42; **53** 24
Fibermux Corporation, **10** 19; **30** 7

Fibic Corp., **18** 118
Fibreboard Corporation, **12** 318; **14** 110; **16 203–05**
FibreChem, Inc., **8** 347
Fibro Tambor, S.A. de C.V., **8** 476
Ficap S.A., **71** 211
Fichet-Bauche SA, **53** 158
Fichtel & Sachs AG, **III** 566; **14** 328; **38** 299
Fidelco Capital Group, **10** 420
Fidelio Software GmbH, **18** 335, 337
Fidelity Exploration & Production Company, **42** 249, 253
Fidelity Federal Savings and Loan, **II** 420
Fidelity Investments Inc., **II 412–13**; **8** 194; **9** 239; **14 188–90 (upd.)**; **18** 552; **19** 113; **21** 147; **22** 52. See also FMR Corp.
Fidelity Leasing Corporation, **42** 312–13
Fidelity National Financial Inc., **54 106–08**
Fidelity National Title, **19** 92
Fidelity Oil Group, **7** 324
Fidenas Investment Ltd., **30** 185
Fides Holding, **21** 146
Field Corporation, **18** 355
Field Enterprises Educational Corporation, **16** 252; **26** 15; **43** 208
Field Enterprises, Inc., **12** 554
Field Group plc, **30** 120
Field Limited Partnership, **22** 441
Field Oy, **10** 113; **50** 43
Fieldale Farms Corporation, **23 191–93**; **25** 185–86
Fieldco Guide Dog Foundation, **42** 207
Fieldcrest Cannon, Inc., **8** 32–33; **9** 213–17; **16** 535; **19** 276, 305; **31 195–200 (upd.)**; **41** 299–301
Fieldstone Cabinetry, **III** 571; **20** 362
Fielmann AG, **31 201–03**
Fiesta Restaurants Inc., **33** 139–40
FIFA. See Fédération Internationale de Football Association.
Fifa International, **39** 58
Fifth Generation Systems Inc., **10** 509
Fifth Third Bancorp, **9** 475; **11** 466; **13** 221–23; **31 204–08 (upd.)**
50-Off Stores. See LOT$OFF Corporation.
Le Figaro. See Société du Figaro S.A.
Figgie International Inc., **7 176–78**; **24** 403–04
Figi's Inc., **9** 218, 220
FII Limited, **38** 197
Fil-Mag Group, **29** 461
Fila–Fabbrica Italiana Lapis ed Affini S.p.A., **69** 129
Fila Holding S.p.A., **20 216–18**; **39** 60; **52 120–24 (upd.)**
Filene's. See The May Department Stores Company.
Filene's Basement. See Value City Department Stores, Inc.
FileNet Corporation, **62 140–43**
Filergie S.A., **15** 355
Fili Enterprises, Inc., **70 94–96**
Filipacchi Medias S.A. See Hachette Filipacchi Medias S.A.
Filiz Lastex, S.A., **15** 386
Filles S.A. de C.V., **7** 115; **25** 126
Film Roman, Inc., **58 122–24**
Films for the Humanities, Inc., **22** 441
Filofax Inc., **41** 120, 123
Filter Queen-Canada, **17** 234
Filterfresh Corporation, **39** 409

Filtertek, Inc., **24** 425
Filtrona International Ltd., **31** 77
Filtros Baldwin de Mexico, **17** 106
Filtros Continental, **17** 106
Fimalac S.A., **37 143–45**
Fimaser, **21** 101
Fimestic, **21** 101
FINA, Inc., **7 179–81**; **26** 368
Finaler. See Leroux S.A.S.
Finalrealm Limited, **42** 404
Finance Oil Corp., **49** 304
Financial Computer Services, Inc., **11** 111
Financial Data Services, Inc., **11** 111
Financial Network Marketing Company, **11** 482
Financial News Network, Inc., **25** 507; **31** 147
Financial Performance Corporation. See BrandPartners Group, Inc.
Financial Security Assurance Inc., **25** 497
Financial Services Corp., **III** 306–07
Financial Services Corporation of Michigan, **11** 163
Financial Systems, Inc., **11** 111
Financial Technologies International, **17** 497
The Financial Times Group, **46** 337
Financiera Aceptaciones, **19** 189
Financière Leroux. See Leroux S.A.S.
Financière Saint Dominique, **9** 151–52
Finast. See First National Supermarkets, Inc.
Find-A-Home Service, Inc., **21** 96
Findel plc, **60 122–24**
Findlays Spring Natural Mineral Water, **64** 11
Findomestic, **21** 101
Findorff. See J.H. Findorff and Son, Inc.
Fine Art Developments Ltd., **15** 340
Fine Fare, **II** 609, 628–29
Fine Fragrances, **22** 213
Finesco, LLC, **37** 200–01
Finevest Services Inc., **15** 526
Fingerhut Companies, Inc., **V** 148; **9** 218–20; **15** 401; **18** 133; **31** 190; **34** 232; **36 201–05 (upd.)**; **37** 130; **56** 226
Fininvest Group
Fininvest S.p.A., **IV** 587–88; **54** 17, 21, 23; **65** 230–31
The Finish Line, Inc., **29 186–88**; **68 153–56 (upd.)**
FinishMaster, Inc., **17** 310–11; **24 159–61**
Finlay Enterprises, Inc., **16 206–08**
Finmeccanica S.p.A., **13** 28; **23** 83; **36** 34; **50** 197; **52** 115
Finnair Oy, **6** 87–89; **25 157–60 (upd.)**; **33** 50; **61 91–95 (upd.)**
Finnforest Oy, **IV** 316
Finnigan Corporation, **11** 513
Finning International Inc., **69 167–69**
Finnish Chemicals Oy. See Kemira Oyj
Finsa, **II** 196
FinSer Capital Corporation, **17** 262
Finsider, **IV** 125
Firan Motor Coach, Inc., **17** 83
Firearms Training Systems, Inc., **27 156–58**
Fireman's Fund Insurance Company, **III** 214, **250–52**, 263
Firestone Tire and Rubber Co., **8** 80; **9** 247; **15** 355; **17** 182; **18** 320; **20** 259–62; **50** 316. See also Bridgestone Corporation.

Firma Hamburger Kaffee-Import- Geschäft Emil Tengelmann. See Tengelmann Group.
Firma Huter Vorfertigung GmbH, **49** 163
Firmenich International S.A., **60 125–27**
FirmLogic, L.P., **52** 423
The First, **10** 340
First & 42nd, **62** 115
First Acadiana National Bank, **11** 107
First Air. See Bradley Air Services Ltd.
First Albany Companies Inc., **37 146–48**
First Alert, Inc., **28 133–35**
First American. See Bremer Financial Corp.
First American Bank Corporation, **8** 188; **41** 178
The First American Corporation, **52 125–27**
First American Media, Inc., **24** 199
First American National Bank, **19** 378
First American National Bank-Eastern, **11** 111
First Analysis Securities Corporation, **22** 5
First and Merchants, **10** 426
First Atlanta Corporation, **16** 523
First Atlantic Capital, Ltd., **28** 340, 342
First Aviation Services Inc., **49 140–42**
First Bancard, Inc., **11** 106
First BanCorporation, **13** 467
First Bank of Savannah, **16** 522
First Bank System Inc., **11** 130; **12 164–66**; **13** 347–48; **24** 393. See also U.S. Bancorp
First Boston Corp., **II** 426, 434, 441; **9** 378, 386; **12** 439; **13** 152, 342. See also CSFB.
First Brands Corporation, **8 180–82**; **16** 44
First Capital Financial, **8** 229
First Carolina Investors Inc., **17** 357
First Cash Financial Services, Inc., **57 138–40**; **61** 53, 55
First Chicago Corporation, **II 284–87**. See also Bank One Corporation.
First Chicago Venture Capital, **24** 516
First Choice Holidays PLC, **40 185–87**, 284–85
First Cincinnati, Inc., **41** 133
First Commerce Bancshares, Inc., **15 161–63**
First Commerce Corporation, **11 105–07**
First Commercial Savings and Loan, **10** 340
First Constitution Financial Corporation. See The Aristotle Corporation.
First Consumers National Bank, **10** 491; **27** 429
First Data Corporation, **10** 63; **18** 516–18, 537; **24** 393 **30 195–98 (upd.)**; **46** 250; **54** 413
First Data Management Company of Oklahoma City, **11** 112
First Delaware Life Insurance Co., **III** 254
First Deposit Corp. See Providian Financial Corporation.
First Empire State Corporation, **11 108–10**
First Executive Corporation, **III 253–55**
First Express, **48** 177
First Federal Savings & Loan Assoc., **IV** 343; **9** 173
First Federal Savings and Loan Association of Crisp County, **10** 92

First Federal Savings and Loan Association of Hamburg, **10** 91
First Federal Savings and Loan Association of Fort Myers, **9** 476
First Federal Savings and Loan Association of Kalamazoo, **9** 482
First Federal Savings Bank of Brunswick, **10** 92
First Fidelity Bank, N.A., New Jersey, 9 221–23
First Fidelity Bank of Rockville, **13** 440
First Financial Insurance, **41** 178
First Financial Management Corporation, 11 111–13; **18** 542; **25** 183; **30** 195
First Florida Banks, **9** 59
First Hawaiian, Inc., 11 114–16
FIRST HEALTH Strategies, **11** 113
First Healthcare, **14** 242
First Heights, fsa, **8** 437
First Hospital Corp., **15** 122
First Industrial Realty Trust, Inc., 65 146–48
First Insurance Agency, Inc., **17** 527
First International Computer, Inc., 56 129–31
First Interstate Bancorp, **II** 228, **288–90**; **8** 295; **9** 334; **17** 546
First Investment Advisors, **11** 106
First Investors Management Corp., **11** 106
First Leisure Corporation plc. *See* Esporta plc.
First Liberty Financial Corporation, **11** 457
First Line Insurance Services, Inc., **8** 436
First Madison Bank, **14** 192
First Maryland Bancorp, **16** 14
First Mississippi Corporation, 8 183–86. *See also* ChemFirst, Inc.
First Mississippi National, **14** 41
First National Bank, **10** 298; **13** 467
First National Bank and Trust Company, **22** 4
First National Bank and Trust Company of Kalamazoo, **8** 187–88
First National Bank in Albuquerque, **11** 119
First National Bank of Akron, **9** 475
First National Bank of Allentown, **11** 296
First National Bank of Atlanta, **16** 522
First National Bank of Boston, **12** 310; **13** 446
First National Bank of Carrollton, **9** 475
First National Bank of Commerce, **11** 106
First National Bank of Harrington, Delaware. *See* J.C. Penny National Bank.
First National Bank of Hartford, **13** 466
First National Bank of Hawaii, **11** 114
First National Bank of Highland, **11** 109
First National Bank of Houma, **21** 522
The First National Bank of Lafayette, **11** 107
First National Bank of Minneapolis, **22** 426–27
First National Bank of Salt Lake, **11** 118
First National Bank of Seattle, **8** 469–70
First National Bankshares, Inc., **21** 524
First National City Bank, **9** 124; **16** 13
First National Holding Corporation, **16** 522
First National Supermarkets, Inc., **II** 641–42; **9** 452
First Nations Gaming, Ltd., **44** 334
First Nationwide Bank, **8** 30; **14** **191–93**
First Nationwide Holdings Inc., **28** 246

First New England Bankshares Corp., **13** 467
First Nitrogen, Inc., **8** 184
First Nuclear Corporation, **49** 411
First of America Bank Corporation, 8 187–89
First of America Bank-Monroe, **9** 476
First Omni Bank NA, **16** 14; **18** 518; **43** 8
First Options of Chicago, Inc., **51** 148
First Pacific Company Limited, 18 180–82
First Physician Care, Inc., **36** 367
First Pick Stores, **12** 458
First Private Power Corporation, **56** 215
First Quench Retailing Ltd., **52** 416
First Railroad and Banking Company, **11** 111
First Republic Corp., **14** 483
First RepublicBank Corporation, **II** 337; **10** 425–26
First Savings and Loan, **10** 339
First Seattle Dexter Horton National Bank, **8** 470
First Security Bank of Missoula, **35** 197–99
First Security Corporation, 11 117–19; **38** 491
First Signature Bank and Trust Co., **III** 268
First Sport Ltd., **39** 60
1st State Bank & Trust, **9** 474
First State Bank Southwest Indiana, **41** 178–79
First SunAmerican Life Insurance Company, **11** 482
First Team Sports, Inc., 15 396–97; **22 202–04**
First Tennessee National Corporation, 11 120–21; **48 176–79 (upd.)**
First Trust Bank, **16** 14
First Union Corporation, 10 298–300; **24** 482; **37** 148; **57** 415. *See also* Wachovia Corporation.
First USA, Inc., 11 122–24
First USA Paymentech, **24** 393
First Variable Life, **59** 246
First Virginia Banks, Inc., 11 125–26
First Women's Bank of New York, **23** 3
First Worth Corporation, **19** 232
The First Years Inc., 46 191–94
FirstAir Inc., **48** 113
Firstar Corporation, 11 127–29; **33 152–55 (upd.)**
FirstBancorp., **13** 467
FirstGroup plc, **38** 321
FirstMiss, Inc., **8** 185
FirstPage USA Inc., **41** 265
Firth Carpet, **19** 275
Fischbach Corp., **III** 198; **8** 536–37
FISCOT, **10** 337
Fiserv Inc., 11 130–32; **33 156–60 (upd.)**
Fish & Neave, 54 109–12
Fisher & Company, **9** 16
Fisher Broadcasting Co., **15** 164
Fisher-Camuto Corp., **14** 441
Fisher Companies, Inc., 15 164–66
Fisher Controls International, LLC, 13 224–26; **15** 405, 407; **29** 330; **46** 171; **61 96–99 (upd.)**
Fisher Foods, Inc., **II** 602; **9** 451, 452; **13** 237; **41** 11, 13
Fisher Nut, **14** 275
Fisher-Price Inc., 12 167–69; **13** 317; **25** 314, 380; **32 190–94 (upd.)**; **61** 201–03

Fisher Scientific International Inc., 24 162–66; **25** 260
Fishers Agricultural Holdings, **II** 466
Fisk Corporation, 72 132–34
Fiskars Corporation, 33 161–64; **60** 351
Fiskeby Board AB, **48** 344
Fisons plc, 9 224–27; **23 194–97 (upd.)**
Fitch IBCA Inc., **37** 143, 145
Fitch Investor Services, **65** 243–44
Fitch Lovell PLC, **13** 103
Fitchburg Gas and Electric Light, **37** 406
Fitzsimmons Stores Inc., **16** 452
Fitzwilton Public Limited Company, **12** 529; **34** 496
5 & Diner Franchise Corporation, 72 135–37
Five Bros. Inc., **19** 456
Five Star Entertainment Inc., **28** 241
Five Star Group, Inc., **64** 166
546274 Alberta Ltd., **48** 97
FKI Plc, 57 141–44; **69** 52
FKM Advertising, **27** 280
FL Industries Holdings, Inc., **11** 516
Flagler Development Company, **59** 184–85
Flagship Resources, **22** 495
Flagstar Companies, Inc., 10 301–03; **29** 150. *See also* Advantica Restaurant Group, Inc.
Flagstone Hospitality Management LLC, **58** 194
Flair Corporation, **18** 467
Flair Fold, **25** 11
Flambeau Products Corporation, **55** 132
Flanders Corporation, 65 149–51
Flanigan's Enterprises, Inc., 60 128–30
Flapdoodles, **15** 291
Flashes Publishers, Inc., **36** 341
Flatiron Mandolin Company, **16** 239
Flatow, Moore, Bryan, and Fairburn, **21** 33
Flavors Holdings Inc., **38** 294
Fleck Controls, Inc., **26** 361, 363
Fleer Corporation, 10 402; **13** 519; **15 167–69**; **19** 386; **34** 447; **37** 295
Fleet Aerospace Corporation. *See* Magellan Aerospace Corporation.
Fleet Call, Inc., **10** 431–32
Fleet Equity Partners, **62** 325, 327
Fleet Financial Group, Inc., IV 687; **9 228–30**; **12** 31; **13** 468; **18** 535; **38** 13, 393
Fleet Holdings, **28** 503
FleetBoston Financial Corporation, 36 206–14 (upd.)
Fleetway, **7** 244
Fleetwood Enterprises, Inc., III 484–85; **13** 155; **17** 83; **21** 153; **22 205–08 (upd.)**; **33** 399
Fleming Chinese Restaurants Inc., **37** 297
Fleming Companies, Inc., II 624–25, 671; **7** 450; **12** 107, 125; **13** 335–37; **17 178–81 (upd.)**; **18** 506–07; **23** 407; **24** 529; **26** 449; **28** 152, 154; **31** 25; **34** 198; **50** 457
Fleming Foodservice, **26** 504
Fletcher Challenge Ltd., IV 250, 278–80; **19 153–57 (upd.)**; **25** 12; **63** 315
Fletcher Pacific Construction Co. Ltd., **64** 113
Fleury Michon S.A., 39 159–61
Flex Elektrowerkzeuge GmbH, **26** 363
Flex Interim, **16** 421; **43** 308
Flex-O-Lite, **14** 325
Flexi-Van Corporations, **II** 492; **20** 118

Flexsteel Industries Inc., **15** 170–72; **41** 159–62 (upd.)
Flextronics International Ltd., **12** 451; **38** 186–89
Flexys, **16** 462
FLGI Holding Company, **10** 321
Flick Industrial Group. *See* Feldmühle Nobel AG.
Flight One Logistics, Inc., **22** 311
Flight Refuelling Limited. *See* Cobham plc.
FlightSafety International, Inc., **9** 231–33; **29** 189–92 (upd.)
Flint Ink Corporation, **13** 227–29; **41** 163–66 (upd.)
Flip Chip Technologies, LLC, **33** 248
FLIR Systems, Inc., **69** 170–73
Flo-Pak, Inc., **57** 160
Flora Frey GmbH. *See* Vilmorin Clause et Cie
Florafax International, Inc., **37** 162
Floral City Furniture Company, **14** 302–03; **50** 309–10
Flori Roberts, Inc., **11** 208
Florida Crystals Inc., **35** 176–78
Florida Cypress Gardens, Inc., **IV** 623
Florida Distillers Company, **27** 479
Florida East Coast Industries, Inc., **59** 184–86
Florida East Coast Railway, L.L.C., **8** 486–87; **12** 278; **59** 184
Florida Flavors, **44** 137
Florida Frozen Foods, **13** 244
Florida Gaming Corporation, **47** 130–33
Florida Gas Co., **15** 129
Florida Gas Transmission Company, **6** 578
Florida Panthers Hockey Club, Ltd., **37** 33, 35
Florida Power & Light Company. *See* FPL Group, Inc.
Florida Presbyterian College, **9** 187
Florida Progress Corp., **V** 621–22; **23** 198–200 (upd.)
Florida Public Utilities Company, **69** 174–76
Florida Rock Industries, Inc., **23** 326; **46** 195–97
Florida Steel Corp., **14** 156
Florida's Natural Growers, **45** 160–62
FloridaGulf Airlines, **11** 300
Florimex Verwaltungsgesellschaft mbH, **12** 109
Florists' Transworld Delivery, Inc., **28** 136–38
Florsheim Shoe Group Inc., **9** 135, 234–36; **12** 308; **16** 546; **31** 209–12 (upd.)
Flour City International, Inc., **44** 181–83
Flow International Corporation, **56** 132–34
Flow Laboratories, **14** 98
Flow Measurement, **26** 293
Flower Time, Inc., **12** 179, 200
Flowers Industries, Inc., **12** 170–71; **35** 179–82 (upd.). *See also* Keebler Foods Company.
Flowserve Corporation, **33** 165–68
Floyd West & Co., **6** 290
FLSmidth & Co. A/S, **72** 138–40
Fluent, Inc., **29** 4–6
Fluf N'Stuf, Inc., **12** 425
Fluke Corporation, **15** 173–75
Flunch, **37** 22

Fluor Corporation, **I** 569–71, 586; **8** 190–93 (upd.); **12** 244; **26** 433; **34** 164–69 (upd.); **57** 237–38
Fluor Daniel Inc., **41** 148
The Fluorocarbon Company. *See* Furon Company.
Flushing Federal Savings & Loan Association, **16** 346
FlyBE. *See* Jersey European Airways (UK) Ltd.
Flying Boat, Inc. (Chalk's Ocean Airways), **56** 135–37
Flying Colors Toys Inc., **52** 193
Flying Fruit Fantasy, USA, Inc., **57** 56–57
Flying J Inc., **19** 158–60
Flying Tiger Line, **39** 33
FMC Corp., **I** 442–44, 679; **11** 133–35 (upd.); **14** 457; **22** 415; **30** 471; **47** 238
FMR Corp., **8** 194–96; **14** 188; **22** 413; **30** 331; **32** 195–200 (upd.)
FMXI, Inc. *See* Foamex International Inc.
FN Manufacturing Co., **12** 71
FNAC, **21** 224–26; **26** 160
FNC Comercio, **III** 221
FNCB. *See* First National City Bank of New York.
FNH USA, Inc., **58** 147
FNK. *See* Finance Oil Corp.
FNMA. *See* Federal National Mortgage Association.
FNN. *See* Financial News Network.
Foamex International Inc., **17** 182–85; **26** 500
Focal Surgery, Inc., **27** 355
FOCUS, **44** 402
Fodor's Travel Guides, **13** 429
Fog Cutter Capital Group Inc., **64** 124
Fogdog Inc., **36** 347
Fokker. *See* N.V. Koninklijke Nederlandse Vliegtuigenfabriek Fokker.
Fokker Aircraft Corporation of America, **9** 16
Foley & Lardner, **28** 139–42
Folksamerica Holding Company, Inc., **48** 431
Follett Corporation, **12** 172–74; **16** 47; **39** 162–65 (upd.); **43** 61
Follis DeVito Verdi. *See* De Vito/Verdi.
Follum Fabrikker, **63** 314
Fomento de Valores, S.A. de C.V., **23** 170
Fomento Economico Mexicano, S.A. de C.V. *See* Femsa.
Fonda Group, **36** 462
Fondazione Cassa di Risparmio di Venezia, **50** 408
Fondiaria Group, **III** 351
Fonterra Co-Operative Group Ltd., **58** 125–27
Food City, **II** 649–50
The Food Emporium, **64** 125–27
Food Fair, **19** 480
Food 4 Less Supermarkets, Inc., **II** 624; **17** 558–61
Food Giant, **II** 670
Food Ingredients Technologies, **25** 367
Food King, **20** 306
Food Lion LLC, **II** 626–27; **7** 450; **15** 176–78 (upd.), 270; **18** 8; **21** 508; **33** 306; **44** 145; **66** 112–15 (upd.)
Food Machinery Corp. *See* FMC Corp.
Food Source, **58** 290
Food Town Inc., **II** 626–27
Food World, **26** 46; **31** 372

Foodarama Supermarkets, Inc., **28** 143–45
FoodBrands America, Inc., **21** 290; **22** 510; **23** 201–04. *See also* Doskocil Companies, Inc.
FoodLand Distributors, **II** 625, 645, 682
Foodmaker, Inc., **13** 152; **14** 194–96
Foodstuffs, **9** 144
Foodtown, **II** 626; **V** 35; **15** 177; **24** 528
FoodUSA.com, **43** 24
Foodways National, Inc., **12** 531; **13** 383
Foot Locker, Inc., **68** 157–62 (upd.)
Footaction. *See* Footstar, Incorporated.
Foote, Cone & Belding Worldwide, **I** 12–15, 28, 34; **11** 51; **13** 517; **22** 395; **25** 90–91; **66** 116–20 (upd.)
Foote Mineral Company, **7** 386–87
Footquarters, **14** 293, 295
Footstar, Incorporated, **24** 167–69
Foracon Maschinen und Anlagenbau GmbH & Co., **56** 134
Forbes Inc., **30** 199–201
The Ford Foundation, **34** 170–72; **52** 200–01
Ford Motor Company, **I** 164–68; **11** 136–40 (upd.); **36** 215–21 (upd.); **64** 128–34 (upd.)
Ford Motor Company, S.A. de C.V., **20** 219–21
Ford New Holland, Inc. *See* New Holland N.V.
Fording Inc., **45** 80
FORE Systems, Inc., **25** 161–63; **33** 289
Forefront Communications, **22** 194
Forefront Petroleum Company, **60** 160
Foreign & Colonial, **64** 303
Foremost-McKesson Inc. *See* McKesson Corporation.
Foremost Warehouse Corp., **14** 372
FöreningsSparbanken AB, **69** 177–80
Forest City Auto Parts, **23** 491
Forest City Enterprises, Inc., **16** 209–11; **52** 128–31 (upd.)
Forest City Ratner Companies, **17** 318
Forest E. Olson, Inc., **21** 96
Forest Laboratories, Inc., **11** 141–43; **47** 55; **52** 132–36 (upd.)
Forest Oil Corporation, **19** 161–63
Forestal Mininco S.A. *See* Empresas CMPC S.A.
Forestal Quiñenco S.A. *See* Madeco S.A.
Forestry Corporation of New Zealand, **19** 156
Företagsfinans, **25** 464
Forethought Group, Inc., **10** 350
Forever Living Products International Inc., **17** 186–88
Forge Books. *See* Tom Doherty Associates Inc.
Forjas Metalicas, S.A. de C.V. (Formet), **44** 193
Formento Económico Mexicano, S.A. de C.V., **25** 279, 281
Formica Corporation, **10** 269; **13** 230–32
Forming Technology Co., **III** 569; **20** 361
Formonix, **20** 101
Formosa Plastics Corporation, **11** 159; **14** 197–99; **16** 194, 196; **31** 108; **58** 128–31 (upd.)
Formtec Inc., **62** 350
Formulabs, Inc., **52** 307
Formule 1, **13** 364; **27** 10
Forney Fiber Company, **8** 475
Forrester Research, Inc., **54** 113–15

Forstmann Little & Co., I 483; 7 206; 10 321; 12 344, 562; 14 166; 16 322; 19 372–73, 432; 22 32, 60; 30 426; 34 145, 448; 36 523; 38 190–92; 54 372
Fort Bend Utilities Company, 12 269
Fort Garry Brewery, 26 304
Fort Howard Corporation, 8 197–99; 15 305; 22 209. See also Fort James Corporation.
Fort James Corporation, 22 209–12 (upd.); 29 136
Fort Mill Manufacturing Co. See Springs Industries, Inc.
Forte Plc, 15 46; 16 446; 24 195; 29 443; 64 340
Fortis, Inc., 15 179–82; 47 134–37 (upd.); 50 4–6
Fortum Corporation, 30 202–07 (upd.)
Fortum Oil and Gas Oy, 68 125–26
Fortun Foods, 26 59
Fortune Brands, Inc., 19 168; 29 193–97 (upd.); 45 269; 49 153; 51 7; 58 194, 196; 64 3; 68 163–67 (upd.)
Fortune Enterprises, 12 60
Fortunoff Fine Jewelry and Silverware Inc., 26 144–46
Forum Cafeterias, 19 299–300
Fosgate Electronics, 43 322
Foss Maritime Co., 9 509, 511
Fossil, Inc., 17 189–91
Foster & Kleiser, 7 335; 14 331
Foster Forbes, 16 123
Foster Grant. See FosterGrant, Inc.
Foster Management Co., 11 366–67
Foster Medical Corp., 11 282
Foster Poultry Farms, 32 201–04
Foster-Probyn Ltd., 38 501
Foster Sand & Gravel, 14 112
Foster Wheeler Corporation, 6 145–47; 23 205–08 (upd.); 25 82
Foster's Group Limited, 7 182–84; 21 227–30 (upd.); 26 303, 305–06; 36 15; 50 199–203 (upd.), 261
FosterGrant, Inc., 60 131–34
Fougerolle, 27 136, 138
Foundation Computer Systems, Inc., 13 201
Foundation Fieldbus, 22 373
Foundation Health Corporation, 11 174; 12 175–77
Founders Equity Inc., 14 235
Founders of American Investment Corp., 15 247
Fountain Powerboats Industries, Inc., 28 146–48
Four Media Co., 33 403
Four Paws Products, Ltd., 58 60
Four Queens Hotel and Casino. See The Elsinore Corporation.
Four Seasons Hotels Inc., 9 237–38; 29 198–200 (upd.)
Four-Ten Corporation, 58 378
Four Winds, 21 153
4Kids Entertainment Inc., 59 187–89
Fournier Furniture, Inc., 12 301
4P, 30 396–98
Fourth Financial Corporation, 11 144–46; 15 60
Fowler, Roenau & Geary, LLC, 37 224
Fox and Hound English Pub and Grille. See Total Entertainment Restaurant Corporation.
Fox & Jacobs, 8 87

Fox Broadcasting Company, II 156; 9 428; 21 25, 360; 24 517; 25 174, 417–18
Fox Children's Network, 21 26
Fox Entertainment Group, Inc., 43 173–76; 52 4–5
Fox Family Worldwide, Inc., 24 170–72; 63 437. See also ABC Family Worldwide, Inc.
Fox Film Corp. See Twentieth Century Fox Film Corporation.
Fox Grocery Co., II 682
Fox, Inc., 12 359; 25 490
Fox Network, 29 426
Fox Paine & Company L.L.C., 63 410, 412
Fox Paper Company, 8 102
Fox Ridge Homes, 70 208
Fox-Vliet Drug Company, 16 212
Foxboro Company, 13 233–35; 27 81
Foxconn International, Inc. See Hon Hai Precision Industry Co., Ltd.
FoxMeyer Health Corporation, 16 212–14
Foxmoor, 29 163
Foxx Hy-Reach, 28 387
Foxy Products, Inc., 60 287
FP&L. See Florida Power & Light Co.
FPA Corporation. See Orleans Homebuilders, Inc.
FPK LLC, 26 343
FPL Group, Inc., V 623–25; 45 150; 49 143–46 (upd.)
FR Corp., 18 340; 43 282
Fracmaster Ltd., 55 294
Fragrance Corporation of America, Ltd., 53 88
Fragrance Express Inc., 37 271
Framatome SA, 9 10; 19 164–67
Framingham Electric Company, 12 45
Franc-Or Resources, 38 231–32
France-Loisirs, IV 615–16, 619
France Quick, 12 152; 26 160–61; 27 10
France Télécom Group, V 291–93, 471; 9 32; 14 489; 18 33; 21 231–34 (upd.); 25 96, 102; 34 13; 47 214; 52 108; 63 375–77
Franchise Associates, Inc., 17 238
Franchise Business Systems, Inc., 18 207
Franchise Finance Corp. of America, 19 159; 37 351
Francis H. Leggett & Co., 24 527
Franciscan Vineyards, Inc., 34 89; 68 99
Franco-Américaine de Constructions Atomiques, 19 165
Franco-American Food Company. See Campbell Soup Company.
Frank & Pignard SA, 51 35
Frank & Schulte GmbH, 8 496
Frank Dry Goods Company, 9 121
Frank H. Nott Inc., 14 156
Frank Holton Company, 55 149, 151
Frank J. Rooney, Inc., 8 87
Frank J. Zamboni & Co., Inc., 34 173–76
Frank Russell Company, 45 316; 46 198–200
Frank Schaffer Publications, 19 405; 29 470, 472
Frank W. Horner, Ltd., 38 123
Frank's Nursery & Crafts, Inc., 12 178–79; 198–200
Frankel & Co., 39 166–69
Frankenberry, Laughlin & Constable, 9 393
Frankford-Quaker Grocery Co., II 625

Frankfurter Allgemeine Zeitung GmbH, 66 121–24
Franklin Assurances, III 211
Franklin Brass Manufacturing Company, 20 363
Franklin Coach, 56 223
Franklin Container Corp., IV 312; 19 267
Franklin Corp., 14 130; 41 388
Franklin Covey Company, 11 147–49; 37 149–52 (upd.)
Franklin Electric Company, Inc., 43 177–80
Franklin Electronic Publishers, Inc., 23 209–13
The Franklin Mint, 9 428; 37 337–38; 69 181–84
Franklin Mutual Advisors LLC, 52 119, 172
Franklin National Bank, 9 536
Franklin Plastics, 19 414
Franklin Research & Development, 11 41
Franklin Resources, Inc., 9 239–40
Franklin Sports, Inc., 17 243
Franklin Steamship Corp., 8 346
Frans Maas Beheer BV, 14 568
Franzia. See The Wine Group, Inc.
Frape Behr S.A. See Behr GmbH & Co. KG.
Fraser & Chalmers, 13 16
Fraser & Neave Ltd., 54 116–18; 59 58–59
Fray Data International, 14 319
Frazer & Jones, 48 141
FRE Composites Inc., 69 206
Fred Campbell Auto Supply, 26 347
Fred Meyer Stores, Inc., II 669; V 54–56; 18 505; 20 222–25 (upd.); 35 370; 50 455; 64 135–39 (upd.)
Fred Sammons Company of Chicago, 30 77
Fred Schmid Appliance & T.V. Co., Inc., 10 305; 18 532
Fred Usinger Inc., 54 119–21
The Fred W. Albrecht Grocery Co., 13 236–38
Fred Weber, Inc., 61 100–02
Fred's, Inc., 23 214–16; 62 144–47 (upd.)
Freddie Mac, 54 122–25
Fredelle, 14 295
Frederick & Nelson, 17 462
Frederick Atkins Inc., 16 215–17
Frederick Bayer & Company, 22 225
Frederick Gas Company, 19 487
Frederick Manufacturing Corporation, 26 119; 48 59
Frederick's of Hollywood Inc., 16 218–20; 25 521; 59 190–93 (upd.)
Fredrickson Motor Express, 57 277
Free-lance Uitzendburo, 26 240
Freeborn Farms, 13 244
Freedom Communications, Inc., 36 222–26
Freedom Group Inc., 42 10–11
Freedom Technology, 11 486
Freeman Chemical Corporation, 61 111–12
Freeman, Spogli & Co., 17 366; 18 90; 32 12, 15; 35 276; 36 358–59; 47 142–43; 57 11, 242
Freemans. See Sears plc.
FreeMark Communications, 38 269
Freeport-McMoRan Copper & Gold, Inc., IV 81–84; 7 185–89 (upd.); 16 29; 23 40; 57 145–50 (upd.)

Freeport Power, **38** 448
Freezer Queen Foods, Inc., **21** 509
Freezer Shirt Corporation, **8** 406
Freight Car Services, Inc., **23** 306
Freight Outlet, **17** 297
Freixenet S.A., 71 162–64
Frejlack Ice Cream Co., **II** 646; **7** 317
Fremont Canning Company, **7** 196
Fremont Group, **21** 97
Fremont Investors, **30** 268
Fremont Partners, **24** 265
Fremont Savings Bank, **9** 474–75
French Connection Group plc, 41
   167–69
French Fragrances, Inc., 22 213–15; **40**
   170. *See also* Elizabeth Arden, Inc.
French Kier, **I** 568
French Quarter Coffee Co., **27** 480–81
Frequency Electronics, Inc., 61 103–05
Frequency Sources Inc., **9** 324
Fresenius AG, 22 360; **49** 155–56; **56**
   138–42
Fresh America Corporation, 20 226–28
Fresh Choice, Inc., 20 229–32
Fresh Enterprises, Inc., 66 125–27
Fresh Fields, **19** 501
Fresh Foods, Inc., 25 391; **29** 201–03
Fresh Start Bakeries, **26** 58
Freshbake Foods Group PLC, **II** 481; **7** 68;
   25 518; **26** 57
Fretter, Inc., 9 65; **10** 9–10, **304–06**, 502;
   19 124; **23** 52
Freudenberg & Co., 41 170–73
Friction Products Co., **59** 222
Frictiontech Inc., **11** 84
Friday's Front Row Sports Grill, **22** 128
Friden, Inc., **30** 418; **53** 237
Fried, Frank, Harris, Shriver &
   Jacobson, 35 183–86
Fried. Krupp GmbH, IV 85–89, 104,
   128, 203, 206, 222, 234. *See also*
   Thyssen Krupp AG.
Friede Goldman Halter, **61** 43
Friedman, Billings, Ramsey Group, Inc.,
   53 134–37
Friedman's Inc., 29 204–06
Friedrich Grohe AG & Co. KG, 53
   138–41
Friendly Hotels PLC, **14** 107
Friendly Ice Cream Corporation, 30
   208–10; 72 141–44 (upd.)
Friesland Coberco Dairy Foods Holding
   N.V., 59 194–96
Frigidaire Home Products, 13 564; **19**
   361; **22** 28, **216–18**, 349
Frigoscandia AB, **57** 300
Frimont S.p.A, **68** 136
Frisby P.M.C. Incorporated, **16** 475
Frisch's Restaurants, Inc., 35 187–89
Frisdranken Industries Winters B.V., **22**
   515
Frisk Int. Nv, **72** 272
Frito-Lay Company, 22 95; **32** 205–10;
   44 348
Fritz Companies, Inc., 12 180–82
Fritz Gegauf AG. *See* Bernina Holding
   AG.
Fritz W. Glitsch and Sons, Inc. *See* Glitsch
   International, Inc.
Frolic, **16** 545
Frolich Intercon International, **57** 174
Fromagerie d'Illoud. *See* Bongrain SA.
La Fromagerie du Velay, **25** 85
Fromagerie Paul Renard, **25** 85

Fromageries Bel, 19 51; **23 217–19; 25**
   83–84
Fromageries des Chaumes, **25** 84
Fromarsac, **25** 84
Frome Broken Hill Co., **IV** 59
Front Range Pipeline LLC, **60** 88
Frontec, **13** 132
Frontenac Co., **24** 45
Frontier Airlines, Inc., I 103, 118, 124,
   129–30; **11** 298; **22 219–21; 25** 421; **26**
   439–40; **39** 33
Frontier Communications, **32** 216, 218
Frontier Corp., 16 221–23; 18 164
Frontier Electronics, **19** 311
Frontier Expeditors, Inc., **12** 363
Frontier Pacific Insurance Company, **21**
   263
Frontier Vision Partners L.P., **52** 9
FrontLine Capital Group, **47** 330–31
Frontline Ltd., 45 163–65
Frontstep Inc., **55** 258
Frosch Touristik, **27** 29
Frost & Sullivan, Inc., 53 142–44
Frost National Bank. *See* Cullen/Frost
   Bankers, Inc.
Frozen Food Express Industries, Inc., 20
   233–35; 27 404
Fru-Con Holding Corporation, **I** 561; **55** 62
Fruehauf Corp., I 169–70, 480; **7**
   259–60, 513–14; **27** 202–03, 251; **40**
   432
Fruit of the Loom, Inc., 8 200–02; 16
   535; **25 164–67 (upd.); 54** 403
The Frustum Group Inc., **45** 280
Fruth Pharmacy, Inc., 66 128–30
Fry's Electronics, Inc., 68 168–70
Fry's Food Stores, **12** 112
Frye Copy Systems, **6** 599
Frymaster Corporation, 27 159–62
FSA Corporation, **25** 349
FSI International, Inc., 17 192–94. *See
   also* FlightSafety International, Inc.
FSP. *See* Frank Schaffer Publications.
FT Freeport Indonesia, **57** 145
FTD. *See* Florists Transworld Delivery,
   Inc.
F3 Software Corp., **15** 474
FTP Software, Inc., 20 236–38
Fubu, 29 207–09
Fuddruckers, **27** 480–82
Fuel Pipeline Transportation Ltd. *See* Thai
   Airways International.
Fuel Resources Development Co., **6**
   558–59
Fuel Resources Inc., **6** 457
FuelMaker Corporation, **6** 569
Fuji Bank, Ltd., II 291–93, 360–61, 391,
   422, 459, 554; **17** 556–57; **24** 324; **26**
   455; **58** 228
Fuji Electric Co., Ltd., II 22–23, 98, 103;
   13 356; **18** 511; **22** 373; **42** 145; **48**
   180–82 (upd.)
Fuji Gen-Gakki, **16** 202; **43** 171
Fuji Heavy Industries, **I** 207; **9** 294; **12**
   400; **13** 499–501; **23** 290; **36** 240, 243;
   64 151
Fuji Kaolin Co. *See* English China Clays
   Ltd.
Fuji Photo Film Co., Ltd., III 486–89; **7**
   162; **18** 94, **183–87 (upd.)**, 341–42; **36**
   172, 174; **43** 284
Fuji Photo Film USA, Inc., **45** 284
Fuji Seito, **I** 511
Fuji Television, **7** 249; **9** 29

Fuji Xerox. *See* Xerox Corporation.
Fujian Hualong Carburetor, **13** 555
Fujisawa Pharmaceutical Company,
   Ltd., I 635–36; **58 132–34 (upd.)**
Fujitsu-ICL Systems Inc., 11 150–51
Fujitsu Limited, I 455, 541; **III 139–41**,
   164, 482; **6** 217, 240–42; **10** 238; **11**
   308, 542; **13** 482; **14** 512; **16** 139,
   224–27 (upd.); 17 172; **21** 390; **27** 107;
   40 145–50 (upd.); 43 285; **50** 156
Fujitsu Takamisawa, **28** 131
Fukuoka Mitsukoshi Ltd., **56** 242
Fukuoka Paper Co., Ltd., **IV** 285
Fukutake Publishing Co., Ltd., **13** 91, 93
Ful-O-Pep, **10** 250
Fulbright & Jaworski L.L.P., 22 4; **47**
   138–41
Fulcrum Communications, **10** 19
The Fulfillment Corporation of America,
   21 37
Fulham Brothers, **13** 244
Fullbright & Jaworski, **28** 48
Fuller Company. *See* FLSmidth and Co. A/
   S.
Fuller Smith & Turner P.L.C., 38
   193–95
Fulton Bank, **14** 40
Fulton Co., **III** 569; **20** 361
Fulton Manufacturing Co., **11** 535
Fulton Performance Products, Inc., **11** 535
Funai Electric Company Ltd., 62 148–50
Funco, Inc., 20 239–41. *See also*
   GameStop Corp.
Fund American Companies. *See* White
   Mountains Insurance Group, Ltd.
Fundimensions, **16** 337
Funk & Wagnalls, **22** 441
Funnel Cake Factory, **24** 241
Funtastic Limited, **52** 193
Fuqua Enterprises, Inc., 17 195–98
Fuqua Industries Inc., I 445–47; **8** 545;
   12 251; **14** 86; **37** 62; **57** 376–77
Furnishings International Inc., **20** 359, 363;
   39 267
Furniture Brands International, Inc., 31
   246, 248; **39 170–75 (upd.)**
The Furniture Center, Inc., **14** 236
Furon Company, 28 149–51
Furr's Restaurant Group, Inc., 53
   145–48
Furr's Supermarkets, Inc., II 601; **28**
   152–54
Furst Group, **17** 106
Furukawa Electric Co., Ltd., III 490–92;
   15 514; **22** 44
Futronix Corporation, **17** 276
Future Diagnostics, Inc., **25** 384
Future Graphics, **18** 387
Future Now, Inc., 6 245; **12 183–85**
Future Shop Ltd., 62 151–53; 63 63
FutureCare, **50** 123
Futurestep, Inc., **34** 247, 249
Fuyo Group, **72** 249
FWD Corporation, **7** 513
FX Coughlin Inc., **51** 130
Fyffes Plc, 38 196–99, 201
Fytek, S.A. de C.V., **66** 42

G&G Shops, Inc., **8** 425–26
G&K Services, Inc., 16 228–30; 21 115
G&L Inc., **16** 202; **43** 170
G&O Manufacturing Company, Inc. *See*
   TransPro, Inc.
G&R Pasta Co., Inc., **II** 512

G.B. Lewis Company, **8** 359
G. Bruss GmbH and Co. KG, **26** 141
G.C. Industries, **52** 186
G.C. Murphy Company, **9** 21
G.C. Smith, **I** 423
G.D. Searle & Co., I 686–89; III 53; **8** 398, 434; **10** 54; **12 186–89 (upd.);** 16 527; **26** 108, 383; **29** 331; **34 177–82 (upd.); 56** 373, 375
G. Felsenthal & Sons, **17** 106
G.H. Bass & Co., **15** 406; **24** 383
G.H. Besselaar Associates, **30** 151
G.H. Rinck NV, **V** 49; **19** 122–23; **49** 111
G. Heileman Brewing Co., I 253–55, 270; **10** 169–70; **12** 338; **18** 501; **23** 403, 405
G.I.E. Airbus Industrie, I
G.I. Joe's, Inc., 30 221–23 41–43, 49–52, 55–56, 70, 72, 74–76, 107, 111, 116, 121; **9** 458, 460; **11** 279, 363; **12** 190–92 (upd.)
G-III Apparel Group, Ltd., 22 222–24
G.J. Coles & Coy. Ltd., **20** 155
G.J. Hopkins, Inc. *See* The Branch Group, Inc.
G.L. Kelty & Co., **13** 168
G.L. Rexroth GmbH, **III** 566; **38** 298, 300
G. Leblanc Corporation, 55 149–52
G.M. Pfaff AG, **30** 419–20
G.P. Group, **12** 358
G.R. Foods, Inc. *See* Ground Round, Inc.
G.R. Herberger's Department Stores, **19** 324–25; **41** 343–44
G.S. Blodgett Corporation, 15 183–85; 22 350. *See also* Blodgett Holdings, Inc.
GABA Holding AG. *See* Colgate-Palmolive Company.
Gabelli Asset Management Inc., 13 561; **30 211–14.** *See also* Lynch Corporation.
Gables Residential Trust, 49 147–49
GAC. *See* The Goodyear Tire & Rubber Company.
GAC Holdings L.P., **7** 204; **28** 164
Gadzooks, Inc., 18 188–90; 33 203
GAF, I 337–40, 549; **8** 180; **9** 518; **18** 215; **22** 14, **225–29 (upd.); 25** 464
Gage Marketing Group, 26 147–49; 27 21
Gaggenau Hausgeräte GmbH, **67** 81
Gagliardi Brothers, **13** 383
Gaiam, Inc., 41 174–77
Gain Technology, Inc., **10** 505
Gaines Furniture Manufacturing, Inc., **43** 315
Gainsco, Inc., 22 230–32
GalaGen Inc., **65** 216
Galardi Group, Inc., 72 145–47
Galas Harland, S.A., **17** 266, 268
Galavision, Inc., **24** 515–17; **54** 72
Galaxy Aerospace Co. L.P., **69** 216
Galaxy Carpet Mills Inc., **19** 276; **63** 300
Galaxy Energies Inc., **11** 28
Galaxy Nutritional Foods, Inc., 58 **135–37**
Galbreath Escott, **16** 474
The Gale Group, Inc., **34** 437
Gale Research Inc., **8** 526; **23** 440
Galen Health Care, **15** 112; **35** 215–16
Galen Laboratories, **13** 160
Galerías Preciados, **26** 130
Galeries Lafayette S.A., V 57–59; 23 **220–23 (upd.)**
Galey & Lord, Inc., 20 242–45; 66 **131–34 (upd.)**

Gallaher Group Plc, 49 150–54 (upd.)
Gallaher Limited, V 398–400; 19 168–71 **(upd.); 29** 195
Gallatin Steel Company, **18** 380; **24** 144
Galleria Shooting Team, **62** 174
Gallo Winery. *See* E. & J. Gallo Winery.
Gallop Johnson & Neuman, L.C., **26** 348
The Gallup Organization, 37 153–56; 41 196–97
Galoob Toys. *See* Lewis Galoob Toys Inc.
GALP, **48** 117, 119
Galveston *Daily News*, **10** 3
GALVSTAR, L.P., **26** 530
Galway Irish Crystal Ltd. *See* Belleek Pottery Ltd.
Galyan's Trading Company, Inc., 47 **142–44**
Gamax Holding, **65** 230, 232
Gamble-Skogmo Inc., **13** 169; **25** 535
The Gambrinus Company, 29 219; **40** **188–90**
Gambro AB, 49 155–57
Gamebusters, **41** 409
Gamesa, **19** 192
GameStop Corp., 69 185–89 (upd.)
GameTime, Inc., **19** 387; **27** 370–71
GAMI. *See* Great American Management and Investment, Inc.
Gamlestaden, **9** 381–82
Gamma Capital Corp., **24** 3
Gammalink, **18** 143
Gander Mountain, Inc., 20 246–48
Gannett Co., Inc.,
Gannett Company, Inc., IV 612–13, 629–30; **7 190–92 (upd.); 9** 3; **18** 63; **23** 157–58, 293; **24** 224; **25** 371; **30** **215–17 (upd.); 32** 354–55; **41** 197–98; **63** 394; **66 135–38 (upd.)**
Gannett Supply, **17** 282
Gantos, Inc., 17 199–201
The Gap, Inc., V 60–62; 9 142, 360; **11** 499; **18 191–94 (upd.); 24** 27; **25** 47–48; **31** 51–52; **55 153–57 (upd.)**
GAR Holdings, **19** 78
Garamond Press, **23** 100
Garan, Inc., 16 231–33; 64 140–43 **(upd.)**
Garanti Bank, **65** 69
Garantie Mutuelle des Fonctionnaires, **21** 225
Garden Botanika, **11** 41
Garden City Newspapers Inc., **38** 308
Garden Escape, **26** 441
Garden Fresh Restaurant Corporation, **31 213–15**
Garden of Eatin' Inc., **27** 198; **43** 218–19
Garden Ridge Corporation, 27 163–65
Garden State BancShares, Inc., **14** 472
Garden State Life Insurance Company, **10** 312; **27** 47–48
Garden State Paper, **38** 307–08
Gardenburger, Inc., 33 169–71
Gardener's Eden, **17** 548–49
Gardner & Harvey Container Corporation, **8** 267
Gardner Advertising. *See* Wells Rich Green BDDP.
Gardner Cryogenics, **13** 140
Gardner Denver, Inc., 49 158–60
Gardner Merchant Ltd., **11** 325; **29** 442–44
Gardner Rubber Co. *See* Tillotson Corp.
Garelick Farms, Inc., **26** 449
Garena Malhas Ltda., **72** 68
Garfield Weston, **13** 51

Garfinckel, Brooks Brothers, Miller & Rhodes, Inc., **15** 94; **22** 110
Garfinckels, **37** 12
Garland Commercial Industries, Inc. *See* Enodis plc.
Garland-Compton, **42** 328
Garland Publishing, **44** 416
Garmin Ltd., 60 135–37
Garrett, **9** 18; **11** 472
Garrett & Company, **27** 326
Garrett AiResearch, **9** 18
Garrick Investment Holdings Ltd., **16** 293
Garrido y Compania, Inc., **26** 448
Gart Sports Company, 24 173–75
Gartner Group, Inc., 21 235–37; 25 22; **57** 176–77
Garuda Indonesia, 6 90–91; 58 138–41 **(upd.)**
Gary Fisher Mountain Bike Company, **16** 494
Gary Industries, **7** 4
Gary-Williams Energy Corporation, **19** 177
Gas Energy Inc., **6** 457
Gas Light and Coke Company. *See* British Gas plc.
Gas Light Company. *See* Baltimore Gas and Electric Company.
Gas Natural SDG S.A., 49 211; **69** **190–93**
Gas Service Company, **6** 593; **12** 542; **50** 38
Gas Tech, Inc., **11** 513
Gas Utilities Company, **6** 471
Gastar Co. Ltd., **55** 375
Gaston Paper Stock Co., Inc., **8** 476
Gastronome, **70** 322
Gasunie. *See* N.V. Nederlandse Gasunie.
GATC. *See* General American Tank Car Company.
Gate Gourmet International AG, 70 **97–100**
The Gates Corporation, 9 241–43
Gates Distribution Company, **12** 60
Gates Radio Co., **II** 37
Gates Rubber, **26** 349
Gates/FA Distributing Inc., **29** 413–14
Gateway Books, **14** 61
Gateway Corporation Ltd., II 612, **628–30,** 638, 642; **10** 442; **16** 249; **25** 119. *See also* Somerfield plc.
Gateway Foodmarkets Ltd., **II** 628; **13** 26
Gateway, Inc., 27 166–69 (upd.); 63 **153–58 (upd.)**
Gateway International Motorsports Corporation, Inc., **43** 139–40
Gateway State Bank, **39** 381–82
Gateway Technologies, Inc., **46** 387
Gateway 2000, Inc., 10 307–09; 11 240; **22** 99; **24** 31; **25** 531. *See also* Gateway, Inc.
Gatliff Coal Co., **6** 583
Gattini, **40** 215
Gatwick Handling, **28** 157
GATX, 6 394–96; 25 168–71 (upd.); 47 298
Gaultier. *See* Groupe Jean-Paul Gaultier.
Gaumont SA, 25 172–75; 29 369–71
Gaya Motor, P.T. **23** 290
Gaylord Brothers', **60** 109
Gaylord Container Corporation, 8 **203–05; 24** 92
Gaylord Entertainment Company, 11 **152–54; 36 226–29 (upd.); 38** 456
Gaymer Group, **25** 82

Gaz de France, IV 425; V 626–28; 38 407; **40 191–95 (upd.)**
Gazelle Graphics Systems, 28 244; 69 243
Gazprom. *See* OAO Gazprom.
GB Foods Inc., 19 92
GB-Inno-BM. *See* GIB Group.
GB s.a. *See* GIB Group.
GB Stores, Inc., 14 427
gbav Gesellschaft für Boden- und Abfallverwertung, 58 28
GC Companies, Inc., 25 176–78
GCFC. *See* General Cinema Finance Co.
GD Express Worldwide, 27 472, 475; 30 463
GDE Systems, Inc., 17 492
GDF. *See* Gaz de France.
GDI. *See* GO/DAN Industries, Inc.
GDS, 29 412
GE. *See* General Electric Company.
GE Aircraft Engines, 9 244–46
GE Capital Aviation Services, 36 230–33
GE Capital Corporation, 29 428, 430; 63 165
GE Capital Services, 27 276; 49 240
GE Medical Systems, 71 350
GE SeaCo SRL, 29 428, 431
GEA AG, 27 170–74
GEAC Computer Corporation Ltd., 43 181–85
Geant Casino, 12 152
Gear Products, Inc., 48 59
Geberit AG, 49 161–64
Gebrüder Hepp, 60 364
Gebrüder Märklin & Cie. *See* Märklin Holding GmbH.
Gebrüder Sulzer Aktiengesellschaft. *See* Sulzer Brothers Limited.
GEC. *See* General Electric Company.
GECAS. *See* GE Capital Aviation Services.
Gecina SA, 42 151–53
Geco Mines Ltd., 64 297
Gedney. *See* M.A. Gedney Co.
Geerlings & Wade, Inc., 45 166–68
Geest Plc, 38 198, 200–02
Gefco SA, 54 126–28
Geffen Records Inc., 21 26; 23 33; 26 150–52; 43 143
GEHE AG, 27 175–78
Gehl Company, 19 172–74
GEICO Corporation, III 214, 248, 252, 273, 448; 10 310–12; 18 60, 61, 63; 40 196–99 (upd.); 42 31–34
Geiger Bros., 60 138–41
Gelco Corporation, 53 275
Gelco Express, 18 177
Gelco S.R.L. *See* Perfetti Van Melle S.p.A.
Gelco Truck Services, 19 293
Gelman Sciences, Inc. *See* Pall Corporation.
Gelsenberg AG, 7 141
Gelson's, 29 32
Gem State Utilities. *See* Pacific Telecom, Inc.
GEMA (Gesellschaft für musikalische Aufführungs- und mechanische Vervielfältigungsrechte), 70 101–05
Gemaire Distributors, Inc., 52 398–99
GemChem, Inc., 47 20
Gemco, 17 366
Gemcolite Company, 8 178
Gemeinhardt Co., 16 201; 43 170
Gemina S.p.A., 52 121–22
Gemini Group Limited Partnership, 23 10
Gemini Industries, 17 215

Gemini Sound Products Corporation, 58 142–44
Gemplus International S.A., 18 543; 64 144–47
Gemstar-TV Guide International, 43 431
Gen-Probe, Inc., 50 138–39
Gen-X Technologies Inc, 53 285
GenCare Health Systems, 17 166–67
Gencor Ltd., I 423; IV 90–93, 95; 22 233–37 (upd.); 49 353. *See also* Gold Fields Ltd.
GenCorp Inc., 8 206–08; 9 247–49; 13 381; 59 324; 63 6
Gendex Corp., 10 270, 272
Gene Upton Co., 13 166
Genencor International Inc., 44 134, 136
Genender International Incorporated, 31 52
Genentech Inc., I 637–38; 8 209–11 (upd.); 32 211–15 (upd.); 37 112; 38 204, 206; 41 153, 155
General Accident plc, III 256–57, 350. *See also* Aviva PLC.
General American Tank Car Company. *See* GATX Corporation.
General Aniline and Film Corporation. *See* GAF Corporation.
General Aquatics, Inc., 16 297; 56 16–17
General Atlantic Partners, 25 34; 26 94
General Atomics, 57 151–54
General Aviation Corp., 9 16
General Bearing Corporation, 45 169–71
General Binding Corporation, 10 313–14
General Bussan Kaisha, Ltd. *See* TonenGeneral Sekiyu K.K.
General Cable Corporation, 7 288; 8 367; 18 549; 40 200–03
General Casualty Co., III 404
The General Chemical Group Inc., 22 29, 115, 193, 349, 541; 29 114; 37 157–60
General Cigar Holdings, Inc., 27 139–40; 43 204–05; 66 139–42 (upd.)
General Cinema Corporation, I 245–46; IV 624; 12 12–13, 226, 356; 14 87; 19 362; 26 468; 27 481. *See also* GC Companies, Inc.
General Corporation, 9 173
General DataComm Industries, Inc., 14 200–02
General Diaper Corporation, 14 550
General Dynamics Corporation, I 57–60; 10 315–18 (upd.); 40 204–10 (upd.)
General Electric Capital Aviation Services, 48 218–19
General Electric Capital Corporation, 15 257, 282; 19 190; 59 265, 268; 71 306
General Electric Company, II 27–31; 12 193–97 (upd.); 34 183–90 (upd.); 63 159–68 (upd.), 436
General Electric Company, PLC, I 423; II 24–26; 9 9–10; 13 356; 20 290; 24 87; 42 373, 377. *See also* Marconi plc.
General Electric Credit Corporation, 19 293; 20 42
General Electric International Mexico, S.A. de C.V., 51 116
General Electric Mortgage Insurance Company, 52 244
General Electric Railcar Wheel and Parts Services Corporation, 18 4
General Electric Venture Capital Corporation, 9 140; 10 108
General Elevator Corporation, 25 15

General Export Iron and Metals Company, 15 116
General Felt Industries Inc., I 202; 14 300; 17 182–83
General Finance Corp., III 232; 11 16
General Finance Service Corp., 11 447
General Fire Extinguisher Co. *See* Grinnell Corp.
General Foods Corp., I 608, 712; II 530–34, 557, 569; V 407; 7 272–74; 10 551; 12 167, 372; 18 416, 419; 25 517; 26 251; 44 341
General Foods, Ltd., 7 577
General Furniture Leasing. *See* CORT Business Services Corporation.
General Glass Corporation, 13 40
General Growth Properties, Inc., 57 155–57
General Host Corporation, 7 372; 12 178–79, 198–200, 275; 15 362; 17 230–31
General Housewares Corporation, 16 234–36; 18 69
General Injectables and Vaccines Inc., 54 188
General Instrument Corporation, 10 319–21; 17 33; 34 298; 54 68
General Insurance Co. of America. *See* SAFECO Corporation.
General Leisure, 16 33
General Maritime Corporation, 59 197–99
General Medical Corp., 18 469
General Merchandise Services, Inc., 15 480
General Mills, Inc., II 501–03; 10 322–24 (upd.); 36 234–39 (upd.); 44 138–40; 50 293–96; 62 269; 63 250, 252
General Motors Acceptance Corporation, 21 146; 22 55
General Motors Corporation, I 171–73; 10 325–27 (upd.); 36 240–44 (upd.); 64 148–53 (upd.); 65 59, 62
General Nutrition Companies, Inc., 11 155–57; 24 480; 29 210–14 (upd.); 31 347; 37 340, 342; 45 210; 63 331, 335
General Office Products Co., 25 500
General Packing Service, Inc., 19 78
General Parts Inc., 29 86
General Petroleum Authority. *See* Egyptian General Petroleum Corporation.
General Physics Corporation, 13 367; 64 166
General Portland Cement Co., III 704–05; 17 497
General Portland Inc., 28 229
General Printing Ink Corp. *See* Sequa Corp.
General Public Utilities Corporation, V 629–31; 6 484, 534, 579–80; 11 388; 20 73. *See also* GPU, Inc.
General Radio Company. *See* GenRad, Inc.
General Railway Signal Company. *See* General Signal Corporation.
General Re Corporation, III 258–59, 276; 24 176–78 (upd.); 42 31, 35
General Rent A Car, 25 142–43
General Research Corp., 14 98
General Sekiyu K.K., IV 431–33, 555; 16 490. *See also* TonenGeneral Sekiyu K.K.
General Shale Building Materials Inc. *See* Wienerberger AG.
General Signal Corporation, 9 250–52; 11 232

General Spring Products, **16** 321
General Steel Industries Inc., **14** 324
General Supermarkets, **II** 673
General Telephone and Electronics Corp. *See* GTE Corporation.
General Telephone Corporation. *See* GTE Corporation.
General Time Corporation, **16** 483
General Tire, Inc., **8** 206–08, **212–14**; **9** 247–48; **20** 260, 262; **22** 219; **56** 71; **59** 324
General Transistor Corporation, **10** 319
General Turbine Systems, **58** 75
General Utilities Company, **6** 555
General Waterworks Corporation, **40** 449
Generale Bank, II 294–95
Generale Biscuit Glico France S.A. *See* Ezaki Glico Company Ltd.
Générale Biscuit S.A., **II** 475
Générale de Banque, **36** 458
Générale de Mécanique Aéronautique, **I** 46
Générale de Restauration, **49** 126
Générale des Eaux Group, **V 632–34**; **21** 226. *See* Vivendi Universal S.A.
Generale du Jouet, **16** 428
Générale Occidentale, **II** 475; **IV** 614–16
Générale Restauration S.A., **34** 123
Generali. *See* Assicurazioni Generali.
Génération Y2K, **35** 204, 207
Genesco Inc., **14** 501; **17 202–06**; **27** 59
Genesee & Wyoming Inc., **27 179–81**
Genesee Brewing Co., **18** 72; **50** 114
Genesee Iron Works. *See* Wickes Inc.
Genesis Health Ventures, Inc., **18 195–97**; **25** 310. *See also* NeighborCare,Inc.
Genesse Hispania, **60** 246
Genetic Anomalies, Inc., **39** 395
Genetics Institute, Inc., **8 215–18**; **10** 70, 78–80; **50** 538
Geneva Metal Wheel Company, **20** 261
Geneva Pharmaceuticals, Inc., **8** 549; **22** 37, 40
Geneva Rubber Co., **17** 373
Geneva Steel, **7 193–95**
Geneve Corporation, **62** 16
GENEX Services, Inc., **52** 379
Genix Group. *See* MCN Corporation.
Genmar Holdings, Inc., **45 172–75**
Genoc Chartering Ltd, **60** 96
Genosys Biotechnologies, Inc., **36** 431
Genovese Drug Stores, Inc., **18 198–200**; **21** 187; **32** 170; **43** 249
Genpack Corporation, **21** 58
GenRad, Inc., **24 179–83**
Gensec Bank, **68** 333
GenSet, **19** 442
Genstar, **22** 14; **23** 327
Genstar Gypsum Products Co., **IV** 273
Genstar Rental Electronics, Inc., **58** 110
Genstar Stone Products Co., **15** 154; **40** 176
GenSys Power Ltd., **64** 404
GenTek Inc., **37** 157; **41** 236
Gentex Corporation, **26 153–57**; **35** 148–49
Gentex Optics, **17** 50; **18** 392
Genting Bhd., **65 152–55**
GenTrac, **24** 257
Gentry Associates, Inc., **14** 378
Gentry International, **47** 234
Genty-Cathiard, **39** 183–84; **54** 306
Genuardi's Family Markets, Inc., **35 190–92**

Genuin Golf & Dress of America, Inc., **32** 447
Genuine Parts Company, **9 253–55**; **45 176–79 (upd.)**
Genung's, **II** 673
Genus, **18** 382–83
Genzyme Corporation, **13 239–42**; **38 203–07 (upd.)**; **47** 4
Genzyme Transgenics Corp., **37** 44
Geo. H. McFadden & Bro., **54** 89
GEO SA, **58** 218
Geo Space Corporation, **18** 513
GEO Specialty Chemicals, Inc., **27** 117
geobra Brandstätter GmbH & Co. KG, **48 183–86**
Geodis S.A., **67 187–90**
Geofizikai Szolgáltató Kft., **70** 195
Geographics, Inc., **25** 183
GEOINFORM Mélyfúrási Információ Szolgáltató Kft., **70** 195
Geomarine Systems, **11** 202
The Geon Company, **11 158–61**
Geon Industries, Inc. *See* Johnston Industries, Inc.
GeoQuest Systems Inc., **17** 419
Georesources, Inc., **19** 247
Georg Fischer AG Schaffhausen, **38** 214; **61 106–09**
Georg Neumann GmbH, **66** 288
George A. Hormel and Company, **II 504–06**; **7** 547; **12** 123–24; **18** 244. *See also* Hormel Foods Corporation.
George A. Touche & Co., **9** 167
George Booker & Co., **13** 102
George Buckton & Sons Limited, **40** 129
The George F. Cram Company, Inc., **55 158–60**
George H. Dentler & Sons, **7** 429
The George Hyman Construction Company, **8** 112–13; **25** 403
George J. Ball, Inc., **27** 507
George K. Baum & Company, **25** 433
George P. Johnson Company, **60 142–44**
George R. Rich Manufacturing Company. *See* Clark Equipment Company.
George S. May International Company, **55 161–63**
George Smith Financial Corporation, **21** 257
George Weston Limited, **II 631–32**; **36 245–48 (upd.)**; **41** 30, 33
George Wimpey plc, **12 201–03**; **28** 450; **51 135–38 (upd.)**
Georges Renault SA, **III** 427; **28** 40
Georgetown Group, Inc., **26** 187
Georgetown Steel Corp., **IV** 228
Georgia Carpet Outlets, **25** 320
Georgia Cotton Producers Association. *See* Gold Kist Inc.
Georgia Federal Bank, **I** 447; **11** 112–13; **30** 196
Georgia Gas Corporation. *See* Atlanta Gas Light Company
Georgia Gulf Corporation, **9 256–58**; **61 110–13 (upd.)**
Georgia Hardwood Lumber Co.,. *See* Georgia-Pacific Corporation
Georgia Kraft Co., **8** 267–68
Georgia-Pacific Corporation, **IV 281–83**, 288, 304, 345, 358; **9** 256–58, **259–62 (upd.)**; **12** 19, 377; **15** 229; **22** 415, 489; **31** 314; **44** 66; **47 145–51 (upd.)**; **51** 284; **61** 110–11

Georgia Power & Light Co., **6** 447, 537; **23** 28; **27** 20
Georgia Power Company, **38** 446–48; **49** 145
Georgia Steel Supply Company, **70** 294
Georgie Pie, **V** 35
GeoScience Corporation, **18** 515; **44** 422
Geosource Inc., **21** 14; **22** 189
Geotec Boyles Brothers, S.A., **19** 247
Geotecnia y Cimientos SA, **55** 182
Geotek Communications Inc., **21 238–40**
GeoTel Communications Corp., **34** 114
Geothermal Resources International, **11** 271
GeoVideo Networks, **34** 259
Geoworks Corporation, **25** 509
Geraghty & Miller Inc., **26** 23
Gerald Stevens, Inc., **37 161–63**
Gérard, **25** 84
Gerber Products Company, **II 481**; **III** 19; **7** 196–98, 547; **9** 90; **11** 173; **21** 53–55, **241–44 (upd)**; **25** 366; **34** 103; **36** 256
Gerber Scientific, Inc., **12 204–06**
Gerbes Super Markets, Inc., **12** 112
Gerbo Telecommunicacoes e Servicos Ltda., **32** 40
Gerdau S.A., **59 200–03**
Geren Associates. *See* CRSS Inc.
Geriatrics Inc., **13** 49
Gericom AG, **47 152–54**
Gerling-Konzern Versicherungs-Beteiligungs-Aktiengesellschaft, **51 139–43**
Germaine Monteil Cosmetiques Corp., **I** 426
German American Bancorp, **41 178–80**
German-American Car Company. *See* GATX.
The German Society. *See* The Legal Aid Society.
GERPI, **51** 16
Gerrard Group, **61** 270, 272
Gerresheimer Glas AG, **43 186–89**
Gerrity Oil & Gas Corporation, **11** 28; **24** 379–80
Gerry Weber International AG, **63 169–72**
GESA. *See* General Europea S.A.
Gesbancaya, **II** 196
Geschmay Group, **51** 14
Gesellschaft für musikalische Aufführungs-und mechanische Vervielfältigungsrechte. *See* GEMA.
GET Manufacturing Inc., **36** 300
Getchell Gold Corporation, **61** 292
Getronics NV, **39 176–78**
Getty Images, Inc., **31 216–18**
Getty Oil Co., **6** 457; **8** 526; **11** 27; **17** 501; **18** 488; **27** 216; **47** 436. *See also* ChevronTexaco.
Getz Corp., **IV** 137
Gevaert. *See* Agfa Gevaert Group N.V.
Gevity HR, Inc., **63 173–77**
Geyser Peak Winery, **58** 196
GFI Informatique SA, **49 165–68**
GfK Aktiengesellschaft, **49 169–72**
GFL Mining Services Ltd., **62** 164
GFS. *See* Gordon Food Service Inc.
GFS Realty Inc., **II** 633
GGT Group, **44** 198
GHI, **28** 155, 157
Ghirardelli Chocolate Company, **24** 480; **27** 105; **30 218–20**

GI Communications, **10** 321
GI Export Corp. *See* Johnston Industries, Inc.
GIAG, **16** 122
Gianni Versace SpA, 22 238–40
Giant Bicycle Inc., **19** 384
Giant Cement Holding, Inc., 23 224–26
Giant Eagle, Inc., **12** 390–91; **13** 237
Giant Food Inc., II 633–35, 656; **13** 282, 284; **15** 532; **16** 313; **22 241–44 (upd.)**; **24** 462; **60** 307
Giant Industries, Inc., 19 175–77; 61 114–18 (upd.)
Giant Resources, III 729
Giant Stores, Inc., **7** 113; **25** 124
Giant TC, Inc. *See* Campo Electronics, Appliances & Computers, Inc.
Giant Tire & Rubber Company, **8** 126
Giant-Vac Manufacturing Inc., **64** 355
Giant Video Corporation, **29** 503
Giant Wholesale, II 625
GIB Group, V 63–66; 22 478; **23** 231; **26 158–62 (upd.)**
Gibbons, Green, van Amerongen Ltd., II 605; **9** 94; **12** 28; **19** 360
Gibbs Construction, **25** 404
GIBCO Corp., **17** 287, 289
Gibraltar Steel Corporation, 37 164–67
Gibson, Dunn & Crutcher LLP, 36 249–52; 37 292
Gibson Greetings, Inc., 7 24; **12 207–10; 16** 256; **21** 426–28; **22** 34–35; **59** 35, 37
Gibson Guitar Corp., 16 237–40
Gibson McDonald Furniture Co., **14** 236
GIC. *See* The Goodyear Tire & Rubber Company.
Giddings & Lewis, Inc., 8 545–46; **10 328–30; 23** 299; **28** 455
Giftmaster Inc., **26** 439–40
Gil-Wel Manufacturing Company, **17** 440
Gilbane, Inc., 34 191–93
Gilbert & John Greenall Limited, **21** 246
Gilbert Lane Personnel, Inc., **9** 326
Gildon Metal Enterprises, **7** 96
Gilead Sciences, Inc., 54 129–31
Gilkey Bros. *See* Puget Sound Tug and Barge Company.
Gill Interprovincial Lines, **27** 473
Gillett Holdings, Inc., 7 199–201; **11** 543, 545; **43** 437–38
The Gillette Company, III 27–30; 20 249–53 (upd.); 23 54–57; **68 171–76 (upd.)**
Gilliam Furniture Inc., **12** 475
Gilliam Manufacturing Co., **8** 530
Gilliam S.A., **61** 104
Gilman & Ciocia, Inc., 72 148–50
Gilman Paper Co., **37** 178
Gilmore Steel Corporation. *See* Oregon Steel Mills, Inc.
Gilroy Foods, **27** 299
Gimbel Brothers, Inc. *See* Saks Holdings, Inc.
Gimbel's Department Store, I 426–27; **8** 59; **22** 72; **50** 117–18
Gindick Productions, **6** 28
Gingiss Group, **60** 5
Ginn & Co., IV 672; **19** 405
Ginnie Mae. *See* Government National Mortgage Association.
Gino's East, **21** 362
Ginsber Beer Group, **15** 47; **38** 77

Giorgio Armani S.p.A., 45 180–83
Giorgio Beverly Hills, Inc., **26** 384
Giraud Restaurant System Co. Ltd. *See* Odakyu Electric Railway Co., Ltd.
Girbaud, **17** 513; **31** 261
Girl Scouts of the USA, 35 193–96
Giro Sport Designs International Inc., **16** 53; **44** 53–54
GiroCredit Bank, **69** 156
Girod, **19** 50
Girsa S.A., **23** 170
Girvin, Inc., **16** 297
Gist-Brocades Co., III 53; **26** 384
Git-n-Go Corporation, **60** 160
The Gitano Group, Inc., 8 219–21; 20 136 **25** 167; **37** 81
La Giulia Ind. S.P.A., **72** 272
Givaudan SA, 43 190–93
GIW Industries Inc., **62** 217
GJM International Ltd., **25** 121–22
GK Technologies Incorporated, **10** 547
GKH Partners, **29** 295
GKN plc, III 493–96; **38 208–13 (upd.); 42** 47; **47** 7, 9, 279–80
Glacier Bancorp, Inc., 35 197–200
Glacier Park Co., **10** 191
Glacier Water Services, Inc., 47 155–58
Glamar Group plc, **14** 224
Glamis Gold, Ltd., 54 132–35
Glamor Shops, Inc., **14** 93
Glanbia plc, 38 196, 198; **59 204–07**, 364
Glass Glover Plc, **52** 419
Glasstite, Inc., **33** 360–61
GlasTec, II 420
Glastron. *See* Genmar Holdings, Inc.
Glatfelter Wood Pulp Company, **8** 413
Glaxo Holdings plc, I 639–41, 643, 668, 675, 693; **9 263–65 (upd.); 10** 551; **11** 173; **20** 39; **26** 31; **34** 284; **38** 365; **50** 56; **54** 130
GlaxoSmithKline plc, 46 201–08 (upd.)
Gleason Corporation, 24 184–87
Glemby Co. Inc., **70** 262
Glen & Co, I 453
Glen Alden Corp., **15** 247
Glen-Gery Corporation, **14** 249
Glencairn Ltd., **25** 418
Glencore International AG, **52** 71, 73
The Glenlyte Group, **29** 469
Glenlyte Thomas Group LLC, **29** 466
Glenmoor Partners, **70** 34–35
Glenn Advertising Agency, **25** 90
Glenn Pleass Holdings Pty. Ltd., **21** 339
GLF-Eastern States Association, **7** 17
Glico. *See* Ezaki Glico Company Ltd.
The Glidden Company, I 353; **8 222–24; 21** 545
Glimcher Co., **26** 262
Glitsch International, Inc. *See* Foster Wheeler Corp.
Global Access, **31** 469
Global Apparel Sourcing Ltd., **22** 223
Global Berry Farms LLC, 62 154–56
Global BMC (Mauritius) Holdings Ltd., **62** 55
Global Card Holdings Inc., **68** 45
Global Communications of New York, Inc., **45** 261
Global Crossing Ltd., 32 216–19
Global Engineering Company, **9** 266
Global Health Care Partners, **42** 68
Global Industries, Ltd., 37 168–72
Global Information Solutions, **34** 257

Global Interactive Communications Corporation, **28** 242
Global Marine Inc., 9 266–67; 11 87
Global One, **52** 108
Global Outdoors, Inc., 49 173–76
Global Petroleum Albania S.A./Elda Petroleum Sh.P.K., **64** 177
Global Power Equipment Group Inc., 52 137–39
Global Switch International Ltd., **67** 104–05
Global TeleSystems, Inc. *See* Global Crossing Ltd.
Global Vacations Group. *See* Classic Vacation Group, Inc.
Global Van Lines. *See* Allied Worldwide, Inc.
GlobalCom Telecommunications, Inc., **24** 122
GlobaLex, **28** 141
Globalia, **53** 301
GlobalSantaFe Corporation, 48 187–92 (upd.)
Globalstar Telecommunications Limited, **54** 233
GLOBALT, Inc., **52** 339
Globe Business Furniture, **39** 207
Globe Feather & Down, **19** 304
Globe Newspaper Co., **7** 15
Globe Pequot Press, **36** 339, 341
Globe Steel Abrasive Co., **17** 371
Globe Telegraph and Trust Company, **25** 99
Globelle Corp., **43** 368
Globenet, **57** 67, 69
Globetrotter Communications, **7** 199
Globo, **18** 211
Globus. *See* Migros-Genossenschafts-Bund.
Glock Ges.m.b.H., 42 154–56
Gloria Jean's Gourmet Coffees, **20** 83
La Gloria Oil and Gas Company, **7** 102
Glosser Brothers, **13** 394
Glotel plc, 53 149–51
Gloucester Cold Storage and Warehouse Company, **13** 243
Glow-Tec International Company Ltd., **65** 343
Glowlite Corporation, **48** 359
Glycomed Inc., **13** 241; **47** 222
Glyn, Mills and Co., **12** 422
GM. *See* General Motors Corporation.
GM Hughes Electronics Corporation, II 32–36; 10 325. *See also* Hughes Electronics Corporation.
GMARA, II 608
GMR Properties, **21** 257
GNB International Battery Group, **10** 445
GNC. *See* General Nutrition Companies, Inc.
GND Holdings Corp., **7** 204; **28** 164
GNMA. *See* Government National Mortgage Association.
Gnôme & Rhône, **46** 369
The Go-Ahead Group Plc, 28 155–57
GO/DAN Industries, Inc. *See* TransPro, Inc.
Go Fly Ltd., **39** 128
Go-Gro Industries, Ltd., **43** 99
Go Sport. *See* Groupe Go Sport S.A.
Go-Video, Inc. *See* Sensory Science Corporation.
Goal Systems International Inc., **10** 394
goClick. *See* Marchex, Inc.

Godfather's Pizza Incorporated, 11 50; **12** 123; **14** 351; **17** 86; **25 179–81**
Godfrey Co., **II** 625
Godfrey L. Cabot, Inc., **8** 77
Godiva Chocolatier, Inc., 64 154–57
Godsell, **10** 277
Godtfred Kristiansen, **13** 310–11
Goelitz Confectionary. *See* Herman Goelitz, Inc.
GOFAMCLO, Inc., **64** 160
Goggin Truck Line, **57** 277
GoGo Tours, Inc., **56** 203–04
Göhner AG, **6** 491
Gokey Company, **10** 216; **28** 339
Gold Bond Stamp Company. *See* Carlson Companies, Inc.
Gold Corporation, **71** 3–4
Gold Exploration and Mining Co. Limited Partnership, **13** 503
Gold Fields Ltd., IV 94–97; 62 157–64 (upd.)
Gold Kist Inc., 7 432; **17 207–09; 26 166–68**
Gold Lance Inc., **19** 451–52
Gold Lion, **20** 263
Gold Prospectors' Association of America, **49** 173
Gold Star Chili, Inc., **62** 325–26
Gold'n Plump Poultry, 54 136–38
Gold's Gym International, Inc., 71 165–68
Goldblatt's Department Stores, **15** 240–42
Golden Bear International, **33** 103; **42** 433; **45** 300; **68** 245
Golden Belt Manufacturing Co., 16 241–43
Golden Books Family Entertainment, Inc., 28 158–61
Golden Circle Financial Services, **15** 328
Golden Corral Corporation, 10 331–33; 66 143–46 (upd.)
Golden Enterprises, Inc., 26 163–65
Golden Gate Airlines, **25** 421
Golden Gates Disposal & Recycling Co., **60** 224
Golden Grain Macaroni Co., **II** 560; **12** 411; **30** 219; **34** 366
Golden Krust Caribbean Bakery, Inc., 68 177–79
Golden Moores Finance Company, **48** 286
Golden Nugget, Inc. *See* Mirage Resorts, Incorporated.
Golden Ocean Group, **45** 164
Golden Partners, **10** 333
Golden Peanut Company, **17** 207
Golden Poultry Company, **26** 168
Golden Press, Inc., **13** 559–61
Golden Road Motor Inn, Inc. *See* Monarch Casino & Resort, Inc.
Golden Sea Produce, **10** 439
Golden Skillet, **10** 373
Golden State Foods Corporation, 32 220–22
Golden State Newsprint Co. Inc., **IV** 296; **19** 226; **23** 225
Golden State Vintners, Inc., 33 172–74
Golden Telecom, Inc., 59 208–11
Golden West Financial Corporation, 47 159–61
Golden West Homes, **15** 328
Golden West Publishing Corp., **38** 307–08
Golden Youth, **17** 227
Goldenberg Group, Inc., **12** 396
Goldfield Corp., **12** 198

Goldfine's Inc., **16** 36
Goldline Laboratories Inc., **11** 208
The Goldman Sachs Group Inc., II 11, 268, 326, 361, **414–16**, 432, 434, 448; **IV** 611; **9** 378, 441; **10** 423; **12** 405; **13** 95, 448, 554; **15** 397; **16** 195; **20 254–57 (upd.)**, 258; **21** 146; **22** 427–28; **26** 456; **27** 317; **29** 508; **36** 190–91; **38** 289, 291; **51** 358–59, 61; **51 144–48 (upd.)**
Goldner Hawn Johnson & Morrison Inc., **48** 412
Goldome Savings Bank, **11** 110; **17** 488
Goldsmith's, **9** 209
Goldstar Co., Ltd., II 53–54; **12 211–13; 13** 213; **30** 184; **43** 428
Goldwin Golf, **45** 76
Goldwyn Films. *See* Metro-Goldwyn-Mayer Inc.
Goleta National Bank, **33** 5
Golf Card International, **56** 5
Golf Day, **22** 517
The Golub Corporation, 26 169–71
Gomoljak, **14** 250
Gonnella Baking Company, 40 211–13
The Good Guys!, Inc., 10 334–35; 30 224–27 (upd.)
The Good Humor-Breyers Ice Cream Company, 14 203–05; 15 222; **17** 140–41; **32** 474, 476
Good Natural Café, **27** 481
Good Times Restaurants Inc., **8** 303; **63** 370
Good Vibrations, Inc., **28** 345
Good Weather International Inc., **III** 221; **14** 109
Goodbody & Company, **22** 428
Goodbody James Capel, **16** 14
Goodby, Berlin & Silverstein, **10** 484
Goodebodies, **11** 41
Goodfriend. *See* Goody's Family Clothing, Inc.
Goodman Bros. Mfg. Co., **14** 436
Goodman Fielder Ltd., 7 577; **44** 137; **52 140–43; 63** 83, 85
Goodman Holding Company, 42 157–60
GoodMark Foods, Inc., 26 172–74
Goodrich Corporation, 46 209–13 (upd.)
Goodson Newspaper Group, **29** 262
GoodTimes Entertainment Ltd., 31 238; **48 193–95**
Goodwill Industries International, Inc., 15 511; **16 244–46; 66 147–50 (upd.)**
Goodwin & Co., **12** 108
Goodwin, Dannenbaum, Littman & Wingfield, **16** 72
Goody Products, Inc., 12 214–16; 60 131–32
Goody's Family Clothing, Inc., 20 265–67; 64 158–61 (upd.)
The Goodyear Tire & Rubber Company, V 244–48; 8 81, 291–92, 339; **9** 324; **10** 445; **16** 474; **19** 221, 223, 455; **20 259–64 (upd.); 21** 72–74; **59** 87–89
Google, Inc., 50 204–07
Gordon & Gotch. *See* PMP Ltd.
Gordon B. Miller & Co., **7** 256; **25** 254
Gordon Food Service Inc., 8 225–27; 39 179–82 (upd.)
Gordon Jewelry Corporation, **16** 559, 561; **40** 472
Gordon Manufacturing Co., **11** 256
Gordon Publications. *See* Reed Elsevier.
Gordon S. Black Corporation, **41** 197–98

Gordon-Van Cheese Company, **8** 225
Gordy Company, **26** 314
Gorges Foodservice, Inc., **14** 516; **50** 493
Gorgonz Group, Inc., **64** 300
Gorham Silver, **12** 313
Gorilla Sports Club, **25** 42
Gorman Eckert & Co., **27** 299
The Gorman-Rupp Company, 18 201–03; 57 158–61 (upd.)
Gorton's, 13 243–44
The Gosho Co. *See* Kanematsu Corporation.
Goss Holdings, Inc., 43 194–97
Götabanken, **II** 353
Gothenburg Light & Power Company, **6** 580
Gothenburg Tramways Co., **II** 1
Gott Corp., **21** 293
Gottleib Group, **38** 437
Gottschalks, Inc., 18 204–06; 26 130
Gould Electronics, Inc., 11 45; **13** 127, 201; **14 206–08; 21** 43
Goulds Pumps Inc., 24 188–91
Gourmet Award Foods, **29** 480–81
Government Bond Department, **9** 369
Government Employees Insurance Company. *See* GEICO Corporation.
Government Technology Services Inc., **45** 69
Governor and Company of Adventurers of England. *See* Hudson's Bay Company.
The Governor and Company of the Bank of Scotland, 10 336–38
Goya Foods Inc., 22 245–47; 24 516
GP Group Acquisition Limited Partnership, **10** 288; **27** 41–42
GP Strategies Corporation, 64 162–66 (upd.)
GPAA. *See* Gold Prospectors' Association of America.
GPE. *See* General Precision Equipment Corporation.
GPI. *See* General Parts Inc.
GPI, **53** 46
GPM Gas Corporation, **40** 357–58
GPS Pool Supply, **29** 34
GPT, **15** 125
GPU. *See* General Public Utilities Corporation.
GPU, Inc., 27 182–85 (upd.)
Graber Industries, Inc. *See* Springs Industries, Inc.
Grace. *See* W.R. Grace & Co.
Grace Drilling Company, **9** 365
Grace-Sierra Horticultural Products Co., **22** 475
Graco Inc., 19 178–80; 67 191–95 (upd.)
Gradall Industries, Inc., **52** 196
Gradco Systems, Inc., **6** 290
Gradiaz, Annis & Co., **15** 138
Gradmann & Holler, **III** 283
Graf, **23** 219
Graficas e Instrumentos S.A., **13** 234
Graficas Monte Alban S.A., **47** 326
Graftek Press, Inc., **26** 44
Graham Brothers, **27** 267, 269
Graham Container Corp., **8** 477
Graham Corporation, 62 165–67
Gralla, **IV** 687
Grameen Bank, 31 219–22
GrameenPhone, **69** 344–46
Gramercy Pictures, **23** 391
Gramophone Company, **22** 192

Grampian Electricity Supply Company, **13** 457

Gran Central Corporation, **8** 487

Gran Dorado, **48** 315

Granada Group PLC, II 138–40; **17** 353; **24 192–95 (upd.)**, 269; **25** 270; **32** 404; **52** 367

Granada Royale Hometels, **9** 426

Granaria Holdings B.V., 23 183; **66 151–53**

GranCare, Inc., 14 209–11; **25** 310

Grand Bazaar Innovations Bon Marché, **13** 284; **26** 159–60

Grand Casinos, Inc., 20 268–70; **21** 526; **25** 386

Grand Department Store, **19** 510

Grand Home Furnishings. *See* Grand Piano & Furniture Company.

Grand Hotel Krasnapolsky N.V., 23 227–29

Grand Magasin de Nouveautés Fournier d'Annecy, **27** 93

Grand Metropolitan plc, I 247–49, 259, 261; **II** 608, 613–15; **9** 99; **13** 391; **14 212–15 (upd.)**; **15** 72; **17** 69, 71; **20** 452; **21** 401; **26** 58; **33** 276; **34** 121; **35** 438; **42** 223; **43** 215; **56** 46. *See also* Diageo plc.

Grand Ole Opry. *See* Gaylord Entertainment Company.

Grand Piano & Furniture Company, 72 151–53

Grand Prix Association of Long Beach, Inc., **43** 139–40

Grand Rapids Carpet Sweeper Company, **9** 70

Grand Rapids Gas Light Company. *See* MCN Corporation.

Grand Rapids Wholesale Grocery Company, **8** 481

Grand Union Company, II 637, 662; **7 202–04**; **8** 410; **13** 394; **16** 249; **28 162–65 (upd.)**

Grand Valley Gas Company, **11** 28

Grand-Perret, **39** 152–53

Grandes Superficies S.A., **23** 247

Les Grands Magasins Au Bon Marché, **26** 159–60

GrandVision S.A., 43 198–200

Grandy's, **15** 345

Granger Associates, **12** 136

Gränges, **III** 480; **22** 27; **53** 127–28

Granite Broadcasting Corporation, 42 161–64

Granite City Steel Company, **12** 353

Granite Construction Incorporated, 61 119–21

Granite Furniture Co., **14** 235

Granite Rock Company, 26 175–78

Granite State Bankshares, Inc., 37 173–75

Grant Oil Tool Co., **III** 569; **20** 361

Grant Prideco, Inc., 57 162–64

Grant Thornton International, 57 165–67

Grantham, Mayo, Van Otterloo & Co. LLC, **24** 407

Grantree Corp., **14** 4; **33** 398

Granville PLC. *See* Robert W. Baird & Co. Incorporated.

Graphic Controls Corp., **IV** 678

Graphic Industries Inc., 25 182–84; **36** 508

Graphic Research, Inc., **13** 344–45

Graphics Systems Software, **8** 519

Graphix Zone, **31** 238

Grass Valley Group, **8** 518, 520

Grasselli Chemical Company, **22** 225

Grasso Production Management Inc., **37** 289

Grattan Plc. *See* Otto-Versand (Gmbh & Co.).

The Graver Company, **16** 357

Gray Communications Systems, Inc., 24 196–200

Gray Line, **24** 118

Gray Matter Holdings, L.L.C., **64** 300

Gray, Siefert & Co., Inc., **10** 44; **33** 259–60

Graybar Electric Company, Inc., 54 139–42

Grays Harbor Mutual Savings Bank, **17** 530

Greaseater, Ltd., **8** 463–64

Great Alaska Tobacco Co., **17** 80

Great American Bagel and Coffee Co., **27** 482

Great American Broadcasting Inc., **18** 65–66; **22** 131; **23** 257–58

Great American Cookie Company. *See* Mrs. Fields' Original Cookies, Inc.

Great American Entertainment Company, **13** 279; **48** 194

Great American First Savings Bank of San Diego, **II** 420

Great American Insurance Company, **48** 9

Great American Lines Inc., **12** 29

Great American Management and Investment, Inc., 8 228–31; **49** 130

Great American Reserve Insurance Co., **IV** 343; **10** 247

Great American Restaurants, **13** 321

The Great Atlantic & Pacific Tea Company, Inc., II 636–38, 629, 655–56, 666; **13** 25, 127, 237; **15** 259; **16** 63–64, **247–50 (upd.)**; **17** 106; **18** 6; **19** 479–80; **24** 417; **26** 463; **33** 434; **55 164–69 (upd.)**; **64** 125

Great Bagel and Coffee Co., **27** 480–81

Great Harvest Bread Company, 44 184–86

Great Lakes Bancorp, 8 232–33

Great Lakes Carbon Corporation, **12** 99

Great Lakes Chemical Corp., I 341–42; **8** 262; **14 216–18 (upd.)**

Great Lakes Dredge & Dock Company, 69 194–97

Great Lakes Energy Corp., **39** 261

Great Lakes Steel Corp., **8** 346; **12** 352; **26** 528

Great Lakes Transportation LLC, **71** 82

Great Lakes Window, Inc., **12** 397

Great Land Seafoods, Inc., **II** 553

Great Northern Nekoosa Corp., **IV** 282–83; **9** 260–61; **47** 148

Great Northern Railway Company, **6** 596

Great Plains Energy Incorporated, 65 156–60 (upd.)

Great Plains Software Inc., **38** 432

Great Plains Transportation, **18** 226

Great Rigs, Inc., **71** 8–9

Great River Oil and Gas Corporation, **61** 111

Great Shoshone & Twin Falls Water Power Company, **12** 265

The Great Universal Stores plc, V 67–69; **15** 83; **17** 66, 68; **19 181–84**

(upd.); **41** 74, 76; **45** 152; **50** 124. *See also* GUS plc.

Great-West Lifeco Inc., III 260–61; **21** 447. *See also* Power Corporation of Canada.

The Great Western Auction House & Clothing Store, **19** 261

Great Western Bank, **47** 160

Great Western Billiard Manufactory, **III** 442

Great Western Financial Corporation, 10 339–41

Great Western Foam Co., **17** 182

Great World Foods, Inc., **17** 93

Greatbatch Inc., 72 154–56

Greb Industries Ltd., **16** 79, 545

Grebner GmbH, **26** 21

Grede Foundries, Inc., 38 214–17

Greeley Beef Plant, **13** 350

Greeley Gas Company, **43** 56–57

Green Acquisition Co., **18** 107

Green Bay Food Company, **7** 127

The Green Bay Packers, Inc., 32 223–26

Green Capital Investors L.P., **23** 413–14

Green Giant, **14** 212, 214; **24** 140–41

Green Island Cement (Holdings) Ltd. Group, **IV** 694–95

Green Line Investor Services, **18** 553

Green Mountain Coffee, Inc., 31 227–30

Green Power & Light Company. *See* UtiliCorp United Inc.

Green River Electric Corporation, **11** 37

Green Siam Air Services Co., Ltd., **51** 123

Green Tree Financial Corporation, 11 162–63. *See also* Conseco, Inc.

The Greenalls Group PLC, 21 245–47

Greenbacks Inc., **62** 104

Greenberg Traurig, LLP, 65 161–63

The Greenbrier Companies, 19 185–87

Greene King plc, 31 223–26

Greene, Tweed & Company, 55 170–72

Greenfield Healthy Foods, **26** 58

Greenfield Industries Inc., **13** 8

Greenham Construction Materials, **38** 451–52

Greenman Brothers Inc. *See* Noodle Kidoodle.

GreenPoint Financial Corp., 28 166–68

Greensboro Life Insurance Company, **11** 213

Greenville Tube Corporation, **21** 108

Greenwich Associates, **19** 117

Greenwood Mills, Inc., 14 219–21

Greenwood Publishing Group. *See* Reed Elsevier.

Greenwood Trust Company, **18** 478

Greg Manning Auctions, Inc., 60 145–46

Greggs PLC, 65 164–66

Greif Inc., 15 186–88; **66 154–56 (upd.)**

Greiner Engineering Inc., **45** 421

Gresham Insurance Company Limited, **24** 285

GretagMacbeth Holdings AG, **18** 291

Gretel's Pretzels, **35** 56

Gretsch & Brenner, **55** 150

Grévin & Compagnie SA, 56 143–45

Grey Advertising, Inc., 6 26–28; **10** 69; **14** 150; **22** 396; **25** 166, 381

Grey Global Group Inc., 66 157–61 (upd.)

Grey Wolf, Inc., 43 201–03

Greyhound Corp., I 448–50; **8** 144–45; **10** 72; **12** 199; **16** 349; **22** 427; **23** 173–74; **27** 480; **42** 394

Greyhound Lines, Inc., **32** 227–31 (upd.); **48** 319
Greyhound Temporary Services, **25** 432
Griffin Bacal, **25** 381
Griffin Industries, Inc., 70 106–09
Griffin Land & Nurseries, Inc., 43 204–06
Griffin Pipe Products Co., **7** 30–31
Griffin Press Pty. *See* PMP Ltd.
Griffin Wheel Company, **7** 29–30
Griffon Corporation, 34 194–96
Griffon Cutlery Corp., **13** 166
Grigg, Elliot & Co., **14** 555
Grimes Aerospace, **22** 32
Grinnell Corp., 11 198; **13 245–47; 63** 401, 403
Grist Mill Company, 15 189–91; 22 338
Gristede's Foods Inc., 68 31 231–33; 180–83 **(upd.)**
GRM Industries Inc., **15** 247–48
Gro-Mor Company, **60** 160
Grob Horgen AG. *See* Groz-Beckert Group.
Grocery Warehouse, **II** 602
GroceryWorks Holdings, Inc, **68** 369
Grogan-Cochran Land Company, **7** 345
Grohe. *See* Friedrich Grohe AG & Co. KG.
Grolier Inc., **IV** 619; **16 251–54; 43 207–11 (upd.)**
Grolier Interactive, **41** 409
Grolsch. *See* Royal Grolsch NV.
Gross Brothers Laundry. *See* G&K Services, Inc.
Gross Townsend Frank Hoffman, **6** 28
Grosskraftwerk Franken AG, **23** 47
Grossman's Inc., 13 248–50
Grosvenor Casinos Ltd., **64** 320
Ground Round, Inc., 21 248–51
Ground Services Inc., **13** 49
Group Arnault, **32** 146
Group 4 Falck A/S, 42 165–68, 338; **63** 425
Group Health Cooperative, 41 181–84
Group Hospitalization and Medical Services, **10** 161
Group Lotus plc, **13** 357; **62** 268
Group Maeva SA, **48** 316
Group Maintenance America Corp. *See* Encompass Services Corporation.
Group 1 Automotive, Inc., 52 144–46
Group Schneider S.A., **20** 214
Groupe AB, **19** 204
Groupe AG, **III** 201–02
Groupe Air France, 6 92–94. *See also* Air France; Societe Air France.
Groupe Alain Manoukian, 55 173–75
Groupe André, 17 210–12. *See also* Vivarte SA.
Groupe Arnault, **66** 244
Groupe Axime, **37** 232
Groupe Barrière SA, **48** 199
Groupe Bisset, **24** 510
Groupe Bolloré, 37 21; **67 196–99**
Groupe Bourbon S.A., 60 147–49
Groupe Bruxelles Lambert, **26** 368
Groupe Bull. *See* Compagnie des Machines Bull.
Groupe Casino. *See* Casino Guichard-Perrachon S.A.
Groupe Castorama-Dubois Investissements, 23 230–32
Groupe Danone, 14 150; **32 232–36 (upd.); 55** 359; **65** 215–17
Le Groupe Darty, **24** 266, 270

Groupe Dassault Aviation SA, 26 179–82 (upd.); 42 373, 376
Groupe de la Cité, IV 614–16, 617
Groupe DMC (Dollfus Mieg & Cie), 27 186–88
Groupe Fournier SA, 44 187–89
Groupe Go Sport S.A., 39 183–85; 54 308
Groupe Guillin SA, 40 214–16
Groupe Herstal S.A., 58 145–48
Groupe Jean-Claude Darmon, 44 190–92
Groupe Jean Didier, **12** 413
Groupe Jean-Paul Gaultier, **34** 214
Groupe Lagardère S.A., **15** 293; **21** 265, 267
Groupe Lapeyre S.A., 33 175–77
Groupe LDC. *See* L.D.C. S.A.
Groupe Legris Industries, 23 233–35
Groupe Les Echos, 25 283–85
Groupe Limagrain, **70** 344
Groupe Louis Dreyfus S.A., 60 150–53
Groupe Monnoyeur, 72 157–59
Groupe Partouche SA, 48 196–99
Groupe Pechiney, **33** 89
Groupe Pinault-Printemps-Redoute, **19** 306, 309; **21** 224, 226
Groupe Poliet, **66** 363–64
Groupe Poron, **35** 206
Groupe Promodès S.A., 19 326–28
Groupe Rallye, **39** 183–85
Groupe Rothschild, **22** 365
Groupe Rougier SA, 21 438–40
Groupe Roussin, **34** 13
Groupe Salvat, **IV** 619
Groupe SEB, 35 201–03
Groupe Sidel S.A., 21 252–55
Groupe Soufflet SA, 55 176–78; 65 65
Groupe Tetra Laval, **53** 327
Groupe Victoire, **III** 394
Groupe Vidéotron Ltée., 20 271–73
Groupe Yves Saint Laurent, 23 236–39
Groupe Zannier S.A., 35 204–07
Groupement d'Achat AVP SAS, **58** 221
Groupement des Mousquetaires. *See* ITM Entreprises SA.
Groupement Français pour l'Investissement Immobilier, **42** 153
Groupement Laitier du Perche, **19** 50
Groupement pour le Financement de la Construction. *See* Gecina SA.
GroupMAC. *See* Encompass Services Corporation.
Groux Beverage Corporation, **11** 451
Grove Manufacturing Co., **9** 393
Grove Worldwide, Inc., **59** 274, 278
Grow Biz International, Inc., 18 207–10
Grow Group Inc., 12 217–19, 387–88; **59** 332
Growing Healthy Inc., **27** 197; **43** 218
Growth International, Inc., **17** 371
Groz-Beckert Group, 68 184–86
GRS Inns Ltd. *See* Punch Taverns plc.
Grubb & Ellis Company, 21 256–58
Gruma, S.A. de C.V., 19 192; **31 234–36**
Grumman Corp., I 61–63, 67–68, 78, 84, 490, 511; **7** 205; **8** 51; **9** 17, 206–07, 417, 460; **10** 536; **11 164–67 (upd.)**, 363–65, 428; **15** 285; **28** 169
Grundig AG, **12** 162; **13** 402–03; **15** 514; **27** 189–92; **48** 383; **50** 299
Gruner + Jahr AG & Co., **7** 245; **22** 442; **23** 85
Gruntal & Co., L.L.C., 20 274–76
Gruntal Financial Corp., **III** 264

Grupo Acerero del Norte, S.A. de C.V., **22** 286; **42** 6
Grupo Aeropuerto del Sureste, S.A. de C.V., 48 200–02
Grupo Antarctica Paulista. *See* Companhia de Bebidas das Américas.
Grupo Banco Bilbao Vizcaya Argentaria S.A., **54** 147
Grupo Bimbo, S.A. de C.V., **31** 236
Grupo Bufete. *See* Bufete Industrial, S.A. de C.V.
Grupo Cabal S.A., **23** 166
Grupo Campi, S.A. de C.V., **39** 230
Grupo Carso, S.A. de C.V., 14 489; **21 259–61; 63** 383
Grupo Casa Saba, S.A. de C.V., 39 186–89
Grupo Clarín S.A., 67 200–03
Grupo Corvi S.A. de C.V., **7** 115; **25** 126
Grupo Cruzcampo S.A., **34** 202
Grupo Cuervo, S.A. de C.V., **31** 91–92
Grupo Cydsa, S.A. de C.V., 39 190–93
Grupo de Ingenieria Ecologica, **16** 260
Grupo Dina. *See* Consorcio G Grupo Dina, S.A. de C.V.
Grupo Dragados SA, 55 179–82
Grupo DST, **41** 405–06
Grupo Editorial Random House Mondadori S.L., **54** 22
Grupo Elektra, S.A. de C.V., 39 194–97
Grupo Empresarial Angeles, **50** 373
Grupo Eroski, 64 167–70
Grupo Ferrovial, S.A., 40 217–19
Grupo Financiero Asemex-Banpais S.A., **51** 150
Grupo Financiero Banamex S.A., 27 304; **54 143–46; 59** 121
Grupo Financiero Banorte, S.A. de C.V., 51 149–51
Grupo Financiero BBVA Bancomer S.A., 54 147–50
Grupo Financiero Galicia S.A., 63 178–81
Grupo Financiero Inbursa, **21** 259
Grupo Financiero Inverlat, S.A., **39** 188; **59** 74
Grupo Financiero Serfin, S.A., 19 188–90, 474; **36** 63
Grupo Gigante, S.A. de C.V., 34 197–99
Grupo Hecali, S.A., **39** 196
Grupo Herdez, S.A. de C.V., 35 208–10; 54 167
Grupo Hermes, **24** 359
Grupo ICA, **52** 394
Grupo IMSA, S.A. de C.V., 44 193–96
Grupo Industrial Alfa, S.A. de C.V. *See* Alfa, S.A. de C.V.
Grupo Industrial Atenquique, S.A. de C.V., **37** 176
Grupo Industrial Bimbo, 19 191–93; 29 338
Grupo Industrial Durango, S.A. de C.V., 37 176–78
Grupo Industrial Maseca S.A. de C.V. (Gimsa). *See* Gruma, S.A. de C.V.
Grupo Industrial Saltillo, S.A. de C.V., 54 151–54
Grupo Irsa, **23** 171
Grupo Leche Pascual S.A., 59 212–14
Grupo Lladró S.A., 52 147–49
Grupo Marsans, **69** 9, 11–12
Grupo Martins, **59** 361
Grupo Mexico, S.A. de C.V., 40 220–23, 413

Grupo Modelo, S.A. de C.V., 29 218–20
Grupo Nacional Provincial, **22** 285
Grupo Pipsamex S.A., **37** 178
Grupo Portucel Soporcel, 60 154–56
Grupo Posadas, S.A. de C.V., 57 168–70
Grupo Protexa, **16** 210
Grupo Pulsar. *See* Pulsar Internacional S.A.
Grupo Quan, **19** 192–93
Grupo Salinas, **39** 196
Grupo Sanborns S.A. de C.V., **35** 118
Grupo Servia, S.A. de C.V., **50** 209
Grupo TACA, 38 218–20
Grupo Televisa, S.A., 9 429; **18** 211–14;
    19 10; **24** 515–17; **39** 188, 398; **54**
    155–58 **(upd.)**; **57** 121
Grupo TMM, S.A. de C.V., 50 208–11
Grupo Transportación Ferroviaria
    Mexicana, S.A. de C.V., 47 162–64
Grupo Tribasa, **34** 82
Grupo Tudor, **IV** 471
Grupo Xtra, **39** 186, 188
Gruppo Banco di Napoli, **50** 410
Gruppo Buffetti S.p.A., **47** 345–46
Gruppo Coin S.p.A., 41 185–87
Gruppo Editoriale L'Espresso S.p.A., **54**
    19–21
Gruppo GFT, **22** 123
Gruppo IRI, **V** 325–27
Gryphon Development, **24** 237
Gryphon Holdings, Inc., 21 262–64
GS Financial Services L.P., **51** 148
GSD&M Advertising, 44 197–200
GSG&T, Inc. *See* Gulf States Utilities
    Company.
GSG Holdings Ltd., **39** 87
GSI. *See* Geophysical Service, Inc.
GSI Acquisition Co. L.P., **17** 488
GSI Commerce, Inc., 67 204–06
GSR, Inc., **17** 338
GSU. *See* Gulf States Utilities Company.
GT Bicycles, 26 183–85, 412
GT Global Inc. *See* AMVESCAP PLC.
GT Interactive Software, 19 405; **31**
    237–41. *See also* Infogrames
    Entertainment S.A.
GTE Corporation, V 294–98; **9** 49, 171,
    478–80; **10** 19, 97, 431; **11** 500; **14** 259,
    433; **15** 192–97 **(upd.)**; **18** 74, 111, 543;
    22 19; **25** 20–21, 91; **26** 520; **27** 302,
    305; **46** 373; **50** 299. *See also* British
    Columbia Telephone Company; Verizon
    Communications.
GTE Northwest Inc., **37** 124–26
GTECH Holdings, Inc., **27** 381
GTI Corporation, **29** 461–62
GTM-Entrepose, **23** 332
GTM Group, **43** 450, 452; **54** 392
GTO. *See* Global Transport Organization.
GTS Duratek, Inc., **13** 367–68
GTSI. *See* Government Technology
    Services Inc.
GTSI Corp., 57 171–73
GU Markets, **55** 83
Guangzhou Kurabo Chemicals Co. Ltd., **61**
    229
Guangzhou M. C. Packaging, **10** 130
Guangzhou Pearl River Piano Group
    Ltd., 49 177–79
Guangzhou Railway Corporation, **52** 43
Guarantee Life Cos., **69** 368
Guarantee Reserve Life Insurance
    Company, **59** 246
Guaranty Bank & Trust Company, **13** 440
Guaranty Federal Bank, F.S.B., **31** 441

Guaranty Federal Savings & Loan Assoc.,
    IV 343
Guaranty Properties Ltd., **11** 258
Guaranty Savings and Loan, **10** 339
Guaranty Trust Co. *See* J.P. Morgan & Co.
    Incorporated.
Guardforce Limited, **45** 378
Guardian Bank, **13** 468
Guardian Federal Savings and Loan
    Association, **10** 91
Guardian Financial Services, 64 171–74
    (upd.)
Guardian Media Group plc, 53 152–55
Guardian Mortgage Company, **8** 460
Guardian Refrigerator Company. *See*
    Frigidaire Home Products.
Guardian Royal Exchange Plc, 11
    168–70; **33** 319. *See also* Guardian
    Financial Services.
Gubor Schokoladen, **15** 221
Gucci Group N.V., 45 343–44; **50**
    212–16 **(upd.)**; **54** 320; **57** 179
Guccio Gucci, S.p.A., 12 281; **15**
    198–200; **27** 329; **57** 180
GUD Holdings, Ltd., **17** 106; **61** 66
Gudang Garam Tbk, PT, **62** 96–97
Guerbet Group, 46 214–16
Guerdon Homes, Inc., **41** 19
Guerlain, 23 240–42; **33** 272
Guess, Inc., 15 201–03; **17** 466; **23** 309;
    24 157; **27** 329; **68** 187–91 **(upd.)**
Guest, Keen and Nettlefolds plc. *See* GKN
    plc.
Guest Supply, Inc., 18 215–17
Guida, **63** 151
Guidant Corporation, 30 316; **37** 39; **43**
    351; **58** 149–51
Guideoutdoors.com Inc., **36** 446
Guilbert S.A., 42 169–71; **55** 355
Guild Press, Inc., **13** 559
Guild Wineries, **13** 134; **34** 89
Guilford Industries, **8** 270–72
Guilford Mills Inc., 8 234–36; **40** 224–27
    (upd.)
Guilford of Maine, Inc., **29** 246
Guilford Transportation Industries, Inc., **16**
    348, 350
Guillemot Corporation, 41 188–91, 407,
    409
Guillin. *See* Groupe Guillin SA
Guinness Mahon, **36** 231
Guinness Overseas Ltd., **25** 281
Guinness Peat Aviation, **10** 277; **36** 426
Guinness plc, I 250–52; **10** 268, 272, 282; **II**
    610; **9** 100, 449; **10** 399; **13** 454; **18** 62,
    501; **29** 84; **33** 276; **36** 405–06. *See also*
    Diageo plc.
Guinness/UDV, 43 212–16 **(upd.)**; **61**
    324–25
Guitar Center, Inc., 29 221–23; **68**
    192–95 **(upd.)**
Guittard Chocolate Company, 55
    183–85
Guizhou Tyres Inc., **71** 393
Gulco Industries, Inc., **11** 194
Gulf + Western Inc., I 451–53; **IV** 672;
    7 64; **10** 482; **13** 121, 169, 470; **25** 328,
    535; **33** 3; **41** 71; **51** 165
Gulf + Western Industries. *See* Paramount
    Communications.
Gulf Air Company, 27 25; **39** 137–38; **56**
    146–48
Gulf Canada Ltd., **I** 262, 264; **IV** 721; **6**
    478; **9** 391; **13** 557–58

Gulf Canada Resources Ltd., **63** 110
Gulf Coast Sportswear Inc., **23** 65
Gulf Energy Development, **22** 107
Gulf Engineering Co. Ltd., **IV** 131
Gulf Island Fabrication, Inc., 44 201–03
Gulf Marine & Maintenance Offshore
    Service Company, **22** 276
Gulf Oil Chemical Co., **13** 502
Gulf Oil Corp. *See* Chevron.
Gulf Power Company, **38** 446, 448
Gulf Printing Company, **70** 67
Gulf Public Service Company, Inc, **6** 580;
    37 89
Gulf Resources & Chemical Corp., **15** 464
Gulf States Steel, **I** 491
Gulf States Utilities Company, 6 495–97;
    12 99
GulfMark Offshore, Inc., 49 180–82
Gulfstream Aerospace Corporation, 7
    205–06; **13** 358; **24** 465; **28** 169–72
    (upd.); **36** 190–91
Gulfwind Marine USA, **30** 303
Gulistan Holdings Inc., **28** 219
Gulton Industries Inc., **7** 297; **19** 31
Gum Base Asia Ltd., **72** 272
Gump's, **7** 286
Gunder & Associates, **12** 553
Gunderson, Inc. *See* The Greenbrier
    Companies.
Gunfred Group, **I** 387
Gunite Corporation, 23 306; **51** 152–55
The Gunlocke Company, 12 299; **13** 269;
    23 243–45
Gunnebo AB, 53 156–58
Gunnite, **27** 203
Gunther, S.A., **8** 477
Gupta, **15** 492
Gurwitch Bristow Products, LLC, **49** 285
GUS plc, 47 165–70 **(upd.)**; **54** 38, 40
Gustav Schickendanz KG. *See* Karstadt
    Quelle AG.
Gustin-Bacon Group, **16** 8
Guthy-Renker Corporation, 32 237–40
Gutteridge, Haskins & Davey, **22** 138
Gutzeit. *See* W. Gutzeit & Co.
Guy Degrenne SA, 44 204–07
Guy Motors, **13** 286
Guy Pease Associates, **34** 248
Guyenne et Gascogne, 23 246–48
Guyomarc'h, **39** 356
GVN Technologies, **63** 5
GW Utilities Ltd., **I** 264; **6** 478
Gwathmey Siegel & Associates
    Architects LLC, 26 186–88
GWC. *See* General Waterworks
    Corporation.
GWK GmbH, **45** 378
GWR Group plc, 39 198–200
Gymboree Corporation, 15 204–06; **69**
    198–201 **(upd.)**
Gynecare Inc., **23** 190
Gynetics, Inc., **26** 31

H&D. *See* Hinde & Dauch Paper
    Company.
H&D Holdings, **64** 79
H&H Craft & Floral, **17** 322
H & H Plastics Co., **25** 312
H & R Block, Incorporated, 9 268–70;
    25 434; **27** 106, 307; **29** 224–28 **(upd.)**;
    48 234, 236; **52** 316
H.B. Fenn and Company Ltd., **25** 485
H.B. Fuller Company, 8 237–40; **32**
    254–58 **(upd.)**

H.B. Nickerson & Sons Ltd., **14** 339
H.B. Tuttle and Company, **17** 355
H.B. Viney Company, Inc., **11** 211
H. Berlind Inc., **16** 388
H.C. Prange Co., **19** 511–12
H Curry & Sons. *See* Currys Group PLC.
H.D. Lee Company, Inc. *See* Lee Apparel Company, Inc.
H.D. Vest, Inc., 46 217–19
H. Douglas Barclay, **8** 296
H.E. Butt Grocery Company, 13 251–53; 32 259–62 (upd.); 33 307
H.E. Moss and Company Tankers Ltd., **23** 161
H.F. Ahmanson & Company, II 181–82; 10 342–44 (upd.); 28 167; **47** 160
H.F.T. Industrial Ltd., **62** 150
H.G. Anderson Equipment Corporation, **6** 441
H. Gringoire S.A.R.L., 70 234
H.H. Brown Shoe Company, **18** 60, **18** 62
H.H. Cutler Company, **17** 513
H.H. Robertson, Inc., **19** 366
H.H. West Co., **25** 501
H.I.G. Capital L.L.C., **30** 235
H.J. Heinz Company, II 450, 507–09, 547; 7 382, 448, 576, 578; **8** 499; **10** 151; **11 171–73 (upd.); 12** 411, 529, 531–32; **13** 383; **21** 55, 500–01; **22** 147; **25** 517; **27** 197–98; **33** 446–49; **36 253–57 (upd.); 43** 217–18
H.J. Justin & Sons. *See* Justin Industries, Inc.
H.J. Russell & Company, 66 162–65
H.K. Ferguson Company, **7** 355
H.K. Porter Company, Inc., **19** 152
H.L. Green Company, Inc., **9** 448
H.L. Yoh Company. *See* Day & Zimmerman, Inc.
H. Lewis and Sons, **14** 294
H. Lundbeck A/S, 44 208–11
H.M. Byllesby & Company, Inc., **6** 539
H.M. Payson & Co., 69 202–04
H.M. Spalding Electric Light Plant, **6** 592; **50** 37
H. Miller & Sons, Inc., **11** 258
H N Norton Co., **11** 208
H.O. Houghton & Company, **10** 355
H.O. Systems, Inc., **47** 430
H-P. *See* Hewlett-Packard Co.
H.P. Foods, **II** 475
H.P. Hood, **7** 17–18
H.S. Trask & Co. *See* Phoenix Footware Group, Inc.
H. Salt Fish and Chips, **13** 320
H. Samuel Plc, **61** 326
H.T. Cherry Company, **12** 376
H.W. Johns Manufacturing Co. *See* Manville Corp.
H.W. Madison Co., **11** 211
H.W.S. Solutions, **21** 37
The H.W. Wilson Company, 17 152; **23** 440; **66 166–68**
H. Williams and Co., Ltd., **II** 678
Ha-Lo Industries, Inc., 27 193–95
Häagen-Dazs, **II** 631; **10** 147; **14** 212, 214; **19** 116; **24** 140, 141
Haake-Beck Brauerei AG, **9** 86
Haan Crafts Corporation, **62** 18
Haas, Baruch & Co. *See* Smart & Final, Inc.
Haas Publishing Companies, Inc., **22** 442
Haas Wheat & Partners, **15** 357; **65** 258–59

Habersham Bancorp, 25 185–87
Habitat for Humanity International, 36 258–61
Habitat/Mothercare PLC. *See* Storehouse PLC.
Hach Co., **14** 309; **18 218–21**
Hachette Filipacchi Medias S.A., 21 265–67; 33 310
Hachette S.A., **IV 617–19; 10** 288; **11** 293; **12** 359; **16** 253–54; **17** 399; **21** 266; **22** 441–42; **23** 476; **43** 210. *See also* Matra-Hachette S.A.
Haci Omer Sabanci Holdings A.S., 55 186–89
Hacker-Pschorr Brau, **35** 331
Hackman Oyj Adp, 44 204, **212–15**
Hadco Corporation, 24 201–03
Haemocell, **11** 476
Haemonetics Corporation, 20 277–79
Haftpflichtverband der Deutschen Industrie Versicherung auf Gegenseitigkeit V.a.G. *See* HDI (Haftpflichtverband der Deutschen Industrie Versicherung auf Gegenseitigkeit V.a.G.).
Hagemeyer N.V., 18 180–82; **39 201–04; 45** 426; **54** 203
Hagemeyer North America, **63** 289
Haggar Corporation, 19 194–96; 24 158
Haggen Inc., 38 221–23
Hägglunds Vehicle AB, **47** 7, 9
Hahn Automotive Warehouse, Inc., 24 204–06
Hahn Department Stores. *See* Allied Stores Corp.
Hahn, Inc., **17** 9
Haier Group Corporation, 65 167–70
Haile Mines, Inc., **12** 253
The Hain Celestial Group, Inc., 43 217–20 (upd.)
Hain Food Group, Inc., I 514; **27** 196–99; **36** 256
Hair Cuttery. *See* Ratner Companies.
Hake Group, Inc. *See* Matrix Service Company.
Hakone Tozan Railway Co., Ltd., **68** 281
Hakuhodo, Inc., 6 29–31; 16 167; **42 172–75 (upd.)**
Hakunetsusha & Company, **12** 483
HAL Inc., 9 271–73. *See also* Hawaiian Airlines, Inc.
Hale and Dorr, **31** 75
Hale-Halsell Company, 60 157–60
Haleko Hanseatisches Lebensmittel Kontor GmbH, **29** 500
Halewood, **21** 246
Half Price Books, Records, Magazines Inc., 37 179–82
Halfords Ltd., **24** 75
Halkin Holdings plc, **49** 338–39
Hall Bros. Co. *See* Hallmark Cards, Inc.
Hall, Kinion & Associates, Inc., 52 150–52
Hall Laboratories, Inc., **45** 209
Hall-Mark Electronics, **23** 490
La Halle aux Chaussures, **17** 210
Haller, Raymond & Brown, Inc., **II** 10
Hallhuber GmbH, **63** 361, 363
Halliburton Company, III 473, **497–500, 617; 11** 505; **13** 118–19; **17** 417; **25 188–92 (upd.); 55 190–95 (upd.); 59** 378; **62** 201
Hallmark Cards, Inc., IV 620–21; 7 23–25; **12** 207, 209; **16 255–57 (upd.),** 427; **18** 67, 69, 213; **21** 426–28; **22** 33,

36; **24** 44, 516–17; **25** 69, 71, 368; **28** 160; **29** 64; **39** 87; **40 228–32 (upd.); 45** 131; **59** 34, 35, 37
Hallmark Chemical Corp., **8** 386
Hallmark Holdings, Inc., **51** 190
Hallmark Investment Corp., **21** 92
Hallmark Residential Group, Inc., **45** 221
Halo Lighting, **30** 266
Haloid Company. *See* Xerox Corporation.
Halsam Company, **25** 380
Halstead Industries, **26** 4; **52** 258
Halter Marine, **22** 276
Hambrecht & Quist Group, **10** 463, 504; **26** 66; **27** 447; **31** 349
Hambro American Bank & Trust Co., **11** 109
Hambro Countrywide Security, **32** 374
Hambros Bank, **16** 14; **27** 474; **43** 7
Hamburg-Amerikanische-Packetfahrt-Actien-Gesellschaft. *See* Hapag-Lloyd AG.
Hamburgische Electricitaets-Werke AG, **57** 395, 397
Hamelin Group, Inc., **19** 415
Hamer Hammer Service, Inc., **11** 523
Hamersley Holdings, **IV** 59–61
Hamil Textiles Ltd. *See* Algo Group Inc.
Hamilton Beach/Proctor-Silex Inc., 7 369–70; **16** 384; **17 213–15; 24** 435; **43** 289
Hamilton Group Limited, **15** 478
Hamilton Industries, Inc., **25** 261
Hamilton National Bank, **13** 465
Hamilton Oil Corp., **IV** 47; **22** 107
Hamilton Standard, **9** 417
Hamilton/Hall-Mark, **19** 313
Hamish Hamilton, **IV** 659; **8** 526
Hammacher Schlemmer & Company Inc., 21 268–70; 72 160–62 (upd.)
Hammarplast, **13** 493
Hammermill Paper Co., **23** 48–49
Hammers Plastic Recycling, **6** 441
Hammerson plc, IV 696–98; 26 420; **40 233–35**
Hammery Furniture Company, **14** 302–03
Hammes Co., **38** 482
Hamming-Whitman Publishing Co., **13** 559
Hampton Industries, Inc., 20 280–82
Hampton Inns, **9** 425–26
Hampton Roads Food, Inc., **25** 389
Hamworthy Engineering Ltd., **31** 367, 369
Han Comm Inc., **62** 174
Hancock Fabrics, Inc., 16 197–99; 18 222–24
Hancock Holding Company, 15 207–09
Hancock Jaffe Laboratories, **11** 460
Hancock Park Associates. *See* Leslie's Poolmart, Inc.
Hancock Textile Co., Inc., **27** 291
Handleman Company, 15 210–12
Handspring Inc., 49 183–86
Handy & Harman, 23 249–52
Handy Andy Home Improvement Centers, Inc., **16** 210; **26** 160–61
Hanes Corp., **8** 202, 288; **25** 166
Hanes Holding Company, **11** 256; **48** 267
Hang Chong, **18** 114
Hang Seng Bank Ltd., 60 161–63
Hanger Orthopedic Group, Inc., 41 192–95
Haniel & Cie. GmbH, **27** 175
Hanjin Group. *See* Korean Ail Lines Co. Ltd.
Hanjin Shipping Co., Ltd., 50 217–21

Hankook Tyre Manufacturing Company, **V** 255–56; **19** 508
Hankuk Glass Industry Co., **III** 715
Hankyu Corporation, **V** 454–56; **23** 253–56 (upd.)
Hankyu Department Stores, Inc., **V** 70–71; **62** 168–71 (upd.)
Hanley Brick, **14** 250
Hanmi Financial Corporation, **66** 169–71
Hanna Andersson Corp., **49** 187–90
Hanna-Barbera Cartoons Inc., **7** 306; **18** 65; **23** 257–59, 387; **25** 313; **33** 432
Hanna Mining Co., **8** 346–47
Hanna Ore Mining Company, **12** 352
Hannaford Bros. Co., **12** 220–22
Hannen Brauerei GmbH, **9** 100
Hannifin Corporation. *See* Parker Hannifin Corporation.
HANNOVER International AG für Industrieversicherungen, **53** 162
Hannover Papier, **49** 353
Hanover Bank. *See* Manufacturers Hanover Corporation.
Hanover Compressor Company, **59** 215–17
Hanover Direct, Inc., **36** 262–65
Hanover Foods Corporation, **35** 211–14
Hanover House, Inc., **24** 154
Hanover Insurance Company, **63** 29
Hansa Linie, **26** 279–80
Hansen Natural Corporation, **31** 242–45
Hansgrohe AG, **56** 149–52
Hansol Paper Co., **63** 315–16
Hanson Building Materials America Inc., **60** 164–66
Hanson Industries, **44** 257
Hanson PLC, **III** 501–03; **7** 207–10 (upd.); **30** 228–32 (upd.)
Hansvedt Industries Inc., **25** 195
Hanwha Group, **62** 172–75
Hapag-Lloyd AG, **6** 397–99; **42** 283
Happy Air Exchangers Ltd., **21** 499
Happy Kids Inc., **30** 233–35
Haralambos Beverage Corporation, **11** 451
Harbert Corporation, **13** 98; **14** 222–23
HARBIN Samick Corp., **56** 300
Harbison-Walker Refractories Company, **24** 207–09
Harbor Group, **41** 262–63
Harborlite Corporation, **10** 45; **60** 16
Harbour Group, **24** 16
Harco, Inc., **37** 31
Harcourt Brace and Co., **12** 223–26
Harcourt Brace Jovanovich, Inc., **IV** 622–24; **7** 312; **12** 224; **13** 106; **14** 177; **19** 404; **25** 177
Harcourt General, Inc., **12** 226; **20** 283–87 (upd.); **25** 178; **49** 286; **57** 15
Harcros Investment Trust Ltd. *See* Harrisons & Crosfield PLC.
Hard Rock Cafe International, Inc., **12** 227–29; **25** 387; **27** 201; **32** 241–45 (upd.); **37** 191; **41** 308; **64** 320
Hardee's Food Systems Inc., **II** 679; **7** 430; **8** 564; **9** 178; **15** 345; **16** 95; **19** 93; **23** 505; **27** 16–18; **46** 98
Hardin Stockton, **21** 96
Harding Lawson Associates Group, Inc., **16** 258–60
Hardinge Inc., **25** 193–95
Hardman Inc., **III** 699
Hardware Wholesalers Inc. *See* Do it Best Corporation.

Hardy Oil & Gas, **34** 75
HARIBO GmbH & Co. KG, **44** 216–19
Harima Shipbuilding & Engineering Co., Ltd., **I** 511; **III** 533
Harken Energy Corporation, **17** 169–70
Harland and Wolff Holdings plc, **19** 197–200
Harlem Globetrotters International, Inc., **7** 199, 335; **61** 122–24
Harlequin Enterprises Limited, **IV** 587, 590, 617, 619, 672; **19** 405; **29** 470–71, 473; **52** 153–56
Harley-Davidson, Inc., **7** 211–14; **13** 513; **16** 147–49; **21** 153; **23** 299–301; **25** 22, 196–200 (upd.); **40** 31
Harleysville Group Inc., **37** 183–86
Harman International Industries Inc., **15** 213–15; **36** 101; **62** 5
Harmon Industries, Inc., **25** 201–04
Harmon Publishing Company, **12** 231
Harmonic Inc., **43** 221–23
Harmony Gold Mining Company Limited, **63** 182–85
Harmsworth Brothers, **17** 396
Harmsworth Publishing, **19** 118, 120
Harnischfeger Industries, Inc., **8** 241–44; **14** 56; **26** 355; **38** 224–28 (upd.)
Harold's Stores, Inc., **22** 248–50
Harp Lager Ltd., **15** 442; **35** 395, 397
Harper Group Inc., **12** 180; **13** 20; **17** 216–19
Harper House, Inc. *See* Day Runner, Inc.
Harper Robinson and Company, **17** 163
HarperCollins Publishers, **14** 555–56; **15** 216–18; **23** 156, 210; **24** 546; **46** 196
Harpers, Inc., **12** 298; **48** 245
Harpo Inc., **28** 173–75; **30** 270; **66** 172–75 (upd.)
Harrah's Entertainment, Inc., **9** 425–27; **16** 261–63; **27** 200; **43** 224–28 (upd.); **62** 195
Harris & Harris Group, **59** 12
Harris Adacom Corporation B.V., **21** 239
Harris Bankcorp, **46** 55
Harris Corporation, **II** 37–39; **11** 46, 286, 490; **20** 288–92 (upd.); **27** 364
Harris-Emery Co., **19** 510
Harris Financial, Inc., **11** 482
Harris InfoSource International, Inc., **61** 83
Harris Interactive Inc., **41** 196–99
Harris Laboratories, **14** 549
Harris Manufacturing Company, **25** 464
Harris Microwave Semiconductors, **14** 417
Harris Moran Seeds Inc. *See* Vilmorin Clause et Cie.
Harris Oil Company, **17** 170
Harris Pharmaceuticals Ltd., **11** 208
Harris Publications, **13** 179
Harris Publishing. *See* Bernard C. Harris Publishing Company, Inc.
Harris Queensway, **24** 269
Harris Teeter Inc., **23** 260–62; **72** 163–66 (upd.)
Harris Transducer Corporation, **10** 319
Harrison Salinson. *See* Posterscope Worldwide.
Harrisons & Crosfield plc, **III** 696–700. *See also* Elementis plc.
Harrods Holdings, , **21** 353; **45** 188; **47** 171–74
Harron Communications Corporation, **52** 9
Harrow Stores Ltd., **II** 677
Harry and David. *See* Bear Creek Corporation.

Harry London Candies, Inc., **70** 110–12
Harry N. Abrams, Inc., **58** 152–55
Harry Winston Inc., **45** 184–87
Harry's Farmers Market Inc., **23** 263–66
Harry's Premium Snacks, **27** 197; **43** 218
Harsah Ceramics, **25** 267
Harsco Corporation, **8** 245–47; **11** 135; **30** 471. *See also* United Defense Industries, Inc.
Harshaw Chemical Company, **9** 154; **17** 363
Hart Press, **12** 25
Hart Schaffner & Marx. *See* Hartmarx Corporation.
Harte & Co., **7** 308
Harte-Hanks Communications, Inc., **17** 220–22; **63** 186–89 (upd.)
Harter Bank & Trust, **9** 474–75
Hartford Container Company, **8** 359
Hartford Electric Light Co., **13** 183
Hartford Financial Services Group, **41** 64
Hartford Fire Insurance, **11** 198
Hartford Group, **63** 47
Hartford Insurance Group, **22** 428
Hartford Life International Ltd., **63** 179
Hartford Machine Screw Co., **12** 344
Hartford National Bank and Trust Co., **13** 396
Hartford National Corporation, **13** 464, 466–67
Hartmann & Braun, **III** 566; **38** 299
Hartmann Elektronik GmbH, **61** 287
Hartmann Fibre, **12** 377
Hartmann Luggage, **12** 313
Hartmarx Corporation, **8** 248–50; **25** 258; **32** 246–50 (upd.)
The Hartstone Group plc, **14** 224–26
The Hartz Mountain Corporation, **12** 230–32; **46** 220–23 (upd.)
Harvard Private Capital Group Inc., **26** 500, 502
Harvard Sports, Inc., **19** 144
Harvard Table Tennis, Inc., **19** 143–44
Harvard Ventures, **25** 358
Harvest Day, **27** 291
Harvest International, **III** 201
Harvest Partners, Inc., **40** 300; **52** 139
Harvest States Cooperative, **64** 307
Harvestore, **11** 5
Harvey & Thompson, **61** 53
Harvey Benjamin Fuller, **8** 237–38
Harvey Group, **19** 312
Harvey Hotel Corporation, **23** 71, 73
Harvey Norman Holdings Ltd., **56** 153–55
Harveys Casino Resorts, **27** 199–201
Harwood Homes, **31** 386
Harza Engineering Company, **14** 227–28
Has.net, **48** 402
Hasbro, Inc., **III** 504–06; **7** 305; **12** 168–69, 495; **13** 561; **16** 264–68 (upd.); **17** 243; **18** 520–21; **21** 375; **25** 313, 380–81, 487–89; **28** 159; **34** 369; **43** 229–34 (upd.); **52** 192–93, 206;
Haskel International, Inc., **59** 218–20
Haslemere Estates, **26** 420
Hasler Holding AG, **9** 32
Hassenfeld Brothers Inc. *See* Hasbro, Inc.
Hasten Bancorp, **11** 371
Hastings Entertainment, Inc., **29** 229–31
Hastings Filters, Inc., **17** 104
Hastings Manufacturing Company, **17** 106; **56** 156–58
Hatch Grinding, **29** 86, 88

Hatersley & Davidson, **16** 80
Hatfield Jewelers, **30** 408
Hatteras Yachts Inc., **45** 175
Hattori Seiko Co., Ltd. *See* Seiko
    Corporation.
HAULOTTE, **51** 295
Hauni Maschinenbau AG, **60** 193
Hauser, Inc., 46 224–27
Hausted, Inc., **29** 451
Havas, SA, 10 195–96, **345–48; 13**
    203–04; **33 178–82 (upd.); 34** 83. *See*
    also Vivendi Universal Publishing
Haverty Furniture Companies, Inc., 31
    246–49
Havertys, **39** 174
Haviland Candy Co., **15** 325
Haw Par Corporation, **56** 362
Hawaii National Bank, **11** 114
Hawaii World, **62** 276
Hawaiian Airlines Inc., 9 271–73; **22**
    251–53 (upd.); 24 20–22; **26** 339. *See*
    also HAL Inc.
Hawaiian Electric Industries, Inc., 9
    274–77
Hawaiian Tug & Barge, **9** 276
Hawk Corporation, 59 221–23
Hawk Model Co., **51** 368
Hawker Siddeley Group Public Limited
    Company, III 507–10; 8 51; **12** 190
Hawkins Chemical, Inc., 16 269–72
Hawley Group Limited, **12** 10
Hawley Products, **16** 20
Haworth Inc., 8 251–52; **27** 434; **39**
    205–08 (upd.)
Hawthorn Company, **8** 287
Hawthorn-Mellody, **11** 25
Hawthorne Appliance and Electronics, **10**
    9–11
Haxton Foods Inc., **21** 155
Hay Group, **42** 329–30
Hayden Clinton National Bank, **11** 180
Hayden Publications, **27** 499
Hayes Aircraft Corp., **54** 283
Hayes Conyngham & Robinson, **24** 75
Hayes Corporation, 24 210–14; 53 381
Hayes Industries Inc., **16** 7
Hayes Lemmerz International, Inc., 27
    202–04
Hayes Microcomputer Products, **9** 515
Hayes Wheel Company, **7** 258
Hayne, Miller & Swearingen, Inc., **22** 202
Haynes Publishing Group P.L.C., 71
    169–71
Hays Plc, 27 205–07
HAZCO International, Inc., **9** 110
Hazel-Atlas Glass Co., **15** 128
Hazelden Foundation, 28 176–79
Hazeltine, Inc., **II** 20
Hazlenut Growers of Oregon, **7** 496–97
Hazleton Laboratories Corp., **30** 151
Hazlewood Foods plc, 32 251–53
Hazzard and Associates, **34** 248
HBO. *See* Home Box Office Inc.
HBOS, **71** 324–26
HCA—The Healthcare Company, 35
    215–18 (upd.)
HCI. *See* Holland Chemical International.
HCI Construction, **61** 125, 127
HCI Direct, Inc., 55 196–98
HCI Distribution Company, **61** 125–26
HCL America, **10** 505
HCL Sybase, **10** 505
HCR Manor Care, **25** 306, 310
HCS Technology, **26** 496–97

HDI (Haftpflichtverband der Deutschen
    Industrie Versicherung auf
    Gegenseitigkeit V.a.G.), **53** 159–63
HDM Worldwide Direct, **13** 204; **16** 168
HDOS Enterprises, 72 167–69
HdP. *See* Holding di Partecipazioni
    Industriali S.p.A.
HDR Inc., 48 203–05
HDS. *See* Heartland Express, Inc.
Head N.V., 55 199–201
Head Sportswear International, **15** 368; **16**
    296–97; **43** 374
Headrick Outdoor, **27** 280
Heads and Threads, **10** 43
Headwaters Incorporated, 56 159–62
Headway Corporate Resources, Inc., 40
    236–38
Headway Technologies, Inc., **49** 392–93
Heald Machine Co., **12** 67
Healing Arts Publishing, Inc., **41** 177
Healix Health Services Inc., **48** 310
Health & Tennis Corp., **25** 40
Health and Diet Group, **29** 212
Health Care & Retirement Corporation,
    22 254–56; **25** 306, 310
Health Care International, **13** 328
Health Communications, Inc., 72 170–73
Health Development Corp., **46** 432
Health Maintenance Organization of
    Pennsylvania. *See* U.S. Healthcare, Inc.
Health Management Associates, Inc., 56
    163–65
Health Management Center West, **17** 559
Health-Mor Inc. *See* HMI Industries.
Health O Meter Products Inc., 14
    229–31; 15 307
Health Plan of America, **11** 379
Health Plan of Virginia, **III** 389
Health Products Inc., **I** 387
Health Risk Management, Inc., 24
    215–17
Health Services Capital Corporation, **64** 27
Health Services, Inc., **10** 160
Health Systems International, Inc., 11
    174–76; 25 527
Healthcare, L.L.C., **29** 412
Healthcare Products Holdings, Inc., **70** 142
HealthCare USA, **59** 139
HealthCo International, Inc., **19** 290
Healthdyne, Inc., **17** 306–09; **25** 82
Healthmagic, Inc., **29** 412
HealthRider Corporation, **38** 238
HealthRite, Inc., **45** 209
Healthshares L.L.C, **18** 370
Healthsource Inc., **22** 143; **45** 104, 109
HealthSouth Corporation, 33 183–86
    (upd.)
HealthSouth Rehabilitation Corporation,
    14 232–34; **25** 111
Healthtex, Inc., 17 223–25, 513
HealthTrust, **III** 80; **15** 112; **35** 215, 217
Healthy Choice, **12** 531
Hearing Aid Specialists Pty Limited, **56**
    338
The Hearst Corporation, IV 625–27; 12
    358–59; **19 201–04 (upd.); 21** 404; **32**
    3; **46 228–32 (upd.); 51** 218–20; **54** 17,
    22, 74; **56** 119
Heartland Components, **III** 519; **22** 282
Heartland Express, Inc., 13 550–51; **18**
    225–27
Heartland Homes, Inc., **41** 19
Heartland Industrial Partners L.P., **41** 94
Heartland Securities Corp., **32** 145

Heartstream Inc., **18** 423
The Heat Group, 53 164–66
Heatcraft Inc., **8** 320–22
Heatilator Inc., **13** 269
Heating & Cooling Supply, Inc., **52**
    398–99
Heavy Duty Parts, Inc., **19** 37
Hebdo Mag International, Inc. *See* Trader
    Classified Media N.V.
Hebei Longteng Paper Corporation, **63** 316
Hechinger Company, 12 233–36; 28 51
Heckett Technology Services Inc., **8**
    246–47
Heckler & Koch GmbH, **24** 88
Hecla Mining Company, 17 363; **20** 149,
    293–96
Hede Nielsen A/S, **47** 219
Heekin Can Inc., 10 130; **13 254–56**
Heery International, Inc., 58 156–59
Hees International Bancorp Inc. *See*
    Brascan Corporation.
HEFCO, **17** 106
Hefei Rongshida Group Corporation, **22**
    350
Hegenscheidt-MFD GmbH & Co. KG, **53**
    352
HEI Investment Corp., **9** 276
HEICO Corporation, 15 380; **30 236–38;**
    66 327
Heide Park, **55** 378
Heidelberger Druckmaschinen AG, 33
    346; **40 239–41**
Heidelberger Zement AG, 23 325–26; **31**
    250–53
Heidelburger Drueck, **III** 301
Heidemij. *See* Arcadis NV.
Heidi Bakery, **II** 633
Heidrick & Struggles International, Inc.,
    14 464; **28 180–82**
Heights of Texas, fsb, **8** 437
Heijmans N.V., 66 176–78
Heil Company, **28** 103
Heileman Brewing Co. *See* G. Heileman
    Brewing Co.
Heilig-Meyers Company, 14 235–37; 23
    412, 414; **40 242–46 (upd.)**
Heim-Plan Unternehmensgruppe, **25** 455
Heimstatt Bauspar AG, **III** 401
Heineken N.V., I 256–58, 266, 288; **II**
    642; **13 257–59 (upd.); 14** 35; **17** 256;
    18 72; **21** 319; **25** 21–22; **26** 305; **34**
    200–04 (upd.); 59 58–59; **63** 229
Heinrich Bauer North America, **7** 42–43
Heinrich Bauer Verlag, **23** 85–86
Heinrich Koppers GmbH, **IV** 89
Heinz Co. *See* H.J. Heinz Company.
Heinz Deichert KG, **11** 95
Heinz Italia S.p.A., **15** 221
Heisey Glasswork Company, **19** 210
Heitman Properties, **60** 184
HEL&P. *See* Houston Electric Light &
    Power Company.
Helados La Menorquina S.A., **22** 515
Helen of Troy Corporation, 18 228–30
Helen's Arts & Crafts, **17** 321
Helena Rubenstein, Inc., **III** 48; **8** 343–44;
    9 201–02; **30** 188; **46** 277
Helene Curtis Industries, Inc., 8 253–54;
    18 217; **22** 487; **28 183–85 (upd.); 32**
    476
Helikopter Services Group AS, **67** 102
Heliotrope Studios, Inc., **39** 396
Helix Biocore, **11** 458
Hella KGaA Hueck & Co., 66 179–83

Hellenic Petroleum SA, 64 175–77
Heller, Ehrman, White & McAuliffe, 41
  200–02
Heller Financial, Inc., **7** 213; **16** 37; **25**
  198; **63** 165
Hellman & Friedman Capital Partners III,
  L.P., **57** 15
Hellman, Haas & Co. *See* Smart & Final,
  Inc.
Helly Hansen ASA, 18 396; **25 205–07**
Helme Products, Inc., **15** 139
Helmerich & Payne, Inc., 18 231–33
Helmsley Enterprises, Inc., 9 278–80; **39**
  209–12 (upd.)
Helmuth Hardekopf Bunker GmbH, **7** 141
Help-U-Sell, Inc., **III** 304
Helzberg Diamonds, 18 60, 63; **40**
  247–49
Hemelinger Aktienbrauerei, **9** 86
Hemex, **11** 458
Hemlo Gold Mines Inc., 9 281–82; **23** 40,
  42
Henderson Brothers Holdings, Inc., **37** 225
Henderson Land Development Company
  Ltd., 70 113–15
Henderson-Union Electric Cooperative, **11**
  37
Henijean & Cie, **III** 283
Henkel KGaA, III 31–34, 45; **9** 382; **13**
  197, 199; **22** 145, 257; **30** 291; **34** 153,
  205–10 (upd.); **51 223–25**
Henkel Manco Inc., 22 257–59
Henkell & Söhnlein Sektkellereien KG, **51**
  102, 105
Henley Drilling Company, **9** 364
The Henley Group, Inc., I 416; **III**
  511–12; **6** 599–600; **9** 298; **11** 435; **12**
  325; **17** 20; **37** 158
Henlys Group plc, **35** 63, 65
Hennes & Mauritz AB, 29 232–34
Hennessy Company, **19** 272
Henney Motor Company, **12** 159
Henningsen Foods, Inc., **57** 202, 204
Henredon Furniture Industries, **III** 571; **11**
  534; **20** 362; **39** 266
Henri Bendel Inc., **17** 203–04
Henry Broderick, Inc., **21** 96
Henry Denny & Sons, **27** 259
Henry Gordy International, Inc. *See* EXX
  Inc.
Henry Holt & Co., **IV** 622–23; **13** 105; **27**
  223; **35** 451
Henry I. Siegel Co., **20** 136
Henry J. Kaiser Company, Ltd., **28** 200
Henry J. Tully Corporation, **13** 531
The Henry Jones Co-op Ltd., **7** 577
Henry Jones Foods, **7** 182; **11** 212
Henry L. Doherty & Company, **12** 542
Henry Lee Company, **16** 451, 453
Henry, Leonard & Thomas Inc., **9** 533
Henry Meadows, Ltd., **13** 286
Henry Modell & Company Inc., 32
  263–65
Henry Pratt Company, **7** 30–31
Henry S. Miller Companies, **21** 257
Henry Schein, Inc., 29 298; **31 254–56;**
  70 116–19 (upd.)
Henry Willis & Co. *See* Willis Corroon
  Group Plc.
Hensel Phelps Construction Company,
  72 174–77
Hensley & Company, 64 178–80
HEPCO. *See* Hokkaido Electric Power
  Company Inc.

Hepworth plc, **44** 438
Her Majesty's Stationery Office, 7
  215–18
Heraclio Fournier S.A., **62** 383–84
Heraeus Holding GmbH, IV 98–100,
  118; **54 159–63 (upd.)**
Heraeus Surgical, Inc., **67** 228
Herald Publishing Company, **12** 150
Heralds of Liberty, **9** 506
Herbalife International, Inc., 17 226–29;
  18 164; **41 203–06 (upd.)**
Herbert Clough Inc., **24** 176
Herbert W. Davis & Co., **III** 344
Herby's Foods, **36** 163
Herco Technology, **IV** 680
Hercules Inc., I 343–45, 347; **19** 11; **22**
  260–63 (upd.); **28** 195; **30** 36; **66**
  184–88 (upd.)
Hercules Offshore Drilling, **28** 347–48
Hereford Paper and Allied Products Ltd.,
  14 430
Herff Jones, **25** 254
Heritage Bankcorp, **9** 482
Heritage Federal Savings and Loan
  Association of Huntington, **10** 92
Heritage House of America Inc. *See*
  Humana Inc.
Heritage Media Group, **25** 418
Heritage Springfield, **14** 245
Heritage 21 Construction, **60** 56
Herley Industries, Inc., 33 187–89
Herman Goelitz, Inc., 28 186–88
Herman Miller, Inc., 8 251–52, **255–57;**
  39 205–07
Herman's World of Sports, **II** 628–29; **15**
  470; **16** 457; **43** 385
Hermann Pfauter Group, **24** 186
Hermès International S.A., 14 238–40;
  34 211–14 (upd.); **49** 83
Hermosillo, **51** 389
Héroux-Devtek Inc., 69 205–07
Herrburger Brooks P.L.C., **12** 297
Herrick, Waddell & Reed. *See* Waddell &
  Reed, Inc.
Herring-Hall-Marvin Safe Co. of Hamilton,
  Ohio, **7** 145
Hershey Foods Corporation, II 510–12;
  7 300; **11** 15; **12** 480–81; **15** 63–64,
  219–22 (upd.), 323; **27** 38–40; **30**
  208–09; **51 156–60 (upd.)**; **53** 241
F.N. Herstal. *See* Groupe Herstal S.A.
Hertel AG, **13** 297
Hertie Waren- und Kaufhaus GmbH, V
  72–74; 19 234, 237
Herts Pharmaceuticals, **17** 450; **41** 375–76
The Hertz Corporation, I 130; **9 283–85;**
  10 419; **11** 494; **16** 379; **21** 151; **22** 524;
  24 409; **25** 143; **33 190–93 (upd.)**; **36**
  215; **64** 128
Hertz-Penske Leasing. *See* Penske
  Corporation.
Hervillier, **27** 188
Heska Corporation, 39 213–16
Hespeler Hockey Inc., **22** 204
Hess. *See* Amerada Hess Corporation.
Hess Department Stores Inc., **16** 61–62; **19**
  323–24; **41** 343; **50** 107
Hesse Newman & Co. AG, **72** 21
Hesston Corporation, **13** 17; **22** 380
Hetteen Hoist & Derrick. *See* Polaris
  Industries Inc.
Heublein Inc., I 259–61, 281; **7** 266–67;
  14 214; **21** 314–15; **24** 140; **25** 177; **31**
  92; **34** 89

Heuer. *See* TAG Heuer International SA.
Heuga Holdings B.V., **8** 271
Hewden Stuart PLC. *See* Finning
  International Inc.
Hewitt & Tuttle, **17** 355–56
Hewlett-Packard Company, III 142–43;
  6 237–39 (upd.); **28 189–92 (upd.)**; **50**
  222–30 (upd.); **51** 150; **63** 33, 125, 153
Hexal AG, 69 208–10
Hexalon, **26** 420
Hexcel Corporation, 11 475; **27** 50; **28**
  193–95
Heyer-Schulte, **26** 286
Heytesbury Party Ltd., **34** 422
HFC. *See* Household Finance Corporation.
HFS Inc., **21** 97; **22** 54, 56; **53** 275
HG Hawker Engineering Co. Ltd. *See*
  Hawker Siddeley Group PLC.
HGCC. *See* Hysol Grafil Composite
  Components Co.
HH Finch Ltd., **38** 501
HI. *See* Houston Industries Incorporated.
Hi-Bred Corn Company, **9** 410
Hi-Flier, Inc. *See* EXX Inc.
Hi-Lo Automotive, Inc., **26** 348–49
Hi Tech Consignments, **18** 208
Hi-Tek Polymers, Inc., **8** 554
Hibbett Sporting Goods, Inc., 26 189–91;
  70 120–23 (upd.)
Hibbing Taconite Company, **62** 74
Hibernia Corporation, 37 187–90
Hichens Harrison Ltd. *See* Sanlam Ltd.
Hickman Coward & Wattles, **24** 444
Hickory Farms, Inc., 12 178, 199; **17**
  230–32
Hickory Specialties, Inc., **63** 69, 71
Hickorycraft, **III** 571; **20** 362
Hicks & Greist, **6** 40
Hicks, Muse, Tate & Furst, Inc., **24** 106;
  30 220; **36** 423; **55** 202
Hicksgas Gifford, Inc., **6** 529
Hidden Creek Industries, Inc., **16** 397; **24**
  498
HiFi Buys, **30** 465
Higgs International Ltd., **51** 130
High Integrity Systems, **51** 16
High Retail System Co. *See* Takashimaya
  Co., Limited.
Highgate Hotels, Inc., **21** 93
Highland Distillers Ltd., **60** 355
Highland Gold Ltd., **63** 182, 184
Highland Superstores, **9** 65–66; **10** 9–10,
  304–05, 468; **23** 51–52
Highland Telephone Company, **6** 334
Highlander Publications, **38** 307–08
Highmark Inc., I 109; **27 208–11**
Highsmith Inc., 60 167–70
Highteam Public Relations Co. Ltd., **60**
  143
Highveld Steel and Vanadium
  Corporation Limited, 59 224–27
Hilbun Poultry, **10** 250
Hildebrandt International, 29 235–38
Hilex Poly Co., Inc., **8** 477
Hill & Knowlton Inc. *See* WPP Group
  PLC.
Hill 50 Ltd., **63** 182, 184
Hill-Rom Company, **10** 349–50
Hill's Pet Nutrition, Inc., 14 123; **26** 207;
  27 212–14, 390. *See also* Colgate-
  Palmolive Company.
Hillard Oil and Gas Company, Inc., **11** 523
Hillards, PLC, **II** 678

Hillenbrand Industries, Inc., 10 349–51;
16 20
Hiller Aircraft Company, **9** 205; **48** 167
Hiller Group, **14** 286
Hillerich & Bradsby Company, Inc., 24
403; **51 161–64**
The Hillhaven Corporation, **14 241–43;**
16 57, 515, 517; **25** 456
Hillos GmbH, **53** 169
Hills & Dales Railway Co. *See* Dayton
Power & Light Company.
Hills Brothers Inc. *See* Nestlé S.A.
Hills Pet Products, **III** 25
Hills Stores Company, 11 228; **13**
260–61; 21 459; **30** 57
Hillsborough Holdings Corporation. *See*
Walter Industries, Inc.
Hillsdale Machine & Tool Company, **8** 514
Hillsdown Holdings, PLC, II 513–14; 24
218–21 (upd.); 28 490; **41** 252
Hillside Industries Inc., **18** 118
Hilo Electric Light Company, **9** 276
Hilti AG, 53 167–69
Hilton Athletic Apparel, **16** 296–97
Hilton Group plc, 49 191–95 (upd.),
449–50
Hilton Hotels Corporation, III 91–93; 9
95, 426; **19 205–08 (upd.); 21** 91, 93,
182, 333, 363; **23** 482; **27** 10; **54**
345–46; **62 176–79 (upd.)**. *See also*
Hilton Group plc.
Himley Brick, **14** 248
Himolene, Inc., **8** 181
Hinde & Dauch Paper Company, **19** 496
Hinds, Hayden & Eldredge, **10** 135
Hines Horticulture, Inc., 49 196–98
Hino Motors, Ltd., 7 219–21; 21 163,
271–74 (upd.); 23 288
HIP Health Plan, **22** 425
Hipercor, S.A.; **V** 52; **26** 129
Hiram Walker Resources Ltd., I 262–64;
6 478; **18** 41
Hiram Walker-Consumers' Home Ltd. *See*
Consumers' Gas Company Ltd.
Hiram Walker-Gooderham & Worts Ltd.,
29 18
Hire-Purchase Company of Ireland, **16** 13;
43 7
Hiroshima Yakult Co., **25** 449
The Hirsh Company, **17** 279
Hirth-Krause Company. *See* Wolverine
World Wide Inc.
Hirz, **25** 85
Hispanic Broadcasting Corporation, 35
219–22; 41 383, 385
Hispanoil. *See* Hispanica de Petroleos.
History Book Club, **13** 105–06
Hit de Venezuela, **54** 73
HIT Entertainment PLC, 40 250–52
Hit or Miss. *See* The TJX Companies, Inc.
Hitachi, Ltd., I 454–55; III 140, 143,
464, 482; **7** 425; **9** 297; **11** 45, 308; **12**
237–39 (upd.); 14 201; **16** 139; **17** 353,
556; **18** 383; **19** 11; **21** 174–75, 390; **23**
53; **24** 324; **40 253–57 (upd.)**
Hitachi Metals, Ltd., IV 101–02
Hitachi Zosen Corporation, III 513–14;
8 449; **53 170–73 (upd.)**
Hitchiner Manufacturing Co., Inc., 23
267–70
Hi3G, **63** 208
Hjalmar Blomqvist A.B., **II** 639
HL&P. *See* Houston Lighting and Power
Company.

HLH Products, **7** 229
HMI Industries, Inc., 17 233–35
HMO-PA. *See* U.S. Healthcare, Inc.
HMSHost Corp., **49** 31; **63** 322
HMT Technology Corp., **IV** 102
HMV Group plc, 59 228–30; 64 304
Ho-Chunk Inc., 61 125–28
Hoan Products Ltd. *See* Lifetime Hoan
Corporation.
HOB Entertainment, Inc., 37 191–94
Hobart Corporation. *See* KitchenAid, Inc;
Whirlpool Corporation.
Hobart Manufacturing Company, **8** 298
Hobby Lobby Stores Inc., **17** 360
Hobson, Bates & Partners, Ltd., **14** 48
Hochschild, Kohn Department Stores, **II**
673
Hochtief AG, 14 298; **17** 376; **24** 88; **33**
194–97
The Hockey Company, 34 215–18; 70
124–26
Hocking Glass Company, **13** 40
Hockleys Professional Limited, **55** 281
Hodenpyl-Walbridge & Company, **14** 134
Hodgart Consulting. *See* Hildebrandt
International.
Hoechst AG, I 346–48, 605, 632, 669–70;
8 262, 451–53; **13** 262–64; **18 234–37**
(upd.), 401; **21** 544; **22** 32; **25** 376; **34**
284; **35** 455–57; **38** 380; **50** 420; **60** 132
Hoechst Celanese Corporation, 8 562; **11**
436; **12** 118; **13** 118, **262–65; 22** 278;
24 151; **26** 108; **54** 51–52
Hoeganaes Corporation, **8** 274–75
Hoenig Group Inc., 41 207–09
Hoesch AG, IV 103–06
Hofbräubierzentrale GmbH Saarbrücken,
41 222
Hoffman Enclosures Inc., **26** 361, 363
Hoffmann-La Roche & Co. *See* F.
Hoffmann- La Roche & Co.
Hoffritz, **27** 288
Hofmann Herbold & Partner, **34** 249
Hogan & Hartson L.L.P., 44 220–23; 47
445–46
Hogatron, **60** 364
Hogue Cellars, **50** 520
Hohner. *See* Matth. Hohner AG.
Hojalata y Laminas S.A., **19** 10
Hojgaard & Schultz, **38** 436
HOK Group, Inc., 59 231–33
Hokkaido Electric Power Company Inc.
(HEPCO), V 635–37; 58 160–63
(upd.)
Hokuriku Electric Power Company, V
638–40
Hokuyo Sangyo Co., Ltd., **IV** 285
Holberg Industries, Inc., 36 266–69
Holbrook Grocery Co., **II** 682
Holcemca B.V., **51** 29
Holcim, Ltd., **51** 27, 29; **59** 111, 115
Holco BV, **41** 12
Holcroft & Company, **7** 521
Hold Everything, **17** 548–50
Holden Ltd., 62 180–83
Holden Meehan. *See* Bradford & Bingley
PLC.
Holderbank Financière Glaris Ltd., III
701–02; **8** 258–59, 456; **39** 217. *See*
also Holnam Inc
Holding di Partecipazioni Industriali
S.p.A., **52** 120, 122
N.V. Holdingmaatschappij De Telegraaf,
23 271–73

Holec Control Systems, **26** 496
Holes-Webway Company, **40** 44
Holga, Inc., **13** 269
Holgate Toys, **25** 379–80
Holiday Corp., **16** 263; **22** 418; **38** 76; **43**
226
Holiday Inns, Inc., III 94–95; 9 425–26;
10 12; **11** 178, 242; **13** 362; **14** 106; **15**
44, 46; **16** 262; **18** 216; **21** 361–62; **23**
71; **24** 253; **25** 386; **27** 21. *See also* The
Promus Cos., Inc.
Holiday Magic, Inc., **17** 227
Holiday Mart, **17** 124; **41** 114–15
Holiday Rambler Corporation, **7** 213; **25**
198
Holiday RV Superstores, Incorporated,
26 192–95
Holland & Barrett, **13** 103; **31** 346, 348
Holland & Holland, **49** 84
Holland & Knight LLP, 60 171–74
Holland America Line. *See* Carnival
Corporation.
Holland Burgerville USA, 44 224–26
Holland Casino, **23** 229
Holland Chemical International, **59** 391
Holland Electro B.V., **17** 234
Holland Graphic Occasions, **64** 226
Holland Motor Express, **14** 505
Holland Studio Craft, **38** 402
Holland Sweetener Company V.O.F. *See*
Tosoh Corporation.
Hollander Home Fashions Corp., 67
207–09
Hollandse Signaalapparaten, **13** 402; **50**
300
Holley Performance Products Inc., 52
157–60
Hollinger Hardware Limited. *See* Home
Hardware Stores Limited.
Hollinger International Inc., 24 222–25;
32 358; **62 184–88 (upd.)**
Hollingsead International, Inc., **36** 158–60
Holloway-Staubach Corporation. *See* The
Staubach Company.
Holly Corporation, 12 240–42; 61 117
Holly Farms Corp., **7** 422–24; **23** 376–77
Holly Sugar Company. *See* Imperial Holly
Corporation.
Hollywood Casino Corporation, 21
275–77
Hollywood Entertainment Corporation,
25 208–10; 29 504; **31** 339
Hollywood Media Corporation, 58
164–68
Hollywood Park, Inc., 20 297–300
Hollywood Park Race Track, **29** 118
Hollywood Pictures, **II** 174; **30** 487
Holme Roberts & Owen LLP, 28 196–99
Holmen AB, 52 161–65 (upd.)
Holmes International. *See* Miller Industries,
Inc.
Holnam Inc., III 702; **8 258–60; 39**
217–20 (upd.)
Holophane Corporation, 19 209–12; 54
255
Holson Burnes Group, Inc., 14 244–45
Holsten Brauerei AG, **35** 256, 258
Holt and Bugbee Company, 66 189–91
Holt, Rinehart and Winston, Inc., **IV**
623–24; **12** 224
Holt's Cigar Holdings, Inc., 42 176–78
Holthouse Furniture Corp., **14** 236
Holtzbrinck. *See* Verlagsgruppe Georg von
Holtzbrinck.

Holvick Corp., **11** 65

Holvis AG, **15** 229

Holyman Sally Ltd., **29** 431

Holyoke Food Mart Inc., **19** 480

Holzer and Co., **III** 569; **20** 361

Homart Development Co., **57** 156

Homasote Company, 72 178–81

Home & Automobile Insurance Co., **III** 214

Home and Community Care, Inc., **43** 46

Home Box Office Inc., 7 222–24, 528–29; **10** 196; **18** 65; **23** 274–77 **(upd.)**, 500; **25** 498

Home Builders Supply, Inc. *See* Scotty's, Inc.

Home Centers of America, Inc., **18** 286

Home Choice Holdings, Inc., **33** 366–67

The Home Depot, Inc., V 75–76; **18** **238–40 (upd.)**; **19** 248, 250; **21** 356, 358; **22** 477; **23** 232; **26** 306; **27** 416, 481; **31** 20; **35** 11–13; **39** 134; **43** 385; **44** 332–33

Home Entertainment of Texas, Inc., **30** 466

Home Hardware Stores Ltd., 62 189–91

Home Insurance Company, III 262–64

Home Interiors & Gifts, Inc., 15 475, 477; **55** 202–04

Home Nutritional Services, **17** 308

Home Office Reference Laboratory, Inc., **22** 266

Home Products International, Inc., 18 492; **55** 205–07

Home Properties Co., Inc., **21** 95

Home Properties of New York, Inc., 42 **179–81**

Home Quarters Warehouse, Inc., **12** 233, 235

Home Savings of America, **16** 346; **28** 167; **47** 160

The Home School, Inc., **41** 111

Home Shopping Network, Inc., V 77–78; **9** 428; **18** 76; **24** 517; **25** 211–15 **(upd.)**; **26** 441; **33** 322. *See also* HSN.

Home Telephone and Telegraph Company, **10** 201

Home Telephone Company. *See* Rochester Telephone Corporation.

Home Vision Entertainment Inc., **31** 339–40

HomeBase, Inc., II 658; **13** 547–48; **33** **198–201 (upd.)**

HomeBuyers Preferred, Inc., **51** 210

HomeChef, Inc. *See* Viking Range Corporation.

HomeClub Inc. *See* HomeBase, Inc.

HomeFed Bank, **10** 340

Homegrocer.com Inc., **38** 223

Homelite, **21** 175

Homemade Ice Cream Company, **10** 371

Homemakers Furniture. *See* John M. Smyth Co.

HomeMax, Inc., **41** 20

Homes By Oakwood, Inc., **15** 328

Homeserve.net Ltd., **46** 72

Homestake Mining Company, 12 **243–45; 38** 229–32 **(upd.)**

Hometown Auto Retailers, Inc., 44 **227–29**

HomeTown Buffet, Inc. *See* Buffets, Inc

Homette Corporation, **30** 423

Homewood Suites, **9** 425–26

Hominal Developments Inc., **9** 512

Hon Hai Precision Industry Co., Ltd., 59 **234–36**

Hon Industries Inc., 13 266–69; **23** 243–45

Honam Oil Refinery, **II** 53

Honda Giken Kogyo Kabushiki Kaisha. *See* Honda Motor Company Limited.

Honda Motor Company Limited, I **174–76; 10** 352–54 **(upd.)**; **29** 239–42 **(upd.)**; **34** 305–06; **36** 243; **55** 326; **59** 393–94, 397

Honey Bear Tree. *See* Furth Pharmacy. Inc.

Honeywell Inc., II 40–43; **12** 246–49 **(upd.)**; **50** 231–35 **(upd.)**; **63** 161

Hong Kong Dragon Airlines Ltd., 18 114; **66** 192–94

Hong Kong Fortune, **62** 63

Hong Kong Industrial Co., Ltd., **25** 312

Hong Kong Island Line Co., **IV** 718

Hong Kong Mass Transit Railway Corp., **19** 111

Hong Kong Ming Wah Shipping Co., **52** 80

Hong Kong Resort Co., **IV** 718; **38** 320

Hong Kong Telecommunications Ltd., 6 **319–21; 18** 114. *See also* Cable & Wireless HKT.

Hong Kong Telephone Company, **47** 177

Hong Leong Group, **26** 3, 5; **71** 231

Hongkong & Kowloon Wharf & Godown Company, **20** 312

Hongkong and Shanghai Banking **Corporation Limited, II** 296–99; **17** 325; **18** 253; **25** 12. *See also* HSBC Holdings plc.

Hongkong Electric Holdings Ltd., 6 **498–500; 20** 134; **23** 278–81 **(upd.)**; **47** 177

Hongkong Land Holdings Ltd., IV **699–701; 47** 175–78 **(upd.)**

Honolua Plantation Land Company, Inc., **29** 308

Honshu Paper Co., Ltd., IV 284–85, 292, 297, 321, 326; **57** 274–75

Hood Rubber Company, **15** 488–89

Hood Sailmakers, Inc., **10** 215

Hoogovens. *See* Koninklijke Nederlandsche Hoogovens en Staalfabricken NV.

Hook's Drug Stores, **9** 67

Hooker Corp., **19** 324

Hooker Furniture Corp. *See* Bassett Furniture Industries, Inc.

Hooper Holmes, Inc., 22 264–67

Hoorcomfort Nederland B.V., **56** 338

Hoosier Insurance Company, **51** 39

Hoosier Park L.P., **29** 118

Hooters of America, Inc., 18 241–43; **69** 211–14 **(upd.)**

The Hoover Company, 12 158, 250–52; **15** 416, 418; **21** 383; **30** 75, 78; **40** 258–62 **(upd.)**

Hoover Group Inc., **18** 11

Hoover Treated Wood Products, Inc., **12** 396

Hopkinsons Group. *See* Carbo PLC.

Hopkinton LNG Corp., **14** 126

Hopper Soliday and Co. Inc., **14** 154

Hops Restaurant Bar and Brewery, 31 41; **46** 233–36

Hopwood & Company, **22** 427

Horace Mann Educators Corporation, 22 268–70

Horizon Air Industries, Inc. *See* Alaska Air Group, Inc.

Horizon Corporation, **8** 348

Horizon Group Inc., **27** 221

Horizon Healthcare Corporation, **25** 456

Horizon Holidays, **14** 36

Horizon Industries, **19** 275

Horizon Lamps, Inc., **48** 299

Horizon Organic Holding Corporation, 37 195–99

Horizon Travel Group, **8** 527

Horizon/CMS Healthcare Corp., **25** 111, 457; **33** 185

Horizons Laitiers, **25** 85

Hormel Foods Corporation, 18 244–47 **(upd.); 54** 164–69 **(upd.); 59** 102

Horn Venture Partners, **22** 464

Hornbrook, Inc., **14** 112

Horne's, **16** 62

Horsehead Industries, Inc., 51 165–67

Horseshoe Gaming Holding Corporation, 62 192–95

Horsham Corp. *See* TrizecHahn.

Horst Breuer GmbH, **20** 363

Horst Salons Inc., **24** 56

Horten, **47** 107; **50** 117, 119

Hortifrut, S.A., **62** 154

Horton Homes, Inc., 25 216–18

Hoshienu Pharmaceutical Co. Ltd., **58** 134

Hoshino Gakki Co. Ltd., 55 208–11

Hosiery Corporation International. *See* HCI Direct, Inc.

Hospal SA, **49** 156

Hospira, Inc., 71 172–74

Hospital Central Services, Inc., 56 **166–68**

Hospital Corporation of America, III **78–80; 15** 112; **23** 153; **27** 237; **53** 345. *See also* HCA - The Healthcare Company.

Hospital Cost Consultants, **11** 113

Hospital Management Associates, Inc. *See* Health Management Associates, Inc.

Hospital Products, Inc., **10** 534

Hospital Specialty Co., **37** 392

Hospitality Franchise Systems, Inc., 11 **177–79; 14** 106; **17** 236. *See also* Cendant Corporation.

Hospitality Worldwide Services, Inc., 26 **196–98**

Hosposable Products, Inc. *See* Wyant Corporation.

Hoss's Steak and Sea House Inc., 68 **196–98**

Host Communications Inc., **24** 404

Host Marriott Corporation, **21** 366

Host Marriott Services Corp. *See* HMSHost

Hot 'n Now, **16** 96–97

Hot Dog Construction Co., **12** 372

Hot Dog on a Stick. *See* HDOS Enterprises.

Hot Sam Co. *See* Mrs. Fields' Original Cookies, Inc.

Hot Shoppes Inc. *See* Marriott.

Hot Topic, Inc., 33 202–04

Hotel Corporation of America, **16** 337

Hotel Corporation of India, **27** 26

Hotel Properties Ltd., 71 175–77

Hotel Reservations Network, Inc., **47** 420

Hotels By Pleasant, **62** 276

HotJobs.com, Ltd. *See* Yahoo! Inc.

HotRail Inc., **36** 124

HotWired, **45** 200

Houbigant, **37** 270

Houchens Industries Inc., 51 168–70

Houghton Mifflin Company, 10 355–57; **26** 215; **36** 270–74 **(upd.); 46** 441

Houlihan's Restaurant Group, **25** 546

Housatonic Power Co., **13** 182
House of Blues, **32** 241, 244
House of Fabrics, Inc., 16 197–98; **18**
223; **21 278–80**
House of Fraser PLC, 21 353; **37** 6, 8; **45**
188–91; 47 173. *See also* Harrods
Holdings.
House of Miniatures, **12** 264
House of Windsor, Inc., **9** 533
Household International, Inc., II 417–20,
605; **7** 569–70; **8** 117; **10** 419; **16**
487–88; **21 281–86 (upd.); 22** 38, 542;
24 152
Household Rental Systems, **17** 234
Housing Development Finance
Corporation, **20** 313
Housmex Inc., **23** 171
Houston Airport Leather Concessions LLC,
58 369
Houston, Effler & Partners Inc., **9** 135
Houston Electric Light & Power Company,
44 368
Houston Industries Incorporated, V
641–44; 7 376. *See also* Reliant Energy
Inc.
Houston International Teleport, Inc., **11**
184
Houston Oil & Minerals Corp., **11** 440–41
Houston Pipe Line Company, **45** 21
Hoveringham Group, **III** 753; **28** 450
Hoving Corp., **14** 501
Hovnanian Enterprises, Inc., 29 243–45
Howard B. Stark Candy Co., **15** 325
Howard Flint Ink Company, **13** 227
Howard H. Sweet & Son, Inc., **14** 502
Howard Hughes Corporation, **63** 341
Howard Hughes Medical Institute, 39
221–24
Howard Hughes Properties, Ltd., **17** 317
Howard Humphreys, **13** 119
Howard Johnson International, Inc., 17
236–39; 72 182–86 (upd.)
Howard Research and Development
Corporation, **15** 412, 414
Howard, Smith & Levin, **40** 126
Howden. *See* Alexander Howden Group.
Howdy Company, **9** 177
Howe & Fant, Inc., **23** 82
Howe Sound Co., **12** 253
Howmedica, **29** 455
Howmet Corporation, 12 IV 253–55; 22
506
Hoyle Products, **62** 384
Hoyt Archery Company, **10** 216
HP. *See* Hewlett-Packard Company.
HPI Health Care Services, **49** 307–08
HQ Global Workplaces, Inc., **47** 331
HQ Office International, **8** 405; **23** 364
HRB Business Services, **29** 227
Hrubitz Oil Company, **12** 244
HSBC Holdings plc, 12 256–58; 17 323,
325–26; **26 199–204 (upd.); 60** 161–62
HSG. *See* Helicopter Services Group AS.
Hsiang-Li Investment Corp., **51** 123
HSN, 25 411; **64 181–85 (upd.)**
HSS Hire Service Group PLC, **45** 139–41
HTH, **12** 464
HTM Goedkoop, **26** 278–79; **55** 200
H2O Plus, **11** 41
Hua Bei Oxygen, **25** 82
Hua Yang Printing Holdings Co. Ltd., **60**
372
Hub Group, Inc., 26 533; **38 233–35**
Hub Services, Inc., **18** 366

Hubbard Air Transport, **10** 162
Hubbard, Baker & Rice, **10** 126
Hubbard Broadcasting Inc., 24 226–28
Hubbard Construction Co., **23** 332
Hubbell Incorporated, 9 286–87; 31
257–59 (upd.)
Huck Manufacturing Company, **22** 506
Hudepohl-Schoenling Brewing Co., **18** 72;
50 114
Hudson Automobile Company, **18** 492
The Hudson Bay Mining and Smelting
Company, Limited, 12 259–61; 13
502–03; **16** 29
Hudson Foods Inc., 13 270–72
Hudson Housewares Corp., **16** 389
Hudson I.C.S., **58** 53
Hudson Pharmaceutical Corp., **31** 347
Hudson River Bancorp, Inc., 41 210–13
Hudson Software, **13** 481
Hudson's. *See* Target Corporation.
Hudson's Bay Company, V 79–81; 8
525; **12** 361; **25 219–22 (upd.)**
Hue International, **8** 324
Hueppe Duscha, **III** 571; **20** 362
Huffman Manufacturing Company, **7**
225–26
Huffy Bicycles Co., **19** 383
Huffy Corporation, 7 225–27; 26 184,
412; **30 239–42 (upd.)**
Hugerot, **19** 50
Hugh O'Neill Auto Co., **12** 309
Hughes Air West, **25** 421
Hughes Aircraft Corporation, **7** 426–27; **9**
409; **10** 327; **13** 356, 398; **15** 528, 530;
21 201; **23** 134; **24** 442; **25** 86, 223; **30**
175. *See also* GM Hughes Electronics
Corporation.
Hughes Communications, Inc., **13** 398; **18**
211
Hughes Corp., **18** 535
Hughes Electronics Corporation, 25
223–25; 36 240, 243; **38** 175, 375; **46**
327; **54** 72, 74; **64** 151
Hughes Helicopter, **26** 431; **46** 65
Hughes Hubbard & Reed LLP, 44
230–32
Hughes Markets, Inc., 22 271–73
Hughes Network Systems Inc., **21** 239
Hughes Properties, Inc., **17** 317
Hughes Space and Communications
Company, **33** 47–48
Hughes Supply, Inc., 14 246–47; 39 360
Hughes Television Network, **11** 184
Hughes Tool Co. *See* Baker Hughes
Incorporated.
Hugo Boss AG, 48 206–09
Hugo Neu Corporation, **19** 381–82
Hugo Stinnes GmbH, **8** 69, 494–95; **50**
168
Huhtamäki Oyj, 30 396, 398; **64 186–88**
HUK-Coburg, 58 169–73
The Hull Group, L.L.C., **51** 148
Hulman & Company, 44 233–36; 46 245
Hüls A.G., I 349–50; 25 82. *See also*
Degussa-Hüls AG.
Hulton, **17** 397
Hulton Getty, **31** 216–17
Human Services Computing, Inc. *See* Epic
Systems Corporation.
Humana Inc., III 81–83; 15 113; **24**
229–32 (upd.); 35 215–16; **53** 185; **54**
48
The Humane Society of the United
States, 54 170–73

Humanetics Corporation, **29** 213
Humanities Software, **39** 341
Humberside Sea & Land Services, **31** 367
Humble Oil & Refining Company. *See*
Exxon.
Hummel International A/S, 68 199–201
Hummel Lanolin Corporation, **45** 126
Hummel-Reise, **44** 432
Hummer, Winblad Venture Partners, **36**
157; **69** 265
Hummingbird, **18** 313
Humongous Entertainment, Inc., **31**
238–40
Humps' n Horns, **55** 312
Hunco Ltd., **IV** 640; **26** 273
Hungarian-Soviet Civil Air Transport Joint
Stock Company. *See* Malæv Plc.
Hungry Howie's Pizza and Subs, Inc., 25
226–28
Hungry Minds, Inc. *See* John Wiley &
Sons, Inc.
Hunt Consolidated, Inc., 7 228–30; 27
215–18 (upd.)
Hunt Manufacturing Company, 12
262–64
Hunt-Wesson, Inc., 17 240–42; 25 278
Hunter-Douglas, **8** 235
Hunter Fan Company, 13 273–75
Huntingdon Life Sciences Group plc, 42
182–85
Huntington Bancshares Inc., 11 180–82
Huntington Learning Centers, Inc., 55
212–14
Hunton & Williams, 35 223–26
Huntsman Chemical Corporation, 8
261–63; 9 305
Huntstown Power Company Ltd., **64** 404
Hupp Motor Car Company, **8** 74; **10** 261
Hurd & Houghton, **10** 355
Huron Steel Company, Inc., **16** 357
Hurricane Hydrocarbons Ltd., 54
174–77
Huse Food Group, **14** 352
Husky Energy Inc., 47 179–82; 49 203
Husky Oil Ltd., **IV** 695; **18** 253–54; **19**
159
Husqvarna AB, **53** 126–27
Husqvarna Forest & Garden Company, **13**
564
Hussmann Corporation, **I** 457–58; **7**
429–30; **10** 554; **13** 268; **22** 353–54; **67**
299
Hutcheson & Grundy, **29** 286
Hutchinson-Mapa, **IV** 560
Hutchinson Technology Incorporated, 18
248–51; 63 190–94 (upd.)
Hutchison Microtel, **11** 548
Hutchison Whampoa Limited, 18 114,
252–55; 25 101; **47** 181; **49 199–204**
(upd.)
Huth Inc., **56** 230
Huth Manufacturing Corporation, **10** 414
Hüttenwerke Kayser AG, **62** 253
Huttepain, **61** 155
Huttig Building Products, **31** 398, 400
Huttig Sash & Door Company, **8** 135
HVB Group, 59 237–44 (upd.)
Hvide Marine Incorporated, 22 274–76
HWI. *See* Hardware Wholesalers, Inc.
Hy-Form Products, Inc., **22** 175
Hy-Vee, Inc., 36 275–78; 42 432
Hyatt-Clark Industries Inc., **45** 170

Hyatt Corporation, III 96–97; 9 426; **16 273–75 (upd.); 22** 101; **23** 482; **48** 148; **64** 393, 395
Hyatt Legal Services, **20** 435; **29** 226
Hyco-Cascade Pty. Ltd. *See* Cascade Corporation.
Hycor Biomedical Inc. *See* Stratagene Corporation.
Hyde Athletic Industries, Inc., 17 243–45. *See* Saucony Inc.
Hyde Company, A.L., **7** 116–17
Hyder Investments Ltd., **51** 173
Hyder plc, 34 219–21; 52 375
Hydra Computer Systems, Inc., **13** 201
Hydrac GmbH, **38** 300
Hydril Company, 46 237–39
Hydro-Aire Incorporated, **8** 135
Hydro Carbide Corp., **19** 152
Hydro-Carbon Light Company, **9** 127
Hydro Electric, **19** 389–90; **49** 363–64
Hydro-Electric Power Commission of Ontario, **6** 541; **9** 461
Hydro Med Sciences, **13** 367
Hydro-Quebéc, 6 501–03; 32 266–69 (upd.)
Hydrocarbon Technologies, Inc., **56** 161
Hydrodynamic Cutting Services, **56** 134
Hyer Boot, **19** 232
Hygeia Sciences, Inc., **8** 85, 512
Hygrade Foods, **14** 536
Hygrade Operators Inc., **55** 20
Hylsa. *See* Hojalata y Laminas S.A.
Hylsamex, S.A. de C.V., 39 225–27
Hynix Semiconductor Inc., **56** 173
Hyper Shoppes, Inc., **II** 670; **18** 507; **50** 456–57
Hypercom Corporation, 27 219–21
Hyperion Software Corporation, 22 277–79
Hypermart USA, **8** 555–56
Hyplains Beef, **7** 175
Hypo-Bank. *See* Bayerische Hypotheken- und Wechsel-Bank AG.
Hypobaruk, **III** 348
Hyponex Corp., **22** 475
Hyster Company, 17 246–48; 33 364
Hyster-Yale Materials Handling, Inc., **I** 424; **7** 369–71
Hyundai Group, I 207, 516; **III 515–17; 7 231–34 (upd.); 9** 350; **10** 404; **13** 280, 293–94; **23** 353; **25** 469; **29** 264, 266; **47** 279; **56 169–73 (upd.); 64** 106

I Can't Believe It's Yogurt, Inc., **17** 474; **35** 121
I Pellettieri d'Italia S.p.A., **45** 342
I. Appel, **30** 23
I.B. Kleinert Rubber Company, **37** 399
I.C. Isaacs & Company, 31 260–62
I.D. Systems, Inc., **11** 444
I-DIKA Milan SRL, **12** 182
I. Feldman Co., **31** 359
I.G. Farbenindustrie AG, 8 108–09; **11** 7; **13** 262; **21** 544; **26** 452; **59** 15. *See also* BASF A.G.; Bayer A.G.; Hoechst A.G.
I.M. Pei & Associates. *See* Pei Cobb Freed & Partners Architects LLP.
I. Magnin Inc., **8** 444; **15** 86; **24** 422; **30** 383; **31** 191, 193
I.N. Kote, **IV** 116; **19** 219
I.N. Tek, **IV** 116; **19** 219
I-X Corp., **22** 416
IAC/InterActiveCorp., **64** 181
Iacon, Inc., **49** 299, 301

IAL. *See* International Aeradio Limited.
IAM/Environmental, **18** 11
Iams Company, 26 205–07; 27 213
IAN S.A. *See* Viscofan S.A.
IAWS Group plc, 46 405; **49 205–08**
IBANCO, **26** 515
Ibanez. *See* Hoshino Gakki Co. Ltd.
IBC Group plc, **58** 189, 191
IBC Holdings Corporation, **12** 276
IBCA. *See* International Banking and Credit Analysis.
Iberdrola, S.A., V 608; **47** 110; **49 209–12**
Iberia Líneas Aéreas De España S.A., 6 95–97; **33** 18; **36 279–83 (upd.)**
IBERIABANK Corporation, 37 200–02
Iberpistas. *See* Abertis Infraestructuras, S.A.
Iberswiss Catering. *See* Iberia.
IBH Holding AG, **7** 513
IBJ. *See* The Industrial Bank of Japan Ltd.
IBM. *See* International Business Machines Corporation.
IBM Foods, Inc., **51** 280
IBP, Inc., II 515–17; 7 525; **21 287–90 (upd.); 23** 201
IBS Conversions Inc., **27** 492
Ibstock Brick Ltd., 37 203–06 (upd.)
Ibstock plc, 14 248–50
IC Designs, Inc., **48** 127
IC Industries Inc., I 456–58; 7 430; **10** 414, 553; **18** 3; **22** 197; **43** 217. *See also* Whitman Corporation.
ICA AB, II 639–40
ICA Fluor Daniel, S. de R.L. de C.V., **41** 148
ICA Mortgage Corporation, **8** 30
Icahn Capital Corp., **35** 143
Icarus Consulting AG, **29** 376
ICEE-USA, **24** 240
Iceland Group plc, 33 205–07. *See also* The Big Food Group plc.
Icelandair, 52 166–69
Icelandic Air, **49** 80
ICF Kaiser International, Inc., 28 200–04
ICH Corporation, **19** 468
Ichikoh Industries Ltd., **26** 154
ICI. *See* Imperial Chemical Industries plc.
ICI Canada, **22** 436
ICL plc, II 65, 81; **III** 141, 164; **6 240–42; 11** 150; **16** 226
ICM Mortgage Corporation, **8** 436
ICN Pharmaceuticals, Inc., 52 170–73
Icon Health & Fitness, Inc., 38 236–39
Icon International, **24** 445
iConcepts, Inc., **39** 95
Icot Corp., **18** 543
Icreo Co., Ltd., **72** 125
ICS. *See* International Care Services.
ICS, **26** 119
ID, Inc., **9** 193
id Software, **31** 237–38; **32** 9
Idaho Power Company, 12 265–67
IDB Communications Group, Inc., 11 183–85; 20 48; **27** 301, 307
IDC, **25** 101
Ideal Basic Industries, **III** 701–02; **8** 258–59; **12** 18
Ideal Corp., **23** 335
Ideal Loisirs Group, **23** 388
Ideas Publishing Group, **59** 134
IDEC Pharmaceuticals Corporation. *See* Biogen Idec Inc.

Idemitso Petrochemicals, **8** 153
Idemitsu Kosan Co., Ltd., IV 434–36, 476, 519; **49 213–16 (upd.); 63** 308, 311–12
Identification Business, Inc., **18** 140
Identix Inc., 44 237–40
IDEO Inc., 65 171–73
IDEXX Laboratories, Inc., 23 282–84
IDG Books Worldwide, Inc., 27 222–24. *See also* International Data Group, Inc.
IDG Communications, Inc, **7** 238
IDG World Expo Corporation, **7** 239
IDI, **22** 365
IDI Temps, **34** 372
iDine Rewards Network. *See* Rewards Network Inc.
IDO. *See* Nippon Idou Tsushin.
Ido Bathroom Ltd., **51** 324
IDS Ltd., **22** 76
IDT Corporation, 34 222–24; 58 124; **63** 44
IDX Systems Corporation, 64 189–92
IEC Electronics Corp., 42 186–88
Iecsa S.A. *See* Sideco Americana S.A.
IEL. *See* Industrial Equity Ltd.
IFC Disposables, Inc., **30** 496–98
IFF. *See* International Flavors & Fragrances Inc.
IFIL, **27** 515; **71** 309
IFM, **25** 85
Ifö Sanitär AB, **51** 324
IG. *See* Integrated Genetics.
IG Farben. *See* I.G. Farbenindustrie AG.
IG Holdings, **27** 430
IGA, **II** 624, 649, 668, 681–82; **7** 451; **15** 479; **18** 6, 9; **25** 234
Igemar. *See* Pesquera Iquique-Guanaye S.A.
iGetSmart.com, Inc. *See* Workflow Management, Inc.
Iggesund Paperboard AB, **52** 161, 164
Igloo Products Corp., 21 291–93; 22 116
IGT-International, **10** 375–76
IGT-North America, **10** 375
IHC Caland N.V., 71 178–80
IHI. *See* Ishikawajima Harima Heavy Industries.
IHOP Corporation, 17 249–51; 19 435, 455; **58 174–77 (upd.)**
IIS, **26** 441
IJ Holdings Corp., **45** 173
IK Coach, Ltd., **23** 290
IKEA International A/S, V 82–84; 26 161, **208–11 (upd.)**
IKON Office Solutions, Inc., 50 236–39
Il Fornaio (America) Corporation, 27 225–28**
Il Giornale, **13** 493
Ilaco, **26** 22
ILC Dover Inc., **63** 318
ILFC. *See* International Lease Finance Corporation.
Ilitch Holdings Inc., 37 207–210; 46 130
Illco Toy Co. USA, **12** 496
Illinois Bell Telephone Company, 14 251–53; 18 30
Illinois Central Corporation, I 456; **8** 410; **10** 553; **11 186–89**
Illinois Lock Company, **48** 142
Illinois Power Company, 6 504–07; 49 119, 121
Illinois Steel Co., **8** 114
Illinois Tool Works Inc., III 518–20; 22 280–83 (upd.); 44 193

Illinova Energy Partners, **27** 247
Illuminet Holdings Inc., **47** 430
illycaffè SpA, 50 240–44
Ilwaco Telephone and Telegraph Company. *See* Pacific Telecom, Inc.
ILX Resorts Incorporated, 65 174–76
Ilyushin, **24** 60
IMA Bancard, Inc., **24** 395
Imabari, **25** 469
Image Business Systems Corp., **11** 66
Image Industries, Inc., **25** 320–21
Image Technologies Corporation, **12** 264
Imageline Inc., **25** 348
ImageTag Inc., **49** 290
Imaginarium Toy Centers, Inc., **57** 374
Imagine Entertainment, **43** 144
Imagine Foods, Inc., 50 245–47
Imagine Manufacturing Solutions Inc., **48** 410
ImagiNet, **41** 97
Imaging Technologies, **25** 183
Imaje, S.A., **28** 104
IMAKE Software and Services, Inc., **49** 423–24
IMall Inc., **26** 441
Imasa Group, **IV** 34
Imasco Limited, I 514; **II** 605; **V 401–02**; **49** 367–68
Imation Corporation, 20 301–04; 33 348; **61** 368. *See also* 3M Company.
Imatra Steel Oy Ab, 55 215–17
Imatran Voima Oy. *See* Fortum Corporation
Imax Corporation, 21 362; **28 205–08**; **46** 422
IMC. *See* Intertec Marine Corporation.
IMC Fertilizer Group, Inc., 8 264–66
IMC Global Inc., **57** 149
Imcera Group, Inc., **8** 264, 266
ImClone Systems Inc., 58 178–81
IMCO Recycling, Incorporated, 32 270–73
IMED Corp., **III** 511–12; **38** 364
Imerys S.A., 40 176, **263–66 (upd.)**
Imetal S.A., IV 107–09
IMG. *See* International Management Group.
Imhoff Industrie Holding GmbH, **53** 315
IMI plc, 9 288–89; 29 364
IMIWeb Bank, **50** 410
Imlo, **26** 22
Immeon Networks LLC, **54** 407
Immersion Corporation, **28** 245
Immobilier Batibail, **42** 152
Immunex Corporation, 8 26; **14 254–56**; **50** 421, **248–53 (upd.)**, 538
Immuno Therapeutics, Inc., **25** 382
Imo Industries Inc., 7 235–37; 27 229–32 (upd.)
Imo Pump, **58** 67
Impala Platinum Holdings Ltd., **IV** 91–93; **63** 38–39
Impark Limited, **42** 433
IMPATH Inc., 45 192–94
Imperial and International Communications Limited, **25** 100
Imperial Airways. *See* British Overseas Airways Corporation.
Imperial Business Forms, **9** 72
Imperial Chemical Industries plc, I 351–53; IV 698; **7** 209; **8** 179, 222, 224; **9** 154, 288; **10** 436; **11** 97, 361; **12** 347; **17** 118; **18** 50; **21** 544; **44** 116–17;

49 268, 270; **50** 57, 90, 178–79, **50 254–58 (upd.)**; **63** 49
Imperial Commodities Corporation. *See* Deli Universal NV.
Imperial Feather Company, **19** 304
Imperial Group Ltd., **III** 503; **7** 209; **17** 238
Imperial Holly Corporation, 12 268–70. *See also* Imperial Sugar Company.
Imperial Japanese Government Steel Works, **17** 349–50
Imperial Metal Industries Ltd. *See* IMI plc.
Imperial Oil Limited, IV 437–39; 25 229–33 (upd.);
Imperial Outdoor, **27** 280
Imperial Packing Co. *See* Beech-Nut Nutrition Corporation.
Imperial Paper, **13** 169
Imperial Parking Corporation, 58 182–84
Imperial Premium Finance, **III** 264
Imperial Products, Inc., **62** 289
Imperial Savings Association, **8** 30–31
Imperial Sports, **19** 230
Imperial Sugar Company, 32 274–78 (upd.); 54 168
Imperial Tobacco Company. *See* B.A.T. Industries PLC.
Imperial Tobacco Group PLC, 50 116–18, **259–63**
Implantes Y Sistemas Medicos, Inc., **72** 262
Implats. *See* Impala Platinum Holdings Ltd.
IMPO Import Parfumerien, **48** 116
Imported Auto Parts, Inc., **15** 246
Impressions Software, **15** 455
Imprimis, **8** 467
Impulse Airlines Pty Ltd. *See* Qantas Airways Ltd.
Impulse Designs, **31** 435–36
IMRA America Inc., **48** 5
Imreg, **10** 473–74
IMRS. *See* Hyperion Software Corporation.
IMS Health, Inc., 57 174–78; 59 129–30
IMS International, Inc., **10** 105
IMX Pharmaceuticals, **59** 285
In Focus Systems, Inc., 22 287–90
In Home Health, Inc., **25** 306, 309–10
In-N-Out Burger, 19 213–15
In-Sink-Erator, II 19; **66 195–98**
INA Corporation. *See* CIGNA Corporation.
INA-Holding Schaeffler KG, **62** 129
InaCom Corporation, 13 176, **276–78**; **19** 471
Inalca S.p.A. *See* Cremonini S.p.A.
Incentive Group, **27** 269
Inchcape PLC, III 521–24; 16 276–80 (upd.); 50 264–68 (upd.); 54 378; **59** 260
INCO-Banco Indústria e Comércio de Santa Catarina, **13** 70
Inco Limited, IV 110–12; 39 338; **45 195–99 (upd.)**
Incon Research Inc., **41** 198
InControl Inc., **11** 460
Incredible Universe, **12** 470; **17** 489; **36** 387
Incyte Genomics, Inc., 52 174–77
Indemnity Insurance Company. *See* CIGNA Corporation.
Indentimat Corp., **14** 542
Independent Breweries Company, **9** 178

Independent Delivery Services, Inc., **37** 409
Independent Election Corp. of America, **47** 37
Independent Exhibitions Ltd., **27** 362
Independent Grocers Alliance. *See* IGA.
Independent Lock Co., **13** 166
Independent News & Media PLC, 61 129–31
Independent Petrochemical, **14** 461
Independent Stave Company, **28** 223
Independent Torpedo Company, **25** 73
India Exotics, Inc., **22** 133
Indian Airlines Corporation. *See* Air-India.
Indian Airlines Ltd., 46 240–42
Indian Archery and Toy Corp., **19** 142–43
Indian Iron & Steel Company Ltd. *See* Steel Authority of India Ltd.
Indian Oil Corporation Ltd., IV 440–41, 483; **48 210–13 (upd.)**
Indiana Bearings, Inc., **13** 78
Indiana Bell Telephone Company, Incorporated, 14 257–61; 18 30
Indiana Board and Filler Company, **12** 376
Indiana Electric Corporation, **6** 555
Indiana Energy, Inc., 27 233–36
Indiana Gaming Company, **21** 40
Indiana Gas & Water Company, **6** 556
Indiana Group, **I** 378
Indiana Parts and Warehouse, **29** 86, 88
Indiana Power Company, **6** 555
Indiana Protein Technologies, **55** 233
Indiana Tube Co., **23** 250
Indianapolis Air Pump Company, **8** 37
Indianapolis Brush Electric Light & Power Company, **6** 508
Indianapolis Cablevision, **6** 508–09
Indianapolis Light and Power Company, **6** 508
Indianapolis Motor Speedway Corporation, 9 16; **46 243–46**
Indianapolis Power & Light Company, **6** 508–09
Indianapolis Pump and Tube Company, **8** 37
IndianOil Companies. *See* Indian Oil Corporation Ltd.
Indigo Books & Music Inc., 58 185–87
Indigo NV, 26 212–14, 540–41
Indigo Systems Corp. *See* FLIR Systems, Inc.
The Inditex Group. *See* Industria de Diseño Textil S.A.
Indo Mobil Ltd., **48** 212
Indola Cosmetics B.V., **8** 16
Indresco, Inc., **22** 285; **52** 215
Induba, S.A. de C.V., **39** 230
Induban, **II** 196
Indura SA Industria Y Commercio, **25** 82
Indus International Inc., 70 127–30
Industri Kapital, **27** 269; **68** 125–26
Industri Kapital 2000 Ltd., **64** 17
Industria de Diseño Textil S.A. (Inditex), 64 193–95
Industrial & Commercial Bank, **56** 363
Industrial Air Products, **19** 380–81
Industrial Air Tool, **28** 387
Industrial Airsystems Inc., **56** 247
Industrial Bancorp, **9** 229
Industrial Bank of Japan, Ltd., II 300–01, 310–11, 338, 369, 433, 459; **17** 121; **58** 228
Industrial Bank of Scotland, **10** 337
Industrial Chemical and Equipment, **16** 271

Industrial Circuits, **IV** 680
Industrial Computer Corp., **11** 78
Industrial Development Corp. of Zambia
    Ltd., **IV** 239–41
Industrial Development Corporation, **57**
    185
Industrial Devices Inc., **48** 359
Industrial Equity Ltd., **17** 357
Industrial Exportadora Famian, S.A. de
    C.V., **62** 353
Industrial Gases Lagos, **25** 82
Industrial Instrument Company. *See*
    Foxboro Company.
Industrial Light & Magic, **12** 322; **50** 320
Industrial Mutual Insurance, **III** 264
Industrial National Bank, **9** 229
Industrial Powder Coatings, Inc., **16** 475
Industrial Publishing Company, **9** 413; **27**
    361
Industrial Resources, **6** 144
Industrial Services Group, Inc., **56** 161
Industrial Services of America, Inc., 46
    247–49
Industrial Shows of America, **27** 362
Industrial Tectonics Corp., **18** 276
Industrial Tires Limited, **65** 91
Industrial Trade & Consumer Shows Inc.
    See Maclean Hunter Publishing Limited.
Industrial Trust Co. of Wilmington, **25** 540
Industrial Trust Company, **9** 228
Industrias Bachoco, S.A. de C.V., 39
    228–31
Industrias del Atlantico SA, **47** 291
Industrias Nacobre, **21** 259
Industrias Negromex, **23** 170
Industrias Penoles, S.A. de C.V., 22
    284–86
Industrias Resistol S.A., **23** 170–71
Industrie Natuzzi S.p.A., 18 256–58
Industrie Zignago Santa Margherita
    S.p.A., 67 210–12, 246, 248
Les Industries Ling, **13** 443
Industriförvaltnings AB Kinnevik, **26**
    331–33; **36** 335
AB Industrivärden, **32** 397
Induyco. *See* Industrias y Confecciones,
    S.A.
Indy Lighting, **30** 266
Indy Racing League, **37** 74
Inelco Peripheriques, **10** 459
Inespo, **16** 322
Inexco Oil Co., **7** 282
Infineon Technologies AG, 50 269–73; 57
    323
Infinity Broadcasting Corporation, 11
    190–92; 22 97; **23** 510; **28** 72; **35** 232;
    48 214–17 (upd.)
Infinity Enterprises, Inc., **44** 4
Infinity Partners, **36** 160
INFLEX, S.A., **8** 247
Inflight Sales Group Limited, **11** 82; **29**
    511
InfoAsia, **28** 241
Infocom, **32** 8
InfoCure Corporation. *See* AMICAS, Inc.
Infogrames Entertainment S.A., 35
    227–30; 41 407; **66** 16, 19
Infonet Services Corporation. *See*
    Belgacom.
Infoplan, **14** 36
Informa Group plc, 58 188–91
Informatics General Corporation, **11** 468;
    25 86

Information Access Company, 12
    560–62; **17 252–55; 34** 438. *See also*
    The Thomson Corporation.
Information and Communication Group, **14**
    555
Information Associates Inc., **11** 78
Information Builders, Inc., 14 16; **22**
    291–93
Information Consulting Group, **9** 345
Information, Dissemination and Retrieval
    Inc., **IV** 670
Information Holdings Inc., 47 183–86
Information International. *See* Autologic
    Information International, Inc.
Information Management Reporting
    Services. *See* Hyperion Software
    Corporation.
Information Management Science
    Associates, Inc., **13** 174
Information Please LLC, **26** 216
Information Resources, Inc., 10 358–60;
    13 4; **25** 366
Information Spectrum Inc., **57** 34
Informix Corporation, 10 361–64, 505;
    30 243–46 (upd.)
Infoseek Corporation, **27** 517; **30** 490
InfoSoft International, Inc. *See* Inso
    Corporation.
Infostrada S.p.A., **38** 300
Infosys Technologies Ltd., 38 240–43
Infotech Enterprises, Ltd., **33** 45
Infotechnology Inc., **25** 507–08
Infotel, Inc., **52** 342
Inframetrics, Inc., **69** 171
Infun, S.A., **23** 269
ING Australia Limited, **52** 35, 39
ING, B.V., **14** 45, 47; **69** 246, 248
Ing. C. Olivetti & C., S.p.A., III 144–46;
    10 499; **16** 122; **25** 33. *See also* Olivetti
    S.p.A
ING Groep N.V., **63** 15
Ingalls Quinn and Johnson, **9** 135
Ingalls Shipbuilding, Inc., 12 28, **271–73;**
    36 78–79; **41** 42
Ingear, **10** 216
Ingefico, S.A., **52** 301
Ingenico—Compagnie Industrielle et
    Financière d'Ingénierie, 46 250–52
Ingenious Designs Inc., **47** 420
Ingersoll-Rand Company, III 473,
    525–27; **10** 262; **13** 27, 523; **15** 187,
    223–26 (upd.); 22 542; **33** 168; **34** 46;
    55 218–22 (upd.)
Ingka Holding B.V. *See* IKEA
    International A/S.
Ingleby Enterprises Inc. *See* Caribiner
    International, Inc.
Inglenook Vineyards, **13** 134; **34** 89
Ingles Markets, Inc., 20 305–08
Inglis Ltd. *See* Whirlpool Corporation.
Ingram Book Group, **30** 70
Ingram Industries, Inc., 10 518–19; **11**
    193–95; 13 90, 482; **49 217–20 (upd.);**
    52 178. *See also* Ingram Micro Inc.
Ingram Micro Inc., 24 29; **52 178–81**
AB Ingredients, **II** 466
Ingredients Technology Corp., **9** 154
Ingres Corporation, **9** 36–37; **25** 87
Ingwerson and Co., **II** 356
INH. *See* Instituto Nacional de
    Hidrocarboros.
Inha Works Ltd., **33** 164
INI. *See* Instituto Nacional de Industria.
Initial Electronics, **64** 198

Initial Security, 64 196–98
Initial Towel Supply. *See* Rentokil Initial
    Plc.
Inktomi Corporation, 41 98; **45 200–04**
Inland Container Corporation, IV
    341–42; **7** 528; **8 267–69**
Inland Motors Corporation, **18** 291
Inland Paperboard and Packaging, Inc., **31**
    438
Inland Pollution Control, **9** 110
Inland Steel Industries, Inc., IV 113–16,
    158, 703; **7** 447; **13** 157; **15** 249–50; **17**
    351; **19** 9, **216–20 (upd.)**, 311, 381; **23**
    35; **30** 254; **40** 269, 381; **41** 4
Inland Valley, **23** 321
Inmac, Inc., **16** 373
Inmobiliaria e Inversiones Aconcagua S.A.,
    71 143
Inmos Ltd., **11** 307; **29** 323
Inmotel Inversiones, **71** 338
InnCOGEN Limited, **35** 480
The Inner-Tec Group, **64** 198
InnerCity Foods Joint Venture Company,
    16 97
Inno-BM, **26** 158, 161
Inno-France. *See* Societe des Grandes
    Entreprises de Distribution, Inno-France.
Innova International Corporation, **26** 333
Innovacom, **25** 96
Innovation, **26** 158
Innovative Marketing Systems. *See*
    Bloomberg L.P.
Innovative Pork Concepts, **7** 82
Innovative Products & Peripherals
    Corporation, **14** 379
Innovative Software Inc., **10** 362
Innovative Sports Systems, Inc., **15** 396
Innovative Valve Technologies Inc., **33**
    167
Innovex Ltd. *See* Quintiles Transnational
    Corporation.
Inovoject do Brasil Ltda., **72** 108
Inpaco, **16** 340
Inpacsa, **19** 226
Inprise/Borland Corporation, **33** 115
Input/Output, Inc., **11** 538
INS. *See* International News Service.
Insa, **55** 189
Insalaco Markets Inc., **13** 394
Inserra Supermarkets, 25 234–36
Insight Enterprises, Inc., 18 259–61
Insight Marques SARL IMS SA, **48** 224
Insignia Financial Group, Inc. *See* CB
    Richard Ellis Group, Inc.
Insilco Corporation, 12 472; **16 281–83;**
    23 212; **36** 469–70
Insley Manufacturing Co., **8** 545
Inso Corporation, 26 215–19; 36 273
Inspiration Resources Corporation, **12** 260;
    13 502–03
Inspirations PLC, **22** 129
Insta-Care Holdings Inc., **16** 59
Insta-Care Pharmacy Services, **9** 186
Instant Auto Insurance, **33** 3, 5
Instant Interiors Corporation, **26** 102
Instapak Corporation, **14** 429
Instinet Corporation, 34 225–27; 48
    227–28
Institute de Development Industriel, **19** 87
Institute for Professional Development, **24**
    40
Institute for Scientific Information, **8** 525,
    528
Institution Food House. *See* Alex Lee Inc.

Institutional Financing Services, **23** 491

Instituto Bancario San Paolo di Torino, **50** 407

Instituto Nacional de Industria, I 459–61

Instromet International, **22** 65

Instrument Systems Corp. *See* Griffon Corporation.

Instrumentarium Corp., **13** 328; **25** 82; **71** 349

Instrumentation Laboratory Inc., **III** 511–12; **22** 75

Instrumentation Scientifique de Laboratoire, S.A., **15** 404; **50** 394

Insurance Auto Auctions, Inc., 23 148, **285–87**

Insurance Company of North America. *See* CIGNA Corporation.

Insurance Company of the Southeast, Ltd., **56** 165

Insurance Partners L.P., **15** 257

InsurMark, **72** 149

InSync Communications, **42** 425

Intabex Holdings Worldwide, S.A., **27** 126

Intalco Aluminum Corp., **12** 254

Intamin, **17** 443

Intarsia Corp., **38** 187

Intat Precision Inc., **48** 5

Integra-A Hotel and Restaurant Company, **13** 473

Integral Corporation, **14** 381; **23** 446; **33** 331

Integrated Business Information Services, **13** 5

Integrated Computer Systems. *See* Learning Tree International Inc.

Integrated Defense Technologies,

Integrated Defense Technologies, Inc., 44 423; **54 178–80**

Integrated Genetics, **8** 210; **13** 239; **38** 204, 206

Integrated Health Services, Inc., **11** 282

Integrated Medical Systems Inc., **12** 333; **47** 236

Integrated Resources, Inc., **11** 483; **16** 54; **19** 393

Integrated Silicon Solutions, Inc., **18** 20; **43** 17; **47** 384

Integrated Software Systems Corporation, **11** 469

Integrated Systems Engineering, Inc., **51** 382

Integrated Systems Operations. *See* Xerox Corporation.

Integrated Systems Solutions Corp., **9** 284; **11** 395; **17** 264

Integrated Telecom Technologies, **14** 417

Integris Europe, **49** 382, 384

Integrity Inc., 44 241–43

Integrity Life Insurance, **III** 249

Intel Corporation, II 44–46; 10 365–67 (upd.); 36 123, **284–88 (upd.); 38** 71, 416; **41** 408; **43** 14–16; **47** 153; **50** 53–54, 225; **63** 123–24

Intelcom Support Services, Inc., **14** 334

Intelicom Solutions Corp., **6** 229

Intelig, **57** 67, 69

IntelliCorp, Inc., 9 310; **31** 298; **45 205–07**

Intelligent Electronics, Inc., 6 243–45; 12 184; **13** 176, 277

Intelligent Interactions Corp., **49** 421

Intelligent Software Ltd., **26** 275

Intelligraphics Inc., **33** 44

Intellimetrics Instrument Corporation, **16** 93

Intellisys, **48** 257

Inter American Aviation, Inc. *See* SkyWest, Inc.

Inter-American Satellite Television Network, **7** 391

Inter-City Gas Ltd., **19** 159

Inter-City Products Corporation, **52** 399

Inter-City Wholesale Electric Inc., **15** 385

Inter-Comm Telephone, Inc., **8** 310

Inter-Continental Hotels and Resorts, **38** 77

Inter-Europa Bank in Hungary, **50** 410

Inter-Island Airways, Ltd., **22** 251; **24** 20

Inter-Island Steam Navigation Co. *See* Hawaiian Airlines.

Inter Island Telephone. *See* Pacific Telecom, Inc.

Inter Link Foods PLC, 61 132–34

Inter-Ocean Corporation, **16** 103; **44** 90

Inter Parfums Inc., 35 235–38

Inter-Regional Financial Group, Inc., 15 231–33. *See also* Dain Rauscher Corporation.

Inter Techniek, **16** 421

Interactive Computer Design, Inc., **23** 489, 491

InterActive Corporation, **71** 136–37

Interactive Media CCSP AG, **61** 350

Interactive Search Holding. *See* Ask Jeeves, Inc.

Interactive Systems, **7** 500

InterAd Holdings Ltd., **49** 422

Interamericana de Talleras SA de CV, **10** 415

Interbake Foods, **II** 631

InterBold, **7** 146; **11** 151

Interbrand Corporation, 70 131–33

Interbrás, **IV** 503

Interbrew S.A., 16 397; **17 256–58; 25** 279, 282; **26** 306; **34** 202; **38** 74, 78; **50 274–79 (upd.); 59** 299

Interceramic. *See* Internacional de Ceramica, S.A. de C.V.

Interchemical Corp., **13** 460

Intercity Food Services, Inc., **II** 663

Interco Incorporated, III 528–31; 9 133, 135, 192, 234–35; **10** 184; **12** 156, 306–08; **22** 49; **29** 294; **31** 136–37, 210; **39** 146; **51** 120. *See also* Furniture Brands International, Inc.

Intercontessa AG, **35** 401; **36** 294

Intercontinental Apparel, **8** 249

Intercontinental Electronics Corp. *See* IEC Electronics Corp.

Intercontinental Mortgage Company, **8** 436

Intercontinentale, **III** 404

Intercord, **22** 194

Intercorp Excelle Foods Inc., 64 199–201

Intercostal Steel Corp., **13** 97

Interdesign, **16** 421

InterDigital Communications Corporation, 61 135–37

Interdiscount/Radio TV Steiner AG, **48** 116

Interealty Corp., **43** 184

Interep National Radio Sales Inc., 35 231–34

Interessen Gemeinschaft Farbenwerke. *See* I.G. Farbenindustrie AG.

Interface Group, **13** 483

Interface, Inc., 8 270–72; 18 112; **29 246–49 (upd.)**

Interferon Sciences, Inc., **13** 366–67

InterFirst Bancorp, Inc., **9** 482

Interglas S.A., **22** 515

Intergram, Inc., **27** 21

Intergraph Corporation, 6 246–49; 10 257; **24 233–36 (upd.); 53** 267

INTERIM Services, Inc. *See* Spherion Corporation.

Interinvest S.A., **33** 19; **69** 11

Interlabor, **16** 420–21

Interlabor Interim, **43** 308

The Interlake Corporation, 8 273–75; 38 210

Interlake Steamship Company, **15** 302

Intermaco S.R.L., **43** 368

Intermagnetics General Corp., **9** 10

Intermarché. *See* ITM Entreprises SA.

Intermark, Inc., **12** 394; **34** 338–39

Intermec Technologies Corporation, 72 187–91

Intermedia, **25** 499

Intermedics, **III** 633; **11** 458–59; **12** 325–26; **40** 66–67

Intermet Corporation, 32 279–82

Intermodal Engineering Co. Ltd., **56** 181

Intermountain Health Care, Inc., 27 237–40

Internacional de Ceramica, S.A. de C.V., 53 174–76

International Aeradio Limited, **47** 352

International Aero Engines, **9** 418

International Agricultural Corporation, **8** 264–65

International Air Service Co., **24** 21

International Airline Support Group, Inc., 55 223–25

International Alliance Services, Inc. *See* Century Business Services, Inc.

International Bank of Japan, **17** 122

International Banking and Credit Analysis (IBCA), **37** 144

International Banking Corp., **9** 123

International Banking Technologies, Inc., **11** 113

International Basic Economy Corporation, **13** 103

International Beauty Supply, Ltd. *See* L.L. Knickerbocker Co., Inc.

International Beverage Corporation. *See* Clearly Canadian Beverage Corporation.

International Brewing Holdings Pty., **21** 229; **50** 201

International Brotherhood of Teamsters, 37 211–14

International Business Directories, Inc., **26** 484

International Business Machines Corporation, III 147–49; 6 250–53 (upd.); 30 247–51 (upd.); 63 195–201 (upd.); 64 65

International Care Services. *See* Extendicare Health Services, Inc.

International Cellucotton Products Co. *See* Kimberly-Clark Corporation.

International Cementers Inc., **25** 74

International Communication Materials, Inc., **18** 387

International Computers. *See* ICL plc.

International Controls Corporation, 10 368–70

International Corona Corporation, **12** 244

International Creative Management, Inc., 38 161; **43 235–37**

International Dairy Queen, Inc., 7 266; **10 371–74; 39 232–36 (upd.)**

International Data Group, Inc., 7 238–40; **12** 561; **25 237–40 (upd.)**; **27** 222

International Distillers & Vintners Ltd., **31** 92

International Engineering Company, Inc., **7** 355

International Enviroguard Systems, Inc., **57** 7–8

International Epicure, **12** 280

International Factoring Corp., **II** 436; **61** 249

International Family Entertainment Inc., 13 279–81; **52** 85

International Finance Corp., **19** 192

International Financial Systems Limited, **62** 141

International Flavors & Fragrances Inc., 9 290–92; **38 244–48 (upd.)**

International Fuel Cells Inc., **39** 394

International Game Technology, 10 375–76; **24** 37 **25** 313; **41 214–16 (upd.)**; **54** 14–15

International Group, **13** 277

International Harvester Co. See Navistar International Corporation.

International Home Foods, Inc., **42** 94; **64** 61

International Hotel Group, **59** 296

International House of Pancakes. See IHOP Corporation.

International Hydron, **10** 47; **13** 367

International Imaging Limited, **29** 58

International Industries, **17** 249

International Insurance Company of Hannover Ltd., **53** 162

International Lease Finance Corporation, **III** 198; **36** 231; **48 218–20**

International Light Metals Corp., **IV** 163

International MacGregor, **27** 269

International Management Group, 18 262–65

International Marine Services, **22** 276

International Match, **12** 463

International Milling. See International Multifoods Corporation.

International Mineral & Chemical, Inc., **8** 265–66

International Minerals and Chemical Corporation, **19** 253

International Multifoods Corporation, 7 241–43; **12** 125; **14** 515; **21** 289; **23** 203; **25 241–44 (upd.)**; **28** 238; **50** 493

International Music Co., **16** 202; **43** 171

International News Service, **IV** 626–27; **19** 203; **25** 507

International Nickel Co. of Canada, Ltd. See Inco Limited.

International Nutrition Laboratories, **14** 558

International Olympic Committee, 44 244–47

International Organization of Consumers Unions, **26** 98

International Paper Company, **IV** 16, 245, **286–88**, 289, 326; **8** 267; **11** 76, 311; **15 227–30 (upd.)**; **16** 349; **17** 446; **23** 48–49, 366, 368; **26** 444; **30** 92, 94; **32** 91, 346; **47 187–92 (upd.)**; **63** 267–69

International Parts Corporation, **10** 414; **56** 230

International Periodical Distributors, **34** 5

International Permalite, **22** 229

International Petroleum Co., Ltd. See Standard Oil Co. of New Jersey.

International Pipeline Services, Inc., **51** 248

International Playing Card Company, **62** 384

International Playtex, Inc., **12** 93; **62** 88

International Power PLC, 50 280–85 (upd.)

International Processing Corporation, **50** 123

International Products Corporation. See The Terlato Wine Group.

International Proteins Corporation, **21** 248

International Publishing Corp., **23** 350; **49** 407

International Raw Materials, Ltd., **31** 20

International Rectifier Corporation, **31 263–66**; **71 181–84 (upd.)**

International Roofing Company, **22** 13–14

International Sealants Corporation, **8** 333

International Shipbreaking Ltd. L.L.C., 67 213–15

International Shipholding Corporation, Inc., 27 241–44

International Silver Company, **12** 472; **14** 482–83

International SMC Ltd., **60** 278

International Specialty Products, Inc., **22** 225, 228–29

International Speedway Corporation, 19 221–23; **32** 439

International Stores, **I** 427

International Supply Consortium, **13** 79

International Talent Group, **25** 281

International Talent Management, Inc. See Motown Records Company L.P.

International Telcell Group, **7** 336

International Telecommunications Satellite Organization, **46** 328

International Telephone & Telegraph Corporation, **I 462–64**; **11 196–99 (upd.)**

International Television Corporation Entertainment Group, **23** 391

International Thomson Organisation Ltd. See The Thomson Corporation.

International Thomson Organization Ltd., **23** 92

International Total Services, Inc., 37 215–18

The International Tourist Corporation, **68** 281

International Utilities Corp., **6** 444

International Wind Systems, **6** 581

International Wine & Spirits Ltd., **9** 533

International Wire Works Corp., **8** 13

International Wireless Inc., **21** 261

Internationale Nederlanden Group, **24** 88

Internet Shopping Network, **26** 441

Interocean Management Corp., **9** 509–11

Interpac Belgium. See Belgacom.

Interpretive Data Systems Inc. See IDX Systems Corporation.

Interprovincial Pipe Line Ltd. See Enbridge Inc.

The Interpublic Group of Companies, Inc., **I 16–18**, 31, 36; **14** 315; **16** 70, 72, 167; **20** 5; **22 294–97 (upd.)**; **23** 478; **28** 66–67; **32** 142; **42** 107; **51** 259

Interra Financial. See Dain Rauscher Corporation.

InterRedec, Inc., **17** 196

Interscience, **17** 271

Interscope Communications, Inc., **23** 389, 391; **27** 121

Interscope Music Group, 31 267–69; **69** 350

Intersec, Inc., **27** 21

Interstate & Ocean Transport, **6** 577

Interstate Assurance Company, **59** 246–47

Interstate Bakeries Corporation, 7 320; **12 274–76**; **27** 310; **38 249–52 (upd.)**

Interstate Brick Company, **6** 568–69

Interstate Electric Manufacturing Company. See McGraw Electric Company.

Interstate Finance Corp., **11** 16

Interstate Financial Corporation, **9** 475

Interstate Hotels & Resorts Inc., 58 192–94

Interstate Iron and Steel Company. See Republic Engineered Steels, Inc.

Interstate Logos, Inc. See Lamar Advertising Company.

Interstate Paint Distributors, Inc., **13** 367

Interstate Power Company, **6** 555, 605; **18** 404

Interstate Properties Inc., **45** 15–16

Interstate Public Service Company, **6** 555

Interstate Supply Company. See McGraw Electric Company.

Interstate United Corporation, **II** 679; **13** 435

InterTAN, Inc. See Circuit City Stores, Inc.

Intertec Design, Inc., **34** 371–72

Intertec Publishing Corp., **22** 441

Intertechnique SA, **36** 530

Interturbine Holland, **19** 150

Intertype Corp., **II** 37

Intervideo TV Productions-A.B., **II** 640

Intervision Express, **24** 510

InterVU Inc. See Akamai Technologies, Inc.

InterWest Partners, **16** 418

Intimate Brands, Inc., 24 237–39' 29 357

InTouch Systems, Inc., **43** 118

Intrac Handelsgesellschaft mbH, **7** 142

Intraco Corp., **56** 157–58

Intrado Inc., 63 202–04

The Intrawest Corporation, 15 234–36; **31** 67; **43** 438

Intrepa L.L.C. See Manhattan Associates, Inc.

Intrepid Corporation, **16** 493

Intrigue Technologies, Inc., **69** 245

IntroGene B.V., **13** 241

Intuit Inc., 13 147; **14 262–64**; **23** 457; **33 208–11 (upd.)**

Invacare Corporation, 11 200–02, 486; **47 193–98 (upd.)**

Invenex Laboratories, **17** 287

Invensys PLC, 50 286–90 (upd.)

Invento Products Corporation, **21** 269

Invep S.p.A., **10** 150

Inverfal S.A., **69** 312

Inverness Medical Innovations, Inc., 45 208; **63 205–07**

Inverness Medical Technology, Inc., **45** 210

Inversale, **9** 92

Inversiones Financieras del Sud S.A., **63** 120–21

Inversiones Freire Ltda., **71** 139, 141

Inversiones y Desarrollo Los Andes S.A., **69** 142

INVESCO PLC. See AMVESCAP PLC.

Invesgen S.A., **26** 129

Investcorp SA, 15 200; **24** 195, 420; **25**
  205, 207; **57 179–82; 63** 49–50
Investimentos Itaú S.A., **19** 33
Investor AB, 63 208–11
Investors Bank and Trust Company, **18** 152
Investors Diversified Services, Inc., **II** 398;
  8 348–49; **10** 43–45, 59, 62; **21** 305; **25**
  248; **38** 42
Investors Management Corp., **10** 331
Investors Overseas Services, **10** 368–69
InvestorsBancorp, **53** 222, 224
Investrónica S.A., **26** 129
Invista Capital Management, **III** 330
Invitrogen Corporation, 52 182–84
Invivo Corporation, 52 185–87
The Invus Group, Ltd., **33** 449
Iomega Corporation, 18 509–10; **21**
  294–97
IONA Technologies plc, 43 238–41
Ionia S.A., **64** 379
Ionics, Incorporated, 52 188–90
Ionpure Technologies Corporation. *See*
  Eastern Enterprises.
Iowa Beef Packers, **21** 287
Iowa Beef Processors, **II** 516–17; **13** 351
Iowa Mold Tooling Co., Inc., **16** 475
Iowa Public Service Company, **6** 524–25
IP Services, Inc., **IV** 597
IP Timberlands Ltd., **IV** 288
IP&L. *See* Illinois Power & Light
  Corporation.
Ipalco Enterprises, Inc., 6 508–09; **53** 18
IPC. *See* International Publishing Corp.
IPC Communications, Inc., **15** 196
IPC Magazines Limited, 7 244–47
IPD. *See* International Periodical
  Distributors.
IPEC Holdings Ltd., **27** 474–75
Iphotonics Inc., **48** 369
Ipiranga S.A., 67 216–18
Ipko-Amcor, **14** 225
IPL Energy Inc. *See* Enbridge Inc.
IPS Praha a.s., **38** 437
IPS Publishing, **39** 341–42
Ipsen International Inc., 72 192–95
IPSOA Editore, **14** 555
Ipsos SA, 24 355; **48 221–24**
Ipswich Bancshares Inc., **55** 52
iQuantic Buck, **55** 73
IQUE, Inc., **21** 194
Irby-Gilliland Company, **9** 127
Irdeto, **31** 330
Irex Corporation, **59** 382–83
IRI. *See* Instituto per la Ricostruzione
  Industriale.
Irideon, Inc., **35** 435
Iridian Asset Management LLC, **52** 172
Iris Associates, Inc., **25** 299, 301
Irish Agricultural Wholesale Society Ltd.
  See IAWS Group plc.
Irish Air. *See* Aer Lingus Group plc.
Irish Life & Permanent Plc, 59 245–47
Irish Life Assurance Company, **16** 14; **43** 7
Irkut Corporation, 68 202–04
Iron and Steel Industrial Corporation, **59**
  224
Iron and Steel Press Company, **27** 360
Iron Cliffs Mining Company, **13** 156
Iron Mountain Forge, **13** 319
Iron Mountain, Inc., 33 212–14
Iron Ore Company of Canada, **8** 347
Ironside Technologies Inc., **72** 197
IronUnits LLC, **62** 74
Iroquois Gas Corporation, **6** 526

**IRSA Inversiones y Representaciones
  S.A., 63** 119–21, **212–15**
**Irvin Feld & Kenneth Feld Productions,
  Inc., 15 237–39.** *See also* Feld
  Entertainment, Inc.
Irving Tanning Company, **17** 195
Irving Trust Coompany, **22** 55
Irwin Lehrhoff Associates, **11** 366
Irwin Toy Limited, 14 265–67
Isabela Shoe Corporation, **13** 360
Isagro S.p.A., **26** 425
Isbank. *See* Turkiye Is Bankasi A.S.
Iscor. *See* Iron and Steel Industrial
  Corporation.
Iscor Limited, 57 183–86
Isdin, **60** 246
**Isetan Company Limited, V 85–87; 36
  289–93 (upd.)**
**Ishikawajima-Harima Heavy Industries
  Co., Ltd., I** 508, 511; **III** 532–33; **9**
  293; **41** 41; **63** 223
Ishizaki Honten, **III** 715
Isis Distributed Systems, Inc., **10** 501
Island Air, **24** 22
Island Def Jam Music, **57** 359
The Island ECN, Inc., 48 225–29
Island Equipment Co., **19** 381
Island Pictures Corp., **23** 389
Island Records, **23** 389
Islands Restaurants, **17** 85–87
Isle of Capri Casinos, Inc., 33 41; **41
  217–19**
Isokauf. *See* SIG plc.
Isosceles PLC, **II** 628–29; **24** 270; **47**
  367–68
Isotec Communications Incorporated, **13**
  213
Ispat Inland Inc., 40 267–72 (upd.), 381
Ispat International N.V., 30 252–54
**Israel Aircraft Industries Ltd., 69
  215–17**
Israel Chemicals Ltd., 55 226–29
ISS A/S, 49 221–23, 376
ISS International Service System, Inc., **8**
  271
ISS Securitas, **42** 165, 167
ISSI. *See* Integrated Silicon Solutions Inc.
Istante Vesa s.r.l., **22** 239
Istituto Farmacologico Serono S.p.A. *See*
  Serono S.A.
Istituto Mobiliare Italiano S.p.A., **50** 407,
  409
**Istituto per la Ricostruzione Industriale
  S.p.A., I** 465–67; **11** 203–06; **13** 28,
  218
Isuzu Motors, Ltd., 7 8, 219; **9** 293–95;
  10 354; **23** 288–91 (upd.); **36** 240, 243;
  57 187–91 (upd.); 64 151
Isuzu Motors of Japan, **21** 6
IT Group, **28** 203
IT International, **V** 255
IT-Software Companies, **48** 402
Italcimenti Group, **40** 107–08
Italianni's, **22** 128
Italstate. *See* Societa per la Infrastrutture e
  l'Assetto del Territorio.
Italtel, **V** 326–27
Italware, **27** 564
Itaú. *See* Banco Itaú S.A.
Itaú Winterthur Seguradura S.A., **III** 404
Itaúsa. *See* Investimentos Itaú S.A.
Itek Corp., **I** 486; **11** 265

Itel Corporation, 9 49, 296–99; **15** 107;
  22 339; **26** 519; **47** 37; **69** 196–97,
  268–69
**Items International Airwalk Inc., 17
  259–61**
Ithaca Gas & Electric. *See* New York State
  Electric and Gas.
ITI Education Corporation, **29** 472
ITM Entreprises SA, 36 294–97
Ito Gofuku Co. Ltd. *See* Matsuzakaya
  Company Limited.
Ito-Yokado Co., Ltd., II 661; **V 88–89;
  32** 414, 416–17; **42 189–92 (upd.)**
Itochu and Renown, Inc., **12** 281
ITOCHU Corporation, 19 9; **32 283–87
  (upd.); 34** 231; **42** 342; **63** 346
Itochu Housing, **38** 415
Itochu of Japan, **14** 550
Itoh. *See* C. Itoh & Co.
Itoham Foods Inc., II 518–19; **61 138–40
  (upd.)**
Itokin, **III** 48
Itoman & Co., **26** 456
Itron, Inc., 64 202–05
The Itsy Bitsy Entertainment Company, **51**
  309
ITT. *See* International Telephone and
  Telegraph Corporation.
ITT Aerospace, **33** 48
ITT Automotive Inc. *See* Valeo.
**ITT Educational Services, Inc., 33
  215–17**
ITT Sheraton Corporation, III 98–101;
  23 484; **54** 345–47. *See also* Starwood
  Hotels & Resorts Worldwide, Inc.
ITT World Directories, **27** 498, 500
iTurf Inc., **29** 142–43
ITV PLC, **71** 368
ITW. *See* Illinois Tool Works Inc.
ITW Devcon, **12** 7
IU International, **23** 40
IURA Edition, **14** 556
IV Therapy Associates, **16** 440
IVACO Industries Inc., **11** 207
Ivanhoe, Inc., **II** 662, 664; **57** 157
IVAX Corporation, 11 207–09; 41
  420–21; **55 230–33 (upd.)**
IVC Industries, Inc., 45 208–11
Ives Trains, **16** 336
iVillage Inc., 46 232, **253–56**
Ivy and Mader Philatelic Auctions, Inc., **60**
  146
Ivy Mortgage Corp., **39** 380, 382
Iwata Air Compressor, **III** 427
Iwerks Entertainment, Inc., 33 127; **34
  228–30**
**IXC Communications, Inc., 29 250–52;
  37** 127
IXI Ltd., **38** 418–19
IYG Holding Company of Japan, **7** 492; **32**
  414, 417
The IZOD Gant Corporation, **24** 385
Izod Lacoste, **9** 156–57
Izukyu Corporation, **47** 408
Izumi Fudosan. *See* Sumitomo Reality &
  Development Co., Ltd.

J&E Davy, **16** 14
J&G Meakin, **12** 529
**J & J Snack Foods Corporation, 24
  240–42**
J&L Industrial Supply, **13** 297
J&L Steel. *See* Jones & Laughlin Steel
  Corp.

J & M Laboratories, **48** 299
J&R Electronics Inc., 26 224–26
J&W Hardie Ltd., **62** 347
J. & W. Seligman & Co. Inc., 17 498; **61 141–43**
J.A. Baldwin Manufacturing Company, **17** 106; **61** 65
J.A. Jones, Inc., 16 284–86; 17 377
J. Alexander's Corporation, 65 177–79
J.B. Hudson & Son, **18** 136
J.B. Hunt Transport Services Inc., 12 277–79; 15 440; **26** 533; **50** 209; **63** 237
J.B. Ivey & Company. *See* Dillard's Inc.
J.B. Lippincott & Company, **14** 554–56; **33** 460
J.B. McLean Publishing Co., Ltd. *See* Maclean Hunter Publishing Limited.
J.B. Williams Company, **8** 63
J.B. Wolters Publishing Company, **14** 554
J. Baker, Inc., 13 361; **31 270–73**
J. Beres & Son, **24** 444–45
J Bibby & Sons, **I** 424
J Bibby Agriculture Limited, **13** 53
J. Boag & Son Limited, **57** 306
J. Bulova Company. *See* Bulova Corporation.
J. Byrons, **9** 186
J.C. Baxter Co., **15** 501
J.C. Hillary's, **20** 54
J.C. McCormic, Inc., **58** 334
J.C. Penney Company, Inc., V 90–92; 18 269–73 (upd.); 43 245–50 (upd.)
J.C. Potter Sausage Company, **57** 56–57
J. Crew Group Inc., 12 280–82; 25 48; **34 231–34 (upd.); 36** 472
J.D. Bassett Manufacturing Co. *See* Bassett Furniture Industries, Inc.
J.D. Edwards & Company, 14 268–70; 38 431
J.D. Power and Associates, 9 166; **32 297–301**
J. D'Addario & Company, Inc., 48 230–33
J.E. Nolan, **11** 486
J.E. Sirrine. *See* CRSS Inc.
J.E. Smith Box & Printing Co., **13** 441
J. Edward Connelly Associates, Inc., **22** 438
J. Evershed & Son, **13** 103
J.F. Corporation. *See* Isetan Company Limited.
J.F. Shea Co., Inc., 55 234–36
J.H. Findorff and Son, Inc., 60 175–78
J.H. Heafner Co., **20** 263
J.H. Westerbeke Corp. *See* Westerbeke Corporation.
J.H. Whitney & Company, **9** 250; **32** 100
J. Homestock. *See* R.H. Macy & Co.
J. Horner's, **48** 415
J.I.C. Group Limited, **61** 233
J.I. Case Company, I 148; **10 377–81; 13** 17; **22** 380. *See also* CNH Global N.V.
JJ. Farmer Clothing Inc., **51** 320–21
J.J. Kenney Company, Inc., **51** 244
The J. Jill Group, Inc., 35 239–41
J.K. Armsby Co., **7** 130–31
J.K. Starley and Company Ltd, **7** 458
J.L. Clark, Inc. *See* Clarcor Inc.
J.L. French Automotive Castings, Inc. *See* Onex Corporation.
J.L. Hammett Company, 72 196–99
J.L. Hudson Company. *See* Target Corporation.

J.L. Shiely Co. *See* English China Clays Ltd.
J.L. Wright Company, **25** 379
J. Levin & Co., Inc., **13** 367
J.M. Brunswick & Brothers, **III** 442
J.M. Douglas & Company Limited, **14** 141
J.M. Huber Corporation, **40** 68
J.M. Kohler Sons Company, **7** 269
The J.M. Smucker Company, 11 210–12
J.M. Tull Metals Co., Inc., **IV** 116; **15** 250; **19** 219
J.M. Voith AG, 33 222–25
J. Mandelbaum & Sons, **19** 510
J-Mar Associates, **31** 435–36
J.P. Heilwell Industries, **II** 420
J.P. Morgan & Co. Incorporated, II 329–32; 9 386; **11** 421; **12** 165; **13** 13; **16** 25, 375; **19** 190; **26** 66, 500; **30 261–65 (upd.); 33** 464; **35** 74; **36** 151–53; **50** 30
J.P. Morgan Chase & Co., 38 253–59 (upd.)
J.P. Stevens Inc., **8** 234; **12** 404; **16** 533–35; **17** 75; **19** 420; **27** 468–69; **28** 218; **62** 283
J.R. Brown & Sharpe. *See* Brown & Sharpe Manufacturing Co.
J.R. Geigy S.A., **8** 108–10; **39** 72
J.R. Simplot Company, 16 287–89; 21 508; **26** 309; **60 179–82 (upd.)**
J Sainsbury plc, **II** 657–59, 677–78; **10** 442; **11** 239, 241; **13 282–84 (upd.); 17** 42; **21** 335; **22** 241; **32** 253; **38 260–65 (upd.); 56** 316
J. Sears & Company. *See* Sears plc.
J. Spiegel and Company. *See* Spiegel, Inc.
J.U. Dickson Sawmill Inc. *See* Dickson Forest Products, Inc.
J.W. Bateson, **8** 87
J.W. Charles Financial Services Inc., **25** 542
J.W. Childs Associates, L.P., **46** 220; **64** 119
J.W. Childs Equity Partners LP, **40** 274
J.W. Foster and Sons, Inc. *See* Reebok International Ltd.
J.W. Spear, **25** 314
J.W. Wassall Ltd. *See* Wassall PLC.
J. Walter Thompson Co. *See* JWT Group Inc.
J. Weingarten Inc., **7** 203; **28** 163
J. Wiss & Sons Co., **II** 16
J.Z. Sales Corp., **16** 36
J. Zinmeister Co., **II** 682
Jabil Circuit, Inc., 36 298–301
Jacintoport Corporation, **7** 281
Jack Daniel Distillery, **10** 180
Jack Daniel's. *See* Brown-Forman Corporation.
Jack Eckerd Corp., **16** 160; **19** 467
Jack Frain Enterprises, **16** 471
Jack Henry and Associates, Inc., 17 262–65
Jack Houston Exploration Company, **7** 345
Jack in the Box, Inc. *See* Foodmaster, Inc.
Jack Schwartz Shoes, Inc., 18 266–68
Jackpot Enterprises Inc., 21 298–300; 24 36
Jackson & Perkins. *See* Bear Creek Corporation.
Jackson Cushion Spring Co., **13** 397
Jackson Furniture of Danville, LLC, **48** 246
Jackson Hewitt, Inc., 48 234–36

Jackson Ice Cream Co., **12** 112
Jackson Mercantile Co. *See* Jitney-Jungle Stores of America, Inc.
Jackson National Life Insurance Company, 8 276–77; 48 327
Jackson Purchase Electric Cooperative Corporation, **11** 37
Jaco Electronics, Inc., 19 311; **30 255–57**
Jacob Holm & Sons A/S, **22** 263
Jacob Leinenkugel Brewing Company, 12 338; **28 209–11; 59** 68
Jacobs Brake Manufacturing Company, **7** 116–17
Jacobs Engineering Group Inc., 6 148–50; 26 220–23 (upd.)
Jacobs Suchard (AG), **II** 520–22, 540, 569; **15** 64; **29** 46–47. *See also* Kraft Jacobs Suchard AG.
Jacobson Stores Inc., 21 301–03
Jacoby & Meyers, **20** 435
Jacor Communications, Inc., 23 292–95; 24 108; **27** 339; **35** 220
Jacques Borel International, **II** 641; **10** 12; **49** 126
Jacques Chocolaterie S.A., **53** 315
Jacuzzi Inc., 7 207, 209; **23 296–98**
Jade Accessories, **14** 224
Jade KK, **25** 349
Jadepoint, **18** 79–80
Jafco Co. Ltd., **49** 433
Jafra Cosmetics, **15** 475, 477
Jagenberg AG, **9** 445–46; **14** 57
Jaguar Cars, Ltd., 11 140; **13** 219, 285–87, 414; **36** 198, 217; **64** 132
JAI Parabolic Spring Ltd., **III** 582
JAIX Leasing Company, **23** 306
JAKKS Pacific, Inc., 52 191–94
JAL. *See* Japan Air Lines.
Jalate Inc., 25 245–47
Jaluzot & Cie. *See* Pinault-Printemps-Redoute S.A.
Jamaica Water Supply Company. *See* JWP Inc.
Jamar Company, **64** 30, 32
Jamba Juice Company, 47 199–202
James Beattie plc, 43 242–44
James Burn/American, Inc., **17** 458
James C. Heintz Company, **19** 278
James Ericson, **III** 324
James Felt Realty, Inc., **21** 257
James Fison and Sons. *See* Fisons plc.
James G. Fast Company. *See* Angelica Corporation.
James Galt & Co. Ltd., **60** 124
James Hardie Industries N.V., 26 494; **56 174–76**
James Heekin and Company, **13** 254
James Industries, Inc., **61** 298
James McNaughton Ltd., **IV** 325
James Publishing Group, **17** 272
James R. Osgood & Company, **10** 356
James River Corporation of Virginia, IV 289–91; 8 483; **22** 209; **29** 136. *See also* Fort James Corporation.
James Talcott, Inc., **11** 260–61
James Wellbeloved, **39** 354, 356
James Wholesale Company, **18** 7
Jamestown Insurance Co. Ltd., **55** 20
Jamestown Publishers, **22** 522
Jamesway Corporation, **13** 261; **23** 177
Jamie Scott, Inc., **27** 348
Jamieson & Co., **22** 428
Jan Bell Marketing Inc. *See* Mayor's Jewelers, Inc.

Janata Bank, **31** 219
Janco Overseas Limited, **59** 261
Jane Jones Enterprises, **16** 422; **43** 309
Jane's Information Group, **8** 525
Janesville Electric, **6** 604
Janin, S.A., **36** 163
Janna Systems Inc., **38** 433
Janson Publications, **22** 522
JanSport, Inc., 70 134–36
N.V. Janssen M&L, **17** 147
JANT Pty. Ltd., **IV** 285
Jantzen Inc. *See* VF Corporation.
Janus Capital Group Inc., 57 192–94
Japan Advertising Ltd., **16** 166
**Japan Airlines Company, Ltd., I 104–06;
    24 399–400; 32 288–92 (upd.); 49 459**
Japan Brewery. *See* Kirin Brewery
    Company, Limited.
**Japan Broadcasting Corporation, 7
    248–50; 9 31**
Japan Creative Tours Co., **I** 106
Japan Elanco Company, Ltd., **17** 437
Japan Energy Corporation, **13** 202; **14** 206,
    208; **59** 375
Japan Food Corporation, **14** 288
**Japan Leasing Corporation, 8 278–80;
    11 87**
Japan Medico, **25** 431
**Japan Pulp and Paper Company
    Limited, IV 292–93**, 680
Japan Rifex Co., Ltd., **64** 261
Japan Telecom, **7** 118; **13** 482
Japan Telegraphic Communication
    Company (Nihon Denpo-Tsushin Sha),
    16 166
Japan Tobacco Inc., V 403–04; 30 387;
    46 257–60 (upd.)
Japan Trustee Services Bank Ltd., **53** 322
Japan Try Co., **III** 758
Japan Vilene Company Ltd., **41** 170–72
Japanese Electronic Computer Co., **III** 140
Japanese National Railway, **43** 103
Japonica Partners, **9** 485
Jara Enterprises, Inc., **31** 276
Jarden Corporation, **62** 365, 381
Jardinay Manufacturing Corp., **24** 335
**Jardine Matheson Holdings Limited, I
    468–71; 18** 114; **20 309–14 (upd.)**
Jarvis plc, 39 237–39
Jas. D. Easton Archery. *See* Easton Sports,
    Inc.
Jas. I. Miller Co., **13** 491
Jason Incorporated, 23 299–301; 52 138
Jasper Corporation. *See* Kimball
    International, Inc.
JAT, **27** 475
Jato, **II** 652
Jauch & Hübener, **14** 279
Java Software, **30** 453
Javelin Software Corporation, **10** 359
Jax, **9** 452
Jay Cooke and Co., **9** 370
Jay Jacobs, Inc., 15 243–45
Jay's Washateria, Inc., **7** 372
Jayco Inc., 13 288–90
**Jazz Basketball Investors, Inc., 55
    237–39**
Jazzercise, Inc., 45 212–14
JB Oxford Holdings, Inc., 32 293–96
JB Pawn, Inc., **57** 139
JBA Holdings PLC, **43** 184
JBL, **22** 97
JCB, **14** 321
JCJL. *See* Java-China-Japan Line.

JCT Wireless Technology Company, **61**
    233
JD Wetherspoon plc, 30 258–60
JDS Uniphase Corporation, 34 235–37
**The Jean Coutu Group (PJC) Inc., 46
    261–65**
Jean-Jacques, **19** 50
Jean Lassale. *See* Seiko Corporation.
Jean Lincet, **19** 50
Jean-Philippe Fragrances, Inc. *See* Inter
    Parfums, Inc.
Jeanmarie Creations, Inc., **18** 67, 69
Jeanneau SA, **55** 56
Jefferies Group, Inc., 25 248–51
Jefferson Bancorp, Inc., **37** 201
Jefferson National Life Group, **10** 247
**Jefferson-Pilot Corporation, 11 213–15;
    29 253–56 (upd.)**
Jefferson Properties, Inc. *See* JPI.
**Jefferson Smurfit Group plc, IV 294–96;
    16** 122; **19 224–27 (upd.); 49 224–29
    (upd.).** *See also* Smurfit-Stone Container
    Corporation.
Jefferson Standard Life Insurance, **11**
    213–14
Jefferson Ward, **12** 48–49
Jefferson Warrior Railroad Company, **III**
    767; **22** 546
JEGTCO. *See* Japan Electricity Generation
    and Transmission Company (JEGTCO).
Jeld-Wen, Inc., 33 409; **45 215–17**
Jem Development, **17** 233
Jenkens & Gilchrist, P.C., 65 180–82
Jenn-Air Corporation. *See* Maytag
    Corporation.
Jennie-O Foods, **II** 506; **54** 166–67
Jennifer Convertibles, Inc., 31 274–76
Jenny Craig, Inc., 10 382–84; 12 531; **29
    257–60 (upd.)**
Jeno's, **13** 516; **26** 436
Jenoptik AG, 33 218–21; 53 167
Jenson, Woodward & Lozier, Inc., **21** 96
JEORA Co., **IV** 564
Jepson Corporation, **8** 230
Jeri-Jo Knitwear, Inc., **27** 346, 348
Jerome Foods, Inc., **54** 168
Jerome Increase Case Machinery Company.
    See J.I. Case Company.
Jerrico Inc., **27** 145
Jerrold Corporation, **10** 319–20
Jerry Bassin Inc., **17** 12–14
Jerry's Famous Deli Inc., 24 243–45
Jerry's Restaurants, **13** 320
Jersey Central Power & Light Company,
    27 182
**Jersey European Airways (UK) Ltd., 61
    144–46**
Jersey Standard. *See* Standard Oil Co. of
    New Jersey.
Jerusalem Post Publications Limited, **62**
    188
Jervis B. Webb Company, 24 246–49
JESCO Inc. *See* The Yates Companies, Inc.
Jesse Jones Sausage Co. *See* GoodMark
    Foods, Inc.
**Jet Airways (India) Private Limited, 65
    14–15; 183–85**
Jet Set Corporation, **18** 513
JetBlue Airways Corporation, 44 248–50
**Jetro Cash & Carry Enterprises Inc., 38
    266–68**
Jetstar Airways Pty Ltd. *See* Qantas
    Airways Ltd.
Jeumont-Schneider Industries, **9** 10

Jevic Transportation, Inc., **45** 448
Jewel Companies, Inc., **II** 605; **6** 531; **12**
    63; **18** 89; **22** 38; **26** 476; **27** 291
Jewel Food Stores, **7** 127–28; **13** 25
JFD-Encino, **24** 243
JFE Steel Corporation, **67** 85
JFW Distributing Company. *See* Spartan
    Stores Inc.
JG Industries, Inc., 15 240–42
Jheri Redding Products, Inc., **17** 108
JHT, Inc., **39** 377
Jiamusi Combine Harvester Factory, **21**
    175
Jiangsu General Ball & Roller Co., Ltd.,
    45 170
JIB Group plc, **20** 313
Jiffy Auto Rental, **16** 380
Jiffy Convenience Stores, **II** 627
Jiffy Lube International, Inc., **IV** 490; **21**
    541; **24** 339; **25** 443–45; **50** 353
Jiffy Mixes, **29** 109–10
Jiffy Packaging, **14** 430
Jiji, **16** 166
Jil Sander A.G., **45** 342, 344
**Jillian's Entertainment Holdings, Inc., 40
    273–75**
**Jim Beam Brands Worldwide, Inc., 14
    271–74; 29** 196; **58 194–96 (upd.)**
Jim Cole Enterprises, Inc., **19** 247
**The Jim Henson Company, 23 302–04;
    45** 130
Jim Hjelm's Private Collection, Ltd. *See*
    JLM Couture, Inc.
The Jim Pattison Group, 37 219–22
Jim Walter Corporation. *See* Walter
    Industries, Inc.
Jimmy Carter Work Project. *See* Habitat
    for Humanity International.
Jintan Taionkei Co. *See* Terumo
    Corporation.
**Jitney-Jungle Stores of America, Inc., 27
    245–48**
JJB Sports plc, 32 302–04
JLA Credit, **8** 279
JLG Industries, Inc., 52 195–97
JLL. *See* Jones Lang LaSalle Incorporated.
JLM Couture, Inc., 64 206–08
JMB Internacionale S.A., **25** 121
JMB Realty Corporation, IV 702–03.
    See also Amfac/JMB Hawaii L.L.C.
Jno. H. Swisher & Son. *See* Swisher
    International Group Inc.
JNR. *See* Japan National Railway.
Jo-Gal Shoe Company, Inc., **13** 360
Jo-Ann Stores, Inc., 72 200–03 (upd.)
Joanna Cotton Mills, **14** 220
Jobete Music. *See* Motown Records
    Company L.P.
JobWorks Agency, Inc., **16** 50
**Jockey International, Inc., 12 283–85; 34
    238–42 (upd.)**
Joe Alexander Press, **12** 472; **36** 469
Joe's American Bar & Grill, **20** 54
Joe's Crab Shack, **15** 279
JOFA AB. *See* The Hockey Company.
**The Joffrey Ballet of Chicago, 52
    198–202**
Joh. A. Benckiser GmbH, **36** 140
John A. Frye Shoe Company, **V** 376; **8** 16;
    26 397–98; **36** 24
John A. Pratt and Associates, **22** 181
John Alden Life Insurance, **10** 340
**John B. Sanfilippo & Son, Inc., 14
    274–76**

John Brown plc, I 572–74
John Carr Group, **31** 398–400
John Charcol. *See* Bradford & Bingley
    PLC.
John Chatillon & Sons Inc., **29** 460
John Crane International, **17** 480
John Crosland Company, **8** 88
**The John D. and Catherine T.
    MacArthur Foundation, 34** 243–46
John Deere. *See* Deere & Company.
John F. Jelke Company, **9** 318
John Fairfax Holdings Limited, 7
    251–54
John Frieda Professional Hair Care Inc.,
    70 137–39
John H. Harland Company, 17 266–69
John H.R. Molson & Bros. *See* The
    Molson Companies Limited.
John Hancock Financial Services, Inc.,
    42 193–98 (upd.)
**John Hancock Mutual Life Insurance
    Company, III** 265–68, 332, 400; **IV**
    283; **13** 530; **25** 528
John Holroyd & Co. of Great Britain, **7**
    236
John Labatt Ltd. *See* Labatt Brewing
    Company Limited.
John Laing plc, I 575–76, 588; **51**
    171–73 (upd.)
John Lewis Partnership plc, V 93–95; **42**
    199–203 (upd.)
John M. Hart Company, **9** 304
John M. Smyth Co., **15** 282
John McConnell & Co., **13** 102
John Menzies plc, 39 240–43
John Morrell and Co., **21** 111
The John Nuveen Company, 21 304–06;
    22 492, 494–95
John Oster Manufacturing Company. *See*
    Sunbeam-Oster.
John Paul Mitchell Systems, 24 250–52
John Pew & Company, **13** 243
John Q. Hammons Hotels, Inc., 24
    253–55
John R. Figg, Inc., **II** 681
John Rogers Co., **9** 253
John Sands, **22** 35
John Schroeder Lumber Company, **25** 379
John Sexton & Co., **26** 503
John Strange Paper Company, **8** 358
John Swire & Sons Ltd. *See* Swire Pacific
    Ltd.
John W. Danforth Company, 48 237–39
John Wanamaker, **22** 110
John Wiley & Sons, Inc., 17 270–72; **65**
    186–90 (upd.)
John Yokley Company, **11** 194
John Zink Company, **22** 3–4; **25** 403
Johnny Rockets Group, Inc., 31 277–81
Johns Manville Corporation, 7 293; **11**
    420; **19** 211–12; **61** 307–08; **64** 209–14
    (upd.)
Johnsen, Jorgensen and Wettre, **14** 249
Johnson. *See* Axel Johnson Group.
Johnson & Higgins, 14 277–80
Johnson and Howe Furniture Corporation,
    33 151
Johnson & Johnson, III 35–37; **8** 281–83
    (upd.); 36 302–07 (upd.); **37** 110–11,
    113; **41** 154–55; **46** 104; **55** 122–23; **63**
    205–06
Johnson Brothers, **12** 528

Johnson Controls, Inc., III 534–37; **13**
    398; **16** 184, 322; **26** 227–32 (upd.); **59**
    248–54 (upd.)
Johnson Engineering Corporation, **37** 365
Johnson Matthey PLC, II 390; **IV** 23,
    117–20; 16 28, 290–94 (upd.), 439; **49**
    230–35 (upd.); 50 33
Johnson Products Co., Inc., **11** 208; **31** 89
Johnson Publishing Company, Inc., 28
    212–14; 72 204–07 (upd.)
Johnson Wax. *See* S.C. Johnson & Son,
    Inc.
Johnson Worldwide Associates, Inc., 24
    530; **28** 215–17, 412
Johnsonville Sausage L.L.C., 63 216–19
Johnston Coca-Cola Bottling Company of
    Chattanooga, **13** 163–64
Johnston Industries, Inc., 15 246–48
Johnston, Lemon & Co., **53** 134
Johnston Press plc, 35 242–44
Johnston Sport Architecture Inc., **63** 91
Johnstown America Industries, Inc., 23
    305–07
Johnstown Sanitary Dairy, **13** 393
Joint Environment for Digital Imaging, **50**
    322
Joker S.A., **56** 103
Jolly Time. *See* American Pop Corn
    Company.
Jonathan Logan Inc., **13** 536
Jonell Shoe Manufacturing Corporation, **13**
    360
Jones & Babson, Inc., **14** 85
Jones & Johnson, **14** 277
Jones & Laughlin Steel Corp., **I** 489–91;
    IV 228
Jones Apparel Group, Inc., 11 216–18;
    27 60; **30** 310–11; **39** 244–47 (upd.),
    301, 303; **62** 284
Jones Brothers Tea Co., **7** 202
Jones, Day, Reavis & Pogue, 33 226–29
Jones Environmental, **11** 361
Jones Financial Companies, L.P. *See*
    Edward Jones.
Jones Intercable, Inc., 14 260; **17** 7; **21**
    307–09; 24 123; **25** 212
Jones Janitor Service, **25** 15
Jones Lang LaSalle Incorporated, 49
    236–38
Jones Medical Industries, Inc., 24
    256–58; 34 460
Jones Motor Co., **10** 44
Jones-Rodolfo Corp. *See* Cutter & Buck,
    Inc.
Jones Soda Co., 69 218–21
Jonkoping & Vulcan, **12** 462
Jordache Enterprises, Inc., 15 201–02;
    23 308–10
The Jordan Company LP, 70 140–42
Jordan Industries, Inc., 36 308–10
Jordan Valley Electric Cooperative, **12** 265
Jos. A. Bank Clothiers, Inc., II 560; **12**
    411; **31** 282–85
The Joseph & Feiss Company, **48** 209
Joseph Leavitt Corporation, **9** 20
Joseph Littlejohn & Levy, **27** 204; **53** 241
Joseph Lumber Company, **25** 379
Joseph Malecki Corp., **24** 444–45
Joseph Schlitz Brewing Company, **25** 281
Joseph T. Ryerson & Son, Inc., 15
    249–51; 19 381. *See also* Ryerson Tull,
    Inc.
Joseph Transportation Inc., **55** 347
Josephson International, **27** 392; **43** 235

Joshin Denki, **13** 481
Joshua's Christian Bookstores, **31** 435–36;
    51 132
Josiah Wedgwood and Sons Limited. *See*
    Waterford Wedgewood plc..
Jostens, Inc., 7 255–57; **25** 252–55
    (upd.); 36 470
Jotcham & Kendall Ltd. *See* Seddon Group
    Ltd.
JOULÉ Inc., 58 197–200
Journal Register Company, 29 261–63
Journal Star Printing Company, **64** 237
Journey's End Corporation, **14** 107
Jove Publications, Inc., **IV** 623; **12** 224
Jovi, **II** 652
Joy Planning Co., **III** 533
Joy Technologies Inc., **II** 17; **26** 70; **38**
    227
Joyce International, Inc., **16** 68
JP Foodservice Inc., **24** 445
JP Household Supply Co. Ltd., **IV** 293
JP Planning Co. Ltd., **IV** 293
JP Realty Inc., **57** 157
JPF Holdings, Inc. *See* U.S. Foodservice.
JPI, 49 239–41
JPS Automotive L.P., **17** 182–84
JPS Textile Group, Inc., 28 218–20
JPT Publishing, **8** 528
JR & F SA, **53** 32
JR Central, **43** 103
Jr. Food Stores, Inc., **51** 170
JR Tokai, **43** 103
JSC MMC Norilsk Nickel, 48 300–02
JT Aquisitions, **II** 661
JTL Corporation, **13** 162–63
JTN Acquisition Corp., **19** 233
JTS Corporation. *See* Atari Corporation.
Judel Glassware Co., Inc., **14** 502
Judge & Dolph, Ltd. *See* Wirtz
    Corporation.
The Judge Group, Inc., 51 174–76
Judson Dunaway Corp., **12** 127
Judson Steel Corp., **13** 97
Jugend & Volk, **14** 556
Juice Works, **26** 57
Jujamcyn, **24** 439
Jujo Paper Co., Ltd., IV 297–98
JuJu Media, Inc., **41** 385
Julius Baer Holding AG, 52 203–05
Julius Garfinckel & Co., Inc., **22** 110
Julius Meinl International AG, 53
    177–80
Jumbo Food Stores. *See* Shoppers Food
    Warehouse Corp.
Jumping-Jacks Shoes, Inc., **17** 390
Junghans Uhren, **10** 152
Juniper Networks, Inc., 43 251–55
Juno Lighting, Inc., 30 266–68
Juno Online Services, Inc., 38 269–72.
    See also United Online, Inc.
Juovo Pignone, **13** 356
Jupiter National, **15** 247–48; **19** 166
Jupiter Partners II, **62** 265
Jupiter Tyndall, **47** 84
Jurgensen's, **17** 558
Juristförlaget, **14** 556
Jurys Doyle Hotel Group plc, 64 215–17
Jusco Car Life Company, **23** 290
JUSCO Co., Ltd., V 96–99; **11** 498; **36**
    419; **43** 386. *See also* AEON Co., Ltd.
Jusco Group, **31** 430
Just Born, Inc., 32 305–07
Just For Feet, Inc., 19 228–30
Just Squeezed, **31** 350

Just Toys, Inc., **29** 476
Justin Industries, Inc., 19 231–33
Juventus F.C. S.p.A, 44 387–88; **53** 181–83
JVC. *See* Victor Company of Japan, Ltd.
JW Aluminum Company, **22** 544
JW Bernard & Zn., **39** 203
JWD Group, Inc., **48** 238
JWP Inc., 9 300–02; 13 176. *See also* EMCOR Group Inc.
JWT Group Inc., I 19–21, 23. *See also* WPP Group plc.
JZC. *See* John Zink Company.

K&B Inc., 12 286–88; 17 244
K&F Manufacturing. *See* Fender Musical Instruments.
K & G Men's Center, Inc., 21 310–12; 48 286
K&K Insurance Group, **26** 487
K&K Toys, Inc., **23** 176
K&M Associates L.P., **16** 18; **43** 19
K & R Warehouse Corporation, **9** 20
K-C Aviation, **III** 41; **16** 304; **43** 258
K-Graphics Inc., **16** 306; **43** 261
K-Group, **27** 261
K-H Corporation, **7** 260
K Shoes Ltd., **52** 57–58
K-Swiss, Inc., 33 243–45
K-tel International, Inc., 21 325–28
K-III Holdings. *See* Primedia Inc.
K.F. Kline Co., **7** 145; **22** 184
K.H.S. Musical Instrument Co. Ltd., **53** 214
K.H. Wheel Company, **27** 202
K. Hattori & Co., Ltd. *See* Seiko Corporation.
K.J. International Inc., **70** 74, 76
k.k. Staatsbahnen. *See* $$Österreichische Bundesbahnen GmbH.
K Line. *See* Kawasaki Kisen Kaisha, Ltd.
K-Line Pharmaceuticals Ltd. *See* Taro Pharmaceutical Industries Ltd.
K.O. Lester Co., **31** 359, 361
K.P. American, **55** 305
K.W. Muth Company, **17** 305
KA Teletech, **27** 365
Ka Wah AMEV Insurance, **III** 200–01
Kabelvision AB, **26** 331–33
Kable News Company. *See* AMREP Corporation.
Kable Printing Co., **13** 559
Kaepa, **16** 546
Kafte Inc., **28** 63
Kagle Home Health Care, **11** 282
Kagoshima Central Research Laboratory, **21** 330
Kahan and Lessin, **II** 624–25
Kaiser + Kraft GmbH, **27** 175
Kaiser Aluminum & Chemical Corporation, IV 121–23; 12 377; **8** 348, 350; **22** 455; **50** 104. *See also* ICF Kaiser International, Inc.
Kaiser Foundation Health Plan, Inc., 53 184–86
Kaiser Packaging, **12** 377
Kaiser Permanente Corp. *See* Kaiser Foundation Health Plan, Inc.
Kaiser Steel, **IV** 59
Kaiser's Kaffee Geschäft AG, **27** 461
Kajaani Oy, **IV** 350
Kajima Corporation, I 577–78; 51 177–79
Kal Kan Foods, Inc., 22 298–300

Kalamazoo Limited, **50** 377
Kaldveer & Associates, **14** 228
Kaliningradnefteprodukt, **48** 378
Kalitta Group, **22** 311
Kalua Koi Corporation, **7** 281
Kaman Corporation, 12 289–92; 16 202; **42 204–08 (upd.); 43** 171
Kaman Music Corporation, 68 205–07
Kamewa Group, **27** 494, 496
Kaminski/Engles Capital Corp. *See* Suiza Foods Corporation.
Kammer Valves, A.G., **17** 147
Kampgrounds of America, Inc., 33 230–33
Kamps AG, 44 251–54
Kana Software, Inc., 51 180–83
Kanagawa Chuo Kotsu Co., Ltd., **68** 281
Kanda Shokai, **16** 202; **43** 171
Kanders Florida Holdings, Inc., **27** 50
Kane Foods, **III** 43
Kane-Miller Corp., **12** 106
Kanebo, Ltd., 53 187–91
Kanematsu Corporation, IV 442–44; 24 259–62 (upd.)
Kangaroo. *See* Seino Transportation Company, Ltd.
Kanoldt, **24** 75
Kanpai Co. Ltd., **55** 375
The Kansai Electric Power Company, Inc., V 645–48; 62 196–200 (upd.)
Kansallis-Osake-Pankki, II 302–03
Kansas City Ingredient Technologies, Inc., **49** 261
Kansas City Power & Light Company, 6 510–12, 592; **12** 541–42; **50** 38. *See also* Great Plains Energy Incorporated.
Kansas City Securities Corporation, **22** 541
Kansas City Southern Industries, Inc., 6 400–02; 26 233–36 (upd.); 29 333; **47** 162; **50** 208–09; **57** 194
Kansas City White Goods Company. *See* Angelica Corporation.
Kansas Fire & Casualty Co., **III** 214
Kansas Public Service Company, **12** 541
Kansas Sand and Concrete, Inc., **72** 233
Kansas Utilities Company, **6** 580
The Kantar Group, **48** 442
Kanzaki Paper Manufacturing Co., **IV** 285, 293
Kao Corporation, III 38–39; 16 168; **20 315–17 (upd.); 51** 223–25
Kaolin Australia Pty Ltd. *See* English China Clays Ltd.
Kapalua Land Company, Ltd., **29** 307–08
Kaplan Educational Centers, **12** 143
Kaplan, Inc., 42 209–12, 290
Kaplan Musical String Company, **48** 231
Kapok Computers, **47** 153
Karan Co. *See* Donna Karan Company.
Karastan Bigelow, **19** 276
Karl Kani Infinity, Inc., 49 242–45
Karl Schmidt Unisia, Inc., **56** 158
Karlsberg Brauerei GmbH & Co KG, 41 220–23
Karmelkorn Shoppes, Inc., **10** 371, 373; **39** 232, 235
Karrosseriewerke Weinsberg GmbH. *See* ASC, Inc.
Karstadt Aktiengesellschaft, V 100–02; 19 234–37 (upd.)
Karstadt Quelle AG, 57 195–201 (upd.)
Karsten Manufacturing Corporation, 51 184–86
Kasai Securities, **II** 434

Kasco Corporation, **28** 42, 45
Kash n' Karry Food Stores, Inc., 20 318–20; 44 145
Kashi Company, **50** 295
Kashima Chlorine & Alkali Co., Ltd., **64** 35
Kasmarov, **9** 18
Kaspare Cohn Commercial & Savings Bank. *See* Union Bank of California.
Kasper A.S.L., Ltd., 40 276–79
Kasuga Radio Company. *See* Kenwood Corporation.
Kasumi Co., Ltd., **68** 9
Kat-Em International Inc., **16** 125
Katabami Kogyo Co. Ltd., **51** 179
kate spade LLC, 68 208–11
Katharine Gibbs Schools Inc., **22** 442
Katherine Beecher Candies, Inc. *See* Warrell Corporation.
Kathy's Ranch Markets, **19** 500–01
Katies, **V** 35
Kativo Chemical Industries Ltd., **8** 239; **32** 256
Katy Industries Inc., I 472–74; 14 483–84; **16** 282; **51 187–90 (upd.)**
Katz Communications, Inc., 6 32–34
Katz Media Group, Inc., 35 232, 245–48
Kaufhalle AG, **V** 104; **23** 311; **41** 186–87
Kaufhof Warenhaus AG, V 103–05; 23 311–14 (upd.)
Kaufman and Broad Home Corporation, 8 284–86; 11 481–83. *See also* KB Home.
Kaufmann Department Stores, Inc. *See* The May Department Stores Company.
Kaufring AG, 35 249–52
Oy Kaukas Ab. *See* UPM-Kymmene
Kaukauna Cheese Inc., **23** 217, 219
Kauppiaitten Oy, **8** 293
Kawamata, **11** 350
Kawasaki Heavy Industries, Ltd., I 75; **III 538–40**, 756; **7** 232; **8** 72; **23** 290; **59** 397; **63 220–23 (upd.)**
Kawasaki Kisen Kaisha, Ltd., V 457–60; 56 177–81 (upd.)
Kawasaki Steel Corporation, IV 30, **124–25**, 154, 212–13; **13** 324; **19** 8
Kawecki Berylco Industries, **8** 78
Kawsmouth Electric Light Company. *See* Kansas City Power & Light Company.
Kay-Bee Toy Stores, 15 252–53; 16 389–90; **50** 99. *See also* KB Toys.
Kay Home Products, **17** 372
Kay Jewelers Inc., **61** 327
Kaydon Corporation, 18 274–76
Kaye, Scholer, Fierman, Hays & Handler, **47** 436
Kayex, **9** 251
Kaynar Manufacturing Company, **8** 366
Kayser Aluminum & Chemicals, **8** 229
Kayser Roth Corp., **8** 288; **22** 122
Kaytee Products Incorporated, **58** 60
KB Home, 45 218–22 (upd.)
AO KB Impuls, **48** 419
KB Investment Co., Ltd., **58** 208
KB Toys, 35 253–55 (upd.)
KBLCOM Incorporated, **V** 644
KC. *See* Kenneth Cole Productions, Inc.
KC Holdings, Inc., **11** 229–30
KCI Konecranes International, **27** 269
KCPL. *See* Kansas City Power & Light Company.
KCS Industries, **12** 25–26

KCSI. *See* Kansas City Southern
  Industries, Inc.
KCSR. *See* Kansas City Southern Railway.
KD Acquisition Corporation, **34** 103–04
KD Manitou, Inc. *See* Manitou BF S.A.
KDI Corporation, **56** 16–17
KDT Industries, Inc., **9** 20
Keane, Inc., 38 431; **56 182–86**
Keck's. *See* Decorator Industries Inc.
The Keds Corp., **37** 377, 379
Keebler Foods Company, 35 181; **36
  311–13; 50** 295
Keegan Management Co., **27** 274
Keene Packaging Co., **28** 43
KEG Productions Ltd., **IV** 640; **26** 272
Keil Chemical Company, **8** 178
**Keio Teito Electric Railway Company, V
  461–62**
The Keith Companies Inc., 54 181–84
Keith Prowse Music Publishing, **22** 193
**Keithley Instruments Inc., 16 299–301;
  48** 445
Kelco, **34** 281
Kelda Group plc, 45 223–26
Keliher Hardware Company, **57** 8
Kelkoo S.A. *See* Yahoo! Inc.
Keller Builders, **43** 400
Keller-Dorian Graveurs, S.A., **17** 458
Kelley & Partners, Ltd., **14** 130
Kelley Drye & Warren LLP, 40 280–83
Kellock, **10** 336
**Kellogg Brown & Root, Inc., 62 201–05
  (upd.)**
Kellogg Company, II 523–26, 530, 560;
  12 411; **13** 3, **291–94 (upd.); 15** 189; **18**
  65, 225–26; **22** 336, 338; **25** 90; **27** 39;
  29 30, 110; **50 291–96 (upd.); 63** 249,
  251–52
Kellogg Foundation, **41** 118
Kellwood Company, 8 287–89; 59 268;
  62 210
Kelly & Cohen, **10** 468
Kelly-Moore Paint Company, Inc., 56
  99, **187–89**
Kelly Nason, Inc., **13** 203
Kelly Services, Inc., 6 35–37, 140; **9** 326;
  16 48; **25** 356, 432; **26 237–40 (upd.);**
  40 236, 238; **49** 264–65
The Kelly-Springfield Tire Company, 8
  290–92; 20 260, 263
Kelsey-Hayes Group of Companies, 7
  258–60; 27 249–52 (upd.)
Kelso & Co., **12** 436; **19** 455; **21** 490; **33**
  92; **63** 237; **71** 145–46
Kelty Pack, Inc., **10** 215
Kelvinator Inc., **17** 487
Kelvinator of India, Ltd., **59** 417
KemaNobel, **9** 380–81; **13** 22
Kemet Corp., 14 281–83
Kemi Oy, **IV** 316
Kemira Oyj, 70 143–46
Kemper Corporation, III 269–71, 339;
  15 254–58 (upd.); 22 495; **33** 111; **42**
  451
Kemper Financial Services, **26** 234
Kemper Snowboards, **22** 460
Kencraft, Inc., **71** 22–23
Kendall International, Inc., IV 288; **11
  219–21; 14** 121; **15** 229; **28** 486
Kendall-Jackson Winery, Ltd., 28 111,
  221–23
Kenetech Corporation, 11 222–24
Kenhar Corporation. *See* Cascade
  Corporation.

Kenmore Air Harbor Inc., 65 191–93
**Kennametal, Inc., 13 295–97; 68 212–16
  (upd.)**
Kennecott Corporation, IV 192, 288,
  576; **7 261–64; 10** 262; **12** 244; **27
  253–57 (upd.); 35** 135; **38** 231. *See also*
  Rio Tinto PLC.
Kennedy Automatic Products Co., **16** 8
Kennedy-Wilson, Inc., 60 183–85
Kenner Parker Toys, Inc., **9** 156; **12** 168;
  14 266; **16** 337; **25** 488–89
Kenneth Cole Productions, Inc., 22 223;
  25 256–58
Kenneth O. Lester, Inc., **21** 508
Kenny Rogers' Roasters, **22** 464; **29** 342,
  344
Kenroy International, Inc., **13** 274
Kensey Nash Corporation, 71 185–87
Kensington Associates L.L.C., **60** 146
Kent Electronics Corporation, 17 273–76
Kentrox Industries, **30** 7
Kentucky Electric Steel, Inc., 31 286–88
Kentucky Fried Chicken. *See* KFC
  Corporation.
Kentucky Institution for the Education of
  the Blind. *See* American Printing House
  for the Blind.
**Kentucky Utilities Company, 6 513–15;
  11** 37, 236–38; **51** 217
Kenwood Corporation, 19 360; **23** 53; **31
  289–91**
Kenwood Silver Company, Inc., **31** 352
Kenwood Winery, 68 146
Kenyon & Eckhardt Advertising Agency,
  25 89–91
Kenyon Corp., **18** 276
Kenzo, **25** 122
Keo Cutters, Inc., **III** 569; **20** 360
Keolis SA, 51 191–93
Kepco. *See* Korea Electric Power
  Corporation; Kyushu Electric Power
  Company Inc.
Keppel Tatlee, **56** 363
Keramik Holding AG Laufen, 51 194–96
Kern County Land Co., **10** 379
Kernite SA, **8** 386
Kernkraftwerke Lippe-Ems, **V** 747
Kerr Concrete Pipe Company, **14** 250
Kerr Corporation, 14 481
Kerr Drug Stores, **32** 170
Kerr Group Inc., 10 130; **24 263–65; 30**
  39
Kerr-McGee Corporation, IV 445–47; 13
  118; **22 301–04 (upd.); 63** 441; **68
  217–21 (upd.)**
Kerry Group plc, 27 258–60
Kerry Properties Limited, 22 305–08; 24
  388
**Kerzner International Limited, 69
  222–24 (upd.)**
Keski-Suomen Tukkukauppa Oy, **8** 293
**Kesko Ltd (Kesko Oy), 8 293–94; 27
  261–63 (upd.)**
Kessler Rehabilitation Corporation. *See*
  Select Medical Corporation.
Ketchikan Paper Company, **31** 316
Ketchum Communications Inc., 6 38–40
Kettle Chip Company (Australia), **26** 58
Kettle Foods Inc., 26 58; **48 240–42**
Kettle Restaurants, **29** 149
**Kewaunee Scientific Corporation, 25
  259–62**
Kewpie Kabushiki Kaisha, 57 202–05
Key Computer Laboratories, Inc., **14** 15

Key Industries, Inc., **26** 342
Key Pharmaceuticals, Inc., **11** 207; **41** 419
Key Safety Systems, Inc., 63 224–26
Key Tronic Corporation, 14 284–86
KeyCorp, 8 295–97; 11 110; **14** 90
Keyes Fibre Company, 9 303–05
KeyLabs, **65** 34–35
Keypage. *See* Rural Cellular Corporation.
Keypoint Technology Corporation. *See*
  ViewSonic Corporation.
KeySpan Energy Co., 27 264–66
Keystone Consolidated Industries, Inc., **19**
  467
Keystone Foods Corporation, **10** 443
Keystone Frozen Foods, **17** 536
Keystone Health Plan West, Inc., **27** 211
Keystone Insurance and Investment Co., **12**
  564
**Keystone International, Inc., 11 225–27;
  28** 486
Keystone Life Insurance Co., **III** 389; **33**
  419
Keystone Paint and Varnish, **8** 553
Keystone Portland Cement Co., **23** 225
Keystone Savings and Loan, **II** 420
Keystone Tube Inc., **25** 8
Keytronics, **18** 541
KFC Corporation, 7 265–68; 10 450; **21
  313–17 (upd.); 23** 115, 117, 153; **32**
  12–14; **58** 383–84
KFF Management, **37** 350
Kforce Inc., 71 188–90
KHBB, **16** 72
KHD AG. *See* Klöckner-Humboldt-Deutz
  AG.
KHD Konzern, III 541–44
KHF Finland Oy, **70** 126
KHL. *See* Koninklijke Hollandsche Lloyd.
KI, 57 206–09
**Kia Motors Corporation, 12 293–95; 29
  264–67 (upd.); 56** 173
Kiabi Europe, 37 22–23; **66 199–201**
Kian Dai Wools Co. Ltd., **53** 344
Kickers Worldwide, **35** 204, 207
Kidd, Kamm & Co., **21** 482
Kidde Inc., I 475–76; 23 297; **39 344–46**
Kidde plc, 44 255–59 (upd.); 50 133–35
Kidder, Peabody & Co., **II** 31, 207, 430; **7**
  310; **12** 197; **13** 465–67, 534; **16** 322;
  22 406
Kiddie Products, Inc. *See* The First Years
  Inc.
Kids ''R'' Us. *See* Toys ''R'' Us.
Kids Foot Locker, **14** 293, 295
Kidz Biz Ltd., **52** 193
Kiehl's Since 1851, Inc., 52 209–12
Kien, **13** 545
Kienzle Apparate GmbH, **III** 566; **38** 299
Kierulff Electronics, **10** 113; **50** 42
Kieser Verlag, **14** 555
Kiewit Diversified Group Inc. *See* Level 3
  Communications, Inc.
Kiewit Materials. *See* Rinker Group Ltd.
Kiewit-Murdock Investment Corp., **15** 129
Kijkshop/Best-Sellers, **13** 545
**Kikkoman Corporation, 14 287–89; 47
  203–06 (upd.)**
Kilgore Federal Savings and Loan Assoc.,
  IV 343
Killington, Ltd., **28** 21
Kilpatrick's Department Store, **19** 511
KIM Holdings, Inc., **66** 204
**Kimball International, Inc., 12 296–98;
  48 243–47 (upd.)**

Kimbell Inc., **II** 684
Kimberly-Clark Corporation, **III** 40–41;
IV 254, 297–98, 329, 648, 665; **8** 282;
15 357; **16 302–05 (upd.)**; **17** 30, 397;
18 147–49; **19** 284, 478; **22** 209; **43**
256–60 (upd.); **52** 301–02; **54** 185, 187
Kimberly-Clark de México, S.A. de
C.V., **54** 185–87
Kimco Realty Corporation, **11 228–30**
Kimowelt Medien, **39** 13
Kincaid Furniture Company, **14** 302–03
Kindai Golf Company, **32** 447
Kinden Corporation, **7** 303
Kinder Morgan, Inc., **45 227–30**
KinderCare Learning Centers, Inc., **13**
298–300; **34** 105; **35** 408
Kindergard Corporation, **57** 230
Kineret Acquisition Corp. *See* The Hain
Celestial Group, Inc.
Kinetek, Inc., **70** 142
Kinetic Concepts, Inc., **20 321–23**
King & Spalding, **23 315–18**
The King Arthur Flour Company, **31**
292–95
King Bearing, Inc., **13** 79
King Cullen, **II** 644
King Features Syndicate, **IV** 626; **19** 201,
203–04; **46** 232
King Folding Box Co., **13** 441
King Hickory, **17** 183
King Kullen Grocery Co., Inc., **15**
259–61; **19** 481; **24** 528
King Pharmaceuticals, Inc., **54 188–90**
King Ranch, Inc., **14 290–92**; **60 186–89**
(upd.)
King-Seeley, **16** 487
King Soopers Inc., **12** 112–13
King World Productions, Inc., **9 306–08**;
28 174; **30 269–72 (upd.)**
King's Lynn Glass, **12** 528
Kingbird Media Group LLC, **26** 80
Kingfisher plc, **V 106–09**; **10** 498; **19**
123; **24 266–71 (upd.)**; **27** 118, 120; **28**
34, 36; **49** 112–13
Kings, **24** 528
Kings County Research Laboratories, **11**
424
Kings Mills, Inc., **13** 532
Kings Super Markets, **24** 313, 316
Kingston Technology Corporation, **20**
324–26; **38** 441
Kinki Nippon Railway Company Ltd., **V**
463–65
Kinki Piping Company Ltd., **60** 236
Kinko's Inc., **12** 174; **16 306–08**; **18**
363–64; **43 261–64 (upd.)**
Kinnevik. *See* Industriförvaltnings AB
Kinnevik.
Kinney Corporation, **23** 32; **24** 373
Kinney National Service Inc., **25** 140
Kinney Shoe Corp., **11** 349; **14 293–95**
Kinney Tobacco Co., **12** 108
Kinoshita Sansho Steel Co., **I** 508
Kinpo Electronic, **23** 212
Kinross Gold Corporation, **36 314–16**
Kinson Resources Inc., **27** 38
Kintana, Inc., **59** 295
Kintec Corp., **10** 97
Kirby. *See* Scott Fetzer Company.
Kirby Corporation, **18 277–79**; **22** 275;
66 202–04 (upd.)
Kirch Gruppe, **10** 196; **35** 452
KirchMedia GmbH & Co., **54** 295–98
KirchPayTV, **46** 402

Kirin Brewery Company, Limited, **I**
265–66, 282; **10** 78, 80; **13** 258, 454; **20**
28; **21 318–21 (upd.)**; **36** 404–05; **52**
31–32; **54** 227, 229–30; **57** 305; **63**
227–31 (upd.)
Kirk Stieff Company, **10** 181; **12** 313
Kirkland & Ellis LLP, **65 194–96**
Kirkland Messina, Inc., **19** 392, 394
Kirsch Co., **II** 16
Kirschner Manufacturing Co., **16** 296
Kirshenbaum Bond + Partners, Inc., **57**
210–12
Kirsten Modedesign GmbH & Co. KG, **53**
195
Kirtland Capital Partners, **67** 312–13
Kit Manufacturing Co., **18 280–82**
Kita Consolidated, Ltd., **16** 142
Kitchell Corporation, **14 296–98**
KitchenAid, **8 298–99**
Kitchenbell, **III** 43
Kittery Electric Light Co., **14** 124
Kittinger, **10** 324
Kitty Hawk, Inc., **22 309–11**
Kiwi International Airlines Inc., **20**
327–29
Kiwi Packaging, **IV** 250
Kiwi Polish Co., **15** 507
KJJ. *See* Klaus J. Jacobs Holdings.
KJPCL. *See* Royal Interocean Lines.
KKR. *See* Kohlberg Kravis Roberts & Co.
KLA Instruments Corporation, **11**
231–33; **20** 8
KLA-Tencor Corporation, **45 231–34**
(upd.)
Klaus J. Jacobs Holdings, **29** 46–47; **71** 46
Klaus Steilmann GmbH & Co. KG, **53**
192–95
KLC/New City Televentures, **25** 269
Klein Bicycles, **16** 495
Klein Sleep Products Inc., **32** 426
Kleiner, Perkins, Caufield & Byers, **10**
15, 504; **14** 263; **16** 418; **27** 447; **53**
196–98
Kleinwort Benson Group PLC, **II**
421–23; **22** 55. *See also* Dresdner
Kleinwort Wasserstein.
Klement's Sausage Company, **61 147–49**
Kline Manufacturing, **II** 16
KLLM Transport Services, **27** 404
KLM Royal Dutch Airlines. *See*
Koninklijke Luftvaart Maatschappij N.V.
Klöckner-Humboldt-Deutz AG. *See* KHD
Konzern.
Klöckner-Werke AG, **IV 126–28**; **19** 64;
39 125; **58 201–05 (upd.)**
Klondike, **14** 205
Kloof Gold Mining Company Ltd., **62** 164
Klopman International, **12** 118
Klüber Lubrication München KG, **41** 170
Kluwer Publishers, **IV** 611; **14** 555
Klynveld Main Goerdeler, **10** 387
Klynveld Peat Marwick Goerdeler. *See*
KPMG International.
KM&G. *See* Ketchum Communications
Inc.
Kmart Canada Co., **25** 222
Kmart Corporation, **V 110–12**; **18**
283–87 (upd.); **47 207–12 (upd.)**
Kmart Mexico, **36** 139
KMC Enterprises, Inc., **27** 274
KMI Corporation, **55** 302
KMI Europe, Inc., **68** 207
KN. *See* Kühne & Nagel Group.
KN Energy. *See* Kinder Morgan, Inc.

Kna-Shoe Manufacturing Company, **14**
302; **50** 309
Knape & Vogt Manufacturing
Company, **17 277–79**
Knapp Communications Corporation, **II**
656; **13** 180; **24** 418
Knapp-Monarch, **12** 251
Knauf, **III** 736
K'Nex Industries, Inc., **52 206–08**
KNI Retail A/S, **12** 363
Knickerbocker Trust Company, **13** 465
Knife River Coal Mining Company, **7**
322–25
Knife River Corporation, **42** 249, 253
Knight-Ridder, Inc., **IV** 628–30, 670; **15**
262–66 (upd.); **18** 323; **38** 307; **63** 394;
67 219–23 (upd.)
Knight Trading Group, Inc., **70 147–49**
Knight Transportation, Inc., **64 218–21**
Knightsbridge Capital Corporation, **59** 192
Knightsbridge Partners, **26** 476
Knightway Promotions Ltd., **64** 346
KNILM, **24** 397
Knogo Corp., **11** 444; **39** 78
Knoll Group Inc., **I** 202; **14 299–301**
Knorr-Bremse, **11** 31
Knorr Co. *See* C.H. Knorr Co.
Knorr Foods Co., Ltd., **28** 10
Knott's Berry Farm, **18 288–90**; **22** 130
Knowledge Learning Corporation, **51**
197–99; **54** 191
Knowledge Systems Concepts, **11** 469
Knowledge Universe, Inc., **54 191–94**,
215–16
KnowledgeWare Inc., **9 309–11**; **27** 491;
31 296–98 (upd.); **45** 206
Knox County Insurance, **41** 178
Knox Reeves Advertising Agency, **25** 90
Knoxville Glove Co., **34** 159
Knoxville Paper Box Co., Inc., **13** 442
KNP BT. *See* Buhrmann NV.
KNP Leykam, **49** 352, 354
KNSM. *See* Koninklijke Nederlandsche
Stoomboot Maatschappij.
Knudsen & Sons, Inc., **11** 211
Knudsen Foods, **27** 330
Knutson Construction, **25** 331
KOA. *See* Kampgrounds of America, Inc.
Koala Corporation, **44 260–62**
Kobacker Co., **18** 414–15
Kobe Hankyu Company Ltd., **62** 170
Kobe Shipbuilding & Engine Works, **II** 57
Kobe Steel, Ltd., **I** 511; **IV** 16, **129–31**,
212–13; **8** 242; **11 234–35**; **13** 297; **19**
238–41 (upd.); **38** 225–26
Kobelco America Inc., **19** 241
Kobelco Middle East, **IV** 131
Kobold. *See* Vorwerk & Co.
Kobrand Corporation, **24** 308; **43** 402
Koç Holding A.S., **I 478–80**; **27** 188; **54**
195–98 (upd.)
Koch Enterprises, Inc., **29 215–17**
Koch Industries, Inc., **IV 448–49**; **20**
330–32 (upd.); **21** 108; **22** 3
Koch-Light Laboratories, **13** 239; **38**
203–04
Kockos Brothers, Inc., **II** 624
Kodak. *See* Eastman Kodak Company.
Kodansha Ltd., **IV 631–33**; **38 273–76**
(upd.)
Koehring Company, **8** 545; **23** 299
Koehring Cranes & Excavators, **7** 513
Koei Real Estate Ltd. *See* Takashimaya
Co., Limited.

Koenig & Bauer AG, **64** 222–26
Koenig Plastics Co., **19** 414
Kogaku Co., Ltd., **48** 295
Kohl's Corporation, **9** 312–13; **22** 72; **30** 273–75 (upd.); **50** 117–18; **63** 146
Kohl's Food Stores, Inc., **I** 426–27; **16** 247, 249
Kohlberg & Co., **52** 159
Kohlberg Kravis Roberts & Co., **24** 272–74; **56** 190–94 (upd.)
Kohler Company, **7** 269–71; **10** 119; **24** 150; **32** 308–12 (upd.); **53** 176
Kohler Mix Specialties, Inc., **25** 333
Kohn Pedersen Fox Associates P.C., **57** 213–16
Kokkola Chemicals Oy, **17** 362–63
Kokomo Gas and Fuel Company, **6** 533
Kokusai Kigyo Co. Ltd., **60** 301
Kolb-Lena, **25** 85
Kolker Chemical Works, Inc., **7** 308
The Koll Company, **8** 300–02; **21** 97; **25** 449
Kollmorgen Corporation, **18** 291–94
Kölnische Rückversicherungs- Gesellschaft AG, **24** 178
Komag, Inc., **11** 234–35
Komatsu Ltd., **III** 453, 473, 545–46; **15** 92; **16** 309–11 (upd.); **52** 213–17 (upd.)
Kompass Allgemeine Vermögensberatung, **51** 23
Konan Camera Institute, **III** 487
Kone Corporation, **27** 267–70; **67** 8
Kongl. Elektriska Telegraf-Verket. *See* Swedish Telecom.
Konica Corporation, **III** 547–50; **30** 276–81 (upd.); **43** 284
König Brauerei GmbH & Co. KG, **35** 256–58 (upd.)
Koninklijke Ahold N.V., **II** 641–42; **12** 152–53; **16** 312–14 (upd.)
Koninklijke Bols Wessanen, N.V., **29** 480–81; **57** 105
Koninklijke Grolsch BV. *See* Royal Grolsch NV.
Koninklijke Hoogovens NV. *See* Koninklijke Nederlandsche Hoogovens en Staalfabrieken NV.
Koninklijke Java-China Paketvaart Lijnen. *See* Royal Interocean Lines.
NV Koninklijke KNP BT. *See* Buhrmann NV.
Koninklijke KPN N.V. *See* Royal KPN N.V.
Koninklijke Luchtvaart Maatschappij N.V., **I** 107–09, 119, 121; **6** 105, 109–10; **14** 73; **28** 224–27 (upd.)
Koninklijke Nederlandsche Hoogovens en Staalfabrieken NV, **IV** 132–34; **49** 98, 101
Koninklijke Nederlandsche Stoomboot Maatschappij, **26** 241
N.V. Koninklijke Nederlandse Vliegtuigenfabriek Fokker, **I** 54–56, 75, 82, 107, 115, 121–22; **28** 327–30 (upd.)
Koninklijke Nedlloyd N.V., **6** 403–05; **26** 241–44 (upd.)
Koninklijke Numico N.V. *See* Royal Numico N.V.
Koninklijke Paketvaart Maatschappij, **26** 242
Koninklijke Philips Electronics N.V., **50** 297–302 (upd.)

Koninklijke PTT Nederland NV, **V** 299–301; **27** 471–72, 475. *See also* Royal KPN NV.
Koninklijke Van Ommeren, **22** 275
Koninklijke Vendex KBB N.V. (Royal Vendex KBB N.V.), **62** 206–09 (upd.)
Koninklijke Wessanen nv, **II** 527–29; **54** 199–204 (upd.)
Koninklijke West-Indische Maildienst, **26** 242
Konishiroku Honten Co., Ltd., **III** 487, 547–49
Konrad Hornschuch AG, **31** 161–62
Koo Koo Roo, Inc., **25** 263–65
Kookmin Bank, **58** 206–08
Koop Nautic Holland, **41** 412
Koor Industries Ltd., **II** 47–49; **22** 501; **25** 266–68 (upd.); **54** 363; **68** 222–25 (upd.)
Koors Perry & Associates, Inc., **24** 95
Koortrade, **II** 48
Kop-Coat, Inc., **8** 456
Kopin Corp., **13** 399
Köpings Mekaniska Verkstad, **26** 10
Koppel Steel, **26** 407
Koppers Industries, Inc., **I** 354–56; **17** 38–39; **26** 245–48 (upd.)
Koracorp Industries Inc., **16** 327
Koramic Roofing Products N.V., **70** 363
Korbel Champagne Cellers. *See* F. Korbel & Bros. Inc.
Körber AG, **60** 190–94
Korea Automotive Fuel Systems Ltd., **13** 555
Korea Automotive Motor Corp., **16** 436; **43** 319
Korea Electric Power Corporation (Kepco), **56** 195–98
Korea Ginseng Corporation. *See* KT&G Corporation.
Korea Independent Energy Corporation, **62** 175
Korea Steel Co., **III** 459
Korea Tobacco & Ginseng Corporation. *See* KT&G Corporation.
Korean Air Lines Co. Ltd., **6** 98–99; **24** 443; **27** 271–73 (upd.); **46** 40
Korean Development Bank, **III** 459
Korean Life Insurance Company, Ltd., **62** 175
Koret of California, Inc., **62** 210–13
Kori Kollo Corp., **23** 41
Korn/Ferry International, **34** 247–49
Koro Corp., **19** 414
Korrekt Gebäudereinigung, **16** 420; **43** 307
KorrVu, **14** 430
Kortbetalning Servo A.B., **II** 353
Kortgruppen Eurocard-Köpkort A.B., **II** 353
Korvettes, E.J., **14** 426
Kos Pharmaceuticals, Inc., **63** 232–35
Koss Corporation, **38** 277–79
Kosset Carpets, Ltd., **9** 467
Kotobukiya Co., Ltd., **V** 113–14; **56** 199–202 (upd.)
Kowa Metal Manufacturing Co., **III** 758
Koyland Ltd., **64** 217
KPM. *See* Koninklijke Paketvaart Maatschappij.
KPMG International, **7** 266; **10** 115, 385–87; **29** 176; **33** 234–38 (upd.)
KPN. *See* Koninklijke PTT Nederland N.V.
KPR Holdings Inc., **23** 203

KPS Special Situations Fund, L.P., **69** 360–62
Kraft Foods Inc., **II** 530–34; **7** 272–77 (upd.); **45** 235–44 (upd.); **48** 331; **63** 83, 86
Kraft Foodservice, **26** 504; **31** 359–60
Kraft Jacobs Suchard AG, **26** 249–52 (upd.)
Kraftco Corporation, **14** 204
KraftMaid Cabinetry, Inc., **72** 208–10
Kragen Auto Supply Co. *See* CSK Auto Corporation.
Kramer, **III** 48
Kramer Guitar, **29** 222
Kramer Machine and Engineering Company, **26** 117
Krames Communications Co., **22** 441, 443
Kransco, **25** 314; **61** 392
Krasnapolsky Restaurant and Wintergarden Company Ltd., **23** 228
Kraus-Anderson, Incorporated, **36** 317–20
Krause Publications, Inc., **35** 259–61
Krause's Furniture, Inc., **27** 274–77
Krauss-Maffei AG, **I** 75; **III** 566; **14** 328; **38** 299
Kredietbank N.V., **II** 304–05; **59** 246
Kreditanstalt für Wiederaufbau, **29** 268–72
Kreher Steel Co., **25** 8
Krelitz Industries, Inc., **14** 147
Kresge Foundation. *See* Kmart Corporation.
Kreuger & Toll, **12** 462–63
Kreymborg, **13** 544–45
Krislex Knits, Inc., **8** 235
Krispy Kreme Doughnut Corporation, **21** 322–24; **61** 150–54 (upd.)
Kristall, **62** 10
Kroenke Sports Enterprises, **51** 97
Kroeze, **25** 82
The Kroger Company, **II** 643–45; **15** 267–70 (upd.); **65** 197–202 (upd.)
Kroll Inc., **57** 217–20
Kronans Droghandel, **72** 258
Krone AG, **33** 220
Kronos, Inc., **18** 295–97; **19** 468
Krovtex, **8** 80
Kroy Tanning Company, **17** 195
KRS Corporation, **57** 202–04
Krueger Insurance Company, **21** 257
Krueger International. *See* KI.
Kruger Inc., **17** 280–82
Kruidvat, **54** 265–67
Krumbhaar Chemical Inc., **14** 308
Krung Thai Bank Public Company Ltd., **69** 225–27
Krupp AG. *See* Fried. Krupp GmbH; Thyssen Krupp AG.
Krupp Widia GmbH, **12** 66
Kruse International, **32** 162
The Krystal Company, **33** 239–42
KSB AG, **62** 214–18
KT&G Corporation, **62** 219–21
KT Contract Services, **24** 118
KTR. *See* Keio Teito Electric Railway Company.
K2 Inc., **16** 295–98; **22** 481, 483; **23** 474; **43** 389
KU Energy Corporation, **6** 513, 515; **11** 236–38
Kubota Corporation, **III** 551–53; **10** 404; **12** 91, 161; **21** 385–86; **24** 324; **39** 37; **40** 134

Kudelski Group SA, 44 263–66
Kuehne & Nagel International AG, V
    466–69; 53 199–203 (upd.)
Kuhlman Corporation, 20 333–35
Kühn + Bayer, 24 165
Kühne & Nagel International AG, V
    466–69
Kulicke and Soffa Industries, Inc., 33
    246–48
Kulka Smith Inc., 13 398
Kumagai Gumi Co., I 579–80
Kumba Resources, 57 183, 186
Kumon Institute of Education Co., Ltd.,
    72 211–14
Kunkel Industries, 19 143
KUNPETROL Kiskunhalasi Szolgáltató
    Kft., 70 195
Kunz-Holding GmbH & Co., 53 216
Kuo International Ltd., I 566; 44 153
Kuok Group, 28 84; 57 292, 294; 71
    331–32
Kuoni Travel Holding Ltd., 40 284–86
The Kuppenheimer Company, 8 248–50;
    32 247
Kurabo Industries Ltd., 61 229
Kuraray Co., Ltd., 72 363
Kurt Möller Verlag, 7 42
Kurushima Dockyard, II 339
Kurzweil Technologies, Inc., 51 200–04
KUS. See Karl Schmidt Unisia, Inc.
The Kushner-Locke Company, 25
    269–71
Kuwait Airways Corporation, 68 226–28
Kuwait Aviation Fueling Co., 55 243
Kuwait Investment Office, II 198; IV 380,
    452; 27 206
Kuwait Petroleum Corporation, IV
    450–52; 18 234; 38 424; 55 240–43
    (upd.)
Kvaerner ASA, 20 313; 31 367, 370; 36
    321–23
KW, Inc. See Coca-Cola Bottling Company
    of Northern New England, Inc.
Kwik-Fit Holdings plc, 54 205–07
Kwik Save Group plc, 11 239–41; 13 26;
    47 368
Kwik Shop, Inc., 12 112
Kwikasair Ltd., 27 473
KWIM. See Koninklijke West-Indische
    Maildienst.
Kyivstar GSM, 69 344, 346
Kymmene Corporation, IV 299–303. See
    also UPM-Kymmene Corporation.
Kyocera Corporation, II 50–52; 7 118;
    21 329–32 (upd.); 67 41–42
Kyodo, 16 166
Kyodo Dieworks Thailand Co., III 758
Kyodo Kako, IV 680
Kyodo Kokusan K.K., 21 271
Kyoei Mutual Fire and Marine Insurance
    Co., III 273
Kyoei Steel, 59 202
Kyosai Trust Co. See Yasuda Trust and
    Banking Company, Limited.
Kyotaru Co., 66 270–71
Kyoto Ceramic Co., Ltd. See Kyocera
    Corporation.
Kyowa Hakko Kogyo Co., Ltd., III
    42–43; 45 94; 48 248–50 (upd.)
Kyowa Seeds, 70 346
Kyushu Electric Power Company Inc., V
    649–51; 17 349
Kywan Petroleum Ltd., 13 556
KYZ International, 9 427

KZO, 13 21

L & G, 27 291
L&H. See Lernout and Hauspie.
L. & H. Sales Co., 16 389
L. and J.G. Stickley, Inc., 50 303–05
L&W Supply Corp., III 764
L E Lundbergföretagen AB, 52 161, 164
L-3 Communications Holdings, Inc., 48
    251–53; 54 234
L.A. Dreyfus Company, 58 378
L.A. Gear, Inc., 8 303–06; 11 349; 31
    413; 32 313–17 (upd.)
L.A. Mex. See Checkers Drive-Up
    Restaurants Inc.
L.A. T Sportswear, Inc., 26 257–59
L.B. Foster Company, 33 255–58
L. Bosendorfer Klavierfabrik, A.G., 12 297
L.D.C. SA, 61 155–57
L.D. Canocéan, 25 104
The L.D. Caulk Company, 10 271
L. Fish, 14 236
L.G. Balfour Company, 12 472; 19
    451–52; 36 469
L. Greif & Bro. Inc., 17 203–05
L. Grossman and Sons. See Grossman's
    Inc.
L.J. Knowles & Bros., 9 153
L.J. Melody & Co., 21 97
L.K. Liggett Company, 24 74
L. Kellenberger & Co. AG, 25 194
L.L. Bean, Inc., 9 190, 316; 10 388–90;
    12 280; 19 333; 21 131; 22 173; 25 48,
    206; 29 278; 36 180, 420; 38 280–83
    (upd.)
The L.L. Knickerbocker Co., Inc., 25
    272–75
L. Luria & Son, Inc., 19 242–44
L.M. Ericsson. See Telefonaktiebolaget LM
    Ericsson.
L-O-F Glass Co. See Libbey-Owens-Ford
    Glass Co.
L. Prang & Co., 12 207
L.S. Holding, Inc., 60 204
L.S. Starrett Company, 13 301–03; 64
    227–30 (upd.)
L.W. Pierce Co., Inc. See Pierce Leahy
    Corporation.
L.W. Singer, 13 429
La Banque Suisse et Française. See Crédit
    Commercial de France.
La Barge Mirrors, III 571; 20 362
La Cadena Investments, 64 364
La Cerus, IV 615
La Choy Food Products Inc., 17 241; 25
    276–78
La Cinq, IV 619
La Cloche d'Or, 25 85
La Crosse Telephone Corporation, 9 106
La Cruz del Campo S.A., 9 100
La Fromagerie du Velay, 25 85
La Grange Foundry, Inc., 39 31
La Halle aux Chaussures, 17 210
La Joya, 51 389
La Madeleine French Bakery & Café, 33
    249–51
La Maison du Jambon, 58 218
La Martiniere Groupe, 58 152
La Mesa RV Center, Inc., 69 230
La Oroya, 22 286
La Petite Academy, 13 299
La Pizza Loca Inc., 44 86
La Poste, V 270–72; 47 213–16 (upd.)

The La Quinta Companies, 42 213–16
    (upd.)
La Quinta Inns, Inc., 11 242–44; 21 362
La Redoute S.A., 19 306, 309
La Rinascente, 12 153
La-Ru Truck Rental Company, Inc., 16 386
La Ruche Meridionale, 12 153
La Senza Corporation, 66 205–07
La 7, 47 345, 347
La Societe Anonyme Francaise Holophane,
    19 211
La Supercalor S.P.A. See De'Longhi S.p.A.
La Vie Claire, 13 103
La-Z-Boy Incorporated, 14 302–04; 50
    309–13 (upd.)
LAB. See Lloyd Aereo de Bolivia.
The Lab, 37 263
LaB Investing Co. L.L.C, 37 224
LaBakelite S.A., I 387
LaBarge Inc., 41 224–26
Labatt Brewing Company Limited, I
    267–68; 18 72; 25 279–82 (upd.); 26
    303, 306
Labatt U.S.A., 54 212–14
L'Abeille SA, 61 44–45
Labelcraft, Inc., 8 360
LaBelle Iron Works, 7 586
LabOne, Inc., 48 254–57
Labor Ready, Inc., 29 273–75
Labor W. See Sennheiser Electronic GmbH
    and Co. AG.
Laboratoire L. Lafon, 45 94
Laboratoires de Biologie Végétale Yves
    Rocher, 35 262–65
Laboratoires Goupil, III 48
Laboratoires Roche Posay, III 48
Laboratorio Chile S.A., 55 233
Laboratorios Elmor S.A., 55 233
Laboratorios Liade S.A., 24 75
Laboratorium Wennebostel. See Sennheiser
    Electronic GmbH and Co. AG.
Laboratory Corporation of America
    Holdings, 42 217–20 (upd.)
LaBranche & Co. Inc., 37 223–25
Labsphere, Inc., 48 446
Labtronics, Inc., 49 307–08
Laci Le Beau Tea, 49 275–76
Lacks Enterprises Inc., 61 158–60
Laclede Steel Company, 15 271–73
Lacombe Electric. See Public Service
    Company of Colorado.
LaCrosse Footwear, Inc., 18 298–301;
    161–65 (upd.)
Lacto Ibérica, 23 219
Lactos, 25 85
Lacy Diversified Industries, Ltd., 24
    159–61
Ladbroke Group PLC, II 141–42; 19
    208; 21 333–36 (upd.); 42 64; 49
    449–50. See also Hilton Group plc.
Ladd and Tilton, 14 527–28
LADD Furniture, Inc., 12 299–301; 23
    244
Ladd Petroleum Corp., II 30
LADECO. See Iberia.
Ladenburg, Thalmann & Co. Inc., 17 346
Ladenso, IV 277
Ladish Co., Inc., 30 282–84
Lady Foot Locker, V 226; 14 293, 295
Lady Lee, 27 291
Laerdal Medical, 18 423
Lafarge Cement UK, 54 208–11 (upd.)

Lafarge Coppée S.A., **III** 703–05; **8** 258; **10** 422–23; **23** 333; **59** 111–12, 115; **64** 380

Lafarge Corporation, **24** 332; **28** 228–31

Lafayette Manufacturing Co., **12** 296

Lafayette Radio Electronics Corporation, **9** 121–22

Lafuma S.A., **39** 248–50

LAG&E. See Los Angeles Gas and Electric Company.

LaGard Inc., **20** 363

Lagardère Groupe SCA, **16** 254; **24** 84, 88; **34** 83

Laidlaw Inc., **39** 19, 21

Laidlaw Transportation, Inc., **6** 410; **32** 227, 231

Laing's Properties Ltd. See John Laing plc.

L'Air Liquide SA, **I** 357–59; **11** 402; **47** 217–20 (upd.)

Laiterie Centrale Krompholtz, **25** 84

Laiterie de la Vallée du Dropt, **25** 84

Laiterie Ekabe, **19** 50

SA Laiterie Walhorn Molkerel, **19** 50

Laiteries Prairies de l'Orne, **19** 50

Lake Erie Screw Corp., **11** 534, 536

Lake Odessa Machine Products, **18** 494

Lake Pacific Partners, LLC, **55** 124

Lake Superior & Ishpeming Railroad Company, **62** 74

Lake Superior Consolidated Mines Company, **17** 355–56

Lake Superior Paper Industries, **26** 363

Lakehead Pipe Line Partners, L.P., **43** 155

Lakeland Industries, Inc., **45** 245–48

Laker Airways, **24** 399

Lakes Entertainment, Inc., **51** 205–07

The Lakeside Publishing and Printing Co. See R.R. Donnelley & Sons Co.

Lakestone Systems, Inc., **11** 469

Lakewood Animal Hospital, Inc., **58** 354

Lalique, **55** 309

Lam Research Corporation, **IV** 213; **11** 245–47; **18** 383; **31** 299–302 (upd.)

Lam Son Sugar Joint Stock Corporation (Lasuco), **60** 195–97

Lamar Advertising Company, **27** 278–80; **70** 150–53 (upd.)

The Lamaur Corporation, **41** 227–29

Lamb Technicon Corp., **I** 486

Lamb Weston, Inc., **23** 319–21

Lambda Electronics Inc., **32** 411

Lambert Brothers, Inc., **7** 573

Lambert Brussels Financial Corporation. See Drexel Burnham Lambert Incorporated.

Lambert Frères, **33** 339

Lambert Kay Company, **8** 84

Lambert Rivière, **41** 340

Lamborghini. See Automobili Lamborghini S.p.A.

Lamkin Brothers, Inc., **8** 386

Lamons Metal Gasket Co., **11** 535

Lamontagne Ltd., **II** 651

Lamonts Apparel, Inc., **15** 274–76

Lampadaires Feralux, Inc., **19** 472

Lamplight Farms Inc. See W.C. Bradley Co.

The Lamson & Sessions Co., **13** 304–06; **61** 166–70 (upd.)

Lamson Corporation, **7** 145; **49** 159

Lan Chile S.A., **31** 303–06; **33** ; **59** 172

Lanca, **14** 224

Lancair International, Inc., **67** 224–26

Lancaster Colony Corporation, **8** 307–09; **57** 354–55; **61** 171–74 (upd.)

Lancaster Financial Ltd., **14** 472

Lancaster National Bank, **9** 475

Lancaster Press, **23** 102

Lance, Inc., **14** 305–07; **41** 230–33 (upd.); **56** 365–66

Lancel, **27** 487, 489

Lancer Corporation, **21** 337–39

Lancey Investissement SAS, **58** 221

Lanchester Motor Company, Ltd., **13** 286

Land O'Lakes, Inc., **II** 535–37; **7** 339; **13** 351; **21** 340–43 (upd.)

Land-O-Sun Dairies, L.L.C., **26** 449

Land Securities PLC, **IV** 704–06; **49** 246–50 (upd.); **54** 38

Landauer, Inc., **51** 208–10

Lander Company, **21** 54

Landis International, Inc., **10** 105–06

Landmark Banks, **10** 426

Landmark Business Products, Inc., **61** 254

Landmark Communications, Inc., **12** 302–05; **22** 442; **52** 401–02; **55** 244–49 (upd.)

Landmark Financial Services Inc., **11** 447

Landmark Theatre Corporation, **70** 154–56

Landmark Union Trust, **18** 517

Landoll, Inc., **22** 522

Landry's Restaurants, Inc., **15** 277–79; **65** 203–07 (upd.)

Lands' End, Inc., **9** 314–16; **12** 280; **16** 37; **19** 333; **26** 439; **27** 374, 429; **29** 276–79 (upd.); **56** 311, 313

Landstar System, Inc., **26** 533; **63** 236–38

Lane Bryant, Inc., **64** 231–33

The Lane Co., Inc., **12** 306–08

Lane Drug Company, **12** 132

Lane, Piper, and Jaffray, Inc. See Piper Jaffray Companies.

Lane Publishing Co., **IV** 676; **7** 529

Laneco, Inc., **II** 682

Lang Exploratory Drilling, **26** 42

Langdon Rieder Corp., **21** 97

Lange International S.A., **15** 462; **43** 375–76

Langen Packaging Inc., **51** 249, 251

Langenpac NV, **51** 249–50

Langford Labs, **8** 25

Lanier Business Products, Inc., **8** 407; **20** 290

Lanman Companies, Inc., **23** 101

Lannet Data Communications Ltd., **18** 345–46; **26** 275–77

Lanoga Corporation, **62** 222–24

LAPE. See Líneas Aéreas Postales Españolas.

Lapeyre S.A. See Groupe Lapeyre S.A.

LaPine Technology, **II** 51; **21** 331

Lapp, **8** 229

Lara, **19** 192

Larami Corp., **14** 486

Lareco, **26** 22

Largardère Groupe, **43** 210

Largo Entertainment, **25** 329

Largo Music Publishing, **55** 250

Lariat Petroleum, **65** 262

Larousse Group. See Groupe de la Cité.

Larry Flynt Publishing Inc., **31** 307–10

Larry H. Miller Group, **29** 280–83

Larry's Food Products, **36** 163

Larsen Company, **7** 128

Larson Boats. See Genmar Holdings, Inc.

Las Vegas Gas Company, **19** 411

Las Vegas Sands, Inc., **50** 306–08

LaSalle Investment Management, Inc., **49** 238

LaSalle Machine Tool, Inc., **13** 7–8

LaSalle Partners, **49** 28

LaSalle Steel Corporation, **28** 314

LaSalles & Koch Co., **8** 443

Lasco Shipping Co., **19** 380

Laser Tech Color, **21** 60

Laserscope, **67** 227–29

LaserSoft, **24** 349

LaSiDo Inc., **58** 209–11

Lasky's, **24** 269

Lasmo, **IV** 455, 499; **65** 316–17

Lason, Inc., **31** 311–13

Lassonde Industries Inc., **68** 229–31

Lasuco. See Lam Son Sugar Joint Stock Corporation.

Latcom, Inc., **55** 302

Latham & Watkins, **33** 252–54; **37** 292

Latin Communications Group Inc., **41** 151

Latin Percussion, Inc. See Kaman Music Corporation.

Latitude Communications, **22** 52

Latrobe Brewing Company, **25** 281; **54** 212–14

Latrobe Steel Company, **8** 529–31

Lattice Semiconductor Corp., **16** 315–17; **43** 17

Lauda Air Luftfahrt AG, **48** 258–60

Lauder Chemical, **17** 363

Laura Ashley Holdings plc, **13** 307–09; **37** 226–29 (upd.)

Laura Scudders, **7** 429; **44** 348

Laureate Enterprises Inc., **64** 190

Laurel Glen, **34** 3, 5

Laurel Pipe Line Company. See Buckeye Partners, L.P.

The Laurel Pub Company Limited, **59** 255–57

Laurel Technologies Partnership, **58** 101

Laurent-Perrier SA, **42** 221–23

Laurentian Group, **48** 290

Laurus N.V., **65** 208–11

Lauson Engine Company, **8** 515

LaVista Equipment Supply Co., **14** 545; **60** 326

Lavold, **16** 421; **43** 308

Lavoro Bank AG. See Banca Nazionale del Lavoro SpA.

Lawn Boy Inc., **7** 535–36; **8** 72; **26** 494

Lawrenceburg Gas Company. See Cincinnati Gas & Electric Company.

The Lawson Co., **7** 113; **25** 125

Lawson Inc., **41** 113, 115

Lawson Software, **38** 284–88

Lawter International Inc., **14** 308–10; **18** 220

Lawyers Cooperative, **8** 527–28

Layer Five, **43** 252

Layne & Bowler Pump, **11** 5

Layne Christensen Company, **19** 245–47; **26** 71

Layton Homes Corporation, **30** 423

Lazard Freres & Co., **IV** 23, 79, 658–59; **7** 287, 446; **10** 399; **12** 165, 391, 547, 562

Lazard LLC, **38** 289–92

Lazare Kaplan International Inc., **21** 344–47

Lazio. See Societá Sportiva Lazio SpA.

Lazy Days RV Center, Inc., **69** 228–30

LBO Holdings, **15** 459

LBS Communications, **6** 28
LCI International, Inc., 16 318–20
LCIE, **55** 79
LCP Hotels. *See* CapStar Hotel Co.
LDB Corporation, 53 204–06
LDC. *See* L.D.C. S.A.
LDC, 68 232–34
LDCom Networks, **60** 151
LDDS-Metro Communications, Inc., 8 310–12
LDDS WorldCom, Inc., **16** 467–68
LDI. *See* Lacy Diversified Industries, Ltd.
LDMA-AU, Inc., **49** 173
LDS Health Services Corporation, **27** 237
Le Bon Marché. *See* Bon Marché.
Le Buffet System-Gastronomie, **V** 74
Le Chameau, **39** 250
Le Chateau Inc., 63 239–41
Le Clerc, **21** 225–26
Le Cordon Bleu S.A., II 609; **45** 88; **45** 88; **67 230–32**
Le Courviour S.A., **10** 351
Le Monde S.A., 33 308–10
Le Riche Group Ltd., **61** 44, 46
Le Rocher, Compagnie de Reassurance, **III** 340
Le Touquet's, SA, **48** 197
Lea & Perrins, **II** 475
Lea County Gas Co., **6** 580
Lea Lumber & Plywood Co., **12** 300
Lea Manufacturing, **23** 299
Leach McMicking, **13** 274
Leadra Design Inc., **59** 164
Leaf Candy Company, **64** 187
Leaf North America, **51** 159
Leahy & Co. *See* Pierce Leahy Corporation.
Lean Cuisine, **12** 531
Leap Wireless International, Inc., 69 231–33
LeapFrog Enterprises, Inc., 54 191, 193, **215–18; 61** 203
Lear Corporation, 16 321–23; 71 191–95 (upd.)
Lear Inc., **8** 49, 51
Lear Romec Corp., **8** 135
Lear Siegler Inc., I 481–83; 8 313; **13** 169, 358, 398; **19** 371–72; **30** 426; **44** 308
Learjet Inc., 8 313–16; 9 242; **27 281–85 (upd.)**
Learning Centers Inc., **51** 198
The Learning Company Inc., 24 275–78, 480; **29** 74, 77; **41** 409; **61** 202
Learning Tree International Inc., 24 279–82
LeaRonal, Inc., 23 322–24
Lease International SA, **6** 358
Leaseway Personnel Corp., **18** 159
Leaseway Transportation Corp., 12 309–11
Leatherback Industries, **22** 229
Leatherman Tool Group, Inc., 51 211–13
Lebhar-Friedman, Inc., 55 250–52
Leblanc Corporation. *See* G. Leblanc Corporation.
LeBoeuf, Lamb, Greene & MacRae, L.L.P., 29 284–86
Lebr Associates Inc., **25** 246
Lech Brewery, **24** 450
Leche Pascual Group. *See* Grupo Leche Pascual S.A.
Lechmere Inc., 10 391–93

Lechters, Inc., 11 248–50; 39 251–54 (upd.)
Leclerc. *See* Association des Centres Distributeurs E. Leclerc.
LeCroy Corporation, 41 234–37
Lectorum Publications, **29** 426
Ledcor Industries Limited, 46 266–69
Lederle Laboratories, **14** 254, 256, 423; **27** 115; **50** 248, 250
Lederle Standard Products, **26** 29
Ledesma Sociedad Anónima Agrícola Industrial, 62 225–27
Lee Ackerman Investment Company, **18** 513
Lee Apparel Company, Inc., 8 317–19; **17** 512, 514
The Lee Company. *See* VF Corporation.
Lee Cooper Group Ltd., **49** 259
Lee Enterprises, Incorporated, 11 251–53; 47 120; **64 234–37 (upd.)**
Lee International, **24** 373
Lee National Corporation, **26** 234
Lee Optical, **13** 390
Lee Rubber and Tire Corp., **16** 8
Lee Way Holding Co., **14** 42
Lee's Famous Recipe Chicken, **58** 323
Leeann Chin, Inc., 30 285–88
Leeds & Northrup Company, **28** 484; **63** 401
Lees Carpets, **17** 76
Leewards Creative Crafts Inc., **17** 322
Leeway International Company Ltd., **68** 69
Lefrak Organization Inc., 8 357; **26 260–62**
Legacy Homes Ltd., **26** 290
Legacy Hotels Real Estate Investment Trust, **69** 163
Legal & General Group plc, III 272–73; **24 283–85 (upd.); 30** 494; **33** 319
The Legal Aid Society, 48 261–64
Legal Technologies, Inc., **15** 378
Legault and Masse, **II** 664
Legent Corporation, 10 394–96; 14 392
Legetojsfabrikken LEGO Billund A/S. *See* Lego A/S.
Legg Mason, Inc., 11 493; **33 259–62**
Leggett & Platt, Inc., 9 93; **11 254–56;** **48 265–68 (upd.)**
Leggett Stores Inc., **19** 48
Lego A/S, 12 495; **13 310–13; 40 287–91 (upd.); 52** 206
Legrand SA, 21 348–50
Lehigh Acquisition Corp., **34** 286
Lehigh Portland Cement Company, 23 325–27; 31 252
Lehman Brothers, **14** 145; **22** 445; **25** 301; **38** 411; **48** 59
Lehman Merchant Bank Partners, **19** 324
Lehmer Company. *See* Centel Corporation.
Lehser Communications, Inc., **15** 265
Leica Camera AG, 35 266–69
Leica Microsystems Holdings GmbH, 35 270–73
Leigh-Mardon Security Group, **30** 44
Leighton Holdings Ltd., **19** 402
Leinenkugel Brewing Company. *See* Jacob Leinenkugel Brewing Company.
Leiner Health Products Inc., 34 250–52
The Leisure Company, **34** 22
Leisure Concepts, Inc., **59** 187–89
Leisure System Inc., **12** 359
Leitz. *See* Esselte Worldwide.
LeMaster Litho Supply, **13** 228
Lemmerz Holding GmbH, **27** 202, 204

Lemmon Co., **54** 363
Lempereur, **13** 297
Lend Lease Corporation Limited, IV 707–09; 17 283–86 (upd.); 47 410; **52 218–23 (upd.)**
Lender's Bagel, **32** 69
Lending Textiles, **29** 132
Lenel Systems International Inc., **24** 510
Lennar Corporation, 11 257–59
Lennon's, **II** 628
Lennox Industries, Inc., **22** 6
Lennox International Inc., 8 320–22; 28 232–36 (upd.)
Lenoir Furniture Corporation, **10** 183
Lenox, Inc., 10 179, 181; **12 312–13; 18** 69; **38** 113
Lens, Inc., **30** 267–68
LensCrafters Inc., 13 391; **17** 294; **23 328–30; 43** 199; **52** 227, 229
Lentheric, **I** 426
L'Entreprise Jean Lefebvre, 23 331–33
Leo Burnett Company, Inc., I 22–24, 25, 31, 37; **11** 51, 212; **12** 439; **20 336–39 (upd.)**
Leo d'Or Trading Co. Ltd., **56** 242
The Leo Group, **32** 140; **40** 140
Léon Gaumont et Cie. *See* Gaumont SA.
Leonard Bernstein Music Publishing Company, **23** 391
Leonard Development Group, **10** 508
Leonard Green & Partners LP, **12** 477–78; **24** 173
Leonard Machinery Corp., **16** 124
Leonard Parker Company, **26** 196
Leonard Silver, **14** 482
Leonardi Manufacturing, **48** 70
Leonardo Editore, **IV** 587
Leprino Foods Company, 28 237–39; 59 204
Lerner Plastics, **9** 323
Lernout and Hauspie, **51** 202
Leroux S.A.S., 65 212–14
Leroy Merlin SA, **23** 230; **37** 24; **54 219–21**
Les Abeilles International SA, **60** 149
Les Boutiques San Francisco, Inc., 62 228–30
Les broderies Lesage, **49** 83
Les Echos. *See* Groupe Les Echos.
Les Grands Magasins Au Bon Marché: Etablissements Vaxelaire-Claes, **26** 159–60
Les Industries Ling, **13** 443
Les Papeteries du Limousin, **19** 227
Les Schwab Tire Centers, 50 314–16
Lesaffre et Compagnie, **52** 305
Lesco Inc., 19 248–50
The Leslie Fay Companies, Inc., 8 323–25
The Leslie Fay Company, Inc., 39 255–58 (upd.); 40 276–77
Leslie Paper, **IV** 288
Leslie's Poolmart, Inc., 18 302–04
Lesser-Goldman, **II** 18
Lester Ink and Coatings Company, **13** 228
Lester of Minnesota, Inc., **62** 55
Lestrem Group, **IV** 296; **19** 226
Létang et Rémy, **44** 205
Lettuce Entertain You Enterprises, **38** 103
Leucadia National Corporation, 11 260–62; 71 196–200 (upd.)
Leumi & Company Investment Bankers Ltd., **60** 50
Leuna-Werke AG, **7** 142

Leupold & Stevens, Inc., 52 224–26
Level Five Research, Inc., **22** 292
Level 13 Entertainment, Inc., **58** 124
Level 3 Communications, Inc., 67
    233–35
Levenger Company, 63 242–45
Lever Brothers Company, 9 291,
    317–19; **14** 314. *See also* Unilever.
Leverage Group, **51** 99
Levernz Shoe Co., **61** 22
Levi Strauss & Co., II 634, 669; **V**
    362–65; **9** 142; **12** 430; **16** 324–28
    (upd.), 509, 511; **17** 512; **19** 196; **23**
    422; **24** 158; **25** 47; **57** 283–84, 86
Leviathan Gas Pipeline Company, **21** 171
Levine, Huntley, Vick & Beaver, **6** 28
Leviton Manufacturing Co., Inc., **54** 372
Levitt Corp., **21** 471
Levitt Industries, **17** 331
Levitt Investment Company, **26** 102
Levitz Furniture Inc., 15 280–82; **23** 412,
    414
Levolor Hardware Group, **53** 37
Levtex Hotel Ventures, **21** 363
Levy. *See* Chas. Levy Company LLC.
Levy Home Entertainment, LLC, **60** 83, 85
Levy Restaurants L.P., 26 263–65
Lew Liberbaum & Co., **27** 197
The Lewin Group, Inc., **21** 425
Lewis and Marks, **16** 27; **50** 32
Lewis Batting Company, **11** 219
Lewis Galoob Toys Inc., 16 329–31
Lewis Group Ltd., **58** 54–55
Lewis Homes, **45** 221
Lewis Refrigeration Company, **21** 500
Lex Electronics, **10** 113; **50** 42
Lex Service plc, **19** 312; **50** 42
Lexecon, Inc., **26** 187
Lexington Furniture Industries, **III** 571; **20**
    362
Lexington Ice Company, **6** 514
Lexington Utilities Company, **6** 514; **11**
    237
LEXIS-NEXIS Group, 17 399; **18** 542;
    21 70; **31** 388, 393; **33** 263–67
Lexitron, **II** 87
Lexmark International, Inc., 9 116; **10**
    519; **18** 305–07; **30** 250
Leybold GmbH, **IV** 71; **48** 30
Leyland Motor Corporation, **7** 459
LF International, Inc., **59** 259
LFC Financial, **10** 339
LFC Holdings Corp. *See* Levitz Furniture
    Inc.
LFE Corp., **7** 297
LG&E Energy Corporation, 6 516–18;
    18 366–67; **50** 172; **51** 214–17 (upd.)
LG Chemical Ltd., **26** 425
LG Electronics Inc., **13** 572, 575; **43** 428
LG Group, **18** 124; **34** 514, 517–18
LG Semiconductor, **56** 173
LGT Asset Management. *See* AMVESCAP
    PLC.
Lhomme S.A., **8** 477
Li & Fung Limited, 59 258–61
Liaison Agency, **31** 216–17
Lianozovo Dairy, **48** 438
Libbey Inc., 49 251–54
Libbey-Owens-Ford Company, **III** 640–42,
    714–15, 731; **7** 292; **16** 7–9; **22** 434; **23**
    83; **26** 353; **31** 355
Libeltex, **9** 92
Liber, **14** 556
Liberty Bank of Buffalo, **9** 229

Liberty Brokerage Investment Company,
    10 278
Liberty Can and Sign Company, **17**
    105–06
The Liberty Corporation, 22 312–14
Liberty Gauge Company, **17** 213
Liberty Hardware Manufacturing
    Corporation, **20** 363
Liberty Life, **IV** 97
Liberty Livewire Corporation, 42
    224–27
Liberty Media Corporation, 18 66; **19**
    282; **25** 214; **34** 224; **42** 114, 224; **47**
    414, 416, 418; **50** 317–19
Liberty Mutual Holding Company, 59
    262–64
Liberty Mutual Insurance Group, **11** 379;
    48 271
Liberty Mutual Savings Bank, **17** 530
Liberty National Insurance Holding
    Company. *See* Torchmark Corporation.
Liberty National Life Insurance Co., **9**
    506–07
Liberty Natural Gas Co., **11** 441
Liberty Property Trust, 57 221–23
Liberty Software, Inc., **17** 264
Liberty Surf UK, **48** 399
Liberty Tax Service, **48** 236
Liberty Travel, Inc., 56 203–06
Librairie Générale Française. *See* Hachette.
Librairie Larousse. *See* Groupe de la Cité.
Librairie Louis Hachette. *See* Hachette.
Librizol India Pvt. Ltd., **48** 212
Libyan National Oil Corporation, IV
    453–55. *See also* National Oil
    Corporation.
Lieberman Enterprises, **24** 349
Liebert Corp., **II** 20
Liebherr Haushaltgerate GmbH, **65** 167
Liebherr-International AG, 64 238–42
Life Assurance Holding Corporation, **71**
    324–26
Life Investors International Ltd., **III** 179;
    12 199
Life Partners Group, Inc., **33** 111
Life Retail Stores. *See* Angelica
    Corporation.
Life Savers Corp., **7** 367; **21** 54
Life Science Research, Inc., **10** 105–07
Life Technologies, Inc., 17 287–89; **52**
    183–184
Life Time Fitness, Inc., 66 208–10
Life Uniform Shops. *See* Angelica
    Corporation.
Lifecycle, Inc., **25** 40
Lifeline Systems, Inc., 32 374; **53** 207–09
LifeLink, **11** 378
Lifemark Corp., **III** 74; **14** 232; **33** 183
LifePoint Hospitals, Inc., 69 234–36
LifeScan Inc., **63** 206
Lifestyle Fitness Clubs, **46** 432
Lifetime Corp., **29** 363–64
Lifetime Entertainment Services, 51
    218–22
Lifetime Foam Products, Inc., **12** 439
Lifetime Hoan Corporation, 27 286–89
Lifeway Foods, Inc., 65 215–17
Ligand Pharmaceuticals Incorporated,
    10 48; **47** 221–23
Liggett & Meyers, **29** 195
Liggett-Ducat, **49** 153
Liggett Group Inc. *See* Vector Group Inc.
Light & Power Company, **12** 265

Light Savers U.S.A., Inc. *See* Hospitality
    Worldwide Services, Inc.
Lightel Inc., **6** 311
Lighthouse, Ltd., **24** 95
Lil' Champ Food Stores, Inc., **36** 359
LILCO. *See* Long Island Lighting
    Company.
Lilia Limited, **17** 449
Lille Bonnières et Colombes, **37** 143–44
Lillian Vernon Corporation, 12 314–15;
    35 274–77 (upd.)
Lillie Rubin, **30** 104–06
Lilliput Group plc, **11** 95; **15** 478
Lilly & Co. *See* Eli Lilly & Co.
Lilly Endowment Inc., 70 157–59
Lilly Industries, **22** 437
Lily Tulip Co., **I** 611; **8** 198
Limhamns Golvindustri AB. *See* Tarkett
    Sommer AG.
The Limited, Inc., V 115–16; **9** 142; **12**
    280, 356; **15** 7, 9; **16** 219; **18** 193, 215,
    217, 410; **20** 340–43 (upd.); **24** 237; **25**
    120–21, 123; **28** 344; **47** 142–43; **61**
    371; **64** 232
LIN Broadcasting Corp., 9 320–22; **11**
    330
Linamar Corporation, 18 308–10
Lincare Holdings Inc., 43 265–67
Lincoln American Life Insurance Co., **10**
    246
Lincoln Automotive, **26** 363
Lincoln Benefit Life Company, **10** 51
Lincoln Center for the Performing Arts,
    Inc., 69 237–41, 295
Lincoln Electric Co., 13 314–16
Lincoln Electric Motor Works, **9** 439
Lincoln Federal Savings, **16** 106
Lincoln Income Life Insurance Co., **10** 246
Lincoln Industrial Corporation, **70** 142
Lincoln Liberty Life Insurance Co., **III** 254
Lincoln Marketing, Inc., **18** 518
Lincoln National Corporation, III
    274–77; **10** 44; **22** 144; **25** 286–90
    (upd.)
Lincoln Property Company, 8 326–28;
    54 222–26 (upd.)
Lincoln Savings, **10** 340
Lincoln Savings & Loan, **9** 199
Lincoln Snacks Company, 24 286–88
Lincoln Telephone & Telegraph
    Company, 14 311–13
LinCom Corp., **8** 327
Lindal Cedar Homes, Inc., 29 287–89
Linde AG, I 581–83; **9** 16, 516; **11**
    402–03; **25** 81; **48** 323; **67** 236–39
    (upd.)
Linde Refrigeration. *See* Carrier
    Corporation.
Lindemans. *See* Southcorp Limited.
Lindex, **II** 640
Lindsay Manufacturing Co., 20 344–46
Lindt & Sprüngli. *See* Chocoladefabriken
    Lindt & Sprüngli AG.
Linear Corporation Bhd, **66** 28
Linear Technology, Inc., 16 332–34
Linens 'n Things, Inc., 13 81–82; **24**
    289–92; **33** 384; **41** 50
Linfood Cash & Carry, **13** 103
Linfood Holdings Ltd., **II** 628–29
Ling Products, **12** 25
Ling-Temco-Vought. *See* LTV Corporation.
Lingerfelt Development Corporation, **57**
    223
Lingerie Time, **20** 143

Linguaphone Group, **43** 204, 206
Linificio e Canapificio Nazionale S.p.A., **67** 210–11, 246–48
Link House Publications PLC, **IV** 687
Link Motor Supply Company, **26** 347
Linmark Westman International Limited, **25** 221–22
Linroz Manufacturing Company L.P., **25** 245
LINT Company, **64** 237
Lintas: Worldwide, 14 314–16
Lintott Engineering, Ltd., **10** 108
Linz, **16** 559
Lion Corporation, III 44–45; 51 223–26 (upd.)
Lion Manufacturing, **25** 40
Lion Match Company, **24** 450
Lion Nathan Limited, 54 227–30, 342; **63** 229
Lion's Head Brewery. *See* The Stroh Brewery Company.
Lionel L.L.C., 12 494; **16 335–38; 18** 524
Lionex Corporation, **13** 46
Lions Gate Entertainment Corporation, 35 278–81
Liontech, **16** 337–38
Lippincott & Margulies, **III** 283
Lippincott-Raven Publishers, **14** 556
Lipschutz Bros., Inc., **29** 511
Lipson Alport Glass & Associates, **27** 195
Lipton. *See* Thomas J. Lipton Company.
Liqui-Box Corporation, 16 339–41
Liquid Ag Systems Inc., **26** 494
Liquid Carbonic, **7** 74, 77
Liquid Gas Company Ltd., **60** 236
Liquid Holdings, Inc., **45** 168
Liquor Barn, **II** 656
Liquorland, **V** 35
Liquorsave, **II** 609–10
LIRCA, **III** 48
Liris, **23** 212
LIRR. *See* The Long Island Rail Road Company.
Liscaya, **II** 196
Listening Library Inc., **31** 379
Lister, **21** 503
Litehouse Inc., 60 198–201
LiTel Communications, Inc., **16** 318
Lithia Motors, Inc., 41 238–40
Lithonia Lighting, Inc., **54** 252, 254–55
LitleNet, **26** 441
Littelfuse, Inc., 26 266–69
Little, Brown & Company, **IV** 675; **7** 528; **10** 355; **36** 270
Little Caesar Enterprises, Inc., 24 293–96 (upd.); 27 481; **63** 133, 136–37. *See also* Ilitch Holdings Inc.
Little Caesar International, Inc., 7 278–79; 7 278–79; **15** 344, 346; **16** 447; **25** 179, 227–28
Little General, **II** 620; **12** 179, 200
Little Giant Pump Company, **8** 515
Little League Baseball, Incorporated, **23** 450
Little Leather Library, **13** 105
Little, Royal, **8** 545; **13** 63
Little Switzerland, Inc., 19 451; **60 202–04**
Little Tikes Company, 12 169; **13 317–19; 62 231–34 (upd.)**
Littlewoods Financial Services, **30** 494
Littlewoods plc, V 117–19; 24 316; **42 228–32 (upd.)**

Litton Industries Inc., I 484–86; III 473, 732; **6** 599; **10** 537; **11 263–65 (upd.)**, 435; **12** 248, 271–72, 538–40; **15** 287; **19** 31, 110, 290; **21** 86; **22** 436; **45** 306; **48** 383. *See also* Avondale Industries.
Litwin Engineers & Constructors, **8** 546
LIVE Entertainment Inc., 18 64, 66; **20 347–49; 24** 349
LiveAquaria.com., **62** 108
Liverpool Daily Post & Echo Ltd., **49** 405
Liverpool Mexico S.A., **16** 216
Living Arts, Inc., **41** 174
Living Centers of America, **13** 49
Living Videotext, **10** 508
LivingWell Inc., **12** 326
Liz Claiborne, Inc., 8 329–31; 16 37, 61; **25** 258, **291–94 (upd.); 55** 136, 138
LKQ Corporation, 71 201–03
Lledo Collectibles Ltd., **60** 372
LLJ Distributing Company. *See* Spartan Stores Inc.
Lloyd Aereo de Bolivia, **6** 97
Lloyd Creative Staffing, **27** 21
Lloyd George Management, **18** 152
Lloyd Instruments, Ltd., **29** 460–61
Lloyd Italico, **III** 351
Lloyd Thompson Group plc, **20** 313
Lloyd Triestino company, **50** 187
Lloyd-Truax Ltd., **21** 499
Lloyd's Electronics, **14** 118
Lloyd's of London, III 278–81; 9 297; **10** 38; **11** 533; **22 315–19 (upd.)**
Lloyds Bank PLC, II 306–09 319, 334, 358; **17** 324–25; **48** 373
Lloyds Chemists plc, **27** 177
Lloyds Life Assurance, **III** 351
Lloyds TSB Group plc, 39 6; **47 224–29 (upd.); 61** 60, 62
LLP Group plc, **58** 189
LM Ericsson. *See* Telefonaktiebolaget LM Ericsson.
LMC Metals, **19** 380
LME. *See* Telefonaktiebolaget LM Ericsson.
LNM Group, **30** 252
Lo-Cost, **II** 609
Lo-Vaca Gathering Co., **7** 553
Loblaw Companies Limited, II 631–32; 19 116; **43 268–72; 51** 301. *See also* George Weston Limited.
Local Data, Inc., **10** 97
Lockhart Corporation, **12** 564
Lockheed Martin Corporation, I 64–66; 11 266–69 (upd.); 15 283–86 (upd.); 21 86; **24** 88; **29** 409; **32** 437; **33** 47–48; **38** 372, 376; **45** 306; **48** 251; **49** 345, 347; **54** 233; **61** 12, 15
Locksmith Publishing Corp., **56** 75
Lockwood Banc Group, Inc., **11** 306
Lockwood Greene Engineers, Inc., **17** 377
Lockwood National Bank, **25** 114
Lockwood Technology, Inc., **19** 179
Loctite Corporation, 8 332–34; 30 289–91 (upd.); 34 209
Lodding Engineering, **7** 521
Lodestar Group, **10** 19
Lodge Plus, Ltd., **25** 430
LodgeNet Entertainment Corporation, 26 441; **28 240–42**
The Lodging Group, **12** 297; **48** 245
Loehmann's Inc., 24 297–99
Loew's, Inc., **31** 99

The Loewen Group, Inc., 16 342–44; 37 67–68; **40 292–95 (upd.)**. *See also* Alderwoods Group Inc.
Loewenstein Furniture Group, Inc., **21** 531–33
Loews Cineplex Entertainment Corp., **37** 64
Loews Corporation, I 487–88; 12 316–18 (upd.), 418; **13** 120–21; **19** 362; **22** 73; **25** 177, 326–28; **36 324–28 (upd.); 41** 70, 72
LOF Plastics, Inc. *See* Libbey-Owens-Ford.
Loffland Brothers Company, **9** 364
Logan's Roadhouse, Inc., 19 287–88; 22 464; **29 290–92; 35** 84; **60** 230–31
Loganair Ltd., 68 235–37
Logic Modeling, **11** 491
Logica plc, 14 317–19; 37 230–33 (upd.)
Logicon Inc., 20 350–52; 45 68, 310
Logility, **25** 20, 22
Logistics.com, Inc. *See* Manhattan Associates, Inc.
Logistics Data Systems, **13** 4
Logistics Industries Corporation, **39** 77
Logistics Management Systems, Inc., **8** 33
Logitech International S.A., 9 116; **28 243–45; 69 242–45 (upd.)**
Logo Athletic, Inc., **35** 363
Logo 7, Inc., **13** 533
Logon, Inc., **14** 377
Lohja Corporation, **61** 295
LoJack Corporation, 48 269–73
Lojas Arapuã S.A., 22 320–22; 61 175–78 (upd.)
Loma Linda Foods, **14** 557–58
Lomak Petroleum, Inc., **24** 380
Lomas & Nettleton Financial Corporation, **III** 249; **11** 122
London & Hull, **III** 211
London & Midland Bank. *See* Midland Bank plc.
London & Overseas Freighters plc. *See* Frontline Ltd.
London & Rhodesia Mining & Land Company. *See* Lonrho Plc.
London and Scottish Marine Oil, **11** 98
London & Western Trust, **39** 90
London Assurance Corp., **55** 331
London Brick Co., **14** 249
London Brokers Ltd., **6** 290
London Buses Limited. *See* London Regional Transport.
London Cargo Group, **25** 82
London Central, **28** 155–56
London Drugs Ltd., 46 270–73
London East India Company, **12** 421
London Electricity, **12** 443; **41** 141
London Fog Industries, Inc., 16 61; **29 293–96**
London Insurance Group, **III** 373; **36** 372
London International Group. *See* SSL International plc.
London Precision Machine & Tool, Ltd., **39** 32
London Records, **23** 390
London Regional Transport, 6 406–08
London Rubber Co., **49** 380
London Scottish Bank plc, 70 160–62
London South Partnership, **25** 497
London Stock Exchange Limited, 34 253–56; 37 131–33
London Transport, **19** 111
Londontown Manufacturing Company. *See* London Fog Industries, Inc.

Lone Star Brewing Co., **I** 255
Lone Star Funds, **59** 106
Lone Star Industries, **23** 326; **35** 154
Lone Star Steakhouse & Saloon, Inc., 21 250; **51** 227–29
Lone Star Technologies, Inc., **22** 3
Lonely Planet Publications Pty Ltd., 55 253–55
Long Distance Discount Services, Inc., **8** 310; **27** 305
Long Distance/USA, **9** 479
Long Island Bancorp, Inc., 16 345–47; 44 33
Long Island Cable Communication Development Company, **7** 63
Long Island College Hospital. *See* Continuum Health Partners, Inc.
Long Island Lighting Company, V 652–54; 27 264
Long Island Power Authority, **27** 265
The Long Island Rail Road Company, 68 238–40
Long John Silver's, 57 224–29 (upd.)
Long John Silver's Restaurants Inc., 13 320–22; **58** 384
Long Lac Mineral Exploration, **9** 282
Long Life Fish Food Products, **12** 230
Long-Term Credit Bank of Japan, Ltd., II 310–11, 338, 369
Long Valley Power Cooperative, **12** 265
The Longaberger Company, 12 319–21; 44 267–70 **(upd.)**
Longchamps, Inc., **38** 385; **41** 388
LongHorn Steaks Inc., **19** 341
Longman Group Ltd., **IV** 611, 658
Longs Drug Stores Corporation, V 120; 25 295–97 **(upd.)**
Longview Fibre Company, 8 335–37; **37** 234–37 **(upd.)**
Lonmin plc, 66 211–16 (upd.)
Lonrho Plc, 10 170; **21** 351–55; **43** 38; **53** 153, 202. *See also* Lonmin plc.
Lookers plc, 71 204–06
Loomis Armored Car Service Limited, **45** 378
Loomis Fargo Group, **42** 338
Loomis Products, Inc., **64** 349
Loop One2, **53** 240
Loose Leaf Metals Co., Inc., **10** 314
Lor-Al, Inc., **17** 10
Loral Corporation, 7 9; **8** 338–40; **9** 323–25; **13** 356; **15** 283, 285; **20** 262; **47** 319
Loral Space & Communications Ltd., 54 231–35 **(upd.)**
Lord & Taylor, **13** 44; **14** 376; **15** 86; **18** 137, 372; **21** 302
L'Oréal, III 46–49; **8** 129–31; 341–44 **(upd.); 11** 41; **23** 238, 242; **31** 418; **46** 274–79 **(upd.); 52** 211
Lorentzen & Wettre AB, **53** 85
Lorillard Industries, **V** 407, 417; **18** 416; **22** 73; **29** 195
Lorimar Telepictures, **II** 177; **25** 90–91, 329
Loronix Inc., **24** 509
Los Angeles Drug Co., **12** 106
Los Angeles Lakers. *See* California Sports, Inc.
Los Lagos Corp., **12** 175
Loss Prevention Inc., **24** 509
Lost Arrow Inc., 22 323–25
LOT Polish Airlines (Polskie Linie Lotnicze S.A.), 33 268–71

LOT$OFF Corporation, 24 300–01
Lotus Cars Ltd., 14 320–22; 62 268
Lotus Development Corporation, 6 254–56; **9** 81, 140; **10** 24, 505; **12** 335; **16** 392, 394; **20** 238; **21** 86; **25** 298–302 **(upd.); 30** 251; **38** 417; **63** 199
Lotus Publishing Corporation, **7** 239; **25** 239
Louart Corporation, **29** 33–34
Loucks, Hoffman & Company, **8** 412
Loudcloud, Inc. *See* Opsware Inc.
Louis Allis, **15** 288
Louis Cruise Lines, **52** 298–99
Louis Dreyfus. *See* Groupe Louis Dreyfus S.A.
Louis Dreyfus Energy Corp., **28** 471
Louis Harris & Associates, Inc., **22** 188
Louis Kemp Seafood Company, **14** 515; **50** 493
Louis Rich, Inc., **12** 372
Louis Vuitton, I 272; **III** 48; **8** 343; **10** 397–99. *See also* LVMH Moët Hennessy Louis Vuitton SA.
Louisiana & Southern Life Insurance Co., **14** 460
Louisiana Bank & Trust, **11** 106
Louisiana Corporation, **19** 301
Louisiana Energy Services, **27** 130
The Louisiana Land and Exploration Company, 7 280–83
Louisiana-Pacific Corporation, IV 304–05; **16** 203; **22** 491; **31** 314–17 **(upd.); 32** 91; **59** 161
Louisville Gas and Electric Company. *See* LG&E Energy Corporation.
Louisville Home Telephone Company, **14** 258
Loup River Public Power District, **29** 352
Louthan Manufacturing Company, **8** 178
LoVaca Gathering Company. *See* The Coastal Corporation.
Love's Travel Stops & Country Stores, Inc., 71 207–09
Lovelace Truck Service, Inc., **14** 42
Loveman's, Inc., **19** 323
Lowe Group, **22** 294
Lowe's Companies, Inc., V 122–23; 11 384; **12** 234, 345; **18** 239; **21** 324, 356–58 **(upd.); 27** 416; **44** 333
Lowell Shoe, Inc., **13** 360
Löwenbräu, **II** 240
Lower Manhattan Development Corporation, **47** 360
Lowes Food Stores. *See* Alex Lee Inc.
Lowney/Moirs, **II** 512
Lowrance Electronics, Inc., 18 311–14
Lowrey's Meat Specialties, Inc., **21** 156
LPL Investment Group, **40** 35–36
LRC International, **69** 303
LRV Corporation, **61** 173
LS Management, Inc., **51** 229
LSG Sky Chefs, Inc., **68** 109
LSI. *See* Lear Siegler Inc.
LSI Logic Corporation, 13 323–25; 18 382; **64** 243–47
LTR Industries, **52** 301–03
LTU Group Holding GmbH, 37 238–41
LTV Aerospace. *See* Vought Aircraft Industries, Inc.
The LTV Corporation, I 489–91; 7 107–08; **8** 157, 315; **10** 419; **11** 166, 364; **12** 124; **17** 357; **18** 110, 378; **19** 466; **24** 302–06 **(upd.); 26** 406; **45** 306; **52** 254; **59** 282

The Lubrizol Corporation, I 360–62; **21** 385–87; **30** 292–95 **(upd.)**
Luby's Cafeteria's, Inc., 17 290–93; **19** 301
Luby's, Inc., 42 233–38 (upd.)
Lucas Bols, **II** 642
Lucas Digital Ltd., **12** 322
Lucas Industries Plc, III 554–57; 27 251
Lucas Ingredients, **27** 258
Lucas-Milhaupt, Inc., **23** 250
LucasArts Entertainment Company, **32** 9
Lucasfilm Ltd., 9 368, 472; **12** 322–24; **22** 459; **34** 350; **38** 70; **50** 320–23 **(upd.)**
LucasVarity plc, **27** 249, 251
Lucchini, **IV** 228
Lucent Technologies Inc., 18 154, 180; **20** 8; **22** 19; **26** 275, 277; **29** 44, 414; **34** 257–60; **36** 122, 124; **41** 289–90; **44** 426; **48** 92; **61** 17; **63** 203
Lucille Farms, Inc., 45 249–51
Lucky Brand Dungarees, **18** 85
Lucky-Goldstar, II 53–54; **13** 574. *See also* Goldstar Co., Ltd.
Lucky Stores Inc., **II** 605, 653; **6** 355; **8** 474; **12** 48; **17** 369, 559; **22** 39; **27** 290–93
Ludi Wap S.A., **41** 409
Ludovico, **25** 85
Lufkin Rule Co., **II** 16
Luftfahrzeug-Betriebs GmbH, **60** 253
Lufthansa. *See* Deutsche Lufthansa AG.
The Luggage Company, **14** 224
Luigino's, Inc., 64 248–50
Luitpold-Werk GmbH & Co., **56** 303
Lukens Inc., 14 323–25; 27 65
LUKOIL. *See* OAO LUKOIL.
Lumac B.V., **I** 387
Lumbermens Building Centers. *See* Lanoga Corporation.
Lumbertown USA, **52** 232
Lumex, Inc., **17** 197
Lumidor Safety Products, **52** 187
La Lumière Economique, **II** 79
Luminar Plc, 40 296–98
Lummus Crest, **26** 496
Lunar Corporation, 29 297–99
Luncheon Voucher, **27** 10
Lund Boat Co. *See* Genmar Holdings, Inc.
Lund Food Holdings, Inc., 22 326–28
Lund International Holdings, Inc., 40 299–301
Lundstrom Jewelers, **24** 319
Lunenburg Sea Products Limited, **14** 339
L'Unite Hermetique S.A., **8** 515
Lunn Poly, **8** 525–26
Lurgei, **6** 599
LURGI. *See* Metallurgische Gesellschaft Aktiengesellschaft.
Lutèce, **20** 26
Lutheran Brotherhood, 31 318–21
Luxair, **49** 80
Luxor, **6** 205; **17** 353
Luxottica SpA, 17 294–96; **23** 328; **43** 96; **49** 301; **52** 227–30 **(upd.); 54** 320. *See also* Casual Corner Group, Inc.
LuxSonor Semiconductor Inc., **48** 92
Luxury Linens, **13** 81–82
Luzianne Blue Plate Foods. *See* Wm. B. Reily & Company Inc.
LVMH Moët Hennessy Louis Vuitton SA, I 272; **19** 86; **24** 137, 140; **33** 272–77 **(upd.); 45** 344; **46** 277; **49** 90,

326; **51** 234–35; **56** 92; **61** 323. *See also* Christian Dior S.A.
LXE Inc., **21** 199–201
Lycos. *See* Terra Lycos, Inc.
Lydall, Inc., 64 251–54
Lykes Corp., **24** 303
Lyn Knight Currency Auctions, Inc, **48** 100
Lynch Corporation, 43 273–76; 301–02
Lynde Company, **16** 269–71
Lynx Express Delivery. *See* Exel plc.
Lyondell Chemical Company, IV 456–57; 10 110; **45 252–55 (upd.)**
Lyonnaise Communications, **10** 196; **25** 497
Lyonnaise des Eaux-Dumez, V 655–57; 23 332. *See also* Suez Lyonnaise des Eaux.
Lyons. *See* J. Lyons & Co. Ltd.
LyphoMed Inc., **17** 287
Lysaght, **24** 143
Lytag Ltd., **31** 398–99

M & C Saatchi, **42** 330
M&C Systems Co Ltd., **62** 245
M&F Worldwide Corp., 38 293–95
M&G Group plc, **48** 328
M and H Valve Co., **55** 266
M&I Bank. *See* Marshall & Ilsley Corporation.
M&J Diesel Locomotive Filter Co., **17** 106
M&M Limited, **7** 299
M and M Manufacturing Company, **23** 143
M&M/Mars, **14** 48; **15** 63–64; **21** 219
M & S Computing. *See* Intergraph Corporation.
M&T Capital Corporation, **11** 109
M/A Com Inc., **14** 26–27
M-Cell Ltd., **31** 329
M-I Drilling Fluids Co., **III** 473; **15** 468
M-R Group plc, **31** 312–13
M-real Oyj, 56 252–55 (upd.)
M-Web Holdings Ltd., **31** 329–30
M.A. Bruder & Sons, Inc., 56 99, 189, **207–09**
M.A. Gedney Co., 51 230–32
M.A. Hanna Company, 8 345–47; 12 352
M.B. McGerry, **21** 94
M.B. Papeles Especiales, S.A., **68** 258
M.D.C., **11** 258
M.E.P.C. Ltd. *See* MEPC PLC.
M.F. Patterson Dental Supply Co. *See* Patterson Dental Co.
M/G Transport Inc. *See* The Midland Company.
M.G. Waldbaum Company, **25** 332–33
M.H. McLean Wholesaler Grocery Company, **8** 380
M.H. Meyerson & Co., Inc., 46 280–83
M.I. Schottenstein Homes Inc., **19** 125–26
M.J. Brock Corporation, **8** 460
M.J. Designs, Inc., **17** 360
M.L.C. Partners Limited Partnership, **22** 459
M. Loeb Ltd., **II** 652
M.M. Warburg. *See* SBC Warburg.
M.P. Burke PLC, **13** 485–86
M.P. Pumps, Inc., **8** 515
M. Polaner Inc., **10** 70; **40** 51–52; **50** 538
M.S. Carriers, Inc., **42** 363, 365
M. Shanken Communications, Inc., 50 324–27
M. Sobol, Inc., **28** 12
M Stores Inc., **II** 664

M.T.G.I. Textile Manufacturers Group, **25** 121
M.W. Carr, **14** 245
M.W. Kellogg Co., **34** 81; **62** 204
MAAG Gear Wheel, **72** 138, 140
Maakauppiaitten Oy, **8** 293–94
Maatschappij tot Exploitatie van de Onderneming Krasnapolsky. *See* Grand Hotel Krasnapolsky N.V.
Maatschappij tot Exploitatie van Steenfabrieken Udenhout, voorheen Weyers, **14** 249
Mabley & Carew, **10** 282
Mabuchi Motor Co. Ltd., 68 241–43
Mabuhay Vinyl Corporation. *See* Tosoh Corporation.
Mac Frugal's Bargains - Closeouts Inc., 17 297–99
Mac-Gray Corporation, 44 271–73
Mac Publications LLC, **25** 240
The Macallan Distillers Ltd., 63 246–48
MacAndrews & Forbes Holdings Inc., II 679; **9** 129; **11** 334; **28 246–49; 30** 138; **38** 293–94; **64** 333
MacArthur Foundation. *See* The John D. and Catherine T. MacArthur Foundation.
Macau Telephone, **18** 114
Macauley & Co. *See* Greif Inc.
MacCall Management, **19** 158
MacDermid Incorporated, 32 318–21
MacDonald Companies, **15** 87
MacDonald Dettwiler and Associates, **32** 436
MacDonald, Halsted, and Laybourne, **10** 127
Mace Security International, Inc., 57 230–32
The Macerich Company, 57 233–35
Macey Furniture Co., **7** 493
Macfield Inc., **12** 502; **62** 374
MacFrugal's Bargains Close-Outs Inc., **29** 312; **50** 98
MacGregor Golf Company, 68 244–46
MacGregor Sporting Goods Inc., **22** 115, 458; **23** 449
Mach Performance, Inc., **28** 147
Machine Vision International Inc., **10** 232
Macintosh. *See* Apple Computer, Inc.
Mack-Cali Realty Corporation, 42 239–41
Mack Trucks, Inc., I 177–79; 9 416; **12** 90; **22 329–32 (upd.); 61 179–83 (upd.)**
Mack-Wayne Plastics, **42** 439
Mackay Envelope Corporation, 45 256–59
MacKenzie & Co., **II** 361
Mackie Designs Inc., 30 406; **33 278–81**
Maclean Hunter Publishing Limited, IV 638–40, 22 442; **23** 98; **26 270–74 (upd.); 30** 388
Maclin Co., **12** 127
Macluan Capital Corporation, **49** 196
The MacManus Group, **32** 140; **40** 140
MacMark Corp., **22** 459
MacMarr Stores, **II** 654
Macmillan & Co. Ltd., **35** 452
MacMillan Bloedel Limited, IV 306–09; 9 391; **19** 444, 446; **25** 12; **26** 445
Macmillan, Inc., 7 284–86; 9 63; **12** 226; **13** 91, 93; **17** 399; **22** 441–42; **23** 350, 503; **25** 484; **27** 222–23
The MacNeal-Schwendler Corporation, 25 303–05
Macon Kraft Co., **11** 421

Macquarie Bank Ltd., 69 246–49
Macrodata, **18** 87
Macromedia, Inc., 50 328–31; 61 124
MACSTEEL Monroe, Inc., **62** 289
Macwhyte Company, **27** 415
Macy's. *See* R.H. Macy & Co., Inc.
Macy's California, **21** 129
Mad Dog Athletics, **19** 385
MADD. *See* Mothers Against Drunk Driving.
Madden's on Gull Lake, 52 231–34
Madeco S.A., 71 210–12
Madeira Wine Company, S.A., 49 255–57
Maderin ECO S.A., **51** 6
Madge Networks N.V., 18 346; **26 275–77**
Madison & Sullivan, Inc., **10** 215
Madison Dearborn Partners LLC, **46** 289; **49** 197; **51** 131, 282, 284; **69** 197
Madison Financial Corp., **16** 145
Madison Foods, **14** 557
Madison Furniture Industries, **14** 436
Madison Gas and Electric Company, 6 605–06; **39 259–62**
Madison-Kipp Corporation, 58 213–16
Madison Resources, Inc., **13** 502
Madrange SA, 58 217–19
MAEFORT Hungarian Air Transport Joint Stock Company, **24** 310
Maersk Oile, **22** 167; **65** 316–17
Maersk Sealand. *See* A.P. Møller - Maersk A/S.
Maes Group Breweries, **II** 475
Maeva Group. *See* Club Mediterranee SA.
Mafco Holdings, Inc., **28** 248; **38** 293–95
Mag Instrument, Inc., 67 240–42
Magazine and Book Services, **13** 48
MagCorp, **28** 198
Magee Company, **31** 435–36
Magella Healthcare Corporation, **61** 284
Magellan Aerospace Corporation, 46 8; **48 274–76**
Magellan Corporation, **22** 403; **60** 137
Magellan et Bergerat., **72** 159
Magic Chef Co. *See* Maytag Corporation.
Magic City Food Products Company. *See* Golden Enterprises, Inc.
Magic Marker, **29** 372
Magic Pantry Foods, **10** 382
Magic Years Child Care, **51** 198
Magicsilk, Inc., **22** 133
MagicSoft Inc., **10** 557
Maglificio di Ponzano Veneto dei Fratelli Benetton. *See* Benetton.
Magma Copper Company, 7 287–90, 385–87; **22** 107
Magma Power Company, 11 270–72
Magna Computer Corporation, **12** 149; **13** 97
Magna Distribuidora Ltda., **43** 368
Magnaflux, **III** 519; **22** 282
Magnavox Co., **13** 398; **19** 393
MagneTek, Inc., 15 287–89; 41 241–44 (upd.)
Magnetic Controls Company, **10** 18
Magnetic Peripherals Inc., **19** 513–14
Magnivision, **22** 35
La Magona d'Italia, **IV** 228
Magro, **48** 63
MAGroup Inc., **11** 123
Magyar Viscosa, **37** 428
Mahalo Air, **22** 252; **24** 22
Maharam Fabric, **8** 455

Mahir & Numan A.S., **48** 154
MAI PLC, **28** 504
MAI Systems Corporation, 10 242; **11**
   273–76; **26** 497, 499
Maid-Rite Corporation, 62 235–38
Maidenform, Inc., 59 265–69 (upd.)
Maidenform Worldwide Inc., 20 352–55
Mail Boxes Etc., 18 315–17; 25 500; **41**
   245–48 (upd.). *See also* U.S. Office
   Products Company.
Mail.com Inc., **38** 271
Mail Coups, Inc., **53** 13
Mail Finance, **53** 239
Mail Marketing Systems Inc., **53** 13
Mail-Well, Inc., 28 250–52. *See also*
   Cenveo Inc.
MailCoups, Inc., **53** 9
Mailson Ferreira da Nobrega, **II** 200
Mailtek, Inc., **18** 518
MAIN. *See* Mid-American Interpool
   Network.
Main Plaza Corporation, **25** 115
Main Street Advertising USA, **IV** 597
Maine & Maritimes Corporation, 56
   210–13
Maine Central Railroad Company, 16
   348–50
Maines Paper & Food Service Inc., 71
   213–15
Mainline Industrial Distributors, Inc., **13** 79
Mainline Travel, **I** 114
Maison Blanche Department Stores Group,
   35 129
Maison de Schreiber and Aronson, **25** 283
Maison de Valérie, **19** 309
Maison Louis Jadot, 24 307–09
Majestic Contractors Ltd., **8** 419–20
Majestic Industries, Inc., **43** 459
Majestic Wine Warehouses Ltd., **II** 656
The Major Automotive Companies, Inc.,
   45 260–62
Major League Baseball, **12** 457
Major SA, **53** 179
Major Video Concepts, **6** 410
Major Video, Inc., **9** 74
Mak van Waay, **11** 453
Makepeace Preserving Co., **25** 365
Makhteshim-Agan Industries Ltd. *See* Koor
   Industries Ltd.
Makita Corporation, 22 333–35; 59
   270–73 (upd.)
Makivik Corporation, **56** 38–39
Makoff R&D Laboratories, **56** 375
Makovsky & Company, **12** 394
Makro Inc., **18** 286
Malama Pacific Corporation, **9** 276
Malapai Resources, **6** 546
Malayan Banking Berhad, 72 215–18
Malaysian Airlines System Berhad, 6
   100–02; 29 300–03 (upd.)
Malcolm Pirnie, Inc., 42 242–44
Malden Mills Industries, Inc., 16 351–53
Malév Plc, 24 310–12; 27 474; **29** 17
Malew Engineering, **51** 354
Malheur Cooperative Electric Association,
   12 265
Malibu, **25** 141
Mall.com, **38** 271
Mallard Bay Drilling, Inc., **28** 347–48
Malleable Iron Works, **II** 34
Mallinckrodt Group Inc., 8 85; **19** 28,
   251–53; **63** 404
Malmö Aviation, **47** 61

Malmö Woodworking Factory. *See* Tarkett
   Sommer AG.
Malone & Hyde, Inc., **II** 625, 670–71; **9**
   52–53; **14** 147; **18** 506; **50** 456–57
Malt-O-Meal Company, 15 189; **22**
   336–38; 63 249–53 (upd.)
Malterie Soufflet. *See* Groupe Soufflet SA
Mama Fu's Noodle House, Inc., **64**
   327–28
Mama's Concept, Inc., **51** 229
Mameco International, **8** 455
Mammoet Transport B.V., 26 241,
   278–80
Man Aktiengesellschaft, III 301, **561–63**
MAN Gutehoffnungshütte AG, **15** 226
Management and Training Corporation,
   28 253–56
Management By Information Inc., **48** 307
Management Decision Systems, Inc., **10**
   358
Management Recruiters International. *See*
   CDI Corp.
Management Science America, Inc., **11** 77;
   25 20
Manchester Board and Paper Co., **19** 77
Manchester United Football Club plc, 30
   296–98; 44 388
Manco, Inc. *See* Henkel Manco Inc.
Mancuso & Co., **22** 116
Mandabach & Simms, **6** 40
Mandalay Pictures, **35** 278–80
Mandalay Resort Group, 32 322–26
   (upd.)
Mandarin, Inc., **33** 128
Mandarin Oriental Hotel Group
   International Ltd., **I** 471; **20** 312
Mandarin Oriental International Limited,
   47 177
Manetta Mills, Inc., **19** 304
Manhattan Associates, Inc., 67 243–45
Manhattan Bagel Inc., **63** 80
Manhattan Card Co., **18** 114
Manhattan Construction Company. *See*
   Rooney Brothers Co.
Manhattan Electrical Supply Co., **9** 517
Manhattan International Limousine
   Network Ltd., **26** 62
Manheim Auctions, Inc. *See* Cox
   Enterprises, Inc.
Manila Electric Company (Meralco), 56
   214–16
Manischewitz Company. *See* B.
   Manischewitz Company.
Manistique Papers Inc., **17** 282
Manitoba Bridge and Engineering Works
   Ltd., **8** 544
Manitoba Rolling Mill Ltd., **8** 544
Manitoba Telecom Services, Inc., 61
   184–87
Manitou BF S.A., 27 294–96
The Manitowoc Company, Inc., 18
   318–21; 59 274–79 (upd.)
Mann Theatres Chain, **25** 177
Mann's Wine Company, Ltd., **14** 288
Mann's Wine Pub Co., Ltd., **47** 206
Mannatech Inc., 33 282–85
Mannesmann AG, III 564–67; 14 326–29
   (upd.); 34 319; **38 296–301 (upd.); 54**
   391, 393. *See also* Vodafone Group
   PLC.
Mannheim Steamroller. *See* American
   Gramophone LLC.
Manning, Selvage & Lee. *See* D'Arcy
   Masius Benton & Bowles, Inc.

Manor AG, **48** 279
Manor Care, Inc., 6 187–90; 14 105–07;
   15 522; **25 306–10 (upd.)**
Manor Healthcare Corporation, **26** 459
Manos Enterprises, **14** 87
Manpower, Inc., 9 326–27; 16 48; **25**
   432; **30 299–302 (upd.); 40** 236, 238;
   44 157; **49** 264–65
Mantrec S.A., **27** 296
Mantua Metal Products. *See* Tyco Toys,
   Inc.
Manufactured Home Communities, Inc.,
   22 339–41; 46 378
Manufacturera Mexicana de Partes de
   Automoviles S.A., **56** 247
Manufacturers and Traders Trust Company,
   11 108–09
Manufacturers Casualty Insurance Co., **26**
   486
Manufacturers Fire Insurance Co., **26** 486
Manufacturers Hanover Corporation, II
   312–14; 9 124; **11** 16, 54, 415; **13** 536;
   14 103; **16** 207; **17** 559; **22** 406; **26** 453;
   38 253. *See also* Chemical Bank.
Manufacturers National Bank of Detroit, **40**
   116
Manufacturing Management Inc., **19** 381
Manutan International S.A., 72 219–21
Manville Corporation, III 706–09, 721; 7
   291–95 (upd.); 10 43, 45; **11** 420–22.
   See also Johns Manville Corporation.
Manweb plc, **19** 389–90; **49** 363–64
MAP. *See* Marathon Ashland Petroleum
   LLC.
MAPCO Inc., IV 458–59; 26 234; **31**
   469, 471
Mapelli Brothers Food Distribution Co., **13**
   350
MAPICS, Inc., 55 256–58
Maple Grove Farms of Vermont, Inc., **40**
   51–52
Maple Leaf Foods Inc., 41 249–53
Maple Leaf Mills, **41** 252
Maple Leaf Sports & Entertainment
   Ltd., 61 188–90
MAPP. *See* Mid-Continent Area Power
   Planner.
Mapra Industria e Comercio Ltda., **32** 40
MAR Associates, **48** 54
Mar-O-Bar Company, **7** 299
Marantha! Music, **14** 499
Marantz Co., **14** 118
Marathon Ashland Petroleum LLC, **49**
   329–30; **50** 49
Marathon Insurance Co., **26** 486
Marathon Oil Co., **13** 458; **49** 328, 330.
   See also United States Steel Corp.
Marauder Company, **26** 433
Marblehead Communications, Inc., **23** 101
Marbodal, **12** 464
Marboro Books, Inc., **10** 136
Marbro Lamp Co., **III** 571; **20** 362
Marc's Big Boy. *See* The Marcus
   Corporation.
Marcade Group. *See* Aris Industries, Inc.
Marcam Coporation. *See* MAPICS, Inc.
Marceau Investments, **II** 356
March-Davis Bicycle Company, **19** 383
March of Dimes, 31 322–25
March Plasma Systems, Inc., **48** 299
Marchand, **13** 27
Marchesi Antinori SRL, 42 245–48
Marchex, Inc., 72 222–24
marchFIRST, Inc., 34 261–64

Marchland Holdings Ltd., **II** 649
Marchon Eyewear, **22** 123
Marciano Investments, Inc., **24** 157
Marcillat, **19** 49
Marco Acquisition Corporation, **62** 268
Marcolin S.p.A., 61 191–94; 62 100
Marcon Coating, Inc., **22** 347
Marconi plc, 33 286–90 **(upd.)**
The Marcus Corporation, 21 359–63
Marcy Fitness Products, Inc., **19** 142, 144
Maremont Corporation, **8** 39–40
Margarete Steiff GmbH, 23 334–37
Marge Carson, Inc., **III** 571; **20** 362
Margo's La Mode, **10** 281–82; **45** 15
Marico Acquisition Corporation, **8** 448, 450
Marie Brizard & Roger International S.A., 22 342–44
Marie Callender's Restaurant & Bakery, Inc., 13 66; **28** 257–59
Marina Mortgage Company, **46** 25
Marine Bank and Trust Co., **11** 105
Marine Computer Systems, **6** 242
Marine Harvest, **13** 103; **56** 257
Marine Manufacturing Corporation, **52** 406
Marine Midland Corp., **9** 475–76; **11** 108; **17** 325
Marine Transport Lines, Inc., **59** 323
Marine United Inc., **42** 361
Marinela, **19** 192–93
MarineMax, Inc., 30 303–05; **37** 396
Marinette Marine Corporation, **59** 274, 278
Marion Brick, **14** 249
Marion Foods, Inc., **17** 434; **60** 268
Marion Laboratories Inc., I 648–49; **8** 149; **9** 328–29; **16** 438; **50** 163
Marion Manufacturing, **9** 72
Marion Merrell Dow, Inc., 9 328–29 (upd.)
Marionet Corp., **IV** 680–81
Marionnaud Parfumeries SA, 51 233–35; **54** 265–66
Marisa Christina, Inc., 15 290–92; **25** 245
Maritime Electric Company, Limited, **15** 182; **47** 136–37
Maritz Inc., 38 302–05
Mark Controls Corporation, **30** 157
Mark Cross, Inc., **17** 4–5
Mark Goldston, **8** 305
Mark IV Industries, Inc., 7 296–98; **21** 418; **28 260–64 (upd.); 61** 66
Mark Travel Corporation, **30** 448
Mark Trouser, Inc., **17** 338
Mark's Work Wearhouse Ltd. *See* Canadian Tire Corporation, Limited.
Markborough Properties, **V** 81; **8** 525; **25** 221
Market Development Corporation. *See* Spartan Stores Inc.
Market Growth Resources, **23** 480
Market National Bank, **13** 465
Marketing Data Systems, Inc., **18** 24
Marketing Equities International, **26** 136
MarketSpan Corp. *See* KeySpan Energy Co.
Märklin Holding GmbH, 70 163–66
Marks and Spencer p.l.c., II 678; **V 124–26; 10** 442; **17** 42, 124; **22** 109, 111; **24** 268, 270; **313–17 (upd.),** 474; **28** 96; **35** 308, 310; **41** 114; **42** 231; **61** 258–59, 261; **62** 342–43
Marks-Baer Inc., **11** 64

Marks Brothers Jewelers, Inc., 24 318–20
Marlene Industries Corp., **16** 36–37
Marley Co., **19** 360
Marley Holdings, L.P., **19** 246
Oy Marli Ab, **56** 103
Marman Products Company, **16** 8
The Marmon Group,
The Marmon Group, Inc., IV 135–38; **16 354–57 (upd.); 70 167–72 (upd.)**
Marmon-Perry Light Company, **6** 508
Marolf Dakota Farms, Inc., **18** 14–15
Marotte, **21** 438
Marpac Industries Inc. *See* PVC Container Corporation.
Marquam Commercial Brokerage Company, **21** 257
Marquette Electronics, Inc., 13 326–28
Marquis Who's Who, **17** 398
Marr S.p.A., **57** 82–84
Marriner Group, **13** 175
Marriot Inc., **29** 442
Marriot Management Services, **29** 444
Marriott Corporation, II 608; **III 102–03,** 248; **7** 474–75; **9** 95, 426; **15** 87; **17** 238; **18** 216; **19** 433–34; **21** 91, 364; **22** 131; **23** 436–38; **27** 334; **38** 386; **41** 82; **64** 340
Marriott International, Inc., 21 182, **364–67 (upd.); 29** 403, 406; **41** 156–58; **52** 415
Mars, Incorporated, 7 299–301; 22 298, 528; **40 302–05 (upd.)**
Marsh & McLennan Companies, Inc., III 282–84; **10** 39; **14** 279; **45** 28, **263–67 (upd.); 53** 64
Marsh Supermarkets, Inc., 17 300–02
Marshall & Ilsley Corporation, 56 217–20
Marshall Amplification plc, 62 239–42
Marshall Die Casting, **13** 225
Marshall Field's, 8 33; **9** 213; **12** 283; **15** 86; **18** 488; **22** 72; **50** 117, 119; **61** 394, 396; **63** 242, 244, **254–63.** *See also* Target Corporation.
Marshall Industries, **19** 311
Marshalls Incorporated, 13 329–31; 14 62
Marship Tankers (Holdings) Ltd., **52** 329
Marstellar, **13** 204
Marstons, **57** 412–13
The Mart, **9** 120
Martank Shipping Holdings Ltd., **52** 329
Martek Biosciences Corporation, 65 218–20
Marten Transport, **27** 404
Martha Lane Adams, **27** 428
Martha Stewart Living Omnimedia, L.L.C., 24 321–23; **47** 211
Martin & Pagenstecher GMBH, **24** 208
Martin-Baker Aircraft Company Limited, 61 195–97
Martin Band Instrument Company, **55** 149, 151
Martin Bros. Tobacco Co., **14** 19
Martin Collet, **19** 50
Martin Dunitz, **44** 416
Martin Gillet Co., **55** 96, 98
Martin Guitar Company. *See* C.F. Martin & Co., Inc.
Martin Hilti Foundation, **53** 167
Martin Industries, Inc., 44 274–77
Martin Marietta Corporation, I 67–69, 416; **IV** 163; **7** 356, 520; **8** 315; **9** 310;

10 162, 199, 484; **11** 166, 277–78, 364; **12** 127, 290; **13** 327, 356; **15** 283; **17** 564; **18** 369; **19** 70; **22** 400; **28** 288. *See also* Lockheed Martin Corporation.
Martin Mathys, **8** 456
Martin Sorrell, **6** 54
Martin Theaters, **14** 86
Martin-Yale Industries, Inc., **19** 142–44
Martin Zippel Co., **16** 389
Martin's, **12** 221
Martindale-Hubbell, **17** 398
Martini & Rossi SpA, 18 41; **63 264–66**
Martinus Nijhoff, **14** 555; **25** 85
Martz Group, 56 221–23
Marubeni Corporation, 24 324–27 (upd.)
Marubeni K.K., I 492–95; **12** 147; **17** 556
Maruetsu, **17** 124; **41** 114
Marui Company Ltd., V 127; **62 243–45 (upd.)**
Marusa Co. Ltd., **51** 379
Maruti Udyog Ltd., **59** 393, 395–97
Maruzen Co., Limited, IV 403–04, 476, 554; **18** 322–24
Maruzen Oil Co., Ltd., **53** 114
Marvel Entertainment Group, Inc., 10 400–02; 18 426, 520–21; **21** 404; **25** 141; **34** 449
Marvin & Leonard Advertising, **13** 511–12
Marvin H. Sugarman Productions Inc., **20** 48
Marvin Lumber & Cedar Company, 10 95; **22 345–47**
Marwick, Mitchell & Company, **10** 385
Marx, **12** 494
Mary Ann Co. Ltd., **V** 89
Mary Ann Restivo, Inc., **8** 323
Mary Ellen's, Inc., **11** 211
Mary Kathleen Uranium, **IV** 59–60
Mary Kay Corporation, 9 330–32; **12** 435; **15** 475, 477; **18** 67, 164; **21** 49, 51; **30 306–09 (upd.)**
Maryland Cup Company, **8** 197
Maryland Medical Laboratory Inc., **26** 391
Maryland National Corp., **11** 287
Maryland National Mortgage Corporation, **11** 121; **48** 177
Maryland Square, Inc., **68** 69
Marzotto S.p.A., 20 356–58; **48** 206–07; **67 246–49 (upd.)**
Masayoshi Son, **13** 481–82
Maschinenfabrik Augsburg-Nürnberg. *See* M.A.N.
Masco Corporation, III 568–71; **11** 385, 534–35; **12** 129, 131, 344; **13** 338; **18** 68; **20 359–63 (upd.); 39 263–68 (upd.)**
Masco Optical, **13** 165
Mase Westpac Limited, **11** 418
Maserati. *See* Officine Alfieri Maserati S.p.A.
Maserati Footwear, Inc., **68** 69
Mashantucket Pequot Gaming Enterprise Inc., 35 282–85
MASkargo Ltd. *See* Maladian Airlines System Bhd.
Masland Corporation, 17 303–05; **19** 408
Mason Best Co., **IV** 343
Masonite International Corporation, 63 267–69
Mass Rapid Transit Corp., **19** 111
Massachusetts Capital Resources Corp., **III** 314
Massachusetts Electric Company, **51** 265

Massachusetts Mutual Life Insurance Company, III 285–87, 305; 25 528; 53 210–13 (upd.)
Massachusetts Technology Development Corporation, 18 570
Massachusetts's General Electric Company, 32 267
Massey Energy Company, 57 236–38
MasTec, Inc., 55 259–63 (upd.)
Master Builders, I 673
Master Cellars Inc., 68 146
Master Electric Company, 15 134
Master Glass & Color, 24 159–60
Master Lock Company, 45 268–71
Master Loom, 63 151
Master Processing, 19 37
Master Products, 14 162
Master Shield Inc., 7 116
Master Tank and Welding Company, 7 541
Master Tek International, Inc., 47 372
MasterBrand Cabinets, Inc., 71 216–18
MasterCard International, Inc., 9 333–35; 18 337, 543; 25 41; 26 515; 41 201; 61 248
Mastercraft Homes, Inc., 11 257
Masters-Jackson, 50 49
Mastex Industries, 29 132
Maszovlet. See Malév Plc.
Matador Records, 22 194
Matairco, 9 27
Matalan PLC, 49 258–60
Matane Pulp & Paper Company, 17 281
Match.com, 71 136
Matchbox Toys Ltd., 12 168
MatchLogic, Inc., 41 198
Matco Tools, 7 116
Material Management and Services Inc., 28 61
Material Sciences Corporation, 54 331; 63 270–73
Mathematica, Inc., 22 291
Mather Metals, III 582
Mathews Conveyor Co., 14 43
Matra, IV 617–19; 13 356; 17 354; 24 88
Matra Aerospace Inc., 22 402
Matra-Hachette S.A., 15 293–97 (upd.); 21 267. See also European Aeronautic Defence and Space Company EADS N.V.
Matria Healthcare, Inc., 17 306–09
Matrix Science Corp., 14 27
Matrix Service Company, 65 221–23
Matsumoto Medical Instruments, Inc., 11 476; 29 455
Matsushita Electric Industrial Co., Ltd., II 55–56, 58, 61, 91–92, 102, 117–19, 361, 455; 10 286, 389, 403, 432; 11 487; 12 448; 13 398; 18 18; 20 81; 26 511; 33 432; 36 399–400, 420; 64 255–58 (upd.)
Matsushita Electric Works, Ltd., III 710–11; 7 302–03 (upd.); 12 454; 16 167; 27 342
Matsushita Kotobuki Electronics Industries, Ltd., 10 458–59
Matsuzakaya Company Ltd., V 129–31; 64 259–62 (upd.)
Matt Prentice Restaurant Group, 70 173–76
Mattatuck Bank & Trust Co., 13 467
Mattel, Inc., 7 304–07; 12 168–69, 495; 13 560–61; 15 238; 16 428; 17 243; 18 520–21; 25 311–15 (upd.), 381, 488; 27 20, 373, 375; 28 159; 29 74, 78; 32 187;

34 369–70; 52 192–93; 61 198–203 (upd.), 390, 392
Matth. Hohner AG, 53 214–17
Matthew Bender & Company, Inc., IV 677; 7 94; 14 97; 17 486
Matthews International Corporation, 29 304–06
Matthews Paint Co., 22 437
Matussière et Forest SA, 58 220–22
Maui Electric Company, 9 276
Maui Land & Pineapple Company, Inc., 29 307–09
Maui Tacos International, Inc., 49 60
Mauna Loa Macadamia Nut Corporation, 64 263–65
Maus Frères SA, 19 307; 48 277–79
Maverick Tube Corporation, 59 280–83
Max & Erma's Restaurants Inc., 19 258–60
Max Factor & Co., 12 314
Max-Grundig-Stiftung, 27 190–91
Max Media Properties LLC, 25 419
Max Television Co., 25 418
Maxco Inc., 17 310–11; 24 159, 160
Maxell Corp., 14 534
Maxfield Candy Company. See Alpine Confections, Inc.
Maxi-Papier-Markt, 10 498; 24 270
Maxi Vac, Inc., 9 72
Maxicare Health Plans, Inc., III 84–86; 25 316–19 (upd.); 44 174
Maxie's of America, 25 389
The Maxim Group, 25 88, 320–22
Maxim Integrated Products, Inc., 16 358–60
MAXIMUS, Inc., 43 277–80
Maxis Software, 13 115
Maxoptix Corporation, 10 404
Maxpro Sports Inc., 22 458
Maxpro Systems, 24 509–10
Maxtor Corporation, 10 403–05, 459, 463–64
Maxus Energy Corporation, 7 308–10; 10 191
Maxvalu Hokkaido Co., Ltd., 68 9
Maxwell Communication Corporation plc, IV 611, 641–43; 7 286, 311–13 (upd.), 343; 10 288; 13 91–93; 23 350; 39 49; 47 326; 49 408
Maxwell Shoe Company, Inc., 30 310–12
Maxwell Travel Inc., 33 396
MAXXAM Inc., 8 348–50
Maxxcom Inc., 63 290–91
Maxxim Medical Inc., 12 325–27
May & Speh Inc., 35 17
The May Department Stores Company, V 132–35; 8 288; 11 349; 12 55, 507–08; 13 42, 361; 15 275; 16 62, 160, 206–07; 18 414–15; 19 261–64 (upd.); 23 345; 27 61, 291, 346, 348; 33 471, 473; 46 284–88 (upd.); 60 3; 63 259–61, 263
May International. See George S. May International Company.
Mayer & Schweitzer, 26 66
Mayer, Brown, Rowe & Maw, 47 230–32
Mayfield Dairy Farms, Inc., 7 128
Mayflower Group Inc., 6 409–11; 15 50
Mayo Foundation, 9 336–39; 13 326; 34 265–69 (upd.)
Mayor's Jewelers, Inc., 41 254–57
Mays + Red Spot Coatings, LLC, 55 321

Maytag Corporation, III 572–73; 12 252, 300; 21 141; 22 218, 348–51 (upd.); 23 244; 42 159; 43 166; 61 36
Mazda Motor Corporation, II 4, 361; 9 340–42; 11 86; 13 414; 16 322; 23 338–41 (upd.); 36 215; 63 274–79 (upd.); 64 128, 133
Mazel Stores, Inc., 29 310–12
MB Group. See Novar plc.
MBB. See Messerschmitt-Bölkow-Blohm.
MBC. See Middle East Broadcasting Centre, Ltd.
MBC Holding Company, 40 306–09
MBE. See Mail Boxes Etc.
MBG Marketing, 62 154
MBNA Corporation, 11 123; 12 328–30; 33 291–94 (upd.)
MC Distribution Services, Inc., 35 298
MC Sporting Goods. See Michigan Sporting Goods Distributors Inc.
MCA Inc., II 143–45; 10 286; 11 557; 17 317; 21 23, 25–26; 22 131, 194; 25 411; 26 151, 314; 33 431; 52 191; 64 257. See also Universal Studios.
McAfee Associates. See Network Associates, Inc.
McAlister's Corporation, 66 217–19
MCall, 64 57
The McAlpin Company, 19 272
McAndrew & Forbes Holdings Inc., 23 407; 26 119
McArthur Glen Realty, 10 122; 33 59
MCC. See Maxwell Communications Corporation; Morris Communications Corporation.
McCain Foods, 41 252
McCall Pattern Company, 22 512; 23 99
McCall Printing Co., 14 460
McCall's Corp., 23 393
McCann-Erickson Worldwide, 14 315; 16 167; 18 68; 22 294
McCann-Erickson Hakuhodo, Ltd., 42 174
McCarthy Building Companies, Inc., 48 280–82
McCarthy Milling, II 631; 27 245–47
McCaw Cellular Communications, Inc., 6 274, 322–24; 7 15; 9 320–21; 10 433; 15 125, 196; 27 341, 343–44; 29 44, 61; 36 514–15; 43 447; 49 71–72. See also AT&T Wireless Services, Inc.
McClain Industries, Inc., 51 236–38
McClatchy Newspapers, Inc., 23 156, 158, 342–44
McCleary, Wallin and Crouse, 19 274
McClintic-Marshall, 7 49
The McCloskey Corporation, 8 553
The McClure Syndicate, 25 138
McColl-Frontenac Petroleum Inc., IV 439; 25 232
McComb Manufacturing Co., 8 287
McCormack & Dodge, IV 605; 11 77
McCormick & Company, Incorporated, 7 314–16; 17 104, 106; 21 497; 27 297–300 (upd.); 36 185, 188; 63 84; 64 414
McCormick & Schmick's Seafood Restaurants, Inc., 71 219–21
McCown De Leeuw & Co., 16 510; 71 363–64
McCoy Corporation, 58 223–25
McCracken Brooks, 23 479; 25 91
McCrory Stores, 9 447–48
McCulloch Corp., 8 348–49

McCullough Environmental Services, **12** 443

McDermott International, Inc., III 558–60; 37 242–46 (upd.)

McDonald's Corporation, II 646–48; 7 317–19 (upd.); 26 281–85 (upd.); 63 280–86 (upd.)

McDonnell Douglas Corporation, I 70–72; 11 277–80 (upd.); 12 190–91; 13 356; **15** 283; **16** 78, 94; **18** 368; **32** 81, 83, 85; **63** 397

McDougal, Littell & Company, **10** 357

McDowell Energy Center, **6** 543

McDowell Furniture Company, **10** 183

McDuff, **10** 305

McElligott Wright Morrison and White, **12** 511

McFadden Holdings L.P., **27** 41

MCG PCS Inc., **69** 233

McGaughy, Marsha 584, **634–37**, 643, 656, 674; **10** 62; **12** 359; **13** 417; **18 325–30 (upd.)**; **26** 79; **27** 360

McGaw Inc., **11** 208

McGraw-Edison Co., **II** 17, 87

McGraw Electric Company. *See* Centel Corporation.

The McGraw-Hill Companies, Inc., IV 584, 634–37, 643, 656, 674; 12 359; **13** 417; **18 325–30 (upd.)**; **26** 79; **27** 360; **51 239–44 (upd.)**

McGregor Corporation, **26** 102

McGrew Color Graphics, **7** 430

MCI. *See* Manitou Costruzioni Industriali SRL; Melamine Chemicals, Inc.

MCI WorldCom, Inc., V 302–04; 27 301–08 (upd.)

McIlhenny Company, 20 364–67

McIlwraith McEachern Limited, **27** 474

McJunkin Corporation, 13 79; **28** 61; **63 287–89**

McKechnie plc, 34 270–72

McKee Foods Corporation, 7 320–21; 27 309–11 (upd.)

McKenna Metals Company, **13** 295–96

McKesson Corporation, I 496–98, 713; II 652; **8** 464; **9** 532; **11** 91; **12 331–33 (upd.)**; **16** 43; **18** 97; **37** 10; **41** 340; **47 233–37 (upd.)**

McKesson General Medical, **29** 299

McKinsey & Company, Inc., 9 343–45; 10 175; **13** 138; **18** 68; **25** 34; **26** 161

McLain Grocery, **II** 625

McLane America, Inc., **29** 481

McLane Company, Inc., 8 556; **13 332–34; 36** 269

McLaren Consolidated Cone Corp., **7** 366

McLean Clinic, **11** 379

McLeodUSA Incorporated, 32 327–30; 38 192

McLouth Steel Products, **13** 158

MCM Electronics, **9** 420

McMahan's Furniture Co., **14** 236

MCMC. *See* Minneapolis Children's Medical Center.

McMenamins Pubs and Breweries, 65 224–26

McMoCo, **7** 187

McMoRan, **7** 185, 187

McMullen & Yee Publishing, **22** 442

McMurtry Manufacturing, **8** 553

MCN Corporation, 6 519–22; 13 416; **17** 21–23; **45** 254

McNeil Corporation, **26** 363

McNeil Laboratories. *See* Johnson & Johnson

MCO Holdings Inc., **8** 348–49

MCorp, **10** 134; **11** 122

McPaper AG, **29** 152

McPherson's Ltd., 66 220–22

McQuay International. *See* AAF-McQuay Incorporated.

McRae's, Inc., **19** 324–25; **41** 343–44

MCS, Inc., **10** 412

MCSi, Inc., 41 258–60

MCT Dairies, Inc., **18** 14–16

MCTC. *See* Medical Center Trading Corporation.

McTeigue & Co., **14** 502

McWane Corporation, 55 264–66

McWhorter Inc., **8** 553; **27** 280

MD Distribution Inc., **15** 139

MD Foods (Mejeriselskabet Danmark Foods), **48** 35

MDC. *See* Mead Data Central, Inc.

MDC Partners Inc., 63 290–92

MDI Entertainment, LLC, **64** 346

MDP. *See* Madison Dearborn Partners LLC.

MDS/Bankmark, **10** 247

MDU Resources Group, Inc., 7 322–25; 42 249–53 (upd.)

Mead & Mount Construction Company, **51** 41

The Mead Corporation, IV 310–13, 327, 329, 342–43; 8 267; **9** 261; **10** 406; **11** 421–22; **17** 399; **19 265–69 (upd.)**; **20** 18; **33** 263, 265

Mead Data Central, Inc., 7 581; **10 406–08**. *See also* LEXIS-NEXIS Group.

Mead John & Co., **19** 103

Mead Packaging, **12** 151

Meade County Rural Electric Cooperative Corporation, **11** 37

Meade Instruments Corporation, 41 261–64

Meadow Gold Dairies, Inc., **II** 473

Meadowcraft, Inc., 29 313–15

Means Services, Inc., **II** 607

Measurement Specialties, Inc., 71 222–25

Measurex Corporation, **8** 243; **14** 56; **38** 227

Mebetoys, **25** 312

MEC. *See* Mitsubishi Estate Company, Limited.

MECA Software, Inc., **18** 363

Mecair, S.p.A., **17** 147

MECAR S.A. *See* The Allied Defense Group.

Mecca Bingo Ltd., **64** 320

Mecca Bookmakers, **49** 450

Mecca Leisure PLC, **12** 229; **32** 243

Meccano S.A., **52** 207

Mechanics Exchange Savings Bank, **9** 173

Mecklermedia Corporation, 24 328–30; 26 441; **27** 360, 362

Meconic, **49** 230, 235

Medal Distributing Co., **9** 542

Medallion Pictures Corp., **9** 320

Medar, Inc., **17** 310–11

Medco Containment Services Inc., 9 346–48; 11 291; **12** 333; **44** 175

Medeco Security Locks, Inc., **10** 350

Medford, Inc., **19** 467–68

Medi Mart Drug Store Company. *See* The Stop & Shop Companies, Inc.

Media Arts Group, Inc., 42 254–57

Media Exchange International, **25** 509

Media General, Inc., III 214; 7 326–28; 18 61; **23** 225; **38 306–09 (upd.)**

Media Groep West B.V., **23** 271

Media News Corporation, **25** 507

Media Play. *See* Musicland Stores Corporation.

MediaBay, **41** 61

Mediacom Communications Corporation, 25 373; **69 250–52**

Mediamark Research, **28** 501, 504

Mediamatics, Inc., **26** 329

MediaNews Group, Inc., 70 177–80

MediaOne Group Inc. *See* U S West, Inc.

Mediaplex, Inc., **49** 433

Mediaset SpA, 50 332–34

Media24. *See* Naspers Ltd.

Medic Computer Systems LLC, **16** 94; **45** 279–80

Medical Arts Press, Inc., **55** 353, 355

Medical Care America, Inc., **15** 112, 114; **35** 215–17

Medical Center Trading Corporation, **70** 182

Medical China Publishing Limited, **51** 244

Medical Development Corp. *See* Cordis Corp.

Medical Development Services, Inc., **25** 307

Medical Economics Data, **23** 211

Medical Equipment Finance Corporation, **51** 108

Medical Indemnity of America, **10** 160

Medical Information Technology Inc., 64 266–69

Medical Innovations Corporation, **21** 46

Medical Learning Company, **51** 200, 203

Medical Management International, Inc., 65 227–29

Medical Marketing Group Inc., **9** 348

Medical Service Assoc. of Pennsylvania. *See* Pennsylvania Blue Shield.

Medical Tribune Group, **IV** 591; **20** 53

Medicare-Glaser, **17** 167

Medicine Bow Coal Company, **7** 33–34

Medicine Shoppe International. *See* Cardinal Health, Inc.

Medicis Pharmaceutical Corporation, 59 284–86

Medicor, Inc., **36** 496

Medicus Intercon International. *See* D'Arcy Masius Benton & Bowles, Inc.

Medifinancial Solutions, Inc., **18** 370

MedImmune, Inc., 35 286–89

Medinol Ltd., **37** 39

Mediobanca Banca di Credito Finanziario SpA, **11** 205; **65** 86, 88, 230–31

Mediocredito Toscano, **65** 72

Mediolanum S.p.A., 65 230–32

The Mediplex Group, Inc., **11** 282

Medis Health and Pharmaceuticals Services Inc., **II** 653

Medite Corporation, **19** 467–68

MEDITECH. *See* Medical Information Technology Inc.

Meditrust, 11 281–83

Medline Industries, Inc., 61 204–06

MedPartners, Inc. *See* Caremark Rx, Inc.

Medsep Corporation, **72** 265

Medtech, Ltd., **13** 60–62

Medtronic, Inc., 8 351–54; 11 459; **18** 421; **19** 103; **22** 359–61; **26** 132; **30 313–17 (upd.)**; **37** 39; **43** 349; **67 250–55 (upd.)**

Medusa Corporation, 8 135; **24** 331–33; **30** 156
Mega Bloks, Inc., 61 207–09
The MEGA Life and Health Insurance Co., **33** 418–20
MEGA Natural Gas Company, **11** 28
MegaBingo, Inc., **41** 273, 275
Megafoods Stores Inc., 13 335–37; **17** 560
Megahouse Corp., **55** 48
MegaKnowledge Inc., **45** 206
Megasong Publishing, **44** 164
Megasource, Inc., **16** 94
Meggitt PLC, 34 273–76; **48** 432, 434
MEGTEC Systems Inc., **54** 331
MEI Diversified Inc., **18** 455; **70** 262
Mei Foo Investments Ltd., **IV** 718; **38** 319
Meier & Frank Co., 23 345–47
Meierjohan-Wengler Inc., **56** 23
Meijer Incorporated, 7 329–31; **15** 449; **17** 302; **27** 312–15 (upd.)
Meiji Milk Products Company, Limited, II 538–39
Meiji Mutual Life Insurance Company, III 288–89
Meiji Seika Kaisha Ltd., II 540–41; **64** 270–72 (upd.)
Meinecke Muffler Company, **10** 415
Meineke Discount Muffler Shops, **38** 208
Meis of Illiana, **10** 282
Meisel. See Samuel Meisel & Co.
Meisenzahl Auto Parts, Inc., **24** 205
Meister, Lucious and Company, **13** 262
Meiwa Manufacturing Co., **III** 758
Mel Farr Automotive Group, 20 368–70
Melaleuca Inc., 31 326–28
Melamine Chemicals, Inc., 27 316–18
Melbourne Engineering Co., **23** 83
Meldisco. See Footstar, Incorporated.
Melitta Unternehmensgruppe Bentz KG, 53 218–21
Mello Smello. See The Miner Group International.
Mellon Bank Corporation, II 315–17, 342, 402; **9** 470; **13** 410–11; **18** 112
Mellon Financial Corporation, 42 76; **44** 278–82 (upd.); **55** 71
Mellon Indemnity Corp., **24** 177
Mellon Stuart Building Services, Inc., **51** 248
Mellon-Stuart Co., I 584–85; **14** 334
Melmarkets, **24** 462
Meloy Laboratories, Inc., **11** 333
Melroe Company, **8** 115–16; **34** 46
Melville Corporation, V 136–38; **9** 192; **13** 82, 329–30; **14** 426; **15** 252–53;, **16** 390; **19** 449; **21** 526; **23** 176; **24** 167, 290; **35** 253; **57** 368. See also CVS Corporation.
Melvin Simon and Associates, Inc., 8 355–57; **26** 262. See also Simon Property Group, Inc.
MEM, **37** 270–71
Memco, **12** 48
Memorial Sloan-Kettering Cancer Center, 57 239–41
Memphis International Motorsports Corporation Inc., **43** 139–40
Memphis Retail Investors Limited Partnership, **62** 144
Memry Corporation, 72 225–27
The Men's Wearhouse, Inc., 17 312–15; **21** 311; **48** 283–87 (upd.)

Menasha Corporation, 8 358–61; **59** 287–92 (upd.)
Menck, **8** 544
Mendocino Brewing Company, Inc., 60 205–07
The Mennen Company, **14** 122; **18** 69; **35** 113
Mental Health Programs Inc., **15** 122
The Mentholatum Company Inc., 32 331–33
Mentor Corporation, 26 286–88
Mentor Graphics Corporation, 8 519; **11** 46–47, **284–86**, 490; **13** 128; **69** 340, 342
MEPC plc, IV 710–12
Mepco/Electra Inc., **13** 398
MeraBank, **6** 546
Meralco. See Manila Electric Company.
MERBCO, Inc., **33** 456
Mercantile Bancorporation Inc., **33** 155
Mercantile Bankshares Corp., 11 287–88
Mercantile Credit Co., **16** 13
Mercantile Estate and Property Corp. Ltd. See MEPC PLC.
Mercantile Stores Company, Inc., V 139; **19** 270–73 (upd.)
Mercator & Noordstar N.V., **40** 61
Mercator Software, **59** 54, 56
Mercedes Benz. See DaimlerChrysler AG
Mercer International Inc., 64 273–75
Merchant Bank Services, **18** 516, 518
Merchant Distributors, Inc., **20** 306
Merchant Investors. See Sanlam Ltd.
Merchants & Farmers Bank of Ecru, **14** 40
Merchants Bank & Trust Co., **21** 524
Merchants Distributors Inc. See Alex Lee Inc.
Merchants Home Delivery Service, **6** 414
Merchants National Bank, **9** 228; **14** 528; **17** 135
Merck & Co., Inc., I 650–52; **III** 299; **8** 154, 548; **10** 213; **11** 9, 90, **289–91** (upd.); **12** 325, 333; **14** 58, 422; **15** 154; **16** 440; **20** 39, 59; **26** 126; **34** 280–85 (upd.); **36** 91, 93, 305; **38** 380; **44** 175; **47** 236; **50** 56, 138–39; **58** 180–81; **63** 235
Mercury Air Group, Inc., 20 371–73
Mercury Asset Management (MAM), **14** 420; **40** 313
Mercury Communications, Ltd., 7 332–34; **10** 456; **11** 547–48; **25** 101–02; **27** 365
Mercury Drug Corporation, 70 181–83
Mercury General Corporation, 25 323–25
Mercury, Inc., **8** 311
Mercury Interactive Corporation, 59 293–95
Mercury International Ltd., **51** 130
Mercury Mail, Inc., **22** 519, 522
Mercury Marine Group, 68 247–51
Mercury Records, **13** 397; **23** 389, 391
Mercury Telecommunications Limited, **15** 67, 69
Mercy Air Service, Inc., **53** 29
Meredith Corporation, 11 292–94; **17** 394; **18** 239; **23** 393; **29** 316–19 (upd.)
Merfin International, **42** 53
Merial, **34** 284
Merico, Inc., **36** 161–64
Merida, **50** 445, 447
Meridian Bancorp, Inc., 11 295–97; **17** 111, 114

Meridian Emerging Markets Ltd., **25** 509
Meridian Gold, Incorporated, 47 238–40
Meridian Healthcare Ltd., **18** 197; **59** 168
Meridian Industrial Trust Inc., **57** 301
Meridian Investment and Development Corp., **22** 189
Meridian Oil Inc., **10** 190–91
Meridian Publishing, Inc., **28** 254
Merillat Industries, LLC, 13 338–39; **69** 253–55 (upd.)
Merisant Worldwide, Inc., 70 184–86
Merisel, Inc., 10 518–19; **12** 334–36; **13** 174, 176, 482
Merit Distribution Services, **13** 333
Merit Medical Systems, Inc., 29 320–22; **36** 497
Merit Tank Testing, Inc., **IV** 411
Merita/Cotton's Bakeries, **38** 251
Meritage Corporation, 26 289–92; **62** 327
MeritaNordbanken, **40** 336
Meritor Automotive Inc. See ArvinMeritor Inc.
Merix Corporation, 36 329–31
Merkur Direktwerbegesellschaft, **29** 152
Merlin Gérin, **19** 165
Merpati Nusantara Airlines. See Garuda Indonesia.
Merrell, **22** 173
Merrell Dow, **16** 438
Merriam-Webster Inc., 70 187–91
Merrill Corporation, 18 331–34; **47** 241–44 (upd.)
Merrill Gas Company, **9** 554
Merrill Lynch & Co., Inc., II 424–26; **III** 340, 440; **7** 130; **8** 94; **9** 125, 187, 239, 301, 386; **11** 29, 122, 348, 557; **13** 44, 125, **340–43** (upd.), 448–49, 512; **14** 65; **15** 463; **16** 195; **17** 137; **21** 68–70; **22** 404–06, 542; **23** 370; **25** 89–90, 329; **29** 295; **32** 14, 168; **40** 310–15 (upd.); **49** 130; **50** 419
Merrill Lynch Capital Partners, **47** 363
Merrill, Pickard, Anderson & Eyre IV, **11** 490
Merrill Publishing, **IV** 643; **7** 312; **9** 63; **29** 57
Merrimack Services Corp., **37** 303
Merry-Go-Round Enterprises, Inc., 8 362–64; **24** 27
Merry Group. See Boral Limited.
Merry Maids. See ServiceMaster Inc.
Merryhill Schools, Inc., **37** 279
The Mersey Docks and Harbour Company, 30 318–20
Mervyn's California, 10 409–10; **13** 526; **27** 452; **39** 269–71 (upd.). See also Target Corporation.
Merz + Co., **52** 135
Mesa Air Group, Inc., 32 334–37 (upd.)
Mesa Airlines, Inc., 11 298–300
Mesa Petroleum, **11** 441; **27** 217
Mesaba Holdings, Inc., 22 21; **28** 265–67
Messerschmitt-Bölkow-Blohm GmbH., I 46, 51–52, 55, **73–75**; **11** 267; **24** 86; **52** 113
Messner, Vetere, Berger, Carey, Schmetterer, **13** 204
Mesta Machine Co., **22** 415
Mestek, Inc., 10 411–13
Met Food Corp. See White Rose Food Corp.
Met-Mex Penoles. See Industrias Penoles, S.A. de C.V.

META Group, Inc., **37** 147
Metaframe Corp., **25** 312
Metal Box plc, I 604–06; 20 108. *See also* Novar plc.
Metal-Cal. *See* Avery Dennison Corporation.
Metal Casting Technology, Inc., **23** 267, 269
Metal Office Furniture Company, **7** 493
AB Metal Pty Ltd, **62** 331
Metalcorp Ltd, **62** 331
Metales y Contactos, **29** 461–62
Metaleurop S.A., 21 368–71
MetalExchange, **26** 530
Metall Mining Corp., **27** 456
Metallgesellschaft AG, IV 139–42, 229; **16 361–66 (upd.)**
MetalOptics Inc., **19** 212
Metalúrgica Gerdau. *See* Gerdau S.A.
Metalurgica Mexicana Penoles, S.A. *See* Industrias Penoles, S.A. de C.V.
Metaphase Technology, Inc., **10** 257
Metatec International, Inc., 47 245–48
Metcalf & Eddy Companies, Inc., **6** 441; **32** 52
Metcash Trading Ltd., 58 226–28
Meteor Film Productions, **23** 391
Meteor Industries Inc., 33 295–97
Methane Development Corporation, **6** 457
Methanex Corporation, 12 365; **19** 155–56; **40 316–19**
Methode Electronics, Inc., 13 344–46
MetLife. *See* Metropolitan Life Insurance Company.
MetMor Financial, Inc., **III** 293; **52** 239–40
Meto AG, **39** 79
MetPath, Inc., **III** 684; **26** 390
Metra Corporation. *See* Wärtsilä Corporation.
Metra Steel, **19** 381
Metragaz, **69** 191
Metrastock Ltd., **34** 5
Metric Constructors, Inc., **16** 286
Metric Systems Corporation, **18** 513; **44** 420
Metris Companies Inc., 25 41; **56 224–27**
Metro AG, 23 311; **50 335–39**
Metro Distributors, Inc., **14** 545
Metro-Goldwyn-Mayer Inc., 25 173, 253, **326–30 (upd.); 33** 120
Metro Holding AG, **38** 266
Metro Information Services, Inc., 36 332–34
Metro International SA, **36** 335
Metro-Mark Integrated Systems Inc., **11** 469
Metro-North Commuter Railroad Company, **35** 292
Metro Pacific, **18** 180, 182
Metro-Richelieu Inc., **II** 653
Metro Southwest Construction. *See* CRSS Inc.
Metro Support Services, Inc., **48** 171
Metrocall, Inc., 18 77; **39** 25; **41 265–68**
Metrol Security Services, Inc., **32** 373
Metroland Printing, Publishing and Distributing Ltd., **29** 471
Metromail Corp., **IV** 661; **18** 170; **38** 370
Metromedia Companies, 7 91, 335–37; **14 298–300**
Metromedia Company, 61 210–14 (upd.)
Metronic AG, **64** 226
Metroplex, LLC, **51** 206

Metropolis Intercom, **67** 137–38
Metropolitan Baseball Club Inc., 39 272–75
Metropolitan Broadcasting Corporation, **7** 335
Metropolitan Clothing Co., **19** 362
Metropolitan Distributors, **9** 283
Metropolitan Edison Company, **27** 182
Metropolitan Financial Corporation, 12 165; **13 347–49**
Metropolitan Furniture Leasing, **14** 4
Metropolitan Life Insurance Company, II 679; **III 290–94,** 313, 329, 337, 339–40; **IV** 283; **6** 256; **8** 326–27; **11** 482; **22** 266; **25** 300; **42** 194; **45** 249, 411; **52 235–41 (upd.); 54** 223–25
The Metropolitan Museum of Art, 55 267–70
Metropolitan Opera Association, Inc., 40 320–23
Metropolitan Reference Laboratories Inc., **26** 391
Metropolitan Tobacco Co., **15** 138
Metropolitan Transportation Authority, 35 290–92
MetroRed, **57** 67, 69
Metrostar Management, **59** 199
METSA, Inc., **15** 363
Metsä-Serla Oy, IV 314–16. *See also* M-real Oyj.
Metsec plc, **57** 402
Metso Corporation, 30 321–25 (upd.)
Mettler-Toledo International Inc., 30 326–28
Mettler United States Inc., **9** 441
Metwest, **26** 391
Metz Baking Company, **36** 164
Metzdorf Advertising Agency, **30** 80
Metzeler Kautschuk, **15** 354
Mexican Metal Co. *See* Industrias Penoles, S.A. de C.V.
Mexican Restaurants, Inc., 41 269–71
Meyer Brothers Drug Company, **16** 212
Meyer Corporation, **27** 288
Meyerland Company, **19** 366
Meyers Motor Supply, **26** 347
Meyers Parking, **18** 104
The Meyne Company, **55** 74
Meyr Melnhof Karton AG, **41 325–27**
M4 Data (Holdings) Ltd., **62** 293
M40 Trains Ltd., **51** 173
MFS Communications Company, Inc., 11 301–03; 14 253; **27** 301, 307
MG&E. *See* Madison Gas & Electric.
MG Holdings. *See* Mayflower Group Inc.
MG Ltd., **IV** 141
MGD Graphics Systems. *See* Goss Holdings, Inc.
MGIC Investment Corp., 45 320; **52 242–44**
MGM. *See* McKesson General Medical.
MGM Grand Inc., 17 316–19; 18 336–37
MGM Mirage. *See* Mirage Resorts, Incorporated.
MGM Studios, **50** 125
MGM/UA Communications Company, II 146–50, 408; **IV** 676; **12** 73, 316, 323; **15** 84; **17** 316. *See also* Metro-Goldwyn-Mayer Inc.
MGN. *See* Mirror Group Newspapers Ltd.
MGT Services Inc. *See* The Midland Company.
MH Alshaya Group, **28** 96
MH Media Monitoring Limited, **26** 270

MHI Group, Inc., **13** 356; **16** 344
MHS Holding Corp., **26** 101
MHT. *See* Manufacturers Hanover Trust Co.
MI. *See* Masco Corporation.
MI S.A., **66** 244
Mi-Tech Steel Inc., **63** 359–60
Miami Computer Supply Corporation. *See* MCSi, Inc.
Miami Power Corporation. *See* Cincinnati Gas & Electric Company.
Miami Subs Corp., **29** 342, 344
Micamold Electronics Manufacturing Corporation, **10** 319
Mich-Wis. *See* Michigan Wisconsin Pipe Line.
Michael Anthony Jewelers, Inc., 24 334–36
Michael Baker Corporation, 14 333–35; 51 245–48 (upd.)
MICHAEL Business Systems Plc, **10** 257
Michael C. Fina Co., Inc., 52 245–47
Michael Foods, Inc., 25 331–34; 39 319–321
Michael Joseph, **IV** 659
Michael Page International plc, 45 272–74; 52 317–18
Michael's Fair-Mart Food Stores, Inc., **19** 479
Michaels Stores, Inc., 17 320–22; 71 226–30 (upd.)
MichCon. *See* MCN Corporation.
Michelin. *See* Compagnie Générale des Établissements Michelin.
Michie Co., **33** 264–65
Michigan Automotive Compressor, Inc., **III** 638–39
Michigan Automotive Research Corporation, **23** 183
Michigan Bell Telephone Co., 14 336–38; 18 30
Michigan Carpet Sweeper Company, **9** 70
Michigan Consolidated Gas Company. *See* MCN Corporation.
Michigan International Speedway. *See* Penske Corporation.
Michigan Livestock Exchange, **36** 442
Michigan Motor Freight Lines, **14** 567
Michigan National Corporation, 11 304–06; 18 517
Michigan Oil Company, **18** 494
Michigan Packaging Company. *See* Greif Inc.
Michigan Seamless Tube Company. *See* Quanex Corporation.
Michigan Shoe Makers. *See* Wolverine World Wide Inc.
Michigan Sporting Goods Distributors, Inc., 72 228–30
Michigan Spring Company, **17** 106
Michigan Steel Corporation, **12** 352
Michigan Tag Company, **9** 72
Michigan Wisconsin Pipe Line, **39** 260
Mick's Inc., **30** 329
Mickey Shorr Mobile Electronics, **10** 9–11
Micro Contract Manufacturing Inc., **44** 441
Micro D, Inc., **11** 194
Micro Decisionware, Inc., **10** 506
Micro Focus Inc., **27** 491
Micro Magic, Inc., **43** 254
Micro Metallics Corporation, **64** 297
Micro Peripherals, Inc., **18** 138
Micro Power Systems Inc., **14** 183
Micro Switch, **14** 284

Micro/Vest, **13** 175
Micro Warehouse, Inc., 16 371–73
Micro-Controle, **71** 248
MicroAge, Inc., 16 367–70; **29** 414
Microamerica, **12** 334
Microban Products Company, **27** 288
MicroBilt Corporation, **11** 112
Microcar SA, **55** 54, 56
MicroClean Inc, **50** 49
Microcom, Inc., **26** 93; **50** 227
Microcomputer Asset Management
    Services, **9** 168
Microcomputer Systems, **22** 389
Microdot Inc., 8 365–68, 545
Microfral, **14** 216
MicroFridge, **44** 273
Micromass Ltd., **43** 455
Micromedex, **19** 268
Micron Technology, Inc., 11 307–09; **29**
    323–26 (upd.)
Micropolis Corp., **10** 403, 458, 463
MicroPro International Corp. *See* The
    Learning Company Inc.
Microprocessor Systems, **13** 235
Microprose Inc., **24** 538
Micros Systems, Inc., 18 335–38
Microsensor Systems Inc., **43** 366
Microsoft Corporation, 6 257–60; **27**
    319–23 (upd.); **63** 64, **293–97 (upd.)**;
    64 78
Microtek, Inc., **22** 413
MicroUnity Systems Engineering Inc., **50**
    53
Microware Surgical Instruments Corp., **IV**
    137
Microwave Communications, Inc. *See* MCI
    Telecom.
Mid-America Capital Resources, Inc., **6**
    508
Mid-America Dairymen, Inc., 7 338–40;
    11 24; **22** 95; **26** 448
Mid-America Interpool Network, **6** 602
Mid-America Packaging, Inc., **8** 203
Mid-America Tag & Label, **8** 360
Mid Bus Inc., **33** 107
Mid-Central Fish and Frozen Foods Inc., **II**
    675
Mid-Continent Computer Services, **11** 111
Mid-Continent Life Insurance Co., **23** 200
Mid-Continent Telephone Corporation. *See*
    Alltel Corporation.
Mid-Georgia Gas Company, **6** 448
Mid-Illinois Gas Co., **6** 529
Mid-Michigan Music Co., **60** 84
Mid-Pacific Airlines, **9** 271; **24** 21–22
Mid-Packaging Group Inc., **19** 78
Mid-South Towing, **6** 583
Mid-States Development, Inc., **18** 405
Mid-Valley Dairy, **14** 397
MidAmerican Communications
    Corporation, **8** 311
Midas Inc., 56 228–31 (upd.)
Midas International Corporation, 10
    414–15, 554; **24** 337
MIDCO, **III** 340
Middle East Broadcasting Centre, Ltd., **25**
    506, 508
Middle East Tube Co. Ltd., **25** 266
Middle South Utilities. *See* Entergy
    Corporation.
Middle Wisconsin Power, **6** 604
The Middleby Corporation, 22 352–55;
    61 34
Middlesex Water Company, 45 275–78

Middleton Aerospace, **48** 275
The Middleton Doll Company, 53
    222–25
Middleton Packaging, **12** 377
Middletown Manufacturing Co., Inc., **16**
    321
Middletown National Bank, **13** 467
Midland Advertising & Design, Inc., **56**
    332
Midland Bank plc, II 318–20; **9** 505; **12**
    257; **14** 169; **17 323–26 (upd.)**; **19** 198;
    26 202; **33** 395
Midland Brick, **14** 250
The Midland Company, 65 233–35
Midland Enterprises Inc. *See* Eastern
    Enterprises.
Midland Group. *See* Regency Centers
    Corporation.
Midland Independent Newspaper plc, **23**
    351
Midland International, **8** 56–57
Midland Investment Co., **II** 7
Midland National Bank, **11** 130
Midland-Ross Corporation, **14** 369
Midland Southwest Corp., **8** 347
Midland Steel Products Co., **13** 305–06
Midland United, **6** 556; **25** 89
Midland Utilities Company, **6** 532
Midlands Electricity, **13** 485
Midlantic Corp., **13** 411
Midlantic Hotels Ltd., **41** 83
Midrange Performance Group, **12** 149
Midway Airlines Corporation, 6 105,
    120–21; **33 301–03**
Midway Games, Inc., 25 335–38
Midway Manufacturing Company, **15** 539
Midwest Agri-Commodities Company, **11**
    15; **32** 29
Midwest Biscuit Company, **14** 306
Midwest Com of Indiana, Inc., **11** 112
Midwest Express Holdings, Inc., 35
    293–95; **43** 258
Midwest Federal Savings & Loan
    Association, **11** 162–63
Midwest Financial Group, Inc., **8** 188
Midwest Foundry Co., **IV** 137
Midwest Grain Products, Inc., 49 261–63
Midwest Manufacturing Co., **12** 296
Midwest Realty Exchange, Inc., **21** 257
Midwest Resources Inc., 6 523–25
Midwest Staffing Systems, **27** 21
Midwest Steel Corporation, **13** 157
Midwest Suburban Publishing Inc., **62** 188
Midwest Synthetics, **8** 553
Midwinter, **12** 529
Miele & Cie. KG, 56 232–35
MIG Realty Advisors, Inc., **25** 23, 25
Migros-Genossenschafts-Bund, 68
    252–55
Miguel Galas S.A., **17** 268
MIH Limited, 31 329–32
Mikasa, Inc., 28 268–70
Mike-Sell's Inc., 15 298–300
Mikemitch Realty Corp., **16** 36
Mikohn Gaming Corporation, 39 276–79
Mikon, Ltd., **13** 345
Milac, **27** 259
Milacron, Inc., 53 226–30 (upd.)
Milan A.C., S.p.A., **44** 387
Milbank, Tweed, Hadley & McCloy, 27
    324–27
Milchem, Inc., **63** 306
Mile-Hi Distributing, **64** 180
Miles Inc., **22** 148

Miles Kimball Co., **9** 393
Miles Laboratories, I 653–55, 674, 678;
    14 558
Milgram Food Stores Inc., **II** 682
Milgray Electronics Inc., **19** 311; **47** 41
Milk Producers, Inc., **11** 24
Milk Specialties Co., **12** 199
Mill-Power Supply Company, **27** 129–30
Millea Holdings Inc., 64 276–81 (upd.)
Millennium & Copthorne Hotels plc, 71
    231–33
Millennium Chemicals Inc., **30** 231; **45**
    252, 254; **71** 149–50
Millennium Materials Inc. *See* Dyson
    Group PLC.
Millennium Pharmaceuticals, Inc., 47
    249–52
Miller Automotive Group, **52** 146
Miller Brewing Company, I, 254–55,
    257–58, **269–70**, 283, 290–91; **10** 100;
    11 421; **12 337–39 (upd.)**, 372; **13** 258;
    15 429; **17** 256; **18** 70, 72, 418, 499,
    501; **21** 230; **22** 199, 422; **26** 303, 306;
    27 374; **28** 209–10; **34** 36–37; **44** 342;
    50 202. *See also* SABMiller plc.
Miller Companies, **17** 182
Miller Container Corporation, **8** 102
Miller Exploration Company. *See* Edge
    Petroleum Corporation.
Miller Freeman, Inc., **IV** 687; **27** 362; **28**
    501, 504
Miller Group Ltd., **22** 282
Miller Industries, Inc., 26 293–95
Miller, Mason and Dickenson, **III** 204–05
Miller Plant Farms, Inc., **51** 61
Miller Publishing Group, LLC, 57
    242–44
Miller, Tabak, Hirsch & Co., **13** 394; **28**
    164
Millet, **39** 250
Millet's Leisure. *See* Sears plc.
Millicom, **11** 547; **18** 254
Milliken & Co., V 366–68; **8** 270–71; **17**
    327–30 (upd.); **29** 246
Milliken, Tomlinson Co., **II** 682
Milliman USA, 66 223–26
Millipore Corporation, 9 396; **23** 284; **25**
    339–43; **43** 454
Mills Clothing, Inc. *See* The Buckle, Inc.
Millway Foods, **25** 85
Milne & Craighead, **48** 113
Milne Fruit Products, Inc., **25** 366
Milnot Company, 46 289–91; **51** 47
Milpark Drilling Fluids, Inc., **63** 306
Milsco Manufacturing Co., **23** 299, 300
Milton Bradley Company, 17 105; **21**
    372–75; **25** 380
Milton Light & Power Company, **12** 45
Milton Roy Co., **8** 135
Milupa S.A., **37** 341
Milwaukee Brewers Baseball Club, 37
    247–49
Milwaukee Cheese Co. Inc., **25** 517
Milwaukee Electric Railway and Light
    Company, **6** 601–02, 604–05
Milwaukee Electric Tool, **28** 40
Mimi's Cafés. *See* SWH Corporation.
Minatome, **IV** 560
Mindpearl, **48** 381
Mindport, **31** 329
Mindset Corp., **42** 424–25
Mindspring Enterprises, Inc., **36** 168
Mine Safety Appliances Company, 31
    333–35

The Miner Group International, 22 356–58
Minera Loma Blanca S.A., **56** 127
Mineral Point Public Service Company, **6** 604
Minerales y Metales, S.A. *See* Industrias Penoles, S.A. de C.V.
Minerals & Metals Trading Corporation of India Ltd., IV 143–44
Minerals and Resources Corporation Limited. *See* Minorco.
Minerals Technologies Inc., 11 310–12; 52 248–51 (upd.)
Minerec Corporation, **9** 363
Minerva SA, **72** 289
Minerve, **6** 208
Minet Group, **III** 357; **22** 494–95
MiniScribe, Inc., **10** 404
Minitel, **21** 233
Minivator Ltd., **11** 486
Minneapolis Children's Medical Center, **54** 65
Minneapolis-Honeywell Regulator Co., **8** 21; **22** 427
Minneapolis Steel and Machinery Company, **21** 502
Minnehoma Insurance Company, **58** 260
Minnesota Brewing Company. *See* MBC Holding Company.
Minnesota Linseed Oil Co., **8** 552
Minnesota Mining & Manufacturing Company, I 387, 499–501; IV 8 35, 369–71 (upd.); 11 494; 13 326; 22 427; 25 96, 372; 26 296–99 (upd.). *See also* 3M Company.
Minnesota Paints, **8** 552–53
Minnesota Power & Light Company, 11 313–16
Minnesota Power, Inc., 34 286–91 (upd.)
Minnesota Sugar Company, **11** 13
Minnetonka Corp., **III** 25; **22** 122–23
Minntech Corporation, 22 359–61
Minn-Dak Farmers Cooperative, **32** 29
Minolta Co., Ltd., III 574–76; 18 93, 186, **339–42 (upd.); 43 281–85 (upd.)**
Minorco, **IV** 97; **16** 28, 293
Minstar Inc., **11** 397; **15** 49; **45** 174
Minton China, **38** 401
The Minute Maid Company, 28 271–74, 473; 32 116
Minuteman International Inc., 46 292–95
Minyard Food Stores, Inc., 33 304–07
Mippon Paper, **21** 546; **50** 58
Miquel y Costas Miquel S.A., 68 256–58
Miracle Food Mart, **16** 247, 249–50
Miracle-Gro Products, Inc., **22** 474
Miraflores Designs Inc., **18** 216
Mirage Resorts, Incorporated, 6 209–12; 15 238; **28 275–79 (upd.); 29** 127; **43** 82
Miraglia Inc., **57** 139
Miramax Film Corporation, 64 282–85
Mirant, **39** 54, 57
Mircali Asset Management, **III** 340
Mircor Inc., **12** 413
Mirror Group Newspapers plc, 7 341–43; 23 348–51 (upd.); 49 408; **61** 130
Misceramic Tile, Inc., **14** 42
Misr Airwork. *See* AirEgypt.
Misr Bank of Cairo, **27** 132
Misrair. *See* AirEgypt.
Miss Erika, Inc., **27** 346, 348

Miss Selfridge. *See* Sears plc.
Misset Publishers, **IV** 611
Mission Group. *See* SCEcorp.
Mission Jewelers, **30** 408
Mission Valley Fabrics, **57** 285
Mississippi Chemical Corporation, 8 183; **27** 316; **39 280–83**
Mississippi Gas Company, **6** 577
Mississippi Power Company, **38** 446–47
Mississippi River Corporation, **10** 44
Mississippi River Recycling, **31** 47, 49
Mississippi Valley Title Insurance Company, **58** 259–60
Missoula Bancshares, Inc., **35** 198–99
Missouri Book Co., **10** 136
Missouri Fur Company, **25** 220
Missouri Gaming Company, **21** 39
Missouri Gas & Electric Service Company, **6** 593
Missouri Pacific Railroad, **10** 43–44
Missouri Public Service Company. *See* UtiliCorp United Inc.
Missouri Utilities Company, **6** 580
Mist Assist, Inc. *See* Ballard Medical Products.
Mistik Beverages, **18** 71
Misys PLC, 45 279–81; 46 296–99
Mitchel & King Skates Ltd., **17** 244
Mitchell Energy and Development Corporation, 7 344–46; 61 75
Mitchell Home Savings and Loan, **13** 347
Mitchell International, **8** 526
Mitchells & Butlers PLC, 59 296–99
MiTek Industries Inc., **IV** 259
MiTek Wood Products, **IV** 305
Mitel Corporation, 15 131–32; **18 343–46**
MitNer Group, **7** 377
MITRE Corporation, 26 300–02
Mitre Sport U.K., **17** 204–05
MITROPA AG, 37 250–53
Mitsubishi Aircraft Co., **9** 349; **11** 164
Mitsubishi Bank, Ltd., II 321–22; 15 41; **16** 496, 498; **50** 498. *See also* Bank of Tokyo-Mitsubishi Ltd.
Mitsubishi Chemical Corporation, 56 236–38 (upd.)
Mitsubishi Chemical Industries Ltd., I 363–64; 11 207
Mitsubishi Corporation, I 261, 502–04; IV 285, 518, 713; **6** 499; **7** 82, 233, 590; **9** 294; **12 340–43 (upd.); 17** 349, 556; **24** 359; **27** 511
Mitsubishi Electric Corporation, II 57–59, 68, 73, 94, 122; 18 18; **23** 52–53; **43** 15; **44 283–87 (upd.)**
Mitsubishi Estate Company, Limited, IV 713–14; 58 303; **61 215–18 (upd.)**
Mitsubishi Foods, **24** 114
Mitsubishi Group, **7** 377; **21** 390
Mitsubishi Heavy Industries, Ltd., III 577–79; 7 347–50 (upd.); 8 51; **9** 349–50; **10** 33; **13** 507; **15** 92; **24** 359; **40 324–28 (upd.); 63** 95
Mitsubishi International Corp., **16** 462
Mitsubishi Kasei Corp., **14** 535
Mitsubishi Kasei Vinyl Company, **49** 5
Mitsubishi Materials Corporation, III 712–13; 38 463
Mitsubishi Motors Corporation, 7 219; **8** 72, 374; **9 349–51; 23 352–55 (upd.); 34** 128, 136; **57 245–49 (upd.); 64** 100
Mitsubishi Oil Co., Ltd., IV 460–62, 479, 492

Mitsubishi Rayon Co. Ltd., V 369–71
Mitsubishi Shipbuilding Co. Ltd., **9** 349
Mitsubishi Trust & Banking Corporation, II 323–24
Mitsui & Co., Ltd., 7 303; **13** 356; **24** 325, **488–89; 27** 337; **28 280–85 (upd.)**
Mitsui Bank, Ltd., II 325–27, 328, 372; **III** 295–97; **17** 556. *See also* Sumitomo Mitsui Banking Corporation.
Mitsui Bussan K.K., I 505–08; II 392; **III** 295–96; **9** 352–53. *See also* Mitsui & Co., Ltd.
Mitsui Group, **9** 352; **16** 84; **20** 310; **21** 72
Mitsui Light Metal Processing Co., **III** 758
Mitsui Marine and Fire Insurance Company, Limited, III 209, **295–96**
Mitsui Mining & Smelting Co., Ltd., IV 145–46, 147–48
Mitsui Mining Company, Limited, IV 147–49
Mitsui Mutual Life Insurance Company, III 297–98; **39 284–86 (upd.)**
Mitsui-no-Mori Co., Ltd., **IV** 716
Mitsui O.S.K. Lines, Ltd., V 473–76; 26 278–80
Mitsui Petrochemical Industries, Ltd., I 390, 516; **9 352–54**
Mitsui Real Estate Development Co., Ltd., IV 715–16
Mitsui Toatsu, **9** 353–54
Mitsui Trust & Banking Company, Ltd., II 328
Mitsukoshi Ltd., I 508; **V 142–44; 14** 502; **41** 114; **47** 391; **56 239–42 (upd.)**
Mity Enterprises, Inc., 38 310–12
Mizuho Financial Group Inc., 58 229–36 (upd.)
Mizuno Corporation, 25 344–46
MJ Pharmaceuticals Ltd., **57** 346
MK-Ferguson Company, **7** 356
MLC. *See* Medical Learning Company.
MLC Ltd., **IV** 709; **52** 221–22
MLH&P. *See* Montreal Light, Heat & Power Company.
MLT Vacations Inc., **30** 446
MM Merchandising Munich, **54** 296–97
MMAR Group Inc., **19** 131
MMC Networks Inc., **38** 53, 55
MML Investors Services, **III** 286; **53** 213
MMS America Corp., **26** 317
MNC Financial. *See* MBNA Corporation.
MNC Financial Corp., **11** 447
MND Drilling, **7** 345
MNet, **11** 122
MNS, Ltd., 65 236–38
Mo och Domsjö AB, IV 317–19. *See also* Holmen AB
MOB, **56** 335
Mobil Corporation, IV 93, 295, 363, 386, 401, 403, 406, 423, 428, 454, **463–65,** 466, 472–74, 486, 492, 504–05, 515, 517, 522, 531, 538–39, 545, 554–55, 564, 570–71; **6** 530; **7** 171, **351–54 (upd.); 8** 552–53; **9** 546; **10** 440; **12** 348; **16** 489; **17** 363, 415; **19** 140, 225, 297; **21 376–80 (upd.); 24** 496, 521; **25** 232, 445; **26** 369; **32** 175, 179, 181; **45** 50; **50** 416. *See also* Exxon Mobil Corporation.
Mobil Oil Australia, **24** 399
Mobil Oil Indonesia, **56** 273
Mobile America Housing Corporation. *See* American Homestar Corporation.
Mobile Corporation, **25** 232

Mobile Mini, Inc., 21 476; **58 237–39**
**Mobile Telecommunications
  Technologies Corp.,** V 277–78; 16 74;
  18 347–49
Mobile TeleSystems OJSC, 48 419; 59
  300–03
Mobilefone, Inc., 25 108
MobileMedia Corp., 39 23, 24
MobileStar Network Corp., 26 429
Mochida Pharaceutical Co. Ltd., II 553
Modar, 17 279
Mode 1 Communications, Inc., 48 305
Modell's Shoppers World, 16 35–36
Modell's Sporting Goods. See Henry
  Modell & Company Inc.
Modeluxe Linge Services SA, 45 139–40
Modem Media, 23 479
Modern Furniture Rentals Inc., 14 4; 27
  163
Modern Handling Methods Ltd., 21 499
Modern Merchandising Inc., 19 396
Modern Times Group AB, 36 335–38
Modern Woodmen of America, 66
  227–29
Modernistic Industries Inc., 7 589
Modine Manufacturing Company, 8
  372–75; 56 243–47 (upd.)
Modis Professional Services. See MPS
  Group, Inc.
MoDo. See Mo och Domsjö AB.
MoDo Paper AB, 28 446; 52 164
Moe's Southwest Grill, LLC, 64 327–28
Moen Incorporated, 12 344–45
Moët-Hennessy, I 271–72; 10 397–98; 23
  238, 240, 242. See also LVMH Moët
  Hennessy Louis Vuitton SA.
Mogen David. See The Wine Group, Inc.
The Mogul Metal Company. See Federal-
  Mogul Corporation.
Mohasco Corporation, 15 102; 26 100–01
Mohawk & Hudson Railroad, 9 369
Mohawk Carpet Corp., 26 101
Mohawk Industries, Inc., 19 274–76; 31
  199; 63 298–301 (upd.)
Mohawk Rubber Co. Ltd., V 256; 7 116;
  19 508
Mohegan Tribal Gaming Authority, 37
  254–57
Mohr-Value Stores, 8 555
Mojave Foods Corporation, 27 299
Mojo MDA Group Ltd., 11 50–51; 43 412
Moksel. See A. Moskel AG.
Mokta. See Compagnie de Mokta.
MOL. See Mitsui O.S.K. Lines, Ltd.
MOL Rt, 70 192–95
Molabe S.A. Espagne. See Leroux S.A.S.
Molerway Freight Lines, Inc., 53 250
Molex Incorporated, 11 317–19; 14 27;
  54 236–41 (upd.)
Molfino Hermanos SA, 59 365
Molinera de México S.A. de C.V., 31 236
Molinos Nacionales C.A., 7 242–43; 25
  241
Molinos Río de la Plata S.A., 61 219–21
Molins plc, 51 249–51
Moll Plasticrafters, L.P., 17 534
Molloy Manufacturing Co., III 569; 20
  360
Mölnlycke AB, 36 26
The Molson Companies Limited, I
  273–75, 333; 7 183–84; 12 338; 13 150,
  199; 21 320; 23 404; 25 279; 26 303–07
  (upd.); 36 15
Molycorp, IV 571; 24 521

Momentus Group Ltd., 51 99
Mon-Dak Chemical Inc., 16 270
Mon-Valley Transportation Company, 11
  194
Mona Meyer McGrath & Gavin, 47 97
MONACA. See Molinos Nacionales C.A.
Monaco Coach Corporation, 31 336–38
Monadnock Paper Mills, Inc., 21 381–84
Monarch Air Lines, 22 219
Monarch Casino & Resort, Inc., 65
  239–41
The Monarch Cement Company, 72
  231–33
Monarch Development Corporation, 38
  451–52
Monarch Foods, 26 503
Mondadori. See Arnoldo Monadori Editore
  S.p.A.
Mondex International, 18 543
Mondi Foods BV, 41 12
Moneris Solutions Corp., 46 55
Monet Jewelry, 9 156–57
Money Access Service Corp., 11 467
Money Management Associates, Inc., 53
  136
Monfort, Inc., 13 350–52
Monitor Dynamics Inc., 24 510
Monitor Group Inc., 33 257
Monk-Austin Inc., 12 110
Monmouth Pharmaceuticals Ltd., 16 439
Monnaie de Paris, 62 246–48
Monneret Industrie, 56 335
Monnoyeur Group. See Groupe
  Monnoyeur.
Monogram Aerospace Fasteners, Inc., 11
  536
Monogram Models, 25 312
Monolithic Memories Inc., 16 316–17, 549
Monon Corp., 13 550
Monongahela Power, 38 40
Monoprix. See Galeries Lafayette S.A.
Monro Muffler Brake, Inc., 24 337–40
Monroe Savings Bank, 11 109
Monrovia Nursery Company, 70 196–98
Monsanto Company, I 365–67; 8 398; 9
  318, 355–57 (upd.), 466; 12 186; 13
  225; 16 460–62; 17 131; 18 112; 22
  107; 23 170–71; 26 108; 29 327–31
  (upd.); 33 135; 34 179; 41 306; 52 312;
  53 261; 59 149; 60 227; 61 97
Monsoon plc, 39 287–89
Monster Cable Products, Inc., 69 256–58
Mont Blanc, 17 5; 27 487, 489
Montabert S.A., 15 226
Montan TNT Pty Ltd., 27 473
Montana Alimentaria S.p.A., 57 82
Montana Coffee Traders, Inc., 60
  208–10
Montana-Dakota Utilities Co., 7 322–23;
  37 281–82; 42 249–50, 252
Montana Group, 54 229
Montana Mills Bread Co., Inc., 61 153
The Montana Power Company, 6 566; 7
  322; 11 320–22; 37 280, 283; 44
  288–92 (upd.); 50 367
Montana Refining Company, 12 240–41
Montana Resources, Inc., IV 34
Montaup Electric Co., 14 125
MontBell America, Inc., 29 279
Monte Paschi Vita, 65 71–72
Montedison S.p.A., I 368–69; 14 17; 22
  262; 24 341–44 (upd.); 36 185–86, 188
Montefina, IV 499; 26 367
Montell N.V., 24 343

Monterey Homes Corporation. See
  Meritage Corporation.
Monterey Mfg. Co., 12 439
Monterey Pasta Company, 58 240–43
Monterey's Acquisition Corp., 41 270
Monterey's Tex-Mex Cafes, 13 473
Monterrey, Compania de Seguros sobre la
  Vida. See Seguros Monterrey.
Monterrey Group, 19 10–11, 189
Montgomery Elevator Company, 27 269
Montgomery Ward & Co., Incorporated,
  V 145–48; 8 509; 9 210; 10 10, 116,
  172, 305, 391, 393, 490–91; 12 48, 309,
  315, 335, 430; 13 165; 15 330, 470; 17
  460; 18 477; 20 263, 374–79 (upd.),
  433; 22 535; 25 144; 27 428–30; 43 292
Montiel Corporation, 17 321
Montinex, 24 270
Montreal Engineering Company, 6 585
Montreal Mining Co., 17 357
Montres Rolex S.A., 8 477; 13 353–55;
  19 452; 34 292–95 (upd.)
Montrose Capital, 36 358
Montrose Chemical Company, 9 118, 119
Montupet S.A., 63 302–04
Monumental Corp., III 179
Moody's Corporation, IV 605; 16 506;
  19 133; 22 189; 61 81–83; 65 242–44
Moody's Investors Service,
Moog Inc., 13 356–58
Mooney Aerospace Group Ltd., 52
  252–55
Mooney Chemicals, Inc. See OM Group,
  Inc.
Moonlight Mushrooms, Inc. See Sylvan,
  Inc.
Moonstone Mountaineering, Inc., 29 181
Moore and McCormack Co. Inc., 19 40
Moore Corporation Limited, IV 644–46,
  679; 15 473; 16 450; 36 508
Moore Gardner & Associates, 22 88
The Moore Group Ltd., 20 363
Moore-Handley, Inc., 39 290–92
Moore McCormack Resources Inc., 14 455
Moore Medical Corp., 17 331–33
Moquin Breuil. See Smoby International
  SA.
Moran Group Inc., II 682
Moran Health Care Group Ltd., 25 455
Moran Towing Corporation, Inc., 15
  301–03
Morana, Inc., 9 290
Moretti-Harrah Marble Co. See English
  China Clays Ltd.
Morgan & Banks Limited, 30 460
Morgan Construction Company, 8 448
Morgan Edwards, II 609
Morgan Engineering Co., 8 545
Morgan Grampian Group, IV 687
Morgan Grenfell Group PLC, II 427–29;
  59 182–83, 255. See also Deutsche
  Bank AG.
The Morgan Group, Inc., 46 300–02
Morgan Guaranty Trust Company. See J.P.
  Morgan & Co. Incorporated.
Morgan, J.P. & Co. Inc. See J.P. Morgan
  & Co. Incorporated.
Morgan, Lewis & Bockius LLP, 29
  332–34
Morgan, Lewis, Githens & Ahn, Inc., 6
  410
Morgan Schiff & Co., 29 205

Morgan Stanley Dean Witter & Company, **33** 311–14 (upd.); **38** 289, 291, 411
Morgan Stanley Group, Inc., **II** 430–32; **IV** 447, 714; **9** 386; **11** 258; **12** 529; **16** 374–78 (upd.); **18** 448–49; **20** 60, 363; **22** 404, 407; **25** 542; **30** 353–55; **34** 496; **36** 153
Moria Informatique, **6** 229
Morinaga & Co. Ltd., 61 222–25
Morino Associates, **10** 394
Mormac Marine Group, **15** 302
Morning Star Technologies Inc., **24** 49
Morning Sun, Inc., **23** 66
Morningstar Inc., 68 259–62
Morningstar Storage Centers LLC, **52** 311
Morris Air, **24** 455; **71** 346
Morris Communications Corporation, 36 339–42
Morris Motors, **7** 459
Morris Travel Services L.L.C., 26 308–11
Morrison & Co. Ltd., **52** 221
Morrison Homes, Inc., **51** 138
Morrison Knudsen Corporation, 7 355–58; **11** 401, 553; **28** 286–90 (upd.); **33** 442; **50** 363. See also The Washington Companies.
Morrison Machine Products Inc., **25** 193
Morrison Restaurants Inc., 11 323–25; **18** 464
Morse Equalizing Spring Company, **14** 63
Morse Industrial, **14** 64
Morse Shoe Inc., 13 359–61
Morse's Ltd., **70** 161
Mortgage Associates, **9** 229
Mortgage Guaranty Insurance Corp. See MGIC Investment Corp.
Mortgage Resources, Inc., **10** 91
Morton Foods, Inc., **27** 258
Morton International Inc., 9 358–59 (upd.), 500–01; **16** 436; **22** 505–06; **43** 319
Morton Thiokol Inc., I 370–72; **19** 508; **28** 253–54. See also Thiokol Corporation.
Morton's Restaurant Group, Inc., 28 401; **30** 329–31
Mos Magnetics, **18** 140
MOS Technology, **7** 95
Mosby-Year Book, Inc., **IV** 678; **17** 486
Moseley, Hallgarten, Estabrook, and Weeden, **III** 389
Mosher Steel Company, **7** 540
Mosinee Paper Corporation, 15 304–06. See also Wausau-Mosinee Paper Corporation.
Moskatel's, Inc., **17** 321
Moss Bros Group plc, 51 252–54
Moss-Rouse Company, **15** 412
Mossgas, **IV** 93
Mossimo, Inc., 27 328–30
Mostek Corp., **11** 307–08; **13** 191; **20** 175; **29** 323
Mostjet Ltd. See British World Airlines Ltd.
Móstoles Industrial S.A., **26** 129
Mostra Importaciones S.A., **34** 38, 40
Motel 6, 10 13; **13** 362–64; **56** 248–51 (upd.). See also Accor SA
Mother Karen's, **10** 216
Mothercare Stores, Inc., **16** 466
Mothercare UK Ltd., 17 42–43, 334–36

Mothers Against Drunk Driving (MADD), 51 255–58
Mothers Work, Inc., 18 350–52
Motif Inc., **22** 288
Motion Designs, **11** 486
Motion Factory, Inc., **38** 72
Motion Picture Association of America, **37** 353–54
Motion Picture Corporation of America, **25** 326, 329
Motiva Enterprises LLC, **41** 359, 395
MotivePower. See Wabtec Corporation.
The Motley Fool, Inc., 40 329–31
Moto Photo, Inc., 45 282–84
Moto S.p.A., **57** 84
Moto-Truc Co., **13** 385
Motor Cargo Industries, Inc., 35 296–99; **58** 262
Motor Club of America Insurance Company, **44** 354
Motor Coaches Industries International Inc., **36** 132
Motor Parts Industries, Inc., **9** 363
Motor Wheel Corporation, **20** 261; **27** 202–04
Motorcar Parts & Accessories, Inc., 47 253–55
Motoren-und-Turbinen-Union, **I** 151; **9** 418; **15** 142; **34** 128, 131, 133
Motorola, Inc., II 60–62; **7** 119, 494, 533; **8** 139; **9** 515; **10** 87, 365, 367, 431–33; **11** 45, 308, 326–29 (upd.), 381–82; **12** 136–37, 162; **13** 30, 356, 501; **17** 33, 193; **18** 18, 74, 76, 260, 382; **19** 391; **20** 8, 439; **22** 17, 19, 288, 542; **26** 431–32; **27** 20, 341–42, 344; **33** 47–48; **34** 296–302 (upd.); **38** 188; **43** 15; **44** 97, 357, 359; **45** 346, 348; **47** 318, 320, 385; **48** 270, 272
Motown Records Company L.P., II 145; **22** 194; **23** 389, 391; **26** 312–14
Mott's Inc., 57 250–53
Moulinex S.A., 22 362–65
Mound Metalcraft. See Tonka Corporation.
Mount. See also Mt.
Mount Hood Credit Life Insurance Agency, **14** 529
Mount Isa Mines, **IV** 61
Mount Vernon Group, **8** 14
Mount Washington Hotel. See MWH Preservation Limited Partnership.
Mountain Fuel Supply Company. See Questar Corporation.
Mountain High Casino. See Ameristar Casinos, Inc.
Mountain Pass Canning Co., **7** 429
Mountain Safety Research, **18** 445–46
Mountain States Mortgage Centers, Inc., 29 335–37
Mountain States Power Company. See PacifiCorp.
Mountain States Wholesale, **II** 602; **30** 25
Mountain Valley Indemnity Co., **44** 356
Mountain West Bank, **35** 197
Mountleigh PLC, **16** 465
Mouvement des Caisses Desjardins, 48 288–91
Movado Group, Inc., 28 291–94
Mövenpick Holdings, **63** 328
Movie Gallery, Inc., 31 339–41
Movie Star Inc., 17 337–39
Movies To Go, Inc., **9** 74; **31** 57
Movil@ccess, S.A. de C.V., **39** 25, 194
Moving Co. Ltd. See Marui Co., Ltd.

The Moving Picture Company, **15** 83; **50** 124, 126
The Mowry Co., **23** 102
MP3.com, **43** 109
MPB Corporation, **8** 529, 531
MPI. See Michael Page International plc.
MPRG. See Matt Prentice Restaurant Group.
MPS Group, Inc., 49 264–67
MPW Industrial Services Group, Inc., 53 231–33
Mr. Bricolage S.A., 37 258–60
Mr. Coffee, Inc., 14 229–31; **15** 307–09; **17** 215; **27** 275; **39** 406
Mr. D's Food Centers, **12** 112
Mr. Donut, **21** 323
Mr. Gasket Inc., 11 84; **15** 310–12
Mr. Gatti's Inc., **15** 345; **53** 204–06
Mr. Goodbuys, **13** 545
Mr. M Food Stores, **7** 373
Mr. Maintenance, **25** 15
Mr. Payroll Corporation, **20** 113; **61** 52–54
MRD Gaming, **51** 206–07
M-real Oyj, 56 252–55 (upd.)
MRJ Technology Solutions, **54** 396
MRN Radio Network, **19** 223
Mrs. Baird's Bakeries, 29 338–41
Mrs. Fields' Original Cookies, Inc., 27 331–35
Mrs. Giles Country Kitchens, **63** 69, 71
Mrs. Paul's Kitchens. See Campbell Soup Company.
Mrs. Smith's Frozen Foods. See Kellogg Company
Mrs. Winner's Chicken & Biscuits, **58** 324
MS-Relais GmbH. See Matsushita Electric Works, Ltd.
MSAS Cargo International. See Excel plc.
MSC. See Material Sciences Corporation.
MSC Industrial Direct Co., Inc., 71 234–36
MSE Corporation, **33** 44
MSI Data Corp., **10** 523; **15** 482
M6. See Métropole Télévision.
MSL Industries, **10** 44
MSNBC, **28** 301
MSP, Inc., **57** 231
MSR. See Mountain Safety Research.
MSU. See Middle South Utilities.
Mt. See also Mount.
Mt. Beacon Insurance Co., **26** 486
Mt. Goldsworthy Mining Associates, **IV** 47
Mt. Olive Pickle Company, Inc., 44 293–95
Mt. Summit Rural Telephone Company, **14** 258
Mt. Vernon Iron Works, **II** 14
MTA. See Metropolitan Transportation Authority.
MTC. See Management and Training Corporation.
MTel. See Mobile Telecommunications Technologies Corp.
MTG. See Modern Times Group AB.
MTM Entertainment Inc., **13** 279, 281
MTR Foods Ltd., 55 271–73
MTS Inc., 37 261–64
MTV, **31** 239
MTV Asia, **23** 390
MTVi Group, **37** 194
Muehlens KG, **48** 422
Mueller Co. See Tyco International Ltd.
Mueller Furniture Company, **8** 252; **39** 206

Mueller Industries, Inc., 7 359–61; **52** 256–60 (upd.)
Muench Woodworking, Inc., **68** 133
Muffler Corporation of America, **56** 230
Mulberry Group PLC, 71 237–39
Mule-Hide Products Co., **22** 15
Mullen Advertising Inc., 13 513; **51** 259–61
Mullens & Co., **14** 419
Multex Systems, **21** 70
Multi-Color Corporation, 53 234–36
Multi Restaurants, **II** 664
Multibank Inc., **11** 281
Multicanal S.A., **67** 200–01
Multicare Companies. *See* NeighborCare, Inc.
Multicom Publishing Inc., **11** 294
Multiflex, Inc., **63** 318
Multilink, Inc., **27** 364–65
MultiMed, **11** 379
Multimedia Cablevision Inc. *See* Gannett Company, Inc.
Multimedia Games, Inc., 41 272–76
Multimedia, Inc., IV 591; **11** 330–32; **30** 217
Multimedia Security Services, Inc., **32** 374
Multiplex, **67** 104–06
MultiScope Inc., **10** 508
Multitech International. *See* Acer Inc.
Multiview Cable, **24** 121
Mündener Gummiwerke GmbH, **68** 289
Munford, Inc., **17** 499
Munich Re (Münchener Rückversicherungs-Gesellschaft Aktiengesellschaft in München), III 202, 299–301, 400–01; **35** 34, 37; **46** 303–07 (upd.); **63** 411–12
Munising Woodenware Company, **13** 156
Munksjö, **19** 227
Munsingwear, Inc. *See* PremiumWear, Inc.
Munson Transportation Inc., **18** 227
Munster and Leinster Bank Ltd., **16** 13
Mura Corporation, **23** 209
Murata, **37** 347
Murdock Madaus Schwabe, 26 315–19, 470
Murfin Inc., **8** 360
Murmic, Inc., **9** 120
Murphey Favre, Inc., **17** 528, 530
Murphy Family Farms Inc., 7 477; **21** 503; **22** 366–68; **46** 84
Murphy Oil Corporation, 7 362–64; **32** 338–41 (upd.)
Murphy-Phoenix Company, **14** 122
Murphy's Pizza. *See* Papa Murphy's International, Inc.
Murray Inc., **19** 383
Murtaugh Light & Power Company, **12** 265
Muscatine Journal, **11** 251
Muse, Cordero, Chen, **41** 89
Musgrave Group Plc, 57 254–57; **58** 102, 104; **59** 93
Music and Video Club, **24** 266, 270
Music-Appreciation Records, **13** 105
Music Corporation of America. *See* MCA Inc.
Music Go Round, **18** 207–09
Music Man Co., **16** 202; **43** 170; **56** 116
Music Plus, **9** 75
Musical America Publishing, Inc., **22** 441
Musician's Friend, Inc. *See* Guitar Center, Inc.

Musicland Stores Corporation, 9 360–62; **11** 558; **19** 417; **37** 263; **38** 313–17 (upd.); **63** 63
Musicmatch, Inc. *See* Yahoo! Inc.
MusicNet, Inc., **53** 282
MusicNow, Inc. *See* Circuit City Stores, Inc.
Musitek, **16** 202; **43** 170
Muskegon Gas Company. *See* MCN Corporation.
Muskegon Wire, **55** 305
Mutual & Federal, **61** 270, 272
Mutual Benefit Life Insurance Company, III 243, 302–04
Mutual Broadcasting System, **23** 509
Mutual Gaslight Company. *See* MCN Corporation.
Mutual Life Insurance Company of New York, III 305–07, 316, 321, 380
Mutual Marine Office Inc., **41** 284
Mutual of Omaha, **III** 365; **25** 89–90; **27** 47
Mutual Papers Co., **14** 522
Mutual Savings & Loan Association, **III** 215; **18** 60
Muzak, Inc., 7 90–91; **18** 353–56; **35** 19–20
Muzzy-Lyon Company. *See* Federal-Mogul Corporation.
MVC. *See* Music and Video Club.
MVF. *See* Mission Valley Fabrics.
MVR Products Pte Limited, **47** 255
MWA. *See* Modern Woodmen of America.
MWH Preservation Limited Partnership, 65 245–48
Mwinilunga Canneries Ltd., **IV** 241
MXL Industries, Inc., **13** 367; **64** 166
Myanmar Brewery Ltd., **59** 60
Mycalkyushu Corporation. *See* AEON Co., Ltd.
Myco-Sci, Inc. *See* Sylvan, Inc.
Mycogen Corporation, 21 385–87
Mycrom, **14** 36
Myer Emporium Ltd., **20** 156
Myers Industries, Inc., 19 277–79
Mygind International, **8** 477
Mylan Laboratories Inc., I 656–57; **20** 380–82 (upd.); **59** 304–08 (upd.)
Myojo Cement Co. Ltd., **60** 301
Myrna Knitwear, Inc., **16** 231
Myrurgia S.A., **60** 246

N.A. Woodworth, **III** 519; **22** 282
N. Boynton & Co., **16** 534
N.C. Cameron & Sons, Ltd., **11** 95
N.C. Monroe Construction Company, **14** 112
N.E.M., **23** 228
N.E. Restaurant Co. Inc. *See* Bertucci's Corpration.
N.F. Smith & Associates LP, 70 199–202
N.H. Geotech. *See* New Holland N.V.
N.L. Industries, **19** 212
N M Electronics, **II** 44
N M Rothschild & Sons Limited, 24 267; **39** 293–95
N. Shure Company, **15** 477
N.V. *see under first word of company name*
N.Y.P. Holdings Inc., **12** 360
Na Pali, S.A. *See* Quiksilver, Inc.
Naamloze Vennootschap tot Exploitatie van het Café Krasnapolsky. *See* Grand Hotel Krasnapolsky N.V.

Nabari Kintetsu Gas Company Ltd., **60** 236
Nabisco Brands, Inc., II 475, 512, 542–44; **7** 128, 365–67; **12** 167; **25** 366. *See also* RJR Nabisco.
Nabisco Foods Group, 7 365–68 (upd.); **9** 318; **14** 48; **24** 358. *See also* Kraft Foods Inc.
Nabisco Holdings Corporation, **25** 181; **42** 408; **44** 342
Nabisco Ltd., **24** 288
Nabors Industries, Inc., 9 363–65
Nacamar Internet Services, **48** 398
NACCO Industries, Inc., 7 369–71; **17** 213–15, 246, 248
Nacional de Drogas, S.A. de C.V., **39** 188
NACO Finance Corp., **33** 398
Naco-Nogales, **51** 389
Nadler Sportswear. *See* Donnkenny, Inc.
Naegele Outdoor Advertising Inc., **36** 340
Naf Naf SA, 44 296–98
NAFI Corp. *See* Chris-Craft Industries, Inc.
Nagasakiya Co., Ltd., V 149–51; **69** 259–62 (upd.)
Nagasco, Inc., **18** 366
Nagase & Co., Ltd., 8 376–78; **61** 226–30 (upd.)
Nagase-Landauer, Ltd., **51** 210
Nagel Meat Markets and Packing House, **II** 643
Nagoya Mitsukoshi Ltd., **56** 242
NAI. *See* Natural Alternatives International, Inc.; Network Associates, Inc.
NAI Technologies, Inc., **58** 101
Naiman Co., **25** 449
Nairn Linoleum Co., **18** 116
Nakano Vinegar Co. Ltd., **26** 58
Nalco Chemical Corporation, I 373–75; **12** 346–48 (upd.)
Nalge Co., **14** 479–80
NAM. *See* Nederlandse Aardolie Maatschappij.
Nam Tai Electronics, Inc., 61 231–34
Name Development Ltd. *See* Marchex, Inc.
Namibia Breweries Ltd., **33** 75
NAMM. *See* North American Medical Management Company, Inc.
Namor Productions, **58** 124
Namur Re S.A., **51** 143
Nan Ya Plastics Corp., **14** 197–98; **58** 130
NANA Regional Corporation, **7** 558
Nance Petroleum Corporation, **63** 347
Nancy's Notions. *See* Tacony Corporation.
Nanfang South China Motor Corp., **34** 132
Nantucket Allserve, Inc., 22 369–71
Nantucket Corporation, **6** 226
Nantucket Mills, **12** 285; **34** 240
NAPA. *See* National Automotive Parts Association.
NAPC. *See* North American Philips Corp.
Napocor. *See* National Power Corporation.
NAPP Systems, Inc., **11** 253
Napster, Inc., 69 263–66
Narragansett Electric Company, **51** 265
NAS. *See* National Audubon Society.
NASA. *See* National Aeronautics and Space Administration.
NASCAR. *See* National Association for Stock Car Auto Racing.
NASD, 54 242–46 (upd.)
NASDAQ, **37** 132
Nash DeCamp Company, **23** 356–57
Nash Finch Company, 8 379–81; **11** 43; **23** 356–58 (upd.); **40** 80; **65** 249–53 (upd.)

Nashua Corporation, 8 382–84; **61** 280
The Nashville Network, **11** 153
Nashville Speedway USA, Inc., **43** 139–41
Naspers Ltd., 66 230–32
NASRIN Services LLC, **64** 346
Nassco Holdings Inc., **36** 79
Nasu Nikon Co., Ltd., **48** 295
Nat Robbins, **37** 269–70
NaTec Ltd. *See* CRSS Inc.
Nathan's Famous, Inc., 29 342–44
National, **10** 419
The National Academy of Television Arts
    & Sciences, **55** 3
National Acme Company. *See* Acme-
    Cleveland Corp.
National Advertising Company, **27** 280
National Aeronautics and Space
    Administration, **11** 201, 408; **12** 489; **37**
    364–65
National Air Transport Co., **9** 416; **11** 427
National Allied Publications. *See* DC
    Comics Inc.
National Aluminum Company, **11** 38
National American Corporation, **33** 399
National Amusements Inc., 28 295–97
National Association for Stock Car Auto
    Racing, 32 342–44
National Association of Securities
    Dealers, Inc., 10 416–18. *See also*
    NASD.
National Audubon Society, 26 320–23
National Auto Credit, Inc., 16 379–81
National Automotive Fibers, Inc. *See*
    Chris- Craft Industries, Inc.
National Automotive Parts Association, **26**
    348
National Bancard Corporation, **11** 111–13
National Bancorp of Arizona, **12** 565
National Bank for Cooperatives, **8** 489–90
National Bank of Arizona, **53** 378
National Bank of Commerce, **9** 536; **11**
    105–06; **13** 467
National Bank of Commerce Trust &
    Savings Association, **15** 161
National Bank of Greece, 41 277–79
The National Bank of Jacksonville, **9** 58
National Bank of New Zealand, **II** 308; **19**
    155
National Bank of Washington, **13** 440
National BankAmericard Inc. *See* Visa
    International.
National Basketball Association, **12** 457
National Beverage Corp., 26 324–26; **55**
    146. *See also* Faygo Beverages Inc.
National Binding Company, **8** 382
National BioSystems, **47** 37
National Bridge Company of Canada, Ltd.,
    8 544
National Broadcasting Company, Inc., II
    151–53; 6 164–66 (upd.); **10** 173; **17**
    149–50; **19** 201, 210; **21** 24; **23** 120; **28**
    298–301 (upd.); **30** 99; **32** 3; **33** 324;
    34 186; **42** 161, 163. *See also* General
    Electric Company.
National Building Society, **10** 6–7
National Cable & Manufacturing Co., **13**
    369
National Cable Television Association, **18**
    64
National Can Corp., I 607–08; **13** 255
National Car Rental System, Inc., 10
    373, **419–20; 22** 524; **25** 93, 143. *See*
    also Republic Industries, Inc.
National Carriers Ltd. *See* Exel plc.

National Cash Register Company. *See*
    NCR Corporation.
National Cement Co., **35** 419; **70** 343
National Cheerleaders Association, **15**
    516–18
National Chemsearch Corp. *See* NCH
    Corporation.
National Child Care Centers, Inc., **II** 607
National City Bancorporation, **56** 219
National City Bank, **9** 475
National City Corp., 9 475; **15** 313–16
National Coach, **56** 223
National Comics Publications. *See* DC
    Comics Inc.
National Commercial Bank, **11** 108; **12**
    422; **13** 476
National Components Industries, Inc., **13**
    398
National Convenience Stores
    Incorporated, 7 372–75; **20** 140
National Cranberry Association. *See* Ocean
    Spray Cranberries, Inc.
National Dairy Products Corp., **14** 204
National Data Corporation, **24** 393
National Demographics & Lifestyles Inc.,
    10 461
National Discount Brokers Group, Inc.,
    28 302–04
National Disinfectant Company. *See* NCH
    Corporation.
National Distillers and Chemical
    Corporation, I 376–78; **8** 439–41; **9**
    231; **10** 181; **30** 441. *See also* Quantum
    Chemical Corp.
National Drive-In Grocery Corporation, **7**
    372
National Drug Ltd., **II** 652
National Economic Research Associates,
    III 283
National Education Association, **9** 367
National Educational Corporation, **26** 95
National Educational Music Co. Ltd., 47
    256–58
National Electric Company, **11** 388
National Employers Life Assurance Co.
    Ltd., **13** 539
National Endowment for the Arts, **52** 15
National Enquirer, **10** 287–88
National Envelope Corporation, 32
    345–47
National Equipment Services, Inc., 57
    258–60
National Executive Service. *See* Carey
    International, Inc.
National Express Group PLC, 50 340–42
National Express Laboratories, Inc., **10** 107
National Family Opinion. *See* NFO
    Worldwide, Inc.
National Farmers Organization, **53** 260
National Fence Manufacturing Co., Inc., **45**
    327
National Fidelity Life Insurance Co., **10**
    246
National Fidelity Life Insurance Co. of
    Kansas, **IV** 343
National Financial Partners Corp., 65
    254–56
National Fire & Marine Insurance Co., **III**
    213–14; **42** 32
National Football League, 12 457; **29**
    345–47; **37** 294
National Freight Consortium plc. *See* Exel
    plc.
National Fuel Gas Company, 6 526–28

National Geographic Society, 9 366–68;
    30 332–35 (upd.); **42** 115, 117
National Golf Properties, Inc. *See*
    American Golf Corporation
National Grape Co-operative
    Association, Inc., 20 383–85
National Grid Company, **50** 280–81,
    361–362
National Grid Group plc, **11** 399–400; **12**
    349; **13** 484; **45** 298–99; **47** 122
National Grid Transco plc, **66** 283
National Grid USA, 51 262–66 (upd.)
National Grocers of Ontario, **II** 631
National Guardian Corp., **18** 33
National Gypsum Company, 10 421–24
National Health Laboratories
    Incorporated, 11 333–35. *See also*
    Laboratory Corporation of America
    Holdings.
National Healthcare Resources, Inc. *See*
    Concentra Inc.
National Heritage Academies, Inc., 60
    211–13
National Hockey League, 35 300–03
National Home Centers, Inc., 44
    299–301
National Housing Systems, Inc., **18** 27
National ICEE Corporation, **24** 242
National Indemnity Co., **III** 213–14; **42**
    32–33
National India Rubber Company, **9** 228
National Inking Appliance Company, **14** 52
National Instruments Corporation, 22
    372–74
National Integrity Life Insurance, **III** 249
National Intergroup, Inc., V 152–53; **12**
    354; **16** 212. *See also* FoxMeyer Health
    Corporation.
National Iranian Oil Company, IV
    466–68; **47** 342; **61** 235–38 (upd.)
National Journal Group Inc., 67 256–58
National Key Company. *See* Cole National
    Corporation.
National Law Publishing Company, Inc.,
    32 35
National Lead Co., **21** 489
National Leisure Group, **47** 421
National Liability and Fire Insurance Co.,
    III 214
National Liberty Corp., **III** 218–19
National Life Insurance Co. of Canada, **III**
    243
National Linen Service, **54** 251, 254
National Living Centers, **13** 49
National Lumber Co. *See* National Home
    Centers, Inc.
National Magazine Company Limited, **19**
    201
National Marine Service, **6** 530
National Market System, **9** 369
National Media Corporation, 27 336–40
National Medical Care, **22** 360
National Medical Enterprises, Inc., III
    87–88; **10** 252; **14** 233; **33** 185. *See also*
    Tenet Healthcare Corporation.
National Mobility Corp., **30** 436
The National Motor Bearing Company. *See*
    Federal-Mogul Corporation.
The National Motor Club of America, Inc.,
    33 418
National Mutual Life Assurance of
    Australasia, **III** 249
National Office Furniture, **12** 297

National Oil Corporation, 66 233–37 (upd.)
National Oilwell, Inc., 54 247–50
National Old Line Insurance Co., III 179
National Organization for Women, Inc., 55 274–76
National Paper Co., 8 476
National Parks Transportation Company, 25 420–22
National Patent Development Corporation, 7 45; 13 365–68; 25 54. See also GP Strategies Corporation.
National Periodical Publications. See DC Comics Inc.
National Permanent Mutual Benefit Building Society, 10 6
National Petroleum Refiners of South Africa, 47 340
National Pharmacies, 9 346
National Picture & Frame Company, 24 345–47
National Pig Development Co., 46 84
National Postal Meter Company, 14 52
National Power Corporation, 56 214–15
National Power PLC, 11 399–400; 12 349–51; 13 458, 484. See also International Power PLC.
National Presto Industries, Inc., 16 382–85; 43 286–90 (upd.)
National Processing, Inc., 24 394
National Propane Corporation, 8 535–37
National Public Radio, 19 280–82; 47 259–62 (upd.)
National Publishing Company, 41 110
National Quotation Bureau, Inc., 14 96–97
National R.V. Holdings, Inc., 32 348–51
National Railroad Passenger Corporation (Amtrak), 22 375–78; 66 238–42 (upd.)
National Ready Mixed, 70 343
National Realty Trust. See NRT Incorporated.
National Record Mart, Inc., 29 348–50
National Register Publishing Co., 17 399; 23 442
National Reinsurance Corporation. See General Re Corporation.
National Research Corporation, 8 397
National Restaurants Management, Inc., 38 385–87
National Revenue Corporation, 22 181
National Rifle Association of America, 37 265–68
National Rubber Machinery Corporation, 8 298
National Sanitary Supply Co., 13 149–50; 16 386–87
National Satellite Paging, 18 348
National School Studios, 7 255; 25 252
National Science Foundation, 9 266
National Sea Products Ltd., 14 339–41
National Security Containers LLC, 58 238
National Semiconductor Corporation, II 63–65; 6 261–63; 9 297; 11 45–46, 308, 463; 16 332; 18 18; 19 312; 26 327–30 (upd.); 43 15; 69 267–71 (upd.)
National Service Industries, Inc., 11 336–38; 54 251–55 (upd.)
National Shoe Products Corp., 16 17
National Slicing Machine Company, 19 359
National-Southwire Aluminum Company, 11 38; 12 353

National Stamping & Electric Works, 12 159
National Standard Co., IV 137; 13 369–71
National Starch and Chemical Company, 32 256–57; 49 268–70
National Steel and Shipbuilding Company, 7 356
National Steel Corporation, IV 163, 236–37, 572; V 152–53; 8 346, 479–80; 12 352–54; 26 527–29. See also FoxMeyer Health Corporation.
National Student Marketing Corporation, 10 385–86
National System Company, 9 41; 11 469
National Tea, II 631–32
National Technical Laboratories, 14 52
National TechTeam, Inc., 41 280–83
National Telecommunications of Austin, 8 311
National Telephone and Telegraph Corporation. See British Columbia Telephone Company.
National Telephone Co., 7 332, 508
National Thoroughbred Racing Association, 58 244–47
National Trading Manufacturing, Inc., 22 213
National Transcommunications Ltd. See NTL Inc.
National Union Electric Corporation, 12 159
National Utilities & Industries Corporation, 9 363
National Westminster Bank PLC, II 333–35; 13 206
National Wine & Spirits, Inc., 49 271–74
Nationale-Nederlanden N.V., III 308–11; 50 11
Nationar, 9 174
NationsBank Corporation, 10 425–27; 11 126; 13 147; 18 516, 518; 23 455; 25 91, 186; 26 348, 453. See also Bank of America Corporation
NationsRent, 28 388
Nationwide Cellular Service, Inc., 27 305
Nationwide Credit, 11 112
Nationwide Group, 25 155
Nationwide Income Tax Service, 9 326
Nationwide Logistics Corp., 14 504
Nationwide Mutual Insurance Co., 26 488
NATIOVIE, II 234
Native Plants, III 43
NATM Buying Corporation, 10 9, 468
Natomas Company, 7 309; 11 271
Natref. See National Petroleum Refiners of South Africa.
Natrol, Inc., 49 275–78
Natronag, IV 325
NatSteel Electronics Ltd., 48 369
NatTeknik, 26 333
Natudryl Manufacturing Company, 10 271
Natural Alternatives International, Inc., 49 279–82
Natural Gas Clearinghouse. See NGC Corporation.
Natural Gas Corp., 19 155
Natural Gas Pipeline Company, 6 530, 543; 7 344–45
Natural Gas Service of Arizona, 19 411
Natural Ovens Bakery, Inc., 72 234–36
Natural Selection Foods, 54 256–58
Natural Wonders Inc., 14 342–44
NaturaLife International, 26 470

Naturalizer. See Brown Shoe Company, Inc.
The Nature Company, 10 215–16; 14 343; 26 439; 27 429; 28 306
The Nature Conservancy, 26 323; 28 305–07, 422
Nature's Sunshine Products, Inc., 15 317–19; 26 470; 27 353; 33 145
Nature's Way Products Inc., 26 315
Naturin GmbH. See Viscofan S.A.
Naturipe Berry Growers, 62 154
Natuzzi Group. See Industrie Natuzzi S.p.A.
NatWest Bancorp, 38 393
NatWest Bank. See National Westminster Bank PLC.
Naugles, 7 506
Nautica Enterprises, Inc., 16 61; 18 357–60; 25 258; 27 60; 44 302–06 (upd.)
Nautilus International, Inc., 13 532; 25 40; 30 161
Navaho Freight Line, 16 41
Navajo LTL, Inc., 57 277
Navajo Refining Company, 12 240
Navajo Shippers, Inc., 42 364
Navan Resources, 38 231
Navarre Corporation, 22 536; 24 348–51
Navigant International, Inc., 47 263–66
Navigation Mixte, III 348
Navire Cargo Gear, 27 269
Navisant, Inc., 49 424
Navistar International Corporation, I 180–82, 525, 527; 10 428–30 (upd.); 17 327; 33 254. See also International Harvester Co.
NAVTEQ Corporation, 69 272–75
Navy Exchange Service Command, 31 342–45
Navy Federal Credit Union, 33 315–17
Naxon Utilities Corp., 19 359
Naylor, Hutchinson, Vickers & Company. See Vickers PLC.
NBC. See National Broadcasting Company, Inc.
NBC Bankshares, Inc., 21 524
NBC/Computer Services Corporation, 15 163
NBD Bancorp, Inc., 9 476; 11 339–41, 466. See also Bank One Corporation.
NBTY, Inc., 31 346–48
NCA Corporation, 9 36, 57, 171
NCB. See National City Bank of New York.
NCC Industries, Inc., 59 267
NCC L.P., 15 139
NCH Corporation, 8 385–87
nChip, 38 187–88
NCL Holdings. See Genting Bhd.
NCNB Corporation, II 336–37; 12 519; 26 453
NCO Group, Inc., 42 258–60
NCR Corporation, III 150–53; IV 298; V 263; 6 264–68 (upd.); 9 416; 11 62, 151, 542; 12 162, 148, 246, 484; 16 65; 29 44; 30 336–41 (upd.); 36 81
NCS. See Norstan, Inc.
NCS Healthcare Inc., 67 262
NCTI (Noise Cancellation Technologies Inc.), 19 483–84
nCube Corp., 14 15; 22 293
ND Marston, III 593
NDB. See National Discount Brokers Group, Inc.

NDL. *See* Norddeutscher Lloyd.
NE Chemcat Corporation, **72** 118
NEA. *See* Newspaper Enterprise Association.
Nearly Me, **25** 313
Neatherlin Homes Inc., **22** 547
Nebraska Bell Company, **14** 311
Nebraska Book Company, Inc., 65 257–59
Nebraska Cellular Telephone Company, **14** 312
Nebraska Furniture Mart, **III** 214–15; **18** 60–61, 63
Nebraska Light & Power Company, **6** 580
Nebraska Power Company, **25** 89
Nebraska Public Power District, 29 351–54
NEBS. *See* New England Business Services, Inc.
NEC Corporation, II 66–68, 73, 82, 91, 104, 361; **6** 287; **9** 42, 115; **10** 257, 366, 463, 500; **11** 46, 308, 490; **13** 482; **16** 139; **18** 382–83; **19** 391; **21** 388–91 **(upd.); 25** 82, 531; **36** 286, 299–300; **47** 320; **57** 261–67 **(upd.)**
Neckermann Versand AG. *See* Karstadt AG.
Nedcor, **61** 270–71
Nederland Line. *See* Stoomvaart Maatschappij Nederland.
Nederlander Organization, **24** 439
Nederlands Talen Institut, **13** 544
Nederlandsche Electriciteits Maatschappij. *See* N.E.M.
Nederlandsche Handel Maatschappij, **26** 242
Nederlandsche Heidenmaatschappij. *See* Arcadis NV.
Nederlandsche Kunstzijdebariek, **13** 21
N.V. Nederlandse Gasunie, V 658–61; **38** 407
Nedlloyd Group. *See* Koninklijke Nedlloyd N.V.
NedMark Transportation Services. *See* Polar Air Cargo Inc.
Neeco, Inc., **9** 301
Needham Harper Worldwide. *See* Omnicom Group Inc.
Needlecraft, **II** 560; **12** 410
Needleworks, Inc., **23** 66
Neenah Foundry Company, 68 263–66
Neenah Printing, **8** 360
NEES. *See* New England Electric System.
Neff Corp., 32 352–53
Neff GmbH, **67** 81
Negromex, **23** 171–72
NEI. *See* Northern Engineering Industries PLC.
Neico International, Inc., **67** 226
NeighborCare, Inc., 67 259–63 **(upd.)**
Neighborhood Restaurants of America, **18** 241
Neilson/Cadbury, **II** 631
Neiman Bearings Co., **13** 78
The Neiman Marcus Group, Inc., 12 355–57; 15 50, 86, 291; **17** 43; **21** 302; **25** 177–78; **27** 429; **49** 283–87 **(upd.); 52** 45–46
Neisner Brothers, Inc., **9** 20
NEL Equity Services Co., **III** 314
Nelson Bros., **14** 236
Nelson Entertainment Group, **47** 272
Nelson Publications, **22** 442

NEMF. *See* New England Motor Freight, Inc.
Neo Products Co., **37** 401
Neodata, **11** 293
Neopost S.A., 53 237–40
Neos, **21** 438
Neoterics Inc., **11** 65
Neozyme I Corp., **13** 240
Nepera, Inc., **16** 69
Neptun Maritime Oyj, **29** 431
Neptune Orient Lines Limited, 47 267–70; **61** 30
NER Auction Group, **23** 148
NERCO, Inc., 7 376–79
NES. *See* National Equipment Services, Inc.
Nesco Inc., **28** 6, 8
Nescott, Inc., **16** 36
Nespak SpA, **40** 214–15
Neste Oy, IV 469–71; **61** 346. *See also* Fortum Corporation
Nestlé S.A., II 545–49; **7** 380–84 **(upd.); 28** 308–13 **(upd.); 71** 240–46 **(upd.)**
Net Investment S.A., **63** 180
NetApp. *See* Network Appliance, Inc.
NetCom Systems AB, 26 331–33
NetCreations, **47** 345, 347
NetEffect Alliance, **58** 194
Netezza Corporation, 69 276–78
Netflix, Inc., 58 248–51
Netherlands Trading Co. *See* Nederlandse Handel Maatschappij.
NetHold B.V., **31** 330
NetLabs, **25** 117
NetMarket Company, **16** 146
NetPlane Systems, **36** 124
Netron, **II** 390
Netscape Communications Corporation, 15 320–22; **35** 304–07 **(upd.); 44** 97; **50** 328–30; **57** 37
NetStar Communications Inc., **24** 49; **35** 69
Nettingsdorfer, **19** 227
Nettle Creek Corporation, **19** 304
Netto, **11** 240
Net2Phone Inc., **34** 224
NetWest Securities, **25** 450
Network Appliance, Inc., 58 252–54
Network Associates, Inc., 25 119, 347–49
Network Communications Associates, Inc., **11** 409
Network Solutions, Inc., **47** 430
Network Ten, **35** 68–69
NetZero Inc. *See* United Online, Inc.
Netzip Inc., **53** 282
Neuberger Berman Inc., 57 268–71
Neuer Markt, **59** 153
Neuro Navigational Corporation, **21** 47
Neutrogena Corporation, 17 340–44; **36** 305
Nevada Bell Telephone Company, 14 345–47
Nevada Community Bank, **11** 119
Nevada Natural Gas Pipe Line Co., **19** 411
Nevada Power Company, 11 342–44; **12** 265
Nevada Savings and Loan Association, **19** 412
Nevada Southern Gas Company, **19** 411
Nevada State Bank, **53** 378
Neversink Dyeing Company, **9** 153
Nevex Software Technologies, **42** 24, 26
New Access Communications, **43** 252
New America Publishing Inc., **10** 288
New Asahi Co., **I** 221

New Balance Athletic Shoe, Inc., 17 245; **25** 350–52; **68** 267–70 **(upd.)**
New Bauhinia Limited, **53** 333
New Bedford Gas & Edison Light Co., **14** 124–25
New Belgium Brewing Company, Inc., 68 271–74
New Brunswick Scientific Co., Inc., 45 285–87
New Century Equity Holdings Corporation, **72** 39
New Century Network, **13** 180; **19** 204, 285
New City Releasing, Inc., **25** 269
New CORT Holdings Corporation. *See* CORT Business Services Corporation.
New Daido Steel Co., Ltd., **IV** 62–63
New Dana Perfumes Company, 37 269–71
New Departure, **9** 17
New Dimension Software, Inc., **55** 67
New England Audio Company, Inc. *See* Tweeter Home Entertainment Group, Inc.
New England Business Services, Inc., 18 361–64
New England Confectionery Co., 15 323–25
New England CRInc, **8** 562
New England Electric System, V 662–64. *See also* National Grid USA.
New England Gas & Electric Association, **14** 124–25
New England Life Insurance Co., **III** 261
New England Motor Freight, Inc., **53** 250
New England Mutual Life Insurance Co., III 312–14
New England Network, Inc., **12** 31
New England Paper Tube Co., **54** 58
New England Power Association. *See* National Grid USA.
New Found Industries, Inc., **9** 465
New Galveston Company, Inc., **25** 116
New Hampshire Gas & Electric Co., **14** 124
New Hampton Goldfields Ltd., **63** 182, 184
New Hampton, Inc., **27** 429
New Haven District Telephone Company. *See* Southern New England Telecommunications Corporation.
New Haven Electric Co., **21** 512
New Holland N.V., 22 379–81. *See also* CNH Global N.V.
New Horizon Manufactured Homes, Ltd., **17** 83
New Hotel Showboat, Inc. *See* Showboat, Inc.
New Impriver NV. *See* Punch International N.V.
New Jersey Bell, **9** 321
New Jersey Educational Music Company. *See* National Educational Music Co. Ltd.
New Jersey Resources Corporation, 54 259–61
New Jersey Shale, **14** 250
New Jersey Tobacco Co., **15** 138
New Laoshan Brewery, **49** 418
New Line Cinema, Inc., 47 271–74; **57** 35
New London City National Bank, **13** 467
New Look Group plc, 35 308–10
New Market Development Company. *See* Cousins Properties Inc.
New Materials Ltd., **48** 344

New Mather Metals, **III** 582
New Mitsui Bussan, **III** 296
New Orleans Canal and Banking Company, **11** 105
New Orleans Saints LP, 58 255–57
The New Piper Aircraft, Inc., 44 307–10
New Plan Realty Trust, 11 345–47
New Process Company, **25** 76–77
New South Wales Health System, **16** 94
New Street Capital Inc., 8 388–90 (upd.). *See also* Drexel Burnham Lambert Incorporated.
New Sulzer Diesel, **III** 633
New Times, Inc., 45 288–90
New Toyo Group, **19** 227
New Trading Company. *See* SBC Warburg.
New UPI Inc., **25** 507
New Valley Corporation, 17 345–47
New Vanden Borre, **24** 266–70
New Ventures Realty Corporation, **58** 272
New World Coffee-Manhattan Bagel, Inc., **32** 15
New World Communications Group, **22** 442; **28** 248
New World Development Company Limited, IV 717–19; 8 500; 38 318–22 (upd.)
New World Entertainment, **17** 149
New World Hotel (Holdings) Ltd., **13** 66
New World Pasta Company, 53 241–44
New World Restaurant Group, Inc., 44 311–14
New York Air, **I** 103, 118, 129
New York Capital Bank, **41** 312
New York Central Railroad Company, **9** 228; **10** 43–44, 71–73; **17** 496
New York City Health and Hospitals Corporation, 60 214–17
New York City Off-Track Betting Corporation, 51 267–70
New York City Transit Authority, **8** 75
New York Daily News, 32 357–60
New York Electric Corporation. *See* New York State Electric and Gas.
New York Envelope Co., **32** 346
New York Evening Enquirer, **10** 287
New York Eye and Ear Infirmary. *See* Continuum Health Partners, Inc.
New York Fabrics and Crafts, **16** 197
New York Gas Light Company. *See* Consolidated Edison Company of New York.
New York Health Care, Inc., 72 237–39
New York Life Insurance Company, III 315–17; 45 291–95 (upd.); 63 14
New York Magazine Co., **12** 359
New York Marine and Gotham Insurance, **41** 284
New York Philharmonic. *See* Philharmonic-Symphony Society of New York, Inc.
New York Presbyterian Hospital. *See* NewYork-Presbyterian Hospital.
New York Quotation Company, **9** 370
New York Restaurant Group, Inc., 32 361–63
New York Sports Clubs. *See* Town Sports International, Inc.
New York State Electric and Gas Corporation, 6 534–36
New York Stock Exchange, Inc., 9 369–72; 10 416–17; 34 254; 39 296–300 (upd.); 54 242
New York Telephone Co., **9** 321

The New York Times Company, IV 647–49; 15 54; **19 283–85 (upd.); 23** 158; **32** 508; **57** 243; **61 239–43 (upd.)**
New York Trust Co., **I** 378
New York Zoological Society. *See* Wildlife Conservation Society.
New York's Bankers Trust Co., **12** 107
New Zealand Aluminum Smelters, **IV** 59
New Zealand Countrywide Banking Corporation, **10** 336
Newa Insurance Co. Ltd., **64** 280
Newark Electronics Co., **9** 420
Newbridge & Gilbert, **56** 285
Newco Waste Systems. *See* Browning-Ferris Industries, Inc.
Newcor, Inc., 40 332–35; 65 143, 145
Newcrest Mining Ltd., **IV** 47; **22** 107
Newell Co., 9 373–76; 12 216; **13** 40–41; **22** 35; **25** 22; **61** 173
Newell Rubbermaid Inc., 49 253; **52 261–71 (upd.); 53** 37, 40; **62** 231
Newfield Exploration Company, 65 260–62
Newfoundland Brewery, **26** 304
Newfoundland Energy, Ltd., **17** 121
Newfoundland Light & Power Co. *See* Fortis, Inc.
Newfoundland Processing Ltd. *See* Newfoundland Energy, Ltd.
Newhall Land and Farming Company, 14 348–50
Newman's Own, Inc., 37 272–75
Newmark & Lewis Inc., **23** 373
Newmont Mining Corporation, IV 33, 171, 576; 7 287–89, 385–88; 12 244; **16** 25; **23** 40; **38** 231–32; **40** 411–12; **50** 30
Newnes, **17** 397
Newpark Resources, Inc., 63 305–07
Newport Corporation, 71 247–49
Newport News Shipbuilding Inc., 13 372–75; 38 323–27 (upd.); 41 42; **45** 306
News & Observer Publishing Company, **23** 343
News America Publishing Inc., 12 358–60; 27 42; **37** 408
News Communications & Media Plc, **35** 242
News Corporation Limited, IV 650–53; 7 389–93 (upd.); 46 308–13 (upd.); 52 4; **60** 66
News Extracts Ltd., **55** 289
News International Corp., **20** 79
News of the World Organization (NOTW), **46** 309
Newsco NV, **48** 347
Newsfoto Publishing Company, **12** 472; **36** 469
Newspaper Co-op Couponing, **8** 551
Newspaper Enterprise Association, **7** 157–58
Newsquest plc, 32 354–56
Newth-Morris Box Co. *See* Rock-Tenn Company.
Newtherm Oil Burners, Ltd., **13** 286
Newton Yarn Mills, **19** 305
NewYork-Presbyterian Hospital, 59 309–12
Nexans SA, 54 262–64
Nexar Technologies, Inc., **22** 409
NEXCOM. *See* Navy Exchange Service Command.
Nexity S.A., 66 243–45

NeXstar Pharmaceuticals Inc., **54** 130
NeXT Incorporated, **34** 348
Next Media Ltd., 61 244–47
Next plc, 6 25; **29 355–57**
Nextel Communications, Inc., 10 431–33; 21 239; **26** 389; **27 341–45 (upd.)**
Nextera Enterprises, Inc., **54** 191, 193
NEXTLINK Communications, Inc., **38** 192
NextNet Wireless, Inc. *See* Clearwire, Inc.
Neyveli Lignite Corporation Ltd., 65 263–65
NFC Castings Inc., **68** 265
NFC plc, 6 412–14; 14 547. *See also* Exel plc.
NFL Properties, Inc., **22** 223
NFO Worldwide, Inc., 24 352–55
NFT Distribution Limited, **61** 258, 260–61
NGC. *See* National Grid Company.
NGC Corporation, 18 365–67. *See also* Dynegy Inc.
NGI International Precious Metals, Ltd., **24** 335
NGK Insulators Ltd., 67 264–66
NH Hoteles, 71 114–15
NHB Group Ltd. *See* MasterBrand Cabinets, Inc.
NHK. *See* Japan Broadcasting Corporation.
NHK Spring Co., Ltd., III 580–82
NI Industries, **20** 362
Ni-Med, **50** 122
Niagara Corporation, 28 314–16
Niagara First Savings and Loan Association, **10** 91
Niagara Mohawk Holdings Inc., 45 296–99 (upd.)
Niagara Mohawk Power Corporation, V 665–67; 6 535; **25** 130; **51** 265
Niagara of Wisconsin, **26** 362–63
Nice Day, Inc., **II** 539
Nice Systems, **11** 520
NiceCom Ltd., **11** 520
Nichido Fire and Marine Insurance Co. *See* Millea Holdings Inc.
Nichii Co., Ltd., V 154–55; 15 470; **36** 418
Nichimen Corporation, IV 150–52, 154; **10** 439; **24 356–59 (upd.)**
Nichimo Sekiyu Co. Ltd., **IV** 555; **16** 490
Nichirei Corporation, 70 203–05
Nicholas Turkey Breeding Farms, **13** 103
Nichols & Company, **8** 561
Nichols Aluminum-Golden, Inc., **62** 289
Nichols-Homeshield, **22** 14
Nichols plc, 44 315–18
Nichols Research Corporation, 18 368–70
Nicholson File Co., **II** 16
Nicholson Graham & Jones, **28** 141
Nickelodeon, **25** 381
Nickerson Machinery Company Inc., **53** 230
Nicklaus Companies, 45 300–03
Nicolet Instrument Company, **11** 513
Nicolon N.V. *See* Royal Ten Cate N.V.
NICOR Inc., 6 529–31
Nidec Corporation, 59 313–16
Nielsen, **10** 358
Nielsen Marketing Research. *See* A.C. Nielsen Company.
Niemann Chemie, **8** 464
Niesmann & Bischoff, **22** 207
Nieuw Rotterdam, **27** 54
NIF Ventures Co. Ltd., **55** 118

Nigerian National Petroleum Corporation, IV 472–74; **72 240–43 (upd.)**
Nigerian Shipping Operations, **27** 473
Nihon Keizai Shimbun, Inc., IV 654–56
Nihon Kohden Corporation, **13** 328
Nihon Lumber Land Co., III 758
Nihon Noyaku Co., **64** 35
Nihon Sugar, I 511
Nihon Synopsis, **11** 491
Nihon Timken K.K., **8** 530
Nihon Waters K.K., **43** 456
Nihron Yupro Corp. *See* Toto Ltd.
NII. *See* National Intergroup, Inc.
NIKE, Inc., V 372–74; **8 391–94 (upd.)**; **36 343–48 (upd.)**
Nikkei. *See* Nihon Keizai Shimbun, Inc.
Nikkei Shimbun Toei, **9** 29
Nikkelverk, **49** 136
Nikken Global Inc., **32 364–67**
Nikko International Hotels, I 106
The Nikko Securities Company Limited, II 433–35; **9 377–79 (upd.)**
Nikko Trading Co., I 106
Nikolaiev, **19** 49, 51
Nikon Corporation, III 583–85; **9** 251; **12** 340; **18** 93, 186, 340, 342; **43** 282; **48 292–95 (upd.)**
Nilpeter, **26** 540, 542
Niman Ranch, Inc., **67 267–69**
Nimbus CD International, Inc., **20 386–90**
9 Telecom, **24** 79
Nine West Group Inc., **11 348–49**; **14** 441; **23** 330; **39** 247, **301–03 (upd.)**
98 Cents Clearance Centers, **62** 104
99¢ Only Stores, **25 353–55**
Ningbo General Bearing Co., Ltd., **45** 170
Nintendo Co., Ltd., III 586–88; **7 394–96 (upd.)**; **10** 124–25, 284–86, 483–84; **13** 403; **15** 539; **16** 168, 331; **18** 520; **23** 26; **28 317–21 (upd.)**; **31** 237; **38** 415; **50** 83; **67 270–76 (upd.)**
Nintendo of America, **24** 4
NIOC. *See* National Iranian Oil Company.
Nippon Breweries Ltd. *See* Sapporo Breweries Ltd.
Nippon Cable Company, **15** 235
Nippon Credit Bank, II 338–39; **38** 439
Nippon Del Monte Corporation, **47** 206
Nippon Densan Corporation. *See* Nidec Corporation.
Nippon Educational Television (NET). *See* Asahi National Broadcasting Company, Ltd.
Nippon Electric Company, Limited. *See* NEC Corporation.
Nippon Express Company, Ltd., V 477–80; **64 286–90 (upd.)**
Nippon-Fisher, **13** 225
Nippon Foundation Engineering Co. Ltd., **51** 179
Nippon Gakki Co., Ltd. *See* Yamaha Corporation.
Nippon Global Tanker Co. Ltd., **53** 116
Nippon Gyomo Sengu Co. Ltd., IV 555
Nippon Hatsujo Kabushikikaisha. *See* NHK Spring Co., Ltd.
Nippon Helicopter & Aeroplane Transport Co., Ltd. *See* All Nippon Airways Company Limited.
Nippon Hoso Kyokai. *See* Japan Broadcasting Corporation.
Nippon Idou Tsushin, **7** 119–20

Nippon International Container Services, **8** 278
Nippon Interrent, **10** 419–20
Nippon K.K. *See* Nikon Corporation.
Nippon Kogaku K.K. *See* Nikon Corporation.
Nippon Kogyo Co. Ltd. *See* Nippon Mining Co. Ltd.
Nippon Kokan K.K. *See* NKK Corporation.
Nippon Life Insurance Company, III 273, 288, **318–20**; **60 218–21 (upd.)**
Nippon Light Metal Company, Ltd., IV 153–55
Nippon Meat Packers, Inc., II 550–51; **61** 139
Nippon Mining Co., Ltd., IV 475–77; **14** 207
Nippon Mitsubishi Oil Corporation, **49** 216
Nippon Motorola Manufacturing Co., II 62
Nippon Oil Company, Limited, IV 478–79; **19** 74
Nippon Oil Corporation, **63 308–13 (upd.)**
Nippon Paint Co., Ltd, **11** 252
Nippon Paper Industries Co., Ltd., **57** 101
Nippon Phonogram, **23** 390
Nippon Polaroid Kabushiki Kaisha, **7** 437; **18** 570
Nippon Reizo Co. *See* Nichirei Corporation.
Nippon Sanso Corp., **16** 486, 488
Nippon Seiko K.K., III 589–90; **47** 278
Nippon Sekiyu Co. *See* Nippon Oil Company, Limited.
Nippon Sheet Glass Company, Limited, III 714–16
Nippon Shinpan Co., Ltd., II 436–37, 442; **8** 118; **61 248–50 (upd.)**
Nippon Steel Chemical Co., **10** 439
Nippon Steel Corporation, IV 116, 130, **156–58**, 184, 212, 228, 298; **6** 274; **14** 369; **17 348–51 (upd.)**, 556; **19** 219; **24** 370; **67** 284
Nippon Suisan Kaisha, Limited, II 552–53
Nippon Telegraph and Telephone Corporation, II 51, 62; III V 305–07; **7** 118–20; **10** 119; **13** 482; **16** 224; **21** 330; **25** 301; **27** 327, 365; **50** 129; **51 271–75 (upd.)**
Nippon Television, **7** 249; **9** 29
Nippon Tire Co., Ltd. *See* Bridgestone Corporation.
Nippon Unipac Holding, **57** 101
Nippon Yusen Kabushiki Kaisha (NYK), V 481–83; **72 244–48 (upd.)**
Nippon Yusoki Company, Ltd., **13** 501
Nippondenso Co., Ltd., III 591–94. *See also* DENSO Corporation.
NIPSCO Industries, Inc., **6 532–33**
NiSource, Inc., **38** 81
Nissan Motor Acceptance Corporation, **22** 207
Nissan Motor Co., Ltd., I 183–84; III 750; **7** 111, 120, 219; **9** 243, 340–42; **10** 353; **11** 50–51, **350–52 (upd.)**; **16** 167; **17** 556; **23** 338–40, 289; **24** 324; **27** 203; **34** 133, **303–07 (upd.)**; **59** 393–94
Nissan Trading Company, Ltd., **13** 533
Nissay Dowa General Insurance Company Ltd., **60** 220
Nisshin Flour Milling Company, Ltd., II 554. *See also* Nisshin Seifun Group Inc.

Nisshin Seifun Group Inc., **66 246–48 (upd.)**
Nisshin Steel Co., Ltd., IV 159–60; **7** 588
Nissho Iwai K.K., I 509–11; **8** 75; **15** 373; **25** 449; **27** 107
Nissui. *See* Nippon Suisan Kaisha.
Nitches, Inc., **53 245–47**
Nitroglycerin AB, **13** 22
Nitroglycerin Ltd., **9** 380
Nittetsu Curtainwall Corp., III 758
Nittetsu Sash Sales Corp., III 758
Nittsu. *See* Nippon Express Co., Ltd.
Niugini Mining Ltd., **23** 42
Nixdorf Computer AG, III 154–55; **12** 162; **14** 169; **26** 497. *See also* Wincor Nixdorf Holding GmbH.
Nixdorf-Krein Industries Inc. *See* Laclede Steel Company.
Nizhny Novgorod Dairy, **48** 438
NKI B.V., **71** 178–79
NKK Corporation, IV 161–63, 212–13; **28 322–26 (upd.)**; **53** 170, 172
NL Industries, Inc., **10 434–36**; **19** 466–68
NLG. *See* National Leisure Group.
NLI Insurance Agency Inc., **60** 220
NLM City-Hopper, I 109
NM Acquisition Corp., **27** 346
NMC Laboratories Inc., **12** 4
NMT. *See* Nordic Mobile Telephone.
NNG. *See* Northern Natural Gas Company.
No-Leak-O Piston Ring Company, **10** 492
No-Sag Spring Co., **16** 321
Noah's New York Bagels. *See* Einstein/Noah Bagel Corporation.
Nob Hill Foods, **58** 291
Nobel Drilling Corporation, **26** 243
Nobel Industries AB, **9 380–82**; **16** 69. *See also* Akzo Nobel N.V.
Nobel Learning Communities, Inc., **37 276–79**
Noble Affiliates, Inc., **11 353–55**; **18** 366
Noble Broadcast Group, Inc., **23** 293
Noble Roman's Inc., **14 351–53**
Nobles Industries, **13** 501
Noblesville Telephone Company, **14** 258
Nobleza Piccardo SAICF, **64 291–93**
Noblitt-Sparks Industries, Inc., **8** 37–38
Nobody Beats the Wiz. *See* Cablevision Electronic Instruments, Inc.
Nocibé SA, **54 265–68**
Nocona Belt Company, **31** 435–36
Nocona Boot Co. *See* Justin Industries, Inc.
Noel Group, Inc., **24** 286–88
NOF Corporation, **72 249–51**
NOK Corporation, **41** 170–72
Nokia Corporation, II 69–71; IV 296; **6** 242; **15** 125; **17** 33, **352–54 (upd.)**; **18** 74, 76; **19** 226; **20** 439; **38 328–31 (upd.)**; **47** 318–19; **50** 510; **52** 317; **52** 333
Nokian Tyres PLC, **59** 91
NOL Group. *See* Neptune Orient Lines Limited.
Noland Company, **35 311–14**
Nolo.com, Inc., **49 288–91**
Nolte Mastenfabriek B.V., **19** 472
Noma Industries, **11** 526
Nomai Inc., **18** 510
Nomura Bank of Japan, **34** 221
Nomura Holdings, Inc., **49** 451
Nomura Securities Company, Limited, II 438–41; **9 383–86 (upd.)**; **39** 109
Nomura Toys Ltd., **16** 267; **43** 232

Non-Fiction Book Club, **13** 105
Non-Stop Fashions, Inc., **8** 323
Noodle Kidoodle, 16 388–91
Noodles & Company, Inc., 55 277–79
Nooter Corporation, 61 251–53
NOP Research Group, **28** 501, 504
Nopco Chemical Co., **7** 308
Nopri. *See* GIB Group.
Nor-Cal Engineering Co. GmbH, **18** 162
Nora Industrier A/S, **18** 395
Norampac Inc., **71** 95
Norand Corporation, **9** 411; **72** 189
Noranda Inc., IV 164–66; 7 397–99
   (upd.); 9 282; **26** 363; **49** 136; **64**
   294–98 (upd.)
Norandex, **16** 204
Norbro Corporation. *See* Stuart
   Entertainment Inc.
Norcal Pottery Products, Inc., **58** 60
Norcal Waste Systems, Inc., 60 222–24
Norcen Energy Resources, Ltd., **8** 347
Norco Plastics, **8** 553
Norcon, Inc., **7** 558–59
Norcore Plastics, Inc., **33** 361
Nordbanken, **9** 382
Norddeutsche Affinerie AG, 62 249–53
Norddeutscher-Lloyd. *See* Hapag-Lloyd
   AG.
Nordea AB, 40 336–39
Nordic Baltic Holding. *See* Nordea AB.
Nordica S.r.l., **10** 151; **15** 396–97; **53** 24
NordicTrack, 10 215–17; **22 382–84; 38**
   238. *See also* Icon Health & Fitness, Inc.
Nordson Corporation, 11 356–58; 48
   296–99 (upd.)
Nordstrom, Inc., V 156–58; **11** 349; **13**
   494; **14** 376; **17** 313; **18 371–74 (upd.);**
   21 302; **22** 173; **67 277–81 (upd.)**
Nordwestdeutsche Kraftwerke AG. *See*
   PreussenElektra AG.
Norelco, **17** 110
Norelco Consumer Products Co., 12 439;
   26 334–36
Norelec, **27** 138
Norex Leasing, Inc., **16** 397
Norfolk Carolina Telephone Company, **10**
   202
Norfolk Southern Corporation, V
   484–86; 12 278; **22** 167; **29 358–61**
   (upd.)
Norfolk Steel, **13** 97
Norge Co., **18** 173–74; **43** 163–64
Noric Corporation, **39** 332
Norinchukin Bank, II 340–41
Norlin, **16** 238–39
Norm Thompson Outfitters, Inc., 47
   275–77
Norma AS. *See* Autoliv, Inc.
Norman BV, **9** 93; **33** 78
Normandy Mining Ltd., **23** 42
Normark Corporation. *See* Rapala-Normark
   Group, Ltd.
Norment Security Group, Inc., **51** 81
Normond/CMS, **7** 117
Norrell Corporation, 25 356–59
Norris Cylinder Company, **11** 535
Norris Grain Co., **14** 537
Norris Oil Company, **47** 52
Norshield Corp., **51** 81
Norsk Helikopter AS. *See* Bristow
   Helicopters Ltd.
Norsk Hydro ASA, 10 437–40; 35
   315–19 (upd.); 36 322; **61** 345–46

Norsk Rengjorings Selskap a.s., **49** 221
Norske Skogindustrier ASA, 63 314–16
Norstan, Inc., 16 392–94
Norstar Bancorp, **9** 229
Nortek, Inc., 14 482; **22** 4; **26** 101; **34**
   308–12; 37 331
Nortel Inversora S.A., **63** 375–77
Nortel Networks Corporation, 36 349–54
   (upd.); 50 130; **72** 129–31
Nortex International, **7** 96; **19** 338
North African Petroleum Ltd., IV 455
North American Aviation, **7** 520; **9** 16; **11**
   278, 427
North American Carbon, **19** 499
North American Cellular Network, **9** 322
North American Coal Corporation, **7**
   369–71
North American Company, **6** 552–53,
   601–02
North American Dräger, **13** 328
North American Energy Conservation, Inc.,
   35 480
North American InTeleCom, Inc., **IV** 411
North American Light & Power Company,
   12 541
North American Medical Management
   Company, Inc., **36** 366
North American Mogul Products Co. *See*
   Mogul Corp.
North American Philips Corporation, **19**
   393; **21** 520
North American Plastics, Inc., **61** 112
North American Printing Ink Company, **13**
   228
North American Rockwell Corp., **10** 173
North American Site Developers, Inc., **69**
   197
North American Systems, **14** 230
North American Training Corporation. *See*
   Rollerblade, Inc.
North American Van Lines. *See* Allied
   Worldwide, Inc.
North American Watch Company. *See*
   Movado Group, Inc.
North Atlantic Energy Corporation, **21** 411
North Atlantic Laboratories, Inc., **62** 391
North Atlantic Packing, **13** 243
North Atlantic Trading Company Inc.,
   65 266–68
North British Rubber Company, **20** 258
North Broken Hill Peko, **IV** 61
North Carolina Motor Speedway, Inc., **19**
   294
North Carolina National Bank Corporation.
   See NCNB Corporation.
North Carolina Natural Gas Corporation, **6**
   578
North Carolina Shipbuilding Co., **13** 373
North Central Financial Corp., **9** 475
North Central Utilities, Inc., **18** 405
North East Insurance Company, **44** 356
North Eastern Bricks, **14** 249
The North Face, Inc., 8 169; **18 375–77;**
   25 206; **41** 103; **54** 400
North Fork Bancorporation, Inc., 44 33;
   46 314–17
North New York Savings Bank, **10** 91
North of Scotland Hydro-Electric Board,
   19 389
North Pacific Group, Inc., 61 254–57
North Pacific Paper Corp., **IV** 298
North Ridge Securities Corporation, **72**
   149–50
North Sea Ferries, **26** 241, 243

North Sea Oil and Gas, **10** 337
North Shore Gas Company, **6** 543–44
North Shore Land Co., **17** 357
North Star Container, Inc., **59** 290
North Star Egg Case Company, **12** 376
North Star Marketing Cooperative, **7** 338
North Star Mill, **12** 376
North Star Steel Company, 13 138; **18**
   378–81; 19 380; **40** 87
North Star Transport Inc., **49** 402
North Star Tubes, **54** 391, 393
North Star Universal, Inc., **25** 331, 333
North State Supply Company, **57** 9
North Supply, **27** 364
The North West Company, Inc., 12
   361–63; 25 219–20
North-West Telecommunications. *See*
   Pacific Telecom, Inc.
North West Water Group plc, 11
   359–62. *See also* United Utilities PLC.
Northbridge Financial Corp., **57** 137
Northbrook Corporation, **24** 32
Northbrook Holdings, **22** 495
Northcliffe Newspapers, **19** 118
Northeast Federal Corp., **13** 468
Northeast Petroleum Industries, Inc., **11**
   194; **14** 461
Northeast Savings Bank, **12** 31; **13** 467–68
Northeast Utilities, V 668–69; 13
   182–84; **21** 408, 411; **48 303–06 (upd.);**
   55 313, 316
Northeastern New York Medical Service,
   Inc., **III** 246
Northern Animal Hospital Inc., **58** 355
Northern Arizona Light & Power Co., **6**
   545
Northern California Savings, **10** 340
Northern Dairies, **10** 441
Northern Drug Company, **14** 147
Northern Electric Company. *See* Northern
   Telecom Limited.
Northern Energy Resources Company. *See*
   NERCO, Inc.
Northern Engineering Industries Plc. *See*
   Rolls-Royce Group PLC.
Northern Fibre Products Co., **I** 202
Northern Foods plc, 10 441–43; 61
   258–62 (upd.)
Northern Illinois Gas Co., **6** 529–31
Northern Indiana Power Company, **6** 556
Northern Indiana Public Service Company,
   6 532–33
Northern Infrastructure Maintenance
   Company, **39** 238
Northern Leisure, **40** 296–98
Northern Light Electric Company, **18**
   402–03
Northern National Bank, **14** 90
Northern Natural Gas Co. *See* Enron
   Corporation.
Northern Pacific Corp., **15** 274
Northern Pacific Railroad, **14** 168; **26** 451
Northern Paper, **I** 614
Northern Pipeline Construction Co., **19**
   410, 412
Northern Rock plc, 33 318–21
Northern Star Co., **25** 332
Northern States Power Company, V
   670–72; 18 404; **20 391–95 (upd.)**
Northern Stores, Inc., **12** 362
Northern Sugar Company, **11** 13
Northern Telecom Limited, III 164; **V**
   271; **V 308–10; 6** 242, 307, 310; **9** 479;
   10 19, 432; **11** 69; **12** 162; **14** 259; **16**

392, 468; **17** 353; **18** 111; **20** 439; **22** 51; **25** 34; **27** 342; **47** 318–20. *See also* Nortel Networks Corporation.
Northern Trust Company, 9 387–89
Northfield Metal Products, **11** 256
Northgate Computer Corp., **16** 196
Northland. *See* Scott Fetzer Company.
Northland Cranberries, Inc., 38 332–34
Northland Publishing, **19** 231
NorthPrint International, **22** 356
Northrop Corporation, I 49, 55, 59, 76–77, 80, 84, 197, 525; **9** 416, 418; **10** 162; **11** 164, 166, 266, 269, **363–65 (upd.);**
Northrop Grumman Corporation, 41 43; **45** 304–12 **(upd.); 49** 444
NorthStar Computers, **10** 313
Northwest Airlines Inc., I 112–14, 125, 127; **6** 103–05 **(upd.),** 123; **9** 273; **11** 266, 315; **12** 191, 487; **21** 141, 143; **22** 252; **26** 337–40 **(upd.),** 441; **27** 20; **28** 226, 265–66; **30** 447; **31** 419–20; **33** 50–51, 302; **52** 90, 93. *See also* Mesaba Holdings, Inc.
Northwest Engineering Co. *See* Terex Corporation.
Northwest Express. *See* Bear Creek Corporation.
Northwest Industries. *See* Chicago and North Western Holdings Corporation.
Northwest Instruments, **8** 519
Northwest Linen Co., **16** 228
Northwest Natural Gas Company, 45 313–15
Northwest Outdoor, **27** 280
Northwest Paper Company, **8** 430
Northwest Steel Rolling Mills Inc., **13** 97
Northwest Telecommunications Inc., **6** 598
NorthWestern Corporation, 37 280–83
Northwestern Engraving, **12** 25
Northwestern Financial Corporation, **11** 29
Northwestern Flavors LLC, **58** 379
Northwestern Manufacturing Company, **8** 133
Northwestern Mutual Life Insurance Company, III 321–24, 352; **45** 316–21 **(upd.); 46** 198; **52** 243–44; **67** 328–29
Northwestern National Bank, **16** 71
Northwestern National Life Insurance Co., **14** 233
Northwestern Public Service Company, **6** 524
Northwestern States Portland Cement Co., **III** 702
Northwestern Telephone Systems. *See* Pacific Telecom, Inc.
Norton Company, 8 395–97; **22** 68; **26** 70
Norton Healthcare Ltd., **11** 208
Norton McNaughton, Inc., 25 245; **27** 346–49
Norton Opax PLC, **IV** 259; **34** 140
Norton Professional Books. *See* W.W. Norton & Company, Inc.
Norton Simon Industries, **22** 513
Norwales Development Ltd., **11** 239
Norwalk Truck Lines, **14** 567
NORWEB plc, **13** 458; **24** 270
Norwegian Caribbean Line, **27** 90
Norweld Holding A.A., **13** 316
Norwest Bank, **19** 412
Norwest Corp., **16** 135
Norwest Mortgage Inc., **11** 29; **54** 124

Norwich & Peterborough Building Society, 55 280–82
Norwich-Eaton Pharmaceuticals, **III** 53; **8** 434; **26** 383
Norwich Pharmaceuticals, **9** 358
Norwich Union Fire Insurance Society, Ltd., **III** 273, 404
Norwich Winterthur Group, **III** 404
Norwood Company, **13** 168
Norwood Promotional Products, Inc., 26 341–43
Nostell Brick & Tile, **14** 249
Notre Capital Ventures II, L.P., **24** 117
Nouveaux Loisirs. *See* Éditions Gallimard.
Nouvelle Compagnie Havraise Pénninsulaire, **27** 514
Nouvelle Elastelle, **52** 100–01
Nouvelles Galeries Réunies, **10** 205; **19** 308; **27** 95
Nova Corporation, **18** 365–67; **24** 395; **49** 120–21
Nova Corporation of Alberta, V 673–75; **12** 364–66
Nova Information Systems, **24** 393
Nova Mechanical Contractors, **48** 238
Nova Pharmaceuticals, **14** 46
Nova Scotia Steel Company, **19** 186
NovaCare, Inc., 11 366–68; **14** 233; **33** 185; **41** 194
Novacor Chemicals Ltd., 12 364–66
Novaction Argentina SA, **48** 224
Novagas Clearinghouse Ltd., **18** 367; **49** 120
Novalta Resources Inc., **11** 441
Novamax Technologies Inc., **34** 209
Novanet Semiconductor, **36** 124
Novapak Corporation. *See* PVC Container Corporation.
Novar plc, 49 292–96 **(upd.)**
Novara plc, **60** 123
Novartis AG, 18 51; **34** 284; **39** 304–10 **(upd.); 50** 58, 90; **55** 285
Novatec Plastics Corporation. *See* PVC Container Corporation.
Novation, **53** 346–47
Novell, Inc., 6 269–71; **23** 359–62 **(upd.); 25** 50–51, 117, 499; **33** 113, 115; **34** 442–43; **38** 418–19
Novellus Systems, Inc., 18 382–85
Noven Pharmaceuticals, Inc., 55 283–85
Novgorodnefteprodukt, **48** 378
Novo Industri A/S, I 658–60, 697
Novo Nordisk A/S, 61 263–66 **(upd.)**
Novobord, **49** 353
Novotel. *See* Accor SA.
NOVUM. *See* Industrie Natuzzi S.p.A.
NOVUS Financial Corporation, **33** 314
NOW. *See* National Organization for Women, Inc.
Nowsco Well Services Ltd., **25** 73
Noxell Corporation, **III** 53; **8** 434; **26** 384
NPBI International B.V., **56** 141
NPC International, Inc., 40 340–42
The NPD Group, Inc., 68 275–77
NPI-Omnipoint Wireless LLC, **63** 132
NPR. *See* National Public Radio, Inc.
NPS Waste Technologies, **13** 366
NRC Handelsblad BV, **53** 273
NRF B.V., **56** 247
NRG Energy, Inc., **11** 401; **50** 363
NRT Incorporated, 58 76–77; **61** 267–69
NS. *See* Norfolk Southern Corporation.
NS Group, **31** 287
NS Petites Inc., **8** 323

NSF International, 72 252–55
NSG Information System Co., **III** 715
NSK. *See* Nippon Seiko K.K.
NSK Ltd., **42** 384
NSK-Warner, **14** 64
NSMO. *See* Nederlandsche Stoomvart Maatschappij Oceaan.
NSN Network Services, **23** 292, 294
NSP. *See* Northern States Power Company.
NSU Werke, **10** 261
NTC Electronics Inc., **64** 198
NTC Publishing Group, **22** 519, 522
NTCL. *See* Northern Telecom Limited.
NTL Inc., 65 269–72
NTN Corporation, III 595–96; **28** 241; **47** 278–81 **(upd.)**
NTRON, **11** 486
NTT. *See* Nippon Telegraph and Telephone Corp.
NTTPC. *See* Nippon Telegraph and Telephone Public Corporation.
NU. *See* Northeast Utilities.
Nu-Era Gear, **14** 64
The Nu-Gro Corporation. *See* United Industries Corporation.
Nu-kote Holding, Inc., 18
Nu Skin Enterprises, Inc., 27 350–53; **31** 327 386–89
Nuance Group, **63** 361, 363
Nuclear Electric, **6** 453; **11** 399–401; **12** 349; **13** 484; **50** 280–81, 361–63; **66** 282
Nuclear Power International, **19** 166
Nucor Corporation, 7 400–02; **13** 143, 423; **14** 156; **18** 378–80; **19** 380; **21** 392–95 **(upd.); 26** 407; **52** 326
Nucorp Energy, **II** 620; **59** 280–81
NUG Optimus Lebensmittel-Einzelhandelgesellschaft mbH, **V** 74
NUMAR Corporation, **25** 192
NUMMI. *See* New United Motor Manufacturing, Inc.
Nuovo Pignone, **69** 146, 148–49
NUR Touristic GmbH. *See* Karstadt AG.
Nurotoco Inc. *See* Roto-Rooter Service Company.
The Nut Company NV, **66** 153
Nutmeg Industries, Inc., **17** 513
Nutraceutical International Corporation, 37 284–86
NutraSweet Company, 8 398–400; **26** 108; **29** 331
Nutreco Holding N.V., 56 256–59
Nutrena, **II** 617; **13** 137
Nutri-Foods International, **18** 467–68
NutriSystem, Inc., 71 250–53
Nutrition for Life International Inc., 22 385–88
Nutron Industries, **58** 75
Nuveen. *See* John Nuveen Company.
NV Dagblad De Telegraaf. *See* N.V. Holdingmaatschappij De Telegraaf.
NVIDIA Corporation, 54 269–73
NVR Inc., 8 401–03; **70** 206–09 **(upd.)**
NWA, Inc. *See* Northwest Airlines Corporation.
NWK. *See* Nordwestdeutsche Kraftwerke AG.
NWS BANK plc, **10** 336–37
NWT Air, **56** 39
NY Waterway. *See* Port Imperial Ferry Corporation.
NYC OTB Racing Network, **51** 269

NYHC Newco Paxxon, Inc. *See* New York Health Care, Inc.
NYK. *See* Nippon Yusen Kabushiki Kaisha (NYK).
Nyland Mattor, **25** 464
NYLCare Health Plans, **45** 293–94
NYLife Care Health Plans, Inc., **17** 166
Nylon de Mexico, S.A., **19** 10, 12
NYMAGIC, Inc., 41 284–86
Nymofil, Ltd., **16** 297
NYNEX Corporation, V 311–13; 6 340; **11** 19, 87; **13** 176; **25** 61–62, 102; **26** 520. *See also* Verizon Communications.
NYRG. *See* New York Restaurant Group, Inc.
NYSE. *See* New York Stock Exchange.
NYSEG. *See* New York State Electric and Gas Corporation.
NZI Corp., **III** 257

O&K Rolltreppen, **27** 269
O&Y. *See* Olympia & York Developments Ltd.
O.B. McClintock Co., **7** 144–45
O.C. Tanner Co., 69 279–81
O.G. Wilson, **16** 560
O. Kraft & Sons, **12** 363
O.N.E. Color Communications L.L.C., **29** 306
O-Pee-Chee, **34** 447–48
O.S. Designs Inc., **15** 396
O.Y.L. Industries Berhad, **26** 3, 5
Oak Creek Homes Inc., **41** 18
Oak Harbor Freight Lines, Inc., 53 248–51
Oak Hill Investment Partners, **11** 490
Oak Hill Sportswear Corp., **17** 137–38
Oak Industries Inc., 21 396–98
Oak Technology, Inc., 22 389–93
OakBrook Investments, LLC, **48** 18
Oakhurst Dairy, 60 225–28
Oakley, Inc., 18 390–93; 49 297–302 (upd.)
OakStone Financial Corporation, **11** 448
Oaktree Capital Management, LLC, 71 254–56
OakTree Health Plan Inc., **16** 404
Oakville, **7** 518
Oakwood Homes Corporation, 13 155; 15 326–28
OAO AVTOVAZ. *See* AVTOVAZ Joint Stock Company.
OAO Gazprom, 42 261–65
OAO LUKOIL, 40 343–46
OAO NK YUKOS, 47 282–85; 49 304
OAO Severstal. *See* Severstal Joint Stock Company.
OAO Siberian Oil Company (Sibneft), 49 303–06
OAO Tatneft, 45 322–26
Oasis Group P.L.C., **10** 506
OASYS, Inc., **18** 112
Obayashi Corporation, **44** 154; **72** 94–96
ÖBB. *See* Österreichische Bundesbahnen GmbH.
Oberheim Corporation, **16** 239
Oberland, **16** 122
Obi, **23** 231
Obie Media Corporation, 56 260–62
Object Design, Inc., **15** 372
O'Boy Inc. *See* Happy Kids Inc.
O'Brien Kreitzberg, Inc., **25** 130
Observer AB, 55 286–89
Obunsha, **9** 29

OCBC. *See* Overseas-Chinese Banking Corporation.
Occidental Bank, **16** 497; **50** 497
Occidental Chemical Corporation, **19** 414; **45** 254; **71** 149
Occidental Life Insurance Company, **26** 486–87; **41** 401
Occidental Overseas Ltd., **11** 97; **50** 179
Occidental Petroleum Corporation, IV 480–82; 25 360–63 (upd.); 71 257–61 (upd.)
Occidental Petroleum Great Britain Inc., **21** 206
Océ N.V., 24 360–63
Ocean Combustion Services, **9** 109
Ocean Drilling and Exploration Company. *See* ODECO.
Ocean Group plc, 6 415–17. *See also* Exel plc.
Ocean Pacific Apparel Corporation, **51** 321
Ocean Reef Management, **19** 242, 244
Ocean Scientific, Inc., **15** 380
Ocean Specialty Tankers Corporation, **22** 275
Ocean Spray Cranberries, Inc., 7 403–05; 10 525; **19** 278; **25 364–67 (upd.); 38** 334
Ocean Steam Ship Company. *See* Malaysian Airlines System BHD.
Ocean Transport & Trading Ltd., **6** 417
Oceaneering International, Inc., 63 317–19
Oceania Football Confederation, **27** 150
Oceanic Steam Navigation Company, **19** 197; **23** 160
Oceans of Fun, **22** 130
Ocelet Industries Ltd., **25** 232
O'Charley's Inc., 19 286–88; 60 229–32 (upd.)
OCL. *See* Overseas Containers Ltd.
Oclassen Pharmaceuticals Inc., **56** 375
Octagon Group Ltd., **51** 173
Octane Software, **49** 124
Octek, **13** 235
Octel Messaging, 14 217, 354–56; 16 394; **41 287–90 (upd.)**
Octopus Publishing, **IV** 667; **17** 398
Ocular Sciences, Inc., 65 273–75
Oculinum, Inc., **10** 48
Odakyu Electric Railway Co., Ltd., V 487–89; 68 278–81 (upd.)
Odd Job Trading Corp., **29** 311–12
Odda Smelteverk A/S, **25** 82
Odeco Drilling, Inc., **7** 362–64; **11** 522; **12** 318; **32** 338, 340
Odegard Outdoor Advertising, L.L.C., **27** 280
Odetics Inc., 14 357–59
Odhams Press Ltd., **IV** 259, 666–67; **7** 244, 342; **17** 397–98
ODL, Inc., 55 290–92
ODM, **26** 490
ODME. *See* Toolex International N.V.
Odwalla, Inc., 31 349–51
Odyssey Holdings, Inc., **18** 376
Odyssey Partners Group, **II** 679; **V** 135; **12** 55; **13** 94; **17** 137; **28** 218
Odyssey Press, **13** 560
Odyssey Publications Inc., **48** 99
Odyssey Re Group, **57** 136–37
OEA. *See* Autoliv, Inc.
OEC Medical Systems, Inc., 27 354–56
Oelwerken Julias Schindler GmbH, **7** 141
OEN Connectors, **19** 166

Ofek Securities and Investments Ltd., **60** 50
Off Wall Street Consulting Group, **42** 313
Office Depot, Inc., 8 404–05; 10 235, 497; **12** 335; **13** 268; **15** 331; **18** 24, 388; **22** 154, 412–13; **23 363–65 (upd.); 27** 95; **34** 198; **43** 293; **65 276–80 (upd.)**
Office Electronics, Inc., **65** 371
Office Mart Holdings Corporation, **10** 498
Office Systems Inc., **15** 407
The Office Works, Inc., **13** 277; **25** 500
OfficeMax Inc., 8 404; **15 329–31; 18** 286, 388; **20** 103; **22** 154; **23 364–65; 43 291–95 (upd.)**
Official Airline Guides, Inc., **IV** 643; **7** 312, 343; **17** 399
Officine Alfieri Maserati S.p.A., 11 104; **13** 28, **376–78**
Offset Gerhard Kaiser GmbH, **IV** 325
The Offshore Company, **6** 577; **37** 243
Offshore Food Services Inc., **I** 514
Offshore Logistics, Inc., 37 287–89
Offshore Transportation Corporation, **11** 523
O'Gara Company, **57** 219
Ogden Corporation, I 512–14, 701; **6 151–53**, 600; **7** 39; **25** 16; **27** 21, 196; **41** 40–41; **43** 217; **59** 321. *See also* Covanta Energy Corporation.
Ogden Food Products, **7** 430
Ogden Gas Co., **6** 568
Ogden Ground Services, **39** 240, 242
Ogilvy & Mather Worldwide, **22** 200; **71** 158–59
Ogilvy Group Inc., I 25–27, 31, 37, 244; **9** 180. *See also* WPP Group.
Oglebay Norton Company, 17 355–58
Oglethorpe Power Corporation, 6 537–38
Oh la la!, **14** 107
Ohbayashi Corporation, I 586–87
The Ohio Art Company, 14 360–62; 59 317–20 (upd.)
Ohio Ball Bearing. *See* Bearings Inc.
Ohio Barge Lines, Inc., **11** 194
Ohio Bell Telephone Company, 14 363–65; 18 30
Ohio Boxboard Company, **12** 376
Ohio Brass Co., **II** 2
Ohio Casualty Corp., 11 369–70
Ohio Coatings Company, **58** 363
Ohio Crankshaft Co. *See* Park-Ohio Industries Inc.
Ohio Edison Company, V 676–78
Ohio Farmers Insurance Company. *See* Westfield Group.
Ohio Mattress Co., **12** 438–39
Ohio Pizza Enterprises, Inc., **7** 152
Ohio-Sealy Mattress Mfg. Co., **12** 438–39
Ohio Valley Electric Corporation, **6** 517
Ohio Ware Basket Company, **12** 319
Ohlmeyer Communications, **I** 275; **26** 305
OHM Corp., **17** 553
Ohmeda. *See* BOC Group plc.
Ohmite Manufacturing Co., **13** 397
Oil and Natural Gas Commission, IV 483–84
Oil and Solvent Process Company, **9** 109
Oil-Dri Corporation of America, 20 396–99
Oil Drilling, Incorporated, **7** 344
Oil Dynamics Inc., **43** 178

Oil Equipment Manufacturing Company, **16** 8

Oil Shale Corp., **7** 537

Oilfield Industrial Lines Inc., **I** 477

Oilinvest. *See* National Oil Corporation.

Oji Paper Co., Ltd., **IV** 320–22; **57** 272–75 (upd.)

Ojibway Press, **57** 13

OJSC Wimm-Bill-Dann Foods, **48** 436–39

OK Turbines, Inc., **22** 311

Okay, **68** 143

O'Keefe Marketing, **23** 102

Oki Electric Industry Company, Limited, **II** 72–74; **15** 125; **21** 390

Okidata, **9** 57; **18** 435

Oklahoma Airmotive, **8** 349

Oklahoma Entertainment, Inc., **9** 74

Oklahoma Gas and Electric Company, **6** 539–40; **7** 409–11

Oklahoma Publishing Company, **11** 152–53; **30** 84

Okura & Co., Ltd., **IV** 167–68

Olan Mills, Inc., **62** 254–56

Oland & Sons Limited, **25** 281

Olathe Manufacturing, **26** 494

OLC. *See* Orient Leasing Co., Ltd.

Old America Stores, Inc., **17** 359–61

Old Chicago. *See* Rock Bottom Restaurants, Inc.

Old Colony Envelope Co., **32** 345–46

Old Country Buffet Restaurant Co. (OCB). *See* Buffets, Inc.

Old Dominion Freight Line, Inc., **57** 276–79

Old Dominion Power Company, **6** 513, 515

Old El Paso, **14** 212; **24** 140–41

Old Harbor Candles, **18** 68

Old Kent Financial Corp., **11** 371–72

Old Mutual PLC, **IV** 535; **61** 270–72

Old National Bancorp, **14** 529; **15** 332–34

Old Navy, Inc., **70** 210–12

Old 97 Company, **60** 287

Old Quaker Paint Company, **13** 471

Old Republic International Corporation, **11** 373–75; **58** 258–61 (upd.)

Old Spaghetti Factory International Inc., **24** 364–66

Old Stone Trust Company, **13** 468

Oldach Window Corp., **19** 446

Oldcastle, Inc., **60** 77; **64** 98

Oldover Corp., **23** 225

Ole's Innovative Sports. *See* Rollerblade, Inc.

Olean Tile Co., **22** 170

Oleochim, **IV** 498–99

OLEX. *See* Deutsche BP Aktiengesellschaft.

Olex Cables Ltd., **10** 445

Olin Corporation, **I** 379–81; **IV** 482; **8** 23; **11** 420; **13** 379–81 (upd.); **16** 68, 297; **32** 319; **63** 8

Olinkraft, Inc., **11** 420; **16** 376

Olive Garden Italian Restaurants, **10** 322, 324; **16** 156–58; **19** 258; **35** 83

Oliver Rubber Company, **19** 454, 456

Olivetti S.p.A., **34** 316–20 (upd.); **38** 300; **63** 379

Olivine Industries, Inc., **II** 508; **11** 172; **36** 255

Olmstead Products Co., **23** 82

OLN. *See* Outdoor Life Network.

Olsten Corporation, **6** 41–43; **9** 327; **29** 362–65 (upd.); **49** 265. *See also* Adecco S.A.

Olympia & York Developments Ltd., **IV** 720–21; **6** 478; **8** 327; **9** 390–92 (upd.); **30** 108

Olympia Arenas, Inc., **7** 278–79; **24** 294

Olympia Brewing, **11** 50

Olympia Entertainment, **37** 207

Olympiaki, **III** 401

Olympic Courier Systems, Inc., **24** 126

Olympic Fastening Systems, **III** 722

Olympic Insurance Co., **26** 486

Olympic Packaging, **13** 443

Olympus Communications L.P., **17** 7

Olympus Optical Company, Ltd., **15** 483

Olympus Partners, **65** 258

Olympus Sport. *See* Sears plc.

Olympus Symbol, Inc., **15** 483

OM Group, Inc., **17** 362–64

OM Gruppen, **59** 154

Omaha Public Power District, **29** 353

Omaha Steaks International Inc., **62** 257–59

Omega Gas Company, **8** 349

Omega Group. *See* MasterBrand Cabinets, Inc.

Omega Protein Corporation, **25** 546

OmegaTech Inc. *See* Martek Biosciences Corporation.

O'Melveny & Myers, **37** 290–93

OMI Corporation, **IV** 34; **9** 111–12; **22** 275; **59** 321–23

Omnes, **17** 419

Omni ApS, **56** 338

Omni Construction Company, Inc., **8** 112–13

Omni Hotels Corp., **12** 367–69

Omni-Pac, **12** 377

Omni Services, Inc., **51** 76

Omnibus Corporation, **9** 283

Omnicad Corporation, **48** 75

Omnicare, Inc., **13** 150; **49** 307–10

Omnicom Group Inc., **I** 28–32, 33, 36; **14** 160; **22** 394–99 (upd.); **23** 478; **43** 410; **64** 73, 350. *See also* TBWA Worldwide.

Omnipoint Communications Inc., **18** 77

OmniSource Corporation, **14** 366–67

OmniTech Consulting Group, **51** 99

Omnitel Pronto Italia SpA, **38** 300

OMNOVA Solutions Inc., **59** 324–26

Omron Corporation, **28** 331–35 (upd.); **53** 46

Omron Tateisi Electronics Company, **II** 75–77

ÖMV Aktiengesellschaft, **IV** 485–87

On Assignment, Inc., **20** 400–02

On Command Video Corp., **23** 135

On Cue, **9** 360

On-Line Systems. *See* Sierra On-Line Inc.

Onan Corporation, **8** 72

Onbancorp Inc., **11** 110

Once Upon A Child, Inc., **18** 207–8

Ondulato Imolese, **IV** 296; **19** 226

1-800-FLOWERS, Inc., **26** 344–46; **28** 137

1-800-Mattress. *See* Dial-A-Mattress Operating Corporation.

180s, L.L.C., **64** 299–301

One For All, **39** 405

One Price Clothing Stores, Inc., **20** 403–05

O'Neal, Jones & Feldman Inc., **11** 142

OneBeacon Insurance Group LLC, **48** 431

Oneida Bank & Trust Company, **9** 229

Oneida County Creameries Co., **7** 202

Oneida Gas Company, **9** 554

Oneida Ltd., **7** 406–08; **31** 352–55 (upd.)

ONEOK Inc., **7** 409–12

Onex Corporation, **16** 395–97; **22** 513; **24** 498; **25** 282; **50** 275; **65** 281–85 (upd.)

OneZero Media, Inc., **31** 240

Onion, Inc., **69** 282–84

Onitsuka Co., Ltd., **57** 52

Online Financial Communication Systems, **11** 112

Only One Dollar, Inc. *See* Dollar Tree Stores, Inc.

Onoda Cement Co., Ltd., **III** 717–19. *See also* Taiheiyo Cement Corporation.

Onomichi, **25** 469

OnResponse.com, Inc., **49** 433

Onsale Inc., **31** 177

Onstead Foods, **21** 501

OnTarget Inc., **38** 432

Ontario Hydro Services Company, **6** 541–42; **9** 461; **32** 368–71 (upd.)

Ontario Power Generation, **49** 65, 67

Ontario Teachers' Pension Plan, **61** 273–75

OnTrack Data International, **57** 219

OnTrak Systems Inc., **31** 301

Onyx Acceptance Corporation, **59** 327–29

Onyx Software Corporation, **53** 252–55

O'okiep Copper Company, Ltd., **7** 385–86

Opel AG. *See* Adam Opel AG.

Open Board of Brokers, **9** 369

Open Cellular Systems, Inc., **41** 225–26

Open Market, Inc., **22** 522

OpenTV, Inc., **31** 330–31

Operadora de Bolsa Serfin. *See* Grupo Financiero Serfin, S.A.

Operon Technologies Inc., **39** 335

Opinion Research Corporation, **35** 47; **46** 318–22

Opp and Micolas Mills, **15** 247–48

Oppenheimer. *See* Ernest Oppenheimer and Sons.

Oppenheimer & Co., Inc., **17** 137; **21** 235; **22** 405; **25** 450; **61** 50

Oppenheimer Wolff & Donnelly LLP, **71** 262–64

Opryland USA, **11** 152–53; **25** 403; **36** 229

Opsware Inc., **49** 311–14

Optel S.A., **17** 331; **71** 211

OPTi Computer, **9** 116

Opti-Ray, Inc., **12** 215

Optical Corporation. *See* Excel Technology, Inc.

Optical Radiation Corporation, **27** 57

Optilink Corporation, **12** 137

Optima Pharmacy Services, **17** 177

Option Care Inc., **48** 307–10

Optische Werke G. Rodenstock, **44** 319–23

OptiSystems Solutions Ltd., **55** 67

Opto-Electronics Corp., **15** 483

Optus Communications, **25** 102

Optus Vision, **17** 150

Opus Group, **34** 321–23

Oracle Corporation, **6** 272–74; **10** 361, 363, 505; **11** 78; **13** 483; **14** 16; **15** 492; **18** 541, 543; **19** 310; **21** 86; **22** 154,

293; **24** 367–71 **(upd.)**; **25** 34, 96–97, 499; **67** 282–87 **(upd.)**
Orange and Rockland Utilities, Inc., **45** 116, 120
Orange Glo International, 53 256–59
Orange Julius of America, **10** 371, 373; **39** 232, 235
Orange Line Bus Company, **6** 604
Orange PLC, **24** 89; **38** 300
Orange Shipbuilding Company, Inc., **58** 70
Orb Books. *See* Tom Doherty Associates Inc.
Orb Estates, **54** 366, 368
ORBIS Corporation, **59** 289
Orbis Entertainment Co., **20** 6
Orbis Graphic Arts. *See* Anaheim Imaging.
Orbital Engine Corporation Ltd., **17** 24
Orbital Sciences Corporation, 22 400–03
Orbitz, Inc., 61 276–78
Orchard Supply Hardware Stores Corporation, 17 365–67; **25** 535
Orchid Biosciences Inc., **57** 309, 311
Orcofi, **III** 48
OrderTrust LLP, **26** 440
Ore-Ida Foods Incorporated, 12 531; **13** 382–83
Orebehoved Fanerfabrik, **25** 464
Oregon Ale and Beer Company, **18** 72; **50** 112
Oregon Chai, Inc., 49 315–17
Oregon Craft & Floral Supply, **17** 322
Oregon Cutting Systems, **26** 119
Oregon Dental Service Health Plan, Inc., 51 276–78
Oregon Metallurgical Corporation, 20 406–08
Oregon Pacific and Eastern Railway, **13** 100
Oregon Steel Mills, Inc., 14 368–70; **19** 380
O'Reilly Automotive, Inc., 26 347–49
Orenda Aerospace, **48** 274
Organic Valley (Coulee Region Organic Produce Pool), 53 260–62
Organización Soriana, S.A. de C.V., 35 320–22
Organizacion Techint, **66** 293–95
Organon, **63** 141
ORI. *See* Old Republic International Corporation.
Orico Life Insurance Co., **48** 328
Oriel Foods, **II** 609
Orient, **21** 122
Orient Express Hotels Inc., **29** 429–30
Orient Leasing. *See* Orix Corporation.
Orient Overseas, **18** 254
Oriental Brewery Co., Ltd., **21** 320
Oriental Precision Company, **13** 213
Oriental Trading Corp., **22** 213
Oriental Yeast Co. *See* Nisshin Seifun Group Inc.
Origin Energy Limited. *See* Boral Limited.
Origin Systems Inc., **10** 285
Origin Technology, **14** 183
Original Arizona Jean Company. *See* J.C. Penney Company, Inc.
Original Cookie Co. *See* Mrs. Fields' Original Cookies, Inc.
Original Musical Instrument Company (O.M.I.), **16** 239
Origins Natural Resources Inc., **30** 190
Orioala, **72** 258
Orion Capital Corporation, **55** 331
Orion Healthcare Ltd., **11** 168

Orion Oyj, **72** 256–59
Orion Personal Insurances Ltd., **11** 168
Orion Pictures Corporation, 6 167–70; **7** 336; **14** 330, 332; **25** 326, 328–29; **31** 100; **61** 212
Orit Corp., **8** 219–20
ORIX Corporation, II 442–43, 259, 348; **44** 324–26 **(upd.)**
Orkem, **IV** 560; **21** 205
Orkin Pest Control, **11** 431–32, 434
Orkla A/S, 18 394–98; **25** 205–07; **36** 266
Orleans Homebuilders, Inc., 62 260–62
Orlimar Golf Equipment Co., **45** 76
Orm Bergold Chemie, **8** 464
Ormco Corporation, **14** 481
ÖROP, **IV** 485–86
Orowheat Baking Company, **10** 250
La Oroya, **22** 286
ORSCO, Inc., **26** 363
Ortho Diagnostic Systems, Inc., **10** 213; **22** 75
Ortho Pharmaceutical Corporation, **10** 79–80; **30** 59–60
Orthodontic Centers of America, Inc., 35 323–26
Orthofix International NV, 72 260–62
Orthopedic Services, Inc., **11** 366
Ortloff Engineers, Ltd., **52** 103–05
Orval Kent Food Company, Inc., **7** 430
Orville Redenbacher/Swiss Miss Foods Co., **17** 241
The Orvis Company, Inc., 28 336–39
Oryx Energy Company, 7 413–15; **68** 220
OSA Technologies. *See* Avocent Corporation.
Osaka Gas Company, Ltd., V 679–81; **60** 233–36 **(upd.)**
Osaka Shinyo Kumiai, **15** 495
Osaka Shosen Kaisha. *See* Mitsui O.S.K. Lines, Ltd.
Osborn Group Inc., **48** 256
Oscar Mayer Foods Corp., 12 123, 370–72
Osco Drug, **II** 604–05
OSF Japan Ltd., **24** 365
Oshawa Group Limited, II 649–50
OshKosh B'Gosh, Inc., 9 393–95; **42** 266–70 **(upd.)**
Oshkosh Electric Power, **9** 553
Oshkosh Gas Light Company, **9** 553
Oshkosh Truck Corporation, 7 416–18; **14** 458
Oshman's Sporting Goods, Inc., 16 560; **17** 368–70; **27** 7
OSi Specialties, Inc., **16** 543; **36** 148–49
OSI Systems, Inc., **71** 348
Osiris Holding Company, **16** 344
OSK. *See* Osaka Shosen Kaisha.
Osmonics, Inc., 18 399–401
Oster. *See* Sunbeam-Oster.
Österreichische Brau-Beteiligungs AG. *See* BBAG Österreichische Brau-Beteiligungs AG.
Österreichische Bundesbahnen GmbH, 6 418–20
Österreichische Länderbank, **23** 37
Österreichische Luftverkehrs AG. *See* Austrian Airlines AG.
Österreichische Mineralölverwaltung AG, **IV** 485
Österreichische Post- und Telegraphenverwaltung, V 314–17

Ostrada Yachts, **55** 54, 56
Ostravar A.S., **38** 77
O'Sullivan Industries Holdings, Inc., 34 313–15
Osuuskunta Metsäliito, **IV** 316
Otagiri Mercantile Co., **11** 95
OTC, **10** 492
Other Options, **29** 400
Otis Company, **6** 579
Otis Elevator Company, Inc., 13 384–86; **27** 267, 268; **29** 422; **39** 311–15 **(upd.)**
Otis Spunkmeyer, Inc., 28 340–42
Otosan, **I** 479–80; **54** 196–97
OTP, Incorporated, **48** 446
OTR Express, Inc., 25 368–70
Otsego Falls Paper Company, **8** 358
Ott and Brewer Company, **12** 312
Ottakar's plc, 64 302–04
Ottawa Fruit Supply Ltd., **II** 662
Ottaway Newspapers, Inc., 15 335–37
Otter Tail Power Company, 18 402–05; **37** 282
Otter-Westelaken, **16** 420; **43** 308
Otto Bremer Foundation. *See* Bremer Financial Corp.
Otto-Epoka mbH, **15** 340
Otto Sumisho Inc., **V** 161
Otto Versand GmbH & Co., V 159–61; **10** 489–90; **15** 338–40 **(upd.)**; **27** 427, 429; **31** 188; **34** 324–28 **(upd.)**; **36** 177, 180
Ottumwa Daily Courier, **11** 251
Ourso Investment Corporation, **16** 344
Outback Steakhouse, Inc., 12 373–75; **34** 329–32 **(upd.)**
Outboard Marine Corporation, III 597–600; **8** 71; **16** 383; **20** 409–12 **(upd.)**; **26** 494; **42** 45; **43** 287; **45** 174
Outdoor Channel, Inc. *See* Global Outdoors, Inc.
The Outdoor Group Limited, **39** 58, 60
Outdoor Research, Incorporated, 67 288–90
Outdoor Systems, Inc., 25 371–73; **27** 278–80; **48** 217
Outdoor World. *See* Bass Pro Shops, Inc.
The Outdoorsman, Inc., **10** 216
Outlet Retail Stores, Inc., **27** 286
Outlook Group Corporation, 37 294–96
Outlook Window Partnership, **19** 446
Outokumpu Metals Group. *See* OM Group, Inc.
Outokumpu Oyj, 38 335–37
Outpost.com. *See* Fry's Electronics, Inc.
Outrigger Enterprises, Inc., 67 291–93
Ovation, **19** 285
Overhead Door Corporation, 70 213–16
Overhill Corporation, 10 382; **51** 279–81
Overland Energy Company, **14** 567
Overland Western Ltd., **27** 473
Overnite Corporation, 58 262–65 **(upd.)**
Overnite Transportation Co., 14 371–73; **28** 492
Overseas-Chinese Banking Corporation, **56** 363
Overseas Insurance Corporation, **58** 272
Overseas Shipholding Group, Inc., 11 376–77
Overseas Telecommunications, Inc., **27** 304
Overseas Union Bank, **56** 362–63
Overture Services, Inc. *See* Yahoo! Inc.
Ovox Fitness Clubs, **46** 432
Owen Healthcare, **50** 122
Owen Owen, **37** 8

Owen Steel Co. Inc., **15** 117
Owens & Minor, Inc., 16 398–401; **68**
    282–85 (upd.)
Owens Corning Corporation, III
    720–23; 8 177; **13** 169; **20 413–17**
    (upd.); 25 535; **30** 283; **35** 98–99; **44**
    127
Owens Country Sausage, Inc., **63** 69–70
Owens-Illinois Inc., I 609–11, 615; **III**
    720–21; **IV** 343; **16** 123; **22** 254; **24** 92;
    26 350–53 (upd.); 42 438; **43** 188; **49**
    253
Owensboro Municipal Utilities, **11** 37
Owosso Corporation, 29 366–68
Oxdon Investments, **II** 664
Oxfam America, **13** 13
Oxford-AnsCo Development Co., **12** 18
Oxford Bus Company, **28** 155–56
Oxford Financial Group, **22** 456
Oxford Health Plans, Inc., 16 402–04
Oxford Industries, Inc., 8 406–08; 24
    158
Oxford Learning Centres, **34** 105
Oxford Paper Co., **10** 289
Oxford Realty Financial Group, Inc., **49** 26
Oxford University Press, **23** 211
Oxirane Chemical Corporation, **64** 35
OXO International, **16** 234
Oxycal Laboratories Inc., **46** 466
OxyChem, **11** 160
Oxygen Business Solutions Pty Limited.
    See Carter Holt Harvey Ltd.
Oxygen Media Inc., **28** 175; **51** 220
Ozark Automotive Distributors, **26** 347–48
Ozark Utility Company, **6** 593; **50** 38
OZM. *See* OneZero Media, Inc.

P&C Foods Inc., 8 409–11; 13 95, 394
P&C Groep N.V., **46** 344
P & F Industries, Inc., 45 327–29
P&F Technologies Ltd., **26** 363
P&G. *See* Procter & Gamble Company.
P&L Coal Holdings Corporation, **45** 333
P & M Manufacturing Company, **8** 386
P & O. *See* Peninsular & Oriental Steam
    Navigation Company.
P.A. Bergner & Company, **9** 142; **15**
    87–88
P.A. Geier Company. *See* Royal Appliance
    Manufacturing Company.
P.A.J.W. Corporation, **9** 111–12
P.A. Rentrop-Hubbert & Wagner
    Fahrzeugausstattungen GmbH, **III** 582
P.C. Richard & Son Corp., 23 372–74
P.D. Associated Collieries Ltd., **31** 369
P.D. Kadi International, **I** 580
P.E.C. Israel Economic Corporation, **24**
    429
P.F. Chang's China Bistro, Inc., 37
    297–99
P.G. Realty, **III** 340
P.H. Glatfelter Company, 8 412–14; **30**
    349–52 (upd.)
P.Ink Press, **24** 430
P.R. Mallory, **9** 179
P.S.L. Food Market, Inc., **22** 549
P.T. Asurasi Tokio Marine Indonesia, **64**
    280
P.T. Bridgeport Perkasa Machine Tools, **17**
    54
P.T. Darya-Varia Laboratoria, **18** 180
P.T. Gaya Motor, **23** 290
P.T. GOLD Martindo, **70** 235

P.T. Indomobil Suzuki International, **59**
    393, 397
P.T. Samick Indonesia, **56** 300
P.T. Satomo Indovyl Polymer, **70** 329
P.T. Unitex, **53** 344
P.V. Doyle Hotels Ltd., **64** 217
P.W. Huntington & Company, **11** 180
P.W.J. Surridge & Sons, Ltd., **43** 132
Paaco Automotive Group, **64** 20
Pabst Brewing Company, **I** 255; **10** 99; **18**
    502; **50** 114
Pac-Am Food Concepts, **10** 178; **38** 102
Pac-Fab, Inc., **18** 161
PAC Insurance Services, **12** 175; **27** 258
PACCAR Inc., I 185–86; **10** 280; **26**
    354–56 (upd.); 40 135
The Pace Consultants, Inc. *See* Jacobs
    Engineering Group Inc.
PACE Entertainment Corp., **36** 423–24
Pace Express Pty. Ltd., **13** 20
Pace Foods Ltd. *See* Campbell Soup
    Company.
Pace Management Service Corp., **21** 91
PACE Membership Warehouse, Inc. *See*
    Kmart Corporation.
Pace Pharmaceuticals, **16** 439
Pacemaker Plastics, Inc., **7** 296
Pacer International, Inc., 54 274–76
Pacer Technology, 40 347–49
Pacer Tool and Mold, **17** 310
Pacific Advantage, **43** 253
Pacific Air Freight, Incorporated. *See*
    Airborne Freight Corp.
Pacific Air Transport, **9** 416
Pacific and European Telegraph Company,
    25 99
Pacific Bell. *See* SBC Communications.
Pacific Car & Foundry Company. *See*
    PACCAR Inc.
Pacific Coast Feather Company, 67 209,
    294–96
Pacific Communication Sciences, **11** 57
Pacific Destination Services, **62** 276
Pacific Dunlop Limited, 10 444–46. *See*
    also Ansell Ltd.
Pacific Electric Light Company, **6** 565; **50**
    365
Pacific Enterprises, V 682–84; **12** 477.
    See also Sempra Energy.
Pacific Finance Corp., **9** 536; **13** 529; **26**
    486
Pacific Forest Products Ltd., **59** 162
Pacific Fur Company, **25** 220
Pacific Gamble Robinson, **9** 39
Pacific Gas and Electric Company, V
    685–87; 11 270; **12** 100, 106; **19** 411;
    25 415. *See also* PG&E Corporation.
Pacific Glass Corp., **48** 42
Pacific Guardian Life Insurance Co., **III**
    289
Pacific Home Furnishings, **14** 436
Pacific Indemnity Corp., **III** 220; **14** 108,
    110; **16** 204
Pacific Integrated Healthcare, **53** 7
Pacific Lighting Corp. *See* Sempra Energy.
Pacific Linens, **13** 81–82
Pacific Link Communication, **18** 180
Pacific Lumber Company, **III** 254; **8**
    348–50
Pacific Magazines and Printing, **7** 392
Pacific Mail Steamship Company. *See* APL
    Limited.
Pacific Media K.K., **18** 101
Pacific Monolithics Inc., **11** 520

Pacific National Insurance Co. *See* TIG
    Holdings, Inc.
Pacific Natural Gas Corp., **9** 102
Pacific Northwest Laboratories, **10** 139
Pacific Northwest Pipeline Corporation, **9**
    102–104, 540; **12** 144
Pacific Northwest Power Company, **6** 597
Pacific Petroleums Ltd., **9** 102
Pacific Plastics, Inc., **48** 334
Pacific Power & Light Company. *See*
    PacifiCorp.
Pacific Pride Bakeries, **19** 192
Pacific Publications, **72** 283–84
Pacific Recycling Co. Inc., **IV** 296; **19** 226;
    23 225
Pacific Resources Inc., **IV** 47; **22** 107
Pacific Sentinel Gold Corp., **27** 456
Pacific/Southern Wine & Spirits, **48** 392
Pacific Stock Exchange, **48** 226
Pacific Sunwear of California, Inc., 28
    343–45; 47 425
Pacific Telecom, Inc., 6 325–28; **25** 101;
    54 62
Pacific Telesis Group, V 318–20; **6** 324;
    9 321; **11** 10–11; **14** 345, 347; **15** 125;
    25 499; **26** 520; **29** 387; **47** 318. *See*
    also SBC Communications.
Pacific Teletronics, Inc., **7** 15
Pacific Towboat. *See* Puget Sound Tug and
    Barge Company.
Pacific Trail Inc., **17** 462; **29** 293, 295–96
Pacific Western Extruded Plastics
    Company. *See* PW Eagle Inc.
Pacific Wine Co., **18** 71; **50** 112
PacifiCare Health Systems, Inc., 11
    378–80
PacifiCorp, Inc., V 688–90; **7** 376–78; **26**
    357–60 (upd.); 27 327, 483, 485; **32**
    372; **49** 363, 366
Package Products Company, Inc., **12** 150
Packaged Ice, Inc., **21** 338; **26** 449
Packaging Corporation of America, 12
    376–78, 397; **16** 191; **51 282–85 (upd.)**
Packard Bell Electronics, Inc., 10 564; **11**
    413; **13 387–89,** 483; **21** 391; **23** 471;
    57 263
Packard Motor Co., **8** 74; **9** 17
Packerland Packing Company, **7** 199, 201
Pacolet Manufacturing Company, **17** 327
Pact, **50** 175
PacTel. *See* Pacific Telesis Group.
Paddock Publications, Inc., 53 263–65
PAFS. *See* Pacific Alaska Fuel Services.
Page, Bacon & Co., **12** 533
Page Boy Inc., **9** 320
Page Plus NV. *See* Punch International
    N.V.
PageAhead Software, **15** 492
Pageland Coca-Cola Bottling Works, **10**
    222
PageMart Wireless, Inc., **18** 164, 166
Paging Network Inc., 11 381–83; 39
    24–25; **41** 266–67
Pagoda Trading Company, Inc. *See* Brown
    Shoe Company, Inc.
Paid Prescriptions, **9** 346
Paige Publications, **18** 66
PaineWebber Group Inc., II 444–46,
    449; **13** 449; **22** 352, **404–07 (upd.),**
    542; **25** 433
Painter Carpet Mills, **13** 169
PairGain Technologies, **36** 299
Paisley Products, **32** 255
La Paix, **III** 273

Pak-a-Sak, **II** 661
Pak Mail Centers, **18** 316
Pak Sak Industries, **17** 310; **24** 160
Pakhoed Holding, N.V., **9** 532; **26** 420; **41** 339–40
Pakistan International Airlines Corporation, 46 323–26
Pakkasakku Oy, **IV** 471
Paknet, **11** 548
Pakway Container Corporation, **8** 268
PAL. *See* Philippine Airlines, Inc.
Palace Station Hotel & Casino. *See* Station Casinos Inc.
Paladar, **56** 116
Palais Royal, Inc., **24** 456
Palazzo Feroni Finanziaria SpA, **62** 313
Palco Industries, **19** 440
Pale Ski & Sports GmbH, **22** 461
Palestine Coca-Cola Bottling Co., **13** 163
The Palestine Post Limited, **62** 188
PALIC. *See* Pan-American Life Insurance Company.
Pall Corporation, 9 396–98; **72 263–66 (upd.)**
Pallas Textiles, **57** 207, 209
Palm Beach Holdings, **9** 157
Palm Harbor Homes, Inc., 39 316–18
Palm, Inc., 34 441, 445; **36 355–57; 38** 433; **49** 184; **54** 312
Palm Management Corporation, 71 265–68
Palm Shipping Inc., **25** 468–70
Palmafina, **IV** 498–99
Palmax, **47** 153
Palmer & Cay, Inc., 69 285–87
Palmer Communications, **25** 418
Palmer G. Lewis Co., **8** 135
Palmolive Co. *See* Colgate-Palmolive Company.
Palo Alto Brewing, **22** 421
Palo Alto Products International, Inc., **29** 6
Palo Alto Research Center, **10** 510
Paloma Industries Ltd., 71 269–71
Palomar Medical Technologies, Inc., 22 408–10; 31 124
PAM Group, **27** 462
Pamida Holdings Corporation, 15 341–43; 58 331
Pampa OTT, **27** 473
The Pampered Chef, Ltd., 18 406–08
Pamplemousse, **14** 225
Pamplin Corp. *See* R.B. Pamplin Corp.
Pan-Alberta Gas Ltd., **16** 11
Pan-American Life Insurance Company, 48 311–13
Pan American World Airways, Inc., I 103–04, 112–13, **115–16,** 121, 124, 126, 129, 132, 248, 530; **9** 231, 417; **10** 561; **11** 266; **12** 191, **379–81 (upd.),** 419; **13** 19; **14** 73; **29** 189; **36** 52–53
Pan Asia Paper Company Ltd., **63** 314–16
Pan European Publishing Co., **IV** 611
Pan Geo Atlas Corporation, **18** 513
Pan Pacific Fisheries, **24** 114
PanAgora Asset Management Inc., **60** 220
Panalpina World Transport (Holding) Ltd., 47 286–88; **49** 81–82
Panamerican Beverages, Inc., 47 289–91; 54 74
PanAmSat Corporation, 18 211, 213; **46 327–29; 54** 157
Panasonic, **9** 180; **10** 125; **12** 470; **43** 427
Panavia Aircraft GmbH, **24** 84, 86–87

Panavision Inc., 24 372–74; **28** 249; **38** 295
PanCanadian Petroleum Ltd., **27** 217; **45** 80
Pancho's Mexican Buffet, Inc., 46 330–32
Panda Management Company, Inc., 35 327–29
Pandair, **13** 20
Pandel, Inc., **8** 271
Pandick Press Inc., **23** 63
PanEnergy Corporation, **27** 128, 131
Panera Bread Company, 44 186, 327–29
Panerai, **27** 489
Panhandle Eastern Corporation, IV 425; **V 691–92; 10** 82–84; **11** 28; **14** 135; **17** 21. *See also* CMS Energy Corp.
Panhandle Oil Corp., **IV** 498
Panhandle Power & Light Company, **6** 580
Panificadora Bimbo, **19** 191
Pannill Knitting Company, **13** 531
Pannon GSM. *See* Telenor ASA.
Panocean Storage & Transport. *See* Exel plc.
Panola Pipeline Co., **7** 228
Panosh Place, **12** 168
Pansophic Systems Inc., **64** 361
Pantera Energy Corporation, **11** 27
Pantheon Books, **13** 429; **31** 376
Panther, **III** 750
Pantone Inc., 53 266–69
The Pantry, Inc., 36 358–60
Pantry Pride Inc., **I** 668; **II** 670, 674; **23** 407–08
Pants Corral, **II** 634
Papa Aldo's Pizza. *See* Papa Murphy's International, Inc.
Papa John's International, Inc., 15 344–46; 71 272–76 (upd.)
Papa Murphy's International, Inc., 54 277–79
Pape and Co., Ltd., **10** 441
Papelera del Besos, **53** 24
La Papelera del Plata S.A. *See* Empresas CMPC S.A.
Papelera General, S.A. de C.V., **39** 188
Papeleria Calparsoro S.A., **IV** 325
Papeles Anoia, S.A., **68** 258
Papeles Venezolanos C.A., **17** 281
Paper Direct, **37** 107–08
The Paper Factory of Wisconsin, Inc., **12** 209
Paper Magic Group, **35** 130–31
Paper Software, Inc., **15** 322
Paper Stock Dealers, Inc., **8** 476
PaperMate, **23** 54
Paperwork Data-Comm Services Inc., **11** 64
Papeteries de Golbey SA, **63** 315
Les Papeteries de la Chapelle-Darblay, **IV** 337
Papeteries de Lancey, 23 366–68
Papeteries de Malaucene S.A.S., **52** 300–01
Les Papeteries du Limousin, **19** 227
Papetti's Hygrade Egg Products, Inc., 25 332–33; **39 319–21**
Papierfabrik Fahrbrucke GmbH, **64** 275
Papierwaren Fleischer, **IV** 325
Papierwerke Waldhof-Aschaffenburg AG. *See* PWA Group
Papyrus Design Group, **15** 455
Par Pharmaceutical Companies, Inc., 65 286–88

Para-Med Health Services. *See* Extendicare Health Services, Inc.
Parachute Press, **29** 426
ParaData Financial Systems, Inc., **57** 416
Parade Gasoline Co., **7** 228
Paradigm Entertainment, **35** 227
Paradise Creations, **29** 373
Paradise Island Resort and Casino. *See* Sun International Hotels Limited.
Paradise Music & Entertainment, Inc., 42 271–74
Paradyne, **22** 19
Paragon Communications, **44** 372
Paragon Corporate Holdings, Inc., **28** 6, 8
Paragon Vineyard Company, **36** 114
Paragren Technologies Inc., **38** 432
Parallax Software Inc., **38** 70
Parametric Integrated Circuits Inc., **63** 33
Parametric Technology Corp., 16 405–07
Parametrics Corp., **25** 134
Paramount Communications Inc., **16** 338; **19** 403–04; **28** 296
Paramount Fire Insurance Co., **26** 486
Paramount Oil Company, **18** 467
Paramount Paper Products, **8** 383
Paramount Pictures Corporation, II 154–56; **IV** 671–72, 675; **7** 528; **9** 119, 428–29; **10** 175; **12** 73, 323; **19** 404; **21** 23–25; **23** 503; **24** 327; **25** 88, 311, 327–29, 418; **31** 99; **35** 279. *See also* Viacom Inc.
Parashop SA, **48** 279
Parasitix Corporation. *See* Mycogen Corporation.
Parasole Restaurant Holdings, Inc., **38** 117
Paravant Inc., **58** 101
Paravision International, **III** 48; **8** 343
PARCO Co., Ltd. *See* Seibu Department Stores, Ltd.
Parents and Children Together, Inc., **64** 311
ParentWatch, **34** 105
Parfums Chanel, **12** 57
Parfums Rochas S.A. *See* Wella AG.
Pargas, **I** 378
Paribas. *See* Banque de Paris et des Pays-Bas, BNP Paribas Group; Compagnie Financiere de Paribas.
Paridoc and Giant, **12** 153
Paris Bourse, **34** 13
Paris Corporation, 22 411–13
Paris Group, **17** 137
Paris Playground Equipment, **13** 319
Parisian, Inc., 14 374–76; **19** 324–25; **41** 343–44
Park Acquisitions, Inc., **38** 308
Park-Brannock Shoe Company, **48** 69
Park Consolidated Motels, Inc., **14** 105
Park Corp., 22 414–16
Park Drop Forge Co. *See* Park-Ohio Industries Inc.
Park Hall Leisure, **II** 140; **24** 194
Park Inn International, **11** 178
Park-Ohio Industries Inc., 17 371–73
Park Ridge Corporation, **9** 284
Park Tower Hotel Co. Ltd., **55** 375
Parkdale State Bank, **25** 114
Parke-Bernet, **11** 453
Parke, Davis & Co. *See* Warner-Lambert Co.
Parker Brothers, **16** 337; **21** 375; **25** 489
Parker Drilling Company, 28 346–48
Parker Drilling Company of Canada, **9** 363

Parker-Hannifin Corporation, III 601–03; **21** 108; **24 375–78 (upd.)**
Parker Lancasters & Orleans, Inc., **62** 262
Parker Pattern Works Co., **46** 293
Parker's Pharmacy, Inc., **15** 524
Parks-Belk Co., **19** 324
Parks Box & Printing Co., **13** 442
The Parkside Group, **68** 244–46
Parkway Distributors, **17** 331
Parlex Corporation, 61 279–81
Parmalat Finanziaria SpA, 50 343–46
Parque Arauco S.A., 72 267–69
Parson and Hyman Co., Inc., **8** 112
Parsons Brinckerhoff, Inc., 34 333–36
The Parsons Corporation, 8 415–17; 56 263–67 (upd.)
Parsons International Trading Business, **27** 195
Parsons Place Apparel Company, **8** 289
Partech, **28** 346, 348
Partek Corporation, **11** 312; **52** 250
Parthénon, **27** 10
Participating Annuity Life Insurance Co., **21** 14
Partlow Corporation, **7** 116
Partouche SA. *See* Groupe Partouche SA.
Parts Plus, **26** 348
Party City Corporation, 54 280–82
PartyLite Gifts, Inc., **18** 67, 69
Pascagoula Lumber Company, **28** 306
Pascale & Associates, **12** 476
Pasha Pillows, **12** 393
Pasminco, **IV** 61
Pasqua Inc., **28** 64
Pasquier Nutrition, **58** 46
Pass & Seymour, **21** 348–49
Passive Power Products, Inc., **32** 41
Pasta Central, **49** 60
Patagonia. *See* Lost Arrow Inc.
Patak Spices Ltd., **18** 247
Patch Rubber Co., **19** 277–78
Patchoque-Plymouth Co., **IV** 371
PATCO. *See* Philippine Airlines, Inc.
Patent Arms Manufacturing Company, **12** 70
Paterno Wines International, **48** 392
Paternoster Stores plc. *See* Kingfisher plc; Woolworth Corporation.
Paterson Candy Ltd., **22** 89
Paterson Zochonis. *See* PZ Cussons plc.
Pâtes Papiers et Textilose. *See* Matussière et Forest SA.
Pathe Communications Co., **IV** 676; **7** 529; **25** 329
Pathé SA, 29 369–71. *See also* Chargeurs International.
Pathfinder Pubs, **57** 411
Pathmark Stores, Inc., II 672–74; **9** 173; **15** 260; **18** 6; **19** 479, 481; **23** 369–71; **33** 436
PathoGenesis Corporation, **36** 119
Patient Care, Inc., **13** 150
Patil Systems, **11** 56
Patina Group. *See* Restaurant Associates Corporation.
Patina Oil & Gas Corporation, 24 379–81
Patino N.V., **17** 380
Pâtisserie Pasquier, **58** 46
Patrick Industries, Inc., 30 342–45
Patrick Raulet, S.A., **36** 164
Patricof & Company, **24** 45
Patriot American Hospitality, Inc., **21** 184
PATS Inc., **36** 159

Patterson Dental Co., 19 289–91
Patterson Industries, Inc., **14** 42
Patterson Pump Company, **57** 159–60
Patterson-UTI Energy, Inc., 55 293–95
Patton Boggs LLP, 71 277–79
Patton Electric Company, Inc., **19** 360
Patton Paint Company. *See* PPG Industries, Inc.
Paul A. Brands, **11** 19
Paul Andra KG, **33** 393
Paul Boechat & Cie, **21** 515
Paul C. Dodge Company, **6** 579
Paul Davril, Inc., **25** 258
Paul H. Rose Corporation, **13** 445
Paul Harris Stores, Inc., 15 245; **18 409–12**
Paul, Hastings, Janofsky & Walker LLP, 27 357–59
Paul Koss Supply Co., **16** 387
Paul Marshall Products Inc., **16** 36
Paul Mueller Company, 65 289–91
Paul Ramsay Group, **41** 323
The Paul Revere Corporation, 12 382–83; 52 379
Paul Revere Insurance, **34** 433
Paul-Son Gaming Corporation, 66 249–51
Paul Wahl & Co., **IV** 277
Paul, Weiss, Rifkind, Wharton & Garrison, 47 292–94
Paulaner Brauerei GmbH & Co. KG, 35 330–33
Pauls Plc, **III** 699
Pavallier, **18** 35
Pavex Construction Company. *See* Granite Rock Company.
Pawnee Industries, Inc., **19** 415
Paxall, Inc., **8** 545
Paxson Communications Corporation, 33 322–26
Pay 'N Pak Stores, Inc., 9 399–401; 16 186–88
Pay 'n Save Corp., **12** 477; **15** 274; **17** 366
Pay Less, **II** 601, 604
Paychex, Inc., 15 347–49; 46 333–36 (upd.)
PayConnect Solutions, **47** 39
Payless Cashways, Inc., 11 384–86; 13 274; **44 330–33 (upd.)**
Payless DIY. *See* The Boots Company PLC.
PayLess Drug Stores, **12** 477–78; **18** 286; **22** 39
Payless ShoeSource, Inc., 13 361; **18 413–15; 26** 441; **69 288–92 (upd.)**
PayPal Inc., 58 266–69
PBF Corp. *See* Paris Corporation.
PBL. *See* Publishing and Broadcasting Ltd.
PBS. *See* Public Broadcasting Stations.
PC Connection, Inc., 37 300–04
PC Globe, Inc., **13** 114
PC Home Publishing, **61** 246
PC Realty, Canada Ltd., **III** 340
PCA. *See* Packaging Corporation of America.
PCA-Budafok Paperboard Ltd., **12** 377
PCA International, Inc., 62 263–65
PCAS. *See* Dynaction S.A.
pcBoat.com, **37** 398
PCI Acquisition, **11** 385
PCI NewCo Inc., **36** 159
PCI Services, Inc. *See* Cardinal Health, Inc.

PCL Construction Group Inc., 50 347–49
PCL Industries Ltd., **IV** 296; **19** 226
PCM Uitgevers NV, 53 270–73
PCO. *See* Corning Inc.
PCS. *See* Potash Corp. of Saskatchewan Inc.
PCS Health Systems Inc., **12** 333; **47** 115, 235–36
PCX. *See* Pacific Stock Exchange.
PDA Engineering, **25** 305
PDA Inc., **19** 290
PDI, Inc., 49 25; **52 272–75**
PDO. *See* Petroleum Development Oman.
PDQ Machine, **58** 75
PDQ Transportation Inc., **18** 226
PDS Gaming Corporation, 44 334–37
PDV America, Inc., **31** 113
PDVSA. *See* Petróleos de Venezuela S.A.
Peabody Coal Company, IV 47, 576; **7** 387–88; **10 447–49**
Peabody Energy Corporation, 45 330–33 (upd.)
Peabody Holding Company, Inc., IV 19, 169–72; **7** 209
Peace Arch Entertainment Group Inc., 51 286–88
Peaches Entertainment Corporation, **24** 502
Peachtree Doors, **10** 95
Peachtree Federal Savings and Loan Association of Atlanta, **10** 92
Peachtree Software Inc., **18** 364
Peak Audio Inc., **48** 92
Peak Oilfield Service Company, **9** 364
The Peak Technologies Group, Inc., 14 377–80
Peapod, Inc., 22 522; **30 346–48**
Pearce-Uible Co., **14** 460
Pearl Health Services, **I** 249
Pearle Vision, Inc., 12 188; **13 390–92; 14** 214; **23** 329; **24** 140; **34** 179
Pearson plc, IV 657–59; **46 337–41 (upd.)**
Peasant Restaurants Inc., **30** 330
Pease Industries, **39** 322, 324
Peat Marwick. *See* KPMG Peat Marwick.
Peavey Electronics Corporation, 16 408–10
Peavey Paper Mills, Inc., **26** 362
PEC Plastics, **9** 92
Pechenganickel MMC, **48** 300
Pechiney S.A., IV 173–75; **12** 253–54; **26** 403; **45 334–37 (upd.)**
PECO Energy Company, 11 387–90. *See also* Exelon Corporation.
Pecom Nec S.A., **72 279–80**
Pediatric Services of America, Inc., 31 356–58
Pediatrix Medical Group, Inc., 61 282–85
Pedigree Petfoods, **22** 298
Peebles Inc., 16 411–13; 43 296–99 (upd.)
Peek & Cloppenburg KG, 46 342–45
Peekskill Chemical Works. *See* Binney & Smith Inc.
Peel-Conner Telephone Works, **II** 24
Peerless, **8** 74; **11** 534
Peerless Gear & Machine Company, **8** 515
Peerless Spinning Corporation, **13** 532
Peerless Systems, Inc., **17** 263
Peet's Coffee & Tea, Inc., 13 493; **18** 37; **38 338–40**
PEI. *See* Process Engineering Inc.

Pei Cobb Freed & Partners Architects LLP, 57 280–82
Peko-Wallsend Ltd., **13** 97
Pelican Homestead and Savings, **11** 107
Pelikan Holding AG, **18** 388
Pella Corporation, 10 95; **12** 384–86; **22** 346; **39** 322–25 (upd.)
Pelmorex, Inc., **52** 402
Pelto Oil Corporation, **14** 455; **44** 362
PEM International Ltd., **28** 350
Pemco Aviation Group Inc., 54 283–86
Pemex. *See* Petróleos Mexicanos.
Pen Computing Group, **49** 10
Penaflor S.A., 66 252–54
Penauille Polyservices SA, 49 318–21
Penda Corp., **19** 415
Pendaflex. *See* Esselte.
Pendaries Petroleum Ltd. *See* Ultra Petroleum Corporation.
Pendle Travel Services Ltd. *See* Airtours Plc.
Pendleton Grain Growers Inc., 64 305–08
Pendleton Woolen Mills, Inc., 42 275–78
Penford Corporation, 55 296–99
Pengrowth Gas Corp., **25** 232
The Penguin Group, **46** 337
Penguin Publishing Co. Ltd., **IV** 659
Penhaligon's, **24** 237
Peninsula Stores, Ltd. *See* Lucky Stores, Inc.
The Peninsular and Oriental Steam Navigation Company, V 490–93; **22** 444; **26** 241, 243; **37** 137; **38** 341–46 (upd.)
Peninsular and Oriental Steam Navigation Company (Bovis Division), I 588–89
Peninsular Power, **6** 602
Peninsular Railroad Company, **17** 440
Penn Advertising, **27** 280
Penn Central Corp., **II** 255; **10** 71, 73, 547; **17** 443; **70** 34
Penn Champ Co., **9** 72
Penn Corp., **13** 561
Penn Cress Ice Cream, **13** 393
Penn Engineering & Manufacturing Corp., 28 349–51
Penn National Gaming, Inc., 33 327–29
Penn Traffic Company, 8 409–10; **13** 95, 393–95
Penn-Western Gas and Electric, **6** 524
Pennaco Hosiery, Inc., **12** 93; **62** 89–91
PennEnergy, **55** 302
Penney's. *See* J.C. Penney Company, Inc.
Pennington Seed, Inc. of Delaware, **58** 60
Pennon Group Plc, 45 338–41
Pennsy Supply, Inc., **64** 98
Pennsylvania Blue Shield, III 325–27. *See also* Highmark Inc.
Pennsylvania Dutch Candies Company. *See* Warrell Corporation.
Pennsylvania Electric Company, **6** 535; **27** 182
Pennsylvania Farm Bureau Cooperative Association, **7** 17–18
Pennsylvania Gas and Water Company, **38** 51
Pennsylvania General Insurance Company, **48** 431
Pennsylvania House, Inc., **10** 324; **12** 301
Pennsylvania International Raceway. *See* Penske Corporation.

Pennsylvania Life Insurance Company, **27** 47
Pennsylvania Power & Light Company, V 693–94; **11** 388
Pennsylvania Pump and Compressor Co., **II** 16
Pennsylvania Railroad, **10** 71–73; **26** 295
Pennsylvania Steel Foundry and Machine Co., **39** 32
Pennsylvania Water & Power Company, **25** 44
Pennwalt Corporation, I 382–84; **12** 18; **21** 205
PennWell Corporation, 55 300–03
Penny Curtiss Baking Co., Inc., **13** 395
Pennzoil Company, IV 488–90, 551, 553; **10** 190; **14** 491, 493; **20** 418–22 (upd.); **23** 40–41; **25** 443, 445; **39** 330; **41** 391, 394; **47** 436
Pennzoil-Quaker State Company, 49 343; **50** 350–55 (upd.)
Penobscot Shoe Company, **70** 221
Penrod Drilling Corporation, **7** 228, 558
Pension Benefit Guaranty Corp., **III** 255; **12** 489
Penske Corporation, V 494–95; **19** 223, 292–94 (upd.); **20** 263
Penske Motorsports, **32** 440
Penske Truck Rental, **24** 445
Pentair, Inc., 7 419–21; **11** 315; **26** 361–64 (upd.); **56** 18
Pental Insurance Company, Ltd., **11** 523
Pentane Partners, **7** 518
Pentastar Transportation Group, Inc. *See* Dollar Thrifty Automotive Group, Inc.
Pentech International, Inc., 14 217; **29** 372–74; **52** 193
Pentes Play, Inc., **27** 370, 372
Pentland Group plc, 20 423–25; **35** 204, 206–07
Penton Media, Inc., 9 414; **27** 360–62; **33** 335–36
Pentzer Corporation. *See* Avista Corporation.
People Express Airlines Inc., I 98, 103, 117–18, 123–24, 129–30; **21** 142; **22** 220
People That Love (PTL) Television, **13** 279
People's Drug Store, **II** 604–05; **22** 37–38
People's Ice and Refrigeration Company, **9** 274
People's Insurance Co., **III** 368
People's Radio Network, **25** 508
People's Trust Company, **49** 412
Peoples, **24** 315–16
Peoples Bancorp, **14** 529
Peoples Bank, **13** 467; **17** 302
Peoples Bank & Trust Co., **31** 207
Peoples Bank of Youngstown, **9** 474
Peoples Energy Corporation, 6 543–44
Peoples Gas Light & Coke Co., **6** 529, 543–44
Peoples Heritage Financial Group, Inc. *See* Banknorth Group, Inc.
Peoples Jewelers of Canada, **16** 561; **40** 472
Peoples National Bank, **41** 178–79
Peoples Natural Gas Company of South Carolina, **6** 576
Peoples Restaurants, Inc., **17** 320–21
Peoples Savings of Monroe, **9** 482
Peoples Security Insurance Co., **III** 219
Peoples Trust of Canada, **49** 411

PeopleServe, Inc., **29** 401
PeopleSoft Inc., 11 78; **14** 381–83; **33** 330–33 (upd.); **38** 432; **59** 77
The Pep Boys—Manny, Moe & Jack, 11 391–93; **16** 160; **26** 348; **36** 361–64 (upd.)
PEPCO. *See* Portland Electric Power Company; Potomac Electric Power Company.
Pepe Clothing Co., **18** 85
Pepper Hamilton LLP, 43 300–03
Pepperell Manufacturing Company, **16** 533–34
Pepperidge Farm, Incorporated. *See* Campbell Soup Company.
The Pepsi Bottling Group, Inc., 40 350–53; **65** 328, 330
PepsiAmericas, Inc., 67 297–300 (upd.)
PepsiCo, Inc., I 276–79; **10** 450–54 (upd.); **38** 347–54 (upd.); **40** 340–42, 350–52; **54** 72–73
Pepsodent Company, **9** 318
Perception Technology, **10** 500
Perdigao SA, 52 276–79; **59** 361
Perdue Farms Inc., 7 422–24, 432; **23** 375–78 (upd.); **32** 203; **64** 386
Perfect Fit Industries, **17** 182–84
Perfect Pizza Holdings, Ltd. *See* Papa John's International, Inc.
Perfect-Ventil GmbH, **9** 413
Perfetti Van Melle S.p.A., 72 270–73
Performance Contracting, Inc., **III** 722; **20** 415
Performance Food Group Company, 31 359–62
Performance Technologies, Inc., **10** 395
Perfumania, Inc., **22** 157
Pergamon Holdings, **15** 83; **50** 125
Pergamon Press, **IV** 611, 641–43, 687; **7** 311–12
Perini Corporation, 8 418–21; **38** 481
The Perkin-Elmer Corporation, 7 425–27; **9** 514; **13** 326
Perkins Bacon & Co., **10** 267
Perkins Cake & Steak, **9** 425
Perkins Coie LLP, 56 268–70
Perkins Engines Ltd., **10** 274; **11** 472; **19** 294; **27** 203
Perkins Family Restaurants, L.P., 22 417–19
Perl Pillow, **19** 304
Perland Environmental Technologies Inc., **8** 420
Permal Group, **27** 276, 513
Permaneer Corp. *See* Spartech Corporation.
Permanent General Companies, Inc., **11** 194
Permanent Pigments Inc., **25** 71
permanent tsb, **59** 245
Permodalan, **III** 699
Pernod Ricard S.A., I 280–81; **21** 399–401 (upd.); **72** 274–77 (upd.)
Pernvo Inc., **I** 387
Perot Systems Corporation, 13 482; **29** 375–78
Perrier, **19** 50
Perrier Corporation of America, **16** 341
Perrier Vittel S.A., **52** 188
Perrigo Company, 12 218, 387–89; **59** 330–34 (upd.)
Perry Brothers, Inc., **24** 149
Perry Capital Corp., **28** 138
Perry Drug Stores Inc., **12** 21; **26** 476

Perry Ellis International, Inc., 16 37; **41** 291–94

Perry Manufacturing Co., **16** 37

Perry Sports, **13** 545; **13** 545

Perry Tritech, **25** 103–05

Perry's Shoes Inc., **16** 36

Perscombinatie, **IV** 611

Pershing & Co., **22** 189

Personal Care Corp., **17** 235

Personal Performance Consultants, **9** 348

Personal Products Company, **8** 511

Personnel Pool of America, **29** 224, 26–27

Perstorp AB, I 385–87; **51** 289–92 **(upd.)**

Pertamina, IV 491–93; **56** 271–74 **(upd.)**

Pertec Computer Corp., **17** 49; **18** 434

Pertech Computers Ltd., **18** 75

Perusahaan Otomobil Nasional Bhd., 62 266–68

Pesquera Iquique-Guanaye S.A., **69** 142

Pet Food & Supply, **14** 385

Pet Foods Plus Inc., **39** 355

Pet Incorporated, 7 428–31; **10** 554; **12** 124; **13** 409; **14** 214; **24** 140; **27** 196; **43** 217; **46** 290

Pet Warehouse Inc., **62** 108

Petaluma Ltd., **54** 227, 229

Petco Animal Supplies, Inc., 29 379–81

Pete's Brewing Company, 18 72, 502; **22** 420–22

Peter Cundill & Associates Ltd., **15** 504

Peter Gast Shipping GmbH, **7** 40; **41** 42

Peter J. Schmitt Co., **13** 394; **24** 444–45

Peter Kiewit Sons' Inc., I 599–600; **III** 198; **8** 422–24; **15** 18; **25** 512, 514

Peter Norton Computing Group, **10** 508–09

Peter Paul/Cadbury, **II** 512; **15** 221; **51** 158

Peter Piper, Inc., 70 217–19

Peterhouse Group PLC. *See* Babcock International Group PLC.

Peters-Revington Corporation. *See* Chromcraft Revington, Inc.

Petersen Cos., **52** 192

Petersen Publishing Company, 21 402–04

Peterson American Corporation, 55 304–06

Peterson Furniture Company, **51** 9

Peterson, Howell & Heather. *See* PHH Arval.

Peterson Soybean Seed Co., **9** 411

Petit Bateau, **35** 263

La Petite Academy, **13** 299

Petite Sophisticate. *See* The United States Shoe Corporation.

Petoseed Co. Inc., **29** 435

Petrie Stores Corporation, 8 425–27

Petrini's, **II** 653

Petro-Canada Limited, IV 494–96; **13** 557; **50** 172

Petro/Chem Environmental Services, Inc., **IV** 411

Petrobrás. *See* Petróleo Brasileiro S.A.

Petrobras Energia Participaciones S.A., 72 278–81

Petrocel, S.A., **19** 12

Petrochemicals Company, **17** 90–91

Petrochemicals Industry Co., **IV** 451; **55** 243

Petrochim, **IV** 498

PetroChina Company Ltd., **46** 86

Petrocorp. *See* Petroleum Company of New Zealand.

PetroCorp, **63** 409

Petroecuador. *See* Petróleos del Ecuador.

PetroFina S.A., IV 455, 495, **497–500**, 576; **7** 179; **26** 365–69 **(upd.)**

Petrogal. *See* Petróleos de Portugal.

Petrol Ofisi Anonim Sirketi, **IV** 564

Petrolane Properties, **17** 558

Petróleo Brasileiro S.A., IV 501–03

Petróleos de Portugal S.A., IV 504–06

Petróleos de Venezuela S.A., II 661; **IV** 391–93, **507–09[ro; 24** 522; **31** 113

Petróleos del Ecuador, IV 510–11

Petróleos Mexicanos, IV 512–14, 528; **19** 10, 295–98 **(upd.)**; **41** 147

Petroleum Authority of Thailand, **IV** 519; **56** 287

Petroleum Development Corp. of the Republic of Korea, **IV** 455

Petroleum Development Oman LLC, IV 515–16

Petroleum Helicopters, Inc., 35 334–36; **37** 288; **39** 8

Petroleum Projects Co., **IV** 414

Petrolgroup, Inc., **6** 441

Petroliam Nasional Bhd (Petronas), 56 275–79 **(upd.)**

Petrolite Corporation, 15 350–52; **57** 65

Petrolszolg Karbantartó és Szolgáltató Kft., **70** 195

Petromex. *See* Petróleos de Mexico S.A.

Petromin Lubricating Oil Co., **17** 415; **50** 416

Petron Corporation, 58 270–72

Petronas, IV 517–20; **21** 501. *See also* Petroliam Nasional Bhd.

PetroNet, **70** 35

Petronor, **IV** 514, 528

Petrossian Inc., 54 287–89

PETsMART, Inc., 14 384–86; **27** 95; **29** 379–80; **41** 295–98 **(upd.)**; **45** 42

Petstuff, Inc., **14** 386; **41** 297

Pettibone Corporation, **19** 365

Petzazz, **14** 386

Peugeot S.A., I 187–88; **11** 104; **26** 11; **50** 197. *See also* PSA Peugeot Citroen S.A.

The Pew Charitable Trusts, 35 337–40

Pez Candy, Inc., 38 355–57

Pfaff-Pegasus of U.S.A. Inc., **15** 385

Pfaltz & Bauer, Inc., **38** 3

The Pfaltzgraff Co. *See* Susquehanna Pfaltzgraff Company.

Pfauter-Maag Cutting Tools, **24** 186

PFCI. *See* Pulte Financial Companies, Inc.

PFD Supply, Inc., **47** 304

Pfeiffer GmbH, **69** 38

PFI Acquisition Corp., **17** 184

Pfister GmbH. *See* FLSmidth & Co. A/S.

Pfizer, Hoechst Celanese Corp., **8** 399

Pfizer Inc., I 367, 661–63, 668; **9** 356, **402–05 (upd.)**; **10** 53–54; **11** 207, 310–11, 459; **12** 4; **17** 131; **19** 105; **38** 358–67 **(upd.)**; **44** 175; **63** 207, 233, 235

Pflueger Corporation, **22** 483

PG&E Corporation, 26 370–73 **(upd.)**; **27** 131. *See also* Portland General Electric.

PGA. *See* The Professional Golfers' Association.

PGG/HSC Feed Company LLC, **64** 307

PHAMIS Inc., **64** 190

Phantom Fireworks. *See* B.J. Alan Co., Inc.

Phaostron Instruments and Electronic Co., **18** 497–98

Phar-Mor Inc., 12 209, 390–92, 477; **18** 507; **21** 459; **22** 157; **50** 457

Pharma Plus Drugmarts, **II** 649–50

Pharma Services Holding Inc. *See* Quintiles Transnational Corporation.

PharmaCare Management Services, Inc., **45** 136

Pharmaceutical Resources, Inc. *See* Par Pharmaceutical Companies, Inc.

Pharmacia & Upjohn Inc., 25 22, **374–78 (upd.)**; **34** 177, 179

Pharmacia A.B., I 664–65

Pharmacia Hospital Products, **56** 81

Pharmaco Dynamics Research, Inc., **10** 106–07

Pharmacom Systems Ltd., **II** 652; **51** 303

Pharmacy Corporation of America, **16** 57

PharmaKinetics Laboratories, Inc., **10** 106

Pharmanex, Inc., **27** 352

Pharmaplan Gruppe, **56** 141

Pharmaprix Ltd., **II** 663; **49** 368

Pharmedix, **11** 207

Pharos, **9** 381

Phat Fashions LLC, 49 322–24

Phelan & Collender, **III** 442

Phelan Faust Paint, **8** 553

Phelps Dodge Corporation, IV 33, **176–79**, 216; **7** 261–63, 288; **19** 375; **28** **352–57 (upd.)**; **40** 411

Phenix Mills Ltd., **II** 662

PHF Life Insurance Co., **IV** 623

PHH Arval, V 496–97; **53** 274–76 **(upd.)**

PHH Monomers, L.L.C., **61** 113

PHI. *See* Pizza Hut, Inc.

Phibro Corporation, **IV** 80; **21** 67

Philadelphia and Reading Corp., **25** 165

Philadelphia Carpet Company, **9** 465

Philadelphia Company, **6** 484, 493

Philadelphia Eagles, 37 305–08

Philadelphia Electric Company, V **695–97**; **6** 450. *See also* Exelon Corporation.

Philadelphia Sports Clubs. *See* Town Sports International, Inc.

Philadelphia Suburban Corporation, 39 326–29

Philco Corp., **13** 402; **50** 299

Phildar, **37** 22

Phildrew Ventures, **44** 147

PhileoAviation Sdn Bhd, **65** 350

Philharmonic-Symphony Society of New York, Inc. (New York Philharmonic), 69 237, 293–97

Philip Environmental Inc., 16 414–16

Philip Morris Companies Inc., II 530–34; **V** **405–07**, 409, 417; **7** 272, 274, 276, 548; **8** 53; **9** 180; **12** 337, 372; **13** 138, 517; **15** 64, 72–73, 137; **18** 72, **416–19 (upd.)**; **19** 112, 369; **20** 23; **22** 73, 338; **23** 427; **26** 249, 251; **29** 46–47; **32** 472, 476; **44** 338–43 **(upd.)**; **50** 144; **52** 16. *See also* Kraft Foods Inc.

Philip Smith Theatrical Enterprises. *See* GC Companies, Inc.

Philipp Brothers Chemicals, Inc., **25** 82

Philipp Holzmann AG, 14 169; **16** 284, 286; **17** 374–77

Philippine Aerospace Development Corporation, **27** 475

Philippine Airlines, Inc., 6 106–08, 122–23; **23** 379–82 **(upd.)**; **27** 464

Philippine National Oil Company, **58** 270

Philips, **V** 339; **10** 269; **22** 194

Philips Electronics N.V., 8 153; **9** 75; **10** 16; **12** 475, 549; **13** 396, **400–03 (upd.)**; **14** 446; **23** 389; **26** 334; **27** 190–92; **32**

373; **34** 258; **37** 121; **47** 383–86. *See also* Koninklijke Philips Electronics N.V.

Philips Electronics North America Corp., 13 396–99; **26** 334

N.V. Philips Gloeilampenfabriken, II 78–80; IV 680; **12** 454. *See also* Philips Electronics N.V.

Philips Medical Systems, **29** 299

Phillip Securities, **16** 14; **43** 8

Phillippe of California, **8** 16; **36** 24

Phillips & Jacobs, Inc., **14** 486

Phillips Colleges Inc., **22** 442; **39** 102

Phillips, de Pury & Luxembourg, 49 325–27

Phillips Foods, Inc., 63 320–22

Phillips Manufacturing Company, **8** 464

Phillips Petroleum Company, IV 414, 445, 453, 498, **521–23**, 567, 570–71, 575; **10** 84, 440; **11** 522; **13** 356, 485; **17** 422; **19** 176; **24** 521; **31** 457; **38** 407; **40 354–59 (upd.); 47** 70. *See also* ConocoPhillips.

Phillips-Van Heusen Corporation, 24 382–85; 55 87

Philmay Holding Inc., **72** 217

Phitech, Inc., **56** 112

PHLCorp., **11** 261

PHM Corp., **8** 461

Phoenicia Glass, **25** 266–67

Phoenix AG, 68 286–89

Phoenix Assurance Co., **III** 370–74; **55** 332

Phoenix Financial Services, **11** 115

Phoenix Footwear Group, Inc., 70 220–22

Phoenix Insurance Co., **III** 389

Phoenix Mecano AG, 61 286–88

Phoenix Microsystems Inc., **13** 8

Phoenix Mutual Life Insurance, **16** 207

Phoenix Technologies Ltd., **13** 482

Phone America of Carolina, **8** 311

Phonogram, **23** 389

Photo Corporation of America. *See* PCA International, Inc.

Photo Research Inc. *See* Excel Technology, Inc.

PhotoChannel Networks, Inc., **45** 283

Photocircuits Corp., **18** 291–93

PhotoDisc Inc., **31** 216, 218

PHP Healthcare Corporation, 22 423–25

Phuket Air Catering Company Ltd. *See* Thai Airways International.

PhyCor, Inc., 36 365–69

Physical Measurements Information, **31** 357

Physician Corporation of America, **24** 231

Physician Sales & Service, Inc., 14 387–89

Physician's Weight Loss Center, **10** 383

Physicians Formula Cosmetics, **8** 512

Physicians Placement, **13** 49

Physio-Control International Corp., 18 420–23; 30 316

Physiotherapy Associates Inc., **29** 453

Piaget, **27** 487, 489

Piaggio & C. S.p.A., 17 24; **20 426–29; 36** 472; **39** 36–37

Piam Pty. Ltd., **48** 364

PIC International Group PLC, 24 386–88 (upd.)

Pic 'N' Save, **17** 298–99

Picard Surgeles, **27** 93

Picault, **19** 50

Piccadilly Cafeterias, Inc., 19 299–302

Pick-N-Pay, **II** 642; **9** 452

Pick Pay, **48** 63

Pick Up Stix. *See* Carlson Restaurants Worldwide.

Pickands Mather, **13** 158

Picker International Corporation, **8** 352; **30** 314

Pickfords Ltd. *See* Exel plc.

Pickfords Removals, **49** 22

PickOmatic Systems, **8** 135

Pickwick International, **9** 360; **38** 315

Piclands Mather, **7** 308

Pico Ski Area Management Company, **28** 21

Picture Classified Network, **IV** 597

PictureTel Corp., 10 455–57; 27 363–66 (upd.)

Piece Goods Shops, **16** 198

Piedmont Coca-Cola Bottling Partnership, **10** 223

Piedmont Natural Gas Company, Inc., 27 367–69

Piedmont Pulp and Paper Co. *See* Westvaco Corporation.

Pier 1 Imports, Inc., 12 179, 200, 393–95; **34 337–41 (upd.); 53** 245

Pierburg GmbH, **9** 445–46

Pierce Leahy Corporation, 24 389–92. *See also* Iron Mountain Inc.

Pierce National Life, **22** 314

Piercing Pagoda, Inc., 29 382–84; 40 472

Pierre & Vacances SA, 48 314–16

Pierre Foods, **13** 270–72; **29** 203

Pietrafesa Corporation, **29** 208

Piezo Electric Product, Inc., **16** 239

Piggly Wiggly Southern, Inc., 13 404–06; 18 6, 8; **21** 455; **22** 127; **26** 47; **27** 245; **31** 406, 408; **32** 260

Pike Street Industries Inc. *See* Marchex, Inc.

Pilgrim House Group, **50** 134

Pilgrim's Pride Corporation, 7 432–33; 23 383–85 (upd.); 39 229

Pilkington plc, II 475; **724–27; 22** 434; **34 342–47 (upd.)**

Pillar Corp., **52** 185

Pilliod Furniture, Inc., **12** 300

Pillowtex Corporation, 19 303–05; 31 200; **41 299–302 (upd.)**

Pillsbury Company, II 555–57; 13 407–09 (upd.); 62 269–73 (upd.)

Pillsbury Madison & Sutro LLP, 29 385–88

Pilot Air Freight Corp., 67 301–03

Pilot Corporation, 49 328–30

Pilot Freight Carriers, **27** 474

Pilsa, **55** 189

PIMCO Advisors, **57** 20

Pin 'n' Save, **50** 98

Pinault-Printemps-Redoute S.A., 15 386; **19 306–09 (upd.); 22** 362; **27** 513; **41** 185–86; **42** 171

Pincus & Co., **7** 305

Pine Tree Casting. *See* Sturm, Ruger & Company, Inc.

Pinecliff Publishing Company, **10** 357

Pinelands, Inc., **9** 119; **26** 33

Pinelands Water Company, **45** 275, 277

Ping An Insurance Company Ltd., **65** 104

Pinguely-Haulotte SA, 51 293–95

Pinkerton's Inc., 9 406–09; 13 124–25; **14** 541; **16** 48; **41** 77, 79. *See also* Securitas AB.

Pinnacle Art and Frame, **31** 436

Pinnacle Books, **25** 483

Pinnacle Distribution, **52** 429

Pinnacle Fitness, **25** 42

Pinnacle Global Group Inc. *See* Sanders Morris Harris Group Inc.

Pinnacle Ltd., **70** 325

Pinnacle West Capital Corporation, 6 545–47; 26 359; **54 290–94 (upd.)**

Pinole Point Steel, **63** 272

Pinto Island Metals Company, **15** 116

Pioneer Asphalt Co., **36** 146–47

Pioneer Bank, **41** 312

Pioneer Concrete Services Ltd. *See* Pioneer International Limited

Pioneer Corporations, **62** 374

Pioneer Cotton Mill, **12** 503

Pioneer Electronic Corporation, III 604–06; 28 358–61 (upd.)

Pioneer Engineering and Manufacturing Co., **55** 32

Pioneer Federal Savings Bank, **10** 340; **11** 115

Pioneer Financial Corp., **11** 447

Pioneer Food Stores Co-op, **24** 528

Pioneer Hi-Bred International, Inc., 9 410–12; 17 131; **21** 387; **41 303–06 (upd.)**

Pioneer International Limited, III 728–30; 28 83

Pioneer Natural Gas Company, **10** 82

Pioneer Natural Resources Company, 59 335–39

Pioneer Outdoor, **27** 280

Pioneer Plastics Corporation, **31** 399–400

Pioneer-Standard Electronics Inc., 13 47; **19 310–14**

Pipasa, **41** 329

Pipe Line Service Company. *See* Plexco.

Pipelife International GmbH, **70** 363

Piper Aircraft Corp., **8** 49–50

Piper Impact, Inc., **62** 289

Piper Jaffray Companies Inc., 22 426–30, 465. *See also* U.S. Bancorp.

Pirelli S.p.A., V 249–51; **10** 319; **15 353–56 (upd.); 16** 318; **21** 73; **28** 262

Piscataquis Canal and Railroad Company, **16** 348

Pisces Inc., **13** 321

Pispalan Werhoomo Oy, **I** 387

Pitman Company, 58 273–75

Pitney Bowes, Inc., III 156–58, 159; **19 315–18 (upd.); 47 295–99 (upd.)**

Pittman Company, **28** 350

Pittsburgh & Lake Angeline Iron Company, **13** 156

Pittsburgh Aluminum Alloys Inc., **12** 353

Pittsburgh Brewing Co., **10** 169–70; **18** 70, 72; **50** 111, 114

Pittsburgh Chemical Co. *See* United States Steel Corp.

Pittsburgh Consolidation Coal Co., **8** 346

Pittsburgh National Corporation. *See* PNC Financial Corporation.

Pittsburgh Paint & Glass. *See* PPG Industries, Inc.

Pittsburgh Plate Glass Co. *See* PPG Industries, Inc.

Pittsburgh Railway Company, **9** 413

Pittsburgh Steel Company, **7** 587

Pittsburgh Steelers Sports, Inc., 66 255–57

The Pittston Company, IV 180–82, 566;
10 44; **19 319–22 (upd.)**. *See also* The
Brink's Company.
Pittway Corporation, 9 413–15; 27
361–62; **28** 133–34; **33 334–37 (upd.)**
Pivot Rules, Inc. *See* Bluefly, Inc.
Pivotpoint, Inc., **55** 258
Pixar Animation Studios, 34 348–51; 63
437
Pixel Semiconductor, **11** 57
Pixelworks, Inc., 69 298–300
Pizitz, Inc., **19** 324
Pizza Dispatch. *See* Dominos's Pizza, Inc.
Pizza Hut Inc., 7 434–35; **21 405–07
(upd.)**
Pizza Inn, Inc., 46 346–49; 16 447; 25
179
PizzaCo, Inc., **7** 152
Pizzeria Uno, **25** 178
PJ's Coffee, **64** 327
PJS Publications, **22** 442
PKbanken, **II** 353
Place Two. *See* Nordstrom, Inc.
Placer Development Ltd., **IV** 19
Placer Dome Inc., 20 430–33; 36 314; 61
289–93 (upd.)
Placid Oil Co., **7** 228
Plaid Holdings Corp., **9** 157
Plain Jane Dress Company, **8** 169
Plains Cotton Cooperative Association,
57 283–86
Plains Dairy, **53** 21
Plainwell Paper Co., Inc., **8** 103
Planar Systems, Inc., 61 294–97
Planet Hollywood International, Inc., 18
424–26; **25** 387–88; **32** 241, 243–44; **41**
307–10 (upd.)
Planet Smoothie Franchises LLC, **64**
327–28
Planet Waves, **48** 232
**Plantation Pipe Line Company, 68
290–92**
Plante & Moran, LLP, 71 280–83
Planters Company, **24** 287
Planters Lifesavers, **14** 274–75
Plas-Techs, Inc., **15** 35
Plastic Coating Corporation, **8** 483
Plastic Containers, Inc., **15** 129; **25** 512
Plastic Engineered Products Company. *See*
Ballard Medical Products.
Plastic Parts, Inc., **19** 277
Plastic-Plate, Inc., **61** 158, 160
Plastics, Inc., **13** 41
Plasto Bambola. *See* BRIO AB.
Plate Glass Group, **24** 450
Plateau Holdings, **12** 260; **13** 502
Platinum Entertainment, Inc., 35 341–44
PLATINUM Technology, Inc., 14 390–92
Plato Learning, Inc., 44 344–47
Platte River Insurance Company, **60** 16
**Play by Play Toys & Novelties, Inc., 26
374–76**
Play It Again Sam (PIAS), **44** 164
Play It Again Sports, **18** 207–08
Playboy Enterprises, Inc., 18 427–30; **48**
148
PlayCore, Inc., 27 370–72
Players International, Inc., 16 263, 275;
19 402; **22** 431–33; **33** 41; **43** 226–27
Playland, **16** 389
Playmates Toys, 23 386–88
Playmaxx, Inc., **55** 132
Playmobil. *See* geobra Brandstätter GmbH
& Co. KG.

Playskool, Inc., 12 169; **13** 317; **25
379–81**
Playtex Products, Inc., 8 511; **15 357–60**;
24 480; **54** 325
Playworld, **16** 389–90
Plaza Coloso S.A. de C.V., **10** 189
PLC. *See* Prescription Learning
Corporation.
Pleasant Company, 25 314; **27 373–75**;
61 202–03. *See also* American Girl, Inc.
Pleasant Holidays LLC, 62 274–76
Pleasurama PLC, **12** 228; **32** 243
Plessey Company, PLC, II 81–82; 33
287–88
Plex Co., Ltd., **55** 48
Plexco, **7** 30–31
Plexus Corporation, 35 345–47
Plezall Wipers, Inc., **15** 502
Plitt Theatres, Inc. *See* Cineplex Odeon
Corporation.
PLIVA d.d., 70 223–25
PLLN C.V. Partnership, **72** 265
Plough Inc. *See* Schering-Plough.
Plum Associates, **12** 270
**Plum Creek Timber Company, Inc., 43
304–06**
Pluma, Inc., 27 376–78
Plumb Tool, **II** 16
Plus Development Corporation, **10** 458–59
Plus Mark, Inc., **7** 24
Plus System Inc., **9** 537
Plus-Ultra, **II** 196
Plus Vita, **36** 162
Pluto Technologies International Inc., **38**
72
Ply Gem Industries Inc., 12 396–98; **23**
225
Plymouth County Electric Co., **14** 124
Plymouth Mills Inc., **23** 66
PMC Contract Research AB, **21** 425
PMI Corporation. *See* Physical
Measurements Information
The PMI Group, Inc., 49 331–33
PMP Ltd., 72 282–84
PMR Corporation. *See* Psychiatric
Solutions, Inc.
PMS Consolidated, **8** 347
PMT Services, Inc., 24 393–95
PN Gaya Motor, **56** 284
PNC Bank Corp., 13 410–12 (upd.); **14**
103; **18** 63; **53** 135
PNC Financial Corporation, II 342–43;
9 476; **17** 114
The PNC Financial Services Group Inc.,
46 350–53 (upd.)
Pneumo Abex Corp., **I** 456–58; **III** 512;
10 553–54; **38** 293–94
Pneumo Dynamics Corporation, **8** 409
PNL. *See* Pacific Northwest Laboratories.
PNM Resources Inc., 51 296–300 (upd.)
PNP. *See* Pacific Northwest Power
Company.
POAS. *See* Türkiye Petrolleri Anonim
Ortakliği
POB Polyolefine Burghausen GmbH, **IV**
487
Pocahontas Foods USA, **31** 359, 361
Pochet SA, 55 307–09
Pocket Books, Inc., **10** 480; **13** 559–60
Poclain Company, **10** 380
Poe & Associates, Inc., **41** 63–64
Pogo Producing Company, 39 330–32
Pohang Iron and Steel Company Ltd.,
IV 183–85; **17** 351. *See also* POSCO.

Pohjan Sellu Oy, **IV** 316
Point Chehalis Packers, **13** 244
Polak & Schwarz Essencefabricken, **9** 290
Poland Spring Natural Spring Water Co.,
31 229
Polar Air Cargo Inc., 60 237–39
Polar Manufacturing Company, **16** 32
Polar S.A., **59** 418
Polar Star Milling Company, **7** 241
Polaris Industries Inc., 12 399–402; **35**
348–53 (upd.); **40** 47, 50
Polaroid Corporation, III 607–09; **7**
436–39 (upd.); **12** 180; **28 362–66**
(upd.); **41** 104, 106; **54** 110
Polbeth Packaging Limited, **12** 377
Polenghi, **25** 84
**Policy Management Systems
Corporation, 11 394–95**
Policy Studies, Inc., 62 277–80
Poliet S.A., 33 175–77, 338–40; **40** 108
Polioles, S.A. de C.V., **19** 10, 12
Politos, S.A. de C.V., **23** 171
Polk Audio, Inc., 34 352–54
Pollenex Corp., **19** 360
Polo Food Corporation, **10** 250
Polo/Ralph Lauren Corporation, 9 157;
12 403–05; 16 61; **25** 48; **62 281–85**
(upd.)
Polser, **19** 49, 51
Polskie Linie Lotnicze S.A. *See* LOT
Polish Airlines.
Poly-Glas Systems, Inc., **21** 65
Poly-Hi Corporation, **8** 359
Polyblend Corporation, **7** 4
Polydesign België, **16** 421
Polydesign Nederland, **16** 421
Polydor B.V., **23** 389
Polydor KK, **23** 390
Polydress Plastic GmbH, **7** 141
Polygon Networks Inc., **41** 73
PolyGram N.V., 13 402; **22** 194; **23**
389–92; **25** 411; **26** 152, 314, 394; **31**
269
Polyken Technologies, **11** 220
Polymer Technologies Corporation, **26** 287
Polyphase Corporation. *See* Overhill
Corporation.
Polysius AG, **IV** 89
**Pomeroy Computer Resources, Inc., 33
341–44**
Pomeroy's, **16** 61; **50** 107
Pommery et Greno, **II** 475
Pompes Guinard S.A., **62** 217
Ponderosa Steakhouse, 7 336; **12** 373; **14**
331; **15 361–64**
Ponderosa System Inc., **12** 199
Pont-à-Mousson S.A., **16** 119, 121–22; **21**
253
Pont Royal SA, **48** 316
Pontiac, **10** 353
Ponto Frio Bonzao, **22** 321
Pontos GmbH, **56** 152
Poof-Slinky, Inc., 61 298–300
Poore Brothers, Inc., 44 348–50
Poorman-Douglas Corporation, **13** 468
Pop.com, **43** 144
Pope & Talbot, Inc., 12 406–08; **61
301–05 (upd.)**
Pope Cable and Wire B.V., **19** 45
Popeye's/Church's, **23** 115, 117
Popeyes Famous Fried Chicken and
Biscuits, Inc., **7** 26–28; **32** 13
Pophitt Cereals, Inc., **22** 337
Poppe Tyson Inc., **23** 479; **25** 91

Poppin' Fresh Pies, Inc., **12** 510
Popsicle, **II** 573; **14** 205
Popular Aviation Company, **12** 560
Popular Club Plan, **12** 280; **34** 232
Popular, Inc., 41 311–13
Popular Merchandise, Inc., **12** 280
**The Porcelain and Fine China
    Companies Ltd., 69 301–03**
Pori, **IV** 350
Poron Diffusion, **9** 394
Poron, S.A., **42** 268–69
Porsche AG, 13 28, 219, **413–15; 31
    363–66 (upd.); 36** 198
Port Arthur Finance Corp., **37** 309
**The Port Authority of New York and
    New Jersey, 47** 359; **48 317–20**
Port Blakely Mill Company, **17** 438
Port Dickson Power Sdn. Bhd., **36** 435–36
**Port Imperial Ferry Corporation, 70
    226–29**
Port of London Authority, **48** 317
Port Stockton Food Distributors, Inc., **16**
    451, 453
Portage Industries Corp., **19** 415
El Portal Group, Inc., **58** 371
Portal Software, Inc., 47 300–03
Portals Water Treatment, **11** 510
Porter-Cable Corporation, **26** 361–63
Porter Chadburn plc, **28** 252
Porter Shoe Manufacturing Company, **13**
    360
Portex, **25** 431
Portia Management Services Ltd., **30** 318
**Portillo's Restaurant Group, Inc., 71
    284–86**
Portland General Corporation, 6 548–51
Portland General Electric, **45** 313; **50** 103
Portland Heavy Industries, **10** 369
Portland Plastics, **25** 430–31
Portland Shipyard LLC. *See* Cascade
    General Inc.
Portland Trail Blazers, 50 356–60
Portland-Zementwerke Heidelberg A.G., **23**
    326
Portnet, **6** 435
Portsmouth & Sunderland, **35** 242, 244
Portucel. *See* Grupo Portucel Soporcel.
Portugal Telecom SGPS S.A., 69 304–07
Portugalia, **46** 398
Portways, **9** 92
Posadas. *See* Grupo Posadas, S.A. de C.V.
POSCO, 57 287–91 (upd.)
Posful Corporation, **68** 9
Positive Response Television, Inc., **27**
    337–38
Post Office Group, V 498–501
Post Properties, Inc., 26 377–79
Postabank és Takarékpénztár Rt., **69** 155,
    157
La Poste, V 470–72
Posterscope Worldwide, 70 230–32
Posti- Ja Telelaitos, 6 329–31
PostScript, **17** 177
Potain SAS, **59** 274, 278
**Potash Corporation of Saskatchewan
    Inc., 18** 51, **431–33; 27** 318; **50** 90
Potlatch Corporation, 8 428–30; 19 445;
    34 355–59 (upd.)
Potomac Edison Company, **38** 39–40
**Potomac Electric Power Company, 6
    552–54; 25** 46
Potter & Brumfield Inc., 11 396–98
Pottery Barn, **13** 42; **17** 548–50

Pottsville Behavioral Counseling Group, **64**
    311
Poulan/Weed Eater. *See* White
    Consolidated Industries Inc.
PowCon, Inc., **17** 534
Powell Duffryn plc, 31 367–70
Powell Energy Products, **8** 321
Powell Group, **33** 32
Powell's Books, Inc., 37 181; **40 360–63**
Power Applications & Manufacturing
    Company, Inc., **6** 441
**Power Corporation of Canada, 36
    370–74 (upd.)**
Power Parts Co., **7** 358
Power Products, **8** 515
Power Team, **10** 492
PowerBar Inc., 44 351–53
Powercor. *See* PacifiCorp.
PowerFone Holdings, **10** 433
Powergen PLC, 11 399–401; 12 349; **13**
    458, 484; **50** 172, 280–81, **361–64
    (upd.)**
Powerhouse Technologies, Inc., 13 485;
    27 379–81
PowerSoft Corp., **11** 77; **15** 374
Powerteam Electrical Services Ltd., **64** 404
Powertel Inc., **48** 130
Powerware Corporation. *See* Eaton
    Corporation.
Pozzi-Renati Millwork Products, Inc., **8**
    135
PP&L. *See* Pennsylvania Power & Light
    Company.
PP&L Global, Inc., **44** 291
PPB Group Berhad, 57 292–95
PPG Industries, Inc., III 722, **731–33; 8**
    222, 224; **16** 120–21; **20** 415; **21** 221,
    223; **22** 147, **434–37 (upd.); 37** 73; **39**
    292
PPI. *See* Precision Pattern Inc.
PPI Two Corporation, **64** 334
PPL Corporation, 41 314–17 (upd.)
PR Holdings, **23** 382
PR Newswire, 35 354–56
Practical and Educational Books, **13** 105
Practical Business Solutions, Inc., **18** 112
PracticeWorks.com, **69** 33–34
Prada Holding B.V., 45 342–45; 50 215
Pragma Bio-Tech, Inc., **11** 424
Prairie Farms Dairy, Inc., 47 304–07
Prairielands Energy Marketing, Inc., **7** 322,
    325
Prakla Seismos, **17** 419
Pranda Jewelry plc, 70 233–35
Prandium Inc., **51** 70
Pratt & Whitney, 7 456; **9** 14, 16–18,
    244–46, **416–18; 10** 162; **11** 299, 427;
    12 71; **13** 386; **14** 564; **24** 312; **39** 313
Pratt Hotel Corporation, **21** 275; **22** 438
Pratt Properties Inc., **8** 349
Pratta Electronic Materials, Inc., **26** 425
Praxair, Inc., 11 402–04; 16 462; **43** 265;
    48 321–24 (upd.)
Praxis Biologics, **8** 26; **27** 115
Praxis Corporation, **30** 499
Pre-Fab Cushioning, **9** 93
Pre Finish Metals Incorporated, **63** 270–71
Pre-Paid Legal Services, Inc., 20 434–37
PreAnalytiX, **39** 335
Precept Foods, LLC, **54** 168
Precise Fabrication Corporation, **33** 257
Precise Imports Corp., **21** 516
Precision Castparts Corp., 15 365–67
Precision Engineered Products, Inc., **70** 142

Precision Games, **16** 471
Precision Husky Corporation, **26** 494
Precision IBC, Inc., **64** 20–21
Precision Interconnect Corporation, **14** 27
Precision LensCrafters, **13** 391
Precision Moulds, Ltd., **25** 312
Precision Optical Industry Company, Ltd.
    See Canon Inc.
Precision Pattern Inc., **36** 159
Precision Power, Inc., **21** 514
Precision Response Corporation, **47** 420
Precision Software Corp., **14** 319
Precision Spring of Canada, Ltd., **55** 305
Precision Stainless Inc., **65** 289
Precision Standard Inc. *See* Pemco
    Aviation Group Inc.
Precision Studios, **12** 529
Precision Tool, Die & Machine Company
    Inc., **51** 116–17
Precision Tube Formers, Inc., **17** 234
Precisionaire. *See* Flanders Corporation.
Precoat Metals, **54** 331
Precor, **III** 610–11
Predica, **II** 266
Predicasts Inc., **12** 562; **17** 254
Prefco Corporation, **57** 56–57
Preferred Medical Products. *See* Ballard
    Medical Products.
Preferred Products, Inc., **II** 669; **18** 504; **50**
    454
PREINCO Holdings, Inc., **11** 532
PREL&P. *See* Portland Railway Electric
    Light & Power Company.
**Premark International, Inc., III 610–12;
    14** 548; **28** 479–80. *See also* Illinois
    Tool Works Inc.
Premcor Inc., 37 309–11
Premier Cement Ltd., **64** 98
Premier Health Alliance Inc., **10** 143
**Premier Industrial Corporation, 9
    419–21; 19** 311
Premier Insurance Co., **26** 487
Premier Medical Services, **31** 357
Premier Milk Pte Ltd., **54** 117
Premier One Products, Inc., **37** 285
Premier Parks, Inc., 27 382–84
Premier Radio Networks, Inc., **23** 292, 294
Premier Rehabilitation Centers, **29** 400
Premier Sport Group Inc., **23** 66
Premiere Labels Inc., **53** 236
Premisteres S.A., **II** 663
**Premium Standard Farms, Inc., 30
    353–55**
PremiumWear, Inc., 30 356–59
Prentice Hall Computer Publishing, **10** 24
Prentice Hall Inc., **I** 453; **IV** 672; **19** 405;
    23 503
Prescott Ball & Turben, **12** 60
Prescott Investors, **14** 303; **50** 311
Prescription Learning Corporation, **7** 256;
    25 253
Présence, **III** 211
Preserver Group, Inc., 44 354–56
President Baking Co., **36** 313
President Casinos, Inc., 22 438–40
President Riverboat Casino-Mississippi
    Inc., **21** 300
Presidents Island Steel & Wire Company.
    See Laclede Steel Company.
Presley Cos., **59** 422
Press Associates, **19** 334
Presses de la Cité. *See* Groupe de la Cité.
Pressman Toy Corporation, 56 280–82
Presstar Printing, **25** 183

Presstek, Inc., 33 345–48
Pressware International, **12** 377
Prestage Farms, 46 83
Prestel Verlag, **66** 123
Prestige et Collections, **III** 48
Prestige Fragrance & Cosmetics, Inc., **22** 158
The Prestige Group plc., **19** 171
Prestige International, **33** 284
Prestige Leather Creations, **31** 435–36
Prestige Properties, **23** 388
Presto Products, Inc., **II** 609–10; **IV** 187; **19** 348; **50** 401
Preston Corporation, 6 421–23; **14** 566, 568
Prestone Products Corp., **22** 32; **26** 349
Prestwick Mortgage Group, **25** 187
Pret A Manger, **63** 280, 284–85
Pretty Good Privacy, Inc., **25** 349
Pretty Neat Corp., **12** 216
Pretty Paper Inc., **14** 499
Pretzel Time. *See* Mrs. Fields' Original Cookies, Inc.
Pretzelmaker. *See* Mrs. Fields' Original Cookies, Inc.
Pretzels Incorporated, **24** 241
Preussag AG, IV 109, 201, 231; **17** 378–82; **21** 370; **28** 454; **42** 279–83 **(upd.); 44** 432
PreussenElektra Aktiengesellschaft, V 698–700; **39** 57
Preval, **19** 49–50
Previews, Inc., **21** 96
PreVision Marketing, Inc., **37** 409
Priam Corporation, **10** 458
Priba, **26** 158, 160
Pribina, **25** 85
Price Chopper Supermarkets. *See* The Golub Corporation.
Price Club. *See* The Price Company.
Price Communications Corporation, 42 284–86
Price Company Ltd. *See* Abitibi-Consolidated, Inc.
The Price Company, II 664; **V** 162–64; **14** 393–94; **34** 198
Price Enterprises, Inc., **14** 395
Price, McCormick & Co., **26** 451
Price Pfister, Inc., 70 236–39
Price Rite, **25** 67
Price Waterhouse LLP, 9 422–24; **14** 245; **26** 439. *See also* PricewaterhouseCoopers
PriceCostco, Inc., 14 393–95
Pricel. *See* Chargeurs.
Priceline.com Incorporated, 57 296–99
Priceline.com Inc., **58** 118–19
Pricesearch Ltd Co, **48** 224
PriceSmart, Inc., 71 287–90
PricewaterhouseCoopers, 29 389–94 **(upd.); 57** 166; **63** 200
PRIDE Enterprises. *See* Prison Rehabilitative Industries and Diversified Enterprises, Inc.
Pride Petroleum Services. *See* DeKalb Genetics Corporation.
Priggen Steel Building Co., **8** 545
Prima Gold International Company Limited. *See* Pranda Jewlry plc.
Prima S.A., **67** 201
Primadonna Resorts Inc., **17** 318
Primagas GmbH, **55** 347
Primark Corp., 10 89–90; **13** 416–18
Primary Coatings, Inc., **51** 190

Prime Capital Services, Inc. *See* Gilman & Ciocia, Inc.
Prime Care International, Inc., **36** 367
Prime Computer, Inc. *See* Computervision Corporation.
Prime Hospitality Corporation, 52 280–83
Prime Motor Inns Inc., **IV** 718; **11** 177; **17** 238
The Prime-Mover Co., **13** 267
Prime Service, Inc., **28** 40
Prime Telecommunications Corporation, **8** 311
PrimeAmerica, **III** 340
Primedex Health Systems, Inc., 25 382–85
Primedia Inc., 7 286; **12** 306; **21** 403–04; **22** 441–43; **23** 156, 158, 344, 417; **24** 274; **56** 192
Primera Group, **71** 151, 153
Primergy Corp., **39** 261
Primerica Corporation, I 612–14; **III** 283 **8** 118; **9** 218–19, 360–61; **11** 29; **15** 464; **27** 47; **36** 202. *See also* American Can Co.
Primerica Financial Services, Inc., **30** 124; **59** 121, 125
PriMerit Bank, **19** 412
PrimeSource, **26** 542
Primestar, **38** 176
PRIMESTAR Partners L.P., **28** 241
PrimeWood, Inc., **61** 398
Primex Fibre Ltd., **IV** 328
Primo Foods Ltd., **7** 430
Prince Co., **II** 473
Prince Gardner Company, **17** 465; **23** 21
Prince Golf International, Ltd., **23** 450
Prince Holding Corporation, **26** 231; **59** 252
Prince of Wales Hotels, PLC, **14** 106; **25** 308
Prince Sports Group, Inc., 15 368–70
Prince Street Technologies, Ltd., **8** 271
Prince William Bank, **II** 337; **10** 425
Princess Cruise Lines, 22 444–46
Princess Hotel Group, **21** 353
Princess Hotels International Inc., **45** 82
Princess Metropole, **21** 354
Princeton Gas Service Company, **6** 529
Princeton Laboratories Products Company, **8** 84; **38** 124
The Princeton Review, Inc., 12 142; **42** 210, 287–90
Princeton Telecommunications Corporation, **26** 38
Princeville Airlines, **24** 22
Principal Health Care, **59** 139
Principal Mutual Life Insurance Company, III 328–30
Pringle Barge Line Co., **17** 357
Print Technologies, Inc., **22** 357
Printex Corporation, **9** 363
PrintNation Inc., **58** 275
Printpack, Inc., 68 293–96
Printrak, A Motorola Company, 44 357–59
Printronix, Inc., 14 377–78; **18** 434–36
Priority Records, **22** 194; **69** 351
Pripps Ringnes, **18** 394, 396–97
Prison Rehabilitative Industries and Diversified Enterprises, Inc. (PRIDE), 53 277–79
Prisunic SA. *See* Pinault-Printemps-Redoute SA.

Pritchard Corporation. *See* Black & Veatch, Inc.
Private Colleges and Universities, Inc., 55 15
PrivatPort, **70** 311
Prize Energy, **59** 336
Pro-Fac Cooperative, Inc., **7** 104–06; **21** 154–55, 157; **69** 66–67, 69, 71
Pro-Lawn, **19** 250
Pro-Line Corporation, **36** 26
Pro-optik AG, **31** 203
Probe Exploration Inc., **25** 232
Process Engineering Inc., **21** 108
Process Systems International, **21** 108
Processing Technologies International. *See* Food Ingredients Technologies.
Procor Limited, **16** 357
Procordia Foods, **18** 396
The Procter & Gamble Company, III 50–53; **8** 431–35 **(upd.); 26** 380–85 **(upd.); 67** 304–11 **(upd.)**
Proctor & Schwartz, **17** 213
Proctor-Silex. *See* Hamilton Beach/Proctor-Silex Inc.
Prodega Ltd. *See* Bon Appetit Holding AG.
Prodigy Communications Corporation, 10 237–38; **12** 562; **13** 92; **27** 517; **34** 360–62; **56** 312
Prodigy Consulting Inc., **51** 198
Product Components, Inc., **19** 415
Production Association Kirishinefteorgsintez, **48** 378
Production Management Companies Inc., **65** 334
Productivity Point International Inc., **54** 192–93
Produits Jaeger, **27** 258
Produits Ronald Inc. *See* Lassonde Industries Inc.
Profarmaco Nobel S.r.l., **16** 69
Professional Bull Riders Inc., 55 310–12
Professional Computer Resources, Inc., **10** 513
Professional Detailing, Inc. *See* PDI, Inc.
Professional Education Systems, Inc., **17** 272; **53** 319
The Professional Golfers' Association of America, 41 318–21
Professional Health Care Management Inc., **14** 209
Professional Health-Care Resources, **50** 123
Professional Underwriters Liability Insurance Company, **55** 128
Proffitt's, Inc., 19 323–25, 510, 512; **63** 147. *See also* Saks Holdings, Inc.
Profile Extrusion Company, **22** 337
Profimatics, Inc., **11** 66
PROFITCo., **II** 231
Progenx, Inc., **47** 221
Progress Development Organisation, **10** 169
Progress Software Corporation, 15 371–74
Progressive Bagel Concepts, Inc. *See* Einstein/Noah Bagel Corporation.
Progressive Corporation, 11 405–07; **29** 395–98 **(upd.)**
Progressive Distributions Systems, **44** 334
Progressive Distributors, **12** 220
Progressive Grocery Stores, **7** 202
Progressive Networks, Inc. *See* RealNetworks, Inc.
Progresso, **I** 514; **14** 212

Project Carriers. *See* Hansa Linie.
Projexions Video Supply, Inc., **24** 96
Projiis, **II** 356
ProLab Nutrition, Inc., **49** 275, 277
Proland, **12** 139
Proler International Corp., **13** 98; **19** 380–81
ProLogis, 57 300–02
Promarkt Holding GmbH, **24** 266, 270
Promeca S.A. de C.V., **72** 262
Promodès SA, **24** 475; **26** 158, 161; **37** 21; **64** 66, 69
Promonte. *See* Telenor ASA.
Promotional Graphics, **15** 474
Promus Companies, Inc., 9 425–27; 15 46; **16** 263; **22** 537; **38** 76–77; **43** 225–26; **62** 179
Propaganda Films, Inc., **23** 389, 391
Property Automation Software Corporation, **49** 290
Prophecy Ltd., **55** 24
ProSiebenSat.1 Media AG, 46 403; 54 295–98
Proskauer Rose LLP, 47 308–10
ProSource Distribution Services, Inc. *See* Onex Corporation.
The Prospect Group, Inc., **11** 188
Prospect Provisions, Inc. *See* King Kullen Grocery Co., Inc.
Protan & Fagertun, **25** 464
Protection One, Inc., 32 372–75
Protective Closures, **7** 296–97
Protective Insurance Company, **51** 37, 39
Protek, **III** 633
Protiviti, **70** 284
Protogene Laboratories Inc., **17** 288
Proton. *See* Perusahaan Otomobil Nasional Bhd.
Protravel S.A., **69** 7
Proveedora de Seguridad del Golfo, S.A. de C.V., **45** 425–26
Provell Inc., 58 276–79 (upd.)
Proventus Handels AB, **35** 362
The Providence Journal Company, 28 367–69; 30 15
La Providence, **III** 210–11
Providence National Bank, **9** 228
The Providence Service Corporation, 64 309–12
Providence Steam and Gas Pipe Co. *See* Grinnell Corp.
Provident Institution for Savings, **13** 467
Provident Life and Accident Insurance Company of America, III 331–33, 404; **57** 234. *See also* UnumProvident Corporation.
Provident National Corporation. *See* PNC Financial Corporation.
Provident Travelers Mortgage Securities Corp., **III** 389
Providian Financial Corporation, 52 62, 284–90 (upd.)
Provigo Inc., II 651–53; 12 413; **51 301–04 (upd.)**
Provimi, **36** 185
Province Healthcare Company, **69** 236
Les Provinces Réunies, **III** 235
Provincetown-Boston Airlines, **I** 118
Provincial Bank of Ireland Ltd., **16** 13
Provincial Engineering Ltd, **8** 544
Provincial Gas Company, **6** 526
Provincial Newspapers Ltd., **28** 502
PROWA, **22** 89
Proximity Technology, **23** 210

Prudential Assurance Company, **24** 314
Prudential Bache Securities, **9** 441
Prudential-Bache Trade Corporation, **II** 51; **21** 331
Prudential Corporation plc, III 334–36; IV 711; **8** 276–77. *See also* Prudential plc.
Prudential Insurance Company of America, III 337–41; 30 360–64 (upd.); 36 77–78; **52** 238–39
Prudential Oil & Gas, Inc. *See* Gulf States Utilities Company.
Prudential Steel Ltd., 59 280, 282
Prudential plc, 48 325–29 (upd.)
Prymetall GmbH & Co. KG, **62** 253
PS Business Parks, Inc., **52** 291
PSA. *See* Pacific Southwest Airlines.
PSA Peugeot Citroen S.A., 7 35; **28 370–74 (upd.); 54** 126
PSB Company, **36** 517
PSCCo. *See* Public Service Company of Colorado.
PSE, Inc., **12** 100
PSF. *See* Premium Standard Farms, Inc.
PSI. *See* Process Systems International.
PSI Resources, 6 555–57
Psion PLC, 45 346–49
Psychiatric Solutions, Inc., 68 297–300
Psychological Corp., **IV** 623; **12** 223
PT Abacus Distribution System Indonesia, **58** 140
PT Aerowisata, **58** 140
PT Astra International Tbk, 56 283–86
PT Bank Buana Indonesia Tbk, 60 240–42
PT Bank MayBank Indocorp, **72** 217
PT Capura Angkasa, **58** 140
PT Components, **14** 43
Ptarmigan Airways Ltd., **56** 39
PTI Communications, Inc. *See* Pacific Telecom, Inc.
PTN Publishing, Inc., **56** 73
PTT Nederland N.V., **27** 472; **30** 393–94
PTT Public Company Ltd., 56 287–90
PTT Telecom BV, **V** 299–301
PTV. *See* Österreichische Post- und Telegraphenverwaltung.
Pubco Corporation, 17 383–85
Publi-Graphics, **16** 168
Public Broadcasting Stations, **29** 426; **51** 309
Public/Hacienda Resorts, Inc. *See* Santa Fe Gaming Corporation.
Public Savings Insurance Co., **III** 219
Public Service Co., **14** 124
Public Service Company of Colorado, 6 558–60
Public Service Company of Indiana. *See* PSI Energy.
Public Service Company of New Hampshire, 21 408–12; 55 313–18 (upd.)
Public Service Company of New Mexico, 6 561–64; 27 486. *See also* PNM Resources Inc.
Public Service Corporation of New Jersey, **44** 360
Public Service Enterprise Group Inc., V 701–03; 44 360–63 (upd.)
Public Service Market. *See* The Golub Corporation.
Public Storage, Inc., 21 476; **52 291–93, 310–11**
Publicaciones Citem, S.A. de C.V., **39** 188

Publicis S.A., 13 204; **19 329–32; 21** 265–66; **23** 478, 480; **25** 91; **33** 180; **39** 166, 168; **42** 328, 331
PubliGroupe, **49** 424
Publishers Clearing House, 23 393–95; 27 20; **64 313–16 (upd.)**
Publishers Group, Inc., 35 357–59
Publishers Paper Co., **IV** 677–78
Publishing and Broadcasting Limited, 19 400–01; **54 299–302**
Publix Super Markets Inc., II 627; **7 440–42; 9** 186; **20** 84, 306; **23** 261; **31 371–74 (upd.); 59** 425
Pubmaster Finance Ltd, **70** 242
Puck Holdings, **35** 474, 476
Puck Lazaroff Inc. *See* The Wolfgang Puck Food Company, Inc.
Pueblo Xtra International, Inc., 47 311–13; 54 73–74
Puerto Rican Aqueduct and Sewer Authority, **6** 441
Puerto Rico Electric Power Authority, 47 314–16
Puget Mill Company, **12** 406–07
Puget Sound Alaska Van Lines. *See* Alaska Hydro-Train.
Puget Sound Energy Inc., 50 365–68 (upd.)
Puget Sound National Bank, **8** 469–70
Puget Sound Power And Light Company, 6 565–67; 50 103
Puig Beauty and Fashion Group S.L., 60 243–46
Pulaski Furniture Corporation, 33 349–52
Pulitzer Inc., 58 280–83 (upd.)
Pulitzer Publishing Company, 15 375–77
Pullman Savings and Loan Association, **17** 529
Pullman Standard, **7** 540
Pulsar Internacional S.A., 21 413–15
Pulse Engineering, Inc., **29** 461
Pulte Corporation, 8 436–38; 22 205, 207
Pulte Homes, Inc., 42 291–94 (upd.)
Puma AG Rudolf Dassler Sport, 35 360–63; 36 344, 346
Pumpkin Masters, Inc., 48 330–32
Punch International N.V., 66 258–60
Punch Taverns plc, 70 240–42
Punchcraft, Inc., **III** 569; **20** 360
Punter Southall. *See* Sanlam Ltd.
Purdue Fredrick Company, **13** 367
Pure-Gar, Inc., **49** 276
Pure Milk Products Cooperative, **11** 24
Pure Resources, Inc., **71** 382
Pure World, Inc., 72 285–87
Purina Mills, Inc., 32 376–79
Puris Inc., **14** 316
Puritan-Bennett Corporation, 13 419–21
Puritan Fashions Corp., **22** 122
Purity Supreme, Inc., **II** 674; **24** 462
Purodenso Co., **III** 593
Purolator Courier, Inc., **6** 390; **16** 397; **18** 177; **25** 148
Purolator Products Company, 21 416–18; 28 263; **61** 66
Puros de Villa Gonzales, **23** 465
Purup-Eskofot, **44** 44
Push Records, Inc., **42** 271
Putnam Investments Inc. *See* Marsh & McLennan Companies, Inc.
Putnam Management Co., **III** 283

Putnam Plastics Corporation. *See* Memry Corporation.
Putt-Putt Golf Courses of America, Inc., 23 396–98
PVC Container Corporation, 67 312–14
PW Eagle, Inc., 48 333–36
PWA Group, IV 323–25; **28** 446. *See also* Svenska Cellulosa.
PWS Holding Corporation, **13** 406; **26** 47
PWT Projects Ltd., **22** 89
PWT Worldwide, **11** 510
PYA/Monarch, **II** 675; **26** 504
Pyramid Breweries Inc., 33 353–55
Pyramid Communications, Inc., **IV** 623
Pyramid Companies, 54 303–05
Pyramid Electric Company, **10** 319
Pyramid Electronics Supply, Inc., **17** 275
Pyramid Technology Corporation, **10** 504; **27** 448
Pyxis. *See* Cardinal Health, Inc.
Pyxis Innovations. *See* Alticor Inc.
PZ Cussons plc, 72 288–90

Q&B Foods Inc., **57** 202–03
Q Lube, Inc., **18** 145; **24** 339
Q.A.S. Quality Airport Services Israel Ltd., **70** 311
Q.E.P. Co., Inc., 65 292–94
Qantas Airways Limited,
Qantas Airways Ltd., 6 109–13; **24** 396–401 (upd.); **68** 301–07 (upd.)
Qatar General Petroleum Corporation, IV 524–26
Qiagen N.V., 39 333–35
Qingdao Haier Refrigerator Co., Ltd., **65** 167, 169
Qintex Australia Ltd., **II** 150; **25** 329
QLT Inc., 71 291–94
QMS Ltd., **43** 284
QO Chemicals, Inc., **14** 217
QSC Audio Products, Inc., 56 291–93
QSP, Inc. *See* The Reader's Digest Association, Inc.
Qtera Corporation, **36** 352
Quad/Graphics, Inc., 19 333–36
Quad Pharmaceuticals, Inc. *See* Par Pharmaceuticals Inc.
Quail Oil Tools, **28** 347–48
Quaker Alloy, Inc., **39** 31–32
Quaker Fabric Corp., 19 337–39
Quaker Oats Company, II 558–60, 575, 684; **12** 167, 169, **409–12 (upd.); 13** 186; **22** 131, 337–38; **25** 90, 314; **27** 197; **30** 219; **31** 282; **34** 363–67 (upd.); **38** 349; **43** 121, 218; **63** 250–52
Quaker State Corporation, 7 443–45; **21** 419–22 (upd.); **25** 90; **26** 349. *See also* Pennzoil-Quaker State Company.
QUALCOMM Incorporated, 20 438–41; **26** 532; **38** 271; **39** 64; **41** 289; **43** 312–13; **46** 410, 422; **47** 317–21 (upd.)
Qualcore, S. de R.L. de C.V., **51** 116
Qualipac, **55** 309
QualiTROL Corporation, **7** 116–17
Quality Assurance International, **72** 255
Quality Aviation Services, Inc., **53** 132
Quality Bakers of America, **12** 170
Quality Chekd Dairies, Inc., 48 337–39
Quality Courts Motels, Inc. *See* Choice Hotels International, Inc.
Quality Dining, Inc., 18 437–40; **63** 80
Quality Food Centers, Inc., 17 386–88; **22** 271, 273

Quality Inns International. *See* Choice Hotels International, Inc.
Quality Markets, Inc., **13** 393
Quality Oil Co., **II** 624–25
Quality Paperback Book Club (QPB), **13** 105–07
Quality Products, Inc., **18** 162
Qualix S.A., **67** 347–48
Quanex Corporation, 13 422–24; **62** 286–89 (upd.)
Quanta Computer Inc., 47 322–24
Quanta Systems Corp., **51** 81
Quanterra Alpha L.P., **63** 347
Quantex Microsystems Inc., **24** 31
Quantronix Corporation. *See* Excel Technology Inc.
Quantum Chemical Corporation, 8 439–41; **11** 441; **30** 231, 441
Quantum Computer Services, Inc. *See* America Online, Inc.
Quantum Corporation, 10 56, 403, **458–59,** 463; **25** 530; **36** 299–300; **62** 290–93 (upd.)
Quantum Health Resources, **29** 364
Quantum Marketing International, Inc., **27** 336
Quantum Offshore Contractors, **25** 104
Quantum Overseas N.V., **7** 360
Quantum Restaurant Group, Inc., **30** 330
Quarex Industries, Inc. *See* Western Beef, Inc.
Quark, Inc., 36 375–79
Quarrie Corporation, **12** 554
Quebec Credit Union League, **48** 290
Quebéc Hydro-Electric Commission. *See* Hydro-Quebéc.
Quebecor Inc., 12 412–14; **19** 333; **26** 44; **29** 471; **47** 325–28 (upd.)
Queen City Broadcasting, **42** 162
Queens Isetan Co., Ltd. *See* Isetan Company Limited.
Queensborough Holdings PLC, **38** 103
Queensland Alumina, **IV** 59
Queensland and Northern Territories Air Service. *See* Qantas Airways Limited.
Queensland Mines Ltd., **III** 729
Quelle Group, V 165–67. *See also* Karstadt Quelle AG.
Quesarias Ibéricas, **23** 219
Quest Aerospace Education, Inc., **18** 521
Quest Diagnostics Inc., 26 390–92
Quest Education Corporation, **42** 212
Quest Pharmacies Inc., **25** 504–05
Questa Oil and Gas Co., **63** 408
Questar Corporation, 6 568–70; **10** 432; **26** 386–89 (upd.)
Questor Management Co. LLC, **55** 31
Questor Partners, **26** 185
The Quick & Reilly Group, Inc., 18 552; **20** 442–44; **26** 65
Quick Pak Inc., **53** 236
Quicken.com. *See* Intuit Inc.
Quickie Designs, **11** 202, 487–88
The Quigley Corporation, 62 294–97
Quik Stop Markets, Inc., **12** 112
Quiksilver, Inc., 18 441–43; **27** 329
QuikTrip Corporation, 36 380–83
Quill Corporation, 28 375–77; **55** 354
Quillery, **27** 138
Quilmes Industrial (QUINSA) S.A., 57 74, 76–77; **67** 315–17
Quilter Sound Company. *See* QSC Audio Products, Inc.
Quimica Geral do Nordeste S.A., **68** 81

Química y Farmacia, S.A. de C.V., **59** 332
Quimicos Industriales Penoles. *See* Industrias Penoles, S.A. de C.V.
Quincy Family Steak House, **II** 679; **10** 331; **19** 287; **27** 17, 19
Quiñenco S.A., **69** 56–57; **70** 61–62
Quintana Roo, Inc., **17** 243, 245; **25** 42
Quintel Communications, Inc., **61** 375
Quintex Australia Limited, **25** 329
Quintiles Transnational Corporation, 21 423–25; **68** 308–12 (upd.)
Quintron, Inc., **11** 475
Quintus Computer Systems, **6** 248
Quixote Corporation, 15 378–80
Quixtar Inc. *See* Alticor Inc.
Quixx Corporation, **6** 580
The Quizno's Corporation, 32 444; **42** 295–98
Quoddy Products Inc., **17** 389, 390
Quotron Systems, Inc., **IV** 670; **9** 49, 125; **30** 127; **47** 37
Quovadx Inc., 70 243–46
QVC Inc., 9 428–29; **10** 175; **12** 315; **18** 132; **20** 75; **24** 120, 123; **58** 284–87 (upd.); **67** 206
Qwest Communications International, Inc., 25 499; **26** 36; **32** 218; **36** 43–44; **37** 126, **312–17; 49** 312; **63** 393
QwikSilver II, Inc., **37** 119

R&B Falcon Corp. *See* Transocean Sedco Forex Inc.
R&B, Inc., 51 305–07
R & B Manufacturing Co., **III** 569; **20** 361
R&D Systems, Inc., **52** 347
R&O Software-Technik GmbH, **27** 492
R&S Home and Auto, **56** 352
R&S Technology Inc., **48** 410
R. and W. Hawaii Wholesale, Inc., **22** 15
R-Anell Custom Homes Inc., **41** 19
R-B. *See* Arby's, Inc.
R-Byte, **12** 162
R-C Holding Inc. *See* Air & Water Technologies Corporation.
R.B. Pamplin Corp., 45 350–52
R.C. Bigelow, Inc., 16 90; **49** 334–36
R.C. Willey Home Furnishings, 72 291–93
R. Cubed Composites Inc., **I** 387
R.E. Funsten Co., **7** 429
R.G. Barry Corp., 17 389–91; **44** 364–67 (upd.)
R.G. Dun-Bradstreet Corp. *See* The Dun & Bradstreet Corp.
R. Griggs Group Limited, 23 399–402; **31** 413–14
R.H. Donnelley Corporation, **61** 81–83
R.H. Macy & Co., Inc., V 168–70; **8** 442–45 (upd.); **10** 282; **11** 349; **13** 42; **15** 281; **16** 206–07, 328, 388, 561; **23** 60; **27** 60, 481; **30** 379–83 (upd.); **31** 190, 192–93; **45** 15; **60** 72
R.H. Stengel & Company, **13** 479
R.J. Reynolds, **I** 261, 363; **II** 544; **7** 130, 132, 267, 365, 367; **9** 533; **13** 490; **14** 78; **15** 72–73; **16** 242; **21** 315; **27** 125; **29** 195; **32** 344. *See also* RJR Nabisco.
R.J. Reynolds Tobacco Holdings, Inc., 30 384–87 (upd.)
R.J. Tower Corporation. *See* Tower Automotive, Inc.
R.K. Brown, **14** 112
R.L. Crain Limited, **15** 473
R.L. Manning Company, **9** 363–64

R.L. Polk & Co., 10 460–62
R-O Realty, Inc., **43** 314
R.P.M., Inc., **25** 228
R.P. Scherer Corporation, I 678–80; **33** 145
R.R. Bowker Co., **17** 398; **23** 440
R.R. Donnelley & Sons Company, IV 660–62, 673; **9** 430–32 (upd.); **11** 293; **12** 414, 557, 559; **18** 331; **19** 333; **38** 368–71 (upd.)
R.S.R. Corporation, **31** 48
R.S. Stokvis Company, **13** 499
R. Scott Associates, **11** 57
R-T Investors LC, **42** 323–24
R. Twining & Co., **61** 395
R.W. Beck, **29** 353
R.W. Harmon & Sons, Inc., **6** 410
RABA PLC, **10** 274
Rabbit Software Corp., **10** 474
Rabobank Group, 26 419; **33** 356–58
RAC. *See* Ravenswood Aluminum Company.
Racal-Datacom Inc., 11 408–10
Racal Electronics PLC, II 83–84; **11** 408, 547; **42** 373, 376; **50** 134
Race Z, Inc. *See* Action Peformance Companies, Inc.
Rachel's Dairy Ltd., **37** 197–98
Racine Hidraulica, **21** 430
Racine Threshing Machine Works, **10** 377
Racing Champions. *See* Action Performance Companies, Inc.
Racing Champions Corporation, 37 318–20
Racing Collectables Club of America, Inc. *See* Action Performance Companies, Inc.
Racket Store. *See* Duckwall-ALCO Stores, Inc.
Rada Corp., **IV** 250
Radian Group Inc., 42 299–301. *See also* Onex Corporation.
Radiant Lamp Corp., **13** 398
Radio & Television Equipment Company (Radio-Tel), **16** 200–01; **43** 168–69
Radio Austria A.G., **V** 314–16
Radio Cap Company. *See* Norwood Promotional Products, Inc.
Radio City Productions, **30** 102
Radio Corporation of America. *See* RCA Corporation.
Radio Flyer Inc., 34 368–70
Radio-Keith-Orpheum, **9** 247; **12** 73; **31** 99
Radio One, Inc., 67 318–21
Radio Receptor Company, Inc., **10** 319
Radio Shack, **II** 106–08; **12** 470; **13** 174
Radio Vertrieb Fürth. *See* Grundig AG.
Radiocel, **39** 194
Radiometer A/S, **17** 287
Radiometrics, Inc., **18** 369
RadioShack Canada Inc., **30** 391
RadioShack Corporation, 36 384–88 (upd.)
Radiotelevision Española, **7** 511
Radisson Hotels Worldwide, **22** 126–27
Radius Inc., 16 417–19
Radix Group, Inc., **13** 20
Radman Inc., **56** 247
RadNet Managed Imaging Services, Inc., **25** 382–84
Radnor Venture Partners, LP, **10** 474
Raet, **39** 177
Raffinerie Tirlemontoise S.A., **27** 436
Raffineriegesellschaft Vohburg/Ingolstadt mbH, **7** 141

RAG AG, 35 364–67; **60** 247–51 (upd.)
Rag Shops, Inc., 30 365–67
Ragan Outdoor, **27** 280
Ragazzi's, **10** 331
Ragdoll Productions Ltd., 51 308–11
Ragnar Benson Inc., **8** 43–43
Rail Link, Inc., **27** 181
Rail Van Global Logistics, **54** 276
Railroad Enterprises, Inc., **27** 347
RailTex, Inc., 20 445–47
Railtrack Group PLC, 39 238; **50** 369–72
Railway Maintenance Equipment Co., **14** 43
Rainbow Home Shopping Ltd. *See* Otto-Versand (GmbH & Co.).
Rainbow Media, **47** 421
Rainbow Programming Holdings, **7** 63–64
Rainbow Valley Orchards, **54** 257
RainbowBridge Communications, Inc., **25** 162
Raincoast Book Distribution, **34** 5
Rainer Pulp & Paper Company, **17** 439
Rainfair, Inc., **18** 298, 300
Rainforest Café, Inc., 25 386–88; **32** 241, 244
Rainier Brewing Company, 23 403–05
Rainier Pulp and Paper Company. *See* Rayonier Inc.
Rainy River Forest Products, Inc., **26** 445
Rajastan Breweries, Ltd., **18** 502
Raky-Danubia, **IV** 485
Ralcorp Holdings, Inc., **13** 293, 425, 427; **15** 189, 235; **21** 53, 56; **22** 337; **36** 238; **43** 438; **50** 294; **55** 96; **63** 251
Raleigh UK Ltd., 65 295–97
Raley's Inc., 14 396–98; **58** 288–91 (upd.)
Ralli International, **IV** 259
Rally's, 68 25 389–91; 313–16 (upd.)
Rallye SA, 12 154; **54** 306–09; **59** 107
Ralph & Kacoo's. *See* Piccadilly Cafeterias, Inc.
Ralph Lauren. *See* Polo/Ralph Lauren Corportion.
The Ralph M. Parsons Company. *See* The Parsons Corporation.
Ralph Wilson Plastics, **III** 610–11
Ralph's Industries, **31** 191
Ralphs Grocery Company, 35 368–70
Ralston Purina Company, I 608, **II** 560, **561**–63, 617; **7** 209, 396, 547, 556; **8** 180; **9** 180; **12** 276, 411, 510; **13** 137, 270, 293, **425**–27 (upd.); **14** 194–95, 558; **18** 312; **21** 56; **23** 191; **50** 294. *See also* Ralcorp Holdings, Inc.
Ramada International Hotels & Resorts, **IV** 718; **9** 426; **11** 177; **13** 66; **21** 366; **25** 309; **28** 258; **38** 320; **52** 281
Rambol, **25** 84
Rampage Clothing Co., **35** 94
Ramparts, Inc., **57** 159
Ramsay Youth Services, Inc., 41 322–24
Ranbar Packing, Inc. *See* Western Beef, Inc.
Ranbaxy Laboratories Ltd., 70 247–49
Ranchers Packing Corp. *See* Western Beef, Inc.
Rand Capital Corp., **35** 52–53
Rand McNally & Company, 28 378–81; **53** 122
Randall's Food Markets, Inc., 40 364–67
Randgold & Exploration, **63** 182–83

Random House, Inc., 13 113, 115, 178, 428–30; **14** 260; **31** 375–80 (upd.); **42** 287; **54** 17, 22
Randon Meldkamer, 43 307
Randstad Holding n.v., 16 420–22; **43** 307–10 (upd.)
Range Resources Corporation, 45 353–55
The Rank Group plc, II 157–59; **14** 399–402 (upd.); **64** 317–21 (upd.)
Ranks Hovis McDougall Limited, II 564–65; **28** 382–85 (upd.)
Ransburg Corporation, **22** 282
Ransom and Randolph Company, **10** 271
Ransom Industries LP, **55** 266
RAO Unified Energy System of Russia, 45 356–60
Rapala-Normark Group, Ltd., 30 368–71
Rapides Bank & Trust Company, **11** 107
Rapidforms, Inc., **35** 130–31
Rare Hospitality International Inc., 19 340–42
RAS. *See* Riunione Adriatica di Sicurtà SpA.
Rascal House, **24** 243
Raskas Foods, Inc. *See* Shearer's Foods, Inc.
Rathbone Brothers plc, 70 250–53
Ratin A/S, **49** 376
Rational GmbH, **22** 354
Ratner Companies, 72 294–96
Ratti Vallensasca, **25** 312
Raufast et Fils, **35** 205
Rauma-Repola Oy. *See* Metso Corporation
Raumtechnik Messebau & Event Marketing GmbH, **60** 143
Rauscher Pierce Refsnes, Inc., **15** 233
Raven Industries, Inc., 33 359–61
Raven Press, **14** 555
Ravenna Metal Products Corp., **12** 344
Ravensburger AG, 64 322–26
Ravenseft Properties Ltd. *See* Land Securities PLC.
Ravenswood Aluminum Company, **52** 72–73
RAVIcad, **18** 20; **43** 17
Raving Brands, Inc., 64 327–29
Rawlings Sporting Goods Co., Inc., 7 177; **23** 449; **24** 402–04
Rawls Brothers Co., **13** 369
Ray Industries, **22** 116
Ray Simon, **24** 94
Ray Strauss Unlimited, **22** 123
Raychem Corporation, III 492; **8** 446–47; **63** 404; **72** 226
Raymar Book Corporation, **11** 194
Raymond International Inc., **28** 201
Raymond James Financial Inc., 69 308–10
Raymond, Trice & Company, **14** 40
Raynet Corporation, **8** 447
Rayonese Textile, Inc., **29** 140
Rayonier Inc., 24 405–07
Rayovac Corporation, 13 431–34; **17** 105; **23** 497; **24** 480; **39** 336–40 (upd.)
Raytech Corporation, 61 306–09
Raytheon Aircraft Holdings Inc., 46 354–57
Raytheon Company, II 85–87; **8** 51, 157; **11** 411–14 (upd.); **12** 46; **14** 223; **17** 419, 553, 564; **21** 200; **23** 181; **24** 88; **25** 223; **36** 190–91; **38** 372–77 (upd.); **42** 373, 376; **48** 252
Razel S.A., **55** 62

Razorback Acquisitions, **19** 455
Razorfish, Inc., 37 321–24
RB&W Corp., **17** 372
RBC Dominion Securities, **25** 12
RCA Corporation, II 88–90; III 569; **6** 334; **7** 520; **8** 157; **9** 283; **10** 173; **11** 318, 411; **12** 204, 208, 454, 544, 548; **13** 106, 398, 429, 506, 573; **14** 357, 436; **16** 549; **17** 29; **20** 361; **21** 151; **22** 541; **23** 181; **26** 358, 511; **28** 349; **31** 376; **34** 186, 516; **38** 373; **57** 309–10
RCA Global Communications, Inc., **27** 304
RCG International, Inc., **III** 344
RCM Technologies, Inc., 34 371–74
RCN Corporation, 70 254–57
RDMS Direct Marketing BV, **53** 362
RDO Equipment Company, 33 362–65
RE/MAX International, Inc., 59 344–46
REA. *See* Railway Express Agency.
Rea & Derick, **II** 605
Rea Construction Company, **17** 377
React-Rite, Inc., **8** 271
Read-Rite Corp., 10 403–04, **463–64; 18** 250
The Reader's Digest Association, Inc., IV 663–64; **17** 392–95 (upd.); **71 295–99 (upd.)**
Reader's Garden Inc., **22** 441
Reading Etc., **72** 172
Reading International Inc., 70 258–60
Reading Railroad, **9** 407
Ready Mixed Concrete, **28** 82
Real Color Displays, **53** 117
Real Decisions, **21** 236
Real Estate Maintenance, **25** 15
Real Fresh, **25** 85
Real Goods Trading Company, **41** 177
Real-Share, Inc., **18** 542
Real Times, Inc., 66 261–65
Real Turismo, S.A. de C.V., 50 373–75
RealCom Communications Corporation, **15** 196
Realeum, Inc., **58** 11
Reality Group Limited, **47** 165, 169
The Really Useful Group, 23 390; **26** 393–95; **34** 422
RealNetworks, Inc., 53 280–82
Realty Development Co. *See* King Kullen Grocery Co., Inc.
Realty Investment Group, **25** 127
Realty Parking Properties II L.P., **18** 104
Reavis & McGrath, **47** 139
Rebekah W. Harkness Foundation, **52** 199
Recaro North America Inc., **26** 231
Reckitt & Colman plc, II 566–67; 15 46, 360; **18** 556; **22** 148; **27** 69
Reckitt Benckiser plc, 42 302–06 (upd.)
Reckson Associates Realty Corp., 47 329–31
Record Bar / Licorice Pizza, **9** 361
Record Merchandisers. *See* Entertainment UK.
Record World Inc., **9** 361
Recordati S.p.A., **52** 135
Recording for the Blind & Dyslexic, 51 312–14
Recoton Corp., 15 381–83
Recoupe Recycling Technologies, **8** 104
Recovery Centers of America, **III** 88
Recovery Engineering, Inc., 25 392–94
Recreational Equipment, Inc., 18 444–47; 71 300–03 (upd.)
Recticel S.A., **17** 182–84

Recubrimientos Interceramic, S.A. de C.V., **53** 175
Recycled Paper Greetings, Inc., 21 426–28
RED, **44** 164
Red & White, **II** 682
The Red Adair Company, **37** 171
Red Ant Entertainment, **17** 14
Red Apple Group, Inc., 23 406–08; 24 528–29; **31** 231; **68** 180–81
Red Ball, Inc., **18** 300
Red Brick Systems Inc., **30** 246
Red Bull GmbH, 31 244; **60 252–54**
Red Carpet Food Systems, **39** 409
Red Chisinau, **51** 389
Red-E-Food Systems, Inc. *See* Del Taco, Inc.
Red Food Stores, Inc., **19** 327–28
Red Hat, Inc., 45 361–64
Red House Books Ltd., **29** 426
Red Kap. *See* VF Corporation.
Red L Foods, **13** 244
Red Line HealthCare Corporation, **47** 236
Red Lion Entertainment, **29** 503
Red Lobster Inns of America, **16** 156–58
Red Lobster Restaurants, **19** 258
Red Oak Consulting, **42** 244
Red Owl Stores, Inc., **II** 670; **18** 506; **50** 456
Red Pepper Software Co., **59** 77
Red River Commodities, Inc. *See* Deli Universal NV.
Red Robin Gourmet Burgers, Inc., 56 294–96
Red Roof Inns, Inc., 13 363; **18 448–49; 21** 362
Red Rooster, **V** 35
Red Spot Paint & Varnish Company, 55 319–22
Red Star Express, **14** 505
Red Storm, **41** 409
Red Televisiva Megavision S.A., **67** 136–38
The Red Wing Co., Inc., **28** 382; **55** 96, 98
Red Wing Pottery Sales, Inc., 52 294–96
Red Wing Shoe Company, Inc., 9 433–35; 30 372–75 (upd.)
Redbook Florists Service, **28** 138
Redbook Publishing Co., **14** 460
Reddy Ice, **II** 661
Redgate Communications, **26** 19
Redhook Ale Brewery, Inc., 31 381–84
Reditab S.p.A., **12** 109
Redken Laboratories, **8** 131; **24** 251
Redland Plasterboard, **28** 83
Redland plc, III 734–36; 14 249, 739; **15** 154; **37** 205
Redlaw Industries Inc., **15** 247
Redman Industries, Inc., **17** 81, 83
La Redoute, S.A. *See* Pinault-Printemps-Redoute SA.
Redrow Group plc, 31 385–87
Redwood Design Automation, **11** 47; **16** 520
Redwood Fire & Casualty Insurance Co., **III** 214
Redwood Systems, **48** 112
Reebok International Ltd., V 375–77; 8 171, 303–04, 393; **9** 134–35, **436–38** (upd.); **11** 50–51, 349; **13** 513; **14** 8; **17** 244–45, 260; **18** 266; **19** 112; **22** 173; **25** 258, 352, 450; **26 396–400 (upd.); 36** 346
Reed & Barton Corporation, 67 322–24

Reed & Ellis, **17** 439
Reed & Gamage, **13** 243
Reed Elsevier plc, 19 268; **23** 271, 273; **31 388–94 (upd.); 32** 354; **33** 263, 265–66, 458; **34** 438; **43** 92–93
Reed-Hycalog, **57** 162, 164
Reed International PLC, IV 270, 642, **665–67**, 711; **7** 244–45, 343; **10** 407; **12** 359; **17 396–99 (upd.); 23** 350; **49** 408
Reeder Light, Ice & Fuel Company, **6** 592; **50** 38
Reeds Jewelers, Inc., 22 447–49
Reese Finer Foods, Inc., **7** 429
Reese Products, **III** 569; **11** 535; **20** 361
Reeves Banking and Trust Company, **11** 181
Reeves Brothers, **17** 182
Reeves Pulley Company, **9** 440
Refco, Inc., **10** 251; **22** 189
Reference Software International, **10** 558
Refinaria de Petróleo Ipiranga S.A., **67** 216
Reflectone Inc. *See* CAE USA Inc.
Reflex Winkelmann & Pannhoff GmbH, **18** 163
Refractarios Mexicanos, S.A. de C.V., **22** 285
Refrigeração Paraná S.A., **22** 27
Refrigerantes do Oeste, SA, **47** 291
Regal-Beloit Corporation, 18 450–53
Regal Entertainment Group, 59 340–43
Regal Inns, **13** 364
Regal International, **71** 232
Regal Manufacturing Co., **15** 385
Regency Centers Corporation, 71 304–07
Regency Health Services Inc., **25** 457
Regency International, **10** 196
Regeneration Technologies, Inc., **68** 379
Regenerative Environmental Equipment Company, Inc., **6** 441
Regeneron Pharmaceuticals Inc., **10** 80
Regent Carolina Corporation, **37** 226
Regent Communications Inc., **23** 294
Regent International Hotels Limited, **9** 238; **29** 200
Régie Autonome des Pétroles, **IV** 544–46; **21** 202–04
Régie des Télégraphes et Téléphones. *See* Belgacom.
Régie Nationale des Usines Renault, I 145, 148, 178–79, 183, **189–91**, 207, 210; **7** 566–67; **11** 104; **12** 91; **15** 514; **19** 50; **22** 331; **50** 197. *See also* Renault SA.
Regional Bell Operating Companies, **15** 125; **18** 111–12, 373
Regis Corporation, 18 454–56; 70 261–65 (upd.)
Register & Tribune Co. *See* Cowles Media Company.
Regnecentralen AS, **III** 164
Rego Supermarkets and American Seaway Foods, Inc., **9** 451; **13** 237
Rehab Hospital Services Corp., **III** 88; **10** 252
RehabClinics Inc., **11** 367
Rehrig Manufacturing, **51** 35
REI. *See* Recreational Equipment, Inc.
REI Ltd. *See* CB Richard Ellis Group, Inc.
Reich, Landman and Berry, **18** 263
Reichart Furniture Corp., **14** 236
Reichhold Chemicals, Inc., 8 554; **10 465–67**
Reidman Corporation, **41** 65

Reidsville Fashions, Inc., **13** 532
Reiman Publications. *See* The Reader's
  Digest Association, Inc.
Reimersholms, **31** 458–60
Reims Aviation, **8** 92; **27** 100
Rein Elektronik, **10** 459
Reinsurance Agency, **III** 204–05
Reisland GmbH, **15** 340
Reiue Nationale des Usines Renault, **7** 220
Rekkof Restart NV, **28** 327
Relational Courseware, Inc., **21** 235–36
Relational Database Systems Inc., **10**
  361–62
Relational Technology Inc., **10** 361
Relationship Marketing Group, Inc., **37** 409
Release Technologies, **8** 484
Reliable Life Insurance Company, **58** 259
Reliable Stores Inc., **14** 236
Reliance Electric Company, 9 439–42
Reliance Group Holdings, Inc., III
  342–44
Reliance National Indemnity Company, **18**
  159
Reliance Steel & Aluminum Company,
  19 343–45; **70** 266–70 (upd.)
Reliant Energy Inc., 44 368–73 (upd.)
ReLife Inc., **14** 233; **33** 185
Reliv International, Inc., 58 292–95
Relocation Central. *See* CORT Business
  Services Corporation.
Rembrandt Group Ltd., **IV** 93, 97; **50** 144
Remedy Corporation, 58 296–99
RemedyTemp, Inc., 20 448–50
Remgro, **IV** 97
Remington Arms Company, Inc., 12
  415–17; **40** 368–71 (upd.)
Remington Products Company, L.L.C.,
  42 307–10
Remington Rand, **III** 126, 148, 151,
  165–66, 642; **10** 255; **12** 416; **19** 430
Remmele Engineering, Inc., **17** 534
Rémy Cointreau S.A., 20 451–53
Remy Martin, **48** 348–49
REN Corp. USA, Inc., **13** 161
REN Corporation, **49** 156
Renaissance Communications Corp., **22**
  522; **63** 393
Renaissance Connects, **16** 394
Renaissance Cosmetics Inc. *See* New Dana
  Perfumes Co.
Renaissance Energy Ltd., **47** 181
Renaissance Hotel Group N.V., **38** 321
Renaissance Learning Systems, Inc., 39
  341–43
Renal Care Group, Inc., 72 297–99
Renal Systems, Inc. *See* Minntech
  Corporation.
Renault Argentina S.A., 67 325–27
Renault S.A., 26 11, 401–04 (upd.); **34**
  303, 306; **61** 181–82; **63** 302, 304
Rendeck International, **11** 66
Rendic International, **13** 228
René Garraud. *See* Wella AG.
Renfro Corp., **25** 167
Rengo Co., Ltd., IV 326
Renishaw plc, 46 358–60
RENK AG, 37 325–28
Reno Air Inc., 23 409–11; **24** 400; **28** 25
Reno de Medici S.p.A., 41 325–27
Réno-Dépôt Inc., **26** 306
Reno Technologies, **12** 124
Rent-A-Center, Inc., 22 194; **24** 485; **33**
  366, 368; **45** 365–67
Rent-Way, Inc., 33 366–68

Rental Service Corporation, 28 386–88
Renters Choice Inc. *See* Rent-A-Center,
  Inc.
Rentokil Initial Plc, 34 43; **47** 332–35; **49**
  375–77; **64** 197
Rentrak Corporation, 35 371–74
Rentz, **23** 219
Renwick Technologies, Inc., **48** 286
Reo Products. *See* Lifetime Hoan
  Corporation.
Repairmaster Canada, Inc., **53** 359
Repco Ltd., **15** 246
Replacement Enterprises Inc., **16** 380
Repligen Inc., **13** 241
Repola Ltd., **19** 465; **30** 325
Repola Oy, **IV** 316, 347, 350
Repsol S.A., IV 527–29; **16** 423–26
  (upd.); 49 211
Repsol-YPF S.A., 40 372–76 (upd.)
Repubblica, **IV** 587
Republic Airlines, **25** 421; **28** 265
Republic Aviation Corporation, **9** 205–07;
  48 167
Republic Broadcasting Corp., **23** 292
Republic Corp., **I** 447
Republic Engineered Steels, Inc., 7
  446–47 **26** 405–08 (upd.)
Republic Freight Systems, **14** 567
Republic Industries, Inc., 24 12; **26**
  409–11, 501
Republic Insurance, **III** 404
Republic National Bank, **19** 466
Republic New York Corporation, 11
  415–19
Republic Pictures, **9** 75
Republic Powdered Metals, Inc., **8** 454
Republic Steel Corp. *See* Republic
  Engineered Steels, Inc.
Republic Supply Co., **63** 288
Res-Care, Inc., 29 399–402
Research Analysis Corporation, **7** 15
Research Cottrell, Inc., **6** 441
Research Genetics, Inc., **52** 183–84
Research in Motion Ltd., 54 310–14
Research Publications, **8** 526
Réseau Ferré de France, 57 328, 332; **66**
  266–68
Resecenter, **55** 90
Resem SpA, **I** 387
Reserve Mining Co., **17** 356
Reservoir Productions, **17** 150
Residence Inns, **9** 426
Residential Funding Corporation, **10** 92–93
Resin Exchange, **19** 414
ResNet Communications Inc., **28** 241
Resolution Systems, Inc., **13** 201
Resolution Trust Corp., **10** 117, 134; **11**
  371; **12** 368
Resona Holdings Inc., **53** 322
Resorts International, Inc., 12 418–20;
  19 402; **26** 462; **56** 135
Resorts World Bhd. *See* Genting Bhd.
Resource America, Inc., 42 311–14
Resource Associates of Alaska, Inc., **7** 376
The Resource Club, **32** 80
Resource Electronics, **8** 385
Resource Group International, **25** 207
ReSource NE, Inc., **17** 553
reSOURCE PARTNER, INC., **22** 95
Respond Industries, Inc., **51** 76
Response Oncology, Inc., 27 385–87
Restaurant Associates Corporation, 66
  269–72
The Restaurant Company, **22** 417

Restaurant Enterprises Group Inc., **14** 195
Restaurant Property Master, **19** 468
Restaurants Les Pres Limitée, **II** 652
Restaurants Universal Espana S.A., **26** 374
Restaurants Unlimited, Inc., 13 435–37;
  23 127–29
Restoration Hardware, Inc., 30 376–78
Resurgens Communications Group, **7** 336;
  8 311; **27** 306
Retail Association Pskovnefteprodukt, **48**
  378
Retail Concepts Inc., **55** 174
Retail Credit Company. *See* Equifax.
Retail Systems Consulting, Inc., **24** 395
Retail Ventures Inc., **14** 427; **24** 26
Retequattro, **19** 19
Retirement and Health Services
  Corporation, **57** 128
Retirement Care Associates Inc., **25** 457
Retirement Systems of Alabama, **52** 387
Retorte Ulrich Scharrer GmbH, **62** 253
Reuben H. Donnelley Corp. *See* The Dunn
  & Bradstreet Corp.
Reuters Group PLC, 63 323–27 (upd.)
Reuters Holdings PLC, IV 259, 652, 654,
  656, **668–70; 10** 277, 407; **21** 68–70; **22**
  450–53 (upd.); 34 11, 227
Revco D.S., Inc., V 171–73; **9** 67, 187; **12**
  4; **16** 560; **19** 357; **32** 169–70; **45** 136
Revell-Monogram Inc., 16 427–29; **25**
  71; **27** 14
Revere Copper and Brass Co. *See* The Paul
  Revere Corporation.
Revere Foil Containers, Inc., **12** 377
Revere Furniture and Equipment Company,
  14 105; **25** 307
Revere Ware Corporation, 22 454–56
Revlon Inc., III 54–57; **17** 400–04 (upd.);
  64 330–35 (upd.)
Rewards Network Inc., 70 271–75 (upd.)
Rewe-Beteiligungs-Holding National
  GmbH, **53** 179; **54** 295–96
Rewe Group, **37** 241
Rewe-Liebbrand, **28** 152
Rex Pulp Products Company, **9** 304
Rex Re Insurance Ltd., **51** 143
REX Stores Corp., 10 468–69; **19** 362
Rexall Drug & Chemical Co., **13** 525; **14**
  547
Rexall Drug Co., **50** 487
Rexall Sundown, Inc., **37** 340, 342
Rexam PLC, 32 380–85 (upd.); **45** 337;
  50 122
Rexel, Inc., 15 384–87
Rexene Products Co., **IV** 457
Rexham Inc., **IV** 259; **8** 483–84
Rexnord Corporation, 14 43; **21** 429–32;
  37 30; **55** 324
Reycan, **49** 104
Reydel Industries, **23** 95–96
Reyes Holdings, Inc., **24** 388
The Reynolds and Reynolds Company,
  17 142, 144; **50** 376–79
Reynolds Electric Co., **22** 353
Reynolds Metals Company, IV 186–88;
  12 278; **19** 346–48 (upd.); **21** 218; **22**
  455; **25** 22; **56** 9, 11
RF Communications, **II** 38
RF Micro Devices, Inc., 43 311–13
RF Monolithics Inc., **13** 193
RFC Franchising LLC, 68 317–19
RFF. *See* Réseau Ferré de France.
RFI Group, Inc., **54** 275
RGI. *See* Rockefeller Group Inc.

RHC Holding Corp., **10** 13; **13** 364; **27** 11
RHD Holdings, **23** 413
Rheem Manufacturing, **25** 368; **52** 398–99; **71** 269–70
Rheem South Africa Ltd., **59** 226
Rheinische Metallwaaren- und Maschinenfabrik AG, **9** 443–44
Rheinische Zuckerwarenfabrik GmbH, **27** 460
Rheinmetall Berlin AG, 9 443–46
Rheinstahl Union Brueckenbau, **8** 242
Rhenus-Weichelt AG. *See* Schenker-Rhenus AG.
RHI AG, 53 283–86
RHI Entertainment Inc., **16** 257
Rhino Entertainment Company, 18 457–60; **70** 276–80 (upd.)
RHM. *See* Ranks Hovis McDougall.
Rhodes & Co., **8** 345
Rhodes Inc., 23 412–14
Rhodia SA, 38 378–80
Rhône Moulage Industrie, **39** 152, 154
Rhône-Poulenc S.A., I 388–90, 670, 672, 692; **8** 153, 452; **9** 358; **10** 470–72 (upd.); **16** 438; **21** 466; **23** 194, 197; **34** 284; **38** 379
RhoxalPharma Inc., **69** 209
Rhymney Iron Company, **31** 369
Rica Foods, Inc., 41 328–30
Ricardo Gallo. *See* Vidrala S.A.
Riccar, **17** 124; **41** 114
Riccardo's Restaurant, **18** 538
Riceland Foods, Inc., **27** 390
Rich Products Corporation, 7 448–49; **38** 381–84 (upd.)
Rich's Inc., **9** 209; **10** 515; **31** 191
Richard A. Shaw, Inc., **7** 128
Richard D. Irwin Inc. *See* Dow Jones & Company, Inc.
Richard P. Simmons, **8** 19
Richard R. Dostie, Inc. *See* Toll Brothers Inc.
Richards & O'Neil LLP, **43** 70
The Richards Group, Inc., 58 300–02
Richardson Company, **36** 147
Richardson Electronics, Ltd., 17 405–07
Richardson Industries, Inc., 62 298–301
Richardson-Vicks Company. *See* The Procter & Gamble Company
Richardson's, **21** 246
Richfood Holdings, Inc., 7 450–51; **50** 458
Richland Co-op Creamery Company, **7** 592
Richland Gas Company, **8** 349
Richmond American Homes of Florida, Inc., **11** 258
Richmond Carousel Corporation, **9** 120
Richmond Cedar Works Manufacturing Co., **12** 109; **19** 360
Richmond Corp., **15** 129
Richmond Paperboard Corp., **19** 78
Richmond Pulp and Paper Company, **17** 281
Richton International Corporation, 39 344–46
Richtree Inc., 63 328–30
Richway, **10** 515
Richwood Building Products, Inc., **12** 397
Richwood Sewell Coal Co., **17** 357
Rickards, Roloson & Company, **22** 427
Rickel Home Centers, **II** 673
Ricky Shaw's Oriental Express, **25** 181

Ricoh Company, Ltd., III 159–61; **8** 278; **18** 386, 527; **19** 317; **21** 122; **24** 429; **36** 389–93 (upd.)
Ricola Ltd., 62 302–04
Ricolino, **19** 192
Riddarhyttan Resources AB. *See* Agnico-Eagle Mines Limited.
Riddell Inc., **33** 467
Riddell Sports Inc., 22 457–59; **23** 449
Ridder Publications. *See* Knight-Ridder, Inc.
Ride, Inc., 22 460–63
Ridge Tool Co., **II** 19
Ridgewell's Inc., **15** 87
Ridgewood Properties Inc., **12** 394
Ridgway Co., **23** 98
Ridgway Color, **13** 227–28
Ridley Corporation Ltd., 62 305–07
Riedel-de Haën AG, **22** 32; **36** 431
Rieke Corp., **III** 569; **11** 535; **20** 361
The Riese Organization, 38 385–88
Rieter Holding AG, 42 315–17
Riggin & Robbins, **13** 244
Riggs National Corporation, 13 438–40
Right Associates, **27** 21; **44** 156
Right Management Consultants, Inc., 42 318–21
Right Source, Inc., **24** 96
RightPoint, Inc., **49** 124
RightSide Up, Inc., **27** 21
Rijnhaave Information Systems, **25** 21
Rike's, **10** 282
Riken Corp., **10** 493
Riken Kagaku Co. Ltd., **48** 250
Riklis Family Corp., 9 447–50; **12** 87; **13** 453; **38** 169; **43** 355
Rinascente S.p.A., 71 308–10
Ring King Visibles, Inc., **13** 269
Ring Ltd., **43** 99
Ringier America, **19** 333
Ringköpkedjan, **II** 640
Ringling Bros., Barnum & Bailey Circus, **25** 312–13
Ringnes Bryggeri, **18** 396
Rini-Rego Supermarkets Inc., **13** 238
Rini Supermarkets, **9** 451; **13** 237
Rinker Group Ltd., 65 298–301
Rio de Janeiro Refrescos S.A., **71** 140
Rio Grande Industries, Inc., **12** 18–19
Rio Grande Servaas, S.A. de C.V., **23** 145
Rio Sportswear Inc., **42** 269
Rio Sul Airlines. *See* Varig, SA.
Rio Tinto plc, II 628; **IV** 58–61, 189–91, 380; **19** 349–53 (upd.); **21** 352; **27** 253; **42** 395; **50** 380–85 (upd.)
Riocell S.A., **57** 47
Riordan Freeman & Spogli, **13** 406
Riordan Holdings Ltd., **10** 554; **67** 298
Ripotot, **68** 143
Riser Foods, Inc., 9 451–54; **13** 237–38
Risk Management Partners Ltd., **35** 36
Risk Planners, **II** 669
Ritchie Bros. Auctioneers Inc., 41 331–34
Rite Aid Corporation, V 174–76; **9** 187, 346; **12** 221, 333; **16** 389; **18** 199, 286; **19** 354–57 (upd.); **23** 407; **29** 213; **31** 232; **32** 166, 169–70; **63** 331–37 (upd.)
Rite-Way Department Store, **II** 649
Riteway Distributor, **26** 183
Rittenhouse Financial Services, **22** 495
Ritter Co. *See* Sybron Corp.
Ritter Sport. *See* Alfred Ritter GmbH & Co. KG.

Ritter's Frozen Custard. *See* RFC Franchising LLC.
Ritz Camera Centers, 18 186; **34** 375–77
The Ritz-Carlton Hotel Company, L.L.C., 9 455–57; **29** 403–06 (upd.); **71** 311–16 (upd.)
Ritz Firma, **13** 512
Riunione Adriatica di Sicurtà SpA, III 345–48
Riva Group Plc, **53** 46
The Rival Company, 17 215; **19** 358–60
Rivarossi, **16** 337
Rivaud Group, **29** 370
River Boat Casino, **9** 425–26
River City Broadcasting, **25** 418
River North Studios. *See* Platinum Entertainment, Inc.
River Oaks Furniture, Inc., 43 314–16
River Ranch Fresh Foods—Salinas, Inc., **41** 11
River Thames Insurance Co., Ltd., **26** 487
Riverdeep Group plc, **41** 137
Riverside Chemical Company, **13** 502
Riverside Furniture, **19** 455
Riverside Insurance Co. of America, **26** 487
Riverside Iron Works, Ltd., **8** 544
Riverside National Bank of Buffalo, **11** 108
Riverside Press, **10** 355–56
Riverside Publishing Company, **36** 272
Riverwood International Corporation, 7 294; **11** 420–23; **48** 340–44 (upd.)
Riviana Foods, **27** 388–91
Riyadh Armed Forces Hospital, **16** 94
Rizzoli Publishing, **23** 88
RJMJ, Inc., **16** 37
RJR Nabisco Holdings Corp., I 261; **II** 370, 426, 477–78, 542–44; **V** 408–10, 415; **7** 130, 132, 277, 596; **9** 469; **12** 82, 559; **13** 342; **14** 214, 274; **17** 471; **22** 73, 95, 441; **23** 163; **24** 273; **30** 384; **32** 234; **33** 228; **36** 151, 153; **46** 259; **49** 77–78; **56** 190–92; **63** 84. *See also* R.J Reynolds Tobacco Holdings Inc., Nabisco Brands, Inc.; R.J. Reynolds Industries, Inc.
RK Rose + Krieger GmbH & Co. KG, **61** 286–87
RKO. *See* Radio-Keith-Orpheum.
RKO-General, Inc., **8** 207
RLA Polymers, **9** 92
RMC Group p.l.c., III 737–40; **34** 378–83 (upd.)
RMH Teleservices, Inc., 42 322–24
RMP International, Limited, **8** 417
Roadhouse Grill, Inc., 22 464–66; **57** 84
Roadmaster Industries, Inc., 16 430–33; **22** 116
Roadmaster Transport Company, **18** 27; **41** 18
RoadOne. *See* Miller Industries, Inc.
Roadstone-Wood Group, **64** 98
Roadway Express, Inc., 25 395–98 (upd.)
Roadway Services, Inc., V 502–03; **12** 278, 309; **14** 567; **15** 111
Roanoke Capital Ltd., **27** 113–14
Roanoke Electric Steel Corporation, 45 368–70
Roanoke Fashions Group, **13** 532
Robb Engineering Works, **8** 544
Robbins & Myers Inc., 13 273; **15** 388–90
Robeco Group, **26** 419–20

Roberds Inc., 19 361–63
Robert Allen Companies, **III** 571; **20** 362
Robert Benson, Lonsdale & Co. Ltd. *See*
    Dresdner Kleinwort Wasserstein.
Robert Bosch GmbH, I 392–93, 411; **13**
    398; **16** 434–37 (upd.); **22** 31; **43**
    317–21 (upd.); **67** 80–82
Robert E. McKee Corporation, **6** 150
Robert Fleming Holdings Ltd., **I** 471; **11**
    495
Robert Gair Co., **15** 128
Robert Garrett & Sons, Inc., **9** 363
Robert Half International Inc., 18
    461–63; **70** 281–84 (upd.)
Robert Hall Clothes, Inc., **13** 535
Robert Hansen Trucking Inc., **49** 402
Robert Johnson, **8** 281–82
Robert McLane Company. *See* McLane
    Company, Inc.
Robert McNish & Company Limited, **14**
    141
Robert Mondavi Corporation, 15
    391–94; **39** 45; **50** 386–90 (upd.); **54**
    343
Robert Skeels & Company, **33** 467
Robert Stigwood Organization Ltd., **23** 390
Robert W. Baird & Co. Incorporated,
    III 324; **7** 495; **67** 328–30
Robert Watson & Co. Ltd., **I** 568
Robert Wood Johnson Foundation, 35
    375–78
Robertet SA, 39 347–49
Roberts Express, **V** 503
Roberts Pharmaceutical Corporation, 16
    438–40
Roberts Trading Corporation, **68** 99
Robertson Animal Hospital, Inc., **58** 355
Robertson Building Products, **8** 546
Robertson-Ceco Corporation, 8 546; **19**
    364–66
Robertson, Stephens & Co., **22** 465
Robin Hood Flour Mills, Ltd., **7** 241–43;
    25 241
Robin International Inc., **24** 14
Robinair, **10** 492, 494
Robinson & Clark Hardware. *See* Clarcor
    Inc.
Robinson Helicopter Company, 51
    315–17
Robinson Industries, **24** 425
Robinson Smith & Robert Haas, Inc., **13**
    428
Robinson Way, **70** 160–61
Robinson's Japan Co. Ltd. *See* Ito-Yokado
    Co., Ltd.
Robinsons Soft Drinks Limited, **38** 77
Robot Manufacturing Co., **16** 8
Robotic Simulations Limited, **56** 134
Robotic Vision Systems, Inc., **16** 68
ROC. *See* Royal Olympic Cruise Lines Inc.
Roccade, **39** 177
Roch, S.A., **23** 83
Roche Biomedical Laboratories, Inc., 8
    209–10; **11** 424–26. *See also* Laboratory
    Corporation of America Holdings.
Roche Bioscience, 14 403–06 (upd.)
Roche Holding AG, **30** 164; **32** 211,
    213–14; **37** 113; **50** 421
Rocher Soleil, **48** 315
Rochester Gas And Electric
    Corporation, 6 571–73
Rochester Group, Inc., **60** 267
Rochester Instrument Systems, Inc., **16** 357

Rochester Telephone Corporation, 6
    332–34; **12** 136; **16** 221
Röchling Industrie Verwaltung GmbH, **9**
    443
Rock Bottom Restaurants, Inc., 25
    399–401; **68** 320–23 (upd.)
Rock Island Plow Company, **10** 378
Rock of Ages Corporation, 37 329–32
Rock Systems Inc., **18** 337
Rock-Tenn Company, 13 441–43; **59**
    347–51 (upd.)
Rockcor Inc., **I** 381; **13** 380
Rockcote Paint Company, **8** 552–53
The Rockefeller Foundation, 34 384–87;
    52 15
Rockefeller Group International Inc., 58
    303–06
Rocket Chemical Company. *See* WD-40
    Company.
Rockford Corporation, 43 322–25
Rockford Products Corporation, 55
    323–25
Rockhaven Asset Management, LLC, **48**
    18
Rocking Horse Child Care Centers of
    America Inc. *See* Nobel Learning
    Communities, Inc.
Rockland Corp., **8** 271
Rockland React-Rite, Inc., **8** 270
Rockower of Canada Ltd., **II** 649
Rockport Company. *See* Reebok
    International Ltd.
Rockresorts, Inc., **22** 166
RockShox, Inc., 26 412–14; **65** 325–27
Rockwell Automation, 43 326–31 (upd.)
Rockwell International Corporation, I
    78–80; **6** 263; **7** 420; **8** 165; **9** 10; **10**
    279–80; **11** 268, 278, 427–30 (upd.),
    473; **12** 135, 248, 506; **13** 228; **18** 369;
    22 51, 53, 63–64; **32** 81, 84–85; **33** 27;
    35 91; **36** 121–22; **39** 30; **44** 357
Rocky Mexico, Inc., **62** 353
Rocky Mountain Bankcard, **24** 393
Rocky Mountain Financial Corporation, **13**
    348
Rocky River Power Co. *See* Connecticut
    Light and Power Co.
Rocky Shoes & Boots, Inc., 26 415–18
Rod's Food Products, **36** 163
Rodale, Inc., 47 336–39 (upd.)
Rodale Press, Inc., 22 443; **23** 415–17; **54**
    22
Rodamco N.V., IV 698; **26** 419–21
Rodel, Inc., **26** 425
Röder & Co., **34** 38, 40
Rodeway Inns of America, **11** 242; **25** 309
Rodgers Instrument Corporation, **38** 391
Rodney Square Management Corp., **25** 542
Rodven Records, **23** 391
Roederstein GmbH, **21** 520
Roegelein Co., **13** 271
Roger Cleveland Golf Company, **15** 462;
    43 375–76
Roger Williams Foods, **II** 682
Rogers & Co., **63** 17–18
Rogers & Oling, Inc., **17** 533
Rogers & Phillips, Inc., **56** 383
Rogers CanGuard, Inc., **32** 374
Rogers Communications Inc., 30 388–92
    (upd.); **50** 275. *See also* Maclean Hunter
    Publishing Limited.
Rogers Corporation, 61 310–13
Rogue Wave Software, Inc. *See* Quovadix
    Inc.

Rohde & Schwarz GmbH & Co. KG, 39
    350–53
Rohe Scientific Corp., **13** 398
Röhm and Haas Company, I 391–93; **14**
    182–83; **26** 422–26 (upd.)
ROHN Industries, Inc., 22 467–69
Rohölgewinnungs AG, **IV** 485
Rohr Gruppe, **20** 100
Rohr Incorporated, 9 458–60; **11** 165
The Rokke Group, **16** 546; **32** 100; **59** 431
Rokko Warehouse & Transport Co. Ltd.,
    56 181
Rolamentos FAG Ltda., **62** 132
Roland Berger & Partner GmbH, 37
    333–36
Roland Corporation, 38 389–91
Roland Murten A.G., 7 452–53
Roland NV, **41** 340
Rolex. *See* Montres Rolex S.A.
Roll International Corporation, 37
    337–39
Rollerblade, Inc., 15 395–98; **22** 202–03;
    34 388–92 (upd.)
Rolling Stones Records, **23** 33
Rollins Burdick Hunter Company, **III** 204;
    45 27
Rollins, Inc., 11 431–34
Rollo's, **16** 95
Rolls-Royce Allison, 29 407–09 (upd.)
Rolls-Royce Motors Ltd., I 194–96; **9**
    16–18, 417–18; **11** 403; **21** 435
Rolls-Royce plc, I 81–83; **7** 454–57
    (upd.); **9** 244; **11** 268; **12** 190; **13** 414;
    21 433–37 (upd.); **24** 85; **27** 495–96;
    46 358–59; **47** 7, 9
Rolls-Royce Group PLC, 67 331–36
    (upd.)
Rolm Corp., **III** 149; **18** 344; **22** 51; **34**
    512
Rolodex Electronics, **23** 209, 212
Rolscreen. *See* Pella Corporation.
Romacorp, Inc., 58 307–11
Rome Network, Inc., **24** 95
Romeike Ltd., **55** 289
Romper Room Enterprises, Inc., **16** 267
Ron Tonkin Chevrolet Company, 55
    326–28
Ronco, Inc., 15 399–401; **21** 327
Rondel's, Inc., **8** 135
Ronel, **13** 274
Roni-Linda Productions, Inc., **27** 347
Ronnebyredds Trävaru, **25** 463
Ronrico, **58** 195
Ronson PLC, 49 337–39
Ronzoni Foods Corp., **15** 221
Roombar S.A., **28** 241
Rooms To Go Inc., 28 389–92
Rooney Brothers Co., 25 402–04
Roosevelt Hospital. *See* Continuum Health
    Partners, Inc.
Roots Canada Ltd., 27 194; **42** 325–27
Roper Industries, Inc., 15 402–04; **25** 89;
    50 391–95 (upd.)
Ropert Group, **18** 67
Ropes & Gray, 40 377–80
RoProperty Services BV. *See* Rodamco
    N.V.
Rorer Group, I 666–68; **12** 4; **16** 438; **24**
    257
Rosaen Co., **23** 82
Rosarita Food Company, **25** 278
Rose & Co., **26** 65
Rose Acre Farms, Inc., 60 255–57
Rose Art Industries, 58 312–14

Rose Exterminator Company, **25** 15

Rose Forgrove Ltd., **51** 249, 251

Rose Foundation, **9** 348

Rose's Stores, Inc., 13 261, **444–46; 23** 215

Rosebud Dolls Ltd., **25** 312

Roseburg Forest Products Company, 58 315–17

Rosehaugh, **24** 269

RoseJohnson Incorporated, **14** 303; **50** 311

Rosemount Estates. *See* Southcorp Limited.

Rosemount Inc., 13 226; **15 405–08; 46** 171; **61** 98

Rosen Enterprises, Ltd., **10** 482

Rosenbluth International Inc., 14 407–09

Rosenfeld Hat Company. *See* Columbia Hat Company.

Rosengrens Produktions AB, **53** 158

Rosenmund-Guèdu, **31** 158

Rosenthal A.G., **34** 493, 496

Rosewood Financial, Inc., **24** 383

Roshco, Inc., **27** 288

Roslyn Bancorp, **46** 316

Ross Carrier Company, **8** 115

Ross Clouston, **13** 244

Ross Stores, Inc., 17 408–10; 43 332–35 (upd.)

Rossendale Combining Company, **9** 92

Rossignol Ski Company, Inc. *See* Skis Rossignol S.A.

Rostelecom, **59** 208–11

Rostocker Brauerei VEB, **9** 87

Rostvertol plc, 62 308–10

Roswell Public Service Company, **6** 579

Rotadisk, **16** 7

Rotary International, 31 395–97

Rotec Zug AG, **57** 402

Rotelcom Data Inc., **6** 334; **16** 222

Rotem Amfert Negev Ltd., **55** 229

Roth Co., **16** 493

Roth Freres SA, **26** 231; **59** 252

Rothmans International BV, **33** 82

Rothmans International p.l.c., IV 93; **V 411–13; 27** 488

Rothmans UK Holdings Limited, 19 367–70 (upd.)

Rothschild Financial Corporation, **13** 347

Roto-Rooter, Inc., 13 149–50; **15 409–11; 16** 387; **61 314–19 (upd.)**

Rotor Tool Co., **II** 16

Rotork plc, 46 361–64

Rotterdam Beleggings (Investment) Consortium. *See* Robeco.

The Rottlund Company, Inc., 28 393–95

Rouge Steel Company, 8 448–50

Roughdales Brickworks, **14** 249

Rougier. *See* Groupe Rougier, SA.

Roularta Media Group NV, 48 345–47

Round Hill Foods, **21** 535

Round Table, **16** 447

Roundy's Inc., 14 410–12; 58 318–21 (upd.)

Rouse & Associates, **57** 221–23

The Rouse Company, 15 412–15; 63 338–41 (upd.)

Roussel Uclaf, I 669–70; **8 451–53 (upd.); 18** 236; **19** 51; **25** 285; **38** 379

Routh Robbins Companies, **21** 96

Roux Séguéla Cayzac & Goudard. *See* Euro RSCG Worldwide S.A.

Rover Group Ltd., 7 458–60; 11 31, 33; **14** 36; **21 441–44 (upd.); 24** 87–88; **38** 83, 85–86

Rowan Companies, Inc., 43 336–39

Rowe & Pitman, **14** 419

Rowe Price-Fleming International, Inc., **11** 495

Rowell Welding Works, **26** 433

Rowenta. *See* Groupe SEB.

Rowland Communications Worldwide, **42** 328, 331

Rowntree and Co., **27** 104

Rowntree Mackintosh PLC, II 548, **568–70; 7** 383; **28** 311

Roxell, N.V., **43** 129

Roxoil Drilling, **7** 344

Roy and Charles Moore Crane Company, **18** 319

Roy F. Weston, Inc., 33 369–72

Royal & Sun Alliance Insurance Group plc, 55 329–39 (upd.)

Royal Ahold N.V. *See* Koninklijke Ahold N.V.

Royal Appliance Manufacturing Company, 15 416–18; 17 233

The Royal Bank of Canada, II 344–46; **21 445–48 (upd.)**

Royal Bank of Ireland Ltd., **16** 13

The Royal Bank of Scotland Group plc, 10 336–37; **12 421–23; 38** 13, **392–99 (upd.); 42** 76

Royal Bankgroup of Acadiana, Inc., **37** 201

Royal Canin S.A., 39 354–57

Royal Caribbean Cruises Ltd., 22 444–46; **470–73; 27** 29

Royal China and Porcelain Companies Inc. *See* The Porcelain and Fine China Companies Ltd.

Royal Copenhagen A/S, **9** 99

Royal Crown Company, Inc., 8 536–37; **14** 32–33; **23 418–20; 52** 97. *See also* Cott Corporation.

Royal Data, Inc. *See* King Kullen Grocery Co., Inc.

Royal Doulton plc, IV 659; **14 413–15; 34** 497; **38 400–04 (upd.)**

Royal Dutch Petroleum Company, IV 530–32, 657; **24** 496. *See also* Shell Transport and Trading Company p.l.c.

Royal Dutch/Shell Group, IV 530–32; **7** 481–82; **17** 417; **19** 73, 75; **21** 203; **22** 237; **24** 520; **41** 356–57, 359; **49 340–44 (upd.); 57** 152, 237; **59** 372

Royal Exchange Assurance Corp., **III** 369–71, 373

Royal Farms, **24** 528

Royal Food Products, **24** 528–29; **36** 163

Royal Gist-brocades NV, **56** 95

Royal Grolsch NV, 54 315–18

Royal Industries, Inc., **19** 371

Royal Insurance Holdings plc, III 349–51

Royal International Optical Inc. *See* U.S. Vision, Inc.

Royal Interocean Lines. *See* Koninklijke Nedlloyd N.V.

Royal Jackson, **14** 236

Royal KPN N.V., 30 393–95, 461, 463

Royal Mail Group, **6** 416; **19** 198

Royal Nedlloyd. *See* Koninklijke Nedlloyd N.V.

Royal Nepal Airline Corporation, 41 335–38

Royal Netherlands Steamship Company. *See* KNSM.

Royal Numico N.V., 33 145, 147; **37 340–42**

Royal Olympic Cruise Lines Inc., 52 297–99

Royal Orchid Holidays. *See* Thai Airways International.

Royal Ordnance plc, **13** 356; **24** 87–88

Royal Packaging Industries Van Leer N.V., 9 305; **30 396–98; 64** 188

Royal Pakhoed N.V., **9** 532

Royal PTT Post, **30** 463

Royal Robbins, Inc. *See* Phoenix Footwear Group, Inc.

Royal Securities Company, **6** 585

Royal Sporting House Pte. Ltd., **21** 483

Royal Ten Cate N.V., 68 324–26

Royal Vendex KBB N.V. *See* Koninklijke Vendex KBB N.V. (Royal Vendex KBB N.V.).

Royal Vopak NV, 41 339–41

Royal Wessanen. *See* Koninklijike Wessanen.

Royal Worcester Spode Ltd. *See* The Porcelain and Fine China Companies Ltd.

Royale Belge, **III** 177, 200, 394

Royale Inns of America, **25** 307

Royce Electronics, **III** 569; **18** 68; **20** 361

Royce Laboratories Inc., **56** 375

Royster-Clark, Inc., **13** 504

RPB Venture Capital Corporation, **72** 217

RPG (Aventis) S.A. *See* Ranbaxy Laboratories Ltd.

RPI. *See* Research Polymers International.

RPISA. *See* Refinaria de Petróleo Ipiranga S.A.

RPM Inc., 8 454–57; 36 394–98 (upd.); 51 369

RSA Security Inc., 46 365–68; 47 430

RSC. *See* Rental Service Corporation.

RSI Corp., 8 141–42; **30** 160

RSO Records, **23** 390

RSV, **26** 496

RTI Group, **58** 366

RTL Group SA, 41 29; **44 374–78**

RTL-Véeronique, **IV** 611

RTM Restaurant Group, 58 322–24

RTR Funding LLC, **70** 275

RTS Packaging, LLC, **59** 347, 350

RTW Air Service(s) Pte. Ltd., **51** 123

RTZ Corporation PLC, IV 189–92; 7 261, 263; **27** 256. *See also* Rio Tinto plc.

Rubber Latex Limited, **9** 92

Rubbermaid Incorporated, III 613–15; 12 168–69; **13** 317–18; **19** 407; **20** 262, **454–57 (upd.); 21** 293; **28** 479; **31** 160–61; **34** 369. *See also* Newell Rubbermaid Inc.

Rubicon Group plc, **32** 50

Rubio's Restaurants, Inc., 35 379–81

Rubo Lederwaren, **14** 225

Ruby Tuesday, Inc., 18 464–66; 71 317–20 (upd.)

Rubyco, Inc., **15** 386

La Ruche Meridionale, **12** 153

Ruddick Corporation, **23** 260; **72** 163, 165

Rudolf Wolff & Co. Ltd., **64** 297

Ruel Smith Transportation Services, Inc., **39** 66

Ruff Hewn, **25** 48

Rug Corporation of America, **12** 393

The Rugby Group plc, 31 398–400; 34 380

Ruger Corporation, **19** 431

Ruhrgas AG, V 704–06; 38 405–09 (upd.)
Ruhrkohle AG, IV 193–95. *See also* RAG AG.
Ruiz Food Products, Inc., 53 287–89
Rumasa, **69** 165
Runnymede Construction Co., **8** 544
Runo-Everth Treibstoff und Ol AG, **7** 141
Rural Cellular Corporation, 43 340–42
Rural/Metro Corporation, 28 396–98; 39 22
Rush Communications, 33 373–75. *See also* Phat Fashions LLC.
Rush Enterprises, Inc., 64 336–38
Russ Berrie and Company, Inc., 12 424–26
Russell Associates Inc. *See* Pall Corporation.
Russell Corporation, 8 458–59; 30 399–401 (upd.)
Russell Electric, **11** 412
Russell Kelly Office Services, Inc. *See* Kelly Services Inc.
Russell Reynolds Associates Inc., 38 410–12
Russell Stover Candies Inc., 12 427–29
Russian Avionics Design Bureau CJSC, **68** 204
Rust Craft Greeting Cards Incorporated, **12** 561
Rust International Inc., 6 599–600; 11 435–36
Rust-Oleum Corporation, **36** 396
Rütgers AG, **60** 250
Rütgerswerke AG, **8** 81
Ruth's Chris Steak House, 28 399–401; 37 297
Rutherford Hill Winery, **48** 392
RWE Group, V 707–10; 33 194, 196; 50 396–400 (upd.); 59 135–37
RxAmerica, **22** 40; **25** 297
Ryan Aeronautical, **I** 525; **10** 522; **11** 428
Ryan Aircraft Company, **9** 458
Ryan Beck & Co., Inc., 66 273–75
Ryan Homes, Inc. *See* NVR Inc.
Ryan Insurance Company, **III** 204; **45** 26
Ryan Milk Company of Kentucky, **7** 128
Ryan's Family Steak Houses, Inc., 15 419–21; 19 287; **22** 464
Ryan's Restaurant Group, Inc., 68 327–30 (upd.)
Ryanair Holdings plc, 35 382–85
Ryder System, Inc., V 504–06; 13 192; **19** 293; **24 408–11 (upd.); 25** 93, 144; **28** 3; **41** 37
Ryecroft Foods Limited, **61** 387–88
Ryerson Tull, Inc., 19 216; **40** 269, **381–84 (upd.)**
Rykoff-Sexton, Inc., **21** 497; **26** 503, 505
The Ryland Group, Inc., 8 460–61; 19 126; **37 343–45 (upd.)**
Ryobi Ltd., **I** 202
Ryohin Keikaku Co., Ltd., **36** 420
Ryoshoku Ltd., 72 300–02
Rypper Corp., **16** 43
Rysher Entertainment, **22** 162; **25** 329
The Ryvita Company Limited, **II** 466; **13** 52; **41** 31

S&A Restaurant Corp., **7** 336; **10** 176; **14** 331; **15** 363; **38** 100–01
S&C Electric Company, 15 422–24
S&H. *See* Sperry and Hutchinson Co.
S&H Diving Corporation, **6** 578

S&K Famous Brands, Inc., 23 421–23
S&P. *See* Standard & Poor's Corporation.
S&V Screen Inks, **13** 227–28
S&W Fine Foods, **12** 105
S + T Gesellschaft fur Reprotechnik mbH, **29** 306
S.A.C.I. Falabella, 69 311–13
S.A. CARFUEL, **12** 152
S.A. Cockerill Sambre. *See* Cockerill Sambre Group.
S.A. de C.V., **29** 461
S.A. des Ateliers d'Aviation Louis Breguet. *See* Groupe Dassault Aviation SA.
s.a. GB-Inno-BM. *See* GIB Group.
S.A. Greetings Corporation, **22** 35
S.A. Innovation—Bon Marché N.V., **26** 160
S.A. Schonbrunn & Co., **14** 18
S.B. Irving Trust Bank Corp., **II** 218
S.B. Penick & Co., **8** 548
S.C. Johnson & Son, Inc., III 58–59; 8 130; **10** 173; **12** 126–28; **17** 215; **21** 386; **28** 215, **409–12 (upd.)**
S-C-S Box Company, **8** 173
S.D. Cohn & Company, **10** 455; **27** 364
S.E. Rykoff & Co., **26** 503
S.G. Warburg and Co. *See* SBC Warburg.
S. Grumbacher & Son. *See* The Bon-Ton Stores, Inc.
S.H. Kress & Co., **17** 203–04
S.I.P., Co., **8** 416
S-K-I Limited, 15 457–59
S.K. Wellman Ltd., **14** 81; **59** 222
S. Kuhn & Sons, **13** 221
S.P. Richards Co., **45** 177–79
S Pearson & Son Ltd. *See* Pearson plc
S.R. Dresser Manufacturing Co. *See* Dresser Industries, Inc.
S.S. Kresge Company. *See* Kmart Corporation.
S.S. Pierce Company, **60** 267
S.S.V. Inc., **36** 420
S.T. Cooper & Sons, **12** 283
S.T. Dupont Company, **23** 55
S.W.M. Chard, **27** 259
SA Alliance Air, **28** 404
SA Express, **28** 404
Sa SFC NV, **18** 162–63
SAA. *See* South African Airways.
SAA (Pty) Ltd., 28 402–04
SAAB. *See* Svenska Aeroplan Aktiebolaget.
Saab Automobile AB, 32 386–89 (upd.); 36 242–43; **63** 211; **64** 150
Saab-Scania A.B., **I** 197–98, 210; **10** 86; **11 437–39 (upd.); 16** 322; **34** 117
Saarberg-Konzern, IV 196–99. *See also* RAG AG.
Saarstahl AG, **IV** 228
Saatchi & Saatchi plc, I 33–35; 6 229; **14** 49–50; **16** 72; **21** 236; **22** 296; **33** 65, 67; **328–31 (upd.); 64** 351
SAB. *See* South African Breweries Ltd.
SAB WABCO International AB, **53** 85
Saban Entertainment, **24** 171
Sabanci Group, **54** 197–98
Sabanci Holdings. *See* Haci Omer Sabanci Holdings A.S.
Sabaté Diosos SA, 48 348–50
Sabela Media, Inc., **49** 423
Sabena S.A./N.V., 18 80; **33** 49, 51, **376–79; 34** 398
Saber Energy, Inc., **7** 553–54
Saber Software Corp., **25** 348

Sabi International Ltd., **22** 464
Sabian Ltd., **38** 68
SABIC. *See* Saudi Basic Industries Corporation.
SABIM Sable, **12** 152
Sabine Transportation Company. *See* Kirby Corporation.
SABMiller plc, 59 352–58 (upd.)
SABO Maschinenfabrik AG, **21** 175
Sabratek Corporation, 29 410–12
SABRE Group Holdings, Inc., 25 144; **26 427–30; 28** 22; **52** 23
Sabre Interactive, **46** 434
Sacer, **31** 127–28
Sach Bicycle Components. *See* SRAM Corporation.
Sachs-Dolmer G.m.b.H., **22** 334
Sacilor. *See* Usinor S.A.
Sacks Industries, **8** 561
OY Saco AB, **23** 268
SACOR, **IV** 250, 504–06
Sacramento Savings & Loan Association, **10** 43, 45
Saddlebag Lake Resorts, Inc., **63** 23
SADE Ingenieria y Construcciones S.A., **38** 435, 437
Sadia S.A., 59 359–62
SAE Magnetics Ltd., **18** 250
Safe Flight Instrument Corporation, 71 321–23
SAFECO Corporation, III 352–54; 10 44
Safeguard Scientifics, Inc., 10 232–34, 473–75; 27 338
Safelite Glass Corp., 19 371–73
Safer, Inc., **21** 385–86
Safeskin Corporation, 18 467–70
Safety Components International, Inc., 63 342–44
Safety 1st, Inc., 24 412–15; 46 192; **59** 164
Safety-Kleen Corp., 8 462–65
Safety Rehab, **11** 486
Safety Savings and Loan, **10** 339
Safeway Inc., II 654–56; 24 273, **416–19 (upd.)**
Safeway PLC, 50 401–06 (upd.)
Saffa SpA, **41** 325–26
Saffil Ltd. *See* Dyson Group PLC.
Safilo SpA, 40 155–56; 54 319–21
SAFR. *See* Société Anonyme des Fermiers Reúnis.
Saga. *See* Sociedad Andina de Grandes Almeneces.
Saga Communications, Inc., II 608; **27** 226, **392–94**
Saga Petroleum ASA, **35** 318
Sagami Optical Co., Ltd., **48** 295
Sagamore Insurance Company, **51** 37–39
The Sage Group, 43 343–46
Sagebrush Sales, Inc., **12** 397
Sagebrush Steakhouse, **29** 201
SAGEM S.A., 37 346–48
Saginaw Dock & Terminal Co., **17** 357
Sagitta Arzneimittel, **18** 51; **50** 90
Sahara Casino Partners L.P., **19** 379
Sahara Resorts. *See* Santa Fe Gaming Corporation.
SAI. *See* Stamos Associates Inc.
Sai Baba, **12** 228
Saia Motor Freight Line, Inc., **6** 421–23; **45** 448
Saibu Gas, **IV** 518–19
SAIC. *See* Science Applications International Corporation.

SAIC Velcorex, **12** 153; **27** 188
Saiccor, **IV** 92; **49** 353
Sainrapt et Brice, **9** 9
Sainsbury's. *See* J Sainsbury PLC.
St. Alban Boissons S.A., **22** 515
St. Andrews Insurance, **III** 397
Saint-Gobain. *See* Compagnie de Saint
  Gobain S.A.
Saint-Gobain Weber. *See* Weber et Broutin
  France.
St. Ives Laboratories Inc., **36** 26
St Ives plc, 34 393–95
St. James Associates, **32** 362–63
St. James's Place Capital, plc, 71 324–26
The St. Joe Company, 31 422–25
St. Joe Corporation, **59** 185
St. Joe Gold, **23** 40
St. Joe Minerals Corp., **8** 192
St. Joe Paper Company, 8 485–88
St. John Knits, Inc., 14 466–68
St. Jude Medical, Inc., 11 458–61; 43
  347–52 (upd.)
St. Laurent Paperboard Inc., **30** 119
St. Lawrence Cement Inc., **III** 702; **8**
  258–59
Saint Louis Bread Company, **18** 35, 37; **44**
  327
St. Louis Concessions Inc., **21** 39
St. Louis Music, Inc., 48 351–54
St. Louis Post-Dispatch LLC, **58** 283
St. Luke's-Roosevelt Hospital Center. *See*
  Continuum Health Partners, Inc.
St. Martin's Press, **25** 484–85; **35** 452
St. Mary Land & Exploration Company,
  60 189; **63 345–47**
St. Michel-Grellier S.A., **44** 40
St. Paul Bank for Cooperatives, 8
  489–90
St. Paul Book and Stationery, Inc., **47** 90
The St. Paul Companies, III 355–57; 15
  257; **21** 305; **22** 154, **492–95 (upd.)**
St. Paul Fire and Marine Insurance Co. *See*
  The St. Paul Companies, Inc.
St. Paul Venture Capital Inc., **34** 405–06
St. Regis Paper Co., **10** 265; **12** 377
Saipem S.p.A. *See* ENI S.p.A.
SAirGroup, **29** 376; **33** 268, 271; **37** 241;
  46 398; **47** 287
SAirLogistics, **49** 80–81
Saison Group, **V** 184–85, 187–89; **36**
  417–18, 420; **42** 340–41
Sakae Printing Co., Ltd., **64** 261
Sako Ltd., **39** 151
Saks Fifth Avenue, **15** 291; **18** 372; **21**
  302; **22** 72; **25** 205; **27** 329; **50** 117–19;
  57 179–80
Saks Holdings, Inc., 24 420–23
Saks Inc., 41 342–45 (upd.)
Sakura Bank. *See* Sumitomo Mitsui
  Banking Corporation.
Salant Corporation, 12 430–32; 27 445;
  51 318–21 (upd.)
Sale Knitting Company. *See* Tultex
  Corporation.
Salem Broadcasting, **25** 508
Salem Carpet Mills, Inc., **9** 467
Salem Sportswear, **25** 167
Salick Health Care, Inc., 21 544, 546; **50**
  58; **53 290–92**
Salient Partners & Pinnacle Trust Co., **70**
  287
Salim Group, **18** 180–81
Salinas Equipment Distributors, Inc., **33**
  364

Sallie Mae. *See* SLM Holding Corp.;
  Student Loan Marketing Association.
Sally Beauty Company, Inc., 8 15–17; **36**
  23–26; **60 258–60**
Salmon River Power & Light Company, **12**
  265
Salomon Brothers Inc., **28** 164
Salomon Inc., II 426, 432, 434, 441,
  447–49; III 221, 215, 721; **IV** 137; **7**
  114; **9** 378–79, 386; **11** 35, 371; **13** 331,
  447–50 (upd.) Inc.; **18** 60, 62; **19** 293;
  21 67; **22** 102; **23** 472–74; **25** 12, 125;
  42 34
Salomon Smith Barney, **30** 124
Salomon Worldwide, 20 458–60; 33 7.
  See also adidas-Salomon AG.
Salon Cielo and Spa. *See* Ratner
  Companies.
Salon Plaza. *See* Ratner Companies.
Salt River Project, 19 374–76
Salton, Inc., 30 402–04
Salvagnini Company, **22** 6
The Salvation Army USA, 15 510–11; **32**
  390–93
Salvatore Ferragamo Italia S.p.A., 62
  311–13
Salzgitter AG, IV 200–01; 17 381
SAM. *See* Sociedad Aeronáutica de
  Medellín, S.A.
Sam & Libby Inc., **30** 311
Sam Ash Music Corporation, 30 405–07
Sam Goody, **9** 360–61; **63** 65
Sam's Club, 8 555–57; **12** 221, 335; **13**
  548; **14** 393; **15** 470; **16** 64; **25** 235; **40**
  385–87; 41 254–56
Samancor Ltd., **IV** 92–93
Samaritan Senior Services Inc., **25** 503
Samas-Groep N.V., **47** 91
Sambo's, **12** 510
Samcor Glass. *See* Corning Inc.
Samedan Oil Corporation, **11** 353
Sames, S.A., **21** 65–66
Samick Musical Instruments Co., Ltd.,
  56 297–300
Samim, **IV** 422
Sammy Corp., **54** 16
Samna Corp., **6** 256; **25** 300
Sampoerna PT, **62** 96–97
Sampson's, **12** 220–21
Samson Technologies Corp., **30** 406
Samsonite Corporation, 13 311, 451–53;
  16 20–21; **38** 169; **43 353–57 (upd.)**
Samsung-Calex, **17** 483
Samsung Display Co., Ltd., **59** 81
Samsung Electronics Co., Ltd., 14
  416–18; 18 139, 260; **41 346–49 (upd.)**
Samsung Group, I 515–17; 13 387; **29**
  207–08; **62** 68–69
Samuel Austin & Son Company, **8** 41
Samuel Cabot Inc., 53 293–95
Samuel Meisel & Company, Inc., **11**
  80–81; **29** 509, 511
Samuel, Son & Co. Ltd., **24** 144
Samuels Jewelers Incorporated, 30
  408–10
San Antonio Public Service Company. *See*
  City Public Service.
San Diego Gas & Electric Company, V
  711–14; 6 590; **11** 272; **25** 416. *See also*
  Sempra Energy.
San Francisco Baseball Associates, L.P.,
  55 340–43
San Francisco Maillots, **62** 228

San Francisco Mines of Mexico Ltd., **22**
  285
San Gabriel Light & Power Company, **16**
  496; **50** 496
San Giorgio Macaroni Inc., **53** 242
San Jose Water Company. *See* SJW
  Corporation.
San Miguel Corporation, 15 428–30; 23
  379; **57 303–08 (upd.); 63** 227
San Paolo IMI S.p.A., **63** 52–53
Sanborn Hermanos, S.A., 20 461–63; 21
  259
Sanborn Manufacturing Company, **30** 138
The Sanctuary Group PLC, 69 314–17
Sandals Resorts International, 65 302–05
Sandcastle 5 Productions, **25** 269–70
Sanders Associates, Inc., **9** 324; **13** 127–28
Sanders Morris Harris Group Inc., 70
  285–87
Sanderson Computers, **10** 500
Sanderson Farms, Inc., 15 425–27
Sandia National Laboratories, 49 345–48
Sandiacre Packaging Machinery Ltd., **51**
  249–50
Sandoz Ltd., I 671–73; 7 315, 452; **8**
  108–09, 215; **10** 48, 199; **11** 173; **12**
  388; **15** 139; **18** 51; **22** 475; **27** 299; **50**
  90. *See also* Novartis AG.
Sandoz Nutrition Corp., **24** 286
SandPoint Corp., **12** 562; **17** 254
Sandusky Plastics, Inc., **17** 157
Sandusky Portland Cement Company, **24**
  331
Sandvik AB, IV 202–04; 32 394–98
  (upd.)
Sandwell, Inc., **6** 491
Sandwich Chef, Inc. *See* Wall Street Deli,
  Inc.
Sandy's Pool Supply. *See* Leslie's
  Poolmart, Inc.
Sanford C. Bernstein Inc., **63** 27
Sanford-Brown College, Inc., **41** 419–20
Sanichem Manufacturing Company, **16** 386
Sanitary Farm Dairies, Inc., **7** 372
Sanitation Systems, Inc. *See* HMI
  Industries.
Sanitec Corporation, 51 322–24
Sanko Peterson Corporation, **55** 306
Sankyo Company, Ltd., I 674–75; 56
  301–04 (upd.)
Sanlam Ltd., 68 331–34
SANlight Inc., **62** 293
Sano Corporation, **63** 142
Sanofi Group, I 676–77; 21 205; **23** 236,
  238, 242; **35** 262–63, 265
The Sanofi-Synthélabo Group, 49 349–51
  (upd.)
SanomaWSOY Corporation, 51 325–28
Sanpaolo IMI S.p.A., 50 407–11
Sanrio Company, Ltd., 38 413–15
Sansone Group, **69** 120
Santa Ana Savings and Loan, **10** 339
Santa Ana Wholesale Company, **16** 451
Santa Barbara Restaurant Group, Inc.,
  37 349–52
The Santa Cruz Operation, Inc., 38
  416–21
Santa Fe Gaming Corporation, 19
  377–79
Santa Fe Gold Corporation, **38** 232
Santa Fe Industries, **12** 19; **28** 498
Santa Fe International Corporation, 38
  422–24

Santa Fe Pacific Corporation, **V 507–09**; **24** 98. *See also* Burlington Northern Santa Fe Corporation.
Santa Fe Railway, **12** 278; **18** 4
Santa Fe Snyder Corp., **61** 75
Santa Fe Southern Pacific Corp., **III** 512; **6** 150, 599; **22** 491
Santa Isabel S.A., **69** 94
Santa Margherita S.p.A. *See* Industrie Zignago Santa Margherita S.p.A.
Santa Rosa Savings and Loan, **10** 339
Santal, **26** 160
Santiago Land Development Corporation, **58** 20
Santone Industries Inc., **16** 327
Sanus Corp. Health Systems, **III** 317
Sanwa Bank, Ltd., **II 347–48**; **15** 43, **431–33 (upd.)**
Sanwa USA Inc., **70** 213
Sanyo Chemical Manufacturing Co., **III** 758
Sanyo Electric Co., Ltd., **II 91–92**; **III** 569; **14** 535; **20** 361; **36 399–403 (upd.)**
Sanyo-Kokusaku Pulp Co., Ltd., **IV 327–28**
Sanyo Semiconductor, **17** 33
Sanyo White Cement Co. Ltd., **60** 301
SAP AG, **11** 78; **16 441–44**; **25** 34; **26** 496, 498; **43 358–63 (upd.)**
SAP America Inc., **38** 431–32
SAPAC. *See* Société Parisienne d'Achats en Commun.
Sapeksa, **55** 189
Sapirstein Greeting Card Company. *See* American Greetings Corporation.
Sappi Limited, **49 352–55**
Sapporo Breweries Limited, **I 282–83**; **13 454–56 (upd.)**; **20** 28–29; **21** 319–20; **36 404–07 (upd.)**; **52** 32
SAPRA-Landauer Ltd., **51** 210
Saputo Inc., **59 363–65**
Sara Lee Corporation, **II 571–73**; **15 434–37 (upd.)**; **54 322–27 (upd.)**; **63** 218
Saracen's Head Brewery, **21** 245
Saratoga Partners, **24** 436
Sarawak Trading, **14** 448
Sargent & Lundy, **6** 556
SARL, **12** 152
Sarma, **26** 159–61
Sarmag, **26** 161
Sarnoff Corporation, **57 309–12**, 333, 335
Saros Corp., **15** 474; **62** 141
Sarotti GmbH, **53** 315
Sarpe, **IV** 591
Sarrió S.A., **41** 325–26
Sartek Industries Inc., **44** 441
The SAS Group, **34 396–99 (upd.)**
SAS Institute Inc., **10 476–78**; **38** 432; **64** 361
Saskatchewan Oil and Gas Corporation, **13** 556–57
Sasol Limited, **IV 533–35**; **47 340–44 (upd.)**
Sasu Ldc Sable, **68** 234
SAT. *See* Stockholms Allmänna Telefonaktiebolag.
Satcom Group of Companies, **32** 40
Satellite Business Systems, **21** 14; **23** 135; **27** 304
Satellite Software International, **10** 556
Satellite Television PLC, **23** 135

Satellite Transmission and Reception Specialist Company, **11** 184
Saturn Corporation, **7 461–64**; **21 449–53 (upd.)**; **22** 154; **36** 242; **64** 150
Saturn Industries, Inc., **23** 489
SATV. *See* Satellite Television PLC.
Satyam, **59** 129
Saucona Iron Co., **7** 48
Saucony Inc., **35 386–89**
Sauder Woodworking Co., **12 433–34**; **35 390–93 (upd.)**
Saudi Arabian Airlines, **6 114–16**; **27** 132, **395–98 (upd.)**
Saudi Arabian Oil Company, **IV 536–39**; **17 411–15 (upd.)**; **50 412–17 (upd.)**. *See also* Arabian American Oil Co.
Saudi Arabian Parsons Limited, **8** 416
Saudi Basic Industries Corporation (SABIC), **58 325–28**
Saudi Refining Inc., **IV** 539; **17** 414
Saudia. *See* Saudi Arabian Airlines.
Sauer-Danfoss Inc., **61 320–22**
Saunders, Karp, and Megrue, LP, **26** 190; **28** 258; **70** 121
Sauza, **31** 92
Sav-on Drug, **II** 605; **12** 477
Sav-X, **9** 186
Sava Group, **20** 263
Savacentre Ltd., **II** 658; **13** 284
Savage, **19** 430
Savannah Electric & Power Company, **38** 448
Savannah Foods & Industries, Inc., **7 465–67**; **32** 274, 277; **35** 178
Savannah Gas Company, **6** 448; **23** 29
Save & Prosper Group, **10** 277
Save-A-Lot, **II** 682; **11** 228
Save Mart, **14** 397; **27** 292
Save.com, **37** 409
Savia S.A. de C.V., **29** 435
Savio, **IV** 422
Oy Savo-Karjalan Tukkuliike, **8** 293
Savoy Group, **24** 195
Savoy Industries, **12** 495
Savoy Pictures Entertainment Inc., **25** 214
Sawdust Pencil Company, **29** 372
Sawgrass Asset Management, LLC, **48** 18
Sawhill Tubular Products, **41** 3
Sawtek Inc., **43 364–66 (upd.)**; **63** 398
Sawyer Electrical Manufacturing Company, **11** 4
Sawyer Industries, Inc., **13** 532
Sawyer Research Products, Inc., **14** 81
Saxby, S.A., **13** 385
Saxon Oil, **11** 97
Saxon Petroleum, Inc., **19** 162
Saxonville USA, **61** 254, 256
SB Acquisitions, Inc., **46** 74
SBAR, Inc., **30** 4
Sbarro, Inc., **16 445–47**; **19** 435; **27** 146; **64 339–42 (upd.)**
SBC Communications Inc., **32 399–403 (upd.)**
SBC Transportation, Inc. *See* Schwebel Baking Company.
SBC Warburg, **14 419–21**; **15** 197
SBC Warburg Dillon Read, **52** 355
Sberbank, **62 314–17**
SBI. *See* State Bank of India.
SBK Entertainment World, Inc., **22** 194; **24** 485; **26** 187
SBM Group, **71** 178–79
SBS Broadcasting, **61** 58
SBS Technologies, Inc., **25 405–07**

SCA. *See* Svenska Cellulosa AB.
SCA Services, Inc., **9** 109
SCAC. *See* Société Commercial d'Affrètements et de Combustibles.
Scaldia Paper BV, **15** 229
Scali, McCabe & Sloves, **71** 158
Scan Screen, **IV** 600
SCANA Corporation, **6 574–76**; **19** 499; **56 305–08 (upd.)**
Scanair, **34** 397–98
Scancem, **38** 437
Scandic Hotels AB, **49** 193
Scandinavian Airlines System, **I 119–20**, 121; **25** 159; **26** 113; **27** 26; **31** 305; **33** 50; **38** 105. *See also* The SAS Group.
Scandinavian Broadcasting System SA, **53** 325
ScanDust, **III** 625
Scania-Vabis. *See* Saab-Scania AB.
ScanSource, Inc., **29 413–15**
Scantron Corporation, **17** 266–68
Scarborough Public Utilities Commission, **9 461–62**
Scaturro Supermarkets, **24** 528
SCB Computer Technology, Inc., **29 416–18**
SCEcorp, **V 715–17**; **6** 590. *See also* Edison International.
Scenic Airlines, Inc., **25** 420, 423
Scenographic Designs, **21** 277
SCG Corporation, **56** 323
Schäfer, **31** 158
Schaper Mfg. Co., **12** 168
Schauman Wood Oy, **IV** 277, 302
Schawk, Inc., **24 424–26**
SCHC, Inc. *See* Shoe Carnival Inc.
Scheels All Sports Inc., **63 348–50**
Scheid Vineyards Inc., **66 276–78**
Schein Pharmaceutical Inc., **13** 77; **56** 375
Schell Brewing. *See* August Schell Brewing Company Inc.
Schenker Deutschland AG, **59** 391
Schenker-Rhenus Ag, **6 424–26**
Schenley Distilleries Inc., **68** 99
Schenley Industries Inc., **9** 449; **24** 140
Scherer. *See* R.P. Scherer.
Schering A.G., **I 681–82**, 684, 701; **10** 214; **14** 60; **16** 543; **36** 92, 148; **50 418–22 (upd.)**
Schering-Plough Corporation, **I 683–85**; **11** 142, 207; **14** 58, 60, **422–25 (upd.)**; **36** 91–92; **45** 382; **49 356–62 (upd.)**; **63** 232–33
Schiavi Homes, Inc., **14** 138
Schibsted ASA, **31 401–05**
Schick Products, **41** 366
Schick Shaving, **38** 363, 365
Schick-Wilkinson Sword. *See* Wilkinson Sword Ltd.
Schieffelin & Somerset Co., **61 323–25**
Schindler Holding AG, **27** 267; **29 419–22**
Schlitz Brewing Co., **I** 255, 268, 270, 291, 600; **10** 100; **12** 338; **18** 500; **23** 403
Schlotzsky's, Inc., **36 408–10**
Schlumberger Limited, **III 616–18**; **13** 323; **17 416–19 (upd.)**; **25** 191; **43** 91, 338; **45** 418; **49** 305; **59** 217, **366–71 (upd.)**
SchlumbergerSema. *See* Atos Origin S.A.
Schmalbach-Lubeca-Werke A.G., **15** 128
Schmermund Verpackungstechnik GmbH, **60** 193
Schmid, **19** 166

Schmitt Music Company, 40 388–90
Schneider National, Inc., 36 411–13; **47** 318–19; **63** 237
Schneider S.A., II 93–94; **18** 471–74 (upd.); **19** 165–66; **37** 39
Schneiderman's Furniture Inc., 28 405–08
Schnitzer Steel Industries, Inc., 19 380–82
Schnoll Foods, **24** 528
Schnuck Markets, Inc., **60** 256; **63** 129
Schober Direktmarketing, **18** 170
Schocken Books, **13** 429
Schoeller & Co. Bank AG, **59** 239
Schoeller & Hoesch Group, **30** 349, 352
Schoenfeld Industries, **16** 511
Scholastic Corporation, 10 479–81; **29** 143, **423–27 (upd.)**
Scholl Inc., **49** 359, 380
Schöller, **27** 436, 439
School Specialty, Inc., 68 335–37
School-Tech, Inc., 62 318–20
Schorghuber, **70** 61
Schott Brothers, Inc., 67 337–39
Schott Corporation, 53 296–98
Schottenstein Stores Corp., 14 426–28; **19** 108; **24** 26; **38** 475. *See also* American Eagle Outfitters, Inc.
Schreiber Foods, Inc., 72 303–06
Schreiber Frères. *See* Groupe Les Echos.
Schrock Cabinet Company, **13** 564
Schroders plc, 42 332–35
Schroders Ventures, **18** 345
Schroff Inc., **26** 361, 363
Schubach, **30** 408
Schubert & Salzer GmbH, **42** 316
Schuck's Auto Supply. *See* CSK Auto Corporation.
Schuff Steel Company, 26 431–34
Schuitema, **II** 642; **16** 312–13
Schuler Chocolates, **15** 65
Schuler Homes, Inc., **58** 84
Schuller International, Inc., **11** 421
Schultz Sav-O Stores, Inc., 21 454–56; **31** 406–08
Schultz, Snyder & Steele Lumber Company, **61** 254, 256
Schuykill Energy Resources, **12** 41
Schwabe-Verlag, **7** 42
Schwabel Corporation, **19** 453
Schwan's Sales Enterprises, Inc., 7 468–70; **26** 435–38 (upd.)
Schwartz Iron & Metal Co., **13** 142
Schwarze Pumpe, **38** 408
Schwebel Baking Company, 72 307–09
Schweitzer-Mauduit International, Inc., 16 304; **43** 258; **52** 300–02
Schweizerische Post-, Telefon- und Telegrafen-Betriebe, V 321–24
Schweizerische Ruckversicherungs-Gesellschaft. *See* Swiss Reinsurance Company.
Schweppes Ltd. *See* Cadbury Schweppes PLC.
Schwinn Cycle and Fitness L.P., 16 494; **19** 383–85; **26** 412; **47** 95
The Schwinn GT Co., **26** 185
Schwitzer, **II** 420
SCI. *See* Service Corporation International; Société Centrale d'Investissement.
SCI 169 Rue de Rennes, **53** 32
SCI Systems, Inc., 9 463–64; **12** 451
Scicon International, **14** 317; **49** 165
SciCor Inc., **30** 152

Science Applications International Corporation, 15 438–40; **59** 399–400
Scientific-Atlanta, Inc., 6 335–37; **45** 371–75 (upd.); **54** 406
Scientific Communications, Inc., **10** 97
Scientific Data Systems, **10** 365
Scientific Games Corporation, 20 48; **64** 343–46 (upd.)
Scientific Materials Company, **24** 162
Scientific Research Products, Inc. of Delaware, **60** 287
Scioto Bank, **9** 475
Scitex Corporation Ltd., 15 148, 229; **24** 427–32; **26** 212; **43** 150; **48** 123
Scitor, **52** 108
SCLC, Inc. *See* Shoe Carnival Inc.
SCM Corp., **8** 223–24; **17** 213
SCO. *See* Santa Cruz Operation, Inc.
SCOA Industries, Inc., **13** 260
Scopus Technology Inc., **38** 431
SCOR S.A., III 394; **20** 464–66
The Score Board, Inc., 19 386–88
Score Entertainment. *See* Donruss Playoff L.P.
Score! Learning, Inc., **42** 211
Scot Lad Foods, **14** 411
Scotch House Ltd., **19** 181
Scotia Securities, **II** 223
Scotiabank. *See* The Bank of Nova Scotia.
Scotsman Industries, Inc., II 420; **16** 397; **20** 467–69
Scott-Ballantyne Company. *See* Ballantyne of Omaha, Inc.
Scott Communications, Inc., **10** 97
Scott Fetzer Company, III 214; **12** 435–37, 554–55; **17** 233; **18** 60, 62–63; **42** 33
Scott Graphics, **8** 483
Scott Health Care, **28** 445
Scott Holdings, **19** 384
Scott Paper Company, IV 325, 327, 329–31; **8** 483; **16** 302, 304; **17** 182; **18** 181; **29** 333; **31** 409–12 (upd.); **43** 258
Scott Transport, **27** 473
Scotti Brothers, **20** 3
Scottish & Newcastle plc, 15 441–44; **35** 394–97 (upd.); **50** 201, 277; **59** 255, 296, 299
Scottish and Southern Energy plc, 66 279–84 (upd.)
Scottish Amicable plc, **48** 328
Scottish Brick, **14** 250
Scottish Electric, **6** 453
Scottish Hydro-Electric PLC, 13 457–59. *See also* Scottish and Southern Energy plc.
Scottish Inns of America, Inc., **13** 362
Scottish Media Group plc, 32 404–06; **41** 350–52
Scottish Mutual plc, **39** 5–6
Scottish Nuclear, Ltd., **19** 389
Scottish Power plc, 49 363–66 (upd.)
Scottish Radio Holding plc, 41 350–52
Scottish Sealand Oil Services Ltd., **25** 171
Scottish Universal Investments, **45** 189
ScottishPower plc, 19 389–91; **27** 483, 486
ScottishTelecom plc, **19** 389
The Scotts Company, 22 474–76; **68** 343, 345
Scotty's, Inc., 12 234; **22** 477–80; **26** 160–61
Scovill Fasteners Inc., 22 364; **24** 433–36
SCP Pool Corporation, 39 358–60

Scranton Corrugated Box Company, Inc., **8** 102
Scranton Plastics Laminating Corporation, **8** 359
Screen Actors Guild, 72 310–13
Screg Group, **I** 563; **24** 79; **31** 128
Scriha & Deyhle, **10** 196
Scripps-Howard, Inc. *See* The E.W. Scripps Company.
Scrivner Inc., **17** 180
SCS Interactive, **44** 261
Scudder Kemper Investments. *See* Zurich Financial Services.
SD-Scicon plc, **24** 87
SD Warren, **49** 352–53
SDA Systems Inc., **48** 75
SDB Espan, **51** 16
SDGE. *See* San Diego Gas & Electric Company.
SDK Health Care Information Systems, **16** 94
SDL PLC, 67 340–42
SDV. *See* Groupe Bolloré.
Sea Containers Ltd., 29 428–31
Sea-Land Service Inc., **9** 510–11; **22** 164, 166
Sea Life Centre Aquariums, **10** 439
Sea Star Line, **41** 399
Sea World Property Trust, **58** 359
Seabee Corp., **18** 276
Seaboard Air Line Railroad. *See* CSX Corporation.
Seaboard Corporation, 36 414–16
Seaboard Finance Company, **13** 63
Seaboard Surety Company, **III** 357; **22** 494
Seabourn Cruise Lines, **6** 368; **27** 90, 92
Seabrook Farms Co., **24** 527–28
Seabulk Offshore International. *See* Hvide Marine Incorporated.
SeaCat Corporation, **59** 282
Seacat-Zapata Off-Shore Company, **18** 513
Seafield Capital Corporation. *See* LabOne, Inc.
Seafield Estate and Consolidated Plantations Berhad, **14** 448
Seafirst. *See* Seattle First National Bank, Inc.
SeaFirst Corp., **II** 228; **17** 462
Seagate Technology, Inc., 8 466–68; **9** 57; **10** 257, 403–04, 459; **11** 56, 234; **13** 483; **18** 250; **25** 530; **34** 400–04 (upd.); **45** 429
The Seagram Company Ltd., I 284–86; **7** 155; **18** 72; **21** 26, 401; **22** 194; **23** 125; **25** 266, 268, 366, 408–12 (upd.); **26** 125, 127, 152; **28** 475; **29** 196; **31** 269; **33** 375, 424, 432; **46** 438; **47** 418–20; **50** 114
Seagull Energy Corporation, 11 440–42
Seahawk Services Ltd., **37** 289
Seal Products, Inc., **12** 264
Seal Sands Chemicals, **16** 69
Sealaska Corporation, 60 261–64
Sealed Air Corporation, 14 429–31; **57** 313–17 (upd.)
Sealed Power Corporation, I 199–200; **10** 492–94. *See also* SPX Corporation.
SeaLite Sciences, Inc., **52** 171
Sealright Co., Inc., 17 420–23; **64** 186–87
SealRite Windows, **19** 446
Sealtest, **14** 205
Sealy Inc., 12 438–40; **28** 416; **34** 407

Seaman Furniture Company, Inc., 28 389; **32 407–09**
Sean John Clothing, Inc., 70 288–90
Seaquist Manufacturing Corporation, **9** 413–14; **33** 335–36; **69** 38
Searle & Co. *See* G.D. Searle & Co.
Sears Canada Inc., **25** 221
Sears Logistics Services, **18** 225–26
Sears plc, V 177–79
Sears, Roebuck and Co., V 180–83; 18 475–79 (upd.); **56 309–14 (upd.); 57** 11
Sears Roebuck de México, S.A. de C.V., 20 470–72; 21 259; **34** 340
Seashore Transportation Co., **13** 398
SEAT. *See* Sociedad Española de Automoviles de Turismo.
Seat Pagine Gialle S.p.A., 47 345–47
Seatrain International, **27** 474
Seattle Brewing and Malting Company. *See* Rainier Brewing Company.
Seattle City Light, 50 423–26
Seattle Coffee Company, **32** 12, 15
Seattle Electric Company, **6** 565; **50** 365–66
Seattle FilmWorks, Inc., 20 473–75
Seattle First National Bank Inc., 8 469–71
Seattle Times Company, 15 445–47
Seaview Oil Co., **IV** 393
Seaway Express, **9** 510
Seaway Food Town, Inc., 9 452; **15** 448–50
SeaWest, **19** 390
SEB Group. *See* Skandinaviska Enskilda Banken AB.
SEB S.A. *See* Groupe SEB.
Sebastian International, **48** 422
Sebastiani Vineyards, Inc., 28 413–15; 39 421
Seco Products Corporation, **22** 354
Secon GmbH, **13** 160
Second Harvest, 29 432–34
Second National Bank of Bucyrus, **9** 474
Second National Bank of Ravenna, **9** 474
Secoroc, **III** 427
Le Secours, **III** 211
SecPac. *See* Security Pacific Corporation.
Secure Horizons, **11** 378–79
Secure Networks, Inc., **25** 349
Securicor Plc, 11 547; **45 376–79**
Securitas AB, 41 77, 80; **42** 165–66, **336–39**
Securities Industry Automation Corporation, **9** 370
Securities Management & Research, Inc., **27** 46
Security Bancorp, **25** 186–87
Security Capital Corporation, 17 424–27; **21** 476; **48** 330–31; **49** 28–29
Security Capital Group, **56** 58–59
Security Data Group, **32** 373
Security Dynamics Technologies, Inc., **46** 367
Security Express, **10** 269
Security Life and Annuity Company, **11** 213
Security Management Company, **8** 535–36
Security National Corp., **10** 246
Security Pacific Corporation, II 349–50, 422; **III** 366; **8** 45, 48; **11** 447; **17** 137
Security Trust Company, **9** 229, 388
Security Union Title Insurance Co., **10** 43–44

SED International Holdings, Inc., 43 367–69
Sedat Eldem, **13** 475
SEDCO, **17** 418
Seddon Group Ltd., 67 343–45
Sedgwick Group PLC, **I** 427; **10** 38
Sedgwick Sales, Inc., **29** 384
SEDTCO Pty., **13** 61
See's Candies, Inc., 30 411–13
Seeburg Corporation, **15** 538
Seed Restaurant Group Inc., **13** 321; **27** 145
Seed Solutions, Inc., **11** 491; **69** 341
Seeman Brothers. *See* White Rose, Inc.
SEEQ Technology, Inc., **9** 114; **13** 47; **17** 32, 34; **64** 246
Sega Enterprises, Ltd., **28** 320
Sega of America, Inc., 7 396; **10** 124–25, 284–86, **482–85; 18** 520; **50** 157
Sega of Japan, **24** 4
Sego Milk Products Company, **7** 428
Seguros Comercial America, **21** 413
Seguros Monterrey Aetna, **19** 189; **45** 294
Seguros Serfin S.A., **25** 290
Segway LLC, 48 355–57
Seibels, Bruce & Co., **11** 394–95
Seibert-Oxidermo, Inc., **55** 321
Seibu Allstate Life Insurance Company, Ltd., **27** 31
Seibu Department Stores, Ltd., V 184–86; **42 340–43 (upd.)**
Seibu Group, **36** 417–18; **47** 408–09
Seibu Railway Co. Ltd., V 510–11
Seibu Saison, **6** 207
Seifu Co. Ltd., **48** 250
Seigle's Home and Building Centers, Inc., 41 353–55
Seiko Corporation, III 619–21; 17 428–31 (upd.); **72 314–18 (upd.)**
Seiko Instruments USA Inc., **23** 210
Seikosha Co., **64** 261
Seimi Chemical Co. Ltd., **48** 41
Seino Transportation Company, Ltd., 6 427–29
Seismograph Service Limited, **11** 413; **17** 419
Seita, 23 424–27. *See also* Altadis S.A.
Seitel, Inc., 47 348–50
The Seiyu, Ltd., V 187–89; 36 417–21 (upd.); **63** 427, 431
Seizo-sha, **12** 483
Sekisui Chemical Co., Ltd., III 741–43; 72 319–22 (upd.)
Selat Marine Services, **22** 276
Selby Shoe Company, **48** 69
Select Comfort Corporation, 34 405–08
Select Energy, Inc., **48** 305
Select-Line Industries, **9** 543
Select Medical Corporation, 65 306–08
Select Theatres Corp. *See* Shubert Organization Inc.
Selection Trust, **IV** 380, 565
Selectour SA, 53 299–301
Selectronics Inc., **23** 210
Selectrons Ltd., **41** 367
Selena Coffee Inc., **39** 409
Selenia, **I** 467; **38** 374
Self Auto, **23** 232
The Self-Locking Carton Company, **14** 163
Self-Service Drive Thru, Inc., **25** 389
Self Service Restaurants, **II** 613
Selfix, Inc. *See* Home Products International, Inc.
Selfridges Plc, 34 409–11

Selig Chemical Industries, **54** 252, 254
Seligman & Latz, **18** 455
Selkirk Communications Ltd., **26** 273
Sells-Floto, **32** 186
The Selmer Company, Inc., 19 392–94, 426, 428; **55** 113
Seltel International Inc., **35** 246
Sema plc, **59** 370
Semarca, **11** 523
Sematech, **18** 384, 481
SembCorp Logistics Ltd., **53** 199, 203
Sembler Company, **11** 346
SEMCO Energy, Inc., 44 379–82
Semi-Tech Global, **30** 419–20
Seminis, Inc., 21 413; **29 435–37**
Seminole Electric Cooperative, **6** 583
Seminole Fertilizer, **7** 537–38
Seminole National Bank, **41** 312
Semitic, Inc., **33** 248
Semitool, Inc., 18 480–82
Sempra Energy, 25 413–16 (upd.)
Semrau and Sons, **II** 601
Semtech Corporation, 32 410–13
Sencel Aero Engineering Corporation, **16** 483
Seneca Foods Corporation, 17 432–34; **60 265–68 (upd.)**
Senega, **63** 365
Sengstacke Enterprises. *See* Real Times LLC.
Senior Corp., **11** 261
Sennheiser Electronic GmbH & Co. KG, 66 285–89
Sensi, Inc., **22** 173
Sensient Technologies Corporation, 52 303–08 (upd.)
Sensormatic Electronics Corp., 11 443–45; **39** 77–79
Sensory Science Corporation, 37 353–56
Sentinel Foam & Envelope Corporation, **14** 430
Sentinel Savings and Loan, **10** 339
Sentry, **II** 624
Sentry Insurance Company, **10** 210
La Senza Corporation, 66 205–07
Sepal, Ltd., **39** 152, 154
AB Separator. *See* Alfa-Laval AB
SEPECAT, **24** 86
Sephora SA, **51** 234–35; **54** 265–67
SEPI. *See* Sociedad Estatal de Participaciones Industriales.
Sepracor Inc., 45 380–83
Sept, **IV** 325
Sequa Corporation, 13 460–63; 54 328–32 (upd.)
Sequel Corporation, **41** 193
Sequent Computer Systems Inc., **10** 363
Sequoia Athletic Company, **25** 450
Sequoia Pharmacy Group, **13** 150
Sera-Tec Biologicals, Inc. *See* Rite Aid Corporation.
Seragen Inc., **47** 223
Serco Group plc, 47 351–53
Sereg Valves, S.A., **17** 147
Serewatt AG, **6** 491
Serologicals Corporation, 63 351–53
Serono S.A., 47 354–57
Serta, Inc., 28 416–18
Serval Marketing, **18** 393
Servam Corp., **7** 471–73
Service and Systems Solutions Ltd., **64** 404
Service America Corp., 7 471–73; 27 480–81
Service Co., Ltd., **48** 182

Service Control Corp. *See* Angelica Corporation.
Service Corporation International, 6 293–95; 16 343–44; **37** 66–68; **51 329–33 (upd.)**
Service Corporation of America, **17** 552
Service Games Company, **10** 482
Service Master L.P., **34** 153
Service Merchandise Company, Inc., V 190–92; 6 287; **9** 400; **19 395–99 (upd.)**
Service Products Buildings, Inc. *See* Turner Construction Company.
Service Q. General Service Co., **I** 109
The ServiceMaster Company, 6 44–46; 23 428–31 (upd.); 68 338–42 (upd.)
Services Maritimes des Messageries Impériales. *See* Compagnie des Messageries Maritimes.
ServiceWare, Inc., **25** 118
Servicios de Corte y Confeccion, S.A. de C.V., **64** 142
Servicios Financieros Quadrum S.A., **14** 156
Servisair Plc, **49** 320
Servisco, **II** 608
ServiStar Coast to Coast Corporation. *See* TruServ Corporation.
ServoChem A.B., **I** 387
Servomation Corporation, **7** 472–73
Servomation Wilbur. *See* Service America Corp.
Servoplan, S.A., **8** 272
SES Staffing Solutions, **27** 21
Sesame Street Book Club, **13** 560
Sesamee Mexicana, **48** 142
Sessler Inc., **19** 381
Setagaya Industry Co., Ltd., **48** 295
SETCAR, **14** 458
Seton Scholl. *See* SSL International plc.
Seven Arts Limited, **25** 328
7-Eleven, Inc., 32 414–18 (upd.); 36 358
Seven-Eleven Japan Co. *See* Ito-Yokado Co., Ltd.
Seven Generation, Inc., **41** 177
Seven Hills Paperboard, LLC, **59** 350
Seven Network Limited, **25** 329
Seven-Up Co., **18** 418
SevenOne Media, **54** 297
Sevenson Environmental Services, Inc., 42 344–46
Seventh Street Corporation, **60** 130
Severn Trent PLC, 12 441–43; 38 425–29 (upd.)
Severonickel Combine, **48** 300
Seversky Aircraft Corporation, **9** 205
Severstal Joint Stock Company, 65 309–12
Sewell Plastics, Inc., **10** 222
Sextant In-Flight Systems, LLC, **30** 74
Seymour Electric Light Co., **13** 182
Seymour International Press Distributor Ltd., **IV** 619
Seymour Press, **IV** 619
Seymour Trust Co., **13** 467
SF Bio, **52** 51
SF Recycling & Disposal, Inc., **60** 224
SFI Group plc, 51 334–36
SFIC Holdings (Cayman) Inc., **38** 422
SFIM Industries, **37** 348
SFNGR. *See* Nouvelles Galeries Réunies.
SFS Bancorp Inc., **41** 212
SFX Broadcasting Inc., **24** 107

SFX Entertainment, Inc., 36 422–25; 37 383–84
SG Racing, Inc., **64** 346
SGC. *See* Supermarkets General Corporation.
SGE. *See* Vinci.
SGI, 29 438–41 (upd.)
SGL Carbon Group, **40** 83; **46** 14
SGLG, Inc., **13** 367
SGS-Thomson Microelectronics, **54** 269–70
Shakespeare Company, 16 296; **22 481–84**
Shakey's Pizza, **16** 447
Shaklee Corporation, 12 444–46; 17 186; **38** 93; **39 361–64 (upd.)**
Shalco Systems, **13** 7
Shampaine Industries, Inc., **37** 399
Shamrock Advisors, Inc., **8** 305
Shamrock Broadcasting Inc., **24** 107
Shamrock Capital L.P., **7** 81–82
Shamrock Holdings, **9** 75; **11** 556; **25** 268
Shamrock Oil & Gas Co., **7** 308
Shan-Chih Business Association, **23** 469
Shana Corporation, **62** 142
Shandong Nichirei Foods Company Ltd. *See* Nichirei Corporation.
Shandwick International, **47** 97
Shanggong Co. Ltd., **65** 134
Shanghai Asia Pacific Co., **59** 59
Shanghai Baosteel Group Corporation, 71 327–30
Shanghai Crown Maling Packaging Co. Ltd., **13** 190
Shanghai Dajiang, **62** 63
Shanghai General Bearing Co., Ltd., **45** 170
Shanghai International Finance Company Limited, **15** 433
Shanghai Kyocera Electronics Co., Ltd., **21** 331
Shanghai Petrochemical Co., Ltd., 18 483–85; 21 83; **45** 50
Shanghai Shesuo UNF Medical Diagnostic Reagents Co., **61** 229
Shanghai Tobacco, **49** 150, 153
Shangri-La Asia Ltd., 71 331–33
Shanks Group plc, 45 384–87
Shannon Aerospace Ltd., 36 426–28
Shannon Group, Inc., **18** 318, 320; **59** 274, 277
Shansby Group, **27** 197; **43** 218; **64** 265
Shanshin Engineering Company Ltd., **60** 236
Share Drug plc, **24** 269
Shared Financial Systems, Inc., **10** 501
Shared Medical Systems Corporation, 14 432–34
Shared Technologies Inc., **12** 71
Shared Use Network Systems, Inc., **8** 311
ShareWave Inc., **48** 92
Shari Lewis Enterprises, Inc., **28** 160
Sharmoon, **63** 151
Sharon Steel Corp., **7** 360–61; **8** 536; **13** 158, 249; **47** 234
Sharp Corporation, II 95–96; III 14, 428, 455, 480; **6** 217, 231; **11** 45; **12 447–49 (upd.); 13** 481; **16** 83; **21** 123; **22** 197; **40 391–95 (upd.)**
Sharp Water, Inc., **56** 62
The Sharper Image Corporation, 10 486–88; 23 210; **26** 439; **27** 429; **62 321–24 (upd.)**
Sharples Separator Company, **64** 17

Shasta Beverages. *See* National Beverage Corp.
Shato Holdings, Ltd., **60** 357
Shaw Communications Inc., **26** 274; **35** 69
The Shaw Group, Inc., 50 427–30; 64 372
Shaw Industries, Inc., 9 465–67; 19 274, 276; **25** 320; **40 396–99 (upd.)**
Shaw's Supermarkets, Inc., II 658–59; **23** 169; **56 315–18**
Shawell Precast Products, **14** 248
Shea Homes. *See* J.F. Shea Co., Inc.
Shearer's Foods, Inc., 72 323–25
Shearman & Sterling, 32 419–22; 35 467
Shearson Hammill & Company, **22** 405–06
Shearson Lehman Brothers Holdings Inc., I 202; **II** 398–99, 450, 478; **8** 118; **9 468–70 (upd.); 10** 62–63; **11** 418; **12** 459; **15** 124, 463–64
Shearson Lehman Hutton Group, **49** 181
Shearson Lehman Hutton Holdings Inc., II 339, 445, **450–52; 9** 125; **10** 59, 63; **17** 38–39
Shedd's Food Products Company, **9** 318
Sheffield Exploration Company, **28** 470
Sheffield Forgemasters Group Ltd., **39** 32
Sheffield Silver Company, **67** 322–23
Shekou Container Terminal, **16** 481; **38** 345
Shelby Insurance Company, **10** 44–45
Shelby Steel Processing Co., **51** 238
Shelby Williams Industries, Inc., 14 435–37
Shelco, **22** 146
Sheldahl Inc., 23 432–35
Shelf Life Inc. *See* King Kullen Grocery Co., Inc.
Shell. *See* Royal Dutch/Shell Group; Shell Oil Company; Shell Transport and Trading Company p.l.c.
Shell Canada Limited, **32** 45
Shell Chemical Corporation, **IV** 531–32, 540; **8** 415; **24** 151
Shell Forestry, **21** 546; **50** 58
Shell France, **12** 153
Shell Oil Company, IV 540–41; 6 457; **8** 261–62; **11** 522; **14** 25, **438–40 (upd.); 17** 417; **19** 175–76; **21** 546; **22** 274; **24** 520; **25** 96, 232, 469; **26** 496; **41 356–60 (upd.)**, 395; **45** 54
Shell Transport and Trading Company p.l.c., IV 530–32, 564; **31** 127–28; **50** 58, 355. *See also* Royal Dutch Petroleum Company; Royal Dutch/Shell.
Shell Western E & P, **7** 323
Sheller-Globe Corporation, I 201–02; 17 182
Shells Seafood Restaurants, Inc., 43 370–72
Shelly Brothers, Inc., **15** 65
Shenzhen Namtek Co., Ltd., **61** 232–33
Shepherd Hardware Products Ltd., **16** 357
Shepherd Neame Limited, 30 414–16
Shepherd Plating and Finishing Company, **13** 233
Shepler Equipment Co., **9** 512
Sheraton Corp. of America, **III** 98–99; **11** 198; **13** 362–63; **21** 91
Sherborne Group Inc./NH Holding Inc., **17** 20
Sherbrooke Paper Products Ltd., **17** 281
Sheridan Bakery, **II** 633
Sherr-Gold, **23** 40

Sherritt Gordon Mines, **7** 386–87; **12** 260
The Sherwin-Williams Company, III 744–46; **13** 469–71 (upd.)
Sherwood Brands, Inc., 53 302–04
Sherwood Equity Group Ltd. *See* National Discount Brokers Group, Inc.
Sherwood Medical Group, **I** 624; **10** 70; **50** 538
Sherwood Securities, **66** 308
Shiara Holdings, Inc., **53** 88
Shidler Group. *See* First Industrial Realty Trust, Inc.
Shieh Chi Industrial Co., **19** 508
Shields & Co., **9** 118
Shihen Technical Corporation, **60** 272
Shihlin Electric & Engineering Group, **49** 460
Shikoku Electric Power Company, Inc., V 718–20; **60** 269–72 (upd.)
Shiley, Inc., **38** 361
Shillito's, **31** 192
Shimano Inc., 64 347–49
Shimizu Construction Company Ltd., **44** 153
Shin-Nihon Glass Co., **I** 221
Shinko Rayon Ltd. *See* Mitsubishi Rayon Co., Ltd.
Shinko Securities Co. Ltd., **58** 235
Shintech, **11** 159–60
Shinwa Pharmaceutical Co. Ltd., **48** 250
Shionogi & Co., Ltd., III 60–61; **11** 90, 290; **17** 435–37 (upd.)
Ship 'n Shore, **9** 156–57
Shipley Co. Inc., **26** 425
Shipper Group, **16** 344
Shipstad & Johnson's Ice Follies, **25** 313
Shiseido Company, Limited, III 62–64; **8** 341, 343; **22** 485–88 (upd.)
Shizuoka Itaku Co., Ltd., **64** 261
SHL Systemhouse Inc., **27** 305
Shobiz, Inc., **60** 143
Shochiku Company Ltd., **28** 461
Shockley Electronics, **20** 174
Shoe Carnival Inc., 14 441–43; **72** 326–29 (upd.)
Shoe Supply, Inc., **22** 213
Shoe-Town Inc., **23** 310
Shoe Works Inc., **18** 415
Shonac Corp., **14** 427
Shonco, Inc., **18** 438
Shoney's, Inc., 7 474–76; **14** 453; **19** 286; **23** 436–39 (upd.); **29** 290–91; **59** 104–06
Shop 'n Save Warehouse Foods Inc., **63** 129
Shop At Home Network LLC. *See* The E.W. Scripps Company.
SHOP Channel, **64** 185
Shop Rite Foods Inc. *See* Big V Supermarkets, Inc.
ShopKo Stores Inc., II 669–70; **18** 505–07; **21** 457–59; **50** 455–57; **58** 329–32 (upd.)
Shoppers Drug Mart Corporation, 49 367–70
Shoppers Food Warehouse Corporation, 16 159, 161; **66** 290–92
Shoppers World Stores, Inc. *See* LOT$OFF Corporation.
ShopRite. *See* Foodarama Supermarkets, Inc.
Shopwell/Food Emporium, **II** 638; **16** 247, 249
ShopWise.com Inc., **53** 13

Shore Manufacturing, **13** 165
Shorewood Packaging Corporation, 28 419–21; **47** 189
Shorouk Airways, **68** 227
Short Brothers, **24** 85
Shoseido Co., **17** 110
Shotton Paper Co. Ltd., **IV** 350
Showa Aluminum Corporation, **8** 374
Showa Denko, **IV** 61
Showa Marutsutsu Co. Ltd., **8** 477
Showa Products Company, **8** 476
Showa Shell Sekiyu K.K., IV 542–43; **59** 372–75 (upd.)
ShowBiz Pizza Time, Inc., 12 123; **13** 472–74; **15** 73; **16** 447. *See also* CEC Entertainment, Inc.
Showboat, Inc., 19 400–02; **43** 227
Showcase of Fine Fabrics, **16** 197
Showco, Inc., **35** 436
Showscan Entertainment Inc., **34** 230
Showscan Film Corporation, **28** 206
Showtime, **7** 222–23; **9** 74; **23** 274–75, 391, 503; **25** 329–30
Shred-It Canada Corporation, 56 319–21
Shreve and Company, **12** 312
Shreveport Refrigeration, **16** 74
Shriners Hospitals for Children, 69 318–20
Shu Uemura, **III** 43
Shubert Organization Inc., 24 437–39
Shubrooks International Ltd., **11** 65
Shuffle Master Inc., 51 337–40
Shuford Mills, Inc., **14** 430
Shugart Associates, **8** 466; **22** 189
Shulman Transport Enterprises Inc., **27** 473
Shure Inc., 60 273–76
Shurfine International, **60** 302
Shurgard Storage Centers, Inc., 21 476; **52** 293, 309–11
Shuttleworth Brothers Company. *See* Mohawk Industries, Inc.
Shuwa Corp., **22** 101; **36** 292
SHV Holdings N.V., 14 156; **55** 344–47
SI Holdings Inc., **10** 481; **29** 425
The Siam Cement Public Company Limited, 56 322–25
Siam Makro, **62** 63
SIAS, **19** 192
SIATA S.p.A., **26** 363
SIB Financial Services, **39** 382
Sibco Universal, S.A., **14** 429
Sibel, **48** 350
Siberian Moloko, **48** 438
Sibneft. *See* OAO Siberian Oil Company.
Siboney Shoe Corp., **22** 213
SiCAP AG, **58** 338
SICC. *See* Univision Communications Inc.
Sichuan Changhong Electric Co. Ltd., **63** 36
Sichuan Station Wagon Factory, **38** 462
Sick's Brewery, **26** 304
Siclet, **25** 84
Sicma Aero Seat, **36** 529
Sideco Americana S.A., 67 346–48
Sidel. *See* Groupe Sidel S.A.
Siderar S.A.I.C., 66 293–95
Siderca S.A.I.C., **41** 405–06
Sidley Austin Brown & Wood, 40 400–03
Sidney Frank Importing Co., Inc., 69 321–23
Siebe plc. *See* BTR Siebe plc.
Siebel Group, **13** 544–45

Siebel Marketing Group, **27** 195
Siebel Systems, Inc., 38 430–34
Siebert Financial Corp., 32 423–25
Siegel & Gale, 64 350–52
Siemens AG, II 97–100; **III** 154–55, 466, 482, 516; **7** 232; **9** 11, 32, 44; **10** 16, 363; **11** 59, 196, 235, 397–98, 460; **12** 546; **13** 402; **14** 169, 444–47 (upd.); **16** 392; **18** 32; **19** 166, 313; **20** 290; **22** 19, 373–74; **23** 389, 452, 494–95; **24** 88; **33** 225, 288; **57** 318–23 (upd.)
Siemens Solar Industries L.P., **44** 182
The Sierra Club, 28 422–24
Sierra Designs, Inc., **10** 215–16
Sierra Health Services, Inc., 15 451–53
Sierra Leone External Telegraph Limited, **25** 100
Sierra Nevada Brewing Company, 70 291–93
Sierra On-Line, Inc., 13 92, 114; **14** 263; **15** 454–56; **16** 146; **29** 75; **41** 361–64 (upd.)
Sierra Pacific Industries, 22 489–91
Sierra Precision, **52** 187
Sierrita Resources, Inc., **6** 590
Siete Oil and Gas Co., **63** 346
SIFCO Industries, Inc., 41
Sifo Group AB. *See* Observer AB.
SIG plc, 71 334–36
Sight & Sound Entertainment, **35** 21
Sigma-Aldrich Corporation, I 690–91; **36** 429–32 (upd.)
Sigma Alimentos, S.A. de C.V., **19** 11–12
Sigma Network Systems, **11** 464
Signal Companies, Inc. *See* AlliedSignal Inc.
Signal Corporation, **54** 395–96
Signal Galaxies, **13** 127
Signal Oil & Gas Inc., **7** 537; **11** 278; **19** 175
Signal Pharmaceutical Inc. *See* Celgene Corporation.
Signalite, Inc., **10** 319
SignalSoft, **63** 202
Signature Bank, **54** 36
Signature Brands USA Inc., **28** 135; **30** 139
Signature Corporation, **22** 412–13
Signature Flight Support Services Corporation, **47** 450
Signature Health Care Corp., **25** 504
Signet Banking Corporation, 11 446–48
Signet Communications Corp., **16** 195
Signet Group PLC, 61 326–28
Signetics Co., **11** 56; **18** 383; **44** 127
Signode Industries, **III** 519; **22** 282
Sika Finanz AG, **28** 195
Sikes Corporation, **III** 612
Sikorsky Aircraft Corporation, 9 416; **24** 440–43; **41** 368; **46** 65
SIL&P. *See* Southern Illinois Light & Power Company.
SILA. *See* Swedish Intercontinental Airlines.
Silband Sports Corp., **33** 102
Silenka B.V., **III** 733; **22** 436
Silex. *See* Hamilton Beach/Proctor-Silex Inc.
Silgan Holdings Inc., **26** 59
Silhouette Brands, Inc., 55 348–50
Silicon Beach Software, **10** 35
Silicon Compiler Systems, **11** 285
Silicon Energy Corporation, **64** 205
Silicon Engineering, **18** 20; **43** 17

Silicon Graphics Inc., **9** 471–73; **10** 119, 257; **12** 323; **15** 149, 320; **16** 137, 140; **20** 8; **25** 96; **28** 320; **38** 69; **43** 151; **50** 322. *See also* SGI.
Silicon Light Machines Corporation, **48** 128
Silicon Magnetic Systems, **48** 128
Silicon Microstructures, Inc., **14** 183
Silit, **60** 364
Silk-Epil S.A., **51** 58
Silkies, **55** 196
Silknet Software Inc., **51** 181
Silo Electronics, **16** 73, 75
Silo Holdings, **9** 65; **23** 52
Silo Inc., **V** 50; **10** 306, 468; **19** 123; **49** 112
Silver Burdett Co., **IV** 672, 675; **7** 528; **19** 405
Silver Cinemas Inc., **71** 256
Silver City Airways. *See* British World Airlines Ltd.
Silver City Casino. *See* Circus Circus Enterprises, Inc.
Silver Dollar Mining Company, **20** 149
Silver Dolphin, **34** 3, 5
Silver Furniture Co., Inc., **15** 102, 104
Silver King Communications, **25** 213
Silver Screen Partners, **II** 174
Silverado Banking, **9** 199
Silverado Partners Acquisition Corp., **22** 80
Silverline, Inc., **16** 33
Silvermans Menswear, Inc., **24** 26
SilverPlatter Information Inc., 23 440–43
Silvershoe Partners, **17** 245
Silverstar Ltd. S.p.A., **10** 113; **50** 42
Silverstein Properties, Inc., 47 358–60; 48 320
Simco S.A., 37 357–59
Sime Darby Berhad, 14 448–50; 36 433–36 (upd.)
Simeira Comercio e Industria Ltda., **22** 320
SIMEL S.A., **14** 27
Simer Pump Company, **19** 360
SIMEST, **24** 311
Simi Winery, Inc., **34** 89
Simicon Co., **26** 153
Simkins Industries, Inc., **8** 174–75
Simmons Company, 34 407; **47 361–64**
Simon & Schuster Inc., IV 671–72; **13** 559; **19 403–05 (upd.)**; **23** 503; **28** 158
Simon de Wit, **II** 641
Simon DeBartolo Group Inc., **26** 146; **27** 401; **57** 234
Simon Engineering, **11** 510
Simon Marketing, Inc., **19** 112, 114
Simon Property Group, Inc., 27 399–402; **49** 414
Simon Transportation Services Inc., 27 403–06
Simons Inc., **26** 412
Simple Shoes, Inc., **22** 173
Simplex Industries, Inc., **16** 296
Simplex Technologies Inc., 21 460–63
Simplex Wire and Cable Co. *See* Tyco International Ltd.
Simplicity Manufacturing, Inc., 64 353–56
Simplicity Pattern Company, **I** 447; **8** 349; **23** 98; **29** 134
Simpson Investment Company, 17 438–41
Simpson Marketing, **12** 553

Simpson Thacher & Bartlett, **27** 327; **39 365–68**
Simpson Timber Company. *See* PW Eagle Inc.
Simpsons. *See* Hudson's Bay Company.
SIMS Deltec, Inc. *See* Deltec, Inc.
Sims Telephone Company, **14** 258
Simsmetal USA Corporation, **19** 380
SimuFlite, **II** 10
Simula, Inc., 41 368–70
Simulaids, Inc., **62** 18
SINA Corporation, 69 324–27
Sinai Kosher Foods, **14** 537
Sinclair Broadcast Group, Inc., 25 417–19; **47** 120
Sinclair Paint Company, **12** 219
Sinfor Holding, **48** 402
Sing Tao Holdings Ltd., **29** 470–71
Singapore Airlines Ltd., 6 117–18; **12** 192; **20** 313; **24** 399; **26** 115; **27** 26, **407–09 (upd.)**, 464, 466; **38** 26
Singapore Alpine Electronics Asia Pte. Ltd., **13** 31
Singapore Candle Company, **12** 393
Singapore Petroleum Co., **IV** 452
Singapore Shinei Sangyo Pte Ltd., **48** 369
Singapore Technologies Engineering Ltd., **61** 43
Singapore Telecom, **18** 348
Singer & Friedlander Group plc, 41 371–73
Singer Company, **9** 232; **11** 150; **13** 521–22; **19** 211; **22** 4; **26** 3; **29** 190. *See also* Bicoastal Corp.
The Singer Company N.V., 30 417–20 (upd.)
Singer Hardware & Supply Co., **9** 542
Singer Sewing Machine Co., **12** 46
Singer Supermarkets, **25** 235
The Singing Machine Company, Inc., 60 277–80
Singular Software, **9** 80
Sinister Games, **41** 409
Sinkers Inc., **21** 68
Sino Life Insurance Co., **64** 280
Sinochem. *See* China National Chemicals Import and Export Corp.
Sinopec. *See* China National Petroleum Corporation.
Sintel, S.A., **19** 256
Sioux City Gas and Electric Company, **6** 523–24
Sioux City Newspapers, **64** 237
SIP. *See* Società Italiana per L'Esercizio delle Telecommunicazioni p.A.
Siporex, S.A., **31** 253
Sir Speedy, Inc., 16 448–50; **33** 231
SIRCOMA, **10** 375
SIREM, **23** 95
The Sirena Apparel Group Inc., **25** 245
Sirius Satellite Radio, Inc., 69 328–31
Sirloin Stockade, **10** 331
Sirrine. *See* CRSS Inc.
Sirte Oil Company. *See* Natinal Oil Corporation.
Siskin Steel & Supply Company, 70 294–96
Sisters Chicken & Biscuits, **8** 564
Sisters of Bon Secours USA. *See* Bon Secours Health System, Inc.
SIT-Siemens. *See* Italtel.
SITA Telecommunications Holdings. *See* Equant N.V.
Sitca Corporation, **16** 297

Sithe Energies, Inc., **24** 327
Sitintel, **49** 383
Sitmar Cruises, **22** 445
Six Continents PLC, **54** 315; **59** 298
Six Flags, Inc., 17 442–44; 54 333–40 (upd.)
Six Industries, Inc., **26** 433
61 Going to the Game!, **14** 293
Sixt AG, 39 369–72
Sizeler Property Investors Inc., **49** 27
Sizzler International Inc. *See* Worldwide Restaurant Concepts, Inc.
SJB Equities, Inc., **30** 53
SJW Corporation, 70 297–99
The SK Equity Fund, L.P., **23** 177
Skånska Ättiksfabriken A.B. *See* Perstorp AB.
Skadden, Arps, Slate, Meagher & Flom, 10 126–27; **18 486–88**; **27** 325, 327
Skaggs-Albertson's Properties, **II** 604
Skaggs Companies, **22** 37
Skaggs Drug Centers, Inc., **II** 602–04; **7** 20; **27** 291; **30** 25–27; **65** 22
Skagit Nuclear Power Plant, **6** 566
Skalli Group, 67 349–51
Skandia America Reinsurance Corp., **57** 135–36
Skandia Insurance Company, Ltd., 25 85; **50 431–34**
Skandinaviska Enskilda Banken AB, II 351–53, 365–66; **56 326–29 (upd.)**
Skanska AB, IV 204; **25** 463; **32** 396; **38 435–38**
Skanza Mammoet Transport Sdn Bhd, **26** 280
Skechers U.S.A. Inc., 31 413–15; **62** 47
Sketchley plc, **19** 124
SKF. *See* Aktiebolaget SKF.
SKF Industries Inc. *See* AB Volvo.
Ski-Doo. *See* Bombardier Inc.
Skidmore, Owings & Merrill LLP, 13 475–76; **69 332–35 (upd.)**
Skil-Craft Playthings, Inc., **13** 560
Skillern, **16** 560
Skillware, **9** 326
Skis Rossignol S.A., 15 460–62; 43 373–76 (upd.)
Skoda Auto a.s., 39 373–75
SKODA Group, **37** 399–400
SKS Group, **20** 363
SKW Nature's Products, Inc., **25** 332
Sky Chefs, Inc., **16** 397; **65** 282–84
Sky Climber Inc., **11** 436
Sky Merchant, Inc., **V** 78
Skyband, Inc., **12** 359
SkyBox International Inc., **15** 72–73
Skylight, **25** 508
Skyline Chili, Inc., 62 325–28
Skyline Corporation, 30 421–23
Skyline Homes, **17** 82
Skyline Transportation, **57** 277
SkyMall, Inc., 26 439–41; 28 241
Skypak, **27** 474
Skyservice Airlines Inc., **42** 327
SkyTel Corp., **18** 349; **23** 212
Skywalker Sound, **12** 322; **50** 320
Skyway Airlines, **11** 299; **32** 335; **35** 293–94
SkyWest, Inc., 25 420–24
Skyy Spirits, LLC, **57** 105–06
Sl. Aves Ldc España, **68** 234
SL Green Realty Corporation, 44 383–85
SL Holdings. *See* Finlay Enterprises, Inc.

Slade Gorton & Company, **13** 243
Slater Co. Foods, **II** 607
Slater Electric, **21** 349
Slater Systems, Inc., **13** 48
Slater, Walker, **63** 76
Slautterback Corporation, **48** 299
Slavneft, **49** 306
SLCN Ltd., **64** 205
Sleeman Breweries of Canada, **50** 115
Sleepy's Inc., 32 426–28
SLI, Inc., 48 358–61
Slim Jim, Inc. See GoodMark Foods, Inc.
Slim-Fast Foods Company, 12 531; **18**
  489–91; 27 196; **66 296–98 (upd.)**
Slingerland Drum Company, **16** 239
Slinky, Inc. See Poof-Slinky, Inc.
Slip-X Safety Treads, **9** 72
SLJFB Vedrenne, **22** 344
SLM Holding Corp., 25 425–28 (upd.)
SLM International Inc. See The Hockey
  Company.
Sloan's Supermarkets Inc. See Gristede's
  Sloan's, Inc.
Sloman Neptun Schiffahrts, **26** 279
Slope Indicator Company, **26** 42
Sloss Industries Corporation. See Walter
  Industries, Inc.
Slots-A-Fun. See Circus Circus Enterprises,
  Inc.
Slough Estates PLC, IV 722–25; 50
  435–40 (upd.)
Slovak Air Services S.R.O., **66** 51
Slovenská Konzultacná Firma S.R.O. V
  Likvidácii, **66** 51
Slovenská Sporitelna a.s., **69** 156
AB Small Business Investment Co., Inc.,
  13 111–12
Small Tube Products, Inc., **23** 517
Small World Productions, **65** 136
SMALLCO, **III** 340
Smalley Transportation Company. See
  Preston Corporation.
SMAN. See Societe Mecanique
  Automobile du Nord.
Smart & Final, Inc., 12 153–54; **16**
  451–53
Smart Choice Automotive Group, **64**
  20–21
Smart Communications, **18** 180, 182
Smart Products, **44** 261
Smart Shirts Ltd., **8** 288–89
Smart Talk Network, Inc., **16** 319
SmartCash, **18** 543
SmartForce PLC, 43 377–80
SmarTTarget Marketing, **36** 342
SMBC. See Sumitomo Mitsui Banking
  Corporation.
Smead Manufacturing Co., 17 445–48
Smed International, **39** 207
SMG. See Scottish Media Group.
SMH. See Sanders Morris Harris Group
  Inc.; The Swatch Group SA.
SMI Industries, **25** 15
Smiles Holdings Ltd., **38** 501
Smirnoff, **14** 212; **18** 41
Smit International, **26** 241
Smith and Bell Insurance, **41** 178, 180
Smith & Butterfield Co., Inc., **28** 74
Smith & Hawken, Ltd., 68 343–45
Smith & Nephew plc, 17 449–52; 41
  374–78 (upd.)
Smith & Wesson Corporation, 30
  424–27
Smith & Weston, **19** 430

Smith & Wollensky Operating Corp., **32**
  362
Smith Barney Inc., I 614; **6** 410; **10** 63;
  13 328; **15 463–65; 19** 385; **20** 360; **22**
  406; **59** 121, 125–26
Smith Cattleguard. See Smith-Midland
  Corporation.
Smith Corona Corp., 13 477–80; 14 76;
  23 210
Smith International, Inc., 15 466–68; 59
  368, **376–80 (upd.)**
Smith McDonell Stone and Co., **14** 97
Smith Meter Co., **11** 4
Smith-Midland Corporation, 56 330–32
Smith New Court PLC, **13** 342; **40** 313
Smith Packaging Ltd., **14** 429
Smith Parts Co., **11** 3
Smith Sport Optics Inc., **54** 319–20
Smith Transfer Corp., **II** 607–08; **13** 49
Smith Wall Associates, **32** 145
Smith's Food & Drug Centers, Inc., 8
  472–74; **17** 558, 561; **24** 36; **26** 432; **57**
  324–27 (upd.)
Smithfield Foods, Inc., 7 477–78,
  524–25; **22** 509, 511; **43** 25, **381–84**
  (upd.); 46 83
SmithKline Beckman Corporation, I
  692–94. See also GlaxoSmithKline plc.
SmithKline Beecham plc, III 65–67; 32
  429–34 (upd.). See also
  GlaxoSmithKline plc.
SmithMart. See N.F. Smith & Asociates
  LP.
Smiths Group plc, **56** 83
Smiths Industries PLC, 25 429–31
Smithsonian Institution, 27 410–13
Smithway Motor Xpress Corporation, 39
  376–79
Smitty's Super Valu Inc., **12** 391; **17**
  560–61
Smittybilt, Incorporated, **40** 299–300
Smoby International SA, 56 333–35
Smoothie Island, **49** 60
Smorgon Steel Group Ltd., 62 329–32
SMP Clothing, Inc., **22** 462
Smucker. See The J.M. Smucker Company.
Smurfit Companies. See Jefferson Smurfit
  Group plc.
Smurfit-Stone Container Corporation,
  26 442–46 (upd.)
SN Repal. See Société Nationale de
  Recherche de Pétrole en Algérie.
Snack Ventures Europe, **10** 324; **36** 234,
  237
Snake River Sugar Company, **19** 468
Snam. See Società Nazionale Metanodotti.
Snam Montaggi, **IV** 420
Snam Progetti, **IV** 420, 422
Snap-On, Incorporated, 27 414–16
  (upd.); 32 397
Snap-on Tools Corporation, 7 479–80;
  25 34
Snapper Inc., **64** 355
Snapple Beverage Corporation, 11
  449–51; 12 411; **24** 480; **27** 153; **31**
  243; **34** 366; **39** 383, 386
Snapps Drive-Thru, **25** 389
Snappy Car Rental, Inc. See Republic
  Industries, Inc.
SnapTrack Inc., **63** 203
SNC-Lavalin Group Inc., 72 330–33
SNCF. See Société Nationale des Chemins
  de Fer Français.
SNE Enterprises, Inc., **12** 397

SNEA. See Société Nationale Elf
  Aquitaine.
Snecma Group, 17 482; **46 369–72**
Snell & Wilmer L.L.P., 28 425–28
Snell Acoustics, **22** 99
Snelling Personnel Services, **52** 150
SNET. See Southern New England
  Telecommunications Corporation.
SNMC Management Corporation, **11** 121;
  48 177
Snoqualmie Falls Plant, **6** 565
Snow Brand Milk Products Company,
  Ltd., II 574–75; 48 362–65 (upd.)
Snow White Dairies Inc. See Dairy Mart
  Convenience Stores, Inc.
Snowy Mountains Hydroelectric Authority,
  13 118
Snyder Communications, **35** 462, 465
Snyder Group Company, **56** 294
Snyder Oil Company, **24** 379–81; **45** 354
Snyder's of Hanover, **35** 213
SnyderGeneral Corp. See AAF-McQuay
  Incorporated.
Soap Opera Magazine, **10** 287
Socal. See Standard Oil Company
  (California).
Socamel-Rescaset, **40** 214, 216
Socar, Incorporated, **45** 370
Socata. See EADS SOCATA.
Sochiku, **9** 30
Sociade Intercontinental de Compressores
  Hermeticos SICOM, S.A., **8** 515
La Sociale di A. Mondadori & C. See
  Arnoldo Mondadori Editore S.P.A.
Sociedad Aeronáutica de Medellín, S.A.,
  36 53
Sociedad Andina de Grandes Almeneces,
  69 312
Sociedad Anónima Viña Santa Rita, **67**
  136–37
Sociedad Anonimo de Electricidad, **72** 278
Sociedad de Inversiones Internacionales
  Parque Arauco S.A., **72** 269
Sociedad Española Zig Zag, S.A., **68** 258
Sociedad Estatal de Participaciones
  Industriales, **69** 11
Sociedad Financiera Mexicana, **19** 189
Sociedad Macri S.A., **67** 346
Sociedade Anónima Concessionária de
  Refinacao em Portugal. See SACOR.
Sociedade de Vinhos da Herdade de
  Espirra-Produçao e Comercializaçao de
  Vinhos, S.A., **60** 156
Società Anonima Lombarda Fabbrica
  Automobili, **13** 27
Societa Esercizio Fabbriche Automobili e
  Corse Ferrari, **13** 219
Società Finanziaria Idrocarburi, **69** 148
Società Finanziaria Telefonica per
  Azioni, V 325–27
Societa Industria Meccanica Stampaggio
  S.p.A., **24** 500
Societa Italiana Gestione Sistemi Multi
  Accesso. See Alitalia—Linee Aeree
  Italiana, S.P.A.
Società Italiana per L'Esercizio delle
  Telecommunicazioni p.A., **V** 325–27
Società Meridionale Finanziaria, **49** 31
Società Sportiva Lazio SpA, 44 386–88
Société Africaine de Déroulage des Ets
  Rougier, **21** 439
Société Air France, 27 417–20 (upd.).
  See also Groupe Air France.

Société Alsacienne de Magasins SA, **19** 308

Societe Anonima Italiana Ing. Nicola Romeo & Company, **13** 27

Societe Anonomie Alfa Romeo, **13** 28

Societe Anonyme Automobiles Citroen. *See* PSA Peugeot Citroen S.A.

Société Anonyme Belge des Magasins Prisunic-Uniprix, **26** 159

Société Anonyme des Assurances Générales. *See* Assurances Générales de France.

Société Anonyme des Fermiers Reúnis, **23** 219

Société Anonyme Française du Ferodo. *See* Valeo.

La Societe Anonyme Francaise Holophane, **19** 211

Societe Anonyme Francaise Timken, **8** 530

Société Anonyme Telecommunications, **III** 164

Société, Auxiliaire d'Entrepreses SA, **13** 206

Société BIC, S.A., **8** 60–61; **23** 55–57

Société Centrale d'Investissement, **29** 48

Société Civil des Mousquetaires. *See* ITM Entreprises SA.

Société Civile Valoptec, **21** 222

Société Commercial d'Affrètements et de Combustibles, **67** 198

Societe Commerciale Citroen, **7** 36

Société Congolaise des Grands Magasins Au Bon Marché, **26** 159

Société d'Emboutissage de Bourgogne. *See* Groupe SEB.

Société d'Exploitation AOM Air Liberté SA (AirLib), 53 305–07

Société d'Investissement de Travaux Publics, **31** 128

Société de Collecte des Prodicteirs de Preval, **19** 50

Société de Développements et d'Innovations des Marchés Agricoles et Alimentaires. *See* SODIMA.

Société de Diffusion de Marques. *See* SODIMA.

Société de Diffusion Internationale Agro-Alimentaire. *See* SODIAAL.

Société de Fiducie du Québec, **48** 289

Société des Caves de Roquefort, **24** 444

Société des Caves et des Producteurs Reunis de Roquefort, **19** 49

Société des Ciments Français, **33** 339

Société des Etablissements Gaumont. *See* Gaumont SA.

Société des Fibres de Carbone S.A., **51** 379

Société des Grandes Entreprises de Distribution, Inno-France, **V** 58

Société des Immeubles de France, **37** 357, 359

Société des Magasins du Casino, **59** 109

Société des Moteurs Gnôme, **46** 369

Société du Figaro S.A., 60 281–84

Société du Louvre, 27 421–23

Société Economique de Rennes, **19** 98

Société European de Semi-Remorques, **7** 513

Société Européenne de Production de L'avion E.C.A.T. *See* SEPECAT.

Société Française de Casinos, **48** 198

Société General de Banque, **17** 324

Société Générale, II 354–56; 9 148; **13** 203, 206; **19** 51; **33** 118–19; **42 347–51 (upd.); 47** 411–12

Société Générale de Banque. *See* Generale Bank.

Société Générale de Belgique S.A. *See* Generale Bank.

Société Générale des Entreprises. *See* Vinci.

Société Générale du Telephones, **21** 231

Societe-Hydro-Air S.a.r.L., **9** 27

Société Industrielle Belge des Pétroles, **IV** 498–99

Société Internationale Pirelli S.A., **V** 250

Société Laitière Vendômoise, **23** 219

Société Luxembourgeoise de Navigation Aérienne S.A., 64 357–59

Societe Mecanique Automobile de l'Est/du Nord, **7** 37

Société Nationale de Programmes de Télévision Française 1. *See* Télévision Française 1.

Société Nationale des Chemins de Fer Français, V 512–15; 57 328–32 (upd.); 67 187–88

Société Nationale des Pétroles d'Aquitaine, **21** 203–05

Société Nationale Elf Aquitaine, IV 544–47; 7 481–85 (upd.)

Société Norbert Dentressangle S.A., 67 352–54

Société Nouvelle d'Achat de Bijouterie, **16** 207

Société Nouvelle des Etablissements Gaumont. *See* Gaumont SA.

Société Parisienne d'Achats en Commun, **19** 307

Société Parisienne Raveau-Cartier, **31** 128

Société pour l'Étude et la Realisation d'Engins Balistiques. *See* SEREB.

Société pour le Financement de l'Industrie Laitière, **19** 51

Société Samos, **23** 219

Société Savoyarde des Fromagers du Reblochon, **25** 84

Société Succursaliste S.A. d'Approvisonnements Guyenne et Gascogne. *See* Guyenne et Gascogne.

Société Suisse de Microelectronique & d'Horlogerie. *See* The Swatch Group SA.

Société Tefal. *See* Groupe SEB.

Société Tunisienne de l'Air-Tunisair, 49 371–73

Societe Vendeenne des Embalages, **9** 305

Society Corporation, 9 474–77

Socma. *See* Sociedad Macri S.A.

SOCO Chemical Inc., **8** 69

Socony. *See* Standard Oil Co. (New York).

Socony-Vacuum Oil Company. *See* Mobil Corporation.

Socpresse, **60** 281

Sodak Gaming, Inc., **9** 427; **41** 216

Sodexho Alliance SA, 23 154; **29 442–44; 47** 201

Sodiaal S.A., 19 50; **36 437–39 (upd.)**

SODIMA, II 576–77. *See also* Sodiaal S.A.

Sodimac S.A., **69** 312

La Sodis. *See* Éditions Gallimard.

Sodiso, **23** 247

Soeker Exploration & Production Pty, Ltd., **59** 336–37

Soekor, **IV** 93

Sofamor Danek Group, Inc. *See* Medtronic, Inc.

Soffo, **22** 365

Soficom, **27** 136

SOFIL. *See* Société pour le Financement de l'Industrie Laitière.

Sofimex. *See* Sociedad Financiera Mexicana.

Sofitam, S.A., **21** 493, 495

Sofitels. *See* Accor SA.

Sofora Telecomunicaciones S.A., **63** 377

Soft Lenses Inc., **25** 55

Soft Sheen Products, Inc., 31 416–18; 46 278

Soft*Switch, **25** 301

Softbank Corp., 12 562; **13 481–83; 16** 168; **27** 516, 518; **36** 523; **38 439–44 (upd.); 68** 260

Softimage Inc., **38** 71–72

SoftKat. *See* Baker & Taylor, Inc.

SoftKey Software Products Inc., **24** 276

Softsel Computer Products, **12** 334–35

SoftSolutions Technology Corporation, **10** 558

Software AG, **11** 18

Software Development Pty., Ltd., **15** 107

Software Dimensions, Inc. *See* ASK Group, Inc.

Software, Etc., **13** 545

The Software Group Inc., **23** 489, 491

Software Plus, Inc., **10** 514

Software Publishing Corp., **14** 262

Softwood Holdings Ltd., **III** 688

Sogara S.A., **23** 246–48

Sogedis, **23** 219

Sogo Co., **42** 342

Sohio Chemical Company, **13** 502

Soil Teq, Inc., **17** 10

Soilserv, Inc. *See* Mycogen Corporation.

Sol Meliá S.A., 71 337–39

Sola International Inc., 71 340–42

Solair Inc., **14** 43; **37** 30–31

La Solana Corp., **IV** 726

Solar Electric Corp., **13** 398

Solaray, Inc., **37** 284–85

Solect Technology Group, **47** 12

Solectron Corporation, 12 161–62, **450–52; 38** 186, 189; **46** 38; **48 366–70 (upd.)**

Solera Capital, **59** 50

Solid Beheer B.V., **10** 514

Solid Cement Corporation, **59** 115

Solite Corp., **23** 224–25

Söll, **40** 96, 98

Sollac, **24** 144; **25** 96

Solley's Delicatessen and Bakery, **24** 243

Solo Serve Corporation, 23 177; **28 429–31**

SOLOCO Inc., **63** 305

Soloman Brothers, **17** 561

Solomon Smith Barney Inc., **22** 404

Solomon Valley Milling Company, **6** 592; **50** 37

Solon Automated Services, **II** 607

Solsound Industries, **16** 393

Soltam, **25** 266

Solutia Inc., 29 330; **52 312–15**

Solvay & Cie S.A., I 394–96; 21 464–67 (upd.)

Solvay Animal Health Inc., **12** 5

Solvay S.A., 61 329–34 (upd.)

Solvent Resource Recovery, Inc., **9** 109

Solvents Recovery Service of New Jersey, Inc., **8** 464

SOMABRI, **12** 152

SOMACA, **12** 152

Somali Bank, **31** 220

Someal, **27** 513, 515

Somerfield plc, 47 365–69 (upd.)

Somerville Electric Light Company, **12** 45

Somerville Packaging Group, **28** 420

Sommer-Allibert S.A., 19 406–09; 22 49; **25** 462, 464

Sommers Drug Stores, **9** 186

Sonat Exploration Company, **63** 366

Sonat, Inc., 6 577–78; 22 68

Sonatrach, 65 313–17 (upd.)

Sonecor Systems, **6** 340

Sonera Corporation, 50 441–44. *See also* TeliaSonera AB.

Sonergy, Inc., **49** 280

Sonesta International Hotels Corporation, 44 389–91

Sonet Media AB, **23** 390

SONI Ltd., **64** 404

Sonic Corp., 37 14 451–53; 16 387; **360–63 (upd.)**

Sonic Duo, **48** 419

Sonic Innovations Inc., 56 336–38

Sonic Restaurants, **31** 279

Sonnen Basserman, **II** 475

SonnenBraune, **22** 460

Sonoco Products Company, 8 475–77; 12 150–51; **16** 340

Sonofon. *See* Telenor ASA.

The Sonoma Group, **25** 246

Sonor GmbH, **53** 216

SonoSite, Inc., 56 339–41

Sony Corporation, II 101–03, 440; **III** 141, 143, 340, 658; **7** 118; **9** 385; **10** 86, 119, 403; **11** 46, 490–91, 557; **12** 75, 161, 448, **453–56 (upd.); 13** 399, 403, 482, 573; **14** 534; **16** 94; **17** 533; **18** 18; **19** 67; **20** 439; **21** 129; **22** 194; **24** 4; **25** 22; **26** 188, 433, 489, 511; **28** 241; **30** 18; **31** 239; **40 404–10 (upd.); 43** 15; **47** 318–20, 410; **63** 36; **64** 256–57

Sony Ericsson Mobile Communications AB, **61** 137

Soo Line Corporation. *See* Canadian Pacific Ltd.

Soo Line Mills, **II** 631

Sooner Trailer Manufacturing Co., **29** 367

Soparind, **25** 83–85

Sope Creek, **30** 457

Sophus Berendsen A/S, 49 374–77

SOPORCEL, **34** 38–39

Soporcel-Sociedade Portuguesa de Papel, S.A., **60** 156

Sorbents Products Co. Inc., **31** 20

Sorbus, **6** 242

Soreal, **8** 344

Sorenson Research Company, **36** 496

Sorg Paper Company. *See* Mosinee Paper Corporation.

Soriana. *See* Organización Soriana, S.A. de C.V.

Sorin S.p.A., **61** 70, 72

Soros Fund Management LLC, 27 198; **28 432–34; 43** 218

Sorrento, Inc., 19 51; **24 444–46; 26** 505

SOS Staffing Services, 25 432–35

Sosa, Bromley, Aguilar & Associates. *See* D'Arcy Masius Benton & Bowles, Inc.

Soterra, Inc., **15** 188

Sotetsu Rosen, **72** 301

Sotheby's Holdings, Inc., 11 452–54; 15 98–100; **29 445–48 (upd.); 32** 164; **39** 81–84; **49** 325

Soufflet SA. *See* Groupe Soufflet SA.

Sound Advice, Inc., 41 379–82

Sound of Music Inc. *See* Best Buy Co., Inc.

Sound Trek, **16** 74

Sound Video Unlimited, **16** 46; **43** 60

Sound Warehouse, **9** 75

Souplantation Incorporated. *See* Garden Fresh Restaurant Corporation.

The Source Enterprises, Inc., 65 318–21

Source One Mortgage Services Corp., **12** 79

Source Perrier, **7** 383; **24** 444

Sourdough Bread Factory. *See* Matt Prentice Restaurant Group.

Souriau, **19** 166

South African Airways Ltd., **27** 132. *See also* Transnet Ltd.

The South African Breweries Limited, I 287–89; **24 447–51 (upd.); 26** 462. *See also* SABMiller plc.

South African Transport Services. *See* Transnet Ltd.

South Asia Tyres, **20** 263

South Australian Brewing Company, **54** 228, 341

South Bend Toy Manufacturing Company, **25** 380

South Carolina Electric & Gas Company. *See* SCANA Corporation.

South Carolina National Corporation, **16** 523, 526

South Carolina Power Company, **38** 446–47

South Central Bell Telephone Co. *See* BellSouth Corporation.

South Central Railroad Co., **14** 325

South Coast Gas Compression Company, Inc., **11** 523

South Coast Terminals, Inc., **16** 475

South Dakota Public Service Company, **6** 524

South Florida Neonatology Associates, **61** 284

South Fulton Light & Power Company, **6** 514

South Jersey Industries, Inc., 42 352–55

South of Scotland Electricity Board, **19** 389–90

South Overseas Fashion Ltd., **53** 344

South Sea Textile, **III** 705

South Wales Electric Company, **34** 219

South West Water Plc. *See* Pennon Group Plc.

South Western Electricity plc, **38** 448; **41** 316

South-Western Publishing Co., **8** 526–28

Southam Inc., 7 486–89; 15 265; **24** 223; **36** 374

Southco, **II** 602–03; **7** 20–21; **30** 26

Southcorp Holdings Ltd., **17** 373; **22** 350

Southcorp Limited, 54 341–44

Southdown, Inc., 14 454–56; 59 114–15

Southdown Press. *See* PMP Ltd.

Southeast Bank of Florida, **11** 112

Southeast Public Service Company, **8** 536

Southeastern Freight Lines, Inc., **53** 249

Southeastern Personnel. *See* Norrell Corporation.

Southern and Phillips Gas Ltd., **13** 485

Southern Australia Airlines, **24** 396

Southern Bank, **10** 426

Southern Bearings Co., **13** 78

Southern Bell, **10** 202

Southern Blvd. Supermarkets, Inc., **22** 549

Southern Box Corp., **13** 441

Southern California Edison Co. *See* Edison International.

Southern California Financial Corporation, **27** 46

Southern California Fruit Growers Exchange. *See* Sunkist Growers, Inc.

Southern California Gas Co., **25** 413–14, 416

Southern Casualty Insurance Co., **III** 214

The Southern Company, V 721–23; 38 445–49 (upd.)

Southern Cooker Limited Partnership, **51** 85

Southern Cotton Co., **24** 488

Southern Cross Paints, **38** 98

Southern Discount Company of Atlanta, **9** 229

Southern Electric PLC, 13 484–86. *See also* Scottish and Southern Energy plc.

Southern Electric Supply Co., **15** 386

Southern Electronics Corp. *See* SED International Holdings, Inc.

Southern Equipment & Supply Co., **19** 344

Southern Financial Bancorp, Inc., 56 342–44

Southern Forest Products, Inc., **6** 577

Southern Gage, **III** 519; **22** 282

Southern Graphic Arts, **13** 405

Southern Guaranty Cos., **III** 404

Southern Idaho Water Power Company, **12** 265

Southern Indiana Gas and Electric Company, 13 487–89

Southern Lumber Company, **8** 430

Southern Manufacturing Company, **8** 458

Southern Minnesota Beet Sugar Cooperative, **32** 29

Southern National Bankshares of Atlanta, **II** 337; **10** 425

Southern Natural Gas Co., **6** 577

Southern Nevada Power Company, **11** 343

Southern Nevada Telephone Company, **11** 343

Southern New England Telecommunications Corporation, 6 338–40

Southern Oregon Broadcasting Co., **7** 15

Southern Pacific Communications Corporation, **9** 478–79

Southern Pacific Rail Corp. *See* Union Pacific Corporation.

Southern Pacific Transportation Company, V 516–18; 12 278; **26** 235; **37** 312

Southern Peru Copper Corp.,

Southern Peru Copper Corporation, IV 3; **40** 220, 222, 411–13

Southern Phenix Textiles Inc., **15** 247–48

Southern Power Company. *See* Duke Energy Corporation.

Southern Recycling Inc., **51** 170

Southern Science Applications, Inc., **22** 88

Southern States Cooperative Incorporated, 36 440–42

Southern Sun Hotel Corporation. *See* South African Breweries Ltd.; Sun International Hotels Limited.

Southern Telephone Company, **14** 257

Southern Union Company, 12 542; **27 424–26**

Southern Video Partnership, **9** 74

Southern Water plc, **19** 389–91; **49** 363, 365–66

Southgate Medical Laboratory System, **26** 391

Southington Savings Bank, **55** 52

The Southland Corporation, II 620, **660–61**; **7** 114, 374, **490–92 (upd.)**; **9** 178; **13** 333, 525; **23** 406–07; **25** 125; **26** 447; **31** 231; **50** 487. *See also* 7-Eleven, Inc.

Southland Mobilcom Inc., **15** 196

Southland Paper, **13** 118

Southland Royal Company, **27** 86

Southland Royalty Co., **10** 190

Southmark Corp., **11** 483; **33** 398

Southport, Inc., **44** 203

Southtrust Corporation, 11 455–57

Southwest Airlines Co., 6 119–21; **24 452–55 (upd.)**; **71 343–47 (upd.)**

Southwest Airmotive Co., **II** 16

Southwest Convenience Stores, LLC, **26** 368

Southwest Converting, **19** 414

Southwest Enterprise Associates, **13** 191

Southwest Forest Industries, **IV** 334

Southwest Gas Corporation, 19 410–12

Southwest Hide Co., **16** 546

Southwest Property Trust Inc., **52** 370

Southwest Sports Group, **51** 371, 374

Southwest Water Company, 47 370–73

Southwestern Bell Corporation, V 328–30; **6** 324; **10** 431, 500; **14** 489; **17** 110; **18** 22. *See also* SBC Communications Inc.

Southwestern Bell Publications, **26** 520

Southwestern Electric Power Co., 21 468–70

Southwestern Gas Pipeline, **7** 344

Southwestern Illinois Coal Company, **7** 33

Southwestern Public Service Company, 6 579–81

Southwestern Textile Company, **12** 393

Southwire Company, Inc., 8 478–80; **12** 353; **23 444–47 (upd.)**

Souvall Brothers, **8** 473

Souza Cruz S.A., 65 322–24

Souza Pinto Industria e Comercio de Artefatos de Borracha Ltda., **71** 393

Sovereign Corp., **III** 221; **14** 109; **37** 84

Soviba, **70** 322

Sovintel, **59** 209, 211

Sovran Financial, **10** 425–26

Sovran Self Storage, Inc., 66 299–301

SovTransavto, **6** 410

Soyco Foods, Inc., **58** 137

SP Pharmaceuticals, LLC, **50** 123

SP Reifenwerke, **V** 253

SP Tyres, **V** 253

Space Control GmbH, **28** 243–44

Space Craft Inc., **9** 463

Space Data Corporation, **22** 401

Space Systems Corporation. *See* Orbital Sciences Corporation.

Space Systems/Loral, **9** 325

Spacehab, Inc., 37 364–66

Spacelabs Medical, Inc., 71 348–50

Spacesaver Corporation, **57** 208–09

Spaghetti Warehouse, Inc., 25 436–38

Spagnesi, **18** 258

Spago. *See* The Wolfgang Puck Food Company, Inc.

Spalding & Evenflo, **24** 530

Spalding, Inc., **17** 243; **23** 449; **54** 73

Spanco Yarns, **62** 375

Spangler Candy Company, 44 392–95

Spanish Broadcasting System, Inc., 41 383–86

Spanish International Communications Corp. *See* Univision Communications Inc.

SPAO, **39** 184

Spar Aerospace Limited, 32 435–37

SPAR Handels AG, 35 398–401; **36** 296; **63** 431

Sparbanken Bank, **18** 543

SPARC International, **7** 499

Spare Change, **10** 282

SpareBank 1 Gruppen, **69** 177, 179

Sparks Computerized Car Care Centers, **25** 445

Sparks-Withington Company. *See* Sparton Corporation.

Sparrow Records, **22** 194

Sparta, Inc., **18** 369

Sparta Surgical Corporation, **33** 456

Spartan Communications, **38** 308–09

Spartan Industries, Inc., **45** 15

Spartan Insurance Co., **26** 486

Spartan Motors Inc., 14 457–59

Spartan Stores Inc., II 679–80; **8 481–82**; **10** 302; **14** 412; **66 302–05 (upd.)**

Spartech Corporation, 9 92; **19 413–15**; **33** 78–79

Sparton Corporation, 18 492–95

SPCM, Inc., **14** 477

Spear, Leeds & Kellogg, 51 148; **66 306–09**

Spec's Music, Inc., 19 416–18

Special Agent Investigators, Inc., **14** 541

Special Foods, **14** 557

Special Project Films, Inc., **58** 124

Special Zone Limited, **26** 491

Specialized Bicycle Components Inc., 19 384; **50 445–48**

Specialty Brands Inc., **25** 518

Specialty Coatings Inc., 8 483–84

Specialty Equipment Companies, Inc., 25 439–42

Specialty Foods Corporation, **29** 29, 31

Specialty Products & Insulation Co., 59 381–83

Specialty Products Co., **8** 386

Specialty Restaurant Group, LLC, **71** 319

Specialty Retailers, Inc., **24** 456

Spectra-Physics, Inc. *See* Newport Corporation.

Spectra Star, Inc., **18** 521

Spectradyne, **28** 241

Spectral Dynamics Corporation. *See* Scientific- Atlanta, Inc.

Spectron MicroSystems, **18** 143

Spectrum Brands. *See* United Industries Corporation.

Spectrum Club, **25 448–50**

Spectrum Communications Holdings International Limited, **24** 95

Spectrum Concepts, **10 394–95**

Spectrum Control, Inc., 67 355–57

Spectrum Data Systems, Inc., **24** 96

Spectrum Dyed Yarns of New York, **8** 559

Spectrum Health Care Services, **13** 48

Spectrum Medical Technologies, Inc., **22** 409

Spectrum Numismatics International, Inc., **60** 146

Spectrum Organic Products, Inc., 68 346–49

Spectrum Technology Group, Inc., **7** 378; **18** 112

Spectrumedia, **21** 361

Speech Design GmbH, **62** 38–39

Speed-O-Lac Chemical, **8** 553

SpeeDee Oil Change and Tune-Up, 25 443–47

Speedway Motorsports, Inc., 32 438–41

Speedway SuperAmerica LLC, **49** 330

Speedy Auto Glass, **30** 501

Speedy Europe, **54** 207

Speedy Muffler King, **10** 415; **24** 337, 339

Speizman Industries, Inc., 44 396–98

Spelling Entertainment, 14 460–62; **35 402–04 (upd.)**

Spenard Builders Supply. *See* Lanoga Corporation.

Spencer & Spencer Systems, Inc., **18** 112

Spencer Gifts, Inc., **15** 464

Spencer Stuart and Associates, Inc., 14 463–65

Sperry & Hutchinson Co., **12** 299; **23** 243–44

Sperry Aerospace Group, **6** 283

Sperry Corporation, **III** 165–66, 329, 642; **8** 92; **12** 39; **13** 511; **16** 137; **18** 386, 542; **22** 379. *See also* Unisys Corporation.

Sperry New Holland. *See* New Holland N.V.

Sperry Top-Sider, Inc., **37** 377, 379

Spezialpapierfabrik Blankenstein GmbH, **64** 275

Sphere Drake Holdings Ltd., **57** 136

Sphere Inc., **8** 526; **13** 92

Sphere SA, **27** 9

Spherion Corporation, 45 272, 274; **52 316–18**

Spider Software, Inc., **46** 38

Spie. *See* Amec Spie S.A.

Spie Batignolles SA, **13** 206; **24** 79

Spiegel, Inc., 8 56–58; **10** 168, **489–91**; **11** 498; **9** 190, 219; **13** 179; **27 427–31 (upd.)**; **34** 232; **36** 177, 180

SPIEGEL-Verlag Rudolf Augstein GmbH & Co. KG, 44 399–402

Spike's Holding, Inc. *See* The Finish Line, Inc.

Spin Master, Ltd., 61 335–38

SpinCircuit Inc., **38** 188

Spinelli Coffee Co., **51** 385

Spinnaker Exploration Company, 72 334–36

Spinnaker Industries, Inc., **43** 276

Spinnaker Software Corp., **24** 276

Spirax-Sarco Engineering plc, 59 384–86

SPIRE Corporation, **14** 477

Spire, Inc., **25** 183

Spirella Company of Great Britain Ltd. *See* Coats plc.

Spirit Airlines, Inc., 31 419–21

Spirit Cruises, **29 442–43**

Spliethoff, **26** 280

SPN Resources, LLC, **65** 334

Spode. *See* The Porcelain and Fine China Companies Ltd.

Spoerle Electronic, **10** 113; **50** 42

Spokane Falls Electric Light and Power Company. *See* Edison Electric Illuminating Company.

Spokane Falls Water Power Company, **6** 595

Spokane Natural Gas Company, **6** 597

Spokane Street Railway Company, **6** 595

Spokane Traction Company, **6** 596
Spom Japan, **IV** 600
Spon Press, **44** 416
Spoornet, **6** 435
Sporis, **27** 151
Sporloisirs S.A., **9** 157
Sport Chalet, Inc., 16 454–56
Sport Developpement SCA, **33** 10
Sport Maska Inc., **70** 126
Sport Supply Group, Inc., 22 458–59; **23** 448–50; **30** 185
Sporting Dog Specialties, Inc., **14** 386
Sportland, **26** 160
Sportmagazine NV, **48** 347
Sportmart, Inc., 15 469–71. *See also* Gart Sports Company.
Sports & Co. *See* Hibbett Sporting Goods, Inc.
Sports & Recreation, Inc., 15 470; **17** 453–55
The Sports Authority, Inc., 15 470; **16** 457–59; **17** 453; **18** 286; **24** 173; **43** 385–88 (upd.)
The Sports Club Company, 25 448–51
Sports Experts Inc., **II** 652
Sports Holdings Corp., **34** 217
Sports Inc., **14** 8; **33** 10
Sports Plus, **44** 192
Sports-Tech Inc., **21** 300
Sports Traders, Inc., **18** 208
Sportservice Corporation, **7** 133–35
The Sportsman's Guide, Inc., 36 443–46
Sportstown, Inc., **15** 470
Sportsystems Corporation, **7** 133, 135
Spotless Group Limited, **62** 391
Sprague Devices, Inc., **11** 84
Sprague Technologies, **21** 520
Spraysafe, **29** 98
Sprecher & Schuh, **9** 10
Spreckels Sugar Company, Inc., **32** 274, 277
Spring Co., **21** 96, 246
Spring Forge Mill, **8** 412
Spring Group plc, **54** 191–93
Spring Grove Services, **45** 139–40
Spring Valley Brewery. *See* Kirin Brewery Company, Limited.
Springer Verlag GmbH & Co., **IV** 611, 641
Springfield Bank, **9** 474
Springfield Gas Light Company, **38** 81
Springhouse Corp. *See* Reed Elsevier.
Springmaid International, Inc., **19** 421
Springs Industries, Inc., V 378–79; **19** 419–22 (upd.); **29** 132; **31** 199
Sprint Canada Inc., **44** 49
Sprint Communications Company, L.P., 9 478–80; **10** 19, 57, 97, 201–03; **11** 183, 185, 500–01; **18** 32, 164–65, 569–70; **22** 19, 162; **24** 120, 122; **25** 102; **26** 17; **27** 365; **36** 167. *See also* Sprint Corporation; US Sprint Communications.
Sprint Corporation, 46 373–76 (upd.)
Sprint PCS, **33** 34, 36–37; **38** 433
Sprocket Systems, **50** 320
Sprout Group, **37** 121
Sprout-Matador A.S., **51** 25
SPS Technologies, Inc., 30 428–30
SPSS Inc., 64 360–63
SPT Telecom. *See* Cesky Telecom, a.s.
Spun Yarns, Inc., **12** 503
Spur Oil Co., **7** 362

SPX Corporation, 10 492–95; **47** 374–79 **(upd.)**
SPZ, Inc., **26** 257
SQ Software, Inc., **10** 505
SQL Solutions, Inc., **10** 505
Square D Company, **18** 473
Square Industries, **18** 103, 105
Squibb Beech-Nut. *See* Beech-Nut Nutrition Corp.
Squibb Corporation, I 695–97; **8** 166; **16** 438–39. *See also* Bristol-Myers Squibb Company.
Squire Fashions Inc. *See* Norton McNaughton of Squire, Inc.
SR. *See* Southern Railway.
SRAM Corporation, 65 325–27
SRC Holdings Corporation, 67 358–60
SRI International, Inc., 10 139; **57** 309, 311, **333–36**
SRI Strategic Resources Inc., **6** 310
SS&C Technologies Inc., **66** 225
SS Cars, Ltd. *See* Jaguar Cars, Ltd.
SS Lazio. *See* Società Sportiva Lazio SpA.
SSA. *See* Stevedoring Services of America Inc.
Ssangyong Cement Industrial Co., Ltd., III 747–50; **61** 339–43 **(upd.)**
Ssangyong Motor Company, **34** 132
SSC Benelux & Company, **52** 310–11
SSDS, Inc., **18** 537; **43** 433
SSI Medical Services, Inc., **10** 350
SSL International plc, 49 378–81
SSMC Inc., **II** 10
SSP Company, Inc., **17** 434
St. *See under* Saint
Staal Bankiers, **13** 544
STAAR Surgical Company, 57 337–39
Stackpole Fibers, **37** 427
Stadia Colorado Corporation, **18** 140
Stadt Corporation, **26** 109
Staefa Control System Limited. *See* Elektrowatt AG.
Staff Builders Inc. *See* ATC Healthcare, Inc.
Staff International, **40** 157
StaffAmerica, Inc., **16** 50
Stafford-Lowdon, **31** 435
Stage Stores, Inc., 24 456–59
Stagecoach Holdings plc, 30 431–33; **55** 103
Stags' Leap Winery, **22** 80
Stahl-Urban Company, **8** 287–88
Stahlwerke Südwestfalen AG, **IV** 89
Stainless Fabrication Inc., **65** 289
Stakis plc, **49** 193
Stamford Drug Group, **9** 68
Stamford FHI Acquisition Corp., **27** 117
Stamos Associates Inc., **29** 377
Stamps.com Inc., **34** 474
Stanadyne Automotive Corporation, 37 367–70
Stanadyne, Inc., **7** 336; **12** 344
StanCorp Financial Group, Inc., 56 345–48
Standard & Poor's Corp., **IV** 482, 636–37; **12** 310; **25** 542
Standard Aircraft Equipment, **II** 16
Standard Alaska, **7** 559
Standard Bank, **17** 324
Standard Box Co., **17** 357
Standard Brands, **7** 365, 367; **18** 538
Standard Car Truck, **18** 5
Standard Chartered plc, II 357–59; 386; **10** 170; **47** 227; **48** 371–74 **(upd.)**

Standard Commercial Corporation, 12 110; **13** 490–92; **27** 126; **62** 333–37 **(upd.)**
The Standard Companies, Inc., **58** 374
Standard Electric Time Company, **13** 233
Standard Electrica, **II** 13
Standard Federal Bank, 9 481–83
Standard Fruit and Steamship Co. of New Orleans, **31** 168
Standard Gauge Manufacturing Company, **13** 233
Standard Gypsum Corp., **19** 77
Standard Insert Co., **28** 350
Standard Kollsman Industries Inc., **13** 461
Standard Life & Accident Insurance Company, **27** 47–48
Standard Life Assurance Company, III 358–61
Standard Life Insurance Company, **11** 481
The Standard Life Insurance Company of New York, **56** 345
Standard Microsystems Corporation, 11 462–64
Standard Motor Products, Inc., 40 414–17
Standard of America Life Insurance Co., **III** 324
Standard of Georgia Insurance Agency, Inc., **10** 92
Standard Oil Co., **7** 169–72, 263, 414; **8** 415; **10** 110, 289; **14** 21; **25** 230; **27** 129. *See also* Exxon Corporation; Mobil Corporation.
Standard Oil Co. (California). *See* ChevronTexaco Corporation
Standard Oil Co. (Indiana). *See* Amoco Corporation.
Standard Oil Co. (New York), **IV** 485, 504, 537, 549, 558; **7** 171. *See also* Mobil Corporation.
Standard Oil Co. of New Jersey, **IV** 415–16, 419, 431–33, 438, 460, 463–64, 488, 522, 531, 537–38, 544, 558, 565, 571; **7** 170–72, 253, 351; **13** 124; **17** 412–13; **24** 521
Standard Oil Co. of Ohio, **IV** 452, 463, 522, 571; **7** 171, 263; **12** 309; **24** 521
Standard Pacific Corporation, 52 319–22
Standard Plastics, **25** 312
Standard Printing Company, **19** 333
Standard Process & Engraving, Inc., **26** 105
Standard Products Company, **19** 454
Standard Rate & Data Service, **7** 286
Standard Register Co., 15 472–74
Standard Screw Co., **12** 344
Standard Shares, **9** 413–14
Standard Steel Propeller, **9** 416; **10** 162
Standard Telephone and Radio, **II** 13
Standard Telephones and Cables, Ltd., **6** 242
Standard Tin Plate Co., **15** 127
Standard-Vacuum Oil Co. *See* Mobil Corporation.
Standex International Corporation, 16 470–71; **17** 456–59; **44** 403–06 **(upd.)**
Standish Industries Inc., **61** 295
Stanhome Inc., 9 330; **11** 94–96; **15** 475–78
Stanhome Worldwide Direct Selling, **35** 262, 264
STANIC, **69** 145, 148
Stankiewicz GmbH. *See* Phoenix AG

Stanley Furniture Company, Inc., 34 412–14
Stanley Home Products, Incorporated. *See* Stanhome Inc.
Stanley Leisure plc, 66 310–12
Stanley Mining Services, Ltd., **19** 247
Stanley Smith Security. *See* Initial Security.
The Stanley Works, III 626–29; 7 480; **9** 543; **13** 41; **20 476–80 (upd.)**
StanMont, Inc., **24** 425
Stant Corporation, **15** 503, 505
StanWest Equities, Inc., **56** 348
Staples, Inc., 8 404–05; **10 496–98; 18** 24, 388; **20** 99; **22** 154; **23** 363, 365; **24** 270; **55 351–56 (upd.)**
Star, **10** 287–88
Star Air Service. *See* Alaska Air Group, Inc.
Star Alliance, **26** 113; **33** 51; **38** 36
Star Banc Corporation, 11 465–67; 13 222; **31** 206. *See also* Firstar Corporation.
Star Building Systems, Inc., **19** 366
Star Cruises Ltd. *See* Genting Bhd.
Star Engraving, **12** 471
Star Enterprises, Inc., **6** 457
Star Finishing Co., **9** 465
Star Laboratories Inc., **24** 251
Star Markets Company, Inc., **23** 169; **56** 317
Star Medical Europe B.V., **56** 338
Star Medical Technologies, Inc., **22** 409; **31** 124
Star Paper Tube, Inc., **19** 76–78
Star Sportwear Manufacturing Corp., **29** 294
Star Systems, Inc., **52** 88
Starber International, **12** 181
Starbucks Corporation, 13 493–94; 18 37; **22** 370; **25** 178, 501; **28** 63; **34 415–19 (upd.); 36** 156–57; **37** 181; **38** 340; **40** 152–53; **44** 313; **50** 97; **63** 87
Starcraft Corporation, 13 113; **30 434–36; 66 313–16 (upd.)**
Stardent Computer Inc., **III** 553; **26** 256
Starfish Software, **23** 212
Stark Record and Tape Service. *See* Camelot Music, Inc.
Starkey Laboratories, Inc., 52 323–25
StarKist Foods. *See* H.J. Heinz Company.
Starlen Labs, Ltd., **31** 346
Starlight Networks, Inc., **27** 366
Starline Optical Corp., **22** 123
Starpointe Savings Bank, **9** 173
Starrett Corporation, 21 471–74
Star's Discount Department Stores, **16** 36
Startech Semiconductor Inc., **14** 183
Startel Corp., **15** 125
Starter Corp., 12 457–458
Starwood Capital, **29** 508
Starwood Hotels & Resorts Worldwide, Inc., 33 217; **54 345–48**
The Stash Tea Company, 50 449–52
State Bank of Albany, **9** 228
State Bank of India, 63 354–57
State Farm Insurance Companies, **27** 30; **29** 397; **39** 155
State Farm Mutual Automobile Insurance Company, III 362–64; 10 50; **22** 266; **23** 286; **25** 155; **41** 313; **51 341–45 (upd.)**
State Finance and Thrift Company, **14** 529

State Financial Services Corporation, 51 346–48
State Leed, **13** 367
State Mutual Life Assurance Company, **63** 29
State-o-Maine, **18** 357–59
State Savings Bank and Trust Co., **11** 180; **42** 429
State Street Corporation, 8 491–93; 57 340–44 (upd.)
Staten Island Advance Corp. *See* Advance Publications Inc.
Staten Island Bancorp, Inc., 39 380–82
Stater Bros. Holdings Inc., 17 558; **64** 364–67
Statex Petroleum, Inc., **19** 70
Static, Inc., **14** 430
Static Snowboards, Inc., **51** 393
Station Casinos Inc., 25 452–54
Stationers Distributing Company, **14** 523
Stationers, Inc., **28** 74
Statoil ASA, 54 97; **61** 238, **344–48 (upd.)**
StatScript Management Services, **26** 73
The Staubach Company, 62 338–41
Stauffer Chemical Company, **8** 105–07; **21** 545
Stauffer Communications, Inc., **36** 339–41
Stax Records, **23** 32
STC PLC, III 141, **162–64; 25** 497; **36** 351
Stead & Miller, **13** 169
Steak & Ale, **7** 336; **12** 373
The Steak n Shake Company, 14 130–31; **41 387–90**
Steam Boiler Works, **18** 318
Steamboat Ski and Resort Corporation, **28** 21
Stearns & Foster, **12** 439
Stearns Catalytic World Corp., **II** 87; **11** 413
Stearns Coal & Lumber, **6** 514
Stearns, Inc., 43 389–91
Stearns Manufacturing Co., **16** 297
Steego Auto Paints, **24** 160
Steel Authority of India Ltd., IV 205–07; 66 317–21 (upd.)
Steel Co. of Canada Ltd. *See* Stelco Inc.
Steel Dynamics, Inc., 18 380; **26** 530; **52 326–28**
Steel Technologies Inc., 63 358–60
Steelcase Inc., 7 493–95; 8 251–52, 255, 405; **25** 500; **27 432–35 (upd.); 39** 205–07
Steely, **IV** 109
Steen Production Services, Inc., **51** 248
Steenfabriek De Ruiterwaard, **14** 249
Steenkolen Handelsvereniging NV, **39** 176; **50** 335
Stefanel SpA, 63 361–63
Stefany, **12** 152
Stegbar Pty Ltd., **31** 398–400
Steger Furniture Manufacturing Co., **18** 493
Steiff. *See* Margarete Steiff GmbH.
Steil, Inc., **8** 271
Steilman Group. *See* Klaus Steilmann GmbH & Co. KG.
Stein Mart Inc., 19 423–25; 72 337–39 (upd.)
Stein Printing Company, **25** 183
Stein Robaire Helm, **22** 173
Steinbach Inc., **14** 427
Steinbach Stores, Inc., **19** 108

Steinberg Incorporated, II 652–53, **662–65**
Steinberger, **16** 239
Steiner Corporation (Alsco), 53 308–11
Steinheil Optronik GmbH, **24** 87
Steinmüller Verwaltungsgesellschaft. *See* Vereinigte Elektrizitaswerke Westfalen AG
Steinway & Sons, **16** 201; **43** 170
Steinway Musical Properties, Inc., 19 392, 394, **426–29; 55** 111, 114
Stelco Inc., IV 208–10; 24 144; **51 349–52 (upd.)**
Stella Bella Corporation, **19** 436
Stella D'Oro Company, **7** 367
Stellar Systems, Inc., **14** 542
Stelmar Shipping Ltd., 52 329–31
Stelux Manufacturing Company, **13** 121; **41** 71
Stelwire Ltd., **51** 352
Stena AB, **25** 105; **29** 429–30
Stena Line AB, **38** 345
Stena-Sealink, **37** 137
Stens Corporation, **48** 34
Stentor Canadian Network Management, **6** 310
Stenval Sud, **19** 50
Stepan Company, 30 437–39
The Stephan Company, 60 285–88
Stephen F. Whitman & Son, Inc., **7** 429
Stephens Inc., **67** 129–30
Stephenson Clarke and Company, **31** 368–69
Sterchi Bros. Co., **14** 236
Steria SA, 49 382–85
Stericycle Inc., 33 380–82
STERIS Corporation, 29 449–52
Sterling Capital Partners, **57** 56–57
Sterling Chemicals, Inc., 16 460–63; 27 117
Sterling Drug Inc., I 698–700
Sterling Electronics Corp., 18 496–98; 19 311
Sterling Engineered Products, **III** 640, 642; **16** 9
Sterling European Airlines A/S, 70 300–02
Sterling Forest Corp., **III** 264
Sterling House Corp., **42** 4
Sterling Inc., **61** 326–27
Sterling Industries, **13** 166
Sterling Manhattan, **7** 63
Sterling Organics Ltd., **12** 351; **50** 282
Sterling Software, Inc., 11 468–70; 31 296
Sterling Stores Co. Inc., **24** 148
Sterling Winthrop, **7** 164; **36** 174; **49** 351
Stern & Stern Textiles, **11** 261
Stern Bros. Investment Bank, **19** 359
Stern Bros., LLC, **37** 224
Stern Publishing, **38** 478
Stern's, **9** 209
Sternco Industries, **12** 230–31
STET. *See* Società Finanziaria Telefonica per Azioni.
Stet Hellas, **63** 378–79
Steuben Glass. *See* Corning Inc.
Stevcoknit Fabrics Company, **8** 141–43
Steve's Ice Cream, **16** 54–55
Stevedoring Services of America Inc., 28 435–37; 50 209–10
Steven Madden, Ltd., 37 371–73
Stevens Linen Associates, Inc., **8** 272
Stevens Sound Proofing Co., **7** 291

Stevens, Thompson & Runyan, Inc. *See* CRSS Inc.

Stevens Water Monitoring Systems, **52** 226

Stew Leonard's, 56 349–51

Stewart and Richey Construction Co., **51** 170

Stewart & Stevenson Services Inc., 11 471–73

Stewart Enterprises, Inc., 16 344; **20 481–83; 37** 67

Stewart Systems, Inc., **22** 352–53

Stewart, Tabori & Chang, **58** 155

Stewart's Beverages, 39 383–86

Steyr Walzlager, **III** 625

Stichting Continuiteit AMEV, **III** 202

Stickley. *See* L. and J.G. Stickley, Inc.

Stieber Rollkupplung GmbH, **14** 63

Stihl. *See* Andreas Stihl AG & Co. KG.

Stilecraft, **24** 16

Stillwater Mining Company, 47 380–82

Stilwell Financial Inc. *See* Janus Capital Group Inc.

Stimson & Valentine, **8** 552

Stimsonite Corporation, **49** 38

Stinnes AG, 8 68–69, **494–97; 23** 68–70, **451–54 (upd.); 33** 195; **59 387–92 (upd.)**

Stirling Group plc, 62 342–44

STM Systems Corp., **11** 485

STMicroelectronics NV, 52 332–35

Stock Clearing Corporation, **9** 370

Stock Yards Packing Co., Inc., 37 374–76

Stockholder Systems Inc., **11** 485

Stockpack Ltd., **44** 318

Stoddard International plc, 72 340–43

Stoelting Brothers Company, **10** 371

Stokely Van Camp, **II** 560, 575; **12** 411; **22** 338

Stokvis/De Nederlandsche Kroon Rijwiefabrieken, **13** 499

Stoll-Moss Theatres Ltd., 34 420–22

Stollwerck AG, 53 312–15

Stolt-Nielsen S.A., 42 356–59; 54 349–50

Stolt Sea Farm Holdings PLC, 54 349–51

Stone & Webster, Inc., 13 495–98; 64 368–72 (upd.)

Stone-Consolidated Corporation, **25** 9, 12

Stone Container Corporation, IV 332–34; 8 203–04; **15** 129; **17** 106; **25** 12. *See also* Smurfit-Stone Container Corporation.

Stone Manufacturing Company, 14 469–71; 43 392–96 (upd.)

Stonega Coke & Coal Co. *See* Westmoreland Coal Company.

Stoner Associates. *See* Severn Trent PLC.

Stonington Partners, **19** 318

StonyBrook Services Inc., **24** 49

Stonyfield Farm, Inc., 55 357–60

Stoody Co., **19** 440

Stoof, **26** 278–79

Stoomvaart Maatschappij Nederland. *See* Koninklijke Nedlloyd N.V.

The Stop & Shop Supermarket Company, II 666–67; **24 460–62 (upd.); 68 350–53 (upd.)**

Stop N Go, **7** 373; **25** 126

Stoppenbauch Inc., **23** 202

Stora Enso Oyj, 36 128, **447–55 (upd.)**

Stora Kopparbergs Bergslags AB, IV 335–37, 340; **12** 464; **28** 445–46. *See also* Stora Enso Oyj.

Storage Dimensions Inc., **10** 404

Storage Technology Corporation, 6 275–77; 12 148, 161; **16** 194; **28** 198

Storage USA, Inc., 21 475–77

Storebor Brux Company, **52** 406

Storehouse PLC, II 658; **13** 284; **16 464–66; 17** 42–43, 335; **24** 75

Storer Communications, **7** 91–92, 200–1; **24** 122

Storm Technology, **28** 245

Storybook, Inc., **70** 52

Storz Instruments Co., **25** 56; **27** 115

Stouffer Corp., 8 498–501; 28 238

Stowe Machine Co., Inc., **30** 283

STP, **19** 223; **26** 349

STRAAM Engineers. *See* CRSS Inc.

Straits Steamship Co. *See* Malaysian Airlines System.

Stran, **8** 546

StrataCom, Inc., 11 59; **16 467–69; 34** 113

Stratagene Corporation, 70 303–06

Stratasys, Inc., 67 361–63

Strategic Implications International, Inc., **45** 44

Strategix Solutions, **43** 309

StrategyOne, **62** 115

Stratford Corporation, **15** 103; **26** 100

Stratos Boat Co., Ltd., **III** 600

Stratton Oakmont Inc., **37** 372–73; **46** 282

Stratton Ski Corporation, **15** 235

Stratus Computer, Inc., 10 499–501

Straus-Frank Company, **29** 86, 88

Strauss Discount Auto, 56 352–54

Strauss-Elite Group, 68 354–57

Strawberries, **30** 465

Strayer Education, Inc., 53 316–19

Stream International Inc., **48** 369

Stream Machine Co., **48** 92

Streamline Holdings, **39** 237–38

StreamScapes Media, **51** 286, 288

Street & Smith Publications, Inc., **13** 178

The Stride Rite Corporation, 8 502–04; 9 437; **33** 244; **37 377–80 (upd.)**

Strintzis Lines Shipping S.A., **64** 45

Strix Ltd., 51 353–55

Strobbe Graphics NV. *See* Punch International N.V.

Stroehmann Bakeries, **II** 631

The Stroh Brewery Company, I 255, **290–92; 13** 10–11, 455; **18** 72, **499–502 (upd.); 22** 422; **23** 403, 405; **36** 14–15

Strombecker Corporation, 60 289–91

Stromeyer GmbH, **7** 141

Strong Electric Corporation, **19** 211

Strong International, **27** 57

Stroock & Stroock & Lavan LLP, 40 418–21

Strouds, Inc., 33 383–86

Structural Dynamics Research Corporation, **10** 257

Structural Fibers, Inc. *See* Essef Corporation.

Structural Iberica S.A., **18** 163

Struebel Group, **18** 170

Strydel, Inc., **14** 361; **59** 320

Stryker Corporation, 10 351; **11 474–76; 29 453–55 (upd.)**

Stuart & Sons Ltd., **34** 493, 496

Stuart C. Irby Company, 58 333–35

Stuart Entertainment Inc., 16 470–72

Stuart Hall Co., **17** 445

Stuart Medical, Inc., **10** 143; **16** 400

Stuckey's, Inc., **7** 429

Studebaker-Packard, **9** 118; **10** 261

Student Loan Marketing Association, II 453–55. *See also* SLM Holding Corp.

StudioCanal, **48** 164–65

Studley Products Inc., **12** 396

Stuffit Co., **IV** 597

Stuller Settings, Inc., 35 405–07

Sturbridge Yankee Workshop, Inc., **10** 216

Sturgeon Bay Shipbuilding and DryDock Company, **18** 320

Sturm, Ruger & Company, Inc., 19 430–32

Stussy, Inc., 55 361–63

Style Magazine BV, **48** 347

Styleclick.com, Inc., **47** 420

Stylus Writing Instruments, **27** 416

SU214, **28** 27, 30

Suave Shoe Corporation. *See* French Fragrances, Inc.

Sub-Zero Freezer Co., Inc., 31 426–28

Suber Suisse S.A., **48** 350

Subic Bay Energy Co., Ltd, **56** 290

The SubLine Company, Inc., **53** 340

SubLogic, **15** 455

SUBperior Distribution Systems, Inc., **53** 340

Suburban Coastal Corporation, **10** 92

Suburban Light and Power Company, **12** 45

Suburban Propane Partners, L.P., 30 440–42

Suburban Savings and Loan Association, **10** 92

Subway, 15 56–57; **32 442–44.** *See also* Doctor's Associates Inc.

Successories, Inc., 30 443–45

Sucden. *See* Compagnie Financière Sucres et Denrées.

Sucesora de Jose Puig y Cia C.A., **60** 246

Suchard Co. *See* Jacobs Suchard.

Sudamericana Holding S.A., **63** 180

Sudbury Inc., 16 473–75; 17 373

Sudbury River Consulting Group, **31** 131

Südzucker AG, 27 436–39

Suez Lyonnaise des Eaux, 36 456–59 (upd.); 38 321; **40** 447, 449; **42** 386, 388; **45** 277; **47** 219

Suez Oil Processing Co., **IV** 413–14; **51** 113

Suffolk County Federal Savings and Loan Association, **16** 346

Sugar Entertainment, **51** 288

Sugar Land State Bank, **25** 114

Sugar Mount Capital, LLC, **33** 355

Sugarland Industries. *See* Imperial Holly Corporation.

SugarLoaf Creations, Inc. *See* American Coin Merchandising, Inc.

Sugarloaf Mountain Corporation, **28** 21

Suge Knight Films, Inc., **69** 350–51

The Suit Company, **51** 253

Suito Sangyo Co., Ltd. *See* Seino Transportation Company, Ltd.

SUITS. *See* Scottish Universal Investments.

Suiza Foods Corporation, 25 512, 514; **26 447–50; 37** 197; **38** 381

Sukhoi Design Bureau Aviation Scientific-Industrial Complex, 24 463–65

Sullivan & Cromwell, 26 451–53; 27 327; **47** 437

Sullivan-Schein Dental Products Inc. *See* Henry Schein Inc.

Sullivan, Stauffer, Colwell & Bayles, **14** 314

Sulpetro Limited, **25** 232

Sulzer Ltd., III 630–33; 68 358–62 (upd.)

Sumergrade Corporation, **19** 304; **41** 300

Suminoe Textile Co., **8** 235

Sumisei Secpac Investment Advisors, **III** 366

Sumisho Electronics Co. Ltd., **18** 170

Sumitomo Bank, Limited, II 360–62; IV, 726; **9** 341–42; **18** 170; **23** 340; **26** **454–57 (upd.)**

Sumitomo Chemical Company Ltd., I **397–98; II** 361

Sumitomo Corporation, I 518–20; III 43, 365; **V** 161; **7** 357; **11 477–80 (upd.),** 490; **15** 340; **17** 556; **18** 170; **28** 288; **36** 420; **45** 115

Sumitomo Electric Industries, II 104–05

Sumitomo Heavy Industries, Ltd., III **634–35; 10** 381; **42 360–62 (upd.)**

Sumitomo Life Insurance Company, III **365–66; 60 292–94 (upd.)**

Sumitomo Metal Industries, Ltd., I 390; **II** 361; **IV 211–13,** 216; **10** 463–64; **11** 246; **24** 302

Sumitomo Metal Mining Co., Ltd., IV **214–16; 9** 340; **23** 338

Sumitomo Mitsui Banking Corporation, **51 356–62 (upd.)**

Sumitomo Realty & Development Co., **Ltd., IV 726–27**

Sumitomo Rubber Industries, Ltd., V **252–53; 20** 263

Sumitomo Trading, **45** 8

The Sumitomo Trust & Banking **Company, Ltd., II 363–64; IV** 726; **53** **320–22 (upd.)**

Summa Corporation, **9** 266; **17** 317; **50** 306

Summa International, **56** 284

Summer Paper Tube, **19** 78

SummerGate Inc., **48** 148

Summers Group Inc., **15** 386

The Summit Bancorporation, 14 472–74

Summit Constructors. *See* CRSS Inc.

Summit Family Restaurants Inc., 19 89, 92, **433–36**

Summit Gear Company, **16** 392–93

Summit Management Co., Inc., **17** 498

Summit Screen Inks, **13** 228

Summit Systems Inc., **45** 280

Summit Technology Inc., **30** 485

Sumolis, **54** 315, 317

Sun Aire, **25** 421–22

Sun Alliance Group PLC, III 296, **369–74,** 400; **37** 86. *See also* Royal & Sun Alliance Insurance Group plc.

Sun Apparel Inc., **39** 247

Sun Capital Partners Inc., **63** 79

Sun Chemical Corp. *See* Sequa Corp.

Sun Communities Inc., 46 377–79

Sun Company, Inc., IV 548–50; 7 114, 414; **11** 484; **12** 459; **17** 537; **25** 126. *See also* Sunoco, Inc.

Sun Country Airlines, I 114; **30 446–49**

Sun-Diamond Growers of California, 7 **496–97.** *See also* Diamond of California.

Sun Distributors L.P., 12 459–461

Sun Electric, **15** 288

Sun Electronics, **9** 116

Sun Equities Corporation, **15** 449

Sun-Fast Color, **13** 227

Sun Federal, **7** 498

Sun Federal Savings and Loan Association of Tallahassee, **10** 92

Sun Financial Group, Inc., **25** 171

Sun Fire Coal Company, **7** 281

Sun Foods, **12** 220–21

Sun Gro Horticulture Inc., **49** 196, 198

Sun Healthcare Group Inc., 25 455–58; **61** 205

Sun International Hotels Limited, 12 420; **26 462–65; 37** 254–55. *See also* Kerzner International Limited.

Sun Kyowa, **III** 43

Sun Life Group of America, **11** 482

Sun Live Co., **56** 201

Sun-Maid Growers of California, **7** 496–97

Sun Mark, Inc., **21** 483

Sun Media, **27** 280; **29** 471–72; **47** 327

Sun Men's Shop Co., Ltd. *See* Nagasakiya Co., Ltd.

Sun Microsystems, Inc., 7 498–501; 30 **450–54 (upd.); 36** 80–81; **38** 416, 418; **43** 238–40

Sun Oil Co., **IV** 371, 424, 548–50; **7** 413–14; **11** 35; **18** 233; **19** 162; **36** 86–87. *See also* Sunoco, Inc.

Sun Optical Co., Ltd. . *See* Nagasakiya Co., Ltd.

Sun Pac Foods, **45** 161

Sun Pharmaceutical Industries Ltd., 24 480; **57 345–47**

Sun Shades 501 Ltd., **21** 483

Sun Ship, **IV** 549

Sun Sportswear, Inc., 17 460–63; 23 65–66

Sun State Marine Services, Inc. *See* Hvide Marine Incorporated.

Sun Techno Services Co., Ltd. *See* Nagasakiya Co., Ltd.

Sun Technology Enterprises, **7** 500

Sun Television & Appliances Inc., 10 **502–03; 19** 362

Sun Valley Equipment Corp., **33** 363

SunAir, **11** 300

SunAmerica Inc., 11 481–83

Sunbeam-Oster Co., Inc., 9 484–86; 14 230; **16** 488; **17** 215; **19** 305; **22** 3; **28** 135, 246; **30** 136; **42** 309

Sunbelt Beverage Corporation, **32** 520

Sunbelt Coca-Cola, **10** 223

Sunbelt Nursery Group, Inc., **12** 179, 200, 394

Sunbelt Rentals Inc., **34** 42

Sunbird. *See* Nagasakiya Co., Ltd.

Sunburst Hospitality Corporation, 26 **458–61**

Sunburst Technology Corporation, **36** 273

Sunburst Yarns, Inc., **13** 532

Sunclipse Inc., **IV** 250

Sunco N.V., **22** 515

Suncoast Motion Picture Company, **9** 360; **63** 65

SunCor Development Company, **6** 546–47

Suncor Energy Inc., 33 167; **54 352–54**

Sundance Publishing, **IV** 609; **12** 559

Sundor Group, **54** 213

Sundstrand Corporation, 7 502–04; 21 **478–81 (upd.); 61** 320–21

Sundt Corp., 24 466–69

Sundwig Eisenhütte Maschinenfabrik GmbH & Co., **51** 25

SunGard Data Systems Inc., 11 484–85

Sunglass Hut International, Inc., 18 393; **21 482–84; 52** 227, 230

Sunkiss Thermoreactors, **21** 65

Sunkist Growers, Inc., 7 496; **25** 366; **26** **466–69; 47** 63

Sunkus & Associates, **49** 427

Sunkus Co. Ltd. *See* Nagasakiya Co., Ltd.

Sunlight Services Group Limited, **45** 139

Sunlit Industries, **44** 132

Sunnybrook Farms, **25** 124

Sunnyside Feedmill, **60** 316

Sunoco, Inc., 28 438–42 (upd.)

SunQuest HealthCare Corp. *See* Unison HealthCare Corporation.

Sunquest Information Systems Inc., **45** 279, 281

Sunray DX Oil Co., **7** 414

The Sunrider Corporation, 26 316, **470–74; 27** 353

SunRise Imaging, **44** 358

Sunrise Inc., **55** 48

Sunrise Medical Inc., 11 202, **486–88**

Sunrise Test Systems, **11** 491

Sunsations Sunglass Company, **21** 483

Sunshine Biscuit Co., **35** 181; **36** 313

Sunshine Bullion Co., **25** 542

Sunshine Jr. Stores, Inc., **17** 170

Sunshine Mining Company, **20** 149

SunSoft Inc., **7** 500; **43** 238

Sunstate Airlines Pty Ltd. *See* Qantas Airways Ltd.

Sunsweet Growers, **7** 496

Suntory Ltd., 13 454; **21** 320; **36** 404; **65** **328–31**

SunTrust Banks Inc., 23 455–58; 33 293

Sunward Technologies, Inc., **10** 464

Supasnaps, **V** 50

Supelco, Inc., **36** 431

Super Bazars, **26** 159

Super D Drugs, **9** 52

Super Dart. *See* Dart Group Corporation.

Super 8 Motels, Inc., **11** 178

Super Food Services, Inc., 15 479–81; 18 8

Super Oil Seals & Gaskets Ltd., **16** 8

Super 1 Stores. *See* Brookshire Grocery Company.

Super Quick, Inc., **7** 372

Super Rite Foods, Inc., **V** 176; **19** 356; **63** 334

Super Sagless Spring Corp., **15** 103

Super Sol Ltd., **41** 56–57

Super Store Industries, **14** 397

Super Valu Stores, Inc., II 632, **668–71;** **7** 450; **8** 380; **14** 411; **17** 180; **23** 357–58. *See also* SUPERVALU INC.

Superb Manufacturing, **60** 56

Superbrix, **14** 248

La Supercalor S.P.A. *See* De'Longhi S.p.A.

Supercuts Inc., 26 475–78

Superdrug plc. *See* Rite Aid Corporation.

Superfast Ferries SA, **64** 45

Superior Bearings Company. *See* Federal-Mogul Corporation.

Superior Energy Services, Inc., 65 **332–34**

Superior Foam and Polymers, Inc., **44** 261

Superior Healthcare Group, Inc., **11** 221

Superior Industries International, Inc., 8 **505–07**

Superior Oil Co., **49** 137

Superior Recycled Fiber Industries, **26** 363

Superior Transfer, **12** 309

Superior Uniform Group, Inc., 30 **455–57**

SuperMac Technology Inc., **16** 419

Supermarchés GB, **26** 159
Supermarchés Montréal, **II** 662–63
Supermarkets General Holdings Corporation, II 672–74; **16** 160; **23** 369–70. *See also* Pathmark Stores, Inc.
Supermart Books, **10** 136
Supersaver Wholesale Clubs, **8** 555
Supersnaps, **19** 124
SuperStation WTBS. *See* Turner Broadcasting System, Inc.
Supertest Petroleum Corporation, **9** 490
SUPERVALU INC., 18 503–08 **(upd.); 21** 457–57; **22** 327; **50** 453–59 **(upd.); 58** 319–20, 329
Supervalue Corp., **13** 393
SupeRx, **II** 644
Supplyon AG, **48** 450
Suprema Specialties, Inc., 27 440–42
Supreme International Corporation, 27 443–46; **30** 358; **41** 291
Supreme Life Insurance Company of America. *See* Johnson Publishing Company, Inc.
Supron Energy Corp., **15** 129
Surapon Nichirei Foods Company Ltd. *See* Nichirei Corporation.
Surety Life Insurance Company, **10** 51
SureWay Air Traffic Corporation, **24** 126
Surgical Health Corporation, **14** 233
Surgical Plastics, **25** 430–31
Surgimedics Inc., **68** 379
OAO Surgutneftegaz, 48 375–78
Suroflex GmbH, **23** 300
Surpass Software Systems, Inc., **9** 81
Surplus Software, **31** 176
Surrey Free Inns plc. *See* SFI Group plc.
Surridge Dawson Ltd. *See* Dawson Holdings PLC.
Survey Research Group, **10** 360
SurVivaLink, **18** 423
Susan Bristol, **16** 61
Susan Kay Cosmetics. *See* The Cosmetic Center, Inc.
SuSE Linux AG, **45** 363
Susie's Casuals, **14** 294
Susquehanna Pfaltzgraff Company, 8 508–10
Sussex Group, **15** 449
Sussex Trust Company, **25** 541
Sutherland Lumber Co., **19** 233
Sutter Corp., **15** 113
Sutter Health, **12** 175–76
Sutter Home Winery Inc., 16 476–78
Sutton & Towne, Inc., **21** 96
Sutton Laboratories, **22** 228
Sutton Publishing Limited. *See* Haynes Publishing Group P.L.C.
Suunto Oy, **41** 14, 16
Suzannah Farms, **7** 524
Suzhou Elevator Company, **29** 420
Suzuki Motor Corporation, 7 110; **8** 72; **9** 487–89; **23** 290, 459–62 **(upd.); 36** 240, 243; **39** 38; **59** 393–98 **(upd.); 61** 10
Suzy Shier Limited. *See* La Senza Corporation.
Svea Choklad A.G., **II** 640
AB Svensk Färgämnesindustri, **50** 55
Svensk Filmindustrie, **52** 49, 51
Svensk Golvindustri, **25** 463
Svensk Pantbelåning, **61** 53
Svenska Aeroplan Aktiebolaget. *See* Saab-Scania AB.
Svenska Aller AB, **72** 62

Svenska Cellulosa Aktiebolaget SCA, IV 325, 336, **338–40,** 667; **17** 398; **28** 443–46 **(upd.); 52** 163
Svenska Handelsbanken AB, II 365–67; **50** 460–63 **(upd.)**
Svenska Kullagerfabriken A.B. *See* AB Volvo.
Svenska Stålpressnings AB, **26** 11
Sverdrup Corporation, 14 475–78
SVF. *See* Société des Vins de France.
SVIDO, **17** 250
SWA. *See* Southwest Airlines.
SWALEC. *See* Scottish and Southern Energy plc.
Swales & Associates, Inc., 69 336–38
Swallow Airplane Company, **8** 49; **27** 98
Swallow Sidecar and Coach Building Company, **13** 285
Swan, **10** 170
Swank Inc., 17 464–66
Swarovski International Holding AG, 40 422–25
The Swatch Group SA, 7 532–33; **25** 481; **26** 479–81
Swearingen Aircraft Company, **9** 207; **48** 169
Swedish Ericsson Group, **17** 353
Swedish Match AB, 39 387–90 **(upd.)**
Swedish Match S.A., 9 381; **12** 462–64; **23** 55; **25** 464
Swedish Ordnance-FFV/Bofors AB, **9** 381–82
Swedish Telecom, V 331–33
SwedishAmerican Health System, 51 363–66
Sweedor, **12** 464
Sweeney Specialty Restaurants, **14** 131
Sweeney's, **16** 559
Sweet & Maxwell, **8** 527
Sweet Candy Company, 60 295–97
Sweet Life Foods Inc., **18** 507; **50** 457
Sweet Stripes, Inc. *See* Bobs Candies, Inc.
Sweet Traditions LLC, **21** 323
Sweetheart Cup Company, Inc., 36 460–64
Swenson Granite Company, Inc., **37** 331
Swett & Crawford Group, **III** 357; **22** 494
SWH Corporation, 70 307–09
Swift & Company, 13 351; **17** 124; **41** 114; **55** 364–67; **60** 187
Swift Adhesives, **10** 467
Swift Denim Group, **66** 134
Swift Energy Company, 63 364–66
Swift Independent Packing Co., **13** 350, 352; **42** 92
Swift Textiles, Inc., **12** 118; **15** 247
Swift Transportation Co., Inc., 26 533; **33** 468; **42** 363–66; **64** 218
Swinerton Inc., 43 397–400
Swing-N-Slide, Inc. *See* PlayCore, Inc.
Swingline, Inc., **7** 3–5
Swire Pacific Ltd., I 521–22; **16** 479–81 **(upd.); 18** 114; **57** 348–53 **(upd.); 59** 261
Swisher International Group Inc., 14 17–19; **23** 463–65; **27** 139
Swiss Air Transport Company Ltd., I 121–22; **24** 312; **27** 409; **33** 49, 51, 271
Swiss Banca de Gottardo, **26** 456
Swiss Bank Corporation, II 368–70, 378–79; **14** 419–20; **52** 354. *See also* UBS AG.
Swiss Barry Callebaut AG, **53** 315
Swiss Broadcasting Corporation, **53** 325

Swiss Federal Railways (Schweizerische Bundesbahnen), V 519–22
Swiss International Air Lines Ltd., 48 379–81
Swiss Life, **52** 357–58
Swiss Reinsurance Company (Schweizerische Rückversicherungs-Gesellschaft), III 375–78; **15** 13; **21** 146; **45** 110; **46** 380–84 **(upd.)**
Swiss Saurer AG, **39** 39, 41
Swiss Telecom PTT. *See* Swisscom AG.
Swiss Time Australia Pty Ltd, **25** 461
Swiss Volksbank, **21** 146–47
Swissair Associated Co., **34** 397–98; **36** 426
Swissair Group, **47** 286–87; **49** 80–81
SwissCargo, **49** 81
Swisscom AG, 58 336–39
Swissport International Ltd., 70 310–12
Switchboard Inc., **25** 52
SXI Limited, **17** 458
Sybase, Inc., 10 361, 504–06; **11** 77–78; **15** 492; **25** 96; **27** 447–50 **(upd.)**
SyberVision, **10** 216
Sybra, Inc., **19** 466–68
Sybron International Corp., 14 479–81; **19** 289–90
Sycamore Networks, Inc., 45 388–91
SYCOM, Inc., **18** 363
Sydney Electricity, **12** 443
Sydney FM Facilities Pty. Limited, **58** 359
SYDOOG, Inc., **64** 160
Sydsvenska Kemi AB, **51** 289
Sykes Enterprises, Inc., 45 392–95
Syllogic B.V., **29** 376
Sylvan, Inc., 22 496–99
Sylvan Lake Telephone Company, **6** 334
Sylvan Learning Systems, Inc., 13 299; **34** 439; **35** 408–11; **55** 213
Sylvania Companies, **7** 161; **8** 157; **11** 197; **13** 402; **23** 181; **50** 299
Symantec Corporation, 10 507–09; **25** 348–49
Symbian Ltd., **45** 346, 348
Symbios Logic Inc., **19** 312; **31** 5
Symbiosis Corp., **10** 70; **50** 538
Symbol Technologies, Inc., 10 363, 523–24; **15** 482–84
Symphony International, **14** 224
Syms Corporation, 29 456–58
Symtron Systems Inc., **37** 399–400
Symtronix Corporation, **18** 515
Syn-Optics, Inc., **29** 454
Synavant Inc. *See* Dendrite International, Inc.
Synbiotics Corporation, **23** 284
Syncordia Corp., **15** 69
Syncro Ltd., **51** 89
Syncrocom, Inc., **10** 513
Syncrude Canada Limited, **25** 232
Synercom Technology Inc., **14** 319
Synercon Corporation, **25** 538
Synergen Inc., **13** 241
Synergy Dataworks, Inc., **11** 285
Synergy Software Inc., **31** 131
Synetic, Inc., **16** 59
Synfloor SA, **25** 464
Synopsys, Inc., 11 489–92; **18** 20; **43** 17; **69** 339–43 **(upd.)**
SynOptics Communications, Inc., 10 194, 510–12; **11** 475; **16** 392; **22** 52
Synovus Financial Corp., 12 465–67; **18** 516–17; **52** 336–40 **(upd.)**
Synrad, Inc. *See* Excel Technology, Inc.

Syntex Corporation, I 701–03; III 53; 8 216–17, 434, 548; 10 53; 12 322; 26 384; 50 321
Syntex Pharmaceuticals Ltd., 21 425
Synthecolor S.A., 8 347
Synthetic Blood Corp., 15 380
Synthetic Pillows, Inc., 19 304
Synthomer. See Yule Catto & Company plc.
Syntron, Inc., 18 513–15
SyQuest Technology, Inc., 18 509–12
Syracuse China, 8 510
Syratech Corp., 14 482–84; 27 288
Syroco, 14 483–84
SYSCO Corporation, II 675–76; 9 453; 16 387; 18 67; 24 470–72 (upd.), 528; 26 504; 47 457; 58 241
SYSCO Security Systems, Inc., 51 81
Syscon Corporation, 38 227
Sysorex Information Systems, 11 62
SysScan, V 339
Systech Environmental Corporation, 28 228–29
System Designers plc. See SD-Scicon plc.
System Fuels, Inc., 11 194
System Parking West, 25 16
System Software Associates, Inc., 10 513–14
Systematic Business Services, Inc., 48 256–57
Systematics Inc., 6 301; 11 131
Systemax, Inc., 52 341–44
Systembolaget, 31 459–60
Systems & Computer Technology Corp., 19 437–39
Systems and Services Company. See SYSCO Corporation.
Systems Center, Inc., 11 469
Systems Construction Ltd., II 649
Systems Development Corp., 25 117
Systems Engineering and Manufacturing Company, 11 225
Systems Engineering Labs (SEL), 11 45; 13 201
Systems Exploration Inc., 10 547
Systems Marketing Inc., 12 78
Systron Donner Corp. See BEI Technologies, Inc.
Systronics, 13 235
Sytner Group plc, 45 396–98
Syufy Enterprises. See Century Theatres, Inc.
Szabo, II 608

T. and J. Brocklebank Ltd., 23 160
T&N PLC, 26 141
T-Fal. See Groupe SEB.
T/Maker, 9 81
T-Netix, Inc., 46 385–88
T-Online International AG, 61 349–51
T-Shirt Brokerage Services, Inc., 26 257
T-Tech Industries, 26 363
T.G.I. Friday's, 10 331; 19 258; 20 159; 21 250; 22 127; 44 349
T.J. Falgout, 11 523
T.J. Maxx. See The TJX Companies, Inc.
T.L. Smith & Company, 21 502
T. Marzetti Company, 57 354–56; 60 199–200; 61 172, 174
T. Rowe Price Associates, Inc., 10 89; 11 493–96; 34 423–27 (upd.)
T.S. Farley, Limited, 10 319
T. Wear Company S.r.l., 25 121

TA Associates Inc., 10 382; 32 146; 54 361
TA Logistics, 49 402
TA Media AG, 15 31
TA Triumph-Adler AG, 48 382–85
TAB Products Co., 17 467–69
Tabacalera, S.A., V 414–16; 17 470–73 (upd.). See also Altadis S.A.
TABCORP Holdings Limited, 44 407–10
Table Supply Meat Co. See Omaha Steaks International Inc.
Tabletop Holdings, 70 185
TACA. See Grupo TACA.
Tachikawa Bus Co., Ltd., 68 281
Taco Bell Corp., 7 267, 505–07; 9 178; 13 336, 494; 14 453; 15 486; 16 96–97; 17 537; 21 315, 485–88 (upd.); 25 178; 58 385
Taco Cabana, Inc., 23 466–68; 72 344–47 (upd.)
Taco John's International Inc., 15 485–87; 63 367–70 (upd.)
Tacony Corporation, 70 313–15
Taft Broadcasting Co. See Great American Broadcasting Inc.
TAG Heuer International SA, 7 554; 25 459–61
Tag Mex, Inc., 62 353
TAG Pharmaceuticals, Inc., 22 501; 54 363
Taggarts Motor Group. See Lookers plc.
Taguchi Automobile. See Seino Transportation Company, Ltd.
Tahoe Joe's, Inc., 32 102 32 249
TAI, Ltd., 34 397
Taiba Corporation, 8 250
Taiheiyo Bank, 15 495
Taiheiyo Cement Corporation, 60 298–301 (upd.)
Taiko Trading Co. Ltd., 51 179
Taikoo Motors Limited, 57 352
Taio Paper Mfg. Co., Ltd. See Daio Paper Co., Ltd.
Taisho Marine and Fire Insurance Co., Ltd., III 209, 295–96
Taisho Pharmaceutical, II 361
Taittinger S.A., 27 421; 43 401–05
Taiwan Aerospace Corp., 11 279; 24 88
Taiwan Auto Glass, III 715
Taiwan Power Company, 22 89
Taiwan Semiconductor Manufacturing Company Ltd., 18 20; 22 197; 43 17; 47 383–87
Taiyo Fishery Company, Limited, II 578–79
Taiyo Kobe Bank, Ltd., II 371–72
Taiyo Kogyo Corporation, 35 98, 100
Taiyo Nippon Kisen Co. Ltd., 56 181
Taka-Q, 72 4
Takanashi Milk Products Ltd., 37 197
Takara Holdings Inc., 25 488; 62 345–47
Takarazuka Hankyu Company Ltd., 62 170
Takashimaya Company, Limited, V 193–96; 41 114; 47 388–92 (upd.)
Take-Two Interactive Software, Inc., 46 389–91
Takeda Chemical Industries, Ltd., I 704–06; 46 392–95 (upd.)
Takeda Riken, 11 504
Takihyo, 15 145
Takkyubin, V 537
Tako Carton Plant Ltd., 56 255
Talanx AG, 53 162
The Talbots, Inc., 11 497–99; 12 280; 31 429–32 (upd.)

Talcott National Corporation, 11 260–61
Talegen Holdings Inc., 26 546
Talent Net Inc., 44 164
Taliq Corp., III 715
Talisman Energy Inc., 9 490–93; 47 393–98 (upd.)
Talk America Holdings, Inc., 70 316–19
TALK Corporation, 34 48
Talk Miramax Books, 64 285
Talk Radio Network, Inc., 23 294
Talkline, 63 371–72
Talley Industries, Inc., 10 386; 16 482–85
Tally Corp., 18 434
Talmadge Farms, Inc., 20 105
Taltex Ltd., 51 379
TAM Linhas Aéreas S.A., 68 363–65
Tama. See Hoshino Gakki Co. Ltd.
Tamarind International Inc., 62 342, 344
Tamarkin Co., 12 390
Tambrands Inc., 8 511–13; 12 439; 15 359–60, 501; 16 303; 26 384; 37 394
Tamco, 12 390; 19 380
Tamedia AG, 53 323–26
Tamfelt Oyj Abp, 62 348–50
Tamglass Automotive OY, 22 436
Tampa Electric Company, 6 582–83
Tampax Inc. See Tambrands Inc.
Tampimex Oil, 11 194
TAMSA. See Tubos de Acero de Mexico, S.A.
Tandem Computers, Inc., 6 278–80; 10 499; 11 18; 14 318; 26 93; 29 477–79; 50 227
Tandon, 25 531
Tandy Corporation, II 106–08; 9 43, 115, 165; 10 56–57, 166–67, 236; 12 468–70 (upd.); 13 174; 14 117; 16 84; 17 353–54; 24 502; 25 531; 26 18; 34 198; 49 183; 63 122. See also RadioShack Corporation.
Tandycrafts, Inc., 31 433–37
Tangent Industries, 15 83; 50 124
Tanger Factory Outlet Centers, Inc., 49 386–89
Tangiers International. See Algo Group Inc.
Tangram Rehabilitation Network, Inc., 29 401
Tanimura & Antle, 54 257
Tanks Oil and Gas, 11 97; 50 178
Tanne-Arden, Inc., 27 291
Tanner-Brice Company, 13 404
Tantalum Mining Corporation, 29 81
TAP—Air Portugal Transportes Aéreos Portugueses S.A., 46 396–99 (upd.)
Tapemark Company Inc., 64 373–75
Tapiola Insurance, IV 316
Tapis-St. Maclou, 37 22
Tappan. See White Consolidated Industries Inc.
Tara Foods, II 645
Target Corporation, 10 515–17; 27 451–54 (upd.); 61 352–56 (upd.); 63 254, 262
Target Marketing and Promotions, Inc., 55 15
Target Marketing Systems Inc., 64 237
Target Rock Corporation, 35 134–36
Tarkett Sommer AG, 12 464; 25 462–64
Tarmac America, 64 379–80
Tarmac plc, III 751–54; 14 250; 28 447–51 (upd.); 36 21

Taro Pharmaceutical Industries Ltd., 65 335–37
TAROM S.A., 64 376–78
Tarragon Oil and Gas Ltd. *See* Unocal Corporation.
Tarragon Realty Investors, Inc., 45 399–402
Tarrant Apparel Group, 62 351–53
Tarsa, **63** 151
TASC. *See* Analytical Sciences Corp.
Taser International, Inc., 62 354–57
Tasman Pulp and Paper Co. Ltd. *See* Fletcher Challenge Ltd.
Tastee Freeze, **39** 234
Tasty Baking Company, 14 485–87; **35** 412–16 (upd.)
Tasukara Company Ltd., **62** 170
TAT European Airlines, **14** 70, 73; **24** 400
Tata Airlines. *See* Air-India Limited.
Tata Enterprises, **III** 43
Tata Industries, **20** 313; **21** 74
Tata Iron & Steel Co. Ltd., IV 217–19; **44** 411–15 (upd.)
Tate & Lyle PLC, II 580–83; **7** 466–67; **13** 102; **42** 367–72 (upd.)
Tatham Corporation, **21** 169, 171
Tatham/RSCG, **13** 204
Tati SA, 25 465–67
Tatneft. *See* OAO Tatneft.
Tattered Cover Book Store, 43 406–09
Tatung Co., 13 387; **23** 469–71
Taurus Exploration, **21** 208
Taurus Programming Services, **10** 196
TaurusHolding GmbH & Co. KG, 46 400–03
Tax Management, Inc., **23** 92
Taylor & Francis Group plc, 44 416–19
Taylor Aircraft Corporation, **44** 307
Taylor Corporation, 36 465–67; **37** 108
Taylor Guitars, 48 386–89
Taylor Made Golf Co., 23 270, 472–74; **33** 7
Taylor Material Handling, **13** 499
Taylor Medical, **14** 388
Taylor Nelson Sofres plc, 34 428–30; **37** 144
Taylor Petroleum, Inc., **17** 170
Taylor Publishing Company, 12 471–73; **25** 254; **36** 468–71 (upd.)
Taylor Woodrow plc, I 590–91; **13** 206; **38** 450–53 (upd.)
Tayto Ltd., **22** 515
Tazo Tea Company, **50** 450
TB Wood's Corporation, 56 355–58
TBC Corp., **20** 63
TBS. *See* Turner Broadcasting System, Inc.
TBWA Advertising, Inc., 6 47–49; **22** 394
TBWA\Chiat\Day, 43 410–14 (upd.)
TC Advertising. *See* Treasure Chest Advertising, Inc.
TC Debica, **20** 264
TCA. *See* Air Canada.
TCBC. *See* Todays Computers Business Centers.
TCBY Enterprises Inc., 17 474–76
TCF. *See* Tokyo City Finance.
TCF Financial Corporation, 47 399–402
TCH Corporation, **12** 477
TCI. *See* Tele-Communications, Inc.
TCI Communications, **29** 39
TCI Inc., **33** 92–93
TCI International Inc., **43** 48
TCM Investments, Inc., **49** 159

TCPL. *See* TransCanada PipeLines Ltd.
TCS Management Group, Inc., **22** 53
TCW Capital, **19** 414–15
TD Bank. *See* The Toronto-Dominion Bank.
TDC A/S, 63 371–74
TDK Corporation, II 109–11; **IV** 680; **17** 477–79 (upd.); **49** 390–94 (upd.)
TDL Group Ltd., 46 404–06
TDL Infomedia Ltd., **47** 347
TDS. *See* Telephone and Data Systems, Inc.
Teachers Insurance and Annuity Association, III 379–82; **22** 268; **35** 75; **47** 331; **49** 413
Teachers Insurance and Annuity Association-College Retirement Equities Fund, 45 403–07 (upd.)
Teachers Service Organization, Inc., **8** 9–10
Team America, **9** 435
Team Penske. *See* Penske Corporation.
Team Rental Group. *See* Budget Group, Inc.
Teams, Inc., **37** 247
Teamsters Central States Pension Fund, **19** 378
Teamsters Union, **13** 19
TearDrop Golf Company, 32 445–48
Tech Data Corporation, 10 518–19
Tech/Ops Landauer, Inc. *See* Landauer, Inc.
Tech Pacific International, **18** 180; **39** 201, 203
Tech-Sym Corporation, 18 513–15; **44** 420–23 (upd.)
Tech Textiles, USA, **15** 247–48
Techalloy Co., **IV** 228
Techgistics, **49** 403
Techint Group, **63** 385
Technair Packaging Laboratories, **18** 216
TECHNE Corporation, 52 345–48
Technical Ceramics Laboratories, Inc., **13** 141
Technical Coatings Co., **13** 85; **38** 96–97
Technical Materials, Inc., **14** 81
Technical Olympic USA, **46** 180
Technicare, **11** 200
Technicolor Inc., **28** 246
Technicon Instruments Corporation, **III** 56; **11** 333–34; **22** 75
Technifax, **8** 483
Techniques d'Avant-Garde. *See* TAG Heuer International SA.
Technisch Bureau Visser, **16** 421
Technitrol, Inc., 29 459–62
Technology Management Group, Inc., **18** 112
Technology Resources International Ltd., **18** 76
Technology Venture Investors, **11** 490; **14** 263
Technophone Ltd., **17** 354
Techserviceavia, CJSC, **68** 204
Techsource Services, Inc., **60** 185
TechTeam Europe, Ltd., **41** 281
Teck Corporation, 9 282; **27** 455–58
Tecnacril Ltda, **51** 6
Tecnamotor S.p.A. *See* Tecumseh Products Company.
Tecneco, **IV** 422
Tecnipapel-Sociedade de Transformaçao e Distribuiçao de Papel, Lda, **60** 156
Tecnipublicaciones, **14** 555

Tecnost S.p.A., **34** 319
TECO Energy, Inc., 6 582–84
Tecom Industries, Inc., **18** 513–14
Tecomar S.A., **50** 209
Tecsa, **55** 182
Tecstar Inc. *See* Starcraft Corporation.
Tectrix Fitness Equipment, Inc., **49** 108
Tecumseh Products Company, 8 514–16; **71** 351–55 (upd.)
Ted Bates, Inc., **10** 69; **16** 71–72; **50** 537
Teddy's Shoe Store. *See* Morse Shoe Inc.
Tee Vee Toons, Inc., 57 357–60
Teekay Shipping Corporation, 25 468–71
Teepak International, **55** 123
Tees and Hartlepool, **31** 367, 369
Tefal. *See* Groupe SEB.
TEFSA, **17** 182
TEIC. *See* B.V. Tabak Export & Import Compagnie.
Teijin Limited, I 511; **V** 380–82; **61** 357–61 (upd.)
Teikoku Jinken. *See* Teijin Limited.
Teikoku Oil Co., Ltd., **63** 312
Tejas Gas Co., **41** 359
Tejas Snacks LP, **44** 349
Tejon Ranch Company, 35 417–20
Teklogix International, **45** 346, 348
Tekmunc A/S, **17** 288
Teknekron Infoswitch Corporation, **22** 51
Teknika Electronics Corporation, **43** 459
Tekno Books, **58** 167
Tekrad, Inc. *See* Tektronix, Inc.
Tektronix, Inc., 8 517–21; **10** 24; **11** 284–86; **36** 331; **38** 71; **39** 350, 353; **41** 235; **61** 294–95; **63** 396–97
Tel-A-Data Limited, **11** 111
TelAutograph Corporation, **29** 33–34
Telcon. *See* Telegraph Construction and Maintenance Company.
Telcordia Technologies, Inc., 59 399–401
Tele-Communications, Inc., II 160–62, 167; **10** 484, 506; **11** 479; **13** 280; **15** 264–65; **17** 148; **18** 64–66, 211, 213, 535; **19** 282; **21** 307, 309; **23** 121, 502; **24** 6, 120; **25** 213–14; **26** 33; **28** 241; **38** 120; **42** 114–15; **43** 433; **50** 317
Tele Consulte, **14** 555
Tele Danmark. *See* TDC A/S.
Télé Luxembourg, **44** 376
Tele-Response and Support Services, Inc., **53** 209
Telebook, **25** 19
Telec Centre S.A., **19** 472
TeleCheck Services, **18** 542
TeleCheck Services, Inc., **11** 113
TeleChef, **33** 387, 389
Teleco Oilfield Services Inc., **6** 578; **22** 68
TeleColumbus, **11** 184
Telecom Argentina S.A., 63 375–77
Telecom Australia, 6 341–42
Telecom Canada. *See* Stentor Canadian Network Management.
Telecom Corporation of New Zealand Limited, 54 355–58
Telecom Eireann, 7 508–10. *See also* eircom plc.
Telecom Finland, **57** 363
Telecom FL AG, **58** 338
Telecom Italia Mobile S.p.A., 63 378–80
Telecom Italia S.p.A., 15 355; **24** 79; **34** 316, 319; **43** 415–19; **47** 345–46; **57** 67, 69
Telecom New Zealand, **18** 33

Telecom-900, **59** 303

Telecom One, Inc., **29** 252

Telecom Personal S.A., **63** 376

Telecom*USA, **27** 304

Telecom XXI, **59** 303

TelecomAsia, **62** 63

Telecommunications of Jamaica Ltd., **25** 101

Telecomunicaçoes do Paraná. *See* Brasil Telecom Participaçoes S.A.

Telecredit, Inc., **6** 25

Telectronic Pacing Systems, **10** 445

Teledyne Inc., **I** 486, **523–25**; **10** 262–63, 365, **520–22 (upd.)**; **11** 265; **13** 387; **17** 109; **18** 369; **29** 400; **35** 136

Teledyne Technologies Inc., **62 358–62 (upd.)**

Teleflora LLC, **19** 12; **21** 259; **28** 138; **37** 337

Telefonaktiebolaget LM Ericsson, **V 334–36**; **46 407–11 (upd.)**

Telefónica de Argentina S.A., **61 362–64**; **63** 214, 375–77

Telefónica de España, S.A., **V 337–40**; **43** 422

Telefonica Moviles, **69** 304, 306

Telefónica S.A., **46** 172, **412–17 (upd.)**; **61** 362

Telefonos de Mexico S.A. de C.V., **14 488–90**; **63 381–84 (upd.)**

Téléfrance, **25** 174

telegate AG, **18** 155; **47** 345, 347

Teleglobe Inc., **14** 512

Telegraph Construction and Maintenance Company, **25** 98–100

Telegraphic Service Company, **16** 166

Telekomunikacja Polska SA, **18** 33; **50 464–68**

Telelistas Editors Ltda., **26** 520

TeleMarketing Corporation of Louisiana, **8** 311

Telemarketing Investments, Ltd., **8** 311

Telematics International Inc., **18** 154, 156

Télémécanique, **19** 166

Telemundo Communications Group Inc., **III** 344; **24** 516; **63** 161, 166

Telenet Communications, **18** 32

Telenet Information Services, **47** 37

Telenor ASA, **31** 221; **57** 364; **69 344–46**

Teleos Communications Inc., **26** 277

Telepar. *See* Brasil Telecom Participaçoes S.A.

Telephone and Data Systems, Inc., **9 494–96**, 527–529; **31** 449

Telephone Company of Ireland, **7** 508

Telephone Exchange Company of Indianapolis, **14** 257

Telephone Management Corporation, **8** 310

Telephone Utilities, Inc. *See* Pacific Telecom, Inc.

Telephone Utilities of Washington. *See* Pacific Telecom, Inc.

TelePizza S.A., **33 387–89**

Teleport Communications Group. *See* AT&T Corporation.

Teleprompter Corp., **7** 222; **10** 210; **18** 355

Telerate Systems Inc., **IV** 603, 670; **10** 276–78; **21** 68; **47** 102–03

Telerent Europe. *See* Granada Group PLC.

TeleRep. *See* Cox Enterprises, Inc.

TeleRoss LLC, **59** 209–211

Telesat Cable TV, Inc., **23** 293

Telesis Oil and Gas, **6** 478

Telesistema, **18** 212

Telesistema Mexico. *See* Grupo Televisa.

TeleSite, U.S.A., Inc., **44** 442

TeleSphere, **8** 310; **60** 62

Telesystems SLW Inc., **10** 524

Teletrade Inc., **60** 146

Telettra S.p.A., **V** 326; **9** 10; **11** 205

Teletype Corp., **14** 569

Televimex, S.A., **18** 212

Television de Mexico, S.A., **18** 212

Television Española, S.A., **7 511–12**; **18** 211

Télévision Française 1, **23 475–77**

Television Sales and Marketing Services Ltd., **7** 79–80

Teleway Japan, **7** 118–19; **13** 482

Telex Corporation, **II** 87; **13** 127

TeleZüri AG, **53** 324

Telfin, **V** 339

Telia AB. *See* TeliaSonera AB.

Telia Mobitel, **11** 19; **26** 332

TeliaSonera AB, **57 361–65 (upd.)**

Telihoras Corporation, **10** 319

Telinq Inc., **10** 19

Telios Pharmaceuticals, Inc., **11** 460; **17** 288

Tellabs, Inc., **11 500–01**; **40 426–29 (upd.)**; **45** 390; **54** 69; **63** 4

TELMARK, Inc., **57** 284

Telmex. *See* Teléfonos de México S.A. de C.V.

Telpar, Inc., **14** 377

Telport, **14** 260

Telrad Networks Ltd., **68** 222, 225

Telstra Corporation Limited, **50 469–72**

Teltrend, Inc., **57** 409

Telxon Corporation, **10 523–25**

Tembec Inc., **IV** 296; **19** 226; **66 322–24**

Temerlin McClain, **23** 479; **25** 91

TEMIC TELEFUNKEN, **34** 128, 133, 135

Temp Force, **16** 421–22; **43** 308

Temple, Barker & Sloan/Strategic Planning Associates, **III** 283

Temple Frosted Foods, **25** 278

Temple Inks Company, **13** 227

Temple-Inland Inc., **IV 341–43**; **8** 267–69; **31 438–42 (upd.)**

Templeton, **II** 609

TEMPO Enterprises, **II** 162

Tempo-Team, **16** 420; **43** 307

Tempur-Pedic Inc., **54 359–61**

Tempus Expeditions, **13** 358

Tempus Group plc, **48** 442

TemTech Ltd., **13** 326

Ten Cate. *See* Royal Ten Cate N.V.

Ten Speed Press, **27** 223

Tenacqco Bridge Partnership, **17** 170

Tenaris SA, **63 385–88**

Tenby Industries Limited, **21** 350

Tencor Instruments, Inc. *See* KLA-Tencor Corporation.

Tender Loving Care Health Care Services Inc., **64** 39

Tenet Healthcare Corporation, **55 368–71 (upd.)**

TenFold Corporation, **35 421–23**

Tengelmann Group, **II** 636–38; **16** 249–50; **27 459–62**; **35** 401; **55** 164

Tengelmann Warenhandelsgesellschaft OHG, **47** 107

Tennant Company, **13 499–501**; **33 390–93 (upd.)**

Tenneco Inc., **I** 182, **526–28**; **IV** 152, 283, 371, 499; **6** 531; **10** 379–80, 430,

526–28 (upd.); **11** 440; **12** 91, 376; **13** 372–73; **16** 191, 461; **19** 78, 483; **21** 170; **22** 275, 380; **24** 358; **38** 325, 380; **40** 134; **45** 354; **51** 282–84; **65** 260–61

Tennessee Book Company, **11** 193

Tennessee Eastman Corporation. *See* Eastman Chemical Company.

Tennessee Gas Pipeline Co., **14** 126

Tennessee Gas Transmission Co., **13** 496; **14** 125

Tennessee Insurance Company, **11** 193–94

Tennessee Paper Mills Inc. *See* Rock-Tenn Company.

Tennessee Restaurant Company, **9** 426; **30** 208–9; **72** 141–42

Tennessee River Pulp & Paper Co., **12** 376–77; **51** 282–83

Tennessee Trifting, **13** 169

Tennessee Valley Authority, **22** 10; **38** 447; **50 473–77**

Tennessee Woolen Mills, Inc., **19** 304

Teoma Technologies, Inc., **65** 51–52

TEP. *See* Tucson Electric Power Company.

Tequila Sauza, **31** 91

Tequilera de Los Altos, **31** 92

TeraBeam Networks Inc., **41** 261, 263–64

Teradata Corporation. *See* NCR Corporation.

Teradyne, Inc., **11 502–04**

Terex Corporation, **7 513–15**; **8** 116; **40 430–34 (upd.)**

Teril Stationers Inc., **16** 36

The Terlato Wine Group, **48 390–92**

Terminix International, **11** 433; **25** 16

Terra Industries, Inc., **13** 277, **502–04**

Terra Lycos, Inc., **43 420–25**; **46** 416

Terracor, **11** 260–61

Terragrafics, **14** 245

Terrain King, **32** 26

Terre Haute Electric, **6** 555

Terre Lune, **25** 91

Terrena L'Union CANA CAVAL, **70 320–22**

Territory Ahead, Inc., **29** 279

Terumo Corporation, **48 393–95**

Tesa, S.A., **23** 82

TESC. *See* The European Software Company.

Tesco plc, **II** 677–78; **24 473–76 (upd.)**; **68 366–70 (upd.)**

Tesoro Bolivia Petroleum Company, **25** 546

Tesoro Petroleum Corporation, **7 516–19**; **45 408–13 (upd.)**

Tesseract Inc., **11** 78; **33** 331

Tessman Seed, Inc., **16** 270–71

The Testor Corporation, **8** 455; **51 367–70**

Tetra Pak International SA, **53 327–29**

Tetra Plastics Inc. *See* NIKE, Inc.

Tetra Tech, Inc., **29 463–65**

Tettemer & Associates. *See* The Keith Companies.

Teva Pharmaceutical Industries Ltd., **22 500–03**; **47** 55; **54 362–65 (upd.)**

Tex-Mex Partners L.C., **41** 270

Texaco Canada Inc., **25** 232

Texaco Inc., **IV 551–53**; **14 491–94 (upd.)**; **41 391–96 (upd.)**. *See also* ChevronTexaco Corporation.

Texas Air Corporation, **I 123–24**, 127, 130; **12** 489; **35** 427

Texas Almanac, **10** 3

Texas Bus Lines, **24** 118

Texas Coffee Traders, **60** 210
Texas Eastern Corp., **11** 97, 354; **14** 126; **50** 179
Texas Eastern Transmission Company, **11** 28
Texas Gas Resources Corporation, **22** 166
Texas Homecare, **21** 335
Texas Industries, Inc., 8 522–24; **13** 142–43
Texas Instruments Incorporated, II 112–15; **11** 505–08 (upd.); **46** 418–23 (upd.)
Texas International Airlines, **21** 142
Texas Metal Fabricating Company, **7** 540
Texas-New Mexico Utilities Company, **6** 580
Texas Pacific Group Inc., 36 472–74
Texas Public Utilities, **II** 660
Texas Rangers Baseball, 51 371–74
Texas Roadhouse, Inc., 69 347–49
Texas Super Duper Markets, Inc., **7** 372
Texas Timberjack, Inc., **51** 279–81
Texas Trust Savings Bank, **8** 88
Texas United Insurance Co., **III** 214
Texas Utilities Company, V 724–25; **12** 99; **25** 472–74 (upd.); **35** 479
Texasgulf Inc., **13** 557; **18** 433
Texboard, **IV** 296; **19** 226
Texstar Petroleum Company, **7** 516
Texstyrene Corp., **IV** 331
Têxtil Santa Catarina Ltda., **72** 68
Textile Diffusion, **25** 466
Textile Paper Tube Company, Ltd., **8** 475
Textile Rubber and Chemical Company, **15** 490
Textron Inc., I 529–30; **II** 420; **8** 93, 157, 315, 545; **9** 497, 499; **11** 261; **12** 251, 382–83, 400–01; **13** 63–64; **17** 53; **21** 175; **22** 32; **27** 100; **34** 431–34 (upd.); **35** 350–51; **46** 65
Textron Lycoming Turbine Engine, 9 497–99
Texwood Industries, Inc., **20** 363
TFC. *See* Times Fiber Communications, Inc.
TFH Publications, Inc., **58** 60
TFM. *See* Grupo Transportación Ferroviaria Mexicana, S.A. de C.V.
TFN Group Communications, Inc., **8** 311
TF1. *See* Télévision Française 1
TFP, Inc., **44** 358–59
TFS. *See* Total Filtration Services, Inc.
TG Credit Service Co. Ltd., **55** 375
TGEL&PCo. *See* Tucson Gas, Electric Light & Power Company.
TH:s Group, **10** 113; **50** 43
Tha Row Records, 69 350–52 (upd.)
Thai Airways International Public Company Limited, 6 122–24; **27** 463–66 (upd.)
Thai Lube Blending Co., **56** 290
Thai Nylon Co. Ltd., **53** 344
Thai Union International Inc., **24** 116
Thalassa International, **10** 14; **27** 11
Thales S.A., 42 373–76; **47** 9; **49** 165, 167
Thames Trains, **28** 157
Thames Water plc, 11 509–11; **22** 89
Thameslink, **28** 157
THAW. *See* Recreational Equipment, Inc.
Theatrical Syndicate, **24** 437
Thelem SA, **54** 267
Therm-o-Disc, **II** 19
Therm-X Company, **8** 178
Thermacore International Inc., **56** 247

Thermador Corporation, **67** 82
Thermadyne Holding Corporation, 19 440–43
Thermal Dynamics, **19** 441
Thermal Energies, Inc., **21** 514
Thermal Power Company, **11** 270
Thermal Snowboards, Inc., **22** 462
Thermal Transfer Ltd., **13** 485
ThermaStor Technologies, Ltd., **44** 366
Thermo BioAnalysis Corp., 25 475–78
Thermo Electron Corporation, 7 520–22; **11** 512–13; **13** 421; **24** 477; **25** 475–76; **52** 389
Thermo Fibertek, Inc., 24 477–79
Thermo Instrument Systems Inc., 11 512–14; **25** 475–77
Thermo King Corporation, 13 505–07
Thermoform Plastics, Inc., **56** 378–79
Thermoforming USA, **16** 339
Thermogas Co., **35** 175
Thermolase Corporation, **22** 410
Thermos Company, 16 486–88
TheStreet.com, **34** 125
THHK Womenswear Limited, **53** 333
ThiemeMeulenhoff BV, **53** 273
Thies Companies, **13** 270
Thiess Dampier Mitsui, **IV** 47
Things Remembered, **13** 165–66
Think Entertainment, **II** 161
Think Technologies, **10** 508
Thiokol Corporation, 8 472; **9** 358–59, 500–02 (upd.); **12** 68; **22** 504–07 (upd.)
Third Age Inc., **71** 137
Third Coast Capital, Inc., **51** 109
Third National Bank. *See* Fifth Third Bancorp.
Third National Bank of Dayton, **9** 475
Third Wave Publishing Corp. *See* Acer Inc.
ThirdAge.com, **49** 290
Thirteen/WNET. *See* Educational Broadcasting Corporation.
Thistle Group, **9** 365
Thistle Hotels PLC, 54 366–69
THM Biomedical Inc. *See* Kensey Nash Corporation.
Thom McAn. *See* Melville Corporation.
Thomas & Betts Corporation, 11 515–17; **14** 27; **54** 370–74 (upd.)
Thomas & Howard Co., **II** 682; **18** 8
Thomas and Judith Pyle, **13** 433
Thomas Bros. Maps, **28** 380
Thomas Cook Group Ltd., **17** 325; **57** 195
Thomas Cook Travel Inc., 9 503–05; **33** 394–96 (upd.); **42** 282
Thomas De La Rue and Company, Ltd., **44** 357–58
Thomas H. Lee Co., 11 156, 450; **14** 230–31; **15** 309; **19** 371, 373; **24** 480–83; **25** 67; **28** 134; **30** 219; **32** 362; **52** 95; **56** 225
Thomas Industries Inc., 29 466–69
Thomas J. Lipton Company, II 609, 657; **11** 450; **14** 495–97; **16** 90; **32** 474
Thomas Jefferson Life Insurance Co., **III** 397
Thomas Kinkade Galleries. *See* Media Arts Group, Inc.
Thomas Linnell & Co. Ltd., **II** 628
Thomas Nationwide Transport. *See* TNT.
Thomas Nationwide Transport Limited. *See* TNT Post Group N.V.
Thomas Nelson Inc., 8 526; **14** 498–99; **24** 548; **38** 454–57 (upd.)
Thomas Publishing Company, 26 482–85

Thomas Y. Crowell, **IV** 605
Thomaston Mills, Inc., 27 467–70
Thomasville Furniture Industries, Inc., 12 474–76; **28** 406; **31** 248; **39** 170, 174
Thompson and Formby, **16** 44
Thompson Aircraft Tire Corp., **14** 42
Thompson-Hayward Chemical Co., **13** 397
Thompson Medical Company. *See* Slim-Fast Nutritional Foods International Inc.
Thompson Nutritional Products, **37** 286
Thompson PBE Inc., **24** 160–61
Thomsen Greenhouses and Garden Center, Incorporated, 65 338–40
Thomson BankWatch Inc., **19** 34
Thomson-Brandt, **II** 13, 116–17; **9** 9
The Thomson Corporation, 8 525–28; **10** 407; **12** 361, 562; **17** 255; **22** 441; **34** 435–40 (upd.); **44** 155
Thomson International, **37** 143
Thomson-Jenson Energy Limited, **13** 558
THOMSON multimedia S.A., 18 126; **36** 384; **42** 377–80 (upd.)
Thomson-Ramo-Woolridge. *See* TRW Inc.
Thomson S.A., II 31, 116–17; **7** 9; **13** 402; **50** 300; **59** 81. *See also* THOMSON multimedia S.A.
Thomson Travel Group, **27** 27
Thonet Industries Inc., **14** 435–36
Thor Industries, Inc., 39 391–94
Thorn Apple Valley, Inc., 7 523–25; **12** 125; **22** 508–11 (upd.); **23** 203
Thorn EMI plc, I 52, 411, 531–32; **19** 390; **24** 87; **26** 151; **40** 105; **59** 228. *See also* EMI plc; Thorn plc.
Thorn plc, 24 484–87
Thorncraft Inc., **25** 379
Thorndike, Doran, Paine and Lewis, Inc., **14** 530
Thornhill Inc., **64** 217
Thornton Baker. *See* Grant Thornton International.
Thornton Stores, **14** 235
Thorntons plc, 46 424–26
Thoroughgood, **II** 658
Thorpe Park, **55** 378
Thorsen Realtors, **21** 96
Thos. & Wm. Molson & Company. *See* The Molson Companies Limited.
Thousand Trails, Inc., 13 494; **33** 397–99
Thousands Springs Power Company, **12** 265
THQ, Inc., 39 395–97; **52** 191
Threads for Life, **49** 244
Threadz, **25** 300
Three-Diamond Company. *See* Mitsubishi Shokai.
The 3DO Company, 10 286; **43** 426–30
3 Guys, **II** 678, **V** 35
3 Maj, **25** 469
Three Ring Asia Pacific Beer Co., Ltd., **49** 418
Three Rivers Pulp and Paper Company, **17** 281
Three Score, **23** 100
3 Suisses International, **12** 281
3Com Corporation, 10 237; **11** 518–21; **20** 8, 33; **26** 276; **34** 441–45 (upd.); **36** 122, 300, 357; **49** 184. *See also* Palm, Inc.
3D Planet SpA, **41** 409
3dfx Interactive Inc., **54** 269–71
3Dlabs, **57** 78, 80
3i, **70** 21
3M Company, 61 365–70 (upd.)

360 Youth Inc., **55** 15
360networks inc., **46** 268
Threshold Entertainment, **25** 270
Thrift Drug, **V** 92
Thrift Mart, **16** 65
ThriftiCheck Service Corporation, **7** 145
Thriftimart Inc., **12** 153; **16** 452
Thriftway Food Drug, **21** 530
Thriftway Foods, **II** 624
Thrifty Corporation, **25** 413, 415–16; **55** 58
Thrifty PayLess, Inc., 12 477–79; 18 286; **19** 357
Thrifty Rent-A-Car. *See* Dollar Thrifty Automotive Group, Inc.
Throwing Corporation of America, **12** 501
Thrustmaster S.A., **41** 190
Thummel Schutze & Partner, **28** 141
Thunder Bay Press, **34** 3–5
Thüringer Schokoladewerk GmbH, **53** 315
Thurmond Chemicals, **27** 291
Thurston Motor Lines Inc., **12** 310
Thyssen AG, IV 195, 221–23, 228; **8** 75–76; **14** 169
Thyssen Krupp AG, 28 104, 452–60 (upd.); 42 417
Thyssen-Krupp Stahl AG, **26** 83
Thyssengas, **38** 406–07
TI. *See* Texas Instruments.
TI Corporation, **10** 44
TI Group plc, 17 480–83
TIAA-CREF. *See* Teachers Insurance and Annuity Association-College Retirement Equities Fund.
Tianjin Automobile Industry Group, **21** 164
Tianjin Bohai Brewing Company, **21** 230; **50** 202
Tianjin Paper Net, **62** 350
Tibbett & Britten Group plc, 32 449–52
Tiber Construction Company, **16** 286
Tichenor Media System Inc., **35** 220
Ticketmaster Corp., 13 508–10; 25 214; **36** 423–24
Ticketmaster Group, Inc., 37 381–84 (upd.); 47 419, 421
Ticketron, **13** 508–09; **24** 438; **37** 381–82
TicketsWest.com, **59** 410, 412
Tichnor & Fields, **10** 356
Ticor Title Insurance Co., **10** 45
Tidel Systems, **II** 661; **32** 416
Tidewater Inc., 11 522–24; 37 385–88 (upd.);59 402
Tidewater Utilities, Inc., **45** 275, 277
Tidi Wholesale, **13** 150
TIE. *See* Transport International Express.
Tien Wah Press (Pte.) Ltd., **IV** 600
Tierco Group, Inc., **27** 382
Tierney & Partners, **23** 480
Tiffany & Co., 12 312; **14 500–03; 15** 95; **19** 27; **26** 145; **27** 329; **41** 256; **57** 179–80; **60** 202
TIG Holdings, Inc., 26 486–88; 57 136–37
Tiger Accessories, **18** 88
Tiger Aspect Productions Ltd., 72 348–50
Tiger International, Inc., **17** 505; **18** 178; **42** 141
Tiger Management Associates, **13** 158, 256
Tiger Oats, **I** 424
TigerDirect, Inc., **52** 342–44
Tigon Corporation, **41** 288
Tiki Corp., **69** 365
Tilcon Capaldi, Inc., **64** 98

Tilden Interrent, **10** 419
Tile & Coal Company, **14** 248
Tilia Inc., 62 363–65
Tilley Endurables, Inc., 67 364–66
Tillinghast, Nelson & Warren Inc., **32** 459
Tillotson Corp., 14 64; **15 488–90**
TIM. *See* Telecom Italia Mobile S.p.A.
Tim Horton's Restaurants. *See* TDL Group Ltd.; Wendy's Inc.
Timber Lodge Steakhouse, Inc., **37** 351–52
Timber Realization Co., **IV** 305
The Timberland Company, 11 349; **13 511–14; 17** 245; **19** 112; **22** 173; **25** 206; **54 375–79 (upd.)**
Timberline Software Corporation, 15 491–93
TIMCO. *See* Triad International Maintenance Corp.
Time Distribution Services, **13** 179
Time Electronics, **19** 311
Time Industries, **26** 445
Time-Life Books, Inc. *See* AOL Time Warner Inc.
Time Life Music, **44** 242
Time Out Group Ltd., 68 371–73
Time Saver Stores, Inc., **12** 112; **17** 170
Time-Sharing Information, **10** 357
Time Warner Inc., IV 673–76; 7 526–30 (upd.). *See also* AOL Time Warner Inc.
Timeplex, **9** 32
Times Fiber Communications, Inc., **40** 35–36
The Times Mirror Company, IV 677–78; 14 97; **17 484–86 (upd.); 21** 404; **22** 162, 443; **26** 446; **35** 419; **63** 393–94
Times Newspapers, **8** 527
Times Publishing Group, **54** 116, 118
Timeshare Resale Brokers Inc. *See* ILX Resorts Incorporated.
TIMET. *See* Titanium Metals Corporation.
Timex Corporation, 25 479–82 (upd.)
Timex Enterprises Inc., 7 531–33; 10 152; **12** 317; **25** 22
The Timken Company, 7 447; **8 529–31; 15** 225; **42 381–85 (upd.); 55** 221–22
Timothy Whites, **24** 74
Tioga Gas Plant Inc., **55** 20
Tioxide Group plc, **44** 117, 119
Tip Top Drugstores plc, **24** 269
Tip Top Tailors, **29** 162
TIPC Network. *See* Gateway 2000.
Tiphook PLC, **13** 530
Tipton Centers Inc., **V** 50; **19** 123; **49** 112
Tiscali SpA, 48 396–99
TISCO. *See* Tata Iron & Steel Company Ltd.
Tishman Speyer Properties, L.P., 47 403–06
Tissue Technologies, Inc., **22** 409
Titan Acquisition Corporation, **51** 34, 36
Titan Cement Company S.A., 64 379–81
The Titan Corporation, 36 475–78; 45 68, 70
Titan Manufacturing Company, **19** 359
Titan Sports, Inc., **52** 192
Titanium Metals Corporation, 10 434; **21 489–92**
Titanium Technology Corporation, **13** 140
Titleist. *See* Acushnet Company.
TITISA, **9** 109
Titmuss Sainer Dechert. *See* Dechert.
Tivoli Audio, **48** 85
Tivoli Systems, Inc., **14** 392
TJ International, Inc., 19 444–47

The TJX Companies, Inc., V 197–98; 13 548; **14** 426; **19 448–50 (upd.); 29** 106; **57 366–69 (upd.)**
TKR Cable Co., **15** 264
TKT. *See* Transkaryotic Therapies Inc.
TL Enterprises, Inc., **56** 5
TLC Associates, **11** 261
TLC Beatrice International Holdings, Inc., 22 512–15
TLC Gift Company, **26** 375
TLO, **25** 82
TMB Industries, **24** 144
TMC Industries Ltd., **22** 352
TML Information Services Inc., **9** 95
TMNI International Inc., **70** 275
TMP Worldwide Inc., 30 458–60
TMS, Inc., **7** 358
TMS Marketing, **26** 440
TMS Systems, Inc., **10** 18
TMT. *See* Trailer Marine Transport.
TMW Capital Inc., **48** 286
TN Technologies Inc., **23** 479
TNI Funding I Inc., **70** 275
TNT Crust, Inc., **23** 203
TNT Freightways Corporation, 14 504–06
TNT Grading Inc., **50** 348
TNT Limited, V 523–25
TNT Post Group N.V., 27 471–76 (upd.); 30 393, **461–63 (upd.).** *See also* TPG N.V.
Toa Medical Electronics Ltd., **22** 75
Toa Tanker Co. Ltd., **IV** 555
Toastmaster, **17** 215; **22** 353
Tobacco Group PLC, **30** 231
Tobacco Products Corporation, **18** 416
Tobias, **16** 239
Tobu Railway Co Ltd, 6 430–32
TOC Retail Inc., **17** 170
Tocom, Inc., **10** 320
Today's Man, Inc., 20 484–87; 21 311
Todays Computers Business Centers. *See* Intelligent Electronics, Inc.
The Todd-AO Corporation, 33 400–04. *See also* Liberty Livewire Corporation.
Todd Shipyards Corporation, 7 138; **14 507–09**
Todhunter International, Inc., 27 477–79
Todito.com, S.A. de C.V., **39** 194, 196
Toei Co. Ltd., **9** 29–30; **28** 462
Tofaş, **I** 479–80; **54** 196–97
Tofte Industrier, **63** 315
Toftejorg Group, **64** 18
Tofutti Brands, Inc., 64 382–84
Togo's Eatery, **29** 19
Toho Co., Ltd., 24 327; **28** 461–63; **61** 360
Tohoku Alps, **II** 5
Tohoku Anritsu Co., Ltd. *See* Anritsu Corporation.
Tohokushinsha Film Corporation, **18** 429
Tohoku Electric Power Company, Inc., V 726–28
Tokai Aircraft Co., Ltd. *See* Aisin Seiki Co., Ltd.
The Tokai Bank, Limited, II 373–74; 15 494–96 (upd.)
Tokai Kogyo Co. Ltd., **I** 615; **48** 42
Tokheim Corporation, 21 493–95
Tokio Marine and Fire Insurance Co., Ltd., III 383–86. *See also* Millea Holdings Inc.
Tokiwa shokai Ltd., **64** 261

Tokos Medical Corporation, **17** 306, 308–09

Tokushima Automobile Service Company Inc., **60** 272

Tokyo Broadcasting System, **7** 249; **9** 29; **16** 167

Tokyo City Finance, **36** 419–20

Tokyo Disneyland, **6** 176

Tokyo Electric Power Company, V 729–33

Tokyo Electronic Corp., **11** 232

Tokyo Gas and Electric Industrial Company, **9** 293

Tokyo Gas Co., Ltd., V 734–36; 55 372–75 (upd.)

Tokyo Ishikawajima Shipbuilding and Engineering Company, **9** 293

Tokyo Maritime Agency Ltd., **56** 181

Tokyo Motors. *See* Isuzu Motors, Ltd.

Tokyo Stock Exchange, **34** 254

Tokyo Telecommunications Engineering Corp. *See* Tokyo Tsushin Kogyo K.K.

Tokyu Corporation, V 526–28; 47 407–10 (upd.)

Tokyu Department Store Co., Ltd., V 199–202; 32 453–57 (upd.)

Tokyu Land Corporation, IV 728–29

Toledo Edison Company. *See* Centerior Energy Corporation.

Toledo Milk Processing, Inc., **15** 449

Toledo Scale Corp., **9** 441; **30** 327

Toll Brothers Inc., 15 497–99; 70 323–26 (upd.)

Tollgrade Communications, Inc., 44 424–27

Tom Brown, Inc., 37 389–91

Tom Doherty Associates Inc., 25 483–86

Tom Snyder Productions, **29** 470, 472

Tom Thumb, **40** 365–66

Tom Thumb-Page, **16** 64

Tom's Foods Inc., 66 325–27

Tom's of Maine, Inc., 45 414–16

Toman Corporation, **19** 390

The Tomatin Distillery Co., Ltd., **62** 347

Tombstone Pizza Corporation, 13 515–17

Tomcan Investments Inc., **53** 333

Tomen Corporation, IV 224–25; 19 256; 24 488–91 (upd.)

Tomkins-Johnson Company, **16** 8

Tomkins plc, 11 525–27; 28 382, 384; 30 424, 426; 44 428–31 (upd.); 56 78–79

Tomlee Tool Company, **7** 535; **26** 493

Tommy Armour Golf Co., **32** 446–47

Tommy Bahama. *See* Viewpoint International, Inc.

Tommy Hilfiger Corporation, 16 61; 20 488–90; 25 258; 53 330–33 (upd.)

Tomy Company Ltd., 65 341–44

Tone Brothers, Inc., 21 496–98; 63 83, 85

Tone Coca-Cola Bottling Company, Ltd., **14** 288; **47** 206

Tonen Corporation, IV 554–56; 16 489–92 (upd.)

TonenGeneral Sekiyu K.K., 54 380–86 (upd.)

Tong Yang Cement Corporation, 62 366–68

Tonka Corporation, 12 169; 14 266; 16 267; 25 380, 487–89; 43 229, 232

Tonkin, Inc., **19** 114

Tony Lama Company Inc., **19** 233

Tony Roma's, A Place for Ribs Inc. *See* Romacorp, Inc.

Tony Stone Images, **31** 216–17

Too, Inc., 61 371–73

Toohey, **10** 170

Toolex International N.V., 26 489–91

Tootsie Roll Industries Inc., 12 480–82; 15 323

Top End Wheelchair Sports, **11** 202

Top Green International, **17** 475

Top Tool Company, Inc., **25** 75

Topack Verpackungstechnik, **60** 193

The Topaz Group, Inc., 62 369–71

Topco Associates LLC, 17 78; 60 302–04

Topkapi, **17** 101–03

Toppan Printing Co., Ltd., IV 679–81; 58 340–44 (upd.)

Topps Company, Inc., 13 518–20; 19 386; 34 446–49 (upd.)

Topps Markets, **16** 314

Tops Appliance City, Inc., 17 487–89

Tops Markets LLC, 60 305–07

TopTip, **48** 116

Topy Industries, Limited, **8** 506–07

Tor Books. *See* Tom Doherty Associates Inc.

Toray Industries, Inc., V 383–86; 17 287; 51 375–79 (upd.)

Torchmark Corporation, 9 506–08; 11 17; 22 540–43; 33 405–08 (upd.)

Torfeaco Industries Limited, **19** 304

The Toro Company, 7 534–36; 26 492–95 (upd.)

Toromont Industries, Ltd., 21 499–501

Toronto and Scarborough Electric Railway, **9** 461

The Toronto-Dominion Bank, II 375–77, 456; 16 13–14; 18 551–53; 21 447; 43 7; 49 395–99 (upd.)

Toronto Electric Light Company, **9** 461

Toronto Maple Leafs. *See* Maple Leaf Sports & Entertainment Ltd.

Toronto Raptors. *See* Maple Leaf Sports & Entertainment Ltd.

Toronto Sun Publishing Company. *See* Sun Media.

Torrent Systems, Inc., **59** 56

The Torrington Company, 13 521–24

Torrington National Bank & Trust Co., **13** 467

Torstar Corporation, 7 488–89; 29 470–73; 52 155. *See also* Harlequin Enterprises Limited.

Toscany Co., **13** 42

Tosco Corporation, 7 537–39; 12 240; 20 138; 24 522; 36 359; 40 358; 63 113

Toshiba Corporation, I 533–35; II 62, 68, 73, 99, 102, 118, 122, 326, 440; III 298, 461, 533, 604; 6 287; 7 529; 9 7, 181; 10 518–19; 11 46, 328; 12 454, 483–86 (upd.), 546; 13 324, 399, 482; 14 117, 446; 16 5, 167; 17 533; 18 18, 260; 21 390; 22 193, 373; 23 471; 40 435–40 (upd.); 43 15; 47 153–54; 57 321

Toshin Kaihatsu Ltd. *See* Takashimaya Co., Limited.

Toshin Paper Co., Ltd., **IV** 285

Tosoh Corporation, 70 327–30

Tostem. *See* Toyo Sash Co., Ltd.

Total Audio Visual Services, **24** 95

Total Beverage Corporation, **16** 159, 161

Total Compagnie Française des Pétroles S.A., IV 498, 504, 515, 525, 544–47, 557–61; **7** 481–84; **13** 557; **21** 203. *See also* TOTAL S.A.

Total Entertainment Restaurant Corporation, 46 427–29

Total Exploration S.A., **11** 537

Total Filtration Services, Inc., **61** 66

Total Fina Elf S.A., 47 342, 365, 368; 50 478–86 (upd.); 56 63, 65

Total Global Sourcing, Inc., **10** 498

Total Home Entertainment (THE), **39** 240, 242

Total Petroleum Corporation, **21** 500

TOTAL S.A., 24 492–97 (upd.), 522; 25 104; 26 369; 61 238

Total System Services, Inc., 12 465–66; 18 168, 170, 516–18; 52 336

Totem Resources Corporation, 9 509–11

Totino's Finer Foods, **26** 436

TOTO LTD., III 755–56; 28 464–66 (upd.)

Touch America Inc., **37** 127; **44** 288

Touch-It Corp., **22** 413

Touche Remnant Holdings Ltd., **II** 356

Touche Ross. *See* Deloitte Touche Tohmatsu International.

Touchstone Films. *See* The Walt Disney Company.

Le Touquet's, SA, **48** 197

Tourang Limited, **7** 253

Touristik Union International GmbH. and Company K.G., II 163–65; 46 460. *See also* Preussag AG.

Tourtime America, **56** 223

Toval Japon, **IV** 680

Towa Optical Manufacturing Company, **41** 261–63

Tower Air, Inc., 28 467–69

Tower Automotive, Inc., 24 498–500

Tower Records, **9** 361; **10** 335; **11** 558; **30** 224. *See also* MTS Inc.

Towers, **II** 649

Towers Perrin, 32 458–60

Towle Manufacturing Co., **14** 482–83; **18** 69

Town & Country Corporation, 7 372; 16 546; 19 451–53; 25 254

Town Sports International, Inc., 46 430–33

Townsend Hook, **IV** 296, 650, 652; **19** 226

Townsends, Inc., 64 385–87

Toxicol Laboratories, Ltd., **21** 424

The Toxicology Group, LLC. *See* NOF Corporation.

Toy Biz, Inc., 10 402; 18 519–21; 54 58

Toy Liquidators, **13** 541–43; **50** 99

Toy Park, **16** 390

Toyad Corp., **7** 296

Toymax International, Inc., 29 474–76; 52 193

Toyo Ink Manufacturing, **26** 213

Toyo Kogyo, **II** 361

Toyo Microsystems Corporation, **11** 464

Toyo Pulp Co., **IV** 322

Toyo Rayon. *See* Toray Industries, Inc.

Toyo Sash Co., Ltd., III 757–58

Toyo Seikan Kaisha Ltd., I 615–16

Toyo Soda Manufacturing Co. *See* Tosoh Corporation.

Toyo Tire & Rubber Co., **V** 255–56; **9** 248

Toyo Toki Co., Ltd. *See* Toto.

Toyo Trust and Banking Co., **17** 349

Toyoda Automatic Loom Works, Ltd., III 636–39

Toyota Industrial Equipment, **27** 294, 296

Toyota Motor Corporation, I 203–05; 6
514; **7** 111, 118, 212, 219–21; **8** 315; **9**
294, 340–42; **10** 407; **11** 351, 377, 487,
528–31 (upd.); 14 321; **15** 495; **21** 162,
273; **23** 289–90, 338–40; **25** 198; **34**
303, 305–06; **38 458–62 (upd.); 56** 284,
286; **59** 393–94
Toyota Tsusho America, Inc., **13** 371
Toys 'R' Us, Inc., V 203–06; 10 235,
284, 484; **12** 178; **13** 166; **14** 61; **15**
469; **16** 389–90, 457; **18 522–25 (upd.);**
24 412; **25** 314; **31** 477–78; **37** 129; **43**
385; **57 370–75 (upd.)**
TP Transportation, **39** 377
TPA. *See* Aloha Airlines Incorporated.
TPCR Corporation. *See* The Price
Company.
TPG N.V., 64 388–91 (upd.)
Trac Inc., **44** 355
Trace International Holdings, Inc., **17**
182–83; **26** 502
Tracinda Corporation, **25** 329–30
Tracker Marine. *See* Bass Pro Shops, Inc.
Tracker Services, Inc., **9** 110
Traco International N.V., **8** 250; **32** 249
Tracor Inc., 10 547; **17 490–92; 26** 267
Tractebel S.A., 20 491–93. *See also* Suez
Lyonnaise des Eaux.
Tractor Supply Company, 57 376–78
Tradax, **II** 617; **13** 137
Trade Development Bank, **11** 415–17
Trade Secret Development Corp. *See* Regis
Corporation.
Trade Source International, **44** 132
Trade Waste Incineration, Inc., **9** 109
Trade-Winds Environmental Restoration,
Inc., **62** 389
Trader Classified Media N.V., 57 379–82
Trader Joe's Company, 13 525–27; 41
422; **50 487–90 (upd.)**
Trader Media Group, **53** 152
Trader Publications, Inc., **IV** 597
Trader Publishing Company, **12** 302
Traders Group Ltd., **11** 258
Trading Cove Associates. *See* Kerzner
International Limited.
Trading Post Group Pty Ltd., **57** 381
The Trading Service, **10** 278
Traex Corporation, **8** 359
Trafalgar House Investments Ltd., **IV** 259,
711; **20** 313; **23** 161; **24** 88; **36** 322
Trafalgar House PLC, **47** 178
TrafficLeader. *See* Marchex, Inc.
Traffix, Inc., 61 374–76
Trafford Park Printers, **53** 152
Trafiroad NV, **39** 239
Trailer Bridge, Inc., 41 397–99
Trailways Lines, Inc., **I** 450; **9** 425; **32** 230
Trak Auto Corporation, **16** 159–62
TRAK Communications Inc., **44** 420
TRAK Microwave Corporation, **18** 497,
513
Trammell Crow Company, IV 343; **8**
326–28, **532–34; 49** 147–48; **54**
222–24; **57** 27, **383–87 (upd.); 58**
11–13
Trane Company. *See* American Standard
Companies, Inc.
Trans-Canada Air Lines. *See* Air Canada.
Trans Colorado, **11** 299
Trans-Continental Leaf Tobacco Company,
(TCLTC) **13** 491
Trans Continental Records, **52** 430
Trans Freight Lines, **27** 473–74

Trans International Airlines, **41** 402
Trans Louisiana Gas Company, **43** 56–57
Trans-Lux Corporation, 51 380–83
Trans-Mex, Inc. S.A. de C.V., **42** 365
Trans-Natal Coal Corp., **IV** 93
Trans Ocean Products, **8** 510
Trans-Pacific Airlines. *See* Aloha Airlines
Incorporated.
Trans-Resources Inc., **13** 299
Trans Thai-Malaysia, **56** 290
Trans Union Corp., **IV** 137; **6** 25; **28** 119
Trans Western Publishing, **25** 496
Trans World Airlines, Inc., I 125–27,
132; **II** 679; **6** 130; **9** 17, 232; **10**
301–03; **11** 277, 427; **12** 381, **487–90**
(upd.); 14 73; **15** 419; **22** 22, 219; **26**
439; **29** 190; **35 424–29 (upd.); 52** 21,
90, 168
Trans-World Corp., **19** 456; **47** 231
Trans World Entertainment
Corporation, 24 501–03; 68 374–77
(upd.)
Trans World International, **18** 262–63
Trans World Life Insurance Company, **27**
46–47
Trans World Music, **9** 361
Trans World Seafood, Inc., **13** 244
Transaction Systems Architects, Inc., 29
477–79
Transaction Technology, **12** 334
TransAlta Utilities Corporation, 6
585–87
Transamerica—An AEGON Company,
41 400–03 (upd.)
Transamerica Corporation, I 536–38; III
344; **7** 236–37; **8** 46; **11** 273, 533; **13**
528–30 (upd.); 21 285; **25** 328; **27** 230;
46 48. *See also* TIG Holdings, Inc.
Transamerica Pawn Holdings. *See*
EZCORP Inc.
Transamerica Retirement Services, **63** 176
TransAmerican Waste Industries Inc., **41**
414
Transat. *See* Compagnie Générale
Transatlantique (Transat).
Transatlantic Holdings, Inc., III 198; **11**
532–33; 15 18
Transatlantische Gruppe, **III** 404
Transax, **63** 102
TransBrasil S/A Linhas Aéreas, 31
443–45; **46** 398
TransCanada PipeLines Limited, I 264;
V 737–38; 17 22–23
Transco Energy Company, V 739–40; 18
366. *See also* The Williams Companies.
Transcontinental and Western Air Lines, **9**
416; **12** 487
Transcontinental Gas Pipe Line
Corporation. *See* Transco Energy
Company.
Transcontinental Services Group N.V., **16**
207
TransCor America, Inc., **23** 154
Transelco, Inc., **8** 178
Transfer Drivers, Inc., **46** 301
Transfracht, **6** 426
Transiciel SA, 48 400–02
Transit Homes of America, Inc., **46** 301
Transit Mix Concrete and Materials
Company, **7** 541
Transitions Optical Inc., **21** 221, 223
Transitron, **16** 332
Transkaryotic Therapies Inc., **54** 111

Transking Inc. *See* King Kullen Grocery
Co., Inc.
Transkrit Corp., **IV** 640; **26** 273
Translittoral, **67** 353
Transmanche-Link, **13** 206–08; **37** 135
Transmedia Network Inc., 20 494–97.
See also Rewards Network Inc.
Transmedica International, Inc., **41** 225
Transmisiones y Equipos Mecanicos, S.A.
de C.V., **23** 171
Transmitter Equipment Manufacturing Co.,
13 385
TransMontaigne Inc., 28 470–72
Transmontane Rod and Gun Club, **43**
435–36
Transnet Ltd., 6 433–35
Transocean Sedco Forex Inc., 45 417–19;
59 368
Transpac, **IV** 325
Transport Corporation of America, Inc.,
49 400–03
Transport International Pool, **58** 239
Transportacion Ferroviaria Mexicana, **50**
209
Transportacion Maritima Mexicana S.A. de
C.V., **12** 279; **26** 236; **47** 162; **50** 208
Transportation Technologies Industries Inc.,
51 155
Transportation.com, **45** 451
Transportes Aéreas Centro-Americanos.
See Grupo TACA.
Transportes Aereos Portugueses, S.A., 6
125–27. *See also* TAP—Air Portugal
Transportes Aéreos Portugueses S.A.
Transportes Aeromar, **39** 188
TransPro, Inc., 71 356–59
Transrack S.A., **26** 363
Transue & Williams Steel Forging Corp.,
13 302
Transway International Corp., **10** 369
Transworld Communications, **35** 165
Transworld Corp., **14** 209
Transworld Drilling Company Limited. *See*
Kerr-McGee Corporation.
The Tranzonic Companies, 8 512; **15**
500–02; 37 392–95
Trapper's, **19** 286
Trasgo, S.A. de C.V., **14** 516; **50** 493
Travel Air Manufacturing Company, **8** 49;
27 97
Travel Inc., **26** 309
Travel Information Group, **17** 398
Travel Ports of America, Inc., 17 493–95
Travelers/Aetna Property Casualty Corp.,
63 14
Travelers Bank & Trust Company, **13** 467
Travelers Book Club, **13** 105
Travelers Corporation, III 387–90; 15
463 124. *See also* Citigroup Inc.
Travelers/Aetna Property Casualty Corp.,
21 15
Travelocity.com, Inc., 46 434–37; 58
118–20
Travers Morgan Ltd., **42** 183
Travis Boats & Motors, Inc., 37 396–98
Travis Perkins plc, 34 450–52
Travocéan, **25** 104
TRC. *See* Tennessee Restaurant Company.
TRC Companies, Inc., 32 461–64
TRE Corp., **23** 225
Treadco, Inc., 16 39; **19** 38, **454–56**
Treasure Chest Advertising Company,
Inc., 21 60; **32 465–67**
Treasure House Stores, Inc., **17** 322

Treatment Centers of America, **11** 379
Trebuhs Realty Co., **24** 438
Tredegar Corporation, 10 291; **52** 349–51; **59** 24
Tree of Life, Inc., 29 480–82
Tree Sweet Products Corp., **12** 105; **26** 325
Tree Tavern, Inc., **27** 197
Trefoil Capital Investors, L.P., **8** 305
Trego Systems Inc., **64** 190
Trek Bicycle Corporation, 16 493–95; **19** 384–85
Trelleborg A.B., **IV** 166
Tremec. *See* Transmisiones y Equipos Mecanicos, S.A. de C.V.
Tremont Corporation, **21** 490
Trencherwood Plc, **45** 443
Trend International Ltd., **13** 502
Trend-Lines, Inc., 22 516–18
Trends Magazine NV, **48** 347
Trendwest Resorts, Inc., 12 439; **33** 409–11. *See also* Jeld-Wen, Inc.
TrentonWorks Limited. *See* The Greenbrier Companies.
Tresco, **8** 514
Trevor Sorbie of America, Inc., **60** 287
Trex Company, Inc., 71 360–62
Tri-City Federal Savings and Loan Association, **10** 92
Tri-City Utilities Company, **6** 514
Tri-County National Bank, **9** 474
Tri-Marine International Inc., **24** 116
Tri-Miller Packing Company, **7** 524
Tri-Sonics, Inc., **16** 202; **43** 170
Tri-State Baking, **53** 21
Tri-State Improvement Company. *See* Cincinnati Gal & Electric Company.
Tri-State Publishing & Communications, Inc., **22** 442
Tri-State Recycling Corporation, **15** 117
Tri-Union Seafoods LLC, **24** 116
Tri Valley Growers, 32 468–71
Tri-Village Developments BV, **58** 359
Triad, **14** 224
Triad Artists Inc., **23** 514
Triad International Maintenance Corp., **13** 417
Triad Nitrogen, Inc., **27** 316, 318
Triad Systems Corp., **38** 96
The Triangle Group, **16** 357
Triangle Industries Inc., **I** 614; **14** 43
Triangle Pharmaceuticals, Inc., **54** 131
Triangle Publications, Inc., **12** 359–60
Triangle Sheet Metal Works, Inc., **45** 327
Triarc Companies, Inc., 8 535–37; **13** 322; **14** 32–33; **34** 453–57 (upd.); **39** 383, 385; **57** 227; **58** 324
Triax Midwest Associates L.P. *See* Mediacom Communications Corporation.
Tribe Computer Works. *See* Zoom Technologies, Inc.
Tribune Company, IV 682–84; **10** 56; **11** 331; **22** 519–23 (upd.); **26** 17; **32** 358–59; **38** 306; **42** 133; **63** 389–95 (upd.)
Tricap Restructuring Fund, **59** 162
Trick & Murray, **22** 153
Trico Products Corporation, 15 503–05
Tricon Global Restaurants, Inc., **21** 313, 317, 405, 407, 485; **40** 342; **57** 228. *See also* Yum! Brands Inc.
Tridel Enterprises Inc., 9 512–13
Trident Data Systems, **54** 396
Trident II, Inc., **64** 253
Trident NGL Holdings Inc., **18** 365, 367

Trident Seafoods Corporation, 56 359–61
Tridon Ltd., **69** 206
Trifari, Krussman & Fishel, Inc., **9** 157
Trigen Energy Corporation, 6 512; **42** 386–89
Trigon Industries, **13** 195; **14** 431
Trilan Developments Ltd., **9** 512
Trilogy Fabrics, Inc., **16** 125
Trilogy Retail Enterprises L.P., **58** 186
Trilon Financial Corporation, II 456–57
Trimac Ltd., **25** 64
TriMas Corp., III 571; **11** 534–36; **20** 359, 362; **39** 266
Trimble Navigation Limited, 40 441–43
Trimel Corp., **47** 54
Trinc Company, **59** 320
TriNet Corporate Realty Trust, Inc., **65** 146
Trinidad and Tobago External Telecommunications Company, **25** 100
Trinidad-Tesoro Petroleum Company Limited, **7** 516, 518
Trinity Beverage Corporation, **11** 451
Trinity Broadcasting, **13** 279
Trinity Capital Opportunity Corp., **17** 13
Trinity Distributors, **15** 139
Trinity Industries, Incorporated, 7 540–41
Trinity Mirror plc, 49 404–10 (upd.)
TRINOVA Corporation, III 640–42, 731; **13** 8; **16** 7, 9
Triple Five Group Ltd., 49 411–15
Triple P N.V., 26 496–99
Trippe Manufacturing Co., **10** 474; **24** 29
TriQuest-Nypro Plastics, **60** 264
TriQuint Semiconductor, Inc., 63 396–99
Trisko Jewelry Sculptures, Ltd., 57 388–90
TriStar Pictures, **II** 136–37; **12** 75, 455; **23** 275; **28** 462. *See also* Columbia TriStar Motion Pictures Companies.
Triton Bioscience, **III** 53; **26** 384
Triton Cellular Partners, L.P., **43** 341
Triton Energy Corporation, 11 537–39; **55** 20
Triton Group Ltd., **I** 447; **31** 287; **34** 339
Triton Systems Corp., **22** 186
Triumph-Adler. *See* TA Triumph-Adler AG.
Triumph American, Inc., **12** 199
Triumph Films, **25** 174
Triumph, Finlay, and Philips Petroleum, **11** 28
Triumph Group, Inc., 21 153; **31** 446–48
Triumph LOR, Inc., **63** 305–06
Triumph Motorcycles Ltd., 53 334–37
Trivest, Inc., **21** 531–32
Trix Modelleisenbahn GmbH & Co. KG, **70** 166
Trizec Corporation Ltd., 9 84–85; **10** 529–32
TrizecHahn, **37** 311; **63** 341
TRM Copy Centers Corporation, 18 526–28
Troll, **13** 561
Trolley Barn Brewery Inc., **25** 401
Tropical Marine Centre, **40** 128–29
Tropical Shipping, Inc., **6** 529, 531
Tropical Sportswear Int'l Corporation, **42** 120
Tropicana Products, Inc., 25 366; **28** 271, 473–77; **38** 349; **45** 160–62
Trotter, Inc., **49** 108
Trotter-Yoder & Associates, **22** 88

Trottner-McJunkin SA de CV, **63** 287–88
Trouw Nutrition USA, **56** 258
Troxel Cycling, **16** 53
Troy & Nichols, Inc., **13** 147
Troy Design Group, **55** 32
Troy Metal Products. *See* KitchenAid.
Troyfel Ltd., **III** 699
TRT Communications, Inc., **6** 327; **11** 185
Tru-Run Inc., **16** 207
Tru-Stitch, **16** 545
Tru-Trac Therapy Products, **11** 486
Truck Components Inc., **23** 306
Trudeau Marketing Group, Inc., **22** 386
True Form Foundations Corporation, **59** 267
True North Communications Inc., 23 478–80; **25** 91. *See also* Foote, Cone & Belding Worldwide.
True Temper Hardware Co., **30** 241–42
True Value Hardware Stores. *See* TruServ Corporation.
Trugg-Hansa Holding AB, **III** 264
TruGreen, **23** 428, 430
Truitt Bros., **10** 382
Trump Organization, 16 262; **23** 481–84; **43** 225; **64** 392–97 (upd.)
Trunkline Gas Company, **6** 544; **14** 135
Trunkline LNG Co., **IV** 425
Trus Joist Corporation. *See* TJ International, Inc.
TruServ Corporation, 24 504–07
Trussdeck Corporation. *See* TJ International, Inc.
Trust Company of the West, **19** 414; **42** 347
Trustcorp, Inc., **9** 475–76
Trusted Information Systems, Inc., **25** 349
Trusthouse Forte PLC, III 104–06; **16** 446
TRW Inc., I 539–41; **11** 68, 540–42 (upd.); **14** 510–13 (upd.); **16** 484; **17** 372; **18** 275; **19** 184; **23** 134; **24** 480; **26** 141; **28** 119; **32** 437; **33** 47; **34** 76; **43** 311, 313; **45** 152
TRW Vehicle Safety Systems Inc., **41** 369
Tryart Pty. Limited, **7** 253
TSA. *See* Transaction Systems Architects, Inc.
TSB Group plc, 12 491–93; **16** 14
TSC. *See* Tractor Supply Company.
TSI Inc., **38** 206
TSI Soccer Corporation, **29** 142–43
Tsingtao Brewery Group, 49 416–20
TSMC. *See* Taiwan Semiconductor Manufacturing Company Ltd.
TSO. *See* Teacher's Service Organization, Inc.
TSO Financial Corp., **II** 420; **8** 10
Tsogo Sun Gaming & Entertainment, **17** 318
TSP. *See* Tom Snyder Productions.
TSR Inc., **24** 538
Tsuang Hine Co., **III** 582
Tsubakimoto-Morse, **14** 64
Tsurusaki Pulp Co., Ltd., **IV** 285
Tsutsunaka Plastic Industry Co., **8** 359
TSYS. *See* Total System Services, Inc.
TT Acquisitions, Inc., **56** 361
TTK. *See* Tokyo Tsushin Kogyo K.K.
TTX Company, 6 436–37; **66** 328–30 (upd.)
Tubby's, Inc., 53 338–40
Tube Fab Ltd., **17** 234
Tube Forming, Inc., **23** 517

Tube Reducing Corp., **16** 321
Tube Service Co., **19** 344
Tubed Chemicals Corporation, **27** 299
Tuborg, **9** 99
**Tubos de Acero de Mexico, S.A.
   (TAMSA), 41 404–06**
Tuboscope, **42** 420
Tucker, Lynch & Coldwell. *See* CB
   Commercial Real Estate Services Group,
   Inc.
TUCO, Inc., **8** 78
**Tucson Electric Power Company, 6
   588–91; 42** 388
Tucson Gas & Electric, **19** 411–12
**Tuesday Morning Corporation, 18
   529–31; 70 331–33 (upd.)**
Tuff Stuff Publications, **23** 101
TUI. *See* Touristik Union International
   GmbH. and Company K.G.
TUI Group GmbH, 42 283; **44 432–35**
Tuileries et Briqueteries d'Hennuyeres et
   de Wanlin, **14** 249
TUJA, **27** 21
Tully's Coffee Corporation, 51 384–86
Tultex Corporation, 13 531–33
Tumbleweed, Inc., 33 412–14
Tunhems Industri A.B., **I** 387
Tunisair. *See* Société Tunisienne de l'Air-
   Tunisair.
**Tupolev Aviation and Scientific
   Technical Complex, 24 58–60**
Tupperware Corporation, 15 475, 477;
   17 186; **18** 67; **28 478–81**
Turbine Engine Asset Management LLC,
   28 5
TurboLinux Inc., **45** 363
Turcot Paperboard Mills Ltd., **17** 281
Turk Telecom, **63** 378, 380
**Turkish Airlines Inc. (Türk Hava Yollari
   A.O.), 72 351–53**
Turkish Petroleum Co. *See* Türkiye
   Petrolleri Anonim Ortakliği.
Turkiye Is Bankasi A.S., 61 377–80
**Türkiye Petrolleri Anonim Ortakliği, IV
   562–64**
**Turner Broadcasting System, Inc., II
   166–68; IV** 676; **6 171–73 (upd.); 7** 64,
   99, 306, 529; **23** 33, 257; **25** 313, 329,
   498; **30** 100; **47** 272; **57** 40; **66 331–34
   (upd.)**
**Turner Construction Company, 66
   335–38**
**The Turner Corporation, 8 538–40; 23
   485–88 (upd.); 25** 402; **33** 197
Turner Entertainment Co., **18** 459
Turner Glass Company, **13** 40
Turner Network Television, **21** 24
Turnstone Systems, **44** 426
TURPAS. *See* Türkiye Petrolleri Anonim
   Ortakliği
Turtle Wax, Inc., 15 506–09; 16 43; **26**
   349
Tuscarora Inc., 17 155; **29 483–85**
The Tussauds Group, 55 376–78
Tutogen Medical, Inc., 68 378–80
Tutt Bryant Industries PLY Ltd., **26** 231
Tuttle, Oglebay and Company. *See*
   Oglebay Norton Company.
TV & Stereo Town, **10** 468
TV Asahi, **7** 249
TV Azteca, S.A. de C.V., 39 194–95,
   398–401
TV Food Network, **22** 522
TV Guide, Inc., 43 431–34 (upd.)

TVA. *See* Tennessee Valley Authority.
TVE. *See* Television Española, S.A.
TVE Holdings, **22** 307
TVH Acquisition Corp., **III** 264
TVI, Inc., 15 510–12
TVN Entertainment Corporation, **32** 239
TVS Entertainment PLC, **13** 281
TVSN Ltd., **64** 185
TVT Records. *See* Tee Vee Toons, Inc.
TVW Enterprises, **7** 78
TW Services, Inc., II 679–80; 10 301–03
TWA. *See* Trans World Airlines;
   Transcontinental & Western Airways.
TWC. *See* The Weather Channel, Inc.
Tweco Co., **19** 441
Tweeds, **12** 280
**Tweeter Home Entertainment Group,
   Inc., 30 464–66; 41** 379, 381
**Twentieth Century Fox Film
   Corporation, II 169–71; 12** 322, 359;
   15 23, 25, 234; **25** 327, **490–94 (upd.);
   43** 173
"21" International Holdings, **17** 182
21 Invest International Holdings Ltd., **14**
   322
21st Century Food Products. *See* Hain
   Food Group, Inc.
21st Century Mortgage, **18** 28
21st Century Telecom Services, Inc. *See*
   RCN Corporation.
Twenty-third Publications, **49** 48
**24 Hour Fitness Worldwide, Inc., 71
   363–65**
24/7 Real Media, Inc., 49 421–24
TWI. *See* Trans World International.
Twin City Wholesale Drug Company, **14**
   147
Twin Disc, Inc., 21 502–04
Twin Hill Acquisition Company, Inc., **48**
   286
Twinings Tea, **41** 31
Twinlab Corporation, 34 458–61
Twinpak, **IV** 250
Two Guys, **12** 49
II-VI Incorporated, 69 353–55
2ndhead Oy, **51** 328
21st Century Mortgage, **41** 18, 20
TWW Plc, **26** 62
TXEN, Inc., **18** 370
TxPort Inc., **13** 8
Ty Inc., 33 415–17
**Tyco International Ltd., III 643–46; 28
   482–87 (upd.); 63 400–06 (upd.)**
Tyco Submarine Systems Ltd., **32** 217
Tyco Toys, Inc., 12 494–97; 13 312, 319;
   18 520–21; **25** 314
Tyler Corporation, 23 489–91
Tymnet, **18** 542
**Tyndale House Publishers, Inc., 57
   391–94**
Tyndall's Formal Wear, **60** 5
Tyrolean Airways, **9** 233; **33** 50
Tyskie Brewery, **24** 450
Tyson Foods, Inc., II 584–85; 7 422–23,
   432; **14 514–16 (upd.); 21** 535; **23** 376,
   384; **26** 168; **39** 229; **50 491–95 (upd.);
   64** 386

U.B. TUFF., **67** 339
U.C.L.A.F. *See* Roussel-Uclaf.
U-Haul International Inc. *See* Amerco.
U.K. Corrugated, **IV** 296; **19** 226
U.S. *See also* US.
U.S. Aggregates, Inc., 42 390–92

U.S. Appliances, **26** 336
U.S. Bancorp, 12 165; **14 527–29; 36
   489–95 (upd.)**
U.S. Bank of Washington, **14** 527
U.S. Banknote Company, **30** 43
U.S. Bearings Company. *See* Federal-
   Mogul Corporation.
U.S. Billing, Inc. *See* Billing Concepts
   Corp.
U.S. Biomedicals Corporation, **27** 69
U.S. Bioscience, Inc., **35** 286, 288
U.S. Borax, Inc., 42 393–96
U.S. Brass, **24** 151
U.S. Can Corporation, 30 474–76
**U.S. Cellular Corporation, 31 449–52
   (upd.)**
U.S. Computer of North America Inc., **43**
   368
U.S. Delivery Systems, Inc., 22 153,
   531–33; 47 90. *See also* Velocity
   Express Corporation.
U.S. Electrical Motors, **II** 19
U.S. Elevator Corporation, **19** 109–11
U.S. Envelope, **19** 498
U.S. Foodservice, 26 503–06; 37 374, 376
U.S. Generating Company, **26** 373
U.S. Geological Survey, **9** 367
U.S. Graphite. *See* Wickes Inc.
U.S. Guarantee Co., **III** 220; **14** 108
U.S. Healthcare, Inc., 6 194–96; 21 16
U.S. Home Corporation, 8 541–43
U.S. Industries, Inc., **7** 208; **18** 467; **23**
   296; **24** 150; **27** 288
U.S. Intec, **22** 229
U.S. International Reinsurance, **III** 264
U.S. Investigations Services Inc., **35** 44
U.S. Journal Training, Inc., **72** 172
U.S. Lawns, **31** 182, 184
U.S. Lines, **III** 459; **11** 194
U.S. Lock Corporation, **9** 543; **28** 50–52
U.S. Long Distance Corp. *See* Billing
   Concepts Corp.
**U.S. News and World Report Inc., 30
   477–80**
**U.S. Office Products Company, 25
   500–02; 41** 69, 247; **47** 91
U.S. Overall Company, **14** 549
U.S. Physical Therapy, Inc., 65 345–48
U.S. Plywood Corp. *See* United States
   Plywood Corp.
U.S. RingBinder Corp., **10** 313–14
U.S. Robotics Corporation, 9 514–15; 20
   8, 69; **22** 17; **24** 212; **34** 444; **36** 122,
   357; **48** 369; **49** 184; **66 339–41 (upd.)**
U.S. Rubber Company, **10** 388
**U.S. Satellite Broadcasting Company,
   Inc., 20 505–07**
U.S. Shoe Corporation, **43** 98; **44** 365
U.S. Smelting Refining and Mining, **7** 360
U.S. Software Inc., **29** 479
U.S. Steel Corp. *See* United States Steel
   Corp.
U.S. Telephone Communications, **9** 478
**U.S. Timberlands Company, L.P., 42
   397–400**
U.S. Time Corporation, **13** 120
U.S. Trust Corp., 17 496–98
U.S. Vanadium Co., **9** 517
U.S. Venture Partners, **15** 204–05
U.S. Vision, Inc., 66 342–45
U S West, Inc., V 341–43; 11 12, 59,
   547; **25** 101, **495–99 (upd.); 32** 218; **36**
   43; **37** 124–27
U.S. Windpower, **11** 222–23

U.S. Xpress Enterprises, Inc., **18** 159
U-Tote'M, **II** 620; **7** 372
UA. *See* Metro- Goldwyn-Mayer Inc., MGM/UA Communications Company; United Artists Corp.
UAA. *See* EgyptAir.
UAL Corporation, 34 462–65 (upd.); 52 22, 25
UAP. *See* Union des Assurances de Paris.
UAP Inc., **45** 179
UARCO Inc., **15** 473–74
UAT. *See* UTA.
UAW (International Union, United Automobile, Aerospace and Agricultural Implement Workers of America), 72 354–57
Ube Industries, Ltd., III 759–61; 38 463–67 (upd.)
Ubi Soft Entertainment S.A., 41 188–89, **407–09**
Ubique Ltd, **25** 301
UBL Educational Loan Center, **42** 211
UBS AG, 52 352–59 (upd.); 59 141, 144–45
UCAR International, Inc., **40** 83
UCI, **25** 173
Udo Fischer Co., **8** 477
UDRT. *See* United Dominion Realty Trust, Inc.
UDV. *See* United Distillers and Vintners.
Ueda Kotsu Company, **47** 408
UETA Inc., **29** 510–11
Ufa Sports, **44** 190
UFJ Bank, **61** 250
Ugg Holdings, Inc., **22** 173
UGI. *See* United Gas Improvement.
UGI Corporation, 12 498–500
Ugine S.A., 20 498–500
Ugly Duckling Corporation, 22 524–27. *See also* DriveTime Automotive Group Inc.
Uhlmans Inc., **24** 458
UI International, **6** 444
UIB. *See* United Independent Broadcasters, Inc.
UICI, 33 418–21
Uinta Co., **6** 568
Uintah National Corp., **11** 260
UIS Co., **13** 554–55; **15** 324
Uitgeversmaatschappij Elsevier. *See* Reed Elsevier.
Uitzendbureau Amstelveen. *See* Randstad Holding n.v.
UJB Financial Corp., **14** 473
UKF. *See* Unie van Kunstmestfabrieken.
Ukrop's Super Market's, Inc., 39 402–04
UL. *See* Underwriters Laboratories, Inc.
Ullrich Copper, Inc. *See* Foster Wheeler Corp.
Ullstein Langen Müller, **IV** 591
ULN. *See* Union Laitière Normande.
Ulstein Holding ASA, **27** 494
Ulster Television PLC, 71 366–68
Ultimate Electronics, Inc., 18 532–34; **21** 33; **24** 52, 269; **69 356–59 (upd.)**
Ultra Mart, **16** 250
Ultra Pac, Inc., 24 512–14
Ultra Petroleum Corporation, 71 369–71
UltraCam. *See* Ultrak Inc.
UltraCare Products, **18** 148
Ultrak Inc., 24 508–11
Ultralar, **13** 544
Ultralife Batteries, Inc., 58 345–48

Ultramar Diamond Shamrock Corporation, IV 565–68; 31 453–57 (upd.)
Ultrametl Mfg. Co., **17** 234
Umacs of Canada Inc., **9** 513
Umberto's of New Hyde Park Pizzeria, **16** 447
Umbro Holdings Ltd. *See* Stone Manufacturing Company.
UMC. *See* United Microelectronics Corp.
UMG. *See* Universal Music Group.
UMI Company, **29** 58
NV Umicore SA, 47 411–13
Umpqua River Navigation Company, **13** 100
Unadulterated Food Products, Inc., **11** 449
UNAT, **III** 197–98
Unbrako Socket Screw Company Ltd., **30** 429
Uncas-Merchants National Bank, **13** 467
Uncle Ben's Inc., 22 528–30
Under Armour Performance Apparel, 61 381–83
Underwood, **24** 269
Underwriter for the Professions Insurance Company, **55** 128
Underwriters Laboratories, Inc., 30 467–70
Underwriters Reinsurance Co., **10** 45
Unefon, S.A., **39** 194, 196
UNELCO. *See* Union Electrica de Canarias S.A.
Unelec, Inc., **13** 398
UNG. *See* United National Group, Ltd.
Ungaro SA, **62** 313
Uni-Cast. *See* Sturm, Ruger & Company, Inc.
Uni Europe, **III** 211
Uni-Marts, Inc., 17 499–502
Uni-President Group, **49** 460
Unibail SA, 40 444–46
Unibank, **40** 336; **50** 149–50
Unic. *See* GIB Group.
Unicapital, Inc., **15** 281
Unicare Health Facilities, **6** 182; **25** 525
Unicco Security Services, **27** 22
Unice, **56** 335
UNICEF. *See* United Nations International Children's Emergency Fund (UNICEF).
Unicel. *See* Rural Cellular Corporation.
Unicer, **9** 100
Unichem, **25** 73
Unichema International, **13** 228
Unicom Corporation, 29 486–90 (upd.). *See also* Exelon Corporation.
Unicon Producing Co., **10** 191
Unicoolait, **19** 51
UNICOR. *See* Federal Prison Industries, Inc.
Unicord Company, **24** 115; **64** 60
UniCorp, **8** 228
UniCredito Italiano, **50** 410
Uniden, **14** 117
Unidrive, **47** 280
UniDynamics Corporation, **8** 135
Uniface Holding B.V., **10** 245; **30** 142
Unifi, Inc., 12 501–03; 62 372–76 (upd.)
Unified Energy System of Russia. *See* RAO Unified Energy System of Russia.
Unified Western Grocers, **31** 25
UniFirst Corporation, 16 228; **21** 115, **505–07**
Uniflex Corporation, **53** 236
Uniforce Services Inc., **40** 119

Unigate PLC, II 586–87; 28 488–91 (upd.); 29 150. *See also* Uniq Plc.
Unigesco Inc., **II** 653
Uniglory, **13** 211
Unigro. *See* Laurus N.V.
Unigroup, **15** 50
UniHealth America, **11** 378–79
Unijoh Sdn, Bhd, **47** 255
Unik S.A., **23** 170–171
Unilab Corp., **26** 391
Unilever PLC/Unilever N.V., II 588–91; III 52, 495; **7 542–45 (upd.)**, 577; **8** 105–07, 166, 168, 341, 344; **9** 449; **11** 205, 421; **13** 243–44; **14** 204–05; **18** 395, 397; **19** 193; **21** 219; **22** 123; **23** 242; **26** 306; **28** 183, 185; **30** 396–97; **32 472–78 (upd.); 36** 237; **49** 269; **57** 301
Unilife Assurance Group, **III** 273
UniLife Insurance Co., **22** 149
Unilog SA, 42 401–03
Uniloy Milacron Inc., **53** 230
UniMac Companies, **11** 413
Unimetal, **30** 252
Uninsa, **I** 460
Union Aéromaritime de Transport. *See* UTA.
Union Bag–Camp Paper Corp. *See* Union Camp Corporation.
Union Bank. *See* State Street Boston Corporation.
Union Bank of California, 16 496–98. *See also* UnionBanCal Corporation.
Union Bank of New York, **9** 229
Union Bank of Scotland, **10** 337
Union Bank of Switzerland, II 378–79; 21 146. *See also* UBS AG.
Union Bay Sportswear, **17** 460
Union Biscuits. *See* Leroux S.A.S.
Union Camp Corporation, IV 344–46; 8 102; **39** 291; **47** 189; **63** 269
Union Carbide Corporation, I 390, **399–401**, 582, 666; **7** 376; **8** 180, 182, 376; **9** 16, **516–20 (upd.); 10** 472; **11** 402–03; **12** 46; **13** 118; **14** 281–82; **16** 461; **17** 159; **43** 265–66; **48** 321; **55** 380
Union Cervecera, **9** 100
Union Colliery Company. *See* Union Electric Company.
Union Commerce Corporation, **11** 181
Union Commerciale, **19** 98
Union Corporation. *See* Gencor Ltd.
Union des Assurances de Paris, II 234; **III** 201, **391–94**
Union des Coopératives Bressor, **25** 85
Union des Cooperatives Laitières. *See* Unicoolait.
Union des Mines, **52** 362
Union des Transports Aériens. *See* UTA.
Union Electric Company, V 741–43; 26 451. *See also* Ameren Corporation.
Unión Electrica Fenosa. *See* Unión Fenosa S.A.
Union Equity Co-Operative Exchange, **7** 175
Unión Fenosa, S.A., 51 387–90; 56 216
Union Financiera, **19** 189
Union Financière de France Banque SA, 52 360–62
Union Fork & Hoe Company. *See* Acorn Products, Inc.
Union Gas & Electric Co., **6** 529
l'Union Générale des Pétroles, **IV** 560
Union Hardware, **22** 115

Union Laitière Normande. *See* Compagnie Laitière Européenne.
Union Levantina de Seguros, **III** 179
Union Light, Heat & Power Company. *See* Cincinnati Gas & Electric Company.
Union Minière. *See* NV Umicore SA.
Union Mutual Life Insurance Company. *See* UNUM Corp.
Union National Bank of Wilmington, **25** 540
Union of European Football Association, **27** 150
Union of Food Co-ops, **II** 622
Union Oil Co., **9** 266
Union Oil Co. of California. *See* Unocal Corporation.
Union Pacific Corporation, V 529–32; 12 18–20, 278; **14** 371–72; **28 492–500 (upd.); 36** 43–44; **58** 262
Union Pacific Resources Group, **52** 30
Union Pacific Tea Co., **7** 202
Union Paper & Co. AS, **63** 315
Union Planters Corporation, 54 387–90
Union Power Company, **12** 541
Union Pub Company, **57** 411, 413
Union Savings and Loan Association of Phoenix, **19** 412
Union Savings Bank, **9** 173
Union Savings Bank and Trust Company, **13** 221
Union Steamship Co. of New Zealand Ltd., **27** 473
Union Sugar, **II** 573
Union Suisse des Coopératives de Consommation. *See* Coop Schweiz.
Union Tank Car Co., **IV** 137
Union Telecard Alliance, LLC, **34** 223
Union Telephone Company, **14** 258
Union Texas Petroleum Holdings, Inc., 7 379; **9 521–23**
Union Trust Co., **9** 228; **13** 222
The Union Underwear Company, **8** 200–01; **25** 164–66
Union Verwaltungsgesellschaft mbH, **66** 123
Unionamerica, Inc., **III** 243; **16** 497; **50** 497
UnionBanCal Corporation, 50 496–99 (upd.)
UnionBay Sportswear Co., **27** 112
Unione Manifatture, S.p.A., **19** 338
Uniphase Corporation. *See* JDS Uniphase Corporation.
Uniplex Business Software, **41** 281
Uniq Plc, **52** 418, 420
Unique Casual Restaurants, Inc., 27 480–82
Unique Pub Company, **59** 182
Uniroy of Hempstead, Inc. *See* Aris Industries, Inc.
Uniroyal Chemical Corporation, **36** 145
Uniroyal Corp., **8** 503; **11** 159; **20** 262
Uniroyal Goodrich, **42** 88
Uniroyal Holdings Ltd., **21** 73
Unishops, Inc. *See* Aris Industries, Inc.
Unison HealthCare Corporation, 25 503–05
Unisource Worldwide, Inc., **47** 149
Unistar Radio Networks, **23** 510
Unisys Corporation, III 165–67; 6 281–83 (upd.); 8 92; **9** 32, 59; **12** 149, 162; **17** 11, 262; **18** 345, 386, 434, 542; **21** 86; **36 479–84 (upd.)**
Unit Corporation, 63 407–09

Unit Group plc, **8** 477
Unitech plc, **27** 81
United Acquisitions, **7** 114; **25** 125
United Advertising Periodicals, **12** 231
United AgriSeeds, Inc., **21** 387
United Air Express. *See* United Parcel Service of America Inc.
United Air Fleet, **23** 408
United Aircraft and Transportation Co., **9** 416, 418; **10** 260; **12** 289; **21** 140
United Airlines, I 118, 124, **128–30; II** 680; **6 128–30 (upd.)**, 131, 388–89; **9** 271–72, 283, 416, 549; **10** 199, 301, 561; **11** 299; **12** 192, 381; **14** 73; **22** 199, 220; **24** 21, 22; **25** 146, 148, 421–23; **26** 113, 440; **27** 20; **29** 507; **38** 105; **52** 386; **55** 10–11. *See also* UAL Corporation.
United Alaska Drilling, Inc., **7** 558
United Alloy Steel Company, **26** 405
United-American Car, **13** 305
United American Insurance Company of Dallas, **9** 508; **33** 407
United Arab Airlines. *See* EgyptAir.
United Artists Corp., **IV** 676; **9** 74; **12** 13; **13** 529; **14** 87; **21** 362; **23** 389; **26** 487; **36** 47; **41** 402. *See also* MGM/UA Communications Company; Metro-Goldwyn-Mayer Inc.
United Artists Theatre Circuit, Inc., **37** 63–64; **59** 341
United Australian Automobile Industries, **62** 182
United Auto Group, Inc., 26 500–02; 68 381–84 (upd.)
United Biscuits (Holdings) plc, II 592–94; 26 59; **36** 313; **42 404–09 (upd.); 64** 270
United Brands Company, II 595–97; 7 84–85; **12** 215; **21** 110, 112; **25** 4; **60** 132
United Breweries International, Ltd., **60** 207
United Breweries Ltd. *See* Carlsberg A/S.
United Broadcasting Corporation Public Company Ltd., **31** 330
United Building Centers. *See* Lanoga Corporation.
United Business Media plc, 52 363–68 (upd.)
United Cable Television Corporation, **9** 74; **18** 65; **43** 431
United Capital Corporation, **56** 136
The United Center. *See* Wirtz Corporation.
United Central Oil Corporation, **7** 101
United Cigar Manufacturers Company,. *See* Culbro Corporation.
United Cities Gas Company, **43** 56, 58
United Communications Systems, Inc. **V** 346
United Computer Services, Inc., **11** 111
United Consolidated Industries, **24** 204
United Corp., **10** 44
United Defense Industries, Inc., 30 471–73; 66 346–49 (upd.)
United Distillers and Vintners. *See* Diageo plc.
United Distillers Glenmore, Inc., **34** 89
United Dominion Industries Limited, IV 288; **8 544–46; 16 499–502 (upd.); 47** 378; **57** 87
United Dominion Realty Trust, Inc., 52 369–71

United Electric Light and Water Co., **13** 182
United Electronic Services, Inc., **72** 29
United Engineers & Constructors, **11** 413
United Express, **11** 299
United Factors Corp., **13** 534–35
United Federal Savings and Loan of Waycross, **10** 92
United Financial Corporation, **12** 353
United Financial Group, Inc., **8** 349
United 5 and 10 Cent Stores, **13** 444
United Foods, Inc., 21 508–11
United Fruit Co., **7** 84–85; **21** 110–11; **44** 152
United Funds, Inc., **22** 540–41
United Gas and Electric Company of New Albany, **6** 555
United Gas and Improvement Co., **13** 182
United Gas Improvement Co., **6** 523; **11** 388
United Graphics, **12** 25
United Grocers, **II** 625
United Health, Inc. *See* Extendicare Health Services, Inc.
United HealthCare Corporation, 9 524–26; 24 229, 231. *See also* Humana Inc.
The United Illuminating Company, 21 512–14
United Image Entertainment, **18** 64, 66
United Industrial Corporation, 37 399–402
United Industrial Syndicate, **8** 545
United Industries Corporation, 68 385–87
United Information Systems, Inc., **V** 346
United International Holdings Inc., **28** 198
United Investors Life Insurance Company, **22** 540; **33** 407
United Iron & Metal Co., **14** 156
United Jewish Communities, 33 422–25
United Kingdom Hotel Investments Ltd., **64** 217
United Knitting, Inc., **21** 192, 194
United Life & Accident Insurance Co., **III** 220–21; **14** 109
United Life Insurance Company, **12** 541
United Light and Power, **6** 511
United Machinery Co., **15** 127
United Match Factories, **12** 462
United Media, **22** 442
United Merchandising Corp., **12** 477
United Merchants & Manufacturers, Inc., 13 534–37; 31 160
United Meridian Corporation, **8** 350
United Microelectronics Corporation, **22** 197; **47** 384, 386; **67** 38
United Mortgage Servicing, **16** 133
United National Group, Ltd., 63 410–13
United Nations International Children's Emergency Fund (UNICEF), 58 349–52
United Natural Foods, Inc., 32 479–82
United Natural Gas Company, **6** 526
United Netherlands Navigation Company. *See* Vereenigde Nederlandsche Scheepvaartmaatschappij.
United News & Media plc, 28 501–05 (upd.); 35 354. *See also* United Business Media plc.
United Newspapers plc, IV 685–87. *See also* United Business Media plc.
United of Omaha, **III** 365
United Office Products, **11** 64

United Online, Inc., **71** 372–77 (upd.)
United Optical, **10** 151
United Overseas Bank Ltd., **56** 362–64
United Pacific Financial Services, **III** 344
United Pacific Life Insurance Co., **III** 343–44
United Pan-Europe Communications NV, **47** 414–17
United Paper Mills Ltd., **IV** 316, 347–50. *See also* UPM-Kymmene Corporation.
United Paramount Network, **25** 418–19; **26** 32; **31** 109
United Parcel Service, Inc., **63** 414–19
United Parcel Service of America Inc., **V** 533–35; **11** 11; **12** 309, 334; **13** 19, 416; **14** 517; **17** 503–06 (upd.); **18** 82, 177, 315–17; **25** 148, 150, 356; **27** 471, 475; **34** 473; **39** 33; **41** 245; **42** 140; **49** 460
United Pet Group, Inc. *See* United Industries Corporation.
United Plantations Berhad. *See* Aarhus United A/S.
United Power and Light Corporation, **12** 541
United Presidential Life Insurance Company, **12** 524, 526
United Press International, Inc., **16** 166; **25** 506–09
United Railways & Electric Company, **25** 44
United Refining Co., **23** 406, 408
United Rentals, Inc., **28** 386, 388; **34** 466–69; **48** 272
United Resources, Inc., **21** 514
United Retail Group Inc., **33** 426–28
United Retail Merchants Stores Inc., **9** 39
United Road Services, Inc., **69** 360–62
United Satellite Television, **10** 320
United Savings of Texas, **8** 349
United Scientific Holdings, **47** 8
United Service Organizations, **60** 308–11
United Servomation, **7** 471–72
United Shipping & Technology, Inc., **49** 440
United Shirt Shops, Inc. *See* Aris Industries, Inc.
United Skates of America, **8** 303
United Software Consultants Inc., **11** 65
United States Aluminum Co., **17** 213
United States Aviation Underwriters, Inc., **24** 176
United States Can Co., **15** 127, 129
United States Cellular Corporation, **9** 494–96, 527–29. *See also* U.S. Cellular Corporation.
United States Electric Light and Power Company, **25** 44
The United States Electric Lighting Company, **11** 387
United States Fidelity and Guaranty Co. *See* USF&G Corporation.
United States Filter Corporation, **20** 501–04; **38** 168, 170; **52** 189
United States Football League, **29** 347
United States Gypsum Co. *See* USG Corporation.
United States Health Care Systems, Inc. *See* U.S. Healthcare, Inc.
United States Mail Steamship Co., **23** 160
United States Medical Finance Corp., **18** 516, 518
United States National Bancshares, **25** 114
United States National Bank of Galveston. *See* Cullen/Frost Bankers, Inc.

United States National Bank of Oregon, **14** 527
The United States National Bank of Portland, **14** 527–28
United States Pipe and Foundry Company, **62** 377–80
United States Playing Card Company, **62** 381–84
United States Plywood Corp., **13** 100
United States Postal Service, **10** 60; **14** 517–20; **34** 470–75 (upd.); **42** 140
United States Satellite Broadcasting Company Inc., **24** 226; **38** 176
United States Security Trust Co., **13** 466
United States Shoe Corporation, **V** 207–08; **17** 296, 390; **23** 328; **39** 301; **52** 229
United States Steel Corporation, **I** 491; **IV** 572–74; **6** 514; **7** 70–73, 401–02, 549–51; **10** 32; **11** 194; **12** 353–54; **17** 356; **18** 378; **26** 405, 451; **50** 500–04 (upd.); **54** 247–48
United States Surgical Corporation, **10** 533–35; **13** 365; **21** 119–20; **28** 486; **34** 476–80 (upd.)
United States Tobacco Company, **9** 533
United Stationers Inc., **14** 521–23; **25** 13; **36** 508
United Steel Mills Ltd., **25** 266
United Supers, **II** 624
United Technologies Automotive Inc., **15** 513–15
United Technologies Corporation, **I** 84–86; **9** 18, 418; **10** 536–38 (upd.); **11** 308; **12** 289; **13** 191, 384–86; **22** 6; **34** 371–72, 432, 481–85 (upd.); **39** 311, 313
United Telecommunications, Inc., **V** 344–47; **8** 310; **9** 478–80; **10** 202; **12** 541
United Telephone Company, **7** 508; **14** 257
United Telephone Company of the Carolinas, **10** 202
United Telephone of Indiana, **14** 259
United Telephone System, Inc., **V** 346
United Television, Inc., **9** 119; **26** 32
United Thermal Corp., **42** 388
United Truck Lines, **14** 505
United Utilities, Inc., **10** 202
United Utilities PLC, **52** 372–75 (upd.)
United Van Lines, **14** 37; **15** 50
United Video Satellite Group, **18** 535–37. *See also* TV Guide, Inc.
United Water Resources, Inc., **40** 447–50; **45** 277
United Way of America, **36** 485–88
United Westburne Inc., **19** 313
United Wholesale Grocery Company. *See* Spartan Stores Inc.
United-A.G. Cooperative Inc., **65** 252
Unitel Communications Inc., **6** 311; **44** 49; **46** 401; **47** 136
Unitika Ltd., **V** 387–89; **53** 341–44 (upd.)
Unitil Corporation, **37** 403–06
Unitog Co., **16** 228; **19** 457–60; **21** 115; **51** 76
Unitpool, **70** 311
Unitransa, **27** 474
Unitrin Inc., **16** 503–05
Unitron Medical Communications, **29** 412
Unity Cellular Systems, Inc. *See* Rural Cellular Corporation.
Unity Financial Corp., **19** 411

Univar Corporation, **8** 99; **9** 530–32; **12** 333; **41** 340; **55** 297
Univas, **13** 203 **23** 171
Univasa, **39** 229
Univel Inc., **38** 418
Universal Belo Productions, **10** 5
Universal Cheerleaders Association. *See* Varsity Spirit Corp.
Universal Cigar Corp., **14** 19
Universal Compression, Inc., **59** 402–04
Universal Consumer Products Group, **30** 123
Universal Controls, Inc., **10** 319
Universal Cooler Corp., **8** 515
Universal Corporation, **V** 417–18; **48** 403–06 (upd.)
Universal Electronics Inc., **39** 405–08
Universal Foods Corporation, **7** 546–48; **21** 498. *See also* Sensient Technologies Corporation.
Universal Footcare Products Inc., **31** 255
Universal Forest Products, Inc., **10** 539–40; **59** 405–09 (upd.)
Universal Frozen Foods, **23** 321
Universal Genève, **13** 121
Universal Guaranty Life Insurance Company, **11** 482
Universal Health Services, Inc., **6** 191–93
Universal Industries, Inc., **10** 380; **13** 533
Universal International, Inc., **25** 353, 355, 510–11
Universal Juice Co., **21** 55
Universal Leaf Tobacco Company. *See* Universal Corporation.
Universal Manufacturing, **25** 167
Universal Marking Systems, **25** 331
Universal Match, **12** 464
Universal Matchbox Group, **12** 495
Universal Music Group, **22** 194; **26** 152; **37** 193
Universal Pictures. *See* Universal Studios, Inc.
Universal Press Syndicate, **10** 4; **40** 38
Universal Records, **27** 123
Universal Reinsurance Corporation, **58** 20
Universal Resources Corporation, **6** 569; **26** 388
Univeral Shoes, Inc., **22** 213
Universal Studios Florida, **14** 399
Universal Studios, Inc., **12** 73; **21** 23–26; **25** 411; **33** 429–33; **47** 419–21
Universal Tea Co., Inc., **50** 449
Universal Telephone, **9** 106
Universal Textured Yarns, **12** 501
Universe Tankships, **59** 198
UNIVERSELLE Engineering U.N.I. GmbH, **60** 194
University HealthSystem Consortium, **53** 346
University of Phoenix, **24** 40
Univisa, **24** 516
Univision Communications Inc., **18** 213; **24** 515–18; **41** 150–52; **54** 72–73, 158
Unix System Laboratories Inc., **25** 20–21; **38** 418
UNM. *See* United News & Media plc.
Uno-e Bank, **48** 51
Uno Restaurant Holdings Corporation, **18** 538–40; **70** 334–37 (upd.)
Uno-Ven, **IV** 571; **24** 522
Unocal Corporation, **IV** 569–71; **24** 519–23 (upd.); **71** 378–84 (upd.)
Unova Manufacturing Technologies Inc., **72** 69, 71

UNR Industries, Inc. *See* ROHN Industries, Inc.
Unterberg Harris, **25** 433
UNUM Corp., **13** 538–40
UnumProvident Corporation, **52** 376–83 **(upd.)**
Uny Co., Ltd., **II** 619; **V** 209–10, 154; **13** 545; **36** 419; **49** 425–28 **(upd.)**
UOB. *See* United Overseas Bank Ltd.
UPC. *See* United Pan-Europe Communications NV.
UPI. *See* United Press International.
Upjohn Company, **I** 707–09; **III** 53; **8** 547–49 **(upd.)**; **10** 79; **12** 186; **13** 503; **14** 423; **16** 440. *See also* Pharmacia & Upjohn Inc.
UPM-Kymmene Corporation, **19** 461–65; **25** 12; **30** 325; **50** 505–11 **(upd.)**
UPN. *See* United Paramount Network.
Upper Deck Company, LLC, **34** 448; **37** 295
Upper Peninsula Power Co., **53** 369
UPS. *See* United Parcel Service, Inc.
UPS Aviation Technologies, Inc., **60** 137
UPSHOT, **27** 195
Urban Outfitters, Inc., **14** 524–26
Urbaser SA, **55** 182
URS Corporation, **45** 420–23
URSI. *See* United Road Services, Inc.
Urwick Orr, **II** 609
US. *See also* U.S.
US Airways Express, **32** 334; **38** 130
US Airways Group, Inc., **28** 506–09 **(upd.)**; **33** 303; **52** 24–25, 384–88 **(upd.)**
US Industrial Chemicals, Inc., **8** 440
US Industries Inc., **30** 231
US Monolithics, **54** 407
US 1 Industries, **27** 404
US Order, Inc., **10** 560, 562
US Repeating Arms Co., **58** 147
US Sprint Communications Company. *See* Sprint Communications Company, L.P.
US Telecom, **9** 478–79
US West Communications Services, Inc. *See* Regional Bell Operating Companies.
USA Cafes, **14** 331
USA Floral Products Inc., **27** 126
USA Interactive, Inc., **47** 418–22 **(upd.)**; **58** 117, 120
USA Networks Inc., **25** 330, 411; **33** 432; **37** 381, 383–84; **43** 422
USA Security Systems, Inc., **27** 21
USA Truck, Inc., **42** 410–13
USAA, **10** 541–43; **62** 385–88 **(upd.)**
USAir Group, Inc., **I** 131–32; **III** 215; **6** 131–32 **(upd.)**; **11** 300; **14** 70, 73; **18** 62; **21** 143; **24** 400; **26** 429; **42** 34. *See also* US Airways Group, Inc.
USANA, Inc., **27** 353; **29** 491–93
USCC. *See* United States Cellular Corporation.
USCP-WESCO Inc., **II** 682
Usego AG., **48** 63
USF&G Corporation, **III** 395–98; **11** 494–95; **19** 190. *See also* The St. Paul Companies.
USFL. *See* United States Football League.
USFreightways Corporation, **27** 475; **49** 402
USG Corporation, **III** 762–64; **26** 507–10 **(upd.)**
USH. *See* United Scientific Holdings.

Usinger's Famous Sausage. *See* Fred Usinger Inc.
Usinor SA, **42** 414–17 **(upd.)**
Usinor Sacilor, **IV** 226–28; **22** 44; **24** 144; **26** 81, 84; **54** 393
USLD Communications Corp. *See* Billing Concepts Corp.
USM, **10** 44
USO. *See* United Service Organizations.
Usource LLC, **37** 406
USPS. *See* United States Postal Service.
USSC. *See* United States Surgical Corporation.
USSI. *See* U.S. Software Inc.
UST Inc., **9** 533–35; **42** 79; **50** 512–17 **(upd.)**
UST Wilderness Management Corporation, **33** 399
Usutu Pulp Company, **49** 353
USV Pharmaceutical Corporation, **11** 333
USWeb/CKS. *See* marchFIRST, Inc.
USX Corporation, **IV** 572–74; **7** 193–94, 549–52 **(upd.)**. *See also* United States Steel Corporation.
UT Starcom, **44** 426
Utag, **11** 510
Utah Construction & Mining Co., **14** 296
Utah Federal Savings Bank, **17** 530
Utah Gas and Coke Company, **6** 568
Utah Medical Products, Inc., **36** 496–99
Utah Mines Ltd., **IV** 47; **22** 107
Utah Power and Light Company, **9** 536; **12** 266; **27** 483–86. *See also* PacifiCorp.
UTI Energy, Inc. *See* Patterson-UTI Energy, Inc.
Utilicom, **6** 572
Utilicorp United Inc., **6** 592–94. *See also* Aquila, Inc.
UtiliTech Solutions, **37** 88
Utility Constructors Incorporated, **6** 527
Utility Engineering Corporation, **6** 580
Utility Fuels, **7** 377
Utility Line Construction Service, Inc., **59** 65
Utility Service Affiliates, Inc., **45** 277
Utility Services, Inc., **42** 249, 253
Utility Supply Co. *See* United Stationers Inc.
UTV. *See* Ulster Television PLC.
Utz Quality Foods, Inc., **72** 358–60
UUNET, **38** 468–72
UV Industries, Inc., **7** 360; **9** 440
Uwajimaya, Inc., **60** 312–14

V.L. Churchill Group, **10** 493
VA Linux Systems, **45** 363
VA TECH ELIN EBG GmbH, **49** 429–31
VA Technologie AG, **57** 402
Vacheron Constantin, **27** 487, 489
Vaco, **38** 200, 202
Vaculator Division. *See* Lancer Corporation.
Vacuum Metallurgical Company, **11** 234
Vacuum Oil Co. *See* Mobil Corporation.
Vadoise Vie, **III** 273
VAE AG, **57** 402
VAE Nortrak Cheyenne Inc., **53** 352
Vail Associates, Inc., **11** 543–46; **31** 65, 67
Vail Resorts, Inc., **43** 435–39 **(upd.)**
Vaillant GmbH, **44** 436–39
Val Corp., **24** 149

Val-Pak Direct Marketing Systems, Inc., **22** 162
Val Royal LaSalle, **II** 652
Valassis Communications, Inc., **8** 550–51; **37** 407–10 **(upd.)**
Valcom, **13** 176
ValCom Inc. *See* InaCom Corporation.
Valdi Foods Inc., **II** 663–64
Vale do Rio Doce Navegacao SA—Docenave, **43** 112
Vale Harmon Enterprises, Ltd., **25** 204
Vale Power Company, **12** 265
Valenciana de Cementos, **59** 112
Valentine & Company, **8** 552–53
Valentino, **67** 246, 248
Valeo, **23** 492–94; **66** 350–53 **(upd.)**
Valero Energy Corporation, **7** 553–55; **71** 385–90 **(upd.)**
Valhi, Inc., **10** 435–36; **19** 466–68
Valid Logic Systems Inc., **11** 46, 284; **48** 77
Vality Technology Inc., **59** 56
Vallen Corporation, **45** 424–26
Valley Bank of Helena, **35** 197, 199
Valley Bank of Maryland, **46** 25
Valley Bank of Nevada, **19** 378
Valley Crest Tree Company, **31** 182–83
Valley Deli Inc., **24** 243
Valley Fashions Corp., **16** 535
Valley Federal of California, **11** 163
Valley Fig Growers, **7** 496–97
Valley Media Inc., **35** 430–33
Valley National Bank, **II** 420
Valley of the Moon, **68** 146
Valley-Todeco, Inc., **13** 305–06
Valleyfair, **22** 130
Vallourec SA, **54** 391–94
Valmet Corporation, **III** 647–49; **IV** 350, 471. *See also* Metso Corporation.
Valmont Industries, Inc., **13** 276; **19** 50, 469–72
Valois S.A. *See* AptarGroup, Inc.
Valores Industriales S.A., **19** 10, 12, 189, 473–75; **29** 219
The Valspar Corporation, **8** 552–54; **32** 483–86 **(upd.)**
Valtek International, Inc., **17** 147
Value America, **29** 312
Value City Department Stores,
Value City Department Stores, Inc., **29** 311; **38** 473–75
Value Foods Ltd., **11** 239
Value Giant Stores, **12** 478
Value House, **II** 673
Value Investors, **III** 330
Value Line, Inc., **16** 506–08
Value Merchants Inc., **13** 541–43
Value Rent-A-Car, **9** 350; **23** 354
ValueClick, Inc., **49** 432–34
Valueland, **8** 482
ValueVision International, Inc., **22** 534–36; **27** 337
ValuJet, Inc. *See* AirTran Holdings, Inc.
Valvtron, **11** 226
VAMED Gruppe, **56** 141
Van Ameringen-Haebler, Inc., **9** 290
Van Camp Seafood Company, Inc., **7** 556–57. *See also* Chicken of the Sea International.
Van Cleef & Arpels Inc., **26** 145
Van de Kamp's, Inc., **7** 430
Van der Moolen Holding NV, **37** 224
Van Dorn Company, **13** 190
Van Houtte Inc., **39** 409–11

Van Kirk Chocolate, **7** 429
Van Kok-Ede, **II** 642
Van Leer Containers Inc., **30** 397
Van Leer Holding, Inc., **9** 303, 305
Van Leer N.V. *See* Royal Packaging
 Industries Van Leer N.V.; Greif Inc.
Van Mar, Inc., **18** 88
Van Nostrand Reinhold, **8** 526
Van Ommeren, **41** 339–40
Van Sickle, **IV** 485
Van Waters & Rogers, **8** 99; **41** 340
Van Wezel, **26** 278–79
Van Wijcks Waalsteenfabrieken, **14** 249
Van's Aircraft, Inc., 65 349–51
Vanadium Alloys Steel Company
 (VASCO), **13** 295–96
Vanant Packaging Corporation, **8** 359
Vance International Airways, **8** 349
Vance Publishing Corporation, 64
 398–401
Vanderbilt Mortgage and Finance, **13** 154
Vanessa and Biffi, **11** 226
The Vanguard Group, Inc., 14 530–32;
 34 486–89 (upd.)
Vanguard Health Systems Inc., 70
 338–40
Vanguard International Semiconductor
 Corp., **47** 385
Vanity Fair. *See* VF Corporation.
Vans, Inc., 16 509–11; **17** 259–61; **47**
 423–26 (upd.)
Vanstar, **13** 176
Vantage Analysis Systems, Inc., **11** 490
Vantage Components. *See* Bell
 Microproducts Inc.
Vantive Corporation, **33** 333; **38** 431–32
Varco International, Inc., 42 418–20
Varco-Pruden, Inc., **8** 544–46
Vare Corporation, **8** 366
Vari-Lite International, Inc., 35 434–36
Varian Associates Inc., 12 504–06
Varian, Inc., 48 407–11 (upd.)
Varibus Corporation. *See* Gulf States
 Utilities Company.
Variflex, Inc., 51 391–93
Variform, Inc., **12** 397
VARIG S.A. (Viação Aérea Rio-
 Grandense), 6 133–35; **26** 113; **29**
 494–97 (upd.); 31 443–45; **33** 19
Varity Corporation, III 650–52; **7** 258,
 260; **19** 294; **27** 203, 251
Varlen Corporation, 16 512–14
Varney Speed Lines. *See* Continental
 Airlines, Inc.
Varo, **7** 235, 237
Varsity Spirit Corp., 15 516–18; **22** 459
Varta AG, 9 180–81; **23** 495–99
Vascoloy-Ramet, **13** 295
VASP (Viaçao Aérea de Sao Paulo), **31**
 444–45
Vasset, S.A., **17** 362–63
Vast Solutions, **39** 24
Vastar Resources, Inc., 24 524–26; **38**
 445, 448
Vattenfall AB, 57 395–98
Vaughan Harmon Systems Ltd., **25** 204
Vaughan Printers Inc., **23** 100
Vaungarde, Inc., **22** 175
Vauxhall, **19** 391
VBB Viag-Bayernwerk-Beteiligungs-
 Gesellschaft mbH, **IV** 232; **50** 170
VCA Antech, Inc., 58 353–55
VCH Publishing Group. *See* John Wiley &
 Sons, Inc.

VDM Nickel-Technologie AG, **IV** 89
VEAG, **57** 395, 397
Veba A.G., I 542–43; **IV** 199, 455, 508; **8**
 69, 494–495; **15** 519–21 (upd.); **23** 69,
 451, 453–54; **24** 79; **25** 102; **26** 423; **32**
 147; **59** 389–91; **62** 14. *See also* E.On
 AG.
Vebego International BV, 49 435–37
VECO International, Inc., 7 558–59
Vector Automotive Corporation, **13** 61
Vector Casa de Bolsa, **21** 413
Vector Gas Ltd., **13** 458
Vector Group Ltd., 35 437–40 (upd.)
Vector Video, Inc., **9** 74
Vectra Bank Colorado, **53** 378
Vectura Holding Company L.L.C., **69** 197
Veda International, **54** 395–96
Vedelectric, **13** 544
Vedior NV, 35 441–43; **44** 5; **62** 208
Veeco Instruments Inc., 32 487–90
Veeder-Root Company, **7** 116–17
VeggieTales. *See* Big Idea Productions,
 Inc.
Veit Companies, 43 440–42
Vel-Tex Chemical, **16** 270
Velcarta S.p.A., **17** 281
Velcro Industries N.V., 19 476–78; **72**
 361–64
Velda Farms, Inc., **26** 448
VeloBind, Inc., **10** 314
Velocity Express Corporation, 49 438–41
Velva-Sheen Manufacturing Co., **23** 66
Vemar, **7** 558
Venator Group Inc., 35 444–49 (upd.).
 See also Foot Locker Inc.
Vencemos, **20** 124
Vencor, Inc., IV 402; **14** 243; **16** 515–17;
 25 456
Vendex International N.V., 10 136–37;
 13 544–46; **26** 160; **46** 187, 189. *See
 also* Koninklijke Vendex KBB N.V.
 (Royal Vendex KBB N.V.).
Vendôme Luxury Group plc, 27 487–89;
 29 90, 92
Vendors Supply of America, Inc., **7**
 241–42; **25** 241
Venetian Casino Resort, LLC, 47
 427–29
Venevision, **54** 72–73, 75
Venevision, **24** 516, 517
Ventshade Company, **40** 299–300
Ventura, **29** 356–57
Venture Out RV, **26** 193
Venture Stores Inc., 12 507–09
Ventures Limited, **49** 137
Venturi, Inc., **9** 72
Veolia Environnement SA, **66** 68
Vepco. *See* Virginia Electric and Power
 Company.
Vera Imported Parts, **11** 84
Verafumos Ltd., **12** 109
Veragon Corporation. *See* Drypers
 Corporation.
Veratex Group, **13** 149–50
Veravision, **24** 510
Verbatim Corporation, 14 533–35
Verbundnetz Gas AG, **38** 408
Verd-A-Fay, **13** 398
Verdugt, **70** 143, 145
Vereinigte Elektrizitäts und Bergwerke
 A.G. *See* VEBA A.G.
Vereinigte Elektrizitätswerke Westfalen
 AG, IV 195; **V** 744–47
Vereinigte Glanzstoff-Fabriken, **13** 21

Vereinigte Industrie-Unternehmungen
 Aktiengesellschaft. *See* VIAG
Vereinigte Papierwerke Schickedanz AG,
 26 384
Vereinigte Stahlwerke AG, **14** 327
Verenigde Bedrijven Bredero, **26** 280
Verenigde Nederlandse Uitgeverijen. *See*
 VNU N.V.
Verenigde Spaarbank Groep. *See* VSB
 Groep.
Veri-Best Baking Co., **56** 29
Veridian Corporation, 54 395–97
Verifact Inc. (IVI), **46** 251
VeriFone, Inc., 15 321; **18** 541–44; **27**
 219–21; **28** 191; **50** 227
Verilyte Gold, Inc., **19** 452
VeriSign, Inc., 47 430–34
Verispan LLC, **68** 308
Veritas Capital Fund L.P., **44** 420, 423; **59**
 192
Veritas Capital Management, L.L.C., **54**
 178
Veritas Capital Partners, **26** 408
Veritas Software Corporation, 45
 427–31
Veritec Technologies, Inc., **48** 299
Veritus Inc., **27** 208–09
Verity Inc., 68 388–91
Verizon Communications, **43** 443–49
 (upd.)
Verizon Wireless, Inc., **42** 284; **63** 131
Verlagsgruppe Georg von Holtzbrinck
 GmbH, **15** 158, 160; **25** 485; **35** 450–53
Verlagsgruppe Märkische Verlags- und
 Druckgesellschaft mbH, **66** 123
Vermeer Manufacturing Company, 17
 507–10
Vermont General Insurance Company, **51**
 248
Vermont Pure Holdings, Ltd., 51 394–96
The Vermont Teddy Bear Co., Inc., 36
 500–02
Verneuil Holding Co, **21** 387
Vernitron Corporation, **18** 293
Vernon and Nelson Telephone Company.
 See British Columbia Telephone
 Company.
Vernon Savings & Loan, **9** 199
Vernors, Inc., **25** 4
Verreries Brosse S.A.S., **67** 210, 212
Verreries Pochet et du Courval, **55** 309
Versace. *See* Gianni Versace SpA.
Versatec Inc., **13** 128
Versatile Farm and Equipment Co., **22** 380
Versax, S.A. de C.V., **19** 12
Verson Allsteel Press Co., **21** 20, 22
Vert Baudet, **19** 309
Vertex Data Science Limited, **52** 372,
 374–75
Vertical Technology Industries, **14** 571
Verticom, **25** 531
Verve Records, **23** 389
Vesa Energy, **57** 397
Vessel Management Services, Inc., **28** 80
Vestek Systems, Inc., **13** 417
Vestro, **19** 309
Vesuvius USA Corporation, **8** 179
Veszpremtej, **25** 85
Veterinary Cos. of America, **III** 25
VEW AG, 39 412–15
Vexlar, **18** 313
VF Corporation, V 390–92; **17** 511–14
 (upd.); 54 398–404 (upd.)
VH Serviços e Construçoes Ltda., **72** 68

VHA Inc., 53 345–47
VHA Long Term Care, 23 431
VH1 Inc., 23 503
VI-Jon Laboratories, Inc., 12 388
Via Cariane. See Keolis SA.
Via-Générale de Transport et d'Industrie
SA, 28 155
Via Verde, 64 57
ViaAfrika. See Naspers Ltd.
Viacao Aerea Rio Grandense of South
America. See VARIG, SA.
Viacom Enterprises, 7 336
Viacom Inc., 23 274–76, 500–03 (upd.);
24 106, 327; 26 32; 28 295; 30 101; 31
59, 109; 35 402; 48 214; 51 218–19; 67
367–71 (upd.)
Viacom International Inc., 7 222–24,
530, 560–62; 9 429; 10 175; 19 403
Viag AG, IV 229–32, 323; 25 332; 32
153; 43 188–89; 59 252. See also E.On
AG.
Viajes El Corte Inglés, S.A., 26 129
VIASA. See Iberia.
ViaSat, Inc., 54 405–08
Viasoft Inc., 27 490–93; 59 27
VIASYS Healthcare, Inc., 52 389–91
Viasystems Group, Inc., 67 372–74
Viatech Continental Can Company, Inc.,
25 512–15 (upd.)
Vibracoustic GmbH & Co. KG, 68 289
Vicat S.A., 70 341–43
Vickers Inc., III 640, 642; 13 8; 23 83
Vickers plc, 21 435; 27 494–97; 47 9
VICOM, 48 415
Vicon Industries, Inc., 44 440–42
VICORP Restaurants, Inc., 12 510–12;
48 412–15 (upd.)
Victoire Delage, 62 229
Victor Company, 10 483
Victor Company of Japan, Ltd., II
118–19; 12 454; 26 511–13 (upd.)
Victor Equipment Co., 19 440
Victor Value, II 678
Victoria & Co., 39 247
Victoria Coach Station. See London
Regional Transport.
Victoria Creations Inc., 13 536
Victoria Group, 44 443–46 (upd.)
VICTORIA Holding AG, III 399–401.
See also Victoria Group.
Victoria Ward, Limited, 57 157
Victoria's Secret. See The Limited, Inc.
Victorinox AG, 21 515–17
Victory Refrigeration Company, 22 355
Victory Savings and Loan, 10 339
Victory Supermarket. See Big V
Supermarkets, Inc.
Vidal Sassoon, 17 110
Video Concepts, 9 186
Video Independent Theatres, Inc., 14 86
Video Library, Inc., 9 74
Video News International, 19 285
Video Superstores Master Limited
Partnership, 9 74
Video Trend, 60 84
VideoFusion, Inc., 16 419
Videotex Network Japan, IV 680
Videotron, 25 102
VideV, 24 509
Vidrala S.A., 67 375–77
La Vie Claire, 13 103
Vie de France Yamazaki Inc., 58 380–82
Vielle Montaign, 22 285

Vienna Sausage Manufacturing Co., 14
536–37
Viessmann Werke GmbH & Co., 37
411–14
Vietnam International Assurance Co., 64
280
Vietnam LPG Co., Ltd., 56 290
View-Master/Ideal Group, 12 496
Viewer's Edge, 27 429
Viewpoint International, Inc., 66 354–56
ViewSonic Corporation, 72 365–67
ViewStar Corp., 20 103
Viewtel, 14 36
ViewTrade Holding Corp., 46 282
Vigilant Insurance Co., III 220; 14 108; 37
83
Vigoro, 22 340
Viking, IV 659
Viking Building Products, 22 15
Viking Computer Services, Inc., 14 147
Viking Consolidated Shipping Corp, 25
470
Viking Direct Limited, 10 545
Viking Foods, Inc., 8 482; 14 411
Viking Industries, 39 322, 324
Viking Office Products, Inc., 10 544–46
Viking Penguin, IV 611
Viking Press, 12 25
Viking Pump Company, 21 499–500
Viking Range Corporation, 66 357–59
Viking Star Shipping, Inc. See Teekay
Shipping Corporation.
Viktor Achter, 9 92
Village Inn. See VICORP Restaurants, Inc.
Village Roadshow Ltd., 58 356–59
Village Super Market, Inc., 7 563–64
Village Voice Media, Inc., 38 476–79
Villager, Inc., 11 216; 39 244
Villazon & Co., 27 139
Villeroy & Boch AG, 37 415–18
Vilmorin Clause et Cie, 70 344–46
VILPAC, S.A., 26 356
AO VimpelCom, 48 416–19; 59 300
Vimto. See Nichols plc.
Vin & Spirit AB, 31 458–61; 58 197
Viña Concha y Toro S.A., 45 432–34
Vina San Pedro S.A., 70 62–63
Vinci, 27 54; 43 450–52; 49 44
Vincor International Inc., 50 518–21
Viner Bros., 16 546
Vinewood Companies, 53 232
Vingaarden A/S, 9 100
Vining Industries, 12 128
Viniprix SA, 10 205; 19 309; 27 95
Vinita Rock Company, 50 49
Vinland Web-Print, 8 360
Vinson & Elkins L.L.P., 28 48; 30
481–83; 47 139–40, 447
Vintage Petroleum, Inc., 42 421–23
Vintage Yarns, 62 374
Vintners International, 34 89
Vinton Studios, 63 420–22
Vipond, Inc., 64 31
Vipont Pharmaceutical, III 25; 14 122
VIPS, 11 113
Viratec Thin Films, Inc., 22 347
Virco Manufacturing Corporation, 17
515–17
Virgin Atlantic Airlines. See Virgin Group
PLC.
Virgin Express, 35 384

Virgin Group PLC, 12 513–15; 14 73; 18
80; 22 194; 24 486; 29 302; 32 491–96
(upd.); 50 125
The Virgin Islands Telephone Co., 19 256
Virgin Music Group Worldwide, 52 429
Virgin Retail Group Ltd., 9 75, 361; 37
262
Virginia Eastern Shore Sustainable
Development Corporation, 28 307
Virginia Electric and Power Company. See
Dominion Resources, Inc.
Virginia Fibre Corporation. See Greif Inc.
Virginia Laminating, 10 313
Virginia Mason Medical Center, 41 183
Virginia National Bankshares, 10 426
Virginia Railway and Power Company
(VR&P). See Dominion Resources, Inc.
Viridian Group plc, 64 402–04
Viridor Waste Limited, 45 338
Visa. See Valores Industriales S.A.
Visa International, 9 536–38; 26 514–17
(upd.); 41 200–01; 61 249
Viscofan S.A., 70 347–49
Vishay Intertechnology, Inc., 11 516; 21
518–21
Visible Impact Target Company, 62 82
Visio Corporation, 63 296
Vision Centers, 12 188
Vision Hardware Group. See Acorn
Products, Inc.
Vision Technologies Kinetics Inc., 61 43
Vision Technology Group Ltd., 19 124; 49
113
Visionware Ltd., 38 419
Visionworks, 9 186
Viskase Companies, Inc., 17 157, 159; 55
379–81
Vista Alegre, 69 303
Vista Bakery, Inc., 14 306; 56 365–68
Vista Chemical Company, I 402–03
Vista Concepts, Inc., 11 19
Vista Resources, Inc., 17 195
Vista 2000, Inc., 36 444
Vistana, Inc., 22 537–39; 26 464
Visual Action Holdings plc, 24 96, 374
Visual Information Technologies, 11 57
VISX, Incorporated, 30 484–86
Vita-Achter, 9 92
Vita Liquid Polymers, 9 92
Vita Plus Corporation, 60 315–17
Vitafoam Incorporated, 9 93; 33 78
Vital Health Corporation, 13 150
Vital Processing Services LLC, 18 516,
518
Vital S.A., 71 140
Vitalink Communications Corp., 11 520;
34 444
Vitalink Pharmacy Services, Inc., 15
522–24; 25 309–10
Vitalscheme, 38 426
VitalWorks, Inc. See AMICAS, Inc.
Vitamin Shoppe Industries, Inc., 60
318–20
Vitamin World, 31 346–48
Vitesse Semiconductor Corporation, 32
497–500
Vitex Foods, 10 382
Vitoria-Minas Railroad, 43 111
Vitramon, Inc., 54 371–72
Vitro Corp., 8 178; 10 547–48; 17 492
Vitro Corporativo S.A. de C.V., 34
490–92
Vitro S.A., 19 189

VIVA, **23** 390
Vivarte SA, 54 409–12 **(upd.)**
Vivendi Universal S.A., 29 369, 371; **32**
  52, 54; **33** 178, 181; **34** 83, 85; **38** 168,
  170; **40** 408; **41** 361; **43** 450, 452; **44**
  190; **46** 438–41 **(upd.);** **47** 420–21; **48**
  164–65; **63** 166
Vivendia, **40** 449
Vivesvata Iron and Steel Ltd., **IV** 207
Vivra, Inc., 15 119; **18** 545–47
VKI Technologies Inc., **39** 409
Vladivostok Dairy, **48** 438
Vlasic Foods International Inc., 25
  516–19
VLSI Technology, Inc., 11 246; **16**
  518–20; **31** 300
VMG Products. *See* Drypers Corporation.
VMX Inc., **14** 355; **41** 289
VND, **III** 593
VNG. *See* Verbundnetz Gas AG.
VNS. *See* Vereenigde Nederlandsche
  Scheepvaartmaatschappij.
VNU N.V., 27 361, 498–501; **38** 8
Vobis Microcomputer, **20** 103; **23** 311
VocalTec, Inc., **18** 143
Vodac, **11** 548
Vodacom World Online Ltd, **48** 399
Vodafone Group Plc, 11 547–48; **34** 85;
  36 503–06 **(upd.);** **38** 296, 300
Vodapage, **11** 548
Vodata, **11** 548
Vodavi Technology Corporation, **13** 213
Voest-Alpine Stahl AG, IV 233–35; **31**
  47–48
voestalpine AG, 57 399–403 **(upd.)**
Vogel Peterson Furniture Company, **7** 4–5
Vogoro Corp., **13** 503
Voice Data Systems, **15** 125
Voice Powered Technology International,
  Inc., **23** 212
Voice Response, Inc., **11** 253
VoiceStream Wireless Corporation, **48** 130
Voith Sulzer Papiermaschinen GmbH. *See*
  J.M. Voith AG.
Volition, Inc., **39** 395
Volkswagen Aktiengesellschaft, I 206–08;
  7 8; **10** 14; **11** 104, 549–51 **(upd.);** **13**
  413; **14** 169; **19** 484; **26** 12; **27** 11, 496;
  31 363–65; **32** 501–05 **(upd.);** **34** 55,
  130; **39** 373–74
Volt Information Sciences Inc., 26
  518–21
Volume Distributors. *See* Payless
  ShoeSource, Inc.
Volume Service Company. *See* Restaurants
  Unlimited, Inc.
Volume Shoe Corporation. *See* Payless
  ShoeSource,Inc.
Volunteer Leather Company, **17** 202, 205
Volunteer State Life Insurance Co., **III**
  221; **37** 84
Volunteers of America, Inc., 66 360–62
AB Volvo, **I** 209–11; **7** 565–68 **(upd.);** **26**
  9–12 **(upd.);** **67** 378–83 **(upd.)**
Volvo-Penta, **21** 503
Von Maur Inc., 64 405–08
von Roll, **6** 599
Von Ruden Manufacturing Co., **17** 532
Von's Grocery Co., **8** 474; **17** 559
The Vons Companies, Incorporated, II
  655; **7** 569–71; **12** 209; **24** 418; **28**
  510–13 (upd.); **35** 328
VOP Acquisition Corporation, **10** 544

Vornado Realty Trust, 20 508–10; **39**
  211; **45** 14–16; **47** 360
Voroba Hearing Systems, **25** 56
Vortex Management, Inc., **41** 207
Vorwerk & Co., 27 502–04
Vosper Thornycroft Holding plc, 41
  410–12
Vossloh AG, 53 348–52
Votainer International, **13** 20
Vought Aircraft Industries, Inc., 11 364;
  45 309; **49** 442–45
Vox, **58** 195
Voyager Communications Inc., **24** 5
Voyager Ltd., **12** 514
Voyageur Travel Insurance Ltd., **21** 447
VR&P. *See* Virginia Railway and Power
  Company.
Vratislavice A.S., **38** 77
VRG International. *See* Roberts
  Pharmaceutical Corporation.
Vriesco Plastics B.V., **53** 221
Vroom & Dreesmann, **13** 544–46
VS Services, **13** 49
VSA. *See* Vendors Supply of America, Inc.
VSB Groep, **III** 199, 201
VSD Communications, Inc., **22** 443
VSEL, **24** 88
VSK Group. *See* The Allied Defense
  Group, Inc.
VSM. *See* Village Super Market, Inc.
VST. *See* Vision Technology Group Ltd.
Vtel Corporation, **10** 456; **27** 365
VTR Incorporated, **16** 46; **43** 60
Vu-Tech Communications, Inc., **48** 54
Vulcan Materials Company, 7 572–75;
  12 39; **25** 266; **41** 147, 149; **52** 392–96
  (upd.)
Vulcan Ventures Inc., **32** 145; **43** 144
Vulcraft, **7** 400–02
VW&R. *See* Van Waters & Rogers.
VWR Textiles & Supplies, Inc., **11** 256
VWR United Company, **9** 531
Vycor Corporation, **25** 349
Vyvx, **31** 469

W&A Manufacturing Co., LLC, **26** 530
W&F Fish Products, **13** 103
W & J Sloane Home Furnishings Group,
  35 129
W de Argentina–Inversiones S.L., **63** 377
W.A. Krueger Co., **19** 333–35
W.A. Whitney Company, 53 353–56
W. Atlee Burpee & Co., 11 198; **27**
  505–08
W.B Doner & Co., 10 420; **12** 208; **28**
  138; **56** 369–72
W.B. Saunders Co., **IV** 623–24
W.C. Bradley Co., 18 516; **69** 363–65
W.C.G. Sports Industries Ltd. *See* Canstar
  Sports Inc.
W.C. Smith & Company Limited, **14** 339
W. Duke Sons & Company, **27** 128
W.E. Andrews Co., Inc., **25** 182
W.E. Dillon Company, Ltd., **21** 499
W.F. Kaiser, **60** 364
W.F. Linton Company, **9** 373
W.G. Yates & Sons Construction
  Company. *See* The Yates Companies,
  Inc.
W.H. Brady Co., 17 518–21
W.H. Gunlocke Chair Co. *See* Gunlocke
  Company.
W.H. Smith & Son (Alacra) Ltd., **15** 473
W H Smith Group PLC, V 211–13

W.L. Gore & Associates, Inc., 14
  538–40; **26** 417; **60** 321–24 **(upd.)**
W.M. Bassett Furniture Co. *See* Bassett
  Furniture Industries, Inc.
W.O. Daley & Company, **10** 387
W.P. Carey & Co. LLC, 49 446–48
W.R. Bean & Son, **19** 335
W.R. Berkley Corp., 15 525–27
W.R. Breen Company, **11** 486
W.R. Case & Sons Cutlery Company. *See*
  Zippo Manufacturing Company.
W.R. Grace & Company, I 547–50; **11**
  216; **12** 337; **13** 149, 502, 544; **14** 29;
  16 45–47; **17** 308, 365–66; **21** 213, 507,
  526; **22** 188, 501; **25** 535; **35** 38, 40; **43**
  59–60; **49** 307; **50** 78, 522–29 **(upd.);**
  54 363
W. Rosenlew, **IV** 350
W.S. Barstow & Company, **6** 575
W.T. Grant Co., **16** 487
W.T. Rawleigh, **17** 105
W.W. Grainger, Inc., V 214–15; **26**
  537–39 (upd.); **68** 392–95 **(upd.)**
W.W. Kimball Company, **12** 296; **18** 44
W.W. Norton & Company, Inc., 28
  518–20
Waban Inc., **V** 198; **13** 547–49; **19** 449.
  See also HomeBase, Inc.
Wabash National Corp., 13 550–52
Wabash Valley Power Association, **6** 556
Wabtec Corporation, 40 451–54
Wachbrit Insurance Agency, **21** 96
Wachovia Bank of Georgia, N.A., 16
  521–23
Wachovia Bank of South Carolina, N.A.,
  16 524–26
Wachovia Corporation, 10 425; **12** 16,
  516–20; **16** 521, 524, 526; **23** 455; **46**
  442–49 **(upd.)**
Wachtell, Lipton, Rosen & Katz, 47
  435–38
The Wackenhut Corporation, 13 124–25;
  14 541–43; **28** 255; **41** 80; **63** 423–26
  (upd.)
Wacker-Chemie GmbH, 35 454–58
Wacker Oil Inc., **11** 441
Waco Aircraft Company, **27** 98
Wacoal Corp., 25 520–24
Waddell & Reed, Inc., 22 540–43; **33**
  405, 407
Wade Smith, **28** 27, 30
Wadsworth Inc., **8** 526
WaferTech, **18** 20; **43** 17; **47** 385
Waffle House Inc., 14 544–45; **60** 325–27
  (upd.)
Wagenseller & Durst, **25** 249
Waggener Edstrom, 42 424–26
The Wagner & Brown Investment Group, **9**
  248
Wagner Castings Company, **16** 474–75
Wagner Litho Machinery Co., **13** 369–70
Wagner Spray Tech, **18** 555
Wagonlit Travel, **22** 128; **55** 90
Wagons-Lits, **27** 11; **29** 443; **37** 250–52
Waha Oil Company. *See* Natinal Oil
  Corporation.
AB Wahlbecks, **25** 464
Waitaki International Biosciences Co., **17**
  288
Waitrose Ltd. *See* John Lewis Partnership
  plc.
Wakefern Food Corporation, II 672; **7**
  563–64; **18** 6; **25** 66, 234–35; **28** 143;
  33 434–37

Wako Shoji Co. Ltd. *See* Wacoal Corp.
Wal-Mart de Mexico, S.A. de C.V., 35 322, **459–61 (upd.)**
Wal-Mart Stores, Inc., V 216–17; 8 555–57 (upd.); 26 522–26 (upd.); 63 427–32 (upd.); 64 36, 38
Walbridge Aldinger Co., 38 480–82
Walbro Corporation, 13 553–55
Walchenseewerk AG, 23 44
Waldbaum, Inc., II 638; **15** 260; **16** 247, 249; **19 479–81; 24** 528
Walden Book Company Inc., 10 136–37; **16** 160; **17 522–24; 25** 30
Waldorf Corporation, 59 350
Wales & Company, 14 257
Walgreen Co., V 218–20; 9 346; **18** 199; **20 511–13 (upd.); 21** 186; **24** 263; **32** 166, 170; **45** 133, 137; **65 352–56 (upd.)**
Walk Haydel & Associates, Inc., 25 130
Walk Softly, Inc., 25 118
Walker & Lee, 10 340
Walker Dickson Group Limited, 26 363
Walker Digital, 57 296–98
Walker Interactive Systems, 11 78; 25 86
Walker Manufacturing Company, 19 482–84
Walkers Snack Foods Ltd., 70 350–52
Walkins Manufacturing Corp., III 571; 20 362
Walkup's Merchant Express Inc., 27 473
Wall Drug Store, Inc., 40 455–57
Wall Street Deli, Inc., 33 438–41
Wallace & Tiernan Group, 11 361; 52 374
The Wallace Berrie Company. *See* Applause Inc.
Wallace Computer Services, Inc., 36 507–10
Wallace International Silversmiths, 14 482–83
Wallbergs Fabriks A.B., 8 14
Wallin & Nordstrom. *See* Nordstrom, Inc.
Wallis. *See* Sears plc.
Wallis Arnold Enterprises, Inc., 21 483
Wallis Tractor Company, 21 502
Walnut Capital Partners, 62 46–47
Walrus, Inc., 18 446
Walsin-Lihwa, 13 141
The Walt Disney Company, II 172–74; 6 174–77 (upd.); **30 487–91 (upd.); 63** 433–38 (upd.); **64** 282
Walter Bau, 27 136, 138
Walter E. Heller, 17 324
Walter Herzog GmbH, 16 514
Walter Industries, Inc., III 765–67; 22 544–47 (upd.); **72 368–73 (upd.)**
Walter Wilson, 49 18
Walter Wright Mammoet, 26 280
Walton Manufacturing, 11 486
Walton Monroe Mills, Inc., 8 558–60
Wang Global, 39 176–78
Wang Laboratories, Inc., III 168–70; 6 284–87 (upd.); **8** 139; **9** 171; **10** 34; **11** 68, 274; **12** 183; **18** 138; **19** 40; **20** 237
WAP, 26 420
Waples-Platter Co., II 625
Warbasse-Cogeneration Technologies Partnership, 35 479
Warburg Pincus, 9 524; 14 42; 24 373; 61 403
Warburg USB, 38 291
Warburtons Bakery Cafe, Inc., 18 37
Ward's Communications, 22 441
Wards. *See* Circuit City Stores, Inc.

Waremart. *See* WinCo Foods.
WARF. *See* Wisconsin Alumni Research Foundation.
Waring and LaRosa, 12 167
The Warnaco Group Inc., 9 156; **12** 521–23; **22** 123; **25** 122, 523; **46** 450–54 (upd.); **51** 30. *See also* Authentic Fitness Corp.
Warner & Swasey Co., 8 545
Warner Communications Inc., II 175–77, 452; **IV** 673, 675–76; **7** 526, 528–30 **8** 527; **9** 44–45, 119, 469; **10** 196; **11** 557; **12** 495–96; **17** 65, 149, 442–43; **21** 23–25, 360; **22** 519, 522; **23** 23–24, 390, 501; **24** 373; **25** 327–28, 418–19, 498; **26** 102, 151; **61** 202. *See also* AOL Time Warner Inc.
Warner Cosmetics, III 48; 8 129
Warner Electric, 58 67
Warner-Lambert Co., I 710–12; 7 596; **8** 62–63; **10 549–52 (upd.); 12** 480, 482; **13** 366; **16** 439; **20** 23; **25** 55, 366; **34** 284; **38** 366; **56** 303
Warner Roadshow Film Distributors Greece SA, 58 359
Warners' Stellian Inc., 67 384–87
Warrantech Corporation, 53 357–59
Warrell Corporation, 68 396–98
Warren Apparel Group Ltd., 39 257
Warren Bancorp Inc., 55 52
Warren Bank, 13 464
Warren Frozen Foods, Inc., 61 174
Warren, Gorham & Lamont, 8 526
Warren Oilfield Services, 9 363
Warren Petroleum, 18 365, 367; 49 121
Warrick Industries, 31 338
Warrington Products Ltd. *See* Canstar Sports Inc.
Warrior River Coal Company, 7 281
Warwick Chemicals, 13 461
Warwick International Ltd., 13 462
Warwick Valley Telephone Company, 55 382–84
Wasatch Gas Co., 6 568
Wascana Energy Inc., 13 556–58
Washburn Graphics Inc., 23 100
The Washington Companies, 33 442–45
Washington Duke Sons & Co., 12 108
Washington Federal, Inc., 17 525–27
Washington Football, Inc., 35 462–65
Washington Gas Light Company, 19 485–88
Washington Inventory Service, 30 239
Washington Mills Company, 13 532
Washington Mutual, Inc., 17 528–31
Washington National Corporation, 11 482; **12 524–26**
Washington Natural Gas Company, 9 539–41
The Washington Post Company, III 214; IV 688–90; 11 331; **18** 60, 61, 63; **20** 515–18 (upd.); **23** 157–58; **42** 31, 33–34, 209–10
Washington Public Power Supply System, 50 102
Washington Railway and Electric Company, 6 552–53
Washington Scientific Industries, Inc., 17 532–34
Washington Specialty Metals Corp., 14 323, 325
Washington Sports Clubs. *See* Town Sports International, Inc.
Washington Steel Corp., 14 323, 325

Washington Water Power Company, 6 566, 595–98; **50** 103–04, 366. *See also* Avista Corporation.
Washtenaw Gas Company. *See* MCN Corporation.
Wassall Plc, 18 548–50
Wasserstein Perella Partners, II 629; 17 366
Waste Connections, Inc., 46 455–57
Waste Control Specialists LLC, 19 466, 468
Waste Holdings, Inc., 41 413–15
Waste Management, Inc., V 752–54; 6 600; **9** 73, 108–09; **11** 435–36; **18** 10; **50** 61; **60** 343
Water Engineering, 11 360
Water Pik Technologies, Inc., 34 498–501
Water Street Corporate Recovery Fund, 10 423
The Waterbury Companies, 16 482
Waterford Foods Plc, 59 206
Waterford Wedgwood Holdings PLC, IV 296; **12 527–29**
Waterford Wedgwood plc, 34 493–97 (upd.); 38 403
Waterhouse Investor Services, Inc., 18 551–53; 49 397
Waterlow and Sons, 10 269
Waterman Marine Corporation, 27 242
The Waterman Pen Company. *See* BIC Corporation.
WaterPro Supplies Corporation. *See* Eastern Enterprises.
Waters Corporation, 43 453–57
Waterstone's, 42 444. *See also* HMV Group plc.
Waterstreet Inc., 17 293
Watkins-Johnson Company, 15 528–30
Watkins-Strathmore Co., 13 560
Watney Mann and Truman Brewers, 9 99
Watsco Inc., 52 397–400
Watson & Philip. *See* Alldays plc.
Watson Group, 55 52
Watson-Haas Lumber Company, 33 257
Watson-Marlow Bredel, 59 384
Watson Pharmaceuticals Inc., 16 527–29; **56 373–76 (upd.)**
Watson-Triangle, 16 388, 390
Watson Wyatt Worldwide, 42 427–30
Watt & Shand, 16 61; 50 107
Watt AG, 6 491
Watt Electronic Products, Limited, 10 319
The Watt Stopper, 21 348, 350
Wattie Industries, 52 141
Wattie's Ltd., 7 576–78; 11 173
Watts Industries, Inc., 19 489–91
Watts of Lydney Group Ltd., 71 391–93
Watts/Silverstein, Inc., 24 96
Waukesha Engine Servicenter, 6 441
Waukesha Foundry Company, 11 187
Wausau Sulphate Fibre Co. *See* Mosinee Paper Corporation.
Wausau-Mosinee Paper Corporation, 60 328–31 (upd.)
Wavelength Corporate Communications Pty Limited, 24 95
Waverly, Inc., 10 135; **16 530–32; 19** 358
Waverly Pharmaceutical Limited, 11 208
Wawa Inc., 17 535–37
The Wawanesa Mutual Insurance Company, 68 399–401
Waxman Industries, Inc., 9 542–44; 20 362; **28** 50–51

Wayco Foods, **14** 411
Waycross-Douglas Coca-Cola Bottling, **10** 222
Wayfinder Group Inc., **51** 265
Waymaker Oy, **55** 289
Wayne Home Equipment. *See* Scott Fetzer Company.
Wayne Oakland Bank, **8** 188
WB. *See* Warner Communications Inc.
WBI Holdings, Inc., **42** 249, 253
WCI Holdings Corporation, **V** 223; **13** 170; **41** 94
WCK, Inc., **14** 236
WCM Beteilingungs- und Grundbesitz AG, **58** 202, 205
WCPS Direct, Inc., **53** 359
WCRS Group plc. *See* Aegis Group plc.
WCT Live Communication Limited, **24** 95
WD-40 Company, 18 554–57
We Energies. *See* Wisconsin Energy Corporation.
Wear-Ever, **17** 213
WearGuard, **13** 48
The Weather Channel Companies, 52 401–04; **55** 244. *See also* Landmark Communications, Inc.
The Weather Department, Ltd., **10** 89
Weather Guard, **IV** 305
Weatherford International, Inc., 39 416–18; **57** 164; **59** 403
Weathers-Lowin, Leeam, **11** 408
Webb & Knapp, **10** 43
Webb Corbett and Beswick, **38** 402
Webber Gage Co., **13** 302
Webber Oil Company, 61 384–86
WeBco International LLC, **26** 530
Webco Securities, Inc., **37** 225
Weber, **16** 488
Weber Aircraft Inc., **41** 369
Weber et Broutin France, 66 363–65
Weber Metal, **30** 283–84
Weber-Stephen Products Co., 40 458–60
Weblock, **I** 109
WebLogic Inc., **36** 81
WebMD Corporation, 65 357–60
Webtron Corp., **10** 313
Webvan Group Inc., **38** 223
Wedgwood. *See* Waterford Wedgewood Holdings PLC.
Weeres Industries Corporation, 52 405–07
Weetabix Limited, 61 387–89
Wegener NV, 53 360–62
Wegert Verwaltungs-GmbH and Co. Beteiligungs-KG, **24** 270
Wegmans Food Markets, Inc., 9 545–46; **24** 445; **41** 416–18 (upd.)
Weichenwerk Brandenburg GmbH, **53** 352
Weider Health and Fitness, Inc., **38** 238
Weider Nutrition International, Inc., 29 498–501; **33** 146–47; **34** 459; **61** 222, 224
Weider Sporting Goods, **16** 80
Weifang Power Machine Fittings Ltd., **17** 106
Weight Watchers Gourmet Food Co., **43** 218
Weight Watchers International Inc., 10 383; **12** 530–32; **13** 383; **27** 197; **33** 446–49 (upd.)
Weil Ceramics & Glass, **52** 148
Weil, Gotshal & Manges LLP, 55 385–87
Weiner's Stores, Inc., 33 450–53

Weingut Robert Weil, **65** 328, 330
Weirton Steel Corporation, IV 236–38; **7** 447, 598; **8** 346, 450; **10** 31–32; **12** 352, 354; **26** 407, **527–30 (upd.)**
Weis Markets, Inc., 15 531–33
The Weitz Company, Inc., 42 431–34
Welbilt Corp., 19 492–94; **27** 159
Welborn Transport Co., **39** 64, 65
Welch Engineering Ltd. *See* Swales & Associates, Inc.
Welch's, **25** 366
Welco Feed Manufacturing Company, **60** 316
Welcome Wagon International Inc., **16** 146
Weldless Steel Company, **8** 530
Wella AG, III 68–70; **48** 420–23 (upd.)
Welland Pipe Ltd., **51** 352
Wellborn Paint Manufacturing Company, **56** 98
Wellby Super Drug Stores, **12** 220
WellChoice, Inc., 67 388–91 (upd.)
Wellcome Foundation Ltd., I 713–15; **8** 210, 452; **9** 265; **10** 551; **32** 212. *See also* GlaxoSmithKline plc.
Wellcome Trust, **41** 119
Weller Electric Corp., **II** 16
Wellington Management Company, **14** 530–31; **23** 226
Wellington Sears Co., **15** 247–48
Wellman, Inc., 8 561–62; **21** 193; **52** 408–11 (upd.); **64** 86
Wellmark, Inc., **10** 89
Wellness Co., Ltd., **IV** 716
WellPath Community Health Plans, Inc., **59** 140
WellPoint Health Networks Inc., 25 525–29
Wellrose Limited, **53** 333
Wells Aircraft, **12** 112
Wells Fargo & Company, II 380–84, 319, 395; **10** 59–60; **12** 165, **533–37 (upd.)**; **17** 325; **18** 60, 543; **19** 411; **22** 542; **25** 434; **27** 292; **32** 373; **38** 44, **483–92 (upd.)**; **41** 200–01; **46** 217; **54** 124. *See also* American Express Company.
Wells Fargo HSBC Trade Bank, **26** 203
Wells-Gardner Electronics Corporation, 43 458–61
Wells Rich Greene BDDP, 6 50–52
Wells' Dairy, Inc., 36 511–13
Wellspring Associates L.L.C., **16** 338
Wellspring Resources LLC, **42** 429
Welsh Associated Collieries Ltd., **31** 369
Welsh, Carson, Anderson & Stowe, **65** 128–30; **71** 117–19
Welsh Water. *See* Hyder plc.
Wendel Investissement, **57** 381
Wendy's International, Inc., 8 563–65; **23** 504–07 (upd.); **47** 439–44 (upd.)
Wenger S.A., **21** 515
Wenmac Corp., **51** 368
Wenner Media, Inc., 32 506–09
Werco, Inc., **54** 7
Werkhof GmbH, **13** 491; **62** 336
Werknet, **16** 420; **43** 308
Werner Baldessarini Design GmbH, **48** 209
Werner Die & Stamping, **69** 38
Werner Enterprises, Inc., 26 531–33
Werner International, **III** 344; **14** 225
Wertheim Schroder & Company, **17** 443
Weru Aktiengesellschaft, 18 558–61; **49** 295

Wesco Financial Corp., **III** 213, 215; **18** 62; **42** 32–34
Wesco Food Co., **II** 644
Wescot Decisison Systems, **6** 25
Wesley Jessen VisionCare Inc., **65** 274
Wesper Co., **26** 4
Wesray and Management, **17** 213
Wesray Capital Corporation, **13** 41; **17** 443; **47** 363
Wesray Corporation, **22** 55
Wesray Holdings Corp., **13** 255
Wesray Transportation, Inc., **14** 38
Wessanen. *See* Koninklijke Wessanen nv.
Wessanen USA, **29** 480
Wesson/Peter Pan Foods Co., **17** 241
West Australia Land Holdings, Limited, **10** 169
West Bend Co., 14 546–48; **16** 384; **43** 289
West Coast Entertainment Corporation, 29 502–04
West Coast Grocery Co., **II** 670; **18** 506; **50** 456
West Coast Machinery, **13** 385
West Coast Power Company, **12** 265
West Coast Restaurant Enterprises, **25** 390
West Coast Savings and Loan, **10** 339
West Company, **53** 298
West Corporation, 42 435–37
West End Family Pharmacy, Inc., **15** 523
West Fraser Timber Co. Ltd., 17 538–40
West Georgia Coca-Cola Bottlers, Inc., **13** 163
West Group, 34 438, 502–06 (upd.)
West Harrison Gas & Electric Company. *See* Cincinnati Gas & Electric Company.
West Los Angeles Veterinary Medical Group, Inc., **58** 355
West Lynn Creamery, Inc., **26** 450
West Marine, Inc., 17 541–43; **37** 398
West Missouri Power Company. *See* UtiliCorp United Inc.; Aquilla, Inc.
West Newton Savings Bank, **13** 468
West Newton Telephone Company, **14** 258
West One Bancorp, 11 552–55; **36** 491
West Penn Electric. *See* Allegheny Power System, Inc.
West Penn Power Company, **38** 38–40
West Pharmaceutical Services, Inc., 42 438–41
West Point-Pepperell, Inc., 8 566–69; **9** 466; **15** 247; **25** 20; **28** 218. *See also* WestPoint Stevens Inc.; JPS Textile Group, Inc.
West Publishing Co., 7 579–81; **10** 407; **33** 264–65. *See also* The West Group.
West Shore Pipe Line Company, **70** 35
West Side Printing Co., **13** 559
West TeleServices Corporation. *See* West Corporation.
West Texas LPG Pipeline Limited Partnership, **70** 35
West Texas Utilities Company, **6** 580
West Union Corporation, **22** 517
West Virginia Bearings, Inc., **13** 78
West Virginia Pulp and Paper Co. *See* Westvaco Corporation.
Westaff Inc., 33 454–57
WestAir Holding Inc., **11** 300; **25** 423; **32** 336
Westamerica Bancorporation, 17 544–47
Westar Energy, Inc., 57 404–07 (upd.)
Westbrae Natural, Inc., **27** 197–98; **43** 218
Westburne Group of Companies, **9** 364

Westchester County Savings & Loan, **9** 173

Westchester Specialty Group, Inc., **26** 546

Westclox Seth Thomas, **16** 483

WestCoast Hospitality Corporation, 59 410–13

Westcon Group, Inc., 67 392–94

Westcor Realty, **57** 235

Westcorp Financial Services. *See* WFS Financial Inc.

Westcott Communications Inc., **22** 442

Westdeutsche Landesbank Girozentrale, II 385–87; **33** 395; **46 458–61 (upd.)**; **47** 83

Westec Corporation. *See* Tech-Sym Corporation.

Westell Technologies, Inc., 57 408–10

Westerbeke Corporation, 60 332–34

Western Aerospace Ltd., **14** 564

Western Air Express, **9** 17

Western Air Lines, **I** 98, 100, 106; **21** 142; **25** 421–23

Western Areas Ltd., **61** 292

Western Atlas Inc., III 473; **12 538–40**; **17** 419; **57** 64

Western Australian Specialty Alloys Proprietary Ltd., **14** 564

Western Auto, **19** 223; **57** 11

Western Auto Supply Co., **8** 56; **11** 392

Western Automatic Machine Screw Co., **12** 344

Western Bank, **17** 530

Western Beef, Inc., 22 548–50

Western Bingo, **16** 471

Western Company of North America, 15 534–36; **25** 73, 75

Western Crude, **11** 27

Western Data Products, Inc., **19** 110

Western Digital Corp., 10 403, 463; **11** 56, 463; **25 530–32**

Western Edison, **6** 601

Western Electric Co., **II** 57, 66, 88, 101, 112; **7** 288; **11** 500–01; **12** 136; **13** 57; **49** 346

Western Electric Manufacturing Company, **54** 139

Western Empire Construction. *See* CRSS Inc.

Western Equities, Inc. *See* Tech-Sym Corporation.

Western Family Foods, **47** 457; **53** 21

Western Federal Savings & Loan, **9** 199

Western Fire Equipment Co., **9** 420

Western Forest Products Ltd., **59** 161

Western Gas Resources, Inc., 45 435–37

Western Geophysical, **12** 538–39

Western Glucose Co., **14** 17

Western Graphics Corporation, **58** 314

Western Hotels Inc. *See* Westin Hotels and Resorts Worldwide.

Western Inland Lock Navigation Company, **9** 228

Western International Communications, **35** 68

Western International Media, **22** 294

Western International University, **24** 40

Western Kentucky Gas Company, **43** 56–57

Western Kraft Corp., **8** 476

Western Life Insurance Co., **III** 356; **22** 494

Western Light & Telephone Company. *See* Western Power & Gas Company.

Western Light and Power. *See* Public Service Company of Colorado.

Western Lithograph Company. *See* Consolidated Graphics, Inc.

Western Massachusetts Co., **13** 183

Western Medical Services, **33** 456

Western Merchandise, Inc., **8** 556

Western Merchandisers, Inc., **29** 229–30

Western Mining Corp., **IV** 61, 95

Western Mortgage Corporation, **16** 497; **50** 497

Western National Life Company, **10** 246; **14** 473

Western Natural Gas Company, **7** 362

Western Newell Manufacturing Company. *See* Newell Co.

Western Pacific, **22** 220

Western Pacific Industries, **10** 357

Western Pioneer, Inc., **18** 279

Western Platinum, **21** 353

Western Platinum Ltd. *See* Lomin plc.

Western Playing Card Co., **13** 559

Western Power & Gas Company. *See* Centel Corporation.

Western Printing and Lithographing Company, **19** 404

Western Public Service Corporation, **6** 568

Western Publishing Group, Inc., 13 114, **559–61**; **15** 455; **25** 254, 313; **28** 159; **29** 76

Western Reflections LLC, **55** 291

Western Reserve Bank of Lake County, **9** 474

Western Reserve Telephone Company. *See* Alltel Corporation.

Western Reserves, **12** 442

Western Resources, Inc., 12 541–43; **27** 425; **32** 372–75

Western Rosin Company, **8** 99

The WesterN SizzliN Corporation, 10 331; **19** 288; **60 335–37**

Western Slope Gas, **6** 559

Western States Fire Protection Company, **64** 30–32

Western Steel Group, **26** 407

Western Steer Family Restaurant, **10** 331; **18** 8

Western Telegraph Company, **25** 99

Western Telephone Company, **14** 257

Western Union Corporation, **9** 536; **10** 263; **12** 9; **14** 363; **15** 72; **17** 345–46; **21** 25; **24** 515

Western Union Financial Services, Inc., 54 413–16

Western Vending, **13** 48; **41** 22

Western Wireless Corporation, 36 514–16

Westfälische Metall-Industrie Aktien-Gesellschaft. *See* Hella KGaA Hueck & Co.

Westfälische Transport AG, **6** 426

Westfield Group, 57 156; **69 366–69**

Westin Hotel Co., **9** 283, **547–49**; **21** 91; **54** 345–47

Westin Hotels and Resorts Worldwide, 29 505–08 (upd.)

Westinghouse Air Brake Company. *See* Wabtec Corporation.

Westinghouse Cubic Ltd., **19** 111

Westinghouse Electric Corporation, I 4, 7, 19, 22, 28, 33, 82, 84–85, 524; **II 120–22**; **6** 556; **9** 12, 17, 128, 162, 245, 417, 439–40, 553; **10** 280, 536; **11** 318; **12** 194, **544–47 (upd.)**; **13** 230, 398,

402, 506–07; **14** 300–01; **16** 8; **17** 488; **18** 320, 335–37, 355; **19** 164–66, 210; **21** 43; **26** 102; **27** 269; **28** 69; **33** 253; **36** 327; **41** 366; **45** 306; **48** 217; **50** 299; **57** 319, 321–22. *See also* CBS Radio Group.

WestJet Airlines Ltd., 38 493–95

WestLB. *See* Westdeutsche Landesbank Girozentrale.

Westmark Mortgage Corp., **13** 417

Westmark Realty Advisors, **21** 97

Westmark Systems, Inc., **26** 268

Westminster Press Ltd. *See* Pearson plc.

Westmoreland Coal Company, 7 582–85

Weston Bakeries, **II** 631

Weston Engineering, **53** 232

Weston Foods Inc. *See* George Weston Limited.

Weston Pharmaceuticals, **V** 49; **19** 122–23; **49** 111–12

Weston Presidio, **49** 189; **65** 257, 259

Weston Resources, **II** 631–32

Westpac Banking Corporation, II 388–90; **17** 285; **48 424–27 (upd.)**

WestPoint Stevens Inc., 16 533–36; **21** 194; **28** 219. *See also* JPS Textile Group, Inc.

Westport Resources Corporation, 63 439–41

Westport Woman, **24** 145

Westvaco Corporation, IV 351–54; **19 495–99 (upd.)**

The Westwood Group, **20** 54

Westwood One, Inc., 17 150; **23 508–11**; **69** 282

Westwood Pharmaceuticals, **III** 19

Westworld Resources Inc., **23** 41

Westwynn Theatres, **14** 87

The Wet Seal, Inc., 18 562–64; **70 353–57 (upd.)**

Wet'n Wild Inc., **64** 94

Wetterau Incorporated, II 645, 681–82; **7** 450; **18** 507; **32** 222; **50** 457

Wexpro Company, **6** 568–69

Weyco Group, Incorporated, 32 510–13

Weyerhaeuser Company, IV 298, 304, 308, **355–56**, 358; **8** 428, 434; **9 550–52 (upd.)**; **19** 445–46, 499; **22** 489; **26** 384; **28 514–17 (upd.)**; **31** 468; **32** 91; **42** 397; **49** 196–97

Weyman-Burton Co., **9** 533

WFP. *See* Western Forest Products Ltd.

WFS Financial Inc., 70 358–60

WFSC. *See* World Fuel Services Corporation.

WGBH Educational Foundation, 66 366–68

WGM Safety Corp., **40** 96–97

WH Smith PLC, 42 442–47 (upd.)

Wham-O, Inc., 61 390–93

Wharf Holdings Limited, **12** 367–68; **18** 114

Whatman plc, 46 462–65

Wheat, First Securities, **19** 304–05

Wheaton Industries, 8 570–73

Wheaton Science Products, 60 338–42 (upd.)

Wheatsheaf Investment, **27** 94

Wheel Horse, **7** 535

Wheel Restaurants Inc., **14** 131

Wheel to Wheel Inc., **66** 315

Wheelabrator Technologies, Inc., V 754; **6 599–600**; **11** 435; **60 343–45 (upd.)**

Wheeled Coach Industries, Inc., **33** 105–06

Wheeling-Pittsburgh Corporation, 7 586–88; **58** 360–64 (upd.)
Whemco, **22** 415
Where Magazines International, **57** 242
Wherehouse Entertainment Incorporated, 9 361; **11 556–58**; **29** 350; **35** 431–32
WHI Inc., **14** 545; **60** 326
Whippoorwill Associates Inc., **28** 55
Whirl-A-Way Motors, **11** 4
Whirlpool Corporation, III 653–55; **8** 298–99; **11** 318; **12** 252, 309, **548–50** (upd.); **13** 402–03, 563; **15** 403; **18** 225–26; **22** 218, 349; **23** 53; **25** 261; **50** 300, 392; **59 414–19** (upd.)
Whirlwind, Inc., **7** 535
Whistler Corporation, **13** 195
Whitaker-Glessner Company, **7** 586
Whitaker Health Services, III 389
Whitbread PLC, I 293–94; **20 519–22** (upd.); **52 412–17** (upd.); **59** 182–83, 255
Whitby Pharmaceuticals, Inc., **10** 289
White & Case LLP, **35 466–69**
White Automotive, **10** 9, 11
White Brothers, **39** 83, 84
White Castle System, Inc., **12 551–53**; **33** 239; **36 517–20** (upd.)
White Consolidated Industries Inc., III 573; **8** 298; **12** 252; **13 562–64**; **22** 216–17
White Discount Department Stores, **16** 36
The White House, Inc., **60 346–48**
White Miller Construction Company, **14** 162
White Mountain Freezers, **19** 360
White Mountains Insurance Group, Ltd., **48 428–31**
White-New Idea, **13** 18
White Oil Corporation, **7** 101
White Rock Corp., **27** 198; **43** 218
White-Rodgers, II 19
White Rose, Inc., **12** 106; **24 527–29**
White Star Line, **23** 161
White Swan Foodservice, II 625
White Tractor, **13** 17
White Wave, **43 462–64**
White-Westinghouse. *See* White Consolidated Industries Inc.
Whitehall Company Jewellers, **24** 319
Whitehall Labs, **8** 63
Whitewater Group, **10** 508
Whitewear Manufacturing Company. *See* Angelica Corporation.
Whitman Corporation, **7** 430; **10** 414–15, **553–55** (upd.); **11** 188; **22** 353–54; **27** 196; **43** 217. *See also* PepsiAmericas, Inc.
Whitman Education Group, Inc., **41 419–21**
Whitman Publishing Co., **13** 559–60
Whitman's Chocolates, **7** 431; **12** 429
Whitmire Distribution. *See* Cardinal Health, Inc.
Whitney Group, **40** 236–38
Whitney Holding Corporation, **21 522–24**
Whitney National Bank, **12** 16
Whitney Partners, L.L.C., **40** 237
Whittaker Corporation, I 544–46; III 389, 444; **34** 275; **48 432–35** (upd.)
Whittard of Chelsea Plc, **61 394–97**
Whittle Communications L.P., IV 675; **7** 528; **13** 403; **22** 442

Whittman-Hart Inc. *See* marchFIRST, Inc.
Whitworth Brothers Company, **27** 360
Whole Foods Market, Inc., **19** 501–02; **20 523–27**; **41** 422–23; **47** 200; **50 530–34** (upd.)
Wholesale Cellular USA. *See* Brightpoint, Inc.
The Wholesale Club, Inc., **8** 556
Wholesale Depot, **13** 547
Wholesale Food Supply, Inc., **13** 333
Wholesome Foods, L.L.C., **32** 274, 277
Wholly Harvest, **19** 502
WHSC Direct, Inc., **53** 359
WHX Corporation, **58** 360
Whyte & Mackay Distillers Ltd., V 399; **19** 171; **49** 152
Wicanders Group, **48** 119
Wicat Systems, **7** 255–56; **25** 254
Wicell Research Institute, **65** 367
Wichita Industries, **11** 27
Wickes Inc., I 453, 483; V 221–23; **10** 423; **13** 169–70; **15** 281; **17** 365–66; **19** 503–04; **20** 415; **25 533–36** (upd.); **41** 93
Wicor, Inc., **54** 419
Wielkopolski Bank Kredytowy, **16** 14
Wiener Städtische, **58** 169
Wienerberger AG, **70 361–63**
Wienerwald Holding, **17** 249
Wiesner, Inc., **22** 442
Wight Nurseries. *See* Monrovia Nursery Company.
Wilbert, Inc., **56 377–80**
Wilbur Chocolate Company, **66 369–71**
Wild by Nature. *See* King Cullen Grocery Co., Inc.
Wild Harvest, **56** 317
Wild Leitz G.m.b.H., **23** 83
Wild Oats Markets, Inc., **19 500–02**; **29** 213; **41 422–25** (upd.)
WildBlue Communications Inc., **54** 406
Wildlife Conservation Society, **31 462–64**
Wildlife Land Trust, **54** 172
Wildwater Kingdom, **22** 130
Wiles Group Ltd. *See* Hanson PLC.
Wiley Manufacturing Co., **8** 545
Oy Wilh. Schauman AB. *See* UPM-Kymmene
Wilhelm Weber GmbH, **22** 95
Wilhelm Wilhelmsen Ltd., **7** 40; **41** 42
Wilkins Department Store, **19** 510
Wilkinson, Gaddis & Co., **24** 527
Wilkinson Sword Ltd., **12** 464; **38** 365; **60 349–52**
Willamette Falls Electric Company. *See* Portland General Corporation.
Willamette Industries, Inc., IV 357–59; **13** 99, 101; **16** 340; **28** 517; **31 465–68** (upd.)
Willbros Group, Inc., **56 381–83**
Willcox & Gibbs Sewing Machine Co., **15** 384
Willetts Manufacturing Company, **12** 312
Willey Brothers, Inc. *See* BrandPartners Group, Inc.
William B. Tanner Co., **7** 327
William Barnet and Son, Inc., III 246
William Benton Foundation, **7** 165, 167
The William Brooks Shoe Company. *See* Rocky Shoes & Boots, Inc.
William Byrd Press Inc., **23** 100
William Carter Company, **17** 224
William Cory & Son Ltd., **6** 417

William E. Pollack Government Securities, II 390
William E. Wright Company, **9** 375
William Esty Company, **16** 72
William George Company, **32** 519
William Grant & Sons Ltd., **22** 343; **60 353–55**
William Hewlett, **41** 117
William Hill Organization Limited, **49 449–52**
William Hodges & Company, **33** 150
William Hollins & Company Ltd., **44** 105
William J. Hough Co., **8** 99–100
William L. Bonnell Company, Inc., **66 372–74**
William Lyon Homes, **59 420–22**
William Morris Agency, Inc., **23 512–14**; **43** 235–36
William Morrow & Company, **19** 201
William Odhams Ltd., **7** 244
William P. Young Contruction, **43** 400
William Penn Cos., III 243, 273
William Penn Life Insurance Company of New York, **24** 285
William Press, I 568
William S. Kimball & Co., **12** 108
William Southam and Sons, **7** 487
William Underwood Co., **7** 430
William Zinsser & Co.,
William Zinsser & Company, Inc., **8** 456; **58 365–67**
Williams & Connolly LLP, **47 445–48**
Williams & Glyn's Bank Ltd., **12** 422
Williams & Wilkins. *See* Waverly, Inc.
Williams Communications Group, Inc., **6** 340; **25** 499; **34 507–10**
The Williams Companies, Inc., IV 575–76; **27** 307; **31 469–72** (upd.)
Williams Deacon's Bank, **12** 422
Williams Electronics, **12** 419
Williams Electronics Games, Inc., **15** 539
Williams Gold Refining Co., **14** 81
The Williams Manufacturing Company, **19** 142–43
Williams/Nintendo Inc., **15** 537
Williams Oil-O-Matic Heating Corporation, **12** 158; **21** 42
Williams plc, **44** 255
Williams Printing Company. *See* Graphic Industries Inc.
Williams Scotsman, Inc., **65 361–64**
Williams-Sonoma, Inc., **13** 42; **15** 50; **17 548–50**; **27** 225, 429; **44 447–50** (upd.)
Williamsburg Restoration, Incorporated, **53** 106
Williamson-Dickie Manufacturing Company, **14** 549–50; **45 438–41** (upd.)
Williamsport Barber and Beauty Corp., **60** 287
Willie G's, **15** 279
Willis Corroon Group plc, **25 537–39**
Willis Stein & Partners, **21** 404; **58** 318, 321
Williston Basin Interstate Pipeline Company, **7** 322, 324. *See also* WBI Holdings, Inc.
Willor Manufacturing Corp., **9** 323
Wilmington Coca-Cola Bottling Works, Inc., **10** 223
Wilmington Trust Corporation, **25 540–43**
Wilsdorf & Davis, **13** 353–54

Wilshire Real Estate Investment Trust Inc., **30** 223

Wilshire Restaurant Group Inc., **13** 66; **28** 258

Wilson Bowden Plc, 45 442–44

Wilson Brothers, **8** 536

Wilson Foods Corp., **12** 124; **22** 510

Wilson Greatbatch Technologies Ltd. *See* Greatbatch Inc.

Wilson Jones Company, **7** 4–5

Wilson Learning Group, **17** 272; **65** 188–89

Wilson-Maeulen Company, **13** 234

Wilson Sonsini Goodrich & Rosati, 34 511–13

Wilson Sporting Goods Company, 13 317; **16** 52; **23** 449; **24** 403, **530–32**; **25** 167; **41** 14–16

Wilson's Supermarkets, **12** 220–21

Wilsons The Leather Experts Inc., 21 525–27; 58 368–71 (upd.)

WilTel Communications, Inc., **71** 199

WilTel Network Services, **27** 301, 307

Wimbledon Tennis Championships. *See* The All England Lawn Tennis & Croquet Club.

Wimpey International Ltd., **13** 206

Win-Chance Foods, **II** 508; **36** 255

Win Schuler Foods, **25** 517

Wincanton plc, 52 418–20

Winchell's Donut Houses Operating Company, L.P., II 680; **60 356–59**

WinCo Foods Inc., 60 360–63

Wincor Nixdorf Holding GmbH, 69 370–73 (upd.)

Wind River Systems, Inc., 37 419–22

Windmere Corporation, 16 537–39. *See also* Applica Incorporated.

Windmere-Durable Holdings, Inc., **30** 404

WindowVisions, Inc., **29** 288

Windsong Exports, **52** 429

Windsor Forestry Tools, Inc., **48** 59

Windsor Manufacturing Company, **13** 6

Windsor Trust Co., **13** 467

Windstar Sail Cruises. *See* Carnival Corporation.

Windsurfing International, **23** 55

Windswept Environmental Group, Inc., 62 389–92

Windward Capital Partners, **28** 152, 154

The Wine Group, Inc., 39 419–21

Wine World, Inc., **22** 78, 80

Winegard Company, 56 384–87

Winfire, Inc., **37** 194

Wingate Partners, **14** 521, 523

Winget Ltd. *See* Seddon Group Ltd.

Wings & Wheels, **13** 19

Wings Luggage, Inc., **10** 181

WingspanBank.com, **38** 270

Winkelman Stores, Inc., **8** 425–26

Winlet Fashions, **22** 223

Winn-Dixie Stores, Inc., II 626–27, 670, **683–84**; **7** 61; **11** 228; **15** 178; **16** 314; **18** 8; **21** 528–30 **(upd.)**; **34** 269; **59** 423–27 **(upd.)**

Winnebago Industries Inc., 7 589–91; 22 207; **27 509–12 (upd.)**

Winners Apparel Ltd. *See* The TJX Companies, Inc.

Winning International, **21** 403

WinsLoew Furniture, Inc., 21 531–33

Winston & Strawn, 35 470–73

Winston Furniture Company, Inc., **21** 531–33

Winston Group, **10** 333

Winter Hill Frozen Foods and Services, **55** 82

WinterBrook Corp., **26** 326

Winterflood Securities Limited, **39** 89, 91

Wintershall AG, **IV** 485; **38** 408

Winterthur Group, III 402–04; **68** 402–05 **(upd.)**

Winthrop Lawrence Corporation, **25** 541

Winton Engines, **10** 273

Winyah Concrete & Block, **50** 49

Wipro Limited, 43 465–68

Wire and Cable Specialties Corporation, **17** 276

Wire and Plastic Products PLC. *See* WPP Group PLC.

Wireless Hong Kong. *See* Hong Kong Telecommunications Ltd.

Wireless LLC, **18** 77

Wireless Management Company, **11** 12

Wiron Prefabricados Modulares, S.A., **65** 363

Wirtz Corporation, 72 374–76

Wisconsin Alumni Research Foundation, 65 365–68

Wisconsin Bell, Inc., 14 551–53; 18 30

Wisconsin Central Transportation Corporation, 24 533–36

Wisconsin Dairies, 7 592–93

Wisconsin Energy Corporation, 6 601–03, 605; **54 417–21 (upd.)**

Wisconsin Gas Company, **17** 22–23

Wisconsin Power and Light, **22** 13; **39** 260

Wisconsin Public Service Corporation, 6 604–06; **9 553–54**. *See also* WPS Resources Corporation.

Wisconsin Steel, **10** 430; **17** 158–59

Wisconsin Tissue Mills Inc., **8** 103

Wisconsin Toy Company. *See* Value Merchants Inc.

Wisconsin Wire and Steel, **17** 310; **24** 160

Wise Foods, Inc., **22** 95

Wise Solutions, Inc. *See* Altiris, Inc.

Wiser's De Luxe Whiskey, **14** 141

Wispark Corporation, **6** 601, 603

Wisser Service Holdings AG, **18** 105

Wisvest Corporation, **6** 601, 603

WiSys Technology Foundation, **65** 367

Witco Corporation, I 404–06; **16 540–43 (upd.)**

Wite-Out Products, Inc., **23** 56–57

Witech Corporation, **6** 601, 603

Withington Company. *See* Sparton Corporation.

Wittgensteiner Kliniken Gruppe, **56** 141

Wittington Investments Ltd., **13** 51

The Wiz. *See* Cablevision Electronic Instruments, Inc.

Wizards of the Coast Inc., 24 537–40; 43 229, 233

WizardWorks Group, Inc., **31** 238–39

WL Ross & Co., **67** 125

WLIW-TV. *See* Educational Broadcasting Corporation.

WLR Foods, Inc., 14 516; **21 534–36; 50** 494

Wm. B. Reily & Company Inc., 58 372–74

WM Investment Company, **34** 512

Wm. Morrison Supermarkets PLC, 38 496–98

Wm. Underwood Company, **40** 53

Wm. Wrigley Jr. Company, 7 594–97; 58 375–79 (upd.)

WMC, Limited, 43 469–72

WMF. *See* Württembergische Metallwarenfabrik AG (WMF).

WMS Industries, Inc., 15 537–39; 53 363–66 **(upd.)**

WMX Technologies Inc., 11 435–36; **17** 551–54; **26** 409

Wolf Furniture Enterprises, **14** 236

Wolfe & Associates, **25** 434

Wolfe Industries, Inc., **22** 255

Wolff Printing Co., **13** 559

Wolfgang Puck Worldwide, Inc., 26 534–36; 70 364–67 (upd.)

Wolohan Lumber Co., **19** 503–05; **25** 535

Wolseley plc, 64 409–12

Wolters Kluwer NV, IV 611; **14 554–56; 31** 389, 394; **33 458–61 (upd.)**

The Wolverhampton & Dudley Breweries, PLC, 57 411–14

Wolverine Equities Company, **62** 341

Wolverine Insurance Co., **26** 487

Wolverine Tube Inc., 23 515–17

Wolverine World Wide, Inc., 16 544–47; 17 390; **32** 99; **44** 365; **59 428–33 (upd.)**

Womack Development Company, **11** 257

Womacks Saloon and Gaming Parlor, **53** 91

Womble Carlyle Sandridge & Rice, PLLC, 52 421–24

Women's Specialty Retailing Group. *See* Casual Corner Group, Inc.

Women's World, **15** 96

Wometco Coca-Cola Bottling Co., **10** 222

Wometco Coffee Time, **I** 514

Wometco Enterprises, **I** 514

Wonderware Corp., **22** 374

Wong International Holdings, **16** 195

Wood Hall Trust plc, I 592–93; **50** 200

Wood-Metal Industries, Inc. *See* Wood-Mode, Inc.

Wood-Mode, Inc., 23 518–20

Wood River Oil and Refining Company, **11** 193

Wood Shovel and Tool Company, **9** 71

Wood, Struthers & Winthrop, Inc., **22** 189

Wood Wyant Inc., **30** 496–98

Woodbridge Winery, **50** 388

Woodbury Co., **19** 380

Woodcock, Hess & Co., **9** 370

Woodcraft Industries Inc., 61 398–400

Woodhill Chemical Sales Company, **8** 333

Woodland Publishing, Inc., **37** 286

Woodlands, **7** 345–46

Woodmen of the World Life Insurance Society, **66** 227–28

Woods Equipment Company, **32** 28

Woodside Petroleum, **63** 440

Woodside Travel Trust, **26** 310

Woodville Appliances, Inc., **9** 121

Woodward-Clyde Group Inc., **45** 421

Woodward Foodservice Ltd. *See* The Big Food Group plc.

Woodward Governor Company, 13 565–68; 49 453–57 (upd.)

Woodworkers Warehouse, **22** 517

Woolco Department Stores. *See* Woolworth Corporation.

Woolrich Inc., 62 393–96

The Woolwich plc, 30 492–95; 64 50

Woolworth Corporation, 6 344; **V** 224–27; **8** 509; **14** 293–95; **17** 42, 335;

20 528–32 (upd.); 25 22. *See also* Kingfisher plc; Venator Group Inc.

Woolworth Holdings. *See* Kingfisher plc.

Woolworth's Ltd., II 656. *See also* Kingfisher plc.

Wooster Preserving Company, 11 211

Worcester Gas Light Co., 14 124

Worcester Wire Works, 13 369

Word, Inc., 14 499; 38 456

Word Publishing, 71 401

WordPerfect Corporation, 6 256; 10 519, 556–59; 12 335; 25 300; 41 281. *See also* Corel Corporation.

WordStar International, 15 149; 43 151. *See also* The Learning Company Inc.

Work Wear Corp., II 607; 16 229

Workflow Management, Inc., 65 369–72

Working Assets Funding Service, 43 473–76

Working Title Films, 23 389

Workman Publishing Company, Inc., 70 368–71

Workscape Inc., 42 430

World Acceptance Corporation, 57 415–18

World Airways, 10 560–62; 28 404

World Bank Group, 33 462–65

World Book Group. *See* Scott Fetzer Company.

World Book, Inc., 12 554–56

World Championship Wrestling (WCW), 32 516

World Color Press Inc., 12 557–59; 19 333; 21 61

World Commerce Corporation, 25 461

World Communications, Inc., 11 184

World Duty Free Americas, Inc., 29 509–12 (upd.)

World Duty Free plc, 33 59

World Film Studio, 24 437

World Flight Crew Services, 10 560

World Foot Locker, 14 293

World Fuel Services Corporation, 47 449–51

World Gift Company, 9 330

World International Holdings Limited, 12 368

World Machinery Company, 45 170–71

World Minerals Inc., 60 16

World Online, 48 398–39

World Poker Tour, LLC, 51 205, 207

World Publications, LLC, 8 423; 65 373–75

World Savings and Loan, 19 412; 47 159–60

World Service Life Insurance Company, 27 47

World Trade Corporation. *See* International Business Machines Corporation.

World Trans, Inc., 33 105

World Wrestling Federation Entertainment, Inc., 32 514–17

World Yacht Enterprises, 22 438

The World's Biggest Bookstore, 58 185

World's Finest Chocolate Inc., 39 422–24

WorldCom, Inc., 14 330, 332; 18 33, 164, 166; 29 227; 38 269–70, 468; 46 376; 61 212; 71 372–73. *See also* MCI WorldCom, Inc.

WorldCorp, Inc., 10 560–62

WorldGames, 10 560

WorldMark, The Club, 33 409

Worlds of Fun, 22 130

Worlds of Wonder, Inc., 25 381; 26 548

Worldview Systems Corporation, 26 428; 46 434

WorldWay Corporation, 16 41

Worldwide Fiber Inc., 46 267

Worldwide Insurance Co., 48 9

Worldwide Logistics, 17 505

Worldwide Restaurant Concepts, Inc., 47 452–55

Worldwide Semiconductor Manufacturing Co., 47 386

Worldwide Underwriters Insurance Co., III 218–19

Wormald International Ltd., 13 245, 247; 63 403

Worms et Cie, 27 275–76, 513–15

Worth Corp., 27 274

Worthen Banking Corporation, 15 60

Worthington Foods, Inc., 14 557–59; 33 170

Worthington Industries, Inc., 7 598–600; 8 450; 21 537–40 (upd.)

Woven Belting Co., 8 13

WP Spinnaker Holdings, Inc. *See* Spinnaker Exploration Company.

WPL Holdings, 6 604–06

WPM. *See* Wall Paper Manufacturers.

WPP Group plc, 6 53–54; 22 201, 296; 23 480; 48 440–42 (upd.); 66 157, 160, 378. *See also* Ogilvy Group Inc.

WPS Resources Corporation, 53 367–70 (upd.)

Wrafton Laboratories Ltd., 59 332

Wrather Corporation, 18 354

Wrenn Furniture Company, 10 184

WRG. *See* Wells Rich Greene BDDP.

Wright & Company Realtors, 21 257

Wright Aeronautical, 9 16

Wright Company, 9 416

Wright Group, 22 519, 522

Wright Manufacturing Company, 8 407

Wright Medical Group, Inc., 61 401–05

Wright Plastic Products, 17 310; 24 160

Wrightson Limited, 19 155

WS Atkins Plc, 45 445–47

WSGC Holdings, Inc., 24 530

WSI. *See* Weather Services International.

WSI Corporation, 10 88–89

WSM Inc., 11 152

WSMC. *See* Worldwide Semiconductor Manufacturing Co.

WSMP, Inc., 29 202

WTD Industries, Inc., 20 533–36

Wurlitzer Co., 17 468; 18 45

Württembergische Metallwarenfabrik AG (WMF), 60 364–69

WVPP. *See* Westvaco Corporation.

WVT Communications. *See* Warwick Valley Telephone Company.

WWG Industries, Inc., 22 352–53

WWT, Inc., 58 371

WWTV, 18 493

Wyandotte Chemicals Corporation, 18 49

Wyant Corporation, 30 496–98

Wycombe Bus Company, 28 155–56

Wyeth, 50 535–39 (upd.)

Wyeth-Ayerst Laboratories, 25 477; 27 69

Wyle Electronics, 14 560–62; 19 311

Wyly Corporation, 11 468

Wyman-Gordon Company, 14 563–65; 30 282–83; 41 367

Wynkoop Brewing Company, 43 407

Wynn's International, Inc., 22 458; 33 466–70

Wyse Technology, Inc., 10 362; 15 540–42

X-Acto, 12 263

X-Chem Oil Field Chemicals, 8 385

X-Rite, Inc., 48 443–46

XA Systems Corporation, 10 244

Xaos Tools, Inc., 10 119

Xaver Fendt GmbH & Co. KG. *See* AGCO Corporation.

XCare.net, Inc. *See* Quovadx Inc.

Xcor International, 15 538; 53 364–65

Xeikon NV, 26 540–42; 66 260

Xenell Corporation, 48 358

Xenia National Bank, 9 474

Xenotech, 27 58

Xeron, Inc., 56 62

Xerox Corporation, III 171–73; 6 288–90 (upd.); 26 543–47 (upd.); 69 374–80 (upd.)

Xetra, 59 151

Xiamen Airlines, 33 99

Xilinx, Inc., 16 317, 548–50; 18 17, 19; 19 405; 43 15–16

Xing Technology Corp., 53 282

XM Satellite Radio Holdings, Inc., 69 381–84

XMR, Inc., 42 361

XP, 27 474

Xpect First Aid Corp., 51 76

Xpert Recruitment, Ltd., 26 240

Xpress Automotive Group, Inc., 24 339

XR Ventures LLC, 48 446

XRAL Storage and Terminaling Co., IV 411

Xros, Inc., 36 353

XTO Energy Inc., 52 425–27

XTRA Corp., 18 67

Xtra Limited New Zealand, 54 355–57

XTX Corp., 13 127

Xuzhuo Liebherr Concrete Machinery Co. Ltd., 64 241

Xynetics, 9 251

Xytek Corp., 13 127

Yacimientos Petrolíferos Fiscales Sociedad Anónima. *See* Repsol-YPF SA.

Yageo Corporation, 16 551–53

Yahoo! Inc., 25 18; 27 516–19; 70 372–75 (upd.)

Yakovlev, 24 60

Yale and Valor, PLC, 50 134–35

Yamagata Enterprises, 26 310

Yamaha Corporation, III 366, 599, 656–59; 11 50; 12 401; 16 410, 554–58 (upd.); 17 25; 18 250; 19 428; 22 196; 33 28; 40 461–66 (upd.); 49 178

Yamaha Motor Co., Ltd., 59 393, 397

Yamaha Musical Instruments, 16 202; 43 170

Yamaichi Capital Management, 42 349

Yamaichi Securities Company, Limited, II 458–59; 9 377

Yamamotoyama Co., Ltd., 50 449

Yamano Music, 16 202; 43 171

Yamanouchi Consumer Inc., 39 361

Yamanouchi Pharmaceutical Co., Ltd., 12 444–45; 38 93

Yamato Transport Co. Ltd., V 536–38; 49 458–61 (upd.)

Yamazaki Baking Co., Ltd., IV 152; 24 358; 58 380–82

Yanbian Industrial Technology Training Institute, 12 294

Yangzhou Motor Coach Manufacturing Co., **34** 132
The Yankee Candle Company, Inc., 37 423–26; 38 192
Yankee Energy Gas System, Inc., **13** 184
Yankee Gas Services Company, **48** 305
YankeeNets LLC, 35 474–77
Yankton Gas Company, **6** 524
Yarmouth Group, Inc., **17** 285
Yasuda Fire and Marine Insurance Company, Limited, III 405–07, 408; **45** 110
Yasuda Mutual Life Insurance Company, II 446; **III 408–09; 22** 406–07; **39 425–28 (upd.)**
The Yasuda Trust and Banking Company, Limited, II 391–92; 17 555–57 (upd.)
Yates-Barco Ltd., **16** 8
Yates Circuit Foil, **IV** 26
The Yates Companies, Inc., 62 397–99
Yearbooks, Inc., **12** 472
Yeargin Construction Co., **II** 87; **11** 413
Yellow Cab Co., **10** 370; **24** 118
Yellow Corporation, 14 566–68; 45 448–51 (upd.)
Yellow Freight System, Inc. of Deleware, V 539–41; 12 278
YES! Entertainment Corporation, 10 306; **26 548–50**
Yesco Audio Environments, **18** 353, 355
Yeti Cycles Inc., **19** 385
YGK Inc. *See* Cincinnati Gas & Electric Company.
Yhtyneet Paperitehtaat Oy. *See* United Paper Mills Ltd.
YKK, **19** 477
YMCA of the USA, 31 473–76
Ymos A.G., **IV** 53; **26** 83
YOCREAM International, Inc., 47 456–58
Yogen Fruz World-Wide, Inc. *See* CoolBrands International Inc.
Yokado Co. Ltd. *See* Ito-Yokado Co. Ltd.
Yoko Sangyo Co., **64** 35
Yokogawa Electric Works, Limited, **13** 234
Yokohama Bottle Plant, **21** 319
The Yokohama Rubber Co., Ltd., V 254–56; 19 506–09 (upd.)
Yokohama Tokyu Deppartment Store Co., Ltd., **32** 457
Yondenko Corporation, **60** 272
Yongpyong Resort Co., **61** 342
Yoosung Enterprise Co., Ltd., **23** 269
Yoplait S.A. *See* Sodiaal S.A.
The York Bank and Trust Company, **16** 14; **43** 8
The York Group, Inc., 50 540–43
York International Corp., 13 569–71; 22 6
York Manufacturing Co., **13** 385
York Research Corporation, 35 478–80
York Safe & Lock Company, **7** 144–45; **22** 184
York Steak House, **16** 157
York Wastewater Consultants, Inc., **6** 441
Yorkshire Energies, **45** 21
Yorkshire Group, **61** 133
Yorkshire Television Ltd., **IV** 659
Yorkshire-Tyne Tees Television, **24** 194
Yorkshire Water Services Ltd. *See* Kelda Group plc.
Young & Co.'s Brewery, P.L.C., 38 499–502

Young & Rubicam, Inc., I 36–38; 22 551–54 (upd.); 66 375–78 (upd.)
Young & Selden, **7** 145
Young Broadcasting Inc., 40 467–69; 42 163
Young Chang Akki Company, **51** 201
Young Innovations, Inc., 44 451–53
Young Readers of America, **13** 105
Young's Market Company, LLC, 32 518–20
Youngblood Truck Lines, **16** 40
Youngjin Pharmaceutical, **62** 221
Youngs Drug Products Corporation, **8** 85; **38** 124
Youngstown Sheet & Tube, **I** 490–91; **13** 157
Younkers, Inc., 19 324–25, **510–12; 41** 343–44
Your Communications Limited, **52** 372, 374
Youth Centre Inc., **16** 36
Youth Services International, Inc., 21 541–43; 30 146
Youthtrack, Inc., **29** 399–400
Yoxall Instrument Company, **13** 234
YPF Sociedad Anónima, IV 577–78. *See also* Repsol-YPF S.A.
Yside Investment Group, **16** 196
YTT. *See* Yorkshire-Tyne Tees Television.
The Yucaipa Cos., 17 558–62; 22 39; **32** 222; **35** 369
Yugraneft, **49** 306
Yukon Pacific Corporation, **22** 164, 166
YUKOS, **49** 305–06. *See also* OAO NK YUKOS.
Yule Catto & Company plc, 54 422–25
Yum! Brands Inc., 57 228; 58 383–85
Yutaka Co., Ltd., **55** 48
Yves Bertelin SAS., **72** 35
Yves Rocher. *See* Laboratoires de Biologie Végétale Yves Rocher.
Yves Soulié, **II** 266
YWCA of the U.S.A., 45 452–54

Z Media, Inc., **49** 433
Z-Spanish Media Corp., **35** 220; **41** 151
Z.C. Mines, **IV** 61
Zagara's Inc., **35** 190–91
Zahnfabrik Weinand Sohne & Co. G.m.b.H., **10** 271
Zale Corporation, 16 206, **559–61; 17** 369; **19** 452; **23** 60; **40 470–74 (upd.)**
Zambezi Saw Mills (1968) Ltd., **IV** 241
Zambia Breweries, **25** 281
Zambia Industrial and Mining Corporation Ltd., IV 239–41
Zamboni. *See* Frank J. Zamboni & Co., Inc.
Zanders Feinpapiere AG, **IV** 288; **15** 229
Zanussi, **III** 480; **22** 27; **53** 127
Zany Brainy, Inc., 31 477–79; 36 502
Zap, Inc., **25** 546
Zapata Corporation, 17 157, 160; **25 544–46; 63** 343–44
Zapata Gulf Marine Corporation, **11** 524
Zaring Premier Homes, **41** 133
Zastron Electronic (Shenzhen) Co. Ltd., **61** 233
Zatarain's, Inc., 64 413–15
Zausner, **25** 83
Zayre Corp., **9** 20–21; **13** 547–48; **29** 106; **30** 55–56; **33** 198. *See also* The TJX Companies, Inc.
ZCE Platinum, **63** 40

ZCMI. *See* Zion's Cooperative Mercantile Institution.
ZDF, **41** 28–29
ZDNet, **36** 523
Zealand Mines S.A., **23** 41
Zebco Corp. *See* W.C. Bradley Co.
Zebra Technologies Corporation, 14 378, **569–71; 53 371–74 (upd.)**
Zecco, Inc., **6** 441
Zee Medical, Inc., **47** 235
ZeFer, **63** 151
Zell Bros., **16** 559
Zell/Chilmark Fund LP, **12** 439; **19** 384
Zellers. *See* Hudson's Bay Company.
Zellstoff-und Papierfabrik Rosenthal Gmbh & Co KG., **64** 275
Zellweger Telecommunications AG, **9** 32
Zeneca Group PLC, 21 544–46. *See also* AstraZeneca PLC.
Zengine, Inc., **41** 258–59
Zenit Bank, **45** 322
Zenith Data Systems, Inc., 10 563–65
Zenith Electronics Corporation, II 123–25; 10 563; **11** 62, 318; **12** 183; **13** 109, 398, **572–75 (upd.); 18** 421; **34 514–19 (upd.)**
Zenith Media, **42** 330–31
Zentralsparkasse und Kommerzialbank Wien, **23** 37
Zentronics, **19** 313
Zep Manufacturing Company, **54** 252, 254
Zeppelin Luftschifftechnik GmbH, **48** 450
Zerex, **50** 48
Zergo Holdings, **42** 24–25
Zero Corporation, 17 563–65
Zero First Co Ltd., **62** 245
Zero Plus Dialing, Inc. *See* Billing Concepts Corp.
Zetor s.p., **21** 175
Zeus Components, Inc., **10** 113; **50** 43
Zexel Valeo Compressor USA Inc. *See* Valeo.
ZF Friedrichshafen AG, 48 447–51
Zhenjiang Zhengmao Hitachi Zosen Machinery Co. Ltd., **53** 173
Zhong Yue Highsonic Electron Company, **62** 150
Zhongbei Building Material Products Company, **26** 510
Zhongde Brewery, **49** 417
Ziebart International Corporation, 30 499–501; 66 379–82 (upd.)
The Ziegler Companies, Inc., 24 541–45; 63 442–48 (upd.)
Ziff Communications Company, 7 239–40; **12** 359, **560–63; 13** 483; **16** 371; **17** 152, 253; **25** 238, 240; **41** 12
Ziff Davis Media Inc., 36 521–26 (upd.); 47 77, 79. *See also* CNET Networks, Inc.
Ziff-Davis Publishing Co., **38** 441
Zignago Vetro S.p.A., **67** 210–12
Zila, Inc., 46 466–69
Zilber Ltd., **13** 541
Zildjian. *See* Avedis Zildjian Co.
Zilkha & Company, **12** 72
ZiLOG, Inc., 15 543–45; 72 377–80 (upd.)
Zimmer Holdings, Inc., 45 455–57
Zimmer Inc., **10** 156–57; **11** 475
Zinc Products Company, **30** 39
Zindart Ltd., 60 370–72
Zingerman's Community of Businesses, 68 406–08

Zinsser. *See* William Zinsser & Company, Inc.

Zion Foods, **23** 408

Zion's Cooperative Mercantile Institution, 33 471–74

Zions Bancorporation, 12 564–66; **24** 395; **53 375–78 (upd.)**

Zippo Manufacturing Company, 18 565–68; **71 394–99 (upd.)**

Zipps Drive-Thru, Inc., **25** 389

Zippy Mart, **7** 102

Zodiac S.A., 36 527–30

Zody's Department Stores, **9** 120–22

Zolfo Cooper LLC, **57** 219

Zoll Foods, **55** 366

Zoll Medical, **18** 423

Zoloto Mining Ltd., **38** 231

Zoltek Companies, Inc., 37 427–30

Zomba Records Ltd., 52 428–31

Zondervan Corporation, 24 546–49; **71 400–04 (upd.)**

Zones, Inc., 67 395–97

Zoom Technologies, Inc., 53 379–82 (upd.)

Zoom Telephonics, Inc., 18 569–71

Zortech Inc., **10** 508

Zotos International, Inc., **III** 63; **17** 110; **22** 487; **41** 228

ZPT Radom, **23** 427

ZS Sun Limited Partnership, **10** 502

Zuari Cement, **40** 107, 109

Zuellig Group N.A., Inc., **46** 226

Zuivelcooperatie De Seven Provincien UA, **59** 194

Zuka Juice, **47** 201

Zumtobel AG, 50 544–48

Zurich Financial Services, 40 59, 61; **42 448–53 (upd.)**

Zurich Insurance Group, **15** 257; **25** 154, 156

Zürich Versicherungs-Gesellschaft, III 410–12. *See also* Zurich Financial Services

Zurn Industries, Inc., **24** 150

Zvezda Design Bureau, **61** 197

Zwarovski, **16** 561

Zweckform Büro-Produkte G.m.b.H., **49** 38

Zycad Corp., **11** 489–91; **69** 340–41

Zycon Corporation, **24** 201

Zygo Corporation, 42 454–57

ZymoGenetics Inc., **61** 266

Zytec Corporation, 19 513–15. *See also* Artesyn Technologies Inc.

INDEX TO INDUSTRIES

Index to Industries

ACCOUNTING

American Institute of Certified Public Accountants (AICPA), 44
Andersen, 29 (upd.); 68 (upd.)
Automatic Data Processing, Inc., 47 (upd.)
Deloitte Touche Tohmatsu International, 9; 29 (upd.)
Ernst & Young, 9; 29 (upd.)
Grant Thornton International, 57
KPMG International, 33 (upd.)
L.S. Starrett Co., 13
McLane Company, Inc., 13
NCO Group, Inc., 42
Paychex, Inc., 46 (upd.)
Plante & Moran, LLP, 71
PricewaterhouseCoopers, 9; 29 (upd.)
Robert Wood Johnson Foundation, 35
Univision Communications Inc., 24

ADVERTISING & OTHER BUSINESS SERVICES

ABM Industries Incorporated, 25 (upd.)
Ackerley Communications, Inc., 9
ACNielsen Corporation, 13; 38 (upd.)
Acsys, Inc., 44
Adecco S.A., 36 (upd.)
Adia S.A., 6
Administaff, Inc., 52
Advo, Inc., 6; 53 (upd.)
Aegis Group plc, 6
Affiliated Computer Services, Inc., 61
AHL Services, Inc., 27
Alloy, Inc., 55
Amdocs Ltd., 47
American Building Maintenance Industries, Inc., 6
The American Society of Composers, Authors and Publishers (ASCAP), 29
Amey Plc, 47
Analysts International Corporation, 36
The Arbitron Company, 38
Ariba, Inc., 57
Armor Holdings, Inc., 27
Ashtead Group plc, 34
The Associated Press, 13
Bain & Company, 55
Barrett Business Services, Inc., 16
Barton Protective Services Inc., 53
Bates Worldwide, Inc., 14; 33 (upd.)
Bearings, Inc., 13
Berlitz International, Inc., 13
Big Flower Press Holdings, Inc., 21
Billing Concepts, Inc., 72 (upd.)
Boron, LePore & Associates, Inc., 45
The Boston Consulting Group, 58
Bozell Worldwide Inc., 25
BrandPartners Group, Inc., 58
Bright Horizons Family Solutions, Inc., 31
Broadcast Music Inc., 23
Buck Consultants, Inc., 55
Bureau Veritas SA, 55
Burns International Services Corporation, 13; 41 (upd.)

Cambridge Technology Partners, Inc., 36
Campbell-Mithun-Esty, Inc., 16
Cannon Design, 63
Capita Group PLC, 69
Career Education Corporation, 45
Carmichael Lynch Inc., 28
Cazenove Group plc, 72
CDI Corporation, 54 (upd.)
Central Parking Corporation, 18
Century Business Services, Inc., 52
Chancellor Beacon Academies, Inc., 53
ChartHouse International Learning Corporation, 49
Chiat/Day Inc. Advertising, 11
Chicago Board of Trade, 41
Chisholm-Mingo Group, Inc., 41
Christie's International plc, 15; 39 (upd.)
Cintas Corporation, 21
COMFORCE Corporation, 40
Command Security Corporation, 57
Computer Learning Centers, Inc., 26
Concentra Inc., 71
Corporate Express, Inc., 47 (upd.)
CORT Business Services Corporation, 26
Cox Enterprises, Inc., 22 (upd.)
Creative Artists Agency LLC, 38
Cyrk Inc., 19
Dale Carnegie Training, Inc., 28
D'Arcy Masius Benton & Bowles, Inc., 6; 32 (upd.)
Dawson Holdings PLC, 43
DDB Needham Worldwide, 14
Deluxe Corporation, 22 (upd.)
Dentsu Inc., I; 16 (upd.); 40 (upd.)
Deutsch, Inc., 42
Deutsche Post AG, 29
DHL Worldwide Network S.A./N.V., 69 (upd.)
DoubleClick Inc., 46
Drake Beam Morin, Inc., 44
The Dun & Bradstreet Corporation, 61 (upd.)
Earl Scheib, Inc., 32
eBay Inc., 67 (upd.)
EBSCO Industries, Inc., 17
Ecology and Environment, Inc., 39
Edelman, 62
Edison Schools Inc., 37
Education Management Corporation, 35
Electro Rent Corporation, 58
Employee Solutions, Inc., 18
Ennis Business Forms, Inc., 21
Equifax Inc., 6; 28 (upd.)
Equity Marketing, Inc., 26
ERLY Industries Inc., 17
Euro RSCG Worldwide S.A., 13
Expedia, Inc., 58
Fallon Worldwide, 22; 71 (upd.)
FileNet Corporation, 62
Fiserv, Inc., 33 (upd.)
FlightSafety International, Inc., 29 (upd.)
Florists' Transworld Delivery, Inc., 28
Foote, Cone & Belding Worldwide, I; 66 (upd.)

Forrester Research, Inc., 54
Frankel & Co., 39
Franklin Covey Company, 37 (upd.)
Frost & Sullivan, Inc., 53
Gage Marketing Group, 26
The Gallup Organization, 37
GEMA (Gesellschaft für musikalische Aufführungs- und mechanische Vervielfältigungsrechte), 70
George P. Johnson Company, 60
George S. May International Company, 55
Gevity HR, Inc., 63
GfK Aktiengesellschaft, 49
Glotel plc, 53
Grey Global Group Inc., 6; 66 (upd.)
Group 4 Falck A/S, 42
Groupe Jean-Claude Darmon, 44
GSD&M Advertising, 44
GSI Commerce, Inc., 67
Gwathmey Siegel & Associates Architects LLC, 26
Ha-Lo Industries, Inc., 27
Hakuhodo, Inc., 6; 42 (upd.)
Hall, Kinion & Associates, Inc., 52
Handleman Company, 15
Harte-Hanks, Inc., 63 (upd.)
Havas SA, 33 (upd.)
Hays Plc, 27
Headway Corporate Resources, Inc., 40
Heidrick & Struggles International, Inc., 28
Hildebrandt International, 29
IKON Office Solutions, Inc., 50
IMS Health, Inc., 57
Interbrand Corporation, 70
Interep National Radio Sales Inc., 35
International Brotherhood of Teamsters, 37
International Management Group, 18
International Total Services, Inc., 37
The Interpublic Group of Companies, Inc., I; 22 (upd.)
Ipsos SA, 48
Iron Mountain, Inc., 33
ITT Educational Services, Inc., 33
J.D. Power and Associates, 32
Jackson Hewitt, Inc., 48
Japan Leasing Corporation, 8
Jostens, Inc., 25 (upd.)
JOULÉ Inc., 58
JWT Group Inc., I
Katz Communications, Inc., 6
Katz Media Group, Inc., 35
Keane, Inc., 56
Kelly Services Inc., 6; 26 (upd.)
Ketchum Communications Inc., 6
Kforce Inc., 71
Kinko's Inc., 16; 43 (upd.)
Kirshenbaum Bond + Partners, Inc., 57
Kohn Pedersen Fox Associates P.C., 57
Korn/Ferry International, 34
Kroll Inc., 57
Labor Ready, Inc., 29
Lamar Advertising Company, 27; 70 (upd.)
Le Cordon Bleu S.A., 67
Learning Tree International Inc., 24

ADVERTISING & OTHER BUSINESS SERVICES (*continued*)

Leo Burnett Company Inc., I; 20 (upd.)
Lintas: Worldwide, 14
Mail Boxes Etc., 18; 41 (upd.)
Manhattan Associates, Inc., 67
Manpower, Inc., 30 (upd.)
Marchex, Inc., 72
marchFIRST, Inc., 34
Maritz Inc., 38
MAXIMUS, Inc., 43
MDC Partners Inc., 63
Mediaset SpA, 50
Milliman USA, 66
Moody's Corporation, 65
MPS Group, Inc., 49
Mullen Advertising Inc., 51
Napster, Inc., 69
National Equipment Services, Inc., 57
National Media Corporation, 27
NAVTEQ Corporation, 69
Neopost S.A., 53
New England Business Services, Inc., 18
New Valley Corporation, 17
NFO Worldwide, Inc., 24
Nobel Learning Communities, Inc., 37
Norrell Corporation, 25
Norwood Promotional Products, Inc., 26
The NPD Group, Inc., 68
O.C. Tanner Co., 69
Obie Media Corporation, 56
Observer AB, 55
The Ogilvy Group, Inc., I
Olsten Corporation, 6; 29 (upd.)
Omnicom Group, I; 22 (upd.)
On Assignment, Inc., 20
1-800-FLOWERS, Inc., 26
Opinion Research Corporation, 46
Oracle Corporation, 67 (upd.)
Orbitz, Inc., 61
Outdoor Systems, Inc., 25
Paris Corporation, 22
Paychex, Inc., 15
PDI, Inc., 52
Pei Cobb Freed & Partners Architects LLP, 57
Penauille Polyservices SA, 49
Phillips, de Pury & Luxembourg, 49
Pierce Leahy Corporation, 24
Pinkerton's Inc., 9
Plante & Moran, LLP, 71
PMT Services, Inc., 24
Posterscope Worldwide, 70
Priceline.com Incorporated, 57
Publicis S.A., 19
Publishers Clearing House, 23; 64 (upd.)
Quintiles Transnational Corporation, 68 (upd.)
Quovadx Inc., 70
Randstad Holding n.v., 16; 43 (upd.)
RemedyTemp, Inc., 20
Rental Service Corporation, 28
Rentokil Initial Plc, 47
Rewards Network Inc., 70 (upd.)
The Richards Group, Inc., 58
Right Management Consultants, Inc., 42
Ritchie Bros. Auctioneers Inc., 41
Robert Half International Inc., 18
Roland Berger & Partner GmbH, 37
Ronco, Inc., 15
Russell Reynolds Associates Inc., 38
Saatchi & Saatchi, I; 42 (upd.)
Securitas AB, 42
ServiceMaster Limited Partnership, 6
Shared Medical Systems Corporation, 14
Sir Speedy, Inc., 16

Skidmore, Owings & Merrill LLP, 13; 69 (upd.)
SmartForce PLC, 43
SOS Staffing Services, 25
Sotheby's Holdings, Inc., 11; 29 (upd.)
Spencer Stuart and Associates, Inc., 14
Spherion Corporation, 52
Steiner Corporation (Alsco), 53
Strayer Education, Inc., 53
Superior Uniform Group, Inc., 30
Sykes Enterprises, Inc., 45
Sylvan Learning Systems, Inc., 35
TA Triumph-Adler AG, 48
Taylor Nelson Sofres plc, 34
TBWA\Chiat\Day, 6; 43 (upd.)
Thomas Cook Travel Inc., 33 (upd.)
Ticketmaster Group, Inc., 13; 37 (upd.)
TMP Worldwide Inc., 30
TNT Post Group N.V., 30
Towers Perrin, 32
Trader Classified Media N.V., 57
Traffix, Inc., 61
Transmedia Network Inc., 20
Treasure Chest Advertising Company, Inc., 32
TRM Copy Centers Corporation, 18
True North Communications Inc., 23
24/7 Real Media, Inc., 49
Tyler Corporation, 23
U.S. Office Products Company, 25
UniFirst Corporation, 21
United Business Media plc, 52 (upd.)
United News & Media plc, 28 (upd.)
Unitog Co., 19
Valassis Communications, Inc., 37 (upd.)
ValueClick, Inc., 49
Vebego International BV, 49
Vedior NV, 35
W.B Doner & Co., 56
The Wackenhut Corporation, 14; 63 (upd.)
Waggener Edstrom, 42
Warrantech Corporation, 53
Wells Rich Greene BDDP, 6
Westaff Inc., 33
Whitman Education Group, Inc., 41
William Morris Agency, Inc., 23
Williams Scotsman, Inc., 65
Workflow Management, Inc., 65
WPP Group plc, 6; 48 (upd.)
Xerox Corporation, 69 (upd.)
Young & Rubicam, Inc., I; 22 (upd.); 66 (upd.)

AEROSPACE

A.S. Yakovlev Design Bureau, 15
Aerojet-General Corp., 63
Aeronca Inc., 46
Aerosonic Corporation, 69
The Aerospatiale Group, 7; 21 (upd.)
Alliant Techsystems Inc., 30 (upd.)
Antonov Design Bureau, 53
Aviacionny Nauchno-Tehnicheskii Komplex im. A.N. Tupoleva, 24
Avions Marcel Dassault-Breguet Aviation, I
B/E Aerospace, Inc., 30
Banner Aerospace, Inc., 14
Beech Aircraft Corporation, 8
Bell Helicopter Textron Inc., 46
The Boeing Company, I; 10 (upd.); 32 (upd.)
Bombardier Inc., 42 (upd.)
British Aerospace plc, I; 24 (upd.)
CAE USA Inc., 48
Canadair, Inc., 16
Cessna Aircraft Company, 8
Cirrus Design Corporation, 44

Cobham plc, 30
Daimler-Benz Aerospace AG, 16
DeCrane Aircraft Holdings Inc., 36
Ducommun Incorporated, 30
EADS SOCATA, 54
EGL, 59
Empresa Brasileira de Aeronáutica S.A. (Embraer), 36
European Aeronautic Defence and Space Company EADS N.V., 52 (upd.)
Fairchild Aircraft, Inc., 9
Fairchild Dornier GmbH, 48 (upd.)
First Aviation Services Inc., 49
G.I.E. Airbus Industrie, I; 12 (upd.)
General Dynamics Corporation, I; 10 (upd.); 40 (upd.)
GKN plc, 38 (upd.)
Goodrich Corporation, 46 (upd.)
Groupe Dassault Aviation SA, 26 (upd.)
Grumman Corporation, I; 11 (upd.)
Grupo Aeropuerto del Sureste, S.A. de C.V., 48
Gulfstream Aerospace Corporation, 7; 28 (upd.)
HEICO Corporation, 30
International Lease Finance Corporation, 48
Irkut Corporation, 68
Israel Aircraft Industries Ltd., 69
N.V. Koninklijke Nederlandse Vliegtuigenfabriek Fokker, I; 28 (upd.)
Lancair International, Inc., 67
Learjet Inc., 8; 27 (upd.)
Lockheed Martin Corporation, I; 11 (upd.); 15 (upd.)
Loral Space & Communications Ltd., 54 (upd.)
Magellan Aerospace Corporation, 48
Martin Marietta Corporation, I
Martin-Baker Aircraft Company Limited, 61
McDonnell Douglas Corporation, I; 11 (upd.)
Meggitt PLC, 34
Messerschmitt-Bölkow-Blohm GmbH., I
Moog Inc., 13
Mooney Aerospace Group Ltd., 52
The New Piper Aircraft, Inc., 44
Northrop Grumman Corporation, I; 11 (upd.); 45 (upd.)
Orbital Sciences Corporation, 22
Pemco Aviation Group Inc., 54
Pratt & Whitney, 9
Raytheon Aircraft Holdings Inc., 46
Robinson Helicopter Company, 51
Rockwell International Corporation, I; 11 (upd.)
Rolls-Royce Allison, 29 (upd.)
Rolls-Royce plc, I; 7 (upd.); 21 (upd.)
Rostvertol plc, 62
Safe Flight Instrument Corporation, 71
Sequa Corp., 13
Shannon Aerospace Ltd., 36
Sikorsky Aircraft Corporation, 24
Smiths Industries PLC, 25
Snecma Group, 46
Société Air France, 27 (upd.)
Spacehab, Inc., 37
Spar Aerospace Limited, 32
Sukhoi Design Bureau Aviation Scientific-Industrial Complex, 24
Sundstrand Corporation, 7; 21 (upd.)
Swales & Associates, Inc., 69
Teledyne Technologies Inc., 62 (upd.)
Textron Lycoming Turbine Engine, 9
Thales S.A., 42
Thiokol Corporation, 9; 22 (upd.)

United Technologies Corporation, I; 10 (upd.)
Van's Aircraft, Inc., 65
Vought Aircraft Industries, Inc., 49
Whittaker Corporation, 48 (upd.)
Woodward Governor Company, 49 (upd.)
Zodiac S.A., 36

AIRLINES

Aer Lingus Group plc, 34
Aeroflot—Russian International Airlines, 6; 29 (upd.)
Aerolíneas Argentinas S.A., 33; 69 (upd.)
Air Berlin GmbH & Co. Luftverkehrs KG, 71
Air Canada, 6; 23 (upd.); 59 (upd.)
Air China, 46
Air Jamaica Limited, 54
Air Mauritius Ltd., 63
Air New Zealand Limited, 14; 38 (upd.)
Air Pacific Ltd., 70
Air Sahara Limited, 65
Air Wisconsin Airlines Corporation, 55
Air-India Limited, 6; 27 (upd.)
AirTran Holdings, Inc., 22
Alaska Air Group, Inc., 6; 29 (upd.)
Alitalia-Linee Aeree Italiana, S.p.A., 6; 29 (upd.)
All Nippon Airways Company Limited, 6; 38 (upd.)
Aloha Airlines, Incorporated, 24
America West Holdings Corporation, 6; 34 (upd.)
American Airlines, I; 6 (upd.)
AMR Corporation, 28 (upd.); 52 (upd.)
Amtran, Inc., 34
Arrow Air Holdings Corporation, 55
A/S Air Baltic Corporation, 71
AS Estonian Air, 71
Asiana Airlines, Inc., 46
Atlantic Coast Airlines Holdings, Inc., 55
Atlantic Southeast Airlines, Inc., 47
Atlas Air, Inc., 39
Austrian Airlines AG (Österreichische Luftverkehrs AG), 33
Aviacionny Nauchno-Tehnicheskii Komplex im. A.N. Tupoleva, 24
Avianca Aerovías Nacionales de Colombia SA, 36
Bahamas Air Holdings Ltd., 66
Banner Aerospace, Inc., 37 (upd.)
Braathens ASA, 47
Bradley Air Services Ltd., 56
Bristow Helicopters Ltd., 70
British Airways PLC, I; 14 (upd.); 43 (upd.)
British Midland plc, 38
British World Airlines Ltd., 18
Cargolux Airlines International S.A., 49
Cathay Pacific Airways Limited, 6; 34 (upd.)
Ceské aerolinie, a.s., 66
Chautauqua Airlines, Inc., 38
China Airlines, 34
China Eastern Airlines Co. Ltd., 31
China Southern Airlines Company Ltd., 33
Comair Holdings Inc., 13; 34 (upd.)
Continental Airlines, Inc., I; 21 (upd.); 52 (upd.)
Corporación Internacional de Aviación, S.A. de C.V. (Cintra), 20
Delta Air Lines, Inc., I; 6 (upd.); 39 (upd.)
Deutsche Lufthansa AG, I; 26 (upd.); 68 (upd.)
Eastern Airlines, I
easyJet Airline Company Limited, 39
EgyptAir, 6; 27 (upd.)

El Al Israel Airlines Ltd., 23
The Emirates Group, 39
EVA Airways Corporation, 51
Finnair Oyj, 6; 25 (upd.); 61 (upd.)
Flying Boat, Inc. (Chalk's Ocean Airways), 56
Frontier Airlines, Inc., 22
Garuda Indonesia, 6
Groupe Air France, 6
Grupo TACA, 38
Gulf Air Company, 56
HAL Inc., 9
Hawaiian Airlines, Inc., 22 (upd.)
Hong Kong Dragon Airlines Ltd., 66
Iberia Líneas Aéreas de España S.A., 6; 36 (upd.)
Icelandair, 52
Indian Airlines Ltd., 46
Japan Air Lines Company Ltd., I; 32 (upd.)
Jersey European Airways (UK) Ltd., 61
Jet Airways (India) Private Limited, 65
JetBlue Airways Corporation, 44
Kenmore Air Harbor Inc., 65
Kitty Hawk, Inc., 22
Kiwi International Airlines Inc., 20
Koninklijke Luchtvaart Maatschappij, N.V. (KLM Royal Dutch Airlines), I; 28 (upd.)
Korean Air Lines Co., Ltd., 6; 27 (upd.)
Kuwait Airways Corporation, 68
Lan Chile S.A., 31
Lauda Air Luftfahrt AG, 48
Loganair Ltd., 68
LOT Polish Airlines (Polskie Linie Lotnicze S.A.), 33
LTU Group Holding GmbH, 37
Malév Plc, 24
Malaysian Airlines System Berhad, 6; 29 (upd.)
Mesa Air Group, Inc., 11; 32 (upd.)
Mesaba Holdings, Inc., 28
Midway Airlines Corporation, 33
Midwest Express Holdings, Inc., 35
Northwest Airlines Corporation, I; 6 (upd.); 26 (upd.)
Offshore Logistics, Inc., 37
Pakistan International Airlines Corporation, 46
Pan American World Airways, Inc., I; 12 (upd.)
Panalpina World Transport (Holding) Ltd., 47
People Express Airlines, Inc., I
Petroleum Helicopters, Inc., 35
Philippine Airlines, Inc., 6; 23 (upd.)
Preussag AG, 42 (upd.)
Qantas Airways Ltd., 6; 24 (upd.); 68 (upd.)
Reno Air Inc., 23
Royal Nepal Airline Corporation, 41
Ryanair Holdings plc, 35
SAA (Pty) Ltd., 28
Sabena S.A./N.V., 33
The SAS Group, 34 (upd.)
Saudi Arabian Airlines, 6; 27 (upd.)
Scandinavian Airlines System, I
Singapore Airlines Ltd., 6; 27 (upd.)
SkyWest, Inc., 25
Société d'Exploitation AOM Air Liberté SA (AirLib), 53
Société Luxembourgeoise de Navigation Aérienne S.A., 64
Société Tunisienne de l'Air-Tunisair, 49
Southwest Airlines Co., 6; 24 (upd.); 71 (upd.)
Spirit Airlines, Inc., 31
Sterling European Airlines A/S, 70
Sun Country Airlines, 30

Swiss Air Transport Company, Ltd., I
Swiss International Air Lines Ltd., 48
TAM Linhas Aéreas S.A., 68
TAP—Air Portugal Transportes Aéreos Portugueses S.A., 46
TAROM S.A., 64
Texas Air Corporation, I
Thai Airways International Public Company Limited, 6; 27 (upd.)
Tower Air, Inc., 28
Trans World Airlines, Inc., I; 12 (upd.); 35 (upd.)
TransBrasil S/A Linhas Aéreas, 31
Transportes Aereos Portugueses, S.A., 6
Turkish Airlines Inc. (Türk Hava Yollari A.O.), 72
TV Guide, Inc., 43 (upd.)
UAL Corporation, 34 (upd.)
United Airlines, I; 6 (upd.)
US Airways Group, Inc., I; 6 (upd.); 28 (upd.); 52 (upd.)
VARIG S.A. (Viação Aérea Rio-Grandense), 6; 29 (upd.)
WestJet Airlines Ltd., 38

AUTOMOTIVE

AB Volvo, I; 7 (upd.); 26 (upd.); 67 (upd.)
Adam Opel AG, 7; 21 (upd.); 61 (upd.)
ADESA, Inc., 71
Advance Auto Parts, Inc., 57
Aisin Seiki Co., Ltd., 48 (upd.)
Alfa Romeo, 13; 36 (upd.)
Alvis Plc, 47
America's Car-Mart, Inc., 64
American Motors Corporation, I
Applied Power Inc., 32 (upd.)
Arnold Clark Automobiles Ltd., 60
ArvinMeritor, Inc., 8; 54 (upd.)
Asbury Automotive Group Inc., 60
ASC, Inc., 55
Autocam Corporation, 51
Autoliv, Inc., 65
Automobiles Citroen, 7
Automobili Lamborghini Holding S.p.A., 13; 34 (upd.)
AutoNation, Inc., 50
AVTOVAZ Joint Stock Company, 65
Bajaj Auto Limited, 39
Bayerische Motoren Werke AG, I; 11 (upd.); 38 (upd.)
Bendix Corporation, I
Blue Bird Corporation, 35
Bombardier Inc., 42 (upd.)
Borg-Warner Automotive, Inc., 14; 32 (upd.)
The Budd Company, 8
Canadian Tire Corporation, Limited, 71 (upd.)
CarMax, Inc., 55
CARQUEST Corporation, 29
Caterpillar Inc., 63 (upd.)
Chrysler Corporation, I; 11 (upd.)
CNH Global N.V., 38 (upd.)
Consorcio G Grupo Dina, S.A. de C.V., 36
CSK Auto Corporation, 38
Cummins Engine Company, Inc., I; 12 (upd.); 40 (upd.)
Custom Chrome, Inc., 16
Daihatsu Motor Company, Ltd., 7; 21 (upd.)
Daimler-Benz A.G., I; 15 (upd.)
DaimlerChrysler AG, 34 (upd.); 64 (upd.)
Dana Corporation, I; 10 (upd.)
Deere & Company, 42 (upd.)
Delphi Automotive Systems Corporation, 45
Don Massey Cadillac, Inc., 37

AUTOMOTIVE (*continued*)

Donaldson Company, Inc., 49 (upd.)
Douglas & Lomason Company, 16
DriveTime Automotive Group Inc., 68 (upd.)
Ducati Motor Holding S.p.A., 30
Eaton Corporation, I; 10 (upd.)
Echlin Inc., I; 11 (upd.)
Edelbrock Corporation, 37
Faurecia S.A., 70
Federal-Mogul Corporation, I; 10 (upd.); 26 (upd.)
Ferrari S.p.A., 13; 36 (upd.)
Fiat SpA, I; 11 (upd.); 50 (upd.)
FinishMaster, Inc., 24
Ford Motor Company, I; 11 (upd.); 36 (upd.); 64 (upd.)
Ford Motor Company, S.A. de C.V., 20
Fruehauf Corporation, I
General Motors Corporation, I; 10 (upd.); 36 (upd.); 64 (upd.)
Gentex Corporation, 26
Genuine Parts Company, 9; 45 (upd.)
GKN plc, 38 (upd.)
Group 1 Automotive, Inc., 52
Harley-Davidson Inc., 7; 25 (upd.)
Hastings Manufacturing Company, 56
Hayes Lemmerz International, Inc., 27
The Hertz Corporation, 33 (upd.)
Hino Motors, Ltd., 7; 21 (upd.)
Holden Ltd., 62
Holley Performance Products Inc., 52
Hometown Auto Retailers, Inc., 44
Honda Motor Company Limited (Honda Giken Kogyo Kabushiki Kaisha), I; 10 (upd.); 29 (upd.)
Hyundai Group, 56 (upd.)
Insurance Auto Auctions, Inc., 23
Isuzu Motors, Ltd., 9; 23 (upd.); 57 (upd.)
Kawasaki Heavy Industries, Ltd., 63 (upd.)
Kelsey-Hayes Group of Companies, 7; 27 (upd.)
Key Safety Systems, Inc., 63
Kia Motors Corporation, 12; 29 (upd.)
Kwik-Fit Holdings plc, 54
Lazy Days RV Center, Inc., 69
Lear Corporation, 71 (upd.)
Lear Seating Corporation, 16
Les Schwab Tire Centers, 50
Lithia Motors, Inc., 41
LKQ Corporation, 71
Lookers plc, 71
Lotus Cars Ltd., 14
Lund International Holdings, Inc., 40
Mack Trucks, Inc., I; 22 (upd.); 61 (upd.)
The Major Automotive Companies, Inc., 45
Masland Corporation, 17
Mazda Motor Corporation, 9; 23 (upd.); 63 (upd.)
Mel Farr Automotive Group, 20
Metso Corporation, 30 (upd.)
Midas Inc., 10; 56 (upd.)
Mitsubishi Motors Corporation, 9; 23 (upd.); 57 (upd.)
Monaco Coach Corporation, 31
Monro Muffler Brake, Inc., 24
Montupet S.A., 63
National R.V. Holdings, Inc., 32
Navistar International Corporation, I; 10 (upd.)
Nissan Motor Co., Ltd., I; 11 (upd.); 34 (upd.)
O'Reilly Automotive, Inc., 26
Officine Alfieri Maserati S.p.A., 13
Oshkosh Truck Corporation, 7
Paccar Inc., I
PACCAR Inc., 26 (upd.)

Pennzoil-Quaker State Company, IV; 20 (upd.); 50 (upd.)
Penske Corporation, 19 (upd.)
The Pep Boys—Manny, Moe & Jack, 11; 36 (upd.)
Perusahaan Otomobil Nasional Bhd., 62
Peugeot S.A., I
Piaggio & C. S.p.A., 20
Porsche AG, 13; 31 (upd.)
PSA Peugeot Citroen S.A., 28 (upd.)
R&B, Inc., 51
Regie Nationale des Usines Renault, I
Renault Argentina S.A., 67
Renault S.A., 26 (upd.)
Republic Industries, Inc., 26
The Reynolds and Reynolds Company, 50
Robert Bosch GmbH., I; 16 (upd.); 43 (upd.)
RockShox, Inc., 26
Rockwell Automation, 43 (upd.)
Rolls-Royce plc, I; 21 (upd.)
Ron Tonkin Chevrolet Company, 55
Rover Group Ltd., 7; 21 (upd.)
Saab Automobile AB, 32 (upd.)
Saab-Scania A.B., I; 11 (upd.)
Safelite Glass Corp., 19
Safety Components International, Inc., 63
Saturn Corporation, 7; 21 (upd.)
Sealed Power Corporation, I
Sheller-Globe Corporation, I
Sixt AG, 39
Skoda Auto a.s., 39
Spartan Motors Inc., 14
SpeeDee Oil Change and Tune-Up, 25
SPX Corporation, 10; 47 (upd.)
Standard Motor Products, Inc., 40
Superior Industries International, Inc., 8
Suzuki Motor Corporation, 9; 23 (upd.); 59 (upd.)
Sytner Group plc, 45
Tower Automotive, Inc., 24
Toyota Motor Corporation, I; 11 (upd.); 38 (upd.)
TransPro, Inc., 71
Triumph Motorcycles Ltd., 53
TRW Inc., 14 (upd.)
Ugly Duckling Corporation, 22
United Auto Group, Inc., 26; 68 (upd.)
United Technologies Automotive Inc., 15
Valeo, 23; 66 (upd.)
Volkswagen Aktiengesellschaft, I; 11 (upd.); 32 (upd.)
Walker Manufacturing Company, 19
Winnebago Industries Inc., 7; 27 (upd.)
Woodward Governor Company, 49 (upd.)
ZF Friedrichshafen AG, 48
Ziebart International Corporation, 30; 66 (upd.)

BEVERAGES

A & W Brands, Inc., 25
Adolph Coors Company, I; 13 (upd.); 36 (upd.)
AG Barr plc, 64
Allied Domecq PLC, 29
Allied-Lyons PLC, I
Anchor Brewing Company, 47
Anheuser-Busch Companies, Inc., I; 10 (upd.); 34 (upd.)
Asahi Breweries, Ltd., I; 20 (upd.); 52 (upd.)
Asia Pacific Breweries Limited, 59
August Schell Brewing Company Inc., 59
Bacardi Limited, 18
Baltika Brewery Joint Stock Company, 65
Banfi Products Corp., 36
Baron Philippe de Rothschild S.A., 39

Bass PLC, I; 15 (upd.); 38 (upd.)
BBAG Osterreichische Brau-Beteiligungs-AG, 38
Beringer Blass Wine Estates Ltd., 22; 66 (upd.)
The Boston Beer Company, Inc., 18; 50 (upd.)
Brauerei Beck & Co., 9; 33 (upd.)
Britannia Soft Drinks Ltd. (Britvic), 71
Brown-Forman Corporation, I; 10 (upd.); 38 (upd.)
Budweiser Budvar, National Corporation, 59
Cadbury Schweppes PLC, 49 (upd.)
Canandaigua Brands, Inc., 13; 34 (upd.)
Cantine Giorgio Lungarotti S.R.L., 67
Carlsberg A/S, 9; 29 (upd.)
Carlton and United Breweries Ltd., I
Casa Cuervo, S.A. de C.V., 31
Cerveceria Polar, I
The Chalone Wine Group, Ltd., 36
Clearly Canadian Beverage Corporation, 48
Click Wine Group, 68
Coca Cola Bottling Co. Consolidated, 10
The Coca-Cola Company, I; 10 (upd.); 32 (upd.); 67 (upd.)
Companhia de Bebidas das Américas, 57
Compania Cervecerias Unidas S.A., 70
Constellation Brands, Inc., 68 (upd.)
Corby Distilleries Limited, 14
Cott Corporation, 52
D.G. Yuengling & Son, Inc., 38
Davide Campari-Milano S.p.A., 57
Dean Foods Company, 21 (upd.)
Delicato Vineyards, Inc., 50
Deschutes Brewery, Inc., 57
Distillers Company PLC, I
Double-Cola Co.-USA, 70
Dr Pepper/Seven Up, Inc., 9; 32 (upd.)
E. & J. Gallo Winery, I; 7 (upd.); 28 (upd.)
Eckes AG, 56
Embotelladora Andina S.A., 71
Empresas Polar SA, 55 (upd.)
F. Korbel & Bros. Inc., 68
Faygo Beverages Inc., 55
Federico Paternina S.A., 69
Ferolito, Vultaggio & Sons, 27
Florida's Natural Growers, 45
Foster's Group Limited, 7; 21 (upd.); 50 (upd.)
Freixenet S.A., 71
Fuller Smith & Turner P.L.C., 38
G. Heileman Brewing Company Inc., I
The Gambrinus Company, 40
Geerlings & Wade, Inc., 45
General Cinema Corporation, I
Golden State Vintners, Inc., 33
Grand Metropolitan PLC, I
Green Mountain Coffee, Inc., 31
The Greenalls Group PLC, 21
Greene King plc, 31
Grupo Modelo, S.A. de C.V., 29
Guinness/UDV, I; 43 (upd.)
The Hain Celestial Group, Inc., 43 (upd.)
Hansen Natural Corporation, 31
Heineken N.V., I; 13 (upd.); 34 (upd.)
Heublein, Inc., I
Hiram Walker Resources, Ltd., I
illycaffè SpA, 50
Imagine Foods, Inc., 50
Interbrew S.A., 17; 50 (upd.)
Jacob Leinenkugel Brewing Company, 28
JD Wetherspoon plc, 30
Jim Beam Brands Worldwide, Inc., 58 (upd.)
Jones Soda Co., 69
Karlsberg Brauerei GmbH & Co KG, 41

Kendall-Jackson Winery, Ltd., 28
Kikkoman Corporation, 14
Kirin Brewery Company, Limited, I; 21
  (upd.); 63 (upd.)
König Brauerei GmbH & Co. KG, 35
  (upd.)
Labatt Brewing Company Limited, I; 25
  (upd.)
Latrobe Brewing Company, 54
Laurent-Perrier SA, 42
Lion Nathan Limited, 54
The Macallan Distillers Ltd., 63
Madeira Wine Company, S.A., 49
Maison Louis Jadot, 24
Marchesi Antinori SRL, 42
Marie Brizard & Roger International S.A.,
  22
Martini & Rossi SpA, 63
MBC Holding Company, 40
Mendocino Brewing Company, Inc., 60
Miller Brewing Company, I; 12 (upd.)
The Minute Maid Company, 28
Mitchells & Butlers PLC, 59
Moët-Hennessy, I
The Molson Companies Limited, I, 26
  (upd.)
Montana Coffee Traders, Inc., 60
Mott's Inc., 57
National Beverage Corp., 26
National Grape Cooperative Association,
  Inc., 20
National Wine & Spirits, Inc., 49
New Belgium Brewing Company, Inc., 68
Nichols plc, 44
Ocean Spray Cranberries, Inc., 25 (upd.)
Odwalla, Inc., 31
Oregon Chai, Inc., 49
Panamerican Beverages, Inc., 47
Parmalat Finanziaria SpA, 50
Paulaner Brauerei GmbH & Co. KG, 35
Peet's Coffee & Tea, Inc., 38
Penaflor S.A., 66
The Pepsi Bottling Group, Inc., 40
PepsiAmericas, Inc., 67 (upd.)
PepsiCo, Inc., I; 10 (upd.); 38 (upd.)
Pernod Ricard S.A., I; 21 (upd.); 72 (upd.)
Pete's Brewing Company, 22
Philip Morris Companies Inc., 18 (upd.)
Pyramid Breweries Inc., 33
Quilmes Industrial (QUINSA) S.A., 67
R.C. Bigelow, Inc., 49
Rainier Brewing Company, 23
Red Bull GmbH, 60
Redhook Ale Brewery, Inc., 31
Rémy Cointreau S.A., 20
Robert Mondavi Corporation, 15; 50 (upd.)
Royal Crown Company, Inc., 23
Royal Grolsch NV, 54
SABMiller plc, 59 (upd.)
San Miguel Corporation, 57 (upd.)
Sapporo Breweries Limited, I; 13 (upd.);
  36 (upd.)
Scheid Vineyards Inc., 66
Schieffelin & Somerset Co., 61
Scottish & Newcastle plc, 15; 35 (upd.)
The Seagram Company Ltd., I; 25 (upd.)
Sebastiani Vineyards, Inc., 28
Shepherd Neame Limited, 30
Sidney Frank Importing Co., Inc., 69
Sierra Nevada Brewing Company, 70
Skalli Group, 67
Snapple Beverage Corporation, 11
The South African Breweries Limited, I;
  24 (upd.)
Southcorp Limited, 54
Starbucks Corporation, 13; 34 (upd.)
The Stash Tea Company, 50

Stewart's Beverages, 39
The Stroh Brewery Company, I; 18 (upd.)
Suntory Ltd., 65
Sutter Home Winery Inc., 16
Taittinger S.A., 43
Takara Holdings Inc., 62
The Terlato Wine Group, 48
Todhunter International, Inc., 27
Triarc Companies, Inc., 34 (upd.)
Tsingtao Brewery Group, 49
Tully's Coffee Corporation, 51
Van Houtte Inc., 39
Vermont Pure Holdings, Ltd., 51
Vin & Spirit AB, 31
Viña Concha y Toro S.A., 45
Vincor International Inc., 50
Whitbread and Company PLC, I
William Grant & Sons Ltd., 60
The Wine Group, Inc., 39
The Wolverhampton & Dudley Breweries,
  PLC, 57
Young & Co.'s Brewery, P.L.C., 38

BIOTECHNOLOGY

Amersham PLC, 50
Amgen, Inc., 10; 30 (upd.)
ArQule, Inc., 68
Biogen Idec Inc., 71 (upd.)
Biogen Inc., 14; 36 (upd.)
Caliper Life Sciences, Inc., 70
Cambrex Corporation, 44 (upd.)
Centocor Inc., 14
Charles River Laboratories International,
  Inc., 42
Chiron Corporation, 10; 36 (upd.)
Covance Inc., 30
CryoLife, Inc., 46
Cytyc Corporation, 69
Delta and Pine Land Company, 33
Dionex Corporation, 46
Embrex, Inc., 72
Enzo Biochem, Inc., 41
Eurofins Scientific S.A., 70
Genentech, Inc., 32 (upd.)
Genzyme Corporation, 38 (upd.)
Gilead Sciences, Inc., 54
Howard Hughes Medical Institute, 39
Huntingdon Life Sciences Group plc, 42
IDEXX Laboratories, Inc., 23
ImClone Systems Inc., 58
Immunex Corporation, 14; 50 (upd.)
IMPATH Inc., 45
Incyte Genomics, Inc., 52
Inverness Medical Innovations, Inc., 63
Invitrogen Corporation, 52
The Judge Group, Inc., 51
Life Technologies, Inc., 17
Martek Biosciences Corporation, 65
Medtronic, Inc., 30 (upd.)
Millipore Corporation, 25
Minntech Corporation, 22
Mycogen Corporation, 21
New Brunswick Scientific Co., Inc., 45
Qiagen N.V., 39
Quintiles Transnational Corporation, 21
Seminis, Inc., 29
Serologicals Corporation, 63
Sigma-Aldrich Corporation, 36 (upd.)
Starkey Laboratories, Inc., 52
STERIS Corporation, 29
Stratagene Corporation, 70
TECHNE Corporation, 52
Waters Corporation, 43
Whatman plc, 46
Wisconsin Alumni Research Foundation,
  65
Wyeth, 50 (upd.)

CHEMICALS

A. Schulman, Inc., 8
Aceto Corp., 38
Air Products and Chemicals, Inc., I; 10
  (upd.)
Airgas, Inc., 54
Akzo Nobel N.V., 13
Albemarle Corporation, 59
AlliedSignal Inc., 22 (upd.)
American Cyanamid, I; 8 (upd.)
American Vanguard Corporation, 47
ARCO Chemical Company, 10
Asahi Denka Kogyo KK, 64
Atanor S.A., 62
Atochem S.A., I
Avecia Group PLC, 63
Baker Hughes Incorporated, 22 (upd.); 57
  (upd.)
Balchem Corporation, 42
BASF Aktiengesellschaft, I; 18 (upd.); 50
  (upd.)
Bayer A.G., I; 13 (upd.); 41 (upd.)
Betz Laboratories, Inc., I; 10 (upd.)
The BFGoodrich Company, 19 (upd.)
BOC Group plc, I; 25 (upd.)
Brenntag AG, 8; 23 (upd.)
Burmah Castrol PLC, 30 (upd.)
Cabot Corporation, 8; 29 (upd.)
Caliper Life Sciences, Inc., 70
Cambrex Corporation, 16
Catalytica Energy Systems, Inc., 44
Celanese Corporation, I
Celanese Mexicana, S.A. de C.V., 54
Chemcentral Corporation, 8
Chemi-Trol Chemical Co., 16
Church & Dwight Co., Inc., 29
Ciba-Geigy Ltd., I; 8 (upd.)
The Clorox Company, 22 (upd.)
Croda International Plc, 45
Crompton Corporation, 9; 36 (upd.)
Cytec Industries Inc., 27
Degussa-Hüls AG, 32 (upd.)
DeKalb Genetics Corporation, 17
The Dexter Corporation, I; 12 (upd.)
Dionex Corporation, 46
The Dow Chemical Company, I; 8 (upd.);
  50 (upd.)
DSM N.V., I; 56 (upd.)
Dynaction S.A., 67
E.I. du Pont de Nemours & Company, I; 8
  (upd.); 26 (upd.)
Eastman Chemical Company, 14; 38 (upd.)
Ecolab Inc., I; 13 (upd.); 34 (upd.)
Elementis plc, 40 (upd.)
Engelhard Corporation, 72 (upd.)
English China Clays Ltd., 15 (upd.); 40
  (upd.)
Enterprise Rent-A-Car Company, 69 (upd.)
Equistar Chemicals, LP, 71
ERLY Industries Inc., 17
Ethyl Corporation, I; 10 (upd.)
Ferro Corporation, 8; 56 (upd.)
Firmenich International S.A., 60
First Mississippi Corporation, 8
Formosa Plastics Corporation, 14; 58
  (upd.)
Fort James Corporation, 22 (upd.)
G.A.F., I
The General Chemical Group Inc., 37
Georgia Gulf Corporation, 9; 61 (upd.)
Givaudan SA, 43
Great Lakes Chemical Corporation, I; 14
  (upd.)
Guerbet Group, 46
H.B. Fuller Company, 32 (upd.)
Hauser, Inc., 46
Hawkins Chemical, Inc., 16

CHEMICALS (*continued*)

Henkel KGaA, 34 (upd.)
Hercules Inc., I; 22 (upd.); 66 (upd.)
Hoechst A.G., I; 18 (upd.)
Hoechst Celanese Corporation, 13
Huls A.G., I
Huntsman Chemical Corporation, 8
IMC Fertilizer Group, Inc., 8
Imperial Chemical Industries PLC, I; 50 (upd.)
International Flavors & Fragrances Inc., 9; 38 (upd.)
Israel Chemicals Ltd., 55
Kemira Oyj, 70
Koppers Industries, Inc., I; 26 (upd.)
L'Air Liquide SA, I; 47 (upd.)
Lawter International Inc., 14
LeaRonal, Inc., 23
Loctite Corporation, 30 (upd.)
Lubrizol Corporation, I; 30 (upd.)
Lyondell Chemical Company, 45 (upd.)
M.A. Hanna Company, 8
MacDermid Incorporated, 32
Mallinckrodt Group Inc., 19
MBC Holding Company, 40
Melamine Chemicals, Inc., 27
Methanex Corporation, 40
Minerals Technologies Inc., 52 (upd.)
Mississippi Chemical Corporation, 39
Mitsubishi Chemical Corporation, I; 56 (upd.)
Mitsui Petrochemical Industries, Ltd., 9
Monsanto Company, I; 9 (upd.); 29 (upd.)
Montedison SpA, I
Morton International Inc., 9 (upd.)
Morton Thiokol, Inc., I
Nagase & Company, Ltd., 8
Nalco Chemical Corporation, I; 12 (upd.)
National Distillers and Chemical Corporation, I
National Sanitary Supply Co., 16
National Starch and Chemical Company, 49
NCH Corporation, 8
Nisshin Seifun Group Inc., 66 (upd.)
NL Industries, Inc., 10
Nobel Industries AB, 9
NOF Corporation, 72
Norsk Hydro ASA, 35 (upd.)
Novacor Chemicals Ltd., 12
NutraSweet Company, 8
Occidental Petroleum Corporation, 71 (upd.)
Olin Corporation, I; 13 (upd.)
OM Group, Inc., 17
OMNOVA Solutions Inc., 59
Penford Corporation, 55
Pennwalt Corporation, I
Perstorp AB, I; 51 (upd.)
Petrolite Corporation, 15
Pioneer Hi-Bred International, Inc., 41 (upd.)
Praxair, Inc., 11
Quantum Chemical Corporation, 8
Reichhold Chemicals, Inc., 10
Rhodia SA, 38
Rhône-Poulenc S.A., I; 10 (upd.)
Robertet SA, 39
Rohm and Haas Company, I; 26 (upd.)
Roussel Uclaf, I; 8 (upd.)
RPM, Inc., 36 (upd.)
RWE AG, 50 (upd.)
The Scotts Company, 22
SCP Pool Corporation, 39
Sequa Corp., 13
Shanghai Petrochemical Co., Ltd., 18
Sigma-Aldrich Corporation, 36 (upd.)

Solutia Inc., 52
Solvay S.A., I; 21 (upd.); 61 (upd.)
Stepan Company, 30
Sterling Chemicals, Inc., 16
Sumitomo Chemical Company Ltd., I
Takeda Chemical Industries, Ltd., 46 (upd.)
Terra Industries, Inc., 13
Teva Pharmaceutical Industries Ltd., 22
Tosoh Corporation, 70
Total Fina Elf S.A., 24 (upd.); 50 (upd.)
Ube Industries, Ltd., 38 (upd.)
Union Carbide Corporation, I; 9 (upd.)
United Industries Corporation, 68
Univar Corporation, 9
The Valspar Corporation, 32 (upd.)
Vista Chemical Company, I
Witco Corporation, I; 16 (upd.)
Yule Catto & Company plc, 54
Zeneca Group PLC, 21

CONGLOMERATES

A.P. Møller - Maersk A/S, 57
Accor SA, 10; 27 (upd.)
AEG A.G., I
Alcatel Alsthom Compagnie Générale d'Electricité, 9
Alco Standard Corporation, I
Alexander & Baldwin, Inc., 40 (upd.)
Alfa, S.A. de C.V., 19
Alleghany Corporation, 60 (upd.)
Allied Domecq PLC, 29
Allied-Signal Inc., I
AMFAC Inc., I
The Anschutz Corporation, 36 (upd.)
Antofagasta plc, 65
APi Group, Inc., 64
Aramark Corporation, 13
ARAMARK Corporation, 41
Archer-Daniels-Midland Company, I; 11 (upd.)
Arkansas Best Corporation, 16
Associated British Ports Holdings Plc, 45
BAA plc, 33 (upd.)
Barlow Rand Ltd., I
Barratt Developments plc, 56 (upd.)
Bat Industries PLC, I
Berjaya Group Bhd., 67
Berkshire Hathaway Inc., 42 (upd.)
Bond Corporation Holdings Limited, 10
Brascan Corporation, 67
BTR PLC, I
Bunzl plc, 31 (upd.)
Burlington Northern Santa Fe Corporation, 27 (upd.)
Business Post Group plc, 46
C. Itoh & Company Ltd., I
C.I. Traders Limited, 61
Cargill, Incorporated, 13 (upd.); 40 (upd.)
CBI Industries, Inc., 7
Charoen Pokphand Group, 62
Chemed Corporation, 13
Chesebrough-Pond's USA, Inc., 8
China Merchants International Holdings Co., Ltd., 52
Cisneros Group of Companies, 54
CITIC Pacific Ltd., 18
CJ Corporation, 62
Colgate-Palmolive Company, 71 (upd.)
Colt Industries Inc., I
Compagnie Financiere Richemont AG, 50
The Connell Company, 29
Cox Enterprises, Inc., 67 (upd.)
Cristalerias de Chile S.A., 67
CSR Limited, 28 (upd.)
Daewoo Group, 18 (upd.); 57 (upd.)
Dallah Albaraka Group, 72
De Dietrich & Cie., 31

Deere & Company, 21 (upd.)
Delaware North Companies Incorporated, 7
Desc, S.A. de C.V., 23
The Dial Corp., 8
Dr. August Oetker KG, 51
EBSCO Industries, Inc., 40 (upd.)
El Corte Inglés Group, 26 (upd.)
Elders IXL Ltd., I
Empresas Copec S.A., 69
Engelhard Corporation, 21 (upd.); 72 (upd.)
Farley Northwest Industries, Inc., I
Fimalac S.A., 37
First Pacific Company Limited, 18
Fisher Companies, Inc., 15
Fletcher Challenge Ltd., 19 (upd.)
Florida East Coast Industries, Inc., 59
FMC Corporation, I; 11 (upd.)
Fortune Brands, Inc., 29 (upd.); 68 (upd.)
Fraser & Neave Ltd., 54
Fuqua Industries, Inc., I
General Electric Company, 34 (upd.); 63 (upd.)
Genting Bhd., 65
GIB Group, 26 (upd.)
Gillett Holdings, Inc., 7
The Gillette Company, 68 (upd.)
Granaria Holdings B.V., 66
Grand Metropolitan PLC, 14 (upd.)
Great American Management and Investment, Inc., 8
Greyhound Corporation, I
Groupe Bolloré, 67
Groupe Louis Dreyfus S.A., 60
Grupo Carso, S.A. de C.V., 21
Grupo Clarín S.A., 67
Grupo Industrial Bimbo, 19
Grupo Industrial Saltillo, S.A. de C.V., 54
Gulf & Western Inc., I
Haci Omer Sabanci Holdings A.S., 55
Hagemeyer N.V., 39
Hankyu Corporation, 23 (upd.)
Hanson PLC, III; 7 (upd.)
Hanwha Group, 62
Hawk Corporation, 59
Hitachi Zosen Corporation, 53 (upd.)
Hitachi, Ltd., I; 12 (upd.); 40 (upd.)
Ho-Chunk Inc., 61
Hutchison Whampoa Limited, 18; 49 (upd.)
Hyundai Group, 56 (upd.)
IC Industries, Inc., I
Ilitch Holdings Inc., 37
Inchcape PLC, 16 (upd.); 50 (upd.)
Industria de Diseño Textil S.A. (Inditex), 64
Industrie Zignago Santa Margherita S.p.A., 67
Ingram Industries, Inc., 11; 49 (upd.)
Instituto Nacional de Industria, I
International Controls Corporation, 10
International Telephone & Telegraph Corporation, I; 11 (upd.)
Investor AB, 63
Istituto per la Ricostruzione Industriale, I
ITOCHU Corporation, 32 (upd.)
J.R. Simplot Company, 60 (upd.)
Jardine Matheson Holdings Limited, I; 20 (upd.)
Jason Incorporated, 23
Jefferson Smurfit Group plc, 19 (upd.)
The Jim Pattison Group, 37
Jordan Industries, Inc., 36
Justin Industries, Inc., 19
Kanematsu Corporation, 24 (upd.)
Kao Corporation, 20 (upd.)
Katy Industries, Inc., I
Kesko Ltd. (Kesko Oy), 8; 27 (upd.)

Kidde plc, I; 44 (upd.)
King Ranch, Inc., 60 (upd.)
Knowledge Universe, Inc., 54
Koç Holding A.S., I; 54 (upd.)
Koninklijke Nedlloyd N.V., 26 (upd.)
Koor Industries Ltd., 25 (upd.); 68 (upd.)
Körber AG, 60
K2 Inc., 16
The L.L. Knickerbocker Co., Inc., 25
Lancaster Colony Corporation, 8; 61 (upd.)
Larry H. Miller Group, 29
Lear Siegler, Inc., I
Lefrak Organization Inc., 26
Leucadia National Corporation, 11; 71 (upd.)
Linde AG, 67 (upd.)
Litton Industries, Inc., I; 11 (upd.)
Loews Corporation, I; 12 (upd.); 36 (upd.)
Loral Corporation, 8
LTV Corporation, I
LVMH Moët Hennessy Louis Vuitton SA, 33 (upd.)
The Marmon Group, Inc., 70 (upd.)
Marubeni Corporation, I; 24 (upd.)
MAXXAM Inc., 8
McKesson Corporation, I
McPherson's Ltd., 66
Melitta Unternehmensgruppe Bentz KG, 53
Menasha Corporation, 8
Metallgesellschaft AG, 16 (upd.)
Metromedia Company, 7; 61 (upd.)
Minnesota Mining & Manufacturing Company (3M), I; 8 (upd.); 26 (upd.)
Mitsubishi Corporation, I; 12 (upd.)
Mitsubishi Heavy Industries, Ltd., 40 (upd.)
Mitsui & Co., Ltd., I; 28 (upd.)
The Molson Companies Limited, I; 26 (upd.)
Montedison S.p.A., 24 (upd.)
NACCO Industries, Inc., 7
Nagase & Co., Ltd., 61 (upd.)
National Service Industries, Inc., 11; 54 (upd.)
New World Development Company Limited, 38 (upd.)
Nichimen Corporation, 24 (upd.)
Nichirei Corporation, 70
Nissho Iwai K.K., I
Norsk Hydro A.S., 10
Novar plc, 49 (upd.)
Ogden Corporation, I
Onex Corporation, 16; 65 (upd.)
Orkla A/S, 18
Park-Ohio Industries Inc., 17
Pentair, Inc., 7
Petrobras Energia Participaciones S.A., 72
Philip Morris Companies Inc., 44 (upd.)
Poliet S.A., 33
Powell Duffryn plc, 31
Power Corporation of Canada, 36 (upd.)
PPB Group Berhad, 57
Preussag AG, 17
The Procter & Gamble Company, 67 (upd.)
PT Astra International Tbk, 56
Pubco Corporation, 17
Pulsar Internacional S.A., 21
R.B. Pamplin Corp., 45
The Rank Organisation Plc, 14 (upd.)
Red Apple Group, Inc., 23
Roll International Corporation, 37
Rubbermaid Incorporated, 20 (upd.)
Samsung Group, I
San Miguel Corporation, 15
Sara Lee Corporation, 15 (upd.); 54 (upd.)
Schindler Holding AG, 29
Sea Containers Ltd., 29

Seaboard Corporation, 36
Sealaska Corporation, 60
Sequa Corporation, 54 (upd.)
ServiceMaster Inc., 23 (upd.)
SHV Holdings N.V., 55
Sideco Americana S.A., 67
Sime Darby Berhad, 14; 36 (upd.)
Société du Louvre, 27
Standex International Corporation, 17; 44 (upd.)
Stinnes AG, 23 (upd.)
Sudbury Inc., 16
Sumitomo Corporation, I; 11 (upd.)
Swire Pacific Limited, I; 16 (upd.); 57 (upd.)
Talley Industries, Inc., 16
Tandycrafts, Inc., 31
TaurusHolding GmbH & Co. KG, 46
Teijin Limited, 61 (upd.)
Teledyne, Inc., I; 10 (upd.)
Tenneco Inc., I; 10 (upd.)
Textron Inc., I; 34 (upd.)
Thomas H. Lee Co., 24
Thorn Emi PLC, I
Thorn plc, 24
TI Group plc, 17
Time Warner Inc., IV; 7 (upd.)
Tokyu Corporation, 47 (upd.)
Tomen Corporation, 24 (upd.)
Tomkins plc, 11; 44 (upd.)
Toshiba Corporation, I; 12 (upd.); 40 (upd.)
Tractebel S.A., 20
Transamerica—An AEGON Company, I; 13 (upd.); 41 (upd.)
The Tranzonic Cos., 15
Triarc Companies, Inc., 8
Triple Five Group Ltd., 49
TRW Inc., I; 11 (upd.)
Tyco International Ltd., 63 (upd.)
Unilever, II; 7 (upd.); 32 (upd.)
Unión Fenosa, S.A., 51
United Technologies Corporation, 34 (upd.)
Universal Studios, Inc., 33
Valhi, Inc., 19
Valores Industriales S.A., 19
Veba A.G., I; 15 (upd.)
Vendôme Luxury Group plc, 27
Viacom Inc., 23 (upd.); 67 (upd.)
Virgin Group, 12; 32 (upd.)
W.R. Grace & Company, I; 50
Walter Industries, Inc., 72 (upd.)
The Washington Companies, 33
Watsco Inc., 52
Wheaton Industries, 8
Whitbread PLC, 20 (upd.)
Whitman Corporation, 10 (upd.)
Whittaker Corporation, I
Wirtz Corporation, 72
WorldCorp, Inc., 10
Worms et Cie, 27
Yamaha Corporation, 40 (upd.)

CONSTRUCTION

A. Johnson & Company H.B., I
ABC Supply Co., Inc., 22
Abertis Infraestructuras, S.A., 65
Abrams Industries Inc., 23
Aegek S.A., 64
Amec Spie S.A., 57
AMREP Corporation, 21
Anthony & Sylvan Pools Corporation, 56
Asplundh Tree Expert Co., 59 (upd.)
ASV, Inc., 34; 66 (upd.)
The Austin Company, 8
Autoroutes du Sud de la France SA, 55
Balfour Beatty plc, 36 (upd.)

Baratt Developments PLC, I
Barton Malow Company, 51
Bauerly Companies, 61
Beazer Homes USA, Inc., 17
Bechtel Group, Inc., I; 24 (upd.)
Bellway Plc, 45
BFC Construction Corporation, 25
Bilfinger & Berger AG, I; 55 (upd.)
Bird Corporation, 19
Black & Veatch LLP, 22
Boral Limited, 43 (upd.)
Bouygues S.A., I; 24 (upd.)
The Branch Group, Inc., 72
BRISA Auto-estradas de Portugal S.A., 64
Brown & Root, Inc., 13
Bufete Industrial, S.A. de C.V., 34
Building Materials Holding Corporation, 52
Bulley & Andrews, LLC, 55
CalMat Co., 19
Cavco Industries, Inc., 65
Centex Corporation, 8; 29 (upd.)
Chugach Alaska Corporation, 60
Cianbro Corporation, 14
The Clark Construction Group, Inc., 8
Colas S.A., 31
D.R. Horton, Inc., 58
Day & Zimmermann, Inc., 31 (upd.)
Dick Corporation, 64
Dillingham Construction Corporation, I; 44 (upd.)
Dominion Homes, Inc., 19
The Drees Company, Inc., 41
Dycom Industries, Inc., 57
E.W. Howell Co., Inc., 72
Edw. C. Levy Co., 42
Eiffage, 27
Ellerbe Becket, 41
EMCOR Group Inc., 60
Empresas ICA Sociedad Controladora, S.A. de C.V., 41
Encompass Services Corporation, 33
Engle Homes, Inc., 46
Environmental Industries, Inc., 31
Eurotunnel PLC, 13
Fairclough Construction Group PLC, I
Fleetwood Enterprises, Inc., 22 (upd.)
Fluor Corporation, I; 8 (upd.); 34 (upd.)
Forest City Enterprises, Inc., 52 (upd.)
Fred Weber, Inc., 61
George Wimpey plc, 12; 51 (upd.)
Gilbane, Inc., 34
Granite Construction Incorporated, 61
Granite Rock Company, 26
Great Lakes Dredge & Dock Company, 69
Grupo Dragados SA, 55
Grupo Ferrovial, S.A., 40
H.J. Russell & Company, 66
Habitat for Humanity International, 36
Heery International, Inc., 58
Heijmans N.V., 66
Hensel Phelps Construction Company, 72
Hillsdown Holdings plc, 24 (upd.)
Hochtief AG, 33
Horton Homes, Inc., 25
Hospitality Worldwide Services, Inc., 26
Hovnanian Enterprises, Inc., 29
IHC Caland N.V., 71
J.A. Jones, Inc., 16
J.F. Shea Co., Inc., 55
J.H. Findorff and Son, Inc., 60
Jarvis plc, 39
JLG Industries, Inc., 52
John Brown PLC, I
John Laing plc, I; 51 (upd.)
John W. Danforth Company, 48
Kajima Corporation, I; 51 (upd.)
Kaufman and Broad Home Corporation, 8

CONSTRUCTION (*continued*)

KB Home, 45 (upd.)
Kellogg Brown & Root, Inc., 62 (upd.)
Kitchell Corporation, 14
The Koll Company, 8
Komatsu Ltd., 16 (upd.)
Kraus-Anderson, Incorporated, 36
Kumagai Gumi Company, Ltd., I
L'Entreprise Jean Lefebvre, 23
Ledcor Industries Limited, 46
Lennar Corporation, 11
Lincoln Property Company, 8
Lindal Cedar Homes, Inc., 29
Linde A.G., I
MasTec, Inc., 55
Matrix Service Company, 65
McCarthy Building Companies, Inc., 48
Mellon-Stuart Company, I
Michael Baker Corp., 14
Morrison Knudsen Corporation, 7; 28
   (upd.)
New Holland N.V., 22
Newpark Resources, Inc., 63
NVR Inc., 70 (upd.)
NVR L.P., 8
Ohbayashi Corporation, I
Opus Group, 34
Orleans Homebuilders, Inc., 62
The Parsons Corporation, 56 (upd.)
PCL Construction Group Inc., 50
The Peninsular & Oriental Steam
   Navigation Company (Bovis Division), I
Perini Corporation, 8
Peter Kiewit Sons' Inc., 8
Philipp Holzmann AG, 17
Post Properties, Inc., 26
Pulte Homes, Inc., 8; 42 (upd.)
Pyramid Companies, 54
Redrow Group plc, 31
Rinker Group Ltd., 65
RMC Group p.l.c., 34 (upd.)
Rooney Brothers Co., 25
The Rottlund Company, Inc., 28
The Ryland Group, Inc., 8; 37 (upd.)
Sandvik AB, 32 (upd.)
Schuff Steel Company, 26
Seddon Group Ltd., 67
Shorewood Packaging Corporation, 28
Simon Property Group, Inc., 27
Skanska AB, 38
Skidmore, Owings & Merrill LLP, 69
   (upd.)
SNC-Lavalin Group Inc., 72
Standard Pacific Corporation, 52
Stone & Webster, Inc., 64 (upd.)
Sundt Corp., 24
Swinerton Inc., 43
Taylor Woodrow plc, I; 38 (upd.)
Thyssen Krupp AG, 28 (upd.)
Toll Brothers Inc., 15; 70 (upd.)
Trammell Crow Company, 8
Tridel Enterprises Inc., 9
Turner Construction Company, 66
The Turner Corporation, 8; 23 (upd.)
U.S. Aggregates, Inc., 42
U.S. Home Corporation, 8
VA TECH ELIN EBG GmbH, 49
Veit Companies, 43
Walbridge Aldinger Co., 38
Walter Industries, Inc., 22 (upd.)
The Weitz Company, Inc., 42
Willbros Group, Inc., 56
William Lyon Homes, 59
Wilson Bowden Plc, 45
Wood Hall Trust PLC, I
The Yates Companies, Inc., 62

CONTAINERS

Ball Corporation, I; 10 (upd.)
BWAY Corporation, 24
Clarcor Inc., 17
Continental Can Co., Inc., 15
Continental Group Company, I
Crown Cork & Seal Company, Inc., I; 13
   (upd.); 32 (upd.)
Gaylord Container Corporation, 8
Golden Belt Manufacturing Co., 16
Greif Inc., 15; 66 (upd.)
Grupo Industrial Durango, S.A. de C.V.,
   37
Hanjin Shipping Co., Ltd., 50
Inland Container Corporation, 8
Kerr Group Inc., 24
Keyes Fibre Company, 9
Libbey Inc., 49
Liqui-Box Corporation, 16
The Longaberger Company, 12
Longview Fibre Company, 8
The Mead Corporation, 19 (upd.)
Metal Box PLC, I
Molins plc, 51
National Can Corporation, I
Owens-Illinois, Inc., I; 26 (upd.)
Packaging Corporation of America, 51
   (upd.)
Primerica Corporation, I
PVC Container Corporation, 67
Reynolds Metals Company, 19 (upd.)
Royal Packaging Industries Van Leer N.V.,
   30
Sealright Co., Inc., 17
Shurgard Storage Centers, Inc., 52
Smurfit-Stone Container Corporation, 26
   (upd.)
Sonoco Products Company, 8
Thermos Company, 16
Toyo Seikan Kaisha, Ltd., I
U.S. Can Corporation, 30
Ultra Pac, Inc., 24
Viatech Continental Can Company, Inc., 25
   (upd.)
Vidrala S.A., 67
Vitro Corporativo S.A. de C.V., 34

DRUGS/PHARMACEUTICALS

A.L. Pharma Inc., 12
Abbott Laboratories, I; 11 (upd.); 40 (upd.)
Akorn, Inc., 32
Alpharma Inc., 35 (upd.)
ALZA Corporation, 10; 36 (upd.)
American Home Products, I; 10 (upd.)
American Pharmaceutical Partners, Inc., 69
AmerisourceBergen Corporation, 64 (upd.)
Amersham PLC, 50
Amgen, Inc., 10
Amylin Pharmaceuticals, Inc., 67
Andrx Corporation, 55
Astra AB, I; 20 (upd.)
AstraZeneca PLC, 50 (upd.)
Barr Pharmaceuticals, Inc., 26; 68 (upd.)
Bayer A.G., I; 13 (upd.)
Berlex Laboratories, Inc., 66
Biovail Corporation, 47
Block Drug Company, Inc., 8
Bristol-Myers Squibb Company, III; 9
   (upd.); 37 (upd.)
C.H. Boehringer Sohn, 39
Caremark Rx, Inc., 10; 54 (upd.)
Carter-Wallace, Inc., 8; 38 (upd.)
Celgene Corporation, 67
Cephalon, Inc., 45
Chiron Corporation, 10
Chugai Pharmaceutical Co., Ltd., 50
Ciba-Geigy Ltd., I; 8 (upd.)

D&K Wholesale Drug, Inc., 14
Discovery Partners International, Inc., 58
Dr. Reddy's Laboratories Ltd., 59
Elan Corporation PLC, 63
Eli Lilly and Company, I; 11 (upd.); 47
   (upd.)
Endo Pharmaceuticals Holdings Inc., 71
Eon Labs, Inc., 67
Express Scripts Inc., 44 (upd.)
F. Hoffmann-La Roche Ltd., I; 50 (upd.)
Fisons plc, 9; 23 (upd.)
Forest Laboratories, Inc., 52 (upd.)
FoxMeyer Health Corporation, 16
Fujisawa Pharmaceutical Company Ltd., I
G.D. Searle & Co., I; 12 (upd.); 34 (upd.)
GEHE AG, 27
Genentech, Inc., I; 8 (upd.)
Genetics Institute, Inc., 8
Genzyme Corporation, 13
Glaxo Holdings PLC, I; 9 (upd.)
GlaxoSmithKline plc, 46 (upd.)
Groupe Fournier SA, 44
H. Lundbeck A/S, 44
Hauser, Inc., 46
Heska Corporation, 39
Hexal AG, 69
Hospira, Inc., 71
Huntingdon Life Sciences Group plc, 42
ICN Pharmaceuticals, Inc., 52
IVAX Corporation, 55 (upd.)
Johnson & Johnson, III; 8 (upd.)
Jones Medical Industries, Inc., 24
The Judge Group, Inc., 51
King Pharmaceuticals, Inc., 54
Kos Pharmaceuticals, Inc., 63
Kyowa Hakko Kogyo Co., Ltd., 48 (upd.)
Leiner Health Products Inc., 34
Ligand Pharmaceuticals Incorporated, 47
Marion Merrell Dow, Inc., I; 9 (upd.)
McKesson Corporation, 12; 47 (upd.)
Medicis Pharmaceutical Corporation, 59
MedImmune, Inc., 35
Merck & Co., Inc., I; 11 (upd.)
Miles Laboratories, I
Millennium Pharmaceuticals, Inc., 47
Monsanto Company, 29 (upd.)
Moore Medical Corp., 17
Murdock Madaus Schwabe, 26
Mylan Laboratories Inc., I; 20 (upd.); 59
   (upd.)
National Patent Development Corporation,
   13
Natrol, Inc., 49
Natural Alternatives International, Inc., 49
Novartis AG, 39 (upd.)
Noven Pharmaceuticals, Inc., 55
Novo Nordisk A/S, I; 61 (upd.)
Omnicare, Inc., 49
Par Pharmaceutical Companies, Inc., 65
Perrigo Company, 59 (upd.)
Pfizer Inc., I; 9 (upd.); 38 (upd.)
Pharmacia & Upjohn Inc., I; 25 (upd.)
PLIVA d.d., 70
QLT Inc., 71
The Quigley Corporation, 62
Quintiles Transnational Corporation, 21
R.P. Scherer, I
Ranbaxy Laboratories Ltd., 70
Roberts Pharmaceutical Corporation, 16
Roche Bioscience, 14 (upd.)
Rorer Group, I
Roussel Uclaf, I; 8 (upd.)
Sandoz Ltd., I
Sankyo Company, Ltd., I; 56 (upd.)
The Sanofi-Synthélabo Group, I; 49 (upd.)
Schering AG, I; 50 (upd.)

Schering-Plough Corporation, I; 14 (upd.); 49 (upd.)
Sepracor Inc., 45
Serono S.A., 47
Shionogi & Co., Ltd., 17 (upd.)
Sigma-Aldrich Corporation, I; 36 (upd.)
SmithKline Beecham plc, I; 32 (upd.)
Solvay S.A., 61 (upd.)
Squibb Corporation, I
Sterling Drug, Inc., I
Sun Pharmaceutical Industries Ltd., 57
The Sunrider Corporation, 26
Syntex Corporation, I
Takeda Chemical Industries, Ltd., I
Taro Pharmaceutical Industries Ltd., 65
Teva Pharmaceutical Industries Ltd., 22; 54 (upd.)
The Upjohn Company, I; 8 (upd.)
Vitalink Pharmacy Services, Inc., 15
Warner-Lambert Co., I; 10 (upd.)
Watson Pharmaceuticals Inc., 16; 56 (upd.)
The Wellcome Foundation Ltd., I
Zila, Inc., 46

ELECTRICAL & ELECTRONICS

ABB ASEA Brown Boveri Ltd., II; 22 (upd.)
ABB Ltd., 65 (upd.)
Acer Inc., 16
Acuson Corporation, 10; 36 (upd.)
ADC Telecommunications, Inc., 30 (upd.)
Adtran Inc., 22
Advanced Micro Devices, Inc., 30 (upd.)
Advanced Technology Laboratories, Inc., 9
Agere Systems Inc., 61
Agilent Technologies Inc., 38
Aiwa Co., Ltd., 30
AKG Acoustics GmbH, 62
Akzo Nobel N.V., 41 (upd.)
Alliant Techsystems Inc., 30 (upd.)
AlliedSignal Inc., 22 (upd.)
Alpine Electronics, Inc., 13
Alps Electric Co., Ltd., II
Altera Corporation, 18; 43 (upd.)
Altron Incorporated, 20
Amdahl Corporation, 40 (upd.)
American Power Conversion Corporation, 24; 67 (upd.)
American Technical Ceramics Corp., 67
Amkor Technology, Inc., 69
AMP Incorporated, II; 14 (upd.)
Amphenol Corporation, 40
Amstrad plc, 48 (upd.)
Analog Devices, Inc., 10
Analogic Corporation, 23
Anam Group, 23
Anaren Microwave, Inc., 33
Andrew Corporation, 10; 32 (upd.)
Anritsu Corporation, 68
Apex Digital, Inc., 63
Apple Computer, Inc., 36 (upd.)
Applied Power Inc., 32 (upd.)
Arrow Electronics, Inc., 10; 50 (upd.)
Ascend Communications, Inc., 24
Astronics Corporation, 35
Atari Corporation, 9; 23 (upd.); 66 (upd.)
Atmel Corporation, 17
AU Optronics Corporation, 67
Audiovox Corporation, 34
Ault Incorporated, 34
Autodesk, Inc., 10
Avnet Inc., 9
AVX Corporation, 67
Bang & Olufsen Holding A/S, 37
Barco NV, 44
Bell Microproducts Inc., 69
Benchmark Electronics, Inc., 40

Bicoastal Corporation, II
Blonder Tongue Laboratories, Inc., 48
BMC Industries, Inc., 59 (upd.)
Bogen Communications International, Inc., 62
Bose Corporation, 13; 36 (upd.)
Boston Acoustics, Inc., 22
Bowthorpe plc, 33
Braun GmbH, 51
Broadcom Corporation, 34
Bull S.A., 43 (upd.)
Burr-Brown Corporation, 19
C-COR.net Corp., 38
Cabletron Systems, Inc., 10
Cadence Design Systems, Inc., 48 (upd.)
Cambridge SoundWorks, Inc., 48
Canon Inc., 18 (upd.)
Carbone Lorraine S.A., 33
Carl-Zeiss-Stiftung, 34 (upd.)
CASIO Computer Co., Ltd., 16 (upd.); 40 (upd.)
CDW Computer Centers, Inc., 52 (upd.)
Checkpoint Systems, Inc., 39
Chubb, PLC, 50
Cirrus Logic, Inc., 48 (upd.)
Cisco Systems, Inc., 34 (upd.)
Citizen Watch Co., Ltd., 21 (upd.)
Clarion Company Ltd., 64
Cobham plc, 30
Cobra Electronics Corporation, 14
Coherent, Inc., 31
Cohu, Inc., 32
Compagnie Générale d'Électricité, II
Conexant Systems, Inc., 36
Cooper Industries, Inc., II
Cray Research, Inc., 16 (upd.)
Cree Inc., 53
CTS Corporation, 39
Cubic Corporation, 19
Cypress Semiconductor Corporation, 20; 48 (upd.)
Dai Nippon Printing Co., Ltd., 57 (upd.)
Daktronics, Inc., 32
Dallas Semiconductor Corporation, 13; 31 (upd.)
De La Rue plc, 34 (upd.)
Dell Computer Corporation, 31 (upd.)
DH Technology, Inc., 18
Digi International Inc., 9
Discreet Logic Inc., 20
Dixons Group plc, 19 (upd.)
Dolby Laboratories Inc., 20
DRS Technologies, Inc., 58
Dynatech Corporation, 13
E-Systems, Inc., 9
Electronics for Imaging, Inc., 15; 43 (upd.)
Emerson, II; 46 (upd.)
Emerson Radio Corp., 30
ENCAD, Incorporated, 25
Equant N.V., 52
Equus Computer Systems, Inc., 49
ESS Technology, Inc., 22
Everex Systems, Inc., 16
Exabyte Corporation, 40 (upd.)
Exar Corp., 14
Exide Electronics Group, Inc., 20
Fisk Corporation, 72
Flextronics International Ltd., 38
Fluke Corporation, 15
Foxboro Company, 13
Frequency Electronics, Inc., 61
Fuji Electric Co., Ltd., II; 48 (upd.)
Fujitsu Limited, 16 (upd.); 42 (upd.)
Funai Electric Company Ltd., 62
Gateway, Inc., 63 (upd.)
General Atomics, 57
General Dynamics Corporation, 40 (upd.)

General Electric Company, II; 12 (upd.)
General Electric Company, PLC, II
General Instrument Corporation, 10
General Signal Corporation, 9
GenRad, Inc., 24
GM Hughes Electronics Corporation, II
Goldstar Co., Ltd., 12
Gould Electronics, Inc., 14
Grundig AG, 27
Guillemot Corporation, 41
Hadco Corporation, 24
Hamilton Beach/Proctor-Silex Inc., 17
Harman International Industries Inc., 15
Harris Corporation, II; 20 (upd.)
Hayes Corporation, 24
Herley Industries, Inc., 33
Hewlett-Packard Company, 28 (upd.); 50 (upd.)
Holophane Corporation, 19
Hon Hai Precision Industry Co., Ltd., 59
Honeywell Inc., II; 12 (upd.); 50 (upd.)
Hubbell Incorporated, 9; 31 (upd.)
Hughes Supply, Inc., 14
Hutchinson Technology Incorporated, 18; 63 (upd.)
Hypercom Corporation, 27
IDEO Inc., 65
IEC Electronics Corp., 42
Imax Corporation, 28
In Focus Systems, Inc., 22
Indigo NV, 26
Ingram Micro Inc., 52
Integrated Defense Technologies, Inc., 54
Intel Corporation, II; 10 (upd.)
Intermec Technologies Corporation, 72
International Business Machines Corporation, III; 6 (upd.); 30 (upd.); 63 (upd.)
International Rectifier Corporation, 31; 71 (upd.)
Itel Corporation, 9
Jabil Circuit, Inc., 36
Jaco Electronics, Inc., 30
JDS Uniphase Corporation, 34
Johnson Controls, Inc., 59 (upd.)
Juno Lighting, Inc., 30
Katy Industries, Inc., 51 (upd.)
Keithley Instruments Inc., 16
Kemet Corp., 14
Kent Electronics Corporation, 17
Kenwood Corporation, 31
Kimball International, Inc., 48 (upd.)
Kingston Technology Corporation, 20
KitchenAid, 8
KLA-Tencor Corporation, 45 (upd.)
KnowledgeWare Inc., 9
Kollmorgen Corporation, 18
Konica Corporation, 30 (upd.)
Koninklijke Philips Electronics N.V., 50 (upd.)
Koor Industries Ltd., II
Koss Corporation, 38
Kudelski Group SA, 44
Kulicke and Soffa Industries, Inc., 33
Kyocera Corporation, II
LaBarge Inc., 41
The Lamson & Sessions Co., 61 (upd.)
Lattice Semiconductor Corp., 16
LeCroy Corporation, 41
Legrand SA, 21
Linear Technology, Inc., 16
Littelfuse, Inc., 26
Loral Corporation, 9
Lowrance Electronics, Inc., 18
LSI Logic Corporation, 13; 64
Lucent Technologies Inc., 34
Lucky-Goldstar, II

ELECTRICAL & ELECTRONICS
(*continued*)

Lunar Corporation, 29
Mackie Designs Inc., 33
MagneTek, Inc., 15; 41 (upd.)
Marconi plc, 33 (upd.)
Marquette Electronics, Inc., 13
Matsushita Electric Industrial Co., Ltd., II
Maxim Integrated Products, Inc., 16
Measurement Specialties, Inc., 71
Merix Corporation, 36
Methode Electronics, Inc., 13
Mitel Corporation, 18
MITRE Corporation, 26
Mitsubishi Electric Corporation, II; 44
(upd.)
Molex Incorporated, 54 (upd.)
Monster Cable Products, Inc., 69
Motorola, Inc., II; 11 (upd.); 34 (upd.)
N.F. Smith & Associates LP, 70
Nam Tai Electronics, Inc., 61
National Instruments Corporation, 22
National Presto Industries, Inc., 16; 43
(upd.)
National Semiconductor Corporation, II; 26
(upd.); 69 (upd.)
NEC Corporation, II; 21 (upd.); 57 (upd.)
Nexans SA, 54
Nintendo Co., Ltd., 28 (upd.)
Nokia Corporation, II; 17 (upd.); 38 (upd.)
Nortel Networks Corporation, 36 (upd.)
Northrop Grumman Corporation, 45 (upd.)
Oak Technology, Inc., 22
Oki Electric Industry Company, Limited, II
Omron Corporation, II; 28 (upd.)
Otter Tail Power Company, 18
Palm, Inc., 36
Palomar Medical Technologies, Inc., 22
Parlex Corporation, 61
The Peak Technologies Group, Inc., 14
Peavey Electronics Corporation, 16
Philips Electronics N.V., II; 13 (upd.)
Philips Electronics North America Corp.,
13
Pioneer Electronic Corporation, 28 (upd.)
Pioneer-Standard Electronics Inc., 19
Pitney Bowes Inc., 47 (upd.)
Pittway Corporation, 9
Pixelworks, Inc., 69
Planar Systems, Inc., 61
The Plessey Company, PLC, II
Plexus Corporation, 35
Polk Audio, Inc., 34
Potter & Brumfield Inc., 11
Premier Industrial Corporation, 9
Protection One, Inc., 32
Quanta Computer Inc., 47
Racal Electronics PLC, II
RadioShack Corporation, 36 (upd.)
Radius Inc., 16
Raychem Corporation, 8
Rayovac Corporation, 13
Raytheon Company, II; 11 (upd.); 38
(upd.)
RCA Corporation, II
Read-Rite Corp., 10
Reliance Electric Company, 9
Research in Motion Ltd., 54
Rexel, Inc., 15
Richardson Electronics, Ltd., 17
Ricoh Company, Ltd., 36 (upd.)
The Rival Company, 19
Rockford Corporation, 43
Rogers Corporation, 61
S&C Electric Company, 15
SAGEM S.A., 37
St. Louis Music, Inc., 48

Sam Ash Music Corporation, 30
Samsung Electronics Co., Ltd., 14; 41
(upd.)
SANYO Electric Co., Ltd., II; 36 (upd.)
Sarnoff Corporation, 57
ScanSource, Inc., 29
Schneider S.A., II; 18 (upd.)
SCI Systems, Inc., 9
Scientific-Atlanta, Inc., 45 (upd.)
Scitex Corporation Ltd., 24
Seagate Technology, Inc., 34 (upd.)
Semtech Corporation, 32
Sennheiser Electronic GmbH & Co. KG,
66
Sensormatic Electronics Corp., 11
Sensory Science Corporation, 37
SGI, 29 (upd.)
Sharp Corporation, II; 12 (upd.); 40 (upd.)
Sheldahl Inc., 23
Shure Inc., 60
Siemens AG, II; 14 (upd.); 57 (upd.)
Silicon Graphics Incorporated, 9
Smiths Industries PLC, 25
Solectron Corporation, 12; 48 (upd.)
Sony Corporation, II; 12 (upd.); 40 (upd.)
Spectrum Control, Inc., 67
SPX Corporation, 47 (upd.)
Sterling Electronics Corp., 18
STMicroelectronics NV, 52
Strix Ltd., 51
Stuart C. Irby Company, 58
Sumitomo Electric Industries, Ltd., II
Sun Microsystems, Inc., 30 (upd.)
Sunbeam-Oster Co., Inc., 9
Synopsys, Inc., 69 (upd.)
SyQuest Technology, Inc., 18
Tandy Corporation, II; 12 (upd.)
Tatung Co., 23
TDK Corporation, II; 17 (upd.); 49 (upd.)
Tech-Sym Corporation, 18
Technitrol, Inc., 29
Tektronix, Inc., 8
Teledyne Technologies Inc., 62 (upd.)
Telxon Corporation, 10
Teradyne, Inc., 11
Texas Instruments Inc., II; 11 (upd.); 46
(upd.)
Thales S.A., 42
Thomas & Betts Corporation, 54 (upd.)
THOMSON multimedia S.A., II; 42 (upd.)
The Titan Corporation, 36
Tops Appliance City, Inc., 17
Toromont Industries, Ltd., 21
Trans-Lux Corporation, 51
Trimble Navigation Limited, 40
TriQuint Semiconductor, Inc., 63
Tweeter Home Entertainment Group, Inc.,
30
Ultimate Electronics, Inc., 69 (upd.)
Ultrak Inc., 24
Universal Electronics Inc., 39
Varian Associates Inc., 12
Veeco Instruments Inc., 32
VIASYS Healthcare, Inc., 52
Viasystems Group, Inc., 67
Vicon Industries, Inc., 44
Victor Company of Japan, Limited, II; 26
(upd.)
Vishay Intertechnology, Inc., 21
Vitesse Semiconductor Corporation, 32
Vitro Corp., 10
VLSI Technology, Inc., 16
Wells-Gardner Electronics Corporation, 43
Westinghouse Electric Corporation, II; 12
(upd.)
Wincor Nixdorf Holding GmbH, 69 (upd.)
Wyle Electronics, 14

Xerox Corporation, 69 (upd.)
Yageo Corporation, 16
York Research Corporation, 35
Zenith Data Systems, Inc., 10
Zenith Electronics Corporation, II; 13
(upd.); 34 (upd.)
Zoom Telephonics, Inc., 18
Zumtobel AG, 50
Zytec Corporation, 19

ENGINEERING & MANAGEMENT SERVICES

AAON, Inc., 22
Aavid Thermal Technologies, Inc., 29
Alliant Techsystems Inc., 30 (upd.)
Altran Technologies, 51
Amey Plc, 47
Analytic Sciences Corporation, 10
Arcadis NV, 26
Arthur D. Little, Inc., 35
The Austin Company, 8; 72 (upd.)
Babcock International Group PLC, 69
Balfour Beatty plc, 36 (upd.)
Brown & Root, Inc., 13
Bufete Industrial, S.A. de C.V., 34
C.H. Heist Corporation, 24
CDI Corporation, 6
CH2M Hill Ltd., 22
The Charles Stark Draper Laboratory, Inc.,
35
Coflexip S.A., 25
Corrections Corporation of America, 23
CRSS Inc., 6
Dames & Moore, Inc., 25
DAW Technologies, Inc., 25
Day & Zimmermann Inc., 9; 31 (upd.)
Donaldson Co. Inc., 16
Dycom Industries, Inc., 57
Edwards and Kelcey, 70
EG&G Incorporated, 8; 29 (upd.)
Eiffage, 27
Essef Corporation, 18
FKI Plc, 57
Fluor Corporation, 34 (upd.)
Forest City Enterprises, Inc., 52 (upd.)
Foster Wheeler Corporation, 6; 23 (upd.)
Framatome SA, 19
Georg Fischer AG Schaffhausen, 61
Gilbane, Inc., 34
Great Lakes Dredge & Dock Company, 69
Grupo Dragados SA, 55
Halliburton Company, 25 (upd.)
Harding Lawson Associates Group, Inc., 16
Harza Engineering Company, 14
HDR Inc., 48
HOK Group, Inc., 59
ICF Kaiser International, Inc., 28
IHC Caland N.V., 71
Jacobs Engineering Group Inc., 6; 26
(upd.)
The Judge Group, Inc., 51
JWP Inc., 9
The Keith Companies Inc., 54
Klöckner-Werke AG, 58 (upd.)
Kvaerner ASA, 36
Layne Christensen Company, 19
The MacNeal-Schwendler Corporation, 25
Malcolm Pirnie, Inc., 42
McDermott International, Inc., 37 (upd.)
McKinsey & Company, Inc., 9
Michael Baker Corporation, 51 (upd.)
Nooter Corporation, 61
Oceaneering International, Inc., 63
Ogden Corporation, 6
Opus Group, 34
Parsons Brinckerhoff, Inc., 34
The Parsons Corporation, 8; 56 (upd.)

RCM Technologies, Inc., 34
Renishaw plc, 46
Rosemount Inc., 15
Roy F. Weston, Inc., 33
Royal Vopak NV, 41
Rust International Inc., 11
Sandia National Laboratories, 49
Sandvik AB, 32 (upd.)
Sarnoff Corporation, 57
Science Applications International
    Corporation, 15
Serco Group plc, 47
Siegel & Gale, 64
Siemens AG, 57 (upd.)
SRI International, Inc., 57
Stone & Webster, Inc., 13; 64 (upd.)
Sulzer Ltd., 68 (upd.)
Susquehanna Pfaltzgraff Company, 8
Sverdrup Corporation, 14
Tech-Sym Corporation, 44 (upd.)
Tetra Tech, Inc., 29
Thyssen Krupp AG, 28 (upd.)
Towers Perrin, 32
Tracor Inc., 17
TRC Companies, Inc., 32
Underwriters Laboratories, Inc., 30
United Dominion Industries Limited, 8; 16
    (upd.)
URS Corporation, 45
VA TECH ELIN EBG GmbH, 49
VECO International, Inc., 7
Vinci, 43
Willbros Group, Inc., 56
WS Atkins Plc, 45

ENTERTAINMENT & LEISURE

A&E Television Networks, 32
Aardman Animations Ltd., 61
ABC Family Worldwide, Inc., 52
Academy of Television Arts & Sciences,
    Inc., 55
Acclaim Entertainment Inc., 24
Activision, Inc., 32
AEI Music Network Inc., 35
Affinity Group Holding Inc., 56
Airtours Plc, 27
Alaska Railroad Corporation, 60
All American Communications Inc., 20
The All England Lawn Tennis & Croquet
    Club, 54
Alliance Entertainment Corp., 17
Alternative Tentacles Records, 66
Alvin Ailey Dance Foundation, Inc., 52
Amblin Entertainment, 21
AMC Entertainment Inc., 12; 35 (upd.)
American Golf Corporation, 45
American Gramaphone LLC, 52
American Skiing Company, 28
Ameristar Casinos, Inc., 33; 69 (upd.)
AMF Bowling, Inc., 40
Anaheim Angels Baseball Club, Inc., 53
Anchor Gaming, 24
AOL Time Warner Inc., 57 (upd.)
Applause Inc., 24
Aprilia SpA, 17
Argosy Gaming Company, 21
Aristocrat Leisure Limited, 54
The Art Institute of Chicago, 29
Artisan Entertainment Inc., 32 (upd.)
Asahi National Broadcasting Company,
    Ltd., 9
Aspen Skiing Company, 15
Aston Villa plc, 41
The Athletics Investment Group, 62
Atlanta National League Baseball Club,
    Inc., 43
The Atlantic Group, 23

Autotote Corporation, 20
Aztar Corporation, 13
Bad Boy Worldwide Entertainment Group,
    58
Baker & Taylor Corporation, 16; 43 (upd.)
Bally Total Fitness Holding Corp., 25
Baltimore Orioles L.P., 66
The Baseball Club of Seattle, LP, 50
The Basketball Club of Seattle, LLC, 50
Bertelsmann A.G., 15 (upd.); 43 (upd.)
Bertucci's Inc., 16
Big Idea Productions, Inc., 49
BigBen Interactive S.A., 72
Blockbuster Inc., 9; 31 (upd.)
Boca Resorts, Inc., 37
Bonneville International Corporation, 29
Booth Creek Ski Holdings, Inc., 31
Boston Celtics Limited Partnership, 14
Boston Professional Hockey Association
    Inc., 39
The Boy Scouts of America, 34
Boyne USA Resorts, 71
British Broadcasting Corporation Ltd., 7;
    21 (upd.)
The British Museum, 71
British Sky Broadcasting Group plc, 20; 60
    (upd.)
Cablevision Systems Corporation, 7
California Sports, Inc., 56
Callaway Golf Company, 45 (upd.)
Canterbury Park Holding Corporation, 42
Capital Cities/ABC Inc., II
Carlson Companies, Inc., 22 (upd.)
Carlson Wagonlit Travel, 55
Carmike Cinemas, Inc., 14; 37 (upd.)
Carnival Corporation, 6; 27 (upd.)
The Carsey-Werner Company, L.L.C., 37
CBS Inc., II; 6 (upd.)
Cedar Fair, L.P., 22
Central European Media Enterprises Ltd.,
    61
Central Independent Television, 7; 23
    (upd.)
Century Casinos, Inc., 53
Century Theatres, Inc., 31
Championship Auto Racing Teams, Inc.,
    37
Chicago Bears Football Club, Inc., 33
Chicago National League Ball Club, Inc.,
    66
Chris-Craft Industries, Inc., 31 (upd.)
Chrysalis Group plc, 40
Churchill Downs Incorporated, 29
Cinar Corporation, 40
Cineplex Odeon Corporation, 6; 23 (upd.)
Cinram International, Inc., 43
Cirque du Soleil Inc., 29
Classic Vacation Group, Inc., 46
Cleveland Indians Baseball Company, Inc.,
    37
ClubCorp, Inc., 33
Colonial Williamsburg Foundation, 53
Colorado Baseball Management, Inc., 72
Columbia Pictures Entertainment, Inc., II
Columbia TriStar Motion Pictures
    Companies, 12 (upd.)
Comcast Corporation, 7
Compagnie des Alpes, 48
Continental Cablevision, Inc., 7
Corporation for Public Broadcasting, 14
Cox Enterprises, Inc., 22 (upd.)
Cranium, Inc., 69
Crown Media Holdings, Inc., 45
Cruise America Inc., 21
Cunard Line Ltd., 23
Dallas Cowboys Football Club, Ltd., 33
Dave & Buster's, Inc., 33

Death Row Records, 27
Denver Nuggets, 51
The Detroit Lions, Inc., 55
The Detroit Pistons Basketball Company,
    41
Detroit Tigers Baseball Club, Inc., 46
dick clark productions, inc., 16
DIRECTV, Inc., 38
Dover Downs Entertainment, Inc., 43
DreamWorks SKG, 43
E! Entertainment Television Inc., 17
edel music AG, 44
Educational Broadcasting Corporation, 48
Edwards Theatres Circuit, Inc., 31
Elektra Entertainment Group, 64
Elsinore Corporation, 48
Elvis Presley Enterprises, Inc., 61
Empire Resorts, Inc., 72
Endemol Entertainment Holding NV, 46
Equity Marketing, Inc., 26
ESPN, Inc., 56
Esporta plc, 35
Euro Disney S.C.A., 20; 58 (upd.)
Europe Through the Back Door Inc., 65
Fair Grounds Corporation, 44
Family Golf Centers, Inc., 29
FAO Schwarz, 46
Fédération Internationale de Football
    Association, 27
Feld Entertainment, Inc., 32 (upd.)
Film Roman, Inc., 58
First Choice Holidays PLC, 40
First Team Sports, Inc., 22
Fisher-Price Inc., 32 (upd.)
Florida Gaming Corporation, 47
4Kids Entertainment Inc., 59
Fox Entertainment Group, Inc., 43
Fox Family Worldwide, Inc., 24
GameStop Corp., 69 (upd.)
Gaumont SA, 25
Gaylord Entertainment Company, 11; 36
    (upd.)
GC Companies, Inc., 25
Geffen Records Inc., 26
Gibson Guitar Corp., 16
Girl Scouts of the USA, 35
Global Outdoors, Inc., 49
GoodTimes Entertainment Ltd., 48
Granada Group PLC, II; 24 (upd.)
Grand Casinos, Inc., 20
The Green Bay Packers, Inc., 32
Grévin & Compagnie SA, 56
Groupe Partouche SA, 48
Grupo Televisa, S.A., 54 (upd.)
Hallmark Cards, Inc., 40 (upd.)
Hanna-Barbera Cartoons Inc., 23
Hard Rock Cafe International, Inc., 32
    (upd.)
Harlem Globetrotters International, Inc., 61
Harpo Inc., 28; 66 (upd.)
Harrah's Entertainment, Inc., 16; 43 (upd.)
Harveys Casino Resorts, 27
Hasbro, Inc., 43 (upd.)
Hastings Entertainment, Inc., 29
The Hearst Corporation, 46 (upd.)
The Heat Group, 53
Hilton Group plc, III; 19 (upd.); 49 (upd.)
HIT Entertainment PLC, 40
HOB Entertainment, Inc., 37
Hollywood Casino Corporation, 21
Hollywood Entertainment Corporation, 25
Hollywood Media Corporation, 58
Hollywood Park, Inc., 20
Home Box Office Inc., 7; 23 (upd.)
Horseshoe Gaming Holding Corporation,
    62
Imax Corporation, 28

ENTERTAINMENT & LEISURE
(continued)

Indianapolis Motor Speedway Corporation, 46
Infinity Broadcasting Corporation, 48 (upd.)
Infogrames Entertainment S.A., 35
Integrity Inc., 44
International Creative Management, Inc., 43
International Family Entertainment Inc., 13
International Game Technology, 41 (upd.)
International Olympic Committee, 44
International Speedway Corporation, 19
The Intrawest Corporation, 15
Irvin Feld & Kenneth Feld Productions, Inc., 15
Isle of Capri Casinos, Inc., 41
iVillage Inc., 46
Iwerks Entertainment, Inc., 34
Jackpot Enterprises Inc., 21
Japan Broadcasting Corporation, 7
Jazz Basketball Investors, Inc., 55
Jazzercise, Inc., 45
Jillian's Entertainment Holdings, Inc., 40
The Jim Henson Company, 23
The Joffrey Ballet of Chicago, 52
Jurys Doyle Hotel Group plc, 64
Juventus F.C. S.p.A, 53
K'Nex Industries, Inc., 52
Kampgrounds of America, Inc. (KOA), 33
Kerzner International Limited, 69 (upd.)
King World Productions, Inc., 9; 30 (upd.)
Knott's Berry Farm, 18
Kuoni Travel Holding Ltd., 40
The Kushner-Locke Company, 25
Ladbroke Group PLC, II; 21 (upd.)
Lakes Entertainment, Inc., 51
Landmark Theatre Corporation, 70
Las Vegas Sands, Inc., 50
Lego A/S, 13; 40 (upd.)
Liberty Livewire Corporation, 42
Liberty Media Corporation, 50
Liberty Travel, Inc., 56
Life Time Fitness, Inc., 66
Lifetime Entertainment Services, 51
Lincoln Center for the Performing Arts, Inc., 69
Lionel L.L.C., 16
Lions Gate Entertainment Corporation, 35
LIVE Entertainment Inc., 20
LodgeNet Entertainment Corporation, 28
Lucasfilm Ltd., 12; 50 (upd.)
Luminar Plc, 40
Manchester United Football Club plc, 30
Mandalay Resort Group, 32 (upd.)
Maple Leaf Sports & Entertainment Ltd., 61
The Marcus Corporation, 21
Märklin Holding GmbH, 70
Mashantucket Pequot Gaming Enterprise Inc., 35
MCA Inc., II
McMenamins Pubs and Breweries, 65
Media General, Inc., 7
Mediaset SpA, 50
Mega Bloks, Inc., 61
Metro-Goldwyn-Mayer Inc., 25 (upd.)
Metromedia Companies, 14
Métropole Télévision, 33
Metropolitan Baseball Club Inc., 39
The Metropolitan Museum of Art, 55
Metropolitan Opera Association, Inc., 40
MGM Grand Inc., 17
MGM/UA Communications Company, II
Midway Games, Inc., 25

Mikohn Gaming Corporation, 39
Milwaukee Brewers Baseball Club, 37
Miramax Film Corporation, 64
Mizuno Corporation, 25
Mohegan Tribal Gaming Authority, 37
Monarch Casino & Resort, Inc., 65
Motown Records Company L.P., 26
Movie Gallery, Inc., 31
Multimedia Games, Inc., 41
Muzak, Inc., 18
National Amusements Inc., 28
National Association for Stock Car Auto Racing, 32
National Broadcasting Company, Inc., II; 6 (upd.)
National Football League, 29
National Hockey League, 35
National Public Radio, Inc., 19; 47 (upd.)
National Rifle Association of America, 37
National Thoroughbred Racing Association, 58
Navarre Corporation, 24
Navigant International, Inc., 47
New Line Cinema, Inc., 47
New Orleans Saints LP, 58
New York City Off-Track Betting Corporation, 51
News Corporation Limited, 46 (upd.)
Nicklaus Companies, 45
Nintendo Company, Ltd., 28 (upd.); 67 (upd.)
O'Charley's Inc., 19
Orion Pictures Corporation, 6
Outrigger Enterprises, Inc., 67
Paradise Music & Entertainment, Inc., 42
Paramount Pictures Corporation, II
Pathé SA, 29
Paul-Son Gaming Corporation, 66
PDS Gaming Corporation, 44
Peace Arch Entertainment Group Inc., 51
Penn National Gaming, Inc., 33
Philadelphia Eagles, 37
Philharmonic-Symphony Society of New York, Inc. (New York Philharmonic), 69
Pierre & Vacances SA, 48
Pittsburgh Steelers Sports, Inc., 66
Pixar Animation Studios, 34
Platinum Entertainment, Inc., 35
Play by Play Toys & Novelties, Inc., 26
Players International, Inc., 22
Pleasant Holidays LLC, 62
PolyGram N.V., 23
Poof-Slinky, Inc., 61
Portland Trail Blazers, 50
Powerhouse Technologies, Inc., 27
Premier Parks, Inc., 27
President Casinos, Inc., 22
Preussag AG, 42 (upd.)
Princess Cruise Lines, 22
Professional Bull Riders Inc., 55
The Professional Golfers' Association of America, 41
Promus Companies, Inc., 9
ProSiebenSat.1 Media AG, 54
Publishing and Broadcasting Limited, 54
Putt-Putt Golf Courses of America, Inc., 23
Radio One, Inc., 67
Ragdoll Productions Ltd., 51
Rainforest Cafe, Inc., 25
The Rank Group plc, II; 64 (upd.)
Rawlings Sporting Goods Co., Inc., 24
The Really Useful Group, 26
Regal Entertainment Group, 59
Rentrak Corporation, 35
Rhino Entertainment Company, 18; 70 (upd.)
Ride, Inc., 22

Rollerblade, Inc., 34 (upd.)
Roularta Media Group NV, 48
Royal Caribbean Cruises Ltd., 22
Royal Olympic Cruise Lines Inc., 52
RTL Group SA, 44
Rush Communications, 33
S-K-I Limited, 15
Salomon Worldwide, 20
San Francisco Baseball Associates, L.P., 55
The Sanctuary Group PLC, 69
Santa Fe Gaming Corporation, 19
Schwinn Cycle and Fitness L.P., 19
Scientific Games Corporation, 64 (upd.)
Scottish Radio Holding plc, 41
Seattle FilmWorks, Inc., 20
Sega of America, Inc., 10
Selectour SA, 53
SFX Entertainment, Inc., 36
Showboat, Inc., 19
Shubert Organization Inc., 24
Shuffle Master Inc., 51
The Singing Machine Company, Inc., 60
Sirius Satellite Radio, Inc., 69
Six Flags, Inc., 17; 54 (upd.)
Smithsonian Institution, 27
Società Sportiva Lazio SpA, 44
Sony Corporation, 40 (upd.)
Speedway Motorsports, Inc., 32
Spelling Entertainment Group, Inc., 14
Spin Master, Ltd., 61
The Sports Club Company, 25
Stanley Leisure plc, 66
Station Casinos Inc., 25
Stoll-Moss Theatres Ltd., 34
Stuart Entertainment Inc., 16
TABCORP Holdings Limited, 44
Take-Two Interactive Software, Inc., 46
Tee Vee Toons, Inc., 57
Tele-Communications, Inc., II
Television Española, S.A., 7
Texas Rangers Baseball, 51
Tha Row Records, 69 (upd.)
Thomas Cook Travel Inc., 9
The Thomson Corporation, 8
Thousand Trails, Inc., 33
THQ, Inc., 39
Ticketmaster Corp., 13
Tiger Aspect Productions Ltd., 72
The Todd-AO Corporation, 33
Toho Co., Ltd., 28
Tomy Company Ltd., 65
The Topps Company, Inc., 34 (upd.)
Touristik Union International GmbH. and Company K.G., II
Town Sports International, Inc., 46
Toy Biz, Inc., 18
Trans World Entertainment Corporation, 24
Travelocity.com, Inc., 46
Tribune Company, 63 (upd.)
TUI Group GmbH, 44
Turner Broadcasting System, Inc., II; 6 (upd.); 66 (upd.)
The Tussauds Group, 55
Twentieth Century Fox Film Corporation, II; 25 (upd.)
24 Hour Fitness Worldwide, Inc., 71
Ubi Soft Entertainment S.A., 41
Ulster Television PLC, 71
United Pan-Europe Communications NV, 47
United States Playing Card Company, 62
Universal Studios, Inc., 33
Univision Communications Inc., 24
USA Interactive, Inc., 47 (upd.)
Vail Resorts, Inc., 11; 43 (upd.)
Venetian Casino Resort, LLC, 47
Viacom Inc., 7; 23 (upd.)

Village Roadshow Ltd., 58
Vinton Studios, 63
Vivendi Universal S.A., 46 (upd.)
The Walt Disney Company, II; 6 (upd.); 30 (upd.); 63 (upd.)
Warner Communications Inc., II
Washington Football, Inc., 35
West Coast Entertainment Corporation, 29
WGBH Educational Foundation, 66
Wham-O, Inc., 61
Wherehouse Entertainment Incorporated, 11
Whitbread PLC, 52 (upd.)
Wildlife Conservation Society, 31
William Hill Organization Limited, 49
Wilson Sporting Goods Company, 24
Wizards of the Coast Inc., 24
WMS Industries, Inc., 53 (upd.)
World Wrestling Federation Entertainment, Inc., 32
XM Satellite Radio Holdings, Inc., 69
YankeeNets LLC, 35
YES! Entertainment Corporation, 26
YMCA of the USA, 31
Young Broadcasting Inc., 40
Zomba Records Ltd., 52

FINANCIAL SERVICES: BANKS

Abbey National plc, 10; 39 (upd.)
Abigail Adams National Bancorp, Inc., 23
ABN AMRO Holding, N.V., 50
Algemene Bank Nederland N.V., II
Allianz AG, 57 (upd.)
Allied Irish Banks, plc, 16; 43 (upd.)
Almanij NV, 44
Amalgamated Bank, 60
AMCORE Financial Inc., 44
American Residential Mortgage Corporation, 8
AmSouth Bancorporation, 12; 48 (upd.)
Amsterdam-Rotterdam Bank N.V., II
Anchor Bancorp, Inc., 10
Apple Bank for Savings, 59
Astoria Financial Corporation, 44
Australia and New Zealand Banking Group Limited, II; 52 (upd.)
Banca Commerciale Italiana SpA, II
Banca Fideuram SpA, 63
Banca Intesa SpA, 65
Banca Monte dei Paschi di Siena SpA, 65
Banca Nazionale del Lavoro SpA, 72
Banco Bilbao Vizcaya Argentaria S.A., II; 48 (upd.)
Banco Bradesco S.A., 13
Banco Central, II
Banco Comercial Português, SA, 50
Banco de Chile, 69
Banco do Brasil S.A., II
Banco Espírito Santo e Comercial de Lisboa S.A., 15
Banco Itaú S.A., 19
Banco Santander Central Hispano S.A., 36 (upd.)
Bank Austria AG, 23
Bank Brussels Lambert, II
Bank Hapoalim B.M., II; 54 (upd.)
Bank Leumi le-Israel B.M., 60
Bank of America Corporation, 46 (upd.)
Bank of Boston Corporation, II
Bank of China, 63
Bank of East Asia Ltd., 63
Bank of Ireland, 50
Bank of Mississippi, Inc., 14
Bank of Montreal, II; 46 (upd.)
Bank of New England Corporation, II
The Bank of New York Company, Inc., II; 46 (upd.)
The Bank of Nova Scotia, II; 59 (upd.)
Bank of the Philippine Islands, 58
Bank of Tokyo-Mitsubishi Ltd., II; 15 (upd.)
Bank One Corporation, 10; 36 (upd.)
BankAmerica Corporation, II; 8 (upd.)
Bankers Trust New York Corporation, II
Banknorth Group, Inc., 55
Banque Nationale de Paris S.A., II
Barclays plc, II; 20 (upd.); 64 (upd.)
BarclaysAmerican Mortgage Corporation, 11
Barings PLC, 14
Barnett Banks, Inc., 9
BayBanks, Inc., 12
Bayerische Hypotheken- und Wechsel-Bank AG, II
Bayerische Vereinsbank A.G., II
Beneficial Corporation, 8
BNP Paribas Group, 36 (upd.)
Boatmen's Bancshares Inc., 15
Bremer Financial Corp., 45
Brown Brothers Harriman & Co., 45
Canadian Imperial Bank of Commerce, II; 61 (upd.)
Capitalia S.p.A., 65
Carolina First Corporation, 31
Casco Northern Bank, 14
The Chase Manhattan Corporation, II; 13 (upd.)
Cheltenham & Gloucester PLC, 61
Chemical Banking Corporation, II; 14 (upd.)
Citicorp, II; 9 (upd.)
Citigroup Inc., 30 (upd.); 59 (upd.)
Citizens Financial Group, Inc., 42
Close Brothers Group plc, 39
Commercial Credit Company, 8
Commercial Federal Corporation, 12; 62 (upd.)
Commerzbank A.G., II; 47 (upd.)
Compagnie Financiere de Paribas, II
Continental Bank Corporation, II
CoreStates Financial Corp, 17
Countrywide Credit Industries, Inc., 16
Crédit Agricole, II
Crédit Lyonnais, 9; 33 (upd.)
Crédit National S.A., 9
Credit Suisse Group, II; 21 (upd.); 59 (upd.)
Credito Italiano, II
Cullen/Frost Bankers, Inc., 25
CUNA Mutual Group, 62
The Dai-Ichi Kangyo Bank Ltd., II
The Daiwa Bank, Ltd., II; 39 (upd.)
Danske Bank Aktieselskab, 50
Dauphin Deposit Corporation, 14
DEPFA BANK PLC, 69
Deposit Guaranty Corporation, 17
Deutsche Bank AG, II; 14 (upd.); 40 (upd.)
Dexia Group, 42
Dime Savings Bank of New York, F.S.B., 9
Donaldson, Lufkin & Jenrette, Inc., 22
Dresdner Bank A.G., II; 57 (upd.)
Emigrant Savings Bank, 59
Erste Bank der Osterreichischen Sparkassen AG, 69
European Investment Bank, 66
Fifth Third Bancorp, 13; 31 (upd.)
First Bank System Inc., 12
First Chicago Corporation, II
First Commerce Bancshares, Inc., 15
First Commerce Corporation, 11
First Empire State Corporation, 11
First Fidelity Bank, N.A., New Jersey, 9
First Hawaiian, Inc., 11
First Interstate Bancorp, II
First Nationwide Bank, 14
First of America Bank Corporation, 8
First Security Corporation, 11
First Tennessee National Corporation, 11; 48 (upd.)
First Union Corporation, 10
First Virginia Banks, Inc., 11
Firstar Corporation, 11; 33 (upd.)
Fleet Financial Group, Inc., 9
FleetBoston Financial Corporation, 36 (upd.)
FöreningsSparbanken AB, 69
Fourth Financial Corporation, 11
The Fuji Bank, Ltd., II
Generale Bank, II
German American Bancorp, 41
Glacier Bancorp, Inc., 35
Golden West Financial Corporation, 47
The Governor and Company of the Bank of Scotland, 10
Grameen Bank, 31
Granite State Bankshares, Inc., 37
Great Lakes Bancorp, 8
Great Western Financial Corporation, 10
GreenPoint Financial Corp., 28
Grupo Financiero Banamex S.A., 54
Grupo Financiero Banorte, S.A. de C.V., 51
Grupo Financiero BBVA Bancomer S.A., 54
Grupo Financiero Galicia S.A., 63
Grupo Financiero Serfin, S.A., 19
H.F. Ahmanson & Company, II; 10 (upd.)
Habersham Bancorp, 25
Hancock Holding Company, 15
Hang Seng Bank Ltd., 60
Hanmi Financial Corporation, 66
Hibernia Corporation, 37
The Hongkong and Shanghai Banking Corporation Limited, II
HSBC Holdings plc, 12; 26 (upd.)
Hudson River Bancorp, 41
Huntington Bancshares Inc., 11
HVB Group, 59 (upd.)
IBERIABANK Corporation, 37
The Industrial Bank of Japan, Ltd., II
Irish Life & Permanent Plc, 59
J Sainsbury plc, 38 (upd.)
J.P. Morgan & Co. Incorporated, II; 30 (upd.)
J.P. Morgan Chase & Co., 38 (upd.)
Japan Leasing Corporation, 8
Julius Baer Holding AG, 52
Kansallis-Osake-Pankki, II
KeyCorp, 8
Kookmin Bank, 58
Kredietbank N.V., II
Kreditanstalt für Wiederaufbau, 29
Krung Thai Bank Public Company Ltd., 69
Lloyds Bank PLC, II
Lloyds TSB Group plc, 47 (upd.)
Long Island Bancorp, Inc., 16
Long-Term Credit Bank of Japan, Ltd., II
Macquarie Bank Ltd., 69
Malayan Banking Berhad, 72
Manufacturers Hanover Corporation, II
Marshall & Ilsley Corporation, 56
MBNA Corporation, 12
Mediolanum S.p.A., 65
Mellon Bank Corporation, II
Mellon Financial Corporation, 44 (upd.)
Mercantile Bankshares Corp., 11
Meridian Bancorp, Inc., 11
Metropolitan Financial Corporation, 13
Michigan National Corporation, 11
Midland Bank PLC, II; 17 (upd.)

FINANCIAL SERVICES: BANKS
(continued)

The Mitsubishi Bank, Ltd., II
The Mitsubishi Trust & Banking
  Corporation, II
The Mitsui Bank, Ltd., II
The Mitsui Trust & Banking Company,
  Ltd., II
Mizuho Financial Group Inc., 58 (upd.)
Mouvement des Caisses Desjardins, 48
N M Rothschild & Sons Limited, 39
National Bank of Greece, 41
National City Corp., 15
National Westminster Bank PLC, II
NationsBank Corporation, 10
NBD Bancorp, Inc., 11
NCNB Corporation, II
Nippon Credit Bank, II
Nordea AB, 40
Norinchukin Bank, II
North Fork Bancorporation, Inc., 46
Northern Rock plc, 33
Northern Trust Company, 9
NVR L.P., 8
Old Kent Financial Corp., 11
Old National Bancorp, 15
PNC Bank Corp., II; 13 (upd.)
The PNC Financial Services Group Inc., 46
  (upd.)
Popular, Inc., 41
PT Bank Buana Indonesia Tbk, 60
Pulte Corporation, 8
Rabobank Group, 33
Republic New York Corporation, 11
Riggs National Corporation, 13
The Royal Bank of Canada, II; 21 (upd.)
The Royal Bank of Scotland Group plc,
  12; 38 (upd.)
The Ryland Group, Inc., 8
St. Paul Bank for Cooperatives, 8
Sanpaolo IMI S.p.A., 50
The Sanwa Bank, Ltd., II; 15 (upd.)
SBC Warburg, 14
Sberbank, 62
Seattle First National Bank Inc., 8
Security Capital Corporation, 17
Security Pacific Corporation, II
Shawmut National Corporation, 13
Signet Banking Corporation, 11
Singer & Friedlander Group plc, 41
Skandinaviska Enskilda Banken AB, II; 56
  (upd.)
Société Générale, II; 42 (upd.)
Society Corporation, 9
Southern Financial Bancorp, Inc., 56
Southtrust Corporation, 11
Standard Chartered plc, II; 48 (upd.)
Standard Federal Bank, 9
Star Banc Corporation, 11
State Bank of India, 63
State Financial Services Corporation, 51
State Street Corporation, 8; 57 (upd.)
Staten Island Bancorp, Inc., 39
The Sumitomo Bank, Limited, II; 26 (upd.)
Sumitomo Mitsui Banking Corporation, 51
  (upd.)
The Sumitomo Trust & Banking Company,
  Ltd., II; 53 (upd.)
The Summit Bancorporation, 14
SunTrust Banks Inc., 23
Svenska Handelsbanken AB, II; 50 (upd.)
Swiss Bank Corporation, II
Synovus Financial Corp., 12; 52 (upd.)
The Taiyo Kobe Bank, Ltd., II
TCF Financial Corporation, 47
The Tokai Bank, Limited, II; 15 (upd.)
The Toronto-Dominion Bank, II; 49 (upd.)

TSB Group plc, 12
Turkiye Is Bankasi A.S., 61
U.S. Bancorp, 14; 36 (upd.)
U.S. Trust Corp., 17
UBS AG, 52 (upd.)
Union Bank of California, 16
Union Bank of Switzerland, II
Union Financière de France Banque SA, 52
Union Planters Corporation, 54
UnionBanCal Corporation, 50 (upd.)
United Overseas Bank Ltd., 56
USAA, 62 (upd.)
Wachovia Bank of Georgia, N.A., 16
Wachovia Bank of South Carolina, N.A.,
  16
Washington Mutual, Inc., 17
Wells Fargo & Company, II; 12 (upd.); 38
  (upd.)
West One Bancorp, 11
Westamerica Bancorporation, 17
Westdeutsche Landesbank Girozentrale, II;
  46 (upd.)
Westpac Banking Corporation, II; 48 (upd.)
Whitney Holding Corporation, 21
Wilmington Trust Corporation, 25
The Woolwich plc, 30
World Bank Group, 33
The Yasuda Trust and Banking Company,
  Ltd., II; 17 (upd.)
Zions Bancorporation, 12; 53 (upd.)

**FINANCIAL SERVICES:
NON-BANKS**

A.B. Watley Group Inc., 45
A.G. Edwards, Inc., 8; 32 (upd.)
ACE Cash Express, Inc., 33
Advanta Corporation, 8; 38 (upd.)
Ag Services of America, Inc., 59
Alliance Capital Management Holding
  L.P., 63
Allmerica Financial Corporation, 63
Ambac Financial Group, Inc., 65
America's Car-Mart, Inc., 64
American Express Company, II; 10 (upd.);
  38 (upd.)
American General Finance Corp., 11
American Home Mortgage Holdings, Inc.,
  46
Ameritrade Holding Corporation, 34
AMVESCAP PLC, 65
Arthur Andersen & Company, Société
  Coopérative, 10
Avco Financial Services Inc., 13
Aviva PLC, 50 (upd.)
Bear Stearns Companies, Inc., II; 10
  (upd.); 52 (upd.)
Benchmark Capital, 49
Bill & Melinda Gates Foundation, 41
Bozzuto's, Inc., 13
Bradford & Bingley PLC, 65
Capital One Financial Corporation, 52
Carnegie Corporation of New York, 35
Cash America International, Inc., 20; 61
  (upd.)
Cattles plc, 58
Cendant Corporation, 44 (upd.)
Certegy, Inc., 63
Cetelem S.A., 21
The Charles Schwab Corporation, 8; 26
  (upd.)
Citfed Bancorp, Inc., 16
Coinstar, Inc., 44
Comerica Incorporated, 40
Commercial Financial Services, Inc., 26
Concord EFS, Inc., 52
Coopers & Lybrand, 9
Cramer, Berkowitz & Co., 34

Credit Acceptance Corporation, 18
Cresud S.A.C.I.F. y A., 63
CS First Boston Inc., II
Dain Rauscher Corporation, 35 (upd.)
Daiwa Securities Group Inc., II; 55 (upd.)
Datek Online Holdings Corp., 32
The David and Lucile Packard Foundation,
  41
Dean Witter, Discover & Co., 12
Deutsche Börse AG, 59
Dow Jones Telerate, Inc., 10
Dresdner Kleinwort Wasserstein, 60 (upd.)
Drexel Burnham Lambert Incorporated, II
The Dreyfus Corporation, 70
DVI, Inc., 51
E*Trade Financial Corporation, 20; 60
  (upd.)
Eaton Vance Corporation, 18
Edward D. Jones & Company L.P., 66
  (upd.)
Edward Jones, 30
Euronext Paris S.A., 37
Experian Information Solutions Inc., 45
Fair, Isaac and Company, 18
Fannie Mae, 45 (upd.)
Federal National Mortgage Association, II
Fidelity Investments Inc., II; 14 (upd.)
First Albany Companies Inc., 37
First Data Corporation, 30 (upd.)
First USA, Inc., 11
FMR Corp., 8; 32 (upd.)
Forstmann Little & Co., 38
Fortis, Inc., 15
Frank Russell Company, 46
Franklin Resources, Inc., 9
Freddie Mac, 54
Friedman, Billings, Ramsey Group, Inc., 53
Gabelli Asset Management Inc., 30
Gilman & Ciocia, Inc., 72
The Goldman Sachs Group Inc., II; 20
  (upd.); 51 (upd.)
Grede Foundries, Inc., 38
Green Tree Financial Corporation, 11
Gruntal & Co., L.L.C., 20
Grupo Financiero Galicia S.A., 63
H & R Block, Incorporated, 9; 29 (upd.)
H.D. Vest, Inc., 46
H.M. Payson & Co., 69
Hoenig Group Inc., 41
Household International, Inc., II; 21 (upd.)
Ingenico—Compagnie Industrielle et
  Financière d'Ingénierie, 46
Instinet Corporation, 34
Inter-Regional Financial Group, Inc., 15
Investcorp SA, 57
The Island ECN, Inc., 48
Istituto per la Ricostruzione Industriale
  S.p.A., 11
J. & W. Seligman & Co. Inc., 61
Janus Capital Group Inc., 57
JB Oxford Holdings, Inc., 32
Jefferies Group, Inc., 25
John Hancock Financial Services, Inc., 42
  (upd.)
The John Nuveen Company, 21
Jones Lang LaSalle Incorporated, 49
The Jordan Company LP, 70
Kansas City Southern Industries, Inc., 26
  (upd.)
Kleiner, Perkins, Caufield & Byers, 53
Kleinwort Benson Group PLC, II
Knight Trading Group, Inc., 70
Kohlberg Kravis Roberts & Co., 24; 56
  (upd.)
KPMG Worldwide, 10
La Poste, 47 (upd.)
LaBranche & Co. Inc., 37

Lazard LLC, 38
Legg Mason, Inc., 33
Lilly Endowment Inc., 70
London Scottish Bank plc, 70
London Stock Exchange Limited, 34
M.H. Meyerson & Co., Inc., 46
MacAndrews & Forbes Holdings Inc., 28
MasterCard International, Inc., 9
MBNA Corporation, 33 (upd.)
Merrill Lynch & Co., Inc., II; 13 (upd.); 40 (upd.)
Metris Companies Inc., 56
Morgan Grenfell Group PLC, II
Morgan Stanley Dean Witter & Company, II; 16 (upd.); 33 (upd.)
Mountain States Mortgage Centers, Inc., 29
NASD, 54 (upd.)
National Association of Securities Dealers, Inc., 10
National Auto Credit, Inc., 16
National Discount Brokers Group, Inc., 28
National Financial Partners Corp., 65
Navy Federal Credit Union, 33
Neuberger Berman Inc., 57
New Street Capital Inc., 8
New York Stock Exchange, Inc., 9; 39 (upd.)
The Nikko Securities Company Limited, II; 9 (upd.)
Nippon Shinpan Co., Ltd., II; 61 (upd.)
Nomura Securities Company, Limited, II; 9 (upd.)
Norwich & Peterborough Building Society, 55
Oaktree Capital Management, LLC, 71
Old Mutual PLC, 61
Ontario Teachers' Pension Plan, 61
Onyx Acceptance Corporation, 59
ORIX Corporation, II; 44 (upd.)
PaineWebber Group Inc., II; 22 (upd.)
PayPal Inc., 58
The Pew Charitable Trusts, 35
Piper Jaffray Companies Inc., 22
Pitney Bowes Inc., 47 (upd.)
Providian Financial Corporation, 52 (upd.)
The Prudential Insurance Company of America, 30 (upd.)
The Quick & Reilly Group, Inc., 20
Rathbone Brothers plc, 70
Raymond James Financial Inc., 69
Resource America, Inc., 42
Robert W. Baird & Co. Incorporated, 67
Ryan Beck & Co., Inc., 66
Safeguard Scientifics, Inc., 10
St. James's Place Capital, plc, 71
Salomon Inc., II; 13 (upd.)
Sanders Morris Harris Group Inc., 70
Sanlam Ltd., 68
SBC Warburg, 14
Schroders plc, 42
Shearson Lehman Brothers Holdings Inc., II; 9 (upd.)
Siebert Financial Corp., 32
SLM Holding Corp., 25 (upd.)
Smith Barney Inc., 15
Soros Fund Management LLC, 28
Spear, Leeds & Kellogg, 66
State Street Boston Corporation, 8
Student Loan Marketing Association, II
T. Rowe Price Associates, Inc., 11; 34 (upd.)
Teachers Insurance and Annuity Association-College Retirement Equities Fund, 45 (upd.)
Texas Pacific Group Inc., 36
Total System Services, Inc., 18
Trilon Financial Corporation, II

United Jewish Communities, 33
The Vanguard Group, Inc., 14; 34 (upd.)
VeriFone, Inc., 18
Visa International, 9; 26 (upd.)
Wachovia Corporation, 12; 46 (upd.)
Waddell & Reed, Inc., 22
Washington Federal, Inc., 17
Waterhouse Investor Services, Inc., 18
Watson Wyatt Worldwide, 42
Western Union Financial Services, Inc., 54
WFS Financial Inc., 70
Working Assets Funding Service, 43
World Acceptance Corporation, 57
Yamaichi Securities Company, Limited, II
The Ziegler Companies, Inc., 24; 63 (upd.)
Zurich Financial Services, 42 (upd.)

FOOD PRODUCTS

A. Moksel AG, 59
Agway, Inc., 7
Ajinomoto Co., Inc., II; 28 (upd.)
Alabama Farmers Cooperative, Inc., 63
The Albert Fisher Group plc, 41
Alberto-Culver Company, 8
Aldi Group, 13
Alfred Ritter GmbH & Co. KG, 58
Alpine Confections, Inc., 71
Alpine Lace Brands, Inc., 18
American Crystal Sugar Company, 11; 32 (upd.)
American Foods Group, 43
American Italian Pasta Company, 27
American Maize-Products Co., 14
American Pop Corn Company, 59
American Rice, Inc., 33
Amfac/JMB Hawaii L.L.C., 24 (upd.)
Annie's Homegrown, Inc., 59
Archer-Daniels-Midland Company, 32 (upd.)
Archway Cookies, Inc., 29
Arcor S.A.I.C., 66
Arla Foods amba, 48
Arnott's Ltd., 66
Associated British Foods plc, II; 13 (upd.); 41 (upd.)
Associated Milk Producers, Inc., 11; 48 (upd.)
Atlantic Premium Brands, Ltd., 57
August Storck KG, 66
Aurora Foods Inc., 32
Awrey Bakeries, Inc., 56
B&G Foods, Inc., 40
The B. Manischewitz Company, LLC, 31
Bahlsen GmbH & Co. KG, 44
Balance Bar Company, 32
Baltek Corporation, 34
Barilla G. e R. Fratelli S.p.A., 17; 50 (upd.)
Barry Callebaut AG, 71 (upd.)
Bear Creek Corporation, 38
Beatrice Company, II
Beech-Nut Nutrition Corporation, 21; 51 (upd.)
Ben & Jerry's Homemade, Inc., 10; 35 (upd.)
Berkeley Farms, Inc., 46
Besnier SA, 19
Bestfoods, 22 (upd.)
Bettys & Taylors of Harrogate Ltd., 72
Birds Eye Foods, Inc., 69 (upd.)
Blue Bell Creameries L.P., 30
Blue Diamond Growers, 28
Bob's Red Mill Natural Foods, Inc., 63
Bobs Candies, Inc., 70
Bonduelle SA, 51
Bongrain SA, 25
Booker PLC, 13; 31 (upd.)

Borden, Inc., II; 22 (upd.)
Boyd Coffee Company, 53
Brach and Brock Confections, Inc., 15
Brake Bros plc, 45
Bridgford Foods Corporation, 27
Brigham's Inc., 72
Brioche Pasquier S.A., 58
Brothers Gourmet Coffees, Inc., 20
Broughton Foods Co., 17
Brown & Haley, 23
Bruce Foods Corporation, 39
Bruegger's Corporation, 63
BSN Groupe S.A., II
Bumble Bee Seafoods L.L.C., 64
Bunge Ltd., 62
Burns, Philp & Company Ltd., 63
Bush Boake Allen Inc., 30
Bush Brothers & Company, 45
C.H. Robinson Worldwide, Inc., 40 (upd.)
Cadbury Schweppes PLC, II; 49 (upd.)
Cagle's, Inc., 20
Cal-Maine Foods, Inc., 69
Calavo Growers, Inc., 47
Calcot Ltd., 33
Campbell Soup Company, II; 7 (upd.); 26 (upd.); 71 (upd.)
Campofrío Alimentación S.A., 59
Canada Packers Inc., II
Cargill Inc., 13 (upd.)
Carnation Company, II
The Carriage House Companies, Inc., 55
Carroll's Foods, Inc., 46
Carvel Corporation, 35
Castle & Cooke, Inc., II; 20 (upd.)
Cattleman's, Inc., 20
Celestial Seasonings, Inc., 16
Central Soya Company, Inc., 7
Chelsea Milling Company, 29
Chicken of the Sea International, 24 (upd.)
Chiquita Brands International, Inc., 7; 21 (upd.)
Chock Full o'Nuts Corp., 17
Chocoladefabriken Lindt & Sprüngli AG, 27
Chr. Hansen Group A/S, 70
CHS Inc., 60
Chupa Chups S.A., 38
Clif Bar Inc., 50
Cloetta Fazer AB, 70
The Clorox Company, 22 (upd.)
Clougherty Packing Company, 72
Coca-Cola Enterprises, Inc., 13
Cold Stone Creamery, 69
Coleman Natural Products, Inc., 68
Community Coffee Co. L.L.C., 53
ConAgra Foods, Inc., II; 12 (upd.); 42 (upd.)
The Connell Company, 29
ContiGroup Companies, Inc., 43 (upd.)
Continental Grain Company, 10; 13 (upd.)
CoolBrands International Inc., 35
CPC International Inc., II
Cranswick plc, 40
CSM N.V., 65
Cumberland Packing Corporation, 26
Curtice-Burns Foods, Inc., 7; 21 (upd.)
Czarnikow-Rionda Company, Inc., 32
Dairy Crest Group plc, 32
Dalgety, PLC, II
Danisco A/S, 44
Dannon Co., Inc., 14
Darigold, Inc., 9
Dawn Food Products, Inc., 17
Dean Foods Company, 7; 21 (upd.)
DeKalb Genetics Corporation, 17
Del Monte Foods Company, 7; 23 (upd.)
Di Giorgio Corp., 12

FOOD PRODUCTS (continued)

Diageo plc, 24 (upd.)
Diamond of California, 64 (upd.)
Dippin' Dots, Inc., 56
Dole Food Company, Inc., 9; 31 (upd.); 68 (upd.)
Domino Sugar Corporation, 26
Doskocil Companies, Inc., 12
Dot Foods, Inc., 69
Dreyer's Grand Ice Cream, Inc., 17
The Earthgrains Company, 36
Emge Packing Co., Inc., 11
Empresas Polar SA, 55 (upd.)
Eridania Béghin-Say S.A., 36
ERLY Industries Inc., 17
Eskimo Pie Corporation, 21
Ezaki Glico Company Ltd., 72
Farley's & Sathers Candy Company, Inc., 62
Farmland Foods, Inc., 7
Farmland Industries, Inc., 48
Ferrero SpA, 54
Fieldale Farms Corporation, 23
Fleer Corporation, 15
Fleury Michon S.A., 39
Florida Crystals Inc., 35
Flowers Industries, Inc., 12; 35 (upd.)
Fonterra Co-Operative Group Ltd., 58
FoodBrands America, Inc., 23
Foster Poultry Farms, 32
Fred Usinger Inc., 54
Fresh America Corporation, 20
Fresh Foods, Inc., 29
Friesland Coberco Dairy Foods Holding N.V., 59
Frito-Lay Company, 32
Fromageries Bel, 23
Fyffes Plc, 38
Galaxy Nutritional Foods, Inc., 58
Gardenburger, Inc., 33
Geest Plc, 38
General Mills, Inc., II; 10 (upd.); 36 (upd.)
George A. Hormel and Company, II
George Weston Limited, 36 (upd.)
Gerber Products Company, 7; 21 (upd.)
Ghirardelli Chocolate Company, 30
Givaudan SA, 43
Glanbia plc, 59
Global Berry Farms LLC, 62
Godiva Chocolatier, Inc., 64
Gold Kist Inc., 17; 26 (upd.)
Gold'n Plump Poultry, 54
Golden Enterprises, Inc., 26
Gonnella Baking Company, 40
Good Humor-Breyers Ice Cream Company, 14
Goodman Fielder Ltd., 52
GoodMark Foods, Inc., 26
Gorton's, 13
Goya Foods Inc., 22
Great Harvest Bread Company, 44
Grist Mill Company, 15
Groupe Danone, 32 (upd.)
Groupe Soufflet SA, 55
Gruma, S.A. de C.V., 31
Grupo Herdez, S.A. de C.V., 35
Grupo Leche Pascual S.A., 59
Guittard Chocolate Company, 55
H.J. Heinz Company, II; 11 (upd.); 36 (upd.)
The Hain Celestial Group, Inc., 27; 43 (upd.)
Hanover Foods Corporation, 35
HARIBO GmbH & Co. KG, 44
Harry London Candies, Inc., 70
The Hartz Mountain Corporation, 12
Hazlewood Foods plc, 32

Herman Goelitz, Inc., 28
Hershey Foods Corporation, II; 15 (upd.); 51 (upd.)
Hill's Pet Nutrition, Inc., 27
Hillsdown Holdings plc, II; 24 (upd.)
Horizon Organic Holding Corporation, 37
Hormel Foods Corporation, 18 (upd.); 54 (upd.)
Hudson Foods Inc., 13
Hulman & Company, 44
Hunt-Wesson, Inc., 17
Iams Company, 26
IAWS Group plc, 49
IBP, Inc., II; 21 (upd.)
Iceland Group plc, 33
Imagine Foods, Inc., 50
Imperial Holly Corporation, 12
Imperial Sugar Company, 32 (upd.)
Industrias Bachoco, S.A. de C.V., 39
Intercorp Excelle Foods Inc., 64
International Multifoods Corporation, 7; 25 (upd.)
Interstate Bakeries Corporation, 12; 38 (upd.)
Itoham Foods Inc., II; 61 (upd.)
J & J Snack Foods Corporation, 24
The J.M. Smucker Company, 11
J.R. Simplot Company, 16
Jacobs Suchard A.G., II
Jim Beam Brands Co., 14
John B. Sanfilippo & Son, Inc., 14
Johnsonville Sausage L.L.C., 63
Julius Meinl International AG, 53
Just Born, Inc., 32
Kal Kan Foods, Inc., 22
Kamps AG, 44
Keebler Foods Company, 36
Kellogg Company, II; 13 (upd.); 50 (upd.)
Kerry Group plc, 27
Kettle Foods Inc., 48
Kewpie Kabushiki Kaisha, 57
Kikkoman Corporation, 14; 47 (upd.)
The King Arthur Flour Company, 31
King Ranch, Inc., 14
Klement's Sausage Company, 61
Koninklijke Wessanen nv, II; 54 (upd.)
Kraft Foods Inc., 45 (upd.)
Kraft General Foods Inc., II; 7 (upd.)
Kraft Jacobs Suchard AG, 26 (upd.)
Krispy Kreme Doughnuts, Inc., 21; 61 (upd.)
L.D.C. SA, 61
La Choy Food Products Inc., 25
Lam Son Sugar Joint Stock Corporation (Lasuco), 60
Lamb Weston, Inc., 23
Lance, Inc., 14; 41 (upd.)
Land O'Lakes, Inc., II; 21 (upd.)
Lassonde Industries Inc., 68
LDC, 68
Ledesma Sociedad Anónima Agrícola Industrial, 62
Leprino Foods Company, 28
Leroux S.A.S., 65
Lifeway Foods, Inc., 65
Lincoln Snacks Company, 24
Litehouse Inc., 60
Lucille Farms, Inc., 45
Luigino's, Inc., 64
M.A. Gedney Co., 51
Madrange SA, 58
Malt-O-Meal Company, 22; 63 (upd.)
Maple Leaf Foods Inc., 41
Mars, Incorporated, 7; 40 (upd.)
Maui Land & Pineapple Company, Inc., 29
Mauna Loa Macadamia Nut Corporation, 64

McCormick & Company, Incorporated, 7; 27 (upd.)
McIlhenny Company, 20
McKee Foods Corporation, 7; 27 (upd.)
Meiji Milk Products Company, Limited, II
Meiji Seika Kaisha, Ltd., II
Merisant Worldwide, Inc., 70
Michael Foods, Inc., 25
Mid-America Dairymen, Inc., 7
Midwest Grain Products, Inc., 49
Mike-Sell's Inc., 15
Milnot Company, 46
Molinos Río de la Plata S.A., 61
Monfort, Inc., 13
Morinaga & Co. Ltd., 61
Mrs. Baird's Bakeries, 29
Mt. Olive Pickle Company, Inc., 44
MTR Foods Ltd., 55
Murphy Family Farms Inc., 22
Nabisco Foods Group, II; 7 (upd.)
Nantucket Allserve, Inc., 22
Nathan's Famous, Inc., 29
National Presto Industries, Inc., 43 (upd.)
National Sea Products Ltd., 14
Natural Ovens Bakery, Inc., 72
Natural Selection Foods, 54
Nestlé S.A., II; 7 (upd.); 28 (upd.); 71 (upd.)
New England Confectionery Co., 15
New World Pasta Company, 53
Newhall Land and Farming Company, 14
Newman's Own, Inc., 37
Niman Ranch, Inc., 67
Nippon Meat Packers, Inc., II
Nippon Suisan Kaisha, Limited, II
Nisshin Seifun Group Inc., II; 66 (upd.)
Northern Foods plc, 10; 61 (upd.)
Northland Cranberries, Inc., 38
Nutraceutical International Corporation, 37
NutraSweet Company, 8
Nutreco Holding N.V., 56
NutriSystem, Inc., 71
Oakhurst Dairy, 60
Ocean Spray Cranberries, Inc., 7; 25 (upd.)
OJSC Wimm-Bill-Dann Foods, 48
Omaha Steaks International Inc., 62
Ore-Ida Foods Incorporated, 13
Organic Valley (Coulee Region Organic Produce Pool), 53
Oscar Mayer Foods Corp., 12
Otis Spunkmeyer, Inc., 28
Overhill Corporation, 51
Papetti's Hygrade Egg Products, Inc., 39
Parmalat Finanziaria SpA, 50
Pendleton Grain Growers Inc., 64
Penford Corporation, 55
PepsiCo, Inc., I; 10 (upd.); 38 (upd.)
Perdigao SA, 52
Perdue Farms Inc., 7; 23 (upd.)
Perfetti Van Melle S.p.A., 72
Pet Incorporated, 7
Petrossian Inc., 54
Pez Candy, Inc., 38
Philip Morris Companies Inc., 18 (upd.)
Phillips Foods, Inc., 63
PIC International Group PLC, 24 (upd.)
Pilgrim's Pride Corporation, 7; 23 (upd.)
The Pillsbury Company, II; 13 (upd.); 62 (upd.)
Pioneer Hi-Bred International, Inc., 9
Pizza Inn, Inc., 46
Poore Brothers, Inc., 44
PowerBar Inc., 44
Prairie Farms Dairy, Inc., 47
Premium Standard Farms, Inc., 30
The Procter & Gamble Company, III; 8 (upd.); 26 (upd.)

Punch Taverns plc, 70
Purina Mills, Inc., 32
Quaker Oats Company, II; 12 (upd.); 34 (upd.)
Quality Chekd Dairies, Inc., 48
Ralston Purina Company, II; 13 (upd.)
Ranks Hovis McDougall Limited, II; 28 (upd.)
Reckitt Benckiser plc, II; 42 (upd.)
Rica Foods, Inc., 41
Rich Products Corporation, 7; 38 (upd.)
Richtree Inc., 63
Ricola Ltd., 62
Ridley Corporation Ltd., 62
Riviana Foods Inc., 27
Roland Murten A.G., 7
Rose Acre Farms, Inc., 60
Rowntree Mackintosh, II
Royal Numico N.V., 37
Ruiz Food Products, Inc., 53
Russell Stover Candies Inc., 12
Sadia S.A., 59
Sanderson Farms, Inc., 15
Saputo Inc., 59
Sara Lee Corporation, II; 15 (upd.); 54 (upd.)
Savannah Foods & Industries, Inc., 7
Schlotzsky's, Inc., 36
Schreiber Foods, Inc., 72
Schwan's Sales Enterprises, Inc., 7
Schwebel Baking Company, 72
See's Candies, Inc., 30
Seminis, Inc., 29
Seneca Foods Corporation, 60 (upd.)
Sensient Technologies Corporation, 52 (upd.)
Shearer's Foods, Inc., 72
Silhouette Brands, Inc., 55
Skalli Group, 67
Slim-Fast Foods Company, 66 (upd.)
Smithfield Foods, Inc., 7; 43 (upd.)
Snow Brand Milk Products Company, Ltd., II; 48 (upd.)
Sodiaal S.A., 36 (upd.)
SODIMA, II
Sorrento, Inc., 24
Spangler Candy Company, 44
Spectrum Organic Products, Inc., 68
Stock Yards Packing Co., Inc., 37
Stollwerck AG, 53
Stolt Sea Farm Holdings PLC, 54
Stolt-Nielsen S.A., 42
Stonyfield Farm, Inc., 55
Stouffer Corp., 8
Strauss-Elite Group, 68
Südzucker AG, 27
Suiza Foods Corporation, 26
Sun-Diamond Growers of California, 7
Sunkist Growers, Inc., 26
Supervalu Inc., 18 (upd.); 50 (upd.)
Suprema Specialties, Inc., 27
Sweet Candy Company, 60
Swift & Company, 55
Sylvan, Inc., 22
T. Marzetti Company, 57
Taiyo Fishery Company, Limited, II
Tasty Baking Company, 14; 35 (upd.)
Tate & Lyle PLC, II; 42 (upd.)
TCBY Enterprises Inc., 17
TDL Group Ltd., 46
Terrena L'Union CANA CAVAL, 70
Thomas J. Lipton Company, 14
Thorn Apple Valley, Inc., 7; 22 (upd.)
Thorntons plc, 46
TLC Beatrice International Holdings, Inc., 22
Tofutti Brands, Inc., 64

Tom's Foods Inc., 66
Tombstone Pizza Corporation, 13
Tone Brothers, Inc., 21
Tootsie Roll Industries Inc., 12
Townsends, Inc., 64
Tri Valley Growers, 32
Trident Seafoods Corporation, 56
Tropicana Products, Inc., 28
Tyson Foods, Inc., II; 14 (upd.); 50 (upd.)
U.S. Foodservice, 26
Uncle Ben's Inc., 22
Unigate PLC, II; 28 (upd.)
United Biscuits (Holdings) plc, II; 42 (upd.)
United Brands Company, II
United Foods, Inc., 21
Universal Foods Corporation, 7
Utz Quality Foods, Inc., 72
Van Camp Seafood Company, Inc., 7
Vienna Sausage Manufacturing Co., 14
Vilmorin Clause et Cie, 70
Vista Bakery, Inc., 56
Vlasic Foods International Inc., 25
Walkers Snack Foods Ltd., 70
Warrell Corporation, 68
Wattie's Ltd., 7
Weetabix Limited, 61
Wells' Dairy, Inc., 36
White Wave, 43
Wilbur Chocolate Company, 66
Wimm-Bill-Dann Foods, 48
Wisconsin Dairies, 7
WLR Foods, Inc., 21
Wm. B. Reily & Company Inc., 58
Wm. Wrigley Jr. Company, 7; 58 (upd.)
World's Finest Chocolate, 39
Worthington Foods, Inc., 14
Yamazaki Baking Co., Ltd., 58
YOCREAM International, Inc., 47
Zatarain's, Inc., 64

FOOD SERVICES & RETAILERS

Advantica Restaurant Group, Inc., 27 (upd.)
AFC Enterprises, Inc., 32 (upd.)
Affiliated Foods Inc., 53
Albertson's, Inc., II; 7 (upd.); 30 (upd.); 65 (upd.)
Aldi Group, 13
Alex Lee Inc., 18; 44 (upd.)
Allen Foods, Inc., 60
America's Favorite Chicken Company, Inc., 7
American Stores Company, II
Andronico's Market, 70
Applebee's International, Inc., 14; 35 (upd.)
ARA Services, II
Arby's Inc., 14
Arden Group, Inc., 29
Argyll Group PLC, II
Ark Restaurants Corp., 20
Asahi Breweries, Ltd., 20 (upd.)
ASDA Group Ltd., II; 28 (upd.); 64 (upd.)
Associated Grocers, Incorporated, 9; 31 (upd.)
Association des Centres Distributeurs E. Leclerc, 37
Atlanta Bread Company International, Inc., 70
Au Bon Pain Co., Inc., 18
Auchan, 37
Auntie Anne's, Inc., 35
Autogrill SpA, 49
Avado Brands, Inc., 31
Back Bay Restaurant Group, Inc., 20
Back Yard Burgers, Inc., 45

Bashas' Inc., 33
Bear Creek Corporation, 38
Benihana, Inc., 18
Bertucci's Corporation, 64 (upd.)
Bettys & Taylors of Harrogate Ltd., 72
Big Bear Stores Co., 13
The Big Food Group plc, 68 (upd.)
Big V Supermarkets, Inc., 25
Big Y Foods, Inc., 53
Blimpie International, Inc., 15; 49 (upd.)
Bob Evans Farms, Inc., 9; 63 (upd.)
Bob's Red Mill Natural Foods, Inc., 63
Boddie-Noell Enterprises, 68
Bon Appetit Holding AG, 48
Boston Market Corporation, 12; 48 (upd.)
Briazz, Inc., 53
Brinker International, Inc., 10; 38 (upd.)
Brookshire Grocery Company, 16
Bruegger's Corporation, 63
Bruno's Supermarkets, Inc., 7; 26 (upd.); 68 (upd.)
Buca, Inc., 38
Budgens Ltd., 59
Buffalo Wild Wings, Inc., 56
Buffets, Inc., 10; 32 (upd.)
Burger King Corporation, II; 17 (upd.); 56 (upd.)
C & S Wholesale Grocers, Inc., 55
C.H. Robinson, Inc., 11
Caffè Nero Group PLC, 63
California Pizza Kitchen Inc., 15
Captain D's, LLC, 59
Cargill, Inc., II
Caribou Coffee Company, Inc., 28
Carlson Companies, Inc., 22 (upd.)
Carlson Restaurants Worldwide, 69
Carr-Gottstein Foods Co., 17
Casey's General Stores, Inc., 19
Casino Guichard-Perrachon S.A., 59 (upd.)
CBRL Group, Inc., 35 (upd.)
CEC Entertainment, Inc., 31 (upd.)
Chart House Enterprises, Inc., 17
Checkers Drive-Up Restaurants Inc., 16
The Cheesecake Factory Inc., 17
Chi-Chi's Inc., 13; 51 (upd.)
Chicago Pizza & Brewery, Inc., 44
Chick-fil-A Inc., 23
Chipotle Mexican Grill, Inc., 67
Church's Chicken, 66
Cinnabon Inc., 23
The Circle K Corporation, II
CKE Restaurants, Inc., 19; 46 (upd.)
Coborn's, Inc., 30
Cold Stone Creamery, 69
Compass Group PLC, 34
Comptoirs Modernes S.A., 19
Consolidated Products Inc., 14
Controladora Comercial Mexicana, S.A. de C.V., 36
Cooker Restaurant Corporation, 20; 51 (upd.)
The Copps Corporation, 32
Cosi, Inc., 53
Cost-U-Less, Inc., 51
Coto Centro Integral de Comercializacion S.A., 66
Cracker Barrel Old Country Store, Inc., 10
Cremonini S.p.A., 57
Culver Franchising System, Inc., 58
D'Agostino Supermarkets Inc., 19
Dairy Mart Convenience Stores, Inc., 7; 25 (upd.)
Darden Restaurants, Inc., 16; 44 (upd.)
Dean & DeLuca, Inc., 36
Del Taco, Inc., 58
Delhaize "Le Lion" S.A., 44
DeMoulas / Market Basket Inc., 23

FOOD SERVICES & RETAILERS
(continued)

DenAmerica Corporation, 29
Deschutes Brewery, Inc., 57
Diedrich Coffee, Inc., 40
Dierbergs Markets Inc., 63
Distribución y Servicio D&S S.A., 71
Doctor's Associates Inc., 67 (upd.)
Dominick's Finer Foods, Inc., 56
Domino's, Inc., 7; 21 (upd.); 63 (upd.)
Donatos Pizzeria Corporation, 58
Eateries, Inc., 33
Edeka Zentrale A.G., II; 47 (upd.)
Einstein/Noah Bagel Corporation, 29
El Chico Restaurants, Inc., 19
El Pollo Loco, Inc., 69
Elior SA, 49
Elmer's Restaurants, Inc., 42
Embers America Restaurants, 30
Etablissements Economiques du Casino
    Guichard, Perrachon et Cie, S.C.A., 12
Famous Dave's of America, Inc., 40
Fatburger Corporation, 64
Fazoli's Systems, Inc., 27
Fili Enterprises, Inc., 70
5 & Diner Franchise Corporation, 72
Flagstar Companies, Inc., 10
Flanigan's Enterprises, Inc., 60
Fleming Companies, Inc., II
The Food Emporium, 64
Food Lion LLC, II; 15 (upd.); 66 (upd.)
Foodarama Supermarkets, Inc., 28
Foodmaker, Inc., 14
The Fred W. Albrecht Grocery Co., 13
Fresh Choice, Inc., 20
Fresh Enterprises, Inc., 66
Fresh Foods, Inc., 29
Friendly Ice Cream Corporation, 30; 72
    (upd.)
Frisch's Restaurants, Inc., 35
Fuller Smith & Turner P.L.C., 38
Furr's Restaurant Group, Inc., 53
Furr's Supermarkets, Inc., 28
Galardi Group, Inc., 72
Garden Fresh Restaurant Corporation, 31
Gate Gourmet International AG, 70
The Gateway Corporation Ltd., II
Genuardi's Family Markets, Inc., 35
George Weston Limited, II; 36 (upd.)
Ghirardelli Chocolate Company, 30
Giant Food Inc., II; 22 (upd.)
Godfather's Pizza Incorporated, 25
Golden Corral Corporation, 10; 66 (upd.)
Golden Krust Caribbean Bakery, Inc., 68
Golden State Foods Corporation, 32
The Golub Corporation, 26
Gordon Food Service Inc., 8; 39 (upd.)
The Grand Union Company, 7; 28 (upd.)
The Great Atlantic & Pacific Tea
    Company, Inc., II; 16 (upd.); 55 (upd.)
Greggs PLC, 65
Gristede's Foods Inc., 31; 68 (upd.)
Ground Round, Inc., 21
Groupe Promodès S.A., 19
Guyenne et Gascogne, 23
H.E. Butt Grocery Co., 13; 32 (upd.)
Haggen Inc., 38
Hannaford Bros. Co., 12
Hard Rock Cafe International, Inc., 12
Harris Teeter Inc., 23; 72 (upd.)
Harry's Farmers Market Inc., 23
HDOS Enterprises, 72
Hickory Farms, Inc., 17
Holberg Industries, Inc., 36
Holland Burgerville USA, 44
Hooters of America, Inc., 18; 69 (upd.)
Hops Restaurant Bar and Brewery, 46

Hoss's Steak and Sea House Inc., 68
Hotel Properties Ltd., 71
Houchens Industries Inc., 51
Hughes Markets, Inc., 22
Hungry Howie's Pizza and Subs, Inc., 25
Hy-Vee, Inc., 36
ICA AB, II
Iceland Group plc, 33
IHOP Corporation, 17; 58 (upd.)
Il Fornaio (America) Corporation, 27
In-N-Out Burger, 19
Ingles Markets, Inc., 20
Inserra Supermarkets, 25
Inter Link Foods PLC, 61
International Dairy Queen, Inc., 10; 39
    (upd.)
ITM Entreprises SA, 36
Ito-Yokado Co., Ltd., 42 (upd.)
J Sainsbury plc, II; 13 (upd.); 38 (upd.)
J. Alexander's Corporation, 65
Jamba Juice Company, 47
JD Wetherspoon plc, 30
Jerry's Famous Deli Inc., 24
Jitney-Jungle Stores of America, Inc., 27
John Lewis Partnership plc, 42 (upd.)
Johnny Rockets Group, Inc., 31
KFC Corporation, 7; 21 (upd.)
King Kullen Grocery Co., Inc., 15
Koninklijke Ahold N.V. (Royal Ahold), II;
    16 (upd.)
Koo Koo Roo, Inc., 25
The Kroger Co., II; 15 (upd.); 65 (upd.)
The Krystal Company, 33
Kwik Save Group plc, 11
La Madeleine French Bakery & Café, 33
Landry's Restaurants, Inc., 15; 65 (upd.)
The Laurel Pub Company Limited, 59
Laurus N.V., 65
LDB Corporation, 53
Leeann Chin, Inc., 30
Levy Restaurants L.P., 26
Little Caesar Enterprises, Inc., 7; 24 (upd.)
Loblaw Companies Limited, 43
Logan's Roadhouse, Inc., 29
Lone Star Steakhouse & Saloon, Inc., 51
Long John Silver's, 13; 57 (upd.)
Luby's, Inc., 17; 42 (upd.)
Lucky Stores, Inc., 27
Lund Food Holdings, Inc., 22
Madden's on Gull Lake, 52
Maid-Rite Corporation, 62
Maines Paper & Food Service Inc., 71
Marie Callender's Restaurant & Bakery,
    Inc., 28
Marsh Supermarkets, Inc., 17
Matt Prentice Restaurant Group, 70
Max & Erma's Restaurants Inc., 19
McAlister's Corporation, 66
McCormick & Schmick's Seafood
    Restaurants, Inc., 71
McDonald's Corporation, II; 7 (upd.); 26
    (upd.); 63 (upd.)
Megafoods Stores Inc., 13
Meijer Incorporated, 7
Metcash Trading Ltd., 58
Metromedia Companies, 14
Mexican Restaurants, Inc., 41
The Middleby Corporation, 22
Minyard Food Stores, Inc., 33
MITROPA AG, 37
Monterey Pasta Company, 58
Morrison Restaurants Inc., 11
Morton's Restaurant Group, Inc., 30
Mrs. Fields' Original Cookies, Inc., 27
Musgrave Group Plc, 57
Nash Finch Company, 8; 23 (upd.); 65
    (upd.)

Nathan's Famous, Inc., 29
National Convenience Stores Incorporated,
    7
New World Restaurant Group, Inc., 44
New York Restaurant Group, Inc., 32
Noble Roman's Inc., 14
Noodles & Company, Inc., 55
NPC International, Inc., 40
O'Charley's Inc., 19; 60 (upd.)
Old Spaghetti Factory International Inc., 24
The Oshawa Group Limited, II
Outback Steakhouse, Inc., 12; 34 (upd.)
P&C Foods Inc., 8
P.F. Chang's China Bistro, Inc., 37
Palm Management Corporation, 71
Pancho's Mexican Buffet, Inc., 46
Panda Management Company, Inc., 35
Panera Bread Company, 44
Papa John's International, Inc., 15; 71
    (upd.)
Papa Murphy's International, Inc., 54
Pathmark Stores, Inc., 23
Peapod, Inc., 30
Penn Traffic Company, 13
Performance Food Group Company, 31
Perkins Family Restaurants, L.P., 22
Peter Piper, Inc., 70
Petrossian Inc., 54
Phillips Foods, Inc., 63
Piccadilly Cafeterias, Inc., 19
Piggly Wiggly Southern, Inc., 13
Pizza Hut Inc., 7; 21 (upd.)
Planet Hollywood International, Inc., 18;
    41 (upd.)
Players International, Inc., 22
Ponderosa Steakhouse, 15
Portillo's Restaurant Group, Inc., 71
Provigo Inc., II; 51 (upd.)
Publix Super Markets Inc., 7; 31 (upd.)
Pueblo Xtra International, Inc., 47
Quality Dining, Inc., 18
Quality Food Centers, Inc., 17
The Quizno's Corporation, 42
Rally's, 25; 68 (upd.)
Ralphs Grocery Company, 35
Randall's Food Markets, Inc., 40
Rare Hospitality International Inc., 19
Raving Brands, Inc., 64
Red Robin Gourmet Burgers, Inc., 56
Restaurant Associates Corporation, 66
Restaurants Unlimited, Inc., 13
RFC Franchising LLC, 68
Richfood Holdings, Inc., 7
Richtree Inc., 63
The Riese Organization, 38
Riser Foods, Inc., 9
Roadhouse Grill, Inc., 22
Rock Bottom Restaurants, Inc., 25; 68
    (upd.)
Romacorp, Inc., 58
Roundy's Inc., 58 (upd.)
RTM Restaurant Group, 58
Rubio's Restaurants, Inc., 35
Ruby Tuesday, Inc., 18; 71 (upd.)
Ruth's Chris Steak House, 28
Ryan's Restaurant Group, Inc., 15; 68
    (upd.)
Safeway PLC, II; 24 (upd.); 50 (upd.)
Santa Barbara Restaurant Group, Inc., 37
Sbarro, Inc., 16; 64 (upd.)
Schlotzsky's, Inc., 36
Schultz Sav-O Stores, Inc., 21
Schwan's Sales Enterprises, Inc., 26 (upd.)
Seaway Food Town, Inc., 15
Second Harvest, 29
See's Candies, Inc., 30
Seneca Foods Corporation, 17

Service America Corp., 7
SFI Group plc, 51
Shaw's Supermarkets, Inc., 56
Shells Seafood Restaurants, Inc., 43
Shoney's, Inc., 7; 23 (upd.)
ShowBiz Pizza Time, Inc., 13
Skyline Chili, Inc., 62
Smart & Final, Inc., 16
Smith's Food & Drug Centers, Inc., 8; 57
  (upd.)
Sodexho Alliance SA, 29
Somerfield plc, 47 (upd.)
Sonic Corporation, 14; 37 (upd.)
The Southland Corporation, II; 7 (upd.)
Spaghetti Warehouse, Inc., 25
SPAR Handels AG, 35
Spartan Stores Inc., 8
Stater Bros. Holdings Inc., 64
The Steak n Shake Company, 41
Steinberg Incorporated, II
Stew Leonard's, 56
The Stop & Shop Supermarket Company,
  II; 68 (upd.)
Subway, 32
Super Food Services, Inc., 15
Supermarkets General Holdings
  Corporation, II
Supervalu Inc., II; 18 (upd.); 50 (upd.)
SWH Corporation, 70
SYSCO Corporation, II; 24 (upd.)
Taco Bell Corp., 7; 21 (upd.)
Taco Cabana, Inc., 23; 72 (upd.)
Taco John's International, Inc., 15; 63
  (upd.)
TelePizza S.A., 33
Tesco PLC, II
Texas Roadhouse, Inc., 69
Tops Markets LLC, 60
Total Entertainment Restaurant
  Corporation, 46
Trader Joe's Company, 13; 50 (upd.)
Travel Ports of America, Inc., 17
Tree of Life, Inc., 29
Triarc Companies, Inc., 34 (upd.)
Tubby's, Inc., 53
Tully's Coffee Corporation, 51
Tumbleweed, Inc., 33
TW Services, Inc., II
Ukrop's Super Market's, Inc., 39
Unique Casual Restaurants, Inc., 27
United Natural Foods, Inc., 32
Uno Restaurant Corporation, 18
Uno Restaurant Holdings Corporation, 70
  (upd.)
Uwajimaya, Inc., 60
Vail Resorts, Inc., 43 (upd.)
VICORP Restaurants, Inc., 12; 48 (upd.)
Village Super Market, Inc., 7
The Vons Companies, Incorporated, 7; 28
  (upd.)
Waffle House Inc., 14; 60 (upd.)
Wakefern Food Corporation, 33
Waldbaum, Inc., 19
Wall Street Deli, Inc., 33
Wawa Inc., 17
Wegmans Food Markets, Inc., 9; 41 (upd.)
Weis Markets, Inc., 15
Wendy's International, Inc., 8; 23 (upd.);
  47 (upd.)
The WesterN SizzliN Corporation, 60
Wetterau Incorporated, II
White Castle System, Inc., 12; 36 (upd.)
White Rose, Inc., 24
Whittard of Chelsea Plc, 61
Whole Foods Market, Inc., 50 (upd.)
Wild Oats Markets, Inc., 19; 41 (upd.)

Winchell's Donut Houses Operating
  Company, L.P., 60
WinCo Foods Inc., 60
Winn-Dixie Stores, Inc., II; 21 (upd.); 59
  (upd.)
Wm. Morrison Supermarkets PLC, 38
Wolfgang Puck Worldwide, Inc., 26, 70
  (upd.)
Worldwide Restaurant Concepts, Inc., 47
Young & Co.'s Brewery, P.L.C., 38
Yucaipa Cos., 17
Yum! Brands Inc., 58
Zingerman's Community of Businesses, 68

HEALTH & PERSONAL CARE PRODUCTS

Akorn, Inc., 32
ALARIS Medical Systems, Inc., 65
Alberto-Culver Company, 8
Alco Health Services Corporation, III
Allergan, Inc., 10; 30 (upd.)
American Safety Razor Company, 20
American Stores Company, 22 (upd.)
Amway Corporation, III; 13 (upd.)
Atkins Nutritionals, Inc., 58
Aveda Corporation, 24
Avon Products, Inc., III; 19 (upd.); 46
  (upd.)
Bally Total Fitness Holding Corp., 25
Bausch & Lomb Inc., 7; 25 (upd.)
BeautiControl Cosmetics, Inc., 21
Becton, Dickinson & Company, I; 11
  (upd.)
Beiersdorf AG, 29
Big B, Inc., 17
Bindley Western Industries, Inc., 9
Block Drug Company, Inc., 8; 27 (upd.)
The Body Shop International plc, 53 (upd.)
The Boots Company PLC, 24 (upd.)
Bristol-Myers Squibb Company, III; 9
  (upd.)
C.R. Bard Inc., 9
Candela Corporation, 48
Cardinal Health, Inc., 18; 50 (upd.)
Carson, Inc., 31
Carter-Wallace, Inc., 8
Caswell-Massey Co. Ltd., 51
CCA Industries, Inc., 53
Chattem, Inc., 17
Chesebrough-Pond's USA, Inc., 8
Chronimed Inc., 26
Church & Dwight Co., Inc., 68 (upd.)
Cintas Corporation, 51 (upd.)
The Clorox Company, III
CNS, Inc., 20
Colgate-Palmolive Company, III; 14 (upd.);
  35 (upd.)
Combe Inc., 72
Conair Corp., 17
Connetics Corporation, 70
Cordis Corp., 19
Cosmair, Inc., 8
Coty, Inc., 36
Cybex International, Inc., 49
Cytyc Corporation, 69
Dade Behring Holdings Inc., 71
Datascope Corporation, 39
Del Laboratories, Inc., 28
Deltec, Inc., 56
Dentsply International Inc., 10
DEP Corporation, 20
DePuy, Inc., 30
The Dial Corp., 23 (upd.)
Direct Focus, Inc., 47
Drackett Professional Products, 12
Elizabeth Arden, Inc., 8; 40 (upd.)

Empi, Inc., 26
Enrich International, Inc., 33
The Estée Lauder Companies Inc., 9; 30
  (upd.)
Ethicon, Inc., 23
Forest Laboratories, Inc., 11
Forever Living Products International Inc.,
  17
French Fragrances, Inc., 22
Gambro AB, 49
General Nutrition Companies, Inc., 11; 29
  (upd.)
Genzyme Corporation, 13
The Gillette Company, III; 20 (upd.)
Groupe Yves Saint Laurent, 23
Guerlain, 23
Guest Supply, Inc., 18
Guidant Corporation, 58
Hanger Orthopedic Group, Inc., 41
Helen of Troy Corporation, 18
Helene Curtis Industries, Inc., 8; 28 (upd.)
Henkel KGaA, III
Henry Schein, Inc., 31; 70 (upd.)
Herbalife International, Inc., 17; 41 (upd.)
Inter Parfums Inc., 35
Invacare Corporation, 11
IVAX Corporation, 11
IVC Industries, Inc., 45
The Jean Coutu Group (PJC) Inc., 46
John Paul Mitchell Systems, 24
Johnson & Johnson, III; 8 (upd.); 36 (upd.)
Kanebo, Ltd., 53
Kao Corporation, III
Kendall International, Inc., 11
Kensey Nash Corporation, 71
Kimberly-Clark Corporation, III; 16 (upd.);
  43 (upd.)
Kyowa Hakko Kogyo Co., Ltd., III
L'Oréal SA, III; 8 (upd.); 46 (upd.)
Laboratoires de Biologie Végétale Yves
  Rocher, 35
The Lamaur Corporation, 41
Lever Brothers Company, 9
Lion Corporation, III; 51 (upd.)
Luxottica SpA, 17
Mannatech Inc., 33
Mary Kay Corporation, 9; 30 (upd.)
Maxxim Medical Inc., 12
Medco Containment Services Inc., 9
Medline Industries, Inc., 61
Medtronic, Inc., 8; 67 (upd.)
Melaleuca Inc., 31
The Mentholatum Company Inc., 32
Mentor Corporation, 26
Merck & Co., Inc., 34 (upd.)
Merit Medical Systems, Inc., 29
Nature's Sunshine Products, Inc., 15
NBTY, Inc., 31
NeighborCare, Inc., 67 (upd.)
Neutrogena Corporation, 17
New Dana Perfumes Company, 37
Nikken Global Inc., 32
NutriSystem, Inc., 71
Nutrition for Life International Inc., 22
Ocular Sciences, Inc., 65
OEC Medical Systems, Inc., 27
Orion Oyj, 72
Patterson Dental Co., 19
Perrigo Company, 12
Physician Sales & Service, Inc., 14
Playtex Products, Inc., 15
The Procter & Gamble Company, III; 8
  (upd.); 26 (upd.); 67 (upd.)
PZ Cussons plc, 72
Relìv International, Inc., 58
Revlon Inc., III; 17 (upd.)
Roche Biomedical Laboratories, Inc., 11

HEALTH & PERSONAL CARE PRODUCTS (*continued*)

S.C. Johnson & Son, Inc., III
Safety 1st, Inc., 24
Schering-Plough Corporation, 14 (upd.)
Shaklee Corporation, 39 (upd.)
Shionogi & Co., Ltd., III
Shiseido Company, Limited, III; 22 (upd.)
Slim-Fast Nutritional Foods International, Inc., 18
Smith & Nephew plc, 17
SmithKline Beecham PLC, III
Soft Sheen Products, Inc., 31
Sola International Inc., 71
Spacelabs Medical, Inc., 71
STAAR Surgical Company, 57
Sunrise Medical Inc., 11
Tambrands Inc., 8
Terumo Corporation, 48
Tom's of Maine, Inc., 45
The Tranzonic Companies, 37
Turtle Wax, Inc., 15
Tutogen Medical, Inc., 68
United States Surgical Corporation, 10; 34 (upd.)
USANA, Inc., 29
Utah Medical Products, Inc., 36
VHA Inc., 53
VIASYS Healthcare, Inc., 52
VISX, Incorporated, 30
Vitamin Shoppe Industries, Inc., 60
Water Pik Technologies, Inc., 34
Weider Nutrition International, Inc., 29
Wella AG, III; 48 (upd.)
West Pharmaceutical Services, Inc., 42
Wright Medical Group, Inc., 61
Wyeth, 50 (upd.)
Zila, Inc., 46
Zimmer Holdings, Inc., 45

HEALTH CARE SERVICES

Acadian Ambulance & Air Med Services, Inc., 39
Adventist Health, 53
Advocat Inc., 46
Alterra Healthcare Corporation, 42
Amedysis, Inc., 53
The American Cancer Society, 24
American Healthways, Inc., 65
American Lung Association, 48
American Medical Association, 39
American Medical International, Inc., III
American Medical Response, Inc., 39
American Red Cross, 40
AMERIGROUP Corporation, 69
AmeriSource Health Corporation, 37 (upd.)
AmSurg Corporation, 48
Applied Bioscience International, Inc., 10
Assisted Living Concepts, Inc., 43
ATC Healthcare Inc., 64
Beverly Enterprises, Inc., III; 16 (upd.)
Bon Secours Health System, Inc., 24
C.R. Bard, Inc., 65 (upd.)
Caremark Rx, Inc., 10; 54 (upd.)
Children's Comprehensive Services, Inc., 42
Children's Hospitals and Clinics, Inc., 54
Chronimed Inc., 26
COBE Laboratories, Inc., 13
Columbia/HCA Healthcare Corporation, 15
Community Health Systems, Inc., 71
Community Psychiatric Centers, 15
CompDent Corporation, 22
CompHealth Inc., 25
Comprehensive Care Corporation, 15
Continental Medical Systems, Inc., 10
Continuum Health Partners, Inc., 60

Coventry Health Care, Inc., 59
Easter Seals, Inc., 58
Erickson Retirement Communities, 57
Express Scripts Incorporated, 17
Extendicare Health Services, Inc., 6
Eye Care Centers of America, Inc., 69
FHP International Corporation, 6
Fresenius AG, 56
Genesis Health Ventures, Inc., 18
GranCare, Inc., 14
Group Health Cooperative, 41
Hazelden Foundation, 28
HCA - The Healthcare Company, 35 (upd.)
Health Care & Retirement Corporation, 22
Health Management Associates, Inc., 56
Health Risk Management, Inc., 24
Health Systems International, Inc., 11
HealthSouth Corporation, 14; 33 (upd.)
Highmark Inc., 27
The Hillhaven Corporation, 14
Hooper Holmes, Inc., 22
Hospital Central Services, Inc., 56
Hospital Corporation of America, III
Howard Hughes Medical Institute, 39
Humana Inc., III; 24 (upd.)
Intermountain Health Care, Inc., 27
Jenny Craig, Inc., 10; 29 (upd.)
Kinetic Concepts, Inc. (KCI), 20
LabOne, Inc., 48
Laboratory Corporation of America Holdings, 42 (upd.)
Lifeline Systems, Inc., 53
LifePoint Hospitals, Inc., 69
Lincare Holdings Inc., 43
Manor Care, Inc., 6; 25 (upd.)
March of Dimes, 31
Matria Healthcare, Inc., 17
Maxicare Health Plans, Inc., III; 25 (upd.)
Mayo Foundation, 9; 34 (upd.)
Medical Management International, Inc., 65
Memorial Sloan-Kettering Cancer Center, 57
Merit Medical Systems, Inc., 29
National Health Laboratories Incorporated, 11
National Medical Enterprises, Inc., III
New York City Health and Hospitals Corporation, 60
New York Health Care, Inc., 72
NewYork-Presbyterian Hospital, 59
NovaCare, Inc., 11
NSF International, 72
Option Care Inc., 48
Orthodontic Centers of America, Inc., 35
Oxford Health Plans, Inc., 16
PacifiCare Health Systems, Inc., 11
Palomar Medical Technologies, Inc., 22
Pediatric Services of America, Inc., 31
Pediatrix Medical Group, Inc., 61
PHP Healthcare Corporation, 22
PhyCor, Inc., 36
Primedex Health Systems, Inc., 25
The Providence Service Corporation, 64
Psychiatric Solutions, Inc., 68
Quest Diagnostics Inc., 26
Ramsay Youth Services, Inc., 41
Renal Care Group, Inc., 72
Res-Care, Inc., 29
Response Oncology, Inc., 27
Rural/Metro Corporation, 28
Sabratek Corporation, 29
St. Jude Medical, Inc., 11; 43 (upd.)
Salick Health Care, Inc., 53
Select Medical Corporation, 65
Shriners Hospitals for Children, 69
Sierra Health Services, Inc., 15
Smith & Nephew plc, 41 (upd.)

The Sports Club Company, 25
SSL International plc, 49
Stericycle Inc., 33
Sun Healthcare Group Inc., 25
SwedishAmerican Health System, 51
Tenet Healthcare Corporation, 55 (upd.)
Twinlab Corporation, 34
U.S. Healthcare, Inc., 6
U.S. Physical Therapy, Inc., 65
Unison HealthCare Corporation, 25
United HealthCare Corporation, 9
United Nations International Children's Emergency Fund (UNICEF), 58
United Way of America, 36
Universal Health Services, Inc., 6
Vanguard Health Systems Inc., 70
VCA Antech, Inc., 58
Vencor, Inc., 16
VISX, Incorporated, 30
Vivra, Inc., 18
Volunteers of America, Inc., 66
WellPoint Health Networks Inc., 25
YWCA of the U.S.A., 45

HOTELS

Accor S.A., 69 (upd.)
Amerihost Properties, Inc., 30
Ameristar Casinos, Inc., 69 (upd.)
Aztar Corporation, 13; 71 (upd.)
Bass PLC, 38 (upd.)
Boca Resorts, Inc., 37
Boyd Gaming Corporation, 43
Boyne USA Resorts, 71
Bristol Hotel Company, 23
The Broadmoor Hotel, 30
Caesars World, Inc., 6
Candlewood Hotel Company, Inc., 41
Carlson Companies, Inc., 22 (upd.)
Castle & Cooke, Inc., 20 (upd.)
Cedar Fair, L.P., 22
Cendant Corporation, 44 (upd.)
Choice Hotels International Inc., 14
Circus Circus Enterprises, Inc., 6
Club Mediterranée S.A., 6; 21 (upd.)
Compagnia Italiana dei Jolly Hotels S.p.A., 71
Doubletree Corporation, 21
Extended Stay America, Inc., 41
Fairmont Hotels & Resorts Inc., 69
Fibreboard Corporation, 16
Four Seasons Hotels Inc., 9; 29 (upd.)
Fuller Smith & Turner P.L.C., 38
Gables Residential Trust, 49
Gaylord Entertainment Company, 11; 36 (upd.)
Granada Group PLC, 24 (upd.)
Grand Casinos, Inc., 20
Grand Hotel Krasnapolsky N.V., 23
Grupo Posadas, S.A. de C.V., 57
Helmsley Enterprises, Inc., 9
Hilton Hotels Corporation, III; 19 (upd.); 49 (upd.); 62 (upd.)
Holiday Inns, Inc., III
Hospitality Franchise Systems, Inc., 11
Hotel Properties Ltd., 71
Howard Johnson International, Inc., 17; 72 (upd.)
Hyatt Corporation, III; 16 (upd.)
ILX Resorts Incorporated, 65
Interstate Hotels & Resorts Inc., 58
ITT Sheraton Corporation, III
JD Wetherspoon plc, 30
John Q. Hammons Hotels, Inc., 24
Kerzner International Limited, 69 (upd.)
The La Quinta Companies, 11; 42 (upd.)
Ladbroke Group PLC, 21 (upd.)
Landry's Restaurants, Inc., 65 (upd.)

Las Vegas Sands, Inc., 50
Madden's on Gull Lake, 52
Mandalay Resort Group, 32 (upd.)
Manor Care, Inc., 25 (upd.)
The Marcus Corporation, 21
Marriott International, Inc., III; 21 (upd.)
McMenamins Pubs and Breweries, 65
Millennium & Copthorne Hotels plc, 71
Mirage Resorts, Incorporated, 6; 28 (upd.)
Monarch Casino & Resort, Inc., 65
Motel 6, 13; 56 (upd.)
MWH Preservation Limited Partnership, 65
Omni Hotels Corp., 12
Park Corp., 22
Players International, Inc., 22
Preussag AG, 42 (upd.)
Prime Hospitality Corporation, 52
Promus Companies, Inc., 9
Real Turismo, S.A. de C.V., 50
Red Roof Inns, Inc., 18
Resorts International, Inc., 12
The Ritz-Carlton Hotel Company, L.L.C.,
    9; 29 (upd.); 71 (upd.)
Sandals Resorts International, 65
Santa Fe Gaming Corporation, 19
The SAS Group, 34 (upd.)
SFI Group plc, 51
Shangri-La Asia Ltd., 71
Showboat, Inc., 19
Sol Meliá S.A., 71
Sonesta International Hotels Corporation,
    44
Starwood Hotels & Resorts Worldwide,
    Inc., 54
Sun International Hotels Limited, 26
Sunburst Hospitality Corporation, 26
Thistle Hotels PLC, 54
Trusthouse Forte PLC, III
Vail Resorts, Inc., 43 (upd.)
WestCoast Hospitality Corporation, 59
Westin Hotels and Resorts Worldwide, 9;
    29 (upd.)
Whitbread PLC, 52 (upd.)
Young & Co.'s Brewery, P.L.C., 38

INFORMATION TECHNOLOGY

A.B. Watley Group Inc., 45
Acxiom Corporation, 35
Adaptec, Inc., 31
Adobe Systems Incorporated, 10; 33 (upd.)
Advanced Micro Devices, Inc., 6
Agence France-Presse, 34
Agilent Technologies Inc., 38
Akamai Technologies, Inc., 71
Aldus Corporation, 10
Allen Systems Group, Inc., 59
AltaVista Company, 43
Altiris, Inc., 65
Amdahl Corporation, III; 14 (upd.); 40
    (upd.)
Amdocs Ltd., 47
America Online, Inc., 10; 26 (upd.)
American Business Information, Inc., 18
American Management Systems, Inc., 11
American Software Inc., 25
AMICAS, Inc., 69
Amstrad PLC, III
Analytic Sciences Corporation, 10
Analytical Surveys, Inc., 33
Anker BV, 53
Ansoft Corporation, 63
Anteon Corporation, 57
AOL Time Warner Inc., 57 (upd.)
Apollo Group, Inc., 24
Apple Computer, Inc., III; 6 (upd.)
The Arbitron Company, 38
Ariba, Inc., 57

Asanté Technologies, Inc., 20
Ascential Software Corporation, 59
AsiaInfo Holdings, Inc., 43
ASK Group, Inc., 9
Ask Jeeves, Inc., 65
ASML Holding N.V., 50
AST Research Inc., 9
ASM L Holding N.V., 50
At Home Corporation, 43
AT&T Bell Laboratories, Inc., 13
AT&T Corporation, 29 (upd.)
AT&T Istel Ltd., 14
Atos Origin S.A., 69
Attachmate Corporation, 56
Autologic Information International, Inc.,
    20
Automatic Data Processing, Inc., III; 9
    (upd.)
Autotote Corporation, 20
Avid Technology Inc., 38
Avocent Corporation, 65
Aydin Corp., 19
Baan Company, 25
Baltimore Technologies Plc, 42
Banyan Systems Inc., 25
Battelle Memorial Institute, Inc., 10
BBN Corp., 19
BEA Systems, Inc., 36
Bell and Howell Company, 9; 29 (upd.)
Bell Industries, Inc., 47
Billing Concepts Corp., 26
Bloomberg L.P., 21
Blue Martini Software, Inc., 59
BMC Software, Inc., 55
Boole & Babbage, Inc., 25
Booz Allen & Hamilton Inc., 10
Borland International, Inc., 9
Bowne & Co., Inc., 23
Brite Voice Systems, Inc., 20
Broderbund Software, 13; 29 (upd.)
BTG, Inc., 45
Bull S.A., 43 (upd.)
Business Objects S.A., 25
C-Cube Microsystems, Inc., 37
CACI International Inc., 21; 72 (upd.)
Cadence Design Systems, Inc., 11
Caere Corporation, 20
Cahners Business Information, 43
CalComp Inc., 13
Cambridge Technology Partners, Inc., 36
Candle Corporation, 64
Canon Inc., III
Cap Gemini Ernst & Young, 37
Caribiner International, Inc., 24
Catalina Marketing Corporation, 18
CDC Corporation, 71
CDW Computer Centers, Inc., 16
Cerner Corporation, 16
Cheyenne Software, Inc., 12
CHIPS and Technologies, Inc., 9
Ciber, Inc., 18
Cincom Systems Inc., 15
Cirrus Logic, Incorporated, 11
Cisco Systems, Inc., 11
Citizen Watch Co., Ltd., 21 (upd.)
Citrix Systems, Inc., 44
CNET Networks, Inc., 47
Cogent Communications Group, Inc., 55
Cognizant Technology Solutions
    Corporation, 59
Cognos Inc., 44
Commodore International Ltd., 7
Compagnie des Machines Bull S.A., III
Compaq Computer Corporation, III; 6
    (upd.); 26 (upd.)
Complete Business Solutions, Inc., 31
CompuAdd Computer Corporation, 11
CompuCom Systems, Inc., 10

CompUSA, Inc., 35 (upd.)
CompuServe Interactive Services, Inc., 10;
    27 (upd.)
Computer Associates International, Inc., 6;
    49 (upd.)
Computer Data Systems, Inc., 14
Computer Sciences Corporation, 6
Computervision Corporation, 10
Compuware Corporation, 10; 30 (upd.); 66
    (upd.)
Comshare Inc., 23
Conner Peripherals, Inc., 6
Control Data Corporation, III
Control Data Systems, Inc., 10
Corbis Corporation, 31
Corel Corporation, 15; 33 (upd.)
Corporate Software Inc., 9
Cray Research, Inc., III
CTG, Inc., 11
Cybermedia, Inc., 25
Dassault Systèmes S.A., 25
Data Broadcasting Corporation, 31
Data General Corporation, 8
Datapoint Corporation, 11
Dell Computer Corp., 9
Dendrite International, Inc., 70
Deutsche Börse AG, 59
Dialogic Corporation, 18
DiamondCluster International, Inc., 51
Digex, Inc., 46
Digital Equipment Corporation, III; 6
    (upd.)
Digital River, Inc., 50
Dimension Data Holdings PLC, 69
Documentum, Inc., 46
The Dun & Bradstreet Corporation, IV; 19
    (upd.)
Dun & Bradstreet Software Services Inc.,
    11
DynCorp, 45
E.piphany, Inc., 49
EarthLink, Inc., 36
ECS S.A, 12
Edmark Corporation, 14; 41 (upd.)
Egghead Inc., 9
El Camino Resources International, Inc., 11
Electronic Arts Inc., 10
Electronic Data Systems Corporation, III;
    28 (upd.)
Electronics for Imaging, Inc., 43 (upd.)
EMC Corporation, 12; 46 (upd.)
Encore Computer Corporation, 13
Environmental Systems Research Institute
    Inc. (ESRI), 62
Epic Systems Corporation, 62
EPIQ Systems, Inc., 56
Evans & Sutherland Computer Corporation,
    19
Exabyte Corporation, 12
Experian Information Solutions Inc., 45
F5 Networks, Inc., 72
First Financial Management Corporation,
    11
Fiserv Inc., 11
FlightSafety International, Inc., 9
FORE Systems, Inc., 25
Franklin Electronic Publishers, Inc., 23
FTP Software, Inc., 20
Fujitsu Limited, III; 42 (upd.)
Fujitsu-ICL Systems Inc., 11
Future Now, Inc., 12
Gartner Group, Inc., 21
Gateway, Inc., 10; 27 (upd.)
GEAC Computer Corporation Ltd., 43
Gericom AG, 47
Getronics NV, 39
GFI Informatique SA, 49

INFORMATION TECHNOLOGY
(*continued*)

Google, Inc., 50
GSI Commerce, Inc., 67
GT Interactive Software, 31
Guthy-Renker Corporation, 32
Handspring Inc., 49
Hewlett-Packard Company, III; 6 (upd.)
Hyperion Software Corporation, 22
ICL plc, 6
Identix Inc., 44
IDX Systems Corporation, 64
IKON Office Solutions, Inc., 50
Imation Corporation, 20
Indus International Inc., 70
Infineon Technologies AG, 50
Information Access Company, 17
Information Builders, Inc., 22
Information Resources, Inc., 10
Informix Corporation, 10; 30 (upd.)
Infosys Technologies Ltd., 38
Ing. C. Olivetti & C., S.p.a., III
Inktomi Corporation, 45
Inso Corporation, 26
Intel Corporation, 36 (upd.)
IntelliCorp, Inc., 45
Intelligent Electronics, Inc., 6
Intergraph Corporation, 6; 24 (upd.)
International Business Machines
    Corporation, III; 6 (upd.); 30 (upd.); 63
    (upd.)
Intrado Inc., 63
Intuit Inc., 14; 33 (upd.)
Iomega Corporation, 21
IONA Technologies plc, 43
J.D. Edwards & Company, 14
Jack Henry and Associates, Inc., 17
Janus Capital Group Inc., 57
The Judge Group, Inc., 51
Juniper Networks, Inc., 43
Juno Online Services, Inc., 38
Kana Software, Inc., 51
Keane, Inc., 56
KLA Instruments Corporation, 11
Knight Ridder, Inc., 67 (upd.)
KnowledgeWare Inc., 31 (upd.)
Komag, Inc., 11
Kronos, Inc., 18
Kurzweil Technologies, Inc., 51
Lam Research Corporation, 11
Landauer, Inc., 51
Lason, Inc., 31
Lawson Software, 38
The Learning Company Inc., 24
Learning Tree International Inc., 24
Legent Corporation, 10
LEXIS-NEXIS Group, 33
Logica plc, 14; 37 (upd.)
Logicon Inc., 20
Logitech International S.A., 28; 69 (upd.)
LoJack Corporation, 48
Lotus Development Corporation, 6; 25
    (upd.)
The MacNeal-Schwendler Corporation, 25
Macromedia, Inc., 50
Madge Networks N.V., 26
MAI Systems Corporation, 11
MAPICS, Inc., 55
Maxtor Corporation, 10
Mead Data Central, Inc., 10
Mecklermedia Corporation, 24
Medical Information Technology Inc., 64
Mentor Graphics Corporation, 11
Mercury Interactive Corporation, 59
Merisel, Inc., 12
Metatec International, Inc., 47
Metro Information Services, Inc., 36

Micro Warehouse, Inc., 16
Micron Technology, Inc., 11; 29 (upd.)
Micros Systems, Inc., 18
Microsoft Corporation, 6; 27 (upd.); 63
    (upd.)
Misys plc, 45; 46
MITRE Corporation, 26
Morningstar Inc., 68
The Motley Fool, Inc., 40
National Semiconductor Corporation, 6
National TechTeam, Inc., 41
Navarre Corporation, 24
NAVTEQ Corporation, 69
NCR Corporation, III; 6 (upd.); 30 (upd.)
Netezza Corporation, 69
Netscape Communications Corporation, 15;
    35 (upd.)
Network Appliance, Inc., 58
Network Associates, Inc., 25
Nextel Communications, Inc., 10
NFO Worldwide, Inc., 24
Nichols Research Corporation, 18
Nimbus CD International, Inc., 20
Nixdorf Computer AG, III
Novell, Inc., 6; 23 (upd.)
NVIDIA Corporation, 54
Océ N.V., 24
Odetics Inc., 14
Onyx Software Corporation, 53
Opsware Inc., 49
Oracle Corporation, 6; 24 (upd.); 67 (upd.)
Orbitz, Inc., 61
Packard Bell Electronics, Inc., 13
Parametric Technology Corp., 16
PC Connection, Inc., 37
PeopleSoft Inc., 14; 33 (upd.)
Perot Systems Corporation, 29
Pitney Bowes Inc., III
PLATINUM Technology, Inc., 14
Policy Management Systems Corporation,
    11
Policy Studies, Inc., 62
Portal Software, Inc., 47
Primark Corp., 13
The Princeton Review, Inc., 42
Printrak, A Motorola Company, 44
Printronix, Inc., 18
Prodigy Communications Corporation, 34
Progress Software Corporation, 15
Psion PLC, 45
Quantum Corporation, 10; 62 (upd.)
Quark, Inc., 36
Racal-Datacom Inc., 11
Razorfish, Inc., 37
RCM Technologies, Inc., 34
RealNetworks, Inc., 53
Red Hat, Inc., 45
Remedy Corporation, 58
Renaissance Learning Systems, Inc., 39
Reuters Group PLC, 22 (upd.); 63 (upd.)
The Reynolds and Reynolds Company, 50
Ricoh Company, Ltd., III
RSA Security Inc., 46
SABRE Group Holdings, Inc., 26
The Sage Group, 43
The Santa Cruz Operation, Inc., 38
SAP AG, 16; 43 (upd.)
SAS Institute Inc., 10
SBS Technologies, Inc., 25
SCB Computer Technology, Inc., 29
Schawk, Inc., 24
SDL PLC, 67
Seagate Technology, Inc., 8
Siebel Systems, Inc., 38
Sierra On-Line, Inc., 15; 41 (upd.)
SilverPlatter Information Inc., 23
SINA Corporation, 69

SmartForce PLC, 43
Softbank Corp., 13; 38 (upd.)
SPSS Inc., 64
Standard Microsystems Corporation, 11
STC PLC, III
Steria SA, 49
Sterling Software, Inc., 11
Storage Technology Corporation, 6
Stratus Computer, Inc., 10
Sun Microsystems, Inc., 7; 30 (upd.)
SunGard Data Systems Inc., 11
Sybase, Inc., 10; 27 (upd.)
Sykes Enterprises, Inc., 45
Symantec Corporation, 10
Symbol Technologies, Inc., 15
Synopsys, Inc., 11; 69 (upd.)
System Software Associates, Inc., 10
Systems & Computer Technology Corp.,
    19
T-Online International AG, 61
Tandem Computers, Inc., 6
TenFold Corporation, 35
Terra Lycos, Inc., 43
The Thomson Corporation, 34 (upd.)
3Com Corporation, 11; 34 (upd.)
The 3DO Company, 43
Timberline Software Corporation, 15
Traffix, Inc., 61
Transaction Systems Architects, Inc., 29
Transiciel SA, 48
Triple P N.V., 26
Ubi Soft Entertainment S.A., 41
Unilog SA, 42
Unisys Corporation, III; 6 (upd.); 36 (upd.)
United Business Media plc, 52 (upd.)
United Online, Inc., 71 (upd.)
UUNET, 38
Verbatim Corporation, 14
Veridian Corporation, 54
VeriFone, Inc., 18
VeriSign, Inc., 47
Veritas Software Corporation, 45
Verity Inc., 68
Viasoft Inc., 27
Volt Information Sciences Inc., 26
Wang Laboratories, Inc., III; 6 (upd.)
WebMD Corporation, 65
West Group, 34 (upd.)
Westcon Group, Inc., 67
Western Digital Corp., 25
Wind River Systems, Inc., 37
Wipro Limited, 43
Wolters Kluwer NV, 33 (upd.)
WordPerfect Corporation, 10
Wyse Technology, Inc., 15
Xerox Corporation, III; 6 (upd.); 26 (upd.)
Xilinx, Inc., 16
Yahoo! Inc., 27; 70 (upd.)
Zapata Corporation, 25
Ziff Davis Media Inc., 36 (upd.)
Zilog, Inc., 15

INSURANCE

AEGON N.V., III; 50 (upd.)
Aetna Inc., III; 21 (upd.); 63 (upd.)
AFLAC Incorporated, 10 (upd.); 38 (upd.)
Alexander & Alexander Services Inc., 10
Alfa Corporation, 60
Alleanza Assicurazioni S.p.A., 65
Alleghany Corporation, 10
Allianz AG, III; 15 (upd.); 57 (upd.)
Allmerica Financial Corporation, 63
The Allstate Corporation, 10; 27 (upd.)
AMB Generali Holding AG, 51
American Family Corporation, III
American Financial Group Inc., III; 48
    (upd.)

American General Corporation, III; 10 (upd.); 46 (upd.)
American International Group, Inc., III; 15 (upd.); 47 (upd.)
American National Insurance Company, 8; 27 (upd.)
American Premier Underwriters, Inc., 10
American Re Corporation, 10; 35 (upd.)
N.V. AMEV, III
Aon Corporation, III; 45 (upd.)
Assicurazioni Generali SpA, III; 15 (upd.)
Assurances Générales de France, 63
Atlantic American Corporation, 44
Aviva PLC, 50 (upd.)
Axa, III
AXA Colonia Konzern AG, 27; 49 (upd.)
B.A.T. Industries PLC, 22 (upd.)
Baldwin & Lyons, Inc., 51
Bâloise-Holding, 40
Benfield Greig Group plc, 53
Berkshire Hathaway Inc., III; 18 (upd.)
Blue Cross and Blue Shield Association, 10
Brown & Brown, Inc., 41
Business Men's Assurance Company of America, 14
Capital Holding Corporation, III
Catholic Order of Foresters, 24
China Life Insurance Company Limited, 65
ChoicePoint Inc., 65
The Chubb Corporation, III; 14 (upd.); 37 (upd.)
CIGNA Corporation, III; 22 (upd.); 45 (upd.)
Cincinnati Financial Corporation, 16; 44 (upd.)
CNA Financial Corporation, III; 38 (upd.)
Commercial Union PLC, III
Connecticut Mutual Life Insurance Company, III
Conseco Inc., 10; 33 (upd.)
The Continental Corporation, III
Debeka Krankenversicherungsverein auf Gegenseitigkeit, 72
The Doctors' Company, 55
Empire Blue Cross and Blue Shield, III
Enbridge Inc., 43
Engle Homes, Inc., 46
The Equitable Life Assurance Society of the United States Fireman's Fund Insurance Company, III
ERGO Versicherungsgruppe AG, 44
Erie Indemnity Company, 35
Fairfax Financial Holdings Limited, 57
Farm Family Holdings, Inc., 39
Farmers Insurance Group of Companies, 25
Fidelity National Financial Inc., 54
The First American Corporation, 52
First Executive Corporation, III
Foundation Health Corporation, 12
Gainsco, Inc., 22
GEICO Corporation, 10; 40 (upd.)
General Accident PLC, III
General Re Corporation, III; 24 (upd.)
Gerling-Konzern Versicherungs-Beteiligungs-Aktiengesellschaft, 51
Great-West Lifeco Inc., III
Gryphon Holdings, Inc., 21
Guardian Financial Services, 64 (upd.)
Guardian Royal Exchange Plc, 11
Harleysville Group Inc., 37
HDI (Haftpflichtverband der Deutschen Industrie Versicherung auf Gegenseitigkeit V.a.G.), 53
The Home Insurance Company, III
Horace Mann Educators Corporation, 22
Household International, Inc., 21 (upd.)

HUK-Coburg, 58
Irish Life & Permanent Plc, 59
Jackson National Life Insurance Company, 8
Jefferson-Pilot Corporation, 11; 29 (upd.)
John Hancock Financial Services, Inc., III; 42 (upd.)
Johnson & Higgins, 14
Kaiser Foundation Health Plan, Inc., 53
Kemper Corporation, III; 15 (upd.)
Legal & General Group plc, III; 24 (upd.)
The Liberty Corporation, 22
Liberty Mutual Holding Company, 59
Lincoln National Corporation, III; 25 (upd.)
Lloyd's of London, III; 22 (upd.)
The Loewen Group Inc., 40 (upd.)
Lutheran Brotherhood, 31
Marsh & McLennan Companies, Inc., III; 45 (upd.)
Massachusetts Mutual Life Insurance Company, III; 53 (upd.)
The Meiji Mutual Life Insurance Company, III
Mercury General Corporation, 25
Metropolitan Life Insurance Company, III; 52 (upd.)
MGIC Investment Corp., 52
The Midland Company, 65
Millea Holdings Inc., 64 (upd.)
Mitsui Marine and Fire Insurance Company, Limited, III
Mitsui Mutual Life Insurance Company, III; 39 (upd.)
Modern Woodmen of America, 66
Munich Re (Münchener Rückversicherungs-Gesellschaft Aktiengesellschaft in München), III; 46 (upd.)
The Mutual Benefit Life Insurance Company, III
The Mutual Life Insurance Company of New York, III
Nationale-Nederlanden N.V., III
New England Mutual Life Insurance Company, III
New York Life Insurance Company, III; 45 (upd.)
Nippon Life Insurance Company, III; 60 (upd.)
Northwestern Mutual Life Insurance Company, III; 45 (upd.)
NYMAGIC, Inc., 41
Ohio Casualty Corp., 11
Old Republic International Corporation, 11; 58 (upd.)
Oregon Dental Service Health Plan, Inc., 51
Palmer & Cay, Inc., 69
Pan-American Life Insurance Company, 48
The Paul Revere Corporation, 12
Pennsylvania Blue Shield, III
The PMI Group, Inc., 49
Preserver Group, Inc., 44
Principal Mutual Life Insurance Company, III
The Progressive Corporation, 11; 29 (upd.)
Provident Life and Accident Insurance Company of America, III
Prudential Corporation PLC, III
The Prudential Insurance Company of America, III; 30 (upd.)
Prudential plc, 48 (upd.)
Radian Group Inc., 42
Reliance Group Holdings, Inc., III
Riunione Adriatica di Sicurtà SpA, III
Royal & Sun Alliance Insurance Group plc, 55 (upd.)

Royal Insurance Holdings PLC, III
SAFECO Corporaton, III
The St. Paul Companies, Inc., III; 22 (upd.)
SCOR S.A., 20
Skandia Insurance Company, Ltd., 50
StanCorp Financial Group, Inc., 56
The Standard Life Assurance Company, III
State Farm Mutual Automobile Insurance Company, III; 51 (upd.)
State Financial Services Corporation, 51
Sumitomo Life Insurance Company, III; 60 (upd.)
The Sumitomo Marine and Fire Insurance Company, Limited, III
Sun Alliance Group PLC, III
SunAmerica Inc., 11
Svenska Handelsbanken AB, 50 (upd.)
Swiss Reinsurance Company (Schweizerische Rückversicherungs-Gesellschaft), III; 46 (upd.)
Teachers Insurance and Annuity Association-College Retirement Equities Fund, III; 45 (upd.)
Texas Industries, Inc., 8
TIG Holdings, Inc., 26
The Tokio Marine and Fire Insurance Co., Ltd., III
Torchmark Corporation, 9; 33 (upd.)
Transatlantic Holdings, Inc., 11
The Travelers Corporation, III
UICI, 33
Union des Assurances de Pans, III
United National Group, Ltd., 63
Unitrin Inc., 16
UNUM Corp., 13
UnumProvident Corporation, 52 (upd.)
USAA, 10
USF&G Corporation, III
Victoria Group, 44 (upd.)
VICTORIA Holding AG, III
W.R. Berkley Corp., 15
Washington National Corporation, 12
The Wawanesa Mutual Insurance Company, 68
WellChoice, Inc., 67 (upd.)
Westfield Group, 69
White Mountains Insurance Group, Ltd., 48
Willis Corroon Group plc, 25
Winterthur Group, III; 68 (upd.)
The Yasuda Fire and Marine Insurance Company, Limited, III
The Yasuda Mutual Life Insurance Company, III; 39 (upd.)
"Zürich" Versicherungs-Gesellschaft, III

LEGAL SERVICES

Akin, Gump, Strauss, Hauer & Feld, L.L.P., 33
American Bar Association, 35
American Lawyer Media Holdings, Inc., 32
Amnesty International, 50
Andrews Kurth, LLP, 71
Arnold & Porter, 35
Baker & Hostetler LLP, 40
Baker & McKenzie, 10; 42 (upd.)
Baker and Botts, L.L.P., 28
Bingham Dana LLP, 43
Brobeck, Phleger & Harrison, LLP, 31
Cadwalader, Wickersham & Taft, 32
Chadbourne & Parke, 36
Cleary, Gottlieb, Steen & Hamilton, 35
Clifford Chance LLP, 38
Coudert Brothers, 30
Covington & Burling, 40
Cravath, Swaine & Moore, 43
Davis Polk & Wardwell, 36
Debevoise & Plimpton, 39

LEGAL SERVICES (*continued*)

Dechert, 43
Dewey Ballantine LLP, 48
Dorsey & Whitney LLP, 47
Fenwick & West LLP, 34
Fish & Neave, 54
Foley & Lardner, 28
Fried, Frank, Harris, Shriver & Jacobson, 35
Fulbright & Jaworski L.L.P., 47
Gibson, Dunn & Crutcher LLP, 36
Greenberg Traurig, LLP, 65
Heller, Ehrman, White & McAuliffe, 41
Hildebrandt International, 29
Hogan & Hartson L.L.P., 44
Holland & Knight LLP, 60
Holme Roberts & Owen LLP, 28
Hughes Hubbard & Reed LLP, 44
Hunton & Williams, 35
Jenkens & Gilchrist, P.C., 65
Jones, Day, Reavis & Pogue, 33
Kelley Drye & Warren LLP, 40
King & Spalding, 23
Kirkland & Ellis LLP, 65
Latham & Watkins, 33
LeBoeuf, Lamb, Greene & MacRae, L.L.P., 29
The Legal Aid Society, 48
Mayer, Brown, Rowe & Maw, 47
Milbank, Tweed, Hadley & McCloy, 27
Morgan, Lewis & Bockius LLP, 29
O'Melveny & Myers, 37
Oppenheimer Wolff & Donnelly LLP, 71
Patton Boggs LLP, 71
Paul, Hastings, Janofsky & Walker LLP, 27
Paul, Weiss, Rifkind, Wharton & Garrison, 47
Pepper Hamilton LLP, 43
Perkins Coie LLP, 56
Pillsbury Madison & Sutro LLP, 29
Pre-Paid Legal Services, Inc., 20
Proskauer Rose LLP, 47
Ropes & Gray, 40
Shearman & Sterling, 32
Sidley Austin Brown & Wood, 40
Simpson Thacher & Bartlett, 39
Skadden, Arps, Slate, Meagher & Flom, 18
Snell & Wilmer L.L.P., 28
Stroock & Stroock & Lavan LLP, 40
Sullivan & Cromwell, 26
Vinson & Elkins L.L.P., 30
Wachtell, Lipton, Rosen & Katz, 47
Weil, Gotshal & Manges LLP, 55
White & Case LLP, 35
Williams & Connolly LLP, 47
Wilson Sonsini Goodrich & Rosati, 34
Winston & Strawn, 35
Womble Carlyle Sandridge & Rice, PLLC, 52

MANUFACTURING

A-dec, Inc., 53
A. Schulman, Inc., 49 (upd.)
A.B.Dick Company, 28
A.O. Smith Corporation, 11; 40 (upd.)
A.T. Cross Company, 17; 49 (upd.)
A.W. Faber-Castell Unternehmensverwaltung GmbH & Co., 51
AAF-McQuay Incorporated, 26
AAON, Inc., 22
AAR Corp., 28
Aarhus United A/S, 68
ABB Ltd., 65 (upd.)
ABC Rail Products Corporation, 18
Abiomed, Inc., 47
ACCO World Corporation, 7; 51 (upd.)

Acme United Corporation, 70
Acme-Cleveland Corp., 13
Acorn Products, Inc., 55
Acushnet Company, 64
Acuson Corporation, 36 (upd.)
Adams Golf, Inc., 37
Adolf Würth GmbH & Co. KG, 49
Advanced Circuits Inc., 67
AEP Industries, Inc., 36
Ag-Chem Equipment Company, Inc., 17
AGCO Corporation, 13; 67 (upd.)
Agfa Gevaert Group N.V., 59
Ahlstrom Corporation, 53
Airgas, Inc., 54
Aisin Seiki Co., Ltd., III
AK Steel Holding Corporation, 41 (upd.)
AKG Acoustics GmbH, 62
Aktiebolaget Electrolux, 22 (upd.)
Aktiebolaget SKF, III; 38 (upd.)
Alamo Group Inc., 32
ALARIS Medical Systems, Inc., 65
Alberto-Culver Company, 36 (upd.)
Aldila Inc., 46
Alfa Laval AB, III; 64 (upd.)
Allen Organ Company, 33
Allen-Edmonds Shoe Corporation, 61
Alliant Techsystems Inc., 8; 30 (upd.)
The Allied Defense Group, Inc., 65
Allied Healthcare Products, Inc., 24
Allied Products Corporation, 21
Allied Signal Engines, 9
AlliedSignal Inc., 22 (upd.)
Allison Gas Turbine Division, 9
Alltrista Corporation, 30
Alps Electric Co., Ltd., 44 (upd.)
Alticor Inc., 71 (upd.)
Alvis Plc, 47
Amer Group plc, 41
American Axle & Manufacturing Holdings, Inc., 67
American Biltrite Inc., 43 (upd.)
American Business Products, Inc., 20
American Cast Iron Pipe Company, 50
American Greetings Corporation, 59 (upd.)
American Homestar Corporation, 18; 41 (upd.)
American Locker Group Incorporated, 34
American Power Conversion Corporation, 67 (upd.)
American Standard Companies Inc., 30 (upd.)
American Technical Ceramics Corp., 67
American Tourister, Inc., 16
American Woodmark Corporation, 31
Ameriwood Industries International Corp., 17
Amerock Corporation, 53
Ameron International Corporation, 67
AMETEK, Inc., 9
AMF Bowling, Inc., 40
Ampacet Corporation, 67
Ampex Corporation, 17
Amway Corporation, 30 (upd.)
Analogic Corporation, 23
Anchor Hocking Glassware, 13
Andersen Corporation, 10
The Andersons, Inc., 31
Andreas Stihl AG & Co. KG, 16; 59 (upd.)
Andritz AG, 51
Ansell Ltd., 60 (upd.)
Anthem Electronics, Inc., 13
Apasco S.A. de C.V., 51
Apex Digital, Inc., 63
Applica Incorporated, 43 (upd.)
Applied Films Corporation, 48
Applied Materials, Inc., 10; 46 (upd.)
Applied Micro Circuits Corporation, 38

Applied Power Inc., 9; 32 (upd.)
AptarGroup, Inc., 69
ARBED S.A., 22 (upd.)
Arctco, Inc., 16
Arctic Cat Inc., 40 (upd.)
Ariens Company, 48
The Aristotle Corporation, 62
Armor All Products Corp., 16
Armstrong World Industries, Inc., III; 22 (upd.)
Artesyn Technologies Inc., 46 (upd.)
ArvinMeritor, Inc., 54 (upd.)
Asahi Glass Company, Ltd., 48 (upd.)
Ashley Furniture Industries, Inc., 35
ASICS Corporation, 57
ASML Holding N.V., 50
Astronics Corporation, 35
ASV, Inc., 34; 66 (upd.)
Atlas Copco AB, III; 28 (upd.)
Atwood Mobil Products, 53
AU Optronics Corporation, 67
Aurora Casket Company, Inc., 56
Avedis Zildjian Co., 38
Avery Dennison Corporation, 17 (upd.); 49 (upd.)
Avocent Corporation, 65
Avondale Industries, 7; 41 (upd.)
AVX Corporation, 67
B.J. Alan Co., Inc., 67
Badger Meter, Inc., 22
Baker Hughes Incorporated, III
Baldor Electric Company, 21
Baldwin Piano & Organ Company, 18
Baldwin Technology Company, Inc., 25
Balfour Beatty plc, 36 (upd.)
Ballantyne of Omaha, Inc., 27
Ballard Medical Products, 21
Bally Manufacturing Corporation, III
Baltek Corporation, 34
Baltimore Aircoil Company, Inc., 66
Bandai Co., Ltd., 55
Barmag AG, 39
Barnes Group Inc., 13; 69 (upd.)
Barry Callebaut AG, 29
Bassett Furniture Industries, Inc., 18
Bath Iron Works, 12; 36 (upd.)
Beckman Coulter, Inc., 22
Beckman Instruments, Inc., 14
Becton, Dickinson & Company, 36 (upd.)
Behr GmbH & Co. KG, 72
BEI Technologies, Inc., 65
Beiersdorf AG, 29
Bel Fuse, Inc., 53
Belden Inc., 19
Bell Sports Corporation, 16; 44 (upd.)
Belleek Pottery Ltd., 71
Beloit Corporation, 14
Bénéteau SA, 55
Benjamin Moore & Co., 13; 38 (upd.)
BenQ Corporation, 67
Berger Bros Company, 62
Bernina Holding AG, 47
Berry Plastics Corporation, 21
Berwick Offray, LLC, 70
BIC Corporation, 8; 23 (upd.)
BICC PLC, III
Billabong International Ltd., 44
The Bing Group, 60
Binks Sames Corporation, 21
Binney & Smith Inc., 25
Biomet, Inc., 10
BISSELL Inc., 9; 30 (upd.)
The Black & Decker Corporation, III; 20 (upd.); 67 (upd.)
Black Diamond Equipment, Ltd., 62
Blodgett Holdings, Inc., 61 (upd.)
Blount International, Inc., 12; 48 (upd.)

Blue Nile Inc., 61
Blyth Industries, Inc., 18
BMC Industries, Inc., 17; 59 (upd.)
Bodum Design Group AG, 47
Boral Limited, 43 (upd.)
Borden, Inc., 22 (upd.)
Borg-Warner Automotive, Inc., 14
Borg-Warner Corporation, III
Boston Scientific Corporation, 37
Bou-Matic, 62
The Boyds Collection, Ltd., 29
Brannock Device Company, 48
Brass Eagle Inc., 34
Bridgeport Machines, Inc., 17
Briggs & Stratton Corporation, 8; 27 (upd.)
BRIO AB, 24
British Vita plc, 33 (upd.)
Brother Industries, Ltd., 14
Brown & Sharpe Manufacturing Co., 23
Brown-Forman Corporation, 38 (upd.)
Broyhill Furniture Industries, Inc., 10
Brunswick Corporation, III; 22 (upd.)
BSH Bosch und Siemens Hausgeräte
  GmbH, 67
BTR Siebe plc, 27
Buck Knives Inc., 48
Buckeye Technologies, Inc., 42
Bucyrus International, Inc., 17
Bugle Boy Industries, Inc., 18
Building Materials Holding Corporation, 52
Bulgari S.p.A., 20
Bulova Corporation, 13; 41 (upd.)
Bundy Corporation, 17
Burelle S.A., 23
Burton Snowboards Inc., 22
Bush Boake Allen Inc., 30
Bush Industries, Inc., 20
Butler Manufacturing Company, 12; 62
  (upd.)
C&J Clark International Ltd., 52
C.F. Martin & Co., Inc., 42
C.R. Bard, Inc., 65 (upd.)
California Cedar Products Company, 58
California Steel Industries, Inc., 67
Callaway Golf Company, 15; 45 (upd.)
Campbell Scientific, Inc., 51
Cannondale Corporation, 21
Caradon plc, 20 (upd.)
The Carbide/Graphite Group, Inc., 40
Carbo PLC, 67 (upd.)
Carbone Lorraine S.A., 33
Cardo AB, 53
Carl-Zeiss-Stiftung, III; 34 (upd.)
Carma Laboratories, Inc., 60
Carrier Corporation, 7; 69 (upd.)
Carter Holt Harvey Ltd., 70
Cascade Corporation, 65
Cascade General, Inc., 65
CASIO Computer Co., Ltd., III; 40 (upd.)
Catalina Lighting, Inc., 43 (upd.)
Caterpillar Inc., III; 15 (upd.); 63 (upd.)
Cavco Industries, Inc., 65
CEMEX S.A. de C.V., 59 (upd.)
Central Garden & Pet Company, 58 (upd.)
Central Sprinkler Corporation, 29
Centuri Corporation, 54
Century Aluminum Company, 52
Cenveo Inc., 71 (upd.)
Ceradyne, Inc., 65
Cessna Aircraft Company, 27 (upd.)
Champion Enterprises, Inc., 17
Chanel SA, 12; 49 (upd.)
The Charles Machine Works, Inc., 64
Chart Industries, Inc., 21
Chittenden & Eastman Company, 58
Chris-Craft Industries, Inc., 31 (upd.)
Christian Dalloz SA, 40

Christofle SA, 40
Chromcraft Revington, Inc., 15
Ciments Français, 40
Cincinnati Lamb Inc., 72
Cincinnati Milacron Inc., 12
Cinram International, Inc., 43
Circon Corporation, 21
Cirrus Design Corporation, 44
Citizen Watch Co., Ltd., III
CLARCOR Inc., 17; 61 (upd.)
Clark Equipment Company, 8
Clayton Homes Incorporated, 13; 54 (upd.)
The Clorox Company, 22 (upd.)
CNH Global N.V., 38 (upd.)
Coach, Inc., 45 (upd.)
COBE Cardiovascular, Inc., 61
Cobra Golf Inc., 16
Cockerill Sambre Group, 26 (upd.)
Cohu, Inc., 32
Colas S.A., 31
The Coleman Company, Inc., 30 (upd.)
Colfax Corporation, 58
Collins & Aikman Corporation, 41 (upd.)
Collins Industries, Inc., 33
Colorado MEDtech, Inc., 48
Colt's Manufacturing Company, Inc., 12
Columbia Sportswear Company, 19
Columbus McKinnon Corporation, 37
Compagnie de Saint-Gobain, 64 (upd.)
CompuDyne Corporation, 51
Conair Corporation, 69 (upd.)
Concord Camera Corporation, 41
Congoleum Corp., 18
Conn-Selmer, Inc., 55
Conrad Industries, Inc., 58
Conso International Corporation, 29
Consorcio G Grupo Dina, S.A. de C.V., 36
Constar International Inc., 64
Converse Inc., 9
Cooper Cameron Corporation, 58 (upd.)
The Cooper Companies, Inc., 39
Cooper Industries, Inc., 44 (upd.)
Cordis Corporation, 46 (upd.)
Corning Inc., 44 (upd.)
Corrpro Companies, Inc., 20
Corticeira Amorim, Sociedade Gestora de
  Participaço es Sociais, S.A., 48
Crane Co., 8; 30 (upd.)
Cranium, Inc., 69
Creative Technology Ltd., 57
Creo Inc., 48
CRH plc, 64
Crosman Corporation, 62
Crown Equipment Corporation, 15
CTB International Corporation, 43 (upd.)
Cuisinart Corporation, 24
Culligan Water Technologies, Inc., 12; 38
  (upd.)
Cummins Engine Company, Inc., 40 (upd.)
CUNO Incorporated, 57
Curtiss-Wright Corporation, 10; 35 (upd.)
Cutter & Buck Inc., 27
Cybex International, Inc., 49
Dade Behring Holdings Inc., 71
Daewoo Group, III
Daikin Industries, Ltd., III
Daisy Outdoor Products Inc., 58
Danaher Corporation, 7
Daniel Industries, Inc., 16
Danisco A/S, 44
Day Runner, Inc., 41 (upd.)
DC Shoes, Inc., 60
De'Longhi S.p.A., 66
Dearborn Mid-West Conveyor Company,
  56
Decora Industries, Inc., 31
Decorator Industries Inc., 68

DeCrane Aircraft Holdings Inc., 36
Deere & Company, III; 42 (upd.)
Defiance, Inc., 22
Dell Inc., 63 (upd.)
DEMCO, Inc., 60
Denby Group plc, 44
Denison International plc, 46
DENSO Corporation, 46 (upd.)
Department 56, Inc., 14
DePuy Inc., 37 (upd.)
Detroit Diesel Corporation, 10
Deutsche Babcock A.G., III
Deutz AG, 39
Devro plc, 55
Dial-A-Mattress Operating Corporation, 46
Diebold, Incorporated, 7; 22 (upd.)
Diesel SpA, 40
Dixon Industries, Inc., 26
Dixon Ticonderoga Company, 12; 69
  (upd.)
Djarum PT, 62
DMI Furniture, Inc., 46
Donaldson Company, Inc., 49 (upd.)
Donnelly Corporation, 12; 35 (upd.)
Dorel Industries Inc., 59
Douglas & Lomason Company, 16
Dover Corporation, III; 28 (upd.)
Dresser Industries, Inc., III
Drew Industries Inc., 28
Drexel Heritage Furnishings Inc., 12
Drypers Corporation, 18
Ducommun Incorporated, 30
Duncan Toys Company, 55
Dunn-Edwards Corporation, 56
Duracell International Inc., 9; 71 (upd.)
Durametallic, 21
Duriron Company Inc., 17
Dürkopp Adler AG, 65
Duron Inc., 72
Dürr AG, 44
Dynea, 68
Dyson Group PLC, 71
EADS SOCATA, 54
Eagle-Picher Industries, Inc., 8; 23 (upd.)
The Eastern Company, 48
Eastman Kodak Company, III; 7 (upd.); 36
  (upd.)
Easton Sports, Inc., 66
Eaton Corporation, 67 (upd.)
ECC International Corp., 42
Ecolab Inc., 34 (upd.)
Eddie Bauer Inc., 9
EDO Corporation, 46
EG&G Incorporated, 29 (upd.)
Ekco Group, Inc., 16
Elamex, S.A. de C.V., 51
Elano Corporation, 14
Electrolux AB, III; 53 (upd.)
Eljer Industries, Inc., 24
Elscint Ltd., 20
Encompass Services Corporation, 33
Energizer Holdings, Inc., 32
Enesco Corporation, 11
Engineered Support Systems, Inc., 59
English China Clays Ltd., 40 (upd.)
Enodis plc, 68
Ernie Ball, Inc., 56
Escalade, Incorporated, 19
Esselte, 64
Esselte Leitz GmbH & Co. KG, 48
Essilor International, 21
Esterline Technologies Corp., 15
Ethan Allen Interiors, Inc., 12; 39 (upd.)
The Eureka Company, 12
Everlast Worldwide Inc., 47
Excel Technology, Inc., 65
EXX Inc., 65

MANUFACTURING (*continued*)

Fabbrica D' Armi Pietro Beretta S.p.A., 39
Facom S.A., 32
FAG—Kugelfischer Georg Schäfer AG, 62
Faiveley S.A., 39
Falcon Products, Inc., 33
Fanuc Ltd., III; 17 (upd.)
Farah Incorporated, 24
Farmer Bros. Co., 52
Fastenal Company, 42 (upd.)
Faultless Starch/Bon Ami Company, 55
Featherlite Inc., 28
Fedders Corporation, 18; 43 (upd.)
Federal Prison Industries, Inc., 34
Federal Signal Corp., 10
Fellowes Manufacturing Company, 28
Fender Musical Instruments Company, 16;
  43 (upd.)
Ferro Corporation, 56 (upd.)
Figgie International Inc., 7
Firearms Training Systems, Inc., 27
First Alert, Inc., 28
First Brands Corporation, 8
First International Computer, Inc., 56
The First Years Inc., 46
Fisher Controls International, LLC, 13; 61
  (upd.)
Fisher Scientific International Inc., 24
Fisher-Price Inc., 12; 32 (upd.)
Fiskars Corporation, 33
Fisons plc, 9
Flanders Corporation, 65
Fleetwood Enterprises, Inc., III; 22 (upd.)
Flexsteel Industries Inc., 15; 41 (upd.)
Flextronics International Ltd., 38
Flint Ink Corporation, 41 (upd.)
FLIR Systems, Inc., 69
Florsheim Shoe Company, 9
Flour City International, Inc., 44
Flow International Corporation, 56
Flowserve Corporation, 33
FLSmidth & Co. A/S, 72
Fort James Corporation, 22 (upd.)
FosterGrant, Inc., 60
Fountain Powerboats Industries, Inc., 28
Foxboro Company, 13
Framatome SA, 19
Frank J. Zamboni & Co., Inc., 34
Franklin Electric Company, Inc., 43
The Franklin Mint, 69
Freudenberg & Co., 41
Friedrich Grohe AG & Co. KG, 53
Frigidaire Home Products, 22
Frymaster Corporation, 27
FSI International, Inc., 17
Fuji Photo Film Co., Ltd., III; 18 (upd.)
Fujisawa Pharmaceutical Company, Ltd.,
  58 (upd.)
Fuqua Enterprises, Inc., 17
Furniture Brands International, Inc., 39
  (upd.)
Furon Company, 28
The Furukawa Electric Co., Ltd., III
G. Leblanc Corporation, 55
G.S. Blodgett Corporation, 15
Gardner Denver, Inc., 49
The Gates Corporation, 9
GE Aircraft Engines, 9
GEA AG, 27
Geberit AG, 49
Gehl Company, 19
Gemini Sound Products Corporation, 58
Gemplus International S.A., 64
GenCorp Inc., 8; 9 (upd.)
General Atomics, 57
General Bearing Corporation, 45
General Cable Corporation, 40

General Dynamics Corporation, 40 (upd.)
General Housewares Corporation, 16
Genmar Holdings, Inc., 45
geobra Brandstätter GmbH & Co. KG, 48
Georg Fischer AG Schaffhausen, 61
The George F. Cram Company, Inc., 55
Georgia Gulf Corporation, 61 (upd.)
Gerber Scientific, Inc., 12
Gerresheimer Glas AG, 43
Giddings & Lewis, Inc., 10
The Gillette Company, 20 (upd.)
GKN plc, III; 38 (upd.)
Gleason Corporation, 24
The Glidden Company, 8
Global Power Equipment Group Inc., 52
Glock Ges.m.b.H., 42
Goodman Holding Company, 42
Goodrich Corporation, 46 (upd.)
Goody Products, Inc., 12
The Gorman-Rupp Company, 18; 57 (upd.)
Goss Holdings, Inc., 43
Goulds Pumps Inc., 24
Graco Inc., 19; 67 (upd.)
Graham Corporation, 62
Grant Prideco, Inc., 57
Greatbatch Inc., 72
Greene, Tweed & Company, 55
Greif Inc., 66 (upd.)
Griffin Industries, Inc., 70
Griffon Corporation, 34
Grinnell Corp., 13
Groupe André, 17
Groupe Guillin SA, 40
Groupe Herstal S.A., 58
Groupe Legis Industries, 23
Groupe SEB, 35
Grow Group Inc., 12
Groz-Beckert Group, 68
Grupo Cydsa, S.A. de C.V., 39
Grupo IMSA, S.A. de C.V., 44
Grupo Industrial Saltillo, S.A. de C.V., 54
Grupo Lladró S.A., 52
Guangzhou Pearl River Piano Group Ltd.,
  49
Gulf Island Fabrication, Inc., 44
Gunite Corporation, 51
The Gunlocke Company, 23
Guy Degrenne SA, 44
H.B. Fuller Company, 8; 32 (upd.)
Hach Co., 18
Hackman Oyj Adp, 44
Haemonetics Corporation, 20
Haier Group Corporation, 65
Halliburton Company, III
Hallmark Cards, Inc., 40 (upd.)
Hansgrohe AG, 56
Hanson PLC, 30 (upd.)
Hardinge Inc., 25
Harland and Wolff Holdings plc, 19
Harmon Industries, Inc., 25
Harnischfeger Industries, Inc., 8; 38 (upd.)
Harsco Corporation, 8
Hartmarx Corporation, 32 (upd.)
The Hartz Mountain Corporation, 46 (upd.)
Hasbro, Inc., III; 16 (upd.)
Haskel International, Inc., 59
Hastings Manufacturing Company, 56
Hawker Siddeley Group Public Limited
  Company, III
Haworth Inc., 8; 39 (upd.)
Head N.V., 55
Headwaters Incorporated, 56
Health O Meter Products Inc., 14
Heekin Can Inc., 13
HEICO Corporation, 30
Heidelberger Druckmaschinen AG, 40
Hella KGaA Hueck & Co., 66

Henkel Manco Inc., 22
The Henley Group, Inc., III
Heraeus Holding GmbH, 54 (upd.)
Herman Miller, Inc., 8
Hermès International S.A., 34 (upd.)
Héroux-Devtek Inc., 69
Hillenbrand Industries, Inc., 10
Hillerich & Bradsby Company, Inc., 51
Hillsdown Holdings plc, 24 (upd.)
Hilti AG, 53
Hitachi Zosen Corporation, III
Hitchiner Manufacturing Co., Inc., 23
HMI Industries, Inc., 17
The Hockey Company, 70
Hollander Home Fashions Corp., 67
Holnam Inc., 8
Holson Burnes Group, Inc., 14
Home Products International, Inc., 55
HON INDUSTRIES Inc., 13
The Hoover Company, 12; 40 (upd.)
Hoshino Gakki Co. Ltd., 55
Huffy Corporation, 7; 30 (upd.)
Huhtamäki Oyj, 64
Hummel International A/S, 68
Hunt Manufacturing Company, 12
Hunter Fan Company, 13
Hydril Company, 46
Hyster Company, 17
Hyundai Group, III; 7 (upd.)
Icon Health & Fitness, Inc., 38
IDEO Inc., 65
Igloo Products Corp., 21
Illinois Tool Works Inc., III; 22 (upd.)
Imatra Steel Oy Ab, 55
IMI plc, 9
Imo Industries Inc., 7; 27 (upd.)
In-Sink-Erator, 66
Inchcape PLC, III; 16 (upd.); 50 (upd.)
Industrie Natuzzi S.p.A., 18
Infineon Technologies AG, 50
Ingalls Shipbuilding, Inc., 12
Ingersoll-Rand Company Ltd., III; 15
  (upd.); 55 (upd.)
Insilco Corporation, 16
Interco Incorporated, III
Interface, Inc., 8
The Interlake Corporation, 8
Internacional de Ceramica, S.A. de C.V.,
  53
International Controls Corporation, 10
International Flavors & Fragrances Inc., 38
  (upd.)
International Game Technology, 10
Invacare Corporation, 47 (upd.)
Invensys PLC, 50 (upd.)
Invivo Corporation, 52
Ionics, Incorporated, 52
Ipsen International Inc., 72
Irwin Toy Limited, 14
Ishikawajima-Harima Heavy Industries Co.,
  Ltd., III
Itron, Inc., 64
J. D'Addario & Company, Inc., 48
J.I. Case Company, 10
J.M. Voith AG, 33
Jabil Circuit, Inc., 36
Jacuzzi Inc., 23
JAKKS Pacific, Inc., 52
James Hardie Industries N.V., 56
JanSport, Inc., 70
Japan Tobacco Inc., 46 (upd.)
Jayco Inc., 13
Jeld-Wen, Inc., 45
Jenoptik AG, 33
Jervis B. Webb Company, 24
JLG Industries, Inc., 52
John Frieda Professional Hair Care Inc., 70

Johns Manville Corporation, 64 (upd.)
Johnson Controls, Inc., III; 26 (upd.); 59 (upd.)
Johnson Matthey PLC, 49 (upd.)
Johnson Worldwide Associates, Inc., 28
Johnstown America Industries, Inc., 23
Jones Apparel Group, Inc., 11
Jostens, Inc., 7; 25 (upd.)
K'Nex Industries, Inc., 52
Kaman Corporation, 12; 42 (upd.)
Kaman Music Corporation, 68
Karsten Manufacturing Corporation, 51
Kasper A.S.L., Ltd., 40
Katy Industries, Inc., 51 (upd.)
Kawasaki Heavy Industries, Ltd., III; 63 (upd.)
Kaydon Corporation, 18
KB Toys, 35 (upd.)
Kelly-Moore Paint Company, Inc., 56
Kenmore Air Harbor Inc., 65
Kennametal Inc., 68 (upd.)
Keramik Holding AG Laufen, 51
Kerr Group Inc., 24
Kewaunee Scientific Corporation, 25
Key Safety Systems, Inc., 63
Key Tronic Corporation, 14
Keystone International, Inc., 11
KHD Konzern, III
KI, 57
Kimball International, Inc., 12; 48 (upd.)
Kit Manufacturing Co., 18
Knape & Vogt Manufacturing Company, 17
Knoll Group Inc., 14
Koala Corporation, 44
Kobe Steel, Ltd., IV; 19 (upd.)
Koch Enterprises, Inc., 29
Koenig & Bauer AG, 64
Kohler Company, 7; 32 (upd.)
Komatsu Ltd., III; 16 (upd.); 52 (upd.)
Kone Corporation, 27
Konica Corporation, III
KraftMaid Cabinetry, Inc., 72
KSB AG, 62
Kubota Corporation, III; 26 (upd.)
Kuhlman Corporation, 20
Kyocera Corporation, 21 (upd.)
L-3 Communications Holdings, Inc., 48
L. and J.G. Stickley, Inc., 50
L.B. Foster Company, 33
L.S. Starrett Company, 64 (upd.)
La-Z-Boy Incorporated, 14; 50 (upd.)
Lacks Enterprises Inc., 61
LADD Furniture, Inc., 12
Ladish Co., Inc., 30
Lafarge Cement UK, 28; 54 (upd.)
Lafuma S.A., 39
Lakeland Industries, Inc., 45
Lam Research Corporation, 31 (upd.)
The Lamson & Sessions Co., 13; 61 (upd.)
Lancer Corporation, 21
The Lane Co., Inc., 12
Laserscope, 67
LaSiDo Inc., 58
LeapFrog Enterprises, Inc., 54
Lear Corporation, 71 (upd.)
Leatherman Tool Group, Inc., 51
Leggett & Platt, Inc., 11; 48 (upd.)
Leica Camera AG, 35
Leica Microsystems Holdings GmbH, 35
Lennox International Inc., 8; 28 (upd.)
Lenox, Inc., 12
Leupold & Stevens, Inc., 52
Lexmark International, Inc., 18
Liebherr-International AG, 64
Linamar Corporation, 18
Lincoln Electric Co., 13

Lindal Cedar Homes, Inc., 29
Lindsay Manufacturing Co., 20
Little Tikes Company, 13; 62 (upd.)
Loctite Corporation, 8
Logitech International S.A., 28; 69 (upd.)
The Longaberger Company, 12; 44 (upd.)
Louis Vuitton, 10
Lucas Industries PLC, III
Luxottica SpA, 52 (upd.)
Lydall, Inc., 64
Lynch Corporation, 43
M&F Worldwide Corp., 38
M.A. Bruder & Sons, Inc., 56
Mabuchi Motor Co. Ltd., 68
MacAndrews & Forbes Holdings Inc., 28
Mace Security International, Inc., 57
MacGregor Golf Company, 68
Mackay Envelope Corporation, 45
Madeco S.A., 71
Madison-Kipp Corporation, 58
Mag Instrument, Inc., 67
Maidenform, Inc., 59 (upd.)
Mail-Well, Inc., 28
Makita Corporation, 22; 59 (upd.)
MAN Aktiengesellschaft, III
Manitou BF S.A., 27
The Manitowoc Company, Inc., 18; 59 (upd.)
Mannesmann AG, III; 14 (upd.)
Marcolin S.p.A., 61
Margarete Steiff GmbH, 23
Marisa Christina, Inc., 15
Mark IV Industries, Inc., 7; 28 (upd.)
Märklin Holding GmbH, 70
The Marmon Group, 16 (upd.)
Marshall Amplification plc, 62
Martin Industries, Inc., 44
Martin-Baker Aircraft Company Limited, 61
Marvin Lumber & Cedar Company, 22
Mary Kay, Inc., 30 (upd.)
Masco Corporation, III; 20 (upd.); 39 (upd.)
Masonite International Corporation, 63
Master Lock Company, 45
MasterBrand Cabinets, Inc., 71
Material Sciences Corporation, 63
Matsushita Electric Industrial Co., Ltd., 64 (upd.)
Mattel, Inc., 7; 25 (upd.); 61 (upd.)
Matth. Hohner AG, 53
Matthews International Corporation, 29
Maverick Tube Corporation, 59
Maxco Inc., 17
Maxwell Shoe Company, Inc., 30
Maytag Corporation, III; 22 (upd.)
McClain Industries, Inc., 51
McDermott International, Inc., III
McKechnie plc, 34
McWane Corporation, 55
Meade Instruments Corporation, 41
Meadowcraft, Inc., 29
Measurement Specialties, Inc., 71
Medtronic, Inc., 67 (upd.)
Meggitt PLC, 34
Meiji Seika Kaisha Ltd., 64 (upd.)
Memry Corporation, 72
Menasha Corporation, 59 (upd.)
Merck & Co., Inc., 34 (upd.)
Mercury Marine Group, 68
Merillat Industries Inc., 13
Merillat Industries, LLC, 69 (upd.)
Mestek Inc., 10
Metso Corporation, 30 (upd.)
Mettler-Toledo International Inc., 30
Michael Anthony Jewelers, Inc., 24
Microdot Inc., 8

The Middleton Doll Company, 53
Midwest Grain Products, Inc., 49
Miele & Cie. KG, 56
Mikasa, Inc., 28
Mikohn Gaming Corporation, 39
Milacron, Inc., 53 (upd.)
Miller Industries, Inc., 26
Milton Bradley Company, 21
Mine Safety Appliances Company, 31
Minolta Co., Ltd., III; 18 (upd.); 43 (upd.)
Minuteman International Inc., 46
Mitsubishi Heavy Industries, Ltd., III; 7 (upd.)
Mity Enterprises, Inc., 38
Mobile Mini, Inc., 58
Modine Manufacturing Company, 8; 56 (upd.)
Moen Incorporated, 12
Mohawk Industries, Inc., 19; 63 (upd.)
Molex Incorporated, 11
The Monarch Cement Company, 72
Monnaie de Paris, 62
Monster Cable Products, Inc., 69
Montres Rolex S.A., 13; 34 (upd.)
Montupet S.A., 63
Motorcar Parts & Accessories, Inc., 47
Moulinex S.A., 22
Movado Group, Inc., 28
Mr. Coffee, Inc., 15
Mr. Gasket Inc., 15
Mueller Industries, Inc., 7; 52 (upd.)
Multi-Color Corporation, 53
Nashua Corporation, 8
National Envelope Corporation, 32
National Gypsum Company, 10
National Oilwell, Inc., 54
National Picture & Frame Company, 24
National Semiconductor Corporation, 69 (upd.)
National Standard Co., 13
National Starch and Chemical Company, 49
Natrol, Inc., 49
Natural Alternatives International, Inc., 49
NCR Corporation, 30 (upd.)
Neenah Foundry Company, 68
Neopost S.A., 53
New Balance Athletic Shoe, Inc., 25
New Holland N.V., 22
Newcor, Inc., 40
Newell Rubbermaid Inc., 9; 52 (upd.)
Newport Corporation, 71
Newport News Shipbuilding Inc., 13; 38 (upd.)
Nexans SA, 54
NGK Insulators Ltd., 67
NHK Spring Co., Ltd., III
Nidec Corporation, 59
NIKE, Inc., 36 (upd.)
Nikon Corporation, III; 48 (upd.)
Nintendo Company, Ltd., III; 7 (upd.); 67 (upd.)
Nippon Seiko K.K., III
Nippondenso Co., Ltd., III
NKK Corporation, 28 (upd.)
NOF Corporation, 72
NordicTrack, 22
Nordson Corporation, 11; 48 (upd.)
Nortek, Inc., 34
Norton Company, 8
Norton McNaughton, Inc., 27
Novellus Systems, Inc., 18
NTN Corporation, III; 47 (upd.)
Nu-kote Holding, Inc., 18
O'Sullivan Industries Holdings, Inc., 34
Oak Industries Inc., 21
Oakley, Inc., 49 (upd.)

MANUFACTURING (*continued*)

Oakwood Homes Corporation, 15
ODL, Inc., 55
The Ohio Art Company,14; 59 (upd.)
Oil-Dri Corporation of America, 20
180s, L.L.C., 64
Oneida Ltd., 7; 31 (upd.)
Optische Werke G. Rodenstock, 44
Orange Glo International, 53
Orthofix International NV, 72
Osmonics, Inc., 18
Otis Elevator Company, Inc., 13; 39 (upd.)
Outboard Marine Corporation, III; 20 (upd.)
Outdoor Research, Incorporated, 67
Overhead Door Corporation, 70
Owens Corning Corporation, 20 (upd.)
Owosso Corporation, 29
P & F Industries, Inc., 45
Pacer Technology, 40
Pacific Coast Feather Company, 67
Pacific Dunlop Limited, 10
Pall Corporation, 9; 72 (upd.)
Palm Harbor Homes, Inc., 39
Paloma Industries Ltd., 71
Panavision Inc., 24
Park Corp., 22
Parker-Hannifin Corporation, III; 24 (upd.)
Parlex Corporation, 61
Patrick Industries, Inc., 30
Paul Mueller Company, 65
Pechiney SA, IV; 45 (upd.)
Pella Corporation, 12; 39 (upd.)
Penn Engineering & Manufacturing Corp., 28
Pentair, Inc., 26 (upd.)
Pentech International, Inc., 29
The Perkin-Elmer Corporation, 7
Peterson American Corporation, 55
Phillips-Van Heusen Corporation, 24
Phoenix AG, 68
Phoenix Mecano AG, 61
Physio-Control International Corp., 18
Pilkington plc, 34 (upd.)
Pinguely-Haulotte SA, 51
Pioneer Electronic Corporation, III
Pitney Bowes, Inc., 19
Pittway Corporation, 33 (upd.)
Planar Systems, Inc., 61
PlayCore, Inc., 27
Playmates Toys, 23
Playskool, Inc., 25
Pleasant Company, 27
Ply Gem Industries Inc., 12
Pochet SA, 55
Polaris Industries Inc., 12; 35 (upd.)
Polaroid Corporation, III; 7 (upd.); 28 (upd.)
The Porcelain and Fine China Companies Ltd., 69
PPG Industries, Inc., 22 (upd.)
Prada Holding B.V., 45
Pranda Jewelry plc, 70
Praxair, Inc., 48 (upd.)
Precision Castparts Corp., 15
Premark International, Inc., III
Pressman Toy Corporation, 56
Presstek, Inc., 33
Price Pfister, Inc., 70
Prince Sports Group, Inc., 15
Printpack, Inc., 68
Printronix, Inc., 18
Puig Beauty and Fashion Group S.L., 60
Pulaski Furniture Corporation, 33
Pumpkin Masters, Inc., 48
Punch International N.V., 66
Pure World, Inc., 72

Puritan-Bennett Corporation, 13
Purolator Products Company, 21
PVC Container Corporation, 67
PW Eagle, Inc., 48
Q.E.P. Co., Inc., 65
QSC Audio Products, Inc., 56
Quixote Corporation, 15
R. Griggs Group Limited, 23
Racing Champions Corporation, 37
Radio Flyer Inc., 34
Raleigh UK Ltd., 65
Rapala-Normark Group, Ltd., 30
Raven Industries, Inc., 33
Raychem Corporation, 8
Rayovac Corporation, 39 (upd.)
Raytech Corporation, 61
Recovery Engineering, Inc., 25
Red Spot Paint & Varnish Company, 55
Red Wing Pottery Sales, Inc., 52
Red Wing Shoe Company, Inc., 9
Reed & Barton Corporation, 67
Regal-Beloit Corporation, 18
Reichhold Chemicals, Inc., 10
Remington Arms Company, Inc., 12; 40 (upd.)
Remington Products Company, L.L.C., 42
RENK AG, 37
Revell-Monogram Inc., 16
Revere Ware Corporation, 22
Revlon Inc., 64 (upd.)
Rexam PLC, 32 (upd.)
Rexnord Corporation, 21
RF Micro Devices, Inc., 43
Rheinmetall Berlin AG, 9
RHI AG, 53
Richardson Industries, Inc., 62
Riddell Sports Inc., 22
Rieter Holding AG, 42
River Oaks Furniture, Inc., 43
RMC Group p.l.c., 34 (upd.)
Roadmaster Industries, Inc., 16
Robbins & Myers Inc., 15
Robertson-Ceco Corporation, 19
Rock-Tenn Company, 59 (upd.)
Rockford Products Corporation, 55
RockShox, Inc., 26
Rockwell Automation, 43 (upd.)
Rogers Corporation, 61
Rohde & Schwarz GmbH & Co. KG, 39
ROHN Industries, Inc., 22
Rohr Incorporated, 9
Roland Corporation, 38
Rollerblade, Inc., 15; 34 (upd.)
Rolls-Royce Group PLC, 67 (upd.)
Ronson PLC, 49
Roper Industries, Inc., 15; 50 (upd.)
Rose Art Industries, 58
Roseburg Forest Products Company, 58
Rotork plc, 46
Royal Appliance Manufacturing Company, 15
Royal Canin S.A., 39
Royal Doulton plc, 14; 38 (upd.)
RPM, Inc., 8; 36 (upd.)
Rubbermaid Incorporated, III
Russ Berrie and Company, Inc., 12
S.C. Johnson & Son, Inc., 28 (upd.)
Sabaté Diosos SA, 48
Safe Flight Instrument Corporation, 71
Safeskin Corporation, 18
Safety Components International, Inc., 63
Safilo SpA, 54
Salant Corporation, 12; 51 (upd.)
Salton, Inc., 30
Samick Musical Instruments Co., Ltd., 56
Samsonite Corporation, 13; 43 (upd.)
Samuel Cabot Inc., 53

Sandvik AB, 32 (upd.)
Sanitec Corporation, 51
Sanrio Company, Ltd., 38
Sauder Woodworking Company, 12; 35 (upd.)
Sauer-Danfoss Inc., 61
Sawtek Inc., 43 (upd.)
Schindler Holding AG, 29
Schlumberger Limited, III
School-Tech, Inc., 62
Schott Corporation, 53
Scotsman Industries, Inc., 20
Scott Fetzer Company, 12
The Scotts Company, 22
Scovill Fasteners Inc., 24
Sealed Air Corporation, 14; 57 (upd.)
Sealy Inc., 12
Segway LLC, 48
Seiko Corporation, III; 17 (upd.); 72 (upd.)
Select Comfort Corporation, 34
The Selmer Company, Inc., 19
Semitool, Inc., 18
Sequa Corp., 13
Serta, Inc., 28
Severstal Joint Stock Company, 65
Shakespeare Company, 22
Shanghai Baosteel Group Corporation, 71
The Shaw Group, Inc., 50
Shelby Williams Industries, Inc., 14
Sherwood Brands, Inc., 53
Shimano Inc., 64
Shorewood Packaging Corporation, 28
Shuffle Master Inc., 51
Shurgard Storage Centers, Inc., 52
SIFCO Industries, Inc., 41
Simmons Company, 47
Simplicity Manufacturing, Inc., 64
Simula, Inc., 41
The Singer Company N.V., 30 (upd.)
The Singing Machine Company, Inc., 60
Skis Rossignol S.A., 15; 43 (upd.)
Skyline Corporation, 30
SLI, Inc., 48
Smead Manufacturing Co., 17
Smith & Wesson Corporation, 30
Smith Corona Corp., 13
Smith International, Inc., 15
Smith-Midland Corporation, 56
Smiths Industries PLC, 25
Smoby International SA, 56
Snap-On, Incorporated, 7; 27 (upd.)
Sola International Inc., 71
Sonic Innovations Inc., 56
SonoSite, Inc., 56
Spacelabs Medical, Inc., 71
Sparton Corporation, 18
Specialized Bicycle Components Inc., 50
Specialty Equipment Companies, Inc., 25
Specialty Products & Insulation Co., 59
Spectrum Control, Inc., 67
Speizman Industries, Inc., 44
Spin Master, Ltd., 61
Spirax-Sarco Engineering plc, 59
SPS Technologies, Inc., 30
SPX Corporation, 47 (upd.)
SRC Holdings Corporation, 67
Stanadyne Automotive Corporation, 37
Standex International Corporation, 17
Stanley Furniture Company, Inc., 34
The Stanley Works, III; 20 (upd.)
Starcraft Corporation, 66 (upd.)
Stearns, Inc., 43
Steel Authority of India Ltd., 66 (upd.)
Steel Dynamics, Inc., 52
Steel Technologies Inc., 63
Steelcase, Inc., 7; 27 (upd.)

Steinway Musical Properties, Inc., 19
Stelco Inc., 51 (upd.)
The Stephan Company, 60
Stewart & Stevenson Services Inc., 11
STMicroelectronics NV, 52
Stratasys, Inc., 67
Strombecker Corporation, 60
Stryker Corporation, 11; 29 (upd.)
Sturm, Ruger & Company, Inc., 19
Sub-Zero Freezer Co., Inc., 31
Sudbury Inc., 16
Sulzer Brothers Limited (Gebruder Sulzer Aktiengesellschaft), III
Sumitomo Heavy Industries, Ltd., III; 42 (upd.)
Susquehanna Pfaltzgraff Company, 8
Swank Inc., 17
Swarovski International Holding AG, 40
The Swatch Group SA, 26
Swedish Match AB, 12; 39 (upd.)
Sweetheart Cup Company, Inc., 36
Sybron International Corp., 14
Syratech Corp., 14
Systemax, Inc., 52
TAB Products Co., 17
Tacony Corporation, 70
TAG Heuer International SA, 25
Taiheiyo Cement Corporation, 60 (upd.)
Taiwan Semiconductor Manufacturing Company Ltd., 47
Tarkett Sommer AG, 25
Taser International, Inc., 62
Taylor Guitars, 48
Taylor Made Golf Co., 23
TB Wood's Corporation, 56
TDK Corporation, 49 (upd.)
TearDrop Golf Company, 32
Tecumseh Products Company, 8; 71 (upd.)
Tektronix, Inc., 8
Tempur-Pedic Inc., 54
Tenaris SA, 63
Tennant Company, 13; 33 (upd.)
Terex Corporation, 7; 40 (upd.)
The Testor Corporation, 51
Tetra Pak International SA, 53
Thales S.A., 42
Thermadyne Holding Corporation, 19
Thermo BioAnalysis Corp., 25
Thermo Electron Corporation, 7
Thermo Fibertek, Inc., 24
Thermo Instrument Systems Inc., 11
Thermo King Corporation, 13
Thiokol Corporation, 22 (upd.)
Thomas & Betts Corp., 11
Thomas Industries Inc., 29
Thomasville Furniture Industries, Inc., 12
Thor Industries, Inc., 39
3M Company, 61 (upd.)
Thyssen Krupp AG, 28 (upd.)
Tilia Inc., 62
Timex Corporation, 7; 25 (upd.)
The Timken Company, 8; 42 (upd.)
Titan Cement Company S.A., 64
TJ International, Inc., 19
Todd Shipyards Corporation, 14
Tokheim Corporation, 21
Tomy Company Ltd., 65
Tong Yang Cement Corporation, 62
Tonka Corporation, 25
Toolex International N.V., 26
The Topaz Group, Inc., 62
Topps Company, Inc., 13
Toray Industries, Inc., 51 (upd.)
The Toro Company, 7; 26 (upd.)
The Torrington Company, 13
TOTO LTD., 28 (upd.)
Town & Country Corporation, 19

Toymax International, Inc., 29
Toyoda Automatic Loom Works, Ltd., III
TransPro, Inc., 71
Tredegar Corporation, 52
Trek Bicycle Corporation, 16
Trex Company, Inc., 71
Trico Products Corporation, 15
TriMas Corp., 11
Trinity Industries, Incorporated, 7
TRINOVA Corporation, III
TriQuint Semiconductor, Inc., 63
Trisko Jewelry Sculptures, Ltd., 57
Triumph Group, Inc., 31
Tubos de Acero de Mexico, S.A. (TAMSA), 41
Tultex Corporation, 13
Tupperware Corporation, 28
Twin Disc, Inc., 21
II-VI Incorporated, 69
Ty Inc., 33
Tyco International Ltd., III; 28 (upd.)
Tyco Toys, Inc., 12
U.S. Robotics Corporation, 9; 66 (upd.)
Ube Industries, Ltd., 38 (upd.)
Ultralife Batteries, Inc., 58
United Defense Industries, Inc., 30; 66 (upd.)
United Dominion Industries Limited, 8; 16 (upd.)
United Industrial Corporation, 37
United States Filter Corporation, 20
United States Pipe and Foundry Company, 62
Unitika Ltd., 53 (upd.)
Unitog Co., 19
Utah Medical Products, Inc., 36
VA TECH ELIN EBG GmbH, 49
Vaillant GmbH, 44
Vallourec SA, 54
Valmet Corporation (Valmet Oy), III
Valmont Industries, Inc., 19
The Valspar Corporation, 8
Vari-Lite International, Inc., 35
Varian, Inc., 48 (upd.)
Variflex, Inc., 51
Varity Corporation, III
Varlen Corporation, 16
Varta AG, 23
Velcro Industries N.V., 19; 72
Vermeer Manufacturing Company, 17
Viasystems Group, Inc., 67
Vickers plc, 27
Victorinox AG, 21
Vidrala S.A., 67
Viessmann Werke GmbH & Co., 37
ViewSonic Corporation, 72
Viking Range Corporation, 66
Villeroy & Boch AG, 37
Virco Manufacturing Corporation, 17
Viscofan S.A., 70
Viskase Companies, Inc., 55
Vita Plus Corporation, 60
Vitro Corporativo S.A. de C.V., 34
voestalpine AG, 57 (upd.)
Vorwerk & Co., 27
Vosper Thornycroft Holding plc, 41
Vossloh AG, 53
W.A. Whitney Company, 53
W.C. Bradley Co., 69
W.H. Brady Co., 17
W.L. Gore & Associates, Inc., 14; 60 (upd.)
W.W. Grainger, Inc., 26 (upd.); 68 (upd.)
Wabash National Corp., 13
Wabtec Corporation, 40
Walbro Corporation, 13
Walter Industries, Inc., 72 (upd.)

Washington Scientific Industries, Inc., 17
Wassall Plc, 18
Waterford Wedgwood plc, 12; 34 (upd.)
Waters Corporation, 43
Watts Industries, Inc., 19
Watts of Lydney Group Ltd., 71
WD-40 Company, 18
Weber-Stephen Products Co., 40
Weeres Industries Corporation, 52
Welbilt Corp., 19
Wellman, Inc., 8; 52 (upd.)
Weru Aktiengesellschaft, 18
West Bend Co., 14
Westell Technologies, Inc., 57
Westerbeke Corporation, 60
Western Digital Corp., 25
Wheaton Science Products, 60 (upd.)
Wheeling-Pittsburgh Corporation, 58 (upd.)
Whirlpool Corporation, III; 12 (upd.); 59 (upd.)
White Consolidated Industries Inc., 13
Wilbert, Inc., 56
Wilkinson Sword Ltd., 60
William L. Bonnell Company, Inc., 66
William Zinsser & Company, Inc., 58
Williamson-Dickie Manufacturing Company, 45 (upd.)
Wilson Sporting Goods Company, 24
Wincor Nixdorf Holding GmbH, 69 (upd.)
Windmere Corporation, 16
Winegard Company, 56
WinsLoew Furniture, Inc., 21
WMS Industries, Inc., 15; 53 (upd.)
Wolverine Tube Inc., 23
Wood-Mode, Inc., 23
Woodcraft Industries Inc., 61
Woodward Governor Company, 13; 49 (upd.)
Wright Medical Group, Inc., 61
Württembergische Metallwarenfabrik AG (WMF), 60
Wyant Corporation, 30
Wyman-Gordon Company, 14
Wynn's International, Inc., 33
X-Rite, Inc., 48
Xerox Corporation, 69 (upd.)
Yamaha Corporation, III; 16 (upd.)
The York Group, Inc., 50
York International Corp., 13
Young Innovations, Inc., 44
Zebra Technologies Corporation, 53 (upd.)
Zero Corporation, 17
ZiLOG, Inc., 72 (upd.)
Zindart Ltd., 60
Zippo Manufacturing Company, 18; 71 (upd.)
Zodiac S.A., 36
Zygo Corporation, 42

MATERIALS

AK Steel Holding Corporation, 19
American Biltrite Inc., 16
American Colloid Co., 13
American Standard Inc., III
Ameriwood Industries International Corp., 17
Apasco S.A. de C.V., 51
Apogee Enterprises, Inc., 8
Asahi Glass Company, Limited, III
Asbury Carbons, Inc., 68
Bairnco Corporation, 28
Bayou Steel Corporation, 31
Blessings Corp., 19
Blue Circle Industries PLC, III
Bodycote International PLC, 63
Boral Limited, III
British Vita PLC, 9

MATERIALS (*continued*)

Brush Engineered Materials Inc., 67
California Steel Industries, Inc., 67
Callanan Industries, Inc., 60
Cameron & Barkley Company, 28
Carborundum Company, 15
Carl-Zeiss-Stiftung, 34 (upd.)
Carlisle Companies Incorporated, 8
Carter Holt Harvey Ltd., 70
Cemex SA de CV, 20
Century Aluminum Company, 52
CertainTeed Corporation, 35
Chargeurs International, 21 (upd.)
Chemfab Corporation, 35
Cold Spring Granite Company Inc., 16; 67 (upd.)
Compagnie de Saint-Gobain S.A., III; 16 (upd.)
Cookson Group plc, III; 44 (upd.)
Corning Incorporated, III
CSR Limited, III
Dal-Tile International Inc., 22
The David J. Joseph Company, 14
The Dexter Corporation, 12 (upd.)
Dyckerhoff AG, 35
Dyson Group PLC, 71
ECC Group plc, III
Edw. C. Levy Co., 42
84 Lumber Company, 9; 39 (upd.)
ElkCorp, 52
English China Clays Ltd., 15 (upd.); 40 (upd.)
Envirodyne Industries, Inc., 17
Feldmuhle Nobel A.G., III
Fibreboard Corporation, 16
Florida Rock Industries, Inc., 46
Foamex International Inc., 17
Formica Corporation, 13
GAF Corporation, 22 (upd.)
The Geon Company, 11
Giant Cement Holding, Inc., 23
Gibraltar Steel Corporation, 37
Granite Rock Company, 26
Groupe Sidel S.A., 21
Harbison-Walker Refractories Company, 24
Harrisons & Crosfield plc, III
Heidelberger Zement AG, 31
Hexcel Corporation, 28
''Holderbank'' Financière Glaris Ltd., III
Holnam Inc., 39 (upd.)
Holt and Bugbee Company, 66
Homasote Company, 72
Howmet Corp., 12
Ibstock Brick Ltd., 14; 37 (upd.)
Imerys S.A., 40 (upd.)
Internacional de Ceramica, S.A. de C.V., 53
International Shipbreaking Ltd. L.L.C., 67
Joseph T. Ryerson & Son, Inc., 15
Lafarge Coppée S.A., III
Lafarge Corporation, 28
Lehigh Portland Cement Company, 23
Manville Corporation, III; 7 (upd.)
Material Sciences Corporation, 63
Matsushita Electric Works, Ltd., III; 7 (upd.)
McJunkin Corporation, 63
Medusa Corporation, 24
Mitsubishi Materials Corporation, III
Nippon Sheet Glass Company, Limited, III
North Pacific Group, Inc., 61
OmniSource Corporation, 14
Onoda Cement Co., Ltd., III
Owens-Corning Fiberglass Corporation, III
Pilkington plc, III; 34 (upd.)
Pioneer International Limited, III
PPG Industries, Inc., III

Redland plc, III
Rinker Group Ltd., 65
RMC Group p.l.c., III
Rock of Ages Corporation, 37
The Rugby Group plc, 31
Schuff Steel Company, 26
Sekisui Chemical Co., Ltd., III; 72 (upd.)
Severstal Joint Stock Company, 65
Shaw Industries, 9
The Sherwin-Williams Company, III; 13 (upd.)
The Siam Cement Public Company Limited, 56
SIG plc, 71
Simplex Technologies Inc., 21
Siskin Steel & Supply Company, 70
Solutia Inc., 52
Sommer-Allibert S.A., 19
Southdown, Inc., 14
Spartech Corporation, 19
Ssangyong Cement Industrial Co., Ltd., III; 61 (upd.)
Steel Technologies Inc., 63
Sun Distributors L.P., 12
Tarmac PLC, III
Tarmac plc, 28 (upd.)
TOTO LTD., III; 28 (upd.)
Toyo Sash Co., Ltd., III
Tuscarora Inc., 29
U.S. Aggregates, Inc., 42
Ube Industries, Ltd., III
United States Steel Corporation, 50 (upd.)
USG Corporation, III; 26 (upd.)
Vicat S.A., 70
voestalpine AG, 57 (upd.)
Vulcan Materials Company, 7; 52 (upd.)
Wacker-Chemie GmbH, 35
Walter Industries, Inc., III
Waxman Industries, Inc., 9
Weber et Broutin France, 66
Wienerberger AG, 70
Wolseley plc, 64
Zoltek Companies, Inc., 37

MINING & METALS

A.M. Castle & Co., 25
Aggregate Industries plc, 36
Agnico-Eagle Mines Limited, 71
Aktiebolaget SKF, 38 (upd.)
Alcan Aluminium Limited, IV; 31 (upd.)
Alcoa Inc., 56 (upd.)
Alleghany Corporation, 10
Allegheny Ludlum Corporation, 8
Alrosa Company Ltd., 62
Altos Hornos de México, S.A. de C.V., 42
Aluminum Company of America, IV; 20 (upd.)
AMAX Inc., IV
AMCOL International Corporation, 59 (upd.)
Amsted Industries Incorporated, 7
Anglo American Corporation of South Africa Limited, IV; 16 (upd.)
Anglo American PLC, 50 (upd.)
Aquarius Platinum Ltd., 63
ARBED S.A., IV; 22 (upd.)
Arch Mineral Corporation, 7
Armco Inc., IV
ASARCO Incorporated, IV
Ashanti Goldfields Company Limited, 43
Atchison Casting Corporation, 39
Barrick Gold Corporation, 34
Battle Mountain Gold Company, 23
Benguet Corporation, 58
Bethlehem Steel Corporation, IV; 7 (upd.); 27 (upd.)
BHP Billiton, 67 (upd.)

Birmingham Steel Corporation, 13; 40 (upd.)
Boart Longyear Company, 26
Bodycote International PLC, 63
Boral Limited, 43 (upd.)
British Coal Corporation, IV
British Steel plc, IV; 19 (upd.)
Broken Hill Proprietary Company Ltd., IV, 22 (upd.)
Brush Engineered Materials Inc., 67
Brush Wellman Inc., 14
Buderus AG, 37
Carpenter Technology Corporation, 13
Chaparral Steel Co., 13
Christensen Boyles Corporation, 26
Cleveland-Cliffs Inc., 13; 62 (upd.)
Coal India Ltd., IV; 44 (upd.)
Cockerill Sambre Group, IV; 26 (upd.)
Coeur d'Alene Mines Corporation, 20
Cold Spring Granite Company Inc., 16; 67 (upd.)
Cominco Ltd., 37
Commercial Metals Company, 15; 42 (upd.)
Companhia Vale do Rio Doce, IV; 43 (upd.)
CONSOL Energy Inc., 59
Corporacion Nacional del Cobre de Chile, 40
Corus Group plc, 49 (upd.)
CRA Limited, IV
Cyprus Amax Minerals Company, 21
Cyprus Minerals Company, 7
Daido Steel Co., Ltd., IV
De Beers Consolidated Mines Limited/De Beers Centenary AG, IV; 7 (upd.); 28 (upd.)
Degussa Group, IV
Dofasco Inc., IV; 24 (upd.)
Echo Bay Mines Ltd., IV; 38 (upd.)
Engelhard Corporation, IV
Falconbridge Limited, 49
Fansteel Inc., 19
Fluor Corporation, 34 (upd.)
Freeport-McMoRan Copper & Gold, Inc., IV; 7 (upd.); 57 (upd.)
Fried. Krupp GmbH, IV
Gencor Ltd., IV, 22 (upd.)
Geneva Steel, 7
Gerdau S.A., 59
Glamis Gold, Ltd., 54
Gold Fields Ltd., IV; 62 (upd.)
Grupo Mexico, S.A. de C.V., 40
Handy & Harman, 23
Hanson Building Materials America Inc., 60
Hanson PLC, 30 (upd.)
Harmony Gold Mining Company Limited, 63
Hecla Mining Company, 20
Hemlo Gold Mines Inc., 9
Heraeus Holding GmbH, IV
Highveld Steel and Vanadium Corporation Limited, 59
Hitachi Metals, Ltd., IV
Hoesch AG, IV
Homestake Mining Company, 12; 38 (upd.)
Horsehead Industries, Inc., 51
The Hudson Bay Mining and Smelting Company, Limited, 12
Hylsamex, S.A. de C.V., 39
IMCO Recycling, Incorporated, 32
Imerys S.A., 40 (upd.)
Imetal S.A., IV
Inco Limited, IV; 45 (upd.)
Industrias Penoles, S.A. de C.V., 22
Inland Steel Industries, Inc., IV; 19 (upd.)

Intermet Corporation, 32
Iscor Limited, 57
Ispat Inland Inc., 30; 40 (upd.)
Johnson Matthey PLC, IV; 16 (upd.)
JSC MMC Norilsk Nickel, 48
Kaiser Aluminum & Chemical Corporation, IV
Kawasaki Heavy Industries, Ltd., 63 (upd.)
Kawasaki Steel Corporation, IV
Kennecott Corporation, 7; 27 (upd.)
Kentucky Electric Steel, Inc., 31
Kerr-McGee Corporation, 22 (upd.)
Kinross Gold Corporation, 36
Klockner-Werke AG, IV
Kobe Steel, Ltd., IV; 19 (upd.)
Koninklijke Nederlandsche Hoogovens en Staalfabrieken NV, IV
Laclede Steel Company, 15
Layne Christensen Company, 19
Lonmin plc, 66 (upd.)
Lonrho Plc, 21
The LTV Corporation, 24 (upd.)
Lukens Inc., 14
Magma Copper Company, 7
The Marmon Group, IV; 16 (upd.)
Massey Energy Company, 57
MAXXAM Inc., 8
Meridian Gold, Incorporated, 47
Metaleurop S.A., 21
Metallgesellschaft AG, IV
Minerals and Metals Trading Corporation of India Ltd., IV
Minerals Technologies Inc., 11; 52 (upd.)
Mitsui Mining & Smelting Co., Ltd., IV
Mitsui Mining Company, Limited, IV
Mueller Industries, Inc., 52 (upd.)
National Steel Corporation, 12
NERCO, Inc., 7
Newmont Mining Corporation, 7
Neyveli Lignite Corporation Ltd., 65
Niagara Corporation, 28
Nichimen Corporation, IV
Nippon Light Metal Company, Ltd., IV
Nippon Steel Corporation, IV; 17 (upd.)
Nisshin Steel Co., Ltd., IV
NKK Corporation, IV; 28 (upd.)
Noranda Inc., IV; 7 (upd.); 64 (upd.)
Norddeutsche Affinerie AG, 62
North Star Steel Company, 18
Nucor Corporation, 7; 21 (upd.)
Oglebay Norton Company, 17
Okura & Co., Ltd., IV
Oregon Metallurgical Corporation, 20
Oregon Steel Mills, Inc., 14
Outokumpu Oyj, 38
Park Corp., 22
Peabody Coal Company, 10
Peabody Energy Corporation, 45 (upd.)
Peabody Holding Company, Inc., IV
Pechiney SA, IV; 45 (upd.)
Peter Kiewit Sons' Inc., 8
Phelps Dodge Corporation, IV; 28 (upd.)
The Pittston Company, IV; 19 (upd.)
Placer Dome Inc., 20; 61 (upd.)
Pohang Iron and Steel Company Ltd., IV
POSCO, 57 (upd.)
Potash Corporation of Saskatchewan Inc., 18
Quanex Corporation, 13; 62 (upd.)
RAG AG, 35; 60 (upd.)
Reliance Steel & Aluminum Co., 19
Republic Engineered Steels, Inc., 7; 26 (upd.)
Reynolds Metals Company, IV
Rio Tinto PLC, 19 (upd.); 50 (upd.)
RMC Group p.l.c., 34 (upd.)
Roanoke Electric Steel Corporation, 45

Rouge Steel Company, 8
The RTZ Corporation PLC, IV
Ruhrkohle AG, IV
Ryerson Tull, Inc., 40 (upd.)
Saarberg-Konzern, IV
Salzgitter AG, IV
Sandvik AB, IV
Saudi Basic Industries Corporation (SABIC), 58
Schnitzer Steel Industries, Inc., 19
Severstal Joint Stock Company, 65
Shanghai Baosteel Group Corporation, 71
Siderar S.A.I.C., 66
Smorgon Steel Group Ltd., 62
Southern Peru Copper Corporation, 40
Southwire Company, Inc., 8; 23 (upd.)
Steel Authority of India Ltd., IV
Stelco Inc., IV
Stillwater Mining Company, 47
Sumitomo Metal Industries, Ltd., IV
Sumitomo Metal Mining Co., Ltd., IV
Tata Iron & Steel Co. Ltd., IV; 44 (upd.)
Teck Corporation, 27
Tenaris SA, 63
Texas Industries, Inc., 8
Thyssen AG, IV
The Timken Company, 8; 42 (upd.)
Titanium Metals Corporation, 21
Tomen Corporation, IV
Total Fina Elf S.A., 50 (upd.)
U.S. Borax, Inc., 42
Ugine S.A., 20
NV Umicore SA, 47
Usinor SA, IV; 42 (upd.)
Usinor Sacilor, IV
VIAG Aktiengesellschaft, IV
Voest-Alpine Stahl AG, IV
Vulcan Materials Company, 52 (upd.)
Walter Industries, Inc., 22 (upd.)
Weirton Steel Corporation, IV; 26 (upd.)
Westmoreland Coal Company, 7
Wheeling-Pittsburgh Corp., 7
WMC, Limited, 43
Worthington Industries, Inc., 7; 21 (upd.)
Zambia Industrial and Mining Corporation Ltd., IV

PAPER & FORESTRY

Abitibi-Consolidated, Inc., IV; 25 (upd.)
Albany International Corporation, 51 (upd.)
Amcor Limited, IV; 19 (upd.)
American Greetings Corporation, 59 (upd.)
American Pad & Paper Company, 20
Aracruz Celulose S.A., 57
Arjo Wiggins Appleton p.l.c., 34
Asplundh Tree Expert Co., 20; 59 (upd.)
Avery Dennison Corporation, IV
Badger Paper Mills, Inc., 15
Beckett Papers, 23
Bemis Company, Inc., 8
Bohemia, Inc., 13
Boise Cascade Corporation, IV; 8 (upd.); 32 (upd.)
Bowater PLC, IV
Bunzl plc, IV
Canfor Corporation, 42
Caraustar Industries, Inc., 19; 44 (upd.)
Carter Lumber Company, 45
Cascades Inc., 71
Champion International Corporation, IV; 20 (upd.)
Chesapeake Corporation, 8; 30 (upd.)
Consolidated Papers, Inc., 8; 36 (upd.)
Crane & Co., Inc., 26
Crown Vantage Inc., 29
CSS Industries, Inc., 35
Daio Paper Corporation, IV

Daishowa Paper Manufacturing Co., Ltd., IV; 57 (upd.)
Deltic Timber Corporation, 46
Dillard Paper Company, 11
Doman Industries Limited, 59
Domtar Inc., IV
DS Smith Plc, 61
Empresas CMPC S.A., 70
Enso-Gutzeit Oy, IV
Esselte Pendaflex Corporation, 11
Federal Paper Board Company, Inc., 8
FiberMark, Inc., 37
Fletcher Challenge Ltd., IV
Fort Howard Corporation, 8
Fort James Corporation, 22 (upd.)
Georgia-Pacific Corporation, IV; 9 (upd.); 47 (upd.)
Groupe Rougier SA, 21
Grupo Portucel Soporcel, 60
Guilbert S.A., 42
Holmen AB, 52 (upd.)
Honshu Paper Co., Ltd., IV
International Paper Company, IV; 15 (upd.); 47 (upd.)
James River Corporation of Virginia, IV
Japan Pulp and Paper Company Limited, IV
Jefferson Smurfit Group plc, IV; 49 (upd.)
Jujo Paper Co., Ltd., IV
Kimberly-Clark Corporation, 16 (upd.); 43 (upd.)
Kimberly-Clark de México, S.A. de C.V., 54
Kruger Inc., 17
Kymmene Corporation, IV
Longview Fibre Company, 8; 37 (upd.)
Louisiana-Pacific Corporation, IV; 31 (upd.)
M-real Oyj, 56 (upd.)
MacMillan Bloedel Limited, IV
Matussière et Forest SA, 58
The Mead Corporation, IV; 19 (upd.)
Mercer International Inc., 64
Metsa-Serla Oy, IV
Miquel y Costas Miquel S.A., 68
Mo och Domsjö AB, IV
Monadnock Paper Mills, Inc., 21
Mosinee Paper Corporation, 15
Nashua Corporation, 8
National Envelope Corporation, 32
NCH Corporation, 8
Norske Skogindustrier ASA, 63
Oji Paper Co., Ltd., IV
P.H. Glatfelter Company, 8; 30 (upd.)
Packaging Corporation of America, 12
Papeteries de Lancey, 23
Plum Creek Timber Company, Inc., 43
Pope & Talbot, Inc., 12; 61 (upd.)
Potlatch Corporation, 8; 34 (upd.)
PWA Group, IV
Rayonier, 24
Rengo Co., Ltd., IV
Reno de Medici S.p.A., 41
Rexam PLC, 32 (upd.)
Riverwood International Corporation, 11; 48 (upd.)
Rock-Tenn Company, 13; 59 (upd.)
Rogers Corporation, 61
St. Joe Paper Company, 8
Sanyo-Kokusaku Pulp Co., Ltd., IV
Sappi Limited, 49
Schweitzer-Mauduit International, Inc., 52
Scott Paper Company, IV; 31 (upd.)
Sealed Air Corporation, 14
Sierra Pacific Industries, 22
Simpson Investment Company, 17
Specialty Coatings Inc., 8

PAPER & FORESTRY (*continued*)

Stone Container Corporation, IV
Stora Enso Oyj, 36 (upd.)
Stora Kopparbergs Bergslags AB, IV
Svenska Cellulosa Aktiebolaget SCA, IV;
    28 (upd.)
Tapemark Company Inc., 64
Tembec Inc., 66
Temple-Inland Inc., IV; 31 (upd.)
Thomsen Greenhouses and Garden Center,
    Incorporated, 65
TJ International, Inc., 19
U.S. Timberlands Company, L.P., 42
Union Camp Corporation, IV
United Paper Mills Ltd. (Yhtyneet
    Paperitehtaat Oy), IV
Universal Forest Products, Inc., 10; 59
    (upd.)
UPM-Kymmene Corporation, 19; 50 (upd.)
Wausau-Mosinee Paper Corporation, 60
    (upd.)
West Fraser Timber Co. Ltd., 17
Westvaco Corporation, IV; 19 (upd.)
Weyerhaeuser Company, IV; 9 (upd.); 28
    (upd.)
Wickes Inc., 25 (upd.)
Willamette Industries, Inc., IV; 31 (upd.)
WTD Industries, Inc., 20

PERSONAL SERVICES

AARP, 27
ADT Security Services, Inc., 12; 44 (upd.)
Africare, 59
Alderwoods Group, Inc., 68 (upd.)
Ambassadors International, Inc., 68 (upd.)
American Civil Liberties Union (ACLU),
    60
American Retirement Corporation, 42
American Society for the Prevention of
    Cruelty to Animals (ASPCA), 68
Arthur Murray International, Inc., 32
Association of Junior Leagues International
    Inc., 60
Berlitz International, Inc., 39 (upd.)
Bonhams 1793 Ltd., 72
Boys & Girls Clubs of America, 69
The Brink's Company, 58 (upd.)
Caritas Internationalis, 72
Carriage Services, Inc., 37
CDI Corporation, 54 (upd.)
ChildrenFirst, Inc., 59
Childtime Learning Centers, Inc., 34
Chubb, PLC, 50
Corinthian Colleges, Inc., 39
Correctional Services Corporation, 30
CUC International Inc., 16
Curves International, Inc., 54
Davis Service Group PLC, 45
DeVry Incorporated, 29
Educational Testing Service, 12; 62 (upd.)
eHarmony.com Inc., 71
Feed The Children, Inc., 68
The Ford Foundation, 34
Franklin Quest Co., 11
Gold's Gym International, Inc., 71
Goodwill Industries International, Inc., 16;
    66 (upd.)
GP Strategies Corporation, 64 (upd.)
Greg Manning Auctions, Inc., 60
Gunnebo AB, 53
The Humane Society of the United States,
    54
Huntington Learning Centers, Inc., 55
Imperial Parking Corporation, 58
Initial Security, 64
Jazzercise, Inc., 45

The John D. and Catherine T. MacArthur
    Foundation, 34
Kaplan, Inc., 42
KinderCare Learning Centers, Inc., 13
Knowledge Learning Corporation, 51
Kumon Institute of Education Co., Ltd., 72
The Loewen Group Inc., 16; 40 (upd.)
Mace Security International, Inc., 57
Management and Training Corporation, 28
Manpower, Inc., 9
Michael Page International plc, 45
Mothers Against Drunk Driving (MADD),
    51
National Heritage Academies, Inc., 60
National Organization for Women, Inc., 55
Prison Rehabilitative Industries and
    Diversified Enterprises, Inc. (PRIDE), 53
Recording for the Blind & Dyslexic, 51
Regis Corporation, 18; 70 (upd.)
Robert Half International Inc., 70 (upd.)
The Rockefeller Foundation, 34
Rollins, Inc., 11
Rosenbluth International Inc., 14
Rotary International, 31
The Salvation Army USA, 32
Screen Actors Guild, 72
Service Corporation International, 6; 51
    (upd.)
The ServiceMaster Company, 68 (upd.)
SOS Staffing Services, 25
Stewart Enterprises, Inc., 20
Supercuts Inc., 26
24 Hour Fitness Worldwide, Inc., 71
UAW (International Union, United
    Automobile, Aerospace and Agricultural
    Implement Workers of America), 72
United Service Organizations, 60
Weight Watchers International Inc., 12; 33
    (upd.)
The York Group, Inc., 50
Youth Services International, Inc., 21
YWCA of the U.S.A., 45

PETROLEUM

Abu Dhabi National Oil Company, IV; 45
    (upd.)
Agway, Inc., 21 (upd.)
Alberta Energy Company Ltd., 16; 43
    (upd.)
Amerada Hess Corporation, IV; 21 (upd.);
    55 (upd.)
Amoco Corporation, IV; 14 (upd.)
Anadarko Petroleum Corporation, 10; 52
    (upd.)
ANR Pipeline Co., 17
Anschutz Corp., 12
Apache Corporation, 10; 32 (upd.)
Aral AG, 62
Arctic Slope Regional Corporation, 38
Ashland Inc., 19; 50 (upd.)
Ashland Oil, Inc., IV
Atlantic Richfield Company, IV; 31 (upd.)
Baker Hughes Incorporated, 22 (upd.); 57
    (upd.)
Belco Oil & Gas Corp., 40
Benton Oil and Gas Company, 47
Berry Petroleum Company, 47
BHP Billiton, 67 (upd.)
Bill Barrett Corporation, 71
BJ Services Company, 25
Blue Rhino Corporation, 56
BP p.l.c., 45 (upd.)
The British Petroleum Company plc, IV; 7
    (upd.); 21 (upd.)
British-Borneo Oil & Gas PLC, 34
Broken Hill Proprietary Company Ltd., 22
    (upd.)

Burlington Resources Inc., 10
Burmah Castrol PLC, IV; 30 (upd.)
Callon Petroleum Company, 47
Caltex Petroleum Corporation, 19
ChevronTexaco Corporation, IV; 19 (upd.);
    47 (upd.)
Chiles Offshore Corporation, 9
China National Petroleum Corporation, 46
Chinese Petroleum Corporation, IV; 31
    (upd.)
CITGO Petroleum Corporation, IV; 31
    (upd.)
The Coastal Corporation, IV; 31 (upd.)
Compañia Española de Petróleos S.A.
    (Cepsa), IV; 56 (upd.)
Comstock Resources, Inc., 47
Conoco Inc., IV; 16 (upd.)
ConocoPhillips, 63 (upd.)
CONSOL Energy Inc., 59
Cooper Cameron Corporation, 20 (upd.)
Cosmo Oil Co., Ltd., IV; 53 (upd.)
Crown Central Petroleum Corporation, 7
DeepTech International Inc., 21
Den Norse Stats Oljeselskap AS, IV
Denbury Resources, Inc., 67
Deutsche BP Aktiengesellschaft, 7
Devon Energy Corporation, 61
Diamond Shamrock, Inc., IV
Dynegy Inc., 49 (upd.)
E.On AG, 50 (upd.)
Edge Petroleum Corporation, 67
Egyptian General Petroleum Corporation,
    IV; 51 (upd.)
El Paso Corporation, 66 (upd.)
Elf Aquitaine SA, 21 (upd.)
Empresa Colombiana de Petróleos, IV
Enbridge Inc., 43
Energen Corporation, 21
ENI S.p.A., 69 (upd.)
Enron Corporation, 19
ENSCO International Incorporated, 57
Ente Nazionale Idrocarburi, IV
Enterprise Oil PLC, 11; 50 (upd.)
Entreprise Nationale Sonatrach, IV
Equitable Resources, Inc., 54 (upd.)
Exxon Corporation, IV; 7 (upd.); 32 (upd.)
Exxon Mobil Corporation, 67 (upd.)
Ferrellgas Partners, L.P., 35
FINA, Inc., 7
Flying J Inc., 19
Forest Oil Corporation, 19
OAO Gazprom, 42
General Sekiyu K.K., IV
Giant Industries, Inc., 19; 61 (upd.)
Global Industries, Ltd., 37
Global Marine Inc., 9
GlobalSantaFe Corporation, 48 (upd.)
Grey Wolf, Inc., 43
Halliburton Company, 25 (upd.); 55 (upd.)
Hanover Compressor Company, 59
Hellenic Petroleum SA, 64
Helmerich & Payne, Inc., 18
Holly Corporation, 12
Hunt Consolidated, Inc., 7; 27 (upd.)
Hurricane Hydrocarbons Ltd., 54
Husky Energy Inc., 47
Idemitsu Kosan Co., Ltd., 49 (upd.)
Idemitsu Kosan K.K., IV
Imperial Oil Limited, IV; 25 (upd.)
Indian Oil Corporation Ltd., IV; 48 (upd.)
Ipiranga S.A., 67
Kanematsu Corporation, IV
Kerr-McGee Corporation, IV; 22 (upd.); 68
    (upd.)
Kinder Morgan, Inc., 45
King Ranch, Inc., 14
Koch Industries, Inc., IV; 20 (upd.)

Koppers Industries, Inc., 26 (upd.)
Kuwait Petroleum Corporation, IV; 55 (upd.)
Libyan National Oil Corporation, IV
The Louisiana Land and Exploration Company, 7
OAO LUKOIL, 40
Lyondell Petrochemical Company, IV
MAPCO Inc., IV
Maxus Energy Corporation, 7
McDermott International, Inc., 37 (upd.)
Meteor Industries Inc., 33
Mitchell Energy and Development Corporation, 7
Mitsubishi Oil Co., Ltd., IV
Mobil Corporation, IV; 7 (upd.); 21 (upd.)
MOL Rt, 70
Murphy Oil Corporation, 7; 32 (upd.)
Nabors Industries, Inc., 9
National Iranian Oil Company, IV; 61 (upd.)
National Oil Corporation, 66 (upd.)
Neste Oy, IV
Newfield Exploration Company, 65
NGC Corporation, 18
Nigerian National Petroleum Corporation, IV; 72 (upd.)
Nippon Oil Corporation, IV; 63 (upd.)
OAO NK YUKOS, 47
Noble Affiliates, Inc., 11
Occidental Petroleum Corporation, IV; 25 (upd.); 71 (upd.)
Oil and Natural Gas Commission, IV
ÖMV Aktiengesellschaft, IV
Oryx Energy Company, 7
Parker Drilling Company, 28
Patina Oil & Gas Corporation, 24
Patterson-UTI Energy, Inc., 55
Pennzoil-Quaker State Company, IV; 20 (upd.); 50 (upd.)
Pertamina, IV; 56 (upd.)
Petro-Canada Limited, IV
Petrobras Energia Participaciones S.A., 72
PetroFina S.A., IV; 26 (upd.)
Petróleo Brasileiro S.A., IV
Petróleos de Portugal S.A., IV
Petróleos de Venezuela S.A., IV
Petróleos del Ecuador, IV
Petróleos Mexicanos, IV; 19 (upd.)
Petroleum Development Oman LLC, IV
Petroliam Nasional Bhd (Petronas), IV; 56 (upd.)
Petron Corporation, 58
Phillips Petroleum Company, IV; 40 (upd.)
Pioneer Natural Resources Company, 59
Pogo Producing Company, 39
Premcor Inc., 37
PTT Public Company Ltd., 56
Qatar General Petroleum Corporation, IV
Quaker State Corporation, 7; 21 (upd.)
Range Resources Corporation, 45
Repsol-YPF S.A., IV; 16 (upd.); 40 (upd.)
Resource America, Inc., 42
Rowan Companies, Inc., 43
Royal Dutch/Shell Group, IV; 49 (upd.)
RWE AG, 50 (upd.)
St. Mary Land & Exploration Company, 63
Santa Fe International Corporation, 38
Sasol Limited, IV; 47 (upd.)
Saudi Arabian Oil Company, IV; 17 (upd.); 50 (upd.)
Schlumberger Limited, 17 (upd.); 59 (upd.)
Seagull Energy Corporation, 11
Seitel, Inc., 47
Shanghai Petrochemical Co., Ltd., 18
Shell Oil Company, IV; 14 (upd.); 41 (upd.)

Showa Shell Sekiyu K.K., IV; 59 (upd.)
OAO Siberian Oil Company (Sibneft), 49
Smith International, Inc., 59 (upd.)
Société Nationale Elf Aquitaine, IV; 7 (upd.)
Sonatrach, 65 (upd.)
Spinnaker Exploration Company, 72
Statoil ASA, 61 (upd.)
Suburban Propane Partners, L.P., 30
Sun Company, Inc., IV
Suncor Energy Inc., 54
Sunoco, Inc., 28 (upd.)
Superior Energy Services, Inc., 65
OAO Surgutneftegaz, 48
Swift Energy Company, 63
Talisman Energy Inc., 9; 47 (upd.)
OAO Tatneft, 45
Tesoro Petroleum Corporation, 7; 45 (upd.)
Texaco Inc., IV; 14 (upd.); 41 (upd.)
Tidewater Inc., 37 (upd.)
Tom Brown, Inc., 37
Tonen Corporation, IV; 16 (upd.)
TonenGeneral Sekiyu K.K., 54 (upd.)
Tosco Corporation, 7
TOTAL S.A., IV; 24 (upd.)
TransMontaigne Inc., 28
Transocean Sedco Forex Inc., 45
Travel Ports of America, Inc., 17
Triton Energy Corporation, 11
Türkiye Petrolleri Anonim Ortakliği, IV
Ultra Petroleum Corporation, 71
Ultramar Diamond Shamrock Corporation, IV; 31 (upd.)
Union Texas Petroleum Holdings, Inc., 9
Unit Corporation, 63
Universal Compression, Inc., 59
Unocal Corporation, IV; 24 (upd.); 71 (upd.)
USX Corporation, IV; 7 (upd.)
Valero Energy Corporation, 7; 71 (upd.)
Varco International, Inc., 42
Vastar Resources, Inc., 24
Vintage Petroleum, Inc., 42
Wascana Energy Inc., 13
Weatherford International, Inc., 39
Webber Oil Company, 61
Western Atlas Inc., 12
Western Company of North America, 15
Western Gas Resources, Inc., 45
Westport Resources Corporation, 63
The Williams Companies, Inc., IV; 31 (upd.)
World Fuel Services Corporation, 47
XTO Energy Inc., 52
YPF Sociedad Anonima, IV

PUBLISHING & PRINTING

A.B.Dick Company, 28
A.H. Belo Corporation, 10; 30 (upd.)
Advance Publications Inc., IV; 19 (upd.)
Advanced Marketing Services, Inc., 34
Advanstar Communications, Inc., 57
Affiliated Publications, Inc., 7
Agence France-Presse, 34
American Banknote Corporation, 30
American Girl, Inc., 69
American Greetings Corporation, 7, 22 (upd.)
American Media, Inc., 27
American Printing House for the Blind, 26
Andrews McMeel Universal, 40
The Antioch Company, 40
AOL Time Warner Inc., 57 (upd.)
Arandell Corporation, 37
Archie Comics Publications, Inc., 63
Arnoldo Mondadori Editore S.p.A., IV; 19 (upd.); 54 (upd.)

The Associated Press, 31 (upd.)
The Atlantic Group, 23
Axel Springer Verlag AG, IV; 20 (upd.)
Banta Corporation, 12; 32 (upd.)
Bauer Publishing Group, 7
Bayard SA, 49
Berlitz International, Inc., 13
Bernard C. Harris Publishing Company, Inc., 39
Bertelsmann A.G., IV; 15 (upd.); 43 (upd.)
Big Flower Press Holdings, Inc., 21
Blue Mountain Arts, Inc., 29
Bobit Publishing Company, 55
Bonnier AB, 52
Book-of-the-Month Club, Inc., 13
Bowne & Co., Inc., 23
Broderbund Software, 13; 29 (upd.)
Brown Printing Company, 26
Burda Holding GmbH. & Co., 23
The Bureau of National Affairs, Inc., 23
Butterick Co., Inc., 23
Cadmus Communications Corporation, 23
Cahners Business Information, 43
Carl Allers Etablissement A/S, 72
CCH Inc., 14
Central Newspapers, Inc., 10
Champion Industries, Inc., 28
Cherry Lane Music Publishing Company, Inc., 62
ChoicePoint Inc., 65
The Christian Science Publishing Society, 55
The Chronicle Publishing Company, Inc., 23
Chrysalis Group plc, 40
CMP Media Inc., 26
Commerce Clearing House, Inc., 7
Concepts Direct, Inc., 39
Condé Nast Publications, Inc., 13; 59 (upd.)
Consolidated Graphics, Inc., 70
Consumers Union, 26
The Copley Press, Inc., 23
Courier Corporation, 41
Cowles Media Company, 23
Cox Enterprises, Inc., IV; 22 (upd.)
Crain Communications, Inc., 12; 35 (upd.)
Current, Inc., 37
Cygnus Business Media, Inc., 56
Dai Nippon Printing Co., Ltd., IV; 57 (upd.)
Daily Mail and General Trust plc, 19
Dawson Holdings PLC, 43
Day Runner, Inc., 14
DC Comics Inc., 25
De La Rue plc, 10; 34 (upd.)
DeLorme Publishing Company, Inc., 53
Deluxe Corporation, 7; 22 (upd.)
Dennis Publishing Ltd., 62
Dex Media, Inc., 65
Donruss Playoff L.P., 66
Dorling Kindersley Holdings plc, 20
Dover Publications Inc., 34
Dow Jones & Company, Inc., IV; 19 (upd.); 47 (upd.)
The Dun & Bradstreet Corporation, IV; 19 (upd.)
Duplex Products Inc., 17
The E.W. Scripps Company, IV; 7 (upd.); 28 (upd.); 66 (upd.)
The Economist Group Ltd., 67
Éditions Gallimard, 72
Edmark Corporation, 14
Electronics for Imaging, Inc., 43 (upd.)
Elsevier N.V., IV
EMAP plc, 35
EMI Group plc, 22 (upd.)

PUBLISHING & PRINTING (continued)

Encyclopaedia Britannica, Inc., 7; 39 (upd.)
Engraph, Inc., 12
Enquirer/Star Group, Inc., 10
Entravision Communications Corporation, 41
Essence Communications, Inc., 24
F&W Publications, Inc., 71
Farm Journal Corporation, 42
Farrar, Straus and Giroux Inc., 15
Flint Ink Corporation, 13
Follett Corporation, 12; 39 (upd.)
Forbes Inc., 30
Frankfurter Allgemeine Zeitung GmbH, 66
Franklin Electronic Publishers, Inc., 23
Freedom Communications, Inc., 36
Gannett Company, Inc., IV; 7 (upd.); 30 (upd.); 66 (upd.)
Geiger Bros., 60
Gibson Greetings, Inc., 12
Golden Books Family Entertainment, Inc., 28
Goss Holdings, Inc., 43
Graphic Industries Inc., 25
Gray Communications Systems, Inc., 24
Grolier Incorporated, 16; 43 (upd.)
Groupe de la Cite, IV
Groupe Les Echos, 25
Grupo Clarín S.A., 67
Grupo Televisa, S.A., 54 (upd.)
Guardian Media Group plc, 53
The H.W. Wilson Company, 66
Hachette, IV
Hachette Filipacchi Medias S.A., 21
Hallmark Cards, Inc., IV; 16 (upd.); 40 (upd.)
Harcourt Brace and Co., 12
Harcourt Brace Jovanovich, Inc., IV
Harcourt General, Inc., 20 (upd.)
Harlequin Enterprises Limited, 52
HarperCollins Publishers, 15
Harris Interactive Inc., 41
Harry N. Abrams, Inc., 58
Harte-Hanks Communications, Inc., 17
Havas SA, 10; 33 (upd.)
Haynes Publishing Group P.L.C., 71
Hazelden Foundation, 28
Health Communications, Inc., 72
The Hearst Corporation, IV; 19 (upd.); 46 (upd.)
Her Majesty's Stationery Office, 7
N.V. Holdingmaatschappij De Telegraaf, 23
Hollinger International Inc., 24; 62 (upd.)
Houghton Mifflin Company, 10; 36 (upd.)
IDG Books Worldwide, Inc., 27
Independent News & Media PLC, 61
Informa Group plc, 58
Information Holdings Inc., 47
International Data Group, Inc., 7; 25 (upd.)
IPC Magazines Limited, 7
John Fairfax Holdings Limited, 7
John H. Harland Company, 17
John Wiley & Sons, Inc., 17; 65 (upd.)
Johnson Publishing Company, Inc., 28; 72 (upd.)
Johnston Press plc, 35
Jostens, Inc., 25 (upd.)
Journal Register Company, 29
Kaplan, Inc., 42
Kinko's, Inc., 43 (upd.)
Knight Ridder, Inc., 67 (upd.)
Knight-Ridder Inc., IV; 15 (upd.)
Kodansha Ltd., IV; 38 (upd.)
Krause Publications, Inc., 35
Landmark Communications, Inc., 12; 55 (upd.)

Larry Flynt Publishing Inc., 31
Le Monde S.A., 33
Lebhar-Friedman, Inc., 55
Lee Enterprises Inc., 11; 64 (upd.)
LEXIS-NEXIS Group, 33
Lonely Planet Publications Pty Ltd., 55
M. Shanken Communications, Inc., 50
Maclean Hunter Publishing Limited, IV; 26 (upd.)
Macmillan, Inc., 7
Martha Stewart Living Omnimedia, L.L.C., 24
Marvel Entertainment Group, Inc., 10
Matra-Hachette S.A., 15 (upd.)
Maxwell Communication Corporation plc, IV; 7 (upd.)
McClatchy Newspapers, Inc., 23
The McGraw-Hill Companies, Inc., IV; 18 (upd.); 51 (upd.)
Mecklermedia Corporation, 24
Media General, Inc., 38 (upd.)
MediaNews Group, Inc., 70
Menasha Corporation, 59 (upd.)
Meredith Corporation, 11; 29 (upd.)
Merriam-Webster Inc., 70
Merrill Corporation, 18; 47 (upd.)
Miller Publishing Group, LLC, 57
The Miner Group International, 22
Mirror Group Newspapers plc, 7; 23 (upd.)
Moore Corporation Limited, IV
Morris Communications Corporation, 36
Multimedia, Inc., 11
Naspers Ltd., 66
National Audubon Society, 26
National Geographic Society, 9; 30 (upd.)
National Journal Group Inc., 67
New Times, Inc., 45
New York Daily News, 32
The New York Times Company, IV; 19 (upd.); 61 (upd.)
News America Publishing Inc., 12
News Corporation Limited, IV; 7 (upd.)
Newsquest plc, 32
Next Media Ltd., 61
Nihon Keizai Shimbun, Inc., IV
Nolo.com, Inc., 49
Oji Paper Co., Ltd., 57 (upd.)
Onion, Inc., 69
Ottaway Newspapers, Inc., 15
Outlook Group Corporation, 37
Pantone, Inc., 53
PCM Uitgevers NV, 53
Pearson plc, IV; 46 (upd.)
PennWell Corporation, 55
Penton Media, Inc., 27
Petersen Publishing Company, 21
Plato Learning, Inc., 44
Playboy Enterprises, Inc., 18
Pleasant Company, 27
PMP Ltd., 72
PR Newswire, 35
Primedia Inc., 22
The Providence Journal Company, 28
Publishers Group, Inc., 35
Publishing and Broadcasting Limited, 54
Pulitzer Inc., 15; 58 (upd.)
Quad/Graphics, Inc., 19
Quebecor Inc., 12; 47 (upd.)
R.L. Polk & Co., 10
R.R. Donnelley & Sons Company, IV; 9 (upd.); 38 (upd.)
Rand McNally & Company, 28
Random House, Inc., 13; 31 (upd.)
Ravensburger AG, 64
The Reader's Digest Association, Inc., IV; 17 (upd.); 71 (upd.)
Real Times, Inc., 66

Recycled Paper Greetings, Inc., 21
Reed Elsevier plc, IV; 17 (upd.); 31 (upd.)
Reuters Group PLC, IV; 22 (upd.); 63 (upd.)
Rodale, Inc., 23; 47 (upd.)
Rogers Communications Inc., 30 (upd.)
St Ives plc, 34
SanomaWSOY Corporation, 51
Schawk, Inc., 24
Schibsted ASA, 31
Scholastic Corporation, 10; 29 (upd.)
Scott Fetzer Company, 12
Scottish Media Group plc, 32
Seat Pagine Gialle S.p.A., 47
Seattle Times Company, 15
The Sierra Club, 28
Simon & Schuster Inc., IV; 19 (upd.)
Sir Speedy, Inc., 16
SkyMall, Inc., 26
Société du Figaro S.A., 60
Softbank Corp., 13
The Source Enterprises, Inc., 65
Southam Inc., 7
SPIEGEL-Verlag Rudolf Augstein GmbH & Co. KG, 44
Standard Register Co., 15
Tamedia AG, 53
Taylor & Francis Group plc, 44
Taylor Corporation, 36
Taylor Publishing Company, 12; 36 (upd.)
Thomas Nelson, Inc., 14; 38 (upd.)
Thomas Publishing Company, 26
The Thomson Corporation, 8; 34 (upd.)
Time Out Group Ltd., 68
The Times Mirror Company, IV; 17 (upd.)
Tom Doherty Associates Inc., 25
Toppan Printing Co., Ltd., IV; 58 (upd.)
The Topps Company, Inc., 34 (upd.)
Torstar Corporation, 29
Trader Classified Media N.V., 57
Tribune Company, IV, 22 (upd.); 63 (upd.)
Trinity Mirror plc, 49 (upd.)
Tyndale House Publishers, Inc., 57
U.S. News and World Report Inc., 30
United Business Media plc, 52 (upd.)
United News & Media plc, IV; 28 (upd.)
United Press International, Inc., 25
Valassis Communications, Inc., 8
Value Line, Inc., 16
Vance Publishing Corporation, 64
Verlagsgruppe Georg von Holtzbrinck GmbH, 35
Village Voice Media, Inc., 38
VNU N.V., 27
Volt Information Sciences Inc., 26
W.W. Norton & Company, Inc., 28
Wallace Computer Services, Inc., 36
The Washington Post Company, IV; 20 (upd.)
Waverly, Inc., 16
Wegener NV, 53
Wenner Media, Inc., 32
West Group, 7; 34 (upd.)
Western Publishing Group, Inc., 13
WH Smith PLC, V; 42 (upd.)
Wolters Kluwer NV, 14; 33 (upd.)
Workman Publishing Company, Inc., 70
World Book, Inc., 12
World Color Press Inc., 12
World Publications, LLC, 65
Xeikon NV, 26
Zebra Technologies Corporation, 14
Ziff Davis Media Inc., 12; 36 (upd.)
Zondervan Corporation, 24; 71 (upd.)

REAL ESTATE

Alexander's, Inc., 45

Alico, Inc., 63
AMB Property Corporation, 57
Amfac/JMB Hawaii L.L.C., 24 (upd.)
Apartment Investment and Management
   Company, 49
Archstone-Smith Trust, 49
Associated Estates Realty Corporation, 25
AvalonBay Communities, Inc., 58
Berkshire Realty Holdings, L.P., 49
Boston Properties, Inc., 22
Bramalea Ltd., 9
British Land Plc, 54
Canary Wharf Group Plc, 30
CapStar Hotel Company, 21
CarrAmerica Realty Corporation, 56
Castle & Cooke, Inc., 20 (upd.)
Catellus Development Corporation, 24
CB Commercial Real Estate Services
   Group, Inc., 21
CB Richard Ellis Group, Inc., 70 (upd.)
Chateau Communities, Inc., 37
Chelsfield PLC, 67
Cheung Kong (Holdings) Limited, IV; 20
   (upd.)
Clayton Homes Incorporated, 54 (upd.)
Colonial Properties Trust, 65
The Corcoran Group, Inc., 58
Cousins Properties Incorporated, 65
Del Webb Corporation, 14
Developers Diversified Realty Corporation,
   69
Duke Realty Corporation, 57
EastGroup Properties, Inc., 67
The Edward J. DeBartolo Corporation, 8
Enterprise Inns plc, 59
Equity Office Properties Trust, 54
Equity Residential, 49
Erickson Retirement Communities, 57
Fairfield Communities, Inc., 36
First Industrial Realty Trust, Inc., 65
Forest City Enterprises, Inc., 16; 52 (upd.)
Gecina SA, 42
General Growth Properties, Inc., 57
Griffin Land & Nurseries, Inc., 43
Grubb & Ellis Company, 21
The Haminerson Property Investment and
   Development Corporation plc, IV
Hammerson plc, 40
Harbert Corporation, 14
Helmsley Enterprises, Inc., 39 (upd.)
Henderson Land Development Company
   Ltd., 70
Home Properties of New York, Inc., 42
Hongkong Land Holdings Limited, IV; 47
   (upd.)
Hyatt Corporation, 16 (upd.)
ILX Resorts Incorporated, 65
IRSA Inversiones y Representaciones S.A.,
   63
J.F. Shea Co., Inc., 55
JMB Realty Corporation, IV
Jones Lang LaSalle Incorporated, 49
JPI, 49
Kaufman and Broad Home Corporation, 8
Kennedy-Wilson, Inc., 60
Kerry Properties Limited, 22
Kimco Realty Corporation, 11
The Koll Company, 8
Land Securities PLC, IV; 49 (upd.)
Lefrak Organization Inc., 26
Lend Lease Corporation Limited, IV; 17
   (upd.); 52 (upd.)
Liberty Property Trust, 57
Lincoln Property Company, 8; 54 (upd.)
The Loewen Group Inc., 40 (upd.)
The Macerich Company, 57
Mack-Cali Realty Corporation, 42

Manufactured Home Communities, Inc., 22
Maui Land & Pineapple Company, Inc., 29
Maxco Inc., 17
Meditrust, 11
Melvin Simon and Associates, Inc., 8
MEPC plc, IV
Meritage Corporation, 26
The Middleton Doll Company, 53
Mitsubishi Estate Company, Limited, IV;
   61 (upd.)
Mitsui Real Estate Development Co., Ltd.,
   IV
The Nature Conservancy, 28
New Plan Realty Trust, 11
New World Development Company Ltd.,
   IV
Newhall Land and Farming Company, 14
Nexity S.A., 66
NRT Incorporated, 61
Olympia & York Developments Ltd., IV; 9
   (upd.)
Park Corp., 22
Parque Arauco S.A., 72
Perini Corporation, 8
Post Properties, Inc., 26
ProLogis, 57
Public Storage, Inc., 52
Railtrack Group PLC, 50
RE/MAX International, Inc., 59
Reading International Inc., 70
Reckson Associates Realty Corp., 47
Regency Centers Corporation, 71
Rockefeller Group International Inc., 58
Rodamco N.V., 26
The Rouse Company, 15; 63 (upd.)
Shubert Organization Inc., 24
The Sierra Club, 28
Silverstein Properties, Inc., 47
Simco S.A., 37
SL Green Realty Corporation, 44
Slough Estates PLC, IV; 50 (upd.)
Sovran Self Storage, Inc., 66
Starrett Corporation, 21
The Staubach Company, 62
Storage USA, Inc., 21
Sumitomo Realty & Development Co.,
   Ltd., IV
Sun Communities Inc., 46
Tanger Factory Outlet Centers, Inc., 49
Tarragon Realty Investors, Inc., 45
Taylor Woodrow plc, 38 (upd.)
Tejon Ranch Company, 35
Tishman Speyer Properties, L.P., 47
Tokyu Land Corporation, IV
Trammell Crow Company, 8; 57 (upd.)
Trendwest Resorts, Inc., 33
Tridel Enterprises Inc., 9
Trizec Corporation Ltd., 10
The Trump Organization, 23; 64 (upd.)
Unibail SA, 40
United Dominion Realty Trust, Inc., 52
Vistana, Inc., 22
Vornado Realty Trust, 20
W.P. Carey & Co. LLC, 49
William Lyon Homes, 59

RETAIL & WHOLESALE

A-Mark Financial Corporation, 71
A.C. Moore Arts & Crafts, Inc., 30
A.T. Cross Company, 49 (upd.)
Aaron Rents, Inc., 14; 35 (upd.)
Abatix Corp., 57
ABC Appliance, Inc., 10
ABC Carpet & Home Co. Inc., 26
Abercrombie & Fitch Co., 15
Academy Sports & Outdoors, 27
Ace Hardware Corporation, 12; 35 (upd.)

Action Performance Companies, Inc., 27
ADESA, Inc., 71
Adolfo Dominguez S.A., 72
AEON Co., Ltd., 68 (upd.)
After Hours Formalwear Inc., 60
Alabama Farmers Cooperative, Inc., 63
Alain Afflelou SA, 53
Alba-Waldensian, Inc., 30
Alberto-Culver Company, 36 (upd.)
Albertson's, Inc., 65 (upd.)
Alldays plc, 49
Allders plc, 37
Allou Health & Beauty Care, Inc., 28
Alrosa Company Ltd., 62
Alticor Inc., 71 (upd.)
Amazon.com, Inc., 25; 56 (upd.)
AMERCO, 67 (upd.)
American Coin Merchandising, Inc., 28
American Eagle Outfitters, Inc., 24; 55
   (upd.)
American Furniture Company, Inc., 21
American Girl, Inc., 69 (upd.)
American Stores Company, 22 (upd.)
AmeriSource Health Corporation, 37 (upd.)
Ames Department Stores, Inc., 9; 30 (upd.)
Amscan Holdings, Inc., 61
Amway Corporation, 13; 30 (upd.)
The Anderson-DuBose Company, 60
The Andersons, Inc., 31
AnnTaylor Stores Corporation, 13; 37
   (upd.); 67 (upd.)
Appliance Recycling Centers of America,
   Inc., 42
Arbor Drugs Inc., 12
Arcadia Group plc, 28 (upd.)
Army and Air Force Exchange Service, 39
Art Van Furniture, Inc., 28
ASDA Group plc, 28 (upd.)
Ashworth, Inc., 26
Au Printemps S.A., V
Audio King Corporation, 24
Authentic Fitness Corporation, 20; 51
   (upd.)
Auto Value Associates, Inc., 25
Autobytel Inc., 47
AutoNation, Inc., 50
AutoZone, Inc., 9; 31 (upd.)
AVA AG (Allgemeine Handelsgesellschaft
   der Verbraucher AG), 33
Aveda Corporation, 24
Aviation Sales Company, 41
AWB Ltd., 56
B. Dalton Bookseller Inc., 25
Babbage's, Inc., 10
Baby Superstore, Inc., 15
Baccarat, 24
Bachman's Inc., 22
Bailey Nurseries, Inc., 57
Banana Republic Inc., 25
Barnes & Noble, Inc., 10; 30 (upd.)
Barnett Inc., 28
Barney's, Inc., 28
Bass Pro Shops, Inc., 42
Bear Creek Corporation, 38
Bearings, Inc., 13
bebe stores, inc., 31
Bed Bath & Beyond Inc., 13; 41 (upd.)
Belk Stores Services, Inc., V; 19 (upd.)
Belk, Inc., 72 (upd.)
Ben Bridge Jeweler, Inc., 60
Benetton Group S.p.A., 67 (upd.)
Bergdorf Goodman Inc., 52
Bergen Brunswig Corporation, V; 13 (upd.)
Bernard Chaus, Inc., 27
Best Buy Co., Inc., 9; 23 (upd.); 63 (upd.)
Bhs plc, 17
Big Dog Holdings, Inc., 45

RETAIL & WHOLESALE (*continued*)

Big 5 Sporting Goods Corporation, 55
The Big Food Group plc, 68 (upd.)
Big Lots, Inc., 50
Big O Tires, Inc., 20
Birkenstock Footprint Sandals, Inc., 42 (upd.)
Birthdays Ltd., 70
Black Box Corporation, 20
Blacks Leisure Group plc, 39
Blair Corporation, 25; 31 (upd.)
Bloomingdale's Inc., 12
Blue Nile Inc., 61
Blue Square Israel Ltd., 41
Bluefly, Inc., 60
Blyth Industries, Inc., 18
The Body Shop International PLC, 11
The Bombay Company, Inc., 10; 71 (upd.)
The Bon Marché, Inc., 23
The Bon-Ton Stores, Inc., 16; 50 (upd.)
Booker Cash & Carry Ltd., 68 (upd.)
Books-A-Million, Inc., 14; 41 (upd.)
The Boots Company PLC, V; 24 (upd.)
Borders Group, Inc., 15; 43 (upd.)
Boscov's Department Store, Inc., 31
Bozzuto's, Inc., 13
Bradlees Discount Department Store Company, 12
Brambles Industries Limited, 42
Bricorama S.A., 68
Brioni Roman Style S.p.A., 67
Broder Bros. Co., 38
Brooks Brothers Inc., 22
Brookstone, Inc., 18
Brown Shoe Company, Inc., 68 (upd.)
The Buckle, Inc., 18
Buhrmann NV, 41
Build-A-Bear Workshop Inc., 62
Building Materials Holding Corporation, 52
Burdines, Inc., 60
Burlington Coat Factory Warehouse Corporation, 10; 60 (upd.)
Burt's Bees, Inc., 58
The Burton Group plc, V
Buttrey Food & Drug Stores Co., 18
buy.com, Inc., 46
C&A, V; 40 (upd.)
C&J Clark International Ltd., 52
Cabela's Inc., 26; 68 (upd.)
Cablevision Electronic Instruments, Inc., 32
Cache Incorporated, 30
Caldor Inc., 12
Calloway's Nursery, Inc., 51
Camaïeu S.A., 72
Camelot Music, Inc., 26
Campeau Corporation, V
Campo Electronics, Appliances & Computers, Inc., 16
Car Toys, Inc., 67
Carrefour SA, 10; 27 (upd.); 64 (upd.)
Carson Pirie Scott & Company, 15
Carter Hawley Hale Stores, Inc., V
Carter Lumber Company, 45
Cartier Monde, 29
Casual Corner Group, Inc., 43
Casual Male Retail Group, Inc., 52
Catherines Stores Corporation, 15
Cato Corporation, 14
CDW Computer Centers, Inc., 16
Celebrate Express, Inc., 70
Celebrity, Inc., 22
Cencosud S.A., 69
Central Garden & Pet Company, 23
Cenveo Inc., 71 (upd.)
Chadwick's of Boston, Ltd., 29
Charlotte Russe Holding, Inc., 35
Charming Shoppes, Inc., 38

Chas. Levy Company LLC, 60
ChevronTexaco Corporation, 47 (upd.)
Chiasso Inc., 53
The Children's Place Retail Stores, Inc., 37
Christian Dior S.A., 49 (upd.)
Christopher & Banks Corporation, 42
Cifra, S.A. de C.V., 12
The Circle K Company, 20 (upd.)
Circuit City Stores, Inc., 9; 29 (upd.); 65 (upd.)
Clare Rose Inc., 68
Clinton Cards plc, 39
The Clothestime, Inc., 20
CML Group, Inc., 10
Co-operative Group (CWS) Ltd., 51
Coach, Inc., 45 (upd.)
Coborn's, Inc., 30
Coinmach Laundry Corporation, 20
Coldwater Creek Inc., 21
Cole National Corporation, 13
Cole's Quality Foods, Inc., 68
Coles Myer Ltd., V; 20 (upd.)
Collectors Universe, Inc., 48
Columbia House Company, 69
Comdisco, Inc., 9
Compagnie Financière Sucres et Denrées S.A., 60
CompUSA, Inc., 10
Computerland Corp., 13
Concepts Direct, Inc., 39
Conn's, Inc., 67
The Container Store, 36
Controladora Comercial Mexicana, S.A. de C.V., 36
Coop Schweiz Genossenschaftsverband, 48
Corby Distilleries Limited, 14
Corporate Express, Inc., 22; 47 (upd.)
Cortefiel S.A., 64
The Cosmetic Center, Inc., 22
Cost Plus, Inc., 27
Costco Wholesale Corporation, V; 43 (upd.)
Cotter & Company, V
County Seat Stores Inc., 9
Courts Plc, 45
CPI Corp., 38
Crate and Barrel, 9
Croscill, Inc., 42
Crowley, Milner & Company, 19
Crown Books Corporation, 21
Cumberland Farms, Inc., 17
CVS Corporation, 45 (upd.)
Daffy's Inc., 26
The Daiei, Inc., V; 17 (upd.); 41 (upd.)
The Daimaru, Inc., V; 42 (upd.)
Dairy Mart Convenience Stores, Inc., 25 (upd.)
Daisytek International Corporation, 18
Damark International, Inc., 18
Dart Group Corporation, 16
Darty S.A., 27
David Jones Ltd., 60
David's Bridal, Inc., 33
Dayton Hudson Corporation, V; 18 (upd.)
Deb Shops, Inc., 16
Debenhams Plc, 28
Deli Universal NV, 66
dELiA*s Inc., 29
Department 56, Inc., 34 (upd.)
Designer Holdings Ltd., 20
Deveaux S.A., 41
DFS Group Ltd., 66
Dick's Sporting Goods, Inc., 59
Diesel SpA, 40
Digital River, Inc., 50
Dillard Department Stores, Inc., V; 16 (upd.)

Dillard's Inc., 68 (upd.)
Dillon Companies Inc., 12
Discount Auto Parts, Inc., 18
Discount Drug Mart, Inc., 14
Dixons Group plc, V; 19 (upd.); 49 (upd.)
Do it Best Corporation, 30
Dollar Tree Stores, Inc., 23; 62 (upd.)
Donna Karan International Inc., 56 (upd.)
The Dress Barn, Inc., 24; 55 (upd.)
Drs. Foster & Smith, Inc., 62
Drug Emporium, Inc., 12
Du Pareil au Même, 43
Duane Reade Holding Corp., 21
Duckwall-ALCO Stores, Inc., 24
Dunnes Stores Ltd., 58
Duron Inc., 72
Duty Free International, Inc., 11
Dylex Limited, 29
E-Z Serve Corporation, 17
Eagle Hardware & Garden, Inc., 16
eBay Inc., 32
Eckerd Corporation, 9; 32 (upd.)
Eddie Bauer, Inc., 36 (upd.)
Edgars Consolidated Stores Ltd., 66
Edward Hines Lumber Company, 68
Egghead.com, Inc., 31 (upd.)
Eileen Fisher Inc., 61
El Corte Inglés Group, V
The Elder-Beerman Stores Corp., 10; 63 (upd.)
Electrocomponents PLC, 50
Electronics Boutique Holdings Corporation, 72
Ellett Brothers, Inc., 17
EMI Group plc, 22 (upd.)
Empresas Almacenes Paris S.A., 71
Ermenegildo Zegna SpA, 63
ESCADA AG, 71
Etablissements Franz Colruyt N.V., 68
Ethan Allen Interiors, Inc., 39 (upd.)
EToys, Inc., 37
Euromarket Designs Inc., 31 (upd.)
Evans, Inc., 30
Eye Care Centers of America, Inc., 69
EZCORP Inc., 43
Family Christian Stores, Inc., 51
Family Dollar Stores, Inc., 13; 62 (upd.)
Farmacias Ahumada S.A., 72
Fastenal Company, 14; 42 (upd.)
Faultless Starch/Bon Ami Company, 55
Fay's Inc., 17
Federated Department Stores, Inc., 9; 31 (upd.)
Fielmann AG, 31
Fila Holding S.p.A., 20; 52 (upd.)
Findel plc, 60
Fingerhut Companies, Inc., 9; 36 (upd.)
The Finish Line, Inc., 29; 68 (upd.)
Finlay Enterprises, Inc., 16
Finning International Inc., 69
First Cash Financial Services, Inc., 57
Fleming Companies, Inc., 17 (upd.)
Florsheim Shoe Group Inc., 9; 31 (upd.)
FNAC, 21
Follett Corporation, 12
Foot Locker, Inc., 68 (upd.)
Footstar, Incorporated, 24
Fortunoff Fine Jewelry and Silverware Inc., 26
Frank's Nursery & Crafts, Inc., 12
Fred Meyer Stores, Inc., V; 20 (upd.); 64 (upd.)
Fred's, Inc., 23; 62 (upd.)
Frederick Atkins Inc., 16
Frederick's of Hollywood, Inc., 59 (upd.)
Fretter, Inc., 10
Friedman's Inc., 29

Fruth Pharmacy, Inc., 66
Fry's Electronics, Inc., 68
Funco, Inc., 20
Future Shop Ltd., 62
G.I. Joe's, Inc., 30
Gadzooks, Inc., 18
Gaiam, Inc., 41
Galeries Lafayette S.A., V; 23 (upd.)
Galyan's Trading Company, Inc., 47
GameStop Corp., 69 (upd.)
Gander Mountain, Inc., 20
Gantos, Inc., 17
The Gap, Inc., V; 18 (upd.); 55 (upd.)
Garden Ridge Corporation, 27
Gart Sports Company, 24
GEHE AG, 27
General Binding Corporation, 10
General Host Corporation, 12
Genesco Inc., 17
Genovese Drug Stores, Inc., 18
Genuine Parts Company, 45 (upd.)
Gerald Stevens, Inc., 37
Giant Food Inc., 22 (upd.)
GIB Group, V; 26 (upd.)
Glacier Water Services, Inc., 47
The Good Guys, Inc., 10; 30 (upd.)
Goodwill Industries International, Inc., 16
Goody's Family Clothing, Inc., 20; 64 (upd.)
Gottschalks, Inc., 18
Grand Piano & Furniture Company, 72
GrandVision S.A., 43
Graybar Electric Company, Inc., 54
The Great Universal Stores plc, V; 19 (upd.)
Griffin Land & Nurseries, Inc., 43
Grossman's Inc., 13
Groupe Alain Manoukian, 55
Groupe Castorama-Dubois Investissements, 23
Groupe DMC (Dollfus Mieg & Cie), 27
Groupe Go Sport S.A., 39
Groupe Lapeyre S.A., 33
Groupe Monnoyeur, 72
Groupe Zannier S.A., 35
Grow Biz International, Inc., 18
Grupo Casa Saba, S.A. de C.V., 39
Grupo Elektra, S.A. de C.V., 39
Grupo Eroski, 64
Grupo Gigante, S.A. de C.V., 34
Gruppo Coin S.p.A., 41
GT Bicycles, 26
GTSI Corp., 57
Gucci Group N.V., 15; 50 (upd.)
Guilbert S.A., 42
Guitar Center, Inc., 29; 68 (upd.)
GUS plc, 47 (upd.)
Gymboree Corporation, 69 (upd.)
Hahn Automotive Warehouse, Inc., 24
Hale-Halsell Company, 60
Half Price Books, Records, Magazines Inc., 37
Hallmark Cards, Inc., 40 (upd.)
Hammacher Schlemmer & Company Inc., 21; 72 (upd.)
Hancock Fabrics, Inc., 18
Hankyu Department Stores, Inc., V; 62 (upd.)
Hanna Andersson Corp., 49
Hanover Compressor Company, 59
Hanover Direct, Inc., 36
Harold's Stores, Inc., 22
Harrods Holdings, 47
Harry Winston Inc., 45
Harvey Norman Holdings Ltd., 56
Hasbro, Inc., 43 (upd.)
Haverty Furniture Companies, Inc., 31

Hechinger Company, 12
Heilig-Meyers Company, 14; 40 (upd.)
Helzberg Diamonds, 40
Hennes & Mauritz AB, 29
Henry Modell & Company Inc., 32
Hensley & Company, 64
Hertie Waren- und Kaufhaus GmbH, V
Hibbett Sporting Goods, Inc., 26; 70 (upd.)
Highsmith Inc., 60
Hills Stores Company, 13
Hines Horticulture, Inc., 49
HMV Group plc, 59
The Hockey Company, 34
Holiday RV Superstores, Incorporated, 26
Holt's Cigar Holdings, Inc., 42
The Home Depot, Inc., V; 18 (upd.)
Home Hardware Stores Ltd., 62
Home Interiors & Gifts, Inc., 55
Home Shopping Network, Inc., V; 25 (upd.)
HomeBase, Inc., 33 (upd.)
Hot Topic, Inc., 33
House of Fabrics, Inc., 21
House of Fraser PLC, 45
HSN, 64 (upd.)
Hudson's Bay Company, V; 25 (upd.)
IKEA International A/S, V; 26 (upd.)
InaCom Corporation, 13
Indigo Books & Music Inc., 58
Insight Enterprises, Inc., 18
International Airline Support Group, Inc., 55
Intimate Brands, Inc., 24
Isetan Company Limited, V; 36 (upd.)
Ito-Yokado Co., Ltd., V; 42 (upd.)
J&R Electronics Inc., 26
J. Baker, Inc., 31
The J. Jill Group, Inc., 35
J.C. Penney Company, Inc., V; 18 (upd.); 43 (upd.)
J.L. Hammett Company, 72
Jack Schwartz Shoes, Inc., 18
Jacobson Stores Inc., 21
Jalate Inc., 25
James Beattie plc, 43
Jay Jacobs, Inc., 15
Jennifer Convertibles, Inc., 31
Jetro Cash & Carry Enterprises Inc., 38
JG Industries, Inc., 15
JJB Sports plc, 32
Jo-Ann Stores, Inc., 72 (upd.)
John Lewis Partnership plc, V; 42 (upd.)
JUSCO Co., Ltd., V
Just For Feet, Inc., 19
K & B Inc., 12
K & G Men's Center, Inc., 21
K-tel International, Inc., 21
Karstadt Aktiengesellschaft, V; 19 (upd.)
Kash n' Karry Food Stores, Inc., 20
Kasper A.S.L., Ltd., 40
kate spade LLC, 68
Kaufhof Warenhaus AG, V; 23 (upd.)
Kaufring AG, 35
Kay-Bee Toy Stores, 15
Kiabi Europe, 66
Kiehl's Since 1851, Inc., 52
Kingfisher plc, V; 24 (upd.)
Kinney Shoe Corp., 14
Kmart Corporation, V; 18 (upd.); 47 (upd.)
Knoll Group Inc., 14
Kohl's Corporation, 9; 30 (upd.)
Koninklijke Vendex KBB N.V. (Royal Vendex KBB N.V.), 62 (upd.)
Kotobukiya Co., Ltd., V; 56 (upd.)
Krause's Furniture, Inc., 27
Krispy Kreme Doughnuts, Inc., 61 (upd.)
L. and J.G. Stickley, Inc., 50

L. Luria & Son, Inc., 19
L.A. T Sportswear, Inc., 26
L.L. Bean, Inc., 38 (upd.)
La Senza Corporation, 66
La-Z-Boy Incorporated, 14; 50 (upd.)
Lamonts Apparel, Inc., 15
Lands' End, Inc., 9; 29 (upd.)
Lane Bryant, Inc., 64
Lanoga Corporation, 62
Laura Ashley Holdings plc, 37 (upd.)
Lazare Kaplan International Inc., 21
Le Chateau Inc., 63
Lechmere Inc., 10
Lechters, Inc., 11; 39 (upd.)
LensCrafters Inc., 23
Leroy Merlin SA, 54
Les Boutiques San Francisco, Inc., 62
Lesco Inc., 19
Leslie's Poolmart, Inc., 18
Leupold & Stevens, Inc., 52
Levenger Company, 63
Levitz Furniture Inc., 15
Lewis Galoob Toys Inc., 16
Li & Fung Limited, 59
Lifetime Hoan Corporation, 27
Lillian Vernon Corporation, 12; 35
The Limited, Inc., V; 20 (upd.)
Linens 'n Things, Inc., 24
Little Switzerland, Inc., 60
Littlewoods plc, V; 42 (upd.)
Liz Claiborne, Inc., 25 (upd.)
LKQ Corporation, 71
Loehmann's Inc., 24
Lojas Arapuã S.A., 22; 61 (upd.)
London Drugs Ltd., 46
Longs Drug Stores Corporation, V; 25 (upd.)
Lookers plc, 71
Lost Arrow Inc., 22
LOT$OFF Corporation, 24
Love's Travel Stops & Country Stores, Inc., 71
Lowe's Companies, Inc., V; 21 (upd.)
Luxottica SpA, 52 (upd.)
Mac Frugal's Bargains - Closeouts Inc., 17
Mac-Gray Corporation, 44
Manutan International S.A., 72
MarineMax, Inc., 30
Marionnaud Parfumeries SA, 51
Marks and Spencer p.l.c., V; 24 (upd.)
Marks Brothers Jewelers, Inc., 24
Marshall Field's, 63
Marshalls Incorporated, 13
Marui Company Ltd., V; 62 (upd.)
Maruzen Co., Limited, 18
Mary Kay, Inc., 30 (upd.)
Matalan PLC, 49
Matsuzakaya Company Ltd., V; 64 (upd.)
Maus Frères SA, 48
The Maxim Group, 25
The May Department Stores Company, V; 19 (upd.); 46 (upd.)
Mayor's Jewelers, Inc., 41
Mazel Stores, Inc., 29
McCoy Corporation, 58
McJunkin Corporation, 63
McKesson Corporation, 47 (upd.)
McLane Company, Inc., 13
MCSi, Inc., 41
Media Arts Group, Inc., 42
Meier & Frank Co., 23
Meijer Incorporated, 27 (upd.)
Melville Corporation, V
The Men's Wearhouse, Inc., 17; 48 (upd.)
Menard, Inc., 34
Mercantile Stores Company, Inc., V; 19 (upd.)

RETAIL & WHOLESALE (continued)

Mercury Drug Corporation, 70
Merry-Go-Round Enterprises, Inc., 8
Mervyn's California, 10; 39 (upd.)
Metro AG, 50
Michael C. Fina Co., Inc., 52
Michaels Stores, Inc., 17; 71 (upd.)
Michigan Sporting Goods Distributors, Inc., 72
Micro Warehouse, Inc., 16
MicroAge, Inc., 16
Migros-Genossenschafts-Bund, 68
Mitsukoshi Ltd., V; 56 (upd.)
MNS, Ltd., 65
Monrovia Nursery Company, 70
Monsoon plc, 39
Montgomery Ward & Co., Incorporated, V; 20 (upd.)
Moore-Handley, Inc., 39
Morse Shoe Inc., 13
Moss Bros Group plc, 51
Mothers Work, Inc., 18
Moto Photo, Inc., 45
Mr. Bricolage S.A., 37
MSC Industrial Direct Co., Inc., 71
MTS Inc., 37
Mulberry Group PLC, 71
Musicland Stores Corporation, 9; 38 (upd.)
Nagasakiya Co., Ltd., V; 69 (upd.)
Nash Finch Company, 65 (upd.)
National Educational Music Co. Ltd., 47
National Home Centers, Inc., 44
National Intergroup, Inc., V
National Record Mart, Inc., 29
National Wine & Spirits, Inc., 49
Natural Wonders Inc., 14
Navy Exchange Service Command, 31
Nebraska Book Company, Inc., 65
Neff Corp., 32
NeighborCare, Inc., 67 (upd.)
The Neiman Marcus Group, Inc., 12; 49 (upd.)
Netflix, Inc., 58
New Look Group plc, 35
Next plc, 29
Nichii Co., Ltd., V
NIKE, Inc., 36 (upd.)
Nine West Group Inc., 11
99¢ Only Stores, 25
Nocibé SA, 54
Noland Company, 35
Noodle Kidoodle, 16
Nordstrom, Inc., V; 18 (upd.); 67 (upd.)
Norelco Consumer Products Co., 26
Norm Thompson Outfitters, Inc., 47
North Pacific Group, Inc., 61
The North West Company, Inc., 12
Norton McNaughton, Inc., 27
Nu Skin Enterprises, Inc., 27
Oakley, Inc., 49 (upd.)
Office Depot, Inc., 8; 23 (upd.); 65 (upd.)
OfficeMax, Inc., 15; 43 (upd.)
Olan Mills, Inc., 62
Old America Stores, Inc., 17
Old Navy, Inc., 70
One Price Clothing Stores, Inc., 20
Orchard Supply Hardware Stores Corporation, 17
Organización Soriana, S.A. de C.V., 35
The Orvis Company, Inc., 28
OshKosh B'Gosh, Inc., 42 (upd.)
Oshman's Sporting Goods, Inc., 17
Ottakar's plc, 64
Otto Versand (GmbH & Co.), V; 15 (upd.); 34 (upd.)
Owens & Minor, Inc., 16; 68 (upd.)
P.C. Richard & Son Corp., 23

Pamida Holdings Corporation, 15
The Pampered Chef, Ltd., 18
The Pantry, Inc., 36
Parisian, Inc., 14
Party City Corporation, 54
Paul Harris Stores, Inc., 18
Pay 'N Pak Stores, Inc., 9
Payless Cashways, Inc., 11; 44 (upd.)
Payless ShoeSource, Inc., 18; 69 (upd.)
PCA International, Inc., 62
Pearle Vision, Inc., 13
Peebles Inc., 16; 43 (upd.)
Peet's Coffee & Tea, Inc., 38
Petco Animal Supplies, Inc., 29
Petrie Stores Corporation, 8
PETsMART, Inc., 14; 41 (upd.)
Phar-Mor Inc., 12
Pier 1 Imports, Inc., 12; 34 (upd.)
Piercing Pagoda, Inc., 29
Pilot Corporation, 49
Pinault-Printemps Redoute S.A., 19 (upd.)
Pitman Company, 58
Pomeroy Computer Resources, Inc., 33
Powell's Books, Inc., 40
The Price Company, V
PriceCostco, Inc., 14
PriceSmart, Inc., 71
Proffitt's, Inc., 19
Provell Inc., 58 (upd.)
Provigo Inc., 51 (upd.)
Publishers Clearing House, 64 (upd.)
Puig Beauty and Fashion Group S.L., 60
Purina Mills, Inc., 32
Quelle Group, V
QuikTrip Corporation, 36
Quill Corporation, 28
QVC Inc., 58 (upd.)
R.C. Willey Home Furnishings, 72
R.H. Macy & Co., Inc., V; 8 (upd.); 30 (upd.)
RadioShack Corporation, 36 (upd.)
Rag Shops, Inc., 30
Raley's Inc., 14; 58 (upd.)
Rallye SA, 54
Rapala-Normark Group, Ltd., 30
Ratner Companies, 72
RDO Equipment Company, 33
Reckitt Benckiser plc, 42 (upd.)
Recoton Corp., 15
Recreational Equipment, Inc., 18; 71 (upd.)
Reeds Jewelers, Inc., 22
Reliance Steel & Aluminum Company, 70 (upd.)
Rent-A-Center, Inc., 45
Rent-Way, Inc., 33
Restoration Hardware, Inc., 30
Revco D.S., Inc., V
REX Stores Corp., 10
Rhodes Inc., 23
Richton International Corporation, 39
Riklis Family Corp., 9
Rinascente S.p.A., 71
Rite Aid Corporation, V; 19 (upd.); 63 (upd.)
Ritz Camera Centers, 34
Roberds Inc., 19
Rocky Shoes & Boots, Inc., 26
Rogers Communications Inc., 30 (upd.)
Rooms To Go Inc., 28
Roots Canada Ltd., 42
Rose's Stores, Inc., 13
Ross Stores, Inc., 17; 43 (upd.)
Roundy's Inc., 14
Rush Enterprises, Inc., 64
Ryoshoku Ltd., 72
S&K Famous Brands, Inc., 23
S.A.C.I. Falabella, 69

Saks Inc., 24; 41 (upd.)
Sally Beauty Company, Inc., 60
Sam Ash Music Corporation, 30
Sam's Club, 40
Samuels Jewelers Incorporated, 30
Sanborn Hermanos, S.A., 20
SanomaWSOY Corporation, 51
Scheels All Sports Inc., 63
Schmitt Music Company, 40
Schneiderman's Furniture Inc., 28
School Specialty, Inc., 68
Schottenstein Stores Corp., 14
Schultz Sav-O Stores, Inc., 31
The Score Board, Inc., 19
Scotty's, Inc., 22
SCP Pool Corporation, 39
Seaman Furniture Company, Inc., 32
Sean John Clothing, Inc., 70
Sears plc, V
Sears Roebuck de México, S.A. de C.V., 20
Sears, Roebuck and Co., V; 18 (upd.); 56 (upd.)
SED International Holdings, Inc., 43
Seibu Department Stores, Ltd., V; 42 (upd.)
Seigle's Home and Building Centers, Inc., 41
The Seiyu, Ltd., V; 36 (upd.)
Selfridges Plc, 34
Service Merchandise Company, Inc., V; 19 (upd.)
7-Eleven, Inc., 32 (upd.)
Shaklee Corporation, 12
The Sharper Image Corporation, 10; 62 (upd.)
Shoe Carnival Inc., 14; 72 (upd.)
ShopKo Stores Inc., 21; 58 (upd.)
Shoppers Drug Mart Corporation, 49
Shoppers Food Warehouse Corporation, 66
SIG plc, 71
Signet Group PLC, 61
SkyMall, Inc., 26
Sleepy's Inc., 32
Smith & Hawken, Ltd., 68
Solo Serve Corporation, 28
Sophus Berendsen A/S, 49
Sound Advice, Inc., 41
Southern States Cooperative Incorporated, 36
Spartan Stores Inc., 66 (upd.)
Spec's Music, Inc., 19
Spiegel, Inc., 10; 27 (upd.)
Sport Chalet, Inc., 16
Sport Supply Group, Inc., 23
Sportmart, Inc., 15
Sports & Recreation, Inc., 17
The Sports Authority, Inc., 16; 43 (upd.)
The Sportsman's Guide, Inc., 36
Stage Stores, Inc., 24
Stanhome Inc., 15
Staples, Inc., 10; 55 (upd.)
Starbucks Corporation, 34 (upd.)
Starcraft Corporation, 30
Stefanel SpA, 63
Stein Mart Inc., 19; 72 (upd.)
Stinnes AG, 8
The Stop & Shop Companies, Inc., 24 (upd.)
Storehouse PLC, 16
Strauss Discount Auto, 56
Stride Rite Corporation, 8
Strouds, Inc., 33
Stuller Settings, Inc., 35
Successories, Inc., 30
Sun Television & Appliances Inc., 10
Sunglass Hut International, Inc., 21

Supreme International Corporation, 27
Swarovski International Holding AG, 40
Syms Corporation, 29
Systemax, Inc., 52
Takashimaya Company, Limited, V; 47
   (upd.)
The Talbots, Inc., 11; 31 (upd.)
Target Corporation, 61 (upd.)
Target Stores, 10; 27 (upd.)
Tati SA, 25
Tattered Cover Book Store, 43
Tech Data Corporation, 10
Tengelmann Group, 27
Tesco plc, 24 (upd.); 68 (upd.)
Thomsen Greenhouses and Garden Center,
   Incorporated, 65
Thrifty PayLess, Inc., 12
Tiffany & Co., 14
The Timberland Company, 54 (upd.)
The TJX Companies, Inc., V; 19 (upd.); 57
   (upd.)
Today's Man, Inc., 20
Tokyu Department Store Co., Ltd., V; 32
   (upd.)
Too, Inc., 61
Topco Associates LLC, 60
Tops Appliance City, Inc., 17
Total Fina Elf S.A., 50 (upd.)
Toys ''R'' Us, Inc., V; 18 (upd.); 57 (upd.)
Tractor Supply Company, 57
Trans World Entertainment Corporation, 68
   (upd.)
Travis Boats & Motors, Inc., 37
Travis Perkins plc, 34
Trend-Lines, Inc., 22
TruServ Corporation, 24
Tuesday Morning Corporation, 18; 70
   (upd.)
Tupperware Corporation, 28
TVI, Inc., 15
Tweeter Home Entertainment Group, Inc.,
   30
U.S. Vision, Inc., 66
Ultimate Electronics, Inc., 18; 69 (upd.)
Ultramar Diamond Shamrock Corporation,
   31 (upd.)
Uni-Marts, Inc., 17
United Rentals, Inc., 34
The United States Shoe Corporation, V
United Stationers Inc., 14
Universal International, Inc., 25
Uny Co., Ltd., V; 49 (upd.)
Urban Outfitters, Inc., 14
Uwajimaya, Inc., 60
Vallen Corporation, 45
Valley Media Inc., 35
Value City Department Stores, Inc., 38
Value Merchants Inc., 13
ValueVision International, Inc., 22
Vans, Inc., 47 (upd.)
Venator Group Inc., 35 (upd.)
Vendex International N.V., 13
Venture Stores Inc., 12
The Vermont Teddy Bear Co., Inc., 36
VF Corporation, 54 (upd.)
Viewpoint International, Inc., 66
Viking Office Products, Inc., 10
Vivarte SA, 54 (upd.)
Von Maur Inc., 64
Vorwerk & Co., 27
W. Atlee Burpee & Co., 27
W.W. Grainger, Inc., V
Waban Inc., 13
Wacoal Corp., 25
Wal-Mart de Mexico, S.A. de C.V., 35
   (upd.)

Wal-Mart Stores, Inc., V; 8 (upd.); 26
   (upd.); 63 (upd.)
Walden Book Company Inc., 17
Walgreen Co., V; 20 (upd.); 65 (upd.)
Wall Drug Store, Inc., 40
Warners' Stellian Inc., 67
Weiner's Stores, Inc., 33
West Marine, Inc., 17
Western Beef, Inc., 22
The Wet Seal, Inc., 18; 70 (upd.)
Weyco Group, Incorporated, 32
WH Smith PLC, V; 42 (upd.)
The White House, Inc., 60
Whole Foods Market, Inc., 20
Wickes Inc., V; 25 (upd.)
Williams Scotsman, Inc., 65
Williams-Sonoma, Inc., 17; 44 (upd.)
Wilsons The Leather Experts Inc., 21; 58
   (upd.)
Wolohan Lumber Co., 19
Wolverine World Wide, Inc., 59 (upd.)
Woolworth Corporation, V; 20 (upd.)
World Duty Free Americas, Inc., 29 (upd.)
The Yankee Candle Company, Inc., 37
Young's Market Company, LLC, 32
Younkers, Inc., 19
Zale Corporation, 16; 40 (upd.)
Zany Brainy, Inc., 31
Ziebart International Corporation, 30
Zion's Cooperative Mercantile Institution,
   33
Zones, Inc., 67

RUBBER & TIRE

Aeroquip Corporation, 16
Bandag, Inc., 19
The BFGoodrich Company, V
Bridgestone Corporation, V; 21 (upd.); 59
   (upd.)
Canadian Tire Corporation, Limited, 71
   (upd.)
Carlisle Companies Incorporated, 8
Compagnie Générale des Établissements
   Michelin, V; 42 (upd.)
Continental AG, V; 56 (upd.)
Continental General Tire Corp., 23
Cooper Tire & Rubber Company, 8; 23
   (upd.)
Elementis plc, 40 (upd.)
General Tire, Inc., 8
The Goodyear Tire & Rubber Company,
   V; 20 (upd.)
The Kelly-Springfield Tire Company, 8
Les Schwab Tire Centers, 50
Myers Industries, Inc., 19
Pirelli S.p.A., V; 15 (upd.)
Safeskin Corporation, 18
Sumitomo Rubber Industries, Ltd., V
Tillotson Corp., 15
Treadco, Inc., 19
Ube Industries, Ltd., 38 (upd.)
The Yokohama Rubber Co., Ltd., V; 19
   (upd.)

TELECOMMUNICATIONS

A.H. Belo Corporation, 30 (upd.)
Abertis Infraestructuras, S.A., 65
Acme-Cleveland Corp., 13
ADC Telecommunications, Inc., 10
Adelphia Communications Corporation, 17;
   52 (upd.)
Adtran Inc., 22
Advanced Fibre Communications, Inc., 63
AEI Music Network Inc., 35
AirTouch Communications, 11
Alcatel S.A., 36 (upd.)
Alliance Atlantis Communications Inc., 39

ALLTEL Corporation, 6; 46 (upd.)
American Tower Corporation, 33
Ameritech Corporation, V; 18 (upd.)
Amstrad plc, 48 (upd.)
AO VimpelCom, 48
AOL Time Warner Inc., 57 (upd.)
Arch Wireless, Inc., 39
ARD, 41
Ascom AG, 9
Aspect Telecommunications Corporation,
   22
AT&T Bell Laboratories, Inc., 13
AT&T Corporation, V; 29 (upd.); 68 (upd.)
AT&T Wireless Services, Inc., 54 (upd.)
BCE Inc., V; 44 (upd.)
Beasley Broadcast Group, Inc., 51
Belgacom, 6
Bell Atlantic Corporation, V; 25 (upd.)
Bell Canada, 6
BellSouth Corporation, V; 29 (upd.)
BET Holdings, Inc., 18
BHC Communications, Inc., 26
Blackfoot Telecommunications Group, 60
Bonneville International Corporation, 29
Bouygues S.A., 24 (upd.)
Brasil Telecom Participações S.A., 57
Brightpoint, Inc., 18
Brite Voice Systems, Inc., 20
British Columbia Telephone Company, 6
British Telecommunications plc, V; 15
   (upd.)
Broadwing Corporation, 70
BT Group plc, 49 (upd.)
C-COR.net Corp., 38
Cable & Wireless HKT, 30 (upd.)
Cable and Wireless plc, V; 25 (upd.)
Cablevision Systems Corporation, 30 (upd.)
The Canadian Broadcasting Corporation
   (CBC), 37
Canal Plus, 10; 34 (upd.)
CanWest Global Communications
   Corporation, 35
Capital Radio plc, 35
Carlton Communications PLC, 15; 50
   (upd.)
Carolina Telephone and Telegraph
   Company, 10
Carrier Access Corporation, 44
CBS Corporation, 28 (upd.)
CBS Television Network, 66 (upd.)
Centel Corporation, 6
Centennial Communications Corporation,
   39
Central European Media Enterprises Ltd.,
   61
Century Communications Corp., 10
Century Telephone Enterprises, Inc., 9; 54
   (upd.)
Cesky Telecom, a.s., 64
Chancellor Media Corporation, 24
Charter Communications, Inc., 33
China Telecom, 50
Chris-Craft Industries, Inc., 9
The Christian Broadcasting Network, Inc.,
   52
Chrysalis Group plc, 40
Chugach Alaska Corporation, 60
CIENA Corporation, 54
Cincinnati Bell, Inc., 6
Citadel Communications Corporation, 35
Clear Channel Communications, Inc., 23
Clearwire, Inc., 69
Cogent Communications Group, Inc., 55
COLT Telecom Group plc, 41
Comcast Corporation, 24 (upd.)
Comdial Corporation, 21

TELECOMMUNICATIONS (*continued*)

Commonwealth Telephone Enterprises, Inc., 25
Comsat Corporation, 23
Comverse Technology, Inc., 15; 43 (upd.)
Corning Inc., 44 (upd.)
Craftmade International, Inc., 44
Cumulus Media Inc., 37
DDI Corporation, 7
Deutsche Telekom AG, V; 48 (upd.)
Dialogic Corporation, 18
Directorate General of Telecommunications, 7
DIRECTV, Inc., 38
Discovery Communications, Inc., 42
Dobson Communications Corporation, 63
DSC Communications Corporation, 12
EchoStar Communications Corporation, 35
ECI Telecom Ltd., 18
eircom plc, 31 (upd.)
Electric Lightwave, Inc., 37
Electromagnetic Sciences Inc., 21
Emmis Communications Corporation, 47
Energis plc, 47
Entercom Communications Corporation, 58
Entravision Communications Corporation, 41
Equant N.V., 52
Eschelon Telecom, Inc., 72
ESPN, Inc., 56
Eternal Word Television Network, Inc., 57
EXCEL Communications Inc., 18
Executone Information Systems, Inc., 13
Expand SA, 48
4Kids Entertainment Inc., 59
Fox Family Worldwide, Inc., 24
France Télécom Group, V; 21 (upd.)
Frontier Corp., 16
Gannett Co., Inc., 30 (upd.)
Garmin Ltd., 60
General DataComm Industries, Inc., 14
Geotek Communications Inc., 21
Getty Images, Inc., 31
Global Crossing Ltd., 32
Golden Telecom, Inc., 59
Granite Broadcasting Corporation, 42
Gray Communications Systems, Inc., 24
Groupe Vidéotron Ltée., 20
Grupo Televisa, S.A., 18; 54 (upd.)
GTE Corporation, V; 15 (upd.)
Guthy-Renker Corporation, 32
GWR Group plc, 39
Harmonic Inc., 43
Havas, SA, 10
Hispanic Broadcasting Corporation, 35
Hong Kong Telecommunications Ltd., 6
Hubbard Broadcasting Inc., 24
Hughes Electronics Corporation, 25
IDB Communications Group, Inc., 11
IDT Corporation, 34
Illinois Bell Telephone Company, 14
Indiana Bell Telephone Company, Incorporated, 14
Infineon Technologies AG, 50
Infinity Broadcasting Corporation, 11
InterDigital Communications Corporation, 61
IXC Communications, Inc., 29
Jacor Communications, Inc., 23
Jones Intercable, Inc., 21
Koninklijke PTT Nederland NV, V
Landmark Communications, Inc., 55 (upd.)
LCI International, Inc., 16
LDDS-Metro Communications, Inc., 8
Leap Wireless International, Inc., 69
Level 3 Communications, Inc., 67
LIN Broadcasting Corp., 9

Lincoln Telephone & Telegraph Company, 14
LodgeNet Entertainment Corporation, 28
Loral Space & Communications Ltd., 54 (upd.)
Manitoba Telecom Services, Inc., 61
Mannesmann AG, 38
MasTec, Inc., 19; 55 (upd.)
McCaw Cellular Communications, Inc., 6
MCI WorldCom, Inc., V; 27 (upd.)
McLeodUSA Incorporated, 32
Mediacom Communications Corporation, 69
Mercury Communications, Ltd., 7
Metrocall, Inc., 41
Metromedia Companies, 14
Métropole Télévision, 33
MFS Communications Company, Inc., 11
Michigan Bell Telephone Co., 14
MIH Limited, 31
MITRE Corporation, 26
Mobile Telecommunications Technologies Corp., 18
Mobile TeleSystems OJSC, 59
Modern Times Group AB, 36
The Montana Power Company, 44 (upd.)
Multimedia, Inc., 11
National Broadcasting Company, Inc., 28 (upd.)
National Grid USA, 51 (upd.)
NCR Corporation, 30 (upd.)
NetCom Systems AB, 26
Nevada Bell Telephone Company, 14
New Valley Corporation, 17
Nexans SA, 54
Nextel Communications, Inc., 27 (upd.)
Nippon Telegraph and Telephone Corporation, V; 51 (upd.)
Norstan, Inc., 16
Nortel Networks Corporation, 36 (upd.)
Northern Telecom Limited, V
NTL Inc., 65
NYNEX Corporation, V
Octel Messaging, 14; 41 (upd.)
Ohio Bell Telephone Company, 14
Olivetti S.p.A., 34 (upd.)
Österreichische Post- und Telegraphenverwaltung, V
Pacific Telecom, Inc., 6
Pacific Telesis Group, V
Paging Network Inc., 11
PanAmSat Corporation, 46
Paxson Communications Corporation, 33
PictureTel Corp., 10; 27 (upd.)
Portugal Telecom SGPS S.A., 69
Posti- ja Telelaitos, 6
Price Communications Corporation, 42
ProSiebenSat.1 Media AG, 54
Publishing and Broadcasting Limited, 54
QUALCOMM Incorporated, 20; 47 (upd.)
QVC Network Inc., 9
Qwest Communications International, Inc., 37
RCN Corporation, 70
Research in Motion Ltd., 54
RMH Teleservices, Inc., 42
Rochester Telephone Corporation, 6
Rogers Communications Inc., 30 (upd.)
Royal KPN N.V., 30
Rural Cellular Corporation, 43
Saga Communications, Inc., 27
Sawtek Inc., 43 (upd.)
SBC Communications Inc., 32 (upd.)
Schweizerische Post-, Telefon- und Telegrafen-Betriebe, V
Scientific-Atlanta, Inc., 6; 45 (upd.)
Seat Pagine Gialle S.p.A., 47

Securicor Plc, 45
Sinclair Broadcast Group, Inc., 25
Sirius Satellite Radio, Inc., 69
Società Finanziaria Telefonica per Azioni, V
Sonera Corporation, 50
Southern New England Telecommunications Corporation, 6
Southwestern Bell Corporation, V
Spanish Broadcasting System, Inc., 41
Spelling Entertainment, 35 (upd.)
Sprint Corporation, 9; 46 (upd.)
StrataCom, Inc., 16
Swedish Telecom, V
Swisscom AG, 58
Sycamore Networks, Inc., 45
SynOptics Communications, Inc., 10
T-Netix, Inc., 46
Talk America Holdings, Inc., 70
TDC A/S, 63
Telcordia Technologies, Inc., 59
Telecom Argentina S.A., 63
Telecom Australia, 6
Telecom Corporation of New Zealand Limited, 54
Telecom Eireann, 7
Telecom Italia Mobile S.p.A., 63
Telecom Italia S.p.A., 43
Telefonaktiebolaget LM Ericsson, V; 46 (upd.)
Telefónica de Argentina S.A., 61
Telefónica S.A., V; 46 (upd.)
Telefonos de Mexico S.A. de C.V., 14; 63 (upd.)
Telekomunikacja Polska SA, 50
Telenor ASA, 69
Telephone and Data Systems, Inc., 9
Télévision Française 1, 23
TeliaSonera AB, 57 (upd.)
Tellabs, Inc., 11; 40 (upd.)
Telstra Corporation Limited, 50
Tiscali SpA, 48
The Titan Corporation, 36
Tollgrade Communications, Inc., 44
TV Azteca, S.A. de C.V., 39
U.S. Satellite Broadcasting Company, Inc., 20
U S West, Inc., V; 25 (upd.)
U.S. Cellular Corporation, 9; 31 (upd.)
United Pan-Europe Communications NV, 47
United Telecommunications, Inc., V
United Video Satellite Group, 18
USA Interactive, Inc., 47 (upd.)
Verizon Communications, 43 (upd.)
ViaSat, Inc., 54
Vivendi Universal S.A., 46 (upd.)
Vodafone Group PLC, 11; 36 (upd.)
The Walt Disney Company, 63 (upd.)
Watkins-Johnson Company, 15
The Weather Channel Companies, 52
West Corporation, 42
Western Union Financial Services, Inc., 54
Western Wireless Corporation, 36
Westwood One, Inc., 23
Williams Communications Group, Inc., 34
The Williams Companies, Inc., 31 (upd.)
Wipro Limited, 43
Wisconsin Bell, Inc., 14
Working Assets Funding Service, 43
XM Satellite Radio Holdings, Inc., 69
Young Broadcasting Inc., 40
Zoom Technologies, Inc., 53 (upd.)

TEXTILES & APPAREL

Abercrombie & Fitch Co., 35 (upd.)
adidas-Salomon AG, 14; 33 (upd.)

Adolfo Dominguez S.A., 72
Alba-Waldensian, Inc., 30
Albany International Corp., 8
Algo Group Inc., 24
American Safety Razor Company, 20
Amoskeag Company, 8
Angelica Corporation, 15; 43 (upd.)
AR Accessories Group, Inc., 23
Aris Industries, Inc., 16
ASICS Corporation, 57
Authentic Fitness Corporation, 20; 51
  (upd.)
Banana Republic Inc., 25
Bata Ltd., 62
Benetton Group S.p.A., 10; 67 (upd.)
Bill Blass Ltd., 32
Birkenstock Footprint Sandals, Inc., 12
Blair Corporation, 25
Brazos Sportswear, Inc., 23
Brioni Roman Style S.p.A., 67
Brooks Brothers Inc., 22
Brooks Sports Inc., 32
Brown Group, Inc., V; 20 (upd.)
Bugle Boy Industries, Inc., 18
Burberry Ltd., 17; 41 (upd.)
Burke Mills, Inc., 66
Burlington Industries, Inc., V; 17 (upd.)
Calcot Ltd., 33
Calvin Klein, Inc., 22; 55 (upd.)
Candie's, Inc., 31
Canstar Sports Inc., 16
Capel Incorporated, 45
Capezio/Ballet Makers Inc., 62
Carhartt, Inc., 30
Cato Corporation, 14
Chargeurs International, 21 (upd.)
Charming Shoppes, Inc., 8
Cherokee Inc., 18
Chic by H.I.S, Inc., 20
Chico's FAS, Inc., 45
Chorus Line Corporation, 30
Christian Dior S.A., 19; 49 (upd.)
Christopher & Banks Corporation, 42
Cia Hering, 72
Cintas Corporation, 51 (upd.)
Claire's Stores, Inc., 17
Coach Leatherware, 10
Coats plc, V; 44 (upd.)
Collins & Aikman Corporation, 13
Columbia Sportswear Company, 19; 41
  (upd.)
Concord Fabrics, Inc., 16
Cone Mills LLC, 8; 67 (upd.)
Converse Inc., 31 (upd.)
Cotton Incorporated, 46
Courtaulds plc, V; 17 (upd.)
Croscill, Inc., 42
Crown Crafts, Inc., 16
Crystal Brands, Inc., 9
Culp, Inc., 29
Cygne Designs, Inc., 25
Dan River Inc., 35
Danskin, Inc., 12; 62 (upd.)
Deckers Outdoor Corporation, 22
Delta and Pine Land Company, 59
Delta Woodside Industries, Inc., 8; 30
  (upd.)
Designer Holdings Ltd., 20
The Dixie Group, Inc., 20
Dogi International Fabrics S.A., 52
Dolce & Gabbana SpA, 62
Dominion Textile Inc., 12
Donna Karan International Inc., 15; 56
  (upd.)
Donnkenny, Inc., 17
Duck Head Apparel Company, Inc., 42
Dunavant Enterprises, Inc., 54

Dyersburg Corporation, 21
Ecco Sko A/S, 62
The Echo Design Group, Inc., 68
Edison Brothers Stores, Inc., 9
Eileen Fisher Inc., 61
Ellen Tracy, Inc., 55
Eram SA, 51
Ermenegildo Zegna SpA, 63
ESCADA AG, 71
Esprit de Corp., 8; 29 (upd.)
Etam Developpement SA, 44
Etienne Aigner AG, 52
Evans, Inc., 30
Fab Industries, Inc., 27
Fabri-Centers of America Inc., 16
Fat Face Ltd., 68
Fieldcrest Cannon, Inc., 9; 31 (upd.)
Fila Holding S.p.A., 20
Florsheim Shoe Group Inc., 31 (upd.)
Fossil, Inc., 17
Frederick's of Hollywood Inc., 16
French Connection Group plc, 41
Fruit of the Loom, Inc., 8; 25 (upd.)
Fubu, 29
G&K Services, Inc., 16
G-III Apparel Group, Ltd., 22
Galey & Lord, Inc., 20; 66 (upd.)
Garan, Inc., 16; 64 (upd.)
Gerry Weber International AG, 63
Gianni Versace SpA, 22
Giorgio Armani S.p.A., 45
The Gitano Group, Inc. 8
Greenwood Mills, Inc., 14
Groupe DMC (Dollfus Mieg & Cie), 27
Groupe Yves Saint Laurent, 23
Gucci Group N.V., 15; 50 (upd.)
Guess, Inc., 15; 68 (upd.)
Guilford Mills Inc., 8; 40 (upd.)
Gymboree Corporation, 15; 69 (upd.)
Haggar Corporation, 19
Hampton Industries, Inc., 20
Happy Kids Inc., 30
Hartmarx Corporation, 8
The Hartstone Group plc, 14
HCI Direct, Inc., 55
Healthtex, Inc., 17
Helly Hansen ASA, 25
Hermès S.A., 14
The Hockey Company, 34
Hugo Boss AG, 48
Hummel International A/S, 68
Hyde Athletic Industries, Inc., 17
I.C. Isaacs & Company, 31
Industria de Diseño Textil S.A., 64
Interface, Inc., 8; 29 (upd.)
Irwin Toy Limited, 14
Items International Airwalk Inc., 17
J. Crew Group, Inc., 12; 34 (upd.)
JLM Couture, Inc., 64
Jockey International, Inc., 12; 34 (upd.)
Johnston Industries, Inc., 15
Jones Apparel Group, Inc., 39 (upd.)
Jordache Enterprises, Inc., 23
Jos. A. Bank Clothiers, Inc., 31
JPS Textile Group, Inc., 28
K-Swiss, Inc., 33
Karl Kani Infinity, Inc., 49
Kellwood Company, 8
Kenneth Cole Productions, Inc., 25
Kinney Shoe Corp., 14
Klaus Steilmann GmbH & Co. KG, 53
Koret of California, Inc., 62
L.A. Gear, Inc., 8; 32 (upd.)
L.L. Bean, Inc., 10; 38 (upd.)
LaCrosse Footwear, Inc., 18; 61 (upd.)
Laura Ashley Holdings plc, 13
Lee Apparel Company, Inc., 8

The Leslie Fay Company, Inc., 8; 39 (upd.)
Levi Strauss & Co., V; 16 (upd.)
Liz Claiborne, Inc., 8
London Fog Industries, Inc., 29
Lost Arrow Inc., 22
Maidenform, Inc., 20; 59 (upd.)
Malden Mills Industries, Inc., 16
Marzotto S.p.A., 20; 67 (upd.)
Milliken & Co., V; 17 (upd.)
Mitsubishi Rayon Co., Ltd., V
Mossimo, Inc., 27
Mothercare UK Ltd., 17
Movie Star Inc., 17
Mulberry Group PLC, 71
Naf Naf SA, 44
Nautica Enterprises, Inc., 18; 44 (upd.)
New Balance Athletic Shoe, Inc., 25; 68
  (upd.)
Nike, Inc., V; 8 (upd.)
Nine West Group, Inc., 39 (upd.)
Nitches, Inc., 53
The North Face, Inc., 18
Oakley, Inc., 18
OshKosh B'Gosh, Inc., 9; 42 (upd.)
Oxford Industries, Inc., 8
Pacific Sunwear of California, Inc., 28
Peek & Cloppenburg KG, 46
Pendleton Woolen Mills, Inc., 42
Pentland Group plc, 20
Perry Ellis International, Inc., 41
Phat Fashions LLC, 49
Phoenix Footwear Group, Inc., 70
Pillowtex Corporation, 19; 41 (upd.)
Plains Cotton Cooperative Association, 57
Pluma, Inc., 27
Polo/Ralph Lauren Corporation, 12; 62
  (upd.)
Prada Holding B.V., 45
PremiumWear, Inc., 30
Puma AG Rudolf Dassler Sport, 35
Quaker Fabric Corp., 19
Quiksilver, Inc., 18
R.G. Barry Corporation, 17; 44 (upd.)
Recreational Equipment, Inc., 18
Red Wing Shoe Company, Inc., 30 (upd.)
Reebok International Ltd., V; 9 (upd.); 26
  (upd.)
Rieter Holding AG, 42
Rollerblade, Inc., 15
Royal Ten Cate N.V., 68
Russell Corporation, 8; 30 (upd.)
St. John Knits, Inc., 14
Salant Corporation, 51 (upd.)
Salvatore Ferragamo Italia S.p.A., 62
Saucony Inc., 35
Schott Brothers, Inc., 67
Shaw Industries, Inc., 40 (upd.)
Shelby Williams Industries, Inc., 14
Skechers U.S.A. Inc., 31
Sophus Berendsen A/S, 49
Springs Industries, Inc., V; 19 (upd.)
Starter Corp., 12
Stefanel SpA, 63
Steiner Corporation (Alsco), 53
Steven Madden, Ltd., 37
Stirling Group plc, 62
Stoddard International plc, 72
Stone Manufacturing Company, 14; 43
  (upd.)
The Stride Rite Corporation, 8; 37 (upd.)
Stussy, Inc., 55
Sun Sportswear, Inc., 17
Superior Uniform Group, Inc., 30
Tamfelt Oyj Abp, 62
Tarrant Apparel Group, 62
Teijin Limited, V
Thomaston Mills, Inc., 27

TEXTILES & APPAREL (*continued*)

Tilley Endurables, Inc., 67
The Timberland Company, 13; 54 (upd.)
Tommy Hilfiger Corporation, 20; 53 (upd.)
Too, Inc., 61
Toray Industries, Inc., V
Tultex Corporation, 13
Under Armour Performance Apparel, 61
Unifi, Inc., 12; 62 (upd.)
United Merchants & Manufacturers, Inc.,
 13
United Retail Group Inc., 33
Unitika Ltd., V
Vans, Inc., 16; 47 (upd.)
Varsity Spirit Corp., 15
VF Corporation, V; 17 (upd.); 54 (upd.)
Walton Monroe Mills, Inc., 8
The Warnaco Group Inc., 12; 46 (upd.)
Wellman, Inc., 8; 52 (upd.)
West Point-Pepperell, Inc., 8
WestPoint Stevens Inc., 16
Weyco Group, Incorporated, 32
Williamson-Dickie Manufacturing
 Company, 14
Wolverine World Wide, Inc., 16; 59 (upd.)
Woolrich Inc., 62

TOBACCO

Altadis S.A., 72 (upd.)
American Brands, Inc., V
B.A.T. Industries PLC, 22 (upd.)
British American Tobacco PLC, 50 (upd.)
Brooke Group Ltd., 15
Brown & Williamson Tobacco
 Corporation, 14; 33 (upd.)
Culbro Corporation, 15
Dibrell Brothers, Incorporated, 12
DIMON Inc., 27
800-JR Cigar, Inc., 27
Gallaher Group Plc, V; 19 (upd.); 49 (upd.)
General Cigar Holdings, Inc., 66 (upd.)
Holt's Cigar Holdings, Inc., 42
Imasco Limited, V
Imperial Tobacco Group PLC, 50
Japan Tobacco Incorporated, V
KT&G Corporation, 62
Nobleza Piccardo SAICF, 64
North Atlantic Trading Company Inc., 65
Philip Morris Companies Inc., V; 18 (upd.)
R.J. Reynolds Tobacco Holdings, Inc., 30
 (upd.)
RJR Nabisco Holdings Corp., V
Rothmans UK Holdings Limited, V; 19
 (upd.)
Seita, 23
Souza Cruz S.A., 65
Standard Commercial Corporation, 13; 62
 (upd.)
Swisher International Group Inc., 23
Tabacalera, S.A., V; 17 (upd.)
Universal Corporation, V; 48 (upd.)
UST Inc., 9; 50 (upd.)
Vector Group Ltd., 35 (upd.)

TRANSPORT SERVICES

Abertis Infraestructuras, S.A., 65
Aéroports de Paris, 33
Air Express International Corporation, 13
Airborne Freight Corporation, 6; 34 (upd.)
Alamo Rent A Car, Inc., 6; 24 (upd.)
Alaska Railroad Corporation, 60
Alexander & Baldwin, Inc., 10
Allied Worldwide, Inc., 49
AMCOL International Corporation, 59
 (upd.)
Amerco, 6

AMERCO, 67 (upd.)
American Classic Voyages Company, 27
American President Companies Ltd., 6
Anschutz Corp., 12
APL Limited, 61 (upd.)
Aqua Alliance Inc., 32 (upd.)
Arriva PLC, 69
Atlas Van Lines, Inc., 14
Attica Enterprises S.A., 64
Avis Rent A Car, Inc., 6; 22 (upd.)
BAA plc, 10
Bekins Company, 15
Berliner Verkehrsbetriebe (BVG), 58
Bollinger Shipyards, Inc., 61
Boyd Bros. Transportation Inc., 39
Brambles Industries Limited, 42
The Brink's Company, 58 (upd.)
British Railways Board, V
Broken Hill Proprietary Company Ltd., 22
 (upd.)
Buckeye Partners, L.P., 70
Budget Group, Inc., 25
Budget Rent a Car Corporation, 9
Burlington Northern Santa Fe Corporation,
 V; 27 (upd.)
C.H. Robinson Worldwide, Inc., 40 (upd.)
Canadian National Railway Company, 71
 (upd.)
Canadian National Railway System, 6
Canadian Pacific Railway Limited, V; 45
 (upd.)
Cannon Express, Inc., 53
Carey International, Inc., 26
Carlson Companies, Inc., 6
Carolina Freight Corporation, 6
Celadon Group Inc., 30
Central Japan Railway Company, 43
Chargeurs, 6
CHC Helicopter Corporation, 67
Chicago and North Western Holdings
 Corporation, 6
Christian Salvesen Plc, 45
Coach USA, Inc., 24; 55 (upd.)
Coles Express Inc., 15
Compagnie Générale Maritime et
 Financière, 6
Consolidated Delivery & Logistics, Inc., 24
Consolidated Freightways Corporation, V;
 21 (upd.); 48 (upd.)
Consolidated Rail Corporation, V
CR England, Inc., 63
Crowley Maritime Corporation, 6; 28
 (upd.)
CSX Corporation, V; 22 (upd.)
Danzas Group, V; 40 (upd.)
Deutsche Bahn AG, V; 46 (upd.)
DHL Worldwide Network S.A./N.V., 6; 24
 (upd.); 69 (upd.)
Dollar Thrifty Automotive Group, Inc., 25
Dot Foods, Inc., 69
East Japan Railway Company, V; 66 (upd.)
EGL, Inc., 59
Emery Air Freight Corporation, 6
Emery Worldwide Airlines, Inc., 25 (upd.)
Enterprise Rent-A-Car Company, 6
Eurotunnel Group, 37 (upd.)
EVA Airways Corporation, 51
Evergreen International Aviation, Inc., 53
Evergreen Marine Corporation (Taiwan)
 Ltd., 13; 50 (upd.)
Executive Jet, Inc., 36
Exel plc, 51 (upd.)
Expeditors International of Washington
 Inc., 17
Federal Express Corporation, V
FedEx Corporation, 18 (upd.); 42 (upd.)
Fritz Companies, Inc., 12

Frontline Ltd., 45
Frozen Food Express Industries, Inc., 20
Garuda Indonesia, 58 (upd.)
GATX Corporation, 6; 25 (upd.)
GE Capital Aviation Services, 36
Gefco SA, 54
General Maritime Corporation, 59
Genesee & Wyoming Inc., 27
Geodis S.A., 67
The Go-Ahead Group Plc, 28
The Greenbrier Companies, 19
Greyhound Lines, Inc., 32 (upd.)
Groupe Bourbon S.A., 60
Grupo TMM, S.A. de C.V., 50
Grupo Transportación Ferroviaria
 Mexicana, S.A. de C.V., 47
GulfMark Offshore, Inc., 49
Hanjin Shipping Co., Ltd., 50
Hankyu Corporation, V; 23 (upd.)
Hapag-Lloyd AG, 6
Harland and Wolff Holdings plc, 19
Harper Group Inc., 17
Heartland Express, Inc., 18
The Hertz Corporation, 9
Holberg Industries, Inc., 36
Hospitality Worldwide Services, Inc., 26
Hub Group, Inc., 38
Hvide Marine Incorporated, 22
Illinois Central Corporation, 11
International Shipholding Corporation, Inc.,
 27
J.B. Hunt Transport Services Inc., 12
John Menzies plc, 39
Kansas City Southern Industries, Inc., 6; 26
 (upd.)
Kawasaki Kisen Kaisha, Ltd., V; 56 (upd.)
Keio Teito Electric Railway Company, V
Keolis SA, 51
Kinki Nippon Railway Company Ltd., V
Kirby Corporation, 18; 66 (upd.)
Knight Transportation, Inc., 64
Koninklijke Nedlloyd Groep N.V., 6
Kuehne & Nagel International AG, V; 53
 (upd.)
La Poste, V; 47 (upd.)
Landstar System, Inc., 63
Leaseway Transportation Corp., 12
London Regional Transport, 6
The Long Island Rail Road Company, 68
Maine Central Railroad Company, 16
Mammoet Transport B.V., 26
Martz Group, 56
Mayflower Group Inc., 6
Mercury Air Group, Inc., 20
The Mersey Docks and Harbour Company,
 30
Metropolitan Transportation Authority, 35
Miller Industries, Inc., 26
Mitsui O.S.K. Lines, Ltd., V
Moran Towing Corporation, Inc., 15
The Morgan Group, Inc., 46
Morris Travel Services L.L.C., 26
Motor Cargo Industries, Inc., 35
National Car Rental System, Inc., 10
National Express Group PLC, 50
National Railroad Passenger Corporation
 (Amtrak), 22; 66 (upd.)
Neptune Orient Lines Limited, 47
NFC plc, 6
Nippon Express Company, Ltd., V; 64
 (upd.)
Nippon Yusen Kabushiki Kaisha (NYK),
 V; 72 (upd.)
Norfolk Southern Corporation, V; 29 (upd.)
Oak Harbor Freight Lines, Inc., 53
Ocean Group plc, 6

Odakyu Electric Railway Co., Ltd., V; 68 (upd.)
Oglebay Norton Company, 17
Old Dominion Freight Line, Inc., 57
OMI Corporation, 59
Österreichische Bundesbahnen GmbH, 6
OTR Express, Inc., 25
Overnite Corporation, 14; 58 (upd.)
Overseas Shipholding Group, Inc., 11
Pacer International, Inc., 54
The Peninsular and Oriental Steam Navigation Company, V; 38 (upd.)
Penske Corporation, V
PHH Arval, V; 53 (upd.)
Pilot Air Freight Corp., 67
Plantation Pipe Line Company, 68
Polar Air Cargo Inc., 60
The Port Authority of New York and New Jersey, 48
Port Imperial Ferry Corporation, 70
Post Office Group, V
Preston Corporation, 6
RailTex, Inc., 20
Railtrack Group PLC, 50
Réseau Ferré de France, 66
Roadway Express, Inc., V; 25 (upd.)
Royal Olympic Cruise Lines Inc., 52
Royal Vopak NV, 41
Ryder System, Inc., V; 24 (upd.)
Santa Fe Pacific Corporation, V
Schenker-Rhenus AG, 6
Schneider National, Inc., 36
Securicor Plc, 45
Seibu Railway Co. Ltd., V
Seino Transportation Company, Ltd., 6
Simon Transportation Services Inc., 27
Smithway Motor Xpress Corporation, 39
Société Nationale des Chemins de Fer Français, V; 57 (upd.)
Société Norbert Dentressangle S.A., 67
Southern Pacific Transportation Company, V
Stagecoach Holdings plc, 30
Stelmar Shipping Ltd., 52
Stevedoring Services of America Inc., 28
Stinnes AG, 8; 59 (upd.)
Stolt-Nielsen S.A., 42
Sunoco, Inc., 28 (upd.)
Swift Transportation Co., Inc., 42
The Swiss Federal Railways (Schweizerische Bundesbahnen), V
Swissport International Ltd., 70
Teekay Shipping Corporation, 25
Tibbett & Britten Group plc, 32
Tidewater Inc., 11; 37 (upd.)
TNT Freightways Corporation, 14
TNT Post Group N.V., V; 27 (upd.); 30 (upd.)
Tobu Railway Co Ltd, 6
Tokyu Corporation, V
Totem Resources Corporation, 9
TPG N.V., 64 (upd.)
Trailer Bridge, Inc., 41
Transnet Ltd., 6
Transport Corporation of America, Inc., 49
TTX Company, 6; 66 (upd.)
U.S. Delivery Systems, Inc., 22
Union Pacific Corporation, V; 28 (upd.)
United Parcel Service of America Inc., V; 17 (upd.)
United Parcel Service, Inc., 63
United Road Services, Inc., 69
United States Postal Service, 14; 34 (upd.)
USA Truck, Inc., 42
Velocity Express Corporation, 49
Werner Enterprises, Inc., 26
Wincanton plc, 52
Wisconsin Central Transportation Corporation, 24
Yamato Transport Co. Ltd., V; 49 (upd.)
Yellow Corporation, 14; 45 (upd.)
Yellow Freight System, Inc. of Delaware, V

UTILITIES

AES Corporation, 10; 13 (upd.); 53 (upd.)
Aggreko Plc, 45
Air & Water Technologies Corporation, 6
Alberta Energy Company Ltd., 16; 43 (upd.)
Allegheny Energy, Inc., V; 38 (upd.)
Ameren Corporation, 60 (upd.)
American Electric Power Company, Inc., V; 45 (upd.)
American States Water Company, 46
American Water Works Company, Inc., 6; 38 (upd.)
Aquila, Inc., 50 (upd.)
Arkla, Inc., V
Associated Natural Gas Corporation, 11
Atlanta Gas Light Company, 6; 23 (upd.)
Atlantic Energy, Inc., 6
Atmos Energy Corporation, 43
Avista Corporation, 69 (upd.)
Baltimore Gas and Electric Company, V; 25 (upd.)
Bay State Gas Company, 38
Bayernwerk AG, V; 23 (upd.)
Bewag AG, 39
Big Rivers Electric Corporation, 11
Black Hills Corporation, 20
Bonneville Power Administration, 50
Boston Edison Company, 12
Bouygues S.A., 24 (upd.)
British Energy Plc, 49
British Gas plc, V
British Nuclear Fuels plc, 6
Brooklyn Union Gas, 6
Calpine Corporation, 36
Canadian Utilities Limited, 13; 56 (upd.)
Cap Rock Energy Corporation, 46
Carolina Power & Light Company, V; 23 (upd.)
Cascade Natural Gas Corporation, 9
Centerior Energy Corporation, V
Central and South West Corporation, V
Central Hudson Gas and Electricity Corporation, 6
Central Maine Power, 6
Central Vermont Public Service Corporation, 54
Centrica plc, 29 (upd.)
Chesapeake Utilities Corporation, 56
Chubu Electric Power Company, Inc., V; 46 (upd.)
Chugoku Electric Power Company Inc., V; 53 (upd.)
Cincinnati Gas & Electric Company, 6
CIPSCO Inc., 6
Citizens Utilities Company, 7
City Public Service, 6
Cleco Corporation, 37
CMS Energy Corporation, V, 14
The Coastal Corporation, 31 (upd.)
Cogentrix Energy, Inc., 10
The Coleman Company, Inc., 9
The Columbia Gas System, Inc., V; 16 (upd.)
Commonwealth Edison Company, V
Commonwealth Energy System, 14
Companhia Energética de Minas Gerais S.A. CEMIG, 65
Connecticut Light and Power Co., 13
Consolidated Edison, Inc., V; 45 (upd.)
Consolidated Natural Gas Company, V; 19 (upd.)
Consumers Power Co., 14
Consumers Water Company, 14
Consumers' Gas Company Ltd., 6
Covanta Energy Corporation, 64 (upd.)
Dalkia Holding, 66
Destec Energy, Inc., 12
The Detroit Edison Company, V
Dominion Resources, Inc., V; 54 (upd.)
DPL Inc., 6
DQE, Inc., 6
DTE Energy Company, 20 (upd.)
Duke Energy Corporation, V; 27 (upd.)
E.On AG, 50 (upd.)
Eastern Enterprises, 6
Edison International, 56 (upd.)
El Paso Electric Company, 21
El Paso Natural Gas Company, 12
Electrabel N.V., 67
Electricidade de Portugal, S.A., 47
Electricité de France, V; 41 (upd.)
Electricity Generating Authority of Thailand (EGAT), 56
Elektrowatt AG, 6
Enbridge Inc., 43
ENDESA S.A., V; 46 (upd.)
Enron Corporation, V; 46 (upd.)
Enserch Corporation, V
Ente Nazionale per L'Energia Elettrica, V
Entergy Corporation, V; 45 (upd.)
Environmental Power Corporation, 68
Equitable Resources, Inc., 6; 54 (upd.)
Exelon Corporation, 48 (upd.)
Florida Progress Corporation, V; 23 (upd.)
Florida Public Utilities Company, 69
Fortis, Inc., 15; 47 (upd.)
Fortum Corporation, 30 (upd.)
FPL Group, Inc., V; 49 (upd.)
Gas Natural SDG S.A., 69
Gaz de France, V; 40 (upd.)
General Public Utilities Corporation, V
Générale des Eaux Group, V
GPU, Inc., 27 (upd.)
Great Plains Energy Incorporated, 65 (upd.)
Gulf States Utilities Company, 6
Hawaiian Electric Industries, Inc., 9
Hokkaido Electric Power Company Inc. (HEPCO), V; 58 (upd.)
Hokuriku Electric Power Company, V
Hongkong Electric Holdings Ltd., 6; 23 (upd.)
Houston Industries Incorporated, V
Hyder plc, 34
Hydro-Québec, 6; 32 (upd.)
Iberdrola, S.A., 49
Idaho Power Company, 12
Illinois Bell Telephone Company, 14
Illinois Power Company, 6
Indiana Energy, Inc., 27
International Power PLC, 50 (upd.)
IPALCO Enterprises, Inc., 6
The Kansai Electric Power Company, Inc., V; 62 (upd.)
Kansas City Power & Light Company, 6
Kelda Group plc, 45
Kenetech Corporation, 11
Kentucky Utilities Company, 6
KeySpan Energy Co., 27
Korea Electric Power Corporation (Kepco), 56
KU Energy Corporation, 11
Kyushu Electric Power Company Inc., V
LG&E Energy Corporation, 6; 51 (upd.)
Long Island Lighting Company, V
Lyonnaise des Eaux-Dumez, V

UTILITIES (continued)

Madison Gas and Electric Company, 39
Magma Power Company, 11
Maine & Maritimes Corporation, 56
Manila Electric Company (Meralco), 56
MCN Corporation, 6
MDU Resources Group, Inc., 7; 42 (upd.)
Middlesex Water Company, 45
Midwest Resources Inc., 6
Minnesota Power, Inc., 11; 34 (upd.)
The Montana Power Company, 11; 44 (upd.)
National Fuel Gas Company, 6
National Grid USA, 51 (upd.)
National Power PLC, 12
Nebraska Public Power District, 29
N.V. Nederlandse Gasunie, V
Nevada Power Company, 11
New England Electric System, V
New Jersey Resources Corporation, 54
New York State Electric and Gas, 6
Neyveli Lignite Corporation Ltd., 65
Niagara Mohawk Holdings Inc., V; 45 (upd.)
NICOR Inc., 6
NIPSCO Industries, Inc., 6
North West Water Group plc, 11
Northeast Utilities, V; 48 (upd.)
Northern States Power Company, V; 20 (upd.)
Northwest Natural Gas Company, 45
NorthWestern Corporation, 37
Nova Corporation of Alberta, V
Oglethorpe Power Corporation, 6
Ohio Edison Company, V
Oklahoma Gas and Electric Company, 6
ONEOK Inc., 7
Ontario Hydro Services Company, 6; 32 (upd.)
Osaka Gas Company, Ltd., V; 60 (upd.)
Otter Tail Power Company, 18
Pacific Enterprises, V
Pacific Gas and Electric Company, V
PacifiCorp, V; 26 (upd.)
Panhandle Eastern Corporation, V
PECO Energy Company, 11
Pennon Group Plc, 45
Pennsylvania Power & Light Company, V
Peoples Energy Corporation, 6
PG&E Corporation, 26 (upd.)
Philadelphia Electric Company, V
Philadelphia Suburban Corporation, 39
Piedmont Natural Gas Company, Inc., 27
Pinnacle West Capital Corporation, 6; 54 (upd.)
PNM Resources Inc., 51 (upd.)
Portland General Corporation, 6
Potomac Electric Power Company, 6
Powergen PLC, 11; 50 (upd.)
PPL Corporation, 41 (upd.)
PreussenElektra Aktiengesellschaft, V
PSI Resources, 6
Public Service Company of Colorado, 6
Public Service Company of New Hampshire, 21; 55 (upd.)
Public Service Company of New Mexico, 6
Public Service Enterprise Group Inc., V; 44 (upd.)
Puerto Rico Electric Power Authority, 47
Puget Sound Energy Inc., 6; 50 (upd.)
Questar Corporation, 6; 26 (upd.)
RAO Unified Energy System of Russia, 45
Reliant Energy Inc., 44 (upd.)
Rochester Gas and Electric Corporation, 6
Ruhrgas AG, V; 38 (upd.)
RWE AG, V; 50 (upd.)
Salt River Project, 19

San Diego Gas & Electric Company, V
SCANA Corporation, 6; 56 (upd.)
Scarborough Public Utilities Commission, 9
SCEcorp, V
Scottish and Southern Energy plc, 66 (upd.)
Scottish Hydro-Electric PLC, 13
Scottish Power plc, 19; 49 (upd.)
Seattle City Light, 50
SEMCO Energy, Inc., 44
Sempra Energy, 25 (upd.)
Severn Trent PLC, 12; 38 (upd.)
Shikoku Electric Power Company, Inc., V; 60 (upd.)
SJW Corporation, 70
Sonat, Inc., 6
South Jersey Industries, Inc., 42
The Southern Company, V; 38 (upd.)
Southern Electric PLC, 13
Southern Indiana Gas and Electric Company, 13
Southern Union Company, 27
Southwest Gas Corporation, 19
Southwest Water Company, 47
Southwestern Electric Power Co., 21
Southwestern Public Service Company, 6
Suez Lyonnaise des Eaux, 36 (upd.)
TECO Energy, Inc., 6
Tennessee Valley Authority, 50
Texas Utilities Company, V; 25 (upd.)
Thames Water plc, 11
Tohoku Electric Power Company, Inc., V
The Tokyo Electric Power Company, Incorporated, V
Tokyo Gas Co., Ltd., V; 55 (upd.)
TransAlta Utilities Corporation, 6
TransCanada PipeLines Limited, V
Transco Energy Company, V
Trigen Energy Corporation, 42
Tucson Electric Power Company, 6
UGI Corporation, 12
Unicom Corporation, 29 (upd.)
Union Electric Company, V
The United Illuminating Company, 21
United Utilities PLC, 52 (upd.)
United Water Resources, Inc., 40
Unitil Corporation, 37
Utah Power and Light Company, 27
UtiliCorp United Inc., 6
Vattenfall AB, 57
Vereinigte Elektrizitätswerke Westfalen AG, V
VEW AG, 39
Viridian Group plc, 64
Warwick Valley Telephone Company, 55
Washington Gas Light Company, 19
Washington Natural Gas Company, 9
Washington Water Power Company, 6
Westar Energy, Inc., 57 (upd.)
Western Resources, Inc., 12
Wheelabrator Technologies, Inc., 6
Wisconsin Energy Corporation, 6; 54 (upd.)
Wisconsin Public Service Corporation, 9
WPL Holdings, Inc., 6
WPS Resources Corporation, 53 (upd.)

WASTE SERVICES

Allied Waste Industries, Inc., 50
Allwaste, Inc., 18
Appliance Recycling Centers of America, Inc., 42
Azcon Corporation, 23
Berliner Stadtreinigungsbetriebe, 58
Brambles Industries Limited, 42

Browning-Ferris Industries, Inc., V; 20 (upd.)
Chemical Waste Management, Inc., 9
Copart Inc., 23
E.On AG, 50 (upd.)
Ecology and Environment, Inc., 39
Industrial Services of America, Inc., 46
Ionics, Incorporated, 52
ISS A/S, 49
Kelda Group plc, 45
MPW Industrial Services Group, Inc., 53
Newpark Resources, Inc., 63
Norcal Waste Systems, Inc., 60
Pennon Group Plc, 45
Philip Environmental Inc., 16
Roto-Rooter, Inc., 15; 61 (upd.)
Safety-Kleen Corp., 8
Sevenson Environmental Services, Inc., 42
Severn Trent PLC, 38 (upd.)
Shanks Group plc, 45
Shred-It Canada Corporation, 56
Stericycle Inc., 33
TRC Companies, Inc., 32
Veit Companies, 43
Waste Connections, Inc., 46
Waste Holdings, Inc., 41
Waste Management, Inc., V
Wheelabrator Technologies, Inc., 60 (upd.)
Windswept Environmental Group, Inc., 62
WMX Technologies Inc., 17

GEOGRAPHIC INDEX

Geographic Index

Algeria

Sonatrach, IV; 65 (upd.)

Argentina

Aerolíneas Argentinas S.A., 33; 69 (upd.)
Arcor S.A.I.C., 66
Atanor S.A., 62
Coto Centro Integral de Comercializacion S.A., 66
Cresud S.A.C.I.F. y A., 63
Grupo Clarín S.A., 67
Grupo Financiero Galicia S.A., 63
IRSA Inversiones y Representaciones S.A., 63
Ledesma Sociedad Anónima Agrícola Industrial, 62
Molinos Río de la Plata S.A., 61
Nobleza Piccardo SAICF, 64
Penaflor S.A., 66
Petrobras Energia Participaciones S.A., 72
Quilmes Industrial (QUINSA) S.A., 67
Renault Argentina S.A., 67
Sideco Americana S.A., 67
Siderar S.A.I.C., 66
Telecom Argentina S.A., 63
Telefónica de Argentina S.A., 61
YPF Sociedad Anonima, IV

Australia

Amcor Limited, IV; 19 (upd.)
Ansell Ltd., 60 (upd.)
Aquarius Platinum Ltd., 63
Aristocrat Leisure Limited, 54
Arnott's Ltd., 66
Australia and New Zealand Banking Group Limited, II; 52 (upd.)
AWB Ltd., 56
BHP Billiton, 67 (upd.)
Billabong International Ltd., 44
Bond Corporation Holdings Limited, 10
Boral Limited, III; 43 (upd.)
Brambles Industries Limited, 42
Broken Hill Proprietary Company Ltd., IV; 22 (upd.)
Burns, Philp & Company Ltd., 63
Carlton and United Breweries Ltd., I
Coles Myer Ltd., V; 20 (upd.)
CRA Limited, IV
CSR Limited, III; 28 (upd.)
David Jones Ltd., 60
Elders IXL Ltd., I
Foster's Group Limited, 7; 21 (upd.); 50 (upd.)
Goodman Fielder Ltd., 52
Harvey Norman Holdings Ltd., 56
Holden Ltd., 62
James Hardie Industries N.V., 56
John Fairfax Holdings Limited, 7
Lend Lease Corporation Limited, IV; 17 (upd.); 52 (upd.)
Lion Nathan Limited, 54
Lonely Planet Publications Pty Ltd., 55
Macquarie Bank Ltd., 69

McPherson's Ltd., 66
Metcash Trading Ltd., 58
News Corporation Limited, IV; 7 (upd.); 46 (upd.)
Pacific Dunlop Limited, 10
Pioneer International Limited, III
PMP Ltd., 72
Publishing and Broadcasting Limited, 54
Qantas Airways Ltd., 6; 24 (upd.); 68 (upd.)
Ridley Corporation Ltd., 62
Rinker Group Ltd., 65
Smorgon Steel Group Ltd., 62
Southcorp Limited, 54
TABCORP Holdings Limited, 44
Telecom Australia, 6
Telstra Corporation Limited, 50
Village Roadshow Ltd., 58
Westpac Banking Corporation, II; 48 (upd.)
WMC, Limited, 43

Austria

AKG Acoustics GmbH, 62
Andritz AG, 51
Austrian Airlines AG (Österreichische Luftverkehrs AG), 33
Bank Austria AG, 23
BBAG Osterreichische Brau-Beteiligungs-AG, 38
Erste Bank der Osterreichischen Sparkassen AG, 69
Gericom AG, 47
Glock Ges.m.b.H., 42
Julius Meinl International AG, 53
Lauda Air Luftfahrt AG, 48
ÖMV Aktiengesellschaft, IV
Österreichische Bundesbahnen GmbH, 6
Österreichische Post- und Telegraphenverwaltung, V
Red Bull GmbH, 60
RHI AG, 53
VA TECH ELIN EBG GmbH, 49
voestalpine AG, IV; 57 (upd.)
Wienerberger AG, 70
Zumtobel AG, 50

Bahamas

Bahamas Air Holdings Ltd., 66
Kerzner International Limited, 69 (upd.)
Sun International Hotels Limited, 26
Teekay Shipping Corporation, 25

Bahrain

Gulf Air Company, 56
Investcorp SA, 57

Bangladesh

Grameen Bank, 31

Belgium

Agfa Gevaert Group N.V., 59
Almanij NV, 44

Bank Brussels Lambert, II
Barco NV, 44
Belgacom, 6
C&A, 40 (upd.)
Cockerill Sambre Group, IV; 26 (upd.)
Delhaize "Le Lion" S.A., 44
DHL Worldwide Network S.A./N.V., 69 (upd.)
Electrabel N.V., 67
Etablissements Franz Colruyt N.V., 68
Generale Bank, II
GIB Group, V; 26 (upd.)
Groupe Herstal S.A., 58
Interbrew S.A., 17; 50 (upd.)
Kredietbank N.V., II
PetroFina S.A., IV; 26 (upd.)
Punch International N.V., 66
Roularta Media Group NV, 48
Sabena S.A./N.V., 33
Solvay S.A., I; 21 (upd.); 61 (upd.)
Tractebel S.A., 20
NV Umicore SA, 47
Xeikon NV, 26

Bermuda

Bacardi Limited, 18
Central European Media Enterprises Ltd., 61
Frontline Ltd., 45
Jardine Matheson Holdings Limited, I; 20 (upd.)
Sea Containers Ltd., 29
Tyco International Ltd., III; 28 (upd.); 63 (upd.)
White Mountains Insurance Group, Ltd., 48

Brazil

Aracruz Celulose S.A., 57
Banco Bradesco S.A., 13
Banco Itaú S.A., 19
Brasil Telecom Participaçoes S.A., 57
Cia Hering, 72
Companhia de Bebidas das Américas, 57
Companhia Energética de Minas Gerais S.A. CEMIG, 65
Companhia Vale do Rio Doce, IV; 43 (upd.)
Empresa Brasileira de Aeronáutica S.A. (Embraer), 36
Gerdau S.A., 59
Ipiranga S.A., 67
Lojas Arapua S.A., 22; 61 (upd.)
Perdigao SA, 52
Petróleo Brasileiro S.A., IV
Sadia S.A., 59
Souza Cruz S.A., 65
TAM Linhas Aéreas S.A., 68
TransBrasil S/A Linhas Aéreas, 31
VARIG S.A. (Viaçâo Aérea Rio-Grandense), 6; 29 (upd.)

Canada

Abitibi-Consolidated, Inc., V; 25 (upd.)

Canada (*continued*)

Abitibi-Price Inc., IV
Agnico-Eagle Mines Limited, 71
Air Canada, 6; 23 (upd.); 59 (upd.)
Alberta Energy Company Ltd., 16; 43 (upd.)
Alcan Aluminium Limited, IV; 31 (upd.)
Alderwoods Group, Inc., 68 (upd.)
Algo Group Inc., 24
Alliance Atlantis Communications Inc., 39
Bank of Montreal, II; 46 (upd.)
Bank of Nova Scotia, The, II; 59 (upd.)
Barrick Gold Corporation, 34
Bata Ltd., 62
BCE Inc., V; 44 (upd.)
Bell Canada, 6
BFC Construction Corporation, 25
Biovail Corporation, 47
Bombardier Inc., 42 (upd.)
Bradley Air Services Ltd., 56
Bramalea Ltd., 9
Brascan Corporation, 67
British Columbia Telephone Company, 6
Campeau Corporation, V
Canada Packers Inc., II
Canadair, Inc., 16
Canadian Broadcasting Corporation (CBC), The, 37
Canadian Imperial Bank of Commerce, II; 61 (upd.)
Canadian National Railway Company, 71 (upd.)
Canadian National Railway System, 6
Canadian Pacific Railway Limited, V; 45 (upd.)
Canadian Tire Corporation, Limited, 71 (upd.)
Canadian Utilities Limited, 13; 56 (upd.)
Canfor Corporation, 42
Canstar Sports Inc., 16
CanWest Global Communications Corporation, 35
Cascades Inc., 71
CHC Helicopter Corporation, 67
Cinar Corporation, 40
Cineplex Odeon Corporation, 6; 23 (upd.)
Cinram International, Inc., 43
Cirque du Soleil Inc., 29
Clearly Canadian Beverage Corporation, 48
Cognos Inc., 44
Cominco Ltd., 37
Consumers' Gas Company Ltd., 6
CoolBrands International Inc., 35
Corby Distilleries Limited, 14
Corel Corporation, 15; 33 (upd.)
Cott Corporation, 52
Creo Inc., 48
Discreet Logic Inc., 20
Dofasco Inc., IV; 24 (upd.)
Doman Industries Limited, 59
Dominion Textile Inc., 12
Domtar Inc., IV
Dorel Industries Inc., 59
Dylex Limited, 29
Echo Bay Mines Ltd., IV; 38 (upd.)
Enbridge Inc., 43
Extendicare Health Services, Inc., 6
Fairfax Financial Holdings Limited, 57
Fairmont Hotels & Resorts Inc., 69
Falconbridge Limited, 49
Finning International Inc., 69
Fortis, Inc., 15; 47 (upd.)
Four Seasons Hotels Inc., 9; 29 (upd.)
Future Shop Ltd., 62
GEAC Computer Corporation Ltd., 43
George Weston Limited, II; 36 (upd.)
Great-West Lifeco Inc., III

Groupe Vidéotron Ltée., 20
Harlequin Enterprises Limited, 52
Hemlo Gold Mines Inc., 9
Héroux-Devtek Inc., 69
Hiram Walker Resources, Ltd., I
Hockey Company, The, 34; 70
Hollinger International Inc., 62 (upd.)
Home Hardware Stores Ltd., 62
Hudson Bay Mining and Smelting Company, Limited, The, 12
Hudson's Bay Company, V; 25 (upd.)
Hurricane Hydrocarbons Ltd., 54
Husky Energy Inc., 47
Hydro-Québec, 6; 32 (upd.)
Imasco Limited, V
Imax Corporation, 28
Imperial Oil Limited, IV; 25 (upd.)
Imperial Parking Corporation, 58
Inco Limited, IV; 45 (upd.)
Indigo Books & Music Inc., 58
Intercorp Excelle Foods Inc., 64
Intrawest Corporation, The, 15
Irwin Toy Limited, 14
Jean Coutu Group (PJC) Inc., The, 46
Jim Pattison Group, The, 37
Kinross Gold Corporation, 36
Kruger Inc., 17
La Senza Corporation, 66
Labatt Brewing Company Limited, I; 25 (upd.)
LaSiDo Inc., 58
Lassonde Industries Inc., 68
Le Chateau Inc., 63
Ledcor Industries Limited, 46
Les Boutiques San Francisco, Inc., 62
Linamar Corporation, 18
Lions Gate Entertainment Corporation, 35
Loblaw Companies Limited, 43
Loewen Group, Inc., The, 16; 40 (upd.)
London Drugs Ltd., 46
Maclean Hunter Publishing Limited, IV; 26 (upd.)
MacMillan Bloedel Limited, IV
Magellan Aerospace Corporation, 48
Manitoba Telecom Services, Inc., 61
Maple Leaf Foods Inc., 41
Maple Leaf Sports & Entertainment Ltd., 61
Masonite International Corporation, 63
MDC Partners Inc., 63
Mega Bloks, Inc., 61
Methanex Corporation, 40
Mitel Corporation, 18
Molson Companies Limited, The, I; 26 (upd.)
Moore Corporation Limited, IV
Mouvement des Caisses Desjardins, 48
National Sea Products Ltd., 14
Noranda Inc., IV; 7 (upd.); 64 (upd.)
Nortel Networks Corporation, 36 (upd.)
North West Company, Inc., The, 12
Northern Telecom Limited, V
Nova Corporation of Alberta, V
Novacor Chemicals Ltd., 12
Olympia & York Developments Ltd., IV; 9 (upd.)
Onex Corporation, 16; 65 (upd.)
Ontario Hydro Services Company, 6; 32 (upd.)
Ontario Teachers' Pension Plan, 61
Oshawa Group Limited, The, II
PCL Construction Group Inc., 50
Peace Arch Entertainment Group Inc., 51
Petro-Canada Limited, IV
Philip Environmental Inc., 16
Placer Dome Inc., 20; 61 (upd.)

Potash Corporation of Saskatchewan Inc., 18
Power Corporation of Canada, 36 (upd.)
Provigo Inc., II; 51 (upd.)
QLT Inc., 71
Quebecor Inc., 12; 47 (upd.)
Research in Motion Ltd., 54
Richtree Inc., 63
Ritchie Bros. Auctioneers Inc., 41
Rogers Communications Inc., 30 (upd.)
Roots Canada Ltd., 42
Royal Bank of Canada, The, II; 21 (upd.)
Saputo Inc., 59
Scarborough Public Utilities Commission, 9
Seagram Company Ltd., The, I; 25 (upd.)
Shoppers Drug Mart Corporation, 49
Shred-It Canada Corporation, 56
SNC-Lavalin Group Inc., 72
Southam Inc., 7
Spar Aerospace Limited, 32
Spin Master, Ltd., 61
Steinberg Incorporated, II
Stelco Inc., IV; 51 (upd.)
Suncor Energy Inc., 54
Talisman Energy Inc., 9; 47 (upd.)
TDL Group Ltd., 46
Teck Corporation, 27
Tembec Inc., 66
Thomson Corporation, The, 8; 34 (upd.)
Tilley Endurables, Inc., 67
Toromont Industries, Ltd., 21
Toronto-Dominion Bank, The, II; 49 (upd.)
Torstar Corporation, 29
TransAlta Utilities Corporation, 6
TransCanada PipeLines Limited, V
Tridel Enterprises Inc., 9
Trilon Financial Corporation, II
Triple Five Group Ltd., 49
Trizec Corporation Ltd., 10
Van Houtte Inc., 39
Varity Corporation, III
Vincor International Inc., 50
Wascana Energy Inc., 13
Wawanesa Mutual Insurance Company, The, 68
West Fraser Timber Co. Ltd., 17
WestJet Airlines Ltd., 38

Cayman Islands

Garmin Ltd., 60
United National Group, Ltd., 63

Chile

Banco de Chile, 69
Cencosud S.A., 69
Compania Cervecerias Unidas S.A., 70
Corporacion Nacional del Cobre de Chile, 40
Cristalerias de Chile S.A., 67
Distribución y Servicio D&S S.A., 71
Embotelladora Andina S.A., 71
Empresas Almacenes Paris S.A., 71
Empresas CMPC S.A., 70
Empresas Copec S.A., 69
Farmacias Ahumada S.A., 72
Lan Chile S.A., 31
Madeco S.A., 71
Parque Arauco S.A., 72
S.A.C.I. Falabella, 69
Viña Concha y Toro S.A., 45

China

Air China, 46
Asia Info Holdings, Inc., 43
Bank of China, 63

China Eastern Airlines Co. Ltd., 31
China Life Insurance Company Limited, 65
China National Petroleum Corporation, 46
China Southern Airlines Company Ltd., 33
China Telecom, 50
Chinese Petroleum Corporation, IV; 31 (upd.)
Guangzhou Pearl River Piano Group Ltd., 49
Haier Group Corporation, 65
Li & Fung Limited, 59
Shanghai Baosteel Group Corporation, 71
Shanghai Petrochemical Co., Ltd., 18
SINA Corporation, 69
Tsingtao Brewery Group, 49
Zindart Ltd., 60

Colombia

Avianca Aerovías Nacionales de Colombia SA, 36
Empresa Colombiana de Petróleos, IV

Croatia

PLIVA d.d., 70

Czech Republic

Budweiser Budvar, National Corporation, 59
Ceské aerolinie, a.s., 66
Cesky Telecom, a.s., 64
Skoda Auto a.s., 39

Denmark

A.P. Møller - Maersk A/S, 57
Aarhus United A/S, 68
Arla Foods amba, 48
Bang & Olufsen Holding A/S, 37
Carl Allers Etablessement A/S, 72
Carlsberg A/S, 9; 29 (upd.)
Chr. Hansen Group A/S, 70
Danisco A/S, 44
Danske Bank Aktieselskab, 50
Ecco Sko A/S, 62
FLSmidth & Co. A/S, 72
Group 4 Falck A/S, 42
H. Lundbeck A/S, 44
Hummel International A/S, 68
IKEA International A/S, V; 26 (upd.)
ISS A/S, 49
Lego A/S, 13; 40 (upd.)
Novo Nordisk A/S, I; 61 (upd.)
Sophus Berendsen A/S, 49
Sterling European Airlines A/S, 70
TDC A/S, 63

Ecuador

Petróleos del Ecuador, IV

Egypt

EgyptAir, 6; 27 (upd.)
Egyptian General Petroleum Corporation, IV; 51 (upd.)

El Salvador

Grupo TACA, 38

Estonia

AS Estonian Air, 71

Fiji

Air Pacific Ltd., 70

Finland

Ahlstrom Corporation, 53
Amer Group plc, 41
Dynea, 68
Enso-Gutzeit Oy, IV
Finnair Oyj, 6; 25 (upd.); 61 (upd.)
Fiskars Corporation, 33
Fortum Corporation, 30 (upd.)
Hackman Oyj Adp, 44
Huhtamäki Oyj, 64
Imatra Steel Oy Ab, 55
Kansallis-Osake-Pankki, II
Kemira Oyj, 70
Kesko Ltd. (Kesko Oy), 8; 27 (upd.)
Kone Corporation, 27
Kymmene Corporation, IV
M-real Oyj, 56 (upd.)
Metsa-Serla Oy, IV
Metso Corporation, 30 (upd.)
Neste Oy, IV
Nokia Corporation, II; 17 (upd.); 38 (upd.)
Orion Oyj, 72
Outokumpu Oyj, 38
Posti- ja Telelaitos, 6
Sanitec Corporation, 51
SanomaWSOY Corporation, 51
Sonera Corporation, 50
Stora Enso Oyj, 36 (upd.)
Tamfelt Oyj Abp, 62
United Paper Mills Ltd. (Yhtyneet Paperitchtaat Oy), IV
UPM-Kymmene Corporation, 19; 50 (upd.)
Valmet Corporation (Valmet Oy), III

France

Accor S.A., 10; 27 (upd.); 69 (upd.)
Aéroports de Paris, 33
Aerospatiale Group, The, 7; 21 (upd.)
Agence France-Presse, 34
Alain Afflelou SA, 53
Alcatel S.A., 9; 36 (upd.)
Altran Technologies, 51
Amec Spie S.A., 57
Association des Centres Distributeurs E. Leclerc, 37
Assurances Générales de France, 63
Atochem S.A., I
Atos Origin S.A., 69
Au Printemps S.A., V
Auchan, 37
Automobiles Citroen, 7
Autoroutes du Sud de la France SA, 55
Avions Marcel Dassault-Breguet Aviation, I
Axa, III
Baccarat, 24
Banque Nationale de Paris S.A., II
Baron Philippe de Rothschild S.A., 39
Bayard SA, 49
Bénéteau SA, 55
Besnier SA, 19
BigBen Interactive S.A., 72
BNP Paribas Group, 36 (upd.)
Bonduelle SA, 51
Bongrain SA, 25
Bouygues S.A., I; 24 (upd.)
Bricorama S.A., 68
Brioche Pasquier S.A., 58
BSN Groupe S.A., II
Bull S.A., 43 (upd.)
Bureau Veritas SA, 55
Burelle S.A., 23
Business Objects S.A., 25
Camaïeu S.A., 72
Canal Plus, 10; 34 (upd.)
Cap Gemini Ernst & Young, 37
Carbone Lorraine S.A., 33

Carrefour SA, 10; 27 (upd.); 64 (upd.)
Casino Guichard-Perrachon S.A., 59 (upd.)
Cetelem S.A., 21
Chanel SA, 12; 49 (upd.)
Chargeurs International, 6; 21 (upd.)
Christian Dalloz SA, 40
Christian Dior S.A., 19; 49 (upd.)
Christofle SA, 40
Ciments Français, 40
Club Mediterranée S.A., 6; 21 (upd.)
Coflexip S.A., 25
Colas S.A., 31
Compagnie de Saint-Gobain, III; 16 (upd.); 64 (upd.)
Compagnie des Alpes, 48
Compagnie des Machines Bull S.A., III
Compagnie Financiere de Paribas, II
Compagnie Financière Sucres et Denrées S.A., 60
Compagnie Générale d'Électricité, II
Compagnie Générale des Établissements Michelin, V; 42 (upd.)
Compagnie Générale Maritime et Financière, 6
Comptoirs Modernes S.A., 19
Crédit Agricole, II
Crédit Lyonnais, 9; 33 (upd.)
Crédit National S.A., 9
Dalkia Holding, 66
Darty S.A., 27
Dassault Systèmes S.A., 25
De Dietrich & Cie., 31
Deveaux S.A., 41
Dexia Group, 42
Du Pareil au Même, 43
Dynaction S.A., 67
EADS SOCATA, 54
ECS S.A, 12
Éditions Gallimard, 72
Eiffage, 27
Electricité de France, V; 41 (upd.)
Elf Aquitaine SA, 21 (upd.)
Elior SA, 49
Eram SA, 51
Eridania Béghin-Say S.A., 36
Essilor International, 21
Etablissements Economiques du Casino Guichard, Perrachon et Cie, S.C.A., 12
Etam Developpement SA, 44
Euro Disney S.C.A., 20; 58 (upd.)
Euro RSCG Worldwide S.A., 13
Eurofins Scientific S.A., 70
Euronext Paris S.A., 37
Expand SA, 48
Facom S.A., 32
Faiveley S.A., 39
Faurecia S.A., 70
Fimalac S.A., 37
Fleury Michon S.A., 39
FNAC, 21
Framatome SA, 19
France Télécom Group, V; 21 (upd.)
Fromageries Bel, 23
G.I.E. Airbus Industrie, I; 12 (upd.)
Galeries Lafayette S.A., V; 23 (upd.)
Gaumont SA, 25
Gaz de France, V; 40 (upd.)
Gecina SA, 42
Gefco SA, 54
Générale des Eaux Group, V
Geodis S.A., 67
GFI Informatique SA, 49
GrandVision S.A., 43
Grévin & Compagnie SA, 56
Groupe Air France, 6
Groupe Alain Manoukian, 55
Groupe André, 17

France (*continued*)

Groupe Bolloré, 67
Groupe Bourbon S.A., 60
Groupe Castorama-Dubois Investissements, 23
Groupe Danone, 32 (upd.)
Groupe Dassault Aviation SA, 26 (upd.)
Groupe de la Cite, IV
Groupe DMC (Dollfus Mieg & Cie), 27
Groupe Fournier SA, 44
Groupe Go Sport S.A., 39
Groupe Guillin SA, 40
Groupe Jean-Claude Darmon, 44
Groupe Lapeyre S.A., 33
Groupe Legris Industries, 23
Groupe Les Echos, 25
Groupe Louis Dreyfus S.A., 60
Groupe Monnoyeur, 72
Groupe Partouche SA, 48
Groupe Promodès S.A., 19
Groupe Rougier SA, 21
Groupe SEB, 35
Groupe Sidel S.A., 21
Groupe Soufflet SA, 55
Groupe Yves Saint Laurent, 23
Groupe Zannier S.A., 35
Guerbet Group, 46
Guerlain, 23
Guilbert S.A., 42
Guillemot Corporation, 41
Guy Degrenne SA, 44
Guyenne et Gascogne, 23
Hachette, IV
Hachette Filipacchi Medias S.A., 21
Havas, SA, 10; 33 (upd.)
Hermès International S.A., 14; 34 (upd.)
Imerys S.A., 40 (upd.)
Imetal S.A., IV
Infogrames Entertainment S.A., 35
Ingenico—Compagnie Industrielle et Financière d'Ingénierie, 46
ITM Entreprises SA, 36
Keolis SA, 51
Kiabi Europe, 66
L'Air Liquide SA, I; 47 (upd.)
L'Entreprise Jean Lefebvre, 23
L'Oréal SA, III; 8 (upd.); 46 (upd.)
L.D.C. SA, 61
La Poste, V; 47 (upd.)
Laboratoires de Biologie Végétale Yves Rocher, 35
Lafarge Coppée S.A., III
Lafuma S.A., 39
Laurent-Perrier SA, 42
Lazard LLC, 38
LDC, 68
Le Cordon Bleu S.A., 67
Le Monde S.A., 33
Legrand SA, 21
Leroux S.A.S., 65
Leroy Merlin SA, 54
LVMH Möet Hennessy Louis Vuitton SA, I; 10; 33 (upd.)
Lyonnaise des Eaux-Dumez, V
Madrange SA, 58
Maison Louis Jadot, 24
Manitou BF S.A., 27
Manutan International S.A., 72
Marie Brizard & Roger International S.A., 22
Marionnaud Parfumeries SA, 51
Matra-Hachette S.A., 15 (upd.)
Matussière et Forest SA, 58
Metaleurop S.A., 21
Métropole Télévision, 33
Monnaie de Paris, 62
Montupet S.A., 63

Moulinex S.A., 22
Mr. Bricolage S.A., 37
Naf Naf SA, 44
Neopost S.A., 53
Nexans SA, 54
Nexity S.A., 66
Nocibé SA, 54
Papeteries de Lancey, 23
Pathé SA, 29
Pechiney SA, IV; 45 (upd.)
Penauille Polyservices SA, 49
Pernod Ricard S.A., I; 21 (upd.); 72 (upd.)
Peugeot S.A., I
Pierre & Vacances SA, 48
Pinault-Printemps Redoute S.A., 19 (upd.)
Pinguely-Haulotte SA, 51
Pochet SA, 55
Poliet S.A., 33
PSA Peugeot Citroen S.A., 28 (upd.)
Publicis S.A., 19
Rallye SA, 54
Regie Nationale des Usines Renault, I
Rémy Cointreau S.A., 20
Renault S.A., 26 (upd.)
Réseau Ferré de France, 66
Rhodia SA, 38
Rhône-Poulenc S.A., I; 10 (upd.)
Robertet SA, 39
Roussel Uclaf, I; 8 (upd.)
Royal Canin S.A., 39
Sabaté Diosos SA, 48
SAGEM S.A., 37
Salomon Worldwide, 20
Sanofi-Synthélabo Group, The, I; 49 (upd.)
Schneider S.A., II; 18 (upd.)
SCOR S.A., 20
Seita, 23
Selectour SA, 53
Simco S.A., 37
Skalli Group, 67
Skis Rossignol S.A., 15; 43 (upd.)
Smoby International SA, 56
Snecma Group, 46
Société Air France, 27 (upd.)
Société d'Exploitation AOM Air Liberté SA (AirLib), 53
Société du Figaro S.A., 60
Société du Louvre, 27
Société Générale, II; 42 (upd.)
Société Nationale des Chemins de Fer Français, V; 57 (upd.)
Société Nationale Elf Aquitaine, IV; 7 (upd.)
Société Norbert Dentressangle S.A., 67
Sodexho Alliance SA, 29
Sodiaal S.A., 36 (upd.)
SODIMA, II
Sommer-Allibert S.A., 19
Steria SA, 49
Suez Lyonnaise des Eaux, 36 (upd.)
Taittinger S.A., 43
Tati SA, 25
Télévision Française 1, 23
Terrena L'Union CANA CAVAL, 70
Thales S.A., 42
THOMSON multimedia S.A., II; 42 (upd.)
Total Fina Elf S.A., IV; 24 (upd.); 50 (upd.)
Transiciel SA, 48
Ubi Soft Entertainment S.A., 41
Ugine S.A., 20
Unibail SA, 40
Unilog SA, 42
Union des Assurances de Pans, III
Union Financière de France Banque SA, 52
Usinor SA, IV; 42 (upd.)
Valeo, 23; 66 (upd.)

Vallourec SA, 54
Vicat S.A., 70
Vilmorin Clause et Cie, 70
Vinci, 43
Vivarte SA, 54 (upd.)
Vivendi Universal S.A., 46 (upd.)
Weber et Broutin France, 66
Worms et Cie, 27
Zodiac S.A., 36

Germany

A. Moksel AG, 59
A.W. Faber-Castell Unternehmensverwaltung GmbH & Co., 51
Adam Opel AG, 7; 21 (upd.); 61 (upd.)
adidas-Salomon AG, 14; 33 (upd.)
Adolf Würth GmbH & Co. KG, 49
AEG A.G., I
Air Berlin GmbH & Co. Luftverkehrs KG, 71
Aldi Group, 13
Alfred Ritter GmbH & Co. KG, 58
Allianz AG, III; 15 (upd.); 57 (upd.)
AMB Generali Holding AG, 51
Andreas Stihl AG & Co. KG, 16; 59 (upd.)
Aral AG, 62
ARD, 41
August Storck KG, 66
AVA AG (Allgemeine Handelsgesellschaft der Verbraucher AG), 33
AXA Colonia Konzern AG, 27; 49 (upd.)
Axel Springer Verlag AG, IV; 20 (upd.)
Bahlsen GmbH & Co. KG, 44
Barmag AG, 39
BASF Aktiengesellschaft, I; 18 (upd.); 50 (upd.)
Bauer Publishing Group, 7
Bayer A.G., I; 13 (upd.); 41 (upd.)
Bayerische Hypotheken- und Wechsel-Bank AG, II
Bayerische Motoren Werke AG, I; 11 (upd.); 38 (upd.)
Bayerische Vereinsbank A.G., II
Bayernwerk AG, V; 23 (upd.)
Behr GmbH & Co. KG, 72
Beiersdorf AG, 29
Berliner Stadtreinigungsbetriebe, 58
Berliner Verkehrsbetriebe (BVG), 58
Bertelsmann A.G., IV; 15 (upd.); 43 (upd.)
Bewag AG, 39
Bilfinger & Berger AG, I; 55 (upd.)
Brauerei Beck & Co., 9; 33 (upd.)
Braun GmbH, 51
Brenntag AG, 8; 23 (upd.)
BSH Bosch und Siemens Hausgeräte GmbH, 67
Buderus AG, 37
Burda Holding GmbH. & Co., 23
C&A Brenninkmeyer KG, V
C.H. Boehringer Sohn, 39
Carl-Zeiss-Stiftung, III; 34 (upd.)
Commerzbank A.G., II; 47 (upd.)
Continental AG, V; 56 (upd.)
Daimler-Benz Aerospace AG, 16
DaimlerChrysler AG, I; 15 (upd.); 34 (upd.); 64 (upd.)
Debeka Krankenversicherungsverein auf Gegenseitigkeit, 72
Degussa Group, IV
Degussa-Huls AG, 32 (upd.)
Deutsche Babcock A.G., III
Deutsche Bahn AG, 46 (upd.)
Deutsche Bank AG, II; 14 (upd.); 40 (upd.)
Deutsche BP Aktiengesellschaft, 7
Deutsche Bundesbahn, V
Deutsche Bundespost TELEKOM, V
Deutsche Börse AG, 59

Deutsche Lufthansa AG, I; 26 (upd.); 68 (upd.)
Deutsche Post AG, 29
Deutsche Telekom AG, 48 (upd.)
Deutz AG, 39
Dr. August Oetker KG, 51
Dresdner Bank A.G., II; 57 (upd.)
Dürkopp Adler AG, 65
Dürr AG, 44
Dyckerhoff AG, 35
E.On AG, 50 (upd.)
Eckes AG, 56
Edeka Zentrale A.G., II; 47 (upd.)
edel music AG, 44
ERGO Versicherungsgruppe AG, 44
ESCADA AG, 71
Esselte Leitz GmbH & Co. KG, 48
Etienne Aigner AG, 52
FAG—Kugelfischer Georg Schäfer AG, 62
Fairchild Dornier GmbH, 48 (upd.)
Feldmuhle Nobel A.G., III
Fielmann AG, 31
Frankfurter Allgemeine Zeitung GmbH, 66
Fresenius AG, 56
Freudenberg & Co., 41
Fried. Krupp GmbH, IV
Friedrich Grohe AG & Co. KG, 53
GEA AG, 27
GEHE AG, 27
GEMA (Gesellschaft für musikalische Aufführungs- und mechanische Vervielfältigungsrechte), 70
geobra Brandstätter GmbH & Co. KG, 48
Gerling-Konzern Versicherungs-Beteiligungs-Aktiengesellschaft, 51
Gerresheimer Glas AG, 43
Gerry Weber International AG, 63
GfK Aktiengesellschaft, 49
Groz-Beckert Group, 68
Grundig AG, 27
Hansgrohe AG, 56
Hapag-Lloyd AG, 6
HARIBO GmbH & Co. KG, 44
HDI (Haftpflichtverband der Deutschen Industrie Versicherung auf Gegenseitigkeit V.a.G.), 53
Heidelberger Druckmaschinen AG, 40
Heidelberger Zement AG, 31
Hella KGaA Hueck & Co., 66
Henkel KGaA, III; 34 (upd.)
Heraeus Holding GmbH, IV; 54 (upd.)
Hertie Waren- und Kaufhaus GmbH, V
Hexal AG, 69
Hochtief AG, 33
Hoechst A.G., I; 18 (upd.)
Hoesch AG, IV
Hugo Boss AG, 48
HUK-Coburg, 58
Huls A.G., I
HVB Group, 59 (upd.)
Infineon Technologies AG, 50
J.M. Voith AG, 33
Jenoptik AG, 33
Kamps AG, 44
Karlsberg Brauerei GmbH & Co KG, 41
Karstadt Aktiengesellschaft, V; 19 (upd.)
Karstadt Quelle AG, 57 (upd.)
Kaufhof Warenhaus AG, V; 23 (upd.)
Kaufring AG, 35
KHD Konzern, III
Klaus Steilmann GmbH & Co. KG, 53
Klöckner-Werke AG, IV; 58 (upd.)
Koenig & Bauer AG, 64
König Brauerei GmbH & Co. KG, 35 (upd.)
Körber AG, 60
Kreditanstalt für Wiederaufbau, 29

KSB AG, 62
Leica Camera AG, 35
Leica Microsystems Holdings GmbH, 35
Linde AG, I; 67 (upd.)
LTU Group Holding GmbH, 37
MAN Aktiengesellschaft, III
Mannesmann AG, III; 14 (upd.); 38 (upd.)
Margarete Steiff GmbH, 23
Märklin Holding GmbH, 70
Matth. Hohner AG, 53
Melitta Unternehmensgruppe Bentz KG, 53
Messerschmitt-Bölkow-Blohm GmbH., I
Metallgesellschaft AG, IV; 16 (upd.)
Metro AG, 50
Miele & Cie. KG, 56
MITROPA AG, 37
Munich Re (Münchener Rückversicherungs-Gesellschaft Aktiengesellschaft in München), III; 46 (upd.)
Nixdorf Computer AG, III
Norddeutsche Affinerie AG, 62
Optische Werke G. Rodenstock, 44
Otto Versand GmbH & Co., V; 15 (upd.); 34 (upd.)
Paulaner Brauerei GmbH & Co. KG, 35
Peek & Cloppenburg KG, 46
Philipp Holzmann AG, 17
Phoenix AG, 68
Porsche AG, 13; 31 (upd.)
Preussag AG, 17; 42 (upd.)
PreussenElektra Aktiengesellschaft, V
ProSiebenSat.1 Media AG, 54
Puma AG Rudolf Dassler Sport, 35
PWA Group, IV
Qiagen N.V., 39
Quelle Group, V
RAG AG, 35; 60 (upd.)
Ravensburger AG, 64
RENK AG, 37
Rheinmetall Berlin AG, 9
Robert Bosch GmbH, I; 16 (upd.); 43 (upd.)
Rohde & Schwarz GmbH & Co. KG, 39
Roland Berger & Partner GmbH, 37
Ruhrgas AG, V; 38 (upd.)
Ruhrkohle AG, IV
RWE AG, V; 50 (upd.)
Saarberg-Konzern, IV
Salzgitter AG, IV
SAP AG, 16; 43 (upd.)
Schenker-Rhenus AG, 6
Schering AG, I; 50 (upd.)
Sennheiser Electronic GmbH & Co. KG, 66
Siemens AG, II; 14 (upd.); 57 (upd.)
Sixt AG, 39
SPAR Handels AG, 35
SPIEGEL-Verlag Rudolf Augstein GmbH & Co. KG, 44
Stinnes AG, 8; 23 (upd.); 59 (upd.)
Stollwerck AG, 53
Südzucker AG, 27
T-Online International AG, 61
TA Triumph-Adler AG, 48
Tarkett Sommer AG, 25
TaurusHolding GmbH & Co. KG, 46
Tengelmann Group, 27
Thyssen Krupp AG, IV; 28 (upd.)
Touristik Union International GmbH. and Company K.G., II
TUI Group GmbH, 44
Vaillant GmbH, 44
Varta AG, 23
Veba A.G., I; 15 (upd.)
Vereinigte Elektrizitätswerke Westfalen AG, V

Verlagsgruppe Georg von Holtzbrinck GmbH, 35
VEW AG, 39
VIAG Aktiengesellschaft, IV
Victoria Group, III; 44 (upd.)
Viessmann Werke GmbH & Co., 37
Villeroy & Boch AG, 37
Volkswagen Aktiengesellschaft, I; 11 (upd.); 32 (upd.)
Vorwerk & Co., 27
Vossloh AG, 53
Wacker-Chemie GmbH, 35
Wella AG, III; 48 (upd.)
Weru Aktiengesellschaft, 18
Westdeutsche Landesbank Girozentrale, II; 46 (upd.)
Wincor Nixdorf Holding GmbH, 69 (upd.)
Württembergische Metallwarenfabrik AG (WMF), 60
ZF Friedrichshafen AG, 48

Ghana

Ashanti Goldfields Company Limited, 43

Greece

Aegek S.A., 64
Attica Enterprises S.A., 64
Hellenic Petroleum SA, 64
National Bank of Greece, 41
Royal Olympic Cruise Lines Inc., 52
Stelmar Shipping Ltd., 52
Titan Cement Company S.A., 64

Hong Kong

Bank of East Asia Ltd., 63
Cable & Wireless HKT, 30 (upd.)
Cathay Pacific Airways Limited, 6; 34 (upd.)
CDC Corporation, 71
Cheung Kong (Holdings) Limited, IV; 20 (upd.)
China Merchants International Holdings Co., Ltd., 52
CITIC Pacific Ltd., 18
First Pacific Company Limited, 18
Hang Seng Bank Ltd., 60
Henderson Land Development Company Ltd., 70
Hong Kong Dragon Airlines Ltd., 66
Hong Kong Telecommunications Ltd., 6
Hongkong and Shanghai Banking Corporation Limited, The, II
Hongkong Electric Holdings Ltd., 6; 23 (upd.)
Hongkong Land Holdings Limited, IV; 47 (upd.)
Hutchison Whampoa Limited, 18; 49 (upd.)
Kerry Properties Limited, 22
Nam Tai Electronics, Inc., 61
New World Development Company Limited, IV; 38 (upd.)
Next Media Ltd., 61
Playmates Toys, 23
Shangri-La Asia Ltd., 71
Singer Company N.V., The, 30 (upd.)
Swire Pacific Limited, I; 16 (upd.); 57 (upd.)
Tommy Hilfiger Corporation, 20; 53 (upd.)

Hungary

Malév Plc, 24
MOL Rt, 70

Iceland

Icelandair, 52

India

Air Sahara Limited, 65
Air-India Limited, 6; 27 (upd.)
Bajaj Auto Limited, 39
Coal India Limited, IV; 44 (upd.)
Dr. Reddy's Laboratories Ltd., 59
Indian Airlines Ltd., 46
Indian Oil Corporation Ltd., IV; 48 (upd.)
Infosys Technologies Ltd., 38
Jet Airways (India) Private Limited, 65
Minerals and Metals Trading Corporation
  of India Ltd., IV
MTR Foods Ltd., 55
Neyveli Lignite Corporation Ltd., 65
Oil and Natural Gas Commission, IV
Ranbaxy Laboratories Ltd., 70
State Bank of India, 63
Steel Authority of India Ltd., IV; 66 (upd.)
Sun Pharmaceutical Industries Ltd., 57
Tata Iron & Steel Co. Ltd., IV; 44 (upd.)
Wipro Limited, 43

Indonesia

Djarum PT, 62
Garuda Indonesia, 6; 58 (upd.)
PERTAMINA, IV
Pertamina, 56 (upd.)
PT Astra International Tbk, 56
PT Bank Buana Indonesia Tbk, 60

Iran

National Iranian Oil Company, IV; 61
  (upd.)

Ireland

Aer Lingus Group plc, 34
Allied Irish Banks, plc, 16; 43 (upd.)
Baltimore Technologies Plc, 42
Bank of Ireland, 50
CRH plc, 64
DEPFA BANK PLC, 69
Dunnes Stores Ltd., 58
eircom plc, 31 (upd.)
Elan Corporation PLC, 63
Fyffes Plc, 38
Glanbia plc, 59
Harland and Wolff Holdings plc, 19
IAWS Group plc, 49
Independent News & Media PLC, 61
IONA Technologies plc, 43
Irish Life & Permanent Plc, 59
Jefferson Smurfit Group plc, IV; 19 (upd.);
  49 (upd.)
Jurys Doyle Hotel Group plc, 64
Kerry Group plc, 27
Musgrave Group Plc, 57
Ryanair Holdings plc, 35
Shannon Aerospace Ltd., 36
Telecom Eireann, 7
Waterford Wedgwood plc, 34 (upd.)

Israel

Amdocs Ltd., 47
Bank Hapoalim B.M., II; 54 (upd.)
Bank Leumi le-Israel B.M., 60
Blue Square Israel Ltd., 41
ECI Telecom Ltd., 18
El Al Israel Airlines Ltd., 23
Elscint Ltd., 20
Israel Aircraft Industries Ltd., 69
Israel Chemicals Ltd., 55

Koor Industries Ltd., II; 25 (upd.); 68
  (upd.)
Scitex Corporation Ltd., 24
Strauss-Elite Group, 68
Taro Pharmaceutical Industries Ltd., 65
Teva Pharmaceutical Industries Ltd., 22; 54
  (upd.)

Italy

Alfa Romeo, 13; 36 (upd.)
Alitalia-Linee Aeree Italiana, S.p.A., 6; 29
  (upd.)
Alleanza Assicurazioni S.p.A., 65
Aprilia SpA, 17
Arnoldo Mondadori Editore S.p.A., IV; 19
  (upd.); 54 (upd.)
Assicurazioni Generali SpA, III; 15 (upd.)
Autogrill SpA, 49
Automobili Lamborghini Holding S.p.A.,
  13; 34 (upd.)
Banca Commerciale Italiana SpA, II
Banca Fideuram SpA, 63
Banca Intesa SpA, 65
Banca Monte dei Paschi di Siena SpA, 65
Banca Nazionale del Lavoro SpA, 72
Barilla G. e R. Fratelli S.p.A., 17; 50
  (upd.)
Benetton Group S.p.A., 10; 67 (upd.)
Brioni Roman Style S.p.A., 67
Bulgari S.p.A., 20
Cantine Giorgio Lungarotti S.R.L., 67
Capitalia S.p.A., 65
Compagnia Italiana dei Jolly Hotels S.p.A.,
  71
Credito Italiano, II
Cremonini S.p.A., 57
Davide Campari-Milano S.p.A., 57
De'Longhi S.p.A., 66
Diesel SpA, 40
Dolce & Gabbana SpA, 62
Ducati Motor Holding S.p.A., 30
ENI S.p.A., 69 (upd.)
Ente Nazionale Idrocarburi, IV
Ente Nazionale per L'Energia Elettrica, V
Ermenegildo Zegna SpA, 63
Fabbrica D' Armi Pietro Beretta S.p.A., 39
Ferrari S.p.A., 13; 36 (upd.)
Ferrero SpA, 54
Fiat SpA, I; 11 (upd.); 50 (upd.)
Fila Holding S.p.A., 20; 52 (upd.)
Gianni Versace SpA, 22
Giorgio Armani S.p.A., 45
Gruppo Coin S.p.A., 41
Guccio Gucci, S.p.A., 15
illycaffè SpA, 50
Industrie Natuzzi S.p.A., 18
Industrie Zignago Santa Margherita S.p.A.,
  67
Ing. C. Olivetti & C., S.p.a., III
Istituto per la Ricostruzione Industriale
  S.p.A., I; 11
Juventus F.C. S.p.A., 53
Luxottica SpA, 17; 52 (upd.)
Marchesi Antinori SRL, 42
Marcolin S.p.A., 61
Martini & Rossi SpA, 63
Marzotto S.p.A., 20; 67 (upd.)
Mediaset SpA, 50
Mediolanum S.p.A., 65
Montedison SpA, I; 24 (upd.)
Officine Alfieri Maserati S.p.A., 13
Olivetti S.p.A., 34 (upd.)
Parmalat Finanziaria SpA, 50
Perfetti Van Melle S.p.A., 72
Piaggio & C. S.p.A., 20
Pirelli S.p.A., V; 15 (upd.)
Reno de Medici S.p.A., 41

Rinascente S.p.A., 71
Riunione Adriatica di Sicurtè SpA, III
Safilo SpA, 54
Salvatore Ferragamo Italia S.p.A., 62
Sanpaolo IMI S.p.A., 50
Seat Pagine Gialle S.p.A., 47
Società Finanziaria Telefonica per Azioni,
  V
Società Sportiva Lazio SpA, 44
Stefanel SpA, 63
Telecom Italia Mobile S.p.A., 63
Telecom Italia S.p.A., 43
Tiscali SpA, 48

Jamaica

Air Jamaica Limited, 54

Japan

AEON Co., Ltd., 68 (upd.)
Aisin Seiki Co., Ltd., III; 48 (upd.)
Aiwa Co., Ltd., 30
Ajinomoto Co., Inc., II; 28 (upd.)
All Nippon Airways Co., Ltd., 6; 38 (upd.)
Alpine Electronics, Inc., 13
Alps Electric Co., Ltd., II; 44 (upd.)
Anritsu Corporation, 68
Asahi Breweries, Ltd., I; 20 (upd.); 52
  (upd.)
Asahi Denka Kogyo KK, 64
Asahi Glass Company, Ltd., III; 48 (upd.)
Asahi National Broadcasting Company,
  Ltd., 9
ASICS Corporation, 57
Bandai Co., Ltd., 55
Bank of Tokyo-Mitsubishi Ltd., II; 15
  (upd.)
Bridgestone Corporation, V; 21 (upd.); 59
  (upd.)
Brother Industries, Ltd., 14
C. Itoh & Company Ltd., I
Canon Inc., III; 18 (upd.)
CASIO Computer Co., Ltd., III; 16 (upd.);
  40 (upd.)
Central Japan Railway Company, 43
Chubu Electric Power Company, Inc., V;
  46 (upd.)
Chugai Pharmaceutical Co., Ltd., 50
Chugoku Electric Power Company Inc., V;
  53 (upd.)
Citizen Watch Co., Ltd., III; 21 (upd.)
Clarion Company Ltd., 64
Cosmo Oil Co., Ltd., IV; 53 (upd.)
Dai Nippon Printing Co., Ltd., IV; 57
  (upd.)
Dai-Ichi Kangyo Bank Ltd., The, II
Daido Steel Co., Ltd., IV
Daiei, Inc., The, V; 17 (upd.); 41 (upd.)
Daihatsu Motor Company, Ltd., 7; 21
  (upd.)
Daikin Industries, Ltd., III
Daimaru, Inc., The, V; 42 (upd.)
Daio Paper Corporation, IV
Daishowa Paper Manufacturing Co., Ltd.,
  IV; 57 (upd.)
Daiwa Bank, Ltd., The, II; 39 (upd.)
Daiwa Securities Group Inc., II; 55 (upd.)
DDI Corporation, 7
DENSO Corporation, 46 (upd.)
Dentsu Inc., I; 16 (upd.); 40 (upd.)
East Japan Railway Company, V; 66 (upd.)
Ezaki Glico Company Ltd., 72
Fanuc Ltd., III; 17 (upd.)
Fuji Bank, Ltd., The, II
Fuji Electric Co., Ltd., II; 48 (upd.)
Fuji Photo Film Co., Ltd., III; 18 (upd.)
Fujisawa Pharmaceutical Company, Ltd., I;
  58 (upd.)

Fujitsu Limited, III; 16 (upd.); 42 (upd.)
Funai Electric Company Ltd., 62
Furukawa Electric Co., Ltd., The, III
General Sekiyu K.K., IV
Hakuhodo, Inc., 6; 42 (upd.)
Hankyu Department Stores, Inc., V; 23 (upd.); 62 (upd.)
Hino Motors, Ltd., 7; 21 (upd.)
Hitachi, Ltd., I; 12 (upd.); 40 (upd.)
Hitachi Metals, Ltd., IV
Hitachi Zosen Corporation, III; 53 (upd.)
Hokkaido Electric Power Company Inc. (HEPCO), V; 58 (upd.)
Hokuriku Electric Power Company, V
Honda Motor Company Limited, I; 10 (upd.); 29 (upd.)
Honshu Paper Co., Ltd., IV
Hoshino Gakki Co. Ltd., 55
Idemitsu Kosan Co., Ltd., IV; 49 (upd.)
Industrial Bank of Japan, Ltd., The, II
Isetan Company Limited, V; 36 (upd.)
Ishikawajima-Harima Heavy Industries Co., Ltd., III
Isuzu Motors, Ltd., 9; 23 (upd.); 57 (upd.)
Ito-Yokado Co., Ltd., V; 42 (upd.)
ITOCHU Corporation, 32 (upd.)
Itoham Foods Inc., II; 61 (upd.)
Japan Airlines Company, Ltd., I; 32 (upd.)
Japan Broadcasting Corporation, 7
Japan Leasing Corporation, 8
Japan Pulp and Paper Company Limited, IV
Japan Tobacco Inc., V; 46 (upd.)
Jujo Paper Co., Ltd., IV
JUSCO Co., Ltd., V
Kajima Corporation, I; 51 (upd.)
Kanebo, Ltd., 53
Kanematsu Corporation, IV; 24 (upd.)
Kansai Electric Power Company, Inc., The, V; 62 (upd.)
Kao Corporation, III; 20 (upd.)
Kawasaki Heavy Industries, Ltd., III; 63 (upd.)
Kawasaki Kisen Kaisha, Ltd., V; 56 (upd.)
Kawasaki Steel Corporation, IV
Keio Teito Electric Railway Company, V
Kenwood Corporation, 31
Kewpie Kabushiki Kaisha, 57
Kikkoman Corporation, 14; 47 (upd.)
Kinki Nippon Railway Company Ltd., V
Kirin Brewery Company, Limited, I; 21 (upd.); 63 (upd.)
Kobe Steel, Ltd., IV; 19 (upd.)
Kodansha Ltd., IV; 38 (upd.)
Komatsu Ltd., III; 16 (upd.); 52 (upd.)
Konica Corporation, III; 30 (upd.)
Kotobukiya Co., Ltd., V; 56 (upd.)
Kubota Corporation, III; 26 (upd.)
Kumagai Gumi Company, Ltd., I
Kumon Institute of Education Co., Ltd., 72
Kyocera Corporation, II; 21 (upd.)
Kyowa Hakko Kogyo Co., Ltd., III; 48 (upd.)
Kyushu Electric Power Company Inc., V
Lion Corporation, III; 51 (upd.)
Long-Term Credit Bank of Japan, Ltd., II
Mabuchi Motor Co. Ltd., 68
Makita Corporation, 22; 59 (upd.)
Marubeni Corporation, I; 24 (upd.)
Marui Company Ltd., V; 62 (upd.)
Maruzen Co., Limited, 18
Matsushita Electric Industrial Co., Ltd., II; 64 (upd.)
Matsushita Electric Works, Ltd., III; 7 (upd.)
Matsuzakaya Company Ltd., V; 64 (upd.)

Mazda Motor Corporation, 9; 23 (upd.); 63 (upd.)
Meiji Milk Products Company, Limited, II
Meiji Mutual Life Insurance Company, The, III
Meiji Seika Kaisha Ltd., II; 64 (upd.)
Millea Holdings Inc., 64 (upd.)
Minolta Co., Ltd., III; 18 (upd.); 43 (upd.)
Mitsubishi Bank, Ltd., The, II
Mitsubishi Chemical Corporation, I; 56 (upd.)
Mitsubishi Corporation, I; 12 (upd.)
Mitsubishi Electric Corporation, II; 44 (upd.)
Mitsubishi Estate Company, Limited, IV; 61 (upd.)
Mitsubishi Heavy Industries, Ltd., III; 7 (upd.); 40 (upd.)
Mitsubishi Materials Corporation, III
Mitsubishi Motors Corporation, 9; 23 (upd.); 57 (upd.)
Mitsubishi Oil Co., Ltd., IV
Mitsubishi Rayon Co., Ltd., V
Mitsubishi Trust & Banking Corporation, The, II
Mitsui & Co., Ltd., 28 (upd.)
Mitsui Bank, Ltd., The, II
Mitsui Bussan K.K., I
Mitsui Marine and Fire Insurance Company, Limited, III
Mitsui Mining & Smelting Co., Ltd., IV
Mitsui Mining Company, Limited, IV
Mitsui Mutual Life Insurance Company, III; 39 (upd.)
Mitsui O.S.K. Lines, Ltd., V
Mitsui Petrochemical Industries, Ltd., 9
Mitsui Real Estate Development Co., Ltd., IV
Mitsui Trust & Banking Company, Ltd., The, II
Mitsukoshi Ltd., V; 56 (upd.)
Mizuho Financial Group Inc., 58 (upd.)
Mizuno Corporation, 25
Morinaga & Co. Ltd., 61
Nagasakiya Co., Ltd., V; 69 (upd.)
Nagase & Co., Ltd., 8; 61 (upd.)
NEC Corporation, II; 21 (upd.); 57 (upd.)
NGK Insulators Ltd., 67
NHK Spring Co., Ltd., III
Nichii Co., Ltd., V
Nichimen Corporation, IV; 24 (upd.)
Nichirei Corporation, 70
Nidec Corporation, 59
Nihon Keizai Shimbun, Inc., IV
Nikko Securities Company Limited, The, II; 9 (upd.)
Nikon Corporation, III; 48 (upd.)
Nintendo Co., Ltd., III; 7 (upd.); 28 (upd.); 67 (upd.)
Nippon Credit Bank, II
Nippon Express Company, Ltd., V; 64 (upd.)
Nippon Life Insurance Company, III; 60 (upd.)
Nippon Light Metal Company, Ltd., IV
Nippon Meat Packers, Inc., II
Nippon Oil Corporation, IV; 63 (upd.)
Nippon Seiko K.K., III
Nippon Sheet Glass Company, Limited, III
Nippon Shinpan Co., Ltd., II; 61 (upd.)
Nippon Steel Corporation, IV; 17 (upd.)
Nippon Suisan Kaisha, Limited, II
Nippon Telegraph and Telephone Corporation, V; 51 (upd.)
Nippon Yusen Kabushiki Kaisha (NYK), V; 72 (upd.)
Nippondenso Co., Ltd., III

Nissan Motor Company Ltd., I; 11 (upd.); 34 (upd.)
Nisshin Seifun Group Inc., II; 66 (upd.)
Nisshin Steel Co., Ltd., IV
Nissho Iwai K.K., I
NKK Corporation, IV; 28 (upd.)
NOF Corporation, 72
Nomura Securities Company, Limited, II; 9 (upd.)
Norinchukin Bank, II
NTN Corporation, III; 47 (upd.)
Odakyu Electric Railway Co., Ltd., V; 68 (upd.)
Ohbayashi Corporation, I
Oji Paper Co., Ltd., IV; 57 (upd.)
Oki Electric Industry Company, Limited, II
Okura & Co., Ltd., IV
Omron Corporation, II; 28 (upd.)
Onoda Cement Co., Ltd., III
ORIX Corporation, II; 44 (upd.)
Osaka Gas Company, Ltd., V; 60 (upd.)
Paloma Industries Ltd., 71
Pioneer Electronic Corporation, III; 28 (upd.)
Rengo Co., Ltd., IV
Ricoh Company, Ltd., III; 36 (upd.)
Roland Corporation, 38
Ryoshoku Ltd., 72
Sankyo Company, Ltd., I; 56 (upd.)
Sanrio Company, Ltd., 38
Sanwa Bank, Ltd., The, II; 15 (upd.)
SANYO Electric Company, Ltd., II; 36 (upd.)
Sanyo-Kokusaku Pulp Co., Ltd., IV
Sapporo Breweries, Ltd., I; 13 (upd.); 36 (upd.)
Seibu Department Stores, Ltd., V; 42 (upd.)
Seibu Railway Co. Ltd., V
Seiko Corporation, III; 17 (upd.); 72 (upd.)
Seino Transportation Company, Ltd., 6
Seiyu, Ltd., The, V; 36 (upd.)
Sekisui Chemical Co., Ltd., III; 72 (upd.)
Sharp Corporation, II; 12 (upd.); 40 (upd.)
Shikoku Electric Power Company, Inc., V; 60 (upd.)
Shimano Inc., 64
Shionogi & Co., Ltd., III; 17 (upd.)
Shiseido Company, Limited, III; 22 (upd.)
Showa Shell Sekiyu K.K., IV; 59 (upd.)
Snow Brand Milk Products Company, Ltd., II; 48 (upd.)
Softbank Corp., 13; 38 (upd.)
Sony Corporation, II; 12 (upd.); 40 (upd.)
Sumitomo Bank, Limited, The, II; 26 (upd.)
Sumitomo Chemical Company Ltd., I
Sumitomo Corporation, I; 11 (upd.)
Sumitomo Electric Industries, Ltd., II
Sumitomo Heavy Industries, Ltd., III; 42 (upd.)
Sumitomo Life Insurance Company, III; 60 (upd.)
Sumitomo Marine and Fire Insurance Company, Limited, The, III
Sumitomo Metal Industries, Ltd., IV
Sumitomo Metal Mining Co., Ltd., IV
Sumitomo Mitsui Banking Corporation, 51 (upd.)
Sumitomo Realty & Development Co., Ltd., IV
Sumitomo Rubber Industries, Ltd., V
Sumitomo Trust & Banking Company, Ltd., The, II; 53 (upd.)
Suntory Ltd., 65
Suzuki Motor Corporation, 9; 23 (upd.); 59 (upd.)

Japan (*continued*)

Taiheiyo Cement Corporation, 60 (upd.)
Taiyo Fishery Company, Limited, II
Taiyo Kobe Bank, Ltd., The, II
Takara Holdings Inc., 62
Takashimaya Company, Limited, V; 47 (upd.)
Takeda Chemical Industries, Ltd., I; 46 (upd.)
TDK Corporation, II; 17 (upd.); 49 (upd.)
Teijin Limited, V; 61 (upd.)
Terumo Corporation, 48
Tobu Railway Co Ltd, 6
Toho Co., Ltd., 28
Tohoku Electric Power Company, Inc., V
Tokai Bank, Limited, The, II; 15 (upd.)
Tokio Marine and Fire Insurance Co., Ltd., The, III
Tokyo Electric Power Company, Incorporated, The, V
Tokyo Gas Co., Ltd., V; 55 (upd.)
Tokyu Corporation, V; 47 (upd.)
Tokyu Department Store Co., Ltd., V; 32 (upd.)
Tokyu Land Corporation, IV
Tomen Corporation, IV; 24 (upd.)
Tomy Company Ltd., 65
TonenGeneral Sekiyu K.K., IV; 16 (upd.); 54 (upd.)
Toppan Printing Co., Ltd., IV; 58 (upd.)
Toray Industries, Inc., V; 51 (upd.)
Toshiba Corporation, I; 12 (upd.); 40 (upd.)
Tosoh Corporation, 70
TOTO LTD., III; 28 (upd.)
Toyo Sash Co., Ltd., III
Toyo Seikan Kaisha, Ltd., I
Toyoda Automatic Loom Works, Ltd., III
Toyota Motor Corporation, I; 11 (upd.); 38 (upd.)
Ube Industries, Ltd., III; 38 (upd.)
Unitika Ltd., V; 53 (upd.)
Uny Co., Ltd., V; 49 (upd.)
Victor Company of Japan, Limited, II; 26 (upd.)
Wacoal Corp., 25
Yamaha Corporation, III; 16 (upd.); 40 (upd.)
Yamaichi Securities Company, Limited, II
Yamato Transport Co. Ltd., V; 49 (upd.)
Yamazaki Baking Co., Ltd., 58
Yasuda Fire and Marine Insurance Company, Limited, The, III
Yasuda Mutual Life Insurance Company, The, III; 39 (upd.)
Yasuda Trust and Banking Company, Ltd., The, II; 17 (upd.)
Yokohama Rubber Co., Ltd., The, V; 19 (upd.)

Kuwait

Kuwait Airways Corporation, 68
Kuwait Petroleum Corporation, IV; 55 (upd.)

Latvia

A/S Air Baltic Corporation, 71

Libya

National Oil Corporation, IV; 66 (upd.)

Liechtenstein

Hilti AG, 53

Luxembourg

ARBED S.A., IV; 22 (upd.)
Cargolux Airlines International S.A., 49
Gemplus International S.A., 64
RTL Group SA, 44
Société Luxembourgeoise de Navigation Aérienne S.A., 64
Tenaris SA, 63

Malaysia

Berjaya Group Bhd., 67
Genting Bhd., 65
Malayan Banking Berhad, 72
Malaysian Airlines System Berhad, 6; 29 (upd.)
Perusahaan Otomobil Nasional Bhd., 62
Petroliam Nasional Bhd (Petronas), IV; 56 (upd.)
PPB Group Berhad, 57
Sime Darby Berhad, 14; 36 (upd.)

Mauritius

Air Mauritius Ltd., 63

Mexico

Alfa, S.A. de C.V., 19
Altos Hornos de México, S.A. de C.V., 42
Apasco S.A. de C.V., 51
Bufete Industrial, S.A. de C.V., 34
Casa Cuervo, S.A. de C.V., 31
Celanese Mexicana, S.A. de C.V., 54
CEMEX S.A. de C.V., 20; 59 (upd.)
Cifra, S.A. de C.V., 12
Consorcio G Grupo Dina, S.A. de C.V., 36
Controladora Comercial Mexicana, S.A. de C.V., 36
Corporación Internacional de Aviación, S.A. de C.V. (Cintra), 20
Desc, S.A. de C.V., 23
Editorial Televisa, S.A. de C.V., 57
Empresas ICA Sociedad Controladora, S.A. de C.V., 41
Ford Motor Company, S.A. de C.V., 20
Gruma, S.A. de C.V., 31
Grupo Aeropuerto del Sureste, S.A. de C.V., 48
Grupo Carso, S.A. de C.V., 21
Grupo Casa Saba, S.A. de C.V., 39
Grupo Cydsa, S.A. de C.V., 39
Grupo Elektra, S.A. de C.V., 39
Grupo Financiero Banamex S.A., 54
Grupo Financiero Banorte, S.A. de C.V., 51
Grupo Financiero BBVA Bancomer S.A., 54
Grupo Financiero Serfin, S.A., 19
Grupo Gigante, S.A. de C.V., 34
Grupo Herdez, S.A. de C.V., 35
Grupo IMSA, S.A. de C.V., 44
Grupo Industrial Bimbo, 19
Grupo Industrial Durango, S.A. de C.V., 37
Grupo Industrial Saltillo, S.A. de C.V., 54
Grupo Mexico, S.A. de C.V., 40
Grupo Modelo, S.A. de C.V., 29
Grupo Posadas, S.A. de C.V., 57
Grupo Televisa, S.A., 18; 54 (upd.)
Grupo TMM, S.A. de C.V., 50
Grupo Transportación Ferroviaria Mexicana, S.A. de C.V., 47
Hylsamex, S.A. de C.V., 39
Industrias Bachoco, S.A. de C.V., 39
Industrias Penoles, S.A. de C.V., 22
Internacional de Ceramica, S.A. de C.V., 53

Kimberly-Clark de México, S.A. de C.V., 54
Organización Soriana, S.A. de C.V., 35
Petróleos Mexicanos, IV; 19 (upd.)
Pulsar Internacional S.A., 21
Real Turismo, S.A. de C.V., 50
Sanborn Hermanos, S.A., 20
Sears Roebuck de México, S.A. de C.V., 20
Telefonos de Mexico S.A. de C.V., 14; 63 (upd.)
Tubos de Acero de Mexico, S.A. (TAMSA), 41
TV Azteca, S.A. de C.V., 39
Valores Industriales S.A., 19
Vitro Corporativo S.A. de C.V., 34
Wal-Mart de Mexico, S.A. de C.V., 35 (upd.)

Nepal

Royal Nepal Airline Corporation, 41

Netherlands

ABN AMRO Holding, N.V., 50
AEGON N.V., III; 50 (upd.)
Akzo Nobel N.V., 13; 41 (upd.)
Algemene Bank Nederland N.V., II
Amsterdam-Rotterdam Bank N.V., II
Arcadis NV, 26
ASML Holding N.V., 50
Baan Company, 25
Buhrmann NV, 41
CNH Global N.V., 38 (upd.)
CSM N.V., 65
Deli Universal NV, 66
DSM N.V., I; 56 (upd.)
Elsevier N.V., IV
Endemol Entertainment Holding NV, 46
Equant N.V., 52
European Aeronautic Defence and Space Company EADS N.V., 52 (upd.)
Friesland Coberco Dairy Foods Holding N.V., 59
Getronics NV, 39
Granaria Holdings B.V., 66
Grand Hotel Krasnapolsky N.V., 23
Gucci Group N.V., 50
Hagemeyer N.V., 39
Head N.V., 55
Heijmans N.V., 66
Heineken N.V., I; 13 (upd.); 34 (upd.)
IHC Caland N.V., 71
Indigo NV, 26
Ispat International N.V., 30
Koninklijke Ahold N.V. (Royal Ahold), II; 16 (upd.)
Koninklijke Luchtvaart Maatschappij, N.V. (KLM Royal Dutch Airlines), I; 28 (upd.)
Koninklijke Nederlandsche Hoogovens en Staalfabrieken NV, IV
Koninklijke Nedlloyd N.V., 6; 26 (upd.)
Koninklijke Philips Electronics N.V., 50 (upd.)
Koninklijke PTT Nederland NV, V
Koninklijke Vendex KBB N.V. (Royal Vendex KBB N.V.), 62 (upd.)
Koninklijke Wessanen nv, II; 54 (upd.)
KPMG International, 10; 33 (upd.)
Laurus N.V., 65
Mammoet Transport B.V., 26
MIH Limited, 31
N.V. AMEV, III
N.V. Holdingmaatschappij De Telegraaf, 23
N.V. Koninklijke Nederlandse Vliegtuigenfabriek Fokker, I; 28 (upd.)
N.V. Nederlandse Gasunie, V

Nationale-Nederlanden N.V., III
New Holland N.V., 22
Nutreco Holding N.V., 56
Océ N.V., 24
PCM Uitgevers NV, 53
Philips Electronics N.V., II; 13 (upd.)
PolyGram N.V., 23
Prada Holding B.V., 45
Qiagen N.V., 39
Rabobank Group, 33
Randstad Holding n.v., 16; 43 (upd.)
Rodamco N.V., 26
Royal Dutch/Shell Group, IV; 49 (upd.)
Royal Grolsch NV, 54
Royal KPN N.V., 30
Royal Numico N.V., 37
Royal Packaging Industries Van Leer N.V.,
   30
Royal Ten Cate N.V., 68
Royal Vopak NV, 41
SHV Holdings N.V., 55
TNT Post Group N.V., V, 27 (upd.); 30
   (upd.)
Toolex International N.V., 26
TPG N.V., 64 (upd.)
Trader Classified Media N.V., 57
Triple P N.V., 26
Unilever N.V., II; 7 (upd.); 32 (upd.)
United Pan-Europe Communications NV,
   47
Vebego International BV, 49
Vedior NV, 35
Velcro Industries N.V., 19
Vendex International N.V., 13
VNU N.V., 27
Wegener NV, 53
Wolters Kluwer NV, 14; 33 (upd.)

Netherlands Antilles

Orthofix International NV, 72
Velcro Industries N.V., 72

New Zealand

Air New Zealand Limited, 14; 38 (upd.)
Carter Holt Harvey Ltd., 70
Fletcher Challenge Ltd., IV; 19 (upd.)
Fonterra Co-Operative Group Ltd., 58
Telecom Corporation of New Zealand
   Limited, 54
Wattie's Ltd., 7

Nigeria

Nigerian National Petroleum Corporation,
   IV; 72 (upd.)

Norway

Braathens ASA, 47
Den Norse Stats Oljeselskap AS, IV
Helly Hansen ASA, 25
Kvaerner ASA, 36
Norsk Hydro ASA, 10; 35 (upd.)
Norske Skogindustrier ASA, 63
Orkla A/S, 18
Schibsted ASA, 31
Statoil ASA, 61 (upd.)
Stolt Sea Farm Holdings PLC, 54
Telenor ASA, 69

Oman

Petroleum Development Oman LLC, IV

Pakistan

Pakistan International Airlines Corporation,
   46

Panama

Panamerican Beverages, Inc., 47
Willbros Group, Inc., 56

Peru

Southern Peru Copper Corporation, 40

Philippines

Bank of the Philippine Islands, 58
Benguet Corporation, 58
Manila Electric Company (Meralco), 56
Mercury Drug Corporation, 70
Petron Corporation, 58
Philippine Airlines, Inc., 6; 23 (upd.)
San Miguel Corporation, 15; 57 (upd.)

Poland

LOT Polish Airlines (Polskie Linie
   Lotnicze S.A.), 33
Telekomunikacja Polska SA, 50

Portugal

Banco Comercial Português, SA, 50
Banco Espírito Santo e Comercial de
   Lisboa S.A., 15
BRISA Auto-estradas de Portugal S.A., 64
Corticeira Amorim, Sociedade Gestora de
   Participaço es Sociais, S.A., 48
Electricidade de Portugal, S.A., 47
Grupo Portucel Soporcel, 60
Madeira Wine Company, S.A., 49
Petróleos de Portugal S.A., IV
Portugal Telecom SGPS S.A., 69
TAP—Air Portugal Transportes Aéreos
   Portugueses S.A., 46
Transportes Aereos Portugueses, S.A., 6

Puerto Rico

Puerto Rico Electric Power Authority, 47

Qatar

Qatar General Petroleum Corporation, IV

Romania

TAROM S.A., 64

Russia

A.S. Yakovlev Design Bureau, 15
Aeroflot—Russian International Airlines, 6;
   29 (upd.)
Alrosa Company Ltd., 62
AO VimpelCom, 48
Aviacionny Nauchno-Tehnicheskii
   Komplex im. A.N. Tupoleva, 24
AVTOVAZ Joint Stock Company, 65
Baltika Brewery Joint Stock Company, 65
Golden Telecom, Inc., 59
Irkut Corporation, 68
JSC MMC Norilsk Nickel, 48
Mobile TeleSystems OJSC, 59
OAO Gazprom, 42
OAO LUKOIL, 40
OAO NK YUKOS, 47
OAO Siberian Oil Company (Sibneft), 49
OAO Surgutneftegaz, 48
OAO Tatneft, 45
OJSC Wimm-Bill-Dann Foods, 48
RAO Unified Energy System of Russia, 45
Rostvertol plc, 62
Sberbank, 62
Severstal Joint Stock Company, 65
Sukhoi Design Bureau Aviation Scientific-
   Industrial Complex, 24

Saudi Arabia

Dallah Albaraka Group, 72
Saudi Arabian Airlines, 6; 27 (upd.)
Saudi Arabian Oil Company, IV; 17 (upd.);
   50 (upd.)
Saudi Basic Industries Corporation
   (SABIC), 58

Scotland

Arnold Clark Automobiles Ltd., 60
Distillers Company PLC, I
General Accident PLC, III
Governor and Company of the Bank of
   Scotland, The, 10
Royal Bank of Scotland Group plc, The,
   12
Scottish & Newcastle plc, 15
Scottish Hydro-Electric PLC, 13
Scottish Media Group plc, 32
ScottishPower plc, 19
Stagecoach Holdings plc, 30
Standard Life Assurance Company, The,
   III

Singapore

Asia Pacific Breweries Limited, 59
Creative Technology Ltd., 57
Flextronics International Ltd., 38
Fraser & Neave Ltd., 54
Hotel Properties Ltd., 71
Neptune Orient Lines Limited, 47
Singapore Airlines Ltd., 6; 27 (upd.)
United Overseas Bank Ltd., 56

South Africa

Anglo American Corporation of South
   Africa Limited, IV; 16 (upd.)
Barlow Rand Ltd., I
De Beers Consolidated Mines Limited/De
   Beers Centenary AG, IV; 7 (upd.); 28
   (upd.)
Dimension Data Holdings PLC, 69
Edgars Consolidated Stores Ltd., 66
Gencor Ltd., IV; 22 (upd.)
Gold Fields Ltd., IV; 62 (upd.)
Harmony Gold Mining Company Limited,
   63
Highveld Steel and Vanadium Corporation
   Limited, 59
Iscor Limited, 57
Naspers Ltd., 66
SAA (Pty) Ltd., 28
Sanlam Ltd., 68
Sappi Limited, 49
Sasol Limited, IV; 47 (upd.)
South African Breweries Limited, The, I;
   24 (upd.)
Transnet Ltd., 6

South Korea

Anam Group, 23
Asiana Airlines, Inc., 46
CJ Corporation, 62
Daewoo Group, III; 18 (upd.); 57 (upd.)
Electronics Co., Ltd., 14
Goldstar Co., Ltd., 12
Hanjin Shipping Co., Ltd., 50
Hanwha Group, 62
Hyundai Group, III; 7 (upd.); 56 (upd.)
Kia Motors Corporation, 12; 29 (upd.)
Kookmin Bank, 58
Korea Electric Power Corporation (Kepco),
   56
Korean Air Lines Co., Ltd., 6; 27 (upd.)
KT&G Corporation, 62

South Korea (*continued*)

Lucky-Goldstar, II
Pohang Iron and Steel Company Ltd., IV
POSCO, 57 (upd.)
Samick Musical Instruments Co., Ltd., 56
Samsung Electronics Co., Ltd., I; 41 (upd.)
Ssangyong Cement Industrial Co., Ltd., III;
   61 (upd.)
Tong Yang Cement Corporation, 62

Spain

Abertis Infraestructuras, S.A., 65
Adolfo Dominguez S.A., 72
Altadis S.A., 72 (upd.)
Banco Bilbao Vizcaya Argentaria S.A., II;
   48 (upd.)
Banco Central, II
Banco do Brasil S.A., II
Banco Santander Central Hispano S.A., 36
   (upd.)
Campofrío Alimentación S.A, 59
Chupa Chups S.A., 38
Compañia Española de Petróleos S.A.
   (Cepsa), IV; 56 (upd.)
Cortefiel S.A., 64
Dogi International Fabrics S.A., 52
El Corte Inglés Group, V; 26 (upd.)
ENDESA S.A., V; 46 (upd.)
Federico Paternina S.A., 69
Freixenet S.A., 71
Gas Natural SDG S.A., 69
Grupo Dragados SA, 55
Grupo Eroski, 64
Grupo Ferrovial, S.A., 40
Grupo Leche Pascual S.A., 59
Grupo Lladró S.A., 52
Iberdrola, S.A., 49
Iberia Líneas Aéreas de España S.A., 6; 36
   (upd.)
Industria de Diseño Textil S.A., 64
Instituto Nacional de Industria, I
Miquel y Costas Miquel S.A., 68
Puig Beauty and Fashion Group S.L., 60
Repsol-YPF S.A., IV; 16 (upd.); 40 (upd.)
Sol Meliá S.A., 71
Tabacalera, S.A., V; 17 (upd.)
Telefónica S.A., V; 46 (upd.)
TelePizza S.A., 33
Television Española, S.A., 7
Terra Lycos, Inc., 43
Unión Fenosa, S.A., 51
Vidrala S.A., 67
Viscofan S.A., 70

Sweden

A. Johnson & Company H.B., I
AB Volvo, I; 7 (upd.); 26 (upd.); 67 (upd.)
Aktiebolaget Electrolux, 22 (upd.)
Aktiebolaget SKF, III; 38 (upd.)
Alfa Laval AB, III; 64 (upd.)
Astra AB, I; 20 (upd.)
Atlas Copco AB, III; 28 (upd.)
Autoliv, Inc., 65
Bonnier AB, 52
BRIO AB, 24
Cardo AB, 53
Cloetta Fazer AB, 70
Electrolux AB, III; 53 (upd.)
FöreningsSparbanken AB, 69
Gambro AB, 49
Gunnebo AB, 53
Hennes & Mauritz AB, 29
Holmen AB, 52 (upd.)
ICA AB, II
Investor AB, 63
Mo och Domsjö AB, IV

Modern Times Group AB, 36
NetCom Systems AB, 26
Nobel Industries AB, 9
Nordea AB, 40
Observer AB, 55
Perstorp AB, I; 51 (upd.)
Saab Automobile AB, I; 11 (upd.); 32
   (upd.)
Sandvik AB, IV; 32 (upd.)
SAS Group, The, 34 (upd.)
Scandinavian Airlines System, I
Securitas AB, 42
Skandia Insurance Company, Ltd., 50
Skandinaviska Enskilda Banken AB, II; 56
   (upd.)
Skanska AB, 38
Stora Kopparbergs Bergslags AB, IV
Svenska Cellulosa Aktiebolaget SCA, IV;
   28 (upd.)
Svenska Handelsbanken AB, II; 50 (upd.)
Swedish Match AB, 39 (upd.)
Swedish Telecom, V
Telefonaktiebolaget LM Ericsson, V; 46
   (upd.)
TeliaSonera AB, 57 (upd.)
Vattenfall AB, 57
Vin & Spirit AB, 31

Switzerland

ABB ASEA Brown Boveri Ltd., II; 22
   (upd.)
ABB Ltd., 65 (upd.)
Adecco S.A., 36 (upd.)
Adia S.A., 6
Arthur Andersen & Company, Société
   Coopérative, 10
Ascom AG, 9
Bâloise-Holding, 40
Barry Callebaut AG, 29; 71 (upd.)
Bernina Holding AG, 47
Bodum Design Group AG, 47
Bon Appetit Holding AG, 48
Chocoladefabriken Lindt & Sprüngli AG,
   27
Ciba-Geigy Ltd., I; 8 (upd.)
Compagnie Financiere Richemont AG, 50
Coop Schweiz Genossenschaftsverband, 48
Credit Suisse Group, II; 21 (upd.); 59
   (upd.)
Danzas Group, V; 40 (upd.)
De Beers Consolidated Mines Limited/De
   Beers Centenary AG, IV; 7 (upd.); 28
   (upd.)
Elektrowatt AG, 6
F. Hoffmann-La Roche Ltd., I; 50 (upd.)
Fédération Internationale de Football
   Association, 27
Firmenich International S.A., 60
Gate Gourmet International AG, 70
Geberit AG, 49
Georg Fischer AG Schaffhausen, 61
Givaudan SA, 43
Holderbank Financière Glaris Ltd., III
International Olympic Committee, 44
Jacobs Suchard A.G., II
Julius Baer Holding AG, 52
Keramik Holding AG Laufen, 51
Kraft Jacobs Suchard AG, 26 (upd.)
Kudelski Group SA, 44
Kuehne & Nagel International AG, V; 53
   (upd.)
Kuoni Travel Holding Ltd., 40
Liebherr-International AG, 64
Logitech International S.A., 28; 69 (upd.)
Maus Frères SA, 48
Mettler-Toledo International Inc., 30
Migros-Genossenschafts-Bund, 68

Montres Rolex S.A., 13; 34 (upd.)
Nestlé S.A., II; 7 (upd.); 28 (upd.); 71
   (upd.)
Novartis AG, 39 (upd.)
Panalpina World Transport (Holding) Ltd.,
   47
Phoenix Mecano AG, 61
Ricola Ltd., 62
Rieter Holding AG, 42
Roland Murten A.G., 7
Sandoz Ltd., I
Schindler Holding AG, 29
Schweizerische Post-, Telefon- und
   Telegrafen-Betriebe, V
Serono S.A., 47
STMicroelectronics NV, 52
Sulzer Ltd., III; 68 (upd.)
Swarovski International Holding AG, 40
Swatch Group SA, The, 26
Swedish Match S.A., 12
Swiss Air Transport Company, Ltd., I
Swiss Bank Corporation, II
Swiss Federal Railways (Schweizerische
   Bundesbahnen), The, V
Swiss International Air Lines Ltd., 48
Swiss Reinsurance Company
   (Schweizerische Rückversicherungs-
   Gesellschaft), III; 46 (upd.)
Swisscom AG, 58
Swissport International Ltd., 70
TAG Heuer International SA, 25
Tamedia AG, 53
Tetra Pak International SA, 53
UBS AG, 52 (upd.)
Union Bank of Switzerland, II
Victorinox AG, 21
Winterthur Group, III; 68 (upd.)
Zurich Financial Services, 42 (upd.)
Zürich Versicherungs-Gesellschaft, III

Taiwan

Acer Inc., 16
AU Optronics Corporation, 67
BenQ Corporation, 67
China Airlines, 34
Directorate General of Telecommunications,
   7
EVA Airways Corporation, 51
Evergreen Marine Corporation (Taiwan)
   Ltd., 13; 50 (upd.)
First International Computer, Inc., 56
Formosa Plastics Corporation, 14; 58
   (upd.)
Hon Hai Precision Industry Co., Ltd., 59
Quanta Computer Inc., 47
Taiwan Semiconductor Manufacturing
   Company Ltd., 47
Tatung Co., 23
Yageo Corporation, 16

Thailand

Charoen Pokphand Group, 62
Electricity Generating Authority of
   Thailand (EGAT), 56
Krung Thai Bank Public Company Ltd., 69
Pranda Jewelry plc, 70
PTT Public Company Ltd., 56
Siam Cement Public Company Limited,
   The, 56
Thai Airways International Public
   Company Limited, 6; 27 (upd.)
Topaz Group, Inc., The, 62

Tunisia

Société Tunisienne de l'Air-Tunisair, 49

Turkey

Haci Omer Sabanci Holdings A.S., 55
Koç Holding A.S., I; 54 (upd.)
Turkish Airlines Inc. (Türk Hava Yollari
  A.O.), 72
Turkiye Is Bankasi A.S., 61
Türkiye Petrolleri Anonim Ortakliği, IV

Ukraine

Antonov Design Bureau, 53

United Arab Emirates

Abu Dhabi National Oil Company, IV; 45
  (upd.)
Emirates Group, The, 39

United Kingdom

Aardman Animations Ltd., 61
Abbey National plc, 10; 39 (upd.)
Aegis Group plc, 6
AG Barr plc, 64
Aggregate Industries plc, 36
Aggreko Plc, 45
Airtours Plc, 27
Albert Fisher Group plc, The, 41
All England Lawn Tennis & Croquet Club,
  The, 54
Alldays plc, 49
Allders plc, 37
Allied Domecq PLC, 29
Allied-Lyons PLC, I
Alvis Plc, 47
Amersham PLC, 50
Amey Plc, 47
Amnesty International, 50
Amstrad plc, III; 48 (upd.)
AMVESCAP PLC, 65
Anglo American PLC, 50 (upd.)
Anker BV, 53
Antofagasta plc, 65
Arcadia Group plc, 28 (upd.)
Argyll Group PLC, II
Arjo Wiggins Appleton p.l.c., 34
Arriva PLC, 69
ASDA Group Ltd., II; 28 (upd.); 64 (upd.)
Ashtead Group plc, 34
Associated British Foods plc, II; 13 (upd.);
  41 (upd.)
Associated British Ports Holdings Plc, 45
Aston Villa plc, 41
AstraZeneca PLC, 50 (upd.)
AT&T Istel Ltd., 14
Avecia Group PLC, 63
Aviva PLC, 50 (upd.)
BAA plc, 10; 33 (upd.)
Babcock International Group PLC, 69
Balfour Beatty plc, 36 (upd.)
Barclays plc, II; 20 (upd.); 64 (upd.)
Barings PLC, 14
Barratt Developments plc, I; 56 (upd.)
Bass PLC, I; 15 (upd.); 38 (upd.)
Bat Industries PLC, I; 20 (upd.)
Belleek Pottery Ltd., 71
Bellway Plc, 45
Benfield Greig Group plc, 53
Bettys & Taylors of Harrogate Ltd., 72
Bhs plc, 17
BICC PLC, III
Big Food Group plc, The, 68 (upd.)
Birthdays Ltd., 70
Blacks Leisure Group plc, 39
Blue Circle Industries PLC, III
BOC Group plc, I; 25 (upd.)
Body Shop International plc, The, 11; 53
  (upd.)
Bodycote International PLC, 63

Bonhams 1793 Ltd., 72
Booker Cash & Carry Ltd., 13; 31 (upd.);
  68 (upd.)
Boots Company PLC, The, V; 24 (upd.)
Bowater PLC, IV
Bowthorpe plc, 33
BP p.l.c., 45 (upd.)
Bradford & Bingley PLC, 65
Brake Bros plc, 45
Bristow Helicopters Ltd., 70
Britannia Soft Drinks Ltd. (Britvic), 71
British Aerospace plc, I; 24 (upd.)
British Airways PLC, I; 14 (upd.); 43
  (upd.)
British American Tobacco PLC, 50 (upd.)
British Broadcasting Corporation Ltd., 7;
  21 (upd.)
British Coal Corporation, IV
British Energy Plc, 49
British Gas plc, V
British Land Plc, 54
British Midland plc, 38
British Museum, The, 71
British Nuclear Fuels plc, 6
British Petroleum Company plc, The, IV; 7
  (upd.); 21 (upd.)
British Railways Board, V
British Sky Broadcasting Group plc, 20; 60
  (upd.)
British Steel plc, IV; 19 (upd.)
British Telecommunications plc, V; 15
  (upd.)
British Vita plc, 9; 33 (upd.)
British World Airlines Ltd., 18
British-Borneo Oil & Gas PLC, 34
BT Group plc, 49 (upd.)
BTR PLC, I
BTR Siebe plc, 27
Budgens Ltd., 59
Bunzl plc, IV; 31 (upd.)
Burberry Ltd., 17; 41 (upd.)
Burmah Castrol PLC, IV; 30 (upd.)
Burton Group plc, The, V
Business Post Group plc, 46
C&J Clark International Ltd., 52
C.I. Traders Limited, 61
Cable and Wireless plc, V; 25 (upd.)
Cadbury Schweppes PLC, II; 49 (upd.)
Caffè Nero Group PLC, 63
Canary Wharf Group Plc, 30
Capita Group PLC, 69
Capital Radio plc, 35
Caradon plc, 20 (upd.)
Carbo PLC, 67 (upd.)
Carlton Communications PLC, 15; 50
  (upd.)
Cartier Monde, 29
Cattles plc, 58
Cazenove Group plc, 72
Central Independent Television, 7; 23
  (upd.)
Centrica plc, 29 (upd.)
Chelsfield PLC, 67
Cheltenham & Gloucester PLC, 61
Christian Salvesen Plc, 45
Christie's International plc, 15; 39 (upd.)
Chrysalis Group plc, 40
Chubb, PLC, 50
Clifford Chance LLP, 38
Clinton Cards plc, 39
Close Brothers Group plc, 39
Co-operative Group (CWS) Ltd., 51
Coats plc, V; 44 (upd.)
Cobham plc, 30
COLT Telecom Group plc, 41
Commercial Union PLC, III
Compass Group PLC, 34

Cookson Group plc, III; 44 (upd.)
Corus Group plc, 49 (upd.)
Courtaulds plc, V; 17 (upd.)
Courts Plc, 45
Cranswick plc, 40
Croda International Plc, 45
Daily Mail and General Trust plc, 19
Dairy Crest Group plc, 32
Dalgety, PLC, II
Davis Service Group PLC, 45
Dawson Holdings PLC, 43
De La Rue plc, 10; 34 (upd.)
Debenhams Plc, 28
Denby Group plc, 44
Denison International plc, 46
Dennis Publishing Ltd., 62
Devro plc, 55
Diageo plc, 24 (upd.)
Dixons Group plc, V; 19 (upd.); 49 (upd.)
Dorling Kindersley Holdings plc, 20
Dresdner Kleinwort Wasserstein, 60 (upd.)
DS Smith Plc, 61
Dyson Group PLC, 71
easyJet Airline Company Limited, 39
ECC Group plc, III
Economist Group Ltd., The, 67
Electrocomponents PLC, 50
Elementis plc, 40 (upd.)
EMAP plc, 35
EMI Group plc, 22 (upd.)
Energis plc, 47
English China Clays Ltd., 15 (upd.); 40
  (upd.)
Enodis plc, 68
Enterprise Inns plc, 59
Enterprise Oil PLC, 11; 50 (upd.)
Esporta plc, 35
Eurotunnel Group, 13; 37 (upd.)
Exel plc, 51 (upd.)
Fairclough Construction Group PLC, I
Fat Face Ltd., 68
Findel plc, 60
First Choice Holidays PLC, 40
Fisons plc, 9; 23 (upd.)
FKI Plc, 57
French Connection Group plc, 41
Fuller Smith & Turner P.L.C., 38
Gallaher Group Plc, 49 (upd.)
Gallaher Limited, V; 19 (upd.)
Gateway Corporation Ltd., The, II
Geest Plc, 38
General Electric Company PLC, II
George Wimpey PLC, 12; 51 (upd.)
GKN plc, III; 38 (upd.)
GlaxoSmithKline plc, I; 9 (upd.); 46 (upd.)
Glotel plc, 53
Go-Ahead Group Plc, The, 28
Granada Group PLC, II; 24 (upd.)
Grand Metropolitan PLC, I; 14 (upd.)
Great Universal Stores plc, The, V; 19
  (upd.)
Greenalls Group PLC, The, 21
Greene King plc, 31
Greggs PLC, 65
Guardian Financial Services, 64 (upd.)
Guardian Media Group plc, 53
Guardian Royal Exchange Plc, 11
Guinness/UDV, I; 43 (upd.)
GUS plc, 47 (upd.)
GWR Group plc, 39
Hammerson plc, 40
Hammerson Property Investment and
  Development Corporation plc, The, IV
Hanson PLC, III; 7 (upd.); 30 (upd.)
Harrisons & Crosfield plc, III
Harrods Holdings, 47
Hartstone Group plc, The, 14

United Kingdom (*continued*)

Hawker Siddeley Group Public Limited Company, III
Haynes Publishing Group P.L.C., 71
Hays Plc, 27
Hazlewood Foods plc, 32
Her Majesty's Stationery Office, 7
Hillsdown Holdings plc, II; 24 (upd.)
Hilton Group plc, 49 (upd.)
HIT Entertainment PLC, 40
HMV Group plc, 59
House of Fraser PLC, 45
HSBC Holdings plc, 12; 26 (upd.)
Huntingdon Life Sciences Group plc, 42
Ibstock Brick Ltd., 14; 37 (upd.)
ICL plc, 6
IMI plc, 9
Imperial Chemical Industries PLC, I; 50 (upd.)
Imperial Tobacco Group PLC, 50
Inchcape PLC, III; 16 (upd.); 50 (upd.)
Informa Group plc, 58
Inter Link Foods PLC, 61
International Power PLC, 50 (upd.)
Invensys PLC, 50 (upd.)
IPC Magazines Limited, 7
J Sainsbury plc, II; 13 (upd.); 38 (upd.)
James Beattie plc, 43
Jarvis plc, 39
JD Wetherspoon plc, 30
Jersey European Airways (UK) Ltd., 61
JJB Sports plc, 32
John Brown PLC, I
John Laing plc, I; 51 (upd.)
John Lewis Partnership plc, V; 42 (upd.)
John Menzies plc, 39
Johnson Matthey PLC, IV; 16 (upd.); 49 (upd.)
Johnston Press plc, 35
Kelda Group plc, 45
Kennecott Corporation, 7; 27 (upd.)
Kidde plc, 44 (upd.)
Kingfisher plc, V; 24 (upd.)
Kleinwort Benson Group PLC, II
Kvaerner ASA, 36
Kwik-Fit Holdings plc, 54
Ladbroke Group PLC, II; 21 (upd.)
Lafarge Cement UK, 54 (upd.)
Land Securities PLC, IV; 49 (upd.)
Laura Ashley Holdings plc, 13; 37 (upd.)
Laurel Pub Company Limited, The, 59
Legal & General Group plc, III; 24 (upd.)
Littlewoods plc, V; 42 (upd.)
Lloyd's of London, III; 22 (upd.)
Lloyds TSB Group plc, II; 47 (upd.)
Loganair Ltd., 68
Logica plc, 14; 37 (upd.)
London Regional Transport, 6
London Scottish Bank plc, 70
London Stock Exchange Limited, 34
Lonmin plc, 66 (upd.)
Lonrho Plc, 21
Lookers plc, 71
Lotus Cars Ltd., 14
Lucas Industries PLC, III
Luminar Plc, 40
Macallan Distillers Ltd., The, 63
Madge Networks N.V., 26
Manchester United Football Club plc, 30
Marconi plc, 33 (upd.)
Marks and Spencer p.l.c., V; 24 (upd.)
Marshall Amplification plc, 62
Martin-Baker Aircraft Company Limited, 61
Matalan PLC, 49
Maxwell Communication Corporation plc, IV; 7 (upd.)

McKechnie plc, 34
Meggitt PLC, 34
MEPC plc, IV
Mercury Communications, Ltd., 7
Mersey Docks and Harbour Company, The, 30
Metal Box PLC, I
Michael Page International plc, 45
Midland Bank PLC, II; 17 (upd.)
Millennium & Copthorne Hotels plc, 71
Mirror Group Newspapers plc, 7; 23 (upd.)
Misys plc, 45; 46
Mitchells & Butlers PLC, 59
Molins plc, 51
Monsoon plc, 39
Morgan Grenfell Group PLC, II
Moss Bros Group plc, 51
Mothercare UK Ltd., 17
Mulberry Group PLC, 71
N M Rothschild & Sons Limited, 39
National Express Group PLC, 50
National Power PLC, 12
National Westminster Bank PLC, II
New Look Group plc, 35
Newsquest plc, 32
Next plc, 29
NFC plc, 6
Nichols plc, 44
North West Water Group plc, 11
Northern Foods plc, 10; 61 (upd.)
Northern Rock plc, 33
Norwich & Peterborough Building Society, 55
Novar plc, 49 (upd.)
NTL Inc., 65
Ocean Group plc, 6
Old Mutual PLC, 61
Ottakar's plc, 64
Pearson plc, IV; 46 (upd.)
Peninsular & Oriental Steam Navigation Company (Bovis Division), The, I
Peninsular and Oriental Steam Navigation Company, The, V; 38 (upd.)
Pennon Group Plc, 45
Pentland Group plc, 20
PIC International Group PLC, 24 (upd.)
Pilkington plc, III; 34 (upd.)
Plessey Company, PLC, The, II
Porcelain and Fine China Companies Ltd., The, 69
Post Office Group, V
Posterscope Worldwide, 70
Powell Duffryn plc, 31
Powergen PLC, 11; 50 (upd.)
Prudential plc, 48 (upd.)
Psion PLC, 45
Punch Taverns plc, 70
PZ Cussons plc, 72
R. Griggs Group Limited, 23
Racal Electronics PLC, II
Ragdoll Productions Ltd., 51
Railtrack Group PLC, 50
Raleigh UK Ltd., 65
Rank Group plc, The, II; 14 (upd.); 64 (upd.)
Ranks Hovis McDougall Limited, II; 28 (upd.)
Rathbone Brothers plc, 70
Really Useful Group, The, 26
Reckitt Benckiser plc, II; 42 (upd.)
Redland plc, III
Redrow Group plc, 31
Reed Elsevier plc, IV; 17 (upd.); 31 (upd.)
Renishaw plc, 46
Rentokil Initial Plc, 47
Reuters Group PLC, IV; 22 (upd.); 63 (upd.)

Rexam PLC, 32 (upd.)
Rio Tinto PLC, 19 (upd.); 50 (upd.)
RMC Group p.l.c., III; 34 (upd.)
Rolls-Royce Group PLC, 67 (upd.)
Rolls-Royce plc, I; 7 (upd.); 21 (upd.)
Ronson PLC, 49
Rothmans UK Holdings Limited, V; 19 (upd.)
Rotork plc, 46
Rover Group Ltd., 7; 21 (upd.)
Rowntree Mackintosh, II
Royal & Sun Alliance Insurance Group plc, 55 (upd.)
Royal Bank of Scotland Group plc, The, 38 (upd.)
Royal Doulton plc, 14; 38 (upd.)
Royal Dutch Petroleum Company/ The Shell Transport and Trading Company p.l.c., IV
Royal Insurance Holdings PLC, III
RTZ Corporation PLC, The, IV
Rugby Group plc, The, 31
Saatchi & Saatchi PLC, I
SABMiller plc, 59 (upd.)
Safeway PLC, 50 (upd.)
Sage Group, The, 43
St. James's Place Capital, plc, 71
Sanctuary Group PLC, The, 69
SBC Warburg, 14
Schroders plc, 42
Scottish & Newcastle plc, 35 (upd.)
Scottish and Southern Energy plc, 66 (upd.)
Scottish Power plc, 49 (upd.)
Scottish Radio Holding plc, 41
SDL PLC, 67
Sea Containers Ltd., 29
Sears plc, V
Securicor Plc, 45
Seddon Group Ltd., 67
Selfridges Plc, 34
Serco Group plc, 47
Severn Trent PLC, 12; 38 (upd.)
SFI Group plc, 51
Shanks Group plc, 45
Shepherd Neame Limited, 30
SIG plc, 71
Signet Group PLC, 61
Singer & Friedlander Group plc, 41
Slough Estates PLC, IV; 50 (upd.)
Smith & Nephew plc, 17;41 (upd.)
SmithKline Beecham plc, III; 32 (upd.)
Smiths Industries PLC, 25
Somerfield plc, 47 (upd.)
Southern Electric PLC, 13
Spirax-Sarco Engineering plc, 59
SSL International plc, 49
St Ives plc, 34
Standard Chartered plc, II; 48 (upd.)
Stanley Leisure plc, 66
STC PLC, III
Stirling Group plc, 62
Stoddard International plc, 72
Stoll-Moss Theatres Ltd., 34
Stolt-Nielsen S.A., 42
Storehouse PLC, 16
Strix Ltd., 51
Sun Alliance Group PLC, III
Sytner Group plc, 45
Tarmac plc, III; 28 (upd.)
Tate & Lyle PLC, II; 42 (upd.)
Taylor & Francis Group plc, 44
Taylor Nelson Sofres plc, 34
Taylor Woodrow plc, I; 38 (upd.)
Tesco plc, II; 24 (upd.); 68 (upd.)
Thames Water plc, 11
Thistle Hotels PLC, 54

Thorn Emi PLC, I
Thorn plc, 24
Thorntons plc, 46
TI Group plc, 17
Tibbett & Britten Group plc, 32
Tiger Aspect Productions Ltd., 72
Time Out Group Ltd., 68
Tomkins plc, 11; 44 (upd.)
Travis Perkins plc, 34
Trinity Mirror plc, 49 (upd.)
Triumph Motorcycles Ltd., 53
Trusthouse Forte PLC, III
TSB Group plc, 12
Tussauds Group, The, 55
Ulster Television PLC, 71
Ultramar PLC, IV
Unigate PLC, II; 28 (upd.)
Unilever PLC, II; 7 (upd.); 32 (upd.)
United Biscuits (Holdings) plc, II; 42
  (upd.)
United Business Media plc, 52 (upd.)
United News & Media plc, IV; 28 (upd.)
United Utilities PLC, 52 (upd.)
Vendôme Luxury Group plc, 27
Vickers plc, 27
Virgin Group, 12; 32 (upd.)
Viridian Group plc, 64
Vodafone Group PLC, 11; 36 (upd.)
Vosper Thornycroft Holding plc, 41
Walkers Snack Foods Ltd., 70
Wassall Plc, 18
Waterford Wedgwood Holdings PLC, 12
Watson Wyatt Worldwide, 42
Watts of Lydney Group Ltd., 71
Weetabix Limited, 61
Wellcome Foundation Ltd., The, I
WH Smith PLC, V, 42 (upd.)
Whatman plc, 46
Whitbread PLC, I; 20 (upd.); 52 (upd.)
Whittard of Chelsea Plc, 61
Wilkinson Sword Ltd., 60
William Grant & Sons Ltd., 60
William Hill Organization Limited, 49
Willis Corroon Group plc, 25
Wilson Bowden Plc, 45
Wincanton plc, 52
Wm. Morrison Supermarkets PLC, 38
Wolseley plc, 64
Wolverhampton & Dudley Breweries, PLC,
  The, 57
Wood Hall Trust PLC, I
Woolwich plc, The, 30
WPP Group plc, 6; 48 (upd.)
WS Atkins Plc, 45
Young & Co.'s Brewery, P.L.C., 38
Yule Catto & Company plc, 54
Zeneca Group PLC, 21
Zomba Records Ltd., 52

United States

A & E Television Networks, 32
A & W Brands, Inc., 25
A-dec, Inc., 53
A-Mark Financial Corporation, 71
A. Schulman, Inc., 8; 49 (upd.)
A.B. Watley Group Inc., 45
A.B.Dick Company, 28
A.C. Moore Arts & Crafts, Inc., 30
A.G. Edwards, Inc., 8; 32
A.H. Belo Corporation, 10; 30 (upd.)
A.L. Pharma Inc., 12
A.M. Castle & Co., 25
A.O. Smith Corporation, 11; 40 (upd.)
A.T. Cross Company, 17; 49 (upd.)
AAF-McQuay Incorporated, 26
AAON, Inc., 22
AAR Corp., 28

Aaron Rents, Inc., 14; 35 (upd.)
AARP, 27
Aavid Thermal Technologies, Inc., 29
Abatix Corp., 57
Abbott Laboratories, I; 11 (upd.); 40 (upd.)
ABC Appliance, Inc., 10
ABC Carpet & Home Co. Inc., 26
ABC Family Worldwide, Inc., 52
ABC Rail Products Corporation, 18
ABC Supply Co., Inc., 22
Abercrombie & Fitch Co., 15; 35 (upd.)
Abigail Adams National Bancorp, Inc., 23
Abiomed, Inc., 47
ABM Industries Incorporated, 25 (upd.)
Abrams Industries Inc., 23
Academy of Television Arts & Sciences,
  Inc., 55
Academy Sports & Outdoors, 27
Acadian Ambulance & Air Med Services,
  Inc., 39
Acclaim Entertainment Inc., 24
ACCO World Corporation, 7; 51 (upd.)
ACE Cash Express, Inc., 33
Ace Hardware Corporation, 12; 35 (upd.)
Aceto Corp., 38
Ackerley Communications, Inc., 9
Acme United Corporation, 70
Acme-Cleveland Corp., 13
ACNielsen Corporation, 13; 38 (upd.)
Acorn Products, Inc., 55
Acsys, Inc., 44
Action Performance Companies, Inc., 27
Activision, Inc., 32
Acushnet Company, 64
Acuson Corporation, 10; 36 (upd.)
Acxiom Corporation, 35
Adams Golf, Inc., 37
Adaptec, Inc., 31
ADC Telecommunications, Inc., 10; 30
  (upd.)
Adelphia Communications Corporation, 17;
  52 (upd.)
ADESA, Inc., 71
Administaff, Inc., 52
Adobe Systems Inc., 10; 33 (upd.)
Adolph Coors Company, I; 13 (upd.); 36
  (upd.)
ADT Security Services, Inc., 12; 44 (upd.)
Adtran Inc., 22
Advance Auto Parts, Inc., 57
Advance Publications Inc., IV; 19 (upd.)
Advanced Circuits Inc., 67
Advanced Fibre Communications, Inc., 63
Advanced Marketing Services, Inc., 34
Advanced Micro Devices, Inc., 6; 30 (upd.)
Advanced Technology Laboratories, Inc., 9
Advanstar Communications, Inc., 57
Advanta Corporation, 8; 38 (upd.)
Advantica Restaurant Group, Inc., 27
  (upd.)
Adventist Health, 53
Advo, Inc., 6; 53 (upd.)
Advocat Inc., 46
AEI Music Network Inc., 35
AEP Industries, Inc., 36
Aerojet-General Corp., 63
Aeronca Inc., 46
Aeroquip Corporation, 16
Aerosonic Corporation, 69
AES Corporation, The, 10; 13 (upd.); 53
  (upd.)
Aetna Inc., III; 21 (upd.); 63 (upd.)
AFC Enterprises, Inc., 32
Affiliated Computer Services, Inc., 61
Affiliated Foods Inc., 53
Affiliated Publications, Inc., 7
Affinity Group Holding Inc., 56

AFLAC Incorporated, 10 (upd.); 38 (upd.)
Africare, 59
After Hours Formalwear Inc., 60
Ag Services of America, Inc., 59
Ag-Chem Equipment Company, Inc., 17
AGCO Corporation, 13; 67 (upd.)
Agere Systems Inc., 61
Agilent Technologies Inc., 38
Agway, Inc., 7; 21 (upd.)
AHL Services, Inc., 27
Air & Water Technologies Corporation, 6
Air Express International Corporation, 13
Air Methods Corporation, 53
Air Products and Chemicals, Inc., I; 10
  (upd.)
Air Wisconsin Airlines Corporation, 55
Airborne Freight Corporation, 6; 34 (upd.)
Airgas, Inc., 54
AirTouch Communications, 11
AirTran Holdings, Inc., 22
AK Steel Holding Corporation, 19; 41
  (upd.)
Akamai Technologies, Inc., 71
Akin, Gump, Strauss, Hauer & Feld,
  L.L.P., 33
Akorn, Inc., 32
Alabama Farmers Cooperative, Inc., 63
Alamo Group Inc., 32
Alamo Rent A Car, Inc., 6; 24 (upd.)
ALARIS Medical Systems, Inc., 65
Alaska Air Group, Inc., 6; 29 (upd.)
Alaska Railroad Corporation, 60
Alba-Waldensian, Inc., 30
Albany International Corporation, 8; 51
  (upd.)
Albemarle Corporation, 59
Alberto-Culver Company, 8; 36 (upd.)
Albertson's, Inc., II; 7 (upd.); 30 (upd.); 65
  (upd.)
Alco Health Services Corporation, III
Alco Standard Corporation, I
Alcoa Inc., 56 (upd.)
Aldila Inc., 46
Aldus Corporation, 10
Alex Lee Inc., 18; 44 (upd.)
Alexander & Alexander Services Inc., 10
Alexander & Baldwin, Inc., 10; 40 (upd.)
Alexander's, Inc., 45
Alfa Corporation, 60
Alico, Inc., 63
All American Communications Inc., 20
Alleghany Corporation, 10; 60 (upd.)
Allegheny Energy, Inc., 38 (upd.)
Allegheny Ludlum Corporation, 8
Allegheny Power System, Inc., V
Allen Foods, Inc., 60
Allen Organ Company, 33
Allen Systems Group, Inc., 59
Allen-Edmonds Shoe Corporation, 61
Allergan, Inc., 10; 30 (upd.)
Alliance Capital Management Holding
  L.P., 63
Alliance Entertainment Corp., 17
Alliant Techsystems Inc., 8; 30 (upd.)
Allied Defense Group, Inc., The, 65
Allied Healthcare Products, Inc., 24
Allied Products Corporation, 21
Allied Signal Engines, 9
Allied Waste Industries, Inc., 50
Allied Worldwide, Inc., 49
AlliedSignal Inc., I; 22 (upd.)
Allison Gas Turbine Division, 9
Allmerica Financial Corporation, 63
Allou Health & Beauty Care, Inc., 28
Alloy, Inc., 55
Allstate Corporation, The, 10; 27 (upd.)
ALLTEL Corporation, 6; 46 (upd.)

United States (*continued*)

Alltrista Corporation, 30

Allwaste, Inc., 18

Aloha Airlines, Incorporated, 24

Alpharma Inc., 35 (upd.)

Alpine Confections, Inc., 71

Alpine Lace Brands, Inc., 18

AltaVista Company, 43

Altera Corporation, 18; 43 (upd.)

Alternative Tentacles Records, 66

Alterra Healthcare Corporation, 42

Alticor Inc., 71 (upd.)

Altiris, Inc., 65

Altron Incorporated, 20

Aluminum Company of America, IV; 20 (upd.)

Alvin Ailey Dance Foundation, Inc., 52

ALZA Corporation, 10; 36 (upd.)

Amalgamated Bank, 60

AMAX Inc., IV

Amazon.com, Inc., 25; 56 (upd.)

AMB Property Corporation, 57

Ambac Financial Group, Inc., 65

Ambassadors International, Inc., 68 (upd.)

Amblin Entertainment, 21

AMC Entertainment Inc., 12; 35 (upd.)

AMCOL International Corporation, 59 (upd.)

AMCORE Financial Inc., 44

Amdahl Corporation, III; 14 (upd.); 40 (upd.)

Amdocs Ltd., 47

Amedysis, Inc., 53

Amerada Hess Corporation, IV; 21 (upd.); 55 (upd.)

Amerco, 6

AMERCO, 67 (upd.)

Ameren Corporation, 60 (upd.)

America Online, Inc., 10; 26 (upd.)

America West Holdings Corporation, 6; 34 (upd.)

America's Car-Mart, Inc., 64

America's Favorite Chicken Company, Inc., 7

American Airlines, I; 6 (upd.)

American Axle & Manufacturing Holdings, Inc., 67

American Banknote Corporation, 30

American Bar Association, 35

American Biltrite Inc., 16; 43 (upd.)

American Brands, Inc., V

American Building Maintenance Industries, Inc., 6

American Business Information, Inc., 18

American Business Products, Inc., 20

American Cancer Society, The, 24

American Cast Iron Pipe Company, 50

American Civil Liberties Union (ACLU), 60

American Classic Voyages Company, 27

American Coin Merchandising, Inc., 28

American Colloid Co., 13

American Crystal Sugar Company, 9; 32 (upd.)

American Cyanamid, I; 8 (upd.)

American Eagle Outfitters, Inc., 24; 55 (upd.)

American Electric Power Company, Inc., V; 45 (upd.)

American Express Company, II; 10 (upd.); 38 (upd.)

American Family Corporation, III

American Financial Group Inc., III; 48 (upd.)

American Foods Group, 43

American Furniture Company, Inc., 21

American General Corporation, III; 10 (upd.); 46 (upd.)

American General Finance Corp., 11

American Girl, Inc., 69 (upd.)

American Golf Corporation, 45

American Gramaphone LLC, 52

American Greetings Corporation, 7; 22 (upd.); 59 (upd.)

American Healthways, Inc., 65

American Home Mortgage Holdings, Inc., 46

American Home Products, I; 10 (upd.)

American Homestar Corporation, 18; 41 (upd.)

American Institute of Certified Public Accountants (AICPA), 44

American International Group, Inc., III; 15 (upd.); 47 (upd.)

American Italian Pasta Company, 27

American Lawyer Media Holdings, Inc., 32

American Locker Group Incorporated, 34

American Lung Association, 48

American Maize-Products Co., 14

American Management Systems, Inc., 11

American Media, Inc., 27

American Medical Association, 39

American Medical International, Inc., III

American Medical Response, Inc., 39

American Motors Corporation, I

American National Insurance Company, 8; 27 (upd.)

American Pad & Paper Company, 20

American Pharmaceutical Partners, Inc., 69

American Pop Corn Company, 59

American Power Conversion Corporation, 24; 67 (upd.)

American Premier Underwriters, Inc., 10

American President Companies Ltd., 6

American Printing House for the Blind, 26

American Re Corporation, 10; 35 (upd.)

American Red Cross, 40

American Residential Mortgage Corporation, 8

American Retirement Corporation, 42

American Rice, Inc., 33

American Safety Razor Company, 20

American Skiing Company, 28

American Society for the Prevention of Cruelty to Animals (ASPCA), 68

American Society of Composers, Authors and Publishers (ASCAP), The, 29

American Software Inc., 25

American Standard Companies Inc., III; 30 (upd.)

American States Water Company, 46

American Stores Company, II; 22 (upd.)

American Technical Ceramics Corp., 67

American Tourister, Inc., 16

American Tower Corporation, 33

American Vanguard Corporation, 47

American Water Works Company, Inc., 6; 38 (upd.)

American Woodmark Corporation, 31

AMERIGROUP Corporation, 69

Amerihost Properties, Inc., 30

AmeriSource Health Corporation, 37 (upd.)

AmerisourceBergen Corporation, 64 (upd.)

Ameristar Casinos, Inc., 33; 69 (upd.)

Ameritech Corporation, V; 18 (upd.)

Ameritrade Holding Corporation, 34

Ameriwood Industries International Corp., 17

Amerock Corporation, 53

Ameron International Corporation, 67

Ames Department Stores, Inc., 9; 30 (upd.)

AMETEK, Inc., 9

AMF Bowling, Inc., 40

Amfac/JMB Hawaii L.L.C., I; 24 (upd.)

Amgen, Inc., 10; 30 (upd.)

AMICAS, Inc., 69

Amkor Technology, Inc., 69

Amoco Corporation, IV; 14 (upd.)

Amoskeag Company, 8

AMP Incorporated, II; 14 (upd.)

Ampacet Corporation, 67

Ampex Corporation, 17

Amphenol Corporation, 40

AMR Corporation, 28 (upd.); 52 (upd.)

AMREP Corporation, 21

Amscan Holdings, Inc., 61

AmSouth Bancorporation, 12; 48 (upd.)

Amsted Industries Incorporated, 7

AmSurg Corporation, 48

Amtran, Inc., 34

Amway Corporation, III; 13 (upd.); 30 (upd.)

Amylin Pharmaceuticals, Inc., 67

Anadarko Petroleum Corporation, 10; 52 (upd.)

Anaheim Angels Baseball Club, Inc., 53

Analog Devices, Inc., 10

Analogic Corporation, 23

Analysts International Corporation, 36

Analytic Sciences Corporation, 10

Analytical Surveys, Inc., 33

Anaren Microwave, Inc., 33

Anchor Bancorp, Inc., 10

Anchor Brewing Company, 47

Anchor Gaming, 24

Anchor Hocking Glassware, 13

Andersen, 10; 29 (upd.); 68 (upd.)

Anderson-DuBose Company, The, 60

Andersons, Inc., The, 31

Andrew Corporation, 10; 32 (upd.)

Andrews Kurth, LLP, 71

Andrews McMeel Universal, 40

Andronico's Market, 70

Andrx Corporation, 55

Angelica Corporation, 15; 43 (upd.)

Anheuser-Busch Companies, Inc., I; 10 (upd.); 34 (upd.)

Annie's Homegrown, Inc., 59

AnnTaylor Stores Corporation, 13; 37 (upd.); 67 (upd.)

ANR Pipeline Co., 17

Anschutz Corporation, The, 12; 36 (upd.)

Ansoft Corporation, 63

Anteon Corporation, 57

Anthem Electronics, Inc., 13

Anthony & Sylvan Pools Corporation, 56

Antioch Company, The, 40

AOL Time Warner Inc., 57 (upd.)

Aon Corporation, III; 45 (upd.)

Apache Corporation, 10; 32 (upd.)

Apartment Investment and Management Company, 49

Apex Digital, Inc., 63

APi Group, Inc., 64

APL Limited, 61 (upd.)

Apogee Enterprises, Inc., 8

Apollo Group, Inc., 24

Applause Inc., 24

Apple Bank for Savings, 59

Apple Computer, Inc., III; 6 (upd.); 36 (upd.)

Applebee's International Inc., 14; 35 (upd.)

Appliance Recycling Centers of America, Inc., 42

Applica Incorporated, 43 (upd.)

Applied Bioscience International, Inc., 10

Applied Films Corporation, 48

Applied Materials, Inc., 10; 46 (upd.)

Applied Micro Circuits Corporation, 38

Applied Power, Inc., 9; 32 (upd.)

AptarGroup, Inc., 69
Aqua Alliance Inc., 32 (upd.)
Aquila, Inc., 50 (upd.)
AR Accessories Group, Inc., 23
ARA Services, II
ARAMARK Corporation, 13; 41 (upd.)
Arandell Corporation, 37
Arbitron Company, The, 38
Arbor Drugs Inc., 12
Arby's Inc., 14
Arch Mineral Corporation, 7
Arch Wireless, Inc., 39
Archer-Daniels-Midland Company, I; 11 (upd.); 32 (upd.)
Archie Comics Publications, Inc., 63
Archstone-Smith Trust, 49
Archway Cookies, Inc., 29
ARCO Chemical Company, 10
Arctco, Inc., 16
Arctic Cat Inc., 40 (upd.)
Arctic Slope Regional Corporation, 38
Arden Group, Inc., 29
Argosy Gaming Company, 21
Ariba, Inc., 57
Ariens Company, 48
Aris Industries, Inc., 16
Aristotle Corporation, The, 62
Ark Restaurants Corp., 20
Arkansas Best Corporation, 16
Arkla, Inc., V
Armco Inc., IV
Armor All Products Corp., 16
Armor Holdings, Inc., 27
Armstrong World Industries, Inc., III; 22 (upd.)
Army and Air Force Exchange Service, 39
Arnold & Porter, 35
ArQule, Inc., 68
Arrow Air Holdings Corporation, 55
Arrow Electronics, Inc., 10; 50 (upd.)
Art Institute of Chicago, The, 29
Art Van Furniture, Inc., 28
Artesyn Technologies Inc., 46 (upd.)
Arthur D. Little, Inc., 35
Arthur Murray International, Inc., 32
Artisan Entertainment Inc., 32 (upd.)
ArvinMeritor, Inc., 8; 54 (upd.)
Asanté Technologies, Inc., 20
ASARCO Incorporated, IV
Asbury Automotive Group Inc., 60
Asbury Carbons, Inc., 68
ASC, Inc., 55
Ascend Communications, Inc., 24
Ascential Software Corporation, 59
Ashland Inc., 19; 50 (upd.)
Ashland Oil, Inc., IV
Ashley Furniture Industries, Inc., 35
Ashworth, Inc., 26
ASK Group, Inc., 9
Ask Jeeves, Inc., 65
Aspect Telecommunications Corporation, 22
Aspen Skiing Company, 15
Asplundh Tree Expert Co., 20; 59 (upd.)
Assisted Living Concepts, Inc., 43
Associated Estates Realty Corporation, 25
Associated Grocers, Incorporated, 9; 31 (upd.)
Associated Milk Producers, Inc., 11; 48 (upd.)
Associated Natural Gas Corporation, 11
Associated Press, The, 13; 31 (upd.)
Association of Junior Leagues International Inc., 60
AST Research Inc., 9
Astoria Financial Corporation, 44
Astronics Corporation, 35

ASV, Inc., 34; 66 (upd.)
At Home Corporation, 43
AT&T Bell Laboratories, Inc., 13
AT&T Corporation, V; 29 (upd.); 68 (upd.)
AT&T Wireless Services, Inc., 54 (upd.)
Atari Corporation, 9; 23 (upd.); 66 (upd.)
ATC Healthcare Inc., 64
Atchison Casting Corporation, 39
Athletics Investment Group, The, 62
Atkins Nutritionals, Inc., 58
Atlanta Bread Company International, Inc., 70
Atlanta Gas Light Company, 6; 23 (upd.)
Atlanta National League Baseball Club, Inc., 43
Atlantic American Corporation, 44
Atlantic Coast Airlines Holdings, Inc., 55
Atlantic Energy, Inc., 6
Atlantic Group, The, 23
Atlantic Premium Brands, Ltd., 57
Atlantic Richfield Company, IV; 31 (upd.)
Atlantic Southeast Airlines, Inc., 47
Atlas Air, Inc., 39
Atlas Van Lines, Inc., 14
Atmel Corporation, 17
Atmos Energy Corporation, 43
Attachmate Corporation, 56
Atwood Mobil Products, 53
Au Bon Pain Co., Inc., 18
Audio King Corporation, 24
Audiovox Corporation, 34
August Schell Brewing Company Inc., 59
Ault Incorporated, 34
Auntie Anne's, Inc., 35
Aurora Casket Company, Inc., 56
Aurora Foods Inc., 32
Austin Company, The, 8; 72 (upd.)
Authentic Fitness Corporation, 20; 51 (upd.)
Auto Value Associates, Inc., 25
Autobytel Inc., 47
Autocam Corporation, 51
Autodesk, Inc., 10
Autologic Information International, Inc., 20
Automatic Data Processing, Inc., III; 9 (upd.); 47 (upd.)
AutoNation, Inc., 50
Autotote Corporation, 20
AutoZone, Inc., 9; 31 (upd.)
Avado Brands, Inc., 31
AvalonBay Communities, Inc., 58
Avco Financial Services Inc., 13
Aveda Corporation, 24
Avedis Zildjian Co., 38
Avery Dennison Corporation, IV; 17 (upd.); 49 (upd.)
Aviation Sales Company, 41
Avid Technology Inc., 38
Avis Rent A Car, Inc., 6; 22 (upd.)
Avista Corporation, 69 (upd.)
Avnet Inc., 9
Avocent Corporation, 65
Avon Products, Inc., III; 19 (upd.); 46 (upd.)
Avondale Industries, 7; 41 (upd.)
AVX Corporation, 67
Awrey Bakeries, Inc., 56
Aydin Corp., 19
Azcon Corporation, 23
Aztar Corporation, 13; 71 (upd.)
B&G Foods, Inc., 40
B. Dalton Bookseller Inc., 25
B. Manischewitz Company, LLC, The, 31
B.J. Alan Co., Inc., 67
B/E Aerospace, Inc., 30
Babbage's, Inc., 10

Baby Superstore, Inc., 15
Bachman's Inc., 22
Back Bay Restaurant Group, Inc., 20
Back Yard Burgers, Inc., 45
Bad Boy Worldwide Entertainment Group, 58
Badger Meter, Inc., 22
Badger Paper Mills, Inc., 15
Bailey Nurseries, Inc., 57
Bain & Company, 55
Bairnco Corporation, 28
Baker & Hostetler LLP, 40
Baker & McKenzie, 10; 42 (upd.)
Baker & Taylor Corporation, 16; 43 (upd.)
Baker and Botts, L.L.P., 28
Baker Hughes Incorporated, III; 22 (upd.); 57 (upd.)
Balance Bar Company, 32
Balchem Corporation, 42
Baldor Electric Company, 21
Baldwin & Lyons, Inc., 51
Baldwin Piano & Organ Company, 18
Baldwin Technology Company, Inc., 25
Ball Corporation, I; 10 (upd.)
Ballantyne of Omaha, Inc., 27
Ballard Medical Products, 21
Bally Manufacturing Corporation, III
Bally Total Fitness Holding Corp., 25
Baltek Corporation, 34
Baltimore Aircoil Company, Inc., 66
Baltimore Gas and Electric Company, V; 25 (upd.)
Baltimore Orioles L.P., 66
Banana Republic Inc., 25
Bandag, Inc., 19
Banfi Products Corp., 36
Bank of America Corporation, 46 (upd.)
Bank of Boston Corporation, II
Bank of Mississippi, Inc., 14
Bank of New England Corporation, II
Bank of New York Company, Inc., The, II; 46 (upd.)
Bank One Corporation, 10; 36 (upd.)
BankAmerica Corporation, II; 8 (upd.)
Bankers Trust New York Corporation, II
Banknorth Group, Inc., 55
Banner Aerospace, Inc., 14; 37 (upd.)
Banta Corporation, 12; 32 (upd.)
Banyan Systems Inc., 25
BarclaysAmerican Mortgage Corporation, 11
Barnes & Noble, Inc., 10; 30 (upd.)
Barnes Group Inc., 13; 69 (upd.)
Barnett Banks, Inc., 9
Barnett Inc., 28
Barney's, Inc., 28
Barr Pharmaceuticals, Inc., 26; 68 (upd.)
Barrett Business Services, Inc., 16
Barton Malow Company, 51
Barton Protective Services Inc., 53
Baseball Club of Seattle, LP, The, 50
Bashas' Inc., 33
Basketball Club of Seattle, LLC, The, 50
Bass Pro Shops, Inc., 42
Bassett Furniture Industries, Inc., 18
Bates Worldwide, Inc., 14; 33 (upd.)
Bath Iron Works, 12; 36 (upd.)
Battelle Memorial Institute, Inc., 10
Battle Mountain Gold Company, 23
Bauerly Companies, 61
Bausch & Lomb Inc., 7; 25 (upd.)
Baxter International Inc., I; 10 (upd.)
Bay State Gas Company, 38
BayBanks, Inc., 12
Bayou Steel Corporation, 31
BBN Corp., 19
BEA Systems, Inc., 36

United States (*continued*)

Bear Creek Corporation, 38
Bear Stearns Companies, Inc., II; 10 (upd.); 52 (upd.)
Bearings, Inc., 13
Beasley Broadcast Group, Inc., 51
Beatrice Company, II
BeautiControl Cosmetics, Inc., 21
Beazer Homes USA, Inc., 17
bebe stores, inc., 31
Bechtel Group, Inc., I; 24 (upd.)
Beckett Papers, 23
Beckman Coulter, Inc., 22
Beckman Instruments, Inc., 14
Becton, Dickinson & Company, I; 11 (upd.); 36 (upd.)
Bed Bath & Beyond Inc., 13; 41 (upd.)
Beech Aircraft Corporation, 8
Beech-Nut Nutrition Corporation, 21; 51 (upd.)
BEI Technologies, Inc., 65
Bekins Company, 15
Bel Fuse, Inc., 53
Belco Oil & Gas Corp., 40
Belden Inc., 19
Belk Stores Services, Inc., V; 19 (upd.)
Belk, Inc., 72 (upd.)
Bell and Howell Company, 9; 29 (upd.)
Bell Atlantic Corporation, V; 25 (upd.)
Bell Helicopter Textron Inc., 46
Bell Industries, Inc., 47
Bell Microproducts Inc., 69
Bell Sports Corporation, 16; 44 (upd.)
BellSouth Corporation, V; 29 (upd.)
Beloit Corporation, 14
Bemis Company, Inc., 8
Ben & Jerry's Homemade, Inc., 10; 35 (upd.)
Ben Bridge Jeweler, Inc., 60
Benchmark Capital, 49
Benchmark Electronics, Inc., 40
Bendix Corporation, I
Beneficial Corporation, 8
Benihana, Inc., 18
Benjamin Moore & Co., 13; 38 (upd.)
Benton Oil and Gas Company, 47
Bergdorf Goodman Inc., 52
Bergen Brunswig Corporation, V; 13 (upd.)
Berger Bros Company, 62
Beringer Blass Wine Estates Ltd., 66 (upd.)
Beringer Wine Estates Holdings, Inc., 22
Berkeley Farms, Inc., 46
Berkshire Hathaway Inc., III; 18 (upd.); 42 (upd.)
Berkshire Realty Holdings, L.P., 49
Berlex Laboratories, Inc., 66
Berlitz International, Inc., 13; 39 (upd.)
Bernard C. Harris Publishing Company, Inc., 39
Bernard Chaus, Inc., 27
Berry Petroleum Company, 47
Berry Plastics Corporation, 21
Bertucci's Corporation, 16; 64 (upd.)
Berwick Offray, LLC, 70
Best Buy Co., Inc., 9; 23 (upd.); 63 (upd.)
Bestfoods, 22 (upd.)
BET Holdings, Inc., 18
Bethlehem Steel Corporation, IV; 7 (upd.); 27 (upd.)
Betz Laboratories, Inc., I; 10 (upd.)
Beverly Enterprises, Inc., III; 16 (upd.)
BFGoodrich Company, The, V; 19 (upd.)
BHC Communications, Inc., 26
BIC Corporation, 8; 23 (upd.)
Bicoastal Corporation, II
Big B, Inc., 17
Big Bear Stores Co., 13

Big Dog Holdings, Inc., 45
Big 5 Sporting Goods Corporation, 55
Big Flower Press Holdings, Inc., 21
Big Idea Productions, Inc., 49
Big Lots, Inc., 50
Big O Tires, Inc., 20
Big Rivers Electric Corporation, 11
Big V Supermarkets, Inc., 25
Big Y Foods, Inc., 53
Bill & Melinda Gates Foundation, 41
Bill Barrett Corporation, 71
Bill Blass Ltd., 32
Billing Concepts Corp., 26
Billing Concepts, Inc., 72 (upd.)
Bindley Western Industries, Inc., 9
Bing Group, The, 60
Bingham Dana LLP, 43
Binks Sames Corporation, 21
Binney & Smith Inc., 25
Biogen Idec Inc., 71 (upd.)
Biogen Inc., 14; 36 (upd.)
Biomet, Inc., 10
Bird Corporation, 19
Birds Eye Foods, Inc., 69 (upd.)
Birkenstock Footprint Sandals, Inc., 12; 42 (upd.)
Birmingham Steel Corporation, 13; 40 (upd.)
BISSELL Inc., 9; 30 (upd.)
BJ Services Company, 25
Black & Decker Corporation, The, III; 20 (upd.); 67 (upd.)
Black & Veatch LLP, 22
Black Box Corporation, 20
Black Diamond Equipment, Ltd., 62
Black Hills Corporation, 20
Blackfoot Telecommunications Group, 60
Blair Corporation, 25; 31
Blessings Corp., 19
Blimpie International, Inc., 15; 49 (upd.)
Block Drug Company, Inc., 8; 27 (upd.)
Blockbuster Inc., 9; 31 (upd.)
Blodgett Holdings, Inc., 61 (upd.)
Blonder Tongue Laboratories, Inc., 48
Bloomberg L.P., 21
Bloomingdale's Inc., 12
Blount International, Inc., 12; 48 (upd.)
Blue Bell Creameries L.P., 30
Blue Bird Corporation, 35
Blue Cross and Blue Shield Association, 10
Blue Diamond Growers, 28
Blue Martini Software, Inc., 59
Blue Mountain Arts, Inc., 29
Blue Nile Inc., 61
Blue Rhino Corporation, 56
Bluefly, Inc., 60
Blyth Industries, Inc., 18
BMC Industries, Inc., 17; 59 (upd.)
BMC Software, Inc., 55
Boart Longyear Company, 26
Boatmen's Bancshares Inc., 15
Bob Evans Farms, Inc., 9; 63 (upd.)
Bob's Red Mill Natural Foods, Inc., 63
Bobit Publishing Company, 55
Bobs Candies, Inc., 70
Boca Resorts, Inc., 37
Boddie-Noell Enterprises, Inc., 68
Boeing Company, The, I; 10 (upd.); 32 (upd.)
Bogen Communications International, Inc., 62
Bohemia, Inc., 13
Boise Cascade Corporation, IV; 8 (upd.); 32 (upd.)
Bollinger Shipyards, Inc., 61
Bombay Company, Inc., The, 10; 71 (upd.)

Bon Marché, Inc., The, 23
Bon Secours Health System, Inc., 24
Bon-Ton Stores, Inc., The, 16; 50 (upd.)
Bonneville International Corporation, 29
Bonneville Power Administration, 50
Book-of-the-Month Club, Inc., 13
Books-A-Million, Inc., 14; 41 (upd.)
Boole & Babbage, Inc., 25
Booth Creek Ski Holdings, Inc., 31
Booz Allen & Hamilton Inc., 10
Borden, Inc., II; 22 (upd.)
Borders Group, Inc., 15; 43 (upd.)
Borg-Warner Automotive, Inc., 14; 32 (upd.)
Borg-Warner Corporation, III
Borland International, Inc., 9
Boron, LePore & Associates, Inc., 45
Boscov's Department Store, Inc., 31
Bose Corporation, 13; 36 (upd.)
Boston Acoustics, Inc., 22
Boston Beer Company, Inc., The, 18; 50 (upd.)
Boston Celtics Limited Partnership, 14
Boston Consulting Group, The, 58
Boston Edison Company, 12
Boston Market Corporation, 12; 48 (upd.)
Boston Professional Hockey Association Inc., 39
Boston Properties, Inc., 22
Boston Scientific Corporation, 37
Bou-Matic, 62
Bowne & Co., Inc., 23
Boy Scouts of America, The, 34
Boyd Bros. Transportation Inc., 39
Boyd Coffee Company, 53
Boyd Gaming Corporation, 43
Boyds Collection, Ltd., The, 29
Boyne USA Resorts, 71
Boys & Girls Clubs of America, 69
Bozell Worldwide Inc., 25
Bozzuto's, Inc., 13
Brach and Brock Confections, Inc., 15
Bradlees Discount Department Store Company, 12
Branch Group, Inc., The, 72
BrandPartners Group, Inc., 58
Brannock Device Company, 48
Brass Eagle Inc., 34
Brazos Sportswear, Inc., 23
Bremer Financial Corp., 45
Briazz, Inc., 53
Bridgeport Machines, Inc., 17
Bridgford Foods Corporation, 27
Briggs & Stratton Corporation, 8; 27 (upd.)
Brigham's Inc., 72
Bright Horizons Family Solutions, Inc., 31
Brightpoint, Inc., 18
Brink's Company, The, 58 (upd.)
Brinker International, Inc., 10; 38 (upd.)
Bristol Hotel Company, 23
Bristol-Myers Squibb Company, III; 9 (upd.); 37 (upd.)
Brite Voice Systems, Inc., 20
Broadcast Music Inc., 23
Broadcom Corporation, 34
Broadmoor Hotel, The, 30
Broadwing Corporation, 70
Brobeck, Phleger & Harrison, LLP, 31
Broder Bros. Co., 38
Broderbund Software, Inc., 13; 29 (upd.)
Brooke Group Ltd., 15
Brooklyn Union Gas, 6
Brooks Brothers Inc., 22
Brooks Sports Inc., 32
Brookshire Grocery Company, 16
Brookstone, Inc., 18
Brothers Gourmet Coffees, Inc., 20

Broughton Foods Co., 17
Brown & Brown, Inc., 41
Brown & Haley, 23
Brown & Root, Inc., 13
Brown & Sharpe Manufacturing Co., 23
Brown & Williamson Tobacco
  Corporation, 14; 33 (upd.)
Brown Brothers Harriman & Co., 45
Brown Printing Company, 26
Brown Shoe Company, Inc., V; 20 (upd.);
  68 (upd.)
Brown-Forman Corporation, I; 10 (upd.);
  38 (upd.)
Browning-Ferris Industries, Inc., V; 20
  (upd.)
Broyhill Furniture Industries, Inc., 10
Bruce Foods Corporation, 39
Bruegger's Corporation, 63
Bruno's Supermarkets, Inc., 7; 26 (upd.);
  68 (upd.)
Brunswick Corporation, III; 22 (upd.)
Brush Engineered Materials Inc., 67
Brush Wellman Inc., 14
BTG, Inc., 45
Buca, Inc., 38
Buck Consultants, Inc., 55
Buck Knives Inc., 48
Buckeye Partners, L.P., 70
Buckeye Technologies, Inc., 42
Buckle, Inc., The, 18
Bucyrus International, Inc., 17
Budd Company, The, 8
Budget Group, Inc., 25
Budget Rent a Car Corporation, 9
Buffalo Wild Wings, Inc., 56
Buffets, Inc., 10; 32 (upd.)
Bugle Boy Industries, Inc., 18
Build-A-Bear Workshop Inc., 62
Building Materials Holding Corporation, 52
Bulley & Andrews, LLC, 55
Bulova Corporation, 13; 41 (upd.)
Bumble Bee Seafoods L.L.C., 64
Bundy Corporation, 17
Bunge Ltd., 62
Burdines, Inc., 60
Bureau of National Affairs, Inc.,The 23
Burger King Corporation, II; 17 (upd.); 56
  (upd.)
Burke Mills, Inc., 66
Burlington Coat Factory Warehouse
  Corporation, 10; 60 (upd.)
Burlington Industries, Inc., V; 17 (upd.)
Burlington Northern Santa Fe Corporation,
  V; 27 (upd.)
Burlington Resources Inc., 10
Burns International Services Corporation,
  13; 41 (upd.)
Burr-Brown Corporation, 19
Burt's Bees, Inc., 58
Burton Snowboards Inc., 22
Bush Boake Allen Inc., 30
Bush Brothers & Company, 45
Bush Industries, Inc., 20
Business Men's Assurance Company of
  America, 14
Butler Manufacturing Company, 12; 62
  (upd.)
Butterick Co., Inc., 23
Buttrey Food & Drug Stores Co., 18
buy.com, Inc., 46
BWAY Corporation, 24
C & S Wholesale Grocers, Inc., 55
C-COR.net Corp., 38
C-Cube Microsystems, Inc., 37
C.F. Martin & Co., Inc., 42
C.H. Heist Corporation, 24

C.H. Robinson Worldwide, Inc., 11; 40
  (upd.)
C.R. Bard, Inc., 9; 65 (upd.)
Cabela's Inc., 26; 68 (upd.)
Cabletron Systems, Inc., 10
Cablevision Electronic Instruments, Inc., 32
Cablevision Systems Corporation, 7; 30
  (upd.)
Cabot Corporation, 8; 29 (upd.)
Cache Incorporated, 30
CACI International Inc., 21; 72 (upd.)
Cadence Design Systems, Inc., 11; 48
  (upd.)
Cadmus Communications Corporation, 23
Cadwalader, Wickersham & Taft, 32
CAE USA Inc., 48
Caere Corporation, 20
Caesars World, Inc., 6
Cagle's, Inc., 20
Cahners Business Information, 43
Cal-Maine Foods, Inc., 69
Calavo Growers, Inc., 47
CalComp Inc., 13
Calcot Ltd., 33
Caldor Inc., 12
California Cedar Products Company, 58
California Pizza Kitchen Inc., 15
California Sports, Inc., 56
California Steel Industries, Inc., 67
Caliper Life Sciences, Inc., 70
Callanan Industries, Inc., 60
Callaway Golf Company, 15; 45 (upd.)
Callon Petroleum Company, 47
Calloway's Nursery, Inc., 51
CalMat Co., 19
Calpine Corporation, 36
Caltex Petroleum Corporation, 19
Calvin Klein, Inc., 22; 55 (upd.)
Cambrex Corporation, 16; 44 (upd.)
Cambridge SoundWorks, Inc., 48
Cambridge Technology Partners, Inc., 36
Camelot Music, Inc., 26
Cameron & Barkley Company, 28
Campbell Scientific, Inc., 51
Campbell Soup Company, II; 7 (upd.); 26
  (upd.); 71 (upd.)
Campbell-Mithun-Esty, Inc., 16
Campo Electronics, Appliances &
  Computers, Inc., 16
Canandaigua Brands, Inc., 13; 34 (upd.)
Candela Corporation, 48
Candie's, Inc., 31
Candle Corporation, 64
Candlewood Hotel Company, Inc., 41
Cannon Design, 63
Cannon Express, Inc., 53
Cannondale Corporation, 21
Canterbury Park Holding Corporation, 42
Cap Rock Energy Corporation, 46
Capel Incorporated, 45
Capezio/Ballet Makers Inc., 62
Capital Cities/ABC Inc., II
Capital Holding Corporation, III
Capital One Financial Corporation, 52
CapStar Hotel Company, 21
Captain D's, LLC, 59
Car Toys, Inc., 67
Caraustar Industries, Inc., 19; 44 (upd.)
Carbide/Graphite Group, Inc., The, 40
Carborundum Company, 15
Cardinal Health, Inc., 18; 50 (upd.)
Career Education Corporation, 45
Caremark Rx, Inc., 10; 54 (upd.)
Carey International, Inc., 26
Cargill, Incorporated, II; 13 (upd.); 40
  (upd.)
Carhartt, Inc., 30

Caribiner International, Inc., 24
Caribou Coffee Company, Inc., 28
Carlisle Companies Incorporated, 8
Carlson Companies, Inc., 6; 22 (upd.)
Carlson Restaurants Worldwide, 69
Carlson Wagonlit Travel, 55
Carma Laboratories, Inc., 60
CarMax, Inc., 55
Carmichael Lynch Inc., 28
Carmike Cinemas, Inc., 14; 37 (upd.)
Carnation Company, II
Carnegie Corporation of New York, 35
Carnival Corporation, 6; 27 (upd.)
Carolina First Corporation, 31
Carolina Freight Corporation, 6
Carolina Power & Light Company, V; 23
  (upd.)
Carolina Telephone and Telegraph
  Company, 10
Carpenter Technology Corporation, 13
CARQUEST Corporation, 29
Carr-Gottstein Foods Co., 17
CarrAmerica Realty Corporation, 56
Carriage House Companies, Inc., The, 55
Carriage Services, Inc., 37
Carrier Access Corporation, 44
Carrier Corporation, 7; 69 (upd.)
Carroll's Foods, Inc., 46
Carsey-Werner Company, L.L.C., The, 37
Carson Pirie Scott & Company, 15
Carson, Inc., 31
Carter Hawley Hale Stores, Inc., V
Carter Lumber Company, 45
Carter-Wallace, Inc., 8; 38 (upd.)
Carvel Corporation, 35
Cascade Corporation, 65
Cascade General, Inc., 65
Cascade Natural Gas Corporation, 9
Casco Northern Bank, 14
Casey's General Stores, Inc., 19
Cash America International, Inc., 20; 61
  (upd.)
Castle & Cooke, Inc., II; 20 (upd.)
Casual Corner Group, Inc., 43
Casual Male Retail Group, Inc., 52
Caswell-Massey Co. Ltd., 51
Catalina Lighting, Inc., 43 (upd.)
Catalina Marketing Corporation, 18
Catalytica Energy Systems, Inc., 44
Catellus Development Corporation, 24
Caterpillar Inc., III; 15 (upd.); 63 (upd.)
Catherines Stores Corporation, 15
Catholic Order of Foresters, 24
Cato Corporation, 14
Cattleman's, Inc., 20
Cavco Industries, Inc., 65
CB Commercial Real Estate Services
  Group, Inc., 21
CB Richard Ellis Group, Inc., 70 (upd.)
CBI Industries, Inc., 7
CBRL Group, Inc., 35 (upd.)
CBS Corporation, II; 6 (upd.); 28 (upd.)
CBS Television Network, 66 (upd.)
CCA Industries, Inc., 53
CCH Inc., 14
CDI Corporation, 6; 54 (upd.)
CDW Computer Centers, Inc., 16; 52
  (upd.)
CEC Entertainment, Inc., 31 (upd.)
Cedar Fair, L.P., 22
Celadon Group Inc., 30
Celanese Corporation, I
Celebrate Express, Inc., 70
Celebrity, Inc., 22
Celestial Seasonings, Inc., 16
Celgene Corporation, 67
Cendant Corporation, 44 (upd.)

United States (*continued*)

Centel Corporation, 6
Centennial Communications Corporation, 39
Centerior Energy Corporation, V
Centex Corporation, 8; 29 (upd.)
Centocor Inc., 14
Central and South West Corporation, V
Central Garden & Pet Company, 23; 58 (upd.)
Central Hudson Gas and Electricity Corporation, 6
Central Maine Power, 6
Central Newspapers, Inc., 10
Central Parking Corporation, 18
Central Soya Company, Inc., 7
Central Sprinkler Corporation, 29
Central Vermont Public Service Corporation, 54
Centuri Corporation, 54
Century Aluminum Company, 52
Century Business Services, Inc., 52
Century Casinos, Inc., 53
Century Communications Corp., 10
Century Telephone Enterprises, Inc., 9; 54 (upd.)
Century Theatres, Inc., 31
Cenveo Inc., 71 (upd.)
Cephalon, Inc., 45
Ceradyne, Inc., 65
Cerner Corporation, 16
CertainTeed Corporation, 35
Certegy, Inc., 63
Cessna Aircraft Company, 8; 27 (upd.)
Chadbourne & Parke, 36
Chadwick's of Boston, Ltd., 29
Chalone Wine Group, Ltd., The, 36
Champion Enterprises, Inc., 17
Champion Industries, Inc., 28
Champion International Corporation, IV; 20 (upd.)
Championship Auto Racing Teams, Inc., 37
Chancellor Beacon Academies, Inc., 53
Chancellor Media Corporation, 24
Chaparral Steel Co., 13
Charles Machine Works, Inc., The, 64
Charles River Laboratories International, Inc., 42
Charles Schwab Corporation, The, 8; 26 (upd.)
Charles Stark Draper Laboratory, Inc., The, 35
Charlotte Russe Holding, Inc., 35
Charming Shoppes, Inc., 8; 38
Chart House Enterprises, Inc., 17
Chart Industries, Inc., 21
Charter Communications, Inc., 33
ChartHouse International Learning Corporation, 49
Chas. Levy Company LLC, 60
Chase Manhattan Corporation, The, II; 13 (upd.)
Chateau Communities, Inc., 37
Chattem, Inc., 17
Chautauqua Airlines, Inc., 38
Checkers Drive-Up Restaurants Inc., 16
Checkpoint Systems, Inc., 39
Cheesecake Factory Inc., The, 17
Chelsea Milling Company, 29
Chemcentral Corporation, 8
Chemed Corporation, 13
Chemfab Corporation, 35
Chemi-Trol Chemical Co., 16
Chemical Banking Corporation, II; 14 (upd.)
Chemical Waste Management, Inc., 9

Cherokee Inc., 18
Cherry Lane Music Publishing Company, Inc., 62
Chesapeake Corporation, 8; 30 (upd.)
Chesapeake Utilities Corporation, 56
Chesebrough-Pond's USA, Inc., 8
ChevronTexaco Corporation, IV; 19 (upd.); 47 (upd.)
Cheyenne Software, Inc., 12
Chi-Chi's Inc., 13; 51 (upd.)
Chiasso Inc., 53
Chiat/Day Inc. Advertising, 11
Chic by H.I.S, Inc., 20
Chicago and North Western Holdings Corporation, 6
Chicago Bears Football Club, Inc., 33
Chicago Board of Trade, 41
Chicago National League Ball Club, Inc., 66
Chick-fil-A Inc., 23
Chicken of the Sea International, 24 (upd.)
Chico's FAS, Inc., 45
Children's Comprehensive Services, Inc., 42
Children's Hospitals and Clinics, Inc., 54
Children's Place Retail Stores, Inc., The, 37
ChildrenFirst, Inc., 59
Childtime Learning Centers, Inc., 34
Chiles Offshore Corporation, 9
Chipotle Mexican Grill, Inc., 67
CHIPS and Technologies, Inc., 9
Chiquita Brands International, Inc., 7; 21 (upd.)
Chiron Corporation, 10; 36 (upd.)
Chisholm-Mingo Group, Inc., 41
Chittenden & Eastman Company, 58
Chock Full o' Nuts Corp., 17
Choice Hotels International Inc., 14
ChoicePoint Inc., 65
Chorus Line Corporation, 30
Chris-Craft Industries, Inc., 9; 31 (upd.)
Christensen Boyles Corporation, 26
Christian Broadcasting Network, Inc., The, 52
Christian Science Publishing Society, The, 55
Christopher & Banks Corporation, 42
Chromcraft Revington, Inc., 15
Chronicle Publishing Company, Inc., The, 23
Chronimed Inc., 26
Chrysler Corporation, I; 11 (upd.)
CHS Inc., 60
CH2M Hill Ltd., 22
Chubb Corporation, The, III; 14 (upd.); 37 (upd.)
Chugach Alaska Corporation, 60
Church & Dwight Co., Inc., 29; 68 (upd.)
Church's Chicken, 66
Churchill Downs Incorporated, 29
Cianbro Corporation, 14
Ciber, Inc., 18
CIENA Corporation, 54
CIGNA Corporation, III; 22 (upd.); 45 (upd.)
Cincinnati Bell, Inc., 6
Cincinnati Financial Corporation, 16; 44 (upd.)
Cincinnati Gas & Electric Company, 6
Cincinnati Lamb Inc., 72
Cincinnati Milacron Inc., 12
Cincom Systems Inc., 15
Cinnabon Inc., 23
Cintas Corporation, 21; 51 (upd.)
CIPSCO Inc., 6
Circle K Company, The, II; 20 (upd.)

Circon Corporation, 21
Circuit City Stores, Inc., 9; 29 (upd.); 65 (upd.)
Circus Circus Enterprises, Inc., 6
Cirrus Design Corporation, 44
Cirrus Logic, Inc., 11; 48 (upd.)
Cisco Systems, Inc., 11; 34 (upd.)
Citadel Communications Corporation, 35
Citfed Bancorp, Inc., 16
CITGO Petroleum Corporation, IV; 31 (upd.)
Citicorp, II; 9 (upd.)
Citigroup Inc., 30 (upd.); 59 (upd.)
Citizens Financial Group, Inc., 42
Citizens Utilities Company, 7
Citrix Systems, Inc., 44
City Public Service, 6
CKE Restaurants, Inc., 19; 46 (upd.)
Claire's Stores, Inc., 17
CLARCOR Inc., 17; 61 (upd.)
Clare Rose Inc., 68
Clark Construction Group, Inc., The, 8
Clark Equipment Company, 8
Classic Vacation Group, Inc., 46
Clayton Homes Incorporated, 13; 54 (upd.)
Clear Channel Communications, Inc., 23
Clearwire, Inc., 69
Cleary, Gottlieb, Steen & Hamilton, 35
Cleco Corporation, 37
Cleveland Indians Baseball Company, Inc., 37
Cleveland-Cliffs Inc., 13; 62 (upd.)
Click Wine Group, 68
Clif Bar Inc., 50
Clorox Company, The, III; 22 (upd.)
Clothestime, Inc., The, 20
Clougherty Packing Company, 72
ClubCorp, Inc., 33
CML Group, Inc., 10
CMP Media Inc., 26
CMS Energy Corporation, V, 14
CNA Financial Corporation, III; 38 (upd.)
CNET Networks, Inc., 47
CNS, Inc., 20
Coach USA, Inc., 24; 55 (upd.)
Coach, Inc., 10; 45 (upd.)
Coastal Corporation, The, IV; 31 (upd.)
COBE Cardiovascular, Inc., 61
COBE Laboratories, Inc., 13
Coborn's, Inc., 30
Cobra Electronics Corporation, 14
Cobra Golf Inc., 16
Coca Cola Bottling Co. Consolidated, 10
Coca-Cola Company, The, I; 10 (upd.); 32 (upd.); 67 (upd.)
Coca-Cola Enterprises, Inc., 13
Coeur d'Alene Mines Corporation, 20
Cogent Communications Group, Inc., 55
Cogentrix Energy, Inc., 10
Cognizant Technology Solutions Corporation, 59
Coherent, Inc., 31
Cohu, Inc., 32
Coinmach Laundry Corporation, 20
Coinstar, Inc., 44
Cold Spring Granite Company, 16
Cold Spring Granite Company Inc., 67 (upd.)
Cold Stone Creamery, 69
Coldwater Creek Inc., 21
Cole National Corporation, 13
Cole's Quality Foods, Inc., 68
Coleman Company, Inc., The, 9; 30 (upd.)
Coleman Natural Products, Inc., 68
Coles Express Inc., 15
Colfax Corporation, 58

Colgate-Palmolive Company, III; 14 (upd.); 35 (upd.); 71 (upd.)
Collectors Universe, Inc., 48
Collins & Aikman Corporation, 13; 41 (upd.)
Collins Industries, Inc., 33
Colonial Properties Trust, 65
Colonial Williamsburg Foundation, 53
Colorado Baseball Management, Inc., 72
Colorado MEDtech, Inc., 48
Colt Industries Inc., I
Colt's Manufacturing Company, Inc., 12
Columbia Gas System, Inc., The, V; 16 (upd.)
Columbia House Company, 69
Columbia Sportswear Company, 19; 41 (upd.)
Columbia TriStar Motion Pictures Companies, II; 12 (upd.)
Columbia/HCA Healthcare Corporation, 15
Columbus McKinnon Corporation, 37
Comair Holdings Inc., 13; 34 (upd.)
Combe Inc., 72
Comcast Corporation, 7; 24 (upd.)
Comdial Corporation, 21
Comdisco, Inc., 9
Comerica Incorporated, 40
COMFORCE Corporation, 40
Command Security Corporation, 57
Commerce Clearing House, Inc., 7
Commercial Credit Company, 8
Commercial Federal Corporation, 12; 62 (upd.)
Commercial Financial Services, Inc., 26
Commercial Metals Company, 15; 42 (upd.)
Commodore International Ltd., 7
Commonwealth Edison Company, V
Commonwealth Energy System, 14
Commonwealth Telephone Enterprises, Inc., 25
Community Coffee Co. L.L.C., 53
Community Health Systems, Inc., 71
Community Psychiatric Centers, 15
Compaq Computer Corporation, III; 6 (upd.); 26 (upd.)
CompDent Corporation, 22
CompHealth Inc., 25
Complete Business Solutions, Inc., 31
Comprehensive Care Corporation, 15
CompuAdd Computer Corporation, 11
CompuCom Systems, Inc., 10
CompuDyne Corporation, 51
CompUSA, Inc., 10; 35 (upd.)
CompuServe Interactive Services, Inc., 10; 27 (upd.)
Computer Associates International, Inc., 6; 49 (upd.)
Computer Data Systems, Inc., 14
Computer Learning Centers, Inc., 26
Computer Sciences Corporation, 6
Computerland Corp., 13
Computervision Corporation, 10
Compuware Corporation, 10; 30 (upd.); 66 (upd.)
Comsat Corporation, 23
Comshare Inc., 23
Comstock Resources, Inc., 47
Comverse Technology, Inc., 15; 43 (upd.)
ConAgra Foods, Inc., II; 12 (upd.); 42 (upd.)
Conair Corporation, 17; 69 (upd.)
Concentra Inc., 71
Concepts Direct, Inc., 39
Concord Camera Corporation, 41
Concord EFS, Inc., 52
Concord Fabrics, Inc., 16

Condé Nast Publications, Inc., 13; 59 (upd.)
Cone Mills LLC, 8; 67 (upd.)
Conexant Systems, Inc., 36
Congoleum Corp., 18
Conn's, Inc., 67
Conn-Selmer, Inc., 55
Connecticut Light and Power Co., 13
Connecticut Mutual Life Insurance Company, III
Connell Company, The, 29
Conner Peripherals, Inc., 6
Connetics Corporation, 70
ConocoPhillips, IV; 16 (upd.); 63 (upd.)
Conrad Industries, Inc., 58
Conseco, Inc., 10; 33 (upd.)
Conso International Corporation, 29
CONSOL Energy Inc., 59
Consolidated Delivery & Logistics, Inc., 24
Consolidated Edison, Inc., V; 45 (upd.)
Consolidated Freightways Corporation, V; 21 (upd.); 48 (upd.)
Consolidated Graphics, Inc., 70
Consolidated Natural Gas Company, V; 19 (upd.)
Consolidated Papers, Inc., 8; 36 (upd.)
Consolidated Products Inc., 14
Consolidated Rail Corporation, V
Constar International Inc., 64
Constellation Brands, Inc., 68 (upd.)
Consumers Power Co., 14
Consumers Union, 26
Consumers Water Company, 14
Container Store, The, 36
ContiGroup Companies, Inc., 43 (upd.)
Continental Airlines, Inc., I; 21 (upd.); 52 (upd.)
Continental Bank Corporation, II
Continental Cablevision, Inc., 7
Continental Can Co., Inc., 15
Continental Corporation, The, III
Continental General Tire Corp., 23
Continental Grain Company, 10; 13 (upd.)
Continental Group Company, I
Continental Medical Systems, Inc., 10
Continuum Health Partners, Inc., 60
Control Data Corporation, III
Control Data Systems, Inc., 10
Converse Inc., 9; 31 (upd.)
Cooker Restaurant Corporation, 20; 51 (upd.)
Cooper Cameron Corporation, 20 (upd.); 58 (upd.)
Cooper Companies, Inc., The, 39
Cooper Industries, Inc., II; 44 (upd.)
Cooper Tire & Rubber Company, 8; 23 (upd.)
Coopers & Lybrand, 9
Copart Inc., 23
Copley Press, Inc., The, 23
Copps Corporation, The, 32
Corbis Corporation, 31
Corcoran Group, Inc., The, 58
Cordis Corporation, 19; 46 (upd.)
CoreStates Financial Corp, 17
Corinthian Colleges, Inc., 39
Corning Inc., III; 44 (upd.)
Corporate Express, Inc., 22; 47 (upd.)
Corporate Software Inc., 9
Corporation for Public Broadcasting, 14
Correctional Services Corporation, 30
Corrections Corporation of America, 23
Corrpro Companies, Inc., 20
CORT Business Services Corporation, 26
Cosi, Inc., 53
Cosmair, Inc., 8
Cosmetic Center, Inc., The, 22

Cost Plus, Inc., 27
Cost-U-Less, Inc., 51
Costco Wholesale Corporation, V; 43 (upd.)
Cotter & Company, V
Cotton Incorporated, 46
Coty, Inc., 36
Coudert Brothers, 30
Countrywide Credit Industries, Inc., 16
County Seat Stores Inc., 9
Courier Corporation, 41
Cousins Properties Incorporated, 65
Covance Inc., 30
Covanta Energy Corporation, 64 (upd.)
Coventry Health Care, Inc., 59
Covington & Burling, 40
Cowles Media Company, 23
Cox Enterprises, Inc., IV; 22 (upd.); 67 (upd.)
CPC International Inc., II
CPI Corp., 38
CR England, Inc., 63
Cracker Barrel Old Country Store, Inc., 10
Craftmade International, Inc., 44
Crain Communications, Inc., 12; 35 (upd.)
Cramer, Berkowitz & Co., 34
Crane & Co., Inc., 26
Crane Co., 8; 30 (upd.)
Cranium, Inc., 69
Crate and Barrel, 9
Cravath, Swaine & Moore, 43
Cray Research, Inc., III; 16 (upd.)
Creative Artists Agency LLC, 38
Credit Acceptance Corporation, 18
Cree Inc., 53
Crompton Corporation, 9; 36 (upd.)
Croscill, Inc., 42
Crosman Corporation, 62
Crowley Maritime Corporation, 6; 28 (upd.)
Crowley, Milner & Company, 19
Crown Books Corporation, 21
Crown Central Petroleum Corporation, 7
Crown Crafts, Inc., 16
Crown Equipment Corporation, 15
Crown Media Holdings, Inc., 45
Crown Vantage Inc., 29
Crown, Cork & Seal Company, Inc., I; 13; 32 (upd.)
CRSS Inc., 6
Cruise America Inc., 21
CryoLife, Inc., 46
Crystal Brands, Inc., 9
CS First Boston Inc., II
CSK Auto Corporation, 38
CSS Industries, Inc., 35
CSX Corporation, V; 22 (upd.)
CTB International Corporation, 43 (upd.)
CTG, Inc., 11
CTS Corporation, 39
Cubic Corporation, 19
CUC International Inc., 16
Cuisinart Corporation, 24
Culbro Corporation, 15
Cullen/Frost Bankers, Inc., 25
Culligan Water Technologies, Inc., 12; 38 (upd.)
Culp, Inc., 29
Culver Franchising System, Inc., 58
Cumberland Farms, Inc., 17
Cumberland Packing Corporation, 26
Cummins Engine Company, Inc., I; 12 (upd.); 40 (upd.)
Cumulus Media Inc., 37
CUNA Mutual Group, 62
Cunard Line Ltd., 23
CUNO Incorporated, 57

United States (*continued*)

Current, Inc., 37
Curtice-Burns Foods, Inc., 7; 21 (upd.)
Curtiss-Wright Corporation, 10; 35 (upd.)
Curves International, Inc., 54
Custom Chrome, Inc., 16
Cutter & Buck Inc., 27
CVS Corporation, 45 (upd.)
Cybermedia, Inc., 25
Cybex International, Inc., 49
Cygne Designs, Inc., 25
Cygnus Business Media, Inc., 56
Cypress Semiconductor Corporation, 20; 48 (upd.)
Cyprus Amax Minerals Company, 21
Cyprus Minerals Company, 7
Cyrk Inc., 19
Cytec Industries Inc., 27
Cytyc Corporation, 69
Czarnikow-Rionda Company, Inc., 32
D&K Wholesale Drug, Inc., 14
D'Agostino Supermarkets Inc., 19
D'Arcy Masius Benton & Bowles, Inc., VI; 32 (upd.)
D.G. Yuengling & Son, Inc., 38
D.R. Horton, Inc., 58
Dade Behring Holdings Inc., 71
Daffy's Inc., 26
Dain Rauscher Corporation, 35 (upd.)
Dairy Mart Convenience Stores, Inc., 7; 25 (upd.)
Daisy Outdoor Products Inc., 58
Daisytek International Corporation, 18
Daktronics, Inc., 32
Dal-Tile International Inc., 22
Dale Carnegie Training, Inc., 28
Dallas Cowboys Football Club, Ltd., 33
Dallas Semiconductor Corporation, 13; 31 (upd.)
Damark International, Inc., 18
Dames & Moore, Inc., 25
Dan River Inc., 35
Dana Corporation, I; 10 (upd.)
Danaher Corporation, 7
Daniel Industries, Inc., 16
Dannon Co., Inc., 14
Danskin, Inc., 12; 62 (upd.)
Darden Restaurants, Inc., 16; 44 (upd.)
Darigold, Inc., 9
Dart Group Corporation, 16
Data Broadcasting Corporation, 31
Data General Corporation, 8
Datapoint Corporation, 11
Datascope Corporation, 39
Datek Online Holdings Corp., 32
Dauphin Deposit Corporation, 14
Dave & Buster's, Inc., 33
Davey Tree Expert Company, The, 11
David and Lucile Packard Foundation, The, 41
David J. Joseph Company, The, 14
David's Bridal, Inc., 33
Davis Polk & Wardwell, 36
DAW Technologies, Inc., 25
Dawn Food Products, Inc., 17
Day & Zimmermann Inc., 9; 31 (upd.)
Day Runner, Inc., 14; 41 (upd.)
Dayton Hudson Corporation, V; 18 (upd.)
DC Comics Inc., 25
DC Shoes, Inc., 60
DDB Needham Worldwide, 14
Dean & DeLuca, Inc., 36
Dean Foods Company, 7; 21 (upd.)
Dean Witter, Discover & Co., 12
Dearborn Mid-West Conveyor Company, 56
Death Row Records, 27

Deb Shops, Inc., 16
Debevoise & Plimpton, 39
Dechert, 43
Deckers Outdoor Corporation, 22
Decora Industries, Inc., 31
Decorator Industries Inc., 68
DeCrane Aircraft Holdings Inc., 36
DeepTech International Inc., 21
Deere & Company, III; 21 (upd.); 42 (upd.)
Defiance, Inc., 22
DeKalb Genetics Corporation, 17
Del Laboratories, Inc., 28
Del Monte Foods Company, 7; 23 (upd.)
Del Taco, Inc., 58
Del Webb Corporation, 14
Delaware North Companies Incorporated, 7
dELiA*s Inc., 29
Delicato Vineyards, Inc., 50
Dell Inc., 9; 31 (upd.); 63 (upd.)
Deloitte Touche Tohmatsu International, 9; 29 (upd.)
DeLorme Publishing Company, Inc., 53
Delphi Automotive Systems Corporation, 45
Delta Air Lines, Inc., I; 6 (upd.); 39 (upd.)
Delta and Pine Land Company, 33; 59
Delta Woodside Industries, Inc., 8; 30 (upd.)
Deltec, Inc., 56
Deltic Timber Corporation, 46
Deluxe Corporation, 7; 22 (upd.)
DEMCO, Inc., 60
DeMoulas / Market Basket Inc., 23
DenAmerica Corporation, 29
Denbury Resources, Inc., 67
Dendrite International, Inc., 70
Denison International plc, 46
Dentsply International Inc., 10
Denver Nuggets, 51
DEP Corporation, 20
Department 56, Inc., 14; 34 (upd.)
Deposit Guaranty Corporation, 17
DePuy Inc., 30; 37 (upd.)
Deschutes Brewery, Inc., 57
Designer Holdings Ltd., 20
Destec Energy, Inc., 12
Detroit Diesel Corporation, 10
Detroit Edison Company, The, V
Detroit Lions, Inc., The, 55
Detroit Pistons Basketball Company, The, 41
Detroit Tigers Baseball Club, Inc., 46
Deutsch, Inc., 42
Developers Diversified Realty Corporation, 69
Devon Energy Corporation, 61
DeVry Incorporated, 29
Dewey Ballantine LLP, 48
Dex Media, Inc., 65
Dexter Corporation, The, I; 12 (upd.)
DFS Group Ltd., 66
DH Technology, Inc., 18
DHL Worldwide Express, 6; 24 (upd.)
Di Giorgio Corp., 12
Dial Corp., The, 8; 23 (upd.)
Dial-A-Mattress Operating Corporation, 46
Dialogic Corporation, 18
Diamond of California, 64 (upd.)
Diamond Shamrock, Inc., IV
DiamondCluster International, Inc., 51
Dibrell Brothers, Incorporated, 12
dick clark productions, inc., 16
Dick Corporation, 64
Dick's Sporting Goods, Inc., 59
Diebold, Incorporated, 7; 22 (upd.)
Diedrich Coffee, Inc., 40

Dierbergs Markets Inc., 63
Digex, Inc., 46
Digi International Inc., 9
Digital Equipment Corporation, III; 6 (upd.)
Digital River, Inc., 50
Dillard Paper Company, 11
Dillard's Inc., V; 16 (upd.); 68 (upd.)
Dillingham Construction Corporation, I; 44 (upd.)
Dillon Companies Inc., 12
Dime Savings Bank of New York, F.S.B., 9
DIMON Inc., 27
Dionex Corporation, 46
Dippin' Dots, Inc., 56
Direct Focus, Inc., 47
DIRECTV, Inc., 38
Discount Auto Parts, Inc., 18
Discount Drug Mart, Inc., 14
Discovery Communications, Inc., 42
Discovery Partners International, Inc., 58
Dixie Group, Inc., The, 20
Dixon Industries, Inc., 26
Dixon Ticonderoga Company, 12; 69 (upd.)
DMI Furniture, Inc., 46
Do it Best Corporation, 30
Dobson Communications Corporation, 63
Doctor's Associates Inc., 67 (upd.)
Doctors' Company, The, 55
Documentum, Inc., 46
Dolby Laboratories Inc., 20
Dole Food Company, Inc., 9; 31 (upd.); 68 (upd.)
Dollar Thrifty Automotive Group, Inc., 25
Dollar Tree Stores, Inc., 23; 62 (upd.)
Dominick's Finer Foods, Inc., 56
Dominion Homes, Inc., 19
Dominion Resources, Inc., V; 54 (upd.)
Domino Sugar Corporation, 26
Domino's Pizza, Inc., 7; 21 (upd.)
Domino's, Inc., 63 (upd.)
Don Massey Cadillac, Inc., 37
Donaldson Company, Inc., 16; 49 (upd.)
Donaldson, Lufkin & Jenrette, Inc., 22
Donatos Pizzeria Corporation, 58
Donna Karan International Inc., 15; 56 (upd.)
Donnelly Corporation, 12; 35 (upd.)
Donnkenny, Inc., 17
Donruss Playoff L.P., 66
Dorsey & Whitney LLP, 47
Doskocil Companies, Inc., 12
Dot Foods, Inc., 69
Double-Cola Co.-USA, 70
DoubleClick Inc., 46
Doubletree Corporation, 21
Douglas & Lomason Company, 16
Dover Corporation, III; 28 (upd.)
Dover Downs Entertainment, Inc., 43
Dover Publications Inc., 34
Dow Chemical Company, The, I; 8 (upd.); 50 (upd.)
Dow Jones & Company, Inc., IV; 19 (upd.); 47 (upd.)
Dow Jones Telerate, Inc., 10
DPL Inc., 6
DQE, Inc., 6
Dr Pepper/Seven Up, Inc., 9; 32 (upd.)
Drackett Professional Products, 12
Drake Beam Morin, Inc., 44
DreamWorks SKG, 43
Drees Company, Inc., The, 41
Dress Barn, Inc., The, 24; 55 (upd.)
Dresser Industries, Inc., III
Drew Industries Inc., 28

Drexel Burnham Lambert Incorporated, II
Drexel Heritage Furnishings Inc., 12
Dreyer's Grand Ice Cream, Inc., 17
Dreyfus Corporation, The, 70
DriveTime Automotive Group Inc., 68
  (upd.)
DRS Technologies, Inc., 58
Drs. Foster & Smith, Inc., 62
Drug Emporium, Inc., 12
Drypers Corporation, 18
DSC Communications Corporation, 12
DTE Energy Company, 20 (upd.)
Duane Reade Holding Corp., 21
Duck Head Apparel Company, Inc., 42
Duckwall-ALCO Stores, Inc., 24
Ducommun Incorporated, 30
Duke Energy Corporation, V; 27 (upd.)
Duke Realty Corporation, 57
Dun & Bradstreet Corporation, The, IV; 19
  (upd.); 61 (upd.)
Dun & Bradstreet Software Services Inc.,
  11
Dunavant Enterprises, Inc., 54
Duncan Toys Company, 55
Dunn-Edwards Corporation, 56
Duplex Products Inc., 17
Duracell International Inc., 9; 71 (upd.)
Durametallic, 21
Duriron Company Inc., 17
Duron Inc., 72
Duty Free International, Inc., 11
DVI, Inc., 51
Dycom Industries, Inc., 57
Dyersburg Corporation, 21
Dynatech Corporation, 13
DynCorp, 45
Dynegy Inc., 49 (upd.)
E! Entertainment Television Inc., 17
E*Trade Financial Corporation, 20; 60
  (upd.)
E. & J. Gallo Winery, I; 7 (upd.); 28 (upd.)
E.I. du Pont de Nemours & Company, I; 8
  (upd.); 26 (upd.)
E.piphany, Inc., 49
E-Systems, Inc., 9
E.W. Howell Co., Inc., 72
E.W. Scripps Company, The, IV; 7 (upd.);
  28 (upd.); 66 (upd.)
E-Z Serve Corporation, 17
Eagle Hardware & Garden, Inc., 16
Eagle-Picher Industries, Inc., 8; 23 (upd.)
Earl Scheib, Inc., 32
Earthgrains Company, The, 36
EarthLink, Inc., 36
Easter Seals, Inc., 58
Eastern Airlines, I
Eastern Company, The, 48
Eastern Enterprises, 6
EastGroup Properties, Inc., 67
Eastman Chemical Company, 14; 38 (upd.)
Eastman Kodak Company, III; 7 (upd.); 36
  (upd.)
Easton Sports, Inc., 66
Eateries, Inc., 33
Eaton Corporation, I; 10 (upd.); 67 (upd.)
Eaton Vance Corporation, 18
eBay Inc., 32; 67 (upd.)
EBSCO Industries, Inc., 17; 40 (upd.)
ECC International Corp., 42
Echlin Inc., I; 11 (upd.)
Echo Design Group, Inc., The, 68
EchoStar Communications Corporation, 35
Eckerd Corporation, 9; 32 (upd.)
Ecolab, Inc., I; 13 (upd.); 34 (upd.)
Ecology and Environment, Inc., 39
Eddie Bauer, Inc., 9; 36 (upd.)
Edelbrock Corporation, 37

Edelman, 62
Edge Petroleum Corporation, 67
Edison Brothers Stores, Inc., 9
Edison International, 56 (upd.)
Edison Schools Inc., 37
Edmark Corporation, 14; 41 (upd.)
EDO Corporation, 46
Education Management Corporation, 35
Educational Broadcasting Corporation, 48
Educational Testing Service, 12; 62 (upd.)
Edw. C. Levy Co., 42
Edward D. Jones & Company L.P., 30; 66
  (upd.)
Edward Hines Lumber Company, 68
Edward J. DeBartolo Corporation, The, 8
Edwards and Kelcey, 70
Edwards Theatres Circuit, Inc., 31
EG&G Incorporated, 8; 29 (upd.)
Egghead.com, Inc., 9; 31 (upd.)
EGL, Inc., 59
eHarmony.com Inc., 71
84 Lumber Company, 9; 39 (upd.)
800-JR Cigar, Inc., 27
Eileen Fisher Inc., 61
Einstein/Noah Bagel Corporation, 29
Ekco Group, Inc., 16
El Camino Resources International, Inc., 11
El Chico Restaurants, Inc., 19
El Paso Corporation, 66 (upd.)
El Paso Electric Company, 21
El Paso Natural Gas Company, 12
El Pollo Loco, Inc., 69
Elamex, S.A. de C.V., 51
Elano Corporation, 14
Elder-Beerman Stores Corp., The, 10; 63
  (upd.)
Electric Lightwave, Inc., 37
Electro Rent Corporation, 58
Electromagnetic Sciences Inc., 21
Electronic Arts Inc., 10
Electronic Data Systems Corporation, III;
  28 (upd.)
Electronics Boutique Holdings Corporation,
  72
Electronics for Imaging, Inc., 15; 43 (upd.)
Elektra Entertainment Group, 64
Eli Lilly and Company, I; 11 (upd.); 47
  (upd.)
Elizabeth Arden, Inc., 8; 40 (upd.)
Eljer Industries, Inc., 24
ElkCorp, 52
Ellen Tracy, Inc., 55
Ellerbe Becket, 41
Ellett Brothers, Inc., 17
Elmer's Restaurants, Inc., 42
Elsinore Corporation, 48
Elvis Presley Enterprises, Inc., 61
Embers America Restaurants, 30
Embrex, Inc., 72
EMC Corporation, 12; 46 (upd.)
EMCOR Group Inc., 60
Emerson, II; 46 (upd.)
Emerson Radio Corp., 30
Emery Worldwide Airlines, Inc., 6; 25
  (upd.)
Emge Packing Co., Inc., 11
Emigrant Savings Bank, 59
Emmis Communications Corporation, 47
Empi, Inc., 26
Empire Blue Cross and Blue Shield, III
Empire Resorts, Inc., 72
Employee Solutions, Inc., 18
ENCAD, Incorporated, 25
Encompass Services Corporation, 33
Encore Computer Corporation, 13
Encyclopaedia Britannica, Inc., 7; 39 (upd.)
Endo Pharmaceuticals Holdings Inc., 71

Energen Corporation, 21
Energizer Holdings, Inc., 32
Enesco Corporation, 11
Engelhard Corporation, IV; 21 (upd.); 72
  (upd.)
Engineered Support Systems, Inc., 59
Engle Homes, Inc., 46
Engraph, Inc., 12
Ennis Business Forms, Inc., 21
Enquirer/Star Group, Inc., 10
Enrich International, Inc., 33
Enron Corporation, V; 19; 46 (upd.)
ENSCO International Incorporated, 57
Ensearch Corporation, V
Entercom Communications Corporation, 58
Entergy Corporation, V; 45 (upd.)
Enterprise Rent-A-Car Company, 6; 69
  (upd.)
Entravision Communications Corporation,
  41
Envirodyne Industries, Inc., 17
Environmental Industries, Inc., 31
Environmental Power Corporation, 68
Environmental Systems Research Institute
  Inc. (ESRI), 62
Enzo Biochem, Inc., 41
Eon Labs, Inc., 67
Epic Systems Corporation, 62
EPIQ Systems, Inc., 56
Equifax, Inc., 6; 28 (upd.)
Equistar Chemicals, LP, 71
Equitable Life Assurance Society of the
  United States, III
Equitable Resources, Inc., 6; 54 (upd.)
Equity Marketing, Inc., 26
Equity Office Properties Trust, 54
Equity Residential, 49
Equus Computer Systems, Inc., 49
Erickson Retirement Communities, 57
Erie Indemnity Company, 35
ERLY Industries Inc., 17
Ernie Ball, Inc., 56
Ernst & Young, 9; 29 (upd.)
Escalade, Incorporated, 19
Eschelon Telecom, Inc., 72
Eskimo Pie Corporation, 21
ESPN, Inc., 56
Esprit de Corp., 8; 29 (upd.)
ESS Technology, Inc., 22
Essef Corporation, 18
Esselte, 64
Esselte Pendaflex Corporation, 11
Essence Communications, Inc., 24
Estée Lauder Companies Inc., The, 9; 30
  (upd.)
Esterline Technologies Corp., 15
Eternal Word Television Network, Inc., 57
Ethan Allen Interiors, Inc., 12; 39 (upd.)
Ethicon, Inc., 23
Ethyl Corporation, I; 10 (upd.)
EToys, Inc., 37
Eureka Company, The, 12
Euromarket Designs Inc., 31 (upd.)
Europe Through the Back Door Inc., 65
Evans & Sutherland Computer Corporation,
  19
Evans, Inc., 30
Everex Systems, Inc., 16
Evergreen International Aviation, Inc., 53
Everlast Worldwide Inc., 47
Exabyte Corporation, 12; 40 (upd.)
Exar Corp., 14
EXCEL Communications Inc., 18
Excel Technology, Inc., 65
Executive Jet, Inc., 36
Executone Information Systems, Inc., 13
Exelon Corporation, 48 (upd.)

United States (*continued*)

Exide Electronics Group, Inc., 20
Expedia, Inc., 58
Expeditors International of Washington Inc., 17
Experian Information Solutions Inc., 45
Express Scripts Inc., 17; 44 (upd.)
Extended Stay America, Inc., 41
EXX Inc., 65
Exxon Corporation, IV; 7 (upd.); 32 (upd.)
Exxon Mobil Corporation, 67 (upd.)
Eye Care Centers of America, Inc., 69
EZCORP Inc., 43
F&W Publications, Inc., 71
F. Korbel & Bros. Inc., 68
Fab Industries, Inc., 27
Fabri-Centers of America Inc., 16
Fair Grounds Corporation, 44
Fair, Isaac and Company, 18
Fairchild Aircraft, Inc., 9
Fairfield Communities, Inc., 36
Falcon Products, Inc., 33
Fallon McElligott Inc., 22
Fallon Worldwide, 71 (upd.)
Family Christian Stores, Inc., 51
Family Dollar Stores, Inc., 13; 62 (upd.)
Family Golf Centers, Inc., 29
Famous Dave's of America, Inc., 40
Fannie Mae, 45 (upd.)
Fansteel Inc., 19
FAO Schwarz, 46
Farah Incorporated, 24
Farley Northwest Industries, Inc., I
Farley's & Sathers Candy Company, Inc., 62
Farm Family Holdings, Inc., 39
Farm Journal Corporation, 42
Farmer Bros. Co., 52
Farmers Insurance Group of Companies, 25
Farmland Foods, Inc., 7
Farmland Industries, Inc., 48
Farrar, Straus and Giroux Inc., 15
Fastenal Company, 14; 42 (upd.)
Fatburger Corporation, 64
Faultless Starch/Bon Ami Company, 55
Fay's Inc., 17
Faygo Beverages Inc., 55
Fazoli's Systems, Inc., 27
Featherlite Inc., 28
Fedders Corporation, 18; 43 (upd.)
Federal Express Corporation, V
Federal National Mortgage Association, II
Federal Paper Board Company, Inc., 8
Federal Prison Industries, Inc., 34
Federal Signal Corp., 10
Federal-Mogul Corporation, I; 10 (upd.); 26 (upd.)
Federated Department Stores Inc., 9; 31 (upd.)
FedEx Corporation, 18 (upd.); 42 (upd.)
Feed The Children, Inc., 68
Feld Entertainment, Inc., 32 (upd.)
Fellowes Manufacturing Company, 28
Fender Musical Instruments Company, 16; 43 (upd.)
Fenwick & West LLP, 34
Ferolito, Vultaggio & Sons, 27
Ferrellgas Partners, L.P., 35
Ferro Corporation, 8; 56 (upd.)
F5 Networks, Inc., 72
FHP International Corporation, 6
FiberMark, Inc., 37
Fibreboard Corporation, 16
Fidelity Investments Inc., II; 14 (upd.)
Fidelity National Financial Inc., 54
Fieldale Farms Corporation, 23
Fieldcrest Cannon, Inc., 9; 31 (upd.)

Fifth Third Bancorp, 13; 31 (upd.)
Figgie International Inc., 7
FileNet Corporation, 62
Fili Enterprises, Inc., 70
Film Roman, Inc., 58
FINA, Inc., 7
Fingerhut Companies, Inc., 9; 36 (upd.)
Finish Line, Inc., The, 29; 68 (upd.)
FinishMaster, Inc., 24
Finlay Enterprises, Inc., 16
Firearms Training Systems, Inc., 27
Fireman's Fund Insurance Company, III
First Albany Companies Inc., 37
First Alert, Inc., 28
First American Corporation, The 52
First Aviation Services Inc., 49
First Bank System Inc., 12
First Brands Corporation, 8
First Cash Financial Services, Inc., 57
First Chicago Corporation, II
First Commerce Bancshares, Inc., 15
First Commerce Corporation, 11
First Data Corporation, 30 (upd.)
First Empire State Corporation, 11
First Executive Corporation, III
First Fidelity Bank, N.A., New Jersey, 9
First Financial Management Corporation, 11
First Hawaiian, Inc., 11
First Industrial Realty Trust, Inc., 65
First Interstate Bancorp, II
First Mississippi Corporation, 8
First Nationwide Bank, 14
First of America Bank Corporation, 8
First Security Corporation, 11
First Team Sports, Inc., 22
First Tennessee National Corporation, 11; 48 (upd.)
First Union Corporation, 10
First USA, Inc., 11
First Virginia Banks, Inc., 11
First Years Inc., The, 46
Firstar Corporation, 11; 33 (upd.)
Fiserv Inc., 11; 33 (upd.)
Fish & Neave, 54
Fisher Companies, Inc., 15
Fisher Controls International, LLC, 13; 61 (upd.)
Fisher Scientific International Inc., 24
Fisher-Price Inc., 12; 32 (upd.)
Fisk Corporation, 72
5 & Diner Franchise Corporation, 72
Flagstar Companies, Inc., 10
Flanders Corporation, 65
Flanigan's Enterprises, Inc., 60
Fleer Corporation, 15
FleetBoston Financial Corporation, 9; 36 (upd.)
Fleetwood Enterprises, Inc., III; 22 (upd.)
Fleming Companies, Inc., II; 17 (upd.)
Flexsteel Industries Inc., 15; 41 (upd.)
FlightSafety International, Inc., 9; 29 (upd.)
Flint Ink Corporation, 13; 41 (upd.)
FLIR Systems, Inc., 69
Florida Crystals Inc., 35
Florida East Coast Industries, Inc., 59
Florida Gaming Corporation, 47
Florida Progress Corporation, V; 23 (upd.)
Florida Public Utilities Company, 69
Florida Rock Industries, Inc., 46
Florida's Natural Growers, 45
Florists' Transworld Delivery, Inc., 28
Florsheim Shoe Group Inc., 9; 31 (upd.)
Flour City International, Inc., 44
Flow International Corporation, 56
Flowers Industries, Inc., 12; 35 (upd.)
Flowserve Corporation, 33

Fluke Corporation, 15
Fluor Corporation, I; 8 (upd.); 34 (upd.)
Flying Boat, Inc. (Chalk's Ocean Airways), 56
Flying J Inc., 19
FMC Corporation, I; 11 (upd.)
FMR Corp., 8; 32 (upd.)
Foamex International Inc., 17
Foley & Lardner, 28
Follett Corporation, 12; 39 (upd.)
Food Emporium, The, 64
Food Lion LLC, II; 15 (upd.), 66 (upd.)
Foodarama Supermarkets, Inc., 28
FoodBrands America, Inc., 23
Foodmaker, Inc., 14
Foot Locker, Inc., 68 (upd.)
Foote, Cone & Belding Worldwide, I; 66 (upd.)
Footstar, Incorporated, 24
Forbes Inc., 30
Ford Foundation, The, 34
Ford Motor Company, I; 11 (upd.); 36 (upd.); 64 (upd.)
FORE Systems, Inc., 25
Forest City Enterprises, Inc., 16; 52 (upd.)
Forest Laboratories, Inc., 11; 52 (upd.)
Forest Oil Corporation, 19
Forever Living Products International Inc., 17
Formica Corporation, 13
Forrester Research, Inc., 54
Forstmann Little & Co., 38
Fort Howard Corporation, 8
Fort James Corporation, 22 (upd.)
Fortune Brands, Inc., 29 (upd.); 68 (upd.)
Fortunoff Fine Jewelry and Silverware Inc., 26
Fossil, Inc., 17
Foster Poultry Farms, 32
Foster Wheeler Corporation, 6; 23 (upd.)
FosterGrant, Inc., 60
Foundation Health Corporation, 12
Fountain Powerboats Industries, Inc., 28
4Kids Entertainment Inc., 59
Fourth Financial Corporation, 11
Fox Entertainment Group, Inc., 43
Fox Family Worldwide, Inc., 24
Foxboro Company, 13
FoxMeyer Health Corporation, 16
FPL Group, Inc., V; 49 (upd.)
Frank J. Zamboni & Co., Inc., 34
Frank Russell Company, 46
Frank's Nursery & Crafts, Inc., 12
Frankel & Co., 39
Franklin Covey Company, 11; 37 (upd.)
Franklin Electric Company, Inc., 43
Franklin Electronic Publishers, Inc., 23
Franklin Mint, The, 69
Franklin Resources, Inc., 9
Fred Meyer Stores, Inc., V; 20 (upd.); 64 (upd.)
Fred Usinger Inc., 54
Fred W. Albrecht Grocery Co., The, 13
Fred Weber, Inc., 61
Fred's, Inc., 23; 62 (upd.)
Freddie Mac, 54
Frederick Atkins Inc., 16
Frederick's of Hollywood, Inc., 16; 59 (upd.)
Freedom Communications, Inc., 36
Freeport-McMoRan Copper & Gold, Inc., IV; 7 (upd.); 57 (upd.)
French Fragrances, Inc., 22
Frequency Electronics, Inc., 61
Fresh America Corporation, 20
Fresh Choice, Inc., 20
Fresh Enterprises, Inc., 66

Fresh Foods, Inc., 29
Fretter, Inc., 10
Fried, Frank, Harris, Shriver & Jacobson, 35
Friedman's Inc., 29
Friedman, Billings, Ramsey Group, Inc., 53
Friendly Ice Cream Corporation, 30; 72 (upd.)
Frigidaire Home Products, 22
Frisch's Restaurants, Inc., 35
Frito-Lay Company, 32
Fritz Companies, Inc., 12
Frontier Airlines, Inc., 22
Frontier Corp., 16
Frost & Sullivan, Inc., 53
Frozen Food Express Industries, Inc., 20
Fruehauf Corporation, I
Fruit of the Loom, Inc., 8; 25 (upd.)
Fruth Pharmacy, Inc., 66
Fry's Electronics, Inc., 68
Frymaster Corporation, 27
FSI International, Inc., 17
FTP Software, Inc., 20
Fubu, 29
Fujitsu-ICL Systems Inc., 11
Fulbright & Jaworski L.L.P., 47
Funco, Inc., 20
Fuqua Enterprises, Inc., 17
Fuqua Industries, Inc., I
Furniture Brands International, Inc., 39 (upd.)
Furon Company, 28
Furr's Restaurant Group, Inc., 53
Furr's Supermarkets, Inc., 28
Future Now, Inc., 12
G&K Services, Inc., 16
G-III Apparel Group, Ltd., 22
G. Heileman Brewing Company Inc., I
G. Leblanc Corporation, 55
G.A.F., I
G.D. Searle & Company, I; 12 (upd.); 34 (upd.)
G.I. Joe's, Inc., 30
G.S. Blodgett Corporation, 15
Gabelli Asset Management Inc., 30
Gables Residential Trust, 49
Gadzooks, Inc., 18
GAF Corporation, 22 (upd.)
Gage Marketing Group, 26
Gaiam, Inc., 41
Gainsco, Inc., 22
Galardi Group, Inc., 72
Galaxy Nutritional Foods, Inc., 58
Galey & Lord, Inc., 20; 66 (upd.)
Gallup Organization, The, 37
Galyan's Trading Company, Inc., 47
Gambrinus Company, The, 40
GameStop Corp., 69 (upd.)
Gander Mountain, Inc., 20
Gannett Company, Inc., IV; 7 (upd.); 30 (upd.); 66 (upd.)
Gantos, Inc., 17
Gap, Inc., The, V; 18 (upd.); 55 (upd.)
Garan, Inc., 16; 64 (upd.)
Garden Fresh Restaurant Corporation, 31
Garden Ridge Corporation, 27
Gardenburger, Inc., 33
Gardner Denver, Inc., 49
Gart Sports Company, 24
Gartner Group, Inc., 21
Gates Corporation, The, 9
Gateway, Inc., 10; 27 (upd.); 63 (upd.)
GATX Corporation, 6; 25 (upd.)
Gaylord Container Corporation, 8
Gaylord Entertainment Company, 11; 36 (upd.)
GC Companies, Inc., 25

GE Aircraft Engines, 9
GE Capital Aviation Services, 36
Geerlings & Wade, Inc., 45
Geffen Records Inc., 26
Gehl Company, 19
GEICO Corporation, 10; 40 (upd.)
Geiger Bros., 60
Gemini Sound Products Corporation, 58
GenCorp Inc., 8; 9
Genentech, Inc., I; 8 (upd.); 32 (upd.)
General Atomics, 57
General Bearing Corporation, 45
General Binding Corporation, 10
General Cable Corporation, 40
General Chemical Group Inc., The, 37
General Cigar Holdings, Inc., 66 (upd.)
General Cinema Corporation, I
General DataComm Industries, Inc., 14
General Dynamics Corporation, I; 10 (upd.); 40 (upd.)
General Electric Company, II; 12 (upd.); 34 (upd.); 63 (upd.)
General Growth Properties, Inc., 57
General Host Corporation, 12
General Housewares Corporation, 16
General Instrument Corporation, 10
General Maritime Corporation, 59
General Mills, Inc., II; 10 (upd.); 36 (upd.)
General Motors Corporation, I; 10 (upd.); 36 (upd.); 64 (upd.)
General Nutrition Companies, Inc., 11; 29 (upd.)
General Public Utilities Corporation, V
General Re Corporation, III; 24 (upd.)
General Signal Corporation, 9
General Tire, Inc., 8
Genesco Inc., 17
Genesee & Wyoming Inc., 27
Genesis Health Ventures, Inc., 18
Genetics Institute, Inc., 8
Geneva Steel, 7
Genmar Holdings, Inc., 45
Genovese Drug Stores, Inc., 18
GenRad, Inc., 24
Gentex Corporation, 26
Genuardi's Family Markets, Inc., 35
Genuine Parts Company, 9; 45 (upd.)
Genzyme Corporation, 13; 38 (upd.)
Geon Company, The, 11
George A. Hormel and Company, II
George F. Cram Company, Inc., The, 55
George P. Johnson Company, 60
George S. May International Company, 55
Georgia Gulf Corporation, 9; 61 (upd.)
Georgia-Pacific Corporation, IV; 9 (upd.); 47 (upd.)
Geotek Communications Inc., 21
Gerald Stevens, Inc., 37
Gerber Products Company, 7; 21 (upd.)
Gerber Scientific, Inc., 12
German American Bancorp, 41
Getty Images, Inc., 31
Gevity HR, Inc., 63
Ghirardelli Chocolate Company, 30
Giant Cement Holding, Inc., 23
Giant Food Inc., II; 22 (upd.)
Giant Industries, Inc., 19; 61 (upd.)
Gibraltar Steel Corporation, 37
Gibson Greetings, Inc., 12
Gibson Guitar Corp., 16
Gibson, Dunn & Crutcher LLP, 36
Giddings & Lewis, Inc., 10
Gilbane, Inc., 34
Gilead Sciences, Inc., 54
Gillett Holdings, Inc., 7
Gillette Company, The, III; 20 (upd.); 68 (upd.)

Gilman & Ciocia, Inc., 72
Girl Scouts of the USA, 35
Gitano Group, Inc., The, 8
Glacier Bancorp, Inc., 35
Glacier Water Services, Inc., 47
Glamis Gold, Ltd., 54
Gleason Corporation, 24
Glidden Company, The, 8
Global Berry Farms LLC, 62
Global Crossing Ltd., 32
Global Industries, Ltd., 37
Global Marine Inc., 9
Global Outdoors, Inc., 49
Global Power Equipment Group Inc., 52
GlobalSantaFe Corporation, 48 (upd.)
GM Hughes Electronics Corporation, II
Godfather's Pizza Incorporated, 25
Godiva Chocolatier, Inc., 64
Gold Kist Inc., 17; 26 (upd.)
Gold'n Plump Poultry, 54
Gold's Gym International, Inc., 71
Golden Belt Manufacturing Co., 16
Golden Books Family Entertainment, Inc., 28
Golden Corral Corporation, 10; 66 (upd.)
Golden Enterprises, Inc., 26
Golden Krust Caribbean Bakery, Inc., 68
Golden State Foods Corporation, 32
Golden State Vintners, Inc., 33
Golden West Financial Corporation, 47
Goldman Sachs Group Inc., The, II; 20 (upd.); 51 (upd.)
Golub Corporation, The, 26
Gonnella Baking Company, 40
Good Guys, Inc., The, 10; 30 (upd.)
Good Humor-Breyers Ice Cream Company, 14
Goodman Holding Company, 42
GoodMark Foods, Inc., 26
Goodrich Corporation, 46 (upd.)
GoodTimes Entertainment Ltd., 48
Goodwill Industries International, Inc., 16; 66 (upd.)
Goody Products, Inc., 12
Goody's Family Clothing, Inc., 20; 64 (upd.)
Goodyear Tire & Rubber Company, The, V; 20 (upd.)
Google, Inc., 50
Gordon Food Service Inc., 8; 39 (upd.)
Gorman-Rupp Company, The, 18; 57 (upd.)
Gorton's, 13
Goss Holdings, Inc., 43
Gottschalks, Inc., 18
Gould Electronics, Inc., 14
Goulds Pumps Inc., 24
Goya Foods Inc., 22
GP Strategies Corporation, 64 (upd.)
GPU, Inc., 27 (upd.)
Graco Inc., 19; 67 (upd.)
Graham Corporation, 62
GranCare, Inc., 14
Grand Casinos, Inc., 20
Grand Piano & Furniture Company, 72
Grand Union Company, The, 7; 28 (upd.)
Granite Broadcasting Corporation, 42
Granite Construction Incorporated, 61
Granite Rock Company, 26
Granite State Bankshares, Inc., 37
Grant Prideco, Inc., 57
Grant Thornton International, 57
Graphic Industries, Inc., 25
Gray Communications Systems, Inc., 24
Graybar Electric Company, Inc., 54
Great American Management and Investment, Inc., 8

United States (*continued*)

Great Atlantic & Pacific Tea Company, Inc., The, II; 16 (upd.); 55 (upd.)
Great Harvest Bread Company, 44
Great Lakes Bancorp, 8
Great Lakes Chemical Corporation, I; 14 (upd.)
Great Lakes Dredge & Dock Company, 69
Great Plains Energy Incorporated, 65 (upd.)
Great Western Financial Corporation, 10
Greatbatch Inc., 72
Grede Foundries, Inc., 38
Green Bay Packers, Inc., The, 32
Green Mountain Coffee, Inc., 31
Green Tree Financial Corporation, 11
Greenberg Traurig, LLP, 65
Greenbrier Companies, The, 19
Greene, Tweed & Company, 55
GreenPoint Financial Corp., 28
Greenwood Mills, Inc., 14
Greg Manning Auctions, Inc., 60
Greif Inc., 15; 66 (upd.)
Grey Advertising, Inc., 6
Grey Global Group Inc., 66 (upd.)
Grey Wolf, Inc., 43
Greyhound Lines, Inc., I; 32 (upd.)
Griffin Industries, Inc., 70
Griffin Land & Nurseries, Inc., 43
Griffon Corporation, 34
Grinnell Corp., 13
Grist Mill Company, 15
Gristede's Foods Inc., 31; 68 (upd.)
Grolier Incorporated, 16; 43 (upd.)
Grossman's Inc., 13
Ground Round, Inc., 21
Group 1 Automotive, Inc., 52
Group Health Cooperative, 41
Grow Biz International, Inc., 18
Grow Group Inc., 12
Grubb & Ellis Company, 21
Grumman Corporation, I; 11 (upd.)
Gruntal & Co., L.L.C., 20
Gryphon Holdings, Inc., 21
GSD&M Advertising, 44
GSI Commerce, Inc., 67
GT Bicycles, 26
GT Interactive Software, 31
GTE Corporation, V; 15 (upd.)
GTSI Corp., 57
Guangzhou Pearl River Piano Group Ltd., 49
Guccio Gucci, S.p.A., 15
Guess, Inc., 15; 68 (upd.)
Guest Supply, Inc., 18
Guidant Corporation, 58
Guilford Mills Inc., 8; 40 (upd.)
Guitar Center, Inc., 29; 68 (upd.)
Guittard Chocolate Company, 55
Gulf & Western Inc., I
Gulf Island Fabrication, Inc., 44
Gulf States Utilities Company, 6
GulfMark Offshore, Inc., 49
Gulfstream Aerospace Corporation, 7; 28 (upd.)
Gunite Corporation, 51
Gunlocke Company, The, 23
Guthy-Renker Corporation, 32
Gwathmey Siegel & Associates Architects LLC, 26
Gymboree Corporation, 15; 69 (upd.)
H & R Block, Incorporated, 9; 29 (upd.)
H.B. Fuller Company, 8; 32 (upd.)
H.D. Vest, Inc., 46
H.E. Butt Grocery Company, 13; 32 (upd.)
H.F. Ahmanson & Company, II; 10 (upd.)

H.J. Heinz Company, II; 11 (upd.); 36 (upd.)
H.J. Russell & Company, 66
H.M. Payson & Co., 69
H.W. Wilson Company, The, 66
Ha-Lo Industries, Inc., 27
Habersham Bancorp, 25
Habitat for Humanity International, 36
Hach Co., 18
Hadco Corporation, 24
Haemonetics Corporation, 20
Haggar Corporation, 19
Haggen Inc., 38
Hahn Automotive Warehouse, Inc., 24
Hain Celestial Group, Inc., The, 27; 43 (upd.)
HAL Inc., 9
Hale-Halsell Company, 60
Half Price Books, Records, Magazines Inc., 37
Hall, Kinion & Associates, Inc., 52
Halliburton Company, III; 25 (upd.); 55 (upd.)
Hallmark Cards, Inc., IV; 16 (upd.); 40 (upd.)
Hamilton Beach/Proctor-Silex Inc., 17
Hammacher Schlemmer & Company Inc., 21; 72 (upd.)
Hampton Industries, Inc., 20
Hancock Fabrics, Inc., 18
Hancock Holding Company, 15
Handleman Company, 15
Handspring Inc., 49
Handy & Harman, 23
Hanger Orthopedic Group, Inc., 41
Hanmi Financial Corporation, 66
Hanna Andersson Corp., 49
Hanna-Barbera Cartoons Inc., 23
Hannaford Bros. Co., 12
Hanover Compressor Company, 59
Hanover Direct, Inc., 36
Hanover Foods Corporation, 35
Hansen Natural Corporation, 31
Hanson Building Materials America Inc., 60
Happy Kids Inc., 30
Harbert Corporation, 14
Harbison-Walker Refractories Company, 24
Harcourt Brace and Co., 12
Harcourt Brace Jovanovich, Inc., IV
Harcourt General, Inc., 20 (upd.)
Hard Rock Cafe International, Inc., 12; 32 (upd.)
Harding Lawson Associates Group, Inc., 16
Hardinge Inc., 25
Harlem Globetrotters International, Inc., 61
Harley-Davidson Inc., 7; 25 (upd.)
Harleysville Group Inc., 37
Harman International Industries Inc., 15
Harmon Industries, Inc., 25
Harmonic Inc., 43
Harnischfeger Industries, Inc., 8; 38 (upd.)
Harold's Stores, Inc., 22
Harper Group Inc., 17
HarperCollins Publishers, 15
Harpo Inc., 28; 66 (upd.)
Harrah's Entertainment, Inc., 16; 43 (upd.)
Harris Corporation, II; 20 (upd.)
Harris Interactive Inc., 41
Harris Teeter Inc., 23; 72 (upd.)
Harry London Candies, Inc., 70
Harry N. Abrams, Inc., 58
Harry Winston Inc., 45
Harry's Farmers Market Inc., 23
Harsco Corporation, 8
Harte-Hanks, Inc., 17; 63 (upd.)
Hartmarx Corporation, 8; 32 (upd.)

Hartz Mountain Corporation, The, 12; 46 (upd.)
Harveys Casino Resorts, 27
Harza Engineering Company, 14
Hasbro, Inc., III; 16 (upd.); 43 (upd.)
Haskel International, Inc., 59
Hastings Entertainment, Inc., 29
Hastings Manufacturing Company, 56
Hauser, Inc., 46
Haverty Furniture Companies, Inc., 31
Hawaiian Airlines, Inc., 22 (upd.)
Hawaiian Electric Industries, Inc., 9
Hawk Corporation, 59
Hawkins Chemical, Inc., 16
Haworth Inc., 8; 39 (upd.)
Hayes Corporation, 24
Hayes Lemmerz International, Inc., 27
Hazelden Foundation, 28
HCA - The Healthcare Company, 35 (upd.)
HCI Direct, Inc., 55
HDOS Enterprises, 72
HDR Inc., 48
Headwaters Incorporated, 56
Headway Corporate Resources, Inc., 40
Health Care & Retirement Corporation, 22
Health Communications, Inc., 72
Health Management Associates, Inc., 56
Health O Meter Products Inc., 14
Health Risk Management, Inc., 24
Health Systems International, Inc., 11
HealthSouth Corporation, 14; 33 (upd.)
Healthtex, Inc., 17
Hearst Corporation, The, IV; 19 (upd.); 46 (upd.)
Heartland Express, Inc., 18
Heat Group, The, 53
Hechinger Company, 12
Hecla Mining Company, 20
Heekin Can Inc., 13
Heery International, Inc., 58
HEICO Corporation, 30
Heidrick & Struggles International, Inc., 28
Heilig-Meyers Company, 14; 40 (upd.)
Helen of Troy Corporation, 18
Helene Curtis Industries, Inc., 8; 28 (upd.)
Heller, Ehrman, White & McAuliffe, 41
Helmerich & Payne, Inc., 18
Helmsley Enterprises, Inc., 9; 39 (upd.)
Helzberg Diamonds, 40
Henkel Manco Inc., 22
Henley Group, Inc., The, III
Henry Modell & Company Inc., 32
Henry Schein, Inc., 31; 70 (upd.)
Hensel Phelps Construction Company, 72
Hensley & Company, 64
Herbalife International, Inc., 17; 41 (upd.)
Hercules Inc., I; 22 (upd.); 66 (upd.)
Herley Industries, Inc., 33
Herman Goelitz, Inc., 28
Herman Miller, Inc., 8
Hershey Foods Corporation, II; 15 (upd.); 51 (upd.)
Hertz Corporation, The, 9; 33 (upd.)
Heska Corporation, 39
Heublein, Inc., I
Hewlett-Packard Company, III; 6 (upd.); 28 (upd.); 50 (upd.)
Hexcel Corporation, 28
Hibbett Sporting Goods, Inc., 26; 70 (upd.)
Hibernia Corporation, 37
Hickory Farms, Inc., 17
Highmark Inc., 27
Highsmith Inc., 60
Hildebrandt International, 29
Hill's Pet Nutrition, Inc., 27
Hillenbrand Industries, Inc., 10
Hillerich & Bradsby Company, Inc., 51

Hillhaven Corporation, The, 14
Hills Stores Company, 13
Hilton Hotels Corporation, III; 19 (upd.); 62 (upd.)
Hines Horticulture, Inc., 49
Hispanic Broadcasting Corporation, 35
Hitchiner Manufacturing Co., Inc., 23
HMI Industries, Inc., 17
Ho-Chunk Inc., 61
HOB Entertainment, Inc., 37
Hoechst Celanese Corporation, 13
Hoenig Group Inc., 41
Hogan & Hartson L.L.P., 44
HOK Group, Inc., 59
Holberg Industries, Inc., 36
Holiday Inns, Inc., III
Holiday RV Superstores, Incorporated, 26
Holland & Knight LLP, 60
Holland Burgerville USA, 44
Hollander Home Fashions Corp., 67
Holley Performance Products Inc., 52
Hollinger International Inc., 24
Holly Corporation, 12
Hollywood Casino Corporation, 21
Hollywood Entertainment Corporation, 25
Hollywood Media Corporation, 58
Hollywood Park, Inc., 20
Holme Roberts & Owen LLP, 28
Holnam Inc., 8; 39 (upd.)
Holophane Corporation, 19
Holson Burnes Group, Inc., 14
Holt and Bugbee Company, 66
Holt's Cigar Holdings, Inc., 42
Homasote Company, 72
Home Box Office Inc., 7; 23 (upd.)
Home Depot, Inc., The, V; 18 (upd.)
Home Insurance Company, The, III
Home Interiors & Gifts, Inc., 55
Home Products International, Inc., 55
Home Properties of New York, Inc., 42
Home Shopping Network, Inc., V; 25 (upd.)
HomeBase, Inc., 33 (upd.)
Homestake Mining Company, 12; 38 (upd.)
Hometown Auto Retailers, Inc., 44
HON INDUSTRIES Inc., 13
Honda Motor Company Limited, I; 10 (upd.); 29 (upd.)
Honeywell Inc., II; 12 (upd.); 50 (upd.)
Hooper Holmes, Inc., 22
Hooters of America, Inc., 18; 69 (upd.)
Hoover Company, The, 12; 40 (upd.)
Hops Restaurant Bar and Brewery, 46
Horace Mann Educators Corporation, 22
Horizon Organic Holding Corporation, 37
Hormel Foods Corporation, 18 (upd.); 54 (upd.)
Horsehead Industries, Inc., 51
Horseshoe Gaming Holding Corporation, 62
Horton Homes, Inc., 25
Hospira, Inc., 71
Hospital Central Services, Inc., 56
Hospital Corporation of America, III
Hospitality Franchise Systems, Inc., 11
Hospitality Worldwide Services, Inc., 26
Hoss's Steak and Sea House Inc., 68
Hot Topic, Inc., 33
Houchens Industries Inc., 51
Houghton Mifflin Company, 10; 36 (upd.)
House of Fabrics, Inc., 21
Household International, Inc., II; 21 (upd.)
Houston Industries Incorporated, V
Hovnanian Enterprises, Inc., 29
Howard Hughes Medical Institute, 39
Howard Johnson International, Inc., 17; 72 (upd.)

Howmet Corp., 12
HSN, 64 (upd.)
Hub Group, Inc., 38
Hubbard Broadcasting Inc., 24
Hubbell Incorporated, 9; 31 (upd.)
Hudson Foods Inc., 13
Hudson River Bancorp, Inc., 41
Huffy Corporation, 7; 30 (upd.)
Hughes Electronics Corporation, 25
Hughes Hubbard & Reed LLP, 44
Hughes Markets, Inc., 22
Hughes Supply, Inc., 14
Hulman & Company, 44
Humana Inc., III; 24 (upd.)
Humane Society of the United States, The, 54
Hungry Howie's Pizza and Subs, Inc., 25
Hunt Consolidated, Inc., 27 (upd.)
Hunt Manufacturing Company, 12
Hunt Oil Company, 7
Hunt-Wesson, Inc., 17
Hunter Fan Company, 13
Huntington Bancshares Inc., 11
Huntington Learning Centers, Inc., 55
Hunton & Williams, 35
Huntsman Chemical Corporation, 8
Hutchinson Technology Incorporated, 18; 63 (upd.)
Hvide Marine Incorporated, 22
Hy-Vee, Inc., 36
Hyatt Corporation, III; 16 (upd.)
Hyde Athletic Industries, Inc., 17
Hydril Company, 46
Hypercom Corporation, 27
Hyperion Software Corporation, 22
Hyster Company, 17
I.C. Isaacs & Company, 31
Iams Company, 26
IBERIABANK Corporation, 37
IBP, Inc., II; 21 (upd.)
IC Industries, Inc., I
ICF Kaiser International, Inc., 28
ICN Pharmaceuticals, Inc., 52
Icon Health & Fitness, Inc., 38
Idaho Power Company, 12
IDB Communications Group, Inc., 11
Identix Inc., 44
IDEO Inc., 65
IDEXX Laboratories, Inc., 23
IDG Books Worldwide, Inc., 27
IDT Corporation, 34
IDX Systems Corporation, 64
IEC Electronics Corp., 42
Igloo Products Corp., 21
IHOP Corporation, 17; 58 (upd.)
IKON Office Solutions, Inc., 50
Il Fornaio (America) Corporation, 27
Ilitch Holdings Inc., 37
Illinois Bell Telephone Company, 14
Illinois Central Corporation, 11
Illinois Power Company, 6
Illinois Tool Works Inc., III; 22 (upd.)
ILX Resorts Incorporated, 65
Imagine Foods, Inc., 50
Imation Corporation, 20
IMC Fertilizer Group, Inc., 8
ImClone Systems Inc., 58
IMCO Recycling, Incorporated, 32
Immunex Corporation, 14; 50 (upd.)
Imo Industries Inc., 7; 27 (upd.)
IMPATH Inc., 45
Imperial Holly Corporation, 12
Imperial Sugar Company, 32 (upd.)
IMS Health, Inc., 57
In Focus Systems, Inc., 22
In-N-Out Burger, 19
In-Sink-Erator, 66

InaCom Corporation, 13
Incyte Genomics, Inc., 52
Indiana Bell Telephone Company, Incorporated, 14
Indiana Energy, Inc., 27
Indianapolis Motor Speedway Corporation, 46
Indus International Inc., 70
Industrial Services of America, Inc., 46
Infinity Broadcasting Corporation, 11; 48 (upd.)
Information Access Company, 17
Information Builders, Inc., 22
Information Holdings Inc., 47
Information Resources, Inc., 10
Informix Corporation, 10; 30 (upd.)
Ingalls Shipbuilding, Inc., 12
Ingersoll-Rand Company Ltd., III; 15 (upd.); 55 (upd.)
Ingles Markets, Inc., 20
Ingram Industries, Inc., 11; 49 (upd.)
Ingram Micro Inc., 52
Initial Security, 64
Inktomi Corporation, 45
Inland Container Corporation, 8
Inland Steel Industries, Inc., IV; 19 (upd.)
Inserra Supermarkets, 25
Insight Enterprises, Inc., 18
Insilco Corporation, 16
Inso Corporation, 26
Instinet Corporation, 34
Insurance Auto Auctions, Inc., 23
Integrated Defense Technologies, Inc., 54
Integrity Inc., 44
Intel Corporation, II; 10 (upd.); 36 (upd.)
IntelliCorp, Inc., 45
Intelligent Electronics, Inc., 6
Inter Parfums Inc., 35
Inter-Regional Financial Group, Inc., 15
Interbrand Corporation, 70
Interco Incorporated, III
InterDigital Communications Corporation, 61
Interep National Radio Sales Inc., 35
Interface, Inc., 8; 29 (upd.)
Intergraph Corporation, 6; 24 (upd.)
Interlake Corporation, The, 8
Intermec Technologies Corporation, 72
Intermet Corporation, 32
Intermountain Health Care, Inc., 27
International Airline Support Group, Inc., 55
International Brotherhood of Teamsters, 37
International Business Machines Corporation, III; 6 (upd.); 30 (upd.); 63 (upd.)
International Controls Corporation, 10
International Creative Management, Inc., 43
International Dairy Queen, Inc., 10; 39 (upd.)
International Data Group, Inc., 7; 25 (upd.)
International Family Entertainment Inc., 13
International Flavors & Fragrances Inc., 9; 38 (upd.)
International Game Technology, 10; 41 (upd.)
International Lease Finance Corporation, 48
International Management Group, 18
International Multifoods Corporation, 7; 25 (upd.)
International Paper Company, IV; 15 (upd.); 47 (upd.)
International Rectifier Corporation, 31; 71 (upd.)
International Shipbreaking Ltd. L.L.C., 67

United States (*continued*)

International Shipholding Corporation, Inc., 27

International Speedway Corporation, 19

International Telephone & Telegraph Corporation, I; 11 (upd.)

International Total Services, Inc., 37

Interpublic Group of Companies, Inc., The, I; 22 (upd.)

Interscope Music Group, 31

Interstate Bakeries Corporation, 12; 38 (upd.)

Interstate Hotels & Resorts Inc., 58

Intimate Brands, Inc., 24

Intrado Inc., 63

Intuit Inc., 14; 33 (upd.)

Invacare Corporation, 11; 47 (upd.)

Inverness Medical Innovations, Inc., 63

Invitrogen Corporation, 52

Invivo Corporation, 52

Iomega Corporation, 21

Ionics, Incorporated, 52

IPALCO Enterprises, Inc., 6

Ipsen International Inc., 72

Iron Mountain, Inc., 33

Irvin Feld & Kenneth Feld Productions, Inc., 15

Island ECN, Inc., The, 48

Isle of Capri Casinos, Inc., 41

Ispat Inland Inc., 40 (upd.)

Itel Corporation, 9

Items International Airwalk Inc., 17

Itron, Inc., 64

ITT Educational Services, Inc., 33

ITT Sheraton Corporation, III

IVAX Corporation, 11; 55 (upd.)

IVC Industries, Inc., 45

iVillage Inc., 46

Iwerks Entertainment, Inc., 34

IXC Communications, Inc., 29

J & J Snack Foods Corporation, 24

J&R Electronics Inc., 26

J. & W. Seligman & Co. Inc., 61

J. Alexander's Corporation, 65

J. Baker, Inc., 31

J. Crew Group Inc., 12; 34 (upd.)

J. D'Addario & Company, Inc., 48

J. Jill Group, Inc., The, 35

J.A. Jones, Inc., 16

J.B. Hunt Transport Services Inc., 12

J.C. Penney Company, Inc., V; 18 (upd.); 43 (upd.)

J.D. Edwards & Company, 14

J.D. Power and Associates, 32

J.F. Shea Co., Inc., 55

J.H. Findorff and Son, Inc., 60

J.I. Case Company, 10

J.L. Hammett Company, 72

J.M. Smucker Company, The, 11

J.P. Morgan & Co. Incorporated, II; 30 (upd.)

J.P. Morgan Chase & Co., 38 (upd.)

J.R. Simplot Company, 16; 60 (upd.)

Jabil Circuit, Inc., 36

Jack Henry and Associates, Inc., 17

Jack Schwartz Shoes, Inc., 18

Jackpot Enterprises Inc., 21

Jackson Hewitt, Inc., 48

Jackson National Life Insurance Company, 8

Jaco Electronics, Inc., 30

Jacob Leinenkugel Brewing Company, 28

Jacobs Engineering Group Inc., 6; 26 (upd.)

Jacobson Stores Inc., 21

Jacor Communications, Inc., 23

Jacuzzi Inc., 23

JAKKS Pacific, Inc., 52

Jalate Inc., 25

Jamba Juice Company, 47

James River Corporation of Virginia, IV

JanSport, Inc., 70

Janus Capital Group Inc., 57

Jason Incorporated, 23

Jay Jacobs, Inc., 15

Jayco Inc., 13

Jazz Basketball Investors, Inc., 55

Jazzercise, Inc., 45

JB Oxford Holdings, Inc., 32

JDS Uniphase Corporation, 34

Jefferies Group, Inc., 25

Jefferson-Pilot Corporation, 11; 29 (upd.)

Jeld-Wen, Inc., 45

Jenkens & Gilchrist, P.C., 65

Jennifer Convertibles, Inc., 31

Jenny Craig, Inc., 10; 29 (upd.)

Jerry's Famous Deli Inc., 24

Jervis B. Webb Company, 24

JetBlue Airways Corporation, 44

Jetro Cash & Carry Enterprises Inc., 38

JG Industries, Inc., 15

Jillian's Entertainment Holdings, Inc., 40

Jim Beam Brands Worldwide, Inc., 14; 58 (upd.)

Jim Henson Company, The, 23

Jitney-Jungle Stores of America, Inc., 27

JLG Industries, Inc., 52

JLM Couture, Inc., 64

JMB Realty Corporation, IV

Jo-Ann Stores, Inc., 72 (upd.)

Jockey International, Inc., 12; 34 (upd.)

Joffrey Ballet of Chicago, The 52

John B. Sanfilippo & Son, Inc., 14

John D. and Catherine T. MacArthur Foundation, The, 34

John Frieda Professional Hair Care Inc., 70

John H. Harland Company, 17

John Hancock Financial Services, Inc., III; 42 (upd.)

John Nuveen Company, The, 21

John Paul Mitchell Systems, 24

John Q. Hammons Hotels, Inc., 24

John W. Danforth Company, 48

John Wiley & Sons, Inc., 17; 65 (upd.)

Johnny Rockets Group, Inc., 31

Johns Manville Corporation, 64 (upd.)

Johnson & Higgins, 14

Johnson & Johnson, III; 8 (upd.); 36 (upd.)

Johnson Controls, Inc., III; 26 (upd.); 59 (upd.)

Johnson Publishing Company, Inc., 28; 72 (upd.)

Johnson Worldwide Associates, Inc., 28

Johnsonville Sausage L.L.C., 63

Johnston Industries, Inc., 15

Johnstown America Industries, Inc., 23

Jones Apparel Group, Inc., 11; 39 (upd.)

Jones, Day, Reavis & Pogue, 33

Jones Intercable, Inc., 21

Jones Lang LaSalle Incorporated, 49

Jones Medical Industries, Inc., 24

Jones Soda Co., 69

Jordache Enterprises, Inc., 23

Jordan Company LP, The, 70

Jordan Industries, Inc., 36

Jos. A. Bank Clothiers, Inc., 31

Joseph T. Ryerson & Son, Inc., 15

Jostens, Inc., 7; 25 (upd.)

JOULÉ Inc., 58

Journal Register Company, 29

JPI, 49

JPS Textile Group, Inc., 28

Judge Group, Inc., The, 51

Juniper Networks, Inc., 43

Juno Lighting, Inc., 30

Juno Online Services, Inc., 38

Just Born, Inc., 32

Just For Feet, Inc., 19

Justin Industries, Inc., 19

JWP Inc., 9

JWT Group Inc., I

K & B Inc., 12

K & G Men's Center, Inc., 21

K'Nex Industries, Inc., 52

K-Swiss, Inc., 33

K-tel International, Inc., 21

Kaiser Aluminum & Chemical Corporation, IV

Kaiser Foundation Health Plan, Inc., 53

Kal Kan Foods, Inc., 22

Kaman Corporation, 12; 42 (upd.)

Kaman Music Corporation, 68

Kampgrounds of America, Inc. 33

Kana Software, Inc., 51

Kansas City Power & Light Company, 6

Kansas City Southern Industries, Inc., 6; 26 (upd.)

Kaplan, Inc., 42

Karl Kani Infinity, Inc., 49

Karsten Manufacturing Corporation, 51

Kash n' Karry Food Stores, Inc., 20

Kasper A.S.L., Ltd., 40

kate spade LLC, 68

Katy Industries, Inc., I; 51 (upd.)

Katz Communications, Inc., 6

Katz Media Group, Inc., 35

Kaufman and Broad Home Corporation, 8

Kaydon Corporation, 18

KB Home, 45 (upd.)

KB Toys, 15; 35 (upd.)

Keane, Inc., 56

Keebler Foods Company, 36

Keith Companies Inc., The, 54

Keithley Instruments Inc., 16

Kelley Drye & Warren LLP, 40

Kellogg Brown & Root, Inc., 62 (upd.)

Kellogg Company, II; 13 (upd.); 50 (upd.)

Kellwood Company, 8

Kelly Services Inc., 6; 26 (upd.)

Kelly-Moore Paint Company, Inc., 56

Kelly-Springfield Tire Company, The, 8

Kelsey-Hayes Group of Companies, 7; 27 (upd.)

Kemet Corp., 14

Kemper Corporation, III; 15 (upd.)

Kendall International, Inc., 11

Kendall-Jackson Winery, Ltd., 28

Kenetech Corporation, 11

Kenmore Air Harbor Inc., 65

Kennametal Inc., 68 (upd.)

Kennedy-Wilson, Inc., 60

Kenneth Cole Productions, Inc., 25

Kensey Nash Corporation, 71

Kent Electronics Corporation, 17

Kentucky Electric Steel, Inc., 31

Kentucky Utilities Company, 6

Kerr Group Inc., 24

Kerr-McGee Corporation, IV; 22 (upd.); 68 (upd.)

Ketchum Communications Inc., 6

Kettle Foods Inc., 48

Kewaunee Scientific Corporation, 25

Key Safety Systems, Inc., 63

Key Tronic Corporation, 14

KeyCorp, 8

Keyes Fibre Company, 9

KeySpan Energy Co., 27

Keystone International, Inc., 11

KFC Corporation, 7; 21 (upd.)

Kforce Inc., 71

KI, 57

Kidde, Inc., I
Kiehl's Since 1851, Inc., 52
Kikkoman Corporation, 47 (upd.)
Kimball International, Inc., 12; 48 (upd.)
Kimberly-Clark Corporation, III; 16 (upd.); 43 (upd.)
Kimco Realty Corporation, 11
Kinder Morgan, Inc., 45
KinderCare Learning Centers, Inc., 13
Kinetic Concepts, Inc. (KCI), 20
King & Spalding, 23
King Arthur Flour Company, The, 31
King Kullen Grocery Co., Inc., 15
King Pharmaceuticals, Inc., 54
King Ranch, Inc., 14; 60 (upd.)
King World Productions, Inc., 9; 30 (upd.)
Kingston Technology Corporation, 20
Kinko's, Inc., 16; 43 (upd.)
Kinney Shoe Corp., 14
Kirby Corporation, 18; 66 (upd.)
Kirkland & Ellis LLP, 65
Kirshenbaum Bond + Partners, Inc., 57
Kit Manufacturing Co., 18
Kitchell Corporation, 14
KitchenAid, 8
Kitty Hawk, Inc., 22
Kiwi International Airlines Inc., 20
KLA-Tencor Corporation, 11; 45 (upd.)
Kleiner, Perkins, Caufield & Byers, 53
Klement's Sausage Company, 61
Kmart Corporation, V; 18 (upd.); 47 (upd.)
Knape & Vogt Manufacturing Company, 17
Knight Ridder, Inc., 67 (upd.)
Knight Trading Group, Inc., 70
Knight Transportation, Inc., 64
Knight-Ridder, Inc., IV; 15 (upd.)
Knoll Group Inc., 14
Knott's Berry Farm, 18
Knowledge Learning Corporation, 51
Knowledge Universe, Inc., 54
KnowledgeWare Inc., 9; 31 (upd.)
Koala Corporation, 44
Koch Enterprises, Inc., 29
Koch Industries, Inc., IV; 20 (upd.)
Kohl's Corporation, 9; 30 (upd.)
Kohlberg Kravis Roberts & Co., 24; 56 (upd.)
Kohler Company, 7; 32 (upd.)
Kohn Pedersen Fox Associates P.C., 57
Koll Company, The, 8
Kollmorgen Corporation, 18
Komag, Inc., 11
Koo Koo Roo, Inc., 25
Koppers Industries, Inc., I; 26 (upd.)
Koret of California, Inc., 62
Korn/Ferry International, 34
Kos Pharmaceuticals, Inc., 63
Koss Corporation, 38
Kraft Foods Inc., II; 7 (upd.); 45 (upd.)
KraftMaid Cabinetry, Inc., 72
Kraus-Anderson, Incorporated, 36
Krause Publications, Inc., 35
Krause's Furniture, Inc., 27
Krispy Kreme Doughnuts, Inc., 21; 61 (upd.)
Kroger Company, The, II; 15 (upd.); 65 (upd.)
Kroll Inc., 57
Kronos, Inc., 18
Krystal Company, The, 33
K2 Inc., 16
KU Energy Corporation, 11
Kuhlman Corporation, 20
Kulicke and Soffa Industries, Inc., 33
Kurzweil Technologies, Inc., 51
Kushner-Locke Company, The, 25

L-3 Communications Holdings, Inc., 48
L. and J.G. Stickley, Inc., 50
L. Luria & Son, Inc., 19
L.A. Gear, Inc., 8; 32 (upd.)
L.A. T Sportswear, Inc., 26
L.B. Foster Company, 33
L.L. Bean, Inc., 10; 38 (upd.)
L.L. Knickerbocker Co., Inc., The, 25
L.S. Starrett Company, 13; 64 (upd.)
La Choy Food Products Inc., 25
La Madeleine French Bakery & Café, 33
La Quinta Companies, The, 11; 42 (upd.)
La-Z-Boy Incorporated, 14; 50 (upd.)
LaBarge Inc., 41
LabOne, Inc., 48
Labor Ready, Inc., 29
Laboratory Corporation of America Holdings, 42 (upd.)
LaBranche & Co. Inc., 37
Lacks Enterprises Inc., 61
Laclede Steel Company, 15
LaCrosse Footwear, Inc., 18; 61 (upd.)
LADD Furniture, Inc., 12
Ladish Co., Inc., 30
Lafarge Corporation, 28
Lakeland Industries, Inc., 45
Lakes Entertainment, Inc., 51
Lam Research Corporation, 11; 31 (upd.)
Lamar Advertising Company, 27; 70 (upd.)
Lamaur Corporation, The, 41
Lamb Weston, Inc., 23
Lamonts Apparel, Inc., 15
Lamson & Sessions Co., The, 13; 61 (upd.)
Lancair International, Inc., 67
Lancaster Colony Corporation, 8; 61 (upd.)
Lance, Inc., 14; 41 (upd.)
Lancer Corporation, 21
Land O'Lakes, Inc., II; 21 (upd.)
Landauer, Inc., 51
Landmark Communications, Inc., 12; 55 (upd.)
Landmark Theatre Corporation, 70
Landry's Restaurants, Inc., 65 (upd.)
Landry's Seafood Restaurants, Inc., 15
Lands' End, Inc., 9; 29 (upd.)
Landstar System, Inc., 63
Lane Bryant, Inc., 64
Lane Co., Inc., The, 12
Lanoga Corporation, 62
Larry Flynt Publishing Inc., 31
Larry H. Miller Group, 29
Las Vegas Sands, Inc., 50
Laserscope, 67
Lason, Inc., 31
Latham & Watkins, 33
Latrobe Brewing Company, 54
Lattice Semiconductor Corp., 16
Lawson Software, 38
Lawter International Inc., 14
Layne Christensen Company, 19
Lazare Kaplan International Inc., 21
Lazy Days RV Center, Inc., 69
LCI International, Inc., 16
LDB Corporation, 53
LDDS-Metro Communications, Inc., 8
Leap Wireless International, Inc., 69
LeapFrog Enterprises, Inc., 54
Lear Corporation, 71 (upd.)
Lear Seating Corporation, 16
Lear Siegler, Inc., I
Learjet Inc., 8; 27 (upd.)
Learning Company Inc., The, 24
Learning Tree International Inc., 24
LeaRonal, Inc., 23
Leaseway Transportation Corp., 12
Leatherman Tool Group, Inc., 51
Lebhar-Friedman, Inc., 55

LeBoeuf, Lamb, Greene & MacRae, L.L.P., 29
Lechmere Inc., 10
Lechters, Inc., 11; 39 (upd.)
LeCroy Corporation, 41
Lee Apparel Company, Inc., 8
Lee Enterprises Inc., 11; 64 (upd.)
Leeann Chin, Inc., 30
Lefrak Organization Inc., 26
Legal Aid Society, The, 48
Legent Corporation, 10
Legg Mason, Inc., 33
Leggett & Platt, Inc., 11; 48 (upd.)
Lehigh Portland Cement Company, 23
Leiner Health Products Inc., 34
Lennar Corporation, 11
Lennox International Inc., 8; 28 (upd.)
Lenox, Inc., 12
LensCrafters Inc., 23
Leo Burnett Company Inc., I; 20 (upd.)
Leprino Foods Company, 28
Les Schwab Tire Centers, 50
Lesco Inc., 19
Leslie Fay Companies, Inc., The, 8; 39 (upd.)
Leslie's Poolmart, Inc., 18
Leucadia National Corporation, 11; 71 (upd.)
Leupold & Stevens, Inc., 52
Level 3 Communications, Inc., 67
Levenger Company, 63
Lever Brothers Company, 9
Levi Strauss & Co., V; 16 (upd.)
Levitz Furniture Inc., 15
Levy Restaurants L.P., 26
Lewis Galoob Toys Inc., 16
LEXIS-NEXIS Group, 33
Lexmark International, Inc., 18
LG&E Energy Corporation, 6; 51 (upd.)
Libbey Inc., 49
Liberty Corporation, The, 22
Liberty Livewire Corporation, 42
Liberty Media Corporation, 50
Liberty Mutual Holding Company, 59
Liberty Property Trust, 57
Liberty Travel, Inc., 56
Life Technologies, Inc., 17
Life Time Fitness, Inc., 66
Lifeline Systems, Inc., 53
LifePoint Hospitals, Inc., 69
Lifetime Entertainment Services, 51
Lifetime Hoan Corporation, 27
Lifeway Foods, Inc., 65
Ligand Pharmaceuticals Incorporated, 47
Lillian Vernon Corporation, 12; 35 (upd.)
Lilly Endowment Inc., 70
Limited, Inc., The, V; 20 (upd.)
LIN Broadcasting Corp., 9
Lincare Holdings Inc., 43
Lincoln Center for the Performing Arts, Inc., 69
Lincoln Electric Co., 13
Lincoln National Corporation, III; 25 (upd.)
Lincoln Property Company, 8; 54 (upd.)
Lincoln Snacks Company, 24
Lincoln Telephone & Telegraph Company, 14
Lindal Cedar Homes, Inc., 29
Lindsay Manufacturing Co., 20
Linear Technology, Inc., 16
Linens 'n Things, Inc., 24
Lintas: Worldwide, 14
Lionel L.L.C., 16
Liqui-Box Corporation, 16
Litehouse Inc., 60
Lithia Motors, Inc., 41

United States (*continued*)

Littelfuse, Inc., 26
Little Caesar Enterprises, Inc., 7; 24 (upd.)
Little Tikes Company, 13; 62 (upd.)
Litton Industries, Inc., I; 11 (upd.)
LIVE Entertainment Inc., 20
Liz Claiborne, Inc., 8; 25 (upd.)
LKQ Corporation, 71
Lockheed Martin Corporation, I; 11 (upd.);
    15 (upd.)
Loctite Corporation, 8; 30 (upd.)
LodgeNet Entertainment Corporation, 28
Loehmann's Inc., 24
Loews Corporation, I; 12 (upd.); 36 (upd.)
Logan's Roadhouse, Inc., 29
Logicon Inc., 20
LoJack Corporation, 48
London Fog Industries, Inc., 29
Lone Star Steakhouse & Saloon, Inc., 51
Long Island Bancorp, Inc., 16
Long Island Lighting Company, V
Long Island Rail Road Company, The, 68
Long John Silver's, 13; 57 (upd.)
Longaberger Company, The, 12; 44 (upd.)
Longs Drug Stores Corporation, V; 25
    (upd.)
Longview Fibre Company, 8; 37 (upd.)
Loral Space & Communications Ltd., 8; 9;
    54 (upd.)
Lost Arrow Inc., 22
LOT$OFF Corporation, 24
Lotus Development Corporation, 6; 25
    (upd.)
Louisiana Land and Exploration Company,
    The, 7
Louisiana-Pacific Corporation, IV; 31
    (upd.)
Love's Travel Stops & Country Stores,
    Inc., 71
Lowe's Companies, Inc., V; 21 (upd.)
Lowrance Electronics, Inc., 18
LSI Logic Corporation, 13; 64
LTV Corporation, The, I; 24 (upd.)
Lubrizol Corporation, I; 30 (upd.)
Luby's, Inc., 17; 42 (upd.)
Lucasfilm Ltd., 12; 50 (upd.)
Lucent Technologies Inc., 34
Lucille Farms, Inc., 45
Lucky Stores, Inc., 27
Luigino's, Inc., 64
Lukens Inc., 14
Lunar Corporation, 29
Lund Food Holdings, Inc., 22
Lund International Holdings, Inc., 40
Lutheran Brotherhood, 31
Lydall, Inc., 64
Lynch Corporation, 43
Lyondell Chemical Company, IV; 45
    (upd.)
M&F Worldwide Corp., 38
M. Shanken Communications, Inc., 50
M.A. Bruder & Sons, Inc., 56
M.A. Gedney Co., 51
M.A. Hanna Company, 8
M.H. Meyerson & Co., Inc., 46
Mac Frugal's Bargains - Closeouts Inc., 17
Mac-Gray Corporation, 44
MacAndrews & Forbes Holdings Inc., 28
MacDermid Incorporated, 32
Mace Security International, Inc., 57
Macerich Company, The, 57
MacGregor Golf Company, 68
Mack Trucks, Inc., I; 22 (upd.); 61 (upd.)
Mack-Cali Realty Corporation, 42
Mackay Envelope Corporation, 45
Mackie Designs Inc., 33
Macmillan, Inc., 7

MacNeal-Schwendler Corporation, The, 25
Macromedia, Inc., 50
Madden's on Gull Lake, 52
Madison Gas and Electric Company, 39
Madison-Kipp Corporation, 58
Mag Instrument, Inc., 67
Magma Copper Company, 7
Magma Power Company, 11
MagneTek, Inc., 15; 41 (upd.)
MAI Systems Corporation, 11
Maid-Rite Corporation, 62
Maidenform, Inc., 20; 59 (upd.)
Mail Boxes Etc., 18; 41 (upd.)
Mail-Well, Inc., 28
Maine & Maritimes Corporation, 56
Maine Central Railroad Company, 16
Maines Paper & Food Service Inc., 71
Major Automotive Companies, Inc., The,
    45
Malcolm Pirnie, Inc., 42
Malden Mills Industries, Inc., 16
Mallinckrodt Group Inc., 19
Malt-O-Meal Company, 22; 63 (upd.)
Management and Training Corporation, 28
Mandalay Resort Group, 32 (upd.)
Manhattan Associates, Inc., 67
Manitowoc Company, Inc., The, 18; 59
    (upd.)
Mannatech Inc., 33
Manor Care, Inc., 6; 25 (upd.)
Manpower, Inc., 9; 30 (upd.)
Manufactured Home Communities, Inc., 22
Manufacturers Hanover Corporation, II
Manville Corporation, III; 7 (upd.)
MAPCO Inc., IV
MAPICS, Inc., 55
March of Dimes, 31
Marchex, Inc., 72
marchFIRST, Inc., 34
Marcus Corporation, The, 21
Marie Callender's Restaurant & Bakery,
    Inc., 28
MarineMax, Inc., 30
Marion Laboratories, Inc., I
Marisa Christina, Inc., 15
Maritz Inc., 38
Mark IV Industries, Inc., 7; 28 (upd.)
Marks Brothers Jewelers, Inc., 24
Marmon Group, The, IV; 16 (upd.)
Marmon Group, Inc., The, 70 (upd.)
Marquette Electronics, Inc., 13
Marriott International, Inc., III; 21 (upd.)
Mars, Incorporated, 7; 40 (upd.)
Marsh & McLennan Companies, Inc., III;
    45 (upd.)
Marsh Supermarkets, Inc., 17
Marshall & Ilsley Corporation, 56
Marshall Field's, 63
Marshalls Incorporated, 13
Martek Biosciences Corporation, 65
Martha Stewart Living Omnimedia, L.L.C.,
    24
Martin Industries, Inc., 44
Martin Marietta Corporation, I
Martz Group, 56
Marvel Entertainment Group, Inc., 10
Marvin Lumber & Cedar Company, 22
Mary Kay Corporation, 9; 30 (upd.)
Masco Corporation, III; 20 (upd.); 39
    (upd.)
Mashantucket Pequot Gaming Enterprise
    Inc., 35
Masland Corporation, 17
Massachusetts Mutual Life Insurance
    Company, III; 53 (upd.)
Massey Energy Company, 57
MasTec, Inc., 19; 55 (upd.)

Master Lock Company, 45
MasterBrand Cabinets, Inc., 71
MasterCard International, Inc., 9
Material Sciences Corporation, 63
Matria Healthcare, Inc., 17
Matrix Service Company, 65
Matt Prentice Restaurant Group, 70
Mattel, Inc., 7; 25 (upd.); 61 (upd.)
Matthews International Corporation, 29
Maui Land & Pineapple Company, Inc., 29
Mauna Loa Macadamia Nut Corporation,
    64
Maverick Tube Corporation, 59
Max & Erma's Restaurants Inc., 19
Maxco Inc., 17
Maxicare Health Plans, Inc., III; 25 (upd.)
Maxim Group, The, 25
Maxim Integrated Products, Inc., 16
MAXIMUS, Inc., 43
Maxtor Corporation, 10
Maxus Energy Corporation, 7
Maxwell Shoe Company, Inc., 30
MAXXAM Inc., 8
Maxxim Medical Inc., 12
May Department Stores Company, The, V;
    19 (upd.); 46 (upd.)
Mayer, Brown, Rowe & Maw, 47
Mayflower Group Inc., 6
Mayo Foundation, 9; 34 (upd.)
Mayor's Jewelers, Inc., 41
Maytag Corporation, III; 22 (upd.)
Mazel Stores, Inc., 29
MBC Holding Company, 40
MBNA Corporation, 12; 33 (upd.)
MCA Inc., II
McAlister's Corporation, 66
McCarthy Building Companies, Inc., 48
McCaw Cellular Communications, Inc., 6
McClain Industries, Inc., 51
McClatchy Newspapers, Inc., 23
McCormick & Company, Incorporated, 7;
    27 (upd.)
McCormick & Schmick's Seafood
    Restaurants, Inc., 71
McCoy Corporation, 58
McDermott International, Inc., III; 37
    (upd.)
McDonald's Corporation, II; 7 (upd.); 26
    (upd.); 63 (upd.)
McDonnell Douglas Corporation, I; 11
    (upd.)
McGraw-Hill Companies, Inc., The, IV; 18
    (upd.); 51 (upd.)
MCI WorldCom, Inc., V; 27 (upd.)
McIlhenny Company, 20
McJunkin Corporation, 63
McKee Foods Corporation, 7; 27 (upd.)
McKesson Corporation, I; 12; 47 (upd.)
McKinsey & Company, Inc., 9
McLane Company, Inc., 13
McLeodUSA Incorporated, 32
McMenamins Pubs and Breweries, 65
MCN Corporation, 6
MCSi, Inc., 41
McWane Corporation, 55
MDU Resources Group, Inc., 7; 42 (upd.)
Mead Corporation, The, IV; 19 (upd.)
Mead Data Central, Inc., 10
Meade Instruments Corporation, 41
Meadowcraft, Inc., 29
Measurement Specialties, Inc., 71
Mecklermedia Corporation, 24
Medco Containment Services Inc., 9
Media Arts Group, Inc., 42
Media General, Inc., 7; 38 (upd.)
Mediacom Communications Corporation,
    69

MediaNews Group, Inc., 70
Medical Information Technology Inc., 64
Medical Management International, Inc., 65
Medicis Pharmaceutical Corporation, 59
MedImmune, Inc., 35
Meditrust, 11
Medline Industries, Inc., 61
Medtronic, Inc., 8; 30 (upd.); 67 (upd.)
Medusa Corporation, 24
Megafoods Stores Inc., 13
Meier & Frank Co., 23
Meijer Incorporated, 7; 27 (upd.)
Mel Farr Automotive Group, 20
Melaleuca Inc., 31
Melamine Chemicals, Inc., 27
Mellon Bank Corporation, II
Mellon Financial Corporation, 44 (upd.)
Mellon-Stuart Company, I
Melville Corporation, V
Melvin Simon and Associates, Inc., 8
Memorial Sloan-Kettering Cancer Center, 57
Memry Corporation, 72
Men's Wearhouse, Inc., The, 17; 48 (upd.)
Menard, Inc., 34
Menasha Corporation, 8; 59 (upd.)
Mendocino Brewing Company, Inc., 60
Mentholatum Company Inc., The, 32
Mentor Corporation, 26
Mentor Graphics Corporation, 11
Mercantile Bankshares Corp., 11
Mercantile Stores Company, Inc., V; 19 (upd.)
Mercer International Inc., 64
Merck & Co., Inc., I; 11 (upd.); 34 (upd.)
Mercury Air Group, Inc., 20
Mercury General Corporation, 25
Mercury Interactive Corporation, 59
Mercury Marine Group, 68
Meredith Corporation, 11; 29 (upd.)
Meridian Bancorp, Inc., 11
Meridian Gold, Incorporated, 47
Merillat Industries Inc., 13
Merillat Industries, LLC, 69 (upd.)
Merisant Worldwide, Inc., 70
Merisel, Inc., 12
Merit Medical Systems, Inc., 29
Meritage Corporation, 26
Merix Corporation, 36
Merrell Dow, Inc., I; 9 (upd.)
Merriam-Webster Inc., 70
Merrill Corporation, 18; 47 (upd.)
Merrill Lynch & Co., Inc., II; 13 (upd.); 40 (upd.)
Merry-Go-Round Enterprises, Inc., 8
Mervyn's California, 10; 39 (upd.)
Mesa Air Group, Inc., 11; 32 (upd.)
Mesaba Holdings, Inc., 28
Mestek Inc., 10
Metatec International, Inc., 47
Meteor Industries Inc., 33
Methode Electronics, Inc., 13
Metris Companies Inc., 56
Metro Information Services, Inc., 36
Metro-Goldwyn-Mayer Inc., 25 (upd.)
Metrocall, Inc., 41
Metromedia Company, 7; 14; 61 (upd.)
Metropolitan Baseball Club Inc., 39
Metropolitan Financial Corporation, 13
Metropolitan Life Insurance Company, III; 52 (upd.)
Metropolitan Museum of Art, The, 55
Metropolitan Opera Association, Inc., 40
Metropolitan Transportation Authority, 35
Mexican Restaurants, Inc., 41
MFS Communications Company, Inc., 11
MGIC Investment Corp., 52

MGM Grand Inc., 17
MGM/UA Communications Company, II
Michael Anthony Jewelers, Inc., 24
Michael Baker Corporation, 14; 51 (upd.)
Michael C. Fina Co., Inc., 52
Michael Foods, Inc., 25
Michaels Stores, Inc., 17; 71 (upd.)
Michigan Bell Telephone Co., 14
Michigan National Corporation, 11
Michigan Sporting Goods Distributors, Inc., 72
Micro Warehouse, Inc., 16
MicroAge, Inc., 16
Microdot Inc., 8
Micron Technology, Inc., 11; 29 (upd.)
Micros Systems, Inc., 18
Microsoft Corporation, 6; 27 (upd.); 63 (upd.)
Mid-America Dairymen, Inc., 7
Midas Inc., 10; 56 (upd.)
Middleby Corporation, The, 22
Middlesex Water Company, 45
Middleton Doll Company, The, 53
Midland Company, The, 65
Midway Airlines Corporation, 33
Midway Games, Inc., 25
Midwest Express Holdings, Inc., 35
Midwest Grain Products, Inc., 49
Midwest Resources Inc., 6
Mikasa, Inc., 28
Mike-Sell's Inc., 15
Mikohn Gaming Corporation, 39
Milacron, Inc., 53 (upd.)
Milbank, Tweed, Hadley & McCloy, 27
Miles Laboratories, I
Millennium Pharmaceuticals, Inc., 47
Miller Brewing Company, I; 12 (upd.)
Miller Industries, Inc., 26
Miller Publishing Group, LLC, 57
Milliken & Co., V; 17 (upd.)
Milliman USA, 66
Millipore Corporation, 25
Milnot Company, 46
Milton Bradley Company, 21
Milwaukee Brewers Baseball Club, 37
Mine Safety Appliances Company, 31
Miner Group International, The, 22
Minerals Technologies Inc., 11; 52 (upd.)
Minnesota Mining & Manufacturing Company (3M), I; 8 (upd.); 26 (upd.)
Minnesota Power, Inc., 11; 34 (upd.)
Minntech Corporation, 22
Minute Maid Company, The, 28
Minuteman International Inc., 46
Minyard Food Stores, Inc., 33
Mirage Resorts, Incorporated, 6; 28 (upd.)
Miramax Film Corporation, 64
Mississippi Chemical Corporation, 39
Mitchell Energy and Development Corporation, 7
MITRE Corporation, 26
Mity Enterprises, Inc., 38
MNS, Ltd., 65
Mobil Corporation, IV; 7 (upd.); 21 (upd.)
Mobile Mini, Inc., 58
Mobile Telecommunications Technologies Corp., 18
Modern Woodmen of America, 66
Modine Manufacturing Company, 8; 56 (upd.)
Moen Incorporated, 12
Mohawk Industries, Inc., 19; 63 (upd.)
Mohegan Tribal Gaming Authority, 37
Molex Incorporated, 11; 54 (upd.)
Monaco Coach Corporation, 31
Monadnock Paper Mills, Inc., 21
Monarch Casino & Resort, Inc., 65

Monarch Cement Company, The, 72
Monfort, Inc., 13
Monro Muffler Brake, Inc., 24
Monrovia Nursery Company, 70
Monsanto Company, I; 9 (upd.); 29 (upd.)
Monster Cable Products, Inc., 69
Montana Coffee Traders, Inc., 60
Montana Power Company, The, 11; 44 (upd.)
Monterey Pasta Company, 58
Montgomery Ward & Co., Incorporated, V; 20 (upd.)
Moody's Corporation, 65
Moog Inc., 13
Mooney Aerospace Group Ltd., 52
Moore Medical Corp., 17
Moore-Handley, Inc., 39
Moran Towing Corporation, Inc., 15
Morgan Group, Inc., The, 46
Morgan Stanley Dean Witter & Company, II; 16 (upd.); 33 (upd.)
Morgan, Lewis & Bockius LLP, 29
Morningstar Inc., 68
Morris Communications Corporation, 36
Morris Travel Services L.L.C., 26
Morrison Knudsen Corporation, 7; 28 (upd.)
Morrison Restaurants Inc., 11
Morse Shoe Inc., 13
Morton International Inc., 9 (upd.)
Morton Thiokol, Inc., I
Morton's Restaurant Group, Inc., 30
Mosinee Paper Corporation, 15
Mossimo, Inc., 27
Motel 6, 13; 56 (upd.)
Mothers Against Drunk Driving (MADD), 51
Mothers Work, Inc., 18
Motley Fool, Inc., The, 40
Moto Photo, Inc., 45
Motor Cargo Industries, Inc., 35
Motorcar Parts & Accessories, Inc., 47
Motorola, Inc., II; 11 (upd.); 34 (upd.)
Motown Records Company L.P., 26
Mott's Inc., 57
Mountain States Mortgage Centers, Inc., 29
Movado Group, Inc., 28
Movie Gallery, Inc., 31
Movie Star Inc., 17
MPS Group, Inc., 49
MPW Industrial Services Group, Inc., 53
Mr. Coffee, Inc., 15
Mr. Gasket Inc., 15
Mrs. Baird's Bakeries, 29
Mrs. Fields' Original Cookies, Inc., 27
MSC Industrial Direct Co., Inc., 71
Mt. Olive Pickle Company, Inc., 44
MTS Inc., 37
Mueller Industries, Inc., 7; 52 (upd.)
Mullen Advertising Inc., 51
Multi-Color Corporation, 53
Multimedia Games, Inc., 41
Multimedia, Inc., 11
Murdock Madaus Schwabe, 26
Murphy Family Farms Inc., 22
Murphy Oil Corporation, 7; 32 (upd.)
Musicland Stores Corporation, 9; 38 (upd.)
Mutual Benefit Life Insurance Company, The, III
Mutual Life Insurance Company of New York, The, III
Muzak, Inc., 18
MWH Preservation Limited Partnership, 65
Mycogen Corporation, 21
Myers Industries, Inc., 19
Mylan Laboratories Inc., I; 20 (upd.); 59 (upd.)

United States (*continued*)

N.F. Smith & Associates LP, 70
Nabisco Foods Group, II; 7 (upd.)
Nabors Industries, Inc., 9
NACCO Industries, Inc., 7
Nalco Chemical Corporation, I; 12 (upd.)
Nantucket Allserve, Inc., 22
Napster, Inc., 69
NASD, 54 (upd.)
Nash Finch Company, 8; 23 (upd.); 65 (upd.)
Nashua Corporation, 8
Nathan's Famous, Inc., 29
National Amusements Inc., 28
National Association for Stock Car Auto Racing, 32
National Association of Securities Dealers, Inc., 10
National Audubon Society, 26
National Auto Credit, Inc., 16
National Beverage Corp., 26
National Broadcasting Company, Inc., II; 6 (upd.); 28 (upd.)
National Can Corporation, I
National Car Rental System, Inc., 10
National City Corp., 15
National Convenience Stores Incorporated, 7
National Discount Brokers Group, Inc., 28
National Distillers and Chemical Corporation, I
National Educational Music Co. Ltd., 47
National Envelope Corporation, 32
National Equipment Services, Inc., 57
National Financial Partners Corp., 65
National Football League, 29
National Fuel Gas Company, 6
National Geographic Society, 9; 30 (upd.)
National Grape Cooperative Association, Inc., 20
National Grid USA, 51 (upd.)
National Gypsum Company, 10
National Health Laboratories Incorporated, 11
National Heritage Academies, Inc., 60
National Hockey League, 35
National Home Centers, Inc., 44
National Instruments Corporation, 22
National Intergroup, Inc., V
National Journal Group Inc., 67
National Media Corporation, 27
National Medical Enterprises, Inc., III
National Oilwell, Inc., 54
National Organization for Women, Inc., 55
National Patent Development Corporation, 13
National Picture & Frame Company, 24
National Presto Industries, Inc., 16; 43 (upd.)
National Public Radio, Inc., 19; 47 (upd.)
National R.V. Holdings, Inc., 32
National Railroad Passenger Corporation (Amtrak), 22; 66 (upd.)
National Record Mart, Inc., 29
National Rifle Association of America, 37
National Sanitary Supply Co., 16
National Semiconductor Corporation, II; VI, 26 (upd.); 69 (upd.)
National Service Industries, Inc., 11; 54 (upd.)
National Standard Co., 13
National Starch and Chemical Company, 49
National Steel Corporation, 12
National TechTeam, Inc., 41
National Thoroughbred Racing Association, 58

National Wine & Spirits, Inc., 49
NationsBank Corporation, 10
Natrol, Inc., 49
Natural Alternatives International, Inc., 49
Natural Ovens Bakery, Inc., 72
Natural Selection Foods, 54
Natural Wonders Inc., 14
Nature Conservancy, The, 28
Nature's Sunshine Products, Inc., 15
Nautica Enterprises, Inc., 18; 44 (upd.)
Navarre Corporation, 24
Navigant International, Inc., 47
Navistar International Corporation, I; 10 (upd.)
NAVTEQ Corporation, 69
Navy Exchange Service Command, 31
Navy Federal Credit Union, 33
NBD Bancorp, Inc., 11
NBTY, Inc., 31
NCH Corporation, 8
NCNB Corporation, II
NCO Group, Inc., 42
NCR Corporation, III; 6 (upd.); 30 (upd.)
Nebraska Book Company, Inc., 65
Nebraska Public Power District, 29
Neenah Foundry Company, 68
Neff Corp., 32
NeighborCare, Inc., 67 (upd.)
Neiman Marcus Group, Inc., The, 12; 49 (upd.)
NERCO, Inc., 7
Netezza Corporation, 69
Netflix, Inc., 58
Netscape Communications Corporation, 15; 35 (upd.)
Network Appliance, Inc., 58
Network Associates, Inc., 25
Neuberger Berman Inc., 57
Neutrogena Corporation, 17
Nevada Bell Telephone Company, 14
Nevada Power Company, 11
New Balance Athletic Shoe, Inc., 25; 68 (upd.)
New Belgium Brewing Company, Inc., 68
New Brunswick Scientific Co., Inc., 45
New Dana Perfumes Company, 37
New England Business Services, Inc., 18
New England Confectionery Co., 15
New England Electric System, V
New England Mutual Life Insurance Company, III
New Jersey Resources Corporation, 54
New Line Cinema, Inc., 47
New Orleans Saints LP, 58
New Piper Aircraft, Inc., The, 44
New Plan Realty Trust, 11
New Street Capital Inc., 8
New Times, Inc., 45
New Valley Corporation, 17
New World Pasta Company, 53
New World Restaurant Group, Inc., 44
New York City Health and Hospitals Corporation, 60
New York City Off-Track Betting Corporation, 51
New York Daily News, 32
New York Health Care, Inc., 72
New York Life Insurance Company, III; 45 (upd.)
New York Restaurant Group, Inc., 32
New York State Electric and Gas, 6
New York Stock Exchange, Inc., 9; 39 (upd.)
New York Times Company, The, IV; 19 (upd.); 61 (upd.)
Newcor, Inc., 40
Newell Rubbermaid Inc., 9; 52 (upd.)

Newfield Exploration Company, 65
Newhall Land and Farming Company, 14
Newman's Own, Inc., 37
Newmont Mining Corporation, 7
Newpark Resources, Inc., 63
Newport Corporation, 71
Newport News Shipbuilding Inc., 13; 38 (upd.)
News America Publishing Inc., 12
NewYork-Presbyterian Hospital, 59
Nextel Communications, Inc., 10; 27 (upd.)
NFO Worldwide, Inc., 24
NGC Corporation, 18
Niagara Corporation, 28
Niagara Mohawk Holdings Inc., V; 45 (upd.)
Nichols Research Corporation, 18
Nicklaus Companies, 45
NICOR Inc., 6
NIKE, Inc., V; 8 (upd.); 36 (upd.)
Nikken Global Inc., 32
Niman Ranch, Inc., 67
Nimbus CD International, Inc., 20
Nine West Group, Inc., 11; 39 (upd.)
99¢ Only Stores, 25
NIPSCO Industries, Inc., 6
Nitches, Inc., 53
NL Industries, Inc., 10
Nobel Learning Communities, Inc., 37
Noble Affiliates, Inc., 11
Noble Roman's Inc., 14
Noland Company, 35
Nolo.com, Inc., 49
Noodle Kidoodle, 16
Noodles & Company, Inc., 55
Nooter Corporation, 61
Norcal Waste Systems, Inc., 60
NordicTrack, 22
Nordson Corporation, 11; 48 (upd.)
Nordstrom, Inc., V; 18 (upd.); 67 (upd.)
Norelco Consumer Products Co., 26
Norfolk Southern Corporation, V; 29 (upd.)
Norm Thompson Outfitters, Inc., 47
Norrell Corporation, 25
Norstan, Inc., 16
Nortek, Inc., 34
North Atlantic Trading Company Inc., 65
North Face, Inc., The, 18
North Fork Bancorporation, Inc., 46
North Pacific Group, Inc., 61
North Star Steel Company, 18
Northeast Utilities, V; 48 (upd.)
Northern States Power Company, V; 20 (upd.)
Northern Trust Company, 9
Northland Cranberries, Inc., 38
Northrop Grumman Corporation, I; 11 (upd.); 45 (upd.)
Northwest Airlines Corporation, I; 6 (upd.); 26 (upd.)
Northwest Natural Gas Company, 45
NorthWestern Corporation, 37
Northwestern Mutual Life Insurance Company, III; 45 (upd.)
Norton Company, 8
Norton McNaughton, Inc., 27
Norwood Promotional Products, Inc., 26
NovaCare, Inc., 11
Novell, Inc., 6; 23 (upd.)
Novellus Systems, Inc., 18
Noven Pharmaceuticals, Inc., 55
NPC International, Inc., 40
NPD Group, Inc., The, 68
NRT Incorporated, 61
NSF International, 72
Nu Skin Enterprises, Inc., 27
Nu-kote Holding, Inc., 18

Nucor Corporation, 7; 21 (upd.)
Nutraceutical International Corporation, 37
NutraSweet Company, 8
NutriSystem, Inc., 71
Nutrition for Life International Inc., 22
NVIDIA Corporation, 54
NVR Inc., 8; 70 (upd.)
NYMAGIC, Inc., 41
NYNEX Corporation, V
O.C. Tanner Co., 69
Oak Harbor Freight Lines, Inc., 53
Oak Industries Inc., 21
Oak Technology, Inc., 22
Oakhurst Dairy, 60
Oakley, Inc., 18; 49 (upd.)
Oaktree Capital Management, LLC, 71
Oakwood Homes Corporation, 15
Obie Media Corporation, 56
Occidental Petroleum Corporation, IV; 25
   (upd.); 71 (upd.)
Ocean Spray Cranberries, Inc., 7; 25 (upd.)
Oceaneering International, Inc., 63
O'Charley's Inc., 19; 60 (upd.)
Octel Messaging, 14; 41 (upd.)
Ocular Sciences, Inc., 65
Odetics Inc., 14
ODL, Inc., 55
Odwalla, Inc., 31
OEC Medical Systems, Inc., 27
Office Depot, Inc., 8; 23 (upd.); 65 (upd.)
OfficeMax, Inc., 15; 43 (upd.)
Offshore Logistics, Inc., 37
Ogden Corporation, I; 6
Ogilvy Group, Inc., The, I
Oglebay Norton Company, 17
Oglethorpe Power Corporation, 6
Ohio Art Company, The, 14; 59 (upd.)
Ohio Bell Telephone Company, 14
Ohio Casualty Corp., 11
Ohio Edison Company, V
Oil-Dri Corporation of America, 20
Oklahoma Gas and Electric Company, 6
Olan Mills, Inc., 62
Old America Stores, Inc., 17
Old Dominion Freight Line, Inc., 57
Old Kent Financial Corp., 11
Old National Bancorp, 15
Old Navy, Inc., 70
Old Republic International Corporation, 11;
   58 (upd.)
Old Spaghetti Factory International Inc., 24
Olin Corporation, I; 13 (upd.)
Olsten Corporation, 6; 29 (upd.)
OM Group, Inc., 17
Omaha Steaks International Inc., 62
O'Melveny & Myers, 37
OMI Corporation, 59
Omni Hotels Corp., 12
Omnicare, Inc., 49
Omnicom Group, I; 22 (upd.)
OmniSource Corporation, 14
OMNOVA Solutions Inc., 59
On Assignment, Inc., 20
180s, L.L.C., 64
One Price Clothing Stores, Inc., 20
1-800-FLOWERS, Inc., 26
Oneida Ltd., 7; 31 (upd.)
ONEOK Inc., 7
Onion, Inc., 69
Onyx Acceptance Corporation, 59
Onyx Software Corporation, 53
Opinion Research Corporation, 46
Oppenheimer Wolff & Donnelly LLP, 71
Opsware Inc., 49
Option Care Inc., 48
Opus Group, 34
Oracle Corporation, 6; 24 (upd.); 67 (upd.)

Orange Glo International, 53
Orbital Sciences Corporation, 22
Orbitz, Inc., 61
Orchard Supply Hardware Stores
   Corporation, 17
Ore-Ida Foods Incorporated, 13
Oregon Chai, Inc., 49
Oregon Dental Service Health Plan, Inc.,
   51
Oregon Metallurgical Corporation, 20
Oregon Steel Mills, Inc., 14
O'Reilly Automotive, Inc., 26
Organic Valley (Coulee Region Organic
   Produce Pool), 53
Orion Pictures Corporation, 6
Orleans Homebuilders, Inc., 62
Orthodontic Centers of America, Inc., 35
Orvis Company, Inc., The, 28
Oryx Energy Company, 7
Oscar Mayer Foods Corp., 12
OshKosh B'Gosh, Inc., 9; 42 (upd.)
Oshkosh Truck Corporation, 7
Oshman's Sporting Goods, Inc., 17
Osmonics, Inc., 18
O'Sullivan Industries Holdings, Inc., 34
Otis Elevator Company, Inc., 13; 39 (upd.)
Otis Spunkmeyer, Inc., 28
OTR Express, Inc., 25
Ottaway Newspapers, Inc., 15
Otter Tail Power Company, 18
Outback Steakhouse, Inc., 12; 34 (upd.)
Outboard Marine Corporation, III; 20
   (upd.)
Outdoor Research, Incorporated, 67
Outdoor Systems, Inc., 25
Outlook Group Corporation, 37
Outrigger Enterprises, Inc., 67
Overhead Door Corporation, 70
Overhill Corporation, 51
Overnite Corporation, 14; 58 (upd.)
Overseas Shipholding Group, Inc., 11
Owens & Minor, Inc., 16; 68 (upd.)
Owens Corning Corporation, III; 20 (upd.)
Owens-Illinois, Inc., I; 26 (upd.)
Owosso Corporation, 29
Oxford Health Plans, Inc., 16
Oxford Industries, Inc., 8
P&C Foods Inc., 8
P & F Industries, Inc., 45
P.C. Richard & Son Corp., 23
P.F. Chang's China Bistro, Inc., 37
P.H. Glatfelter Company, 8; 30 (upd.)
Paccar Inc., I; 26 (upd.)
Pacer International, Inc., 54
Pacer Technology, 40
Pacific Coast Feather Company, 67
Pacific Enterprises, V
Pacific Gas and Electric Company, V
Pacific Sunwear of California, Inc., 28
Pacific Telecom, Inc., 6
Pacific Telesis Group, V
PacifiCare Health Systems, Inc., 11
PacifiCorp, V; 26 (upd.)
Packaging Corporation of America, 12; 51
   (upd.)
Packard Bell Electronics, Inc., 13
Paddock Publications, Inc., 53
Paging Network Inc., 11
PaineWebber Group Inc., II; 22 (upd.)
Pall Corporation, 9; 72 (upd.)
Palm Harbor Homes, Inc., 39
Palm Management Corporation, 71
Palm, Inc., 36
Palmer & Cay, Inc., 69
Palomar Medical Technologies, Inc., 22
Pamida Holdings Corporation, 15
Pampered Chef, Ltd., The, 18

Pan American World Airways, Inc., I; 12
   (upd.)
Pan-American Life Insurance Company, 48
Panamerican Beverages, Inc., 47
PanAmSat Corporation, 46
Panavision Inc., 24
Pancho's Mexican Buffet, Inc., 46
Panda Management Company, Inc., 35
Panera Bread Company, 44
Panhandle Eastern Corporation, V
Pantone Inc., 53
Pantry, Inc., The, 36
Papa John's International, Inc., 15; 71
   (upd.)
Papa Murphy's International, Inc., 54
Papetti's Hygrade Egg Products, Inc., 39
Par Pharmaceutical Companies, Inc., 65
Paradise Music & Entertainment, Inc., 42
Parametric Technology Corp., 16
Paramount Pictures Corporation, II
Paris Corporation, 22
Parisian, Inc., 14
Park Corp., 22
Park-Ohio Industries Inc., 17
Parker Drilling Company, 28
Parker-Hannifin Corporation, III; 24 (upd.)
Parlex Corporation, 61
Parsons Brinckerhoff, Inc., 34
Parsons Corporation, The, 8; 56 (upd.)
Party City Corporation, 54
Pathmark Stores, Inc., 23
Patina Oil & Gas Corporation, 24
Patrick Industries, Inc., 30
Patterson Dental Co., 19
Patterson-UTI Energy, Inc., 55
Patton Boggs LLP, 71
Paul Harris Stores, Inc., 18
Paul, Hastings, Janofsky & Walker LLP,
   27
Paul Mueller Company, 65
Paul Revere Corporation, The, 12
Paul, Weiss, Rifkind, Wharton & Garrison,
   47
Paul-Son Gaming Corporation, 66
Paxson Communications Corporation, 33
Pay 'N Pak Stores, Inc., 9
Paychex, Inc., 15; 46 (upd.)
Payless Cashways, Inc., 11; 44 (upd.)
Payless ShoeSource, Inc., 18; 69 (upd.)
PayPal Inc., 58
PC Connection, Inc., 37
PCA International, Inc., 62
PDI, Inc., 52
PDS Gaming Corporation, 44
Peabody Coal Company, 10
Peabody Energy Corporation, 45 (upd.)
Peabody Holding Company, Inc., IV
Peak Technologies Group, Inc., The, 14
Peapod, Inc., 30
Pearle Vision, Inc., 13
Peavey Electronics Corporation, 16
PECO Energy Company, 11
Pediatric Services of America, Inc., 31
Pediatrix Medical Group, Inc., 61
Peebles Inc., 16; 43 (upd.)
Peet's Coffee & Tea, Inc., 38
Pei Cobb Freed & Partners Architects LLP,
   57
Pella Corporation, 12; 39 (upd.)
Pemco Aviation Group Inc., 54
Pendleton Grain Growers Inc., 64
Pendleton Woolen Mills, Inc., 42
Penford Corporation, 55
Penn Engineering & Manufacturing Corp.,
   28
Penn National Gaming, Inc., 33
Penn Traffic Company, 13

United States (*continued*)

Pennsylvania Blue Shield, III
Pennsylvania Power & Light Company, V
Pennwalt Corporation, I
PennWell Corporation, 55
Pennzoil-Quaker State Company, IV; 20 (upd.); 50 (upd.)
Penske Corporation, V; 19 (upd.)
Pentair, Inc., 7; 26 (upd.)
Pentech International, Inc., 29
Penton Media, Inc., 27
People Express Airlines, Inc., I
Peoples Energy Corporation, 6
PeopleSoft Inc., 14; 33 (upd.)
Pep Boys—Manny, Moe & Jack, The, 11; 36 (upd.)
Pepper Hamilton LLP, 43
Pepsi Bottling Group, Inc., The, 40
PepsiAmericas, Inc., 67 (upd.)
PepsiCo, Inc., I; 10 (upd.); 38 (upd.)
Perdue Farms Inc., 7; 23 (upd.)
Performance Food Group Company, 31
Perini Corporation, 8
Perkin-Elmer Corporation, The, 7
Perkins Coie LLP, 56
Perkins Family Restaurants, L.P., 22
Perot Systems Corporation, 29
Perrigo Company, 12; 59 (upd.)
Perry Ellis International, Inc., 41
Pet Incorporated, 7
Petco Animal Supplies, Inc., 29
Pete's Brewing Company, 22
Peter Kiewit Sons' Inc., 8
Peter Piper, Inc., 70
Petersen Publishing Company, 21
Peterson American Corporation, 55
Petrie Stores Corporation, 8
Petroleum Helicopters, Inc., 35
Petrolite Corporation, 15
Petrossian Inc., 54
PETsMART, Inc., 14; 41 (upd.)
Pew Charitable Trusts, The, 35
Pez Candy, Inc., 38
Pfizer Inc., I; 9 (upd.); 38 (upd.)
PG&E Corporation, 26 (upd.)
Phar-Mor Inc., 12
Pharmacia & Upjohn Inc., I; 25 (upd.)
Phat Fashions LLC, 49
Phelps Dodge Corporation, IV; 28 (upd.)
PHH Arval, V; 53 (upd.)
Philadelphia Eagles, 37
Philadelphia Electric Company, V
Philadelphia Suburban Corporation, 39
Philharmonic-Symphony Society of New York, Inc. (New York Philharmonic), 69
Philip Morris Companies Inc., V; 18 (upd.); 44 (upd.)
Philips Electronics North America Corp., 13
Phillips, de Pury & Luxembourg, 49
Phillips Foods, Inc., 63
Phillips Petroleum Company, IV; 40 (upd.)
Phillips-Van Heusen Corporation, 24
Phoenix Footwear Group, Inc., 70
PHP Healthcare Corporation, 22
PhyCor, Inc., 36
Physician Sales & Service, Inc., 14
Physio-Control International Corp., 18
Piccadilly Cafeterias, Inc., 19
PictureTel Corp., 10; 27 (upd.)
Piedmont Natural Gas Company, Inc., 27
Pier 1 Imports, Inc., 12; 34 (upd.)
Pierce Leahy Corporation, 24
Piercing Pagoda, Inc., 29
Piggly Wiggly Southern, Inc., 13
Pilgrim's Pride Corporation, 7; 23 (upd.)
Pillowtex Corporation, 19; 41 (upd.)

Pillsbury Company, The, II; 13 (upd.); 62 (upd.)
Pillsbury Madison & Sutro LLP, 29
Pilot Air Freight Corp., 67
Pilot Corporation, 49
Pinkerton's Inc., 9
Pinnacle West Capital Corporation, 6; 54 (upd.)
Pioneer Hi-Bred International, Inc., 9; 41 (upd.)
Pioneer Natural Resources Company, 59
Pioneer-Standard Electronics Inc., 19
Piper Jaffray Companies Inc., 22
Pitman Company, 58
Pitney Bowes Inc., III; 19; 47 (upd.)
Pittsburgh Steelers Sports, Inc., 66
Pittston Company, The, IV; 19 (upd.)
Pittway Corporation, 9; 33 (upd.)
Pixar Animation Studios, 34
Pixelworks, Inc., 69
Pizza Hut Inc., 7; 21 (upd.)
Pizza Inn, Inc., 46
Plains Cotton Cooperative Association, 57
Planar Systems, Inc., 61
Planet Hollywood International, Inc., 18; 41 (upd.)
Plantation Pipe Line Company, 68
Plante & Moran, LLP, 71
Platinum Entertainment, Inc., 35
PLATINUM Technology, Inc., 14
Plato Learning, Inc., 44
Play by Play Toys & Novelties, Inc., 26
Playboy Enterprises, Inc., 18
PlayCore, Inc., 27
Players International, Inc., 22
Playskool, Inc., 25
Playtex Products, Inc., 15
Pleasant Company, 27
Pleasant Holidays LLC, 62
Plexus Corporation, 35
Plum Creek Timber Company, Inc., 43
Pluma, Inc., 27
Ply Gem Industries Inc., 12
PMI Group, Inc., The, 49
PMT Services, Inc., 24
PNC Financial Services Group Inc., The, II; 13 (upd.); 46 (upd.)
PNM Resources Inc., 51 (upd.)
Pogo Producing Company, 39
Polar Air Cargo Inc., 60
Polaris Industries Inc., 12; 35 (upd.)
Polaroid Corporation, III; 7 (upd.); 28 (upd.)
Policy Management Systems Corporation, 11
Policy Studies, Inc., 62
Polk Audio, Inc., 34
Polo/Ralph Lauren Corporation, 12; 62 (upd.)
PolyGram N.V., 23
Pomeroy Computer Resources, Inc., 33
Ponderosa Steakhouse, 15
Poof-Slinky, Inc., 61
Poore Brothers, Inc., 44
Pope & Talbot, Inc., 12; 61 (upd.)
Popular, Inc., 41
Port Authority of New York and New Jersey, The, 48
Port Imperial Ferry Corporation, 70
Portal Software, Inc., 47
Portillo's Restaurant Group, Inc., 71
Portland General Corporation, 6
Portland Trail Blazers, 50
Post Properties, Inc., 26
Potlatch Corporation, 8; 34 (upd.)
Potomac Electric Power Company, 6
Potter & Brumfield Inc., 11

Powell's Books, Inc., 40
PowerBar Inc., 44
Powerhouse Technologies, Inc., 27
PPG Industries, Inc., III; 22 (upd.)
PPL Corporation, 41 (upd.)
PR Newswire, 35
Prairie Farms Dairy, Inc., 47
Pratt & Whitney, 9
Praxair, Inc., 11; 48 (upd.)
Pre-Paid Legal Services, Inc., 20
Precision Castparts Corp., 15
Premark International, Inc., III
Premcor Inc., 37
Premier Industrial Corporation, 9
Premier Parks, Inc., 27
Premium Standard Farms, Inc., 30
PremiumWear, Inc., 30
Preserver Group, Inc., 44
President Casinos, Inc., 22
Pressman Toy Corporation, 56
Presstek, Inc., 33
Preston Corporation, 6
Price Communications Corporation, 42
Price Company, The, V
Price Pfister, Inc., 70
PriceCostco, Inc., 14
Priceline.com Incorporated, 57
PriceSmart, Inc., 71
PricewaterhouseCoopers, 9; 29 (upd.)
Primark Corp., 13
Prime Hospitality Corporation, 52
Primedex Health Systems, Inc., 25
Primedia Inc., 22
Primerica Corporation, I
Prince Sports Group, Inc., 15
Princess Cruise Lines, 22
Princeton Review, Inc., The, 42
Principal Mutual Life Insurance Company, III
Printpack, Inc., 68
Printrak, A Motorola Company, 44
Printronix, Inc., 18
Prison Rehabilitative Industries and Diversified Enterprises, Inc. (PRIDE), 53
Procter & Gamble Company, The, III; 8 (upd.); 26 (upd.); 67 (upd.)
Prodigy Communications Corporation, 34
Professional Bull Riders Inc., 55
Professional Golfers' Association of America, The, 41
Proffitt's, Inc., 19
Progress Software Corporation, 15
Progressive Corporation, The, 11; 29 (upd.)
ProLogis, 57
Promus Companies, Inc., 9
Proskauer Rose LLP, 47
Protection One, Inc., 32
Provell Inc., 58 (upd.)
Providence Journal Company, The, 28
Providence Service Corporation, The, 64
Provident Life and Accident Insurance Company of America, III
Providian Financial Corporation, 52 (upd.)
Prudential Insurance Company of America, The, III; 30 (upd.)
PSI Resources, 6
Psychiatric Solutions, Inc., 68
Pubco Corporation, 17
Public Service Company of Colorado, 6
Public Service Company of New Hampshire, 21; 55 (upd.)
Public Service Company of New Mexico, 6
Public Service Enterprise Group Inc., V; 44 (upd.)
Public Storage, Inc., 52
Publishers Clearing House, 23; 64 (upd.)
Publishers Group, Inc., 35

Publix Supermarkets Inc., 7; 31 (upd.)
Pueblo Xtra International, Inc., 47
Puget Sound Energy Inc., 6; 50 (upd.)
Pulaski Furniture Corporation, 33
Pulitzer Inc., 15; 58 (upd.)
Pulte Corporation, 8
Pulte Homes, Inc., 42 (upd.)
Pumpkin Masters, Inc., 48
Pure World, Inc., 72
Purina Mills, Inc., 32
Puritan-Bennett Corporation, 13
Purolator Products Company, 21
Putt-Putt Golf Courses of America, Inc., 23
PVC Container Corporation, 67
PW Eagle, Inc., 48
Pyramid Breweries Inc., 33
Pyramid Companies, 54
Q.E.P. Co., Inc., 65
QSC Audio Products, Inc., 56
Quad/Graphics, Inc., 19
Quaker Fabric Corp., 19
Quaker Oats Company, The, II; 12 (upd.); 34 (upd.)
Quaker State Corporation, 7; 21 (upd.)
QUALCOMM Incorporated, 20; 47 (upd.)
Quality Chekd Dairies, Inc., 48
Quality Dining, Inc., 18
Quality Food Centers, Inc., 17
Quanex Corporation, 13; 62 (upd.)
Quantum Chemical Corporation, 8
Quantum Corporation, 10; 62 (upd.)
Quark, Inc., 36
Quest Diagnostics Inc., 26
Questar Corporation, 6; 26 (upd.)
Quick & Reilly Group, Inc., The, 20
Quigley Corporation, The, 62
Quiksilver, Inc., 18
QuikTrip Corporation, 36
Quill Corporation, 28
Quintiles Transnational Corporation, 21; 68 (upd.)
Quixote Corporation, 15
Quizno's Corporation, The, 42
Quovadx Inc., 70
QVC Inc., 9; 58 (upd.)
Qwest Communications International, Inc., 37
R&B, Inc., 51
R.B. Pamplin Corp., 45
R.C. Bigelow, Inc., 49
R.C. Willey Home Furnishings, 72
R.G. Barry Corporation, 17; 44 (upd.)
R.H. Macy & Co., Inc., V; 8 (upd.); 30 (upd.)
R.J. Reynolds Tobacco Holdings, Inc., 30 (upd.)
R.L. Polk & Co., 10
R.P. Scherer, I
R.R. Donnelley & Sons Company, IV; 9 (upd.); 38 (upd.)
Racal-Datacom Inc., 11
Racing Champions Corporation, 37
Radian Group Inc., 42
Radio Flyer Inc., 34
Radio One, Inc., 67
RadioShack Corporation, 36 (upd.)
Radius Inc., 16
Rag Shops, Inc., 30
RailTex, Inc., 20
Rainforest Cafe, Inc., 25
Rainier Brewing Company, 23
Raley's Inc., 14; 58 (upd.)
Rally's, 25; 68 (upd.)
Ralphs Grocery Company, 35
Ralston Purina Company, II; 13 (upd.)
Ramsay Youth Services, Inc., 41
Rand McNally & Company, 28

Randall's Food Markets, Inc., 40
Random House, Inc., 13; 31 (upd.)
Range Resources Corporation, 45
Rapala-Normark Group, Ltd., 30
Rare Hospitality International Inc., 19
Ratner Companies, 72
Raven Industries, Inc., 33
Raving Brands, Inc., 64
Rawlings Sporting Goods Co., Inc., 24
Raychem Corporation, 8
Raymond James Financial Inc., 69
Rayonier Inc., 24
Rayovac Corporation, 13; 39 (upd.)
Raytech Corporation, 61
Raytheon Aircraft Holdings Inc., 46
Raytheon Company, II; 11 (upd.); 38 (upd.)
Razorfish, Inc., 37
RCA Corporation, II
RCM Technologies, Inc., 34
RCN Corporation, 70
RDO Equipment Company, 33
RE/MAX International, Inc., 59
Read-Rite Corp., 10
Reader's Digest Association, Inc., The, IV; 17 (upd.); 71 (upd.)
Reading International Inc., 70
Real Times, Inc., 66
RealNetworks, Inc., 53
Reckson Associates Realty Corp., 47
Recording for the Blind & Dyslexic, 51
Recoton Corp., 15
Recovery Engineering, Inc., 25
Recreational Equipment, Inc., 18; 71 (upd.)
Recycled Paper Greetings, Inc., 21
Red Apple Group, Inc., 23
Red Hat, Inc., 45
Red Robin Gourmet Burgers, Inc., 56
Red Roof Inns, Inc., 18
Red Spot Paint & Varnish Company, 55
Red Wing Pottery Sales, Inc., 52
Red Wing Shoe Company, Inc., 9; 30 (upd.)
Redhook Ale Brewery, Inc., 31
Reebok International Ltd., V; 9 (upd.); 26 (upd.)
Reed & Barton Corporation, 67
Reeds Jewelers, Inc., 22
Regal Entertainment Group, 59
Regal-Beloit Corporation, 18
Regency Centers Corporation, 71
Regis Corporation, 18; 70 (upd.)
Reichhold Chemicals, Inc., 10
Reliance Electric Company, 9
Reliance Group Holdings, Inc., III
Reliance Steel & Aluminum Company, 19; 70 (upd.)
Reliant Energy Inc., 44 (upd.)
Reliv International, Inc., 58
Remedy Corporation, 58
RemedyTemp, Inc., 20
Remington Arms Company, Inc., 12; 40 (upd.)
Remington Products Company, L.L.C., 42
Renaissance Learning Systems, Inc., 39
Renal Care Group, Inc., 72
Reno Air Inc., 23
Rent-A-Center, Inc., 45
Rent-Way, Inc., 33
Rental Service Corporation, 28
Rentrak Corporation, 35
Republic Engineered Steels, Inc., 7; 26 (upd.)
Republic Industries, Inc., 26
Republic New York Corporation, 11
Res-Care, Inc., 29
Resorts International, Inc., 12

Resource America, Inc., 42
Response Oncology, Inc., 27
Restaurant Associates Corporation, 66
Restaurants Unlimited, Inc., 13
Restoration Hardware, Inc., 30
Revco D.S., Inc., V
Revell-Monogram Inc., 16
Revere Ware Corporation, 22
Revlon Inc., III; 17 (upd.); 64 (upd.)
Rewards Network Inc., 70 (upd.)
REX Stores Corp., 10
Rexel, Inc., 15
Rexnord Corporation, 21
Reynolds and Reynolds Company, The, 50
Reynolds Metals Company, IV; 19 (upd.)
RF Micro Devices, Inc., 43
RFC Franchising LLC, 68
Rhino Entertainment Company, 18; 70 (upd.)
Rhodes Inc., 23
Rica Foods, Inc., 41
Rich Products Corporation, 7; 38 (upd.)
Richards Group, Inc., The, 58
Richardson Electronics, Ltd., 17
Richardson Industries, Inc., 62
Richfood Holdings, Inc., 7
Richton International Corporation, 39
Riddell Sports Inc., 22
Ride, Inc., 22
Riese Organization, The, 38
Riggs National Corporation, 13
Right Management Consultants, Inc., 42
Riklis Family Corp., 9
Riser Foods, Inc., 9
Rite Aid Corporation, V; 19 (upd.); 63 (upd.)
Ritz Camera Centers, 34
Ritz-Carlton Hotel Company, L.L.C., The, 9; 29 (upd.); 71 (upd.)
Rival Company, The, 19
River Oaks Furniture, Inc., 43
Riverwood International Corporation, 11; 48 (upd.)
Riviana Foods Inc., 27
RJR Nabisco Holdings Corp., V
RMH Teleservices, Inc., 42
Roadhouse Grill, Inc., 22
Roadmaster Industries, Inc., 16
Roadway Express, Inc., V; 25 (upd.)
Roanoke Electric Steel Corporation, 45
Robbins & Myers Inc., 15
Roberds Inc., 19
Robert Half International Inc., 18; 70 (upd.)
Robert Mondavi Corporation, 15; 50 (upd.)
Robert W. Baird & Co. Incorporated, 67
Robert Wood Johnson Foundation, 35
Roberts Pharmaceutical Corporation, 16
Robertson-Ceco Corporation, 19
Robinson Helicopter Company, 51
Roche Bioscience, 11; 14 (upd.)
Rochester Gas and Electric Corporation, 6
Rochester Telephone Corporation, 6
Rock Bottom Restaurants, Inc., 25; 68 (upd.)
Rock of Ages Corporation, 37
Rock-Tenn Company, 13; 59 (upd.)
Rockefeller Foundation, The, 34
Rockefeller Group International Inc., 58
Rockford Corporation, 43
Rockford Products Corporation, 55
RockShox, Inc., 26
Rockwell Automation, 43 (upd.)
Rockwell International Corporation, I; 11 (upd.)
Rocky Shoes & Boots, Inc., 26
Rodale Press, Inc., 23

United States (*continued*)

Rodale, Inc., 47 (upd.)
Rogers Corporation, 61
Rohm and Haas Company, I; 26 (upd.)
ROHN Industries, Inc., 22
Rohr Incorporated, 9
Roll International Corporation, 37
Rollerblade, Inc., 15; 34 (upd.)
Rollins, Inc., 11
Rolls-Royce Allison, 29 (upd.)
Romacorp, Inc., 58
Ron Tonkin Chevrolet Company, 55
Ronco, Inc., 15
Rooms To Go Inc., 28
Rooney Brothers Co., 25
Roper Industries, Inc., 15; 50 (upd.)
Ropes & Gray, 40
Rorer Group, I
Rose Acre Farms, Inc., 60
Rose Art Industries, 58
Rose's Stores, Inc., 13
Roseburg Forest Products Company, 58
Rosemount Inc., 15
Rosenbluth International Inc., 14
Ross Stores, Inc., 17; 43 (upd.)
Rotary International, 31
Roto-Rooter, Inc., 15; 61 (upd.)
Rottlund Company, Inc., The, 28
Rouge Steel Company, 8
Roundy's Inc., 14; 58 (upd.)
Rouse Company, The, 15; 63 (upd.)
Rowan Companies, Inc., 43
Roy F. Weston, Inc., 33
Royal Appliance Manufacturing Company, 15
Royal Caribbean Cruises Ltd., 22
Royal Crown Company, Inc., 23
RPM, Inc., 8; 36 (upd.)
RSA Security Inc., 46
RTM Restaurant Group, 58
Rubbermaid Incorporated, III; 20 (upd.)
Rubio's Restaurants, Inc., 35
Ruby Tuesday, Inc., 18; 71 (upd.)
Ruiz Food Products, Inc., 53
Rural Cellular Corporation, 43
Rural/Metro Corporation, 28
Rush Communications, 33
Rush Enterprises, Inc., 64
Russ Berrie and Company, Inc., 12
Russell Corporation, 8; 30 (upd.)
Russell Reynolds Associates Inc., 38
Russell Stover Candies Inc., 12
Rust International Inc., 11
Ruth's Chris Steak House, 28
Ryan Beck & Co., Inc., 66
Ryan's Restaurant Group, Inc., 15; 68 (upd.)
Ryder System, Inc., V; 24 (upd.)
Ryerson Tull, Inc., 40 (upd.)
Ryland Group, Inc., The, 8; 37 (upd.)
S&C Electric Company, 15
S&K Famous Brands, Inc., 23
S-K-I Limited, 15
S.C. Johnson & Son, Inc., III; 28 (upd.)
Saatchi & Saatchi, 42 (upd.)
Sabratek Corporation, 29
SABRE Group Holdings, Inc., 26
Safe Flight Instrument Corporation, 71
SAFECO Corporaton, III
Safeguard Scientifics, Inc., 10
Safelite Glass Corp., 19
Safeskin Corporation, 18
Safety Components International, Inc., 63
Safety 1st, Inc., 24
Safety-Kleen Corp., 8
Safeway Inc., II; 24 (upd.)
Saga Communications, Inc., 27

St. Joe Company, The, 31
St. Joe Paper Company, 8
St. John Knits, Inc., 14
St. Jude Medical, Inc., 11; 43 (upd.)
St. Louis Music, Inc., 48
St. Mary Land & Exploration Company, 63
St. Paul Bank for Cooperatives, 8
St. Paul Companies, Inc., The, III; 22 (upd.)
Saks Inc., 24; 41 (upd.)
Salant Corporation, 12; 51 (upd.)
Salick Health Care, Inc., 53
Sally Beauty Company, Inc., 60
Salomon Inc., II; 13 (upd.)
Salt River Project, 19
Salton, Inc., 30
Salvation Army USA, The, 32
Sam Ash Music Corporation, 30
Sam's Club, 40
Samsonite Corporation, 13; 43 (upd.)
Samuel Cabot Inc., 53
Samuels Jewelers Incorporated, 30
San Diego Gas & Electric Company, V
Sandals Resorts International, 65
Sanders Morris Harris Group Inc., 70
Sanderson Farms, Inc., 15
Sandia National Laboratories, 49
Santa Barbara Restaurant Group, Inc., 37
Santa Cruz Operation, Inc., The, 38
Santa Fe Gaming Corporation, 19
Santa Fe International Corporation, 38
Santa Fe Pacific Corporation, V
Sara Lee Corporation, II; 15 (upd.); 54 (upd.)
Sarnoff Corporation, 57
SAS Institute Inc., 10
Saturn Corporation, 7; 21 (upd.)
Saucony Inc., 35
Sauder Woodworking Company, 12; 35 (upd.)
Sauer-Danfoss Inc., 61
Savannah Foods & Industries, Inc., 7
Sawtek Inc., 43 (upd.)
Sbarro, Inc., 16; 64 (upd.)
SBC Communications Inc., 32 (upd.)
SBS Technologies, Inc., 25
SCANA Corporation, 6; 56 (upd.)
ScanSource, Inc., 29
SCB Computer Technology, Inc., 29
SCEcorp, V
Schawk, Inc., 24
Scheels All Sports Inc., 63
Scheid Vineyards Inc., 66
Schering-Plough Corporation, I; 14 (upd.); 49 (upd.)
Schieffelin & Somerset Co., 61
Schlotzsky's, Inc., 36
Schlumberger Limited, III; 17 (upd.); 59 (upd.)
Schmitt Music Company, 40
Schneider National, Inc., 36
Schneiderman's Furniture Inc., 28
Schnitzer Steel Industries, Inc., 19
Scholastic Corporation, 10; 29 (upd.)
School Specialty, Inc., 68
School-Tech, Inc., 62
Schott Brothers, Inc., 67
Schott Corporation, 53
Schottenstein Stores Corp., 14
Schreiber Foods, Inc., 72
Schuff Steel Company, 26
Schultz Sav-O Stores, Inc., 21; 31 (upd.)
Schwan's Sales Enterprises, Inc., 7; 26 (upd.)
Schwebel Baking Company, 72
Schweitzer-Mauduit International, Inc., 52
Schwinn Cycle and Fitness L.P., 19

SCI Systems, Inc., 9
Science Applications International Corporation, 15
Scientific Games Corporation, 64 (upd.)
Scientific-Atlanta, Inc., 6; 45 (upd.)
Score Board, Inc., The, 19
Scotsman Industries, Inc., 20
Scott Fetzer Company, 12
Scott Paper Company, IV; 31 (upd.)
Scotts Company, The, 22
Scotty's, Inc., 22
Scovill Fasteners Inc., 24
SCP Pool Corporation, 39
Screen Actors Guild, 72
Seaboard Corporation, 36
Seagate Technology, Inc., 8; 34 (upd.)
Seagull Energy Corporation, 11
Sealaska Corporation, 60
Sealed Air Corporation, 14; 57 (upd.)
Sealed Power Corporation, I
Sealright Co., Inc., 17
Sealy Inc., 12
Seaman Furniture Company, Inc., 32
Sean John Clothing, Inc., 70
Sears, Roebuck and Co., V; 18 (upd.); 56 (upd.)
Seattle City Light, 50
Seattle FilmWorks, Inc., 20
Seattle First National Bank Inc., 8
Seattle Times Company, 15
Seaway Food Town, Inc., 15
Sebastiani Vineyards, Inc., 28
Second Harvest, 29
Security Capital Corporation, 17
Security Pacific Corporation, II
SED International Holdings, Inc., 43
See's Candies, Inc., 30
Sega of America, Inc., 10
Segway LLC, 48
Seigle's Home and Building Centers, Inc., 41
Seitel, Inc., 47
Select Comfort Corporation, 34
Select Medical Corporation, 65
Selmer Company, Inc., The, 19
SEMCO Energy, Inc., 44
Seminis, Inc., 29
Semitool, Inc., 18
Sempra Energy, 25 (upd.)
Semtech Corporation, 32
Seneca Foods Corporation, 17; 60 (upd.)
Sensient Technologies Corporation, 52 (upd.)
Sensormatic Electronics Corp., 11
Sensory Science Corporation, 37
Sepracor Inc., 45
Sequa Corporation, 13; 54 (upd.)
Serologicals Corporation, 63
Serta, Inc., 28
Service America Corp., 7
Service Corporation International, 6; 51 (upd.)
Service Merchandise Company, Inc., V; 19 (upd.)
ServiceMaster Company, The, 6; 23 (upd.); 68 (upd.)
7-11, Inc., 32 (upd.)
Sevenson Environmental Services, Inc., 42
SFX Entertainment, Inc., 36
SGI, 29 (upd.)
Shakespeare Company, 22
Shaklee Corporation, 12; 39 (upd.)
Shared Medical Systems Corporation, 14
Sharper Image Corporation, The, 10; 62 (upd.)
Shaw Group, Inc., The, 50
Shaw Industries, Inc., 9; 40 (upd.)

Shaw's Supermarkets, Inc., 56
Shawmut National Corporation, 13
Shearer's Foods, Inc., 72
Shearman & Sterling, 32
Shearson Lehman Brothers Holdings Inc., II; 9 (upd.)
Shelby Williams Industries, Inc., 14
Sheldahl Inc., 23
Shell Oil Company, IV; 14 (upd.); 41 (upd.)
Sheller-Globe Corporation, I
Shells Seafood Restaurants, Inc., 43
Sherwin-Williams Company, The, III; 13 (upd.)
Sherwood Brands, Inc., 53
Shoe Carnival Inc., 14; 72 (upd.)
Shoney's, Inc., 7; 23 (upd.)
ShopKo Stores Inc., 21; 58 (upd.)
Shoppers Food Warehouse Corporation, 66
Shorewood Packaging Corporation, 28
ShowBiz Pizza Time, Inc., 13
Showboat, Inc., 19
Shriners Hospitals for Children, 69
Shubert Organization Inc., 24
Shuffle Master Inc., 51
Shure Inc., 60
Shurgard Storage Centers, Inc., 52
Sidley Austin Brown & Wood, 40
Sidney Frank Importing Co., Inc., 69
Siebel Systems, Inc., 38
Siebert Financial Corp., 32
Siegel & Gale, 64
Sierra Club, The, 28
Sierra Health Services, Inc., 15
Sierra Nevada Brewing Company, 70
Sierra On-Line, Inc., 15; 41 (upd.)
Sierra Pacific Industries, 22
SIFCO Industries, Inc., 41
Sigma-Aldrich Corporation, I; 36 (upd.)
Signet Banking Corporation, 11
Sikorsky Aircraft Corporation, 24
Silhouette Brands, Inc., 55
Silicon Graphics Incorporated, 9
SilverPlatter Information Inc., 23
Silverstein Properties, Inc., 47
Simmons Company, 47
Simon & Schuster Inc., IV; 19 (upd.)
Simon Property Group, Inc., 27
Simon Transportation Services Inc., 27
Simplex Technologies Inc., 21
Simplicity Manufacturing, Inc., 64
Simpson Investment Company, 17
Simpson Thacher & Bartlett, 39
Simula, Inc., 41
Sinclair Broadcast Group, Inc., 25
Singing Machine Company, Inc., The, 60
Sir Speedy, Inc., 16
Sirius Satellite Radio, Inc., 69
Siskin Steel & Supply Company, 70
Six Flags, Inc., 17; 54 (upd.)
SJW Corporation, 70
Skadden, Arps, Slate, Meagher & Flom, 18
Skechers USA Inc., 31
Skidmore, Owings & Merrill LLP, 13; 69 (upd.)
Skyline Chili, Inc., 62
Skyline Corporation, 30
SkyMall, Inc., 26
SkyWest, Inc., 25
SL Green Realty Corporation, 44
Sleepy's Inc., 32
SLI, Inc., 48
Slim-Fast Foods Company, 18; 66 (upd.)
SLM Holding Corp., 25 (upd.)
Smart & Final, Inc., 16
SmartForce PLC, 43
Smead Manufacturing Co., 17

Smith & Hawken, Ltd., 68
Smith & Wesson Corporation, 30
Smith Barney Inc., 15
Smith Corona Corp., 13
Smith International, Inc., 15; 59 (upd.)
Smith's Food & Drug Centers, Inc., 8; 57 (upd.)
Smith-Midland Corporation, 56
Smithfield Foods, Inc., 7; 43 (upd.)
SmithKline Beckman Corporation, I
Smithsonian Institution, 27
Smithway Motor Xpress Corporation, 39
Smurfit-Stone Container Corporation, 26 (upd.)
Snap-On, Incorporated, 7; 27 (upd.)
Snapple Beverage Corporation, 11
Snell & Wilmer L.L.P., 28
Society Corporation, 9
Soft Sheen Products, Inc., 31
Sola International Inc., 71
Solectron Corporation, 12; 48 (upd.)
Solo Serve Corporation, 28
Solutia Inc., 52
Sonat, Inc., 6
Sonesta International Hotels Corporation, 44
Sonic Corp., 14; 37 (upd.)
Sonic Innovations Inc., 56
Sonoco Products Company, 8
SonoSite, Inc., 56
Soros Fund Management LLC, 28
Sorrento, Inc., 24
SOS Staffing Services, 25
Sotheby's Holdings, Inc., 11; 29 (upd.)
Sound Advice, Inc., 41
Source Enterprises, Inc., The, 65
South Jersey Industries, Inc., 42
Southdown, Inc., 14
Southern Company, The, V; 38 (upd.)
Southern Financial Bancorp, Inc., 56
Southern Indiana Gas and Electric Company, 13
Southern New England Telecommunications Corporation, 6
Southern Pacific Transportation Company, V
Southern States Cooperative Incorporated, 36
Southern Union Company, 27
Southland Corporation, The, II; 7 (upd.)
Southtrust Corporation, 11
Southwest Airlines Co., 6; 24 (upd.); 71 (upd.)
Southwest Gas Corporation, 19
Southwest Water Company, 47
Southwestern Bell Corporation, V
Southwestern Electric Power Co., 21
Southwestern Public Service Company, 6
Southwire Company, Inc., 8; 23 (upd.)
Sovran Self Storage, Inc., 66
Spacehab, Inc., 37
Spacelabs Medical, Inc., 71
Spaghetti Warehouse, Inc., 25
Spangler Candy Company, 44
Spanish Broadcasting System, Inc., 41
Spartan Motors Inc., 14
Spartan Stores Inc., 8; 66 (upd.)
Spartech Corporation, 19
Sparton Corporation, 18
Spear, Leeds & Kellogg, 66
Spec's Music, Inc., 19
Specialized Bicycle Components Inc., 50
Specialty Coatings Inc., 8
Specialty Equipment Companies, Inc., 25
Specialty Products & Insulation Co., 59
Spectrum Control, Inc., 67
Spectrum Organic Products, Inc., 68

SpeeDee Oil Change and Tune-Up, 25
Speedway Motorsports, Inc., 32
Speizman Industries, Inc., 44
Spelling Entertainment, 14; 35 (upd.)
Spencer Stuart and Associates, Inc., 14
Spherion Corporation, 52
Spiegel, Inc., 10; 27 (upd.)
Spinnaker Exploration Company, 72
Spirit Airlines, Inc., 31
Sport Chalet, Inc., 16
Sport Supply Group, Inc., 23
Sportmart, Inc., 15
Sports & Recreation, Inc., 17
Sports Authority, Inc., The, 16; 43 (upd.)
Sports Club Company, The, 25
Sportsman's Guide, Inc., The, 36
Springs Industries, Inc., V; 19 (upd.)
Sprint Corporation, 9; 46 (upd.)
SPS Technologies, Inc., 30
SPSS Inc., 64
SPX Corporation, 10; 47 (upd.)
Squibb Corporation, I
SRAM Corporation, 65
SRC Holdings Corporation, 67
SRI International, Inc., 57
STAAR Surgical Company, 57
Stage Stores, Inc., 24
Stanadyne Automotive Corporation, 37
StanCorp Financial Group, Inc., 56
Standard Commercial Corporation, 13; 62 (upd.)
Standard Federal Bank, 9
Standard Microsystems Corporation, 11
Standard Motor Products, Inc., 40
Standard Pacific Corporation, 52
Standard Register Co., 15
Standex International Corporation, 17; 44 (upd.)
Stanhome Inc., 15
Stanley Furniture Company, Inc., 34
Stanley Works, The, III; 20 (upd.)
Staples, Inc., 10; 55 (upd.)
Star Banc Corporation, 11
Starbucks Corporation, 13; 34 (upd.)
Starcraft Corporation, 30; 66 (upd.)
Starkey Laboratories, Inc., 52
Starrett Corporation, 21
Starter Corp., 12
Starwood Hotels & Resorts Worldwide, Inc., 54
Stash Tea Company, The, 50
State Farm Mutual Automobile Insurance Company, III; 51 (upd.)
State Financial Services Corporation, 51
State Street Corporation, 8; 57 (upd.)
Staten Island Bancorp, Inc., 39
Stater Bros. Holdings Inc., 64
Station Casinos Inc., 25
Staubach Company, The, 62
Steak n Shake Company, The, 41
Stearns, Inc., 43
Steel Dynamics, Inc., 52
Steel Technologies Inc., 63
Steelcase, Inc., 7; 27 (upd.)
Stein Mart Inc., 19; 72 (upd.)
Steiner Corporation (Alsco), 53
Steinway Musical Properties, Inc., 19
Stepan Company, 30
Stephan Company, The, 60
Stericycle Inc., 33
STERIS Corporation, 29
Sterling Chemicals, Inc., 16
Sterling Drug, Inc., I
Sterling Electronics Corp., 18
Sterling Software, Inc., 11
Stevedoring Services of America Inc., 28
Steven Madden, Ltd., 37

United States (*continued*)

Stew Leonard's, 56
Stewart & Stevenson Services Inc., 11
Stewart Enterprises, Inc., 20
Stewart's Beverages, 39
Stillwater Mining Company, 47
Stock Yards Packing Co., Inc., 37
Stone & Webster, Inc., 13; 64 (upd.)
Stone Container Corporation, IV
Stone Manufacturing Company, 14; 43
  (upd.)
Stonyfield Farm, Inc., 55
Stop & Shop Supermarket Company, The,
  II; 24 (upd.); 68 (upd.)
Storage Technology Corporation, 6
Storage USA, Inc., 21
Stouffer Corp., 8
StrataCom, Inc., 16
Stratagene Corporation, 70
Stratasys, Inc., 67
Stratus Computer, Inc., 10
Strauss Discount Auto, 56
Strayer Education, Inc., 53
Stride Rite Corporation, The, 8; 37 (upd.)
Stroh Brewery Company, The, I; 18 (upd.)
Strombecker Corporation, 60
Stroock & Stroock & Lavan LLP, 40
Strouds, Inc., 33
Stryker Corporation, 11; 29 (upd.)
Stuart C. Irby Company, 58
Stuart Entertainment Inc., 16
Student Loan Marketing Association, II
Stuller Settings, Inc., 35
Sturm, Ruger & Company, Inc., 19
Stussy, Inc., 55
Sub-Zero Freezer Co., Inc., 31
Suburban Propane Partners, L.P., 30
Subway, 32
Successories, Inc., 30
Sudbury Inc., 16
Suiza Foods Corporation, 26
Sullivan & Cromwell, 26
Summit Bancorporation, The, 14
Summit Family Restaurants, Inc. 19
Sun Communities Inc., 46
Sun Company, Inc., IV
Sun Country Airlines, 30
Sun Distributors L.P., 12
Sun Healthcare Group Inc., 25
Sun Microsystems, Inc., 7; 30 (upd.)
Sun Sportswear, Inc., 17
Sun Television & Appliances Inc., 10
Sun-Diamond Growers of California, 7
SunAmerica Inc., 11
Sunbeam-Oster Co., Inc., 9
Sunburst Hospitality Corporation, 26
Sundstrand Corporation, 7; 21 (upd.)
Sundt Corp., 24
SunGard Data Systems Inc., 11
Sunglass Hut International, Inc., 21
Sunkist Growers, Inc., 26
Sunoco, Inc., 28 (upd.)
Sunrider Corporation, The, 26
Sunrise Medical Inc., 11
SunTrust Banks Inc., 23
Super Food Services, Inc., 15
Supercuts Inc., 26
Superior Energy Services, Inc., 65
Superior Industries International, Inc., 8
Superior Uniform Group, Inc., 30
Supermarkets General Holdings
  Corporation, II
SUPERVALU Inc., II; 18 (upd.); 50 (upd.)
Suprema Specialties, Inc., 27
Supreme International Corporation, 27
Susquehanna Pfaltzgraff Company, 8
Sutter Home Winery Inc., 16

Sverdrup Corporation, 14
Swales & Associates, Inc., 69
Swank Inc., 17
SwedishAmerican Health System, 51
Sweet Candy Company, 60
Sweetheart Cup Company, Inc., 36
SWH Corporation, 70
Swift & Company, 55
Swift Energy Company, 63
Swift Transportation Co., Inc., 42
Swinerton Inc., 43
Swisher International Group Inc., 23
Sybase, Inc., 10; 27 (upd.)
Sybron International Corp., 14
Sycamore Networks, Inc., 45
Sykes Enterprises, Inc., 45
Sylvan Learning Systems, Inc., 35
Sylvan, Inc., 22
Symantec Corporation, 10
Symbol Technologies, Inc., 15
Syms Corporation, 29
Synopsys, Inc., 11; 69 (upd.)
SynOptics Communications, Inc., 10
Synovus Financial Corp., 12; 52 (upd.)
Syntex Corporation, I
SyQuest Technology, Inc., 18
Syratech Corp., 14
SYSCO Corporation, II; 24 (upd.)
System Software Associates, Inc., 10
Systemax, Inc., 52
Systems & Computer Technology Corp.,
  19
T-Netix, Inc., 46
T. Marzetti Company, 57
T. Rowe Price Associates, Inc., 11; 34
  (upd.)
TAB Products Co., 17
Taco Bell Corp., 7; 21 (upd.)
Taco Cabana, Inc., 23; 72 (upd.)
Taco John's International, Inc., 15; 63
  (upd.)
Tacony Corporation, 70
Take-Two Interactive Software, Inc., 46
Talbots, Inc., The, 11; 31 (upd.)
Talk America Holdings, Inc., 70
Talley Industries, Inc., 16
Tambrands Inc., 8
Tandem Computers, Inc., 6
Tandy Corporation, II; 12 (upd.)
Tandycrafts, Inc., 31
Tanger Factory Outlet Centers, Inc., 49
Tapemark Company Inc., 64
Target Corporation, 10; 27 (upd.); 61
  (upd.)
Tarragon Realty Investors, Inc., 45
Tarrant Apparel Group, 62
Taser International, Inc., 62
Tasty Baking Company, 14; 35 (upd.)
Tattered Cover Book Store, 43
Taylor Corporation, 36
Taylor Guitars, 48
Taylor Made Golf Co., 23
Taylor Publishing Company, 12; 36 (upd.)
TB Wood's Corporation, 56
TBWA\Chiat\Day, 6; 43 (upd.)
TCBY Enterprises Inc., 17
TCF Financial Corporation, 47
Teachers Insurance and Annuity
  Association-College Retirement Equities
  Fund, III; 45 (upd.)
TearDrop Golf Company, 32
Tech Data Corporation, 10
Tech-Sym Corporation, 18; 44 (upd.)
TECHNE Corporation, 52
Technitrol, Inc., 29
TECO Energy, Inc., 6
Tecumseh Products Company, 8; 71 (upd.)

Tee Vee Toons, Inc., 57
Tejon Ranch Company, 35
Tektronix, Inc., 8
Telcordia Technologies, Inc., 59
Tele-Communications, Inc., II
Teledyne Technologies Inc., I; 10 (upd.);
  62 (upd.)
Telephone and Data Systems, Inc., 9
Tellabs, Inc., 11; 40 (upd.)
Telxon Corporation, 10
Temple-Inland Inc., IV; 31 (upd.)
Tempur-Pedic Inc., 54
Tenet Healthcare Corporation, 55 (upd.)
TenFold Corporation, 35
Tennant Company, 13; 33 (upd.)
Tenneco Inc., I; 10 (upd.)
Tennessee Valley Authority, 50
Teradyne, Inc., 11
Terex Corporation, 7; 40 (upd.)
Terlato Wine Group, The, 48
Terra Industries, Inc., 13
Tesoro Petroleum Corporation, 7; 45 (upd.)
Testor Corporation, The, 51
Tetra Tech, Inc., 29
Texaco Inc., IV; 14 (upd.); 41 (upd.)
Texas Air Corporation, I
Texas Industries, Inc., 8
Texas Instruments Inc., II; 11 (upd.); 46
  (upd.)
Texas Pacific Group Inc., 36
Texas Rangers Baseball, 51
Texas Roadhouse, Inc., 69
Texas Utilities Company, V; 25 (upd.)
Textron Inc., I; 34 (upd.)
Textron Lycoming Turbine Engine, 9
Tha Row Records, 69 (upd.)
Thermadyne Holding Corporation, 19
Thermo BioAnalysis Corp., 25
Thermo Electron Corporation, 7
Thermo Fibertek, Inc., 24
Thermo Instrument Systems Inc., 11
Thermo King Corporation, 13
Thermos Company, 16
Thiokol Corporation, 9; 22 (upd.)
Thomas & Betts Corporation, 11; 54 (upd.)
Thomas Cook Travel Inc., 9; 33 (upd.)
Thomas H. Lee Co., 24
Thomas Industries Inc., 29
Thomas J. Lipton Company, 14
Thomas Nelson, Inc., 14; 38 (upd.)
Thomas Publishing Company, 26
Thomaston Mills, Inc., 27
Thomasville Furniture Industries, Inc., 12
Thomsen Greenhouses and Garden Center,
  Incorporated, 65
Thor Industries, Inc., 39
Thorn Apple Valley, Inc., 7; 22 (upd.)
Thousand Trails, Inc., 33
THQ, Inc., 39
3Com Corporation, 11; 34 (upd.)
3DO Company, The, 43
3M Company, 61 (upd.)
Thrifty PayLess, Inc., 12
Ticketmaster Group, Inc., 13; 37 (upd.)
Tidewater Inc., 11; 37 (upd.)
Tiffany & Co., 14
TIG Holdings, Inc., 26
Tilia Inc., 62
Tillotson Corp., 15
Timberland Company, The, 13; 54 (upd.)
Timberline Software Corporation, 15
Time Warner Inc., IV; 7 (upd.)
Times Mirror Company, The, IV; 17 (upd.)
Timex Corporation, 7; 25 (upd.)
Timken Company, The, 8; 42 (upd.)
Tishman Speyer Properties, L.P., 47
Titan Corporation, The, 36

Titanium Metals Corporation, 21
TJ International, Inc., 19
TJX Companies, Inc., The, V; 19 (upd.); 57 (upd.)
TLC Beatrice International Holdings, Inc., 22
TMP Worldwide Inc., 30
TNT Freightways Corporation, 14
Today's Man, Inc., 20
Todd Shipyards Corporation, 14
Todd-AO Corporation, The, 33
Todhunter International, Inc., 27
Tofutti Brands, Inc., 64
Tokheim Corporation, 21
Toll Brothers Inc., 15; 70 (upd.)
Tollgrade Communications, Inc., 44
Tom Brown, Inc., 37
Tom Doherty Associates Inc., 25
Tom's Foods Inc., 66
Tom's of Maine, Inc., 45
Tombstone Pizza Corporation, 13
Tone Brothers, Inc., 21
Tonka Corporation, 25
Too, Inc., 61
Tootsie Roll Industries Inc., 12
Topco Associates LLC, 60
Topps Company, Inc., The, 13; 34 (upd.)
Tops Appliance City, Inc., 17
Tops Markets LLC, 60
Torchmark Corporation, 9; 33 (upd.)
Toro Company, The, 7; 26 (upd.)
Torrington Company, The, 13
Tosco Corporation, 7
Total Entertainment Restaurant Corporation, 46
Total System Services, Inc., 18
Totem Resources Corporation, 9
Tower Air, Inc., 28
Tower Automotive, Inc., 24
Towers Perrin, 32
Town & Country Corporation, 19
Town Sports International, Inc., 46
Townsends, Inc., 64
Toy Biz, Inc., 18
Toymax International, Inc., 29
Toys ''R'' Us, Inc., V; 18 (upd.); 57 (upd.)
Tracor Inc., 17
Tractor Supply Company, 57
Trader Joe's Company, 13; 50 (upd.)
Traffix, Inc., 61
Trailer Bridge, Inc., 41
Trammell Crow Company, 8; 57 (upd.)
Trans World Airlines, Inc., I; 12 (upd.); 35 (upd.)
Trans World Entertainment Corporation, 24; 68 (upd.)
Trans-Lux Corporation, 51
Transaction Systems Architects, Inc., 29
Transamerica—An AEGON Company, I; 13 (upd.); 41 (upd.)
Transatlantic Holdings, Inc., 11
Transco Energy Company, V
Transmedia Network Inc., 20
TransMontaigne Inc., 28
Transocean Sedco Forex Inc., 45
Transport Corporation of America, Inc., 49
TransPro, Inc., 71
Tranzonic Companies, The, 37
Travel Ports of America, Inc., 17
Travelers Corporation, The, III
Travelocity.com, Inc., 46
Travis Boats & Motors, Inc., 37
TRC Companies, Inc., 32
Treadco, Inc., 19
Treasure Chest Advertising Company, Inc., 32
Tredegar Corporation, 52

Tree of Life, Inc., 29
Trek Bicycle Corporation, 16
Trend-Lines, Inc., 22
Trendwest Resorts, Inc., 33
Trex Company, Inc., 71
Tri Valley Growers, 32
Triarc Companies, Inc., 8; 34 (upd.)
Tribune Company, IV; 22 (upd.); 63 (upd.)
Trico Products Corporation, 15
Trident Seafoods Corporation, 56
Trigen Energy Corporation, 42
TriMas Corp., 11
Trimble Navigation Limited, 40
Trinity Industries, Incorporated, 7
TRINOVA Corporation, III
Triple Five Group Ltd., 49
TriQuint Semiconductor, Inc., 63
Trisko Jewelry Sculptures, Ltd., 57
Triton Energy Corporation, 11
Triumph Group, Inc., 31
TRM Copy Centers Corporation, 18
Tropicana Products, Inc., 28
True North Communications Inc., 23
Trump Organization, The, 23; 64 (upd.)
TruServ Corporation, 24
TRW Inc., I; 11 (upd.); 14 (upd.)
TTX Company, 6; 66 (upd.)
Tubby's, Inc., 53
Tucson Electric Power Company, 6
Tuesday Morning Corporation, 18; 70 (upd.)
Tully's Coffee Corporation, 51
Tultex Corporation, 13
Tumbleweed, Inc., 33
Tupperware Corporation, 28
Turner Broadcasting System, Inc., II; 6 (upd.); 66 (upd.)
Turner Construction Company, 66
Turner Corporation, The, 8; 23 (upd.)
Turtle Wax, Inc., 15
Tuscarora Inc., 29
Tutogen Medical, Inc., 68
TV Guide, Inc., 43 (upd.)
TVI, Inc., 15
TW Services, Inc., II
Tweeter Home Entertainment Group, Inc., 30
Twentieth Century Fox Film Corporation, II; 25 (upd.)
24 Hour Fitness Worldwide, Inc., 71
24/7 Real Media, Inc., 49
Twin Disc, Inc., 21
Twinlab Corporation, 34
II-VI Incorporated, 69
Ty Inc., 33
Tyco Toys, Inc., 12
Tyler Corporation, 23
Tyndale House Publishers, Inc., 57
Tyson Foods, Inc., II; 14 (upd.); 50 (upd.)
U S West, Inc., V; 25 (upd.)
U.S. Aggregates, Inc., 42
U.S. Bancorp, 14; 36 (upd.)
U.S. Borax, Inc., 42
U.S. Can Corporation, 30
U.S. Cellular Corporation, 31 (upd.)
U.S. Delivery Systems, Inc., 22
U.S. Foodservice, 26
U.S. Healthcare, Inc., 6
U.S. Home Corporation, 8
U.S. News and World Report Inc., 30
U.S. Office Products Company, 25
U.S. Physical Therapy, Inc., 65
U.S. Robotics Corporation, 9; 66 (upd.)
U.S. Satellite Broadcasting Company, Inc., 20
U.S. Timberlands Company, L.P., 42
U.S. Trust Corp., 17

U.S. Vision, Inc., 66
UAL Corporation, 34 (upd.)
UAW (International Union, United Automobile, Aerospace and Agricultural Implement Workers of America), 72
UGI Corporation, 12
Ugly Duckling Corporation, 22
UICI, 33
Ukrop's Super Market's, Inc., 39
Ultimate Electronics, Inc., 18; 69 (upd.)
Ultra Pac, Inc., 24
Ultra Petroleum Corporation, 71
Ultrak Inc., 24
Ultralife Batteries, Inc., 58
Ultramar Diamond Shamrock Corporation, 31 (upd.)
Uncle Ben's Inc., 22
Under Armour Performance Apparel, 61
Underwriters Laboratories, Inc., 30
Uni-Marts, Inc., 17
Unicom Corporation, 29 (upd.)
Unifi, Inc., 12; 62 (upd.)
UniFirst Corporation, 21
Union Bank of California, 16
Union Camp Corporation, IV
Union Carbide Corporation, I; 9 (upd.)
Union Electric Company, V
Union Pacific Corporation, V; 28 (upd.)
Union Planters Corporation, 54
Union Texas Petroleum Holdings, Inc., 9
UnionBanCal Corporation, 50 (upd.)
Unique Casual Restaurants, Inc., 27
Unison HealthCare Corporation, 25
Unisys Corporation, III; 6 (upd.); 36 (upd.)
Unit Corporation, 63
United Airlines, I; 6 (upd.)
United Auto Group, Inc., 26; 68 (upd.)
United Brands Company, II
United Defense Industries, Inc., 30; 66 (upd.)
United Dominion Industries Limited, 8; 16 (upd.)
United Dominion Realty Trust, Inc., 52
United Foods, Inc., 21
United HealthCare Corporation, 9
United Illuminating Company, The, 21
United Industrial Corporation, 37
United Industries Corporation, 68
United Jewish Communities, 33
United Merchants & Manufacturers, Inc., 13
United National Group, Ltd., 63
United Nations International Children's Emergency Fund (UNICEF), 58
United Natural Foods, Inc., 32
United Online, Inc., 71 (upd.)
United Parcel Service of America Inc., V; 17 (upd.)
United Parcel Service, Inc., 63
United Press International, Inc., 25
United Rentals, Inc., 34
United Retail Group Inc., 33
United Road Services, Inc., 69
United Service Organizations, 60
United States Cellular Corporation, 9
United States Filter Corporation, 20
United States Pipe and Foundry Company, 62
United States Playing Card Company, 62
United States Postal Service, 14; 34 (upd.)
United States Shoe Corporation, The, V
United States Steel Corporation, 50 (upd.)
United States Surgical Corporation, 10; 34 (upd.)
United Stationers Inc., 14
United Technologies Automotive Inc., 15

United States (*continued*)

United Technologies Corporation, I; 10 (upd.); 34 (upd.)
United Telecommunications, Inc., V
United Video Satellite Group, 18
United Water Resources, Inc., 40
United Way of America, 36
Unitil Corporation, 37
Unitog Co., 19
Unitrin Inc., 16
Univar Corporation, 9
Universal Compression, Inc., 59
Universal Corporation, V; 48 (upd.)
Universal Electronics Inc., 39
Universal Foods Corporation, 7
Universal Forest Products, Inc., 10; 59 (upd.)
Universal Health Services, Inc., 6
Universal International, Inc., 25
Universal Studios, Inc., 33
Univision Communications Inc., 24
Uno Restaurant Corporation, 18
Uno Restaurant Holdings Corporation, 70 (upd.)
Unocal Corporation, IV; 24 (upd.); 71 (upd.)
UnumProvident Corporation, 13; 52 (upd.)
Upjohn Company, The, I; 8 (upd.)
Urban Outfitters, Inc., 14
URS Corporation, 45
US Airways Group, Inc., I; 6 (upd.); 28 (upd.); 52 (upd.)
USA Interactive, Inc., 47 (upd.)
USA Truck, Inc., 42
USAA, 10; 62 (upd.)
USANA, Inc., 29
USF&G Corporation, III
USG Corporation, III; 26 (upd.)
UST Inc., 9; 50 (upd.)
USX Corporation, IV; 7 (upd.)
Utah Medical Products, Inc., 36
Utah Power and Light Company, 27
UtiliCorp United Inc., 6
Utz Quality Foods, Inc., 72
UUNET, 38
Uwajimaya, Inc., 60
Vail Resorts, Inc., 11; 43 (upd.)
Valassis Communications, Inc., 8; 37 (upd.)
Valero Energy Corporation, 7; 71 (upd.)
Valhi, Inc., 19
Vallen Corporation, 45
Valley Media Inc., 35
Valmont Industries, Inc., 19
Valspar Corporation, The, 8; 32 (upd.)
Value City Department Stores, Inc., 38
Value Line, Inc., 16
Value Merchants Inc., 13
ValueClick, Inc., 49
ValueVision International, Inc., 22
Van Camp Seafood Company, Inc., 7
Van's Aircraft, Inc., 65
Vance Publishing Corporation, 64
Vanguard Group, Inc., The, 14; 34 (upd.)
Vanguard Health Systems Inc., 70
Vans, Inc., 16; 47 (upd.)
Varco International, Inc., 42
Vari-Lite International, Inc., 35
Varian, Inc., 12; 48 (upd.)
Variflex, Inc., 51
Varlen Corporation, 16
Varsity Spirit Corp., 15
Vastar Resources, Inc., 24
VCA Antech, Inc., 58
VECO International, Inc., 7
Vector Group Ltd., 35 (upd.)
Veeco Instruments Inc., 32

Veit Companies, 43
Velocity Express Corporation, 49
Venator Group Inc., 35 (upd.)
Vencor, Inc., 16
Venetian Casino Resort, LLC, 47
Venture Stores Inc., 12
Verbatim Corporation, 14
Veridian Corporation, 54
VeriFone, Inc., 18
VeriSign, Inc., 47
Veritas Software Corporation, 45
Verity Inc., 68
Verizon Communications, 43 (upd.)
Vermeer Manufacturing Company, 17
Vermont Pure Holdings, Ltd., 51
Vermont Teddy Bear Co., Inc., The, 36
VF Corporation, V; 17 (upd.); 54 (upd.)
VHA Inc., 53
Viacom Inc., 7; 23 (upd.); 67 (upd.)
ViaSat, Inc., 54
Viasoft Inc., 27
VIASYS Healthcare, Inc., 52
Viasystems Group, Inc., 67
Viatech Continental Can Company, Inc., 25 (upd.)
Vicon Industries, Inc., 44
VICORP Restaurants, Inc., 12; 48 (upd.)
Vienna Sausage Manufacturing Co., 14
Viewpoint International, Inc., 66
ViewSonic Corporation, 72
Viking Office Products, Inc., 10
Viking Range Corporation, 66
Village Super Market, Inc., 7
Village Voice Media, Inc., 38
Vinson & Elkins L.L.P., 30
Vintage Petroleum, Inc., 42
Vinton Studios, 63
Virco Manufacturing Corporation, 17
Visa International, 9; 26 (upd.)
Vishay Intertechnology, Inc., 21
Viskase Companies, Inc., 55
Vista Bakery, Inc., 56
Vista Chemical Company, I
Vistana, Inc., 22
VISX, Incorporated, 30
Vita Plus Corporation, 60
Vitalink Pharmacy Services, Inc., 15
Vitamin Shoppe Industries, Inc., 60
Vitesse Semiconductor Corporation, 32
Vitro Corp., 10
Vivra, Inc., 18
Vlasic Foods International Inc., 25
VLSI Technology, Inc., 16
Volt Information Sciences Inc., 26
Volunteers of America, Inc., 66
Von Maur Inc., 64
Vons Companies, Incorporated, The, 7; 28 (upd.)
Vornado Realty Trust, 20
Vought Aircraft Industries, Inc., 49
Vulcan Materials Company, 7; 52 (upd.)
W. Atlee Burpee & Co., 27
W.A. Whitney Company, 53
W.B Doner & Co., 56
W.C. Bradley Co., 69
W.H. Brady Co., 17
W.L. Gore & Associates, Inc., 14; 60 (upd.)
W.P. Carey & Co. LLC, 49
W.R. Berkley Corp., 15
W.R. Grace & Company, I; 50 (upd.)
W.W. Grainger, Inc., V; 26 (upd.); 68 (upd.)
W.W. Norton & Company, Inc., 28
Waban Inc., 13
Wabash National Corp., 13
Wabtec Corporation, 40

Wachovia Bank of Georgia, N.A., 16
Wachovia Bank of South Carolina, N.A., 16
Wachovia Corporation, 12; 46 (upd.)
Wachtell, Lipton, Rosen & Katz, 47
Wackenhut Corporation, The, 14; 63 (upd.)
Waddell & Reed, Inc., 22
Waffle House Inc., 14; 60 (upd.)
Waggener Edstrom, 42
Wakefern Food Corporation, 33
Wal-Mart Stores, Inc., V; 8 (upd.); 26 (upd.); 63 (upd.)
Walbridge Aldinger Co., 38
Walbro Corporation, 13
Waldbaum, Inc., 19
Walden Book Company Inc., 17
Walgreen Co., V; 20 (upd.); 65 (upd.)
Walker Manufacturing Company, 19
Wall Drug Store, Inc., 40
Wall Street Deli, Inc., 33
Wallace Computer Services, Inc., 36
Walt Disney Company, The, II; 6 (upd.); 30 (upd.); 63 (upd.)
Walter Industries, Inc., II; 22 (upd.); 72 (upd.)
Walton Monroe Mills, Inc., 8
Wang Laboratories, Inc., III; 6 (upd.)
Warnaco Group Inc., The, 12; 46 (upd.)
Warner Communications Inc., II
Warner-Lambert Co., I; 10 (upd.)
Warners' Stellian Inc., 67
Warrantech Corporation, 53
Warrell Corporation, 68
Warwick Valley Telephone Company, 55
Washington Companies, The, 33
Washington Federal, Inc., 17
Washington Football, Inc., 35
Washington Gas Light Company, 19
Washington Mutual, Inc., 17
Washington National Corporation, 12
Washington Natural Gas Company, 9
Washington Post Company, The, IV; 20 (upd.)
Washington Scientific Industries, Inc., 17
Washington Water Power Company, 6
Waste Connections, Inc., 46
Waste Holdings, Inc., 41
Waste Management, Inc., V
Water Pik Technologies, Inc., 34
Waterhouse Investor Services, Inc., 18
Waters Corporation, 43
Watkins-Johnson Company, 15
Watsco Inc., 52
Watson Pharmaceuticals Inc., 16; 56 (upd.)
Watson Wyatt Worldwide, 42
Watts Industries, Inc., 19
Wausau-Mosinee Paper Corporation, 60 (upd.)
Waverly, Inc., 16
Wawa Inc., 17
Waxman Industries, Inc., 9
WD-40 Company, 18
Weather Channel Companies, The 52
Weatherford International, Inc., 39
Webber Oil Company, 61
Weber-Stephen Products Co., 40
WebMD Corporation, 65
Weeres Industries Corporation, 52
Wegmans Food Markets, Inc., 9; 41 (upd.)
Weider Nutrition International, Inc., 29
Weight Watchers International Inc., 12; 33 (upd.)
Weil, Gotshal & Manges LLP, 55
Weiner's Stores, Inc., 33
Weirton Steel Corporation, IV; 26 (upd.)
Weis Markets, Inc., 15
Weitz Company, Inc., The, 42

Welbilt Corp., 19
WellChoice, Inc., 67 (upd.)
Wellman, Inc., 8; 52 (upd.)
WellPoint Health Networks Inc., 25
Wells Fargo & Company, II; 12 (upd.); 38 (upd.)
Wells Rich Greene BDDP, 6
Wells' Dairy, Inc., 36
Wells-Gardner Electronics Corporation, 43
Wendy's International, Inc., 8; 23 (upd.); 47 (upd.)
Wenner Media, Inc., 32
Werner Enterprises, Inc., 26
West Bend Co., 14
West Coast Entertainment Corporation, 29
West Corporation, 42
West Group, 34 (upd.)
West Marine, Inc., 17
West One Bancorp, 11
West Pharmaceutical Services, Inc., 42
West Point-Pepperell, Inc., 8
West Publishing Co., 7
Westaff Inc., 33
Westamerica Bancorporation, 17
Westar Energy, Inc., 57 (upd.)
WestCoast Hospitality Corporation, 59
Westcon Group, Inc., 67
Westell Technologies, Inc., 57
Westerbeke Corporation, 60
Western Atlas Inc., 12
Western Beef, Inc., 22
Western Company of North America, 15
Western Digital Corp., 25
Western Gas Resources, Inc., 45
Western Publishing Group, Inc., 13
Western Resources, Inc., 12
WesterN SizzliN Corporation, The, 60
Western Union Financial Services, Inc., 54
Western Wireless Corporation, 36
Westfield Group, 69
Westin Hotels and Resorts Worldwide, 9; 29 (upd.)
Westinghouse Electric Corporation, II; 12 (upd.)
Westmoreland Coal Company, 7
WestPoint Stevens Inc., 16
Westport Resources Corporation, 63
Westvaco Corporation, IV; 19 (upd.)
Westwood One, Inc., 23
Wet Seal, Inc., The, 18; 70 (upd.)
Wetterau Incorporated, II
Weyco Group, Incorporated, 32
Weyerhaeuser Company, IV; 9 (upd.); 28 (upd.)
WFS Financial Inc., 70
WGBH Educational Foundation, 66
Wham-O, Inc., 61
Wheaton Industries, 8
Wheaton Science Products, 60 (upd.)
Wheelabrator Technologies, Inc., 6; 60 (upd.)
Wheeling-Pittsburgh Corporation, 7; 58 (upd.)
Wherehouse Entertainment Incorporated, 11
Whirlpool Corporation, III; 12 (upd.); 59 (upd.)
White & Case LLP, 35
White Castle System, Inc., 12; 36 (upd.)
White Consolidated Industries Inc., 13
White House, Inc., The, 60
White Rose, Inc., 24
Whitman Corporation, 10 (upd.)
Whitman Education Group, Inc., 41
Whitney Holding Corporation, 21
Whittaker Corporation, I; 48 (upd.)
Whole Foods Market, Inc., 20; 50 (upd.)

Wickes Inc., V; 25 (upd.)
Wilbert, Inc., 56
Wilbur Chocolate Company, 66
Wild Oats Markets, Inc., 19; 41 (upd.)
Wildlife Conservation Society, 31
Willamette Industries, Inc., IV; 31 (upd.)
William L. Bonnell Company, Inc., 66
William Lyon Homes, 59
William Morris Agency, Inc., 23
William Zinsser & Company, Inc., 58
Williams & Connolly LLP, 47
Williams Communications Group, Inc., 34
Williams Companies, Inc., The, IV; 31 (upd.)
Williams Scotsman, Inc., 65
Williams-Sonoma, Inc., 17; 44 (upd.)
Williamson-Dickie Manufacturing Company, 14; 45 (upd.)
Wilmington Trust Corporation, 25
Wilson Sonsini Goodrich & Rosati, 34
Wilson Sporting Goods Company, 24
Wilsons The Leather Experts Inc., 21; 58 (upd.)
Winchell's Donut Houses Operating Company, L.P., 60
WinCo Foods Inc., 60
Wind River Systems, Inc., 37
Windmere Corporation, 16
Windswept Environmental Group, Inc., 62
Wine Group, Inc., The, 39
Winegard Company, 56
Winn-Dixie Stores, Inc., II; 21 (upd.); 59 (upd.)
Winnebago Industries Inc., 7; 27 (upd.)
WinsLoew Furniture, Inc., 21
Winston & Strawn, 35
Wirtz Corporation, 72
Wisconsin Alumni Research Foundation, 65
Wisconsin Bell, Inc., 14
Wisconsin Central Transportation Corporation, 24
Wisconsin Dairies, 7
Wisconsin Energy Corporation, 6; 54 (upd.)
Wisconsin Public Service Corporation, 9
Witco Corporation, I; 16 (upd.)
Wizards of the Coast Inc., 24
WLR Foods, Inc., 21
Wm. B. Reily & Company Inc., 58
Wm. Wrigley Jr. Company, 7; 58 (upd.)
WMS Industries, Inc., 15; 53 (upd.)
WMX Technologies Inc., 17
Wolfgang Puck Worldwide, Inc., 26, 70 (upd.)
Wolohan Lumber Co., 19
Wolverine Tube Inc., 23
Wolverine World Wide, Inc., 16; 59 (upd.)
Womble Carlyle Sandridge & Rice, PLLC, 52
Wood-Mode, Inc., 23
Woodcraft Industries Inc., 61
Woodward Governor Company, 13; 49 (upd.)
Woolrich Inc., 62
Woolworth Corporation, V; 20 (upd.)
WordPerfect Corporation, 10
Workflow Management, Inc., 65
Working Assets Funding Service, 43
Workman Publishing Company, Inc., 70
World Acceptance Corporation, 57
World Bank Group, 33
World Book, Inc., 12
World Color Press Inc., 12
World Duty Free Americas, Inc., 29 (upd.)
World Fuel Services Corporation, 47
World Publications, LLC, 65

World Wrestling Federation Entertainment, Inc., 32
World's Finest Chocolate Inc., 39
WorldCorp, Inc., 10
Worldwide Restaurant Concepts, Inc., 47
Worthington Foods, Inc., 14
Worthington Industries, Inc., 7; 21 (upd.)
WPL Holdings, Inc., 6
WPS Resources Corporation, 53 (upd.)
Wright Medical Group, Inc., 61
WTD Industries, Inc., 20
Wyant Corporation, 30
Wyeth, 50 (upd.)
Wyle Electronics, 14
Wyman-Gordon Company, 14
Wynn's International, Inc., 33
Wyse Technology, Inc., 15
X-Rite, Inc., 48
Xerox Corporation, III; 6 (upd.); 26 (upd.); 69 (upd.)
Xilinx, Inc., 16
XM Satellite Radio Holdings, Inc., 69
XTO Energy Inc., 52
Yahoo! Inc., 27; 70 (upd.)
Yankee Candle Company, Inc., The, 37
YankeeNets LLC, 35
Yates Companies, Inc., The, 62
Yellow Corporation, 14; 45 (upd.)
Yellow Freight System, Inc. of Delaware, V
YES! Entertainment Corporation, 26
YMCA of the USA, 31
YOCREAM International, Inc., 47
York Group, Inc., The, 50
York International Corp., 13
York Research Corporation, 35
Young & Rubicam, Inc., I; 22 (upd.); 66 (upd.)
Young Broadcasting Inc., 40
Young Innovations, Inc., 44
Young's Market Company, LLC, 32
Younkers, Inc., 19
Youth Services International, Inc., 21
Yucaipa Cos., 17
Yum! Brands Inc., 58
YWCA of the United States, 45
Zale Corporation, 16; 40 (upd.)
Zany Brainy, Inc., 31
Zapata Corporation, 25
Zatarain's, Inc., 64
Zebra Technologies Corporation, 14; 53 (upd.)
Zenith Data Systems, Inc., 10
Zenith Electronics Corporation, II; 13 (upd.); 34 (upd.)
Zero Corporation, 17
Ziebart International Corporation, 30; 66 (upd.)
Ziegler Companies, Inc., The, 24; 63 (upd.)
Ziff Davis Media Inc., 12; 36 (upd.)
Zila, Inc., 46
ZiLOG, Inc., 15; 72 (upd.)
Zimmer Holdings, Inc., 45
Zingerman's Community of Businesses, 68
Zion's Cooperative Mercantile Institution, 33
Zions Bancorporation, 12; 53 (upd.)
Zippo Manufacturing Company, 18; 71 (upd.)
Zoltek Companies, Inc., 37
Zondervan Corporation, 24; 71 (upd.)
Zones, Inc., 67
Zoom Technologies, Inc., 18; 53 (upd.)
Zygo Corporation, 42
Zytec Corporation, 19

Vatican City

Caritas Internationalis, 72

Venezuela

Cerveceria Polar, I
Cisneros Group of Companies, 54
Empresas Polar SA, 55 (upd.)
Petróleos de Venezuela S.A., IV

Vietnam

Lam Son Sugar Joint Stock Corporation
    (Lasuco), 60

Virgin Islands

Little Switzerland, Inc., 60

Wales

Hyder plc, 34
Iceland Group plc, 33
Kwik Save Group plc, 11

Zambia

Zambia Industrial and Mining Corporation
    Ltd., IV

NOTES ON CONTRIBUTORS

Notes on Contributors

BRENNAN, Gerald E. California-based writer.

COHEN, M. L. Novelist and business writer living in Paris.

COVELL, Jeffrey L. Seattle-based writer.

DINGER, Ed. Bronx-based writer and editor.

GARIEPY, Jennifer. Editor and artist in Detroit, Michigan.

GREENLAND, Paul R. Illinois-based writer and researcher; author of two books and former senior editor of a national business magazine; contributor to *The Encyclopedia of Chicago History, The Encyclopedia of Religion,* and the *Encyclopedia of American Industries.*

HALASZ, Robert. Former editor in chief of *World Progress* and *Funk & Wagnalls New Encyclopedia Yearbook*; author, *The U.S. Marines* (Millbrook Press, 1993).

HAUSER, Evelyn. Researcher, writer and marketing specialist based in Arcata, California; expertise includes historical and trend research in such topics as globalization, emerging industries and lifestyles, future scenarios, biographies, and the history of organizations.

INGRAM, Frederick C. Utah-based business writer who has contributed to *GSA Business, Appalachian Trailway News,* the *Encyclopedia of Business,* the *Encyclopedia of Global Industries,* the *Encyclopedia of Consumer Brands,* and other regional and trade publications.

LEMIEUX, Gloria A. Researcher and writer living in Nashua, New Hampshire.

MONTGOMERY, Bruce P. Curator and director of historical collection, University of Colorado at Boulder.

ROTHBURD, Carrie. Writer and editor specializing in corporate profiles, academic texts, and academic journal articles.

STANSELL, Christina M. Writer and editor based in Louisville, Kentucky.

UHLE, Frank. Ann Arbor-based writer; movie projectionist, disc jockey, and staff member of *Psychotronic Video* magazine.

WILOCH, Thomas. Author whose most recent title is *Crime: A Serious American Problem* (2005); regular contributor to *Rain Taxi Review of Books*; associate editor with *Sidereality.*